Immigration Law and Practice in the United Kingdom

Volume 1

Immigration Law and Practice in the United Kingdom

Ninth edition

Volume 1

General Editors

Ian A Macdonald QC
Garden Court Chambers

Ronan Toal
Garden Court Chambers

and a team of specialist Contributing Editors

Members of the LexisNexis Group worldwide

United Kingdom	LexisNexis, a Division of Reed Elsevier (UK) Ltd, Lexis House, 30 Farringdon Street, London EC4A 4HH, and London House, 20-22 East London Street, Edinburgh EH7 4BQ
Australia	Reed International Books Australia Pty Ltd trading as LexisNexis, Chatswood, New South Wales
Austria	LexisNexis Verlag ARD Orac GmbH & Co KG, Vienna
Benelux	LexisNexis Benelux, Amsterdam
Canada	LexisNexis Canada, Markham, Ontario
China	LexisNexis China, Beijing and Shanghai
France	LexisNexis SA, Paris
Germany	LexisNexis GmbH, Dusseldorf
Hong Kong	LexisNexis Hong Kong, Hong Kong
India	LexisNexis India, New Delhi
Italy	Giuffrè Editore, Milan
Japan	LexisNexis Japan, Tokyo
Malaysia	Malayan Law Journal Sdn Bhd, Kuala Lumpur
New Zealand	LexisNexis New Zealand Ltd, Wellington
Singapore	LexisNexis Singapore, Singapore
South Africa	LexisNexis, Durban
USA	LexisNexis, Dayton, Ohio

First edition 1983, Second edition 1987, Third edition 1991, Fourth edition 1995, Fifth edition 2001, Sixth edition 2005, Seventh edition 2008, Eighth edition 2010, Ninth edition 2014

© Reed Elsevier (UK) Ltd 2014

Published by LexisNexis

ISBN 978-1-4057-9047-5

ISBN 978-1-4057-9942-3

9 781405 790475

9 781405 799423

ISBN for this volume: 9781405790475

ISBN for the set: 9781405799423

Printed and bound by CPI Group (UK) Ltd, Croydon, CR0 4YY

Contributors

General Editors

Ian A Macdonald QC
Garden Court Chambers

Ronan Toal
Garden Court Chambers

Contributors

Navtej Ahluwalia
Garden Court Chambers

Ali Bandegani
Garden Court Chambers

Adrian Berry
Garden Court Chambers

Michelle Brewer
Garden Court Chambers

Rebecca Chapman
Garden Court Chambers

Kathryn Cronin
Garden Court Chambers

Jared Ficklin
Garden Court North Chambers

Helen Foot
Garden Court Chambers

Hannah Graves
Solicitor at Fisher Jones Greenwood

Contributors

Alex Grigg

Garden Court Chambers

Raza Halim

Garden Court Chambers

Stephanie Harrison QC

Garden Court Chambers

Alison Harvey

Immigration Law Practitioners' Association

Louise Hooper

Garden Court Chambers

Bijan Hoshi

Garden Court Chambers

Vijay Jagadesham

Garden Court North Chambers

David Jones

Garden Court Chambers

Peter Jorro

Garden Court Chambers

Patrick Lewis

Garden Court Chambers

Shu Shin Luh

Garden Court Chambers

Lucy Mair

Garden Court North Chambers

Joseph Markus

Garden Court North Chambers

Maria Moodie

Garden Court Chambers

Sonali Naik

Garden Court Chambers

Greg O'Ceallaigh

Garden Court Chambers

Rory O'Ryan

Garden Court North Chambers

Bryony Poynor

Garden Court Chambers

Desmond Rutledge

Garden Court Chambers

Sadat Sayeed

Garden Court Chambers

Abigail Smith

Garden Court Chambers

Kerry Smith

Garden Court North Chambers

Mark Symes

Garden Court Chambers

Rajeev Thacker

Garden Court Chambers

Anthony Vaughan

Garden Court Chambers

Camille Warren

Garden Court North Chambers

Amanda Weston

Garden Court Chambers

Jo Wilding

Garden Court Chambers

Natalie Wilkins

Garden Court North Chambers

Colin Yeo

Garden Court Chambers

Preface

This has been one of the most trying editions to produce, mostly because of the amount of new material since the last edition, but also because there has been such a radical reshaping of some of the fundamental parts of immigration law.

Let us start with removals and appeals. The Immigration Appeals Act 1969 was passed in response to the report of the Wilson Committee on Immigration Appeals, set up in 1966 and chaired by Sir Roy Wilson QC.[1] The report had been commissioned to provide Commonwealth citizens (but not aliens) with appeals against exclusion, removal and other decisions affecting immigrants. In January 1973 the right of appeal was extended to aliens as well as Commonwealth citizens and included an appeal against deportation. Paragraph 85 got to the heart of the matter, stating that the right of appeal is to provide 'a sense of protection against oppression and injustice, and . . . reassurance against fears of arbitrary action on the part of the Immigration Service' and to ensure a more consistent and rational decision-making process.

Other judicial voices have also made it clear that 'The right of access to justice . . . is a fundamental and constitutional principle of a legal system'[2] and 'a right of access to a tribunal or other adjudicative mechanism established by the state is just as important and fundamental as a right of access to the ordinary courts'.[3] Two important features of a Tribunal appeal are that (a) it is suspensive, meaning that the possibility of removal is suspended until the appeal process is exhausted, and (b) it allows there to be a reconsideration by the Tribunal of the facts by calling witnesses to give live evidence and to produce fresh documentary evidence within certain limits set out in the immigration laws. A Tribunal appeal is, therefore, quite different and more far reaching than judicial review.

Over the years there has been an expansion of appeal rights,[4] coupled with legal aid and assistance to appellants. However, since 2002 there has been a slow whittling down of appeal rights and their suspensive effect by successive governments. This has culminated in the radical changes proposed by the Immigration Act 2014 and being put into effect by successive commencement orders. These involve a root and branch change to the power of removal and to the appellate system, as we have known and used it for so many years. The changes are not only far reaching but also mark a set back to one of the fundamental and constitutional principles of our legal system.

The timing of the commencement orders with the transitional provisions contained in them has meant that we have felt obliged to delay the publication of Volume 1 so that we could properly revise some of our chapters in the light of these developments.

Immigration law is such a moving tapestry of change that it is in fact very difficult not to be already out of date on or soon after our publication date on at least one topic. But we felt that the changes to the powers of removal and to the ambit of appeal rights are of such importance that we needed to be as up to date as possible. Thus the delay in publishing Volume 1 until early 2015.

As well as changing removal powers and rights of appeal, the Immigration Act 2014 accelerates the process of drawing ever more state and non-state actors into the apparatus of immigration control. The effect is to create a society that is suspicious of and hostile to people perceived to be migrants, an aim recently and chillingly articulated by the government when it explained its refusal to support operations to rescue drowning migrants from the Mediterranean on the basis that to do so would encourage others.[5] Now landlords, banks, health practitioners, and driving licensors are turned into quasi-immigration officers because they are required by the Act to regulate access to their property and services according to the immigration status of their would-be tenants, customers, patients and licensees. The danger is the Act will further the creation of a class of outlaws and promote widespread discrimination by these new regulators who, out of fear of being penalised for providing assistance to outlaws, will refuse their services to those who look like or talk like migrants or have foreign names. The Act also adds to the information gathering and information sharing powers of the state.

Other notable changes since the publication of the last Supplement have been the changes to the availability of legal aid in immigration cases for both Tribunal appeals, such as they now are, and to judicial review. We now have over 50 immigration specialist barristers in Garden Court and Garden Court North. All but two of the contributors to this edition are from these two chambers. Many spend a large chunk of their time speaking at training conferences and passing their knowledge and experience to other practitioners. Many also take part with other practitioners in ILPA training sessions. All this effort to try and keep practitioners abreast of the law is of diminished value if our learning and experience cannot be brought to the benefit of immigration clients because they no longer have access to justice in the absence of available legal aid.

Legal aid is not a topic that we have dealt with in previous editions other than in passing. In this edition we have covered legal aid in a separate section of Chapter 1, prepared by Alison Harvey the Legal Director of the Immigration Law Practitioners' Association.

Although the new family and 'private life' rules were first introduced as long ago as July 2012, they are dealt with for the first time in this edition of the book together with the increasingly important list of relevant cases. But we still have to live with the dreadful lettering/numbering of the paragraphs in Appendix FM (thankfully not followed in Appendix FM S-E). We have it on good authority that the lady in the Home Office who drafted the rules makes no admission whatsoever that she had anything to do with the lettering/numbering. But whoever was responsible, it is one more example of an ongoing process of making immigration law impossibly complex and impenetrable.

Article 8 of the European Convention on Human Rights so far as it applies to immigration and asylum now appears to have two or possibly three sets of identities – first of all there are the Immigration Rules, first introduced in July 2012 and repeatedly altered thereafter. Then there is the Immigration Act 2014 and last but not least the autonomous meaning applicable to all signatory countries to the Convention and referred to in section 6 of the Human Rights Act 1998. It would appear that these identities sometimes cross paths; they sometimes coincide; and they sometimes run in separate but parallel paths. The Courts have been trying to make sense of it all since the 2012 rule changes. Now the Immigration Act 2014 has added its own statutory interpretation. It is all very confusing. We try to give guidance in the chapters of this edition.

We have included a new Chapter on human trafficking. It is a subject that has attracted increasing attention from international, European and domestic legislators, courts and policy makers as well as from UN bodies and international and national NGOs. This is having an impact on the legal framework for controlling immigration as well as on the protective obligations that the UK has towards migrants who may have been trafficked and may still be being trafficked.

A number of changes have been made to the Chapter numbers. The former Chapters 3 and 4 are now contained in one Chapter 3. This means that ex Chapters 5-9 become 4-8; ex Chapter 9A (students) becomes Chapter 9. Chapters 10, 11 and 12 remain the same, the new chapter on trafficking comes in as Chapter 13. So all the following chapters cease to be Chapters 13-21 and become Chapters 14-22.

We would like to thank Alison Harvey of ILPA and all the other contributors who are listed after this Preface, and who have given up so much of their time to do either bits of chapters or in some cases to supervise the editing of whole chapters. We would also like to thank Tania Poscotis for co-ordinating the whole process in chambers and who liaised with our publishers. We would also like to thank Brigid and Cameron Baillie and Amarjit Ahluwalia and William Toal for their support and forbearance during the whole process of writing and editing.

The law is stated as at 1 November 2014.

Ian Macdonald QC
Ronan Toal
5 December 2014

[1] 1967 Cmnd 3387

[2] R (on the application of Anufrijeva) v Secretary of State for the Home Department [2003] UKHL 36, [2004] 1 AC 604, per Lord Steyn at para 26.

[3] R (Asifa Saleem) v Secretary of State for the Home Department [2000] EWCA Civ 186, [2000] 4 All ER 814, per Hale LJ

[4] Such as the suspensive right of appeal for nearly all asylum seekers under the Asylum and Immigration Appeals Act 1993, the setting up of SIAC under the Special Immigration Appeals Commission Act 1997, and the right to argue human rights breaches under section 6 of the Human Rights Act 1998, when it came into force in 2000.

[5] Baroness Anelay, Minister of State, Foreign Office, House of Lords Hansard, 15.10.2014 WA 41

Contents

Contents

Contents

Contents

Contents

Contents

Contents

Contents

Contents

VOLUME 2

For the full contents listing, see Volume 2

Table of Statutes

Table of Statutory Instruments

Table of Immigration Rules

Table of Conventions and Agreements

Table of Conventions and Agreements

Table of European Legislation

Secondary Legislation

Decisions

Table of Cases

A

Table of Cases

B

C

F

I

Table of Cases

M

Table of Cases

N

O

Table of Cases

Table of Cases

Table of Cases

Table of Cases

Table of Cases

Table of Cases

Table of Cases

Table of Cases

S

Table of Cases

T

U

V

W

Z

Decisions of the European Court of Justice are listed below numerically. These decisions are also included in the preceding alphabetical list.

Table of Cases

Table of Cases

Table of Cases

C-483/09 and C-1/10: Guyez and Sanchez (Salmeron) v Spain (X and Y Intervening) [2011] ECR I-8263, [2013] All ER (EC) 446, [2012] 1 WLR 2672, [2012] 1 CMLR 667, [2012] 1 FLR 268, [2011] All ER (D) 85 (Sep), ECJ 6.80
C-516/09: Borger v Tiroler Gebietskrankenkasse [2011] ECR I-1493, [2011] All ER (D) 132 (Mar), ECJ 6.95
C-7/10: Staatssecretaris van Justitie v Kahveci (Tayfun) [2012] 2 CMLR 1071, ECJ
.... 6.207
C-9/10: Staatssecretaris van Justitie v Inan [2012] 2 CMLR 1071, ECJ 6.207
C-69/10: Samba Diouf v Ministre du Travail, de l'Emploi et de l'Immigration [2011] ECR I-7151, [2012] 1 CMLR 204, ECJ 12.15
C-186/10: Oguz v Secretary of State for the Home Department [2011] ECR I-6957, [2012] 1 WLR 709, [2012] ICR 335, (2011) Times, 21 November, [2011] All ER (D) 96 (Aug), ECJ 6.212
C-187/10: Unal (Baris) v Staatssecretaris van Justitie [2011] ECR I-9045, [2012] ICR D1, [2011] All ER (D) 33 (Oct), ECJ 6.199
C-411/10: NS v Secretary of State for the Home Department (Amnesty International Ltd and the AIRE Centre (Advice on Individual Rights in Europe) (UK)) [2013] QB 102, [2012] All ER (EC) 1011, [2012] 3 WLR 1374, [2012] 29 LS Gaz R 28, [2012] All ER (D) 12 (Jul), ECJ 6.3, 6.61, 7.10, 7.52, 12.20, 12.78, 12.147, 12.157, 12.158, 12.160, 12.164
C-424/10: Ziolkowski v Land Berlin [2014] All ER (EC) 314, [2013] 3 CMLR 1013, [2012] Imm AR 421, [2012] INLR 467, ECJ 6.7, 6.19, 6.21, 6.38, 6.163, 14.63, 14.64
C-425/10: Szeja v Land Berlin [2014] All ER (EC) 314, [2013] 3 CMLR 1013, [2012] Imm AR 421, [2012] INLR 467, ECJ 6.7, 6.21, 6.38, 6.163, 14.63, 14.64
C-493/10: ME v Refugee Applications Comr (Amnesty International Ltd and the AIRE Centre (Advice on Individual Rights in Europe) (UK)) [2013] QB 102, [2012] All ER (EC) 1011, [2012] 3 WLR 1374, [2012] 29 LS Gaz R 28, [2012] All ER (D) 12 (Jul), ECJ 6.3, 6.61, 7.10, 12.78
C-497/10 PPU: Mercredi v Chaffe [2012] Fam 22, [2010] ECR I-14309, [2011] 3 WLR 1229, [2011] 1 FLR 1293, [2011] Fam Law 351, ECJ 4.7, 11.11
C-522/10: Reichel-Albert v Deutsche Rentenverichtserung Nordbayern [2012] 3 CMLR 1135, [2012] All ER (D) 289 (Jul), ECJ 6.95
C-620/10: Migrationsverket v Kastrati [2013] 1 WLR 1, ECJ 12.166
C-4/11: Federal Republic of Germany v Puid (Kaveh) [2014] QB 346, [2014] 2 WLR 98, [2013] All ER (D) 198 (Nov), ECJ 12.160, 12.166, 12.172
C-15/11: Sommer (Leopold) v Landesgeschäftsstelle des Arbeitsmarktservice Wien (21 June 2012, unreported), ECJ 6.26
C-40/11: Iida v Stadt Ulm [2013] Fam 121, [2014] All ER (EC) 619, [2013] 2 WLR 788, [2013] 1 CMLR 1289, [2012] All ER (D) 204 (Nov), ECJ 6.83, 6.85, 6.92, 6.175
C-71/11: Bundesrepublik Deutschland v Y [2013] All ER (EC) 1144, [2013] 1 CMLR 175, [2012] All ER (D) 51 (Sep), ECJ 12.34, 12.72
C-83/11: Secretary of State for the Home Department v Rahman [2013] QB 249, [2014] All ER (EC) 340, [2013] 2 WLR 230, [2012] 3 CMLR 1315, [2012] All ER (D) 48 (Sep), ECJ 6.140
C-99/11: Bundesrepublik Deutschland v Z [2013] All ER (EC) 1144, [2013] 1 CMLR 175, [2012] All ER (D) 51 (Sep), ECJ 12.34, 12.72
C-147/11: Secretary of State for Work and Pensions v Czop [2013] Imm AR 104, [2013] PTSR 334, [2012] All ER (D) 65 (Sep), ECJ 6.7, 14.69
C-148/11: Secretary of State for Work and Pensions v Punakova [2013] PTSR 334, [2012] All ER (D) 65 (Sep), ECJ 6.7
C-221/11: Demirkan v Germany [2014] 1 CMLR 39, ECJ 6.213
C-245/11: K v Bundesasylamt [2013] 1 WLR 883, [2012] All ER (D) 137 (Nov), ECJ
.... 12.163, 12.172
C-249/11: Byankov v Glaven sekretar na Ministerstvo na vatreshnite raboti [2013] QB 423, [2013] 2 WLR 293, [2013] 1 CMLR 451, [2012] All ER (D) 47 (Oct), ECJ 6.151
C-256/11: Dereci v Bundesministerium für Inneres [2011] ECR I-11315, [2012] All ER (EC) 373, [2012] 1 CMLR 1311, ECJ . 6.74, 6.75, 6.76, 6.79, 6.80, 6.82, 6.83, 6.84, 6.92, 6.144, 6.175, 6.212, 7.102, 16.101
C-268/11: Gulbahce v Freie und Hanestadt Hamburg [2013] ICR 389, [2012] All ER (D) 182 (Nov), ECJ 6.199

Chapter 1

INTRODUCING IMMIGRATION LAW

INTRODUCTION

1.1 This is the 31st anniversary of the publication of this work and the ninth edition. When I wrote the first edition all the earlier immigration statutes had been appealed there were two main Acts of parliament, one, consisting of 35 sections and 4 schedules, one of which had already been repealed – the original Immigration Act 1971. The second was the British Nationality Act 1981 and the day on which it came into force coincided with the UK joining what was then called the European Common Market. The Immigration Rules extended to 40 pages, including a two page table of contents. Then there seven statutory Instruments covering 37 pages. There was quite a lot of case law. But the point is that it was all very manageable. Now there are 17 statutes. Only one has been repealed. The original HC 395, when it was laid before Parliament in 1994 was 80 pages long. There have been over 100 rule changes since then and the amended HC 395 has become increasingly complex. The July 2014 consolidated version which is available on line from the GOV.UK website extends to 1,490 pages, 775 in the main part and 715 in the Appendices. It is at least still one document even though the numbering uses every letter of the alphabet in every combination as add-ons both before and after the numerals.

1.2 This not a intended as a whine. It is to highlight the problem of writing a text book which can keep pace with all the changes that take place on an almost daily basis. Judges, practitioners, immigration officers and government officials are inundated with information.[1] Our task is to understand and collate all this material in the ensuing chapters. We have always used this chapter as a short summary of the development of modern immigration law, giving a short account of the statutes as they were enacted, the sources of immigration law and the key personnel. We then deal with features of immigration law, which crop up within many of the main subject areas, such as discrimination and fee charging. In this edition we deal for the first time with legal aid, without which all this agglomeration of skills and knowledge counts for so much less than it should, because our clients are becoming less and less able to access the knowledge and experience embodied in this work.

¹   In *DP (United States of America) v Secretary of State for the Home Department* [2012] EWCA Civ 365, para 14 Longmore LJ lamented, with good reason, the absolute whirlwind which litigants and judges now feel themselves in due to the speed with which the law, practice and policy change in this field of law. Quoted with approval by Lord Hope in *R (on the application of Alvi) v Secretary of State for the Home Department* [2012] UKSC 33, [2012] 4 All ER 1041 at para 11.

A BRIEF HISTORY OF IMMIGRATION LAW

1.3 The first of the modern immigration laws was the Aliens Act 1905, which was then updated during World War I (1914–18) and eventually became the Aliens Order 1953. This provided a system of work permits for aliens seeking employment in the UK, registration with the police and deportation for the public good. It applied only to aliens but not commonwealth citizens. At that time all British subjects or commonwealth citizens (terms used interchangeably) as set out in the British Nationality Act 1948 were free to come to and go from the UK as they wished under what might well be described as a Common Law right of abode.¹

¹   See *DPP v Bhagwan* [1972] AC 60, [1970] 3 All ER 97, HL.

Aliens, British subjects and the prerogative¹

¹   (1608) 2 State Tr 559.

1.4 Aliens have, at least since Calvin's case¹, been distinguished from British subjects, who later morphed into Commonwealth citizens. Recent use of the term 'aliens' by the senior judiciary has somewhat lost sight of this distinction and uses the term to mean all those who are subject to immigration control.² Even to-day 'foreign criminals', defined by statute as those who are not British citizens for the purposes of automatic deportation, is still a distinct category from the term 'aliens' which is still defined by reference to nationality law. Furthermore aliens have traditionally been divided into alien friends and alien enemies³. Alien enemies have no civil rights or privileges unless they are here under the protection and by the permission of the Crown. Alien friends, on the other hand, have long since been treated in reference to civil rights as if they were British subjects.⁴ Friendly aliens were never controlled by the prerogative power, at least since the 1770s. In a directive issued to all British missions in 1852, the Foreign Secretary, Earl Granville, made it clear that:

'By the existing laws of Great Britain, all foreigners have the unrestricted right of entrance and residence in this country . . . No foreigner, as such, can be sent out of the country by the Executive Government, except persons removed by treaties with other States, confirmed by Act of Parliament, for the mutual surrender of criminal offenders.'[5]

2   See *G1 v Secretary of State for the Home Department* [2012] EWCA Civ 867.
3   Following a critical review of the history section of this book's 5th edition, Dr Prakash Shah very kindly drew our attention to a number of academic Articles and books, including Dr Christopher Vincenzi's important Article *Aliens and the judicial review of Immigration Law* (1985) Pub L 93, which we have used heavily in this section, as well as his own book *Refugees, Race and The Legal Concept of Asylum in Britain* (Cavendish Publishing 2000), which we have also used.
4   *Porter v Freudenberg* [1915] 1 KB 857, per Lord Reading CJ, dictum approved in Ertel Bieber & Co v Rio Tinto Co [1918] AC 260, at 268. Contrast *Silvester's Case* (1701) 7 Mod 150 (alien enemy), cited by Vincenzi, p 107.
5   State Papers, vol 42 (1852–1853), quoted by Vincenzi at p 107, Shah, below, at p 24, and B Porter *The Refugee Question in Mid Victorian Politics* (Cambridge CUP 1979) p 149.

1.5 Immediately prior to the Aliens Act 1905, friendly aliens were as free to come to Britain as British subjects and could not be removed or deported by executive act. That was why the Act was enacted. According to Dr Vincenzi, every removal or exclusion of aliens during the previous 200 years or more had been taken to Parliament for authorisation, whether temporary in effect[1] or permanent.[2] Likewise the Foreign Deserters Act 1852 and the Extradition Act 1870 'enabled' the Crown to hand over deserters and fugitive offenders to foreign powers. In none of these statutes, passed while the country was at peace, is there any mention of a Crown prerogative relating to aliens, or any reservation of one.[3] The first appearance of a reservation is in the Aliens Restriction Act 1914, passed on the outbreak of World War I,[4] intended to preserve the Crown's undoubted prerogative power in relation to enemy aliens.[5] The Immigration Act 1971 contains a similar power, never used but clearly intending to preserve the same powers.

1   For example, Aliens Act 1793 33 George III c 4; Aliens Act 1848 11 & 12 Victoria c 20.
2   For example, the Aliens Act 1905, the Aliens Restriction Act 1914. For a full history see Prakash Shah, ch 3.
3   Vincenzi at p 107.
4   Aliens Restriction Act 1914 s 1(6).
5   See *R v Commandant of Knockaloe Camp, ex p Forman* (1917) 82 JP 41.

1.6 In the Supreme Court it was pointed out in *Munir*[1] with Lord Dyson stating:

'These inferences are supported by the fact that, when promoting the 1971 Act, the Government made it clear that it intended that the use of the prerogative should be limited to controlling the entry of enemy aliens into the United Kingdom.'

He then referred to the debate in parliament on 3.8.71 which made this clear.[2] In *Alvi*[3] Lord Hope went further and said:

'But it is hard to see how that provision, which may have been thought appropriate 40 years ago, can have any practical effect today. One has only to think of the possibility of a challenge under article 5 of the European Convention on Human Rights, which declares that no one shall be deprived of his liberty save in accordance with a procedure prescribed by law. The old order, under which such a sweeping power could be exercised at will by the executive, is now long gone.'

1   *R (on the application of Munir) v Secretary of State for the Home Department (Joint Council for the Welfare of Immigrants intervening)* [2012] UKSC 32, at para 32.

2   Hansard (HL Debates) 3 August 1971, Col 1046-1047.
3   *R (on the application of Alvi) v Secretary of State for the Home Department* [2012] UKSC 33, at para 30.

1.7 Dicta in the Privy Council cases of *Musgrove v Chun Teeong Toy, Attorney General for Canada v Cain* and in the Scottish case of *Johnstone v Pedlar* which support the existence of a prerogative power in relation to all aliens,[1] and further dicta in the mid- twentieth century cases of *R v Governor of Brixton Prison, ex p Soblen* and *Schmidt v Secretary of State for the Home Department*, which contain very firm assertions of the existence of such a power,[2] are not matched by the practice or views of successive British governments. In any event, as Lord Hope made clear in Alvi, at paras 28–30, above, they have long since been replaced by statute.

1   *Musgrove v Chun Teeong Toy* [1891] AC 272, 282; *A-G for Canada v Cain* [1906] AC 542, 546, and *Johnstone v Pedlar* [1921] 2 AC 262, 283, where Lord Atkinson said: 'Aliens, whether friendly or enemy, can be lawfully prevented from entering this country and can be expelled from it . . .'
2   *R v Bottrill, ex p Kuechenmeister* [1947] 1 KB 41, at p 51, per Scott LJ, *R v Governor of Brixton Prison, ex p Soblen* [1963] 2 QB 243, 300, CA and *Schmidt v Secretary of State for Home Affairs* [1969] 2 Ch 149, 168. See also *R (on the application of BAPIO Action Ltd) v Secretary of State for the Home Department* [2008] UKHL 27, [2008] 1 AC 1003, para 4, per Lord Bingham.

1.8 These older decisions have been given detailed scrutiny by Dr Vincenzi in his Article and are found wanting. We need not repeat his telling deconstruction here. Undoubtedly the *Musgrove* judgment has been identified as a turning point in legal thinking[1]. At about the same time the US Supreme Court, drawing inspiration from *Vattel*, in the case of a Japanese national, declared that according to international law a State had the discretion to admit whomsoever it saw fit.[2] This view has proved persistent to the present day, influencing a judicial perception at that time that excluded aliens were not deserving of a detailed scrutiny of their claims. Dr Shah goes further.[3] He says:

'What is significant is that such case law developed as a result of the exclusion of particular racial groups (blacks, Japanese, Chinese and South Asian) that were not deserving of an equal right of free movement, and that judges in legal systems across the Anglo-Saxon world tended to accommodate legislative demands to exclude such people.'

We shall come back to the modern application of the Prerogative when we deal with the Prerogative as a source of immigration law at **1.33**, below

1   At the time it gave rise to a lively academic debate: see Craies 'The Right of Aliens to Enter British territory' (1890) 6 Law Quarterly Revue 27–41 and Haycraft 'Alien Legislation and The Prerogative of the Crown' (1897) 13 Law Quarterly Review 165–168; Shah p 28. Referred to by Shah p 28.
2   *Nishimura Ekiu v United States of America* 142 US 651 at 659. Cited by Shah at p 29. See also Richard Plender *International Migration Law* (2nd edn, 1988) p 64ff. In these judicial pronouncements, the views of international jurists who took a less tenacious perspective were totally ignored; Plender pp 72–75.
3   Shah, p 29.

1.9 The position of British subjects is also important. The traditional view is that their situation stood in direct contrast to that of aliens.[1] It is said that at common law all British subjects had a right of abode in the UK. Prior to 1962 they enjoyed this right whether they lived in the UK or elsewhere, and whether or not they were citizens of the United Kingdom and Colonies (CUKCs). Under the British Nationality Act 1948 British subjects were also known as 'Commonwealth citizens' and the two terms were interchangeable until 1983.[2] British Protected Persons were not British subjects and, therefore, had no right of abode, but they were under British protection.[3] In *DPP v Bhagwan*[4] Lord Diplock referred to this right of abode:

'Prior to the passing of the Commonwealth Immigrants Act 1962, the Respondent as a British Subject had the right at common law to enter the United Kingdom without let or hindrance when and where he pleased and to remain here as long as he liked. That right he still retained in 1967 save insofar as it was restricted or qualified by the provisions of the Act.'[5]

This was first time such a right had been mentioned in any case, and it was made without any reference to authority. So far as we know there is none. However, bearing in mind Sir Robert Megarry's famous quote about the difference between directly enforceable nominate rights and liberties:

'England . . . is a country where everything is permitted except what is expressly forbidden.'[6]

and applying it to Lord Diplock's speech, it is possible to read his 'right' as no more than one aspect or consequence of the British subject's right not to be restrained without lawful authority and an expression of the situation, as it existed under the British Nationality Act 1948, under which all CUKCs had a right to come freely to the UK and go from it. But here is the rub. As we have seen, friendly aliens were in exactly the same position, at least until 1891.[7] They could not be restrained except by lawful authority. It was already well established by 1772 that an alien in territorial waters who was in the process of being forcibly removed from the country could secure his or her release by *habeas corpus*, as in *Somerset v Stewart*,[8] where Lord Mansfield ordered the release of an African-born slave being detained on board a ship bound for the American colonies.[9] So, as Dr Vincenzi argues, 'the more accurate way of describing the position of both subjects and aliens would be to say that neither has rights of entry into the United Kingdom as such, at common law, only a freedom from restraint, in the absence of statutory authority, at the port of entry'.[10] With these qualifications we can accept Lord Diplock's dictum, but, if we are right, it also means that friendly aliens still retained that right 'save insofar as it was restricted or qualified' by statute, but they could not be made subject to coercive deportation.[11]

---

[1]   This was the view taken in the first five editions of this book, We quoted Calvin's Case (1608) 2 State Tr 559; *Musgrove v Chun Teeong Toy* [1891] AC 272; and *A-G for Canada v Cain; A-G for Canada v Gilhula* [1906] AC 542. It was an easy assumption to make, given that at the time of the passing of the British Nationality Act 1948 aliens were controlled by the Aliens Order 1953, but no restrictions were placed on British subjects or Commonwealth citizens, as they were also called: British Nationality Act 1948, s 1(2).

[2]   British Nationality Act 1948, s 1(2); British Nationality Act 1981, s 51.

[3]   British Nationality Act 1948, s 1(3); *R v Secretary of State for the Home Department, ex p Thakrar* [1974] QB 684, [1974] 2 All ER 261, CA; *R v Chief Immigration Officer, Gatwick Airport, ex p Singh (Harjendar)* [1987] Imm AR 346, QBD.

[4]   [1972] AC 60, [1970] 3 All ER 97, HL.

[5]   [1970] 3 All ER 97 at 99.

[6]   Sir Robert Megarry VC in *Malone v Metropolitan Police Comr* [1979] Ch 344, at 366, cited at Vincenzi, op cit, p 97.

[7]   *Musgrove v Chun Teeong Toy* [1891] AC 272, above.

8   *R v Knowles, ex parte Somerset* (1772) 20 State Tr 1; (1772) Lofft 1; *R v Lesley (or Leslie)* (1860) Bell CC 220; *Ex p Lo Pak* (1888) IX NSWR 221 (application for *habeas corpus*, in which the Prerogative was raised by the Crown, but rejected by the High Court of New South Wales as a bad return); *Ex p Leong Kum* (1888) IX NSWR 250. These cases are all cited by Vincenzi op cit, at p 98.

9   There the lawyers representing Somerset had a field day, achieving degrees of high-flown eloquence rarely seen in a court. Mansfield, however, dithered. Eventually he gave judgment granting *habeas corpus* and discharging the prisoner. Unfortunately there is no official version of his judgment. As a result legal academics have argued for years over precisely what legal precedent was set in the case: see for example, Jerome Nadelhaft, The Somersett Case and Slavery: Myth, Reality and Representation; Edward Fiddes, 'Lord Mansfield and the Sommersett Case', 50 LQR 499 (1934); James Oldham, '*New Light of Mansfield and Slavery*', 27 Journal of British Studies 45 (1988).

10 Vincenzi, op cit, pp 98–99.

11 The passage of the judgment in *Somersett* in the published law report does not appear to refer to the removal from the country of slaves by force, whereas the same passage in the informal report by letter to The Times does (quoted in Simon Schama, *Rough Crossings – Britain, The Slaves and The American Revolution* (BBC Books, 2006). In this version of his judgment Lord Mansfield repeated and recognised the judgment of Lord Hardwicke, sitting as Chancellor on 19 October 1749 in *Pearne v Lisle* (1749) Amb 75, 27 ER 47, which had confirmed that slaves were mere items of property (Hardwicke described them as 'like stock on a farm') who were not emancipated either by becoming a Christian or by entry into England, and that possession of them could be recovered by the legal action of trover, and that their master might legally compel them to leave England with him, but he held that a foreigner cannot be imprisoned here on the authority of any law existing in his own country; and the power claimed by this return was never in use here; no master ever was allowed here to take a slave by force to be sold abroad because he had deserted from his service, or for any other reason whatever; we cannot say the cause set forth by this return is allowed or approved of by the laws of this kingdom, therefore the man must be discharged. The case was, therefore decided on the basis that coercive deportation of a foreigner was not allowed by the laws of England. This narrow interpretation was confirmed by Lord Mansfield in a later judgment. In 1785, he expressed the view in *R v Inhabitants of Thames Ditton* (1785) 4 Doug 300, 99 ER 891 that all the *Somersett* case decided was that a slave could not be forcibly removed from England against his will, which would support the account of his judgment given in The Times letter, and is the strongest argument for a limited scope to the decision. It should further be noted that in at least one of the cases which the abolitionist, James Sharpe won, prior to *Somersett's* case, he did so on the grounds that coercive deportation of a foreigner was unlawful: in 1768, he had helped bring a suit against the owners of the female slave who had shipped her back to the West Indies notwithstanding that she had married a freed black. Invoking the unlawfulness of coercive transportation, Sharp and his lawyer managed to secure a judgment demanding the return, cost paid, of the woman: see Schama, *Rough Crossings – Britain, The Slaves and The American Revolution*, as above.

1.10 Do these matters have any bearing on what is happening to-day? In nearly all the case law under the ECHR, involving the removal of immigrants or asylum seekers, references are made to the right which sovereign States possess under international law to regulate the entry of aliens into their territory. Undoubtedly this right exists, but it is a right, which requires regulation in accordance with applicable constitutional principles and which applies subject to any treaty obligation of a State or rule of the State's domestic law which may apply to the exercise of that control.[1] In Strasbourg cases the court makes frequent reference to this right, always making it clear that it is subject to any treaty obligations the State has entered into.[2] The British courts do the same, but usually excluding mention that the right requires regulation by law or stating that it may in part at least be controlled by an exercise of the prerogative, which, unless regulated by statute, gives the Crown an unfettered discretion over aliens.[3] The significance of the reference to the international law right in the Strasbourg case law is twofold. First the need to uphold and protect the individual's Convention rights is a qualification or limitation upon the exercise of immigration control.[4] Secondly, in the case of qualified rights, the exigencies of immigration control may call into play one or more of the public interests, economic wellbeing, prevention of crime and so on, named in Article 8(2) and the other qualified rights. However, if immigration law is seen as some kind of extension to an unfettered prerogative power, it is all too easy to give it undue weight in determining the issue of proportionality. In rejecting human rights claims to enter or remain in the UK for family or private life reasons, the Secretary of State invariably makes the point that Article 8 of ECHR does not guarantee a person or their family the right to choose to live in the United Kingdom. Well, sometimes it does; sometimes it does not. Where the choice of where to live is an issue, the right of a state to control immigration is not the answer to it. The issue is whether it is reasonable in all the particular circumstances of the case to expect family or private life to take place in the country of origin. Where the family is already settled in the UK the right to choose where to live is not the issue; more likely the issue is whether interference with established family life is necessary in the interests of preventing crime and so forth. The objection to the over-emphasis on the right to live in Britain is that it risks becoming a factor on its own in favour of interference and creating a presumption in favour of refusing a human rights claim. In short, it becomes an additional factor weighing against the applicant. In our view there can be no presumptive non-breach of Article 8 by reason of the public international law right to control immigration into a sovereign state's territory.

[1] See eg per Lord Slynn in *R (on the application of Saadi) v Secretary of State for the Home Department* [2002] UKHL 41, [2002] 1 WLR 3131, para 31.

[2] *Vilvarajah v United Kingdom* (1991) 14 EHRR 248, para 102; *Chahal v United Kingdom* (1996) 23 EHRR 413, para 73; *D v United Kingdom* (1997) 24 EHRR 423, para 46; *Bensaid v United Kingdom* (2001) 33 EHRR 205, para 32; *Boultif v Switzerland* (2001) 33 EHRR 1179, para 46.

[3] *R (on the application of Saadi) v Secretary of State for the Home Department* [2002] UKHL 41, [2002] 1 WLR 3131, at para 31: *R (on the application of Ullah) v Special Adjudicator* [2004] UKHL 26, [2004] 2 AC 323 at para 6; *Odelola v Secretary of State for the Home Department* [2009] UKHL 25, [2010] Imm AR 59, per Lord Brown at paras 12 and 35. In *European Roma Rights Centre v Immigration Officer at Prague Airport (United Nations High Commissioner for Refugees intervening)* [2004] UKHL 55, [2005] 2 WLR 1, at para 9 Lord Bingham quoted with approval a reference by Sir William Holdsworth (A History of English Law, Vol X, pp 395–396) to a judgment by Jeffreys CJ in *East India Co v Sandys (Case of Monopolies)* (1685) 10 State Tr 371, at 530–531, when he said: 'I conceive the King had an absolute power to forbid foreigners, whether merchants or others, from coming within his dominions, both in times of war and in times of peace, according to his royal will and pleasure; and therefore gave safe-conducts to merchants strangers, to come in, at all ages, and at his pleasure commanded them out again.' This 17th century authority, seen then as part of the absolute power of the sovereign, predates the much more cogent position taken nearly a century later when the issues of coercive deportation and slavery merged to produce a fairly emphatic denial of the power to forcibly remove an alien slave from this country. It would be a shame to have to fight the battles of the 17th century between royal absolutism and the sovereignty of Parliament all over again.'

[4] It also has to be remembered in what context these questions of a state's right to control immigration first arose. It is derived from the case of *Abdulaziz, Cabales and Balkandali v United Kingdom* (1985) 7 EHRR 471. That case was dealing with persons who had yet to establish any kind of residence or immigration status in the UK but who wished to join their spouses who were already there. The phrase arose because of the British government's submission that the ECHR had no application at all in immigration cases, a submission which the court rejected. Since then the Supreme Court decision in *R (on the application of Aguilar Quila) v Secretary of State for the Home Department* [2011] UKSC 45, per Lord Wilson at paragraphs 42 and 43, specifically disavows and declines to follow the case of *Abdulaziz* on

the proposition that Article 8 imposes no general obligation on a state to facilitate the choice made by a married couple to reside in it.

Commonwealth Immigrants Act 1962

1.11 Commonwealth citizens aka British subjects were first made subject to statutory immigration control in the UK by the Commonwealth Immigrants Act 1962. They were never on any view subject to control prior to this under any prerogative power.[1] This Act was brought into force mainly as a result of a campaign against black Commonwealth citizens already here. The Act made a distinction between CUKCs and citizens of independent Commonwealth countries, and based control upon the kind of passport held by the would-be immigrant. All Commonwealth citizens became subject to immigration control except the following:

(a) persons born in the UK;

(b) holders of UK passports issued by the UK government as opposed to those issued on behalf of the government of a Crown colony or of some other part of the Commonwealth;[2]

(c) other persons included in the passport of one of the persons excluded from immigration control under (a) or (b) above.

---

[1] Whatever may be the position with regard to aliens, which we have discussed above, the absence of any prerogative power in relation to Commonwealth immigration is unchallenged. In order to manage this new statutory control the government began publishing Immigration Rules in relation to Commonwealth citizens. Their issue had nothing to do with the prerogative. They were administrative acts in the exercise of the Secretary of State's statutory powers, giving guidance on how he or she would exercise these new statutory powers. It is therefore something of a surprise that in *Odelola v Secretary of State for the Home Department* [2009] UKHL 25, [2010] Imm AR 59, Lord Brown should state at para 35 that: 'The Secretary of State's Immigration Rules, as and when promulgated, indicate how it is proposed to exercise the prerogative power of immigration control'. In para 35 Lord Brown appears to base his view on a reading of section 33(5) of the Immigration Act 1971, a section which preserves a prerogative power in relation only to aliens. In our view, as already argued above, it is the preservation of an undoubted prerogative power retained to deal with hostile aliens in time of war. On any view it can have no application to immigration control over Commonwealth citizens. Perhaps the best way to deal with it is to treat it as an ill-considered obiter dictum. Nevertheless, it is of some concern to see that prerogative power still lurks in this area of law like the undead in Transylvania. For a different view of the Immigration Rules, see Lord Hope at para 6 in *Odelola* and the judgment of Sedley LJ in *Secretary of State for the Home Department v Pankina* [2010] EWCA Civ 719, (2010) Times, 20 July, although he appears to classify Immigration Rules in their original form as an exercise of the prerogative power because they do not derive from any empowering primary legislation (a point which is at the very least highly debatable, given that since 1905 Immigration Rules have always been formulated in the exercise of statutory, not prerogative, powers), and so could not be subordinate legislation (para 17), this is quite peripheral to the core of the judgment which is about the need for Immigration Rules, if they are indeed rules of law, to have parliamentary scrutiny and not be creatures of some untrammelled Crown prerogative (paras 18–19).

[2] Commonwealth Immigrants Act 1962, s 1(2) and (3); *R v Secretary of State for the Home Department, ex p Bhurosah (Shadeo)* [1968] 1 QB 266, [1967] 3 All ER 831, CA. Other exemptions from control were given to diplomats (s 17(1)); certain members of Commonwealth armed forces (s 17(2)); persons exempted by the Secretary of State for the Home Department (Commonwealth Immigrants (Control of Immigration) Exemption Order 1965, SI 1965/153); and persons who landed in the UK and spent 28 days without submitting to examination by immigration officers (Commonwealth Immigrants Act 1962, Sch 1, para 1(2),

as amended by Commonwealth Immigrants Act 1968, s 4; and see *R v Governor of Brixton Prison, ex p Ahsan (or Ahsen or Ahson)* [1969] 2 QB 222, [1969] 2 All ER 347).

1.12 In short, CUKCs were exempted from control, except those who were born in Crown Colonies and obtained their passports there. CUKCs who were born in independent Commonwealth countries and who retained that status after independence were exempted from control provided they had a UK passport. A passport issued by the High Commissioner would normally qualify. This category of CUKC comprised, among others, large sections of the Asian community in Kenya, who had expressly been given the option of UK citizenship by the Kenya Independence Act 1963 on exactly the same basis as the European settlers. Similar provisions had been made when Uganda became independent. Under the Commonwealth Immigrants Act 1962 all of these persons were entitled to come to Britain as of right, and many did so, because of the policy of Kenyanisation adopted by the Kenyan government and a similar policy of preference to their own citizens adopted by other East African countries.[1]

[1]   On 'The Legal Basis for the Asian Exodus from Kenya' see Alan H Smith in *Law Guardian* (November 1970). It should also be noted that Asians who opted for Kenyan citizenship rather than UK citizenship after independence were unaffected. Those who opted for UK citizenship, however, clearly did so because they assumed (rightly at the time) that it offered greater security. See further Plender *International Migration Law* (2nd edn, 1988) pp 88–93 and 156.

Commonwealth Immigrants Act 1968

1.13 The Commonwealth Immigrants Act 1968 sought to change all this. Its aim was to bring the East African Asians under immigration control;[1] its method was to divide holders of UK passports into two separate categories, those who could enter Britain without restriction and those who could not. A CUKC, who was the holder of a UK passport issued by the UK government, was now subject to immigration control unless he or she, or at least one parent or grandparent, was born, adopted, naturalised or registered as a CUKC in the UK. Ancestral connection to the UK became the key factor in determining which CUKCs were subject to immigration control. The intention was to keep out East African Asians and it was not difficult to see that the mechanism for doing this was the section defining the necessary ancestral connection. The immediate precedent was to be found in the British Nationality Act 1964, the main aim of which had been to preserve the right to resume UK citizenship to white settlers in Africa who were then under pressure to assume the citizenship of newly-independent African countries. It is a formula which enables politicians and officials to proclaim that there was nothing racist about such laws. In 1971 the requirement of an ancestral connection was further refined by the enactment of the 'patrial' section in the Immigration Act 1971. When British nationality was reformed by the British Nationality Act 1981, 'patriality' was replaced by an extended definition of 'British citizenship', which we look at in CHAPTER 2 below, where we note that some, but not all, of the discrepancies of the 1981 Act are being remedied by the provisions of the British Overseas Territory Act 2002, in relation to former British Dependant Territories Citizens (BDTCs) at section 4B of the British Nationality Act 1981, inserted by section 12 of the Nationality Immigration and Asylum Act 2002. But there is still long way to go before we can speak of a single meaningful

British nationality.

1   See in particular *East African Asians v United Kingdom* (1973) 3 EHRR 76, paras 76, 83–84, 96.

1.14 By the time of the Commonwealth Immigrants Act 1968, the UK had already granted individuals the right to petition the European Commission on Human Rights in Strasbourg over alleged breaches of their human rights, a right whose first exercise was by Commonwealth immigrants, with mixed success.[1] But it was the Asian CUKCs excluded from their country of nationality by the 1968 Act who really began the trend of using the ECHR to seek redress for immigration grievances. Their common law right to enter the UK freely was replaced by a discretionary scheme of special vouchers. Many also lost the right to remain and work in the countries where they were living. Some became destitute. But when they tried to enter Britain they found themselves being shuttlecocked in and out, or being kept in prison.[2] The International Commission of Jurists criticised the 1968 Act at the time of its passing as a violation of international law.[3]

1   *Alam (Mohammed) v United Kingdom (Application 2991/66)*; *Singh (Harbajan) v United Kingdom (Application 2992/66)* (1967) Times, 12 October.
2   'Return to Sender, Report on Shuttlecocks' (September 1970) JCWI, p 1.
3   Bulletin No 34, pp 36–37.

1.15 In *East African Asians v United Kingdom*[1] complaints by a large number of applicants, that their human rights had been infringed by the operation of the 1968 Act, were upheld, and in particular the Commission found as a fact that, notwithstanding the neutrality of the language of the statute, it had racial motives and targeted a racial group, and that the racial discrimination in its operation constituted degrading treatment.[2] The special voucher system continued until March 2002, when it was abolished. Under provisions of the Nationality and Immigration Act 2002 any remaining British nationals who have no other citizenship can register as British citizens.[3] The huge opposition to the 1962 and 1968 Acts, and the real sense of grievance within the immigrant communities, may have been among the factors leading to the setting up of the Committee on Immigration Appeals,[4] whose report led to the Immigration Appeals Act 1969. The 1969 Act gave appeal rights only to Commonwealth citizens (these were extended to aliens by the Immigration Act 1971), and instituted the two-tier system of appeal which survived until 4 April 2005, when the two tiers were amalgamated into one, but which created a reconsideration procedure which evolved into something not that different from the old two-tier system.[5] A two-tier appellate system has now been re-established by the Tribunals, Courts and Enforcement Act 2007.

1   (1973) 3 EHRR 76.
2   (1973) 3 EHRR 76, at paras 197, 202 and 207.
3   Nationality, Immigration and Asylum Act 2002, s 12; British Overseas Territories Act 2002, ss 3, 4. See **2.21** below.
4   Chaired by Rir Roy Wilson QC, Cmd 3387.
5   See *AM (Serbia) v Secretary of State for the Home Department* [2007] EWCA Civ 16, [2007] INLR 211.

1.16 The Immigration Act 1971 repealed all previous legislation, with minor exceptions, and spelled the end of large-scale primary immigration for settlement from the 'new Commonwealth'. The benefits of the right of abode had shrunk to a small, exclusive, largely white group of 'patrials', defined by their connection to the UK through their ancestry. On the same day that the 1971 Act came into force, 1 January 1973, the Treaty of Rome provisions came into force in the UK, giving rights of free movement for work and establishment in business or self-employment to all citizens of the EEC's Member States.[1] The 1971 Act virtually assimilated Commonwealth citizens with aliens, although the former had some residual benefits: some were eligible for the right of abode (which aliens could never have, except on naturalisation), or for exemption from deportation on fulfilling certain residence requirements; and there was a standstill clause preventing the rules on settlement from becoming more restrictive than those enjoyed before 1973 (which operated mainly to exclude Commonwealth citizens seeking family reunion from having to comply with maintenance and accommodation requirements). The standstill clause was repealed in 1988. Commonwealth citizens, in addition, have never had to register with the police. Constitutional innovations brought by the Act, unprecedented in peacetime, included the introduction of powers of administrative detention[2] and, by requiring individuals to prove their British citizenship,[3] reversed the principle of *habeas corpus* that it is for the state to justify deprivation of liberty.[4]

[1] At that time France, Germany, Belgium, Netherlands, Luxembourg, Ireland and Italy.
[2] Immigration Act 1971, Schs 2 and 3.
[3] Immigration Act 1971, s 3(8).
[4] Secretary of State for the *Home Department v Pankina* [2010] EWCA Civ 719, (2010) Times, 20 July.

1.17 The concept of patriality was introduced to entrench the division between persons with the right of abode and those who needed leave to enter. All aliens were non-patrial, as were some Commonwealth citizens and some UK citizens. Thus the harmony between nationality and free movement was destroyed between 1962 and 1971. The British Nationality Act of 1981 attempted to re-align nationality with immigration rights, and in doing so created further confusion and anger. The 1981 Act created out of the former UK and Colonies citizenship several different types of British nationality, only the first of which, British citizenship, carried the right of abode. The other 'citizens', British Dependent Territories citizens, British Overseas citizens (BOCs), British subjects without citizenship, and British Nationals Overseas, remained subject to immigration control. The return of Hong Kong to Chinese control in 1997, and the resulting dramatic reduction in the numbers of British Dependent Territories citizens and British Nationals (Overseas) with no other citizenship, enabled the government to offer some of the remaining British Dependent (now Overseas) Territories citizens and British Nationals (Overseas) British citizenship.[1] The other main category of former CUKCs given lesser citizenship status by the 1981 Act, the BOCs, a category with no right of entry anywhere, may now register as British citizens if they have no other nationality.[2]

[1] British Nationality (Hong Kong) Act 1997; White Paper *Partnership for Progress and Prosperity* (1999); British Overseas Territories Act 2002, ss 3, 4.
[2] Nationality, Immigration and Asylum Act 2002, s 12.

1.18 The politics of immigration and race continued to play a decisive role in developing the law in the 1970s and 1980s. Rules on family settlement became tighter and ever more strictly applied, with virginity tests for brides from the Indian sub-continent causing a furore in the late 1970s[1] and the primary purpose rule[2] keeping husbands out throughout the 1980s and 1990s. The 'standstill' clause preventing the application of harsher rules to Commonwealth settlement after 1973 was repealed in 1988,[3] and appeal rights on deportation were curtailed for those who had been in the UK for less than seven years.[4] By the mid-1980s the first visa controls had been imposed on Commonwealth citizens,[5] and these were swiftly followed by the first carriers' liability measure, the Immigration (Carriers' Liability) Act 1987, pushed through in response to the arrival of visa-less Tamils fleeing Sri Lanka.

[1] See Yellowlees report on medical examination of immigrants, 15 December 1980.
[2] HC 394, para 50 (1980); the burden of proof shifted to the couple to prove that the primary purpose was not settlement in HC 66, para 54 (1982).
[3] Immigration Act 1988, s 1.
[4] Immigration Act 1988, s 5.
[5] India, Sri Lanka, Bangladesh, Ghana, Nigeria.

1.19 The introduction of visa controls on Commonwealth citizens, and of carrier sanctions, were the first domestic manifestation of a pan-European policy to deal with the increasing numbers of asylum seekers arriving in Europe, and it is asylum which has become the big issue in the past two decades. Britain and most European countries had signed up to the 1951 Refugee Convention and its 1967 Protocol. But when Britain and Europe sought unskilled migrant labour during the fifties and sixties to rebuild their ravaged infrastructure and economy, their governments neither knew nor cared what the migrants' motives were. Many who came from Africa and Asia may have been eligible for refugee status under the Convention, but so long as migration for work was possible, asylum was not an issue. The closing of all avenues of migration (save for the highly educated or talented, through the work permit scheme, and the wealthy, through the business and independent means categories) took away a possible escape route when upheavals, sudden regime change, breakdowns and murderous civil wars left devastation in the home country. Asylum became the big issue. Developments in immigration law in the 1980s and 1990s reflected the battle between the exclusionary imperatives of European immigration policy to the poor countries of the world, on the one hand, and the humanitarian imperatives of international human rights law on the other. Visa controls and carrier sanctions were thus calculated to stop refugees and others arriving in Europe. Non-British and non-EU travellers from 'refugee-producing' countries required visas and could not get them.[1] Airlines would not sell tickets to those without visas. Thus the trade in false passports and documents began, and the trafficking trade, with which many of the laws of the 1990s and the early years of the new century deal.

[1] A person is not a 'refugee' under the 1951 Refugee Convention unless he or she is outside his or her own country, and so it is impossible to obtain a 'refugee visa'. For the territorial limitations of the Refugee Convention see *European Roma Rights Centre v Immigration Officer at Prague Airport (United Nations High Commissioner for Refugees intervening)* [2004] UKHL 55, [2005] 2 WLR 1 (**12.9** and **12.36** below).

1.20 The Immigration Act 1971 did not deal with asylum, and rules made under it merely recorded that full account was to be taken of the UK's obligations under the 1951 Refugee Convention when a person seeking to enter or being removed claimed asylum or indicated a fear of persecution. This changed with the Asylum and Immigration Appeals Act 1993, which, with new Immigration Rules introduced in 1994 and asylum procedure rules, made up a statutory scheme for asylum determination and appeals. The scheme gave effect to the developing inter-governmental initiatives in the EEC, in particular the Dublin Convention 1990[1] and the London Resolutions 1992[2] which indicated a common approach to asylum seekers who had travelled through 'safe third countries', or whose claims were otherwise believed to be manifestly ill-founded. On the one hand, the 1993 Act gave in-country appeal rights to all asylum seekers, including those who had travelled through a 'safe' third country, although appeals in such cases were subject to an accelerated procedure. On the other hand, the 1993 Act began the process of placing asylum seekers in a class apart, subjecting them to mass fingerprinting and to separate and inferior provision in the fields of housing and social security. The 1993 Act also removed appeal rights from visitors and other groups defined by the purpose or length of their proposed stay, or by their lack of appropriate documents or other qualifying conditions. It also replaced the right to seek judicial review of Immigration Appeal Tribunal final determinations by a direct appeal to the Court of Appeal on a point of law.

[1] Convention determining the State responsible for examining applications for asylum lodged in one of the Member States of the European Communities, Dublin, 15 June 1990.
[2] Resolution on a harmonised approach to questions concerning host third countries (SN 4823/92 WGI 1283 AS 147); Resolution on manifestly unfounded applications for asylum (SN 4822/92 WGI 1282 ASIM 146), adopted 30 November 1992 and 1 December 1992 by immigration ministers of the EU States; in *Key texts on Justice and Home Affairs in the EU* Vol 1 (1976–1993) (1997) Statewatch Publications.

1.21 The Asylum and Immigration Act 1996 reduced the rights of immigrants and asylum seekers, without any compensatory improvements. Accelerated appeal procedures were extended from third-country cases to whole new categories of asylum seekers.[1] The 1996 Act responded to widespread concern among adjudicators about the admissibility procedures of several European countries, particularly Italy, France and Belgium, by abolishing the suspensive appeal in the case of removal of asylum seekers to an EU destination, leading to a series of judicial review challenges.[2] The 1996 Act also introduced employer sanctions to ensure that those subject to prohibitions on taking employment did not work, provisions which remained in force until 2008, although subject to very light touch enforcement where employers are concerned.[3] But the other, more shocking, change was the wholesale removal from entitlement to basic subsistence benefits of virtually everyone subject to immigration control except for port asylum claimants. Regulations to this effect were introduced in February 1996,[4] but were declared *ultra vires* in their application to asylum seekers in July 1996, because they 'necessarily contemplate for some a life so destitute that . . . no civilised nation can tolerate it . . . . Something so uncompromisingly draconian can only be achieved by primary legislation'.[5] The government duly obliged, enacting the condemned regulation as section 11 of the 1996 Act.

[1] The 'white list' of so-called safe countries under the Asylum (Designated Countries of Destination and Designated Safe Third Countries) Order 1996, SI 1996/2671, included Pakistan, from which women, Ahmadis, Christians and political activists had been found to be refugees. See *Ahmed (Iftikhar) v Secretary of State for the Home Department* [2000] INLR 1

(Ahmadis); *Islam v Secretary of State for the Home Department (United Nations High Comr for Refugees intervening); R v Immigration Appeal Tribunal, ex p Shah (United Nations High Comr for Refugees intervening)* [1999] 2 AC 629, [1999] INLR 144, HL (women). The designation of Pakistan was held unlawful in *R (on the application of Javed) v Secretary of State for the Home Department* upheld [2001] EWCA Civ 789, [2002] QB 129.

2   See eg *R v Secretary of State for the Home Department, ex p Canbolat* [1997] Imm AR 442; *Kerrouche (Mohammed) v Secretary of State for the Home Department [1997] Imm AR 610* [1997] Imm AR 610; *Iyadurai v Secretary of State for the Home Department* [1998] Imm AR 470; *R v Secretary of State for the Home Department, ex p Adan* [1999] Imm AR 521, CA; affd [2001] INLR 44, HL: see Chapter 12 below.

3   See **14.90** below for the current position. The new law kicks in for all employment starting on or after 29 February 2008 and the 1996 sanctions will continue to apply to any earlier employment: see the Immigration, Asylum and Nationality Act 2006 (Commencement No 8 and Transitional and Saving Provisions) Order 2008, SI 2008/310, art 5 and the transitional provisions in the UK Borders Act 2007 (Commencement No 2 and Transitional Provisions) Order 2008, SI 2008/309, art 5.

4   Social Security (Persons from Abroad) Miscellaneous Amendments Regulations 1996, SI 1996/30.

5   *R v Secretary of State for Social Security, ex p Joint Council for the Welfare of Immigrants* [1997] 1 WLR 275, per Simon Brown LJ.

1.22 In the same year, the lack of due process afforded to those liable to removal on national security grounds came in for condemnation by the ECHR in *Chahal v United Kingdom*.[1] The extra-statutory advisory panel, whose recommendation did not bind the Secretary of State, and before which there was a right to appear but not to know the basis for removal, was not a 'court', and did not provide an effective remedy for possible breaches of Article 3 of the ECHR involved in the removal of such persons. The judgment led to the setting up of the Special Immigration Appeals Commission and a system of special advocates by the Special Immigration Appeals Commission Act 1997, which provides a parallel appeal system for 'national security' cases aiming both to safeguard the rights of the subject and to pay due regard to security concerns. In 2001, after the September 11 atrocities in New York the Anti-terrorism Crime and Security Act 2001 gave SIAC jurisdiction to hear appeals from foreign nationals who had been detained for an indefinite period without trial and on the basis that they had been certified as suspected international terrorists linked to Al Qaeda under the Anti-terrorism Crime and Security Act 2001. This lasted until December 2004, when the House of Lords held that the whole system of indefinite detention of foreign nationals was unlawful under ECHR law as being discriminatory and disproportionate, and quashed the derogation order which had allowed it to happen.[2] The legislation has now lapsed and has been replaced by new laws which no longer come within the ambit of immigration law.[3] SIAC will now continue with its former immigration appellate jurisdiction, hearing appeals which involve issues of national security. Because of its special nature we deal with it in a separate chapter (see Chapter 21), with a particular, though not exclusive, focus on the deportation of suspected terrorists to countries where they would normally be expected to face torture or other inhuman and degrading treatment contrary to Article 3 of the European Convention on Human Rights (ECHR).

1   (1996) 23 EHRR 413.

2   *A v Secretary of State for the Home Department; X v Secretary of State for the Home Department* [2004] UKHL 56, [2005] 2 WLR 87. Derogation from Article 5 of the ECHR was made under Article 15.

3   Prevention of Terrorism Act 2005, which enacts a system of control orders for suspected terrorists, British or foreign, on the basis of reasonable suspicion.

1.23 Then came seven Acts, which form the bulk of modern immigration and asylum law and have been the source material for much of this and previous editions – the Immigration and Asylum Act 1999 (IAA 1999), the Nationality Immigration and Asylum Act 2002 (NIAA 2002), the Asylum and Immigration (Treatment of Claimants, etc) Act 2004, the Immigration, Asylum and Nationality Act 2006 (IAN 2006), the UK Borders Act 2007, the Criminal Justice and Immigration Act 2008 and the Borders, Citizenship and Immigration Act 2009. In addition, there have been important changes in the family part of immigration through the implementation of the Civil Partnership Act 2002, which came into effect in December 2005 and far-reaching changes in adoption law. The Tribunals, Courts and Enforcement Act 2007 has remade the jurisdiction dealing with immigration appeals and some judicial review. Together these Acts constitute a vast reorganisation of the law and practice in the field of immigration, asylum and to a lesser extent nationality. The changes have not been introduced in any coherent fashion, but bit by bit, changing something one year and then re-amending it later, or worse still, giving the Secretary of State power to amend by statutory instrument. The 1999 Act, like its 2002 successor, is a vast and rambling piece of legislation, spreading over several fields. Perhaps its main innovation was the introduction of a new system of asylum support and a new Home Office organisation to run it, called the National Asylum Support Service or NASS,[1] which has been embellished by the later Acts. Apart from its section 2, which makes it a criminal offence for an asylum seeker to attend an interview without a passport or other identity document without a reasonable excuse,[2] and its ss 19–25, which restricted the right to marry. The main claim to fame of the 2004 Act was its recasting of the immigration appellate authority into a one tier Asylum and Immigration Tribunal and consigning adjudicators to the dustbin of history. The Asylum and Immigration Tribunal has now joined adjudicators there, replaced by the First-tier Tribunal and the Upper Tribunal. The last four Immigration Acts are also a hotch potch of different measures, but have at their heart four main themes:

(1)   tidying up measures;
(2)   removing and restricting rights of appeal;
(3)   creating a new system of employer sanctions to stop illegal working by migrants; and
(4)   monitoring, surveillance, and more co-ordinated policing of migrants old and new on the basis of seeking out crime, people smuggling and terrorism, and collecting vast new data bases on all third country nationals (ie those who are not British or EEA citizens) and placing their details in a special ID card, referred in the UK Borders Act 2007 as a 'biometric immigration document' (BID).

We give a brief overview of these and further new legislative initiatives in the following paragraphs together with the recent legislation which has fundamentally changed family law and family immigration law and recast appeal rights by the red pen approach – scoring out everything which has been built up so carefully over 50 years and leaving only a small rump of asylum, human rights and discrimination appeals. Nasty, unnecessary and an affront, one might say, to the rule of law, or, maybe, an attempt to shuffle off genuine points of law to judicial review, often without any possibility of legal aid, as we describe below, but to stick a great big protective shield around the fact-finding of immigration officials, whether good or bad.[3]

[1] Immigration and Asylum Act 1999, Part V and Schs 5–7.
[2] See Chapter 14, below.
[3] Senior immigration officials may in some cases conduct an administrative review over the findings of first-tier officials, but the independence and efficacity of this system is sufficiently unclear that it will require a report of the independent Chief Inspector of the UK Border Agency once the new system has been in operation for one year: see **1.78** below.

RECENT IMMIGRATION, NATIONALITY AND ASYLUM STATUTES

Civil partnership and adoption

1.24 The Civil Partnership Act 2004 came into force on 5 December 2005. Civil partnerships are a new legal relationship which can be registered by two people of the same sex and give couples legal recognition for their relationship. From 5 December 2005, the Immigration Rules were amended so as to put civil partners on the same footing as spouses for immigration purposes. The rule amendments made by HC 582 are to ensure that civil partners and proposed civil partners are afforded the same treatment as spouses and fiancés throughout. The Marriage (Same Sex Couples) Act 2013, which came into force in England and Wales on 29 March 2014, enables same-sex couples to marry and/or to convert their civil partnership into marriage.[1] In Scotland these changes were brought about by the Marriage and Civil Partnership (Scotland) Act 2014, which took effect on 16 December 2013. The second major change has been in the field of inter-country adoptions. The Adoption and Children Act 2002 came into force on 30 December 2005 and replaced most of the Adoption (Intercountry Aspects) Act 1999 which had previously governed this area.[1] The Children and Adoption Act 2006 also received Royal Assent on 21 June 2006. It contains a number of provisions about inter-country adoption, including a statutory framework for the suspension of inter-country adoption from specified countries where there are concerns about adoption practices in that country and increases the restrictions on bringing recently adopted children into the UK. These new provisions came into force on 2 August 2007. See Chapter 10 for more details.

[1] These changes negate the decision in *Wilkinson v Kitzinger* [2006] EWHC 2022 (Fam), [2006] HRLR 36, where a same same-sex marriage valid in Canada was treated as a civil partnership. The Northern Ireland Executive has stated that it does not intend to introduce legislation allowing for same-sex marriage in Northern Ireland. Same-sex marriages from other jurisdictions are there treated as civil partnerships.
[1] The Adoption (Intercountry Aspects) Act 1999 was repealed, save for sections 1, 2 and 7 and Schedule 1 has been replaced by Chapter 6 of the Adoption and Children Act 2002. The 2002 Act also amended the inter-country adoption provisions in the Adoption Act 1976.

The Immigration, Asylum and Nationality Act 2006

1.25 The Immigration, Asylum and Nationality Act 2006 (IAN 2006) received the Royal Assent on 30 March 2006. The government began to implement its provisions in June 2006, with further implementation taking place much later. The Act is arranged under six headings:

- **Appeals.** The main changes to the appeal system were the new restrictions on appeals against refusals of entry clearance to dependants and family visitors and by holders of entry clearance who are refused entry at a port of entry. These provisions have since been repealed by the Immigration Act 2014.
- **Employer sanctions.** A new scheme of civil penalties was to be introduced for employers who employ people who have no right to work or no right to work for that employer. There was also a more measured criminal sanction which is no longer an offence of strict liability and would eventually replace section 8 of the Asylum and Immigration Act 1996. This is dealt with in Chapter 15.
- **Information.** Vast new information-gathering and information sharing powers were introduced, which was aimed at creating a more integrated and co-operative machinery of border control.
- **Claimants and applicants.** There is a hotch potch of changes under this heading, including modifications of local authority powers to provide support and housing for asylum seekers, powers to enable the Secretary of State to regulate the provision of goods and services for those in section 4 housing and to make 'integration loans' more accessible to both refugees and other categories of migrant. There were also minor changes to nationality law.
- **Miscellaneous.** This widens the power to arrest pending deportation (section 53); introduces a statutory construction of Article 1(F)(c) of the Refugee Convention (section 54); directs the AIT on how to deal with the Secretary of State's certificates of non-application of the Refugee Convention (section 55); widens the power to deprive of British citizenship (section 56); introduces a new power to deprive someone of the right of abode (section 57); brings in a new requirement of 'good character' for the over 10's in order to qualify for registration as a British citizen; and allows detainees to be employed at less than the minimum wage.
- **General.** This contains the usual end of statute things like money, commencement, territorial reach and citation. The two schedules deal with consequential amendments and repeals.

There have been some eight Commencement Orders and one amending Commencement Order.[1]

---

[1] All, except the following sections have been brought into force: ss 12, 13, 34, 35, 39, 44, and parts of Schedules 1 and 3. See the Immigration, Asylum and Nationality Act 2006 (Commencement No 8) Order 2008, SI 2008/310 for a table of the provisions that have already commenced with their commencement date as well as the new starting dates and the saving and transitional provisions set out in this Order.

UK Borders Act 2007

1.26 The UK Borders Act 2007 received the Royal Assent on 30 October 2007, but its provisions, apart from s 17, did not come in to force automatically but have depended on the making of Commencement Orders.[1] The Act deals with a miscellany of matters as follows:

- **Powers at ports.** Sections 1–4 provide for the Secretary of State to designate suitably qualified immigration officers acting at ports in England and Wales and Northern Ireland to have the power to detain suspected criminals for up to three hours pending the arrival of the police.

- **Biometric registration.** Sections 5 and 6 confer a power to make regulations to require those subject to immigration control to apply for a document recording external physical characteristics – a 'biometric immigration document' (BID), which can then be used in specified circumstances where a question arises about a person's status in relation to nationality or immigration. The Act also deals with the consequences of non-compliance with this compulsory registration.

- **Treatment of claimants.** This part of the Act contains a mixed bag of changes. Section 16 increases the number of conditions which can be attached to a limited leave to enter or remain under s 3(1)(c) of the Immigration Act 1971 to include a reporting and/or residency condition.[2] Section 17 provides that an asylum-seeker remains eligible for support during an appeal related to his or her asylum claim. Section 18 provides for a power of arrest without warrant by immigration officers of those suspected of offences relating to asylum support fraud. Section 19 cuts down the giving of post-decision evidence in an appeal against the refusal of a points-based application, which only applied to the Highly Skilled Migrants Programme (see Chapter 10). Section 20 extends the government's fee collecting powers to allow over-cost charges in connection with the sponsorship of migrants and cross-subsidies between certain in-country services and between certain in-country and overseas services. Section 21 makes provision for the Secretary of State to issue a code of practice to keep children safe from harm while they are in the UK.

- **Enforcement.** This part of the Act introduces a new offence of assaulting an immigration officer; gives immigration officers new powers to seize cash deal with the conditions under which cash may be seized and allows detained property to be forfeited and disposed of not just to the police but also to the Secretary of State.[3] More powers of arrest are given to immigration officers in cases of illegal employment and the Act widens the ambit of the offence of facilitating an asylum-seeker's entry to the UK and extends the territorial reach of the various facilitation offences. Similar changes are made to widen the ambit and extend the territorial reach of existing trafficking for exploitation offences. See Chapter 14 for more details.

- **Automatic deportation of criminals.** This is the part of the Act which is most media driven and has received the widest publicity. Sections 32–39 detail the conditions and procedure under which a foreign national prisoner will be automatically deported. They specify those foreign nationals subject to compulsory deportation and the sentences that will trigger it. See Chapter 15 for more details.

- **Information.** Sections 40 to 43 deal with the information sharing arrangements between the Border and Immigration Agency (BIA) (now the UKBA), HM Revenue and Customs (HMRC) and Revenue and

Customs Prosecution Office. The Act includes safeguards to protect confidentiality and wrongful disclosure. Sections 44 to 46 allow an immigration officer, a police constable or a designated police civilian to search premises for evidence of an arrested individual's nationality and to retain and copy these documents.

- **Border and Immigration Inspectorate.** Sections 48 to 56 establish a single independent inspectorate for the (BIA) (now the UKBA). This replaced the existing inspecting bodies. See below for more details.
- **Senior President of Tribunals.** Section 56 adds cases coming before the Asylum and Immigration Tribunal to the reporting remit of the Senior President of Tribunals under s 43(3) of the Tribunals, Courts and Enforcement Act 2007.

The UK Borders Act 2007 extends to the whole of the UK, with three exceptions, ss 1–4 relating to powers of detention for immigration officers at ports, s 25 relating to forfeiture of property, and s 31(1) and (2) relating to trafficking offences. These will only apply to England, Wales and Northern Ireland, but not Scotland. Provision of the Act may be extended to any of the Channel Islands or to the Isle of Man by Order in Council.

[1] For commencement orders see under Part 2 of this work.
[2] A condition under s 3(1)(c)(iv) and (v) of the Immigration Act 1971 (general provisions for regulation and control) may be added to leave given before the passing of the 2007 Act; UK Borders Act 2007 (Commencement No 1 and Transitional Provisions) Order 2008, SI 2008/99, art 3.
[3] Regulations made under s 26(5) of the 2007 Act may have effect in relation to property which came into the possession of an immigration officer or the Secretary of State before the passing of the 2007 Act: UK Borders Act 2007 (Commencement No 1 and Transitional Provisions) Order 2008, SI 2008/99, art 4.

Criminal Justice and Immigration Act 2008

1.27 The Criminal Justice and Immigration Act 2008 created a new special immigration status, never and never likely to be brought into force.[1] It allowed the Secretary of State to designate to this status a foreign criminal and his or her family members,[2] where the foreign criminal is liable to deportation, but cannot be removed from the UK because of s 6 of the Human Rights Act 1998. A number of people were to be excluded from the ambit of the new provisions:

(i)   those with the right of abode in the UK;
(ii) those whose designation the Secretary of State thinks would breach either (a) the UK's obligations under the Refugee Convention, or (b) the person's rights under the EC law.[3]

The Act also makes further provision for the repatriation of prisoners by amending the Repatriation of Prisoners Act 1984, by enabling a British escort to deliver a prisoner to a point of arrival in the receiving country and paving the way for the UK to ratify the Additional Protocol to the Council of Europe Convention on the Transfer of Sentenced Persons which provides for the transfer of prisoners without their consent where the prisoner is to be deported at the end of the sentence or where a prisoner has fled from one jurisdiction to another in order to avoid imprisonment.[4]

[1] Criminal Justice and Immigration Act 2008, ss 130–137 and Sch 27, para 36. For more details, see Blackstone's Guide to the Criminal Justice and Immigration Act 2008, edited by Maya Sikand. These provisions are not yet in force.
[2] Criminal Justice and Immigration Act 2008, s 130(1)–(3).
[3] Criminal Justice and Immigration Act 2008, s 130(4) and (5).
[4] Criminal Justice and Immigration Act 2008, ss 93–96, brought into force on 14 July 2008 by the Criminal Justice and Immigration Act 2008 (Commencement No 2 and Transitional and Saving Provisions) Order 2008, SI 2008/1586.

Borders, Citizenship and Immigration Act 2009

1.28 The Borders, Citizenship and Immigration Act 2009 contains extensive provision in Part 1 for amalgamating Immigration and Customs functions. Part 2 makes significant changes to the acquisition of British citizenship by naturalisation and to the right of abode. Part 3 amended section 3 of the Immigration Act 1971 enabling a condition to be imposed on a grant of leave to enter or remain restricting the studies that an individual may undertake. This means that any changes of study would need Home Office permission, thereby reversing an important part of the very sensible Court of Appeal decision in *Obed (Omerenma) v Secretary of State for the Home Department*.[1] It also extends powers for finger-printing those liable to automatic deportation and immigration officers' powers of detention. Part 4 makes provision for the transfer of claims for judicial review of decisions refusing to accept fresh asylum or human rights claims from the Administrative Court to the Upper Tribunal.[2] It also amends the definition of 'trafficking people for exploitation' in section 4(4) of the 2004 Act and it imposes a duty on the Secretary of State to make arrangements ensuring that functions under the Immigration Acts are carried out having regard to the need to safeguard and promote the welfare of children who are in the UK.

[1] [2008] EWCA Civ 747, [2008] Imm AR 747. This case has now been superseded by the introduction of Tier 4 (General Student) Migrant provisions: see chapter 9, below.
[2] The Borders, Citizenship and Immigration Act 2009 (Commencement No 2) Order 2011, SI 2011/1741, brought into force s 53 (transfer of certain immigration judicial review applications) on 8 August 2011. The earlier Borders, Citizenship and Immigration Act 2009 (Commencement No 1) Order 2009, SI 2009/2731, brought into force ss 42–49(1) and parts of the Sch on 2 November 2009 and 13 January 2010; s 55 and part of s 56 on 2 November 2009; and ss 51 and 54 on 10 November 2009.

The Identity Documents Act 2010

1.29 The Identity Documents Act 2010 repeals entirely the Identity Cards Act 2006 and abolishes ID Cards and the National Identity Register, but re-enacts the provisions of section 21 of the 2006 Act relating to the possession of false identity documents etc, with improper intention. The 2006 Act also made provision relating specifically to passports. The 2006 Act provided a power to enable biographical checks to be made for the purposes of verifying information supplied by an applicant for a British passport. It also provided a statutory basis to enable cross-subsidisation of fees for different types of passports and passport services (by amending the Consular Fees Act 1980). The 2010 Act re-enacts these provisions so far as they relate to documents other than ID cards. However, the abolition of identity cards does not mean that the parallel provisions under immigration legislation for identity cards for foreign nationals is also abolished. It is not.

European Union Act 2011

1.30 The European Union Act 2011 imposes restrictions relating to amendments of the two main EU Treaties; the Treaty on European Union (TEU) and the Treaty on the Functioning of the European Union TFEU and to other changes relating to restrictions relating to decisions made under TEU or TFEU. Some changes can only become part of UK law if the changes have been approved by referendum and the Act sets out provisions for the holding of such referenda. More details are in Chapter 8.

Crime and Courts Act 2013

1.31 Part 3 of the Crime and Courts Act 2013 deals with immigration appeals. First, it enables simultaneous service in one document of a decision to refuse to vary leave with a decision to remove, with the result that both appeals can be heard at the same time. Secondly, it abolished altogether the full right of appeal for family visitors refused a visa – one of the most successful grounds of appeal hitherto. They can only appeal now on human right or race discriminations grounds – grounds unlikely to be available to more than a handful of such visitors. Sections 53 and 54 restrict the right of appeal of (i) persons whose presence in the UK is certified by the Secretary of State, acting in person, as no longer conducive to the public good; and (ii) of persons under a deportation order made on the grounds that the person's removal from the United Kingdom would be in the interests of national security.

Immigration Act 2014

1.32 The Immigration Act 2014 was expressly designed to create an ever more hostile environment for migrants who abuse the system, thereby potentially punishing all migrants, and to reduce appeal rights and lower the chance of successful appeals without provisions for improving the quality of decision making. Key provisions include:

- Part 1: along with Schedule 1, creates new enforcement and removal powers[1], as well as restrictions on bail applications within 14 days of scheduled removal and within 28 days of a previous application without a proven change of circumstances[2];
- Part 2 drastically reduces appeal rights and seeks to control judges' consideration of Article 8 ECHR[3];
- Part 3, creates wide-ranging limitations on access to residential tenancies (along with Schedule 3), all but emergency health services, bank accounts and driving licences for those who cannot prove they have (or do not require) leave to remain and seeks to outsource immigration control to numerous private citizens and businesses.

- Part 4, alongside Schedules 4, 5 and 6 creates new duties and powers of reporting and investigation of 'suspicious' marriages where one party could potentially gain an immigration advantage.
- Part 5 and Schedule 7 contain provisions about the Office of the Immigration Services Commissioner and Northern Ireland's Police Ombudsman.
- Part 6 contains provisions for the SSHD to deprive naturalised British nationals of citizenship if she deems their presence in the UK not conducive to the public good. It also finally resolves the position whereby a small group of people born between 1983 and 2006 to unmarried British fathers and non-British mothers were not entitled to British citizenship[4]. It also expands the SSHD's powers to charge fees for 'functions in connection with immigration or nationality'[5].

Doubts about the compliance of various parts of the Act with the ECHR and discrimination law have been expressed by (among others) the Joint Committee on Human Rights in its legislative scrutiny of the Bill.[6]

[1] See chapter 16, below on Removal and other expulsion.
[2] See Chapter 17 on Detention and Bail.
[3] See Chapter 18 and 19 on Rights of appeal.
[4] Immigration Act 2014, s 65, inserting ss 4D to 4J into the British Nationality Act 1981.
[5] See Chapter 3 at **3.38–3.39**
[6] www.publications.parliament.uk/pa/jt201314/jtselect/jtrights/102/10202.htm Joint Committee on Human Rights–Eighth Report; Legislative Scrutiny: Immigration Bill, printed 11 December 2013.

SOURCES OF IMMIGRATION LAW AND PRACTICE

The prerogative

1.33 The prerogative powers of the Secretary of State for the Home Department are another source of immigration law. Section 33(5) of the Immigration Act 1971 states that the Act 'shall not be taken to supersede or impair any power exercisable by Her Majesty in relation to aliens by virtue of her prerogative'. A similar reservation was made in the Aliens Restriction Act 1914, which was passed at the beginning of World War I. The view then was that it referred to a prerogative power to deal with enemy aliens, and it is now settled law, as indicated at **1.7** above that this is also the full and correct ambit of the reservation in the Immigration Act 1971.[1] The issue of passports to British citizens involves a quite separate prerogative power, which we describe at **2.107–2.108** below. The prerogative power was more recently discussed in the House of Lords in *R (on the application of Bancoult) v Secretary of State for Foreign and Commonwealth Affairs*,[2] where Lord Hoffmann, giving a majority opinion, said:

'The Crown has no authority to transport anyone beyond the seas except by statutory authority. At common law, any subject of the Crown has the right to enter and remain in the United Kingdom whenever and for as long as he pleases: see *R v Bhagwan* [1972] AC 60. The Crown cannot remove this right by an exercise of the prerogative. That is because since the 17th century the prerogative has not empowered the Crown to change English common or statute law. In a ceded colony, however, the Crown has plenary legislative authority. It can make or unmake the law of the land.'

For further comment, see **2.25**, below.

1   A contrary view expressed by Lord Brown in *Odelola v Secretary of State for the Home Department*, [2009] UKHL 25, [2010] Imm AR 59, at para 35 has been authoritatively dismissed as wrong by Lord Dyson in *R (on the application of Munir) v Secretary of State for the Home Department (Joint Council for the Welfare of Immigrants intervening)* [2012] UKSC 32, at paras 23–33 and by Lord Hope in *R (on the application of Alvi) v Secretary of State for the Home Department* [2012] UKSC 33 at para 32.
2   [2008] UKHL 61, [2008] 4 All ER 1055.

1.34 Normally the Secretary of State must abide by the Immigration Rules, but he or she may depart from them by making a decision more beneficial to an applicant, by overruling an immigration official, granting someone discretionary leave to remain when the Immigration Rules say he or she should go, or adopting a policy that people of a particular class or nationality should get leave outside the Immigration Rules, or granting a general amnesty. The source of this well recognised discretion – prerogative or statute – has caused some difficulty. Our view has consistently been that it derives from the Secretary of State's statutory powers, and, in particular, from the discretion under section 4(1) of the Immigration Act 1971, which is a very broad discretion, not made subject to the Immigration Rules. The Secretary of State can, therefore, waive a requirement of the Rules in an individual case as a matter of statutory discretion. We felt it would be introducing an arcane, inaccurate and unnecessary spin on immigration law to call policy guidance outside the Immigration Rules exercises of prerogative power. But there are dicta in two cases which suggest that the power to treat an immigrant more favourably than the Rules dictate derives from prerogative rather than statute,[1] as if it was a revival of the ancient prerogative of the Crown as the 'fountain of justice'.[2] In *Ahmed and Patel*[3] the parties were agreed that the Secretary of State was using prerogative powers in the formulation and application of extra-statutory policies such as those on long residence or marriage and children in relation to removal. But the court held that a Treaty entered into by the executive, such as the ECHR or the UN Convention on the Rights of the Child, could have no greater effect in relation to the exercise of a discretion under the prerogative than in the case of a statutory discretion.[4]

These cases have been referred to by the Supreme Court in *Munir* and held to be wrongly decided. In Lord Dyson's judgment, with which all other members of the Court agreed, the Secretary of State is given a wide discretion under sections 3, 3A, 3B and 3C of the IA 1971 to control the grant and refusal of leave to enter or to remain. The language of these provisions, especially section 3(1)(b) and (c), could not be wider. He, therefore, concluded that the Secretary of State is authorised by the 1971 Act to make policies setting out the principles by which she may, as a matter of discretion, grant concessions in individual cases to those seeking leave to enter or remain in the United Kingdom. The old quandary between a statutory or Prerogative fountain of justice appears to have been settled.[5]

1   *R v Secretary of State for the Home Department, ex p Kaur (Rajinder)* [1987] Imm AR 278, DC; *R v Secretary of State for the Home Department, ex p Ounejma* [1989] Imm AR 75. In *R v Secretary of State for the Home Department, ex p Northumbria Police Authority* [1989] QB 26 Purchas LJ approved of this kind of residual use of the prerogative power, stating that:

   'where the executive action is directed towards the benefit or protection of the individual, it is unlikely that its use will attract the intervention of the courts . . . Before the courts will hold that such executive action is contrary to legislation, express and unequivocal terms must be found in the statute which deprive the individual from receiving the benefit or protection intended by the exercise of the Prerogative power.'

2   See Chitty, Treatise on the Law of the Prerogative of the Crown (1820) ch 7; *R v Secretary of State for the Home Department, ex p Northumbria Police Authority* [1989] QB 26, [1988] 1 All ER 556 at 563, CA.
3   *R v Secretary of State for the Home Department, ex p Ahmed; R v Secretary of State for the Home Department, ex p Patel* [1998] INLR 570.
4   See also *R (on the application of Acan) v Immigration Appeal Tribunal* [2004] EWHC 297 (Admin), [2004] All ER (D) 193 (Feb), where Gibbs J held that it was unnecessary to decide whether exceptional leave was granted outside the terms of the Act, under the prerogative, or within the Act but outside the rules.
5   *R (on the application of Munir) v Secretary of State for the Home Department (Joint Council for the Welfare of Immigrants intervening)* [2012] UKSC 32 at paras 43–45; adopted in *R (on the application of Alvi) v Secretary of State for the Home Department* [2012] UKSC 33, at para 25.

1.35 It is old established law that the exercise of a prerogative power can be suspended, or abrogated, by an Act of Parliament.[1] So a statute which operates in the field of prerogative may exclude the possibility of exercising prerogative powers. Where a complete and exhaustive code is to be found in the statute, or in the case of immigration and nationality law, in a whole host of statutory and other parliamentary approved powers deriving from the statutory powers, any powers under the prerogative, which would otherwise have applied, are excluded entirely.[2] Any exercise of a prerogative power in a manner, or for a purpose, which is inconsistent with the statute will be an abuse of power.[3] However, at the time of *Munir and Alvi* the Home Office seemed to love the Prerogative and sought to apply it in those and other immigration and nationality situations. An example, is *G1 v Secretary of State for the Home Department*[4], decided by the Court of Appeal 14 days before *Munir*. G had been born in Sudan and gained British citizenship. He left the UK after being charged with a public order offence. The Secretary of state made an order under the BNA 1981, s 40(2) depriving G of British citizenship on the ground of the public good, because of G's alleged involvement in terrorism-related activities. G launched a statutory appeal against that decision to the Special Immigration Appeals Commission (SIAC). It was held inter alia that the Crown had prerogative power to exclude an alien unless the power was abrogated or modified by the relevant statutory provisions. The Court held that these provisions did not abrogate the prerogative power. The repeal of section 40A(6) extinguished the suspension of the secretary of state's statutory power under the 1981 Act to make a section 40(2) order while an appeal against deprivation was pending or could be brought. The reliance on prerogative power, was, however, gratuitous and quite unnecessary, because G's right of appeal was wholly dealt with by statute which allowed him an out of country appeal but not one in country. Secondly, his exclusion from the UK was also wholly covered by statutory power and the Immigration Rules as the Court clearly recognised in its other holdings, including that on EU law. Another decision as far as the Prerogative is concerned which ought to be consigned to the dustbin of history.

1   *A-G v De Keyser's Royal Hotel Ltd* [1920] AC 508, per Lord Atkinson at pp 539–540. See now per Lord Hope in *R (on the application of Alvi) v Secretary of State for the Home Department* [2012] UKSC 33, at para 28; and Lord Dyson in *R (on the application of Munir) v Secretary of State for the Home Department (Joint Council for the Welfare of Immigrants intervening)* [2012] UKSC 32, at para 33.

2   See, eg, *Mitchell, Re, Hatton v Jones* [1954] Ch 525.
3   *R v Secretary of State for the Home Department, ex p Fire Brigades Union* [1995] 2 AC 513, per Lord Nicholls of Birkenhead at p 576.
4   [2012] EWCA Civ 867.

1.36 The prerogative powers in relation to national security affected immigration law adversely until very recently, overriding normally applicable Immigration Rules[1] or the obligations under the 1951 Refugee Convention.[2] The courts retained no more than a nominal power to quash the decision on normal judicial review grounds.[3] But this changed following (i) the *Chahal* case,[4] where the European Court held that the applicant's rights not to be subjected to torture, inhuman and degrading treatment (under Article 3 of the ECHR) overrode any interests of national security; and (ii) the enactment of the Special Immigration Appeals Commission Act 1997, passed as a direct response to the European Court in *Chahal*, which set up the Special Immigration Appeals Commission to hear appeals involving national security. We deal with these in later chapters. The higher courts have made it clear that, in deciding whether a decision or action is lawful, it is the subject matter, not the source of the power, which is determinative,[5] and have recently shown a willingness to entertain challenges to decisions in prerogative areas traditionally held not justiciable, such as foreign relations,[6] defence[7] and declaring war.[8] The issue of whether a power derives from prerogative or statute is now largely of historical interest.[9]

1   *R v Secretary of State for the Home Department, ex p Hosenball* [1977] 3 All ER 452, [1977] 1 WLR 766, CA; *NSH v Secretary of State for the Home Department* [1988] Imm AR 389, CA; *R v Secretary of State for the Home Department, ex p Chahal* [1994] Imm AR 107, CA.
2   Although the Secretary of State was under an obligation to asylum seekers lawfully in the UK to balance their interests under the 1951 Refugee Convention against the interests of national security: see *NSH v Secretary of State for the Home Department* above; *Ex p Chahal* above.
3   See *The Zamora* [1916] 2 AC 77, PC; the speech of Lord Atkin in *Liversidge v Anderson* [1942] AC 206, [1941] 3 All ER 338, HL; *Council of Civil Service Unions v Minister for the Civil Service* [1985] AC 374 at 420–423, HL, per Lord Roskill; *Hussain v Secretary of State for the Home Department* [1993] Imm AR 353, CA; *Ex p Hosenball* above; *NSH v Secretary of State for the Home Department* above; *Chahal* above.
4   *Chahal v United Kingdom* (1996) 23 EHRR 413, ECtHR.
5   *Council of Civil Service Unions v Minister for the Civil Service* [1985] AC 374, *R (on the application of Abbasi) v Secretary of State for Foreign and Commonwealth Affairs* [2002] EWCA Civ 1598.
6   *R (on the application of Abbasi) v Secretary of State for Foreign and Commonwealth Affairs* [2002] EWCA Civ 1598, (2002) Times, 8 November (failure to intervene in the detention of British nationals in Guantánamo).
7   *R (on the application of Bancoult) v Secretary of State for Foreign and Commonwealth Affairs* [2001] QB 1067 (expulsion of Ilois from their homes for defence purposes, where the Divisional Court concluded that the British Indian Ocean Territory Order 1965 was made under prerogative rather than statutory power, but that the prerogative power did not permit the Queen to exile her subjects from the territory where they belong).
8   *R (on the application of Campaign for Nuclear Disarmament) v Prime Minister* [2002] EWHC 2777 (Admin), (2002) Times, 27 December.
9   See *Council of Civil Service Unions* case, fn 5 above; *R (on the application of Acan) v Immigration Appeal Tribunal* [2004] EWHC 297 (Admin), [2004] All ER (D) 193 (Feb) at **1.58** fn 4 below.

Ancillary and Incidental Administrative Powers

1.37 In *R (on the application of New London College Ltd) v Secretary of State for the Home Department* [2013] UKSC 51 the case concerned the categorisation of a complete and self-contained regulatory code for sponsoring educational institutions. The Crown relied on some alternative, unidentified source of such powers, derived neither from the prerogative nor from any specific provision in the Act, but from the general responsibilities of the Secretary of State in this field.[1] The Court said there was no need to decide this controversial issue.[2] The majority view was that the statutory power of the Secretary of State to administer the system of immigration control must necessarily extend to a range of ancillary and incidental administrative powers not expressly spelt out in the Act, including the vetting of sponsors. Lord Sumption, who gave the majority judgment, said (paras 29):

'If the Secretary of State is entitled (as she plainly is) to prescribe and lay before Parliament rules for the grant of leave to enter or remain in the United Kingdom which depend upon the migrant having a suitable sponsor, then she must be also be entitled to take administrative measures for identifying sponsors who are and remain suitable, even if these measures do not themselves fall within section 3(2) of the Act.

This right is not of course unlimited. The Secretary of State cannot adopt measures for identifying suitable sponsors which are inconsistent with the Act or the Immigration Rules. Without specific statutory authority, she cannot adopt measures which are coercive; or which infringe the legal rights of others (including their rights under the Human Rights Convention); or which are irrational or unfair or otherwise conflict with the general constraints on administrative action imposed by public law.

She has not transgressed any of these limitations by operating a system of approved Tier 4 sponsors. It is not coercive. There are substantial advantages for sponsors in participating, but they are not obliged to do so. The rules contained in the Tier 4 Guidance for determining whether applicants are suitable to be sponsoring institutions, are in reality conditions of participation, and sponsors seeking the advantages of a licence cannot complain if they are required to adhere to them.'

Lord Carnwath took issue with the width of this power, as explained by Lord Sumption and agreed by the other judges (paras 35–38). He sought to treat the licensing process as linked to the specific provisions for regulating entry under section 1(4), but not to the general system of immigration control under the Act.

[1] The Crown did not, however, rely on a doctrine which has been referred to as a 'Third Source' of authority, by which the Crown possesses some general administrative powers to carry on the ordinary business of government which are not exercises of the royal prerogative and do not require statutory authority: See B V Harris, 'The "Third Source" of Authority for Government Action Revisited' (2007) 123 LQR 225. The extent of these powers and their exact juridical basis are controversial. In *R v Secretary of State for Health, ex p C* [2000] 1 FLR 627 and *R (on the application of Shrewsbury and Atcham Borough Council) v Secretary of State for Communities and Local Government* [2008] EWCA Civ 148, [2008] 3 All ER 548, the Court of Appeal held that the basis of the power was the Crown's status as a common law corporation sole, with all the capacities and powers of a natural person subject only to such particular limitations as were imposed by law. In *R (on the application of Hooper) v Secretary of State for Work and Pensions* [2005] UKHL 29, [2005] 1 WLR 1681, para 47 Lord Hoffmann had previously indicated that he thought there was 'a good deal of force' in this analysis.

[2] Lord Sumption at para 28. He questioned the validity of the analogy between a corporation sole and a natural person, stating that it was open to question whether the analogy with a

natural person is really apt in the case of public or governmental action. Lord Carnwath (para 34) was more scathing. The Crown, he said, was wise not to seek to rely on the 'third source' for the reasons given in his judgment for the majority in the *Shrewsbury* case [2008] 3 All ER 548, 562-4 and pointed out that this sensitive issue had also been the subject of recent consideration by the House of Lords Select Committee on the Constitution: *The pre-emption of Parliament* HL Paper 165 – 1 May 2013).

Immigration statutes and the orders and regulations made under them

1.38 The main sources of immigration and asylum law are the Immigration Act 1971 and the amending and other statutes described in the previous sections.[1] The 1971 Act still contains the rule-making power and used to contain the appeal powers, until these were revamped under the Nationality, Immigration and Asylum Act 2002. They have subsequently been further amended and are now to be severely limited by the Immigration Act 2014. The succession of statutes all provide for implementing Orders and Regulations, usually to be made by statutory instrument, sometimes by Order in Council. The Immigration and Asylum Act 1999 has so far been the worst offender. On a rough count there were twelve instances of powers to make Orders by statutory instrument; 26 for regulations; seven for rules; seven codes of practice will apply; two sets of directions; one Order in Council; and one set of arrangements.[2] Not all these powers have been used, but the list of Orders and Regulations, covering a very wide span, is formidable. All are subject to change. All are now available on the internet to check the up-to-date position. The key rules are still The Statement of Immigration Rules, made under the 1971 Act and usually published as a House of Commons paper (currently HC 395, as amended many times), setting out the criteria for entry and stay in the various immigration categories

The 1971 Act received the Royal Assent on 28 October 1971. Section 3(2) came into force on 1 January 1973.[3] Draft Immigration Rules had been published and were available during the debates on the Bill in Parliament. On 23 October 1972 the Secretary of State laid two sets of Immigration Rules before Parliament: a Statement of Immigration Rules for Control on Entry (Cmnd 4606); and a Statement of Immigration Rules for Control after Entry (Cmnd 4792). These statements were disapproved after a debate in the House of Commons on 22 November 1972. But they were the rules under which the Act was administered until two new sets of rules, one for Commonwealth citizens and the other for foreign nationals, were laid on 23 January 1973.[2] The current Immigration Rules have their origin in a Statement of Changes in the Immigration Rules (HC 395) which was laid before Parliament on 23 May 1994.

[1] There is very little left of the Immigration Act 1988 and the Asylum and Immigration Act 1996, and the Asylum and Immigration Appeals Act 1993 has been wholly repealed and replaced by the Nationality, Immigration and Asylum Act 2002, which in turn has been extensively amended.

[2] The Nationality, Immigration and Asylum Act 2002 originally had 15 instances of powers to make Orders and two dozen for regulations, with two Lord Chancellor's rules, a code of practice and two sets of guidance.

[3] The 1971 Act came into force on 1 January 1973: SI 1972/1514.

The Immigration Rules

1.39 A consolidated version of the current Immigration Rules is available on the Home Office website, and the most recent Statements of Changes are also available separately.[1] Since the last edition, there have been 37 such changes. In addition to Immigration Rules there are also the rules of procedure for immigration and asylum appeals[2] and the regulations for the service of notices in connection with appeals.[3] The validity of these subordinate rules and regulations may be challenged.[4] The rules, Orders, Codes of Practice and Regulations all have some statutory foundation, but in addition to them there is a whole collection of Guidance notes and internal instructions, issued by the UKBA (UKVI) section of the Home Office and by the Foreign and Commonwealth Office.[5] Finally, there are information documents on: carriers' liability,[6] and civil penalty information for vehicle operators travelling to the UK.[6]

[1] See www.gov.uk/government/collections/immigration-rules
[2] See volume 2, App 4, including Asylum and Immigration Tribunal (Procedure) Rules 2005, SI 2005/230, as amended. There are separate rules for fast track appeals: Asylum and Immigration Tribunal (Fast Track Procedure) Rules 2005, SI 2005/560.
[3] See volume 3, App 5; Immigration (Notices) Regulations 2003, SI 2003/658.
[4] In *R v Immigration Appeal Tribunal, ex p Begum (Manshoora)* [1986] Imm AR 385, QBD, a provision of an Immigration Rule was held so unreasonable as to be invalid. A procedure rule met the same fate in *R v Secretary of State for the Home Department, ex p Saleem (Asifa)* [2000] INLR 413, and designation of a safe country in a statutory instrument in *R (on the application of Javed) v Secretary of State for the Home Department* [2001] EWHC 7 (Admin), (2001) Times, 9 February; affd [2001] EWCA Civ 789, [2002] QB 129. In *FP (Iran) and MB (Libya) v Secretary of State for the Home Department* [2007] EWCA Civ 13, a Procedure Rule compelling the Tribunal to hear an appeal in a party's absence was held to be ultra vires and in *AM (Serbia) v Secretary of State for the Home Department* [2007] EWCA Civ 16 a Procedure Rule which prevented enlargement of the grounds for reconsideration of a decision of the Tribunal was held to be irrational. See also *R v Secretary of State for Social Security, ex p Joint Council for the Welfare of Immigrants* [1997] 1 WLR 275. The Human Rights Act 1998 s 6(1), (2) offers further scope for challenge on the basis that the rule or regulation in question infringes ECHR rights and is not required to do so by the primary legislation. If the primary legislation requires the infringement, the High Court can make a declaration of incompatibility under s 4(4): cf *International Transport Roth GmbH v Secretary of State for the Home Department* [2002] EWCA Civ 158, [2003] QB 728; *A v Secretary of State for the Home Department* [2004] UKHL 56, [2005] 2 WLR 87. See Chapter 9 below.
[5] See www.gov.uk/immigration-operational-guidance. A list is set out at **1.53** below.
[6] See Chapter 33: Immigration (carriers' liability) Act 1987 (immigration directorate instructions) first published 11 December 2013, available at: www.gov.uk/government/collections/chapter-33-immigration-carriers-liability-act-1987-immigration-directorate-instructions.

1.40 The Immigration Rules are 'detailed statements by a minister of the Crown as to how the Crown proposes to exercise its executive power to control immigration'.[1] They have a legal status which is 'not merely unusual[2] but unique'.[3] They are not delegated legislation;[4] whilst the Immigration Act 1971 makes provision about what the Rules must contain[5] and about how parliamentary approval of the Rules is to be obtained[6] they do not derive from any empowering legislation.[7] Immigration Rules existed before the enactment of the 1971 Act and the Act regulates rather than authorises the making and changing of the rules.[8]

[1] *Odelola v Secretary of State for the Home Department* [2009] UKHL 25, [2009] 1 WLR 1230, at para 6, *per* Lord Hoffmann.
[2] The word used by Lord Hoffmann in *Odelola*.
[3] *Secretary of State for the Home Department v Pankina* [2010] EWCA Civ 719.

[4]   See the authorities reviewed in *MO (Nigeria) v Secretary of State for the Home Department* [2008] EWCA Civ 308 as well as the judgment in the House of Lords.

[5]   Section 1(4).

[6]   Section 3(2).

[7]   *Pankina* (fn 3 above). See also Lord Neuberger's judgment in *Odelola* (fn 4 above) at para 45f: 'neither section Immigration Act 1971, s 1(4) and 3(2)] purports to be the source of the power' to make Immigration Rules which are 'non-statutory in origin'.

[8]   Sedley LJ's phrase in *Pankina*, fn 3 above.

1.41 However, the Rules are more than just statements of policy that can be adduced in evidence in order to identify relevant considerations to which a decision maker should have had regard. They have acquired 'a status of quasi-law'.[1] The Tribunal is required to allow an appeal against an immigration decision if it is not in accordance with the law 'including Immigration Rules'[2] so that the rules are both 'a code to be followed and a source of legal rights'.[3] Constitutional principle forbids the executive to make law without the authority of Parliament.[4] That is why the 1971 Immigration Act requires statements of the Immigration Rules or any changes to the Rules to be laid before Parliament which may disapprove them by negative resolution within 40 days of the Rules being laid.[5] If Parliament disapproves the Rules, they are not thereby invalidated but the Secretary of State has to make such further changes to the Rules as appear to be necessary in the circumstances.[6] On the other hand, the absence of a negative resolution gives the Rules the parliamentary authority that is required by their quasi-legal status.[7] The statutory and constitutional requirements that the Rules have parliamentary approval as well as the requirement of legal certainty mean that substantive criteria affecting individuals' status and entitlements so far as entry and stay of those requiring leave to enter or remain must be included within the Rules;[8] Thus a significant feature of the implementation of the 'points based system' whereby the Immigration Rules made reference to 'policy guidance' setting out criteria that a student applicant was required by the Rules to satisfy was held to be unlawful for falling foul of these principles.[9] However, where rules are made to supplement the rules on entry and stay and are contained in Guidance laying down the conditions of sponsorship licences for educational institutions and employers, the legal situation may be quite different,[10] as we shall see.

[1]   Sedley LJ's phrase in *Pankina*, fn 3 above.

[2]   Nationality, Immigration and Asylum Act 2002, s 86(3)(a).

[3]   *Pankina*, fn 3 above. See also, for example, *Pearson v Immigration Appeal Tribunal* [1978] Imm AR 212 where the Court of Appeal held that the Rules had the force of law for those hearing immigration appeals.

[4]   *Case of Proclamations* (1611) 12 Co Rep 74, cited in *Pankina*, fn 3 above.

[5]   Immigration Act 1971, s 3(2).

[6]   Immigration Act 1971, s 3(2); *R v Secretary of State for the Home Department, ex p Hosenball* [1977] 1 WLR 766 and *Odelola v Secretary of State for the Home Department* [2009] UKHL 25, Lord Brown para 33.

[7]   *Pankina*, fn 3 above.

[8]   See *R (on the application of Alvi) v Secretary of state for the Home Department* [2012] UKSC 33, where it was held that any requirement in immigration guidance or codes of practice which, if not satisfied by the migrant, would lead to an application for leave to enter or remain being refused was a 'rule' within the meaning of the Immigration Act 1971, s 3(2) and should be laid before Parliament.

[9]   *Pankina*, above. In that case, the Immigration Rules required an individual applying for leave to remain to have held £800 for a period to be specified in policy guidance in order to satisfy the requirement of the rules that the applicant be able to maintain him or herself. The court decided that because the specification of a period was done by policy guidance, not the rules, holding the money for a period (as opposed just to having it at the time of making an

application for leave to remain) was not a criterion that an individual could be required to satisfy. The *Pankina* test was not accepted by the Supreme Court as providing sufficient certainty and was fine tuned in *Alvi* [2012] UKSC 33 to provide greater certainty.

10   See *R (on the application of New London College Ltd) v Secretary of State for the Home Department; R (on the application of West London Vocational Training College) v Secretary of State for the Home Department* [2013] UKSC 51, [2013] 4 All ER 195, at para 29.

1.42 There are few statutory or other restrictions as to the content of the Rules.[1] Section 1(4) of the 1971 Act provides that the Rules must include provisions for the admission of persons coming for employment and study, and as visitors or dependants. There is no similar requirement for 'after entry' rules. Section 3(2) of the 1971 Act expressly provides that in framing the Rules there is no need to have uniform provisions as regards admission of persons for employment, study or as visitors or dependants and account may be taken of citizenship or nationality. The rule making power is subject to the provisions of the Human Rights Act 1998 which make it unlawful for public authorities to act in a way which is incompatible with a right protected by the ECHR,[2] and to the provisions of the Equality Act 2010 which prohibits racial discrimination by public authorities.[3]

1   The Asylum and Immigration Appeals Act 1993, s 2 provides that nothing in the Immigration Rules shall lay down any practice which would be contrary to the 1951 Refugee Convention. Before its repeal by Immigration Act 1988, s 1, s 1(5) of the 1971 Act imposed mandatory and negative obligations on the rule-making power of the Secretary of State for the Home Department, by providing that the Rules should be so framed that Commonwealth citizens settled in the UK on 1 January 1973, and their wives and children, were no less free to come into and go from the UK than if the 1971 Act had not been passed. In *R v Immigration Appeal Tribunal, ex p Haque, Ruhul* [1987] Imm AR 587 the Court of Appeal held that an Immigration Rule infringing the mandatory and negative obligations contained in s 1(5) was *ultra vires* and void, but that could not lead to a resurrection of any of the pre-1973 rules. For standstill clauses in EC law, see *R (on the application of Tum) v Secretary of State for the Home Department, R (on the application of Dari) v Secretary of State for the Home Department* [2003] EWHC 2745 (Admin), [2004] 1 CMLR 1091, upheld [2004] EWCA Civ 788, [2004] INLR 442; referred to the ECJ at [2004] UKHL.
2   Human Rights Act 1998, s 6(1).
3   Race Relations Act 1976, s 19B(2) and (3) and s 19C(2) and (3), as amended by the Race Relations (Amendment) Act 2000. For a broad outline of the new statutory hat governing public authorities under the Equalities Act 2010, see **1.81** ff and the Government Equality Office's *A Summary Guide for Public Sector Organisations*.

1.43 The fact that the Rules are not subordinate legislation means that they cannot be impugned on conventional *ultra vires* grounds but as an exercise of public power they can be challenged for abuse of power or for violation of human rights; the possibility of such a challenge being brought is not precluded by the fact that the Rules have received parliamentary approval (in the sense that no negative resolution was made after they were laid before Parliament).[1] Abuse of power might include imposition by the rules of a requirement on officials to do what the legislation does not allow or an unlawful fetter on the discretion of the immigration official or if they unlawfully delegate a discretionary power. Such challenges have been made unsuccessfully in relation to rules which provide for mandatory refusal of leave for those arriving in the UK without a proper visa or entry clearance.[2] A rule may be challenged on the basis that it is unreasonable, in the sense of being partial or unequal in its operation as between classes; manifestly unjust; made in bad faith; or involving such oppressive or gratuitous interference with the rights of those affected by it as could find no justification in the minds of reasonable persons.[3] In *R v*

Immigration Appeal Tribunal, ex p Manshoora Begum a provision in one of the family rules was struck down on this ground.[4] On the other hand, there have been two recent developments which have given rise to some concern. When the Special Voucher System was abolished, the government made it clear that no new applications would be received after the date they announced the abolition of the scheme, even although the Immigration Rules remained in existence for some time afterwards to deal with outstanding applications made prior to the announced date of abolition. This left many people stranded (see Chapter 2, below). In the second case, the criteria for renewal of leave for highly skilled migrants were changed – the bar was heightened, but the old rules were deleted on the day after the laying of the new rules before Parliament and the new rules only came into force 27 days later, making it impossible to apply for an extension under the existing criteria and leaving an estimated 6000 people likely to fail the new criteria (see Chapter 10).

[1] *Secretary of State for the Home Department v Pankina* [2010] EWCA Civ 719.
[2] *R v Secretary of State for the Home Department, ex p Kaur (Rajinder)* [1987] Imm AR 278, DC; *R v Secretary of State for the Home Department, ex p Hassan* [1989] Imm AR 75, DC.
[3] Per Lord Russell CJ in *Kruse v Johnson* [1898] 2 QB 91. Applied in *R v Immigration Appeal Tribunal, ex p Begum (Manshoora)* [1986] Imm AR 385, QBD. In *R v Immigration Appeal Tribunal, ex p Begum (Hasna)* [1995] Imm AR 249, QBD the court held that HC 251, para 3, dealing with polygamous marriages (now HC 395, para 278), was not ultra vires.
[4] *R v Immigration Appeal Tribunal, ex p Begum (Manshoora)* [1986] Imm AR 385, QBD.

1.44 Where changes are made to the Immigration Rules, it is sometimes difficult to establish whether the old or new rules apply. The transitional provisions in the current Rules, HC 395, which provide that applications extant prior to their coming into force would be decided under the previous rules, do not unfortunately create a general principle applicable to the later amendments made to HC 395. However, the House of Lords has held that absent specific transitional provisions to the contrary, applications are to be decided in accordance with the Rules in force at the time the decision is made, not those in force at the time of the application.[1] Transitional provisions may themselves give rise to problems of interpretation.[2] There is a further practical problem. The consolidated version of the rules published in the GOV.UK website does not indicate, when or where a rule change has been made and they do not refer anywhere in the consolidated version to the particular Statement of change or any transitional provisions in it; so it is very difficult to check, often many years later, which rules should have applied to a particular decision and whether it was the correct decision. In Part 2 of this volume we indicate throughout the rules, the when and where rule changes have taken place. We believe this is unique to Butterworth texts on immigration law.

[1] *Odelola v Secretary of State for the Home Department* [2009] UKHL 25.
[2] For reported decisions on transitional provisions see *Shamseddin v Secretary of State for the Home Department* [1981] Imm AR 66; *Kamry v Secretary of State for the Home Department* [1981] Imm AR 118; *Secretary of State for the Home Department v Pope* [1987] Imm AR 10; *Minah Begum v Secretary of State for the Home Department* [1990] Imm AR 38; *Pardeepan v Secretary of State for the Home Department* [2000] INLR 447. See also Chapter 19 below.

1.45 On appeal, the Tribunal is always concerned to see whether immigration officials have followed the Immigration Rules applicable to the case. If they have failed to do so, the appeal must be allowed.[1] Even after the IA 2014 appeal changes have come into effect this exercise will still be necessary in judicial review applications. Much of the case law of the courts and tribunals is concerned with the interpretation of the Immigration Rules which 'like any other question of construction . . . depends on the language of the rule, construed against the relevant background. That involves a consideration of the Immigration Rules as a whole and the function which they serve in the administration of immigration policy'.[2] In *Odelola v Secretary of State for the Home Department*[3] it was said that the Immigration Rules are not the law of the land but essentially statements of administrative policy; an indication of how at any particular time the Secretary of State will exercise his or her discretion with regard to the grant of leave to enter or remain. Owing to the complexity and obscurity of immigration policy, construing a rule may necessitate 'a trawl through Hansard or formal Home Office correspondence as well as through the comparatively complex rules themselves' in order to elucidate their meaning, so that one senior judge commented that he was 'left perplexed and concerned how any individual whom the Rules affect can discover what the policy of the Secretary of State actually is at any particular time'.[4] Although statements of the Secretary of State's policy are contained elsewhere than the Rules, the Immigration Directorate Instructions for example, are generally not a legitimate source for interpreting a rule,[5] they may be relied upon if the language of the rule is genuinely ambiguous.[6]

1 Nationality, Immigration and Asylum Act 2002, s 86(3)(a), amended by Asylum and Immigration (Treatment of Claimants, etc) Act 2004, Sch 2, para 18.
2 *Odelola v Secretary of State for the Home Department* [2009] UKHL 25, [2009] 1 WLR 1230.
3 [2009] UKHL 25, [2009] 1 WLR 1230; [2010] ImmAR 59.
4 *Adedoyin v Secretary of State for the Home Department* [2010] EWCA Civ 773 (Longmore LJ).
5 *Mahad (previously referred to as AM) (Ethiopia) v Entry Clearance Officer* [2009] UKSC 16.
6 *Adedoyin v Secretary of State for the Home Department* (fn 4 above). In cases of ambiguity the court may not only rely on the IDI, but also on statements and assurances given in Parliament by ministers and on clarifications given in correspondence to such bodies as the ILPA.

1.46 If the rule allows the immigration official a discretion, the Tribunal can currently review the exercise of that discretion and decide that it ought to have been exercised differently.[1] If, however, the wording of the rule is in mandatory terms Modern Guidance or an IDI which instructs case workers to exercise a discretion in deciding cases under the rule, this is classed as a policy or concession outside the Rules and the only challenge on appeal is on the basis that the decision is not in accordance with the law.[2] This in turn means that the key date is the date of the UKBA decision so that only IDIs or Modern Guidance operative at that date (not ones that come into effect after the decision and by the time of the hearing of an appeal) apply.[3] As immigration law becomes more sophisticated, the Immigration Rules tend to be drafted in a more comprehensive and prescriptive form leaving less scope for the exercise of discretion by the decision maker.[4] The current Rules make it mandatory to refuse entry clearance, leave to enter, or a variation sought for a purpose not covered by the Rules,[5] putting at risk all those whose immigration status is, and remains, regulated outside the Rules, such as carers of UK-based relatives, and asylum seekers granted exceptional or discretionary leave. However, more and more concessionary policies have been incorporated into the Rules since October 2000, in accordance with the requirements of consistency and transparency mandated by the ECHR.[6]

[1] Under NIAA 2002, ss 84(1)(f) and 86(3)(b).
[2] Under NIAA 2002, ss 84(1)(e) and 86(3)(a); *SA (Long residence concession) Bangladesh* [2009] UKAIT 00051; *MD (Jamaica) v Secretary of State for the Home Department* [2010] EWCA Civ 213.
[3] *AG (Policies; executive discretion; Tribunal's powers) Kosovo* [2008] UKAIT 00082; *SA (long residence concession)*, fn 2 above.
[4] For a discussion of the appellate jurisdiction under the old rules, see the fourth edition at **2.51**.
[5] HC 395, paras 320(1) and 322(1). See also *Somasundaram v Entry Clearance Officer* [1990] Imm AR 16.
[6] Former policies incorporated into the Immigration Rules before *Pankina* and *Alvi* include, for example, those on domestic workers in private households (now HC 395, paras 159A–H, inserted by Cm 5597 on 27 August 2002); access rights to a UK-based child (now HC 395, paras 246–248F, substituted and inserted by Cm 4851 on 2 October 2000); long residence (now HC 276A–D, inserted by HC 538 on 31 March 2003); and Gurkhas and foreign or Commonwealth citizens discharged from HM forces (now HC 395, paras 276F–276Q, inserted by HC 1112 on 18 October 2004).

1.47 Although the rules are in mandatory terms, there is still a discretion outside the rules, which it may be necessary for the Secretary of state to consider exercising. In *R (on the application of Kobir) v Secretary of State for the Home Department)*[1] the Court held that although the Secretary of State had acted lawfully and within the Immigration Rules in refusing a student further leave to remain, 'it was manifestly unfair and unreasonable for the Defendant not to have looked very carefully indeed at the full history with a view to exercising her discretion outside the rules rather than simply refusing it within the rules.' Likewise *R (on the application of Forrester) v Secretary of State for the Home Department* the fact that the refusal was correct according to the rules, that was not the end of the matter because the Secretary of State had a discretion which had to be exercised intelligently and 'with a modicum of common sense and humanity.'[2]

[1] [2011] EWHC 2515 (Admin), [2011] All ER (D) 43 (Oct) at paragraph 27.
[2] [2008] EWHC 2307 (Admin). *R (on the application of Walker) v Secretary of State for the Home Department* [2010] EWHC 2473 (Admin), [2010] All ER (D) 05 (Nov) considered.

1.48 Prior to the rule changes in July 2012 there had been discussion for some time about the relationship of the Immigration Rules with the requirements of the Human Rights Act 1998. This has focussed on two main topics; first, on deference and the margin of appreciation to contracting states and their immigration policies[1] and, second, on whether the rules represented a policy yardstick by which to settle the balance between the public interest and individual rights especially in determining the issue of proportionality in family and private right claims under ECHR, Article 8.[2] More recently a new issue has arisen and probably died an early death – whether the rules should be interpreted so as to be consistent with the provisions in the ECHR. In *R (on the application of Syed) v Secretary of State for the Home Department*[3] the Court of Appeal rejected an argument that the Immigration Rules should, so far as is relevant to the particular case, be read and given effect under section 3 of the Human Rights Act 1998 so as to make them compatible with the appli-cant's rights under Article 8 of the European Convention on Human Rights. Clearly, if this view was accepted, it would require the court to modulate the very many paragraphs of the Immigration Rules whose application to a particular case was perceived to produce a decision which infringed an applicant's Article 8 rights. This would not only be impracticable, but would present subordinate caseworkers with a near impossible task. In applying the rules, however, the Secretary of State must have regard to and respect Convention rights whether or not the rules explicitly introduce them.[4] But this does not decide that the Immigration Rules are to be construed so as to be compliant with Article 8 of the Convention. Then there are the issues raised, first in the July 2012 immigration rule changes in HC 194 and secondly in the statutory changes contained in the IA 2014, regarding the proper balance to be struck in Article 8 ECHR cases between the public interest and private rights. These are not for discussion in Chapter 1 but in Chapters 7 (ECHR) and Chapter 19 (Appeal).

[1] See **7.21** regarding deference and **7.35–7.36** regarding the margin of appreciation.
[2] See the most radical exposition of this view in the Court of Appeal judgment in *Huang v Secretary of State for the Home Department* [2005] EWCA Civ 105, [2006] QB 1, [2005] 3 All ER 435, to the effect that the policy expressed in the Immigration Rules and supplementary instructions should be treated as having 'struck the balance between the public interest and the private right' that is required by Article 8, save in a 'truly exceptional case'; so that the assessment of proportionality becomes merely the determination of whether a case is 'truly exceptional'. This view was rejected and put to rest when the case went to the HL *Huang v Secretary of State for the Home Department* [2007] UKHL 11, [2007] 2 AC 167, [2007] 4 All ER 15.
[3] [2011] EWCA Civ 1059, 155 Sol Jo (no 34) 31 (7 September 2011).
[4] *Secretary of State for the Home Department v Pankina* [2010] EWCA Civ 719, [2011] Q.B. 376,, at para44; *R (on the application of BAPIO Action Ltd) v Secretary of State for the Home Department* [2007] EWCA Civ 1139, [2007] All ER (D) 172 (Nov).

1.49 The debate about the legal status of the Immigration Rules has been given a twist by the enactment of section 50 of the IAN 2006. This section gave the Secretary of State the power to use the Immigration Rules to prescribe the procedures to be followed in making applications for leave. New rules have now been made.[1] This novel way of proceeding replaced section 31A of the Immigration Act 1971 which required a statutory instrument to set out the procedures for making immigration applications for leave, variations of leave and so forth, and section 25 of the Asylum and Immigration (Treatment of Claimants, etc) Act 2004 which dealt with applications for permission to marry. The enactment in section 50 gives a boost to the holding in *Pankina*[2] that the Immigration Rules have acquired 'a status of quasi-law', a status which is unique. In *Pankina*, as we have already indicated, the Court of Appeal went on to hold that, so far as entry to and stay in the UK was concerned anything which was 'in the nature of a rule' had to be laid before Parliament in the form of a Statement of Changes and anything which had not been so laid could not be relied on as part of the Immigration Rules. In *Alvi* the Supreme Court upheld the *Pankina* decision, but modified the test for deciding whether something was a rule or mere guidance[3]

[1] HC 395, paras 34–34J. It should also be noted that when prescribed application forms were first made compulsory in 1996, it was done under the Immigration Rules (HC 395, para 32, as amended by HC 329, effective from 3 June 1996) without statutory aurority. In *R v Secretary of State for the Home Department, ex p Immigration Law Practitioners Association* [1997] Imm AR 189, Collins J held that the statutory power under s 3(2) of the Immigration Act 1971 was broad enough to allow the Secretary of State to redefine how an application should be made.
[2] *R (on the application of BAPIO Action Ltd) v Secretary of State for the Home Department* [2007] EWCA Civ 1139.

[3] *R (on the application of Alvi) v Secretary of State for the Home Department* [2012] UKSC 33 (18 July 2012). Lord Hope [53] agreed with lord Dyson [94] that any requirement which, if not satisfied, will lead to an application for leave to enter or to remain being refused is a rule within the meaning of section 3(2).

1.50 It should be noted, however, that there is still some question over the extent to which 'veracity checks' on Sponsors amount to a 'rule'. In *Pokhriyal*[1], where no points were awarded because the SSHD took issue over the confirmation of academic progression in the Confirmation of Acceptance of Studies (CAS), the Court of Appeal held that 'Whether a particular course constitutes academic progress . . . involves a value judgment. Paragraph 120B of Appendix A makes it clear that it is for the college, not the Secretary of State, to carry out the assessment. It is unsurprising that colleges are trusted to make this particular decision. The colleges have the requisite expertise'. Thus the SSHD could not go behind the confirmation of academic progress in the CAS, though the Court left open the question of whether the SSHD could do so in cases of fraud or a 'plainly inappropriate' assessment. In the later case of *Global Vision College Ltd*[2], Beatson LJ held that veracity checks carried out by the ECO as to the content of the CAS did not have the status of a 'rule' which had to be laid, but rather went to a question of evidential weight to be given to the document, thus the applicant could lawfully be denied points for a valid CAS if there was a discrepancy over how English language ability had been assessed by the college. The Court of Appeal sought to distinguish *Pokhriyal* in the Global Vision College case on the basis that there was no discrepancy between the evidence of the applicants and the college in *Pokhriyal*, without explaining how that was consistent with the decision in *Alvi* that even checks to be carried out by a sponsor (in relation to the 'resident labour market test') should be contained in the Rules.[3] How relevant these cases are now is doubtful, because what the government has done is to insert 'genuine application' and 'genuine intention' tests for various Tier 1 applications, in areas in which the UKBA and UK Visas are most concerned with credibility issues.[4]

[1] *R (on the application of Pokhriyal) v Secretary of State for the Home Department* [2013] EWCA Civ 1568.
[2] *R (on the application of Global Vision College Ltd) v Secretary of State for the Home Department* [2014] EWCA Civ 659.
[3] See Lord Dyson at para 104-106, Lord Clarke at 124 and Lord Wilson at 131.
[4] See Tier 1 (General) Migrants; See Appendix A, Attributes for Tier 1 (General) Migrants, para 19(h) – (l); for Tier 1 (Entrepreneur) Migrant at HC 359 para 245DB (f) – (i); for Tier 2 (Minister of Religion) Migrants at para 245HB (m).

1.51 The Immigration Rules also play a very important role in judicial review where the decisions of UKBA officials are challenged in the Administrative Court. In this context, the Rules are not rules of law, because they are not made by statutory instrument but are described in the Immigration Act 1971 as rules of practice to be followed in the administration of the Act for regulating entry to and stay in the UK. This characterisation of the rules has a number of consequences:

(i)   the language of the Rules is that of the administrator rather than that of the parliamentary draftsman. Often, they are no more than descriptive. They are, therefore, to be given a purposive rather than a strict construction unless, the words used are wholly unambiguous;[1]

(ii) the power to make any decision on entry, stay or deportation comes from the 1971 Act, not the Rules, and is unfettered.² In particular, it is not made subject to the Immigration Rules;³

(iii) the existence of a residuary discretion outside the Rules means that the Secretary of State can make some Rules mandatory without risk of unlawfully fettering his or her discretion, because in each case, he or she can decide whether to depart from the Rules.⁴ It is probably also why an immigration officer who gives leave mistakenly is not acting outside his or her authority;⁵

(iv) the Rules are not binding on the Administrative Court in the way that statutes are. Indeed, as we have seen, in exceptional cases, the court may strike out a Rule as being wholly or in part invalid for unreasonableness or unnecessary infringement of human rights.⁶ In most cases however, the court is concerned with the interpretation, rather than the *vires* of the Rules.

¹ *Alexander v Immigration Appeal Tribunal* [1982] 2 All ER 766, [1982] 1 WLR 1076, HL; *Singh v Immigration Appeal Tribunal* [1986] 2 All ER 721, [1986] Imm AR 352, HL; *R v Immigration Appeal Tribunal, ex p Rahman* [1987] Imm AR 313, CA; *Singh (Gurdev) v Immigration Appeal Tribunal* [1988] Imm AR 510, CA; *R v Immigration Appeal Tribunal, ex p Begum (Manshoora)* [1986] Imm AR 385, QBD; *R v Immigration Appeal Tribunal, ex p Zanib Bibi* [1987] Imm AR 392, QBD; *Bombay Entry Clearance Officer v De Noronha* [1995] Imm AR 341, CA; *R v Secretary of State for the Home Department, ex p Ali (Arman)* [2000] INLR 89.
² Immigration Act 1971, s 4(1).
³ See **1.34** ff above for a discussion on the source of the residuary discretion.
⁴ See *Pearson v Immigration Appeal Tribunal* [1978] Imm AR 212, CA; per Banks LJ in *R v Port of London Authority, ex p Kynoch Ltd* [1919] 1 KB 176 at 184, CA; *British Oxygen Co Ltd v Minister of Technology* [1971] AC 610, [1970] 3 All ER 165, HL. A good example of a fettering of discretion is *R v LCC, ex p Corrie* [1918] 1 KB 68 – a decision of the London County Council to refuse all further permits, without exception, to distribute literature in London public parks. In considering the exercise of the discretion outside the Immigration Rules, the Secretary of State is entitled to act so as to ensure that generally speaking the Rules are followed, to ensure fairness between applicants: *R v Secretary of State for the Home Department, ex p Ahmed* [1995] Imm AR 210, CS.
⁵ See *R v Secretary of State for the Home Department, ex p Ram* [1979] 1 All ER 687, [1979] 1 WLR 148.
⁶ *R v Immigration Appeal Tribunal, ex p Manshoora Begum* [1986] Imm AR 385; *R v Secretary of State for the Home Department, ex p Dhahan* [1988] Imm AR 257, QBD; *R v Secretary of State for the Home Department, ex p Saleem (Asifa)* [2000] INLR 413, CA. The Court of Appeal held in Huang v Secretary of State for the Home Department [2005] EWCA Civ 105, [2006] QB 1 that the Immigration Rules, in prescribing which classes of aliens (sic) will in the ordinary way be allowed to enter the UK and which will not, had themselves struck the balance between public interest and private right for the general run of cases, so that the courts would accord very considerable respect for the balance so struck (paras 57–58, per Laws LJ). However, this reasoning was rejected by the House of Lords in *Huang v Secretary of State for the Home Department* [2007] UKHL 11 which said 'it is a premise of the statutory scheme enacted by Parliament that an applicant may fail to qualify under the rules yet may have a valid claim by virtue of article 8'. See further the discussion in Chapter 8.

Decisions of the Tribunal and courts

1.52 The most voluminous source of immigration and asylum law is the case law of the higher courts, the former Immigration Appeal Tribunal (IAT) and the Asylum and Immigration Tribunal (AIT) and now the Upper Tribunal of the Immigration and Asylum Chamber (UT (IAC), on the meaning, effect, and application of the primary and subordinate legislation, the Immigration Rules, the Refugee Convention, ECHR, European Community Law, and Home Office policies outside the Rules. Decisions of the House of Lords, the Supreme Court and Court of Appeal are binding on those courts and on the lower courts and tribunals. Decisions of the Court of Sessions are binding on the Tribunals, which have a universal UK jurisdiction and are of persuasive authority in the higher courts of England and Wales. Decisions of the English and Welsh High Court also bind the First Tier Tribunal (IAC). Tribunal decisions are not strictly binding, but in 2001 the then President, Mr Justice Collins, instituted a system of key decisions, known as starred cases, decided by legal panels, which are meant to be binding on the Tribunal in subsequent cases, in order to end the previously common situation where there were conflicting decisions by different Tribunals.[1] The starred cases system was later followed by the system of 'Country Guideline' cases (referred to in Chapter 18 below)[2] and finally, the system of 'Reported' cases introduced in 2003. The current Practice Direction[3] brings the three systems together, and has exhaustive directions on their citation. It stipulates that no unreported decision of the Tribunal may be cited unless either a member of the family of the current appellant was a party or the appellate authority has given permission: the conditions for obtaining permission are very stringent indeed.[4] Reported decisions of the Upper Tribunal (IAC), often anonymised and referred to by their neutral citation, are available in electronic form on the Upper Tribunal website or through BAILII and the Electronic Immigration Network.[5] Administrative Court, Court of Appeal, Supreme Court and House of Lords decisions are all available online. With two competing sets of specialist immigration law reports, the official websites, BAILII and the EIN, more decisions of importance are now reported or otherwise available to practitioners than ever before. In this situation we have retained some unreported cases from previous editions, although we have tried to purge the text of references to old and largely inaccessible unreported Tribunal decisions. In addition to the reports of decisions of domestic courts, there is a growing body of European decisions from both Luxembourg[6] and Strasbourg.[7] We refer to these in the text, and to Commonwealth case law, all of which is widely available in electronic form.[8]

[1] The Tribunal should follow an earlier starred decision unless it is satisfied that the decision is clearly wrong: *Sepet v Secretary of State for the Home Department* [2001] EWCA Civ 681, [2001] INLR 33, per Laws LJ, para 99. Starred IAT and Tribunal decisions are binding unless inconsistent with other binding authority: Asylum and Immigration Tribunal Practice Directions 2005, 18.1.

[2] For the status of a Tribunal determination marked 'CG' see Chapter 12 – Asylum. A list of current CG cases is maintained on the Tribunal website, with which the parties will be expected to be conversant: see Chapter 18 below.

[3] Practice Directions: Immigration and Asylum Chambers of the First-tier Tribunal and the Upper Tribunal, 10 February 2010.

[4] Practice Directions, para 11.2ff. See Chapter 19.

[5] The Upper Tribunal website: //tribunalsdecisions.service.gov.uk/utiac/, contains all reported and country guidance IAT and Upper Tribunal cases. BAILII (British and Irish Legal Information Institute), www.bailii.org, is a free website with a vast database of cases from the Tribunal, the higher courts, and Irish and Commonwealth law. The Electronic Immigration Network website is at www.ein.org and its public resources homepage is an excellent gateway into most websites which immigration practitioners would need.

[6] ECJ judgments and Opinions are available on the Internet at www.curia.eu.int.

[7] ECtHR judgments are available at www.echr.coe.int.

[8] The New Zealand refugee cases are at www.refugee.org.nz. Australian cases are on AUSTLII (sister to BAILII). Canadian and South African cases can be found through a Google search of

the relevant court. There are some specialist websites on refugee law, such as www.refugec aselaw.org.

Immigration operational guidance

1.53 There are 14 different Guidance topics for immigration and nationality law on: www.gov.uk/immigration-operational-guidance

- Asylum policy
- Business and commercial caseworker guidance
- Enforcement
- Entry clearance guidance
- European casework instructions
- Fees and forms
- Immigration directorate instructions
- Immigration Rules
- Modernised guidance
- Nationality instructions
- Non-compliance with the biometric registration regulations
- Rights and responsibilities
- Sponsorship
- Stateless guidance

These above Guidances[1] are not part of any statute, or statutory instrument, and they are not part of the Immigration Rules. The Secretary of State is not entitled by guidance or instructions to his or her officers to restrict the rights which would otherwise exist under legislation and the Immigration Rules. So it follows that the guidance is of relevance in any challenge to a decision by way of appeal or judicial review, only if it exactly reflect the contents of legislation and the Immigration Rules or if it is more generous than the combination of those other sources.[2] Generally guidance cannot be relied on to interpret the Immigration Rules[3] unless the rule is genuinely ambiguous[4] but they may explain the purpose of the rule and the context in which it is intended to operate.[5] The IDIs have been held to give rise to a legitimate expectation that any policy approach that they contain will be followed[6] and the Secretary of State has an obligation to place before the Tribunal any policy material that may be of relevance to an issue in an appeal.[7] IDIs are instructions to immigration officers, who although having clear statutory duties in relation to leave to enter, can be given instructions by the Secretary of State.[8] It has been held that Entry Clearance Officers (ECOs) could have no duty imposed on them by the IDIs, which do not apply to ECOs, but only to Immigration Officers,[9] but it is doubtful if this would apply to Modern Guidance. In *R (on the application of NA (Iraq)) v Secretary of State for Foreign and Commonwealth Affairs*[10] it was held that under the Immigration Rules as then operating it was for the ECO to take the decision on the validity of a passport and, although he or she may be given guidance by the Secretary of State, he or she could not be instructed what a decision should be. Nevertheless, there are occasions when the Tribunal or court may need to interpret guidance to see in what situations it applies.[11] Home Office policies, although not based on statute, delegated legislation, or the Immigration Rules, can make a decisive difference in determining the legality of Home Office actions, particularly in the area of detention, as we see in Chapter 17.[12] In *US (Nepal) v Secretary of State for the Home Department*[13] the Court of Appeal found that the AIT had erred in law when it failed to look at relevant IDIs which set out a more generous and liberal policy in relation to abused domestic workers. For cases where there was an apparent conflict between the policy set out in the IDI, dealing with in country applications and that set out in SET 12, dealing with overseas applications, see *UR (policy; executive discretion; remittal) Nepal*[14] and *CT (Gurkhas:policy) Nepal*.[15]

[1] According to the government this website is in process of being rebuilt with new services and redesigned existing ones. GOV.UK refer to the service as a Beta service, which presumably means that it is not yet Alpha standard, because it is not completely finished but it will still do everything it's designed to do. Beta services will sometimes be available at the same time as an older, existing service and will run alongside it. This would obviously be the case as regards the IDIs and Modern Guidance. Some of the IDIs date back to 2002 but others are more recent and certainly gives off an aura of near redundancy.

[2] *JL (Domestic violence: evidence and procedure) India* [2006] UKAIT 00058 and *FH (Bangladesh) v Secretary of State for the Home Department* [2009] EWCA Civ 385.

[3] *Mahad (previously referred to as AM) (Ethiopia) v Entry Clearance Officer* [2009] UKSC 16, [2010] INLR 268; *MD (Jamaica) v Secretary of State for the Home Department* [2010] EWCA Civ 213; *OS (10 years' lawful residence) Hong Kong* [2006] UKAIT 00031.

[4] *Adedoyin v Secretary of State for the Home Department* [2010] EWCA Civ 773.

[5] *ZT (Kosovo) v Secretary of State for the Home Department* [2009] UKHL 6, [2009] 1 WLR 348, per Lord Hope

[6] *R v Secretary of State for the Home Department, ex p Chew; R v Secretary of State for the Home Department, ex p Popatia* [2000] EWHC 556 QB.

[7] *AA (Afghanistan) v Secretary of State for the Home Department* [2007] EWCA Civ 12, (2007) Times, 2 February, [2007] All ER (D) 250 (Jan).

[8] See the Immigration Act 1971, s 4(1) and Sch 1, para 1 and *Mahad v Entry Clearance Officer*, at fn 3 above.

[9] *MN (Non-recognised adoptions: unlawful discrimination?) India* [2007] UKAIT 00015 (12 February 2007).

[10] [2007] EWCA Civ 759, (2007) Times, 29 August, [2007] All ER (D) 409 (Jul).

[11] *KL (Student: IDI 'warning' about progress) India* [2007] UKAIT 00005 (12 January 2007).

[12] For a recent example, see the very carefully constructed judgment of Wyn Williams J in *R (on the application of S) v Secretary of State for the Home Department* [2007] EWHC 1654 (Admin), [2007] All ER (D) 290 (Jul) where the Admin Court was deciding the legality of the detention of a minor.

[13] [2009] EWCA Civ 208, [2009] All ER (D) 217 (Jan).

[14] [2010] UKUT 480 (IAC).

[15] [2011] UKUT 53 (IAC) (11 February 2011).

Administrative policy outside the Immigration Rules

1.54 The Immigration Rules are not a comprehensive code of all the practices regulating entry into the UK. There are still gaps, but where these are clearly within the definition of rules they will need to have been converted into rules within HC 395. This has now largely been done. Immigration rules, however, only deal with those relating to entry to and stay in the UK and do not include rules and practices which are necessary extensions to the system of immigration control, including a range of ancillary and incidental administrative powers not expressly spelt out in the Act, including the vetting of sponsors.[1] However, the Secretary of State cannot adopt measures which are inconsistent with the Act or the Immigration Rules. Without specific statutory authority, she cannot adopt measures which are coercive; or which infringe the legal rights of others (including their rights under the Human

Rights Convention); or which are irrational or unfair or otherwise conflict with the general constraints on administrative action imposed by public law.[2] Other policies deal with such matters as detention under immigration powers. A failure to take such a practice or policy into account, or a misinterpretation or misapplication, might well open the decision to a successful challenge, either on appeal on the basis that the decision is not in accordance with the law,[3] or on judicial review on the basis that it is unreasonable or unfair.[4] The existence of the policy may give rise to a legitimate expectation that it will be invoked in the applicant's favour, whether or not it has been published.[5] The application of an unpublished policy not to release a person in immigration detention in circumstances where the published policy indicated that there would be a release was held unfair in *Nadarajah and Amirthanathan*.[6] In *R (on the application of Lumba) v Secretary of State for the Home Department; R (on the application of Mighty) v Secretary of State for the Home Department*[7] it was held that the Secretary of State for the Home Department was liable for the false imprisonment of two foreign national prisoners pending their deportation, as she had applied an unlawful policy when exercising her power of detention. However, they were entitled to nominal damages only as they would have been detained if the published policy had been applied. For more details see Chapter 18.

[1] See *R (on the application of New London College Ltd) v Secretary of State for the Home Department* [2013] UKSC 51, at para 29.

[2] Ibid, at para 29.

[3] *Abdi (Dhudi Saleban) v Secretary of State for the Home Department* [1996] Imm AR 148, CA; *Hersi, Uslusow, Nur, Warsame and Kahie v Secretary of State for the Home Department* [1996] Imm AR 569 at 580, CA, per Otton LJ.

[4] *A-G of Hong Kong v Ng Yuen Shiu* [1983] 2 AC 629, [1983] 2 All ER 346, PC; *R v Secretary of State for the Home Department, ex p Khan* [1985] 1 All ER 40, [1984] 1 WLR 1337, CA; *R v Immigration Appeal Tribunal, ex p Bastiampillai* [1983] 2 All ER 844, [1983] Imm AR 1; *Khan (Asif Mahmood) v Immigration Appeal Tribunal* [1984] Imm AR 68, CA.

[5] *R (on the application of Rashid) v Secretary of State for the Home Department* [2004] EWHC 2465 (Admin), [2004] All ER (D) 316 (Oct), para 51. For older cases see *Gyeabour v Secretary of State for the Home Department* [1989] Imm AR 94; *Ahmed v Secretary of State for the Home Department, Patel v Secretary of State for the Home Department* [1999] Imm AR 22, CA (marriage and deportation); *R v Secretary of State for the Home Department, ex p Najem* [1999] Imm AR 107, QBD (travel documents; grounds for grant of exceptional leave to remain); *Warsame v Entry Clearance Officer, Nairobi* [2000] Imm AR 155, CA (Somali family reunion); *R v Secretary of State for the Home Department, ex p Singh (Tarlok)* [2000] Imm AR 508, QBD (children and deportation).

[6] *R (on the application of Amirthanathan) v Secretary of State for the Home Department; Nadarajah v Secretary of State for the Home Department* [2003] EWCA Civ 1768, [2004] INLR 139.

[7] [2011] UKSC 12.

1.55 However, in *Rashid*,[1] the Court ordered the Secretary of State to grant indefinite leave to remain to the claimant asylum seeker who had been wrongly denied the benefit of a policy even though the policy had by then been withdrawn. The Court did so notwithstanding the '*Ravichandran* principle'[2] that asylum claims should be determined in accordance with the circumstances, including policies, existing at the time the asylum decision is made. It did so because of its finding that there had been 'conspicuous unfairness amounting to an abuse of power'. The Court found 'conspicuous unfairness amounting to an abuse of power' because of the 'flagrant and prolonged incompetence' of the Secretary of State (refusing asylum in circumstances where the policy required a grant; successfully defending the refusal on appeal by pursuing a case antithetical to the policy and failing to offer an explanation for the incompetence once it came to light) and because others in the same circumstances as the claimant were granted asylum. The decision in *Rashid* was further explained in *R (on the application of S) v Secretary of State for the Home Department*.[3] Carnwath LJ said[4] that in *Rashid* there were two distinct questions. The first was whether the historical decisions denying the claimant the benefit of the policy were legally flawed. The second was what if any legal relevance the historical illegality had in relation to the decision of the Secretary of State under challenge which was not to rectify the historical error by putting the claimant in the position he would have been in had the withdrawn policy been applied. The existence of a historical 'abuse of power' was not 'a magic ingredient, able to achieve remedial results which other forms of illegality cannot match' but a concept underlying and characterising other particular forms of illegality. It did not make any difference whether the illegality resulted from bad faith, bad luck or sheer muddle: 'it is the unlawfulness, not the cause of it, which justifies the Court's intervention'. The unlawfulness justifying the Court's intervention related to the Secretary of State's current exercise of his remedial powers in respect of the past illegality. Having been asked by the claimant to grant indefinite leave to remain to remedy the failure to apply the policy, a factor that was relevant to the Secretary of State's exercise of the discretion was the correction of injustice. That that was a relevant consideration was 'implicit in the principles of fairness and consistency which underlay the whole statutory scheme'. In an extreme case, as *Rashid* was, the Court could hold that the unfairness was so obvious and the remedy so plain that the only way in which the Secretary of State's discretion could reasonably be exercised was by the grant of indefinite leave. The Court applied the same principles to the case that was before it; there the historical illegality was the Secretary of State's fettering of his discretion as a result of entering a Public Service Agreement with the Treasury whereby 'old' asylum claims such as the claimants were to be left in a back-log of cases and only new claims for asylum were to be determined. Consequently, by the time a decision was made on the claimant's asylum claim, the policy which would have resulted in his getting indefinite leave to remain had been withdrawn. The Court held that the Secretary of State now had the power to correct that historical illegality and should do so by reconsidering the claimant's case with the expectation that, absent countervailing considerations, he would be granted indefinite leave to remain. Where a claimant was denied the benefit of the policy of granting exceptional leave to remain to failed Afghan asylum seekers because the Secretary of State wrongly but not unlawfully or irrationally found him not to be Afghan he was not entitled to be put in the position he would have been in had the Secretary of State made the correct finding as to his nationality.[5] The Court refused judicial review in another application brought in reliance on *Rashid* and concerned with failure to give an Afghan the benefit of the same policy.[6] The application was refused as being an abuse of process because of the absence of evidence to explain the delay of years between the relevant policy being made public and the claimant seeking a remedy from the Secretary of State in respect of the failure to apply the policy. The Court also said that in the absence of a history of cumulative errors of the kind there had been in *Rashid* it would not in any event have found an 'abuse of power'. In the light of *R (on the application of S) v Secretary of State for the Home Department* however, which the Court did not consider, it is at least questionable whether that is right.

1   *R (on the application of Rashid) v Secretary of State for the Home Department* [2004] EWHC
     2465 (Admin), [2004] All ER (D) 316 (Oct), per Davis J He reached this conclusion on the
     basis that the policy was in universal and unqualified terms, admitting of no exception, and
     that the Secretary of State had no good reason for failing to apply it to the claimant at the
     relevant time. In those circumstances it would be substantively unfair to allow the Secretary
     of State to rely on the change of circumstances to deny the claimant the benefit of it. At the
     time of writing, the Secretary of State's appeal to the Court of Appeal was pending.
2   Referring to *Ravichandran (Senathirajah) v Secretary of State for the Home Department*
     [1996] Imm AR 97.
3   *R (on the application of S) v Secretary of State for the Home Department* [2007] EWCA Civ
     546, 151 Sol Jo LB 858.
4   In a judgment with which Moore-Bick LJ and Lightman J agreed.
5   *DS (Afghanistan) v Secretary of State for the Home Department* [2007] EWCA Civ 774.
6   *R (on the application of ZK (Afghanistan)) v Secretary of State for the Home Department*
     [2007] EWCA Civ 615.

European Union law

1.56 On the same day that the Immigration Act 1971 came into effect, the
UK's membership of the EC (now the EU) also took effect. Joining the Common Market, as it was then known, has meant that the development of
domestic immigration law has gone hand in hand with that of EU law on free
movement rights. Since then EU law has expanded to take in third-country
immigration, expulsion and asylum issues. New Directives, such as the
Qualification Directive[1] now give a European law dimension to asylum law
and are explained in Chapter 12. Free movement rights have been modernised
and consolidated into the Citizens' Directive,[2] and have been transposed into
UK domestic law by the Immigration (European Economic Area) Regulations
2006.[3] The Treaty of Lisbon came into force on 1 December 2009 and has
produced new consolidated versions of the two main Treaties, the Treaty on
European Union (TEU) and the Treaty on the Functioning of the European
Union (TFEU), which replaces the Treaty Establishing the European Community (TEC). So there is now only a European Union and no longer a
European Community. The ECJ is now renamed the Court of Justice of the
European Union (CJEU). The consolidated TEU now provides that the ECHR
and the principles set out in the Charter of Fundamental Rights of the
European Union are recognised by the EU and now have the same legal value
as the Treaties.[4] The EU has now joined the ECHR.[5] All these matters are dealt
with in Chapter 6. Reports of decisions of the ECJ are published on the
internet[6] and in the European Court Reports (ECR).[7]

1   Directive 2004/83/EC.
2   Directive 2004/38/EC.
3   SI 2006/1003. See further Chapter 6.
4   Treaty on European Union, as consolidated by the Treaty of Lisbon, art 6 (ex Art F); *Elliniki
     Radiophonia Tileorass-AE v Pliroforissis and Kouvelas* [1991] ECR I-2925, ECJ.
5   As above, art 6 (ex art 6 TEU).
6   At: curia.europa.eu/
7   The official reports published by the ECJ registry.

The European Convention of Human Rights

1.57 The ECHR and its case law, consisting mainly of judgments of the European Court of Human Rights in Strasbourg and (previously) opinions of the European Commission on Human Rights,[1] has long been a necessary part of the immigration lawyer's library and we have dealt with its very considerable impact on immigration law in this and all of the previous editions of this work. See Chapter 7. The case law is to be found on the court's website, which also gives access to press releases of forthcoming cases and summaries of recent decisions;[2] in the printed decisions of the ECtHR or the EComHR (the Series A reports); the case law summaries published by the court; and the commercially published Human Rights Law Digest (for decisions of the Committee of Ministers up to 1998), the European Human Rights Reports and the European Human Rights Law Review.

[1]   Abolished by Protocol 11 of the ECHR as from 1 November 1998.
[2]   At www.echr.coe.int/ECHR/EN/Header/Case-Law/Hudoc/Hudoc+database/

The Convention Relating to the Status of Refugees

1.58 The Convention Relating to the Status of Refugees (Geneva, 1951) and its 1967 Protocol (collectively the Refugee Convention) and the very considerable body of UK and foreign case law are key sources of asylum law, to be read with the provisions of the UK statutes and rules which give effect to the Convention in this country.[1] The Convention is a primary source of asylum law and its provisions are now construed routinely by the courts. In doing so, the courts use a number of UNHCR materials as aids to interpretation, in particular the UNHCR *Handbook*[2] and Executive Committee (ExCom) recommendations and conclusions. These may also be relevant to the exercise of a broad discretion, even though they are not themselves the source of obligations and duties.[3] Although the Convention is an international instrument, there is no supra-national court which can provide an international interpretation of its provisions. This may be one reason why the government has seen fit to introduce statutory definitions of various terms contained in the Convention, which on any reading appear to narrow the scope of the Convention application to those seeking refuge in the UK.[4] Because of the lack of a supra-national court, any examination of a particular provision by the UK courts will involve looking at a wide range of case law from different countries. Some familiarity with the leading case law of countries such as Canada, the US, New Zealand and Australia has been, and no doubt will continue to be, essential for those practising in this field. Much of this case law is available on the Internet through the Electronic Immigration Network and other websites.[5]

[1]   Asylum and Immigration Appeals Act 1993, s 2; see **1.20** above.
[2]   UNHCR Handbook on Procedures and Criteria for Determining Refugee Status (1979), 'the Handbook'.
[3]   See Chapter 12 below.
[4]   The Immigration, Asylum and Nationality Act 2006, ss 54 and 55 dictate how Article 1F(c) of the Refugee Convention (exclusion for acts contrary to the principles and purposes of the United Nations) is to be construed and applied and how issues relating to exclusion from Refugee status and expulsion of refugees are to be determined by the tribunal. The purposes and principles of the UN which are set out in the Preamble, Article 1 and 2 of the UN Charter are vague and unusual if not unsuitable for the characterisation of individual acts of a criminal

nature: see The European Council on Refugees and Exiles (ECRE), *Position on Exclusion from Refugee Status* (March 2004). Section 54 imposes a statutory interpretation of Article 1(F)(c) to include acts of committing, preparing or instigating terrorism and of encouraging or inducing others to commit, prepare or instigate terrorism, where the acts include inchoate offences and, where, notwithstanding given the lack of consensus within the international community as to its exact definition and constituent elements, terrorism is given the domestic UK definition contained in section 1 of the Terrorism Act 2000, thereby excluding protection for those who engage in liberation struggles or resistance to illegal occupations. This is contrary to the principle that 'the Convention must be interpreted as an international instrument, not a domestic statute, in accordance with the rules prescribed by the Vienna Convention on the Law of Treaties' (*Januzi v Secretary of State for the Home Department; Hamid v Secretary of State for the Home Department; Gaafar v Secretary of State for the Home Department; Mohammed v Secretary of State for the Home Department* [2006] UKHL 5, [2006] 3 All ER 305, [2006] 2 WLR 397, per Lord Bingham, para 4). The Nationality, Immigration and Asylum Act 2002, s 72 gives a definition of 'particularly serious crime' for the purpose of Article 33(2) of the Refugees Convention and dictates how issues relating to the expulsion of refugees are to be determined by the Tribunal. For further details, see Chapter 12, below.

5   The Electronic Immigration Network website is at: www.ein.org.

Other International treaties and obligations

1.59 Until the last decade, international instruments other than the Refugee Convention and the ECHR have played a rather background role in immigration and asylum, because they were not part of domestic law and their role as sources of immigration law was either very obscure or barely counted. For example, there are a number of Conventions which have led to the adoption of particular provisions in the Immigration Rules, such as the rule providing for settlement after four years (now changed to five in domestic law) in employment, which derives from the International Labour Organisation Convention regarding Migration for Employment, or the long residence concession, which derives from the European Convention on Establishment. With the incorporation of the ECHR into British law, UK courts and tribunals have developed their own human rights jurisprudence, which as we have noted in Chapter 8 does not always march hand in hand with Strasbourg case law. A number of other human rights instruments and the case law built round them is both relevant and helpful. These have already played a role in the development of Strasbourg jurisprudence. They are recognised as important aids to construction in the Convention itself. Article 53 provides that nothing in the Convention shall be construed as limiting or derogating from any of the human rights and fundamental freedoms under any other agreement to which any High Contracting Party is a party. These include the International Covenant on Civil and Political Rights (ICCPR) and decisions of the UN Human Rights Committee set up to receive complaints under this Covenant; the International Covenant on Economic, Social and Cultural Rights; the Convention on the Rights of the Child (UNCRC);[1] the Convention for the Elimination of all Forms of Racial Discrimination; the Convention on the Elimination of all Forms of Discrimination Against Women; the UN Convention Against Torture and Other Cruel, Inhuman and Degrading Treatment; the European Convention for the Prevention of Torture and Inhuman and Degrading Treatment or Punishment; and the UN Body of Principles on All Forms of Detention (1988). Perhaps the most striking developments are those in relation to children[2] and trafficked persons.[3]

In *R (on the appplication of Dehn (Courtney)) v Secretary of State for the Home Department*[4] it was held that any claim based upon an inconsistency between the Convention and domestic law was unarguable given that the Convention has no direct effect in UK law. In *AK v Secretary of State for the Home Department*[5] the Court of Appeal accepted that a failure to consider the 1954 Convention relating to the Status of Stateless Persons, which was a relevant consideration regarding the grant of discretionary leave to remain, could be litigated under section 82 of the Nationality Immigration and Asylum Act 2002 on the ground that the decision was 'otherwise not in accordance with the law' within section 84(1)(e), but it could not be pursued if it had not been raised before the Secretary of State and absent it being the subject of any published policy. On the other hand, it was made clear in *Habte v Secretary of State for the Home Department*[6] that the mere fact that someone is stateless does not give rise to a well-founded fear of persecution such as to justify refugee status – what has to be considered is whether the consequences of the refusal to allow someone to return, or of statelessness, amounts to persecution for a Convention reason.

1   In *R (on the application of S) v Secretary of State for the Home Department* [2007] EWHC 1654 (Admin), [2007] All ER (D) 290 (Jul) where the Admin Court was deciding the legality of the detention of a minor, the court used the UNCRC as an aid to construing Article 5 of the ECHR and ruled that the reservation made by the UK government was not and was not intended to permit the UK government to enact legislation or apply legislation so as to remove or alter the provisions of the convention which proscribe the circumstances in which it is permissible to detain children.
2   See *ZH (Tanzania) v Secretary of State for the Home Department* [2011] UKSC 4, [2011] 2 AC 166, [2011] 2 All ER 783 per Lady Hale at paras.
3   See our new Chapter 13 on trafficking.
4   [2012] EWHC 2676 (Admin). The Convention in issue was the UN Convention upon the Elimination or Reduction of Future Statelessness.
5   *AK v Secretary of State for the Home Department* [2006] EWCA Civ 1117 (31 July 2006).
6   *Habte v Secretary of State for the Home Department* [2006] EWCA Crim 1490 (7 November 2006).

THE PERSONNEL OF IMMIGRATION CONTROL

1.60 Control of immigration and asylum, as we have just seen, is administered within the framework of the Immigration Act 1971 and subsequent primary and subordinate legislation, EC law, the 1951 Refugee Convention, the ECHR and, of course, the Immigration Rules. All this has created a lot of officials and has placed onerous responsibilities and duties on airlines and other carriers, road hauliers, employers, local authorities, marriage registrars and others. It has generated a whole industry of advisers, some more caring, scrupulous and competent than others. The purpose of the remainder of this chapter is to describe the key elements of the administration of immigration control, by looking at the principal personnel and the main sources and limits of their power. At one level it is all about the Home Office, immigration officers, airlines and immigration advisers. But at another level it is about power, legality, and the particular tools of the trade of a very large and powerful administrative organisation.

The Home Office and Secretary of State for the Home Department

1.61 The Home Office is responsible for nationality, passports and immigration control. The Secretary of State for the Home Department is the minister in charge. But the statutes make no express reference to either. The Immigration Act 1971 refers only to the Secretary of State. Under Schedule 1 to the Interpretation Act 1978 it is provided that in every Act the expression 'Secretary of State' shall mean 'one of Her Majesty's principal Secretaries of State for time being'. In practice, it is the Secretary of State for the Home Department (the Home Secretary) who is in overall control and has the last word.[1] In Scotland it might be thought that the powers would be exercisable by the Secretary of State for Scotland, but it has been held that this is not so, and the Home Secretary in London can validly order someone who is within the Scottish jurisdiction to be deported,[2] or in some cases, admitted.[3] The administration of immigration control is not, however, entirely run by the Home Secretary: entry clearance officers in overseas posts are usually attached to the Foreign and Commonwealth Office,[4] and the Lord Chancellor is responsible for appointing judges of the First-tier and Upper Tribunals.[5] Until 1 April 2007 the Immigration and Nationality Directorate (IND) ran the show[6] and comprised an asylum section, an appeals directorate, the National Asylum Support Service (NASS) and managed migration, which includes all non-asylum casework, work permits and British nationality.[7]

[1] *Pearson v Immigration Appeal Tribunal* [1978] Imm AR 212, CA.
[2] *Agee v Murray* (23 February 1977, unreported), CS, per Lord Kincraig. However, the appointment of immigration officers and medical inspectors in Scotland is transferred to Scottish ministers: Scotland Act 1998 (Transfer of Functions to the Scottish Ministers) Order 1999, SI 1999/1750.
[3] In 2000 the Home Secretary ordered the admission of boxer Mike Tyson, who had a conviction for rape, to enable him to box in Scotland, a decision upheld in *R v Secretary of State for the Home Department, ex p Bindel* [2001] Imm AR 1, QBD.
[4] The Home office and Foreign Office have formed a Joint Entry Clearance Unit (JECU) which is responsible for coordination of entry clearance policy and practice.
[5] Tribunals, Courts and Enforcement Act 2007, Sch 2, paras 1(1) and 2(1).
[6] Since internal reorganisation in 2003.
[7] There is/was a bewildering array of departments and units within these Home Office departments, all referred to by acronym, such as RESCU, DEPMU, WICU, OASIS and NEAT, respectively (so far as we can ascertain) Resettlement and Coordination Unit; Detainee Escorting and Population Management Unit; Warnings Index Computerised Unit (reporting on overstayers); Operational Advisory Services for Immigration Service; and NASS Eligibility and Assessment Team). We have attempted to list as many of these acronyms as possible in a glossary: see Appendix 8.

UK Visas and Immigration

1.62 On 1 April 2007, the Border and Immigration Agency (BIA) was launched as a Home Office shadow agency. It replaced the old IND and has since become the UKBA. Its launch was accompanied by great fanfare and market speak.[1] The government spin doctors assured us it was not a 'big bang' nor a trial. Instead it was being 'rolled out' – like a new lawn, purchased from the local garden centre. During the 'roll-out' period there would be a mix of old and new branded items in circulation and a move to an organisation with a reputation for being fair, effective, transparent and trusted'. The first act in this brave new world was an announcement that new increases in immigration fees would take effect on 2 April 2007 for all those coming to the UK to work, stay, or study.[2] However, the BIA lasted just over a year and was replaced by the new UK Border Agency (UKBA), established as a shadow agency of the Home Office on 3 April 2008. The UKBA brought together under one umbrella the work of the Border and Immigration Agency, UK Visas and parts of HM Revenue and Customs at the border, and has worked closely with the police and other law enforcement agencies on issues of border control and security. One part of UKBA became effectively a new frontier police force, with a range of enforcement powers similar to the actual police, but it also incorporated the functions of immigration officers and the departmental officials in the Home Office immigration sections. It has now been split up into the UK Visas and Immigration and a Border agency, the earlier division of functions now place within distinct organisational sections of the Home Office. Details of the new structure GOV.UK are to be found in Chapter 14.

[1]   See, for example, letter to ILPA and other organisations from the Operations and Transition Director of Managed Migration, dated 3 April 2007.
[2]   See Chapter 3 at **3.26** for fees.

1.63 Within the Home Office there was previously a clear division of responsibility between the Secretary of State and immigration officers – under section 4(1) of the Immigration Act 1971, immigration officers are responsible for giving leave to enter and the Secretary of State for giving leave to remain or varying leave – but this clear division has been blurred by section 62 of the 2002 Act, which allows the Secretary of State to give leave to enter. The Secretary of State also has responsibility for making the Immigration Rules and laying them before Parliament,[1] and for making various Orders, rules and regulations under the 1971 Act and the other Immigration statutes. The various tasks of the Secretary of State are normally carried out by responsible departmental officials operating within normal *Carltona* principles,[2] but certain decisions such as the exclusion of persons on grounds of national security must be taken by the Secretary of State in person.[3] The signing of deportation orders is normally done by the Secretary of State in person, reflecting the significance of his or her decision.[4] In *R v Secretary of State for the Home Department, ex p Oladehinde*[5] the House of Lords held that although immigration officers had independent statutory powers, they were members of the Home Office and accordingly the Secretary of State could devolve decisions to deport to them. Since the formation of UKBA the division of immigration officers and departmental officials still exists but it has probably become even more blurred.

[1]   Immigration Act 1971, s 3(2).
[2]   *Carltona Ltd v Works Comrs* [1943] 2 All ER 560, CA.
[3]   Immigration and Asylum Act 1999, ss 60(9), 62(4), 64(2).
[4]   Earlier rules reflected this: HC 251, para 175, but not the current Immigration Rules. See per Woolf LJ in *R v Secretary of State for the Home Department, ex p Oladehinde; R v Secretary of State for the Home Department, ex p Alexander* [1990] 2 WLR 1195 at 1202, DC; further *Re Khan (Amanullah)* [1986] Imm AR 485, QBD.
[5]   [1991] 1 AC 254, [1990] 3 All ER 393, HL. See also *Jazayeri* [2001] UKIAT 00014, [2001] INLR 489.

1.64 The Secretary of State for the Home Department is expected to carry out his or her functions in accordance with the established principles of administrative law and not to do anything which breaches any person's human rights.[1]

As a public authority he or she must not discriminate unlawfully on racial and an ever-widening range of grounds set out in the Equality Act 2010,[2] although discrimination on grounds of age, disability, nationality or ethnic or national origin and religion or belief in certain areas of immigration law is permissible.[3] He or she must keep within the limits of the statutory powers, under which decisions are taken, and must exercise prerogative powers fairly (see **2.112** below). In situations covered by the Immigration Rules, the Secretary of State must act in accordance with them, unless it be to make a decision more favourable to an immigrant (see **1.34** above). The Secretary of State is now fully susceptible to control by the courts and may be restrained by interim or final injunctions and is guilty of contempt of court if he or she breaches an injunction or undertaking given to the court.[4]

1   Human Rights Act 1998, s 6.
2   Equality Act 2010, s 29(6).
3   See the Equality Act 2010, Sch 3, paras 15A-19 and the discussion below at **1.69**.
4   *Re M* [1994] 1 AC 377, sub nom *M v Home Office* [1993] 3 All ER 537, HL.

Immigration officers

1.65 Immigration officers are part of the immigration service, which consists of immigration officers, chief immigration officers and immigration inspectors, all of whom are appointed by the Secretary of State under the Immigration Act 1971.[1] They have their own statutory functions as immigration officers, but they are also civil servants[2] and can, therefore, be asked to make decisions to deport on behalf of the Secretary of State.[3] Their functions are to examine those who arrive in this country[4] and to grant, refuse, suspend or cancel leave to enter.[5] They also have important policing functions under ss 28A–K of, and Schs 2 and 3 to, the 1971 Act, Part VII of the Immigration and Asylum Act 1999 and s 14 of the Asylum and Immigration (Treatment of Claimants, etc) Act 2004. The policing function has been progressively added to in legislation stretching from the IAN Act 2006, the UK Borders Act 2007, the Borders Citizenship and Immigration Act 2009 and most recently by the Immigration Act 2014.[6] It is probably true to say that their function of granting leave to enter has now been greatly diminished by the practise of moving the grant of any leave over six months to overseas posts, by combining the grant of entry clearance in these cases with leave to enter, but this loss of function is more than compensated by their increasing role of policing Britain's borders and working more closely with police and intelligence services to stop the entry of alleged criminals, terrorists and people smugglers. Amongst other things, it is a criminal offence to obstruct immigration officers in carrying out their functions under the 1971 Act,[7] or to assault them.[8]

1   Immigration Act 1971, Sch 2, para 1(2). The paragraph enables customs officers to be employed as immigration officers by arrangement with the Commissioner of Customs and Excise. In Scotland, immigration officers are appointed by the Scottish ministers: Scotland Act 1998 (Transfer of Functions to the Scottish Ministers) Order 1999, SI 1999/1750.
2   See per Woolf LJ in *R v Secretary of State for the Home Department, ex p Oladehinde; R v Secretary of State for the Home Department, ex p Alexander* [1990] 2 WLR 1195 at 1203.
3   *R v Secretary of State for the Home Department, ex p Oladehinde* [1991] 1 AC 254, [1990] 3 All ER 393, HL. See also *Jazayeri* [2001] UKIAT 00014, [2001] INLR 489.
4   And at Eurostar stations, on Eurostar and in ports at Dover, Calais, Boulogne and Dunkirk, to be extended to Belgian ports: see modifications made to Immigration Act 1971, Sch 2 by the

Channel Tunnel (International Arrangements) Order 1993, SI 1993/1813 as amended; Nationality, Immigration and Asylum (Juxtaposed Controls) Order 2003, SI 2003/2818. See further **3.157** ff below.
5   Immigration Act 1971, Sch 2, paras 2–6, as amended by the Immigration (Leave to Enter and Remain) Order 2000, SI 2000/1161. In doing so they are entitled to mark passports: *R v Secretary of State for the Home Department, ex p Raju* [1986] Imm AR 348, QBD.
6   See ss 1 and 2 (extended removal powers under substituted s 10 of the Immigration and Asylum Act 1999, and s 4 (new enforcement powers under Sch 1).
7   Immigration Act 1971, s 26(1)(g).
8   UK Borders Act 2007, ss 22 and 23. For this and other criminal offences, see Chapter 14 below.

1.66 In exercising their statutory functions immigration officers must act in accordance with the law, the Immigration Rules, and any instructions given to them by the Secretary of State for the Home Department, provided these are not inconsistent with the Immigration Rules,[1] and they must not do anything which breaches a person's human rights[2] or constitutes unlawful discrimination.[3] The need to act in accordance with the law and the Immigration Rules is consistent with the general principles of administrative law and includes the duty to act fairly, which we look at in more detail below. But it also derives quite specifically from section 86(3) of the Nationality, Immigration and Asylum Act 2002,[4] which requires the Asylum and Immigration Tribunal to allow an appeal if the decision is not in accordance with the law, including the Immigration Rules. Uncertainty still hangs over the extent of the Tribunal's jurisdiction in respect of a decision which is *Wednesbury* unreasonable, taken in bad faith or unfairly (see Chapter 19 below), but this does not affect the clear restraints placed upon the immigration officer's powers and the manner in which they must be exercised. It appears that immigration officers share the Secretary of State's discretion to depart from the Rules in a manner favourable to the immigrant,[5] an issue the court left open in *Ex p Ounejma*.[6]

1   Immigration Act 1971, Sch 2, para 1(3).
2   Human Rights Act 1998, s 6.
3   As to which, see **1.67**.
4   Previously Immigration and Asylum Act 1999, Sch 4, para 21, and before that, Immigration Act 1971, s 19(1)(a)(i).
5   See Immigration Act 1971, s 4(1), **1.34**, **1.51** and **1.53** above.
6   [1989] Imm AR 75.

1.67 In exercising their statutory functions immigration officers must act in accordance with the law, the Immigration Rules, and any instructions given to them by the Secretary of State for the Home Department, provided these are not inconsistent with the Immigration Rules,[1] and they must not do anything which breaches a person's human rights[2] or constitutes unlawful discrimination.[3] The need to act in accordance with the law and the Immigration Rules is consistent with the general principles of administrative law and includes the duty to act fairly. Older cases, like ex *Ex p Safira Begum*[4] are no longer representative of the immigration officer's proper functions, but others making it clear that the officer must act honestly and fairly.[5] In *Mughal* the Court of Appeal set out the position which is still relevant today. Immigration Officers must both give the entrant a real opportunity of satisfying the immigration officer that he or she should be admitted, and where the officers' suspicions are aroused they must make them known to the immigrant and give him or her a chance to explain,[6] unless it is so obvious that that there is unlikely to be an exculpatory explanation.[7] It appears that immigration officers share the Secretary of State's discretion to depart from the Rules in a manner favourable to the immigrant,[8] an issue the court left open in *Ex p Ounejma*.[9]

[1] Immigration Act 1971, Sch 2, para 1(3).
[2] Human Rights Act 1998, s 6.
[3] As to which, see **1.67**.
[4] *R v Secretary of State for the Home Department, ex p Begum (Safira)* (1976) Times, 27 May, QBD (no obligation on immigration officers to make any inquiries on their own initiative in an attempt to assist would-be entrants; they could merely stand at their bench and wait for intending entrants to say what they had to say).
[5] *Re HK (infant)* [1967] 2 QB 617 at 630, per Lord Parker CJ; *Arif (Mohamed) (an infant), Re* [1968] Ch 643, sub nom *A (an infant), Re, Hanif v Secretary of State for Home Affairs* [1968] 2 All ER 145, CA; *R v Chief Immigration Officer, Lympne Airport, ex p Singh (Amrik)* [1969] 1 QB 333, [1968] 3 All ER 163.
[6] *R v Secretary of State for the Home Department, ex p Mughal* [1974] QB 313, per Lord Denning at p 325 and Scarman LJ at p 331 CA. See also *R v Secretary of State for the Home Department, ex p Ramnial* [1983] LS Gaz R 30, DC (a simple inquiry of the Home Office would have revealed a Home Office report that a woman passenger's marriage was genuine); see also *R v Secretary of State for the Home Department, ex p Moon* (1995) Times, 8 December (unfair not to give a visa applicant an opportunity to deal with objections to his admission).
[7] *R v Immigration Officer, ex p Ajekukor* [1982] Imm AR 3, DC (woman passenger with forged stamp in her passport and could give no explanation).
[8] See Immigration Act 1971, s 4(1).
[9] [1989] Imm AR 75.

Police

1.68 Although immigration officers have taken over much of the policing of immigration control with the powers given to them under Part VII of the IAA 1999 and section 14 of the Asylum and Immigration (Treatment of Claimants, etc) Act 2004, the police retain a considerable role. They are responsible for the registration of foreign nationals[1] and remain jointly responsible for the enforcement of those parts of the criminal law, including immigration offences, which involve immigration. Like immigration officers, they have powers under the IA 1971 to arrest suspected overstayers, illegal entrants and absconders for the purposes of administrative detention,[2] as well as immigration offenders.[3] They can arrest illegal entrants and others, and can obtain warrants for the search and arrest of such persons.[4] In addition to these powers, the police may be used for the service of documents such as decisions to deport, and have been used in the collection of information about the home circumstances of sponsors wishing to bring relatives and family into this country and on applicants for naturalisation. Immigration law makes a distinction between police acting in the execution of the Immigration Acts (ie performing an administrative function given to them under the Acts) and police exercising common law powers to investigate crime.[5]

[1] Immigration Act 1971, s 4(3); Immigration (Registration with Police) Regulations 1972, SI 1972/1758 (amended on many occasions only in respect of the fee for issue of a certificate of registration).
[2] Immigration Act 1971, Sch 2, para 17.
[3] Immigration Act 1971, s 28A(1), as amended by Immigration and Asylum Act 1999 (arrest without warrant for certain immigration offences).
[4] Immigration Act 1971, s 28B.
[5] *R v Clarke* [1985] AC 1037, [1985] 2 All ER 777, HL.

Entry clearance officers

1.69 The citizens of approximately 100 countries now need visas even for a visit to the UK, and visas or entry clearance have long been required for citizens of every non-EEA country who wish to come to the UK for work, business, study or family reunion. Now visas or entry clearances are required for everyone, except certain British nationals,[1] who seeks entry for more than six months for whatever purpose, but the entry clearance or visa will now also be a leave to enter. Visas and entry clearances are granted by entry clearance officers.[2] Entry clearance is defined in the IA 1971[3] but there is no mention of entry clearance officers, as such, in the Immigration Acts, which is surprising in view of the vitally important role they play in granting entry clearances which operate as leave to enter.[4] However, the Immigration Rules HC 395 place entry clearance officers in an equivalent position to immigration officers vis-à-vis the application of the rules.[5] They are also under obligation to act in accordance with the UK's obligations under the ECHR and for the purpose of the Human Rights Act 1998 they are 'public authorities'.[6] They are also subject to the prohibition on unlawful discrimination on the grounds set out in statute, in particular, on grounds of nationality or ethnic or national origin, unless this is permitted by specific ministerial authorisation.[7] All the requirements of legality and fairness set out above in relation to immigration officers apply with equal force to entry clearance officers.[8] One aspect of their role and status was highlighted by the Court of Appeal decision in *NA (Iraq)* which dealt with instructions issued to visa officers about the recognition of a certain category of Iraqi passport of dubious authenticity.[9] The Court held that it was for each ECO to make the final decision, not the Secretary of State. He or she could give guidance, but the final decision had to be that of the ECO.

[1] These are (i) a British Dependent Territories citizen; (ii) a British National (Overseas); (iii) a British Overseas citizen; (iv) a British protected person; (v) a British subject by virtue of Section 30(a) of the British Nationality Act 1981: HC 395, para 16. They can come without an entry clearance, ask for entry for more than six months and be given leave up to six months, and be told to apply for the end of this period to the Home Office for an extension.

[2] See *R v Secretary of State for the Home Department, ex p Phansopkar* [1976] QB 606, [1975] 3 All ER 497, CA. In many cases entry clearance officers refer applications back to London for decision. But see *R(on the application of NA (Iraq)) v Secretary of State for Foreign and Commonwealth Affairs* [2007] EWCA Civ 759, at para 18 to the effect that unless the Immigration Rules make the contrary clear the decision on a visa or EC application is that of the ECOs, using their individual judgment under the rules, not that of the Secretary of State.

[3] Under IA 1971, s 34(1) 'entry clearance' means a visa, entry certificate or other document which, in accordance with the immigration rules, is to be taken as evidence or the requisite evidence of a person's eligibility, though not a British citizen, for entry into the United Kingdom (but does not include a work permit).

[4] Immigration Act 1971, s 3A, inserted by Immigration and Asylum Act 1999, s 1; Immigration (Leave to Enter and Remain) Order 2000, SI 2000/1161, arts 2–4.

[5] Under HC 395, para 16 26. An application for entry clearance is to be considered in accordance with the Rules governing the grant or refusal of leave to enter. Where appropriate, the term 'Entry Clearance Officer' should be substituted for 'Immigration Officer'.

[6] Human Rights Act 1998, s 6.

[7] Equality Act 2010, s 29(6) and Schedule 3, paragraphs 15A-19. See *European Roma Rights Centre v Immigration Officer at Prague Airport (United Nations High Commissioner for Refugees intervening)* [2004] UKHL 55, [2005] 2 WLR 1, where the House of Lords held that the operation conducted by UK immigration officials at Prague Airport in an attempt to stop Roma people coming to the UK to claim asylum was unlawful under both domestic and international law.

[8] *Kumar v Entry Clearance Officer, New Delhi* [1985] Imm AR 242; *R v Secretary of State for the Home Department, ex p Moon* (1995) Times, 8 December, QBD.

NA (Iraq) (R on the application of) v The Secretary of State for the Foreign and Common Wealth Affairs [2007] EWCA Civ 759 (26 July 2007).

Chief Inspector of the UK Border Agency

1.70 Following a Home Office Immigration and Nationality Directorate Review undertaken in July 2006, the Government sought views on proposals about setting up a single inspection body to replace the many different inspection and advisory bodies, already in existence – the Immigration Race Monitor, Independent Monitor of Certification of Claims as Unfounded, The Accommodation Centres Monitor, and the Independent Monitor for entry clearance refusals. The problem identified was that there was no assessment of overall effectiveness, no assessment of enforcement, no assessment of overall decision making, no assessment of access to information and limited assessment of treatment. Following this consultation the Government proposed a new independent inspectorate to carry out inspections across the whole system of immigration control at home and abroad and to report. It also proposed abolishing the Advisory Panel on Country Information, Monitor of Accommodation Centres, Race Monitor and Certification Monitor. The UK Borders Act 2007, section 48 (powers came into force on 1 April 2008) provided the statutory framework for the Chief Inspector of the UK Border Agency. Since then there have been important and enlightening Reports on various aspects of immigration control, available on the Independent Inspector's web site at: www.icinspector.independent.gov.uk.

Additional duties are cast on the Chief Inspector by section 16 of the Immigration Act 2014 in the light of the replacement of the independent immigration appeal system in place for over 50 years. He or she must produce a report commissioned by the Home Secretary on whether the substitution of administrative reviews conducted by immigration staff on decisions made by other immigration staff in place of the established appeal system is effective and independent, independent being given a very restricted meaning by section 16(1)(c) meaning 'independent' in terms of their separation from the original decision-maker.

The first Chief Inspector, John Vine, is known as the man who holds Britain's border controls to account. He has published more than 50 reports during his near six-year tenure, including findings that exposed huge backlogs in the now-defunct UK Border Agency. His reports brought a rigorous and determined approach to the role of scrutinising the UK's borders and have highlighted flaws in the Home Office's immigration regime.[1] Keith Vaz, chair of the home affairs select committee has expressed concerns about the number of reports that the Independent Inspector had produced which had not been published by the Home Office and said that all of these must be released.[2]

John Vine is to step down on 31 December 2014, seven months earlier than planned. The Home Office have indicated that the Independent Chief Inspector of Borders and Immigration currently has a separate website but will soon be incorporated into GOV.UK; see now: www.gov.uk/government/organisations/chief-inspector-of-the-uk-border-agency.
See *Guardian*, 1 August 2014.

Private security firms

1.71 A source of increasing concern is the involvement of the private sector in the detention and removal of immigrants. Private security companies have been involved for decades in the running of immigration detention centres. Concerns about the treatment of detainees, and of those being removed from the UK, have emerged from time to time, but are more difficult to investigate than if the establishments and officers concerned were under the direct control of the Secretary of State.[1] In *Quaquah v Group 4 and the Home Office*,[2] the High Court struck out a claim in tort against the Home Office for events at Campsfield House detention centre in 1997 which resulted in the prosecution of the plaintiff, holding that the Home Office was not liable for the tortious actions of an independent contractor to whom it had delegated the running of a detention centre, provided it exercised reasonable care over the selection of that contractor. The 1999 and 2002 Acts have established a regulatory regime at removal centres, but have also given staff employed by the private companies extensive disciplinary powers, including the use of reasonable force, and powers of entry into premises, search and seizure when accompanying an immigration officer.[3] The companies concerned are however 'public authorities' when exercising these functions.[4] The Secretary of State may intervene in the running of a contracted out removal centre if the manager has lost control of the centre or any part of it, or appears likely to, or in the interests of safety or prevention of damage to property.[5]

In a recent inquest in May 2013 into the death of Jimmy Mubenga on a British Airways flight to Angola on 12 October 2010 where he had been forcibly taken to be deported, the G4S security guard in charge of restraining him was asked to read out a string of racist jokes he received and forwarded using his mobile phone. These 'jokes' aggressively targeting black men, Pakistanis and Muslims but, he said, did not reflect his beliefs or influence his treatment of the deportees he removed from the UK. He was obviously less moved by the evidence given by over 20 passengers who said they heard Mubenga repeatedly cry out during the struggle that he could not breath. He died of asphyxiation. The Inquest found that his death was an unlawful killing.

[1] One of the companies which runs a number of removal centres, GSL (a former subsidiary of Group 4) has been the subject of at least three official inquiries, including one into the events at Yarl's Wood on 14 February 2002 which led to the centre burning down; an inquiry into allegations of racism and abuse at Yarl's Wood, where the Prisons Ombudsman found the incidence of force 'disproportionate', and an ongoing inquiry into racism and abuse at Oakington Immigration Reception Centre and at Heathrow during escort of deportees, depicted by a BBC programme, 'Asylum Undercover' in March 2005 (see ministerial statement by Des Browne, Hansard 3.3.05, Col 95WS). Despite this record, the company has been awarded the contract to design, build and run the accommodation centres established under Part 2 of the Nationality, Immigration and Asylum Act 2002 (see IND website).

[2] *Quaquah v Group 4 (Total Security) and the Home Office* (01/TLQ/0340) (23 May 2001, unreported).

[3] See Immigration and Asylum Act 1999, ss 147–157; Schs 11–13; Nationality, Immigration and Asylum Act 2002, s 64.

[4] Human Rights Act 1998, s 6; this was conceded in *Quaquah v Group 4*, fn 2 above.

[5] Immigration and Asylum Act 1999, s 151.

Airlines and other carriers

1.72 Airlines and other carriers which bring passengers to the UK have responsibilities for checking passengers' passports and visas and now perform public law duties and have public law powers in respect of immigration control beyond any rights and liabilities arising from the contract of carriage.[1] The Immigration Act 1971 and the Immigration and Asylum Act 1999 make special provision for them. First, they are generally expected to call or, in the case of trains, stop only at specified ports of entry or terminal control points.[2] There they are under a duty to co-operate with the immigration authorities in ensuring that passengers embark and disembark in designated controlled areas and observe the conditions and restrictions which apply.[3] During the journey they must supply passengers with landing or embarkation cards as required.[4] The captain of a ship or aircraft and the manager of a train arriving in the UK is required to stop passengers disembarking, except in accordance with the arrangements made for their examination by immigration officers,[5] and is required to furnish immigration officers with lists of passengers and crew members and other passenger information,[6] arrival times of ships, trains or aircraft expected to carry non-EEA nationals,[7] and copies of passengers' documents,[8] as required.

[1] See generally 5 *Halsbury's Laws* (4th edn) para 301ff; Carriage by Air Act 1961.
[2] IA 1971, Sch 2, para 26(1), modified in relation to Channel Tunnel trains by the Channel Tunnel (International Arrangements) Order 1993, SI 1993/1813, Sch 4 para 1(11)(r).
[3] IA 1971, Sch 2, para 26(2), as modified for the Channel Tunnel by SI 1993/1813.
[4] IA 1971, Sch 2, para 5, modified in relation to Channel Tunnel trains by SI 1993/1813, para 1(11)(g); Immigration (Landing and Embarkation Cards) Order 1972, SI 1972/1666, as amended by SI 1975/65.
[5] IA 1971, Sch 2, para 27(1), modified in relation to Channel Tunnel trains by SI 1993/1813, para 1(11)(r).
[6] IA 1971, Sch 2, paras 27(2) and 27B, inserted by Immigration and Asylum Act 1999, s 18, modified in relation to Channel Tunnel trains by SI 2000/913; Immigration (Particulars of Passengers and Crew) Order 1972, SI 1972/1667, as amended; Immigration (Passenger Information) Order 2000, SI 2000/912.
[7] IA 1971, Sch 2, para 27C, inserted by Immigration and Asylum Act 1999, s 19, modified in relation to Channel Tunnel trains by SI 2000/913.
[8] IA 1971, Sch 2, para 27B(4A), inserted by Asylum and Immigration (Treatment of Claimants, etc) Act 2004, s 16, not yet in force at time of writing.

1.73 Carriers or their agents may be required to remove or make arrangements for the removal from the UK of any passengers who are refused leave to enter or are illegal entrants.[1] Normally the cost of removal will fall on the carrier, but in the case of passengers refused admission there is a two-month time limit for the giving of directions for their removal, after which the cost of removal falls on the Secretary of State for the Home Department.[2] Carriers are also liable to pay up to 14 days' detention costs for those refused leave to enter, illegal entrants and certain crew members who overstay their shore leave.[3] The costs of detaining illegal entrants by deception is not payable, however, unless their leave was cancelled within 24 hours of the conclusion of their examination.[4] In the case of deportees, the owners or agents of any ship, train or aircraft or the captain are required to comply with the directions given by the Secretary of State for the removal of the person from the UK.[5] The captain of a ship or aircraft, or a train manager, may also be required to prevent the escape of a person placed on board pending removal from the UK and has power to detain such person in custody for this purpose.[6] Breaches of their respective duties under the Immigration Act 1971 by either the owners, their agents or the captain or manager may make them liable to criminal penalties under section 27 of the 1971 Act.[7] If passengers arrive in the UK without proper documentation, the carrier may, in addition to the cost of removal and detention, be liable to pay a penalty of up to £2000.[8] Carriers' liability is treated in detail in CHAPTER 15 below.

[1] Immigration Act 1971, Sch 2, paras 8–9, modified in relation to Channel Tunnel trains by SI 1993/1813, Sch 4, para 1(11)(h)–(l); see also *R v Immigration Officer, ex p Shah* [1982] 2 All ER 264, [1982] 1 WLR 544; *Singh (Parshotam) v Secretary of State for the Home Department* [1989] Imm AR 469, CA.

[2] IA 1971, Sch 2, paras 8(2) and 10(3).

[3] IA 1971, Sch 2, paras 19(1) and 20(1), as amended by Asylum and Immigration Act 1996, Sch 2, paras 8, 9, modified in relation to Channel Tunnel trains by SI 1993/1813, Sch 4, para 1(11)(q).

[4] IA 1971, Sch 2, para 20(1A), inserted by Asylum and Immigration Act 1996, Sch 2, para 9(2).

[5] IA 1971, Sch 3, para 1(1) and (2), modified in relation to Channel Tunnel trains by SI 1993/1813, Sch 4, para 1(12).

[6] IA 1971, Sch 2, para 16(4) and Sch 3, para 1(3), modified in relation to Channel Tunnel trains by SI 1993/1813, Sch 4, para 1(11)(p), 1(12).

[7] Modified in relation to Channel Tunnel trains by SI 1993/1813, Sch 4, para 1(9).

[8] Immigration and Asylum Act 1999, s 40(2), substituted by Nationality, Immigration and Asylum Act 2002 s 125, Sch 8.

Sponsors

1.74 Sponsors used only to feature in the Immigration Rules in relation to overseas students 'sponsored' by their government or other institution and in connection with family visits and family reunion, and they barely got a mention in our main chapters. However, this has now all changed. They are now key players in the government's points based immigration scheme (PBS). We describe this in relation to students in CHAPTER 9 and in relation to employment in CHAPTER 10. Sponsorship carries with it very onerous duties, with regard to student registration and attendance records which have to be kept on a password controlled computer system shared with UK Visas.[1] Without getting a sponsorship licence no educational institutions can enrol overseas students and no employer can employ overseas workers and staff. Yet given the enormous detailed provisions regulating sponsorship, a feature of the sponsorship scheme is that none of the application processes and none of the detailed regulation or sanctions is spelt out in statute, delegated regulation or Immigration Rules and none of the Guidance is subject to parliamentary control or supervision. However, as set out above at **1.49** the Supreme Court has given its approval to the means of control on the basis that the system of immigration control must necessarily extend to a range of ancillary and incidental administrative powers not expressly spelt out in the Act, including the vetting of sponsors.[2]

[1] See CHAPTER 9.

[2] *R (on the application of New London College Ltd) v Secretary of State for the Home Department* [2013] UKSC 51, at para 29.

Marriage and civil partnership registrars

1.75 Section 24 of the Immigration and Asylum Act 1999 imposes a duty on registrars to whom notice of marriage has been given, and those who have attested a declaration accompanying the notice, to report to the Secretary of State for the Home Department any suspicion on reasonable grounds that a marriage or civil partnership is, or will be, a sham.[1] This whole business is now much more rigorously controlled by the Immigration Act 2014. A more extensive system of reporting suspicions about proposed marriages and civil partnerships and investigating them is set out in sections 48 to 52 and Schedule 4, with extensions to Scotland and Northern Ireland in section 53. Section 55(2) substitutes the definition in section 24 of the Immigration and Asylum Act 1999 with a new definition of a 'sham marriage' and 'sham partnership' and adds to the personnel involved in registration of marriages and civil partnerships, who are now under a duty to report suspected sham marriages or civil partnerships. It is all highly regulated. See further CHAPTER 11.

[1] Immigration and Asylum Act 1999, s 24 (in force from 1 January 2001) and s 24A (in force from 15 April 2005). Section 24(3) – the registrar concerned must report his suspicion to the Secretary of State without delay and in such form and manner as may be prescribed by regulations. See also the Reporting of Suspicious Marriages and Registration of Marriages (Miscellaneous Amendments) Regulations 2000, SI 2000/3164 (in Northern Ireland, SI 2000/3233). As regards civil partnerships, see Reporting of Suspicious Civil Partnerships Regulations 2005, SI 2005/3174.

Immigration advisers

Unqualified practitioners

1.76 The Immigration and Asylum Act 1999 made provision for the regulation of immigration advisers and service providers, following widespread public concern at the incompetent and sometimes unscrupulous advisers who were active in this field, taking advantage of the vulnerability and lack of proficiency in the English language of their clients. The scheme of Part V of the 1999 Act focuses on non-legally qualified advisers, but there is scope for control of professionally qualified practitioners, should the professional bodies fail.[1] It is now unlawful for any person to provide immigration advice or services[2] unless he or she is (i) registered by the Immigration Services Commissioner or by an equivalent body in the EEA; (ii) authorised to practice by a designated professional body in the UK or the EEA; (iii) a Crown officer or employee of a government department acting in that capacity; (iv) exempt under the terms of the 1999 Act; or (v) works for or under the supervision of any of the above.[3] Voluntary bodies such as immigration aid units, and publicly funded bodies like CABs must apply for exemption, and have to comply with the requirements of the scheme. The Commissioner has developed a Code of Standards and Guidance on Competences detailing the regulatory requirements for organisations seeking exemption.[4] Advisers charging for their services must register with the Commissioner, and will need to show that they are capable of complying with the Commissioner's Rules and Codes of Standards.[5] Registration may be at level 1 (generalist advice), level 2 (detailed advice) or level 3 (specialist advice), according to a competence assessment by the Commissioner. The fees for registration depend on the

level of competence and the number of advisers.[6] Those authorised to practice
by a designated professional body whose members are regulated by that body
(eg the Bar Council or the Law Society)[7] do not need to apply for exemption
or registration, and nor does anyone working under the supervision of such a
person. Contravention of the prohibition on unqualified advice or services is
an offence,[8] as is advertising services which the adviser is not registered to
provide. The Immigration Act 2014 now contains provisions which amend to
some extent and recast some of the powers of the Commissioner. These are set
out in Schedule 7 of the Act, brought into being by section 63.

1   Section 86A of IAA 1999, inserted by the Legal Services Act 2007 has not yet been brought
    into force.
2   As defined in Immigration and Asylum Act 1999, s 82.
3   IAA 1999, s 84. The provisions of s 84 do not apply to educational institutions, students'
    unions acting on behalf of their members and health sector bodies: Immigration and Asylum
    Act 1999 (Part V Exemption: Educational Institutions and Health Sector Bodies) Order 2001,
    SI 2001/1403.
4   Under the Immigration and Asylum Act 1999, Sch 5, para 3.
5   IAA 1999, Sch 5, paras 1–3.
6   The current fees are £555 for first or continuing registration of a level one adviser, and
    otherwise range from £1700 for first registration of an organisation with 1–4 advisers (£1,250
    for continuing registration) to £2,300 and £2,050 respectively for an organisation with ten or
    more advisers: Immigration Services Commissioner (Registration Fee) Order 2004, SI
    2004/802, arts 4, 5.
7   IAA 1999, s 86.
8   IAA 1999, s 91.

Professionally qualified practitioners

1.77 Concern has also been voiced about members of the legal profession,
both by the Lord Chancellor and the Legal Aid Board, the predecessor to the
Legal Services Commission. In 1998 the Lord Chancellor's Advisory Committee on Legal Education and Conduct reported that immigration law was an
area where solicitors and barristers lack both knowledge and expertise,
involving as it did many non-traditional sources such as the quantity of
administrative guidance, with some of which many practitioners were unfamiliar.[1] The Legal Aid Board went further, complaining of a significant increase
in poor quality, ill-supervised and sometimes unnecessary work.[2] To meet the
criticisms, there have been several reforms, including franchising and immigration contracts, which involve solicitors demonstrating compliance with key
quality criteria; and the Law Society's setting up of a specialist panel of
immigration practitioners who meet fairly rigorous criteria of competence and
proper case management. The most recent initiative has been the Law
Society's Accreditation Scheme. From August 2005, no publicly funded work
may be undertaken by a practitioner who is not accredited.[3] In *R v K*,[4]
the Court of Appeal dealt with a barrister who had been called to the Bar but
was not able to obtain a place in chambers. He went on to provide legal
services for clients in various areas of the law. He provided the requisite details
of his activities to the Bar Council and he made his status clear to those with
whom he dealt. He fell within, and had complied with, the conditions set out
in the Code of Conduct of the Bar of England and Wales, para 206.1.
Nevertheless, the court held that he was not qualified to provide immigration
advice or services for the purposes of the Immigration and Asylum Act 1999,

s 84 and upheld his conviction under s 91 of that Act.

1   Advisory Committee on Legal Education and Conduct, Improving the quality of immigration advice and representation: A report (July 1998).
2   Legal Aid Board (now Legal Services Commission) *Access to quality services in the immigration category* (May 1999). We deal in CHAPTER 19 below with funding of immigration and asylum appeals.
3   Accreditation, like registration of unqualified advisers, is at three levels. The Legal Services Act 1999, s 4(8) enables the Legal Service Commission to require accreditation of those providing publicly funded legal services. For details of accreditation scheme, see the Law Society's website.
4   [2008] EWCA Crim 1900, [2009] 1 All ER 510.

The Legal Services Commission

1.78 The Legal Services Commission (LSC) provides public funding for legal services from the Community Legal Service Fund. We set out below the current position of legal aid[1]. This paragraph, so far as relevant is dealt with there.

1   See **1.108** ff.

MISCELLANEOUS PRINCIPLES OF UK IMMIGRATION LAW

Principles of UK immigration law and practice

1.79 This book is not a book about the British constitution, nor a book on human rights or social security law, or family or criminal law, but it does impinge on all these other areas of law. It deals mainly with public law but not exclusively. It intersects with many areas of law and includes a sizeable chunk of EU law but it has its own terms and some of its concepts and principles. In this section we deal with both of these.

Territorial and personal application

1.80 When we talk about UK immigration law and practice what territory are we dealing with? The UK consists of Great Britain (Scotland, England and Wales) plus Northern Ireland. In general UK immigration laws apply to the whole of the UK. Each statute sets out its territorial application. Where the statute enables subordinate legislation to be made, the resulting orders and regulations often have territorial application to the whole of the UK but in some cases separate subordinate legislation needs to be made in respect of, for example, Northern Ireland or Scotland. It also has a territorial reach to the Channel Islands and the Isle of Man (The Islands), which have always retained a large element of internal autonomy from the rest of the UK especially in matters of tax and residence and employment. The territorial reach of immigration law is achieved through Schedule 4 of the Immigration Act 1971 and Orders in Council made to apply specific parts of UK immigration law to the different Islands. We deal with this in CHAPTER 5.

Personal application

1.81 UK immigration law and practice has a much wider personal reach. The right of abode depends on a nationality and nationality law has for a long time had a wide personal reach, to people born, for example, or descended from those born in the Falkland Islands or Gibraltar, who now automatically become citizens by birth or descent, as we explain in CHAPTER 2. BDTCs are enabled to become British nationals and thereby acquire a right of abode under UK immigration law and practice, which of course, affects every person who comes to the UK whether as a tourist, for other temporary purposes, or for a more permanent reason, whether to join family already here or to make the UK their main home and to work here. Nationality laws, Immigration Rules, human rights laws and European Community law set out their personal and material application. They are what the bulk of this book is about but there are also some curiosities which touch on the territorial, personal and material applications of immigration law.

IMMIGRATION AND DISCRIMINATION

Introduction

1.82 Discrimination is an expanding field with new legislation at domestic and European levels having developed the protections not only on grounds of race and gender, but also of age, sexual orientation, religion or belief and disability. The Equality Act 2010, which largely came into force on October 1 2010, contains the relevant domestic provisions. In EU law equality and prevention of discrimination are enshrined in chapter three of the Charter of Fundamental Rights of the European Union. The Charter consolidated the fundamental rights applicable at EU level in June 1999 but had no binding legal effect until the Lisbon Treaty amended it to give it the same legal effect as the treaties from December 2007. The Charter has been highly influential in the opinions of the Advocates-General and the decisions of the European Court and has undoubtedly played a role in driving forward domestic protection from discrimination. Negotiations are ongoing towards an EU Article 13 Equal Treatment Directive which, if passed, would have to be transposed into UK law and would cover goods and services in the four grounds not yet covered in EU law, ie age, sexual orientation, religion or belief and disability. The EU Citizens' Directive imposes a duty of non-discrimination on Member States in relation to access of EU citizens and their family members and extended family members to the rights set out in the Directive. See paragraphs 20 and 31 of the preamble. It is noteworthy that the 2010 Act does not extend the prohibition on age discrimination in access to goods and services to those under 18, although the current proposals for the Directive would do so. However, the BCIA 2009, s 55 does impose a new duty on the Secretary of State to ensure that immigration, asylum, nationality and customs functions are discharged having regard to the need to safeguard and promote the welfare of children who are in the UK.[1] This follows on from the government's announcement in 2008 that it was withdrawing the immigration reservation to the UN Convention on the Rights of the Child.[2]

1   Entered into force 2 November 2009, Borders, Citizenship and Immigration Act 2009 (Commencement No 1) Order 2009, SI 2009/2731.
2   It should be noted that recent government pledges to end the immigration detention of children are in practice often fulfilled by separating children from their parents, placing the children in care while continuing to detain parents.

1.83 The Equality Act 2010 received Royal Assent on 8 April 2010 and its main provisions came into force on 1 October 2010.[1] It replaces previous legislation (such as the Race Relations Act 1976 and the Disability Discrimination Act 1995) but covers the same groups that were protected by existing equality legislation. It additionally extends its ambit and scope so as to provide protection to groups having characteristics not previously covered, so that protected characteristics will include: age, disability, gender reassignment, race, religion or belief, sex, sexual orientation, marriage and civil partnership and pregnancy and maternity. Immigration authorities are responsible for facilitating legal migration to and from the UK and preventing illegal migration. Their immigration duties involve receiving and processing applications for entry clearance, granting leave to remain and so forth; or they may be involved in immigration searches, arrests, or raids of premises. In general, they are covered by equality law in carrying out these various functions. In broad terms, this means that, under the Equality Act, they may not either discriminate against persons because of a protected characteristic, or harass or victimise them and must make reasonable adjustments if someone is disabled so that that person can access the service on the same terms as non-disabled people. But there are some areas where what might otherwise be unlawful discrimination is allowed because of specific exceptions relating to immigration..

1   See the Equality Act 2010 (Commencement No 4, Savings, Consequential, Transitional, Transitory and Incidental Provisions and Revocation) Order 2010, SI 2010/2317, which brought most of the Act into force.

Discrimination by public authorities

1.84 Once the relevant protected characteristic has been identified, and the type of unlawful treatment decided upon, the scheme of the 2010 Act requires consideration of the relevant sphere of activity. For present purposes, we are concerned with section 29, which deals with discrimination by service providers and persons exercising a public function. It is unlawful, by virtue of section 29(6) for a person to do anything that amounts to discrimination, harassment or victimisation when it is exercising a public function that is not the provision of a service to the public or to a section of the public. Section 31(4) states that a public function is a function of a public nature for the purposes of the Human Rights Act 1998. The definition is accordingly a broad one and will include private persons who are exercising the coercive powers of the state, such as companies running detention centres. Sections 29(1) to (5) impose a similar prohibition against discrimination upon 'service providers', which is defined as a person who is providing a service to the public or a section of the public.

1.85 Accordingly, whilst slightly convoluted, it can be seen that bodies exercising public functions are potentially liable for discrimination (including victimisation and harassment) on two bases. First, where they come within the definition of service providers and second, where the function being exercised is one that does not come within the ambit of the provision of a service. This will not make any practical difference since, in the immigration field, much of what is done will not amount to the provision of a service but will amount to the body exercising public functions making decisions about the rights and status of an individual.[1]

[1] *Gichura v Home Office* [2008] EWCA Civ 697, [2008] ICR 1287. This is discussed at **1.94**, below

1.86 Whilst there is no exhaustive list of public functions (contrast the list of public authorities set out in Schedule 19 to the Act for the purpose of determining who is subject to the equality duty), the wide definition taken from the Human Rights Act means that it will cover all central and local government bodies who deal with immigration matters. This will include but is not limited to the Home Office, the Foreign Office, and local authorities involved in providing for asylum seekers.

1.87 It should be noted, however, that these bodies are exempt from a claims under section 29, in certain respects. So, a claim for unlawful discrimination, victimisation or harassment cannot be brought by a person under 18 who is relying upon the protected characteristic of age, nor at all by those over or under 18 on the basis of the protected characteristic of marriage and civil partnership.[1] Furthermore, Schedule 3, Part 4 of the Act provides an immunity from liability where the protected characteristic is disability or religion or belief and the decisions relate to entry clearance, leave to enter or remain and variations or cancellations of leave.[2]

[1] Equality Act 2010. s 29.
[2] Equality Act 2010, Sch 3, paras 16 and 17. Reference should be made to the specific paragraphs for the precise decisions that come within their scope.

1.88 Further immunity from liability is provided in claims of age discrimination[1] and discrimination on the grounds of nationality and ethnic or national origins where a minister of the Crown is acting personally under certain immigration legislation or a person is acting under a relevant authorisation.[2] These authorisations are considered in more detail below. However, it should be noted that immigration officers are not immune from liability on these grounds (age and nationality and ethnic or national origins) when they are involved in the investigation and prosecution of offences under Part III of the Immigration Act 1971 or exercising a power of arrest under section 14 of the Asylum and Immigration (Treatment of Claimants, etc) Act 2004.[3]

[1] Equality Act 2010, para 15 of Sch 3, Part 4.
[2] Ibid, para 17 – but not race or colour.
[3] See the decision of the House of Lords in *YL v Birmingham City Council (Secretary of State for Constitutional Affairs intervening)* [2007] UKHL 27, [2007] 3 WLR 112. See, however, in *Gichura v Home Office* [2008] EWCA Civ 697, [2008] ICR 1287] the Claimant was a disabled person and detained at an immigration removal centre. He brought a claim complaining about the conditions of his detention, alleging various forms of discrimination, including an allegation of a failure to make reasonable adjustments. The Court of Appeal found that the treatment of the claimant by the detention centre came within the provision of

services. The importance of this decision has diminished somewhat, since the case was decided under the Disability Discrimination Act 1995 and there was no distinct liability for public authorities. It is nevertheless useful as an authority as to the scope of the services provisions in the 2010 Act.

The working of discrimination law

1.89 One of the aims of the Equality Act 2010 was to bring together all the different strands of discrimination, contained in other pieces of legislation, and consolidate them so that they apply, with some exception to all of the so-called protected characteristics. Accordingly, in broad terms, the 2010 Act works by defining discrimination in general terms (as well as other prohibited conduct) and then explaining how it applies to the protected characteristics as well as the particular fields in which the relevant treatment is outlawed (employment, education, public functions and so on). The types of unlawful treatment covered are direct, indirect, victimisation and harassment. Extended discussion of these concepts is beyond the scope of this work but they can be summarised as follows:

- direct discrimination occurs when one person (A) treats another (B) less favourably on the basis of a protected characteristic possessed by B;
- indirect discrimination occurs when one person (A) applies to another (B) a provision, criterion or practice (PCP), that PCP is applied to all, whether or not they possess the protected characteristic that B has, it puts or would put, persons with whom B shares the characteristic at a particular disadvantage when compared with persons with whom B does not share it, it puts, or would put, B at that disadvantage, and A cannot show it to be a proportionate means of achieving a legitimate aim;
- victimisation occurs when one person (A) subjects another (B) to a detriment because that other person has done a protected act or A believes that B has done a protected act; the term protected act is defined in the legislation but most commonly arises where B has made a complaint of discrimination and is treated less favourably as a consequence; and
- harassment occurs where a person (A) engages in unwanted conduct related to another's protected characteristic, and (b) the conduct has the purpose or effect of (violating B's dignity or creating an intimidating, hostile, degrading, humiliating or offensive environment for B.

1.90 A number of points are worth making:

(1) The law surrounding disability discrimination is more complex than that in relation to the other protected characteristics and reference should be made to a specialist textbook for a detailed treatment. As well as the unlawful conduct outlined above, the legislation additionally refers to two other forms of discrimination which are not mirrored in respect of the other protected characteristics. The first is 'reason related discrimination', where the reason for the less favourable treatment is related to a person's disability, for example, the disadvantaging of an immigration detainee who is unable to use certain facilities due to mobility difficulties, where those difficulties are attributable to a

disability. The second is the duty to make reasonable adjustments, which arises where a disabled person is put at a substantial disadvantage in relation to relevant matters in comparison to those who are not disabled.[1] This is a wide-ranging duty and is intended to ensure that public authorities and service providers take positive steps to act so as to place those with disabilities on an equal footing with those who are not disabled.[2]

(2)   Motivation is irrelevant in determining discrimination[3] and a person may be liable for an unlawful act even if acting from benign motives.[4] Decisions made on the basis of stereotypical assumptions, most likely to arise in cases involving race and sexual orientation, are unlawful. So, in *R (European Roma Rights Centre) v Immigration Officer at Prague Airport*[5] the governments of the UK and Czech Republic introduced a special pre-clearance immigration control scheme at Prague airport, the aim of which was to reduce the numbers of those seeking asylum in the UK, the majority of such individuals being Roma. The House of Lords drew the inference that those of Roma origin were subject to more intrusive questioning and treated with more scepticism than others wishing to travel. This amounted to direct discrimination on racial grounds.[6] Such acts of discrimination may also violate Article 14 of the ECHR.[7]

(3)   Although dual discrimination appears in the Act, at section 14, this provision has not been brought into force. It was intended to deal with the situation where a person is treated less favourably on the combined effect of two protected characteristics. However, the government decided, in 2011, not to take any steps to bring this provision into force.[8].

(4)   The issue of stereotyping and the making of generic assumptions was also an issue in *AA and ors (Sectors-based work: general principles) Bangladesh*.[9] Here, the applicants challenged decisions to refuse entry clearance despite their having obtained permits under a work scheme. The AIT held that it was quite wrong for an ECO to assume that because the sectors-based work permit scheme offered only seasonal employment, it was quite wrong to assume that the application was being made only in order to enable the applicant to overstay or to do so on the basis of the country from which the applicants came. The poverty of the country from which the applicant comes was not of relevance to the ECO's decision. Rather, each applicant was entitled to a decision of his or her case on the merits.

(5)   In certain circumstances the defence of illegality may defeat a complaint by employees that their employer has committed the tort of having discriminated against the employee by dismissing him or her contrary to section 39(2)(c) of the 2010 Act. However, in *Hounga v Allen*[10] the Supreme Court held that in the particular circumstances it was wrong to reject the employee's discrimination claim on grounds of illegality.

[1]   Equality Act 2010 s 20.
[2]   See ibid, ss 20–21
[3]   *Nagarajan v London Regional Transport* [2000] 1 AC 501.
[4]   *James v Eastleigh Borough Council* [1990] 2 AC 751. Although the question of intention will be relevant to an award of damages in cases of indirect discrimination; see ss 119(5)(b) (county and sheriff courts) and 124(4) (employment tribunals) of the 2010 Act.

⁵ *European Roma Rights Centre v Immigration Officer at Prague Airport (United Nations High Comr for Refugees intervening)* [2004] UKHL 55, [2005] 2 AC 1.

⁶ Some members of the House of Lords seemed to doubt the reasoning in the *Roma Rights case* in the later case of *R (on the application of Gillan) v Metropolitan Police Comr* [2006] UKHL 12, [2006] 2 AC 307. However, any expressions of disagreement were clearly *obiter* since the issue of discrimination was not before the House in *Gillan*.

⁷ See *A v Secretary of State for the Home Department; X v Secretary of State for the Home Department* [2004] UKHL 56, [2005] 2 AC 68 where the House of Lords held that the indefinite detention of foreign nationals was unlawful. The decisive factor was the acceptance by the security services that British nationals (who could not be interned) were also as likely to be engaged in terrorist activity as foreign nationals. Contrast this with *Saadi v United Kingdom*, [2007] Imm AR 38 where a Chamber of the European Court of Human Rights held that there was no violation of Article 5(1) of the Convention, whether taken by itself or in conjunction with Article 14, when asylum-seekers were held for a period of seven days under the fast-track procedure in order to determine their claims. The Grand Chamber agreed with the decision on 29 January 2008: [2008] ECHR 80.

⁸ The Government Equalities Office confirmed that the dual discrimination provisions under the Equality Act 2010 will not be implemented in April 2011 as originally planned. See www.personneltoday.com/hr/equality-act-2010-dual-discrimination-provisions-delayed.

⁹ *AA (Sectors-based work: general principles) Bangladesh* [2006] UKAIT 00026.

¹⁰ [2014] UKSC 47, [2014] 4 All ER 595, [2014] 1 WLR 2889.

The ministerial authorisations

1.91 As discussed above, the Equality Act 2010 permits discrimination in relation to age, nationality and ethnic or national origins where a Minister of the Crown is acting personally or a person is acting under a Ministerial Authorisation. Eleven such authorisations[1] are currently in force, all of which relate to nationality and ethnic or national origins. They cover, amongst other things, examination of passengers seeking entry, prioritisation of asylum claims, permission to work outside the Immigration Rules and fingerprint comparison.[2] This licence to discriminate has been rightly criticised by some commentators[3] and the independent race monitor previously pointed to the risk that the authorisations become self-fulfilling by encouraging scepticism about the nationalities involved.[4] The courts have made it clear that the ability to grant authorisations must be subject to strict control and, in *R (on the application of the Tamil Information Centre) v Secretary of State for the Home Department*, Forbes J held unlawful a ministerial authorisation which allowed immigration officers to discriminate when examining passengers on the basis of intelligence or statistics, because it improperly delegated the analysis of the intelligence and statistics, and the decision to discriminate, to officers, when this should have been exercised personally by the Secretary of State.[5]

¹ They can be found at www.gov.uk/government/uploads/system/uploads/attachment_data/file /262793/annex-ee.pdf

² A general provision appears at Annex EE4 applying to asylum applicants claiming to be of a nationality which appears in the 'Top Ten list'. A separate provision which previously appeared at Annex EE9 for individuals claiming to be from North Korea, for comparison with fingerprints held by South Korean authorities, has now disappeared.

³ Ann Dummett, 'The Immigration Exceptions in the Race Relation (Amendment) Act 2000', ILPA, 2001.

⁴ See paragraph 2.35 of her 2005–06 annual reports, available at: www.ociukba.homeoffice.g ov.uk/files/race-monitor-annual-reports/irn-ann-rpt-0506.pdf. The Race Monitor post was absorbed into that of the Chief Inspector of the UK Border Agency In April 2008.

⁵ [2002] EWHC 2155 (Admin), (2002) Times, 30 October

1.92 Of particular note are authorisations EE8 and EE9, made in 2011, and applying to Great Britain and Northern Island. This permits, on the basis of nationality, greater scrutiny of applications for transit visas and entry clearance, more rigorous examination by an immigration officer, the declining or cancellation of leave prior to arrival in the United Kingdom and greater priority to the setting of removal directions. The nationalities which are subject to this differential treatment are, however, not known, since they are kept on a list that is personally approved by a Home Office minister. An attempt to obtain, on freedom of information grounds, the list of nationalities covered by the authorisation has been rebuffed on public interest grounds.[1]

[1] See: www.whatdotheyknow.com/request/63859/response/168979/attach/2/FOI%20request%2017943%20Reply.pdf.

1.93 The EHRC also has power, pursuant to section 14 of the Equality Act 2006, to publish codes of practice in connection with any matter addressed by the Equality Act 2010. A failure to observe any such code does not of itself render a person liable to proceedings but any provision that a court or tribunal considers to be relevant to a question arising in proceedings shall be taken into account when determining that question.[1] This means that a failure to comply with a code can be specifically raised in immigration proceedings. A code of practice has been published in relation to the provision of services and the carrying out of public functions[2] but there is no code in relation to the public sector equality duty. The EHRC has, however, published technical guidance in relation to that duty[3].

[1] Section 15(4) of the Equality Act 2006.
[2] Equality Act 2010 Code of Practice – Services, public functions and associations, available at:www.equalityhumanrights.com/sites/default/files/publication_pdf/servicescode.pdf.
[3] Available at: www.equalityhumanrights.com/legal-and-policy/legislation/equality-act-2010/equality-act-codes-practice-and-technical-guidance.

Determination of discrimination issues in asylum and immigration cases

1.94 Section 114(1)(a) of the Equality Act 2010 provides that a claim, under Part 3 of the Act, which includes public authorities and service providers, that a person has committed an act of unlawful discrimination, is ordinarily to be brought in the county court. However, section 114(2) provides that such a claim cannot be brought where it falls within the scope of section 115. This covers relevant decisions taken by an 'immigration authority' where the issue of discrimination was or could have been raised in the immigration proceedings or it was raised and decided against the applicant. An 'immigration authority' means the Secretary of State, an immigration officer or a person responsible for the grant or refusal of entry clearance,. Section 115 precludes the bringing of a claim in the county court, where there is an appeal concerning a relevant decision e relating to leave to enter or remain or an appeal under section 2D of the Special Immigration Appeals Commission Act 1997[1]. There is nothing in the Equality Act 2010 which suggests that the parties are bound, in subsequent civil proceedings, by any finding of discrimination made in immigration proceedings. However, in accordance with the ordinary principles of issue estoppel, it is likely that the Secretary of State would be bound by such a finding.[2] Furthermore, there is nothing in the 2010 Act to prevent an applicant from bringing a county court claim if his or her immigration claim is not dealt with in the context of the immigration appeal.[3] A six month time limit applies to the bringing of a county court discrimination claim, although this can be extended where it is just and equitable to do so.[4] Where the applicant has obtained a favourable decision on discrimination in the immigration proceedings, this time limit starts running from the day after which the bar on proceedings in the county court was lifted. Finally, although there is nothing in the domestic discrimination legislation which requires a decision maker to read down a statute or part of a statute for discriminatory effects, where discrimination affects access to Convention Rights as set out in Article 14 ECHR, the supremacy of EU law may require the domestic legislation to be read down.

[1] Normally appeals go to the First Tier Tribunal (IAC) (the 'FTT'), but where national security etc is involved they go to SIAC; see Chapters 19, 20and 22, below.
[2] See *Johnson v Gore Wood & Co (a firm)* [2000] UKHL 65, [2002] 2 AC 1.
[3] See *R (on the application of Bibi) v Secretary for the Home Department* [2005] EWHC 386 (Admin), [2005] 1 WLR 3214 and *Emunefe v Secretary of State for the Home Department* [2005] EWCA Civ 2002, [2005] INLR 587. See also section 115(7) of the 2010 Act which deals with when an appeal is to be treated as 'pending' for the purposes of section 115(1).
[4] See Equality Act 2010, s 118(1), (5).

1.95 It is open to FTT or the Upper Tribunal (IAC) or SIAC to allow an appeal solely on the basis that there has been unlawful discrimination.[1] However, the AIT has held that such a finding of discrimination does not automatically lead to success in the appeal if, having identified the unlawful factor, the immigration judge can independently conclude that the decision was in accordance with the law.[2]

[1] Section 84(1)(b) of the Nationality, Immigration and Asylum Act 2002.
[2] *CS (Jamaica) (Race Discrimination etc)*[2006] UKAIT 00004, [2006] Imm AR 289.

The public sector equality duty

1.96 Section 149 of the Equality Act 2010 imposes a duty on various public authorities, including government departments, to have regard to the need to eliminate discrimination, harassment and victimisation and any other conduct prohibited by the 2010 Act, to advance equality of opportunity and foster good relations between persons who share a relevant protected characteristic and those who do not. However, schedule 18 provides exceptions to the public sector equality duty. Paragraph 2(1) deals with exceptions in relation to the exercise of immigration and nationality functions. The protected characteristics of age, race or religion or belief are excluded from the section 149 duties in this field, 'race' meaning race only so far as it relates to nationality or ethnic or national origins. Immigration and nationality functions are those performed in the exercise of various specified domestic and EU immigration and nationality laws, but not to the powers to arrest and search as they relate to criminal offences set out in sections 28A and 28K of the IA 1971. Regulations made under the 2010 Act[1] impose a duty upon certain public authorities to publish documents which demonstrate compliance with the section 149 duty. They are also required to publish equality objectives. Such equality objectives have been published by the Home Office[2], and deal with numerous matters relating to immigration and asylum, albeit not in great detail.

1 www.gov.uk/government/uploads/system/uploads/attachment_data/file/98859/equality-object
   ives.pdf.
2 Equality Act 2010 (Specific Duties) Regulations 2011, SI 2011//2260.

1.97 It should be noted that the equality duty does not give rise to a cause of
action in private law[1]. However, judicial review is available, for example,
where it is alleged that a public authority has failed to have regard to the
section 149 duty. So, in a different context, the Secretary of State for Work and
Pensions was found to have had insufficient regard to that duty when closing
the Independent Living Fund, which provided monies to individuals with
disabilities to assist them with their needs and attain a greater degree of
independence. The Secretary of State was required to retake his decision.[2]

1 See section 156.
2 *Bracking v Secretary of State for Work and Pensions* [2013] **EWCA Civ 1345.**

1.98 There is no longer any obligation upon public authorities, as there
previously was under the race relations legislation[1], to carry out an equality
impact assessment when carrying out their functions. However, the fact that
there has been such an assessment may be an important way of demonstrating
that a public authority has complied with the section 149 duty.[2]

1 See *R (on the application of C) v Secretary of State for Justice* [2008] EWCA Civ 882,
   [2009] QB 657.
2 See, for example, and in a different context, *R (on the application of LH) v Shropshire Council*
   [2014] EWCA Civ 404 where a local authority successfully relied upon an equality impact
   assessment as evidence that it had considered the needs of disabled persons when deciding to
   close a day centre.

1.99 The Equality and Human Rights Commission has power, under section 31 of the Equality Act 2006, to make assessments as to a public
authority's compliance with the public sector equality duty. If it considers that
there has been a failure to comply with the duty it may, under section 32, issue
a compliance notice.

1.100 Section 1 of the Equality Act 2010 creates a very wide duty, applicable
across all the protected characteristics, to reduce socio-economic inequality.
However, the government has indicated that it does not propose to bring this
provision into force.[1]

1 The Guardian.com, 17 November 2010, announced that Theresa May was scrapping the legal
   requirement to reduce inequality introduced by Harriet Harman under Labour and dismissed
   by the Home Secretary as 'ridiculous': 'we are scrapping Harman's law for good.' One
   commentator thought it was worrying that 'the coalition's plan for tackling inequalities seems
   based on sanction by embarrassment, rather than law.' See www.theguardian.com/society
   /2010/nov/17/theresa-may-scraps-legal-requirement-inequality.

Article 14 ECHR

1.101 Article 14 of the ECHR prohibits discrimination specifically in relation
to the other Convention Rights. For more details see CHAPTER 6. It can only be
argued where there is sufficient nexus between the claimed discrimination and
one of the Convention rights but it is not always necessary for the substantive

right itself to have been breached in order for Article 14 to be engaged.[1] The courts should approach the question of breaches of Article 14 not by following a step-by-step approach but by reference to 'the real issue in the case, which was why the complainant had been treated as she had been treated'.[2] A recent example of an Article 14 case is *R (on the application of Johnson) v Secretary of State for the Home Department*,[3] where there was a breach of art 14 read with art 8 where the deportation was sought of a Jamaican citizen who would have been a British citizen, and therefore would not have been liable to deportation, if he had not been born out of wedlock. The fact that he was not a British citizen because of his illegitimacy and could be deported, unlike comparators in exactly the same position but whose parents were married, meant that he was being unjustifiably treated differently on the ground that he was born illegitimate.

[1]   See, for example, *M v Secretary of State for Work and Pensions* [2006] UKHL 11, [2006] 2 AC 91, [2006] 4 All ER 929.
[2]   *R (on the application of Carson) v Secretary of State for Work and Pensions* [2005] UKHL 37.
[3]   [2014] EWHC 2386 (Admin).

GLOSSARY OF KEY TERMS

1.102 Some of the key terms of immigration law can be very confusing to someone not familiar with their usage – terms such as Control on and after entry, Entry to the UK and Arrival in the UK, Visa and entry clearance, Leave to enter and Leave to remain, Limited and Indefinite leave, Temporary admission, Conditions attached to limited leave, Residence, Right of abode, Cancellation, Curtailment, Suspension and Revocation of leave. We deal in outline with some of these terms all of which are further explained in the succeeding chapters.

Control on and after entry – When Immigration Rules were first published there were two sets, one dealing with control of entry, and the other with control after entry. The rules tied in with the provisions of section 4(1) of the Immigration Act 1971, where a clear division was established between leave to enter and leave to remain and to the different functions of Immigration Officers and the immigration staff at the Home Office. Immigration officers granted leave to enter. (It is true that immigration officers can be given instructions by the Secretary of State as part of his or her statutory powers under Schedule 2 of the Immigration Act 1971, but in the end the decision on entry was still formally that of the immigration officer). The Immigration Staff at the Home Office gave leave to remain. That clarity of distinction has gone. The first muddying of the waters was when the House of Lords approved new administrative arrangements, whereby immigration officers were permitted to take deportation decisions, the House of Lords holding that not withstanding their statutory functions as immigration officers, they were also departmental officers of the Home Office, therefore, within the *Carltona* doctrine.[1] Later, the Secretary of State acquired powers to make decisions on entry.[2] The third and most important change started in 2000 with the power given to ECOs at British posts overseas to give leave to enter when granting an entry clearance or a visa.[3] The effect of all this is to move the borders of the UK to the relevant British post overseas where all decisions on leave to enter will be taken, except for visitors and others seeking short-term leave of six months or less. So the main focus on leave to enter is now on ECOs and the function of immigration officers becomes less one of checking passports at the ports of entry (which they still do) and more on border security where they now become part of a unified border security force.[4]

1   *R v Secretary of State for the Home Department ex p Oladahinde* [1991] 1 AC 254.
2   See **3.3** below.
3   Now anyone seeking leave to enter for more than six months must obtain prior entry clearance before travelling to the UK, even if that person is not a visa national. The only exceptions are the subordinate class of British nationals; they can travel without an entry clearance but will not be given more than six months at the port of entry and will therefore have to apply before the end of this period for their further leave and will have to pay the appropriate fee.
4   See **1.65** above.

1.103 There are a number of terms used in the control of entry to the UK:

(i)   *Visa and entry clearance* – 'entry clearance' means a visa, entry certificate or other document which, in accordance with the Immigration Rules, is to be taken as evidence or the requisite evidence of a person's eligibility, though not a British citizen, for entry into the UK (but does not include a work permit). Entry clearance takes the form of a visa (for visa nationals) or an entry certificate (for non visa nationals) *Visa nationals* are nationals of countries whose citizens require a visa for all travel to the UK, unless they are coming to the UK as returning residents. Visa countries are listed in Appendix 1 of the Immigration Rules. *Non visa nationals* do not a visa to visit the UK, but will need entry clearance, if they are coming for longer than six months. Nowadays an entry clearance may double up as leave to enter the UK (Immigration (Leave to Enter and Remain) Order 2000, SI 2000/1161, art 3). See CHAPTER 3.

(ii)   'Work permit' means a permit indicating, in accordance with the Immigration Rules, that a person named in it is eligible, though not a British citizen, for entry into the UK for the purpose of taking employment. But someone who obtains a work permit must also obtain entry clearance and leave to enter.

Leave

(i)   'Leave' – leave is a domestic term of UK immigration law, originally known as leave to land (under the Aliens Order 1953), now split into *leave to enter* or *leave to remain*. Certain nationalities are required to obtain leave to enter before they arrive in the UK – that is, they effectively require permission to travel to as well as permission to enter the UK. Those nationalities obliged to obtain leave before arrival are termed visa nationals.

(ii)   *Leave to enter* is a quite technical term because of the provisions of section 11 of the Immigration Act 1971 which distinguishes *arrival* at a port of entry and *entry* and between arrival and *temporary admission* (see CHAPTER 3). An entry which by-passes immigration control is an illegal entry and one which crosses the only land border between the UK and another State (Ireland) is also an entry which may or may not be illegal (footnote). Any leave before entry is leave to enter and any leave after entry is leave to remain.

(iii)   'Limited leave' – leave to enter or remain may be for a *limited* or *indefinite* period (footnote). If it is a leave for a limited period, it may have *conditions* attached to it relating to employment and so forth (see Chapter 3) and in the case of some foreign nationals a requirement to register with the police.

(iv)   'Indefinite leave' – is leave for an indefinite period which can be cancelled or revoked and which can lapse if the person is away from the UK for longer than two years (we deal with these matters in Chapters 3, and 6). The leave system is a permissive system of immigration control. Someone who requires leave under UK domestic law and who fails to get it will become an illegal entrant, but not all those who are subject to immigration control require leave to enter before they can come to the UK. There are certain exemptions from the leave system given, for example, to diplomats or other international functionaries working for the UN and other organisations. There are also exemptions for crew members of ships and aircraft who are simply stopping over before rejoining their ship or flight. Then there is the whole system of admission by citizens of the EU who are given rights of entry to another member state without having to obtain any permission or leave. See Immigration Act 1988, section 7. Not all EU citizens can remain in the UK. Although all citizens of the EU can come to the UK without leave for a three-month period, not all of them can remain thereafter without obtaining leave.

(v)   'Temporary admission' – persons liable to detention or detained under paragraph 16 of Schedule 2 to the Immigration Act 1971, for example, because they are required to come back for further examination by an immigration officer, may, under the written authority of an immigration officer, be *temporarily admitted* to the UK without being detained or be released from detention. This is known as *temporary admission*. It is useful to consider that the presence of persons granted temporary admission is tolerated but not formally approved. As temporary admission serves to allow the person to live in the community and avoid immigration detention it is often equated to bail. Persons who have not otherwise entered the UK are deemed not to do so as long as they are temporarily admitted while liable to detention. We deal with this in more detail in Chapter 3.

Cancellation, suspension and revocation of leave

1.105 Immigration legislation is confusing on the issue of cancellation, curtailment and revocation of leave. These different terms are used for the same or a similar process – a decision to take away leave that has been granted.

(i)   'Cancellation' and 'suspension' of leave – where leave has been granted on an entry clearance and, on arrival in the UK, the immigration officer wishes to examine the passenger further, he or she can suspend the person's leave until the examination is complete (Immigration Act 1971, Sch 2, para 2A). On completion of the examination of such a passenger, the immigration officer can then cancel the leave for specified reasons set out in paragraph 2A. If the passenger arrives without having obtained leave before arrival and leave to enter is granted, the immigration officer may then, at any time before the end of 24 hours from the conclusion of the examination, give the passenger a notice in writing cancelling the earlier leave to enter. In cases of cancellation the authority of a Chief Immigration Officer or of an Immigration Inspector must always be obtained.

(ii) 'Curtailment of leave' – a person's leave may be varied by restricting its duration and thereby curtailing it.[1] Details of the practice of curtailing leave are contained in the Immigration Rules.[2] Curtailment is discretionary and in the IDI guidance is given on its use.[3]

(iii) 'Revocation of indefinite leave' is now possible for a number of reasons under section 76 of the Nationality, Immigration and Asylum Act 2002, covering those liable to deportation but who cannot be deported for legal reasons, because they are likely to face ill-treatment engaging Article 3 of the ECHR if removed.[4] Revocation of indefinite leave attracts an in country right of appeal under NIAA 2002, s 82(2)(f).[5]

[1] Immigration Act 1971, s 3(3)(a).
[2] HC 395, paras 323, incorporating paragraphs 322(2)–(5), 339A(i)-(vi), and 339G(i)-(vi).
[3] See IDI, Ch 9, s 5 'Variation of Stay: Curtailment' states: 'It should be borne in mind that the curtailment provisions are discretionary. Therefore curtailment should not follow automatically if one of the above criteria applies. When curtailing a person's leave the burden of proof rests with the Secretary of State. Careful consideration should accordingly be given to all the person's circumstances.'
[4] NIAA 2002, s 76 covers refugees excluded from protection by Article 33(2) of the Refugee Convention (commission of a particularly serious crime and representing danger to community), who cannot be deported because they are likely to face ill-treatment engaging Article 3 of the ECHR, if removed; those who obtained indefinite leave to remain by deception but who cannot be removed for similar reasons or for practical reasons (s 76(2)); and refugees whose voluntary act (eg returning home or taking another nationality) attracts the cessation clauses art 1C(1)–(4) of the Refugee Convention (s 76(3), see **12.84** below).
[5] In such cases a new section 3D of the Immigration Act 1971, inserted by IAN 2006, s 11(5), will extend the revoked leave and replace the provisions in section 82(3) of the NIAA 2002, which use a different mechanism to achieve the same result, namely, that curtailment or revocation should not take effect while an appeal is pending. The right of appeal against removal under NIAA 2002, s 82(2)(g) now applies to a decision to remove by way of directions under the Act of 1999, s 10(1)(ba) (IAN 2006, s 2). This will give the person a separate right of appeal at each of the two decision stages: the first at the revocation stage and the second at the stage when the decision to remove is taken.

Revocation of asylum and humanitarian protection

1.106 Revocation of asylum and humanitarian protection

(i) 'Revocation of asylum' – the grant of asylum may be reviewed during the initial period of five years leave or when the person applies for indefinite leave to remain or on the expiry of the five year period. Such a review may result in asylum being *revoked* or not renewed if the Secretary of State is satisfied that the person's refugee status has ceased[1] or the person should have been[2] or is to be excluded from being a refugee[3] or the use of deception was decisive for the grant of asylum[4] or there are reasonable grounds for regarding the person as a danger to the security of the UK[5] or the person, having been convicted of a particularly serious crime constitutes a danger to the community of the UK.[6] The Immigration Rules use only the single term, referring to asylum being 'revoked', in all of these situations and do not make any distinction between 'cancellation of refugee status' (where circumstances come to light that indicate that the person should not have been recognised as a refugee in the first place) and 'revocation of refugee status' (where the seriousness of a refugee's subsequent conduct warrants revocation of status).

(ii)   'Revocation of humanitarian protection' – humanitarian protection will be revoked or will not be renewed if: the circumstances which led to the grant of humanitarian protection have ceased to exist or have changed to such an extent that protection is no longer required or there are other reasons similar to those needed for the revocation of asylum.[7]

(iii)   'Revocation of UK Residence Permits' (UKRP) – as soon as someone is granted asylum or humanitarian protection, they and members of their family are issued with a UKRP valid for five years.[8] If a grant of asylum or humanitarian protection is revoked, the UKRP may also be revoked.[9]

(iv)   'Effect of revocation on leave' – revocation of asylum or humanitarian protection does not by itself bring a person's leave to enter or remain to an end or render the person removable. If a refugee has limited leave, the leave may be curtailed if asylum or humanitarian protection is revoked[10] If asylum or humanitarian leave was obtained by deception with a consequential grant of leave, in the case of leave to enter (including indefinite leave to enter) the leave may be disregarded and directions can be given for the person's removal[11] or in the case of leave to remain (including indefinite leave to remain), removal directions can be given which invalidate the leave.[12]

(v)   'Special immigration status' – the Secretary of State may designate a person for 'special immigration status' if the person is a 'foreign criminal' as defined or a family member of a 'foreign criminal'.[13] The effect of such designation is that the person has neither leave to enter nor remain in the UK although, whilst subject to immigration control is not in the UK in breach of the immigration laws.

[1]   HC 395, para 339A(i)–(vi). Asylum will not normally be revoked on the 'voluntary cessation grounds' (reavailment of protection; reacquistion of nationality; acquisition of another nationality or restablishment in the country of feared persecution) if it was granted over five years previously unless there are exceptional circumstances. See CHAPTER 12, below, for further details.

[2]   The UNHCR Handbook on Procedures and Criteria for Determining Refugee Status at paragraphs 117 and 141 acknowledges that refugee status may be cancelled if information comes to light indicating that an individual should have been excluded.

[3]   HC 395, para 339A(vii) referring to exclusion in accordance with regulation 7 of the Refugee or Person in Need of International Protection (Qualification) Regulations 2006, SI 2006/2525 which provides that a person is not a refugee if he or she falls within the scope of Articles 1D, Article 1E, or Article 1F (exclusion of persons in respect of whom there are serious reasons to consider that they have committed a crime against peace, war crimes, crimes against humanity, a serious non-political crime or acts contrary to the purposes and principles of the UN) of the Refugee Convention.

[4]   HC 395, para 339A(viii).

[5]   HC 395, para 339A(ix).

[6]   HC 395, para 339A(x), reflecting Article 33(2) of the Refugee Convention and Article 21(2)(b) of Council Directive 2004/83/EC (The Qualification Directive).

[7]   HC 395, para 339G(i)–(vi).

[8]   HC 395, para 339Q(i) and (ii).

[9]   HC 395, para 339Q(iv).

[10]   As a matter of policy, revocation of asylum will normally result in curtailment of any extant limited leave with a view to removing the person concerned. Nevertheless, if a person's refugee

status is revoked, consideration should be given to whether he or she qualifies for humanitarian protection or discretionary leave. See CHAPTER 12 below.

[11] Immigration and Asylum Act 1999, s 10(1)(b) and (8).

[12] NIAA 2002, s 76(6). There is a right of appeal against the decision to revoke under sections 82(1), (2)(f). NIAA 2002, s 76(3) makes provision for a person's indefinite leave (as well as that of his or her dependants' unless they are refugees in their own rights) to be revoked if the 'voluntary cessation clauses' apply. This section 76(3) power of revocation can be exercised in respect of leave granted before the provision came into force but only in reliance on any action taken by the refugee after it came into force. See further Chapter 12 below.

[13] See Criminal Justice and Immigration Bill 2008, cls 115–122 and Sch 22. Under these clauses a 'foreign criminal' is a person who has been convicted of a 'particularly serious crime' within the meaning of Article 33(2) of the Refugee Convention as construed by NIAA 2002, s 72 or a person to whom Article 1F of the Refugee Convention applies. Conditions may be imposed by the Secretary of State or an immigration officer relating to residence, employment or occupation or reporting. A person subject to 'special immigration status' may be supported by the Secretary of State under a modified asylum support regime.

Status

1.107 Status is an important concept in immigration law. The term is not defined in immigration legislation. It is however a term generally used by immigration officers, practitioners and judges. The term refers to the person's immigration identity. This immigration identity comprises both an assertion concerning whether their presence in the UK is lawful and their categorisation under the rules – whether as a visitor, student of family member. If a person is, for example, said to have the status of a work permit holder, this implies firstly that the person's presence here is lawful and that he/she will have been permitted entry subject to the conditions imposed on work permit entrants. To those who have knowledge of immigration law and practice, the short-hand reference to a person's immigration status, provides a reference to the nature and the conditions of their entry and stay. A person may have dependent immigration status. For example persons admitted as spouses/children or partners are dependent on the immigration status of their partner/parent until they obtain settlement.[1] If the sponsor/partner is found to have obtained entry unlawfully, or doubts are raised about the validity of the marriage or the relationship, or if the relationship breaks down, or the new arrival has recourse to public funds, an extension of stay may be refused or existing leave curtailed.[2] Persons are said to have settled status when they have 'indefinite leave to enter or remain.' Other important examples of status in immigration law are those of ordinary residence,[3] nationality and domicile. Nationality identifies the person's political status; domicile shows a person's civil status. British nationality in the form of British citizenship gives a right of abode and therefore freedom from immigration control.[4] Nationality may also be important in family proceedings.[5] Domicile is an important status in determining the validity of a marriage and is an important connecting factor in other areas of private international law. For example, a person may be 'habitually resident' or 'ordinarily resident' in more than one place at a time, or may have no habitual residence at all. By contrast, a person must always have a domicile but can only have one domicile at a time. If a new domicile is obtained by choice, the previous domicile is no longer applicable.[6] The requirement of an intention to remain permanently distinguishes domicile from mere residence and in particular from ordinary residence.[7]

[1] See **11.45**, below.

2   But once spouses and unmarried partners have been granted settlement and have settled status they may not normally be deprived of it, whether or not the marriage or relationship lasts, and cannot be removed from the UK, unless the Home Office can demonstrate that deception was used in seeking (whether successfully or not) to obtain settlement (see Immigration and Asylum Act 1999, s 10(1)(b)), or they are the subject of a deportation order, which invalidates any leave to remain, including indefinite leave (see Immigration Act 1971, s 5(1). See **11.45**, below.

3   On 'ordinary residence', see *Shah v Barnet London Borough Council* [1983] 2 AC 309; see **4.5** above.

4   See Chapter 2, above.

5   If the parties in family litigation have different nationalities, it can be important to consider the nationality or potential nationalities of their children, in order to facilitate family contact in a home country or to guard against the child's abduction. See **11.6**. Nationality issues can also arise in care and wardship cases. See **11.7**.

6   *Moorhouse Ltd v Lord* (1863) 10 HL Cas 272 at 285 per Lord Chelmsford. See also discussion in *Mark v Mark* [2005] UKHL 42, [2005] INLR 614 at para 37.

7   See further **11.26**.

LEGAL AID FOR IMMIGRATION, ASYLUM AND NATIONALITY WORK

1.108 The schemes in England and Wales, in Scotland and in Northern Ireland, are very different. It is the scheme in England and Wales that has undergone the greatest changes in recent years and it is the main focus of this part. Changes are anticipated in both Scotland and Northern Ireland.

Legal Aid in Scotland

1.109 Legal aid is administered by the Scottish Legal Aid Board in accordance with the scheme set out in the Legal Aid (Scotland) Act 1986 and the Civil Legal Aid (Scotland) Regulations 2002[1]. Applications for legal aid can be made by any firm of solicitors that has registered with the Board and has obtained a compliance certificate from the Law Society of Scotland. Thus a firm can do exclusively legal aid work, or just the occasional case. The majority of the population in Scotland meets the means test for legal aid, although household income will determine the contribution that the individual makes, right up to 100%. The benefits in such cases are not having to pay up front and not being at risk of the other sides' costs. Funding covers immigration and asylum cases as well as related matters such as challenges to immigration detention.[2]

1   SSI 2002/494, as amended. See further the *Civil Legal Assistance Handbook*, Scottish Legal Aid Board, January 2014.

2   *A sustainable future for legal aid*, APS Group Scotland, DPPAS12089 (10/11). Published by the Scottish Government, October 2011, see also Scottish Legal Aid Board, Best Value Review, Immigration and Asylum, June 2011.

Legal Aid in Northern Ireland

1.110 Legal Aid is administered by the Northern Ireland Legal Services Commission, a Non Departmental Public Body of the Department of Justice established under the Access to Justice (Northern Ireland) Order 2003[1]. The intention is to transfer the responsibilities of the Commission to an executive agency within the Department called the Legal Services Agency Northern Ireland in autumn 2014. The Law Centre Northern Ireland has been funded to do immigration and asylum work since 1 April 2005 through a grant arrangement with the Northern Ireland Legal Services Commission. Prior to that, the work was funded by the Home Office by way of grant in aid[2]. Section 117 of the Nationality, Immigration and Asylum Act 2002 amended Part 1 of Schedule 1 to the Legal Aid, Advice and Assistance (Northern Ireland) Order 1981[3] to make provision for legal aid before the tribunals and before the Special Immigration Appeals Commission. Initial advice is provided under a legal advice and assistance ('green form') scheme[4].

[1] NISI 2003/435.
[2] Immigration and Asylum Act 1999, s 81.
[3] SI 1981/228 (NI 8).
[4] Ibid. and see further the Northern Ireland Legal Services Commission *A guide to legal aid* v 2 January 2011.

Legal Aid in England and Wales

1.111 The current scheme for the provision of legal aid in England and Wales is based upon the LASPO 2012 which came into force on 1 April 2013[1]. The rationale for cuts to the scope of legal aid made by the Act was that only the most serious cases, for example involving life, liberty, homelessness and abuse of power by the State, would be eligible for legal aid[2]. The first of April 2013 was also the date on which the latest (three year) civil contracts for legal aid took effect. Just nine days later, the Government published *Transforming legal aid: delivering a more credible and efficient system*[3], which proposed extensive further changes to the provision of legal aid in all categories. Following consultation, it is implementing those proposals.

[1] Legal Aid, Sentencing and Punishment of Offenders Act 2012 (Commencement No. 6) SI 2012/453.
[2] Ministry of Justice Consultation, *Proposals for the Reform of Legal Aid in England and Wales*, CP 12/10, November 2010, at paragraphs 4.7–4.29.
[3] CP 14/2013, 9 April 2013.

1.112 The Act replaced the Legal Services Commission with the Legal Aid Agency, an executive agency of the Ministry of Justice.[1] The Act made provision for a Director of Legal Aid Casework with responsibility for making decisions on funding in individual cases, giving effect to the statutory scheme.[2] Appeals against decisions of the Director lie to Independent Cost Assessors.[3]

[1] Legal Aid, Sentencing and Punishment of Offenders Act 2012, s 38.
[2] Ibid, s 4.
[3] These are established under the powers in s 2(1) of the Legal Aid, Sentencing and Punishment of Offenders Act 2012.

1.113 Both the Act and the subsequent changes continue to be shaped by litigation. Most controversial is the proposal for a residence test for legal aid.[1] This proposes to restrict legal aid to those lawfully present in the UK on the date of application and who have been lawfully present in the UK for a continuous period of 12 months at any date prior to the date of application. One of the most significant aspects of the proposal is that it would affect legal aid for judicial review. Draft regulations implementing this change and making provision for certain exceptions[2], were approved by the House of Commons[3] but, following the Government's defeat in *R (on the application of the Public*

Law Project) v Secretary of State for Justice[4], were withdrawn before they could be debated by the House of Lords. It was held that the regulations were *ultra vires* the enabling powers of the Act, since they did not limit legal on the basis of need[5] and were discriminatory in circumstances where the discrimination could not be justified[6]. The case is under appeal. At the time of writing immigration status is not a bar to receipt of legal aid and legal aid for persons under immigration control is provided on the same terms as it would be provided to anyone else.[7]

[1]   Transforming legal aid: delivering a more credible and efficient system, op.cit., Chapter 3.
[2]   The Legal Aid, Sentencing and Punishment of Offenders Act 2012 (Amendment of Schedule 1) Order 2014.
[3]   HC Fifth Delegated Legislation Committee 1 July 2014, cols 3-22.
[4]   [2014] EWHC 2365 (Admin).
[5]   Paragraph 50 of the judgment.
[6]   Paragraph 88 of the judgment.
[7]   See below for the discussion of the specific exclusions from legal aid for judicial review for immigration cases under the Legal Aid, Sentencing and Punishment of Offenders Act 2012, Sch 1, Pt 1, para 19. The exclusion is, however, based on the type of case, not the type of claimant.

1.114 Transitional provision was made in The Legal Aid, Sentencing and Punishment of Offenders Act 2012 (Consequential, Transitional and Saving Provisions) Regulations 2013[1]. Cases started on or before 31 March 2013 continue to be funded under the old laws until the file is closed for funding purposes or until the individual no longer meets the criteria for funding. When the file is closed will depend on the type of funding. An applicant granted funding to make an initial application for leave in the UK continues to be funded until work funded as 'controlled work' has concluded. A person whose case is before the higher courts, funded as 'licensed' work, continues to be funded until that stage of the case has concluded. Thus if a case is, for example, remitted from the Court of Appeal to the Upper Tribunal, funding ceases at the point of remittal. If a controlled work case transfers to a new provider after 1 April 2013 funding is subject to the current regime. Thus the transfer may cause a person to lose funding. By contrast, licensed cases continue to be funded.

[1]   SI 2013/534 as amended by The Legal Aid, Sentencing and Punishment of Offenders Act 2012 (Consequential, Transitional and Saving Provisions) (Amendment) Regulations 2013 (SI 2013/621).

1.115 To receive legal aid, a person's case must be within the scope of legal aid or funded on an exceptional basis and individual tests as to the person's means[1] and as to the merits of the case[2] must be satisfied. Persons in receipt of certain benefits[3] and of asylum support[4] are passported through the means test, but otherwise evidence must be provided. The merits test for controlled cases is that the Director of Legal Aid Casework must be satisfied that the prospects of success are very good, good or moderate.[5] The alternative is that the case is of significant wider public interest or of overwhelming importance to the individual or that the substance of the case relates to a breach of Convention rights and, as of 27 January 2014, that the prospects of success are unclear.[6] Prior to that date, in such cases the prospects of success could be unclear or borderline.[7]

1. The Civil Legal Aid (Financial Resources and Payment of Services) Regulations 2013, SI 2013/480; see further the Standard Civil Contract General Specification, April 2013 and the Guide to Determining Financial Eligibility for Controlled Work and Family Mediation April 2014 v1.
2. The Civil Legal Aid (Merits Criteria) Regulations 2013, SI 2013/104 amended by the Civil Legal Aid (Merits Criteria) (Amendment) Regulations 2014, SI 2014/131.
3. The Civil Legal Aid (Financial Resources and Payment for Services) Regulations 2013, SI 2013/480, reg 6(2).
4. SI 2013/480, reg 6(1).
5. SI 2013/104, reg 60(3).
6. SI 2013/104, reg 60(3)(a).
7. See SI 2014/131, reg 3(6).

The Scope of legal aid

1.116 The scheme established by the Legal Aid Sentencing and Punishment of Offenders Act 2012 is that all matters are outside the scope of legal aid unless expressly included by being listed in Schedule 1, Part 1, subject to the limitations and exclusions set out in Part 2 of that Schedule. Representation for appeals is dealt with in Part 3 of Schedule 1. Inclusions are by type of case.

1.117 The Act makes provision for the inclusion of asylum work, defined as claims 'arising from' the 1951 UN Convention Relating to the Status of Refugees[1], Articles 2 and 3 of the European Convention on Human Rights[2], the 'Temporary Protection' Directive[3] or the 'Qualification' Directive.[4] Attendance at asylum interviews is excluded unless provision is made in regulations.[5] Civil Legal Aid (Immigration Interviews) (Exceptions) Regulations[6] provide for attendance at asylum and asylum screening interviews where the client is a child[7] or being treated as a child at the time of the interview by the Secretary of State[8], or at a substantive, as opposed to screening, asylum interview where the person is detained under the 'fast track' or lacks mental capacity.[9]

1. Legal Aid, Sentencing and Punishment of Offenders Act 2012, Sch 1, Pt 1, para 30(1)(a).
2. Ibid, para 30(1)(b).
3. Council Directive 2001/55/EC of 20 July 2001 on minimum standards for giving temporary protection in the event of a mass influx of displaced persons and on measures promoting a balance of efforts between Member States in receiving such persons and bearing the consequences thereof. Legal Aid, Sentencing and Punishment of Offenders Act 2012, para 30(1)(c).
4. Council Directive 2004/83/EC of 29 April 2004 on minimum standards for the qualification and status of third country nationals or stateless persons as refugees or as persons who otherwise need international protection and the content of the protection granted. Legal Aid, Sentencing and Punishment of Offenders Act 2012, Sch 1, Pt 1, para 30(1)(d).
5. Legal Aid, Sentencing and Punishment of Offenders Act 2012, Sch 1, Pt 1, para 30(3).
6. SI 2012/2683.
7. SI 2012/2683, reg 3.
8. SI 2012/2683, reg 3, read with reg 2.
9. SI 2012/2683, reg 4.

1.118 Asylum support cases where accommodation and subsistence are sought are within the scope of legal aid but, from April 2013, cases where only subsistence is sought are no longer within the scope of legal aid[1]. As before the passage of the Legal Aid, Sentencing and Punishment of Offenders Act 2012, legal aid is not available for representation before the First-tier Tribunal (Asylum Support)[2]. Regulations provide that help at court is not appropriate in such cases[3].

[1]   Legal Aid, Sentencing and Punishment of Offenders Act 2013, Sch 1, Pt 1, para 31(1).
[2]   Ibid, read with Pt 3 of that Schedule.
[3]   Civil Legal Aid (Merits Criteria) Regulations 2013, SI 2013/104, reg 23(b).

1.119 In *Gudanaviciene v Director of Legal Aid Casework and the Lord Chancellor*[1] the question arose as to whether family reunion for refugees was a 'matter "arising from" the Refugee Convention and thus within the scope of legal aid'. The High Court held that it was.[2] Clear Ministerial statements as to its exclusion made during the passage of the Legal Aid, Sentencing and Punishment of Offenders Act 2012[3] were not relevant because there was no ambiguity on the face of the legislation.[4] The Legal Aid Agency appealed the judgment but agreed that pending resolution of the appeal it would fund these cases and would not seek subsequently to recoup funding if its appeal succeeded.[5]

[1]   [2014] EWHC 1840 (Admin).
[2]   Paragraph 104 of the judgment.
[3]   Hansard HC Report 31 Oct 2011: Column 651.
[4]   *Gudanaviciene v Director of Legal Aid Casework and the Lord Chancellor* [2014] EWHC 1840 (Admin), para 109.
[5]   Ministry of Justice *Update on Refugee Family Reunion work*, 4 July 2014.

1.120 There is no general inclusion of immigration matters within the scope of legal aid. Instead, specific types of immigration case fall within Schedule 1 to the Legal Aid, Sentencing and Punishment of Offenders Act 2012. Challenges to immigration detention fall within the scope of legal aid: work on an application for bail, temporary release or temporary admission, including challenges to conditions applied on release[1]. So do applications for indefinite leave to remain under the domestic violence immigration rule[2] and for residence permits under EU law on the grounds of retained rights of residence arising from domestic violence.[3] Domestic violence is defined as 'any incident, or pattern of incidents, of controlling, coercive or threatening behaviour, violence or abuse (whether psychological, physical, sexual, financial or emotional) between individuals who are associated with each other'.[4] In such cases, time spent advising and assisting with an application under the Home Office/Department for Work and Pensions Destitute Domestic Violence Concession can be claimed.[5] The scope of legal aid encompasses persons with leave under the Immigration Rules as partners/spouses who have suffered domestic violence, but not children or other family members who have suffered domestic violence. Legal aid is available for work 'in relation to' an application for leave to enter or remain for a trafficked person.[6] The definition of a trafficked person[7] is that there has been conclusive determination under the 'National Referral Mechanism' that a person is victim of trafficking or that there is a 'reasonable grounds determination' under that mechanism that they are a victim and there has been no conclusive determination to say that they are not. A trafficked person is not therefore entitled to legal aid before going to the authorities, unless they begin their case as an asylum case. All proceedings before the Special Immigration Appeals Commission are within the scope of legal aid.[8] They are normally funded as licensed work.[9]

1   Legal Aid, Sentencing and Punishment of Offenders Act 2012, Sch 1, Pt 1, paras 25 to 27.
2   Made under HC 395, paragraph 289A Appendix FM, paragraph DV-ILR.
3   Immigration (European Economic Area) Regulations 2006, SI 2006/1003, regs 10(5) and 15(1). See the Legal Aid, Sentencing and Punishment of Offenders Act 2014, Sch 1, Pt 1, paras 28 to 29.
4   Legal Aid, Sentencing and Punishment of Offenders Act 2012, Sch 1, para 29(4) as amended by The Legal Aid, Sentencing and Punishment of Offenders Act 2012 (Amendment of Schedule 1) Order 2013, SI 2013/748, reg 4.
5   John Facey, Legal Aid Agency to Solange Valdez Ealing Law Centre of 28 January 2014, available from the Immigration Law Practitioners' Association.
6   Legal Aid, Sentencing and Punishment of Offenders Act 2012, Sch 1, Pt 1, para 32. The Civil Legal Aid (Procedures) Regulations 2012, SI 2012/3098 at reg 31(8) prescribes the time period in which an application for funding of licensed work under paragraph 32 must be made.
7   Ibid.
8   Legal Aid, Sentencing and Punishment of Offenders Act 2012, Sch 1, Pt 1, para 24.
9   Legal Aid, Sentencing and Punishment of Offenders Act 2012 Sch 1, Pt 3, paras 21 and 22.

1.121 Advocacy at immigration and asylum appeals and where the subject matter is in scope is within scope[1]. It is unclear therefore why it is specifically provided that asylum, domestic violence and trafficking appeals as defined are within scope.[2] Representation at bail hearings is within scope.[3] Advocacy before the Tribunals is within scope in cases of deprivation of British citizenship[4] and appeals against refusal of applications under regulation 26 Appeal Rights of the European Economic Area Regulations 2006[5] is within scope but only to the extent to which they concern contravention of the Equality Act 2010[6], just one example of how scope may be easy to define on paper but complex where an advocate is on his/her feet before the tribunal. Advocacy in judicial review is within scope with express provision made for judicial review before the Upper Tribunal.[7] However, in immigration, and immigration alone, there are restrictions on legal aid for judicial review. The source of these can be traced to suggestions made by a subcommittee of the Judges' Council of England and Wales in response to the Ministry of Justice Consultation, *Proposals for the Reform of Legal Aid in England and Wales*[8] and the evidence of Sir Anthony May, then President of the Queen's Bench division, before the House of Commons' Justice Select Committee.[9] Where there has been an appeal hearing or determination of the same, or substantially the same, issue within twelve months and the decision was not in favour of the appellant, an immigration judicial review will not be within the scope of legal aid.[10] Similarly, where an appeal against removal has been decided within twelve months of judicial review being sought against removal, legal aid will not be available for the judicial review.[11] There is specific protection for 'fresh claim' judicial reviews[12] and for judicial reviews of certification under section 94 (Unfounded Human Rights or Asylum Claims) or section 96 (Certification on the basis of an earlier right of appeal) of the Nationality, Immigration and Asylum Act 2002. Provision is made to prescribe conditions relating to the period between a person's being given notice of removal directions and the proposed time for removal and/or the reasons for proposing that period that would being the matter back within the scope of legal aid, but no such conditions have been prescribed.[13]

1   Legal Aid, Sentencing and Punishment of Offenders Act 2012, Sch 1, Pt 3, para 11(b) (First–tier Tribunal), and para 15 read with paragraph 11(b) (Upper Tribunal), para 1 (Supreme Court), para 2 (Court of Appeal), para 3 (High Court).

2   Legal Aid, Sentencing and Punishment of Offenders Act 2012, Sch 1, Pt 3, para 13 (first-tier Tribunal) and para 15 read with para 13 (Upper Tribunal).
3   Legal Aid, Sentencing and Punishment of Offenders Act 2012, Sch 1, Pt 3, para 11(a).
4   Legal Aid, Sentencing and Punishment of Offenders Act 2012, Sch 1, Pt 3, para 12(a).
5   SI 2006/1003.
6   Legal Aid, Sentencing and Punishment of Offenders Act 2012, Sch 1, Pt 3, para 12(b).
7   Legal Aid, Sentencing and Punishment of Offenders Act 2012, Sch 1, Pt 3, paras 18 and 19.
8   CP 12/10, November 2010, for the Government response to the consultation, discussing the subcommittee of the Judges' Council response, see *Legal Aid Reform in England and Wales: the Government Response*, presented to Parliament by the Lord Chancellor and Secretary of State for Justice by Command of Her Majesty, June 2011, paragraphs 13 to 17.
9   House of Commons Justice Select Committee, *Government's proposed reform of legal aid*, Third Report of Session 2010–11, HC 681-1, 30 March 2011.
10   Legal Aid, Sentencing and Punishment of Offenders Act 2012, Sch 1, Pt 1, para 19(5).
11   Legal Aid, Sentencing and Punishment of Offenders Act 2012, Sch 1, Pt 1, para 19(6).
12   Legal Aid, Sentencing and Punishment of Offenders Act 2012, Sch 1, Pt 1, para 19(7)(a), with the judicial reviews defined as judicial reviews of a negative decision on an asylum application (defined by reference to Council Directive 2005/85/EC of 1 December 2005 on minimum standards on procedures in Member States for granting and withdrawing refugee status) against which there is no right of appeal to the First-tier Tribunal.
13   Legal Aid, Sentencing and Punishment of Offenders Act 2012, Sch 1, Pt 1, para 19(8).

Connected matters

1.122 A connected matter is one in which part of the work needing to be done in the matter is within the scope of legal aid and part is out of scope. Under the Legal Aid, Sentencing and Punishment of Offenders Act 2012[1] the Lord Chancellor can make provision though regulations for legal aid for legal services that would otherwise be out of scope where these are 'in connection with' services in scope. However, the Civil Legal Aid (Connected Matters) Regulations 2013[2] provide only for legal aid for civil legal services in relation to the identification of a proposed defendant or respondent[3] including services related to trust law, company or partnership law and business cases that would otherwise be excluded[4]. Other connected matters must be paid for privately, done pro bono, or not done. This creates ethical dilemmas and tensions with codes of professional conduct for legal representatives where the client cannot pay and there is no capacity to do the work pro bono. Even where there is capacity to work pro bono this does not provide a complete solution to the problem of connected matters because without legal aid there may be no way to fund application and appeal fees or to fund disbursements.

1   Schedule 1, Part 1, paragraph 46.
2   SI 2013/451.
3   Ibid., paragraph 3.
4   By the Legal Aid, Sentencing and Punishment of Offenders Act 2012, Sch 1, Pt 1, paras 11, 13 and 14 respectively.

Exceptional Cases

1.123 There is a provision to grant legal aid in exceptional cases where failure to provide legal aid would amount to a breach of a person's human rights or of EU law.[1] Part 8 of the Civil Legal Services (Procedures) Regulations 2012[2] deals with exceptional funding. An application for exceptional funding must be made by a provider with a contract with the Legal Aid Agency to provide legal services, unless the 'effective administration of justice'[3] test is satisfied in which case an individual case contract[4] may be given.[5] The regulations specify that providers do not have delegated powers to grant exceptional funding.[6]

[1] Legal Aid, Sentencing and Punishment of Offenders Act 2012, s 10; see HL Report, 21 Nov 2011: Column 821 and HL Report 5 Mar 2012: Column 1570.
[2] SI 2012/3098.
[3] SI 2012/3098, reg 31(5).
[4] SI 2012/3098, reg 2.
[5] SI 2012/3098, reg 67(1)(b).
[6] SI 2012/3098, reg 66.

1.124 The Lord Chancellor's Exceptional Funding Guidance (non-inquests)[1] cites *Maaouia v France*[2] as authority for the proposition that immigration cases are not covered by the right to a fair trial protected by Article 6(1) of the European Convention on Human Rights as they do not involve a determination of civil rights and obligations. The guidance does contemplate funding where not to fund would be a breach of other articles of the European Convention on Human Rights but indicates that the Lord Chancellor does not consider there to be anything in current case law that 'would put the State under a legal obligation to provide legal aid in immigration proceedings in order to meet the procedural requirements of Article 8 ECHR'.[3] However, while *Airey v Ireland*[4] and *P, C and S v United Kingdom*[5] were both family law cases, there is nothing in the case law that suggests that a different approach to rights other than rights under Article 6 should be taken in immigration cases. The guidance does contemplate that Article 47 of the Charter of Fundamental Rights of the European Union might be in point, but considers that this will only be in those very rare cases that are within the scope of EU law but do not involve a determination of civil rights and obligations.

[1] At paragraph 59.
[2] *Maaouia v France (Application 39652/98)* (2000) 33 EHRR 10(2000) 33 EHRR 103737, 9 BHRC 29 BHRC 20505, (2001) 33 EHRR 42. *Eskelinen v Finland* (2007) 45 EHRR 43 13 is also mentioned.
[3] Lord Chancellor's Exceptional Funding Guidance (non-inquests) paragraph 60.
[4] (1979) 2 EHRR 305.
[5] (2002) 35 EHRR 31.

1.125 As of 1 December 2013, according to figures that the Ministry of Justice statisticians compelled a reluctant Legal Aid Agency to publish[1], there had been a mere three grants of exceptional funding in immigration, 147 refusals, 34 rejections and one case withdrawn.[2] The rest of the 187 applications were pending. Only 35 grants had been made in total, 21 of which were for inquests, always funded by means of grants of exceptional funding, if funded at all. Where granted, exceptional funding is granted only to the extent determined to be necessary to avoid a breach of human rights.[3] For example, it may be concluded that if a lawyer prepares a case for the tribunal, that the person can represent themselves at the hearing. Where an application for exceptional funding is refused there is a right to apply, within 14 days, for a review Director of Legal Aid Casework.[4]

[1] See the minutes of the Legal Aid Agency/ Law Society Civil Contracts Consultative Group for evidence of the resistance to publication.
[2] Ad hoc statistical release: Exceptional Case Funding Application and Determination statistics: April 2013 to December 2013, Ministry of Justice 13 March 2014.
[3] Lord Chancellor's Exceptional Funding Guidance, paragraph 35.

⁴   Civil Legal Aid (Procedure) Regulations 2012, SI/2012/3098, reg 69.

1.126 The exceptional funding regime was the subject of a legal challenge in *Gudanaviciene v Director of Legal Aid Casework and the Lord Chancellor*.[1] The challenge succeeded in the High Court. The Lord Chancellor's Guidance was held to be defective in setting too high a threshold and in failing to recognise that Article 8 of the European Convention on Human Rights 'does apply even in immigration cases and, despite the exclusion of Article 6, carries with it procedural requirements which must be taken into account.'[2]. The Home Office appealed. The appeal is pending. A residence test for judicial review would have implications for challenges to refusals to provide funding.

¹   [2014] EWHC 1840 (Admin).
²   Ibid, paragraph 51.

Tenders and contracts

1.127 Legal aid in England and Wales is based on a system of exclusive contracting whereby 'providers' bid by area of law for 'matter starts' which they can use for 'controlled work'. A fixed number of matter starts were available for the 2013 contract and tenders were competitive. Those who won a contract are not restricted in the number of judicial review cases or cases before the higher courts that they can do. The detailed specifications, both for civil law as a whole and for individual categories, supplement the legislation. There is very limited scope for individual case contracts for matters funded on an exceptional basis that do not align with any area of work within the scope of legal aid.[1]

¹   See reg 31(5) of the Civil Legal Aid (Procedures) Regulations 2012, SI 2012/3098.

1.128 Specific contracts (an 'Exclusive Schedule Arrangement') are let for Immigration Removal Centres, whether the work concerns the asylum de-tained fast-track or advice surgeries funded in the centres. Only in very limited circumstances can those not funded under such contracts represent persons deprived of their liberty under immigration act powers: where the detainee is a close family member of an existing client, or is him/herself an existing client and five hours work exclusive of travel and waiting has been done prior to incarceration.[1] There are no equivalent contracts for the prison estate and the indigent held in prison service establishments, including under Immigration Act powers, are reliant on providers holding contracts making the journey to their place of incarceration.

¹   2013 Standard Civil Contract Specification Category Specific Rules, Immigration and Asylum specification, regs 8.6 and 8.46.

1.129 For funding purposes work is divided into controlled work and licensed work.[1] Controlled work is subdivided into legal help and controlled legal representation. Legal help is the work done on the initial stages of a case up until proceedings are issued: advice on what application can be made, the making of that application and consideration of the decision. Controlled legal representation is work done on appeal to the First-tier and Upper Tribunal including applications to the Tribunal for permission to appeal. Since 2007, controlled work has been paid by a system of 'graduated fixed fees' whereby a fixed amount is paid for work at each stage of the case, exclusive of disbursements.[2] There are limited exceptions which are paid at hourly rates, for example in the case of an unaccompanied child seeking asylum.[3] Some of these exceptions are subject to a cap on payment, for example initial advice on asylum prior to a claim for asylum being made where no asylum claim is made in which that provider is acting.[4] Where a case falls under the graduated fixed fee scheme, if the work done on the case, exclusive of disbursements, is three times that nominally represented by the fixed fee, the 'escape' threshold has been reached and case will be paid at hourly rates.[5]

Disbursements limits for certain experts are set out in the Civil Legal Aid (Remuneration) Regulations 2013 as amended[6] and prior authority must be obtained to exceed these. Prior authority need not routinely be sought where the expert is not one specified but often is, to protect against a dispute about payment at a later stage. In immigration and asylum controlled work counsel's fees are treated as profit costs, not as disbursements. This is an exception to the general treatment of counsel's fees as disbursements. The obligation on a provider to satisfy him/herself of a client's financial eligibility for legal aid is an ongoing one and is onerous.[7] Both income and resources form part of the calculation as do the income and resources of a partner, unless she or he has a contrary interest in the matter for which funding is being provided. For controlled work, the resources of a parent, guardian or person responsible for, or contributing substantially toward, the maintenance of a child is taken into account, unless there is a conflict of interest or unless it would appear inequitable to do so (for example in the case of a foster carer). The Director of Legal Aid casework may take into account all or part of the resources of a person who is, or is likely, substantially to be maintaining a person or whose resources have been or are likely to be made available to that person or to persons whose resources are taken account in their case.[8]

[1]   The Civil Legal Aid (Remuneration) Regulations 2013, SI 2013/422, reg 2(1).
[2]   The Civil Legal Aid (Remuneration) Regulations 2013, SI 2013/422, reg 6(2) and Sch 1.
[3]   2013 Standard Civil Contract Specification Category Specific Rules, Immigration and Asylum specification, regulation 8.77(i).
[4]   2013 Standard Civil Contract Specification Category Specific Rules, Immigration and Asylum specification, regulations 8.77(g) and 8.80.
[5]   2013 Standard Civil Contract Specification Category Specific Rules, Immigration and Asylum specification, paragraphs 8.72 to 8.76.
[6]   SI 2013/422, Sch 5.
[7]   2013 Standard Civil Contract Specification General, paragraphs 3.23-3.25.
[8]   Legal Aid Agency, Controlled work: Guide to Determining Financial Eligibility for Controlled Work and Family Mediation April 2014 v1.

1.130 The Civil Legal Aid (Remuneration) (Amendment) (No 3) Regulations 2014[1] changed the basis of funding of judicial review cases with effect from 22 April 2014. Payment for work done on the case between issue of proceedings and grant of permission was made conditional on either permission being granted or the Lord Chancellor's considering it reasonable to make payment, taking into account why no costs order was made, the extent to which the outcome sought was obtained and the strength of the application at issue. There is concern that this will make lawyers more reluctant to take judicial review work and limit the amount of judicial review work that they can do at any one time.

[1]   SI 2014/607.

1.131 Not all work done by immigration practitioners falls within the immigration contract. For example, work on asylum support cases falls within the housing category.[1] Judicial review work can be done under a public law contract or a contract under the particular area of law in which a judicial review is sought.[2] Claims for compensation from traffickers and employment law claims against traffickers can only be brought using the 'Miscellaneous' allocation of cases[3], for which each provider holds only a very limited number of matter starts.

[1]   Legal Aid Agency Category Definitions to 2013, paragraph 28(h).
[2]   Ibid, paragraph 13.
[3]   Ibid, paragraph 37.

1.132 Requirements under the contract are that the person claiming legal aid be accredited under the Law Society's Immigration and Asylum Accreditation Scheme[1]. Accreditation can be at probationer level, levels 1 or 2 and level 2 advisors can further be accredited as supervisors.

[1]   2013 Standard Civil Contract Specification Category Specific Rules, Immigration and Asylum specification, regulation 8.15(a).

Administration

1.133 The scheme is bureaucratic and places a heavy administrative burden on firms doing legal aid work. The main forms are first those concerned with financial eligibility for legal aid. The MEANS1 form is used to assess eligibility, with certain exceptions and supplements. The exceptions are that MEANS2 is used for persons passported into legal aid by their receipt of certain benefits, that MEANS3 is used where a person is outside the UK and that MEANS4 is used where the applicant is under 16. The supplementary forms are MEANS1P for remand or serving prisoners and FORM L17, a statement of earnings form to be used in the absence of payslips. Form CW1 is used for advice or assistance provided under legal help, CW2 for appeals to the Tribunal, CW3B for the extension of matters paid at hourly rates[1] and CW3C for extensions for disbursements in fixed fee cases. An App6 is used to apply for funding for emergency cases. In Exceptional Funding cases an additional (not alternative) form must be completed, Civ ECF.

[1]   CW3A for extensions under paragraph 8.77(a) of the Immigration Specification, viz. hourly rates cases opened prior to 1 April 2013.

Chapter 2

RIGHT OF ABODE AND CITIZENSHIP

INTRODUCTION

2.1 British citizenship, broadly speaking, now largely determines who obtains the right of abode in UK domestic law and who obtains the right of free movement and residence as a European Union citizen. However, the meaning of 'British citizen' for the purpose of the right of abode and freedom from immigration control in the UK domestic context is different from the meaning of 'British national' under international human rights law or UK national for the purpose of free movement and residence under EU law. In this chapter we explain the link between British nationality, British citizenship and the right of abode as provided for in the British Nationality Act 1981 and the Immigration Act 1971 and refer to the additional and, in particular cases, easier means of acquiring British citizenship following the enactment of the British Overseas Territories Act 2002 and the Nationality, Immigration and Asylum Act 2002. The meaning of UK national for EU law purposes is explained in Chapter 4. The following abbreviations are used in this chapter:

AI(TC)A 2004	Asylum and Immigration (Treatment of Claimants, etc) Act 2004
BC	British citizen
BCIA 2009	Borders, Citizenship and Immigration Act 2009
BDTC	British Dependent Territories citizen (now renamed BOTC)
BNA 1981	British Nationality Act 1981 (into force on 1 January 2083)
BN(O)	British National (Overseas)
BOC	British Overseas citizen
BOTA 2002	British Overseas Territories Act 2002 (main parts in force 26 February 2003)
BOTC	British overseas territories citizen (previously named BDTC)
BPP	British Protected Person
CUKC	Citizen of the United Kingdom and Colonies
FTT	First Tier Tribunal (Immigration and Asylum Chamber)
UT	Upper Tribunal (Immigration and Asylum Chamber)
NI	Nationality Instructions
IA 2014	Immigration Act 2014
IAN 2006	Immigration, Asylum and Nationality Act 2006
NIAA 2002	Nationality, Immigration and Asylum Act 2002
SIAC	Special Immigration Appeal Commission
UKBA 2007	UK Borders Act 2007

UKPH	UK passport holder
UKRP	UK residence permit

2.2 Under the Borders, Citizenship and Immigration Act 2009, Part 2 (Citizenship), proposed alterations were enacted relating to the acquisition of British citizenship by birth, registration and naturalisation. However, with the change of government in 2010, an announcement was made by the Home Secretary on 5 November 2010 that she had decided not to bring the naturalisation provisions of the Borders, Citizenship and Immigration Act 2009 into force and that they would be repealed. These changes have never been put into practice and are no longer relevant. Further changes to the right of abode result from the provisions relating to nationality in the Immigration Act 2014. The Act has sought to rectify a long standing complaint that persons whose mother and father were not married at the time of their birth lost out on acquiring British citizenship by birth and descent. These changes are discussed below at **2.49–2.50**. The other changes involve an extension of the Home Secretary's powers to deprive a person of their British nationality by reversing the Supreme Court decision in *Al-Jedda*[1] Nothing, however, has been done in any of the more recent legislation to abolish the distinctions, discussed in this chapter, between different classes of British nationals, very few of whom, apart from British citizens, have the right of abode. This is despite the recommendations made in the report 'Citizenship: Our Common Bond' by Lord Goldsmith QC.[2] The marginalisation of British nationals without a right of abode began to be unravelled in a piecemeal way so far as BOCs and BOTCs were concerned in 2002[3] but there are no plans to take this process any further, notwithstanding that the current statutory provisions, arguably, fall short of the standards set by international public law and common law standards.[4] The 'civis britannicus sum' concept so central to the British Nationality Act 1948 is not, it seems, going to be revived.

[1] *Secretary of State for the Home Department v Al -Jedda* [2013] UKSC 62, [2014] AC 253, [2014] INLR 131, [2014] 1 All ER 356, [2014] Imm AR 229, [2013] 3 WLR 1006.
[2] 11 March 2008, p 6.
[3] See the discussion on the BOTA 2002 and the NIAA 2002 at **2.16** ff.
[4] Sir William Holdsworth, *A History of English Law*, vol X, p 393, states: 'The Crown has never had a prerogative power to prevent its subjects from entering the kingdom, or to expel them from it,' cited by Lord Bingham in his dissenting judgment in *R (on the application of Bancoult) v Secretary of State for Foreign and Commonwealth Affairs* [2008] UKHL 61, [2009] AC 453, [2008] 4 All ER 1055 at para 70. Plender,*International Migration Law* (1988, 2nd edn), ch 4, p 133 states: 'The principle that every state must admit its own nationals to its territory is accepted so widely that its existence as a rule of law is virtually beyond dispute . . .'.

THE RIGHT OF ABODE

2.3 When British nationality was reorganised by the British Nationality Act 1948 (in force 1 January 1949), possession of British nationality (British subject/Commonwealth citizen status) gave an automatic right of abode to all such persons, not just Citizens of the UK and Colonies (CUKCs). At that time, the right of abode was purely a common law concept. After Commonwealth immigration control was introduced in 1962, the right of abode became a status of enormous importance. Between 1962 and 1973, when the Immigration Act 1971 came into force, it remained purely a common law concept, subject to such derogations as were required by clear provisions of the Commonwealth Immigrants Act 1962[1] and the modifications made to that Act by the Commonwealth Immigrants Act 1968. After 1973 it took on an additional, statutory form that constrained the operation of the common law right, and became quite separate in statute law from the broad concept of British nationality and the status of British subject/Commonwealth citizen which went with it. But the definition of persons who had a right of abode was still linked to one or more of the categories of British subject/Commonwealth citizen. It is therefore necessary to look at the outlines of British nationality law. Although there is no prerogative power to expel British nationals from a territory to which they belonged, in the *Bancoult case*, the majority in the House of Lords upheld the British government's decision to remove the Chagossians from the Chagos Islands (part of the British Indian Ocean Territory, a British overseas territory) to make way for the American base at Diego Garcia. Section 3 of the Colonial Laws Validity Act 1865 made it clear that no colonial law was to be void or inoperative on the ground of repugnancy to the law of England, unless it was repugnant to the provisions of some Act of Parliament which was made applicable to the colony by express words or necessary intendment and so power to expel from a ceded colony given by an Order in Council was not invalid and the decision to expel was neither unreasonable nor a breach of a legitimate expectation.[2]

[1] *DPP v Bhagwan* [1972] AC 60, [1970] 3 All ER 97, HL. See further Sir William Holdsworth, *A History of English Law*, vol X, p 393, cited in **2.2**, fn 4 above; Laws LJ, in para 39 of his judgment in *R (on the application of Bancoult) v Secretary of State for Foreign and Commonwealth Affairs* [2001] QB 1067 ('*Bancoult (1)*'), which the Secretary of State accepted, stated: 'For my part I would certainly accept that a British subject enjoys a constitutional right to reside in or return to that part of the Queen's dominions of which he is a citizen. Sir William Blackstone says in *Commentaries on the Laws of England* (1809, 15th edn), vol 1, p 137: 'But no power on earth, except the authority of Parliament, can send any subject of England *out of* the land against his will; no, not even a criminal.' Compare Chitty, A Treatise on the law of the Prerogatives of the Crown and the Relative Duties and Rights of the Subject (1820), pp 18, 21. Lord de Grey CJ in *Fabrigas v Mostyn* (1773) 20 St Tr 81 at col 181. See further Lord Bingham's dissenting speech in *Bancoult* at para 70 and Lord Rogers at para 89 who said: 'On the basis of these various authorities it appears to me certainly arguable that there is a "fundamental principle" of English law that no citizen should be exiled or banished from a British colony and sent to a foreign country.'

[2] *R (on the application of Bancoult) v Secretary of State for Foreign and Commonwealth Affairs* [2008] UKHL 61, [2009] AC 453, [2008] 4 All ER 1055 per Lord Rogers at para 96.

2.4 Under the Immigration Act 1971, section 1(1) it is provided that all those who are expressed to have the right of abode in the UK shall be free to live in, and to come and go into and from, the UK without let or hindrance except such as may be required by the Act to enable their right to be established or as may be otherwise lawfully imposed on any person. For example, they may be asked to produce their passports on entry,[1] and they may be refused entry if they do not have the requisite passport or certificate to prove their entitlement. Under section 3(9) of the 1971 Act, as currently in force,[2] a person seeking to enter the UK and claiming to have the right of abode there shall prove it by:

(a)   a United Kingdom passport describing him as a British citizen;
(b)   a United Kingdom passport describing him as a British subject with the right of abode in the United Kingdom; or
(c)   a certificate of entitlement.

There are two groups of people who have a right of abode:

(1)	BCs;[3] and
(2)	Commonwealth citizens who for the purpose of the Immigration Act 1971 are treated as BCs.

By virtue of the right of abode, all these people are free from immigration control and cannot be deported or (except by extradition) removed,[4] unless they are unable to prove their status. The possession of British citizenship confers a status on the holder, and normally it can only be acquired by a strict application of nationality law through automatic acquisition or by entitlement upon application (by a minister or governor) or the exercise of a discretion (by a minister or governor). This means that there is normally no room for the grant of citizenship by a representation from an immigration official or member of the staff at a British High Commission or consulate that a person is entitled to it, unless possibly that person is acting on behalf of a minister or governor who has authority to grant citizenship.[5]

[1]	Immigration Act 1971, s 1(1) and Sch 2, paras 2 and 3. For the equivalent EU law requirement see *Re Wijsenbeek* C-378/97 [1999] ECR I-6207, [2001] 2 CMLR 1403, ECJ.
[2]	Substituted by the Immigration, Asylum and Nationality Act 2006, s 30, in force 16 June 2006 by SI 2006/1497, art 3, Schedule. For the definition of a 'certificate of entitlement' and a 'UK Passport', see Immigration Act 1971, s 33(1). In respect of a 'certificate of entitlement', see also the Nationality, Immigration and Asylum Act 2002, s 10(1)–(4), (6) in force on Royal Assent on 7 November 2002 by s 162(2)(c) and (5)(b) in force 21 December 2006 by SI 2006/3144, art 2; see also Immigration (Certificate of Entitlement to Right of Abode in the United Kingdom) Regulations 2006, SI 2006/3145, in force 21 December 2006; see also below at **2.23**. Paragraphs 12–14 of the Immigration Rules (HC 395 as amended) do not reflect the version of s 3(9) of the Immigration Act 1971 currently in force.
[3]	These include dual nationals, who may be travelling on the passport of another country.
[4]	Immigration Act 1971, ss 2, 3(1), (5) and (6); Immigration and Asylum Act 1999, s 10. But an infant child's right of abode in the UK means more than merely a right to choose to live in the UK on his/her majority, and precludes a local authority from discharging its support responsibilities in a way that encourages or in practice enforces the expulsion of the child before the effect of his/her citizenship has been decided by the proper authority for that purpose. *Obiter* per Buxton LJ, paras 15–21 of *M v Islington London Borough Council* [2004] EWCA Civ 235, [2004] 4 All ER 709, where the local authority's attempt to discharge its responsibility under the Children Act 1989 to the British child of a woman unlawfully in the UK by offering the child's mother tickets for both of them to go to Guyana, the mother's country of nationality, was quashed on different grounds.
[5]	*Christodoulidou v Secretary of State for the Home Department* [1985] Imm AR 179; *Gowa v A-G* (1984) 129 Sol Jo 131, CA, upheld in HL on different grounds: [1985] 1 WLR 1003.

2.5 For the avoidance of doubt, ID Cards under the Identity Cards Act 2006 describing a person as a British citizen or as a British subject with the right of abode in the United Kingdom, are no longer prescribed to prove the right of abode in the UK for the purposes of entry to the UK; s 3(9) of the Immigration Act 1971 has been amended by the Identity Documents Act 2010 to reflect the repeal of the 2006 Act, from 21 January 2011.

2.6 The right of abode must be distinguished from: (1) rights of free movement within the common travel area comprising the UK, Channel Islands, Isle of Man and the Republic of Ireland; (2) exemptions from immigration control conferred on diplomats and others; (3) EU rights of free movement and residence; and (4) settlement or indefinite leave to remain granted to persons who are subject to immigration control and do not have the right of abode. The distinctions are to some extent technical and artificial, but behind them lies the difference between different degrees of immigration control and coming or going without let or hindrance.

2.7 What has to be understood is that essentially the right of abode stems from the status of citizenship and is an automatic benefit of it, whereas the other rights (common travel, free movement, exemption, settlement) flow from separate quite specific provisions of the Immigration Act 1971. Only EU law is comparable. Since 1993 the right of free movement and residence within the European Union is for the first time tied to a European citizenship status, and a fledgling European Union right of abode is discernible. Who benefits from the right of abode under UK law cannot be understood until we have dealt with the main provisions of citizenship and nationality law.

Right of abode and international human rights law

2.8 Protocol 4 of the European Convention on Human Rights (ECHR) contains provisions which give the nationals of signatory States rights which are akin to the right of abode in UK domestic law. First, it provides that no-one shall be deprived of the right to enter the territory of the State of which he or she is a national.[1] Secondly, no-one shall be expelled, by means of a collective or individual measure, from the territory of the State of which he or she is a national.[2] Thirdly, once lawfully in the country, everyone (not just nationals) has a right to move freely throughout the territory, to choose a residence and to leave the country,[3] subject to such restrictions as are in accordance with the law and are necessary in a democratic society in the interests of national security or public safety, for the maintenance of public order, the prevention of crime, the protection of health and morals or for the protection of the rights and freedoms of others.[4] However, the right of abode in UK domestic law is not conferred on all British nationals and so there are important groups of British nationals, who do not enjoy its benefits. Protocol 4 would give them a broadly equivalent right to the right of abode, which is the principal reason why it has not been ratified so far by the British government and is not likely to be in any near future.[5] Notwithstanding this, the principles of the Protocol are still important for UK immigration law. First, the wording of Article 3(2) 'no-one shall *be deprived of* the right to enter . . . .' (our emphasis) is posited on the existence of a right of entry of nationals.[6] This reflects the position in international human rights law, under which there is a duty on a State to admit its own nationals.[7] Secondly, notwithstanding the non-ratification of Protocol 4 by the UK, the ECHR and all the human rights contained in it (including the Protocols) are part of the *corpus* and general principles of EU law,[8] and may therefore be used in the construction of EU law.[9] Thirdly, the government is gradually moving into line with the international human rights position by a series of law changes which have extended the territorial reach of British citizenship to all British overseas territories (save one) (and so to most BOTCs) and have conferred a much more extensive entitlement to registration as a BC on certain BOCs, British subjects, BN(O)s and BPPs.[10]

---

[1] ECHR, Protocol 4, art 3(2).
[2] ECHR, Protocol 4, art 3(1).
[3] ECHR, Protocol 4, art 2(1) and (2). Notification of overseas travel plans by a sex offender was not a ban on the right of exit and, not therefore a breach of either ECHR or art 4 of the

Citizen's Directive 2004/38/EC: see *R (on the application of F) v Secretary of State for Justice; R (on the application of Thompson) v Secretary of State for Justice* [2008] EWHC 317 (Admin) at **2.9**, fn 5, below.

4 ECHR, Protocol 4, art 2(3).

5 See Laurie Fransman 'Human Rights and British Nationality' in Butterworths *A Guide to the Human Rights Act 1998* (1999) pp 134 ff; see also 'Citizenship: Our Common Bond' (March 2008) Lord Goldsmith QC, Chapter 3, para 17.

6 See *East African Asians v United Kingdom* (1973) 3 EHRR 76, para 242, per Professor JES Fawcett.

7 See eg the UN International Covenant on Civil and Political Rights 1966 (ICCPR), art 12(4) which provides that no one shall be arbitrarily deprived of the right to enter his own country. For texts see Brownlie and Goodwin-Gill *Basic Documents on Human Rights* (4th edn, 2002) OUP. See further Universal Declaration of Human Rights, art 13(2), Brownlie and Goodwin-Gill *op cit*; Fransman fn 5 above, para 3.1. This right has in fact been relied on by the British government in arguing (unsuccessfully) against the application of EU law to the return to the UK of a British national who has gone to another Member State of the EU in the exercise of her free movement rights: *R v Immigration Appeal Tribunal and Surinder Singh, ex p Secretary of State for the Home Department* [1992] Imm AR 565, ECJ, at 22, quoted in *Fransman* above. The UK signed the ICCPR on 16 September 1968 and ratified it on 20 May 1976. However, upon ratification the UK entered the following reservation in respect of art 12(4): 'The Government of the United Kingdom reserve the right to continue to apply such immigration legislation governing entry into, stay in and departure from the United Kingdom as they may deem necessary from time to time and, accordingly, their acceptance of article 12 (4) and of the other provisions of the Covenant is subject to the provisions of any such legislation as regards persons not at the time having the right under the law of the United Kingdom to enter and remain in the United Kingdom. The United Kingdom also reserves a similar right in regard to each of its dependent territories'.

8 Consolidated Treaty on European Union, art 6 (ex art 6TEU), OJ C 83/13 (30 March 2010); *Elliniki Radiophonia Tiléorassi AE v Pliroforissis and Kouvelas* [1994] ECR I-2951 ECJ; *B v Secretary of State for the Home Department* [2000] Imm AR 478, paras 13–14.

9 In the referred application of *Manjit Kaur* it was argued that art 3(2) of Protocol 4 could and should be used as an aid to the construction of art 8 of EC Treaty (now art 20 of the Treaty on the Functioning of the European Union (ex art 17 TEC), so as to entitle a BOC to enter and remain in the UK. This question was not dealt with in the judgment of the court: see Case C-192/99: *R (on the application of Kaur) v Secretary of State for the Home Department* [2001] ECR I-237, [2001] All ER (EC) 250, ECJ. See also Case C-34/09 *Ruiz Zambrano v Office National de l'emploi* [2011] All ER (EC) 491, [2011] 2 CMLR 1197, ECJ, discussed in fuller detail in Chapter 5, below.

10 See the BOTA 2002, ss 3 and 4, the NIAA 2002, s 12 and the BCIA 2009, s 44, as discussed below at **2.16–2.20**.

Restrictions on the right of abode

2.9 The statutory definition of the right of abode refers to 'let or hindrance' which may be lawfully imposed on any person. The extent of this exception is uncertain and untested, but is thought to include the following six restrictions:

(i) lawful imprisonment and other restrictions (eg bail conditions restricting residence) imposed by criminal courts in the exercise of their normal jurisdiction;[1]

(ii) lawful detention and other restrictions imposed under other statutory powers, for example, under the Mental Health Act 1983. This will include non-derogable Control Orders imposed under the Prevention of Terrorism Act 2005 and geographical restrictions imposed under Anti-Social Behaviour Orders (ASBOs) introduced by the Crime and Disorder Act 1998 and amended many times since;[2]

(iii)   restrictions lawfully imposed on the movement of children by an order of a court in matrimonial, wardship and Children Act 1989 proceedings;[3]

(iv)   restraints imposed by the issue of a writ *'ne exeat regno'*, restraining the subject from leaving the kingdom, now largely superseded by injunction;[4]

(v)   restrictions, other than normal bail conditions, requiring surrender of a passport and a ban on foreign travel. This concerns measures taken, for example to deal with football hooliganism and foreign travel by paedophiles;[5]

(vi)   restrictions on entry of polygamous wives.[6]

[1]   See *R v Saunders*: Case 175/78 [1980] QB 72, [1979] 2 All ER 267 at 275, ECJ where a similar exemption with regard to EC free movement provisions is discussed. Any loss of liberty must also be justifiable under ECHR, art 5: see 7.62 below.

[2]   See Maya Sikand, ASBOs: A Practitioner's Guide to Defending Anti-social Behaviour Orders (2006) LAG.

[3]   See *Re Arif (Mohamed) (an infant)* [1968] Ch 643, sub nom *Re A (an infant), Harif v Secretary of State for Home Affairs* [1968] 2 All ER 145, CA.

[4]   For discussion of the writ *'Ne exeat regno'* see the fourth edition of this work at 6.6.

[5]   Section 86 of the Sexual Offences Act 2003 falls short of a ban on leaving the country but gives the Secretary of State power to make regulations for sexual offenders to give the police their travel details for travel outside the UK. Under the Sexual Offences Act 2003 (Travel Notification Requirements) Regulations 2004, SI 2004/1220, sex offenders were subject to, among other things, travel notification requirements. The relevant statutory provisions required an offender who intended to leave the United Kingdom for a period of three days or longer to specify the date on which he would leave the UK, the country to which he would travel and his point of arrival in that country and, if more than one country, his point of arrival in each such additional country, the identity of any carrier or carriers he intended to use, details of his accommodation for his first night outside the UK, the date on which he intended to return and the point of arrival. Under s 82 these would last for an indefinite period in the case of someone sentenced to a period in excess of 30 months. In *R (on the application of F (by his litigation friend F) and Thompson) v Secretary of State for the Home Department* [2006] UKHL 11, [2006] 2 AC 91, [2006] 4 All ER 929, the Supreme Court held that the Sexual Offences Act 2003, s 82 was incompatible with art 8 ECHR in subjecting certain sex offenders to notification requirements indefinitely without the opportunity for review.

[6]   Immigration Act 1988, s 2. The restrictions do not prevent a wife who entered the UK in that capacity before 1 August 1988 from returning to this country, or from being issued with a certificate of entitlement or entry clearance enabling her to do so, irrespective of the presence in the UK of other wives. Nor do they apply to a wife who has been in the UK at any time since her marriage if she was then the only wife to have entered, or been cleared for entry to, the UK.

2.10 An example of lawful restrictions which may be imposed on the right of abode is contained in the much amended Football Spectators Act 1989.[1] Under this Act banning orders may be imposed on those convicted of a football related offence or who have at any time caused or contributed to violence or disorder in the UK or abroad, where the Court is satisfied that there are reasonable grounds to believe that the banning order will help prevent violence and disorder at football matches.[2] So far as matches abroad are concerned, the subjects of banning orders are prevented from travelling by having to surrender their passports and to report to their local police stations over the period of the match or tournament.[3] A second example of restraints on foreign travel is where courts can issue travel restriction orders in cases of drug trafficking offenders leaving prison.[4] In all these cases there is also a power to require the surrender of passports under the Criminal Justice and Police Act 2001. A third example is contained in the Sexual Offences Act 2003. Under section 114 the police may apply for a foreign travel order to prevent convicted paedophiles from travelling outside the UK, if this is necessary for the purpose of protecting children from serious sexual harm from the defendant outside the UK. No provision is made for the surrender of passports or ID cards.

[1]   See Football Spectators Act 1989, as amended, especially ss 14–14J. Note also amendments which took place as from April 6 2007 under the Violent Crime Reduction Act 2006, s 52(2) and Sch 3. Relevant parts, as amended, are contained in Archbold *Criminal Pleading Evidence and Practice* (2010) Sweet & Maxwell, paras 5-824–833 and Second Supplement. Prior to the World Cup in South Africa in 2010 3,143 people were banned from travelling for the duration of the tournament, which, according to the police, played a major part in the good behaviour of England fans: *Guardian* 25 June 2010.
[2]   Football Spectators Act 1989 as amended, ss 14A and 14B. An order under the Act preventing BCs from leaving the UK to attend international football matches is not a 'penalty' within Article 7 ECHR and is not in breach of it: *Gough v Chief Constable of the Derbyshire Constabulary; R (on the application of Miller) v Leeds Magistrates' Court; Lilley v DPP* [2001] 554 EWHC (Admin) , [2002] QB 459, [2001] 4 All ER 289.
[3]   Football Spectators Act 1989, ss 14(4)(b) and 14E(3).
[4]   Criminal Justice and Police Act 2001, ss 33–37. See further *R v Mee* [2004] Crim LR 487, CA (the discretion to impose an order has to be exercised for the purpose of reducing the risk of re-offending and has to be proportionate) and *R v Gee (Stewart Carl)* [2009] EWCA Crim 1843.

2.11 Section 2 of the Immigration Act 1988 applies to women who acquired the right of abode through their polygamous marriage to a former CUKC, British subject or Commonwealth citizen who became a BC on commencement of the BNA 1981.[1] It provides that such a woman may not enter the UK in exercise of the right of abode, or be granted a certificate of entitlement, if another of the man's wives (or widows) has entered the UK or been granted a certificate of entitlement on the basis of the marriage.[2]

[1]   It does not apply to women who married and came to the UK before the coming into force of the Act: Immigration Act 1988, s 2(1)(b), (the burden of proving these facts is on them: s 2(5)); or to women who first came to the UK after the Act, when they were the only spouse: IA 1988, s 2(4).
[2]   Entry as a visitor or as an illegal entrant is to be disregarded: Immigration Act 1988, s 2(7). The ban also applies if an application for a certificate of entitlement is pending from another wife or widow: IA 1988, s 2(9).

The right of abode 1973 to 1983

2.12 Immediately prior to 1 January 1983 the statutory right of abode depended on whether or not a person was 'patrial' as defined in the Immigration Act 1971, s 2. On and after that date (when the BNA 1981 came into force) it depends on the definition of 'British citizen' set out in the new section 2(2). Under pre-1983 law, patriality was conferred on certain citizens of the UK and Colonies (CUKCs) and certain other Commonwealth citizens (ie citizens of independent Commonwealth countries and British subjects without citizenship). The BNA 1981 redefined British nationality and divided up former CUKCs, re-classifying them into three new categories of citizenship (BC, BDTC and BOC) and, additionally, changed the definition of those who have the right of abode. Under the Immigration Act 1971, before amendment, the following, broadly speaking, were patrials:

(i)   CUKCs by birth, adoption, naturalisation or registration in the UK or Islands;[1]

(ii)   CUKCs with similar connections to the UK through a parent or grandparent;[2]

(iii)   CUKCs who had at any time settled and had been ordinarily resident in the UK or Islands for five years;[3]

(iv)   Commonwealth citizens with a parent born or legally adopted in the UK or Islands;[4]

(v)   Commonwealth women who become patrial through marriage.[5]

[1] Immigration Act 1971, old s 2(1)(a).
[2] Immigration Act 1971, old s 2(1)(b).
[3] Immigration Act 1971, old s 2(1)(c).
[4] Immigration Act 1971, old s 2(1)(d).
[5] Immigration Act 1971, old s 2(2).

RIGHT OF ABODE AFTER BRITISH NATIONALITY ACT 1981

2.13 Under the new provisions of the IA 1971, s 2, as substituted in its entirety by the BNA 1981 and applying on and after 1 January 1983, the old category of 'patrials' was swept away.[1] Those who have the right of abode are defined in terms of British citizenship. But this has been given a special extended meaning for the purpose of the IA 1971. 'British citizens' has one meaning for nationality purposes (eg getting a UK passport as a British citizen) and a somewhat different meaning in the amended section 2 of the 1971 Act, which preserves the right of abode for those Commonwealth citizens who were not CUKCs but had the status of 'patrial' immediately prior to 1 January 1983. They are classed as 'British citizens' for immigration control purposes under the amended section 2. They consist of those who were previously patrial under the old section 2(1)(d) of the IA 1971 because one of their parents was born or legally adopted in the UK or Islands and those women who became patrials through marriage. The original text of section 2 of the 1971 Act is printed with the updated Act in Appendix 1 of this book.

[1] BNA 1981, s 39.

2.14 Those who have the right of abode under the post-1983 definition of British citizenship under the amended section 2 of the IA 1971 are:

(i)   Those who automatically became BCs on the coming into force of the BNA 1981.[1] These will include all the former CUKCs who prior to commencement had a right of abode because they were 'patrials', ie CUKCs born, adopted, registered or naturalised in the UK, those with the necessary ancestral connections with the UK, and those who were ordinarily resident here for five years free of immigration restrictions;[2]

(ii)   Commonwealth citizens[3] who immediately before commencement had the right of abode by virtue of having a parent who was born in the UK under the old section 2(1)(d) of the IA 1971; and

(iii)   Women Commonwealth citizens who immediately before commencement had a right of abode under the old section 2(2) of the 1971 Act by virtue of their marriage to a patrial.

Since only CUKCs who became BCs obtained an automatic right of abode under the BNA 1981, this meant that resident CUKCs who were free from immigration conditions and who would previously (ie prior to 1 January

1983) have expected to become patrial after five years' ordinary residence in the UK,[4] lost out. If they merely became British Dependent Territories citizens or British Overseas citizens, they lost the automatic right to acquire patrial status after five years' ordinary residence. In its place, they obtained a right to register as BCs if they met the requirements of section 4 of the BNA 1981. This applies to all BDTCs (now known as BOTCs), BN(O)s, BOCs, British subjects under the Act, and BPPs who have spent the last five years in the UK (without absence for more than 450 days during the whole period and 90 days in the final 12 months), have been in the UK without restriction on the period for which they may remain in the final 12 months and have not been in breach of the immigration laws during the five-year period.[5] This way of acquiring the right of abode will be of diminished importance in view of the new rights to become BCs under the two Acts of 2002 (see below **2.16**).

[1] BNA 1981, s 11.
[2] IA 1971, s 2(1)(c), before amendment.
[3] Commonwealth citizens are all those who are citizens of the countries set out in BNA 1981, Sch 3.
[4] IA 1971, s 2(1)(c), before amendment.
[5] See BNA 1981, s 4; NB there is provision for the exercise of discretion (i) where the requirements are not met and (ii) where a person has been in Crown service. Further, where a person was settled in the UK immediately prior to 1 January 1983, there is a dispensation from the requirement to have been in the UK at the beginning of the period.

2.15 The second main change made by the BNA 1981 was that women Commonwealth citizens no longer automatically obtained a right of abode by marriage to British national men. Since 1 January 1983 they must naturalise as BCs under section 6 of the 1981 Act, if they are to acquire a right of abode. The third main change is that Commonwealth citizens born after commencement of the 1981 Act will not obtain a right of abode by virtue of having a parent born or legally adopted in the UK or Islands, as used to happen under the old section 2(1)(d) of the IA 1971, as originally in force. Commonwealth citizens born after commencement of the 1981 Act will only obtain a right of abode in the UK if they acquire British citizenship by descent, naturalisation, registration (as British nationals who are not British citizens), registration (as children) or because they are BOTCs who benefited from the provisions of the BOTA 2002.[1] Fourthly, it should be noted that Commonwealth citizens born before 1 January 1983 (the commencement date of the 1981 Act) who were patrial do not lose this status, provided they have not ceased to be Commonwealth citizens in the meanwhile.[2] Commonwealth citizens who were not patrials had a five-year window to register as BCs after completing five years' ordinary residence, but this entitlement ended in 1988.[3]

[1] Under BNA 1981, s 2(1), BC status can now be acquired by descent from either the mother or the father, and the old rules under the British Nationality Act 1948, which prevented an illegitimate child inheriting the father's status have now been swept away by the NIAA 2002: BNA 1948, s 50(9), as amended by NIAA 2002, s 9(1) so as to substitute BNA 1981, s 50(9), (9A)–(9C), in force for persons born on and after 1 July 2006 by NIAA 2002, s 162 and SI 2006/1498, art 2; see also British Nationality (Proof of Paternity) Regulations 2006, SI 2006/1496.
[2] IA 1971, s 2(1)(b), as amended.
[3] BNA 1981, s 7(1).

RIGHT OF ABODE AFTER THE TWO ACTS OF 2002

2.16 In 1983 BDTCs from Gibraltar and the Falkland Islands were granted privileged access to British citizenship, not available to other BDTCs, especially those from Hong Kong.[1] By 1997 Hong Kong had reverted to China and limited safeguards had been put in place to protect the British connections of the people of Hong Kong (see **2.22** below). This cleared the way for fuller integration into full British citizenship of the people from the remaining dependent territories. In 1999 the government published a White Paper, proposing to extend full access to the UK to all remaining BDTCs.[2] This has now been done in the BOTA 2002 as from 21 May 2002[3] (save for those from the British Sovereign Base Areas in Cyprus). Meanwhile moves to ease the position of other residual groups of British nationals and BPPs were taking place and resulted in significant nationality provisions in Part I of the NIAA 2002, much of which came into force on 30 April 2003: see **2.21** below.

[1]   BNA 1981, s 5 (Gibraltar); British Nationality (Falkland Islands) Act 1983 (Falkland Islands).
[2]   *Partnership for Progress and Prosperity – Britain and the Overseas Territories*, Cm 4264, March 1999.
[3]   British Overseas Territories Act 2002 (Commencement) Order 2002, SI 2002/1252.

2.17 Sections 1 and 2 of BOTA 2002 deal solely with name changes. All references in statutes and subordinate legislation to a Dependent Territory are changed to British overseas territory and BDTCs become BOTCs. These changes took effect as soon as the Act came into force on 26 February 2002. The substantive changes put all BOTCs on a similar footing as the Falkland Islanders as from commencement on 21 May 2002.[1] Section 3 confers British citizenship, and thereby a right of abode in the UK, on anyone who was a BOTC immediately before commencement, automatically, without their having to make any kind of application.[2] The one exception to this rule concerns persons who are BOTCs by virtue only of a connection with the Sovereign Base Areas in Cyprus, which remains outside the 'qualifying territories' (ie all the other British overseas territories) for all purposes connected with the Act.[3] An important amendment made during the passage of the Bill deals with the special position of the British Indian Ocean Territory islanders, the Ilois, who come from the Chagos Islands. During the late 1960s and early 1970s, 2000 of these islanders were forced by the British government to leave their homes to make way for a US military base on the largest island, Diego Garcia. They went to Mauritius or other Indian Ocean Islands. This had the effect that many of those born while the Ilois were in exile from their islands would not qualify for British citizenship under the main provisions of the BOTA 2002. In 2001 the High Court held that the forced exile and exclusion from their homelands was unlawful.[4] There was, therefore a grave injustice to rectify, and, by way of some meagre recompense for their expulsion from their homeland, special provision was made in section 6 of the Act to close the important loophole that meant that they would not otherwise become British citizens under the BOTA 2002, s 3. Exceptionally section 6 extends the automatic acquisition of British citizenship to those islanders, who were born outside the British Indian Ocean Territory on or after 26 April 1969 and before 1 January 1983 (who had not acquired CUKC status by descent from their fathers) and who had been unable to inherit their mother's CUKC status (where she had been born in the British Indian Ocean Territory) under the discriminatory provisions of nationality law in force under the British Nationality Act 1948 at the time of their birth.

Where such persons were not already BCs or BOTCs, they became British citizens. Additionally, if they were not already BOTCs, they also automatically acquired that status. Thus, depending on their particular circumstances, the section makes them BCs[5] and/or BOTCs[6] and thus puts them in the same position as the other beneficiaries of the new law.

[1] British Overseas Territories Act 2002 (Commencement) Order 2002, SI 2002/1252.
[2] British Overseas Territories Act 2002, s 3(1). The person becomes a BC by descent if he or she was a BOTC by descent: BOTA 2002, s 3(3).
[3] BOTA 2002, s 3(2). See further Cyprus Act 1960, s 2(1) and Sovereign Base Areas of Akrotiri and Dhekelia (Boundaries) Order in Council 1962, SI 1962/396, as amended by SI 1966/1415; and Sovereign Base Areas of Akrotiri and Dhekelia Order in Council 1960, SI 1960/1369, as amended by SI 1966/1415.
[4] *R (on the application of Bancoult) v Secretary of State for Foreign and Commonwealth Affairs* [2001] QB 1067, [2001] 2 WLR 1219.
[5] BOTA 2002, s 6(1). They become BCs by descent: BOTA 2002, s 6(2).
[6] BOTA 2002, s 6(3), (4).

2.18 So far we have dealt with the position of those who were BOTCs immediately before commencement. Section 5 and Schedule 1 of the BOTA 2002 deal with the position after commencement. In essence, the Schedule extends the territorial application of British nationality law in respect of the acquisition of British citizenship by birth, adoption, descent and the registration of minors, to all British overseas territories other than the Sovereign Base Areas in Cyprus from the time of the 'appointed day', which is 21 May 2002.[1] The territories to which the new provisions apply are referred to as 'qualifying territories'.[2] Thus British citizenship is acquired by birth, abandonment or adoption in a qualifying territory after the appointed day on exactly the same basis as in the UK under section 1 of the BNA 1981.[3] It extends to the qualifying territories the same principles of acquisition of citizenship by descent contained in section 2 of the BNA 1981[4] and allows for registration of minors born outside the UK and a qualifying territory on the basis of ancestral connection to the UK and prior parental presence in the UK or a qualifying territory, and, in the case of stateless minors, if they merely have the ancestral connection.[5]

[1] British Overseas Territories Act 2002 (Commencement) Order 2002, SI 2002/1252 (made under BOTA 2002 s 8(2)).
[2] There are 13 qualifying overseas territories: Anguilla; Bermuda; British Antarctic Territory; British Indian Ocean Territory; (British) Virgin Islands; Cayman Islands; Falkland Islands; Gibraltar; Montserrat; Pitcairn, Henderson, Ducie and Oeno Islands; St Helena, Ascension and Tristan da Cunha; South Georgia and the South Sandwich Islands; Turks and Caicos Islands; South Georgia and the South Sandwich Islands and the Sovereign Base Areas of Akrotiri and Dhekelia (in Cyprus). The latter are a British overseas territory, but not a qualifying territory: see BOTA 2002, Sch 1, para 5(2), inserting the definition of 'qualifying territory' into s 50(1) of BNA 1981. The list of British overseas territories is set out in BNA 1981, Sch 6.
[3] BNA 1981, s 1, as amended by BOTA 2002, Sch 1, para 1.
[4] BNA 1981, s 2, as amended by BOTA 2002, Sch 1, para 2.
[5] BNA 1981, s 3(2) and (3), as amended by BOTA 2002, Sch 1, para 3.

2.19 Despite the far-reaching effect of the changes brought about by the BOTA 2002 in respect of the additional acquisition of British citizenship by BOTCs, a small number of persons will continue to keep or to acquire BOTC status without having any other citizenship status. For example, there are all those connected to the Sovereign Base Areas in Cyprus. They are and will continue to be solely BOTCs.[1] Then there are those who were born stateless in either the UK or a British overseas territory (including the Sovereign Base Areas in Cyprus). They are entitled to register as BCs or BOTCs if they have spent a specified amount of time in either the UK or a British overseas territory (no matter which) during the five years prior to the date of their application to register.[2] If the majority of that time was spent in the UK, they become a BC; if not they become a BOTC. The application can be made anytime up to the age of 22. A previous requirement that applicants have reached the age of 10 has been repealed.[3] Then there are those who acquire BOTC status by naturalisation or registration under Part II of the BNA 1981 on or after 21 May 2002. Such persons do not automatically become BCs by virtue of the BOTA 2002. Except for those connected to the Sovereign Base Areas in Cyprus and those who have renounced their British citizenship, any remaining BOTCs will be able to apply for discretionary registration as BCs under the new section 4A of BNA 1981.[4] People who only have BOTC status because of their connection to the Cyprus bases and people who have renounced their BC status will only be able to acquire or reacquire BC status, if they come to the UK and live here for five years[5] or they can persuade the Secretary of State to register them as a BC under the discretionary power to register minors under section 3(1) of the BNA 1981. Only then will they have the right of abode in the UK.

[1] The Sovereign Bases are contained in the list of British overseas territories in BNA 1981, Sch 6, and those connected with the Bases will have acquired BDTC status by virtue of one of the provisions set out in BNA 1981, ss 15–23 prior to 26 February 2002. That status became BOTC under BOTA 2002, s 1(1).

[2] Under BNA 1981, Sch2, para 3, as amended by NIAA 2002, s 8, which came into force on 1 April 2003: see NIAA 2002, s 162(4) and SI 2003/754, art 2(2).

[3] By BOTA 2002, s 8.

[4] Inserted by BOTA 2002, s 4.

[5] BNA 1981, s 4. Registration under BNA 1981, s 4A, inserted by BOTA 2002, s 4 is available to all BOTCs except those who are BOTCs *only* by virtue of a connection with the Cyprus Bases. If they have the status by virtue of a connection with another British overseas territory, eg, because one their parents was born there, they can apply straight away for discretionary registration under s 4A, which came into force on 21 May 2002: British Overseas Territories Act 2002 (Commencement) Order 2002, SI 2002/1252 (made under BOTA 2002, s 8(2)).

2.20 Although BOTA 2002 widens the number of territories a connection with which qualifies a person for acquiring British citizenship, the right of abode does not have an equivalent territorial scope. It still remains a right confined to the territory of the UK.[1] The position of people who wish to move from one British overseas territory to another or from the UK to one of the British overseas territories is not dealt with in UK legislation but in the local immigration law of each territory. One possibility for the future is that the position will be regulated by reviving and adapting the common law right of abode;[2] another is that it will remain a matter for local law. BOTA 2002 applies to the UK, the Channel Islands, the Isle of Man, and all the British overseas territories.[3] It should not be difficult for Parliament to clarify or alter the position. If you have a universal British citizenship covering a wide stretch of territories, it may be no great matter to enact that there is a right of abode with the same territorial reach, subject to the consent of the legislatures of the British overseas territories.

[1] Immigration Act 1971, s 1(1).

2   *DPP v Bhagwan* [1972] AC 60, [1970] 3 All ER 97, HL. See further *R (on the application of Bancoult) v Secretary of State for Foreign and Commonwealth Affairs* [2008] UKHL 61, [2009] AC 453, [2008] 4 All ER 1055.
3   BOTA 2002, s 8(4).

2.21 A number of provisions in the NIAA 2002 widen the scope for acquiring BC status and, therefore, the right of abode in the UK. The amendments to the provisions relating to the registration of stateless children are referred to in **2.18** above. The other changes are as follows:

(i)   *Legitimacy.* Section 50(9) of BNA 1981 defined the relationship between father and child in a way which meant that a child born illegitimate did not have a father for nationality purposes, unless the child was legitimated by the subsequent marriage of the parents. Section 9 of NIAA 2002 amends section 50(9) as from 1 July 2006.[1] The effect of the section is to allow those proved to be fathers, by DNA testing or otherwise, to be recognised as the fathers of their illegitimate children, born on or after 1 July 2006, for nationality purposes.[2] Other differences in the treatment of legitimate and illegitimate children were also removed on 1 July 2006.[3] People previously not recognised as BCs will by now have benefited from this legislation and have been able to acquire the right of abode, previously denied to them. But those who came before 2006 were left stranded. The Immigration Act 2014 has now enacted legislation (not yet in force) to give those people the same benefits and access to the right of abode. We deal with the new legislation at **2.49** below;

(ii) *Registration of BOCs, BN(O)s, BPPs and British Subjects.* After the ending of the special voucher scheme[4] without warning on 5 March 2002, many BOCs were left without the possibility of acquiring leave and thereafter a right of abode in the UK and were unable to do so in any other country, because they had no other nationality. The same was true of BPPs and British subjects. Section 4B of the BNA 1981, inserted by section 12 of the NIAA 2002,[5] now gives each of these groups an entitlement to register as BCs provided they have no other citizenship or nationality and have not after 4 July 2002 (the date when the new provision was made public) renounced, voluntarily relinquished or lost through action or inaction any other citizenship or nationality.[6] The benefit of this provision was extended to BN(O)s by the BCIA 2009, although for them the relevant day is 19 March 2009 rather than 4 July 2002.[7]

(iii) *Special voucher scheme.* The scheme was introduced in 1968 in recognition of the specific hardship being suffered at that time by UKPHs and their dependants, who were under political pressure to leave their countries of residence in former British colonies in East Africa, but who held no other citizenship and had nowhere else to go. These included BOCs,[8] BPPs, most of whom derived their status from a connection with former British Protectorates or former Trust Territories but did not become citizens of these countries, and British subjects born before 1 January 1949 who had that status by reason of their connection with former British India but who had not become citizens of India or Pakistan when those countries became independent (usually, in the case of persons of Asian ethnic origin, because they were not living in one for those countries at that time).[9] Under the scheme, heads of household could apply for vouchers to come to the UK for settlement with their families, including dependent children who were over 18.[10] After the scheme was brought to an abrupt halt in March 2002, no further applications by potential voucher holders or their dependants were to be entertained.[11] As a result, a number of people were left stranded, particularly dependent children, many of whom will not be able to take advantage of the provisions of the NIAA 2002 described in (ii) above.[12]

(iv) *Discrimination.* Prior to 1983, a British woman who had married a foreign national and was living abroad could not pass on her CUKC status to her foreign born children. To be CUKC they would need to have been born in the UK. In an identical situation children of a CUKC father, who lived abroad with his foreign wife, became British by descent.[13] On 6 February 1979 a policy was introduced to register the children born outside the UK to British mothers so long as the children were under 18. But not everyone knew of the practice and many missed the opportunity. Then the BNA 1981 provided for the first time that citizenship could descend through either the mother or the father.[14] But this still left many people born overseas to British mothers prior to 1983 without British citizenship. On enactment, under the new section 4C of the BNA 1981, such people, if born after 7 February 1961 and before 1983, in circumstances where they would have become CUKCs by descent under s 5 of the British Nationality Act 1948 had their mother been their father, and if they would thereby have had a right of abode under s 2 of the Immigration Act 1971 (as in force immediately prior to 1983) were entitled to register as BCs.[15] Notwithstanding these changes, some discrimination remained. Those born abroad to British mothers on or before 7 February 1961 still did not have the right to register. Further, those who may have acquired CUKC status by descent but by provisions other than s 5 of the 1948 Act were not catered for. To meet those objections, s 45 of the BCIA 2009 amended s 4C of the BNA 1981 so that the requirement to be born after 7 February 1961 is removed and a range of other provisions for acquisition by descent under the 1948 Act in addition to s 5 are brought within the ambit of the amended s 4C of the BNA 1981.[16] A stark case of discrimination arose as a result of illegitimacy in *R (Johnson).*[17]

1   NIAA 2002, s 9 came into force on 1 July 2006: the Nationality, Immigration and Asylum Act 2002 (Commencement No 11) Order 2006, SI 2006/1498 under NIAA 2002, s 162(1); for effect see s 162(5). The section does not have retrospective effect, and children born before its coming into force will have to rely on the policy of discretionary registration of such children under s 3(1) of the BNA 1981, see Nationality Instructions, Vol 1, Ch 9, para 9.

2   See British Nationality (Proof of Paternity) Regulations 2006, SI 2006/1496. For fuller details, see **2.48** below.

3   BNA 1981, ss 3(6)(c) and 17(6)(c) (registration of the children of BCs and BOTCs by descent).

4   A quota scheme introduced when CUKCs were stripped of their entitlement to enter the UK by the Commonwealth Immigrants Act 1968: see Sixth edition of this work at **8.85** ff.

5   NIAA 2002, s 12 came into force on 30 April 2003: see SI 2003/754, art 2(1), Sch 1.

6   A failure to take timeous action to get rid of his Indian citizenship in 2001 meant that there was no benefit to be gained once the deadline of 4 July 2002 had passed: *Senanayake v Secretary of State for the Home Department* [2005] EWCA Civ 1530, [2005] All ER (D) 215 (Nov). In *R (on the application of Vagh (Minaxi)) v Secretary of State for the Home Department* [2013] EWCA Civ 1253 the Court of Appeal held that the Secretary of State had been entitled to refuse to register a British overseas citizen as a British citizen under the British

Nationality Act 1981, s 4B, which allows BOC's to register as BC's if they were without other citizenship, but a person could not renounce their other citizenship after 4 July 2002 (s 4B(2)(c)). The Court held that it was not possible to be satisfied that all the requirements of s 4B(2)(c) had been fulfilled because the applicant had come to the UK on an Indian passport, which she claimed had been issued in error, but had failed to provide an explanation of that error from the Indian authorities.

7   BCIA 2009, s 44, amending BNA 1981, s 4B, in force 13 January 2010 by SI 2009/2731, art 4. The majority of Hong Kong BDTCs, prior to the return of Hong Kong to China on 1 July 1997, were ethnically Chinese and regarded by China as Chinese nationals. Non-Chinese ethnic minorities, who were otherwise stateless on the return of Hong Kong to China having lost BDTC status on 1 July 1997, either became BN(O)s on application before 1 July 1997 or became BOCs by default on that date. Prior to amendment, s 4B of the BNA 1981 provided for stateless BOCs to register as BCs but this provision did not apply to stateless BN(O)s. Some of the latter were able, subject to satisfaction of an ordinary residence test with respect to Hong Kong, to apply for registration as a BC under the British Nationality (Hong Kong) Act 1997, s 1. However, those who were unable to meet that ordinary residence test were, effectively, stateless as BN(O) status has never conferred the functional benefits of nationality so that a person could belong to, and live and work in, a country. This amendment enables such persons to register as BCs and thus gives them a functional nationality and a right of abode.

8   When those countries became independent, many of the residents of Asian origin did not acquire local citizenship and retained their CUKC citizenship after independence. Under the BNA 1981 they became BOCs.

9   In 1980, it was estimated that there were at least 50,000 persons in this situation. (See evidence of Alison Bennett, referred to in fn 10 below).

10 Several thousand BOCs and other UKPHs took advantage of the scheme and settled in the UK in the 1990s and 1980s. Further details of the scheme were given by Alison Bennett, the Assistant Director of the Managed Migration Strategy and Review Directorate, whose evidence is concisely set out in *HT (Special Voucher Holder – dependants) India* [2007] UKAIT 00031.

11 *PP and SP (paragraph 252 – effect of deletion) India* [2005] UKAIT 00141; *RM (Special Vouchers – representation) India* [2005] UKIAT 00067, (that was later upheld by the Court of Appeal in *Modhvadiya* [2005] EWCA Civ 1340; and *HT (Special Voucher Holder – dependants) India* [2007] UKAIT 00031.

12 But see also *NH (India) v Entry Clearance Officer* [2007] EWCA Civ 1330, [2008] INLR 154; *RO (India) v Entry Clearance Officer* [2008] EWCA Civ 1525, [2008] All ER (D) 292 (Oct) and *Patel v Entry Clearance Officer (Mumbai)* [2010] EWCA Civ 17 for the attempts of the children of BOCs to secure leave to enter and remain in the UK by reference to ECHR, art 8.

13 See British Nationality Act 1948, s 5.

14 BNA 1981, s 2.

15 As inserted by NIAA 2002, s 13, which came into force on 30 April 2003: see SI 2003/754, art 2(1), Sch 1. The change was preceded by a concessionary policy allowing discretionary registration of children born abroad to British mothers between 1961 and 1979: see Home Office to ILPA 3 October 2003.

16 In force 13 January 2010 by SI 2009/2731, art 4. For a detailed consideration of the complicated way in which s 4C of the BNA 1981 has been amended and now operates, see I Macdonald QC, L Fransman QC, et al, *Blackstone's Guide to the Borders, Citizenship and Immigration Act 2009* (2010) OUP, paras 6.50–6.93. As regards the operation of s 4C of the British Nationality Act 1981, see also, Fransman's British Nationality Law (3rd edn, 2011), 17.7.

17 *R (on the application of Johnson) v Secretary of State for the Home Department* [2014] EWHC 2386 (Admin) where it was held that there had been a breach of the ECHR Article 14 read in conjunction with Article 8 where the deportation was sought of a Jamaican citizen who would have been a British citizen, and therefore would not have been liable to deportation, if he had not been born out of wedlock. The fact that he was not a British citizen because of his illegitimacy and could be deported, unlike comparators in exactly the same position but whose parents were married, meant that he was being unjustifiably treated differently on the ground that he was born illegitimate.

HONG KONG AND THE RIGHT OF ABODE

2.22 At the time of the handover of Hong Kong to the People's Republic of China in 1997, there were some 3.2 million BDTCs, most having acquired that status by virtue of their birth in Hong Kong, but others by registration or naturalisation. In the run-up to the handover three significant changes were made.[1] First, the British Nationality (Hong Kong) Act 1990 made provision for some 50,000 selected key people to be awarded British citizenship and, therefore the right of abode in the UK, even though many of them had little intention of taking up their option. This affected an elite of selected people. Secondly, it was made clear that British Dependent Territories citizenship which was based on a Hong Kong connection would come to an end on handover. The Hong Kong (British Nationality) Order 1986 enacted that BDTCs who had that citizenship only by virtue of a Hong Kong connection, would cease to be such citizens on 1 July 1997,[2] and that Hong Kong would then be removed from the list of Dependent Territories.[3] Thirdly, the same Order created a new category of citizenship to be known as British National (Overseas).[4] It was open to all BDTCs who were to lose their BDTC status on handover, but would apply only to those who registered. Those who did not register, and who would otherwise have become stateless, became BOCs.[5] The advantages to being a BN(O) or a BOC were fourfold. First, the statuses would continue after handover. Secondly, all BN(O)s and BOCs are Commonwealth citizens.[6] Thirdly, BN(O)s and BOCs are able to use a British travel document after that date and were in fact able to keep and use their passports showing BDTC citizenship. Fourthly, if the holder of BN(O) or BOC status comes to the UK to live, he or she has a right to register as a BC after five years under section 4(1) of the BNA 1981. The great disadvantage is that by losing BDTC status, none of the Hong Kong BDTCs can take advantage of the new rights of BOTCs to register as BCs under the BOTA 2002. Section 14 of the NIAA 2002 makes it clear that there is no way back into BOTC status by registration under the BNA 1981 for those who would have to rely on a Hong Kong connection. Indeed, it seems very likely that the removal of some 3.2 million potential BCs of Chinese origin paved the way for the new liberalism of the 2002 Acts.

[1] For fuller details see the 4th edition of this work at 6.82–6.88.
[2] Hong Kong (British Nationality) Order 1986, SI 1986/948, art 3.
[3] SI 1986/948, art 5.
[4] SI 1986/948, art 4.
[5] SI 1986/948, art 6.
[6] BNA 1981, s 37(1)(a). BN(O)s now number about 3.5 million. They continue to receive consular and passport services from HMG.: *Six-monthly report on Hong Kong 1 January – 30 June 2009* (Cm 7694) at para 60.

PROVING ENTITLEMENT TO RIGHT OF ABODE

2.23 Proving entitlement to British citizenship and, therefore, to a right of abode has been a matter of particular statutory concern. Under section 3(8) of the Immigration Act 1971 it is provided that when any question arises under the Immigration Acts whether or not a person is a BC, it lies on the person asserting the claim to prove it. This will arise when people apply for a passport or a certificate of entitlement or pass through immigration control in the course of their travel to the UK. Section 3(9) makes provision for the means of proof for someone seeking to enter the UK and claiming a right of abode. The section has been reformatted by section 30 of the IAN 2006,[1] which makes a number of amendments to the documents that can be used to prove a right of abode. The full list now is:

(a)   a UK passport describing the person as a British citizen;
(b)   a UK passport[2] describing that person as a British subject with the right of abode in the UK; or
(c)   a certificate of entitlement.[3]

In substance what the amendment does is to remove the now redundant reference to a passport issued to a 'citizen of the UK and Colonies', as this category has not existed since 1 January 1983, when the British Nationality Act 1981 came into force. The procedure for applying for a certificate of entitlement had been unregulated, except as regards fees and a right of appeal against refusal,[4] and there was no case law or immigration rules to give guidance as there is, for example, in the case of entry certificates (see **3.66**). However, section 10 of NIAA 2002 gave the Secretary of State powers to make regulations to provide a statutory foundation for the control of certificates of entitlement. The regulations made by the Secretary of State in the exercise of the powers conferred by NIAA 2002, s 10(1) are the Immigration (Certificate of Entitlement to Right of Abode in the United Kingdom) Regulations 2006, SI 2006/3145 ('the 2006 Regulations').[5] These provide among other things that a certificate will only be issued where a person does not 'hold' (see fn 6) another specified document, such as: (i) a United Kingdom passport describing him as a British citizen; or (ii) a United Kingdom passport describing him as a British subject with the right of abode in the United Kingdom; that he or she is not a person for whom the exercise of the right of abode is restricted under section 2 of the Immigration Act 1988 (in relation to polygamy); and that he or she is not a person who has been deprived of the right of abode.[6] They also specify the authority to whom an application must be made and the form of application.[7] By regulation 8 a certificate of entitlement ceases to have effect on the expiry of the passport or travel document to which it is affixed. By regulation 9 a certificate of entitlement may be revoked where the person specified is satisfied that the person in possession of the certificate (whether or not this is the person to whom the certificate was issued) is the 'holder' of a specified document listed (see above), is a person whose exercise of the right of abode is restricted under section 2 of the IA 1988 (in relation to polygamy) or is a person who has been deprived of the right of abode. By regulation 10 a certificate issued before the 2006 Regulations came into force ceases to have effect on the expiry of the passport or travel document to which it is affixed. The Explanatory Memorandum accompanying the 2006 Regulations records that section 10 was ' . . . introduced due to concern that the lack of regulation made the process of obtaining certificates of entitlement vulnerable to fraud' (4.2) and that the ' . . . Government was reacting to concern on the part of officials tasked with considering applications and policing entry to the United Kingdom that the lack of regulation made the process and its outcome uniquely vulnerable to fraud' (7.1). Certificates of entitlement are statutory creations and the person applying for one either fulfils the statutory conditions or cannot do so. If a person does not satisfy those conditions, no action by or on behalf of the Secretary of State by error or estoppel can operate so as to confer that right.[8] Furthermore, there is no right of appeal against the cancellation or revocation of a certificate of entitlement found to have been issued in error.[9] Fees for certificates of entitlement are specified in regulations under IAN 2006, s 51(3).[10]

[1] In force on 16 June 2006: Immigration, Asylum and Nationality Act 2006 (Commencement No 1) Order 2006, SI 2006/1497, art 3, Schedule.

[2] Under the previous version of section 3(9) the passport had to be a current one, though this is certainly not required by the words of the current statute. See *Akewushola v Secretary of State for the Home Department* [1999] INLR 433, CA.

[3] Under section 39(8) of the British Nationality Act 1981, a certificate of patriality issued under the 1971 Act and in force before 1 January 1983 is regarded as a certificate of entitlement unless, on that date, the holder ceased to have the right of abode. The certificate of confirmation of right of abode, a non-statutory document no longer in use, was issued for a brief period before commencement of the Immigration Act 1988 to dual nationals whose British citizenship gave them a claim to right of abode but who had opted to travel on non-British passports. For the current definition of a 'certificate of entitlement' and a 'UK Passport' see Immigration Act 1971, s 33(1).

[4] NIAA 2002, s 82(2)(c).

[5] NIAA 2002, s 10(2), as amended by IAN 2006, s 50(5) and Sch 2. In respect of a 'certificate of entitlement' and the statutory provision now made in the Nationality, Immigration and Asylum Act 2002, s 10 (1)–(4), (6) is in force from Royal Assent on 7 November 2002 by s 162(2)(c), and sub-s (5)(b) came into force on 21 December 2006 by SI 2006/3144, art 2; see also Immigration (Certificate of Entitlement to Right of Abode in the United Kingdom) Regulations 2006, SI 2006/3145 in force 21 December 2006. Paragraphs 12–14 of the Immigration Rules (HC 395 of 1993–94 as amended) do not reflect the version of s 3(9) of the Immigration Act 1971 currently in force.

[6] SI 2006/3145, reg 6. In *SL (Certificate of Entitlement – holds a passport) Malaysia* [2010] UKUT 164 (IAC) the Upper Tribunal (Blake J, President, Eshun SIJ) held that 'hold' is 'to have possession or control of something' and that 'a person who has lost a document and cannot retrieve it or produce it cannot be said to hold what they do not have'.

[7] SI 2006/3145, regs 3 and 4.

[8] See *Christodoulido v Secretary of State for the Home Department* [1985] Imm AR 179.

[9] *Gold* [1985] Imm AR 66, IAT.

[10] See the Immigration and Nationality (Fees) (Amendment) Order 2008, SI 2008/166, art 6, and the Immigration and Nationality (Cost Recovery Fees) Regulations 2010, SI 2010/228, reg 20. The current fee for an application outside the UK is £220 and for an application inside the UK is £143.

Certificates of Entitlement

2.24 The Immigration (Certificate of Entitlement to Right of Abode in the United Kingdom) (Amendment) Regulations 2011, SI 2011/2682, came into force on 12 December 2011. They amend the procedure under the 2006 Regulations by which a person can apply for and obtain a Certificate of Entitlement. Under these Regulations an application can now be made from any of the Channel Islands or the Isle of Man and may be made either to the Secretary of State for the Home Department or to the Lieutenant-Governor. There is now a discretion to waive the requirement in regulation 4(1)(c) of the 2006 Regulations in relation to a particular document if the official dealing with the application is satisfied that it is appropriate to do so in the particular case and is otherwise satisfied that the applicant has the right of abode in the UK. These new Regulations also make it clear that a certificate of entitlement is an alternative means of proving that a person has a right of abode and should not be issued to someone who has:

(i)   a UK passport describing the person as a British citizen;

(ii)   a UK passport describing that person as a British subject with the right of abode in the UK; or

(iii)   a certificate of entitlement.

If someone is found to have one of these other documents, the certificate can be revoked. For the avoidance of doubt, ID Cards under the Identity Cards Act 2006 describing a person as a British citizen or as a British subject with the right of abode in the United Kingdom, are no longer prescribed to prove the right of abode in the UK for the purposes of entry to the UK; section 3(9) of the Immigration Act 1971 has been amended by the Identity Documents Act 2010 to reflect the repeal of the 2006 Act, from 21 January 2011.

2.25 In most cases proving a right of abode is not a problem and involves collecting the necessary birth, marriage or death certificates and applying for a passport or a certificate of entitlement.[1] The problem areas arise where:

(i)   persons cannot prove an essential ingredient of the claim to British citizenship, such as their place of birth, their parent's nationality at the relevant time, or that a birth certificate relates to them;

(ii)   the Home Office or immigration officer disputes the validity of an existing full UK passport or certificate of entitlement.

In the first situation the burden remains throughout on the applicant.[2] In the second case the burden of proving any alleged fraud or deception will be on the Home Office or immigration officer, and since the allegation involves fraud or deception, proof will need to be by a preponderance of probability.[3]

---

[1]   Certified copies of documents are acceptable as an alternative to original documentation submitted in support of nationality applications: IND to ILPA 7 February 2002, although under the 2006 Regulations original documents are required. The Passport Office holds cassettes containing the name, date of birth and passport number of all passport holders from 1898 onwards, and is prepared to disclose its records in the public interest provided the subject of the records is dead and sufficient information is provided to enable a search. This would normally be full name and date of birth, and sometimes passport number and/or date of issue: Home Office (Record Management Services) to James & Co Solicitors, 15 August 2003.

[2]   *Re Bamgbose* [1990] Imm AR 135, CA; *Mokuolo v Secretary of State for the Home Department* [1989] Imm AR 51, CA. On an application for a declaration of British citizenship, the High Court will assess the facts for itself: *R (on the application of Harrison) v Secretary of State for the Home Department* [2003] EWCA Civ 432, [2003] INLR 284.

[3]   *R v Secretary of State for the Home Department, ex p Obi* [1997] 1 WLR 1498, [1997] Imm AR 420; *Khawaja v Secretary of State for the Home Department* [1984] AC 74, [1983] 1 All ER 765, HL. See **2.103** below.

Deprivation of the right of abode

2.26 Section 57(1) of IAN 2006 inserts a new section 2A into the Immigration Act 1971,[1] which confers on the Secretary of State a power to make an order removing a right of abode in the UK from a person, where that right is derived from being a Commonwealth citizen (in practice, that is from possessing citizenship of another Commonwealth country or being a British subject) and he thinks it would be conducive to the public good to remove or exclude that person from the UK. The Secretary of State may also make an order revoking the order for deprivation.[2] Section 57(2) also amends s 82(2) of the NIAA to provide a right of appeal against the decision to deprive a person of their right of abode, either to the First-tier Tribunal (Immigration and Asylum Chamber) or to the Special Immigration Appeals Commission (SIAC).[3]

[1]   In force on 16 June 2006: Immigration, Asylum and Nationality Act 2006 (Commencement No 1) Order 2006, SI 2006/1497.
[2]   IAN 2006, s 57(3).
[3]   Section 57(2) inserts a new section 82(2)(ib) into NIAA 2002.

OUTLINES OF BRITISH NATIONALITY LAW

2.27 The right of abode started out as a right unambiguously linked to a broad concept of British nationality which included citizens of independent Commonwealth countries as well as those of the UK and Colonies. It then became something much narrower, as British nationality was split up into more distinct species of citizenship. Now citizens of independent Commonwealth countries are out of the nationality equation, except for a small exceptional group, who still have a right of abode, as we have seen. Otherwise the tendency is towards an eventual consolidation of all the different sub-categories of British nationality back into a single British citizenship, where the right of abode will once more be a concomitant right of British national status (although the recommendations made in the report 'Citizenship: Our Common Bond' by Lord Goldsmith QC,[1] that were directed to this issue, have not been taken up). To understand this trend and the processes by which BCs achieve their status, it is necessary to look at the outlines of British nationality law and the changes that have taken place since 1948.[2]

[1]   11 March 2008, p 6.
[2]   We do so only to identify the right of abode. Anyone wishing to deal with the wider issues of nationality should consult Fransman's *British Nationality Law* (3rd edn, 2011).

2.28 Before the British Nationality Act 1948, the status of British subject belonged to all those who owed allegiance to the Crown in whichever Crown territory they were born. An additional category was the status of British Protected Person, that is to say people who had placed themselves (or had been placed) under the protection of the British Crown without becoming the subjects of the Sovereign. Unlike British subjects, their position was regulated by prerogative rather than common law. They were neither Commonwealth citizens nor aliens under the 1948 Act and are not so also under the BNA 1981, as we shall see at **2.45** below. With the break-up of the British empire and the creation of separate citizenships in the self-governing dominions, it was thought necessary to devise citizenship laws which were appropriate to a number of self-governing units within a unified Commonwealth. The principle of separate citizenships for each of the self-governing units was expressly recognised, but at the same time the universal status of 'British subject' or 'Commonwealth citizen' was retained. For our purposes, the point about having the status of British subject or Commonwealth citizen (the two terms then had the same meaning under the 1948 Act)[1] was that it gave an unqualified common law right of abode to such persons in the UK.[2] Aliens alone were subject to immigration control.

[1] British Nationality Act 1948, s 1(2). Now, all British subjects are Commonwealth citizens, but not vice versa: see BNA 1981, s 37.
[2] *DPP v Bhagwan* [1972] AC 60, [1970] 3 All ER 97, HL.

2.29 Although entry to the UK for British subjects was unrestricted, this did not mean that the same thing applied to independent Commonwealth countries or to colonial territories. The opposite was the case, and had been so for many years. In fact the mechanisms of immigration control introduced for the UK in 1962 had been tried and tested many years earlier in the dominion territories in attempts to keep out Chinese, Japanese and Indian migrants.[1] But at the time of the entry into force of the British Nationality Act 1948 on 1 January 1949, the status of British subject or Commonwealth citizen gave an unrestricted right of entry to the UK. When immigration controls were later imposed by the Commonwealth Immigrants Act 1962 and its amending Act of 1968,[2] the method used was to make subdivisions within the three main categories of Commonwealth citizen:

- CUKCs
- citizens of independent Commonwealth countries
- British subject without citizenship.

Initially, under the 1962 Act the dividing line between a continuing right of abode and being subject to immigration control depended on the place of issue of the person's British passport. Under the 1968 Act, the need for an ancestral connection to the UK was introduced, cutting across and undermining ties to Britain of British nationality. By the time of the Immigration Act 1971, birth in and ancestral connection to the UK were the principal distinctions between 'patrials' and 'non-patrials'.[3] Patrials had a right of abode; non-patrials were subject to control. Possession of British nationality no longer qualified British nationals for the right of abode in their country of nationality. The BNA 1981 formally reconnected the right of abode to British citizenship, but only by creating the hierarchy of British nationalities that placed British citizenship at the top and subordinated other forms of British nationality such as BDTC, BOC, etc.

[1] See the third edition of this work, pp 12–15.
[2] Commonwealth Immigrants Act 1968.
[3] There were other ways of acquiring patriality, eg by residence in the UK or marriage to a patrial: see Immigration Act 1971, s 2 (before amendment).

2.30 Throughout the period from commencement of the British Nationality Act 1948 to the commencement of the Immigration Act 1971 all classes of British subject/Commonwealth citizen were to be distinguished from: (i) Irish citizens; (ii) aliens, ie all foreigners other than Irish citizens, and (iii) BPPs. So far as aliens and BPPs are concerned, they could never became 'patrial' under the Immigration Act 1971 unless they had dual nationality[1] or acquired the status of CUKC through marriage or naturalisation. Some Irish citizens were Commonwealth citizens and could therefore be patrial, though this was really an unimportant category because Ireland was part of the common travel area and later a Member State of the EEC. The right of abode of an Irish citizen, therefore, usually only arose when there was an issue of deportation.

1   The status of BPP was not inconsistent with that of CUKC and so a person could be both CUKC and BPP – a sort of domestic dual nationality: *Motala v A-G* [1992] 1 AC 281, [1992] Imm AR 112, HL, overruling CA [1991] 2 All ER 312 at 315.

Dual nationality

2.31 Some countries forbid their citizens to have dual nationality, but this is not the case in the UK. So the fact that a person has another nationality, and travels under another country's passport, does not mean that he or she was not a CUKC under the British Nationality Act 1948 or, under the BNA 1981, is not a BC. For example, there are large numbers of persons living in Malaysia and Singapore who are citizens of those countries and BOCs at the same time. Indeed, the 1981 Act quite clearly confers dual nationality on possibly quite large numbers of persons. For example, as we shall see, CUKCs who were patrial through five years' residence in the UK became BCs on commencement, but may have become, by virtue of their connection to a dependent territory, BOTCs as well or, in other cases, BOCs.[1] Under the pre-1983 patriality provisions of the Immigration Act 1971, one category of patrial citizens was Commonwealth citizens with a parent born in the UK.[2] This provision was intended for holders of Australian, New Zealand, and other 'old' Commonwealth passports, but in fact if their fathers were born in the UK they had dual nationality – Australian or New Zealand by birth and CUKC by descent through their father. Under the 1981 Act, British citizenship can descend through the mother as well as the father and this has created large numbers of Commonwealth citizens who have dual nationality. However, there are limits. British citizenship is a unitary concept, which does not give rise to classes of such citizenship, such as citizenship otherwise than by citizenship by descent. So BCs by descent cannot use the process of naturalisation under BNA 1981 to become full BCs, who can transmit their citizenship to their children.[3]

1   This sort of domestic double nationality was expressly approved of by the House of Lords in *Motala v A-G* [1992] 1 AC 281, [1992] Imm AR 112, HL; see further *Patel v Secretary of State for the Home Department* [1993] Imm AR 509, CA. In both these cases it was held that a BPP could simultaneously be a CUKC.
2   Immigration Act 1971, s 2(1)(d).
3   *R (on the application of Ullah) v Secretary of State for the Home Department* [2001] EWCA Civ 659, [2002] QB 525, [2001] Imm AR 439, CA.

CITIZENSHIP UNDER BRITISH NATIONALITY ACT 1948

2.32 In order to understand the concept and status of 'British citizen', it is necessary to go back to the three main classifications of British national used in the British Nationality Act 1948. But beware! In this part of this chapter we set out what is at best a very brief summary. For fuller treatment it is essential to refer to a specialist textbook on British nationality law.[1]

1   See Fransman's *British Nationality Law* (3rd edn, 2011), which contains a full account and texts of the relevant provisions of every Commonwealth country as well as the UK.

Citizens of Commonwealth countries

2.33 Each independent Commonwealth country has its own citizenship laws which determine who are citizens of that country. The list of countries is set out in Schedule 3 to the BNA 1981, as amended. Once a country achieves political independence with its own constitution and laws, the determination of its citizenship is no longer a matter for UK law[1] or the UK Parliament. All UK law determines is that for the purposes of UK law citizens of independent Commonwealth countries are Commonwealth citizens. Nothing more. To find out whether someone is or becomes a citizen of an independent Commonwealth country it is always necessary to look at that country's own citizenship laws. Depending upon the answer to that question, UK nationality law may have something to say about that person's status, for example, whether they remain BCs or not.

[1] See *Oppenheimer v Cattermole* [1976] AC 249, [1975] 1 All ER 538, HL. Although the question of whether a person is a citizen of a Commonwealth country is under English private international law a matter for the law of that country, one English court has determined that question as one of purely domestic English law when it affects a claim to British citizenship, even though it reached a conclusion different from that of the governing authorities of the country concerned: *Bibi (Mahaboob) v Secretary of State for the Home Department* [1987] Imm AR 340, CA.

2.34 The difficulties do not arise so much with regard to persons born in a Commonwealth country after independence,[1] but with those born before independence and living there or in the UK at the time of independence. CUKCs who acquired their citizenship through connection with a colony may have lost that citizenship when the colony became independent. This often happened through the operation of statute, without the person realising it. A person from Grenada or St Lucia might have been a UK citizen with the right of abode as a result of five years' ordinary residence one day and have ceased to be so on the next day following independence. In all cases where there is a history of this kind it is necessary to examine the particular statute that granted independence and the new citizenship laws of the newly independent country, in order to find out who lost and who retained their status as a CUKC.[2] On decolonisation the usual provision was that any persons who acquired citizenship of the new Commonwealth (or non-Commonwealth) country lost their former citizenship of the UK and Colonies, unless they had a parent or grandparent who was born in the UK or in a country which remained a colony at that time. But the formulations differed from country to country. In order to discover whether a person acquired citizenship of the new country, it is always necessary to examine the constitution or citizenship laws of the new country. In East Africa, some CUKCs were specifically permitted to retain their UK citizenship.[3] At the time of decolonisation, these CUKCs were free from immigration control, although they continued to live in East Africa. In 1968, however, they became subject to immigration control under the Commonwealth Immigrants Act 1968. So when living in East Africa was made difficult or they were expelled, they had nowhere to go. This is the source of what was referred to as the 'problem' of the East African Asians.[4]

[1] Although there is always a question of whether such persons are BCs or some other citizen by descent.
[2] See Fransman *British Nationality Law* (3rd edn, 2011), where all the independence statutes and Commonwealth citizenship laws are gathered.

[3] For the position in Kenya see *Mohammed (AA) v Secretary of State for the Home Department* [1979–80] Imm AR 103.

[4] See *East African Asians v United Kingdom* (1973) 3 EHRR 76.

Citizens of the UK and Colonies (CUKCs)

Birth

2.35 Under the British Nationality Act 1948 a person born in the UK and Colonies before or after commencement (1 January 1949) became a CUKC by birth, unless the person's father was a foreign diplomat or an enemy alien and the birth occurred in enemy-occupied territory.[1] Thus those born in the Channel Islands of a German father during the 1939–45 war would not have become British subjects at birth and would not become CUKCs on 1 January 1949.

[1] British Nationality Act 1948, ss 4 and 12(1)(a).

Adoption

2.36 Adopted children could also acquire citizenship. In England and Wales the Adoption Acts of 1949 and 1976 and in Scotland the Adoption (Scotland) Act 1978 provided that a child adopted in the UK by a CUKC became a CUKC, if not already one, from the date of the adoption order. In the case of a joint adoption, where the adopting parents had different nationalities, the child only became a CUKC if that was the male adopter's nationality. An adoption outside the UK did not confer the British nationality of the adoptive parent.[1]

[1] *R v Secretary of State for the Home Department, ex p Brassey and Brassey* [1989] FCR 423, [1989] Imm AR 258, DC.

Descent

2.37 Citizenship by birth in the UK or colonies was the most common method of acquiring the status of CUKC. This was citizenship by *jus soli* (country of birth). But English law also recognises the *jus sanguinis* (citizenship by descent).[1] Persons born outside British territory could therefore be CUKCs by descent if their father was such a citizen[2] at the time of the person's birth.[3] This applied in general to persons born before and after 1948.[4] However, for persons born after 1948 the right to become a CUKC by descent was limited where the person's father himself acquired this citizenship by descent.[5]

[1] See British Nationality Bill 1948 (Cm 7326) p 9.
[2] British Nationality Act 1948, s 5(1).
[3] *R v Immigration Appeal Tribunal, ex p Uddin (Shafique)* [1989] Imm AR 391, QBD.
[4] British Nationality Act 1948, s 12(2).
[5] For exceptions, such as registration at a British consulate, see British Nationality Act 1948, s 5(1)(a)–(d) and (2).

2.38 Citizenship by descent could only be acquired through the father under the British Nationality Act 1948, never through the mother, and not if the child was illegitimate. An illegitimate child was not considered to be the child of its father for nationality purposes unless legitimated by the subsequent marriage of its parents.[1] A legitimate child born after the death of his or her father would acquire the status of the father at the time of the father's death.[2]

1 British Nationality Act 1948, ss 32(2) and 23.
2 British Nationality Act 1948, s 24.

Registration

2.39 An important method of acquiring the status of CUKC after 1948 was by registration. In some cases it was a right; in others it was within the Secretary of State's discretion. Registration was only open to Commonwealth citizens, citizens of the Republic of Ireland, their children, and to women, whether alien or Commonwealth, who married CUKCs. Registration could be completed in the UK or outside. In the UK it was done by the Secretary of State, in the Colonies usually by the Governor and in Commonwealth countries by the British High Commissioner.[1] With the coming into force of successive Immigration Acts between 1962 and 1973 the right of Commonwealth citizens to register was much changed from the originally enacted position in 1948.[2] For women married to CUKCs the right was almost an absolute one, unless they had gained the right to registration by fraudulent or other criminal means.[3]

1 British Nationality Act 1948, s 8.
2 See fourth edition 6.21–6.23.
3 British Nationality Act 1948, s 6 and see *R v Secretary of State for the Home Department, ex p Puttick* [1981] QB 767, [1981] 1 All ER 776.

Naturalisation

2.40 Naturalisation was the mechanism under the British Nationality Act 1948 by which aliens and BPPs could become CUKCs, although the residence requirements differed.[1] The grant was a matter of discretion. Decisions were unappealable and section 26 of the 1948 Act provided that no reasons need be given and the decision was not reviewable in any court. The same ouster clause was inserted in the BNA 1981,[2] which we examine at **2.87** below.

1 British Nationality Act 1948, s 10 and Sch 2 as amended by Commonwealth Immigrants Act 1962, s 20(2).
2 BNA 1981, s 44(2).

Loss of citizenship of the UK and Colonies

2.41 The status of CUKC, as we have seen, could be acquired in a number of ways. It could also be lost. This happened in three ways. The first was the most common:

(i)   CUKCs connected with a Crown colony could lose their citizenship when the colony became independent;[1]
(ii)   Persons having dual nationality or acquiring a new nationality could lose their UK citizenship by making a declaration of renunciation;[2]
(iii) CUKCs could be deprived of their UK citizenship by the Secretary of State for the Home Department if they had acquired it by registration

or naturalisation.[3]

1 See *Motala v A-G* [1992] 1 AC 281, [1992] Imm AR 112, HL; *Patel v Secretary of State for the Home Department* [1993] Imm AR 508, CA; *R v Secretary of State for Foreign and Commonwealth Affairs, ex p Shah* [1993] Imm AR 261, QBD; *Patel v Secretary of State for the Home Department* [1988] Imm AR 521, IAT; *Liew v Secretary of State for the Home Department* [1989] Imm AR 62, IAT.
2 British Nationality Act 1948, s 19.
3 British Nationality Act 1948, s 20, which conferred a right to a hearing before an independent tribunal (called a committee of inquiry). A naturalisation or registration could be of no effect and s 20 would not come into play if the applicant could not prove that he was the person named in the certificate: *R v Secretary of State for the Home Department, ex p Akhtar (Parvaz)* [1981] QB 46, [1980] 2 All ER 735.

Resumption of citizenship

2.42 Resumption of citizenship following renunciation was governed by section 1(1) of the British Nationality Act 1964. A person who was obliged to renounce their CUKC status in order to avoid being deprived of another citizenship (a circumstance which arose when a number of Commonwealth countries became independent) and had a qualifying connection with the UK and colonies or a protectorate or protected State or, if a woman, had been married to such a person, was able to apply for registration.

British subject without citizenship

2.43 The British Nationality Acts 1948 and 1965 created a number of residual categories of British subject. These were people who were neither citizens of independent Commonwealth countries nor CUKCs.[1] They were:

(a) British subjects without citizenship, who consisted of:
    (i) persons who were regarded by the British Nationality Act 1948 as potential citizens of an independent Commonwealth country, but who did not become citizens of that country when they passed citizenship laws;[2] and
    (ii) persons who are declared to be British subjects without citizenship. They are persons who before 1 January 1949 ceased, on the loss of British nationality by a parent, to be a British subject and, but for this, would have become British subjects without citizenship;[3]
(b) married women who registered as British subjects under the 1965 Act.[4] These are alien women who married a man who was within one or other of the residual categories of British subject;
(c) Irish citizens born before 1949 who were also British subjects and remained such if they wrote to the Home Secretary and claimed to remain such.[5]

The BNA 1981 continues these categories of citizenship and refers to them as British subjects under the Act.[6] Under both the 1948 and 1981 Acts, they are Commonwealth citizens.[7] Clearly they are a diminishing group, who now lose their British subject status if they acquire any other citizenship or nationality in whatever circumstances.[8]

1 See Ann Dummett *Citizenship and Nationality* (1976) Runnymede Trust, p 23. The BNA 1965 was an Act to provide for the acquisition of the status of British subject by women, who had

been married to British subjects without citizenship by virtue of ss 13 or 16 of BNA 1948. It was repealed by BNA 1981, with some savings, as of 1 January 1983, by s 52(7), (8), Sch 8, para 1(2) and Sch 9.

2   British Nationality Act 1948, s 13. Such persons did not become CUKCs under s 13(2) of the 1948 Act as might have been supposed because of the definition of citizenship law in s 32(8) of that Act.

3   BNA 1948, s 16.

4   BNA 1965, s 1.

5   BNA 1948, s 2.

6   BNA 1981, ss 30 and 31.

7   BNA 1948, s 1(2) and BNA 1981, s 37(1)(a).

8   BNA 1981, s 35. Irish citizens who obtained British subject status as former citizens of Eire are exempt from this automatic loss provision.

BECOMING A BRITISH CITIZEN

2.44 The BNA 1981 recast British citizenship and replaced the existing definition of patriality by an entirely new section 2 of the Immigration Act 1971. This defined the right of abode in terms of the new categories of citizenship. The right of abode and British citizenship are now more or less equated. To understand who has the right of abode it is therefore necessary to know what became of CUKCs and who become BCs. The 1981 Act divided CUKCs into three new categories of citizenship:[1]

- British citizens
- British Dependent Territories citizens
- British Overseas citizens.

The Hong Kong (British Nationality) Order 1986[2] added another citizenship: that of British National (Overseas). Other categories of Commonwealth citizens are virtually unaltered. Irish citizens who are British subjects and British subjects without citizenship are referred to as British subjects under the Act. The overall category of 'Commonwealth citizen' is retained. So under the 1981 Act Commonwealth citizens comprise:[3]

- British citizens;
- British Dependent Territories (now British overseas territories) citizens;
- British Nationals (Overseas);
- British Overseas citizens;
- British subjects under the 1981 Act;
- Citizens of independent Commonwealth countries.

1   BNA 1981, s 51(3).

2   SI 1986/948, in force 1 July 1987.

3   BNA 1981, ss 37, 51 (as amended by British Overseas Territories Act 2002, s 2) and SI 1986/948, art 7(3).

2.45 BPPs are not Commonwealth citizens,[1] but they are also excluded from the definition of aliens.[2] Traditionally they were excluded from being classed as British nationals in domestic law[3] or being treated as UK nationals under ECHR law,[4] but they have been equated with British Dependent Territories (now overseas territories) citizens, BN(O)s, BOCs, and British subjects under the 1981 Act as having a right to register as BCs after five years' residence in the UK,[5] and now have a right to register as BCs alongside BN(O)s, BOCs and British subjects, provided they have no other nationality (see **2.21** above). They are increasingly being included in modern legislation in the list of UK nationals.[6]

1   BNA 1981, s 38.
2   BNA 1981, s 50(1).
3   *R v Secretary of State for the Home Department, ex p Thakrar* [1974] QB 684, [1974] 2 All ER 261, CA.
4   *East African Asians v United Kingdom* (1973) 3 EHRR 76.
5   BNA 1981, s 4.
6   See L Fransman 'A Right to British Nationality' in Butterworth's *A Guide to the Human Rights Act 1998* (1999) p 131 where he cites definitions of UK nationals in Antarctic Act 1994, s 31(1), Chemical Weapons Act 1996, s 3(4), and Outer Space Act 1996, s 2(2). A BPP is included in the definition of a UK national in the International Criminal Court Act 2001, s 67(1).

Becoming a British citizen on commencement of the 1981 Act

CUKCs

2.46 With two exceptions, a person who immediately before commencement of the BNA 1981 was a CUKC and had the right of abode under the Immigration Act 1971 became a BC upon commencement.[1] The two exceptions are:

(i)   an illegitimate or legitimate (and formerly) stateless person, wherever born, who was the child of a CUKC mother, who (ie the person not his or her mother) became a CUKC by registration under the British Nationality (No 2) Act 1964; unless his or her mother became a British citizen on commencement or that person had been any time settled in the UK at the end of a five-year period of ordinary residence in which case he or she was also a British citizen;[2]

(ii)   a British subject without citizenship who became a CUKC by registration outside the UK by reason of an ancestral connection with the UK.[3]

1   BNA 1981, s 11(1).
2   BNA 1981, s 11(2). Such a person is likely to have become a BOTC (BNA 1981, s 23(1)) or a BOC (s 26). If the person was already resident in the UK but had not completed five years' residence, he or she had a right to register as a BC on completion of the five years under BNA 1981, s 4.
3   BNA 1981, s 11(3); see also British Nationality Act 1948, s 12(6)–(8). Such a person may in fact have qualified for a right of abode by another route, eg by completing five years' ordinary residence in the UK prior to 1983, and thus qualifying as patrials under the former s 2(1)(c) of the Immigration Act 1971. If they did not qualify under the pre-1983 regime and are resident in the UK, they qualify to register as BCs on completion of five years' residence under BNA 1981, s 4.

Falkland Islanders

2.47 Persons from the Falkland Islands who would normally have become BOTCs on commencement in fact also became BCs, if immediately before commencement:

(i)   they were CUKCs born, naturalised or registered in the Falkland Islands; or

(ii)   one of their parents was such a CUKC or would have been but for their death; or

(iii)   in the case of a woman she was at any time married to a man who benefits from provisions (i) or (ii) above.[1]

[1]   British Nationality (Falkland Islands) Act 1983, s 1(1).

Becoming a British citizen after commencement

Birth in the UK or an Overseas Territory

2.48 The BNA 1981 abolished citizenship by birth in the UK, pure and simple. Children born in the UK after commencement of the BNA 1981 will only become BCs if one of their parents is a BC, is settled in the UK[1] or, following amendments made by the BCIA 2009, is a member of the armed forces.[2] Children born in the Falkland Islands after commencement of the BNA 1981 also became BCs, if one of their parents was a BC or was settled in the Falkland Islands at the time of the birth, but, rather surprisingly, that legislation did not extend the acquisition of this status, where the only British link was that one or both parents were settled in the UK.[3] This has now been remedied. The provisions of the BNA 1981 are now extended to all persons born in a qualifying territory (meaning an overseas territory other than the Sovereign Base Areas in Cyprus), if one of their parents is a BC or is settled in the UK or that territory (or following amendments made by the BCIA 2009, a member of the armed forces, see above) at the time of the birth.[4] One gap in the new law concerns the baby born in a qualifying territory, whose qualifying parent or parents is or are settled in a different qualifying territory at the time of the birth. This person does not become a BC, because neither parent is settled in 'that territory'.[5] As originally enacted, the BNA 1981 allowed a child to trace entitlement through either parent, provided that the child was legitimate or had been legitimised by the subsequent marriage of its parents. Subject to the provision made by section 47 of BNA 1981 for legitimation following the parents' marriage, an illegitimate child could only trace entitlement through his or her mother.[6] This has now changed with the coming into force of section 9 of the NIAA 2002. Illegitimacy is no longer to be a bar to tracing nationality through the father. Following amendment, for the purposes of the BNA 1981, a child's father is (a) the husband, at the time of the child's birth, of the woman who gives birth to the child, (b) the person identified as the father by section 28 of the Human Fertilisation and Embryology Act 1990 or section 35 or 36 of the Human Fertilisation and Embryology Act 2008, (c) a person treated as a parent of the child under section 42 or 43 of the Human Fertilisation and Embryology Act 2008 or, where none of the above apply, (d) a person who satisfies requirements prescribed in regulations as to proof of paternity.[7] The regulations that have been made prescribe that paternity is proved where (i) the person is named as the father of the child in a birth certificate issued within one year of the date of the child's birth or (ii) a person satisfies the Secretary of State that he is the father of the child. In respect of the latter, the Secretary of State may have regard to any evidence including DNA test reports and court orders. The new provisions will have effect in relation to a child born on or after 1 July 2006.[8]

For those born before this date, the old practice remains.[9]

1   BNA 1981, s 1.
2   BICA 2009, s 42(1), (2), inserting s 1(1A) into BNA 1981, in force from 13 January 2010 by SI 2009/2731, art 4(a). A member of the armed forces is defined in BNA 1981, s 50(1A), (1B), inserted by BCIA 2009, s 49(1).
3   British Nationality (Falkland Islands) Act 1983, s 1(2), which is repealed and incorporated into the amendments made to BNA 1981 by BOTA 2002 as from 21 May 2002: SI 2002/1252, art 2(c). See above **2.16**.
4   BNA 1981, s 1, as amended by BOTA 2002, s 5 and Sch 1. Commencement of the Sch 2 amendments took place on 21 May 2002, the appointed day under SI 2002/1252, art 2(a).
5   BNA 1981, s 1(1)(b), as amended above.
6   BNA 1981, s 50(9), before amendment by NIAA 2002, s 9. The illegitimacy rules were held not to be in breach of art 8 or of art 8 read with art 14 of ECHR: *R (on the application of Montana) v Secretary of State for the Home Department* [2001] 1 WLR 552, CA.
7   The requirements to be satisfied are those prescribed by regulations made by the Secretary of State under the newly in force section 50(9A) and (9B) of BNA 1981, as inserted by the NIAA 2002, s 9(1), in force 1 July 2006 by SI 2006/1498, art 2, and as amended by the Human Fertilisation and Embryology Act 2008, s 56, Sch 6, Pt 1, para 22, in force 6 April 2009 by SI 2009/479, art 6(1)(d).
8   Section 9 of NIAA 2002 and the British Nationality (Proof of Paternity) Regulations 2006, SI 2006/1496, made under section 50(9B) of the BNA 1981. The regulations came into force on 1 July 2006 (via the Nationality, Immigration and Asylum Act 2002 (Commencement No 11) Order 2006, SI 2006/4918).
9   In fact the Secretary of State for the Home Department could always use his or her discretion under BNA 1981, s 3(1) to register as a BC the illegitimate child of a British father. Since March 2000, IND policy has been to register the illegitimate child of a BC father where: (a) they are satisfied about paternity; (b) they are satisfied that the father is a BC; (c) they have the consent of all those with parental responsibility; (d) they are satisfied that the conditions for registration would have been met if the child had been legitimate and (e) there is no reason to refuse on character grounds: Nationality Instructions (NI) Ch 9, para 9. The NI give guidance on the evidence needed to prove paternity.

Children born out of wedlock before 2006

2.49 Two recent cases illustrate the effect of the denial in nationality law prior to 1 July 2006 that for nationality purposes an unwed father is the natural 'father' of his child born out of wedlock. In *R (on the application of Johnson) v Secretary of State for the Home Department*[1] the Claimant, a Jamaican citizen, was facing deportation to Jamaica. He had been born out of wedlock to a father who was British. He claimed that his deportation was a breach of ECHR Article 14 read in conjunction with Article 8. He said he would have been a British citizen, and therefore would not have been liable to deportation, if he had not been born out of wedlock. The fact that he was not a British citizen because of his illegitimacy and could be deported, unlike comparators in exactly the same position but whose parents were married, meant that he was being unjustifiably treated differently on the ground that he was born illegitimate. His claim was upheld by the Court. A quite different sort of case, *MB (Bangladesh) v Secretary of State for The Home Department*[2], illustrates how difficult it is to prove the citizenship by descent. In this case of a young girl of 12 years from her British father (of Bangladeshi origin) who had three wives (one since dead), when he entered into a marriage ceremony with the girl's mother, a Bangladeshi national. The father then died. The court goes through very carefully all the hoops that the girl and her mother have to go through before they might succeed. Not all of these had been considered by the UT, and, as it had become clear that the case now came down to the issue of legitimacy, it was remitted to the Upper Tribunal for redetermination on all the evidence relating to that issue. If the new law had been in force none of this would have been necessary. All the Appellant would have had to prove is that her father was her natural father.

1   [2014] EWHC 2386 (Admin).
2   [2013] EWCA Civ 220.

Immigration Act 2014 changes

2.50 The position of children born after 1 July 2006 was addressed by section 9 of the NIAA 2002 and is referred to at **12.22** above. The position of children born before 1 July 2006 where the mother and natural father[1] were not married at the time of the child's birth has now been addressed by primary legislation. Section 65 of the Immigration Act 2014 inserts new sections 4E to 4J into the BNA 1981 to provide for registration as a British citizen for a specified group of persons born before 1 July 2006, who were unable to acquire British citizenship, because their parents were unmarried at the time of their birth. In particular, they provide an entitlement to be registered for those who would have become British automatically had their parents been married at the time of their birth and for those who would currently have an entitlement to registration but for the fact that their parents were not married at the time of their birth.[2] This legislation may rectify the discrimination claim upheld in the High Court case of *Johnson* on the basis of nationality.[3]

1   'Natural father' is someone who satisfies the requirements as to proof of paternity prescribed in regulations under section 50(9B) of the 1981 Act: BNA 1981, s 4J and see also British Nationality (Proof of Paternity) Regulations 2006, SI 2006/1496.
2   Section 65 has not (as of December 2014) been brought into force.
3   *R (on the application of Johnson) v Secretary of State for the Home Department* [2014] EWHC 2386 (Admin), where the deportation was sought of a Jamaican citizen who would have been a British citizen, and therefore would not have been liable to deportation, if he had not been born out of wedlock. The fact that he was not a British citizen because of his illegitimacy and could be deported, unlike comparators in exactly the same position but whose parents were married, meant that he was being unjustifiably treated differently on the ground that he was born illegitimate.

2.51 New section 4E of the BNA 1981 stipulates the general conditions to be met for the purposes of sections 4E to 4I of the British Nationality Act 1981. They are that:

(a)   the person ('P') was born before 1 July 2006;
(b)   at the time of P's birth, P's mother—
   (i)   was not married, or
   (ii)   was married to a person other than P's natural father;
(c)   no person is treated as the father of P under section 28 of the Human Fertilisation and Embryology Act 1990; and
(d)   P has never been a British citizen.

2.52 New section 4F entitles P to be registered as a British citizen if P meets the general conditions in section 4E and would be entitled to be registered as a British citizen under the specified registration provisions of the 1981 Act had P's mother been married to P's natural father at the time of his or her birth.

Under section 4F the specified registration provisions are contained in the BNA 1981 at:

(i)   section 1(3);
(ii)   section 3(2);
(iii)   section 3(5);
(iv)   paragraph 4 of Schedule 2; and
(v)   paragraph 5 of Schedule 2.

We deal with each of these specified registration provisions in the next paragraph.

2.53 Section 1(3) of the BNA1981 provides that where a person is born in the UK he or she is entitled to register, if, while he or she is a minor, the father or mother becomes a British citizen or settled in the UK. The IA 2014 does not extend this provision to the right to register under section 1(3A) of the BNA 1981, which applies to a person born in the UK where, during the child's minority, his or her father or mother becomes a member of the armed forces.

Section 3(2) of the BNA 1981 is a bit more complicated. It provides that, where a person is born outside the UK and a 'qualified territory',[1] he or she is entitled, on an application made, while the person is still a minor, to be registered as a British citizen if the following requirements are fulfilled in the case of either that person's father or his mother ('the parent in question').[2] These requirements are:

(a)   that the parent in question was a British citizen by descent at the time of the person's birth;
(b)   that the father or mother of the parent in question (ie the person's grandparent)
        (i)   was a British citizen otherwise than by descent at the time of the birth of P's parent; or
        (ii)   became a British citizen otherwise than by descent at the commencement of the BNA 1981, or would have become such a citizen otherwise than by descent at commencement but for his or her death; and
(c)   that during a three year period, with absences of no more than 270 days, ending with a date no later than the date of P's birth, the parent in question was in the UK or a qualifying territory at the beginning of that period.

Section 3(5) of the BNA 1981 also deals with a person born outside the UK. It provides that if a person was born outside the UK and the qualifying territories, he or she is entitled, during his or her minority, to be registered as a British citizen if:

(a)   at the time of the person's birth that person's father or mother was a British citizen by descent; and
(b)   the person and that person's father and mother were in the United Kingdom or a qualifying territory for a three year period with no more than 270 days absence, ending with the date of the application;[3] and
(c)   the consent of his father and mother to the registration has been signified in the prescribed manner.[4]

Paragraphs 4 and 5 of Schedule 2 deal respectively with:

(a)   the right to register stateless children born outside UK and a Qualifying Territory, if parent is a British citizen; and

(b)   the right to register children born stateless before commencement of 1981 Act.

¹ Birth outside a 'qualifying territory', means not born in any British Overseas Territory other than the Sovereign Base Areas of Akrotiri and Dhekalia in Cyprus. Other than the Bases, the British overseas territories are: Anguilla; Bermuda; British Antarctic Territory; British Indian Ocean Territory; Cayman Islands; Falkland Islands; Gibraltar; Montserrat; Pitcairn Henderson, Ducie and Oeno Islands; St Helena, Ascension and Tristan Da Cunha; South Georgia and South Sandwich Islands; Turks and Caicos Islands; and the Virgin Islands.

² BNA 1981, s 3(2). In the case of a person born stateless, only the requirements specified in paragraphs (a) and (b) need be fulfilled.

³ If his father or mother died, or their marriage or civil partnership was terminated, on or before the date of the application, or his father and mother were legally separated on that date, the references to his father and mother in paragraph (b) should be read either as references to his father or as references to his mother: BNA 1981, s 3(6)(a).

⁴ If his father or mother died on or before that date, the reference to his father and mother in paragraph (c) of that subsection shall be read as a reference to either of them: BNA 1981, s 3(6)(b). Section 4F(4) provides a power for the Secretary of State to waive the need for any or all of the parental consents to be given if the relevant registration provision is s 3(5) of the BNA 1981.

2.54 New section 4G of the BNA 1981 entitles a person to be registered as a British citizen if the person meets the general conditions in section 4E and if, at any time after commencement of the 1981 Act, the person would automatically have become a British citizen at birth under the 1981 Act or the British Nationality (Falkland Islands) Act 1983, had the person's mother been married to the person's natural father at the time of the person's birth. If the person would have acquired British citizenship by descent at birth he or she will acquire British citizenship by descent on registration. If P is under the age of 18, no application may be made unless the consent of P's natural father and mother to the registration has been signified in the prescribed manner. But section 4G(5) of the BNA 1981 gives the Secretary of State a discretion to waive the need for any or all of the consents required under subsection (3) as read with subsection (4) to be waived in a particular case.

2.55 New section 4H of the BNA 1981 deals with CUKCs who were unable to become a British citizen at commencement of the 1981 Act. It entitles a person to be registered as a British citizen if the person meets the general conditions in section 4E, was a CUKC immediately before commencement of the 1981 Act and would automatically have become a British citizen under the 1981 Act had the person's mother been married to the person's natural father at the time of the person's birth. If the person would have automatically acquired British citizenship by descent he or she will acquire British citizenship by descent on registration.

2.56 New section 4I of the BNA 1981 deals with other persons unable to become a British citizen at commencement of the 1981 Act. It entitles a person to be registered as a British citizen if the person meets the general conditions in section 4E, is an 'eligible former British national' or an 'eligible non-British national' and would have automatically become a British citizen under the 1981 Act had the person's mother been married to the person's natural father at the time of the person's birth.¹

P is an 'eligible former British national' if P was not a CUKC immediately before commencement of the 1981 Act and either:

(a)   P ceased to be a British subject or a CUKC by virtue of the commencement of any independence legislation, but would not have done so had P's mother been married to P's natural father at the time of P's birth, or

(b)   P was a British subject who did not automatically become a CUKC at commencement of the British Nationality Act 1948 by the operation of any provision of it, but would have done so had P's mother been married to P's natural father at the time of P's birth.[2]

P is an 'eligible non-British national' if:

(a)   P was never a British subject or CUKC; and

(b)   had P's mother been married to P's natural father at the time of P's birth, P would have automatically become a British subject or CUKC:

    (i)   at birth, or

    (ii)   as the child of male British subject who became a CUKC if the father became such a citizen by virtue of paragraph 3 of Schedule 3 to the British Nationality Act 1948.[3]

If the person would have automatically acquired British citizenship by descent at commencement of the BNA 1981 Act he or she will acquire British citizenship by descent on registration.[4] Section 4J contains supplementary provisions, in particular to stipulate that a person's 'natural father' is someone who satisfies the requirements as to proof of paternity prescribed in regulations under section 50(9B) of the BNA 1981.

[1]   BNA 1981, s 4I(1).
[2]   BNA 1981, s 4I(2).
[3]   BNA 1981, s 4I(3).
[4]   BNA 1981, s 4I(4).

Tracing entitlement through a parent

2.57 A child may trace entitlement to British citizenship through a parent who died before his or her birth. Under the BNA 1981 the definition of 'parent' includes the parent of a child born posthumously. The status of the mother or father shall be the status of the parent in question at the time of that parent's death.[1]

[1]   BNA 1981, s 48.

2.58 Where a child wishes to trace entitlement through its parent, it is the status of the parent at the time of the birth, or in the case of posthumous children, at the time of the death, which counts. If the parent becomes a BC, for example by registration, naturalisation or operation of law, after the birth of the child, the child does not automatically become a BC by birth but is entitled to be registered as such on making an application under section 1(3) of the BNA 1981.

2.59 There are two alternatives to having a parent who is a BC. The first alternative is to have a parent who at the time of the child's birth is settled in the UK or in a qualifying territory (meaning a British overseas territory other than the Sovereign Base Areas in Cyprus: **2.17** above). Under section 50(2) of the BNA 1981 a person is settled for the purposes of the Act if he or she is 'ordinarily resident in the United Kingdom or a British overseas territory . . . without being subject under the immigration laws to any restriction on the period for which he may remain'.[1] Section 50(3) of the 1981 Act excludes from this definition people who are in the UK as diplomats, international functionaries or as members of Commonwealth or visiting armed forces and are exempt from immigration control.[2] In some cases persons who have been entitled to a diplomatic exemption may be able to bestow British citizenship on their children born in the UK if they were settled in the UK before they took up their diplomatic posts.[3] The second alternative is to have a parent who at the time of the birth is serving in the armed forces: see **2.46** above.

---

[1] Freedom from immigration restrictions and conditions is the first requirement of settlement. Ordinary residence is the second requirement. This is discussed in detail at 4.5–4.6 below. Section 50(5) of the BNA 1981 provides that a person is not to be treated as ordinarily resident in the UK when he or she is in the UK or a British overseas territory in breach of the immigration laws. The 'immigration laws' are defined by BNA 1981, s 50(1) in relation to the UK as meaning the Immigration Act 1971 and 'any law for purposes similar to that Act which is for the time being or has at any time been in force in any part of the UK'. The current definition of being in breach of immigration laws is found in s 50A of the BNA 1981, inserted by BCIA 2009, s 48(1), in force 13 January 2010 by SI 2009/2731, art 4(g).

[2] See Immigration Act 1971, s 8(3) and (4)(b) and (c). But Gurkhas serve in the UK as members of the home forces.

[3] BNA 1981, s 50(4).

2.60 From this short account it can be seen that disputes about whether a child's parents were 'settled' in the UK or a British overseas territory at the time of the birth may be a contentious issue when determining the nationality of the child.[1] In relation to the UK, the government recognised that doubts about parents' immigration status might arise many years after the birth of the child, and so modified the effect of the rule by providing for citizenship by registration for children born in the UK whose parents could not meet the settlement requirement. So section 1(4) of the BNA 1981 provides that a person born in the UK who has not been out of the country for more than 90 days in each of the first ten years of his or her life may register as a BC at any time. The immigration status of the person is irrelevant, and his or her residence may have been lawful or unlawful.[2] Registration as a BC under s 1(4) can occur in adulthood. It is also provided that where a child's parents become settled after the birth of the child, that child gets an automatic right to be registered as a UK citizen under section 1(3) of the 1981 Act. The application for registration under s 1(3) must be made while the child is still a minor. Under s 1(3A) of the 1981 Act, inserted by the BCIA 2009, provision is made for a person born in the UK (on or after 13 January 2010) to be entitled to register as a BC, if while a minor, his mother or father becomes a member of the armed forces and an application is made for his registration.[3] Limited provision is also made for people born in the UK who would otherwise be stateless. In some cases they automatically become BCs and in other cases they may register.[4] These registration provisions only apply to persons born in the UK. However, as a result of BOTA 2002, the Secretary of State has a general discretion to register any BOTC as a BC, other than those who are BOTCs only by virtue of a connection with the Sovereign Base Areas in Cyprus or who have previously renounced their British citizenship.[5]

[1] This is particularly so where EEA nationals are involved: see Fransman's *British Nationality Law* (3rd edn, 2011), para 13.2.2.
[2] Nationality Instructions, Vol 1, Ch 8, para 8.1 (Entitlement: UK-born person).
[3] In force 13 January 2010 by SI 2009/2731, art 4(a).
[4] BNA 1981, s 36 and Sch 2, paras 1 and 3.
[5] BNA 1981, s 4A, as inserted by BOTA 2002, s 4.

Abandoned infants

2.61 Where a newborn infant has been found abandoned in the UK, after commencement of the BNA 1981, section 1(2) provides that the qualifying conditions for citizenship in section 1(1) are deemed to apply to that child unless the contrary is shown. The same applies to babies abandoned in the Falkland Islands at any time after commencement of the 1981 Act and to other British overseas territories (other than the Sovereign Base Areas in Cyprus) at any time after the appointed day for the commencement of that part of BOTA 2002.[1] There is no definition of 'newborn' in the Act and this must be construed as a matter of fact by the Secretary of State and possibly the courts.[2] Children who have been found abandoned but are patently not newborn may be registered under section 3(1) at the minister's discretion.

[1] British Nationality (Falkland Islands) Act 1983, s 1(3) as from commencement of the BNA 1981; repealed and incorporated into the BNA 1981, s 1 (2), as amended by BOTA 2002, Sch 1 as from 21 May 2002 (SI 2002/1252).
[2] Of course, the precise age of the child is unlikely to be known by the very circumstances of abandonment. In the committee stages of the British Nationality Bill the minister suggested that a child of about 12 months might be considered to be newborn in certain circumstances; it would be the minister's intention to give the phrase a generous interpretation: HC Official Report (5th series) col 212, 26 February 1981, 6th sitting; see also Nationality Instructions, Vol 1, Ch 3, para 3.5.2.2.

Adoption and Parental Orders

2.62 Under the BNA 1981 as enacted, an adoption order made in a UK court automatically confers British citizenship on a child who is not a BC, where at least one of the adopters is a BC, but an adoption order abroad has no such effect.[1] The Adoption (Intercountry Aspects) Act 1999 amended the law in order to give effect to the 1993 Hague Convention on Protection of Children and Co-operation in respect of Intercountry Adoption.[2] In relation to nationality, it implements Article 26(2) of the Convention which requires a Contracting State, where an adoption has the effect of terminating a pre-existing legal parent-child relationship, to ensure that:

> 'the child shall enjoy in the receiving State, and any other Contracting State where the adoption is recognised, rights equivalent to those resulting from adoptions having this effect in each such State'.

The amendment, which came into force on 1 June 2003,[3] ensures that the adopted child enjoys the same status from the making of a Convention adoption order as he or she would if the adoption was made in the UK. Further amendments were made by the British Overseas Territories Act 2002 and the Adoption and Children Act 2002. Amended section 1(5), (5A) of the BNA

1981 now provides that a child without British citizenship, who is adopted either in any UK court (or, on or after the appointed day (21 May 2002), any court in a qualifying territory – that is the British overseas territories other than the Sovereign Base Areas in Cyprus) or under a Convention adoption effected under the law of a country or territory outside the United Kingdom,[4] automatically acquires British citizenship. This is subject to two requirements:[5] first, that at least one of the adoptive parents is a BC at the time the adoption order is made or the Convention adoption is effected; and secondly, in the case of a Convention adoption, the adopter or, in the case of an adoption by a married couple, both of the adopters are habitually resident in the UK or in a designated territory (no territories have yet been designated). The 1999 Act does not extend to Northern Ireland, but covers the whole of the British Islands, including the Channel Islands and the Isle of Man. However, an adoption order made in Northern Ireland would qualify to confer citizenship, as an adoption order made by a court 'in the United Kingdom'.[6]

1 BNA 1981, s 1(5) and (6). See Adoption Act 1976; Adoption (Scotland) Act 1978; Adoption (Northern Ireland) Order 1987. The courts are aware of the immigration consequences of adoption and regard them as a relevant factor, and have held that benefits from the acquisition of British nationality which occur during childhood are benefits to which 'first consideration' should be given under s 6 of the Adoption Act 1976: Re B (Adoption Order: Nationality) Re [1999] 2 AC 136, [1999] Imm AR 277, HL; but see also *ASB and KBS v MQS (Secretary of State for the Home Department intervening)* [2009] EWHC 2491 (Fam), [2010] 1 FLR 748, [2010] Fam Law 9 where *Re B* was considered in a case under the Adoption and Children Act 2002 and the changes it introduced, such as the child's welfare being the court's 'paramount consideration' and something that had to be considered 'throughout his life'. Home Office policy is to register children adopted by BCs overseas in the circumstances set out in the NI, Vol 1, Ch 9, para 9.8, or where adoption was demonstrably in the child's best interests. For the provisions of the Immigration Rules dealing with the admission of adopted children to join their parents in this country see Chapter 11 below.
2 The Convention is printed as the Adoption (Intercountry Aspects) Act 1999, Sch 1.
3 BNA 1981, s 1(5) as substituted by Adoption (Intercountry Aspects) Act 1999, s 7: SI 2003/362, art 2(a), see also further amendments made to s 1(5), (5A) by the British Overseas Territories Act 2002, s 5, Sch 1, para 1(1), (4), in force 21 May 2002 by SI 2002/12, art 2(a), and the Adoption and Children Act 2002, s 137(3), (4), in force 30 December 2005, by SI 2005/2213, art 2(m).
4 'Convention adoption' is an adoption effected under the law of a Convention country outside the British Islands and certified under art 23(1) of the Convention: see the Adoption and Children Act 2002, s 66(1)(c), in force 30 December 2005, by SI 2005/2213, art 2(d).
5 BNA 1981, s 1(5A), as inserted by Adoption (Intercountry Aspects) Act 1999, s 7 and as amended by the Adoption and Children Act 2002, s 137(3), (4), in force 30 December 2005, by SI 2005/2213, art 2(m).
6 Adoption (Intercountry Aspects) Act 1999, s 18(4) and (5).

2.63 From 6 April 2010, a parental order under section 54 of the Human Fertilisation and Embryology Act 2008 will, subject to satisfaction of the remaining requirement (British citizenship of one or more persons obtaining the order), operate so as to confer British citizenship as, in section 1(5), (5A) of the BNA 1981. The reference to an order authorising the adoption of a minor is to be read as including a reference to a parental order in respect of a minor, and the reference to the adopter or, in the case of a joint adoption, one of the adopters is to be read as including a reference to one of the persons who obtained the parental order.[1]

1 Human Fertilisation and Embryology Act 2008, s 54; Human Fertilisation and Embryology (Parental Orders) Regulations 2010, SI 2010/985, reg 5, Sch 4.

Adoption in the British Overseas Territories

2.64 Adoption in the Falkland Islands and other qualifying overseas territories is being brought into line with the provisions operating in the UK, so as to confer British citizenship on minors who are adopted by BCs in those territories.[1] The complication is that there is a gap between the start of the BOTA changes and the coming into force of the Adoption (Intercountry Aspects) Act 1999. BOTA started operating on 21 May 2002 and the 1999 Act on 1 June 2003. It has, therefore, been necessary for the legislators to make provision for BOTA 2002 coming into force first. The two amendments to BNA 1981, section 1(5) come to the same thing,[2] by ensuring that a minor who is not a BC, will automatically become one where an adoption order is made on or after the appointed day (ie 21 May 2002) by any court in a qualifying territory. However, Convention adoptions (effected under the law of a country or territory outside the United Kingdom) only confer British citizenship on minors adopted abroad by parents living in a British overseas territory after 1 June 2003, and in such cases the adoptive parents will have to have been habitually resident in the UK (or from 30 December 2005 a designated territory, although no territories have yet been designated, so habitual residence of the adopters in an overseas territory will not yet suffice).[3]

[1]   British Nationality (Falkland Islands) Act 1983, s 1(4) conferred BC status, where an adoption order was made in any court in the Falklands. On the appointed day (21 May 2002) it was repealed and replaced by the general provision for qualifying territories (meaning all British overseas territories other than the Sovereign Bases in Cyprus): BOTA 2002, ss 5, 7 and Sch 1, paras 1(4) and (5).
[2]   BNA 1981, s 1(5) as substituted by the Adoption (Intercountry Aspects) Act 1999, s 7 and amended successively by BOTA, Sch 1, paras 1(4) and (5) and the Adoption and Children Act 2002, s 137(3), (4), in force 30 December 2005, by SI 2005/2213, art 2(m).
[3]   BNA 1981, s 1(5A)(b), as inserted by Adoption (Intercountry Aspects) Act 1999, s 7 and and as amended by the Adoption and Children Act 2002, s 137(3), (4), in force 30 December 2005, by SI 2005/2213, art 2(m).

Descent

2.65 Where a child is born outside the UK, the BNA 1981 as enacted provides for automatic transmission of citizenship from parent to child for just one generation.[1] The Act provides that persons born overseas after commencement automatically become BCs from birth if their mother or father was a BC otherwise than by descent at the time of their birth, or was in Crown or similar designated service outside the UK or was working for a Community institution somewhere outside the UK.[2] But children born after 21 May 2002, the appointed day under the BOTA 2002, in one of the qualifying overseas territories to a parent, who is a BC by descent, will no longer be subject to the 'one generation' rule; in fact these children will be BCs by birth, although their children born overseas (ie outside the UK or a qualifying territory) will be subject to the descent rules. Similarly, under the BOTA amendments, Crown and other designated services is given a broader definition and the 'one generation' rule will not apply to BCs in such Crown or other designated service, where recruitment has taken place in the UK or a qualifying territory.[3] The 'one generation' rule may nevertheless produce some harsh results and so citizenship by descent is complemented by a scheme of registration to alleviate its deficiencies.[4]

1 BNA 1981, s 2. Citizenship by descent is defined in the BNA 1981, s 14. See further British Nationality (Hong Kong) Act 1997, s 2. It should also be noted that BOTCs, who become BCs under s 3 of the BOTA 2002 and were BOTCs by descent immediately before commencement of that section, are BCs by descent, unless they have become BCs otherwise than by descent: see the BOTA 2002, s 3(3).

2 BNA 1981, s 2(1)(b) and (4). Detailed provisions relating to designated service are now contained in the British Citizenship (Designated Service) Order 2006, SI 2006/1390 (as amended by SI 2007/744). In respect of the Welsh Assembly Government, provision is made by the Government of Wales Act 2006 (Consequential Modifications, Transitional Provisions and Saving) Order 2009, SI 2009/2958), Part 2, art 1(2), in force 6 November 2009. The British Overseas Territories Citizenship (Designated Service) (Amendment) Order 2008, SI 2008/1240 amends the British Dependent Territories Citizenship (Designated Service) Order 1982 so as to remove service for the Hong Kong Tourist Association and the Hong Kong Trade Development Council from the types of service designated as qualifying an individual born outside the British overseas territories as a British overseas territories citizen.

3 BNA 1981, s 2, as amended by the BOTA 2002, Sch 1, para 2.

4 BNA 1981, ss 3(2)–(6), 4D. See also the amendments to these provisions in the BOTA 2002, Sch 1, para 3. In *R (on the application of Ullah) v Secretary of State for the Home Department* [2001] EWCA Civ 659, [2002] QB 525, [2001] Imm AR 439, the Court of Appeal held that a BC by descent cannot naturalise so as to confer citizenship on future children born abroad.

Registration

2.66 Under the BNA 1981 previous entitlements to register as CUKCs were swept away either immediately the Act came into force or after a transitional period and were generally replaced by naturalisation, except for minors, where registration is still available in a variety of circumstances,[1] and for residual classes of British nationals and BPPs resident in the UK who wish to upgrade to BCs.[2] Registration for these citizens is an entitlement, provided all the conditions are fulfilled, but the Secretary of State has a discretion to waive unfulfilled conditions in the 'special circumstances of any particular case'.[3] To qualify the person must have been in the UK for a period of five years prior to the application without being in breach of the immigration laws and must have had no restrictions attached to the period for which he might remain in the twelve months prior to the application.[4] This provision continues to operate, but has been largely overtaken for one class of British nationals by the automatic grant of British citizenship to BOTCs by BOTA 2002 and by the new right to register as a BC given by section 12 of NIAA 2002 to BOCs, British subjects under the Act and BPPs (ie BNA 1981, s 4B), extended to include BN(O)s by BCIA 2009, s 44, unless they have another nationality: see **2.16–2.21**. It will obviously still be of use to those who cannot qualify under BOTA 2002, or because of dual nationality. Under s 4D of the 1981 Act, inserted by BCIA 2009, provision is made for a person born outside the UK (on or after 13 January 2010) to be entitled to register as a BC if at the time of his birth his mother or father was a member of the armed forces serving outside the UK and the qualifying territories (the British overseas territories other than the Sovereign Base Areas in Cyprus), and if he is a minor on application, the consent of his parents has been obtained.[5] Section 41A of the BNA 1981, inserted by BCIA 2009, s 47(1),[6] requires most applicants for British nationality by registration to satisfy the Secretary of State that they are 'of good character' before nationality may be granted. Exceptions will continue to be made where the applicant has an entitlement to registration deriving from the 1961 UN Convention on the Reduction of Statelessness or is entitled to registration as a BC under section 4B of BNA 1981 which gives registration entitlements to certain BOCs, BN(O)s, British subjects and BPPs without other citizenship, or is aged below 10 on the date of the application.[7]

[1]   For registration of those born in the UK see **2.48** and **2.50** above. Additionally, children born abroad to BCs by descent are entitled to register as BCs subject to various conditions: BNA 1981, s 3(2), 3(5). There is provision for discretionary registration in s 3(1). Home Office policy is to register the illegitimate children of BC fathers (NI, Vol 1, Ch 9, s 9), the second- or subsequent generation children born abroad to BCs on long-term business or service overseas (Ch 9, s 10); mentally disabled minors (Ch 9, s 11) and minors needing British citizenship to follow a particular career (eg police, armed forces or civil service) (Ch 9, s 13). The main general criteria for discretionary registration are that the child's future should clearly be seen to lie in the UK, that there are close connections (either through a parent or otherwise) and that a child of 13 or over has lived in the UK for two years. See further NI Ch 9. The consent of the court is needed if the child is a ward, and the consent of all those with parental responsibility where Children Act orders have been made: NI, Vol 1, Ch 9, ss 17, 20–22.

[2]   BNA 1981, s 4.

[3]   BNA 1981, s 4. For the circumstances when residence conditions will be waived see NI, Vol 1, Ch 12 Annex A.

[4]   Having no restrictions attached to leave will usually mean having indefinite leave to remain, but it can also include having an exemption from control or even being in breach: see NI, Vol 1, Ch 12 Annex A. The circumstances in which a person is in the UK in breach of the immigration laws are currently exhaustively set out in BNA 1981, s 50A, inserted by BCIA 2009, s 48(1), in force 13 January 2010 by SI 2009/2731, art 4(g). In respect of the period prior to 13 January 2010, the circumstances were to be found in NIAA 2002, s 11(2); see **2.56** fn 4 below, and there are some saving provisions in respect of that period in BCIA 2009, s 48(3)–(5).

[5]   In force 13 January 2010 by SI 2009/2731, art 4(e).

[6]   In force 13 January 2010 by SI 2009/2731, art 4(f). Prior to this provision for the 'good character' test was made by IAN 2006, s 58(1), which came into force on 4 December 2006 by virtue of SI 2006/2838. Before that, such a requirement only applied to those seeking to acquire British nationality by naturalisation: see **2.67** below.

[7]   BNA 1981, s 41A(5).

NATURALISATION

2.67 Substantial changes were due to be made to the law governing naturalisation, following amendments made to section 6 and Schedule 1 to the BNA 1981 by the Borders, Citizenship and Immigration Act 2009. On 5 November 2010, the Home Secretary announced that she had decided not to bring the naturalisation provisions of the Borders, Citizenship and Immigration Act 2009 into force and that they would be repealed. They are no longer of any relevance. The continuing law is that an application for naturalisation can be made under section 6(1) of the BNA 1981 or, in the case of persons (men or women) married to, or civil partners of, BCs, under section 6(2). There is a residence qualification, which is different in each case. In the non-marriage or non-civil partnership cases the applicant must have been in the UK for five years without any absences in excess of 450 days.[1] In the case of spouses and civil partners the period of required residence is three years with no absence in excess of 270 days.[2] Absences in excess of those number of days may be ignored at the Secretary of State's discretion.[3] Similarly, although the rule is that the applicant must not have been in breach of the immigration laws during either residence period,[4] breaches may be overlooked.[5] A condition which cannot be waived is that the applicant must have been physically present in the UK on a date five (or three) years before the making of the application.[6] In addition to the requirement of a fixed period of residence in the UK, the applicant must also be free from any restrictions on his or her length of stay in the UK.[7] A spouse can apply immediately after receiving indefinite leave, but others must normally wait 12 months, although the Home Secretary may ignore this requirement in a suitable case.[8] There is no requirement that a person be 'settled' in the UK to be naturalised.[9] Applicants other than spouses or civil partners must also intend, if naturalised, to live principally in the UK or work in Crown or similar service, or for a UK-established company.[10] It used to be the normal practice of the government to treat any person resident in the UK in exercise of a right conferred by the EC Treaty, as extended by the European Economic Area Agreement 1992, as being a person with unrestricted stay in the UK, for these purposes.[11] This was changed by Regulation 8 of the EEA Regulations[12] which contained a very limited definition of EEA nationals who were to be regarded as free from a time restriction on their stay. Regulation 15 of the Immigration (European Economic Area) Regulations 2006[13] now sets out those who have a permanent right of residence. It includes EEA nationals and members of their families who have resided in the UK under the new regulations for a continuous period of five years and those who have acquired a permanent right of residence in less than five years in specified circumstances. See further Chapter 6.

1 BNA 1981, Sch 1, para 1(2)(a).
2 BNA 1981, Sch 1, para 3.
3 BNA 1981, Sch 1 paras 1(2)(a), 2(a), 3(a) and 4(b). Criteria for the exercise of discretion to waive excess absence are set out in NI, Vol 1, Ch 18 Annex B, paras 4 and 5.
4 BNA 1981, Sch 1, paras 1(2)(d) and 3(d). What is meant by 'in breach of the immigration laws' is now exhaustively set out in BNA 1981, s 50A, introduced by BCIA 2009, s 48(1), in force from 13 January 2010 by SI 2009/2731, art 4(g). In respect of the period prior to 13 January 2010, the circumstances were to be found in NIAA 2002, s 11(2) and there are some saving provisions in respect of that period in BCIA 2009, s 48(3)–(5). In respect of the introduction of a statutory definition of 'in breach of the immigration laws' by NIAA 2002, s 11(2), although the provision was not intended to change the law (see Lord Filkin, Parliamentary Under-Secretary of State for the Home Office in *Hansard* HL Report, 8 July 2002, vol 637, no 165, col 550), it and its successor s 50A of the BNA 1981 may in fact do so in respect of EEA nationals, who will be treated as being in the UK in breach of the immigration laws, if they have neither an entitlement to be here under European Union law nor permission to be here. The NI (Vol 2: General Information: EEA and Swiss Nationals, paras 10–11) state that EEA nationals remaining in the UK without rights of residence under Community law (now EU law) or leave under the 1971 Act are to be regarded as subject to restrictions on the period for which they can remain, but are not to be regarded as in breach of the immigration laws. One effect of NIAA 2002, s 11(3) and now BNA 1981, s 50A(6), which applies Immigration Act 1971, s 11(1) for the purposes of each respective section, is to ensure that a person is not to be treated as being in breach of the immigration laws at any time when he or she was still in the immigration control area or had been detained or temporarily admitted pending a decision on his or her eligibility to enter. This had been Home Office policy where a person on temporary admission pending admission was granted leave to enter, but not where he or she was removed. Overstaying by an asylum seeker after a claim is not treated as residence in breach: NI, Vol 1, Ch 18 Annex B, para 9.9. The application of s 11(1) of the 1971 Act affects the legality of a person's residence in the UK, but not the calculation of the duration of their stay: see Beverley Hughes MP, Minister of State in the Home Office to Fiona Mactaggart MP, 18 July 2002. For a summary of the position, see 5.10 below.
5 BNA 1981, Sch 1, paras 2(d) and 4(b). See Fransman, para 16.7.3.5. For policy on disregarding breaches see NI, Vol 1, Ch 18, Annex B, para 8.
6 BNA 1981, Sch 1, para 1(2)(a), 3(a). Where an applicant misses the requirement by three months or less, the application may be returned to be re-signed and re-dated to arrive on a date when it can be met: NI, Vol 1, Ch 18, Annex B para 3.
7 BNA 1981, Sch 1, paras 1(2)(c) and 3(c).
8 BNA 1981, Sch 1, para 2(c).
9 Freedom from restrictions will normally mean that the person is also settled, but it does not have to; it could mean residence pursuant to an exemption from control, or residence in breach

of control (which can be waived): NI, Vol 1, Ch 18 Annex B. Irish nationals are considered to be free from time limits on their stay and therefore do not require ILR: Home office to Law Centre (Northern Ireland) 20 March 2003.

[10] BNA 1981, Sch 1, para 1(1)(d). For the meaning of UK-established company see *R v Secretary of State for the Home Department, ex p Mehta* [1992] Imm AR 512. Normally the UKVI expects evidence that employment will continue for five years as a reasonable minimum alternative to an intention to make a permanent home in the UK: NI, Vol 1, Ch 18 Annex F, para 7. An employee of a multinational company seconded to an associate non-UK registered company (parent or subsidiary) would be expected to have a contract of employment with the UK-established company or will be regarded as one of its own career staff: NI, Vol 1, Ch 18 Annex F, para 5.

[11] The UK Passport Agency continued to accept EC nationals exercising EC Treaty rights as 'settled': see Fransman, para 13.2.5.5, and Immigration and Nationality Directorate letter to Walthamstow CAB, 6 December 1999. Prospective applicants were advised to apply for indefinite leave to remain under the Immigration Rules as a precautionary measure.

[12] Immigration (European Economic Area) Regulations 2000, SI 2000/2326, reg 8 provided that, essentially, retired workers and self-employed people and those with permission to stay indefinitely, and their family members, are to be regarded as not subject to a restriction on their length of stay.

[13] SI 2006/1003.

2.68 Additional requirements for naturalisation were introduced by the NIAA 2002.[1] As a result, previous differences between the naturalisation of spouses and non-spouses, other than the residence requirements referred to in the previous paragraph, have gone. In addition, naturalisation under s 6(2) of the BNA 1981, that is the three-year route, has been extended to civil partners.[2] Under provisions in force from commencement of the BNA 1981, firstly, all applicants have to show that they are of full age and capacity,[3] and of good character.[4]

[1] NIAA 2002, ss 1–3 and Sch 1; BNA 1981, Sch 1, para 1(2)(c).
[2] Inserted by the Civil Partnership Act 2004, s 261(1), Sch 27, para 72, in force 5 December 2005 by SI 2005/3175, art 2(2).
[3] Mental illness or disability does not disqualify, but the person 'should be able to grasp, however dimly, the purpose of the application': NI, VOL 1, Ch 18 Annex A. BNA 1981, s 49 now gives the Secretary of State a discretion to waive the 'full capacity' requirement, if it is the applicant's best interests: IAN 2006, s 49. The provision also applies to renunciation and resumption of citizenship. Section 49 came into force on 31 August 2006 by SI 2006/2226.
[4] The Secretary of State is entitled to adopt a high standard in assessing 'good character' for naturalisation, and need not limit it to criminal convictions: *R v Secretary of State for the Home Department, ex p Fayed* [2001] Imm AR 134. The Home Office would not consider applicants to be of good character if there was information on file to suggest that they did not respect and were not prepared to abide by the law (ie were, or were suspected of being, involved in crime), or their financial affairs were not in order (eg failure to pay taxes for which they were liable), or their activities were notorious and cast serious doubt on their standing in the local community, or they had practised deceit, eg in their dealings with the Home Office, DSS, Inland Revenue or Customs and Excise: NI, Vol 1 Ch 18 Annex D. See also *R (on the application of Kokularamaran) v Secretary of State for the Home Department* [2010] EWHC 3512 (Admin): as regards good character, it was doubtful that knowledge engaged personal responsibility in the way put forward in the guidance associated with war crimes. Article 1F of the Refugee Convention was different, but in relation to the commission of war crimes there was a connection; and see also *R (on the application of Chockalingam Thamby) v Secretary of State for the Home Department* [2011] EWHC 1763 (Admin), [2011] NLJR 1027, 175 CL&J 438 as regards the need for a reasonable opportunity to make representations in relation to the concerns of the Secretary of State for the Home Department regarding past involvement in the LTTE and regarding what she believed was a deliberate misstatement in his application form.

Good Character

2.69 There is no definition of Good Character in the British Nationality Act 1981 and therefore no statutory guidance as to how this requirement should be interpreted or applied. However, nationality law makes clear that the Good Character test is to be applied to all persons over the age of ten who apply for naturalisation or registration as a British citizen, except:

(a)   where an application is made under statelessness provisions in Schedule 2 of the British Nationality Act 1981 or;

(b)   where an application is made under section 4B of the BNA 1981 from an eligible applicant which allows:

    (a)   a British Overseas citizen,

    (b)   British subject under this Act,

    (c)   British protected person, or

    (d)   British National (Overseas) to register if they would be stateless if they did not have their nationality status under one of these categories.[1] The decision maker will not normally consider a person to be of good character if there is information to suggest:

    (i)   They have not respected and/or are not prepared to abide by the law. For example, they have been convicted of a crime or there are reasonable grounds to suspect (ie it is more likely than not) they have been involved in crime. For further information on the criminality element

    (ii)   They have been involved in or associated with war crimes, crimes against humanity or genocide, terrorism or other actions that are considered not to be conducive to the public good. For further information on this particular element,

    (iii)   Their financial affairs were not in appropriate order. For example, they have failed to pay taxes for which they were liable.

    (iv)   Their activities were notorious and cast serious doubt on their standing in the local community.

    (v)   They had been deliberately dishonest or deceptive in their dealings with the UK Government.

    (vi)   They have assisted in the evasion of immigration control;

    (vii)   They have previously been deprived of citizenship.

This is a non-exhaustive list. If the person does not clearly fall into one of the categories outlined above but there are doubts about their character, the decision maker may still refuse the application. They may also request an interview in order to make an overall assessment.[2] The Nationality Instructions set out in Vol 1, Annex D, Chapter 18 give a very thorough and detailed Guidance on the Good Character requirement mainly focused on criminal convictions but also dealing in more detail with each of the above categories of bad character.

[1]   NI Vol 1, ch 18, Annex D, para 1.2; BNA 1981, s 4B.
[2]   NI ch 18, Annex D, para 1.3.

2.70 In *Fayed (No 2)*[1] Nourse LJ described the requirements for good character as a concept that cannot be defined as a single standard to which all rational beings would subscribe. It is no part of the function of the courts, he said, to discourage ministers of the Crown from adopting a high standard in matters which have been assigned to their judgment by Parliament, provided only that it is one which can reasonably be adopted in the circumstances.

As regards the Nationality Instructions, they have received considerable attention in more recent case law. In *SK (Sri Lanka)*[2] Burnton LJ said that:

' . . . it is unnecessary to give the Nationality Instructions anything other than their plain and ordinary meaning. Since this suffices for the purposes of the Secretary of State in this appeal, we did not hear argument as to whether they are to be interpreted objectively, or whether, as the Secretary of State contends, she is entitled to place her own interpretation on them, subject to the requirement of rationality. My strong provisional view . . . is that the Secretary of State is not free to decide what they mean.' [35]

He went on to say that the Nationality Instructions are in the main practical instructions to decision-makers as to how they are to go about deciding whether to be satisfied that an applicant for naturalisation has shown that he or she is of good character rather than policy guidance. However, his provisional view is that this did not give the Secretary of State a free hand. His strong provisional view was that the Secretary of State is not free to decide what the Nationality Instructions decide [36].

[1] *R v Secretary of State for the Home Department, ex p Al-Fayed* [2001] Imm AR 134.
[2] *Secretary of State for Home Department v SK (Sri Lanka)* [2012] EWCA Civ 16 (Former 'more than ordinary' member of the LTTE in Sri Lanka granted asylum and indefinite leave to remain: see further below at **2.72**).

Crimes against humanity and war crimes

2.71 Refusals of naturalisation on national security grounds, refusals because of involvement in war crimes and crimes against humanity have been very much on the increase. In *AHK v Secretary of State for the Home Department; AM v Secretary of State for the Home Department; AS v Secretary of State for the Home Department*[1]. Ouseley J indicated that there were over 40 cases currently before the Administrative Court, where naturalisation had been refused and the Secretary of State was unwilling to give reasons for the refusal as doing so would be harmful to national security. At the same time there has been an increase in deprivation cases on these grounds.[2] The landscape has greatly changed and is no doubt in the process of further development.

[1] *AHK v Secretary of State for the Home Department; AM v Secretary of State for the Home Department; AS v Secretary of State for the Home Department* [2013] EWHC 1426, [2013] All ER (D) 128 (Jun).
[2] See **2.92** above.

2.72 *SK (Sri Lanka)*[1] deals with war crimes and the distinction between obtaining asylum and obtaining naturalisation in case where the applicant for naturalistion has been involved in organisations which have been responsible for war crimes or crimes against humanity. SK was a former 'more than ordinary' member of the LTTE in Sri Lanka. He had twice been involved in battles in the aftermath of which the LTTE murdered prisoners of war. It is not in doubt that the murder of prisoners of war is a war crime. The Court of

Appeal held that the Secretary of State was entitled to conclude that SK, if not involved in war crimes, in the sense of personally carrying out such murders, was associated with such crimes.[2] In naturalisation applications applicants should be refused if their activities cast 'serious doubts' on their good character. Serious doubts will be cast if applicants have been involved in or associated with war crimes, crimes against humanity or genocide or have supported the commission of war crimes, crimes against humanity or genocide or have supported groups whose main purpose or mode of operation consisted of the committing of these crimes even if that support did not make any direct contribution to the groups' war crimes or crimes against humanity and genocide. The NI Guidance applicable in this case provided [para 8.6] that in certain cases membership of a particular group may be sufficient to determine that an applicant has been supportive of, and in some cases complicit in, war crimes or crimes against humanity committed by that group. In such cases consideration will be given to the length of membership and the degree to which the group employed war crimes or crimes against humanity to achieve its ends.

[1]   *Secretary of State for Home Department v SK (Sri Lanka)* [2012] EWCA Civ 16.
[2]   sSee NI, para 5.1 of Annex D as operative at the material time.

2.73 Because SK had been granted asylum, it was argued that not granting him citizenship was an abuse of process. In rejecting this argument Burnton LJ said that naturalisation and asylum are different things, involving the conferment of different rights and the imposition of different obligations on the applicant, and different rights and obligations on the part of the host state or country of proposed nationality. The grant of asylum, he said, does not involve any obligation to grant naturalisation. The questions that arise for decision in the two contexts are different, although similar. In relation to asylum, it is whether 'there are serious reasons for considering' that the respondent has committed 'a crime against peace, a war crime' and so on; see *R (on the application of JS (Sri Lanka)) v Secretary of State for the Home Department*[1]. The test is objective, and the onus of establishing the serious reasons is on the Secretary of State. The 'reasons' must point to personal involvement in the relevant criminal activity [30].

> 'In relation to naturalisation, on the other hand, the test is whether the Secretary of State is satisfied that the applicant is of good character. It is for the applicant to so satisfy the Secretary of State. Furthermore, while the Secretary of State must exercise her powers reasonably, essentially the test for disqualification from citizenship is subjective. If the Secretary of State is not satisfied that an applicant is of good character, and has good reason not to be satisfied, she is bound to refuse naturalisation. For these reasons too a decision in one context is not binding in the other.' [31]

Despite the importance of citizenship, the judge did not find it surprising that the test for exclusion from the Refugee Convention is more stringent than the test for exclusion from naturalisation [33].

[1]   [2010] UKSC 15, [2011] 1 AC 184. See also *MH v Secretary of State for the Home Department* [2008] EWHC 2525 (Admin), per Blake J at paras 46-49.

2.74 Fraud in earlier immigration applications may of itself be a reason for refusing a later application for naturalisation. In *Kurmekaj*[1] it was held that the Secretary of State had been entitled to refuse an application for naturalisation on the basis of good character where the applicant's earlier immigration applications, which had led to him being able to make the naturalisation application, had been based on fraud. The judge rejected the argument that the deception of an applicant was not relevant in the context of good character for an application for naturalisation where the applicant had been deceitful when claiming asylum, but was later granted indefinite leave to remain under a family concession and not on the basis of his refugee status. The court applied *SK (Sri Lanka)*[2]. There was no good reason why the earlier deception, although it had no bearing on the later grant of indefinite leave to remain, should not be taken into consideration for the purposes of good character. a decision-maker was not confined to considering fraud only within the immigration and naturalisation process and to no other dealings with the state.

[1]   *R (on the application of Kurmekaj) v Secretary of State for the Home Department* [2014] EWHC 1701 (Admin).
[2]   *Secretary of State for Home Department v SK (Sri Lanka)* [2012] EWCA Civ 16.

2.75 Iranian conscripts have had considerable difficulty in overcoming the stigma of the crimes against humanity carried out during their military service, even although they have come to the UK, obtained asylum and have lived blameless lives during many years since fleeing from the heartless grip on their lives in their own country. A particularly troubling case is the decision in *Amirifard*,[1] where a national of Iran, having been conscripted into military service, was sent to work as a guard in Shiraz prison. Due to his duties there he developed a depressive illness as a result of witnessing torture and executions in the prison. After a year, he could not bear it any longer, and went absent without leave. He was caught and given military detention for one month, and ordered to undertake an additional four months of conscription. He was then transferred to Lajavardi prison in Shiraz where he witnessed prison guards torturing prisoners, he was guarding a section of the prison which contained mainly university students detained without trial. They started a riot and he refused an order to shoot at them. He was threatened by the prison chief, and hit on the head and chest with a rifle. He was seriously injured and lost consciousness. He was then detained in a prison cell for 24 days, and subjected to torture. Fearing that he was going to be killed, he managed to escape from the car when he was being taken to court. He eventually made his way to the UK, where he was granted asylum. However, when he applied for naturalisation he was turned down on the basis that he was not of good character. His application for judicial review failed. The court held [57] that when all the evidence was taken into account, in particular the active part which the Claimant played, over a period of years, in guarding prisoners subjected to crimes against humanity, the Defendant concluded that the Claimant had not sufficiently disassociated himself from the regime. This was not an irrational conclusion. Nor was the Defendant's decision irrational in light of the fact that the Claimant had demonstrated his good conduct whilst in the UK for some eleven years. It is unlikely that the Defendant overlooked this factor. However, it was unlikely to have been sufficient to overcome the Defendant's doubts about his character as a result of his activities in Iran [58]. Is this a case which highlights the limitations of judicial review? if so, it also shows the need to have an appeal against refusal of nationality in which the Tribunal has competence to find that the discretion should have been exercised differently.

1   R *(on the application of Amirifard) v Secretary of State for the Home Department* [2013] EWHC 279 (Admin).

2.76 In R *(on the application of DA (Iran)) v Secretary of State for the Home Department*[1] the Court of Appeal approved the Secretary of State's distinction between disassociation from crimes against humanity, committed during conscripted army service in Iran, and fleeing the country for reasons of self-preservation. The Court of Appeal held that the Secretary of State had been justified in refusing naturalisation to an Iranian national on the ground that his association with crimes against humanity during his compulsory military service in Iran 15 years previously meant that he was not of sufficiently good character. A finding that his escape from the regime had been an act of self-preservation rather than one of disassociation was not, on the evidence, irrational (see paras 19–22 of judgment).

1   [2014] EWCA Civ 654.

Criminality and good character

2.77 The main changes in the NI's guidance on criminality and the good character requirement is summarised below:

*   Applications made on or after 13 December 2012 which feature a criminal conviction will no longer be assessed against the Rehabilitation of Offenders Act 1974. Instead they will be measured against a new set of sentencing limits.
*   Where an application features a sentence of four years or more in prison this can never fall outside a sentencing threshold. Such an application for citizenship will likely be refused.
*   Police cautions will be looked at in determining whether someone meets the good character requirement.
*   There will be greater scope to discount some disciplinary military offences when deciding nationality applications from serving and former members of HM Forces.

For full details of the changes that have been made in terms of the assessment of good character, please see the following updated guidance on the Home Office website.[1]

1   www.gov.uk/government/uploads/system/uploads/attachment_data/file/270533/ch18annexd.pdf

2.78 Where an application features a conviction and was been made on or before 12 December 2012, caseworkers must have regard to the provisions of the Rehabilitation of Offenders Act 1974. Under the Rehabilitation of Offenders Act 1974, a conviction becomes 'spent' after a specified rehabilitation period, which will vary depending on the sentence imposed. The advice to caseworkers is that spent convictions should not be taken into account in assessing the character requirement.

2.79 From the 1 October 2012, certain immigration and nationality decisions became exempt from section 4 of the Rehabilitation of Offenders Act 1974[1].

However, the Rehabilitation of Offenders (Northern Ireland) Order 1978 still applies to applicants who reside in Northern Ireland. This means that the fact a conviction is spent will be relevant to these applications. In England and Wales the concept of a conviction becoming 'spent' no longer applies when making an assessment of good character. Therefore, when dealing with nationality applications made on or after 13 December 2012, the Guidance advises caseworkers that they should refuse an individual who has a conviction within the relevant sentence based threshold as detailed in the table set out in the Guidance[2].

	Sentence	Impact
1	4 years or more imprisonment.	Application will normally be refused, regardless of when the conviction occurred.
2	Between 12 months and 4 Years' imprisonment	Application will normally be refused unless 15 years have passed since the end of the sentence.
3	Up to 12 months' imprisonment.	Applications will normally be refused unless 7 years have passed since the end of the sentence.
4	A non-custodial sentence or other out of court disposal that is recorded on a person's criminal record	Applications will normally be refused if the conviction occurred in the last 3 years.

As can be seen from the above table this short guide starts with the four year plus sentence, which is an automatic 'no', to a non-custodial offence where there should normally only be a refusal if the conviction occurred in the last three years. In other words at one end of the spectrum there are circumstances where an individual has a conviction that will always result in a mandatory refusal, regardless of when the conviction took place, such as someone given a life sentence. The intermediate sentences mean that a 15 or 7-year period must have elapsed since the end of the sentences. At the other end of the spectrum are what can only be regarded as minor offences. It is these that have caused difficulties and led to litigation.[3]

[1] As to the disapplication of the Rehabilitation of Offenders Act 1974, s 4(1)–(3) see UK Borders Act 2007, s 56A, as inserted by LASPO 2012, s 140.
[2] NI ch 18, Annex D, s 2.1.
[3] See *R (on the application of Khan) v Secretary of State for the Home Department* (2013) QBD (Admin) (Holman J) 30/04/2013 (driving while using a mobile phone. Secretary of State entitled to refuse application for British citizenship on the ground that applicant was not of good character.

2.80 Previous NI Guidance suggested[1] that where the applicant is of good character in all other respects caseworkers should normally be prepared to overlook a single minor unspent conviction resulting in:

(a)   a bind-over order;
(b)   absolute or conditional discharge;[2]
(c)   admonition;
(d)   a relatively small fine or compensation order;

(e)   a fixed penalty notice; and
(f)   Scottish fiscal fines.[3]

Although the Guidance has been altered these basic conclusions, in our view, still hold good but have to be read with the qualifications now contained in the current Guidance which we set out below.

[1]   Former NI, ch 18, Section 3.5.2 and 3.6.4.
[2]   In *Omenma (Conditional discharge – not a conviction of an offence)* [2014] UKUT 00314 (IAC) the UT held that the effect of section 14(1) of the Powers of Criminal Courts (Sentencing) Act 2000 is that offences resulting in an absolute or conditional discharge are not to be deemed criminal offences; so a person who has received a conditional or absolute discharge does not make a false representation if the answer is 'no' when asked if he has ever been 'convicted' of an offence.
[3]   Fixed penalty notices and fiscal fines are not classed as convictions and as such do not come within a sentence based threshold; see further below.

2.81 A fine will be considered a 'non-custodial offence' as will other out of court disposals that are recorded on a person's criminal record. Even where a person does not have a fine within the last three years, the decision maker may still conclude that a person is not of good character – and therefore refuse an application – if they have received multiple disposals of this kind that show a pattern of offending.[1]

[1]   NI ch 18, Annex D, s 3.1.

2.82 Fixed Penalty Notices, Penalty Charge Notices and Penalty Notices for Disorder are imposed by the Police or other authorised enforcement officers for traffic violations, and environmental or civil violations. Receiving one does not form part of a person's criminal record as there is no admission of guilt. So the decision maker will not normally consider them when assessing good character, but will do so unless the person has:

(a)   failed to pay and there were criminal proceedings as a result; or
(b)   received numerous fixed penalty notices which would suggest a pattern of behaviour that calls into question their character.[1]

[1]   NI ch 18, Annex D, s 3.2.

2.83 A caution (simple or conditional), warning or reprimand are all examples of an 'out of court disposal' that are recorded on a person's criminal record. Even where a person does not have a caution, warning or reprimand within the last three years, the decision maker may still refuse an application if the person has received multiple disposals of this kind that show a pattern of offending.[1]

[1]   NI ch 18, Annex D, s 3.3.

2.84 Where a Community Sentence is imposed the offence is to be treated as a 'non-custodial offence' and is recorded on a person's criminal record. It will normally cease to count towards bad character for the purposes of naturalisation after three years. However, even where a person does not have a community sentence within the last three years, the decision maker may still conclude that a person is not of good character – and therefore refuse an application – if they have received multiple disposals of this kind that show a pattern of offending.[1]

[1]   NI ch 18, Annex D, s 3.4.

Scottish Law

2.85 It is possible under section 202 of the Criminal Procedure (Scotland) Act 1995 for a court to defer sentence after conviction for a period and on such conditions as it determines. A deferred sentence is not, of itself, a sentence. That is only imposed at the end of the process when the offender returns to court.[1] The decision maker might consider placing the application on hold until the person is sentenced. Under section 246 of the Criminal Procedure (Scotland) Act 1995 a court may, if it appears to meet the justice of the case, dismiss with an admonition any person convicted by the court of any offence. Admonition will be treated as a non-custodial offence or other out of court disposal that is recorded on a person's criminal record.[2] A caution in Scotland is entirely different from that in England and Wales. In Scotland, it is a sum of money or a bond that has to be deposited with the court as 'caution' for good behaviour. The sum or bond can be forfeited if there is further offending. A Scottish caution will be treated as a non-custodial offence or other out of court disposal that is recorded on a person's criminal record.[3] Procurator Fiscal Fines occur where an alleged offence is reported to the Procurator Fiscal and they decide to offer to have the allegation dealt with outside of court and without getting a criminal conviction. The offer will allow the alleged offender to pay a sum of money as a 'fiscal fine' or as compensation to someone affected by the alleged offence. If the offender agrees to pay the fine, they will not be prosecuted. Fiscal fines are not convictions. The decision maker will not consider them when assessing good character[4].

[1]   NI ch 18, Annex D, s 2.3.1.
[2]   NI ch 18, Annex D, s 2.3.2.
[3]   NI ch 18, Annex D, s 2.3.3.
[4]   NI ch 18, Annex D, s 2.2.4.

KNOWLEDGE OF ENGLISH AND THE WAY OF LIFE IN THE UK

2.86 It is now necessary for spouses and civil partners as well as non-spouse/civil partner applicants to have sufficient knowledge of the English, Welsh or Scottish Gaelic language[1] and sufficient knowledge about life in the UK, unless it would be unreasonable to expect the applicant to fulfil either requirement because of age or physical or mental condition.[2] Regulations have now been made to deal with knowledge of English and knowledge of life in Britain.[3] Successful applicants, provided they are of full age, will now have to take an oath or affirmation of allegiance and pledge loyalty to the UK and democracy at a citizenship ceremony.[4] Details of this are set out in a new section 42 and Sch 5 to the BNA 1981.[5] The citizenship ceremony applies to adults being registered as BCs as well as those who are naturalised.[6] Registration or naturalisation are contingent on payment of a fee,[7] and new fees have recently been set for registration and naturalisation, including a fee for the citizenship ceremony.[8]

1   BNA 1981, Sch 1, paras 1(1)(c), 3(e), as amended by NIAA 2002, s 2(1)(a). The form of the
    Welsh oath and affirmation is set out in the Citizenship Oath and Pledge (Welsh Language)
    Order 2007, SI 2007/1484.
2   BNA 1981, Sch 1, paras 1(1)(ca) and 2(e), 3(e) and 4 as amended.
3   The British Nationality (General) (Amendment) Regulations 2005, SI 2005/2785 amend the
    British Nationality (General) Regulations 2003, SI 2003/548, with effect from 1 November
    2005 (1 May 2006 in the Channel Islands and the Isle of Man), and the British Nationality
    (General) (Amendment) Regulations 2010, SI 2010/677 make further amendments to the
    latter from 1 April 2010. The 2003 Regulations make provision for determining whether a
    person has sufficient knowledge of the English language and to make provision for determin-
    ing whether a person has sufficient knowledge about life in the UK for the purposes of such an
    application. Copies of the citizenship materials for ESOL (English for speaker of other
    languages) learners and other information may be obtained from: www.niace.org.uk/project
    s/esolcitizenship/.
4   NIAA 2002, s 3 and Sch 1, substituting BNA 1981, s 42 and Sch 5 and adding new ss 42A and
    42B. See also British Nationality (General) Regulations 2003, SI 2003/548, as amended by SI
    2003/3158, SI 2004/1726, SI 2004/2109.
5   Inserted by NIAA 2002, Sch 1.
6   BNA 1981, s 42(1) as substituted.
7   Asylum and Immigration (Treatment of Claimants, etc) Act 2004, s 42 allows the Secretary
    of State to prescribe fees for applications under the BNA 1981 which exceed the administrative
    costs of determining the application, and reflect benefits believed likely to accrue if the
    application is successful.
8   For more details see **3.26** ff, above.

Challenging registration and naturalisation decisions

2.87 In some registrations and in all naturalisations, the award of British
citizenship is discretionary.[1] The Nationality Instructions now provide guidelines on the way in which that discretion should be exercised, but there is no
appeal to the First-tier Tribunal (Immigration and Asylum Chamber) and, until
recently, the Secretary of State was not obliged to give reasons for any refusal
and his decision on such applications was not subject to 'appeal to or review
in' any court.[2] That has all changed. Currently, although there is still no right
of appeal against refusal to register or naturalise as a BC, reasons for any
refusal must be given and the ouster clause has gone.[3] So a decision can be and
is being challenged on all judicial review grounds, not just lack of jurisdiction
or unfairness.

1   The Secretary of State is not authorised to discriminate on grounds of nationality, ethnic or
    national origin: see chapter 1 discrimination at **1.82** ff and *R (on the application of
    Ramalingum (Sheena)) v Secretary of State for the Home Department* [2009] EWHC 453
    (Admin), [2009] All ER (D) 178 (Mar) where it was held that the Secretary of State had not
    discriminated on grounds of nationality in refusing to register a child as a BC under s 3(1) of
    the BNA 1981, where her parents were not British citizens and merely held ILR. The
    applicable policy forming the basis for the decision was found to be based on two factors: the
    need for family cohesion and the requirement to establish the closeness of a family's ties to the
    UK. See also *R (on the application of Johnson) v Secretary of State for the Home Department*
    [2014] EWHC 2386 (Admin) it was held that there had been a breach of the ECHR Article 14
    read in conjunction with Article 8; **2.50**, above.
2   BNA 1981, s 44 (2) and (3). Ouster clauses, however, have never usually been able to oust
    challenges on the basis of (i) lack of jurisdiction; see *Anismanic Ltd v Foreign Compensa-
    tion Commission* [1969] 2 AC 147 at 171B–D, HL; *A-G v Ryan* [1980] AC 718, PC; *South
    East Asia Fire Bricks Sdn Bhd v Non-Metallic Mineral Products Manufacturing Employees
    Union* [1981] AC 363, [1980] 2 All ER 689, PC; *Re Racal Communications Ltd* [1981] AC
    374, [1980] 2 All ER 634, HL; *Gowa v A-G* [1985] 1 WLR 1003, HL; *R v Secretary of State
    for the Home Department, ex p Mehta* [1992] Imm AR 512, QBD (very restricted view of the

meaning of a company 'established in the United Kingdom' wrong and s 44(2) did not oust court's jurisdiction to say so); or (ii) lack of fairness; see *A-G v Ryan* above; *R v Secretary of State for the Home Department, ex p Fayed* [1997] 1 All ER 228, CA. For the principles to be applied when deciding whether to appoint a Special Advocate in an application for judicial review where the Secretary of State has refused to give reasons on public interest grounds, having refused an application for naturalisation on grounds of a want of good character, see *AHK v Secretary of State for the Home Department* [2009] EWCA Civ 287, [2009] 1 WLR 2049.

3   NIAA 2002, s 7. Judicial review is the only proper route of challenging an erroneous refusal of registration: *Harrison v Secretary of State for the Home Department* [2005] EWHC 706 (Ch).

Loss of British citizenship

2.88 Under the scheme of the BNA 1981 those connected with a dependent territory (now British overseas territory) had their CUKC status re-classified and became British Dependent Territories citizens (now BOTCs) and not BCs by virtue of their connection with that territory.[1] But this process has run its course. Loss of citizenship for BOTCs and BCs who enjoy such status solely by virtue of a connection to a British overseas territory, will now only occur if that overseas territory became an independent country. New legislation would be required. Under current law, loss of British citizenship can occur in two ways:

(i)   by renunciation, where BCs (or other British nationals) with dual nationality or about to acquire another nationality renounce their British citizenship (or other form of British nationality) by a declaration of renunciation;[2]

(ii)   by deprivation, where the Secretary of State for the Home Department makes an order depriving someone of British citizenship (or any other form a British nationality). Previously this only applied to those who have acquired it by registration or naturalisation,[3] but now there is a new power to deprive persons who acquired British citizenship at birth, provided this does not make that person stateless.[4]

1   BNA 1981, s 23; although such persons may also have become BCs if, for example, they had a parent or grandparent with a relevant connection to the UK so as to establish a right of abode in the UK (under the Immigration Act 1971 as in force prior to 1 January 1983).
2   BNA 1981, s 12 (BCs), s 24 (BDTCs/BOTCs), s 29 (BOCs), and s 34 (British subjects). See also the British Protectorates, Protected States and Protected Persons Order 1982, SI 1982/1070, art 11 (BPPs) and the Hong Kong (British Nationality) Order 1986, SI 1986/948, art 7(10) (BN(O)s).
3   BNA 1981, s 40.
4   BNA 1981, s 40(2), as substituted by NIAA 2002, s 4(1) which came into force on 1 April 2003: SI 2003/754 and as further substituted by IAN 2006, s 56(1), in force 16 June 2006 by SI 2006/1497, art 3, Schedule.

Renunciation and resumption of citizenship

2.89 Renunciation of citizenship can only take place if the person renouncing already has or will acquire within the next six months another citizenship or nationality.[1] If the result of the renunciation would be to render the applicant stateless, the renunciation is of no effect. However, if the applicant can overcome this obstacle, renunciation is a fairly straightforward matter, provided the prescribed procedure is followed.[2] Merely making an informal declaration of renunciation, for example, where someone becomes a citizen of the USA, is not enough. There is also a fee to be paid.[3] Once renounced, can British citizenship be resumed? And in what circumstances? This is a more difficult question.

[1]   BNA 1981, s 12(3) (which also applies to ss 24, 29 and 34 and the Hong Kong (British Nationality) Order 1986, SI 1986/948, art 7(10) and is mirrored in the British Protectorates, Protected States and Protected Persons Order 1982, SI 1982/1070, art 11.
[2]   See British Nationality (General) Regulations 2003, SI 2003/548, paras 8, 9 and Sch 5.
[3]   The Immigration and Nationality (Cost Recovery Fees) Regulations 2014, SI 2014/581, Sch 4. The fee is £144. It should be noted that these fees are reviewed annually and new Cost Recovery Fees Regulations will replace those of the previous year.

2.90 Where a person had acquired the right to resume citizenship as a CUKC (under the British Nationality Act 1964), the BNA 1981 gave a right to register either as a BC or as a BDTC, provided that the person had what was known as 'an appropriate qualifying connection' either with the UK (for BCs) or with a British Dependent Territory (now British Overseas Territory) (for BDTCs, now BOTCs).[1] These were people, as we have seen at **2.43** above, with a qualifying connection to the UK or a colony, who had been obliged to renounce their CUKC status in order to avoid being refused or deprived of citizenship of a newly independent Commonwealth country. For them, registration is a right. For other people who renounced their CUKC status, registration as a BC or BOTC is still a possibility, if they have the appropriate qualifying connection, but at the discretion of the Home Secretary.[2] Although these are transitional provisions for people who had renounced their CUKC status prior to commencement of the BNA 1981, they continue to operate today, and the number of potential beneficiaries has been widened by section 5 of the NIAA 2002, which allows resumption of citizenship by all spouses of those with an appropriate qualifying connection, and not just wives, as before.[3] However, the Act of 2002 does nothing about the fact that qualifying connections can be gained only by the person or through his or her father or the father's father. They cannot be acquired through the maternal line.

[1]   BNA 1981, s 10(1) (BCs) and s 22(1) (BDTCs/BOTCs). The meaning of 'an appropriate qualifying connection' in ss 10(4), 22(4) was considered in *R v Secretary of State for the Home Department, ex p Patel and Wahid* [1991] Imm AR 25, QBD.
[2]   BNA 1981, s 10(2) (BCs) and s 22(2) (BDTCs/BOTCs). Registration may be appropriate where the purpose of renunciation was to acquire a spouse's citizenship, and the marriage has now ended, or to acquire another citizenship to assist in a career, and the person now wishes to return or come to the UK for settlement: NI Ch 16.
[3]   BNA 1981, s 10(1) and (2) (BCs) and s 22(1) and (2) (BDTCs/BOTCs), as amended. The amendments to the BNA 1981 apply to all applications made after 7 November 2002 as well as to applications made, but not determined by this date: NIAA 2002, s 162(3).

2.91 A person who makes a declaration of renunciation after the BNA 1981 came into force is entitled to resume citizenship only if the renunciation of British citizenship was necessary in order to retain or acquire some other citizenship or nationality.[1] This resumption is achieved by an application to the Secretary of State for the Home Department for registration by a person of full capacity. In addition to the right to resume under section 13(1) of the BNA 1981, there is also a general discretion to allow resumption under section 13(3).[2]

[1]   BNA 1981, s 13(1).

[2]   The discretion is intended primarily to benefit those who renounced citizenship in order to acquire the nationality of a spouse or civil partner or to assist in a career, and the marriage or career has now ended and the person wishes to remain in or return to the UK for settlement: NI, Vol 1 Ch 17, para 17.5.2.

Deprivation of citizenship

2.92 When the 1981 Act was in Committee the Minister stated that there had been twelve deprivations under s 20 of the 1948 Act – five for spying, five on[1] criminal grounds and two for fraud or misrepresentation. He then explained that 63 registrations had been annulled under the Sultan Mahwood/Parvez Akhtar rulings. It is understood that there were then no deprivations of citizenship from the 1960s until 2006. In 2009 2 people were deprived of their citizenship (1 while out of the country). In 2010 5 people were deprived all while out of the country.[2]. How many nullity case there have been is unknown to us, but there have been further reported cases, discussed below, and very clear and careful NIs place considerable emphasis on this aspect deprivation. But they also make clear that whether nullity action is appropriate will depend on the nature, quality and extent of any fraud, deception or concealment[3].

[1]   Official Reports 7 May 1981cc 1841ff.
[2]   Letter of Linda Bateman, UKBA Nationality Team; Fransman, op cit 19.5 and 19.5.1.
[3]   NI vol 1, ch 55.5.

2.93 The grounds upon which a BC (or any other British national) may be deprived of citizenship under the BNA 1981, as amended by the NIAA 2002 as from 1 April 2003, the IAN 2006 as from 16 June 2006, and the Immigration Act 2014 as from 28 July 2014 are as follows:

(a)   the Secretary of State is satisfied that doing so is 'conducive to the public good' (section 40(2)) and the person would not be left stateless as a result (section 40(4)).[1]

(b)   Where the Secretary of State is satisfied-regardless of whether or not it will render them stateless – that naturalised citizens have conducted themselves in a manner seriously prejudicial to the vital interests of the UK and she has reasonable grounds to believe that the person is able, under the law of a country or territory outside the UK, to become a national of such a country or territory.[2]

(c)   where the Secretary of State is satisfied that registration or naturalisation has been obtained by fraud, false representation or concealment of material facts.[3]

[1]   BNA 1981, s 40(2) and (6). BNA 1981, ss 40, 40A were substituted (1.4.2003) for s 40 by the Nationality, Immigration and Asylum Act 2002), ss 4(1), (4), s 162 (with s 159); SI 2003/754, art. 2(1), Sch. 1 (with arts 3, 4, Sch 2 (as amended by SI 2003/1040, art 2 and SI 2003/1339, art 4)). Thereafter s 40(2) was inserted (16.6.2006) by IAN 2006, ss 56(1), 62; SI 2006/1497, art. 3, Sch. On commencement of the BNA 1981, s 40(3)(a) provided the basis for deprivation of British citizenship on grounds of conduct by a person who had registered or naturalised as a citizen, where he 'has shown himself by act or speech to be disloyal or disaffected towards Her Majesty'; s 40(3)(b) and (c) provided additional conduct-based reasons for deprivation. From 1 April 2003, the NIAA 2002, s 4(1) substituted a new s 40 into the BNA 1981 and imposed a new conduct-based test where the Secretary of State is satisfied that the person has done anything 'seriously prejudicial to the vital interests' of the United Kingdom or a British overseas territory. From 16 June 2006 the test introduced by the IAN 2006 was further substituted for that introduced by the NIAA 2002. The present wording replaces the phrase

'seriously prejudicial to the vital interests', which is taken from the European Convention on Nationality (Strasbourg, 6 September 1997), which the government had, at one time, intended to sign and ratify but then decided not to do so, see JCHR HC 132-I Ev (Q87 and Q88), per Michael Wills MP, Human Rights Minister.
2   BNA 1981, s 40(4A), inserted by IA 2014, s 66.
3   BNA 1981, s 40(3) as substituted. See below.

Conducive to the public good

2.94 In the Nationality Instructions 'Conduciveness to the Public Good' means depriving in the public interest on the grounds of involvement in terrorism, espionage, serious organised crime, war crimes or unacceptable behaviours [Nis vol1 ch 55.4]. The first two provisions above mean that those acquiring British citizenship by birth or descent may be deprived of citizenship, provided that they would not thereby become stateless. Naturalised citizens face more draconian powers and can be made stateless if the Secretary of State has reasonable grounds to believe that the person can obtain another nationality at some undefined stage in the future. How the power will pan out is difficult to predict. There are very few cases to which these provisions apply – less than 30 cases in the recent past. Then there is third way, recently applied by the Home Office and endorsed by the Court of Appeal. Even if on a de facto basis the person deprived of his or her citizenship is no longer recognised by his country of origin as being one of their citizens, and will in fact end up with all the attributes and disadvantages of statelessness, it now appears to be accepted that the Secretary of State can circumvent this obvious fact by doing their own exercise of determining what the law in the country of origin should be and then coming to the conclusion that the man is a de jure citizen of that country after all. The de jure view of statelessness has support in the case of *Hamza*.[1] It has been taken further in the case of *B2 v Secretary of State for the Home Department*.[2] B2 was a Vietnamese by birth. He had come to the UK aged 12 and had acquired British citizenship. Later he converted to Islam and was suspected of involvement in terrorist activities. The Secretary of State took steps to deprive him of his British citizenship. The issue was whether this decision rendered him stateless. Inquiries of the Vietnamese government said he was no longer a Vietnamese citizen. The Court of Appeal, however took a different view. The word 'stateless' in section 40(4) meant de jure stateless, not de facto stateless.[2] The Court held that if it was clear that, under the law of a foreign state, an individual was a national of that foreign state, then he was not de jure stateless. If the Government of that foreign state chose to act contrary to its own law, it could render the individual de facto stateless, but the English courts had to respect the rule of law and could not characterise the individual as de jure stateless. The combined effect of the secretary of state's order and the subsequent responses of the Vietnamese Government was therefore to render B de facto stateless, but not de jure stateless (see paras 81–93 of judgment).

1   *Hamza v Secretary of State for the Home Department* [2006] EWCA Civ 400, [2006] All ER (D) 173 (Apr). *See Alison Harvey* 'The "de facto" Statelessness debate' (2010) IANL Vol 24, No 3.257.
2   [2013] EWCA Civ 616.

2.95 In the *Al-Jeddah* case[1] the the Secretary of State deprived Mr Al-Jedda of British citizenship pursuant to her powers under the BNA Act 1981 by order dated 14 December 2007. On 11 January 2008 Mr Al-Jedda appealed to the Special Immigration Appeals Commission ('SIAC'), one of his grounds of appeal being that the Secretary of State's order would render him stateless and was therefore void. Eventually after a long period of litigation his appeal came to the Court of Appeal and the Supreme Court. The issue was whether the Secretary of State was correct in arguing that if, on 14 December 2007, Mr Al-Jedda had not been an Iraqi national, it had been open to him to regain it by application and that it had been his failure to make the application, rather than her order, which had made him stateless. Both Courts rejected that argument. The Supreme Court held that from a plain reading of the statute and surrounding guidance, it was clear that the question was simply whether the person held another nationality at the date of the order depriving him of his British citizenship. The secretary of State has now reversed this decision by the insertion of a new subsection 40(4A) into the BNA 1981. The decision has also been undermined by the latest in the Al-Jedda saga, where in late 2013, the Iraqi Ministry of Foreign Affairs provided Notes Verbales stating that an Iraqi passport obtained by J in 2008 was genuine (J claimed it was a fake) and that he was an Iraqi national. In the light of this evidence SIAC held that the recent deprivation order had not rendered J stateless.[2]

1   *Secretary of State for the Home Department v Al -Jedda* [2013] UKSC 62, [2014] AC 253, [2014] INLR 131, [2014] 1 All ER 356, [2014] Imm AR 229, [2013] 3 WLR 1006.
2   *Al-Jedda v Secretary of State for the Home Department* (2014) Sp Imm App Comm 18/07/2014.

Nationality obtained by fraud, false representation or concealment of material fact

2.96 Under section 40(3) and (6) of the BNA Act 1981, deprivation may take place, where the person acquired the citizenship or status as a result of his or her registration or naturalisation on or after 1 January 1983 or before that date, and the registration or naturalisation was obtained by means of fraud; or false representation; or the concealment of any material fact (section 40(3))[1]. The Nationality Instructions provide that 'false representation' means a representation which was dishonestly made by the applicant not some third party, innocent mistake would not give rise to a power to make an order of deprivation under this provision.[2] 'concealment of any material fact' means operative concealment, ie concealment of a material fact would have led to the refusal of the citizenship application [55.1.3.2], such as undisclosed convictions or other information which would have affected the individual's ability to meet the good character requirement' [55.3.1.1]. 'Fraud' encompasses either of the above.[3]

1   BNA 1981, s 40(6), as substituted by the NIAA 2002, s 4(1). In *TB (Bangladesh) v Entry Clearance Officer* [2007] EWCA Civ 740, [2007] All ER (D) 267 (Jul) at para 13 the Court of Appeal thought it was highly unlikely that the power of deprivation subsists beyond the citizen's death, nor did it have retrospective effect. For a further description of the various factors to be taken into account, see Fransman, op cit at 19.5.2ff.
2   NI, vol 1, ch 55.4.1.
3   NI, vol 1, ch 55.4.

2.97 In *R (on the application of Hicks) v Secretary of State for the Home Department*[1] H was an Australian citizen who had been seized in Afghanistan and was being held at Guantanamo Bay by the US authorities. He satisfied the conditions for British citizenship by descent from his mother under the BNA 1981, section 4C and, accordingly, applied for registration as a BC. The Secretary of State proposed to grant British citizenship but at the same time to make an order depriving H of citizenship under section 40 of the 1981 Act. The Court of Appeal held that the deprivation would not be lawful since the conduct of H in Afghanistan, where he was alleged to have trained with terrorists, could not constitute disloyalty or disaffection towards the UK, for the purposes of the BNA 1981, section 40(3)(a) as originally enacted, a State of which he was not then a citizen, to which he owed no duty and on which he made no claim.[2]

[1] [2006] EWCA Civ 400, [2006] All ER (D) 173 (Apr).
[2] The Court of Appeal held that s 40(3)(a) of the BNA 1981, as originally enacted, did contemplate circumstances in which conduct before grant of citizenship could provide grounds for revocation of citizenship, as did its statutory predecessors. An allegiance might also arise, the breach of which might constitute disloyalty or disaffection, without the person being a citizen: *Joyce v DPP* [1946] AC 347, [1946] 1 All ER 186, 31 Cr App Rep 57, HL, considered.

2.98 In the NIs caseworkers are instructed that they should consider the impact of deprivation on the individual's rights under the European Convention on Human Rights (ECHR). In particular they should consider whether deprivation and/or removal would interfere with the person's private and family life and, if so, whether such action would nevertheless be proportionate. In some cases it might be appropriate to remove citizenship but allow the person to remain in the UK. In such cases they should consider granting leave in accordance with guidance on family and private life [NI vol 1, ch 55.7.11.6]-[55.7.11.7]. Similarly caseworkers should consider the impact of deprivation on the individual's rights under European law and whether it would nevertheless be proportionate to make a deprivation order. In some cases deprivation may be appropriate but they may need to allow a reasonable period of time before depriving, so that a person can make arrangements to continue or replace the benefits gained from European citizenship. For example, where a person was exercising EU rights as a student overseas and would need time to complete his or her course [55.7.11.7].

2.99 It has been held that the procedural protection provided by ECHR, art 6 does not apply to an appeal against the decision to deprive a person of his or her British citizenship, as the appeal will not determine civil rights and obligations, so as to engage art 6(1).[1] However, the decision may none the less be considered on appeal in order to determine whether there was any breach of either art 3 or art 8 ECHR rights, as well, of course, to determine whether the underlying decision that deprivation was conducive to the public good should be upheld.[2] The decision to deprive a person of the nationality of an EU Member State where that person is also an EU citizen, is not precluded by art 20 of the Treaty on the Functioning of the European Union (ex art 17 of TEC) (ie the provision conferring EU citizenship), where the nationality has been acquired through naturalisation but by deception, provided that the principle of proportionality is observed.[3]

[1] *Al-Jedda v Secretary of State* SC/66/2008 (22 October 2008), SIAC.
[2] *Al-Jedda v Secretary of State* SC/66/2008 (7 April 2009), SIAC.
[3] *Rottmann (Janko) v Freistaat Bayern* C-135/08 CJEU (Grand Chamber), [2010] All ER (EC) 635, ECJ. The application of this case to someone deprived of his British citizenship while he

was living in Sudan and wished to have his appeal in the UK was given short shrift by the Court of Appeal in *G1 v Secretary of state for the Home Department* [2012] EWCA Civ 867 at para 37.

The nullity cases

2.100 Decisions of the courts under the former section 40 of the BNA 1981 and its predecessor, section 20 of the British Nationality Act 1948, drew a distinction between deprivation, which requires a positive act by the Secretary of State for the Home Department, and cases where the Secretary of State can treat the registration or naturalisation as of no effect.[1] In *Mahmood*,[2] the applicant had obtained entry into the UK and subsequently registration as a CUKC by assuming the identity of a dead man. The Court of Appeal held that he had never become a CUKC. In *Akhtar*[3] the applicant had obtained his registration as a CUKC on the basis that he was the son of WA, but WA later denounced him and said he was not his son. The Court of Appeal held that, since the applicant could not prove that he was the son of WA as claimed in the certificate of registration or that he was the person named in the certificate, he could not rely on it. The court preferred to rest their decision on an absence of proof, rather than on a distinction between void and voidable registrations. In *Ejaz*,[4] the applicant was naturalised as a BC on the basis of her marriage, but it later turned out that her husband had never become a BC. The Secretary of State claimed that her naturalisation was a nullity on the ground that the Secretary of State has no power to grant naturalisation where the husband is not in fact a BC. The Court of Appeal rejected that argument and held that she became a BC as from the date on which her certificate of naturalisation was granted under BNA 1981, section 42(5) and remained such unless and until the Secretary of State invoked the deprivation machinery under section 40. In cases of registration the same rule applies; so the date of registration and not the date of application determines when citizenship is granted.[5] In *TB (Bangladesh) v Entry Clearance Officer*,[6] the Court of Appeal distinguished *Ejaz* on the basis that she had obtained a certificate of naturalisation, whereas the claimant and her children, in the present case had no certificate, but were claiming through marriage or descent from the husband/father, derivative claims which had no value because he had obtained registration by adopting a false identity. 'It is important', said the Court 'to distinguish adoption of a pseudonym from advancement of a false identity.' And the registration he had obtained was not in his name but in that of the man whose identity he had assumed. *Mahmood* and *Akhtar*, therefore applied.

[1] The NI, Vol 1, Ch 55, draw a distinction between deprivation and nullity, the latter, broadly, being impersonation cases, the former, broadly, where some other fraud was practised to obtain citizenship.

[2] *R v Secretary of State for the Home Department, ex p Mahmood (Sultan)* [1981] QB 58n, [1980] 3 WLR 312n, CA.

[3] *R v Secretary of State for the Home Department, ex p Akhtar (Parvaz)* [1981] QB 46, [1980] 2 All ER 735, CA.

[4] *R v Secretary of State for the Home Department, ex p Ejaz* [1994] QB 496, [1994] 2 All ER 436, CA.

[5] *R v Secretary of State for the Home Department, ex p Bibi (Amina)* [1995] Imm AR 185, QBD.

[6] [2007] EWCA Civ 740, [2007] All ER (D) 267 (Jul).

2.101 There has been something of a revival in the use of the nullity concept, notwithstanding its dubious jurisprudential basis and its re-introduction of a civil law concept into public law – a matter which was trenchantly rejected in relation to leave obtained by deception by the House of Lords in *Khawaja*[1], confining it, however, to cases of identity fraud. In *Kaziu & Others*[2] the court decided that the key characteristics of identity were name, date of birth, and nationality, or country and place of birth. That reflected the information on the naturalisation certificate. Those were the necessary ingredients for the Secretary of State to check the identity of someone who sought naturalisation. It was also clear that for nullification the grant had to have been obtained by fraud. So, innocent errors in the detail of date of birth, perhaps of name, or the innocent use of pseudonyms, misunderstandings as to nationality, or country and place of birth, which were not uncommon, did not make a nullity of citizenship. Where the grant of nationality was a nullity, the effect was that the person had no right of appeal since he or she was not being deprived of their citizenship status obtained as a result of registration or naturalisation; but had never obtained it at all. A person could not be deprived of that which he or she had never obtained. There was a distinction between nullification and deprivation. Nullification left no room for the exercise of any discretion; the grant either was or was not a nullity. The question of whether a grant of citizenship was a nullity was a question of precedent fact, for the court, and not one for the reasonable judgment of the Secretary of State for the Home Department. It was not enough for the secretary of state to say that there were reasonable grounds for concluding that an applicant had obtained nationality by impersonation and so it was a nullity; if disputed, she had to prove it and the court had to find that that was a matter of fact.

[1] *Khawaja v Secretary of State for the Home Department* [1983] UKHL 8, [1984] 1 AC 74 per Lord Bridge, with whom three of the other members of the House agreed at para 92. He said: 'I think there are dangers in introducing maxims of the common law as to the effect of fraud on common law transactions and still greater dangers in seeking to apply the concepts of "void" and "voidable". In a number of recent cases in your Lordship's House it has been pointed out that these transplants from the field of contract do not readily take root in the field of public law. This is well illustrated in the judgment of the Court of Appeal in the instant case . . . . where Donaldson LJ . . . . spoke of the appellant's leave as "voidable ab initio", which I find . . . an impossibly difficult legal category to comprehend.'

[2] *R (on the application of Kaziu) v Secretary of State for the Home Department* [2014] EWHC 832 (Admin). See also NI, vol 1, ch 55.8 and 55.9. The Court considered the earlier Admin Court decision in *R (on the application of Kadria) v Secretary of State for the Home Department* [2010] EWHC 3405 (Admin) where the Court may have come to the right decision on the facts but was wrong to hold that the secretary of state had been entitled in those circumstances to treat the grants as nullities, and her decisions in that regard were not otherwise outside the generous margin of decision-making to which she was entitled.

2.102 While it is easy to see the policy choices the Court has to make, the final answer of the Court leaves quite untouched the wholly unsatisfactory jurisprudential basis of these two earlier decisions. Does an identity fraud always render void a registration or naturalisation (*Mahmood*)? Or is it that the fraudster cannot prove against the word (in that case) of his angry and punitive father that the certificate in fact relates to him (*Akhtar*)? If the applicant's description does not match that of the person described in the registration or certificate of naturalisation, does that not mean that the person using an alias or pseudonym will also lose out? The irony of the whole situation, as perusal of the judgment in *Akhtar* demonstrates, is that the husband/father would have had no difficulty in obtaining a work voucher, because, unlike work permits, they were not tied to a particular job or a particular employer. All he probably saved was the cost of a return trip from his village in the Sylhet to Dacca to get his own voucher. And why should the deprivation procedure with its own appeal be whittled down to the point where it is so diminished as to be virtually non-existent?

Disputed claims to citizenship

2.103 As noted at **2.23** above, section 3(8) of the Immigration Act 1971 places the burden of proving a claim to British citizenship on the claimant, and section 3(9) provides the means of doing so for persons seeking to enter the UK – by production of a UK passport or certificate of entitlement to the right of abode in the UK. In cases of disputed citizenship, where the applicant has neither the requisite UK passport nor a certificate of entitlement, section 3(8) of the 1971 Act has been crucial.[1] In such cases the court has expressly rejected the argument that other evidence (such as the applicant's British visitor's passport or birth certificate) is prima facie proof of citizenship so as to shift the burden to the immigration authorities to disprove citizenship.[2] On the other hand where the claimant is able to produce the required means of proof, the position is different.

In *Sinha*[3] S claimed to be a British citizen. He was in possession of four British passports, the earliest of which had been issued in 1978. The first passports had been issued in a Muslim name (M). S's case was that he had changed his name by deed poll in 2000 to the name of his wife, who was Hindu, and children. S contended that he was the person formerly known as M and a British citizen The basis of the respondent's refusal to renew the passport was that S had produced in support a forged naturalisation certificate, but they accepted that the issue was not one of the rationality of the decision but whether S was M and a British citizen. The judge held that taken together S's evidence more than satisfied the burden of showing that he was M and a British citizen and entitled to a passport, and it outweighed the respondent's evidence and the forged certificate.

In *Ex p Obi*[4] Sedley J held that the production of a genuine UK passport, issued to the applicant and describing him as a BC, discharges the burden of proof and there was no need for further proof, even though the Secretary of State for the Home Department called into question the applicant's identity. This, however, does not stop the Home Office trying to rebut the presumption of citizenship created by the passport by trying to prove that it or the certificate of registration or naturalisation, on which the passport has been issued, was obtained by fraud, false representation or concealment of a material fact.

At that point *Khawaja* will have a bearing. The burden of proving that citizenship or a certificate of entitlement was obtained by fraud will be on the Home Office and must be proved to a high degree of probability.[5] In *Obi* there was no question but that the passport was issued to the applicant. In such cases, it will clearly be for the Secretary of State to put the machinery of deprivation into motion and to prove that the conditions for a deprivation under section 40(3) are satisfied. But where there is an allegation of impersonation, it remains to be seen whether the Secretary of State will seek to assert that registration or naturalisation did not take effect since it was issued to a person other than the applicant, as in Akhtar,[6] or will invoke the deprivation procedure on the basis that citizenship was obtained by fraud. Although a disputed claim for citizenship may be resolved by an application to the Administrative Court for a declaration, and in such proceedings the Court will resolve the dispute on the merits by deciding the precedent facts for itself,[7] the appeal procedure is likely to be more convenient where available.

[1]   *Minta v Secretary of State for the Home Department* [1992] Imm AR 380; *Re Bamgbose* [1990] Imm AR 135, CA; *Mokuolo v Secretary of State for the Home Department* [1989] Imm AR 51, CA.
[2]   In both *Minta* and *Bamgbose* (fn 1 above), the Court of Appeal held that *Khawaja v Secretary of State for the Home Department* [1984] AC 74, [1983] 1 All ER 765, HL has no bearing on the question of British citizenship, which is expressly dealt with by section 3(8).
[3]   *R (on the application of Sinha) v Secretary of State for the Home Department QBD (Admin)* [2013] EWHC 711 (Admin), [2013] All ER (D) 101 (Apr).
[4]   *R v Secretary of State for the Home Department, ex p Obi* [1997] Imm AR 420, QBD.
[5]   *Khawaja v Secretary of State for the Home Department* [1984] AC 74. See Minta, above; *R v Secretary of State for the Home Department, ex p Rouse and Shrimpton* (13 November 1985, unreported), QBD and more recently *R (on the application of Broni-Appiah) v Secretary of State for the Home Department* [2009] EWHC 2596 (Admin).
[6]   *R v Secretary of State for the Home Department, ex p Akhtar (Parvaz)* [1981] QB 46, [1980] 2 All ER 735, CA.
[7]   *R (on the application of Harrison) v Secretary of State for the Home Department* [2003] EWCA Civ 432, [2003] INLR 284, where a New Zealander claimed that his father was born on a British-registered vessel, making him a BC. His claim for a declaration that he was a BC or had a right to register as such was struck out at [2005] EWHC 706 (Ch).

APPEALS

Refusal to register or naturalise

2.104   No appeal lies against the refusal of the Secretary of State for the Home Department to register or naturalise a person as a BC. The only remedy is, therefore, by way of judicial review. But in disputed claims to citizenship and right of abode an appeal to the First-tier Tribunal (Immigration and Asylum Chamber) is possible. A right of appeal is available to those who are refused a certificate of entitlement.[1] The appellant is entitled to appeal while he or she is in the UK, where the application was made in the UK.[2] Under the previous appeal regime, the appellate authority treated passport refusals and disputed claims to a right of abode as constituting certificate of entitlement appeals even though no formal request for a certificate has been made.[3] It is doubtful if such a view would hold good today and it is, therefore, advisable to apply for a certificate of entitlement in all cases of doubt or dispute over citizenship or entitlement to a right of abode. This view is reinforced by the provisions of the NIAA 2002, which have provided for greater formality in applications for certificates of entitlement.[4] Secondly, there is a variety of other possible appeals, where the issue of disputed citizenship or right of abode may also arise from one of the other appealable immigration decisions.[5] Occasionally, the ambit of the appeal will be limited to dealing with whether the passport is a forgery or the person seeking to enter is the same as the person described in the passport, and will not permit the appellant to prove his or her citizenship or right of abode by any admissible means.[6]

1   Nationality, Immigration and Asylum Act 2002, s 82(2)(c); its precursors were Immigration
    Act 1971, s 13(2) and Immigration and Asylum Act 1999, s 59.
2   NIAA 2002, s 92(2).
3   Under Immigration Act 1971, s 13(2); see *Secretary of State for the Home Department v
    Antoniades* [1993] Imm AR 57; *Menon v Entry Clearance Officer*, Kuala Lumpur [1993] Imm
    AR 577.
4   NIAA 2002, s 10, which gives power to make regulations governing the application for and
    granting of certificates of entitlement; see the Immigration (Certificate of Entitlement to Right
    of Abode in the United Kingdom) Regulations 2006, SI 2006/3145 and see **2.23** above. The
    Immigration (Certificate of Entitlement to Right of Abode in the United Kingdom) Regulations
    2006, SI 2006/3145 have been amended by the Immigration (Certificate of Entitlement to
    Right of Abode in the United Kingdom) (Amendment) Regulations 2011, SI 2011/2682 from
    12 December 2011.
5   Ie, one of the decisions set out in NIAA 2002, s 82(2), eg refusal of leave to enter or refusal
    of entry clearance.
6   *Akewushola v Secretary of State for the Home Department* [1999] INLR 433, CA.

SIAC appeal or Judicial Review

2.105 In *R (on the application of Ignaoua) v Secretary of State for the Home
Department*[1] X, a Tunisian national, had sought judicial review of the
secretary of state's decision to exclude him from the United Kingdom, while Y
and Z, who came from Colombia and Algeria respectively, had sought judicial
review of refusals of their applications for naturalisation. The secretary of state
subsequently certified those decisions under the Special Immigration Appeals Commission Act 1997, section 2C (in X's case) and section 2D (in the
cases of Y and Z). Those provisions covered decisions which were made
wholly or partly in reliance on information which, in the secretary of
state's opinion, should not be made public in the interests of national security,
the relationship between the UK and another country or otherwise in the
public interest.

Under section 2C(2) and section 2D(2), the non-EEA national could apply to
the Special Immigration Appeals Commission (SIAC) to have the decision set
aside. The two judge Divisional Court held that the proceedings should
continue, with SIAC being asked to make a declaration under the Justice and
Security Act 2013, section 6 permitting a closed-material procedure. They said
that the balance of advantage, in fairness and in the effective administration of
justice, lay in staying the judicial reveiw proceedings. The Court applied Court
of Appeal decisions in the same case, *Ignaoua*, and in *K*.[2] Having a court with
SIAC's experience and expertise in establishing whether material should be
protected or not, and in handling the material if it was made it appropriate to
stay judicial review proceedings, thereby enabling claimants to apply to the
SIAC to have the relevant decisions set aside under section 2C(2) or
section 2D(2).

1   *R (on the application of Ignaoua) v Secretary of State for the Home Department* [2014]
    EWHC 1382 (Admin). See also *AHK v Secretary of State for the Home Department* [2013]
    EWHC 1426 (Admin), where the High Court held that after public interest immunity
    certificates were granted covering the material which provided the basis for the Home
    Secretary's refusal to grant a number of claimants naturalisation as British citizens because she
    was not satisfied as to their good character, claims for judicial review of that decision became
    untriable.

² *R (on the application of Ignaoua) v Secretary of State for the Home Department* [2013] EWCA Civ 1498, [2014] 1 WLR 651 and its guidance in *R (on the application of K) v Secretary of State for the Home Department* [2014] EWCA Civ 151, [2014] 3 All ER 437. Both cases pointed to the suitability of the SIAC route as an alternative remedy and hence to the application of the principle that judicial review in the Administrative Court should not be pursued instead.

Appeal against deprivation decision

2.106 Previously, the only remedy in a case of deprivation was a right of inquiry before a specially-appointed committee of inquiry.[1] Now there is a right of appeal to the First-tier Tribunal (Immigration and Asylum Chamber), with the possibility of an appeal to the Upper Tribunal and thereafter to the Court of Appeal or the Court of Session.[2] In national security cases there is provision for cases to be heard by the Special Immigration Appeals Commission.[3]. As we have seen above, the power to deprive a person their British citizenship has since 1 April 2003 been contained in a completely revised s 40 and a new s 40A which gives a right of appeal. An essential provision of the deprivation power is contained in section 40(5) which provides that before making an order under this section in respect of a person the Secretary of State must give the person written notice specifying—

(a)   that the Secretary of State has decided to make an order,

(b)   the reasons for the order, and

(c)   the person's right of appeal under section 40A(1) or under section 2B of the Special Immigration Appeals Commission Act 1997

A right of appeal to the FTT against a decision to make an order under section 40(2) (not the order itself) is given by section 40A(1) of the 1981 Act. By section 40A(2), and section 2B of the Special Immigration Appeals Commission Act 1997, such an appeal is to SIAC in a case where the Secretary of State certifies that the decision has been made wholly or partly in reliance on information which should not be made public in the interests of national security.

¹ BNA 1981, s 40(6)–(9) as enacted. See British Citizenship (Deprivation) Rules 1982, SI 1982/988. There were similar provisions for the deprivation of British Dependent Territories citizenship in s 40 and British Dependent Territories Citizenship (Deprivation) Rules 1982, SI 1982/989.
² BNA 1981, s 40A, as inserted by NIAA 2002, s 4 (1) and as amended by (i) Asylum and Immigration (Treatment of Claimants, etc) Act 2004, Sch 2, para 4(a) from 4 April 2005 by SI 2005/565; (ii) IAN 2006, s 14, Sch 1, para 13, in force 31 August 2006 by SI 2006/2226, art 3, Sch 1; (iii) IAN 2006, ss 56(2), 61, Sch 3, in force 16 June 2006, SI 2006/1497, art 3, Schedule; and (iv) SI 2010/21, from 15 February 2010; see also the Tribunals, Courts and Enforcement Act 2007, ss 11 and 13.
³ Special Immigration Appeals Commission Act 1997, s 2B, inserted by NIAA 2002, s 4(2), and amended by AI(TC)A 2004, s 26(7), Sch 2, Pt 1, paras 10, 11, in force 4 April 2005 by SI 2005/565, art 2(d).

The ambit of a deprivation appeal

2.107 There are two important UT decisions on the ambit of the deprivation appeal. In *Arusha & Demushi (deprivation of citizenship - delay)*[1] the Tribunal held:

(1)   that the absence of prescribed grounds can only mean that the Tribunal is to have a wide ranging power to consider, by way of appeal not a review, what the decision in an appellant's case should have been. The Tribunal has to ask itself 'does the evidence in the case establish that citizenship was obtained by fraud?' If it does then it has to ask 'do the other circumstances of the case point to discretionary deprival?'

(2)   that the Tribunal will be concerned with the facts as it finds them and not with the Secretary of State's view of them.

(3)   that an appellant can raise general human rights grounds but they must be framed to deal with the breach alleged to be caused by the decision to deprive the appellant of his nationality, and giving effect to that decision, and not framed to deal with the fiction that the appellant would be removed [paras 11 to 14].

The second case is *Deliallisi (British citizen: deprivation appeal: Scope)*[2] the UT held that:

•   an appeal under section 40A of the BNA 1981 against a decision to deprive a person of British citizenship requires the Tribunal to consider whether the Secretary of State's discretionary decision to deprive should be exercised differently. This will involve (but not be limited to) ECHR Article 8 issues, as well as the question whether deprivation would be a disproportionate interference with a person's EU rights.

•   As regards the ECHR, if, on the facts, the appellate tribunal is satisfied that depriving an appellant of British citizenship would constitute a disproportionate interference with the Article 8 rights of that person or his or her family[3] the appellate tribunal must re-exercise discretion by finding in favour of the appellant. However, in a case where Article 8(2) is not engaged, because the consequences of deprivation are not found to have consequences of such gravity as to engage that Article, the Tribunal must still consider whether discretion should be exercised differently. This is because the scope of a section 40A appeal is wider than Article 8 [37].

•   As regards EU law, the Tribunal, having referred to the European Court of Justice decisions in *Rottmann* and *Zambrano*,[4] stated that where a person affected by a deprivation decision has made actual use of rights flowing from EU citizenship, in particular, the right to work in another EU State, then the effect of removing such citizenship may well have a greater practical impact, compared with the position where such rights have not been exercised. Depending on the circumstances, that degree of impact may well require a greater degree of justification on the part of the national authorities, as regards their deprivation decision.[5]

•   Although, unlike section 84(1)(g) of the NIAA 2002, section 40A of the BNA 1981 does not involve any statutory hypothesis that the appellant will be removed from the United Kingdom in consequence of the deprivation decision, this does not mean that removal as a consequence of deprivation is automatically excluded from the factors to be considered by the Tribunal hearing a section 40A appeal. Removal will be relevant if, and insofar as the Tribunal finds, as a matter of fact, that in the circumstances of the particular case, it is a reasonably foreseeable consequence of depriving the person of British citizenship.

- A person who, immediately before becoming a British citizen, had indefinite leave to remain in the United Kingdom, does not automatically become entitled to such leave, upon being deprived of such citizenship. It is not compatible with the scheme of that Act to regard indefinite leave to remain (or any other sort of leave) as having some sort of vestigial existence, whilst the person concerned remains a British citizen.

1   [2012] UKUT 80 (IAC). It should be noted that during the passage of the Bill for the Nationality, Immigration and Asylum Act 2002, which inserted s 40A into the BNA 1981, the Minister of State, Lord Filkin, gave this assurance to Lord Avebury (Hansard, 8 July 2002, column 508): 'The appellate body will be able not only to remove [sic; presumably "review"] the legality of the Secretary of State's decision, but also to hear arguments at his discretion on whether or not the right to deprive should have been exercised differently.'
2   [2013] UKUT 439(IAC).
3   This means those persons whose position falls to be examined on the principles identified in *Beoku-Betts* [2008] UKHL 39.
4   *Rottmann (Janko) v Freistaat Bayern*: C-135/08 [2010] QB 761, [2010] ECR I-1449, ECJ; *Ruiz Zambrano v Office National de l'Emploi (ONEm)*: C-34/09 [2012] QB 265, [2011] ECR I-1177, ECJ.
5   [2013] UKUT 439(IAC) at para 42.

Suspensive effect of an appeal

2.108 An appeal under section 40A of the 1981 Act was given a particular suspensive effect by section 40A(6), as follows which provided that:

'an order under s 40 may not be made in respect of a person while an appeal under this section or s 2B of the Special Immigration Appeals Commission Act 1997 (a) has been instituted and has not yet been finally determined, withdrawn or abandoned, or (b) could be brought (ignoring any possibility of an appeal out of time with permission).'

Section 40A(6) was however repealed by Schedule 4 to the Asylum and Immigration (Treatment of Claimants, etc) Act 2004 (the 2004 Act). This meant that the deprivation order can be made before the appellant's appeal rights have been exhausted. A new section 40A(3) of the 1981 Act has been substituted and makes provision for a direction to be made, if the appeal is successful, for an order under section 40 above to be treated as having had no effect. So if the Secretary of State waits till the person goes abroad, then makes the deprivation order, the person has no British nationality and will not be able to return for an in country appeal. This process got the seal of approval from the Court of Appeal in *G1 v Secretary of State for the Home Department*[1].

However, in *L1 v Secretary of State for the Home Department*[2] L, born in Sudan, had obtained British citizenship in 2003. In reliance on closed material indicating that he was a terrorist, it was proposed in May 2010 that he be excluded from the United Kingdom under the Crown's prerogative power, and deprived of British nationality under section 40(2). In June 2010, the secretary of state authorised a proposal that the exclusion and deprivation process should wait until L next travelled out of the UK because it was easier to refuse him re-entry than to enforce his departure. The court held that where the Secretary of State had deliberately waited until a suspected terrorist had left the country before setting in train the procedure under the British Nationality Act 1981 section 40(2) to deprive him of his British nationality, the SIAC ought to have granted him an extension of time to appeal under the Special Immigration Appeals Commission (Procedure) Rules 2003, SI 2003/1034, rule 8(5). In deliberately opting to circumvent proper procedure, the Secretary of State had brought the service difficulties upon herself, and the fact that the appellant was a man who posed national security concerns did not militate against his right of appeal.

It should be noted that in both these case the Secretary of State relied on a Prerogative power to exclude aliens from the UK. We have already criticised *GI* at **1.35** above; it was a decision made shortly before the landmark decisions of the Supreme Court in *Munir* and *Alvi*. Once a deprivation Order has been made the appellant is no longer a British citizen and no longer has a right of abode. There are ample statutory powers to exclude such a person from the UK without delving into some pre Civil War powers operated by a king who was wedded to the absolutism of his powers. In any event, this is a power confined to aliens. So what is the Secretary of State going to do when she has to deal with a Pakistan, Sri Lanka or Bangladesh national, all of whom are Commonwealth citizens not aliens? Charles 1 will be singing in his grave, now that he is so well remembered.

[1] [2012] EWCA Civ 867.
[2] [2013] EWCA Civ 906.

BRITISH PASSPORTS AND IDENTITY CARDS

A prerogative power

2.109 Travellers may be refused a British passport because their citizenship is not recognised. We have dealt with the remedies for this situation in the last section. But passports may also be withheld from BCs for a variety of reasons, and this will obviously affect their ability to travel and, therefore, to enjoy the benefits of their statutory right of abode. In *R (on the application of Ali) v Secretary of State for the Home Department*[1] Burnett J had emphasised that, given the seriousness of refusing a passport to someone who had previously been issued with one, the secretary of state had to advance cogent reasons for such a refusal. In *R (on the application of Fayad (Nazem)) v Secretary of State for the Home Department*[2] McKenna J held that the Secretary of State had advanced cogent reasons why she was yet to make a decision on F's application for a new passport. She had legitimate concerns as to the circumstances in which F, whose parents were both Lebanese yet apparently went to Sierra Leone a couple of months before F's birth and left taking F with them to return to the Lebanon a year or so after his birth, came to obtain his first British overseas passport and the lack of documentation supplied in support of the application for that document at the time. In *Begum (Rangis) v Secretary of State for the Home Department*[3] the Secretary of State for the Home Department had erred in refusing to issue a British passport to a woman who claimed to have acquired British citizenship by descent. The correct standard of proof in establishing citizenship was the normal civil standard of the balance of probabilities, not 'beyond reasonable doubt', as had been applied by Her Majesty's Passport Office.

[1] [2012] EWHC 3379 (Admin).

2   [2014] EWHC 2556 (Admin).
3   [2014] EWHC 2968 (Admin).

2.110 The power to issue passports is not statutory but is derived from the prerogative.[1] Passports are issued by the UK Identity and Passport Service, which is an executive agency of the Home Office, often referred to as the Passport Office. Overseas they are issued by British consulates, British High Commissions and British overseas territory authorities. A passport is not an entry clearance document for the purposes of an appeal under section 82(2) of NIAA 2002 or its statutory precursors. Thus where a person succeeds in proving a disputed relationship and by reason of that relationship is a BC by descent, the appellate authority cannot require the entry clearance officer to issue a passport, only a certificate of entitlement.[2] On the other hand, for the purposes of entry a passport is proof that the holder has a right of abode.[3] It is, therefore, a very valuable and essential document. Yet, so far no court or tribunal has been willing to sanction the existence of any implied duty to order the issue of a passport.

1   Wade and Forsyth do not regard this as a true prerogative power for the highly questionable reason that the grant or cancellation of a passport involves no direct legal consequences; see Administrative Law (10th edn, 2009) OUP, pp 289–90. This may be based on an early judicial view of a passport as a document merely to be used for purposes of consular protection: see *R v Brailsford* [1905] 2 KB 730 at 745. In *R v Secretary of State for Foreign and Commonwealth Affairs, ex p Everett* [1989] QB 811, [1989] 1 All ER 655, CA O'Connor LJ said it was a prerogative power.
2   Kassun (Khatoori) (4272).
3   Immigration Act 1971, s 3(9). See *R v Secretary of State for the Home Department, ex p Obi* [1997] Imm AR 420, QBD.

Identity cards

2.111 Under the Identity Cards Act 2006, provision was made for the issue of identity cards ('ID cards') to all UK residents and individuals, who have resided in the UK, for example, or are proposing to enter the UK. The Identity Documents Act 2010 repealed the Identity Cards Act 2006 from 21 January 2011 but re-enacted provisions in sections 25 and 26 of the 2006 Act (possession of false identity documents) and section 38 of the 2006 Act (verifying information provided with passport applications). The amendments made to the Consular Fees Act 1980 by section 36 of the 2006 Act, were also retained by section 1 and Schedule of the 2010 Act.

Verification of information in passport applications

2.112 Section 38 of the Identity Cards Act 2006 enables background information to be required in order to verify the identity of passport applicants or to make a decision to withdraw a passport.[1] Under the 2006 Act this information may be obtained from a Minister of the Crown; a government department; a Northern Ireland department; and the National Assembly for Wales.[2] Other bodies can be added to this list by statutory order. The bodies added by order are the Registrar General for England and Wales, the Registrar General for Scotland, the Registrar General for Northern Ireland, and any credit reference agency which, at the time when the particular requirement is imposed is a party to a contract for the supply of information for the purposes of the Secretary of State carrying out functions under the Act.[3] A failure to comply with the duty to give information is enforceable in civil proceedings.[4] As indicated at **2.109** above, these requirements are retained in the Identity Documents Act 2010 for all identity documents other than ID cards.[5]

[1]   This will help improve the security and reliability of the passport issuing process in advance of the introduction of similar provisions in s 9 of the Identity Cards Act 2006 to require information for the validation of applications for identity cards.

[2]   Identity Cards Act 2006, s 38 (3)(a) to (d).

[3]   Identity Cards Act 2006, s 38(3)(e); see Identity Cards Act 2006 (Information and Code of Practice on Penalties) Order 2009, SI 2009/2570, in force 24 September 2009.

[4]   Under art 7 of SI 2009/2570 this may be: (a) for an injunction; (b) for specific performance of a statutory duty under s 45 of the Court of Session Act 1988; or (c) for any other appropriate remedy or relief.

[5]   The Identity Documents Act 2010 repealed the Identity Cards Act 2006 from 21 January 2011 but re-enacted provisions in section 38 of the 2006 Act (verifying information provided with passport applications).

2.113 It was stated in the House of Lords in 1958: 'No British subject has a legal right to a passport. The grant of a UK passport is a royal prerogative exercised through Her Majesty's ministers and in particular the Foreign Secretary.'[1] Details of how the prerogative was usually exercised were given to the House. These reasons were amplified in 1974 and 1981.[2] There are five reasons for refusal or withdrawal of a passport. These are:

(a)   minors being taken out of the jurisdiction illegally, or contrary to the wishes of a parent or other person awarded parental rights;

(b)   applicants wishing to leave the country where there is good evidence to believe that they wish to avoid prosecution;

(c)   applicants whose conduct is so demonstrably undesirable that continued enjoyment of passport facilities is contrary to the public interest;[3]

(d)   persons repatriated at the public expense who have not refunded the cost of their repatriation;[4]

(e)   persons for whose arrest a warrant has been issued in the UK[5] or who are wanted for serious crime in the UK.[6]

[1]   209 HL Official Report (5th series) col 860 (PQ). See David W Williams 'Without Let or Hindrance' [1973] NLJ 605; JUSTICE Going abroad.

[2]   See 881 HC Official Report (5th series) written answers col 265, 15 November 1974; 416 HL Official Report (5th series) written answers col 558, 22 January 1981.

[3]   Only about 20 people were denied passports on political grounds between 1945 and 1968. Then there were the exceptional cases during the Rhodesian rebellion; see 764 HC Official Report (5th series) col 1107, 14 May 1968. BCs who had been held at Guantánamo as suspected international terrorists had passports withdrawn or refused on their release and repatriation to the UK, although it is not clear why. See *Guardian* 17 February 2005.

[4]   This was said to occur only once or twice a year and the practice was confirmed in 792 HC Official Report (5th series) col 232. In 1968 it was stated in a parliamentary question that 2,400 passports had been impounded since 1951 (764 HC Official Report (5th series) col 183); a later debate in the House of Commons revealed that the overwhelming majority of these 2,400 refusals or withdrawals were people who had run out of money on holiday and handed in their passports to get their fares home paid: 764 HC Official Report (5th series) col 1107, 14 May 1968; see further David W Williams 'Without Let or Hindrance' [1973] NLJ 605.

[5]   *R v Secretary of State for Foreign and Commonwealth Affairs, ex p Everett* [1989] QB 811, [1989] 1 All ER 655, CA.

[6]   It is not clear how far (b) and (e) overlap.

Challenging refusals

2.114 Since it is now possible to challenge decisions taken under the prerogative on judicial review,[1] it is also possible to challenge a refusal to issue a passport. In *Ex p Everett*,[2] the Court of Appeal held that the Secretary of State for Foreign and Commonwealth Affairs was entitled to refuse a passport, but had to give reasons for doing so. In the cases cited in paragraph **2.106** the courts have now made it clear that these reasons must be cogent reasons. Where the refusal was because of an outstanding arrest warrant, the applicant should be told when and where the warrant was issued and what for. When notifying the applicant he or she should be told to tell the Secretary of State of any exceptional grounds for issuing a passport, for example, when the applicant was ill in a foreign country. Everett focuses on the need to give reasons after the decision is made, but there may now also be cases where it will be necessary as a matter of fairness for the passport office to indicate areas of concern to applicants before the decision in sufficient detail to enable them to make representations.[3]

[1] *Council of Civil Service Unions v Minister for the Civil Service* [1985] AC 374, [1984] 3 All ER 935 at 948, 951 and 956, HL. See further *R v Secretary of State for the Home Department, ex p Bentley* [1994] QB 349, [1993] 4 All ER 442 (challenge to the prerogative of mercy).

[2] *R v Secretary of State for Foreign and Commonwealth Affairs, ex p Everett* [1989] QB 811, [1989] 1 All ER 655, CA.

[3] *R v Secretary of State for the Home Department, ex p Fayed* [1997] 1 All ER 228, CA; *R (on the application of Ali) v Secretary of State for the Home Department* [2012] EWHC 3379 (Admin); *R (on the application of Fayad (Nazem)) v Secretary of State for the Home Department* [2014] EWHC 2556 (Admin); *Begum (Rangis) v Secretary of State for the Home Department* [2014] EWHC 2968 (Admin). Above **2.106**.

A new approach

2.115 Today an unfettered prerogative power to refuse a passport is probably a thing of the past. First, a passport is not just a document to be used for the individual's protection as a British subject.[1] It may also be needed to give effect to the statutory right under section 1 of the Immigration Act 1971 to leave or enter the UK. Further, in EU law there is a right of exit, contained in art 4 of Directive 2004/38/EC, providing for an obligation to allow British nationals (who are UK nationals for EU purposes) to leave the country in pursuit of their free movement rights (see Chapter 6 below). In our view neither the statutory right under s 1 of the 1971 Act nor the right to reside in another EU country in pursuit of free movement rights can be impeded by the refusal of the passport or other suitable identity document, except on public policy grounds within the terms of Directive 2004/38/EC, Chapter VI.

[1] *Per Lord Alverstone in R v Brailsford* [1905] 2 KB 730 at 745.

2.116 The question is whether a passport can be withheld for travel outside the EU. We have already referred to Articles 2(2) and 3(2) of the Fourth Protocol of the ECHR at **2.8** above.[1] However, there is a much older common law right of a British subject to come and go without let or hindrance referred to in *DPP v Bhagwan*.[2] This echoes Blackstone's view that an Englishman had a right at common law to leave the realm, subject only to the restraints of the writ *ne exeat regno*[3] The right is now a statutory right, set out in section 1(1) of the Immigration Act 1971. However, without a passport it is largely useless. Does this mean that there is now a concomitant right to a passport, which can only be withheld in the limited circumstances to which section 1(1) relates?[4] Or are the restraints set out in the parliamentary answers referred to in **2.111** above ones which can be lawfully imposed? Everett was argued on the basis that such restraints were not to be questioned and the only issue dealt with in that case was unfairness. *Rangis Begum*, above seems to go further. The Passport Office had got the standard of proof wrong and on the facts they should issue the passport. The question must be open to further argument in a future case.

[1] Identical provisions on the right to leave are contained in art 12(2) and (3) of the UN International Covenant on Civil and Political Rights 1966. Britain is a party to this but not to the optional protocol which gives individuals a right to complain to the Human Rights Committee. The Covenant may give a right of complaint but it has not been incorporated into UK municipal law and it is, therefore, thought unlikely that it could found a judicial review challenge on any refusal or withdrawal of a passport. For text see Brownlie and Goodwin-Gill, *Basic Documents on Human Rights* (4th edn, 2002) OUP.

[2] [1972] AC 60, [1970] 3 All ER 97; see also *R (on the application of Bancoult) v Secretary of State for Foreign and Commonwealth Affairs* [2008] UKHL 61, [2009] AC 453, per Lord Mance at paras 151, 152 and 154.

[3] See 2.9 above.

[4] See 2.10 above.

Chapter 3

CONTROL OF ENTRY AND STAY

INTRODUCTION

3.1 The following abbreviations are used in this chapter:

BIA	Borders and immigration Agency
CTA	Common Travel Area
ECGs	Entry Clearance Guidance available on www.ukvisas.gov.uk/en/ecg
ECO	Entry Clearance Officer
IAA 1999	Immigration and Asylum Act 1999
AA(ToC) 2004	Asylum and Immigration (Treatment of Claimants etc) Act 2004
IAN 2006	Immigration Asylum and Nationality Act 2006
IA 2014	Immigration Act 2014
IDI	Immigration Directory Instructions
NIAA	Nationality, Immigration and Asylum Act 2002
TFEU	Treaty on the Functioning of the European Union
TEC	Treaty establishing the European Community, now re-place by TFEU
TEU	Treaty on European Union now consolidated and re-numbered in part by the Treaty of Lisbon on 1 December 2009

In all past editions we have kept to the distinction between control on entry (Chapter 3) and control after entry (Chapter 4). When the 1971 Act came into force in 1973 there were four sets of immigration rules – rules on entry and rules after entry for Commonwealth citizens (HC 79 and 80) and the same for EEC and non-Commonwealth citizens (HC 81 and 82). In 1979 the rules were consolidated into one document but the sharp distinction between on entry and after entry control was maintained right up until the original version of HC 395 came into effect on 1 October 1994. Nowadays there is a considerable overlap between the rules on entry and those for after entry and we think that one chapter fits the bill better than two.

3.2 Section 4(1) of the Immigration Act 1971, as originally enacted made a clear distinction between leave to enter and leave to remain and made it clear that in general immigration officers were responsible for leave to enter and the Secretary of State's officials for leave to remain. However, these distinctions have become blurred, as immigration officers have taken on functions of varying leave at ports and the Secretary of State has taken responsibility for specified applications for leave to enter.

3.3 In *Oladahinde*[1] the House of Lords held that, although immigration officers held a distinct statutory office, they were still employees of the Home Office and the Secretary of State could, accordingly, devolve making decisions to deport to them. In the same way immigration officers may be asked to exercise the Secretary of State's power to vary someone's leave at the port on return to the UK, if that leave has not lapsed by the person's departure from the common travel area.[2] Later legislation further blurred the distinction. First, the Secretary of State now has the power to prescribe circumstances in which he or she may grant leave to enter.[3] Second, the Immigration (Leave to Enter) Order 2001[4] provides that the Secretary of State may give or refuse leave to enter to (and exercise other examination, detention and removal powers in respect of) a person who has made a claim for asylum, a person who has made a claim that it would be contrary to the UK's obligations under the ECHR for him to be removed, and a person who seeks leave to enter for a purpose not covered by the Immigration Rules.[5] Nevertheless, despite these changes, the basic rule remains that, once someone has entered the UK, the power to give leave to remain or to vary any leave is to be exercised by the Secretary of State.[6] It should also be noted that in Schedule 2, paragraph 2(3) it is made very clear that immigration officers should act in accordance with such instructions (not inconsistent with the immigration rules) as may be given them by the Secretary of State, when exercising their immigration functions.

[1] *Oladahinde v Secretary of State for the Home Department* [1991] 1 AC 254, [1990] 3 All ER 393, HL. For the latest on delegation, see *DPP v Haw* [2007] EWHC 1931 (Admin), [2007] NLJR 1198.

[2] HC 395, para 31A, inserted by HC 704. The Immigration (Leave to Enter and Remain) Order 2000, SI 2000/1161, art 13(6) allows the Secretary of State to vary leave while the person is abroad.

[3] Immigration Act 1971, s 3A(7), inserted by Immigration and Asylum Act 1999, s 1. SI 2000/1161, SI 2001/2590 (below) and SI 2004/475 were made under the powers conferred by the section. Section 3A enables the Secretary of State to give or refuse leave to enter where an immigration officer has begun but not completed an examination. The most obvious application of the order is in relation to asylum claimants, whose claims are not dealt with by immigration officers at the port but referred to the Home Office. The provision enables Home Office civil servants to take the immigration decision (grant or refusal of leave to enter) at the same time as granting or refusing asylum, instead of (as before) having to return the papers to the port for the immigration officer to issue the relevant decision. The order includes consequential provisions designed to deal with the '24-hour rule', for which see **3.89** below.

[4] SI 2001/2590.

[5] SI 2001/2590, arts 2 and 3.

[6] Immigration Act 1971, s 4(1). We discuss below the point at which someone who arrives in this country is treated as having entered: see **3.56**. This very clear distinction was thrown into confusion by the Divisional Court in *Singh v Hammond* [1987] 1 All ER 829, [1987] 1 WLR 283 – a case which has not been followed and was confined to its particular facts. The distinction was crucial in *R v Naillie* [1993] AC 674, HL.

3.4 The permissive system of immigration control which was represented by these two kinds of permission – leave to enter and leave to remain – stands in contrast to the rights-based system of European free movement law.[1] Under the domestic system of immigration control envisaged by the Immigration Act 1971 as originally enacted, rights belonged to those outside immigration control, through the right of abode or the common travel area, while the entry of those requiring leave was a matter of discretion. It is now settled law that this discretion derives from statute and not prerogative.[2]

[1] We deal with after-entry control of EEA nationals in CHAPTER 6 below.
[2] See *Munir and Alvi*, See further CHAPTER 1 at 1.33.

Part I COMMON FEATURES OF LEAVE

Residence permits

3.5 The European Union institutions not only make laws governing the free movement rights of EU citizens and their families; increasingly Community law sets common norms and standards governing the entry and stay of third country nationals and refugee claimants, through Directives, Regulations and Joint Actions. The UK Government opted in to the Residence Permit Scheme[1] in 2002, and began implementing the provisions in stages, from 13 November 2003. A residence permit is an authorisation issued by a Member State of the European Union allowing a non-EEA national to stay legally in its territory. The EC Council Regulation provides that all such authorisations should be in a uniform format.[2] From February 2004, all leave to remain in the UK for more than six months has been in the form of a residence permit. Furthermore the Home Office now requires everyone who wishes to stay in the UK for longer than six months, other than British nationals who do not have a right of abode in the UK, to obtain prior entry clearance, which will be in the same form as the residence permit, for the full period of the proposed stay. As regards leave to remain the UK has now adopted measures to make a Biometric Immigration Document ('BID') compulsory for certain categories of foreign nationals in accordance with further EU requirements contained in Council Regulation (EC) No 380/2008 on residence permits. We deal with BIDs below at **3.58**.

[1] Council Regulation (EC) No 1030/2002 of 13 June 2002 laying down a uniform format for residence permits for third country nationals, OJ L157, 15.6.02.
[2] The residence permit is a sticker containing security features, which goes into the holder's passport.

3.6 The use of residence permit vignettes instead of leave stamps coincided with the shift of the entry procedure from UK ports of entry to overseas posts in consulates, Embassies and High Commissions. From 13 November 2003, under Phase 1 of the Home Office scheme, 'specified nationals'[1] were required to have an entry clearance for the purpose for which they sought entry, if it was for longer than six months. Phase 2 came into force on 13 November 2005 by the rule changes in HC 645. It requires everyone who wishes to stay in the UK for longer than six months to obtain prior entry clearance, even if they are non-visa nationals. The category of 'specified nationals' has gone. Now all non-visa nationals who are seeking to come to the UK for more than six months have to seek prior entry clearance, which doubles up as a leave to enter[2] and must be able to present a valid passport endorsed with the appropriate entry clearance.[3] An exception is made for British Nationals (Overseas), British Overseas citizens, British Protected persons and British subjects under the British Nationality Act 1981.[4] Without an entry clearance, such British nationals who wish to stay longer than six months will be given six months' leave, provided that they are not seeking entry for a purpose for which entry clearance is needed irrespective of whether the person is a non-visa national.[5] They will then need to apply for a UK residence permit before the end of that period. At the time of these changes a new rule was introduced in November 2005 which provides that Immigration officers cannot grant leave to enter for more than six months at the port.[6] Residence permit vignettes should not be confused with the various residence documents issued to EEA and Swiss nationals under the Immigration (EEA) Regulations SI 2006/1003, as amended.

[1]   Ie, nationals of Australia, Canada, Hong Kong, Japan, Malaysia, New Zealand, Singapore, South Africa, South Korea and USA seeking to enter the UK as students or work permit holders for six months or more. See now deleted rules at HC 395, para 6, as amended by HC 1224 and the List of countries contained in a now deleted Appendix 3.
[2]   HC 395, para 25A, inserted by HC 704 (28.7.00).
[3]   HC 395, para 24(ii), as substituted by HC 645 (9.11.05).
[4]   Ibid.
[5]   HC 395, para 23B, inserted by HC 645 (9.11.05).
[6]   HC 395, para 23A, inserted by HC 645 (9.11.05).

Biometric Documents and information

3.7 The Immigration (Biometric Registration) Regulations 2008, made under ss 5 and 6 of the UK Borders Act 2007,[1] and now supplemented by five further Regulations,[2] inaugurated the start of compulsory ID cards for non EEA or Swiss nationals (referred to for brevity as foreign nationals). The documents are referred to interchangeably as biometric immigration documents (BID) or biometric registration documents (BRD). They take the form of a credit card with a chip containing biometric data. Originally the Regulations only applied to limited groups, starting with spouses and partners and students, when they applied for leave to remain.[3] Now they apply to those seeking entry clearance and to such groups as refugees.[4] Section 5(7) of the 2007 Act provides that Regulations may not require a person to carry a biometric immigration document at all times.

[1]   See ss 5 and 6 of the UK Borders Act 2007, as amended. The original name was a biometric immigration document ('BID'). The creation of BIDs enabled the UK to comply with Regulation 380/2008 which requires residence permits to be issued in a uniform format in the form of a card that contains an embedded chip that stores biometric features of the holder, although that Regulation applied to the Schengen group of countries and was not binding on the UK (HoC WA 10.7.08 col 1770W), See further Council Regulation (EC) No 2252/2004.
[2]   See Immigration (Biometric Registration) Regulations 2008, SI 2008/3048; Immigration (Biometric Registration) (Amendment) Regulations 2009, SI 2009/819; and Immigration (Biometric Registration) (Amendment No 2) Regulations 2009, SI 2009/3321; Immigration (Biometric Registration) (Amendment) Regulations 2010, SI 2010/2958 [which covered Tier 1 (General) Migrant; Tier 1 (Entrepreneur) Migrant; Tier 1 (Investor) Migrant; Tier 1 (Post-Study Work) Migrant; and a Tier 5 (Temporary Worker) Migrant] and Immigration (Biometric Registration) (Amendment) Regulations 2012, SI 2012/594.

[3]   SI 2009/819 added eight new categories: (i) students under PBS Tier 4, applying to extend their leave to study in the UK; (ii) an academic visitor who is applying to extend his leave so that his total stay in the UK is more than six months, up to a total period of 12 months; (iii) a visitor for private medical treatment, needing an extension to complete his or her medical treatment; (iv) a domestic worker in a private household applying to extend his or her employment leave; (v) Commonwealth citizens, who have a British grandparent, and can demonstrate their United Kingdom ancestry; (vi) a retired person of independent means and his or her dependants; (vii) a sole representative of an overseas company; and (viii) a person in the UK who applies to replace his/her passport which contains a stamp, sticker or other attachment showing a limited leave to enter or remain. SI 2009/3321 amended the sole representative category to representatives of overseas businesses in line with immigration rule changes Cm 7701 in October 2009.

[4]   Immigration (Biometric Registration) (Amendment) Regulations 2012, SI 2012/594.

3.8 The Immigration (Biometric Registration) (Amendment) Regulations 2012, SI 2012/594 have extended the need for migrants to the UK to have a BRD. For the first time those seeking recognition as refugees or stateless persons and those needing humanitarian protection are included.[1] An application must be made on the form or in the manner specified for that purpose (if one is specified) in the immigration rules.[2] A completely new Regulation 3 deals with those already in the UK. It applies to those who make an application;

(a)   for limited leave to remain for a period which, together with any preceding period of leave to enter or remain, exceeds a cumulative total of 6 months leave in the United Kingdom;

(b)   for indefinite leave to remain;

(c)   to replace a stamp, sticker or other attachment in a passport or other document which indicated that he had been granted limited or indefinite leave to enter or remain in the United Kingdom;

(d)   to replace a letter which indicated that he had been granted limited or indefinite leave to enter or remain in the United Kingdom;

(e)   to be recognised as a refugee or a person in need of humanitarian protection;

(f)   to be recognised as a stateless person in accordance with Article 1 of the Stateless Convention;

(g)   for a Convention Travel Document, Stateless Person's Travel Document or a Certificate of Travel and does not already hold a valid biometric immigration document; or

(h)   as the dependant of a person who is making an application in accordance with sub-paragraph (a), (b), (e) or (f)

In addition, under the substituted regulation 3(3) a person who has been notified on or after 1st December 2012 that the Secretary of State has decided to grant him or her leave to remain, which taken with the previous leave will exceed 6 months, and was not required to apply for a biometric immigration document in respect of that leave, will be required to apply for a BRD.

[1]   Immigration (Biometric Registration) (Amendment) Regulations 2012, SI 2012/594, Reg 3(5).
[2]   In addition to the Reg 3 requirements, above, refugee seekers etc are required to use their BRD when making their above applications: Reg 21(1)(da), as amended by SI 2012/594.

3.9 As regards those persons who are making an application outside the UK, the need to have and use a biometric immigration document is now extended to those who make an application for entry clearance.[1] This applies not just to the main applicant but also to his or her dependants.[2]

¹ Inserted by Immigration (Biometric Registration) (Amendment) Regulations 2012, SI 2012/594 Reg 21(1)(d).
² Ibid reg 21(1)(db).

3.10 Those who apply will be photographed and fingerprinted,[1] unless they are an unaccompanied child under the age of 16.[2] Under reg 9 the government can use this biometric information for seven specified government functions including the prevention, investigation or prosecution of crime, but the photographs and fingerprints must be destroyed or made inaccessible if the person turns out to be a British[3] citizen or Commonwealth citizen with a right of abode under s 2(1)(b) of the Immigration Act 1971. At the end of the application process the successful applicant will be issued with a biometric immigration document (BID), which can contain up to 19 separate pieces of personal information.[4] Once issued with the new ID card, applicants may be asked to surrender other immigration or nationality documents in their possession.[5] The Regulations also contain powers to require the surrender of an ID card, or to order its cancellation and impose obligations on the holder to give notice to the Secretary of State that certain things have happened and to apply for a replacement document in certain circumstances.[6]

¹ SI 2008/3048, regs 5 and 8.
² SI 2008/3048, reg 7.
³ SI 2008/3048, regs 11 and 12.
⁴ SI 2008/3048, regs 13 and 15.
⁵ SI 2008/3048, reg 14.
⁶ SI 2008/3048, regs 16–20.

3.11 Non-compliance with the requirement to apply for an ID card can be met with immigration sanctions or a civil penalty. Under the Regulations there are a number of immigration sanctions. These include refusing to issue a biometric immigration document, refusing or rejecting an immigration application, cancelling or varying (by curtailment) existing leave. Then there are the civil penalties. Sections 9(1) of the UK Borders Act 2007 enables the Secretary of State to impose a civil penalty regime where a person fails to comply with a requirement of the Regulations. A Code of Practice about the sanctions for non-compliance with the biometric registration regulations has also come into force.[1] It establishes the circumstances when the Secretary of State may impose a civil penalty, and the amount of any civil penalty notice issued. It also sets out when an immigration sanction will be imposed rather than a civil penalty.

¹ The Immigration (Biometric Registration) (Civil Penalty Code of Practice) Order 2008, SI 2008/3049.

3.12 Closely connected to biometric documents are two earlier statutory provisions making it compulsory for for applicants for leave to supply specified information about their external physical characteristics and to give their fingerprints – sections 141–144 of the IAA 1999, as amended (fingerprints and external physical characteristics, including details of the iris and other parts of the eye) and section 126 of NIAA 2002 (external physical characteristics). Section 126 permits the Secretary of State to make Regulations requiring specified physical information to be provided by applicants for entry clearance, leave to enter or remain and variations of such leave in circumstances set out in the section.[1]

[1]   Section 126 (2)(a)-(c) The current Regulations are Immigration (Provision of Physical Data) Regulations 2006, SI, 2006/1743.

3.13 The IA 2014 amends section 126(2) of the 2002 Act to include applications by foreign nationals for Direct Airside Transit Visas (DATVs) and application for a residence or other document evidencing the right of non EEA nationals to enter and reside in the UK.[1] Subsection 4(fa) of section 126 provides for biometric information[2] submitted as part of an application to be recorded on any document issued as a consequence of that application and a document is given the same broad interpretation as in section 15 (1)(d) of the 2007 Act to include a card or sticker or any electronic method of recording.[3] Section 12 of the IA 2014 amends section 15 of the 2007 Act to define biometric information for the purposes of that provision as information about a person's external physical characteristics, such as fingerprints and features of a person's eye.[4] Where the meaning of biometric information is to encompass information beyond those features, the Secretary of State is to specify the physical characteristics in an order. However, they may only be features which can be obtained and recorded by an external examination of the person and cannot include information about a person's DNA. The order is subject to the affirmative resolution procedure. Where a person has failed to comply with a requirement of regulations made under section 5 of the 2007 Act to have a biometric immigration document to be used in connection with an application or claim. New subsection 7(2A) of the 2007 Act enables the Secretary of State to require an application or claim to be disregarded or refused.[5]

[1]   Section 126(2)(d) and (e), inserted by IA 2014, s 8(2).
[2]   Inserted by IA 2014, s 8(3).
[3]   Inserted by IA 2014, s 8(4).
[4]   This definition is extended by para 12(4) to Sch 2 of the IA 2014, which makes corresponding amendments to other enactments providing for powers to require the provision of biometric information.
[5]   Inserted by s 11 of the IA 2014.

3.14 Section 13 of the IA 2014 has extended safeguards for children during examinations under the Immigration Act 1971, Schedule 2, Paragraph 4 and when being detained under paragraph 18 by immigration officials. It amends paragraphs 4 and 18 of Schedule 2 to ensure that persons aged under 16 are not required to provide biometric information under that Schedule, unless the requirement is authorised by a chief immigration officer, and the information is provided in the presence of an adult who is a parent or guardian or someone who takes responsibility for the child at the time.

3.15 Section 14 deals with the use and retention of biometric information by the introduction of amended powers to retain. There is a new section 8 of the 2007 Act. It requires the Secretary of State to make provision about the use and retention of biometric information provided pursuant to regulations made under section 5 of the 2007 Act. They may provide that biometric information 'may be retained' only if it is necessary to retain it for use in connection with the exercise of functions in relation to immigration or nationality,[1] But the regulations may include provision permitting the use of retained biometric information for non-immigration purposes, such as the prevention of crime and disorder or the protection of national security,[2] and they may also be retained in accordance with another power.[3] The regulations must include provision about the destruction of biometric information and must require the Secretary of State to take all reasonable steps to ensure that information is destroyed if its retention is no longer necessary for an immigration or nationality purpose and in all cases where the Secretary of State is satisfied that a person is a British citizen or a Commonwealth citizen with the right of abode.[4]. The requirement to destroy biometric information extends to copies, whether held electronically or otherwise.[5] Where destruction is carried out the applicant is entitled to a certificate to that effect.[6]

[1] Section 8(2) of the UK Borders Act 2007, as inserted by IA 2014, s 14.
[2] Section 8(3) of the UK Borders Act 2007, as inserted by IA 2014, s 14.
[3] Section 8(7) of the UK Borders Act 2007, as inserted by IA 2014, s 14.
[4] Section 8(5) of the UK Borders Act 2007, as inserted by IA 2014, s 14.
[5] Section 8(6) of the UK Borders Act 2007, as inserted by IA 2014, s 14.
[6] Section 8 (8)) of the UK Borders Act 2007, as inserted by IA 2014, s 14.

3.16 Section 10 of the IA 2014 amends section 41 of the 1981 British Nationality Act to require an application for registration or naturalisation as a British citizen to be accompanied by biometric information to be set out in regulations. The amendments to section 41 of the 1981 Act, are made so so that the references to 'authorised person' and 'biometric information' have the same definitions as those contained in section 126 of the 2002 Act. It also provides that the safeguards in relation to taking biometric information from children under the age of 16, which are set out in the IAA1999, apply equally to regulations made under the 1981 Act. It also provides a limited exception to the requirement, contained in section 8(5)(b) of the 2007 Act, that biometric information be destroyed as soon as reasonably practicable once a person becomes a British citizen to enable photographs submitted as part of a citizenship application to be retained until that person is issued with their first British passport.

On line applications

3.17 Paragraphs A34 to 34G of the Immigration Rules lay down the procedure for making a valid application in relation to immigration. Applications can be made by post or in person by making an appointment at a Public Enquiry Office. From 13 February 2012, an online application was permitted for applicants seeking leave to remain as a Tier 2 or Tier 5 Migrant or their family members.[1] HC 760 amended paragraph A34 to remove the requirement that online applications are confined to Tier I and 5 applicants. This is a technical change to allow online applications to be made under other provisions of the Immigration Rules, where this service is in future offered by the UK Border Agency. The availability of an online service does not prevent an application which can be made online to be made by post, although appointments with the Public enquiry office must be made via the online process.[2] Since then on-line applications have almost become *de rigeur* for visa applications[3] as well as extensions of leave in the UK, but applicants and their advisers will need to check that the service is operating. Applicants can apply online for a UK visa to visit, work, study or join a family member or partner (eg spouse) already in the UK.

1 HC 1733, para 1, inserting new para A34.
2 HC 760, explanatory Memorandum, para 7.62 to 7.63.
3 Anyone coming to the UK from abroad to visit, work, study or to join a family member or partner must apply online. In countries, where online application cannot be made, a whole set of VAF forms must be used: see www.gov.uk/government/collections/uk-visa-forms#forms-fo r-a-visa-to-come-to-the-uk.

3.18 An applicant may submit an application online where this option is available on the visas and immigration pages of the gov.uk website. Under HC359 paragraph 34 an application for leave to remain in the United Kingdom under these Rules must be made either by completing the relevant online application process[1] in accordance with paragraph A34(iii) or by using the specified[2] application form in accordance with paragraphs 34A to 34D. The online applicant must also pay any specified fee and provide biometric information, if the online application process requires it.[3] Online applicants may also be required to attend a Home Office public enquiry office within 45 working days of submission of their online application, and be ready to comply with any specified requirements in relation to the provision of biometric information and documents specified as mandatory.[4] A failure to comply with all the requirements of paragraph 34(iii) will mean that the online application will be invalid and will not be considered.[5]

1 'The relevant online application process' means the application process accessible via the visas and immigration pages of the gov.uk website and identified there as relevant for applications for leave to remain in the immigration category under which the applicant wishes to apply.
2 'Specified' in relation to the relevant online application process means specified in the online guidance accompanying that process.
3 HC 395, para 34(iii)(b) and (c)
4 HC 395, para 34(iii)(d).
5 HC 395, para 34(iv).

Compulsory application forms

3.19 Compulsory application forms for immigration applications made in the UK were first introduced in 1996. They were prescribed under the Immigration Rules in operation at that time – para 32 of HC 395 as amended by para 2 of HC 329. This continued until August 2003, when application forms and procedures were prescribed by Regulations made under section 31A of the Immigration Act 1971.[1]

1 These were Immigration (Leave to Remain) (Prescribed Forms and Procedures) Regulations 2003, SI 2003/1712, which came into force on 1 August 2003, amended in 2004 by SI 2004/581 as from 1 April 2004, further amended by SI 2004/ as from 25 October 2004, and then then revoked in 2005 and replaced by SI 2005/771, which came into force on 1 April 2005, and which was revoked and replaced from 15 September 2005 by SI 2005/2385. These in turn were revoked and replaced by SI 2006/1421 which came into force on 22 June 2006, which was twice amended in 2006 by 2006 SI/1548 and /2899, before being revoked and replaced in turn by SI 2007/882 which came into force on 2 April 2007. These provisions may still be relevant in advising and determining long residence claims.

3.20 The Immigration, Asylum and Nationality Act 2006 (IAN 2006) changed all this. Section 50(1) gave the Secretary of State powers to use the immigration rules to specify compulsory application forms. He or she could now make immigration rules requiring a specified procedure to be followed when making an application or claim in connection with immigration. The rules can require specified forms to be used, specified information and documents to be provided, and they can direct the manner in which a fee is to be paid as well as providing for the consequences of non-compliance. On 29 February 2008, section 50(3)(a) of the IAN 2006 swept away the old powers under section 31A of the Immigration Act 1971 and the Immigration (Leave to Remain) (Prescribed Forms and Procedures) Regulations 2007 ceased to have effect. Section 50(2) of the 2006 Act allows new or revised application forms to be specified administratively. There is no longer any need for Regulations. Initially specified forms were only been compulsory for applications for leave to remain in the United Kingdom. The 2008 changes meant that forms could be specified for immigration applications over the whole range of applications and claims, including those made overseas (Explanatory Statement to HC 321, para 7.31).

3.21 The application must be made either by completing the relevant online application process if available, in accordance with HC 395 paragraph A34(iii) or by using the specified application form in accordance with paragraphs 34A to 34D. Applications for visas overseas are now also covered in the rules. The UK 'visa forms' part of the Home Office website states that anyone coming to the UK from abroad to visit, work, study or to join a family member or partner must apply online, which means using an online application process specified in the online guidance accompanying that process. In countries, where online application cannot be made, a whole set of VAF forms must be used.[1] So, as with the BRD system, compulsion is imposed in a more indirect way overseas than it is for applications made in the UK. It is to be found in the online Guidance accompanying the relevant online process. Except in countries without proper online facilities, an online application is 'specified' and becomes compulsory. The application must be made in accordance with the requirements of paragraph A34(iii). Otherwise the application is invalid. In applications made in-country in the UK, an application is 'specified' if the provisions of pargraph 34 are satisfied and invalidity comes from a failure to comply with the much more detailed requirements of paragraph 34A: see para 3.

[1]   See   www.gov.uk/government/collections/uk-visa-forms#forms-for-a-visa-to-come-to-the-uk For example, if the main reason a person is applying to come to the UK is as a tourist or to visit friends he or she must complete VAF1A; a family visitor must complete VAF1B; a business visitor/prospective entrepreneur must complete VAF1C; a student visitor, must complete VAF1D; an academic visitor must complete VAF1E; to get married or register for marriage/civil partnership, a person must complete VAF1F; a visitor in transit must complete VAF1H; a sports visitor must complete VAF1J; and an entertainment visitor must complete VAF1K. If the visit to the UK is for any other reason, the applicant for a visa must complete VAF1A.

3.22 HC 395, paras 34–34F provide for the compulsory use of specified forms to make applications for leave to remain and for indefinite leave and prescribe the procedures for making applications by post, in person, by courier and online. They provide for the procedure which is to apply where an applicant wishes to vary the application. They set out the rules for determining the date when an application is made and provide that if a request is made for the return of a passport for travel outside the common travel area, the application will be treated as withdrawn, unless the person is a Tier 2 migrant or a Tier

5 migrant who is supported by a Certificate of Sponsorship by a Premium Sponsor.[1] When new forms are prescribed (which happens with bewildering frequency) there are transitional provisions for applications or claims made with the old and, therefore, wrong form. Applicants have a 21 day window during which the use the old form is overlooked.[2] If a form is not specified, UK Visas cannot consider an application as invalid under the immigration rules, as the provisions of paragraph 34A do not apply.[3] However if a specified fee is not paid in full it may still be invalid under the relevant fees regulations.[4] An example of an application type that does not have a specified form is the application to confirm rights of residence under European law.

[1]   HC 395 para 34J and 34K.
[2]   HC 395, para 34I
[3]   Modern Guidance leave to remain and specified forms, Specified forms and procedures p50.
[4]   See The Immigration and Nationality (Fees) Regulations 2014, SI 2014/922, reg 11, discussed at 3.36, below.

3.23 The application must be completed as required, and signed by the applicant, or, in the case of a minor, by the parent or legal guardian, and must be accompanied by the documents and photographs specified in the form.[1] Online applications require completion of the confirmation box by the applicant or the applicant's adviser and the forms direct the manner in which mandatory photographs and documents are to be sent.[2] Since November 2008 an applicant has been able to submit an application online where this option is available on the UKBA's (now UK Visas) website, and since October 2010 it has been compulsory for an application for a Tier 2, Tier 4 or Tier 5 (Temporary Worker) sponsorship licence to be made online, and it cannot be sent by pre-paid post.[3]

[1]   Immigration (Leave to Remain) (Prescribed Forms and Procedures) Regulations 2007, 2007/882, reg 16. Now HC 395, para 34A(vi).
[2]   HC 395, para 34A (vii).
[3]   HC 395, para 34B(iv), inserted by Cm 7944.

3.24 The formal requirements for successful completion of an application form are now contained in HC 395, para 34A. Paragraph 34C makes it quite clear that an application or claim which does not comply with the require-ments of para 34A is invalid and will not be considered. This is a more rigid stance than earlier regulations would suggest.[1] There are transitional arrange-ments for applications made before 29 February 2008 and these may still be relevant, for example, when tracing continuity of residence under the long stay rules.[2] Currently there is some leeway where a new form is introduced and the applicant uses the old form.[3] But there is no allowance made for formal non-compliance. This is a very good reason for making an application well before the expiry date of a leave giving the applicant a second chance to put things right before it is too late. The alternative is litigation. The Immigration Rules make it clear that there will be no consideration of the application and so no decision and no appeal. Some early decisions under the old law suggest the thrust of such challenges. In *Derouiche*,[4] the Tribunal found that the wording of the form FLR(S) was misleading and imprecise and that, since it had to be used by applicants who may not speak or understand English, rejection of an application for a minor non-compliance was unfair and unjust. In *Ravichandran and Jeyeanthan*[5] the Court of Appeal indicated that whether an application or notice of refusal was invalid because of a failure to comply with statutory requirements about its content was a much more nuanced question than much of the case law suggested, and that in each case the court or tribunal should concentrate on what the rules intended should be the just consequence of non-compliance. The first question is whether there has been substantial compliance with the procedural requirements, even if there has not been strict compliance. The second is whether the non-compliance is capable of being waived, and if so, whether it has been. That will not arise in this situation, which is predicated on the Secretary of State's refusal to waive the non-compliance. The third is what are the consequences of non-compliance.[6]

1   If the application is rejected, it will be considered a valid application at the date of its original submission provided any defects have been promptly remedied. This was the effect of SI 2007/882, reg 17.
2   See HC 395 paras 276A–276d.
3   HC 395, para 34I.
4   *Derouiche v Secretary of State for the Home Department* [1998] INLR 286.
5   *R v Immigration Appeal Tribunal, ex p Jeyeanthan*; *Ravichandran v Secretary of State for the Home Department* [2000] Imm AR 10, [2000] INLR 241, at 247. See **20.59** below.
6   *Ravichandran* above, per Woolf MR at 17.

3.25 In more recent decisions the court has shown a willingness in a suitable case to contrast formal procedural compliance with substantial compliance with the requirements for leave to enter or remain, In *R (on the application of Kanwal) v Secretary of State for the Home Department*[1], the need for formal compliance triumphed. An application for leave to remain, made in time but using an old application form, was held to be invalid and was not rectified by the later submission of the correct form. The correct form having been submitted after the leave expired, the application for leave to remain was properly treated by the Home Office as out of time. In *R (on the application of Forrester) v Secretary of State for the Home Department*[2], A, lawfully in the country, married a man settled in the UK for some 38 years. She sent in her prescribed form accompanied by a cheque. The cheque bounced and the Home Office rejected her application because the proper fee had not been paid. A submitted a fresh application but this was out of time and the Home Office refused her extension of leave and threatened her with criminal penalties for overstaying if she failed to up sticks and leave the country. The issue was whether form triumphed over substance. Sullivan J was quite clear about where the court stood.

'The defendant is given a discretion, and she is given a discretion on the basis that it will be exercised with a modicum of intelligence, common sense and humanity. It might be asked, in these circumstances, what possible reason there could have been for not exercising the discretion in this claimant's favour' [para 7].

'One would have thought that anyone standing back and looking at this case would have concluded that such a decision was manifestly disproportionate and unreasonable' [para 9].

'It is one thing to say that one should have a fair and firm immigration policy, it is quite another to say that one should have an immigration policy which is utterly inflexible and rigid and pays not the slightest regard to the particular circumstances of the individual case' [para 13].

1   [2007] EWHC 2803 (Admin).

[2] [2008] EWHC 2307 (Admin).

Fees

3.26 This section sets out the power to set fees and the basis on which they are made. We have moved 'Fees' from Chapter 1 (last edition) to this chapter, because fees are part of the basic machinery of control and because the payment of the fees up front is essential to validate an application for entry clearance[1] or leave to enter or remain. We have included nationality fee powers as well, because they dovetail so much with immigration fees, but we will not be referring to various current charges made under different Regulations or Orders in Council, as the case may be, simply because they are subject to rapid change and are easily available on-line and with application forms. The practice now is that the Fees Regulations are updated and revised every year. Because of this we do not, as a rule, refer to actual fees for particular applications.

[1]   In the case of entry clearance this proposition depends on the continuing validity of HC 395, para 30, which links the validity of an entry clearance application to paying fees under the Consular Fees Act 1980, something which may no longer happen. See **3.29** below.

3.27 Fees for applications, work permits, certificates and passports now feature as an important element in immigration control, particularly as the amount charged has increased spectacularly beyond the rate of inflation. The policy behind this is to try to recoup as far as possible the full cost of administration and enforcement. The government's original stated aim was to deliver a self-financing managed migration programme by 2008, where possible, to reduce reliance on the public purse and to generate income to support the ongoing modernisation of immigration services: The Explanatory Memorandum to the Immigration (Application Fees) Order 2005, 2005/582 at para 7.1. On 9 September 2010 the Minister of State announced a further increase in immigration fees to take effect on 1 October 2010, as a measure needed to reduce the budget deficit. These included more than doubling the fees for dependants and further increases to nationality fees which then exceeded the unit cost of processing applications by up to 437%. There is now little constraint on who can be charged and how much. In its September 2009 Charging Consultation document, UKBA refers to nationality and citizenship fees being set above the cost of delivery to reflect the 'value of the product', a phrase which makes clear the Agency's view of citizenship as a commodity available to those who can afford it. The charging of all fees is regulated by statute and subordinate legislation. Fees must be set in accordance with these measures.[1]

[1]   The key statutory powers which we refer to in more detail below are; s 1 of the Consular Fees Act 1980; s 42 of the Asylum and Immigration (Treatment of Claimants, etc) Act 2004, as amended, by the UK Borders Act 2007; ss 51 and 52 of IAN 2006 and Immigration Act 2014.

3.28 Section 5 of IAA 1999 gave the Secretary of State the power to charge fees for applications for leave to remain and variation of leave, subject to Treasury consent. Fees were set in accordance with the Finance (No 2) Act 1987. Under section 102, which is still operating, government bodies are given a power to specify functions and matters which can be taken into account when exercising their power to fix a fee or charge. In relation to immigration and nationality, this power was extended by section 42 of the Asylum and Immigration (Treatment of Claimants, etc) Act 2004 (2004 Act) to enable fees to be set at a level exceeding the administrative costs, and reflecting the benefits deemed likely to accrue to successful applicants. As regards overseas applications a different regime operated. An Order in Council under the Consular Fees Act 1980 could prescribe fees. As originally enacted the 2004 Act enabled the Secretary of State to prescribe fees, with the consent of the Treasury, for:

(a)   applications in relation to Nationality under section 41(2) of the British Nationality Act 1981;

(b)   applications for leave to remain and variation of leave under section 5 of the IAA 1999; and

(c)   certificates of entitlement, work permits etc under sections 10 and 122 of the NIAA 2002.

They could prescribe an amount which:

(a)   exceeded the administrative costs of determining the application or undertaking the process; and

(b)   reflected the benefits likely to accrue to the applicant who was successful in his or her application.[1]

The amount of consular fees could be calculated in much the same way.[2]

---

[1]   Asylum and Immigration (Treatment of Claimants, etc) Act 2004, s 42(1).
[2]   Asylum and Immigration (Treatment of Claimants, etc) Act 2004, s 42 (3).

3.29 Section 5 was then replaced by sections 51 and 52 of the IAN 2006, which attempted to consolidate the fee fixing power for a wide range of immigration and nationality services performed both in the UK and outside it. Section 51(1) provides that the Secretary of State may by order require an application or claim in connection with immigration or nationality (whether or not under an enactment) to be accompanied by a specified fee. Section 51 also gives the Secretary of State the power to make orders which may confer a discretion to reduce, waive or refund all or part of a fee and make provisions as regards the consequences of a failure to pay a fee.[1] Once an order is made specifying that a particular fee may be charged, section 51(3) the provides for regulations to be made specifying the amount of the fee. At the same time IAN 2006 amended section 42 of the Asylum and Immigration (Treatment of Claimants, etc) Act 2004 linking its provisions on the range of specified immigration and nationality applications and processes in the UK to section 51. Section 52 allows fees to be imposed under the powers in section 51 in relation to a thing whether it was done wholly or partly outside the UK.[2] At this stage both consular and domestic fees could be fixed by a section 51 Order and in both cases fees could be set to exceed the administrative costs and to reflect the benefits deemed likely to accrue to successful applicants. This meant that the cost of a visa or settlement application for an adult dependant had leapt almost 300% by April 2010.[3]

---

[1]   IAN 2006, s 51(3), which came into force on 31 January 2007 (by virtue of SI 2007/182).
[2]   These new powers were enacted without prejudice to section 1 of the Consular Fees Act 1980 or any other power to charge a fee, including section 102 of the Finance (No 2) Act 1987, with a saving power for Orders made under that section in respect of a power repealed by IAN 2006, Sch 2.

³ The then Immigration Minister, Phil Woolas, confirmed the fee was way above the administrative costs of dealing with the application. Damian Green MP (later a Conservative Immigration Minister) said during the debate: ' . . . a threefold increase, which seems to suggest that the visa cost is meant to be a deterrent'. A more recent statement put the taxpayer at the forefront. In the Explanatory Memorandum to the 2011 Fees Order, SI 2011/445 at para 7.2: 'The existing fees regime is based on the principle that those who benefit from the border and immigration system should bear a higher share of the cost of running the system. A number of new fees are being introduced to ensure that the contribution the UK tax payer is asked to make continues to fall.'

3.30 So far as Orders and Regulations are concerned, the statutory regime is quite clear. There are two important features:

(i) Section 51(1) and (2) of the 2006 Act stipulate that regulations under section 51(3) may only set charges if an Order specifying the applications, services and processes that may be charged for is made beforehand. This Order is made in order to allow new fees to be introduced. In other words regulations under section 51(3) may only set charges if an Order specifying the applications, services and processes that may be charged for is made beforehand. So you need an Order followed by regulations. This system is carried over into the changes proposed by the IA 2014.

(ii) When it comes to Regulations, there are nearly always two distinct sets: Immigration and Nationality (Fees) Regulations and Immigration and Nationality (Cost Recovery Fees) Regulations. Why two sets? It all goes back to section 42(7) of the Asylum and Immigration (Treatment of Claimants, etc) Act 2004. Once the Order has been made fees may be set:

   (a) at or below the administrative cost of making the application (in which case the regulations setting the fees are subject to the negative resolution procedure);

   (b) at an amount above the administrative cost of making the application (in which case the regulations setting the fees are subject to the affirmative resolution procedure¹); or

   (c) can contain an element of cross subsidisation of other applications which are charged below the administrative cost (in which case the regulations setting the fees are again subject to the affirmative resolution procedure²).

The upshot is that the Cost Recovery Fees Regulations can only cover fees being set at or below the administrative cost (para(a) above) and the Fees Regulations deal with those referred to at paras (b) and (c). This will now change when section 68 of the Immigration Act 2014 comes into effect. Section 74 sets out the parliamentary procedure in respect of various order- and regulation-making powers provided for in the Act. It provides that a fees order within the meaning of section 68 has to be approved by a resolution of each House (section 74(2)(j)), but that a statutory instrument containing any other order or regulation than those mentioned in s 74(2) made by the Secretary of State under the Act is subject to a negative resolution in either House. So in future we need only expect one Order and one set of Regulations.

¹ Section 42(1) and (7) of the Asylum and Immigration (Treatment of Claimants, etc) Act 2004.
² Section 42(2A) and (7) of the Asylum and Immigration (Treatment of Claimants, etc) Act 2004.

3.31 While the Consular Fees Act 1980 remains in force, it is now largely obsolete in relation to immigration and nationality fees. When the UKBA was formed following an announcement by the Prime Minister on 25 July 2007 and a Cabinet Office Report,[1] UK Visas, then under FCO departmental control, was merged with the then-newly created Border and Immigration Agency, and the port of entry functions of Revenue and Customs (HMRC). The upshot was that UKBA's International Group, under the aegis of the Home Office, now carried out the UK visa functions previously carried out by UK Visas. As a logical consequence, entry clearance functions for which consular fees were formerly charged now fell within remit of the Home Office rather than the FCO and there was no longer any need to have two different fee structures running in parallel.

[1] 'Security in a Global Hub: Establishing the UK's new border arrangements' 14 November 2007 (available at www.cabinetoffice.gov.uk/media/cabinetoffice/corp/assets/publications/rep orts/border_review.pdf).

3.32 The first big change came in 2011 with the coming into force of the Immigration and Nationality (Fees) Order 2011.[1] This Order did three main things. First it replaced the Immigration and Nationality (Fees) Order 2007, the main enabling power allowing the Secretary of State to make regulations under section 51(3) of the IAN 2006 to fix fees and charges in relation to applications, services and processes connected with immigration and nationality. The 2011 Order incorporated the provisions of the replaced 2007 Order in order to produce a consolidated fees Order going back to 15 March 2007. Second, the Order allowed fees regulations to specify new types of charge and this process has been continued in successive amendments to the Order in 2013 and 2014.[2] Thirdly, this Order allowed the regulations implementing the new fees to set fees for consular services relating to immigration and nationality – fees were then dealt with in the Consular Fees Order 2010, made under section 1 of the Consular Fees Act 1980. The UKBA (as it then was) were being given the power in this Order to move fees relating to immigration and nationality matters from the Consular Fees Order 2010 into Regulations made under section 51(3) of the 2006 Act.

[1] SI 2011/445.
[2] Immigration and Nationality (Fees) (Amendment) Order 2013, SI 2013/249; Immigration and Nationality (Fees) (Amendment) Order 2014, SI 2014/205. Recent regulations have included Immigration and Nationality (Fees) Regulations 2013, SI 2013/749, Immigration and Nationality (Fees) (Amendment) Regulations 2013, SI 2013/249; Immigration and Nationality (Cost Recovery Fees) Regulations 2013, SI 2013/617; Immigration and Nationality (Fees) Regulations 2014, SI 2014/922 and Immigration and Nationality (Cost Recovery Fees) Regulations 2014, SI 2014/581.

3.33 The Fees Amendment Order 2013 was the first amendment of the 2011 Order. It was all about developing optional premium services.[1] The government wanted to move from the situation where an applicant would either pay the standard application fee, making their application by post or online or alternatively pay a higher application fee and make an application in person. The idea put forward was to simplify the charging structure and widen te scope to develop and offer new optional services in the future, by having a single application fee 'for each product', with an option to pay a separate premium fee if the applicant wished to use an alternative application method. The proposed changes would also apply to sponsors under the PBS, giving those with Premium Sponsor Status the range of optional premium services. In view of these high sounding proposals, the resulting Fees Regulations were a bit flat except for some of the more flamboyant increase for optional premium sponsorship status for Tier 2 and 5 sponsors with £25,000 for the big sponsors and £8,000 for the small fry. This compares with the ordinary fee of £1,500 for those who take their place in the queue. The Cost Recovery Fees Regulations 2013 where more modest fees predominated and rises were limited to 3%.

[1]   See Explanatory Memorandum to SI/249, paras 7.3-7.5.

3.34 The Fees Amendment Order 2014 widens the scope for premium services. The new powers will mean that the Home Office will have the flexibility to offer and charge for providing an optional premium service for any application type where it is able to offer the service. Also, the Home Office may choose to offer this service at an alternative location other than at the old Public Enquiry Offices (PEOs), now more aptly renamed as Premium Service Centres. Instead the premium service applicant can meet the immigration official at an alternative location such as business premises or a University campus. In addition to these changes the government hopes the regulations will be able to garner in more money in fees. Other changes are:

- setting optional charges for services and processes provided by 'commercial partners' to support visa applications;
- charging for 'optional premium added-value services' provided by UK Border Force, such as the Registered Traveller scheme;
- extending existing processes for reviewing refusal decisions by making charges for conducting reviews of refused applications where the right of appeal has been taken away from the applicant by the IA 2014. To fill the gap, the Home Office say: 'We want to be able to charge for conducting this review.'
- enable charging for residence and registration documentation issued to European Economic Area (EEA) nationals, their non EEA family members and other non EEA nationals with a derivative right of residence in the UK under the 2006 Immigration (EEA) Regulations.

3.35 The upshot of all these changes is that applicants and claimants are now faced with extending charges and mounting fees. However, the policy that those who gain most from entry and stay in the UK should pay more does offer hope that there might be a greater willingness of government to be more flexible with waiver, reduction and refunding of fees not just for the indigent but for those who are particularly vulnerable or are faced with real hardship. Although there is an express power under section 51(3)(c) of the IAN 2006 to make regulations with a discretion to reduce, waive or refund fees it is only recently that any attempt to give flesh and bones to these powers has begun to take place.

Fees Regs SI 2014/92, reduction and waiver

3.36 The Fees Regulations are updated each year, so that the 2014 Regulations revoked the 2013 Regulations which in turn revoked the 2012 Regulations and so on. Each has a clause which makes it clear that where the Regulations specify a fee which must accompany the application, the application will not be validly made unless it is accompanied by the correct fee.[1] Each set of Regulations contains a list of exceptions from the need to pay a fee. Using the 2014 Regulations as a kind of benchmark, fees for and in connection with applications for leave to remain in the UK are set out in Tables 1–3. Table 4 provides for exceptions to the requirement to pay fees, but makes no provision to confer a discretion on the Secretary of State to waive or reduce any fees in Tables 1-3. This in stark contrast to fees for entry clearance to come to the UK, where there is a discretion to waive fees,[2] There is also a discretion to waive or reduce fees for those looking for premium services or seeking to expedite their applications or to buy into special optional services available for the fees set out in Tables 14 and 15.[3] On what basis this discretion will be exercised is unclear, but it seems unlikely that it will be destitution. Yet when we look at the list of exceptions in Table 4[4] and put on one side the more obvious candidates, including such applications as those under Article 3 ECHR and Refugee Convention, other human rights applications, stateless people, Turkish nationals under the EC Association Agreement, and children in receipt of local authority assistance, the remaining exceptions each have destitution as the one of their key and central features. These are: 4.2 Applications for leave to remain under the Destitution Domestic Violence Concession;[5] and 4.3 Applications for leave to remain as a victim of domestic violence,[6] where at the time of making the application the applicant appears to the Secretary of State to be destitute. The exceptions for entry clearance are very much shorter and cover:[7] Officials of Her Majesty's Government made in connection with their official duty; Dependants of refugees or persons granted humanitarian protection;[8] and Applications under the EC Association Agreement with Turkey.

1   Fees Regulations 2014, SI 2014/922, reg 11.
2   Fees Regulations 2014, SI 2014/922, Sch 2, Table 9, 9.1 and Sch 5, Table 13, 13.2 (Entry Clearance for Channel Islands).
3   Fees Regulations 2014, 2014 SI 2014/922, Sch 6, para 3 and Sch 7, para 3.
4   Fees Regulations 2014, SI 2014/922, Table 4 (Exceptions in respect of fees for applications for leave to remain in the United Kingdom).
5   The Destitution Domestic Violence Concession enables destitute applicants who intend to apply for indefinite leave to remain in the United Kingdom as a victim of domestic violence to be provided with access to public funds pending resolution of their application. This policy is published at www.ukba.homeoffice.gov.uk/sitecontent/documents/residency/FAQs-DDV-concession.pdf.
6   Under HC 395, paragraph 289A or Appendix FM or Appendix Armed Forces.
7   Fees Regulations 2014, 2014 SI 2014/022, Table 8 (Exceptions in respect of fees for applications for entry clearance to enter the United Kingdom).
8   These applications are made under HC 395, paragraphs 352A to 352FI.

3.37 The development of waivers and reductions (and exceptions for leave to remain) are recent. In *R (on the application of Omar) v Secretary of State for the Home Department*[1] the issue was whether the Secretary of State acted unlawfully on 12 July 2010 in refusing to accept the claimant's application for an extension of discretionary leave without a fee. This involved a challenge to the *vires* of the relevant regulations, which at that time provided for a fee but did not confer a discretion on the Secretary of State to waive the fee in the case of an applicant who seeks leave on human rights grounds but cannot afford the fee because he is either destitute or in receipt only of NASS support. By Regulation 30 of the 2010 Fees Regulations, it was provided that where an application which is required to be accompanied by a specified fee is made without that fee 'the application is not validly made'. Beatson J found against the secretary of State.

'. . . The Secretary of State, as a public official, is under a duty to make and interpret rules in the light of section 3 of the Human Rights Act. The requirement in regulations 6 and 30 of the 2010 Fees Regulations that, in this class of case, a fee must be paid, there is no provision for waiver and an application without a fee "is not validly made" must, in the light of section 3, be read subject to a qualification that the specified fee is not due where to require it to be paid would be incompatible with a person's Convention rights.'

Following this decision a new set of IDI's were issued in September 2013.[2] Applicants will qualify for a fee waiver only where they can demonstrate on the basis of evidence provided that they are destitute, or where there are exceptional circumstances. Destitution was defined as follows:

'Consistent with the provision of support to asylum seekers and their dependants under section 95 of the Immigration and Asylum Act 1999, a person is destitute if a) They do not have adequate accommodation or any means of obtaining it (whether or not their other essential living needs are met); or b) They have adequate accommodation or the means of obtaining it, but cannot meet their other essential living needs.'

A new IDI Section 4 – Charging – refunds/ex-gratia payments and fee exemptions in immigration applications and claims is currently (August 2014) under review. New guidance will be published shortly.

[1] [2012] EWHC 3448 (Admin).
[2] IDI Chapter 1a: Applications for Fee Waiver and Refunds.

Immigration Act 2014 changes

3.38 The Immigration Act 2014 has a short section under Part 6 of the Act dealing with immigration and nationality fees. It makes for the consolidation of the main functions of Fees Orders and Fees Regulations contained in current laws, but also greatly extends the ambit of the Fees system by including all sorts of additional matters which can be used to calculate how much immigration and nationality applicants will have to pay. The bad news is that fees will inevitably continue to rise. The other bad news is that although the 2014 Act continues the statutory power enshrined in section 51 of the IAN 2006 to reduce and waive fees[1] and the Fees Regulations may still provide for a waiver, reduction or refund of all or a part of a fee, there is still no widespread use of the powers beyond assisting the indigent, as we have seen, above.

Another feature of the amended regime is that from now on there is going to be a single consolidated system, meaning the death knell of the Consular Fees Act 1980 as the legislative source of the power to levy fees outside the UK in immigration and Nationality cases.[2] Section 69(2) of the 2014 Act provides expressly that a fee under section 68 may relate to something done outside the United Kingdom. Second, the old reason for having two sets of Regulations – the Fees Regulations and the Cost Recovery Fees) Regulations, explained at **3.30**, above, has gone, since all Regulations to be made under section 68 of the

2014 are subject to the negative resolution procedure and only the Fees Orders are subject to the need for an affirmative resolution of both Houses of Parliament. From now on there need only be one set of Regulations.

¹ Immigration Act 2014, s 68(10).
² It should be noted that s 68 is without prejudice to s 1 of the Consular Fees Act 1980: s 69 (5)(a). This means that ll existing fees set under the Act continue to have validity and that the fee setting functions of the Act outside of the immigration and nationality fields continue to operate.

3.39 Section 68(1) provides for the Secretary of State to make Orders enabling fees to be charged for the exercise of 'functions' in connection with immigration and nationality.¹ The use of the term 'functions' is intended to simplify the legislation, ensuring that there is no longer a need to decide which category a particular activity falls into. Functions can be delivered overseas, at the border or within the UK. They can be delivered by the Secretary of State, her officers, agents, commercial partners or any person acting on her behalf.² The section also provides that the existing legislative structure, we have described above, consisting of a power contained in primary legislation and exercised by way of a Fees Order and Fees Regulations is maintained.³ Chargeable functions will be set out in a fees order; and fee amounts set out in Fees Regulations which will be subject to the negative resolution procedure.⁴ A Fees Order made under section 68 is subject to the affirmative resolution procedure.⁵ Section 68(9) consolidates the matters that can already be taken into account under existing legislation when setting certain fees – administrative costs, benefits and the costs of other functions – and extends these to include international comparisons (fees set by other countries for similar functions), the promotion of economic growth and mutual or reciprocal arrangements with other countries. It also ensures that these matters may be considered in relation to fees for all relevant functions. 'Costs' may include the costs of the Secretary of State or any other person performing a function (for example, a commercial provider exercising functions pursuant to a contract with the department). Subsection (9) ensures that those who use the immigration and nationality system continue to pay their fair share towards its continued running and that fees and any future fee changes can be targeted to promote economic growth, including reducing fees in some categories or offering fast-track services for visitors and economically valuable migrants.⁶ Under section 70 provision is made for additional fees above and beyond those charged under relevant Fees Orders to be charged for attendance services at a location outside of the UK, which are optional and bespoke services, provided in addition to other chargeable services.

¹ IA 2014, s 68 (1).
² IA 2014 Explanatory Notes, para 432.
³ IA 2014, s 68 (2) to (7). The Fees Order must specify the way that fees will be set. Fees must be charged either as a fixed amount; calculated using an hourly rate; as a combination of these; or by way of another factor (subs (4)). The order must also specify the maximum amount that may be charged in respect of the fixed element of the fee and a minimum level of fixed fee may be specified for particular functions (subs (5)). Where fees are set by reference to an hourly rate or other factor the fees order must specify how the fee or fee part is to be calculated (subs (6)). Fees for all functions will be set out in Fees Regulations (subs (7)).
⁴ IA 2014, s 68(7) and (8).
⁵ See IA 2014, s 74.
⁶ IA 2014, Explanatory Notes, para 438.

Medical examinations and Tuberculosis tests

3.40 Whether a person is seeking entry clearance at an overseas post or has just landed in the UK, the power to require him or her to submit to medical test or examination by a medical inspector is the same.[1] On landing in the UK the decision will be made by an immigration officer. At the overseas post it will be done by the entry clearance officer. HC 395, paragraph 39 provides that the ECO has the same discretion as an Immigration Officer to refer applicants for entry clearance for medical examination and the same principles will apply to the decision whether or not to issue an entry clearance. The power to direct a person to submit to medical examination may also be exercised by the Secretary of State, in a case where the Secretary of State is taking a decision on an asylum or human rights application or an application outside the rules.[2]

[1] Immigration Act 1971, Sch 2, para 2(2) and (3).
[2] Immigration (Leave to Enter) Order 2001, SI 2001/2590, arts 2 and 3.

3.41 Putting tuberculosis on one side, the immigration rules set out the situations where a reference to a medical inspector is expected to be made. First, the rules provide that a person who intends to remain in the United Kingdom for more than six months should normally be referred to the Medical Inspector for examination.[1] Secondly, a passenger who produces a medical certificate will be advised to hand it to the Medical Inspector. Thirdly, passengers mentioning health or medical treatment as a reason for their visit, or who appear not to be in good mental or physical health, should also be referred to the medical inspector.[2] Immigration officers have a discretion, which should be exercised sparingly, to refer for examination in any other case[3]. Fourth, Doctors should be used only to determine whether there are medical reasons for refusing admission or making admission subject to a requirement that the person has further examination or treatment. It is quite wrong to use doctors for other purposes in the administration of immigration control[4]. Fifth, refusal to undergo a medical examination is a ground for refusal of leave to enter except where the person is a returning resident[5]. Sixth, Immigration officers may require any person on board or disembarking from an aircraft to produce a valid international vaccination certificate, and may detain anyone who embarked in a local infected area and who is unable to produce such a certificate to await the arrival of a medical inspector, for up to three hours. A person who appears verminous or is suspected of having an infectious disease may also be detained.[6] Seventh, Passengers requiring urgent medical treatment should be required to submit to further examination; those may be sent to hospital by the medical officer taken to hospital before any examination by an Immigration officer but remain liable to examination and to the requirement to obtain leave to enter[7].

[1] HC 395, para 36 An Immigration officer will normally waive the requirement for medical examination for passengers intending to remain longer than six months if they are returning from short visits abroad, or are passengers of international repute or good standing, or are teachers coming for authorised employment, or are students sponsored by the British Council (who will have had a medical before being granted a scholarship), or dependants of US Forces (who will have had a medical before leaving the US), or where the medical inspector is not immediately available, or in any other case where the immigration officer feels it unnecessary: Medical Issues (entry clearance guidance) paragraph MED9. Examination may also be waived for passengers coming for private medical treatment sponsored by their government or those seeking entry clearance for private medical treatment, unless the circumstances are particularly sensitive: Medical Issues (entry clearance guidance) paragraph MED13

² HC 395, para 36.
³ The Modernised Guidance: General Grounds for refusal, Version 16.0, section 1 that a person who is 'bodily dirty' or has scabies or lice infestation could be referred.
⁴ In 1979, after the 'virginity testing' scandal, the Secretary of State gave instructions that medical inspectors should not be asked to examine passengers to establish whether they have borne children or have had sexual relations. In 1982 the Secretary of State gave further instructions that medical inspectors should not be asked to X-ray persons for the purpose of assessing their age. A woman should not be referred for confirmation of a suspected pregnancy unless there is strong evidence that the purpose of her visit is to take advantage of NHS facilities: Medical Issues (entry clearance guidance) paragraph MED14. But seeking to take such advantage is not a ground for refusal of entry. So what is the point of referral? The purpose of referral is unclear.
⁵ HC 395, paras 38 and 320(17).
⁶ Under the Public Health (Aircraft) Regulations 1979, SI 1979/1434 as amended 2007.
⁷ Public Health (Aircraft) Regulations 1979 SI 1979/1434 as amended 2007, reg 9.

3.42 Where the Medical Inspector advises that any person seeking entry is suffering from a specified disease or condition which may interfere with their ability to support themselves or their dependants, two important factors which the immigration officer must take into account in deciding whether to admit that person will be the Medical Inspector's assessment of the likely course of treatment and whether a person seeking entry for private medical treatment has sufficient means at his disposal.[1]

¹ HC 395, para 37.

3.43 A returning resident should not be refused leave to enter or have existing leave to enter or remain cancelled on medical grounds. But there are three situations where the Immigration Officer should give the passenger a notice requiring him or her to report to the Medical Officer of Environmental Health designated by the Medical Inspector with a view to further examination and any necessary treatment.[1] These are:

(i)   where that person would be refused leave to enter or have existing leave cancelled on medical grounds if he or she were not a returning resident;
(ii)   where it is decided on compassionate grounds not to exercise the power to refuse leave to enter or to cancel existing leave to enter or remain, or
(iii) in any other case where the Medical Inspector so recommends.

¹ HC 395, para 38.

3.44 More detailed provisions exist for the detection of tuberculosis. The UK has had a longstanding policy of screening new entrants from high incidence tuberculosis countries intending to remain for over six months. Screening has been conducted at ports of entry and, since October 2005, pre-entry in some high incidence tuberculosis countries. On 21 May 2012 the government announced its intention to expand upon the pre-entry screening programme as that allows for more extensive screening. Entry clearance applicants intending to come to the UK for over six months from countries where pre-entry screening is available will be required to present a certificate from a designated screening provider, listed in Appendix T Part 2, confirming that screening has been conducted and that the applicant is not suffering from active pulmonary tuberculosis.[1] Where tuberculosis is detected, the applicant will be required to undertake treatment and further screening before any entry clearance application can be made.

[1]   HC 395, para A39, as amended.

3.45 HC 395, paragraph B39 imposes these requirements on returning residents returning after two years absence, and existing paragraph A39 has been replaced with a new paragraph by Cm 8599, taking effect on 30 April 2013. This extends the reach of screening requirements not just to any person from a country listed in Appendix T Part 1 making an application for entry clearance to come to the UK for more than six months but also to fiancé(e) or proposed civil partner coming for a lesser period.[1] Appendix T, as amended, contains a list of the specified countries where screening is compulsory and of the clinics authorised to carry out this screening. It has been amended continuously from 2012[2] with a massively extended reach in the two rule changes taking effect on 31 December 2013.[3]

[1]   Applying for leave to enter under Section EC-P: Entry clearance as a partner under Appendix FM or leave to enter under paragraphs 290-291 in Part 8 of HC 395.
[2]   HC 395, paras A39 and B39, inserted into the rules by HC 565 taking effect on 6.9.12, amended by HC 847, as from 31.12.12; HC 967, taking effect on 28.2.13.
[3]   HC 901 and 938, taking effect on 31.12.13, HC 1130, taking effect on 31 March 2014.

Conditions attached to and relating to limited leave

3.46 Leave to enter or remain may be granted for a limited or indefinite period of time. The time limits imposed in the case of limited leave will vary from a few months to several years, depending on the category of applicant.[1] These are dealt with in the later chapters dealing with the different groups of migrant/immigrant. In certain cases the period of leave will be less than the normal length because of the particular circumstances of the case or because of restricted returnability, which we deal with in the next but one paragraph. If limited leave is given, it may be subject to conditions. There are three types of condition affecting limited leave:

(1)   there are the conditions attached to the leave itself under section 3(2) of the Immigration Act 1971;

(2)   there is the requirement to register with the police where a condition of registration is attached to the person's leave; and

(3)   there are written undertakings taken, usually from family sponsors, to accommodate and maintain without recourse to public funds.

The immigration officer may require a person arriving in the UK and granted leave to enter to submit to a medical examination after entry, but this is not a condition of leave under the 1971 Act.[2]

[1]   Immigration Act 1971, s 3(1)(b): leave may be limited in time (eg six months) or to a period of employment: see *R v Immigration Appeal Tribunal, ex p Coomasaru* [1983] 1 All ER 208, [1983] 1 WLR 14, CA.
[2]   See Immigration Act 1971, Sch 2, para 7, above **3.57**.

Conditions under section 3(1)

3.47 The conditions which can be imposed under section 3(1)(c) of the 1971 Act[1] are if the person is given limited leave to enter or remain in the United Kingdom, it may be given subject to all or any of the following conditions, namely:

(i) a condition restricting his or her employment or occupation in the United Kingdom;

(ii) a condition requiring him or her to maintain and accommodate themselves, and any of their dependants, without recourse to public funds; < . . . >

(iii) a condition requiring him or her to register with the police;

(iv) a condition requiring him or her to report to an immigration officer or the Secretary of State; and

(v) a condition about residence.[2]

Under section 3(3) it is provided that in the case of a limited leave to enter or remain in the UK:

(a) a person's leave may be varied, whether by restricting, enlarging or removing the limit on its duration, or by adding, varying or revoking conditions, but if the limit on its duration is removed, any conditions attached to the leave shall cease to apply; and

(b) the limitation on and any conditions attached to a person's leave (whether imposed originally or on a variation) shall, if not superseded, apply also to any subsequent leave he may obtain after an absence from the United Kingdom within the period limited for the duration of the earlier leave.

[1] Para (c) was substituted by the Asylum and Immigration Act 1996, s 12(1), Sch 2, para 1(1).
[2] Para (c)(iv) and (v) were inserted by the UK Borders Act 2007, s 16. Date in force: 31 January 2008: see SI 2008/99, art 2(g); for transitional provisions see art 3 thereof.

3.48 Conditions should not be imposed by reason only of the foreigner's nationality, although this very much depends on the terms of a Ministerial Authorisation made under the Equality Act. However, differential treatment of persons with particular nationalities currently operates. The Ministerial Authorisation which subjects persons of a particular nationality to more rigorous scrutiny, questioning and treatment by the immigration authorities. For a detailed examination of this see **1.91**.

Restricted Returnability

3.49 The leave to enter or remain in the UK of the holder of a passport or travel document whose permission to enter another country has to be exercised before a given date may be restricted so as to terminate at least twomonths before that date.[1] The period of leave to enter or remain may also be restricted if the person's passport or travel document is endorsed with a restriction on the period for which he or she may remain outside his country of normal residence.[2] The holder of a travel document issued by the Home Office should not be given leave to enter or remain for a period extending beyond the validity of that document,[3] but exceptions are made for those who:

(i)   are eligible for admission for settlement or to a spouse or civil partner; and[4]

(ii)   qualify for the removal of the time limit on their stay and will be returnable to another country if allowed to remain in the United Kingdom for a further period.

Where someone cannot show that he or she will be admitted to another country if admitted for a stay in the UK[5] or will not be returnable to another country if allowed to stay in the UK for a further period of leave,[6] their application for leave to enter or remain may be refused under the general grounds of refusal.[7]

[1]   HC 395, para 21.
[2]   HC 395, para 22.
[3]   HC 395, para 23.
[4]   Under HC 395, para 282.
[5]   See HC 395, para 320(13).
[6]   HC 395, para 322(8).
[7]   3.132 below.

Registration with the police

3.50 Under the Immigration Act 1971 the government has power by statutory instrument to make any group of immigrants register with the police. The present policy is to limit this to aliens,[1] but this can be changed at any time, subject to annulment in Parliament.[2] The current regulations are the Immigration (Registration with Police) Regulations 1972 as amended[3] and the applicable immigration rules are HC 395 paragraphs 325 and 326. Under these rules only 'relevant foreign nationals' over 16 years of age are required to register, if they are a national or citizen of a country or territory listed in Appendix 2 to the Immigration Rules;[4] a stateless person; or a person holding a non-national travel document who is given leave to stay in the UK for more than six months.[5] A condition requiring registration with the police should normally be imposed on any relevant foreign national who is given limited leave to enter or remain in the UK for more than six months or a limited leave which has the effect of allowing the person to remain in the UK for longer than six months, reckoned from the date of that person's arrival, whether or not the condition was imposed at that time or later.[6] The requirement to register can be imposed by an entry clearance officer (ECO), a Home Office officer, a Border Force officer, or a caseworker on behalf of the Secretary of State and may be imposed.[7] Applicant must report to the police within seven days of obtaining their leave (in the UK), arriving in the country if imposed by an ECO or Border Force officer or receiving their biometric residence permits.[8]

Once registered, the police will give the applicant a police registration certificate (PRC) which shows they have complied with the requirement to register.[9]

[1]   An alien means a person who is neither a Commonwealth citizen nor a BPP nor a citizen of the Republic of Ireland: British Nationality Act 1981, s 50(1), as applied by SI 1972/1758, reg 2.
[2]   Immigration Act 1971, s 4(3). The Police Federation opposed the registration with police of Commonwealth citizens under the 1971 Act. It cannot have been because of the administrative burden, because only 15 new personnel would have been required: see 813 HC Official Report (5th series) col 51.

3   SI 1972/1758, amended on many occasions in respect of the fee for issue of a certificate of registration. The fee for registration now stands at £34: see the Immigration (Registration with Police) (Amendment) Regulations 1995, SI 1995/2928.
4   The countries listed in Appendix 2 are: Afghanistan, Algeria, Argentina, Armenia, Azerbaijan, Bahrain, Belarus, Bolivia, Brazi, China, Colombia, Cuba, Egypt,Georgia, Iran, Iraq, Israel, Jordan, Kazakhstan, Kuwait, Kyrgyzstan, Lebanon, Libya, Moldova, Morocco, North Korea, Oman, Palestine, Peru, Qatar, Russia, Saudi Arabia, Sudan, Syria, Tajikistan, Tunisia, Turkey, Turkmenistan, United Arab Emirates, Ukraine, Uzbekistan, Yemen.
5   HC 395, para 325, substituted by HC 194 from 4 February 2005.
6   HC 395, para 326(1), substituted by HC 194 from 4 February 2005.
7   Modern Guidance – Police registration – version 9.0 Valid from 25 February 2014 p 1.
8   Ibid pp 8–9.
9   Ibid, pp 5–6.

3.51 In addition the rules contain a further list of exempted persons who do not have to register even if they are relevant foreign nationals. According to HC 395, paragraph 326(2) a condition to register with the police should not normally be imposed on a seasonal agricultural worker; a private servant in a diplomatic household; a minister of religion, missionary or member of a religious order; on the basis of marriage or civil partnership to a person settled in the UK or as the unmarried same-sex partner of a person settled in the UK; a person exercising access rights to a child resident in the UK; the parent of a child at school; or following the grant of asylum. The Modern Guidance contains a fuller list of exempted persons who do not have to register.[1] The Modern Guidance deals with a miscellaneous group of persons whose need to register is not clear.[2] Dependants aged 16 or over need to register with the police if they are a dependant of someone who needs to register, and meet the criteria of those who need to registration. A person with dual nationality only needs to register with the police if both nationalities they hold are listed in Appendix 2 of the Immigration Rules. Turkish nationals who hold travel documents issued by the Turkish Republic of Northern Cyprus need to register with the police unless they are Citizens of the Republic of Cyprus, which is now an EU country. A person who holds a passport issued by the Special Administrative Region of either Hong Kong or Macao is classed as a Chinese national and needs to register.

EEA nationals and their non-EEA family members are not required to register, because they do not require leave to enter and such a condition would be contrary to free movement rights under EC law.

Registration involves going to the local police station within seven days of the requirement to register[3] and giving detailed particulars, including name, address, marital status, details of employment or occupation, including employer's name and address, a photograph, and paying the registration fee.[4] While the person is required to register, changes of address must be notified to the police within seven days, and changes in marital status, nationality and employment or occupation within eight days of the change.[5] In return the foreign national receives from the police a certificate of registration. The requirement to register continues in the case of relevant foreign nationals until they are granted indefinite leave to remain.

Someone who, without reasonable excuse, fails to comply with any of the registration requirements, ie fails to register or fails to notify a change of particulars, commits a criminal offence under section 26(1)(f) of the Immigration Act 1971. This is a summary offence with a six-month time limit. It is continuous up to the time when limited leave expires, but once the period of leave has expired, the registration regulations cease to apply, although offences against the regulation committed prior to the date of expiry of leave might still be prosecuted within the six-month time limit.[6] Additionally, such a person may not be granted further leave to remain, having breached the conditions of leave,[7] and may be summarily removed under s 10 of the Immigration and Asylum Act 1999.[8]

[1] The list is as follows: those granted indefinite leave to enter or remain; spouses, civil partners, unmarried partners, and same-sex partners of people settled here who are granted leave to enter or remain in the UK on that basis; a recognized refugee; family members of European Economic Area (EEA) and Swiss nationals; seasonal agricultural workers; Tier 5 temporary workers sponsored as an overseas government employee, or private servant in a diplomatic household; Tier 2 ministers of religion; those exercising access rights to a child resident in the UK; parents of a child at school in the UK granted leave to enter or remain on that basis; dependants of a person who is not required to register (except dependants of off-shore workers); members of non-NATO (North Atlantic Treaty Organisation) forces admitted for courses at British military establishments or with private companies (Course F); Community Service Volunteers; Civilian components of NATO forces; Non-visa nationals who are employees of contractors to United States of America; (USA) armed forces in the UK; Non-visa nationals who are employees of the American Battle Monuments Commission. See Modern Guidance – Police registration – version 9.0 Valid from 25 February 2014, p 7.
[2] Modern Guidance Guidance – Police registration – version 9.0 Valid from 25 February 2014 pp 8–9
[3] SI 1972/1758, reg 5.
[4] See 3.50 fn 3 above. A further fee is not payable on re-registration by a relevant foreign national who keeps his police registration certificate on leaving the UK and returns within a year: IDI Jan 04, Ch 10, s 1, para 4.3.
[5] SI 1972/1758, reg 7 (changes of residence or address) and 8 (other changes).
[6] *R v Naik* (1978) Times, 26 July, CA.
[7] Under HC 395, para 322(3); see 4.44 and 4.50 above.
[8] See Chapter 17 below.

Undertakings

3.52 A sponsor of a person seeking leave to enter or remain in the United Kingdom may be asked to give an undertaking in writing to be responsible for that person's maintenance, accommodation and (as appropriate) personal care for the period of any leave granted, including any further variation or for a period of 5 years from date of grant where indefinite leave to enter or remain is granted.[1] Under the Social Security Administration Act 1992 and the Social Security Administration (Northern Ireland) Act 1992, the Department of Social Security or, as the case may be, the Department of Health and Social Services in Northern Ireland, may seek to recover from the person giving such an undertaking any income support paid to meet the needs of the person in respect of whom the undertaking has been given. Under the Immigration and Asylum Act 1999 the Home Office may seek to recover from the person giving such an undertaking amounts attributable to any support provided under section 95 of the Immigration and Asylum Act 1999 (support for asylum seekers) to, or in respect of, the person in respect of whom the undertaking has been given. Failure by the sponsor to maintain that person in accordance with the undertaking, may also be an offence under section 105 of the Social Security Administration Act 1992 and/or under section 108 of the Immigration and Asylum Act 1999 if, as a consequence, asylum support and/or income support is provided to, or in respect of, that person. Failure to enter into such an undertaking or failure to honour its terms may lead to a refusal of leave under the general grounds for refusal under paragraph 322 (6) and (7). See **3.132** below.

[1] HC 395, para 35.

Notice of decisions to grant or refuse leave to enter or remain

3.53 Under section 3A the Secretary of State may by order make further provision with respect to the giving, refusing or varying of leave to enter the United Kingdom, including the imposition of conditions. A similar power is given under section 3B with respect to the giving, refusing or varying of leave to remain in the United Kingdom. Under section 4(1) of the Immigration Act 1971 the power to give or refuse leave to enter and the power to give or refuse leave to remain or to vary any leave is to be exercised by notice in writing given to the person affected.[1] Currently service of immigration refusal decisions which attract a right of appeal is provided for in the Immigration (Notices) Regulations 2003.[2] Those regulations require the Secretary of State to undertake reasonable steps to ensure that an individual receives notice of such a decision and sets out the range of methods which may be used to do so. Where reasonable steps have been taken but the Secretary of State has not been able to serve the notice on the individual or their legal representative the Regulations state that the decision will have effect from the point that it is served on the individual's file.[3] Where a notice is served to file in this way a copy of the notice must be given to a person as soon as possible if they are subsequently located.[4] The Immigration (Leave to Enter and Remain) (Amendment) Order 2013[5] puts in place similar provisions for immigration decisions which do not attract a right of appeal, such as decisions to:

- curtail leave such that the individual has leave remaining
- refuse an application to vary leave which is made and decided before the individual's leave expires
- refuse an application for leave which is made by an individual who has no valid leave at the point of application

Under article 8ZA a notice in writing giving or refusing leave to enter or remain, varying or refusing to vary leave can be given in different ways:

(a) given by hand;
(b) sent by fax;
(c) by post;
(d) by Email;
(e) by document exchange; or
(f) sent by courier.[6]

If no postal or Email address for correspondence has been provided, the notice may be sent to by post to the last known address of the person or their representative.[7] Where attempts to give notice in accordance with article 8ZA (2) or (3) are not possible or have failed, the notice shall be deemed to have been given, when the decision-maker places the notice on file.[8] Where a notice is served to file in this way a copy of the notice must be given to a person as soon as possible if they are subsequently located.[9]

[1] There are two exceptions: (i) where other arrangements have been allowed by or under the 1971 Act; and (ii) where an order made by an SI has been made that the powers under section 3(3)(a) may be exercised generally in respect of any class of persons.

[2] SI 2003/658.

[3] Notice Regulations, reg 7(2).

[4] Ibid, reg 7(3).

[5] SI 2013/1749 into force 12th July 2013. The Order amends the Immigration (Leave to Enter and Remain) Order 2000 by substituting art 8 and inserting new arts 8ZA and 8ZB. art 8, as amended, continues to make provision concerning oral notice giving or refusing leave to enter the United Kingdom as a visitor under the immigration rules for a period not exceeding six months. Notice sent electronically or by fax is now dealt with in article 8ZA.

[6] Article 8ZB sets out the circumstances where notice is deemed to have been given to the person affected.

[7] Ibid, art 8ZA(3)(i) and (ii).

[8] Art 8ZA(4).

[9] Art 8ZA(5).

3.54 The 2013 Order has been prompted by the position of students, particularly those who have been left bereft of a place of study when their College has had its sponsorship licence revoked. Currently, when a PBS sponsor loses their sponsor licence or they notify the Home Office that they have withdrawn sponsorship from an individual, the Home Office considers whether it would be appropriate to curtail leave to 60 days, giving the individual an opportunity to regularise their stay or leave the United Kingdom. In the recent case of *Syed (curtailment of leave – notice)*[1] the Upper Tribunal found that, in the absence of an Order covering service of non-appealable decisions, such a decision must be served under section 4 of the Immigration Act 1971 and the Secretary of State must communicate the notice to the person, in order for it to have effect. According to the government the primary policy objective is to enable the effective service of decisions to curtail leave of migrants who are sponsored under the Points Based System (PBS).[2] Clearly it is designed to catch the student who wants to disappear, but it also wrecks the lives and hopes of the honest and ambitious student who is a victim of the withdrawal of sponsorship from his or her College. Worst still, a piece of legislation aimed to catch students turfed out of their college is now applied across the whole spectrum of leave applicants without a right of appeal.

[1] [2013] UKUT 00144 IAC.

[2] Explanatory Statement to the 2013 Order, para 7(3).

Part II – ENTRY

3.55 Leave to enter is the cornerstone of UK immigration law. No one may enter the UK without leave except:

(i) British citizens and Commonwealth citizens who have a proven right of abode;[1]

(ii) persons arriving from Ireland or another part of the common travel area, in circumstances where leave is not required;[2]

(iii) persons exempt from control, such as diplomats, crew members and others;[3]

(iv)   persons exempt from the requirement of leave under EC law, as enacted in section 7 of the Immigration Act 1988 and applied also to EEA and Swiss nationals (see the Immigration (European Economic Area) Regulations 2006).[4]

(v)   Transfer of overseas prisoner to give evidence in court or assist a criminal investigation.[5]

[1]   Immigration Act 1971, ss 3(1), 2(1)(b), 2(2). See CHAPTER 2 above.
[2]   Immigration Act 1971, s 9; Immigration (Control of Entry through Republic of Ireland) Order 1972, SI 1972/1610 as amended. Proposals effectively to disband the CTA were dropped from the Borders, Citizenship and Immigration Act 2009. See CHAPTER 5 below.
[3]   Immigration Act 1971, s 8. For the full list see the Diplomatic Service Procedures, Entry Clearance, Volume 1, General Instructions (DSP), available on the UK Visas website, Ch.5 and annexe 5.1. See also CHAPTER 5 below.
[4]   Immigration (European Economic Area) Regulations 2006, SI 2006/1003, regs 5 and 6, which refers to 'qualified persons' (EEA and Swiss nationals entering the UK as jobseekers, workers, or self-employed persons, the self-sufficient and students See CHAPTER 6 below.
[5]   Criminal Justice (International Co-operation) Act 1990, s 6.

Arrival and entry

3.56 Leave to enter used only to be granted or refused on arrival in the UK. Arrival and entry are two distinct concepts in immigration law. Section 11 of the Immigration Act 1971 defines the point at which someone who arrives in this country is treated as having entered. First, it provides that persons arriving by ship or aircraft are not deemed to 'enter' unless and until they disembark[1]. Secondly, on disembarkation they are still deemed not to have entered so long as they remain in any part of the port which has been approved for use for immigration control. They only enter once they pass through immigration control. Thirdly, they will still not be treated as having entered if they are detained pending examination or removal or are temporarily admitted or released while liable to such detention[2]. This is of practical importance given the increasing use and length of temporary admission, and means that a person on temporary admission may be physically in the UK for years, and may have married and had children, but has not 'entered' for the purposes of section 11 and will still require leave to enter[3]. In *R v Javaherifard*[4] the Court of Appeal explained that section 11 has no application to entry by land; on those who disembark from a boat otherwise than at a port enter on disembarkation, and those who disembark at a port which has no designated immigration area; and that section 11 does not apply to those who have already entered the UK overland or on an earlier disembarkation.

[1]   Immigration Act 1971, s 11(1). For those coming by train through the Channel Tunnel, they 'enter' the UK when they leave a designated control area or stay on a through train after it has ceased to be in a control area: Immigration Act 1971, s 11(1), as modified by Channel Tunnel (International Arrangements) Order 1993, SI 1993/1813, Sch 4, para 1(5). See also, in relation to frontier controls between the UK, France and Belgium, the Channel Tunnel (Miscellaneous Provisions) Order 1994, SI 1994/1405, art 7.
[2]   Immigration Act 1971, s 11(1) as amended by the Nationality, Immigration and Asylum Act 2002 to include detention by the Secretary of State under s 62 and temporary admission under s 68 of that Act.
[3]   See **3.86**, below. In *R (on the application of Yiadom) v Secretary of State for the Home Department*: C-357/98 [2001] All ER (EC) 267, [2001] INLR 300, the ECJ condemned the 'fiction' of temporary admission, holding that an EU national so admitted was entitled to the safeguards attending expulsion on refusal of leave to enter: see **6.194** below. A period of

temporary admission can count as lawful residence for the purpose of naturalisation under the British Nationality Act 1981: see the Nationality, Immigration and Asylum Act 2002, s 11(3).
4   *R v Javaherifard and Miller* [2005] EWCA Crim 3231, [2006] Imm AR 185; [2006] INLR 302.

3.57 Leave to enter may be granted for a limited or indefinite period.[1] If limited leave is given, it may be subject, as we have set out above, to conditions[2] restricting employment or occupation in the UK; requiring the holder to maintain and accommodate himself or herself and any dependants without recourse to public funds; requiring him or her to register with the police or to report to an Immigration Officer or the Secretary of State; or it may be subject to a condition about residence.[3] Conditions will not be imposed by reason of the foreigner's nationality.[4] Indefinite leave to enter (or remain) may not be made subject to any conditions. Where a peron leaves the country and his or her leave does not lapse, any conditions attached to the leave are suspended for such time as the holder is out of the country.[5]

1   Immigration Act 1971, s 3(1)(b): leave may be limited in time (eg six months) or to a period of employment: see *R v Immigration Appeal Tribunal, ex p Coomasaru* [1983] 1 All ER 208, [1983] 1 WLR 14, CA.
2   The Immigration Officer may require a person arriving in the UK and granted leave to enter to submit to a medical examination after entry, under the Immigration Act 1971, Sch 2, para 7, but this is not a condition of leave under the 1971 Act.
3   Immigration Act 1971, s 3(1)(c), as amended by the UK Borders Act 2007, s 16; see Immigration Rules HC 395 (as amended by HC 194 from 4 February 2005), paras 325–326 and Appendix 2 (listing 'relevant foreign nationals' subject to registration requirements).
4   Unless there is a valid Ministerial Authority
5   Immigration (Leave to Enter and Remain) Order 2000, SI 2000//1162 art 13(4)(b).

3.58 Now, however, leave to enter will be granted and refused in the country of departure in many cases. The Immigration (Leave to Enter and Remain) Order 2000[1], made under section 3A of the Immigration Act 1971[2], provides that leave to enter may be given or refused before the person leaves for or arrives in the UK. In most cases, entry clearance obtained at a British post abroad will operate as advance leave to enter[3]. However, there are other cases of advance leave or refusal of leave to enter, such as the pre-entry clearance scheme operated at airports of countries whose nationals did not require visas[4]. The 'juxtaposed controls' whereby UK immigration officers examine passengers seeking entry at French and Belgian ports do not operate by means of advance leave to enter, however, but by modifying the meaning of 'arrival' and 'entry' to include embarkation ports, called 'control zones'[5]. We deal with this and the controls operating in connection with the Channel Tunnel at **3.75** below.

1   SI 2000/1161.
2   Inserted by Immigration and Asylum Act 1999, s 1.
3   Immigration (Leave to Enter and Remain) Order 2000, SI 2000/1161, art 2.
4   See the landmark *European Roma Rights Centre* case [2004] UKHL 55, [2005] 2 WLR 1, where Czech Roma asylum seekers coming to the UK were subjected to intensive questioning and higher refusal rate (conducted without reference to a relevant ministerial authorisation under the Race Relations Act 1976, s 19D). The House of Lords held that 'the operation was inherently and systemically discriminatory and unlawful' (see per Lady Hale at para 97).
5   Through the Channel Tunnel (International Arrangements) Order 1993, SI 1993/1813, as amended, the Channel Tunnel (Miscellaneous Provisions) Order 1994, SI 1994/1405 and the Nationality, Immigration and Asylum Act 2002, s 141.

Entry clearance

3.59 As a general rule visa nationals need a visa or entry clearance whatever their purpose in seeking to come to the UK and non-EEA non-visa nationals need entry clearance if they are seeking to come for a longer period than six months;[1] this entry clearance will operate as an advance leave to enter; the new system came into force on 13 November 2005.[2] Entry clearances under the Immigration Act 1971 consist of visas for visa nationals and entry certificates for non-visa nationals.[3] British Nationals (Overseas), a British overseas territories citizen, a British Overseas citizen, and a British protected person or a person who under the British Nationality Act 1981 is a British subject do not need a visa or entry clearance, even if they are seeking entry for a period exceeding six months or is seeking entry for a purpose for which prior entry clearance is required under these Rules.[4] An entry clearance may be for a single journey or for multiple visits. A multiple entry visa is available for frequent visitors and is usually valid for a period of two years, although it may have a five or ten-year validity.[5] The Immigration (Leave to Enter and Remain) Order 2000 provides that a visit visa which has effect as leave to enter is good for multiple entries within the period of its validity.[6] When the holder of an entry clearance arrives in the UK, admission is not automatic and entry to the UK may still be refused.[7] Since October 2000, as we have seen at **3.55** above, entry clearance has taken the form of a sticker or 'vignette' affixed to the passport or travel document.

[1] HC 395, para 24; Immigration (Leave to Enter and Remain) Order 2000, SI 2000/1161, arts 2–4 as amended by SI 2004/475.

[2] HC 395, para 25A; Immigration (Leave to Enter and Remain) Order 2000, SI 2000/1161, arts 2–4 as amended by SI 2004/475. The first phase of the scheme, affecting the nationals of ten countries (Australia, Canada, Hong Kong (other than BNOs), Japan, Malaysia, New Zealand, Singapore, South Africa, South Korea and USA), came into force on 13 November 2003 and these rules were superseded by HC 645, which came into force on 13 November 2005.

[3] HC 395, para 25.

[4] HC 395, para 24(ii).

[5] See visitors CHAPTER 8 below at **8.9**.

[6] Immigration (Leave to Enter and Remain) Order 2000, SI 2000/1161, as amended, art 4.

[7] See below, **3.132** for grounds on which leave to enter may be refused to holders of entry clearance.

Who needs entry clearance

3.60 Visa nationals require an entry clearance whatever the purpose of their travel to the UK and will normally be refused entry if they do not have one. The list of visa countries is set out in Appendix 1 to the current Immigration Rules. It also includes persons who hold passports or travel documents issued by the former Soviet Union or by the former Yugoslavia, stateless persons and persons who hold non-national documents.[1] This list is frequently amended and care should be taken to ensure that a particular country has not been added to the list or removed from it.[2] Those visa nationals who do not need a visa are:

(i) returning residents (those with indefinite leave who return within two years of departure from the UK);[3]

(ii)   those seeking to re-enter during the period of their original leave and for the same purpose, unless it was for a period of six months or less, or was granted by statute;[4]

(iii)   those who obtained a visa and are re-entering the UK within the period of validity of their original visa and for the same purpose, unless it was for a period of six months or less, or was granted by statute;[5]

(iv)   visitors returning to the UK within the period of validity of their visit visa;[6]

(v)   nationals of the People's Republic of China holding passports issued by the Hong Kong or Macao Special Administrative Region;[7]

(vi)   those nationals or citizens of Taiwan who hold a passport by Taiwan that includes the number of the identification card issued by the competent authority in Taiwan in it.[8]

(vii)   those nationals or citizens of Oman, Qatar, the United Arab Emirates, Turkey, Kuwait and Bahrain, who hold diplomatic and special passports issued by their own government when travelling to the UK for a general visit;[9]

(viii)   Subject to specified exceptions, those coming to the Commonwealth Games in Glasgow for the period beginning with 4 August 2014 and ending with 3 September 2014 who hold a Commonwealth Games Identity and Accreditation Cards;[10]

(ix)   those passport holders of Oman, Qatar or the United Arab Emirates who hold and use an Electronic Visa Waiver (EVW) Document in accordance with Appendix 1 paragraphs 3 to 9.

(x)   persons who hold Service, Temporary Service and Diplomatic passports issued by the Holy See in Rome.[11]

(xi)   schoolchildren who are visa nationals living in other EU States travelling in school groups, if the group is accompanied by a teacher and their names are included on the official form to be obtained by the school;[12]

(xii)   foreign seamen settled in the UK who signed on in the UK who are discharging from a vessel or arriving as passengers having signed off abroad, foreign seamen arriving in the UK as crew members for discharge or for temporary shore leave, or those with a seafarer's identity document who come to join a ship in the UK, and aircrew who are to leave within seven days.[13]

In addition to the above there is also a list of international organisations whose employees are exempt from the need for entry clearance. It can be found at 'Exempt (entry clearance guidance) on www.gov.uk/government/uploads/syst em/uploads/attachment_data/file/257790/exempt-organisations-list.pdf. If visa nationals arrive in the UK from Ireland and have no visa for the UK, they must obtain leave to enter.[14] Note that visa nationals will require a visa if they intend to enter the UK en route to another destination[15]

---

[1]   The list is subject to the exceptions listed below. Refugees use non-national travel documents. Those resident in countries signatories to the Council of Europe Agreement on the Abolition of Visas for Refugees 1959 used not to require a visa for visits of three months or less, but the UK suspended its obligations under the Agreement in February 2003, since when such refugees have required visas to enter the UK.

[2]   HC 395, para 24. The imposition of visa requirements on Commonwealth citizens under the Immigration Rule is not ultra vires: *R v Secretary of State for the Home Department, ex p Suresh Kumar* [1986] Imm AR 420, QBD.

[3]   HC 395, as amended, Appendix 1, para 2(a).

4   HC 395, as amended, Appendix 1, para 2(b). See also SI 2000/1161, art 13(2)–(4): for such persons, their original leave now does not lapse when they leave the UK, unless their leave was extended by the Secretary of State and after the extension, only six months or less was left, or it was extended by s 3C Immigration Act 1971. Section 3C has been amended by IAN 2006, s 11, so that, on an application to vary leave, leave will only be extended pending a decision on the application to vary or pending an in-country appeal. Section 11 of IAN 2006 came into force on 31 August 2006: Immigration, Asylum and Nationality Act 2006 (Commencement No 2) Order 2006, SI 2006/2226.

5   HC 395 as amended, Appendix 1, para 2(f) (which seems to add little if anything to para 2(b), fn 3 above); SI 2000/1161, art 13(2)–(4).

6   SI 2000/1161, art 4

7   HC 395 as amended, Appendix 1, para 2(d) and (e), inserted by HC 735 on 16 April 2002.

8   HC 395 as amended, Appendix 1, para 2(h).

9   HC 395 as amended, Appendix 1, para 2(k), (l), (q), (r), (w) and (v).

10 HC 395 as amended, Appendix 1, para 2 (s) and (t).

11 HC 395 as amended, Appendix 1, para 2 (v).

12 IDI (July 08), Ch 1, s 4, para 8, Annex V para 4, July 08, referring to an EU Council Agreement to waive visa requirements. This concession is not incorporated into the rules.

13 See Crew members (entry clearance guidance) Seafarers: CRM01 published Dec 2013, CRM 1-5 Legislation and Seafarers.

14 Immigration (Control of Entry through Republic of Ireland) Order 1972, SI 1972/1610, art 3. See also *R v Secretary of State for the Home Department, ex p Mohan* [1989] Imm AR 436. If they have gone from Ireland to one of the Islands without the appropriate visa, they require leave. If they fail to get it and proceed to the UK, they will be illegal entrants. See Chapter 6 below.

15 Visitors in transit are dealt with at **8.36**, below.

Transit visas

3.61 Transit visas are now dealt with under the heading of 'visitors in transit' at **8.36** below.

3.62 Most non-visa nationals have no need for an entry clearance if they seek leave to enter at the port of entry in the UK for a period not exceeding six months as a visitor or for some other purpose, for which prior entry clearance is not required,[1] or are returning residents[2] or are born in the UK.[3] Entry clearance is mandatory for all other purposes. So, visa nationals and any other person, who is seeking entry for a period exceeding six months or is seeking entry for a purpose for which prior entry clearance is required under these Rules, must have one, save for the five categories of British national, who do not have a right of abode in the UK, British Nationals (Overseas), BOTCs, BOCs, BPPs and persons who under the British Nationality Act 1981 are British subjects.[4] Because of their special status they will continue to be able to travel to the UK without prior entry clearance and apply for leave to enter the UK on arrival. This may be granted, irrespective of the period of time for which the person seeks entry, for a period not exceeding six months[5]

1   HC 395, para 23A, as substituted by HC 645.
2   HC 395, para 18.
3   HC 395, paras 305–306.
4   HC 395, para 24(ii), as amended by HC 645.
5   HC 395, para 23B, inserted by HC 645.

3.63 The fact that entry clearance is made mandatory for almost all purposes in the Immigration Rules is not unlawful. The courts have held that it is not ultra vires the Secretary of State's rule-making power, either as being an unlawful delegation of power to entry clearance officers or as a fetter on the discretionary powers of immigration officers to give or refuse leave to enter under section 4(1) of the Immigration Act 1971.[1] First, the Home secretary, as the rule maker, still has a residual discretion whether or not to make an exception in the circumstances of the particular case.[2] Secondly, the immigration officers' discretion is retained in the new dispensation, where entry clearance operates as leave to enter, through their power to cancel leave.[3]

[1] See *R v Secretary of State for the Home Department, ex p Rofathullah* [1989] QB 219, [1988] Imm AR 514, CA; *R v Secretary of State for the Home Department, ex p Ounejma* [1989] Imm AR 75, DC. See further *R v Secretary of State for the Home Department, ex p Kaur (Rajinder)* [1987] Imm AR 278, DC, a challenge to the vires of rules made under the Commonwealth Immigrants Act 1962.

[2] See *Pearson v Immigration Appeal Tribunal* [1978] Imm AR 212, at 225, per Stephenson LJ, CA; *R v Port of London Authority, ex p Kynoch Ltd* [1919] 1 KB 176, at 184, per Bankes LJ; *British Oxygen Co Ltd Minister of Technology* [1971] AC 610.

[3] Immigration (Leave to Enter and Remain) Order 2000, SI 2000/1161, art 6; HC 395, para 25A (inserted by HC 704); see **3.58** below.

Making an application for entry clearance

3.64 Applications for entry clearance are to be considered in accordance with the provisions of the Immigration Rule relating to the grant or refusal of leave to enter, subject to the Human Rights Act 1998, and the term 'entry clearance officer' may be substituted for the term 'immigration officer' where this is appropriate[1]. To qualify for the grant of an entry clearance as a visitor, family member, business person or whatever, the person must fulfil the requirements of the particular Immigration Rule which deals with that particular type of entrant. But qualifying in this way may not be enough. Entry clearance may still be refused on a number of general grounds which apply across the board. These are described at **3.132** ff below.

[1] HC 395, para 26.

Where to apply

3.65 First, all applicants must be outside the UK and Islands at the time of application[1]. Secondly, the application has to be made to the British Embassy or High Commission, a British Consular post or special authorised person outside the UK and Islands[2]. A list of designated posts is published by the Foreign and Commonwealth Office[3]. A distinction is made between visit entry clearances and others. Visitors, transit passengers and applicants for EEA family permits can apply to any post designated by the Secretary of State to accept applications from that category of applicants.[4] They do not need to be in the country where they live. An application for entry clearance as a Tier 5 (Temporary Worker) Migrant in the creative and sporting sub-category of Tier 5 provided the post has been designated by the Secretary of State to accept such applications and the applicant has been living lawfully in that country for a similar purpose to the activity he or she proposes to undertake in the UK. Applications as a Tier 1 (Exceptional Talent) Migrant or as a Tier 5 (Youth Mobility Scheme) Temporary Migrant may also be made at the post in the country or territory where the applicant is situated at the time of the application, provided the post has been designated by the Secretary of State to accept such applications and the applicant has been living lawfully in that country for a period exceeding six months[5]. All other visa applications have to be made in the country where the applicant 'is living', unless there is no designated post in that country able to receive applications for that purpose from that category of applicants. Then the visa can be applied for and obtained elsewhere[6]. The Entry Clearance Guidance states that 'where they live' means 'wherever the applicant has permission to reside, eg for work or study purposes . . . an applicant who has permission to stay in a country as a visitor for six months, for example, is not a resident.[7] Closure of some embassies following attacks, and heightened security in others, has led to lengthy delays and severe difficulties for applicants in a number of countries.[8] In particular cases, it may be necessary for advisers to contact the Embassy or Consulate concerned to ascertain the prevailing practice but it should normally be sufficient to contact UKVisas (the joint initiative of the FCO and Home Office) in the event of difficulty.[9]

[1]   HC 395, para 28.
[2]   HC 395, para 29.
[3]   See HC 395, para 29. To obtain details of embassies and overseas posts go to www.fco.gov. uk/en/travel-and-living-abroad/find-an-embassy/..
[4]   HC 395, para 29.
[5]   HC 395, para 28A(a) and (b).
[6]   HC 395, para 28. For example, since 1991 Somalis have applied for entry clearance to posts at Addis Ababa and Nairobi. Under the Somali Family Reunion policy which operated until 1994, UK sponsors obtained indications from the Home Office on the likely outcome of visa applications which were then formally made at the post: *see Secretary of State for the Home Department v Dahir and Abdi* [1995] Imm AR 570, CA.
[7]   ECG ECB5, 8 September 2009. See also *R (on the application of Barlas) v Secretary of State for the Home Department* [2007] EWHC 1709 (Admin), [2007] All ER (D) 359 Jun where it was held that the Immigration Rules do not require permanent residence, or some similar long-term status in the relevant country to be enjoyed, before a person can be said to be living there. An unreasonable refusal to entertain an application where an applicant is not living (because of insuperable difficulties in compliance) might be challengeable if fundamental human rights were at issue. See Chapter 7 below.
[8]   Listing the countries, as we have done in previous editions, is interesting but less helpful than checking on the Home Office website.
[9]   See the UK Visas website, fn 3 above.

3.66 Fees are charged for the issue of visas and entry clearances.[1] Under the Immigration Rules an application for entry clearance is not made until any fees have been paid.[2] The level of fees charged for family settlement may be prohibitive in some cases, for example, where a spouse and a number of dependent children seek entry. Fees Regulations may now provide for a waiver or refund of all or a part of a fee.[3] Really prohibitive fees could also constitute a disproportionate obstacle to the right to respect for family life. Refusal by an entry clearance officer to process an application in such circumstances could, we suggest, be susceptible to challenge by way of judicial review.[4]

[1]   For a more detailed account of fees and how they are charged, see **3.26** ff, above.
[2]   HC 395, para 30, reversing *Entry Clearance Officer, Port Louis v Ross* [1992] Imm AR 493, IAT. As currently drafted para 30 only applies to fees payable under the power to levy fees under the Consular Fees Act 1980, whereas fees payable abroad can now be levied under other legislation, particularly s 68 Immigration Act 2014. See above [3.
[3]   Immigration Act 2014, s 68(10).

[4] A consent order was made in *R v British Embassy Addis Ababa, ex p Jama*, CO 3338/1999, on the FCO accepting that the applicant was destitute when this was considered a valid ground within the Diplomatic Services Procedures (DSP) for waiving the fee.

The application

3.67 The date when an application for entry clearance is made is important because, although the key date for judging whether someone is eligible for a visa or entry certificate is usually the date of the decision rather than the date of the application[1], the date of the application may count in certain cases[2]. For example, in the case of a child wishing to join parents who are settled in the UK, eligibility will depend upon the age of the applicant at the time when the application for entry clearance is made, and an application may not be refused solely on account of an applicant becoming over-age between the date of the application and the date of the decision on it[3]. The rules for certain entry clearance applications, like those for variations of leave from persons already in the UK, now prescribe the use of particular forms. Getting the Form wrong or omitting documents does not have the same punishing effect as an in-country leave application because overseas you just have to start again; in-country you may lose a right of appeal or lose continuity of residence However, this creates more uncertainty. It is not clear what element of discretion now applies, for example, where there are local difficulties which make it impossible to enclose the fee with the postal application an exception may be made or where a delay between the receipt of the application and the fee places the applicant outside the rules (eg regarding an age requirement)[4]. Under earlier guidance the date of receipt of the application form would be treated as the material date of application provided that the applicant attended and paid the fee on the appointed day, but such commonsense guidance no longer applies[5]. Applicants, applying to posts in any country, may be required to provide a record of their fingerprints and photographs of their faces. For this to be done they may be required to attend a British Diplomatic mission or Consular post, a Diplomatic mission or Consular post of another state, or other premises nominated for their fingerprints or photographs to be taken[6]. A failure to provide fingerprints or a facial photograph entitles the entry clearance officer to treat the application as invalid[7].

[1] HC 395, para 27.
[2] In *R v Immigration Appeal Tribunal, ex p Rashida Bibi; R v Immigration Appeal Tribunal, ex p Purvez* [1986] Imm AR 61, DC the date of application was used to determine whether the Pakistani wife and children of a Commonwealth citizen settled in the UK on 1 January 1973 should be treated as Commonwealth citizens or aliens. The date of application is often the important date in transitional provisions for new rules and policies.
[3] HC 395, para 27. For some unexplained reason, Children of Tier 1, 2, 4 and 5 are excluded from the benefit of Paragraph 27. These include children of students, of those coming to work and business persons. Imm AR 570.
[4] See HC 395, paras 28 and 28A 30 which deal with the designated post to which an application should or may be made.
[5] The earlier guidance under DSP Ch 8 at para 8.2 no longer exists.
[6] The Immigration (Provision of Physical Data) Regulations 2006, SI 2006/1743 apply to any person applying for entry clearance. Safeguards for children under 16 (required presence of parent or guardian or responsible person) apply under reg 4 of the 2006 Regulations. The 2006 Regulations were amended by the Immigration (Provision of Physical Data) (Amendment) Regulations 2011, SI 2011/1779 to deal with biometric information to be taken from persons accredited for the 2012 London Olympic and Paralympic Games who would

usually be required to apply for a visa and therefore have their biometric information taken as visa nationals but were excused from obtaining such visa. On a more general basis Reg 5 has now allowed fingerprints or a photograph of the face to be taken by an authorised person at place other than a British Diplomatic mission or British Consular post or a Diplomatic mission or Consular Post of another state.

7   SI 2006/1743, reg 7. An application is not invalid if the applicant is a refugee, seeking leave to enter the UK, and presents a convention travel document endorsed with an entry clearance for that journey to the UK. The application will not be treated as invalid but it may be refused if he does not provide a record of his fingerprints or a photograph of his face as required: reg 7(2) and (3).

3.68 Once an application for entry clearance is properly made, it must be considered by the visa or entry clearance officer. Sponsorship and other specified documentation must be in place. In many cases the required documentation is set out in the immigration rules[1] and can also be obtained from the UK visa website.[2] When an ECO cannot make an immediate decision about whether the applicant should be issued with a visa he or she might be asked to attend an interview.[3] Whereas at one time interviews were routine they have now become the exception. The decision to be taken under the Immigration Rules is that of the individual ECO to whom the application for entry clearance is made. It is the ECO who must exercise his or her individual judgment, for example whether a passport is a valid passport. He or she should remember that the Secretary of State is not the decision-maker under the Immigration Rules, as drafted, and, although she is entitled to issue guidance to assist the ECOs in their task, she is not entitled to instruct or direct them as to the decision to be made or to remove or restrict the ECOs' power of decision-making.[4] The position of ECOs is, therefore, different from that of immigration officers, where there is an express statutory obligation to follow instructions from the Secretary of State, providing they are not inconsistent with the Immigration Rules.[5] However, like immigration officers, entry clearance officers have a duty to be fair. Like immigration officers, they are under a duty not to act in a way which breaches a person's fundamental human rights[6], nor in a way which discriminates on grounds of race or colour.[7] If an interview is conducted the entry clearance officer should check that the person being interviewed is well and understands the questions. Unfair questions should not be put. Leading questions do not particularly advance the case against an applicant or assist the interview, but entry clearance officers are carrying out administrative, not judicial, functions and there is, therefore, nothing improper in asking such questions.[8] An entry clearance officer should afford an applicant an opportunity to address any adverse evidence or conclusions which will affect his or her decision.[9] The conduct of different aspects of the entry clearance exercise may be subject to the general scrutiny of the Independent Chief Inspector of the UK Border Agency, if he decides to carry out such an inspection.[10]

1   See, for example, HC 395, Appendix A, paras 41-SD to 45A (Tier 1 Entrepreneurs) or Appendix FM – SE (evidence for family members).
2   See www.gov.uk/immigration-operational-guidance
3   ECG FAQ.
4   *R (on the application of NA (Iraq)) v Secretary of State for Foreign and Commonwealth Affairs* [2007] EWCA Civ 759, which concerned the validity of an 'S series' passport from Iran. See also *R (on the application of Asad) v Secretary of State for Foreign and Commonwealth Affairs* [2007] EWHC 286 (Admin) (9 February 2007), where Goldring J took a rather different view of the use of 'S series' passports.
5   Immigration Act 1971, Sch 2, para 1(3).

6   Human Rights Act 1998, s 6(1).
7   Section 13 of the Equality Act 2010 makes it unlawful for a public authority to do any act
    which constitutes discrimination on the basis of any of the nine protected characteristics; see
    1.84 above. However, Schedule 3, Part 4, paragraph 17 (4)(a) of the Equality Act allows the
    practice of discrimination on nationality grounds under Ministerial Authorisations to con-
    tinue; see **1.82** above. See also Dummett, 'The immigration exemptions in the Race Relations
    (Amendment) Act 2000', ILPA, April 2001. For an example of discrimination, see *CS (Race
    Discrimination etc) Jamaica* [2006] UKAIT 0004, [2006] Imm AR 289, but it did not
    invalidate the ECO's refusal on appeal.
8   *Kumar v Entry Clearance Officer, New Delhi* [1985] Imm AR 242.
9   *R v Secretary of State for the Home Department, ex p Moon* [1997] INLR 165; see also *R v
    Secretary of State for the Home Department, ex p Thirukumar* [1989] Imm AR 270, DC; on
    appeal sub nom *Secretary of State for the Home Department v Thirukumar* [1989] Imm AR
    402, CA; *R v Secretary of State for the Home Department, ex p Fayed* [1997] 1 All ER 228,
    CA.
10 The Reports of the Independent Chief Inspector are available at www.icinspector.independe
    nt.gov.uk.

3.69 Although entry clearance officers are applying the Immigration Rules, this is not a mechanical exercise of applying rules to the facts of applications as presented to them. They are entitled to and do carry out their own investigations.[1] Sometimes these will prove the existence of a relationship previously in doubt, but their inquiries may also prove that an applicant is disqualified in some other way, for example, because a child seeking entry to join a parent has married. Usually entry clearance officers are not precluded from acting on the results of their investigations.[2] Applications may also be referred back to the Home Office for inquiries to be made in the UK, for guidance to be given in a complicated case or because of a special policy.[3] An application should be based on evidence and not suspicion and speculation or be based on a past unsuccessful application, especially where there had been a substantial history of compliance with the Immigration Rules and not overstaying and where after the individual concerned had returned promptly after dismissal of any appeal against the refusal of indefinite leave.[4]

1   *R v Immigration Appeal Tribunal, ex p Hoque and Singh* [1988] Imm AR 216, CA.
2   *R v Immigration Appeal Tribunal, ex p Kobir* [1986] Imm AR 311, QBD. But they should not
    act on anonymous denunciations or statements made by persons who are not prepared for the
    applicant to be aware of their evidence: IDI (Sep 04), Ch 9, s 1, 'Adverse decisions', para 2.2.
    The DSP Ch 8 para 8.14 suggest a slightly different approach to denunciations, ie, not to
    mention them in refusals even where they may have been taken into account.
3   For the circumstances in which referral is likely, see ECG, Chapters 16 and 24.
4   *MM (Nigeria) v Secretary of State for the Home Department* [2007] EWCA Civ 44, per
    Buxton LJ (16 January 2007).

3.70 Where there has already been a successful application but the entry clearance was for some reason not used, and the applicant has had to re-apply, the previous application is strong evidence in favour of the applicant.[1] Where an applicant has successfully appealed against the refusal of entry clearance, it is wholly improper for an attempt to be made to circumvent the immigration judge's decision by pursuing fresh inquiries with a view to denying entry on a different basis, but in such cases entry clearance officers are entitled to ask questions in order to see if there has been a change of circumstances or there has been fraud or deception.[2] All this means that there may be considerable delay before applications are decided. The existence of delay, however, does not invalidate the need for entry clearance,[3] although in a particular case it might give rise to a challenge on the ground of unfairness, and failure to take a decision after a reasonable period of time may be challenged by an application for a mandatory order.

1   *Visa Officer, Islamabad v Channo Bi* [1978] Imm AR 182; *Visa Officer, Islamabad v Begum* [1986] Imm AR 192.
2   *R v Secretary of State for the Home Department, ex p Yousuf* [1989] Imm AR 554, QBD.
3   *R v Secretary of State for the Home Department, ex p Rofathullah* [1989] QB 219, [1988] Imm AR 514, CA.

Revocation of entry clearance

3.71 After an entry clearance has been issued, an entry clearance officer may revoke it[1] if satisfied that:

(i)   whether or not to the holder's knowledge false representations were employed or material facts were not disclosed, either in writing or orally, for the purpose of obtaining the entry clearance; or

(ii)   a change of circumstances since the issue of the entry clearance has removed the basis for admission to the UK, except where the change of circumstances amounts solely to a child coming for settlement becoming over-age since the issue of the entry clearance; or

(iii) the holder's exclusion from the UK would be conducive to the public good.

There is no right of appeal against a decision to revoke or cancel entry clearance[2]. The rule enabling entry clearance to be revoked or cancelled before departure for the UK is similar to immigration officers' powers to refuse leave to enter to an entry clearance holder and is dealt with below[3].

1   HC 395, para 30A, added by HC 329 from 3 June 1996.
2   It is not an immigration decision for the purposes of Nationality, Immigration and Asylum Act 2002, s 82.
3   See **3.132** below.

Entry clearance as leave to enter

3.72 Section 3A of the Immigration Act 1971 (inserted by section 1 of the Immigration and Asylum Act 1999) created 'greater flexibility in the way permission to enter the UK may be granted'[1] by empowering the Secretary of State to make Orders to allow entry clearance to have effect as leave to enter the UK, thereby reducing the role of immigration officers at the port of entry. The Immigration (Leave to Enter and Remain) Order 2000[2] provides that entry clearance will have effect as leave to enter provided it specifies the purpose for which the holder wishes to enter the UK[3] and is endorsed with the conditions to which it is subject,[4] or a statement that it is to have effect as indefinite leave to enter the UK.[5] Entry clearances which do not operate as leave to enter are those endorsed on refugees' Convention travel documents on or after 27 February 2004,[6] certificates of entitlement, EEA family permits, exempt visas[7] and direct airside transit visas.[8] Visit visas are to have effect as leave to enter on an unlimited number of occasions during their period of validity[9] unless issued pursuant to the 'ADS agreement with China.[10] For periods of leave as a visitor see CHAPTER 8, below. Entry clearances for purposes other than visit(s) are, according to the Order, to have effect as leave to enter the UK on one occasion only during the period of their validity,[11] whether that leave to enter is for an indefinite period[12] or endorsed with conditions.[13] In practice, such entry clearances operate as leave to enter on every entry during the period of leave which they grant, since such leave does not lapse on the holder's departure.[14]

[1]   Explanatory notes to the Immigration and Asylum Act 1999, para 7.
[2]   SI 2000/1161, as amended by SI 2001/1544, so that entry clearances will have effect as leave to enter the UK in a controlled zone in France or Belgium and a supplementary control zone in France, and SI 2004/475.
[3]   SI 2000/1161, art 3(2).
[4]   SI 2000/1161, art 3(2)(a).
[5]   SI 2000/1161, art 3(2)(b). For power to refuse on the basis of nationality, see 3.4 above.
[6]   SI 2000/1161, art 3(4), inserted by SI 2004/475. This does not apply to holders of travel documents issued by the UK, who do not require entry clearance.
[7]   Because such passengers do not require leave to enter. See IDI (Jun 02), Ch 1, s 4, para 2.
[8]   Because such passengers do not enter the UK (within the meaning of Immigration Act 1971, s 11(1)). See IDI above, para 2.
[9]   SI 2000/1161, art 4(1). 'Period of validity' is defined in art 4 as 'the period beginning on the day which the entry clearance becomes effective and ending on the day on which it expires'. Most visit visas only run for six months, but can run for up to five years for frequent travellers. Normally the 'valid from' date is the date of issue, but the ECO may delay this date for up to three months to correspond with the date of travel: IDI, Ch 1, s 4, para 4.4. If this has not been done and a visitor had less than six months left on entry to the UK, he or she may be granted a short extension to make up the full six months: IDI, Ch 1, s 9, para 2.7.
[10] Immigration (Leave to Enter and Remain) (Amendment) Order 2005, SI 2005/1159, in force 1 April 2005, limiting visit visas, granted under the Approved Destination Status (ADS) 'tourist groups' agreement with China, to leave to enter on one or two occasions only, as endorsed. Visitors under the ADS agreement above will be granted 30-day visas: HC 395, para 56G, inserted by HC 486 from 5 April 2005.
[11] SI 2000/1161 art 4(3).
[12] SI 2000/1161, art 4(3)(a).
[13] SI 2000/1161, art 4(3)(b). The conditions which can be imposed will be those which can be imposed on leave to enter under Immigration Act 1971, s 3(1)(c), ie restricting employment, precluding recourse to public funds and requiring registration with police.
[14] SI 2000/1161, art 13. See 4.6 below.

3.73 Where entry clearance operates as leave to enter, the immigration officer may examine the holder at the port to decide whether the leave to enter should be cancelled.[1] An immigration officer at the port of entry may cancel an entry clearance, if the holder arrives in the UK before the day on which it becomes effective,[2] or seeks leave to enter for a different purpose.[3] In the former case, if satisfied that the passenger is seeking entry on the same basis and qualifies for leave to enter, the immigration officer may, while cancelling the entry clearance, grant leave to enter.[4] If leave is sought for a different purpose, the immigration officer would normally cancel the entry clearance, unless it is appropriate to grant leave to enter exceptionally without entry clearance.[5] Other criteria for cancellation of entry clearance operating as leave to enter are stricter. For detailed consideration of these grounds see **3.132–3.133** below. Where entry clearance operates as leave to enter, cancellation by an immigration officer on entry currently attracts a right of appeal, which was exercisable from the UK,[6] but no longer is, since section 28 of the Asylum and Immigration (Treatment of Claimants, etc) Act 2004 came into force, in cases where there has been deception or a change of circumstances or entry is sought for a different purpose than that for which the entry clearance was granted.[7] We deal with cancellation of leave and port examinations below. Where entry clearance does not operate as leave to enter (for example, where it is endorsed on a Convention travel document),[8] when the holder seeks leave to enter it may be refused on the same grounds as those on which the entry clearance officer may revoke entry clearance, set out at **3.71** above. These are that false representations were made or material facts not disclosed for the purpose of obtaining entry clearance, or that there has been a relevant change in circumstances or, that exclusion is conducive to the public good: see Part 3, below.

[1] Immigration Act 1971 Sch 2, para 2A (inserted by Immigration and Asylum Act 1999, amended by Nationality, Immigration and Asylum Act 2002).
[2] Immigration (Leave to Enter and Remain) Order 2000, art 6(2)(a); HC 395 para 30C, inserted by HC 704.
[3] SI 2000/1161 art 6(2)(b). In *R (on the application of Boahen) v Secretary of State for the Home Department* [2010] EWCA Civ 585, [2010] All ER (D) 14 (Jun), the Court of Appeal held that an immigration officer at the port of entry has discretionary power to cancel a visa granted overseas on the ground that the purpose of the visit was not the same as stated in the visa granted and to refuse leave to enter the UK.
[4] See IDI (Jun 02), Ch 1, s 4, para 10.3.
[5] See IDI (Jun 02), Ch 1, s 4, para 10.3.
[6] Nationality, Immigration and Asylum Act 2002 s 82(2)(a) read with s 92(3) and Immigration Act 1971, Sch 2, para 2A(8), (9) (inserted by Immigration and Asylum Act 1999, amended by Nationality, Immigration and Asylum Act 2002), prior to amendment by 2004 Act.
[7] Nationality, Immigration and Asylum Act 2002, s 92(3), (3A), (3B) as inserted by s 28 Asylum and Immigration (Treatment of Claimants, etc) Act 2004 from 1 October 2004: SI 2004/2523).
[8] SI 2000/1161, art 3(4).

Extra-territorial immigration control

3.74 We saw at **3.58** above that, quite apart from the entry clearance system and co-existing with it, section 3A of the Immigration Act 1971, inserted by the Immigration and Asylum Act 1999, gave the Secretary of State the power to introduce a scheme enabling immigration officers to grant or refuse leave to enter extra-territorially.[1] The Immigration Rules provide that 'where a person is outside the UK but wishes to travel to the UK an immigration officer may give or refuse him leave to enter . . . '.[2] These provisions were implemented at Prague airport, by agreement with the Czech government, and were used to refuse numbers of Czech Roma would-be passengers leave to enter the UK before they boarded (and to stop them from doing so). The House of Lords held that the system of 'pre-entry clearance' checks as operated at Prague Airport was unlawful and discriminatory, overturning the majority decision in the Court of Appeal.[3]

[1] See Immigration (Leave to Enter and Remain) Order 2000, SI 2000/1161, art 7 (made under Immigration Act 1971, s 3A as inserted).
[2] HC 395, para 17A, inserted by HC 704.
[3] *European Roma Rights Centre v Immigration Officer at Prague Airport (United Nations High Commissioner for Refugees intervening)* [2004] UKHL 55, [2005] 2 WLR 1.

The Channel Tunnel trains and railway station

3.75 The other way in which immigration controls have been made extra-territorial is through provisions which deem parts of Europe as ports of entry for immigration control purposes. These provisions initially related to the Channel Tunnel and related only to Eurostar railway stations but have been expanded to include other ports of embarkation for the UK, such as Boulogne, Calais and Dunkirk in France. What these provisions do is to create UK control areas in French and Belgian territory, either in a train station or at a designated EEA port of embarkation for the UK, effectively part of the UK for immigration purposes. Under various treaties with France and Belgium reciprocal control areas are allocated to French and Belgian immigration authorities.

3.76 The Channel Tunnel Act 1987, passed to implement the Canterbury Treaty of 12 February 1986 between France and the UK, included provision for the construction and operation of the Channel Tunnel; for the incorporation of the British part of the tunnel system into England and the district of Kent and for English law to apply accordingly[1] for the application and enforcement of law in relation to it and otherwise for the regulation of the tunnel system and matters connected with it. The principal order made under the Act, following the first Sangatte Protocol between France and the UK, is the Channel Tunnel (International Arrangements) Order 1993[2] which came into force on 2 August 1993, initially covering arrangements with France, but amended by the Channel Tunnel (Miscellaneous Provisions) Order 1994 so as also to cover Belgium.[3] The Order and its 1994 counterpart enable UK immigration officers to operate on French and Belgian territory and vice versa and allow immigration controls to be carried out on the trains running between London, Calais, Paris and Lille,[4] and Brussels.[5] The Orders extend the powers of immigration officers under the Immigration Act 1971 to carry out immigration control within 'control zones' (and supplementary control zones[6]) within French and Belgian territory.[7] A 'control zone' means that part of French or Belgian territory within which immigration officers (and also the Secretary of State for the Home Department)[8] are empowered to effect immigration and other controls.[9] The provisions of the Immigration Act 1971 are modified in relation to those entering and leaving through the tunnel system, so as to include leaving a control zone in the definition of entry,[10] and to allow examination, and the grant, refusal or cancellation of leave, to take place in control zones as if they were at a port of entry in the UK.[11] From November 2007, the Eurostar to France and Belgium started its journey from St Pancras station via the new terminal at Ebbsworth. These are now designated control areas and Waterloo is removed as a supplementary control zone.[12]

---

[1] Channel Tunnel Act 1987, s 10.

[2] SI 1993/1813, as amended by the Channel Tunnel (Security) Order 1994, SI 1994/570, and the Channel Tunnel (International Arrangements) (Amendment) Orders, SI 1996/2283, SI 2000/913, SI 2000/1775, SI 2001/178, SI 2001/418, SI 2001/1544, SI 2001/3707 and SI 2004/2589 and, by the Channel Tunnel (International Arrangements) (Amendment) Order 2006, SI 2006/2626, the Channel Tunnel (International Arrangements) (Amendment) Order 2007, SI 2007/2907 and the Channel Tunnel (International Arrangements) (Amendment) Order 2009, SI 2009/2081.

[3] Channel Tunnel (Miscellaneous Provisions) Order 1994, SI 1994/1405 in force 1 December 1997 implementing the provisions of the Tripartite Agreement and Protocol made at Brussels 15 December 1993. This has been amended by the Channel Tunnel (Miscellaneous Provisions) (Amendment) Order 2004, SI 2004/2589; the Channel Tunnel (Miscellaneous Provisions) (Amendment) Order 2006, SI 2006/2627; the Channel Tunnel (Miscellaneous Provisions) (Amendment) Order 2007, SI 2007/2908.

4   International Articles, art 7 (set out in SI 1993/1813, Sch 2); SI 1993/1813, art 5A (inserted by SI 2001/1544). Juxtaposed controls at Coquelles were established in 1994 and immigration powers are provided by the Channel Tunnel (International Arrangements) Order 1993. The powers for juxtaposed controls at the Eurostar stations of Paris, Lille and Calais Frethun in France and Waterloo, St Pancras and Ashford, in the UK are provided by Amendment No 3 to that '93 Order, SI 2001/1544 (supplementary Articles, art 2 (set out in Sch 2A). Waterloo is no longer a control zone: se Fn 12 below.

5   Juxtaposed controls were established at Brussels by the Channel Tunnel (Miscellaneous Provisions) Order 1994, SI 1994/1405, and its amendment of 2004 by SI 2004/2589.

6   Following the Additional Protocol to the Sangatte Protocol, signed at Brussels on 29 May 2000 (Cm 5015), supplementary control zones were set up in France, which allowed UK immigration officers in a supplementary zone to use their full powers, including arrest in France, to stop people boarding a through train to the UK and hand them over to the French authorities to be dealt with under French domestic law procedures: Channel Tunnel (International Arrangements) (Amendment No 3) Order 2001, SI 2001/1544, art 3. Secondly, article 4 provides that where a refugee claim or claim for international humanitarian protection is made in France, it should be dealt with by the French authorities and vice versa.

7   International Articles 5, 8, 9 and 10, contained in Sch 2 to SI 1993/1813; Sch 3, para 2(2)(a) as amended by SI 2001/1544; art 4(1) of the Channel Tunnel (Miscellaneous Provisions) Order 1994, SI 1994/1405.The 1994 Order is amended by the Channel Tunnel (Miscellaneous Provisions) (Amendment) Order 2014, SI 2014/409 which underpins a new bilateral Agreement between the UK and Belgium on the administrative arrangements which provide the basis for juxtaposed controls in respect of trains travelling between Belgium and the UK via the Channel Tunnel and France (see Part IV of Schedule 2 to the Order). The Order provides further legal underpinning, sought by Belgium, for the UK operation of immigration controls on stopping trains at the juxtaposed controls in Belgium. It does not confer any new powers on Border Force and the immigration controls on stopping trains in Belgium will continue as they did before: see the Explanatory Memorandum to the 2014 Order. The French Government is not party to the bilateral Agreement but has approved its contents.

8   Immigration Act 1971, s 3A(7) and (8), as inserted by Immigration and Asylum Act 1999, s 1.

9   See art 1(2)(g) of the International Articles in Sch 2 to SI 1993/1813.

10   Immigration Act 1971, s 11, as modified by SI 1993/1813, art 7 and Sch 4.

11   SI 1993/1813, Sch 4, para 1(11)(d), as substituted by SI 2001/1544, art 6(3). The Channel Tunnel (International Arrangements) (Amendment) Order 2006 amends Schedule 4 to the 1993 Order to provide for a modification in the application of section 141 of the Immigration and Asylum Act 1999 (power to take fingerprints) to Paris and Lille stations. The Channel Tunnel (Miscellaneous Provisions) (Amendment) Order 2006 amends the 1994 Order to make the same modification in relation to control zones in Belgium. In addition, it amends the 1994 Order to substitute a reference to the Prevention of Terrorism (Temporary Provisions) Act 1989 with a reference to the Terrorism Act 2004. These Orders are linked to The Nationality, Immigration and Asylum Act 2002 (Juxtaposed Controls) (Amendment Order) 2006, SI 2006/2908, which, inter alia, provides for the power to take fingerprints at juxtaposed controls at the northern French ports of Calais, Dunkirk and Boulogne. See further 3.78 below.

12   The Channel Tunnel (International Arrangements) (Amendment) Order 2007, SI 2007/2907 (in respect of journeys to France), and the Channel Tunnel (Miscellaneous Provisions) (Amendment) Order 2007, SI 2007/2908 (in relation to journeys to Belgium).

Control zones at sea ports

3.77 The project to re-position UK borders on the other side of the Channel continued with section 141 of the Nationality, Immigration and Asylum Act 2002, which gave the Secretary of State wide powers to make orders giving effect to international agreements allowing for UK laws to have effect in EEA ports. The first Treaty to which effect has been given by an order under the section is the Le Touquet Treaty, which was signed on 4 February 2003 and came into force on 1 February 2004.[1] The Order giving effect to it is the Nationality, Immigration and Asylum (Juxtaposed Controls) Order 2003,[2] which provides for additional control zones in ports at Dover, Calais,

Boulogne and Dunkirk.[3] Article 11 of the 2003 Order sets out those provisions of domestic law which are to have effect in a control zone in France.[4] Since 1 February 2004, all UK-bound passengers travelling from Calais and Dunkirk have been subject to UK immigration control before boarding their ferry. Immigration officers grant or refuse leave to enter as if they were in a UK port.[5]

[1] Treaty between the Government of the UK and the Government of France concerning the implementation of frontier controls at the sea ports of both countries on the Channel and North Sea (Cm 5832).

[2] SI 2003/2818 amended, which privatises the power to search vehicles in a UK control zone at a juxtaposed control at Calais, Dunkerque or Boulogne, and to detain persons hidden inside and provides for the taking of fingerprints under s 141 of the Immigration and Asylum Act 1999 in a UK control zone at these same locations.

[3] SI 2003/2818, Sch 1.

[4] These are the Immigration Act 1971; Schs 7 and 8 to the Terrorism Act 2000; the Code of Practice for examining officers under the Terrorism Act 2000; the Immigration (Leave to Enter and Remain) Order 2000, SI 2000/1161; and the Immigration (European Economic Area) Regulations 2000, SI 2000/2326.

[5] Further control zones may be set up at other EEC ports. Negotiations began with the Dutch authorities for similar control zones at ports in the Netherlands but to date no further such zones have been established: see Home Office press release 15 April 2004.

3.78 Since the start of juxtaposed controls between France, Belgium and the UK, further immigration controls have been brought in. When the immigration controls at the juxtaposed controls in France were initially established, no provision was made for the application of section 141 of the Immigration and Asylum Act 1999 – fingerprinting (not to be confused with section 141 of the 2002 Act). At the time it was felt that it would not be necessary to take fingerprints as all persons refused entry to the UK at a UK control zone are handed over to the French authorities and their movements within the UK do not need any management.[1] However the governments obsession with building data banks containing information about more and more people soon took over. It was felt that a bank of physical data could be developed to identify previous offenders who are without paper documentation and that extended use of fingerprinting would support an intelligence led approach to border security.[2] So the Nationality, Immigration and Asylum Act 2002 (Juxtaposed Controls) (Amendment) Order 2006 was brought in to deal with these matters.[3] The effect of this Order is to provide the same powers to take fingerprints under section 141 of the 1999 Act as those available at UK mainland ports. The Channel Tunnel (International Arrangements) (Amendment) Order 2006[4] and the Channel Tunnel (Miscellaneous Provisions) (Amendment) Order 2006[5] give the same powers in the control zones and supplementary controls zones for Eurostar trains traveling between the UK and France and Belgium respectively. In addition SI 2006/2908 now permits the Home Office to contract out to trained personnel employed by private companies the search of ships and vehicles at the French ports, by applying sections 40 and 41 of IAN 2006 to the control areas at these ports.[6]

[1] Explanatory Memorandum to SI 2006/2626 and SI 2006/2627, para 7.

[2] Explanatory Memorandum to SI 2006/2626 and SI 2006/2627, para 7.

[3] SI 2006/2908, art 2, amending art 11(1)(e) of the 1993 Order.

[4] SI 2006/2626.

[5] SI 2006/2627.

[6] Nationality, Immigration and Asylum Act 2002 (Juxtaposed Controls) (Amendment) Order 2006, 2006/2908, art 2, amending article 11(1)(e) of the 1993 Order.

3.79 How do juxtaposed controls work in practice? Clearly there is no problem if a passenger is granted leave to enter. But if he or she is refused, how can any appeal rights be made effective? Although the government has stated that passengers refused entry who have a right of appeal from abroad will be served with a notice of refusal which will include information about the Immigration Advisory Service,[1] it is not clear how the would-be appellant would in practice be able to access any meaningful legal advice from those organisations. Will those whose leave is cancelled, but who have in-country appeal rights, be allowed to board the ferry in order to access those rights? The 2002 Act is not one of the enactments which has effect in control zones; what effect does this omission have on appeal rights? All these matters still await clarification. If the immigration officer requires the passenger to submit to further examination, the powers of detention under the Immigration Act 1971 apply. But what about temporary admission? The Home Office has stated that Immigration Officers operating at juxtaposed controls may consider alternatives to detention, which means either releasing passengers and 'asking them to come back the next day' or 'handing them back to the French authorities'.[2] Article 4 of the Additional Protocol to the Sangatte Protocol provides that an application for asylum made in a control zone to the officers of the 'state of arrival' is to be examined by the authorities of the 'state of departure'.[3] This means that no asylum seekers will reach the UK through Calais or Dunkirk (or the other control zones, including Eurostar stations and trains), unless they enter illegally, since an admission that asylum is sought will result in being handed over to the French authorities, regardless of the reasons for wishing to claim in the UK.[4] One suspects that reducing the number of asylum claimants reaching the UK was the main reason for the whole exercise.[5]

[1] See Consultation Process Report government response to comments on legal representation, which was available on the BIA website several editions ago but cannot now be found.
[2] Note of meeting between the Home Office and NGOs, 13 January 2004.
[3] Set out in Sch 2A, SI 1993/1813 (as amended by SI 2001/1544).
[4] Presumably, however, the Dublin regulation will operate to enable the French authorities to transfer claimants to the UK if they satisfy the criteria (such as having family members in the UK as refugees).
[5] See responses by Refugee Council Jan 2003 (available at www.refugeecouncil.org.uk) and ILPA.

Examination abroad for the grant of leave

3.80 As we have seen above, an immigration officer, whether or not in the UK, may give or refuse a person leave to enter the UK at any time before that person's departure for the UK, or in the course of their journey.[1] To determine whether or not to give leave to enter, and if so for what period and subject to what conditions, the immigration officer may seek the information and documents that he or she would be entitled to obtain in an examination at the port.[2] Since the Immigration Officer examining someone abroad cannot refer the applicant to the port medical inspector, an up-to-date medical report can be requested instead.[3] Failure to provide the information, documents or medical report is a ground for refusal of leave.[4] The Immigration Officer or Secretary of State is authorised to use the power of examination in a discriminatory way against persons of a particular nationality if justified by statistical information indicating that persons of that nationality have an

205

above average refusal rate or have breached immigration laws.[5]

1   Immigration (Leave to Enter and Remain) Order, SI 2000/1161, art 7(1).
2   SI 2000/1161, art 7(2).
3   SI 2000/1161, art 7(3).
4   SI 2000/1161, art 7(4). Presumably it is a discretionary ground. See **3.165** below.
5   Under a Ministerial Authorisation: see Chapter 1.

Examination at the port of entry

Who is examined

3.81 All passengers arriving at a port of entry in the UK (or in a control zone)[1] are required to submit to examination by immigration officers. This applies to British citizens,[2] other citizens of the EEA,[3] and other people who do not require leave to enter. In order to retain these frontier controls, which run counter to the establishment in the EC of a single market without internal frontiers,[4] the UK has negotiated a special protocol to the Consolidated Treaty of the EC.[5] In order to find out who is eligible and if so on what conditions they should be given leave to enter, immigration officers are given power under the Immigration Act 1971 to examine all those who have arrived in the UK by ship, aircraft or train, even if they are merely in transit and do not wish to enter the UK.[6] The purpose of doing so is to establish:

(i)   whether any of them are British citizens (or Commonwealth citizens with a right of abode); and
(ii)   if subject to control, whether they can or cannot enter without leave; and
(iii)   if they may not, whether they have been given leave which is still in force;
(iv)   if not, whether they should be given leave and for what period and on what conditions (if any); or
(v)   should be refused it.

In respect of passengers arriving with leave to enter which is in force but was given before their arrival, the immigration officer's examination is to establish:

(i)   whether there has been such a change in the circumstances of the case that it should be cancelled;
(ii)   whether the leave was obtained as a result of false information given by the passenger or his or her failure to disclose material facts;
(iii)   whether there are medical grounds on which leave should be cancelled;[7]
(iv)   whether it would be conducive to the public good for the leave to be cancelled;[8]
(v)   whether the purpose for which entry is sought is different to the purpose specified in the entry clearance.[9]

It is a criminal offence to refuse to submit to this examination.[10] Ministerial authorisation under the Race Relations Act[11] enables the immigration officer to subject passengers of particular nationalities to a more rigorous examination, require them to submit to further examination, examine and detain their documents, search them, detain them and impose conditions on temporary admission by reason of their nationality.

1   The term includes areas, ports and trains in France and Belgium defined as control zones under the Channel Tunnel (International Arrangements) Order 1993, SI 1993/1813, as amended. See **3.75–3.79** above.
2   Immigration Act 1971, ss 1(1), 3(9).
3   Immigration (European Economic Area) Regulations 2006, SI 2006/1003, reg 11(1) and (2).
4   See art 26 TFEU (formerly art 14 TEC).
5   See Protocol 20 in TFEU on the application of certain aspects of art 26 TFEU (formally art 14 of TEU).
6   Immigration Act 1971, Sch 2, para 2(1); *R v Secretary of State for the Home Department, ex p Connbye* [1987] Imm AR 478, QBD.
7   Immigration Act 1971, Sch 2, para 2A(2), inserted by the Immigration and Asylum Act 1999, Sch 14, para 57.
8   Immigration Act 1971, Sch 2, para 2A(3) as inserted.
9   Immigration Act 1971, Sch 2, para 2A(2A), inserted by Asylum and Immigration (Treatment of Claimants etc) Act 2004, s 18.
10   Immigration Act 1971, s 26(1)(a).
11   Race Relations (Immigration and Asylum) Authorisation 2004, Annexe EE to Ch 1, s 11 of the IDI at: www.ukba.homeoffice.gov.uk/sitecontent/documents/policyandlaw/IDIs/idischapter1. For more details on discrimination, see CHAPTER 1.

3.82 Apart from refugees and passengers relying on provisions of the ECHR, all other travellers to the UK must be in possession of some kind of identity documentation to obtain entry under the Immigration Act 1971 and the Immigration Rules.[1] The main kinds of document needed on arrival at a port of entry are:

• passport or recognised travel document;
• identity card;

A valid national passport or other document 'satisfactorily' establishing identity and nationality must be produced by every passenger arriving at a port of entry if demanded by an immigration officer.[2] Inability to produce such a document may render the passenger liable to prosecution under section 2 of the Asylum and Immigration (Treatment of Claimants etc) Act 2004,[3] but does not, thereby make the passenger an illegal entrant.[4] EC nationals can travel with valid national identity cards instead of passports.[5] If a person has a passport or travel document from a country which either is not recognised as a State by the UK, or is not dealt with as a government by the UK, or does not accept valid UK passports for its own immigration control, or does not comply with international passport practice, the person should normally be refused leave to enter on that ground alone.[6]

1   Those with the right of abode are entitled to come and go without let or hindrance except such as may be required under the Act to enable their right to be established: Immigration Act 1971, s 1(1). If their right of abode is disputed, they must prove it by means of a passport or a certificate of entitlement: s 3(9); HC 395, paras 12, 13.
2   Immigration Act 1971, Sch 2, para 4(2)(a); HC 395, para 11.
3   See **15.39** below.
4   Before the offence was created under the 2004 Act, mere inability to produce a document under Sch 2, para 4 did not render the passenger an illegal entrant: *R v Naillie* [1993] AC 674; [1993] 2 All ER 782, HL. The new offence does not change this, because the decision on entry does not depend on the absence or not of a passport without reasonable excuse, but on whether the person has a claim to enter as an asylum seeker or on some other good ground. See further CHAPTER 17 below.
5   Immigration (European Economic Area) Regulations 2000, SI 2000/2326, reg 12.

6   HC 395, para 320(10). See **3.165** below; note the concessions and the fact that leave may not be cancelled on this ground.

3.83 Passengers in transit to another country outside the common travel area will not normally be given any detailed examination once it is established that they are in transit, have the means and intention of proceeding at once to another country, are assured of entry there and intend to leave the UK within 48 hours.[1] Leave to enter may be given for 48 hours, no more.[2] Transit passengers, however, can be stopped and detained and removed to a different destination.[3] Leave to enter will be refused if an Immigration Officer is not satisfied about the passenger's intentions, means, or that he or she will be admitted to the country of destination.[4]

1   HC 395, para 47.
2   HC 395, paras 48 and 50.
3   HC 395, para 49; Immigration Act 1971, Sch 2, paras 8 and 16. See the case of *Williams, ex p* [1970] Crim LR 102, a black civil rights leader, who was detained in transit while on his way back from China to the US.
4   HC 395, para 49; see *R v Secretary of State for the Home Department, ex p Connhye* [1987] Imm AR 478; affd (1988) Independent, 20 April, CA, where it was held proper for an immigration officer to examine the financial means of a transit passenger.

3.84 In order to assist immigration officers in their task, a duty is cast on all persons who are examined by immigration officers (either on arrival or departure) to answer any questions put to them, say what documents they may be carrying and to produce their passport or other identity document.[1] These may be retained by the immigration officer until either leave to enter is granted or, if it is refused, until the passenger is about to be removed following refusal of leave.[2] Landing cards are also required for all passengers over 16 who are not British citizens, except on journeys within the common travel area.[3] It is a criminal offence to give false information or documents to an immigration officer,[4] or not to give information which is required or to refuse to hand over documents, unless there is a reasonable excuse.[5] There is no duty to volunteer unsolicited information, and a person will not be an illegal entrant if they accidentally and without intention to mislead offer incorrect information, but silence accompanied by conduct can in some circumstances amount to a false representation.[6]

1   Immigration Act 1971, Sch 2, para 4.
2   Immigration Act 1971, Sch 2, para 4(2A). The IDI state that once a passenger has been refused leave to enter, the passport should not be returned before removal unless there is a valid reason (eg to obtain a foreign visa or have it revalidated). The chief immigration officer must be satisfied that there is no risk of the passenger absconding or defacing the passport to frustrate removal: IDI (Sep 04), Ch 9, s 6, para 6.
3   Immigration Act 1971, Sch 2, para 5; Immigration (Landing and Embarkation Cards) Order 1975, SI 1975/65, art 4. They are supplied by the carriers: art 4(2).
4   Immigration Act 1971, s 26(1)(c).
5   Immigration Act 1971, s 26(1)(b). See **15.68** below.
6   See *Khawaja v Secretary of State for the Home Department* [1984] AC 74, [1983] 1 All ER 765, HL. There is no commensurate duty to attend for interview with an entry clearance officer or to provide documents, but failure to do so may result in an adverse inference being drawn (*R v Immigration Appeal Tribunal, ex p Hubbard* [1985] Imm AR 110, QBD) or even in the entry clearance officer deeming the application to have been withdrawn. See also *R v Secretary of State for the Home Department, ex p Awan* [1996] Imm AR 354, QBD. The Asylum and Immigration (Treatment of Claimants, etc) Act 2004, s 8 obliges adverse inferences to be drawn from such failure in the asylum context: see **20.110** below.

3.85 In carrying out their examination, Immigration Officers can search the person, baggage or vehicle of an entrant, and any ship, aircraft or vehicle on which he or she arrived, for any documents that they wish to see[1] and may now require incoming passengers to provide biometric information (such as fingerprints or features of the iris) in order to ascertain whether the passenger in question is the rightful holder of the passport or other document produced.[2] The main use of these powers is to discover whether an entrant possesses documents which might show that the real purpose of coming to the UK is something other than that stated.[3] There are limits on the documents they may take. Like police powers of search and seizure, where, broadly speaking, only documents which are relevant to some crime may be seized, only documents relevant to the discharge of immigration control may be taken by immigration officers.[4] Documents taken may be photocopied or scanned; fingerprints may be taken and stored.[5] The very extensive powers of examination and search referred to here are inappropriate for citizens of the EU and others exercising their rights under EC law. Even if they are making a journey from outside the EU, they do not require leave to enter and extensive examination is unnecessary.[6]

[1]   Immigration Act 1971, Sch 2, para 4(3). The examination powers of immigration officers are now augmented. The Immigration Act 1971, Sch 2, para 4(2A) is replaced by new provisions, under which passports and other documents can be kept for longer periods.
[2]   Immigration Act 1971, Sch 2, paras 4(4) and 4(5), inserted by IAN 2006, s 27, which came into force on 31 August 2006: Immigration, Asylum and Nationality Act 2006 (Commencement No 2) Order 2006, SI 2006/2226.
[3]   A number of refusals have resulted from such searches. See *Baldacchino v Secretary of State for the Home Department* [1972] Imm AR 14 at 15, where the search of the immigrant's baggage was crucial. In *R v Secretary of State for the Home Department, ex p Hindjou (Frieda)* [1989] Imm AR 24, QBD, the immigration officer drew unreasonable inferences from letters found in the passenger's luggage, and the refusal of leave to enter was quashed.
[4]   See (in relation to police powers) *Chic Fashions (West Wales) Ltd v Jones* [1968] 2 QB 299, [1968] 1 All ER 229, CA; *Ghani v Jones* [1970] 1 QB 693, [1969] 3 All ER 1700, CA. For detailed powers of search and seizure see **15.14** below.
[5]   See the Immigration and Asylum Act 1999, ss 141 and 142 and the further provisions in IAN 2006 ss 28 and 29, which came into force on 31 August 2006: Immigration, Asylum and Nationality Act 2006 (Commencement No 2) Order 2006, SI 2006/2226. Also, see the Immigration (Provision of Physical Data) Regulations 2006, SI 2006/1743, which came into force on 4 July 2006, made under the Nationality Immigration and Asylum Act 2002, s 126 and **15.23** below for fingerprinting powers.
[6]   Directive 2004/38/EC (the 'Citizens' Directive) of 29 April 2004 on the right of citizens of the Union and their family members to move and reside freely within the territory of the Member States, CHAPTER 6, below.

Further examination and detention

3.86 An Immigration Officer may want to ask further questions or obtain further information before deciding whether or not to admit a passenger. In that case, he or she may require the passenger to submit to further examination.[1] The passenger may have arrived without an entry clearance where one is required. Normally the decision is that of the Immigration Officer, but the power may also be exercised by the Secretary of State where a passenger makes an asylum or human rights claim, or seeks leave to enter outside the rules, since in such a situation the Secretary of State is empowered to grant or refuse leave to enter.[2] The requirement to submit to further examination must be in writing.[3] In the case of a passenger with advance leave, the leave to enter may be suspended during the examination or pending further examination.[4] The request to submit to further examination does not prevent a transit passenger or a member of a crew from leaving on his or her intended ship, aircraft or train.[5] Passengers arriving without leave, or those whose leave has been suspended, may be detained under the authority of the immigration officer or the Secretary of State pending the examination or further examination and pending a decision to give, refuse or cancel leave to enter.[6] In deciding whether to detain a passenger pending examination or further examination, the immigration officer or Secretary of State is entitled to discriminate on nationality grounds if justified by statistical information.[7] The power of detention is usually enforced without any need to arrest, but a backup power of arrest is available.[8] The passenger may be released on temporary admission (see next paragraph) instead of being detained.[9] Detainees awaiting further examination may be eligible for bail.[10] During interviews a passenger may be represented by a friend or lawyer, but whether the representative can be present at the interview is a matter for the interviewing officer, who must, however, exercise the discretion properly.[11] Where a person who has been released on temporary admission pending a decision fails to report for further examination as required, the Immigration Officer or Secretary of State may direct that the person's examination is concluded and refuse or cancel leave to enter forthwith.[12]

1   Immigration Act 1971, Sch 2, paras 2(3), 2A(5).
2   Immigration (Leave to Enter) Order 2001, SI 2001/2590 (made under s 3A(7) Immigration and Asylum Act 1999), arts 2, 3.
3   Immigration Act 1971, Sch 2, paras 2(3), 2A(5) and 2A(10).
4   Immigration Act 1971, Sch 2, para 2A(7). The suspension of leave must also be in writing: para 2A(10). The Secretary of State does not have the power to suspend leave under SI 2001/2590, probably because it is assumed that asylum and human rights claimants and those seeking leave to enter outside the rules have not obtained advance leave.
5   Immigration Act 1971, Sch 2, para 2(3), 2A(6), SI 1993/1813, Sch 4, para 1(11)(e), (ea), inserted by SI 2000/1775.
6   Immigration Act 1971, Sch 2, para 16(1), (1A) (Immigration Officers); Nationality, Immigration and Asylum Act 2002, s 62 (Secretary of State).
7   Ministerial authorisations made under Race Relations Act 1976, s 19D (inserted by Race Relations (Amendment) Act 2000; see **3.58** above.
8   Immigration Act 1971, Sch 2, para 17. See **15.11** and CHAPTER **18** below.
9   Immigration Act 1971, Sch 2, para 21, applied to the Secretary of State by Immigration (Leave to Enter) Order 2001, SI 2001/2590, art 3.
10 Immigration Act 1971, Sch 2, para 22. See further Chapter 17 below.
11 *R v Secretary of State for the Home Department, ex p Lawson* [1994] Imm AR 58, QBD.
12 Immigration Act 1971, Sch 2, para 21(3), (4), applied to the Secretary of State by Immigration (Leave to Enter) Order 2001, SI 2001/2590, art 3.

Medical examination

3.87 Anyone seeking to enter the UK may be examined by a medical inspector.[1] The power to require further examination applies to medical examinations as well as others.[2] This is dealt with at **3.81** ff, above. If the immigration officer decides to grant leave to enter (or, in the case of advance leave, not to cancel it), but that (on the advice of a medical inspector or other qualified practitioner) a further medical test or examination may be required in the interests of public health, the passenger may be given notice in writing requiring him or her to report to a medical officer for any further tests or examination that person deems necessary.[3] This requirement is not, however, a condition of leave under section 3(1)(c) of the IA 1971, so failure to comply cannot found a decision to remove, or to curtail or refuse to extend leave, as a breach of conditions. Failure to comply with a direction to report to a medical officer of health, or to attend or submit to a medical examination, is, however, a criminal offence.[4] Information regarding the health of the person examined may be disclosed to a health service body, together with the inspector's opinion as to any action which the health service body should take.[5]

[1]   Immigration Act 1971, Sch 2, paras 2(2), 2A(4).
[2]   Immigration Act 1971, Sch 2, paras 2(3), 2A(5).
[3]   IA 1971, Sch 2, para 7.
[4]   IA 1971, s 24(1)(d): see **14.66** below.
[5]   NIAA 2002, s 133.

3.88 As indicated above, the examination powers extend to control zones in France and Belgium under the modifications to the IA 1971 made by the Channel Tunnel international arrangements and the Juxtaposed Controls Order.[1] Immigration officers also have power to board any ship, aircraft or Channel Tunnel train to carry out their examination on board.[2] These powers have been used, sometimes with unfortunate consequences, where large numbers of asylum seekers are expected to arrive from a particular refugee hot spot.[3] Treating passengers in haste has led to asylum claims being overlooked. Secondly, because of the pressure on airlines and the threat of penalties under the carriers' liability provisions in Part II of the Immigration and Asylum Act 1999,[4] there may be a temptation for airlines and ferry captains to prevent a passenger landing and to call in immigration officials to conduct an on-the-spot examination. In both such cases there is a grave risk of the examination being carried out in an unfair manner, and because abuses can be carried out unseen, and the victim may be quietly removed, the power is a dangerous one.[5] It seems to us that the cases where an 'on board' examination is justified must be very few and far between.

[1]   See **3.75–3.79** above.
[2]   IA 1971, Sch 2, para 1(4), as modified in relation to the Channel Tunnel by SI 1993/1813, Sch 4, para 1(11)(a).
[3]   See Alison Stanley 'The Legal Status of International Zones, the British experience' [1992] 6 Immigration & Nationality Law & Practice at 126.
[4]   As amended by the NIAA2002 , s 125 and Sch 8 following the declaration of incompatibility in *International Transport Roth GmbH v Secretary of State for the Home Department* [2002] EWCA Civ 158, [2002] 3 WLR 344, CA.
[5]   These concerns are accentuated by the specific authorisation of nationality-based discrimination in pre- and on-entry controls discussed at **1.94** above.

Examination, decision and the 24-hour rule

3.89 Passengers with advance leave to enter (by means of entry clearance or otherwise) whose leave is not to be suspended or cancelled will emerge from the examination by the immigration officer with no further entry in their passport. Passengers given leave on or after their arrival in the UK need notice of the decision. This may now be done in a variety of ways. Previously, where leave was granted, written notice had to be given to the person affected and this was usually done by a stamp in the passport.[1] The Immigration and Asylum Act 1999 gave the Secretary of State the power to add to the ways in which leave may be given, refused or varied.[2] Leave to enter may now be granted or refused in a number of ways, including by fax, DX and Email,[3] and in the case of visitors by word of mouth face to face or by telephone.[4] Leave to enter may also be given or refused by a notice to a responsible third party,[5] who might include the person appearing to be in charge of a group of people arriving together, a tour operator, a carrier, a control port manager or a British Embassy or consulate official.[6] The notice does not need to name the individuals covered by it, but can describe them by reference to a group.[7] However, if leave is refused orally or to a responsible third party, a notice in writing must be given as soon as practicable, confirming the refusal and giving the reasons.[8] If the refusal attracts a right of appeal under section 82 of the 2002 Act, written notice must be given under the Immigration (Notices) Regulations 2003,[9] and notice under the Notices Regulations is good notice under the Immigration (Leave to Enter and Remain) Order 2000.[10] A notice which is irregular in that it fails to tell of rights of appeal or gives incorrect information is still a good notice under the 1999 Act and its defects can be corrected.[11] Notice need not be signed.[12] If leave to enter is to be granted, this can be done by the immigration officer who carries out the initial examination. But if leave is to be refused, or advance leave cancelled, immigration officers cannot take the decision on their own but must obtain the authority of a chief immigration officer or an immigration inspector in all cases.[13]

[1]   IA 1971, s 4(1). In granting or refusing leave immigration officers are entitled to mark the passport: *R v Secretary of State for the Home Department, ex p Raju* [1986] Imm AR 348, QBD.

[2]   This was achieved by inserting s 3A and 3B into the Immigration Ac t 1971, which allow the secretary of state to make Orders by SI to make further provision with respect to the giving, refusing or varying of leave to enter or remain in the UK; see above **3.132**.

[3]   Immigration (Leave to Enter and Remain) Order 2000, SI 2000/1161, as amended by Immigration (Leave to Enter and Remain) (Amendment) Order 2013, SI 2013/1749 (into force 12th July 2013) arts 8ZA and 8ZB.

[4]   SI 2000/1161, art 8(3).

[5]   SI 2000/1161, art 9(1).

[6]   SI 2000/1161, art 1(3).

[7]   SI 2000/1161, art 9(2).

[8]   SI 2000/1161, art 10(1). In the case of someone who is illiterate or unable to understand the notice, it may be sent to a representative if there is one: *R v Chief Immigration Officer of Manchester Airport, ex p Begum (Insah)* [1972] 1 All ER 6; affd [1973] 1 All ER 594, [1973] 1 WLR 141, CA.

[9]   Currently service of immigration refusal decisions which attract a right of appeal is provided for in the Immigration (Notices) Regulations 2003, SI 2003/658 regs 4(2) and 5(2).

[10]   SI 2000/1161, art 10(2).

[11]   *Labiche v Secretary of State for the Home Department* [1991] Imm AR 263, CA; *R v Secretary of State for the Home Department, ex p Lateef* [1991] Imm AR 334, QBD. See further *R v Secretary of State for the Home Department, ex p Abeywickrema* [1991] Imm AR 535, QBD; *DJ v Secretary of State for the Home Department (Defective Notice of Decision) Iraq* [2004] UKIAT 00194.

[12]   *R v Secretary of State for the Home Department, ex p Kondo* [1992] Imm AR 326, QBD.

[13]   HC 395, para 10.

3.90 After completing the examination of a person arriving in the UK without advance leave and wishing to enter in a capacity attracting limited leave, the immigration authorities normally have 24 hours in which to give their decision, failing which the passenger is deemed to have been given six months' leave to enter with a condition prohibiting employment.[1] This provision, known as the '24-hour rule', used to be of considerable importance before

1988, when failure to give proper notice resulted in the deemed grant of indefinite leave. The effect of the 24-hour rule has been further eroded by Article 12 of the Immigration (Leave to Enter and Remain) Order 2000,[2] which deals with the situation where an examination has begun but has been adjourned for further inquiries, or the applicant has been required to submit to further examination, after which the immigration officer considers that the applicant does not need to be re-interviewed. In such a situation, any notice which is subsequently given in conformity with the requirements of the Order is deemed to comply with the requirement to give notice within 24 hours. The combination of the very limited nature of the deemed six months' leave and the Article 12 provision does away with much of the old case law dealing with when an examination comes to an end and the 24-hour time limit begins to run.[3] In addition, the Immigration Act 1971 provides that if a passenger who is on temporary admission pending further examination fails to report to an immigration officer as required, his or her examination may be treated as concluded and there is no need for notice to comply with the 24-hour rule.[4]

[1] Immigration Act 1971, Sch 2, para 6(1), as amended.
[2] SI 2000/1161, art 12. This provision is applied to the situation where the Secretary of State takes over an examination begun by an immigration officer (eg where the passenger has made an asylum or human rights claim or has sought leave to enter outside the Immigration Rules), by the Immigration (Leave to Enter) Order 2001, art 4.
[3] See the 4th edition of this work, at 3.38–3.41.
[4] Immigration Act 1971, Sch 2, para 21(3), (4).

3.91 The problem remains, however, as to whether any 'examination' at all has taken place. Not everyone passing through immigration control comes face to face with an immigration officer. Not everyone is interrogated. For example, babes in arms, persons on excursions or named in a collective passport may never be spoken to by an immigration officer on their way through immigration control. These situations are now dealt with by the provision that leave, and notice of it, may be given collectively, to the responsible third party in charge of the group.[1] Examination of all passengers is not mandatory, but permissive;[2] the important thing is that leave is granted to all those who need it. The responsible third party includes anyone who appears to be in charge of a group travelling together,[3] and a family is of course a group par excellence. This provision would avoid the result in *Ex p Ghazalgoo*,[4] where a 16-year-old Iranian boy was included on his father's passport. They arrived together at immigration control, but only the father was asked questions. The passport was stamped for the father only and the boy was completely ignored. The court held that there had been no examination of the boy, no leave given to him, and he was an illegal entrant – an absurdly harsh decision.

[1] Immigration Act 1971, Sch 2, para 6(4); SI 2000/1161, art 9.
[2] *R v Secretary of State for the Home Department, ex p Kumar* [1990] Imm AR 265, QBD.
[3] SI 2000/1161, art 1(3).
[4] [1987] Imm AR 448.

Leave given by mistake

3.92 Immigration officers are fallible and do make mistakes. Sometimes they stamp a passport with indefinite leave to enter by mistake. This is what happened in *Ex p Ram*.[1] A mistake had been made, and the applicant was given indefinite leave. The Divisional Court held that the immigration officer had been acting within his powers under section 4 of the Immigration Act 1971; it could not be said in the absence of any fraud or dishonesty on the part of the applicant that he had no authority to act as he did. And so an immigrant, given a leave by mistake, is allowed to keep it. We suggest that the same doctrine applies to a leave granted abroad, since the mistaken grant of leave is not one of the grounds for cancellation of leave when a passenger arrives at the port.[2]

[1] *R v Secretary of State for the Home Department, ex p Ram* [1979] 1 All ER 687, [1979] 1 WLR 148.
[2] For grounds for cancellation of leave: see **3.141** below.

Illegible stamps and date stamps only

3.93 The use of illegible stamps is a thing of the past. So too is the stamping of the passport with a date stamp only. They may be of historical importance in determining the immigration status of someone who came to the country many years ago and had one of these stamps in his or her passport. For these purposes the information and development of the case law can be found in previous issues of this book.

3.94 A person who has been granted leave to enter on arrival may have his or her leave cancelled up to 24 hours after the conclusion of the immigration officer's examination.[1] This happens most frequently when someone is given leave to enter by immigration control and then passes through to customs, who discover large quantities of drugs in his or her baggage.[2] In the same way, a person refused leave to enter at the port may have that refusal cancelled; in this case the 24-hour time limit does not apply, but if indefinite or limited leave is not granted at the same time that the original refusal of leave is cancelled, then six months' leave is deemed granted.[3]

[1] Immigration Act 1971, Sch 2, para 6(2), as amended.
[2] See eg *Villone v Secretary of State for the Home Department* [1979–80] Imm AR 23.
[3] Immigration Act 1971, Sch 2, para 6(3), as amended.

Part III– TEMPORARY ADMISSION

3.95 Under paragraph 16 of Schedule 2 to the Immigration Act 1971 the following non-British persons are liable to be detained and can be detained:

(i)   pending examination and pending a decision to give or refuse leave to enter, if they are seeking leave to enter;[1]

(ii) pending examination and pending a decision to cancel their leave to enter or remain, where they arrive at a port of entry with that leave and it is suspended by an immigration officer;[2]

(iii) pending a decision to remove or pending removal from the UK on reasonable suspicion that they are someone in respect of whom removal directions can be given, because the person has been refused leave to enter,[3] is an illegal entrant,[4] is an overstayer or breacher of conditions attached to his or her leave;[5] or is the member of the family of any of these.[6]

Temporary admission may be given to any of the above persons under Schedule 2, paragraph 21 of the Immigration Act 1971. It is given under the written authority of an immigration officer, and covers both temporarily admission to the United Kingdom without being detained and release from detention; the use of the power is without prejudice to a later exercise of the power to detain.[7] The grant of temporary admission or release is subject to such restrictions as to residence, as to employment or occupation and as to reporting to the police or an immigration officer as may from time to time be notified to the person in writing by an immigration officer.[8] If the person fails at any time to comply with a reporting restriction made with a view to the conclusion of his or her examination under schedule 2, paragraph 2 of the 1971 Act, the examination may be treated as concluded and there will be no obligation to reach a decision on entry within 24 hours.[9]

[1]   Immigration Act 1971, Sch 2, para 16(1).
[2]   IA 1971, Sch 2, para 16(1A) read with paragraph 2A.
[3]   IA 1971, Sch 2, para 8.
[4]   IA 1971, Sch 2, para 9.
[5]   Immigration and Asylum Act 1999, s 10(7).
[6]   Immigration Act 1971, Sch 2, para 10A.
[7]   Immigration Act 1971, Sch 2, para 21(1).
[8]   Immigration Act 1971, Sch 2, para 21(2)
[9]   Immigration Act 1971, Sch 2, para 21(3) and (4).

3.96 Those who have arrived in the UK who have not been given leave to enter are deemed not yet to have entered the UK under the deeming provisions of section 11 of the Immigration Act 1971 (see **3.56** of the main text). The purpose of the deeming provision has been a matter of some debate. Is it to protect someone given temporary admission from being prosecuted for entering the UK without leave under section 24(1)(a) of the 1971 Act? In *Kaya v Haringey London Borough Council*[1] the Court of Appeal took this line, drawing on the speech of Lord Bridge in *Musisi*.[2] In *Szoma v Secretary of State for the Home Department*[3] the House of Lords said they were wrong. The deeming provision was to exclude the person given temporary admission from the rights (in particular the right to seek an extension of leave) given to those granted leave to enter.[4] Lord Brown at paragraph 25 said it would be quite wrong to carry the fiction beyond its originally intended purpose so as to deem a person in fact lawfully here not to be here at all.[5] However, it should be noted that where persons who seek leave to enter but then breach the terms of their temporary admission, they may be treated as an illegal entrant,[6] although in such circumstances the Secretary of State is not *bound* to treat such persons as illegal entrants.[7] They are not, however, entitled to demand treatment as an illegal entrant. They can still be refused entry or given leave to enter (as distinct from leave to remain), and cannot demand to be considered as an illegal entrant for the purposes of deportation policies.[8]

[1]   *Kaya v Haringey London Borough Council* [2001] EWCA Civ 677, [2002] HLR 1, [2001] All ER (D) 15 (May).
[2]   One of the cases decided in *Bugdaycay v Secretary of State for the Home Department* [1987] AC 514, [1987] 1 All ER 940, [1987] 2 WLR 606, [1987] Imm AR 250, HL.
[3]   *Szoma v Secretary of State for the Home Department* [2005] UKHL 64, [2006] 1 AC 564, [2006] 1 All ER 1, [2005] 3 WLR 955 (the case was about whether a person on TA was 'lawfully present' for the purposes of the Social Security (Immigration and Asylum) Consequential Amendment Regulations 2000, SI 2000/636, and was eligible for welfare benefits).

[4] Lord Brown said at paragraph 24 that *Re Musisi* was rightly decided but for the wrong reasons.

[5] This decision is in line with the ECtJ which has rejected the fiction of temporary admission in *R (on the application of Yiadom) v Secretary of State for the Home Department*: C-357/98 [2000] ECR I-9265, [2001] All ER (EC) 267, [2001] 2 CMLR 132, [2000] All ER (D) 1760, ECJ in holding that the safeguards against expulsion of those enjoying Treaty rights apply equally to those physically in the country for a period of time pending a decision on admission. See further 3.55 of the main text.

[6] See *Akhtar v Governor of Pentonville Prison* [1993] Imm AR 424 and *Afunyah v Secretary of State for the Home Department* [1998] Imm AR 201; *SK (illegal entrant: leave to enter) Nigeria* [2007] UKAIT 00003.

[7] In *SK (illegal entrant: leave to enter) Nigeria* [2007] UKAIT 00003, at para 23, the AIT stated that it was wrong in principle and unrealistic to accept that a person who commits any breach of the terms of his temporary admission, however minor, automatically becomes a person who has entered illegally.

[8] *SK*, at para 24: *Afunyah*, above, per Laws LJ.

3.97 Further, time spent on temporary admission does not count either as 'leave' or even 'time spent lawfully in the UK' for the purposes of accruing lawful time in the UK under the Immigration Rules.[1] The Supreme Court has recently held that temporary admission or leave to enter for the purpose of the determination of a claim for asylum did not render a stay lawful for the purposes of Article 32 of the Refugee Convention.[2] However, a period of temporary admission within section 11 of the Immigration Act 1971 will count as a period of lawful residence for the purpose of the long residence rule where leave to enter or remain is subsequently granted.[3]

[1] *Pembele (Paragraph 399(b)(i) – 'valid leave' – meaning)* [2013] UKUT 00310 (IAC).
[2] *R (on the application of ST (Eritrea)) v Secretary of State for the Home Department* [2012] UKSC 12.
[3] HC 395, para 276A(b)(ii).

3.98 Section 67 of NIAA 2002 has made it clear that even those awaiting removal on a long-term basis remain liable to be detained even though it is impossible because of international law obligations to remove them or there are practical difficulties of a kind set out in section 67(2)(b) and (c). This raises a clear implication that the regime of temporary admission or release should ordinarily continue to apply to them. However, recent caselaw developments cast this into doubt, at least for those on temporary admission who cannot be removed due to the UK's legal obligations under international agreements.[1] In *HH (Somalia) v The Secretary of State for the Home Department*[2], the Court of Appeal found that, 'technical obstacles' aside, a risk of serious harm along the route of return was a matter to be considered and determined by the Secretary of State and the tribunal[3]. In J1[4], the Court of Appeal went further and made clear that where there was a risk inherent in the proposed route of return, claimants were entitled to appropriate periods of international protection until the risk abated or an alternate route became available. No longer should detainees languish awaiting safe passage to their country of origin, at least where the delay results from risk instead of administrative impediment. At para 97 Elias LJ said: 'If he is entitled to refugee status or protection from removal on human rights grounds, even if only on the basis that he should be given leave to remain for limited duration, he ought to be given that status or protection from removal at least for the period when his safety is potentially compromised.'

1   Nationality, Immigration and Asylum Act 2002 s 67(2)(a).
2   *HH (Somalia) v Secretary of State for the Home Department* [2010] EWCA Civ 426 (23 April 2010).
3   *HH (Somalia)*, para 81.
4   *J1 v Secretary of State for the Home Department* [2013] EWCA Civ 279 (27 March 2013).

3.99 People with temporary admission may remain physically in the UK for years, and may have married and had children, without leave to enter. In *Khadir*[1] the appellant was Iraqi Kurd who came to the UK clandestinely in the back of a lorry and unsuccessfully claimed asylum. He came from the Kurdish Autonomous Area ('KAA') of northern Iraq and in that area would have no well-founded fear of persecution. However, although he would be safe in the KAA, the Secretary of State had no safe means of enforcing his return there. He claimed he should stop being on temporary admission and should be granted leave to enter. The House of Lords ruled against him. He still remained liable to detention under paragraph 16 of Schedule 2 of the Immigration Act 1971 *pending* removal. The House held that 'pending' meant 'until'. Lord Brown drew a distinction between liability to be detained and the exercise of the power. So persons are 'liable to be detained' within the meaning of Schedule 2 where the power to detain them exists even if it would not be a proper *exercise* of that power actually to do so. This distinction between the *existence* of a power and its *exercise* meant the House was able to distinguish the case law which says that it is unlawful to detain someone pending removal if there is no reasonable prospect of removal.[2] The result is not entirely satisfactory, because it means that 'pending' is used as a preposition (meaning 'until') for the purpose of its existence, but adjectivally for the purpose of its proper exercise by continuing to detain. But there is a certain practicality in the decision, because the House also recognizes that if there comes a point where there is no realistic prospect of removal then leave should be given.

1   *R (on the application of Khadir) v Secretary of State for the Home Department* [2005] UKHL 39, [2006] 1 AC 207, [2005] 4 All ER 114, [2005] 3 WLR 1.
2   *R v Governor of Durham Prison, ex p Singh* [1984] 1 All ER 983, [1984] 1 WLR 704 at 706, QB; *Re Mahmod (Wasfi Suleman)* [1995] Imm AR 311, QB; *R (on the application of I) v Secretary of State for the Home Department* [2002] EWCA Civ 888, [2002] All ER (D) 243 (Jun), [2003] INLR 196; and *Tan Te Lam v Superintendent of Tai A Chau Detention Centre* [1997] AC 97, [1996] 4 All ER 256, [1996] 2 WLR 863, 140 Sol Jo LB 106, PC.

3.100 In *R (on the application of MW) v Secretary of State for the Home Department*,[1] the Court of Appeal followed *Khadir*, holding that temporary admission was not time-limited but could last as long as there was 'some prospect' of removal. A terminal point would come, correspondingly, if and only if it became clear – as it had in *Tan Te Lam v Superintendent of Tai A Chau Detention Centre*[2] – that there was 'simply no possibility' of repatriation. The case still leaves open the 'potentially interesting' argument (per Sedley LJ at para 24; see also Toulson LJ at para 45) that Article 8, ECHR may mean that temporary admission becomes a disproportionate interference with private life by keeping someone on temporary admission for an excessively or indefinitely long period; conceivably, if the Home Secretary is right, even decades.

1   [2009] EWCA Civ 1310, [2010] INLR 489.

[2]   [1997] AC 97, [1996] 4 All ER 256, PC.

3.101 In *S v Secretary of State for the Home Department (sub nom R (on the application of GG) v Secretary of State for the Home Department) (the Afghan highjack case)*,[1] the story was different. The appellants could not be removed to Afghanistan because there they would face torture, imprisonment and death. A panel of three adjudicators had ruled to this effect on 8 June 2004. At that point the men unquestionably qualified under paragraphs 2.6 and 5.1 of the Discretionary Leave API for a grant of six months' discretionary leave. For a long time afterwards the Secretary of State did nothing. Then he changed the text of the API to give himself a new power to enable the men to be 'kept or placed on temporary admission or temporary release'. In a powerful and scathing judgment the Court of Appeal held that temporary admission under paragraph 21 did not extend to this kind of situation. The case was entirely distinguishable from *Khadir*, because here there was no possibility of removal. Furthermore, it was beyond the powers of the Secretary of State to introduce a new category of 'persons temporarily admitted' without Parliamentary sanction. Leave to enter needed to be given. However, these cases were decided before the Qualification Directive[2] which formed the basis for the judgement in *HH (Somalia)*, which in turn led to J1. Those precluded from return for administrative reasons may be kept on temporary admission; those for whom return or the route of return presents a risk, or whose rights would otherwise be violated by removal as in *MS (Ivory Coast)*, must be granted an appropriate form of leave to remain.

[1]   *R (on the application of GG) v Secretary of State for the Home Department)* [2006] EWCA Civ 1157, [2006] All ER (D) 30 (Aug).
[2]   Council Directive 2004/83/EC.

3.102 In *MS (Ivory Coast) v Secretary of State for the Home Department*[1] the Court of Appeal went beyond *Khadir*.[2] The applicant had pending contact proceedings relating to her two children, the duration of which was uncertain. The court held that if she had a valid Article 8 ECHR claim which was for the AIT to decide she should not be kept on temporary admission, but should be granted a discretionary leave to remain as envisaged in the API of January 2006. This could be for quite a short period, whatever was regarded as sufficient to cover the outstanding contact application. It would have been open to the appellant later to apply for the period to be extended should the circumstances so warrant. As noted above in **3.87**, caselaw now strongly supports granting of leave instead of temporary admission where removal is contrary to the UK's international obligations, whether due to risk of persecution or some other violation of fundamental rights.

[1]   *MS (Ivory Coast) MS (Ivory Coast) v Secretary of State for the Home Department* [2007] EWCA Civ 133 where Scott Baker LJ stated at para 79: 'What was not appropriate was to leave her in this country in limbo with temporary admission and the promise not to remove her until her contact application has been concluded. Temporary admission is, as we have explained, a status given to someone liable to be detained pending removal. If the appellant had a valid human rights claim she is not liable to be detained pending removal. And if she has not, she ought to be removed. If she is entitled to discretionary leave to remain she ought to have it for the period the Secretary of State thinks appropriate, together with the advantages that it conveys; and if not she ought not to.'

2 R *(on the application of Khadir) v Secretary of State for the Home Department* [2005] UKHL
   39, [2006] 1 AC 207, [2005] 4 All ER 114, [2005] 3 WLR 1.

Part IV– LEAVE TO REMAIN

Leave to remain

3.103 People who entered the UK illegally and people who have overstayed the duration of their leave, may have their position regularised; they will be given leave to remain, which may be a limited or indefinite leave. Then there are those who entered the UK without any leave to enter, either because they were exempt, or had a right of abode or came in under EC free movement rights. A change in their circumstances may mean that they require leave. So the main categories that may need to seek leave to remain[1] include:

(i) former Commonwealth citizens (mainly CUKCs and British citizens) and Irish citizens who had a right of abode[2] or the benefit of uncontrolled travel under the common travel area,[3] but have lost it by renouncing or losing their nationality;

(ii) citizens of the EEA and Switzerland[4] and members of their families who cease to be entitled to remain under EU free movement law and have not been given leave to enter or remain in the UK;

(iii) members of the crew of a ship or aircraft who have entered lawfully without leave,[5] but wish to remain in the UK;

(iv) diplomats and others exempted under section 8(2) and (3) of the Immigration Act 1971, who are treated as having been given 90 days' leave to remain when they cease to be exempt, and wish to remain longer in the UK;[6]

(v) illegal entrants[7] and overstayers[8] who seek to be allowed to stay.

As with leave to enter, leave to remain may be of limited or indefinite duration, and, if limited, may be subject to conditions[9] (see **3.99**). The only difference is that since leave to remain is granted under different powers from the immigration officers' examination powers under Schedule 2, no requirement to submit to a medical test or examination may be imposed[10] Failure to comply renders a person liable to removal,[11] as well as to potential prosecution.[12] From February 2004 leave to remain which extends a stay to more than six months will take the form of a UK residence permit stuck into the passport.[13]

---

1 Immigration Act 1971, s 3(1)(b).
2 Immigration Act 1971, s 1(1).
3 Immigration Act 1971, s 1(3); Immigration (Control of Entry through the Republic of Ireland) Order 1972, SI 1972/1610, as amended.
4 Immigration Act 1988, s 7(1) and Immigration (European Economic Area) Regulations 2000, SI 2006/1003, as amended by the Immigration (European Economic Area) Regulations 2009, SI 2009/1117.
5 Immigration Act 1971, s 8(1).
6 Immigration Act 1971, s 8A(2), inserted by Immigration and Asylum Act 1999, s 6.
7 Immigration Act 1971, s 33(1).
8 See *JL (Domestic violence: evidence and procedure) (India)* [2006] UKAIT 00058 and *Ishtiaq v Secretary of State for the Home Department* [2007] EWCA Civ 386, per Dyson LJ at 53 et seq.
9 Immigration Act 1971, s 3(1)(c) and 3B(2)(b), inserted by Immigration and Asylum Act 1999, s 2. No further conditions, other than those set out in s 3(1)(c), have been imposed by regulations.

10 See Immigration Act 1971, Sch 2, para 7.
11 Immigration and Asylum Act 1999, s 10.
12 Immigration Act 1971, s 24(1)(b)(ii).
13 See **4.3** above.

3.104 Until the amendments brought about by the Immigration and Asylum Act 1999, a person's leave to enter or remain in the UK lapsed on his or her leaving the common travel area. This meant that many persons with limited leave (as students, for example) who left the UK for a short holiday were refused leave to enter on their return, because they did not have an entry clearance or visa. The provisions of the Immigration (Leave to Enter and Remain) Order 2000[1] have put an end to this anomaly. Leave to enter or remain does not lapse when the holder goes abroad, if it was conferred by an entry clearance (other than a visit visa) or by an immigration officer or the Secretary of State for more than six months.[2] There appear to be two exceptions. First, section 3C of the Immigration Act 1971,[3] which extends leave where an application for further leave is made during the currency of the original leave but not decided before that leave expires, provides that leave extended as a result of that section will lapse if the person leaves the UK.[4] Secondly, where leave has already been varied by the Secretary of State and, following the variation, there is less than six months left, it will lapse on leaving the UK.[5] Students, and everyone who had entry clearance which operated as leave to enter, except for visitors, can leave the country during the period of their leave without worrying that they will be excluded on return. So can those granted leave by the Secretary of State after arrival. Their leave only lapses if it has already expired or they have remained outside the UK for more than two years, if it has not expired by then.[6] But leave granted to a non-specified national by an immigration officer on arrival after 13 November 2003 and before 13 November 2005 would lapse, since such leave could not exceed six months.[7] The position has now been formalised by the introduction of the UK residence permit; holders of a still-valid permit will not have to obtain fresh leave on re-entry.[8]

1 SI 2000/1161, made under Immigration Act 1971, ss 3A and 3B (inserted by Immigration and Asylum Act 1999, ss 1 and 2).
2 Immigration (Leave to Enter and Remain) Order 2000, SI 2000/1161, artArt 13(2). A fiancé(e) visa (HC 395, para 291) should confer non-lapsing leave, since, although it does not exceed six months, it is leave conferred by means of an entry clearance under arts 3 and art 13(2)(a).
3 Immigration Act 1971, s 3C, as substituted by the Nationality, Immigration and Asylum Act 2002, s 118 and as amended by the Immigration, Asylum and Nationality Act 2006 (IAN 2006), s 11, which came into force on 31 August 2006 (brought into force by virtue of the Immigration, Asylum and Nationality Act 2006 (Commencement No 2) Order 2006, SI 2006/2226).
4 Immigration Act 1971, s 3C(3) as substituted.
5 SI 2000/1161, art 13(3). This might apply where a fiancé(e) extends his or her visa because the projected marriage has been delayed.
6 SI 2000/1161, art 13(4).
7 HC 395, para 23A, inserted by HC 1224 and amended by HC 645 which took effect on 13 November 2005. See **3.103** above.
8 It will be those applicants who qualify for non-lapsing leave (by entry clearance other than visit visas, and leave to remain for over six months, who will be given UK residence permits.

Variation of leave to enter or remain

3.105 As we have seen, leave to enter or remain may be either for a limited or an indefinite period.[1] Indefinite leave cannot be varied, but it may lapse,[2] or be revoked.[3] A person in the UK with limited leave may have that leave varied, whether by restricting, enlarging or removing the limit on its duration, or by adding, varying or revoking conditions.[4] The variations of leave may be made by the Secretary of State[5] or by statute.[6] But if the limit on its duration is removed, any conditions attached to the leave shall cease to apply. In other words, when someone is given settlement, with indefinite leave, any conditions restricting or prohibiting employment or recourse to public funds, and any requirements to register with the police, cease to have effect.

[1] Immigration Act 1971, s 3(1)(b).
[2] If the holder remains out of the UK for two years: Immigration (Leave to Enter and Remain) Order 2000, SI 2000/1161, art 13(4)(a).
[3] NIAA 2002, s 76. Where leave is revoked, s 3D of the IA 1971, as inserted by IAN 2006, s 11(5), now extends the person's leave during any period when that person can bring an in-country appeal against the revocation (ignoring any possibility of an appeal out of time with permission) or an in-country appeal against it is pending. See also **4.10** below.
[4] IA 1971, s 3(3). For the list of conditions which may apply to a limited leave, see **3.56**.
[5] Under IA 1971, s 4(1) and the Immigration (Leave to Enter and Remain) Order 2000, SI 2000/1161, art 13(6) and (8). See **3.119** below.
[6] Under IA 1971, s 3C and 3D, as amended. See **3.120** ff below.

3.106 Two particular situations have been highlighted by the immigration rules. First there is the case where a person has arrived in the UK with a leave to enter or remain which is in force but was given to him before his or her arrival in the UK, he or she may apply for variation of that leave, on arrival at the port of entry. An Immigration Officer acting on behalf of the Secretary of State may vary the leave at the port of entry but is not obliged to do so.[1] So long as the immigration officer has not cancelled the person's leave during his or her examination at the port[2] the person seeking variation should apply to the Home office. Second, where a person having left the common travel area, has leave to enter or remain which has not lapsed[3] his leave may be varied (including any condition to which it is subject in such form and manner as permitted for the giving of leave to enter.[4] However, the Secretary of State is not obliged to consider an application for variation of leave to enter or remain from a person outside the United Kingdom.

[1] HC 395 para 31A.
[2] Under IA 1971, Sch 2, para 2A(8)
[3] Under the Immigration (Leave to Enter and Remain) Order 2000, SI 2000/1161, art 13.
[4] HC 395, para 34G.

3.107 Applications for variation of leave or for all time limits to be removed should always be made before the expiry of the existing leave. A late application is inadvisable for at least four reasons:

(i)   The applicant loses the benefit of having his or her leave extended by section 3C of the Immigration Act 1971. This a tremendously important provision, because it extends leave by operation of statute until the Secretary of State has made a decision on the application or until the applicant has exhausted his appeal rights, if he or she has received a refusal. It also offers the applicant the possibility of amending his application, provided he or she does so before the decision of the Secretary of State has reached a decision.[1]

(ii)   the right of appeal is lost;[2] only an application made during the currency of existing leave gives the applicant a right of appeal;

(iii) there is a risk of being removed for overstaying or breach of conditions.[3]

(iv)   a late application may break continuity of lawful residence for the purpose of the long residence rule set out at HC 395, para 276A–276D.

The date of the application is important for three reasons. First, as indicated above, it is essential to apply before the current leave expires if the person is to have a right of appeal under section 82 of the Nationality, Immigration and Asylum Act 2002. Secondly, the date of the application is a decisive date, where the applicant is a child who becomes over-age before the date of the decision.[4] Thirdly, the date of the application is important if there have been rule changes, since in a number of the transitional provisions in the Immigration Rules, this date determines which set of rules applies.[5] HC 395 paragraph 34G provides as follows:

(i)   where the application form is sent by post, the date of posting,[6]

(ii)   where the application form is submitted in person, the date on which it is accepted by a public enquiry office,

(iii) where the application form is sent by courier, the date on which it is delivered to the the Home Office, or

(iv)   where the application is made via the online application process, the date on which the online application is submitted.

Where an application or claim is made no more than 21 days after the date on which a new form is specified under the immigration rules and the applicant uses a form that was permitted for such application or claim immediately prior to the date when the new form is specified, the application or claim shall be deemed to have been made on the specified form.[7]

[1]   IA 1971, s 3C(5) and *JH (Zimbabwe) v Secretary of State for the Home Department* [2009] EWCA Civ 78, [2009] All ER (D) 193 (Feb).

[2]   Section 82(2)(d) and (e) of the NIAA 2002, like the IA 1971, s 14, requires extant leave in order to appeal against refusal to extend it.

[3]   Under the Immigration and Asylum Act 1999, s 10.

[4]   See HC 395, para 27 which applies to entry clearance, but the same principle will apply to applications for leave to remain.

[5]   See eg HC 395, para 4. See also the House of Lords decision in *Odelola v Secretary of State for the Home Department* [2009] UKHL 25, [2009] 1 WLR 1230, [2009] 3 All ER 1061.

[6]   This accords with Home Office past practice to treat an application as having been made on the day of posting rather than the date of receipt: see *Lubetkin v Secretary of State for the Home Department* [1979–80] Imm AR 162.

[7]   HC 395, para 34I.

3.108 HC 395, paragraphs A34 and 34–34F provide for the compulsory use of specified forms to make applications for leave to remain and for indefinite leave and prescribe the procedures for making applications by post, in person, by courier and online. They provide for the procedure which is to apply where an applicant wishes to vary the application. They set out the rules for determining the date when an application is made. The appropriate fee must be enclosed or paid in accordance with the rules; otherwise the application will not be valid. The same applies to the forms which are not properly completed. HC 395, paragraph A34 provides that an application for leave to remain in the United Kingdom must be made either by completing the relevant online application process in accordance with paragraph A34 or by using the specified application form in accordance with paragraphs 34A to 34D. Paragraph 34C(iii) provides that an applicant may submit an application online where this option is available on the visas and immigration pages of the gov.uk website. For particular requirements for leave to remain applications see below; for general details on compulsory forms see **3.19** above.

3.109 An application form is specified when:

(i)   it is posted on the visas and immigration pages of the gov.uk website,

(ii)   it is marked on the form that it is a specified form for the purpose of the immigration rules, and

(iii)   it comes into force on the date specified on the form and/or in any accompanying announcement.[1]

Where a form is specified, the application or claim must be made using the specified form, the fees must be paid using the specified method, mandatory sections must be completed as specified, required biographical information must be obtained and provided as specified.[2] Applications or claims made by post or courier, or submitted in person must be accompanied by properly formatted photographs and documents specified as mandatory and the form must be signed by the applicant[3] and where applicable, the applicant's spouse, civil partner, same-sex partner or unmarried partner.

---

[1]   HC 395 para 34.
[2]   HC 395 para 34A.
[3]   Where the applicant is under the age of eighteen, the form may be signed by the parent or legal guardian of the applicant on his behalf: HC 395, para 34A(vi)(b).

3.110 The two main methods of submitting applications and claims are by prepaid post to the Home Office, or by a personal visit to a public enquiry office. But there are exceptions.[1] First, the public enquiry office cannot be used for an application for:

(a)   limited or indefinite leave to remain as a sole representative or retired person of independent means;

(ba)   limited or indefinite leave to remain as a Tier 1 (Exceptional Talent) Migrant, Tier 1 (Entrepreneur) Migrant, Tier 1 (Investor) Migrant or Tier 1 (Graduate Entrepreneur) Migrant;

(b)   indefinite leave to remain as a victim of domestic violence;

(c)   a certificate of approval for a marriage or civil partnership,

(d)   a Tier 2, Tier 4 or Tier 5 (Temporary Worker) sponsorship licence,

(e)   indefinite leave to remain as a businessperson, investor or innovator,

(f)   an extension of stay or indefinite leave to remain on the basis of long residence in the United Kingdom, or

(g)   a Designated Competent Body endorsement under the Tier 1 (Exceptional Talent) category.

Second, a courier may be used if it is an application for:

(a)   limited or indefinite leave to remain as a sole representative, retired person of independent means or as a Tier 1 Migrant or Tier 2 Migrant;
(b)   limited leave to remain for work permit employment, as a seasonal agricultural worker, or for the purpose of employment under the Sectors Based Scheme;
(c)   indefinite leave to remain as a businessperson, investor or innovator, or
(d)   limited leave to remain as a Tier 5 (Temporary Worker) Migrant.

Third, an applicant may, as we have seen, submit an application online where this option is available on the visas and immigration pages of the gov.uk website. Fourth, an application must be made online, if it is an application for a Tier 2, Tier 4 or Tier 5 (Temporary Worker) sponsorship licence.

[1]   HC 395 para 34B.

3.111 A failure to comply with the requirements in HC 395, paragraph 34A means that such application or claim will be invalid and will not be considered. A notice of invalidity will be given in writing and deemed to be received on the date it is given, except where it is sent by post, in which case it will be deemed to be received on the second day after it was posted excluding any day which is not a business day.[1] Where the main applicant wishes to include applications or claims by any members of his or her family as dependants on his or her application form, the applications or claims of the dependants will be invalid and will not be considered unless:

(i)   the application form expressly permits the applications or claims of dependants to be included, and
(ii)   such dependants are the spouse, civil partner, unmarried or same-sex partner and/or children under the age of 18 of the main applicant.[2]

[1]   HC 395, para 34C.
[2]   HC 395, para 34D.

Consideration and variation of an application for leave to remain

3.112 The Home Office distinguish between an invalid application and a void one. An invalid one is where an applicant fails to use a specified form, where required documents or information is not given or the fee is not paid in the manner specified or at all. These are all matters which are regulated by the immigration rules and the Fees regulations. An application is treated as void when the Home Office cannot process it because the application is inappropriate, for example, an application for limited leave to remain from a person who already has indefinite leave to remain, or leave to remain submitted by a person outside the UK.[1] First, it is a strange and unlikely concept to use in this context; essentially what is being said is that an application is void because it is inappropriate. If it is inappropriate, it should be refused. Secondly, it is based on a flimsy and legally inaccurate premise. As we discuss at **3.104** the Immigration (Leave to Enter and Remain) Order 2000,[2] makes it quite clear that leave with more than six months to run does not lapse on leaving the CTA and there is an express power to vary it. Does that mean an application to do what the law says you can do is inappropriate and void. What nonsense!

[1]   Modern Guidance-Specified forms and procedures p 54.

SI 2000/1161, art 13(2) and (6).

3.113 Normally applications duly made must be considered by the Home Office, although there is no particular order in which applications must be considered. They can be put in a queue or given priority.[1] However, in an extreme case where there has been conspicuous unfairness the position might be different.[2] Top place in the queue can be bought at a price both at home and abroad.[3]. In the UK an applicant can pay £400 extra on top of the normal fees and get a premium service[4] or pay even more (£6,000) and get a super premium service.[5] All properly completed applications must be dealt with by the Secretary of State. There is no power to cancel an application unilaterally.[6] Only a clear, unambiguous request in writing by the applicant for consideration of the application to be discontinued will the application be considered withdrawn.[7] Where an application has been made to vary leave before the expiry of the extant leave, and that leave has been extended by section 3C of the Immigration Act 1971, this does not paint the whole picture. The period between the making of the application to vary the leave and the date of the Secretary of State's decision on that application is very important. During this period it is possible to make a further application, which is capable of being treated as a variation of the first application, even if it is for a different purpose and on a different form.[8] We deal with this further at **3.120** ff below.

[1] *R v Secretary of State for the Home Department, ex p Khasawneh* [1995] Imm AR 315, QBD, where the division of applications into queues and the prioritisation of newer applications under the Asylum and Immigration Appeals Act 1993 were held lawful.

[2] The principle was enunciated in *R (on the application of S) v Secretary of State for the Home Department* [2007] EWCA Civ 546, 151 Sol Jo LB 858, where the historical illegality was the Secretary of State's fettering of his discretion as a result of entering a Public Service Agreement with the Treasury whereby 'old' asylum claims such as the claimants were to be left in a back-log of cases and only new claims for asylum were to be determined. See also *R (on the application of Rashid) v Secretary of State for the Home Department* [2004] EWHC 2465 (Admin), [2004] All ER (D) 316 (Oct), per Davis J. He reached this conclusion on the basis that the policy was in universal and unqualified terms, admitting of no exception.

[3] This happens in the case of visa applications, where a Visa Application Centre (VAC) or Temporary Enrolment Location (TEL) has been contracted by UK Visas and Immigration to offer customers services that include visa applications and biometric collection facilities, See, for example, the priority service in India at www.vfsglobal.co.uk/India/user_pay_services.htm l#3. Similar priority schemes operate in other countries, including China, Egypt, Mexico, Thailand and Bolivia: see www.gov.uk/search?q=priority+visas.

[4] Applicants should check if you're eligible to apply for the premium service. If they are eligible, they need to choose which of the seven premium service centres they want to visit, book an appointment in advance and pay the fee online when they book: www.gov.uk/ukvi-premium -service-centres. Premium service centres were previously called public enquiry offices (PEOs).

[5] The super premium service is an at-home service. It means that a courier will collect the applicant's application forms and documents; then someone will visit him or her to get the person's biometric information (fingerprints and photo) and their signature. A decision on the application will usually be made within 24 hours: for more detail see www.gov.uk/ukvi-pre mium-service-centres/use-the-super-premium-service.

[6] *Dungarwalla v Secretary of State for the Home Department* [1989] Imm AR 476.

[7] See Modern Guidance leave to remain and specified forms, Specified forms and procedures p58 'An applicant can also withdraw their application by making a clear request for consideration of their application to be stopped. If the request is ambiguous, you must confirm the withdrawal request with the applicant. You must only accept this if the request is in writing Page 59 and it is clear.' Page 58.

[8] *JH (Zimbabwe) v Secretary of State for the Home Department* [2009] EWCA Civ 78, [2009] All ER (D) 193 (Feb); Immigration Act 1971, s 3C(5).

3.114 Furthermore, rule 34E of the Immigration Rules now provides that if a person wishes to vary the purpose of an application or claim for leave to remain in the United Kingdom, and an application form is specified for such purpose, then any variation must comply with the requirements of paragraph 34A (as they apply at the date the variation is made. However, in *JH (Zimbabwe)*[1] the Court of Appeal held that the decision whether to prescribe different forms for different types of application is a matter of executive judgment on which the question whether something is a variation should not depend. So the need for a different form does not mean that there is not a variation of the first application in accordance with section 3C(5) of the 1971 Act. In so doing the Court overturned the previous view of the Tribunal that a new application (for example, as an unmarried couple) could not be treated as a variation of the original one (as a student) within the meaning of section 3C(5), since it was an application for an entirely different purpose, which would require a completely different application form and documents. So now a student application can be varied so as to include marriage grounds.

[1] *JH (Zimbabwe) v Secretary of State for the Home Department* [2009] EWCA Civ 78, [2009] All ER (D) 193 (Feb).

3.115 The upshot is that if an application has been made to vary leave before the expiry of the extant leave, and that leave has been extended by section 3C of the Immigration Act 1971, section 3C(4) says that no further application for leave can be made, but this does not paint the whole picture. The period between the making of the application to vary the leave and the date of the Secretary of State's decision on that application is very important. During this period it is possible to make a further application, which is capable of being treated as a variation of the first application, even if it is for a different purpose and on a different form.[1]

[1] *JH (Zimbabwe) v Secretary of State for the Home Department* [2009] EWCA Civ 78.

3.116 There is a clear distinction between a decision on an application and the appeal against that decision. It is now settled law that once an application has been decided it ceases to be an application and there is no longer any application to vary under section 3C(5). So any new information will fall to be dealt with during the course of an appeal rather than as a variation of the original application. Hence once that application has been decided, and the case has gone to an appeal, the new matters have to be included in the grounds of appeal (made timeously or given permission to be varied); otherwise they could not be raised on appeal.[1] There is a duty on the Tribunal[2] to consider any matter raised in a statement made by an appellant in response to a one-stop notice which constituted a ground of appeal of a kind listed in section 84(1) against the decision under appeal which is not restricted to considering grounds that related to the reasons for that decision or to the original grounds of appeal. There is still a general right of appeal against an 'immigration decision'[3] and it was clear that 'decision' in section 85(2) had the same meaning as 'immigration decision' in section 82(1) (see Appeals at 7.8 below). So, not only do the IDI state that there may be little difference in practice between a fresh application and a request to vary an existing application, they go further. A second or third application made while section 3C leave is running cannot be regarded as a request to withdraw the first application, unless this is clearly and unambiguously stated. However, case workers will pose the question the other way round and will ask the applicant whether this is a variation of their grounds.[4] It should be treated as a variation of that original application. The whole subject has been clarified by *JH (Zimbabwe) v Secretary of State for the Home Department*.[5] Two important points arise.[6] First, if the applicant makes it absolutely clear that the new grounds are to be considered instead of the grounds put forward initially, then the original grounds need not be considered. Second, it should not be assumed that an applicant wishes to withdraw the original grounds simply because they appear incompatible with later grounds. For example, if a person asks for leave to remain as a foreign spouse after an initial application to remain as a student, it may well be that both applications should be considered, since it may be necessary to make a decision on the student point as well as the marriage grounds.

[1]   The Court of Appeal in *AS (Afghanistan) v Secretary of State for the Home Department* [2009] EWCA 1076, [2010] 2 All ER 21 upheld this interpretation, which was originally contained in now discontinued IDIs. There was a duty on the Tribunal to consider matters raised by an appellant in so far as they provided grounds for challenging a substantive decision of a kind identified in s 82 that affected the immigration status. Sections 96(2) and 120 and reinforced that interpretation.
[2]   Under the Nationality, Immigration and Asylum Act 2002, s 85(2).
[3]   Under the Nationality, Immigration and Asylum Act 2002, s 82. This will, however, disappear once the Immigration Act 2014, s 15 is in force.
[4]   Modern Guidance leave to remain and specified forms, Specified forms and procedures p54.
[5]   [2009] EWCA Civ 78; The Court of Appeal disapproved of *DA (Section 3C, meaning and effect) Ghana* [2007] UKAIT 00043 (25 April 2007). Old cases such as *R v Immigration Appeal Tribunal, ex p Majid* [1988] Imm AR 315, QBD, where the Secretary of State was held entitled to treat an application as lapsed by being superseded by a later one are now of dubious authority.
[6]   They were previously referred to in the now discontinued IDI (September 2006), Ch 1, s 5, para 4.3. but would appear to be obviously sensible conclusions to draw from the statute and we adopt them.

Withdrawal of an application

3.117 Where a person makes an application and then goes abroad before the application is determined, is it to be treated as withdrawn or does it remain a valid application, which requires a decision by the Home Office? If the applicant has sent in his or her passport with the application, as is required in every single prescribed application,[1] and has to make a request for its return before being able to travel, is the application treated differently from that of the person who has a second passport and can travel without any need to ask for the return of the passport lodged with the Home Office? And will the Home Office ever be prepared to return a person's passport without treating the application as withdrawn? The normal rule is set out in HC 395, paragraph 34J. It provides that where a person whose application or claim for leave to remain is being considered requests the return of his passport for the purpose of travel outside the common travel area, the application for leave shall, provided it has not already been determined, be treated as withdrawn as soon as the passport is returned in response to that request. Case workers are instructed to treat the application as withdrawn regardless of whether or not the applicant later travels. They are also instructed not refund the specified fee, because there will not have been a decision to refuse to vary leave.[2]. Paragraph

34J does not apply to an applicant who applies as a Tier 2 or Tier 5 migrant and whose application is supported by a certificate of sponsorship from a premium sponsor.[3]. These migrants can request their passport for travel purposes and their application will not be treated as withdrawn, although they will still need valid leave in order to re-enter the UK. Another exception will be where the person requests the return of their passport for purposes other than travel (or for travel within the CTA), for example, to open a bank account, take the Life in The UK Test or apply for an identity document not related to travelling outside the CTA[4] Modern Guidance-Specified forms and procedures p58.

The request for return of the passport is the trigger event leading to withdrawal, not travel abroad. In the Modern Guidance case workers are told they must not treat an application as withdrawn if the person does not ask for the return of their passport and travels outside the CTA on another passport, an emergency travel document or illegally, unless they also request the return of their passport for travel outside the CTA.[5] However, there could be serious problems if a person uses a second passport while an application for leave to remain is being considered. It can be a risky business. However, the Modern Guidance is surely in error stating that no application can be made from outside the country for leave to remain or to vary his or her outstanding application and that It would almost certainly be regarded as void.[6]. The Immigration (Leave to Enter and Remain) Order 2000,[7] provides that an original leave of over six months and a varied leave with six months or more to run will not lapse when a person goes outside the common travel area; and it expressly provides for a power to vary leave, even when the applicant is outside the UK. So what is the position? First, there is no immigration rule which deals with the person who has two passports, but in practice the variation application of such a person is not withdrawn by travel outside the CTA on the second passport. Second, although there could be problems getting back in if they sought to re-enter the UK just to continue with their application clearly, the Modern Guidance accepts this will not be the case, where the person has existing valid leave which will not expire before they return, or they are a dual-national with an EU passport that will allow them to re-enter the UK.[8]

An applicant can also withdraw their application by making a clear request for consideration of their application to be stopped. If the request is ambiguous, the case worker must confirm the withdrawal request with the applicant and can only accept this if the request is in writing and it is clear.[9]

The last Labour government indicated that good sense would prevail in the exercise of the Home Office's discretion to treat an application for a variation of leave as withdrawn, if for instance the person left for a good reason.[10] This clarifies the position in a way, but the sheer complication of the rules is likely to lead to inconvenience, hardship and injustice. There are many people who need to travel frequently on business, or for family reasons, but still need to have their application for a variation of leave dealt with without all the inconvenience and complication of it being treated as withdrawn.

[1]   Ie, under Immigration (Leave to Remain) (Prescribed Forms and Procedures) Regulations 2006, SI 2006/1421, as amended by SI 2006/1548, and see Guidance Notes accompanying

application forms (available on Home Office website, www.ind.homeoffice.gov.uk. A certified copy is acceptable provided there is a reasonable explanation for not sending in the original, and the original is sent in later.

2   See Modern Guidance Specified forms and procedures pp 55–56 - 'Withdrawn Applications.'
3   HC 395, para 34K.
4   Modern Guidance-Specified forms and procedures p58
5   Ibid.
6   Modern Guidance-Specified forms and procedures; 'Applications made by people outside UK' pp50–51. The instructions are to void such applications: p51.
7   SI 2000/1161, art 13(1)–(4).
8   Modern Guidance-Specified forms and procedures p 51.
9   Modern Guidance-Specified forms and procedures pp 58-59.
10 See Hansard (HL) 31 October 2002, col 408 (Lord Bassam of Brighton). It was indicated in 'Return passports' on Home Office website, that the Home Office would consider expediting consideration of an application so that the applicant can travel if there is an emergency medical reason such as a family illness abroad, evidence of which must be faxed in English from a doctor or hospital abroad.

3.118 There are three possible scenarios. First, if the applicant has a statutory leave under section 3C it will end in any event when the person leaves the UK.[1] The application for variation of leave will be treated as withdrawn as soon as the passport has been returned in response to the request. The applicant will be forced, at great inconvenience and cost, to apply for entry clearance to get back in. Secondly, there are those whose original leave has not yet expired, when their passport is returned to them, but that leave does not meet the conditions of the Immigration (Leave to Enter and Remain) Order 2000 because the leave has less than six months to run; so, on going outside the common travel area, their leave will lapse and their application for a variation will be treated as withdrawn. They too will have to obtain an entry clearance to get back in. On the other hand, there is a third group with a leave to enter or remain, which has not expired, when they get their passport back. Their leave does not lapse, because it meets the conditions of the Immigration (Leave to Enter and Remain) Order 2000. But because they have asked for their passport back, their application to vary is treated as withdrawn.[2] They can apply to vary from abroad,[3] or on return, at the port,[4] but may (depending on the time left on their non-lapsed leave) prefer to make a fresh variation application once they are back in the UK, after being readmitted on their original leave, unless that leave has by then expired. Where a person, having left the common travel area with leave which remains in force under Article 13 of the 2000 Order, applies from abroad for a variation of that leave, it is not entirely clear whether that leave can be extended under section 3C of the Immigration Act 1971, as amended, if the application for variation was made before their existing leave expired.

1   Immigration Act 1971, s 3C(3), as inserted by NIAA 2002, s 118.
2   Paragraph 34J of HC 395. Section 3C leave will end immediately. See IDI (September 2006), Ch 1, s 5, para 4.1.
3   Immigration (Leave to Enter and Remain) Order 2000, SI 2000/1161, art 13(6) and (8).
4   HC 395, para 31A, inserted by HC 704.

Variation of leave

3.119 On making a decision on an application for leave to remain or a variation of leave, the Secretary of State may vary leave, including any conditions to which it is subject, in such form and manner as permitted by the Immigration Act 1971.[1] Leave may, as we have seen, be varied by restricting it as well as enlarging it. The Immigration (Leave to Enter and Remain) Order 2000 enables the Secretary of State to vary the leave of someone who, having left the common travel area, has a leave to enter or remain, which remains in force.[2] The Order and the Immigration Rules[3] clearly envisage applications for variation being made while the person is outside the UK. However, the Secretary of State is not obliged to consider such applications.[4] Similarly, an immigration officer may grant a variation of leave at the port (or a control zone) on a person's return, but is not obliged to entertain the application.[5] Leave (including any conditions to which it is subject) may be varied in such form and manner as permitted for the giving of leave to enter.[6] This means that, in order to consider whether to vary leave, the Secretary of State (by his or her officers, including immigration officers) has power to seek the information and documents that an immigration officer would be entitled to seek in an examination on arrival.[7]

[1] Immigration Act 1971, s 3(3).
[2] SI 2000/1161, art 13(6) and (8).
[3] HC 395, para 33A, inserted by HC 704.
[4] HC 395, para 33A.
[5] HC 395, para 31A, inserted by HC 704. If the immigration officer declines, a variation application is made to the Home Office in the normal way: HC 395, para 31A. The statutory power to introduce specified forms for these purposes exists but has not yet been used. See Immigration, Asylum and Nationality Act 2006, s 50(2).
[6] SI 2000/1161, art 13(6) and HC 395, para 33A.
[7] SI 2000/1161 art 13(8). For immigration officers' powers of examination see **3.80** above.

Variation of leave by statute

3.120 The time taken to consider applications for leave varies. Some may take a long time, involving lengthy investigations and, possibly, an interview with the applicant and his or her spouse. Others are quite routine and can be dealt with in a straightforward manner without fuss or difficulty. Yet these variations in time can have a serious adverse impact on the subsequent appeal rights of unsuccessful applicants. Under section 82 of the Nationality, Immigration and Asylum Act 2002, as currently operating,[1] there is, in general, a right of appeal where an immigration decision is made in respect of a person, including a refusal to vary a person's leave to enter or remain in the UK if the result of the refusal is that the person has no leave to enter or remain. In the past, delay by the Home Office in reaching a decision until after the person's leave had expired could affect whether there was a subsequent right of appeal.[2] It could also mean that the applicant would become an overstayer whose presence in the UK would be unlawful. These obvious injustices were remedied by making provision for leave to be extended by law if an application to vary leave was submitted before it expired. This is now achieved by section 3C of the 1971 Act.[3] Technically, the leave is 'extended'. To benefit, a person must have existing leave to enter or remain at the time when the application to vary is made.[4] If that leave expires before a decision is taken section 3C extends it during any period when:[5]

(i) the application for variation is neither decided nor withdrawn;

(ii)   an in-country and in-time appeal under section 82 of the 2002 Act may be brought;

(iii)   a section 82 appeal is pending.[6]

However, the original leave is only extended in this way if the application to vary is made to the Secretary of State before the expiry of the original leave.[7] During the period between the making of the application to vary the leave and the date of the Secretary of State's decision on that application it is possible to make a further application, which is capable of being treated as a variation of the first application, even if it is for a different purpose and on a different form.[8] But once the decision on the application to vary leave has been made and notified by the Secretary of State, no further application can be made, even although the appeal process on the first application is underway.[9] However, the ambit of section 3C can be extended during the appeal process by service by the Secretary of State of a section 120 (one stop) notice or curtailed in its ambit, as set out in *JH (Zimbabwe)*, if no section 120 notice is served.[10]

[1]   Once the changes envisaged by the Immigration Act 1971, s 15 come into force, the whole aappeal landscape will change radically.

[2]   See Immigration Act 1971, s 14 (now repealed) and *Suthendran v Immigration Appeal Tribunal* [1977] AC 359, [1977] Imm AR 44.

[3]   Inserted by the Immigration and Asylum Act 1999, s 3, and substituted by Nationality, Immigration and Asylum Act 2003, s 118 in respect of applications made after 1 April 2003 and applications made earlier but outstanding on that date: see Nationality, Immigration and Asylum Act 2002 (Commencement No 4) Order 2003, SI 2003/754, Sch 2, para 2(2), as amended by SI 2003/1040. Formerly, leave was extended by the Immigration (Variation of Leave) Order 1976, or VOLO, and the phrase 'VOLO leave', meaning statutory extension of leave, is still encountered in the case law.

[4]   Immigration Act 1971, s 3C(1) as substituted.

[5]   Immigration Act 1971, s 3C(2) as substituted and amended by IAN 2006, s 11.

[6]   An appeal is pending until it is finally determined, withdrawn or abandoned, and is not finally determined while a further in-time application for reconsideration or appeal may be brought or is pending, or an appeal has been remitted for reconsideration, but an appeal to the Tribunal is treated as abandoned if the appellant leaves the UK, if he or she is granted leave to enter or remain in the UK or a deportation order is made against him or her: Nationality, Immigration and Asylum Act 2002, s 104(1)–(5) as amended by Asylum and Immigration (Treatment of Claimants, etc) Act 2004, Sch 2, para 20. See **20.78** below.

[7]   Immigration Act 1971, s 3C(1)(b) as substituted.

[8]   *JH (Zimbabwe) v Secretary of State for the Home Department* [2009] EWCA Civ 78, [2009] All ER (D) 193 (Feb), disapproving the AIT in *DA (Section 3C, meaning and effect) Ghana* [2007] UKAIT 00043 (25 April 2007); Immigration Act 1971, s 3C(5).

[9]   Immigration Act 1971, s 3C(4).

[10]   *AS (Afghanistan) v Secretary of State for the Home Department* [2009] EWCA 1076, [2010] 2 All ER 21, [2011] 1 WLR 385, per Moore-Bick LJ at [86]. See further on one stop notices at **19.54**.

3.121 Section 3C(2), as amended by section 11 of IAN 2006 as from 31 August 2006[1] lays down the periods during which leave can be extended in cases to which section 3C (1) applies. They are any period when:

(a)   the application for variation is neither decided nor withdrawn,

(b)   an appeal under section 82(1) of the Nationality, Asylum and Immigration Act 2002 could be brought, while the appellant is in the UK against the decision on the application for variation (ignoring any possibility of an appeal out of time with permission), or

(c)   an appeal under that section against that decision brought, while the appellant is in the UK, is pending (within the meaning of section 104 of that Act).

Section 3C(3) enacts that leave extended by virtue of the section shall lapse if the applicant leaves the UK.

There are four matters which require comment.

(1)   The first is the date when an application is decided. Section 3C(6) says that a reference to an application being decided is a reference to notice of the decision being given in accordance with regulations under section 105 of that Act (notice of immigration decision). That meant the Immigration (Notices) Regulations 2003,[2] which deals only with appealable decisions. At first sight subsection (6) appeared to leave the position of unappealable decisions in the cold. However, the Immigration (Continuation of Leave) (Notice) Regulations 2006,[3] makes it clear that decisions which carry no right of appeal require a written notice to be given in accordance with section 4(1) of the Immigration Act 1971. So the decision will be regarded as decided on the date notice under either notice regime is given.

(2)   However there is still one snag. As we have seen at **3.53**, the Immigration (Notices) Regulations 2003 allow deemed service of a Notice if the applicant cannot be located but until 12 July 2013 section 4(1) notices had to be served on the person and there was until then no deemed service. The case of *Syed* changed all that.[4] It led to new regulations dealing among other things with section 4(1) notices and providing that these too can be served to file, if the applicant cannot be located.[5] In either case the applicant can be blissfully unaware that his or her application has been decided and can lose the benefit of section 3C and of the right of appeal, where applicable.

(3)   Since August 2006 section 3C(2)(b) and (c) makes it clear that leave will only be extended when an in country appeal could be brought or is pending. If the only appeal is out of country, the period of extension will end when the refusal decision has been made and notified.

(4)   The period of leave is extended under section 3C(2)(c) so long as the appeal is pending within the meaning of section 104 of the 2002 Act. Under that provision an appeal is pending during the period beginning when it is instituted and ending when it is finally determined etc. It is thought that this must cover the situation where an appeal is allowed and remitted to the Secretary of State to exercise a discretion not yet exercised, or to decide what length of leave should be granted, to make a reference to the European Court of Justice in Luxembourg. More difficult are the cases where there is no right of appeal in country and the applicant starts judicial review proceedings, which are ongoing.

[1]   By virtue of the Immigration, Asylum and Nationality Act 2006 (Commencement No 2) Order 2006, SI 2006/2226.
[2]   SI 2003/658 made under the Nationality, Asylum and Immigration Act 2002, s 105.
[3]   SI 2006/2170, which came into force on 31 August 2006.
[4]   *Syed (curtailment of leave – notice)* [2013] UKUT 00144 IAC. For further discussion see **3.122**.
[5]   The Immigration (Leave to Enter and Remain) (Amendment) Order 2013, SI 2013/1749 into force 12th July 2013. The Order amends the Immigration (Leave to Enter and Remain) Order

2000 by amending art 8 and inserting arts 8ZA, 8ZB and 8ZC. Article 8ZB sets out the circumstances where notice is deemed to have been given to the person affected.

3.122 Extensions of leave under section 3C of the Immigration Act 1971 are examples of an automatic grant or extension of leave by statute.[1] Another concerns diplomats and other beneficiaries of an exemption from immigration control under sections 8(2) and 8(3) of the Immigration Act 1971 Act.[2] When their exemption ended (because they left their post, for example), the position under the pre-1999 Act law was that they were in the UK without leave. Now, by virtue of section 8A of the 1971 Act,[3] they are treated as if they have 90 days' leave to remain from the date when their exemption ends, unless they already had a shorter leave, in which case that leave operates.[4] Then there are those who come from Ireland who do not need leave to enter, but are liable to the imposition of automatic time limits on their stay in the UK and conditions prohibiting their taking employment.[5] Section 9(3) of the IA 1971 provided for the restrictions to have the same effect as if leave had been given under the 1971 Act. So when they apply to extend their leave they will be able to enjoy the benefits of further extended statutory leave under section 3C. In addition, the Secretary of State has powers under sections 3B and 4(1) to make orders by statutory instrument for general variations of leave and the conditions attached to it, in respect of any class of persons. The only Order made so far was one made during the Gulf War in 1991, which required all Iraqi nationals with limited leave to register with the police.[6]

[1]   Note that section 3C has been amended by IAN 2006, s 11 and a new section 3D has been inserted to allow extensions of leave following curtailment or revocation of a leave to enter or remain.
[2]   See CHAPTER 5 below.
[3]   Inserted by Immigration and Asylum Act 1999, s 7.
[4]   Immigration Act 1971, ss 8(2) and (3), and 8A, as amended by the 1999 Act, ss 6 and 7; s 8A(2)(b).
[5]   Under IA 1971, s 9(2) and Immigration (Control of Entry through the Republic of Ireland) Order 1972, SI 1972/1610, art 4(1).
[6]   Immigration (Variation of Leave) Order 1991, SI 1991/77.

Notifying leave decisions

3.123 The Immigration (Leave to Enter and Remain) (Amendment) Order 2013[1] amends the Immigration (Leave to Enter and Remain) Order 2000 to set out the procedures that the Home Office may follow for the giving, refusing or varying of leave by notice in writing in accordance with section 4(1) of the Immigration Act 1971. Service of immigration refusal decisions which attract a right of appeal is provided for in the Immigration (Notices) Regulations 2003.[2] This Order is to set out the rules governing the service of notice for grants of leave and for non-appealable refusal decisions. First there are the visitors, here for a period of no more than six months. Notice can be given orally instead of in writing.[3] Second, a whole new range of methods of serving a written notice regarding non-appealable decision is introduced by new article 8ZA – by hand, fax, post, email, DX, and courier. Thirdly, new article 8ZB deals with deemed service, detailed in **3.53**, above. Fourthly, article 8ZC says no notice need be given to visitors who pass through an automated gate in accordance with article 8A.

¹ SI 2013/1749. The change was prompted by the decision in *Syed (curtailment of leave – notice)* [2013] UKUT 00144 IAC in which the Upper Tribunal found that, in the absence of an Order covering service of non-appealable decisions, such a decision must be served under section 4 of the Immigration Act 1971 and the Secretary of State must communicate the notice to the person, in order for it to have effect. For a fuller discussion see **3.121**, above.
² SI 2003/658, which came into force on 31 August 2006.
³ SI 2000/1161, art 8(1) and (2), as substituted by SI 2013/1749.

What constitutes an extension of leave?

3.124 In complicated cases considerable correspondence may pass between the applicant and the Home Office. Sometimes Home Office letters appear to indicate that an existing leave has been extended, when in fact, this was not the intention of the Home Office. Thus in *R v Immigration Appeal Tribunal, ex p Ahluwalia*¹ the applicant had received a letter from the Home Office in reply to her application for variation of her leave to remain, which stated: 'Meanwhile this acknowledgement may be regarded as authority for the holder to remain in the UK pending a decision on any application made for an extension of stay'. This was held to be leave. By contrast, a letter, which drew the applicant's attention to the statutory protection provided by section 1 of the Immigration Act 1971, 'the appellant will not be required to leave the UK while the appeal is pending', was held not to constitute leave in *R v Immigration Appeal Tribunal, ex p Subramaniam*.² Misunderstandings of this kind are less likely to occur, now that leave is extended by statute under section 3C of IA 1971 automatically pending a decision and any subsequent appeal.³ The previous Home Office practice of granting 28-day leave to enable someone who has withdrawn his or her passport for travel to do so without being treated as an overstayer on embarkation has been withdrawn.⁴ There is now a clearer distinction between a grant of leave and a decision to refrain from removal without granting leave, which leaves people in limbo.⁵

¹ [1979–80] Imm AR 1. See further *Secretary of State for the Home Department v Enorzah* [1975] Imm AR 10.
² [1977] QB 190, [1976] Imm AR 155, CA.
³ See **3.120**, above.
⁴ See eg the discontinued IDI (September 2006), Ch 1, s 5, para 4.1; see also 'Post-Refusal decisions: Variation (Curtailment of Leave to Remain)', on Home Office website. Discharged NATO soldiers are given 28 days' leave to enable them to make an application to remain in the UK or to leave.
⁵ See **3.99**, above, and in particular *R (on the application of Khadir) v Secretary of State for the Home Department* [2005] UKHL 39, [2006] 1 AC 207, [2005] 4 All ER 114 and *S v Secretary of State for the Home Department (sub nom R (on the application of GG) v Secretary of State for the Home Department) (the Afghan highjack case)*, [2006] EWCA Civ 1157, (2006) Times, 9 October. See further Part III of this chapter on temporary admission, above.

'Packing-up time'

3.125 Where an application has been refused and the applicant has been allowed a short period to organise his or her affairs, pack up and leave, the view of Lord Russell in *Suthendran v Immigration Appeal Tribunal*¹ was that such 'packing up time' constituted a fresh grant of leave.² However this view is, we believe, no longer tenable, at least where the Secretary of State makes it clear that the intention is not to grant further leave but merely to assure an applicant that no action will be taken to enforce departure pending the taking of an exam, the selling of a house or the birth of a child.[3] See the previous paragraph.

1 [1977] AC 359 at 372, HL.
2 He repeated his view in *Halil v Davidson* [1979–80] Imm AR 164, HL.
3 See *R v Immigration Appeal Tribunal, ex p Bhanji* [1977] Imm AR 89, CA; *Theori v Secretary of State for the Home Department* [1979–80] Imm AR 126, IAT; *R v Secretary of State for the Home Department, ex p Smith* [1996] Imm AR 331.

Cancellation, curtailment and revocation of leave

3.126 Under section 3B of the Immigration Act 1971[1] the Secretary of State may make provision with respect to the giving, refusing or varying leave to remain, including any appropriate supplemental provision, which may include a power to cancel leave to remain in appropriate cases. Cancellation on arrival of advance leave to enter is similar to the power to refuse entry to someone holding an entry clearance.[2] Then there is an automatic cancellation of leave to enter or remain, when someone becomes an 'excluded person' under section 8B(2) of the Immigration Act 1971.[3] Where a person fails to comply with a requirement to make an application for a biometric immigration document, otherwise known as an identity card, the Secretary of State has power to cancel or vary leave to enter or remain under regulation 23(1)(d) of the Immigration (Biometric Registration) Regulations 2008, SI 2008/3048. Article 13(7) of the Immigration (Leave to Enter and Remain) Order 2000 provides that non-lapsing leave may be cancelled while its holder is outside the UK, in the case of a leave to enter by an immigration officer, and by the Secretary of State in the case of a leave to remain.[4] The power to seek information and documents is the same as that of an immigration officer conducting an examination at the port, with the additional power of calling for a medical report (since there is no power to refer the person abroad to a medical inspector). A failure to provide the requested information, documentation or report is itself a ground for cancellation of leave.[5] The Immigration rules state that an immigration officer at the port may cancel leave to remain,[6] although in fact this may not be correct, since Schedule 2 to the 1971 Act gives immigration officers at the port powers to cancel leave to enter, but they do have power to cancel leave under the general grounds for refusal at HC 395, paragraph 321A which is dealt with in Part V of this chapter.

1 Inserted by Immigration and Asylum Act 1999, s 2.
2 See CHAPTER 3. Under the IA 1971, Sch 2, para 2A(9) such cancellation is treated as a refusal of leave to enter at a time when the person refused had a current entry clearance, except where entry is sought for a different purpose from that in the entry clearance. This ensures an in-country right of appeal: NIAA 2002, s 82(2)(a) read with s 92(3)(a), subject to the exception: see the AI(TC)A 2004, ss 18, 28.
3 Immigration Act 1971, s 8B, inserted by the Immigration and Asylum Act 1999, s 8 (war criminals).
4 SI 2000/1161, art 13(7)(a) and (b).
5 SI 2000/1161, art 13(8), (9).
6 HC 395, para 10B, inserted by HC 704.

Curtailment, revocation and section 3D

3.127 Under section 76 of the Nationality, Immigration and Asylum Act 2002 indefinite leave to remain may be revoked on a number of grounds, but there is no similar express statutory power to cancel or curtail or revoke a limited leave to remain. However, under section 3(3) of the Immigration Act 1971 limited leave may be varied by removing the limit on its duration, which is curtailment by another name. Various circumstances in which this may happen are set out in the Immigration Rules, particularly under paragraphs 322 and 323 which we set out and comment on in Part V below. It should be noted that until leave is curtailed, it remains in force and neither statute nor the Immigration Rules give a power to cancel leave retrospectively.[1] To prevent people becoming overstayers while exercising a right of appeal against a decision to curtail or to revoke leave to enter or remain, section 11 of the Immigration, Asylum and Nationality Act 2006 added section 3D to the Immigration Act 1971. When leave to enter or remain is curtailed or revoked, section 3D extends the leave (in much the same way as section 3C does for applications to vary leave) while an appeal could be brought or is pending. It applies both where a limited leave is curtailed, by a variation which has the result that the person has no leave to enter or remain in the UK, or where an indefinite leave is revoked.[2] Leave is extended to enable an in-country and in-time appeal under section 82(1) of the Nationality, Immigration and Asylum Act 2002 to be brought.[3] The person's extended leave, however, will lapse if he or she leaves the UK.[4] During the period leave is extended, the person is not allowed to make any application for a variation of leave.[5]

[1] *NM (No retrospective cancellation of leave) Zimbabwe* [2007] UKAIT 00002, at para 5.
[2] Immigration Act 1971, s 3D(1).
[3] Immigration Act 1971, s 3D(2).
[4] Immigration Act 1971, s 3D(3).
[5] Immigration Act 1971, s 3D(4). See further IDI (Sep/06), Ch 1, s 5.

Special immigration status

3.128 The Criminal Justice and Immigration Act 2008 created a new special immigration status,[1] The Act allows the Secretary of State to designate a foreign criminal, who is liable to deportation, but cannot be removed from the UK because of section 6 of the Human Rights Act 1998, and his or her family members to this status. This draconian power has never come into force and our previous discussion of it can be found in the previous edition of this work at 4.37 to 4.38.

[1] Criminal Justice and Immigration Act 2008, ss 130–133.

Exercising the discretion to vary leave

3.129 In determining whether to vary leave, refuse to vary it or curtail it, the Secretary of State has to consider not only the formal requirements of the Immigration Rules regarding visitors, students, and so forth, but also certain general rules. Where someone is granted discretionary leave outside the rules, the Secretary of State is entitled to apply the rules when a variation of leave is sought, provided that the wording of the rule fits the applicant's case.[1]

Similarly, in dealing with the formal requirements of the rules, the Secretary of State has a general discretion to vary leave outside the rules, and can for example extend leave for someone whose case falls partly within one category and partly in another ('cross-fertilisation'), but if he or she declines to do so the appellate authority cannot 'bend' the rules itself.[2] In *R v Immigration Appeal Tribunal, ex p Martin*,[3] decided under earlier rules, an Australian woman only had sufficient means to maintain herself if she combined her earnings as a self-employed seamstress with a private income received from her father, but neither source was sufficient by itself. The adjudicator held that she could qualify as a person who 'set up in business' and that her private income could be taken into account, albeit that it was not large enough for her to qualify as a person of independent means. The Tribunal's reversal of this decision was upheld by the Divisional Court, which held that an applicant for an extension of leave must clearly bring herself within one or other of the categories in the Immigration Rules.[4] Sometimes the difficulties in meeting the precise requirements of the rules may be ameliorated by a more liberal interpretation in the Guidance given to officers in the Modern Guidance and what is left of the IDIs. This is allowed. But when the IDIs set bigger hurdles than the rules, this is likely to be unlawful following the Supreme Court decision in *Alvi*.[5]

[1] *Mamon v Immigration Appeal Tribunal* [1988] Imm AR 364, CA in respect of exceptional leave to remain.
[2] 'Bending' the rules is not the same as giving them a construction which accords with their general humanitarian purpose: *R v Immigration Appeal Tribunal, ex p Singh (Swaran)* [1987] Imm AR 563, CA; or with the ECHR: *R v Secretary of State for the Home Department, ex p Ali (Arman)* [2000] INLR 89.
[3] [1972] Imm AR 275.
[4] See further *R v Immigration Appeal Tribunal, ex p Aisha Khatoon Ali* [1979–80] Imm AR 195, qualified by *R v Immigration Appeal Tribunal, ex p Coomasaru* [1983] 1 All ER 208, [1983] 1 WLR 14, CA.
[5] *R (on the application of Alvi) v Secretary of State for the Home Department* [2012] UKSC 33.

3.130 Just as cross-fertilisation of the different categories is allowed to the Secretary of State but not to the Tribunal on appeal, so too it has been held that the appellate authorities cannot construe the Immigration Rules so as to extend the categories of dependent relatives eligible for entry under the rules on family reunion.[1] However, as a public authority, the Tribunal must act compatibly with the ECHR[2] and must construe the rules purposively to give effect to the rights protected by the Convention, which might involve reading words in where necessary.[3]

[1] *Nisa v Secretary of State for the Home Department* [1979–80] Imm AR 20. But see *R v Secretary of State for the Home Department, ex p Ali (Arman)* [2000] INLR 89.
[2] Human Rights Act 1998, s 6; see CHAPTER 7 below.
[3] Human Rights Act 1998, s 3.

Switching into another category of leave

3.131 Prior to 1980, persons in the UK as visitors, students and other temporary entrants could obtain extensions of leave in different capacities without the need to seek an entry clearance from abroad. Since then, the policy has swung between such changes being permitted and then being denied. The current Immigration Rules generally prevent switching categories, but contain some important exceptions. Most importantly this paragraph now has to be read in the light of the changes brought about by the introduction of Tiers 1 to 5 of the points-based system (in the main from 30 June 2008), where extensive switching is now the order of the day. Details are set out in the chapters dealing with these various categories.

Part V – GENERAL GROUNDS FOR REFUSAL, CANCELLATION AND CURTAILMENT OF LEAVE

Introduction

3.132 An application for leave to enter, entry clearance, leave to remain or a variation of leave will be determined according to the detailed Immigration Rules dealing with the particular purpose for which the applicant wishes to come to or remain in the UK – visit, study, business, family reunion and so forth. Qualifying under these rules does not, however, guarantee that leave to enter or to remain will be granted, because under Part 9 of the rules the person may fail on general grounds, relating, broadly, to deception, past conduct, lack of proper documents, non-cooperation with the immigration authorities, restricted returnability, public policy or public health. There are five separate but interconnected grounds for refusal under Part 9:

(i)   refusal or entry clearance or leave to enter Paragraph 320);

(ii)   refusal entry to those who arrive with an entry clearance (321);

(iii)   cancellation of leave overseas or on entry (321A); refusal of leave to remain (322); and

(iv)   curtailment of leave (323).

In some of these general grounds of refusal, the grounds are self- evident and need no further elucidation. In some of the grounds identical or near identical grounds are to be found in both refusals of leave to enter and refusal of leave to remain or are repeated in like form in the cancellation and curtailment grounds or grounds for overturning an entry clearance at the point of entry in to the UK. These rules should be read with HC 395, para 26, which allows the words 'entry clearance officer' to be used for 'immigration officer' where appropriate, and para 39 which gives entry clearance officers the same discretion in relation to medical examinations as immigration officers.

3.133 In this Part of the chapter we set out the main provisions of the rules with little or no comment. We then have a comment section where we single out the key provisions of these rules and comment. The obvious candidates are refusals, cancellations and curtailment for the use of false representations or false documents; failure to disclose material facts; breach of deportation orders; criminal convictions; decisions taken on grounds conducive to the public good; and decisions on medical grounds. In the Modern Guidance A caseworker or entry clearance officer is told that they must consider refusing a person on general grounds if there is any evidence in their background, behaviour, character, conduct or associations that shows they should not enter or remain in the UK for one or more of the grounds set out in paragraphs 320 and 322 of the Immigration Rules. But they are also instructed that they must carefully consider their statutory duty to children, under section 55 of the Borders, Citizenship and Immigration Act 2009, before applying the instructions in the Modern Guidance either to children or people with children.[1]

[1] Guidance-General grounds for refusal Section 1 – version 17.0 p 1, Valid from 04 August 2014.

3.134 In dealing with paragraphs 320 and 322 a distinction is usually made between mandatory and discretionary decisions of immigration officials.[1] The distinction is not as clear cut as it sounds, because even where words like 'is to be refused' are used, a reading of the IDIs or Modernised Guidance, for example, will often show that there is an element of residual discretion remaining, and under public law the doctrine of 'fettering discretion' means that the circumstances of every case have to be considered, and, even if they do not meet the 'mandatory' requirements of a particular rule, a decision must still be taken whether or not to make an exception.[2] The Guidance states that the entry clearance officer must consider if there are any human rights reason or any exceptional, compelling circumstances which would justify giving entry clearance and, if so, refer such a case to the 'referred casework unit'.[3] Nevertheless the distinction remains an important and useful way of classifying things in this area, not least because the ambit of the right of appeal, as we shall see, may depend on whether a discretion is exercised under the Rules or outside them. The first part of HC 395, paragraphs 320 and 322, which states that leave or entry clearance 'is to be refused', is generally regarded as containing mandatory guidance to be followed by immigration officials. The second list in each paragraph, which contains the instruction that leave or entry clearance 'should normally be' refused, is generally regarded as presuming refusal, but leaving a large measure of discretion to the immigration official.[4]

[1] See the Modernised Guidance which makes it clear that even the 'mandatory' grounds are not wholly mandatory: p 4 of General Reasons for Refusing, section 2 – v 1.0 Ext valid from 30 April 2014. This Guidance is to be found at: www.gov.uk/government/collections/general-grounds-for-refusal-modernised-guidance In *JC (Part 9 HC395, burden of proof) China* [2007] UKAIT 00027, the AIT drew this distinction, but also pointed out that in all paragraph 320 cases the burden of proof is on the decision maker to establish the facts relied on, their common thread being that the decision maker must establish a precedent fact.
[2] *AA (Pakistan)* [2008] UKAIT 00003.
[3] Modernised Guidance, p 3 of General Reasons for Refusing, Section 2 (see **3.132** fn 1 above).
[4] In *RM (Kwok On Tong: HC 395 para 320) India)* [2006] UKAIT 00039 (18 April 2006) it was held that only the first seven sub-paragraphs of paragraph 320 prevent the claimant succeeding. Under the later subparagraphs, although the presumption is clearly against entry clearance, there is no bar on a grant of entry clearance. A grant of entry clearance would not, therefore, conflict with the Rules. An Immigration Judge is, therefore, entitled to allow an appeal even if he or she considers that one (or more) of the later subparagraphs apply to the case.

3.135 Part 9 of the rules (and paragraphs 320 and 322 in particular) do not apply in cases where the person seeking entry already has entry clearance because in that situation the grounds for refusing leave to enter, set out below at **3.138**, are more restricted except as regards deception. Many of the grounds are also disapplied in cases involving family membership, long residence and membership of the armed forces. First, paragraph A320 disapplies paragraph 320 (with exceptions) subparagraph (3), (10) and (11)) from an application for entry clearance, leave to enter or leave to remain as a family member under Appendix FM. The exceptions are a failure to produce a valid passport (320 (3)); producing a passport from an unrecognised territory or one otherwise unacceptable (320 (10); and where the person has previously contrived to frustrate the intentions of the immigration rules (320 (11)). Second, Part 9 (except for paragraph 322(1)) which provides for refusal if leave to enter or remain is being sought for a purpose not covered by the rules) does not apply to an application for leave to remain on the grounds of private life under paragraphs 276ADE–276DH. Thirdly, an application for entry clearance, leave to enter or leave to remain by members of the armed forces under Appendix Armed Forces is subject to a selection of subparagraphs from paragraphs 320 and 322 as set out in paragraph B320 (1) and (2). Thirdly, decisions based on these general grounds may be overridden in cases where refusal of entry or entry clearance, refusal of leave to remain, and cancellation or curtailment of leave by a breach of section 6 of the Human Rights Act 1998, a claim for asylum, or a claim that people have been trafficked to the UK. See CHAPTERS 7, 12 and 13, below.

The texts – Setting out the rules

A.   *Entry clearance and entry*

MANDATORY RULES UNDER PARAGRAPH 320

3.136 Entry clearance or leave to enter is to be refused under HC 395, paragraph 320 in the following cases:

(1)			entry is being sought for a purpose not covered by the Rules; the fact that the person seeking entry to the United Kingdom:
(2)		(a)	is currently the subject of a deportation order; or
		(b)	has been convicted of an offence for which they have been sentenced to a period of imprisonment of at least 4 years; or
		(c)	has been convicted of an offence for which they have been sentenced to a period of imprisonment of at least 12 months but less than 4 years, unless a period of 10 years has passed since the end of the sentence; or
		(d)	has been convicted of an offence for which they have been sentenced to a period of imprisonment of less than 12 months, unless a period of 5 years has passed since the end of the sentence.
			Where this paragraph applies, unless refusal would be contrary to the Human Rights Convention or the Convention and Protocol Relating to the Status of Refugees, it will only be in exceptional circumstances that the public interest in maintaining refusal will be outweighed by compelling factors.
(3)			failure to produce a valid national passport or other document satisfactorily establishing identity and nationality;

(4)   failure to show that he or she is acceptable to the immigration authorities in another part of the common travel area to which the applicant wishes to travel;

(5)   failure to produce entry clearance, if one was required;

(6)   the Secretary of State has personally directed that exclusion is conducive to the public good;

(7)   refusal on medical grounds (unless the person is settled in the UK or there are strong compassionate circumstances);

(7A)   where false representations have been made or false documents [or information] have been submitted (whether or not material to the application, and whether or not to the applicant's knowledge), or material facts have not been disclosed, in relation to the application; or in order to obtain documents from the Secretary of State or a third party required in support of the application.[a]

(7B)   where the applicant has previously breached the UK's immigration laws (and was 18 or over at the time of his or her most recent breach) by:

     (a)   overstaying;

     (b)   breaching a condition attached to his leave;

     (c)   being an Illegal entrant;

     (d)   using deception in an application for entry clearance, leave to enter or remain (whether successful or not), unless the applicant:

     unless the applicant:

     (i)   overstayed for 28 days or less and left the UK voluntarily, not at the expense (directly or indirectly) of the Secretary of State;

     (ii)   used deception in an application for entry clearance more than ten years ago;

     (iii)   left the UK voluntarily, not at the expense (directly or indirectly) of the Secretary of State, more than 12 months ago; (iv) left the UK voluntarily, at the expense (directly or indirectly) of the Secretary of State, more than 2 years ago; and the date the person left the UK was no more than 6 months after the date on which the person was given notice of the removal decision, or no more than 6 months after the date on which the person no longer had a pending appeal; whichever is the later;[b]

     (v)   left the UK voluntarily, at the expense (directly or indirectly) of the Secretary of State, more than five years ago, or

     (vi)   was removed or deported from the UK more than ten years ago; (vii) left or was removed from the UK as a condition of a caution issued in accordance with section 22 of the Criminal Justice Act 2003 more than 5 years ago.

> Where more than one breach of the UK's immigration laws has occurred, only the breach which leads to the longest period of absence from the UK will be relevant under this paragraph.

(7D)   failure, without providing a reasonable explanation, to comply with a request made on behalf of the Entry Clearance Officer to attend for interview.

[a]   The refusal of entry clearance under the general grounds of refusal should not be confused with the ability of entry clearance officers to revoke an entry clearance, if, having issued it, they find that it has been obtained fraudulently. Under HC 395, para 30A entry clearance may be revoked on three grounds set out in the paragraph, including the situation where the officer is satisfied that false representations were used or material facts were not disclosed,to obtain the entry clearance, whether or not to the holder's knowledge (30A(i)). The other two grounds involve a change of circumstances since the entry clearance was issued (30A(ii)) and the holder's exclusion from the United Kingdom would be conducive to the public good (30A(iii)).

[b]   Inserted by HC 863 which took effect on 6 April 2011.

DISCRETIONARY RULES UNDER PARAGRAPH 320

3.137 Grounds on which entry clearance or leave to enter should normally be refused under paragraph 320 are as follows:

(8)   failure by a person arriving in the UK to provide information to the immigration officer for the purpose of deciding whether he requires leave to enter and, if so, whether and on what terms leave should be given;

(8A)   failure, by a person outside the UK, to provide information, documents or medical reports required to the immigration officer;

(9)   failure by a returning resident to meet the requirements of paragraph 18 of the Rules;

(10)   production of a passport which is from an unrecognised territory or which is otherwise unacceptable;

(11)   where the applicant has previously contrived in a significant way to frustrate the intentions of these Rules by:

    (i)   overstaying; or

    (ii)   breaching a condition attached to his leave; or

    (iii) being an illegal entrant; or

    (iv) using deception in an application for entry clearance, leave to enter or remain or in order to obtain documents from the Secretary of State or a third party required in support of the application (whether successful or not); and

    there are other aggravating circumstances, such as absconding, not meeting temporary admission/reporting restrictions or bail conditions, using an assumed identity or multiple identities, switching nationality, making frivolous applications or not complying with the re-documentation process

(12)   [deleted];

(13)   failure to satisfy the immigration officer of admissibility to another country after the stay in the UK, unless being admitted for settlement;

(14)   refusal by a sponsor to give an undertaking in writing to be responsible for the applicant's maintenance and accommodation for the period of any leave granted;

(16)   failure, in the case of an unaccompanied child under the age of 18 years other than an asylum seeker, to provide written consent to the application from his parent(s) or legal guardian;

(17)   save in relation to a person settled in the UK, refusal to undergo a medical examination;

(18A)   within the 12 months prior to the date on which the application is decided, the person has been convicted of or admitted an offence for which they received a non-custodial sentence or other out of court disposal that is recorded on their criminal record;

(18B)   (18B) in the view of the Secretary of State:

    (a)   the person's offending has caused serious harm; or

    (b)   the person is a persistent offender who shows a particular disregard for the law.

(19)   exclusion is conducive to the public good, including in the light of the person's character, conduct or associations.

(20)   failure to comply with a requirement relating to the provision of physical data (eg, fingerprints) required by regulations made under s 126 of the Nationality Immigration and Asylum Act 2002.

(21)   [deleted].

(22)   where one or more relevant NHS body has notified the Secretary of State that the person seeking entry or leave to enter has failed to pay a charge or charges with a total value of at least £1000 in accordance with the relevant NHS regulations on charges to overseas visitors.

B   *refusal of entry to those who arrive with an entry clearance*

REFUSAL UNDER PARAGRAPH 321

3.138 Under paragraph 321 a person seeking leave to enter the United Kingdom who holds an entry clearance which was duly issued to him and is still current may be refused leave to enter only where the Immigration Officer is satisfied that:

- false representations were made or false documents or information were submitted (whether or not material to the application, and whether or not to the holder's knowledge) (321 (i)) [this repeats the wording of paragraph 320 (7A)];

- a change of circumstances since the issue of the entry clearance has removed the basis of the holder's claim to admission, except where the change of circumstances amounts solely to the person becoming over age for entry in one of the categories contained in paragraphs 296-316 of the Rules(321(ii)); or
- on grounds which would have led to a refusal under paragraphs 320(2), 320(6), 320(18A), 320(18B) or 320(19) (321(iii)).[1]

---

[1] There is an exception for members of the armed forces where this provision (paragraph 321 (iii)) applies in respect of an entry clearance issued under Appendix Armed Forces. It is to be read as if for 'paragraphs 320(2), 320(6), 320(18A), 320(18B) or 320(19)' it said 'paragraph 8(a), (b), (c) or (g) and paragraph 9(d)'.

C. *Refusing leave to remain*

MANDATORY GROUNDS FOR REFUSING LEAVE TO REMAIN

3.139 General grounds for refusing leave to remain, for refusing to vary leave to remain or enter and for curtailing leave are contained in HC 395, para 322.

The mandatory grounds are:

(1)   the fact that variation of leave to enter or remain is being sought for a purpose not covered by these Rules.

(1A) where false representations have been made or false documents or information have been submitted (whether or not material to the application, and whether or not to the applicant's knowledge), or material facts have not been disclosed, in relation to the application or in order to obtain documents from the Secretary of State or a third party required in support of the application.[a]

(1B) the applicant is, at the date of application, the subject of a deportation order or a decision to make a deportation order;

(1C) where the person is seeking indefinite leave to enter or remain:

    (i)   they have been convicted of an offence for which they have been sentenced to imprisonment for at least 4 years; or

    (ii) they have been convicted of an offence for which they have been sentenced to imprisonment for at least 12 months but less than 4 years, unless a period of 15 years has passed since the end of the sentence; or

    (iii) they have been convicted of an offence for which they have been sentenced to imprisonment for less than 12 months, unless a period of 7 years has passed since the end of the sentence; or

    (iv) they have, within the 24 months prior to the date on which the application is decided, been convicted of or admitted an offence for which they have received a non-custodial sentence or other out of court disposal that is recorded on their criminal record.

---

[a]   [AQ fn text missing]

[b]   [AQ fn text missing]

[a]   See fn 1 at **3.136**, above

3.140 The grounds on which an application for leave to remain or a variation of leave 'should normally' be refused under paragraph 322 are[1]:

(2)   the making of false representations or the failure to disclose any material fact for the purpose of obtaining leave to enter or a previous variation of leave;

(2A) the making of false representations or the failure to disclose any material fact[a] for the purpose of obtaining a document from the Secretary of State that indicates the person has a right to reside in the United Kingdom.

(3)   failure to comply with any conditions of leave;

(4)   failure by the person concerned to maintain or accommodate himself and any dependants without recourse to public funds;

(5)   the undesirability of permitting the person concerned to remain in the light of his or her character, conduct (including convictions which do not fall within paragraph 322(1C),or associations or because of a threat to national security;

(5A) it is undesirable to permit the person concerned to enter or remain in the United Kingdom because, in the view of the Secretary of State:

(a) their offending has caused serious harm; or

(b) they are a persistent offender who shows a particular disregard for the law;

(6)   refusal by a sponsor to give an undertaking in writing to be responsible for maintenance and accommodation or failure to honour such an undertaking;

(7)   failure by the applicant to honour any declaration or undertaking given orally or in writing as to the intended duration and/or purpose of his or her stay;

(8)   failure, except by those who qualify for settlement or who are married to someone settled in the UK, to satisfy the Secretary of State that he or she will be returnable to another country if allowed to remain in the UK for a further period;

(9)   failure to produce within a reasonable time documents or other evidence required by the Secretary of State to establish a claim to remain under the Rules.[a] This has now been amended by HC 104 to include information as well as documents or other evidence. This additional ground for refusing an application could arise where the applicant has failed to provide information requested on the application form or where the applicant has failed to provide information requested in addition to that already provided in the application form;

(10)   failure, without providing a reasonable explanation, to attend for interview;

(11)   failure in the case of a child (other than an asylum seeker) making an application to remain other than in conjunction with his or her parents, to produce written consent to the application from a parent or legal guardian to the Secretary of State, if required to do so.

(12)   where one or more relevant NHS body has notified the Secretary of State that the person seeking leave to remain or a variation of leave to enter or remain has failed to pay a charge or charges with a total value of at least £1000 in accordance with the relevant NHS regulations on charges to overseas visitors.

a   See *R v Secretary of State for the Home Department, ex p Animashaun* [1990] Imm AR 70, QBD. The asylum equivalent of this rule, HC 395, para 340, combined with absurdly short compliance times, led to over a third of asylum claims being rejected on non-compliance grounds at one time, and to widespread anger at the cynical abuse of the procedure by the Secretary of State to inflate refusal figures for political purposes.

1   HC 395, para 322(2)–(11). We retain the numbering of the sub-paragraphs here.

D.   Cancellation of leave

CANCELLATION OF LEAVE UNDER PARAGRAPH 321A

3.141 The following grounds for the cancellation of a person's leave to enter or remain which is in force on his arrival in, or whilst he is outside, the United Kingdom apply:

(1)   a change in the circumstances since the leave was given, meriting cancellation; or

(2)   false representations were made or false documents were submitted or material facts were not disclosed, in relation to the application for leave; or in order to obtain documents in support of the application. [This repeats the wording of paragraph 320 (7A)] or,

(3)   it is undesirable for medical reasons to admit a person, save where that person is settled in the United Kingdom or where the Immigration Officer or the Secretary of State is satisfied that there are strong compassionate reasons justifying admission, or

(4)   where the Secretary of State has personally directed that the exclusion of that person from the United Kingdom is conducive to the public good; or

(4A)   Grounds which would have led to a refusal under paragraphs 320(2), 320(6), 320(18A), 320(18B) or 320(19) if the person concerned were making a new application for leave to enter or remain;[a] or

(5)   The Immigration Officer or the Secretary of State deems the exclusion of the person from the United Kingdom to be conducive to the public good. For example, because the person's conduct (including convictions which do not fall within paragraph 320(2)), character, associations, or other reasons, make it undesirable to grant them leave to enter the United Kingdom; or

(6)   where that person is outside the United Kingdom, failure by that person to supply any information, documents, copy documents or medical report requested by an Immigration Officer or the Secretary of State.

a   Where this sub-paragraph applies in respect of leave to enter or remain granted under Appendix Armed Forces it is to be read as if for paragraphs 320(2), 320(6), 320(18A), 320(18B) or 320(19) said 'paragraph 8(a), (b), (c) or (g) and paragraph 9(d)'.

E. Curtailment of leave

CURTAILMENT UNDER THE IMMIGRATION ACT 1971 AND PARAGRAPHS 322.
323 AND 323A

3.142 An existing leave to enter or remain can be curtailed through the general operation of section 3(3) of the Immigration Act 1971 following the refusal of an application to extend leave. There is also paragraph 323 of the rules, which provides that a person's leave to enter or remain may be curtailed:

(i)   on any of the grounds set out in paragraph 322 (2)–(5) above;

(ii)   if the person ceases to meet the requirements of the Rules under which leave to enter or remain was granted;

(iii) is the dependant of an asylum seeker whose leave to remain was curtailed prior to 2 October 2000 under the now repealed s 7 of the Asylum and Immigration Appeals Act 1993 and he does not qualify for leave in his own right;

(iv)   is someone whose grant of asylum or humanitarian protection is revoked under HC 395, paras 339A (i)–(vi) and 339G (i)–(vi);

(v)   where a person has, within the first six months of being granted leave to enter, committed an offence for which they are subsequently sentenced to a period of imprisonment, or

(vi)   if he was granted his current period of leave as the dependent of a person ("P") and P's leave to enter or remain is being, or has been, curtailed.

3.143 Paragraph 323A[1] created additional situations where leave to remain will be curtailed. It applies to Tier 2, 4 and Tier 5 migrants who no longer have a licensed sponsor for reasons referred to in the circumstances set out in the rule. It also applies to the migrant who fails to commence, or ceases, working for the sponsor, and in the case of a student under Tier 4 fails to show up at his or her school or College; changes college without written permission of UKBA; or ceases studying with the sponsor. Tier 1 (Exceptional Talent) Migrants can have their leave curtailed under paragraph 323B,[2] if the Designated Competent Body withdraws its endorsement of the migrant.[3] Tier 1 (Entrepreneurs) can already have their leave curtailed if they fail to register with the appropriate authority within six months[4] and likewise Tier 1 (Investors) if they fail to invest £750,000 within three months.[5]

[1]   Inserted by HC 1113 with effect from 27 November 2008.
[2]   Inserted by HC 1436 in July 2011.
[3]   See CHAPTER 10.
[4]   HC 395, para 245DE(c).
[5]   HC 395, para 245EE(c).

3.144 The general considerations at points (2)–(5) of paragraph 322 dealing with refusals of leave to remain expressly apply to a variation of leave under the Immigration Act 1971 section 3(3)(a) which has the effect of curtailing the leave.[1] Curtailment of leave is rather more drastic than a refusal to vary it, and it will not be applied automatically where one of the discretionary grounds applies.[2] There is only one situation where curtailment is routinely considered, and that is where a person who is in the UK in a temporary capacity (which requires an intention to leave the UK at the end of the leave) applies for asylum which is refused. If the person does not qualify for humanitarian protection or discretionary leave, was warned of his or her liability to curtailment, and does not qualify for leave under any other provision of the Immigration Rules, leave may be curtailed on the basis that the applicant ceases to meet the requirements of the Immigration Rules (usually the requirement that they intend to leave the UK at the end of their stay). Students in the UK under Tier 4 of the Points Based System should no longer have their leave curtailed on this basis, since the rules no longer contain a requirement that they intend to leave the UK at the end of their studies. Provided that they are genuine students complying with the conditions of their leave, curtailment should not follow a refusal of asylum, though note that there will be no right of appeal under section 82 of the 2002 Act, nor under section 83 unless leave of 12 months or more is granted (in one grant or in aggregate) at the time of or after the refusal.[3] Exceptions are persons married to British citizens or to EEA nationals exercising Treaty rights; holders of leave in a category leading to settlement (work or business); or passengers who are terminally ill. Leave granted as a result of humanitarian protection will normally be curtailed if the protection is revoked, for example because one of the exclusion criteria applies, or if circumstances change such that protection is no longer needed.[4] Where leave is curtailed and there is an in-country right of appeal under the NIAA 2002, section 82(3)(e), section 3D of the IA 1971, inserted by section 11(5) of IAN 2006, extends the 'curtailed' or revoked leave so long as an in-country appeal against revocation or curtailment may be brought or is pending.[5] Notice of curtailment must comply with the Immigration (Notices) Regulations 2003 if curtailment carries a right of appeal.[6]

[1]   See HC 395, para 323. See also Modernised Guidance: Curtailment of leave.
[2]   Curtailment should not follow automatically when the basis of stay no longer exists: Modernised Guidance: Curtailment of leave, Version 11.0 (30 April 2014) p 10, though it will be considered where a relationship, which formed the basis of stay, breaks down (Modernised Guidance p 24). It 'may not be appropriate where a PBS migrant claimed public funds short term in an emergency: Modernised Guidance p 18. Note that, at the time of writing, leave can only be curtailed for false representations or deception in a previous application, but s 1 of the Immigration Act 2014 will, when commenced, bring into effect a new paragraph 323(ia) providing for curtailment of existing leave where deception is used in a current application.
[3]   *MS (Uganda) v Secretary of State for the Home Department* [2014] EWCA Civ 50.
[4]   Asylum decision making guidance: Humanitarian Protection, version 4.0, section 8.
[5]   It replaces the provisions of section 82(3) of the of the Nationality, Immigration and Asylum Act 2002, which used a different mechanism to achieve the same result, namely, that curtailment or revocation should not take effect while an appeal could be made or was pending. The only difference now is that this operates only if it is an in-country appeal. See 3.60, above.
[6]   Modernised Guidance: Curtailment of leave, version 11.0, p111.

Comment on the Texts

A.   Deceivers

3.145 The General Grounds for Refusal in HC 395, paragraph 320, were amended during 2008,[1] so that mandatory refusal of entry clearance or entry applied where false representations had been made or false documents or information were provided or material facts had not been disclosed in order to get an entry clearance (paragraph 320(7A)). This clause in paragraph 320(7A) is repeated in paragraphs 321 (i) (refusal of leave to enter to a person in possession of an entry certificate), 321A(2) (cancellation of leave at the port or outside the UK) and 322(1A) (refusal to grant leave to remain or to vary leave or curtailment of leave). These paragraphs read as follows:

> 'where false representations have been made or false documents or information have been submitted (whether or not material to the application, and whether or not to the applicant's knowledge), or material facts have not been disclosed, in relation to the application or in order to obtain documents from the Secretary of State or a third party required in support of the application.'

The reference to 'false' representations or 'false' documents and information means dishonestly false rather than mistaken.[2] Second, the deliberate deception may or may not be material to the decision; so the question of materiality which is central to the failure to disclose material facts, and which we deal with below, does not arise with regard to false representations, information or documents. Third, deliberate deception may be that of a third party, made without the applicant's knowledge. Fourth, false representations and false documents must relate to the application being considered or the documents being obtained in support of the application and not to any earlier transaction, though it is necessary for the applicant to be truthful about the previous (established) false representations or documents.[3] Fifth, it is still incumbent on the Home Office to prove the case to the requisite standard; for example, prove a representation, its falsity and the fact that it was made for the purpose of obtaining leave or an earlier variation. Where fraud is alleged, the standard of proof will have to be higher.[4]

[1] See HC 321 HC 607 and HC 1113.
[2] *AA(Nigeria) v Secretary of State for the Home Department* [2010] EWCA Civ 773, [2010] Imm AR 704. See also *LD (Article 8-best interests of child) Zimbabwe* [2010] UKUT 278 (IAC), [2011] Imm AR 99.
[3] *R (on the application of Giri) v Secretary of State for the Home Department* [2014] EWHC 1832 (Admin).
[4] *Khawaja v Secretary of State for the Home Department* [1984] AC 74, [1983] Imm AR 139, HL. For a case where the burden of proof made a difference see *MH (Respondent's Bundle: documents not provided) Pakistan* [2010] UKUT 00168 (IAC), [2010] Imm AR 658. The standard required will also be particularly high where the entry clearance has been issued following a successful appeal, where the starting point is a binding decision in favour of the appellant: *R v Secretary of State for the Home Department, ex p Miah* [1983] Imm AR 91, DC; *Ali v Secretary of State for the Home Department* [1984] 1 All ER 1009, [1984] 1 WLR 663, CA. See *also R v Secretary of State for the Home Department, ex p Danaie* [1998] Imm AR 84, CA.

3.146 Under the general grounds for refusal of leave to remain or a variation of leave under paragraph 322, there is, in addition to the mandatory ground set out above, a discretion to refuse further stay for the making of false representations or the failure to disclose any material fact:

(i) for the purpose of obtaining leave to enter or a previous variation of leave or in order to obtain documents in support of the application for leave to enter or a previous variation of leave;[1] or

(ii) for the purpose of obtaining a document from the Secretary of State that indicates the person has a right to reside in the United Kingdom;[2]

Unlike the mandatory ground, which relates to the application being made, these provision include past deceptions and past failures to disclose material facts. Also excluded is past or current third party deception and past or current third party non-diclosure. In accordance with the case law on 320(7A) etc 'false' means dishonestly false and not mistaken.[3] It would also mean that non-disclosure means deliberate no-disclosure with intent to deceive or mislead.[4]

[1] HC 395, para 322(2).
[2] HC 395, para 322(2A).
[3] *AA(Nigeria) v Secretary of State for the Home Department* [2010] EWCA Civ 773, [2010] Imm AR 704.
[4] *Ahmed (general grounds of refusal – material non-disclosure) Pakistan* [2011] UKUT 00351 (IAC).

3.147 There is a problem about what happens after a mandatory refusal or curtailment on grounds of deception. Entry or further stay may be refused and leave may be cancelled or curtailed, because of third party deception, but the consequences of such a decision depend in many cases upon an assertion in other rules or legislation that the relevant deception is that of the migrant and not of some third party. In other words the migrant must be the deceiver or complicit in the third party's deception. For example, if UK Visas wanted to prosecute by virtue of section 24A(1)(a) of the Immigration Act 1971 (inserted by Immigration and Asylum Act 1999, section 28). It is a criminal offence to obtain leave to remain by means which include deception but the deception must be that of the person charged. If the authorities rely on deception in seeking to remove a person under section 10 of the Immigration and Asylum Act 1999, they must prove that it is that person's deception or that the person is complicit in another person's deception.[1] Further, where the entry clearance officer relies on paragraph 320(7B) (d) to refuse an application for entry clearance because of a breach of the UK's immigration laws by using deception in a previous application, it is not enough that false representations were made by someone else. The dishonesty must have been that of the applicant herself and the burden is on the ECO to show that a false statement was deliberately made for the purpose of securing an advantage in immigration terms.[2]

[1] It should be noted that removal as an overstayer under s 10 of 1999 Act or as an illegal entrant under Immigration Act 1971 Sch 2, para 9 would also be available.
[2] *Ozhogina and Tarasova (deception within para 320(7B) – nannies) Russia* [2011] UKUT 00197 (IAC) – the 'Russian nannies case'. For further discussion of 320(7B) see below **3.152**.

3.148 The real problem lies with the rule at paragraph 321A, which deals with a cancellation of a leave contained in an entry clearance which an immigration officer seeks to cancel when the passenger arrives in the UK. Paragraph 321A gives wide discretionary powers to an immigration officers and the Secretary of State. Unlike Paras 320 and 322 it does not have a mandatory bit and a discretionary bit. Here we are not just dealing with powers contained in the immigration rules but ones regulated and, arguably, limited by statute, so that the immigration cannot exercise a discretion under paragraph 321A(2)[1] to cancel leave because of third party deception in which the passenger is not complicit. Under the immigration officer's statutory powers[2] he or she can examine a passenger who arrives with a leave which is in force but was given to the passenger before his or her arrival in the UK. This includes, but is not limited to a leave in the form of an entry clearance. In either case the questioning is limited *inter alia* to seeking to establish whether that leave was obtained as a result of false information given by the passenger or his or her failure to disclose material facts.[3] The language of the schedule makes it clear that the limit of the questioning is to see if it can be established (i) that the passenger has practised deliberate deception, (ii) that the false information was 'material', which it must be, because in the words of the statute, the leave must have been obtained 'as a result of' the false information. If successful it is arguable that the immigration officers are limited to the issues on which they are permitted to examine when they exercise a discretion under paragraph 2A(8) to cancel the passenger's leave to enter. If correct, the wide ambit of paragraph 320(7A) gives has limited application as set out above.

[1] Paragraph 321A was inserted into HC 395 by HC 704 in Jul 2000 and sub-paragraph 2 was substituted by HC 704 in February 2008.
[2] Immigration Act 1971, Sch 2, para 2A(2)(b).
[3] Immigration Act 1971, Sch 2, para 2A92)(b).

B. Non-disclosure of material facts

3.149 Non-disclosure under paragraphs 320(7A), 321(i), 321A(2), and 322(1A). The second part of the main ground for refusing cancelling or curtailing leave in paragraphs 320(7A) (refusal of entry clearance and entry), 321(i) (refusal of leave to enter to a person in possession of an entry certificate), 321A(2) (cancellation of leave at the port or outside the UK) and 322(1A) (refusal to grant leave to remain or to vary leave or curtailment of leave) is the non-disclosure of material facts. Here, the critical question is the meaning of 'material', a concern prompted by the divergence in its meaning arising from illegal entry cases. *In Kaur (Sukhjinder) v Secretary of State for the Home Department*[1] the Court of Appeal again adopted a different approach from that taken in the illegal entry cases, holding that 'material' did not mean 'decisive', as the court had previously held in *Jayakody*,[2] but it was only necessary that the facts not disclosed would be likely to have influenced the decision. All that immigration officers need show is that passengers have failed to disclose facts which they knew or ought to have known would be relevant in considering whether to grant the visa. So where non-disclosure is relied on, the applicant should not be punished for a failure to realise that facts not disclosed were material. Otherwise, one effect of the rule would be to rectify mistakes by immigration officials in granting earlier leave, at the expense of the innocent applicant. This is consistent with the statement of the then Immigration Minister Liam Byrne on 4 April 2008 in response to a letter from the ILPA seeking clarification, inter alia, on 'innocent mistake' within the scope of the mandatory refusal grounds; he stated:

> 'You go on to ask for confirmation that Lord Bassam's comments about the definition of a false document also apply to false representations . . . . The new Rules are intended to cover people who tell lies – either on their own behalf or that of someone else – in an application to the UK Border Agency. They are not intended to catch those who make innocent mistakes in their applications . . . .'

However, for reasons set out the above paragraph, 'material' may have a different meaning in a cancellation exercise conducted under paragraph 321A(2).

[1] [1998] Imm AR 1, CA. See also *Marquez v Immigration Officer, Gatwick North* [1992] Imm AR 354.

251

[2]   *R v Secretary of State for the Home Department, ex p Jayakody* [1982] 1 All ER 461, [1981] Imm AR 205, CA; see also *R v Secretary of State for the Home Department, ex p Ming* [1994] Imm AR 216, QBD.

3.150 In practice the scope of relevant questions is usually determined by those posed in the application form and any oral questions asked at an interview or in examination at the port of entry. Many of the cases revolve around a failure to disclose a criminal conviction or answering 'no' to the question about convictions on the application form[1]. It should be noted that a guilty verdict or plea resulting in an absolute or conditional discharge is not a 'conviction' and those who received such a sentence do not make a false representation if answering 'no' – although they would do so if they denied ever having been 'found guilty' of an offence.[2] In *Ahmed (general grounds of refusal – material non-disclosure) Pakistan*[3] A used his Oyster Card on a train journey, where it was not valid for travel on that route. This led to his receiving a 'Notice of Fine and Collection Order' sent to him by a Magistrates' Court. He paid the fine. It was a criminal conviction, but he genuinely did not realise this and ticked the 'No' box to the question 'do you have a criminal conviction on his application form seeking leave to remain. He was refused leave because he had used deception. In upholding his appeal the Upper Tribunal held that this was a case where there was no essential difference between a false representation and non-disclosure. In many, if not most, cases false representations and material non-disclosure will be opposite sides of the same coin. So if A had failed to disclose a material fact he would also have made a false representation, and vice versa. This meant that in the light of *AA (Nigeria)*[4] A needed to have a dishonest state of mind on the basis that if failure to disclose material facts is also a species of Deception, by parity of reasoning that too requires dishonesty on the part of A.

[1]   What amounts to a criminal conviction is in most cases easy to determine, but there is also a big grey area, which we have dealt with in some detail in dealing with 'good character' in naturalisation cases in CHAPTER 2. Some help is also given by section 14(1) of the Powers of Criminal Courts (Sentencing) Act 2000, which was determinative in *Omenna* below.
[2]   *Omenna (Conditional discharge – not a conviction of an offence)* [2014] UKUT 314 (IAC).
[3]   [2011] UKUT 00351 (IAC).
[4]   *AA(Nigeria) v Secretary of State for the Home Department* [2010] EWCA Civ 773, [2010] Imm AR 704.

3.151 The idea of the amendments to the General Grounds for Refusal from 2008 onwards was to exclude any kind of discretion on the part of the entry clearance officers and thereby to achieve greater consistency in decision making. However, the result was that the rules became so absurdly draconian that the Secretary of State had to think again and modify her stance.[1] This was done by the introduction of 320(7C) disapplying subparagraphs (7A) and (7B) in family reunion situations but introducing subparagraph 320(11), giving a discretion to entry clearance officers to refuse those who had previously contrived in a significant way to frustrate the intentions of the Rules. Paragraph 320(7C) was deleted when Appendix FM took effect in July 2012 and replaced with paragraph A320, providing that paragraphs 320 (save for (3), (10) and (11)) and 322 do not apply to applications under Appendix FM for entry clearance / leave to enter or remain and indefinite leave.

[1]   See Immigration Minister, Liam Byrne MP, Hansard 13 May 2008, cols 1350–1354, or at www.publications.parliament.uk/pa/cm200708/cmhansrd/cm080513/debtext/80513-0028.ht

m#0805147000250. The concessions he announced took effect immediately, but were later inserted into the Immigration Rules.

C. *Refusals because of past breaches*

PENALISING PAST BREACHES UNDER PARA 320(7B)

3.152 HC 359, paragraph 320(7B) applies to those seeking return to the UK, who have been overstayers, illegal entrants, breachers of their conditions of leave or have used deception (eg submitting false documents) in an immigration application; or who have breached their conditions of stay while in the UK (for example by working illegally). Paragraph 320(7B) provides that when someone has previously breached the immigration laws in any one of these ways, there is a time bar in obtaining entry clearance or leave to enter. Under the subparagraph the period is ten years before the applicant can qualify for leave: (i) if the person used deception in an application for entry clearance more than 10 years ago;[1] or (ii) was deported or removed from the UK more than ten years ago.[2] Apart from deportation and deception cases, the period is five years if: (i) the person leaves voluntarily at public expense,[3] or (ii) the person left or was removed from the UK as a condition of a caution issued in accordance with section 22 of the Criminal Justice Act 2003.[4] It is two years, if the person leaves the UK voluntarily at public expense, no more than six months after the date on which he or she was given notice of the removal decision, or no more than six months after the date on which the person no longer had a pending appeal, whichever is the later.[5] It is one year if the person leaves the UK voluntarily, not at the expense (directly or indirectly) of the Secretary of State.[6] There is no gap where a person has overstayed for 28 days or less and leaves the UK voluntarily not at the expense (directly or indirectly) of the Secretary of State.[7] Where more than one breach of the UK's immigration laws has occurred, the only relevant breach is the one which leads to the longest period of absence from the UK.

[1] HC 359, para 320 (7B)(d) (ii).
[2] HC 359, para (7B)(vi).
[3] HC 359, para (7B)(v).
[4] HC 359, para (7B)(vii).
[5] HC 359, para (7B)(iv).
[6] HC 359, para (7B)(iii).
[7] HC 359, para (7B)(i).

D. *Criminal convictions*

MANDATORY REFUSAL UNDER PARAGRAPHS 320(2) AND 322 (1C)

3.153 A similar approach to (7B) has more recently been added to the grounds of refusal under paragraph 320(2) (entry clearance and entry) and under paragraph 322(1C) (applications for indefinite leave). Although the details are different the principles are the same – to bar those with convictions from gaining entry or settlement for indefinite or definite periods of time-an exercise now carried out without any kind of correlation with notions of 'spent' convictions set out in the recently amended Rehabilitation of Offenders Act 1984.

3.154 Under paragraph 320(2) (entry) there is an indefinite bar to getting an entry clearance or leave to enter the UK, if the person has received a prison sentence of four years or more. Those who have had sentences of between 12 months and four years have to wait ten years from the end of their sentence before they can qualify for entry. There is a time bar of five years from the end of their sentence for those who were sentenced less than 12 months. An applicant for entry clearance or leave to enter is to be refused if within 24 months of the date on which the application is decided, the applicant has had a non-custodial sentence or out of court disposal which has been recorded on his or her criminal record. In other words anyone with as much as a conditional discharge or a caution will need to wait for two years before he or she will qualify for leave to enter or an entry clearance. However, if someone with unspent leave goes on holiday abroad and returns within the period left on his or her leave, this paragraph will not apply. Where paragraph 320(2) does apply, it will only be in exceptional circumstances that the public interest in maintaining refusal will be outweighed by compelling factors unless refusal would be contrary to the Human Rights Convention or the refugee Convention and Protocol.

3.155 Where a person is seeking indefinite leave to enter or remain (ILR) Paragraph 322 (1C) provides that:

(i)   they will never qualify for ILR if they have been convicted of an offence for which they have been sentenced to imprisonment for at least 4 years;

(ii)   If they have been convicted of an offence for which they have been sentenced to imprisonment for at least 12 months but less than 4 years, they will not get ILR unless a period of 15 years has passed since the end of the sentence; or

(iii)   if they have been convicted of an offence for which they have been sentenced to imprisonment for less than 12 months, they will not qualify for ILR, unless a period of seven years has passed since the end of their sentence; or

(iv)   if they have, within the 24 months prior to the date on which the application is decided, been convicted of or admitted an offence for which they have received a non-custodial sentence or other out of court disposal that is recorded on their criminal record, they will have to wait until the two year period has expired to qualify.

3.156 These provisions have no relation to the risk posed by non-British criminal or to the nature of his or her criminality and they bear no correlation with the amended provisions of the Rehabilitation of Offenders Act 1974. Although section 139 of the Legal Aid, Sentencing and Punishment of Offenders Act 2012 ('LASPO') amends the Rehabilitation of Offenders Act so as, inter alia, to reduce the rehabilitation periods for various sentences, section 140 inserted a new section 56A into the UK Borders Act 2007, as from 1 October 2012, which provides for no rehabilitation for certain immigration or nationality purposes.[1] Consequently a previous conviction will never become 'spent' for the purposes of applications for leave to remain and in effect becomes 'unspent'. It should also be noted that a guilty verdict or plea leading to an absolute or conditional discharge is not a conviction, by virtue of section 14(1) of the Powers of Criminal Courts (Sentencing) Act 2000; so there is no false representation if a person who received such a discharge ticks 'no' to the question whether they have any convictions.[2]

[1] In one of the most gobbledygook worded sections a simple English explanation of s 56 is that the key provisions of the Rehabilitation Act do not apply in relation to any proceedings in respect of or for the purposes of any immigration decisions to grant or refuse persons leave to enter or remain in the UK or to remove or deport persons from the UK. The same applies to nationality decisions.
[2] *Omenma (Conditional discharge-not a conviction of an offence)* [2014] UKUT 314 (IAC).

DISCRETION TO ADMIT THOSE WITH CRIMINAL CONVICTIONS UNDER DELETED PARAGRAPH 320(18)

3.157 The now-deleted paragraph 320(18) provided for a discretion to admit a person in spite of a criminal record where there were 'strong compassionate circumstances'.[1] In addition there was (and remains) a residual discretion under which a person may be given leave to enter the UK. In the Mike Tyson case,[2] in which Justice for Women challenged the Secretary of State for the Home Department's instruction to admit the heavyweight boxer, who had been sentenced to six years' imprisonment in the US for rape. Sullivan J pointed out that it may be considered that it is in the public interest that that person be permitted to come to the UK, given some learning, entertainment or economic value that he can bring to this country. Whether those advantages are such as to justify an exception being made to the normal rule is a matter, in normal cases, for the immigration officer to decide. But he expressly upheld the general discretion to admit in the absence of strong compassionate circumstances – a discretion belonging both to the immigration officer and to the Secretary of State. Mike Tyson was however refused entry to the UK in December 2013 on the basis of the same conviction, notwithstanding the passage of a further 13 years since the conviction.

[1] For cases in which the old rule still applies, *see F (Para 320(18); type of leave) USA* [2013] UKUT 00309 (IAC).
[2] *R v Secretary of State for the Home Department, ex p Bindel* [2001] Imm AR 1, QBD.

NON-CUSTODIAL SENTENCES UNDER PARAGRAPHS 320(18A), (18B) AND 322 (5A)

3.158 The rules now contain paragraph 320 (18A) and (18B)(entry) and 322(5A) (leave to remain) which provide for discretionary exclusion on the basis of conviction for or admission of an offence within the last 12 months which is recorded on the criminal record albeit with a non-custodial or out of court disposal. It is relevant to the exercise of the discretion whether the person is a persistent offender 'who shows a particular disregard for the law' or the offending 'has caused serious harm'. Those entitled to rely on EU law are much better off, since exclusion must be much more rigorously justified.[1] Care must also be taken to ensure that the right to family life is not interfered with in a manner contrary to Article 8 of the ECHR by taking disproportionate measures which are not necessary in a democratic society (see CHAPTER 7 below). No one claiming asylum can be refused leave to enter on the basis of this or any other general Immigration Rule; the Convention criteria for exclusion must be applied.[2] Similarly, no one claiming a fear of treatment contrary to Article 3 of the ECHR may be refused leave to enter by virtue of this Rule, or any other.[3]

[1] See Council Directive 2004/38/EC and the provisions on restrictions which can be imposed on the rights of entry and residence on grounds of public policy and public security, particularly Article 27 and 28.
[2] See CHAPTER 12, below.
[3] See CHAPTER 7, below.

3.159 The now-deleted paragraph 320(18) provided for a discretion to admit a person in spite of a criminal record where there were 'strong compassionate circumstances'.[1] In addition there was (and remains) a residual discretion under which a person may be given leave to enter the UK. In the Mike Tyson case,[2] in which Justice for Women challenged the Secretary of State for the Home Department's instruction to admit the heavyweight boxer, who had been sentenced to six years' imprisonment in the US for rape. Sullivan J pointed out that it may be considered that it is in the public interest that that person be permitted to come to the UK, given some learning, entertainment or economic value that he can bring to this country. Whether those advantages are such as to justify an exception being made to the normal rule is a matter, in normal cases, for the immigration officer to decide. But he expressly upheld the general discretion to admit in the absence of strong compassionate circumstances – a discretion belonging both to the immigration officer and to the Secretary of State.

[1] For cases in which the old rule still applies, see *F (Para 320(18); type of leave) USA* [2013] UKUT 00309 (IAC).
[2] *R v Secretary of State for the Home Department, ex p Bindel* [2001] Imm AR 1, QBD.

E.   Deportees

BARRIERS TO GETTING LEAVE

3.160 As regards those subject to a current deportation order, they are barred indefinitely from getting leave to enter.[1] Those seeking leave to remain or an extension their stay must be refused (1B) if, at the date of application, they are subject of a deportation order or a decision to make a deportation order.[2] This, of course, is not the whole story. A deportation order prohibits entry to the UK and invalidates any leave a person may have.[3] A deportation order is not invalidated by leave to enter granted in error. However, if the deportation followed a conviction which is spent, refusal is not automatic.[4] A person who is subject to an Irish deportation order is not to be refused for that reason alone. A person wishing to enter must apply for revocation of the deportation order first before applying for entry clearance, otherwise mandatory refusal will apply. The reasons for revocation cannot simply be raised on appeal against a refusal of entry clearance.[5]

[1] HC 395, para 320(2)(a).
[2] HC 395, para 322(1B).
[3] Immigration Act 1971, s 5(1). Where third country nationals who are EEA family members are subject to a current deportation order (however long ago it may have been imposed) seeks entry to the UK as a family member or is in the UK and applies for an EEA residence document,

he or she can only be only be refused under the public policy proviso under the Citizens' Directive, arts 27 and 28 (Directive 38/2004 EC).

4   Modernised Guidance: General Reasons for Refusing, Section 2 of 5 – considering entry clearance (see **3.132** fn 1 above).

5   *Latif (s 120 – revocation of deportation order)* [2012] UKUT 78 (IAC). The same is likely to apply to those with exclusion orders rather than deportation orders: *Campbell (exclusion; Zambrano)* [2013] UKUT 00147 (IAC).

F.   *Frustrating the intentions of immigration rules*

DISCRETION TO REFUSE UNDER PARAGRAPH 320(11)

3.161 Although Paragraph 320(11) provides for a discretionary refusal where the applicant has previously contrived in a significant way to frustrate the intentions of the immigration rules, we deal with it in this section of comment, because of its close association with the 2008 reforms of the mandatory grounds. Originally the intention was to give the immigration authorities a discretion to refuse applicants who are exempt from automatic refusal under paragraph 320(7B) as a result of the various amendments, especially those in the now revoked paragraph 320(7C). It now has a life of its own. It provides for there to be a discretionary refusal where the applicant has previously contrived in a significant way to frustrate the intentions of the Rules by:

(i)   overstaying; or

(ii)   breaching a condition attached to his leave; or

(iii)   being an illegal entrant; or

(iv)   using deception in an application for entry clearance, leave to enter or remain or in order to obtain documents from the Secretary of State or a third party required in support of the application (whether successful or not); and

(v)   there are other aggravating circumstances, such as absconding, not meeting temporary admission/reporting restrictions or bail conditions, using an assumed identity or multiple identities, switching nationality, making frivolous applications or not complying with the re-documentation process.

So there must have been breaches which frustrated the Rules in a significant way plus aggravating circumstances. The examples set out in the rules are not a comprehensive list. More examples are set out in Modern Guidance.[1] There should be no overlap between a 'significant way' and 'aggravating circumstances'; otherwise there would be double counting. Decision makers and Tribunals must 'exercise great care' in deciding to apply paragraph 320(11) to a family member, and must ensure that the aggravating circumstances relied on are 'truly aggravating' otherwise there is a risk of discouraging migrants from making applications to regularise their stay, which would be contrary to the public interest.[2] It should also be noted that for paragraph 320(11) to apply it needs to be shown that the applicant (as opposed to someone acting without his or her knowledge) is responsible for the contrivance.[3]

1   Modernised Guidance: p 43 of General Reasons for Refusing, section 2 – v 16.0 Ext valid from 30 April 2014. See www.ukba.homeoffice.gov.uk/policyandlaw/guidance/modernised-guidan ce/IIM.

2   *PS (paragraph 320(11) discretion: care needed) India* [2010] UKUT 440 (IAC).

3.161 *Control of Entry and Stay*

³   *Mumu v Entry Clearance Officer, Dhaka* [2012] UKUT 00143 (IAC).

G.   Other mandatory grounds for refusal of leave

Seeking leave for a purpose not covered by the rules

3.162 Leave to enter, entry clearance or leave to remain are to be refused if admission or variation is sought for a purpose not covered by the Immigration Rules.[1] The Rules are drafted so narrowly that large numbers of people and purposes are omitted. Although provision is now made for unmarried partners, there is still no provision in the Rules for the admission of certain relatives, such as step-children or step-parents where the natural parent is still alive. Nor is there provision for the admission of the family members of those in the UK with discretionary leave. Earlier rules were silent on these categories, but since 1994 the Rules have provided for mandatory refusal. This does not prevent immigration officers exercising discretion to admit them outside the Rules,[2] but the result was to deprive applicants for entry of an appeal against an adverse decision, unless human rights are engaged.[3] For applicants for leave to remain, it is open to the Secretary of State to allow an application outside the rules. There would be no right of appeal on the merits, but the refusal will be appealable on asylum or human rights grounds if as a result of the refusal, the person has no leave to enter or remain.[4]

¹   HC 395, para 320(1) and 322(1).
²   *Kuku (Aderimi Shakirat) v Secretary of State for the Home Department* [1990] Imm AR 27, CA; Immigration Officer, *Heathrow v Adac-Bosompra* [1992] Imm AR 579, IAT. See IDI (Jun 04), Ch 9, s 2; immigration officers should consider eligibility under any concession as well as under the Rules.
³   See **19.30** below.
⁴   NIAA 2002, ss 82(2)(d), 84(1)(b), (c), (g), 88(4), subject to the provisions of the Immigration Act 2014.

3.163 Other mandatory refusals require little explanation. Passengers who do not satisfy the entry clearance officer or immigration officer of their identity or nationality are to be refused,[1] unless there are strong compassionate or other reasons for granting leave.[2] When they seek leave to enter, whether they are in the UK or abroad, they must submit to examination and produce valid documents establishing identity and nationality.[3] Those who are travelling to another part of the common travel area but are not acceptable to the authorities there must be refused entry to the UK.[4] Those seeking leave to enter (whether in the UK or abroad) who are required to hold entry clearance but do not have one, are to be refused.[5] The Secretary of State for the Home Department may give a personal direction not to grant leave to enter or entry clearance on the ground that exclusion is conducive to the public good.[6] That ground is considered further below, as are medical grounds for exclusion, which are in discretionary terms although categorised with the mandatory grounds (**3.87**).

¹   HC 395, para 320(3).
²   Modernised Guidance: page 3 of General Reasons for Refusing section 2 of 5, p 4 – considering entry clearance – revealing a discretion even in 'mandatory refusal' cases.
³   Immigration Act 1971, Sch 2, para 4 (persons arriving in the UK); Immigration (Leave to Enter and Remain) Order 2000, SI 2000/1161, art 7(2), (4) (persons seeking leave to enter abroad).
⁴   HC 395, para 320(4).

⁵   HC 395, para 320(5).
⁶   HC 395, para 320(6).

The discretionary grounds

3.164 The lists of discretionary grounds, contained in HC 395, paragraphs 320 and 322, give immigration officials a large measure of discretion[1]. Normally the existence of one of these grounds will lead to a refusal of variation, leave to remain, leave to enter or entry clearance but not always. That is where the discretion comes in. The grounds are wide-ranging, and many are self-explanatory. We have already dealt with Paragraphs 322(2) and (2A) (false representations on a previous application), (320(11) (previous breaches of immigration law) and 320(18(a) and (b)) and 322 (5A) (criminal convictions with non-custodial sentences and cautions). We now examine some of the remainder below.

[1]   The Tribunal has underlined the importance of the reviewable discretion in non-mandatory refusals in *R (on the application of Mauritius) v Entry Clearance Officer, Port Louis* [2003] UKIAT 00030.

Unacceptable passports

3.165 The immigration officer may refuse entry to persons using passports issued by governments of entities not recognised by the UK government.[1] Currently these are the Turkish Republic of Northern Cyprus (TRNC), Republic of China (Taiwan), Yemen (Royalist Authorities), Palestine, Iraq (S-, M- and N- series passports), Somali and South African temporary passports. However, the ECG state that Turkish Republic of Northern Cyprus passport holders should not be refused entry under this paragraph, although their passports should not be endorsed. Taiwanese passports may be stamped notwithstanding non-recognition. Palestinian Authority travel documents are acceptable for travel to the UK and may be endorsed, although the IDI hasten to add that 'this does not imply recognition of a separate State of Palestine'.[2]

[1]   HC 395, para 320(10).
[2]   ECG ECB08 which sets out in full those travel documents acceptable for the purposes of entry clearance.

Restricted returnability

3.166 This particular rule applies to those seeking entry to the UK as well as those seeking leave to remain or a variation of their leave. Persons who do not satisfy the immigration official dealing with their application that they would be admitted to another country after a stay in the UK may be refused leave to enter or leave to remain or have an existing leave extended.[1] These two rules expressly exempt persons who are eligible for settlement. Previously the rules had additionally referred expressly to a spouse or civil partner of someone who is settled in the UK, but as from 9 July 2012 spouses and civil partners were deleted from the rules[2] as part of the package that introduced Appendix FM and the other changes to family reunion. Those coming for settlement are to be distinguished from those coming with a view to settlement. The restricted returnability rule applies to all those entering not for settlement but with a view to settlement. It is not disapplied just because the passenger holds an entry clearance.[3] Where a person's returnability to another country is restricted, leave to enter may nevertheless be given, subject to severe limits on the length of stay.[4] Modernised Guidance suggests that this paragraph cannot be used where the person meets the rules for settlement, leave to enter as a spouse leading to settlement or may return elsewhere[5].

[1]   HC 395, para 320(13) and 322(8).
[2]   HC 194, para 108.
[3]   See *R v Secretary of State for the Home Department, ex p Sadiq* [1990] Imm AR 364, QBD.
[4]   See HC 395, paras 21–23 set out at 3, above **3.74**.
[5]   Modernised Guidance: General grounds for refusal section 2, Version 16.0 p 46.

FAILURE TO COMPLY WITH CONDITIONS ATTACHED TO STAY: FURTHER LEAVE

3.167 A failure to comply with conditions attached to stay[1] will lead to refusal of further leave only where a person has shown by his or her conduct that he or she has deliberately and consistently breached conditions of sta.[2]y The fact that a past breach has been overlooked, in the sense that further leave has been granted despite it, does not mean that it has been condoned in the sense of full forgiveness. Thus, where a student had overstayed once but had been given an extension, and had then overstayed a second time, the first overstay could be used to ground a refusal.[3] However, in all cases, the decision must be personal to the applicant and it would still be wrong to refuse a variation solely to deter others from overstaying or breaching their conditions.[4] Conditions attached to stay do not equate with requirements of the rules,[5] and failure to attend classes is not a breach of conditions of leave to remain as a student, although further leave may be refused, or leave curtailed, on the ground that the person no longer satisfies the requirements of the student rules.[6] The Modern Guidance gives prescriptive and inflexible instructions to its case workers, stating that when evidence shows that one or more of the conditions has been broken, case workers must refuse further leave to remain under paragraph 322(3). They state: 'When you consider whether an applicant can have further leave, you may take into account their previous immigration history. When your checks show that an applicant has broken the conditions of their stay, you should refuse further leave to remain under paragraph 322(3)'.[7] This is tick box stuff. There is a whole range of breaches from minor infractions and those committed in ignorance to serious breaches in deliberate disregard for the conditions. But to case workers a breach is a breach – so no extension of leave, no regard to grey areas, no proper discretion and no regard to fairness. Ridiculous.

[1]   HC 395, para 322(3).
[2]   IDI, Ch 9,s 4. Although this section of Ch 9 has been deleted, s 2 deals with a refusal because of past reliance on public funds, and directs caseworkers (i) in all refusals to make sure that they can substantiate any assertion of fact, and are able to show reasonable grounds for not being satisfied on matters of opinion, such as the person's intentions [s 2.2]; and (ii) Once you have obtained sufficient information to make a decision, it is then necessary to . . . consider the exercise of discretion where appropriate [2.3].
[3]   *Secretary of State for the Home Department v Sidique* [1976] Imm AR 69.
[4]   *Lee v Secretary of State for the Home Department* [1975] Imm AR 75.
[5]   For conditions attached to leave see Immigration Act 1971, s 3(3), 3.8 above; for requirements of the rules see the relevant immigration rule.
[6]   *R (on the application of Zhou) v Secretary of State for the Home Department* [2003] EWCA Civ 51, [2003] INLR 211.

   Modern Guidance – *General grounds for refusal, Failure to comply with conditions of stay: leave to remain* p 27.

RECOURSE TO PUBLIC FUNDS: FURTHER LEAVE

3.168 If leave was subject to a condition of no recourse to public funds (which would be stamped in the passport), the previous paragraph could be used to refuse further leave. If no such formal condition was imposed, this paragraph could be relied on to refuse applicants who have failed to maintain and accommodate themselves and any dependants without recourse to public funds.[1] 'Public funds' covers housing under Part VI or VII of the Housing Act 1996 and Part II of the Housing Act 1985 and the equivalent enactments in Scotland and Northern Ireland, attendance allowance, severe disablement allowance, carers' allowance and disability living allowance under Part III, income support, council tax benefit and housing benefit under Part VII, social fund payments under Part VIII and child benefit under Part IX of the Social Security Contributions and Benefits Act 1992, income-based jobseeker's allowance under the Jobseekers Act 1995, state pension credit under the State Pension Credits Act 2002, child tax credit and working tax credit under Part I of the Tax Credits Act 2002, some kinds of Universal Credit, council tax reduction under a council tax reduction scheme and the equivalent benefits in Northern Ireland.[2] The definition is often amended and should be checked in the current version of the Immigration Rules. An applicant is not treated as having recourse to public funds by relying on funds provided to the sponsor in his or her own right, provided that the applicant's presence in the UK has not resulted in increased entitlement for the sponsor,[3] or if he or she is not excluded from specified benefits under section 115 of the Immigration and Asylum Act 1999 by regulations under that section or under section 42 of the Tax Credits Act 2002.[4] Refusal (or curtailment) on this ground might be appropriate if the person is claiming public funds because they are unable to meet the maintenance and accommodation requirements of the relevant rule but not where they would be able to meet the requirements of the rules without the public fund claimed, nor where they received the funds in good faith or through administrative error and not where they are repaying funds paid in error. A failure to declare claiming public funds may amount to a failure to disclose a material fact (assuming that the person was not allowed to claim the particular fund) and claiming in breach of a condition of stay may also lead to refusal.[5] As against this view the Modern Guidance as we have pointed out in the previous paragraph instructs its case workers to take no prisoners on a breach of conditions of leave.

[1]   HC 395, para 322(4).
[2]   HC 395, para 6 as most recently amended by HC 1098 with effect from 1 April 2013.
[3]   HC 395, para 6A, inserted by Cm 4851.
[4]   HC 395, para 6B, inserted by HC 346 above.
[5]   UK Visas Guidance 'Public Funds' p45-46, V12.0 valid from 21 February 2014.

BREACH OF UNDERTAKINGS: FURTHER LEAVE

3.169 An application for variation of leave may be refused:

(a)   if a sponsor refuses to give a written undertaking to be responsible for the maintenance and accommodation in the UK of the applicant and

(b)   if the person concerned has failed to honour any declaration or undertaking given orally or in writing as to the intended duration and/or purpose of that person's stay.[1]

The situation arises most often when a family visitor decides to apply for leave to remain in the UK with the sponsoring family member, having said on arrival or at entry clearance interview that he or she would return home at the end of the visit. A 'declaration' must, we suggest, be something more definite than a mere statement of intention, but exactly what will amount to a 'declaration' or how cogent the evidence must be to prove a 'declaration' is still unclear. So far as 'undertakings' are concerned, Tribunal authorities under earlier rules held that the only undertakings which count are those which amount to false representations. In other words, a genuine change of circumstances since the 'undertaking' will not prevent an extension of leave.[2] This appears to be the way the rule is interpreted by the Home Office in the, guidance, which states that where there is good reason for the applicant's change of mind, such as unforeseen circumstances, leave may be granted; only where there does not appear to be a good reason, and particularly where there is reason to doubt the applicant's future intentions, should leave be refused.[3]

[1]   HC 395, para 322 (5) and (7).
[2]   *Ridha (3060)*, unreported; *Perera (3063)*, unreported.
[3]   Modernised Guidance – General grounds for refusal Section 4 – version 16.0 Ext 30 April 2014, p 49.

MEDICAL GROUNDS FOR REFUSAL

3.170 We have already dealt with the requirements to submit to medical examination at **3.87** above. Entry clearance officers abroad have a discretion to refer intending travellers for medical examination and a power to require a medical report, and leave to enter may be refused if examination is declined or such a report is not produced.[1] Where the medical inspector at the port advises that for medical reasons it is undesirable to admit someone, the immigration officer must refuse leave to enter unless the person is settled here or there are 'strong compassionate reasons justifying admission.'[2] According to the Modernised Guidance, the medical inspector would normally certify that it is undesirable to admit a passenger who is found or suspected to be suffering from pulmonary tuberculosis, venereal disease, leprosy or trachoma, or if the passenger is heavily infested with lice, is bodily dirty or is suffering from scabies.[3] The IDI indicate that medical inspectors may also issue a certificate if the nature of the person's condition would interfere with his or her ability to comply with the no recourse to public funds requirements.[4] The IDI formerly contained various prescriptions as to which conditions should normally cause a person to be certified as undesirable. The modernised guidance is less prescriptive, stating that the Medical Referee should normally refuse in cases of pulmonary tuberculosis, mental disorder or conduct disorder (drug or alcohol addiction, serious sexual aberration) if such as to affect the health of others, ability to maintain self and dependants or need for major medical treatment[5]. The medical officer may also draw to the ECO's attention 'any condition which might require treatment when the applicant is admitted to the

UK'. This is the only action which the MO can take in respect of returning residents, but for others the MO can recommend refusal, defer making a recommendation or draw the ECO's attention to the circumstances of the case.[6] passenger who is diagnosed as suffering from AIDS or HIV infection, or any other serious illness, should not be refused on public health grounds alone unless it specifically appears that public health may be at risk. The guidance requires consideration of whether the person can maintain self and any dependants adequately in light of the illness and whether they appear likely to need medical treatment while in the UK for which they could not afford to pay privately.[7] Since NHS treatment does not count as 'public funds', leave could not be refused to a passenger who otherwise qualifies on the ground that he or she is likely to seek such treatment, and the immigration officer would therefore have to justify refusal of leave or entry clearance to an AIDS or HIV sufferer on other grounds, but leave could be refused for a visit on the basis that the person was intending to travel in order to seek free medical treatment, since they would not be genuinely seeking leave as a visitor[8]. Clearly any refusal on medical grounds would need to comply with anti-discrimination legislation.

[1]   Immigration (Leave to Enter and Remain) Order 2000, SI 2000/1161, art 7(3) and (4); HC 395, paras 39 and 320(17).
[2]   HC 395, para 320(7).
[3]   Modernised Guidance: General grounds for refusal, Version 16.0, section 1, p111–112.
[4]   Modernised Guidance: General grounds for refusal, Version 16.0, section 1, p111–112.
[5]   Medical Issues (entry clearance guidance) Paragraph MED6.
[6]   Medical Issues (entry clearance guidance) Paragraph MED7.
[7]   Medical Issues (entry clearance guidance) Paragraph MED12.
[8]   Medical Issues (entry clearance guidance) Paragraph MED12. For eligibility for NHS treatment, see CHAPTER 14 below.

3.171 The Rule appears to give medical inspectors enormous powers, as refusal is based (a) on the medical inspector's diagnosis and (b) on his or her views on the desirability of admission, and the wording of the Rule is that immigration officers can only overrule the medical inspector if 'strong compassionate grounds' warrant admission. The Tribunal in *Al-Tuwaidji v Chief Immigration Officer, Heathrow* took the view that refusal was mandatory even if independent medical evidence puts into question the diagnosis or advice of the medical inspector. It held that a medical inspector's diagnosis of schizophrenia could not be challenged on appeal, and that in the absence of compassionate circumstances leave should be refused.[1] We suggest that this decision cannot stand today, since it embodies fundamental unfairness,[2] as well as involving unlawful delegation of power from immigration officers to medical inspectors which is not warranted by the terms of the Immigration Act 1971. A better view of HC 395, paragraph 320(7), and one which accords better with the other relevant rule, para 37, would be to treat the medical advice as a factor to be taken into account by immigration officers in the exercise of their own discretion, enabling them to take into account alternative medical diagnosis and opinions as well as the advice of the medical inspector.[3] The Tribunal has in the past mitigated the effect of the mandatory refusal by a liberal interpretation of strong compassionate circumstances warranting admission.[4] The fact that a patient has undergone a cure would itself be a compassionate circumstance.[5]

1   [1974] Imm AR 34. Followed in *Mohazeb v Immigration Officer, Harwich* [1990] Imm AR
    555.
2   See CHAPTER **8** below.
3   See *Pearson v Immigration Appeal Tribunal* [1978] Imm AR 212, CA; *R v Secretary of State
    for the Home Department, ex p Ounejma* [1989] Imm AR 75, QBD where a similar argument
    as regards mandatory entry clearance was rejected. See further *R v Secretary of State for the
    Home Department, ex p Rofathullah* [1989] QB 219, [1988] Imm AR 514, CA. This is also
    the view of the Home Office: see Modernised Guidance: General Reasons for Refusing, Section
    2 (see **3.132** fn 1 above) and Issues (entry clearance guidance) Paragraph MED4 and 7.
4   See *Entry Clearance Officer, Bombay v Sacha* [1973] Imm AR 5.
5   See *Parvez v Immigration Officer, London (Heathrow) Airport* [1979–80] Imm AR 84, and
    Immigration Officer, London (Heathrow) Airport v Bhatti [1979–80] Imm AR 86n.

EXCLUSION FOR THE PUBLIC GOOD

3.172 The Immigration Rules provide for refusal of leave to enter or of entry
clearance, or cancellation of advance leave on arrival, on 'conducive to the
public good' grounds in two distinct situations. Refusal is mandatory where
the Secretary of State for the Home Department personally has so directed.[1]
But even where there is no such direction, leave should normally be refused,[2]
or is to be cancelled,[3] where the immigration officer has information which
makes it seem right to refuse leave to enter, for example, in the light of the
passenger's character, conduct or associations. Refusal on 'conducive grounds'
may thus result from a prior ban imposed by the Secretary of State or from an
on-the-spot decision by an immigration officer. An example of a prior blanket
ban was that imposed on Scientologists in 1968 on the grounds that
Scientology was 'socially harmful' and a 'serious danger to . . . health'.[4]
This ban was only lifted in 1980.[5] The Secretary of State has imposed bans on
notorious racists such as Ku Klux Klan imperial wizard Bill Wilkinson,[6] and on
US Nation of Islam leader Louis Farrakhan.[7] An example of an on-the-spot
refusal is the case where a man is given leave to enter by the immigration
officer and passes through to Customs, where drugs are discovered in his
baggage and he is refused leave on 'conducive' grounds.[8] The Modernised
Guidance suggests other reasons for a refusal on conducive grounds would
include extreme views which might lead to civil unrest or offences by others,
evidence (short of a charge or conviction) of involvement in war crimes, a
threat to national security or a concern that admitting the person could
unfavourably affect foreign policy.

1   HC 395, paras 320(6) and 321A(4).
2   HC 395, para 320(19).
3   HC 395, para 321A(5).
4   769 HC Official Report (5th series) written answers col 189.
5   988 HC Official Report (5th series) written answers col 578. See further Case No 41/74: *Van
    Duyn v Home Office* [1975] Ch 358, [1974] ECR 1337, ECJ.
6   (1978) *Guardian*, 17 February.
7   This ban was upheld by the Court of Appeal in *R (on the application of Farrakhan) v Secretary
    of State for the Home Department* [2002] EWCA Civ 606, [2002] QB 1391, [2002] 3 WLR
    481, [2002] 4 All ER 289, [2002] Imm AR 447, [2002] INLR 257 reversing the judgment of
    Turner J in the Administrative Court ([2001] EWHC Admin 781).
8   *Villone v Secretary of State for the Home Department* [1979–80] Imm AR 23. The IDI (Jun 04,
    Ch 9, s 2, para 21.2–4) used to consider whether refusal would be justified in this situation,
    which would depend on whether the quantity and questioning indicate commercial or personal
    use. The Modernised Guidance contains no such consideration. Other examples might be
    where someone has no criminal record but is suspected to be involved in organised crime (for

someone refused entry on these grounds and because of their criminal record see *R v Immigration Appeal Tribunal, ex p Palacio* [1979–80] Imm AR 178).

3.173 In determining whether a person should be refused admission on 'public good' grounds, the discretion is wide, but the reasons are not to be trivial or light.[1] This, however, has not prevented refusals for possession of trivial amounts of cannabis,[2] or preventing the entry of someone who has been tried and acquitted of a charge of illegal importation of drugs, just because the immigration officer took a different view from the jury.[3] Nor has it prevented the Tribunal suggesting that there is a general rule that it is conducive to the public good to refuse admission to anyone attempting to import opium.[4] The upshot is that in drug smuggling cases, the offender or suspect is unlikely to obtain admission and the Immigration Rules will be administered without regard to any of the principles governing deportation recommendations by a criminal court or decisions to deport by the Home Office. In deception cases, however, there is likely to be a greater cross-reference to the deportation decisions, particularly since the House of Lords held in *R v Immigration Appeal Tribunal, ex p Patel*[5] that past dishonest deception was covered by the power to deem deportation conducive to the public good.[6] Refusal of entry on conducive grounds based on serious deception, past or present, is unlikely to be struck down as unreasonable on a judicial review challenge.[7]

[1] *Scheele v Immigration Officer, Harwich* [1976] Imm AR 1.
[2] *Villone* fn 8, above.
[3] *Nkiti v Immigration Officer, Gatwick* [1989] Imm AR 585, CA. Now, however, the immigration officer must be satisfied 'beyond reasonable doubt' before refusing on the basis that a passenger is a trafficker in pornography, although seizure of material by Customs would constitute prima facie grounds for refusal.
[4] *Khazrai v Immigration Officer, London (Heathrow) Airport* [1981] Imm AR 9.
[5] [1988] AC 910, [1988], 2 All ER 378.
[6] Immigration Act 1971, s 3(5)(a). Knowing use of a forged document may ground refusal under this head as well as under para 320(3): IDI, Ch 9, s 2, para 21.5.
[7] See *R v Secretary of State for the Home Department, ex p Kwapong* [1993] Imm AR 569 (Nigerian with indefinite residence facilitates an illegal entry by bringing with him a child travelling on a false passport); *R v Secretary of State for the Home Department, ex p Sanyaolu* [1993] Imm AR 505 (applicant had obtained his previous leave by saying he was supported by an uncle, when in fact he was working in breach of conditions).

3.174 Before the Tribunal the test is not so stringent. It is dealing with an appeal on the merits and can assess the exercise of discretion by the immigration officer. This means that Tribunal decisions can often throw greater light on the proper exercise by immigration officers of their discretion. In Olufosoye[1] the Tribunal gave guidance on public good refusals, where the holder of a multiple entry visit visa had worked in breach of her leave conditions on a first visit, and was refused entry when she returned to the UK. First, the Tribunal held that where the immigration authorities contended that exclusion was conducive to the public good, whether on a decision to deport or a refusal of leave to enter, it was for them to satisfy the appellate authority that the decision was justified. In so far as the justification consists of deception or other criminal conduct, the standard of proof will be at the higher end of the spectrum of balance of probability. Secondly, in the light of the provisions of HC 395, paragraph 320(11) and (12), it was necessary to prove grounds other than those set out in those paragraphs to justify exclusion as conducive to the public good. The general reasons for refusing the grant of an entry clearance, such as breach of the time limit or conditions of a previous leave, are a different set of criteria from exclusion on conducive grounds, and paragraph 320(19) should not be used as a back door so as to import into paragraph 321 extra grounds for refusing leave to the holder of an entry clearance. Thirdly, the fact that particular conduct would not provide the basis for a decision to deport on conducive grounds was relevant in considering whether the same conduct should lead to a refusal of leave to enter on 'conducive grounds'.[2] Where a decision on conducive grounds is based on conduct which has been the subject of previous investigation or adjudication, the immigration officer should not normally depart from the results of that inquiry.[3]

1   *Olufosoye v Immigration Officer, Heathrow* [1992] Imm AR 141.
2   In *Entry Clearance Officer, Amsterdam* [2002] UKIAT 05532 the IAT did not consider that a history of threats and aggressive behaviour coupled with deception, rendered exclusion conducive to the public good.
3   See *Ali v Secretary of State for the Home Department* [1984] 1 All ER 1009, [1984] 1 WLR 663, CA; see also (in another context) *R v Secretary of State for the Home Department, ex p Danaie* [1998] Imm AR 84.

3.175 Refusal on conducive grounds will normally be made in the light of the passenger's character, conduct or associations, but it need not be confined to reasons of this kind. This was made clear by the Divisional Court in Ajaib Singh.[1] There a man had obtained an entry certificate to come to the UK for marriage. At the time, however, his bride-to-be was only 14½ years old. This had been overlooked by the entry clearance officer, although fully disclosed, but was spotted by the immigration officer on his arrival and leave to enter was refused. If the reason had been merely to correct an executive or administrative error by the entry clearance officer, the Divisional Court suggested that refusal would be wrong. But more was involved. The discretion to refuse on public good grounds was deliberately left in wide terms so that an immigration officer could exercise a wide discretion. The public good rule has thus been invoked to exclude a man who obtained his prior residence status by a marriage of convenience.[2]

1   *R v Immigration Appeal Tribunal, ex p Ajaib Singh* [1978] Imm AR 59. This situation is now covered by HC 395, para 277.
2   *Osama v Immigration Officer, London (Gatwick) Airport* [1978] Imm AR 8. See also *R v Immigration Appeal Tribunal, ex p Cheema* [1982] Imm AR 124, CA.

REFUSAL OF LEAVE TO REMAIN: CHARACTER, CONDUCT OR ASSOCIATIONS
AND REFUSAL OF FURTHER LEAVE OR CURTAILMENT

3.176 Refusal of variation or further leave, or curtailment of existing leave, may occur if it is deemed undesirable to permit the applicant to remain in the UK in the light of his or her character, conduct or associations.[1] We have already dealt with the situation where indefinite leave to remain is to be refused if a person has previous convictions at **3.153** above. Refusal of leave to remain is discretionary under paragraph 322(5). The discretion may be exercised where there are no convictions but there is other reliable evidence to call into question the person's character, conduct or associations, including attempting to enter into a sham marriage for immigration reasons.[2]

1   HC 395, para 322(5).

² Modernised Guidance: General Grounds for Refusal: leave to remain, section 4, Version 16.0, valid from 30 April 2014 at page 30.

F.   EC joint list of persons to be refused entry

3.177 The Schengen Information System, set up under the Schengen Agreements of 1985 and 1990, is a system for the exchange of information concerning persons who for one reason or another – commission of criminal offences, immigration irregularities, football hooliganism, suspected involvement with banned organisations – are considered undesirable for entry into Member States. The UK has opted out of the Schengen acquis which now forms part of the 'framework' of the EU,[1] but it takes part in Schengen co-operation under the terms of the Treaty of Amsterdam, which introduced the provisions of Schengen acquis into the European Union. Schengen acquis allows the United Kingdom and Ireland to take part in the Schengen convention arrangements and they use the Schengen Information System for law enforcement purposes.

It is probable that persons whose names come up on the computer from other Member States are in fact refused on conducive grounds by an operational practice of co-operation which is not fully transparent.

[1] Protocol 19 in TFEU (formerly Protocol 2 to the Consolidated EC Treaty) incorporates the Schengen acquis into the framework of the EU, but acknowledges at art 4 that the UK and Ireland, who are not parties to the Agreements, may at any time request to take part in some or all although they should be allowed to opt in to the provisions of the Schengen acquis.

EXCLUDED PERSONS UNDER INTERNATIONAL OBLIGATIONS

3.178 Section 8B of the Immigration Act 1971 (inserted by section 8 of the Immigration and Asylum Act 1999) provides for mandatory refusal or cancellation of leave to enter of 'excluded persons', defined as persons named or described by UN Resolution or EU Council instrument in designated Orders under the 1971 Act.[1] Such persons are also to be stripped of diplomatic exemption.[2] The Immigration (Designation of Travel Bans) Order 2000[3] provides that persons named by, or under, or described by a designated instrument (as set out in the Schedule) need not be excluded from the UK if admitting them would not be contrary to the obligations in the designated instruments listed in Article 2 of the Order; or if their exclusion breached the UK's obligations under the ECHR or the Geneva Convention. The designated list is contained in Schedule 1 to the Order.[4] Clearly, these provisions are designed to exclude war criminals and persons of that ilk, rather than football hooligans. However, they may well be used to exclude members and supporters of organisations perceived as terrorist under the very wide new definitions on the domestic and European plane, and the designation orders should therefore be monitored with care.

[1] Immigration Act 1971, as amended, s 8B(4).
[2] Immigration Act 1971, s 8B(3).
[3] SI 2000/2724, in force 10 October 2000, as amended.
[4] The schedule in the original Order of 2000 and its amendments have now been replaced by the Schedule to the Immigration (Designation of Travel Bans) (Amendment) Order 2014, SI 2014/1849. This Order amends the Immigration (Designation of Travel Bans) Order 2000 ('the 2000 Order') by substituting the Schedule 1 to this Order for the Schedule to the 2000

Order. Any person named by or under an instrument listed in the new Schedule or falling within a description in such an instrument will be excluded from the United Kingdom (subject to the exceptions specified in article 3 of the 2000 Order). Article 3 of this Order revokes the 2009 Order. The orders are amended frequently: twice in 2013, three times in 2012 and seven in 2011, reflecting UN and EU resolutions.

CHANGE OF CIRCUMSTANCES SINCE ISSUE

3.179 The entry clearance officer or immigration officer may revoke entry clearance[1] or refuse leave to enter, or cancel it if the entry clearance operated as leave to enter, if a change of circumstances since the issue of entry clearance has removed the basis of the holder's claim to admission.[2] This does not include children, including children adopted under recognised adoption procedures, coming to join parents settled in the UK who become over-age between the issue of entry clearance and travelling to the UK.[3] The change of circumstances must be sufficient to remove the basis of the holder's claim to admission, so only decisive changes will suffice, such as marriage by a child seeking entry as a dependant of his or her parents.[4] Other changes may often be a matter of degree and will depend on the facts.[5] Marriage by a dependent child is perhaps the most frequent decisive change, but there has to be a valid marriage and the burden of proving that is on the immigration officer. The fact that a particular entry is sought for a purpose which is not covered by the existing visa does not of itself mean that cancellation of the visa is justified. Collins J found that the revocation of the visa can only properly be put into effect if the material persuades the Immigration Officer that there is now a permanent desire, or permanent intention, not to use the visit visa for proper visits. There is nothing in rule 321A which permits cancellation purely on the basis that there has been a breach of a condition on a previous visit, so that the overstaying again by itself would not justify cancellation of the visa.[6]

Where a decision on entry has been delayed and the entrant has been on temporary admission, the change of circumstances may arise after arrival in the UK. Thus, where an Iranian was a genuine visitor on arrival but decided to remain as a businessman prior to the decision to grant or refuse entry, this was a change of circumstances.[7] Decisions on this provision are sometimes very harsh, as in cases where the sponsor or the accompanying parent dies between the date of issue of the entry clearance and arrival in the UK.[8]

[1]   HC 395, para 30A(ii).
[2]   Immigration Act 1971, Sch 2, para 2A(2)(a) and HC 395, paras 321(ii) and 321A(1).
[3]   HC 395, paras 321(ii) and 310. Paragraph 321 does not apply to children joining parents who are not settled or in a category leading to settlement.
[4]   The burden of proof is on the immigration officer. See *R v Immigration Appeal Tribunal, ex p Begum (Suily)* [1990] Imm AR 226, QBD.
[5]   *Immigration Officer, Heathrow v Salmak* [1991] Imm AR 191, IAT; *Olufosoye v Immigration Officer, Heathrow* [1992] Imm AR 141, IAT. Cancellation of leave to a student who had ceased to attend classes and was working 39 hours a week was upheld by the Tribunal in *B (Nigeria) v CIO Heathrow* [2004] UKIAT 55. The 'non-exhaustive list' in the Entry Clearance Guidance mentions the withdrawal of an offer of employment, the withdrawal of sponsorship, the permanent departure of the sponsor from the UK: Revocation of an Entry Clearance ECB18 at section 18.2.
[6]   *R (on the application of Boahen) v Secretary of State for the Home Department* [2010] EWCA Civ 585, [2010] All ER (D) 14 (Jun).
[7]   Teflisi (3522) unreported.

8   See *Arshad v Immigration Officer, London (Heathrow) Airport* [1977] Imm AR 19; *R v Secretary of State for the Home Department, ex p Begum (Angur)* [1989] Imm AR 302, QBD.

3.180 The current Immigration Rules provide that they do not generally apply to EEA nationals.[1] Curtailment or refusal to renew residence permits or other leave granted to EEA nationals who benefit from the free movement provisions must all be justifiable by reference to EC law and, in particular, to the public policy provisions (see CHAPTER 6 below).

1   HC 395, para 5.

FAILURE TO PAY NHS CHARGES

3.181 With effect from 31 October 2011, HC 1511 further amends the General Grounds for Refusal, by inserting new discretionary grounds for refusal of entry clearance under para 320(22), or refusal of leave to remain, variation of leave to enter or remain or curtailment of leave under para 322(12) on the grounds that one or more relevant NHS bodies has notified the Secretary of State that the person seeking entry, leave to enter, leave to remain or a variation of leave to enter or remain, as the case may be, has failed to pay a charge or charges with a total value of at least £1000 in accordance with the relevant NHS regulations on charges to overseas visitors.[1] The unpaid debts must have been incurred on or after 1 November 2011.[2] Consideration must in all cases be given to whether there are exceptional circumstances or, in the case of leave to remain, an Article 3 claim.[3] Where the debts relate to the main applicant, dependants should also be refused on the same ground. Where the debt relates to a dependant, only the dependant and not the main applicant should be refused, but where the charges relate to a child, the parents are the debtors and so would fall for refusal.[4] Where debts have been paid the paragraph does not apply. Use of the NHS does not mean there are charges, since it is a matter for the treating trust to decide whether to charge.[5]

1   These Regulations are the National Health Service (Charges to Overseas Visitors) Regulations 2011, SI 2011/1556, in force from 1 August 2011, revoking and replacing the equivalent set of regulations from 1989 (SI 1989/306). See further **8.29**, below. Regulation 10 provides that no charge may be made or recovered in respect of any relevant services provided to an overseas visitor where those services are provided in circumstances covered by a reciprocal agreement with a country or territory specified in Schedule 2. The countries set out in that Schedule are Anguilla, Armenia, Australia, Azerbaijan, Barbados, Belarus, Bosnia, British Virgin Islands, Croatia, Falkland Islands, Georgia, Gibraltar, Isle of Man, Israel, Jersey, Kazakhstan, Kyrgyzstan, Macedonia, Moldova, Montenegro, Montserrat, New Zealand, Russia, Serbia, St Helena, Tajikistan, Turkmenistan, Turks and Caicos Islands, Ukraine, and Uzbekistan. For entry to the UK for the purpose of seeking MHS treatment: see **8.29**.
2   Paragraphs 320 (21) and 322(12).
3   Modernised Guidance: General Grounds for refusal V16.0, section 4 (leave to remain) p55-56 and section 2 (entry clearance) p57.
4   Modernised Guidance. Section 4 p55 and Section 2 p57.
5   Modernised Guidance Section 4 p54.

Part VI CONTROL OF DEPARTURE AND MISCELLANEOUS POWERS

Rights of appeal and administrative review of EC refusals

3.182 Right of appeal or what is left of them is dealt with in CHAPTER 19 below. A refusal of entry clearance does, however, give rise to a right to apply for Administrative Review in a number of cases. It is not a very satisfactory remedy, however, since it is based upon the evidence which was before the original decision maker and it lacks the elementary procedures of an appeal. For most people refused entry clearance it is all that they have got, before having to initiate judicial review proceedings in the UK. The Review is currently free of charge. It is carried out by an Entry Clearance Manager (ECM), who has had no part in making the original decision. For example, any refused applicant for entry clearance under PBS may apply for Administrative Review if they believe that the decision made by the ECO was factually incorrect. The reviewer will be able to amend decisions subject to certain limitations.[1] These limitations make the administrative review a pretty tooth-less remedy. The ECM will overturn the original decision if the review finds that:

- the ECO failed to properly consider evidence submitted with the original application;
- the ECO failed to apply the Immigration Rules correctly;
- the ECO made a mistake as to a material fact that could have been established by evidence submitted at the time of the application;
- the ECO failed to give adequate reasons for refusing entry clearance. This will be remedied by a fresh decision giving adequate reasons, although it may still be a refusal.

But will not overturn a decision simply because:

- the ECO reviewed the evidence and exercised his or her discretion in a particular way in accordance with the Immigration Rules and the complaint is that the discretion should have been exercised differently;
- the applicant claims there is a fault with our underlying processes or policies.

In summary the Review is based purely on the evidence submitted with the original application. Essentially the only basis of review is that the Entry Clearance Officer made a factual error or wrongly applied the Immigration Rules when refusing the application. Very often a factual error can only be successfully established by the production of new evidence. But under this scheme no new evidence is allowed and if any is included with the review request it has to be disregarded and the applicant will be advised to make and pay the full fees of a fresh application if they wish that further information to be considered. In other words the sole remedy available is for a very limited range of error on the face of the record.

[1]   Where the complaint refers to matters that are not within the scope of Administrative Review, it will, if appropriate, be dealt with under the normal complaints procedure. If this happens, the person receiving the request will take the appropriate action and advise the applicant accordingly.

Hotel registers

3.183 The Immigration Act 1971 contains power to make regulations requiring hotels and guest houses to keep records of persons staying there,[1] and under the Immigration (Hotel Records) Order 1972, hotels and other premises where lodging or sleeping accommodation is provided for reward must normally keep registers.[2] All visitors over the age of 16 who stay there must on arrival inform the keeper of the premises of their full name and nationality. That applies to everyone. Aliens (non-Commonwealth citizens) must also give passport details and inform the hotel of their next address.[3] The keeper of the premises must record this information and keep it available for inspection for at least 12 months.[4] It is not clear how effective or how necessary is the maintenance of hotel registers.

[1] Immigration Act 1971, s 4(4).
[2] SI 1972/1689.
[3] SI 1972/1689, art 3.
[4] SI 1972/1689, art 5.

3.184 UK immigration law does not expressly recognise a right of departure by British citizens from the UK, though one might be tempted to think that it does, because of the grandiloquent opening to the Immigration Act 1971:[1]

> 'all those who are in this Act expressed to have the right of abode in the United Kingdom shall be free to live in, and to come and go into and from the United Kingdom without let or hindrance . . .'

This, however, is subject to two limitations affecting the right to depart. First, the right to go without let or hindrance is subject to such limits as may be 'lawfully imposed' on any person.[2] Secondly, the right to depart depends upon the person being able to acquire a passport.[3] Although the position in UK law is somewhat obscure, under EC law there is a clearly defined right to depart.[4] British citizens wishing to exercise their right to depart for a Community purpose can invoke these provisions of EC law if they are refused a passport or other travel document valid in the territories of other EC countries. For a full discussion, see **2.112–2.115** above.

[1] Immigration Act 1971, s 1(1).
[2] Immigration Act 1971, s 1(1). See **2.9–2.10** above.
[3] The refusal of a passport is now subject to judicial review: *R v Secretary of State for Foreign and Commonwealth Affairs, ex p Everett* [1989] QB 811, [1989] Imm AR 155, CA. See **2.109** above.
[4] See CHAPTER 6 below.

Right to depart – immigration officers' powers

3.185 There have been big changes in the power of immigration officers to examine non-British departing passengers. Previously this could only be done, whether the passenger was British or not, to establish nationality and identity. Now section 42 of IAN 2006 has amended paragraphs 3 and 16 of Schedule 2 to the Immigration Act 1971 to cover three additional kinds of information:

- whether the passenger's entry to the UK was lawful;

- whether the passenger has complied with any conditions of his or her leave in the UK;
- whether the passenger's return to the UK is prohibited or restricted.[1]

If a cursory investigation into these matters is not enough, the immigration officer can require the passenger to submit to further examination by giving him or her written notice, and can detain him or her for a maximum of 12 hours pending the completion of that further examination.[2] Section 42(4) states that paragraph 21 of Schedule 2 to the 1971 Act, which makes provision for temporary admission, does not apply to the detention of departing passengers. This has presumably been done on the basis that a maximum of 12 hours detention does not make temporary admission necessary. These powers must be so exercised as not to infringe EEA national right to free movement under community law.

[1] IAN 2006, s 42(2).
[2] IAN 2006, s 42(3).

Emergency and safety powers

3.186 Under section 3(7) of the Immigration Act 1971 power is given to make provision for prohibiting nationals or citizens of a particular country from leaving the UK, or from doing so other than at a port of exit or for imposing conditions or restrictions on them when they wish to leave. Such an order can only be made where it appears to Her Majesty proper to do so by reason of restrictions or conditions imposed on British citizens when they want to leave a particular country or territory. Provision may also be made by Order in Council to prohibit all those who do not have the right of abode in the UK from leaving on a ship or aircraft specified or indicated in the prohibition in the interests of safety.[1] Where such an order is in force, an immigration officer has additional powers of examining persons who are leaving or seeking to leave the UK to determine:

(a)   whether any of the provisions of the order apply to them; and
(b)   whether, if so, any power conferred by the order should be exercised in relation to them and in what way.[2]

No such order has been made or is in force since the Immigration Act 1971 came into force.

[1] Immigration Act 1971, s 3(7).
[2] Immigration Act 1971, Sch 2, para 3(2).

Chapter 4

SETTLEMENT AND RETURN

SETTLEMENT

Definition

4.1 The Immigration Act 1971 makes clear at the very outset the qualitative difference between the right of abode, and leave to enter or remain in the territory.[1] Section 1(4) of the Immigration Act 1971 sets out the conditions and restrictions regulating those with only a right to enter or remain as compared to the right of abode, further elaborated upon at section 3 (1) and (3). A person with the right of abode does not need to qualify for admission to the UK under the Immigration Act 1971 or the Immigration Rules. The right to permanent residence, or settled status, does not confer freedom from immigration control. Being 'settled' means being ordinarily resident without being subject under the immigration laws to any restriction on the period of stay.[2] Ordinary residence and being free from restrictions on the length of permitted stay under the Immigration Rules are the two key elements. The word 'settled', therefore, covers persons with a right of abode and those with indefinite leave to enter or remain, provided each is ordinarily resident in the UK. The phrase 'settled in the United Kingdom' is defined by the Immigration Rules to mean that the person concerned is (a) free from any restriction on the period of stay (excluding those exempt from control under section 8), and (b) ordinarily resident in the UK without (c) having entered or remained in breach of immigration laws or, having entered or remained unlawfully, has subsequently entered lawfully or has been granted leave to remain and is so resident.[3]

¹   Immigration Act 1971, ss 1(1)-(2).
²   Immigration Act 1971, s 33(2A), as amended by British Nationality Act 1981, s 39(6) and Sch 4, para 7. See also British Nationality Act 1981, s 50(2)–(4), where a more comprehensive definition (necessary for the purpose of nationality law) is given: see below. For EEA nationals, see **4.15**, below.
³   HC 395, para 6.

4.2 A similar definition of settlement applies for the purposes of the British Nationality Act 1981, except that for nationality purposes residents in the Channel Islands or Isle of Man, as well as in the UK, are included.[1] Persons who are subject to exemptions from immigration control, such as diplomats, consuls, members of visiting forces and so forth, are not normally regarded as 'settled' during any period when they are entitled to exemption.[2] Limited exceptions apply to enable the children of an 'exempted' parent to obtain British citizenship by birth in the UK under section 1 of the British Nationality Act 1981.[3]

¹   British Nationality Act 1981, s 50(1), (2).
²   In those cases where the Act says that 'the provisions of this Act . . . shall not apply', this would mean that the definition of 'settled' in s 33(2A) would also not apply. Whether this is the reason for the accepted view that settled status cannot be achieved during a period of exemption, unless special provision is made, is not entirely clear. See Immigration Act 1971, s 8(5). See also British Nationality Act 1981, s 50(3).
³   Immigration Act 1971, s 8(5A), as amended; British Nationality Act 1981, s 50(4).

No restriction on the period of stay

4.3 Whether a person is free from immigration restrictions on their length of stay is not normally difficult to determine, in those cases where the person is subject to the permissive system of control used in UK domestic law. Thus, a person with a six-month or 12-month leave has a restriction on their period of stay and cannot be regarded as 'settled'. The Immigration Act 1971 distinguishes between a limited leave and indefinite leave,[1] and normally the person must have been granted one or other of them, there being no half-way house between the grant of leave and entry without leave.[2] Limited leave is subject to a time restriction; indefinite leave is not, as section 33(2A) of the Immigration Act 1971 makes clear. The position is different for those with exemptions from immigration control, whom we deal with at **4.4** below, and EEA nationals and their families, who come to Britain under EEA free movement rights. EEA nationals enter as of right and are not, on entry, subject to the normal permissive system of getting a leave to enter. So it was thought they were not subject to any restrictions on their period of stay. But that has changed. First, the Immigration (European Economic Area) Regulations 2000, provided that freedom from restrictions on length of stay only occurred if indefinite permission was granted or in other specified circumstances.[3] Giving a domestic law status in line with indefinite leave was probably necessary in the light of the then current EC directives and regulations on free movement, which only referred to permanent stay in relatively few cases.[4] Since the coming into force of the Citizens' Directive, which does give a permanent right to reside,[5] and its transposition into domestic law under the Immigration (European Economic Area) Regulations 2006[6] the position has changed. It is now provided that for the purposes of the 1971 Act and the British Nationality Act 1981, a person who has a permanent right of residence under regulation 15 of the 2006 Regulations is to be regarded as a person who is in the UK without being subject under the immigration laws to any restriction on the period for which he may remain.[7] But a qualified person, the family member of a qualified person and a family member who has retained the right of residence shall not, by virtue of that status, be so regarded for those purposes.[8]

[1] Immigration Act 1971, s 3(1).
[2] *Mokuolo v Secretary of State for the Home Department* [1989] Imm AR 51, CA.
[3] Immigration (European Economic Area) Regulations 2000, SI 2000/2326, reg 8.
[4] For example, see Directive 73/148, art 4(1) (self-employed); Directive 75/34, art 2.1 (retired persons); Directive 75/34, art 3(2) (family members of deceased self-employed person); Regulation 1250/70, art 3(2) (family members of deceased worker).
[5] Directive 2004/38/EC, arts 16–18.
[6] SI 2006/1003.
[7] SI 2006/1003, Sch 2, para 2(1). For these purposes any holder of a residence permit, which shows permission to remain in the UK permanently, or of a residence document, which shows permission to remain in the UK indefinitely, is to be treated as a person with a permanent right of residence under regulation 15 of the 2006 regulations, if that permit was issued under the 2000 regulations, or applied for under them before 30 April 2006: SI 2006/1003, Sch 4, para 2(4).
[8] SI 2006/1003, Sch 2, para 2(2).

4.4 Indefinite leave used to be notified by letter, which is a valuable document to keep.[1] However, The Immigration (Biometric Registration) (Amendment) Regulations 2012, SI 2012/594 regulation 3 now applies to those who make an application for indefinite leave to remain. It is intended to replace a stamp, sticker or other attachment in a passport or other document which indicated that the holder had been granted limited or indefinite leave to enter or remain in the United Kingdom and to replace a letter which indicated that he had been granted limited or indefinite leave to enter or remain in the United Kingdom. See further CHAPTER 3 at 3.57. All the old problems of illegible stamps in passports or the use of a rectangular stamp with a date but no clear words indicating any sort of leave, limited or unlimited, have gone.

[1] Where a passport is returned with a notice of decision, an overstamp in the passport that read with the notice was unambiguous and incapable of creating any uncertainty did not render the communication of the decision faulty: *B v Secretary of State for the Home Department* [2006] EWCA Civ 582.

Ordinary and habitual residence and domicile

4.5 The term 'ordinarily resident' is used in a number of different statutes, including the Immigration Act 1971[1],the British Nationality Acts 1948 and 1981 and the Immigration Act 2014. The term is also used as a criterion of eligibility for educational and other social services provided by central and local government including access to the National Health Service.[2] A trend towards defining ordinary residence in terms of immigration status in the context of education was rejected in *Shah v Barnet London Borough Council*,[3] where the House of Lords held that an overseas student habitually and normally resident in the UK for study, apart from temporary or occasional absences of long or short duration, was 'ordinarily resident' in the natural and ordinary meaning of those words used in the Education Acts and implementing regulations. Lord Scarman, who gave the leading speech, unhesitatingly subscribed to the view that 'ordinarily resident' referred to persons' abode in a particular place or country which they had adopted voluntarily and for settled purposes as part of the regular order of their life for the time being, whether of short or long duration. There has been a distinct shift away from Lord Scarman's view in subsequent years (see **4.7**), notably through the introduction of a requirement in government regulations that eligibility for a student loan requires that a student be 'settled'[4]. In *R (on the application of Tigere) v Secretary of State for Business, Innovation and Skills and Student Loans Company Ltd*[5] the Court of Appeal held that the Secretary of State's bright-line rule requiring an applicant for a student loan to have indefinite leave to remain was justified where it served the need for certainty and the avoidance of arbitrariness. It was found to be significant that the Education Act 1944, s 1(1) (replicated in the Education Act 1996, s 10) imposed on the Minister of Education a duty 'to promote the education of the people of England and Wales'. The Court rejected the proposition that the Secretary of State ought to adopt a policy to favour persons who were liable to obtain indefinite leave who had not obtained it yet. Further, the Court of Appeal rejected the argument that a period of time spent on temporary admission might constitute a period of 'ordinary residence' where temporary admission cannot be equated with a (positive) immigration status. It was instead described as 'merely a holding position until "status" is determined'. Further, the notion that ordinary residence required a permanent or indefinitely enduring purpose derived from a confusion of ordinary residence with domicile. The 'real home' test did not apply to determining ordinary residence.[6]

[1]   Section 33(2A).
[2]   The power to make charges for medical services given to non-residents was first exercised in 1982 and the current exceptions are set out in the National Health Service (Charges to Overseas Visitors) Regulations 2011, SI 2011/1556, as subsequently amended in 2012. For the purposes of those regulations, overseas visitors are defined as persons 'not ordinarily resident in the United Kingdom'. The phrase 'ordinarily resident' is interpreted by the Department of Health as meaning 'for the time being, living lawfully in the UK on a properly settled basis'. See also Immigration Act 2014, s 39 yet to come into force
[3]   [1983] 2 AC 309, [1983] 1 All ER 226
[4]   Education (Mandatory Awards) Regulations 1997, SI 1997/431, reg 13(1)
[5]   [2014] EWCA Civ 1216.
[6]   See *Stransky v Stransky* [1954] P 428, [1954] 2 All ER 536.

4.6 Thus ordinary residence is to be distinguished from the more traditional concept of domicile, which is used in private international law. Ordinary residence may be acquired without any intention permanently to reside in the country, whereas an intention permanently to remain is essential to the acquisition of a new domicile.[1] Thus persons who come to the UK for a visit and remain for reasons beyond their control may be ordinarily resident though they cannot acquire a domicile of choice because of absence of any necessary intention.[2] At common law, persons may be ordinarily resident although they are liable to removal or deportation under the immigration laws,[3] but it is not clear whether they may be ordinarily resident if their residence in the UK is not voluntary because, for example, they are in prison or a psychiatric institution.[4] A person may be ordinarily resident in two places at one time.[5] It is also clear that ordinary residence is not lost through temporary absences abroad,[6] though clearly this is always a matter of degree. In *R v Hussain*[7] an absence abroad for a period of 20 months was held to break the period of ordinary residence for the purposes of exemption from deportation under the Commonwealth Immigrants Act 1962. On the other hand, in *R v Edgehill*[8] a sentence of less than six months' imprisonment imposed by a foreign court did not prevent a defendant from having been 'ordinarily' and 'continuously' resident here for five years so as to exempt him from deportation under the 1962 Act. In *R v Immigration Appeal Tribunal, ex p Siggins*,[9] a nine-month absence in the US was insufficient to break the period of ordinary residence. In each case the test to apply is whether the applicant intends to return to the UK so that the break in residence is a merely temporary one[10]. Where the applicant intends to reside in a new country for the foreseeable future, ordinary residence in the UK will end.[11]

1 See *Hopkins v Hopkins* [1951] P 116 at 121–122 and *Stransky v Stransky* [1954] P 428 at 437. For a fuller discussion of domicile see CHAPTER 2.
2 *Re Mackenzie* [1941] Ch 69, [1940] 4 All ER 310; and cf *Re Bright, ex p Bright* (1903) 51 WR 342, CA; *R v Denman, ex p Staal* (1917) 86 LJKB 1328; *Pittar v Richardson* (1917) 87 LJKB 59.
3 *Boldrini v Boldrini and Martini* [1932] P 9, CA; *May v May and Lehmann* [1943] 2 All ER 146; *Cruh v Cruh* [1945] 2 All ER 545.
4 See *IRC v Lysaght* [1928] AC 234, per Viscount Sumner at 243; contrast *Re Mackenzie* [1941] Ch 69, per Morton J at 77. Lord Scarman in *Shah v Barnet London Borough Council* [1983] 2 AC 309 at 344, doubted whether imprisonment had the necessary voluntary character to found ordinary residence.
5 *Re Norris, ex p Reynolds* (1888) 4 TLR 452, CA (bankrupt ordinarily resident in Brussels and London); see further *Fox v Stirk and Bristol Electoral Registration Officer* [1970] 2 QB 463, [1970] 3 All ER 7, CA, per Lord Denning MR at 475 (a person may have two residences); *Shah v Barnet* above at 342F.
6 See *Hopkins v Hopkins* [1951] P 116, [1950] 2 All ER 1035; *Stransky v Stransky* [1954] P 428, [1954] 2 All ER 536; *Lewis v Lewis* [1956] 1 All ER 375, [1956] 1 WLR 200; *R v Immigration Appeal Tribunal, ex p Siggins* [1985] Imm AR 14, QBD; *Secretary of State for the Home Department v Haria* [1986] Imm AR 165. The Court of Appeal in *Ikimi v Ikimi* [2001] EWCA Civ 873, [2001] 3 WLR 672 equated 'ordinary residence' with 'habitual residence', and held that it required a degree of continuity.
7 *R v Hussain* (1971) 56 Cr App Rep 165, CA.
8 [1963] 1 QB 593, [1963] 1 All ER 181, CCA.
9 [1985] Imm AR 14, above.
10 The Secretary of State for the Home Department's Immigration Directorate's Instructions, Chapter 19, section 2 (3 December 2013) considers single absences of up to 6 months to be temporary absences that do not require investigation. Longer absences or frequent shorter absences will however precipitate enquiry (para 2.3).
11 *R v Immigration Appeal Tribunal, ex p NG* [1986] Imm AR 23, QBD; *Ex p Siggins* above.

4.7 The question as to where a child is ordinarily or habitually resident, has now been resolved by the Supreme Court[1] who have held that the test for the determination of habitual residence under the Hague Convention, the provisions of Council Regulation (EC) No 2201/2003 and under domestic legislation should be the same. The test set out in *Ex p Nilish Shah per* Lord Scarman should be abandoned in this setting: the Supreme Court held that the test adopted by the CJEU[2] ought to apply, namely 'the place which reflects some degree of integration by the child in a social and family environment'.

That position was reiterated by the Supreme Court in *LC (children) (Reunite International Child Abduction Centre, intervening), Re*[3] where Baroness Hale once more revisited Lord Scarman's speech in *Shah* and 'consign[ed] it to legal history, along with the test which he propounded'. The Court made clear that when determining the question as to whether a child has achieved a sufficient degree of integration into a social and family environment in a country in which she was living so as to be habitually resident there, a relevant factor was the state of mind of a child who was an adolescent or had the maturity of an adolescent during that residence[4]. That notwithstanding, the Court also held that where a child of any age goes lawfully to reside with a parent in a state in which that parent is habitually resident, it will be highly unusual for that child not to acquire habitual residence there too.

1   *A (children) (jurisdiction: return of child), Re* [2013] UKSC 60, [2014] AC 1, [2014] 1 All ER 827, [2013] 3 WLR 761 at paragraphs 35, 54(iii)(v) and 54(v).
2   *A (Area of Freedom, Security and Justice):* Case C-523/07 [2010] Fam 42; [2010] 2 WLR 527, ECJ, affirmed in *Mercredi v Chaffe:* Case C-497/10 PPU) [2012] Fam 22; [2009] ECR I-2805, ECJ, [2011] 3 WLR 1229, ECJ case.
3   [2014] UKSC 1, [2014] 1 All ER 1181, [2014] 2 WLR 124.
4   Lord Scarman had observed in *Shah*, at p 344, that proof of ordinary (or habitual) residence was 'ultimately a question of fact, depending more on the evidence of matters susceptible of objective proof than on evidence as to state of mind'.

Residence in breach of the immigration laws

4.8 For the purposes of immigration and nationality law, ordinary residence contains statutory requirements over and above those found at common law. The Immigration Act 1971 and British Nationality Act 1981 govern questions as to whether a person can be ordinarily resident while in breach of the immigration laws. For purposes of exemption from deportation, once ordinarily resident, a person does not cease to be so while in breach of the immigration laws.[1] But for other Immigration Act purposes, it is expressly provided that a person cannot be ordinarily resident at a time when he or she is in breach of the immigration laws.[2] A similar qualification is made under the British Nationality Act 1981: a person is not to be treated as ordinarily resident for the purposes of that Act when he or she is in the UK in breach of the immigration laws.[3]

1   Immigration Act 1971, s 7(2).
2   Immigration Act 1971, s 33(2).
3   British Nationality Act 1981, s 50(5). Under the British Nationality Act 1948 no such qualification was made, but in *R v Secretary of State for the Home Department, ex p Margueritte* [1983] QB 180, [1982] 3 All ER 909, the Court of Appeal held that lawful presence was imported into the meaning of ordinary residence under that Act, distinguishing *Azam v Secretary of State for the Home Department* [1974] AC 18, [1973] 2 All ER 765, HL where in a number of their Lordships' speeches it was assumed that a person could be ordinarily resident although an illegal entrant.

4.9 For the purposes of nationality law, section 50A of the British Nationality Act 1981 sets out exhaustively the circumstances in which a person would be in the UK in breach of the immigration laws. A person is in the UK in breach of the immigration laws if (and only if) he or she:

(a)   is in the UK;
(b)   does not have the right of abode in the UK within the meaning of section 2 of the Immigration Act 1971;
(c)   does not have leave to enter or remain in the UK (whether or not he or she previously had leave);
(d)   does not have a qualifying Common Travel Area (CTA) entitlement;[1]
(e)   is not entitled to reside in the UK by virtue of any provision made under section 2(2) of the European Communities Act 1972 (whether or not the person was previously entitled);

(f)   is not entitled to enter and remain in the UK as a crew member[2] (whether or not he or she was previously entitled); and

(g)   does not have the benefit of an exemption under section 8(2) to (4) of the Immigration Act 1971 (diplomats, soldiers and other special cases) (whether or not he or she previously had the benefit of an exemption).

A person is not usually to be treated as having been here in breach of the immigration laws during any time when he or she is in the immigration control area or is detained or temporarily admitted pending a decision on his or her eligibility to enter.[3] But although detention or temporary admission of this kind does not affect the legality of someone's presence in the UK, the time spent in this way can be calculated as part of the duration of the time spent in the UK for nationality purposes because the British Nationality Act 1981 merely requires that the person 'was in' or 'was not in' the UK for a specified amount of time.[4]

[1]   A person has a qualifying CTA entitlement if the person: (a) is a citizen of the Republic of Ireland, (b) last arrived in the UK on a local journey (within the meaning of the Immigration Act 1971) from the Republic of Ireland, and (c) on that arrival, was a citizen of the Republic of Ireland and was entitled to enter without the leave by virtue of s 1(3) of the Immigration Act 1971 (entry from common travel area).

[2]   By virtue of the Immigration Act 1971, s 8(1).

[3]   British Nationality Act 1981, s 50A(6), applying Immigration Act 1971, s 11.

[4]   British Nationality Act 1981, Sch 1, para 1(2).

Consequences of being settled

4.10 Settlement brings many advantages. Persons subject to immigration control who are 'settled' have in general a right to permanent residence in the UK, provided they continue living here, although they are potentially liable to deportation, unless they have an exemption,[1] and may be deported if they commit serious crimes or their presence is no longer conducive to the public good for this or some other reason.[2] The Supreme Court have held that anterior indefinite leave to remain is not revived upon the revocation of a deportation order.[3] Revocation of indefinite leave is possible for a number of reasons under the Nationality, Immigration and Asylum Act 2002 (NIAA 2002).[4] Revocation of indefinite leave will no longer attract an in-country right of appeal once sections 15 and 17 of the IA 2014 comes into force, amending sections 82 and 92 or the NIAA 2002[5].

[1]   IA 1971, s 7.

[2]   IA 1971, s 3(5)(a) and (6), and UK Borders Act 2007, s 32.

[3]   *R (on the application of George (Fitzroy)) v Secretary of State for the Home Department* [2014] UKSC 28, [2014] 3 All ER 365, [2014] 1 WLR 1831: The Supreme Court held section 76(1) of the NIAA 2002 (the power to revoke indefinite leave to remain) does not inform the construction of s 5 of the IA 1971. In that case the Secretary of State had made successive grants of time-limited leave.

[4]   See NIAA 2002, s 76.

[5]   NIAA 2002, s 76. Sections 76(2)(b), 76(2)(c), 76(4) and 76(7) are to be repealed by para 3(3)(a), 3(3)(b) and para 7 of Sch 9(1) to the IA 2014.

4.11 Other important consequences of being 'settled' are that persons are liberated from restrictions on employment or occupation, studies, maintenance and accommodation requirements without recourse to public funds, reporting conditions and registration with the police.[1] Another important practical consequence is that the 'settled' person is in a position to call for members of their family and other dependants to join them in the UK: see **4.13**. Having the right to settle leads to eligibility for naturalisation or registration as a British citizen.[2] Settlement enables a parent to qualify his or her child for British citizenship, if the child is born in the UK,[3] although this is not a precondition of registration or naturalisation.[4]

[1] Immigration Act 1971, s 3(1)(c).
[2] BNA 1981, ss 4 and 6.
[3] BNA 1981, ss 1(1) and 50(4).
[4] BNA 1981, ss 4, 6 and Sch 1.

Settlement under the Immigration Rules

4.12 Under the Points Based System ('PBS'), the general requirements to be fulfilled in order to become eligible to apply for settlement[1] are that a person must have spent a continuous period of five years lawfully in the UK[2], been employed continuously throughout the five years[3] on the terms on which such leave was conferred[4], with any absences from the UK during the five years for a purpose that is consistent with the applicant's basis of stay in the UK, including paid annual leave, or for serious or compelling reasons[5]. To qualify for indefinite leave to remain as the Partner of a Relevant Points Based System Migrant, an applicant must meet the requirements found at paragraph 319E of the Rules.

All applications for settlement in categories outside the PBS or the rules covering employment made after 9 July 2012 will be determined by reference to Appendix FM[6]. Such applicants include persons exercising rights of access to a child resident in the United Kingdom, retired persons of independent means (269) and their partner (273D) and children (275A), long residence (276B), private life (276DE), Gurkhas discharged from the British Army (276I) and their spouses or partners and children, foreign or Commonwealth citizens discharged from HM Forces and their spouses or partners and children, spouses or civil partners (287) or (bereaved (295M)) unmarried or same-sex partners (295G) of a person present and settled in the United Kingdom, victims of domestic violence (289A), (adopted (310)) children of (a) parent(s) or a relative present and settled or being admitted for settlement in the United Kingdom (297), parent, grandparent or other dependent relative of a person present and settled in the United Kingdom (317), child, parent, grandparent or other dependent relative of a person with limited leave to enter or remain in the United Kingdom as a refugee or beneficiary of humanitarian protection, or of a former refugee or beneficiary humanitarian protection, who is present and settled in the United Kingdom or now a British Citizen ((319V-Y)). General grounds for refusing an application for indefinite leave to remain are found at paragraph 322(1C). Those grounds for refusal are mandatory.[7]

[1] HC 395, para 245AAA, inserted by HC 1039, to be read with the requirements set out in separate immigration rules with reference to the particular categories of Tier 1 and 2; for example, there has to be a cooling off period for Tier 2 Intra-Company transfers) and there is accelerated ILR (ie less than five years) for Investor Entrepreneur categories in specified situations; for details see CHAPTER 10.
[2] Under HC 395 para 245AAA, a continuous period is an unbroken period with valid leave; a period shall not be considered to have been broken where the applicant has been absent from the UK for a period of 180 days or less in any of the five consecutive 12 month periods

preceding the date of the application for leave to remain; the applicant has existing limited leave to enter or remain upon their departure and return except that where that leave expired no more than 28 days prior to a further application for entry clearance, in which event that period and any period pending the determination of an application made within that 28 day period shall be disregarded; and the applicant has any period of overstaying between periods of entry clearance, leave to enter or leave to remain of up to 28 days and any period of overstaying pending the determination of an application made within that 28 day period disregarded.

3   Except for periods when the applicant had leave as a Tier 1 (General) Migrant, a Tier 1 (Investor) Migrant, a Tier 1 (Entrepreneur) Migrant, a Tier 1 (Exceptional Talent) Migrant, a highly skilled migrant, a Businessperson, an Innovator, an Investor, a self-employed lawyer or a writer, composer or artist.

4   *Inter alia* under the terms of their Certificate of Sponsorship, work permit or in the employment for which they were given leave to enter or remain, except that any breaks in employment in which they applied for leave as a Tier 2 Migrant, or, under Tier 5 Temporary Worker (International Agreement) Migrant as a private servant in a diplomatic household, where in the latter case they applied to enter the UK before 6 April 2012, to work for a new employer shall be disregarded, provided this is within 60 days of the end of their employment with their previous employer or Sponsor.

5   Except for periods where the applicant had leave as a Tier 1(Investor) Migrant, a Tier 1(Entrepreneur) Migrant, a Tier 1(Exceptional Talent) Migrant or a highly skilled migrant.

6   AB 246, HC 194.

7   See Modernised Guidance – General grounds for refusal Section 4 – version 18.0 Valid from 27 August 2014 and CHAPTER 3.

Knowledge of English and British way of life

4.13 As of 28 October 2013 the Secretary of State for the Home Department introduced changes to the requirements made of individuals wishing to apply for settlement or naturalisation as British citizens in demonstrating their knowledge of language and life in the United Kingdom. All applicants for settlement, unless exempt, are expected both to pass the 'Life in the UK' test and to have an English speaking and listening qualification at B1 CEFR or above. A range of English language qualifications are accepted as evidence that an applicant has met the requirement to hold a B1 level speaking and listening qualification[1]. Migrants will not be required to study for their qualification at any particular institution nor to follow any particular curriculum. The Life in the UK test must be taken at a secure test centre. Nationals of majority English speaking countries[2] and those who have obtained a degree taught in English will not be required to show a formal speaking and listening qualification but will be required to pass the Life in the UK test. Adults aged 18 to 65 years applying for settlement, whether as a main applicant or a dependant, will be expected to meet the new 'Knowledge of the English language and life in the UK' requirement. This will include adult children of persons settled in the UK and adult children applying for indefinite leave as a dependant. Those who have a physical or mental condition which severely restricts their ability to learn English and/or communicate and/or take the Life in the UK test will be exempted from these requirements, as will those applying for settlement as spouses or partners who have been victims of domestic violence or whose spouse or partner has died, refugees and those with Humanitarian Protection and those who hold Discretionary Leave to Remain (although this is being kept under review).[3] There are further categories of exemption for those who find these requirements challenging; those categories of persons will be permitted to apply for further periods of limited leave (subject to continuing to meet the other relevant Immigration Rules in their category) to enable them to meet the requirement if they not yet done so[4]. Further concessions apply to individuals who have been in the UK for 15 years with limited leave as a partner, child or parent (under Appendix FM or the transitional arrangements under Part 8), dependants of HM forces personnel and dependants of PBS migrants or work permit holders[5]. A migrant who fulfils the Life in the UK requirement for settlement as it applied on or after 28 October 2013 will not be required to retake any elements in a later application for naturalisation but will be deemed automatically to satisfy the Knowledge of Language and Life Requirement at that later stage. Those who applied for settlement before 28 October 2013 will not be so deemed and will be required to satisfy the new Knowledge of Language and Life Requirement.

[1] Qualifications covering speaking and listening at B1 or above from the Secure English Language Test (SELT) list in the Immigration Rules, Appendix O. The SELT list is available at www.ukba.homeoffice.gov.uk/sitecontent/applicationforms/new-approved-english-tests.pdf ; Qualifications in English for Speakers of Other Languages (ESOL) at Entry level 3, Level 1 or Level 2, that include speaking and listening and that have been regulated by the Office of Qualifications and Examinations Regulation (Ofqual). The qualification must be listed as an ESOL qualification on the Ofqual Register of Regulated Qualifications and have been taken in England, Wales or Northern Ireland. The Ofqual register is available at: register.ofqual.gov. uk/2; a National Qualification in ESOL at Scottish Qualifications Framework (SCQF) levels 4, 5 or 6 awarded by the Scottish Qualifications Authority (SQA) and taken in Scotland.

[2] Antigua and Barbuda, Guyana, Australia, Jamaica, The Bahamas, New Zealand, Barbados, St Kitts and Nevis, Belize, St Lucia, Canada, St Vincent and the Grenadines, Dominica, Trinidad and Tobago, Grenada, United States of America.

[3] 'Knowledge of language and life in the UK for settlement and naturalisation: Statement of Intent, changes to the requirement from October 2013' April 2013

[4] Ibid., partners, children or parents applying under Appendix FM or subject to transitional arrangements under Part 8; those in the UK on the basis of long residence under paragraph 276A; those in the territory on the basis of private life under paragraph 276ADE; those in the UK as dependants of HM forces personnel; and dependants of those who originally entered the UK as PBS migrants or work permit holders.

[5] Ibid.

4.14 Although the grant of settlement after five years in a particular capacity depends upon the exercise of discretion by the Home Office, settlement is normally given as a matter of course where the requirements of the Immigration Rules are satisfied, and before refusing settlement the Secretary of State must remain unsatisfied about one or more of these requirements unless a general ground for refusing indefinite leave is relied on, such as breach of a condition or undertaking or bad character.[1] In such a situation, settlement may only be given as a concession outside the Rules, an exercise of discretion which cannot be reviewed as to its merits on appeal.

[1] The general grounds for refusing variation of leave are set out at paragraph 322(1C): see **4.12** above. The Secretary of State is entitled to delay a decision on an application for indefinite leave to remain, despite the existence of compassionate circumstances, to await the outcome of a police investigation: *R v Secretary of State for the Home Department, ex p Memon (Hina)* [1999] Imm AR 85. This is also reflected in her policy guidance. See further CHAPTER 3.

Position of EEA nationals

4.15 EEA nationals are treated for domestic law purposes as 'settled' in two different ways. First, Directive 2004/38/EC (the Citizens' Directive) consolidates the provisions made in a number of repealed EC Directives, but it also provides for a permanent right of residence in a host Member State, which generally applies after five years residence[1], provided that during this period the individual has been exercising a Treaty right (i.e. living in the United Kingdom as a worker/jobseeker, in self-employment, studying or self-sufficient throughout the five-year period or to have been a family member of such a person or a person with permanent residence).[2] Regulations 15 and 18 of the Immigration (EEA) Regulations 2006,[3] which came into force on 30 April 2006, transpose this right into UK domestic law and apply it to all EEA nationals and their family members. This means that they have a right to indefinite or permanent residence and can qualify for naturalisation. Third-country national family members who acquire permanent residence under the 2006 Regulations can apply for confirmation of their permanent residence status normally acquired after living in the United Kingdom throughout the five year period where her/his EEA national family member has been exercising Treaty rights.

For residence in the United Kingdom to be considered continuous, a person should not be absent from the United Kingdom for more than six months each year. Longer absences for compulsory military service will not affect continuity, nor will a single absence of a maximum of 12 months for important reasons such as pregnancy, child birth, serious illness, study, vocational training or posting overseas. Further, an EEA national may acquire permanent residence in certain circumstances on retirement or as a result of a permanent incapacity to work.[4] Once permanent residence has been acquired there is no requirement for the EEA national to be in the UK in order for the family member to be admitted and to reside. Permanent residence shall be lost if the individual is absent from the UK for two or more years. Those with permanent residence under the EEA Regulations may only be refused admission on serious grounds of public policy or public security. Those who have resided in the UK for more than ten years or who are under 18 years of age may only be refused admission on imperative grounds of public security grounds.

[1] Or less in certain circumstances, see reg 15 of the EEA Regulations, SI 2006/1003; Directive 2004/38/EC, arts 16-18.
[2] Directive 2004/38/EC, arts 16-18.
[3] SI 2006/1003. These have been extensively amended since 2006. See Appendix 5 – Statutory Instruments in Volume 2.
[4] Guidance notes for applying for residence documentation as a European Economic Area (EEA) national or as the family member of an EEA national (Version 01/2014).

Settlement for Refugees and Persons in need of Humanitarian Protection

4.16 A person who has been recognised as a refugee or person in need of humanitarian protection will ordinarily be granted five years limited leave to enter or remain along with any dependants included in the initial claim or before the decision is made. Those persons[1] and their dependants[2] are eligible for settlement (and are entitled to apply one month before the expiry of their previous grant of leave[3]), unless they fall for refusal on general grounds owing to criminal offending[4], even where the deportation criteria are not met or deportation action has not been pursued[5]. Where there are criminal charges pending, applications will be kept on hold pending the outcome of the prosecution. Checks will be made as to whether the individual has travelled back to their country of origin, or the country from which they sought protection, without the knowledge of the Home Office. Positive enquiries may lead to a decision to cancel or cease leave if such journeys have been made on several occasions, for long periods of time or without notifying the Home Office of compelling and compassionate circumstances for doing so. Where the converse of such factors is true it is less likely that consideration would be given to removing protection rights[6]. Pursuant to Article 24 of the Qualification Directive, applicants and/or their dependants who are refused settlement but are still in need of international protection will continue to be granted leave in periods of three years until the individual becomes eligible for settlement.

[1] Paragraphs 339R to 339T set out the requirements to be met for a grant of indefinite leave to remain for persons granted asylum or HP or their dependants granted asylum or humanitarian protection in line.

[2] Paragraphs 352A to 352FJ set out the criteria for persons seeking leave to enter or remain as the child, spouse or partner of a refugee or beneficiary of humanitarian protection (Refugee Family Reunion).

[3] Any applications received by the Secretary of State after the applicant's extant leave has expired will be considered 'out of time', leading to the applicant becoming an overstayer. If the application is only out of time by less than a month or there are 'reasonable mitigating circumstances', the Secretary of State will process the application without more. Application's out of time by over a month will lead to an 'in-depth case review' to consider whether there is a continuing need for protection (API; Settlement Protection, para 3.2.2; 1 October 2013).

[4] HC 628, which came into force on 1 October 2013, introduced new criminality thresholds into the general grounds for refusal of settlement applications from those with refugee leave or humanitarian protection.

[5] A summary of relevant considerations can be found at section 5 of the API: Settlement Protection, 1 October 2013.

[6] API; Settlement Protection, para 4.2.2.

Settlement on the coming into force of the Immigration Act 1971

4.17 There is a further category of persons who were granted indefinite leave by statute. These are all persons who were either settled in the UK before the coming into force of the Immigration Act 1971 on 1 January 1973 or were given unconditional admission or leave to land under the earlier immigration laws. Section 1(2) of the 1971 Act provides that indefinite leave to enter or remain shall be treated as having been given under the 1971 Act to those in the UK at its coming into force, if they were then settled there and not exempt from immigration control. The benefit of section 1(2) only applies to those physically present in the UK on 1 January 1973. Where the protection of that section is claimed, the burden is on the immigrant to show that he or she was settled.[1]

[1] *R v Secretary of State for the Home Department, ex p Mughal* [1974] QB 313, [1973] 3 All ER 796, CA.

4.18 If such persons had not yet become ordinarily resident by 1 January 1973, or they were absent from the UK on that date, they may still rely upon the provisions of section 34(2) and (3) of the Immigration Act 1971. Section 34(2) provides that leave to land by virtue of earlier legislation is to be treated as leave to enter under the Immigration Act 1971. Section 34(3) provides that a person treated as having leave to enter is to be treated as having indefinite leave if that person was not, on 1 January 1973, subject to a condition limiting her or her stay in the UK. These provisions cannot, however, benefit persons who were illegal entrants.[1]

[1]   *Azam v Secretary of State for the Home Department* [1974] AC 18, [1973] 2 All ER 765, HL; *R v Secretary of State for the Home Department, ex p Razak* [1986] Imm AR 44, DC; affd (25 March 1986, unreported), CA; *R v Secretary of State for the Home Department, ex p Miah* [1990] 2 All ER 523, [1989] Imm AR 559, CA; *R v Secretary of State for the Home Department, ex p Khan (Hiram)* [1990] 2 All ER 531, [1990] Imm AR 327, CA.

RETURN TO THE UK

4.19 Under section 3(4) of the Immigration Act 1971, all leave, including indefinite leave,[1] lapses on leaving the common travel area,[2] unless the holder returns in circumstances in which leave to enter is not required, in which case the previous leave, and the conditions attached to it, continue to apply. The section applies equally to visa nationals and those not requiring visas by virtue of their nationality.[3] Prior to the passage of the Immigration and Asylum Act 1999[4] and the making of the Immigration (Leave to Enter and Remain) Order 2000[5] under it, which made it clear that leave did not normally lapse, the exemption from obtaining leave on return applied only to very limited classes of people, such as certain government officials and Commonwealth citizens on day trips to the continent.[6] The automatic lapsing of leave for everyone else gave rise to absurdity and injustice, as students midway through degree courses found themselves barred from re-entering the UK after a mid-term break in Paris, and long-settled immigrants on contracts abroad lost their right of permanent residence when they returned for short visits, because they did not utter the magic words 'returning to resume settlement'. Section 3(4) still remains the general rule, but now has effect subject to the Immigration (Leave to Enter and Remain) Order,[7] whose provisions have enormously eroded its scope. Leave to enter does not lapse on leaving the common travel area, if it was conferred by means of an entry clearance (other than a visit visa), leave to enter or leave to remain if it was for more than six months.[8] We examine below how these new provisions work.

[1]   *Ghassemian and Mirza v Home Office* [1989] Imm AR 42, CA.
[2]   See CHAPTER 5 below.
[3]   *Re Wijesundera* [1989] Imm AR 291, CA; *Kuku (Aderimi Shakirat) v Secretary of State for the Home Department* [1990] Imm AR 27, CA.
[4]   Immigration and Asylum Act 1999, ss 1 and 2, inserting new ss 3A and 3B into the Immigration Act 1971.
[5]   Immigration (Leave to Enter and Remain) Order 2000, SI 2000/1161.
[6]   Immigration Act 1971, s 8(2); Immigration (Exemption from Control) Order 1972, SI 1972/1613, as amended: see **5.49–5.50** below.
[7]   SI 2000/1161, art 13(10).
[8]   SI 2000/1161, art 13(2)(b) and (3).

Travellers on temporary leave

4.20 The effect of the Immigration (Leave to Enter and Remain) Order 2000[1] provisions is that leave to enter and remain given for a period of more than six months and any leave given by an entry clearance (other than a visit visa), however long or short, will remain in force so as to enable students, Tier 5

(Tempory workers) and others on temporary leave to go abroad and return on the same leave and subject to the same conditions (non-lapsing leave). Only visitors,[2] and those given less than six months stay by immigration officials in the UK,[3] will find that their leave lapses on departure. But even those with visit visas gain protection from the Order. Article 4 provides that during the period of validity of a visit visa, the visa, unless it is endorsed as a single entry visa, has the effect of leave to enter on an unlimited number of occasions.[4] On each occasion that the visitor arrives in the UK, he or she is to be treated as having been granted, before arrival, leave to enter for six months, beginning on the date of arrival, if six months or more remain of the visa's period of validity, and for the visa's remaining period of validity if it has less than six months to run.[5] In cases of any form of entry clearance to which article 4(3) of the 2000 Leave to Enter and Remain Order applies, the holder will be treated as having been given indefinite leave for an indefinite period or limited leave, subject to whatever conditions are endorsed on the entry clearance, which will continue in force until the date of expiry of the entry clearance, unless, of course, it has been varied.[6] Thus visa nationals who leave the UK during the period of leave do not need to obtain a further visa to re-enter.

[1] SI 2000/1161.
[2] SI 2000/1161, art 13(2)(a). The visit visa might be a five-year multiple entry one, but visit leave always lapses on departure. See below.
[3] SI 2000/1161, art 13(3).
[4] SI 2000/1161, art 4(1).
[5] SI 2000/1161, art 4(2). Although a visit leave may not exceed six months under the Immigration Rules (HC 395, paras 42 and 52), a visit visa may well have a much longer validity, eg multiple visit visas are usually valid for a period of two years.
[6] SI 2000/1161, art 4(3)(b), subject to the provisions for visits under the ADS agreement with China under Article 4(3A) (added by SI 2005/1159).

4.21 The purpose and likely effect of the provisions is to obviate the need for repeated scrutiny on each return to the UK of those whose application for entry to or stay in the UK has previously been approved by an immigration officer or a Home Office civil servant. Such persons may still be examined at the port on re-entry, but they do not have to establish a case for re-entry, as was the case under the old law.[1] The object of the immigration officer's examination on re-entry is to establish whether leave previously granted is still in force,[2] and if so, whether there has been a change of circumstances such that it should be cancelled;[3] whether it was obtained by false information given by the passenger or by his or her failure to disclose material facts;[4] whether there are medical grounds for the cancellation of leave;[5] whether entry is sought for a purpose other than that for which entry clearance was obtained;[6] or whether cancellation is conducive to the public good.[7] The passenger may be required to submit to further examination,[8] or to be examined by a medical inspector,[9] and the leave may be suspended pending further inquiries.[10] In this event the ordinary powers of detention and temporary admission apply.[11] If leave is cancelled,[12] the passenger will have an in-country right of appeal (until section 15 of the Immigration Act 2014 does away with these appeal rights) against cancellation,[13] unless cancellation is on the ground that the passenger seeks entry for a different purpose from that on the entry clearance.[14] It is noteworthy that for the purposes of cancellation of leave any false information or failure to disclose material facts must be attributable to the passenger and not to any third party.[15]

1   See *Secretary of State for the Home Department v Patel* [1992] Imm AR 486, CA.
2   Ie because it has not lapsed by virtue of art 13 of the Immigration (Leave to Enter and Remain) Order 2000, SI 2000/1161 or because, as a visit leave, it is deemed to have been granted afresh abroad under art 4. Immigration Act 1971 Sch 2, para 2(1)(c)(i), substituted by Immigration and Asylum Act 1999, Sch 14, para 56 (February 14, 2000).
3   Immigration Act 1971, Sch 2, para 2A(2)(a).
4   Immigration Act 1971, Sch 2, para 2A(2)(b).
5   Immigration Act 1971, Sch 2, para 2A(2)(c).
6   Immigration Act 1971, Sch 2, para 2A(2A), inserted by Asylum and Immigration (Treatment of Claimants, etc) Act 2004, s 18 (from 1 October 2004: SI 2004/2325).
7   Immigration Act 1971, Sch 2, para 2A(3).
8   Immigration Act 1971, Sch 2, para 2A(5).
9   Immigration Act 1971, Sch 2, para 2A(4)
10 Immigration Act 1971, Sch 2, para 2A(7).
11 Immigration Act 1971, Sch 2, para 16(1A), 21.
12 Immigration Act 1971, Sch 2, para 2A(8).
13 Immigration Act 1971, Sch 2, para 2A(9) read with Nationality, Immigration and Asylum Act 2002, ss 82(2)(a) and 92(3)(a).
14 Nationality, Immigration and Asylum Act 2002, s 92(3B), inserted by Asylum and Immigration (Treatment of Claimants, etc) Act 2004, s 28 (from 1 October 2004: SI 2004/2325).
15 Immigration Act 1971, Sch 2, para 2A(2)(b).

4.22 The Immigration (Leave to Enter and Remain) Order 2000[1] also provides that leave to enter or remain may be varied (or cancelled) while the holder is abroad.[2] For that purpose, immigration officers (or Home Office officials) may seek information and documents which they would be entitled to obtain in an ordinary immigration examination under Schedule 2 to the Immigration Act 1971,[3] and may require the holder of the leave to supply an up to date medical report.[4] Failure to provide the information, documents or report requested is a ground for cancellation of leave.[5] These provisions enable a person whose continuing leave expires while he or she is abroad, or who wishes to change the basis of leave (say, from student to trainee or spouse) to apply for an extension or variation while abroad.[6] They also enable leave to be cancelled while the holder is abroad if, for example, it was discovered that the passenger had used deception to obtain the leave or cancellation of leave would be conducive to the public good. Furthermore, if The only categories of passenger who do not benefit from the Order are non-visa nationals granted leave to enter as visitors or in some other capacity at the port for six months or less and those granted leave to remain by the Secretary of State which is due to expire in less than six months. These persons' leave lapses on their departure from the common travel area and does not take effect as a new pre-arrival leave to enter under Article 4. Additionally leave lapses if, during the period of leave, the holder remains outside the UK for longer than two years.[7]

1   SI 2000/1161.
2   SI 2000/1161, art 13(6), (7).
3   SI 2000/1161, art 13(8).
4   SI 2000/1161, art 13(8).
5   SI 2000/1161, art 13(9).
6   For rules and practices on withdrawal of an application and for continuation of leave notwithstanding a return of passport see CHAPTER 3 at **3.117–3.118**.
7   SI 2000/1161, art 13(4)(a).

Returning residents

4.23 A variety of returning resident rights are catered for by the Immigration Rules. The two main categories are those who can return freely however long they have been away and those who should return within two years. Once British nationals without the right of abode, such as British Overseas citizens, have been given indefinite leave to enter or remain, they may be in a better position to return to the UK than other returning residents. The Rules reflect the piecemeal history of the imposition of immigration control on British nationals and the quirks of policy and practice in the past.

Holders of UK passports issued in the UK or Ireland

4.24 Paragraph 16 of HC 395 provides that British Dependent Territories citizens, British Nationals (Overseas), British Overseas citizens, British Protected persons, or British Subjects under the British Nationality Act 1981, who can produce a passport issued in the UK and Islands or the Republic of Ireland before 1 January 1973, should be admitted freely unless the passport has been endorsed to show that they were subject to immigration control. This Rule reflects the rights of residual categories of former nationals of the UK and protected persons who were not subject to control prior to the coming into force of the Immigration Act 1971 but who did not become patrial under that Act or British citizens under the British Nationality Act 1981. The Rule seems to require the actual production of the historic passport that gives rise to the right, but if a replacement passport has been endorsed with the right of re-admission, the passport holder should be entitled to rely on that, even if the historic document has been lost; the endorsement in a current passport would give rise to legitimate expectations of admission unless a person's nationality has changed.[1] It may, however, be necessary to produce the historic passport or its replacement to obtain the endorsement in any subsequent passport. A further question arises where the historic passport was issued to a parent but is endorsed with details of a dependent child during its currency; can the child obtain admission years later in reliance on such a document? This remains unclear.

[1] See *Liew v Secretary of State for the Home Department* [1989] Imm AR 62. See further *Lee* (21753) [2000] 6 ILD 1 at 36, IAT.

4.25 British Overseas citizens who hold a UK passport, wherever issued, and can satisfy the immigration officer that they have been given indefinite leave to enter the UK since 1 March 1968, should be given indefinite leave to enter.[1] There is thus no obligation to comply with the two-year rule, and the presence of any intervening limited leave will not prevent such re-admission. Previous versions of this Rule referred to British Overseas citizens 'who have previously been admitted for settlement'. This was held only to cover those who had been admitted at a time when they were subject to immigration control.[2] It would appear that British Protected Person voucher holders who are admitted for settlement will have to comply with the two-year rule in respect of absences abroad.

[1] HC 395, para 17. See IDI, Ch 1, s 3, Annex M.

[2]   *R v Secretary of State for the Home Department, ex p Himalyaishwar* (1984) Times, 21 February, QBD.

Refugees

4.26 Persons recognised as refugees and issued with a Convention travel document must be re-admitted at any time during the validity of the document.[1] They need not comply with the two-year rule.

[1]   1951 Convention relating to the status of refugees (Geneva, 1951) Sch, para 13(1).

Return within two years

4.27 The system of non-lapsing leave described in paras **4.19–4.22** above applies equally to those with indefinite leave to remain, provided that they have not stayed outside the UK for a continuous period of more than two years.[1]

[1]   Immigration (Leave to Enter and Remain) Order 2000, SI 2000/1161, art 13(4)(a).

4.28 Under the Immigration Rules,[1] returning residents must satisfy the immigration officer that they had indefinite leave to enter or remain in the UK when they *last* left, they have not been away longer than two years, they did not receive public assistance towards the cost of leaving, and they *now seek admission for the purpose of settlement*.[2] Under the Immigration (Leave to Enter and Remain) Order 2000[3] a passenger with continuing leave who does not intend to resume ordinary residence may have leave cancelled,[4] but the Home Office has accepted that where there is some continuity of connections or residence, a short return visit should not lead to the cancellation of indefinite leave. The IDI state that:

> 'a person returning temporarily to the United Kingdom is not necessarily a visitor. Many people who have their home in the United Kingdom may spend substantial periods overseas on short term business contracts or for studies and return to the United Kingdom for only a short period during holidays. This will not disqualify a person from readmission as a returning resident provided he is normally resident in the United Kingdom, at the time of admission he considers himself to be domiciled in the United Kingdom, and he has not been away from the United Kingdom for more than two years and he intends to return to the United Kingdom for settlement in the future on completion of her employment, business or studies etc'.[5]

Cancellation will not attract an in-country appeal upon sections 15 and 17 of the Immigration Act 2014 coming into force. However such decisions will be amenable to challenge by way of judicial review proceedings.[6] The onus is on the immigration officer to justify cancelling leave by reference to a change in circumstances. In the vast majority of cases little examination should be necessary. Returning residents may have their leave cancelled if on inquiry it is discovered that the original leave to enter was secured by their deception.[7]

[1]   HC 395, para 18. By para 19A, added by Cm 4851, spouses accompanying members of HM Forces, of British diplomats and of comparable UK-based staff members of the British Council who are serving overseas are exempt from the two-year rule and from the rule preventing travel at public expense (sub-paras (ii) and (iii)).

2   In *Cawte* (HX 00639) the Tribunal held, following *R v Immigration Appeal Tribunal, ex p Coomasaru* [1983] 1 All ER 208, that an appellant could qualify as a returning resident if she intended to return as such, even if she did not tell the immigration officer on arrival. See fn 5 below. See also *Ali Yazidi* (16387) (16 April 1998, unreported), IAT.

3   SI 2000/1161.

4   The IDI, Ch 1, s 3, para 2.2, state that a person who is returning only for a limited period (eg as a visitor) simply so as to show a period of residence here within two years of departure, should not be re-admitted. But see below.

5   IDI, Ch 1, s 3, para 2.2. See also *R v Secretary of State for the Home Department, ex p Chugtai* [1995] Imm AR 559 where Collins J accepted that a person may retain ordinary residence although working outside the UK for a substantial or indefinite period.

6   Permission was granted in *R v Secretary of State for the Home Department, ex p Pearson* (CO 1397/1998) and a grant of leave to enter as a visitor quashed by consent and indefinite leave reinstated.

7   Immigration Act 1971, Sch 2, para 2A(2)(b); see *Sattar v Secretary of State for the Home Department* [1988] Imm AR 190, CA; *Ali (Mohammed Fazor) v Secretary of State for the Home Department* [1988] Imm AR 274, CA; *R v Secretary of State for the Home Department, ex p Musk* (CO 3956/1996) (26 March 1996, unreported), QBD. However, the dicta on the standard of proof may not apply to this situation, since leave is not being merely refused, but cancelled.

Return after two years

4.29 The leave of persons who have been away from the UK longer than two years lapses.[1] Such former residents may nevertheless be admitted for further settlement at the discretion of the immigration authorities under the provisions of HC 395, paragraph 19.[2] One example given is persons who have lived here for most of their lives.[3] But it is only an example, and a combination of a shorter period of residence and family or other ties may be sufficient.[4] Ties in the UK constituting family life or private life for the purposes of Article 8 ECHR would be relevant to the exercise of discretion under this paragraph.[5] In *Buckle*[6] the Tribunal said the question was whether the facts point to an intentional break of residence or not; children are in a special position, as it is less easy for them to make an intentional break (see also **4.7**).

1   Immigration (Leave to Enter and Remain) Order 2000, SI 2000/1161, art 13(4).

2   HC 395, para 19 as inserted by Cm 4851. Annex K of the IDIs sets out the exceptions under which a person who has been away from the United Kingdom for more than two years may be admitted if her ties to this country merit it. Spouses accompanying British soldiers, diplomats or other comparable staff members of the British Council on tours overseas are not obliged to return to the UK within two years: HC 395, para 19A, inserted by Cm 4851.

3   HC 395, para 19. The phrase 'most of his life' does not mean 'most of his adult life': Entry clearance officer, *Kingston, Jamaica v Peart* [1979–80] Imm AR 41.

4   *Costa v Secretary of State for the Home Department* [1974] Imm AR 69.

5   See eg *Forou* (00TH01101) (28 April 2000, unreported), IAT.

6   (15012) IAT, 8 May 1997, 1999 5 ILD No 1, p 29. See also *Gomez (Joffrey)* (00TH02294) (5 October 2000, unreported), where parental obstruction of a young adult's attempts to return to the UK from Ecuador constituted grounds for the exercise of discretion to admit him.

4.30 The purpose of this discretionary Rule is to avoid injustice or undue hardship which might arise from an inflexible application of the two-year rule and 'the discretion must be exercised in a manner to give effect to this purpose'.[1] In *Armat Ali*[2] it was suggested that the guidelines, set out in *Costa's* case,[3] that the person 'must show strong connections with this country by a combination of length of residence and family or other ties' were applicable when the applicant for re-entry had voluntarily stayed away for more than two years, but not where the absence was involuntary. In *Ex p Ademuyiwa*[4] Farquharson J did not dissent from the *Armat Ali* interpretation where the applicant had originally left because of family illness but had remained to engage in business. In considering whether to admit such a person as a returning resident it was held that the immigration officer when exercising her discretion should consider *inter alia* the following factors:

(i) the length of the original residence of the applicant;

(ii) the time the applicant has been outside the UK;

(iii) the reason for the delay beyond the two years – was it through her own wish or no fault of her own? Could she reasonably have been expected to return within two years?;

(iv) why did she go abroad when she did and what were her intentions?;

(v) what are the nature of her family ties here – how close are they, and to what extent has she maintained them in her absence?;

(vi) whether the applicant has a home in this country and if admitted to the UK, would she resume her residency in that home?

The IDI adopt the criteria in *Armat Ali* in giving guidance on when those remaining abroad over two years may be re-admitted. In addition, the instructions set out other more specific circumstances which might apply in favour of an individual as: travel and service abroad with a particular employer prior to returning with her; service abroad for the UK government, as an employee of a quasi/government body, a British company or a United Nations organisation; employment abroad in the public service of a friendly country by a person who could not reasonably be expected to settle in that country permanently; a prolonged period of study abroad by a person who wished to rejoin their family here at the end of their studies; prolonged medical treatment abroad of a kind not available here; and whether the person contacted a post abroad within two years to express their future intention to return to the United Kingdom.[5]

1 On inflexible (application of) policy see Lord Reid's speech in *Eastleigh Borough Council v Betts* [1983] 2 AC 613 at 627H-328B and *R v Secretary of State for the Home Department, ex p Thompson and Venables* [1998] AC 407 *per* Lord Browne at 496G–497C.

2 Ali [1981] Imm AR 51.

3 [1974] Imm AR 69 at 74.

4 *R v Secretary of State for the Home Department, ex p Ademuyiwa* [1986] Imm AR 1, followed by the Tribunal in *Secretary of State for the Home Department v Agyen-Frempong* [1986] Imm AR 108 (upheld by CA at [1988] Imm AR 262).

5 IDI, Ch 1, Annex K, para 2. This is not a realistic option for most people, as there is no formal mechanism to record such an expression of intention and it would be a long, expensive and wasteful journey to the relevant British post.

4.31 In cases where the absence has been prolonged beyond the two years through no fault of the applicant, Tribunal decisions have tended to be favourable to the applicant. Examples are where a passport had to be surrendered because of legal proceedings abroad, and delay caused by illness,[1] accident or civil disturbance.[2] On the other hand, the longer the period which an applicant has remained out of the UK the more difficult it will be to qualify for admission under paragraph 19 of the Immigration Rules.[3]

1 *Khokhar v Visa Officer, Islamabad* [1981] Imm AR 56n.

2 *Gokulsing* (1632) (1978, unreported). See also *Gomez (Joffrey)* (00TH02294) (parental obstruction).

³   *R v Secretary of State for the Home Department, ex p Ademuyiwa* [1986] Imm AR 1, DC;
    Agyen-Frempong [1986] Imm AR 108; *R v Immigration Appeal Tribunal, ex p Saffiullah
    (Muhammad)* [1986] Imm AR 424, DC. An appellant who had been out of the country for six
    years and acquired citizenship of another country on marriage succeeded in *Cawte* (HX00639)
    (8 February 2000, unreported); another away for nearly seven years succeeded because of his
    four children in the UK (*Forou* (00TH01101)).

4.32 Refusal of leave to enter to a returning resident away for over two years
will not attract an in-country right of appeal in the absence of entry clearance¹
but would be challengeable by judicial review. However, an appeal, albeit
outside the country, is often preferable because of the power of the appellate
authority to reverse decisions to refuse entry on the merits in what are often
finely balanced cases.²

¹   Once ss 15 and 17 of the Immigration Act 2014 comes into force, amending s 82 of the NIAA
    2002

²   See comments of Carnwath J in *R v Secretary of State for the Home Department, ex p Musk*
    (CO 3956/1996) (26 March 1996, unreported).

Chapter 5

COMMON TRAVEL AREA, CREW MEMBERS AND EXEMPTED GROUPS

INTRODUCTION

5.1 The following abbreviations are used in this chapter:

CTA   Common travel area

IA 1971   Immigration Act 1971
NIAA 2002   Nationality, Immigration and Asylum Act 2002

This chapter deals with a number of special cases under UK immigration law. First, there are Irish citizens who, because of the common travel area, can come and go more or less as they like, but who are still subject to exclusion, deportation and removal. Then there are the inhabitants of the Channel Islands and the Isle of Man, who nominally have their own immigration control, but whose laws are, in fact, closely integrated with those of the mainland. Like Irish citizens, they too are part of the common travel area. Then there are such anomalous groups as seamen, airline and train crews, diplomats and military personnel. This chapter is about these groups.

COMMON TRAVEL AREA

5.2 The Common Travel Area is a passport-free zone which comprises the Republic of Ireland, the United Kingdom, the Isle of Man, Jersey and Guernsey.[1] The area's internal borders are subject to immigration controls, as we set out below, but only to minimal or non-existent border controls. There has never been a formal agreement between Ireland and the UK regarding the Common Travel Area[2] and passports have never been required in the zone, except during wartime, when travel restrictions were introduced between Britain and Ireland on the outbreak of war in 1939. After the war the Irish re-instated their previous provisions allowing free movement between Ireland and the UK.[3] However, the British declined to do so pending the agreement of a 'similar immigration policy'[4] in both countries. Consequently, the British maintained immigration controls between the island of Ireland and Great Britain up until 1952.[5] Then in 1953, the British began referring to the Common Travel Area in legislation for the first time.[6] The existence of the Common Travel Area has meant that the Republic has been required to follow changes in British immigration policy. This was notably the case in 1962 when Irish law was changed in response to the Commonwealth Immigrants Act 1962. The 1962 Act imposed immigration controls between the UK, UK colonies and independent Commonwealth countries while in the Republic the Aliens Order 1962 replaced Ireland's previous provision exempting all British subjects from immigration control,[7] with one exempting only those born in the UK. The scope of the Irish provisions were much more restrictive than the British legislation. They excluded a large number of people who were not born in the UK but whose right to reside in the UK was not restricted by the 1962 Act. After the BNA 1981, however, it was also less restrictive, in that it excluded from Irish immigration control any persons born in the UK who were not British citizens, for example because neither parent was settled there at the time of the birth. This discrepancy between Britain's definition of a British citizen with a right to abode in the UK and Ireland's definition was not resolved until 1999.[8] Thereafter under Irish law all British citizens – including those from the Isle of Man and Channel Islanders who are excluded from the territorial reach of the EU's Freedom of Movement provisions – became exempt from Irish immigration control and are therefore immune from deportation. With limited exceptions[9], they have never been treated as foreigners under Irish law. While British and Irish citizens enjoy the right to live in each other's countries under European Community law, the provisions which apply to them under the Common Travel Area are generally more far reaching than those which apply to other EEA nationals.

[1] See further Wikipedia, 'The Common Travel Area'; Bernard Ryan, 'The Common Travel Area between Britain and Ireland', (2001) 64 (6) Modern Law Review 855; JM Evans, 'Immigration Act 1971', The Modern Law Review (1972) 35 (5) 508.
[2] See Ryan, op cit. The agreement was referred to in a Dàil debate on 4 June 1925, albeit indirectly, (*Dáil Debates* volume 12 columns 317–318).
[3] By the Aliens Order 1946 (Ireland).
[4] Under Secretary of State for the Home Department, Geoffrey de Freitas, House of Commons Debates volume 478 columns 842–849 (28 July 1950).
[5] House of Commons Debates volume 446 columns 1158–1166 (28 January 1948), volume 463 column 543 (24 March 1948), and volume 478 columns 842–849 (28 July 1959). The existence of the 1952 agreement was conceded in an Irish parliamentary question on 3 June 1980 (*Dáil Debates* volume 321 column 1379).
[6] The Aliens Order 1953.
[7] The Aliens (Exemption) Order 1935 (Ireland).
[8] The Aliens (Exemption) Order 1999 (Ireland) which exempted all (and only) British citizens from immigration control.
[9] The only exception being that between 1962 and 1999 those British citizens born outside the UK were not exempt. See Evans, *History of British nationality law and the Republic of Ireland*.

5.3 The above paragraph indicates that the common travel area ('CTA') predates the development in Europe of free movement rights in the original Common Market and now in the EU. The Single European Act of 1987 envisaged within the EU an internal market 'without internal frontiers'. Although this is not yet fully effective, the adoption into Community law of the Schengen *acquis* by the Treaty of Amsterdam in 1997[1] has brought an EU without internal frontiers even closer, at least for those countries within the EU who have fully signed up. This does not include Ireland and the UK, whose governments have, so far, opted out of this part of the Schengen *acquis*. That is one reason for the continued importance of the common travel area. But it does not just embrace Ireland and the UK. The Channel Islands, Guernsey and Jersey, and the Isle of Man, referred to hereafter as the Islands, are involved as well. Since they are not fully integrated into the EC, the common travel area provides an important ongoing link with the UK, which preserves their special constitutional position, but at the same time operates on the basis of very close harmony between the immigration laws of mainland and Islands.

[1] See CHAPTER 6, 'The Schengen Agreements and abolition of internal borders' at **6.41** ff.

5.4 Until the Immigration Act 1971 (IA 1971), the common travel area was a purely administrative arrangement allowing free travel between Northern Ireland and the Republic of Ireland, between Britain and Ireland, and between these places and the Isle of Man and the Channel Islands. Since 1971 the common travel area has been given full statutory recognition, but this has also meant it has become hedged around by quite complicated rules, as we shall see.

5.5 The first principle of the common travel area is that local journeys within it are exempt from control, but journeys which start from or extend outside it are not. Thus section 1(3) of the IA 1971 provides that, subject to exceptions, arrivals in and departures from the UK on local journeys 'shall not be subject to control under this Act,[1] nor shall a person require leave to enter the UK on so arriving'. A local journey is one which begins and ends in the common travel area and is not made by a ship or aircraft which:

(i) arrives in the UK, but began its voyage from a place outside the common travel area or has called at such a place during its voyage; or

(ii) leaves the UK, but is due to end its voyage at a place outside the common travel area or to call at such a place in the course of its voyage.[2]

The common travel area consists of the UK, the Republic of Ireland, the Channel Islands and the Isle of Man.[3] The Immigration Rules state that a person who has been examined for the purpose of immigration control at the point at which he or she entered the area does not normally require leave to enter any other part of it.[4] However, there are exceptions, most, but not all of which deal with Ireland.[5] The rules also provide that passengers arriving in the UK or seeking to enter through the Channel Tunnel are to be refused leave, if there is reason to believe they are headed for another part of the common travel area where they would not be acceptable to the immigration authorities.[6] Statutory provision is made to change the boundaries of the common travel area if the immigration laws of the Islands get out of line with those of the UK, or for specified purposes in Ireland.[7]

---

[1] 'Control under this Act' refers to the control on entry envisaged by ss 3 and 4 of the IA 1971, by the Immigration (Leave to Enter and Remain) Order 2000, SI 2000/1161, by the Immigration (Leave to Enter) Order 2001, SI 2001/2590, and to the examination provisions in IA 1971, Sch 2, paras 2–7. We refer to it loosely in the text as passport or frontier control, which is to be contrasted with immigration control, to which all non-British citizens are subject irrespective of their right to cross a border without submitting to any passport control or obtaining leave to enter.

[2] IA 1971, s 11(4).

[3] IA 1971, ss 1(3), 11(4) and 33(1).

[4] HC 395, para 15.

[5] IA 1971, s 9(4), Sch 4, para 4 and Immigration (Control of Entry through the Republic of Ireland) Order 1972, SI 1972/1610, as amended, art 3(2).

[6] HC 395, para 320(4).

[7] IA 1971, s 9(5) and (6).

5.6 The IA 1971 clearly intended to retain the notion of a travel area which is free from frontier immigration control. On the other hand, the government did not want the common travel area (especially entry through Ireland) to become a loophole in an otherwise strict immigration control.[1] A compromise is therefore struck between a frontier-free area and the exceptions. The existence of the common travel area means that:

(i) all British and Irish citizens and EEA nationals are free to travel between Ireland, the UK and the Islands without any passport control. This does not mean that there is no immigration control. That still exists, in that Irish citizens and EEA nationals may still be subject to exclusion or to deportation on public policy grounds, and can then be refused entry. We deal with this at 5.8 below;

(ii) immigration controls imposed in the Islands by their immigration officials have effect in the UK and vice versa. Thus third country nationals who have settled status in any of the Islands are free to travel to the UK to take up employment or occupation and residence; there is no such reciprocal arrangement between the UK and the Republic of Ireland, and it is not clear whether third country nationals with settled status in the Republic are free from immigration control within the common travel area;

(iii)   people with limited leave to enter or remain in any of the Islands are free to travel to the UK and to remain there for the remainder of their leave, subject to the same conditions as were imposed by the immigration authorities there;

(iv)   the absence of frontier control is subject to a series of exceptions, which make it necessary to obtain leave, on local travel from both the Islands and Ireland, and there are further exceptions as between the UK and Ireland, including the automatic imposition of limited leave to enter and conditions prohibiting employment;

(v)   the exceptional requirement to obtain leave and the automatic imposition of leave and conditions are complicated and difficult for lay person and specialist to follow, but can have serious consequences. Those who fail to obtain leave become illegal entrants and can be removed.[2] Those who overstay the limited leave, of which they have had no notice,[3] become overstayers and liable to summary removal.[4] No doubt these restrictions stop loopholes, but they also lay serious traps for the unwary and innocent, who can find themselves arrested, held in custody, and removed from the UK.[5]

[1]   See *Qureshi v Harrington* [1970] 1 All ER 262, [1970] 1 WLR 138 (a decision under the Commonwealth Immigrants Act 1962).

[2]   See *R v Governor of Ashford Remand Centre, ex p Bouzagou* [1983] Imm AR 69, CA.

[3]   In the past notice of leave has normally been given by a stamp in the passport: see IA 1971, s 4(1) and Sch 2, para 6, but this is no longer necessarily the case: see CHAPTER 3 above.

[4]   Immigration and Asylum Act 1999, s 10. Prior to 2 October 2000, overstayers were subject to deportation under the IA 1971, s 3(5)(a) (before amendment) which applied to automatic restrictions imposed on travel from Ireland by virtue of s 9(3): see *Kaya* [1991] Imm AR 572.

[5]   *Bouzagou* above.

THE BRITISH IRISH VISA SCHEME

5.7 The Immigration (Control of Entry through Republic of Ireland) (Amendment) Order 2014[1] has been introduced in order to recognise specific types of valid Republic of Ireland visas, and subsequent endorsements conferring permission to land in the Republic, as enabling an Indian or Chinese citizen to travel on to the UK and to remain in the UK for the same duration as the Irish permission to land. This amendment provides the legal basis for the British-Irish Visa Scheme, a joint UK-Ireland initiative aimed at promoting tourism and growth in both states. The previous provisions in the 1972 Order concerning UK visas endorsed with the words 'short visa' are removed as such visas are no longer issued and are obsolete.

According to the explanatory note to the Order the British-Irish Visa Scheme will allow holders of specified Irish biometric visitor visas entry to the UK where they are travelling from the Republic of Ireland on a local journey and in possession of a valid visa and endorsement of leave to land in the Republic. Individuals will be able to remain in the UK until the expiry date of the permission to land in Ireland but are not able to take any occupation for reward or employment. The Scheme supports both the UK's growth agenda – in attracting visitors to combine a visit to Ireland with a visit to the UK – and the security agenda – by working with Ireland to align visa policy and processes greater certainty can be had on who is entering the CTA[2].

The Memorandum says:

'The British-Irish Visa Scheme will be introduced on a phased basis. The rollout of biometrics as part of the Irish visa regime will be gradual. Therefore it is not possible to introduce the Scheme globally from the outset. Chinese and Indian citizens, applying for visas in China and India respectively, will be included in the first phase. A phased approach also allows the infrastructure, including the processes and IT required, to be proved alongside managing the potential volumes. Subject to a joint evaluation with the Republic of Ireland the Scheme will be expanded to include further nationalities in 2015[3].'

The amendments to the Immigration (Control of Entry through Republic of Ireland) Order 1972 also remove obsolete provisions. Article 3(6) and (132) ensures that an automatic permission to enter and stay in the United Kingdom is not conferred on EEA nationals or those exercising EU rights. Article 3(4)(c) ensures that the powers in relation to illegal entrants contained in the 1971 Immigration Act, and other controls, will apply to those subject to EEA exclusion orders.

[1]   SI 2014/2475; entry in force 14 October 2014.
[2]   Explanatory Memorandum, para 7.3.
[3]   Ibid, para 7.5.

The general exceptions within the CTA

5.8 Section 9(4) of the IA 1971 sets out the general exceptions operating within the CTA. These apply to persons arriving in the UK from any other part of the common travel area. They affect deportees, persons banned from the UK for reasons of national security, and those who have been previously refused leave to enter. We deal with each in turn:

(i)   *Deportees*. Section 1(3) of the IA 1971 does not affect the operation of a deportation order.[1] This means that anyone who is subject to a deportation order in Ireland or the Islands is not free to enter the UK. Further provision is made in Schedule 4 for deportation orders made in the Islands to be enforceable by the UK authorities if the deportee comes to Britain.[2] The provision in section 9(4) also means that where an Irish citizen has been deported from the UK, he or she can be refused leave to enter. The exercise of this power must, however, be in accordance with the EC Public Policy Directive (see CHAPTER 6 below). Deportees may be covered by these general exceptions, but illegal entrants, overstayers and breachers of conditions attached to their stay are not. All of these categories are covered as regards the Islands by Schedule 4 to the IA 1971, but as regards Ireland, only illegal entrants are dealt with, as we shall see.[3] Overstayers coming from Ireland and those in breach of their conditions there are still covered by the section 1(3) arrangements, but are likely to be subject to the automatic imposition of a limited leave and conditions.[4]

(ii)   *Exclusion orders notified on arrival*. The existence of the common travel area does not prevent the Secretary of State from banning non-British citizens from the UK for reasons of national security.[5] But under section 9(4) notice of the exclusion order must be given on arrival in the UK and exclusion is limited to cases involving national security.

Where a person is not examined and given the exclusion notice at the time of his or her arrival, that person remains exempt from control under section 1(3) and cannot be removed if encountered in the UK after arrival,[6] unless he or she arrived from the Republic of Ireland when there were directions for the person's exclusion from the UK on public good grounds; in which case the person will be an illegal entrant.[7] Although this power is mainly targeted on Irish citizens, it prevents anyone else who is subject to such a ban from entering the UK through Ireland or the Islands.

(iii)   *Previous refusal of leave to enter the UK.* Where a person has been refused leave to enter the UK at any time in the past and has not subsequently been granted leave, leave to enter is required and may be refused.[8] A grant of subsequent leave need not necessarily be one given by UK immigration officials. For example, if someone has been given leave in one of the Islands, that counts as a leave in the UK, if it is still current.[9] Secondly, if someone has been given an advance leave under the Immigration (Leave to Enter and Remain) Order 2000,[10] that will also count as a subsequent leave and will override this exception to section 1(3) of the IA 1971. Thirdly, EEA nationals exercising their free movement rights do not require leave to enter, and these rights override the provisions in s 9(4)(b) requiring leave to enter, where the person has an outstanding past refusal.[11]

[1]   IA 1971, s 9(4).
[2]   See **5.15** below.
[3]   See **5.9** below.
[4]   See **5.10** below.
[5]   IA 1971, s 9(4).
[6]   See IDI (Apr 04), Ch 1, s 2, paras 2.4 and 2.6.
[7]   Under art 3(1)(b)(iv) of the Immigration (Control of Entry through the Republic of Ireland) Order 1972, SI 1972/1610, a person subject to such a direction, who has entered from the Republic of Ireland, requires leave to enter and will be an illegal entrant, if he or she fails to obtain such leave.
[8]   IA 1971, s 9(4)(b).
[9]   IA 1971, Sch 4, para 4. See **5.15** below.
[10]   SI 2000/1161, in force since 30 July 2000.
[11]   See **5.12** text and fn 1 below.

The Irish exceptions

Situations where leave required

5.9 Section 1(3) of the IA 1971 exempts from control people travelling within the common travel area. However, in addition to the circumstances set out in the previous paragraph, article 3 of the Immigration (Control of Entry Through the Republic of Ireland) Order 1972 makes further exceptions for certain people who enter the UK through the Republic of Ireland.[1] Persons in the following categories may not enter the UK, from the Republic of Ireland, without leave from an immigration officer:

(i)   *transit passengers.* Passengers (by ship or aircraft) from outside the common travel area who have merely stopped in transit in the Republic of Ireland *en route* to the UK, without being given leave to land there, if they catch a local flight or boat to the UK;[2]

299

(ii)   *no visa.* Visa nationals on a local journey from Ireland who have no valid visa for entry into the UK;[3]

(iii)   *illegal entrants to Ireland.* Those who arrive in the UK on a local journey, having entered the Republic unlawfully from a place outside the common travel area;[4]

(iv)   *illegal entrants to the UK.* Persons who entered the UK unlawfully who go to Ireland and then try to return to the UK on a local journey;[5]

(v)   *expired UK leave.* Under the original Order, persons whose limited leave expired whilst in the UK or Islands, did not require leave to enter on returning to the UK from the Republic. Now they do.[6] However, a person who re-entered the UK in these circumstances before 1 August 1979, and who has not left the UK or Islands since, or been given leave to enter or remain, should be given indefinite leave to remain.[7] An overstayer who re-entered after 1 August 1979 without leave is an illegal entrant. Amended article 3(1)(b)(iii) of the Order does not apply to someone who was exempt from UK immigration control and travelled to Ireland after the exemption came to an end,[8] or to cases in which persons whose leave expired whilst in the UK entered the Irish Republic after first going to a place outside the common travel area;[9]

(vi)   *public good exclusions.* As we have seen, any non-British citizen, including Irish citizens, can be barred from entry to the UK, if the Secretary of State directs that there are national security reasons for their exclusion, and this applies whether the person is travelling from Ireland or one of the Islands.[10] In the case of travel from Ireland the power is more extensive. The Secretary of State can bar entry by giving a direction that exclusion is conducive to the public good without any mention of the interests of national security.[11] Anyone who enters in defiance of such a direction is an illegal entrant and can be removed. However, the power can only be exercised against Irish and other EEA nationals in a manner consistent with the scope and procedural requirements of the public policy derogation under EC law (see CHAPTER 6).

Where a person who requires leave by virtue of section 9(4) of the IA 1971, or by article 3 of the 1972 Order, or a person in respect of whom a deportation order is in force, enters or seeks to enter the UK from the Republic of Ireland, the removal powers of the 1971 Act apply with modifications to take into account the land border between the UK and Ireland.[12] In *R v Javaherifard*[13] the Court of Appeal held that entry into the UK occurred at the point where someone crossed the border from the Republic into Northern Ireland and not at the point where they first present a passport. Section 11 of the IA 1971, which deals with entry into the UK has no application to entry by land, only to entries by boat and ship. Although the provision in section 11(2) in relation to the Common Travel Area and local journeys has the effect of making the Act generally neutral in relation to such journeys, it was necessary to exclude them from section 11(1) because someone arriving by ship or air from within the Common Travel Area could otherwise never disembark in law and thus could never enter or be an illegal entrant. Such a person could also move from UK port to UK port until he or she found one where there was no actual control and then enter after a local journey.

1   SI 1972/1610, as amended. The IDI on the common travel area has a flow chart which attempts to set out the position: see IDI Feb 04, Ch 1, s 2, Annex I. See also Annex G for further details.

2   Immigration (Control of Entry Through the Republic of Ireland) Order 1972, SI 1972/1610, as amended, art 3(1)(a). Under the Aliens (Visas) Order 2003, SI 708/2003, aliens arriving in Ireland from outside the common travel area will not be given leave to land, unless they have a valid transit visa, if they are nationals of Afghanistan, Albania, Bulgaria, Cuba, Democratic Republic of Congo, Ethiopia, Eritrea, Federal Republic of Yugoslavia (Serbia and Montenegro), Ghana, Iran, Iraq, Lebanon, Moldova, Nigeria, Romania, Somalia, Sri Lanka, Zimbabwe. See also IDI (Apr 04), Ch 1, Annex G, para 1.1.

3   SI 1972/1610, art 3(1)(b)(i).

4   SI 1972/1610, art 3(1)(b)(ii).

5   SI 1972/1610, art 3(1)(b)(iii).

6   The Immigration (Control of Entry through the Republic of Ireland) (Amendment) Order 1979, in effect 1 August 1979, amending art 3(1)(b)(iii).

7   IDI (Apr 04), Ch 1, Annex G, para 1.5.

8   SI 1972/1610, art 3(1)(b)(iii). *R v Secretary of State for the Home Department, ex p Wuan* [1989] Imm AR 501, QBD.

9   IDI (Apr 04), Ch 1, Annex G, para 1.5.

10   IA 1971, s 9(4)(a).

11   Immigration (Control of Entry through Republic of Ireland) Order 1972, SI 1972/1610, as amended, art 3(1)(b)(iv).

12   See the Immigration (Entry Otherwise than by Sea or Air) Order 2002, SI 2002/1832, art 2 and Schedule.

13   [2005] EWCA Crim 3231, [2006] Imm AR 185.

Automatic time limit and conditions prohibiting employment

5.10 Then there are those (entering the UK from the Republic of Ireland) who do not require leave to enter, but are liable, under article 4 of the 1972 Order, to the imposition of automatic time limits on their stay in the UK and conditions prohibiting their taking employment.[1] Section 9(3) of the IA 1971 provides for the restrictions to have the same effect as if the leave had been given under the Act. So, firstly, they must apply for their leave to be extended before their time limit runs out, if they wish to stay on. Secondly, a refusal to vary or extend the time limit attracts a right of appeal under section 82 of the Nationality Immigration and Asylum Act 2002 (NIAA 2002) if the result of the refusal means that the person has no leave to enter or remain, or there is a variation which has the same result.[2] The imposition of automatic leave and conditions by article 4 of the Order does not apply to persons who:

(i)   have the right of abode;[3]

(ii)   are British or Irish citizens or other EEA nationals;[4]

(iii)   have obtained an advance leave to enter the UK under the Immigration (Leave to Enter and Remain) Order 2000 or have a non-lapsing leave under that Order;[5] or

(iv)   have been excluded from the benefits of the common travel area for any of the reasons set out in **5.8** and **5.9** above.[6]

Automatic restrictions on length of stay and conditions apply to persons:

(a)   who come to the UK on a local journey from Ireland, 'after having . . . entered the Republic . . . on coming from a place outside the common travel area'.[7] They are subject to an automatic time limit on their stay (three months normally, but one month if they have a 'short-visit' visa), and a condition prohibiting them from engaging in any occupation for reward or any employment.[8] If they have a 'short-stay' visa and are over 16, they must also register with the police;[9]

(b) who come to the UK on a local journey, 'after having entered the Republic . . . after leaving the UK' while having a limited leave to be in the UK and this leave has since expired.[10] On their return to the UK from Ireland they become subject to an automatic limit on their stay of seven days[11] and, unless they are EC nationals, to a condition prohibiting them from engaging in any occupation for reward or any employment.[12] If they have a 'short-visit' visa and are over 16, they must also register with the police.[13]

[1] Under IA 1971, s 9(2) and Immigration (Control of Entry through the Republic of Ireland) Order 1972, SI 1972/1610, art 4(1). See IDI, Ch 1, s 2, Annex I for a flow chart illustrating the position.

[2] NIAA 2002, s 82(2)(d) and (e). There is no longer an appeal against the imposition of conditions, or against the grant of a shorter leave than that requested. The effect of the Immigration Act 2014 (when in force) will be that there will no longer be a right of appeal against the refusal to vary or extend the time limit – see CHAPTER 3.

[3] Immigration (Control of Entry through the Republic of Ireland) Order 1972, SI 1972/1610, art 4(1).

[4] According to the IDI (Apr 04), Ch 1, s 2, para 3.1, art 4 of the Order does not apply to EEA nationals. This must be correct, but is it consistent with the very strange wording of art 4(4)(b) and (c)?

[5] SI 2000/1161; Immigration (Control of Entry through the Republic of Ireland) Order 1972, SI 1972/1610, art 4(2), as amended by SI 2000/1776, which together mean that anyone with extant leave granted by the UK authorities is subject to the time limit granted by and conditions imposed by that leave.

[6] SI 1972/1610, art 4(2).

[7] IA 1971, s 9(2)(a); SI 1972/1610, art 4(4).

[8] SI 1972/1610, art 4(4), 4(5), as amended by SI 1980/1859, SI 1985/1854 and SI 1987/2092. art 4(4) contains a very outdated exemption from the employment prohibition for EC nationals other than those of Portugal or Spain, who at that time enjoyed the right of establishment, but not yet the rights of worker movement. There is also an exemption from the condition prohibiting engagement in an occupation, but it is confined to EC nationals and does not extend to all EEA nationals: SI 1972/1610, art 4(4)(b) and (c). These deficiencies do not particularly matter, because the provisions of EC law cover the situation quite adequately: see CHAPTER 6 below.

[9] SI 1972/1610, art 4(6).

[10] IA 1971, s 9(2)(b); SI 1972/1610, art 4(1)(b).

[11] SI 1972/1610, art 4(7).

[12] SI 1972/1610, art 4(4)(b) and (c), as amended: see fn 3 above.

[13] SI 1972/1610, art 4(6).

5.11 There are a number of difficulties and objections to these provisions. First, the words used in section 9(2)(a) of the 1971 Act and article 4 of the 1972 Order are ambiguous. Do the words: 'after having entered the Republic . . . on coming from outside the common travel area' mean 'shortly after'; immediately after'; 'any time after'; or 'a reasonable time after'? On the face of it there would appear to be no limit on the length of time between arrival in Ireland and departure for the UK. So someone who has been settled in Ireland for many years and comes to the UK and stays here for over three months could find herself in serious trouble. Arguably, there is a world of difference between a person who arrives in Dublin, works there for five years and then travels to the UK and someone who only stays there for three days, having come there as part of a package tour. The purpose of the restrictions is to close loopholes, not to set traps for long-time residents of the Republic. The real problem is that in imposing these restrictions, the UK legislators have had no regard for conditions of stay granted by the Irish authorities. There is no reciprocation of leave, as in the case of the UK and the Islands.[1] A person with a limited leave to land in the Republic will, therefore, be subject to the automatic imposition of three months' leave and conditions on arrival in the UK,[2] irrespective of the length of his or her leave in Ireland. But what of the traveller who has been given settlement in the Republic, and who has an immigration status which does not depend on which route he or she came to Ireland, but on the possession or acquisition of a status or on the fulfilment of certain conditions while in the Republic? On the face of the 1971 Act and the 1972 Order, it appears that they are in the same position vis-à-vis UK immigration control as the traveller coming from Ireland with limited leave. However, it is certainly arguable that both section 9(2) of the 1971 Act and article 4(1) of the 1972 Order are referring to local journeys which cannot be regarded as free from immigration control, because they have characteristics which give them a different quality, either because they started outside the common travel and are not, therefore, strictly speaking, local journeys or trips, or because the person's immigration status within the common travel area has become unregularised. The words 'after having . . . entered Ireland' in section 9(2)(a) may thus be read in the context of a longer journey, which started outside the Republic, but which is reasonably close in time to the arrival in the UK. Similarly, the words 'after having . . . left the United Kingdom . . . ' in section 9(2)(b) are to be read as referring to a period of time during which the traveller has an unregularised immigration status in any part of the common travel area. This is why in previous editions of this work, we have argued that 'third country nationals who have settled status in any part of the common travel area (including the Republic) are free to travel to any other part and to take up employment or occupation and residence there'. The question, however, is not free from doubt.

[1]   Under IA 1971, Sch 4. See **5.16** below.
[2]   Under the Immigration (Leave to Enter and Remain) Order 2000, SI 2000/1161, art 4(4).

Effect of EC law on travel from Ireland

5.12 The control on entry provisions of the common travel area outlined above have to be read in conjunction with free movement and residence rights under EC law. It is not just Irish citizens who are affected, but all EEA nationals and members of their families. Where EC law is engaged there is a right to enter without any need for leave under UK domestic law.[1] This right prevails over the common travel area provisions covering travel from Ireland to the UK where there is a conflict. Similarly, where there are conditions imposed prohibiting employment or occupation for gain, they must yield to the requirements of EC law, not in the terms set out in the Control of Entry Order,[2] but on the terms of current EC law.

[1]   *R v Pieck* [1981] QB 571, ECJ. The European Communities Act 1972, s 2, Immigration Act 1988, s 7(1) and Immigration (European Economic Area) Regulations 2006, SI 2006/1003 give effect in domestic UK law to EC law. Regulations 13–15 of the EEA Regulations 2006 make it clear that the right to remain in the UK derives directly from EC law.

The right to enter under EC law is, of course, subject to public policy considerations: see *Shingara v Secretary of State for the Home Department* [1999] Imm AR 257 and **6.191** ff below.

[2]   Immigration (Control of Entry through the Republic of Ireland) Order 1972, SI 1972/1610, art 4(1). See **5.10** text and fns 4 and 7 above.

5.13 *Patmalniece v Secretary of State for Work and Pensions*[1] highlights the importance of the common travel area under EU law in relation to benefits which are dependent upon the claimant having a right to reside in the UK or elsewhere in the Common Travel Area. Special provision is made for Irish citizens under the Protocol on the Common Travel Area. Having first been annexed to the Treaty of Amsterdam, it is now annexed to the post Lisbon Treaties as Protocol (No 20)[1]. It states that the United Kingdom and Ireland 'may continue to make arrangements between themselves relating to the movement of persons between their territories'. In *Patmalniece* the conditions of entitlement to state pension credit prescribed by regulation 2 of the State Pension Credit Regulations 2002, SI 2002/1792, depended on whether the person concerned had a right to reside in the United Kingdom or elsewhere in the Common Travel Area. The issue in the case was whether these conditions were compatible with Article 3(1) of Council Regulation (EC) No 1408/71 and justifiable, even though they were indirectly discriminatory by reason of nationality. The appellant contended that the refusal of state pension credit to a Latvian because she did not have a right to reside in the United Kingdom was prohibited by Article 3(1) of EC Regulation 1408/71 and was discriminatory and unlawful under EU law. One of the appellant's arguments was that the justification for restricting entitlement to those economically or socially integrated within the United Kingdom was undermined by the special treatment of Irish nationals. Counsel argued that it was not open to the UK to give Irish nationals a free pass to state pension credit simply by showing their passports, while starving out nationals of the other Member States. The Supreme Court rejected this argument, holding that the different treatment afforded to Irish nationals is protected by the Protocol on the Common Travel Area, since there is a sufficient connection between the social security arrangements on the part of the UK and Ireland and the aim of promoting free movement between the two countries, for the arrangements in regulation 2 of the 2002 Regulations to attract the protection of Article 2 of the Protocol.

[1]   [2011] UKSC 11, [2011] 3 All ER 1, [2011] 1 WLR 783.
[1]   OJ C 83/293 30.3.2010

Immigration laws in the Islands

5.14 The Channel Islands and the Isle of Man have the same nationality laws as the UK, but have nominally separate immigration laws. In practice the Immigration Acts of 1971 and 1988 extend to the Islands, with modifications, and although the Islands have their own immigration rules (called Directions in Jersey), they closely follow the UK ones.[1] Following the enactment of the Immigration and Asylum Act 1999, further changes were not made to update the Islands' laws and keep them in step until 2003.[2] This is done in the following way:

(i)   Orders in Council extend the provisions of the UK Acts with any necessary changes to each of the Islands. In the case of Guernsey, the Order is the only effective immigration law, but in the case of Jersey the 1937 Loi sur les Etrangers still operates in addition to the extended Immigration Act, and in the Isle of Man employment is controlled by the Control of Employment Act 1975, as amended;

(ii)   machinery is laid down in the Orders and in Schedule 4 to the IA 1971 for decisions taken in the Islands to apply in the UK and vice versa.

The fate of the Isle of Man's first asylum seeker could lie in the hands of Lieutenant Governor. At the moment, if an asylum seeker arrives in the Island via the common travel area, the rule is they are shipped back to the UK or Ireland. It is more complicated in the case of those who may arrive from outside the CTA. As the Island is not a state for the purposes of asylum and has no asylum legislation, it cannot provide asylum in its own right.

[1]   IDI (Jul 04), Ch 1, s 2, Annex H.
[2]   Immigration and Asylum Act 1999 (Jersey) Order 2003, SI 2003/1252, which came into force on 5 June 2003; Immigration and Asylum Act 1999 (Guernsey) Order 2003 SI 2003/2900, which came into force on 11 December 2003. No Order has been made in relation to the Isle of Man and no Orders have been made applying any of the provisions of the NIAA 2002. The UK Borders Act 2007, s 60(4) makes provision for any provision of the Act to be applied by Order in Council to the Channel Islands and the Isle of Man.

5.15 Schedule 4 to the 1971 Act, as amended by the Immigration and Asylum Act 1999, provides inter alia:

(a)   any leave to enter or remain and time limit or conditions attached to it by the immigration authorities in the Isle of Man, Jersey or Guernsey will still apply to a person who subsequently arrives in the UK from one of the islands before the expiry of any time limit;[1]

(b)   in the case of limited leave, application can then be made to the Home Office for further extensions or the revocation of conditions as if the leave and conditions had originated under UK immigration law. If an extension of leave is refused, the normal rights of appeal under UK law apply;[2]

(c)   a deportation order or its equivalent made in one of the Islands operates in the UK, where it has the same effect as a deportation order made in the UK, except where the person is a British citizen, EEA national, member of the family of an EEA national, or the member of the family of a British citizen who is neither a British citizen or EEA national.[3] Except in the case of British citizens (who cannot be deported from the UK),[4] the Secretary of State can decide to enforce an Island deportation against one of these people,[5] but must bear in mind the public order provisions of EC law. These categories of Island deportees can appeal against an adverse decision.[6] From October 2000 the Secretary of State can no longer revoke an Island deportation order which is operating in the UK.[7] It is not unlawful for a deportee to enter the UK in transit to a place outside the UK;[8]

(d)   there are integrated removal powers after a refusal of leave. Anyone refused leave to enter one of the Islands is treated as if they had been refused leave to enter the UK.[9] The Island authorities can arrange for the UK authorities to remove that person;

(e)   there are also integrated removal powers for illegal entrants. Paragraph 4 provides that notwithstanding the principle of travel without leave 'it shall not be lawful for a person who is not a British citizen to enter the UK from any of the Islands where his presence was unlawful under the immigration laws of the Island, unless he is given leave to enter'. So, if someone with leave to enter the UK goes to one of the Islands, and his or her leave then expires, that person's return to the UK, without getting further leave, makes that person an illegal entrant. The same applies to persons who overstay leave given to them in one of the Islands and then travel to the UK.[10]

Immigration officers in the Islands act in liaison with the Immigration Service in the UK.[11]

1   IA 1971, Sch 4, para 1(1) and (2); *Teixeira v Secretary of State for the Home Department* [1989] Imm AR 432.
2   IA 1971, Sch 4, para 1(3).
3   IA 1971, Sch 4, para 3(1) and (2), as amended.
4   IA 1971, Sch 5, para 3(5) and (6).
5   IA 1971, Sch 4, para 3(4), as amended.
6   IA 1971, Sch 4, para 3(7), as amended. The paragraph extends appeal rights under Immigration and Asylum Act 1999, s 80, which was however repealed by Nationality, Immigration and Asylum Act 2002, ss 114, 161, Sch 9, as from 1 April 2003 (SI 2003/754); the equivalent right of appeal is now NIAA 2002, s 82.
7   IA 1971, Sch 4, para 3(3), as amended.
8   IA 1971, Sch 4, para 3(5), as amended.
9   IA 1971, Sch 4, para 1(1).
10 IA 1971, Sch 4, para 4; IDI, Ch 1, s 2, Annex G, para 2.
11 IDI, Ch 1, s 2, Annex H.

5.16 In the Islands the same integration of their laws with those of the UK and other Islands is achieved by the provisions in the various Orders in Council which extend and adapt Schedule 4 to the particular Island. So leave given in the UK continues to operate when someone travels to one of the Islands; UK deportation orders have effect there; and the island authorities can deal with UK or other Island overstayers and illegal entrants.

5.17 This integration nevertheless leaves some areas of autonomy to each of the Islands. Though the content of each Island's immigration law is almost identical to the mainland Immigration Acts of 1971 and 1988, each administers its own controls and therefore retains a large measure of discretion over whom to admit or refuse. This is particularly important in the area of employment, where each Island retains full control over the granting of work permits and is therefore able to fit immigration control into any existing employment restrictions. Apart from the retention of administrative control over immigration, perhaps the most important difference between the laws operating in the Islands and in mainland UK is the continuing absence of any appeal machinery in the Channel Islands. Only the Order in Council for the Isle of Man extends the rights of appeal set out in Part II of the IA 1971. We look at this in the next paragraph.

Isle of Man

5.18 The provisions of the UK Immigration Acts are extended here by the Immigration (Isle of Man) Order 2008.[1] The appointment of immigration officers and the administration of control is under the Lieutenant-Governor. Changes in the Immigration Rules must be laid by Tynwald. Under the 2008 Order, the rights of appeal operating under Part V of the NIAA 2002 are applied with suitable modifications to the Isle of Man, the High Bailiff and Deputy High Bailiff acting as adjudicators.[2]

[1]   SI 2008/680.
[2]   SI 2008/680, art 16(2)(c).

5.19 The Immigration (Isle of Man) (Amendment) Order 2011[1] which came into force on 29 June 2011 makes extensive amendments to the Immigration (Isle of Man) Order 2008, SI 2008/680. Apart from drafting corrections, its effect is to extend to the Isle of Man sections 31, 32, 34, 36, 37 and 39 (disclosure of information) of the Immigration, Asylum and Nationality Act 2006. This includes a duty on ships and aircraft arriving in the Isle to provide passenger information as specified in the extended legislation and sets out provisions relating to shared information among law enforcement agencies and a power by the Governor and the Treasury to issue jointly one or more codes of practice. Then there are powers to make amendments consequential on the Civil Partnership Act 2011 (an Act of Tynwald), the Asylum and Immigration (Treatment of Claimants, etc) Act 2004 (Remedial) Order 2011, SI 2011/1158. The remedial order abolished the Certificate of Approval Scheme under Section 19 of the Asylum and Immigration (Treatment of Claimants, etc) Act 2004,[2] by which persons subject to immigration control, who did not have an entry clearance granted for the purpose of marriage, were required to obtain the permission of the Secretary of State to marry in the United Kingdom. The new Isle of Man Order also provides for the creation of new Departments of the Isle of Man Government.

[1]   SI 2011/1408, made in pursuance of the powers conferred by section 36 of the Immigration Act 1971(a), section 13(5) of the Asylum and Immigration Act 1996(b), section 170(7) of the Immigration and Asylum Act 1999(c), section 163(4) of the Nationality, Immigration and Asylum Act 2002(d), section 49(3) of the Asylum and Immigration (Treatment of Claimants, etc) Act 2004(e) and section 63(3) of the Immigration, Asylum and Nationality Act 2006.
[2]   The scheme had been declared under section 4 of the Human Rights Act 1998 to be incompatible with a Convention right , following the decision in the High Court in *R (on the application of Baiai) v Secretary of State for the Home Department* [2006] EWHC 823 (Admin). This decision was later confirmed in the House of Lords [2008] UKHL 53, [2008] 3 All ER 1094.

5.20 Apart from immigration controls applying to non-British citizens under the extended IA 1971, there is also strict control over the employment in the Isle of Man of anyone who is not an 'Isle of Man worker' as defined by the Control of Employment Act 1975, as amended in 1983. This status is acquired by birth or long residence in the Isle, or descent from or marriage to an Islander. Subject to exceptions, anyone who is not an 'Isle of Man worker' needs a work permit from the Isle of Man Board of Social Security. EC law rights of free movement are excluded.[1]

[1] See *Department of Health and Social Security v Barr and Montrose Holdings Ltd* [1991] 3 CMLR 325, ECJ, for an examination of these provisions applying to a British citizen seeking employment in the Isle of Man.

5.21 In the Isle of Man, entry from the Republic of Ireland is subject to similar restraints to those operating under UK law. The same categories of person who require leave to enter the UK from Ireland require leave to enter the Isle of Man from there.[1] Secondly, an automatic time limit and condition prohibiting employment is imposed on non-British or Irish citizens arriving in the Isle of Man from Ireland, who entered the Republic from a place outside the common travel area; or who left the Isle of Man while having a limited leave to be there and this leave has since expired.

[1] SI 2008/680, art 7; see **5.9** above.

Guernsey

5.22 The UK Immigration Acts are extended here by the Immigration (Guernsey) Order 1993,[1] the Asylum and Immigration Act 1996 (Guernsey) Order 1998,[2] and the Immigration and Asylum Act 1999 (Guernsey) Order 2003, which came into force on 11 December 2003.[3] Control under these Orders is exercised by immigration officers, who have power to give or refuse leave to enter, the Lieutenant-Governor, who has power to vary the length of any leave, and the Board of Administration, which deals with restrictions and prohibitions on employment and registration with the police as well as making the Immigration Rules. These have to be laid before the States of Guernsey. The power to make subordinate Orders under the extended Act is divided between the States and the Lieutenant-Governor. The 1998 Order gave the 1951 Refugee Convention statutory force in Guernsey for the first time.

[1] SI 1993/1796.
[2] SI 1998/1264.
[3] SI 2003/2900. This extends to Guernsey provisions of the IAA 1999 such as the s 3A and 3B insertions into the IA 1971, relating to new forms in which leave can be granted, provisions for administrative removal of overstayers, extended criminal offences, changes to carrier sanctions, greater powers to officials to enter and search premises, to take fingerprints and to detain.

5.23 The Immigration (Guernsey) Order 2011[1] which was made on 12 October 2011 and comes into force in accordance with article 1, which provides that it shall come into force seven days after the day on which it is registered by the Royal Court of Guernsey, extends to Guernsey, with exceptions and modifications, sections 31, 32, 34 and 39 (disclosure of information) of the Immigration, Asylum and Nationality Act 2006 and section 166 of the Immigration and Asylum Act 1999. It also further modifies section 18 of the Immigration and Asylum Act 1999 which was previously extended to Guernsey with modifications by the Immigration and Asylum Act (Guernsey) Order

2003, SI 2003/2900.

1   SI 2011/2444, made in pursuance of the powers conferred by section 63(3) of the Immigration, Asylum and Nationality Act 2006 and section 170(7) of the Immigration and Asylum Act 1999.

5.24 Special provision is made for entry into Guernsey from the Republic of Ireland. The restraints are almost identical to those operating under UK law. Leave to enter Guernsey from Ireland is required for the same category of persons as require leave to enter the UK from there,[1] and similar restrictions are placed on persons arriving in Guernsey from Ireland (1) who entered Ireland from a place outside the common travel area or (2) who left Guernsey having a limited leave to be there and this leave has since expired.

1   SI 1993/1796, art 3, Sch 1; see 5.9 above.

Jersey

5.25 The UK Immigration Acts are extended to the Bailiwick of Jersey by the Immigration (Jersey) Order 1993,[1] the Asylum and Immigration 1996 (Jersey) Order 1998,[2] and the Immigration and the Immigration and Asylum Act 1999 (Jersey) Order 2003.[3] Asylum control is exercised by immigration officers, who have power to give and refuse leave to enter, and by the Lieutenant Governor, who is responsible for after entry control and for making the immigration rules, which are called 'Directions' in Jersey. The Orders are not the Island's only legislation governing the admission and control of non-British citizens. In addition there is the 1937 Loi sur les Etrangers. The administration of control is divided between the States of Jersey Defence Committee, which deals with the regulation of employment and registration with the police, and the Lieutenant-Governor who has overall direction and authority.

1   SI 1993/1797.
2   SI 1998/1070. This gives statutory force to the 1951 Refugee Convention in Jersey for the first time.
3   SI 2003/1252. This extends to Jersey provisions of the IAA 1999 such as the s 3A and 3B insertions into the IA 1971, relating to new forms in which leave can be granted, provisions for administrative removal of overstayers, extended criminal offences, changes to carrier sanctions, greater powers to officials to enter and search premises, to take fingerprints and to detain.

5.26 The extended UK Acts apply to all non-British citizens, alien and Commonwealth, but the 1937 Loi only applies to aliens. Under it no aliens can take jobs in the Island without a work permit, whatever their status on the mainland.[1] They may need a guarantor as a condition of getting a permit[2] and if, within a year of arrival, they become chargeable to the public of the Island they may be removed,[3] with the guarantor, no doubt, having to foot the bill for removal. A register of aliens is kept and it is the duty of aliens over the age of 15 who reside in the Island for over three months to register.[4] In addition to the deportation powers given under the extended Immigration Act, the 1937 Loi expressly retains the powers of 'banishment and of repatriation possessed by the Royal Court of Jersey'.[5] The same provision is made for entry into Jersey from the Republic of Ireland, as applies in the case of Guernsey and the Isle of

Man: see **5.21** and **5.24** above.[6]

1   1937 Loi sur les Etrangers, art 4.
2   1937 Loi sur les Etrangers, art 5.
3   1937 Loi sur les Etrangers, art 8.
4   1937 Loi sur les Etrangers, arts 12(1) and 15.
5   1937 Loi sur les Etrangers, art 24.
6   SI 1993/1797, art 3, Sch 1.

5.27 The Immigration (Jersey) Order 2012[1], which came into force on 10 August 2012, extends to Jersey, with exceptions and modifications, sections 31, 32, 34 and 39 (disclosure of information) of the Immigration, Asylum and Nationality Act 2006. It also modifies section 18 of the Immigration and Asylum Act 1999. The Immigration and Asylum (Jersey) Order 2012[2], which came into force on 3 November 2012, makes minor amendments to Immigration (Jersey) Order 1993, the Asylum and Immigration Act 1996 (Jersey) Order 1998 and Immigration and Asylum Act 1999 (Jersey) 2003 to include reference, where it is said spouse, to spouse or civil partner.

1   SI 2012/1763, made in pursuance of the powers conferred by section 63(3) of the Immigration, Asylum and Nationality Act 2006 and section 170(7) of the Immigration and Asylum Act 1999.
2   SI 2012/2593, made in pursuance of the powers conferred by section 36 of the Immigration Act 1971, section 13(5) of the Asylum and Immigration Act 1996 and section 107(7) of the Immigration and Asylum Act 1999.

The Islands and the EC

5.28 The Channel Islands and the Isle of Man enjoy a special relationship with the EC, as opposed to full membership.[1] But the extent of it is unclear. The Islands are within the definition of the UK for the purpose of British nationality law,[2] and so connection to the Islands as opposed to mainland UK makes not the slightest bit of difference to the acquisition or possession of full British citizenship. Furthermore, Islanders are included in the declaration by the UK government on the meaning of a British national for the purposes of the European Treaties. On the other hand, when Britain joined the Common Market, Channel Islanders and Manxmen were expressly excluded from the free movement provisions of the EEC Treaty by Protocol 3 of the Treaty of Accession of the UK to the Common Market (as it was then known).[3] Under Article 6 of the Protocol, the following definition is given of a Channel Islander and a Manxman:

> 'In this Protocol, Channel Islander or Manxman shall mean any citizen of the United Kingdom and Colonies[4] who holds that citizenship by virtue of the fact that he, a parent or grandparent was born, adopted, naturalised or registered in the island in question; but such a person shall not for this purpose be regarded as a Channel Islander or Manxman if he, a parent or a grandparent was born, adopted, naturalised or registered in the United Kingdom. Nor shall he be so regarded if he has at any time been ordinarily resident in the UK for five years.'

On the basis of this definition, Islanders, although EU citizens, enjoy no free movement rights, unless they have been ordinarily resident in the UK at any time for a period of five years. In practice this provision is either a dead letter or virtually unenforceable. A passport shows place of birth, but does not show places of residence during a person's lifetime, and says nothing about the place of birth of parents or grandparents. The real effect of the Protocol is that it prevents free movement rights into the Islands and thus protects the residence and employment restrictions operating there. This is, we think, the clear effect of Article 3 to the Protocol read with Article 4, as interpreted by the European Court of Justice. Article 4 requires the Islands to apply 'the same treatment to all natural and legal persons of the Community'. This means that they must treat the nationals of other Member States in the same way as they treat British nationals, who have visiting rights by virtue of the common travel area but are subject to restrictions on residence and employment. These restrictions will thus also apply to those from the EEA. The principle of non-discrimination could not, therefore, give employment rights to EEA nationals in the Isle of Man.[5]

[1] Article 227(5) of EC Treaty (now, after amendment, art 299(6)(c)) and Protocol No 3 to Treaty of Accession.
[2] British Nationality Act 1981, s 50(1). They were also part of the UK for the purpose of the 1948 Act: British Nationality Act 1948, s 3(1).
[3] Article 2 of Protocol No 3 to Treaty of Accession. See further CHAPTER 6 below.
[4] For the meaning of 'citizen of the UK and Colonies' see now British Nationality Act 1981, s 51(3)(a), which provides that after 1 January 1983 it means a British citizen, a British Dependent (now Overseas) Territories citizen or a British Overseas citizen.
[5] *Department of Health and Social Security v Barr and Montrose Holdings Ltd* [1991] 3 CMLR 325, ECJ, where the court warned that the exclusion could not be permitted to operate in a discriminatory manner as between those excluded from the right.

5.29 However, in the case of deportation and recommendations for deportation the position is different. In *Camacho A-G of Jersey*[1] the Jersey Court of Appeal dealt with the question of whether an EU national who had been sentenced to six and a half years after conviction of a long series of offences, including the supply of heroin, should be recommended for deportation under the Immigration Act 1971, s 3(6) as applied to Jersey by the Immigration Jersey Order 1993.[2] The Court held that the position in Jersey should be distinguished from that in the UK, because the limitations on deportation under the public policy provisions in Directive 221/64 and now the Citizens' Directive[3] did not apply to Jersey.[4]

The Court also departed from the guidance given in *R v Carmona*[5] that a sentencing court need not consider the ECHR rights of an offender whose offence justifies a recommendation for deportation. The Jersey Court thought it was significant that in Jersey there was no appeal against the actual decision to deport, as in the UK but also took the view that a recommendation which did not take account of the Convention right would lack both utility and realism. The position is the same in Guernsey.[6]

[1] [2007] JCA 145.
[2] SI 1993/1797.
[3] Directive 2004/38/EC.
[4] *Pereira Roque v Lieutenant Governor* [1998] JLR 246, ECJ, followed.
[5] [2006] EWCA Crim 508 at para 22.
[6] *Odette and Odette v Law Officers*, CA (Criminal Appeals 361 and 362 – 28 March 2007), cited in *Camacho*, where the Jersey Court agreed with the outcome, but not necessarily all the reasons: [2007] JCA 145 at para 49.

Entering UK en route to another part of common travel area

5.30 Where passengers arrive in the UK intending to travel on to the Republic of Ireland or one of the Islands, special rules apply. Guidance is contained in the current practice, given in the IDI.

(i)   The Republic of Ireland:

Visas. Where a person needs a visa to enter the Republic, and is not in possession of one, the immigration officer should contact the Department of Justice, Dublin, to establish whether or not the person will be acceptable to the immigration authorities there.[1] If not, leave to enter should be refused under paragraph 320(4) of HC 395.[2]

Visitors, intending to travel to the Republic, who appear acceptable there and who would normally qualify for leave as a visitor if they were intending to remain in the UK for the whole of their stay, may be given leave to enter as a visitor for six months.[3] Those who do not qualify for a full six months' leave, but a refusal is not appropriate, should be granted leave to enter for one month.[4]

Persons who qualify for indefinite leave to enter the UK, who intend to travel to the Republic, should be given such leave.[5]

Persons intending employment in the Republic of Ireland, who are seeking entry to the UK en route to the Republic should be refused leave to enter unless they are in possession of an Irish labour permit or official confirmation that the permit has been or will be granted. Holders of Irish labour permits or other official documentation should be given leave to enter for one month.[6]

Other persons, who are intending to travel to the Republic of Ireland, for example, as a student or a seaman joining a ship in the Republic, and including those resident in the Republic, should be given leave to enter for no more than one month.[7]

(ii)   The Channel Islands and the Isle of Man:

Visas. Unless otherwise exempted from the requirement to produce a visa, visa nationals seeking entry in transit to any of the Islands, who are not in possession of the appropriate visa will normally be refused leave to enter.[8]

Work permit holders, in possession of a permit to take employment in Jersey or Guernsey or the Isle of Man, should be given leave to enter for the validity of the permit if they are non-visa nationals. A copy of the landing card will be forwarded to the Island authorities.[9]

Persons with indefinite leave to enter or remain in any of the Islands should be dealt with under the returning resident provisions of the UK Immigration Rules (HC 395, paras 18 and 19). They should be given indefinite leave to enter if they qualify for admission.[10]

Other returning residents. Persons who have extant leave to enter or remain in the Islands may be given leave to enter for the remaining period, provided that they still qualify for entry.[11]

Other categories. A person travelling to any of the Islands in any other category may be given leave to enter as if he or she were seeking entry to the UK only. Doubtful cases should be referred to the appropriate Island Immigration Department.[12]

1   IDI (Jul 04), Ch 1, Annex H, para 2.1.

² Paragraph 320(4) of the Rules should only be used as a reason for refusal of leave to enter in cases where a passenger seeks entry in transit to another part of the common travel area and there is reason to believe that he is not acceptable there. Before such a passenger is refused entry for that reason the appropriate authority in the Islands or the Republic of Ireland should be contacted: IDI, as above, para 4.

³ IDI, Ch 1, Annex H, para 2.2.

⁴ IDI, Ch 1, Annex H, para 2.2.

⁵ IDI, Ch 1, Annex H, para 2.2.

⁶ IDI, Ch 1, Annex H, para 2.3. Irish work permits are issued by the Minister of Labour, Dublin.

⁷ IDI, Ch 1, Annex H, para 2.4.

⁸ IDI, Ch 1, Annex H, paras 3.1 and 4.1.

⁹ IDI, Ch 1, Annex H, para 3.2. The Isle of Man Department of Trade and Industry issues two types of work permit: (i) those issued under the IA 1971, as extended to the Isle of Man, which are similar in appearance to the work permits issued by Work Permits (UK); and (ii) permits under the Isle of Man Control of Employment Act 1975, which are issued to persons who are not members of the Isle of Man labour force but who are permitted to work in the Isle of Man. A full text of the Act can be found at www.gov.im/media/350949/controlofemploymentact 1975asa_1_.pdf. Persons holding such documents are likely to be British citizens or persons with indefinite leave in the UK. These permits are not relevant to the Immigration Act and are not 'work permits' as defined in section 33(1) of the IA 1971. A person seeking leave to enter or remain in the UK, presenting one of these permits, does not qualify under para 128 of HC 395: see IDI, Ch 5, Annex A, para 11.2.

¹⁰ IDI (Jul 04), Ch 1, Annex H, para 3.3.

¹¹ IDI, Ch 1, Annex H, para 3.4.

¹² IDI, Ch 1, Annex H, para 3.5.

5.31 Leave to enter the UK should not be refused on general grounds, according to the IDI, unless the immigration officer has reason to believe that any passenger arriving in the UK en route to another part of the common travel area would not be acceptable there.¹ Before any refusal, the immigration officer is expected to contact the appropriate immigration authority in the Republic of Ireland or the Islands. Leave may also be refused if the immigration officer believes that the passenger's real intentions are to use his or her documentation to remain in the UK.²

¹ IDI (Jul 04), Ch 1, s 2, Annex H, para 4.

² IDI Ch 1, s 2, Annex H, para 4.

Irish citizens and terrorism laws

5.32 The existence of the common travel area does not mean that Irish citizens are totally exempt from UK immigration control. Citizens of the Republic, unless they also have British citizenship, are subject to immigration control. Though they can normally come to the UK without needing leave to enter, they may, as we have seen, be refused entry as security risks; they may be deported, and cannot then return without leave or until the deportation order is revoked; they may also be refused admission to the UK on EC public policy grounds.¹ Before the peace process in Northern Ireland these were important powers, but could only be used against Irish citizens and did not deal with movement and travel between Northern Ireland and mainland UK. This was dealt with through extensive powers of exclusion or banishment, in order to prevent acts of terrorism, contained in the Prevention of Terrorism (Temporary Provisions) Act 1989. Under this Act the Secretary of State for the Home Department could make an exclusion order against anyone he or she was satisfied was involved in terrorism, including British citizens, who could be restricted to living either in Northern Ireland or in Great Britain (England, Scotland or Wales).[2] The Act also contained draconian powers of arrest and detention, which gave rise to considerable case law.[3]

1   Council Directive (EEC) 64/221. See CHAPTER 6 below.
2   Prevention of Terrorism (Temporary Provisions) Act 1989, ss 5(1), 6(1), 7(1).
3   Prevention of Terrorism (Temporary Provisions) Act 1989, s 14. See the Northern Ireland High Court in *Hanna v Chief Constable of the Royal Ulster Constabulary* [1986] 13 NIJB 71 (Carswell J); *Brogan v United Kingdom* (1988) 11 EHRR 117, where the ECtHR held that four people who had been arrested and detained for periods of at least four days and six hours under the Prevention of Terrorism Act 1984 had been detained in violation of art 5(3) and (5) of the ECHR; *Brannigan and McBride v United Kingdom* (1993) 17 EHRR 539, ECtHR, where the ECtHR upheld the UK government's later derogation from its Convention obligations. As regards the validity of exclusion orders under EC law, see the references in *R v Secretary of State for the Home Department, ex p Gallagher* [1996] 1 CMLR 557, ECJ; and *R v Secretary of State for the Home Department, ex p Adams* [1995] All ER (EC) 177, DC, a reference subsequently withdrawn by CA after revocation of the exclusion order.

5.33 The peace process in Northern Ireland has made the exclusion powers in the 1989 Act redundant and the whole Act has in fact been repealed by the Terrorism Act 2000.[1] Although various special powers are still retained for Northern Ireland, the Secretary of State can no longer make exclusion orders banning suspected terrorists from travel between Northern Ireland, Great Britain and the Republic. The Terrorism Act 2000[2] re-enacts provisions similar to those in the 1989 Act dealing with port and border controls on travel to and from Northern Ireland, using police, immigration and customs officers,[3] who have extensive powers of examination and search of vehicles, aircraft and ships in order to identify people concerned in the commission, preparation or instigation of acts of terrorism.[4] The Anti-Terrorism Crime and Security Act 2001 and the Prevention of Terrorism Act 2005 amend existing powers and provide a whole batch of new ones in relation to terrorism, but continue to use the definition of terrorism contained in the TA 2000.

1   Terrorism Act 2000, Sch 16.
2   In force February 2001.
3   Terrorism Act 2000, s 53 and Sch 7.
4   Terrorism Act 2000, s 40(1)(b). Terrorism is given a very wide definition in s 1 of the Act, which may conflict with international law definitions, particularly as regards 'action' outside the UK: see s 4(4)(a).

CONTROL OF SHIP, AIRCRAFT AND TRAIN CREWS

5.34 Members of the crews of ships, aircraft and Channel Tunnel trains are in fact subject to more rigorous control than other groups of travellers. Their admission, unless they are resident in the UK or qualify in some other capacity, is always temporary – usually dependent on the turnaround time of their ship, aircraft or train – and they are liable to instant removal without time limit or any effective right of appeal if they overstay. But, because they are usually given temporary admission until the next departure of their ship, aircraft or train and do not normally need to obtain the express leave of an immigration officer on arrival, they are an exempt category,[1] and so are dealt with in this chapter.

1   The exemptions arise from the application under UK immigration law of international standards and practices which have been adopted in order to expedite international travel and

to prevent unnecessary delays owing to immigration procedures. Under the 1958 Seafarers' National Identity Documents Convention, parties to the Convention are obliged to admit the holder of a seaman's card for temporary shore leave to enable him to join a ship or to transfer to another. Under the International Labour Organisation (ILO) Convention No 108, seamen with a Convention document do not require a visa when they are travelling as a crew member to or through countries which have ratified the Convention. A list of countries which have ratified the ILO Convention is contained in IDI (Sep 04), Ch 16, s 1, Annex A. For a fuller account, see Goodwin-Gill *International Law and the Movement of Persons between States* (1978), pp 156–159; Turack *The Passport in International Law*, chs 14 and 15.

Meaning of crew member

5.35 Normally there is no difficulty in telling who is a member of the crew of a ship, aircraft or train[1] and who is not. Under section 33(1) of the IA 1971 the crew means all persons 'actually employed in the working or service' of the ship, aircraft or through train or shuttle train, including the captain or train manager.[2] But in one case the tribunal had to decide whether the wives of two ship's officers were members of the crew. In the ship's Articles they were listed as stewardesses, but they were not actually engaged in any duties on board ship and only received pay at a nominal rate. They were East Germans and would normally require a visa. They had none. The immigration officer refused to treat them as crew members or let them enter, and the Immigration Appeal Tribunal agreed with him. In the definition of 'crew' the words 'actually employed' were intended to differentiate between persons who are necessary to the working and service of the ship and others, like these wives, who are supernumerary and carry out no duties.[3]

[1] 'Aircraft' is defined to include hovercraft: IA 1971, s 33(1).
[2] IA 1971, s 33(1), modified in relation to trains by the Channel Tunnel (International Arrangements) Order 1993, SI 1993/1813, Sch 4, para 1(10). Crew members on ships can include croupiers, waiters, hairdressers, painters and repairmen, but not supernumeraries, stowaways or passengers, whose names may have been entered in the ship's Articles as crew: see IDI, Ch 16, s 1, para 3. For detailed guidance on special classes of seamen see IDI, Ch 16, Annex B.
[3] *Diestel* [1979] Imm AR 51. See the Court of Appeal's definition of 'operational staff' of airlines in *Attivor v Secretary of State for the Home Department* [1988] Imm AR 109, CA. The previously published IDI stated that dependants of air crews are not exempt and require leave to enter: IDI, Ch 16, s 2, para 7.

Automatic shore leave or break between flights or trains

5.36 Under section 8(1) of the IA 1971 no leave to enter is normally needed for crew members of a ship who are contracted to leave the UK on the same ship, or air or train crew between flights or trains. Ships' crews are given until their ship departs; air and train crews do not necessarily go out on the same plane or train that they came in on, and are, therefore, in effect given seven days. But if there is a delay in the departure of a particular aircraft, they are entitled to remain until their plane leaves.[1] Visa requirements are waived for visa nationals who arrive and leave as aircrew within seven days.[2] This leave-free entry does not operate in the case of crew members who are subject to deportation orders, who were refused leave on their last visit or who are required to submit to examination by an immigration officer.[3] Air crews whose breaks between flights exceed seven days may also be exempt from the need to obtain leave to enter if they had a limited leave before their last flight and they returned to the UK within the period of that leave.[4] If that happens, the limited leave does not lapse but continues to have effect as before.[5]

1. IA 1971, s 8(1), modified in relation to train crews by Channel Tunnel (International Arrangements) Order 1993, SI 1993/1813, Sch 4, para 1(4). For the government's explanation of this provision see 817 HC Official Report, cols 1006–1007.
2. For the position of seamen, see **5.43** below.
3. IA 1971, s 8(1)(a), (b), and (c), repeated in IDI, Ch 16, s 1, para 2.
4. Immigration (Exemption from Control) Order 1972, SI 1972/1613, art 5(1)(e).
5. IA 1971, s 3(4).

Leave to enter for shore leave or longer breaks

5.37 Crew members of ships or aircraft who wish to enter the UK for longer periods will normally be required to obtain leave, as will deportees, those refused entry on a previous visit[1] and anyone required to submit to examination by an immigration officer, who may decide to examine any or all crew members.[2] Notice granting leave will usually require them to leave on a ship or aircraft specified or indicated in the notice,[3] or within a specified period in accordance with the arrangements to be made for their return home.[4] But where leave is given to enable crew-members to get hospital treatment, they are allowed to stay until completion of the treatment and will then be required to leave the UK in accordance with the arrangements made for their return home.[5] These provisions do not apply to train crews.

1. IA 1971, s 8(1).
2. IA 1971, Sch 2, para 2(1). This will usually happen because the vessel or certain crew members have been identified as problems: IDI, Ch 16, s 1. The requirements for leave to enter for temporary shore leave are set out in IDI, Ch 16, s 1, paras 4 and 5.
3. IA 1971, Sch 2, paras 12(1), 13(1)(a) (transferring to another ship).
4. IA 1971, Sch 2, para 13(1)(c) (repatriation). There is a concession outside the Immigration Rules allowing for air crew of certain airlines to be based in the UK; they may be granted leave for up to 12 months at a time for this purpose and may be joined by family members.
5. IA 1971, Sch 2, para 13(1)(b) (hospital treatment).

Coming to join a ship or aircraft

5.38 Crew members coming to the UK to join a ship or aircraft, hovercraft, hydrofoil or international train service require leave. Notice granting leave will usually require them to leave on a ship or aircraft specified or indicated in the notice.[1] Extensions of stay will only be given if it is necessary to fulfil the purpose for which leave to enter was given or the crew member meets the requirements for an extension of stay as a spouse under HC 395, paragraph 284.[2] Under the Immigration Rules relating to those seeking leave to enter for work permit employment, seafarers joining ships in British waters are required to possess a work permit *unless* they are under contract to join a ship due to leave British waters.[3] This means that, generally speaking, permits will be needed where the ship in question does not leave British waters for a foreign port, or is operating wholly or largely within British waters. Under Guidelines operating from 1 August 1996, work permits were needed for those working on dredgers and boats doing domestic ferry voyages between two UK ports.[4] With effect from 1 June 2000, the existing work permit requirement was extended to include scheduled domestic freight services between UK ports.[5]

1   IA 1971, Sch 2, para 12(1).
2   HC 395, para 324 (there is no equivalent on-entry rule); *Immigration Officer, Heathrow v Ekinci* [1989] Imm AR 346. Since the spouse rule was amended, it can benefit only those whose leave has permitted them to stay for over six months: para 284(i).
3   HC 395, para 128. If a ship is bound for an overseas port, the requirements of para 128 of HC 395 are met and work permits are not required. This should be taken to include scheduled *passenger and freight* vessels leaving British waters, since the period of 'employment' in the UK will be short: IDI, Ch 16, Annex B. The fact that a vessel leaves British waters for a short period will not enable a seafarer to circumvent this requirement.
4   This does not include voyages to the Isle of Man or the Channel Islands: IDI, Ch 16, Annex B. The fact that a vessel leaves British waters for a short period will not enable a seafarer to circumvent the work permit requirement: ibid.
5   There was a grace period of six months from 1 June 2000, so that from 1 January 2001 all non-EEA seafarers working on ships engaged in scheduled domestic freight services must have a valid work permit. The work permit requirements are to be extended to other types of ship which operate solely or mainly in British waters: IDI, Ch 16, Annex B, para 4.1.

Discharged seamen

5.39 Where seamen are discharged from their ship on its arrival in the UK, they do not qualify for automatic shore leave and will require leave to enter. If the immigration officer is satisfied that they have the proper documents, do not intend to take employment (unless transferring to another ship due to leave British waters), intend to leave the UK, have made satisfactory arrangements for their onward travel and there are no general grounds for refusal, leave to enter will normally be given for a limited period pending departure.[1] If they require hospital treatment, the owners or agents must be willing to meet all the costs involved and to arrange for repatriation at the end of the treatment.[2] Discharged seamen may also be given leave to enter as visitors in a suitable case.[3] Visa requirements are waived.[4] Certain seamen who are discharged from their ship on their arrival in the UK are exempt from the need to obtain leave. These are Commonwealth citizens who hold a British seaman's card and Irish citizens if (in either case) they were engaged as crew members of a ship in a place within the common travel area.[5] The assumption behind this exemption is that seamen within this group are based in the UK or Ireland, and will be seeking their next engagement within the common travel area.

1   IDI, Ch 16, s 1, para 5.4.
2   IDI, Ch 16, s 1, paras 5.4 and 5.6.
3   IDI, Ch 16, s 1, para 5.12.
4   IDI, Ch 16, s 1, para 5.5.
5   Immigration (Exemption from Control) Order 1972, SI 1972/1613, art 5(1)(d).

Arrest, detention and removal of crew members

5.40 In each of these cases the temporary nature of the crew members' stay is emphasised and reinforced by the powers given to the immigration service to deal with those who do not comply. Under Schedule 2 to the IA 1971, crew members who remain beyond the time allowed by section 8(1) or by any express leave can be arrested, detained and summarily removed from the UK.[1] Jumping ship is put on a par with illegal immigration or overstaying. In fact the powers may be more severe. Crew members can be arrested, detained and

317

removed not only if they have actually failed to comply, but also if they are 'reasonably suspected' by an immigration officer of intending to do so. The right of appeal which existed under previous legislation was removed by the 2002 Act, but then reinstated.[2] There is no time limit on the exercise of the powers of removal. Someone who jumped ship ten years ago is as liable to removal, it seems, as someone who did so last week. Train crews are liable to removal if they fail to return to their train or remain beyond the time allowed by their exemption under section 8(1).[3]

[1] IA 1971, Sch 2, paras 12(2) and 13(2).
[2] Removal of crew members under IA 1971, Sch 2, paras 12(2) and 13(2) was not an 'immigration decision' conferring a right of appeal under Nationality, Immigration and Asylum Act 2002, s 82 as enacted, but carries a right of appeal under s 82(2)(ia) of that Act, inserted by Asylum and Immigration (Treatment of Claimants, etc) Act 2004, s 31 as from 1 October 2004: SI 2004/2523. However, the effect of the Immigration Act 2014 (when in force) will be again to remove this right of appeal.
[3] IA 1971, Sch 2, para 13(2), modified by the Channel Tunnel (International Arrangements) Order 1993, SI 1993/1813, Sch 4, para 1(11)(n).

Shipwrecked seamen

5.41 Where a ship is wrecked, shipwrecked seamen should normally be given leave to enter.[1] They will usually be cared for by a local shipping agent, the Shipwrecked Mariners Society or the Mission of Seamen. Seamen for this purpose include non-professional seamen.[2]

[1] IDI, Ch 16, s 1, Annex B, para 8.
[2] IDI, Ch 16, s 1, Annex B, para 8.

Seamen's documents

5.42 Seamen's documents may be issued by governments, not only to their own citizens but also to seamen of other countries. Although the holder of a seamen's document is not a national of the issuing country, the document may be accepted as evidence of identity and status and may exempt the holder from visa requirements, if the issuing country is a signatory to the International Labour Organisation Convention No 108.[1] The main effect of the Convention, to which the UK is a party, is that a seaman holding a document to which it applies:

- shall be readmitted to the country which issued the document both during its validity and during a period of at least one year after any date of expiry; and
- does not require a visa when travelling in the course of his duties to or through countries which have ratified the Convention.

The provisions of the Convention cover joining or transferring to a ship, passing in transit to join a ship in another country or for repatriation and temporary shore leave while the ship is in port.[2] Seamen travelling on national passports or holders of documents issued by countries which have not ratified the ILO Convention are subject to the normal visa requirements.[3]

[1] See IDI, Ch16, Annex A, para 6.1.

² A list of the countries which have ratified the Convention as of 31 December 1995 is contained in IDI, Ch 16, Annex A, para 6.1. Seamen travelling on documents issued by former Soviet Union States, other than the Baltic States, arriving without entry clearance should be refused leave to enter: IDI, Ch 16, Annex A, para 6.1.

³ IDI, Ch 16, Annex A, paras 6.1 and 6.5.

The British Seamen's Card

5.43 The British Seamen's Card, which is red in colour, is issued by the Department of Transport and contains a notice that it is a seafarer's document for the purposes of the ILO Convention. It is issued to persons who qualify under the terms of the Merchant Shipping (Seamen's Documents) Regulations 1987.¹ According to the current IDI these are:

- British Citizens with right of abode;
- British passport holders without right of abode but who have indefinite leave to enter;
- Commonwealth citizens with indefinite leave to enter; and
- Irish citizens.

Non-Commonwealth nationals are not entitled to apply for a British Seaman's Card. Persons travelling on British Seamen's Cards are exempt from immigration control when arriving as a member of a crew of a ship, having signed on in the Common Travel Area.²

¹ SI 1987/408, regs 2 to 14. 'British seamen' are defined in Merchant Shipping Act 1995, s 79(3) as 'persons who are not aliens within the meaning of the British Nationality Act 1981 [s 50(1)] and are employed, or ordinarily employed, as masters or seamen'. Under the regulations the cards must be given to persons with a right of abode; to other non-aliens the grant is discretionary: see SI 1987/408, regs 5 and 11. See further IDI Ch 16, Annex A, para 6.2. British seaman's cards should not be confused with British Discharge Books, which are blue in colour and also issued by the Department of Transport to British and foreign seamen employed on UK registered vessels: see Merchant Shipping (Seamen's Documents) Regulations 1987, SI 1987/408, regs 15 to 24, as amended by SI 1999/3281, made under the Merchant Shipping Act 1995 s 80. They should not be endorsed by the immigration officer: IDI, Ch 16, Annex A, para 6.2. Nor should Indian Seamen's Discharge Books: Ch 16, Annex A, para 6.3. UK seamen who are refugees or stateless, are entitled to have their Home Office documents endorsed 'The Convention relating to Seafarers' National Identity Documents dated 13 May 1958 applies to this document': Ch 16, Annex A, para 6.4.

² IDI, Ch 16, Annex A, para 6.2.

GROUPS COVERED BY EXEMPTION ORDER

5.44 Section 8(2) of the IA 1971 enables the Secretary of State to exempt any person or class of persons from all or any of the provisions of the Act relating to those who are not British citizens. The exemption may be conditional or unconditional.¹ Exemptions of classes of persons must be done through statutory instrument, and the relevant exemptions are set out in the Immigration (Exemption from Control) Order 1972, which has been amended several times to add new classes.²

¹ IA 1971, s 8(2). Exemptions under this section and the Order are in addition to diplomatic exemption (covered by s 8(3): **5.48** below), and exemption for armed forces (**5.56** below).

2   Immigration (Exemption from Control) Order 1972, SI 1972/1613, as amended by SI
    1975/617; SI 1977/693; SI 1982/1649; SI 1985/1809; SI 1997/1402; SI 1997/2207.

Consular officers and employees

5.45 Consular officers are appointed by their governments to live in a foreign port or city, chiefly as a representative of their country's commercial interests. They differ from diplomats, who are dealt with at **5.48** ff below. There is also a distinction between full and partial exemption. Full exemption means not only freedom to enter and leave the country freely but also freedom from deportation. Partial exemption means officials are exempt from all control except deportation. Where consular Conventions have been concluded between the UK and another State,[1] full exemption from immigration control is given to any consular officer or employee[2] in the service of that State, and to any member of the family of such a person who forms part of his or her household.[3] Consular employees only get the exemption if they are in the full-time service of the State concerned and are not engaged in the UK in any private occupation for gain.[4]

1   The list of States with which the UK has concluded such Conventions is set out in SI
    1972/1613, but it has not been updated since 1997. For an up-to-date list see IDI, Ch 14, s 1.
2   For definitions see Consular Relations Act 1968, Sch 1, para 1(d), (e).
3   Immigration (Exemption from Control) Order 1972, SI 1972/1613, as amended, art 3(1).
4   SI 1972/1613, art 3(2).

5.46 Exemption from all immigration control except deportation[1] is given under the Immigration (Exemption from Control) Order 1972[2] to the following:

(i)   members of foreign governments on official business and consular officers and employees of States who have not signed a consular convention with the UK;[3]

(ii)   senior officials from international organisations like the International Monetary Fund, International Bank for Reconstruction and Development, International Finance Corporation, International Development Association, the Hong Kong Economic and Trade Office, the Independent International Commission on Decommissioning and the North Atlantic Salmon Conservation Organisation;[4]

(iii)   persons connected with international organisations or international tribunals who attend certain conferences in the UK;[5]

(iv)   representatives of Commonwealth countries attending conferences[6] or performing consular functions;[7]

(v)   officials of the Commonwealth Secretariat who are entitled to limited immunities under Schedule 6 to the Commonwealth Secretariat Act 1966, but not to full diplomatic immunity.[8]

In each of these cases the exemption also applies to any member of the family forming a part of the exempted person's household.[9]

1   Under IA 1971, s 3(5)(a) and (b).
2   SI 1972/1613, made under IA 1971, s 8(2).
3   SI 1972/1613 as amended, art 4(a), (h), (i).
4   SI 1972/1613 as amended, art 4(b), (c), (d), (k), (l), (m).

5   SI 1972/1613 as amended, art 4(g). The IDI have a full list of organisations whose delegates
      would be exempt: IDI, Ch 14, Annex B.
6   SI 1972/1613 as amended, art 4(e).
7   SI 1972/1613 as amended, art 4(f).
8   SI 1972/1613 as amended, art 4(j).
9   SI 1972/1613 as amended, art 4(n). Family members for these purposes include dependent
      offspring over 18 who are still in full-time education, dependent relatives forming part of the
      household abroad and other close relatives with no one else to look after them: IDI, Ch 14, s 1,
      para 6. For the position of unmarried and same-sex partners of consular officials see IDI, Ch
      14, s 1, para 6. There is an issue as to whether family members benefit if the relevant person
      is a British citizen. The Home Office argues that art 4 of the Immigration (Exemption
      from Control) Order 1972, SI 1972/1613 provides exemption from any provisions of the IA
      1971 relating to those who are not British citizens and that British citizens (and therefore their
      families) are not exempt. The alternative view is that a British citizen can be both exempt and
      have a right of abode; and where Parliament wants to limit exemption to non-British citizens
      it uses the formula in art 5 of the 1972 Order: 'the following persons who are not British
      citizens are exempt . . .'.

Other exempted groups

5.47 Under the Immigration (Exemption from Control) Order 1972,[1] made
under section 8(2) of the IA 1971, the following classes of persons, not already
referred to, who are not British citizens, have a limited exemption from the
requirement under section 3(1)(a) of the 1971 Act to obtain leave to enter:[2]

(i)   any Commonwealth citizen included in a collective passport issued in
        the UK or Islands;[3]
(ii)   any Irish or Commonwealth citizens returning from an excursion to
        France, Belgium or the Netherlands who hold a valid identity document
        issued for such excursions;[4]
(iii)   certain holders of a British seamen's card and certain members of the
        crew of an aircraft.[5]

These exemptions do not apply to any person against whom there is a
deportation order in force, or who has previously entered the UK unlawfully
and has not subsequently been given leave to enter or remain.[6] For these
purposes Commonwealth citizens include British Protected persons.[7]

1   SI 1972/1613.
2   SI 1972/1613, art 5. Former citizens of the UK and Colonies (CUKCs) (British Dependent
      Territories and British Overseas citizens) holding a British visitor's passport are expressed to
      be exempt under Article 5(1)(a) of SI 1972/1613, but British visitor's passports have now been
      abolished, so this exemption has been omitted from the main text.
3   SI 1972/1613, art 5(1)(b).
4   SI 1972/1613, art 5(1)(c).
5   SI 1972/1613, art 5(1)(d) and (e). See **5.36** and **5.53** above.
6   SI 1972/1613, art 5(2).
7   SI 1972/1613, art 5(3).

DIPLOMATIC EXEMPTION

5.48 Representatives of foreign governments and of international organisations, such as the UN, and their families are exempt from control under either
the Immigration (Exemption from Control) Order 1972[1] made under
section 8(2) of the IA 1971 or under section 8(3). In some cases full exemption

is given, and in others officials are exempt from all control except deportation. Consular exemption, described at **5.35–5.46** above, is sometimes full exemption, meaning freedom to enter and leave the UK and freedom from deportation during the period of exemption, and sometimes partial, meaning that deportation is still possible. Diplomatic exemption, which we now consider, is always full exemption.

1. SI 1972/1613 as amended.

Diplomats and their staff

5.49 Diplomatic staff carry on the diplomatic relations of the State they represent in the country to which they have been appointed. Members of diplomatic missions and members of their families who form part of their household are fully exempt under section 8(3) of the IA 1971. The Diplomatic Privileges Act 1964 divides those members of diplomatic missions entitled to diplomatic immunity into three categories:

(i)   diplomatic agents, who are heads of the mission and members of their diplomatic staff;

(ii)   members of the administrative and technical staff, consisting of clerical staff, translators, coding clerks, press representatives, etc; and

(iii) members of the service staff, who are chauffeurs, cooks, cleaners, etc[1]

Each of these categories is entitled to differing degrees of immunity from civil and criminal proceedings, but all are exempt from immigration control under section 8(3) of the 1971 Act, except staff recruited in this country. Section 8(3A), as amended by the Immigration and Asylum Act 1999, provides that members of a mission, other than diplomatic agents, are only exempt if (a) they were resident outside the UK, and were not in the UK, when they were offered their post, and (b) they have not ceased to be a member of the mission after having taken up the post.[2]

1. See Diplomatic Privileges Act 1964, Sch 1, para 1.
2. The original s 8(3A) of the IA 1971 was inserted by Immigration Act 1988, s 4. It ensured that foreign nationals in the UK, who took up posts in diplomatic missions, other than as diplomatic agents, were not exempt from immigration control. But there was a lacuna in the law. If these locally recruited people left the UK and then returned while still in post, the original s 8(3A) operated to free them from immigration control on their return. By the Immigration and Asylum Act 1999 amendment, the new s 8(3A) closes this loophole, but at the same time ensures that they do not remain subject to immigration control for ever. A person who has held such a post in the past, but has subsequently left it, and has then been appointed from abroad, will enjoy full diplomatic exemption.

5.50 The distinction between service staff who are exempt from control and other employees of a mission is sometimes difficult to make. In practice the distinguishing feature appears to be whether or not they are liable to pay UK tax. Under Article 37(3) of the Vienna Convention, members of the service staff of the mission are exempt from local taxes. Thus in *Kandiah*[1] the Tribunal held that a messenger working for a mission was not exempt from immigration control where it was a condition of his employment that he paid local taxes.[2] Equally, it is doubtful if a housekeeper in the household of the deputy head of mission would be exempt from control, even if he or she has his or her contract with the government concerned.[3] The service staff of the mission is not the same as the service staff of one of its members. The Tribunal, however, seemed to take a different view in the case of *Florentine*.[4] The private servants of heads of State have total exemption unless the Secretary of State otherwise directs.[5]

[1]   *(2699) unreported.*
[2]   See *Pintucan (16451)* [1999] 1 ILD 27.
[3]   The test of exemption is not the mere fact of being employed at a diplomatic mission. The IDI, Ch 14, Annex A, para 2.1, distinguishes between a servant of the head of the mission paid by the country, and one paid by the head of mission, the latter requiring leave to enter under Tier 5 of the points-based system. arts 1 and 37(4) of the Vienna Convention contained in Sch 1 to the Diplomatic Privileges Act 1964 (and given force of law by s 1 thereof) is not particularly helpful in shedding light on this distinction.
[4]   *(4811) unreported.*
[5]   State Immunity Act 1978, s 20(3). See IDI, Ch 14, s 1, para 2.3. However, the IDI, Ch 14 Annex A, para 2.2 indicates that servants of Heads of State are subject to control and should be treated as domestic servants in private households. We prefer the former guidance, which fits the statutory position.

UN officials

5.51 Persons entitled to like immunity from jurisdiction as is conferred by the Diplomatic Privileges Act 1964 on 'diplomatic agents' are fully exempt from immigration control.[1] Like immunities are conferred on high officers of a number of international organisations, such as the UN, by Orders in Council made under the International Organisations (Immunities and Privileges) Act 1950, as continued by the International Organisations Act 1968, section 12(5), and on senior officers of the Commonwealth Secretariat under the Commonwealth Secretariat Act 1966. The range of employees covered and whether the exemption extends to any member of the person's family forming part of his or her household depends upon the terms of the agreement reached with each organisation.[2]

[1]   IA 1971, s 8(3).
[2]   IDI, Ch 14, s 1, Annex B, para 2. The family has exemption because they obtain like immunity under the relevant agreement, not because of any express mention of a family in IA 1971, s 8(3).

Members of the diplomat's family

5.52 Subject to the above, in all the immunities granted to diplomats and international functionaries, the exemption extends to members of their family who form part of their household.[1] This can be a difficult issue. In *Gupta*[2] the question in issue was whether the widowed sister of an Indian diplomat qualified. She claimed she was entitled to remain here as a member of her brother's family who formed part of his household within the meaning of section 8(3) of the IA 1971. The High Court held that she was exempt from control. The IDI now give some guidance, giving the term a more generous interpretation than that used for persons subject to immigration control and having more in common with the EC definition.[3] It extends to children over 18 who are still in full-time education; dependent relatives forming part of the household abroad; and other close relatives with no one else to look after them.[4] The IDI give a mixed message about unmarried partners (including same sex partners) and they are clearly out of date as far as civil partnerships are concerned not having been updated since 1984). On the one hand unmarried partners are said not to be exempt from control, but may seek leave to enter under the Immigration Rules.[5] On the other hand unmarried partners (common law or same sex relationships) are to be considered as members of households, where the relationship is recognised as durable by the sending State and is one that is akin to marriage and where the parties intend to live together in the UK for the duration of the posting.[6]

[1] See eg IA 1971, s 8(3); Immigration (Exemption from Control) Order 1972, SI 1972/1613, art 3(1)(c) and 4(l).
[2] *Gupta v Secretary of State for the Home Department* [1979–80] Imm AR 52. See *Florentine v Secretary of State for the Home Department* [1987] Imm AR 1.
[3] In Council Regulation (EEC) 1612/68, art 10.
[4] IDI, Ch 14, s 1, para 6.
[5] IDI, Ch 14, s 1, para 9.
[6] IDI, Ch 14, s 1, para 6.

Locally engaged staff (non-diplomats) of diplomatic missions working in the UK

5.53 *Locally engaged staff recruited prior to 1 August 1988.* Under section 8(3) of the IA 1971 (as originally in force) the locally engaged members of missions in the non-diplomatic categories of administrative and technical staff and service staff, and their families, were entitled to exemption from control. The position of persons recruited in the above categories prior to 1 August 1988 is not affected by subsequent amendments of the IA 1971 and their exemption will continue.

Locally engaged staff recruited between 1 August 1988 and 1 March 2000. Under section 8(3) of the IA 1971,[1] missions were able to engage locally only persons in the above categories, whose status allowed them to take employment, or persons whose appointments were notified to the Protocol Department of the Foreign and Commonwealth Office under Article 10 of the Vienna Convention on Diplomatic Relations.[2] If the Foreign and Commonwealth Office were satisfied that the persons were in bona fide employment and entitled to privileges and immunities, employment was permitted.[3] They were, however, subject to control. Staff recruited between 1 August 1988 and 1 March 2000 who had travelled abroad before 1 March 2000 became exempt upon their return by virtue of returning as a member of a diplomatic mission.[4] Locally engaged staff of missions currently in the UK who have not acquired exempt status by travelling abroad before 1 March 2000 are subject to immigration control, and if they travel abroad on or after 1 March 2000, they will remain subject to immigration control upon their return to the UK.[5]

Locally engaged staff recruited after 1 March 2000. Under the new section 8(3A) of the 1971 Act,[6] members of missions other than diplomatic agents will only benefit from exemption if they were resident outside the UK and were not present in the UK when offered a post as a member of a mission; and if they have not ceased to be a member of the mission after taking up the post. However, they do not remain subject to immigration control for ever. A person who has held such a post in the past, but has subsequently left it and has been appointed abroad to the current post, is to be treated like any other member of that mission appointed outside the UK.[7]

1   As amended by the Immigration Act 1988.
2   IDI, Ch 14, s 1, Annex A, para 3.
3   IDI, Ch 14, s 1, Annex A, para 3.
4   IA 1971, s 8(3A), as inserted by Immigration Act 1988.
5   IA 1971, s 8(3A), as substituted by IA 1999, s 6.
6   Originally inserted by the Immigration Act 1988, s 4; then substituted by the Immigration and Asylum Act 1999, s 6.
7   IA 1971, s 8(3A)(b), as amended by IAA 1999. See commentary in *Butterworths Immigration Law Service*, para A[622].

CEASING TO HAVE DIPLOMATIC AND OTHER EXEMPTION

5.54 When diplomats and others exempted under section 8(2) and (3) of the IA 1971 cease to be exempt on or after 1 March 2000, and, as a result, require leave to remain, they are treated as if they had been given leave for a period of 90 days, beginning on the day exemption ceases.[1] If, however, the person already has a leave which expires before the end of the 90-day period, his or her leave is treated as expiring at the end of the shorter period.[2] If the ex-diplomat wishes to remain in the UK, an application to do so will be considered in the normal way under the Immigration Rules.[3] The provisions of section 8A of the IA 1971, together with the new section 8(3A), which came into force on 1 March 2000,[4] disposes of many of the practical problems of diplomatic exemption referred to in the previous editions of this work.[5] The position now is:

(i)   if clearly indicated indefinite leave was given on arrival in the UK, prior to 1 March 2000, and before taking up the diplomatic post, this will remain unaffected by the exemption. Since under section 8(3) 'the provisions of this Act . . . shall not apply . . . so long as' the person remains exempt, such leave will not lapse due to trips overseas,[6] and the former diplomat will be free to remain;[7]

(ii)   a mere rectangular stamp in a passport with a date but no words indicating any sort of leave does not operate as the grant of indefinite leave.[8] Further, a grant of indefinite leave on arrival in the UK is unlikely, since it is now the law that those who come from overseas to take up a diplomatic post become members of the mission on arrival in the UK, and not when they actually take up the appointment or when the appointment is officially notified to the UK government;[9]

(iii)   persons with prior limited leave are dealt with by sections 8(5) and 8A(3)(b) of the 1971 Act. If they wish to remain longer they need to apply before the end of the period of their leave in the normal way;

(iv)   there is uncertainty as to the effect of an express grant of leave (indefinite or limited) given to somebody who is exempt from control as a diplomat.[10]

A period of exemption from immigration control counts towards 'lawful residence' for the purposes of the long residence rule.[11] However, there may be a problem for the spouse of a retired diplomat. After her spouse has ceased his or her functions, the spouse of a diplomat, who is exempt from immigration control is treated as if she had been given leave to remain in the UK for a period of 90 days beginning on the day on which she ceased to be exempt IA 1971,[12] but the AIT has held that this limited form of leave does not entitle the person to switch into leave as a spouse under rule 284 of the Immigration Rules, because that rule is only available to an extension of a leave given 'in accordance with any provisions of' the rules and a statutory extension of leave is not such a leave.[13]

[1]   IA 1971, s 8A(2), inserted by the Immigration and Asylum Act 1999, s 6 and in force on 1 March 2000.

[2]   IA 1971, s 8A(3).

[3]   IDI, Ch 14, s 1, Annex C, para 2.

[4]   SI 2000/168.

[5]   4th edn at para 7.46 ff.

[6]   As would have been the case under IA 1971, s 3(4); the provisions of the Immigration (Leave to Enter and Remain) Order 2000, SI 2000/1161 would now in any event prevent the lapsing of indefinite leave.

[7]   IDI, Ch 14, s 1, para 8.4. For further details of the pre-March 2000 position, see IDI, Ch 14, s 1, Annex D.

[8]   *R v Secretary of State for the Home Department, ex p Bagga* [1990] Imm AR 413, CA.

[9]   *Bagga* above, overruling *R v Governor of Pentonville Prison, ex p Teja* [1971] 2 QB 274, [1971] 2 All ER 11; *R v Lambeth Justices, ex p Yusufu* [1985] Crim LR 510; *Re Osman (No 2)* (21 December 1988, unreported), DC; and *Rahi v Secretary of State for the Home Department* [1987] Imm AR 293 on the issue that immunity depends on notification and acceptance.

[10] One argument is that such leave is ineffective as contrary to s 8(3) of the IA 1971. The opposing argument is that exemption from the requirement to obtain leave does not preclude reliance being placed subsequently on such a leave when the person ceases to be exempt. In practice the Home Office recognises that there has been a pledge of public faith by immigration officials and the grant of leave is usually honoured: IDI, Ch 14, s 1, para 8.5. This does not apply if the leave was limited and expires within three months of the exemption ending: IDI, Ch 14, s 1.

[11] HC 395, para 276A(b)(iii) (inserted by HC 538).

[12] IA 1971, s 8A(2)),

[13] *VA (Formerly exempt persons: leave) Ghana* [2007] UKAIT 00091.

SOVEREIGN IMMUNITY

5.55 The State Immunity Act 1978, s 1 gives statutory effect to the customary international law rules regarding the immunity of states, a sovereign or other head of state and to members of a government department as regards civil but not criminal immunity. The extent of immunity is qualified by section 14, which creates different gradations of immunity. Section 20(1) and (3) widens the immunity of heads of state to include immunity for private acts[1] and makes express provision for exemption from immigration control for a sovereign or other head of state who enjoys immunity under the Act, members of his family and his private servants. Sovereign immunity is based on the rules of customary international law. Essentially it is the combination of two factors: (i) a consequence of the absolute independence of every sovereign authority, and (ii) international comity which induces every sovereign state to respect the independence of every other sovereign state.[2] Although these rules are now regulated in the UK by statute, we consider that decisions of UK and overseas courts and the practices of states very much inform the proper construction of the statutory provisions.[3] Pre-1978 English Court decisions are, therefore relevant in so far as they contain statements of the legal principles identifying the ambit and remit of international law as it affects sovereign immunity, but they are not authority about whether a particular state is still recognised as a sovereign state today. One question which has been a live issue for some time is the position of states within a Federal system. The US position is that because none of the states in the USA have any responsibility for foreign affairs they do not count as sovereign states under international law. However, although this is a widely held view of writers in international law, this is neither the only view nor necessarily the predominant one.[4] In *Mellenger v New Brunswick Development Corpn,* it was held by the Court of Appeal that sovereign immunity extends to the constituent states of a country which has a federal constitution such as a Canadian province.[5] In *R (on the application of HRH Sultan of Pahang) v Secretary of State for the Home Department,*[6] the Court of Appeal found that Pahang is not a State for the purposes of the State Immunity Act 1978. There was no room for some residual common law category of a person who is not a head of state as defined by the SIA but who would otherwise be recognised as a head of state by the common law for the purposes of, inter alia, immigration control. The Court could not question a certificate (subject to its being sufficiently clear and unequivocal) as to the identity of a head of state: that matter was for the executive.

[1] *Bank of Credit and Commerce International (Overseas) Ltd (in liq) v Price Waterhouse (a firm) (Abu Dhabi, third party)* [1997] 4 All ER 108 ('the Abu Dhabi case').

[2] See *The Parlement Belge* [1874–80] All ER Rep 104.

[3] See *Aziz v Aziz* [2007] EWCA Civ 712, [2008] 2 All ER 501, [2007] NLJR 1047, per Lawrence Collins LJ at 88–92). It is also clear that s 20 of the 1978 Act was not intended to confer on heads of state any privileges or immunities beyond those conferred by customary international law: see *R v Bow Street Metropolitan Stipendiary Magistrate, ex p Pinochet (No 3)* [1999] 2 All ER 97, [2000] 1 AC 147, per Lord Browne Wilkinson at p 112 or 203; per Lord Hope at p 145 or 240.

[4] *R (on the application of Alamieyeseigha) v Crown Prosecution Service* [2005] EWHC 2704 (Admin), (2006) Times, 16 January.

[5] [1971] 2 All ER 593, [1971] 1 WLR 604, CA. Lord Denning MR stated as follows:

'The British North America Act 1867 gave Canada a federal constitution. Under it the powers of government were divided between the dominion government and the provincial governments. Some of those powers were vested in the dominion government. The rest remained with the provincial government. Each provincial government, within its own sphere, retained its independence and autonomy directly under the Crown. The Crown is sovereign in New Brunswick for provincial matters, just as it is sovereign in Canada for dominion powers. . . . It follows that the Province of New Brunswick is a sovereign state in its own right, and entitled, if it so wishes, to claim sovereign immunity.' (at p 608G–H).

See further *Bank of Credit and Commerce International (Overseas) Ltd (in liquidation) v Price Waterhouse (a firm) and another (Abu Dhabi and others, third parties)* [1997] 4 All ER 108, which held that Abu Dhabi is a constituent territory of the United Arab Emirates for the purpose of the 1978 Act but the ruler obtained immunity because he was also the President of the UAE as well, as certified to that effect by the Secretary of State; *Swiss Israel Trade Bank v Government of Salta and Banco Provincial de Salta* [1972] 1 Lloyd's Rep 497, where the High Court took a different route and held that the government of Salta, which was one of several Spanish provinces of South America which in 1816 proclaimed their independence, and in 1853 had combined to form the Argentine Republic, was in effect either the government of the Argentine Republic, which was admittedly a sovereign state, or at least a department of the government and, therefore, entitled to immunity.

[6] [2011] EWCA Civ 616, [2011] NLJR 781, (2011) Times, 13 June.

MILITARY PERSONNEL

5.56 Section 8(4) of the IA 1971 also gives a limited exemption to members of the home forces subject to service law,[1] to members of Commonwealth forces training with the home forces and to members of a visiting force, such as

US servicemen, posted in the UK.[2] The exemption is limited since it exempts from control on and after entry, but not from deportation. From 11 July 2013 the MOD requires a person to have five years' legal residency in the UK at the time they apply to join HM Forces (or switch to this category)[3]. A member of the home forces ceases to be exempt on discharge. Upon advance notification of their date of discharge, the Home Office will grant a period of 28 days leave to remain outside the rules to enable the person to submit an application to regularise their position[4]. Where a member of the home forces had leave to enter or remain before they became exempt and that leave period is still valid at that point they cease to be exempt and that leave is automatically resumed[5]. The dependants of those with a military exemption are not themselves exempt. The Immigration Rules distinguish between dependents of members of HM Forces and dependents of non-HM Forces[6]. A partner of a member of HM forces exempt from immigration control must meet an English language requirement and a minimum income financial requirement[7]. Children of members of HM Forces must meet the financial requirement unless either both parents are service personnel, the other parent has died or the sponsor has sole responsibility[8]. This represents a change in the rules intended to align treatment of non-EEA family members of service personnel with the general approach to family immigration[9]. In contrast dependants of non-HM Forces must provide evidence of adequacy of accommodation and maintenance[10]. Leave to enter for dependants will normally be for whichever is the shortest period of five years or the period of the sponsor's enlistment or posting[11].

[1]   This includes Gurkhas as the Brigade of Ghurkas is part of the British Army: Armed Forces: exempt from immigration control (modernised guidance), Dec 2013. Regular (non-reserve) HM Forces personnel are subject to service law at all times whereas a reservist with HM Forces is only exempt whilst deployed or due to be deployed during which time they are subject to service law: Armed Forces: exempt from immigration control (modernised guidance).
[2]   IA 1971, s 8(4) and (6). See *R v Secretary of State for the Home Department, ex p Wuan* [1989] Imm AR 501, QBD.
[3]   Armed Forces: exempt from immigration control (modernised guidance).
[4]   Armed Forces: exempt from immigration control (modernised guidance).
[5]   IA 1971, s 8(5) and Armed Forces (modernised guidance), Dec 2013.
[6]   Appendix Armed Forces. Members of the home forces are as per s 8(4)(a) of IA 1971. Non-HM Forces are members of Commonwealth forces training with home forces (s 8(4)(b)) and members of a visiting force (s 8(4)(c)).
[7]   Appendix Armed Forces, para 23, inserted by HC 803. The language and financial requirements are the same as under Appendix FM.
[8]   Appendix Armed Forces, para 43(h).
[9]   See Explanatory Memorandum to HC 803.
[10] Appendix Armed Forces, para 62.
[11] Appendix Armed Forces, paras 24 and 65.

5.57 Discharged foreign or commonwealth members of HM Forces who have served at least four years or were medically discharged where the cause was attributable to service in HM Forces may apply for leave to enter the UK, limited leave to remain or indefinite leave to remain. Applications made on or after 1 December 2013 will be considered under Appendix Armed Forces[1]. Applicants must satisfy the suitability requirements in paragraphs 8 and 9 of part 2 to Appendix Armed Forces[2] and the general eligibility requirements in paragraph 11.

[1]   HC 395, para 276DI. Paras 276E–276AI continue to apply to applications (i) made before 1 December 2013 under those paragraphs but which have not been decided and (ii) by persons who have been granted entry clearance or limited leave to enter or remain under pa-

ras 276E–276AI before 1 December 2013 and where it is a requirement of Part 7 that leave to enter or remain is extant: HC 395, para 276DL.

2 HC 395, para 276DK. Suitability requirements under Appendix Armed Forces are the same as those under Appendix FM and the following paragraphs from the general grounds of refusal: 320(3), 320(7B), 320(10), 320(11), 321(iii), 321(4A), 322(3) and 323(i). Gurkas and foreign Commonwealth forces who have been discharged who have served at least four years or was medically discharged where the cause was attributable to service in HM Forces are eligible for indefinite leave to remain in the UK, subject to satisfying suitability requirements – see Appendix Armed Forces of the Immigration Rules in respect of all applications on or after 1 December 2013 and Armed Forces: (modernised guidance).

CHILDREN BORN IN THE UK

5.58 Generally speaking, those exempt from control are not to be regarded as settled in the UK,[1] but the British Nationality Act 1981 made provision[2] for the Secretary of State for the Home Department to treat as settled in the UK (for the purposes of section 1 of the 1981 Act) any person or class of person who is exempted by Order from immigration control. This will apply to parents of children born in the UK after 1983, but who do not acquire British citizenship by birth. The 1972 Order as amended provides that where an exempt person (other than a diplomat)[3] becomes a parent of a UK-born child, the parent will be treated as settled (enabling the child to be a British citizen by birth) if he or she had indefinite leave to remain before becoming exempt from control and was ordinarily resident in the UK from that time until the time of the child's birth.[4]

1 IA 1971, s 8(5).
2 British Nationality Act 1981, s 39(4) inserted a new s 8(5A) into the IA 1971.
3 The Article does not apply if a parent has diplomatic immunity under the Diplomatic Privileges Act 1964.
4 Immigration (Exemption from Control) Order 1972, art 6 (inserted by SI 1982/1649).

Chapter 6

EUROPEAN UNION FREE MOVEMENT LAW AND RELATED OBLIGATIONS

INTRODUCTION

6.1 The following abbreviations are used in this chapter:

CJEU   Court of Justice of the European Union
EC   European Community
ECHR   European Convention on Human Rights
ECtHR   European Court of Human Rights
ECJ   European Court of Justice
EEA   European Economic Area
EEC   European Economic Community
EU   European Union
TEC   Treaty establishing the European Communities
TEU   Treaty on the European Union
TFEU   Treaty on the Functioning of the European Union

This chapter is concerned with the impact on immigration law of rights of freedom of movement and associated provisions afforded under the Treaty of Rome 1959 (the EEC Treaty), as amended by the Single European Act 1987, the Treaty on European Union 1993 (the Maastricht Treaty), the Treaty of Amsterdam 1997 and more recently the Treaty of Lisbon which came into force on 1 December 2009.

The UK became a member of the European Communities with effect from 1 January 1973.[1] Since this date the Treaty, and directives and regulations made under it, are binding in the UK by virtue of the European Communities Act 1972.[2] The Act has been amended on many occasions, as new treaties have been signed and there have been accessions of new States to the Community and Union. The more recent amendments have been:

- the European Union (Accessions) Act 2003, which received Royal Assent in November 2003 and marked the accession of the 8 East European countries, Cyprus and Malta;
- the European Union (Accessions) Act 2006 dealing with the accession of the Republic of Bulgaria and Romania; and providing powers to the Secretary of State to make provision about the right of Romanian and Bulgarian nationals to enter or reside in the UK as workers;

- the European Union (Amendment) Act 2008, intended to enable the UK to ratify the Treaty of Lisbon, published as Paper Cm 7294, European Community Series No 13 (2007); and
- the European Union (Approval of Treaty Amendment Decision) Act 2012 dealing with the accession of Croatia on 1 July 2013 and providing for regulations to make provision concerning the entitlement of Croatian nationals to enter or reside in the UK as workers.[3].

The decisions and interpretations on the provisions of the 1972 Act and its amendments by the European Court of Justice (ECJ) (renamed the Court of Justice of the European Union (CJEU)by the Lisbon Treaty) are also binding in the UK.[4]

Contrary to the general policy of the Immigration Act 1971, whose clear purpose is to restrict the right of individuals to enter or remain in the UK, the main characteristic of these freedom of movement provisions is that they grant rights directly to individuals and restrict the powers of the national authority. Interpretation of the Treaties and subordinate legislation by the CJEU tends, therefore, to favour the individual rather than the Member State. This is in sharp contrast to the interpretation of domestic immigration law, which tends to give fuller recognition to the extensive discretionary power of the immigration authorities at the expense of the individual. From its inception, the freedom of movement of persons was characterised as one of the European Economic Community's (EEC's) principal foundations, along with freedom of movement for goods, services and capital.[5]

[1] European Communities Act 1972 (ch 68), as amended.
[2] European Communities Act 1972, s 2.
[3] It should be noted that the government has decided to opt in to the Council Decisions to sign and conclude an agreement to extend the EU-Switzerland free movement agreement to Croatia: written ministerial statement laid before both Houses of Parliament on 12 December 2013.
[4] European Communities Act 1972, s 3; see EC *Commission v Luxembourg (public service employment)* [1997] ECR I-3207, [1996] 3 CMLR 981; Orfinger v Belgium [2000] 1 CMLR 612, ECJ.
[5] See Case 167/73 EC *Commission v France* [1974] ECR 359, [1974] 2 CMLR 216, ECJ; Preamble to Council Regulation (EEC) 1612/68.

6.2 It should be noted that the Lisbon Treaty created, yet again, a consolidated version of the Treaty on European Union (TEU) and the Treaty on the Functioning of the European Union (TFEU), to which are appended the various Protocols.[1] The Official Journal of the EU has produced Tables of Equivalences to help people find their way round the post-Lisbon version of each Treaty. But readers should beware, because not all the ex-Articles are in fact equivalences. In many the substance has also changed. Below, the old treaty provisions are included in parentheses where necessary.

[1] A consolidated version of the TEU and Treaty on the Functioning of the European Union (TFEU), (the re-named TEC) has been published as Command Paper Cm 7310, along with a comparative table of the current EU Treaties as amended by the Treaty of Lisbon (Cm 7311). See further Treaty of Lisbon (Changes in Terminology) Order 2011, SI 2011/1043.

6.3 After 1 November 1993 and the amendments made at Maastricht by the Treaty on European Union (TEU) the EEC became split into two distinct bodies: one known as the European Community (EC), the other formed by the

Member States and known as the European Union (EU) which includes, but is a different body from, the EC. The Treaty of Lisbon has now abolished the EC and everything now comes under the umbrella of the EU. The only thing kept separate, are the two Treaties, both of which have been amended and consolidated. The first is the TEU and the second the TFEU.[1] References to EC law, except where the context requires it, have been changed to references to EU law. A national of a Member State is now, by virtue of that nationality, also a citizen of the EU.[2] The free movement rights of EU citizens and members of their families remain the core of EU law as it affects immigration, but since the first Treaty on European Union in 1993, which set up the structure for inter-governmental co-operation on asylum and immigration of third-country nationals in what became known as the third pillar of the EU, has developed greatly. On 2 October 1997 Member States signed the Treaty of Amsterdam which provided for the integration into the framework of the EU of the Schengen *acquis*[3] and a new Title IV of the EC Treaty, as it was then known (now Title V of the TFEU). This contained the power to make new Community law on immigration and asylum, matters which had previously been dealt with on an inter-governmental basis under the Justice and Home affairs provisions of the Treaty on European Union (the 'third pillar'). This has since resulted in a number of important Directives and CJEU decisions dealing with such matters as asylum and subsidiary protection[4] and penal penalties for illegal immigration.[5]

[1] Selected Articles of the new consolidated versions of both the TEU and the TFEU are set out in Appendix 6. For the full texts see *Butterworths Immigration Law Service*, F[31] (EU Treaty), F[201] (Treaty on European Union). The European Union (Amendment) Act 2008 (c. 7) gives effect to the Lisbon Treaty in the law of the UK. It received Royal Assent on 19 June 2008. The Act incorporates the Treaty by adding it to the treaties listed in the European Communities Act 1972, s 1(2). The actual ratification of the Treaty by the UK took place when the British government deposited the instruments of ratification in Rome on 16 July 2008. Previous challenges to the power of the Secretary of State for Foreign Affairs to conclude the first Treaty of European Union have not been repeated. See *R v Secretary of State for Foreign and Commonwealth Affairs, ex p Rees-Mogg* [1994] QB 552, [1993] 3 CMLR 101. See also Treaty of Lisbon (Changes in Terminology) Order 2011, SI 2011/1043.

[2] Article 20 TFEU (ex art 17 TEC).

[3] The Schengen *acquis* is a body of comprehensive measures on border controls etc, derived from agreement on the gradual abolition of checks at common borders signed by other EC Member States on 14 June 1985 and 19 June 1990. See 6.47 ff below.

[4] EU Council Directive on Minimum standards for determining who qualifies for refugee status or for subsidiary protection status (Qualification Directive), Council Directive 2004/83/EC, which in turn has led to the Refugee or Person in Need of International Protection (Qualification) Regulations 2006, SI 2006/2525 and changes in the Immigration Rules: see CM 6918, amending HC 395. The ECJ now has jurisdiction in these cases: see *Elgafaji v Staatssecretaris van Justitie* Case C-465/07 [2009] ECR I-921, 2009] All ER (EC) 651. See further 12.21–12.22; Also EU Council Directive on minimum standards on procedures in Member States for granting and withdrawing refugee status, Council Directive 2005/85/EC of 1 December 2005, leading to substantial changes in the Immigration Rules by HC 82, laid before Parliament on 19 November 2007. See also the important CJEU decision on unaccompanied minors and the 'Dublin II' Regulation: *R (on the application of MA, BT and DA) v Secretary of State for the Home Department (the AIRE Centre (Advice on Individual Rights in Europe) (UK), intervening)*: Case C-648/11 [2013] 1 WLR 2961, ECJ. Other cases on asylum/subsidiary protection decided by the CJEU include Case C-19/08*Migrationsverket v Petrosian* [2009] 2 CMLR 863, ECJ (implementation of the Dublin Regulation); Case C-465/07 *Elgafaji v Staatssecretaris van Justitie* [2009] All ER (EC) 651, [2009] 1 WLR 2100 (GC) (Art 15(c), Qualification Directive) (GC) (17 February 2009); Case C-175/08 *Abdulla v Bundesrepublik Deutschland* [2011] QB 46, [2010] ECR I-1493 and C-179/08 *Jamal v Bundesrepublik Deutschland* [2011] QB 46, [2010] All ER (EC) 799 (cessation and arts 11 and 7 of Qualification Directive); Case C-31/09 *Nawras Bolbol v Bevandorlasi es Allampol-*

garsagi Hivatal [2010] All ER (D) 133 (Jun) (GC) (Art 1D of Refugee Convention; art 12 of Qualification Directive); *Bundesrepublik Deutschland v B (Vertreter des Bundesinteresses beim Bundesverwaltungsgericht intervening)* C-57/09) and C-101/09) [2010] All ER (D) 96 (Nov) (GC) (exclusion from refugee status); and Joined Cases C-411/10. Joined Cases C-411/10NS *v Secretary of State for the Home Department (Amnesty International Ltd and the AIRE Centre (Advice on Individual Rights in Europe) (UK)) and and C-493/10 ME v Refugee Applications Comr (Amnesty International Ltd and the AIRE Centre (Advice on Individual Rights in Europe) (UK))*[2013] QB 102;[2012] All ER (EC) 1011 and C-493/10 M E and Others v Refugee Applications Commissioner, Minister for Justice, Equality and Law Reform (Dublin II and the position of Greece) (21 December 2011). According to a Paper by Dr Hugo Storey, 'Preliminary references to the Court of Justice of the European Union (CJEU)' (Sept 2010):

'The CJEU sees a particular utility in references being made in the field of asylum and immigration because it is a new area of EU law. Not only are we still in a period when the new asylum-related directives are "bedding-down", but we are shortly to be faced with implementation of "recast" Directives and, further, as a result of the Lisbon Treaty, there is now legal power for the Council (when it chooses) to introduce new EU asylum and immigration law through Regulations, which do not require national transposition.'

See also 'Information Note for National Courts' issued by the ECJ 2009 C/297/01 (5 December 2009). See further CHAPTER **12** below.

5   See European Directive and Framework Decision on the Facilitation of Unauthorised Entry, Transit and Residence, Council Directive 2002/90/EC which is a Directive seeking to harmonise criminal penalties for illegal entry within Member States and having a direct bearing on the ambit of section 25 of the Immigration Act 1971: *Pupino (criminal proceedings against)* Case C-105/03 [2006] QB 83, [2005] ECR I-5285, ECJ. See further **15.49**.

6.4 The former EC Treaty gave powers to the EC and the Member States to enter into Association Agreements with other States.[1] These are binding in EU law. Some were made with Eastern European countries, such as Poland and Hungary, which have now become full members. Of the others, perhaps the most significant for immigration lawyers are the Ankara Agreement 1963 with Turkey, which we deal with at **6.198** below, and the 1992 Agreement on the European Economic Area (EEA) and the 1999 Agreement with Switzerland, both of which we deal with in **6.5** below.

1   Article 217 TFEU (Art 310 TEC).

6.5 Not all these agreements are with individual States. Some are with other international entities. For example, a completely new entity, the European Economic Area (EEA) was created by an agreement made with the former European Free Trade Association countries under the EC Treaty, giving the same free movement rights within the area to both EU nationals and to nationals of Norway, Iceland and Liechtenstein.[1] In June 1999 the EC and Switzerland entered into an agreement intended to extend full free movement rights between the community and Switzerland. It came into force in the UK on 1 June 2002.[2] The Agreement on the European Economic Area 1992 has the force of law in the UK by virtue of the European Economic Area Act 1993, which amends the European Communities Act 1972. The freedom of movement rights under the 1992 Agreement were implemented in UK law as from 20 July 1994 by the European Economic Area Order in Council 1994.[3] This was then replaced from 2 October 2000 by the Immigration (European Economic Area) Regulations 2000 (2000 Regulations),[4] which in turn were replaced by the 2006 Regulations.[5] In this chapter, in considering free movement rights we will often refer to EEA nationals rather than EU nationals, and this will include Swiss nationals, unless separate consideration is required for any particular group. The rights accruing under association agreements will be considered separately in **6.17** ff.

[1]   See European Economic Area Act 1993, applying the Agreement on the European Economic Area signed at Oporto on 2 May 1992, as adjusted by the Protocol signed at Brussels on 17 March 1993 OJ L86 20.4.1995. The implementation of the Agreement was delayed until the ECJ was satisfied that the joint committee established to monitor the Agreement did not impinge on the court's jurisdiction; see ECJ Opinion 1/92 given on 10 April 1992. For the rules of the joint committee and the EEA Court see [1994] 1 CMLR 84. On 1 May 2004 the ten new Member States of the EU became parties to this agreement, ie the Czech Republic, Estonia, Cyprus, Latvia, Lithuania, Hungary, Malta, Poland, Slovenia, and Slovakia: see Accession Treaty, art 2; Act of Accession art 6.

[2]   Agreement between the European Community and the Swiss Confederation on The Free Movement of Persons (30 Apr/02 OJ L114/6). The first effective regulations were the Immigration (Swiss Free Movement of Persons) (No 3) Regulations 2002, SI 2002/1241 which are now repealed, except for provisions relating to posted workers, by the 2006 Regulations which incorporates Switzerland into the definition of an EEA State (reg 2(1)).

[3]   SI 1994/1895.

[4]   SI 2000/2326, as amended.

[5]   SI 2006/1003.

ENLARGEMENT OF THE EU: 2004 ONWARDS

6.6 Prior to 1 May 2004, the Member States of the EU were Austria, Belgium, Denmark, Finland, France, Germany, Greece, Holland, Ireland, Italy, Luxembourg, Portugal, Spain, Sweden and the UK. On 1 May 2004 they were joined by ten new members: the Czech Republic, Estonia, Cyprus, Latvia, Lithuania, Hungary, Malta, Poland, Slovenia, and Slovakia, under an Accession Treaty, signed with the EU, in Athens on 16 April 2003 ('the 2003 Accession Treaty'), which came into force on 1 May 2004. This was followed by the Treaty of Accession of Bulgaria and Romania to the EU ('the 2005 Accession Treaty'), which was signed on 25 April 2005, in Neumünster Abbey, Luxembourg, which entered into force on 1 January 2007. Finally, on 9 December 2011, Croatia signed a Treaty of Accession with the EU Member States in Brussels ('the 2011 Accession Treaty'), which came into force on 1 July 2013. Each Accession Treaty amended earlier Treaties of the European Union, and as such, are an integral part of the constitutional basis of the European Union. Each, as we have seen, are binding in the UK by reason of the European Communities Act 1972 and its successive amendments by the various European Union Acts.

ACCESSION OF A8 STATES, CYPRUS AND MALTA

Introduction and summary of the current position

6.7 Under the 2003 Accession Treaty, nationals of Cyprus and Malta were granted the same rights to work in another Member State as are currently enjoyed by nationals of the existing Member States. However, for the remaining eight accession states ('the A8 states'), the existing EU Member States were permitted to impose transitional provisions to regulate access to their labour market,[1] thereby derogating from the right to free movement of these workers.[2] Those transitional arrangements could be imposed during the seven years following the date of accession, that is, until 30 April 2011. The UK's derogating national measures were the Accession (Immigration and Worker Registration) Regulations 2004.[3] It created a system of worker registration whereby all A8 nationals working in the UK between 1 May 2004 and 30 April 2011 were deemed to be an 'accession state worker requiring registration' unless they fell within a number of exceptions.[4] Accession state workers requiring registration were required to hold a registration certificate for 12 months, after which they could enjoy full access to the UK's labour market. Under regulations 5(2) to (4) such workers generally only had a right of residence in the UK as workers under the 2006 EEA Regulations (SI 2006/1003) during a period in which they were working for an employer for whom they were authorised to work under the workers' registration scheme in Part 3 of the 2004 Regulations. Upon completion of 12 months working in possession of a registration card, the A8 national had full access to the UK labour market. The lawfulness of the scheme was upheld by a majority of the House of Lords in *Zalewska*.[5]

Although the 2004 Regulations were revoked on 1 May 2011 following the expiry of the accession period,[6] an analysis of the 2003 Treaty and the 2004 Regulations are included below since they remain relevant in determining the historic immigration position of A8 nationals before that date who are now, for example, seeking permanent residence under the Immigration (European Economic Area) Regulations 2006, SI 2006/1003.[7]

[1] These are set out in Annexes V, VI, VIII, IX, X, XII, XIII and XIV of the Act of Accession 2003. Chapter 2 of each Annex contains the relevant material on each Member State. Their effect can be demonstrated by examining the agreement with Slovakia in Annex XIV. These are standard rules which apply to each of the eight relevant new Member States, although in fact all the Annex XIV references below are taken from the rules for Slovakia. See further Professor Steve Peers of the University of Essex, who prepared the Statewatch comments on the EU Accession Treaty.

[2] The derogation only applied to free movement of *workers*. It did *not* apply to freedom of establishment (of the self-employed) or movement for any other purpose (as students, pensioners or self-sufficient persons) or the limited temporary movement of workers to provide services, as defined in Article 1 of Directive 96/71/EC (the Posted Workers Directive). Those freedoms applied immediately upon the entry into force of the Accession Treaty.

[3] SI 2004/1219

[4] See **6.11** below. In summary, the exceptions were set out in reg 2 of the 2004 Regulations. For the purposes of reg 2(3), 'legally working' does not include work whilst an asylum seeker on temporary admission or as an overstaying spouse: *Miskovic v Secretary of State for Work and Pensions* [2011] EWCA Civ 16; [2011] 2 CMLR 495. Note that, for workers admitted under UK domestic law (for example, on a work permit) either before or after 1 May 2004, the Annexes of the 2003 Accession Treaty provided that Accession State workers legally employed on that date and admitted for over 12 months for employment will enjoy continued access to the labour market of that Member State (Annex XIV, para 2). The same applied to those admitted to the labour market for a 12-month period after enlargement. So, even though the work permit regime of the particular country restricted employment to a specified job with a specified employer, the Accession State worker was able to change jobs without having to seek further permission from the authorities. Furthermore, it would not have been possible for an existing Member State to remove people on economic grounds if they have already been admitted or were later admitted for longer-term employment during the transitional period. However, this leeway provided by the Annexes does not seem to have filtered through when translated into the worker registration scheme under the UK's 2004 Regulations.

[5] *Zalewska v Department for Social Development (Child Poverty Action Group intervening)* [2008] UKHL 67, [2008] 1 WLR 2602. The correctness of *Zalewska* was re-iterated by the Court of Appeal in *Mirga v Secretary of State for Work and Pensions* [2012] EWCA Civ 1952, notwithstanding subsequent CJEU and Supreme Court authority (see [15]-[31] of the Court of Appeal's judgment).

[6] The Accession (Immigration and Worker Registration) (Revocation, Savings and Consequential Provisions) Regulations 2011, SI 2011/544 give effect to the ending of the accession period in accordance with the 2003 Accession Treaty. Regulation 3 ensures that reg 8 of the 2004 Regulations continues, with an amendment, for one year from the coming into force of these

Regulations to enable the Secretary of State to continue to process applications for registration of employment made by a person who was an accession State national requiring registration on 30 April 2011 and who was working for the relevant employer at the date of application.
[7] Note that periods of lawful residence in the UK by A8 nationals prior to 1 May 2004 under UK domestic law should count as residence 'in accordance with these regulations' for the purposes of Regulation 15(1)(a) of the 2006 Regulations, applying *Ziolkowski v Land Berlin; Szeja v Land Berlin*: Joined Cases C-424/10 and 425/10; [2014] All ER (EC) 314;[2013] 3 CMLR 1013, ECJ, CJEU (itself applied in *Secretary of State for Work and Pensions v Czop; Secretary of State for Work and Pensions v Punakova*: Joined Cases C-147/11 and C-148/11 [2013] PTSR 334, [2012] All ER (D) 65 (Sep), ECJ. See also Case C-162/09 *Lassal*, Case C-325/09 *Maria Dias* and Joined Cases C-424/10. In the light of these cases, the AIT decisions of *JT (Polish workers, time spent in UK) Poland* [2008] UKAIT 00077 and *GN (EEA Regulations: Five years' residence) Hungary* [2007] UKAIT 00073 (which were discussed at 6.18-6.19 of the eighth edition of this work), should not be followed. It may also be that the House of Lords' decision in *Zalewska v Department for Social Development* [2008] UKHL 67;[2009] NI 116;[2009] 2 All ER 319 may also need to be revisited because one of the premises upon which the decision was based was that an A8 state national who did not register did not have access to the income-related benefits system because she had no right to reside in the UK – a proposition which is no longer in accordance with EU law.

6.8 Now that the accession period has come to an end following the revocation of the 2004 Regulations, someone who was an accession State worker requiring registration on 30 April 2011 will be entitled to reside in the UK in accordance with the Immigration (European Economic Area) Regulations 2006, SI 2006/1003 as amended. This is subject to the consequential amendments made to the 2006 Regulations provided by regulation 5 of, and set out in Schedule 2 to, those Regulations. These amendments insert a new regulation 7A which makes provision for how residence by such a person in accordance with the 2004 Regulations should be treated for the purposes of residence under the 2006 Regulations. Regulation 3(4) of the 2006 Regulations provides that the provisions of the 2004 Regulations relied upon in the consequential amendments to the 2006 Regulations continue to apply to the extent necessary to give effect to the amendments.

How the 2003 Accession Treaty operated

6.9 What then was the position under the Accession Treaty of 2003 as regards free movement? First, it granted nationals of Cyprus and Malta the same rights to work in another Member State as were currently enjoyed by nationals of the existing Member States. Secondly, however, nationals of the other eight relevant States (A8 Nationals) were subject to transitional provisions.[1] Thirdly, nationals of the eight new relevant Member States enjoyed free movement rights as regards each other, although these could have been suspended at the Commission's discretion during the first seven years of membership (until 1 May 2011).[2] Fourthly, where the free movement of nationals of one of the relevant new Member States was restricted during any part of the transitional period by any of the existing States, the new Member State could take equivalent measures against the nationals of the Member State or States in question.[3] Fifthly, existing Member States applying national law during the derogation period, could not make their national rules more restrictive than they were on 1 May 2004,[4] but they could introduce, under national law, more liberal rules if they wished, 'including full labour market access'.[5] This is what happened in the UK (see below). From 1 May 2006 such a State could at any time decide to stop relying on national law and apply the full EC rules.[6] It is important to keep in mind that if a Member State only applied national rules which were more liberal, than the EC rules, the interpretation of those rules was presumably outside the jurisdiction of the EU courts, unless they allegedly infringed the Accession Treaty.[7] Even those Member States which applied full free movement of workers had a special safeguard for seven years (until 1 May 2011), if there were serious threats to the standard of living or the level of employment due to disturbances in its labour market.[8]

[1] These are set out in Annexes V, VI, VIII, IX, X, XII, XIII and XIV of the Act of Accession. Chapter 2 of each Annex contains the relevant material on each Member State. Their effect can be demonstrated by examining the agreement with Slovakia in Annex XIV. These are standard rules which apply to each of the eight relevant new Member States, although in fact all the Annex XIV references below are taken from the rules for Slovakia. See further Professor Steve Peers of the University of Essex, who prepared the Statewatch comments on the EU Accession Treaty.

[2] Annex XIV, para 11.

[3] Annex XIV, para 10.

[4] Annex XIV, para 14. This paragraph also obliges existing Member States to give preference to workers from the accession States over third country nationals as regards access to their labour market, and they may not treat non-EU nationals more favourably than workers and their families from the accession States. Equally new Member States cannot treat nationals from existing Member States and their families, who are in the new Member State, less favourably than third country nationals.

[5] Annex XIV, para 12.

[6] Annex XIV, para 12. In fact the Worker's Registration Scheme is to continue until 2009: see written ministerial statement to Parliament, 25 April 2006, by the Home Office Minister, Tony McNulty.

[7] Statewatch Comments, above.

[8] Annex XIV, para 7. However, any decision to suspend free movement rights will be at the discretion of the Commission, whose decision can be overturned by the Council. It is also possible for Member States to apply the safeguard unilaterally 'in urgent and exceptional cases'.

6.10 The scope of the derogation needs to be understood. It only applied to free movement of workers.[1] It did and does *not* apply to freedom of establishment (of the self-employed) or movement for any other purpose (as students, pensioners or self-sufficient persons) or the limited temporary movement of workers to provide services, as defined in Article 1 of Directive 96/71/EC.[2] Those freedoms applied immediately upon the entry into force of the Accession Treaty. Secondly, the derogation from the full free movement of workers and services applied in three distinct stages. There was an initial period of two years after accession, during which period national immigration law or measures resulting from bilateral agreements would apply.[3] (paragraph 2). Prior to the end of this period, ie prior to 1 May 2006, any Member State that had not imposed restrictions on free movement of workers from the eight relevant States, or had relaxed them in the interim, was free to impose them or re-impose them.[4] From 1 May 2006, Member States had either to grant nationals from the eight relevant States the right to move freely for the purpose of work in accordance with Community law, or continue to apply national measures or bilateral agreements for a further three-year period, up to 30 April 2009.[5] If the option to extend the period of derogation until that date was not taken up, full free movement rights applied.[6] After five years, Member States could extend the derogation until the end of a seven-year period (1 May 2011), if they had notified the Commission before then that there were 'serious disturbances of its labour market or threats thereof.'[7] In the absence of any notification the derogation would automatically come to an end. Thirdly, even if full free movement rights did come into play before the end of the seven-year period, an individual Member State, which 'undergoes or foresees disturbances of its labour market which could seriously threaten the standard of living or level of employment in a given region or occupation', could apply to the Commission to suspend worker rights wholly or in part.[8]

[1] Although derogation is allowed from Article 49 of the EC Treaty, which deals with the provision of services (see next fn) free movement of services may operate during the three-month period during which all EU nationals may enter and reside in any othe Member State under Article 6 of the Citizens' Directive.

[2] The derogation only applies to the free movement rights contained in arts 39 and 49 of the EC Treaty (other than those involving the temporary movement of workers), and those rights contained in arts 1–6 of Regulation 1612/68, such as the right to take up an activity as an employed person in another Member State (para 2). Since the provisions of Directive 68/360/EEC cover much the same ground as arts 1–6 of Regulation 1612/68 and cannot be disassociated from them, derogation from those provisions is also allowed by para 9. However, it should also be noted that Directive 68/360/EEC has been repealed by Council Directive 2004/38/EC (the Citizens' Directive) art 38.

[3] Annexe XIV, para 2.

[4] This is the view set out in the Government Guide to the European Union (Accessions) Bill. Paras 2 and 3, however, speak of the 'present Member States . . . ', suggesting a collective rather than individual choice to continue derogation; contrast paras 5 and 7 which speak of ' . . . a Member State . . . '.

[5] Annex XIV, para 3.

[6] Annex XIV, para 3.

[7] Annex XIV, para 5.

[8] The Commission then has two weeks in which to determine the application and decide on the terms of a derogation. See Annex XIV, para 7. There is also provision in art 37 of the Act of Accession for a safeguard to be applied until 1 May 2007, which allows new members to apply for authorisation to take protective measures, including derogations from the rules of the EC Treaty, if they have serious economic difficulties. These could be relevant to freedom of establishment or freedom to provide services as well as the free movement of workers. Article 38 provides for a similar safeguard regarding the 'internal market'.

6.11 What about the free movement of workers who were admitted (for example, on a work permit) under the domestic law of one of the Member States either before or after 1 May 2004? The Annexes provide that Accession State workers legally employed on that date and admitted for over 12 months for employment would enjoy continued access to the labour market of that Member State.[1] The same would apply to those admitted to the labour market for a 12-month period after enlargement.[2] So, even though the work permit regime of the particular country restricted employment to a specified job with a specified employer, the Accession State worker would be able to change jobs without having to seek further permission from the authorities. Furthermore, it would be impossible for an existing Member State to remove people on economic grounds if they had already been admitted or were later admitted for longer-term employment during the transitional period. However, this leeway provided by the Annexes does not seem to have filtered through when translated into the worker registration schemes.

[1] Annex XIV, para 2.

[2] Annex XIV, para 2.

6.12 The position of the worker may be clear, but there is or may be a problem with the position of family members. Since only Articles 1–6 of Regulation 1612/68 (workers' right to take up an activity as an employed person in another Member State and ancillary rights) were expressly made part of the derogation, implicitly, then, the *other* provisions of that Regulation (concerning equal treatment while in employment, (Articles 7–9) family reunion and the right of family members to employment and education) (Articles 10–12) would apply, *if* a Member State authorised an Accession State national to enter its territory as a worker.[1] The EC rules on social security, expulsions and mutual recognition of qualifications will also apply. However, Annex XIV, paragraph 8 modifies the application of Article 11 of Regulation 1612/68 regarding access to employment. Those family members legally residing in an existing Member State with a worker on the date of accession (1 May 2004) would have immediate access to employment if the worker had been authorised to stay there for 12 or more months.[2] Otherwise they would only have access to employment if they had lived there for over 18 months, or from the third year following the date of accession (1 May 2007), whichever comes earlier.[3] It is not expressly stated that the family members would have equal access to the labour market, though this must be inferred from the non-discrimination clause in the Annex[4] and from the general provisions of the EC Treaty.[5] Nevertheless, there is a clear problem with this provision. All eight of the relevant new accession States had previously entered into Association Agreements with the European Communities. In each of these agreements, there was a general clause saying that the legally resident spouse and children of a worker employed in the territory of a Member State should, subject to exceptions, have access to the labour market of that Member State during the period of the worker's authorised employment.[7] No waiting period for access was provided for (although conversely there was no right of family reunion under the Agreements). It follows that for family members joining workers during the first three years following enlargement, their right of access to employment would be more limited than it was before accession, and more limited than it remained for nationals of Romania and Bulgaria prior to their joining the EU.[8]

[1] See Statewatch Comments, above.
[2] Annex XIV, para 8.
[3] Annex XIV, para 8.
[4] Annex XIV, para 14.
[5] EC Treaty art 12 (ex art 6).
[7] See Agreement with Poland, art 37 (1) 2nd indent, printed in *Butterworths Immigration Law Service* F[6001].
[8] See below **6.197** and Statewatch Comments, above.

How the 2003 Accession Treaty operated in UK law

6.13 In order to give effect in UK law to The Accession Treaty, the European Union (Accessions) Act 2003 amends the definitions of 'the treaties' and 'the Community treaties' in the European Communities Act 1972 to include the 2003 Treaty. In broad terms, it did two things. First, it enabled the Accession Treaty to be implemented in UK law, by granting automatic effect to directly applicable Treaty provisions. Secondly, it provided the power to make regulations amending existing UK legislation, to the extent necessary to give nationals of the Czech Republic, Estonia, Latvia, Lithuania, Hungary, Poland, Slovenia and Slovakia ('the eight relevant States') the same rights to work in the UK from 1 May 2004 as those enjoyed by nationals of the States in the European Economic Area (EEA).[1] In fact the Regulations did no such thing, but instead created a complicated registration system.

1   The regulations are the Accession (Immigration and Worker Registration) Regulations 2004, SI 2004/1219. For the purposes of these Regulations the European Economic Area comprised all Member States of the EU, except the UK, together with Norway, Iceland and Liechtenstein prior to the new accessions. Switzerland was not included in the definition in the Regulations, as it is in the Accession (Immigration and Worker Authorisation) Regulations 2006 (see below), although it was catered for in the provisions of the 2004 Regulations.

Registration scheme for workers in accession period

6.14 In order to give force in UK national law to the provisions which regulate the position of nationals from the relevant new Member States of the EU during the transitional period before full free movement rights for workers and their families came into force, the government made Regulations to establish a worker registration scheme for workers from the eight relevant States.[1] They came into force on 1 May 2004. If it is right that in setting up the registration scheme and its ancillary provisions, the UK was applying national law, not EC law, the new scheme would have been outside the jurisdiction of the European Court. The government announced in May 2006 that the registration scheme would continue after 1 May 2006, noting that applicants had helped to fill vacancies in parts of the economy experiencing shortages of labour. The Accession (Immigration and Worker Registration) Regulations 2004[2] defined those who needed to register and were amended a number of times. Regulation 2 of the 2004 Regulations exempted relevant accession State nationals who were family members of Bulgarian and Romanian self-employed and self sufficient persons and students from the need to register under the 2004 Regulations. And relevant accession State nationals who were members of a diplomatic mission, the family members of such a person; or were otherwise entitled to diplomatic immunity were also exempted from the need to register. These changes brought the 2004 Regulations into line with the derogation in the 2003 Accession Treaty.

1   Accession (Immigration and Worker Registration) Regulations 2004, SI 2004/1219.
2   SI 2004/1219.

6.15 Regulation 4 gives effect to the derogation provided for in the Accession Treaty to regulate access to the UK labour market by accession State nationals. Under regulation 4(2), nationals from the relevant accession States who come to the UK to seek work during the transitional period, will not have a right to reside in the UK by virtue of their work seeker status, but will only be able to do so if they are self-sufficient.[1] The idea of this provision is to deter so called 'benefit scroungers'.[2]

1   Accession (Immigration and Worker Registration) Regulations 2004, SI 2004/1219, reg 4(3). 'Self-sufficient person' is defined in the Immigration (European Economic Area) Regulations 2006, SI 2006/1003, reg 4(1)(c).
2   For EEA workers and benefits see CHAPTER 14 below. However, the detailed implications of the accession regime for social security law are beyond the scope of this work, and for a fuller discussion on access to welfare benefits for nationals of accession States see Nicola Rogers and Rick Scannell *Free Movement of Persons in the Enlarged European Union* (Sweet & Maxwell, 2004), ch 28. In *Kaczmarek (Sylwia) v Secretary State for Work and Pensions* [2008] EWCA Civ 1310, [2009] 2 CMLR 85, [2009] PTSR 897, where the Court of Appeal held that a Polish national who had been lawfully resident in the United Kingdom for three years and active as

a student or an employee for most of that time did not have an entitlement to income support under the EC Treaty (Nice) art 12 or art 18.

6.16 Some workers from the relevant new Accession Member States may already have acquired settled or similar status under UK domestic immigration law or they may have had transitional rights under the Accession Treaty as described above. They will not come within the transitional registration scheme, which came into force after 1 May 2004 and was expected to last until 30 April 2009. This is dealt with by regulations 5, 7 and 8.

6.17 Regulation 5 modified the application of the 2000 Regulations to workers from the relevant accession States who were 'Accession State workers requiring registration', as defined in regulation 2.[1] Broadly speaking, the following rules defined those required to register under the transitional regime:

- An 'Accession State worker requiring registration' means a national of a relevant accession State working in the UK during the accession period.[2]
- Someone who, on 30 April 2004, had leave to enter or remain in the UK under the 1971 Act and that leave was not subject to any condition restricting his employment is not an accession State worker requiring registration.[3]
- Someone who was legally working in the UK on 30 April 2004 and had been legally working here without interruption throughout the previous 12 months is not an accession State worker requiring registration.[4]
- Someone who legally works in the UK without interruption for a period of 12 months falling partly or wholly after 30 April 2004 ceases to be an accession State worker requiring registration at the end of that period of 12 months.[5]
- Someone who is a dual national and is also a national of (a) the UK; (b) another EEA State, other than a relevant accession State; or (c) Switzerland is not an accession State worker requiring registration.[6]
- A person is not an Accession State worker requiring registration during any period in which he or she is (a) a posted worker;[7] or (b) a family member[8] of a Swiss or EEA national who is in the UK as (i) a worker, other than as an accession State worker requiring registration; (ii) a self-sufficient person; (iii) a retired person; (v) a self-employed person; or (v) a student.[9]

[1] There is no need to delete the reference to the 2000 Regulations, because in the transitional provisions of the 2006 Regulations it is provided that any period during which a person carried out an activity or was resident in the UK in accordance with the 2000 Regulations shall be treated as a period during which the person carried out that activity or was resident in the UK in accordance with these Regulations for the purpose of calculating periods of activity and residence under these Regulations: Immigration (European Economic Area) Regulations 2006, SI 2006/1003, Sch 4, para 6.
[2] Accession (Immigration and Worker Registration) Regulations 2004, SI 2004/1219, reg 2(1).
[3] SI 2004/1219, reg 2(2).
[4] SI 2004/1219, reg 2(3). Someone, who is 'legally working' is defined in reg 2(7). The meaning of 'without interruption' is contained in reg 2(8). For the purposes of reg 2(3), 'legally working' does not include work whilst an asylum seeker is on temporary admission or an overstaying spouse: *Miskovic v Secretary of State for Work and Pensions* [2011] EWCA Civ 16, [2011] 2 CMLR 495.
[5] SI 2004/1219, reg 2(4). See above fn for the meaning of the key words used.
[6] SI 2004/1219, reg 2(5).
[7] SI 2004/1219, reg 2(6). 'Posted worker' is defined in reg 2(9)(b).

8 'Family member' is defined in SI 2004/1219, reg 2(9)(c).

9 SI 2004/1219, reg 2(6), as amended by the Immigration (European Economic Area) and Accession (Amendment) Regulations 2004, SI 2004/1236, reg 3(2). 'Self sufficient person' is defined in SI 2004/1219, reg 1(2)(j) and SI 2000/2326, reg 3; 'retired person' and 'student' in reg 3 of SI 2000/2326.

6.18 Under regulations 5(2) to (4) those who were 'Accession State workers requiring registration' would generally only have a right of residence in the UK as workers under the 2006 Regulations[1] during a period in which they were working for an employer for whom they were authorised to work under the workers' registration scheme in Part 3 of these Regulations. Whilst they required registration, neither they nor their family members[2] were entitled to have a residence permit or document.[3] However, the Immigration Appeal Tribunal has held that Accession nationals who were in the UK at the date of accession should not be removed unless they pose a threat to public health, public policy or public security.[4]

1 The reference to the 2006 Regulations is explained in fn 1 in the previous paragraph.

2 'Family member' is defined in Accession (Immigration and Worker Registration) Regulations 2004, SI 2004/1219, reg 2(9)(c), as amended by the Immigration (European Economic Area) and Accession (Amendment) Regulations 2004, SI 2004/1236, reg 3(2).

3 SI 2004/1219, reg 5(5) and (6).

4 Ie, on the same grounds as other EEA nationals (see **6.170** ff): *MH (Slovakia)* [2004] UKIAT 00315 'IAT Reported'.

6.19 Part 3 of the Accession Regulations set out the Accession State worker registration scheme, which will apply to Accession State workers requiring registration.[1] Under regulation 7, workers requiring registration, who were already in legal employment on 30 April 2004, could continue to work for the employer concerned without further registration.[2] Workers requiring registration who began work on or after 1 May 2004 had to apply, within one month of beginning working, for a registration certificate (WRC) authorising them to work for the employer concerned if they were to be authorised to work for that employer for more than a month.[3] A WRC is very important. It took effect from its date of issue once received by the worker. It is not retrospective.[4] It helps determine the start date of an A8 state worker's period of lawful employment in the UK. During the time an A8 State worker has been employed by an 'authorised employer', the A8 State worker is treated as a 'qualified person' for the purpose of the 2006 EEA Regulations, but even so, the A8 state worker could not obtain a registration certificate under reg 16 of the 2006 EEA Regulations and his family members were not entitled to a residence card under reg 17 of the 2006 EEA Regulations.[5] Regulation 8 sets out the registration procedure. Workers requiring registration would be issued with a registration card and a registration certificate authorising them to work for the employer concerned. A fee of £50 was charged for the first registration to cover the administrative costs of registration. Regulation 9 made it an offence for an employer to employ a worker who was not authorised under the registration scheme to work for that employer.

The principal purpose of the Scheme was to enable the UK Government to monitor and review the arrangements for access by A8 State nationals to the UK labour market during the accession period. It was not intended to limit or restrict access, although it was intended to encourage those working in the UK illegally to regularise their status.[6] In *Zalewska v Department for Social*

Development[7] the appellant was a Polish worker who had worked over 12 months in Northern Ireland for various employers but had failed to obtain the necessary registration certificate from one of her employers. As a result she was not recognised as having completed 12 months' continuous employment and was not, therefore, entitled to claim Social Security benefit. The case raised the issue of whether the Accession (Immigration and Worker Registration) Regulations 2004 were compatible with Community law or whether the system of requiring A8 workers to have a registration certificate from their employer under the worker registration regulations was disproportionate. The House of Lords divided 3 to 2 against the appellant, the majority holding that the registration scheme was compatible with EU law and the appellant was not, therefore, entitled to her benefit. *Zalewska* was re-affirmed by the Court of Appeal in *Mirga v Secretary of State for Work and Pensions*[8] in which the Court rejected any suggestion that the applicability of the workers registration scheme in any given case could be conditional upon compliance with the principle of proportionality with reference to Article 20 TFEU.

1   Accession (Immigration and Worker Registration) Regulations 2004, SI 2004/1219, regs 7 to 9.
2   SI 2004/1219, reg 7(2)(a).
3   SI 2004/1219, reg 7(2)(b) and (3). Special provision is made in reg 7(4) in relation to seasonal agricultural workers until 31 December 2004.
4   *Szpak v Secretary of State for Work and Pensions* [2013] EWCA Civ 46, in which the Court of Appeal confirmed that the worker had a one-month grace period, under the 2004 Regulations, after commencing work during which he or she was authorised to work. The worker was expected to make the WRC application during that first month and once made within that period, the worker could work lawfully for that employer. However, continuity of residence under the 2004 Regulations would not commence until receipt of the WRC. See also *JL (A8 worker – lawful employment) Poland* [2009] UKAIT 00030, which should be read with caution following *Ziolkowski*.
5   SI 2004/1219, reg 5(5).
6   *Zalewska v Department for Social Development (Child Poverty Action Group intervening)* [2008] UKHL 67, [2009] NI 116, [2009] 2 All ER 319 per Lord Hope of Craighead and at [53]–[54] per Baroness Hale of Richmond.
7   As fn 6 above.
8   [2012] EWCA Civ 1952.

A8 nationals and permanent residence

6.20 The position of A8 nationals as regards permanent residence/indefinite leave in the UK has followed a somewhat chequered path. First, A8 nationals whose country had an Association Agreement with the EU and were admitted to the UK under this Agreement before their country's accession to membership of the EU on 1 May 2004 qualified for indefinite leave if their decisions were made prior to 30 April 2006. This, according to the reasoning of the AIT decision in *JT and Ors (Polish workers, time spent in UK) Poland*[1] was because they were permitted to aggregate the time spent in the UK under the Association Agreement and the Immigration (European Economic Area) Regulations 2000 in calculating the qualifying period for the grant of ILR. But those who had not managed to beat the 30 April 2006 deadline were not so lucky. This date was the date on which the Immigration (European Economic Area) Regulations 2006[2] came into force. Under those Regulations A8 nationals were not entitled to aggregation of time spent under the Association Agreement, as had been the case under the transitional provisions of the 2000

Regulations. Now A8 nationals could only qualify under the 2006 Regulations if they could show that they had 'resided legally for a continuous period of five years in the host Member State' as required by the Citizens' Directive[3] Article 16.1. In *GN (EEA Regulations: Five years' residence) Hungary*[4] the Tribunal held that the word 'legally' in Article 16 is to be construed as a reference to the requirements of European law, rather than 'in accordance with national law'. This meant that time would only begin to run for A8 nationals from 1 May 2004, when they became Union citizens and would not qualify for permanent residence until at the earliest 2009.

[1]   [2008] UKAIT 00077 (31 July 2008).
[2]   SI 2006/1003.
[3]   Directive 2004/38/EC.
[4]   [2007] UKAIT 00073.

6.21 The case law and problem cited above at **6.17–6.19** have now been overtaken by the judgments of the CJEU in Case C-162/09 *Lassal*, Case C-325/09 *Maria Dias* and *Ziolkowski v Land Berlin; Szeja v Land Berlin*: Joined Cases C-424/10 and 425/10 [2014] All ER (EC) 314, [2013] 3 CMLR 1013, ECJ. We discuss these cases at **6.161**, below. The upshot is that *JT (Polish workers, time spent in UK) Poland*[1] and *GN (EEA Regulations: Five years' residence) Hungary*[2], referred to in **6.20**, are no longer reliable authorities and should not be followed. The House of Lords' decision in *Zalewska v Department for Social Development (Child Poverty Action Group intervening)*[3] discussed in **6.19** may also need to be revisited because one of the premises upon which the decision was based was that an A8 state national who did not register did not have access to the income-related benefits system because she had no right to reside in the UK – a proposition which is no longer in accordance with EU law.

[1]   [2008] UKAIT 00077 (31 July 2008).
[2]   [2007] UKAIT 00073.
[3]   [2008] UKHL 67, [2009] NI 116, [2009] 2 All ER 319.

ACCESSION OF BULGARIA AND ROMANIA

6.22 According to the 2001 census, there were 7,500 Romanian-born people and 5,350 Bulgarians living in the UK. It was predicted in Spring 2006 that following Accession around 56,000 Romanian and Bulgarian workers were likely to migrate to Britain following Accession (IPPR).[1] We are indebted to this paper for some of the text which follows. In 2006 the UK government announced it would limit the rights of nationals of Bulgaria and Romania, to work in the UK. In November 2006 the Accession (Immigration and Worker Authorisation) Regulations 2006 were laid before Parliament and came into force on 1 January 2007.[2] The 2006 Accession Regulations make provision in relation to the entitlement of nationals of Bulgaria and Romania to reside and work in the UK on the accession of those States to the European Union. In particular, the Regulations restrict access to the UK labour market by Bulgarian and Romanian nationals. The Accession Treaty for Bulgaria and Romania (signed in Luxembourg on 25 April 2005) provided that existing Member States could, as a derogation from the usual position under European Union free movement law, regulate access to their labour markets by Bulgarian and Romanian nationals.

1   JCWI 'The Accession (Immigration and Worker Authorisation) Regulations 2006: Implications for UK employers and Bulgarian and Romanian ("A2") nationals in the UK,' para 3. In fact, the number of Bulgarians and Romanians applying to work in the UK was 10,420 in May 2007 and had dropped to only 8,205 applications from A2 nationals in the first three months of 2008: UKBA website, 20 May 2008.
2   SI 2006/3317, since amended by the Accession (Immigration and Worker Authorisation) (Amendment) Regulations 2007, SI 2007/475 and the Accession (Worker Authorisation and Worker Registration) (Amendment) Regulations 2007, SI 2007/3012.

6.23 The European Union (Accessions) Act 2006 makes the 2005 Accession Treaty and its provisions part of UK national law and section 2 of the Act gives the Secretary of State the power to make regulations about free movement rights for nationals of those two countries. The Accession (Immigration and Worker Authorisation) Regulations 2006, SI 2006/3317, set up the workers authorisation scheme regulating access to the UK labour market by nationals from the Republic of Bulgaria and Romania and applied during a five-year transitional period that was initially scheduled to end on 31 December 2011 but was extended for a further two years, so that the transitional measures continued to apply until 31 December 2013.[1] This extension was implemented following an assessment by the UK Government's Migration Advisory Committee that, on the basis of the indicators of labour market performance which it has used, the UK labour market was in a state of serious disturbance and that lifting the current restrictions would risk negative impacts on the labour market.[2] If it is right that in setting up the registration scheme and its ancillary provisions, the UK is applying national law, not EU law, the workers registration scheme set up by the 2006 Regulations falls outside the jurisdiction of the Court of Justice of the European Union.

1   The Accession (Immigration and Worker Authorisation) (Amendment) Regulations 2011, SI 2011/2816.
2   See further, 'Review of the transitional restrictions on access of Bulgarian and Romanian national to the UK labour market', Migration Advisory Committeee, November 2011: www.gov.uk\\government\\uploads\\system\\uploads\\attachmentdata\\file\\257232\\transitional-restrictions.pdf.

6.24 From 1 January 2014, the transitional period under the 2005 Accession Act expired with the result that nationals of Bulgaria and Romania who were an accession State worker requiring registration on 31 December 2013 have been entitled to reside in the UK in accordance with the Immigration (European Economic Area) Regulations 2006, SI 2006/1003, as amended ('the EEA Regulations'). They are therefore no longer subject to the worker registration requirements under the Accession Regulations.[1] Importantly, on 1 January 2014, a new Regulation 7B was inserted into the EEA Regulations 2006,[2] which governs how residence in accordance with the Accession Regulations should now be treated under the EEA Regulations. For example, for the purposes of regulation 15 of the EEA Regulations (concerning permanent residence), any period in which the former accession State national subject to worker authorisation was 'legally working' in the UK is treated as being residence 'in accordance with these Regulations' (reg 7B(6)). Also, any Bulgarian or Romanian national subject to worker authorisation who became involuntarily unemployed before 1 January 2014 does not retain the status of 'worker' during that period of unemployment (reg 7B(4)). Notwithstanding the expiry of the transitional arrangements on 1 January 2014, we will nevertheless proceed to examine the 2005 Accession Treaty and the 2006 Accession Regulations in some detail, given their relatively recent expiry and ongoing relevance to the establishment of free movement rights.

[1] Which have been amended so that the Secretary of State's power to issue registration certificates is limited to the 'accession period', defined in reg 1(2)(c) as 1 January 2007 to 31 December 2013. The amendments were made to Regulations 7(2) and 11(1) of the 2006 Accession Regulations by the Immigration (European Economic Area) (Amendment) (No 2) Regulations 2013/3032, Sch 2, para 3(2) and (3) on 1 January 2014.

[2] By the Immigration (European Economic Area) (Amendment) (No 2) Regulations 2013/3032, Sch 1, para 4 (January 1, 2014).

The 2005 Accession Treaty

6.25 The position under the 2005 Accession Treaty is not dissimilar to that which operated for the 'A8' east European members under the 2003 Treaty. In the case of Bulgaria and Romania, Annexes VI and VII to the Act of Accession 2005 provide that during a transitional period of five years (that is from 1 January 2007 to 31 December 2011) the existing Member States could regulate access to their labour markets by Bulgarian and Romanian workers and restrict their accompanying rights of residence, with provision for a Member State to continue to maintain restrictions for a further two years in the case of disturbances to its labour market. However, one of the terms of the derogation is that the restrictions imposed on access to the labour market must not be more restrictive than those prevailing on the date of signature of the Accession Treaty.[1] The restrictions on access to the UK labour market in the 2006 Accession Regulations purported to have been imposed on the basis of that derogation. This has meant that skilled and highly skilled workers have been able to come to the UK to work but access to low-skilled jobs has been restricted to the Seasonal Agricultural Workers Scheme (SAWS) and the Sector Based Scheme (SBS) for food processing. On 18 December 2008, the UKBA website announced that these restrictions on Bulgarians and Romanians would remain.

[1] See Explanatory Memorandum to Accession (Immigration and Worker Authorisation) (Amendment) Regulations 2007, SI 2007/ 475, at para 4. These amendments made changes to the permitted hours students could work, precisely because the 2006 Accession Regulations made greater restrictions than those prevailing before the Accession Treaty.

6.26 The derogation only affected the right of access to the labour market. It did not otherwise affect the rights of Bulgarian and Romanian nationals to all the other benefits of EU membership on the same basis as nationals of existing EU Member States. Thus, they have a right of residence for a period of up to three months under Article 6 of the Citizens' Directive without any formalities other than the requirement to hold a valid identity card or passport.[1] Secondly, although employment might have been restricted, self-employment and establishing a business were not. After the initial three-month period, such persons could stay on and become entitled to a registration certificate, as could the self-sufficient and students,[2] within the terms of Article 7 of the Citizens' Directive.

[1] Council Directive 2004/38/EC; Immigration (European Economic Area) Regulations 2006, SI 2006/1003, reg 11.

2   In Case C-15/11 *11 Sommer (Leopold) v Landesgeschäftsstelle des Arbeitsmarktservice Wien* (21 June 2012, unreported), the Court of Justice of the European Union confirmed that, during the transitional period following Bulgaria's accession to the EU, the conditions of access by Bulgarian students to the labour market of another Member State may not be more restrictive than those applicable to students who are third-country nationals, ie as set down in Council Directive 2004/114/EC of 13 December 2004 (on the conditions of admission of third-country nationals for the purposes of studies, pupil exchange, unremunerated training or voluntary service).

6.27 The family members of those Bulgarians and Romanians who had an extended right of residence could also benefit from the normal EU free movement and residence rights which apply to other EU nationals.[1] Because Bulgarian and Romanian nationals have not required leave to enter following accession, they cannot be classified as overstayers or illegal entrants and were not, after 1 January 2007, unlawfully present in the UK.[2] By opting for self-employment, whether as a cleaner or a plumber, they could escape the complications and sheer bureaucracy of the worker registration scheme. Bulgarians and Romanians could also come to the UK as posted workers sent to work here by their employers back home, but their stay would only be on a temporary basis during the period their employer was performing services in the UK.[3] Bulgaria and Romania have both signed up to an Agreement on the Participation of the Republic of Bulgaria and Romania in the European Economic Area, signed on 25 July 2007.[4]

1   See Council Directive 2004/38/EC, paras 6(2), 7(2) and 16(2).
2   Accession (Immigration and Worker Authorisation) Regulations 2006, SI 2006/3317, reg 8 provided that any directions for removal given before 1 January 2007 shall cease to have effect after that date and any deportation decision shall be treated as a decision which is subject to justification on public policy, public security or public health grounds under regulation 19(3)(b) of the Immigration (European Economic Area) Regulations 2006, SI 2006/1003.
3   For posted workers see **6.103**, below.
4   This has been declared to be an EU Treaty as defined in s 1(2) of the European Communities Act 1972 and is, therefore, part of UK national law: the European Communities (Definition of Treaties) (Agreement on Enlargement of the European Economic Area) Order 2008, SI 2008/297.

UK's implementation of the 2005 Accession Treaty

6.28 Part 1 of the Accession (Immigration and Worker Authorisation) Regulations 2006, SI 2006/3317 contains the general provisions of the Regulations. Regulation 2 defines 'accession State national subject to worker authorisation' as 'a national of Bulgarian or Romania', and such persons were obliged to obtain permission to work in the UK, unless exempted. Regulations 2(2) to 2(13) define those that were exempt from the requirement to obtain such permission. It is a long list. Nationals of Bulgaria or Romania are not (or cease to be) 'accession State nationals subject to worker authorisation':

- if on accession they had leave to enter or remain in the UK under the Immigration Act 1971 without any condition restricting employment or were given such leave subsequent to accession on 1 January 2007;[1]
- if on 31 December 2006 they were in the UK with leave to remain not subject to any condition restricting employment or were given such leave after that date;[2]

- if they were legally working in the UK on 31 December 2006 and had been legally working in the UK without interruption throughout the period of 12 months ending on that date;[3]
- if they have legally worked in the UK without interruption for a period of 12 months falling partly or wholly after 31 December 2006.[4] For A2 nationals who find themselves just short of being able to meet the 12 months' lawful employment requirement, there are no relevant Home Office concessions, nor are these requirements contrary to EU law;[5]
- during any period in which they are also nationals of the UK; or an EEA State, other than Bulgaria or Romania;[6]
- during any period in which they are the spouse or civil partner of a national of the UK or of a person settled in the UK;[7]
- during any period when they are members of a diplomatic mission, the family members of such a person or who are otherwise entitled to diplomatic immunity;[8]
- during any period in which they have a permanent right of residence under regulation 15 of the 2006 EEA Regulations;[9]
- during any period in which they are the family members of Bulgarian's and Romanian's who are 'qualified persons'[10] either as self-employed, self-sufficient persons or students[11] or family members of an EEA national who has a right to reside in the UK under the 2006 EEA Regulations, unless that EEA national is—
  (i) a Bulgarian or Romanian national subject to worker authorisation; or
  (ii) a student who is a Bulgarian or Romanian national who is not an accession State national subject to worker authorisation solely by virtue of falling within the student exemptions contained in the Accession Regulations 2006, reg 2(10) or (10B);[12]
- during any period in which he or she is a highly skilled person and holds a registration certificate that includes a statement that he or she has unconditional access to the UK labour market;[13]
- during any period in which they are in the UK as a student, who does not work for more than 20 hours a week during term time, but may engage in full-time employment (i) during their vacation, (ii) for a period of 4 months on completion of their studies, or (iii) they are in a work placement directly related to a course of vocational training (for example, a sandwich course of study for a nursing qualification), and hold a registration certificate stating that they have access to the UK labour market as set out above;[14]
- during any period in which he or she is a posted worker.[15]

Regulation 12 of the Accession Regulations 2006 defines what is meant by working legally in reg 2(3) and (4) at a time before 1 January 2007 and at a time after that date.

---

[1] Accession (Immigration and Worker Authorisation) Regulations 2006, SI 2006/3317, reg 2(2), as amended by the Accession (Immigration and Worker Authorisation) (Amendment) Regulations 2007, SI 2007/475, reg 2(1)(a).

[2] Regulation 2(2) as amended (with effect from 16 March 2007). See *IP and Ors (A2 national – worker authorisation – exemptions) Bulgaria* [2009] UKAIT 00042, where it was pointed out that exemption from worker authorisation under the 2006 Accession Regulations as amended does not automatically entitle an A2 national to a registration certificate as a qualified person. It only permits him to be considered in the same way as other EEA nationals:

EA (EEA: 3 months residence) Bulgaria [2008] UKAIT 00017 and *SH (A2 nationals-worker authorisation exemption) Bulgaria* [2009] UKAIT 00020 reaffirmed. Exempt A2 nationals can qualify for a registration certificate under any of the sub-categories of qualified person under reg 6 of the Immigration (European Economic Area) Regulations 2006, SI 2006/1003. Non-exempt A2 nationals, by contrast, can only show they are a qualified person under reg 6, as a self-employed person or a self-sufficient person or as a student.

3 Accession Regulations 2006, reg 2(3). In *EA (EEA: 3 months residence) Bulgaria* [2008] UKAIT 00017, a Bulgarian worker in the UK on a work permit before the accession of Bulgaria, whose leave to enter expired two days before his 12 months were reached, could only count the right to 3 months' residence under Article 6 of the Citizens' Directive (reg 13(1) of EEA Regulations 2006, SI 2006/1003) as from the date of Bulgaria's accession and not from the date when his leave to enter expired.

4 Accession Regulations 2006, reg 2(4).

5 *SH (A2 nationals-worker authorisation exemption) Bulgaria* [2009] UKAIT 00020, where it was held that the terms of the exemption afforded by the Accession (European Economic Area) Regulations 2006 to A2 nationals legally working in the United Kingdom at the date of accession (1 January 2007) and for an uninterrupted period of 12 months are not contrary to either the relevant Accession Treaty provisions, nor does it offend the EU law principle of proportionality.

6 Accession Regulations 2006, reg 2(5).

7 Accession Regulations 2006, reg 2(6).

8 Accession Regulations 2006, reg 6A, inserted by the Accession (Worker Authorisation and Worker Registration) (Amendment) Regulations 2007, SI 2007/3012, reg 2(2).

9 Accession Regulations 2006, reg 2(7).

10 Immigration (European Economic Area) Regulations 2006, SI 2006/1003, reg 6(1)(c), (d), or (e).

11 Accession Regulations 2006, reg 2(8), as amended by the Accession (Worker Authorisation and Worker Registration) (Amendment) Regulations 2007, SI 2007/3012, reg 2(2)(b).

12 Accession Regulations 2006, reg 10, as amended by the Accession (Immigration and Worker Authorisation) (Amendment) Regulations 2007, SI 2007/475, reg 2(2)(c).

13 Accession Regulations 2006, reg 2(9). 'Highly skilled person' is defined by the Accession Regulations 2006, reg 4, as amended by the Accession (Worker Authorisation and Worker Registration) (Amendment) Regulations 2007, SI 2007/3012, para 2(4).

14 Accession Regulations 2006, reg 2(10), as amended by the Accession (Immigration and Worker Authorisation) (Amendment) Regulations 2007, SI 2007/475, reg 2(2). These amendments were necessary to make the Regulations compatible with the Accession Treaty.

15 Accession Regulations 2006, reg 2(11). 'Posted worker' means a worker who is posted to the UK, within the meaning of Article 1(3) of Directive 96/71/EC concerning the posting of workers, by an undertaking established in an EEA State.

6.29 Part 2 of the Regulations provides that a Bulgarian or Romanian national subject to the requirement to obtain permission to work will not be treated as a qualified person for the purposes of the 2006 Regulations,[1] and will only enjoy a right to reside on the basis of his or her worker status if he or she is in possession of an accession worker authorisation document and is working in accordance with the conditions set out in that document.[2] It also provides for the issue of a registration certificate, confirming the person has unconditional access to the UK labour market, in the case of a highly skilled person[3] or a Bulgarian or Romanian national who is exempt from the need to obtain a worker authorisation.[4] In the case of a student, the registration card will confirm that he or she has a limited right of access to the labour market.[5]

1 SI 2006/1003.

2 Accession (Immigration and Worker Authorisation) Regulations 2006, SI 2006/3317, reg 6.

3 Accession Regulations 2006, reg 7(2)(b).

4 Accession Regulations 2006, reg 7(3), as amended by the Accession (Immigration and Worker Authorisation) (Amendment) Regulations 2007, SI 2007/ 475, reg 2(4)(a).

5 Accession Regulations 2006, reg 7(6), as amended by by Accession (Immigration and Worker Authorisation) (Amendment) Regulations 2007, SI 2007/ 475, reg 2(4)(c).

6.30 Part 3 of the Regulations sets out the terms on which a worker requiring authorisation to work could obtain such authorisation (regulations 9 to 11 and Schedule 1). The effect of the Regulations is that those Bulgarian and Romanian nationals subject to the worker authorisation requirement were be required to obtain an 'accession worker card', unless they already had been granted leave under the Immigration Act 1971 for this purpose, in which case the 'accession worker authorisation document' was the stamp in the holder's passport, or had been issued with a 'seasonal agricultural work card' under the Seasonal Agricultural Workers Scheme.[1] The details for applying for and being issued an 'accession worker card' are set out in regulations 10 and 11. Schedule 1 is a detailed document in table form, setting out the categories of employment for which an accession worker card may be issued. These follow the provisions of the Immigration Rules under which a Bulgarian or Romanian or any other worker may be granted leave to enter or remain for a purpose that involves employment.[2] Thus where employers sought to employ a Bulgarian or Romanian national in employment, which would, prior to Accession, fall to be dealt with under the work permit arrangements, those employers continued to be required to obtain a letter from the Home Office confirming that the requirements of those arrangements had been met.[3] The individual would then be able to apply for an accession worker card once the employer had received that letter. The 'accession workers card' provided a photo of the worker and details of employer, and the type of work or occupation for which it had been issued.[4]

[1] See Accession (Immigration and Worker Authorisation) Regulations 2006, SI 2006/3317, reg 9(2)–(4).
[2] See CHAPTER 10, below for the various categories of admission in order to take up employment.
[3] Accession Regulations 2006, reg 10(5).
[4] See Accession Regulations 2006, reg 11(3)–(6).

6.31 Regulation 12 created the new offence of employing a Bulgarian or Romanian national who does not have the authority to undertake the employment, but provided the employer with a statutory defence against prosecution if the employer could prove that he or she had seen, copied and retained copies of certain specified documents. Regulation 13 made it an offence for a Bulgarian or Romanian national to take employment without authority. Individuals may be provided with the opportunity to discharge their liability to prosecution through the payment of a fixed penalty. Regulation 14 made it an offence to obtain or seek to obtain an accession worker card by deception.

ACCESSION OF CROATIA

Croatian Accession Treaty 2011

6.32 In common with the 2003 and 2005 Accession Treaties concerning the 'A8' and 'A2' States, the 2011 Croatian Accession Treaty, which came into force on 1 July 2013, permits existing EU Member States to impose restrictions on access to their labour markets until 30 June 2018, by way of transitional measures which apply by virtue of Article 18 of the 2011 Accession Treaty, read with Annex V. Annex V derogates from the principal sources of EU law providing for the free movement of workers[1] for a five-year period.[2] Member States are permitted to extend the transitional period for a further two years, until 30 June 2020, upon notifying the Commission of their intention to do so provided that there are 'serious disturbances of [the Member State's] labour market or threat thereof.'[3] As noted above, in the case of the 'A8' and 'A2' accession states, the UK imposed transitional restrictions for the full seven-year period, invoking the 'serious labour market disturbances' justification. The effect of the derogation in the 2011 Treaty is that Croatian nationals are unable directly to rely on the free movement of workers provisions cited in footnote 1 and must instead comply with national measures governing such access.[4] The 2011 Accession Treaty was given effect in domestic law by the European Union (Croatian Accession and Irish Protocol) Act 2013, section 1.

[1] That is, Article 45 TFEU, Articles 1-6 of Regulation (EU) No 492/2011 (providing for free movement of workers within the EU) and Directive 2004/38/EC ('the Citizens' Directive'). See Annex V, section 2(1).

[2] Annex V, section 2(2) and (3).

[3] Annex V, section 2(5) and (7).

[4] See, by analogy with the 2004 Accession Treaty, *Zalewska v Department for Social Development (Child Poverty Action Group intervening)* [2008] UKHL 67; [2008] 1 WLR 2602. The House of Lords held that the power of Member States to impose such national measures did not, in the case of the 2004 Accession Treaty, given the UK a complete discretion as to the conditions it could impose on Polish nationals but fell to be exercised in accordance with (what was then) Community law, including the principle of proportionality, having regard to the legitimate aim of introducing national measures to give effect to the derogation provided for in the 2004 Accession Treaty. The House of Lords held, by a majority, that the 2004 Accession Regulations to be a proportionate restriction; but note the dissenting opinions of Baroness Hale and Lord Neuberger on that issue.

6.33 The derogations under Annex V of the 2011 Accession Treaty do not affect the rights of Croatian nationals to all of the other benefits of an EU member on the same basis as nationals of existing EU Member States, including, in particular, the initial right of residence for up to three months under Article 6 of the Citizens' Directive upon production of a valid passport/ ID card;[1] and an extended right of residence on the basis of self-employment/establishing a business, living as a self-sufficient person and as a student. By opting for these latter categories entitling the person to an extended right of residence, a Croatian national can avoid the requirement to comply with the workers registration scheme that is set out below. This is because regulation 7 of the 2013 Regulations deems such persons to be 'qualified persons' for the purposes of the 2006 EEA Regulations, and are therefore entitled to a registration certificate under reg 16 of the 2006 Regulations.[2] They can therefore bring into the UK his/her family members on the same terms as other EU nationals in that capacity.[3]

Croatian nationals may also come to the UK as posted workers[4] who are sent to work in the UK by their employer established in another Member State in order to supply services to a UK client. However, their right to remain in the UK on this basis only lasts for so long as they remain a posted worker within the meaning of the Posted Workers Directive.[4] Any period spent in the UK as a posted worker does not count towards the 12 months necessary to escape the workers registration scheme under the Accession of Croatia (Immigration and Worker Authorisation) Regulations 2013, 2013/1460, which are described below.

[1] Council Directive 2004/38/EC; Immigration (European Economic Area) Regulations 2006, SI 2006/1003 ('the 2006 Regulations'), reg 11.

2   Reg 14 of the 2006 Regulations.
3   Council Directive 2004/38/EC, Articles 2 and 3; the 2006 Regulations (op cit), regs 7 and 17.
4   Within the meaning of Article 1 of Directive 96/71/EC (the Posted Workers Directive). Posted
    workers are dealt with at **6.103** below.

National measures: the 2013 Regulations

6.34 The UK's national measures for regulating access to its labour market by Croatian nationals, implementing the derogations contained in Annex V to the 2011 Accession Treaty, are the Accession of Croatia (Immigration and Worker Authorisation) Regulations 2013, SI 2013/1460 ('the 2013 Regulations'), made under section 4 of the European Union (Croatian Accession and Irish Protocol) Act 2013. The 2013 Regulations apply within 'the accession period', which is defined in regulation 1(2) as 'the period beginning with 1 July 2013 and ending with 30 June 2018.' The regulations require any 'accession state national subject to worker authorisation', defined in regulation 2(1), to obtain permission to work (reg 8), and impose criminal penalties on the employee (regulation 16) and employer where there is non-compliance with the worker registration requirements (regulation 11). All Croatian nationals are deemed by regulation 2(1) to be an 'accession state national subject to worker or authorisation' save for any period in which they fall within any of the many exceptions listed in the remainder of reg 2. The exceptions are as follows:

- Regulation 2(2): on 30 June 2013, the worker had leave to enter or remain in the UK under the Immigration Act 1971 that was not subject to any condition restricting his employment (other than a condition restricting his employment as a doctor or dentist in training or as a professional sports person (including as a sports coach)), or is given such leave after that date;[1]
- Regulation 2(3): a Croatian national legally working in the UK on 30 June 2013 and had been legally working in the UK without interruption throughout the preceding period of 12 months ending on that date.[2] A person is defined by regulation 2(5)(a) as having 'legally worked' in the UK during a period falling before 1 July 2013 if: (i) he had leave to enter or remain in the United Kingdom under the 1971 Act for that period, that leave allowed him to work in the United Kingdom, and he was working in accordance with any condition of that leave restricting his employment; or (ii) he was exempt from the provisions of the 1971 Act by virtue of section 8(2) or (3) of that Act (persons exempted by order or membership of diplomatic mission); or (iii) he was entitled to reside in the United Kingdom for that period under the EEA Regulations without the requirement for such leave. By regulation 2(5)(c), a person is treated as having worked in the UK without interruption for a period of 12 months if (i) he was legally working in the United Kingdom at the beginning and end of that period; and (ii) during that period of 12 months, if his work in the United Kingdom was interrupted, any intervening periods of interruption did not exceed 30 days in total;
- Regulation 2(4): a Croatian national who legally works in the UK without interruption for a period of 12 months falling partly or wholly after 30 June 2013.[3] By regulation 2(5)(b), a person working in the UK

355

on or after 1 July 2013 is 'legally working' in the UK during any period in which he: (i) falls within any of sub-paragraphs (6) to (16) or (18) of regulation 2 (see below); or (ii) holds an accession worker authorisation document and is working in accordance with the conditions set out in that document;

- Regulation 2(6): the Croatian national is also a national of the UK or an EEA state other than Croatia, save for any period (falling before 1 January 2014) in which he is also an accession state national subject to worker authorisation within the meaning of regulation 2 of the Accession (Immigration and Worker Authorisation) Regulations 2006 (as amended), relating to Bulgaria and Romania;

- Regulation 2(7): the Croatian national is also an accession states national subject to worker authorisation within the meaning of regulation 2 of the Accession (Immigration and Worker Authorisation) Regulations 2006 (as amended), relating to Bulgaria and Romania, and is working in accordance with those regulations;

- Regulation 2(8): the Croatian national is the spouse, civil partner, unmarried or same-sex partner, or child under 18 of a person who has leave to enter or remain in the United Kingdom under the Immigration Act 1971 and that leave allows him to work in the United Kingdom;

- Regulation 2(9): the Croatian national is the spouse, civil partner, unmarried or same-sex partner of a national of the United Kingdom or a person that is settled in the United Kingdom in accordance with the meaning given in section 33(2A) of the Immigration Act 1971 (as amended);

- Regulation 2(10): the Croatian national is a member of omission or other person mentioned in section 8(3) (member of a diplomatic mission, or other person mentioned in section 8(3) (member of a diplomatic mission, the family member of such a person, or a person otherwise entitled to diplomatic immunity) of the Immigration Act 1971 Act, other than a person who, under section 8(3A) (conditions of membership of a mission) of that Act, does not count as a member of a mission for the purposes of section 8(3);

- Regulation 2(11): the Croatian national is a person who is exempt from all or any of the provisions of the Immigration Act 1971 Act by virtue of an order made under section 8(2) (exemption for persons specified by order) of that Act;

- Regulation 2(12): the Croatian national has a permanent right of residence under regulation 15 of the Immigration (European Economic Area) Regulations 2006 (as amended);

- Regulation 2(13): the Croatian national is a family member (X) of a (non-Croatian) EEA national (Y) who has a right to reside in the United Kingdom, subject to regulation 2(14);

- Regulation 2(14): where Y is an accession State national subject to worker authorisation under the 2013 Regulations or an accession State national subject to worker authorisation within the meaning of regulation 2 of the Accession (Immigration and Worker Authorisation) Regulations 2006 (as amended), relating to Bulgaria and Romania, paragraph (13) only applies where X is the— (a) spouse or civil partner of Y; (b) unmarried or same sex partner of Y; or (c) a direct descendant of Y, Y's spouse or Y's civil partner who is: (i) under 21; or (ii) dependant of Y, Y's spouse or Y's civil partner;

- Regulation 2(15): the Croatian national is a 'highly skilled person' and holds an EEA registration certificate issued in accordance with regulation 7 of the 2013 Regulations, that includes a statement that he has unconditional access to the United Kingdom labour market. A 'highly skilled person' is defined by regulation 3(1) of the 2013 Regulations as a person who (a) meets the requirements specified by the Secretary of State for the purpose of paragraph 245BB(c) (requirements for entry clearance as a Tier 1 (Exceptional Talent) migrant)[4] of the Immigration Rules; or (b) has been awarded one of the following qualifications and applies for an EEA registration certificate within 12 months of being awarded the qualification—(i) a recognised bachelor, masters or doctoral degree; (ii) a postgraduate certificate in education or professional graduate diploma of education; or (iii) a higher national diploma awarded by a Scottish higher education institution. Reg 3(2)-(4) provide the following further definitions: for the purposes of paragraph (1)(b), the qualification must have been awarded by a higher education institution which, on the date of the award, is a 'UK recognised body' or an institution that is not a UK recognised body but which provides full courses that lead to the award of a degree by a UK recognised body. For the purposes of paragraph (1)(b)(iii), to qualify as a higher national diploma from a Scottish institution, a qualification must be at level 8 on the Scottish credit and qualifications framework. A 'UK recognised body' means an institution that has been granted degree awarding powers by a Royal Charter, an Act of Parliament or the Privy Council;
- Regulation 2(16): the Croatian national is in the United Kingdom as a student and either— (a) holds an EEA registration certificate that includes a statement that he is a student who may work in the United Kingdom whilst a student in accordance with the condition set out in paragraph (17) and complies with that condition; or (b) has leave to enter or remain under the Immigration Act 1971 as a student and is working in accordance with any conditions attached to that leave. Regulation 2(17) states that the condition referred to in paragraph (16)(a) is that the student shall not work for more than 20 hours a week unless— (a) he is following a course of vocational training and is working as part of that training; or (b) he is working during his vacation;
- Regulation 2(18): A Croatian national who ceases to be a student at the end of his course of study is not an accession State national subject to worker authorisation during the period of four months beginning with the date on which his course ends provided he holds an EEA registration certificate that was issued to him before the end of the course that includes a statement that he may work during that period;
- Regulation 2(19): A Croatian national is not an accession State national subject to worker authorisation during any period in which he is a posted worker. Regulation 2(20) defines 'posted worker' as a worker who is posted to the United Kingdom, within the meaning of Article 1(3) of the Council Directive 96/71/EC of 16 December 1996 (the

Posted Workers Directive).[5]

1   The insertion of a qualification relating to conditions restricting employment as a doctor or dentist in training or as a professional sports person was made by the Accession of Croatia (Immigration and Worker Authorisation) (Amendment) Regulations 2014, 2014/530, reg 2(3) (April 6, 2014). The insertion was made to avoid any suggestion that a restriction on work as a doctor/ dentist in training and professional sportsperson, which applies to those on Tier 1 leave, amounted to an employment restriction for the purpose of the 2013 Regulations.
2   See **6.35** fn 3.
3   See **6.35** fn 5.
4   Paragraph 245BB was inserted by the Statement of Changes to the Immigration Rules (HC 863) laid before Parliament on 16 March 2011. The requirements specified for the purpose of paragraph 245BB(c) are set out in Appendices A and L of the Immigration Rules.
5   Posted workers are dealt with at **6.103** below.

6.35   Under the 2013 Regulations, an accession state worker subject to worker authorisation can only be treated as a worker under the 2006 EEA Regulations 'in so far as [that status] gives him a right to reside and only during a period in which he holds an accession worker authorisation document and is working in accordance with the conditions set out in that document'.[1] That definition rules out any right of residence when the person is unemployed (for whatever reason and irrespective of the duration of that unemployment) or is seeking work, within the first 12 months of holding the worker authorisation document. An accession state worker subject to worker authorisation who is seeking employment in the UK cannot be treated as a jobseeker for the purposes of the 2006 Regulations.[2] This is to be contrasted with the position of 'highly skilled' persons, as defined in regulation 3 of the 2013 Regulations, who, while seeking employment, are treated as 'qualified persons' by virtue of regulation 7 of the 2013 Regulations. A Croatian national who is not subject to worker authorisation is entitled to an EEA registration certificate, issued under regulation 16 of the 2006 EEA Regulations, which includes a statement that the holder has unconditional access to the UK labour market unless the person is exempt from worker authorisation in reliance on the exceptions in regulation 2(16) or (18) (students).[3] Registration cards issued to students will state the limitations of their access to the labour market.[4] Registration certificates issued to Croatian extended family members (save for unmarried partners) should state that the holder does not have permission to work.[5] Residence cards issued to family members, or extended family members, of accession state nationals subject to worker authorisation, are limited to 12 months from the date of issue and are called 'Accession residence cards'[6] and do not entail a limitation on access to the labour market. Regulation 6 of the 2013 Regulations also makes provision concerning decisions to deport or administratively remove Croatian nationals prior to accession on 1 July 2013. Under regulation 6(1), any decision to administratively remove[7] a Croatian national, or their family member, from the UK before 1 July 2013, ceases to have effect on that date. Under regulation 6(2), decisions to deport a Croatian national or their family members made before 1 July 2013 are treated as being made under the 2006 EEA Regulations, as is any appeal made against that decision.[8]

1   Regulation 5 of the 2013 Regulations. Words inserted by the Accession of Croatia (Immigration and Worker Authorisation) (Amendment) Regulations 2014, 2014/530, reg.2(4), (April 6, 2014).
2   See fn 1.
3   Reg 7(2)-(3) of the 2013 Regulations.

Worker authorisation registration certificates

6.36 Regulation 8(1) of the 2013 Regulations makes authorisation to work in the UK conditional upon possession of an accession worker authorisation document and the requirement that the holder is working in accordance with the conditions set out in that document. The registration certificate takes effect from when it is issued and received by the worker. It is not retrospective.[1] For practical purposes the accession worker authorisation document is either:

- a passport or other travel document endorsed before 1 July 2013 to show that the holder has leave to enter or remain in the UK under the Immigration Act 1971, subject to a condition restricting employment in the UK to a particular employer or category of employment. The endorsement ceases to be a valid accession worker authorisation document upon the expiry of the relevant period of leave to enter or remain; or when the holder ceases working for the employer, or in the employment, specified in the document for over 30 days in total;[2] or

- a worker authorisation registration certificate endorsed with a condition restricting the holder's employment to a particular employer and authorised category of employment. This document ceases to be valid when the document expires; holder ceases working for the employer, or in the authorised category of employment, specified in the document for over 30 days in total; or the document is revoked.[3]

Applications for a worker authorisation registration certificate are governed by Regulations 9 and 10. Applications should be made in respect of employment in the UK, with an approved employer, falling within an authorised category of employment.[4] Regulation 1(2) of the 2013 Regulations define 'authorised category of employment' as (a) employment for which the applicant has been issued by a sponsor with a valid certificate of sponsorship under Tier 2 or Tier 5 of the Points-Based System;[5] or (b) employment as— (i) a representative of an overseas business; (ii) a postgraduate doctor or dentist; or (iii) a domestic worker in a private household. Where the authorised category of employment specified in the application is one for which a certificate of sponsorship is required, the registration certificate is required to state, inter alia, that the holder of the document has a right to engage in supplementary employment (which is limited to 20 hours per week, and must take place outside of the hours when the appellant is contracted to work for the sponsor in the employment the applicant is being sponsored to do).[6] The

Home Office may refuse to grant, or revoke, a worker authorisation certificate if such action is justified on grounds of public policy, public security or public health.[7] The Secretary of State also has powers to refuse applications/revoke registration certificates where the document holder ceases working from the employer, the specified employment ceases for over 30 days, deception was used to obtain the document, or the sponsorship relied upon has been withdrawn.[8]

---

[1] See by analogy the Polish case, under the Accession (Immigration and Worker Registration) Regulations 2004, SI 20014/1219 of *Szpak v Secretary of State for Work and Pensions* [2013] EWCA Civ 46. See also *JL (A8 worker – lawful employment) Poland* [2009] UKAIT 00030, although note that the principal holding of the case which rules out residence on the basis of employment under national law prior to accession is incompatible with the later CJEU cases cited at **6.38** below.

[2] Regulation 8(2)(a), 8(3) and (5) of the 2013 Regulations.

[3] Regulation 8(2)(b) and 8(4) of the 2013 Regulations.

[4] Regulation 9(1) of the 2013 Regulations.

[5] Reg 1(2) further provides that 'Tier 2' and 'Tier 5' shall be construed 'in accordance in paragraph 6 of the Immigration Rules, except that the reference to the grant of leave is to be read as including a reference to the issuing of a worker authorisation registration certificate'. The term 'certificate of sponsorship' is also defined in regulation 1(2) as having, 'the meaning given in paragraph 6 of the Immigration Rules, except that the reference to an application or potential application for entry clearance or leave to enter or remain as a Tier 2 migrant or a Tier 5 migrant is to be read as including a reference to an application or potential application for a worker authorisation registration certificate'. The Points Based System is dealt with more generally at **6.36**.

[6] Regulation 10(2)(c) of the 2013 Regulations.

[7] Regulation 10(3)(a) of the 2013 Regulations.

[8] Regulation 10 (3)(b) of the 2013 Regulations.

6.37 The 2013 Regulations make provision for a range of penalties arising from failure to comply with the worker authorisation requirements. Regulation 11 imposes upon employers who have employed an accession state national subject to worker authorisation who does not hold a valid accession worker authorisation document (or who breaches a condition of that document by undertaking the employment) a civil liability of up to £5000. A defence is available to the employer if it can be shown that the employee produced confirmation of his right to work and the employer took certain steps to verify the validity of that documentation. Regulations 12-13 set down the procedure for objecting to the fine and for an appeal against any adverse determination. Regulation 15 creates a criminal offence of knowingly employing an accession state national subject to worker authorisation who does not hold a valid authorisation document in respect of the employment, for which the maximum sentence is 51 weeks imprisonment (or six months in Scotland or Northern Ireland) and/or a fine, may be imposed. Regulation 16 creates the employee offence of working in the UK during the accession period without holding a valid accession worker authorisation document, for which the maximum sentence is three months imprisonment and/or a fine.

6.38 Permanent residence is dealt with at **6.72** and **6.83** below. However it is relevant to note here that periods of lawful residence in the UK by Croatian nationals prior to 1 January 2014 under UK domestic law should count as residence 'in accordance with these regulations' for the purposes of Regulation 15(1)(a) of the 2006 Regulations, applying *Ziolkowski v Land Berlin; Szeja v Land Berlin*: Joined Cases C-424/10 and 425/10; [2014] All ER (EC) 314,

[2013] 3 CMLR 1013, ECJ. See also Case C-162/09 *Lassal*, Case C-325/09 *Maria Dias* and Joined Cases C-424/10.

INSTITUTIONS OF EU AND SOURCES OF LAW

6.39 From the EEC Treaty (Treaty of Rome), by which the Common Market was first established in 1959, to the Treaty of Lisbon, which amends and consolidates all the intervening Treaties, the the functions of the EU are still distributed among the same key institutions – the European Parliament, the Council, the European Commission, and the Court of Justice of the European Union (formerly the European Court of Justice).[1] Their constitutional functions are set out in brief in the Consolidated version of the Treaty on the European Union (TEU), Title III, at Articles 13–19. The European Parliament shall, jointly with the Council, exercise legislative and budgetary functions.[2] The Council consists of the Heads of State or Government of the Member States, together with its President and the President of the Commission, but in exercising its joint legislative functions it shall consist of a representative of each Member State at ministerial level, who may commit the government of the Member State in question and cast its vote.[3] The Commission's tasks include ensuring the application of the Treaties,[4] and of measures adopted by the institutions pursuant to the Treaties, and overseeing the application of Union law under the control of the Court of Justice of the European Union.[5] One of its main roles is the introduction of new legislation. Union legislative acts can only be adopted on the basis of a Commission proposal, except where the Treaties provide otherwise. The CJEU has the task of interpretation of the Treaties and the acts of EU institutions. Its jurisdiction is to (a) rule on actions brought by a Member State, an institution or a natural or legal person; (b) give preliminary rulings, at the request of courts or tribunals of the Member States, on the interpretation of Union law or the validity of acts adopted by the institutions; and (c) rule in other cases provided for in the Treaties.[6] EU law consists of the totality of legally enforceable obligations; a wider concept is the *acquis communitaire* which includes the actions and opinions of EU institutions.

[1]   See Consolidated version of the TFEU, Pt VI, Title 1, arts 223–281 (ex arts 190(4) and (5) – 281 TEC).
[2]   Consolidated TEU, arts 14 and 16.
[3]   Consolidated TEU, arts 15 and 16.
[4]   Namely the Treaty on the European Union and the Treaty on the Functioning of the European Union.
[5]   Consolidated TEU, art 17.
[6]   Consolidated TEU, art 19.3.

6.40 The sources of EU law, so far as free movement of persons throughout the EU is concerned, are (i) Article 45 TFEU: free movement of workers; (ii) Article 49 TFEU: freedom of establishment (self-employment and setting up/ running a business); (iii) Article 56 (freedom to provide services); (iv) decisions of ECJ and CJEU; (v) Agreements of Association with non-EEA countries; (vi) Article 20 and 21 TFEU: citizenship of the Union; and (vii) Chapters 1 and 2 of Title V to the TFEU which include provision for the abolition of internal border controls (which include the Schengen acquis from which the UK has opted out (see below)), external border controls and a Common European

Asylum System. This Chapter deals principally with (i)-(vii). However, the genesis of (vii), Title V of the TFEU, will briefly be addressed first.

The Schengen Agreements and abolition of internal borders

6.41 The original Schengen Agreement of 14 June 1985[1] had two objectives:

(1)   to reduce common frontier controls by instituting 'a simple visual check on private vehicles crossing the common frontier at a reduced speed without requiring the vehicle to stop';[2]

(2)   to abolish internal controls on all persons, whatever their origins.

The Schengen Convention of 19 June 1990, which came into force on 26 March 1995, aimed to create a zone with only one external border and free movement within it. In order to achieve this, the 1990 Convention established common conditions of entry,[3] including a common visa[4] for non-EU nationals wishing to cross the external borders of the Schengen States.[5]

[1]   See *Butterworths Immigration Law Service*, F[6551].
[2]   Schengen Agreement 1985, art 2.
[3]   Schengen Convention 1990, art 9.
[4]   Schengen Convention 1990, art 10.
[5]   Airports are now considered to be external borders for flights to or from third countries and internal borders for flights between Schengen States. The same applies to seaports. See *Butterworths Immigration Law Service*, F[6508].

6.42 The Schengen Agreements were a forerunner to the adoption by the Community of measures to get rid of all internal borders between participating States.[1] The first Community measure was the insertion of Article 8a into the EEC Treaty[2] by the Single European Act 1987, agreed in late 1985 and came into force in 1987. It required the EC 'To adopt measures with the aim of progressively establishing the internal market over a period expiring on 31 December 1992.'[3] At the time it came into force, it promised more than it could deliver, since the EC lacked competence under the existing Treaty provisions to adopt the necessary measures.[4]

[1]   Elspeth Guild 'Discretion, Competence and Migration in the European Union' (1999) EJML 61 at 82; D O'Keefe 'Free Movement of Persons and the Single Market' (1992) Eur Law Review 17 at 3–13.
[2]   Later Article 7a EEC, which became Article 14 EC and is now Article 26 TFEU.
[3]   The internal market means 'an area without internal frontiers in which the free movement of goods, persons, services and capital is ensured in accordance with the provisions of this Treaty'.
[4]   The Commission tried but failed in its attempt to use art 100 EC for a directive on illegal immigration and employment law: see *Peers* above, p 65.

6.43 This lack of competence was remedied by the Amsterdam Treaty, with its integration of the Schengen – *acquis* into the framework of the EU and introduced the new Title IV – now, after the Lisbon Treaty, Title V of the TFEU – which enabled and required the Community to introduce measures in respect of the movement and residence of third country nationals. The underlying principle remains the completion of the internal market and the abolition of intra-Community borders,[1] although Title IV gives a 'flanking' Community competence to regulate immigration and asylum, but without any clearly defined goals or objectives, other than the establishment of an area of freedom, security and justice.[2] We deal first with the Schengen *acquis* and then with the present Title V.

1   Elspeth Guild 'Discretion, Competence and Migration in the European Union' [1999] EJM & L 61 at 84.
2   Consolidated TFEU, art 67 (ex art 61 and 29 TEC).

Schengen acquis

6.44 The Schengen *acquis* consist of the Schengen Agreement of 14 June 1985, the Schengen Convention 1990, the accession protocols and agreements creating new members of Schengen, and the decisions and declarations adopted by the Schengen Executive Committee, as well as the acts adopted for its implementation.[1] Protocol 2, applied the Schengen *acquis* to the then 13 participating Member States,[2] and brought the provisions of the Schengen *acquis* into the framework of Community law, the original idea being that these provisions would be split up and allocated to the relevant part of the EU and EC Treaties, while at the same time preserving a special 'pick and choose' position for the UK and Ireland.[3] Since then a total of 31 states, including 27 EU states and four non-EU members (Iceland, Norway,[4] Switzerland[5] and Leichtenstein), are subject to all or some of the Schengen rules, and 24 states have fully implemented them so far.[6] Protocol 2 is now Protocol 19, which is annexed to the Consolidated TEU and TFEU.

1   Annexe to Protocol 2 to TEU and TEC; see *Butterworths Immigration Law Service* F[62]–[76]. By Article 39, subsection 1 of the Schengen Borders Code (Regulation (EC) No 562/2006 of the European Parliament and of the Council of 15 March 2006 establishing a Community Code on the rules governing the movement of persons across borders: OJ 2006 L 105/1), Articles 2 to 8 of the Schengen Agreement had been repealed.
2   The then participating Member States were Austria, Belgium, Denmark, France, Finland, Germany, Greece, Italy, Luxembourg, Netherlands, Portugal, Spain and Sweden.
3   See Council Decision 2000/365/EC of 29 May 2000 concerning the request of the UK and Northern Ireland and Council Decision 2002/192/EC of 28 February 2002 concerning the request of Ireland to take part in some of the provisions of the Schengen acquis in OJ 2000 L 131/43 and OJ 2002 L64/20. These provisions are better described as an 'opt out' with the right to opt in; see Peers *EU Justice and Home Affairs Law* (2000), Pearson Education, p 56. However, the UK and Ireland have not had it all their own way and were not allowed to participate in proposals leading to the adoption of Regulation 2007/2004 setting up an Agency relating to the crossing of external border (see *UK and Northern Ireland v Council of the EU* (Case C-77/05) judgment of the Grand Chamber of 18 December 2007) nor Regulation 2252/2004 of 13 December 2004 on standards for security features and biometrics in passports and travel documents issued by Member States (see *United Kingdom and Northern Ireland v European Council*: C-137/05 [2007] ECR I-11459 judgment of the Grand Chamber of 18 December 2007).
4   Protocol 2, art 6. The Council concluded an agreement with Norway and Iceland in 1999 (OJ 1999 L 176/35) setting out procedures for their 'association' with existing Schengen acquis and measures building on it, and together with Ireland and the UK made a separate agreement with Norway and Iceland on the one hand and the UK and Ireland on the other to the extent that the UK and Ireland opted in to the Schengen acquis: see Peers above, p 57.
5   Council Decisions 2004/849/EC and 2004/860/EC of 25 October 2004 between the European Union, the European Community and the Swiss Confederation concerning Switzerland's association with the implementation, application and development of the Schengen acquis (OJ 2004 L 368/26 and L 370/78). In particular, the application of Articles 2(4) and 120 to 125 of the Schengen II Convention is exempted from application in Switzerland according to Annex A Part 1 of Council Decisions 2004/849.
6   Council Decision of 6 December 2007 on the full application of the provisions of the Schengen acquis in the Czech Republic, the Republic of Estonia, the Republic of Latvia, the Republic of

Lithuania, the Republic of Hungary, the Republic of Malta, the Republic of Poland, the Republic of Slovenia and the Slovak Republic. This leaves out Cyprus, Bulgaria, Romania and Croatia.

6.45 In May 1999 the Council agreed on the allocation of all the Schengen *acquis* with the exception of the Schengen Information Services (SIS), which is used by police and customs to prevent crime and by the immigration authorities to control entry and is, therefore, difficult to place in either the Treaty on European Union or the EC Treaty.[1] In dealing with the allocation it was decided that not all the *acquis* would be allocated.[2] For example, the asylum provisions of Schengen had been overtaken by the ratification of the Dublin Convention and did not, therefore, need to be allocated.[3] After allocation, measures building upon the *acquis* became regular parts of EC or EU law with no special rules applying, or as Peers puts it: 'Conceptually, this is the legal equivalent of breaking a large lump of sugar into two separate lumps, and then dissolving these lumps into two separate cups of tea'.[4] In the immigration field, the Schengen acquis thus form a further basis for EU legislation on border controls and the position of third-country nationals within the Union.

[1] Decision of May 1999 (OJ 1999 L 176/17). Peers *EU Justice and Home Affairs Law*, 2000, Pearson Education, p 59. As a result of the failure to allocate the Schengen Information Services provisions the 'default' position operates and they are to be regarded as third pillar Acts based on Title VI of the Treaty on European Union: see Protocol 2, art 2.1.

[2] *Peers* above, p 57.

[3] *Peers* above, p 57.

[4] *Peers* above, p 57.

Title V Programme: the 'area of freedom, security and justice'

6.46 Articles 67-80 TFEU, within Chapters 1 and 2 of Title V (ex Articles 61-69 of Title IV TEC) provide for the enactment of EU legislation to be carried through by the Council in a number of fields, including immigration and asylum. Much of this programme has been implemented and various Directives have come into force in those fields.[1] (Anyone wishing to look at the history of these measures should consult the seventh edition of this work.) The Title is still important because it contains the provisions giving competency to the EU to involve itself in these new fields and to bring the new Directives and Regulations within the jurisdiction of the Court of Justice of the EU.

[1] For present purposes, these include measures under Article 78 TFEU (common policy on asylum and subsidiary protection: the Common European Asylum System, which is addressed in Chapter12; see also fn 4 of 6.3 above) and Article 79 TFEU (common immigration policy). The application of the Schengen acquis to certain Member States seeks to give effect to Articles 26, 67(2) and 77 TFEU (the latter requiring measures to eliminate internal border controls), read with Article 3(2) TEU. Various implementing Regulations and Directives have been made under each of those articles of the TFEU.

UK and Ireland

6.47 However, notwithstanding the integration of the Schengen *acquis* into the framework of the EU and all the new areas of Union competence created by the provisions in the former Title IV, the UK and Ireland decided not to surrender sovereignty over their own systems of immigration control for the time being. Then, in March 1999 the UK government indicated that in principle it would opt into all civil co-operation and asylum measures, along with many concerning immigration and external (but not internal) border control. Opt in and opt out positions were agreed. The mechanisms giving effect to the UK's reservations are contained in what are now Protocols 19, 20 and 21 annexed to the Consolidated TEU and TFEU (prior to the Treaty of Lisbon the relevant Protocols were 2, 3 and 4). In *R (on the application of McCarthy) v Secretary of State for the Home Department* [2012] EWHC 3368 (Admin) the Administrative Court (Haddon Cave J) recently made a reference to the CJEU on the issue of the compliance of the UK's family permits regime, contained in the 2006 EEA Regulations with Article 5 of the Citizens' Directive: [112]. He expressed his own view that there were 'strong grounds' in support of the lawfulness of the requirement on family members of EEA nationals exercising Treaty rights in the UK to obtain a 'family permit' prior to arrival in the UK. He considered that that the requirement was 'reasonable and proportionate', was not an incorrect implementation of the Citizens' Directive, article 5(2) and was likely to be justified in part by Protocol 20 to the TFEU, which was to be 'widely construed'. Haddon Cave J considered that 'there was a palpable risk that the use of fake EU "residence cards" would increase if residence cards were enough to gain access to the UK' ([42]-[51] and [60]).

THE APPLICATION OF EU FREE MOVEMENT LAW

6.48 There are three principal ways in which effect is given to EU law in the domestic legal systems of Member States: (i) the enactment of national measures to give effect to EU law obligations; (ii) the duty of national courts to interpret general legislation to conform with EU obligations; and (iii) finally, the doctrine of direct effect, where aggrieved individuals can rely on the EU law duty as directly applicable, although not specifically so enacted. There is an inter-relationship between the three. In the area of free movement, for example, we find effect being given to EU law by section 7 of the Immigration Act 1988, by the Immigration Rules, and by the 2006 EEA Regulations.[1] At the same time, measures of EU law are directly applicable, in ways we explore below. Thirdly, UK courts are bound by EU jurisprudence to interpret all measures within the field of Union competence in accordance with the principles and policy of the EU obligation giving rise to these measures. This has been described as the 'teleological' principle of construction, frequently at odds with the common law concept of strict statutory construction.[2] Courts must interpret all statutes and inferior measures, whether passed before or after the obligation arose, so that they accord with the requirements of EU law, if it is possible to do so without distortion.[3] This principle of construction has now been adopted for UK courts dealing with human rights by section 3 of the Human Rights Act 1998.[4]

---

[1]   Immigration (European Economic Area) Regulations 2006, SI 2006/1003.

[2]   See Lord Denning in *James Buchanan & Co Ltd v Babco Forwarding and Shipping (UK) Ltd* [1977] 1 All ER 518 at 522, CA; *Freight Transport Association Ltd v London Boroughs Transport Committee* [1991] 3 All ER 915, [1991] 1 WLR 828, HL; *R v Secretary of State for the Home Department, ex p Adams* [1995] All ER (EC) 177, DC.

[3]   *Duke v GEC Reliance Ltd (formerly Reliance Systems Ltd)* [1988] AC 618, [1988] 1 All ER 626, HL; Case C-106/89 *Marleasing SA v La Comercial Internacional de Alimentacion SA* [1990] ECR I-4135, [1992] 1 CMLR 305, ECJ.

[4] It has been described as a 'new canon of interpretation' and 'a strong adjuration' by Lord Cooke in *R v DPP, ex p Kebeline* [1999] 4 All ER 801, at 837.

National measures

6.49 In the UK, the duty of giving effect to EU Treaty rights is achieved by the European Communities Act 1972. The Act has been extensively amended as the Common Market evolved into the European Union. The latest significant amendments are by the European Union (Amendment) Act 2008 (c 7) giving effect to the Lisbon Treaty in the law of the UK. It received Royal Assent on 19 June 2008.[1] The European Economic Area Act 1993 was passed to make provision in respect of the EEA following the Agreement on the European Economic Area of 2 May 1992 and Protocol of 17 March 1993. The 1992 Agreement is a Community Treaty and has direct effect by virtue of the 1972 Act.[2] Section 2 of the European Economic Area Act 1993 makes provision for a consistent application of EU law to the whole of the EEA, and section 3 ensures that implementing Orders in Council, passed under the powers set out in the 1972 Act, apply to the EEA. By section 2 of the European Communities Act 1972, provision is made for regulations and directives of the EU to have effect in the UK. This means that EU legislation is directly applicable in accordance with the principles discussed at **6.45–6.47** above. It creates rights which British courts must protect.

However, the European Union Act 2011 places restrictions on the applicability in UK domestic law of any new Treaties and Decisions relating to the EU. These restrictions consist of (i) primary legislation and a national referendum; (ii) primary legislation without any referendum; and (iii) an affirmative vote in both Houses of Parliament. First, Part 1 of the Act provides that, in future, a referendum would have to be held before the UK could agree to an amendment of the Treaty on European Union ('TEU') or of the Treaty on the Functioning of the European Union ('TFEU'); or before the UK could agree to certain decisions already provided for by TEU and TFEU if these would transfer power or competence from the UK to the EU. It also makes provision for the persons who would be entitled to vote in a referendum and provides that a separate question would need to be framed for each issue requiring a referendum. Secondly, Part 1 provides that an Act of Parliament is required before the UK can agree to a number of other specified decisions in either the European Council or the Council of the European Union ('the Council'). Thirdly, certain other decisions will require motions to be agreed without amendment in both Houses of Parliament before the UK could vote in favour of specified decisions in either the European Council or the Council.

It should also be noted that section 18 of the European Union Act 2011[3] reaffirms that the status of EU law is dependent on its continuing statutory basis, under the European Communities Act in particular. Although section 18 was initially projected to serve as a 'sovereignty clause' by the coalition government, it has been described by Gordon and Dougan as 'lack[ing] any genuine constitutional significance'[4] since Parliament's power to repeal the 1972 Act, were it so minded, 'stems from . . . Parliament's legally unlimited authority, not from section 18 of the EUA'.[5]

1   See www.opsi.gov.uk\\acts.htm for the full text of all relevant statutes. There have also been more minor amendments to include other Treaties since concluded, eg the Treaty of Accession of Croatia in 2011, eg the European Union (Croatian Accession and Irish Protocol) Act 2013, s.3, as of 31 January 2013.
2   See European Communities Act 1972, ss 1 and 2.
3   The Act came into force in July, August and September 2011: European Union Act 2011 (Commencement No 1) Order 2011, SI 2011/1984 and European Union Act 2011 (Commencement No 2) Order 2011, SI 2011/1985.
4   Michael Gordon and Michael Dougan, 'The United Kingdom's European Union Act 2001: "who won the bloody war anyway?"', *European Law Review* (2012) 37(1), 3 at 6-10.
5   Section 18 (Status of EU law dependent on continuing statutory basis) reads, 'Directly applicable or directly effective EU law (that is, the rights, powers, liabilities, obligations, restrictions, remedies and procedures referred to in section 2(1) of the European Communities Act 1972) falls to be recognised and available in law in the United Kingdom only by virtue of that Act or where it is required to be recognised and available in law by virtue of any other Act'.

6.50 The UK government initially sought to implement the free movement directives by provisions in the Immigration Rules relating to EU nationals. But this was woefully inadequate; it left in place the statutory regime of requiring EC nationals to obtain leave to enter, which was a breach of Community law.[1] The right to enter for a EU law purpose flows directly from EU law rather than from permission given by an official. Thus a residence permit issued under EU law is only evidence of this right and not the source of it.[2] Visas and other formalities not envisaged by EU law cannot be required; under EU law the only formal requirement at the frontier is production of a passport or national identity document.[3] This fundamental principle of EU law was eventually given effect in UK statute law by section 7 of the Immigration Act 1988, which expressly absolved EC nationals from the need to obtain leave when exercising enforceable Community law rights,[4] but was not brought into force until the Immigration (European Economic Area) Order 1994 took effect on 20 July 1994,[5] some 23 shameful years after the accession of the UK to the EC.

1   See especially Case C-157/79 R v Pieck [1981] QB 571, [1981] 3 All ER 46, ECJ; Case 321/87 *EC Commission v Belgium* [1989] ECR 997, [1990] 2 CMLR 492, ECJ.
2   *R v Pieck above*; *Commission v Belgium above*; Case C-59/85 *Netherlands v Reed* [1986] ECR 1283, [1987] 2 CMLR 448; Case C-357/89 *Raulin v Minister van Onderwijs en Wetenschappen* [1992] ECR I-1027, [1994] 1 CMLR 227, ECJ. See also Case C-325/09 *Secretary of State for Work and Pensions v Dias (Maria)* [2011] 3 CMLR 1103, ECJ, at [48]–[49].
3   See Citizens' Directive, art 6 and Immigration (European Economic Area) Order Regulations 2006, SI 2006/1003, reg 11, which adds an additional requirement, not sanctioned by EU law, namely the need for family members to produce an EEA family permit, a residence card or permanent residence card in addition to a passport or identity card – another example of the wrangle the UK government is prone to get into over the direct application of EU law.
4   See Immigration Act 1988, s 12(3) and (4) and the Immigration Act 1988 (Commencement No 1) Order 1988, SI 1988/1133, which excluded the coming into force of section 7(1).
5   SI 1994/1923.

The development and doctrine of direct effect

6.51 The doctrine of direct effect began as a way of bringing into effect provisions of the common market Treaties, even though Member States were dragging their feet over completion of timetables set out in the Treaties. Once the timetable for implementation of an EU law measure[1] has expired, the doctrine allows aggrieved individuals or institutions to seek direct implementation of the measure against the State or its emanations if the obligation is sufficiently clear, precise and unconditional to be capable of direct enforcement.[2] This is the so-called vertical direct effect, as opposed to horizontal direct effect, which applies when one private citizen or corporation sues another.[3] Plainly, individuals who have free movement rights or other rights under EU law, which the UK has failed to implement, may invoke the direct applicability of the measure, and thus come within its 'vertical effect'. Individuals who have suffered loss that was caused directly by the State's breach of EU law can claim damages provided that the breach is 'sufficiently serious'.[4] Decisions in the national courts suggest that direct effect may be relied on by organisations such as the Equal Opportunities Commission, as well as individuals aggrieved by particular decisions.[5]

[1] Including Regulations, Directives, Treaty provisions and Decisions – these are addressed below.

[2] Case 26/62 *Algemene Transport-en Expeditie Onderneming van Gend en Loos NV v Nederlandse Belastingadministratie* [1963] ECR 1, [1963] CMLR 105, ECJ; Case 104/81 *Hauptzollamt Mainz v C A Kupferberg & Cie KG* [1982] ECR 3641, [1983] 1 CMLR 1, ECJ; Case 152/84 *Marshall v Southampton and South West Hampshire Area Health Authority* [1986] ECR 723, [1986] 1 CMLR 688, ECJ; Case C-188/89 Foster v British Gas [1991] 2 AC 306, [1991] 2 All ER 705, HL; *Webb v EMO Air Cargo (UK) Ltd* [1992] 4 All ER 929, [1993] 1 WLR 49, HL; Case C-127/92 *Enderby v Frenchay Health Authority* [1994] 1 All ER 495, [1994] 1 CMLR 8, ECJ; *Wahl v Icelandic State (European Commission, intervening)*: E-15/12), [2014] 1 CMLR 807*European Free Trade Association Court* (22 July 2013) [2014] 1 CMLR 29 at [56]. Article 45 TFEU (ex art 39 TEC) may also have horizontal effect: see Case 36/74 Walrave [1974] ECR 1405.

[3] See *Angonese v Cassa di Risparmio di Bolzano SpA*: Case C-281/98 [2000] All ER (EC) 577, where the ECJ stated at para 36 that the prohibition of discrimination in art 39 EC (ex art 48) applies to private persons as well as public bodies; see also Case 36/74 *Walrave and Koch v Association Union Cycliste Internationale* [1974] ECR 1405, para 16 (rules made by private persons or bodies aimed at regulating gainful employment in a collective manner); *Union Royale Belge des Societes de Football Association ASBL v Bosman* [1995] ECR I-4921, at paras 84 and 87 (agreements or acts concluded by private persons or bodies which determine the terms on which professional sportsmen can engage in professional sport); Joined Cases C-51/96 and C-191/97 *Lehtonen v Ligue Francophone de Judo et Disciplines Associées ASBL; Deliège v Ligue Francophone de Judo et Disciplines Associées ASBL* [2000] ECR I-2549, [2002] 2 CMLR 1574, ECJ 11 April 2000 (judo and basketball rules); *Wilander v Tobin* [1997] 2 CMLR 346, CA (rules of Tennis Federation regarding drugs).

[4] *Francovich (C-6/90); Brasserie du Pecheur (C-46/93 & C-48/93); Factortame (C-213/89)*. In *R (on the application of Negassi) v Secretary of State for the Home Department* [2013] EWCA Civ 151, [2013] CMLR 1252, the Court of Appeal held that the SSHD's failure to grant N permission to work pending determination of his fresh asylum claim, as required by Directive 2003/9, art 11, was not 'sufficiently serious' since the SSHD's failure to transpose art 11 resulted from a 'misunderstanding' of new provisions which was not deliberate, cynical or egregious and was not confined to the SSHD (see paras 15-20 of the judgment). A further example of an unsuccessful claim for *Francovich* damages in the asylum context is *R (on the application of Kuchiey) v Secretary of State for the Home Department* [2012] EWHC 3596 (Admin). See also the cases cited at **6.51** fn 3.

[5] *R v Secretary of State for Employment, ex p Equal Opportunities Commission* [1995] 1 AC 1, [1994] 1 All ER 910, HL. The decisions on *locus standi* in judicial review have also established that representative organisations with a proven interest in the subject-matter of the decision may be able to challenge decisions on grounds of Community law: *R v Inspectorate of Pollution, ex p Greenpeace Ltd* [1994] 4 All ER 321, [1994] 1 WLR 570, CA; *R v Secretary of State for the Environment, ex p Friends of the Earth Ltd* [1994] 2 CMLR 760. Thus, organisations such as the Joint Council for the Welfare of Immigrants (JCWI) or the Immigration Law Practitioners' Association (ILPA) could seek judicial review of Immigration Rules that are not in accordance with Community law.

Direct effect of Treaty obligations

6.52 TFEU Articles 45 (workers), 49 (establishment) and 56 (services) (ex Articles 39, 43 and 50 TEC) are all directly effective.[1] Article 20 TEU, the right to citizenship of the Union and its associated rights including free movement, are also directly effective.[2] The free movement provisions contained within these Treaty provisions are subject to important qualifications which give Member States an element of discretion in enforcement, on grounds of public policy, public security or public health. However, the ECJ has ruled that this is no bar to the direct effectiveness of these provisions.[3] There is a distinction between obligations which are sufficiently precise to be binding and those which have the character of a general programme or aspiration. The existence of direct effect turns on the context of the Article in question, so similar words in different measures may result in different interpretations as to direct effect. Thus the provisions for free movement in the EC/Turkish Association Agreement were held not to be capable of direct effect notwithstanding the expiry of the transitional period, whereas the specific decisions of the Association Council established under that Agreement could be if they produced clear and precise obligations not subject to the adoption of any subsequent measure.[4] In *Savas*[5] the court held that a standstill provision in Article 41(1) of the Additional Protocol to the Turkish Agreement was of direct effect, which means that the UK has to apply the 1973 business rules to Turkish business people seeking to establish themselves in the UK. In *El-Yassini*[6] an anti-discrimination clause, Article 40 of the EEC Moroccan Cooperation Agreement, was held to be of direct effect. The ECJ has held that a provision in an agreement with non-member states is directly effective when, regard being had to its wording and the purpose and nature of the agreement, the provision contains a precise and clear obligation which is not subject in its implementation or effects to the adoption of any subsequent measure.[7]

[1] Case 2/74 *Reyners v Belgium* [1974] ECR 631, [1974] 2 CMLR 305, ECJ; Case 33/74 *Van Binsbergen v Bestuur van de Bedrijfsvereniging voor de Metaalnijverheid* [1974] ECR 1299, [1975] 1 CMLR 298, ECJ. If a provision of national law is incompatible with a directly applicable provision of the EEC Treaty and is retained unchanged, this in itself constitutes an infringement of the Treaty: Case 168/85 *EC Commission v Italy* [1986] ECR 2945, [1988] 1 CMLR 580, ECJ; Case 147/86 *EC Commission v Greece* [1988] ECR 1637, [1989] 2 CMLR 845, ECJ. For the superior position of EC law in the UK see Case C-213/89 *R v Secretary of State for Transport, ex p Factortame Ltd (No 2)* [1991] 1 AC 603, [1990] ECR I-2433, ECJ and *(No 3)* [1992] QB 680, [1991] ECR I-3905, ECJ.

[2] *Baumbast and R v Secretary of State for the Home Department*, Case C-413/99 [2002] ECR I-7091.

[3] Case 41/74 *Van Duyn v Home Office (No 2)* [1974] ECR 1337, [1975] 1 CMLR 1, ECJ. See further on direct applicability of arts 59 and 60 EC Case 33/74 *Van Binsbergen v Bestuur van de Bedrijfsvereniging voor de Metaalnijverheid* [1974] ECR 1299, [1975] 1 CMLR 298, ECJ.

[4] Case 12/86 *Demirel v Stadt Schwäbisch Gmünd* [1987] ECR 3719, [1989] 1 CMLR 421, ECJ; Case C-192/89 *Sevince v Staatsecretaris van Justitie* [1990] ECR I-3461, [1992] 2 CMLR 57, ECJ; *R v Secretary of State for the Home Department, ex p Narin* [1990] 2 CMLR 233, CA; Case C-237/91 *Kus v Landeshauptstadt Wiesbaden* [1992] ECR I-6781, [1993] 2 CMLR 887, ECJ. See also Case C-312/91 *Metalsa Srl v Public Prosecutor (Italy)* [1994] 2 CMLR 121, ECJ where the court gave a different interpretation to a provision of the EEC-Austria free trade Agreement identical to the EEC Treaty.

[5] *R v Secretary of State for the Home Department, ex p Savas* Case C-37/98 [2000] 1 WLR 1828; see **6.211** below.

[6] *El-Yassini v Secretary of State for the Home Department* Case C-416/96 [1999] ECR I-1209, ECJ.

7   Case C-432/92 *R v Minister of Agriculture, Fisheries and Food, ex p S P Anastasiou (Pissouri) Ltd* [1995] 1 CMLR 569, ECJ (Original Protocol to EEC Cyprus Association Agreement held to be of direct effect).

Direct effect of regulations and directives

6.53 The position with regulations, directives and decisions is simpler. Under Article 288 TFEU (ex Article 249 TEC), regulations are 'binding in their entirety and take direct effect in each Member State' directives are 'binding as to the result to be achieved' and decisions are 'binding in their entirety. A decision which specifies those to whom it is addressed shall be binding only on them'. As regards regulations, this means that they are to be treated as law, and national courts are bound by them in their entirety. Depending on their proper interpretation, specific provisions may bestow on individuals rights as against other individuals or a Member State.[1] Although there is no mention of directives having direct effect, a series of court decisions has in effect put them on exactly the same footing as regulations in so far as they are sufficiently clear, precise and unconditional to be capable of direct enforcement.[2] In Case 41/74 *Van Duyn v Home Office (No 2)*[3] the ECJ stated that a directive which itself imposed substantive obligations could be directly effective. Otherwise the 'useful effect' of the directive would be weakened. What this means in practice is that directly effective EU law rules are to be enforced by national courts and take precedence over the provisions of national law. This was stated quite clearly by the ECJ in *Rutili v Minister for the Interior*,[4] where the court referred to some of the free movement provisions contained in directives and said:

'The effect of all these provisions, without exception, is to impose duties on Member States, and it is, accordingly, for the courts to give the rules of the Community Law which may be pleaded before them precedence over the provisions of national law'.

[para 16]

1   Case 43/71 *Politi SAS v Ministry for Finance of the Italian Republic* [1971] ECR 1039, para 9; Case 93/71 *Leonesio v Italian Ministry for Agriculture and Forestry* [1972] ECR 287 at 300. See Wyatt and Dashwood, pp 84-88. An example of a Regulation which has been interpreted as not bestowing directly enforceable rights upon individuals is the 'Dublin II' Regulation (Council Regulation (EC) No 343/2003): *R (on the application of AR (Iran)) v Secretary of State for the Home Department* [2013] EWCA Civ 778, [2013] 3 CMLR 40 at [26]-[32]; see also *Abdullahi v Bundesasylamt* (Case C-394/12), CJEU, [2014] 1 WLR 1895.
2   See **6.51** fn 1.
3   [1974] ECR 1337, [1975] 1 CMLR 1, ECJ.
4   Case 36/75 [1975] ECR 1219, [1976] 1 CMLR 140, ECJ. The superiority of Community law to municipal law, both common law and statutory, was exemplified most clearly in *R v Secretary of State for Transport, ex p Factortame Ltd (No 2)* [1991] 1 AC 603, [1991] 1 All ER 70, HL. See further Case C-473/93 *EC Commission v Luxembourg* [1997] ECR I-3207, [1996] 3 CMLR 981, para 37; *Orfinger v Belgium* [2000] 1 CMLR 612, paras 8–10, Belgian Conseil d'Etat.

6.54 In *Re Watson and Belmann*[1] the court spelt out what was meant by the binding effect of both the Treaty provisions on free movement and the implementing regulations and directives:

'Article 48 of the Treaty and the measures adopted by the Community in application thereof implement a fundamental principle of the Treaty, confer on persons whom they concern individual rights which the national courts must protect and take precedence over any national rule which might conflict with them.'

¹ Case 118/75 [1976] ECR 1185, [1976] 2 CMLR 552, ECJ.

Transposing Directives into domestic law

6.55 In dealing with the transposition of the Citizens' Directive[1] into UK national law,[2] the AIT has given useful general guidance on the proper approach of decision-makers and tribunals to EU law, which has been transposed into domestic regulations.[3] Decision-makers have first to apply the relevant national law implementing the particular directive. That is because, whilst a directive is binding as to the result to be achieved, the Treaty leaves to the national authorities the choice of form and methods.[4] Only the failure on the part of a Member State to implement a directive correctly or within the timeframe required by the directive will result in an individual being able to rely for direct effect on the provisions of the directive.[5] For example, in *ZH (Afghanistan) v Secretary of State for the Home Department*[6] the Court of Appeal held that Regulation 12(b)(i) and (ii) of the Immigration EEA Regulations 2006 as then framed were unlawful in that the 2004 Directive did not permit the imposition of prior requirements that must be met by a 'family member' who is a national of a non-member country, eg prior lawful residence in another Member State. In the earlier decision in *R (on the application of Owusu) v Secretary of State for the Home Department*[7] Blake J held that regulation 12(1)(b) represented a failure to transpose the requirements of the Directive 2004/38/EC lawfully into domestic law and immigration judges should ignore it and apply the Directive directly in accordance with the judgment in Metock.[8] The failure of the Home Office to remedy the illegality of regulation 12(1)(b) has at last been remedied nearly three years after the CJEU judgment in *Metock* (25 July 2008) by the Immigration (European Economic Area) (Amendment) Regulations 2011.[9] The sad business of the abject failure of the Home Office to remedy the illegality of regulation 12(1)(b) reminds us that, although domestic regulations are part of national law they have been enacted in order to implement an EU directive and as such, UK tribunals and courts must adopt a Community law approach to their construction, ie that they must be construed as far as possible, in the light of the wording, context and purpose of the Citizens' Directive, paying particular regard to that Directive's purpose, in order to achieve the result pursued.[10] If that is not possible then the directive will override domestic law, as set out above.

¹ Directive 2004/38/EC.
² Immigration (European Economic Area) Regulations 2006, SI 2006/1003.
³ HB (EEA right to reside – Metock) Algeria [2008] UKAIT 00069, at paragraph 1
⁴ Article 288 TFEU.
⁵ Case 152/84 *Marshall v Southampton and South West Hampshire Area Health Authority (Teaching)* [1986] ECR 723.
⁶ [2009] EWCA Civ 1060 (15 October 2009).
⁷ [2009] EWHC 593 (Admin) (21 January 2009).
⁸ *Metock v Minister for Justice, Equality and Law Reform* Case C-127/08 [2009] All ER (EC) 40, [2008] 3 CMLR 1167, ECJ.
⁹ SI 2011/1247, which came into force on 2 June 2011.

[10] Case C-106/89 *Marleasing SA v La Comercial Internacional de Alimentacion SA* [1990] ECR I-4135, para 8, [1992] 1 CMLR 305, ECJ.

THE COURT OF JUSTICE OF THE EUROPEAN UNION (CJEU)

6.56 Where a Member State fails to fulfil an obligation under the EU Treaties, it may be taken to task by the Commission[1] or another Member State[2] before the CJEU. Without going into detail on the available sanctions, one remedy which the CJEU has endorsed is that damages can be awarded to aggrieved individuals, where a Member State fails to implement a directive.[3] Public bodies may also be liable for damages, instead of or in addition to central government.[4]

[1] Article 258, TFEU (ex art 226, TEC).
[2] Article 259, TFEU (ex art 227, TEC).
[3] Case C-6, 9/90 *Francovich and Bonifaci v Italy* [1991] ECR I-5357, [1993] 2 CMLR 66, superseding the dicta to the contrary in *Bourgoin SA v Ministry of Agriculture, Fisheries and Food* [1986] QB 716, [1985] 3 All ER 585. See also Case C-334/92 *Wagner Miret v Fondo de Garanatia Salarial* [1993] ECR I-6911; *R v HM Treasury, ex p British Telecommunications plc* Case C-392/93 [1996] All ER (EC) 411, [1996] 2 CMLR 217, ECJ; C-46 and 48/93 *Brasserie du Pêcheur v Germany, Factortame v UK* [1996] QB 404, [1996] 1 CMLR 889, ECJ; Case C-5/94 *R v Ministry of Agriculture, Fisheries and Food, ex p Hedley Lomas (Ireland) Ltd* [1997] QB 139, [1996] ECR I-2553, ECJ; Case C-178-190/94 *Dillenkofer v Germany* [1997] QB 259, [1996] All ER (EC) 917, ECJ; cf *R v Secretary of State for the Home Department, ex p Gallagher (No 2)* [1996] 2 CMLR 951, CA (damages refused, because no causal link between the violation and exclusion of the EU national).
[4] Case C-424/97 *Haim v Kassenzahnarztliche Vereinigung Nordrhein*, [2000] ECR I-5123, [2002] 1 CMLR 247, ECJ.

Making a reference to CJEU

6.57 The clear effect of the TFEU and the CJEU decisions is that national courts must apply EU law. Where doubtful points about the effect of EU law arise, they can be settled by a reference of the point to the CJEU under Article 267 TFEU (ex Article 234 TEC).[1] A reference can be made by any court or independent tribunal, if it considers that a decision on the question is necessary to enable it to give judgment. In the UK, magistrates' courts, adjudicators and the Immigration Appeal Tribunal have made references,[2] and clearly immigration judges have a discretion to do so.[3] It should be noted that the Asylum and Immigration Tribunal (AIT) at one stage issued a Practice Direction stating that only its President or Deputy President, or a group including either of them, can make a reference under Article 234 of the Treaty.[4] The decision whether to make a reference to the ECJ where a point of EU law requires determination is discretionary, save in courts against whose decisions there is no judicial remedy under national law.[5] Where a reference is inevitable it should be made as soon as possible to avoid extra delay.[6] The criteria for a reference by a national court, other than a final Appeal Court, have been set out by the Master of the Rolls in *R v International Stock Exchange of the United Kingdom and the Republic of Ireland Ltd, ex p Else*:[7]

'If the facts have been found and the Community law issue is critical to the court's final decision, the appropriate course is ordinarily to refer the issue to the Court of Justice itself unless the national court can with complete confidence resolve the issue itself. In considering whether it can with complete confidence resolve the issue itself, the national court must be fully mindful of the differences between national and Community legislation, of the pitfalls which face a national court venturing into what may be an unfamiliar field, of the need for uniform interpretation throughout the Community and of the great advantages enjoyed by the Court of Justice in construing Community instruments. If the national court has any real doubt it should refer.'

1   See CPR Sch 1, RSC Ord 114 for the procedure for a reference in the High Court. A reference need not be made if the question is *acte claire* or the issues can be disposed of without determining the point of EU law: *R v Plymouth Justices, ex p Rogers* [1982] QB 863, [1982] 2 All ER 175, QBD; *Polydor Ltd and RSO Records Inc v Harlequin Record Shops and Simons Records* [1980] 2 CMLR 413, CA; *R v Henn and Darby* [1980] AC 850, [1980] 2 All ER 166, HL; *HP Bulmer Ltd v J Bollinger SA* [1974] Ch 401, [1974] 2 All ER 1226, CA; Case 166/73 *Rheinmühlen Düsseldorf v Einfuhr-und Vorratsstelle für Getreide und Futtermittel* [1974] ECR 33, [1974] 1 CMLR 523, ECJ. Even if the meaning of an instrument seems clear to the national court, it may still make a reference if it considers it appropriate to do so by reason of the importance of the issue raised or otherwise: *CILFIT Srl and Lanificio di Gavardo v Ministry of Health* [1982] ECR 3415. The House of Lords referred the case of *R (on the application of Tum) v Secretary of State for the Home Department* [2004] UKHL (on appeal by the Secretary of State) citing its concern for the numbers of Turkish asylum seekers who benefit from the Court of Appeal's interpretation (at [2004] EWCA Civ 788, [2004] INLR 442) of the standstill provision in the Ankara Agreement. See also CPR, Part 68 and Practice Direction 68, 'References to the European Court', which annexes a 2005 Note by the ECJ entitled 'Information Note: References from National Courts for a Preliminary Ruling'. A more up-to-date Note is the 'Information Note for National Courts' issued by the ECJ, OJ C 2009 C/297/01 (5 December 2009). See also a most informative draft Paper by Dr Hugo Storey, 'Preliminary references to the Court of Justice of the European Union (CJEU)' (Sept 2010); for an exhaustive account see M Broberg and N Fenger, *Preliminary References to the European Court of Justice* (OUP, 2010), see more generally P Craig, G De Burca, *EU Law: Text, Cases and Materials* (4th edn, 2008, OUP).

2   Case 30/77 *R v Bouchereau* [1978] QB 732, [1977] ECR 1999, ECJ (magistrates' court); Case C-356/98 *Kaba v Secretary of State for the Home Department* [2000] All ER (EC) 537, ECJ *(adjudicator)*; Case C-416/96 *El-Yassini v Secretary of State for the Home Department* [1999] ECR I-1209 *(adjudicator)*; *Baumbast* (21263) IAT; Case C-60/00 *Carpenter (Mary) v Secretary of State for the Home Department*[2003] QB 416, [2002] ECR I-6279, ECJ; Case C-200/02 *Chen v Secretary of State for the Home Department* [2005] QB 325, [2005] All ER (EC) 129, ECJ *(adjudicator)*.

3   *R v Immigration Appeal Tribunal, ex p Antonissen* [1992] Imm AR 196; *El-Yassini* above; Case C-195/98 *Österreichischer Gewerkschaftsbund, Gewerkschaft öffentlicher Dienst v Republik Österreich* [2000] ECR I-10497, [2002] 1 CMLR 375, ECJ. See further Dine, Douglas-Good and Derscard, *Procedure in the European Court* (1991) p 55.

4   Asylum and Immigration Tribunal Practice Directions, consolidated version 30 April 2007, at para 2.2(12). This extraordinary Direction was made notwithstanding that all members constitute 'tribunals' within the meaning of Article 234/EC, applying the criteria developed by the ECJ in Case 246/80 *Broekmeulen v Huisarts Registratie Commissie* [1981] ECR 2311 and subsequent rulings. See *ILPA European Update*, Sep/2007, p 2.The AIT Practice Direction is not traceable on the Internet at the time of writing.

5   Article 267, TFEU (ex art 234, TEC). Usually in the UK this is the Supreme Court.

6   *R v Pharmaceutical Society of Great Britain and Secretary of State for Social Services, ex p Association of Pharmaceutical Importers* [1987] 3 CMLR 951, CA.

7   [1993] QB 534 at 545. For the principles on which interim relief may be granted restraining the implementation of a national law pending a reference see *R v HM Treasury, ex p British Telecommunications plc* [1994] 1 CMLR 621.

6.58 In deciding whether to make a reference the main considerations of principle are: that the relevant facts have been found and are substantially agreed; that the point of law will be substantially determinative of the case; that there is not any Community authority addressing the point of EU law; that the issue in question is one of principle and/or of wide-ranging practical importance; that there are no similar cases pending; and that the question is one that is likely at some stage in the life of the case to need referral to the CJEU.[1]

A reference should not normally be made when the EU provision is *acte clair*. *Acte clair* covers situations where the question for interpretation has not previously been put before the court but where there is no real doubt about the proper interpretation of Community law. Nor should a reference normally be made when the case is 'acte éclair'. 'Acte éclair' means situations where, in other cases, the ECJ or the CJEU has already made a decision on the question.[2] In *CILFIT Srl and Lanificio di Gavardo v Ministry of Health*[3] the ECJ required that the national court must not only itself be convinced as to the correct interpretation of Community law, but also 'be convinced that the matter is equally obvious to the courts of the other Member States and to the Court of Justice'. In the English Court the question posed is whether the proposed construction is one which the court can accept 'with complete confidence'[4] such that it is *acte clair*[5] Nor is it right to refer questions that are merely hypothetical or which lack the necessary factual foundation.[6]

One question is whether higher courts can prevent a lower court or tribunal from making or proceeding with a reference? In *Amministrazione delle Finanze dello Stato v Simmenthal SpA*[7] the ECJ ruled that Community law prevents a provision in national law that would hinder a national court in referring a question to the ECJ about the compatibility of national provisions with Community law. In *Mecanarte-Metalurgica da Lagoa Lda v Chefe do Servico da Conferencia, Oporto*[8] the ECJ ruled that other courts than Portugal's constitutional court could make a preliminary reference and said that national courts have the widest possible powers to refer questions to the ECJ if they consider that an interpretation of Community law is necessary in a case before them. Prior to the decision in Case C-210/06 *CARTESIO Oktato es Szolgaltato bt, Civil proceedings concerning*[9] (ECJ) (16 December 2008) the position was that Community law allowed a decision to make a preliminary reference to be overturned by an appellate court according to national rules.[10] *Cartesio* now holds that a national rule under which a lower court is bound by a superior court's interpretation of Community law cannot of itself deprive the lower court of the possibility of making a reference to the ECJ for a preliminary ruling, even when the superior court had denied that a reference was necessary. It was, therefore, solely for the referring court to draw the proper inferences from a judgment delivered on an appeal against its decision to refer and, in particular, to come to a conclusion as to whether it should maintain the reference or amend or withdraw it.

[1] See Storey, 'Preliminary references to the Court of Justice of the European Union (CJEU)', para 47.
[2] See Joined Cases 28-30/62 *Da Costa en Schaake NV v Nederlandse Belastingadministratie* [1963] ECR 31; [1963] CMLR 224, ECJ.
[3] Case 283/81 [1982] ECR 3415 at [16]–[20]; [1983] 1 CMLR 472.
[4] The words of Sir Thomas Bingham MR in *R v International Stock Exchange of the United Kingdom and the Republic of Ireland Ltd, ex p Else* (1982) Ltd [1993] QB 534 at 545D, [1993] 1 All ER 420, CA.
[5] Per Maurice Kaye LJ in *R (on the application of MA, BT and DA) v Secretary of State for the Home Department & AIRE Centre (Intervener)* [2011] EWCA Civ 1446.
[6] Case C-355/97 *Landesgrundverkehrsreferent der Tiroler Landesregierung v Beck Liegen-schaftsverwaltungsgesellschaft mbH* [1999] ECR I-4977 at [18]–[27].
[7] Case 106/77 [1978] ECR 629, [1978] 3 CMLR 263.

8   Case C-348/89 [1991] ECR I-3277.
9   [2009] Ch 354, [2008] ECR I-9641.
10 See *R (on the application of A) v Secretary of State for the Home Department* [2002] EWCA
    Civ 1008, [2002] EuLR 580.

6.59 Modifications were made to the powers of the ECJ as a result of the Treaty of Amsterdam. Article 234 TEC (ex Article 177) remained so far as the free movement provisions in Part III of the EC Treaty were concerned and all courts might make references. But when it came to visas, immigration and asylum under Title IV of the EC Treaty (now Title V TFEU), the powers of national courts to make references were more limited. References could be made under Article s 35[1] and under Article 68(1) EC[2]. Articles 35 and 68 have now been repealed by the Treaty of Lisbon, and references can be made within the ambit of Article 267 (ex article 234 TEC). In legal terms, for a court of final instance there is an obligation to make a reference (Art 267 (ex art 234)) in all situations where a case gives rise to a question of the interpretation or validity of Union law. For all others, although there is discretion, it is discretion governed by law.

1   These were references eg on the validity and interpretation of Framework decisions. See
    Pupino (criminal proceedings against) Case C-105/03 [2006] QB 83; [2005] ECR I-5285, ECJ.
2   These were references seeking rulings on the interpretation of Title IV or of the acts of
    institutions based on it: see *Elgafaji v Staatssecretaris van Justitie* (Case C-465/07)
    [2009] All ER (EC) 651, [2009] 1 WLR 2100, ECJ, referred under both art 68 and 234 EC.

6.60 There are no court costs in making a reference and legal aid is normally granted by the national court but can also be granted by the CJEU. The issue of legal aid was dealt with in some detail in the recent CJEU case *DEB Deutsche Energiehandels – und Beratungsgesellschaft mbH v Bundesrepublik Deutschland*.[1] The European Court held that whether the principle of effectiveness requires legal aid to be granted to legal persons, the detailed procedural rules governing actions for safeguarding an individual's rights under EU law must not make it in practice impossible or excessively difficult to exercise rights conferred by EU law. The court in effect adopts the provisions of ECHR law on legal aid, stating that the right of access to a court constitutes an element which is inherent in the right to a fair trial under Article 6(1) of the ECHR.[2] The court stated that it is for the national court to ascertain whether the conditions for granting legal aid constitute a limitation on the right of access to the courts which undermines the very core of that right. The national court must take into consideration the subject matter of the litigation; whether the applicant has a reasonable prospect of success; the importance of what is at stake for the applicant in the proceedings; the complexity of the applicable law and procedure; and the applicant's capacity to represent himself effectively – in order to assess the proportionality, the national court may also take account of the amount of the costs of the proceedings in respect of which advance payment must be made and whether or not those costs might represent an insurmountable obstacle to access to the courts.

1   Case C-279/09 [2011] 2 CMLR 529.
2   The court also made it clear that in adopting the ECHR rules, art 52(3) of the Charter states
    that, in so far as it contains rights which correspond to those guaranteed by the ECHR, their
    meaning and scope are to be the same as those laid down by the ECHR. The meaning and the
    scope of the guaranteed rights are to be determined not only by reference to the text of
    the ECHR, but also, inter alia, by reference to the case law of the European Court of Human

Rights. The right to an effective remedy indicates that the assessment of the need to grant that aid must be made on the basis of the right of the actual person, whose rights and freedoms, as guaranteed by EU law, have been violated, rather than on the basis of the public interest of society, even if that interest may be one of the criteria for assessing the need for the aid.

The CJEU and The ECtHR

6.61 The European Union is under an obligation, contained in Article 6(3) TEU (ex Article 6(2) TEU), to respect fundamental rights as guaranteed by the ECHR as general principles of Union law. Article 6(1) now also recognises that the rights, freedoms and principles set out in the Charter of Fundamental Rights of the European Union shall have the same legal value as the Treaties (the Charter is further discussed at CHAPTER 7).[1] The Charter and the ECHR are thereby directly within the jurisdiction of the CJEU. The fact that the ECHR rights are now to be regarded as general principles of Union law is arguably a formal rather than a substantive change since the ECJ was already applying the ECHR.[2] However, the ECJ was not bound to follow Strasbourg case law or to have regard to it, and has not always done so.[3] The important change is that Article 6(2), TEU mandates that 'The Union shall accede' to the ECHR, albeit that 'such accession shall not affect the Union's competences as defined in the Treaties'. At the time of writing, that accession has not as yet taken place; however a 'Draft revised agreement on the accession of the European Union to the Convention for the Protection of Human Rights and Fundamental Freedoms' ('the Draft Accession Agreement') has been drawn up by the European Council, which was recently held by the CJEU to be incompatible with EU Treaties.[4] The Draft Accession Agreement will therefore need to undergo amendments before it can become the basis on which the EU becomes a signatory to the ECHR. That accession, when it comes, is therefore likely to have a number of consequences. Prior to the Treaty of Lisbon, ECJ decisions could not be challenged before the Strasbourg court, since Article 34 of the ECHR only allows complaints against one of the High Contracting Parties and not against the EU or Community.[5] According to the Draft Accession Agreement, once the EU accedes to the ECHR, the EU could be made a respondent to proceedings alleging a violation of the Convention. Also, the EU itself, or other EU Member States, could be brought in as co-respondents where, for example, EU law is alleged to be incompatible with the ECHR (Article 3(2)-(3) of the Draft Accession Agreement). However, in the light of the CJEU's *Opinion 2/13*, these provisions are in doubt. On the basis of the Draft Agreement, the logic of the EU's accession to the ECHR is that the Strasbourg Court would be superior to the CJEU in the application of the ECHR; and this superiority would extend to the CJEU's application of fundamental rights, by virtue of Article 52(3) of the Charter of Fundamental Rights and Article 6(3), TEU. Conversely, the CJEU would remain superior to the Strasbourg court in the application of EU law, given, for example, Articles 19, TEU and 6(3) itself. However, given that the Strasbourg Court would have jurisdiction to rule on whether EU measures have violated the ECHR, it is inevitable that the Strasbourg Court would be required to rule on issues of EU law in order to resolve the complaint. While it is difficult to see how such rulings could be binding on the CJEU, the prospect of the Strasbourg court ruling on EU law issues would mark a clear departure from the Court's current practice.[6]

1 Article 6.1 consolidated TEU. See a useful note by Mark Henderson and Alison Pickup in the *ILPA European Update*, March 2012 on using the Charter following Joined Cases C-411/10NS *v Secretary of State for the Home Department (Amnesty International Ltd and the AIRE Centre (Advice on Individual Rights in Europe) (UK))*; ME *v Refugee Applications Commissioner (Amnesty International Ltd and the AIRE Centre (Advice on Individual Rights in Europe) (UK)* [2013] QB 102; [2012] All ER (EC) 1011; [2012] 2 CMLR 9. Note also Mostyn J's reluctant remarks in *R (on the application of AB) v Secretary of State for the Home Department* [2013] EWHC 3453 (Admin) at [10]-[15]. The incorporation of the Charter is subject to Protocol 30 on the application of the Charter to Poland and the UK, which limits the power of the European Court of Justice to make judgments against the UK or Poland on Charter breaches (Protocol 30, Article 1.1) and provides that to the extent that a provision of the Charter refers to national laws and practices, it shall only apply to Poland and the UK to the extent that the rights and principles it contains are recognised in the law and practices of either country (above, Article 2).

2 See the ERT case: *Elliniki Radiophonia Tileorass-AE v Pliroforissis and Kouvelas* Case C-260/89 [1994] 4 CMLR 540, ECJ.

3 Case 374/87 *Orkem v EC Commission* [1989] ECR 3283, ECJ. See Lord Hope 'Human Rights – where are we now?' [2000] EHRLR 439, where he discusses other cases of divergence. In Case 60/00 *Carpenter (Mary) v Secretary of State for the Home Department* [2003] QB 416, [2002] 2 CMLR 1541, the ECJ applied Article 8 and relied in particular on the landmark ECHR decision in *Boultif v Switzerland* (2001) 33 EHRR 1179, [2001] FLR 1228, to howls of derision (misplaced, it would seem) by Buxton LJ in *W (China) v Secretary of State for the Home Department; X (China) v Secretary of State for the Home Department* [2006] EWCA Civ 1494, who at paragraph 22 lamented the fact that those representing the UK did not tell the ECJ about the balance to be struck between Article 8(1) and 8(2) of the ECHR in English domestic law and thereby necessarily distorted the ECJ's assessment of the balance in that case.

4 The Draft Agreement is dated 3 April 2013, accessed via www.coe.int/t/dghl/standardsetting/hrpolicy/accession/Meeting_reports/47_1(2013)008rev2_EN.pdf; the CJEU's ruling is *Opinion 2/13* of the Court, 18 December 2014 (for commentary on the latter, see Steve Peers' 'The CJEU and the EU's accession to the ECHR: a clear and present danger to human rights proctection', on his *EU Analysis Blog*).

5 See further *Matthews v United Kingdom* (1999) 28 EHRR 361.

6 *Matthews*, supra. See also *Dhabie v Italy* (Application No 17120/09), 8 April 2014 (judgment currently only in French), but see case note in*ILPA European Update*, June 2014. In *Dhabie*, the European Court of Human Rights was presented with a petition by a Tunisian man who alleged that Italy had violated the Euro-Mediterranean Association Agreement which provided for equal treatment with EU national workers in, inter alia, access to social security. He had applied for a 'family allowance' but had been refused on the grounds that he was Tunisian not Italian. Italy's Supreme Court refused to make a reference to the CJEU on the interpretation of the Association Agreement. The applicant argued before the Strasbourg Court, inter alia, that the refusal to make a reference was contrary to Article 6(1) ECHR; and that the refusal of Italian authorities to grant him the family allowance discriminated against him on the grounds of his nationality. The Court upheld both complaints, finding that the absence of reasons or reference to CJEU jurisprudence in failing to make a reference was contrary to Article 6(1); and upheld the discrimination complaint. However, it did so only by reference to ECHR principles, and made no attempt to resolve the issues of EU law that formed the substance of the dispute before the Italian courts.

TERRITORIAL, PERSONAL AND MATERIAL SCOPE OF FREE MOVEMENT RIGHTS

6.62 Entitlement to free movement rights depends on the personal and territorial scope of the EU and TFEU Treaties. Thus Article 47 of Council Regulation (EEC) 1612/68), the main regulation dealing with the free movement of workers and their families prior to the Citizens' Directive (now Article 40 of Council Regulation (EU) 492/2011),[1] applies the regulation to the territories of Member States and to their nationals. If someone is within the territorial and personal scope of the EU law provisions, questions then arise regarding rights of entry and residence of workers and their families or persons seeking to establish themselves, or whether and to what extent Member States can discriminate on grounds of nationality or have conditions or requirements which hinder free movement. Rules regarding these questions fall within the material scope of EU law. We shall mainly be concerned with the personal and material scope of the Treaties, but the territorial scope assumes importance with regard to Overseas Countries and Territories, such as the Cayman Islands and places such as the Channel Islands, Isle of Man and Gibraltar.

[1]   In force from 5 April 2011.

Territorial scope

6.63 Article 52 TEU which substantially replaces Article 299(1) TEC, which is repealed (ex Article 227(1)), read with Article 355 TFEU defines the territorial scope of the Treaties and applies them to the territories of each of the Member States.[1] Article 355 TFEU (ex Article 299(2) TEC) provides that the Treaties apply to the French Overseas Departments, the Azores, Madeira and the Canary Islands,[2] but the Council may adopt specific measures aimed at laying down the conditions of application of the Treaty to these regions, including common policies. When Spain joined the Community, Article 25 of the Treaty of Accession[1] applied free movement rights to the Canary Islands, Ceuta and Melilla without derogation, but Andorra is outside EU territory, although there are various agreements, including a co-operation agreement signed in 2005.

[1]   The territorial scope of EU law is established by art 52 TEU and art 355 TFEU, but it should be noted that the territory which applies for free movement rights is not the same as the territory for customs' purposes: See Martin and Guild *Free Movement of Persons in the European Union* (1996), p 48. Article 13 of the 2011 Treaty of Accession of Croatia to the European Union, inserted Croatia into Article 52 TEU.
[2]   The Treaty of Amsterdam amends art 299(2) EC and simplifies the position. In Case 148/77 *Hansen* [1979] 1 CMLR 604, the ECJ held that the provisions of the Treaty and derived rights apply automatically to the French overseas territories from 1 January 1960, inasmuch as they are an integral part of the French Republic, but that it always remains possible subsequently for specific measures to be adopted in order to meet the needs of those territories. This view was upheld in Case C-163/90 *Administration des Douanes et Droits Indirects v Legros* [1992] ECR I-4625, ECJ. In 1964, Council Decision 64/350 applied the Treaty provisions regarding the right of establishment to these territories. In 1968, Decision 68/359 did the same for workers. In the light of *Hansen* and *Legros* and the latest amendments, these decisions seem unnecessary: see further Martin and Guild above, pp 182–183 on the position prior to the Treaty of Amsterdam.
[1]   Treaty of Accession for Spain and Portugal 1985.

6.64 Special arrangements for association with a number of countries and territories, which have special relations with Denmark, France, the Netherlands and the UK, are contained in Part 4 of TFEU – Association of the Overseas Territories in Articles 198 to 204 (ex Articles 182 to 187 TEC). They are, therefore, within the territorial scope of the Treaties for some purposes, although not generally for freedom of movement.[1] The countries and territories are Greenland, British Indian Ocean Territory, British Antarctic Territory, French Southern and Antarctic Territories, Pitcairn, British Virgin Islands,

Bermuda, Cayman Islands and the Falkland Islands.[2] Apart from this list, no other countries or territories having a special relationship with the UK are included.[3] However, the Treaty applies to those European territories for whose external relations a Member State is responsible.[4] This provision covers Gibraltar, and British Dependent (now Overseas) Territories citizens with a Gibraltarian connection who are also covered because those connected with Gibraltar are included in the definition of a UK national for the purposes of the Treaty. But the Treaties do not cover the Sovereign Base Areas of the UK in Cyprus, nor the Faroe Islands.[5] It applies to the Channel Islands and the Isle of Man 'only to the extent necessary to ensure the implementation of the arrangements for those Islands' as set out in Protocol 3 to the Treaty of Accession of the UK to the EC.[6] We have already dealt with the special position of the Islands at **6.62** above. In Italy, the Republic of San Marino is part of the customs territory of the EU, but is a State independent of Italy and for whose external relations Italy is not responsible and is, therefore, outside the territorial scope of the EU. The same applies to the Vatican for the same reasons.[7] Lastly, the EU Treaty applies to the Åland Islands (Finland) in accordance with the arrangements set out in Protocol 2 to the Treaty of Accession for Austria, Finland and Sweden.[8]

[1]   Article 199(5) sets out the right of establishment on a non-discriminatory basis as an objective of association of the overseas territories with the Union. Article 202 states that freedom of movement of workers, along with provisions relating to public health, security or public policy is to be regulated by future rules and procedures made in accordance with the provisions in Article 203.
[2]   Annex II to TFEU. Greenland was defined as an Overseas Country from 1 February 1985 by a Treaty amendment of 13 March 1984 (OJ L89 1.2.85 p 1); see Martin and Guild *Free Movement of Persons in the European Union* (1996), p 48, and is the subject of specific provisions detailed in Protocol 15 to the EC Treaty.
[3]   Article 355(2) TFEU (ex Article 299(3) TEC).
[4]   Article 355(4) TFEU (ex Article 299(4) TEC).
[5]   Article 355(5)(a) and (b) TFEU (ex Article 299(6) TEC.
[6]   Article 355(5)(c) TFEU.
[7]   Martin and Guild Free Movement of Persons in the European Union (1996), p 48.
[8]   Article 355(5)(a) and (b) TFEU (ex Article 299(5) TEC).

6.65 The geographical application of the Treaties is defined in Article 355 TFEU (ex Article 299 EC), as we have seen, but that Article does not preclude EU rules from having effects outside the territories of the Union.[1] The European case law has consistently held that EU law may apply to professional activities pursued outside Union territory, so long as the employment relationship retains a sufficiently close link with the Union. The starting premise is that in an employment relationship between an EU undertaking and a national of another Member State, the rules on freedom of movement for workers (particularly those prohibiting discrimination on grounds of nationality) are in principle applicable. The case law makes it clear that their application in principle is not affected by the fact that the work is carried out abroad (ie, outside the territories of the Union), whether temporarily and occasionally,[2] or permanently and exclusively.[3] The criterion for applying these rules to an employment relationship existing abroad is the existence of a 'sufficiently close link' with the Union. In *Boukhalfa*[4] the Advocate General's opinion was that it was a matter for the national court to determine whether such a link actually exists. This, however, was not endorsed by the ECJ, which concluded that a Belgian woman working in the German embassy in Algeria, who was paid less than her German colleagues, was sufficiently linked to German law as to come within the Community provisions on discrimination. In determining the existence of the link, the CJEU or national court will look at a number of factors, such as whether the employment relationship was entered into by an EU national and an undertaking of another Member State, whether recruitment took place in a Member State, whether the EU worker was established in a Member State at the time of the recruitment, where the employer is established, whether the contract of employment is governed by the law of a Member State and so forth.

1   Case C-214/94 *Boukhalfa v Germany* [1996] 3 CMLR 22, para 14.
2   Case 36/74 *Walrave & Koc v Association Union Cycliste Internationale* [1974] ECR 1405, ECJ; Case 237/83 *Prodest* [1984] ECR 3153, para 6.
3   Case 9/88 *Da Veiga v Staatssecretaries van Justitie* [1989] ECR 2989, [1991] 1 CMLR 217, para 15; Case C-60/93 *Aldewereld v Staatssecretaris van Financien* [1994] ECR I-2991, para 14.
4   *Boukhalfa* fn 1 above.

6.66 The UK's 2006 EEA Regulations,[1] do not address the question of the territorial scope of the EU Treaties, but deal with 'qualified persons' purely in terms of the personal scope of the Treaties. Regulations 11 and 13 give effect in UK domestic law to an initial right of admission and right of residence to all EEA nationals and Regulations 14 and 15 give 'qualified persons' an extended or permanent right of residence purely in terms of the personal scope of the Treaties. They are given only as regards the UK without further definition. The Channel Islands and Isle of Man[2] are within Union territory for customs purposes,[3] but not for free movement and the provision of services. The 2006 Regulations do not address the position of EEA nationals arriving in the UK under free movement rights and moving on to one or other of the Islands. That is dealt with under a different regime (as we have seen in CHAPTER 5 above). Under the various Orders in Council dealing with the Islands it is provided that EEA nationals, who are entitled to enter and remain in the UK by virtue of an enforceable Community (now EU law) right, do not need leave to enter or remain in that particular Island.[4]

1   SI 2006/1003.
2   According to the government website (www.direct.gov.uk) the Crown Dependencies of the Channel Islands and the Isle of Man, formally possessions of the Crown, are not part of the UK but form a 'federacy with it'.
3   EC Treaty, Protocol 3, art 1.
4   Immigration Act 1988, s 7, as applied to the Islands. (See CHAPTER 5, above.)

PERSONAL SCOPE (1) NATIONALS

EU and EEA nationals

6.67 Although Article 45 TFEU (ex Article 39 TEC) refers only to 'workers' and does not contain any words limiting its application to nationals of a Member State, the ECJ and the subsidiary regulations and directives have all made it clear that this provision may only be relied on by nationals of Member States.[1] Articles 49 (ex Article 43 TEC) (right of establishment) and 56 (ex Article 49 TEC) (provision of services) are expressly limited to nationals of Member States. The Citizens' Directive, which has consolidated and codified much of the subsidiary legislation on free movement makes it clear that the free movement of workers only applies to 'Union citizens', which it defines as 'any person having the nationality of a Member State.'[2] To come within the personal scope of EU free movement rights someone must, therefore, be a national of an EU Member State, which now qualifies him or her as an EU citizen under Article 20 TFEU (ex Article 17 TEC). Because the EEA and Swiss Treaties extend EU free movement rights to all EEA and Swiss nationals, being a national of an EEA State or the Swiss Confederation can properly be described as the main requirement to come within the personal scope of free movement rights. In this context, EEA nationals include UK nationals. However, as regards admission to the UK, a different definition of an 'EEA state' is used in UK domestic law. It does not include UK nationals. Under the 2006 Regulations, EEA nationals means nationals of an EEA State. EEA State means (a) a Member State other than the UK; (b) Norway, Iceland and Liechtenstein; or (c) Switzerland.[3]

[1]   Council Regulation (EU) 492/2011, arts 1 and 2 (ex Council Regulation (EEC) 1612/68, arts 1 and 2); Council Directive (EEC) 68/360, art 1, which has now been repealed by Directive 2004/38/EC; Case 283/83 *Caisse d'Allocations Familiales de la Region Parisienne v Meade* [1984] ECR 2631; see Martin and Guild *Free Movement of Persons in the European Union* (1996), p 95.
[2]   Directive 2004/38/EC, art 2(1).
[3]   Immigration (European Economic Area) Regulations 2006, SI 2006/1003, reg 2(1).

6.68 This group broadly corresponds with those who may come within the definitions of a 'qualified person' and their family members in the UK's Immigration (European Economic Area) Regulations 2006,[1] which seeks to transpose into UK domestic law the obligations under the EU Treaties and the EEA and Swiss Agreements as well as the rights in the unrepealed parts of Regulation 1612/68 (now Regulation 492/2011) and the Citizens' Directive. But the comparison is also misleading. A 'qualified person' is any national of an EEA Member State other than the UK, who is in the UK as a jobseeker, a worker, a self-employed person, including those who have reached retirement age or are permanently incapacitated within the meaning of regulation 5, a self-sufficient person, or a student, or a person who has ceased activity. However, neither the Citizens' Directive nor the 2006 Regulations make mention of receivers or providers of services, almost as if the three-month initial period of residence given to all EEA nationals under regulation 11 covers the point. It may do, but this will not always be the case. Provision of services as in a building contract may last longer than three months.[2] Secondly, the Regulations do not cover students who come within the ambit of the unrepealed regulation 12 of Regulation 1612/68 (now regulation 10, EC Regulation 492/2011), who do not have to have comprehensive sickness insurance or sufficient resources not to become a burden on public assistance, as required by the definition of student in regulation 4.[3] Thirdly, neither the Citizens' Directive nor the 2006 Regulations cover all of the case law developments in EU law, particularly relating to developments in the application of Articles 20 or 21 of the TFEU. Fourthly, the 2006 Regulations are a national measure intended to give effect to EU law as regards entry into and stay in the UK and do not, therefore, deal with the free movement rights of UK nationals, who wish to exercise their rights on the territories of other Member States or when they return to the UK,[4] particularly in relation to grants and access to social security and welfare benefits.[5] Finally, where the

Regulations conflict with EU law, the latter prevails.

¹ Immigration (European Economic Area) Regulations 2006, SI 2006/1003 ('the 2006 Regulations'), regs 4, 5 and 6 (qualified persons) and 7–10 (family members).

² It is true that a saving is made for posted workers in Schedule 4 of the Regulations, where we find that the 2000 Regulations and the Regulations amending the 2000 Regulations are not revoked insofar as they are so applied to posted workers;and, accordingly, the 2000 Regulations, as amended, shall continue to apply to posted workers in accordance with the Immigration (Swiss Free Movement of Persons) (No 3) Regulations 2002, SI 2002/1241. But no other mention of services or service provision is made in the Directive or the 2006 Regulations.

³ See Case C-308/89 *Di Leo v Land Berlin* [1990] ECR I-4185, para 13; Case C-459/99 *Mouvement contre le racisme, l'antisémitisme et la xénophobie (MRAX) ASBL v Belgium* [2002] ECR I-6591, 25/7/2002; Case C–413/99 *Baumbast and R v Secretary of State for the Home Department* [2002] ECR I-7091, [2002] 3 CMLR 599, ECJ; *Teixeira v Lambeth London Borough Council* C-480/08 [2010] NLJR 352, ECJ, and *Harrow London Borough Council v Ibrahim* Case C-310/08. [2010] ELR 261, [2010] Times, 26 February, ECJ.

⁴ Note that the *Surinder Singh* situation is dealt with by regulation 9 of the 2006 Regulations. See **6.73** below.

⁵ Case C-19/92 Kraus [1993] ECR I-1663 (obtaining qualifications recognised by EU law); Case C-370/90 *R v Immigration Appeal Tribunal and Surinder Singh, ex p Secretary of State for the Home Department* [1992] ECR I-4265, [1992] 3 All ER 798 (working on the territory of another Member State); Case C-60/00 *Carpenter* [2002] ECR I-6279, [2002] INLR 439 (providing or receiving services on the territory of another Member State). Similarly, all Community nationals, whatever their place of residence or nationality, who have exercised a free movement right and have worked in another Member State come within art 39 (formerly 48) EC and are to be classed as 'workers': see Case C-419/92 *Scholz v Opera Universitaria di Cagliari and Cinzia Porcedda* [1994] ECR I-505, [1994] 1 CMLR 873, ECJ; Case C-443/93 *Vougioukas v Idrima Koinon Asphalisseon (IKA)* [1995] ECR I-4033.

6.69 Only nationals of a State party to the EEA or Swiss Agreements (whom we refer to as EEA nationals) can take direct advantage of free movement rights. But there are circumstances, such as membership of the family or household of an EEA national, that bring collateral or derivative rights of free movement to non-nationals.¹ Nationality is the principal connecting factor so far as natural persons are concerned, but it is inappropriate for companies. Article 54 TFEU (ex Article 48 TEC) therefore provides that a company or firm which has its registered office, central administration or principal place of business within the Community will be treated in the same way as a natural person who is a Community national. Companies so defined have the right of establishment in the territory of another Member State.² In some cases residence in Community territory is required, in addition to nationality. Thus a period of residence in the UK is necessary before British citizens from the Channel Islands and Isle of Man can benefit from the free movement provisions.³ Similarly, nationals of Denmark who are resident in the Faroe Islands are outside the personal scope of the Treaties.⁴

¹ See **6.74** and **6.116** ff below.

² Article 48 EC (ex art 58).

³ See **6.62** above.

⁴ Article 4 of Protocol 2 to Danish Act of Accession; see also art 299(6)(a) EC (ex art 227).

6.70 Whether someone is or is not a national of a Member State depends on each State's municipal law.¹ The criteria for obtaining nationality vary from State to State. In theory each State can unilaterally expand or reduce the scope of the free movement provisions by changing its nationality law. Thus those born in the UK after 1 January 1983 will not automatically acquire the free movement rights they would have done following birth in the UK in the ten years prior to that date.² Equally, it has been possible for Member States on joining the EU to create for EU purposes special definitions of nationality which derive from, but are different to, the normal definition of nationality in that State's municipal law. The issue has not yet presented real problems, except for Germany³ and the UK. In the UK the problem arises because British nationality is subdivided into a number of different citizenships which carry different immigration rights.

In *Rottmann*⁴ the European Court concluded that, although nationality is normally a matter for national courts to deal with, 'the situation of a citizen of the Union who . . . is faced with a decision withdrawing his naturalisation . . . and placing him . . . in a position capable of causing him to lose his status conferred by Article 20 TFEU and the rights attaching thereto falls, by reason of its nature and its consequences, within the ambit of EU law'. Also, in *JO Nigeria*⁵ UTIAC held that an Immigration Judge should not go behind evidence of a certificate of naturalisation as a citizen of European country on the basis of concerns about the bona fides of the marriage that resulted in the naturalisation. UKUT held that it would be contrary to public policy to dispute Italian nationality or the legal validity of the marriage resulting from it.

¹   See *Oppenheimer v Cattermole* [1976] AC 249, [1975] 1 All ER 538, HL; *Stoeck v Public Trustee* [1921] 2 Ch 67; *Bibi (Mahaboob) v Secretary of State for the Home Department* [1987] Imm AR 340, CA. This also accords with the rule of public international law that in general each State may determine who are its nationals: see Plender *International Migration Law* (2nd edn, 1998) p 39ff.

²   British Nationality Act 1981, s 1. The UK joined the Common Market with effect from 1 January 1973.

³   The German definition of citizenship according to its Constitution prevailed for EC purposes, and this extended German nationality not only to East German nationals but also a wider range of persons of German extraction, thus bringing them within the personal scope of free movement rights. German reunification has caused the problem to vanish.

⁴   Case C-135/08 *Rottmann (Janko) v Freistaat Bayern* [2010] QB 761 at [42] [2010] ECR I-1449 at [42], [2010] QB 761, ECJ. In *G1 v Secretary of State for the Home Department* [2012] EWCA Civ 867 the Court of Appeal took clear issue with *Rottmann*. It was to be applied with caution. National citizenship was not within the EU's competence. *Rottmann* could not be applied to require that the adjudication of a decision to deprive a British citizen of citizenship had to be conducted subject to EU law. EU law's relevance to national citizenship depended on EU citizenship being an incident of national citizenship, but that circumstance could not of itself allocate national citizenship to EU competence. The UK Supreme Court will hand down judgment in *B1 v SSHD* in 2015 on similar issues (on appeal from [2013] EWCA Civ 616).

⁵   *JO (foreign marriage - recognition) Nigeria* [2010] UKUT 478 (IAC) (26 January 2011).

UK nationals for EU purposes

6.71 At the time of signing the Treaty of Accession to the EEC, the British government made a declaration on the meaning of a UK national for the purposes of the Treaties.¹ Since then the government has made a further declaration, which took effect on 1 January 1983, when the British Nationality Act 1981 came into force.² So far as the UK is concerned, the term 'national' or 'nationals' in any Community document now means:

(a)   British citizens;

(b)   British subjects under the British Nationality Act 1981³ who have the right of abode in the UK;

(c)   British Dependent (now Overseas) Territories citizens who acquire that citizenship from a connection with Gibraltar.

Two features of the declaration should be noted. First, it excludes those citizens of a Commonwealth country who have obtained the right of abode in the UK, but not British citizenship.[4] Secondly, it includes Gibraltarians, who can move to any other country of the EU although they are not full British citizens. Just as Gibraltarians can move to other Member States, nationals of those States can move to Gibraltar, to whose territory freedom of movement is extended in accordance with Article 355 299(4) EC (ex Article 227(4)). The validity of the UK Declaration was upheld by the ECJ in *R (on the application of Kaur) v Secretary of State for the Home Department.*[5]

[1]   (1972) (Cm 4862) p 118. Under this declaration a UK national was a citizen of the UK and Colonies (CUKC) or a British subject without citizenship, having in either case the right of abode, or a CUKC by connection with Gibraltar.
[2]   28 January 1983, (1983) OJ C 23, p 1, (1983) (Cmd 9062). There may be some doubt as to the legal authority for this declaration. It is a unilateral declaration not a treaty document. It is made without any statutory authority or parliamentary approval. It is not the judgment of a competent court.
[3]   British Nationality Act 1981, ss 30–32.
[4]   Immigration Act 1971, s 2(1)(b).
[5]   Case C-192/99 [2001] All ER (EC) 250.

6.72 Some people may have the nationality of more than one State. Dual nationality does not hinder the enjoyment of fundamental freedoms under Community law where this applies. This will be the case where the person is both a national of a Member State and of a third State or is a national of two Member States at the same time. In *Micheletti* the ECJ held that a Member State may not restrict the effects of the grant of nationality of another Member State by imposing conditions (such as a habitual residence requirement on the territory of the Member State in question) for recognition of that nationality with a view to the exercise of one of the Treaty's fundamental freedoms. Effectively the Member State is precluded from treating a person who is both an EU national and a national of a non-member state as if he or she were not such an EU national.[1] In the UK this issue has arisen most frequently with respect to Irish nationals.[2] In *McCarthy v Secretary of State for the Home Department*[3] the appellant was a dual national (British and Irish), and although it was common ground that her Irish nationality conferred on her the status of an EEA national within the meaning of the 2006 Regulations (regulation 2), it did not help her qualify for a right to permanent residence under Article 16 of the Citizens' Directive, because that required lawful residence which complies with community law requirements specified in the Citizens' Directive. The court referred to the Directive using the words 'host member state', which 'suggests that the Union citizen is a guest, an inappropriate expression for persons in a state of their own nationality'. None of the European case law was cited. The case should be treated as decided per incuriam. In *Avello*,[4] two dual Belgian and Spanish national children who had lived all their lives in Belgium were found by the ECJ to enjoy the status of citizen of the Union conferred by Article 17 EC (now Article 20 TFEU). The court recalled that the scope of the Treaty is not extended to purely internal situations which have no link with Community law. However it considered that as they were nationals of one Member State lawfully resident in the territory of another Member State a link with Community law had been established. The fact that people may not need to rely on their EU nationality to gain admission does not mean that rights incidental to such a claim are ineffective.[5] Where an applicant claims that he or she is a citizen of a particular Member State, the burden of proof is on the applicant and no different principle is imported because of the implications of Community law.[6]

[1] Case C-369/90 *Micheletti v Delegacion del Gobierno en Cantabria* [1992] ECR I-4239; see also Jauler Carrescosa in (1994) 8 INLP 1. This principle was applied in *Chen and Zhu v Secretary of State for the Home Department* C-200/02 [2005] QB 325, [2005] All ER (EC) 129, ECJ to the situation of an infant whose mother went to Ireland to give birth to her child to enable the child to obtain Irish nationality; the child's Irish nationality conferred free movement rights under art 18 EC and Directive 90/364 and it would be contrary to EU law to impose further conditions over and above possession of that nationality.

[2] Thus in *R v Immigration Appeal Tribunal, ex p Aradi* [1987] Imm AR 359, QBD, a dual Irish and British citizen had never been out of the UK in her whole life. Her possession of dual nationality was held, therefore, not to bring into play the more beneficial provisions of EEC law on family reunion in what would otherwise be a purely internal British situation. This authority is not compatible with more recent decisions of the ECJ. More recently in *EN and AN (EEA regulation 12: British Citizens) Kenya* [2008] UKAIT 00028 the AIT held that a dual national (British and Irish) could not benefit from the application of community law either to himself or his third country national spouse, because as a British citizen he was not subject to any of the restrictions on residence in the EEA regulations 2006 and could not, therefore, be regarded as 'residing in the UK in accordance with regulation 12 of these regulations'. This decision is of very dubious authority because: (i) the Tribunal treated reg 12 as a matter of pure UK law, outside the requirements of European Law, which in the light of subsequent case law is clearly erroneous; and (ii) none of the European Court cases on dual nationality, referred to in this paragraph, were cited to or referred to by the AIT.

[3] [2008] EWCA Civ 641, [2008] 3 CMLR 174.

[4] Case C-148/02 *Avello (Carlos Garcia) v Belgium* [2003] ECR I-11613. The Court held that in the particular circumstances of the case Articles 12 of and 17 of the EC Treaty precluded the administrative authority of the Member State in which the children resided from refusing to grant an application for a change of surname made on their behalf, in the case where the purpose of that application is to enable those children to bear the surname to which they are entitled according to the law and tradition of the second Member State.

[5] Cases C-389 and 390/87 *Echternach and Moritz v Minister van Onderwijs en Wetenschappen* [1989] ECR 723, [1990] 2 CMLR 305, ECJ; Case C-370/90 *R v Immigration Appeal Tribunal and Surinder Singh, ex p Secretary of State for the Home Department* [1992] 3 All ER 798, [1992] Imm AR 565, ECJ.

[6] *Surinder Singh* above.

The Surinder Singh situation

6.73 In *Surinder Singh*[1] the European Court held that where a British citizen had exercised Community rights in another part of the EU or the EEA and returned to the UK with non-national family members, he or she was exercising Community as well as national rights of entry, and the family members could not be treated less favourably than required by Community law. The *Surinder Singh* situation is now dealt with by regulation 9 of the 2006 Regulations,[2] which are, in regulation 9(2), that (a) the British citizen ('P') is residing in an EEA State as a worker or self-employed person or was so residing before returning to the United Kingdom; (b) if the family member of P is P's spouse or civil partner, the parties are living together in the EEA State or had entered into the marriage or civil partnership and were living together in the EEA State before the British citizen returned to the United Kingdom;[3] and (c) the centre of P's life has transferred to the EEA State where P resided as a worker or self-employed person. Regulation 9(3) provides for a range of factors to be taken into account in determining whether the 'centre of P's life transferred to another EEA State' including the period of residence, location of principal residence and degree of integration. There is no corresponding provision in the EU Law.[4] However, the regulation makes very narrow provision for UK nationals who may be exercising EU law rights and there is, for example, no provision for the *Carpenter*[5] type of situation, where a UK national was held to be exercising Community rights by providing services in another EU Member State while retaining UK residence. The 2000 Regulations required that where a UK citizen was seeking to bring a non-EEA national family member with him or her on return from another Member State, that family member must be lawfully resident in an EEA State.[6] This requirement is not repeated in the 2006 Regulations.

[1] Case C-370/90 *R v Immigration Appeal Tribunal and Surinder Singh, ex p Secretary of State for the Home Department* [1992] 3 All ER 798, [1992] Imm AR 565, ECJ.

[2] The Immigration (European Economic Area) Regulations 2006, SI 2006/1003. A revised version of reg 9 was inserted as of 1 January 2014: Immigration (European Economic Area) (Amendment) (No 2) Regulations, 2013/3032, Sch1, para 5 (1 January 2014: subject to transitional provisions as specified in SI 2013/3032, Sch 3, para 2.

[3] There is no requirement that the non-EEA national spouse was lawfully present in the EEA State: *HB (EEA right to reside-Metock) Algeria* [2008] UKAIT 00069, applying the principle in *Metock* (Case C-127/08) [2008] 3 CMLR 1167, ECJ.

[4] See *O and B v Minister voor Immigratie, Integratie en Asiel* (Case C-456/12), CJEU, judgment 12 March 2014, [2014] QB 1163. See also Directive 2004/38/EC.

[5] *Carpenter (Mary) v Secretary of State for the Home Department:* C-60/00: C-60/00 [2003] QB 416, [2002] ECR I-6279, ECJ, [2003] All ER (EC) 577, [2003] 2 WLR 267. See also the recent clarification of the scope of *Carpenter* in *S and G v Minister voor Immigratie, Integratie en Asiel* (Case C-457/12), CJEU, judgment 12 March 2014, [2014] QB 1207.

[6] SI 2005/47, reg 2, amending SI 2000/2326, reg 11(2)(b).

Non-nationals and derivative rights of residence

6.74 Non-nationals are normally outside the personal scope of the Treaty provisions relating to citizens and free movement. They do fall within the scope of measures taken under Title V TFEU (formerly Title IV TEC), relating to the EU's common internal and external border control and asylum measures, but these provisions do not generally create free movement rights. But, as always, there are exceptions. These are:

(1)   family members of all EU members travelling from one Member State to another have a new right residence for up to three months 'without any conditions or any formalities'.[1] For a stay of longer than three months, the right applies to family members of qualified persons under the 2006 Regulations.[2] After five years this can become a permanent right of residence;[3]

(2)   family members of EU citizens may have a derivative right of residence where the EU citizen has a recognised right of residence by virtue of directly acquired rights as a citizen under Article 20, TFEU, without being a qualified person under the 2006 Regulations.[4] This is discussed further below from 6.75;

(3)   directors and staff of a company constituted in one Member State and carrying out services in another. A company providing services in another Member State may travel with the whole of its staff for the duration of the work undertaken under the posted workers rule,[5] which we discuss at 6.103 ff below;

(4)   stateless persons and refugees recognised in one Member State, who have been admitted to the territory of another, are entitled to carry with them accrued social security rights in the same way as EU nationals.[6] As regards free movement rights, the Council declared in 1964 that refugees moving from one Member State to another to seek employment should receive 'the most favourable treatment possible', and their entry 'must be given especially favourable consideration'. This declaration has no direct effect and does not bring refugees within the personal scope of the EU, but it is the strongest possible invitation to Member States to take the declaration into account when considering the grant of leave to enter.[7]

---

[1]   Directive 2004/38/EC, art 6, transposed into UK domestic law by the Immigration (European Economic Area) Regulations 2006, SI 2006/1003, reg 13. See Case 131/85 *Gül v Regierungspräsident Düsseldorf* [1986] ECR 1573, [1987] 1 CMLR 501, ECJ. But the Community national member of the family must have exercised free movement rights. Community law has no application to a wholly internal situation: see **6.90** below.

[2]   SI 2006/1003, reg 14(2).

[3]   SI 2006/1003, reg 15(1)(b).

[4]   Case C-34/09 *Ruiz Zambrano v Office National de l'Emploi (ONEm)* [2011] All ER (EC) 491, [2011] 2 CMLR 1197, ECJ, at [41]–[44]; Case C-434/09 *McCarthy v Secretary of State for the Home Department* [2011] All ER (EC) 729; and Case 256/11 *Dereci v Bundesministerium für Inneres* [2011] ECR I-11315, [2012] All ER (EC) 373 at [62]–[65].

[5]   Case C-113/89 *Rush Portuguesa Lda v ONI* [1990] ECR I-1417, [1991] 2 CMLR 818; and Case C-43/93 *Vander Elst v Office des Migrations Internationales* [1994] ECR I-3803.

[6]   Council Regulation (EEC) 1408/71, which deals with social security benefits for migrant workers.

[7]   See further Martin and Guild *Free movement of persons in the European Union* (1996), chapter 21. It is arguable that the Home Office must have regard to the words quoted in deciding whether to admit Convention refugees recognised in another Member State: *R v Secretary of State, ex p Obomalayat* (16 August 1978, unreported), QBD cited in Vaughan *Law of the European Communities* (Butterworths), para 15.363. See further CHAPTER 12 below.

Citizenship of the EU

6.75 In 1992, the Maastricht Treaty introduced European citizenship as a novel and complementary status for all Member State nationals. By granting to every citizen the right to move and reside freely within the territory of the Member States, the Maastricht Treaty recognised the essential role of individuals, *irrespective of whether or not they were economically active*, within the newly created Union.[1] The key provisions are Articles 20 and 21 TFEU:

- Article 20, TFEU (former Article 17, EC) establishes Union citizenship, which is to be held by every person holding the nationality of a Member State. It also states that Union citizens shall enjoy the rights (and be subject to the duties) provided for in the Treaties, including the right to move and reside freely within the territory of the Member States. The rights listed in Article 20 are non-exhaustive and include specified rights such as the right to vote and stand as a candidate in local and European Parliament elections.
- Article 21, TFEU (former Article 18, EC) grants every Union citizen 'the right to move and reside freely within the territory of the Member States'.

The rights contained in Articles 20 and 21 are subject to the conditions and limitations laid down in the Treaties and secondary legislation. In addition to these primary provisions of the Treaty, there is the Citizens Directive (2004/38/EC), to which we refer extensively throughout this Chapter and which lays down detailed provisions concerning the residence and movement rights of Union citizens and their family members. Article 3(1) of that Directive clearly states that it shall apply exclusively to Union citizens 'who move to or reside in a Member State other than that of which they are a national' and to their accompanying family members. In the three main decisions we discuss in the following paragraphs, *Zambrano, McCarthy* and *Dereci*,[2] the key feature was that in none of them had the Union citizens concerned moved from one Member State to another and in each case the CJEU found that Article 3(1) of the Directive, which clearly states that it shall apply exclusively to Union citizens 'who move to or reside in a Member State other than that of which they are a national' and to their accompanying family members, did not apply. So the issues of the right to reside and the right to work were outwith the Citizens Directive, and Articles 20 and 21 were directly in play.

[1] See Opinion of A-G Eleanour Sharpston in Case C-34/09 *Ruiz Zambrano v Office National de l'Emploi (ONEm)* [2011] All ER (EC) 491, [2011] 2 CMLR 1197, ECJ, at [67] (30 September 2010). We are indebted to this Opinion for confronting and in setting out her opinion so clearly on all the issues which were raised in the *Zambrano* reference – something which was not emulated by the Grand Chamber. See further Anja Wiesbrock, *Union Citizenship and the Redefinition of the 'Internal Situations' Rule: The Implications of Zambrano*, 12 *German Law Journal* 2077–2094 (2011), pp 2083–2084 and fn 30, available at www.germanlawjournal.com\\index.php?pageID=11&=1400. We are also indebted to this very illuminating article.

[2] Case C-34/09 *Ruiz Zambrano v Office National de l'Emploi (ONEm)* [2011] All ER (EC) 491, [2011] 2 CMLR 1197; Case C-434/09 *McCarthy v Secretary of State for the Home Department* [2011] All ER (EC) 729; and Case-256/11 *Dereci v Bundesministerium für Inneres* [2011] ECR I-11315, [2012] All ER (EC) 373.

6.76 Under Article 20 it can be seen that each individual citizen enjoys rights and owes duties that together make up a new status and may therefore rely on the rights pertaining to that status, including against their Member State of origin.[1] In a ground-breaking declaration in the case of *Grzelczyk* in 2001 the ECJ stated that this status was 'destined to become the fundamental status of nationals of the Member States'.[2] *Zambrano* put some unexpected flesh and bones on this fundamental status with seismic effect. The shock waves had hardly abated, when *Zambrano* was followed by *McCarthy* and then by *Dereci*, in which the Austrian, Danish, German, Irish, Netherlands, Polish and UK Governments (and the European Commission) argued for a clear reversal of the road map charted by *Zambrano*. We will deal with the upshot of these cases below. They each put into question what precisely Union citizenship entails. Furthermore we cannot ignore the earlier case of *Chen*[3] Some of the points arising are as follows:

- Do the circumstances of a particular case constitute a situation that is 'purely internal' to the Member State concerned, as the seven opposition states contested in *Dereci*, in which EU law has no role to play (see **6.92** below)?

- Or does full recognition of the rights (including the future rights) that necessarily flow from Union citizenship mean that child EU citizens (and possibly other citizens) have a right, based on EU law rather than national law, to reside anywhere within the territory of the Union (including in the Member State of his nationality)?

- Does this right enable them to be joined by members of their family irrespective of the nationality of the family members?

- Or is the right only available if the measures taken by the national authority deprive the EU citizens effectively of their right to move to and reside in another Member State than their own (the current prevailing view)?

- If so, what is the test to determine whether or not they have been or will be deprived of their right of free movement? Is it a test of 'insurmountable obstacles' or 'hardship' or proportionality or reasonableness or some vague form of practicality?

- If the criterion identified by the court in *Dereci* and applied in *Zambrano*[4] is expressed in terms only of the interference with the EU citizen's free movement rights, is it right to conclude that these two cases and *McCarthy* are based on the premise that the substance of the rights attaching to the status of EU citizen under Article 20 does not include the right to respect for family life enshrined in art 7 of the Charter of Fundamental Rights of the European Union and in art 8(1) of the ECHR?[5]

- When considering the criteria for a right of residence under art 20, what if any weight is to be attached to Article 6(3) TEU, which states that fundamental rights, as guaranteed by the ECHR and as they result from the constitutional traditions common to the Member States, *shall constitute general principles of the Union's law*?

- Can these general principles be switched on and off like a light switch to suit the particular case or do they at all times illuminate and guide EU law in its search for the proper ambit and reach of Article 20?

- Finally, there are the Treaty discrimination provisions under Article 18, which the referring court asked about in *Zambrano*, but did not get any answer; do they have any part to play and if so what?

---

1   See Case C-434/09 *McCarthy v Secretary of State for the Home Department* [2011] All ER (EC) 729 at [48] and Case-256/11 *Dereci* at [63].

2   Case C-184/99 *Grzelczyk (Rudy) v Centre Public d'Aide Sociale d'Ottignies-Louvain-la-Neuve* [2001] ECR I-6193, [2003] All ER (EC) 385 at [31], confirmed later in, inter alia, Case C-224/98 *D'Hoop (Marie-Nathalie) v Office National de l'Emploi* [2002] ECR I-6191, [2003] All ER (EC) 527 at [28]; Case C-413/99 *Baumbast and R v Secretary of State for the Home Department* [2002] ECR I-7091, [2002] 3 CMLR 599 at [82]; Joined Cases C-482/01 and C-493/01 *Orfanopoulos and Oliveri v Land Baden-Württemberg* [2004] ECR I-5257 at [65]; Case C-148/02 *Avello (Carlos Garcia) v Belgium* [2003] ECR I-1161, [2004] All ER (EC) 740 at [22]; Case C-200/02 *Chen and Zhu v Secretary of State for the Home Department* [2005] QB 325, [2005] INLR 1 at [25]; Case C-224/02 *Pusa v Osuuspankkien Keskinäinen Vakuutusyhtiö* [2004] ECR I-5763, [2004] All ER (EC) 797 at [16]; Case C-147/03 *European Communities v Austria* [2005] ECR I-5969 at [45], [2006] 3 CMLR 1089; Case C-209/03 *R (on the application of Bidar) v Ealing London Borough Council* [2005] QB 812, [2005] ECR I-2119 at [31]; Case C-403/03 *Schemp v Finanzamt Munchen V* [2005] ECR I-6421 at [15], [2005] STC 1792; Case C-145/04 *Spain v United Kingdom* [2006] ECR I-7917 at [74], [2007] 1 CMLR 87; Case C-50/06 *EU Commission v Netherlands* [2007] ECR I-4383 at [32], [2007] 3 CMLR 168, ECJ; and Case C-524/06 *Heinz Huber v Bundersrepublik*

Deutschland [2008] ECR I-9705 at [69], [2009] All ER (EC) 239, ECJ; Case C-34/09 *Ruiz Zambrano v Office National de l'Emploi (ONEm)* [2011] All ER (EC) 491, [2011] 2 CMLR 1197 at [41]; *Dereci* at [62].
3   Case C-200/02 *Chen and Another v SSHD* [2005] INLR 1
4   See the Opinion of A-G Eleanor Sharpston in *Zambrano*.
5   See A-G's Opinion in *Dereci* at [37].

The Zambrano line of cases

6.77 In *Zambrano*[1] the facts of the case were that Mr Zambrano, a Colombian national, arrived in Belgium in 1999 holding a valid visa issued by the Belgian authorities. He was joined shortly thereafter by his wife, also Colombian. Their subsequent applications for asylum were refused. He made further applications but they were all refused. Eventually he applied for an annulment of those decisions before the Conseil d'Etat, as well as the suspension of an order requiring him to leave the country. The entire procedure stretched over a period of ten years, from his first application for asylum in September 2000 to the procedures before the Conseil d'Etat, which were still pending when the reference for a preliminary ruling was made in September 2010. In the meantime, and despite not possessing a work permit, Mr Zambrano obtained full-time employment with a Belgian company and became a father to two children, both of whom were born in Belgium with Belgian nationality. His illegal employment status was discovered after an unsuccessful application for unemployment benefits.

Even though the case originally referred to the CJEU concerned a dispute over employment-related rights (namely, the access to unemployment benefits), the major issue became the residence rights held by third-country-national family members of Union citizens who have not left their Member States of nationality. The Belgian referring court inquired, firstly, whether Articles 20 or 21 confer a right of residence upon Union citizens in the Member States of their nationality even if they have not previously exercised their free movement rights. This preliminary question was raised in order to come to the major issue of the derivative right of a third-country-national parent. Secondly, the referring court raised the question of human rights protection, concerning discrimination, rights of the child and access to social security and social assistance under Articles 21, 24, and 34 of the Charter of Fundamental Rights. Thirdly, the Belgian court asked about the exemption from the requirement to hold a work permit for the third-country-national parent of a minor child residing in the Member State of the child's nationality. The underlying claim was that of reverse discrimination facing Belgian nationals who have not exercised their free movement rights *vis-à-vis* Union citizens from other Member States and Belgian nationals who had in some way exercised their free movement rights.[2]

In a very short judgment the Grand Chamber of the CJEU combined the three questions into one and avoided answering the questions relating to human rights protection and reverse discrimination. The court held that Article 20, TFEU confers a right of residence and a right to obtain a work permit upon the parents of a minor dependent EU citizen who has never left the Member State of his or her nationality. The ruling is potentially ground-breaking, because it limited the 'internal situation' rule and extended the reach of the primary law provisions on Union citizenship beyond the Citizens Directive 2004/38/EC. It did place limitations on the residence rights of EU citizens under art 20 by holding that it precluded measures taken by the national authority which have the effect on Union citizens of actually or potentially depriving them of *the genuine enjoyment of the substance of the rights conferred by virtue of their status* as a citizen of the Union. On the facts of *Zambrano* it was clear that if the parents were expelled from Belgium, their two children, both EU citizens, would have to leave Union territory and would be deprived of both free movement and residence rights in the territory of the Union. In other words, they would not be able to enjoy the substance of their rights.

---

1   Case C-34/09 *Ruiz Zambrano v Office National de l'Emploi (ONEm)* [2011] All ER (EC) 491, [2011] 2 CMLR 1197, ECJ.
2   See Wiesbrock, 'Union Citizenship and the Redefinition of the "Internal Situations" Rule: The Implications of Zambrano' (2011) 12 *German Law Journal* 2077 at p 2079.

McCarthy

6.78 By applying Article 20, TFEU to the case at hand even though no cross-border movement was involved, the *Zambrano* ruling potentially had major implications for the Member States, extending the reach of EU law to an area that was thought to be the last realm of national discretion when dealing with the situation of family members of Union citizens.[1]

The ambit of the *Zambrano* judgment, however, has been qualified by the subsequent *McCarthy* ruling of the court's Third Chamber. In *McCarthy*, the court was faced with the situation of a dual British-Irish citizen, who was born and had always lived in the UK. She had never argued that she was or had been a worker, self-employed person or self-sufficient person. She was in receipt of State benefits. On 15 November 2002, she married a Jamaican national who lacked leave to remain in the UK under the Immigration Rules of that Member State.

Mrs McCarthy tried to rely on the provisions on EU citizenship in the Citizens Directive to derive a right of residence in the UK for her third-country national spouse, and the questions referred to the court by the UK Supreme Court were confined to questions about the interpretation of Articles 3(1) and 16 of Directive 2004/38/EC. The court reformulated the question to include the applicability of Article 21, TFEU. The court, not surprisingly, held that the Directive did not apply to her case, because by Article 3.1 it shall apply exclusively to Union citizens 'who move to or reside in a Member State other than that of which they are a national' and to their accompanying family members. The court then went on to consider Article 21, TFEU and held that it was not applicable in the case at hand, since:

> 'no element of the situation of Mrs McCarthy, as described by the national court, indicates that the national measure at issue in the main proceedings has the effect of depriving her of the genuine enjoyment of the substance of the rights associated with her status as a Union citizen, or of impeding the exercise of her right to move and reside freely within the territory of the Member States, in accordance with Article 21 TFEU' (at [49])'.

The court distinguished *Zambrano* and *Garcia Avello v Belgium*[2] stating that the national measure at issue had the effect of depriving Union citizens of the genuine enjoyment of the substance of the rights conferred by virtue of that status or of impeding the exercise of their right of free movement and residence within the territory of the Member States. They concluded:

'In those circumstances, the situation of a person such as Mrs McCarthy has no factor linking it with any of the situations governed by European Union law and the situation is confined in all relevant respects within a single Member State' (at [55])'.

Hence, the court clarified that the 'internal situation' rule has not been abandoned, but merely modified. The required link with Union law in a case such as *Zambrano* does not emerge from the link to cross-border movement, but from the Union citizen's deprivation of the genuine enjoyment of the substance of the rights associated with Union citizenship. *McCarthy* thus limits the implications of *Zambrano* for internal situations, by restricting the range of situations to which the judgment can be applied. It follows from a combination of both judgments that a set of requirements have to be fulfilled in order for a situation to fall under the *Zambrano* regime and for a person to enjoy the rights under EU law.[3]

[1]   See Wiesbrock, *Union Citizenship and the Redefinition of the 'Internal Situations' Rule: The Implications of Zambrano*, p 2085. She also points out that the potential implications of abandoning the restriction against relying on the rights derived from Union citizenship in a purely internal situation were immense, as the percentage of Union citizens who exercise their free movement rights is still marginal.

[2]   Case C-148/02 *Avello (Carlos Garcia) v Belgium* [2003] ECR I-1161, [2004] All ER (EC) 740, ECJ.

[3]   Wiesbrock, *Union Citizenship*, p 2086. At p 2087 she also opines that the *McCarthy* judgment clearly rules out the possibility of applying the case by analogy to third-country-national spouses of Union citizens but leaves open a possibility that the ruling equally covers other types of dependency, such as adult children or parents who cannot take care of themselves.

Dereci

6.79 In the later case of *Dereci*[1] the court sought to clarify and at the same time limit the ambit of the Article 20 rights of residence irrespective of cross-border movement. The case concerned five families where third country nationals wished to join family members in Austria, all of whom were Austrian citizens. Mr Dereci was a Turkish national who had entered Austria illegally and was married to an Austrian citizen by whom he had three minor children. The family lived together in the same household. It is to be inferred from the decision that the children would not be required to leave Austria by reason of their father's removal because they had their mother to turn to for support and care. In fact, Mr Dereci succeeded on another point considered by the Court, namely his rights under the Ankara Agreement, a matter which we deal with quite separately.

Other claimants were spouses and adult children of Austrian citizens resident in Austria. There were two common themes: the Austrian citizens had never exercised Treaty rights to move to or reside in another Member State, and the citizens were not financially dependent on the family member facing expulsion.

The main issue in the case was whether the internal situation rule applied, or the principles laid down in *Zambrano*. A long list of Member States, including the UK, submitted that the principles laid down in that case apply to very exceptional situations and that the issues in *Dereci were* substantially different from those in *Zambrano*, claiming that none of the Union citizens in the current case were at risk of having to leave the territory of the EU and thus of being denied the genuine enjoyment of the substance of the rights conferred by virtue of their status as citizens of the Union. Nor, according to the Commission, was there a barrier to the exercise of their free movement rights under EU law.

The court held, as it had in *Zambrano* and *McCarthy*, that the case was outside the ambit of the Citizens Directive and that only Article 20, TFEU was in issue. The court then moved on to this Article. They reminded themselves that the Treaty rules governing freedom of movement for persons and the measures adopted to implement them cannot be applied to situations which have no factor linking them with any of the situations governed by European Union law and which are confined in all relevant respects within a single Member State (at [60]).[2] However, they stated, as the court had in *McCarthy*, that absence of cross-border movement did not, of itself, mean that the situation of EU citizens had to be assimilated to a purely internal situation (at [61]).[3] The court also accepted as a general principle that as nationals of a Member State, family members of the applicants in the main proceedings enjoy the status of Union citizens under Article 20(1), TFEU and may therefore rely on the rights pertaining to that status, including against their Member State of origin[4] (at [63]).

[1] Case 256/11 *Dereci v Bundesministerium fur Inneres* [2011] ECR I-11315; [2012] 1 CMLR 45; [2012] All ER (EC) 373, CJEU (GC).

[2] Referring to Case C-212/06 *Government of the French Community v Flemish Government* [2008] ECR I-1683 at [33], [2009] All ER (EC) 187, ECJ; C-127/08 *Metock v Minister for Justice, Equality and Law Reform* [2009] QB 318, [2008] ECR I-6241 at [77], ECJ; and Case C-434/09 *McCarthy v Secretary of State for the Home Department* [2011] All ER (EC) 729 at [45].

[3] Quoting Case C-403/03 *Schemp v Finanzamt Munchen V* [2005] ECR I-6421 at [22], [2005] STC 1792; and *McCarthy v Secretary of State for the Home Department* [2011] All ER (EC) 729 at [46].

[4] See *McCarthy v Secretary of State for the Home Department* at [48].

6.80 The court then got to the nub of the question – the right of EU citizens under Article 20, TFEU to the genuine enjoyment of the substance of the rights conferred by virtue of that status and the fact that, in *Zambrano* (at [42]), the CJEU held that Article 20 precludes national measures which have the effect of depriving Union citizens of the substance of that right (at [64]). This all happens outside the Citizens Directive (see at [67]) and irrespective of whether the EU citizens have exercised any cross border rights of free movement. The court then sought (at [65]–[69]) to identify the criterion or criteria by which to judge whether there has been or would be a breach of the right to the genuine enjoyment of the substance of the rights conferred by virtue of EU citizenship. The court accepted that the two children in *Zambrano* would, in fact, be unable to exercise the substance of the rights conferred on them by virtue of their status as citizens of the Union if their parents were removed from Belgium; it followed, said the court, that:

'the criterion relating to the denial of the genuine enjoyment of the substance of the rights conferred by virtue of European Union citizen status refers to situations in which the Union citizen has, in fact, to leave not only the territory of the Member State of which he is a national but also the territory of the Union as a whole' (at [66]).

'That criterion is specific in character inasmuch as it relates to situations in which, although subordinate legislation on the right of residence of third country nationals is not applicable, a right of residence may not, exceptionally, be refused to a third country national, who is a family member of a Member State national, as the effectiveness of Union citizenship enjoyed by that national would otherwise be undermined' (at [67]).

'It may seem desirable to a Union citizen to keep his or her family together but that is not sufficient in itself to support the view that the Union citizen will be forced to leave Union territory if such a right is not granted' (at [68]).

The court admitted that there may be *other criteria* on the basis of which the right to residence cannot be refused and indicated that their finding with regard to the *Zambrano* criterion was without prejudice to the question whether, on the basis of other criteria, a right of residence cannot be refused. None of these other possible criteria, however, are discussed or identified, except, 'inter alia, ... the protection of family life'. The court then went on to deal with the right to respect for private and family life and spent several paragraphs sidelining the Charter of Fundamental Rights,[1] and holding that if the domestic court finds that European law applies it can use Article 7 of the Charter but if it does not apply it can use Article 8, ECHR. It then concluded that the question of whether EU or domestic law was applicable was a matter for national courts to decide. At [72] they said:

'in the present case, if the referring court considers, in the light of the circumstances of the disputes in the main proceedings, that the situation of the applicants in the main proceedings is covered by European Union law, it must examine whether the refusal of their right of residence undermines the right to respect for private and family life provided for in Article 7 of the Charter. On the other hand, if it takes the view that that situation is not covered by European Union law, it must undertake that examination in the light of Article 8(1) of the ECHR.'

The court pointed out that the Charter's provisions are, according to Article 51(1) thereof, addressed to the Member States only when they are implementing European Union law. So when the court is called upon to interpret, in the light of the Charter, the law of the European Union it must do so within the limits of the powers conferred on it.[2] If the *Zambrano* protection under Articles 20 or 21 is limited to safeguarding the dependent citizen's free movement rights and that protecting human rights (including family rights) belongs to a separate department outside the competence of EU law, then (i) why mention the Charter, because it will never be available?; and (ii) the fundamentalist view of the reach of Articles 20 and 21 is not exactly how the CJEU left it in *Dereci*. So perhaps the Court is simply anticipating that their decision is not the end of the road.

---

[1] Case 256/11 *Dereci and others v Bundesminister für Inneres* [2011] ECR I-11315, [2012] All ER (EC) 373 at [71]; see also Case C-434/09 *McCarthy v Secretary of State for the Home Department* [2011] All ER (EC) 729 at [51]; and Joined Cases C-483/09 and C-1/10 *Guyez and Sanchez (Salmeron) v Spain (X and Y Intervening)* [2011] ECR I-8263 at [69], [2013] All ER (EC) 446 at [69].

[2] See n 1 above.

Chen

6.81 In Case C-200/02 *Chen and Zhu v Secretary of State for the Home Department*[1] the status of the infant child of Irish nationality was governed by the Citizens' Directive but the status of the mother and primary carer was not, because she could not be described as a dependent family member of a EU national.[2] However, Article 18 EC (now art 21 TFEU) applied with regard to the mother's rights, because she was the primary carer. This is what the Court said:

'45 . . . a refusal to allow the parent, whether a national of a Member State or a national of a non-member country, who is the carer of a child to whom Article 18 EC and Directive 90/364 [not applicable to the mother] grant a right of residence, to reside with that child in the host Member State would deprive the child's right of residence of any useful effect. It is clear that enjoyment by a young child of a right of residence necessarily implies that the child is entitled to be accompanied by the person who is his or her primary carer and accordingly that the carer must be in a position to reside with the child in the host Member State for the duration of such residence (see, mutatis mutandis, in relation to Article 12 of Regulation No 1612/68, Baumbast and R, paragraphs 71 to 75) [my emphasis].

46 For that reason alone, where, as in the main proceedings, Article 18 EC and Directive 90/364 grant a right to reside for an indefinite period in the host Member State to a young minor who is a national of another Member State, those same provisions allow a parent who is that minor's primary carer to reside with the child in the host Member State.'

[1] Case C-200/02 *Chen and Zhu v Secretary of State for the Home Department* [2005] QB 325; [2005] All ER (EC) 129, ECJ.
[2] The Citizens Directive grants rights to EU citizens, and to any 'family member' of such citizens defined as a spouse or partner of the EU citizen, or direct minor and/or dependent descendant or direct dependent ascendant relative of the EU citizen or his/her spouse or partner – but not a non-dependent ascendant relative: Article 2, (2)(d).

Zambrano, McCarthy, Dereci. The upshot

6.82 According to the CJEU, in *Dereci*[1] the criterion relating to the denial of the genuine enjoyment of the substance of the rights of Union citizenship refers to situations in which the citizen *has, in fact, to leave not only the territory of the home member state but also the territory of the Union as a whole* (at [67]). What this means is that as long as the EU national can, or can reasonably be expected, to move to another Member State and exercise treaty rights, including family reunification, he or she cannot claim family reunification in the Home Member State under Articles 20 or 21. Thus expressed the citizenship right of family reunification only applies to EU nationals who move to another Member State or return to their own State after working, being self-employed or self-sufficient elsewhere in another Member State, or who on the facts just cannot, or cannot reasonably be expected, to move (for example because they are small children and their primary carer is being compelled to leave).[2]

However, the *Dereci* exhortation to 'get on your bikes' is said to be without prejudice to Article 8, ECHR (at [69]) and the phrase 'has to leave Union territory' is a bit general and vague. What are the obstacles that make the use of free movement inaccessible to the Union citizen and what is the test? The options which have been suggested[3] for the test whether an EU citizen can move to another Member State are *reasonableness, proportionality, hardship, practical considerations and insurmountable obstacles.* We would prefer to replace reasonableness, proportionality and hardship with reasonable expectation and add on the need to protect family life and unlawful discrimination (both of which would involve proportionality). We are conscious that some of our options may be ahead of their time, but it may be helpful to look more closely at these options.

- First, the test cannot refer to an insurmountable obstacle, because we know that parents with irregular status can move around with their EU national children: *Chen*[4]. It would not have been an insurmountable task for the *Zambrano* parents and children to have moved to another country but they might have had greater difficulty finding work and accommodation or schools for their children; or it might be that they would have to give up their existing work and social contacts. So the test, we suggest, must be lower than insurmountable obstacles.

- At the same time, to constitute an obstacle to free movement within the EU there must, as suggested in the *Dereci* judgment, be something more than a mere desire to keep the family together in the home state. If it is unreasonable to expect a Union citizen and family to relocate their family and private life to another Member State because of the roots put down in the home country including job, career, social network, friendships, schooling and nationality of the home country, then there is an obstacle to free movement within the Union. Here it seems that we come back to the Charter and ECHR.

- The reasonable expectation test is illustrated by the facts of *Zambrano*. The Zambranos could not reasonably be expected to uproot from Belgium and move to another Member State. In their case there would be, in addition to all the above matters, the considerations of the rights of the child under both international instruments and the Charter of Fundamental Rights as well as the factors relevant to Article 8, ECHR listed above. All these considerations we would have thought are situations within the ambit of both national and EU law. Having set the criterion for the *Zambrano* case, the *Dereci* court cannot have meant to abandon the application of EU law to the further interpretation of the criterion they have identified and to leave it entirely to national courts to choose the tests. However, it should be noted, as we discuss below 6.83, that the English domestic courts have adopted a practical approach, asking whether as a matter of reality the citizen child would 'effectively be compelled to leave the UK' – a test, we would suggest, not much different from a reasonable expectation test.

- It is true that the criterion identified by the court in *Dereci* and applied in *Zambrano* is expressed in terms only of the interference with the EU citizen's free movement rights, but it would be wrong, we would suggest, to conclude that these two cases and *McCarthy* have adopted the premise that the substance of the rights attaching to the status of EU citizen under Article 20 does not include the right to respect for family life enshrined in art 7 of the Charter of Fundamental Rights of the European Union and in Article 8 of the ECHR.[5] Our view expressed above is that the criterion identified by *Dereci* cannot *be* properly interpreted without reference to the general principles of EU law as identified in Article 6, TEU.[6] In this connection it should be recalled that the court itself has made clear that the criterion identified for direct Article 20 application to residence is, admittedly, 'without prejudice to the question whether, on the basis of other criteria, inter alia, by virtue of the right to the protection of family life, a right of residence cannot be refused.' (at [69]). This, however, is one for the future.

- In none of the three cases do the CJEU deal with the question of reverse discrimination, but the arguments presented in the Opinion of A-G Sharpston in *Zambrano* are not yet off the agenda, although they do require a bit of a leap forward by the Court from its existing jurisprudence. She suggests (at [146]–[148]) that Article 18, TFEU should be interpreted as prohibiting reverse discrimination caused by the interaction between EU and national law, provided that three prerequisites are fulfilled: (1) The situation of the Union citizen who is residing in his or her own Member State and has not moved must be comparable to that of other citizens of the Union who are in the same Member State and able to invoke Article 21, TFEU; (2) the reverse discrimination must entail a violation of a fundamental right protected under EU law, which is to be established, inter alia, by reference to Strasbourg case law; and (3) national law does not afford adequate fundamental rights protection.[7] Another one for the future.

[1] Case 256/11 *Dereci v Bundesministerium fur Inneres* [2011] ECR I-11315; [2012] All ER (EC) 373, CJEU (GC).

[2] See *ILPA European Update*, December 2011, p 23.

[3] See ibid, p 24.

[4] Case C-200/02 *Chen v Secretary of State for the Home Department* [2005] QB 325, [2005] INLR 1.

[5] This, however, was the view adopted in the Opinion of A-G Mengozzi in *Dereci*, delivered 29 September 2011 at [37].

[6] Under art 6.3, TEU, it is provided that fundamental rights, as guaranteed by the ECHR and as they result from the constitutional traditions common to the Member States, *shall constitute general principles of the Union's law*. These general principles cannot be switched on and off like a light switch to suit the particular case. In determining the ambit and competence of EU law, one cannot pick and choose which general principles are to be or not to be. All are an integral part of EU law.

[7] The example she gives to illustrate her point is: If young children (such as Catherine Zhu) have acquired the nationality of a different Member State from their Member State of residence, their parent(s) will enjoy a derivative right of residence in the host Member State by virtue of art 21, TFEU and the court's ruling in *Chen v Secretary of State for the Home Department*. Diego and Jessica Zambrano have Belgian nationality and reside in Belgium. Can Mr Ruiz Zambrano rely on art 18, TFEU, which prohibits, within the scope of application of the Treaties, 'any discrimination on grounds of nationality', so as to claim the same derivative right of residence?

Iida and O, S & L

6.83 The CJEU further elucidated its approach to Article 20, TFEU in two further cases in 2012: *Iida v Stadt Ulm*[1], and *O, S, L v Maahanmuuttoviratso*.[2] In *Iida* Mr Iida was a Japanese national who married a German national, obtained a residence permit as her spouse, under German law, and worked full-time in Germany. His wife and their daughter moved to Austria where they became resident, while he remained in Germany. Mr Iida and his wife later separated but did not divorce; both maintained parental responsibility for their daughter. Mr Iida later applied for a residence card as the family member of a Union citizen under Article 10 of the Citizens' Directive (2004/38/EC). The CJEU held that he had no entitlement under the Directive, because the right only arose in the Member State in which his wife resided and he had no derived right of residence through Articles 20 and 21, TFEU because such derived rights 'were not autonomous but were derived from the exercise of freedom of movement by an Union citizen' [67]. The Court cited *Chen*,[3] *Eind*[4] and *Dereci*[5], highlighting that the common factor characterising those situations was 'an intrinsic connection with the freedom of movement of a Union citizen which prevents the right of entry and residence from being refused to those nationals (third country nationals) in the Member State of residence of that citizen, in order not to interfere with that freedom' [72]. The Court further observed that on the facts of the case the wife and daughter would not be denied the genuine enjoyment of the substance of the rights deriving from their EU citizen status, nor impeded in the exercise of their right to move and reside freely within the Union, since they had moved to Austria without him, he did not wish to reside in Austria and he in any event had a right of residence in Germany under other provisions.

As Peers and Berneri observe, the CJEU in *Iida* 'implicitly linked the test of the enjoyment of the substance of citizenship rights to the right of free movement and thereby seems to suggest that, when the national measure denying the right of residence to a third country national family member forces the EU citizen to leave the territory of the Union, the substantive right accruing to his/her status that is being violated is the right of free movement'.[6] Peers and Berneri consequently argue that the effect of the Court's judgment is that the 'denial of genuine enjoyment of the substance of Union citizenship' test is met in two alternative ways: 'in order to breach Article 20, TFEU, the national measure should either violate the substance of citizenship rights and force the Union citizen to leave the territory of the Union or impede the latter's right to move and reside within the Union.'[7]

O, S and L v Maahanmuuttovirasto involved three separate cases with a common factual matrix whereby a third country national woman had married a Finnish husband and obtained a permanent residence permit in Finland. Each woman gave birth to a child of Finnish nationality, over whom she had sole custody following divorce from her husband, who continued to live in Finland. Each woman subsequently married a third country national and each had a second child who did not have Finnish nationality. The Finnish Immigration Office refused applications for residence permits for the third country national husbands on the ground that neither had secure means of subsistence. The question referred was whether Article 20, TFEU precluded a Member State from refusing to grant a residence permit to a third country national on the basis of family reunification where that national sought to reside with his spouse, who had sole custody of a child, born of a previous marriage, who was an Union citizen.

The CJEU held that Article 20, TFEU did not preclude the Member State from refusing to grant a residence permit in the circumstances, provided that the refusal did not entail the denial of the Union citizen child's genuine enjoyment of the substance of the rights conferred by Article 20. That question was a matter for the national referring court having regard to the fact that the mothers themselves held permanent residence in Finland and there was no obligation to leave the EU; the mothers had sole custody of the Union citizen child and were part of 'reconstituted families'; and the fact that the EU citizen child was not legally, financially or emotionally dependent on the third country national ([47]-[58]). The Court's reasoning entails the acceptance that the *Zambrano* test could also encompass cases in which there is no blood relationship between the EU citizen and the third country national seeking a right of residence, provided that the 'denial of genuine enjoyment of the substance of Union citizenship' test is met were a residence right to be refused.

1   C-40/11 [2013] Fam 121, [2014] All ER (EC) 619.
2   Cases C-356/11 and C-357/11 [2013] Fam 203, [2013] All ER (EC) 563.
3   Case C-200/02 *Chen and Zhu v Secretary of State for the Home Department* [2005] QB 325, [2005] INLR 1, [2004] ECR I-9925.
4   Case C-291/05 *Minister voor Vreemdelingenzaken en Integratie v Eind* [2007] ECR I-10719, [2008] All ER (EC) 371.
5   Case C-256/11 *Dereci v Bundesministerium fur Inneres* [2011] ECR I-11315, [2012] All ER (EC) 373 CJEU (GC), paras 69-7.
6   Peers and Berneri, 'Iida and O and S: further developments in the immigration status of static EU citizens', (2013) *JIANL* 27(2) 162 at 170-171.
7   Ibid, p 171. For further analysis, see also Reynolds, 'Exploring the "intrinsic connection" between free movement and the genuine enjoyment test: reflections on EU citizenship after Iida', *European Law Review* (2013) 38(3) 376. In a further case, *Ymeraga v Ministre du Travail, de l'Emploi et de l'Immigration* Case C-87/12, 8 May 2013, CJEU (Second Chamber), [2013] 3 CMLR 895, the parents and brother of a Luxembourg national made a claim for residence under the Charter of Fundamental Rights, arts 20 (equality before the law), 21 (non-discrimination), 24 (rights of the child) and 33 (family life). The CJEU gave short shrift to the reference, holding that since art 21 did not apply: the case fell outside the scope of EU law [43] such that the Charter was not engaged. The Court's decision did not, however, prejudge any claim based on the ECHR.

Domestic cases on Article 20, TFEU

6.84 The UK domestic cases applying *Zambrano*, *Dereci* and subsequent CJEU authority have taken, what they say, is a practical approach to the question whether an EU citizen would be forced to leave the EU in the event of the third country national family member being refused a residence permit, and thereby to the test of whether an Article 20 derived right of residence exists. The domestic courts have not expressly adopted the 'reasonable expectation' approach posited at **6.82**, above, nor a test of 'insurmountable obstacles'. The leading case on this issue is *Harrison (Jamaica) v Secretary of State for the Home Department; AB (Morocco) v Secretary of State for the Home Department*[1] (referred for convenience hereafter as '*Harrison*') which concerned the deportation of non-EU nationals convicted of serious criminal offences, who had British children resident since birth in the UK, who were being looked after by their mothers. In *Harrison*, it was accepted on behalf of the appellants that, 'the application of the *Zambrano* test requires a court to focus on the question whether "as a matter of reality" the EU citizen would be obliged to give up residence in the European Union if the non-EU national were to be removed from the European Union', and the appellants also accepted that, 'on the facts of these cases, there was no such de facto compulsion in either appeal.'[2] It was however contended that it was at least arguable that, if the non-EU nationals were to be removed, then that would adversely affect the quality of life of the children, such that Article 20 and 'the *Zambrano* principle' would be engaged. If arguable, then it was not *acte clair*;

and the issue should be referred by the Court of Appeal to the European Court for a definitive ruling. The claimants argued that even if the EU citizen is not 'compelled' to leave the EU in consequence of the third country national's deportation, a derived right could nevertheless arise owing to their diminished quality of life.[3] The Court of Appeal rejected this argument and ruled that the *Zambrano* principle does not arguably extend to 'cover anything short of a situation where the EU citizen is forced to leave the territory of the European Union. If the EU citizen, be it a child or wife, would not in practice[4] be compelled to leave the country if the non-EU family member were to be refused the right of residence', EU law is not engaged [63].

The Court did, however, accept that a diminished quality of life was relevant in determining whether the *Zambrano* principle[5] applied, by accepting that, 'to the extent that the quality or standard of life will be seriously impaired by excluding the non-EU national, that is likely in practice to infringe the right of residence itself because it will effectively compel the EU citizen to give up residence and travel with the non-EU national' and would thereby engage the *Zambrano* principle. The 'practical effect test' is, we would suggest, a test akin to one of reasonable expectation, because the Court accepts that in assessing what in practice might compel the child to leave the Union there are various factors which must be taken into account. Indeed, the Court also noted at [68] the statement by the CJEU in *Dereci* that the fact that family life is adversely affected, or that the non-EU national's presence is desirable for economic reasons, will not 'of themselves' constitute factors capable of triggering the *Zambrano* principle, implying that they might if taken into account with other factors.

[1]   [2012] EWCA Civ 1736; [2013] 2 CMLR 580; [2013] Imm AR 622. *Harrison* has been applied frequently: eg *Fatima v Secretary of State for the Home Department* [2013] EWCA Civ 76; *Hines v Lambeth London Borough Council* [2014] EWCA Civ 660, [2014] HLR 473, endorsing the approach of the lower court which applied a test of whether the British citizen child would 'effectively be compelled to leave the UK' in consequence of a denial of the right of residence [21]; the best interests of the child had to be examined in deciding that issue; and the legality of the test in Regulation 15A(4A)(c) of the 2006 EEA Regulations, addressed at **6.86** below, was affirmed; *R (on the application of Sanneh (Jamil)) v Secretary of State for Work and Pensions and Revenue and Customs Comrs* [2013] EWHC 793 (Admin).

[2]   [55](1) and (2) of *Harrison*.

[3]   [55](3) and (4) of *Harrison*.

[4]   This has been referred to as 'the practical effect' test in another case: *Secretary of State for Work and Pensions v RR* [2013] UKUT 21 (AAC) at para 63.

[5]   See *Ahmed (Amos; Zambrano; reg 15A(3)(c), 2006 EEA Regs)* [2013] UKUT 00089 (IAC) at para 68.

6.85   Other cases on Article 20, TFEU have established that:

- In deportation cases, it is not possible as a matter of EU law to require British/EU citizens to relocate as a family unit outside of the EU or for the SSHD to submit that it would be reasonable for them to do so.[1]
- The *Zambrano* principle potentially applies where the EEA national/Union citizen child of a third-country national is not a national of the host Member State, eg a British citizen child is living in France.[2] This would appear to extend the availability of a derived right beyond the scenario envisaged in Regulation 15A(4A), described below, to extend to the non-EEA parent of an EEA (non-British) child who is not self-sufficient and is living in the UK.

- The *Zambrano* principle can in principle be relied on in entry clearance cases, in both in-country and out-of-country.[3]
- The *Zambrano* principle can also be relied upon by the parent, or other primary carer, of a minor EU national *resident* outside the EU, *who wishes to travel to the UK with the child or children*, as long as it is their intention, to accompany the EU national child or children.[4]

[1] *Sanade (British children – Zambrano – Dereci) India* [2012] UKUT 00048(IAC), at paras 93–95; *Ogundimu (Article 8 – new rules) Nigeria* [2013] UKUT 60 (IAC) at [108]–[112]: confirming the principle at least in cases where a British child is involved.
[2] *Ahmed (Amos; Zambrano; reg 15A(3)(c) 2006 EEA Regs)* [2013] UKUT 00089 (IAC).
[3] *Campbell (exclusion; Zambrano)* [2013] UKUT 00147 (IAC).
[4] *MA and SM (Zambrano: EU children outside EU) Iran* [2013] UKUT 00380 (IAC). See also *Iida v Stadt Ulm*, discussed at **6.83** above.

The 2006 EEA Regulations and derived rights of residence

6.86 By two Statutory Instruments implemented in July and November 2012.[1] which amended the 2006 EEA regulations, the UK Government sought to codify the situations where a derived EU right of residence stems from (i) the *Zambrano* principles; (ii) the linked cases of *Ibrahim* and *Teixeira*); and (iii) a cross border situation within the scope of the Citizens' Directive (the *Chen* situation). SI 2012/1547 amended regulation 11 of, and inserted a new Regulation 15A into, the 2006 EEA Regulations. These rule amendments are not an attempt to transpose the Directive, but to interpret the CJEU case law. If any of the provisions are in conflict with that case law, the case law has to take precedence.[2] Regulation 11 deals inter alia with the right of admission to the UK, where those persons entitled to a derivative right of residence under new Article 15A need to travel to the UK to exercise it. Regulation 15A is entitled 'Derivative right of residence' and has effect subject to transitional provisions specified in Schedule 3 of that SI and came into force on 16 July 2012. The new regulation 15A specifies alternative situations that entitle the child of an EEA national to reside in the UK for the purpose of education and a third country national ('P') to a derivative right to reside in the UK for as long as P satisfies the relevant criteria, and provided that he or she is not an 'exempt person'.[3] The situations are:

(i) Subparagraph (2), which covers the *Chen* situation: (a) P is the primary carer[4] of a relevant EEA national; and (b) the relevant EEA national— (i) is under the age of 18; (ii) is residing in the United Kingdom as a self-sufficient person; and (iii) would be unable to remain in the United Kingdom if P were required to leave; Regualtion 11 covers the situation where P travels to the UK accompanying or to join the EEA child.

(ii) Subparagraphs (3) and (4) give effect to the ECJ judgments in the linked cases of *Ibrahim* and *Teixeira*[5]. In these cases the Court confirmed that the child of a national of a Member State who has entered and resided in a Member State whilst their parent was residing there as a worker[6] can claim a right of residence in the host State. The Court also determined that the primary carer of such a child can reside in that Member State whilst the child is in education[7] and would not be able to continue in education were their primary carer denied a right of residence. Regulation 15A(3) confirms the right of residence of the child, and regulation 15A(4) confirms the right of residence of the primary carer in such a scenario. Regulation 15A(3)(c) is clearly wrong as the case of *Ahmed* shows.[8]

(iii)   Subparagraph (4A) is the *Zambrano situation*:[9] (a) P is the primary carer[10] of a British citizen ('the relevant British citizen'); (b) the relevant British citizen is residing in the United Kingdom; and (c) the relevant British citizen would be unable to reside in the UK or in another EEA State if P were required to leave. Where P is accompanying or coming to join the British citizen in the UK, regulation 11 provides for a right of admission where P 'would be entitled to reside in the UK pursuant to regulation 15A(4A) were P and the British citizen both in the UK.'

(iv)   Subparagraph (5) provides a right of entry and residence for child dependants of a primary carer where a refusal to confer such a right would prevent their primary carer from exercising his or her right of residence: (a) P is under the age of 18; and (b) P's primary carer is entitled to a derivative right to reside in the United Kingdom by virtue of paragraph (2) or (4); and (c) P does not have leave to enter, or remain in, the United Kingdom; and (d) requiring P to leave the United Kingdom would prevent P's primary carer from residing in the United Kingdom.

Even if P satisfies the eligibility criteria set out above, the Secretary of State can refuse to grant confirmation of a derived right of residence where a decision is made under the 2006 Regulations on the basis of public policy, public security or public health, under regulations 19(3)(b) (removal), 20(1) (refusal to issue, revoke or renew a registration certificate/residence card, etc), 20A(1) (cancellation of right of residence); or where a decision has been taken under 21B(2) (abuse of rights or fraud) within the preceding 12 months.[11] Periods of residence accrued pursuant to a derived right of residence under regulation 15A cannot be relied on for the purposes of establishing a right to permanent residence.[12] Those benefiting from a derived right of residence do not enjoy the procedural protections against expulsion that apply to 'qualified persons' under the 2006 Regulations. For such persons, the safeguards of the Public policy, public security proviso do not apply and they may be expelled on grounds 'conducive to the public good'.[13]

[1]   Immigration (European Economic Area) (Amendment) Regulations, 2012/1547 and Immigration (European Economic Area) (Amendment) (No 2) Regulations, 2012/2560.

[2]   See *Ahmed (Amos; Zambrano*; reg 15A(3)(c), 2006 EEA Regulations) [2013] UKUT 00089 (IAC), where the Upper Tribunal held that notwithstanding inability to satisfy new regulation 15A(3)(c) of the Immigration (European Economic Area) Regulations 2006 as amended by SI 2012/1547 with effect from 16 July 2012, the parent of a child of an EEA national who has been employed in the UK when the child was also residing here can have a derived right of residence under art 12 of Regulation 1612/68 (now art 10 of Regulation 492/2011) even though the EEA national parent was no longer a worker in the UK at the time the child commences education: see Case C-480/08 *Teixiera* [2010] EUECJ, 23 February 2010.

[3]   An 'exempt person' is defined in reg 15A as a person (i) who has a right to reside in the United Kingdom as a result of any other provision of these Regulations; (ii) who has a right of abode in the United Kingdom by virtue of section 2 of the 1971 Act; (iii) to whom s 8 of the 1971 Act, or any order made under subsection (2) of that provision, applies; or (iv) who has indefinite leave to enter or remain in the United Kingdom. The 'exempt person' qualification was inserted by the second amendment regulations, SI 2012/2560.

4   'Primary carer' is defined in Reg 15A (7), (7A), (7B) and (8) and the concept is discussed at **6.87** and **6.88** below.

5   Case C-480/08 *Teixeira v Lambeth LBC* [2010] 2 CMLR 50; [2010] ICR 1118; [2010] Imm AR 487, 23 February 2010, ECJ; Case C-310/08*Harrow London Borough Council v Ibrahim* [2010] 2 CMLR 51; [2010] ICR 1118; [2010] Imm AR 474, 23 February 2010.

6   See Reg 15A(6)(b). But note the case of *MDB v Secretary of State for the Home Department* [2012] EWCA Civ 1015, [2012] 3 CMLR 1020, in which the Court of Appeal held that an Italian national had not been 'employed' within the meaning of art 12, notwithstanding that he had worked for ten weeks for eight hours a day during an eleven-year period of residence in the UK, which prevented his Argentinian children and their mother, his wife from benefiting from a derived right under art 12. The Court also underlined that the derived rights were not triggered merely by work seeking. However, the SSHD conceded that, in the light of *Zambrano*, the children and their mother could not be removed; the matter was remitted to the UT on Article 8, ECHR.

7   See Reg 15A(6)(a). See paragraph 3 of the headnote to *Shabani (EEA - jobseekers; nursery education)* [2013] UKUT 00315 (IAC).

8   *Ahmed (Amos; Zambrano; reg 15A(3)(c) 2006 EEA Regs)* [2013] UKUT 00089 (IAC). Note that the case has been referred to the CJEU on a separate issue concerning retained rights of residence: see [2014] EWCA Civ 995. A right of residence derived from art 12, 1612/68 (now art 10, Regulation 492/2011) alone and not from the Citizens Directive will not count for the purposes of accruing permanent residence under that Directive: *Alarape v Secretary of State for the Home Department (AIRE Centre intervening)*: C-529/11 , [2014] All ER (EC) 470, [2013] 1 WLR 2883, CJEU.

9   Subsection 4A was inserted by Immigration (European Economic Area) (Amendment) (No 2) Regulations, 2012/2560, Sch 1, para3(b) and was in force from 8 November 2012.

10 See fn 4 above.

11 These insertions were made by SI 2012/2560.

12 *Bee (permanent/derived rights of residence)* [2013] UKUT 00083 (IAC).

13 See EEA Regulations 2006, reg 21A(3).

The status of the primary carer

6.87 The position of carers has not been given the same attention in the derivative rights cases as the requirements to establish the right. In *Zambrano* both parents were treated as carers, since both were under threat of expulsion. In *Chen* the beneficiary of the derivative right was the parent with primary responsibility for the child, described as the primary carer. In the 2006 EEA Regulations the beneficiary of derivative rights of residence is described as the primary carer throughout but the drafters have obviously felt it necessary to qualify what is meant by the term. The initial definition is straightforward. Under para (7) of reg 15A. P will be regarded as a primary carer of another person if:

(a)   P is a direct relative or a legal guardian of that person; and

(b)   -

    (i)   is the person who has primary responsibility for that person's care; or

    (ii)   shares equally the responsibility for that person's care with one other person who is not an exempt person meaning that he or she does not have a right of abode, indefinite leave to remain, EU residence rights under the Citizens Directive or diplomatic or other exemption from immigration control.

6.88 The problem occurs in the situation where a dependent child is in the UK and his or her non-EEA national parent or carer is to be removed or deported, often after conviction of serious criminal offences. At that point, except where the primary carer or one of joint primary carers is not the object of deportation or removal, the care of the dependent child is in jeopardy. Can he or she stay or must they leave? In that situation the courts have made it clear that a search for an alternative carer is both practical and necessary. The Courts and Tribunals have said more than once that if there is an alternative acceptable carer (but not in local authority care) Article 20 does not apply. In that situation the child's right of residence can be maintained and he or she is not in practice compelled to leave.[1] If there is only one primary carer and that is the person to be removed, the situation may be different and, depending on the facts, it may be a *Zambrano* case.

The Courts have made the position relatively clear and easily understood. This cannot be said about the clumsy and obscure treatment of this issue by the amendments to the 2006 Regulations introduced by SI 2012/2560, which came into force on 8 November 2012. This was before the judgment in *Harrison*. New paragraphs 7A and 7B of regulation 15A provide:

'(7A) Where P is to be regarded as a primary carer of another person by virtue of paragraph (7)(b)(ii) the criteria in paragraphs (2)(b)(iii), (4)(b) and (4A)(c) shall be considered on the basis that both P and the person with whom care responsibility is shared would be required to leave the United Kingdom.

(7B) Paragraph (7A) does not apply if the person with whom care responsibility is shared acquired a derivative right to reside in the United Kingdom as a result of this regulation prior to P assuming equal care responsibility.'

Still further, subsection (8) states that, 'P will not be regarded as having responsibility for a person's care for the purpose of paragraph (7) on the sole basis of a financial contribution towards that person's care'. The criteria referred to in (7A) are those in the *Chen* and *Zambrano* situations, where the relevant British citizen (*Zambrano* cases) or the relevant EEA national (*Chen* cases) would be unable to reside/remain in the UK if P were required to leave. Now it is necessary to assume, even if it is not true, that both primary carers are required to leave. What does this mean? That if both would be required to leave, the child would in practice be compelled to leave also? The amendments are clearly intended to be helpful, but their meaning is somewhat obscure.

[1] See *Harrison (Jamaica) v Secretary of State for the Home Department* [2012] EWCA Civ 1736 (21 December 2012) at para 19; *R (on the application of Sanneh (Jamil)) v Secretary of State for Work and Pensions and Revenue and Customs Comrs* [2013] EWHC 793 (Admin).

MA and SM

6.89 In *MA* and *SM*[1] the Upper Tribunal made it very clear that, in EU law terms, there is no reason why the decision in *Zambrano* could not in principle be relied upon by the parent, or other primary carer, of a minor EU national living outside the EU as long as it is the intention of the parent, or primary carer, to accompany the EU national child to his/her country of nationality.[2] In *MA* and *SM* there were two separate appeals. In *MA* the appeal was allowed on *Zambrano* grounds, because the British husband in the UK was incapable of being a suitable carer due to mental health problems arising from his detention in Iranian prisons. In *SM* the husband in the UK was capable of looking after the British child and so the Court held that *Zambrano* did not apply but decided in very clear terms that there was a breach of SM's Article 8 rights. Was this inquiry either right or necessary? These were entry situations, not concerning removal or deportation. The deportation/removal situation is quite different from the entry clearance one. One is negative. The other is positive. One involves the splitting up of the Union national's family; the other involves the uniting of families and bringing EEA citizen children, together with both their parents. Our view is that, in so far as the Tribunal in *MA* and *SM* required the appellants to show that there was no other available carer, they were wrong. Removing existing care because of deportation is one thing. Requiring no alternative carers as a condition of entry is another.

1   *MA and SM (Zambrano: EU children outside EU) Iran* [2013] UKUT 00380 (IAC).
2   Quoted from *Campbell (exclusion; Zambrano)* [2013] UKUT 00147 (IAC).

Internal situations

6.90 EU law does not apply to 'wholly internal situations', that is, situations in which EU law is not engaged. For example, Article 45, TFEU (ex Article 39 TEC) only applies to situations within the scope of EU law, namely the free movement of workers, and envisages someone moving from one Member State to another to seek or take up employment. Those who have never exercised a free movement right within the EU do not come within Article 45 and cannot be classified as 'workers'. In *R v Saunders*[1] it was held that the free movement provisions of the EC Treaty cannot apply to situations which are wholly internal to a Member State. In *Morson and Jhanjan*[2] this was interpreted to mean that where workers have never exercised a right to free movement within the Community there is no EC link, and the Member State in question cannot be prevented by EC law from refusing entry or stay to the non-EC parents or spouse of a local national. The purely internal situation does not just apply to Article 45 and workers. The provisions on freedom of establishment do not apply to obstacles which affect nationals of Member States on their own territory without any connecting factor to a situation covered by EU law. In the same way Article 56 TFEU (ex Article 49 TEC) cannot be applied to activities which are confined in all respects within a single Member State. Thus a company operating in one Member State with its head office there did not come within Community law by simply extending its activities in that country.[3]

1   Case 175/78 [1980] QB 72, [1979] ECR 1129, ECJ; Case C-206/91 Poirrez [1992] ECR I-6685, ECJ.
2   Case 35, 36/82 *Morson and Jhanjan v Netherlands* [1982] ECR 3723, [1983] 2 CMLR 221, ECJ; Cases C-297/88 and 197/89 *Dzodzi v Belgium* [1990] ECR I-3763. A hypothetical possibility of professional activity in another Member State is not enough: Case 180/83 *Moser v Land Baden-Württemberg* [1984] ECR 2539, ECJ, nor is a mere intention to become an EC worker without any practical steps being taken: *Bouanimba v Secretary of State for the Home Department* [1986] Imm AR 343, IAT. In Case 44/84 *Hurd v Jones* [1986] QB 892, [1986] 2 CMLR 1, ECJ the same principles were applied to a UK national employed at the European Community School. He was the only teacher not granted a tax exemption by the UK government, but the court held that he could not invoke the non-discrimination provisions of what was then art 7 of the Treaty against the UK government because he had never exercised his free movement right and was not, therefore, within the protection of art 48. See further *R v Immigration Appeal Tribunal, ex p Aradi* [1987] Imm AR 359, QBD (but see **6.72** above); *R v Secretary of State for the Home Department, ex p Tombofa* [1988] Imm AR 400, CA. Case 147/87 *Zaoui v CRAM de l'Ile de France* [1987] ECR 5511, [1989] 2 CMLR 646, ECJ. Other examples where the ECJ has held a situation to be wholly internal are Case C-60/91 *Re Morais* [1992] ECR I-2085, [1992] 2 CMLR 533, ECJ (prosecution of a driving instructor); Case C-147/91 *Ministerio Fiscal v Ferrer Laderer* [1992] 3 CMLR 273, ECJ (prosecution of an estate agent); Case C-332/90 *Steen v Deutsche Bundespost* [1992] ECR I-341,

[1992] 2 CMLR 406 (recruitment of a German national to the post office); Case C-153/91 *Petit v Office National des Pensions* [1992] ECR I-4973, [1993] 1 CMLR 476 (adopted child not exercising community rights).
³   Case C-134/94 *Esso Espanola SA v Comunidad Autonoma de Canarias* [1995] ECR I-4223.

6.91 On the other hand, where there is a sufficient link to a situation envisaged by EU law, the matter is no longer purely internal and EU law can be invoked. Where a broadcasting body established itself in another Member State in order to avoid the legislation applicable in the receiving State to domestic broadcasters, its broadcasts were regarded as services within the meaning of Article 49, irrespective of its motive for relocating.¹ Where a national of a Member State has entered into a contract of employment with an employee in another Member State with a view to exercising gainful employment, the situation cannot be called a purely internal one, even if the offer of employment is never taken up. This is what happened in the case of *Bosman*,² a Belgian footballer who was prevented by the Belgian FA's transfer rules from moving to a French club. The ECJ held that this was not an internal situation. Where a worker has exercised the right of free movement within the Community by taking employment in another Member State, he or she is entitled to rely upon Community law on returning to his or her own State.

The decision of the ECJ in *Surinder Singh*³ upheld the conclusion of the Immigration Appeal Tribunal, that where there has been a genuine exercise of Community rights, the returning national and the non-national spouse or relative are entitled to any more favourable treatment provided by Community law, despite the fact that there is also a right of entry under national law. This case was followed in *Kraus v Land Baden-Würtemberg*,⁴ where a German national wished to use a university title received following study in the UK on return to his native Germany. In *Carpenter* the ECJ considered that a national residing in his own Member State could benefit from free movement rights in his own Member State, in that case the right to family reunion, if he was providing services in another Member State, even where that provision of services was on a very temporary and infrequent basis.⁵ In *Jipa*⁶ the Court held that a national of a Member State who has been repatriated from another Member State enjoys the status of a citizen of the Union under Article 17(1) EC (now Article 20, TFEU) and may therefore rely on the right pertaining to that status, including against his Member State of origin, and in particular the right conferred by Article 18 EC (now Article 21, TFEU) to move and reside freely within the territory of the Member States.

¹   Case C-23/93 *TV10 SA v Commissariaat voor de Media* [1994] ECR I-4795, [1995] 3 CMLR 284, ECJ.
²   Case C-415/93 *Union Royale Belge des Societes de Football Association ASBL v Bosman* [1995] ECR I-4921, [1996] 1 CMLR 645, paras 88–91, ECJ.
³   Case C–370/90 *R v Immigration Appeal Tribunal and Surinder Singh, ex p Secretary of State for the Home Department* [1992] ECR I-4265, ECJ, [1992] Imm AR 565.
⁴   Case C-19/92 [1993] ECR I-1663.
⁵   Case C-60/00 *Carpenter (Mary) v Secretary of State for the Home Department* [2002] ECR I-6279, [2002] INLR 439, ECJ.
⁶   Case C-33/07 *Ministerul Administraţiei şi Internelor – Direcţia Generală de Paşapoarte Bucureşti v Jipa* [2008] 3 CMLR 715. See further **6.151**, below.

6.92 Prior to 1993, the sole fact of moving residence from one Member State to another did not constitute a sufficient connecting factor, as the ECJ held in

Werner v Finanzant Aachen-Innenstadt.[1] This case pre-dates the introduction of Article 18 EC (now Article 21, TFEU) which for the first time confers directly on every citizen of the EU the right to move and reside freely within the territory of the Member States without any economic activity needing to be present. The extent to which EU citizenship gives rise to rights of residence for EU nationals and their family members, even in the absence of economic activity or a cross-border element, was discussed above ('EU citizenship' from 6.75. The early case of *Avello* made it clear that the sole fact of residence in another Member State is sufficient to engage Community law.[2] In *Avello* the children wishing to benefit from Community law were not exercising any particular community right but were born in one Member State and had lived there all their lives and, by reason of dual nationality, were nationals of the second state in question. In *Ali v Secretary of State for the Home Department*[3] the Court of Appeal found that the rights under Article 18 EC are expressly stated to be subject to 'the limitations and conditions laid down in this Treaty and by the measures adopted to give it effect' and that this included the various Directives which contain restrictions on the right of residence. However, as noted above, the rule with regard to internal situations has been modified, as we have seen in previous paragraphs by the decision in *Zambrano* concerning the application of residence rights to non-movers under the EU citizen rules in Article 20, TFEU, but the rule has been strongly reasserted subject to these modifications in *McCarthy*, *Dereci* and *Iida*. In *Dereci* the court reminded itself that the Treaty rules governing freedom of movement for persons and the measures adopted to implement them cannot be applied to situations which have no factor linking them with any of the situations governed by EU law and which are confined in all relevant respects within a single Member State.[4] However, the situation of a Union citizen who, like each of the citizens who are family members of the applicants in the main proceedings, has not made use of the right to freedom of movement cannot, for that reason alone, be assimilated to a purely internal situation.[5]

[1]   Case C-112/91 *Werner v Finanzant Aachen-Innenstadt* [1993] ECR I-429.
[2]   C-148/02 *Avello (Carlos Garcia) v Belgium* [2004] All ER (EC) 740; see also C-200/02 *Chen v Secretary of State for the Home Department* (19 October 2004), ECJ, para 19, where the court cited *Avello* in holding that 'the situation of a national of a Member State born in the host Member State, who has not made use of the right to freedom of movement, cannot for that reason alone be assimilated to a purely internal situation'.
[3]   *Ali v Secretary of State for the Home Department* [2006] EWCA Civ 484, [2006] 3 CMLR 326.
[4]   Case C-34/09 *Zambrano v Office national de l'emploi* at [60]. See, further to that effect, Case C-212/06 *Government of the French Community v Flemish Government* [2008] ECR I-1683 at [33], [2009] All ER (EC) 187, ECJ; C-127/08 *Metock v Minister for Justice, Equality and Law Reform* [2009] QB 318, [2008] ECR I-6241 at [77], ECJ; and Case C-434/09 *McCarthy v Secretary of State for the Home Department* [2011] All ER (EC) 729 at [45].
[5]   See Case C-403/03 *Schemp v Finanzamt Munchen V* [2005] ECR I-6421 at [22], [2005] STC 1792; and *McCarthy*, above, at [46].

PERSONAL SCOPE (2) WORKERS

Definition of workers

6.93 A national of an EEA Member State only comes within the personal scope of Article 45 (ex Article 39 TEC) if he or she is a worker. Although

Article 45 refers to 'freedom of movement for workers', 'workers of the Member States' and 'workers of other Member States' and Article 57 TFEU envisages a programme to encourage the exchange of 'young workers', the Treaty does not define the term 'worker'. However, at an early stage of the EEC it was established by the ECJ[1] that the term must have a Community meaning rather than definitions given by laws of individual Member States.[2] Under the EU Treaties, rights of 'workers' are distinguished from those relating to 'establishment' and 'services', and this suggests that a worker is a person employed, actually or potentially, under a contract of employment and is not a self-employed person, who would be eligible to benefit from freedom of establishment under Article 49 TFEU.[3]

[1]   Case 75/63 *Hoekstra (née Unger) v Bestuur der Bedrijfsvereniging voor Detailhandel en Ambachten* [1964] ECR 177 at 184, ECJ.
[2]   Case 17/76 *Brack v Insurance Officer* [1976] ECR 1429 at 1448, ECJ; Case 53/81 *Levin (DM) v Secretary of State for Justice* [1982] ECR 1035 at 1049, ECJ.
[3]   See C Maestripieri *La Libre Circulation Des Personnes et des Services dans la CEE* (1972) p 46. Sometimes it is difficult to distinguish a worker from the self-employed or a service provider. See Case C-106/91 *Ramrath v Ministre de la Justice* [1992] 3 CMLR 173; Case C-202/90 *Ayuntamiento de Sevilla v Recaudadores de Tributas de las Zonas primera y segunda* [1994] 1 CMLR 424, ECJ; Case C-3/87 *R v Ministry of Agriculture, Fisheries and Food, ex p Agegate Ltd* [1990] 2 QB 151, [1990] 1 CMLR 366, ECJ.

6.94 The ECJ made it clear that, since the terms 'worker' and 'activity as an employed person' define the spheres of application of one of the fundamental freedoms guaranteed by the Treaty, they may not be interpreted restrictively.[1] In *Levin*[2] a woman with a part-time job as a hotel chambermaid was a worker. The court held that an income less than the minimum required for subsistence is enough, provided only that the person pursues an activity as an employed person which is effective and genuine, and it does not matter what the motive was for taking it. Thus, contrary to what reg 11(2)(b) of the 2000 Regulations[3] said, an EEA national wife could take part-time employment for the purpose of giving her non-EEA national husband rights under Community law. In *Lawrie-Blum v Land Baden-Württemberg*[4] the ECJ stated that the essential characteristic of the employment relationship is the fact that during a given time one person provides services for and under the direction of another in return for remuneration. This applies to trainees and apprentices if they do work for an employer for pay, however low, even though they are under supervision and the work is preparation for a qualifying exam or to qualify the employee for work elsewhere.[5] Remuneration appears to be the key. However, payment need not be enough to live on or it may be in kind, rather than a formal wage. In *Kempf v Staatssecretaris van Justitie*[6] the court went further. A person may still be a worker even if the pay is so low that he or she needs to supplement it with unemployment benefit or has to apply for sickness benefit during a period of illness, provided that the effectiveness and genuineness of the activities as an employed person are established. In *Steymann v Staatssecretaris van Justitie*[7] a German plumber went to Holland and joined a religious community, which secured its economic independence by commercial activities, such as the operation of a bar, discotheque and launderette. The claimant worked for them and in return was provided with his material needs, including pocket money. The court held that where commercial activity was an inherent part of membership of the community, the upkeep of the member of the community could be regarded as an indirect countervailing charge for their work, even though it was not a formal wage. Provided the work is genuine and effective (which is a question for the national courts) and not purely marginal and incidental, it can be considered an economic activity. The purpose of the work is irrelevant, whether it be of a non-commercial nature, such as State education, or part of the public service.[8] In *R (on the application of Payir) v Secretary of State for the Home Department; R (on the application of Ozturk) v Secretary of State for the Home Department; R (on the application of Akyuz) v Secretary of State for the Home Department,*[9] the Court of Appeal found that students and au pairs were workers within the meaning of European law, and on a reference the European Court upheld this finding and also held that they were in legal employment and eligible to benefit from the Turkish Association Agreement. Playing sport is not usually regarded as an economic activity, but it is in the case of professional or semi-professional sports players, who thereby become workers.[10] The employer need not be an undertaking; all that is required is the existence of or the intention to create an employment relationship.[11]

[1]   Case 53/81 *Levin (DM) v Secretary of State for Justice* [1982] ECR 1035 at 1052, ECJ at [13]; but see Case C-171/91 *Tsiotras v Landeshauptstadt Stuttgart* [1993] ECR 1-2925, ECJ.

[2]   See *Levin* above.

[3]   SI 2000/2326.

[4]   Case 66/85 [1986] ECR 2121, [1987] 3 CMLR 389. Followed in respect of Turkish 'workers' in Case C-36/96 *Gunaydin v Freistaat Bayern* [1997] ECR 1-5143. Employment from 10 up to 18 hours a week has been acceptable in *Kempf* fn 6 below; Case C-171/88 *Rinner-Kühn v FWW Spezial-Gebäudereinigung GmbH & Co KG* [1993] 2 CMLR 932; Case C-I02/88; *Ruzius-Wilbrink v Bestuur van de Bedrijfsvereniging voor Overheidsdiensten* [1991] 2 CMLR 202, ECJ]; Case C-444/93 *Megner and Scheffel v Innungskrankenkasse Vorderpfalz* [1996] All ER (EC) 212, [1996] IRLR 236, ECJ. Low productivity does not prevent a person from being a worker: Case 344/87 *Bettray v Staatssecretaris van Justitie* [1989] ECR 1621, [1991] 1 CMLR 459, ECJ.

[5]   *Gunaydin* above; Case C-27/91 *Union de Recouvrement des Cotisations de Sécurité Sociale et d'Allocations Familiales de la Savoie (URSSAF) v Hostellerie Le Manoir Sàrl* [1991] ECR 1-5531, ECJ (trainee employed over the summer months in a hotel school).

[6]   Case, 139/85 [1986] ECR 1741, [1987] 1 CMLR 764, ECJ.

[7]   Case, 196/87 [1988] ECR 6159, [1989] 1 CMLR 449, ECJ.

[8]   Work which merely constitutes a means of rehabilitation or re-integration of a person into the workforce may not be regarded as effective and genuine: *Bettray* above. The issue of rehabilitative employment will be considered shortly by the ECJ] again in *Trojani v Centre Public d'Aide Sociale de Bruxelles (CPAS)* Case C-456/02 [2004] ECR I-7573, [2004] All ER (EC) 1065 in which a French national carried out chores for some 30 hours a week in a Salvation Army hostel in Brussels where he lived as part of a rehabilitation project.

[9]   *R (on the application of Payir) v Secretary of State for the Home Department; R (on the application of Ozturk) v Secretary of State for the Home Department; R (on the application of Akyuz) v Secretary of State for the Home Department* [2006] EWCA Civ 541, [2006] ICR 1314. See **6.202** below.

[10]   Case C-415/93 *Union Royale Belge des Societes de Football Association ASBL v Bosman* [1996] 1 CMLR 645, ECJ; Case 36/74 *Walrave and Koch v Association Union Cycliste Internationale* [1974] ECR 1405, [1974] 1 CMLR 320, ECJ; Case 13/76 *Donà v Mantero* [1976] ECR 1333 at 1340, ECJ; see also C-438/00 *Deutscher Handballbund eV v Kolpak* [2003] ECR I-4135, [2004] 2 CMLR 909, ECJ.

[11]   *Bosman* above, para 74. In *Barry (Mohammed) v Southwark London Borough Council* [2008] EWCA Civ 1440, [2009] 2 CMLR 269, [2009] ICR 437, the Court of Appeal held that although a Dutch citizen had only been employed as a steward at a tennis tournament in the UK for two weeks within a six-month period it was enough to qualify him as a 'worker' under the Immigration (European Economic Area) Regulations 2006, reg 6(2)(b)(ii) and he was, therefore, eligible for housing assistance pursuant to the Allocation of Housing and Homelessness (Eligibility) (England) Regulations 2006, reg 6(2)(a).

Jobseekers sickness, illness and retirement

6.95 The term 'worker', within the meaning of Article 45 TFEU, does not cover only actual workers, but also job seekers,[1] those between jobs,[2] workers undergoing vocational training in their own field or in some cases retraining in a different field,[3] the involuntarily unemployed, those who are temporarily ill[4] or injured, and retired workers. In relation to the retention of worker status by women who give up work, or seeking work, because of the physical constraints of the late stages of pregnancy and the aftermath of childbirth, the CJEU has recently ruled, in *Saint Prix (Jessy) v Secretary of State for Work and Pensions*[5] that such a woman does retain the status of worker within the meaning of Article 45 TFEU, provided that she returns to work or finds another job within a reasonable period after the birth of her child. What is a reasonable time will depend on all the circumstances, including "the applicable national rules on the duration of maternity leave"[6] and the Court further noted that, for the purpose of calculating the continuous period of five years residence to acquire permanent residence, continuity is not affected by an absence of a maximum of 12 consecutive months for important reasons such as pregnancy and childbirth.[7] The fact that a contract of employment was for a fixed term does not necessarily lead to the conclusion that, once that contract expired, the employee concerned is automatically to be regarded as voluntarily unemployed.[8] In the case of *Bernini*[9] an Italian national who had undergone occupational training in the Netherlands retained the status of worker when undergoing full-time study in Italy where there was a link between the previous occupational activity and the studies in question. In the case law of the CJEU the amount of time given to job seekers to find work is not fixed. The effectiveness of Article 45 is secured if they have a reasonable time in which to do so. Member States may allow them to remain for a reasonable period, but cannot require them to leave at the end of that period, if the person concerned produces evidence that he or she is continuing to seek employment and has genuine chances of being engaged.[10] Workers who have not yet found employment may not be entitled to the fuller rights available to those who have found employment. In particular the right to enjoy the same social and tax advantages may not accrue until employment is found.[11] The conduct of the person concerned before and after the period of employment was not relevant in establishing the status of worker.[12] Under Article 6 of the Citizens' Directive[13] all EEA nationals get a three months' right of residence irrespective of the purpose of their entry. At the end of the three months, they have a right to remain longer if they are workers. There is also an additional safeguard contained in Article 14(4)(b) of the Directive, which provides that where Union citizens entered the territory of the host Member State in order to seek employment, they should not be expelled for as long as they can provide evidence that they are continuing to seek employment and that they have a genuine chance of being engaged. The Directive also covers the situation of those who have been on short fixed term contracts or have been in employment for periods of more than or less than one year.[14] Most of the above EU law rights have been transposed into UK domestic law by the 2006 Regulations.[15] However, the Regulations have recently undergone significant amendments, as is discussed in the following paragraph, in order to restrict the right of access to social security benefits by EEA nationals in the UK who are not in work in various circumstances.

1   Case C-292/89 *R v Immigration Appeal Tribunal, ex p Antonissen* [1991] ECR I-745, [1991] 2 CMLR 373, para 10.
2   Case 75/63 *Hoekstra (née Unger) v Bestuur der Bedrijfsvereniging voor Detailhandel en Ambachten* [1964] ECR 177 at 184, ECJ.
3   Case 39/86 *Lair v University of Hanover* [1988] ECR 3161, [1989] 3 CMLR 545, ECJ, as qualified by Case 197/86 *Brown v Secretary of State for Scotland* [1988] ECR 3205, [1988] 3 CMLR 403, ECJ.
4   *Lair* above. See also *Giangregorio v Secretary of State for the Home Department* [1983] 3 CMLR 472, [1983] Imm AR 104, IAT; *Monteil v Secretary of State for the Home Department* [1983] Imm AR 149, [1984] 1 CMLR 264, IAT. Case C-302/90 *Caisse auxiliaire d'assurance maladie-invalidité (CAAMI) v Faux* [1991] ECR I-4875. The Upper Tribunal has held that illness (for the purposes of Article 7(3)(b) of the Citizens' Directive, and reg 6(2)(a) of the 2006 EEA Regulations) includes mental illness: *JO (qualified person – hospital order – effect) Slovakia* [2012] UKUT 00237(IAC). The key domestic cases on retention of worker status under Regulation 6(2)(a) are: *FMB (Uganda) v Secretary of State for the Home Department* [2010] UKUT 447 (IAC); *Samin v City of Westminster* [2012] EWCA Civ 1468; [2013] 2 CMLR 6; [2013] Imm AR 375; *De Brito (Aurelio) v Secretary of State for the Home Department* [2012] EWCA Civ 709, [2012] 3 CMLR 538. In *Samin*, the Court of Appeal stressed that whether a migrant worker was 'temporarily unable to work as a result of illness or accident' was one of fact, and it would generally be helpful to ask whether there was a realistic prospect of a return to work. See also *Konodyba v Royal Borough of Kensington and Chelsea* [2012] EWCA Civ 982.
5   Case C-507/12, CJEU, First Chamber, 19 June 2014, upon a preliminary reference made by the UK Supreme Court:[2012] UKSC 49. Note that Advocate General Wahl distinguished *Dias* (Case C-325/09 [2011] ECR I-6387) 'with relative ease': see [23]-[24] of his Opinion in *St Prix* dated 12 December 2012; *Dias* was not mentioned at all in the CJEU's judgment.
6   In accordance with Article 8 of Council Directive 92/85/EEC of 19 October 1992 on the introduction of measures to encourage improvements in the safety and health at work of pregnant workers and workers who have recently given birth or are breastfeeding (tenth individual Directive within the meaning of Article 16(1) of Directive 89/391/EEC) (OJ 1992 L 348, p 1). *St Prix* at [42].
7   *St Prix* at [45]. See also *Borger v Tiroler Gebietskrankenkasse* Case C-516/09 [2011] All ER (D) 132 (Mar), ECJ, in which the ECJ held that an EU citizen, on an extended period of unpaid maternity leave, continued to qualify as an 'employed person' within the meaning of art 1(a) of Council Regulation (EEC) No 1408/71 as long as they continued to be covered by a social security scheme mentioned in art 1(a) of the same Regulation; and *Reichel-Albert v Deutsche Rentenverichtserung Nordbayern* (Case C-522/10), [2012] 3 CMLR 48 (German legislation precluding a German national from treating 'child raising periods' for pension purposes that were accrued while in Belgium exercising Treaty rights was discriminatory [42]-[44]).
8   Case C-413/01 *Ninni-Orasche (Franca) v Bundesminister für Wissenschaft, Verkehr and Kunst* [2003] ECR I-13187, [2004] All ER (EC) 765, ECJ
9   Case C-3/90 *Bernini v Minister van Onderwijs en Wetenschappen* [1992] ECR I-1071. For another case on the interrelation of studies and work see Case C-357/89 *Raulin v Minister van Onderwijs en Wetenschappen* [1992] ECR I-1027, [1994] 1 CMLR 227, ECJ.
10 See *EC Commission v Belgium* Case C-344/95 [1997] 2 CMLR 187, ECJ; Case C-292/89 *R v Immigration Appeal Tribunal, ex p Antonissen* [1991] ECR I-745, [1991] 2 CMLR 373. In *AG (EEA-jobseeker - self-sufficient person - proof) Germany* [2007] UKAIT 00075, the AIT held that the six-months' period is a general rule of thumb and that there is no fixed time limit (para 49). Article 14(4)(b), Directive 2004/38/EC.
11 See Council Regulation (EEC) 1612/68, art 7. The directive makes a distinction between work seekers and those who have found employment, although they may be workers for the purpose of art 39.
12 Case C-413/01 *Ninni-Orasche* fn 8 above.
13 Council Directive 2004/38/EC.
14 Directive 2004/38/EC, arts 7(3) and 14.
15 The Immigration (European Economic Area) Regulations 2006, SI 2006/1003, reg 6(2). Regulation 6(2)(b) may not on first sight appear to be a faithful reproduction of the Directive, but it should be noted that sub-paras (a), (b), and (c) are alternatives, not cumulative. From regulation 6(4) a 'jobseeker' appears to be a persons 'who enters the UK in order to seek

employment', whilst a 'worker' is someone already in the UK who is either employed or seeking work: See *Antonissen*, above.

6.96 Following media attention at the end of 2013 concerning the expiry of transitional restrictions on Romanian and Bulgarian workers' access to the UK labour market, the UK Government took steps to respond to public pressure to combat the perceived threat posed by the likely deluge of Romanian and Bulgarian 'benefit tourists' which, in fact, never transpired.[1] The subsequently enacted Immigration (European Economic Area) (Amendment) (No 2) Regulations, 2013/3032 had the effect, among other things, of tightening the eligibility criteria for the retention of worker status and as to qualification as a 'jobseeker' under regulation 6 of the 2006 EEA Regulations. In relation to the retention of worker status where the person is no longer working, the amended regulation 6 still contains the following categories which had already featured, ie regulation 6(2)(a): temporarily unable to work as the result of illness or accident;[2] regulation 6(2)(c): involuntarily unemployed and has embarked on vocational training; and regulation 6(2)(d): voluntarily ceased working and embarked on vocational training that is related to his previous employment. However, the amended regulation 6 also contains the following categories, which relate to retention of worker status by the involuntarily unemployed where employment has lasted for under a year in the UK:

- Regulation 6(2)(b): he is in duly recorded involuntary unemployment after having been employed in the UK for at least one year provided that he (i) has registered as a jobseeker with the relevant employment office; and (ii) satisfies conditions A and B, where:
  — Condition A[3] is that the person— (a) entered the United Kingdom in order to seek employment; or (b) is present in the United Kingdom seeking employment, immediately after enjoying a right to reside pursuant to paragraph (1)(b) to (e) [i.e. worker, self-employed, sef-sufficient person or student] disregarding any period during which worker status was retained pursuant to paragraph (2)(b) or (ba). The use of the word 'immediately' will obviously will make it harder for people to retain worker status where they have gaps between ceasing work and registering as a jobseeker/duly recording involuntary unemployment.[4] Or,
  — Condition B[5] is that the person can provide evidence that he is seeking employment and has a genuine chance of being engaged.
  — Under this category, the person may not retain the status of worker for longer than a continuous period of six months unless 'he can provide compelling evidence that he is continuing to seek employment and has a genuine chance of being engaged'.[6]
- Regulation 6(2)(ba): he is in duly recorded involuntary unemployment after having been employed in the United Kingdom for less than one year, provided that he— (i) has registered as a jobseeker with the relevant employment office; and (ii) satisfies conditions A and B (which are defined above). Such a person may only retain worker status for a maximum of six months[7] and there is no provison to extend this period. At that point, the person may be able to move to the 'jobseeker' category of qualified person under regulation 6(4).

As to retention of the 'jobseeker' status, regulation 6(4) requires that 'conditions A, B and, where relevant, C' are met. Conditions A and B are defined above. Condition C is that the person has had a period of absence from the UK, and the condition applies where the person has, previously, enjoyed a right to reside under regulation 6 as a result of satisfying conditions A and B: (a) in the case of a person to whom paragraph (2)(b) or (ba) applied, for at least six months; or (b) in the case of a jobseeker, for at least 182 days in total, unless the person concerned has, since enjoying the above right to reside, been continuously absent from the United Kingdom for at least 12 months.[8] Where Condition C applies – (a) paragraph (7) does not apply; and (b) Condition B has effect as if 'compelling' were inserted before 'evidence'. A jobseeker satisfying regulation 6(4) is entitled to retain that status for an initial 'relevant period' of 182 days 'minus the cumulative total of any days during which the person concerned previously enjoyed a right to reside as a jobseeker, not including any days prior to a continuous absence from the United Kingdom of at least 12 months.'[9] The jobseeker may retain that status beyond the 'relevant period' only if able to 'provide compelling evidence that he is continuing to seek employment and has a genuine chance of being engaged.'[10] . A discussion of the legality of the changes, as proposed in Autumn 2013, is provided by Elspeth Guild in the *ILPA European Update*, December 2013 (article dated 27 November 2013).

[1] For example, see Andreou, 'The immigration invasion that never was' TheGuardian.com, 2 January 2014.
[2] See cases at fn 4 at **6.95** above.
[3] Regulation 6(5).
[4] This requirement is difficult to square with CJEU case law, such as *Antonissen* (see **6.57** above, fn 3 and **6.95** above) which permits retention of worker status for a reasonable time following a period of employment provided that there is evidence of work seeking and a genuine chance of being engaged.
[5] Regulation 6(6).
[6] Regulation 6(7) and (8).
[7] Regulation 6(2A).
[8] Regulation 6(9) and (10).
[9] Regulation 6(8)(b).
[10] Regulation 6(7).

Employment in the public service

6.97 Article 45(4), TFEU takes account of the legitimate interest of each Member State in the protection of its national interest by restricting employment in the public service to its own nationals.[1] But, since the exercise of this power is a derogation from the fundamental principle that workers in the Union should enjoy freedom of movement without discrimination on nationality grounds, it must be construed in such a way as to limit its scope to what is strictly necessary for safeguarding the interests which that provision allows Member States to protect.[2] According to the established case law, the derogation must be restricted to activities which in themselves are directly and specifically connected with the exercise of official authority.[3] The test is not the status of the civil servant, but whether the employee is responsible for exercising powers conferred by public law or for safeguarding the general interests of the State. There has to be direct and specific participation in the exercise of official authority. The exemption presupposes the existence of a special relationship to the State and the posts excluded are limited to those which, on account of the tasks and responsibilities attaching to them, are likely to have the characteristics of special administrative activities in these areas.[4] Rather surprisingly, the post of head, technical office supervisor, principal supervisor, work supervisor, stock controller, municipal night watchman and municipal architect in Belgium have been held to fall within the meaning of public service.[5] On the other hand, trainee locomotive drivers, loaders, plate-layers, shunters and signallers with the Belgian National Railway, and unskilled workers with a local Belgian railway company, as well as hospital nurses, children's nurses, plumbers, carpenters, electricians and garden hands with the City of Brussels and the Commune of Auderghem have been held to be outside the category.[6] A nurse and trainee teacher, though having the status of civil servant, have also been held outside the exemption.[7] Court officials may be outside the exemption, but not judges.[8] Masters of ships and chief mates of merchant ships with flag flying duties have been held to fall within the exception.[9] In the case of research scientists, only those with duties of management or advising the State on scientific and technical questions would qualify.[10]

[1] Case C-443/93 *Vougioukas v Idrima Koinonikon Asphalisseon (IKA)* [1995] ECR I-4033, ECJ.

[2] Case C-147/86 *EC Commission v Greece* [1989] 2 CMLR 845, para 7, ECJ; Case C-114/97 *EC Commission v Spain* [1999] 2 CMLR 701, para 34, ECJ.

[3] *Commission v Spain* above, para 35; Case 2/74 *Reyners v Belgium* [1974] 2 CMLR 305, para 45, ECJ; Case C-42/92 *Thijssen v Controldienst voor de Vorzekeringen* [1993] ECR I-4047, para 8, ECJ.

[4] Case C-42/92 *Thijssen v Controldienst voor de Verzekeringen* [1993] ECR I-4047, ECJ (insurance commissioners in Belgium not covered by exemption); Case C-4/91 *Bleis v Ministère de l'Education Nationale* [1991] ECR I-5627, [1994] 1 CMLR 793, ECJ (school teachers not exempt); Case C-213/90 *ASTI (Association de Soutien aux Travailleurs Immigrés) v Chambre des Employés Privés* [1991] ECR I-3507, [1993] 3 CMLR 621, ECJ (guilds with policy advisory function not exempt).

[5] Case 149/79 *EC Commission v Belgium (No 2)* [1982] ECR 1845 at 1851, ECJ. But not 'President of a Port Authority': *Haralambidis v Casilli*:C-270/13 [2014] All ER (D) 123 (Sep), ECJ.

[6] *Commission v Belgium* above, at 1852; see also [1980] ECR 3881 at 3898, ECJ.

[7] Case 66/85 *Lawrie-Blum v Land Baden-Württemberg* [1986] ECR 2121, [1987] 3 CMLR 389, at para 28, ECJ (trainee teachers); Case 307/84 *EC Commission v France* [1986] ECR 1725, [1987] 3 CMLR 555, ECJ (nurses in public hospital); Case C-4/91 *Bleis v Ministere de l'Education Nationale* [1991] ECR I-5627, [1994] 1 CMLR 793, para 7, ECJ (secondary school teachers); Case C-259/91 *Allue v Universita degli Studi di Venezia and Universita degli Studi di Parma* [1993] ECR I-4309, ECJ (university teachers); *EC Commission v Luxembourg (public service employment)* Case C-473/93 [1997] ECR I-3207, at para 33–34 (primary school teachers).

[8] Case 2/74 *Reyners v Belgium* [1974] ECR 631 at 655, ECJ. But for insurance commissioners see Case C-42/92 *Thijssen v Controldienst voor de Vorzekeringen* [1993] ECR I-4047, ECJ.

[9] Case C-405/01 *Colegio de Officiales de la Marina Mercante Espanola v Administracion del Estado* [2003] ECR I-10391, ECJ.

[10] *Lawrie-Blum*, above; Case 225/85 *EC Commission v Italy* [1987] ECR 2625, [1988] 3 CMLR 635, ECJ.

6.98 The interests which the public service exception allows Member States to protect are satisfied by the power to restrict the admission of foreign nationals to certain activities in the public service. But Article 45(4) TFEU goes no further than this, and cannot be used to justify discrimination as regards pay or other terms and conditions of employment against non-national workers once they have been admitted to the public service.[1] However, Article 45(4) may allow the exclusion of nationals of other Member States from the benefit of certain promotions or transfers within the public service, if these involve performing functions required to safeguard the general interests of the State.[2]

[1] Case 152/73 *Sotgiu v Deutsche Bundespost* [1974] ECR 153, ECJ; Case 225/85 *EC Commission v Italy* [1988] 3 CMLR 635, ECJ; Case 390/87 *Echternach and Moritz v Minister van Onderwijs en Wetenschappen* [1990] 2 CMLR 305, ECJ; Case 33/88 *Allué and Coonan v Università degli Studi di Venezia* [1991] 1 CMLR 283, ECJ.
[2] See further Martin and Guild *Free movement of persons in the European Union* (1996), pp 44–47.

PERSONAL SCOPE (3) ESTABLISHMENT

6.99 Free movement rights apply to nationals of Member States and thereby to all EEA nationals who wish to establish themselves in another Member State or EEA country in business or as a self-employed person.[1] They apply to natural persons and to companies. The main provision contained in Article 49 TFEU (ex Article 43 TEC) 'prohibits' restrictions on the freedom of establishment by nationals of a Member State in the territory of another Member State, including the setting up of agencies, branches or subsidiaries. Article 49(2) states that the freedom of establishment includes the right to take up and pursue activities as a self-employed person as well as the right to set up and manage undertakings. These measures are implemented by the Citizens' Directive which repealed Council Directive (EEC) 73/148, and incorporated its provisions into the new Directive in a short and simplified form.[2] The Directive is transposed into UK law by the 2006 Regulations.[3] Under regulation 6(3) of the 2006 Regulations, the status of self-employed person is retained by a person no longer in self-employment 'if he is temporarily unable to pursue his activity as a self-employed person as the result of illness or accident.'[4].

[1] The expression 'self-employed' is defined in Case 300/84 *Van Roosmalen v Bestuur van der Bedrijfsvereniging voor de Gezondheid, Geestelijke en Maatschappelijke Belangen* [1986] ECR 3097, [1988] 3 CMLR 471, ECJ and in Case C-268/99 Jany [2001] ECR I-8615. Self-employment in EU law is defined as genuine and effective economic activity carried out outside of a relationship of subordination.
[2] Directive 2004/38/EC, arts 6 and 7.
[3] Immigration (European Economic Area) Regulations 2006, SI 2006/1003, reg 4(1)(b) and 6.
[4] The legal approach to this provision in relation to workers was dealt with above at **6.95** ff.

6.100 Although Article 49 TFEU (ex Article 43 TEC) confers a direct right of establishment free of restrictions based on nationality and non-discriminatory obstacles, it will only be a complete right when each Member State recognises training and educational and professional qualifications, obtained or recognised in other Member States, as equivalent to its own. There is a whole body of EU law dealing with the harmonisation of professional qualifications, their standardisation and mutual recognition which is outside the scope of the present work.[1]

[1] The principal measure is Directive 2005/36/EC (as amended) on the recognition of professional qualifications (7 September 2005). Also note Council Directive 77/249/EEC to facilitate the effective exercise by lawyers of freedom to provide services; and Council Directive 98/5/EC to facilitate the practice of the profession of lawyer on a permanent basis in a Member State other than that in which the qualification was obtained. The European Communities (Lawyer's Practice and Services of Lawyers) (Amendment) Regulations 2008, SI 2008/81, which came into force on 11 February 2008 give effect to the Treaty concerning the Accession

of Bulgaria and Romania to the EU and will allow lawyers in Bulgaria and Romania to practise those professional activities for which they are authorised in their home jurisdiction, in England and Wales, and in Northern Ireland, including on a permanent basis. This will bring them into line with lawyers of other Member States who wish to practise in England and Wales on a temporary or permanent basis.

6.101 Under Article 51 TFEU (ex Article 45 TEC) Member States are allowed to exclude from the equal treatment rule certain official activities, if they are activities which in the Member State are connected, even occasionally, with the exercise of official authority.[1] It is for each Member State to decide what constitutes official authority, but since the exception derogates from the fundamental rule of freedom of establishment, its scope is limited to what is strictly necessary in order to safeguard the interests which it allows the Member State to protect.[2] Setting up a supplementary school, a language school, a music school or a vocational training centre, or giving private tuition from home do not fall within the Article 45 exception.[3] The profession of 'notary' belongs within the exception,[4] but not that of lawyer.[5]

[1]   Article 45 EC (ex art 55). See **6.97** above, regarding employment in the public service.
[2]   Case 147/86 *EC Commission v Greece* [1988] ECR 1637, [1989] 2 CMLR 845, ECJ. See also **6.97** above with respect to excluded categories of workers.
[3]   Commission v Greece above.
[4]   Martin and Guild *Free movement of persons in the European Union* (1996), p 67.
[5]   Case 2/74 *Reyners v Belgium* [1974] ECR 631, [1974] 2 CMLR 305, ECJ. Other activities which have been excluded from the exception are: a lottery concessionaire and activities relating to the design, programming and operation of data systems for the public service (Case C-272/91 *EC Commission v Italy 'Public supply contract 3 – loto'* [1994] ECR I-1409, [1995] 2 CMLR 673, ECJ); activities of traffic accident experts (Case C-306/89 *EC Commission v Greece* [1991] ECR I-5863, [1994] 1 CMLR 803, ECJ); and the post of approved insurance commissioner (Case C-42/92 *Thijssen v Controldienst voor de Vorzekeringen* [1993] ECR I-4047, ECJ).

PERSONAL SCOPE (4) SERVICES

Providing services

6.102 Akin to the right of establishment is the right given by the TFEU Treaty to provide services in another member country. The idea is that persons established in one country, for example, doctors, plumbers, tailors, etc, should be able to provide their services in other member countries. Article 56 TFEU (ex Article 49 TEC) prohibits restrictions on this right. Article 57 TFEU (ex Article 50 TEC) provides that the person providing a service may, in order to do so, temporarily pursue his activity in the State where the service is provided. The Treaty provisions were supplemented by Council Directive (EEC) 73/148, which was repealed by the Citizens' Directive on 30 April 2006.[1] But the Directive is silent on the provision and receipt of services. No reference is made to them. Instead the Directive creates a right for all Union citizens and their families to travel to another Member State and reside there for up to three months without any limitation on the purpose of the visit, under Article 6.[2] All those who wish to travel either to provide or receive services will therefore be covered by the Article 6 right. If they wish to stay longer, (i) they may have to register their presence with the authorities; and (ii) they will only be able to stay on, if they are self employed, exercising a right of establishment or have sufficient resources not to be a burden on the social assistance system of the host Member State during the period of their residence.[3] For visits longer than three months the following rules should be borne in mind. The right to provide services includes the right to travel to the other country and to remain there long enough to perform them.[4] The right applies to companies as well as persons[5] but there are four conditions. First, a service provider, who is a natural person, must be a national of a Member State (an EEA national in our wider context). Secondly, he or she must be 'established' in a Member State.[6] Thirdly, the provision of services must normally involve the engagement by the provider in some sort of economic activity.[7] Fourthly, the right only arises if the provider of the services is established in country A and wishes to travel to country B. Visits to country B are clearly envisaged as temporary. If anything more permanent is intended, the provisions relating to establishment or workers will apply.[8] A Member State may not make the provision of services in its territory subject to compliance with all the conditions required for establishment.[9] Directive 2005/36/EC (the 'Qualifications' Directive) was adopted in September 2005. The Directive will apply to a number of sectors including, for example, doctors, dentists and vets, as well as architects. It will replace the separate Directives that currently exist for the different professions. The basic premise of the Directive is that it will simplify the process for professionals wishing to work in another Member State. Under the new Directive, regulated professionals can provide their services on a 'temporary and occasional' basis in Member States other than their own.

[1]   Directive 2004/38/EC, art 38.
[2]   Directive 2004/38/EC, art 6. These new rights are transposed into UK domestic law for all EEA citizens by the 2006 Regulations: Immigration (European Economic Area) Regulations 2006, SI 2006/1003, regs 13 and 14. Under reg 11 an EEA national must be admitted to the UK if he or she produces on arrival a valid national identity card or passport issued by an EEA State, and is then is entitled to reside in the UK for a period not exceeding three months under reg 13.
[3]   Council Directive 2004/38/EC (the Citizens' Directive) art 7-14 and 16-18.
[4]   See Case 186/87 *Cowan v Trésor Public* [1989] ECR 195 and Case C-68/89 *EC Commission v Netherlands* [1991] ECR I-2637, para 10.
[5]   Articles 48 EC (ex art 58) and 55 EC (ex art 66).
[6]   An employed person, whether in his or her own State or in another, may benefit from art 49 EC as someone 'established': see Case C-106/91 *Ramrath v Ministre de la Justice* [1992] ECR I-3351, [1992] 3 CMLR 173, ECJ; Case 143/87 *Stanton and SA belge d'assurances L'Étoile 1905 v INASTI (Institute national d'assurance sociales pour travailleurs indépendants)* [1988] ECR 3877, [1989] 3 CMLR 761, ECJ.
[7]   Taking part in sporting events may involve engaging in economic activity, and therefore be the provision of services by the organisers of the event, even though those taking part are amateur athletes or players: Cases C-51/96 and 191/97 *Deliège v Ligue Francophone de Judo et Disciplines Associées ASBL* [2000] ECR I-2549, [2002] 2 CMLR 1574, ECJ.
[8]   Case 196/87 *Steymann v Staatssecretaris Van Justitie* [1988] ECR 6159, [1989] 1 CMLR 449, ECJ. See further Case 220/83 *EC Commission v France* [1986] ECR 3663, [1987] 2 CMLR 113, ECJ (co-insurance services); Case C-113/89 *Rush Portuguesa Lda v ONI* [1990] ECR I-1417, [1991] 2 CMLR 818, ECJ.
[9]   See the judgments in Case C-154/89 *EC Commission v France* [1991] ECR I-659, para 12, and in Case C-76/90 *Säger v Dennemeyer & Co Ltd* [1991] ECR I-4221, para 13.

Posted workers

6.103 Where companies carry out contracts in another Member State, they will usually bring with them a mixture of employees. Some will be nationals of Member States (or EEA nationals). They will often qualify as 'workers' and be covered by Article 45 TFEU. But in other cases posted personnel may properly be considered as falling within the scope of Article 56 TFEU rather than Article 45, although it may be difficult to determine which.[1] In either case, the concern (especially in the building trade) is whether the posted workers are being subjected to an exploitative regime. Although normally national legislation in the receiving State is unable to restrict the provision of services, the public interest relating to the social protection of workers may constitute an overriding requirement, justifying such a restriction, if there is insufficient protection in the State where the service provider is established.[2] In the *Rush Portuguesa* case,[3] Portugal was a member of the Community and its citizens and companies established in Portugal could benefit from the right to provide services but not to the right to seek and take up employment because of a five-year derogation by all Member States from this right. The result of the decision was to override the effect of the derogation which made entry of workers a question for domestic immigration law in each country. The Court held that a company established in the EC has the right to transfer its existing labour force to another Member State for the duration of the project, without having to obtain work permits for the posted employees and a failure to do so cannot make the employer liable to penal sanctions, as happened in the *Vander Elst* case,[4] where the principle of posted workers was extended to third country nationals. The issue which arises out of that case is whether the factual situation of the Moroccan workers, namely that they were lawfully employed and resident under local immigration laws in the sending State, Belgium, has become a limiting condition for the exercise of Article 49 rights in the case of posted workers.

[1]   Case C-106/91 *Ramrath v Ministre de la Justice* [1992] ECR I-3351, paras 15–16, ECJ.
[2]   Case C-272/94 *Guiot* [1996] ECR I-1905, ECJ.
[3]   Case C-113/89 *Rush Portuguesa Lda v ONI* [1990] ECR I-1417, [1991] 2 CMLR 818, ECJ.
[4]   Case C-43/93 *Vander Elst v Office des Migrations Internationales* [1994] ECR I-3803, ECJ.

6.104 In *R (on the application of Low) v Secretary of State for the Home Department*[1] the Court of Appeal held that for the purpose of asserting a right to work under Article 49 of the Nice Treaty as a posted worker, lawful residence or employment in the country of establishment was a necessary precondition. Furthermore, it was an abuse to set up an Irish company to employ those who were illegally in the UK and then seek to use Article 49 to 'post' them to cook and wait tables in restaurants where they could not work lawfully if they were directly employed. In *R (on the application of Gransian Ltd) v Secretary of State for the Home Department*[2] Blake J underlined the non-discrimination principle behind these cases. He held that the posting company does not have to undergo the expenses of work permits, fees, other applications which might put it in an uncompetitive position with respect to another company already established in the UK, who can undertake the work and provide the services and commercial activities without such expense. The principle itself is founded upon movement from people who are workers and established in an ongoing enterprise in EU country A, that seek to deliver economic services, or activities, in EU country B, but if there is no prior business established as a genuine and effective commercial undertaking in EU country A, there is nothing which is capable of engaging the non-discrimination principle. So an Irish company has no claim in such circumstances to recruit third country nationals from either outside the EU altogether, or from some other part of it, with whom it has no prior economic relationship and who have not been working for it in an economic capacity prior to the UK-based activity.

¹ [2010] EWCA Civ 4, [2010] 2 CMLR 909, [2010] ICR 755.
² [2008] EWHC 3431 (Admin) (16 December 2008). See further *R (on the application of Yaus Catering Services Ltd (Ireland) v Secretary of State for the Home Department.*[2009] EWHC 2534 (Admin), [2010] Imm AR 252, where it was held that the mere establishment by an individual of a company in Ireland or Cyprus could not create any rights for that individual to work and stay in those countries; *Gransian* Ltd followed.

6.105 Although posted workers do not need work permits, it is unclear whether they enter and reside as of right, although this would seem to be a necessary consequence of the case-law.¹ Given the uncertainty, it seems that at present they may still need to comply with the host State's laws regarding entry.² However, those rules on entry cannot be unnecessarily restrictive. In *European Commission v Luxembourg*³ local immigration laws required posted workers to have a contract of indefinite employment with the service provider entered into at least six months prior to their being posted. Luxembourg sought to justify these limitations on the company's Article 49 rights by reference to social welfare and stability in the labour market. The Court held that went beyond what was necessary and proportionate to monitor the circumstances of the posted workers. The *Commission v Germany*⁴ case was another attempt to monitor the circumstances of posted workers in the sending country. This time the immigration laws of Germany sought to impose a visa requirement on posted workers coming to Germany, requiring them to show that they had been lawfully and habitually employed in the sending State for at least 12 months. The Court once more held that this was disproportionate. Posted workers working for Swiss employers are in a different position; they are given an express right of entry under the EC-Switzerland Free Movement Agreement.⁵ A new Directive regulating the conditions of entry and residence of third country nationals in the framework of an intra-corporate transfer (Directive 2014/66/EU) has been agreed and is to be transposed by 29 November 2016; however, the UK has not opted in to it.

¹ See *Vander Elst*, above, at paras 19–22, where the issue is alluded to but not dealt with. The EEA Regulations 2000, SI 2000/2326 as amended by SI 2002/1241, regs 3(1)(ba) and 12(3) only deal with posted workers employed by Swiss nationals or Swiss undertakings and neatly avoid the issue of posted workers from other Member States.
² This can be inferred from the *Luxembourg, Austria and Germany* cases, where the court held that the conditions of entry were disproportionate, not that they were unlawful. However, see the more recent case of *Essent Energie Produitie BV v Minister van Sociale Zaken en Werkgelegeheid*: C-91/13[2014] All ER (D) 157 (Sep), ECJ.
³ C-445/03 [2004] ECR I-10191, ECJ.
⁴ Work Visa Regime, *Re, European Commission v Germany* C-244/04 at [31]–[32], [44] and [59] [2006] ECR I-885, [2006] 2 CMLR 631, ECJ; *EC Commission v Austria* C-168/04 at [37] and [44]–[45] (21 September 2006, unreported).
⁵ Agreement between the European Community and the Swiss Confederation on The Free Movement of Persons (30 April 2002 OJ L114/6). Article 1 of Annex I of the Agreement provides that 'the Contracting Parties shall allow . . . posted persons within the meaning of Article 17 of this Annex to enter their territory simply upon production of a valid identity card or passport.' Article 17 defines posted persons as ' . . . employees, irrespective of their nationality, of persons providing services, who are integrated into one Contracting Party's regular labour market and posted for the provision of a service in the territory of another Contracting Party . . . ' Under UK domestic law the Immigration (Swiss Free Movement of Persons) (No 3) Regulations 2002, SI 2002/1241 applied the 2000 Regulations (EEA Regulations SI 2000/2326) to posted workers and Sch 3 part 2 of the 2006 Regulations

(SI 2006/1003), para 1 provides that the 2000 Regulations as amended shall continue to apply to posted workers in accordance with the Swiss Free Movement Regulations as if the 2000 Regulations had not been revoked. However, the practice of UK Embassies has been to require posted workers to have been employed for at least one year by the company abroad. In the light of *Commission v Luxembourg* this requirement cannot be strictly applied.

6.106 The Posted Workers Directive intends to ensure the trans-national provision of services under conditions of fair competition and of guaranteed workers' rights.[1] The Directive obliges EEA States to ensure that, whatever the law applicable to the employment relationship may be, the undertakings guarantee workers posted to their territory the terms and conditions of employment that apply to nationals of that territory (Article 3). Thus it regulates the legal framework of working conditions and applicable employment legislation, so as to alleviate concerns that posted workers would not access the same protection as other employees. But it does so not as part of immigration law but as a part of the posted workers' contracts of employment. The Directive applies to both nationals of Member States and third country nationals. In addition to the Directive the EU law principles of non-discrimination and not placing obstacles in the way of free movement also apply.[2] Where the requirements of the host State create obstacles to free movement rights, a breach of Article 45 TFEU may occur without any need to consider whether there has been indirect discrimination on nationality grounds under Article 45(2).[3]

A related problem arose in Case C-341/05 *Laval un Partneri Ltd v Svenska Byggnadsarbetareforbundet*[4] where a Latvian construction company wished to exercise its freedom to provide services in Sweden, in particular by the posting of Latvian workers to one of its Swedish subsidiaries. The Swedish trade union wanted to prevent wage cutting and demanded that the Latvian company should, by way of guarantee, sign the Swedish collective agreement and apply it to its posted workers. Following unsuccessful negotiations and strike action the case was eventually referred to the ECJ, essentially asking the Court whether collective action constitutes a restriction within the meaning of Articles 49 and 56 TEU. The Court held that a failure under Swedish national rules to take into account, irrespective of their content, collective agreements to which companies that post workers to the host Member State are already bound in the Member State in which they are established, gives rise to discrimination against such companies, if they are then treated as if they are the same as national companies which have not concluded a collective agreement. Effectively this is giving the green light to companies which use posted workers to pay their own local rates, which may be lower than in the receiving state, provided they have entered into collective agreements with those workers in the home Member State.

[1] Directive 96/71/EC of the European Parliament and of the Council of 16 December 1996 concerning the posting of workers in the framework of the provision of services, (OJ L 018, 21/01/1997 p 0001–0006).
[2] See Case C-369/96 *Arblade, Criminal proceedings against* [1999] ECR I-8453.
[3] Case C-18/95 *Terhoeve (F C) v Inspecteur van de Belastingdienst Particulieren Ondernemingen Buitenland* [1999] ECR I-345.
[4] C-341/05 [2007] ECR I-11767, [2008] All ER (EC) 166, ECJ. See also Case C-438/05 *International Transport Workers' Federation v Viking Line ABP* [2008] All ER (EC) 127.

Receiving services

6.107 Where the provisions dealing with services broke new ground was in the implementing provisions. Article 1(1)(b) of Council Directive (EEC) 73/148, now repealed by the Citizens' Directive, provided that *recipients* of services, not just providers, are entitled to enter the territory of another Member State to receive services. The far-reaching nature of these provisions was established in the landmark decision in *Luisi and Carbone*.[1] There the ECJ held that the freedom to provide services includes the freedom, for the recipients of the services, to go to another Member State in order to receive a service there, and that tourists, persons receiving medical treatment and persons travelling for the purpose of education and business are to be regarded as recipients of services. This decision was followed by *Cowan v Trésor Public*[2] where it was held that a British tourist to Paris was exercising rights to seek services, and therefore could not be excluded from compensation for criminal injuries on the grounds of nationality. Although the Citizens' Directive provides a new right for any EEA or Swiss citizen to travel to another Member State and reside there for up to three months on production of a passport or identity card (Article 6), the EU law right to travel to another Member State to receive services still holds good and will apply to longer visits, such as those of fee paying students, but is effectively subsumed into Article 6 of the Directive and will mean that, after three months, they may have to show that they are self sufficient within the meaning of Article 7(1)(b) unless they can rely on Article 56 TFEU as a free-standing right operating alongside but autonomous from the Citizens' Directive, which no-one has said is a comprehensive code.[3] As a travel and residence benefit, there is little to gain from an independent right to receive services in the light of the Citizens' Directive, but it may still be useful in terms of discrimination, as the Cowan case shows.

[1]   Joined Cases 286/82 and 26/83 *Luisi and Carbone v Ministero del Tesoro* [1984] ECR 377, [1985] 3 CMLR 52, ECJ. In Case 263/86 *Belgium v Humbel* [1988] ECR 5365, [1989] 1 CMLR 393, the court restricted the principle, so far as students are concerned, to services 'normally provided for remuneration' thus excluding students at state institutions.
[2]   Case 186/87 *Cowan v Trésor Public* [1989] ECR 195, [1990] 2 CMLR 613, ECJ.
[3]   See *Chen and Zhu v Secretary of State for the Home Department*: C-200/02 [2005] QB 325, [2005] All ER (EC) 129.

6.108 The nationality of the provider of services is crucial for the application of Articles 56 and 57 TFEU rights, but in *Svensson* the ECJ held that nationality was irrelevant so far as concerned the recipient of services.[1] Does this mean that a recipient of services, who happens to be a third country national, may move within the EU in order to enable the provider of a service effectively to provide that service? Does the application of Article 49 to third country nationals, as recipients of services, allow them to travel freely to another Member State, if that is an essential element of the provision of the services? It is much more likely that the proposition only holds good when considering the free movement rights of the provider of services, but not vice versa.

[1]   Case C-484/93 [1995] ECR I-3955.

PERSONAL SCOPE (5) STUDENTS, THE SELF-SUFFICIENT, RETIRED AND INCAPACITATED

Students

6.109 The position regarding students has been altered in form, if not in substance, by the Citizens' Directive becoming fully effective as from 30 April 2006. First, the fact that students may be recipients of services is of little help to their situation in view of the repeal of the service provisions of Council Directive 73/148 and their non-replacement in the Citizens' Directive. Secondly, Council Directive 93/96 has been repealed and its provisions replaced by the much simpler provisions of the Citizens' Directive.[1] Thirdly, the 2000 Regulations, which transposed Community law into UK domestic law have been replaced by the 2006 Regulations.[2] Although arts 10 and 11 of Regulation (EEC) 1612/68 on the rights of workers families have been repealed and replaced by the Citizens' Directive,[3] Article 12 of 1612/68, dealing with the educational rights of workers' children has been left unrepealed and is now Article 10 of Regulation 492/2011. This means that dependants of EU workers or the self-employed will still have rights of access to general and vocational education and consequential rights to remain under Article 10 of Regulation 492/2011. Vocational training referred to in Article 166 TFEU (ex Article 150 TEC) has long been an indispensable element in the Union, to be available to nationals of Member States without discrimination.[4] But it was not thought to give a right of entry or general residence.[5] In order to give effect to free movement in the single market, it was considered necessary to make some provision for those who do not enjoy rights under other parts of Community law.

[1] Directive 2004/38/EC, art 7(1)(c) and (d).
[2] Immigration (European Economic Area) Regulations 2006, SI 2006/1003. Students are defined in regulation 4(1)(d) and are 'qualified persons' under reg 6 and entitled to extended free movement rights under reg 14.
[3] Directive 2004/38/EC, art 38.
[4] Case 293/83 *Gravier v City of Liège* [1985] ECR 593, ECJ; *Belgium v Humbel* [1988] ECR 5365; *Blaizot v University of Liège* [1988] ECR 379; Case 42/87 *EC Commission v Belgium, Higher Education Funding, Re* [1988] ECR 5445; Case C-47/93 *EC Commission v Belgium* [1994] ECR I-1593.
[5] The right of residence implied by the non-discrimination requirement is limited to the purpose and duration of the studies: Case C-357/89 *Raulin v Minister van Onderwijs en Wetenschappen* [1992] ECR I-1027. However the decision in the case of *D'hoop (Marie-Nathalie) v Office National de l' Emploi* Case C-224/98 [2002] ECR I-6191, [2003] All ER (EC) 527, ECJ suggests that an EU citizen who moved to another Member State in order to study is exercising a Community law freedom.

6.110 Council Directive (EEC) 93/96 provided for a right of residence during the duration of a course of studies at a recognised educational establishment, if the principal purpose of the enrolment was to follow a vocational training course.[1] Council Directive 93/96 has been repealed and its provisions replaced by the much simpler provisions of the Citizens' Directive. Now all Union citizens have the right of residence on the territory of another Member State for more than three months, and as a student, if they fulfil two main conditions.[2] First, they must be enrolled at a private or public establishment, accredited or financed by the host Member State on the basis of its legislation or administrative practice, for the principal purpose of following a course of study, including vocational training. Secondly, they must have comprehensive sickness insurance cover in the host Member State[3] and assure the relevant national authority, by means of a declaration or by such equivalent means as they may choose, that they have sufficient resources for themselves and their family members not to become a burden on the social assistance system of the host Member State during their period of residence.[4] These provisions of the Directive have been transposed into UK domestic law by the 2006 Regulations.[5] Thus students are defined in regulation 4(1)(d)[6] and are listed as 'qualified persons' under regulation 6 and are thereby entitled to extended free movement rights under regulation 14. It should be noted that regulation 4(4) of the 2006 Regulations imposes a threshold of sufficient resources as being that in excess of 'the maximum level of resources which a British citizen and his family members may possess if he is to become eligible for social assistance under the United Kingdom benefit system' or, if that requirement does not apply, the decision-maker thinks that the resources of the person(s) concerned should be regarded as sufficient having regard to their situation.[7] It should also be noted that if a Union citizen has been studying as only a secondary purpose and work has been his or her principal purpose, he or she has better rights than as a student alone.[8]

---

[1] Council Directive (EEC) 93/96, art 1(1). But see Case C-209/03 *R (on the application of Bidar) v Ealing London Borough Council* [2005] QB 812, [2005] All ER (EC) 687, where the Court held that, while it is permissible for Member States to ensure that assistance to students from other Member States does not become an unreasonable burden, the non-discrimination provisions of the Treaty cover assistance given to students, and were breached by domestic law provisions limiting student grants and loans to those settled in the UK, since this restriction excluded EU citizens who were integrated into the host Member State.

[2] Directive 2004/38/EC, art 7(1)(c).

[3] This criterion is dealt with at **6.114** below.

[4] The ECJ has qualified this last requirement by holding that students are to avoid becoming an 'unreasonable' burden on Member States. A temporary need for social assistance would not cause a student to fall foul of this requirement, particularly if the student had been lawfully resident and studying in the Member State for a substantial length of time: Case C-184/99 *Grzelczyk (Rudy) v Centre Public d'Aide Sociale d'Ottignies-Louvain-la-Neuve* [2003] All ER (EC) 385, [2001] ECR I-6193.

[5] SI 2006/1003.

[6] The definition of a student was recently amended to reflect the fact that the Secretary of State's mechanism of approving private education institutions is not now via the Department for Education Registers of providers but is via a system of accreditation by the Secretary of State for the Home Department. Substituted by Immigration (European Economic Area) (Amendment) Regulations, 2012/1547, Sch 1, para 2(a) (July 16,2012).

[7] Regulation 4(4), amended by Immigration (European Economic Area) (Amendment) Regulations 2011, 2011/1247, reg 2(2) (June 2, 2011). See *Pensionsversicherungsanstalt v Brey* C-140/12, [2014] All ER (EC) 534, [2014] 1 WLR 1080, ECJ on the approach to be taken on the 'unreasonable burden' issue. The Court emphasised the need for the state to carry out a 'comprehensive assessment of the specific burden that would be created' by recourse to any benefits in the individual case. In particular, it was important for the national court to be able to examine such factors as the amount and regularity of the income received, whether the person has been issued with a certificate of residence, and the period during which the benefit applied for was likely to be granted. The issue is not, therefore, a mere application of the binary *KA and Others (Adequacy of maintenance) Pakistan* [2006] UKAIT 00065 test that is used under the Immigration Rules.

[8] A student who works part-time, as many do, has been held to be a worker of free movement by the ECJ in Case C – 294/06 *R (on the application of Payir) v Secretary of State for the Home Department*[2008] ECR I-203, [2009] All ER (EC) 964. When the case was referred, sub nom *R (on the application of Ozturk) v Seratary of State for the Home Department* [2006] EWCA Civ 541, [2007] 1 WLR 508, reported at [2006] ICR 1314, it was made clear that Laws LJ would have taken a very different view from the ECJ.

6.111 Council Directive 93/96 allowing spouses and children to join students has been repealed and its provisions regarding family members of students have been replaced by the much simpler provisions of the Citizens' Directive.[1] Under it students, who fulfil the requirements of Article 7(1)(c) can be joined by a spouse or civil partner and dependent children, subject to the 'sufficient resources' criterion set out above, and do not enjoy the rather more generous family provisions for workers and the self-sufficient.[2] These provisions have been transposed into domestic law by the 2006 Regulations.[3]

1 Directive 2004/38/EC, art 7(1)(d).
2 Directive 2004/38/EC, arts 2(2) and 7(4).
3 Immigration (European Economic Area) Regulations 2006, SI 2006/1003, reg 7(1) and (2).

Students with derived free movement rights

6.112 Article 10 of Regulation 492/2011 (ex Article 12 of 1612/68) dealing with the educational rights of workers' children, provides that the children of EEA nationals who have installed themselves in a Member State during the exercise by one of their parents of rights of residence as a migrant worker are entitled to reside there in order to continue their education and attend general educational courses there. This right continues even though the worker parent has left the host Member State or has ceased to be a migrant worker. Unlike the students we have been describing above, the student's right to continue living in the country while he or she pursues their education is not conditional on either the parent having sufficient resources not to become a burden on the social assistance system of that Member State or having comprehensive sickness insurance. The child's carer if not entitled under his or her own right to reside may obtain a derivative right to reside with the child as carer.[1] See **6.136**, below, for more details. See also **6.84**, above, for details of the new codification in reg 15A(3) of the 2006 EEA Regulations of a derived right based on the *Zambrano* principle, which is very similar, but not identical, to the scenario covered by Article 10 of Regulation 492/2011.

1 See Case C-413/99 *Baumbast and R v Secretary of State for the Home Department* [2002] ECR I-7091, [2002] 3 CMLR 599, ECJ; *v Lambeth London Borough Council* C 480/08 [2010] ECR I-1107, [2010] ICR 1118, ECJ and *Harrow London Borough Council v Ibrahim* C 310/08 [2010] ELR 261, (2010) Times, 26 February, ECJ; and *MDB and Ors (Article 12, 1612/68) Italy* [2010] UKUT 161 (IAC).

The self-sufficient

6.113 Council Directive 90/364, which dealt with nationals of Member States who do not work but have sufficient resources to avoid becoming a burden on the social assistance system of the host Member State, has been repealed and its provisions replaced by the much simpler provisions of the Citizens' Directive. Now all EEA and Swiss citizens have the right of residence on the territory of another Member State for more than three months if they have sufficient resources for themselves and their family members not to become a burden on the social assistance system of the host Member State during their period of residence and have comprehensive sickness insurance cover.[1] The conditions placed on those wishing to exercise this right of residence must be applied in a manner which is proportionate, so that a temporary need for social assistance or failure to provide evidence of sickness insurance may not result in the automatic refusal of the host Member State to recognise the right of residence.[2] These provisions have been transposed into domestic law by the 2006 Regulations.[3] As noted above at **6.109** in relation to students, regulation 4(4) of the 2006 Regulations imposes a threshold of sufficient resources as being that in excess of 'the maximum level of resources which a British citizen and his family members may possess if he is to become eligible for social assistance under the United Kingdom benefit system' or, if that requirement does not apply, the decision-maker thinks that the resources of the person(s) concerned, including any family members, should be regarded as sufficient having regard to their situation.[4]

1   Directive 2004/38/EC, art 7(1)(b).
2   Case C-413/99 Baumbast and R v Secretary of State for the Home Department [2003] INLR 1.
3   Immigration (European Economic Area) Regulations 2006, SI 2006/1003, reg 4(1)(c) and are 'qualified persons' under regulation 6 and entitled to extended free movement rights under regulation 14.
4   Regulation 4(4), amended by Immigration (European Economic Area) (Amendment) Regulations 2011/1247, reg 2(2) (June 2, 2011). See *Pensionsversicherungsanstalt v Brey* C-140/12 [2014] All ER (EC) 534, [2014] 1 WLR 1080, ECJ on the approach to be taken on the 'unreasonable burden' issue. The Court emphasised the need for the state to carry out a 'comprehensive assessment of the specific burden that would be created' by recourse to any benefits in the individual case. In particular, it was important for the national court to be able to examine such factors as the amount and regularity of the income received, whether the person has been issued with a certificate of residence, and the period during which the benefit applied for was likely to be granted.

6.114 The family members who can join the self-sufficient are a spouse or civil partner and any dependent descendants of that person, or the spouse or partner (children and grandchildren) and any of their dependent relatives in the ascending line (ie parents and grandparents).[1] These provisions have been transposed into domestic law by the 2006 Regulations.[2] The right of residence is without conditions restricting or prohibiting employment and the spouse and dependent children are entitled to take employment or self-employment irrespective of whether they are nationals of a Member State. Where the self-sufficient person is an infant child, her parent who is her primary carer is allowed to accompany her in order to give meaning to the child's free movement and residence rights.[3] Regulation 15A(2) of the 2006 Regulations now recognises this derived right of residence for the non-EEA primary carer on the basis of *Chen/Zambrano*: see above at **6.81**. All attempts to establish on the basis of *Chen* that the child will become self-sufficient, by the carer finding employment in the UK after entry, have so far failed in the UK domestic courts.[4] Income from illegal employment in the host Member State on the part of a parent of a 'Chen child cannot create self-sufficiency for that child'.[5] although it is likely that lawful employment can create such self-sufficiency.[6] As to the requirement for comprehensive sickness insurance, the current position of the case law is that, where there are reciprocal arrangements between the UK and the person's own country (whereby the UK Government recovers the costs of NHS treatment from the person's own state, usually on the basis that foreign nationals can access in the UK the equivalent medical treatment that they can access in their own countries), recourse to the NHS will satisfy the comprehensive sickness insurance criterion.[7] However, where there are no such reciprocal arrangements, it will be necessary to have comprehensive private health insurance in place throughout the period of residence in which the criterion applies.[8]

1   Directive 2004/38/EC, art 2 (2) and 7(1)(d).
2   Immigration (European Economic Area) Regulations 2006, SI 2006/1003, reg 7(1). For extended family members who can join a self-sufficient person, see reg 7(3).
3   *Chen and Zhu v Secretary of State for the Home Department* C-200/02 [2005] QB 325, [2005] All ER (EC) 129, ECJ. Following the judgment, new Immigration Rules regulate the entry of the primary carer and relatives of such EEA national self-sufficient children: see HC 395, paras 275C–275E, inserted by HC 164 (in force 1 January 2005).
4   *KY (China) v Secretary of State for the Home Department* [2006] EWCA Civ 1494 (17 November 2006); *Ali (Zacharia) v Secretary of State for the Home Department* [2006] EWCA Civ 484, [2006] 3 CMLR 326; *R (on the application of Catal) v Secretary of State for the Home Department* [2006] EWHC 1882 (Admin); *GM and AM (EU national establishing self-sufficiency) France* [2006] UKAIT 00059, [2007] Imm AR 18.
5   *W (China) and X (China)* [2006] EWCA Civ 1494, discussed by the Upper Tribunal in *Seye (Chen children; employment)* [2013] UKUT 00178 (IAC).
6   *Liu v Secretary of State for the Home Department* [2007] EWCA Civ 1275, *Seye (Chen children; employment)* [2013] UKUT 00178 (IAC). However, lawful employment undertaken by a parent whose leave has been extended under s 3C of the Immigration Act 1971 cannot create self-sufficiency for the '*Chen*' child: see cases in fn 5.
7   *Ahmad v Secretary of State for the Home Department* [2014] EWCA Civ 988 ;[2014] All ER (D) 193 (Jul), 52]–[57]. The SSHD accepted that that was the position: [53]. In *Ahmad*, the Court of Appeal, rather unfairly, declined to assume in the absence of evidence that the UK had reciprocal arrangements with Denmark, or that the Danish national in question, who had been resident in the UK since 2006, was still entitled to state healthcare in Denmark. In truth, the UK has reciprocal arrangements with all EEA states: see Regulation (EC) 883/2004, arts 20 and 27(3); and Directive 2011/24/EU (9 March 2011) and the implementing provision, the National Health Service (Cross-Border Healthcare) Regulations 2013, SI 2013/2269. According to the NHS website (accessed 30 August 2014), the UK also has reciprocal arrangements with Anguilla, Armenia, Australia, Azerbaijan, Barbados, Belarus, Bosnia Herzegovina, British Virgin Islands, Falkland Islands, Georgia, Gibraltar, Isle of Man, Jersey, Kazakhstan, Kyrgyzstan, Macedonia, Moldova, Monserrat, New Zealand, Russia, St Helena, Serbia, Tajikistan, Turkmenistan, Turks and Caicos Islands, Ukraine and Uzbekistan.
8   Note that the Court's position was taken notwithstanding clear statements by the European Commission to the contrary: see [29]–[36] of *Ahmad*, and the Court also rejected arguments based on discrimination [38]–[43], proportionality [44]–[52] and the Charter of Fundamental Rights [67]–[68], and refused to make a reference to the CJEU on the issue. Note the*ILPA European Update*, December 2011 at p 16–19 on this issue.

The retired and incapacitated

6.115 Council Directive 90/365, which dealt with those who have retired or been incapacitated, has been repealed and its provisions replaced by those of the Citizens' Directive. Commission Regulation (EC) No 635/2006 of 25 April 2006 also repeals Regulation (EEC) No 1251/70, which deals with the right to permanent residence of retired and incapacitated workers and frontier workers and with family rights. Its provisions have been replaced by the Citizens' Directive. The result is a complicated and somewhat labyrinthine set of provisions, in this case rather easier to follow in the 2006 Regulations, which is the Secretary of State's best effort to transpose them into UK law. Now the right of permanent residence in the host Member State can be enjoyed before completion of a continuous period of five years of residence by:

(a)   **Retirement** – Workers or self-employed persons who retire from work, having reached the age laid down by the law of that Member State for entitlement to an old age pension or workers who cease paid employment to take early retirement, provided that they have been working in that Member State for at least the preceding twelve months and have resided there continuously for more than three years.[1] The conditions as to length of residence and employment do not apply if the worker's or the self-employed person's spouse or civil partner is a national of the host Member State or has lost the nationality of that Member State by marriage to that worker or self-employed person.[2] This is matched by regulation 5(2) of the 2006 Regulations.[3]

(b) **Incapacity** – Workers or self-employed persons who stop working as a result of permanent incapacity and who have either (i) resided continuously in the host Member State for more than two years;[4] or (ii) the incapacity is the result of an accident at work or an occupational disease that entitles him to a pension payable in full or in part by an institution in the host Member State.[5] The condition as to length of residence does not apply if the worker's or the self-employed person's spouse or civil partner is a national of the host Member State or has lost the nationality of that Member State by marriage to that worker or self-employed person.[6] This is matched by regulation 5(3) of the 2006 Regulations.[7]

(c) **Frontier workers** – Workers or self-employed persons who, after three years of continuous employment and residence in the host Member State, work in an employed or self-employed capacity in another Member State, while retaining their place of residence in the host Member State, to which they return, as a rule, each day or at least once a week.[8] This is matched by regulation 5(4) of the 2006 Regulations.[9]

(d) **Frontier workers** – Who do not qualify for permanent residence in the host state under (c) above, because they cannot satisfy the condition of three years' prior residence and employment in the host state, may qualify under (a) or (b) above by treating their employment in the other Member State as if it had taken place in the host Member State.[10] This is transposed by regulation 5(5) of the 2006 Regulations by reference to the UK (the host country) and another EEA country in a much clearer and understandable way than in the Directive.[11]

(e) **Family members** – Where workers and the self-employed acquire permanent residence in one of the above ways, their family members, irrespective of nationality, are entitled to the same thing.[12] Family members may also acquire the right of permanent residence, if the worker or self-employed person dies while still working but before acquiring permanent residence, but there are three conditions which must be fulfilled: either (i) the worker or self-employed person had resided continuously on the territory of that Member State for two years at the time of his or her death; (ii) the death resulted from an accident at work or an occupational disease; or (iii) the surviving spouse lost the nationality of that Member State following marriage to the worker or self-employed person.[13]

In calculating the period spent in employment, periods of involuntary unemployment, periods not worked for reasons not of the person's own making, and absences from work or cessation of work due to illness or accident are to be regarded as periods of employment.[14]

1 Directive 2004/38/EC, art 17(1)(a). If the law of the host Member State does not grant the right to an old age pension to certain categories of self-employed persons, the age condition shall be deemed to have been met once the person concerned has reached the age of 60.

2 Immigration (European Economic Area) Regulations 2006, SI 2006/1003.

3 Directive 2004/38/EC, art 17(2).

4 It is worth stressing that, under this limb, any applicant who goes off work due to illness/injury before having accrued two years of residence in accordance with the 2006 Regulations, will generally need to show that he/she was only *temporarily* incapacitated at least up until at least the two-year point, since temporary incapacity is the trigger for retention of worker status under Reg 6(2)(a). The failure of the First-tier Tribunal Judge to distinguish between temporary and permanent incapacity lead to the overturning of his decision to allow the appellant's appeal in *De Brito (Aurelio) v Secretary of State for the Home Department* [2012] EWCA Civ 709; [2012] 3 CMLR 538; [2013] INLR 1: see **6.95**, above, fn 4.

5 SI 2006/1003, art 17(1)(b). If such incapacity is the result of an accident at work or an occupational disease entitling the person concerned to a benefit payable in full or in part by an institution in the host Member State, no condition shall be imposed as to length of residence.

6 Directive 2004/38/EC, art 17(2).

7 SI 2006/1003, reg 5(3).

8 Directive 2004/38/EC, art 17(1).

9 SI 2006/1003.

10 Directive 2004/38/EC, art 17(1)(a). The Directive says that, for the purposes of entitlement to the rights referred to in points (a) and (b), periods of employment spent in the Member State in which the person concerned is working should be regarded as having been spent in the host Member State.

11 SI 2006/1003, reg 5(6).

12 Directive 2004/38/EC, art 17(3).

13 Directive 2004/38/EC, art 17(4).

14 Directive 2004/38/EC, art 17(1); SI 2006/1003, reg 5(7).

MEMBERS OF THE FAMILY

Overview of family groups under the Citizens' Directive

6.116 In addition to workers, the self-employed, the self-sufficient and those providing or receiving services, the right of free movement is also given to the spouse, civil partner and some other family members of such persons. This is principally done through the Citizens' Directive.[1] Although the exercise of family rights depends on the exercise of EU law rights by the principal EU family member, in content they are virtually the same as the principal's right to enter, reside in and remain in another EEA country.[2] They are given irrespective of the sex or nationality of the family members. Thus the Pakistani or American husband of a woman who is an EU national is entitled to accompany his wife when she exercises her right, for example, to set up in business, to seek work or to receive or provide services. The provisions in EU law relating to family members are designed to give effect to the free movement rights of the EU national, and are based upon the notion that obstacles to workers being joined by their families and integrated into the host State are obstacles to free movement within the EU.[3] The ECJ has stressed that the integration of EEA nationals and their family members into the host State is a fundamental objective required to ensure that workers and their families resident in a host State enjoy no disadvantage with respect to those who are nationals of the host State.[4] In Case C-308/89 *Di Leo v Land Berlin*[5] (a case involving the right to education for children of EU workers) the court stated:

'the aim of Regulation 1612/68, namely freedom of movement for workers, requires for such freedom to be guaranteed in compliance with the principles of liberty and dignity, the best possible conditions for the integration of the Community worker's family in the society of the host country.'

The ECJ has emphasised the need to give effect to fundamental rights and in particular the right to respect for family life protected by Article 8 of the European Convention on Human Rights:[6]

'Moreover, in accordance with the case-law of the Court, Regulation No 1612/68 must be interpreted in the light of the requirement of respect for family life laid down in Article 8 of the European Convention. That requirement is one of the fundamental rights which, according to settled case-law, are recognised by Community law.'

It is notable that the ECJ fully endorses the approach to Article 8 ECHR taken by the European Court of Human Rights in the case of *Boultif*,[7] and the application of Article 8 by the ECJ has been favourable to applicants.[8]

1   Council Directive 2004/38/EC, which has repealed Articles 10 and 11 of Council Regulation (EEC) 1612/68; Directive 72/194; art 1 of Council Directive (EEC) 73/148; Council Directives (EEC) 75/34 and 75/35; Council Directives (EEC) 90/364 and 90/365 and 93/96. For a full discussion of EC rights of family reunion, see Prof Steve Peers 'Family reunion in Community law', in Walker (ed) *Europe's Area of Freedom, Security and Justice* (2004) OUP.
2   Case 131/85 *Gül v Regierungspräsident Düsseldorf* [1986] ECR 1573, [1987] 1 CMLR 501, ECJ.
3   The recital of the third Preamble to Council Regulation (EEC) 1612/68 recognises that 'freedom of movement constitutes a fundamental right of workers and their families' and the fifth recital affirms that in order for the right to be exercised with freedom and dignity 'equality of treatment shall be secured in fact and in law'. In the Citizens' Directive 2004/38/EC, Recital (2) states that 'The free movement of persons constitutes one of the fundamental freedoms of the internal market'; Recital (5) that 'The right of all Union citizens to move and reside freely within the territory of the Member States should, if it is to be exercised under objective conditions of freedom and dignity, be also granted to their family members', including 'the registered partner if the legislation of the host Member State treats registered partnership as equivalent to marriage'; and Recital (20) that 'In accordance with the prohibition of discrimination on grounds of nationality, all Union citizens and their family members residing in a Member State on the basis of this Directive should enjoy, in that Member State, equal treatment with nationals in areas covered by the Treaty, subject to such specific provisions as are expressly provided for in the Treaty and secondary law.'
4   Case 249/86 *EC Commission v Germany* [1989] ECR 1263, paras 11–12; [1990] 3 CMLR 540; see also *Diatta (Aissatou) v Land Berlin*: 267/83[1985] ECR 567, [1986] 2 CMLR 164, ECJ, paras 14–18 and 20. In the context of pre-existing Association Agreements see Case C-351/95 *Kadiman v Freistaat Bayern* [1997] ECR I-2133, para 30.
5   [1990] ECR I-4185, para 13. See more recently Case C-459/99 *Mouvement contre le racisme, l'antisémitisme et la xénophobie (MRAX) ASBL v Belgium* [2002] ECR I-6591, [2003] 1 WLR 1073.
6   Case C-413/99 *Baumbast and R v Secretary of State for the Home Department* [2002] ECR I-7091, [2003] INLR 1, para 77.
7   *Boultif v Switzerland* (2001) 33 EHRR 1179, [2001] 2 FLR 1228.
8   Case C-60/00 *Carpenter (Mary) v Secretary of State for the Home Department* [2002] ECR I-6279, [2002] INLR 439.

Right of entry and residence of Family groups

6.117 Under the Citizens' Directive all Union citizens have the right to enter another Member State by virtue of having an identity card or valid passport. Family members, whether they have or do not have the nationality of a Member State, enjoy the same rights as the citizen who they have accompanied. There are three categories of family member. The first list consists of spouses and civil partners, and direct descendants under 21 or dependent (children and grandchildren etc) and dependent direct relatives in the ascending line (parents and grandparents etc) of the Union citizen.[1] They have a right of initial residence of three months, which can be extended; but only the spouse and children under 21 or dependent have a right of work, not parents or grandparents, as used to be the case under Article 11 of Regulation 1612/68. Article 10 of Regulation 492/2011 (ex Article 12 of 1612/68) allows the children of an EU national here to be admitted to that state's general educational, apprenticeship and vocational training courses under the same conditions as the nationals of that state, if such children are residing in its territory.

[1] Directive 2004/38/EC, art 2(2). This list is the same as under the old Article 10 of Regulation 1612/68 with the addition of civil partners.

6.118 The second list, referred to as 'other family members' in the Directive and as 'extended family members' in the 2006 Regulations,[1] is catered for in Article 3(2)(a) and (b) of the Directive. These are: (i) family members not falling under the definition in Article 2(2) (the first list) who, in the country from which they have come, are dependants or members of the household of the Union citizen having the primary right of residence; (ii) family members, who have serious health problems which strictly require the personal care of the Union citizen; and (iii) a partner, who is neither spouse nor civil partner, with whom the Union citizen has a durable relationship, duly attested. Under the Directive the host Member State shall facilitate their entry and residence 'in accordance with its own national legislation'.[2]

[1] Directive 2004/38/EC, art 3(2); Immigration (European Economic Area) Regulations 2006, SI 2006/1003, reg 8.
[2] Directive 2004/38/EC, art 3(2).

6.119 The third category arises after residence in the host Member State has occurred. They are referred in the 2006 Regulations as a 'Family Member who has retained a right of residence'.[1] Subject to certain conditions set out in the Directive, the death of the Union citizen, his or her departure from the host Member State, divorce, annulment of marriage or termination of partnership does not affect the right of these family members who are not nationals of a Member State to continue to reside in the Member State in question.[2] These include a widow or widower who has resided in the United Kingdom for at least a year in accordance with the 2006 Regulations and who can show that he or she was a worker, self-employed or self-sufficient or the family member of a person who was and a child of an Union citizen who has died or left the country and he or she is attending an educational course in the UK and continues to do so and the parent of such a child who has custody for him or her (ie *Baumbast*[3] cases). Those whose marriage or civil partnership to a qualified person is terminated but lasted at least three years may also have retained a right of residence if the other criteria in regulation 10(5) are met. These people can also acquire a permanent right of residence under regulation 15(1)(f). Family members, irrespective of their nationality, who acquire the right to reside will be entitled to engage in economic activity on an employed or self-employed basis.

1 The Immigration (European Economic Area) Regulations 2006, SI 2006/1003, reg 10.
2 or domestic violence in relation to EEA family members, see Council Directive 2004/38/EC (Citizens' Directive) art 13(2)(c).
3 *Baumbast and R v Secretary of State for the Home Department::* C-413/99 [2002] ECR I-7091, [2002] 3 CMLR 599, [2003] ICR 1347, ECJ.

6.120 Under the Directive no visa or equivalent formality may be imposed on Union citizens, including family members. Union citizens need an identity card or passport and non-national family members require a passport.[1] Non-national family members shall only be required to have a short-stay visa[2] or its national equivalent or a valid residence card, presumably one issued by any Member State.[3] Where the persons concerned do not have travel documents, the host Member State must afford them every facility in obtaining the requisite documents or having them sent or in otherwise proving their entitlement.[4] Family members of Union citizens who are union citizens need only apply for a registration certificate but may be required to produce certain documents.[5] Those who are not nationals of a Member State must apply for a residence card, which is valid for five years and remains so, despite temporary absences from the host Member State, as set out in the Directive.[6]

1 Directive 2004/38/EC, art 5(1).
2 Regulation 539/2001, in which neither the UK nor Ireland participated.
3 Directive 2004/38/EC, art 5(2).
4 Directive 2004/38/EC, art 5(4).
5 Directive 2004/38/EC, art 8(5).
6 Directive 2004/38/EC, arts 9, 10 and 11.

6.121 Union citizens acquire the right of permanent residence in the host Member State after a five-year period of uninterrupted legal residence, provided that an expulsion decision has not been enforced against them. This right of permanent residence is no longer subject to any conditions.[1] The same rule applies to family members who are not nationals of a Member State and who have legally resided with a Union citizen for a continuous period of five years.[2] Subject to decisions on grounds of public policy, public security and public health, the right of permanent residence is lost only in the event of more than two successive years' absence from the host Member State.[3] The Directive also recognises, in certain circumstances, the right of permanent residence for Union citizens who are workers or self-employed persons and for family members before the five-year period of continuous residence has expired, subject to certain conditions being met,[4] and a right of permanent residence for non-national family Members who have retained a right of residence.[5] For further details regarding permanent residence, see **6.159–6.160** below.

1 Directive 2004/38/EC, art 16(1).
2 Directive 2004/38/EC, art 16(2).
3 Directive 2004/38/EC, art 16(3).
4 Directive 2004/38/EC, art 17.
5 Directive 2004/38/EC, art 18.

Third country national family members

6.122 The provisions relating to the entry and residence of family members and the formalities to be gone through are transposed into the 2006 Regulations, following very closely the requirements of the Directive. Under regulation 11(1) of the 2006 Regulations, EEA nationals have an initial right of admission to the UK on production of a valid national identity card or passport and do not need to produce any other documentation. If they are extended family members, their credentials will be examined for the first time when they apply for a registration certificate and regulation 16(5) and (6) gives immigration officials their first opportunity to conduct an extensive examination of their personal circumstances and to issue a certificate. This provision is clearly drafted with Article 3(2) of the Directive in mind, whose wording is consistent with the task of determining whether someone is within the extended family category being a matter for determination of each Member State's domestic administration.

6.123 Non-EEA national family members coming to the UK and/or the EEA for the first time are admitted under regulation 11(2) if they have a valid passport and an EEA family permit reflecting a right to reside under the 2006 Regulations, or a residence card Family permits are issued under regulation 12 and are issued to family members where the EEA national is already residing here in accordance with the 2006 Regulations or will be doing so within six months, and the family member will be accompanying the EEA national or joining them here. For extended family members, the requirements are the same, save that the entry clearance officer must be satisfied in all the circumstances that it is appropriate to issue the family permit (Regulation 12(2)). The original version of Regulation 12(1)(b) sought to impose a condition of prior lawful residence in the EEA on non-national family members. However, in the case of *Metock*[1] the ECJ held that such an approach was unlawful, and the 2006 Regulations were fully amended to reflect this by 8 November 2012, over four years later.[2]

---

[1] *Metock v Minister for Justice, Equality and Law Reform Case* C-127/08, [2009] QB 318, [2008] ECR I-6241, ECJ. Regulation 12(1) as then framed was clearly unlawful and was amended on 2 June 2011 by Immigration (European Economic Area) (Amendment) Regulations, 2011/1247, reg 2(4).

[2] See Immigration (European Economic Area) (Amendment) Regulations, 2011/1247, reg 2(3) (2 June 2011); Immigration (European Economic Area) (Amendment) Regulations 2012/1547, Sch 1, para 5(c) (16 July 2012): insertion has effect subject to transitional provisions specified in SI 2012/1547, Sch 3); and Immigration (European Economic Area) (Amendment) (No 2) Regulations, 2012/2560, Sch 1, para 1 (November 8, 2012). (See the eighth edition of this work at 6.97-6.97D for a discussion of the issues surrounding the lawfulness of the previous approach of the 2006 Regulations to family members and other family members.)

The ambit of Citizens Directive

6.124 The Citizens' Directive marks out a clear demarcation line between the competence of EU law and that of the domestic law of the Member States. First, the Preamble to the Directive sets out the principles. Paragraph 5 says: 'The right of all Union citizens to move and reside freely within the territory of the Member States should, if it is to be exercised under objective conditions of freedom and dignity, be also granted to their family members, irrespective of nationality.' Secondly, the substantive provisions of the Directive are clear: Article 2 defines who in EU law qualify as members of a Union citizen's family; and Article 3 states that it is their right to enter and reside with the union citizen who is exercising his or her free movement rights. Article 9 addresses the administrative formalities for family members who are not nationals of a Member State. The creation of EU law rights is set within a larger framework of EU competence than the mere reach of the Citizens' Directive. We have already highlighted the *Surinder Singh* situation[1] at 6.73 and shown that EU law goes much wider than the Directive as in the case of *Carpenter*,[2] where a UK national was held to be exercising treaty rights by providing services in other EU Member States while retaining his UK residence, as well as *Zambrano*, see above at 6.77. Not all Union citizens can have their family reunion rights adjudicated by EU law. There needs to be an EU law element to the case which brings it within the competence of Union law, such as an exercise of free movement rights by moving from the territory of one Member State to that of another. Once the EU element is established, EU law, not domestic law, applies. It is a clear boundary, not a very satisfactory one in view of the added importance of Union citizenship, but clear enough and well established enough in the case law.

[1]   *R v Immigration Appeal Tribunal and Surinder Singh, ex p Secretary of State for the Home Department*: C-370/90 [1992] 3 All ER 798, [1992] ECR I-4265, [1992] 3 CMLR 358, ECJ.
[2]   *Carpenter (Mary) v Secretary of State for the Home Department*: C-60/00 [2003] QB 416, [2003] All ER (EC) 577.

SPOUSES AND CIVIL PARTNERS

6.125 Currently, a spouse means a person who is formally contracted in a legal marriage.[1] The legality or validity of a marriage is important. Issues of validity can be quite complicated involving questions of public international law. We deal with these in CHAPTER 11. However, in most cases they are quite straightforward. The production of a marriage certificate issued by a competent authority will, according to the Upper Tribunal, usually be sufficient to prove that the marriage was contracted; that is, the certificate must have been issued according to the registration laws of the country where the marriage took place, and issued by an authority with legal power to create or confirm the facts it attests.[2] Where there is no marriage certificate, the marital relationship may be proved by other evidence such as evidence that the marriage was contracted between the applicant and the qualified person according to the national law of the EEA country of the qualified person's nationality/the country where the marriage took place, showing proper respect for the qualified person's rights under the Treaties.[3]

[1]   Case 59/85 *Netherlands v Reed* [1986] ECR 1283; Compare Case T-65/92 *Arauxo-Dumay v EC Commission* [1993] ECR II-597. See *R v Secretary of State for the Home Department, ex p Lopez (Moreno)* [1997] Imm AR 11, QBD.
[2]   *Kareem (Proxy marriages – EU law)* [2014] UKUT 00024 (IAC).
[3]   *Kareem*, op cit, in which the UT stated, 'Mere production of legal materials from the EEA country or country where the marriage took place will be insufficient evidence because they will rarely show how such law is understood or applied in those countries. Mere assertions as to the effect of such laws will, for similar reasons, carry no weight'. See *also NA (Customary marriage and divorce – evidence) Ghana* [2009] UKAIT 00009.

6.126 In CHAPTER 11 we deal with civil partners in UK domestic immigration and family law. Now the Citizens' Directive has for the first time extended EU law to include civil partners as family members. In Article 2(2)(b) a family member now includes:

> 'the partner with whom the Union citizen has contracted a registered partnership, on the basis of the legislation of a Member State, if the legislation of the host Member State treats registered partnerships as equivalent to marriage and in accordance with the conditions laid down in the relevant legislation of the host Member State.'

If a civil partner subsequently wants to rely on the dissolution of that civil partnership for the purposes of regulation 10(5) of the 2006 Regulations he or she must provide evidence of the formal termination of that civil partnership, not merely the de facto determination.[1] Provision is also made for partners who are unmarried or who are not civil partners but are in durable relationships in Article 3(2)(b), implemented in the 2006 Regulations by regulations 7(1)(a) and 8(5). A civil partner does not include a partner to a civil partnership of convenience.[2]

[1] *WW (EEA Regulations – civil partnership) Thailand* [2009] UKAIT 00014.
[2] Immigration (European Economic Area) Regulations 2006, SI 2006/1003, reg 2(1). See the discussion in the previous paragraph.

Marriages and partnerships of convenience

6.127 The 2000 Regulations did not give any definition, except to exclude 'a party to a marriage of convenience'.[1] At the time this was a controversial limitation the effect of which has never been authoritatively decided.[2] The EC Regulation and Directives referred simply to 'spouse'. Community law did not permit an examination into how the couple met or why they married. The right of residence was to be acknowledged by the host State on production of the documents identified by Community legislation.[3] The furthest the ECJ had gone in this regard was to note that fraudulent conduct or use of Community law to evade national provisions was not permitted.[4] The issue of marriages of convenience has now been largely resolved by the coming into force of the Citizens' Directive and its categorisation of them as an abuse of rights. Under the heading of 'Abuse of rights' Article 35 of the Citizens' Directive provides that Member States may adopt the necessary measures to refuse, terminate or withdraw any right conferred by the Directive in the case of abuse of rights or fraud, such as marriages of convenience. The Article then adds that any such measure must be proportionate and subject to the procedural safeguards provided for in Articles 30 and 31. Thus the right to exclude 'a party to a marriage of convenience' is given, but its exercise is subject to the key procedural safeguards of the replaced Council Directive 64/222 and must be a proportionate exercise of national power. Treating a marriage of convenience as a purely definitional question, as the wording and layout of the 2006 Regulations suggest,[5] is not enough.

[1] SI 2000/2326, reg 2(1). See CHAPTER 11 below.
[2] A Council Resolution on marriages of convenience makes a broad statement of policy against such arrangements and a commitment by Member States to combat their use to obtain admission and residence, but is expressly stated to be 'without prejudice to Community law'.

³   The Member State may only require from the spouse the document on which he or she entered the territory and a document issued by a competent authority proving the relationship. See eg Council Directive (EEC) 68/360, art 4(3).

⁴   Case C-370/90 R v Immigration Appeal Tribunal and Surinder Singh, ex p Secretary of State for the Home Department [1992] Imm AR 565 at 569-570; [1992] ECR I-4265, ECJ, at para 24. This was more recently confirmed in Secretary of State for the Home Department v Akrich, Case C-109/01 [2004] QB 756, [2004] INLR 36, where the ECJ stated that there would be an abuse if Community law were invoked in the context of marriages of convenience entered into in order to circumvent national immigration laws (see para 57).

⁵   Immigration (European Economic Area) Regulations 2006, SI 2006/1003, reg 2(1).

6.128 In *Papajorgji (EEA spouse – marriage of convenience) Greece* [2012] UKUT 00038(IAC) the claimant was an Albanian national born in 1970, who married a Greek national, Mr Papajorgji in 1996 in Greece. In July 2010 she applied to the British consular authorities in Athens for a document enabling her to accompany her husband on a visit to the UK for a few weeks. She downloaded from the appropriate website and completed the 115 questions in the entry clearance application form and submitted her marriage certificate, her passport and evidence confirming that her husband was both a Greek national and intending to accompany her on the visit. Her application was refused on the basis that this was a marriage of convenience because apart from her Greek marriage certificate and a copy of her husband's Greek passport she had not provided any documentary evidence of their marriage, such as photographs of their wedding or their life together or agreements in joint names such as a bank account or a tenancy agreement. She appealed and eventually her case came before the Upper Tribunal.

The appeal turned on the question of burden of proof. Blake J held that (i) there was no burden on an applicant in an EU case until the respondent raised the issue by evidence; (ii) If there was such evidence it was for the applicant to produce evidence to address the suspicions.¹ As far as evidence went the Tribunal agreed that the claimant must establish that she is a family member; but in the ordinary case she does this by producing the basic documents set out in the Directive. Where there is no reason to suspect that the claim is fraudulent, or the marriage one of convenience, that is conclusive of the matter. Regulation 12 of the Immigration (EEA) Regulations 2006 does not in terms require the claimant to prove a negative. She must prove that she is married, but that marriage will not avail if it turns out to be one of convenience. The Judge described the process as one of an evidential burden in the first place on the respondent and then a shift to the claimant in the light of the relevant information, rather than a formal legal burden. He concluded that in the Tribunal's judgment this case from first to last never had any appearance remotely suggesting that the marriage was one of convenience. The decision was flawed and not in accordance with the law.

This was a very clear case where there was no evidence at all to give grounds for suspicion. But there is still a problem. According to EU case law the burden of proof lies on the authorities of the Member States seeking to restrict rights under the Directive.² According to the Commission's Guidance on the Citizens Directive on abuse and fraud,³ the authorities must be able to build a convincing case while respecting all the material safeguards described in the previous section. On appeal, it is for the national courts to verify the existence of abuse in individual cases, evidence of which must be adduced in accordance with the rules of national law, provided that the effectiveness of Community law is not thereby undermined. *Papajorgji* must, therefore, be read as deciding that the legal burden of proof is on the State, but where there is evidence of suspicion the spouse must at least produce the basic documents, such as the marriage certificate. The position, however, is not completely clear. The UT has recently held that appellants are entitled to know the case against them, and are generally entitled to disclosure of documentation generated by the Home Office interviewer of a party to a suspected marriage of convenience: *Miah (interviewer's comments disclosure: fairness)* [2014] UKUT 00515 (IAC).

¹ See further *IS (marriages of convenience) Serbia* [2008] UKAIT 00031 where the AIT concluded that where there is a dispute on the issue the burden of proving that the claimant was a family member under the Immigration (EEA) Regulations and not a party to a marriage of convenience fell on her. In *TC (Kenya) v Secretary of State for the Home Department* [2008] EWCA Civ 543, 17 April 2008 the Court of Appeal affirmed that a marriage of convenience is an abuse of rights within the meaning of EU law and that meant that not every one of the factors set out in Article 28 of the Citizens Directive such as length of residence is relevant in the assessment of whether the claimant is a party to a marriage of convenience.

² Cases C-110/99 *Emsland-Stärke* (para 54) and C-215/03 *Oulane* (para 56).

³ 2 June 2009 COM (2009) 313 Final. See now the Commission's up-to-date *Handbook on addressing the issue of alleged marriages of convenience between EU citizens and non-EU nationals in the context of EU law on free movement of EU citizens*, dated 26 September 2014. The *Handbook* is not legally binding.

6.129 In our opinion, it is inappropriate for national legislation to qualify EU law rights by giving a restrictive definition of spouse when there is no definition of 'marriage of convenience' in the EU directives or regulations, when opinions differ as to the meaning of this phrase and when the proper approach must be through the public policy derogation. In correspondence arising from the parliamentary debate in respect of the Immigration (European Economic Area) Order 1994,¹ the minister offered the following definition:

> 'A marriage of convenience is regarded as a sham marriage which is entered into solely for immigration purposes where the partners have no intention of living with the other as man and wife in a settled and genuine relationship.'²

The implication that cohabitation is necessary to avoid a finding of a marriage of convenience is at odds with EU law, which does not require a couple to live under the same roof, so that a genuine relationship as man and wife can exist irrespective of cohabitation.³ The ECJ's judgment in *Akrich*, suggests that a marriage of convenience is one which is entered into solely for the purpose of circumventing immigration control.⁴ Recital 28 of the Citizen's Directive defines marriages of convenience for the purposes of the Directive as marriages contracted for the sole purpose of enjoying the right of free movement and residence under the Directive that someone would not have otherwise. This is consistent with the public policy approach set out in Article 35 of that Directive. This interpretation was also adopted in the case of *TC (Kenya) v Secretary of State for the Home Department*.⁵ In *Papajorji*, as we have seen, the Upper Tribunal stressed that there is no burden at the outset of an application on a claimant to demonstrate that a marriage to an EEA national is not one of convenience,⁶ but there is an evidential burden on the claimant to address evidence justifying reasonable suspicion that the marriage is entered into for the sole purpose of securing residence rights.⁷ Guidance of the European Commission issued in respect of the Citizens' Directive ((COM) 2009 313) 2 July 2009 is explicit in placing the burden of proof on the State and sets out suggested indicative criteria for and against the proposition that the marriage is one of convenience. The applicable Home Office guidance documents are the *European Operational Policy Team: guidance on suspected marriages/civil partnerships of convenience*, of 12 September 2012 (15/2012) and *European Operational Policy Team: interim guidance on non-compliance in relation to marriage interview*, of 11 February 2013 (02/2013).[8] Note that, under Regulation 21B of the 2006 EEA Regulations, the Secretary of State 'may take' an EEA decision on the grounds of abuse of rights 'where there are reasonable grounds to suspect the abuse of a right to reside and it is proportionate to do so'.[9] In the context of alleged marriages of convenience, it would clearly not be proportionate to take such a decision where the Secretary of State had reasonable grounds, but could not prove with cogent reasons, that the marriage was in fact one of convenience.[10]

1   SI 1994/1895.
2   Lord Annaly to Lord McIntosh, 24 May 1994. This test is stricter than the definition under the previous Immigration Rules (see *R v Immigration Appeal Tribunal, ex p Khan (Mahmud)* [1983] QB 790, [1982] Imm AR 134).
3   See *Diatta (Aissatou) v Land Berlin*: 267/83 [1985] ECR 567, [1986] 2 CMLR 164, ECJ. See further cases supporting the *Diatta* position as regards Directive 2003/38/EC: *PM (EEA - spouse - 'residing with') Turkey* [2011] UKUT 89 (IAC) (7 March 2011), *Samsam (EEA: revocation and retained rights) Syria* [2011] UKUT 165 (IAC) (13 April 2011) and *Amos v Secretary of State for the Home Department* [2011] EWCA Civ 552, [2011] 1 WLR 2952 (12 May 2011).
4   Case C-109/01 *Secretary of State for the Home Department v Akrich* [2004] QB 756, [2004] INLR 36 ECJ, at paras 57 and 61.
5   [2008] EWCA Civ 543, [2008] Imm AR 645.
6   *Papajorgji (EEA spouse – marriage of convenience) Greece* [2012] UKUT 00038 (IAC).
7   *IS (marriages of convenience) Serbia* [2008] UKAIT 00031.
8   The Home Office documents should be read with the detailed analysis thereof in the *ILPA European Update*, September 2013.
9   Added by Immigration (European Economic Area) (Amendment) (No 2) Regulations, 2013/3032, Sch 1, para 18 (January 1, 2014: insertion has effect subject to transitional provisions as specified in SI 2013/3032, Sch 3, para 3).
10 See *Papajorgji* at [38].

Cohabitating couples

6.130 In *Reed v Netherlands*[1] the ECJ ruled that cohabiting but unmarried heterosexual couples could not be included in the definition of spouse. The court acknowledged the need to give a purposive approach to Community legislation, but decided that it could not yet give such a broad interpretation, in the absence of evidence of a clear consensus within the Member States of the Community, to treat common law relationships on the same basis as marriage.[2] In *Reed* it was not argued that an unmarried partner may qualify under the broader provisions of Article 10(2) of Council Regulation (EEC) 1612/68, which refers to 'any other family member'. Instead, the court ruled that since the Netherlands allowed cohabiting partners of Dutch nationals to obtain residence in the country on the basis of the relationship, it violated the principles of non-discrimination to refuse to extend the same benefit to the unmarried partners of EU nationals. The presence of such a partner was recognised as a 'social advantage' for the purposes of the non-discrimination provision of Article 7 of regulation 1612/68.[3] The non-discrimination principle can found a right of residence.[4] Although the Commission hinted in a Communication that the ECJ had not had to rule on the question of cohabiting couples recently, in a 1999 staff case, the Court of First Instance found that cohabiting couples could not be treated as spouses.[5]

1 Case 59/85 *Netherlands v Reed* [1986] ECR 1283, [1987] 2 CMLR 448, ECJ.
2 Two decades later this conclusion should, we suggest, be revisited, given the social developments and increased recognition afforded to cohabiting relationships within the Union.
3 Article 7 of Council Regulation (EEC) 1612/68 (now Article 7 of Regulation 492/2011) prohibits discrimination on the grounds of nationality in respect of the conditions of employment and work (Arts 7(1) and (4)), and provides for equality of treatment in respect of social and tax advantages (Art 7(2)), and in the conditions for access to training in vocational schools and retraining centres (Art 7(3)).
4 See Case C-237/91 *Kus v Landeshauptstadt Wiesbaden* [1992] ECR I-6781, para 28, where the ECJ recognised, in the context of the Turkish Association Agreement, that the right of residence must necessarily be implied to give effect to the non-discrimination provisions.
5 Case T-264/97 *D v Council of the European Union* (28 January 1999, unreported), CFI.

6.131 The Citizen's Directive recognises civil partnerships and gives limited recognition to cohabiting couples. Under Article 3(2)(b) the host member State shall, in accordance with its national legislation, facilitate entry and residence of the partner with whom the Union citizen has a durable relationship, duly attested. Since UK immigration law recognises cohabitation of heterosexual or same sex couples, entry and stay in the UK will take into account the current Immigration Rules (HC 395, Appendix FM (and formerly paragraphs 295D–295L)). The provisions of the Directive are transposed into domestic law under Regulations 8, 11 and 12 of the 2006 Regulations, which provide for entry as an extended family member as the partner of an EEA national (other than a civil partner) who can prove to the decision maker that he or she is in a durable relationship with the EEA national. Home Office guidance (*European Casework Instructions*) specify a range of requirements that are 'normally' to be satisfied, including a period of two years cohabitation in a relationship akin to marriage which has subsisted for at least two years, and an intention to live together permanently, although 'each case must be considered on its merits' and accepts that a durable relationship may exist notwithstanding that the specified factors are not satisfied.[1]

1 *YB (EEA reg 17(4) – proper approach) Ivory Coast* [2008] UKAIT 00062 and *Rose (Automatic deportation – Exception 3) Jamaica* [2011] UKUT 276 (IAC) (at para 24). See also *Dauhoo (EEA Regulations – reg 8(2))* [2012] UKUT 79 (IAC).

Retained rights (i): divorce/termination

6.132 Until the Citizens' Directive the spouse's and civil partner's right of residence was generally dependent on that of the principal, as indeed was that of children.[1] Thus where the worker left the territory permanently, derived rights would generally cease.[2] This will still be the position in the case of a non-EEA national spouse or partner[3] if the relationship breaks up before the couple have lived together for the requisite period of time required by the Directive (usually one year, but it may be less in cases of domestic violence). Now, however, there is a measure of protection under the Directive. In this paragraph we deal with the consequences divorce,[4] annulment and termination of a registered partnership; and in the next section we deal with the death and departure of the principal. First, divorce, annulment of the Union citizen's marriage or termination of his/her registered partnership does not affect the right of residence of his or her family members who are nationals of a Member State. But to acquire the right of permanent residence, the persons concerned must meet the following conditions:

(a)   are workers or self-employed persons in the host Member State;

(b)   are self-sufficient persons, who have sufficient resources not to become a burden on the social assistance system of the host Member State during their period of residence and have comprehensive sickness insurance cover; or

(c)   are genuine students having comprehensive sickness insurance cover in the host Member State and sufficient resources for themselves and their family members not to become a burden on the social assistance system of the host Member State during their period of residence; or

(d)   are family members accompanying or joining a Union citizen who satisfies the conditions referred to in points (a), (b) or (c).[5]

The position of non-EEA nationals is different. They will not lose their residence rights where:

(a)   prior to initiation of the break up of their relationship, by the initiation of divorce, annulment or termination proceedings, the marriage or registered partnership has lasted at least three years, including one year in the host Member State[6] or

(b)   by mutual agreement or by court order, the spouse or partner who is not a national of a Member State has custody of the Union citizen's children; or

(c)   this is warranted by particularly difficult circumstances, such as having been a victim of domestic violence while the marriage or registered partnership was subsisting; or

(d)   by mutual agreement[7] or by court order, the spouse or partner who is not a national of a Member State has the right of access to a minor child, provided that the court has ruled that such access must be in the host Member State, and for as long as is required.[8]

The 2006 Regulations seek to transpose Article 13 of the Citizens' Directive at Regulation 10(5), which requires, in addition to four alternative criteria just set out, that (a) the non-EEA national ceases to be a family member of a qualified person/EEA national with permanent residence upon divorce/termination; (b) the non-EEA national was residing in the UK in accordance with the 2006 Regulations at the date of termination; and (c) the non-EEA national is working, self-employed, self-sufficient or is a family member of an EEA national who is a qualified person on those grounds. In *Amos*,[9] two non-EEA spouses were seeking to remain in the UK following their divorces. Both had separated before the actual divorces. The Court of Appeal detailed the requirements to qualify for a retained right of residence in these circumstances:

•   The court was prepared to assume without deciding that separation short of divorce does not affect the right of the non-national spouse under Article 16 of the Directive if both the EEA national and his or her non-national spouse continue to reside in the same Member State (at [24]). So the effect of the 1985 case of *Diatta*[10] carries over from Regulation 1612/68 to the Citizens Directive, notwithstanding the difference in the wording as between the Regulation and the Directive.

- Secondly, it is only if a spouse and other family members of the EEA national have acquired a right of residence that the question of its retention arises. So a divorced spouse must establish that he or she has the right of residence under Article 6(2) (right of initial three months' residence) or Article 7(2) (right of residence for more than three months) of the Citizens Directive 2004/38 before the question can be determined whether, notwithstanding the divorce, it has been retained by virtue of Article 13 (at [20]).

- Thirdly, if, immediately before divorce, the requirements of Article 7.2 are satisfied, the non-national must then satisfy the requirements of Article 13.2 (at [26]). These are that the marriage or registered partnership has lasted at least three years, including one year in the host Member State.

- Fourthly, to acquire the right of permanent residence, the persons concerned must be able to show throughout a continuous period of five years that they are workers, self-employed persons or self-sufficient, as required by Articles 13.2 and 18 of the Directive.

Note that the criterion in Regulation 10(5)(b), legal residence at the time of divorce/termination, is arguably contrary to Article 13(2) of the Citizens Directive and the question of its lawfulness was referred to the CJEU by the Court of Appeal in *Ahmed v SSHD* on 17 July 2014.[11]

---

1 Cohabitation under the same roof is not necessary. See *Diatta (Aissatou) v Land Berlin*: 267/83 [1985] ECR 567, [1986] 2 CMLR 164, ECJ and the discussion there of family membership. See further cases supporting the *Diatta* position as regards Directive 2003/38/EC: *PM (EEA – spouse – 'residing with') Turkey* [2011] UKUT 89 (IAC) (7 March 2011); *Samsam (EEA: revocation and retained rights) Syria* [2011] UKUT 165 (IAC) (13 April 2011) and *Amos v Secretary of State for the Home Department* [2011] EWCA Civ 552, [2011] 1 WLR 2952 (12 May 2011).

2 In *R v Secretary of State for the Home Department, ex p Sandhu (Amarjit Singh)* [1983] 3 CMLR 131, CA, the couple separated and the applicant's EEC spouse had gone back to Germany. The Court of Appeal in England held that the applicant was no longer within EEC protection and his residence in the UK could, therefore, be curtailed. The House of Lords dismissed an appeal, concluding that the decision in *Diatta* rendered the question *acte claire*. See (1985) Times, 10 May. In *R v Secretary of State for the Home Department, ex p Botta* [1987] 2 CMLR 189, QBD a deportation order was made against the EEC wife of a non-EEC alien, and the English court held that he lost his EEC right of residence as from that moment.

3 See *TB (EEA national: leave to remain?) Nigeria* [2007] UKAIT 00020 (7 February 2007) (the grant of a right of residence to the spouse of an EEA national is dependent on that spouse's relationship with the EEA national – once that relationship terminates then, subject to regulation 10 of the Immigration (European Economic Area) Regulations 2006, SI 2006/1003, that person's right of residence also ceases because he or she then ceases to be the spouse of a qualified person); *DA (EEA, revocation of residence document) Algeria* [2006] UKAIT 00027 (9 March 2006) (if the rights conferred on a worker are no longer being exercised because the worker has left the host state (and, indeed, left the Community), there is nothing inconsistent with Community legislation in bringing to an end the derivative rights of the worker's family member at that point).

4 See *NA (Customary marriage and divorce – evidence) Ghana* [2009] UKAIT 00009: where a partner is relying on a customary marriage and divorce and registration of the dissolution of a customary marriage is not mandatory in the country of origin, a partner does not have to produce proof of registration of a divorce but can rely on alternative evidence, such as a statutory declaration or affidavit from a family member or other person able to confirm the dissolution.

5 Council Directive 2004/38/EC, art 13(1).

6 Reg 10(5) of the 2006 Regulations; *OA (EEA – retained right of residence) Nigeria* [2010] UKAIT 00003: if the couple are separated but not divorced no right of retention arises but a separated spouse can acquire a permanent right of residence under reg 15(1)(b) of the 2006

Regulations if he or she has previously resided in the UK with his or her EEA national spouse for a continuous period of five years in accordance with these Regulations.

7 Note that the 'mutual agreement' limb is not present in Reg 10(5)(d)(iii) of the 2006 Regulations, which means that those precluded from benefiting from a retained right for that reason will need to rely directly on Article 13(2)(d) of the Citizens' Directive if no court order is present.

8 Council Directive 2004/38/EC, art 13(2). art 10(5) – see the criteria in (d). Such family members shall retain their right of residence exclusively on a personal basis. Note the amendments to the 2006 Regulations on this point: Immigration (European Economic Area) (Amendment) Regulations 2012/1547 Sch 1 para 3(c) (July 16, 2012: substitution has effect subject to transitional provisions specified in SI 2012/1547, Sch 3) which add 'EEA national with permanent residence' as an alternative to 'qualified person'.

9 *Amos and Another v Secretary of State for the Home Department* [2011] EWCA Civ 552, [2011] 1 WLR 2952 (12 May 2011).

10 Case 267/83 *Diatta v Land Berlin* [1985] ECR 567.

11 *NA (Pakistan) v Secretary of State for the Home Department* [2014] EWCA Civ 995, which was an appeal by Ms Ahmed from *Ahmed (Amos; Zambrano; reg 15A(3)(c), 2006 EEA Regs)* [2013] UKUT 00089 (IAC) on the dismissal of her appeal on the basis that her ex-husband, a German national, was not living in the UK at the time of the divorce. The UT had relied on *Amos v Secretary of State for the Home Department* [2011] EWCA Civ 552; [2011] 1 WLR 2952 and *Diatta (Aissatou) v Land Berlin:* 267/83 [1986] 2 CMLR 164, [2011] Imm AR 855.

6.133 Where an applicant is unsuccessful under Regulation 10(5) of the 2006 Regulations/Article 13 of the Citizens' Directive, it may still be possible to assert a right of residence if the applicant is the primary carer of the son or daughter of an EEA national worker, on the basis of Article 10 of Regulation 492/2011 (ex Article 12 of Regulation 1612/68),[1] or as a British or other EEA national child under Regulation 15A(2) or (4A) of the 2006 EEA Regulations or as a British or other EEA national child.[2] The situation for couples, who may be separated, divorced or terminated, who still have the task of looking after dependent children or grandchildren has been transformed since the case of *Baumbast and R,*[3] where the ECJ considered the rights of a third country national divorcée and of a third country national whose spouse was working outside the EU. In both cases, their dependent children were resident and being educated in the UK. The ECJ decided that the children, who were the children of an EU national formerly working in the UK, had acquired the right to enter general education and thereby the right to remain for the duration of their studies in the UK through Regulation 12 of Regulation 1612/68 (now Article 10 of Regulation 492/2011). Their mother, who was their primary carer with no other right to remain in the UK, was said to facilitate the exercise of their Community law rights. If unable to remain with her children, this would constitute a breach of Community law having regard to Article 8 of the ECHR. In *Chen*[4] the process was taken further. Here the only family member with EU citizenship was the couple's small child who was born in Ireland and became an Irish national. The mother was the primary carer and funds were provided from the profits of a business in China run by the father. So when the child moved with her mother to the UK she could be treated as a self-sufficient person,[5] who acquired the right to reside in the UK under Article 18(1) EC (para 41). The court held that the mother could not qualify as a family member of her daughter, because she was not dependent on her (paras 43–44), but acquired a derivative right of residence, because it was clear that enjoyment by a young child of a right of residence necessarily implies that the child is entitled to be accompanied by the person who is his or her primary carer and accordingly that the carer must be in a position to reside with the child in the host Member State for the duration of such residence (para 45).[6] Before acquiring the right of permanent residence, non-EEA nationals must be able to show that they are workers or self-employed persons or that they are self-sufficient persons,[7] who have sufficient resources[8] and comprehensive sickness insurance, or that they are members of the family, already constituted in the host Member State, of a person satisfying these requirements.[9] Those relying on derived rights of residence under Regulation 12 of Regulation 1612/68 and its successor or under Regulation 15A of the 2006 Regulations or *Zambrano*, cannot accrue a right of permanent residence.[10]

[1] This was the basis on which Ms Ahmed herself succeeded in *Ahmed (Amos; Zambrano; reg 15A(3)(c), 2006 EEA Regs)* [2013] UKUT 00089 (IAC), which was not appealed to the Court of Appeal by the SSHD (see **6.85** above, fn 2 and fn 8).

[2] See above at **6.85** in relation to Reg 15A, from **6.77** in relation to *Zambrano* et seq, and below from **6.136** in relation to art 10 of Regulation 492/2011 and its predecessor, reg 12 of Regulation 1612/68.

[3] Case C-413/99 *Baumbast and R v Secretary of State for the Home Department* [2003] INLR 1.

[4] Case C-200/02 *Chen and Zhu v Secretary of State for the Home Department*, [2005] QB 325.

[5] Within the meaning of art 1 of Council Directive 90/364/EEC, which is now defined in reg 4(1)(c) of SI 2006/1003.

[6] See, *mutatis mutandis*, in relation to art 12 of Regulation No 1612/68, *Baumbast and R*, paragraphs 71 to 75. However it should be noted that in *Baumbast* there was no need for prior self-sufficiency, because this was not necessary under art 12. In a host of subsequent cases in the UK courts and Tribunal, the lack of prior funds has been a fatal stumbling block. See *KY (China) v Secretary of State for the Home Department* [2006] EWCA Civ 1494 (17 November 2006); *Ali (Zacharia) v Secretary of State for the Home Department* [2006] EWCA Civ 484; *R (on the application of Catal) v Secretary of State for the Home Department* [2006] EWHC 1882 (Admin); *GM and AM (EU national; establishing self-sufficiency) France* [2006] UKAIT 00059, [2007] Imm AR 18.

[7] SI 2006/1003, reg 4(1)(c).

[8] 'Sufficient resources' shall be as defined in art 8(4); Council Directive 2004/38/EC, art 13(2).

[9] See reg 10(6) of the 2006 Regulations.

[10] Eg *Bee and another (permanent/derived rights of residence)* [2013] UKUT 00083 (IAC); *Alarape* CJEU.

Retained rights (ii) death and departure

6.134 Special provision is made in the case of the death or departure of the EEA national with the primary right. If the principal dies or departs from the host Member State, this does not affect the right of residence of her or her family members who are nationals of a Member State, but if they have not obtained permanent residence they can only do so if they meet the following conditions:

(a)   are workers or self-employed persons in the host Member State;

(b)   are self sufficient persons, who have sufficient resources not to become a burden on the social assistance system of the host Member State during their period of residence and have comprehensive sickness insurance cover; or

(c)   are genuine students having comprehensive sickness insurance cover in the host Member State and sufficient resources for themselves and their family members not to become a burden on the social assistance system of the host Member State during their period of residence; or

(d)   are family members accompanying or joining a Union citizen who satisfies the conditions referred to in points (a), (b) or (c).[1]

For family members who are not EEA nationals the position is slightly different. Where the principal dies, the family's right of residence is not affected if they have been residing in the host Member State as family members for at least one year before the Union citizen's death[2] and satisfy the conditions (as if they were EEA nationals) at (a), (b) and (d) above. The student option at (c) above is not available to them.[3] Then there is an echo of *Baumbast*. In Article 12(3) it is provided that in the event of the departure or death of the principal EEA national, there will be no loss of the right of residence of his or her children or of the parent who has actual custody of the children, irrespective of nationality, if the children reside in the host Member State and are enrolled at an educational establishment, for the purpose of studying there, until the completion of their studies.[4] These provisions of the Directive are transposed into domestic law, albeit in a different format, in the 2006 Regulations at regulation 10. In *Okafor*[5] the principal EEA national died leaving children still at school. It was common ground that, before her death in 2007, the mother of the children had not fulfilled any of the conditions in Article 7(1) but the evidence established that both children were at school. This meant that under Article 12(3) of the Directive the children and their father (as the person with custody after the death of the mother) were entitled to retain the right of residence until the completion of the childrens' studies. So they had a retained right of residence under Article 12(3) of the Directive. But the father wanted to go further. He argued that Article 12(3), standing on its own, also provided a route to permanent residence. The court held that it could not do so. Article 12(3) cannot provide, standing on its own, a route for acquiring the right to permanent residence. The right to permanent residence under the 2006 Regulations for the family members of a deceased EEA national arises in the following ways:

- Regulation 15(1)(e): a person who was the family member of a worker or self-employed person and (i) the worker or self-employed person has died; (ii) the family member resided with him immediately before his death; and (iii) the worker or self-employed person had resided continuously in the United Kingdom for at least the two years immediately before his or the death was the result of an accident at work or an occupational disease death.

- Regulation 15(1)(f) a person who—(i) has resided in the United Kingdom in accordance with these Regulations for a continuous period of five years; and (ii) was, at the end of that period, a family member who has retained the right of residence (ie in accordance with Regulation 10 governing retention of the right of residence).

---

[1] Council Directive 2004/38/EC, art 12(1).

[2] Council Directive 2004/38/EC, art 12(2). Such family members shall retain their right of residence exclusively on a personal basis.

[3] Council Directive 2004/38/EC, art 12(2), and just in case anyone should forget they are reminded at the end of the second paragraph of 12(2) that 'sufficient resources' are as defined in Article 8(4). See Reg 10(2) of the 2006 Regs.

[4] See Reg 10(3) and (4) of the 2006 Regs. An educational establishment must mean one referred to in the unrepealed Article 12 of Regulation 1612/68, as the 2006 Regulations make clear: SI 2006/1003, reg 11(7).

[5] *Okafor v Secretary of State for the Home Department* [2011] EWCA Civ 499, [2011] 1 WLR 3071, [2011] NLJR 636 (20 April 2011).

DESCENDANTS: CHILDREN

6.135 There is no definition of descendants in the 2006 Regulations,[1] nor is there any authoritative case law. The notion of descendant is wider than children. It plainly covers all blood children, legitimate or not, and whose parents are divorced or not, as well as grandchildren, great-grandchildren and so forth. The purposive approach to interpretation of Treaty rights would strongly suggest that it would include step-children[2] and adopted children, including children in *de facto* adoptions where there was clear evidence of the assumption of parental responsibility and dependency.[3] In any event the scope should not be less favourable than that provided in domestic law[4] and practice, in order to keep within the non-discrimination provisions. Further children, who are not descendants but who are part of the EEA worker's household, may qualify under Article 3(2) of the Citizens' Directive as other members of the family (see below). In *PG and VG (EEA; 'direct descendants' includes grandchildren) Portugal*[5] held that the ordinary natural meaning of 'direct descendants' in English includes children and grandchildren (to the nth generation), but excludes (great) nieces and nephews; just as 'direct relatives in the ascending line' includes parents and grandparents (with any more remote ancestors who may fortunately still be alive), but excludes (great) aunts and uncles. Article 2(2)(c) of the Directive and Regulation 7(1)(b)(ii) refer to direct descendants of the EEA national or his/her spouse/civil partner who are dependent. The concept of dependency is addressed at **6.139** below.

[1]   SI 2006/1003.
[2]   The ECJ ruled in Case C-275/02 *Ayaz v Land Baden-Wurttemberg* [2004] All ER (D) 188, ECJ that a step-son of a Turkish worker who is under 21 or dependent on the worker is a family member for the purposes of the EC-Turkey Association Agreement.
[3]   See CHAPTER 11 below.
[4]   See Immigration Rules, HC 395, rule 6 where the definition of 'parent' would mean the inclusion of certain step-children, children born outside marriage and certain adoptive children.
[5]   *PG and VG (EEA; 'direct descendants' includes grandchildren) Portugal* [2007] UKAIT 00019 (13 February 2007) at para 4.

6.136 Children of migrant workers, therefore, have rights of residence derived from their EEA national parent under Article 3 of the Citizens' Directive. They also have a right under Article 10 of Regulation 492/2011 (ex Article 12 of Council Regulation (EEC) 1612/68) to be admitted to the host State's general educational and other training and vocational courses under the same conditions as nationals of the host State, if such children are residing in its territory.[1] The Member States also have an obligation 'to encourage all efforts to enable such children to attend these courses under the best possible conditions'.[2] Interpretation of the former Article 12 by the ECJ means that children of migrant workers retain rights of their own under EU law, notwithstanding the departure of their EEA national parent, where they have entered the educational system of the host State at a time when the parent was exercising Treaty rights. Regulation 15A of the 2006 Regulations also partially recognises this set of entitlements: see **6.86** above. In the case of *Echternach and Moritz*[3] a student had entered the general educational system of a host State while his father was working there. The employment of the father in that State ceased and the family left the territory. The student discovered that there were difficulties in proceeding to further education in the country of origin in the light of the qualifications received in the host State. He therefore returned there and entered further education. The court held that he was entitled to a grant under Article 12 of Regulation 1612/68 notwithstanding the departure of the father. The Article 12 right is not, however, freestanding, and the position is different if the child was not installed with his or her parents when they exercised their free movement rights.[4] However the right to remain in education continues even if the EU worker leaves the host Member State and the children remain behind.[5]

[1] Council Regulation (EEC) 1612/68, art 12 covers general measures intended to facilitate educational attendance and not just rules of admission: Case 9/74 *Casagrande v Landeshauptstadt München* [1974] ECR 773, [1974] 2 CMLR 423, ECJ; Case 68/74 *Alaimo v Prefét du Rhône* Case [1975] ECR 109, [1975] 1 CMLR 262, ECJ Case C-389, 390/87 *Echternach* fn 3 below; Case C-308/89 *Di Leo v Land Berlin* [1990] ECR I-4185. This, coupled with art 7(2) non-discrimination, has resulted in broad application of this measure to ensure State assistance for educational purposes, especially the funding of grants: *EC Commission v Belgium* [1988] ECR 5445, including for non-dependent children over the age of 21 as in Case C-7/94 *Landesamt für Ausbildungsförderung Nordrhein-Westfalen v Gaal (Oberbundesanwalt beim Bundesverwaltungsgericht intervening)* [1995] ECR I-1031, ECJ.

[2] Council Regulation (EEC) 1612/68, art 12. Case 42/87 *EC Commission v Belgium: Re Higher Education Funding, Re* [1989] 1 CMLR 457, ECJ. These rights continue after the child is 21 and/or no longer dependent.

[3] Case C-389, 390/87 *Echternach and Moritz v Minister van Onderwijs en Wetenschappen* [1989] ECR 723, [1990] 2 CMLR 305, ECJ.

[4] Thus, a child of a migrant worker was not entitled to an educational grant, although residing in a host Member State where his parents had exercised Community rights before the child's birth: *Brown* [1988] 3205; Case C-7/92 *Gaal* [1995] ECR I-1031. If the child is an EEA national, however, different considerations may apply, in the light of *Chen and Zhu v Secretary of State for the Home Department* C-200/02 (19 October 2004, unreported) and *R (on the application of Bidar) v Ealing London Borough Council* Case C-209/03 [2005] QB 812, [2005] ECR I-2119, ECJ.

[5] Case C-413/99 *Baumbast and R v Secretary of State for the Home Department* [2002] ECR I-7091.

6.137 In the case of *Gal*[1] the Immigration Appeal Tribunal followed *Echternach and Moritz*[2] in holding that children who had entered primary school before the departure of their father had a right to continue their education, notwithstanding the permanent departure of the EEA worker. The right to admission to the educational system implies a right to remain in the UK for this purpose.[3] In *Teixeira v London Borough of Lambeth and Secretary of State for the Home Department*[4] a Portuguese woman had been, but no longer was, a worker in the UK and her daughter had entered primary education here at a time when her mother was not a worker and they were not self-sufficient. The Grand Chamber in *Teixeira v Lambeth London Borough Council*[5] decided that there was nothing in Article 12 which indicated that its scope was limited to situations in which one of the child's parents had the status of migrant worker at the precise moment when the child started his or her education. It was sufficient that he or she was in education in the host State when a parent was exercising rights of residence as a migrant worker. It also held that the right conferred by Article 12 on the child of a migrant worker to pursue, under the best possible conditions, his or her education in the host Member State necessarily implied that that child had the right to be accompanied by the parent who was his or her primary carer. In addition, it held that the right of access to education under Article 12 also extended to higher education even if the child would have attained his or her majority by the time the course was completed if the presence of that parent was still necessary. The Grand Chamber also reached the same conclusion in *Harrow London Bor-*

ough Council v Ibrahim[6] where it also held that the child exercising a right to access education and the parent who was his or her primary carer did not have to satisfy the conditions laid down in Directive 2004/38 and the right was not conditional on their having sufficient resources of their own and comprehensive sickness insurance cover. The case of *Baumbast* confirms the right of children exercising their right to be admitted to the general education system to have installed with them their non-EU national parent who is their primary carer:[7]

'where the children enjoy, under Article 12 of Regulation 1612/68, the right to continue their education in the host Member State although the parents who are their carers are at risk of losing their rights of residence as result, in one case, of a divorce from the migrant worker and, in the other case, of the fact that the parent who pursued the activity of an employed person in the host Member State as a migrant worker has ceased to work there, it is clear that if those parents were refused the right to remain in the host Member State during the period of their children's education that might deprive those children of a right which is granted to them by the Community legislature.'

The decision is consistent with the European Court's well-established position that Council Regulation (EEC) 1612/68 should be interpreted consistently with the rights under Article 8 of the ECHR,[8] and that measures incompatible with the observance of human rights would not be acceptable under EU law.[9] In Case 7/75 *F v Belgium*[10] a handicapped child who is prevented from acquiring the status of a worker because of the handicap and qualifies during minority for benefits for the handicapped, remains entitled to equality of treatment even after attaining the age of 21.

[1] Gal (10620) INLP vol 8(2) 1994 p 69.
[2] Case C-389, 390/87 *Echternach and Moritz v Minister van Onderwijs en Wetenschappen* [1990] 2 CMLR 305, ECJ.
[3] For another instance of such an implication see Case C-237/91 *Kus v Landeshauptstadt Wiesbaden* [1993] 2 CMLR 887, ECJ where a right to a renewal of a work permit for a Turkish national imported a right to renewal of a residence permit.
[4] [2010] ELR 261, (2010) Times, 26 February, ECJ.
[5] Case C-480-08 [2010] ECR I-1107, [2010] ICR 1118, ECJ. See also *Alarape v SSHD* (Case C-529/11) [2013] 1 WLR 2883, CJEU, 8 May 2013.
[6] Case C-310/08, [2010] ELR 261, (2010) Times, 26 February, ECJ
[7] *Baumbast and R v Secretary of State for the Home Department*, Case C-413/99 [2003] INLR 1, para 71. These rights are now reflected in the EEA Regulations, which enable primary carers of dependent children under 19 in full-time education to remain as 'family members' despite divorce or the departure of the EEA spouse: see **6.119** and **6.133** above.
[8] Case 4/73 *Nold (J) KG v EC Commission* [1974] ECR 491, para 13.
[9] Case C-260/89 *Elliniki Radiophonia Tileorass-AE v Pliroforissis and Kouvelas* [1991] ECR I-2925. See for further examples Case 44/79 *Hauer v Land Rheinland-Pflaz* [1979] ECR 3727, para 17; Case 63/83 *R v Kirk* [1984] ECR 2689, para 22; Case C-404/92P *X v EC Commission* [1994] ECR I-4737, para 17; Case C-415/93 *Union Royale Belge des Societes de Football Association ASBL v Bosman* [1995] ECR I-4921, para 79; Case C-199/92P *Hüls AG v EC Commission* [1999] ECR I-1000, paras 149–150; Case C-235/92P *Montecatini SpA v EC Commission* [1999] ECR I-4539, para 37.
[10] Case 7/75 *F v Belgium* [1975] ECR 679, [1975] 2 CMLR 442, ECJ. See also Case C-7/92 *Gaal* [1995] ECR I-1031, [1995] 3 CMLR 17.

6.138 When a child of a worker or self-employed person who is also an EEA national takes up employment, he or she can rely on the provisions of the Treaty and the unrepealed parts of Council Regulation (EEC) 1612/68 even if he or she was born in the host Member State and/or has never exercised free movement rights.[1]

[1] Case 235/87 *Matteucci v Communaute Française de Belgique* [1988] ECR 5589; see also by way of illustration Case C-243/91 *Belgium v Taghavi* [1992] ECR I-4401.

RELATIVES IN THE ASCENDING LINE

6.139 The notion of relatives in the ascending line covers not only the father and mother of the worker and his or her spouse, but also grandparents and great-grandparents and, on the basis of the above analysis, step-parents and adoptive parents. Such dependent direct relatives must be dependent on the EEA national and/or their spouse/partner: the concept of dependency is addressed at **6.142** below. In an interesting twist to the right to install relatives in the ascending line, the ECJ has held that children who exercise a general right of residence under Article 18 EC and Article 7(1)(b) of the Citizens' Directive (as self sufficient persons) have the right to install their parents who are their primary carers, in order to give content to their own rights of residence, following the *Baumbast* principle, despite the fact that the Directive does not expressly provide for relatives in the ascending line and even though the children who are in fact infants, can only be said to be exercising such rights by virtue of their parents being self-sufficient and thereby making the family collectively self-sufficient.[1] Under Regulation 15A(4A) of the 2006 Regulations, a derived right of residence arises for a 'primary carer' of a British citizen residing in the United Kingdom where the British citizen would be unable to reside in the UK or in another EEA State if the primary carer were required to leave. The concept of 'primary carer' is strictly defined but includes 'direct relations', such that a grandparent of a British/EEA national child in the UK is potentially able to fall within that definition, subject to the other requirements of a 'primary carer': see **6.87** above.

[1] Case C-200/02 *Chen and Zhu v Secretary of State for the Home Department* [2005] QB 325, [2005] All ER (EC) 129, ECJ. Primary carers of EEA national self-sufficient children are not included in the EEA Regulations as 'family members' (although the primary carers of children in education under art 12 of Regulation 1612/68 EEC have been included: see **6.137** above), but instead have been made the subject of new Immigration Rules regulating their entry: see HC 395, para 257C–257E, inserted by HC 164 from 1 January 2005.

Extended family members

6.140 Extended family members are now dealt with by the Citizens' Directive and the 2006 Regulations.[1] According to Article 3 of the Directive the host Member State shall, in accordance with its national legislation, facilitate entry and residence for the following persons:

(a) any other family members, irrespective of their nationality, not falling under the 'family member' definition in Article 2(2), who, in the country from which they have come, are dependants or members of the household of the Union citizen having the primary right of residence, or where serious health grounds strictly require the personal care of the family member by the Union citizen;

(b)   the partner with whom the Union citizen has a durable relationship, duly attested. As a matter of procedure the host Member State should undertake an extensive examination of the personal circumstances of the extended family member and in the case of a refusal should give reasons to justify the refusal.[2] Article 3(a) has been transposed into UK law by Regulation 8 of the 2006 Regs, which calls 'other family members' (in the Directive) 'extended family members'. Save for durable relationships and relatives with serious health issues, Regulation 8(2) provides, in relation to dependent relatives generally:

> (2)   A person satisfies the condition in this paragraph if the person is a relative of an EEA national, his spouse or his civil partner and—
>
> (a)   the person is residing in a country other than the United Kingdom and is dependent upon the EEA national or is a member of his household;
>
> (b)   the person satisfied the condition in paragraph (a) and is accompanying the EEA national to the United Kingdom or wishes to join him there; or
>
> (c)   the person satisfied the condition in paragraph (a), has joined the EEA national in the United Kingdom and continues to be dependent upon him or to be a member of his household;

The wording in regulation 8(2) is the result of litigation over many years challenging previous versions of regulation 8(2), which had imposed among other things a requirement that the dependent relative be lawfully resident in another EEA state with their EEA family member prior to seeking entry to the UK.[3] Following the CJEU cases of *Metock*[4] and *Rahman*[5] regulation 8 was amended to remove the requirements of prior lawful residence in an EEA member state;[6] and that such residence was to be in the same state in which the EEA national resides.[7] (A discussion of the issues surrounding the legality of regulation 8(2) as at September 2010 can be found in the eighth edition of this work at 6.140–6.141.) Under the new regulation 8(2), the following principles apply:

- a person can succeed in establishing that he or she is an 'extended family member' in any one of four different ways, each of which requires proving a relevant connection both prior to arrival in the UK, and in the UK: (i) prior dependency and present dependency; (ii) prior membership of a household and present membership of a household; (iii) prior dependency and present membership of a household; or (iv) prior membership of a household and present dependency;[8]
- the requirement that applicants be dependents or members of the household of the EEA national in the country from which they had come was re-affirmed by the Court of Appeal in *Oboh*;[9]
- it is not necessary to have resided in the same state as the Union citizen or to have been a dependant of that citizen shortly before or at the time when the citizen settled in the host member state (*Rahman* at paras 28, 31, 33–35);
- the situation of dependence had to exist in the country from which the other family member concerned came, at the very least at the time when he applied to join the Union citizen on whom he was dependent (*Rahman* at paras 38–40);

- there is no requirement that the extended family member to have arrived in the UK after, or simultaneously with, the EEA national sponsor: *Aladeselu*.[10] The appellants had been in the UK for between 12 and 21 months before the EEA national sponsor's arrival in the UK, and before making their applications, but the Court of Appeal held that the applicants had 'joined' the EEA national sponsor even though they arrived before her (for the purposes of regulation 8(2)(c));

- it is not possible to qualify by showing dependence on, or household membership of, a spouse or partner of an EEA national; *Soares*.[11]

- Subject to there being no abuse of rights, the jurisprudence of the Court of Justice allows for dependency of choice. Whilst the jurisprudence has not to date dealt with dependency of choice in the form of choosing not to live off savings, it has expressly approved dependency of choice in the form of choosing not take up employment (see *Centre Publique d'Aide Social de Courcelles v Lebon* [1987] ECR 2811 (*'Lebon'*) at [22]) and it may be very difficult to discern any principled basis for differentiating between the two different forms of dependency of choice when the test is a question of fact and the reasons why there is dependency are irrelevant: *Lim*;[12]

- being a member of a household requires living for some period of time under the roof of a household, anywhere in the world, that can be said to be that of the EEA national for a time when he or she was an EEA national;[13]

- dependency is dealt with in general at **6.142** below. In summary, dependency means financial support needed to meet essential living requirements.[14] Where able-bodied people of mature years claim to have always been dependent upon remittances from a sponsor, that may invite particular close scrutiny as to why this should be the case;[15]

- once it has been established that the person is an 'extended family member' within the meaning of regulation 8, the Secretary of State must decide whether in all the circumstances a right of entry/residence should be granted, eg under regulation 12(2)(c)/regulation 17(4)(b). This is a matter of discretion, not right. Prior to exercising that discretion, the Secretary of State must conduct an 'extensive examination of the personal circumstances' of the EEA national and the extended family member. when considering the discretion, concerns about abuse of rights, breach of the criminal law in entering the host state, and potential adverse affects on the exercise of Treaty rights by the qualified person, may all come into play, but such considerations are not relevant to deciding whether a person is a dependent OFM/extended family member or a member of the household of an EEA sponsor. EU legislation is to be interpreted in the light of the fundamental principles of EU law and these include the principle of non-discrimination, and excluding large numbers of 'foreign' OFM dependants from the scope of the Directive by the happenstance of international geography would contravene this;

- on an appeal against a refusal of an application made by an extended family member, the Tribunal can only exercise such discretion for itself where the SSHD has already done so; otherwise, a tribunal that has accepted the factual criteria set out in regulation 8 will need to allow the appeal as not in accordance with the law so that the SSHD may exercise her discretion herself first;[16]

- where a family permit has been issued by an Entry Clearance Officer after enquiry under regulation 12 of the 2006 Regs and is used to enter the UK, a subsequent application for a residence card is to be determined under regulation 7(3) of the 2006 Regs. Where the validity of the issue of the family permit is not contested by the Secretary of State and the permit has not been revoked, the issue is whether there has been a material change of circumstances since arrival with the consequence that the claimant no longer qualifies as an extended family member.[17]

[1] Directive 2004/38/EC, art 3 and the Immigration (European Economic Area) Regulations 2006, SI 2006/1003, regs 8 (extended family) and 12 (issue of EEA family permit).

[2] Directive 2004/38/EC, art 3(2).

[3] See, eg *KG and AK (Sri Lanka) v Secretary of State for the Home Department* [2008] EWCA Civ 13.

[4] *Metock v Minister for Justice, Equality and Law Reform* Case C-127/08, [2009] QB 318, [2008] ECR I-6241, ECJ.

[5] *Secretary of State for the Home Department v Rahman* Case C-83/11 [2013] QB 249, CJEU, referred to the CJEU by the Upper Tribunal in *MR (EEA extended family members) Bangladesh* [2010] UKUT 449 (IAC).

[6] Immigration (European Economic Area) (Amendment) Regulations 2011/1247, reg.2(3) (June 2, 2011).

[7] Immigration (European Economic Area) (Amendment) (No 2) Regulations, 2012/2560 Sch 1, para 1 (November 8, 2012).

[8] *Dauhoo (EEA Regulations – reg 8(2))* [2012] UKUT 79 (IAC). See also *Moneke (EEA – OFMs) Nigeria* [2011] UKUT 341 (IAC).

[9] *Oboh v Secretary of State for the Home Department* [2013] EWCA Civ 1525; [2014] 1 WLR 1680; [2014] Imm AR 521.

[10] *Aladeselu v Secretary of State for the Home Department* [2013] EWCA Civ 144; [2013] Imm. AR 780; [2014] INLR 85.

[11] *Soares v Secretary of State for the Home Department* [2013] EWCA Civ 575; [2013] 3 CMLR 847; [2013] Imm. AR 1096. See also *Moneke (EEA – OFMs) Nigeria* [2011] UKUT 341 (IAC).

[12] *Lim (EEA –dependency)* [2013] UKUT 00437 (IAC).

[13] *Moneke.*

[14] See *SM (India) v Entry Clearance Officer (Mumbai)* [2009] EWCA Civ 1426, (2009) Times, 7 December, applying the case of *Centre Public d'Aide Sociale, Courcelles v Lebon* 316/85 [1987] ECR 2811, [1989] 1 CMLR 337, ECJ. See also *Jia v Migrationsverket* C-1/05 [2007] QB 545 at [35]–[37]. The UT recently summarised the test in *Reyes (EEA Regs: dependency)* [2013] UKUT 314 (IAC) at [19].

[15] See *Moneke and others (EEA – OFMs) Nigeria.*

[16] In *FD (EEA discretion: basis of appeal) Algeria* [2007] UKAIT 00049 (12 June 2007), the AIT held that in an extended family appeal it is open to a person in respect of whom a discretion has been exercised to claim that the discretion under the Regulations should have been exercised differently, in which case the Tribunal has jurisdiction to substitute its own view of how the discretion should have been exercised – this is dependent on the Appellant falling within both Article 3(2) and regulation 8. See also *MO (reg 17(4) EEA Regs) Iraq* [2008] UKAIT 00061; *YB (EEA reg 17(4) – proper approach) Ivory Coast* [2008] UKAIT 00062; *Aladeselu (2006 Regs – reg 8) Nigeria* [2011] UKUT 00253 (IAC); *RH (UTIAC – remittals) Jamaica* [2010] UKUT 423 (IAC).

[17] *Ewulo (effect of family permit – OFM)* [2012] UKUT 00238(IAC).

6.141 Notwithstanding the UK's domestic case law on the 'discretionary' nature of family permits/residence cards for other family members under the Citizens' Directive, our view remains that, once the factual question of whether a person is an extended family member, under regulation 8, has been answered, the UK's domestic competence ends, and the person is entitled to documentary confirmation thereof. Part of the underlying rationale of the *Metock* decision, in ruling that prior lawful residence in an EEA country was an unlawful precondition of entry and residence, was to ensure that Member States did not have exclusive competence to control the first entry of a non-EEA family member into community territory (para 66). The Court of Appeal rightly said, in *Bigia v Entry Clearance* Officer,[1] that the outlawing of the prior lawful residence requirement applied to 'other' family members. The clear implication of this is that EU law governs a very important part of the entry and residence of 'other' family members. Then why, and how far, should other family members coming to Europe for the first time to join a Union citizen have to be subject to a discretionary decision as to their entry rather than a right? Why also should someone coming to Europe from a non-EU Member State not need to go through these hoops if the principal Union member is also coming from that country? A major issue in *Metock* was the dividing line between national and Community law competence. If imposing a condition of prior lawful residence in an EU Member State is unlawful, where is the dividing line to be drawn for 'other' family members, given the express grant of national legislative competence in respect of other family members in Article 3(2)? Where does the dividing line fall? These are not easy questions. The 2006 Regulations treat the entry and residence of other family members, wherever they are coming from, as matters of discretion within the competence of national law.[2] A sharp distinction is at all times kept between what we have called list 1 family members and list 2 ones. The Citizens' Directive is different. There is not such a sharp distinction. When the reference is made to 'family member' as defined in Article 2(2), the phrase 'as defined in Article 2(2)' is used. When 'family members' is used without this qualification the reference is to the wider meaning of 'family members' and includes 'other family members' referred to in Article 3(2)(a) and an unmarried 'partner' referred to in Article 3(2)(b). For example Article 8.5 deals with the issue of a registration certificate to 'family members' who are themselves Union citizens and covers not only family members under Article 2(2), but also those under Article 3(2). Article 10 deals with the issue of residence cards to family members who are not Union citizens and covers family members under Article 2(2) as well as under Article 3(2). If 'family members' bears the wider meaning in the context of residence cards and registration certificates, then it is quite clear from Article 9 that the issue of residence cards is mandatory and not discretionary.[3] Thus under the Directive the dividing line between national and EU competence would seem to fall in a quite different place from that fixed by the 2006 Regulations. Under the 2006 Regulations is the area of national competence as wide and all-embracing as it has been expressed by the AIT in AP and FP (Citizens' Directive Article 3(2); discretion; dependence) India,[4] namely, that the only rights given by EU law to the extended family member are procedural and not in any way substantive? We have criticised this conclusion as 'a very odd categorisation'. It may represent the extremism of the Home Office, but it does not seem to us to be in keeping with the Directive at all. We would suggest that under the Directive national competence extends only as far as settling the questions of the genuineness of the relationship, dependency and membership of the household in the country from which the 'other' family member has come, and the degree of bad health and so forth. Once entry has been facilitated other family members come fully under the competence of EU law as regards the issue of registration certificates and residence cards in accordance with Articles 8 and 10 of the Citizens' Directive. However, none of this is clear cut and these issues are in dire need of guidance from the CJEU.

¹ [2009] EWCA Civ 79,
² See reg 12(2) (issue of EEA family permits); reg 16 (5) (issue of registration certificate to EEA nationals); and reg 17(4) (issue of a residence document.
³ However, see *YB (EEA reg 17(4), proper approach) Ivory Coast* [2008] UKAIT 00062 which held that neither the Citizens' Directive (2004/38/EC) nor reg 17(4) of the Immigration (European Economic Area) Regulations 2006 confers on an 'extended family member' of an EEA national exercising Treaty rights a right to a residence card.
⁴ [2007] UKAIT 00048 (13 June 2007).

Dependency

6.142 This issue is relevant to children over 21-years-old of EEA nationals, and their spouse/civil partner, to dependent direct relatives in the ascending line and to extended family members under regulation 8(2) of the 2006 Regulations. Dependency in EU law is a factual question only. There is no need to establish the reason for the dependency nor that it be a dependency of necessity (in contrast to the domestic Immigration Rules).¹ A person may be dependent even if able to take up employment in his or her own right.² The fact that the family member applies for or receives social assistance does not mean that he or she is no longer dependent. To hold otherwise would deny equality of treatment between nationals.³ Furthermore, dependency need not have arisen before admission to the UK.⁴ According to the case law of the Court, the status of a 'dependent' family member is the result of a factual situation characterised by the fact that material support for that family member is provided by the EU national who has exercised his right of free movement or by his spouse or civil partner.⁵ Secondly, there is no need to determine the reasons for recourse to that support or to raise the question whether the person concerned is able to support himself by taking up paid employment.⁶ That interpretation is dictated in particular by the principle according to which the provisions establishing the free movement of workers, which constitute one of the foundations of the Community, must be construed broadly.⁷ Thirdly, in order to determine whether the relatives in the ascending line of the spouse or civil partner of a EU national are dependent on the latter, the host Member State must assess whether, having regard to their financial and social conditions, they are not in a position to support themselves. The need for material support must exist in the State of origin of those relatives or the State whence they came at the time when they apply to join the EEA national.⁸ Fourthly, when exercising their powers in this area Member States must ensure both the basic freedoms guaranteed by the Treaties and the effectiveness of directives containing measures to abolish obstacles to the free movement of persons between those States, so that the exercise by citizens of the European Union and members of their family of the right to reside in the territory of any Member State may be facilitated.⁹ Fifthly, given the lack of precision as to the means of acceptable proof by which the person concerned can establish that he or she is dependent, it must be concluded that evidence may be adduced by any appropriate means.¹⁰ As a result it is not possible to make the possession of a particular document a condition of issuing a residence permit or to say that a mere undertaking from an EEA national or his spouse to support the family member concerned is enough.[11]

[1]   *Lim (EEA – dependency)* [2013] UKUT 00437 (IAC). The UT recently summarised the test in *Reyes* (EEA Regs: dependency) [2013] UKUT 314 (IAC) at [19]. In *AP and FP (Citizens Directive Article 3(2); discretion; dependence) India* [2007] UKAIT 00048 (13 June 2007) the AIT held that the decision in *Jia* was intended to dictate a new understanding of dependence based on need, whatever may have been said in *Lebon, and that* the effect of the decision of the Court in *Jia* is to import into European law a requirement for dependence to be of necessity. However, in *SM (India) v Entry Clearance Officer (Mumbai); OQ (India) and NQ (India) v Entry Clearance Officer (Mumbai)* [2009] EWCA Civ 1426, (2009) Times, 7 December, the Court of Appeal held that *AP and FP* was wrongly decided on this point and should not be followed. It held that there was nothing in *Jia* to suggest that the ECJ was departing from the approach in *Lebon*. The fact that there was no evidence that *OQ and NQ* could not obtain or had even tried to obtain work in India was not relevant for the purposes of the Directive.

[2]   Case 316/85 *Centre Public d'Aide Sociale, Courcelles v Lebon* [1987] ECR 2811.

[3]   In *Lebon* above the assistance was the Belgian 'minimex' and in Case 256/86 *Frascogna v Caisse des dépôts et Consignations* [1987] ECR 3431 at para 7 an old-age allowance.

[4]   In *Lebon*, above where the issue of dependency arose in relation to payment of the Minimex in Belgium, it was not an issue that could have arisen before Mrs Lebon's admission to Belgium, as she was in fact born there. See further *Jia*, para 22, where the Court poses two possible views about the existence of dependency, one likely to arise in the family member's country of origin and the other which could arise at any time after a family member child reaches the age of 21.The facts of the case will determine which test is appropriate.

[5]   See, in relation to Article 10 of Regulation 1612/68 and Article 1 of Council Directive 90/364/EEC, Case 316/85 *Centre Public d'Aide Sociale v Lebon* [1987] ECR 2811, at para 22, and Case C-200/02 *Chen and Zhu v Secretary of State for the Home Department* [2004] ECR I-9925, at para 43, respectively.

[6]   Case C1/05 *Jia v Migrationverket*, at para 36.

[7]   Jia, para 36 and Lebon, paras 22 and 23.

[8]   *Jia*, para 37.

[9]   Jia, para 40 and see, by analogy, Case C-424/98 *European Commission v Italy* [2000] ECR I-4001, para 35.

[10] See Case C-363/89 *Roux v Belgium* [1991] ECR I-273, para 16, and Case C-215/03 *Oulane* [2005] ECR I-1215, para 53.

[11] *Jia*, para 42.

MATERIAL SCOPE (1) DISCRIMINATION AND FREE MOVEMENT

Abolishing discrimination and other obstacles to free movement

6.143 Our principal concern is with the rules relating to entry into and stay in the UK arising from EU rules on free movement. But a large part of free movement law is concerned with the removal of restrictions and obstacles, which put the incomer at a disadvantage as against nationals of the receiving Member State, or simply act as an unjustifiable obstacle to free movement. No account of free movement rights would be complete without some mention of two of the key elements in the material scope of free movement rights, but this is a vast subject with an extensive case law and within the scope of this work we can only highlight the main outlines:

(i)   the abolition of any discrimination based on nationality; and
(ii)   the abolition of non-discriminatory obstacles.

Non-discrimination

6.144 The principle of non-discrimination is one of the fundamental principles of EU law. Article 18 TFEU (ex Article 12 TEC) provides:

> "Within the scope of application of this treaty and without prejudice to special provisions therein any discrimination on the grounds of nationality shall be prohibited."

The Article is in Part II of the TFEU headed 'Non-discrimination and Citizenship of the Union'. It is the express statement of the general principle of equality and is the source of specific provisions elsewhere in the Treaty prohibiting discrimination in different Treaty fields. It applies independently only to situations governed by EU law, where the Treaties contain no specific prohibition of discrimination. In practice, most of the direct beneficiaries of Article 18 (ex Article 12) in the past have been students.[1] In a landmark decision in *Avello*, however, the court held that EU national children resident in another Member State could rely on Article 12 EC not to suffer discrimination on grounds of nationality vis-a-vis the rules governing the change of surnames, a matter that would not normally fall within the competence of Community law at all.[2] All the other areas of free movement contain their own express prohibitions. Article 45 TFEU (ex article 39(2) TEC) outlaws discrimination based on nationality between workers of Member States as regards employment, remuneration, and other conditions of work and employment. Article 7(1) of Council Regulation (EEC) 1612/68 (now Article 7 of Council Regulation (EU) 492/2011) provides for non-discrimination on the grounds of nationality in the field of employment and vocational training,[3] and Article 9 (also Article 9 in the new Regulation) relates to the field of housing.[4] Article 7(2) provides that an EU worker in the territory of a host Member State must enjoy the same 'social and tax advantages' as nationals of the host State. Thus even where there are no EU law rights to a social security benefit, it may be unlawful to provide it to own nationals but not to other EEA nationals.[5] In Collins,[6] the applicant was an Irish citizen who had lived outside the EU for 17 years. His initial claim for Jobseekers' Allowance was rejected on the basis that he did not satisfy the habitual residence test. The court held that although the applicant, as a newly arrived jobseeker, was not a worker within Part II of Regulation 1612/68,[7] access to a benefit such as the jobseekers' allowance, which was intended to assist the applicant seeking work, had to be provided in a non-discriminatory manner. Thus whilst it considered that it might be justifiable to require a link to the employment market of the host State, and that this might be established by a period of residence, there could be no discrimination on the application of any rules on the basis of nationality. Similarly, the Court has interpreted social advantage very broadly. Thus a national provision allowing those who are nationals or permanently settled to be joined by their common law partners has to be extended to EEA workers in the host State.[8] Anti-discrimination provisions are also contained in Articles 43 EC (ex Article 52) (right of establishment) and 54 (ex Article 65) (services). These provisions are extensive in their application and the ECJ's case law is extensive.[9] It covers direct discrimination, where less favourable treatment is given to one set of nationals,[10] and indirect discrimination, where one set of nationals can fulfil more easily conditions applicable to everyone.[11] For the purposes of immigration law the aggregate effect of these various non-discrimination provisions is much wider than the protection of wages and other conditions of employment referred to in Article 45 (or the housing, education and trade union rights dealt with by Regulation 1612/68 and its successor). They are fundamental to the enjoyment of free movement rights. Advocate General Jacobs expressed it thus in his opinion in the case of Phil Collins:[12]

'The nationals of each Member State are entitled to live, work, and do business in other Member States on the same terms as the local population. They must not simply be tolerated as aliens, but welcomed by the authorities of the host State as Community nationals who are entitled, within the scope of application of the Treaty "to all the privileges and advantages enjoyed by the nationals of the host State'. No other aspect of Community law touches the individual more directly or does more to foster the sense of common identity and shared destiny without which 'the ever-closer union among the peoples of Europe" proclaimed by the preamble to the Treaty would be an empty slogan.'

In *Patmalniece v Secretary of State for Works and Pension*[13] the appellant was a Latvian national who was refused state pension credit because she did not have a 'right to reside' in the UK. She argued that applying the right to reside test which British and Irish citizens always pass, but not other EEA nationals, was unlawful under EU law in that it violated the prohibition on nationality-based discrimination found in Article 3 of Regulation 1408/71/EU (now Article 4 of Regulation 883/04/EU). The Supreme Court rejected that argument in a judgment delivered on 16 March 2011. The majority accepted that the test was discriminatory, as it constitutes indirect discrimination, but that indirect discrimination is justified in these circumstances from the need to protect public funds. Lord Walker, dissenting, found that the discrimination was not justified because 'the provisions . . . are probably aimed at discriminating against economically inactive foreign nationals on grounds of nationality' (at [79]).

For a discussion relating to discrimination in connection with reverse discrimination following the *Zambrano, McCarthy* and *Dereci* litigation in the CJEU, see **6.82**, above.

[1] See **6.109** above. As regards the Turkish Association Agreement, see *Sürül v Bundesanstalt für Arbeit* Case C-262/96 [1999] ECR I-2685; **6.209** below. See most recently *D'Hoop (Marie-Nathalie) v Office National de l'Emploi*Case C-224/98 [2002] ECR I-6191; *R (on the application of Bidar) v Ealing London Borough Council*, Case C-209/03 [2005] QB 812, [2005] ECR I-2119, ECJ (non-discrimination provisions of the Treaty breached by domestic law provisions limiting assistance to students to those settled in the UK, excluding integrated EU citizens).

[2] *Avello (Carlos Garcia) v Belgium* Case C-148/02, [2003] ECR I-11613.

[3] Case 293/83 *Gravier v City of Liège* [1985] ECR 593, [1985] 3 CMLR 1, ECJ; Case 235/87 *Matteucci v Communaute Française de Belgique* [1989] 1 CMLR 357, ECJ; Case 24/86 *Blaizot v University of Liège* [1988] ECR 379, [1989] 1 CMLR 57, ECJ; Case 263/86 *Belgium v Humbel* [1989] 1 CMLR 393, ECJ; Case 42/87 *EC Commission v Belgium, Higher Education Funding, Re* [1989] 1 CMLR 457, ECJ; Case 197/86 *Brown v Secretary of State for Scotland* [1988] 3 CMLR 403, ECJ; Case 261/83 *Castelli v ONPTS* [1987] 1 CMLR 465, ECJ; Case 39/86 *Lair v University of Hanover* [1989] 3 CMLR 545, ECJ.

[4] Case 63/86 *EC Commission v Italy, Housing Aid, Re* [1989] 2 CMLR 601, ECJ.

[5] Under art 42 EC (ex art 51) the Council was required to set up a system to enable workers to overcome obstacles with which they might be confronted in national social security rules. It did so by the enactment of Council Regulations (EEC) 1408/71 and 574/72. A notable application of the principle of non-discrimination in social security is Case C-18/90 *Office National de l'Emploi v Kziber* [1991] ECR I-199, ECJ a decision on the Morocco Association

agreement. *Kziber* has been followed by the ECJ in Case C-58/93 *Yousfi v Belgium* [1994] ECR I-1353, ECJ despite attempts by Member States to persuade the court to overturn it.

6   Case C-138/02 *Collins v Secretary of State for Work and Pensions* [2005] QB 145.

7   The concept of 'worker' is not used in Regulation No 1612/68 in a uniform manner. While in Title II of Part I the term covers only persons who have already entered the employment market, in other parts of the same regulation the concept of 'worker' must be understood in a broader sense. The court's case law draws a distinction between Member State nationals who have not yet entered into an employment relationship in the host Member State where they are looking for work and those who are already working in that State or who, having worked there but no longer being in an employment relationship, are nevertheless considered to be workers (see Case 39/86 *Lair v University of Hanover* [1988] ECR 3161, paras 32 and 33). Only those who have already entered the employment market may, on the basis of art 7(2) of Regulation No 1612/68, claim the same social and tax advantages as national workers (see in particular, *Lebon*, cited above, paragraph 26, and Case C-278/94 *EC Commission v Belgium* [1996] ECR I-4307, paragraphs 39 and 40): *Collins*, above at paras 30–32.

8   Case 59/85 *Netherlands v Reed* [1987] 2 CMLR 448, ECJ.

9   See in particular Case 2/74 *Reyners v Belgium* [1974] ECR 631, [1974] 2 CMLR 305, ECJ; Case 33/74 *Van Binsbergen v Bestuur* [1974] ECR 1299, [1975] 1 CMLR 298, ECJ; Case 36/74 *Walrave and Koch v Association Union Cycliste Internationale* [1974] ECR 1405, [1975] 1 CMLR 320, ECJ; Case 11/77 *Patrick v Ministre des Affaires Culturelles* [1977] ECR 1199, [1977] 2 CMLR 523, ECJ; Case 136/78 *Ministère Public v Auer* [1979] ECR 437, [1979] 2 CMLR 373, ECJ; Case 107/83 *Ordre des Avocats au Barreau de Paris v Klopp* [1985] QB 711, [1985] 1 CMLR 99, ECJ; Case 222/86 *Union Nationale des Entraîneurs et Cadres Techniques Professionnels du Football (UNECTEF) v Heylens* [1989] 1 CMLR 901, ECJ. Case C-179/90 *Merci Convenzionali Porto di Genova SpA v Siderurgica Gabriella SpA* [1991] ECR I-5889, ECJ; Case C-360/89 *EC Commission v Italy* [1992] ECR I-3401, ECJ; Case C-419/92 *Scholz v Opera Universitaria di Cagliari* [1994] ECR I-505.

10 See *R v Trinity House London Pilotage Committee, ex p Jensen and Leu* [1985] 2 CMLR 413, QBD; *R v Inner London Education Authority, ex p Hinde* [1985] 1 CMLR 716, QBD; Case C-293/83 *Gravier v City of Liege* [1985] 3 CMLR 1, ECJ.

11 Case 152/73 *Sotgiu v Deutsche Bundespost* [1974] ECR 153, ECJ; Case 1/78 *Kenny v National Insurance Comr* [1978] ECR 1489, [1978] 3 CMLR 651, ECJ; Case 182/83 *Robert Fearon & Co Ltd v Irish Land Commission* [1985] 2 CMLR 228, ECJ; Case 41/84 *Pinna (Pietro) v Caisse d'Allocations Familiales de la Savoie* [1988] 1 CMLR 350; Case 33/88 *Allué and Coonan v Università degli Studi di Venezia* [1989] ECR 1591, [1991] 1 CMLR 283; ECJ; Case C-175/88 *Biehl v Administration des Contributions du Grand-Duché de Luxembourg* [1990] ECR I-1779, [1990] 3 CMLR 143; Case C-204/90 *Bachmann v Belgium* [1992] ECR I-249, [1993] 1 CMLR 785, ECJ.

12 Case C-92/92 *Collins (Phil) v IMTRAT Handelsgesellschaft mbH* [1993] 3 CMLR 773 at 785.

13 [2011] UKSC 11, [2011] 1 WLR 783, [2011] 2 CMLR 1158.

6.145 Article 24(1) of the Citizens' Directive sets out the principle of non-discrimination as regards free movement rights spelt out in the Directive as follows:

> "Subject to such specific provisions as are expressly provided for in the Treaty and secondary law, all Union citizens residing on the basis of this Directive in the territory of the host Member State shall enjoy equal treatment with the nationals of that Member State within the scope of the Treaty. The benefit of this right shall be extended to family members who are not nationals of a Member State and who have the right of residence or permanent residence."

In the *European Parliament v European Council*[1] case, the ECJ considered allegations from the European Parliament that Directive 2003/86/EC, which deals with the right of minor children of third country nationals as respects fundamental rights and, in particular the right to respect for family life under art 8 of the ECHR and contains useful material on the best interests of the child and discrimination on the grounds of age.

[1]   Case C-540/03 *European Parliament v European Council* [2006] 2 FCR 461, [2006] All ER (D) 320 (Jun), ECJ.

6.146 The material scope of any free movement right is usually to be determined by the yardstick of what the local nationals can do. All EEA nationals must be put on the same footing as nationals of the host State. Thus in *Watson and Belman*[1] it was held that although penalties could be imposed for illegally entering or remaining in a country, they must be comparable to penalties attaching to local nationals for breaches of provisions of equal importance and should not be so disproportionate that they become an obstacle to free movement.[2] Clearly the comparison between the position of own nationals and those of another Member State is not an exact one in this kind of situation, and this is always likely to be the case as regards rights of entry or stay. Normally the court does not draw such a distinction when dealing with the grant of a social advantage. Thus in *Sala*[3] the principle of equal treatment precluded the Member State from requiring a national of another Member State to be in possession of a residence permit in order to be granted a social advantage when no such requirement was imposed on its own nationals.[4] However, exceptions to the principle of discrimination have been acknowledged by the court many times on the basis of 'objective discrimination', which arises from the simple fact that certain requirements are necessary for non-nationals or non-residents which would not apply to own nationals, such as the requirement to hold their national driving licence;[5] to notify the appropriate authorities of the person's presence on the territory;[6] or to have a passport or identity document.[7] In *Kaba*[8] the distinction was made and it was said that the UK could rely on 'any objective difference' between the position of its own nationals and those of another Member State so far as the obtaining of settlement was concerned. The distinction between Kaba and a case like Sala is that in Kaba the claimed 'social advantage' was indefinite leave. This was something which no own national either needed to or could acquire. If on the other hand the claimed 'social advantage' was some social security benefit or a family allowance, it could be acquired by own nationals, and like could be compared with like. It should also be noted that the public policy exceptions, allowing exclusion or expulsion on public policy grounds, can by definition only apply to other nationals and not to own nationals, but this does not constitute discrimination.[9]

[1]   Case 118/75 *Re Watson and Belmann* [1976] ECR 1185, [1976] 2 CMLR 552, ECJ. See Case 8/77 *Re Sagulo, Brenca and Bakhouche* [1977] ECR 1495, [1977] 2 CMLR 585, ECJ and Case 157/79 *R v Pieck* [1981] QB 571, [1981] 3 All ER 46, ECJ at paras 12 and 13, where the need to bring the position of workers of other Member States into line with that of local nationals is referred to.
[2]   See further Case 321/87 *EC Commission v Belgium* [1990] 2 CMLR 492, ECJ.
[3]   Case C-85/96 *Sala v Freistaat Bayern* [1998] ECR I-2691, ECJ.
[4]   See further Case C-262/96 *Sürül v Bundesanstalt für Arbeit* [1999] ECR I-2685, ECJ.
[5]   Case 16/78 *Choquet, Re* [1978] ECR 2293.
[6]   Case 118/75 *Watson and Belmann, Re* [1976] ECR 1185, [1976] 2 CMLR 552, ECJ.
[7]   Case 8/77 *Re Sagulo, Brenca and Bakhouche, Re* [1977] ECR 1495, [1977] 2 CMLR 585, ECJ.
[8]   Case C-356/98 [2000] All ER (EC) 537, ECJ.

6.147 Although the wording of Articles 45(2), 49 and 61 TFEU suggests that the principle of equal treatment applies without exception, the ECJ now accepts that in cases of indirect discrimination, where a measure applies to everyone irrespective of nationality, the discrimination may be justified if based on objective considerations independent of the nationality of the workers concerned, and they are proper to the legitimate aim pursued by the national law and not disproportionate.[1] The wide operation of the justification test in indirect discrimination cases can be seen in *R (HC) v Secretary of State for Work and Pensions and others* [2013] EWHC 3874 (Admin) in which the Administrative Court held that the denial of benefits to a third country national with a *Zambrano* derived right of residence, via her EU child, did not amount to unlawful indirect discrimination against them on the grounds of their nationality/immigration status. Supperstone J held that the regulations implementing the restriction were a proportionate means of furthering the legitimate aim of protecting scarce public resources, including from individuals who moved to, or remained in the UK in order to take advantage of its welfare system (see [50]-[68]).

1 Case C-237/94 *O'Flynn v Adjudication Officer* [1996] ECR I-2617. In another line of cases, the test for justification of indirect discrimination is imperative reasons relating to the public interest: Case 33/88 *Allué and Coonan v Università degli Studi di Venezia* [1989] ECR 1591, ECJ; Case C-175/88 *Biehl v Administration des Contributions du Grand-Duché de Luxembourg* [1990] ECR I-1779, ECJ; Case C-204/90 *Bachmann v Belgium* [1992] ECR I-249; Case C-398/92 *Mund and Fester v Hatrex Internationaal Transport* [1994] ECR I-467, ECJ; Case C-80/94 *Wielockx v Inspecteur der Directe Belastingen* [1995] ECR I-2493, ECJ.

Non-discriminatory obstacles to free movement

6.148 This development in the case law, the justification of indirect discrimination, is closely connected to a further development – that of non-discriminatory obstacles to free movement, which gained particular prominence in the *Bosman* case, concerning the effect of football transfer fees on free movement. The concept was borrowed from earlier case law on the freedom of movement of goods, which held that Article 34 TFEU (ex Article 28 TEC) prohibited not only discriminatory measures in relation to the movement of goods, but also unjustifiable non-discriminatory obstacles.[1] In *Kraus*[2] the ECJ held that Articles 48 and 52 (now Articles 46 and 49 TFEU did not permit any national measure relating to the conditions for use of a postgraduate university degree acquired in another Member State, which, even though applied without discrimination on the basis of nationality, was capable of hindering or making less attractive the exercise of fundamental freedoms contained in the Treaty by Community nationals, including nationals of the Member State which had taken the measure. This rather startling innovation was later confirmed and clarified by the court in *Bosman* and *Gebhard*. In *Bosman*[3] the court held that provisions which preclude or deter nationals of a Member State from leaving their country of origin in order to exercise their right of free movement constitute an obstacle to that freedom, even if they apply without regard to the nationality of workers. In *Gebhard*[4] the court held that where national measures are liable to hinder or make less attractive the exercise of fundamental freedoms guaranteed by the Treaty, they must fulfil four conditions: (i) they must be applied in a non-discriminatory manner; (ii) they must be justified by imperative requirements of the general interest; (iii) they must be suitable for securing the attainment of the objective which they pursue; and (iv) they must not go beyond what is necessary in order to attain it. Here the Court was repeating the reasoning already handed down in an earlier decision on the application of Article 59 EC (now Article 56 TFEU).[5] More recently, the ECJ has confirmed that where obstacles to free movement rights have been identified there is no need to consider whether there is indirect discrimination on grounds of nationality.[6] In an extension of its previous case law the Court has held that the inability to enjoy family life can constitute an obstacle the exercise of free movement rights. In Carpenter, the court held that the expulsion by the UK authorities of the non-EU national wife (who was an overstayer) of a British national exercising free movement rights as a service provider in other Member States, would constitute a breach of Community law since she facilitated the exercise of the British national's Treaty rights by looking after his family:[7]

> 'the Community legislature has recognised the importance of ensuring the protection of the family life of nationals of the Member States in order to eliminate obstacles to the exercise of the fundamental freedoms guaranteed by the Treaty . . . It is clear that the separation of Mr and Mrs Carpenter would be detrimental to their family life and, therefore, to the conditions under which Mr Carpenter exercises a fundamental freedom. That freedom could not be fully effective if Mr Carpenter were to be deterred from exercising it by obstacles raised in his country of origin to the entry and residence of his spouse'.

---

[1]   Case 8/74 *Procureur du Roi v Dassonville* [1974] ECR 837, ECJ; later limited in Case C-267/91 Keck [1993] ECR I-6097.
[2]   Case C-19/92 *Kraus v Land Baden-Würtemberg* [1993] ECR I-1663, ECJ.
[3]   Case C-415/93 *Union Royale Belge des Societes de Football Association ASBL v Bosman* [1996] All ER (EC) 97, [1995] ECR I-4921, ECJ.
[4]   Case C-55/94 *Gebhard v Consiglio dell'Ordine degli Avvocati e Procuration di Milano* [1995] ECR I-4165, ECJ.
[5]   Case C-288/89 *Stichting Collectieve Antennevoorziening Gouda v Commissariaat voor de Media* [1991] ECR I-4007, ECJ.
[6]   Case C-18/95 *Terhoeve (F C) v Inspecteur van de Belastingdienst Particulieren Ondernemingen Buitenland* [1999] ECR I-345, ECJ; Case C-337/97 *Meeusen v Hoofddirectie van de Informatie Beheer Groep* [1999] ECR I-3289, ECJ.
[7]   Case C-60/00 *Carpenter (Mary) v Secretary of State for the Home Department* [2002] ECR I-6279, [2002] INLR 439, ECJ.

Reverse discrimination

6.149 Non-discrimination is important for the protection of other EEA nationals coming to the UK and of UK nationals going to other EEA countries. But can it assist UK nationals who suffer discrimination at the hands of the UK Government? This practice is referred to as 'reverse discrimination'.[1] There is clear reverse discrimination by the UK Government in the field of family rights. Other EEA nationals in the UK have few problems in being joined by members of their families. British citizens, on the other hand, have a host of obstacles to overcome posed by the Immigration Rules (Appendix FM in particular): intention to live together, minimum income requirements, sole responsibility, exceptional compassionate circumstances are a few of them. There is no doubt that the non-discrimination provisions can apply to Member States in respect of their own nationals in certain circumstances. This was first recognised in *Knoors*[2] where a Dutch plumber who had practised his trade in Belgium for seven years was refused a permit to practise by the Dutch government on his return to Holland. He claimed that this was contrary to EU law. The ECJ stated that the wording of Article 43 EC (now Article 49 TFEU), which refers to 'nationals of one Member State in the territory of another', did not exclude 'own' nationals from the benefit of EU law or from the application of non-discrimination provisions. An 'own' national could qualify where, by lawful residence on the territory of another Member State, his or her situation has become assimilated to that of any other persons enjoying the rights and liberties guaranteed by the Treaty. A State cannot discriminate against its own nationals who are within the protection of one or other provision of EU law. The principle is now widely accepted[3] and extends to non-discriminatory measures adopted by the home State, which are obstacles to a home national's free movement.[4] The problem in these cases is not 'reverse discrimination' but establishing a link to a provision of Union law, which removes the case from a wholly internal situation.[5]

[1] See D Pickup 'Reverse Discrimination and Freedom of Movement for Workers' (1986) 23 CML Rev 135.
[2] Case 115/78 *Knoors v Secretary of State for Economic Affairs* [1979] ECR 399, [1979] 2 CMLR 357, ECJ, at para 24. In Case 1/78 *Kenny v National Insurance Comr* [1978] ECR 1489, [1978] 3 CMLR 651, ECJ the court held that discrimination by a Member State against its own nationals, as much as discrimination by a Member State against nationals of another Member State, was forbidden. In Case 136/78 *Ministère Public v Auer* [1979] ECR 437, [1979] 2 CMLR 373, ECJ the court indicated at para 28 that EEC nationals were protected against their own State, provided that the other conditions for the application of the rule on which they rely are fulfilled. See further Case 292/86 *Gullung v Conseil de l'Ordre des Avocats du Barreau de Colmar* [1990] 1 QB 234, [1988] 2 CMLR 57, ECJ.
[3] *Union Royale Belge des Societes de Football Association ASBL v Bosman* [1996] All ER (EC) 97 above; Case C-379/92 *Peralta*, criminal proceedings against [1994] ECR I-3453, ECJ.
[4] See **6.143** fn 6, above.
[5] See *Phull v Secretary of State for the Home Department* [1996] Imm AR 72, CA.

6.150 Where there is a link to some provision of EU law and where reverse discrimination applies, the advantage which own nationals can take of it is nevertheless restricted in the circumstances of the criminal law. The ECJ in *Saunders* noted:[1]

'Although the rights conferred upon workers by Article 48 may lead the Member State to amend their legislation, where necessary, even with respect to their own nationals, this provision does not however aim to restrict the power of the Member States to lay down restrictions, within their own territory, on the freedom of movement of all persons subject to their jurisdiction in implementation of domestic criminal law.'

Putting someone in prison after conviction and sentence in the criminal courts is undoubtedly a restriction on that person's freedom of movement, but is not in any way intended to be restricted by any of the free movement provisions. The English High Court extended this rule to extradition procedures and the handover procedure under the Visiting Forces Act 1952.[2] The rationale was explained by Robert Goff LJ in *Ex p Healy*.[3] Using the purposive construction of Article 48 EEC (now Article 45 TFEU) by the ECJ in *Saunders* he stated that Article 48 (now Article 45 TFEU) did not aim to restrict the power of

Member States to lay down restrictions within their own territories on the freedom of movement of all persons subject to their jurisdiction in the implementation of extradition procedure or the handover procedure under the Visiting Forces Acts.

¹ Case 175/78 *R v Saunders* [1979] ECR 1129, [1980] QB 72, ECJ (application of restrictions of domestic criminal law to own national); Case 180/83 *Moser v Land Baden-Württemberg* [1984] 3 CMLR 720, ECJ (denial to own national of access to further education); Case 298/84 *Iorio v Azienda Autonoma delle Ferrovie dello Stato* [1986] 2 CMLR 665, ECJ (dispute by own national with state railway over limited access to trains); Joined Cases 35 and 36/82 *Morson and Jhanjan v Netherlands* [1982] ECR 3723, [1983] 2 CMLR 221, ECJ (own nationals who have never worked outside home country); Case 44/84 *Hurd v Jones, Inspector of Taxes* [1986] QB 892, [1986] 2 CMLR 1, ECJ; Case C-104/91 *Colegio Oficial de Agentes de la Propiedad Immobiliaria v J L Aguirre Borrell* [1992] ECR I-3003 and Joined Cases C-330/90 and 331/90 *Ministerio Fiscal v Brea (A Lopez) and Palacios (C H)* [1992] 2 CMLR 397, ECJ (proceedings against Spanish estate agents).
² *R v Governor of Pentonville Prison, ex p Budlong* [1980] 1 All ER 701; *Re Budlong and Kember* [1980] 2 CMLR 125, DC; *Re Virdee* [1980] 1 CMLR 709, QBD.
³ *R v Governor of Pentonville Prison, ex p Healy* [1984] 3 CMLR 575, DC.

MATERIAL SCOPE (2) RIGHT TO ENTER AND RESIDE

Right to leave own country

6.151 In EU law the right to depart is expressly given to workers and the self-employed and those providing or receiving services. Article 4 of the Citizens' Directive requires Member States to grant all Union citizens and their families the right to leave their territory to travel to another Member State.¹ What this means is that Member States must be prepared to let any EU citizen leave their territory on production of a valid identity card or passport, and on the production of a passport in the case of family members, who are non-EEA nationals. No exit visa or equivalent formality may be imposed on those wishing to leave as set out above.² In *Byankov v Glaven sekretar na Ministerstvo na vatreshnite raboti*³ the CJEU held that a Bulgarian law preventing Bulgarian nationals from exiting Bulgaria on the grounds of indebtedness, thereby restricting their freedom of movement within the EU, and with no regular review, was discriminatory; such restrictions could only be applied on the grounds of public policy, public security or public health. In *Jipa*⁴ the Court held that a national of a Member State who has been repatriated from another Member State enjoys the status of a citizen of the Union under Article 17(1) EC (now Article 20(1) TFEU) and may therefore rely on any right pertaining to that status, including against his Member State of origin, and in particular the right conferred by Article 18 EC (now Article 21 TFEU) to move and reside freely within the territory of the Member States rights. This right can only be restricted on grounds of 'public policy' or 'public security' as provided by Article 27 of the Citizens' Directive. A failure by a Member State or its national courts to examine the personal conduct of a person when restricting, on grounds of public policy or public security, his right to move and reside freely in the territory of the Member States will invalidate any justification of the restriction in question. Member States shall, acting in accordance with their laws, issue to their own nationals, and renew, an identity card or passport stating their nationality.⁵ The passport shall be valid at least for all Member States and for countries through which the holder must pass when travelling between Member States.[6] Where the law of a Member State does not provide for identity cards to be issued, the period of validity of any passport on being issued or renewed shall be not less than five years.[7]

[1] Council Directive 2004/38/EC art 4(1).
[2] Council Directive 2004/38/EC art 4(2).
[3] C-249/11, [2013] QB 423; [2013] 2 WLR 293; [2013] 1 CMLR.
[4] Case C-33/07 *Ministerul Administrației și Internelor – Direcția Generală de Pașapoarte București v Jipa* [2008] 3 CMLR 715, at paras 17, 18, 25, 28 and 30.
[5] Council Directive 2004/38/EC art 4(3).
[6] Council Directive 2004/38/EC art 4(4).
[7] Council Directive 2004/38/EC art 4(4).

Right to arrive, enter and reside

6.152 Various provisions of EU law give rights of entry to nationals of another Member State and these rights are extended to all EEA States by the Agreement on the European Economic Area,[1] and to Switzerland by the EU-Swiss Confederation Agreement on the Free Movement of Persons.[2] Article 45 TFEU (ex Article TEC) clearly gives a right to enter to those seeking work as well as to workers who have definite jobs to go to and this is spelt out in more detail in the subsidiary legislation.[3] A similar right to enter is given, under the Citizens' Directive (2004/38/EC), to business people, the self-employed, and providers and recipients of services, students, the self-sufficient and the retired. All these are referred to by the 2006 Regulations as 'qualified persons'.[4] In addition rights of entry are given to family members,[5] and, under the Swiss Agreement, to posted workers employed by a Swiss national or Swiss undertaking.[6] Under EU law the right involves both entry and internal free movement,[7] and is exercisable by EEA nationals 'simply on production of a valid identity card or passport'.[8] No prior leave to enter or permission is required, because the right to enter flows directly from EU law.[9] Article 5 of the Citizen's Directive also gives what can only be described as a right to arrive. Article 5(4) says that where a Union citizen, or a family member who is not a national of a Member State, does not have the necessary travel documents or visas, the Member State concerned shall, before turning them back, give such persons every reasonable opportunity to obtain the necessary documents or have them brought to them within a reasonable period of time or to corroborate or prove by other means that they are covered by the right of free movement and residence. Article 5(5) says that the person concerned may be required to report his/her presence within its territory within a reasonable and non-discriminatory period of time. Failure to comply with this requirement may make the person concerned liable to proportionate and non-discriminatory sanctions. This is a right which in our day and age of security may be thwarted by airlines who will not let a passenger board if they do not have a visa.

[1] The Agreement on the European Economic Area signed at Oporto on 2 May 1992, as adjusted by the Protocol signed at Brussels on 17 March 1993 OJ L86 20.4.1995.
[2] Agreement between the European Community and the Swiss Confederation on The Free Movement of Persons (30 Apr/02 OJ L114/6).
[3] Article 1 of Council Regulation (EU) 492/2011 (formerly Council Regulation (EEC) 1612/68) refers to the right to take up activity as an employed person and the right to take up available employment in the territory of another Member State on the same priority as the nationals of

that State. The case law has made it clear that the right includes the right to enter to find available employment and to respond to offers of employment.

4   SI 2006/1003, reg 6.
5   See **6.116** ff, above.
6   Agreement between the European Community and the Swiss Confederation on The Free Movement of Persons (above), arts 1 and 17 of Annex 1. See the extension of the Swiss provisions to all EEA posted workers at **6.103** above.
7   Case 36/75 *Rutili v Minister for the Interior* [1975] ECR 1219, [1976] 1 CMLR 140.
8   Council Directive (EEC) 68/360, art 3(1) and 73/148, art 3(1). Recently the ECJ has held that it is contrary to art 49 EC for an EU national to be required in another Member State to present a valid identity card or passport in order to prove their nationality, when that State does not impose a general obligation on its own nationals to provide evidence of identity, and permits them to prove their identity by any means allowed by national law. This is despite the provision in art 3(1) of Directives 73/148 and 68/360. Case C-215/03 *Oulane*, 17 February 2005.
9   Case 157/79 *R v Pieck* [1981] QB 571, [1981] 3 All ER 46, ECJ; Case 321/87 EC *Commission v Belgium* [1990] 2 CMLR 492.

6.153 The 2006 Regulations[1] now include Switzerland. All the rights to enter in the main text are now covered by the Citizens' Directive and the implementing 2006 Regulations.[2] The right to arrive set out in the previous paragraph is also likely to be thwarted on arrival despite the very clear provisions of Article 5. Family members who do not have the nationality of a Member State enjoy the same rights as the citizen who they have accompanied. They may be subject to a short-stay visa requirement.[3] Notwithstanding the progressive regime of arrival and entry contained in the Citizens' Directive, the 2006 Regulations impose quite difficult requirements on the entry of all foreign family members. The short-term visa requirement which under Regulation (EC) No 539/2001 applies only to nationals who require visas to enter EU territory, but under the 2006 Regulations it applies to everyone, even if they come from a non-visa country. In *KA (EEA: family permit; admission) Sudan*[4] it was held that Article 5 of the Citizens' Directive,[5] does not confer an unqualified right of pre-entry, entry or residence on family members of a Union citizen exercising Treaty rights. Family members are required to have an entry visa in accordance with Regulation (EC) No 539/2001 or, where appropriate, with national law. The Tribunal pointed out that the UK has chosen to impose a visa requirement in the form of an EEA family permit regime, and hence if a family member arrives at a UK border without an EEA family permit and seeks admission, he or she must satisfy the entry documents requirement of regulation 11 of the 2006 Regulations. Whether entrants are entitled to a right of admission under reg 11 depends on their being able to produce relevant documentation on that occasion (or within a reasonable period of time thereafter). The premise of all these injunctions is that entry to the UK is a matter of discretionary leave, whereas it is not. It is the exercise of a right conferred by EU law before the passenger has started his or her journey. Forty two years after the UK joined the European Community, the point has not yet sunk in. In *R (McCarthy) v Secretary of State for the Home Department*[6], the Administrative Court (Haddon Cave J) recently expressed the view that there were 'strong grounds' in support of the lawfulness of the requirement on family members of EEA nationals exercising Treaty rights in the UK to obtain a 'family permit', prior to arrival in the UK. He considered that that requirement was 'reasonable and proportionate', and was not an incorrect implementation of the Citizens' Directive, Article 5(2) and was likely to be justified in part by Protocol 20 to the TFEU, which was to be 'widely construed'. Haddon Cave J considered that 'there was a palpable risk that the use of fake EU "residence cards" would increase if residence cards were enough to gain access to the UK' ([42]-[51] and [60]). However, he nevertheless decided that the issue of the compliance of the family permits regime with Article 5 of the Directive was not *acte clair* and made a reference to the CJEU on that point: [112]. On 18 December 2014, the Grand Chamber of the CJEU ruled in Mr McCarthy's favour (Case C-202/13: *R (on the application of McCarthy and Rodriguez) v Secretary of State for the Home Department* Case C202/13), ruling the UK's permit requirement for short-term visits to be incompatible with EU law[7].

1   SI 2006/1003, reg 2(1).
2   SI 2006/1003.
3   Under Regulation (EC) No 539/2001, which the UK does not subscribe to, or under national law. Residence permits will be deemed equivalent to short-stay visas.
4   [2008] UKAIT 00052.
5   Council Directive 2004/38/EC.
6   [2012] EWHC 3368 (Admin).
7   [2014] All ER (D) 229 (Dec), ECJ

6.154 The entitlement to enter is given effect in UK domestic law by section 7 of the Immigration Act 1988 and by the 2006 Regulations, which provide that admission must be granted to EEA nationals if they produce on arrival a valid passport or national identity card issued by another EEA State.[1] This also applies to posted workers,[2] family members provided they have the right documents,[3] and extended family members, provided they qualify under the provisions of UK domestic law and have an EEA family permit.[4] Residence is granted in three stages: an initial right of residence,[5] an extended right of residence,[6] and finally a permanent right of residence.[7] At all of these stages the EEA national and any family or extended family members must satisfy the criteria for an extension and there are various documents which must be issued.[8] A non-EEA national family member travelling to the United Kingdom accompanied by the EEA national family member concerned for the purpose of a visit of not more than three months' duration is entitled to enter, pursuant to regulations 11(2), 12(1) and 13(1) and (2) of the Immigration (European Economic Area) Regulations 2006, read together.[9] Assuming the person has the requisite documents needed for automatic entry they may still be refused entry. Under regulation 19, if exclusion is justified on grounds of public policy, public security or public health and in the case of family members, if they are not accompanied by the EEA national or coming to join him or her or the EEA national has no right to reside under the Regulations. Regulations 22 and 24 incorporate the powers of examination, detention[10] and temporary admission under Schedule 2 to the Immigration Act 1971 for those seeking admission or refused admission who are family members of EEA nationals or EEA nationals who might fall to be excluded from the UK on public policy grounds. In MRAX,[11] a test case brought before the European Court by a Belgian pressure group, the Court considered the right of non-EU national family members of EU nationals exercising Treaty rights to enter a Member State where they were not in possession of the correct visas. The court held that in order that full effect is given to Article 3(2) of Directive 68/360 and Article 3(2) of Directive 73/148 (which stated that Member States are to accord family members of EU nationals exercising Treaty rights every facility for obtaining any necessary visa) a visa must be issued without delay and as far as possible at the place of entry into the territory of the Member State. The right to respect for family life underlay its decision that a Member State may not send back at the border a third country national married to a national of a Member State who attempts to enter the Member State without being in possession of a valid identity card, passport or visa:

> 'In view of the importance which the Community legislature has attached to the protection of family life, it is in any event disproportionate and, therefore, prohibited to send back a third country national married to a national of Member State where he is able to prove his identity and the conjugal ties and there is not evidence to establish that he represents a risk to the requirements of public policy, public security or public health'.[12]

The A-G has reaffirmed in his opinion in *EC Commission v Spain* that Member States may not require prior long-term visas for the entry of third-country national family members and his opinion was upheld by the Court.[13]

[1]   Immigration (European Economic Area) Regulations 2006, SI 2006/1003, reg 11(1).
[2]   SI 2000/2326, regs 12(3) and 13A, as amended and still in force; see SI 2006/1003, Sch 2, Part 2 Savings. As a result, the 2000 Regulations, as amended continue to apply to posted workers.
[3]   SI 2006/1003 reg 11(2).
[4]   SI 2006/1003 reg 12 (2).
[5]   SI 2006/1003, reg 13.
[6]   SI 2006/1003, reg 14.
[7]   SI 2006/1003, reg 15.
[8]   SI 2006/1003, regs 16–18.
[9]   *Bali (Family member: 3 month visit)* [2013] UKUT 00570 (IAC).
[10] In *R (on the application of Nouazli) v Secretary of State for the Home Department* [2013] EWCA Civ 1608, [2014] 1 All ER 1144, the Court of Appeal held that the detention of third country national family member of an EEA national pending deportation under Reg 24(1) of the 2006 EEA Regulations did not amount to unlawful discrimination on the grounds of nationality within the meaning of Article 18 TFEU since it was only concerned with the way in which citizens of the Union were treated in Member States.
[11] Case C-459/99 *Mouvement contre le racisme, l'antisémitisme et la xénophobie (MRAX) ASBL v Belgium* [2002] ECR I-6591.
[12] *MRAX* above, para 61.
[13] *EC Commission v Spain* C-157/03 [2005] ECR 1-2911, ECJ.

Right of residence

6.155 We have referred in the previous paragraph to documentation connected to the right of residence given to Union citizens and members of their families who exercise their free movement rights under the Directive. With the coming into force of the Citizens' Directive there was a change in the documentation needed. First, EEA nationals no longer get a residence permit as confirmation of their right of residence. Under the new regime there are registration certificates (reg 16) and a document certifying permanent residence (reg 18) for EEA nationals, and an EEA family permit and a residence card for family and extended family members (reg 17) and a permanent residence card (reg 18). These requirements of the 2006 Regulations match those of the Citizens' Directive. It is important to note that the residence permit is not the source of rights or a permission to remain, and no-one exercising free movement rights under the Directive or the 2006 Regulations will lose rights through the absence of a residence card or similar document, as their possession is not a precondition for the exercise of the holder's rights or the completion of administrative formalities.[1] The issue of various residence cards is to be completed not later than six months from the date of application.[2] During this period the applicant is allowed to remain in the country concerned. In *YB (EEA reg 17(4), proper approach) Ivory Coast*[3] the AIT held that neither the Citizens' Directive nor reg 17(4) of the 2006 Regulations confers on an 'extended family member' of an EEA national exercising Treaty rights a right to a residence card. Regulation 17(4) makes it discretionary: first, determine whether the person concerned qualifies as an extended family member under regulation 8. Next have regard, as rules of thumb only, to the criteria set out in comparable provisions of the Immigration Rules. In contrast to this absurd litany, our position is that in Articles 8 and 10 of the Directive 'family members' include 'other' family members. Article 10 offers a relatively simple requirement. First, (Article 10(1)) the right off residence 'shall' be evidenced by the issue of a residence document. Secondly, (Article 10(2)(e)) for the card to be issued the following documents must be presented a document issued by the relevant authority in the country of origin or the country from which they are arriving certifying that they are dependants or members of the household of the Union citizen. See also Article 8(5)(e) for a registration certificate where the 'other' family member is an EU citizen. It is also arguable, though not clear that 'family member' referred to in Article 9 also includes other family members, referred to in Article 3(2). See further **6.141** above.

[1]   Council Directive 2004/38/EC art 25(1). See further Case 48/75 Royer, Re [1976] ECR 497, [1976] 2 CMLR 619; Case 8/77 *Sagulo, Brenca and Bakhouche, Re* [1977] ECR 1495, [1977] 2 CMLR 585; *R v Pieck* [1981] QB 571; Case 59/85 *Netherlands v Reed* [1986] ECR 1283, [1987] 2 CMLR 448; Case C-363/89 Roux v Belgium [1991] ECR I-273, at para 9; Case C-459/99 *Mouvement contre le racisme, l'antisémitisme et la xénophobie (MRAX) ASBL v Belgium* [2002] ECR I-6591, at para 74; Case C-138/02 *Collins v Secretary of State for Work and Pensions* [2005] QB 145, para 40. It follows from this that that if a person fails or ceases to exercise community rights that carries no obligation to make a formal revocation of their residence permit – though the family member's right is derived from their spouse, as will be the case for a family member of a qualified person, it does not follow that there must be revocation of their documentation in order for his rights to be revoked: *DA (EEA, revocation of residence document) Algeria* [2006] UKAIT 00027 (9 March 2006). However, note *Sannie v Secretary of State for the Home Department* [2013] EWCA Civ 1638 in which the Court of Appeal upheld a revocation of a residence card where the underlying criteria were not met, approving *Nkrumah (OFM – annulment of residence permit) Ghana* [2011] UKUT 163 (IAC); in preference to *Samsam (Syria) (EEA: revocation and retained rights)* [2011] UKUT 165 (IAC).

[2]   In the Citizens' Directive the six-month time limit is expressly retained for the obtaining of first residence cards (Article 10) and permanent residence cards (Art 20) for family members and for revocation of an expulsion decision (Article 32) (Council Directive 2004/38/EC). As regards a similar provision in Council Directive 2004/38/EC the Commission successfully brought infringement proceedings against Spain for the failure by the Spanish authorities to make decisions on residence permit applications expeditiously and in any event with six months (see Case C-157/03 *EC Commission v Spain* [2005] ECR 1-2911). See further *R (on the application of AFP Boucherit) v Secretary of State for the Home Department* [2011] EWHC 1175 (Admin) (3 March 2011) (no obligation to act reasonably promptly in issuing a permanent residence card to Union citizens under art 19.2 of Directive 2004/38/EC, just because there was a six-month time limit on issuing such a card to family members who are non EEA nationals under art 20.1).

[3]   [2008] UKAIT 00062.

6.156 A residence card/permit performs two functions. It is evidence that the Secretary of State was satisfied at the time it was issued that the holder had rights of residence under EU law, and its continued validity serves to enable third parties, including employers, to be satisfied of the holder's status during the currency of the card. A non-EU national family member may in particular need to prove who he or she is and that he or she has authority to work and reside in the UK for the time being.[1] Residence documentation cannot be arbitrarily cancelled or revoked and, for reasons noted by the Court of Appeal in *Dias* before it reached the CJEU,[2] proof of continued existence of a right of residence cannot be demanded at frequent intervals during its currency. It is trite law that a residence card is the evidence of the right and not the source of it. This has been confirmed by the CJEU in the recent case of *Dias*[3] where the Court held that where a residence card has been issued to Union citizens and members of their families, it is declaratory of residence rights but is not capable of establishing, on its own, that the owner of it has fulfilled the underlying conditions needed to gain permanent residence (work, self-employment or self-sufficiency). However, a residence card may provide some evidence of past lawful status if there is some evidence to support the exercise of Treaty rights, nothing to contradict, and the historic position can no longer be established with precision.[4] Things may have been slightly different under the EEA Regulations in force in February 2004 (the Immigration (European Economic Area) Regulations 2000, where the definition of 'residence document' states that such a document constitutes 'proof of the holder's right of residence in the United Kingdom' and therefore an Immigration Judge was wrong to find there was no evidence of work over a period where such a document had been issued).[5]

In *Nkrumah (OFM - annulment of residence permit) Ghana*[6] the appellant applied to the Home Office in 2008 for an EEA residence card as a member of his sister's extended family within the meaning of regulation 8(2) of the Immigration (EEA) Regulations 2006 ('the Regulations'). On 21 October 2009 a residence card valid for five years until October 2014 was stamped in his passport. The passport was retained in the Home Office until December 2009 when it was sent to the appellant with a letter stating that the application was refused and affording a right of appeal. The Upper Tribunal held that the grant of a residence card in extended family cases is a matter of discretion for the Secretary of State. By analogy with cases of leave to remain, where a residence card is issued, it takes effect when communicated to the applicant: see *Rafiq v Secretary of State for the Home Department*.[7] Where, as here, the residence card is unambiguously stamped in the passport and communicated, it retains its validity as authority to remain unless or until it expires, lapses by reason of prolonged absence or is revoked under regulation 20. It may be revoked if it is shown that it was issued by mistake to someone not entitled to it and it was still open to the Home Office to do so: see further from **6.170**. Where a right of residence is being revoked under regulation 20(1) on public policy grounds, the circumstances are likely to be similar to deportation on conducive grounds or general grounds of refusal of entry where it is clear that the burden lies on the Secretary of State to establish on the civil standard the facts justifying revocation.[8]

1   *Samsam (EEA: revocation and retained rights) Syria* [2011] UKUT 165 (IAC) (13 April 2011), quoting *Secretary of State for Work and Pensions v Maria Dias* [2009] EWCA Civ 31 at [36]. *Samsam* is also cited as *HS Syria*.
2   *Secretary of State for Work and Pensions v Dias (Maria)* [2009] EWCA Civ 31 at [38].
3   Case C-325/09 *Secretary of State for Work and Pensions v Maria Dias* [2011] 3 CMLR 1103. For a full discussion of this case, see **6.162**, below.

4 *Samsam (EEA: revocation and retained rights) Syria* at [29], which must now be read with
   Sannie v Secretary of State for the Home Department [2013] EWCA Civ 1638, [2013] All ER
   (D) 338 (Oct).
5 *Alarape (Article 12, EC Reg 1612/68) Nigeria* [2011] UKUT 413 (IAC) (10 October 2011).
   See CJEU judgment in *Alarape v Secretary of State for the Home Department (AIRE Centre
   intervening)* Case C-529/11 [2014] All ER (EC) 470, [2013] 1 WLR 2883 on a reference by
   the Upper Tribunal, dated 8 May 2013 reported at [2013] 1 WLR. 2883; [2014] All ER (EC)
   470; [2013] 3 CMLR 38; [2013] Imm. A.R. 752; [2013] I.N.L.R. 542 in which the CJEU held
   that that the parent of a child who had reached the age of majority and who had obtained
   access to education on the basis of Article 12 of Council Regulation (EEC) No 1612/68 could
   continue to have a derived right of residence under that article if that child remained in need
   of the presence and care of that parent in order to be able to complete his education; but that
   periods of residence pursuant to that derived right of residence could not be taken into
   consideration for the purposes of the acquisition of those family members to a right of
   permanent residence under the Citizens' Directive.
6 [2011] UKUT 163 (IAC) (4 April 2011). This case was approved in *Sannie v Secretary of State
   for the Home Department* [2013] EWCA Civ 1638 in preference to *Samsam* [2011] UKUT
   00165 (IAC).
7 [1998] INLR 349 at 355.
8 *Samsam (EEA: revocation and retained rights) Syria* at [24]. See *JC (Part 9 HC 395-burden of
   proof) China* [2007] UKAIT 00027. For more detail of the circumstances when a residence
   card may be revoked, see *Samsam*. However, there appears to be no procedure for inquiring
   afresh into the existence of a residence right in the absence of reasonable grounds to suspect
   that no such right exists. The basis of the reasonable suspicion must be demonstrated by the
   Home Office so there is some evidential burden to raise a sufficient doubt to justify further
   inquiry – if the Home Office have reason to believe that the wife has been voluntarily
   unemployed and not exercising other treaty rights of residence in the UK and this is relevant
   to the grant of a residence card, it can raise the issue from its own inquiries.

Types of Residence

6.157 There are five different types of residence provided for by the Citizens
Directive (2004/38/EC), one from Regulations and the others from Treaties or
EU jurisprudence:

Under Article 6 – This applies to Union Citizens and members of their family
as defined in Article 2(2). They have a right of residence up to three months
without conditions or any formalities other than holding an identity card or
passport or, in the case of family members who are non-EEA citizens, a valid
passport.

Under Article 7 – This applies to Union citizens and members of their family,
including those family members who are not nationals of a Member State for
rights of residence for more than three months, subject to the requirement that
a Union Citizen needs to be a worker, self-employed, self-sufficient, or a
student. (Details are set out at **6.1**.)

Under Articles 12 and 13 – There is a retained right of residence for family
members of a Union citizen, when the sponsoring Union citizen dies or departs
from the host country, or there has been a divorce, annulment of marriage or
termination of the registered partnership referred to in art 2(2)(b). Retained
residence can lead to permanent residence under Articles 16 and 18 after five
years' lawful residence in the host Member State. (Details are set out at
6.159–6.160 below.)

Under Article 16 – Union citizens and their family members of whatever
nationality can qualify for permanent residence after five years' continuous

lawful residence as a worker, in self-employment, self-sufficiency or study, as laid down in Chapter III of the Directive. (Details are set out in **6.102–6.103**, above, and **6.159**, below.) Those with a retained right of residence can qualify for permanent residence after residing legally for five consecutive years in the host State.

Under Article 17 – Permanent residence before completion of five years' continuous residence can be acquired by workers or self-employed persons who have retired or have stopped work because of permanent incapacity, and for frontier workers or family members of such persons permanent residence may be given in less than five years. (Details are set out at **6.115** above.)

Under Article 12, Regulation 1612/68 (now Article 10, Regulation 492/2011/EU). Children of workers who are enrolled in school or College have a right to remain in education with a concomitant right of residence, even if the parent from whom they have derived this right has left the host Member State or ceased to be a worker. Their parents/carers may also have a derived right of residence. In retained right of residence following the death or departure of the main EEA sponsor this right is derived from Article 12(3) of the Directive.[1]

Under Article 20 TFEU/general principles of EU law. In the *Chen*,[2] *Teixera*[3] and *Zambrano*[4] situations derived rights of residence for parent/carers do not derive from the Directive or Regulations but from Article 20, TFEU or general principles of EU law. However, the new Regulation 15A of the EEA Regulations now makes provision for a 'derivative right of residence' in certain specified situations, which purports to implement the Article 20 TFEU derived rights stemming from *Zambrano* et seq. In so far as Article 20/other EU law provisions give rise to rights that are not reflected in regulation 15A, such rights can be asserted in direct reliance on the EU legal provision. (More details are set out in **6.77** and **6.112** above.)

[1]   *Okafor v Secretary of State for the Home Department* [2011] EWCA Civ 499, [2011] 1 WLR 3071, [2011] NLJR 636 (20 April 2011).

[2]   Case C-200/02 *Chen and Zhu v Secretary of State for the Home Department* [2005] QB 325, [2005] INLR 1.

[3]   Case C-480/08 *Teixeira v Lambeth London Borough Council* [2010] ICR 1118, [2010] PTSR 1913, [2010] ELR 261, ECJ.

[4]   Case C-34/09 *Ruiz Zambrano v Office National de l'Emploi (ONEm)* [2011] All ER (EC) 491, [2011] 2 CMLR 1197, ECJ.

6.158 Where registration is required, the deadline may not be less than three months from the date of arrival. A registration certificate must be issued immediately and should contain the name and address of the person registering (Article 8(2)). Under the Directive the documentation needed to obtain a registration certificate will vary depending on the particular free movement right being exercised. Member States may only require that:

- *workers and the self employed* present a valid identity card or passport, a confirmation of engagement from the employer or a certificate of employment, or proof that they are self-employed persons;

- *the self-sufficient* present a valid identity card or passport and provide proof that they satisfy the conditions laid down for self sufficiency;

- *students* present a valid identity card or passport, provide proof of enrolment at an accredited establishment and of comprehensive sickness insurance cover and the declaration or equivalent means to show they have sufficient funds. Member States may not require this declaration to refer to any specific amount of resources.

In determining what are 'sufficient resources', Member States must not lay down a fixed amount, but must take into account the personal situation of the person concerned. In all cases the funds needed should be no higher than the threshold below which nationals of the host Member State become eligible for social assistance, or, where this criterion is not applicable, no higher than the minimum social security pension paid by the host Member State (Article 8(4)). Regulation 4(4) of the 2006 Regulations imposes two alternative tests: either that the EEA national has resources in excess of 'the maximum level of resources which a British citizen and his family members may possess if he is to become eligible for social assistance under the United Kingdom benefit system' or, if that requirement does not apply, the decision-maker thinks that the resources of the person(s) concerned should be regarded as sufficient having regard to their situation.[1]

Family members of Union citizens, who are themselves Union citizens, may also be issued a registration certificate and will be required to produce the following documents:

(a)   a valid identity card or passport;
(b)   a document attesting to the existence of a family relationship or of a registered partnership;
(c)   where appropriate, the registration certificate of the Union citizen whom they are accompanying or joining;
(d)   in cases of direct descendants or ascendants, documentary evidence that they meet conditions laid down for their qualifying as 'family members';
(e)   in cases of extended family members falling under Article 3(2)(a) of the Directive, a document issued by the relevant authority in the country of origin or country from which they are arriving, certifying that they are dependants or members of the household of the Union citizen, or proof of the existence of serious health grounds which strictly require the personal care of the family member by the Union citizen;
(f)   in cases of partners who have not married or entered into a civil partnership (Article 3(2)(b)), proof of the existence of a durable relationship with the Union citizen.

These provisions have been transposed into UK domestic law by reg 16 of the 2006 Regulations.[2] In the case of extended family members who are EEA nationals, the Secretary of State uses the registration process as the means of exercising the discretion given to Member States under Article 3(2)(b) and (c) of the Directive to facilitate the entry of extended family members in accordance with its national legislation.[3] Under the 2006 Regulations, the broad rule is that a qualified person is entitled to reside in the UK for so long as he or she remains a qualified person (reg 14(1)) and family members of a qualified person are entitled to reside for so long as they remain family members of the person through whom they qualify for a residence card (see reg 14(2)). Both the Directive[4] and the 2006 Regulations[5] make detailed provision to ensure that a worker or self employed person remains qualified despite periods of sickness or unemployment (see from **6.95** above).

[1]   Regulation 4(4), amended by Immigration (European Economic Area) (Amendment) Regulations 2011, 2011/1247, reg 2(2) (June 2, 2011). See *Pensionsversicherungsanstalt v Brey* (C-140/12) [2014] All ER (EC) 534 , [2014] 1 WLR 1080, CJEU on the approach to be taken on the 'unreasonable burden' issue. The Court emphasised the need for the state to carry out a 'comprehensive assessment of the specific burden that would be created' by recourse to any benefits in the individual case. In particular, it was important for the national court to be able to examine such factors as the amount and regularity of the income received, whether the person has been issued with a certificate of residence, and the period during which the benefit applied for was likely to be granted. The issue is not, therefore, a mere application of the binary *KA (Adequacy of maintenance) Pakistan* [2006] UKAIT 00065 test that is used under the Immigration Rules.
[2]   SI 2006/1003.
[3]   SI 2006/1003, reg 16(5) and (6). For further discussion see **6.35** above.
[4]   Directive 2004/38/EC.
[5]   SI 2006/1003, reg 6(2).

Permanent residence in the UK

6.159 Under the Citizens' Directive, Union citizens who have resided legally for a continuous period of five years in the host Member State shall have the right of permanent residence there (Article 16(1)).[1] This also applies to non-EEA family members who have legally resided with the Union citizen in the host Member State for a continuous period of five years (Article 16(2)). Continuity of residence shall not be affected by temporary absences not exceeding a total of six months a year, or by absences of a longer duration for compulsory military service, or by one absence of a maximum of 12 consecutive months for important reasons such as pregnancy and childbirth, serious illness, study or vocational training, or a posting in another Member State or a third country (Article 16(3));[2] and, once acquired, the right of permanent residence shall be lost only through absence from the host Member State for a period exceeding two consecutive years (Art 16(4)). The UK implementing provisions are set out at regulation 15 of the 2006 EEA Regulations. We dealt above, at **6.115** and **6.134**, with the eligibility for permanent residence of workers who have retired, are permanently incapacitated, or are 'frontier workers', and their family members, including where the worker has died or departed the host Member State. Those who are resident in the UK on the basis of a derivative right of residence under regulation 15A of the 2006 EEA Regulations, on the basis of Article 20 TFEU/the general principles of EU law, or under Article 10 of Regulation 492/2011 (ex Article 12, Regulation 1612/68) cannot qualify for permanent residence on the basis of such rights alone.[3]

[1]   Reflected in regulation 15 of the Immigration (European Economic Area) Regulations 2006/1003.
[2]   In *Babajanov (Continuity of residence - Immigration (EEA) Regulations 2006)* [2013] UKUT 00513 (IAC), the Upper Tribunal noted that the one absence for between 6 and 12 months 'for important reasons' needs to be justified and needs to be for a purpose of a kind comparable for those illustrated (eg pregnancy, childbirth etc) which embrace 'compelling events and/or an activity which by implication is linked to the exercise of treaty rights in the UK. The reason should be sufficiently compelling to require the Union citizen (or family member) to leave the host Member State for a purpose connected with his continued integration in that Member State or for a reason that is triggered by considerations of importance that need to be met

notwithstanding that integration': [17]; 'the purpose of absence of not more than twelve months must be examined in the light of the degree of integration present in the host Member State before the absence and the manner in which that integration has been affected by the absence: [19]. The Upper Tribunal also confirmed that permanent residence is is capable of being established whilst a national of a Member State or a family member of that national is outside the host country provided the reasons for the absence come within Article 16(3) (and reg 3(2))': [17]. Absences are also dealt with below from **6.161** AND **6.162** in the discussion of *Lassal* and *Dias*, and at **6.165** in relation to the issue of the effect of imprisonment on continuity of residence, and the relevance of time spent in prison, for the purposes of accruing permanent residence.

3   *Bee and another (permanent/derived rights of residence)* [2013] UKUT 00083 (IAC); *Alarape v Secretary of State for the Home Department Case* C-529/11, CJEU [2013] 1 WLR 2883.

6.160 A number of recent cases from the CJEU have clarified a number of issues revolving around the vexed question of whether residence under national law/other EU legal provisions (ie other than the Citizens' Directive) count for the purposes of accruing permanent residence thereunder, among others.

Lassal

6.161 In *Lassal*,[1] the appellant, a French national, entered the UK in January 1999 in order to look for work. From September 1999 to February 2005, while she resided in the UK, Ms Lassal was working or seeking work. It was common ground between the parties to the main proceedings that Ms Lassal was a 'worker' for the purposes of EU law from January 1999 to February 2005. In February 2005 she left the UK to visit her mother in France, where she stayed for ten months. In December 2005, she returned to the UK where she sought work. From January to November 2006 she received Job Seeker's Allowance. In November 2006 she applied for Income Support on the basis that she was pregnant. That application was refused on the ground that she had no right to reside in the UK.

She appealed and when the case came to the CA it was referred to the CJEU. For the purposes of Income Support as provided for in the Social Security Contributions and Benefits Act 1992 and the Income Support (General) Regulations, no claimant is to be treated as habitually resident in the UK unless he or she has a 'right to reside' there. It was common ground in the case that the right of permanent residence provided for in Article 16 of Directive 2004/38 constitutes a right to reside for the purposes of Income Support.

The main issue before the CJEU was whether periods of residence, completed before the date of transposition of Directive 2004/38 (the Citizens Directive), in accordance with EU law instruments in operation prior to that date, could be taken into account for the purposes of acquiring the right of permanent residence provided for by Article 16 thereof. The Court of Justice rejected the argument of the UK that only periods of residence either ending on 30 April 2006 or thereafter, or which commence after 30 April 2006, should be taken into account. The court held:

(1)   that continuous periods of residence of five years which were completed before the date of transposition of Directive 2004/38, namely 30 April 2006, in accordance with earlier European Union law instruments,

must be taken into account for the purposes of the acquisition of the right of permanent residence pursuant to Article 16(1) of that Directive; and

(2)   that absences from the host Member State of less than two consecutive years, which occurred before 30 April 2006 but following a continuous period of five years' legal residence completed before that date, are not such as to affect the acquisition of the right of permanent residence pursuant to art 16(1) of the Directive.

1   C-162/09 *Secretary of State for Work and Pensions v Lassal (Child Poverty Action Group intervening)* [2011] All ER (EC) 1169, [2011] 1 CMLR 972, ECJ.

Dias

6.162 In *Dias*[1] Ms Dias was a Portuguese national who had worked in the UK on and off from January 1998 until 2007 when she applied for Income Support. This was refused on the ground that she had no right to reside in the UK. When her case came to the Court of Appeal it was referred to the CJEU. The brief facts were that she entered the UK in January 1998. Her working time and residence can be divided into the following five periods ('the first to fifth periods'): (i) January 1998 to summer 2002: in work; (ii) summer 2002 to 17 April 2003: on maternity leave; (iii) 18 April 2003 to 25 April 2004: not working; (iv) 26 April 2004 to 23 March 2007: in work; and (v) since 24 March 2007: not working. The issues in her case were twofold: (i) the status of residence covered by a validly issued EEA residence permit; and (ii) the effect of gaps in the continuity of the applicant's lawful residence (where the person was out of work, not self-employed or self-sufficient). On 13 May 2000, the Home Office had issued Ms Dias with a residence permit corresponding to the right of residence provided for in art 4 of Directive 68/360 with a period of validity from 13 May 2000 to 13 May 2005. In her case the Court of Justice held that:

(1)   periods of residence completed before 30 April 2006 on the basis solely of a validly issued residence permit cannot be regarded as legal residence for the purposes of acquiring the right of permanent residence under Article 16(1) of Directive 2004/38, unless the person fulfilled the underlying conditions needed to gain permanent residence (work, self-employment or self-sufficiency);[2] this is because the residence permits are declaratory of residence rights but are not capable of establishing, on their own, rights for their holders (at [48]–[55]);

(2)   periods of residence of less than two consecutive years, completed on the basis solely of a residence permit validly issued pursuant to Directive 68/360, without the conditions governing entitlement to a right of residence having been satisfied, which occurred before 30 April 2006 and after a continuous period of five years' legal residence completed prior to that date, are not such as to affect the acquisition of the right of permanent residence under Article 16(1) of Directive 2004/38 (paras [61]–[66]).

Some commentators[3] have suggested that it can be deduced from this decision that the fact that the five-year qualifying period of residence is interspersed with periods of less than two years, which do not count, because the person cannot fulfil the conditions of legal residence (ie not working, not self-employed or self-sufficient), is irrelevant. They argue that as long as any gap is less than two years, the person can aggregate the lawful periods until they come to five years of qualifying residence. That is not what the judgment says. The court has made it quite clear that any gap up to two years must come after completion of the relevant five years' residence. This is in keeping with the analogous situation of absences catered for in art 16(4). Gaps caused by temporary absences not exceeding six months in a year and other specified longer gaps, including one year for pregnancy and childbirth, are permitted by art 6(3) and it is arguable, using the same analogy as in *Dias*, that lawful residence, prior to the completion of the five years, can be interspersed by gaps spent in the UK, which are no longer than those specified in Article 16(3).

[1] Case C-325/09 *Secretary of State for Work and Pensions v Dias (Maria)* [2011] 3 CMLR 1103.

[2] This gives some support to the view expressed in *Amos v Secretary of State for the Home Department* [2011] EWCA Civ 552, [2011] 1 WLR 2952 (12 May 2011) that there is nothing in the Directive or the Regulations or in the decisions of the Court of Justice to detract from the general principle of Community Law that procedural matters are subject to the domestic law of the Member States and the Citizens Directive imposes no evidentiary obligations on Member States and it was for applicants to prove their cases.

[3] See *ILPA European Update*, September 2011.

Ziolkowski and Szeja

6.163 In *Ziolkowski* and *Szeja*[1] involved two Polish nationals who arrived in Germany, in 1988 and 1989 respectively, before Poland's accession to the EU, and obtained the right to reside there on humanitarian grounds and their right to reside was extended regularly on the same grounds under German law. After Poland's accession to the EU they applied for but were refused permanent residence by the national authorities. Could their earlier period of lawful residence under domestic law count towards permanent residence under the Citizens Directive, Article 16.1? In a judgment delivered on 21 December 2011, the court held that it could do so under the principle that the provisions on citizenship of the EU are applicable as soon as they enter into force and must be applied to the present effects of situations arising previously. Consequently, the provisions on permanent residence could be relied upon by Union citizens and applied to the present and future effects of situations arising before the accession of Poland to the EU.

Arnuf Clauder. A further decision on permanent residence and family reunion comes not from the CJEU but from the EFTA Court.[2] The case of *Proceedings Concerning Clauder (Arnuf)*[3] concerned a retired German national who had lived in Liechtenstein since 1992, first as a worker and then as a retired person. He had been granted permanent residence under national law which recognised a permanent residence under art 16 of the Citizens Directive. He and his first wife divorced and he remarried a German national. However, his pension was so low, that when his new wife came to live with him in Liechtenstein, he became eligible for social assistance from Liechtenstein (apparently even if his wife worked). The question was whether Article 16 of the Directive conferred a derived right of residence on the family members of the principal EEA national irrespective of the fact that they do not come within

Article 7(a), (b) or (c) of the Directive (workers self-employed or self-sufficient). The EFTA Court found that:

- The right to permanent residence under Article 16 does not confer an autonomous right of permanent residence on family members, but a right to reside with the beneficiary of a right of permanent residence as a member of his or her family. It is only on satisfying the condition of legal residence in the host state for a continuous period of five years that a family member may acquire an autonomous right to permanent residence.

- In contrast to Article 1 of Directive 90/364/EEC and Article 1 of Directive 90/365/EEC, Directive 2004/38 does not contain a general requirement of sufficient resources. Such a requirement exists neither with regard to workers and self-employed persons nor with regard to persons who have acquired a permanent right of residence pursuant to the Directive.

- Once an EEA national has acquired permanent residence under Article 16 it is no longer a requirement that he or she should have sufficient resources or be economically active and the enjoyment of the right of permanent residence would be impaired and deprived of its full effectiveness if the EEA national were precluded from founding a family because he or she had insufficient resources (at [46]). So the admission and residence of family members in such cases is not subject to a condition that the family should have sufficient resources (at [47]).

The upshot of this case if it is followed by the CJEU is that it would mean that any EEA national who has resided in the UK for the necessary five years to qualify for permanent residence under Article 16 of the Directive (ie as a worker, self-employed or self-sufficient person) and who then becomes dependent on public funds is still entitled to bring his or her family members to the UK whether the family member is an EEA national or a third country national and even though the whole family may be dependent on public funds in order to survive.

[1] Joined Cases C-424/10 and 425/10 *Ziolkowski and Szeja v Land Berlin*. See also *Ogieriakhi v Minister for Justice and Equality and others* (Case-244/13), CJEU, [2014] 1 WLR 3823 on the accrual of residence under Reg 1612/68 by a separated spouse.
[2] Iceland, Liechtenstein and Norway are not EU Member States but belong to the EEA and cannot use the CJEU, but by reason of the EEA Agreement 1992 are bound by the Citizens Directive (2004/38); see **6.5** above.
[3] Case E-4/11 *Proceedings Concerning Clauder (Arnuf)* [2012] 1 CMLR 1 (26 July 2011), EFTA Ct.

6.164 As far as the UK courts are concerned there is a miscellany of new cases:

- In *Samsam (EEA: revocation and retained rights) Syria*[1] the UT said that to gain permanent residence there is no need to have resided for a continuous period of five years in only one category (worker, self-employed, or self-sufficient).
- In *EN (Continuity of residence – family member) Nigeria*[2] it was held that to gain permanent residence under art 16 a family member has to show that not only he but also his Union national spouse has been residing in the UK in accordance with the Regulations for a continuous period of five years – if the continuity of the residence of the Union

national is broken, having taken into account the permitted gaps in residence provided for in reg 3 of the 2006 EEA Regulations, neither the Union national nor the spouse can acquire permanent residence.

- In *Amos v Secretary of State for the Home Department*[3] the Court of Appeal was prepared to assume without deciding that separation short of divorce does not affect the right of the non-national spouse under art 16 of the Directive if both the EEA national and his or her non-national spouse continue to reside in the same Member State (at [24]). So the effect of the 1985 case of *Diatta*[4] carries over from Regulation 1612/68 to the Citizens Directive, notwithstanding the difference in the wording as between the Regulation and the Directive.

- In *PM (EEA – spouse – 'residing with') Turkey*[5] the UT went further and held that the new right of permanent residence granted to Union citizens and their family members was an extension of European Union law of rights granted under previous provisions of Community law – it would accordingly seem most unlikely that a non-national spouse would have to comply with a new restrictive requirement of residence in the household of an EEA national during the five years preceding the acquisition of the right of permanent residence that was not a requirement under the previous law as exemplified in *Diatta*. The fact that spouses or civil partners decide not to live together in a common household may sometimes invite inquiry into the nature of the relationship, though not where there has been genuine matrimonial cohabitation for some time; an inference of marriage of convenience cannot arise solely because a married couple are not living in the same household.

1   *Samsam (EEA: revocation and retained rights) Syria* [2011] UKUT 165 (IAC) (13 April 2011).
2   [2011] UKUT 55 (IAC) (1 February 2011).
3   [2011] EWCA Civ 552, [2011] 1 WLR 2952 (12 May 2011).
4   Case 267/83 *Diatta (Aissatou) v Land Berlin*: 267/83[1985] ECR 567, [1986] 2 CMLR 164, ECJ.
5   [2011] UKUT 89 (IAC) (7 March 2011). This view was endorsed in *Samsam (EEA: revocation and retained rights) Syria*. It applies to both the retained right of residence and the acquisition of the permanent right of residence; proof of cohabitation may be a relevant question to ask to rebut any suggestion of marriage of convenience or that the spouse has permanently left the UK but neither issue is raised in the present case. As long as both parties remain in the UK, and remain married, and the EEA spouse is exercising Treaty rights, the non-EA spouse obtains a right of residence (at [43] and [50]).

6.165 Article 16(3) provides that continuity shall not be affected by temporary absences described at **6.159**, above. The CJEU has confirmed in *Onuekwere v Secretary of State for the Home Department*[1] that periods of time spent in prison by a third country national cannot be taken into account for the purposes of accruing five years lawful residence under Article 16 of the Citizens' Directive; and, furthermore, that any period of imprisonment interrupts continuity of residence, such that periods of lawful residence before and after an episode of imprisonment cannot be aggregated. In other words, a period of imprisonment not only stops the continuity 'clock', upon imprisonment; it 'resets' it, as well. Periods of wrongful detention, pre-trial remand that lead to an acquittal or a non-custodial sentence, or periods of immigration detention should count towards permanent residence if the claimant qualifies before and after the detention in question.[2] An EEA national does not cease to be a qualified person as a result of being detained in a hospital pursuant to an order of the court under the Mental Health Act 1983, having not been convicted of any criminal offence.[3]

[1]   *Onuekwere v Secretary of State for the Home Department* (C-378/12) [2014] 1 WLR 2420; [2014] 2 CMLR 1369; [2014] Imm AR 551. The Upper Tribunal decision referring the case to the CJEU is reported as *Onuekwere (imprisonment – residence)* [2012] UKUT 00269 (IAC). The CJEU's position confirms earlier English authority, eg *Batista (Valentine) v Secretary of State for the Home Department* [2010] EWCA Civ 896, [2010] All ER (D) 323 (Jul) (re deportation on grounds of public order and public security) and *Carvalho v Secretary of State for the Home Department* [2010] EWCA Civ 1406 and *Ogunyemi (imprisonment breaks continuity of residence) Nigeria* [2011] UKUT 164 (IAC) (in relation to permanent residence). Prior to *Onuekwere* (CJEU) it was at least arguable that lawful residence either side of an episode of imprisonment could be aggregated (see, eg *Jarusevicius (EEA Reg 21 – effect of imprisonment)* [2012] UKUT 00120(IAC)), but this possibility is now ruled out.

[2]   *Essa (EEA: rehabilitation/integration)* [2013] UKUT 00316 (IAC). Note that this case amounts to guidance given by Blake J pending the CJEU's decisions in *Onuekwere* and *G* (see **6.179** below, some of which is inconsistent with those judgments. However, some of the points raised in *Essa*, such as this one, remain good law. See also *HR (Portugal) v Secretary of State for the Home Department* [2009] EWCA Civ 371 in which Sedley LJ said at [45] that acquittals following remands in custody will require 'judge made adjustments' to the principle that time spent in prison is not relevant residence.

[3]   *JO (qualified person – hospital order – effect) Slovakia* [2012] UKUT 00237(IAC).

Retained right of residence

6.166   Under Article 12 family Members retain their right of residence in the event of the death or departure from the host Member State of the Union citizen if they meet certain conditions contained in the Article and the same applies under Article 13 in the event of divorce, annulment of marriage or termination of registered partnership. Nationals of member States acquire permanent residence if they become entitled to any of the free movement rights set out in Article 7. Different conditions apply to non-nationals. If they manage to keep their right of residence by meeting these conditions for a period of five years they will acquire permanent residence under Article 18. These provision have been transposed into the 2006 Regulations.[1] There is a difference between the right of permanent residence under Community law and the grant of indefinite or permanent leave to remain under UK domestic immigration law, which led to litigation, but this is now history, given the new right of permanent residence given by Community law (see sixth edition at 6.121).[2]

[1]   Immigration (European Economic Area) Regulations 2006, SI 2006/1003, regs 15 and 18.

[2]   HC 395, paras 255–257 have been deleted subject to the transitional provisions in paragraphs 5 and 8 which continue to apply for the purpose of determining an applications made before 30 April 2006 for an endorsement under either paras 255 or 257A or 257B.

6.167   *Okafor*[1] is a case about retained rights where the principal EEA national died leaving children still at school. It was common ground that before her death in 2007, the mother of the children had not fulfilled any of the conditions in Article 7(1) but the evidence established that both children were at school. This meant that under Article 12(3) of the Directive the children and their father (as the person with custody after the death of the mother) are entitled to retain the right of residence until the completion of the studies. So they had a retained right of residence under Article 12(3) of the Directive. But the father wanted to go further. He argued that Article 12(3), standing on its own, also provided a route to permanent residence. The court held that it could not do so. Article 12(3) cannot provide, standing on its own, a route for acquiring the right to permanent residence.

Amos[2] was a case where two non-EEA spouses were seeking to remain in the UK following their divorces. Both had separated before the actual divorces. The Court of Appeal detailed the requirements to qualify for a retained right of residence in these circumstances:

- The court was prepared to assume without deciding that separation short of divorce does not affect the right of the non-national spouse under art 16 of the Directive if both the EEA national and his or her non-national spouse continue to reside in the same Member State (at [24]). So the effect of the 1985 case of *Diatta*[3] carries over from Regulation 1612/68 to the Citizens Directive, notwithstanding the difference in the wording as between the Regulation and the Directive.
- Secondly, it is only if a spouse and other family members of the EEA national have acquired a right of residence that the question of its retention arises. So a divorced spouse must establish that he or she has the right of residence under art 6(2) (right of initial three months' residence) or art 7(2) (right of residence for more than three months) of the Citizens Directive (2004/38) before the question can be determined whether, notwithstanding the divorce, it has been retained by virtue of art 13 (at [20]).
- Thirdly, if, immediately before divorce, the requirements of art 7.2 are satisfied, the non-national must then satisfy the requirements of art 13.2 (at [26]). These are that the marriage or registered partnership has lasted at least three years, including one year in the host Member State.
- Fourthly, to acquire the right of permanent residence, the persons concerned must be able to show throughout a continuous period of five years that they are workers, self-employed persons or self-sufficient, as required by arts 13.2 and 18 of the Directive.

[1] *Okafor v Secretary of State for the Home Department* [2011] EWCA Civ 499, [2011] 1 WLR 3071, [2011] NLJR 636 (20 April 2011).
[2] *Amos v Secretary of State for the Home Department* [2011] EWCA Civ 552, [2011] 1 WLR 2952 (12 May 2011).
[3] Case 267/83 *Diatta (Aissatou) v Land Berlin*: 267/83 [1985] ECR 567, [1986] 2 CMLR 164, ECJ.

Appeals against adverse decisions

6.168 The right of appeal against an adverse 'EEA decision'[1] is contained in Part 6 of the 2006 Regulations.[2] The appeal lies to the First-tier Tribunal (Immigration and Asylum Chamber), except where it raises interests of national security; or the interests of the relationship between the UK and another country, when it lies to the Special Immigration Appeals Commission (SIAC). Jurisdiction arises from regulation 26; it does not arise from section 82 of the Nationality, Immigration and Asylum Act 2002. EEA nationals may only appeal if they produce a valid national identity card/EEA passport (regulation 26(2)).[3] If a person claims to be in a durable relationship with an EEA national he may only appeal if he produces (a) a passport; and (b) either (i) an EEA family permit; or (ii) sufficient evidence to satisfy *the Secretary* *of State* that he is in *a relationship* with that EEA national (ie it will be necessary to see whether in the refusal letter the SSHD accepts that there is at least a relationship even if it is not accepted to be a durable one). Regulation 26(3) and (3A) impose on family members the burden of satisfying the tribunal of their relationship to the EEA national as a fact precedent to the existence of jurisdiction (although tribunals will in practice hear the appeal substantively on all issues and determine the jurisdictional issues first). Regulation 26(5) empowers the SSHD to certify a ground, thereby preventing them from bringing an appeal, if it has been considered in a previous appeal brought under the 2006 EEA Regulations or under section 82 of the 2002 Act. Regulation 26(7) incorporates specified provisions of the Nationality Immigration and Asylum Act 2002 that are listed in Schedule 1 of the 2006 Regs, which relate to the tribunal's powers in the exercise of the appellate jurisdiction.

1   An EEA decision is defined in reg 2(1) as 'a decision under these Regulations that concerns—(a) a person's entitlement to be admitted to the United Kingdom; (b) a person's entitlement to be issued with or have renewed, or not to have revoked, a registration certificate, residence card, derivative residence card, document certifying permanent residence or permanent residence card; (c) a person's removal from the United Kingdom; or (d) the cancellation, pursuant to reg 20A, of a person's right to reside in the United Kingdom'. It does not include decisions under regs 24AA (human rights considerations and interim orders to suspend removal) or 29AA (temporary admission in order to submit case in person); these are addressed at **6.195** below.
2   SI 2006/1003.
3   Note SSHD's discretion to accept alternative evidence of identity if a person is unable to produce the required evidence due to circumstances beyond their control: reg 29A.

6.169 An appeal can be brought 'in-country' unless specified to the contrary by regulation 27(1),[1] which lists as out of country appeals the following EEA decisions:

(a)   to refuse to admit him to the United Kingdom;
(aa)   to make an exclusion order against him;
(b)   to refuse to revoke a deportation or exclusion order made against him;
(c)   to refuse to issue him with an EEA family permit;[2]
(ca)   to revoke, or to refuse to issue or renew any document under these Regulations where that decision is taken at a time when the relevant person is outside the United Kingdom; or
(d)   to remove him from the United Kingdom after he has entered the United Kingdom in breach of a deportation or exclusion order.

Regulation 27(2) provides that paragraphs 27(1)(a) and (aa) do not apply where the person is in the United Kingdom and:

(a)   the person held a valid EEA family permit, registration certificate, residence card, derivative residence card, document certifying permanent residence, permanent residence card or qualifying EEA State residence card on his arrival in the United Kingdom or can otherwise prove that he is resident in the United Kingdom;
(b)   the person is deemed not to have been admitted to the United Kingdom under regulation 22(3) but at the date on which notice of the decision to refuse to admit him is given he has been in the United Kingdom for at least 3 months; or
(c)   has made an asylum or human rights claim (or both), unless the Secretary of State has certified that the claim or claims is or are clearly unfounded.

Paragraph (1)(d) does not apply where the person has made an asylum or human rights claim (or both), unless the Secretary of State has certified that the claim or claims is or are clearly unfounded.[3] Regulation 29 prohibits the Secretary of State from making removal directions while an appeal is pending, other than for specified decisions (ie under regulation 19(1), (1A) or (1B) in refusal of admission cases; and regulation 19(3)(b) in public policy removal cases). For further details, see **19.49** below.

[1] Note the restraint on the imposition of, and lapsing of extant, removal directions while appeals against certain types of EEA decisions are pending, and the prohibition on detention (unless Reg 24AA applies): Reg 29 (as amended by SI 2013/3032).

[2] *See R (on the application of Abdullah) v Secretary of State for the Home Department* [2009] EWHC 1771 (Admin) (15 June 2009), [2009] EWHC 1771 (Admin).

[3] The provisions of Reg 27 were amended by Immigration (European Economic Area) (Amendment) Regulations 2009/1117, Immigration (European Economic Area) (Amendment) Regulations 2012/1547 and Immigration (European Economic Area) (Amendment) (No 2) Regulations 2013/3032.

EXCLUSION, TERMINATION OF THE RIGHT TO RESIDE AND EXPULSION

Cessation and public policy

6.170 We have seen in the previous section that EU free movement rights granted to the economically active continue whilst that activity is being exercised, with exceptions for retirement and permanent disability. What happens if it stops? An able-bodied EEA national below the age of retirement might cease to be economically active. The question then arises of whether a right to remain ceases to exist or can be terminated by non-renewal of a residence permit, and whether there is a power of expulsion which can then be exercised. In practice, the issue is unlikely to arise except in the case of an EEA national who is looking to long-term reliance on social security and public funds without any prospect of exercising any economic activity provided for by EU law. An EEA national who is self-supporting can qualify under the Citizens' Directive and the 2006 Regulations.[1]

[1] See **6.113–6.114** above. It is only recourse to income support that leads to cessation of qualification.

6.171 In *Antonissen*[1] an EC national who had not worked in the UK had committed drugs offences during the course of his stay, and the question was whether he could rely on Community rights in the deportation appeal. He was held not to be a worker, and therefore had no rights in EC law. There are several early Immigration Appeal Tribunal decisions upholding refusals of admission to EC nationals on the grounds that they had not been working on previous visits to the UK and were not seeking to enter under one of the directives 68/360 or 73/148.[2] Some of these cases must be regarded as unsound in the light of the later ECJ case law defining a 'worker' as including someone genuinely seeking work.

[1] Case C-292/89 [1991] ECR I-745, (1991) 2 CMLR 373, ECJ. It may be that the ruling in *Antonissen* is restricted to the case where an EU national has never obtained employment at all, and different considerations apply as to cesser of qualification after a number of years employment in the host State. See also *Monteil v Secretary of State for the Home Department*

[1983] Imm AR 149, [1984] 1 CMLR 264, IAT; *Lubbersen v Secretary of State for the Home Department* [1984] Imm AR 56, [1984] 3 CMLR 77, IAT.
2   Note that Directives 68/360 or 73/148 have long since been repealed and replaced by the Citizens' Directive'.

Enforcement powers under domestic law

6.172 Parts 4 and 5 of the 2006 Regulations have been substantially amended[1] and now provide for a range of discretionary enforcement powers to deprive persons of documentary proof of EU residence rights, to remove such persons, to 'verify' residence rights, and to restrict appeal rights:

(1)   Regulation 20(1) empowers the Secretary of State to revoke, or refuse to issue or renew, proof of an EU residence right (ie a registration certification, residence card, document certifying permanent residence or a permanent residence card) where such action is justified on the grounds of public policy, public security or public health, or on grounds of abuse of rights in accordance with regulation 21B(2) (which is addressed below). Regulation 20(2)-(5) then makes provision for the revocation/refusal to issue residence documentation where the holder 'ceases to have, or never had, a right of residence under these Regulations'; without applying the public policy proviso (ie justified on grounds of public policy, public security or public health). The Court of Appeal recently upheld the revocation of a residence card before its expiry under regulation 20(2) where the card had been issued by administrative error, without applying the public policy proviso: see *Sannie*.[2] It should also be noted that, where a person cannot be removed under regulation 19(3)(b) and the SSHD considers that she would like to but cannot make a decision under regulation 20(1), eg an EEA national wins their appeal against deportation action in reliance on regulation 21, their right to reside can nevertheless be cancelled under regulation 21A. Most of the above decisions fall within the definition of 'EEA decisions' in regulation 2(1), which give rise to an appeal right under regulation 26. As to the revocation of residence rights of EEA nationals, see **6.175** below.

(2)   Regulation 19 provides for:
  •   Refusal of entry on the grounds of public policy, public security of public health (1).
  •   Refusal of entry to a person subject to a deportation or exclusion order (save for temporary admission under regulation 29AA (ie in order to attend an appeal) – see **6.195** below) (1A).
  •   Refusal of entry if the Secretary of State has 'reasonable grounds to suspect that his admission would lead to the abuse of a right to reside' (1AB).
  •   The making of an exclusion order prohibiting a person from entering the UK (1B) where the public policy proviso is satisfied.
  •   Removal of persons (3) who (a) do not have, or cease to have, the right to reside; or (b) the SSHD has decided that the person's removal is justified applying the public policy proviso in accordance with regulation 21; or (c) removal is justified on the grounds of abuse of rights under regulation 21B(2).

Regulation 21 regulates decisions taken on the basis of public policy, public security and public health: see **6.176** onwards.

1   The principal amending SIs were: 2209/117; 2012/1547; 2012/2560; 2013/3032; and 2014/1976.
2   *Sannie v Secretary of State for the Home Department* [2013] EWCA Civ 1638. There, S accepted that he did not meet the statutory criteria as an extended family member, the SSHD had revoked his residence card on that basis, and S argued on the basis of *Samsam* [2011] UKUT 165 (IAC) – see *Sannie* at [25]–[26] – that it was not possible to revoke in cases of administrative error. The Court of Appeal rejected that argument: [35]–[38] applying *Nkrumah* [2011] UKUT 00163 (IAC).

6.173 It is still uncertain whether an attempt to exclude an EEA national purely on the grounds of ceasing to qualify would be successful without any other aspect of conduct that brings public policy into play. Ceasing to qualify is not like overstaying leave – a clear breach of the conditions of leave which is met with the sanction of removal. They are conceptually quite different. A major difficulty facing the Home Office, which has the burden of proof,[1] would be to identify the moment when a person ceased to qualify. A person may remain a worker even when not actually in work or seeking work, for example, if employment is interrupted by pregnancy, illness, involuntary unemployment or vocational training.[2] Furthermore, the EEA Regulations provide[3] that a person is not to be removed as an automatic consequence of having recourse to the social assistance system in the UK. They also provide that when a decision to remove is made under regulation 19(3)(a) because the person ceases to be qualified, the person is to be treated as if he or she were a person to whom section 10(1)(a) of the Immigration and Asylum Act 1999 Act applied, and section 10 of that Act (removal of certain persons unlawfully in the UK) is to apply accordingly.[4] Where the decision to remove is taken under regulation 19(3)(b) under the public policy proviso, that person is to be treated as if he were a person to whom section 3(5)(a) of the 1971 Act (liability to deportation) applied, and section 5 of that Act (procedure for deportation) and Schedule 3 to that Act (supplementary provision as to deportation) are to apply accordingly.[5] Normally the person is given one month in which to leave, before removal is carried out.[6]

1   See observations of IAT in *Giangregorio v Secretary of State for the Home Department* [1983] Imm AR 104, [1983] 2 CMLR 472, IAT; decision of ECJ in *Antonissen* [1991] 2 CMLR 373.
2   See **6.95** above, and Articles 14–15 of Directive 2004/38. See also *EU Commission v Netherlands*: Case C50/06: [2007] ECR I-4383, [2007] 3 CMLR 168, ECJ.
3   SI 2006/1003, reg 19(4).
4   SI 2006/1003, reg 24(2).
5   SI 2006/1003, reg 24(3).
6   SI 2006/1003, reg 24(6).

6.174 By regulation 20(1A), the making of a removal decision under regulation 19(3) will invalidate a registration certificate, residence card (etc), save during any period in which a right of residence is deemed to continue as a result of regulation 15B(2). Regulation 15B(2) provides for continuation of the right of residence while an appeal under regulation 26 could be brought while the person is in the UK, or is brought and is pending. It should be noted that, for those residing in the UK pursuant to a derivative right of residence under regulation 15A(2), (4), (4A) or (5), those holding a derivative residence card, or those those who have applied for one, regulation 21A imposes a different test wherever Part 4 of the 2006 Regulations makes reference to a decision 'justified on grounds of public policy, public security or public health'. The different test is, by regulation 21A(3)(b), whether the measure is 'conducive to the public good.' Therefore, for example, such persons when facing deportation action will not be able to rely on the more favourable EU law provisions which focus on present risk and rule out reliance on general deterrence etc (as explained below at **6.180** and **6.183**). Regulation 21A also includes references to a person with a derived right of residence and a derivative residence card as falling within the other provisions of Part 4 of the 2006 Regulations.

6.175 The implications of Article 21 TFEU (ex Article 18 TEC) also fall to be considered. The 2006 Regulations[1] deal to some degree with 'derivative rights of residence' based on Articles 20 and 21 TFEU: see **6.85** above. EU nationals have the right to move and reside freely within the territory of Member States, 'subject to the limitations and conditions laid down in this Treaty and the measures adopted to give it effect'.[2] Expulsion of an EU national on the ground that he or she is no longer a qualified person within the meaning of the 2006 Regulations would materially affect the right of residence. In *Baumbast*[3] the ECJ considered the scope of Article 18 EC (now Article 21 TFEU) and the nature of the limitations and conditions referred to in it. The Court pointed out that the Treaty does not require that citizens of the Union pursue an economic activity in order to enjoy the right of citizenship of the Union and certainly access to citizenship rights does not cease when economic activity comes to an end. Whilst Article 21 TFEU refers to the right of citizens to reside within the territory of another Member State being subject to the limitation and conditions laid down in the Treaty and measure adopted to give it effect, those limitations and conditions 'do not prevent the provisions of Article 18(1) EC from conferring on individuals rights which are enforceable by them and which the national courts must protect'.[4] Thus the ECJ held that even if conditions of the general right of residence directive, Directive 90/364, are not strictly met for instance, the right of residence should not be denied for the reason that:

> 'the limitations and conditions laid down in secondary legislation must be applied in compliance with the limits imposed by Community law and in accordance with the general principles of that law, particular the principle of proportionality'.[5]

On the facts, the ECJ considered that as Mr Baumbast has previously worked in the UK he should not be deprived of a right of residence if he failed to provide evidence of sickness insurance as required by Directive 90/364 on general rights of residence. The CJEU's case law on citizenship of the Union, eg *Dereci* and *Iida*, emphasised the importance inherent in Articles 20/21 TFEU of the freedom to move and reside freely throughout the Union: see **6.75** above. In cases where non-British EEA nationals are in the UK at least with the intention of engaging in economic activity it will be very difficult to suggest that the exercise of free movement rights in the future is entirely hypothetical, see *Dereci*, or that removal would not constitute a real obstacle to the exercise of free movement rights (eg *McCarthy* at [52]).

---

[1] SI 2006/1003, reg 15A.
[2] See *R v Secretary of State for the Home Department, ex p Vitale* [1995] NLJR 631.
[3] Case C-413/99 *Baumbast and R v Secretary of State for the Home Department* [2002] ECR I-7091.
[4] *Baumbast* above, para 86.

⁵   *Baumbast* above para 91. See also the discussion of proportionality in the application of restrictions on the right of residence of EU nationals in *Chen and Zhu v Secretary of State for the Home Department* C-200/02, [2005] QB 325.

Public policy, security and health

6.176 Although the provisions of the UK's 2006 EEA Regulations, which make provision for decisions based on the public policy, public security and public health ("the public policy proviso"), were addressed above (see **6.170**) we will consider the basis for those provisions in the Treaties and under the Citizens' Directive. For workers, Article 45(3) TFEU (ex Article 39(3) TEC) says that the free movement provisions, but not the provisions for the abolition of discrimination based on nationality, shall be 'subject to limitations justified on grounds of public policy, public security or public health'. So far as concerns the right of establishment, Article 52 TFEU (ex Article 46(1) TEC) says:

> 'the provisions of this Chapter and measures taken in pursuance thereof shall not prejudice the applicability of provisions laid down by law, regulation or administrative action providing for special treatment for foreign nationals on grounds of public policy, public security or public health.'

So far as services are concerned, Articles 56 and 62 TFEU (ex Articles 49 and 55 TEC) provides that the provisions of Articles 51–54 TFEU (ex Articles 45–48 TEC) apply also to the matters covered in the chapter concerning services. This means that the provisions of Article 52(1) TFEU apply to the provision of services as well as to the right of establishment. Although the wording of the public policy proviso is slightly different as between workers and those relying on the right of establishment, the ECJ has made it clear that in practice there should be no difference.¹ The rights of free movement of the self-sufficient, the retired and vocational students are also subject to the public policy proviso as the Citizens' Directive makes clear.²

¹   Case 48/75 *Royer, Re* [1976] ECR 497, [1976] 2 CMLR 619.
²   See Council Directive 2004/38/EC, art 27(1) which applies to all freedom of movement rights set out in the Directive, including to the residence rights of self-sufficient and retired persons and students respectively.

Implementing the public policy proviso

6.177 The public policy proviso is given effect by the Citizens' Directive, which applies the provisions of Directive 64/221, but also incorporates some of the case law clarifications and developments. It applies to nationals of a Member State who are workers, self-employed persons or providers or recipients of services, and their families. Its provisions are also expressly made to cover those who have ceased to be economically active as a result of retirement or incapacity, to the economically self-sufficient, and to students. The Directive applies to all measures on grounds of public policy, public security or public health concerning entry into, the issue or renewal of residence permits in and expulsion from an EU country.¹ It also applies to restrictions on the right to leave imposed by the country of nationality on nationals who have been repatriated from another Member State.² It does not apply to the application of Article 35 of the Citizens' Directive (dealing with marriages of convenience) which has its own safeguards as set out in the Article.[3] The UK's EEA Regulations make separate provision for 'abuse of rights' decisions[4]: see **6.188** below. The application of the public policy proviso applies to Turkish nationals benefiting from free movement rights under the Ankara agreement[5] see **6.198** to **6.210** below.

[1]   Council Directive 2004/38/EC, arts 7(1), 15(1), and 27(1).
[2]   Case C-33/07 *Ministerul Administraţiei şi Internelor – Direcţia Generală de Paşapoarte Bucureşti v Jipa* [2008] 3 CMLR 715. See **6.151**, above.
[3]   *TC (Kenya) v Secretary of State for the Home Department* [2008] EWCA Civ 543, [2008] All ER (D) 77 (Jun).
[4]   Regulation 21B of the 2006 Regulations on abuse of rights. Regulation 21 of the 2006 Regulations deals generally with decisions taken on the grounds of public policy, public security and public health and keeps close to the language of the Directive.
[5]   By Article 14 of Commission Decision (ECSC) 1/80 under the Ankara Agreement: see C-340/97 *Nazli v Stadt Nürnberg* [2000] ECR I-957, para 63.

6.178   The Directive does not simply reproduce the text of Directive 64/221; it also incorporates changes and clarifications of Community law made by the case law of the European Court. This is most clear from the text of Article 27 which sets out the general principles of the old Directive. It enables Member States to restrict the freedom of movement and residence of Union citizens and their family members, irrespective of nationality, on grounds of public policy, public security or public health, but they can only do these things 'subject to the provisions of this Chapter'. These powers are not absolute. First, these grounds shall not be invoked to serve economic ends. Secondly, measures taken on grounds of public policy or public security shall comply with the principle of proportionality and shall be based exclusively on the personal conduct of the individual concerned. Previous criminal convictions shall not in themselves constitute grounds for taking such measures. Moreover, the personal conduct of the individual concerned must represent a genuine, present and sufficiently serious threat affecting one of the fundamental interests of society. Justifications that are isolated from the particulars of the case or that rely on considerations of general prevention shall not be accepted. Thirdly, careful provision is made for inquiries of other Member States in order to ascertain whether the person concerned represents a danger for public policy or public security, when issuing a registration certificate or a residence card. Fourthly, when someone has been expelled on grounds of public policy, public security, or public health from one Member State provision, the Member State which issued the passport or identity card to the person expelled must allow the holder of the document to re-enter its territory without any formality even if the document is no longer valid or the nationality of the holder is in dispute. In *Rose (Automatic deportation-Exception 3) Jamaica*[1] the UT held that the personal scope of the safeguards against expulsion which art 27 of the Citizens Directive (2004/38/EC) affords to 'family members' does not include 'other family members' (OFMs). Hence Exception 3 to section 32(4) and (5) of the UK Borders Act 2007 which arises where the removal of a foreign criminal from the UK in pursuance of an automatic deportation order would breach the rights of the foreign criminal under the EU treaties cannot be invoked by OFMs. For a critique of this case, see **6.131**

above.

¹ [2011] UKUT 276 (IAC).

6.179 Article 28 deals with protection against expulsion. First, in a paragraph which is reminiscent of the ECHR decision in *Boultif*,[1] it is incumbent upon a Member State, which is considering making an expulsion decision on grounds of public policy or public security, to take into account such factors as how long the individual concerned has resided on its territory, his/her age, state of health, family and economic situation, social and cultural integration into the host Member State and the extent of his or her links with the country of origin.[2] Secondly, a clear distinction is required to be drawn between the three levels of protection against removal introduced in the 2006 Regulations, each level being intended to be more stringent and narrower than the immediately lower test.[3] So the host Member State may not take an expulsion decision:

- against Union citizens or their family members, irrespective of nationality, who have the right of permanent residence on its territory, except on serious grounds of public policy or public security.[4] In order to accrue the necessary five years permanent residence to acquire the enhanced protection of regulation 21(3), it is not possible to take into account periods of time spent in prison; and continuity of residence is broken by any such periods. Neither is it possible to aggregate periods of time accrued prior to, or following, time spent in prison: *Onuekwere v Secretary of State for the Home Department;*[5] and
- against Union citizens, except if the decision is based on *imperative grounds* of public security,[6] as defined by Member States, if they have resided in the host Member State for the previous 10 years or are a minor.[7] In *G v SSHD*, the CJEU confirmed that the ten-year period of residence referred to in that provision must, in principle, be continuous and must be calculated by counting back from the date of the decision ordering the expulsion of the person concerned.[8] The CJEU also confirmed that the ten-year continuous period may in principle be interrupted by a term of imprisonment, even where the person resided in the host Member State for ten years prior to imprisonment. However, it is necessary to undertake an overall assessment to determine whether the integrating links previously forged with the host Member State have been broken by imprisonment, and the fact of a ten-year period of residence prior to imprisonment should be taken into consideration as part of that overall assessment. The Upper Tribunal stated in *Essa* that the longer the residence the greater the degree of integration was likely to be, and the weightier would be the prospects of rehabilitation as a factor against removal.[9] In *HR (Portugal) v Secretary of State for the Home Department*[10] the Court of Appeal held that on the true construction of regulation 21(4)(a) of the 2006 Regulations and Article 28(3) of the Directive, 'residence' meant presence in the United Kingdom in the exercise of the rights and freedoms conferred by the EC Treaty.

¹ *Boultif v Switzerland (Application 54273/00)* [2001] 2 FLR 1228, [2001] ECHR 54273/00, ECtHR.
² Reproduced in the 2006 Regulations, reg 21(6). In *Batista (Valentine) v Secretary of State for the Home Department* [2010] EWCA Civ 896, [2010] All ER (D) 323 (Jul) the Court of

Appeal suggested that common sense would suggest a degree of shared interest between the EEA countries in helping those deemed sufficiently dangerous to justify deportation to progress towards a better form of life. The prospects offered by B's relationship with his girlfriend in the UK might have been fragile, but in Portugal they were practically non-existent, and B was likely to drift back to crime. There was no reason in principle why those points could not be taken into account in the overall balance of proportionality. It was a matter for the tribunal to consider whether they had any materiality in the instant case.

3 *LG and CC (EEA Regs: residence; imprisonment; removal) Italy* [2009] UKAIT 00024.

4 2006 Regulations, reg 21(3). In *Bulale v Secretary of State for the Home Department* [2008] EWCA Civ 806, [2009] QB 536, [2009] 2 WLR 992 the Court of Appeal said that there was no need to refer questions going to the meaning or effect of the word 'serious', as that would be to invite an attempt at definition of a concept that the legislation treats either as indefinable or as sufficient in itself to guide the decisions of Member States.

5 *Onuekwere v Secretary of State for the Home Department* (C-378/12) [2014] 1 WLR 2420; [2014] 2 CM.LR. 1369; [2014] Imm. AR 551. The Upper Tribunal decision referring the case to the CJEU is reported as *Onuekwere (imprisonment – residence)* [2012] UKUT 00269 (IAC). The CJEU's position confirms earlier English authority, eg *Valentine Batista v Secretary of State for the Home Department* [2010] EWCA Civ 896, [2010] All ER (D) 323 (Jul) (re deportation on grounds of public order and public security) and *Carvalho v Secretary of State for the Home Department* [2010] EWCA Civ 1406 and *Ogunyemi (imprisonment breaks continuity of residence) Nigeria* [2011] UKUT 164 (IAC) (in relation to permanent residence). Prior to *Onuekwere* (CJEU) it was at least arguable that lawful residence either side of an episode of imprisonment could be aggregated (see, eg *Jarusevicius (EEA Reg 21 – effect of imprisonment)* [2012] UKUT 00120(IAC)), but this possibility is now ruled out.

6 In *LG (Italy) v Secretary of State for the Home Department* [2008] EWCA Civ 190, [2008] All ER (D) 262 (Mar), the Court of Appeal held that the words 'imperative grounds of public security' in the Citizens' Directive (ie those grounds that permit expulsion of an individual who has been resident in an EEA state for ten years) clearly mandated a very high standard before an EEA national could be deported. They remitted the matter back to the AIT for further legal argument having noted that the Operational Enforcement Manual could not be the last word on the subject and in any event was unclear.

7 2006 Regulations, reg 21(4). In the case of a minor this stringent test does not apply if the expulsion is necessary for the best interests of the child, as provided for in the United Nations Convention on the Rights of the Child of 20 November 1989.

8 *Secretary of State for the Home Department v MG* (Case C-400/12) [2014] 1 WLR 2441, [2014] 2 CMLR 1172, CJEU, referred to the CJEU by the Upper Tribunal in *MG (EU deportation – Article 28(3) – imprisonment) Portugal* [2012] UKUT 00268(IAC). See the UT's explanation of the CJEU ruling in *MG (prison – Article 28(3)(a) of Citizens Directive) Portugal* [2014] UKUT 00392 (IAC).

9 *Essa (EEA: Rehabilitation/Integration)* [2013] UKUT 00316 (IAC); [2013] Imm AR 980. See another pre-*G* case, *FV (Italy) v Secretary of State for the Home Department* [2012] EWCA Civ 1199; [2013] 1 WLR 3339; [2013] 1 All ER 1180; [2012] 3 CMLR 56; [2013] Imm AR 114; [2013] INLR 293. The various cases on this issue prior to *G* need to be read with caution, eg *LG and CC (EEA Regs: residence; imprisonment; removal) Italy* [2009] UKAIT 00024.

10 [2009] EWCA Civ 371, [2010] 1 All ER 144, [2009] 3 CMLR 295.

Procedural safeguards

6.180 In addition to the substantive limitations on the power of Member States to apply the public policy proviso, the Citizens' Directive, also includes important procedural safeguards, such as the right to be told in clear and understandable terms the nature and reasons for the decision and what appeal rights the person has (Articles 30 and 31). In the *Rutili* case[1] the ECJ stated that this provision meant giving the immigrant 'a precise and comprehensive statement of the grounds for the decision' to enable him or her to take effective steps to prepare a defence. In addition to Articles 30 and 31; Article 32 deals with revocation of expulsion or exclusion orders. Article 33 makes important provision about deportation orders against union citizens. First it makes it clear that expulsion orders may not be issued by the host Member State as a penalty or legal consequence of a custodial penalty, unless they conform to the requirements of Articles 27, 28 and 29. Secondly, if an expulsion order is enforced more than two years after it was issued, the Member State is required to check that the individual concerned is currently and genuinely a threat to public policy or public security and must assess whether there has been any material change in the circumstances since the expulsion order was issued. These are very clear indications and are in marked contrast to the deportation policy recently outlined under UK domestic law. See CHAPTER 16 below.

1   In *Rutili v Minister for the Interior* [1975] ECR 1219, [1976] 1 CMLR 140, ECJ, the ECJ stated that this provision meant giving the immigrant 'a precise and comprehensive statement of the grounds for the decision' to enable him or her to take effective steps to prepare a defence.

Early case law on the public policy proviso

6.181 In a series of important early decisions, the ECJ made it clear that (in contrast to the position in UK immigration law) the principle of free movement within the EEA is far more important than any exceptions to it. First, it stipulated that in any case in which a Member State is relying on the public policy proviso, it has to show that the measure in question is justified on the basis of some objective which forms part of public policy, public security or public health.[1] Secondly, the ECJ has repeatedly held that free movement is a fundamental general principle and that the public policy proviso is an exception which, like all derogations from a fundamental principle of the Treaties, should be construed restrictively.[2] Thirdly, the court has repeatedly emphasised that exclusion or expulsion on the ground of public policy should not occur unless the person's 'presence or conduct constitutes a genuine and sufficiently serious threat to public policy'.[3] So the person's presence must not only be a genuine threat to the public policy objective, but also a sufficiently serious one. In *European Commission v Spain*[4] the ECJ held that Spain had breached its obligations under Articles 1–3 of Directive 64/221 by refusing entry into the Schengen area to third country nationals, solely on the basis of an SIS alert, without first verifying whether their presence would constitute a genuine present and sufficiently serious threat to one of the fundamental interests of society.

1   Case 48/75 *Royer, Re* [1976] ECR 497, [1976] 2 CMLR 619, ECJ.
2   Case 41/74 *Van Duyn v Home Office* [1974] ECR 1337; Case 67/74 *Bonsignore v Oberstadtdirektor der Stadt Köln* [1975] ECR 297; Case 36/75 *Rutili v Minister for the Interior* [1975] ECR 1219, [1976] 1 CMLR 140, ECJ; Case 139/85 *Kempf v Staatssecretaris van Justitie* [1986] ECR 1741; Case C-348/96 *Calfa (criminal proceedings against)* [1999] ECR I-11; Case C-340/97 *Nazli v Stadt Nürnberg* [2000] ECR I-957.
3   Case 30/77 *R v Bouchereau* [1977] ECR 1999; *Bonsignore, Calfa, Nazli* above.
4   Case C-503/03 *European Commission v Spain* [2006] ECR I-1097, ECJ.

6.182 Article 3(1) of Council Directive (EEC) 64/221 provided that measures taken on the grounds of public policy or public security should be based exclusively on the personal conduct of the individual concerned and this is repeated in the Citizens' Directive at Article 27(2).[1] What is meant by this was explained in two early cases before the ECJ. In *Van Duyn v Home Office (No 2)*[2] a member of the Church of Scientology challenged her refusal of entry to

Britain under the general ban on scientologists, and her case was referred to the ECJ. The court explored the term 'personal conduct' and concluded that, while a person's past association does not in general suffice, present association 'which reflects participation in the activities of the body or organisation and identification with its aims and designs' may be considered a voluntary act of the person concerned and thus part of his or her personal conduct. Being a member of the Church of Scientology was personal conduct by which the UK government could justify her exclusion from the UK on the ground that her presence was not conducive to the public good. But if the ban or expulsion is for reasons that go much wider than the personal conduct of the person concerned, this may not be allowed. In *Bonsignore*[3] an Italian worker resident in Cologne purchased a Beretta gun from an unidentified source, and while manipulating the gun he accidentally killed his younger brother. He was found guilty by a German court of illegal possession of firearms and causing death by negligence. The German authorities wanted to deport him, but clearly the only reason for doing this was as a general deterrent and not because *Bonsignore* was likely to commit similar offences again. The ECJ held that Article 3(1) of the Directive made it clear that EEC nationals could not be subjected to decisions made on grounds extraneous to their personal and individual cases. Read together with Article 3(2) it barred Member States from expelling EEC nationals in order to deter other aliens from committing identical or similar offences, that is to say for 'general preventive' or 'deterrent' reasons. This reasoning has been upheld in subsequent cases so as to prevent the automatic expulsion of persons committing drugs offences in particular.[4]

[1] Citizens' Directive, Chapter VI, art 27(2) and the Immigration (European Economic Area) Regulations 2006, SI 2006/1003, reg 21.
[2] Case 41/74 [1974] ECR 1337, [1975] Ch 358.
[3] Case 67/74 [1975] ECR 297, [1975] 1 CMLR 472.
[4] Case C-348/96 *Calfa (criminal proceedings against)* [1999] ECR I-11; Case C-340/97 *Nazli v Stadt Nürnberg* [2000] ECR I-957, ECJ.

6.183 Article 3(2) of Council Directive (EEC) 64/221, on which the court relied in *Bonsignore*, provides that previous criminal convictions shall not in themselves constitute grounds for the taking of measures on the grounds of public policy or public security.[1] The *Bonsignore* case makes it clear that exclusion or deportation of an EEA national cannot be justified on the grounds of general deterrence. The Article also means that a country's authorities cannot apply a blanket rule excluding from their territory anyone with a criminal record,[2] and certainly renders inapplicable to EEA nationals Immigration Rules preventing the entry of persons convicted of an extraditable offence unless there are 'strong compassionate reasons'.[3]

[1] Citizens' Directive, Chapter VI and the Immigration (European Economic Area) Regulations 2006, SI 2006/1003, reg 21.
[2] C-441/02 *EC Commission v Germany* (27 April 2006, unreported), ECJ is pending on the question of Germany's mandatory exclusion of persons who have committed certain criminal offences.
[3] See HC 395, r 320(18).

6.184 In *Bonsignore* the court further held that public policy measures should only be applied if there is a likelihood that the offender will commit further offences or in some other way infringe public security or policy. In *R v Bouchereau*,[1] a case concerning a French national who pleaded guilty to drug offences before an English court which wished to recommend him for deportation, the ECJ described the public policy limitation as follows:

> 'In so far as it may justify certain restrictions on the free movement of persons subject to Community law, recourse by a national authority to the concept of public policy presupposes, in any event, the existence, in addition to the perturbation of the social order which any infringement of the law involves, of a genuine and sufficiently serious threat to the requirements of public policy affecting one of the fundamental interests of society.'

The court held that a criminal conviction can be taken into account only in so far as the circumstances which gave rise to the conviction are evidence of personal conduct:

> 'constituting a present threat to the requirements of public policy . . . . Although, in general, a finding that such threat exists implies the existence in the individual concerned of a propensity to act in the same way in the future, it is possible that past conduct alone may constitute such a threat to the requirements of public policy.'

[1]   Case 30/77 *R v Bouchereau* [1978] QB 732, [1977] ECR 1999, ECJ.

6.185 There was uncertainty in the UK case law applying these principles as to whether a propensity to re-offend was required and in what circumstances it might not be required. In considering a recommendation for deportation of a convicted rapist, the Court of Appeal in *R v Secretary of State for the Home Department, ex p Santillo*[1] considered that future risk posed by the possibility of re-offending was required as a matter of Community law and common sense. In *R v Secretary of State for the Home Department, ex p Al-Sabah*[2] the Court of Appeal doubted these remarks, regarding them as inconsistent with *Bouchereau*. In *Marchon*[3] a Portuguese doctor who had been convicted of importing 4.5 kilos of heroin and sentenced to 14 years' imprisonment was held not to need any propensity to re-offend in order to merit deportation on public good grounds. The court regarded this conduct by a doctor as particularly disgraceful, and indicative of a disregard for the basic or fundamental moral tenets of society.

[1]   [1981] QB 778, CA.
[2]   [1992] Imm AR 223, CA.
[3]   *R v Secretary of State for the Home Department, ex p Marchon* [1993] Imm AR 384, CA.

6.186 The confusion has, we believe, been cleared up by more recent ECJ cases such as *Nazli v Stadt Nürnberg*,[1] involving a Turkish worker exercising rights under the Ankara Agreement and Commission Decision (ECSC) 1/80 under it in Germany. Mr Nazli had been convicted of a drugs-related offence in circumstances indicating no propensity to re-offend, but German aliens' law provided for mandatory expulsion after conviction of drugs offences.[2] The court held that a person enjoying Treaty rights and rights analogous to them under the Association Agreement could not be expelled 'as a deterrent to other aliens without the personal conduct of the person concerned giving reason to consider that he will commit other serious offences prejudicial to the requirements of public policy in the host Member State'.[3] Earlier in its judgment the court referred to the requirement that the expulsion measure 'is justified because . . . personal conduct indicates a risk of new and serious prejudice to the requirements of public policy'. This means that in every case the personal conduct of the person involved, and in particular the indications of future risk of threats to public policy, must be assessed.[4] Criminal convictions even for the most heinous crimes will, we suggest, never be enough by themselves. In *BF (Portugal) v Secretary of State for the Home Department*[5] the Court of Appeal considered European Union law, serious crimes and deportation. The proper approach was, ruled Jacob LJ, to determine (1) what was the relevant personal conduct of the person facing expulsion (2) whether that conduct represented a genuine, present and sufficiently serious threat to society and, if so, (3) whether that threat affected one of the fundamental interests of society. Then the Tribunal should stand back and consider (4) whether the deportation of the respondent would be disproportionate in all the circumstances. He added that, as to the judicial duty to give reasons, it is not sufficient for a tribunal to recite all the pieces of evidence and then state a bold conclusion.

[1]   Case C-340/97 [2000] ECR I-957, ECJ.
[2]   See also Case C-348/96 *Calfa (criminal proceedings against)* [1999] 2 CMLR 1138, ECJ, a case involving a tourist expelled for life under Greek law for possession of drugs.
[3]   *Nazli* fn 1 above, para 64.
[4]   In this regard, see *Vasconcelos (risk - rehabilitation)* [2013] UKUT 00378 (IAC) in which the Upper Tribunal emphasised the relevance of statistical assessments of re-offending provided by the National Offender Management Service (NOMS) but that the Tribunal is not bound by such assessments if on the evidence overall a different conclusion is justified.
[5]   [2009] EWCA Civ 923 (28 July 2009), (2009) Times, 18 August.

Proportionality

6.187 Measures taken by Member States in respect of nationals of other Member States must be reasonable and not disproportionate to the gravity of their conduct.[1] As the Court of Appeal observed in *International Traders' Ferry*,[2] proportionality 'requires the court to judge the necessity of the action taken as well as whether it was within the range of courses of action that could reasonably be followed', and it may be a more exacting test than a *Wednesbury* formulation.[3] In *B v Secretary of State for the Home Department*[4] Simon Brown LJ pointed out that even if the deportation of an EC national could be justified by the existence of 'a genuine and sufficiently serious threat to the requirements of public policy affecting one of the fundamental interests of society',[5] the requirement of proportionality was held to mean that deportation 'must be both appropriate and necessary for the attainment of the public policy objective sought—the containment of the threat—and also must not impose an excessive burden on the individual, the deportee'. In that case, which pre-dated the coming into force of the Human Rights Act 1998, the Court of Appeal considered the proportionality of a proposed deportation on public good grounds of an EU national convicted of persistent sexual abuse of his daughter, both through the free movement provisions of the EC Treaty and also through the constitutional requirement to respect fundamental rights as guaranteed by the ECHR, enshrined in Article 6 of the consolidated Treaty on European Union (formerly Article F), which gave statutory force to the case law of the ECHR as applied by the ECJ.[6] It held that although the Tribunal was entitled to find the existence of a relevant threat to the requirements of public policy arising both from the intrinsic seriousness of the appellant's offending and from a propensity to re-offend, the remaining and determinative issue was that of proportionality, which was a matter of law.[7] In the circumstances of the case, given the appellant's extremely long residence in the UK, the court held deportation a disproportionate response. The ECJ has held that the expulsion of EU nationals or their family members for failure to comply with immigration laws or complete formalities would be manifestly disproportionate to the interference with Community law rights.[8] In *R (on the application of Essa) v Upper Tribunal (Immigration & Asylum Chamber)*[9] the Court of Appeal emphasised that, in EEA deportation cases involving Article 8 ECHR, it was necessary to distinguish between the two distinct proportionality evaluations which fell to be determined: one under regulation 21(5)(a) of the 2006 EEA Regulations; and, if it fell to be determined, under Article 8 ECHR. Under the EEA proportionality evaluation, it is necessary in particular to consider explicitly the prospects of rehabilitation as between the UK and the EEA country of nationality and an awareness of the interests of the EU in general which required a comparison of rehabilitation prospects, as required by *Tsakouridis*[10] (see [12]-[15] of *Essa*).

[1]   Citizens' Directive, art 31(3); the Immigration (European Economic Area) Regulations 2006, SI 2006/1003, reg 21(5); *R v Bouchereau* [1978] QB 732 at 743, per Advocate General Warner.

[2]   *R v Chief Constable of Sussex, ex p International Trader's Ferry Ltd* [1997] 2 CMLR 164, CA. The House of Lords upheld the CA's decision that the Chief Constable's refusal to police the port more than twice a week, meaning that export of live animals was restricted on other days because of demonstrators, was a proportionate measure to maintain public order, although it had a restrictive effect on exports, and was therefore justified under Article 36 EC (now art 30): [1999] 1 All ER 129.

[3]   In *Wilander v Tobin* [1997] 2 CMLR 346 the Court of Appeal, holding that mandatory drug testing of sporting competitors was justified by compelling reasons of public interest, observed that proportionality was close to concepts of reasonableness and natural justice, and that the combination of safeguards such as the review body, the appeal committee and the courts made the measure proportionate (assuming without deciding that it restricted art 39 EC free movement rights).

[4]   [2000] Imm AR 478.

[5]   *R v Bouchereau* [1978] QB 732 at 760, [1981] 2 All ER 924n, ECJ.

[6]   Case 260/89 *Elliniki Radiophonia Tileorassi AE v Pliroforissis and Kouvelas* [1991] ECR I-2925.

[7]   *B v Secretary of State for the Home Department*, fn 4 above. This aspect of the judgment has given rise to endless controversy; see **7.21** and **7.41** below.

[8]   Case C-459/99 *Mouvement contre le racisme, l'antisémitisme et la xénophobie (MRAX) ASBL v Belgium* [2002] ECR I-6591, para 90.

[9]   *R (on the application of Essa) v Upper Tribunal (Immigration & Asylum Chamber)* [2012] EWCA Civ 1718; [2013] Imm AR 644.

[10]   *Land Baden-Wurttemberg v Tsakouridis* (C-145/09) [2011] 2 CMLR 11; [2011] CEC 714; [2011] Imm AR 276; [2011] INLR 415; ECJ (Grand Chamber).

Activities which are not illegal

6.188 Although the application of the proviso depends on the personal conduct of the person involved, the ECJ has held that the activities in question need not be illegal for public policy to be invoked; the activities of scientologists which led to the blanket ban on their immigration to the UK in *Van Duyn* are sufficient. The decision in *Van Duyn*[1] indicates that a ban on the immigration of foreign nationals for public policy reasons is not invalidated merely because no such ban has been imposed on its own nationals. Under international law it is not normally possible for a country to ban its own nationals. The decision makes it clear that the application of the public policy proviso to EU immigration law inevitably involves some discrimination against foreign nationals. However, it is doubtful to what extent a host State can take measures on public policy grounds that it cannot take against own nationals. *Rutili v Minister for the Interior*[2] concerned an Italian national who had spent most of his life in Alsace-Lorraine. He was a political activist who had been involved in the 'events' of May 1968 in France, but had never been convicted of any offence. The French Ministry of the Interior made an order banning him from Alsace-Lorraine. The ECJ ruled, amongst other things, that the public policy proviso does not apply to the right to move freely within the territory of a particular Member State, and so a partial residence prohibition, restraining a migrant from working in one part of the territory of a Member State, could only be applied in those circumstances when such a limitation would be justified under national law in the case of a national.

[1]   [1975] Ch 358, [1974] ECR 1337.
[2]   [1975] ECR 1219, [1976] 1 CMLR 140, ECJ.

6.189 Further in *Adoui and Cornuaille*[1] the court considered the applicability of expulsion on grounds relating to prostitution, which was not specifically prohibited by Belgian law. The court noted:

> 'Although Community law does not impose upon the Member States a uniform scale of values as regards the assessment of conduct which may be considered as contrary to public policy, it should nevertheless be stated that conduct may not be considered as being of a sufficiently serious nature to justify restrictions on the admission of nationals of another Member State in a case where the former Member State does not adopt, with respect to the same conduct on the part of its own nationals, repressive measures or other genuine and effective measures intended to combat such conduct.'

Applying this dictum to the Church of Scientology case, it would appear that unless the UK is prepared to take repressive measures on the grounds of adherence to Scientology against all, including own nationals, it is not entitled to refuse admission to EEA nationals on this ground alone.

[1]   Case 115/81 [1982] ECR 1665, [1982] 3 CMLR 631.

'Abuse of rights'

6.190 Article 35 of the Citizens' Directive incorporates the position previously taken by Member States on the basis of Council Resolution of 4 December 1997 on Measures to be Adopted on the Combating of Marriages of Convenience.[1] But Article 35 has a wider ambit. It is headed 'Abuse of rights' and provides:

> 'Member States may adopt the necessary measures to refuse, terminate or withdraw any right conferred by this Directive in the case of abuse of rights or fraud, such as marriages of convenience. Any such measure shall be proportionate and subject to the procedural safeguards provided for in Articles 30 and 31.'

Article 35 appears in a separate chapter of the Directive from the public policy provisions in Articles 27 to 31. In *TC (Kenya) v Secretary of State for the Home Department*[2] the Court of Appeal rejected the appellant's argument that the reference in Article 35 to proportionality and the procedural safeguards in Articles 30 and 31 incorporates the protections included in Articles 27 and 28 and upheld the definitional approach in the EEA Regulations 2006, which simply says that a civil partner and spouse do not include a party to a civil partnership or marriage of convenience.[3] Marriages of convenience specifically are dealt with above at **6.125**.

1 OJ 16.12.1997 C 382/1.
2 [2008] EWCA Civ 543, [2008] All ER (D) 77 (Jun).
3 Immigration (European Economic Area) Regulations 2006, SI 2006/1003, reg 2(1).

6.191 The EEA Regulations now include a new regulation 21B 'Abuse of rights or fraud',[1] which defines the concept as 'including': (a) engaging in conduct which appears to be intended to circumvent the requirement to be a qualified person; (b) attempting to enter the United Kingdom within 12 months of being removed pursuant to regulation 19(3)(a), where the person attempting to do so is unable to provide evidence that, upon re-entry to the United Kingdom, the conditions for any right to reside, other than the initial right of residence under regulation 13, will be met; (c) entering, attempting to enter or assisting another person to enter or attempt to enter, a marriage or civil partnership of convenience; or (d) fraudulently obtaining or attempting to obtain, or assisting another to obtain or attempt to obtain, a right to reside. Regulation 21B(2) gives the Secretary of State a discretion to take an EEA decision on the grounds of abuse of rights 'where there are reasonable grounds to suspect the abuse of a right to reside and it is proportionate to do so'. Regulation 21B(5) states that 'this regulation may not be involved systematically'. An 'abuse of rights' decision under Regulation 21B(2) can be the basis for revocation/denial of a residence document (Regulation 20(1)), denial of entry (Regulation 19(1AB)), a decision to remove (Regulation 19(3)(c)). However an 'abuse of rights' decision is not an 'EEA decision' as defined in regulation 2(1) and is not itself appealable, although there is an administrative remedy in regulation 21B(3), which gives a right to apply (from outside the UK) to have the effect of the decision set aside on grounds of material change in circumstances which justified the decision.

1 Added by Immigration (European Economic Area) (Amendment) (No 2) Regulations 2013/3032 Sch 1, para 18 (January 1, 2014: insertion has effect subject to transitional provisions as specified in SI 2013/3032, Sch 3, para 3).

Public health

6.192 The Citizens' Directive, Chapter VI, art 29 deals with public health and the need to restrict free movement only if there is a risk from diseases with epidemic potential and other infectious diseases or contagious parasitic diseases and sets out the measures which can be taken. It mirrors the previous position. First, the only diseases which justify restrictive measures are diseases with epidemic potential as defined by the relevant instruments of the World Health Organisation and diseases to which section 38 of the Public Health (Control of Disease) Act 1984 applies (detention in hospital of a person with a notifiable disease).[1] Secondly, diseases occurring after a three-month period from the date of arrival are not grounds for expulsion.[2] Thirdly, where there are serious indications that it is necessary, Member States may, within three months of the date of arrival, require persons entitled to the right of residence to undergo, free of charge, a medical examination to certify that they are not suffering from any of the conditions referred to in point 1 above.[3]

1   Citizens' Directive, art 29(1).
2   Citizens' Directive, art 29(2).
3   Citizens' Directive, art 29(3), which also provides that such medical examinations may not be
     required as a matter of routine.

Review and appeal

6.193 The Citizens' Directive, Chapter VI has now replaced Council Directive
(EEC) 64/221 but changes the format. Under the old Directive, Article 8
required Member States to provide for persons relying on EC rights the same
legal remedies in respect of key decisions as were available to nationals of
the State concerned in respect of acts of the administration. In *Shingara and
Radiom v Secretary of State for the Home Department*,[1] the ECJ held that this
does not mean that EEA nationals refused entry should be given the same
rights of appeal as British citizens whose claim is disputed,[2] since nationals of
the Member State have a right of entry which is not comparable with the
situation of a national of another Member State whose exclusion might be
justified on public policy or national security grounds.[3] Under the Citizens'
Directive the comparative yardstick is no longer used. Instead specific safeguards are given, like notification in writing of decisions (Article 30) and access
to specific judicial and administrative redress on fact and law, which will
normally have suspensive effect (Article 31). In all cases the redress procedures
must ensure that the decision is not disproportionate.[4]

1   *R v Secretary of State for the Home Dept, ex p Shingara; R v Secretary of State for the Home
     Dept, ex p Radiom* [1997] 3 CMLR 703.
2   Under Nationality, Immigration and Asylum Act 2002, s 82.
3   Joined Cases C-111/95 and C-65/95 *Shingara v Secretary of State for the Home Department*
     [1997] ECR I-3343; [1997] 3 CMLR 703, ECJ. Other relevant cases under the old Directive
     are *R v Secretary of State for the Home Department, ex p Santillo* [1980] ECR 1585,
     [1980] 2 CMLR 308, ECJ. Case 115/81 *Adoui and Cornuaille v Belgian State* [1982] ECR
     1665; Case C-175/94 *R v Secretary of State for the Home Department, ex p Gallagher*
     [1995] ECR I-4253; [1996] 1 CMLR 557, ECJ.
4   Directive 2004/38/EC, art 31(3).

6.194 In *Yiadom*[1] the ECJ held that the safeguards of Council Directive (EEC)
64/221 did not apply to persons excluded from the territory, ie refused leave
to enter.[2] In that case, the applicant had been on temporary admission under
paragraph 21 of Schedule 2 to the Immigration Act 1971 for seven months
awaiting a decision on leave to enter. The court condemned the fiction of
temporary admission and said that for EC purposes, a decision to remove an
EU national pursuant to a refusal of leave to enter after such a protracted
period on temporary admission was in fact an expulsion decision, and
attracted the appropriate safeguards. It is thought the same will apply under
the Citizens' Directive. In *Shingara* the court held that, since the prohibition of
entry derogated from a fundamental principle and could not therefore be of
indefinite duration, Community nationals were entitled to have their situation
re-examined if they thought the circumstances justifying their refusal of entry
no longer existed.[3]

1   Case C-357/98 R (on the application of Yiadom) v Secretary of State for the Home
     Department [2001] All ER (EC) 267, ECJ.

2   Under Directive 2004/38/EC, art 31, there is an appeal or review of a refusal of entry, but it is likely to be an out-of-country appeal. For further details, see regulations 25–30 of the Immigration (European Economic Area) Regulations 2006, SI 2006/1003 and CHAPTER 19 below.
3   *R v Secretary of State for the Home Department, ex p Shingara* [1997] ECR I-3343, [1997] 3 CMLR 703, ECJ, para 40. See now regs 25–30 of the Immigration (European Economic Area) Regulations 2006, SI 2006/1005 and see CHAPTER 19 below.

Appeal to the First-tier Tribunal

6.195 Regulation 26 of the 2006 EEA Regulations establishes the jurisdiction of the FTT to hear appeals against 'EEA decisions', which are defined in regulation 2(1) and include removal from the UK under regulation 19(3)(b), removals justified on public policy (etc) grounds: see **6.169** above. Decisions taken under regulation 19(3)(b) are treated as decisions to deport under section 3(5)(a) of the Immigration Act 1971, by regulation 24(3). The Immigration (European Economic Area) (Amendment)(No 2) Regulations 2014, SI 2014/1976 introduce significant new changes to appeal rights in regulation 19(3)(b) removal cases, which are commonly called 'EEA deportation' cases. Now, in such cases, an appeal can be submitted before the subject of the decision is removed from the UK, but that *does not* suspend removal action, *except* where:

- the Secretary of State has *not* certified that the person 'would not face a real risk of serious irreversible harm if removed to the country of return before the appeal is finally determined', the grounds of such a certification including that the person 'would not, before the appeal is finally determined, face a real risk of serious irreversible harm if removed' (this test, which is common to all deportation cases following the Immigration Act 2014, is discussed further at **6.170** of this work);[1] or

- where the person has made an application to the courts for an interim order to suspend removal proceedings (ie judicial review) and that application has not yet been determined, or a court has made an interim order to suspend removal: Reg 24AA(4). However, Reg 24AA(4) also provides that there will be *no* such suspension of removal where (a) 'the expulsion decision is based on a previous judicial decision'; (b) where the person 'has had previous access to judicial review'; or (c) where the removal decision is based on imperative grounds of public security. These three categories mirror the words used in Article 31(2) of the Citizens' Directive. The equivalent provisions under the new section 94B of the Nationality Immigration and Asylum Act 2002 are discussed in CHAPTER 19.

Where a person's removal on the basis of regulation 19(3)(a) is enforced, they are entitled to pursue their appeal against removal outside of the UK, but may apply for temporary admission in order to attend the appeal hearing, under regulation 29AA. Under regulation 29AA(3), the Secretary of State 'must' grant that application for temporary admission unless the person's appearance 'may cause serious troubles to public policy or public security.' After the person's attendance at their appeal, regulation 29AA(5) states that the person 'may be removed' pending determination of their appeal, but they may return to the UK to make submissions in person during the remaining stages of the redress procedure under regulation 29AA. Regulation 24A governs applications to revoke a deportation order by a person who is outside the UK[2] following a material change in circumstances.

1   Her discretion to make such a certification is contained in regulation 24AA(2) and (3), and she may do so either in the period between service of the decision and lodging an appeal or after the appeal has been instituted but remains pending: regulation 24AA(1).
2   In *R (on the application of BXS) v Secretary of State for the Home Department* [2014] EWHC 737 (Admin), Michael Fordham QC held that there was no unlawful discrimination in EU or human rights terms for the requirement in Reg 24A that an application for revocation of a deportation order of an EEA national be pursued out of country even where that would not be the case for a non-EEA national, although permission to appeal was granted on this issue. The refusal to revoke was, however, quashed owing to a failure to grapple with the change in circumstances, it betrayed inadequate reasoning and the mere fact that a ground had previously been considered did not lead to the conclusion that the ground should be certified. See the further, unsuccessful challenge to the denial of a suspending appeal right in an EEA revocation case in *R (on the application of Byczek) v Secretary of State for the Home Department* [2014] EWHC 4298 (Admin).

National security cases

6.196 An appeal against an EEA decision lies to the Special Immigration Appeals Commission (SIAC) where:

- Regulation 28(2): the SSHD, acting in person, certifies that the EEA decision was taken (a) wholly or partly in the interests of national security or in the interests of the relationship between the UK and another country; or (b) in accordance with a direction from the SSHD which identifies the person to whom the decision relates and which is given wholly or partly on a grounds in (a). Or,
- Regulation 28(4): where the Secretary of State, acting in person, certifies that the EEA decision was taken wholly or partly in reliance on information which in his opinion should not be made public— (a) in the interests of national security; (b) in the interests of the relationship between the United Kingdom and another country; or (c) otherwise in the public interest.

Following the CJEU's decision in *ZZ v United* Kingdom,[1] it is necessary in SIAC proceedings for the SSHD to provide the essence of the grounds against an appellant, notwithstanding the interests of national security, in order to comply inter alia with the procedural requirements of the Citizens' Directive and the principle of effective judicial protection of EU rights. For more details of appeals to SIAC, see **CHAPTER 22** below.

1   *ZZ (France) v Secretary of State for the Home Department* (Case C-300/11), CJEU 4 June 2013 [2013] QB 1136; [2013] 3 WLR 813; [2014] All ER (EC) 56; [2013] 3 CMLR 46, applied by the Court of Appeal in *ZZ (France) v Secretary of State for the Home Department* [2014] EWCA Civ 7; [2014] 2 WLR 791; [2014] 3 All ER 587; [2014] 2 CMLR 49.

RIGHTS UNDER ASSOCIATION AGREEMENTS

6.197 Article 217 TFEU (ex Article 310 TEC) provides that the EU may conclude with a third State, a union of States or an international organisation, an agreement establishing an association, involving reciprocal rights and obligations, common actions and special procedures. Article 218 TFEU (ex Article 300 TEC) provides that such agreements shall be negotiated by the Commission, and concluded by the Council, after consulting the European Parliament where required. Agreements concluded under these conditions are binding on the institutions of the EU and on Member States.[1] Agreements entered into by both the EU and Member States with a third country are mixed agreements, but do not for that reason cease to be enforceable in EU law.[2] A number of these agreements have implications for immigration rights of nationals of the countries with which such agreements have been concluded.[3] Ten of the twelve new accession States since May 2004 were central and east European countries formerly with association agreements. Now that Bulgaria and Romania have joined, HC 395, paragraphs 211 to 221 have been deleted and only paragraphs 222 to 223A are left to deal with indefinite leave applications from those who established themselves in business or self-employment before their country became one of the new accession States of the EU. The only relevant major Association Agreement left is the Turkish Association Agreement to which we now turn.

[1]   Article 300(2) EC (ex art 228(2)).
[2]   Case 12/86 *Demirel v Stadt Schwäbisch Gmünd* [1987] ECR 3719, [1989] 1 CMLR 421, ECJ.
[3]   There is a vast array of agreements between the European Union and third countries. Many of these include non-discrimination provisions for workers, which do not provide any right of entry to the territory of the Member States but do provide some protection to workers from those third countries already lawfully resident in Member States. For discussion of these agreements see Rogers and Scannell *Free Movement of Persons in the Enlarged European Union* (Sweet & Maxwell, 2004), chapter 15.

TURKISH ASSOCIATION AGREEMENT

Introduction

6.198 On 12 September 1963 at Ankara the EC signed the Turkey EEC Association Agreement, which was supplemented on 23 November 1970 by the Brussels Protocol.[1] These Agreements aimed to establish free movement provisions between Turkey and the EC within 22 years, and this itself was intended as a step towards full Turkish membership of the EC. These aspirations have never been achieved by implementing measures, and full Turkish membership has not yet happened. However, the Agreement provided for a Council of Association on which the various parties are represented.[2] By Article 36 of the 1970 Protocol, the Council of Association is given the power to decide on the rules necessary to implement the progressive stages for the free movement of workers within the 20-year period.[3] The Association Council adopted three decisions: Decisions 2/76 of 20 December 1976, 1/80 of 19 September 1980 and 3/80 of the same date,[4] which for long were unpublished but have become important for Turkish nationals already resident in the EU by reason of a series of decisions of the ECJ starting with the decisions in *Sevince*[5] and *Kus*.[6]

[1]   Association Agreement approved and confirmed on behalf of the Community by Council Decision 64/732/EEC (OJ 1973 C 133, p 1); Additional Protocol approved and confirmed by Council Regulation (EEC) No 2760/72 (OJ 1972 L 293, p 1). A full description of the Association Agreement and its Protocol is not possible within the confines of this volume, but

the reader is referred to Rogers and Scannell *Free Movement of Persons in the Enlarged European Union* (2004); Martin and Guild *Free movement of persons in the European Union* (1996).

2   Ankara Agreement 1963, art 6, OJ C113/2 24.12.1963.
3   Additional Protocol signed at Brussels, 23 November 1970, art 36, OJ C/113/2 24.12.1973. There is also a power to make recommendations in art 38, but it is the rules which are binding.
4   The decisions are not published in the OJ, but are set out in full in Rogers *A Practitioner's Guide to the Turkey-EC Association Agreement*, ILPA (2000, Kluwer).
5   Case C-192/89 *Sevince v Staatssecretaris van Justitie* [1992] 2 CMLR 57.
6   Case C-237/91 *Kus v Landeshaupstadt Wiesbaden* [1993] 2 CMLR 887, ECJ. Followed in *Eroglu v Land Baden-Württemberg*: Case C-355/93 [1994] ECR I-5113, ECJ.

6.199 The decisions of the ECJ in *Demirel*[1] and *Sevince*[2] held that the programme for free movement of persons between Turkey and the EC by the end of 1985 was not itself of direct effect and therefore gave no rights to Turkish nationals to enter the territory of the EC, even though the Turkey-EC Association Agreement was potentially capable of giving rise to individual rights, if the rules on direct effect were met.[3] However, in *Sevince* the court held that some decisions of the Association Council were sufficiently clear and precise as to be capable of direct effect, although the decision in question was of no assistance to the particular applicant in that case because he was not legally employed. It was only in *Kus*[4] that a Turkish worker succeeded in using an Association Council decision to obtain a fresh work and residence permit in reliance on Community law. The crucial provision relied on in *Kus* is Article 6 of Decision 1/80. This provides:

'1.   Subject to Article 7 on free access to employment for members of his family, a Turkish worker duly registered as belonging to the labour force of a Member State:
–   shall be entitled in that Member State, after one year's legal employment, to the renewal of his permit to work for the same employer, if a job is available;
–   shall be entitled in that Member State, after three years of legal employment and subject to the priority to be given to workers of Member States of the Community, to respond to another offer of employment, with an employer of his choice, made under normal conditions and registered with the employment services of that State for the same occupation;
–   shall enjoy free access in that Member State to any paid employment of his choice, after four years of legal employment.'[5]

Once rights are legitimately accrued under Article 6(1), the existence of those rights are no longer dependent on the continuing existence of the circumstances which gave rise to them, since no such condition is laid down by Decision 1/80.[6]

1   [1987] ECR 3719, [1989] 1 CMLR 421, ECJ.
2   Case C-192/89 *Sevince v Staatssecretaris van Justitie* [1992] 2 CMLR 57.
3   Following *Demirel* the Court of Appeal in the UK held that art 12 of the Ankara Agreement of 12 September 1963 gave no free movement rights to Turkish nationals: *R v Secretary of State for the Home Department, ex p Narin* [1990] 2 CMLR 233, CA.
4   [1993] 2 CMLR 887.
5   Decision 1/80, art 6.
6   *Unal (Baris) v Staatssecretaris van Justitie* (Case C-187/10) [2012] ICR D1. It was therefore held in *Unal* that a Turkish worker who has been employed for more than one year under a valid work permit has to be regarded as fulfilling the conditions laid down in the first indent of art 6(1) of Decision No 1/80, even though his residence permit had initially been granted to him for a purpose other than that of engaging in paid employment. See also *Gulbahce v*

Freie und Hanestadt Hamburg (Case C-268/11) [2013] ICR 389, in which extensions of a domestic residence permit on the basis of a relationship which, it later transpired, was not in fact subsisting did not justify withholding the benefits of art 6(1) of the Decision, where the person had accrued one year's legal employment prior to the subsequent extension applications.

Turkish workers

6.200 Article 6(2) of Decision No 1/80 covers interruptions in the periods of legal employment completed by the Turkish worker concerned. If it applies the continuity of a period of employment is not broken and the relevant national authorities are not entitled to call into question the residence of the person concerned in the host Member State. It reads:

'2.   Annual holidays and absences for reasons of maternity or an accident at work or short periods of sickness shall be treated as periods of legal employment. Periods of involuntary unemployment duly certified by the relevant authorities and long absences on account of sickness shall not be treated as periods of legal employment, but shall not affect rights acquired as the result of the preceding period of employment.'

In *Sedef*[1] the Turkish national was employed in the maritime shipping industry for 15 years. He had the same employer for more than one year without interruption, but not up to the end of a period of three years and his periods of employment had been interrupted 17 times on account of the nature of the occupation. Normally under Article 6.1, a Turkish worker who does not yet enjoy the right provided for in the third indent must be engaged in legal employment for one, three or four years respectively, in principle without any interruption. It is in order to temper the severity of the latter rule that Article 6(2) of Decision No 1/80 sets out certain legitimate causes of interruption to employment. Article 6(2) makes a distinction on the basis of the type and length of the periods in which a Turkish worker was not working. The first sentence of that provision relates to periods of inactivity involving generally only a brief cessation of work, such as absences for annual holiday, maternity leave, an accident at work or a short period of sickness, which constitute events which must be regarded as a normal part of any employment relationship. The second sentence of Article 6(2) relates to periods of inactivity due to long-term sickness or involuntary unemployment. That provision provides that periods of inactivity of that type, which result in a longer absence or one the length of which is not predictable. Although they cannot be treated as periods of legal employment, they cannot result in the Turkish worker losing the rights which he or she has already acquired as the result of preceding periods of legal employment. The court, therefore, held that the 17 breaks in Mr Sedef's employment, which were beyond his control, could be described as periods of involuntary unemployment within the meaning of the second sentence of Article 6(2), even though the claimant did not register as a job-seeker as is required in principle by that provision. He could, therefore, validly rely on the third indent of Article 6(1) of that decision to obtain an extension of his residence permit in order to continue in paid employment in that Member State.

[1]   Case C-230/03 *Sedef v Freie und Hansestadt Hamburg*[2006] ECR I-157.

6.201 This right only applies after Turkish nationals have entered a Member State and taken up lawful employment there. It does not grant a right to enter or obtain a work permit, and it does not allow a Turkish worker to move from one Member State to another, so it is different from the rights of EEA nationals to seek and obtain work. It is not a free movement right, but gives Turkish workers a progressive series of rights over a four-year period, leading to their eventual integration into the host State's workforce. In setting out the considerable ambit and scope of these rights, the ECJ considers that Article 6 of Decision 1/80 forms part of and thus constitutes a further stage in securing freedom of movement of workers on the basis of Articles 39 to 41 EC, and so says it is essential to extend so far as possible the principles in the EC Articles to Turkish workers.[1] This is consistent with Article 12 of the Ankara Agreement, which states:

'The contracting parties agree to be guided by Articles 48, 49 and 50 [now Articles 39–41] of the Treaty establishing the Community for the purposes of progressively securing freedom of movement for workers between them.'

Thus 'worker' is given the same meaning as under Article 39 EC.[2] Administrative documents are declaratory and evidential, rather than conditions of entitlement, in the case of Turkish workers, as is the case with residence permits under Article 39.[3] The public policy derogation is interpreted in the same way as under Council Directive (EEC) 64/221.[4] The position of the children of Turkish workers compares with those of workers under the main EC Treaty.[5]

[1] Case C-98/96 *Ertanir v Land Hessen* [1997] ECR I-5179, para 21; Case C-434/93 *Bozkurt v Staatssecretaris van Justitie* [1995] ECR I-1475, paras 14, 19 and 20; Case C-171/95 *Tetik v Land Berlin* [1997] ECR I-329, para 20; Case C-340/97 *Nazli v Stadt Nürnberg* [2000] ECR I-957, ECJ, paras 50–55; Case C-188/00 *Kurtz v Land Baden-Württemburg* [2002] ECR I-10691, ECJ, para 30.
[2] Case C-36/96 *Günaydin v Freistaat Bayern* [1997] ECR I-5143, para 31, ECJ; Case C-98/96 *Ertanir v Land Hessen* [1997] ECR I-5179, ECJ, para 43; Case C-1/97 *Birden v Stadtgemeinde Bremen* [1998] ECR I-7747, ECJ, paras 25 and 28; Case C-188/00 *Kurtz v Land Baden-Württemberg* [2002] ECR I-10691, ECJ, paras 31–32.
[3] *Bozkurt* above; Case C-329/97 *Ergat v Stadt Ulm* [2000] ECR I-1487, ECJ. Cf Case 48/75 *Royer, Re* [1976] ECR 497.
[4] Case C-340/97 *Nazli v Stadt Nürnberg* [2000] ECR I-957, ECJ; *Ergat* above, ECJ.
[5] Case C-210/97 *Akman v Oberkreisdirektor des Rheinische-Bergischen-Kreises* [1998] ECR I-7519, ECJ.

6.202 In *R (on the application of Payir) v Secretary of State for the Home Department*,[1] the European Court dealt with a reference from the English Court of Appeal about whether Turkish students, who are working to pay their fees, and a Turkish au pair are by law entitled to the benefit of Article 6(1) of Decision No 1/80 of the Association Council, which provides that a Turkish worker duly registered as belonging to the labour force of a Member State is entitled to increasing access to the Member State's labour market after one, three and four years of legal employment. In *Birden*[2] the ECJ said that 'the legality of the employment presupposes a stable and secure situation as a member of the labour force of a Member State and, by virtue of this, implies the existence of an undisputed right of residence (paragraph 55)'. In court it was conceded that the students, who each had part time jobs, and the au pair were workers. They were also quite lawfully in the UK and there was nothing illegal about the work they were doing. But the UK government, taking a lead from Laws LJ in the Court of Appeal (paragraphs 27 and 28), queried whether they were engaged in an effective and genuine economic activity which could be classed as 'legal employment' within the meaning of Article 6(1). The European Court gave these arguments short shrift, holding that it must be determined whether the Turkish national meets the objective conditions laid down in Article 6(1), without it being necessary to take into account the reasons for which he or she was first granted the right to enter that territory or any temporal limitations attached to their right to work.[3] The Court held that the reasons for which leave to enter was granted to the Turkish nationals concerned – to enable them to pursue studies or gain experience as an au pair – cannot in themselves prevent the persons concerned from being able to rely on Article 6(1) of Decision No 1/80. The same applies to statements of intention made by those nationals to the effect that they do not wish to remain in the host Member State for more than two years or that they intend to leave it on completion of their studies, and to temporal limitations attaching to their leave to remain. Turkish workers resident in a host Member State, who are posted to a second Member State to provide services, do not cause Decision 1/80 to be engaged in the second state (*Essent Energie Productie BV v Minister van Sociale Zaken en Werkgelegenheid*[4].

[1] Case C-294/06 *R (on the application of Payir) v Secretary of State for the Home Department*; *R (on the application of Ozturk) v Secretary of State for the Home Department*; *R (on the application of Akyuz) v Secretary of State for the Home Department* [2008] ECR I-203, [2009] All ER (EC) 964(see paragraphs 27–30 and 33, 35, 37 and 40–44). The neutral citation in the CA was [2006] EWCA Civ 541, reported at [2006] ICR 1314.

[2] *Birden v Stadtgemeinde Bremen*: C-1/97 [1998] ECR I-7747, [1999] 1 CMLR 420, ECJ. In *R (on the application of Oczelik (Ali)) v Secretary of State for the Home Department* [2009] EWCA Civ 260, [2009] All ER (D) 81 (May), the Court of Appeal held that the time taken to process an application of a Turkish immigrant for indefinite leave to remain in the United Kingdom did not count towards the one-year period of legal employment that would entitle him to remain in the UK under the Association Agreement 1963, art 6(1). Although he was lawfully in the UK, his position was precarious and he did not meet the requirements of community law to be in a stable and secure situation as a member of the UK labour force.

[3] According to settled case law, it is not open to the national authorities to attach conditions to such rights or to restrict their application, as they would otherwise undermine the effect of Decision No 1/80 (see *Günaydin*, paras 37 to 40, and 50; *Birden*, para 19; *Kurz*, para 26; Joined Cases C-317/01 and C-369/01 *Abatay* [2003] ECR I 12301, para 78; and *Sedef*, para 34).

[4] C-91/13[2014] All ER (D) 157 (Sep), ECJ.

6.203 In a series of cases on the application of Article 6 of Decision 1/80, the ECJ has established the following guidelines for Turkish nationals:

(1)   he or she has to be a worker and not self-employed, that is, someone bound by an employment relationship covering a genuine and effective economic activity pursued for the benefit of and under the direction of another for remuneration.[1] It makes no difference to the definition that employment is for the sole purpose of preparing the employee to work elsewhere;[2] is specific work for a specific employer for a limited period;[3] or is a paid apprenticeship.[4] A person may qualify as a worker even although the job is a temporary one to enable recipients of social assistance to integrate into working life and takes place at a cultural centre funded by public money and not in competition with undertakings in the general labour market;[5]

(2)   he or she has to be duly registered as belonging to the labour force ('appartenant au marché regulier' in the French version) of a Member State.[6] This means being in employment which is either located within the territory of a Member State or which retains a sufficiently close link with it, as in the case of an international lorry-driver who has sufficient links with one Member State,[7] or someone employed in the maritime shipping industry.[8] To establish a close link with a particular Member State, it will be necessary to take into account the place where the worker was hired, the territory on which or from which employment is pursued, and the applicable national legislation in the field of employment and social security.[9] A worker will be treated as duly registered if he or she is employed on the same conditions of work and pay as those claimed by workers who pursue identical or similar activities,[10] and complies with the requirements laid down by the rules and regulations in the Member State concerned;[11]

(3)   he or she has to be in legal employment. This means having a stable and secure position in the labour force and an undisputed right of residence.[12] Legal employment is a concept of Community law, which must be defined objectively and uniformly in the light of the spirit and purpose of Article 6 of Decision 1/80.[13] Accordingly, it does not matter that the worker may have been aware of the restrictions imposed by the host State.[14] Employment of less than 12 months may not have sufficient stability to qualify,[15] but the fact that employment contracts are temporary is of no relevance.[16] The immigration status of the Turkish worker is of relevance to the issue of a stable and secure position. Where a worker has obtained his or her residence permit in fraudulent circumstances, he or she will not qualify,[17] nor does one who is resident on a provisional basis awaiting the grant of a residence permit,[18] or someone who is authorised to work while he or she appeals against a decision refusing a right of residence;[19]

(4)   it is settled case law that once Turkish workers have lawfully entered the territory of the host Member State and have entered into lawful employment, as described above, they can enjoy the rights conferred on them by Article 6 (1), irrespective of whether or not the authorities of the host Member State issue a specific administrative document, such as a work permit or residence permit.[20] This is of particular importance once workers have completed four years in employment and are fully integrated into the host Member State (**6.201** above). It also applies to family members after five years' legal residence (**6.207** below);

(5)   it is also settled case-law that Article 6(1) does not make the recognition of any rights, which it confers on Turkish workers, subject to any condition connected with the reason for which the right to enter, work, or reside was initially granted.[21] So if someone is given leave to do an apprenticeship,[22] or was allowed to work while their spouse was in full time education, these circumstances would not prevent them enjoying the rights conferred by Article 6(1);

(6)   Turkish workers are not exempt from paying fees for a residence card by relying on the standstill clause in Article 13 of Decision No1/80, but at the same time Article 13 precludes the introduction of national legislation, which makes the granting of a residence permit or an

extension of the period of validity of such a permit conditional on payment of administrative charges, where the amount of those charges payable by Turkish nationals is disproportionate as compared with the amount required from Community nationals.[23]

[1] Case C-36/96 *Günaydin v Freistaat Bayern* [1997] ECR I-5143, ECJ; Case C-1/97 *Birden v Stadtgemeinde Bremen* [1998] ECR I-7747, ECJ. For the situation of the self-employed, see **6.151** above.
[2] *Günaydin* above.
[3] Case C-98/96 *Ertanir v Land Hessen* [1997] ECR I-5179, ECJ.
[4] Case C-188/00 *Kurz v Land Baden-Württemberg* [2002] ECR I-10691, ECJ.
[5] *Birden* above.
[6] *Kurtz*, above, at paras 37–44; *R (on the application of Payir) v Secretary of State for the Home Department; R (on the application of Ozturk) v Same; R (on the application of Akyuz) v Same*, para 44.
[7] Case C-434/93 *Bozkurt v Staatssecretaris van Justitie* [1995] ECR I-1475, ECJ, at paras 22–23.
[8] Case C-230/03 *Sedef v Freie und Hansestadt Hamburg* [2006] ECR I-157.
[9] *Bozkurt* above.
[10] *Günaydin* above, at para 29.
[11] *Birden* above, at para 33.
[12] Case C-192/89 *Sevince v Staatssecretaris van Justitie* [1990] ECR I-3461, para 30; Case C-237/91 *Kus v Landeshauptstadt* [1992] ECR I-6781, para 12; *Bozkurt* above, para 26; *Birden* paras 47–55, above. Case C-285/95 *Kol v Land Berlin* [1997] ECR I-3069, para 21.
[13] *Ertanir* above, at para 39. In *FS (Breach of conditions: Ankara agreement) Turkey* [2008] UKAIT 00066 the AIT found that the Ankara Agreement does not entitle Turkish nationals to breach conditions of their leave. A Turkish national is not, therefore, entitled to base a claimed entitlement to remain in the United Kingdom on working in breach of conditions of their leave to enter.
[14] *Ertanir* above.
[15] Case C-306/95 *Eker* [1997] ECR I-2697.
[16] *Günaydin*, above at paras 36–40; *Birden*, above at paras 37–39 and 64; *Kurtz, above*, at para 55.
[17] *Kol* above.
[18] *Kus* above, para 21.
[19] *Sevince* above, para 31.
[20] *Bozkurt*, paras 29–30; *Günaydin* paras 36–40; *Ertanir*, para 55; *Birden* para 65; and *Kurtz* para 54.
[21] *Kus* above, paras 21–22; *Günaydin* para 52; *Birden* para 57; and *Kurz* para 56; *Payir* paras 43-44.
[22] For example, *Kurtz*, above.
[23] *Minister voor Vreemdelingenzaken en Integratie v Sahin (T)* Case C-242/06 [2009] ECR I-08465, [2010] 1 CMLR 215.

6.204 Under the first indent of Article 6 of Decision 1/80, workers have to work continuously for the same employer. If they change employers during the first year, they cannot benefit.[1] Similarly, to qualify under the second indent of Article 6, a worker must continue working for the same employer.[2] It is only at the end of three years' continuous employment that a Turkish worker is entitled to accept offers of work from a different employer, but even then he or she must remain in the same occupation as before, and the new employer must respect the right of priority of Community nationals. At the end of four years' employment, the worker can then choose any job in any occupation with any employer. Workers in this position may then voluntarily terminate their existing employment to look for new work on the same conditions as Community work seekers. They must remain duly registered as belonging to the labour force, and this may mean registering with the local employment office as a person seeking employment.[3]

1   Case C-306/95 *Eker* [1997] ECR I-2697.
2   Case C-355/93 *Eroglu v Land Baden-Württemberg* [1994] ECR I-5113.
3   Case C-171/95 *Tetik v Land Berlin* [1997] ECR I-329.

6.205 Article 6(2) of Decision 1/80 deals with continuity of employment. Annual holidays and absences for reasons of maternity or accident at work, or short periods of sickness, are treated as periods of legal employment. Periods of involuntary unemployment, duly certified by the relevant authorities, and long absences on account of sickness, are not treated as periods of legal employment, but do not break continuity. Article 6(2) of the Decision states that they shall not affect rights acquired as the result of the preceding period of employment. The ECJ has held that short interruptions between the expiry of a residence permit and the obtaining of a new one do not affect the Turkish worker's rights.[1] In *Nazli*[2] a lengthy period in prison on remand did not destroy the worker's right of access to employment, and the ECJ held that he continued to have his rights provided he found a job again within a reasonable period after his release. In that case and in Tetik,[3] the court has recognised that once Turkish workers are free to change their jobs under Article 6[4], they should have a reasonable period to seek new employment in the same way as Community nationals.[5]

1   Case C-98/96 *Ertanir v Land Hessen* [1997] ECR I-5179, ECJ.
2   Case C-340/97 [2000] ECR I-957, ECJ, at paras 40–41. A 16 year prison sentence following a drugs conviction meant that the applicant ceased to be duly registered as belonging to the labour force of the UK when he was detained following conviction: *R (on the application of Samaroo) v Secretary of State for the Home Department* [2001] EWCA Civ 1139, [2002] INLR 55, and *R (on the application of Sezek) v Secretary of State for the Home Department* [2001] EWCA Civ 795, [2001] 1 WLR 348, [2001] Imm AR 657.
3   Case C-171/95 [1997] ECR I-329, ECJ, at para 46. See also Case C-188/00 *Kurtz v Land Baden-Württemberg* [2002] ECR I-10691, ECJ, at para 59.
4   *R (on the application of Buer) v Secretary of State for the Home Department*[2014] EWCA Civ 1109, [2015] 1 CMLR 90. The Court of Appeal has recently held that the standstill clause cannot be relied on for the purposes of asserting a right to indefinite leave to remain where the person had already acquired rights under Article 6 (*R (Buer) v SSHD*).
5   See Case C-292/89 *R v Immigration Appeal Tribunal, ex p Antonissen* [1991] ECR I-745, [1991] 2 CMLR 373.

Family members from Turkey

6.206 Article 7 of Decision 1/80 deals with the employment rights of family members of Turkish workers, and has been held to be directly effective.[1] Under Article 7, two distinct rights are given to family members of Turkish workers. First, members of the family of a Turkish worker who is duly registered as belonging to the labour force of a Member State are entitled after a time to take up job offers, if they 'have been authorised to join' him or her: see **6.207**, below.[2] Secondly, children of Turkish workers who have completed a course of vocational training in the host country have a right to take any job once one of their parents has been in legal employment for a certain period: see **6.208** below. We look at each of these entitlements in more detail. These requirements are, however subject to the following: the 'standstill' provision, that prevents any new measures making it more difficult to carry on self-employment or provide services, also apply to family members, and so national measures that make family reunion 'difficult or impossible' will violate the standstill clause: *Dogan v Bundesrepublik Deutschland*[3] (Case-138/13, CJEU, 10 July 2014).

1   Case C-351/95 Kadiman [1997] ECR I-2133.
2   For the definition of 'family' see **6.116–6.117** and **6.130** above. In *Eyup* Case C-69/98 [2000] ECR I-4747, the ECJ declined to hold that a cohabitee could be a member of the family, but held that a Turkish couple who had married, then divorced and later re-married, but who had always lived together, had 'constantly maintained a common legal residence' within the meaning of art 7(1) of Decision 1/80. In *Ayaz* Case C-275/02, 30 September 2004, the ECJ held that family members would include step-children for the purposes of Article 7 of Decision 1/80.
3   C-138/13 [2014] All ER (D) 310 (Jul), ECJ.

6.207 First, the right of family members only arises if they have been authorised by the host State to join the primary worker or were born there.[1] If they have entered for some other purpose it does not arise. Furthermore, there needs to be a period of cohabitation. In *Kadiman*[2] the ECJ held that the words in the first paragraph of Article 7(1) of Decision 1/80, 'authorised to join him', cannot be interpreted as merely requiring the host Member State to have authorised a family member to enter its territory to join a Turkish worker, without at the same time requiring the person concerned to reside there continually with the migrant worker until he or she is entitled to enter the labour market. In other words, there has to be a specified period of cohabitation in a household with the primary worker before any employment rights accrue. These criteria were explained by the CJEU in *Pehlivan*,[3] which concerned a Turkish national, who joined her parents in Holland when she was almost 20-years-old in August 1999. For the next six years she remained in her parents' home, despite getting married and having a child. In 2005 she left her parents' home with her child. The Dutch authorities then withdrew her residence permit with retrospective effect from 2000. Everyone in the case agreed that Ms Pehlivan had lived for three years under her parents' roof from 1999 onwards. The CJEU held that:

- Article 7 of Decision 1/80 provides that the family member of a Turkish worker who has been authorised to join the worker in the Member State is entitled, after three years' legal residence, to respond to any offer of employment. According to the case law of the CJEU, where there is a right to work there is also a concomitant right to reside (at [42]).
- There are only two requirements for a family member like Ms Pehlivan to fulfil: (i) that she is a member of the family of a Turkish worker (which was not disputed); (ii) that she has been authorised to enter the territory of the Member State.
- As Article 7 only gives the family member a right to work after three years, the CJEU has accepted that Member States can require the person to reside with the family for these three years (at [48] and [55]). But after the initial period the right to work entitles the person to move to take employment where it can be found (at [51]).

- Any conditions a Member State might wish to place on the family member's residence during the first three years must not go beyond the objective of the decision (at [53]). Member States are not permitted to modify unilaterally the scope of the system of integration of Turkish workers and their family members in the whole state (at [56]).

Accordingly, the CJEU found that the Dutch rules, which permitted retrospective withdrawal of a residence permit on the grounds that the family link is broken, were unlawful as imposing a new obstacle in the way of Turkish workers and their families (at [57]).

The rather strict three-year cohabitation condition is at odds with the more lax rules for family members under Council Regulation (EEC) 1612/68, and was prompted by fears of the rules being manipulated by sham marriages. Conscious of the harshness of its interpretation, the court stated that allowances can be made if the person's job or training takes him or her away from home. It is for the national court to determine whether the circumstances justify living apart. It remains to be seen whether domestic violence would constitute such a circumstance.[4] Apart from the hurdle of an initial period of cohabitation, family members are entitled to respond to any offers of employment, subject to the priority to be given to workers of Member States, once they have been legally resident for at least three years. After five years they are free to take any job, without any need for employers to give priority to EU workers. At that point they have independent rights of residence, even if they no longer live with the family member they had been authorised to join.[5] During the periods of legal residence absences for reasonable periods and for legitimate reasons, such as holidays, do not break continuity.[6] In *OY (Ankara Agreement; Standstill Clause; Workers Family) Turkey*[7] the AIT held that the standstill clause in the Ankara Agreement does not restrict Member States' ability to regulate control of entry of family members to those national rules in force at the time of accession to the EC. However, in *Pehlivan*, the CJEU re-enforced the principle that Member States are not free to impose additional requirements on the family members of Turkish workers they have admitted. Once the family is united, then members who do not yet have the right to work only have two conditions to fulfil. Member States cannot add new rules or apply retrospective new conditions on the residents of the family members as this will be in breach of the EC Turkey agreement. Family members of Turkish workers who have become nationals of the host Member State (in addition to the worker's Turkish nationality) can still invoke Article 7 of Decision 1/80, notwithstanding that the principal Turkish worker no longer needs to rely upon the Decision.[8] Family members who are third country nationals, and who are the family member of a Turkish worker under Decision 1/80, may invoke in the host Member State the rights arising from that provision, where all the other conditions laid down by the provision have been fulfilled.[9]

---

[1] *Cetinkaya v Land Baden-Wurttemberg* Case C-467/02 ([2004] ECR I-10895).
[2] Case C-351/95 *Kadiman* [1997] ECR I-2133, paras 37–42.
[3] Case C-484/07 *Pehlivan (Fatma) v Staatssecretaris van Justitie* (16 June 2011, unreported).
[4] For domestic violence in relation to EEA family members, see Council Directive 2004/38/EC (Citizens' Directive) art 13(2)(c).
[5] Case C-329/97 Ergat v Stadt Ulm [2000] ECR I-1487, ECJ.
[6] *Kadiman* above, paras 37–42.
[7] *OY (Ankara Agreement; Standstill Clause; Workers Family) Turkey* [2006] UKAIT 00028.

8   *Staatssecretaris van Justitie v Kahveci (Tayfun)* (C-7/10); *Staatssecretaris van Justitie v Inan* (C-9/10), [2012] 2 C.MLR 37. *Kahveci* and *Inan* were family members of Turkish workers and committed criminal offences. The Netherlands revoked K and I's residence permits on the basis that K and I's Turkish family member had by that point acquired Netherlands nationality in addition to their Turkish nationality, which meant that K and I were no longer their family members under Decision 1/80. The Court held that the measure had the effect of undermining the legal status expressly conferred on Turkish nationals by the EEC-Turkish Association Agreement and that an expulsion measure based on Article14(1) of Decision 1/80 might be taken only if the personal conduct of the person concerned indicated a specific risk of new and serious prejudice to the requirements of public policy, having regard to both the principle of proportionality and the fundamental rights of the person concerned.

9   *Dulger v Wetteraukreis* (C-451/11) [2012] 3 CMLR 1201, [2013] ICR 79. The Court's reasoning included the recognition, at [47], that, 'The advantages that family reunification bring to family life, to the quality of the stay and to the integration of the Turkish worker in the Member State where he works and resides are clearly independent of the nationality of the members of his family who are authorised to join him in that State.'

6.208 Under the second paragraph of Article 7 of Decision 1/80, children of Turkish workers who have completed a course of vocational training in the host State are free to take any job, irrespective of the time they have spent there, provided that one of their parents has been legally employed in the Member State concerned for at least three years. In *Eroglu*[1] the court held that the second paragraph of Article 7 gives a Turkish national who satisfies the conditions a right to respond to any offer of employment and to rely on the right in order to obtain a new work permit; secondly that the right necessarily implies a recognition of a right of residence, giving the person an opportunity to look for job opportunities; and thirdly, that the right is not subject to any conditions concerning the ground on which the right to enter and stay was granted. So it was immaterial that the person was given leave to enter the host State as a student and not as a family member. Once a child has completed his or her education and acquired the right, conferred directly by Article 7 (2) of Decision No 1/80, of access to the employment market of the host country, and, as a result, the right to obtain a residence permit for that purpose, it is not necessary that the parent of the child still has the status of worker or continues to reside in that Member State.[2]

1   Case C-355/93 *Eroglu v Land Baden-Württemberg* [1994] ECR I-5113, ECJ.
2   Case C-210/97 *Akman v Oberkreisdirektor des Rheinische-Bergischen-Kreises* [1998] ECR I-7519, ECJ; Case C-329/97 *Ergat v Stadt Ulm* [2000] ECR I-1487, ECJ, at para 44.

6.209 Decisions made under the Turkey Association Agreement also deal with discrimination on grounds of nationality, in relation to education of the children of Turkish workers and as regards social security. Under Article 9 of Decision 1/80, such children are entitled to education on the same footing as own nationals. This accords with the rights such children would have under Article 2 of Protocol 1 of the ECHR, read with Article 14. In *Sürül*[1] the ECJ held that Article 9 of the Decision was of direct effect. The case dealt with Article 3 of Decision 3/80, under which the applicant claimed family allowance in Germany. She was refused on the basis that, although she was lawfully resident, she had only a limited stay. The court held that this was discriminatory, since a Member State cannot impose on Turkish nationals more or stricter controls than those imposed on own nationals, for whom the only requirement was domicile or habitual residence.

1.   Case C-262/96 *Sürül v Bundesanstalt für Arbeit* [1999] ECR I-2685, ECJ. See further joined cases C-102 and 211/98, *Kocak (Ibrahim) v Landesversicherungsanstalt Oberfranken und Mittelfranken; Ramazan v Bundesknappschaft* [2000] ECR I-1287, ECJ.

6.210 The provisions of Decision 1/80 are subject to limitations based on public policy, public security or public health.[1] However, Turkish nationals seeking to defeat deportation/removal on public policy grounds, who benefit from the provisions of that Decision, cannot rely on the enhanced protection available to EEA nationals under the Citizens' Directive (2004/38/EC), which is accrued with increasing residence in the host Member state: *Ziebell*.[2] The Court's reasoning in *Ziebell* included the recognition that the EEC-Turkey Association pursued a purely economic objective and was restricted to the gradual achievement of the free movement of workers. By contrast, the concept of EU citizenship, because it resulted from the fact that a person held the nationality of a Member State and not from his status as a worker, was a feature of EU law that justified the recognition, for EU citizens alone, of guarantees which were considerably strengthened in respect of expulsion, such as those provided for in Article 28(3)(a) of the Directive. In *Nazli*[3] the ECJ held that the same principles applied as in public policy cases under Article 45(3) (ex Article 39 TEC).[4] So a Turkish worker could not be expelled as a deterrent to others without his or her personal conduct giving reason to believe that he or she would commit other serious offences prejudicial to the requirements of public policy in the host Member State. The same applies to family members.[5]

1.   Decision 1/80, art 14(1).
2.   *Ziebell v Land Baden-Wurttemberg* (C-371/08) [2012] 2 CMLR 35. See discussion at **6.176** ff above.
3.   Case C-340/97 *Nazli v Stadt Nürnberg* [2000] ECR I-957, ECJ. See also *Cetinkaya v Land Baden-Wurttemberg* Case C-467/02 ([2004] ECR I-10895).
4.   See *R v Bouchereau* [1978] QB 732.
5.   See Case C-329/97 *Ergat v Stadt Ulm*, [2000] ECR I-1487, ECJ.

Establishment under Turkey Agreement

6.211 As regards establishment, Article 13 of the Ankara Agreement states that the parties agree to be guided by Articles 52 to 56 EC (now 48 to 52 TFEU) for the purpose of abolishing restrictions on the freedom of establishment between them. Article 14 made similar provision for services. Article 41 of the additional Protocol is a standstill provision, which requires the Parties to refrain from introducing between themselves any new restrictions on the freedom of establishment and the freedom to provide services.[1] In *Savas*[2] a Turkish couple who had overstayed their leave in the UK set up a very successful business and wished to regularise their position. The UK authorities wished to deport them. The case was referred to the ECJ, which ruled that Articles 13 and 41(2) did not have direct effect, but that the standstill clause in Article 41(1) prohibited the introduction of new national restrictions. It was for the national court to determine if the rules applied were less favourable than before the time that the Additional Protocol came into force. However, the clause is not in itself capable of conferring upon a Turkish national the benefit of the right of establishment or of residence which goes with it. The upshot of this is that so far as the UK is concerned no rules more onerous than the 1973 business rules (HC 510) will apply to Turkish nationals.

These rules do not make entry clearance a pre-condition of entry[3] and they are very much less onerous than the current rules, containing no minimum capital requirement or a need to create new jobs. In *Tum and Dari*[4] the European Court held that the restrictions contained in the Article 14 applied to both the substantive and the procedural conditions governing admission into the territory of the host state. It therefore applied as much to first entry as to those who had already entered. In the particular case it was irrelevant that the applicants were on temporary admission and had had their asylum applications turned down.

In the domestic courts and the AIT, much of the focus of the cases has been on whether or not an asylum seeker has tried to seek an immigration advantage by fraud. In *Tum and Dari* there were express findings in both the CA and the ECJ that there was no hint of dishonesty or fraud. (It seems to us that many of the reported cases turn on their facts and are listed in a footnote accordingly.[5]) In *Aksoy v Secretary of State for the Home Department*[6] the High Court agreed that much will turn on the particular facts of each case and the particular conclusions reached by the Immigration Judge. It does not follow that simply because a claim for asylum is rejected entry was sought to be obtained by means of a fraudulent story. However, where there is a fraudulent story, it cannot make a difference whether the applicant is someone who gained entry by false representations, or someone who is placed on temporary admission, and then seeks to gain entry by repeating those false assertions in front of an Immigration Judge who rejects them. Thus far, the refusals had turned on whether 'the fraud exception', as it was called applied. But in *R (on the application of LF (Turkey)) v Secretary of State for the Home Department*[7] the Court of Appeal, relying on a dictum at para 64 of the ECJ judgment in *Tum and Dari*,[8] that Community law cannot be relied on for abusive or fraudulent ends, broadened the fraud exception to mean that a Turkish national cannot benefit from his or her own wrongdoing including the historic establishment of a business in violation of his conditions. This has been recently followed by the AIT in *IY (Ankara Agreement-fraud and abuse) Turkey*,[9] in a case where the applicant had left the United Kingdom voluntarily to make an application from overseas under the standstill clause.

[1] For the UK this means no new restrictions after 1 January 1973, the date of the UK's adherence to the EEC. This position contrasts with the former situation under the old Association agreements where restrictions on entry and the need for entry clearance was endorsed by the European Court: see Case C 327/02 *Panayotova v Minister voor Vreemdelingenzaken en Integratie* [2004] ECR I-11055. Under the 1973 rules appellants who wished to establish a business must show that they will be bringing into the country sufficient funds to establish a business that can realistically be expected to support them and where there was no attempt made to satisfy this requirement, an application would fail: *DD (Turkey) v Secretary of State for the Home Department* [2007] EWCA Civ 270 (21 February 2007). See also *R (on the application of Taskale) v Secretary of State for the Home Department* [2006] EWHC 712 (Admin) (17 March 2006 (not irrational for the Secretary of State for the Home Department to refuse an application when the business plan which formed the main documentary thrust of the original application is manifestly of a business which is completely different in scale and ambition to any that actually has been running, particularly when there was an absence of hard financial evidence supporting the application).

[2] Case C-37/98 *R v Secretary of State for the Home Department, ex p Savas* [2000] INLR 398, ECJ; extended to services in Cases C-317/01 and C-369/01 *Abatay and Sahin v Bundesanstalt für Arbeit* [2003] ECR I-12301, ECJ, [2003] 1 All ER (D) 342 (Oct), ECJ, paras 61–67. In R

(on the application of A) v Secretary of State for the Home Department [2002] EWCA Civ 1008 [2003] CMLR 14, 353, the Court of Appeal said Savas settled the position in community law and there was no need to make a further reference to the ECJ on this subject.

3   Thus persons admitted as visitors or for education or other purpose may apply for leave to establish themselves. In *R (on the application of Tum) v Secretary of State for the Home Department* [2004] EWCA Civ 788, the CA held that the Secretary of State was wrong to apply the current business rules to two failed Turkish asylum seekers, who were on temporary admission to the UK, and to refuse them leave to enter. On appeal by the Secretary of State, the House of Lords referred the issue to the ECJ.

4   Case C-16/05 *R (on the application of Tum and Dari) v Secretary of State for the Home Department*[2007] ECR I-7415, [2008] 1 WLR 94, paras 61 and 63. It was also held that there was no evidence that they had relied on the application of the 'standstill' clause in Article 41(1) of the Additional Protocol with the sole aim of wrongfully benefiting from advantages provided for by Community law (para 66).

5   *R (on the application of Taskale) v Secretary of State for the Home Department* [2006] EWHC 712 (Admin) (17 March 2006); *R (on the application of Semsek) v Secretary of State for the Home Department* [2006] EWHC 1486 (Admin) (15 May 2006); *R (on the application of Aslan) v Secretary of State for the Home Department* [2006] EWHC 1855 (Admin) (10 July 2006); *R (on the application of Catal) v Secretary of State for the Home Department* [2006] EWHC 1882 (Admin); *R (on the application of Arslan) v Secretary of State for the Home Department* [2006] EWHC 1877 (Admin) (28 July 2006); *R (on the application of Temiz) v Secretary of State for the Home Department* [2006] EWHC 2450 (Admin). On the issue of the right of appeal and the absence of a need under the 1973 rules to have an entry clearance, see *R (on the application of Arslan) v Secretary of State for the Home Department* [2006] EWHC 1877 (Admin) (28 July 2006); *R (on the application of Parmak) v Secretary of State for the Home Department* [2006] EWHC 244 (Admin) (13 February 2006) and *R (on the application of Kocakgul) v Secretary of State for the Home Department* [2005] EWHC 3171 (Admin) (23 November 2005).

6   [2006] EWHC 1487 (Admin). See also *FS (Breach of conditions: Ankara Agreement) Turkey* [2008] UKAIT 00066.

7   [2007] EWCA Civ 1441, [2007] All ER (D) 257 (Oct). In *Sonmez v Secretary of State for the Home Department* [2009] EWCA Civ 582, [2010] 1 CMLR 186 the court held that LF had been rightly decided.

8   Case C-16/05 *R (on the application of Tum and Dari) v the Secretary of State for the Home Department* [2007] ECR I-7415, [2008] 1 WLR 94, [2007] All ER (D) 115 (Sep) ECJ.

9   [2008] UKAIT 00081. See further *R (on the application of Ustun) v Secretary of State for the Home Department* [2010] EWHC 1517 (Admin); *R (on the application of Ahlat) v Secretary of State for the Home Department* [2009] EWHC 2166 (Admin), [2009] All ER (D) 231 (Oct).

6.212 There have been a number of more recent decisions in Europe and domestically, clarifying how the standstill provisions on self-employed Turkish nationals should operate.

- In *Oguz*[1] the CJEU settled the issue whether Turkish nationals who entered the UK and set themselves up in business while they are in breach of their conditions of entry can still rely on the standstill clause of Article 41 of the Additional Protocol EC-Turkey to establish a right of residence. The court held that:
  - The self-employment rule in the UK's 1972 Immigration Rules may be relied on by a Turkish national who enters into self-employment in breach of a condition of his or her leave not to engage in any business or profession and later applies to the UK national authorities for further leave to remain on the basis of the business which has meanwhile been established (at [46]).
  - The upshot is that Turkish nationals who enter the UK lawfully can immediately set up in business and apply in UKBA to change their status to self-employed under the 1972 Immigration Rules irrespective of the conditions attached to their leave to enter.

- However, this will not apply if the initial entry was unlawful (at [43]).

As a sop to the UKBA, the court also referred to the case law of the court that EU law cannot be relied on for abusive or fraudulent cases and that national courts may on a case-by-case basis (depending on the objective evidence) make a finding of abuse or fraudulent conduct). The court also stated that the standstill clause does not preclude Member States from penalising, within the framework of national law, abuse relating to immigration (at [31]).

- In *Dereci*[2] the CJEU was concerned with the standstill provision in art 41 of the Additional Protocol on access to self-employment. The court held that Austria could amend its laws as much as it liked, but every element of every amendment which makes it easier for a Turkish national to be self-employed can continue to be relied upon by a Turkish national irrespective of the fact that the State changes the law again to make it more restrictive (at [94]). It is irrelevant that at the time of accession/application of the Protocol, national law was less favourable to the Turkish national (at [94]). The court followed its earlier decision in *Toprak and Auguz*.[3]

- In *EK (Ankara Agreement-1972 Rules-construction) Turkey*[4] the UT held that:
  - There is nothing in the 1972 Immigration Rules (HC 510) that provides that a person who cannot come within one of the categories of the Rules is to be refused an extension of stay for that reason alone. Accordingly, it was open to the Home Office to grant an extension of stay as a businesswoman to someone who had entered as an au pair. The finding in *OT (Turkey)*[5] that HC 510 prohibited switching to business status by anyone other than a visitor is not considered correct.
  - HC 510, para 28 does not require a person who had been given leave as a businessman to demonstrate as a pre-condition for the exercise of discretion that in each or any year in which they had been given leave in that capacity they had complied with particular requirements of para 21. Those requirements are directly relevant only to the first application for permission to remain and the first extension of stay. There was no mandatory requirement in the settlement provisions in HC 510 for an applicant to substantiate that in each year since the grant of leave she had maintained herself and her dependants from the profits of the business.
  - There is no precise code in HC 510 distinguishing between maintenance and accommodation and precluding third party contributions to living expenses.

---

[1] Case C-186/10 *Oguz v Secretary of State for the Home Department* (2011) Times, 21 November, ECJ.

[2] Case 256/11 *Dereci and others v Bundesminister für Inneres*.

[3] C-300/09 and C-301/09 *Staatssecretaris van Justitie v Toprak and Auguz* [2011] All ER (D) 11 (Jan), ECJ.

[4] [2010] UKUT 425 (IAC).

[5] [2010] UKUT 330 (IAC).

6.213 The application of the standstill clauses to Turkish nationals providing lawful services is still dictated by the decision in *Soysal*. In that case, Turkish lorry drivers lawfully working for a Turkish company were required to have visas by the German authorities. No such requirement was in force when the Additional Protocol to the EEC-Turkey Association Agreement entered into force. Article 41(1) of the Protocol, which is a standstill clause and provides that the contracting parties are to refrain from introducing between themselves any new restrictions on the freedom of establishment and the freedom to provide services was called in aid. The ECJ held that from the date it entered into force, Article 41(1) precludes the introduction of a requirement that Turkish nationals such as the appellants must have a visa to enter the territory of a Member State in order to provide services there on behalf of an undertaking established in Turkey, since, on that date, such a visa was not required.[1] In *Demirkan*,[2] the CJEU held that the notion of 'freedom to provide services' in the Additional Protocol to the Agreement establishing an Association between the European Economic Community and Turkey Article 41(1) did not encompass freedom for Turkish nationals who were the recipients of services to visit an EU Member State in order to obtain services.

[1]   *Soysal v Germany* C-228/06 [2009] 2 CMLR 1249, ECJ.
[2]   *Demirkan v Germany* (C-221/11) (24 September 2013) [2014] 1 CMLR 39, GC.

Chapter 7

HUMAN RIGHTS LAW

HUMAN RIGHTS LAW SIGNIFICANCE TO IMMIGRATION LAW

7.1 Of the numerous international human rights instruments to which the UK is a party,[1] the European Convention of Human Rights (ECHR)[2] had already become the most significant and most frequently cited source of rights outside the common law well before 2 October 2000, when the Human Rights Act 1998 brought its provisions within the reach of the domestic courts. Since the coming into force of the 1998 Act, the ECHR has taken its place at the heart of UK human rights law. This chapter will look at the Convention, at how the 1998 Act incorporates it, and at some of the incorporated rights as they affect immigration law. It will also look briefly at human rights in the context of European Union law and at other sources of the UK's international human rights obligations.

[1] Of which the most important are the UN Universal Declaration of Human Rights 1948 (UDHR), the UN International Covenant on Civil and Political Rights 1966 (ICCPR), the UN Convention Against Torture 1984 (UNCAT), the UN Convention on the Rights of the Child 1989 (COROC), the Convention on the Elimination of all forms of Discrimination against Women (CEDAW) and the UN Convention against Torture and Inhuman and Degrading Treatment 1984.

[2] To give it its full title, the European Convention for the Protection of Human Rights and Fundamental Freedoms, Rome, 4 November 1950.

HISTORY OF THE ECHR

7.2 The ECHR was produced by the Council of Europe, an inter-governmental body formed in 1949 by ten Member States[1] to foster European unity and reduce the risk of future wars. The Charter of the Council of Europe required Member States to subscribe to the rule of law and to afford human rights and fundamental freedoms to all within their jurisdiction.[2] The Convention was one of the Council's earliest projects. Its two principal objectives were to maintain and further realise human rights and fundamental freedoms, and to foster effective political democracy.[3] It was designed to 'secure the universal and effective recognition and observance' of the rights set out in the Universal Declaration of Human Rights 1948, by making contracting States responsible under public international law for ensuring that their laws and practices gave effect to such rights and creating mechanisms of enforcement if they did not. Article 19 of the Convention set up the Commission and the Court. Article 25 provided that contracting States could recognise individuals' right to petition the Commission and Article 46 provided that they could accept the compulsory jurisdiction of the Court. Article 13 required States to provide an effective remedy in their domestic courts for violation of the rights in the Convention. The Commission has now gone and Articles 25, 44 and 46 of the original Convention have since been repealed and no longer form part of the Convention. The jurisdiction of the court is now compulsory (Art 32) and individuals have a right to apply to the court (Art 34). But the focus of the Convention is still on securing observance by Member States of minimum standards in the protection of the human rights set out in the Convention. Member States are bound by Article 46(1) to abide by the final judgment (or decision) of the court in any case to which they are parties.

Article 26 of the Vienna Convention on the Law of Treaties, expressing customary international law, requires States parties to a treaty to perform it in good faith. The expectation therefore is, and has always been, that a Member State found to have violated the Convention will act promptly to prevent a repetition of the violation, and in this way the primary object of the Convention is served. The Convention has always, however, made provision for affording just satisfaction to the injured party.

[1] Belgium, Denmark, France, Ireland, Italy, Luxembourg, Netherlands, Norway, Sweden and the UK. As of March 2005 there were 46 Member States: Albania, Andorra, Armenia, Austria, Azerbaijan, Belgium, Bosnia and Herzegovina, Bulgaria, Croatia, Cyprus, Czech Republic, Denmark, Estonia, Finland, France, Georgia, Germany, Greece, Hungary, Iceland, Ireland, Italy, Latvia, Liechtenstein, Lithuania, Luxembourg, Malta, Moldova, Monaco, Netherlands, Norway, Poland, Portugal, Romania, Russian Federation, San Marino, Serbia and Montenegro, Slovakia, Slovenia, Spain, Sweden, Switzerland, former Yugoslav Republic of Macedonia, Turkey, Ukraine and the UK.
[2] Statute of the Council of Europe 1949 (Cmd 7778).
[3] See judgment of Lord Steyn in *Brown v Stott (Procurator Fiscal, Dunfermline)* [2003] 1 AC 681, [2001] 2 All ER 97, PC.

7.3 The right of individual petition and the compulsory jurisdiction of the court are the mechanisms behind the success of the ECHR as a living and well-used instrument. The UK did not recognise the right, or submit to the compulsory jurisdiction of the court, until 1966,[1] citing the superiority of British law, concern that a 'flood of fatuous or insincere applications would roll in', causing extra work and adverse publicity,[2] and arguing that 'the State, not the individual, is the proper subject of international law'.[3] The real reason for the delay was Britain's colonial situation—in the course of fighting against the independence movements in the colonies, the UK had issued ten derogations from Article 5 (the right to liberty and security of person) from 1953 to May 1960.[4] Once the right of individual petition was recognised in the UK, it was frequently used to challenge immigration control measures. The very first British case where the individual right of petition was exercised was an immigration case.[5] The UK renewed the right of petition and its submission to the compulsory jurisdiction every five years. Since November 1998, contracting States have been obliged to recognise the right of individual petition and to submit to the compulsory jurisdiction of the court.[6] Further changes in the procedures of the court are set out in new Protocol 14, agreed on 13 May 2004, which was designed to amend and streamline Convention machinery for admission of new cases. More details are at **7.127**.

[1] For the full text of the letters from the UK government see (1966) 15 ICLQ 539.
[2] HC Official Report (5th Series) 23 May 1960, col 174.
[3] HC Official Report (5th Series) 23 May 1960, col 180.
[4] HC Official Report (5th Series) 23 May 1960, col 174 and 182: 'Among emerging communities political agitators thrive, and one may well imagine the use which political agitators would make of the right of individual petition.' See further Ian Macdonald, foreword to *A Guide to the Human Rights Act 1998* 1999 *Butterworths Immigration Law Service* Special Bulletin.
[5] Application 2991/66, *Application 2991/66, Alam (Mohammed) v United Kingdom* (1967) Times, 12 October, relating to the refusal to allow a 12-year-old boy to join his father in the UK. It led to a friendly settlement. This was followed by *Singh (Harbahjan) v United Kingdom* (Application 2992/96), reported at (1967) Times, 12 October. The fact that individual immigrants were invoking the right of individual petition as soon as it became available contributed to the introduction in 1969 of the immigration appellate system. See CHAPTER 19 below.

THE UK AND THE ECHR

7.4 As noted above,[1] the UK government's approach to the ECHR was always ambivalent; on the one hand, it took part in the drafting, and in 1953 accepted that the Convention applied to 42 overseas territories,[2] while on the other, it feared a stream of cases from those same territories if it recognised the right of individual petition. In fact, the first time the UK stood in the dock was an inter-State case, *Ireland v United Kingdom*,[3] which exposed the practices of hooding, wall-standing, exposure to white noise, deprivation of sleep, food and drink inflicted on Republican internees in Northern Ireland, which the ECHR condemned as inhuman and degrading treatment. After the right of individual petition had been recognised, all the early cases were immigration ones,[4] culminating in the *East African Asians* case,[5] where the Commission made a finding of rank racial discrimination, amounting to degrading treatment under Article 3 of ECHR, in the application of the Commonwealth Immigrants' Act 1968, which excluded UK and Colonies citizens from the UK on grounds of race.[6]

---

[1] See 7.3 above. For a fuller description, see the first edition of this work.
[2] Declaration of Her Majesty's Government of 23 October 1953, Cmd 9045. See HC Official Report (5th Series) 23 May 1960, cols 174-181; HC Official Report (5th Series) 19 May 1960 written answers cols 133–134. An irony of the colonial situation was the willingness of the UK government to see guarantees of fundamental rights inserted into the constitutions of the newly independent ex-colonies: see De Smith *Constitutions of the Commonwealth* .
[3] (1978) 2 EHRR 25.
[4] See 7.3 fn 5 above.
[5] (1973) 3 EHRR 76.
[6] 'Publicly to single out a group of persons for differential treatment on the basis of race might in certain circumstances constitute a special form of affront to human dignity, and . . . might be capable of constituting degrading treatment when differential treatment on some other ground would raise no such question': (1973) 3 EHRR 76, para 207.

7.5 Before incorporation of the ECHR, judicial opinion in the UK was divided on the relevance of the Convention to the interpretation of statute and the proper exercise of administrative powers. The arguments are still relevant today in the debate on the permissible application in domestic law of rights under other unincorporated international Conventions. The clash between two rules – the rule that international treaties do not confer rights enforceable in the domestic courts without incorporation,[1] and the presumption that Parliament did not intend to enact laws that were contrary to the UK's international obligations[2] led to a difference between the school of judicial thought which believed that, wherever possible, a statute should be construed in conformity with those obligations (the *Garland*[3] view), and the restrictive school, which held that regard should be had to the Convention only in the construction of ambiguous statutes (the *Brind*[4] view).[5] The *Brind* view prevailed, meaning that the Secretary of State was not obliged to have regard to the Convention when framing rules or directives under primary legislation. Where a statutory administrative power was enacted in general terms, a government official did not need to consult or have regard to the Convention in reaching decisions, since the power was 'unambiguous'.[6] To hold otherwise, the House of Lords ruled, would be to incorporate the Convention through the back door, usurping Parliament's function.[7] Nevertheless, prior to incorporation, the ECHR played a large part in developing the common law and, through it, developing a much more comprehensive review of administrative discretion, where a breach of human right has been involved.[8] There is now an open recognition that a decision which breaches an individual's or group's human rights requires 'justification' and that the degree of justification required must be proportionate to the scale and level and importance of the breach of human rights. But the formulation of the new and developing process shows a reluctance by many of the judges, as yet, to break with the traditional language and categories of public law review. Thus the courts speak of a varying intensity of review depending on the nature of the rights affected—building on the dictum of Lord Bridge in *Bugdaycay*[9] a decade earlier. A similar approach was taken in *Saleem*[10] where the Court of Appeal quashed a procedure rule deeming service of an adjudicator's determination to have been effected regardless of whether it had in fact been received, and held that the right of access to a tribunal is a fundamental right.

[1]   *Malone v Metropolitan Police Comr* [1979] Ch 344 at 379; *J H Rayner (Mincing Lane) ltd v Department of Trade and Industry* [1990] 2 AC 418, 476–7. Article 46 ECHR (the UK's obligation to abide by a judgment of the ECHR), was held to be an international obligation not directly enforceable in the domestic courts in *R v Lyons* [2002] UKHL 44, [2003] 1 AC 976, [2002] 4 All ER 1028 (para 104, per Lord Millett). For the debate on incorporation see the 4th edition of this work, 13.102 fn 2. For a full description of the attitude of the courts see Murray Hunt *Using human rights law in the English courts* (Hart Publishing, 1997). See also Feldman *Civil liberties and human rights in England and Wales* (OUP, 2002); McCrudden *A common law of human rights? Transnational judicial conversations on constitutional rights* 2000 20(4) OJLS 499.

[2]   See *Bennion Statutory Interpretation* (3rd edn); *Salomon v Customs and Excise Comrs* [1967] 2 QB 116, per Diplock LJ; *Waddington v Miah* [1974] 2 All ER 377 where the House of Lords decided, having regard to art 7 ECHR (no retrospective criminality), that the penal provisions of the Immigration Act 1971 were not retrospective.

[3]   *Garland v British Rail Engineering Ltd* [1983] 2 AC 751 at 771, per Lord Diplock (this was, however, a case involving EC law). See also *R v Secretary of State for the Home Department, ex p Simms* [2000] 2 AC 115, where Lord Hoffmann thundered: 'Fundamental rights cannot be overridden by general or ambiguous words. . . .   In the absence of express language or necessary implication, the courts   . . .   presume that even the most general words were intended to be subject to the basic rights of the individual.'

[4]   *R v Secretary of State for the Home Department, ex p Brind* [1991] 1 AC 696 at 748.

[5]   In *Pan American World Airways Inc v Department of Trade* [1976] 1 Lloyd's Rep 257 Scarman LJ said that an international Convention should be consulted in three situations: where Parliament expressly or implicitly requires it; when two courses are reasonably open, only one of which would lead to a result consistent with obligations under the Convention; and where statutory words have to be construed or a legal principle formulated in an area of law where the government has accepted international obligations, as part of the full context or background.

[6]   The Court of Appeal had previously held in *Chundawadra v Immigration Appeal Tribunal* [1988] Imm AR 161 that immigration officers did not have to have regard to the ECHR in deciding whether to grant leave to enter, following Lord Denning's recantation in *Salamat Bibi* [1976] 3 All ER 843, [1976] 1 WLR 979, CA of remarks in *R v Secretary of State for the Home Department, ex p Singh (Bhajan)* [1976] QB 198 to the effect that immigration officers ought to bear in mind the principles stated in the Convention. For a recent application of this principle to the Refugee Convention see *European Roma Rights Centre v Immigration Officer at Prague Airport* [2003] EWCA Civ 666, [2004] QB 811, para 51 (Simon Brown LJ), 98–101 (Laws LJ). The Lords, however, held that the Refugee Convention was incorporated into domestic law.

[7]   But in *R v Secretary of State for the Home Department, ex p Thompson and Venables* [1998] AC 407, the House of Lords held, in relation to the UN Convention on the Rights of the Child, that 'it is legitimate   . . .   to assume that Parliament has not maintained on the

statute book a power capable of being exercised in a manner inconsistent with the treaty obligations of this country' (per Lord Browne-Wilkinson at 499).

[8] For details see the 5th edition of this work at 8.14–8.20; also *R v Secretary of State for the Home Department, ex p Brind* [1991] 1 AC 696 at 748 and 751; *R v Secretary of State for the Home Department, ex p McQuillan* [1995] 4 All ER 400, per Sedley J, who drew on the Article by Sir John Laws 'Is the High Court the Guardian of Fundamental Human Rights?' in (1993) PL 59; Simon Brown LJ's judgment in *R v Secretary of State for Social Security, ex p Joint Council for the Welfare of Immigrants* [1997] 1 WLR 275 at 292: 'So basic are the human rights here at issue that it cannot be necessary to resort to the ECHR to take note of their violation'; *R v Ministry of Defence, ex p Smith* [1996] QB 517 at 554 per Lord Bingham MR (the 'gays in the military' case); *R (on the application of A) v Lord Saville of Newdigate (No 2)* [2001] EWCA Civ 2048, [2002] 1 WLR 129 at para 37 (on anonymity for soldiers testifying to the Saville Inquiry on Bloody Sunday).

[9] The most fundamental right is the individual's right to life, and when an administrative decision under challenge is said to be one which may put the applicant's life at risk, the basis of the decision must surely call for the most anxious scrutiny: *Bugdaycay v Secretary of State for the Home Department* [1987] AC 514, HL.

[10] *R v Secretary of State for the Home Department, ex p Saleem* [2000] 4 All ER 814, [2000] Imm AR 529, [2000] INLR 413, upholding Hooper J at [1999] INLR 621. See also *R v Secretary of State for the Home Department, ex p Simms* [2000] 2 AC 115, 7.5 fn 3 above. But the limits of judicial freedom were drawn in *R v Lyons* [2002] UKHL 44, [2003] 1 AC 976, [2002] 4 All ER 1028, where Lord Hoffmann pointed out that 'If Parliament has plainly laid down the law, it is the duty of the courts to apply it, whether that would involve the Crown in breach of an international treaty or not.'

7.6 The various ways in which the courts may have regard to international obligations are of course still highly relevant. The UK has, after all, international obligations respecting human rights, even fundamental human rights, which are not expressed in the ECHR, of which perhaps the most important are rights of children,[1] the right to work, to shelter and subsistence[2], and to health care[3]. So, while it may be possible to enlarge the scope of some of the rights protected by the ECHR in the domestic courts, by approaching them through the medium of the common law,[4] through the construction rule contained in Article 53 of the ECHR,[5] and by use of Commonwealth jurisprudence,[6] on the other hand it will always be necessary to persuade the courts to have regard to other international obligations which past and present governments have seen fit to sign up to without incorporating them into domestic law.[7] A summary of the relevant principles relating to rights protected by unincorporated Conventions is as follows:

(i) the courts assume that Parliament does not intend to legislate in a manner incompatible with the UK's international legal obligations, and will interpret legislation in a manner consistent with those obligations wherever possible, even where there is no obvious ambiguity:[8]

(ii) when a statute is enacted to fulfil an international obligation, the courts will assume it is intended to be effective for that purpose and will interpret the legislation accordingly;[9]

(iii) where the common law is uncertain or there are gaps in the law, the courts will seek to make a decision which is compatible with international obligations;[10]

(iv) where possible, the courts will exercise their discretion compatibly with international obligations;[11]

(v)   in reviewing the exercise of discretion by public authorities, the courts will subject decisions or actions interfering with fundamental human rights to particularly anxious scrutiny, and such decisions or actions require particularly strong justification if they are not to be regarded as irrational or disproportionate and therefore unlawful;[12]

(vi)   it is part of legal public policy that courts give effect to established rules of international law;[13]

Whether persons having dealings with government bodies have a legitimate expectation that they will be dealt with compatibly with international human rights standards, in the absence of incorporation, is a matter of dispute.[14]

[1]   The Government has appointed a Children's Commissioner to protect children's rights (see Children Act 2004) but has failed to lift the reservation to the UN Convention on the Rights of the Child in respect of immigration and asylum, despite the urging of the Joint Committee on Human Rights: see Joint Committee on Human Rights: Tenth report 2002/3: UN Convention on the Rights of the Child, 24 June 2003 (HL 117/HC 81); Joint Committee on Human Rights: 19th report 2003/4: Children Bill, 21 September 2004 (HL 161/HC 537).

[2]   While the courts have accepted that a complete lack of shelter and subsistence engages art 3 in extreme circumstances (see **7.59** below), there is no free-standing right.

[3]   Similarly, access to health care may engage art 3 or 8 if denial (or withdrawal in the context of expulsion) causes extreme suffering or severe damage to physical or psychological integrity as an aspect of private life (see **7.54** and **7.92** below) but not otherwise. All these rights are contained in the UN's companion to the ICCPR, the International Covenant on Economic, Social and Cultural Rights 1966 (ICESCR), but the ICESCR has no enforcement mechanism at the suit of individuals, although States are monitored and have reporting obligations. The Joint Human Rights Committee identifies gaps in the protection of these rights in its 21st report 2004/5: International Covenant for Economic, Social and Cultural Rights, 2 November 2004 (HL 183/HC 1188). Another right as yet unrecognised by the ECtHR is the right to conscientious objection to military service, accepted by the (non-binding) EU Charter of Rights: see *Sepet and Bulbul* [2001] EWCA Civ 681, upheld by [2003] UKHL 15, [2003] 3 All ER 304.

[4]   In accordance with the injunctions of Lord Lester of Herne Hill QC. See per Lord Steyn in *R v Secretary of State for the Home Department, ex p Thompson and Venables* [1998] AC 407; see also Lord Bingham in *R (on the application of Amin) v Secretary of State for the Home Department* [2003] UKHL 51, [2004] 1 AC 653, para 30. But Sedley LJ's attempt to create a right of privacy by judicial development of the common law, distinct from art 8 ECHR, in *Douglas v Hello! Ltd* [2001] QB 967, was firmly rebuffed in *Wainwright v Home Office* [2001] EWCA Civ 2081, [2002] QB 1334 (paras 97 ff).

[5]   In *T and V v United Kingdom* (1999) 30 EHRR 121 the ECtHR had regard to the UN Convention on the Rights of the Child and the Beijing Rules (a non-binding declaration) to determine the international consensus on the age of criminal responsibility. See also *Jersild v Denmark* (1994) 19 EHRR 1, where the ECtHR took account of art 4 of the International Convention on the Elimination of All Forms of Racial Discrimination and interpreted art 10 ECHR in the light of the International Covenant on Civil and Political rights (ICCPR).

[6]   See eg the discussion in *R (on the application of Pretty) v DPP* [2001] UKHL 61 [2002] 1 AC 800 of Canadian jurisprudence on the principle of personal autonomy, and the citation of Indian case law in support of the right to life in *Amin* (fn 4 above). But caution was expressed by Brooke LJ in *A v Secretary of State for the Home Department* [2002] EWCA Civ 1502, [2004] QB 335 (para 94) about referring to an interpretation of a different human rights charter as a guide to the provisions of the ECHR.

[7]   The House of Lords reiterated in *R v Lyons* [2002] UKHL 44, [2003] 1 AC 976, [2002] 4 All ER 1028 that any customary international law duty (or one arising from an unincorporated international instrument) was overridden by express and unqualified statutory provision; but where no such express prohibition exists, the courts have shown themselves willing to push forward the boundaries to uphold fundamental rights; see eg *R v Secretary of State for the Home Department, ex p Simms* [2000] 2 AC 115. In *R (on the application of Abbasi) v Secretary of State for Foreign and Commonwealth Affairs* [2002] EWCA Civ 1598, (2002) Times, 8 November,, the Court of Appeal held it was not prevented from reviewing the

legitimacy of the actions of a foreign sovereign State where fundamental rights were in play, but that there was no *ius cogens* (peremptory international law norm) requiring the UK's intervention.

8   *Garland v British Rail Engineering* [1983] 2 AC 751; *Litster v Forth Dry Dock and Engineering Co* [1990] 1 AC 546.

9   *R (on the application of Mullen) v Secretary of State for the Home Department* [2002] EWCA Civ 1882, [2003] QB 993.

10 *DPP v Jones* [1999] 2 AC 240, HL.

11 *Rantzen v Mirror Group Newspapers (1986) Ltd* [1994] QB 670, CA.

12 *Bugdaycay v Secretary of State for the Home Department* [1987] AC 514, HL; *R v Secretary of State for the Home Department, ex p Simms* [2000] 2 AC 115, HL; *R v Ministry of Defence, ex p Smith* [1996] QB 517, CA; *R v Secretary of State for the Home Department, ex p Thompson and Venables* [1998] AC 407, HL.

13 *Oppenheimer v Cattermole* [1976] AC 249; *Blathwayt v Baron Cawley* [1976] AC 397; *European Roma Rights Centre v Immigration Officer at Prague Airport* [2004] UKHL 55, [2005] 2 WLR 1 per Lady Hale at paras 98ff.

14 See discussion at **7.32** below.

EC, ECHR AND THE CHARTER OF FUNDAMENTAL RIGHTS

7.7 Prior to the incorporation of the ECHR into British domestic law, it was possible to have full regard to its provisions in the domestic courts in cases involving EC law.[1] Article 6(2) of the revised Treaty on European Union (formerly Article F(2)) required the Union to 'respect fundamental rights as guaranteed by the ECHR and as they result from the constitutional conditions common to the Member States, as general principles of Community law'.[2] This meant that, although the EU was not a party to the ECHR its standards became part of EC law.[3] So all EC law on immigration and asylum under Articles 61–64 of the revised Treaty of the European Communities,[4] and any national law based on it had to be compatible with the Convention.[5] The EU's judicial institutions had to have regard to the Convention in interpreting and formulating the requirements of EC law.[6] Thus, even rights contained in Protocols to which the UK was not a party, such as the right of nationals to enter their own country, are, in our view, part of the *corpus* of law to be taken into account in construing the Treaty.[7]

1   See *Elliniki Radiophonia Tileorass-AE v Pliroforissis and Kouvelas* [1991] ECR I-2925, [1994] 4 CMLR 540, ECJ, the rationale of which is now contained in art 6(2) EU (formerly Art F(2)); see further *B v Secretary of State for the Home Department* [2000] Imm AR 478, CA.

2   This is now Article 6(2) of the new TEU, as consolidated by the Treaty of Lisbon.

3   Case 29/69 *Stauder v City of Ulm* [1969] ECR 419; Case 11/70 *Internationale Handelsgesellschaft mbH v Einfuhr und Vorratstelle für Getreide und Futtermittel* [1970] ECR 1125; Case 4/73 *Nold (J) KG v EC Commission* [1974] ECR 491.

4   These have now been renumbered or replaced in the Treaty on the Functioning of the European Union (TFEU), as consolidated by the Treaty of Lisbon as follows: art 61 (now art 67), art 2 (now art 77), art 63 (now art 8), art 64 (now art 72, para 12 being replaced), art 65 (now art 81), art 66 (now replaced by art 74), arts 67–69 repealed.

5   In *Elliniki Radiophonia* above (the *ERT* case), the Court of Justice held that, when considering national legislation falling within the field of application of EC law, it 'must provide the national court with all the elements of interpretation which are necessary in order to enable it to assess the compatibility of that legislation with the fundamental rights as laid down in particular in the European Convention on Human Rights, the observance of which the Court ensures'.

6   The *ERT* case, fn 1 above.

7   *R v Immigration Appeal Tribunal and Surinder Singh, ex p Secretary of State for the Home Department* [1992] Imm AR 565, ECJ, para 22. In *Jersild v Denmark* (1994) 19 EHRR 1, the ECtHR in effect incorporated art 20(2) of the ICCPR ('Any advocacy of national, racial

or religious hatred that constitutes incitement to discrimination, hostility or violence shall be prohibited by law.') into the interpretation of art 9 and 10 ECHR, an interpretation which would be valid in UK courts, even though the ICCPR is not incorporated into UK law.

7.8 In *Rutili v Ministry for the Interior*[1] the Court of Justice held that the ECHR provisions applied to measures taken by Member States in derogation of free movement rights. Thus an order banning free movement in a part of France could infringe the ECHR, Article 11 right of freedom of association, holding out the possibility that a removal or refusal of entry involving EC free movement rights could be challenged on the basis that it infringes a Convention right such as family life.[2] This possibility was realised in *Carpenter*,[3] where the ECJ held that to require a Philippines wife of a British citizen living in the UK but exercising Treaty rights by conducting frequent business trips to Europe to return to the Philippines to apply for entry clearance to re-join him because her immigration position was irregular was a disproportionate interference with family life.[4] In the domestic context, the Court of Appeal in *B*[5] used the EU route to apply proportionality principles to a decision to deport which was said to infringe the applicant's combined rights of free movement and private life.[6]

[1]   36/75 [1975] ECR 1219. See also *Pecastaing v Belgium*: 98/79 [1980] ECR 691; *Johnston v Chief Constable of the Royal Ulster Constabulary*: 222/84 [1986] ECR 1651; *Dzodzi v Belgium* C-297/88, C-197/89, [1990] ECR I-3763; *Society for the Protection of Unborn Children Ireland Ltd v Grogan* C-159/90, [1991] ECR I-4685.
[2]   See also the opinion of Advocate General Jacobs in *Konstantinidis v Stadt Altensteig-Standesamt*: C-168/91 [1993] 3 CMLR 401.
[3]   *Carpenter (Mary) v Secretary of State for the Home Department* C-60/00, [2002] INLR 439.
[4]   See also *Mouvement contre le racisme, l'antisémitisme et la xénophobie (MRAX) ASBL v Belgium* C-459/99, [2002] ECR I-6591, ECJ.
[5]   *B v Secretary of State for the Home Department* [2000] Imm AR 478, CA.
[6]   See also *R v Secretary of State for Employment, ex p Equal Opportunities Commission* [1995] 1 AC 1, HL.

7.9 The Treaty of Lisbon[1] introduced amendments to the Treaty on European Union and the Treaty establishing the European Community which came into force on 1 December 2009 and have considerable importance in relation to the protection of human rights. The European Union is to accede to the ECHR[2] so that it can be a party to proceedings in the European Court of Human Rights; then accession is made possible by an amendment to the ECHR.[3] Moreover, the Treaty on European Union now provides that the Union 'recognises the rights, freedoms and principles set out in the Charter of Fundamental Rights of the European Union . . . which shall have the same legal value as the Treaties'.[4] The provisions of the Charter[5] apply to the institutions and bodies of the Union and to the Member States 'when they are implementing Union law'.[6] Thus it will apply when the UK takes (or fails to take) action in relation to the rights of movement and residence of EU nationals and their family members; the criteria for recognising refugee status and giving other forms of international protection and the procedures for deciding asylum claims which are among the areas of Union law[7] to which the Charter is applicable. The Charter is to be interpreted 'with due regard to the explanations referred to in the Charter, that set out the sources of those provisions'.[8] The 'explanations' were prepared, and subsequently amended, under the authority of the Praesidium of the Convention which drafted the Charter as a 'tool of interpretation intended to clarify the provisions of the Charter'.[9] The ECHR is the source of many of the rights contained in the Charter but in significant respects the Charter provides wider protection than does the ECHR. For example, Article 47 of the Charter recognises the right to a fair trial protected by Article 6 of the ECHR but unlike Article 6 is not restricted to the determination of civil rights and obligations and criminal charges and it expressly requires the provision of legal aid in so far as necessary to ensure effective access to justice. The Charter also recognises rights that are not or not explicitly recognised by the ECHR, eg the right to asylum,[10] to non-refoulement,[11] the rights of the child,[12] of the elderly,[13] and of those with disabilities[14] and the right to conscientious objection.[15] Whilst the ECHR is clearly one source of the rights contained in the Charter it is evident that the Charter is in turn informing the European Court of Human Rights' interpretation of the ECHR.[16]

[1] Treaty of Lisbon amending the Treaty on European Union and the Treaty establishing the European Community, signed at Lisbon, 13 December 2007, OJ 2007/C 306/01.
[2] New Article 6(2) of the Treaty on European Union, introduced by the Treaty of Lisbon, art 1(8).
[3] Protocol 14 to the ECHR amended Article 59 of the ECHR, with effect from 1 June 2010 so that Article 59(2) of the ECHR provides 'The European Union may accede to this Convention'.
[4] New Article 6(1) of the Treaty on European Union.
[5] Charter of Fundamental Rights of the European Union, Official Journal of the European Communities 2000/C 364/01.
[6] Charter, Article 51(1).
[7] In the form of Directive 2004/28/EC of the European Parliament and of the Council of 29 April 2004 on the right of citizens of the Union and their family members to move and reside freely within the territory of the Member States ('the Citizens Directive') Council Directive 2004/83/EC of 29 April 2004 on minimum standards for the qualification and status of third country nationals or stateless persons as refugees or as persons who otherwise need international protection and the content of the protection granted ('the Qualification Directive') and Council Directive 2005/85/EC of 1 December 2005 on minimum standards on procedures in Member States for granting and withdrawing refugee status ('the Procedures Directive').
[8] New Article 6(1) of the Treaty on European Union.
[9] Explanations relating to the Charter of fundamental rights, Official Journal of the European Union, 2007/C 303/02.
[10] Article 18.
[11] Article 19.
[12] Article 24.
[13] Article 25.
[14] Article 26.
[15] Article 10(2). Recognition of this right should mean that fear of being punished for conscientious objection is by itself sufficient foundation for an asylum claim by contrast to the position before the Charter came into force when want of international recognition of such a right made such a claim untenable: *Sepet and Bulbul v Secretary of State for the Home Department* [2003] UKHL 15, [2003] 3 All ER 304, [2003] 1 WLR 856.
[16] See, for example, *Schalk and Kopf v Austria* [2010] ECHR 995 where the Court held, having regard to Article 9 of the Charter which recognised the 'right to marry and found a family' without specifying the gender of those marrying, that the protection of the right to marry provided by Article 12 of the ECHR was not necessarily restricted any longer to marriages between members of opposite sexes.

7.10 Article 1(1) of a Protocol to the Treaty of Lisbon[1] says that the Charter does not extend the ability of the Court of Justice of the European Union or the UK's domestic courts or tribunals to find that the laws, regulations, administrative provisions, practices or action of the UK are inconsistent with the fundamental rights, freedoms and principles that it reaffirms.[2] However, the preamble to the Protocol records that the Charter 'reaffirms the rights, freedoms and principles recognised in the Union and makes those rights more visible, but does not create new rights or principles'. Article 1(1), read in the light of the preamble, probably means that if a national law or practice is inconsistent with a provision of the Charter then it is also inconsistent with an already existing EU or international law norm.[3] Thus a finding of inconsistency between UK law or practice and the Charter would not amount to an extension of the courts' ability to find illegality of a kind precluded by the Protocol because the Charter merely reaffirms extant rights, freedoms and principles. The Protocol 'is not an opt-out for the United Kingdom; it is an interpretative protocol'.[4] It has been held that, owing to the Protocol, 'the Charter cannot be directly relied on as against the UK'.[5] However, in the course of the appeal against that decision it was made clear that:

> 'the Secretary of State accepts, in principle, that fundamental rights set out in the Charter can be relied on as against the United Kingdom, and submits that the Judge erred in holding otherwise . . . The purpose of the Charter Protocol is not to prevent the Charter from applying to the United Kingdom but to explain its effect'.[6]

The Court of Justice has confirmed that the Protocol on the application of the Charter of fundamental rights of the European Union to Poland and to the United Kingdom does not intend to exempt the UK from the obligation to comply with the provisions of the Charter or to prevent a court of the UK from ensuring compliance.[7]

[1] Protocol on the application of the Charter of fundamental rights of the European Union to Poland and to the United Kingdom OJ 2007/C 306/156.
[2] Article 1(2) of the Protocol.
[3] This is the view of the European Union Committee of the House of Lords expressed in para 5.103 of its report 'The Treaty of Lisbon: an impact assessment' (13 March 2008) HL Paper 62-I.
[4] Evidence of Professor Dashwood to the European Union Committee of the House of Lords, para 5.85 of 'The Treaty of Lisbon: an impact assessment'.
[5] Cranston J in *R (on the application of Saeedi) v Secretary of State for the Home Department* [2010] EWHC 705 (Admin), [2010] NLJR 548.
[6] Paragraph 8 of the Secretary of State's respondent's notice, set out in the judgment adjourning the appeal in *R (on the application of NS) v Secretary of State for the Home Department* [2010] EWCA Civ 990.
[7] Joined Cases C-411/10 and C-493/10 *NS v Secretary of State for the Home Department (Amnesty International Ltd and the AIRE Centre (Advice on Individual Rights in Europe) (UK))* and *ME v Refugee Applications Comr (Amnesty International Ltd and the AIRE Centre (Advice on Individual Rights in Europe) (UK))* ([2013] QB 102, [2012] All ER (EC) 1011, ECJ.

THE HUMAN RIGHTS ACT 1998

7.11 The Human Rights Act 1998 is designed to 'make more directly accessible the rights which British people already enjoy under the Convention'[1] by providing access to those rights through the domestic courts.[2] The two principal mechanisms for giving effect to Convention rights are the interpretative obligation[3] – to interpret all legislation compatibly with the Convention whenever possible – and the obligation imposed on all public authorities, including courts, to act compatibly with Convention rights.[4] Lord Hope expressed the view that the Act would 'subject the entire legal system to a fundamental process of review and, where necessary, reform by the judiciary',[5] but without offending against the sovereignty of Parliament, which is not a public authority[6] and so is exempt from the obligation to act compatibly with the Convention (although there is a clear expectation that it will do so). The interpretative obligation does not affect the validity of primary legislation which is incompatible with the Convention,[7] nor does a declaration of incompatibility affect its validity or oblige Parliament to remedy the incompatibility.[8] The remedy is available but not compulsory. New legislation may be incompatible with the Convention, so long as it declares itself so;[9] and public authorities are not required to act compatibly with the Convention if primary legislation prevents them from doing so. These features of the 1998 Act, designed to reassure those sceptics who feared a shift in the constitutional balance in favour of the judiciary, sets it apart from most Bills of Rights and constitutions, which allow courts to strike down incompatible legislation, and from EC law, which takes precedence over incompatible national law.[10] Much of the debate in the courts since October 2000 has concerned this constitutional balance.

[1] *Thoburn v Sunderland City Council* [2002] EWHC 195 (Admin), [2002] 4 All ER 156 (the 'metric martyrs' case).
[2] *Rights Brought Home* (Cm 3782, 1997) para 1.19. Sedley LJ's phrase is 'patriating' the ECHR rights: see The Hamlyn Lectures *Freedom, Law and Justice* (1999).
[3] Human Rights Act 1998, s 3.
[4] HRA 1998, s 6.
[5] *R v DPP, ex p Kebeline* [1999] 4 All ER 801, 838.
[6] HRA 1998, s 6(3).
[7] See *R v Lyons* [2002] UKHL 44, [2003] 1 AC 976, [2002] 4 All ER 1028, para 27.
[8] HRA 1998, s 4. See in particular the defiant stance of the government, from December 2004, when the House of Lords ruled that indefinite detention under the Anti-terrorism Crime and Security Act 2001 was unlawful under ECHR, until March 2005, when it was able to introduce a regime of control orders under the Prevention of Terrorism Act 2005.
[9] HRA 1998, s 19.
[10] *R v Secretary of State for Transport, ex p Factortame (No 2)* [1991] 1 AC 603, HL.

7.12 The rights protected under the Human Rights Act 1998 are the substantive ECHR rights set out in Articles 2–12 and 14, Articles 1–3 of Protocol 1, and Article 1 of Protocol 13, all as read with Articles 16–18.[1] Article 1 of the Convention, the obligation to secure the Convention rights and freedoms to everyone within the jurisdiction, is effected by the 1998 Act itself. The same reason is given for the omission of Article 13 (the right to an effective remedy for violations of the Convention),[2] and clearly courts' and tribunals' powers should be construed with Article 13 in mind.[3] The rights protected have effect subject to designated derogations and reservations.[4] At the time of the entry into force of the Act, the UK derogated from Article 5(3) (the right of a detained person to be brought before a court),[5] and had a reservation in respect of Article 2 of Protocol 1 (education in conformity with parental convictions).[6] The derogation was revoked in April 2001,[7] only to be replaced by a derogation from Article 5(1) in December 2001 to enable the indefinite detention without trial of suspected international terrorists under the Anti-Terrorism Crime and Security Act 2001, which was in turn withdrawn in 2005.[8] The 1998 Act contains provisions for monitoring derogations and reservations to ensure they are not retained after the need for them has gone.[9] Derogations are to have a life of five years,[10] unless extended by Order.[11] Reservations are to be reviewed after five years and the minister must report to

Parliament on the review.[12] There is scope for amendment of the Act by Order[13] to bring within the Act further rights in Protocols to be ratified, or signed with a view to ratification, in the future.[14]

[1]   Human Rights Act 1998, s 1(1). Article 1 of Protocol 13 (prohibition of death penalty in all circumstances) replaced arts 1 and 2 of Protocol 6 (prohibition of death penalty in peacetime) in the Schedule on 22 June 2004: SI 2004/1574.

[2]   Lord Irvine, 583 HL Official Report (5th series) col 475, 18 November 1997.

[3]   583 HL Official Report (5th series) col 479, 18 November 1997. Article 13 'reflects the long-standing principle of our law that where there is a right there should be a remedy. Parliament's intention was, of course, that the Human Rights Act itself should constitute the UK's compliance with Article 13, but this makes it if anything more important that the courts . . . should satisfy themselves so far as possible that the common law affords adequate control . . . of the legality of official measures which interfere with personal autonomy': *R (on the application of K) v Camden and Islington Health Authority* [2001] EWCA Civ 240, [2002] QB 198. See **7.118** below.

[4]   HRA 1998, s 1(2).

[5]   See HRA 1998, s 14 and Sch 3, Pt I (as originally enacted).

[6]   The reservation was made on 20 March 1952, and shows no signs of being removed. See Human Rights Act 1998, s 15 and Sch 3, Pt II.

[7]   Repealed by SI 2001/1216, art 4.

[8]   In *A v Secretary of State for the Home Department; X v Secretary of State for the Home Department* [2004] UKHL 56, [2005] 2 WLR 87, the House of Lords ruled that the derogation from Article 5 of ECHR was discriminatory and disproportionate, and quashed the derogation order. Part I of Sch 3 to the 1998 Act, containing the derogation, was repealed by the Human Rights Act 1998 (Amendment) Order 2005, SI 2005/1071.

[9]   HRA 1998, ss 16 and 17.

[10] The quashed derogation in *A and X* above had no time limit, so the default provisions of s 16 would have come into play if it had still been in force in December 2006. On the other hand, the indefinite detention provisions of the Anti-terrorism, Crime and Security Act 2001 (ss 21–23), under which A and X were detained, were set to expire 15 months after enactment (14 December 2001) unless extended by order; they were so extended for one year (to 14 March 2004) by the Anti-terrorism, Crime and Security Act 2001 (Continuance in Force of Sections 21–23) Order 2003, SI 2003/691, and for a further year by SI 2004/751.

[11] HRA 1998, s 16(2); the power to make orders under this section is exercisable by statutory instrument subject to affirmative resolution: s 20(4). See SI 2005/1071.

[12] HRA 1998, s 17.

[13] HRA 1998, s 1(4). Orders under this section are also subject to the affirmative resolution procedure under s 20(4).

[14] ECHR, Protocol 4 (rights of nationals and aliens in respect of entry, movement within the territory and expulsion) was signed by the UK in 1963, but never ratified because of concerns about the scope of the obligation giving the right of entry to own nationals. The government did not intend to ratify it, according to Lord Williams of Mostyn, Parliamentary Under-Secretary at the Home Office, during the Committee stage in the House of Lords (583 HL Official Report (5th series) col 504, 18 November 1997). Protocol 7 gives aliens procedural rights on expulsion and deals with double jeopardy, appeal rights and compensation in criminal cases, and with spousal equality in marriage. The government indicated its intention to sign and ratify it in due course during the passage of the Act, but has not done so. Protocol 12 (free-standing right not to be discriminated against) has not been signed or ratified by the UK, but Protocol 13 (prohibition of death penalty in any circumstances) has been, and came into force, so far as the UK is concerned, on 1 February 2004. See fn 1 above.

The importance of Strasbourg case law

7.13 The interpretative obligations are set out in sections 2 and 3 of the HRA 1998. Section 2 requires a court or tribunal determining questions in connection with ECHR rights to take into account the jurisprudence of the ECtHR[1] (and of the Commission before its demise,[2] and of the Committee of Ministers)[3] whenever it was made or given.[4] There is provision under section 2(2) for rules which will indicate how evidence of the relevant jurisprudence is to be given.[5] In practice, Court judgments, Commission opinions and admissibility decisions (of the Commission and now of the court) are the most useful and used jurisprudence. The jurisprudence which must be taken into account is not limited to that on the incorporated Articles; the Lord Chancellor confirmed during the passage of the Act that courts could have regard to jurisprudence on Article 13 of the ECHR, which ought to be of considerable significance for issues such as the intensity of review required by the court.[6]

[1]   Including not only judgments (Arts 29, 42, 44), but also decisions (on admissibility under arts 29 and 35, striking out under art 37, friendly settlement under art 39, and on just satisfaction under art 41), declarations (of admissibility, arts 28 and 45), and advisory opinions under art 47: s 2(1)(a). See further per Lord Bingham in *R (on the application of Ullah) v Special Adjudicator* [2004] UKHL 26, [2004] INLR 381 at para 20; *A-G's Reference (No 4 of 2002); Sheldrake v DPP* [2004] UKHL 43, [2005] 1 AC 264 at para 33 (UK courts must take the lead from Strasbourg).

[2]   Human Rights Act 1998, s 2(1)(b), (c) and 21(2). Before the coming into force of Protocol 11, the Commission made the decision on admissibility under arts 26 and 27 of the (unamended) ECHR, and if the application was declared admissible, would (unless a friendly settlement was reached) prepare a Report stating its opinion on whether the facts found disclosed a breach of the Convention, under art 31. Decisions and opinions of the Commission under the transitional provisions of Protocol 11 are included: s 21(4).

[3]   HRA 1998, s 2(1)(d). The Committee of Ministers, comprising political representatives of the Council of Europe's Member States, took unreasoned decisions on the merits in secret under art 32 of the unamended ECHR, and supervised the implementation of judgments under art 54. The former function has been removed with Protocol 11 and the only reports which will emanate from it under art 46 will be on implementation of judgments. As Grosz *et al* remark (Grosz, Beatson and Duffy *Human Rights: the 1998 Act and the European Convention* (2000, Sweet & Maxwell) at para 2.17), the nature of their past proceedings means little juridical significance can attach to their pronouncements.

[4]   Ie before or after the coming into force either of Protocol 11 or of the Human Rights Act 1998.

[5]   Rules have been made in relation to Scotland only: see Act of Adjournal (Criminal Procedure Rules Amendment No 2) (Human Rights Act 1998) SSI 2000/315 and Act of Sederunt (Rules of the Court of Session Amendment No 6) (Human Rights Act 1998) SSI 2000/316. ECtHR jurisprudence is in practice cited in the same way as other authority.

[6]   See in particular, the observations of the court in *Chahal v United Kingdom* (1996) 23 EHRR 413, paras 153–154; *Smith and Grady v United Kingdom* (1999) 29 EHRR 493, para 136; *Lustig-Prean and Beckett v United Kingdom* (1999) 29 EHRR 548.

7.14 The obligation under section 2 of the Human Rights Act 1998 holds the balance between bringing ECHR rights into UK law and retaining the internal constitutional arrangements of the UK, and its common-law case-by-case jurisprudence, by requiring that the courts take Strasbourg jurisprudence into account rather than making that case law binding.[1] UK courts are thus free to develop their own human rights jurisprudence, mindful always that an aggrieved person still has the right to go to the European Court in Strasbourg, once local remedies have been exhausted.[2] Although the Strasbourg case law is not binding, it is likely to be highly persuasive. The House of Lords has held that in the absence of special circumstances, the courts should follow any 'clear and constant' jurisprudence of the European Court[3] according particular weight to decisions of the Grand Chamber.[4] At the same time it has to be remembered that, since the Convention is a living instrument, to be interpreted purposively[5] and dynamically in the light of current conditions,[6] the ECtHR is not itself bound by its own previous case law.[7] In deciding on the scope and content of the rights protected by the Convention, it will often be fruitful to refer to Privy Council cases and to the jurisprudence of Commonwealth countries, with which the UK shares a legal tradition.[8]

1   A judgment of the ECtHR is binding on the UK, but not directly binding as a matter of domestic law on the courts: *R v Lyons* [2002] UKHL 44, [2003] 1 AC 976, [2002] 4 All ER 1028 at para 105, per Lord Millett. In *R (on the application of Ullah) v Special Adjudicator* [2004] UKHL 26, [2004] INLR 381, Lord Bingham pointed out (para 20) that the Convention was an international instrument whose authoritative interpretation came from the Strasbourg court, and the national court should not without strong reason dilute or weaken the effect of Strasbourg case law. The House of Lords said in *Huang v Secretary of State for the Home Department* [2007] UKHL 11, [2007] 2 AC 67 'while the case law of the Strasbourg court is not strictly binding, it has been held that domestic courts and tribunals should, in the absence of special circumstances, follow the clear and constant jurisprudence of that court' (para 18).

2   *Rights brought home*, para 2.5, Home Secretary Jack Straw at 306 HC Official Report (6th series) col 769, 16 February 1998. 'Our courts must be free to develop human rights jurisprudence . . . and to move out in new directions': Lord Chancellor, 583 HL Official Report (5th series) col 783, 24 November 1997. The Lord Chancellor also said that 'it is possible that [our courts] might give a successful lead to Strasbourg': 583 HL Official Report (5th series) col 514, 18 November 1997. The 'dialogue' between the higher courts and the European Court has ranged from the House of Lords correcting ECtHR misconceptions about English law (see eg *Lyons* (fn 1 above) para 46; *Z v United Kingdom* (2001) 34 EHRR 97, correcting its reasoning in *Osman v United Kingdom* (1998) 29 EHRR 245) to the most careful analysis and adoption of the Strasbourg case law (see *R (on the application of Ullah) v Special Adjudicator* [2004] UKHL 26, [2004] INLR 381 and *R (on the application of Razgar) v Secretary of State for the Home Department* [2004] UKHL 27, [2004] 2 AC 368) and *N v Secretary of State for the Home Department* [2005] UKHL 31, [2005] 2 AC 296.

3   In *R (on the application of Alconbury Developments Ltd) v Secretary of State for the Environment, Transport and the Regions* [2001] UKHL 23, [2003] 2 AC 295 (per Lord Slynn); *R (on the application of Ullah) v Special Adjudicator* [2004] UKHL 26, [2004] INLR 381 at para 20. See also *R (on the application of Anderson) v Secretary of State for the Home Department* [2002] UKHL 46, [2003] 1 AC 837, [2003] UKHRR 112, and *R (on the application of Amin) v Secretary of State for the Home Department* [2003] UKHL 51, [2004] 1 AC 653. The Court of Appeal could find no such 'clear and constant' jurisprudence on the issue of damages for a breach of art 8 ECHR, in *Anufrijeva v Southwark London Borough Council; R (on the application of N) v Secretary of State for the Home Department; R (on the application of M) v Secretary of State for the Home Department* [2003] EWCA Civ 1406, [2004] 1 All ER 833. In *N v Secretary of State for the Home Department* [2003] EWCA Civ 1369, [2004] 1 WLR 1182 Laws LJ reluctantly followed ECtHR jurisprudence on art 3, but gave it a highly restrictive application: see below **7.54**.

4   *R (on the application of Al-Skeini) v Secretary of State for Defence* [2007] UKHL 26, [2007] 3 All ER 685. In *Secretary of State for the Home Department v AF* [2009] UKHL 28, para 70 it was said by Lord Hoffmann, with reference to *A v United Kingdom (Application 3455/05)* (2009) 49 EHRR 625, (2009) Times, 20 February:

> 'It is true that section 2(1) of the Human Rights Act 1998 requires us only to "take into account" decisions of the ECHR. As a matter of domestic law we could take the decision in *A v UK* into account but nevertheless prefer our own view. But the United Kingdom is bound by the Convention as a matter of international law to accept the decisions of the ECtHR on its interpretation. To reject such a decision would almost certainly put this country in breach of the international obligation which it accepted when it acceded to the Convention. I can see no advantage in your Lordships doing so'.

5   The objectives of the ECHR should be taken into account, particularly its aim to give full and practical effect to human rights: *Golder v United Kingdom* (1975) 1 EHRR 524; *Artico v Italy* (1980) 3 EHRR 1. However, the Privy Council's observation in *Boyce (Lennox) and Joseph (Jeffrey) v R* (PC appeal 99/2002, 7 July 2004), on the Barbados Constitution is apposite: 'the living instrument principle has its reasons, logic and limitations. It is not a magic ingredient which can be stirred into the judicial pot, together with 'international obligations', 'generous construction' and other such phrases, sprinkled with a cherished aphorism or two and brewed up into a potion which will make the Constitution mean something it obviously does not.'

6   See **7.33** below. For similar 'dynamic interpretation' in the UK courts see eg *Fitzpatrick v Sterling Housing Association Ltd* [1999] 4 All ER 705, [2000] 1 FLR 271, HL; *Ghaidan v Mendoza* [2004] UKHL 30, [2004] 3 All ER 411, HL.

7   Although for legal certainty and the orderly development of the case law it usually follows its own precedents (*Sheffield and Horsham v United Kingdom* (1998) 27 EHRR 163), in

Goodwin v United Kingdom [2002] 2 FCR 577 the Court departed from the decision in *Sheffield and Horsham* to rule that, in the light of rapidly changing ideas about relationships and marriage, the UK's failure to give recognition to post-operative transsexuals was now in breach of arts 8 and 12.

8   The citation of Commonwealth authority has already become common in human rights cases; see eg *R v Secretary of State for the Home Department, ex p Ahmed and Patel* [1998] INLR 570, approving the Australian case of *Minister for Immigration and Ethnic Affairs v Teoh* (1995) 183 CLR 273. The House of Lords considered New Zealand and Australian law in the post-Goodwin case of *Bellinger v Bellinger* [2003] UKHL 21, [2003] 2 AC 467 (incompatibility of law, not recognising the change of sex of post-operative transsexual, with arts 8 and 12 ECHR), and Canadian law in *R (on the application of Ullah) v Special Adjudicator* [2004] UKHL 26, [2004] INLR 381 (para 23) and *R (on the application of Pretty) v DPP* [2001] UKHL 61, [2002] 1 AC 800 (assisted suicide).

Interpretative obligation to achieve compatibility with Human Rights

7.15 The second interpretative obligation requires all legislation—primary and subordinate, past and future—to be read and given effect so far as possible in a way which is compatible with ECHR rights.[1] This interpretative formula is borrowed from EC law,[2] but is a fundamental break with normal principles of statutory interpretation (the 'true meaning',[3] the 'plain meaning of the words',[4] the 'intention of the legislature',[5] so as to ensure that domestic law in time conforms to the basic human rights norms expressed in the Convention.[6] In cases engaging fundamental rights, the courts must 'strive to find an interpretation of legislation which is consistent with Convention rights so far as the language of the legislation allows, and only in the last resort to conclude that the legislation is simply incompatible with them'.[7] This does not depend on statutory ambiguity, as the House of Lords said it did in *Brind*.[8] In seeking a meaning which will prevent incompatibility, the courts are not bound by previous interpretations,[9] and are becoming accustomed to 'reading in' safeguards by way of provisos to apparently absolute restrictions.[10] They are also learning to 'read down' provisions which are on their face incompatible with Convention rights,[11] by limiting the scope and effect of the words to enable compatibility.[12]

1   Human Rights Act 1998, s 3(1)(a). It does not affect the validity and continuing operation or enforcement of incompatible legislation, however—another balancing mechanism with parliamentary sovereignty: s 3(1)(b) and (c). Although the rule of construction in s 3 applies to all legislation, whenever enacted, it cannot be used to introduce retrospective rights or to change the substantive law retrospectively, so as to apply the Act to events pre-dating it, except in the limited circumstances covered by s 22(4): *Wainwright v Home Office* [2001] EWCA Civ 2081, [2002] 3 WLR 405; see also *R v Lambert* [2001] UKHL 37, [2001] 3 WLR 206, HL; *R v Kansal (No 2)* [2001] UKHL 62, [2002] 2 AC 69; *Pearce v Governing Body of Mayfield Secondary School* [2001] EWCA Civ 1347, [2002] ICR 198.

2   *Marleasing SA v La Comercial Internacional de Alimentacion SA* C-106/89 [1992] 1 CMLR 305, ECJ.

3   In practice this will mean 'a rebuttable presumption in favour of an interpretation consistent with Convention rights': Lord Steyn 'Incorporation and Devolution—A few reflections on the changing scene' [1998] EHRLR 153. A ministerial statement of compatibility under s 19 of the Human Rights Act 1998 (see **7.24** below) will support such a presumption.

4   Bennion *Statutory Interpretation* (4rd edn, 2002) Butterworths, pp 467ff.

5   Bennion above, pp 819ff.

6   *R v DPP, ex p Kebilene* [1999] 4 All ER 801 at 838.

7   583 HL Official Report (5th series) col 535, 18 November 1997.

8   *R v Secretary of State for the Home Department, ex p Brind* [1991] 1 AC 696; see **7.5** above.

9   Starmer *European Human Rights Law* (1999) LAG, p 16.

10   As *in R v A* [2001] UKHL 25, [2001] 1 AC 45, where the House of Lords read in a discretion
     into what on its face was a mandatory requirement to limit cross-examination of a rape victim,
     to ensure compatibility with fair trial rights. In *R (on the application of Zenovics) v Secretary
     of State for the Home Department* [2002] EWCA Civ 273, [2002] INLR 219, the Court of
     Appeal read words into Sch 4, para 9(2) to the Immigration and Asylum Act 1999
     (certification limiting appeal rights) to avoid the unintended effect of depriving an appellant of
     a human rights appeal when the Secretary of State certified his or her asylum claim manifestly
     unfounded. However, the boundary between interpretation and judicial trespass on the
     legislative function was reached in *S (children: care plan), Re* [2002] UKHL 10, [2002] 2 AC
     291, where the House of Lords reversed the Court of Appeal's attempt to write in a mechanism
     for further review of care orders which Parliament had omitted; this was an 'impermissible
     amendment of a statutory scheme which (if necessary for compatibility with the Convention)
     only Parliament could effect'. And in *Bellinger v Bellinger* [2003] UKHL 21, [2003] 2 AC 467
     the House of Lords emphasised that judges' function is to interpret, not to legislate (paras 67,
     per Lord Hope, 98, per Lord Hobhouse). See also *R (on the application of Anderson) v
     Secretary of State for the Home Department* [2002] UKHL 46, [2003] 1 AC 837.
11   See *R v Secretary of State for the Home Department, ex p Pierson* [1998] AC 539 at 573–575,
     per Lord Browne-Wilkinson, 587–590, per Lord Steyn.
12   See eg *R v DPP, ex p Kebilene* [1999] 4 All ER 801, HL; *R v A* [2001] UKHL 25, [2001] 1 AC
     45, at para 44, per Lord Steyn. See further *R v Lambert* [2001] UKHL 37, [2002] 2 AC 545;
     R v Johnstone [2003] UKHL 28, [2003] 1 WLR 1736; and *A-G's Reference (No 4 of 2002);
     Sheldrake v DPP* [2004] UKHL 43, [2005] 1 AC 264, on when (on the same wording) a
     reverse burden of proof on a defendant in a criminal trial should be read as 'evidential' and
     when 'persuasive' to ensure compatibility with art 6 fair trial rights.

7.16 The interpretative obligation also applies to subordinate legislation such
as Immigration Rules.[1] Thus in *Boadi*[2] the Tribunal held that the requirement
that an adopted child has 'lost or broken her ties with her family of origin'
must be read as referring to ties of responsibility, not of affection, to be
compatible with Article 8 ECHR.[3] If it is impossible to interpret a provision in
subordinate legislation in a way which is compatible with ECHR rights, and
there is nothing in the parent Act requiring this incompatibility,[4] the offending
provision may be disapplied or struck down as *ultra vires* the parent Act, as
the Court of Appeal did with the rule preventing access to the Tribunal in
Saleem.[5] However, it should be noted that the Tribunal has no power to strike
down incompatible rules,[6] although it can set aside an immigration decision
which is unlawful as being incompatible with the appellant's Convention
rights, regardless of whether it is in accordance with the rules.[7]

1   In *R v Secretary of State for the Home Department, ex p Ali (Arman)* [2000] INLR 89, Collins
    J interpreted the rules relating to recourse to public funds so as to give effect to art 8 ECHR
    obligations.
2   *Boadi v Entry Clearance Officer, Ghana* [2002] UKIAT 01323, [2003] INLR 54.
3   See also *Abdulla (Intekab)* [2002] UKIAT 07516, where the Tribunal read para 281(v) of the
    Immigration Rules (for admission of spouse, the couple must have no recourse to public funds)
    as allowing the spouse to depend on the sponsor's savings from disability allowance 'to ensure
    compliance with ECHR obligations. To prevent someone qualifying for family reunion solely
    on the basis of inevitable financial hardship could in certain circumstances, particularly where
    disability prevents a sponsor working, amount to disrespect for private and family life or
    discrimination contrary to art 14 with art 8.'
4   For example, if the rules are made in exercise of a general rule-making power such as that
    under the Immigration Act 1971, s 3(2).
5   *R v Secretary of State for the Home Department, ex p Saleem* [2000] 4 All ER 814, [2000]
    Imm AR 529, [2000] INLR 413.
6   See *Pardeepan v Secretary of State for the Home Department* [2000] INLR 447; *Koprinov*
    (01TH00095).
7   Nationality, Immigration and Asylum Act 2002, s 84(1)(c), (g); see *Huang v Secretary of State
    for the Home Department* [2007] UKHL 11, [2007] 2 AC 167.

7.17 If incompatibility of primary legislation cannot be remedied by the new method of construction, or subordinate legislation cannot be read compatibly because the parent Act prevents this, the only remedy is a declaration of incompatibility.[1] A declaration of incompatibility may be made only by the higher courts, ie the High Court, the Court of Appeal, the Privy Council and the House of Lords, and in Scotland the High Court of Judiciary (except when it sits as a trial court) and the Court of Session.[2] The Special Immigration Appeals Commission may make a declaration of incompatibility in a derogation matter.[3] It is a discretionary remedy; the court may decide to leave the incompatibility (although it is hard to reconcile this with its own duty as a public authority to act compatibly with the ECHR, under s 6).[4] If a court is considering making a declaration, the Crown is entitled to notice[5] and to be joined as a party.[6] In another example of the balancing of judicial guardianship of fundamental rights with parliamentary sovereignty, a declaration of incompatibility does not affect the continuing validity, operation and enforcement of the incompatible legislation, nor does it bind the parties.[7] If a minister insisted on action (such as removal) under legislation which has been held incompatible with the Convention, however, it is likely that the court would grant a stay pending parliamentary consideration of a remedial amendment. The declaration empowers, but does not oblige Parliament to remedy the incompatibility,[8] and if Parliament does not do so the victim can apply to the ECtHR as before. Declarations of incompatibility were made in the immigration context in respect of provisions in the Asylum and Immigration (Treatment of Claimants, etc) Act 2004. One provision was declared incompatible with Article 14 of the ECHR on grounds of religion because it exempted those entering an Anglican marriage from the requirement, applicable in respect of other religious marriages, of obtaining permission to marry from the Home Office.[9] The other provision declared incompatible was one which prevented the Secretary of State from investigating a claim that removal of an asylum seeker from the UK to a 'safe third country' would breach Article 3 even if there was apparently persuasive evidence supporting the claim.[10] However, this decision was overturned by the Court of Appeal.[11]

[1]   Human Rights Act 1998, s 4(1)–(4). In the first two years of the Act's operation, nine declarations of incompatibility were made: see 'Two years of the Human Rights Act', in (2003) EHRLR 14–23. Recent cases involve the right of transsexuals to marry (*Bellinger v Bellinger* [2003] UKHL 21, [2003] 2 AC 467) and the rights of mental patients: *R (on the application of M) v Secretary of State for Health* (2003) UKHRR 746. In *International Transport Roth GmbH v Secretary of State for the Home Department* [2002] EWCA Civ 158, [2003] QB 728, the Court of Appeal held the statutory scheme penalising carriers of clandestine entrants (Immigration and Asylum Act 1999, ss 32–37) incompatible with art 6 and Protocol 1, art 1 because of the mandatory and inflexible nature of the penalties, the lack of fair proceedings to challenge penalties and the draconian powers of detention of transporters: see CHAPTER 15 below. Measures denying all support to late asylum claimants (Nationality, Immigration and Asylum Act 2002, s 55) avoided a similar fate by saving provisions enabling support to be given 'to the extent necessary to prevent a breach of an applicant's Convention rights': see *R (on the application of Q) v Secretary of State for the Home Department* [2003] EWCA Civ 364, [2003] UKHRR 607, [2003] 2 All ER 905.

[2]   HRA 1998, s 4(5).

[3]   Anti-terrorism, Crime and Security Act 2001, s 30(2). On an appeal originating from a decision by SIAC under this section in *A v Secretary of State for the Home Department; X v Secretary of State for the Home Department* [2004] UKHL 56, [2005] 2 WLR 87 the House of Lords ruled that the derogation from art 5 ECHR was discriminatory and disproportionate, quashed the Derogation Order and and declared s 23 of the Anti-terrorism, Crime and Security Act 2001, which allowed indefinite detention without trial of foreign nationals, incompatible

with arts 5 and 14 of ECHR, since it addressed only the threat of terrorism posed by non-nationals, while that threat was as likely to emanate from nationals.

⁴ HRA 1998, s 6(3)(a); see below. But in *Bellinger v Bellinger* [2003] UKHL 21, [2003] 2 AC 467, the House of Lords rejected the Crown's submissions to the effect that a declaration was unnecessary since the government was committed to changing the law after the adverse decision of the ECtHR in *Goodwin v United Kingdom* (28957/95) [2002] IRLR 664, holding it desirable 'in a sensitive case that this House, as the court of final appeal in this country, should formally record that the present state of statute law is incompatible with the Convention.'

⁵ HRA 1998, s 5(1).

⁶ HRA 1998, s 5(2). The court will also be sympathetic to public interest organisations applying to be joined as interveners: see **7.25** below.

⁷ HRA 1998, s 4(6). The purpose of the declaration is to put Parliament under pressure to remedy the incompatibility: Lord Chancellor, 583 HL Official Report (5th series) col 546, 18 November 1997. Since the offending legislation continues in force, there can be no award of damages when a declaration is made: *K (a child) (secure accommodation order: right to liberty), Re* [2001] 2 All ER 719, CA, paras 128–130, although costs should be awarded.

⁸ Parliament is not a 'public authority' for the purposes of the Human Rights Act 1998: s 6(3) (except for the judicial committee of the House of Lords: s 6(4)), and has no obligation to act compatibly with the ECHR, save under international law. Detailed description of the mechanism for remedying statutory incompatibility is beyond the scope of this work. In essence, the offending legislation may simply be amended when there is parliamentary time, or in cases where the minister considers there are compelling reasons not to wait, he or she may amend the legislation by an order under s 10, known as a remedial order. HRA 1998, Sch 2 contains the fairly complex procedural requirements for a valid remedial order.

⁹ *R (on the application of Baiai) v Secretary of State for the Home Department* [2006] EWHC 823 (Admin), [2006] 3 All ER 608 and *R (on the application of Baiai) v Secretary of State for the Home Department* [2008] UKHL 53, [2008] 3 All ER 1094 in respect of the Asylum and Immigration (Treatment of Claimants, etc) Act 2004, s 19(1).

¹⁰ *R (on the application of Nasseri) v Secretary of State for the Home Department* [2007] EWHC 1548 (Admin), [2008] 1 All ER 411, in respect of the Asylum and Immigration (Treatment of Claimants, etc) Act 2004, Sch 3, para 3.

¹¹ *R (on the application of Nasseri) v Secretary of State for the Home Department* [2008] EWCA Civ 464, [2009] 1 All ER 116.

The duty on public authorities

7.18 The interpretative obligation is one of the two mechanisms to ensure the compliance of UK law with the ECHR. The other is the obligation on public authorities to act compatibly with the Convention. Section 6 of the Human Rights Act 1998 makes it unlawful for a public authority to act in a way incompatible with a Convention right,¹ unless the authority could not have acted differently because of a provision of primary legislation,² or because it was acting to enforce or give effect to such an (incompatible) provision.³ An act includes a failure to act.⁴ A public authority includes a court or tribunal⁵ but not Parliament (except the House of Lords in its judicial capacity),⁶ and also includes a person⁷ some of whose functions are of a public nature.⁸ The jurisprudence relating to judicial review will be relevant in determining who is a 'public authority',⁹ as will be the Strasbourg jurisprudence on bodies which engage the responsibility of the State for the purposes of the Convention.¹⁰ Purely public authorities such as immigration officers must always act compatibly; private bodies which have private and public functions must do so only in relation to their public functions.¹¹ Thus, while a security company is delivering bullion (a commercial operation) it has no obligation to act compatibly with the Convention;¹² but while it is running a removal centre, it clearly does; it is a public authority in performing this function.¹³ The Court of

Appeal applied a restrictive test in *R (on the application of Heather) v Leonard Cheshire Foundation*,[14] but the House of Lords moved to a more realistic (and generous) approach to the exercise of public functions by private bodies in *Aston Cantlow*.[15] They ruled that a function is a public one when the government has taken responsibility for it in the public interest, and the attribution of public authority responsibilities to private sector bodies is justified on the basis that a private body operating to discharge a government programme is likely to exercise a degree of power and control over the realisation of the individual's Convention rights which in the absence of delegation would be State power and control.[16] Despite this guidance, the lower courts have continued to apply an institutional rather than a functional approach to 'public functions' which, as the Joint Committee on Human Rights[17] has commented, leaves real gaps and inadequacies in human rights protection through inconsistent and restrictive interpretation.[18] However, an airline or other carrier refusing boarding to an inadequately documented passenger performs a commercial, as opposed to a public function on the current interpretation of the law.[19]

1   Human Rights Act 1998, s 6(1).
2   HRA 1998, s 6(2)(a). The provision of primary legislation must of course be read compatibly if possible, and if this is possible, or if the legislation does not compel the authority to act in the way it has, the authority cannot rely on this exception. See *Hampson v Department of Education and Science* [1991] 1 AC 171, [1990] 2 All ER 513, and see discussion in Grosz, Beatson and Duffy, **7.13** fn 3 above.
3   HRA 1998, s 6(2)(b).
4   HRA 1998, s 6(6). This accords with Strasbourg jurisprudence on positive obligations: see **7.34** below. A decision whether or not to prosecute is an 'act' for these purposes: *Brown v Stott* [2001] 2 All ER 97, [2001] 2 WLR 817, PC; *R (on the application of Pretty) v DPP* [2001] UKHL 61, [2002] 1 AC 800 (para 75, per Lord Hope) (refusal to give undertaking not to prosecute is justiciable in exceptional circumstances where the matter cannot be tested at a criminal trial or on appeal). But a failure to make a decision is not a 'decision' for the purpose of an immigration appeal: *Bouras* [2002] UKIAT 00772 (decided under the Immigration and Asylum Act 1999, s 65 which gave a right of appeal against a 'decision relating to . . . entitlement to enter or remain'). Failure to take a decision is challengeable by way of judicial review: see *R v Secretary of State for the Home Department, ex p Phansopkar* [1976] QB 606 (common law).
5   HRA 1998, s 6(3)(a). A 'public authority' does not have to be in the UK, so would include consular officials such as entry clearance officers acting in relation to UK immigration control.
6   HRA 1998, s 6(3), (4). Thus, failure to bring legislation into force (such as the repealed automatic bail provisions of Part 4 of the 1999 Act, which were never brought into force) is not an 'act' capable of being unlawful: HRA 1998, s 6(6).
7   This includes legal persons, ie companies such as Group 4, but probably not unincorporated associations.
8   HRA 1998, s 6(3)(b).
9   A body is 'public' if (for example) the source of its power is statutory or prerogative or it is institutionally or structurally controlled by government, whether the power it exercises is 'governmental in nature' and would be exercised by government if not by the body concerned: *R v Panel on Take-overs and Mergers, ex p Datafin plc* [1987] QB 815.
10   For a useful discussion on the scope of 'public authorities' and 'public functions' see Grosz, Beatson and Duffy (at **7.13** fn 3 above), paras 4.02–4.15.
11   HRA 1998, s 6(5). The Lord Chancellor accepted that a private security company would be exercising public functions in its management of a contracted-out prison: 583 HL Official Report (5th series) col 811, 24 November 1997.
12   *Griffiths v Smith* [1941] AC 170 at 205.
13   Under Immigration and Asylum Act 1999, ss 148–157 and Schs 11–13. The element of compulsion was held important in *R (on the application of A) v Partnerships in Care Ltd* [2002] EWHC 529 (Admin), [2002] 1 WLR 2610, (2002) Times, 23 April where the Court of Appeal held that private sector care providers who were authorised to detain patients under the Mental Health Act 1983 were performing a public function.

[14] [2002] EWCA Civ 366, [2002] 2 All ER 936, holding that a private charitable organisation which houses vulnerable people who have been placed there and funded by a local authority or housing authority is not exercising a public function; the fact that a body performs an activity which otherwise a public authority would be under a duty to perform does not mean such performance is inevitably public, and the role performed by the charity was 'manifestly' not public; it was not standing in the shoes of the public authority, unlike the housing association in *Poplar Housing and Regeneration Community Association Ltd v Donoghue* [2001] EWCA Civ 595, [2002] QB 48, [2001] 4 All ER 604 (a registered social landlord which took transfers of properties from a London borough, which was held to stand in the Council's shoes as a 'public authority'). According to this formulation, landlords contracting with NASS or local authorities to provide accommodation for asylum seekers would not be public authorities for the purposes of the Act.

[15] *Aston Cantlow and Wilmcote with Billesley Parochial Church Council v Wallbank* [2003] UKHL 37 [2003] UKHRR 919, HL.

[16] *Aston Cantlow and Wilmcote with Billesley Parochial Church Council v Wallbank.*

[17] For the Joint Committee on Human Rights see **7.24** below.

[18] Joint Committee on Human Rights, 7th report 2003–4 session, 'The meaning of "public authority" under the Human Rights Act', 3 March 2004, HL 39/HC 382.

[19] See *R v Secretary of State for the Home Department, ex p Hoverspeed* [1999] INLR 591. Even if this was held to be a public function, the carrier might still argue that it is giving effect to provisions of primary legislation, ie the carriers' liability provisions of the Immigration and Asylum Act 1999, s 40 and is therefore not obliged to act compatibly with the ECHR: HRA 1998, s 6(2)(b).

7.19 The requirement that courts and tribunals act compatibly with the ECHR embraces both judicial and procedural or administrative functions of the court. Despite the jurisprudence of the ECtHR indicating that immigration and asylum matters do not relate to 'civil rights and obligations' and so are not within the province of Article 6 ECHR,[1] the legislation on immigration and asylum appeals, and the procedure rules, are clearly intended to reflect Article 6 requirements of due process, openness and fairness.[2] In cases involving human rights, the appellate authorities and the courts thus have a dual function: to review the decision of an immigration officer or the Secretary of State, or of a lower court or tribunal, for compatibility with the Convention, and to act compatibly with the Convention themselves.[3] In the performance of this dual function, the courts are bound to determine for themselves whether the act the appellant complains of is unlawful. This involves determining:

(a)   whether there is a Convention right in play;

(b)   whether any exceptions are permitted in respect of that right under the Convention or whether any reservation or derogation applies;

(c)   if so, whether the exception is provided for by the domestic law (ie the Immigration Acts or the Rules, or any relevant published policy);

(d)   in the case of a qualified right, whether the government has a legitimate aim in applying the exception;

(e)   in such a case, whether the application of the exception is necessary to achieve the legitimate aim, ie is proportionate to it.

[1] *Maaouia v France* (2000) 33 EHRR 1037. See 7.77 below.

[2] The language of the Asylum and Immigration Tribunal (Procedure) Rules 2005, SI 2005/230, r 54, setting out exceptions to the norm of public hearings, mirrors the language of ECHR, art 6(1), for example.

[3] However, the argument that the courts, as an organ of State, are obliged to give effect to the State's international obligations, is a fallacy which would completely undermine the principle that the courts apply domestic law, not international treaties: *R v Lyons* [2002] UKHL 44, [2003] 1 AC 976, [2002] 4 All ER 1028 at para 40, per Lord Hoffmann. The Tribunal has referred to its own function as a public authority in ensuring human rights-compliant decisions in *MNM* (00TH02423) and in *SK* [2002] UKIAT 05613 (starred). But the

requirement that the court, as a public authority, act compatibly with the Convention does not give it a roving commission to detect breaches of human rights not raised by the applicant, or to ignore procedural requirements such as time limits: *Xhezo* (01TH00625) (12 July 2001, unreported), IAT.

Proportionality and deference

7.20 The proportionality test is clearly more rigorous, objective and intrusive (in demanding a greater degree of justification) than the *Wednesbury* test whose borders, even in a human rights case, are set by mere rationality. The ECtHR has repeatedly made clear that, in determining whether a breach of the ECHR can be justified under Articles 8(2) or 10(2), the court's supervision goes beyond ascertaining whether discretion has been exercised reasonably, carefully or in good faith, and requires it to determine whether it was 'proportionate to the legitimate aim pursued' and whether the reasons adduced by the national authorities to justify it are 'relevant and sufficient'.[1] In the 'gays in the military' cases of *Smith and Grady v United Kingdom* and *Lustig-Prean and Beckett*[2] the court held that 'the threshold at which the High Court and Court of Appeal[3] could find the Ministry of Defence policy, of dismissing gays from the army, irrational was placed so high, that it effectively excluded any consideration by the domestic courts of the question of whether the interference with the applicants' rights answered a pressing social need or was proportionate to the national security and public order aims pursued, principles which lie at the heart of the court's analysis of complaints under Article 8 of the Convention'.[4] In *Daly*,[5] Lord Steyn pointed out that 'There is a material difference between the *Wednesbury* and *ex p Smith* grounds of review and the approach of proportionality applicable in respect of review where Convention rights are at stake.' He adopted the threefold test applied in *de Freitas:*[6] whether (i) the legislative objective is sufficiently important to justify limiting a fundamental right; (ii) the measures designed to meet the legislative objective are rationally connected to it; (iii) the means used to impair the right or freedom are no more than is necessary to accomplish the objective, emphasising the importance of the third criterion, that of necessity. The proportionality test, he added, would require attention to be given to the weight of the factors involved and not merely whether they had been taken into consideration: 'It may require the reviewing court to assess the balance which the decision-maker has struck, not merely whether it is within the range of rational or reasonable decisions. It may require attention to be paid to the relative weight accorded to interests and considerations . . . even the heightened scrutiny test developed in ex p *Smith* is not necessarily appropriate to the protection of human rights.'[7] Lord Cooke, concurring, said it was time to bury *Wednesbury* in human rights cases.[8] *Samaroo*[9] was the first post-Human Rights Act attempt of the Court of Appeal to apply the proportionality test as set out in *Daly* in an immigration context. The test was held to be whether the decision-maker has struck 'a fair balance' between the interests of the individual and those of the community, a test which has been followed in countless subsequent cases.[10] In *Huang* in both the House of Lords and the Court of Appeal it was emphasised once more that the proportionality test, not a *Wednesbury* review, was to be applied in human rights cases.[11]

[1]   *Sunday Times Ltd v United Kingdom (No 2)* (1991) 14 EHRR 229; *Hertel v Switzerland* (1998) 28 EHRR 534.

2   (1999) 29 EHRR 493; *Lustig-Prean and Beckett v United Kingdom* (1999) 29 EHRR 548.
3   *R v Ministry of Defence, ex p Smith* [1996] QB 517.
4   *Smith and Grady v United Kingdom* at para 138.
5   *R (on the application of Daly) v Secretary of State for the Home Department* [2001] UKHL 26, [2001] 2 AC 532.
6   *De Freitas v Permanent Secretary of Ministry of Agriculture, Fisheries, Lands and Housing* [1999] 1 AC 69, [1998] 3 WLR 675.
7   *R (on the application of Daly) v Secretary of State for the Home Department* [2001] UKHL 26, [2001] 2 AC 532 at para 27.
8   *Daly* at para 32.
9   *R (on the application of Samaroo) v Secretary of State for the Home Department* [2001] EWCA Civ 1139, [2001] UKHRR 1150, [2002] INLR 55 and *R (on the application of Sezek) v Secretary of State for the Home Department* [2001] EWCA Civ 795, [2002] 1 WLR 348.
10 The test derives from *Sporrong and Lonnroth v Sweden* (1982) 5 EHRR 35, a decision relating to a successful claim under art 1 of Protocol 1 that the complainants' right to peaceful enjoyment of properties they owned in central Stockholm had been blighted by planning laws.
11 *Huang v Secretary of State for the Home Department* [2005] EWCA Civ 105, 149 Sol Jo LB 297; affd [2007] UKHL 11, [2007] 2 AC 167, [2005] EWCA Civ 105, (2005) Sol Jo LB 297, and see **7.21–7.23** below.

7.21 There has been intense debate as to the existence and scope of the 'margin of discretion' or 'discretionary area of judgment' to be afforded to ministers and lower courts by the court reviewing the decision for compatibility with the ECHR,[1] and whether the same margin applies in judicial review and statutory appeal. In *ex p Kebilene*[2] Lord Hope said of the 'discretionary area of judgment':

> 'In this area difficult choices may have to be made by the executive or the legislature between the rights of the individual and the needs of society. In some circumstances it will be appropriate for the court to recognise that there is an area of judgment within which the judiciary will defer, on democratic grounds, to the considered opinion of the elected body or person whose act or decision is said to be incompatible with the Convention . . . It will be easier for such an area of judgment to be recognised where the Convention itself requires a balance to be struck, much less so where the right is stated in terms which are unqualified. It will be easier for it to be recognised where the issues involve questions of social or economic policy, much less so where the rights are of high constitutional importance or are of a kind where the courts are especially well placed to assess the need for protection . . .'

Lord Hope saw this as a constitutional question, marking out the boundaries between the considered opinions of the elected body and those of the judiciary.[3] The constitutional basis of deference, and its flexibility in different contexts, has been emphasised by the Court of Appeal in a string of cases since. In *Roth*[4] Laws LJ said that the reach of deference which judges would pay to the democratic decision-maker, their giving and withholding of it, was the 'second means by which the courts resolve the tension between parliamentary sovereignty and fundamental rights in our intermediate constitution' (the first was the rule of construction under section 3). More deference would be due, he said, to an Act of Parliament than to a decision of the executive; more when the right itself was balanced, more where the subject-matter is peculiarly within executive or legislative constitutional responsibility (such as defence and security of borders, including immigration control[5]), and more or less according to whether the subject matter lies more readily within the potential experience of what he called the democratic powers or the courts.[6] In *Farrakhan*[7] the Court of Appeal emphasised the Secretary of State's relatively wide margin of discretion in immigration cases. This was a judgment which involved the personal decision of the Secretary of State and could, therefore, be classed as the opinion of an elected representative and set apart from more routine immigration decisions. The trend in the domestic case law, however, extends this deference well beyond personal ministerial decisions. Routine decisions to deport and so forth, which used to be the bread and butter of adjudicators, were treated as matters of policy, requiring a large margin of executive discretion to be accorded to the Secretary of State, the high watermark of this trend being the careful deconstruction of proportionality by Dyson LJ in *R (on the application of Samaroo) v Secretary of State for the Home Department*,[8] and its application beyond judicial review to statutory appeal, which we deal with in the next paragraph. The Court of Appeal decision in *Huang* rightly rejected the *Wednesbury* approach and re-armed immigration judges with full power to carry out a merits review on proportionality grounds, not some neo-*Wednesbury* test.

[1]   See Lester and Pannick *Human Rights Law and Practice* (2nd edn, 2004, Butterworths), p 74, para 3.21.
[2]   *R v DPP, ex p Kebilene* [1999] 3 WLR 972, per Lord Hope at 993–994, and see *Brown v Stott* [2001] 2 All ER 97, PC.
[3]   See also Lord Steyn in *Daly* above para 28.
[4]   *International Transport Roth GmbH v Secretary of State for the Home Department* [2002] EWCA Civ 158, [2003] QB 728, paras 83–87.
[5]   It should be noted that 'immigration control' is not just about security of borders, but includes such inclusive and positive policies, such as family stability, the need for migrant workers and the principles of non-discrimination. It is not identified as one of the legitimate public interests identified in any of Articles 8(2), 9(2), 10(2), or 11 (2) of ECHR, although some of these will cover particular aspects of 'immigration control', such as national security, economic well-being and the prevention of crime.
[6]   Thus, deference may be due because of the particular knowledge and expertise of the decision maker; see *R v Chief Constable of Sussex, ex p International Trader's Ferry Ltd* [1999] 2 AC 418 (involving the deployment of scarce police resources, where the court deferred to the considered opinion of the chief constable), or of a tribunal with specialist knowledge of the subject matter: see *B v Secretary of State for the Home Department* [2000] Imm AR 478, paras 24–27, per Sedley LJ. See also Singh, Hunt and Demetriou, 'Is there a role for the "Margin of Appreciation" in national law after the Human Rights Act?' [1999] 1 EHRLR 15–22, which suggests other relevant factors, including whether the aim of the measure under review is to promote other human rights, whether the applicants are particularly vulnerable or eg members of unpopular minorities, and whether the context is one of fairly constant standards throughout democratic societies or one where no discernible standards have yet emerged. And see Clayton and Tomlinson *The Law of Human Rights* (2000, OUP), p 253.
[7]   *R (on the application of Farrakhan) v Secretary of State for the Home Department* [2002] EWCA Civ 606, [2002] QB 1391, [2002] 3 WLR 481, [2002] Imm AR 447, [2002] INLR 257, where the court ascribed the wide margin of discretion (i) to the weight attached by the Strasbourg court to the right under international law to control the entry of aliens and (ii) to the democratic accountability of the Secretary of State.
[8]   *R (on the application of Samaroo) v Secretary of State for the Home Department* [2001] EWCA Civ 1139, [2001] UKHRR 1150, [2002] INLR 55 and *R (on the application of Sezek) v Secretary of State for the Home Department* [2001] EWCA Civ 795, [2002] 1 WLR 348.

7.22 How the requirements of proportionality and due deference were to be applied by the court gave rise to considerable difficulty. A series of decisions from the Court of Appeal[1] and the Administrative Court[2] enabled the Tribunal, in a starred decision, to conclude that an adjudicator 'should normally hold that a decision to remove is unlawful *only when the disproportionality is so great that no reasonable Secretary of State could remove*' (emphasis added).[3] This *Wednesbury* approach to proportionality was rejected by the House of Lords in *Razgar* where their Lordships made it clear that in a statutory appeal, the adjudicator was to exercise an independent judgment on the issue of proportionality, based on all the materials adduced on the appeal.[4]

1   *R (on the application of Mahmood) v Secretary of State for the Home Department* [2001] 1 WLR 840, [2001] Imm AR 229, para 40; *R (on the application of Samaroo) v Secretary of State for the Home Department* [2001] EWCA Civ 1139, [2001] UKHRR 1150, [2002] INLR 55 and *R (on the application of Sezek) v Secretary of State for the Home Department* [2001] EWCA Civ 795, [2002] 1 WLR 348; *Edore v Secretary of State for the Home Department* [2003] EWCA Civ 716, [2003] Imm AR 516, [2003] INLR 361, at para 20.

2   *R (on the application of Ala) v Secretary of State for the Home Department* [2003] EWHC 521 (Admin), [2003] All ER (D) 283 (Mar).

3   *M (Croatia) v Secretary of State for the Home Department* [2004] UKIAT 24, [2004] INLR 327, at para 28. See for a fuller discussion, **7.20–7.23** of the 7th edition of this work.

4   *R (on the application of Razgar) v Secretary of State for the Home Department* [2004] UKHL 27, [2004] 2 AC 368.

7.23 There remain situations where little or no deference is due to the executive or to Immigration Rules. In cases involving Article 3 claims, no deference is paid to the executive's view of what constitutes treatment contrary to Article 3, because the right is absolute and cannot depend on differing interpretations of inhuman treatment or torture.[1] Little or no deference is paid to the Secretary of State's view of the reality of a risk, since 'whether a sufficient risk exists is a question of evaluation and prediction based on evidence; in answering such a question the executive enjoys no constitutional prerogative.[2] In *Turgut*,[3] a case involving an evaluation of likely mistreatment of the appellant on his return to Turkey, the court concluded that 'what has been called the "discretionary area of judgment" . . . is a decidedly narrow one'. The court also affords little deference to the executive in questions of detention.[4]

1   See eg *R (on the application of T) v Secretary of State for the Home Department* [2003] EWCA Civ 1285, [2004] HLR 254. This corresponds with the lack of any margin of appreciation to contracting States on art 3: see Callewaerts, Johann 'Is there a margin of appreciation in the application of arts 2, 3 and 4 of the Convention?' [1998] 19 HRLJ 6–9.

2   *Secretary of State for the Home Department v Rehman* [2001] UKHL 47, [2001] 3 WLR 877, [2002] INLR 92, para 54, per Lord Hoffmann, who (at para 57) contrasted the lack of deference to the executive in answering this question with the assessment of a national security risk, where the appellate body allows a wide margin to the decision maker. See also *R (on the application of A) v Lord Saville of Newdigate (No 2)* [2001] EWCA Civ 2048, [2002] 1 WLR 1249, para 34.

3   *R v Secretary of State for the Home Department, ex p Turgut* [2000] Imm AR 306. This passage was cited in the ECtHR in *Hilal v United Kingdom* (Application 45276/99) (2001) 11 BHRC 354, in support of the court's conclusion that judicial review was an effective remedy for the purposes of art 13 in cases raising asylum or art 3 issues.

4   'Liberty . . . is a right which English law has guarded with jealous care since at least the time of Edward I; [it is] one of the rights of high constitutional importance in which relatively slight deference to the executive is appropriate': *R (on the application of Amirthanathan) v Secretary of State for the Home Department* [2003] EWHC 2595 (Admin) (although the decision in this case was upheld by the Court of Appeal on the narrowest of grounds: see *Nadarajah v Secretary of State for the Home Department* [2003] EWCA Civ 1768). See also *A v Secretary of State for the Home Department; X v Secretary of State for the Home Department* [2004] UKHL 56, [2005] 2 WLR 87 per Lord Bingham at para 36.

Statement of compatibility

7.24 In accordance with the constitutional balance of the Human Rights Act 1998, Parliament is excluded from the definition of a public authority for the purposes of compliance with the ECHR, as noted above, as is any person exercising functions in connection with proceedings in Parliament.[1] A failure to introduce or propose legislation or to make any primary legislation or remedial order is not 'an act' which can be challenged in the courts.[2] The one obligation imposed on ministers is that of stating, before second reading of any Bill, whether in his or her view the Bill's provisions are compatible with the Convention rights (a 'statement of compatibility') or not. The purpose of this is twofold: to ensure that ministers and Parliament address compatibility with the Convention when legislation is debated (which itself makes the legislation more likely to be compatible), and to create a presumption that it is so compatible, in the face of apparently incompatible provisions. The Joint Committee on Human Rights, a Select Committee formed by both Houses of Parliament in July 2001 to consider human rights issues in the UK and proposals for remedial orders under the Act,[3] scrutinises bills and prepares reports on their compatibility with the Convention, enabling ministers to reconsider provisions about which the Committee expresses concern.[4]

[1] Human Rights Act 1998, s 6(3); see **7.18** above.
[2] HRA 1998, s 6(6).
[3] Under HRA 1998, s 10(2).
[4] See the Committee's regular reports on scrutiny of Bills; see also its 5th and 14th reports of 2003/4, on the Asylum and Immigration (Treatment of Claimants) Bill, 10 February 2004 (HL 35/HC 304) and 5 July 2004 (HL 130/HC 828), its 6th report, on the Anti-terrorism, Crime and Security Act 2001, 24 February 2004 (HL 38/HC 381), and its 5th report of 2004/5 on the Identity Cards Bill, 2.2.05 (HL 35/HC 283). JCAR also scrutinises subordinate legislation which raises human rights concerns; see its 22nd report of 2003/4, on the Nationality, Immigration and Asylum Act 2002 (Specification of Particularly Serious Crimes) Order 2004, 3 November 2004 (HL 190/HC 1212).

Who may bring proceedings

7.25 Sections 7–9 of the Human Rights Act were intended to lay down a remedial structure for giving effect to the Convention rights.[1] A victim of an unlawful act may bring proceedings for a breach or proposed breach of an ECHR right under section 7(1) of the Human Rights Act in an appropriate court or tribunal,[2] or may rely on the Convention right in any legal proceedings.[3] The intention behind the subsection appears to be to ensure that Convention rights may be relied on in any legal proceedings, whether brought by the public authority or not, and whether the public authority is a party or not.[4] Section 7(11) gives the minister power to enlarge the jurisdiction of a tribunal hearing a human rights case, both as regards the grounds on which it may allow an appeal and as to the remedies it may afford, but no such enlargement has been ordered in the immigration sphere.

[1] *Brown v Stott* [2001] 2 WLR 817, per Lord Hope at 847B.
[2] Human Rights Act 1998, s 7(1)(a).
[3] HRA 1998, s 7(1)(b). 'Legal proceedings' for the purposes of this sub-section includes proceedings brought by the authority or at its instigation (the most obvious example being a criminal case) and an appeal against the decision of a court or tribunal: s 7(6); *R v Kansal (No 2)* [2001] UKHL 62, [2002] 2 AC 69, [2001] 3 WLR 1562; *Pearce v Governing Body of*

Mayfield School; Macdonald v Advocate-General for Scotland [2003] UKHL 34, [2004] 1 All ER 339, [2003] IRLR 512. It must also include an appeal against the decision of the public authority, eg an immigration appeal.

[4] Where the proceedings were brought by or at the instigation of a public authority, ECHR rights may be relied on even if the unlawful act complained of happened before the Human Rights Act 1998 came into force: s 22(4). But an administrative decision to exclude or expel cannot be categorised as a 'proceeding', much less a 'legal proceeding', and so a decision to refuse entry before the Act came into force on 2 October 2000 could not be impugned after that date on Convention grounds under the Act: see *Pardeepan* [2000] INLR 447, IAT, decided under the provisions of the Commencement Order. The Secretary of State gave an undertaking in that case that human rights claims made after a pre-October 2000 refusal of asylum would attract a separate right of appeal on human rights grounds. In *R (on the application of Mahmood) v Secretary of State for the Home Department* [2001] 1 WLR 840 the Court of Appeal considered and rejected an argument that the Human Rights Act 1998 applied to a pre-October 2000 decision to remove because in substance the challenge was to its future implementation, cf *Chahal v United Kingdom* (1996) 23 EHRR 413; *Nasri v France* (1995) 21 EHRR 458.

7.26 Only a 'victim' of an unlawful act or proposed act may bring proceedings or rely on ECHR rights under section 7 of the Human Rights Act 1998,[1] and 'victim' is to have the same meaning as in the Strasbourg jurisprudence on Article 34 of the ECHR.[2] Article 34 allows applications from 'any person, non-governmental organisation or group of individuals claiming to be the victim of a violation', and includes all those directly affected or potentially affected by an act or omission.[3] But the definition of victim is considerably narrower than the 'sufficient interest' test for standing to bring judicial review proceedings, and precludes public interest organisations such as the Joint Council for the Welfare of Immigrants (JCWI) from challenging rules or policy as contrary to the Convention.[4] The action or decision complained of does not need to have caused prejudice to the person claiming victim status,[5] which means that an organisation of asylum seekers (rather than one assisting them) could bring a challenge to rules which might affect them.[6] The concern that the narrowness of the 'victim' test would inhibit the use of judicial review to raise issues of general importance involving Convention rights[7] has however been allayed to some extent by the courts' readiness to accept intervention by third parties, in particular by public interest organisations.[8] The need to wait or search for a 'victim' in order to remedy an incompatibility affecting thousands is clearly unsatisfactory, however, and there seems no good reason for the restrictive approach to survive in UK jurisprudence. The 'victim' provision has caused some difficulty in statutory appeals, because the wording of the immigration appeal statutes has been held unjustifiably to narrow the scope of the appeal to the sole issue of whether the appellant's Convention rights have been breached, while in Article 8 cases it is often those of UK-based family members which are affected.[9] On this, see **7.48** below. Family members of those to be removed do have standing for judicial review as 'victims' under section 7, however.[10]

[1] Human Rights Act 1998, s 7(1).
[2] HRA 1998, s 7(7).
[3] Under Article 43, those potentially at risk qualify as victims: *Norris v Ireland* (1988) 13 EHRR 186 (victim of legislation penalising homosexual activities even if risk of prosecution under legislation minimal). In *Open Door Counselling and Dublin Well Woman v Ireland* (1992) 15 EHRR 244, the class of victims was all women of childbearing age, since all could be adversely affected by a ban on the dissemination of information about abortion. In *Klass*

v Germany (1978) 2 EHRR 214, the class was all users or potential users of post and telecommunications, who could be adversely affected by secret surveillance. See also *Marckx v Belgium* (1979) 2 EHRR 330.

⁴ As in *R v Secretary of State for Social Security, ex p Joint Council for the Welfare of Immigrants* [1997] 1 WLR 275.

⁵ *Lüdi v Switzerland* (1992) 15 EHRR 173, para 34. See also *Open Door Counselling* fn 3 above.

⁶ In *Segi and Gestoras Pro-Amnistia v Fifteen States of the EU* (6422/02, 9916/02, 23.5.02) the court held that the EU Common Positions 2001/930/CFSP and 2001/931/CFSP which listed the applicant organisations as 'groups involved in terrorist acts' were not directly applicable and gave rise to no binding obligations on the part of Member States, so the situation did not confer on the associations the status of victims of a violation. Clearly, had the lists been adopted in domestic laws, the applicant organisations would have had victim status.

⁷ See Lord Lester, 583 HL Official Report (5th series) cols 823–837, 24 November 1997; Lord Slynn and Lord Lester, vol 585, cols 805–812, 5 February 1998.

⁸ For example, Liberty intervened in *A v Secretary of State for the Home Department; X v Secretary of State for the Home Department* [2004] UKHL 56, [2005] 2 WLR 87 (on whether derogation from art 5 ECHR and internment of foreign terrorist suspects breached arts 5 and 14), Liberty and the Joint Council for the Welfare of Immigrants intervened in *R (on the application of Q) v Secretary of State for the Home Department* [2003] EWCA Civ 364 [2003] 2 All ER 905 (on whether refusal of support under NIAA 2002, s 55 breached art 3 ECHR); the Terrence Higgins Trust in *N v Secretary of State for the Home Department* [2003] EWCA Civ 1369, [2005] UKHL 31 (on whether art 3 was engaged by expulsion of an AIDS sufferer to a country where lack of resources meant no or inadequate treatment). Previously, Amnesty International, the Medical Foundation, Redress, Human Rights Watch and organisations of relatives of the 'disappeared' were allowed to intervene, either orally or by written submissions, in *R v Bow Street Metropolitan Stipendiary Magistrate, ex p Pinochet Ugarte* [1998] 4 All ER 897; *(No 2)* [1999] 1 All ER 577. See also Lord Woolf's endorsement of the Justice/Public Law Project report on public interest interventions in *R v Chief Constable of North Wales Police, ex p AB* [1998] 3 WLR 57 at 66. Public interest organisations may be permitted to intervene in Strasbourg: see *HLR v France* (1997) 26 EHRR 29.

⁹ Nationality, Immigration and Asylum Act 2002, s 84(1)(c) and its predecessor, Immigration and Asylum Act 1999, s 65(1). In *Kehinde* (01TH2668) (starred), a starred Tribunal held that the appellate authority is concerned only with the human rights of the appellant, not of family members. The relationships in that case were found to be without real substance. In *R v Immigration Appeal Tribunal, ex p AC* [2003] EWHC 389 (Admin) [2003] INLR 507, a judicial review of a Tribunal's preliminary ruling that the art 8 rights of the (non-appellant) infant child of a deportee were irrelevant to her appeal, Jack J held (para 33) that the effect of the proposed interference on all those sharing the family life in question must be considered and taken into account, an approach consistent with ECHR jurisprudence (see *McCann v United Kingdom* (1995) 21 EHRR 97; see also Harris, O'Boyle and Warbrick *Law of the European Convention on Human Rights* (Butterworths, 1995), p 637. In art 8 cases on family life, in the Strasbourg jurisprudence, all members of a family are victims). He distinguished between the human rights of other family members, which were not the subject of an appeal, and the impact of deportation on others, which were relevant (para 37).

¹⁰ In *R (on the application of Holub) v Secretary of State for the Home Department* [2001] 1 WLR 1359, the parents of a child whose rights to education were alleged to be breached by proposed removal had standing under the Act.

7.27 Victim status is lost once the breach has been effectively remedied. But partial reparation does not necessarily prevent an applicant from retaining victim status to bring proceedings,¹ and the grant of a temporary or provisional status to someone who claims that removal would violate an ECHR right does not necessarily bring victim status to an end so as to preclude recourse to a court.²

¹ *Chevrol v France* (49646/99), 13 February 2002.

² *Ahmed v Austria* (1996) 24 EHRR 278: a stay on expulsion for a renewable period of a year, with a right of recourse to a court if renewal were refused did not prevent the applicant from arguing that his deportation, if it ever happened, would breach art 3. But cf *Vijayanathan and Pusparajah v France* (1992) 15 EHRR 62, where rejection of asylum claims did not give the

applicant the status of victim because no expulsion measure had been taken; see also *BB v France* (Application 30930/96) (7 September 1998), where the court struck out an art 3 claim over the expulsion of an AIDS sufferer after a compulsory residence order was made.

Just satisfaction

7.28 Article 41 of the Convention, repeating the substance of Article 50 of the original version, now provides:

> 'Just satisfaction
>
> If the court finds that there has been a violation of the Convention or the protocols thereto, and if the internal law of the High Contracting Party concerned allows only partial reparation to be made, the court shall, if necessary, afford just satisfaction to the injured party.'

Article 41 is not one of the Articles scheduled to the Human Rights Act 1998, but it is reflected in section 8 of the Human Rights Act 1998.[1] Under that section a court or tribunal, which finds a breach of the ECHR, is empowered to grant any relief or remedy or make any order within its powers which it considers just and appropriate.[2] However, no award of damages is to be made unless the court is satisfied, taking account of all the circumstances of the particular case, that an award of damages is necessary to afford just satisfaction to the person in whose favour it is made.[3] Often a finding of violation will, in itself, be just satisfaction for the violation.[4] This reflects the point that the focus of the Convention is on the protection of human rights and not the award of compensation.[5] Under section 8(4) of the 1998 Act the domestic court must take into account the principles applied by the European Court of Human Rights in relation to the award of compensation under Article 41 of the Convention. It is, therefore, to Strasbourg that British courts must look for guidance on the award of damages.[6] For the position regarding compensation for detention, see **7.73** below.

[1]   *R (on the application of Greenfield) v Secretary of State for the Home Department* [2005] UKHL 14, [2005] 2 All ER 240.

[2]   Human Rights Act 1998, s 8.

[3]   For the issue of damages under the HRA 1998 see Law Commision Paper No 266 of October 2000. Even the enforceable right to compensation under art 5(5) of the Convention does not mean that compensation must always be awarded; what the Article requires is a mechanism for the judicial determination of a compensation claim for unlawful detention: *Nikolova v Bulgaria* (1999) 31 EHRR 64. See *R (on the application of KB) v Mental Health Review Tribunal and Secretary of State for Health* [2003] EWHC 193 (Admin), [2004] QB 936; *R (on the application of H) v Secretary of State for the Home Department* [2003] UKHL 59, [2004] 2 AC 253.

[4]   See the exhaustive survey of ECtHR jurisprudence in *London Borough Council, R (on the application of N) v Secretary of State for the Home Department, R (on the application of M) v Secretary of State for the Home Department* [2003] EWCA Civ 1406, [2004] 1 All ER 833, in which no 'clear and constant' jurisprudence on the recovery of damages for human rights breaches other than detention was found. For the principles of just satisfaction in the ECHR see Grosz, Beatson and Duffy *Human Rights: The 1998 Act and the European Convention* (2000, Sweet & Maxwell), paras 6.19–21.

[5]   *Greenfield*, above, para 9; *Anufrijeva v Southwark London Borough Council* above, paras 52–53, where the Court of Appeal held that the remedy of damages generally plays a less prominent role in actions based on breaches of the Articles of the Convention, where the concern will usually be to bring the infringement to an end and any question of compensation will be of secondary, if any, importance. It is noteworthy that, in exercising its former jurisdiction under the original art 32, the Committee of Ministers did not, before 1987, award

compensation at all, even where a violation was found: D J Harris, M O'Boyle and C Warbrick
Law of the European Convention on Human Rights (1995, Butterworths), p 699.

6   *Greenfield*, above, para 6.

7.29 The ECtHR has upheld the rule of domestic law that in general no civil
action will lie against a public authority for failure to comply with statutory
duties.[1] In *Wainwright v Home Office*[2] the Court of Appeal sought to grapple
with a claim for damages for a strip-search conducted in breach of Article 8,
but Buxton LJ said it was wholly unclear what the rules of remoteness were in
a claim under the Human Rights Act, whether breaches were actionable *per se*
and what heads of damage and amounts were recoverable. The court sought
to answer some of these questions in *Anufrijeva*[3], in which it gave guidance on
claims for damages for breach of Article 8 rights arising out of maladministration, which it held would only infringe Article 8 where the consequences
were serious, that damages would be awarded on an equitable basis only
where necessary to provide just satisfaction, that awards would be modest and
that claimants should seek other routes, such as ADR or the Ombudsman,
before launching expensive proceedings in the Administrative Court. Awards
under the Act are intended to compensate, not punish, so exemplary damages
would rarely be appropriate.[4]

1   See eg *W v Home Office* [1997] Imm AR 302 (no damages for wrongful administrative acts
causing loss in the absence of negligence, misfeasance or false imprisonment). In *Osman v
United Kingdom* (1998) 29 EHRR 245 the court criticised the 'immunity from suit' of police
and other public authorities, but withdrew the criticism in *Z v United Kingdom*
(2001) 34 EHRR 97, 10 BHRC 384 and *Clunis v United Kingdom* (45049/98) (11 September
2001, unreported) after it was pointed out by the House of Lords that the rule was not a
procedural immunity but a substantive rule of law. See now *ID v Home Office* [2005] EWCA
Civ 38, [2005] All ER (D) 253 (Jan): **18.55** below.

2   [2001] EWCA Civ 2081, [2002] QB 1334.

3   *A London Borough Council, R (on the application of N) v Secretary of State for the Home
Department, R (on the application of M) v Secretary of State for the Home Department* [2003]
EWCA Civ 1406, [2004] 1 All ER 833 – see **7.28** fn 4 above. See also *R (on the application
of Bernard) v Enfield London Borough Council* [2002] EWHC 2282 (Admin), [2003] LGR
423 (award of £10,000 appropriate for 20 months' unsuitable accommodation provided in
breach of art 8 ECHR); *R (on the application of Gezer) v Secretary of State for the Home
Department* [2003] EWHC 860 (Admin), [2003] HLR 972 (dispersal to dangerous area where
family subjected to racial attacks did not attract liability on the facts but if it had, £5,000
would have been appropriate for exacerbation of psychiatric injuries) (the issue of damages
was not dealt with by the Court of Appeal at [2004] EWCA Civ 1730).

4   *Russell v Home Office* [2001] All ER (D) 38 (Mar), QBD.

7.30 As noted above, the Tribunal does not have the power to strike down
Immigration Rules or subordinate legislation,[1] but clearly it has power to
disapply a rule to give effect to fundamental rights in a particular case, deriving
from its duty to allow an appeal against an unlawful decision,[2] and may issue
directions for the grant of entry clearance or leave to remain even if the refusal
appealed against is in accordance with the rules. The section does not allow the
appellate authority to grant a remedy it has no statutory power to grant, such
as damages, although in appropriate cases it may recommend the award of an
ex gratia payment of compensation for violation of Convention rights (the
Secretary of State has a scheme for 'consolatory payments' for maladministration, including delays, causing injustice, set up at the recommendation of
the Parliamentary Ombudsman)[3] but an award of damages is within the

powers of the Administrative Court on judicial review.

1   *Pardeepan*, see **7.16** fn 6 above.
2   Nationality, Immigration and Asylum Act 2002, s 86(3).
3   Disclosed in a statement produced to the court in *R (on the application of Mambakasa) v Secretary of State for the Home Department* [2003] EWHC 319 (Admin), [2003] 18 LS Gaz R 35.

7.31 Section 11 of the Human Rights Act 1998, broader in its terms than Article 53 of the ECHR, ensures that a person's reliance on a Convention right does not restrict any other right or freedom conferred on that person by or under any law having effect in any part of the UK. It has been suggested that one possible interpretation of this section is that it allows reliance on rights conferred by other incorporated or partly incorporated Conventions, such as the Refugee Convention and the UN Convention against Torture, and on unincorporated rights from other Conventions, which have been ratified by the UK, on the basis that the Crown's ratification of, or entry into, a treaty might be capable of giving rise to a legitimate expectation upon which the public in general would be entitled to rely.[1] However, the proposition runs counter to older authority[2] and has been given short and scathing shrift in more recent judicial dicta. In *European Roma Rights Centre*,[3] Laws LJ rejected the idea of incorporation through legitimate expectation as a 'constitutional solecism'. 'We must not,' he warned, 'be seduced by humanitarian claims to a spurious acceptance of a false source of law'.[4] This categoric and persuasive rejection of incorporation by 'legitimate expectation does not undermine the reliance on rights recognised by unincorporated Conventions which the decision maker has purported to recognise and apply to the applicant's case,[5] on rights identified and recognised by the common law,[6] and unincorporated treaties and conventions used as an aid to the interpretation of ECHR rights and freedoms in accordance with Article 53 of the ECHR.[7]

1   See *R v Secretary of State for the Home Department, ex p Ahmed and Patel* [1998] INLR 570, CA where Lord Woolf MR accepted that the entering into a Treaty could give rise to a legitimate expectation that the Secretary of State would act in accordance with the Treaty obligations, and an applicant would be entitled to relief if the Secretary of State, without reason, acted inconsistently with those obligations (at 583G). The Treaty in question was, however, not the ECHR but the UN Convention on the Rights of the Child 1989, which contains express reservations relating to immigration control in respect of the principle that the welfare of the child should be the paramount consideration in court proceedings. He endorsed the judgment of the High Court of Australia in *Minister for Immigration and Ethnic Affairs v Teoh* (1995) 183 CLR 273 to that effect. This approach was followed by the Divisional Court in *R v Uxbridge Magistrates Court, ex p Adimi* [1999] INLR 490 in respect of obligations under the Refugee Convention 1951 not expressly incorporated into UK law by the Asylum and Immigration Appeals Act 1993.
2   In *Chundawadra v Immigration Appeal Tribunal* [1988] Imm AR 161 the Court of Appeal held that ratification of the European Convention on Human Rights created no justiciable legitimate expectation that the Convention's provisions would be complied with. In *R v Secretary of State for the Home Department, ex p Behluli* [1998] Imm AR 407, CA the court came to a like conclusion in relation to the Dublin Convention.
3   *European Roma Rights Centre v Immigration Officer at Prague Airport* [2003] EWCA Civ 666, [2003] INLR 374, at paras 98. The House of Lords confirmed that the Refugee Convention was incorporated into domestic law without resorting to legitimate expectation, at [2004] UKHL 55, [2005] 2 WLR 1.
4   *European Roma Rights Centre* (CA) above paras 99–101. Simon Brown LJ expressed his conclusion in *Adimi* (fn 1 above) as 'superficial and suspect' (para 51).
5   *R v Secretary of State for the Home Department, ex p Launder* [1997] 3 All ER 961.

6   Such as the 'law of common humanity' which prevents foreigners from starving, *R v Eastbourne Inhabitants* (1803) 4 East 103 cited by Simon Brown LJ in *R v Secretary of State for Social Security, ex p Joint Council for the Welfare of Immigrants* [1997] 1 WLR 275.
7   See **7.6** above.

Home Office policy

7.32 To to extent that the Immigration Rules themselves do not afford adequate protection to the human rights of those affected by them,[1] the Home Office gives effect to human rights considerations by a grant of discretionary leave (DL).[2] Formerly, humanitarian protection was granted, outside the Immigration Rules in circumstances where a person was unable to demonstrate a claim for asylum but who would face a serious risk to life or person arising from:

*   the death penalty;
*   unlawful killing;
*   torture, inhuman or degrading treatment or punishment.

Now, the rules make provision for the grant of humanitarian protection.[3] The circumstances in which humanitarian protection may be granted, renewed or revoked are considered in **CHAPTER 12** below. Discretionary leave may be granted to persons who would qualify for asylum or humanitarian protection but have been excluded,[4] and additionally to those with a good Article 3 claim on medical or severe humanitarian grounds, or a good Article 8 claim or where return would breach another ECHR protected right.[5]

1   See the analysis in *Huang v Secretary of State for the Home Department* [2005] EWCA Civ 105, (149) Sol Jo LB 297 at paras 56–7.
2   The criteria for granting, renewing and revoking discretionary leave are set out in the Asylum Policy Instruction 'Discretionary Leave' (undated) and are discussed in **CHAPTER 12**.
3   HSC 395, para 339C–339H.
4   Asylum Policy Instruction 'Discretionary Leave'.
5   As above.

ECHR PRINCIPLES

7.33 The ECHR is based on the obligation of contracting States to give effect to the core values of a democratic society: pluralism, openness and broadmindedness,[1] the rule of law,[2] freedom of expression,[3] and is designed to maintain and promote those values.[4] It is a living instrument which must be interpreted in the light of present-day conditions.[5] This approach, in contrast with that of the common law, decreases the role of precedent as the court re-determines issues in the light of changing conditions.[6] In *Selmouni v France*[7] the court observed that:

'certain acts which were classified in the past as "inhuman and degrading treatment" as opposed to "torture" could be classified differently in future . . . the increasingly high standard being required in the area of the protection of human rights and fundamental liberties correspondingly and inevitably requires greater firmness in assessing breaches of the fundamental values of democratic societies.'

The 'living instrument' or dynamic approach to Convention rights applies with force to areas affected by rapidly changing views of private morality,[8] and in particular to the rights of sexual minorities in the context of protection of private life.[9] It also applies to rights to fair trial, as the requirements of fairness have evolved considerably in the court's case law.[10] We shall consider later the relevance of Article 6 'fair trial' requirements to immigration and asylum cases.[11]

[1] *Handyside v United Kingdom* (1976) 1 EHRR 737, para 49.
[2] See Preamble; *Golder v United Kingdom* (1975) 1 EHRR 524, para 34; *Klass v Germany* (1978) 2 EHRR 214, para 55.
[3] *Handyside v United Kingdom* above.
[4] Preamble; *Kjeldsen, Busk Madsen and Pedersen v Denmark* (1976) 1 EHRR 711, para 53.
[5] *Tyrer v United Kingdom* (1978) 2 EHRR 1, para 31; *Marckx v Belgium* (1979) 2 EHRR 330; *Loizidou v Turkey* (1995) 20 EHRR 99, at para 71. This means that the content and scope of rights might be deepened and broadened over time, see eg *Sutherland v United Kingdom* [1998] EHRLR 117, but not that entirely new rights are created: *Johnston v Ireland* (1986) 9 EHRR 203; *Feldbrugge v Netherlands* (1986) 8 EHRR 425.
[6] See eg *Goodwin v United Kingdom* (28957/95) [2002] IRLR 664 where the court departed from its previous jurisprudence relating to the private lives of transsexuals and found that in the light of present-day conditions there were no longer any significant factors of public interest to weigh against the interest of a transsexual obtaining legal recognition of her gender re-assignment.
[7] (1999) 29 EHRR 403.
[8] *Marckx v Belgium* (1979) 2 EHRR 330.
[9] *Dudgeon v United Kingdom* (1981) 4 EHRR 149; *Smith and Grady v United Kingdom* (1999) 29 EHRR 493, para 97 (homosexuals); *Goodwin v United Kingdom* (fn 6 above).
[10] See *Borgers v Belgium* (1991) 15 EHRR 92, para 24.
[11] See **7.77** below.

7.34 The concept of State responsibility for the protection of fundamental rights is at the heart of the ECHR. States have negative and positive obligations under the Convention: not to interfere with core human rights, and to protect those within their jurisdiction from violations.[1] A positive obligation may also require action to give effect to rights, such as the provision of legal aid to enable access to a court to be effective,[2] or the promotion of family life through the admission of a family member to the country.[3] The positive obligation to protect against killing and torture extends to an effective investigation when individuals have been killed (whether by State agents or private individuals) or when they allege torture.[4] The state also has an obligation to appraise itself of conditions in a country to which it intends to remove individuals otherwise it cannot know, as it must, whether such removal would violate Article 3.[5] In accordance with the ideas expressed in the Preamble and Article 1, the Convention is intended to guarantee rights that are practical and effective, not theoretical and illusory.[6] Thus, rights must not be subject to conditions for their exercise which render them useless.[7]

[1] By, for example, not sending someone to a country where their human rights will be violated: *Soering v United Kingdom* (1989) 11 EHRR 439, or by preventing a death which was eminently foreseeable: *Osman v United Kingdom* (1998) 29 EHRR 245, para 115. See also *A v United Kingdom* (1998) 27 EHRR 611 (prevention of assaults on children by appropriate criminal penalties); *Plattform Ärzte für das Leben v Austria* (1988) 13 EHRR 204, para 32 (dealing with threats of violence by opponents on demonstrations to ensure freedom of assembly).
[2] *Airey v Ireland* (1979) 2 EHRR 305, para 24. See also *Marckx v Belgium* (1979) 2 EHRR 330: 'Fulfilment of a duty under the Convention on occasion necessitates some positive action on the part of the State; in such circumstances the State cannot simply remain passive.'
[3] *Sen v Netherlands* (2003) 36 EHRR 7. The distinction between positive and negative obligations, in the context of family reunion and separation, was held to be of lesser significance by Judge Martens in *Gul v Switzerland* (1996) 22 EHRR 93, see **7.84** below. For

discussion on the relative precision, intensity and scope of negative and positive obligations see *R (on the application of Pretty) v DPP* [2001] UKHL 61, [2002] 1 AC 800; *R (on the application of A) v Lord Saville of Newdigate (No 2)* [2001] EWCA Civ 2048, [2002] 1 WLR 129; *R (on the application of Ullah) v Special Adjudicator* [2004] UKHL 26, [2004] INLR 381 (para 34); see also *R (on the application of Q) v Secretary of State for the Home Department* [2003] EWCA Civ 364, [2004] QB 36. See also *R (on the application of Limbuela) v Secretary of State for the Home Department* [2004] EWCA Civ 540, [2004] QB 440), *R (on the application of Gezer) v Secretary of State for the Home Department* [2004] EWCA Civ 1730, see **7.60** below.

4 *Kaya v Turkey* (1998) 28 EHRR 1; *Gülec v Turkey* (1998) 28 EHRR 121, para 78; *Kaya (Mahmut) v Turkey* (28 March 2000, unreported), ECtHR, para 106–107.

5 *R (on the application of Nasseri) v Secretary of State for the Home Department* [2008] EWCA Civ 464, [2009] 1 All ER 116.

6 *Airey* above; *Golder v United Kingdom* (1975) 1 EHRR 524, paras 28–36.

7 *Winterwerp v Netherlands* (1979) 2 EHRR 387, para 60; *Artico v Italy* (1980) 3 EHRR 1, para 33; *Ashingdane v United Kingdom* (Series A no 93)(1985) 7 EHRR 528, para 57.

7.35 The ECHR allows the State a margin of appreciation in deciding how best to give effect to the rights enshrined in it pursuant to its obligations under Article 1 and Article 13 (provision of effective remedies for violation of the rights).[1] The margin of appreciation has been defined as the degree of latitude accorded to the national authorities and courts in recognition of the fact that 'by reason of their direct and continuous contact with the vital forces of their countries, the national authorities are in principle better placed than an international court to evaluate local needs and conditions'.[2] By conceding a margin of appreciation to each national system, the ECtHR has recognised that the Convention does not need to be applied uniformly by all States, but may vary in its application according to local needs and conditions.[3] The margin applies in relation to justification for derogation[4] from or interference with a Convention right,[5] the scope of positive obligations[6] and in assessing what constitutes objective and reasonable justification for discrimination under Article 14.[7] It reflects the principle of subsidiarity.[8] But the Court must give the final ruling on whether a restriction is reconcilable with protected rights, and its supervision is not limited merely to ascertaining whether a State exercised its discretion reasonably, carefully and in good faith.[9] The limits of the 'margin of appreciation' vary according to the importance of the rights at stake, the purpose pursued by the State and the degree to which opinions within a democratic society may reasonably vary. The limits are wider in cases involving national security,[10] planning policy,[11] tax,[12] social and economic policy,[13] and narrower in the fields of criminal law, free speech and private morality.[14] The technique is not available to the national courts, when they are considering Convention issues arising in their own countries.[15] However, as Lord Hope pointed out in *Kebilene*, something akin to the margin of appreciation may operate in some circumstances in the domestic jurisdiction, because the alleged breach of the Convention may involve an area of judgment within which the judiciary will defer to the considered opinion of the minister or departmental official.[16]

1 'The State has a choice of various means, but a law that fails to satisfy the requirement [protection of family life] violates Article 8': *Marckx v Belgium* above, para 31.

2 *Handyside v United Kingdom* (1976) 1 EHRR 737, paras 48–49; *Buckley v United Kingdom* (1996) 23 EHRR 101, paras 74–75.

3 *R v DPP, ex p Kebilene* [1999] 4 All ER 801 at 844B, per Lord Hope.

4 Ie, in deciding whether a 'public emergency threatens the life of the nation' under art 15: *Ireland v United Kingdom* (1978) 2 EHRR 25, para 207. See **7.42** below.

5 *Handyside* above fn 2.

6   *Abdulaziz, Cabales and Balkandali v United Kingdom* (1985) 7 EHRR 471, para 67; *Osman v United Kingdom* [1999] 1 FLR 193.
7   *Rasmussen v Denmark* (1984) 7 EHRR 371, para 40.
8   Clayton and Tomlinson *The Law of Human Rights* (2000, OUP); R Ryssdall 'The coming of age of the European Convention on Human Rights' [1996] EHRLR 18–27. See further Lord Mackenzie-Stuart 'Subsidiarity – a busted flush?' in Curtin and O'Keefe *Constitutional adjudication in European Community law and national law* (1992, Butterworths).
9   *Sunday Times v United Kingdom* (1979) 2 EHRR 245, para 59.
10 The concept was developed initially to ensure freedom of action for national governments in derogating from the ECHR under art 15: *Lawless v Ireland* 332/57 (1960) 1 EHRR 1, A61.501, 48–49, Commission. See also *Brannigan and McBride v United Kingdom* (1993) 17 EHRR 539.
11 *Buckley v United Kingdom* (1996) 23 EHRR 101, para 129.
12 *Gasus-Dosier-und Fördertechnik GmbH v Netherlands* (1995) 20 EHRR 403.
13 *Hatton v United Kingdom* (Grand Chamber) (2003) 37 EHRR 28.
14 *Smith and Grady v United Kingdom* (1999) 29 EHRR 493.
15 *R v Stratford Justices, ex p Imbert* [1999] 2 Cr App Rep 276 at 286, per Buxton LJ; *R (on the application of Mahmood) v Secretary of State for the Home Department* [2001] 1 WLR 840 at para 31, per Laws LJ.
16 See the majority of the HL in *A v Secretary of State for the Home Department; X v Secretary of State for the Home Department* [2004] UKHL 56, [2005] 2 WLR 87 (on the need for derogation) (7.42 below); *Mahmood* above at para 33; *R (on the application of Daly) v Secretary of State for the Home Department* [2001] UKHL 26, [2001] 2 AC 532. See also Lester and Pannick *Human Rights Law and Practice* (2nd edn, 2004, Butterworths) para 3.21; Tomlinson, fn 8 above, paras 6.32, 6.37, 6.82ff; Singh, Hunt and Demetriou 'Is there a role for the "Margin of Appreciation" in National Law After the Human Rights Act?' [1999] 1 EHRLR 15–22.

7.36 The margin of appreciation involves a recognition by the ECtHR that the ECHR need not be applied uniformly by all States, but may vary according to local needs and conditions. But this is limited in practice by another strand of the Strasbourg jurisprudence, namely the principle that terms such as 'civil rights and obligations',[1] 'criminal charges',[2] 'penalty',[3] 'property', 'law' and 'association'[4] have an autonomous meaning under the Convention[5] and cannot be redefined by States so as to avoid their obligations.[6]

1   *König v Germany* (1978) 2 EHRR 170, para 95. See 7.77 below.
2   *Engel v Netherlands* (1976) 1 EHRR 647, para 82; *Deweer v Belgium* (1980) 2 EHRR 439, para 46. But the fact that, for example, a breach of the peace is categorised as a criminal offence for the purposes of art 5 (*Steel v United Kingdom*) (1998) 28 EHRR 603) does not mean that the UK courts must so characterise it for the purposes of the Police and Criminal Evidence Act: *Williamson v Chief Constable of West Midlands* [2003] EWCA Civ 337, [2004] 1 WLR 14, para 26.
3   *Welch v United Kingdom* (1995) 20 EHRR 247, para 27; *Lauko v Slovakia* (1999) EHRLR 105.
4   *Chassagnou v France* (1999) 7 BHRC 151, 29 EHRR 615, para 100.
5   *Adolf v Austria* (1982) 4 EHRR 313, para 30.
6   This rationalisation of the concept was given in *Chassagnou* fn 4 above.

7.37 There are three kinds of rights protected under the ECHR:

(i)   Absolute rights, which apply without qualification and from which States may not derogate even in time of war or public emergency threatening the life of the nation.[1] These are the right to life,[2] the right not to be condemned to death or executed,[3] the right not to be subjected to torture or to inhuman or degrading treatment or punishment,[4] the right not to be held in slavery or servitude,[5] freedom of conscience[6] and the right not to be punished by retrospective laws.[7]

(ii)   Rights which are written in unqualified terms but which in practice are qualified and limited. They include rights to liberty and security[8] and to fair[9] and open trial,[10] of appeal in criminal matters,[11] to compensation for wrongful conviction,[12] not to be tried or punished twice[13] and the right to education.[14]

(iii)   qualified rights, which may be limited in strictly defined circumstances, and must thus be balanced against, and if necessary may give way to, other public interests. They include rights to family life,[15] to freedom to manifest religion or beliefs,[16] expression,[17] assembly and association,[18] to protection of property,[19] to freedom of movement,[20] the right of aliens to procedural safeguards relating to expulsion,[21] to equality between spouses[22] and the right to enjoy Convention rights and freedoms without discrimination.[23]

[1]   By art 15(1).
[2]   Article 2. But death may be inflicted in self-defence, to effect a lawful arrest or to prevent the escape of a lawfully detained person, or in quelling a riot, if it results from the use of force which is no more than absolutely necessary: see *McCann v United Kingdom* (1995) 21 EHRR 97; *Ogur v Turkey* (Application No 21594/93), 20 May 1999, para 78.
[3]   Protocol 6 (which prohibits the death penalty except in time of war) and Protocol 13 (in force 1 July 2003, 1 February 2004 in UK) (which prohibits the death penalty in all circumstances).
[4]   Article 3. See *Chahal v United Kingdom* (1996) 23 EHRR 413, para 79. So far as art 3 refers to violence, this does not include the lawful use of violence in self defence, making a lawful arrest, or used reasonably for the prevention of crime; per Laws LJ in *R (on the application of Tesema) v Secretary of State for the Home Department; R (on the application of Adam) v Secretary of State for the Home Department; R (on the application of Limbuela) v Secretary of State for the Home Department* [2004] EWCA Civ 540, [2004] QB 1440.
[5]   Article 4(1). See *Ould Barar v Sweden* (1999) 28 EHRR CD 213.
[6]   Article 9. Contrast freedom to *manifest* belief, which is qualified.
[7]   Article 7.
[8]   Article 5, which spells out situations where detention is lawful, and is derogable under art 15, but only a narrow interpretation of the exceptions is consistent with the aim and purpose of the provision, which is to ensure that no-one is arbitrarily deprived of his or her liberty: *Quinn v France* (1995) 21 EHRR 529. Article 1 of Protocol 4 (not ratified by the UK) prohibits imprisonment for debt.
[9]   The right to a fair trial is absolute, but the subsidiary rights contained in it (eg the presumption of innocence) are not: *Brown v Stott (Procurator Fiscal, Dunfermline)* [2001] 2 All ER 97, PC.
[10] Article 6, which provides for less than open justice when circumstances require and is derogable under art 15.
[11] Protocol 7, art 2.
[12] Protocol 7, art 3.
[13] Protocol 7, art 4.
[14] Protocol 1, art 2.
[15] Article 8.
[16] Article 9.
[17] Article 10.
[18] Article 11.
[19] Protocol 1, art 1(2).
[20] Protocol 4, art 2(3). This has not yet been ratified by the UK government.
[21] Protocol 7, art 1(2). This has not yet been ratified by the UK government.
[22] Protocol 7, art 5. This has not yet been ratified by the UK government.
[23] Article 14.

7.38   The right to respect for private and family life, home and correspondence, which is protected by ECHR, Article 8, permits interference which is in accordance with the law, and is necessary in a democratic society in the interests of national security, public safety, the economic well-being of the country, for the prevention of disorder or crime, for the protection of health or morals, or for the protection of the rights and freedoms of others.[1] Other qualified rights permit interference in similar, though not identical, terms. These interests are the legitimate aims which might justify interference with the protected rights. They are exhaustive, not illustrative,[2] and are to be construed strictly.[3] In *Miailhe v France*[4] the ECtHR stated that the exceptions in Article 8(2) are to be interpreted narrowly and the need for them in a given case must be convincingly established. The permitted restrictions must not be applied for any collateral purpose.[5]

[1]   Article 8(2).
[2]   *De Wilde, Ooms and Versyp v Belgium* (1971) 1 EHRR 373; *Golder v United Kingdom* (1975) 1 EHRR 524, para 44. In cases such as *Abdulaziz, Cabales and Balkandali v United Kingdom* (1985) 7 EHRR 471 and *D v United Kingdom* (1997) 24 EHRR 423, the ECtHR has referred to the right of States to control immigration. This undoubted international law right is however not one of the legitimate aims justifying interference with the qualified rights, but in the UK jurisprudence on Article 8 it is sometimes treated as if it were a free-standing 'legitimate aim' rather than a means of promoting one of the listed aims such as economic well-being or the prevention of disorder or crime. See the comment by Lord Phillips MR at para 44 of *R (on the application of Ullah) v Special Adjudicator* [2004] UKHL 26, [2004] INLR 381, not dealt with by the House of Lords when it reversed the Court of Appeal's decision.
[3]   *Sunday Times v United Kingdom* (1979) 2 EHRR 245; *Smith and Grady v United Kingdom* (1999) 29 EHRR 493 ('pandering to the prejudices of members of the population is not a legitimate aim').
[4]   (1993) 16 EHRR 332, para 38; see also *Funke v France* (1993) 16 EHRR 297, para 55; *Klass v Germany* (1978) 2 EHRR 214; *Lustig-Prean and Beckett v United Kingdom* (1999) 29 EHRR 548 (need for particularly serious reasons where restrictions concern a most intimate part of individuals' private life).
[5]   Article 18.

7.39   Once it is established that the interference has a legitimate aim as defined within the relevant Article of the ECHR, assessing permissible interference with or restriction of qualified rights requires consideration of legality and proportionality. An interference which is not in accordance with domestic law will breach the Convention regardless of whether it is justified.[1] But legality, or the requirement that interference with rights is 'in accordance with the law' or 'prescribed by law', does not merely refer back to whether interference is allowed by domestic law[2] but it also relates to 'the quality of the law, requiring it to be compatible with the rule of law, a concept inherent in all Articles of the Convention'.[3] To comply with the rule of law the law itself must be sufficiently accessible[4] and precise[5] to enable the citizen to regulate his or her conduct[6] and avoid all risk of arbitrariness.[7] To conform with the requirements of accessibility and precision, a law conferring discretion must indicate its scope and set out the way discretion is to be exercised.[8] The policy whereby discretionary leave could be withheld from a person who otherwise qualified on Article 8 grounds if Ministers 'decide in view of all the circumstances of the case that it is inappropriate to grant any leave', conferred a discretion that was so broad and open ended that it was not 'in accordance with the law' within the meaning of Article 8(2).[9] For an interference with a protected right to be 'in accordance with the law' there would also have to be adequate legal safeguards against abuse, including scrutiny of the measure by an independent and impartial body competent to review all the relevant questions of fact and law and to determine its lawfulness, even in the context of national security.[10]

[1]   See eg *Poltoratskiy v Ukraine* (38812/97) 29 April 2003; *GK v Poland* (Application 38816/97) (20 January 2004).

2   Including subordinate legislation: *Barthold v Germany* (1985) 7 EHRR 383.

3   *Dougoz v Greece* (2002) 34 EHRR 61, para 55.

4   *Malone v United Kingdom* (1984) 7 EHRR 14; *Halford v United Kingdom* (1997) 24 EHRR
    523. See also *Zamir v United Kingdom* (1983) 40 DR 42, paras 90–91; *Steel v United
    Kingdom* (1998) 28 EHRR 603. For a discussion of the effect of late promulgation of an Act
    of Parliament on the legality of action taken under it see *R (on the application of ZL and VL)
    v Secretary of State for the Home Department* [2003] EWCA Civ 25, [2003] Imm AR 330,
    [2003] INLR 224, sub nom *R (on the application of L) v Secretary of State for the Home
    Department* [2003] All ER 1062, where the Secretary of State certified claims as clearly
    unfounded, depriving asylum seekers of an in-country right of appeal, before the 2002 Act
    containing the certification provisions was published. Home Office internal policy guidelines
    are not 'accessible' unless they are published: *Malone v United Kingdom*. Since 2 October
    2000 (the date the Human Rights Act 1998 came into force), many Home Office discretionary
    policies have been incorporated into the Immigration Rules (eg on unmarried partners, victims
    of domestic violence and domestic workers, while some remaining discretionary policies are
    posted on the Home Office website. But not all: in *R (on the application of Salih) v Secretary
    of State for the Home Department* [2003] EWHC 2273 (Admin), (2003) Times, 13 October
    the Secretary of State's failure to make known to those eligible his policy of providing 'hard
    cases' support to failed asylum seekers was held unlawful having regard to the 'fundamental
    requisite of the rule of law' that the law should be made known. See also *R (on the application
    of Amirthanathan) v Secretary of State for the Home Department* [2003] EWCA Civ 1768,
    [2004] INLR 139, sub nom *Nadarajah v Secretary of State for the Home Department*
    (detention under unpublished policy unlawful).

5   *Amuur v France* (1996) 22 EHRR 533, para 50; *Camenzind v Switzerland* (1997) 28 EHRR
    458, para 45; *Hashman and Harrup v United Kingdom* [2000] Crim LR 185 (bind over to 'be
    of good behaviour' not sufficiently precise).

6   *Sunday Times v United Kingdom* (1979) 2 EHRR 245, para 49. Unwritten law may fulfil these
    criteria: para 47.

7   *Dougoz v Greece* (2002) 34 EHRR 61. Expelling a person from the country whilst he had an
    appeal pending against the expulsion decision when the applicable national law provided that
    he was entitled to reside in the country whilst the appeal was pending was 'not in accordance
    with the law' and therefore breached his right to respect for family life; *Estrikh v Latvia* (2007)
    App No 73819/01.

8   *Silver v United Kingdom* (1983) 5 EHRR 347. See also *Huvig v France* (1990) 12 EHRR 528
    (what is required is detailed rules setting out when intrusive measures may be carried out);
    Leander v Sweden (1987) 9 EHRR 433.

9   *R (on the application of GG) v Secretary of State for the Home Department* [2006] EWHC
    1111 (Admin), (2006) Times, 14 June, approved in *S v Secretary of State for the Home
    Department* [2006] EWCA Civ 1157, applying the principles set out by Lord Bingham in *R
    (on the application of Gillan) v Metropolitan Police Comr* [2006] UKHL 12, [2006] 2 AC 307,
    [2006] 2 WLR 537 as to the meaning of 'prescribed by law' (in Articles 5, 10 and 11 of
    the Convention) and 'in accordance with the law' in Article 8(2).

10 *Lupsa v Romania (Application 10337/04)* [2006] 2 FCR 685, [2006] ECHR 10337/04,
    EctHR, a case concerning deportation on national security grounds where the Court said 'the
    existence of adequate and effective safeguards against abuse, including in particular proce-
    dures for effective scrutiny by the courts is all the more important since a system of secret
    surveillance designed to protect national security entails the risk of undermining or even
    destroying democracy on the ground of defending it'. See also *R (on the application of Purdy)
    v DPP* [2009] UKHL 45, [2010] AC 345, [2009] 4 All ER 1147, [2009] UKHL 45, per Lord
    Hope, para 40.

7.40 The balance between the protection of individual rights and the interests
of the wider community is at the heart of the ECHR,[1] and a fair balance is
achieved when interference with the individual's rights is strictly proportionate
to the legitimate aim pursued in restricting it.[2] As Sedley LJ put it succinctly in
B:[3]

> 'A measure which interferes with a human right must not only be authorised by law
> but must correspond to a pressing social need and go no further than is strictly
> necessary in a pluralistic society to achieve its permitted purpose; or, more shortly,
> must be appropriate and necessary to its legitimate aim.'[4]

The requirement that a restriction on a fundamental right be 'necessary' is strict; 'necessary' is not so flexible a term as 'useful' or 'desirable',[5] and the phrase 'necessary in a democratic society' refers to a pluralistic, tolerant and broadminded society.[6] In *Sunday Times Ltd v United Kingdom (No 2)*[7] the ECtHR stated:

'The court's task, in exercising its supervisory jurisdiction, is not to take the place of the competent national authorities but rather to review under Article 10 the decision they delivered pursuant to their powers of appreciation. This does not mean that the supervision is limited to ascertaining whether the respondent exercised its jurisdiction reasonably and carefully and in good faith; what the court has to do is to look at the interference complained of in the light of the case as a whole and determine whether it was "proportionate to the legitimate aim pursued" and whether the reasons adduced by the national authorities to justify it are "relevant and sufficient".'

[1] *Sporrong and Lönnroth v Sweden* (1982) 5 EHRR 35, para 52.
[2] See **7.20**, above and *Handyside v United Kingdom* (1976) 1 EHRR 737, para 49. For the principle of proportionality see Clayton and Tomlinson (at **7.21** fn 6 above), para 6.40ff; Lester and Pannick *Human Rights Law and Practice* (1999, Butterworths), para 3.10; Grosz, Beatson and Duffy *Human Rights* (2000, Sweet & Maxwell), pp 112–114; Starmer *European Human Rights Law*, pp 169–180; Wadham and Mountfield (1999, Blackstone) *The Human Rights Act* 1998, pp 13–16; De Smith, Woolf and Jowell *Judicial Review of Administrative Action* (5th edn, 1995, Sweet & Maxwell), pp 593–606.
[3] *B v Secretary of State for the Home Department* [2000] Imm AR 478.
[4] Para 17. It was accepted by both parties that the test of proportionality under the ECHR was the same as that in EU law: para 7.
[5] *Chassagnou v France* (1999) 7 BHRC 151.
[6] *Handyside* fn 2 above; *Dudgeon v United Kingdom* (1981) 4 EHRR 149 (criminalisation of homosexual acts disproportionate to aim of protection of morals).
[7] (1991) 14 EHRR 229, para 50. See further *Hertel v Switzerland* (1998) 28 EHRR 534, para 46; *Grigoriades v Greece* (1997) 27 EHRR 464, para 44.

7.41 Factors relevant to assessing the proportionality of a restriction have been held to include the extent of the interference[1] and whether there was a less restrictive alternative;[2] and whether there are fair procedures[3] and safeguards against abuse.[4] The absence of relevant and sufficient reasons for the restriction[5] is likely to result in a finding that the restriction was not necessary or was disproportionate. The principle of proportionality is not limited to the rights in respect of which interference is expressly defined, but also applies, for example, to detention under Article 5,[6] to Article 6 rights,[7] to the prohibition of discrimination in the enjoyment of ECHR rights under Article 14[8] and to the scope of positive obligations under the Convention.[9]

[1] Restrictions which impair the 'very essence' of the right in question will be disproportionate: *F v Switzerland* (1987) 10 EHRR 411, para 40; *Rees v United Kingdom* (1986) 9 EHRR 56, para 50.
[2] *Informationsverein Lentia v Austria* (1993) 17 EHRR 93, para 40; *Campbell v United Kingdom* (1992) 15 EHRR 137. The question of a 'less restrictive alternative' (proportionality as to means) was held irrelevant to cases involving expulsion in *R (on the application of Samaroo) v Secretary of State for the Home Department* [2001] EWCA Civ 1139, [2001] UKHRR 1150, [2002] INLR 55 and *R (on the application of Sezek) v Secretary of State for the Home Department* [2001] EWCA Civ 795, [2002] 1 WLR 348, where the issue is to expel or not.
[3] *W v United Kingdom* (1987) 10 EHRR 29, para 62; *Buckley v United Kingdom* (1996) 23 EHRR 101, para 76.
[4] *Klass v Germany* (1978) 2 EHRR 214, paras 55, 59; *Camenzind v Switzerland* (1997) 28 EHRR 458, para 45.

⁵   *Observer and Guardian v United Kingdom* (1991) 14 EHRR 153, para 59; *Vogt v Germany* (1996) 21 EHRR 205, para 52.
⁶   See **7.37** , fn 8 above.
⁷   Thus the right of access to a court may be limited, but limitation will not be compatible with art 6(1) ECHR unless it pursues a legitimate aim and there is a reasonable relationship of proportionality between the means employed and the aim sought to be achieved: *Ashingdane v United Kingdom* (1985) 7 EHRR 528, para 57.
⁸   'Very weighty reasons would have to be advanced before a difference in treatment on grounds of sex could be considered compatible with the Convention': *Abdulaziz, Cabales and Balkandali v United Kingdom* (1985) 7 EHRR 471, para 78. See **7.123** below.
⁹   See *Powell and Rayner v United Kingdom* (1990) 12 EHRR 355.

Derogation

7.42 Article 15 of the Convention enables Contracting States to derogate from their obligations under the Convention in time of war or other public emergency threatening the life of the nation, to the extent strictly required by the exigencies of the situation. Derogation is never possible from Article 2 (except in relation to deaths resulting from lawful acts of war), or from Articles 3, 4(1) or 7.[1] A Contracting State is obliged to keep the Secretary-General of the Council of Europe fully informed of the measures it has taken in derogation of any of the Convention rights, and the reasons.[2] The cases all involve derogation from rights to liberty (Article 5), and the court has made it clear that, while it accords a significant margin of appreciation to Contracting States, it nevertheless supervises detention very closely to see whether (a) there is an emergency threatening the life of the nation[3] and (b) the derogation is strictly required by the exigencies of the situation.[4]

¹   Article 15(2). There can be no derogation from the prohibition on the death penalty: see Protocol 6 art 3; Protocol 13 art 2.
²   Article 15(3).
³   *A v Secretary of State for the Home Department; X v Secretary of State for the Home Department* [2004] UKHL 56, [2005] 2 WLR 87, where seven Law Lords supported the derogation in principle and one was against (*for:* Lord Bingham at para 29; Lord Hope at para 119 (with reservations); Lord Scott at para 154 (giving the Secretary of State the benefit of very great doubts); Lord Rodger at para 165; Lord Walker at para 208; Lady Hale at p 226; Lord Carswell at para 240; *against:* Lord Hoffmann at para 96. Lord Nicholls said nothing on this, but agreed in general terms with Lords Bingham, Hope and Rodgers). In *Lawless v Ireland (No 3)* (1961) 1 EHRR 15, a case concerned with very a low level of IRA terrorist activity in Ireland and Northern Ireland between 1954 and 1957, the case for derogation was made out. In the *Greek Case* (1969) 12 YB 186 the Government of Greece failed to persuade the Commission that there had been a public emergency threatening the life of the nation. In *Ireland v United Kingdom* (1978) 2 EHRR 25 the parties were agreed that the Article 15 test was satisfied. In *Brannigan and McBride v United Kingdom* (1993) 17 EHRR 539, an IRA case, the court again accepted that there had been a qualifying emergency. In *Aksoy v Turkey* (1996) 23 EHRR 553 the applicant did not contest that a qualifying public emergency existed. In *Marshall v United Kingdom* (10 July 2001, Appn No 41571/98) the applicant relied on the improved security situation in Northern Ireland, but his application was rejected as inadmissible, although the court acknowledged the need to 'address with special vigilance the fact that almost nine years separate the prolonged administrative detention of the applicants Brannigan and McBride from that of the applicant in the case before it'.
⁴   See (in the domestic court) *A v Secretary of State for the Home Department; X v Secretary of State for the Home Department* [2004] UKHL 56, [2005] 2 WLR 87; *Brannigan and McBride v United Kingdom* (1993) 17 EHRR 539; *Aksoy v Turkey* (1996) 23 EHRR 553; *Sen v Turkey* (41478/98) (17 June 2003, unreported), para 25.

Territoriality

7.43 Although human rights issues might arise through detention of asylum seekers and denial of support, for the most part it is the act of expulsion or exclusion which engages human rights in the field of immigration. Both expulsions and exclusions raise the question to what extent the Convention (and the Human Rights Act) protects people from feared human rights violations in their own country. Article 1 ECHR requires Contracting States to 'secure the Convention rights and freedoms to everyone within their juris-diction'.[1] Normally jurisdiction is co-extensive with territory. But there are exceptions. This was made clear in *Bankovic v Belgium* (bombing of Belgrade by NATO held not to engage Convention) where the court accepted that 'from the standpoint of public international law, the jurisdictional competence of a State is primarily territorial',[2] and that acts of the contracting States performed, or producing effects, outside their territories would only in exceptional cases constitute an exercise of jurisdiction by them within the meaning of Article 1 of the Convention.[3] The first exception occurs when the respondent State gains effective control of the relevant territory and its inhabitants abroad as a consequence of military occupation or through the consent, invitation or acquiescence of the government of that territory, and then exercises all or some of the public powers normally to be exercised by that government.[4] Secondly, there are cases involving the activities of its diplomatic or consular agents abroad and on board craft and vessels registered in, or flying the flag of, that State. In these specific situations, customary inter-national law and treaty provisions have recognised the extra-territorial exercise of jurisdiction by the relevant State.[5] Thirdly, there are the cases, familiar to immigration practitioners, where as a result of expulsion or extradition someone is being sent to a country where they face the risk of a human rights violation. This was first made clear by the European Court in *Soering v United Kingdom*,[6] an extradition case, and was then extended to deportation and removal cases.[7] All these cases were Article 3 cases and the question then arose whether the Convention's application was limited to Article 3 or applied to other Articles, where the alleged violations would take place in the receiving country. In two consecutive appeals in *Ullah*[8] and *Razgar*[9] the House of Lords held that, in principle, all the Convention Articles could be engaged by expulsion. They distinguished between domestic cases, where a State is said to have acted within its own territory in a way which infringes the enjoyment of a Convention right within that territory (for example, expulsion which separates someone from family members living in the UK), and foreign cases, in which it is claimed that the conduct of the State in removing a person from its territory (whether by expulsion or extradition) to another territory will lead to a violation of the person's Convention rights in that other territory (for example, through detention, an unfair trial, inability to practice religion, or conditions damaging mental health).[10] The House held that the Strasbourg case law did not preclude reliance on Articles other than Article 3 in a foreign case, but, where the case involved qualified rights, such as those under Articles 8 and 9, it will be necessary to show a real risk of a flagrant denial or gross violation, where the very essence of the right will be completely denied or nullified in the destination country. Various different expressions have been used to describe the test: 'flagrant denial', 'gross violation', 'flagrant violation of the very essence of the right', 'flagrant, gross or fundamental breach', 'gross invasion of [the person's] most fundamental human rights', 'particularly flagrant breaches'. However, all describe the same test which requires 'a flagrant breach of the relevant right, such as will completely deny or nullify the right in the destination country'.[11] The test does not require that every last vestige of the right must be eliminated.[12] The majority in *Razgar* could not rule out such a flagrant breach in relation to the foreseeable consequences to health of removal of asylum claimants to Germany. In *EM (Lebanon)* the House of Lords held that the destruction of the family life between a mother and her child that would follow their removal to Lebanon would be a flagrant violation of their rights to respect for family life, notwithstanding that there might be continuing contact between mother and child.[13] The Tribunal has held that a person outside the territory of the UK cannot normally rely upon Convention rights to claim an entitlement to entry clearance and it is only where the person enjoys family life with someone within the UK that issues under Article 8 might arise.[14] In such circumstances, so the Tribunal says, the only human rights involved are those of the person in the UK and the rights of that person, not being an appellant, cannot be considered by the tribunal; they are enforceable by means of judicial review.[15] We think that that the Tribunal was wrong not to treat decisions on entry clearance applications as one of the instances of extra-territorial jurisdiction acknowledged in *Bankovic*, as being 'cases involving the activities of [the state's] diplomatic or consular agents abroad', bearing in mind that the issuing of visas is plainly an activity of consular agents abroad.[16] We also think that the Tribunal was wrong to regard breach of a non-appellant's human rights as not being justiciable in an appeal to the tribunal.

[1]   Article 1 is not one of the Convention rights set out in Sch 1 to the Human Rights Act 1998; the passage of the Act itself was to give effect to it, and the courts treat it as such.

[2]   *Bankovic v Belgium* (2001) 11 BHRC 435, para 59.

[3]   *Bankovic* above, para 67. In *R (on the application of Abbasi) v Secretary of State for Foreign and Commonwealth Affairs* [2002] EWCA Civ 1598, (2002) Times, 8 November, para 71, 106, where the claimant, held in a 'legal black hole' in Guantánamo Bay, sought a declaration that the British authorities had a duty to assist him diplomatically by making representations to US officials, the court held that nothing in the Convention imposed an enforceable duty to protect citizens from inhuman treatment abroad: it was 'a considerable extension' of the territoriality principle to postulate that the Convention requires a State to take positive action to prevent or mitigate the effects of violations of human rights that take place outside the jurisdiction and for which the State has no responsibility. In *R (on the application of Suresh) v Secretary of State for the Home Department* [2001] EWHC 1028 (Admin), [2002] Imm AR 345, an attempt to seek entry of a leading LTTE member to the UK to prevent his expulsion from Canada to Sri Lanka, where he feared torture, was dismissed on the basis there was no duty on the Secretary of State to prevent a breach of art 3 by another country, either on the basis of the applicant's entry clearance application or because he had family members in the UK.

[4]   *Bankovic v Belgium* above, para 71. See *Loizidou v Turkey* (1995) 20 EHRR 99 (Turkish occupation of northern Cyprus).

[5]   *Bankovic v Belgium* above, para 73. See *Xhavara v Italy and Albania* (39473/98, 11 January 2001 (interception by Italian naval vessel of ship carrying refugees); *Öcalan v Turkey* (46221/99) (2003) 15 BHRC 297 (seizure of suspect abroad). Lord Bingham expressed the greatest doubt whether this included the actions of British immigration officers in Prague in *European Roma Rights Centre v Immigration Officer at Prague Airport (United Nations High Comr for Refugees Intervening)* [2004] UKHL 55, [2005] 1 All ER 527 at para 21. But see *R (on the application of B) v Secretary of State for the Foreign and Commonwealth Affairs* [2004] EWCA Civ 1344, [2005] 2 WLR 618, para 66. And consider the Haitians, intercepted at sea when trying to reach the coast of the US, whose plight was considered in *Sale V, Acting Comr, Immigration and Naturalisation Service v Haitian Centers Council Inc* 509 US 155 (1993), p 183, fn 40. The United States authorities' treatment of them was understandably held by the Inter-American Commission of Human Rights (Report No 51/96, 13 March 1997, para 171) to breach their right to life, liberty and security of their persons as

well as the right to asylum protected by Article XXVII of the American Declaration of the Rights and Duties of Man (para 163. The Commission also found the United States to be in breach of art 33(1) of the Refugee Convention: paras 156–158, a view shared by Blackmun J in his dissent in *Sale*).

6   *Soering v United Kingdom* (1989) 11 EHRR 439.

7   *Cruz Varas v Sweden* (1991) 14 EHRR 1; *Vilvarajah v United Kingdom* (1991) 14 EHRR 248; *Chahal v United Kingdom* (1996) 23 EHRR 413; *D v United Kingdom* (1997) 24 EHRR 423; *HLR v France* (1997) 26 EHRR 29; *Gonzalez v Spain* (Application No 43544/98, 29 June 1999, unreported); *Dehwari v Netherlands* (2000) 29 EHRR CD 74; and *Hilal v United Kingdom* (2001) 33 EHRR 31.

8   *R (on the application of Ullah) v Special Adjudicator* [2004] UKHL 26, [2004] INLR 381.

9   *R (on the application of Razgar) v Secretary of State for the Home Department* [2004] UKHL 27, [2004] 2 AC 368.

10 *Ullah* at paras 7 and 9.

11 *EM (Lebanon) v Secretary of State for the Home Department* [2008] UKHL 64, [2009] 1 All ER 559 in which the divorced appellant, on return to Lebanon would lose custody of her young child for no reason other than that Sharia law as applied automatically awarded custody to the father following a divorce. However, she had not shown that she would not be accorded some rights of access to the child.

12 Lord Carswell, para 53. The House of Lords held that there would be a flagrant breach, even though it had not been shown that all contact between mother and child would be eliminated. At para 41 Lord Bingham said: 'In no meaningful sense could occasional supervised visits by the [mother] to [her child] at a place other than her home, even if ordered (and there was no guarantee that they would be ordered) be described as family life'.

13 *EM (Lebanon) v Secretary of State for the Home Department* [2008] UKHL 64, [2009] 1 All ER 559.

14 *H (Somalia)* [2004] UKIAT 00027; and *Moon (USA)* [2005] UKIAT 00112. In *Tuquabo-Tekle v Netherlands* (2006) App No 60665/00 the respondent government raised the argument that the applicant for entry clearance did not fall within the jurisdiction of the State within the meaning of Article 1 of the ECHR; for procedural reasons the court declined to entertain the issue.

15 *Moon (USA)* – following the line of cases saying that only the appellants' human rights and not the impact of the decision on non-appellants' human rights may be considered on an appeal to the Asylum and Immigration Tribunal. On this issue, see 7.118 below.

16 See the definition of 'consular functions' in Article 5 of the Vienna Convention on Consular Relations, 1963 which says 'Consular functions consist in: . . . (d) issuing . . . visas or appropriate documents to persons wishing to travel to the sending state'.

THE ECHR RIGHTS

7.44 The main ECHR rights of potential relevance in immigration law are: the right to life (Article 2) and the prohibition of the death penalty (Protocol 6, Article 1 and Protocol 13); the prohibition of torture and inhuman or degrading treatment or punishment (Article 3); the prohibition of slavery and forced labour (Article 4); the right to liberty and security (Article 5); the right of access to courts and due process (Article 6); rights to the protection of private and family life (Article 8) and the prohibition of discrimination in the enjoyment of these rights (Article 14). Other rights of some relevance, particularly in asylum appeals, are freedom of conscience, expression and assembly (Articles 9–11).[1] The right to marry and found a family (Article 12) has recently assumed some significance, although it is generally of less relevance than might be supposed. For reasons of space we refer here only to the main Articles of relevance to immigration and asylum law.[2]

1   See 12.46 below for an exposition of the common human rights foundation of the Refugee and Human Rights Conventions.

2   For full coverage of the ECHR see Clayton and Tomlinson *The Law of Human Rights* (2000, OUP); Grosz, Beatson and Duffy *Human Rights: the 1998 Act and the European Convention*

(2000, Sweet & Maxwell); Lester, Pannick and Herberg *Human Rights Law and Practice* (3rd edn, 2009, LexisNexis); Starmer *European Human Rights Law* (1999, LAG). For more detailed coverage of ECHR rights in the immigration context see Blake and Husai *Immigration, asylum and human rights* (2003, OUP).

Right to life

7.45 Article 2 of the ECHR states that:

'1   Everyone's right to life shall be protected by law. No one shall be deprived of his life intentionally save in the execution of a sentence of a court following his conviction of a crime for which this penalty is provided by law.

2   Deprivation of life shall not be regarded as inflicted in contravention of this Article when it results from the use of force which is no more than absolutely necessary:

    (a)   in defence of any person from unlawful violence;

    (b)   in order to effect a lawful arrest or to prevent the escape of a person lawfully detained;

    (c)   in action lawfully taken for the purpose of quelling a riot or insurrection.'

Article 1 of Protocol 13 states that:

'The death penalty shall be abolished. No one shall be condemned to such penalty or executed.'

The Protocol was ratified by the UK and subsequently came into force on 1 February 2004. On 22 June 2004, it replaced Protocol 6, which provided that the death penalty could be used in time of war, in the Schedule of Convention Rights in the Human Rights Act 1998.

7.46 Article 2 of the ECHR is comprised of two substantive duties: a negative obligation not to take life except in clearly defined and strictly limited circumstances; and a positive obligation to take appropriate measures to protect life.[1] Thus, Article 2:

'extends beyond its primary duty to secure the right to life by putting in place effective criminal law provisions to deter the commission of offences against the person backed up by law-enforcement machinery for the prevention, suppression and sanctioning of breaches of such provisions . . . Article 2 may well also imply in certain well-defined circumstances a positive obligation on the authorities to take preventive operational measures to protect an individual whose life is at risk from the criminal acts of another individual.'[2]

As regards the negative duty not to take life, the use of lethal force by agents of the State must be 'absolutely necessary' (Article 2(2)), which is a 'stricter and more compelling test of necessity' than that applicable when determining whether State action is 'necessary in a democratic society' under paragraph 2 of Articles 8 to 11.[3] The positive duty obliges States 'to establish a framework of laws, precautions, procedures and means of enforcement which will, to the greatest extent reasonably practicable, protect life.'[4] It includes an operational duty to protect individuals from risks which are or ought to be known. Thus, it can apply where a person is in custody and the risk derives from self-harm[5] or to acts or omissions in the field of healthcare, in particular where life is put at risk by the denial of healthcare that is available to the general population.[6]

The positive duty also encompasses an obligation to ensure that there exists a judicial system that can effectively investigate alleged breaches of Article 2, as far as reasonably practicable prevent similar breaches occurring in the future and, in particular, 'secure the accountability of agents of the State for their use of lethal force'.[7] This investigative obligation extends to alleged breaches of both the negative and positive duties.[8]

[1] *Pretty v United Kingdom* (2002) 35 EHRR 1, para 39: 'The consistent emphasis in all the cases before the court has been the obligation of the State to protect life'. As Lord Bingham said in *R (on the application of Amin) v Secretary of State for the Home Department* [2003] UKHL 51, [2004] 1 AC 653, para 30: 'A profound respect for the sanctity of human life underpins . . . the jurisprudence under Articles 1 and 2 of the Convention.'

[2] *Osman v United Kingdom* (1998) 29 EHRR 245, para 115. But, see para 116: 'bearing in mind the difficulties involved in policing modern societies, the unpredictability of human conduct and the operational choices which must be made in terms of priorities and resources, such an obligation must be interpreted in a way which does not impose an impossible or disproportionate burden on the authorities'. Thus, Article 2 would be breached only if 'the authorities do not do all that could be reasonably expected of them to avoid a real and immediate risk to life of which they have or ought to have knowledge'.

[3] *Ogur v Turkey* (1999) 31 EHRR 912, para 77. See also *McCann v United Kingdom* (1995) 21 EHRR 97.

[4] *R (on the application of Middleton) v West Somerset Coroner* [2004] UKHL 10, [2004] 2 AC 182, para 2.

[5] *Keenan v United Kingdom* (2001) 33 EHRR 38, paras 88–92. In the domestic context, see *IM (Nigeria) v Secretary of State for the Home Department* [2013] EWCA Civ 1561, [2014] 1 WLR 1870 (the extent of the art 2 positive obligation in the context of an immigration detainee who was on hunger strike).

[6] *Nitecki v Poland* (65653/01) 21 March 2002. Thus, legislation denying life-saving treatment to certain groups such as asylum seekers would be incompatible with art 2. However, in removal cases, there is usually also an art 3 claim which the court prefers to deal with first as it covers much the same ground; see *D v United Kingdom* (1997) 24 EHRR 423. In the domestic context, art 2 was held to be engaged where an HIV positive mother on asylum support was provided with insufficient money to buy formula milk, giving rise to a real risk that she would breast-feed her child and transmit the virus to her: *R (on the application of T) v Secretary of State for Health, Secretary of State for the Home Department* [2002] EWHC 1887 (Admin), para 87.

[7] *Kaya v Turkey* (1998) 28 EHRR 1, para 87; *Güleç v Turkey* (1998) 28 EHRR 121, para 78; *Ciechonska v Poland* (19776/04) 14 June 2011, paras 71, 77. In the domestic context, see *R (on the application of Middleton) v HM Coroner for West Somerset* (fn 4 above).

[8] In *R (on the application of Amin) v Secretary of State for the Home Department* [2003] UKHL 51, [2004] 1 AC 653, para 42 (on the investigative duty where a young offender in detention was killed by a racist cellmate) the House of Lords said that the ECtHR jurisprudence drew no clear dividing line (in terms of the investigate duty) between cases where an agent of the State kills, and those where deficiencies in the system are such that a killing occurs; the guarantees of a public investigation and next-of-kin involvement were minimum requirements. For the investigative duty in the context of NHS negligence see *R (on the application of Khan) v Secretary of State for Health* [2003] EWCA Civ 1129, [2003] 4 All ER 1239 (although note that the House of Lords, *in Re McKerr* [2004] UKHL 12, [2004] 1 WLR 807, disapproved of what the Court of Appeal in *Khan* had said about the retrospective effect of the HRA 1998).

7.47 The prohibition on the death penalty in all circumstances under Article 1 of Protocol 13 of the ECHR, which superceded its partial prohibition (in times of peace) under Protocol 6, was ratified by the UK in 2004.[1] In *Öcalan*[2] the ECtHR considered that the de jure abolition of the death penalty in 43 of the 44 Contracting States and a moratorium in the remaining death penalty State (Russia), the signing by all Contracting States of Protocol 6 and its ratification by 41 States,[3] and the Council of Europe's policy requiring new Member States to undertake to abolish capital punishment as a condition of admission, meant that the territories encompassed by Member States of the Council of Europe comprised a 'zone free of capital punishment': 'Against such a consistent background, it can be said that capital punishment in peacetime has come to be regarded as an unacceptable, if not inhuman, form of punishment which is no longer permissible under Article 2'.[4] But the ECtHR's application of Article 2 to expulsion cases has been inconsistent. In *Bahaddar*[5] the Commission held that expulsion to a real risk of death did not engage the first sentence of Article 2, and would not constitute 'intentional deprivation of life' under the second sentence unless the expelling State 'knowingly puts the person concerned at such high risk of losing his life as for the outcome to be a near-certainty', although if there was a real risk of death, expulsion would amount to inhuman treatment contrary to Article 3.[6] Conversely, a (mere) real risk of being executed upon deportation was sufficient to establish a breach of Article 2 in *Bader*.[7] In *Kaboulov*[8] the court resolved this apparent tension. It observed that where there is a real risk of execution in the receiving State, the positive duty under Article 2 implies an obligation not to expel the individual. Further, if the expelling State knowingly puts the individual concerned at such high risk of losing their life as for the outcome to be a near certainty, such an extradition may be regarded as 'intentional deprivation of life', ie a breach of the negative duty under Article 2(1).[9] In either case the individual must not be returned. Note that the practical application of Article 2 is broader than cases involving a real risk of execution by state actors:

> 'Owing to the importance of the right to life, the Convention may also apply where the danger emanates from persons or groups of persons who are not public officials. However, it must be shown that the risk is real and that the authorities of the receiving State are not able to obviate the risk by providing appropriate protection.'.[10]

The EC 'Qualification Directive' provides, subject to exclusionary provisions, for the subsidiary protection of those showing 'substantial grounds' for believing that they 'would face a real risk' of the death penalty or execution or, in a situation of armed conflict, a serious and individual threat to a civilian's life or person by reason of indiscriminate violence.[11] The Immigration Rules implementing the directive make similar provision but also include those facing 'a real risk' of suffering unlawful killing.[12]

[1]   See 7.45 above. Art 1 of Protocol 13 replaced arts 1 and 2 of Protocol 6 in the Schedule to the HRA 1998 in June 2004: see The Human Rights Act 1998 (Amendment) Order 2004, SI 2004/1574.

[2]   *Öcalan v Turkey* (2003) 37 EHRR 10.

[3]   Apart from Turkey, Armenia and Russia. All Council of Europe Member States bar three have now ratified Protocol 13: Armenia has signed but not ratified the Protocol; Russia and Azerbaijan have not signed it (see Council of Europe Treaty Office website: conventions.coe. int/Treaty/Commun/ChercheSig.asp?NT=187&CM=8&CL=ENG, accessed 24 December 2014).

[4]   *Öcalan v Turkey* (fn 2 above) paras 195–6.

[5]   *Bahaddar v Netherlands* (1998) 26 EHRR 278 (report of Commission adopted, 13 September 1996).

[6]   *Bahaddar v Netherlands* (fn 5 above) paras 76–8. This reasoning was adopted by the Commission in *Dehwari v Netherlands* (2000) 29 EHRR CD 74, para 61 (where there was a real risk that the death penalty would be imposed in Iran).

[7]   *Bader v Sweden* (2008) 46 EHRR 13, para 48. In the domestic context, see also *McLean v High Court of Dublin, Ireland* [2008] EWHC 547 (Admin), [2008] Extradition LR 182.

[8]   *Kaboulov v Ukraine* (2010) 50 EHRR 39 (where, on the basis of objective evidence and assurances from the Kazakhstani authorities, there was not a real risk that the death penalty would be imposed upon extradition to Kazakhstan).

9   *Kaboulov v Ukraine* (fn 8 above) para 99. See also *Al-Saadoon v United Kingdom* (2010) 51 EHRR 212, para 123.
10 *Gonzalez v Spain* (43544/98) 22 June 1999, para 4.
11 Council Directive 2004/83/EC on minimum standards for the qualification and status of third country nationals and stateless persons as refugees or persons who otherwise need international protection (OJ 2004 L304/12), arts 2, 15.
12 HC 395, para 339C.

Exposure to torture or inhuman or degrading treatment or punishment

7.48 Article 3 of the ECHR states that:

> 'No one shall be subjected to torture or to inhuman or degrading treatment or punishment.'

Torture is not defined in the ECHR. It implies deliberately inflicted suffering of particular intensity and cruelty.[1] In the UN Convention Against Torture[2] it comprises three elements: severe pain or suffering, physical or mental; intentionally inflicted for purposes such as obtaining information or a confession or for punishment, for intimidation or coercion or from discrimination; inflicted by or at the instigation of, or with the consent or acquiescence of, a public authority or person acting in an official capacity.[3] But the ECtHR does not require official involvement to find a breach of Article 3.[4] The Convention being a living instrument, acts which were previously classified as inhuman treatment could now be classified as torture, as standards in the protection of human rights and fundamental liberties rise.[5] It may be inflicted gratuitously without any intention to obtain information.[6] Rape has been recognised as torture,[7] and rape of a detainee by a State official is a specially grave and abhorrent form of ill-treatment because of the vulnerability and weakened resistance of the victim.[8] But a finding of torture is not required to found a violation of Article 3:

> 'Ill-treatment [must] attain a minimum level of severity and involve actual bodily injury or intense physical or mental suffering. Where treatment humiliates or debases an individual, showing a lack of respect for, or diminishing his or her human dignity, or arouses feelings of fear, anguish or inferiority capable of breaking an individual's moral and physical resistance, it may be classified as degrading and also fall within the prohibition.'.[9]

Inhuman treatment requires less serious suffering than torture (although the threshold is still high), and it need not be deliberately inflicted.[10] Any use of physical force against a person deprived of his or her liberty which is not made strictly necessary by the person's own conduct is in principle an infringement of their Article 3 rights.[11] What constitutes inhuman treatment will depend on the characteristics of the individual, such as their age, sex and state of health.[12] The ECtHR has held that being an asylum seeker makes an individual particularly vulnerable, underprivileged and in need of special protection and is thus a personal characteristic relevant to determining whether treatment breaches Article 3.[13] A threat of torture, if sufficiently real and immediate, may give rise to such mental suffering as to constitute inhuman treatment,[14] as may a callous disregard for the anguish of relatives of the 'disappeared'.[15] Being kicked, robbed, intimidated, harassed and made to carry out forced labour on many occasions has been characterised as inhuman treatment.[16] Conditions of detention such as physical ill-treatment, severe overcrowding, constant lighting, inadequate sanitation and lack of opportunities for outdoor exercise or human contact, may constitute inhuman treatment,[17] as may subjection to a death sentence,[18] or the agony of waiting on death row.[19] While, in principle, matters of appropriate sentencing largely fall outside the scope of the ECHR, a 'grossly disproportionate' sentence may amount to a violation of Article 3.[20] The detention of an unaccompanied, five-year-old child in an adult immigration detention centre where no one was assigned to look after her and no measures were taken to ensure that she received proper counselling and education assistance from qualified personnel has been found to be inhuman treatment.[21] The authorities are under a particular obligation to protect the health of detainees, and a lack of appropriate medical treatment in custody may amount to treatment contrary to Article 3.[22] The deportation of a five-year-old child without making adequate arrangements for her care on her arrival in the destination country was inhuman treatment.[23] The suffering which flows from naturally occurring illness, physical or mental, may be covered by Article 3 where it is, or risks being, exacerbated by treatment (whether flowing from conditions of detention, expulsion or other measures) for which the authorities can be held responsible.[24] The relatives of a victim of a serious human rights violation may also be a 'victim' of the violation for the purposes of the ECHR if there are 'special factors', such as the closeness or particular circumstances of the relationship and the way in which the State responds to the relative, that distinguish their suffering from the inevitable emotional distress that relatives are likely to suffer in such circumstances.[25] Thus, for example, the infliction of FGM on a daughter might cause suffering of such intensity to her parents as to amount to their persecution or Article 3 ill-treatment[26] as would the suffering of a mother caused by witnessing the slow death of her son from inadequately treated HIV/AIDs whilst imprisoned.[27] The anguish and distress caused to the surviving inhabitants of a village bombed by the authorities could amount to inhuman treatment.[28] Article 3 contains within it a duty to investigate any ill-treatment for which the State may be held responsible.[29]

---

[1] *Ireland v United Kingdom* (1978) 2 EHRR 25 where the 'five techniques' of hooding, wall standing, subjection to noise, sleep deprivation and deprivation of food and drink were held not to occasion suffering of the particular intensity and cruelty implied by the word 'torture', although they constituted inhuman or degrading treatment. See also *Greek Case* (1969) 12 YB 186. In the domestic context, see generally *A v Secretary of State for the Home Department (No 2)* [2005] UKHL 71, [2006] 2 AC 221, [2006] 1 All ER 575 on the nature and extent of the international law and common law prohibition of torture.

[2] Article 1, UN Convention against Torture and other Cruel, Inhuman or Degrading Treatment or Punishment 1984. The prohibition against torture is a ius cogens norm, a binding obligation in international customary law: *R v Bow Street Metropolitan Stipendiary Magistrate, ex p Pinochet Ugarte (No 3)* [2000] 1 AC 147, per Lord Browne-Wilkinson at 203–5.

[3] In the absence of central government, armed factions (eg in Somalia) could be 'public officials': *Elmi v Australia* [1999] INLR 341 (UN Committee Against Torture).

[4] *HLR v France* (1997) 26 EHRR 29, para 40, but see further below 7.53.

[5] *Selmouni v France* (1999) 29 EHRR 403, para 101.

[6] No intention to obtain information is necessary for a finding of torture: *Selmouni v France* (fn 5 above); *R v Secretary of State for the Home Department, ex p Singh* [1999] INLR 632 at 637, although such an intention may turn lesser violence into torture; cf *Denizi v Cyprus* 23 May 2001 (in which beating was not torture as the purpose was not to extract information).

[7] *Aydin v Turkey* (1998) 25 EHRR 251, paras 80–7. A risk of sexual abuse and gang attacks in Jamaica were held to engage art 3 in *A v Secretary of State for the Home Department* [2003] EWCA Civ 175, [2003] All ER (D) 151 (Jan), [2003] INLR 249, para 32. Similarly, in *PS (Sri Lanka) v Secretary of State for the Home Department* [2008] EWCA Civ 1213, para 14, art 3

was engaged because of a real risk that the individual would be targeted for rape by soldiers in Sri Lanka. See also *Livio Zilli*, 'The crime of rape in the case law of the Strasbourg institutions' (2002) 13 Crim LF 2, pp 245–65.

[8] *Aydin v Turkey* (fn 7 above) para 83. See also the judgment of the International War Crimes Tribunal for the former Yugoslavia in *Furundzija* (IT-95-17/1-T) (10 December 1998, unreported).

[9] *Pretty v United Kingdom* (2002) 35 EHRR 1.

[10] The techniques in *Ireland v United Kingdom* (fn 1 above), were held to constitute inhuman treatment since, without causing bodily injury, they caused intense physical and mental suffering and led to psychiatric disturbances during interrogation. In *Tomasi v France* (1993) 15 EHRR 1 a 40-hour interrogation including slapping, kicking, punching, being threatened with a firearm and made to stand for long periods handcuffed or naked was held to constitute inhuman and degrading treatment.

[11] *Ribitsch v Austria* (1995) 21 EHRR 573, para 38: any recourse to physical force against a person deprived of his liberty, not made strictly necessary by his own conduct, diminishes human dignity and is in principle an infringement of art 3 rights. Given that principle, the tribunal erred in law by finding that the treatment a returnee to Zimbabwe claimed to have suffered – being struck across the mouth whilst being interrogated and hearing shouts and groans from other detainees – was not serious enough to breach Article 3: *AA (Zimbabwe) v Secretary of State for the Home Department* [2007] EWCA Civ 149, [2007] All ER (D) 73 (Mar), para 43.

[12] *Tyrer v United Kingdom* (1978) 2 EHRR 1, para 3; *Campbell* and *Cosans v United Kingdom* (1982) 4 EHRR 293, paras 28–30; *Soering v United Kingdom* (1989) 11 EHRR 439, para 100. In *Selçuk and Asker v Turkey* (1998) 26 EHRR 477, para 77, the destruction of the homes and property of two elderly residents of a Turkish village by security forces, 'carried out contemptuously and without respect for the feelings' of the applicants, was held to constitute inhuman treatment.

[13] *MSS v Belgium and Greece* (2011) 53 EHRR 28.

[14] *Campbell and Cosans v United Kingdom* (1982) 4 EHRR 293, para 26.

[15] *Kurt v Turkey* (1998) 27 EHRR 373, paras 130–4; cf *Tanli v Turkey* (2004) 38 EHRR 3, para 159. While a family member of a 'disappeared' person can claim to be a victim of treatment contrary to art 3, the same principle does not usually apply to situations where that person is later found dead: *Sabanchiyeva v Russia* (2014) 58 EHRR 14, para 105.

[16] *Salah Sheekh v Netherlands* (2007) 45 EHRR 1158.

[17] See eg: *Cyprus v Turkey* (1976) 4 EHRR 482 (physical ill-treatment; withholding food and drinking water); *Dougoz v Greece* (2002) 34 EHRR 61 (Art 3 violated through serious overcrowding and lack of sleeping facilities); *Kalashnikov v Russia* (2002) 36 EHRR 587 (cramped and unsanitary detention conditions for an excessive period pre-trial violated art 3); *Van der Ven v Netherlands* (2004) 38 EHRR 46 (conditions in maximum security prison, in particular weekly strip-searching, violated art 3); *Poltoratiskiy v Ukraine* (2003) 39 EHRR 916 (conditions on death row, including a lack of natural light and poor sanitation, amounted to a violation of art 3); *Ryabikin v Russia* (2008) 48 EHRR 1322 (extremely poor detention conditions precluded extradition to Turkmenistan, notwithstanding diplomatic assurances); *Kim v Russia* (2014) Application no 44260/13 (prolonged detention in an overcrowded, unhygienic facility intended only for short-term detention). In the domestic context see: *R (on the application of D) v Secretary of State for the Home Department* [2012] EWHC 2501 (Admin) and *R (on the application of MD) v Secretary of State for the Home Department* [2014] EWHC 2249 (Admin) (in both cases the failure properly to treat the mental illness of a foreign national immigration detainee amounted to a breach of art 3). Solitary confinement is not per se inhuman treatment but is capable of being so depending on the particular conditions, the duration and stringency of the measure, its objective and its effects. Complete sensory and social isolation may be so by virtue of its effect of breaking down the personality: *Ensslin, Baader and Raspe v Germany* (1978) 14 DR 64; see also *Ahmad v United Kingdom* (2013) 56 EHRR 1 (although conditions in super-maximum security prisons in the USA were highly restrictive, they did not constitute complete sensory or social isolation, and so the extradition of the applicants would not violate art 3); cf *Aswat v United Kingdom* (2014) 58 EHRR 1.

[18] In *Öcalan v Turkey* (2003) 37 EHRR 10, the court held that the imposition of a death sentence was inhuman and degrading, and violated art 3 (7.46 above).

[19] *Soering v United Kingdom* (1989) 11 EHRR 439.

[20] *Ahmad v United Kingdom* (fn 17 above) para 237 (on the facts, in particular given the seriousness of the terrorist offences alleged, the sentences faced by the applicants would not be

grossly disproportionate, and so would not violate art 3 upon imposition); see also *Weeks v United Kingdom* (1988) 10 EHRR 293, para 47; *Hussain v United Kingdom* (1996) 22 EHRR 1, para 53; and *Harkins v United Kingdom* (2012) 55 EHRR 19, para 133 in which the court held that gross disproportionality is a strict test. In *Trabelsi v Belgium* (2014) Application no 140/10 extradition to face a whole life sentence in the USA was held to breach Article 3 not because such a sentence was grossly disproportionate in the circumstances but because there was no prospect of release even if circumstances materially changed. Note that the individual circumstances of the applicant are relevant: in *Mouisel v France* (67263/01) 14 November 2002 the continued detention of a prisoner with cancer violated his dignity and caused suffering in excess of that inevitably associated with a custodial sentence and treatment for cancer, giving rise to a violation of art 3.

[21] *Mayeka and Mitunga v Belgium* (2008) 46 EHRR 23. See further 7.86 below.

[22] For statements of this general principle see *Keenan v United Kingdom* (2001) 33 EHRR 38, para 115; *Kudla v Poland* (2002) 35 EHRR 11, para 94. For its application, see eg: *VD v Romania* (7078/02) 16 February 2010 (failure to provide dental treatment violated art 3); *Slyusarev v Russia* (60333/00) 20 April 2010 (failure to provide spectacles violated art 3); *Vasilyev v Russia* (28370/05) 10 January 2012 (failure to provide appropriate orthopaedic footwear violated art 3); *Gülay Çetin v Turkey* (44084/10) 5 March 2013 (detention conditions of a cancer sufferer who ultimately died whilst incarcerated violated art 3).

[23] *Mayeka and Mitunga v Belgium* (fn 21 above).

[24] *Pretty v United Kingdom* (2002) 35 EHRR 1, para 52 (but no positive obligation to sanction actions intended to terminate life can be derived from art 3: para 55).

[25] See eg *Mayeka and Mitunga v Belgium* (fn 21 above) para 51. The mother's experience (in Canada) of her 5-year-old daughter being detained in Belgium and then deported to the Democratic Republic of Congo was found to have been sufficiently severe to render the mother a victim and constitute a breach of her art 3 rights.

[26] *FM (Sudan) CG* [2007] UKAIT 00060, para 161, which applied *Katrinak v Secretary of State for the Home Department* [2001] EWCA Civ 832, [2001] INLR 499. For a recent reiteration of this principle see *AMM and others (conflict; humanitarian crisis; returnees; FGM) Somalia CG* [2011] UKUT 445 (IAC), paras 558–9.

[27] *Salakhov and Islyamova v Ukraine* (2013) Application no 28005/08 (ECHR).

[28] *Benzer and others v Turkey* (2013) Application no 23502/06 (ECHR).

[29] See cases cited at 7.46 fn 7 and fn 8 above. Where an individual is taken into custody in good health but is found to be injured on release, the injuries give rise to a strong presumption of fact and the burden is upon the State to produce evidence to displace it: *Tomasi v France* (fn 10 above) paras 108–11; *Makhauri v Russia* (2010) 50 EHRR 40, para 122.

Degrading treatment

7.49 In the case law on Article 3 of the ECHR, the same treatment (particularly in detention) may be both 'inhuman' and 'degrading', but they are separate concepts. Degrading treatment is treatment which is 'grossly humiliating',[1] or capable of arousing feelings of 'anguish and inferiority capable of humiliating and debasing' the victim.[2] In considering whether treatment or punishment is degrading, the court will have regard to whether the object is to humiliate and debase,[3] but the absence of an intention to degrade does not preclude a finding of degrading treatment.[4] Corporal punishment has been held to constitute degrading punishment.[5] Race discrimination is capable of constituting degrading treatment, as 'publicly to single out a group of persons for differential treatment on the basis of race might . . . constitute a special form of affront to human dignity'.[6]

[1] *East African Asians v United Kingdom* (1973) 3 EHRR 76, para 195.

[2] *Ireland v United Kingdom* (1978) 2 EHRR 25, para 167. See also: *Hurtado v Switzerland* (1994) Series A, 280A (where the Commission found degrading treatment where a detainee was not permitted to change his clothes after he had soiled his trousers); *Gurdogan v Turkey* (1986) 76 DR 9 (smearing excrement on the mouths of Kurdish villagers); *Valašinas v Lithuania* 12 BHRC 266, [2001] Prison LR 36 (a strip search in front of a prison officer of the

opposite sex was held to be degrading). In the domestic context, in *Grant v Ministry of Justice* [2011] EWHC 3379 (QB), the court rejected the argument that prisoners detained without in-cell sanitation (who consequently had to urinate and defecate into plastic buckets) had suffered gross humiliation amounting to degrading treatment. The minimum level of seriousness or severity for art 3 to be engaged had not been reached.

3   *Raninen v Finland* (1998) 26 EHRR 563, para 55; *Keenan v United Kingdom* (2001) 33 EHRR 38, para 109; *MS v United Kingdom* (2012) 55 EHRR 23, para 38.
4   *Peers v Greece* (2001) 33 EHRR 1192, para 74; *Price v UK* (2002) 34 EHRR 53, para 30; *Ramirez Sanchez v France* (2007) 45 EHRR 49, para 118. See **7.67** below.
5   In *Tyrer v United Kingdom* (1978) 2 EHRR 1 (judicial birching of a 15-year-old which was 'institutionalised violence' on someone 'in the power of the authorities'). But cf *Costello-Roberts v United Kingdom* (1993) 19 EHRR 112 where smacking the bottom of a 7-year-old boy in a private school was held not to reach the minimum necessary level of severity. In *A v United Kingdom* (1998) 27 EHRR 611, however, a parent's beating of his 9-year-old stepson, leaving bruising, was held sufficiently serious.
6   *East African Asians v United Kingdom* (fn 1 above) paras 207–8. The Commission said that treatment is degrading if 'it lowers [a person] in rank, position, reputation or character, whether in his own eyes or in the eyes of other people' (para 189), and reaches a certain level of severity. The applicants were being deprived of their livelihood and being left destitute in Africa, and were reduced to the status of second-class citizens by the UK government, which denied them admission to their country of nationality. The 'shuttle-cocking' of refugees – repeated expulsion to a country where admission is not guaranteed – was held to be capable of engaging art 3 in *Giana v Belgium* 21 DR 73 and *Harabi v Netherlands* 46 DR 112. But cf *X and Y v United Kingdom* (5302/71) 11 October 1973 in which Kenyan Asians had gone to India where they were established and had strong family links. Their application was declared inadmissible, since 'unlike their fellow citizens in East Africa they had work and a place to live'. See also *Lalljee v United Kingdom* (1985) 8 EHRR 84 where a quota system for immigration was held not to be degrading. In the domestic context, the Administrative Court held that art 3 might arguably be engaged by a claim that Roma children were at risk of being sent to specially designated schools in the Czech Republic in *R (on the application of Kurecaj) v Secretary of State for the Home Department* [2001] EWHC 1199 (Admin), [2001] All ER (D) 278 (Dec).

7.50 The right not to be tortured or subjected to inhuman or degrading treatment contrary to Article 3 of the ECHR is an unqualified right and can never be balanced or give way to competing considerations. It:

'enshrines one of the fundamental values of democratic societies . . . prohibits in absolute terms torture or inhuman or degrading treatment or punishment, irrespective of the victim's conduct. Unlike most of the substantive clauses of the Convention . . . it makes no provision for exceptions and no derogation from it is permissible even in the event of a public emergency threatening the life of the nation . . . the activities of the individual in question, however undesirable or dangerous, cannot be a material consideration.'.[1]

However, some domestic confusion has been caused by the court's observations in Soering:[2]

'What constitutes inhuman or degrading treatment or punishment depends on all the circumstances of the case. Furthermore, inherent in the whole of the Convention is a search for a fair balance between the demands of the general interests of the community and the requirements of the protection of the individual's fundamental rights. As movement becomes easier and crime takes on a larger international dimension, it is increasingly in the interests of all nations that suspected offenders who flee abroad should be brought to justice. Conversely, the establishment of safe havens for fugitives would not only result in danger for the State obliged to harbour the protected person but also tend to undermine the foundations of extradition. These considerations must also be included among the factors to be taken into account in the interpretation and application of notions of inhuman or degrading treatment or punishment in extradition cases.'.[3]

The court confirmed in *Chahal* that there is no 'balancing' of interests in Article 3 cases:

> 'It should not be inferred from the court's remarks about the risks of undermining the foundations of extradition, as set out in para 89 of [Soering], that there is any room for balancing the risk of ill-treatment against the reasons for expulsion in determining whether a State's responsibility under Article 3 is engaged.'.[4]

The United Kingdom government tried to persuade the court to revisit the *Chahal* principle in Saadi,[5] arguing that criminal prosecution, surveillance and restrictions on individuals' movements were not an adequate substitute for deportation as a means to protect the community in cases concerning international terrorism. In such cases, so it was said, governments should be able to balance the risk to the individual consequent on removal against the gravity of the threat that he or she posed to the community and where there was evidence that an individual threatened national security, correspondingly stronger evidence had to be produced to establish that risk of ill treatment of that individual was such as to prevent the individual's deportation. In response, the court reaffirmed the principles that the protection afforded by Article 3 was absolute; that the conduct of the individual, 'however undesirable or dangerous' could not be taken into account and rejected the proposal that the individual had to discharge a higher standard of proof where there was a threat to national security. Even in such a case, it was 'necessary and sufficient for substantial grounds to have been shown for believing that there is a real risk' of prohibited treatment in the destination country.[6] In *Ahmad* the court again reaffirmed the *Chahal* principle, and found that the same approach must be taken to the assessment of whether the minimum level of severity has been met for the purposes of Article 3 (ie it too 'can only be assessed independently of the reasons for removal or extradition').[7] Further, the court sought unambiguously to preclude any further arguments that Article 3 ill-treatment may be balanced against other factors:

> '[I]n the 22 years since the Soering judgment, in an art 3 case the Court has never undertaken an examination of the proportionality of a proposed extradition or other form of removal from a contracting state. To this extent, the Court must be taken to have departed from the approach contemplated at [89] and [110] of the Soering judgment.'[8]

In *MSS* the court reaffirmed the absolute character of the obligations imposed by Article 3, rejecting an argument that when deciding whether conditions in which asylum seekers were detained breached Article 3, regard should be had to the limited resources available to the State to cope with the disproportionate numbers of asylum seekers entering its territory.[9]

---

[1]   *Chahal v United Kingdom* (1996) 23 EHRR 413, paras 79–80. See also *Ahmed v Austria* (1996) 24 EHRR 278, para 41.

[2]   *Soering v United Kingdom* (1989) 11 EHRR 439.

[3]   *Soering v United Kingdom* (fn 2 above) para 89; see also para 110. For examples of the domestic confusion caused by *Soering*, see both *R (on the application of Ullah) v Special Adjudicator* [2002] EWCA Civ 1856, [2003] INLR 74, para 38 and *N v Secretary of State for the Home Department* [2003] EWCA Civ 1369, [2004] 1 WLR 1182, para 30 in which the Court of Appeal used this passage to hold that the public interest in extradition or immigration control could be a relevant factor in deciding on the severity of ill-treatment in a receiving State which would preclude removal. This issue was not canvassed in *Ullah* when it reached the House of Lords ([2004] UKHL 26, [2004] 2 AC 323), but the judgment of the House of Lords in *N v Secretary of State for the Home Department* ([2005] UKHL 31, [2005] 2 AC 296) clearly had such considerations in mind.

[4]   *Chahal v United Kingdom* (fn 1 above) para 81.

[5]   *Saadi v Italy* (2008) 49 EHRR 730.

[6]   *Saadi v Italy* (fn 5 above) paras 138–40. See also *Sufi* and *Elmi v United Kingdom*
(2011) 54 EHRR 209, paras 212–4. In *Tyrer v United Kingdom* (1978) 2 EHRR 1, para 38
the court held that: 'no local requirement relative to the maintenance of law and order would
entitle any of [the Contracting States] to make use of a punishment contrary to Article 3'. See
also Johan Callewaert 'Is there a margin of appreciation in the application of Articles 2, 3 and
4 of the Convention?' (1998) 19 HRLJ 1, pp 6–9: 'A relativisation of the scope of one of
the Convention's most fundamental rights would not only be both absurd and disturbing; it
would also occur in the very midst of the western community of nations that is fond of
stressing the universality of human rights on the international scene. . . . . If ever there was
an area symbolising such universality, it is . . . the one covered by Article 3.'.

[7]   *Ahmad v United Kingdom* (2013) 56 EHRR 1, para 172.

[8]   *Ahmad v United Kingdom* (fn 7 above) para 173.

[9]   *MSS v Belgium and Greece* (2011) 53 EHRR 28.

7.51 The landmark case of *Soering* established that extradition to a country
where there is a real risk of treatment contrary to Article 3 of the ECHR
engages the UK's responsibility under Article 3.[1] The *Soering* principle has
since been applied to the removal of rejected asylum seekers,[2] the deportation
on national security grounds[3] and, indeed, must be taken to apply to any
forced expulsion.[4] In *Vilvarajah*[5] the court held that the expelling State's responsibility was engaged:

> 'where substantial grounds have been shown for believing that the person concerned
> faces a real risk of being subjected to torture or inhuman or degrading treatment or
> punishment in the country to which he is returned.'.[6]

The assessment of this risk must be thorough, in view of the importance of
Article 3, and is carried out by reference both to the applicant's personal
history and to the human rights conditions in the destination country, in much
the same way as a Refugee Convention assessment.[7] In exceptional cases, the
country evidence may establish serious reasons for believing in the existence of
a practice of systematically ill-treating a particular group; if it does, an
individual need only establish his or her membership of the group in order to
show that removal would violate Article 3.[8] It is also possible for a general
situation of violence to be so extreme that there is a real risk of ill-treatment
simply by virtue of an individual being exposed to such violence on return
(although in practice this threshold is very rarely crossed). In *Sufi* and *Elmi*
the ECtHR held that the level of violence in Mogadishu was of sufficient
intensity to pose a real risk of an Article 3 violation for anyone present in the
city (with the possible exception of those well-connected to powerful persons).
It did so having regard to the methods and tactics used by the parties to the
conflict, including indiscriminate bombardments; the 'unacceptable number'
of civilian casualties; the substantial number of people displaced by the conflict
and the unpredictable and widespread nature of the conflict.[9] Similarly,
exposing an individual to a situation of generalised, extreme poverty can
engage Article 3.[10] Where the general situation is not by itself sufficient, the
'personal circumstances' of the applicant may nevertheless be such that
removal would breach Article 3.[11] The ECtHR has shown its willingness to
review and reverse domestic courts' adverse credibility findings in carrying out
the assessment.[12] The automatic and mechanical application of rigid procedural requirements for asylum claimants is at variance with the protection of

the fundamental values embodied in Article 3.[13]

[1]   *Soering v United Kingdom* (1989) 11 EHRR 439, in which the applicant was awaiting extradition to the US, where he faced the prospect of waiting on death row for many years. The court upheld the principle that the sending State was responsible under art 3 for 'all and any foreseeable consequences of extradition suffered outside their jurisdiction' (para 86).

[2]   In *Cruz Varas v Sweden* (1912) 14 EHRR 1, para 70 the court held that the test in *Soering* applied a fortiori to expulsions as well as extraditions. See also: *Hilal v United Kingdom* (2001) 33 EHRR 31, [2001] INLR 595 (rejection of claim of Tanzanian asylum seeker and decision to remove him breached art 3); *Dzhurayev v Russia* (2013) 57 EHRR 22 (Art 3 violated where Russian agents had been complicit in the rendition of a rejected asylum seeker to Tajikistan, despite the ECtHR having adopted interim measures prohibiting his expulsion pursuant to Rule 39 of its Rules of Court).

[3]   *Chahal v United Kingdom* (1997) 23 EHRR 413. In the domestic context, see *RB (Algeria) v Secretary of State for the Home Department* [2009] UKHL 10, [2010] 2 AC 110, in which the House of Lords considered art 3 in a series of national security cases (note that one of the applicant's complaints was upheld in part in the ECtHR, on the basis that there was a real risk that evidence obtained through torture would not be used in order to try him, in violation of art 6: *Othman (Abu Qatada) v United Kingdom* (2012) 55 EHRR 1).

[4]   In *Pretty v United Kingdom* (2002) 35 EHRR 1, para 52, the ECtHR held that the act of expulsion is 'treatment' within the scope of the negative duty to under Article 3; thus, expulsion which exposes a person to a real risk of ill-treatment abroad is a violation of Article 3. For positive and negative obligations, see **7.34** above.

[5]   *Vilvarajah v United Kingdom* (1992) 14 EHRR 248.

[6]   *Vilvarajah v United Kingdom* (fn 5 above) para 103. See also *Matumbo v Switzerland* (1994) 15 HRLJ 164, a case on the UN Convention Against Torture. This standard of proof—substantial grounds for believing that a real risk of the prohibited harm exists—has been held to be the same to all intents and purposes as that under the *Refugee Convention*: *Kacaj* [2001] INLR 354, [2002] Imm AR 213, para 12 (starred), which was reversed by the Court of Appeal on other grounds ([2002] EWCA Civ 314) but has subsequently been approved in respect of what was said about the standard of proof (eg per Laws LJ in *MH (Iraq) v the Secretary for State for the Home Department* [2007] EWCA Civ 852, para 22).

[7]   See eg *Chahal v United Kingdom* (1996) 23 EHRR 413, paras 96, 117; *Jabari v Turkey* 9 BHRC 1, [2001] INLR 136, paras 40–1. See also *M v Bulgaria* (2014) 58 EHRR 20, in which the court found that a failure properly to scrutinise the applicant's case because it concerned a matter of national security meant that there was no safeguard against arbitrariness and so his removal would violate art 8 (the court considered that there was no need for separate consideration under art 3 because there was no reason to doubt that the State would comply with the decision, ie would not deport the applicant). The historical position is of interest insofar as it may shed light on the current situation and its likely evolution, but it is the present conditions which are decisive: *Ahmed v Austria* (1997) 24 EHRR 278, para 43. The Court of Appeal held in *Hariri v Secretary of State for the Home Department* [2003] EWCA Civ 807, [2003] ACD 97, para 8 (following *Iqbal (Muzafar)* [2002] UKIAT 02239, para 57) that where there is nothing to distinguish the applicant from others, he or she would need to show a 'consistent pattern of gross and systematic violations of fundamental rights' in the destination country to succeed on an art 3 claim. However, in *Batayav v Secretary of State for the Home Department* [2003] EWCA Civ 1489, [2004] INLR 126, para 39, per Sedley LJ, the court emphasised the danger of assimilating 'real risk' to 'probability' by the use of the test in Hariri; see also *R (on the application of Kpangui) v Secretary of State for the Home Department* [2005] EWHC 881 (Admin), para 8, per Munby J: '[the] observations of Sedley LJ in *Batayav* are not mere obiter dicta. They were expressly agreed to, both by Mummery LJ and by me, and represent the unanimous view of the Court of Appeal as to what the law is'. See also the analysis of the Administrative Court in *R (on the application of Evans) v Secretary of State for Defence* [2010] EWHC 1445 (Admin); [2011] ACD 11.

[8]   As in *Salah Sheekh v Netherlands* (2007) 45 EHRR 1158, paras 138–49 in respect of the Ashraf in Somalia. See also *Makhmudzhan Ergashev v Russia* (49747/11) 16 October 2012 in respect of the Uzbek minority in Kyrgyzstan, paras 68–76.

[9]   *Sufi and Elmi v United Kingdom* (2011) 54 EHRR 209 (cf *KAB v Sweden* (886/11) 5 September 2013, [2014] Imm AR 371, in which the court held that the security situation in Mogadishu had improved such that it could no longer be said that anyone there would be at real risk of treatment contrary to art 3). See also *Hirsi Jamaa v Italy* (2012) 55 EHRR 21; *TN v Denmark* (2013) 57 EHRR 11.

[10] *MSS v Belgium and Greece* (2011) 53 EHRR 28, paras 252–64, in which the court held that returning an Afghan asylum seeker to Greece pursuant to the Dublin II Regulation (343/2003) would violate his art 3 rights, inter alia, because of the inadequate living conditions that he would face there (cf *SHH v United Kingdom* (2013) 57 EHRR 18, paras 88–90, which the court distinguished from *MSS* because, in contrast to Greece, Afghanistan was not a contracting state with positive ECHR obligations). In the domestic context see *R (on the application of EM (Eritrea)) v Secretary of State for the Home Department* [2014] UKSC 12, [2014] 2 WLR 409, para 62, in which the parties agreed that the positive obligations under art 3 of ECHR included 'the duty to protect asylum seekers from deliberate harm by being exposed to living conditions (for which the state bears responsibility) which cause ill-treatment.'

[11] *NA v United Kingdom* (2009) 48 EHRR 15, para 113 (in respect of Sri Lanka); *FH v Sweden* (2010) 51 EHRR 42, para 93 (in respect of Iraq); *N v Sweden* (23505/09) 20 July 2010, [2011] Imm AR 38 (in respect of Afghanistan).

[12] See *Hatami v Sweden* (1999) 27 EHRR CD8 paras 95–106. See also: *Hilal v United Kingdom* (fn 2 above) paras 62–8; *Said v Netherlands* (2006) 43 EHRR 14, paras 50–53; *N v Finland* (2006) 43 EHRR 12, paras 152–7. The court also obtains evidence for itself, eg by taking oral evidence in appropriate cases (which it did in *N v Finland*). In cases in which there are conflicting accounts of events, the court will cautiously take the role of a first-instance tribunal of fact, where this is rendered unavoidable by the circumstances of a particular case: *El Masri v the Former Yugoslav Republic of Macedonia* (2013) 57 EHRR 25, para 151; *Dzhurayev v Russia* (fn 2 above) para 128.

[13] *Jabari v Turkey* (fn 7 above) paras 40–1: the imposition of a rigid five-day registration requirement as a condition of having an asylum claim examined prevented scrutiny of a claim based on a fear of inhuman and degrading punishment in Iran for adultery. Note that in *R (on the application of Nasseri) v Secretary of State for the Home Department* [2009] UKHL 23, [2010] 1 AC 1, para 15, Lord Hoffman held that *Jabari* did not give rise to a 'free-standing duty to investigate' where there is 'actually no real risk' of treatment contrary to art 3 in the receiving State (although this analysis must be viewed in light of the subsequent jurisprudence on third-country returns, in particular *R (on the application of EM (Eritrea)) v Secretary of State for the Home Department* [2014] UKSC 12, [2014] 2 WLR 409, see 7.52 below).

7.52 In recent years both the ECtHR and the domestic courts have considered the nature and scope of EU Member States' obligations under Article 3 of the ECHR when seeking to return an asylum seeker to another Member State pursuant to the Dublin II Regulation.[1] The Dublin system operates on the principle that the first Member State in which a person claims asylum – or, in practice, in which their fingerprints are taken and stored on the EU-wide EURODAC database – is responsible for determining the person's claim. Thus, if the person subsequently makes a further asylum claim in another Member State, that Member State may call on the first Member State to take responsibility for the person's claim, and may return the person to the first Member State without first undertaking an assessment of the merits of their claim. In *KRS*[2] the ECtHR declared manifestly ill-founded the applicant's argument that his return to Greece from the UK under the Dublin system would constitute a breach of his Article 3 rights. The court considered that in the absence of proof to the contrary, there was a presumption that Greece would comply with its ECHR obligations. Subsequently, in *MSS*,[3] the court held that the Dublin system return of an asylum seeker from Belgium to Greece would breach his Article 3 rights because he would face a situation of extreme material poverty and deficiencies in the asylum procedure meant that he would face the risk of being returned to Afghanistan without any substantive examination of the merits of his claim taking place.[4] In the domestic context, in *EM (Eritrea)*[5] the Supreme Court considered the test to be applied in cases in which a Dublin system return is proposed and the returnee alleges that his or her Article 3 rights will be breached in the receiving Member State.

The Court of Appeal,[6] seeking to apply the preliminary ruling of the CJEU in *NS*,[7] had determined that in such cases, for return to constitute an Article 3 breach, the returnee must demonstrate that there exist systemic deficiencies in the reception conditions for asylum seekers or the asylum procedure in the receiving Member State. The Supreme Court rejected this conclusion and held that the 'critical test' remained the one established in *Soering*:[8] return is forbidden where it is shown that there is a real risk that the individual would suffer treatment contrary to Article 3 in the receiving Member State.[9] Further, the court held that although there is a presumption that EU Member States will comply with their ECHR obligations, this presumption does not extinguish the need to examine whether, in fact, those obligations would be fulfilled on return.[10] Subsequently, the Grand Chamber held that removing a family to Italy would breach Article 3 following an examination of the individual circumstances that the asylum seekers would be likely to face in the context of deficiencies in Italy's reception arrangements. Particular importance was attached to the need of child asylum seekers for 'special protection', even when accompanied by their parents, meant that in the absence of an assurance from the receiving authorities that those needs would be met, removal would breach Article 3.[11]

[1] Regulation 2003/343/EA. Note that the Dublin III Regulation 604/2013 came into force on 19 July 2013. It operates on the same principle as its predecessor.

[2] *KRS v United Kingdom* (2009) 48 EHRR SE8.

[3] *MSS v Belgium and Greece* (2011) 53 EHRR 28.

[4] *MSS v Belgium and Greece* (fn 3 above) paras 252, 263–4, 321. See *Hussein v Netherlands and Italy* (27725/10) 2 April 2013; *Mohammed v Austria* (2283/12) 6 June 2013 (Chamber judgement); *Tarakhel v Switzerland* (29217/12).

[5] *EM (Eritrea) v Secretary of State for the Home Department* [2014] UKSC 12, [2014] 2 WLR 409.

[6] [2012] EWCA Civ 1336, [2013] 1 WLR 576.

[7] *NS v Secretary of State for the Home Department (Amnesty International Ltd and the AIRE Centre (Advice on Individual Rights in Europe) (UK))*: C-411/10 [2013] QB 102, in which the court held that Member States are precluded from removing asylum seekers pursuant to the Dublin system where they 'cannot be unaware that systemic deficiencies in the asylum procedure and in the reception conditions of asylum seekers in that Member State amount to substantial grounds for believing that the asylum seeker would face a real risk of being subjected to inhuman or degrading treatment within the meaning of Article 4 of the Charter [of Fundamental Rights of the European Union]' (para 94). See also *Abdullahi v Bundesasylamt*: C-394/12 [2014] 1 WLR 1895.

[8] *Soering v United Kingdom* (1989) 11 EHRR 439. See **7.51** above.

[9] *EM (Eritrea) v Secretary of State for the Home Department* (fn 5 above) para 58, per Lord Kerr, with whom Lords Neuberger, Carnwath, Toulson and Hodge agreed.

[10] *EM (Eritrea) v Secretary of State for the Home Department* (fn 5 above) paras 40–1.

[11] *Tarakhel v Switzerland* (2014) Application 29217/12, Grand Chamber.

7.53 Article 3 of the ECHR, read with Article 1, contains a positive obligation to protect against inhuman or degrading treatment emanating from persons or groups who are not public officials, and State responsibility for a breach of Article 3 may be engaged where the framework of law fails to provide adequate protection[1] or where the authorities fail to take reasonable steps to avoid a real risk of ill-treatment about which they knew or ought to have known.[2] In the expulsion context, Article 3 may apply where the risk from non-State actors is real and the authorities of the receiving State are unable to obviate it by providing appropriate protection. The ECtHR jurisprudence suggests that, in order to exclude the responsibility of the UK, the standard of protection required by the receiving State must be such as to remove – 'obviate'

– the real risk of ill-treatment because in the expulsion cases the sole issue is the existence of a real risk of sufficiently serious harm to the applicant. The court does not appear to be concerned with the issue of protection in the receiving State except in relation to its impact on the risk.[3] This brings us to the conflation by the higher English courts (in what is binding authority) of the principle of sufficiency of protection in refugee law with the requirements of Article 3 (and, indeed, Article 2) of the ECHR. In our view there is a conceptual difference between protection under the Refugee Convention 1951, whose rationale and prerequisite is the failure of protection by the individual's own State, and the common responsibility for the observance of human rights underlying the ECHR (see the Preamble), which makes the *Horvath*[4] test inappropriate in the ECHR context. Nevertheless, the House of Lords in *Bagdanavicius*[5] held that in a non-State agent Article 3 case the applicant must demonstrate both a real risk of being subjected to sufficiently serious harm and a failure by the receiving State to provide reasonable protection from that harm, and emphasised the equivalence of the tests under the two Conventions. This conclusion was reached by reference to the way in which the 'Soering principle' has been 'repeatedly re-stated' by the Strasbourg court to the effect that Article 3 would be breached by expelling a person if there is 'a real risk of being subjected to treatment contrary to Article 3 in the receiving country'.[6] It is not enough, so the House of Lords held, that the person should face harm, however serious; he or she must face 'proscribed ill-treatment', and 'Non-State agents do not subject people to torture or the other proscribed forms of ill-treatment, however violently they treat them: what, however, would transform such violent treatment into article 3 ill-treatment would be the state's failure to provide reasonable protection against it'.[7] Thus, the question of whether a person's removal is compatible with Article 3 is to be answered (somewhat surprisingly) not by reference to whether the removing, signatory State would breach its obligations under the ECHR by acting in such a way as to expose the person to real risk of sufficiently serious harm, but rather by reference to whether the recipient State would breach its Article 3 obligations (such obligations being purely notional in the case of non-signatory states). It should be noted that measures taken by the receiving State are required to be effective in practice as well as in theory, and an applicant who can show that remedies in the receiving State are unlikely to be an effective deterrent against non-State harm will have shown that her removal would violate Article 3.[8] The ECtHR has consistently declared that States are entitled to consider whether internal relocation within the receiving State would obviate a real risk of Article 3 ill-treatment on return.[9] However, 'as a precondition of relying on an internal flight alternative, certain guarantees have to be in place: the person to be expelled must be able to travel to the area concerned, to gain admittance and be able to settle there'.

[1]   See *A v United Kingdom* [1998] 3 FCR 597, (1999) 27 EHRR 611, para 22 and *Z v United Kingdom* (2001) 34 EHRR 97, [2001] 2 FCR 246 (both cases in which the UK's failure to provide adequate protection against child abuse violated art 3). The test under art 3 does not require it to be shown that but for the failure of the authorities, the ill-treatment would not have occurred; a failure to take reasonably available measures which could have had a real prospect of altering the outcome or mitigating the harm is sufficient to engage State responsibility: *E v United Kingdom* (2002) 36 EHRR 519, [2002] 3 FCR 700. See also *O'Keeffe v Ireland* (2014) 59 EHRR 15, paras 144–52 (the failure to implement an adequate legal or regulatory framework to protect primary school children against the risk of sexual abuse violated art 3).

[2]   *O'Keeffe v Ireland* (fn 1 above) para 144.

3   See *HLR v France* (1997) 26 EHRR 29, para 40: '[I]t must be shown that the risk is real and that the authorities of the receiving State are not able to obviate the risk by providing appropriate protection'. See also: *Salah Sheekh v Netherlands* (2007) 45 EHRR 1158, [2007] INLR 547, para 137; *Sufi* and *Elmi v United Kingdom* (2011) 54 EHRR 209, para 213.

4   See *Horvath v Secretary of State for the Home Department* [2002] 1 AC 489,[2000] INLR 239 HL, (see CHAPTER 12 below).

5   *R (on the application of Bagdanavicius) v Secretary of State for the Home Department* [2005] UKHL 38, [2005] 2 AC 668, [2005] 4 All ER 263, paras 22–4.. Note the House of Lords left undisturbed Auld LJ's analysis on the sufficiency of protection in the Court of Appeal ([2003] EWCA Civ 1605, [2004] 1 WLR 1207, para 55).

6   *R (on the application of Bagdanavicius) v Secretary of State for the Home Department* (fn 5 above) para 17, citing *Nasimi v Sweden* (38865/02) (16 March 2004).

7   *R (on the application of Bagdanavicius) v Secretary of State for the Home Department* (fn 5 above) paras 23–4.

8   *McPherson v Secretary of State for the Home Department* [2001] EWCA Civ 1955, [2002] INLR 139, para 22. For a discussion of sufficiency of protection in the context of the Refugee Convention, see CHAPTER 12 above.

9   *Sheekh v Netherlands* (2007) 45 EHRR 50, para 141. See also: *Sufi* and *Elmi v United Kingdom* (2011) 54 EHRR 209, para 266; *B v United Kingdom* (2013) 57 EHRR 17, para 91. For a discussion of internal relocation in the context of the Refugee Convention, see CHAPTER 12 above.

Application of Article 3 to illness

7.54 The Strasbourg Court has made it clear that, in the light of the fundamental importance of Article 3 of the ECHR, it may be engaged by expulsion when the source of the harm in the destination country is not human agency at all, but the exacerbation of a naturally occurring severe illness, whether physical or mental, because of inadequate medical provision or the lack of carers in the receiving State.[1] In the 1987 case of *Fadele*[2] the Commission held admissible under Article 3 (as well as Article 8) the refusal of admission to the UK of a Nigerian father with a poor immigration history after the mother of the UK-based children was killed, leading to the children having to move to Nigeria, where they suffered from illness, isolation, lack of education and loss of the facilities they had enjoyed in the UK. A friendly settlement meant that the issues were not adjudicated on their merits, but a decade later, the case of *D* established that expulsion to sufficiently severe harm may engage the expelling State's responsibility under Article 3 where 'the source of the risk of proscribed treatment in the receiving country stems from factors which could not engage, either directly or indirectly, the responsibility of that country, or which, taken alone, do not in themselves infringe the standards of the Article'.[3] In that case, it was held to be in breach of Article 3 to implement a decision to remove a terminal AIDS sufferer from a situation in which he enjoyed treatment and support to a country where there was a serious danger that the conditions of adversity awaiting him would further reduce his already limited life expectancy and subject him to acute mental and physical suffering.[4] The court emphasised the need to subject all the circumstances to rigorous scrutiny, especially the applicant's personal situation in the expelling State.[5] The principle was set out in *SCC v Sweden*:

'Aliens who are subject to expulsion cannot in principle claim any entitlement to remain in the territory of a Contracting State in order to continue to benefit from medical, social or other forms of assistance provided by the expelling State.

However, in exceptional circumstances an implementation of a decision to remove an alien may, owing to compelling humanitarian considerations, result in a violation of Article 3.'.[6]

The principle has been reaffirmed in a number of cases, including *BB*,[7] and *Pretty*.[8] In *Bensaid* the court accepted that the same principles applied to psychiatric illness which, if untreated, would cause acute suffering and damage to psychological and perhaps physical integrity.[9] Whether physical or mental health is at risk, factors which have assumed significance in the court's view have included the severity of the applicant's condition, its prognosis, the assumption of responsibility by the expelling State (by the provision of treatment), the availability (including accessibility and affordability) of appropriate treatment for the condition in the receiving State, whether family support is available, and the likely impact on the individual of withdrawal of treatment.[10]

[1]   See eg *Pretty v United Kingdom* (2002) 35 EHRR 1, para 52.
[2]   *Fadele v United Kingdom* (13078/87) (1990) 1 CD 15.
[3]   *D v United Kingdom* (1997) 24 EHRR 423, para 49.
[4]   *D v United Kingdom* (fn 3 above) paras 52–3.
[5]   *D v United Kingdom* (fn 3 above) para 49.
[6]   *SCC v Sweden* (46553/99) 15 February 2000, para 8.
[7]   *BB v France* (30930/96) 9 March 1998 (Commission), 7 September 1998 (ECtHR), in which the Commission held that the expulsion of a severely ill AIDS sufferer to Zaire would breach art 3 because of the length of time he had lived in France, the assumption of responsibility for his health care by the French authorities and the lack of a treatment programme in Zaire (France undertook not to deport the applicant, rendering substantive consideration by the court otiose). See also: *Tatete v Switzerland* (41874/98) 18 November 1999 (Art 3 claim involving the removal of another AIDS sufferer to Zaire was held admissible; struck out following friendly settlement); *Ahmed v Sweden* (9886/05) 22 February 2007 (Art 3 claim based on the unavailability of HIV treatment in Somalia and Kenya was declared admissible; struck out when, having been granted a residence permit, the applicant decided not to pursue the claim). In *SJ v Belgium* (70055/10) 27 February 2014 an HIV-positive Nigerian national alleges that the complex antiretroviral therapy which guarantees her survival is neither available nor accessible in Nigeria. In its Chamber judgment the court found that her expulsion would not violate art 3 but that she had been deprived of an effective remedy contrary to art 13. The case has been referred to the Grand Chamber to be heard in February 2015. However, a number of health-based claims have been held inadmissible, either because the applicant had no significant symptoms, or because he or she had not shown that treatment or family support would not be available to him or her in the receiving State, so that the risk of the severity of suffering required to engage art 3 was not reached, see eg: *Karara v Finland* (1998) 26 EHRR CD220; *MM v Switzerland* (1999) 27 EHRR CD356; *Karagoz v France* (47531/99) 15 November 2001; *Henao v Netherlands* (13669/03) 24 June 2003; *Ndangoya v Sweden* (17868/03) 22 June 2004; *Amegnigan v Netherlands* (25629/04) 25 November 2004; *X v Norway* (2012) 55 EHRR SE4; *Agalar v Norway* (2012) 54 EHRR SE6; *Ghali v Sweden* (2013) 57 EHRR SE11.
[8]   *Pretty v United Kingdom* (fn 1 above).
[9]   *Bensaid v United Kingdom* (2001) 33 EHRR 205, [2001] INLR 325, para 37 (Algerian schizophrenic fearing relapse on return; failed on its facts because of the availability of treatment and speculative nature of the risk of harm). See also paras 46–7 (on the possible engagement of art 8 in such cases).
[10] See eg *Bensaid v United Kingdom* (fn 9 above), paras 34–41.

7.55 In the domestic context, the extent of Article 3 obligations in this field was defined restrictively by the House of Lords in the case of *N*,[1] a Ugandan AIDS sufferer who had been very ill but whose health had improved considerably with highly active anti-retroviral treatment in the UK, an innovation which had been developed since the time of *D's* case. The evidence indicated that without such treatment, which would not be reliably available or accessible to the appellant in Uganda, her mental and physical health and her life expectancy would collapse, subjecting her to acute suffering and early death. The Court of Appeal, by a majority, had refused to hold that her removal would breach Article 3. The majority advocated a test requiring that the 'humanitarian appeal of the case [be] so powerful that it could not in reason be resisted by the authorities of a civilised State'.[2] On appeal, the House of Lords upheld the Court of Appeal, although on different grounds. Broadly, the judges agreed upon the test to be applied, perhaps most vividly set out in Lady Hale's speech:

> 'the test, in this sort of case, is whether the applicant's illness has reached such a critical stage (ie he is dying) that it would be inhuman treatment to deprive him of the care which he is currently receiving and send him home to an early death unless there is care available there to enable him to meet that fate with dignity.'.[3]

They rejected as unhelpful a test based on humanitarian appeal, acknowledging that it was hard to distinguish on humanitarian grounds between cases of expulsion of the terminally ill, and expulsion of those whose good health depended wholly on treatment which would effectively be ended by the act of expulsion.[4] Their Lordships accepted the humanitarian appeal of all such cases and instead based their dismissal of N's appeal on other considerations. Analysis of post-*D* Strasbourg jurisprudence (which they criticised for its fudging of the criteria applied by the court and of issues of availability of treatment and family support) by Lords Hope and Brown yielded the oft-repeated principle that aliens could not claim any entitlement to remain to benefit from medical or other assistance.[5] What was exceptional in D's case was not the denial of treatment which would ensure his long-term survival (no such treatment existed at that time), but rather the denial of the opportunity to die in dignity, in a caring environment.[6] Article 3 did not require Contracting States to allow aliens to remain for indefinite medical treatment and associated welfare benefits, and to interpret it as imposing such an obligation would be to extend the reach of the ECHR further than Contracting States would be prepared to accept.[7] Thus, by placing their emphasis on the public interest in preventing health tourism, their Lordships developed a test whereby the fact that expulsion will, in reality, be a death sentence is irrelevant. A majority[8] of the Grand Chamber of the ECtHR decided that removal of the applicant in *N v United Kingdom* would not breach Article 3.[9] It reviewed its caselaw and noted that since the decision in *D v United Kingdom* the Court had never found that a proposed removal from a contracting state would violate Article 3 on grounds of the consequences for the applicant's health.[10] The Court had consistently applied the principle that an alien subject to expulsion could not claim any entitlement to remain in order to continue to benefit from medical, social or other forms of assistance and services provided in the expelling state.[11] The fact that his or her life expectancy would be 'significantly reduced' as a result of removal would not be sufficient and 'only in a very exceptional case, where the humanitarian grounds against removal are compelling' might there be a breach of Article 3.[12] It is noteworthy that three judges dissented, on the basis that the majority had introduced a policy balance into the application of Article 3 where other case law made it clear that the prohibition was an absolute one.[13]

[1]   *N v Secretary of State for the Home Department* [2005] UKHL 31, [2005] 2 AC 296.

2 *N v Secretary of State for the Home Department* [2003] EWCA Civ 1369, [2004] 1 WLR 1182, per Laws LJ at para 38. Carnwath J dissented, holding that a combination of adverse factors in the receiving State could engage art 3 at para 52.

3 *N v Secretary of State for the Home Department* (fn 1 above) per Lady Hale at para 69. See also Lords Hope (para 50) and Brown (para 94).

4 *N v Secretary of State for the Home Department* (fn 1 above) per Lord Nicholls at para 13, Lord Hope at para 49, Lord Brown at para 91. Their Lordships accepted that the humanitarian appeal of N's case was very strong: per Lord Nicholls at para 14, Lord Hope at para 20, Lady Hale at para 67, Lord Brown at paras 97–99. Lord Walker agreed at para 55.

5 *N v Secretary of State for the Home Department* (fn 1 above) per Lord Nicholls at para 14, Lord Hope at para 35, Lord Brown at para 91.

6 *N v Secretary of State for the Home Department* (fn 1 above) per Lord Hope at para 36, Lady Hale at para 68, Lord Brown at para 93. Note that Baroness Hale acknowledged at para 70 that there may be 'other exceptional cases, with extreme facts, where the humanitarian considerations are equally compelling' to those in D (see also Lord Nicholls at para 9 and Lord Hope at para 50).

7 *N v Secretary of State for the Home Department* (fn 1 above) per Lord Nicholls at paras 15 and 17, and Lord Brown at para 92. Lord Brown noted that such cases involve a positive obligation of affording treatment as well as a negative obligation of refraining from expulsion (para 88).

8 Fourteen votes to three.

9 *N v United Kingdom* (2008) 47 EHRR 885.

10 *N v United Kingdom* (fn 9 above) para 34.

11 *N v United Kingdom* (fn 9 above) para 42.

12 *N v United Kingdom* (fn 9 above) paras 42–3.

13 *N v United Kingdom* (fn 9 above), Joint Dissenting Opinion of Judges Tulkens, Bonello and Spielmann.

7.56 Article 3 might be breached if removal would not only result in an 'earlier and more wretched death' but also a real risk that the returnee would have no family and friends to look after her and a near certainty of losing what little remained of her eyesight.[1] Where the want of effective treatment in the home country would exacerbate the suffering caused by the illness is a result of government policy intended to repress opposition, rather than just lack of national resources, removal might breach Article 3.[2] The Article 3 threshold might be reached in relation to a child where it would not be met in the same circumstances involving an adult.[3] In *GS and EO (Article 3 – health cases) India*,[4] the Upper Tribunal undertook a thorough analysis of the domestic and Strasbourg jurisprudence, and found that it was 'not . . . altogether satisfactory'.[5] The Tribunal held that in determining whether an individual's circumstances are sufficiently exceptional, the focus must be upon the circumstances in which the individual will find him or herself in the receiving State. Although the threshold is a high one, in order to be exceptional a case does not require unique or even particularly rare circumstances. Circumstances that might enhance an individual's claim and make it more likely that he or she will pass the high threshold include, inter alia, being a child, discriminatory denial of treatment in the receiving State, and the absence of resources through civil war or similar human agency.[6] Where the high Article 3 threshold is not passed, health issues are nonetheless relevant to the question of the proportionality of expulsion under Article 8.[7] It is noteworthy that in *Yoh-Ekale Mwanje v Belgium*[8] six of the seven judges expressed the hope that the Grand Chamber would one day revisit the high threshold in health cases set out in N:

'[S]uch an extreme threshold of seriousness—to be nearing death—is hardly consistent with the letter and spirit of art 3, an absolute right which is among the most fundamental rights of the Convention and which concerns an individual's integrity and dignity. In this regard, the difference between a person on his or her deathbed and a person who everyone acknowledges will die very shortly would appear to us to be minimal in terms of humanity. We hope that the Court may one day review its case law in this respect.'[9]

1   AE (Ivory Coast) v Secretary of State for the Home Department [2008] EWCA Civ 1509, paras 7 and 8..

2   RS (Zimbabwe) v Secretary of State for the Home Department [2008] EWCA Civ 839, 152 Sol Jo (no 30) 30.

3   R (on the application of SQ (Pakistan) v Upper Tribunal Immigration and Asylum Chamber [2013] EWCA Civ 1251, para 17.

4   GS and EO (Article 3 – health cases) India [2012] UKUT 00397 (IAC).

5   GS and EO (Article 3 – health cases) India (fn 4 above) para 86.

6   GS and EO (Article 3 – health cases) India (fn 4 above) para 85. Note that in SHH v United Kingdom (2013) 57 EHRR 18, the court found that the removal to Afghanistan of a rejected asylum seeker did not violate art 3. The future harm emanated not from the intentional acts or omissions of state or non-state actors but from a naturally occurring illness and the lack of sufficient resources to deal with it in Afghanistan. Consequently, the applicable test was the one set out in N v United Kingdom (2008) 47 EHRR 885 (7.55 above) which was not, on the facts, met.

7   See eg: Bensaid v United Kingdom (2001) 33 EHRR 205, [2001] INLR 325, paras 46–7; R (on the application of Razgar) v Secretary of State for the Home Department [2004] UKHL 27, [2004] 2 AC 368, paras 10, 59, 74; MM (Zimbabwe) v Secretary of State for the Home Department [2012] EWCA Civ 279, paras 19–23; GS and EO (Article 3 – health cases) India (fn 4 above) para 86(8); Akhalu (health claim: ECHR Article 8) [2013] UKUT 400 (IAC), para 46; SQ (Pakistan) v Upper Tribunal (Immigration and Asylum Chamber) (fn 3) paras 34, 36, 41–2; AE (Algeria) v Secretary of State for the Home Department [2014] EWCA Civ 653, paras 7–9. (See 7.115 below.) [BH1]

8   Yoh-Ekale Mwanje v Belgium (2013) 56 EHRR 35.

9   Yoh-Ekale Mwanje v Belgium (fn 8 above), Joint Partially Concurring Opinion of Judges Tulkens, Jočienė, Popović, Karakaş, Raimondi and de Albuquerque. In this context see the comments of Maurice Kay LJ in AE (Algeria) v Secretary of State for the Home Department [2014] EWCA Civ 653, para 6 and Blake J in GS and EO (Article 3 – health cases) India [2012] UKUT 00397 (IAC), para 86.

7.57 In principle psychological illness is capable of engaging Article 3 just as physical illness is, particularly where there is a significantly increased risk of suicide because of removal.[1] In the case of J the Court of Appeal confirmed that Article 3 may be breached if there is a real risk of committing suicide as a foreseeable consequence of the decision to remove whether on being informed of the removal decision, in the course of removal or after arrival in the destination country.[2] The court drew a distinction between 'domestic cases' and 'foreign cases'.[3] With regard to the risk of suicide on being informed of an adverse immigration decision and in the course of being removed from the UK (both of which are 'domestic cases'), the tribunal would be entitled to assume that the UK authorities would take all reasonable steps in accordance with its obligations under the Human Rights Act 1998 to protect the individual from self-harm, including by the practice of arranging escorts to accompany the person on removal.[4] Further, a real risk that the person would commit suicide after arrival in the receiving State might not be sufficient to establish an Article 3 breach: what happens to the person on and after arrival is treated as a 'foreign case' (ie one in which the alleged violation takes place outside of the jurisdiction of the sending State), making the Article 3 threshold particularly high.[5] What would have to be shown is 'exceptional circumstances comparable in impact to those of the terminal patient in D'[6] or that 'removal would be an "affront to fundamental humanitarian principles"'.[7] An issue of considerable relevance in this context is whether the removing and the receiving states have effective mechanisms for reducing the suicide risk and whether those mechanisms are accessible to the particular invidual.[8] Although suicide risk cases are rarely successful, in Y the Court of Appeal found that the removal of a brother and sister to Sri Lanka where they had both been tortured and the sister raped; where they subjectively feared similar treatment if returned, notwithstanding that their fear was not objectively well-founded; and where they would have no family or other social support created such a likelihood that they would commit suicide in order to escape isolation and fear that their removal would breach Article 3.[9] In *Balogun* the ECtHR approved of the approach taken in J and noted that in suicide cases, appropriate and adequate steps taken to mitigate the risk will weigh against a conclusion that the high threshold of Article 3 has been reached.[10]

[1]   See eg *Bensaid v United Kingdom* (2001) 33 EHRR 205, [2001] INLR 325; *Y (Sri Lanka) v Secretary of State for the Home Department* [2009] EWCA Civ 362, [2010] INLR 178. See also the UT's obiter comments per Blake J at para 85(9) in *GS and EO (Article 3 – health cases) India* [2012] UKUT 00397 (IAC).

[2]   *J v Secretary of State for the Home Department* [2005] EWCA Civ 629, [2005] Imm. AR 409.

[3]   *J v Secretary of State for the Home Department* (fn 2 above) paras 16–17.

[4]   *J v Secretary of State for the Home Department* (fn 2 above) paras 57, 61–2.

[5]   *J v Secretary of State for the Home Department* (fn 2 above) para 28.

[6]   *AJ (Liberia) v Secretary of State for the Home Department* [2006] EWCA Civ 1736, [2006] All ER (D) 230 (Dec), para 16, referring to *D v United Kingdom* (1997) 24 EHRR 423.

[7]   *R (on the application of Tozlukaya) v Secretary of State for the Home Department* [2006] EWCA Civ 379, [2006] All ER (D) 155 (Apr), para 64, referring to *J v Secretary of State for the Home Department* (fn 2 above). In both *R (Tozlukaya)* and *AJ (Liberia) v Secretary of State for the Home Department* (fn 6 above) the court held that mental illness cases were more closely analogous to physical illness cases than the court had considered them to be in J and that the test set out in *N v Secretary of State for the Home Department* [2005] UKHL 31, [2005] 2 AC 296 was applicable. The difficulties involved in drawing the analogy are considered by Black J in *R (on the application of Kurtaj) v Secretary of State for the Home Department* [2007] EWHC 221 (Admin), [2007] All ER (D) 189 (Feb).

[8]   *J v Secretary of State for the Home Department* (fn 2 above) para 31; *AJ (Liberia) v Secretary of State for the Home Department* (fn 6 above) paras 27–31; *CN (Burundi) v Secretary of State for the Home Department* [2007] EWCA Civ 587, [2007] All ER (D) 192 (Jun), para 27; *Y v Secretary of State for the Home Department* (fn 1 above) para 60.

[9]   *Y v Secretary of State for the Home Department* (fn 1 above). It is noteworthy that the court found that 'self-harm would be the consequence of the acts of the Sri Lankan security forces, not of a naturally occurring illness. It would be, if it were to occur, the product of fear and humiliation brought about by the brutality to which both appellants were subjected before they fled' (para 50). See also *R (on the application of C) v Secretary of State for the Home Department* [2012] EWHC 801 (Admin) (application for judicial review of the Secretary of State's refusal to treat further representations based on suicide risk as a fresh claim granted).

[10]   *Balogun v United Kingdom* (2013) 56 EHRR 3, paras 31–2. On the facts, the court found the applicant's complaint under art 3 to be manifestly ill-founded and thus inadmissible: 'In light of the precautions to be taken by the Government and the existence of adequate psychiatric care in Nigeria, should the applicant require it, the Court is unable to find that the applicant's deportation would result in a real and imminent risk of treatment of such severity as to reach this [high] threshold' (para 34). In the domestic context, see *R (on the application of T (Sri Lanka) v Secretary of State for the Home Department* [2013] EWHC 1093 (Admin).

7.58 Article 3 does not impose an obligation on a state to provide individuals with a home or a particular standard of living. However, if conditions of extreme poverty in which an individual has to live are the fault of the authorities they may give rise to a breach of Article 3. The authorities would be at fault if they had a legal obligation to provide accommodation and support, deriving from some other source such as, in respect of asylum seekers, the EU Reception Directive,[1] but failed to comply with that obligation. In such a case there would be a breach of Article 3 if the consequences were of sufficient severity.[2] Thus, an asylum seeker having to live on the street, with no resources or access to sanitary facilities and without means to provide for his essential living needs because of the government's failure to act in accordance with its obligations thereby suffered degrading treatment.[3] Similarly, if dire humanitarian conditions were predominantly caused by the direct and indirect actions of non-state actors, as opposed to being predominantly attributable to poverty or the state's lack of resources to deal with natural phenomena (such as drought) then they would cause a violation of Article 3 if sufficiently severe.[4] If neither the state nor non-state actors are responsible then such a case would have to be viewed through the restrictive lens of N[5] requiring it to be very exceptional and not merely having effects of sufficient severity before there would be a breach of Article 3.[6]

[1] Council Directive 2003/9/EC of 27 January 2003 on laying down minimum standards for the reception of asylum seekers.
[2] *MSS v Belgium and Greece* (2011) 53 EHRR 28.
[3] *MSS v Belgium and Greece* (2011) 53 EHRR 2.
[4] *Sufi and Elmi v United Kingdom* (2011) 54 EHRR 209.
[5] *N v United Kingdom* (2008) 47 EHRR 885.
[6] The tribunal held that the humanitarian situation in southern Somalia reached that threshold in *AMM and others (conflict; humanitarian crisis; returnees; FGM) Somalia CG* [2011] UKUT 445 (IAC).

7.59 Article 3 of the ECHR is in some respects thus considerably broader in its application than the Refugee Convention.[1] It is capable of being engaged by general conditions in the receiving country;[2] there are no exclusions from Article 3 protection on national security or criminality grounds;[3] there is no need to show that the harm feared is for reasons of the applicant's race, religion, nationality, membership of a particular social group or political opinion;[4] the harm feared need not have the character of 'persecution'[5] or even be attributable to any aggressive action.[6] In *Chahal* the ECtHR said that given the irreversible nature of the harm that might occur if the risk of ill-treatment materialised and the importance the court attaches to Article 3, the notion of an effective remedy under Article 13 required independent scrutiny of the claim that there exist substantial grounds for fearing a real risk of treatment contrary to Article 3.[7]

[1] *R (on the application of Borak) v Secretary of State for the Home Department* [2005] EWCA Civ 110, [2004] Imm AR 768, paras 15–21; *Ryabikin v Russia* (2008) 48 EHRR 1322, para 120; *MP (Sri Lanka) v Secretary of State for the Home Department* [2014] EWCA Civ 829, para 48.
[2] See eg: *Sufi and Elmi v United Kingdom* (2012) 54 EHRR 9; *MSS v Belgium and Greece* (2011) 53 EHRR 28. See para 7.51 above.
[3] See eg: *Chahal v United Kingdom* (1996) 23 EHRR 413; *Ahmad v United Kingdom* (2013) 56 EHRR 1; see also 7.50 above. Whereas under the Refugee Convention, cf eg: *T v Immigration Officer* [1996] AC 742, HL; *KK (Turkey) (Article 1F(c))* [2004] UKIAT 00101, [2004] Imm AR 284; *Al-Sirri v Secretary of State for the Home Department* [2012] UKSC 54, [2013] 1 AC 745. However, note that the EC Qualification Directive (Council Directive 2004/83/EC on minimum standards for the qualification and status of third country nationals and stateless persons as refugees or persons who otherwise need international protection (OJ 2004 L304/12)) art 17 provides for the exclusion from subsidiary protection on grounds akin to those under the Refugee Convention (for which see 12.88 ff below). These provisions are not binding, since the Directive sets out minimum standards of protection, leaving Member States free to be more generous.

4   For 'Convention reasons' under the Refugee Convention see **12.64** below.
5   For 'persecution' under the Refugee Convention see **12.46** below.
6   See eg *D v United Kingdom* (1997) 24 EHRR 423.
7   *Chahal v United Kingdom* (1996) 23 EHRR 413, para 151. See also *A v Netherlands* (4900/06) 20 July 2010, paras 155–8.

7.60 Although Article 3 of the ECHR will mainly be engaged in relation to proposed removal, it also has application in relation to conditions in which asylum seekers are detained,[1] and the manner of their support or the deprivation of all support in the UK.[2] Although the humiliating and degrading voucher system of asylum support was abolished,[3] the denial of all support to asylum seekers not making their claim as soon as practicable[4] has led to a spate of cases dealing with when Article 3 is engaged by destitution.[5] In the leading case of *Q*,[6] the Court of Appeal accepted that the regime imposed on asylum seekers who are denied support by reason of section 55(1) of the NIAA 2002 constitutes 'treatment' within the meaning of Article 3, but held that the degree of degradation that must be demonstrated in order to engage Article 3 is significantly more severe than the statutory definition of 'destitution'.[7] The real risk test was, the court held, applied by the ECtHR in expulsion cases where the removing State would no longer be in a position to influence events; it was not appropriate in the context of the (domestic) provision of support to asylum seekers.[8] The court held that it is not unlawful for the Secretary of State to decline to provide support unless and until it is clear that charitable support is not forthcoming and that the individual is incapable of fending for him- or herself.[9] But where the condition of an applicant verges on that described in *Pretty*[10] (see **7.48** above), section 55(5) permits, and section 6 of the Human Rights Act 1998, section 6 obliges, the Secretary of State to provide support.[11] In *T*,[12] the court said that there was no simple way of deciding when Article 3 would be engaged; each case had to be examined on its facts.[13] Psychiatric illness through sleeping rough and begging, resulting in loss of weight and malnutrition, crossed the line,[14] but living at the airport, amid constant noise and light preventing rest and sleep, and being constantly moved on, did not, since there was shelter, sanitary facilities and the applicant had some money for food.[15] In *Limbuela*[16] the House of Lords – approving the earlier decision of the majority of the Court of Appeal – held that in the generality of cases once it was established that the refusal of support would mean that an individual would become street homeless imminently, little more would be required to establish a breach of Article 3.[17] Lord Hope[18] and Baroness Hale[19] disapproved Laws LJ's dissenting analysis in the Court of Appeal – in which he had posited that Article 3 cases are on a spectrum, with violence authorised by the State but unauthorised by law at one end and decisions made in the exercise of lawful policy which nevertheless expose the individual to a marked degree of suffering at the other[20]– as wrongly introducing considerations of proportionality into the absolute prohibition required by Article 3. Even in relation to acts and omissions pursuant to legitimate government policy, the State is obliged to refrain from conduct that causes suffering of the necessary degree of severity.[21] Lord Brown found much of Laws LJ's analysis useful, not because it was helpful to place Article 3 complaints on a spectrum, but rather because it highlighted the need to look at cases in the round.[22] Note that Article 3 does not impose a duty on to provide support for rejected asylum seekers in circumstances where there is no impediment to returning to their own State (although the principles set out above would also apply to rejected asylum seekers who are not removed because of practical difficulties).[23]

1   For Strasbourg cases where detention conditions of aliens held pending expulsion violated art 3 see eg: *Cyprus v Turkey* (1976) 4 EHRR 482 *Dougoz v Greece* (2002) 34 EHRR 61; *Abdolkhani v Turkey* (50213/08) 27 July 2010, 31 BHRC 1; *Popov v France* (39472/07; 39474/07) 19 January 2012 (Chamber judgment); *Kangaratnam v Belgium* (2012) 55 EHRR 26; *Ahmed (Aden) v Malta* (Application 55352/12) (23 July 2013, unreported) (Chamber judgment). However the threshold is high: see *Zhu v United Kingdom* (2000) 30 EHRR CD106 (18-month detention with racist abuse and intimidation from other prisoners held not sufficiently severe to give rise to arguable breach of art 3 ECHR: manifestly unfounded); see also *ZNS v Turkey* (2012) 55 EHRR 11 paras 81, 86–7. In the domestic context see eg *R (on the application of D) v Secretary of State for the Home Department* [2012] EWHC 2501 (Admin); *R (on the application of S) v Secretary of State for the Home Department* [2014] EWHC 50 (Admin); *R (on the application of MD) v Secretary of State for the Home Department* [2014] EWHC 2249 (Admin). On the control and restraint of migrants during the process of enforced removal, see also: *Shchukin v Cyprus* (14030/03) 29 July 2010; *R (on the application of Z) v Secretary of State for the Home Department* [2013] EWHC 498 (Admin).

2   Note that the common law had paved the way: 'the law of humanity' obliges us to afford relief to foreigners and to prevent them from starving (per Lord Ellenborough CJ in *R v Eastbourne Inhabitants* (1803) 4 East 103 at 107, cited by Simon Brown LJ in *R v Secretary of State for Social Security, ex p Joint Council for the Welfare of Immigrants* [1997] 1 WLR 275, CA, at 292).

3   For the voucher scheme and its effects see the 6th edition of this work, 13.26 and 13.27 text and fn 6.

4   Under Nationality, Immigration and Asylum Act 2002, s 55(1); see CHAPTER 14 below.

5   In *O'Rourke v United Kingdom* (39022/97) 26 June 2001 and *Larioshina v Russia* (56869/00) (23 April 2002, unreported), the ECtHR accepted that in principle both eviction leading to homelessness (*O'Rourke*) and payment of a wholly insufficient pension (*Larioshina*) could raise an issue under art 3, if damage to physical or mental health of sufficient severity was caused, but ruled both applications to be manifestly unfounded on their facts. In the Commission report on *BB v France* (30930/96) 9 March 1998, Cabral Barreto, in a concurring opinion, said: 'I consider that a seriously ill foreigner living in a country as a kind of illegal alien, unable to benefit fully and as of right from the social security regime, is in a situation which fails to meet the requirements of Article 3.'

6   *R (on the application of Q) v Secretary of State for the Home Department* [2003] EWCA Civ 364, [2004] QB 36.

7   *R (on the application of Q) v Secretary of State for the Home Department* (fn 6 above) paras 56, 59.

8   *R (on the application of Q) v Secretary of State for the Home Department* (fn 6 above) para 61.

9   *R (on the application of Q) v Secretary of State for the Home Department* (fn 6 above) para 63.

10 *Pretty v United Kingdom* (2002) 35 EHRR 1.

11 *R (on the application of Q) v Secretary of State for the Home Department* (fn 6 above) paras 62, 119.

12 *R (on the application of T) v Secretary of State for the Home Department* [2003] EWCA Civ 1285, [2004] HLR 254.

13 *R (on the application of T) v Secretary of State for the Home Department* (fn 12 above), para 16.

14 *R (on the application of T) v Secretary of State for the Home Department* (fn 12 above) paras 17–18.

15 *R (on the application of T) v Secretary of State for the Home Department* (fn 12 above) para 19.

16 *R (on the application of Limbuela) v Secretary of State for the Home Department* [2005] UKHL 66, [2006] 1 AC 396.

17 *R (on the application of Limbuela) v Secretary of State for the Home Department* (fn 16 above), per Lord Bingham at paras 7–9, Lord Hope at paras 60–2, Lord Scott at para 72, Lady Hale at para 78 and Lord Brown at para 102.

18 *R (on the application of Limbuela) v Secretary of State for the Home Department* (fn 16 above) para 53.

19 *R (on the application of Limbuela) v Secretary of State for the Home Department* (fn 16 above) para 77.

20 *R (on the application of Limbuela) v Secretary of State for the Home Department* [2004] EWCA Civ 540, [2004] QB 1440, para 70.
21 *R (on the application of Limbuela) v Secretary of State for the Home Department* (fn 16 above) para 53, per Lord Hope.
22 *R (on the application of Limbuela) v Secretary of State for the Home Department* (fn 16 above) para 53.
23 see eg: *R (on the application of Kimani) v Lambeth LBC* [2003] EWCA Civ 1150, [2004] 1 WLR 272; *R (on the application of Kimani) v Lambeth London Borough Council* [2005] EWHC 2950 (Admin); R (on the application of N) v Coventry City Council [2008] EWHC 2786 (Admin); *MK v Secretary of State for the Home Department* [2012] EWHC 1896 (Admin).

Slavery and forced labour

7.61 Article 4 of the ECHR states that:

"1   No one shall be held in slavery or servitude.

2   No one shall be required to perform forced or compulsory labour. For the purposes of this Article the term "forced or compulsory labour" shall not include:

(a)   any work required to be done in the ordinary course of detention imposed according to the provisions of Article 5 of this Convention or during conditional release from such detention;

(b)   any service of a military character or, in the case of conscientious objectors in countries where they are recognised, service exacted instead of compulsory military service;

(c)   any service exacted in case of an emergency or calamity threatening the life or well-being of the community;

(d)   any work or service which forms part of normal civic obligations."

Article 4(1) absolutely prohibits slavery and servitude. The prohibition of slavery, servitude and forced labour is unqualified and enshrines one of the fundamental values of democratic society. In the context of immigration, its principal significance is in relation to trafficking and it is dealt with in the CHAPTER 13 on trafficking in human beings.

Detention

7.62 Article 5 of the ECHR is considered further in CHAPTER 18. It states that:

'1   Everyone has the right to liberty and security of person. No one shall be deprived of his liberty save in the following cases and in accordance with a procedure prescribed by law:

(a)   the lawful detention of a person after conviction by a competent court;

(b)   the lawful arrest or detention of a person for non-compliance with the lawful order of a court or in order to secure the fulfilment of any obligation prescribed by law;

(c)   the lawful arrest or detention of a person effected for the purpose of bringing him before the competent legal authority on reasonable suspicion of having committed an offence or when it is reasonably considered necessary to prevent his committing an offence or fleeing after having done so;

> (d) the detention of a minor by lawful order for the purpose of educational supervision or his lawful detention for the purpose of bringing him before the competent legal authority;
>
> (e) the lawful detention of persons for the prevention of the spreading of infectious diseases, of persons of unsound mind, alcoholics or drug addicts or vagrants;
>
> (f) the lawful arrest or detention of a person to prevent his effecting an unauthorised entry into the country or of a person against whom action is being taken with a view to deportation or extradition.
>
> 2 Everyone who is arrested shall be informed promptly, in a language which he understands, of the reasons for his arrest and of any charge against him.
>
> 3 Everyone arrested or detained in accordance with the provisions of paragraph 1(c) of this Article shall be brought promptly before a judge or other officer authorised by law to exercise judicial power and shall be entitled to trial within a reasonable time or to release pending trial. Release may be conditioned by guarantees to appear for trial.
>
> 4 Everyone who is deprived of his liberty by arrest or detention shall be entitled to take proceedings by which the lawfulness of his detention shall be decided speedily by a court and his release ordered if the detention is not lawful.
>
> 5 Everyone who has been the victim of arrest or detention in contravention of the provisions of this Article shall have an enforceable right to compensation.'

The ECtHR has consistently emphasised the importance of the Article 5 protection as a cornerstone of the rule of law and the need to construe it strictly so as to confine the power of the State to interfere with the liberty of the person in a democracy.[1] The central purpose of the Article, the right to liberty and security of person, is designed to protect against arbitrary detention.[2] This is both a substantive and procedural right. Deprivation of liberty must be in accordance with a procedure prescribed by law and, in the immigration context, is lawful only if its purpose is to prevent the person effecting an unauthorised entry into the country, or with a view to removal.[3]

[1] *Aksoy v Turkey* (1996) 23 EHRR 553; *Brogan v United Kingdom* (1988) 11 EHRR 117.
[2] *Winterwerp v Netherlands* (1979) 2 EHRR 387, paras 37–39, *Aksoy v Turkey* above, para 76. The list of exceptions to the right to liberty secured in ECHR, art 5(1) is an exhaustive one and only a narrow interpretation of those exceptions is consistent with the aim and purpose of that provision, namely to ensure that no one is arbitrarily deprived of his or her liberty: *Quinn v France* (1995) 21 EHRR 529, para 42.
[3] Article 5(1)(f).

7.63 Article 5(1) is concerned with the deprivation of liberty rather than its mere restriction, but the distinction is a matter of degree rather than substance, depending on factors such as the nature of the interference with liberty, its duration and the effect on the individual.[1] Thus, the interference with liberty involved in a short examination at the port to establish identity and qualifications for entry would probably not constitute detention so as to engage Article 5. But an equally short detention for fingerprinting or a compulsory medical examination might attract the protection of the Article, because of the element of compulsion and intrusion on privacy.[2] Restrictions on freedom of movement such as residence conditions imposed on temporary admission[3] probably do not involve sufficient deprivation of liberty to amount to detention,[4] although other Convention rights might be engaged.[5] But restrictions amounting to house arrest or severe restrictions falling short of this with conditions prohibiting access to phones or email, as in the government's recently enacted control orders for suspected terrorists,[6] would be sufficient deprivations of liberty to come within the ambit of Article 5.[7] In *Amuur*[8] the French government argued that asylum seekers held at the 'international zone' of the airport were not detained because they could 'at any time have removed themselves from the sphere of application of the measure'. The argument was rejected by the ECtHR, both on the ground that the 'international zone' was a fiction and was French territory, and that an asylum seeker's decision to remain on the territory to make a claim could not be construed as voluntary detention.[9] Detention must also be fair.[10]

1   *Guzzardi v Italy* (1980) 3 EHRR 333, para 92; *Amuur v France* (1996) 22 EHRR 533, para 42, *Engel v Netherlands* (1976) 1 EHRR 647 at paras 58–59.
2   See eg App 8278/78 18 DR 154.
3   Under Immigration Act 1971, Sch 2, para 21(2)–(2B), under which regulations may prohibit unauthorised absence from designated accommodation.
4   In *Guzzardi v Italy* (1980) 3 EHRR 333 (fn 1 above) compulsory residence of a suspect on a small island under strict police supervision was a deprivation of liberty engaging art 5, while restriction on a larger island subject to a less strict regime was not.
5   Notably art 8, because of restrictions on private life and home resulting from the restrictions.
6   Prevention of Terrorism Act 2005.
7   Interference with liberty short of actual confinement has been held to be a deprivation of liberty, see *Guzzardi v Italy* (fn 4 above. House arrest such as that imposed on a detainee G released on bail by SIAC with conditions as to residence, curfew, tagging surveillance and restrictions on who and how he may contact others (described in *A v Secretary of State for the Home Department; X v Secretary of State for the Home Department* [2004] UKHL 56, [2005] 2 WLR 87 para 35) would also constitute a deprivation of liberty; see also *NC v Italy* (24952/94) at para 33.
8   *Amuur v France* (1996) 22 EHRR 533.
9   *Amuur v France* (1996) 22 EHRR 533, paras 43, 46, 52.
10   *Conka v Belgium* (51564/99) (2002) 11 BHRC 555, where a stratagem securing the arrest and detention for deportation of a large number of Slovak Roma, involving conscious deception to make deprivation of liberty easier (requiring them to report to police on the pretext that files needed to be completed) was held unlawful.

Purpose

7.64 The permissible grounds for detention in Article 5 must be construed strictly and narrowly.[1] The two categories of authorised detention directly relating to those subject to immigration control are contained in Article 5(1)(f) and cover (i) prevention of unauthorised entry and (ii) pending deportation.

Preventing unauthorised entry: on its face this is a limited power restricted to a State's legitimate concern to stop people illegally entering countries and attempting to circumvent immigration control. The words indicate it is to prevent such activity and is not a broad ranging power of prolonged detention pending full determination of a claim to entry, and in particular its exercise must not impair or interfere with the right to seek asylum and the protection of the Refugee and Human Rights Conventions.[2] The use of the power to detain asylum seekers on arrival, and those who, having entered illegally, present themselves at the first opportunity, has proved controversial.[3] On any view these persons are seeking authorised entry to the UK and exercising their right to seek international protection.[4] It is not immediately apparent that the purpose of detention, in these circumstances, is to prevent unauthorised entry, unless there is evidence justifying a belief that the person would abscond or not comply with conditions of release. In *Saadi*[5] the House of Lords, however, ruled that detention on arrival of asylum seekers who present no risk of absconding, for the purpose of speedy determination of a claim for asylum, was within the first limb of Article 5(1)(f).[6] The Lords ruled that:

(i) detention in order to determine the claim for asylum was to prevent unauthorised entry because, (turning the phrase on its head) until the claim was determined and granted, entry was not authorised, and the State has power to detain without violating Article 5, until the application has been considered and entry 'authorised'. The power was wider than to prevent evasion of immigration control, and would include the assessment of the merits of the asylum claim;[7]

(ii) to be permissible under Article 5(1)(f), detention need not be 'necessary' to prevent unauthorised entry, even if there is an alternative means of processing the claim for asylum that does not require confinement [para 37]. Here the court relied on the judgment of the ECtHR in *Chahal*[8] that detention under the second limb of Article 5(1)(f) need not be necessary to ensure deportation; all that was required is action being taken with a view to deportation for the power to detain to be invoked;[9]

(iii) the detention was a proportionate response to the reasonable requirements of immigration control, given the established need for speedy decision making to process large numbers of claimants, taking into account its limited duration of around seven days in reasonable conditions [para 45].

This judgment has in principle given the Article (5)(1)(f) ground for detention the widest possible basis. Once the focus is shifted from unauthorised to authorised entry, anyone presenting themselves at the border is liable to detention under the paragraph, since all are seeking authorised entry whatever their immigration status, whether they are British nationals, are exercising Community law rights, have indefinite leave to remain or some other limited leave, or are foreigners and have no leave at all. It is our view that this could not possibly have been the intention of the framers of Article 5, and resort to the 19th century notion of unrestrained rights 'to regulate the entry of aliens'[10] is not a sufficient basis for a power as broad and wide as this to deprive a person of their liberty. It remains to be seen whether administrative convenience as a ground for detention is allowed to prevail beyond asylum seekers to other categories of lawful entrant. A majority of the ECtHR (3:4) upheld the decision of the House of Lords in *Saadi*.[11] The issue was whether an asylum seeker who presented no risk of absconding could lawfully be detained for reasons of administrative convenience connected with processing his asylum claim, given that Article 5(1)(f) only permitted detention 'to prevent his effecting an unauthorised entry into the country'. The Court held that detention of a person who had not been granted leave to enter or remain could be considered as aimed at preventing unlawful entry simply by virtue of the fact that leave had not been granted. Moreover, there was no requirement that detention should be a 'necessary' means to the end of preventing unlawful entry. Whereas for a person authorised to be at large in a country, deprivation of his or her liberty required a reasonable balance to be struck between the interests of the individual and those of society, no such balance had to be struck for an immigrant who was not 'authorised' to be on the territory. 'All that is required is that the detention should be a genuine part of the process to determine whether the individual should be granted immigration clearance and/or asylum and that it should not otherwise be arbitrary, for example on account of its length'.[12] The Court did find a breach of Article 5(2) because of the failure to provide adequate reasons for the detention.

1   *McVeigh, O'Neill and Evans v United Kingdom* (1981) 25 DR 15.
2   *Amuur v France* (1996) 22 EHRR 533, para 43.
3   See CHAPTER 12 above, and CHAPTER 18 below.
4   See Article 14 of the Universal Declaration of Human Rights.
5   *R (on the application of Saadi) v Secretary of State for the Home Department* [2002] UKHL 41, [2002] 1 WLR 3131, [2002] INLR 523, at para 35.
6   The House of Lords upheld the Court of Appeal's judgment at [2001] EWCA Civ 1512, which reversed that of Collins J, who had found the detention contrary to art 5 at [2001] 1 WLR 356.
7   On the basis that if the claim was 'a pack of lies' the claimant would be seeking unauthorised entry: *Saadi* above, para 36 and 43.
8   *Chahal v United Kingdom* (1996) 23 EHRR 413, para 112.
9   'Necessary' in this context can only go to the vires or power to detain and not to the issue of proportionality, as is illustrated in the judgment in *R (on the application of Saadi) v Secretary of State for the Home Department*, above.
10   *R (on the application of Saadi) v Secretary of State for the Home Department*, above para 31, but see **1.10** above.
11   *Saadi v United Kingdom (Application No 13229/03)* (2006) Times, 3 August, [2006] All ER (D) 125 (Jul), EctHR, upheld by the Grand Chamber.
12   *Saadi v United Kingdom (Application No 13229/03)* at para [45].

Action with a view to deportation

7.65 To justify detention with a view to deportation, all that is required under Article 5 is that 'action is being taken with a view to deportation'.[1] This means that detention need not be necessary to effect removal or to ensure compliance with the enforcement process. In *Chahal v United Kingdom* the ECtHR expressly rejected the idea that Article 5(1)(f) required a connection between detention and the conduct of the person; detention need not be 'reasonably considered necessary, for example, to prevent his committing an offence or fleeing'.[2] However, the power to detain under this provision is limited to circumstances where deportation proceedings are actually in progress and removal can be effected; where the proceedings are being pursued with due diligence; where the overall period of detention is not excessive; and where proper explanation is given for any delay.[3] These Convention restrictions match the limitations on the power to detain in domestic common law. Thus, the detention of a Somali national was held to be outwith Article 5(1)(f) because expulsion to Somalia was practically impossible since the individual did not have the relevant travel documents.[4] In *Chahal* a lengthy detention pending deportation was held not to violate Article 5(1) of the Convention, given the complexity of the issues in the proceedings, which were pursued diligently, and the seriousness of the case, given that it involved national security.[5] The conduct of the detainee is a factor and if he or she has contributed to the length of the detention by delaying proceedings this will be a relevant consideration.[6]

1   *Chahal v United Kingdom* (1996) 23 EHRR 413, para 413.
2   *Chahal* above, at para 112; see also *Bozano v France* (1986) 9 EHRR 297 para 60.
3   *Chahal* above, at para 113. In *Ryabikin v Russia* (2008) App 8320/04 detention for just over 12 months was not justified because extradition proceedings were not being pursued with due diligence.
4   *Ali v Switzerland* (1998) 28 EHRR 304.

⁵   *Chahal* above, at paras 109 and 117.
⁶   *Kolompar v Belgium* (1992) 16 EHRR 197.

Legality

7.66 Article 5 of the ECHR requires that any detention conform to the substantive and procedural rules of national law. A detention which is unlawful in domestic law will necessarily be unlawful under the ECHR.¹ In addition, the provisions for detention must conform to the norms of Convention legality and be sufficiently accessible and precise to prevent arbitrary detention.² This means that they must be formulated with sufficient clarity to enable those affected to understand them and to regulate their conduct accordingly.³ The principle, which underlies Convention legality, is, therefore, legal certainty.⁴ In *Amuur v France* the ECtHR explained that the words in Article 5 'prescribed by law' refer to the quality of the domestic law and other legal rules.⁵ It is in this context that the existence and application of a policy governing detention is of paramount importance. A detailed policy such as that provided in the Enforcement Instructions and Guidance is not an optional extra for the immigration service; it is essential to ensure that the wide power to detain those subject to immigration control is not exercised in an arbitrary fashion. It is also an essential requirement of the common law necessary to meet the demands of fairness and consistency.⁶ The Secretary of State's frequent refrain that his policy is more generous than the Convention is in this respect disingenuous: the policy is a fundamental requirement of compliance with Article 5 and the common law. For this reason a failure to apply stated policy is incompatible with Article 5, as is having unpublished criteria for detention, such as the 1991 and 1994 instructions (now published),⁷ or an undisclosed practice which is inconsistent with stated policy,⁸ or policies whose meaning is not sufficiently clear and foreseeable. Detention may also be arbitrary if insufficient information is provided to the detainees or their representatives to determine the basis of the decision to detain and in order to mount an effective challenge to the decision.⁹

¹   *Raninen v Finland* (1997) 26 EHRR 563 para 46 and *R v Governor of Brockhill Prison, ex p Evans (No 2)* [2000] 3 WLR 843 per Lord Hope.
²   The three requirements of Convention legality have been formulated by the ECtHR as follows: (i) the interference in question must have some basis in domestic law; and (ii) the law must be accessible; and (iii) the law must be formulated so that it is sufficiently foreseeable: *Sunday Times v United Kingdom* (1979) 2 EHRR 245; *Silver v United Kingdom* (1983) 5 EHRR 347; *Malone v United Kingdom* (1984) 7 EHRR 14; *Halford v United Kingdom* (1997) 24 EHRR 523. See also *Zamir v United Kingdom* (1983) 40 DR 42, paras 90–91; *Steel v United Kingdom* (1998) 28 EHRR 603. In *Nadarajah v Secretary of State for the Home Department; R (on the application of Amirthanathan) v Secretary of State for the Home Department* [2003] EWCA Civ 1768, 148 Sol Jo LB 24 the Court of Appeal held that the Secretary of State's policy on detention for removal was not sufficiently accessible, in that his policy of disregarding an intimation of judicial review proceedings when considering whether removal was 'imminent' was not known.
³   *G v Germany* (1989) 60 DR 256 approved in *De Freitas v Permanent Secretary of Ministry of Agriculture, Fisheries, Lands and Housing* [1998] 3 WLR 675.
⁴   *De Freitas v Permanent Secretary of Ministry of Agriculture, Fisheries, Lands and Housing* [1998] 3 WLR 675 per Lord Clyde at 681.
⁵   *Amuur v France* (1996) 22 EHRR 533, para 50; see also *Dougoz v Greece* (2002) 34 EHRR 61, (2001) 10 BHRC 306, paras 56–58.
⁶   See *R (on the application of Alconbury Developments Ltd) v Secretary of State for the Environment, Transport and the Regions* [2001] UKHL 23, [2003] 2 AC 295 at para 143 per

Lord Clyde: 'policies are an essential element in securing the coherent and consistent performance of administrative functions'. For the Enforcement Instructions and Guidance, and the Secretary of State's detention policy, see Chapter 18 below.

7 *Butterworths Immigration Law Service*, D[971]; see Chapter 18 below.
8 *R (on the application of Nadarajah) v Secretary of State for the Home Department, R (Amirthanathan) v Secretary of State for the Home Department* [2003] EWCA Civ 1768.
9 *Alva (Garcia) v Germany* (13 February 2001, unreported).

Proportionate

7.67 For detention not to be considered arbitrary, in accordance with international law principles, it must be necessary and proportionate to its legitimate aim. Detention may be arbitrary if it is disproportionate in its effect on the individual measured against the aim pursued in detaining the person.[1] The concept of proportionality is also at the heart of the common law in relation to detention.[2] In *Amuur*[3] the court accepted some confinement of asylum seekers to enable States to prevent unlawful immigration, but held that States must ensure the presence of suitable safeguards and that the length of confinement was proportionate to the process of examination. Confinement should not 'above all . . . deprive the asylum seeker of the right to gain effective access to the procedure for determining refugee status'.[4] Detention may also be disproportionate if it is used in circumstances where alternatives to incarceration are available[5] and it is not a recourse of last resort.[6] This approach has been applied by the UN Human Rights Committee, applying the equivalent provisions of the International Covenant on Civil and Political Rights, in several cases against Australia.[7] These cases do not appear to have been cited to the Court of Appeal in *Sezek*,[8] when the court stated that 'there is nothing in the Convention nor any authority to support [the] assertion that Mr Sezek's detention is incompatible with Article 5(1)(f) if other ways of preventing him absconding are available'. In *Saadi* the House of Lords considered proportionality as an important aspect of whether the detention under the Oakington regime was compliant with Article 5.[9] The House determined that although alternatives to incarceration were available, they were not as effective as a short period of detention in securing the speedy processing of asylum claims and determining whether or not to authorise entry. Furthermore the limited period of detention in reasonable physical conditions was important in demonstrating that the detention was a proportionate measure balanced against this policy consideration.[10]

1 *Winterwerp v Netherlands* (1979) 2 EHRR 387 and *Caprino v United Kingdom* (1980) 4 EHRR 97 EComHR, para 67. The proportionality test was accepted by the House of Lords in *R (on the application of Saadi) v Secretary of State for the Home Department* [2002] UKHL 41, [2002] 1 WLR 3131, [2002] INLR 523, and in *R v Governor of Brockhill Prison, ex p Evans (No 2)* [2000] 3 WLR 843, and by the Court of Appeal in *A v Secretary of State for the Home Department; X v Secretary of State for the Home Department; Y v Secretary of State for the Home Department* [2002] EWCA Civ 1502, [2003] 2 WLR 564 and (implicitly) in *R (on the application of I) v Secretary of State for the Home Department* [2002] EWCA Civ 888, [2003] INLR 196, [2002] All ER (D) 243 (Jun).
2 See eg *R v Governor of Durham Prison, ex p Singh* [1984] 1 WLR 704, [1983] Imm AR 198, and Chapter 18 below.
3 *Amuur v France* (1996) 22 EHRR 533.
4 *Amuur* at para 43.
5 *Tomasi v France* (1993) 15 EHRR 1.
6 *Litwa v Poland* (26629/95) (2000) 63 BMLR 199, ECtHR, a case involving the detention of a drunk, the court emphasised that 'detention of an individual is such a serious measure that

it is only justified where other, less severe, measures have been considered and found to be insufficient to safeguard the individual or the public interest'.

[7] For example in *A v Australia* [1997] Communication No 560/1993, [1997] 4 BHRC 210, UN HRC, it was held that detention of an asylum seeker can be considered arbitrary if it is 'not necessary in all the circumstances of the case, for example to prevent flight or interference with evidence: the element of proportionality becomes relevant in this context'. See also *B v Australia* (Communication No 1014/2001, 18 September 2003) at para 7.2, where the Committee held that the State had failed to demonstrate that 'there were not less invasive means of achieving the same ends, that is to say compliance with the State's immigration policies by, for example, imposition of reporting obligations, sureties or other conditions'.

[8] *R (on the application of Sezek) v Secretary of State for the Home Department* [2002] 1 WLR 348, at para 13.

[9] *R (on the application of Saadi) v Secretary of State for the Home Department* [2002] UKHL 41, [2002] 1 WLR 3131, [2002] INLR 523 at para 44.

[10] *Saadi* above, at paras 45–47.

7.68 Difficulty has arisen in the domestic courts over the ECtHR's ruling in *Chahal* that detention with a view to deportation did not have to be necessary to prevent the commission of offences or absconding.[1] This was applied to entry by the House of Lords in *Saadi*.[2] However, the question of whether detention is a proportionate measure is a different issue from whether or not Article 5(1)(f) should be construed so as to restrict the use of the power to circumstances where it is demonstrably necessary to achieve those ends. The *Chahal* ruling goes to the *vires* or power to detain, but not to the issue of proportionality. Thus the rejection in *Saadi* of the test of necessity was made in the context of the power to detain; having dealt with that the House of Lords then went on to deal with the question of proportionality.[3] But this does not mean that in any individual case, evidence of effective alternatives to detention will be irrelevant to the overall question of whether, assuming the power to detain exists, its exercise is disproportionate. In *Nadarajah and Amirthanathan*[4] the Court of Appeal appears to have conflated the two issues; whilst it was correct to state that Article 5(1)(f) does not 'itself import the test of proportionality', proportionality is an element of the broader requirement that the detention is prescribed by law and not arbitrary.[5] Outside of the Oakington regime, the detention of someone not facing imminent removal, with no history of absconding or other adverse factors, would in our view be disproportionate.[6]

[1] *Chahal v United Kingdom* (1996) 23 EHRR 413, para 112.

[2] *R (on the application of Saadi) v Secretary of State for the Home Department* [2002] UKHL 41, [2002] 1 WLR 3131, [2002] INLR 523. The House upheld administrative detention for seven days at Oakington Barracks to enable the Secretary of State to process claims, accepting that it was compatible with art 5(1)(f) provided that detention was not continued longer than necessary for this purpose (ie, proportionate to the legitimate aim), but held that detention did not have to be 'necessary' either in the sense that the claimants would otherwise abscond and make an unauthorised entry, or in the sense that the claims could not be investigated without detention.

[3] See above.

[4] *Nadarajah v Secretary of State for the Home Department* [2003] EWCA Civ 1768, [2004] INLR 139.

[5] In *R v Governor of Brockhill Prison, ex p Evans (No 2)* [2000] 4 All ER 15, [2000] 3 WLR 843, the House of Lords considered that a detention that is lawful in domestic law may 'nevertheless be open to criticism on the ground that it is arbitrary because, for example, it was resorted to in bad faith or was not proportionate', referring to *Engel v Netherlands* (1976) 1 EHRR 647 para 58 and *Tsirlis and Kouloumpas v Greece* (1997) 25 EHRR 198, para 56.

[6] In such circumstance the policy would dictate release.

7.69 The conditions and circumstances of detention are also relevant to the question of whether or not the detention is proportionate. There must be 'some relationship between the ground of permitted deprivation of liberty relied upon and the place and conditions of detention',[1] such that it would not be lawful to detain an asylum seeker or immigrant with serious mental health problems in an immigration detention centre. In *Saadi* the physical conditions and relaxed regime at Oakington were important factors in the Lords conclusion that the short period of detention was not disproportionate.[2] Factors such as the age, mental and physical health of the detainee, as well as the actual conditions in the detention centre are all relevant to the question of whether or not the detention is a proportionate measure. In *Dougoz v Greece*[3] the ECtHR found that the detention of an asylum seeker who had been convicted of a series of serious offences and whose expulsion from the territory was ordered violated Article 5 (and 3) in a number of ways: Mr Dougoz was held for a substantial period of time in overcrowded holding cells without adequate health, recreational or social facilities, and in conditions condemned by the Committee for the Prevention of Torture;[4] on his release from the sentence for drug smuggling he was detained by the decision of the deputy prosecutor in a remand centre pending his expulsion, without any independent court decision being taken as to whether he was likely to re-offend;[5] his requests for discretionary release were unanswered and the court that reviewed the decision to expel him did not expressly consider the need to continue to detain him.[6] His detention in these circumstances was held to be arbitrary.

[1]   *Aerts v Belgium* (1998) 29 EHRR 50, para 46 and *Bouamar v Belgium* (1988) 11 EHRR 1.
[2]   *R (on the application of Saadi) v Secretary of State for the Home Department* [2002] UKHL 41, [2002] 1 WLR 3131, [2002] INLR 523.
[3]   *Dougoz v Greece* (2002) 34 EHRR 61, (200)] 10 BHRC 306.
[4]   *Dougoz v Greece* above, at para 46, 48.
[5]   *Dougoz v Greece* at para 56–58.
[6]   *Dougoz v Greece* at para 62, 63.

7.70 Detention, and more often its continuation, may have serious repercussions for the health especially mental health of a detainee and may give rise to a breach of Article 8 or, if more severe, Article 3 of the ECHR.[1] The obligation on the detaining authority is to ensure that 'a person is detained in conditions compatible with respect for human dignity and that the manner and method of the execution of the measure does not subject [the detainee] to distress and hardship of an intensity exceeding the unavoidable level of suffering inherent in detention and that, given the practical demands of imprisonment, [the detainee's] health and wellbeing are adequately secured'.[2] When assessing the conditions of detention account must be taken of the cumulative effect of the conditions.[3]

[1]   *Dougoz v Greece* (above) and *Kalashnikov v Russia* (2002) 36 EHRR 587 paras 101–103 in respect of prison conditions; and more generally *Bensaid v United Kingdom* (2001) 33 EHRR 205.
[2]   *Kalashnikov* para 95, approved by the Court of Appeal in *Batayav v Secretary of State for the Home Department* [2003] EWCA Civ 1489, [2004] INLR 126.
[3]   *Dougoz* para 45 and *Kalashnikov* at para 95. The cases *of Peers v Greece* (2001) 33 EHRR 1192, para 74 and *Price v United Kingdom* (2002) 34 EHRR 53 both concerned conditions of detention which were held to give rise to art 3 violations. Both applicants were disabled prisoners and in neither case was there any intention to inflict suffering or debase the

individual, a factor which is not a necessary condition for an art 3 violation. They were both detained in intolerable conditions, held to constitute degrading treatment.

7.71 In determining whether the detention of immigrants and asylum seekers is arbitrary, the UN Working Group on Arbitrary Detention considers whether the person concerned is able to enjoy all or some of the following guarantees:

(1) to be informed, at least orally, in a language he or she understands, of the grounds for proposed refusal at the border;

(2) to have the detention decision taken by an authorised official with a sufficient level of responsibility;

(3) determination of the lawfulness of the detention by automatic and prompt recourse to a judge or body of equivalent competence, independence and impartiality, or the possibility of appealing to a judge or such a body;

(4) entitlement to review of detention by higher court or equivalent body;

(5) written and reasoned notification of detention measure in a language understood by the applicant;

(6) the possibility of communicating effectively by phone, fax or email with, in particular, a lawyer, consular representative and relatives;

(7) assistance by counsel (of the detainee's choice or officially appointed) through visits in the place of custody and at any hearing;

(8) detention in dedicated detention centres or separation from criminal prisoners;

(9) up-to-date register of those detained with reasons;

(10) not to be held for an excessive or unlimited period, with a maximum statutory period;

(11) information of guarantees provided in disciplinary rules;

(12) procedure for incommunicado detention;

(13) alternatives to administrative detention;

(14) access to places of custody by UNHCR, International Committee of the Red Cross and specialised NGOs.[1]

UNHCR's view of required safeguards in respect of detention of asylum seekers[2] includes (i) prompt and full communication of any order of detention, together with the reasons for the order, and the rights in connection with the order, in a language and in terms they understand; (ii) to be informed of the right to legal counsel. Where possible, they should receive free legal assistance; (iii) to have the decision subjected to an automatic review before a judicial or administrative body independent of the detaining authorities, followed by regular periodic reviews of the necessity to continue detention; (iv) either personally or through a representative, the right to challenge the necessity of the deprivation of liberty at the review hearing.

---

[1] *Civil and political rights, including questions of torture and detention* UN Commission on Human Rights, 55th Session, 18 December 1998, E/CN.4/1999/63, para 69. See also Report on visit to UK and Isle of Man by the Committee for the Prevention of Torture and Inhuman or Degrading Treatment or Punishment, March 2005 (CPT Inf/2005 1).

[2] UNHCR *Guidelines on applicable criteria and standards relating to the detention of asylum seekers* (February 1999), Guideline 5 Butterworths Immigration Law Service, 2C[261]. See also UNHCR EXCOM Conclusion 44 ('Detention of Refugees and Asylum seekers') UN Doc A/AC.96/688.

Articles 5(2) and (4)

7.72 Detention must be adequately reasoned[1] and subject to prompt and regular review by a court to comply with the procedural requirements of ECHR, Article 5(2) and 5(4). Article 5(2) states that anyone arrested or detained must be 'informed promptly, in a language which he understands, of the reasons for the arrest and of any charge against him'. This applies to all cases and not just criminal charges.[2] It requires that the detainee must be told at least the essential legal and factual basis for his detention and something that goes beyond simple reference to the source of the power.[3] Article 5(2) was violated by a document that was inexact as to the facts which were said to justify detention and which referred to a repealed statutory provision, not to its successor which conferred the power under which the individual was detained.[4] The giving of reasons is an essential safeguard against arbitrary detention.

[1]   *X v United Kingdom* (1981) 4 EHRR 188, para 66; *Fox, Campbell and Hartley v United Kingdom* (1990) 13 EHRR 157, para 40.
[2]   *Van der Leer v Netherlands* (1990) 12 EHRR 567, paras 27–29.
[3]   *Fox, et al v United Kingdom* (1990) 13 EHRR 157, paras 40–41.
[4]   *Rusu v Austria* (2008) App No 34082/02.

7.73 Article 5(4) of the ECHR requires speedy access to a court to determine the lawfulness of detention, and release if the detention is not lawful.[1] Its purpose is to ensure judicial supervision of the lawfulness of the measure to which they are subjected.[2] The scope of the supervision and the degree of scrutiny under Article 5(4) depends upon the context and the procedure must give to the individual concerned 'guarantees, appropriate to the kind of deprivation of liberty in question, of [a] judicial procedure the forms of which may vary from one domain to another'.[3] The procedure must be adversarial and ensure equality of arms.[4] In *Chahal v United Kingdom*[5] the ECtHR found a violation of ECHR, art 5(4) because there was no court which could properly review the detention and the national security grounds for it. To meet the requirements of Article 5(4) the review must be wide enough to bear on those conditions which are essential for the lawful detention of a person according to Article 5(1).[6] In *Dougoz v Greece*[7] an Article 5(4) violation was found where release from detention pending deportation was entirely at the discretion of the Minister of Justice with no right of independent review. The court in *Amuur* held that deprivation of liberty is not compatible with the Convention if the courts are unable to review the conditions under which individuals are being held,[8] or to impose a limit on the length of detention or to provide legal, humanitarian or social assistance.[9] The court stressed that 'account should be taken of the fact that detention is applied 'not to those who have committed criminal offences but to aliens who, often fearing for their lives, have fled from their own country'.[10] Failure to keep to a timetable of periodic review may lead to violations of Article 5(4).[11] This has been a problem in domestic jurisdiction, especially with Mental Health Review Tribunals,[12] but the absence of speedy access to a court for immigration bail could also lead to incompatibility with Article 5(4).[13] Volume of applications and workload is not a sufficient justification for delay on the part of judicial bodies in providing access to review.[14] Because the grounds for detention may change over time, periodic review is required.[15] The court must be able to determine the legality of the detention, not merely according to the provisions of domestic law but also those of Convention law.[16] *Habeas corpus* was not an adequate remedy for asylum seekers detained under the Immigration Act 1971, Schedule 2, paragraph 16 prior to the coming into force of the Human Rights Act 1998, because it was concerned merely with the lawfulness of detention under domestic law.[17] A court on a *habeas corpus* application is now required to apply ECHR requirements of legality—including proportionality—to ensure that the decision to detain is compatible with ECHR, Article 5 rights.

[1] *Amuur v France* (1996) 22 EHRR 533, para 43. The court must be able to examine not only whether conditions precedent for detention under domestic law are met (which the High Court does in *habeas corpus*) but also whether detention is necessary or proportionate: *Amuur*, para 53. See also *X v United Kingdom* (1981) 4 EHRR 188; *Brogan v United Kingdom* (1988) 11 EHRR 117, para 65.

[2] *De Wilde, Ooms and Versyp v Belgium* (1971) 1 EHRR 373, para 76. In *Reid (Hutchison) v United Kingdom* (Application 50272/99) [2003] ECHR 50272/99, 37 EHRR 211the imposition on the applicant of the burden of proof that he no longer required to be detained violated art 5(4), as did refusal of access to the detention file which contained documents essential for determining the lawfulness of the detention: see also *Shishkov v Bulgaria* (38822/97).

[3] *De Wilde* above, paras 76–78.

[4] *Sanchez-Reisse v Switzerland* (1986) 9 EHRR 71; *Toth v Austria* (1991) 14 EHRR 551; *Kampanis v Greece* (1995) 21 EHRR 43; *Nikolova v Bulgaria* (Application 31195/96) (1999) 31 EHRR 64); *Garcia v Germany (23541/94)* (13 February 2001, unreported) para 39.

[5] *Chahal v United Kingdom* (1996) 23 EHRR 413. The decision led to the creation of the Special Immigration Appeals Commission; see CHAPTER 22 below.

[6] *Chahal v United Kingdom* above, at para 127.

[7] *Dougoz v Greece* (2002) 34 EHRR 61, (2001) 10 BHRC 306.

[8] *Amuur v France* above. See also *R (on the application of H) v Secretary of State for the Home Department* [2003] UKHL 59, [2004] 2 AC 253, where the House of Lords held that there was a violation of art 5(4), where a Mental Health Review Tribunal ordered a conditional discharge of a patient but the applicant could not be released because the conditions could not be met and the legislation did not allow the Tribunal to reconsider its decision in light of the changed circumstances.

[9] *Amuur* above, para 53.

[10] *Amuur* above, para 43.

[11] In *Sanchez-Reisse v Switzerland* (1986) 9 EHRR 71, 31 days was held not to meet the requirements of speedy review in an extradition case but much shorter periods were held unlawful in *De Jong v Netherlands* (22 May 1984, unreported) Series A No 77 and *GB and MB v Switzerland* (30 November 2000, unreported).

[12] In *R (on the application of C) v Mental Health Review Tribunal* [2001] EWCA Civ 1110, [2002] 1 WLR 176, the Tribunal's practice of listing all hearings of patients detained under the Mental Health Act for a uniform specified period after the date of the request was held in breach of art 5(4) requirements of speedy determination of the lawfulness of the detention. The court held that the Convention requires a hearing within the period reasonably necessary to adjudicate on the application, which will be dependent on the facts of each case.

[13] A system of automatic bail hearings for immigration detainees in Part 3 of the Immigration and Asylum Act 1999, designed to ensure compliance with the procedural requirements of art 5, was never brought into force and was repealed by the Nationality, Immigration and Asylum Act 2002. In this connection, the seven-day bar on bail applications for new arrivals contained in the Immigration Act 1971, and the repeal of the eight- and 36-day automatic bail references means that there is no time requirement on access to the courts. This compares unfavourably with the review afforded to detained criminal suspects (see fn 11, above) and may not be compatible with art 5(4). See UN Working Group on Arbitrary Detention *Report on a visit to the UK on the issue of immigrants and asylum seekers*, E/CN.4/1999/63/Add.3 (1998).

[14] *Bezicheri v Italy* (1989) 12 EHRR 210 para 25.

[15] *Bezicheri*, above.

[16] *Amuur v France* above, paras 50 and 53.

[17] *X v United Kingdom* (1981) 4 EHRR 188, paras 58–61; *Weeks v United Kingdom* (1987) 10 EHRR 293. However, in *Zamir v United Kingdom* (1983) 40 DR 42, para 100,

judicial review was found to be sufficient to establish the lawfulness of detention under art 5(1)(f).

Just satisfaction

7.74 Everyone who has been the victim of arrest or detention in contravention of the provisions of Article 5 of the ECHR must have an enforceable right to compensation.[1] Damages for breaches of section 6 of the Human Rights Act 1998 may not be awarded against a court or Tribunal for judicial acts done in good faith, but there is an exception in section 9(3) of the HRA where the award is for compensation for breaches of Article 5.[2] In *KB v the Mental Health Review Tribunal*[3] the court considered, in the context of significant delay in access to the Mental Health Review Tribunal in breach of Article 5(4), whether an enforceable right to compensation means that damages must always be awarded for any breach of Article 5 and concluded that it does not: damages are not mandatory, even where damage flows from the deprivation of liberty, but discretionary, and a declaration of illegality may be sufficient. The court was unable to identify any clear and constant jurisprudence on the issue but two principles could be discerned namely (i) damages are not recoverable in the absence of a deprivation of liberty[4] and (ii) damages are available for distress.[5] Establishing a deprivation of liberty will be inevitable if the detention is unlawful under Article 5(1) but the more difficult question arises in the context of the absence of appropriate procedural rights as required by Article 5(4). There it will need to be established that the applicant would not have been detained or would have been released sooner had he or she had the benefit of the procedural guarantees.[6] *Chahal v United Kingdom* is an example of this approach where the the ECHR declined to award monetary compensation for the applicant despite finding Article 5(4) breached by the lack of judicial supervision of the detention,[7] and a challenge by judicial review of the Secretary of State's refusal to provide compensation was rejected by the Court of Appeal on the basis that the lack of judicial supervision did not affect the lawfulness of the actual detention.[8]

[1] ECHR, art 5(5). See *W v Home Office* [1997] Imm AR 302.

[2] *R v Governor of Brockhill Prison, ex p Evans (No 2)* [1999] QB 1043 [2000] 3 WLR 843. In *ID v Home Office* [2005] EWCA Civ 38, [2006] 1 All ER 183 the Court of Appeal rejected a claim by the government that immigration officers as well as judges were exempt from civil actions for damages. See CHAPTER 18 below.

[3] *R (on the application of KB) v Mental Health Review Tribunal* [2004] QB 936, [2003] 2 All ER 209.

[4] Although even where there is such deprivation damages may not be recovered: see *Fox, Campbell and Hartley v United Kingdom* (1990) 13 EHRR 157 (merits) and (1991) 14 EHRR 108 (just satisfaction).

[5] *R (on the application of KB) v Mental Health Review Tribunal*, above at paras 41 and 42.

[6] *KB* at paras 41 and 64, applying ECtHR cases including *Nikolova v Bulgaria* (Application 43125/98) (2001) EHRR 3 and *Migon v Poland* (24244/94) and not following other Strasbourg court decisions, where compensation was awarded for frustration and distress without unlawful detention in the context of art 5(4): see *Delbec v France* (43125/98) (18 June 2002, unreported); *LR v France* (33396/96) (27 June 2002, unreported); *DM v France* (041376/98) (27 June 2002, unreported), and *Laidin v France* (43191/98) (5 November 2002, unreported).

[7] *Chahal v United Kingdom* (1996) 23 EHRR 413, para 158.

[8] *R v Secretary of State for the Home Department, ex p Chahal* (1999) Times, 10 November, CA.

7.75 In *R (on the application of KB) v Mental Health Review Tribunal*,[1] the court rejected the Secretary of State's submission on the measure of damages to the effect that a European standard should be applied (which was generally extremely modest)[2] and held that the court is free to depart from the European scale in order to award adequate, but not excessive damages judged by the conditions in the UK.[3] In general those awards should reflect awards made in comparable torts.[4] Thus the level of damages for a breach of Article 5(1) should be no different from those for false imprisonment, and the court should make a global assessment of the loss, drawing a distinction between cases where the person has been detained lawfully for a period and those where the entire period of detention was unlawful.[5] In *Anufrijeva v London Borough of Southwark*[6] the Court of Appeal endorsed the approach of Stanley Burnton in *KB* and ruled that the level of damages awarded in respect of torts did provide some rough guidance, as did the guidance from the Judicial Studies Board, awards made by the Criminal Injuries Compensation Board and the Parliamentary and Local Government Ombudsmen where the consequences of the infringement of human rights are similar. In the past damages have been awarded against the Home Office for unlawful detention on a scale similar to that obtaining in actions against the police.[7] This should continue under the Human Rights Act 1998. It is also strongly arguable that those detained under Immigration Act powers are in a similar category to *Lunt*[8]—they are administrative detainees, who have not been convicted of criminal offences and are otherwise of good character. Incarceration for asylum seekers can be particular distressing because of a previous experience of torture or other abuse and they invariably find it difficult to understand why, when they are seeking sanctuary, they find themselves incarcerated. Exemplary damages were held not to be available for a breach of Article 5 on the basis that section 8(3) of the Human Rights Act 1998 prohibits damages otherwise than by way of compensation and exemplary damages by their very nature are punitive.[9] On this reasoning, however, aggravated damages can be available.

[1] *R (on the application of KB) v Mental Health Review Tribunal* [2003] EWHC 193 (Admin), [2004] QB 936.

[2] See *Curley v United Kingdom* (2000) 31 EHRR 401, referred to at para 44 of *KB*, above.

[3] *R (on the application of KB) v Mental Health Review Tribunal* para 48. See, however, the admonitions of the House of Lords on the need to have regard to the Strasbourg case law in *R (on the application of Greenfield) v Secretary of State for the Home Department* [2005] UKHL 14, [2005] 2 All ER 240, which was a case dealing with an art 6 breach. See **7.28** above.

[4] The court adopted the approach of Sullivan J in *Bernard* and of the Law Commission and rejected Lord Woolf's extra-judicial observation that damages under the HRA should be lower than tort damages, an observation he resiled from in *Anufrijeva v Southwark London Borough Council* [2003] EWCA Civ 1406, [2004] QB 1124 at para 73.

[5] *R (on the application of KB) v Mental Health Review Tribunal*, above at para 53, referring to the cases of *Thompson v Metropolitan Police Comr* [1998] QB 498 at 516 and the approach of the Court of Appeal in *R v Governor of Brockhill Prison, ex p Evans (No 2)* [1999] QB 1043, especially Lord Woolf at 1059–60, which the court found particularly helpful. Damages for 59 additional days imprisonment were increased from £2,000 to £5,000, to reflect the fact that Ms Evans was properly convicted of a serious criminal offence, had adjusted to serving a prison sentence during that period, had no reason to think that she was not properly incarcerated, and had committed a disciplinary offence which was the cause of the additional days. Her position was contrasted with the case of *Lunt v Liverpool City Justices* (5 March 1991, unreported), CA, where a man of previous good character and reputation was imprisoned for default on payment of his rates. In his case an award of £13,500 was increased on appeal to £25,000 for 42 days of false imprisonment, the entire period having been unlawful.

6   *Anufrijeva v Southwark London Borough Council* [2003] EWCA Civ 1406, [2004] QB 1124, at para 74.

7   £17,000 was awarded for detention of a British citizen and her infant child for approximately five days following a successful judicial review of her detention in *R v Secretary of State for the Home Department, ex p Ejaz* [1994] Imm AR 300, CA. The same amount was awarded for a four-day detention over Christmas following a judgment that the refusal of leave to enter on which the detention depended was irrational: *R v Secretary of State for the Home Department, ex p Honegan*, 13 March 1995, QBD. £2,000 was awarded against police for a four-hour detention for immigration status check in *Okot v Metropolitan Police Comr*, 1 September 1995, CLCC (1996) Legal Action February, p 12.

8   *Lunt v Liverpool City Justices* (5 March 1991, unreported), CA, fn 5 above.

9   *R (on the application of KB) v Mental Health Review Tribunal* [2003] EWHC 193 (Admin), [2004] QB 936 at para 60.

7.76 Article 5 is one of the rights from which derogation can be made in time of war or other public emergency threatening the life of the nation.[1] Such a derogation, affecting Article 5(1), was made on 11 November 2001[2] by reference to the events of 11 September 2001, to enable the indefinite detention of suspected international terrorists, alleged to be linked to Al Qaeda.[3] It was quashed by the House of Lords in December 2004 in *A and X*,[4] on the grounds that it was discriminatory and disproportionate.[5] The House made a declaration that the certification provisions of the 2001 Act which allowed indefinite detention were incompatible with Articles 5 and 14 of ECHR. Indefinite detention has now been replaced by 'control orders' which may also infringe Article 5 and require derogation, but these are no longer within the ambit of immigration law.[6]

1   Article 15(1) ECHR. See **7.42** above.

2   See the Human Rights Act 1998 (Designated Derogation) Order 2001, SI 2001/3644; Human Rights Act 1998, Sch 3 (as amended). This refers to UN Security Council Resolution 1373 (2001), which requires Member States to take measures (not including detention) to prevent the commission of terrorist attacks, and to the provisions of the Anti-terrorism, Crime and Security Act 2001.

3   Anti-terrorism, Crime and Security Act 2001, ss 21–23, now expired.

4   *A v Secretary of State for the Home Department; X v Secretary of State for the Home Department* [2004] UKHL 56, [2005] 3 All ER 169.

5   Schedule 3 to the Human Rights Act 1998 was amended to delete the derogation by the Human Rights Act 1998 (Amendment) Order 2005, SI 2005/1071.

6   Prevention of Terrorism Act 2005.

Fair trial

7.77 Article 6 of the ECHR states (so far as relevant) that:

'1   In the determination of his civil rights and obligations or of any criminal charge against him, everyone is entitled to a fair and public hearing within a reasonable time by an independent and impartial tribunal established by law. Judgment shall be pronounced publicly but the press and public may be excluded from all or part of the trial in the interests of morals, public order or national security in a democratic society, where the interests of juveniles or the protection of the private life of the parties so require, or to the extent strictly necessary in the opinion of the court in special circumstances where publicity would prejudice the interests of justice.'

2   Everyone charged with a criminal offence shall be presumed innocent until proved guilty according to law.

3   Everyone charged with a criminal offence has the following minimum rights:

a)   to be informed promptly, in a language which he understands and in detail, of the nature and cause of the accusation against him;

b)   to have adequate time and facilities for the preparation of his defence;

c)   to defend himself in person or through legal assistance of his own choosing or, if he has not sufficient means to pay for legal assistance, to be given it free when the interests of justice so require;

d)   to examine or have examined witnesses against him and to obtain the attendance and examination of witnesses on his behalf under the same conditions as witnesses against him;

e)   to have the free assistance of an interpreter if he cannot understand or speak the language used in court.'

The right to fair administration of justice holds a central place in a democratic society[1] and Article 6 of the ECHR is the most frequently invoked provision of the Convention. Article 6 guarantees rights to a fair and public hearing within a reasonable time by an independent and impartial tribunal established by law in the determination of civil rights and obligations or of criminal charges.[2] In the ECtHR and domestic jurisprudence, the right to a fair trial guaranteed by Article 6 has been held not to apply to decisions about the entry and residence of aliens,[3] nor about the determination of British citizenship,[4] since 'civil rights' is an autonomous concept equated by and large with private law rights as opposed to administrative discretions.[5] The Court of Appeal has held (albeit with some reluctance) that the Qualification Directive[6] does not have the effect of making decisions about refugee status the determination of civil rights and obligations to which article 6 applies.[7] There may, however, be an exception where the immigration decision is said to be in breach of the person's right to peaceful enjoyment of his or her property; in such a case the Administrative Court has held that Article 6 is applicable.[8] Substantive Convention rights such as the right to liberty[9] and family life rights[10] are 'civil rights', even if they involve the exercise of discretion, so that bail hearings and hearings relating to contact with children attract Article 6 guarantees of equality of arms[11] The common law also recognises the rights guaranteed by Article 6 as applicable to cases before the immigration appellate authorities,[12] and provides an equally high standard of procedural protection, at least where human rights issues are engaged by the decision.[13] The fair trial rights conferred by Article 6 apply in relation to decisions concerned with the implementation of European Union law (including decisions on asylum claims and the free movement rights of EU citizens and their family members) because of article 47 of the Charter of Fundamental rights of the European Union.[14] The Explanations relating to the Charter note that Article 47 corresponds to article 6(1) of the ECHR but that 'in community law, the right to a fair hearing is not confined to disputes relating to civil law rights and obligations. That is one of the consequences of the fact that the Community is a community based on the rule of law'.[15]

[1]   *Delcourt v Belgium* (1970) 1 EHRR 355, para 26.

[2]   Article 6(1). Criminal proceedings are proceedings instituted to determine the veracity of an accusation, where the potential outcome is a sanction whose degree and severity belongs to the criminal sphere: *Engel v Netherlands* (1976) 1 EHRR 647; *Ezeh and Connors v United Kingdom* (39665/98, 40086/98) [2004] Crim LR 472. Article 6 has been held to apply to extradition proceedings: *R v Secretary of State for the Home Department, ex p Johnson* [1999] QB 1174, QBD.

3   *Agee v United Kingdom* (1976) 7 DR 164; *P v United Kingdom* (Application 13162/87) (1987) 54 DR 211; *Alam and Khan v United Kingdom* (1967) 10 Yb 478; *Uppal v United Kingdom* (1980) 3 EHRR 391; *Maaouia v France* (2000) 33 EHRR 1047; *Ilic v Croatia (42389/98)* (19 September 2000, unreported). The IAT has held in the starred case of MNM [2000] INLR 576, that art 6 does not apply to asylum appeals and SIAC in the context of refusal of entry in *BY v Secretary of State for the Home Department (SC/65/2007)* 7 November 2008 and the House of Lords in the context of deportation in *RB (Algeria) v Secretary of State for the Home Department* [2009] UKHL 10 held similarly.

4   *S v Switzerland* (1988) 59 DR 256; *Karassev v Switzerland* (314144/96) (14 April 1998, unreported); see *R (on the application of Harrison) v Secretary of State for the Home Department* [2003] EWCA Civ 432, [2003] INLR 284; *Al Jedda v Secretary of State for the Home Department (SC/66/2008)* 22 October 2008 (SIAC).

5   *König v Germany* (1978) 2 EHRR 170. Proceedings classified under national law as being part of 'public law' could come under . . . civil rights if their outcome is decisive for private rights and obligations': *Ferrazzini v Italy* (2001) 34 EHRR 1068. Rights to social security and social assistance have been recognised as 'civil rights' attracting art 6 protection: *Feldbrugge v Netherlands* (1986) 8 EHRR 425; *Salesi v Italy* (1993) 26 EHRR 187; *Schüler-Zgraggen v Switzerland* (1993) 16 EHRR 405. Although the drafting of asylum support provisions (in the Immigration and Asylum Act 1999) is in discretionary terms, the provisions are not genuinely discretionary, and the support received by destitute asylum seekers is a civil right within the meaning of art 6: *R (on the application of Husain) v Asylum Support Adjudicator* [2001] EWHC 852 (Admin), (2001) Times, 15 November.

6   Council Directive 2004/83/EC of 29 April 2004 on minimum standards for the qualification and status of third-country nationals or stateless persons as refugees or as persons who otherwise need international protection and the content of the protection granted.

7   *R (on the application of MK) v Secretary of State for the Home Department* [2010] EWCA Civ 115.

8   *R (on the application of Murungaru) v Secretary of State for the Home Department* [2006] EWHC 2416 (Admin).

9   *Aerts v Belgium* (1998) 5 BHRC 382, 29 EHRR 50. In *A, X and Y* [2002] EWCA Civ 1502, [2005] 3 All ER 169 the Court of Appeal rejected the submission of the appellants that a certificate under s 21 of the Anti-Terrorist Crime and Security Act 2001 amounted to a criminal charge within the meaning of art 6 but confirmed that detention under s 23 of the Act (now lapsed) engaged art 6 civil rights.

10 *W v United Kingdom* (1987) 10 EHRR 29.

11 *Toth v Austria* (1991) 14 EHRR 551, para 84; *Lamy v Belgium* (1989) 11 EHRR 529, para 29.

12 See *R v Secretary of State for the Home Department, ex p Saleem* [2000] 4 All ER 814, [2000] Imm AR 529, [2000] INLR 413.

13 *RB (Algeria) v Secretary of State for the Home Department* [2009] UKHL 10, 153 Sol Jo (no 7) 32.

14 OJ 2000/C 364/01.

15 Explanations relating to the Charter of fundamental rights, OJ 2007/C 303/02.

7.78 The ECHR, Article 6(1) requires independence from the executive and from the parties.[1] The Tribunal's independence does not have to be established by statute; the argument that, because the Home Office appoints asylum support adjudicators and is a party to appeals before them, they do not satisfy the requirement of independence was rejected in *Husain*, where the most important factor ensuring independence was held to be security of tenure.[2] 'Impartiality' requires a lack of either actual bias or the appearance of bias to a fair-minded and informed observer.[3] It has been held that the requirement of impartiality has not been automatically breached when a tribunal has previously been involved in the case at a pre-trial stage,[4] but the presence on the Tribunal of a chair whose refusal of permission to appeal was successfully challenged on judicial review might give rise to concerns under Article 6(1).[5] The ethnicity or nationality of an immigration judge is not on its own a sound basis for a complaint of partiality.[6] A two-tier process in which the first tier is administrative rather than judicial, and not independent and impartial, may satisfy Article 6 requirements where there is the added safeguard of judicial review.[7]

[1] The involvement of the Home Secretary in fixing sentences for mandatory lifers was held incompatible with art 6 independence requirements in *R (on the application of Anderson) v Secretary of State for the Home Department* [2002] UKHL 46, [2002] 4 All ER 1089.

[2] *R (on the application of Husain) v Asylum Support Adjudicator* [2001] EWHC 852 (Admin), (2001) Times, 15 November. Stanley Burnton J indicated the desirability of publishing the adjudicators' terms of employment. See also *Bryan v United Kingdom* (1995) 21 EHRR 342, para 38 (planning inspector in quasi-judicial role appointed by Secretary of State not independent). Cf EU case law: *Adouai and Cornuaille v Belgium* [1982] ECR 1665; *R v Secretary of State for the Home Department, ex p Gallagher* [1994] 3 CMLR 295 (on EC Directive 64/221, art 9).

[3] *Porter v Magill* [2001] UKHL 67, [2002] 1 All ER 465, para 85; *Director-General of Fair Trading v Propietary Association of Great Britain* [2001] EWCA Civ 1217, [2002] 1 All ER 853.

[4] *Bulut v Austria* (1996) 24 EHRR 84, para 33.

[5] The Court of Appeal held in *Mwakulna v Secretary of State for the Home Department* (98/7306/4) 4 March 1999 that this gave rise to no problem, although the Tribunal held in *Huang* (14058) that it would be inappropriate for a member who had made adverse credibility findings to hear the appeal.

[6] *R (on the application of Krishnarajah) v Secretary of State for the Home Department* [2001] EWHC 351 (Admin), [2001] All ER (D) 161 (May) (Tamil asylum seeker's complaint that adjudicator's Sinhalese ethnicity gave rise to danger of bias rejected).

[7] See below.

7.79 The rule of law implies effective judicial control of executive action, such control offering the best guarantees of independence, impartiality and proper procedure.[1] Since the rule of law, central to the Convention and set out in its Preamble, is scarcely conceivable without access to the court, the right to a fair hearing presupposes access to a court.[2] Lack of access to a court to challenge the imposition of carrier sanctions or to seek mitigation was one of the factors rendering the sanction scheme under sections 32–37 Immigration and Asylum Act 1999 incompatible with Article 6 in *International Transport Roth GmbH v Secretary of State for the Home Department*.[3] The right of access is fundamental and cannot be blocked by unnecessary procedural obstacles or restrictions.[4] There must be access to a court of 'full jurisdiction' for compliance with Article 6(1),[5] but an appellate body does not have to be able to remake findings of fact for it to be a court of 'full jurisdiction', so long as it can review the decision-maker's factual findings.[6] In deciding whether the individual's civil rights have been determined by an independent and impartial tribunal established by law, the whole of the adjudication system, including rights of appeal and rights to judicial review, must be considered.[7] Thus, in *R (Q) v Secretary of State for the Home Department*[8] the Court of Appeal held that, although the blocking of the appeal mechanism for asylum support under section 55(10) Nationality, Immigration and Asylum Act 2002 was lawful, since 'judicial review today is capable of affording to an asylum seeker who is denied support . . . recourse to an independent, impartial tribunal which has, in the Strasbourg sense, full jurisdiction' (para 115), the inadequacies of the NASS procedure made it impossible for officials to make an informed decision, and left the court on judicial review equally unable to do so. Thus, the process as a whole, which had to be capable of fairly determining the civil rights in play, did not do so, and was incompatible with Article 6. Article 6 does not necessarily require a statutory right of appeal against all executive decisions, provided that judicial review is available.[9] Where there is no statutory right of appeal, the decision-maker is obliged to give the individual notice of adverse considerations and an opportunity to address them.[10] Access to a court does not necessarily require an oral hearing, and the procedure for statutory review of Tribunal decisions 'on the papers' is compatible with Article 6 requirements.[11] However, ouster of higher courts' jurisdiction over manifest errors of law and breaches of natural justice would represent a fundamental breach of these requirements, and seriously damage the rule of law.[12]

[1]   *Klass v Germany* (1978) 2 EHRR 214, para 55.
[2]   *Golder v United Kingdom* (1975) 1 EHRR 524, paras 34–36.
[3]   [2002] EWCA Civ 158 [2002] 3 WLR 344: see CHAPTER 15.
[4]   *Aït-Mohoub v France* (1998) 30 EHRR 382 (security for costs); *R v Lord Chancellor, ex p Witham* [1998] QB 575 (court fees); *Tinnelly & Sons Ltd v United Kingdom, McElduff v United Kingdom* (1998) 27 EHRR 249 (public interest immunity certificates). Procedural restrictions such as time limits and rules allowing appeals to be determined without a hearing, eg SI 2005/230, r 19 (made under Nationality, Immigration and Asylum Act 2002, s 106) are allowable provided they do not impair the essence of the right, and provided there is effective supervision by judicial review. The previous rules, which permitted determination without consideration of the merits for procedural non-compliance (SI 2003/652, r 45), have not been repeated in the current rules; in our view they certainly impaired the essence of the right.
[5]   *Le Compte, Van Leuven and De Meyere v Belgium* (1981) 4 EHRR 1, para 51.
[6]   See *Kaplan v United Kingdom* (1980) 4 EHRR 64, para 158; *Bryan v United Kingdom* (1995) 21 EHRR 342, para 44, and see discussion in Grosz, Beatson and Duffy, 7.13 fn 3.
[7]   *Tehrani v United Kingdom Central Council for Nursing, Midwifery and Health Visiting* [2001] IRLR 208
[8]   *R (on the application of Q) v Secretary of State for the Home Department* [2003] EWCA Civ 364, [2003] 2 All ER 905, at para 115.
[9]   But in *R (on the application of Husain) v Asylum Support Adjudicator* [2001] EWHC 852 (Admin), (2001) Times, 15 November, para 78. Stanley Burnton J said that where a decision is likely to depend to a substantial extent on disputed questions of primary fact, judicial review would probably not suffice to produce compliance with the Article, since the scope for review of the primary facts is too narrow to be considered 'full jurisdiction' (para 78). 'The courts should lean against accepting judicial review as a substitute for the independence of the tribunal; [otherwise] the incentive for the executive and the legislature to ensure the independence of tribunals is considerably weakened' (para 79). His appears to be a minority view; see the CA's decision in *Q* (fn 8 above).
[10] *R v Secretary of State for the Home Department, ex p Thirukumar* [1989] Imm AR 270; *R v Secretary of State for the Home Department, ex p Fayed* [1997] 1 All ER 228; see also *Q* (fn 8 above).
[11] See the provisions of Nationality, Immigration and Asylum Act 2002, s 103A (inserted by Asylum and Immigration (Treatment of Claimants, etc) Act 2004, s 26), formerly s 101(2), (3).
[12] As was proposed by the Asylum and Immigration (Treatment of Claimants) Bill; see Joint Committee on Human Rights, 5th Report 2003–04, 10 February 2004, HL 35/HC 304; Constitutional Affairs Committee, 2nd report of 2003–2004 on Asylum and Immigration Appeals, 2 March 2004, HC 211.

Legal assistance

7.80 The right of access to a court implies the right to legal assistance when this is compulsory or if it is made necessary by reason of the complexity of the procedure or of the case,[1] or if the applicant is a detainee challenging the legality of his or her detention.[2] It is central to the concept of a fair trial, in civil as in criminal proceedings, that a litigant is not denied the opportunity to present his or her case effectively before the court.[3] In such circumstances, if the applicant cannot pay for legal aid, denial of it can amount to a breach of the right of access to a court.[4] However, as the court has recently ruled in *Steel and Morris v United Kingdom*, whether the provision of legal aid is necessary for a fair hearing must be determined on the basis of the particular facts and circumstances of each case and will depend inter alia upon the importance of what is at stake for the applicant in the proceedings, the complexity of the relevant law and procedure and the applicant's capacity to represent him or herself effectively.[5] The right of access to a court is not, however, absolute and may be subject to restrictions, provided that these pursue a legitimate aim and are proportionate.[6] It may therefore be acceptable to impose conditions on the grant of legal aid based, inter alia, on the financial situation of the litigant or his or her prospects of success in the proceedings.[7] Moreover, it is not incumbent on the State to seek through the use of public funds to ensure total equality of arms between the assisted person and the opposing party, as long as each side is afforded a reasonable opportunity to present his or her case under conditions that do not place him or her at a substantial disadvantage vis-à-vis the adversary.[8] Delays in determination procedures and appeal hearings may violate the right to have a hearing within a reasonable time, particularly where the delay causes prejudice, such as loss of benefits;[9] once again, the ECHR accords with the common law, which has long held that 'justice delayed is justice denied', and mandatory orders are available against foot-dragging.[10] Asylum support appeals have strict time limits in recognition of the need for speed because of the potentially irremediable hardship and injustice to which appellants are subjected by denial of all support.[11]

[1]   *Airey v Ireland* (1979) 2 EHRR 305 para 26. In deciding whether the interests of justice require free legal assistance, the seriousness of the possible consequences of the case and its complexity are relevant: *Benham v United Kingdom* (1996) 22 EHRR 293.

[2]   *Golder v United Kingdom* (1975) 1 EHRR 524; *Airey v Ireland* (1979) 2 EHRR 305; *Megyeri v Germany* (1992) 15 EHRR 584, para 27. See also *A v Australia* (1997) 4 BHRC 210. Legal aid was always available for habeas corpus and judicial review applications (subject to means) and since January 2000 has been available for bail applications under the Immigration Act 1971.

[3]   *Steel and Morris v United Kingdom* (68416/01) (15 February 2005, unreported); *Airey v Ireland* (1979) 2 EHRR 305.

[4]   *Aerts v Belgium* (1998) 29 EHRR 50, para 60, where the ECtHR held that, where the law required legal representation the refusal of legal aid by the Legal Aid Board on the ground that the applicant's challenge to his detention did not appear well-founded impaired the applicant's right of access to a court. Legal aid was made available for all UK immigration appeals in the immigration appellate authority (subject to means and merits tests) from 1 January 2000, although in the Special Immigration Appeals Commission only as from 1 April 2003 (Access to Justice Act 1999, Sch 2, para 2(1)(ha), added by Nationality, Immigration and Asylum Act 2002, s 116). However, there are now concerns that severe legal aid cutbacks are seriously impairing the rights of asylum seekers to effective access; see the Fourth Report 2002–03 of the Constitutional Affairs Committee on Immigration and Asylum: the Government's proposed changes to publicly funded immigration and asylum work, 31 October 2003, HC 1171, and the government's response, printed as an Appendix to the CAC 2nd Special Report 2003–04, 29 January 2004, HC 299.

[5]   *Steel and Morris*, above, at para 61.

[6]   *Steel and Morris*, para 62; see *Ashingdane v United Kingdom*, judgment of 28 May 1985, Series A no 93, pp 24–25, para 57.

[7]   *Steel and Morris*, above, at para 62; *Munro v United Kingdom* (Application 10594/83) (1987) 10 EHRR 516.

[8]   *Steel and Morris*, above, at para 62; see *De Haes and Gijsels v Belgium* (1997) 25 EHRR 1), Reports 1997-1, para 53, and also *McVicar v United Kingdom* (46311/99), paras 51 and 62.

⁹ *Zimmermann and Steiner v Switzerland* (1983) 6 EHRR 17; *Guincho v Portugal* (1984) 7 EHRR 223.

¹⁰ *R v Secretary of State for the Home Department, ex p Phansopkar* [1976] QB 606. The Privy Council has held that where there is no constitutional right to judgment within a reasonable time, a delay in producing a judgment is capable of depriving the individual of the protection of the law (rendering it unlawful) where it meant the judge could no longer produce a proper judgment, or the parties could not obtain from the decision the benefit they should: *Boodhoo and Jagram v A-G of Trinidad and Tobago* [2004] UKPC 17.

¹¹ See Asylum Support Appeals (Procedure) Rules 2000, SI 2000/541 as amended by SI 2003/1735.

7.81 The right to a fair hearing under Article 6 of the ECHR and under the common law embraces the principle of equality of arms, which affords parties a reasonable opportunity of presenting their case to the court under conditions which do not place them at a substantial disadvantage vis-à-vis their opponents.[1] So far as it is relevant in the immigration context, the principle requires adequate reasons for an administrative decision which may be the subject of an appeal,[2] and disclosure of all relevant evidence in the possession of the authorities.[3] In *Quaquah* deportation which would severely hamper a claimant in the preparation of his civil action against the Home Office for malicious prosecution was held to violate the principle of equality of arms.[4]

¹ *Kaufman v Belgium* (1986) 50 DR 98; *Delcourt v Belgium* (1970) 1 EHRR 355; *Neumeister v Austria* (1968) 1 EHRR 91; *De Haes and Gijsels v Belgium* (1997) 25 EHRR 1. The application of retrospective legislation affecting current proceedings was held to be an unacceptable interference by the legislature in the administration of justice designed to influence judicial determination in *Stran Greek Refineries and Stratis Andreadis v Greece* (1994) 19 EHRR 293; see also *Pressos Compania Naviera SA v Belgium* (1995) 21 EHRR 301 (Comm).

² *X v United Kingdom* (1981) 4 EHRR 188, para 66.

³ *Lamy v Belgium* (1989) 11 EHRR 529, para 29; *McMichael v United Kingdom* (1995) 20 EHRR 205, para 82; *Shishkov v Bulgaria* (38822/97).

⁴ *R v Immigration Officer, ex p Quaquah (John)* [2000] INLR 196. The Home Office now generally agrees not to remove litigants whose claims are pending before the UK courts.

7.82 In Special Immigration Appeals Commission cases, and particularly 'derogation' cases involving allegations of suspected international terrorism, the Article 6 guarantees applicable to civil proceedings clearly apply, and it is arguable that the criminal standards might also apply.[1] However, this jurisdiction has now lapsed and the new system of 'control orders' under the Prevention of Terrorism Act 2005, which replaces the indefinite detention regime, is no longer dealt with as an immigration matter but comes under the jurisdiction of the High Court or the Court of Sessions. Our very considerable concerns about the low standard of proof, the presumption of innocence, inequality of arms and the receipt of evidence extracted under torture[2] now belong to a different textbook.

¹ The latter argument was rejected by the Court of Appeal in *A v Secretary of State for the Home Department, X v Secretary of State for the Home Department* [2002] EWCA Civ 1502, [2004] QB 335; see **7.76** fn 4 above.

² *A, B, C, D v Secretary of State for the Home Department* (SC/1, 6, 7, 9, 10/2002) 2 October 2003, paras 83–84, upheld by the Court of Appeal as *A v Secretary of State for the Home Department* [2004] EWCA Civ 1123, and now on appeal to the House of Lords. See Amnesty International 'Justice perverted under the Anti-terrorism, Crime and Security Act 2001', EUR45/029/2003, 11 December 2003.

7.83 In *Soering*[1] the European Court acknowledged that an expulsion could engage Article 6 ECHR in circumstances where the fugitive has suffered or risks suffering a flagrant denial of a fair trial in the receiving country[2]. This view has now been confirmed by the House of Lords in *Ullah*.[3] In *RB (Algeria) v Secretary of State for the Home Department*[4] the House of Lords approved the test formulated by the minority in *Mamatkulov*[5] to the effect that a flagrant denial of justice went beyond 'mere irregularities or lack of safeguards in the trial procedures such as might result in a breach of Article 6 if occurring within the Contracting State itself'. What had to be shown was 'a breach of the principles of fair trial guaranteed by Article 6 which is so fundamental as to amount to a nullification or destruction of the very essence of the right guaranteed by that article'. The House of Lords added the further requirement of a real risk that the flagrant breach of the person's Article 6 rights would result in a serious violation of a substantive right, eg imprisonment following conviction. The Special Immigration Appeals Commission had been entitled to conclude that there would be no 'complete denial of justice' and therefore no breach of Article 6, notwithstanding that the appellant would, following his removal to Jordan, be tried by a tribunal that was not independent. Moreover, the real risk that evidence obtained by torture would be admitted in the proceedings did not necessarily give rise to a flagrant breach of Article 6.[6]

[1] *Soering v United Kingdom* (1989) 11 EHRR 439.
[2] *Soering v United Kingdom* (1989) 11 EHRR 439, para 113. In *Einhorn v France* (71555/01), 16 October 2001, the court, following *Soering*, held that in a case where an applicant had been unfairly convicted *in absentia*, extradition would be likely to raise an issue under art 6 if substantial grounds existed for believing he could not get a retrial and would be imprisoned to serve his sentence. The IAT found no flagrant violation of fair trial rights such as to render the return of a conscientious objector to Israel in breach of art 6 in *Nikulin* [2002] UKIAT 06719; see also *Din (Jamal)* [2002] UKIAT 06585 (Pakistan). See also *Lodhi v Governor of Brixton Prison* [2001] EWHC 178 (Admin 178), [2001] All ER (D) 136 (Mar), DC (extradition case).
[3] *R (on the application of Ullah) v Special Adjudicator* [2004] UKHL 26, [2004] INLR 381.
[4] *RB (Algeria) v Secretary of State for the Home Department* [2009] UKHL 10, 153 Sol Jo (no 7) 32.
[5] *Mamatkulov and Askarov v Turkey* (2005) 41 EHRR 25.
[6] *RB* overturning the decision of the Court of Appeal in respect of evidence obtained by torture.

Family and private life

7.84 Article 8 of the ECHR states that:

'1   Everyone has the right to respect for his private and family life, his home and his correspondence.

2   There shall be no interference by a public authority with the exercise of this right except such as is in accordance with the law and is necessary in a democratic society in the interests of national security, public safety or the economic well-being of the country, for the prevention of disorder or crime, for the protection of health or morals, or for the protection of the rights and freedoms of others.'

Article 8(1) protects the right to respect for four separate rights: to family life, private life, home and correspondence. Only the first two are important for most immigration purposes, although the other two may be relevant on occasion.[1] Article 8 rights will most often be engaged by decisions to refuse entry or to remove or deport someone with relevant ties to the UK, although they may be engaged in other contexts such as detention and asylum support. Article 8(2) qualifies those rights as set out above.

¹ In particular the rights to respect for home and correspondence would be engaged by the search and seizure provisions of Immigration Act 1971, as amended by Pt VII of the Immigration and Asylum Act 1999 and Pt VII of the Nationality, Immigration and Asylum Act 2002.

7.85 A lawful and genuine marriage will be enough to constitute family life between two people,¹ even if the couple are not cohabiting,² but a sham marriage will not give rise to family life.³ A formally invalid marriage believed valid by the parties gives rise to family life.⁴ Although the most important 'family' relationships are those between husband and wife and parent and child, relationships between siblings, between grandparents and grandchildren,⁵ and uncle and nephew⁶ are all potentially within the scope of 'family life',⁷ depending on the strength of the emotional ties. A child born of an existing marital union will usually become part of the family from birth and will only cease to be so in exceptional circumstances,⁸ even where there has been a voluntary separation between the parents and child.⁹ Family life between parent and child does not necessarily terminate upon the child reaching the age of 18.¹⁰ The presumption in favour of family life between parent and child operates between a child and its natural father, provided he continues to have a level of contact with the child.¹¹ Family ties may be established through adoption¹² and fostering¹³ as well as through biological connections. But the Commission has held that Article 8 of the ECHR was not engaged by the deportation of a woman with her children from a country where her parents and sisters lived, on the ground that she and her children formed an independent family unit, so that the relationship with the extended family did not constitute family life.¹⁴

¹ *Abdulaziz, Cabales and Balkandali v United Kingdom* (1985) 7 EHRR 471, para 62.
² *Abdulaziz above; Wakefield v United Kingdom* (1990) 66 DR 251. Cohabitation is not a sine qua non of family life: *Kroon v Netherlands* (1994) 19 EHRR 263; *Berrehab v Netherlands* (1988) 11 EHRR 322, para 21; *Boughanemi v France* (1996) 22 EHRR 228; but will be relevant in deciding whether interference is proportionate: *Söderbäck v Sweden* (1998) 29 EHRR 95.
³ However the definition of a 'sham' marriage in Immigration and Asylum Act 1999, s 24(5) is almost certainly too wide, since many of the marriages caught within it are based on genuine relationships which would in any event attract ECHR, art 8 protection. See **11.47** ff below.
⁴ *A and A v Netherlands* (1992) 72 DR 118. In *R v Secretary of State for the Home Department, ex p Glowacka* (26 June 1997, unreported), QBD, the Home Office agreed to treat the parties to an invalid Roma marriage as if they were validly married for the purposes of refugee family reunion following the grant of permission for judicial review. In relation to polygamous marriages, the ECtHR has held it legitimate on public policy grounds to prevent two wives living together with their husband: *Bibi v United Kingdom* (19628/92).
⁵ *Marckx v Belgium* (1979) 2 EHRR 330, para 45.
⁶ *Boyle v United Kingdom* (1994) 19 EHRR 179, Commission. The boy's father had died and the uncle stayed frequently. See *R (on the application of Lekstaka) v Immigration Appeal Tribunal* [2005] EWHC 745 (Admin), 18 April 2005 (de facto family life with uncle and aunt).
⁷ *Moustaquim v Belgium* (1991) 13 EHRR 802; *X v Germany* (1978) 9 YB 449. Immigration Rules providing for the admission of only certain categories of 'distressed relatives' will need to be read so as to include other categories, not mentioned, to avoid offending against art 8.
⁸ *Berrehab v Netherlands* fn 2 above, para 21; *Ciliz v Netherlands*, [2000] 2 FLR 469, paras 33, 44.
⁹ *Sen v Netherlands* (2003) 36 EHRR 7.

[10] *Etti-Adegbola v Secretary of State for the Home Department* [2009] EWCA Civ 1319, [2009] All ER (D) 71 (Nov)

[11] Even if at the time of the birth the relationship between the parents had ended: *Keegan v Ireland* (1994) 18 EHRR 342. See also *Boughanemi v France* (1996) 22 EHRR 228. The presumption may be defeated in the face of a total lack of interest or contact by the father.

[12] *X v France* (1992) 31 DR 241; *Lebbink v Netherlands* (45582/99) (1 June 2004, unreported; *Pini and Bertani v Romania* (Application 78028/01) 2004) 40 EHRR 312, [2005] 2 FLR 596. The European Court is to consider the compatibility of para 310 of the Immigration Rules HC 395 and the Adoption (Designation of Overseas Adoptions) Act 1973 with the ECHR in *Singh (Pavittar) v United Kingdom* (60148/00), declared admissible on 3 September 2002, on the refusal to grant entry clearance to a child adopted in India (not a designated country under the 1973 Act. But see now *Singh v Entry Clearance Officer, New Delhi* [2004] EWCA Civ 1075, [2004] INLR 515.

[13] *X v Switzerland* (Application 8257/78) (1978) 13 DR 248.

[14] *A and family v Sweden* (1994) 18 EHRR CD 209. See also *Papayianni v United Kingdom* (5269/71) [1974] Imm AR 7, 39 CD 104; cf *Uppal v United Kingdom* (Application 8244/78) (1980) 3 EHRR 391, a case where family life between children, parents, grandparents and married sisters forming a large and close family unit was argued, held admissible and subject of a friendly settlement.

7.86 Whether relationships between adult siblings or adult children and their parents or other adult relatives fall within the scope of Article 8 is a question of fact as to whether there exist ties strong enough to constitute family life within the meaning of the Article.[1] The ties between young adults who have not yet established their own families and their parents, siblings and other close family members may constitute 'family life'.[2] The Court of Appeal has recently noted that domestic and Strasbourg jurisprudence does not establish that there is a general obligation imposed by article 8 to admit parents left behind by migrant, adult children even if the parents cannot be supported without recourse to public funds but it does require individualized, case-by-case consideration.[3] However, the same may be said in respect of any category of family relationship; if an obligation to admit arises under article 8 it does so because of the individual facts, not because the relationship belongs to a particular category. Moreover, it is not enough to consider existing family life; the State must also have regard to potential family life and refrain from inhibiting the development of a real family life in the future.[4] If family ties are found not to constitute 'family life' the court may nevertheless take them into account when considering 'private life'.[5] In the landmark decision of the Court of Appeal in *Singh v Entry Clearance Officer, Delhi*[6] the court recognised that with the enormous social and cultural changes which have taken place in the last decades, much greater flexibility may be applied to what constitutes family life. The appellant was a seven-year-old boy who had been adopted in India by his uncle and aunt who lived in the UK. The adoption had been carried out within the family in accordance with a social, religious and cultural tradition which served a humane purpose. Although the child was still living with his natural parents, there had been a genuine transfer of parental responsibility, and the court held that he had become a member of his adoptive parents' family for the purposes of Article 8 of ECHR. Clearly these cases are fact sensitive. Whether a relationship amounts to 'family life' depends on substance as much as form;[7] so informal heterosexual relationships of sufficient substance and stability have been classified as 'family life,'[8] although stable homosexual relationships have not.[9] However, the Court has now held that owing to the rapid evolution of social attitudes across Member States towards same-sex couples it is artificial to maintain the view that 'in contrast to a different-sex couple, a same-sex couple cannot enjoy family life for the purposes of Article 8. Consequently, the relationship of the applicants, a cohabiting same-sex couple living in a stable de facto partnership falls within the notion of "family life" just as the relationship of a different-sex couple in the same situation would'.[10] Where family members have lived apart for a considerable period of time Article 8 may nevertheless oblige the State to facilitate family reunion and not merely to refrain from interfering with their existing level of contact, particularly in cases involving unaccompanied children[11] and cases where family separation was caused by flight from feared persecution,[12] but even where it was freely chosen.[13] That is because respect for family life requires consideration of how family life might best develop[14] and entails a positive obligation to take measures enabling family ties to be developed.[15]

¹   See *Nasri v France* (1995) 21 EHRR 458; *Beldjoudi v France* (1992) 14 EHRR 801 and *Moustaquim v Belgium* (1991) 13 EHRR 802. In *Advic v United Kingdom* 20 EHRR CD 125, the ECommHR said that art 8 did not cover links between adult brothers living apart for a long period and not dependent on each other, and that there must be more than the normal emotional ties between adult siblings or parents and adult children, for family life to exist within the meaning of art 8. For UK courts and Tribunal application of this restrictive approach see eg *Kugathas v Immigration Appeal Tribunal* [2003] EWCA Civ 31, [2003] INLR 170 (where however there had been too little contact for family life to be real and effective); *R (Serbia and Montenegro)* [2004] UKIAT 78. But in *Senthuran v Secretary of State for the Home Department* [2004] EWCA Civ 950, [2004] 4 All ER 365 the Court of Appeal warned that each case is fact sensitive, and held both the length of time a young adult had been with his family in the UK, and the Secretary of State's unreasonable delay in determining his application, relevant to the existence of family life and the proportionality of any interference with it. See also *R (on the application of Johnson (Renford)) v Secretary of State for the Home Department* [2004] EWHC 1550 (Admin) (para 16). In *Kaya v Germany (Application no 31753/02)*, [2007] 2 FCR 527 the court held that there was family life between an adult son and his parents given that he had lived with his parents until the time of his imprisonment; he continued to write letters to his mother whilst in prison and he 'played a special role' in the family following the accidental death of his brother. A finding that a 23-year-old woman who had lived pretty well continuously with her parents and siblings all her life did not have family life with them 'would have been quite unreal' – *RP (Zimbabwe) v Secretary of State for the Home Department* [2008] EWCA Civ 825, [2008] All ER (D) 135 (Aug). See also *Krasniqi v Secretary of State for the Home Department* [2006] EWCA Civ 391, (2006) Times, 20 April – relationship between two women protected by Article 8, given their traumatic histories; their emotional and mental fragility; the nature of the love and support they offered each other and their shared experience of bringing up a child together. In *R (on the application of Katshunga) v Secretary of State for the Home Department* [2006] EWHC 1208 (Admin), [2006] All ER (D) 71 (May) Gibbs J held that the adult claimant could establish that her removal would breach Article 8 by reference to her relationship with her adult brother upon whom she was particularly dependant owing to her own and her family's traumatic history and her consequent mental illness. See also *Mukarkar v Secretary of State for the Home Department* [2006] EWCA Civ 1045, (2006) Times, 16 August, [2006] All ER (D) 367 (Jul) – the tribunal had been entitled to conclude that refusing leave to remain to a father who was in poor health and dependant upon his family in the UK for support breached Article 8. In *MT (Zimbabwe) v Secretary of State for the Home Department* [2007] EWCA Civ 455 the adjudicator had been entitled to find there was 'family life' between an adult on the one hand and her cousin, his wife and their children on the other, bearing in mind that she had been integrated into his family since the age of 14; the cultural norm that single adult women remain in the family home and their shared experience of violence in Zimbabwe giving rise to a closer bonding process than normal between adults. In *ZB (Pakistan) v Secretary of State for the Home Department* [2009] EWCA Civ 834, [2009] All ER (D) 343 (Jul) the tribunal had erred in law by failing to consider whether the insulin dependent diabetic mother's reliance for care and financial support on her daughter meant that there was 'family life' between them.

²   *AA v United Kingdom* (Application No 8000/08) [2011] NLJR 1336, (2011) Times, 28 September, ECtHR; *Osman v Denmark* (Application No 38058/09) (14 June 2011, unreported).

³ *Odawey v Entry Clearance Officer* [2011] EWCA Civ 840, [2011] All ER (D) 204 (Jul). In that
   case there was in fact no family life or 'at most a weak family life' so that the result was
   unsurprising
⁴ *R (on the application of Fawad Ahmadi) v Secretary of State for the Home Department* [2005]
   EWCA Civ 1721, [2005] All ER (D) 169 (Dec).
⁵ As it did in *Slivenko v Latvia* (Application no 48321/99), [2004] 2 FCR 28.
⁶ *Singh v Entry Clearance Officer, New Delhi* [2004] EWCA Civ 1075, [2004] INLR 515. The
   failure to grant the child entry clearance to come to the UK was a violation of Article 8.
⁷ *Marckx* above, para 31; *Kroon v Netherlands* (1994) 19 EHRR 263; *Attafuah* [2002] UKIAT
   05922.
⁸ *Johnston v Ireland* (1986) 9 EHRR 203; *Marckx v Belgium* above.
⁹ *X v United Kingdom* (1983) 32 DR 220; *S v United Kingdom* (1986) 47 D & R 274, para 2;
   Kerkhoven v Netherlands (19 May 1992, unreported) (relationship between a woman and the
   child of her long-term, same-sex partner not 'family life'). Homosexual relationships have been
   considered instead in the context of private life: *Roosli v Germany* (Application 28318/95)
   (15 May 1996), DR 85, p 149. Most recently in *Karner v Austria* [2003)] 2 FLR 623
   the ECtHR found it 'unnecessary' to consider whether homosexual relationships fell within the
   scope of 'family life'. The European Court of Justice in *Grant v South West Trains Ltd*
   [1998] ECR I-621 has similarly failed to recognise homosexual relationships as constituting
   family life. With the advent of homosexual marriages in European countries such as the
   Netherlands and the wider legal recognition of homosexual relationships it is difficult to see
   that the European courts will be able to maintain this distinction between homosexual and
   heterosexual couples. In *X, Y and Z v United Kingdom* (1997) 24 EHRR 143, the relationship
   between a transsexual, her female partner and their child was '*de facto*' family life. And in the
   UK a stable same-sex partner has been held to be 'part of the family' for the purposes of
   succession to a tenancy: *Fitzpatrick v Sterling Housing Association Ltd* [1999] 4 All ER 705,
   [2000] 1 FLR 271, HL (reversing [1998] Ch 304, CA); in *Ghaidan v Mendoza* [2004] UKHL
   30, [2004] 3 All ER 411, HL a same-sex partner was equated with a spouse. This is another
   area where the common law can fertilise ECtHR jurisprudence in the UK courts.
¹⁰ *PB and JS v Austria* Application No 18984/02, 22 July 2010.
¹¹ *Mayeka and Mitunga v Belgium* (2006) Application No 13178/03.
¹² *Tuquabo-Tekle v Netherlands* (Application No 60665/00) [2005] 3 FCR 649, [2006] 1 FLR
   798, [2006] Fam Law 267, [2005] ECHR 60665/00, ECtHR; *R (on the application of Yussuf)
   v Secretary of State for the Home Department* [2005] EWHC 2847 (Admin), [2005] All ER
   (D) 105 (Nov); *H (Somalia)* [2004] UKIAT 00027.
¹³ *Sen v Netherlands* (2003) 36 EHRR 7.
¹⁴ *Sen and Tuquabo-Tekle*.
¹⁵ *Mehemi v France (2)* (2003) Application No 53470/99 .

7.87 Not every exclusion or removal from the country of residence of the
applicant's family constitutes a breach of the right to respect for family life.
Article 8 of the ECHR does not expressly deal with immigration. Indeed, the
right of a foreigner to enter or remain in a country is not as such guaranteed
by the ECHR, but as the court observed in its landmark decision of *Abdulaziz,
Cabales and Balkandali*, immigration controls have to be exercised consistently with the obligations under the Convention, although the right to family
life is to be seen in the context of the right of States to control the entry of
non-nationals onto their territory and consequently Article 8 does not
oblige States to respect the choice by married couples of their matrimonial
residence or to accept the non-national spouse for settlement in the country.¹
The significance of the proposition for which *Abdulaziz, Cabales and Balkandali v United Kingdom*² is authority, ie that Article 8 does not impose a general
obligation on the part of contracting states to respect the choice by a married
couple of the country in which they are to reside and to admit the non-citizen
spouse for settlement was considered by the Supreme Court in *Quila* where it
was relied on by the Secretary of State to contend that a blanket ban on the
admission of spouses under the age of 21 did not interfere with, let alone
breach Article 8 rights. The court held the principle to be unexceptionable; it

invites a fact-specific investigation which logically falls within the realms of whether the state's obstruction of that choice is justified under paragraph 2 of Article 8.[3] However, *Abdulaziz* should not be followed as authority for the proposition that exclusion of a non-citizen spouse would not interfere with the right to respect for family life if the couple could establish their family life in another country; the Court's more recent case law showed the distinction between positive and negative obligations on which the majority in *Abulaziz* based their decision to have lost its significance in the immigration context.[4] Forcing a married couple to choose either to live separately for the three years it would take for them to meet the age requirement of the Immigration Rules governing the entry of spouses or for the British citizen spouse to leave the UK 'a colossal interference' with the right.[5] 'For the state to make exile for one of the spouses the price of exercising the right to marry and embark on family life requires powerful justification'[6] because 'great weight attaches to the prima facie entitlement to the UK citizen to marry without being forced to choose between separation and exile'.[7] In the years that followed *Abdulaziz* there emerged two types of cases: those involving the expulsion of long-term residents, normally following criminal conviction, and those involving the expulsion or failure to admit third country nationals with family members in the Contracting State. The position of long-term residents would be more easily secured if they had family members in the Contracting State.[8] In considering whether an expulsion amounted to a breach of Article 8, the court would weigh the nature of any offence committed by the applicant and the extent to which links with his country of origin had been severed, although the outcomes generally favoured State control.[9] In cases concerning the expulsion or refusal to admit other third country nationals with close family members in the Contracting State, the family would need to demonstrate that there were 'obstacles' to family life being established elsewhere. In the 1990s the Commission's jurisprudence was extremely tough on this issue; thus even the deportation of the mother of a British citizen child was declared compatible with the ECHR, as the child was of an adaptable age'.[10] In similar vein, the court upheld a refusal to admit a child into a Contracting State where his parents had been granted humanitarian leave to remain, holding that there were no real obstacles to the parents returning to their country of origin.[11] Divorced or separated parents had an apparent advantage, since the non-national parents were likely to encounter obstacles to enjoying their family life with children staying in the State of residence of the other parent, who could not be expected to accompany the non-national abroad[12] or might even be prohibited from doing so by a court order.[13] Removal of a parent from the UK whilst proceedings relating to the care of or contact with his or her child are unresolved is likely to be an interference with a may be a breach of the right to respect for family life.[14]

---

[1]   *Abdulaziz* above, para 68. In *Begum (Husna) v Entry Clearance Officer, Dhaka* [2001] INLR 115, an entry clearance case, the Court of Appeal held that the ability of the family to live together in the country of origin was not always crucial and that family reunion could operate to enable a family member 'left behind' to join family in the UK.

[2]   (1985) 7 EHRR 471.

[3]   *R (on the application of Aquilar Quila) v Secretary of State for the Home Department* [2011] UKSC 45, [2011] 3 WLR 836, [2011] 3 FCR 575.

[4]   *R (on the application of Aquilar Quila) v Secretary of State for the Home Department*, Lord Wilson, para 43; Baroness Hale, para 72 and see for example *Osman v Denmark* (Application No 38058/09) (14 June 2011, unreported).

5 *R (on the application of Aquilar Quila) v Secretary of State for the Home Department*, Lord Wilson, para 32, Baroness Hale, para 72.
6 Sedley LJ in *R (on the application of Aquilar Quila) v Secretary of State for the Home Department* [2010] EWCA Civ 1482.
7 Sedley LJ in *WJ (China) v Secretary of State for the Home Department* [2011] EWCA Civ 183.
8 In *Boughanemi v France* (1996) 22 EHRR 228 the court found the expulsion of a Tunisian national who had lived in France for 20 years since the age of eight, but had been sentenced to less than four years' imprisonment, did not violate art 8 ECHR, cf *Moustaquim v Belgium* (1991) 13 EHRR 802.
9 See for instance *Boujlifa v France* (1997) 30 EHRR 419, where the applicant had lived in France since the age of five and had extensive family there, but had been convicted of armed robbery justifying expulsion; in *Bouchelkia v France* (1997) 25 EHRR 886 the applicant had lived in France since the age of two but a conviction for rape justified his expulsion.
10 *Sorabjee v United Kingdom* (Application 23938/93), 23 October 1995, unpublished. *PP v United Kingdom* (1996) 21 EHRR CD 81; *Jaramillo v United Kingdom* (24865/94).
11 *Gul v Switzerland* (1996) 22 EHRR 93.
12 *Berrehab v Netherlands* (1989) 11 EHRR 322. See also *Ciliz v Netherlands* [2000] 2 FLR 469.
13 As in *Da Silva and Hoogkamer v Netherlands* (2006) Application No 50435/99.
14 *Ciliz v Netherlands* above and see also *MS (Ivory Coast) v Secretary of State for the Home Department* [2007] EWCA Civ 133.

7.88 The emphasis of the case law of the European Court has changed significantly in the last few years. In the court's jurisprudence there has been a considerable softening of the *Abdulaziz* principle on a State's right to control immigration, such that whilst Contracting States are not prohibited by Article 8 from exercising immigration control, the need for fair processes that 'afford due respect to the interests safeguarded by Article 8' is urged upon States.[1] There are now clear principles that emerge from the court's jurisprudence that can be applied to all types of immigration cases, whether long-term residents facing expulsion or those without any other legal entitlement seeking to join or remain with close family members. The court's judgment in *Boultif* lays down guiding principles in assessing the likelihood that a decision will interfere with family life and if so, its proportionality to its legitimate aim:

> 'the court will consider the nature and seriousness of the offence committed by the applicant; the length of the applicant's stay in the country from which he is going to be expelled; the time elapsed since the offence was committed as well as the applicant's conduct in that period; the nationalities of the various persons concerned; the applicant's family situation, such as the length of the marriage; and other factors expressing the effectiveness of a couple's family life; whether the spouse knew about the offence at the time when he or she entered into a family relationship; and whether there are children in the marriage, and if so, their age. Not least, the court will also consider the seriousness of the difficulties which the spouse is likely to encounter in the country of origin, though the mere fact that a person might face certain difficulties in accompanying her or his spouse cannot in itself exclude an expulsion.'[2]

Subsequently, the Court said that it wished to make explicit two further criteria that might already be implicit in the *Boultif* judgment which were:

> 'the best interests and well-being of the children, in particular the seriousness of the difficulties which any children of the applicant are likely to encounter in the country to which the applicant is to be expelled; and the solidity of the social, cultural and family ties with the host country and with the country of destination.'[3]

A decision that interference with family or private life was proportionate but that was taken without identifying and applying the criteria elaborated in *Uner*[4] and *Maslov*[5] would be unlawful.[6] In a later case following *Boultif*, the Court made clear that, in considering the proportionality of deportation as a response to criminal convictions, it will place considerable emphasis on the future threat that a person might pose to public order, rather than confining itself to consideration of the past.[7] The principles and the approach established by these and other cases for assessing whether an interference with a protected right is proportionate are equally applicable whether the person was lawfully resident but faced with deportation or unlawfully present and facing administrative removal. Any differences would relate to weight; on the one hand, more weight may be given to the need to protect society from serious crime; on the other, more weight might be given to family and private life established by a person whilst lawfully present.[8] If family life was established when the persons involved were aware that the applicant's immigration status was insecure or 'precarious', it would only be in exceptional circumstances that removal of the non-national family member would violate Article 8.[9] Exceptional circumstances might include detriment to the welfare of any children affected by the expulsion[10] particularly where the children and other affected family members are nationals of the expelling state;[11] the length of the applicant's residence and the strength of ties in the country of residence, particularly when they have developed whilst the authorities could have but failed to expel the applicant.[12] Exceptional circumstances that would make expulsion a breach of Article 8 may exist even where there are no 'insurmountable obstacles' to the family or private life being enjoyed in the country to which the applicant is to be expelled.[13] Article 8 may also be breached by a state's failure to comply with the procedural safeguards inherent in the provision, in particular, the domestic court's failure to hold a hearing and to receive relevant testimony and the failure to assess the impact of the applicant's expulsion on his family.[14] What is required is that measures affecting fundamental human rights be subject to some form of adversarial proceedings before an independent body competent to review the reasons for the decision and the relevant evidence.[15]

[1]   *Ciliz v Netherlands* [2000] 2 FLR 469, para 66.
[2]   *Boultif v Switzerland* (2001) 33 EHRR 1179; followed in *Amrollahi v Denmark* (56811/00), 11 July 2002, where the applicant was convicted of drugs trafficking offences but had left Iran 15 years earlier and was married to a Danish woman with a child; *Yildiz v Austria* (2003) 36 EHRR 32, where the applicant had been subject of a five-year residence ban following serious traffic offences but had a wife (from whom he was divorced by the time of hearing) and a child in Austria making the residence ban disproportionate; *Mokrani v France* (52206/99), 15 July 2003, where the applicant had been convicted of drugs trafficking offences but his family ties in France meant that removal would breach art 8 ECHR; *Udeh v Switzerland* (2013) Application No 12020/09 where deportation of a man who had been sentenced to 42 months imprisonment for importation of cocaine was said to breach Article 8 having regard to his irreproachable conduct in prison and following his release; his residence for seven and a half years in Switzerland 'a considerable length of time in a person's life'; the likelihood that his removal would result in his daughters being brought up separated from their father who, although divorced from their mother, had contact with them every two weeks. *Boultif* has also been cited with approval by the European Court of Justice in *Carpenter (Mary) v Secretary of State for the Home Department* Case C-60/00 [2003] QB 416.
[3]   *Uner v Netherlands* (Application No 46410/99), [2006] 3 FCR 340 (Grand Chamber). See for example, *Sezen v Netherlands* (2006) App No 50252/99 where deportation of a Turkish man convicted for possession of a large quantity of heroin and who had been resident for only 1 1/2 years at the time of the offence was found to breach Article 8 because it would be a 'radical upheaval' for his wife and in particular, his two children to follow him to Turkey. The children had always lived in the Netherlands and went to school there and had minimal ties with Turkey; they did not even speak Turkish. In *Keles v Germany* (2006) App No 32231/02 the applicant's wife was, like him, a Turkish national and she had been in Germany for only 10

years so could reintegrate into Turkish society. However, the four children of the couple were born in Germany or entered at a young age and even if they spoke Turkish 'would necessarily have to face major difficulties with regard to the different language of instruction and the different curriculum in Turkish schools'. See also *Sen v Netherlands* (2003) 36 EHRR 7 and *Tuquabo-Tekle v Netherlands* (Application No 60665/00), [2005] 3 FCR 649 where similar considerations led to conclusions that refusals to admit children of settled aliens breached Article 8.

4 *Uner v The Netherlands* (Application No 46410/99), (2006) 45 EHRR 421, [2006] 3 FCR 340, ECtHR.

5 *Maslov v Austria* (Application no 1638/03) (2007) 47 EHRR 496, [2007] 1 FCR 707, ECtHR.

6 *HM (Iraq) v Secretary of State for the Home Department* [2010] EWCA Civ 1322. Although *Maslov* was a case about a settled migrant, the fact that a person had been in the country since childhood, albeit unlawfully, was still a 'weighty consideration': see *JO (Uganda) v Secretary of State for the Home Department* [2010] EWCA Civ 10 and *Darko v Secretary of State for the Home Department* [2012] EWCA Civ 39. But see *R (on the application of Akpinar (Irfan)) v Upper Tribunal (Immigration and Asylum Chamber)* [2014] EWCA Civ 937: *Maslov* did not create a rule of law that 'very serious reasons' are required before a settled migrant who had spent all or a substantial part of his or her childhood in the country could be deported.

7 *Yildiz v Austria* (2003) 36 EHRR 32. In *Jakupovic v Austria* [2003] INLR 499, where the applicant joined his mother in Austria four years before the convictions for burglary relied on for expulsion, the court found a violation of art 8, holding that 'very weighty reasons' would be needed to justify the expulsion of a 16-year-old, alone, to a country which had recently experienced armed conflict and where he had no close relatives. In *SE (Zimbabwe) v Secretary of State for the Home Department* [2014] EWCA Civ 256 the Court of Appeal held that, 'absent exceptional circumstances' a person could not rely on the disruption to his or her rehabilitative work with probation officers and other staff to establish that deportation would breach art 8; to do so would be to rely on the deportee's unreformed criminality.

8 *JO (Uganda) and JT (Ivory Coast) v Secretary of State for the Home Department* [2010] EWCA Civ 10.

9 *Jeunesse v The Netherlands* (2014) Application no 12738/10 (Grand Chamber); *Konstatinov v Netherlands* (Application No 16351/03), [2007] 2 FCR 194. In *Omoregie v Norway* (2008) Application No 265/07 the Court gave substantial weight to the fact that for the whole duration of the family life in issue, the husband had no right of residence in Norway and no reasonable expectation of obtaining such a right. His removal would interfere with the right to respect for family life but absent exceptional circumstances and insurmountable obstacles to family life being developed in Nigeria, there was no breach. See also *Y v Russia* (2008) App No 20113/07.

10 *Da Silva and Hoogkamer v Netherlands* (2006) App No 50435/99; *Nunez v Norway* (2014) 58 EHRR 17; *Jeunesse v The Netherlands*.

11 *Jeunesse v The Netherlands*.

12 *Nunez v Norway*; *Jeunesse v The Netherlands*; *Butt v Norway* (2012) Application no 47017/09.

13 *Jeunesse v The Netherlands*; *Butt v Norway*.

14 *Alim v Russia* (2011) (Application No 39417/07).

15 *IR (Sri Lanka) v Secretary of State for the Home Department* [2011] EWCA Civ 704, [2011] 4 All ER 908, [2011] NLJR 918 where the Court of Appeal held that *Al-Nashif v Bulgaria* (2002) 36 EHRR 655 described the procedural protection implicitly required by art 8.

7.89 It is clear that the court, which had in the past rarely found in favour of applicants even where they had close family members in the Contracting State, has lowered the threshold for finding a violation of Article 8 based on obstacles to the family relocating elsewhere in the world – and this appears to be a quite deliberate shift of emphasis, from the right of States to control their borders to their duty to respect their international obligations in doing so.[1] In *Boultif* it recognised that the existence of real difficulties (such as lack of ties or language difficulties) for some family members in the deportee's country of origin, is likely to lead to the conclusion that the family cannot be expected to follow the deportee and that expulsion is a breach of Article 8 unless there are serious public order reasons for it. In *Sen*[2] the court took this one stage further in acknowledging that long-term residents in Contracting States can themselves face obstacles in returning to their countries of origin, in particular, having to give up the settled status and integrated position that they and especially their children had achieved. In such circumstances refusal by a Contracting State to admit a family member who had remained behind in the country of origin, could breach its obligations under Article 8.[3] The duty to admit family members in these circumstances flows from the positive obligation placed on a Contracting State by Article 8 ECHR to foster family life and to consider where family life might best develop, reflecting decisions made in family care cases and echoing what the court had stated in *Ciliz v Netherlands*.[4] Ciliz concerned a divorcé who was attempting to re-establish contact with his child through the courts when the State proposed to remove him for immigration reasons. Confirming its approach to positive obligations under Article 8, the court:

> 'reiterates that the essential object of Article 8 is to protect the individual against arbitrary action by the public authorities. There may in addition be positive obligations inherent in effective "respect" for family life. However the boundaries between the State's positive and negative obligations under this provision do not lend themselves to precise definition. The applicable principles are, nonetheless, similar.'[5]

[1] See *Boultif v Switzerland*, para 48; see also the Concurring Opinion of Judges Baka, Wildhaber and Lorenzen, which lists all the previous case law of the court relating to expulsion where no breach of art 8 ECHR had been found.
[2] *Sen v Netherlands* (2003) 36 EHRR 7.
[3] In *Sen* the excluded family member was a daughter who was nine years old at the time the application was made for her to join the family in the Netherlands. The same principles were applied in *Tuquabo-Tekle v Netherlands* (Application No 60665/00), [2005] 3 FCR 649 with the court similarly finding a breach of Article 8 where the excluded daughter was 15 at the time of the application for family reunion. In the domestic context, see *Begum (Husna) v Entry Clearance Officer, Dhaka* [2001] INLR 115, where the Court of Appeal held that while it may be relevant to a family reunion application that members of the family had chosen to live in the UK, leaving a relative in the country of origin, it was not universally the case that family reunion could not apply.
[4] *Ciliz v Netherlands* {2000} 2 FLR 469, para 66.
[5] See the strong dissenting judgment of Judge Martens in *Gul v Switzerland* (1996) 22 EHRR 93, suggesting that the differences were now indistinguishable.

7.90 The court's recent case law reflects a general acceptance that removal will normally constitute an interference with family life. Rather than requiring the applicant to establish that there would be insurmountable obstacles to family life being established elsewhere, the court has placed the burden of proof on the Contracting State to establish that an expulsion decision or refusal to admit would not constitute an interference with family life. In *Yildiz*[1] the court stated

> 'Nevertheless, the court considers that, as regards the possible effects of the residence ban on his family life, the authorities *failed to establish* whether the second applicant could be expected to follow him to Turkey, in particular whether she spoke Turkish and maintained any links, other than her nationality, with that country.'(our emphasis)'

It is settled law that it is for the State to demonstrate that any interference is in accordance with the law (in both its meanings), corresponds to a pressing social need and is proportionate to the legitimate aim pursued.[2] In *Jakupovic v Austria*[3] the court required 'very weighty reasons' to justify the expulsion of a 16-year-old to a country which had recently experienced armed conflict, where he had no close relatives, separating him from his mother, despite his criminal convictions.

1 *Yildiz v Austria* (2003) 36 EHRR 32.
2 *Moustaquim v Belgium* (1991) 13 EHRR 802; *Beldjoudi v France* (1992) 14 EHRR 801; *Sporrong and Lönnroth v Sweden* (1982) 5 EHRR 35 (para 69); *Cossey v United Kingdom* (1990) 13 EHRR 622.
3 [2003] INLR 499.

7.91 Whilst the focus of *Boultif* and cases that have followed it has been on 'family life', the court had previously begun to take cognisance of the fact that second generation migrants and long-term residents in Contracting States develop whole networks of social ties constituting 'private life'. In *Lamguindaz*,[1] a case involving the proposed deportation on conducive grounds of a Moroccan youth who had lived in the UK since the age of seven, Judge Schermers, in his concurring opinion, said:

> 'Even independent of human rights considerations I doubt whether modern international law permits a State which has educated children of admitted aliens to expel these children when they become a burden. Shifting this burden to the State of origin of the parents is no longer so clearly acceptable under modern international law.'[2]

In *Beldjoudi*[3] Judge Martens, in his concurring opinion, said that 'mere nationality' should not constitute an:

> 'objective and reasonable justification for the existence of a difference as regards the admissibility of expelling someone from what may be called "his own country" . . . . An increasing number of member States of the Council of Europe accept the principle that such "integrated aliens" should be no more liable to expulsion than nationals, an exception being justified if at all, only in very exceptional circumstances.'

However, the Grand Chamber in *Uner* rejected the proposition[4] that the situation of a long resident and highly integrated alien, particularly one born in the country, should be equated with that of a national in relation to the power to expel from the country. Article 8 did not confer an absolute right not to be expelled on any category of alien and deportation was to be seen as a preventative not a punitive measure so that it did not constitute a double punishment.[5] Thus, for example, deportation of a man who had been resident in the UK for 34 years did not breach Article 8.[6] Nevertheless, 'the Court will have regard to the special situation of aliens who have spent most, if not all, their childhood in the host country, were brought up there and received their education there'.[7] The Court would require 'very serious reasons' to justify the expulsion of a settled migrant who had spent all or a major part of his or her youth or childhood in the host country.[8] 'Very serious reasons' were required to justify refusing a residence permit to someone who had spent the 'formative years of her childhood and youth', ie from 7–15 in the contracting state.[9] Thus in *Uner* itself (where the applicant was 12 when he came to the Netherlands) and in the subsequent case of *Kaya*[10] (where the applicant was born in Germany), the Court found that deportation did not breach Article 8. The gravity of the offences (manslaughter and assault by shooting two men of whom one died in *Uner*; aggravated trafficking in human beings and exceptionally brutal assaults on two women in *Kaya*) and the failure of the applicants to produce evidence to show they no longer posed a risk to public safety were decisive considerations. On the other hand, the Court has been willing to treat repeated offending that attracted substantial periods of imprisonment as insufficient to justify deporting a long resident foreigner because it was 'non-violent juvenile delinquency' that was sufficiently mitigated by a period of 11/2 years' good conduct following release from the last period of imprisonment.[11] Where an offence underlying a decision to deport was committed whilst the individual was a minor, the obligation to have regard to the best interests of the child militates against deportation even after the individual has become an adult. That is because the obligation includes facilitating the reintegration of the child offender which may not be achieved if his or her family and social ties are eventually to be severed by deportation.[12] An offence as serious as rape did not justify deportation in circumstances where it was committed whilst the applicant was a minor; he was subsequently assessed as a low risk of reoffending and there had been a significant period of exemplary conduct following the conviction and release from prison.[13] The Court of Appeal has emphasised that whilst Article 8 imposes no absolute bar to removal of long resident non-citizens but that a balance still has to be struck between the interests served by removal of the protected rights, it must be struck with a proper appreciation of the special situation of those who have been in the host country since childhood[14] for whom removal may have more the character of exile than enforced return.[15]

[1] *Lamguindaz v United Kingdom* (1993) 17 EHRR 213.

[2] The government has accepted, in the amended policy DP5/96 relating to the removal of families with children, that children who have lived in the UK for seven years cannot be expected to adapt to life abroad.

[3] *Beldjoudi v France* (1992) 14 EHRR 801.

[4] Contained in, for example, Recommendation Rec (2000)15 of the Committee of Ministers fo the Council of Europe.

[5] *Uner v Netherlands* (Application No 46410/99), [2006] 3 FCR 340. Three judges gave a dissenting judgment in which they said that the position of settled aliens should as far as possible be assimilated to that of nationals.

[6] *Grant v United Kingdom* (Application No 10606/07) [2009] All ER (D) 82 (Jan). The applicant had children in the UK but did not live with any of them and none of them were dependent on him. He was a habitual offender and whilst his offences were not at the 'more serious end of the spectrum of criminal activity', their sheer number, committed over a long period of time and the want of evidence of any attempt to address the drug addiction which lay behind the offending meant that his deportation did not breach Article 8.

[7] *Uner.*

[8] *Maslov v Austria* (Application no 1638/03) [2007] 1 FCR 707 and in the Grand Chamber, [2008] ECHR 546 [2009] INLR 47.

[9] *Osman v Denmark* (2011) (App. No 38058/09).

[10] *Kaya v Germany* (Application No 31753/02), [2007] 2 FCR 527.

[11] *Maslov v Austria* (Application No 1638/03), [2007] 1 FCR 707. The applicant was Bulgarian and had lived in Austria from the age of six. He was sentenced to 18 months' imprisonment on 22 counts that included aggravated gang burglary, extortion and assault. Shortly after his release he was again convicted for a series of burglaries and sentenced to 15 months' imprisonment. The case has been referred to the Grand Chamber.

[12] *Maslov v Austria* [2008] ECHR 546; [2009] INLR 47; *AA v United Kingdom* (Application No 8000/08).

[13] *AA v United Kingdom* (Application No 8000/08) [2011] NLJR 1336, (2011) Times, 28 September, ECtHR.

[14] *JO (Uganda) and JT (Ivory Coast) v Secretary of State for the Home Department* [2010] EWCA Civ 10.

[15] HK *(Turkey) v Secretary of State for the Home Department* [2010] EWCA Civ 583, [2010] All ER (D) 71 (Jun).

7.92 The importance of reviewing deportation and removal decisions in the context of the protection of private life has developed significantly in the Strasbourg jurisprudence. As Judge Martens stated:

'Expulsion severs irrevocably all social ties between the deportee and the community he is living in and . . . the totality of those ties may be said to be part of the concept of private life'[1]

The principle seemed to have been accepted by the court by the late 1990s. In *C v Belgium*,[2] relying on its approach in *Niemietz v Germany*,[3] having looked at the family life of a long-term resident and proposed deportee, it examined his 'private life' in some detail:

'Mr C established real social ties in Belgium. He lived there from the age of 11, went to school there, underwent vocational training there and worked there for a number of years. He accordingly also established a private life there within the meaning of Article 8 (art 8), which encompasses the right for an individual to form and develop relationships with other human beings, including relationships of a professional or business nature (see, mutatis mutandis, the Niemietz v Germany judgment . . . para 29).'[4]

The Grand Chamber (in *Uner*) has now said:

'it must be accepted that the totality of social ties between settled migrants and the community in which they are living constitute part of the concept of "private life" within the meaning of article 8. Regardless of the existence or otherwise of a "family life", therefore, the Court considers that the expulsion of a settled migrant constitutes interference with his or her right to respect for private life. It will depend on the circumstances of the case whether is appropriate for the Court to focus on the "family life" rather than the "private life" aspect'.[5]

In such cases, 'the guiding principles' established in the *Boultif* case and added to in *Uner* are to be applied.[6] In the case of *Slivenko* the Court found that removal of a mother and her adult daughter 'from the country where they had developed uninterruptedly since birth, the network of personal, social and economic relations that make up the private life of every human being' did not interfere with their rights to respect for family life but breached their rights to respect for their private life and also their home.[7] The Court has increasingly emphasized that the factors to be examined in order to assess the proportionality of a measure excluding a settled migrant are the same whether family or private life is engaged so that it may not even be necessary to determine whether a breach is of the right to respect for family life or private life.[8] The domestic courts have recently taken a much more rigorous approach to private life, particularly that of the family members of the person whose removal or deportation is proposed. In *SS (India)* the Court of Appeal held that the Tribunal had erred in law because it had conducted no 'analysis of the social effect on the children of being wrenched from their social milieu in the UK'.[9] Assessing the existence and quality of 'private life' is not a matter of 'simply counting the number of friends that a person has in the UK' but would include, for example, the treatment and care being received by an AIDS sufferer.[10]

[1] *Beldjoudi v France* (1992) 14 EHRR 801. This position was defended by other judges such as Judge Wildhaber in *Nasri v France* (1995) 21 EHRR 458. Judge Morenilla in *Nasri v France*

and Judge De Meyer in *Beldjoudi v France* had gone further and expressed the view that the deportation of an integrated migrant per se would breach art 3 ECHR. Judge Morenilla stated:

'The deportation of such dangerous "non-nationals" may be expedient for a State which in this way rids itself of persons regarded as "undesirable", but it is cruel and inhuman and clearly discriminatory in relation to "nationals" who find themselves in such circumstances. A State which for reasons of convenience, accepts immigrant workers and authorises their residence, becomes responsible for the education and social integration of the children of such immigrants as it is of the children of its "citizens". Where such social integration fails, and the result is anti-social or criminal behaviour, the State is also under a duty to make provision for their social rehabilitation instead of sending them back to their country of origin, which has no responsibility for the behaviour in question and where the possibilities of rehabilitation in a foreign social environment are virtually non-existent. The treatment of offenders whether on the administrative or criminal level should not therefore differ according to the national origin of the parents in a way which – through deportation – makes the sanction more severe in a clearly discriminatory manner.'

²   *C v Belgium* (7 August 1996, unreported), para 25. The application failed on the facts.
³   (1992) 16 EHRR 97.
⁴   This was acknowledged in the domestic context in the case of *R v Immigration Officer, ex p James* (CO 2187/1999) where the Home Office accepted 16 years' residence, a close circle of friends, home and employment in the UK as engaging private life considerations.
⁵   *Uner v Netherlands* (Application No 46410/99), [2006] 3 FCR 340.
⁶   *Uner v Netherlands*.
⁷   *Slivenko v Latvia* (Application No 48321/99), [2004] 2 FCR 28. In *Nnyanzi v United Kingdom* (Application 21878/06) (2008) Times, 23 April, the Court held that whether or not removal of a woman from the UK where she had been for 10 years without leave to remain interfered with her right to respect for private life, such interference was in any event justified.
⁸   *AA v United Kingdom* (Application No 8000/08) [2011] NLJR 1336, (2011) Times, 28 September, ECtHR; *Osman v Denmark* (Application No 38058/09); *Nunez v Norway* (Application No 55597/09).
⁹   *SS (India) v Secretary of State for the Home Department* [2010] EWCA Civ 388.
¹⁰   *DM (Zambia) v Secretary of State for the Home Department* [2009] EWCA Civ 474.

7.93 The right to respect for private life is linked with personal autonomy, physical and psychological integrity, and the guarantee afforded by Article 8 of the ECHR is primarily intended to ensure the development, without outside interference, of the personality of each individual in his or her relations with other human beings.¹ Thus, enforcement action against carers who enable disabled or ill friends or relatives to live an independent and dignified life at home may constitute a disproportionate interference with the private life rights of the person cared for.² Same-sex relationships are an aspect of private life protected by Article 8.³ Although as yet there has been no ECtHR case in which interference with a homosexual relationship by removal or exclusion of a partner has been held to violate the right of respect to private life, now that such relationships are recognised under the UK Immigration Rules as conferring rights of residence in domestic law on a par with cohabiting heterosexual couples,⁴ there can no longer be any justification for a differential approach to interference with these relationships in the domestic courts. In a different context, destitution, isolation and social marginalisation to which late and failed asylum seekers may be subjected, raise issues relating to the right of respect for private life under Article 8.⁵

¹   *Botta v Italy* (1998) 26 EHRR 241, para 32; *Niemietz v Germany* (1992) 16 EHRR 97, para 29.
²   The invaluable role of carers is recognised in the government White Paper *Caring for People* (Cmd 849) and policy guidance *Community Care in the next decade and beyond*. The Home Office policy on carers (set out in the IDI Jun 01, Ch 17, s 2, is heavily restricted in time and, insofar as it insists on institutional care as a viable long-term alternative to allowing family members to remain as carers, may well breach art 8 ECHR. The importance of care provided

by friends or relatives was held to outweigh immigration control considerations in *R v Secretary of State for the Home Department, ex p Zakrocki* [1996] COD 304; cf *R v Secretary of State for the Home Department, ex p Green*, 29 October 1996, QBD, 31 January 1997, CA.

3   *Dudgeon v United Kingdom* (1980) 3 EHRR 40, paras 96–97; *Modinos v Cyprus* (1993) 16 EHRR 485; *Sutherland v United Kingdom* [1998] EHRLR 117; *Smith and Grady v United Kingdom* (1999) 29 EHRR 493.

4   HC 395, as amended by Cm 4851, paras 295A and D.

5   See *Smirnova v Russia* (46133/99, 48183/99) (24 July 2003, unreported), where the court held that the failure of the authorities to return identity papers following the applicant's release from prison, which led to difficulties in obtaining work, medical services etc, was a continuing violation of private life rights. See also *Ahmed v Austria* (1996) 24 EHRR 278, [1998] INLR 65. But cf *Mehemi v France* (53470/99), where no violation was found to arise from the legal limbo of an unenforceable exclusion order.

7.94 In order to comply with Article 8 it is not sufficient for the government merely to refrain from removing a person where such removal would breach his or her right to respect for private or family life; the government also has a positive obligation to confer such immigration status as is necessary to enable the person freely to exercise the right.[1] However, so long as that condition is fulfilled, the positive obligation does not extend to requiring a particular kind of status to be given.[2] In the UK, a person who establishes that removing him or her would violate a Convention right would be entitled to leave to enter or remain[3] and an undertaking not to remove the person whilst such a violation might occur would not be sufficient.[4]

1   *Sisojeva v Latvia* (2007) App No 60654/00, Grand Chamber.

2   *Sisojeva v Latvia*, Grand Chamber, overturning the decision of the former first section (*Sisojeva v Latvia* (2005) App No 60654/00) which was that failure to confer permanent residence and merely to offer regularisation of status on a temporary basis breached the applicants' rights to respect for their private lives. The Grand Chamber held that the government's offer of a five-year residence permit was sufficient. The first section in *Shevanova v Latvia* (2006) App No 58822/00 and *Kaftailova v Latvia* (2006) App No 59643/00 reached similar conclusions but the cases have been referred to the Grand Chamber.

3   *S v Secretary of State for the Home Department* [2006] EWCA Civ 1157. The position may change in respect of some people if the provisions in the Criminal Justice and Immigration Bill creating a 'special immigration status' for 'foreign criminals' and their families are enacted.

4   *MS (Ivory Coast) v Secretary of State for the Home Department* [2007] EWCA Civ 133.

Article 8 in the domestic courts

7.95 In *Razgar*[1] Lord Bingham identified five questions that should be addressed in order to determine whether a decision breaches Article 8. They are:

(1)   Will the proposed removal be an interference by a public authority with the exercise of the applicant's right to respect for his private or (as the case may be) family life?

(2)   If so, will such interference have consequences of such gravity as potentially to engage the operation of Article 8?

(3)   If so, is such interference in accordance with the law?

(4)   If so, is such interference necessary in a democratic society in the interests of national security, public safety or the economic well-being of the country, for the prevention of disorder or crime, for the protection of health or morals, or for the protection of the rights and freedoms of others?

(5)   If so, is such interference proportionate to the legitimate public end sought to be achieved?

Questions (1) and (2) require positive answers and one or more of (3)–(5) requires a negative answer for a breach of Article 8 to be found. The first two questions relate to whether Article 8(1) is engaged. The second of them sets the threshold for Article 8 to be engaged and whilst it requires that the interference be real, it is not otherwise a specially high threshold.[2]

---

1   *R (on the application of Razgar) v Secretary of State for the Home Department* [2004] UKHL 27, [2004] 2 AC 368, [2004] 3 All ER 821.
2   *AG (Eritrea) v Secretary of State for the Home Department* [2007] EWCA Civ 801; [2008] 2 All ER 28; [2007] NLJR 1235. See also *KR (Iraq) v Secretary of State for the Home Department* [2007] EWCA Civ 514, [2007] All ER (D) 426 (May) where Auld LJ observed that it was hard to see why there should be a particularly high threshold for Article 8 to be engaged when the issue was threatened removal from the UK compared with other less draconian interferences and *VW (Uganda) v Secretary of State for the Home Department* [2009] EWCA Civ 5, [2009] All ER (D) 92 (Jan);[2009] Imm AR 436 : the second question 'simply reflects the fact that more than a technical or inconsequential interference with one of the protected rights is needed if Article 8(1) is to be engaged'.

7.96 The leading decisions of the UK courts on Article 8 ECHR in the immigration context are *Huang*,[1] *Chikwamba*,[2] *EB (Kosovo)*[3] and later, *ZH (Tanzania)*[4] and *Quila*.[5] These decisions followed a period where the UK courts took a much more conservative approach to Article 8. A key feature of this period was what amounted to a general presumption that in the absence of 'insurmountable obstacles' to family life being enjoyed outside of the UK, exclusion or removal of a family member would not breach Article 8,[6] nor would a decision made in accordance with the Immigration Rules unless there were truly exceptional circumstances.[7] The House of Lords' judgments in *Huang*, *Chikwamba* and *EB (Kosovo)* decisively put an end to such notions, although since 9 July 2012 the Secretary of State has attempted to restore them by implementing Immigration Rules which seek to define the scope of Article 8.[8] The domestic landscape of Article 8 has been further complicated by the 'public interest considerations' brought into force on 28 July 2014 by the Immigration Act 2014.[9] The combination of the new Rules and primary legislation has given rise to significant controversy as to the precise scope of Article 8 in the immigration context. This has resulted in a series of judgments by the Upper Tribunal and higher courts, displaying a range of different judicial approaches. This body of law is now characterised, unhelpfully in our view, by a proliferation of phrases which all simultaneously attempt to define thresholds and legal tests for the application of Article 8.[10] This is to be contrasted with the period of relative legal certainty that followed the House of Lords decisions in *Huang*, *Chikwamba* and *EB (Kosovo)*.

---

1   *Huang v Secretary of State for the Home Department* [2007] UKHL 11, [2007] 2 AC 167.
2   *R (on the application of Chikwamba) v Secretary of State for the Home Department* [2008] UKHL 40, [2009] 1 All ER 363.
3   *EB (Kosovo) v Secretary of State for the Home Department* [2008] UKHL 41, [2009] AC 1159.
4   *ZH (Tanzania) v Secretary of State for the Home Department* [2011] UKSC 4, [2011] 2 All ER 783, [2011] 2 WLR 148.
5   *R (on the application of Aguilar Quila) v Secretary of State for the Home Department* [2011] UKSC 45; [2012] 1AC, 621.
6   *R (on the application of Mahmood) v Secretary of State for the Home Department* [2001] 1 WLR 840.
7   *Huang v Secretary of State* [2005] EWCA Civ 105, [2006] QB 1.

[8] By virtue of Statement of Changes in Immigration Rules HC 194, new Immigration Rules came into force. See **7.99** below.

[9] Inserting new ss 117A-117D to the Immigration, Nationality and Asylum Act 2002. See **7.104** below.

[10] These include 'exceptional circumstances' (Home Office IDI, 'Family Migration: Appendix FM Section 1.0b, Family Life (as a Partner or Parent) and Private Life: 10 Year Routes'; HC 395, para 398 before amendment by HC 532 on 28 July 2014), 'very exceptional circumstances' (HC 395, para 399D), 'compelling circumstances' (*R (on the application of Nagre) v Secretary of State for the Home Department* [2013] EWHC 720 (Admin); HC 395, para 398), 'very compelling circumstances' (HC 395, para 398; NIAA 2002, s 117C(6)), 'insurmountable obstacles' (HC 395, Appendix FM, EX.1, EX.2; *Nagre*), 'very significant difficulties . . . which could not be overcome' (HC 395, Appendix FM, EX.2), 'very significant obstacles' (HC 395, paras 399A and 276ADE(vi); NIAA 2002, s 117C(4)(c)), 'very serious hardship' (HC 395, Appendix FM, EX.2), 'unjustifiably harsh' (Home Office IDI, 'Family Migration: Appendix FM Section 1.0b, Family Life (as a Partner or Parent) and Private Life: 10 Year Routes'; *Nagre*) and 'unduly harsh' (HC 394, para 399; NIAA 2002, s 117C(5)).

7.97 The decision of the House of Lords in *Huang*[1] which remains the leading authority on Article 8 in the immigration context, is critically important for a number of reasons. First of all, it confirmed that the Tribunal's task is to determine whether an immigration decision is incompatible with a Convention right and therefore unlawful, a task requiring the Tribunal to determine for itself the lawfulness of the immigration decision on the basis of its findings as to the facts, not merely to review the decision of the primary decision maker.[2] Secondly, it reminds the courts of the obligation to follow the clear and constant jurisprudence of the Strasbourg Court unless there are special circumstances such that it should not be followed[3] and highlights the value of that jurisprudence as 'showing where, in many different factual situations, the Strasbourg Court, as the ultimate guardian of Convention rights, has drawn the line, thus guiding national authorities in making their own decisions'.[4] Thirdly, it emphasises that Article 8 exists to protect a 'core value' and that what protection of that value may require necessitates consideration of a very wide range of factors:

'Human beings are social animals. They depend on others. Their family, or extended family, is the group on which many people most heavily depend, socially, emotionally and often financially. There comes a point at which, for some, prolonged and unavoidable separation from this group seriously inhibits their ability to live full and fulfilling lives. Matters such as the age, health and vulnerability of the applicant, the closeness and previous history of the family, the applicant's dependence on the financial and emotional support of the family, the prevailing cultural tradition and conditions in the country of origin and many other factors may all be relevant.'[5]

Fourthly, general principles applicable to the assessment of proportionality[6] apply no less to immigration than to other areas[7]; they require the proportionality of an interference with family life to be assessed by answering the 'ultimate question':

'whether the refusal of leave to enter or remain, in circumstances where the life of the family cannot reasonably be expected to be enjoyed elsewhere, taking full account of all considerations weighing in favour of the refusal, prejudices the family life of the applicant in a manner sufficiently serious to amount to a breach of the fundamental right protected by article 8. If the answer to this question is affirmative, the refusal is unlawful and the authority must so decide.'[8]

Fifthly, it is clear from that formulation of the 'ultimate question' as well as the general analysis of proportionality that the policy expressed in the Immigration Rules and supplementary instructions cannot simply be treated as having 'struck the balance between the public interest and the private right' that is required by Article 8, save in a 'truly exceptional case'[9] so that the assessment of proportionality becomes merely the determination of whether a case is 'truly exceptional'.[10] The suggestion that the Immigration Rules could be so treated was made by analogy with public housing policy which the House of Lords had accepted[11] as striking that balance. However, the analogy was rejected because whereas housing policy represented a genuinely democratic reconciliation of the various competing interests following debate in Parliament in which each of those interests was represented the same could not be said of the Immigration Rules and policies; they were not actively debated in Parliament and the interests of affected non-nationals were not represented.[12] Consequently, an applicant's failure to qualify under the Rules is relevant to the consideration of an Article 8 claim, but as a starting point rather than the conclusion;[13] an applicant may fail to qualify under the Rules but have a valid claim under Article 8.[14] In the light of *Huang*, the Court of Appeal has resiled from the proposition that the Immigration Rules are intended to secure compliance with Article 8 or indeed that they have any overarching purpose other than to articulate the Secretary of State's current policy with regard to immigration control.[15] Sixthly, there are general considerations relating to the effective and consistent operation of immigration control that may weigh in favour of refusal when assessing proportionality:[16]

'the general administrative desirability of applying known rules if a system of immigration control is to be workable, predictable, consistent and fair as between one applicant and another; the damage to good administration and effective control if a system is perceived by applicants internationally to be unduly porous, unpredictable or perfunctory; the need to discourage non-nationals admitted to the country temporarily from believing that they can commit serious crimes and yet be allowed to remain; the need to discourage fraud, deception and deliberate breaches of the law; and so on.'

1   *Huang v Secretary of State for the Home Department* [2007] UKHL 11, [2007] 2 AC 167, [2007] 4 All ER 15.
2   *Huang*, paras 11, 13 and 15. Thus decisions such as *Edore v Secretary of State for the Home Department* [2003] EWCA Civ 716 [2003] 1 WLR 2979 were wrong on that issue.
3   *Huang*, para 18.
4   *Huang*, para 18.
5   *Huang*, para 18.
6   Citing *de Freitas v Permanent Secretary of Ministry of Agriculture, Fisheries, Lands and Housing* [1999] 1 AC 69, 80 where the questions to be asked to decide whether a measure is proportionate are whether '(i) the legislative object is sufficiently important to justify limiting a fundamental right; (ii) the measures designed to meet the legislative objective are rationally connected to it; and (iii) the means used to impair the right or freedom are no more important than is necessary to accomplish the objective'. In addition, citing *R (on the application of Aguilar Quila) v Secretary of State for the Home Department* [2004] UKHL 27 [2004] 2 AC 368, the judgment on proportionality 'must always involve the striking of a fair balance between the rights of the individual and the interests of the community which is inherent in the whole of the Convention. The severity and consequences of the interference will call for careful assessment at this stage'. In many immigration cases, this is usually the only and decisive question, however, with reference to the third question in *de Freitas*, in *R (on the application of Quila and another) v Secretary of State for the Home Department* [2011] UKSC 45, [2011] 3 WLR 836, [2011] 3 FCR 575, Article 8 was said to be breached by the application of an immigration rule that prevented entry by a spouse if the person seeking entry or the sponsor was under the age of 21. That was so because the Secretary of State had failed to discharge the

burden on her of showing that the rule, whose purpose was to deter forced marriages, sufficiently achieved that objective particularly having regard to the effect of the rule on parties to non-forced marriages.

7   *AG (Eritrea) v Secretary of State for the Home Department* [2007] EWCA Civ 801, [2007] NLJR 1235 where the Court, recapitulating various statements of principle generally applicable to the assessment of proportionality, including *de Freitas* said that whilst courts and tribunals need not adopt a set formula for determining proportionality 'they should have proper and visible regard to relevant principles in making a structured decision about it case by case'.

8   *Huang*, para 20.

9   Huang in the Court of Appeal [2005] EWCA Civ 105, [2006] QB 1.

10 'It is not necessary that the appellate immigration authority, directing itself along the lines indicated in this opinion, need ask in addition whether the case meets a test of exceptionality': *Huang*, para 20.

11 In *Kay v Lambeth London Borough Council* [2006] UKHL 10, [2006] 2 AC 465.

12 *Huang*, para 17. The importance of this was underlined by Blake J in *R (on the application of Vu) v Secretary of State for the Home Department* [2008] EWHC 1192 (Admin), [2008] All ER (D) 172 (May).

13 *Huang*, para 6.

14 *Huang*, para 17. See also *R (on the application of Syed) v Secretary of State for the Home Department* [2011] EWCA Civ 1059, 155 Sol Jo (no 34) 31.

15 *AM (Ethiopia) v Entry Clearance Officer* [2008] EWCA Civ 1082, [2008] All ER (D) 150 (Oct), paras 38–39. *Odawey v Entry Clearance Officer* [2011] EWCA Civ 840, para 36, Rix LJ: 'it is perfectly true that article 8 lies beyond the immigration rules and there is no necessity that the rules represent the appropriate balance in a particular case'.

16 *Huang*, para 16 where those considerations are identified. In *FK and OK (Botswana) v Secretary of State for the Home Department* [2013] EWCA Civ 238 Stanley Burnton LJ emphasised that whilst the 'maintenance of effective immigration control' is not itself one of the legitimate aims that may justify interference with a protected right, its maintenance is said to be necessary to preserve the economic well-being of the country; to protect health and morals and for the protection of the rights and freedoms of others.

7.98 In *EB (Kosovo)*[1], the House of Lords emphasised the significance of careful investigation of the relevant facts by the immigration appellate authority, in recognition that the authority's judgment of proportionality will be 'strongly influenced by the particular facts and circumstances of the particular case'.[2] Giving the lead judgment, Lord Bingham made a critically important observation about the nature of the Article 8 exercise:

'there is in general no alternative to making a careful and informed evaluation of the facts of the particular case. The search for a hard-edged or bright-line rule to be applied to the generality of cases is incompatible with the difficult evaluative exercise which article 8 requires.'[3]

This observation has resonance in the context of the attempted 'codification' of Article 8 in both Immigration Rules and primary legislation.

1   *EB (Kosovo) v Secretary of State for the Home Department* [2008] UKHL 41, [2009] 1 AC 1159.

2   *EB (Kosovo)*, paras 9 and 12.

3   *EB (Kosovo)*, para 12.

7.99 On 9 July 2012, by virtue of Statement of Changes in Immigration Rules HC 194, new Immigration Rules came into force. These Rules make provision for applications for leave to remain on 'the grounds of private life' (paras 276ADE–276DH), applications for entry and stay based on family life (Appendix FM) and Article 8 claims arising in the context of deportation (paras 398–399B). The government announced that these Rules 'would reflect fully the factors which can weigh for or against an Article 8 claim' and that they would for the 'first time reflect the views of the Government and Parliament as to how Article 8 should, as a matter of public policy, be qualified in the public interest in order to safeguard the economic well-being of the UK by controlling immigration and to protect the public from foreign criminals.'[1] While the Rules provide greater specificity as to the matters which the Secretary of State regards as attracting the greatest weight in respect of the public interest, references in them to 'exceptional circumstances' or 'insurmountable obstacles' are simply legal requirements within the Rules rather than legal tests within Article 8.[2] Where the Rules apply, cases should first be considered under them, but where the requirements of the Rules are not met it is necessary to go on to make an assessment of Article 8 applying the criteria established by case law.[3] The criteria in the Rules do not accord with the criteria for an Article 8 assessment established by the existing case law, and there can be no presumption that the Rules will normally be conclusive of Article 8 or that a fact sensitive inquiry is not normally needed.[4] The more the new Rules restrict otherwise relevant and weighty considerations from being taken into account, the less regard will be had to them in the assessment of proportionality.[5] Established criteria such as the best interests of children are not reflected in Appendix FM.[6]

[1] Home Office 'Statement of Intent: Family Migration', June 2012.
[2] *MF (Article 8 – new rules) Nigeria* [2012] UKUT 393 (IAC); *Haleemudeen v Secretary of State for the Home Department* [2014] EWCA Civ 558 per Beatson LJ at para 40: 'These new provisions in the Immigration Rules are a central part of the legislative and policy context in which the interests of immigration control are balanced against the interests and rights of people who have come to this country and wish to settle in it. Overall the Secretary of State's policy as to when an interference with an Article 8 right will be regarded as disproportionate is more particularised in the new Rules than it had previously been.'
[3] *Secretary of State for the Home Department v Izuazu* [2013] UKUT 45 (IAC), para 41.
[4] *Izuazu*, paras 52 and 67.
[5] *Izuazu*, para 52.
[6] *Izuazu*, para 52.

7.100 Paragraph EX.1 of Appendix FM and paragraph 276ADE were not unlawful for being inherently incompatible with Article 8,[1] nor is paragraph 276ADE *ultra vires* section 3(2) of the Immigration Act 1971.[2] The minimum financial requirements in Appendix FM were not in principle a disproportionate interference with a UK-based partner's rights under Article 8, although they might be in a particular factual situation.[3] Similarly, the requirement imposed by the rules that a spouse demonstrate sufficient knowledge of the English language was not in principle a disproportionate interference with family life rights, albeit that application of the rule might breach Article 8 in the case of a particular family's circumstances.[4]

[1] *R (on the application of Nagre) v Secretary of State for the Home Department* [2013] EWHC 720 (Admin).
[2] *R (on the application of Amin) v Secretary of State for the Home Department* [2014] EWHC 2322 (Admin)
[3] *R (on the application of MM (Lebanon)) v Secretary of State for the Home Department* [2014] EWCA Civ 985. Aikens LJ at paras 141–153 held that the aims of the minimum income policy were sufficiently important to justify limiting those rights, there was a rational connection between the sums required and the policy aim and that the Secretary of State had demonstrated that the interference was the minimum necessary and struck a fair balance between the interests of the groups concerned and the community in general. The court would not impose

its own view unless the levels chosen could be characterised as irrational, inherently unjust or inherently unfair. Further, the provisions in Appendix FM precluding reliance on third party funding were not irrational (para 154).

⁴ *R (on the application of Bibi) v Secretary of State for the Home Department (Liberty and Joint Council for the Welfare of Immigrants, intervening)* [2013] EWCA Civ 322, paras 30, 32.

7.101 *In MF (Nigeria)*¹ the Court of Appeal held that the new deportation provisions provide a 'complete code'. Where paragraphs 399–399A do not apply, for the public interest in deportation to be outweighed by 'other factors' the rules require a deportee to demonstrate 'very compelling circumstances over and above those described in paragraphs 399 and 399A'.² The Court of Appeal held that this residual test contained within the 'complete code' constituted by the deportation rules involved the application of a proportionality test required by the Strasbourg jurisprudence,³ including factors such as best interests of the children and the *Maslov*⁴ principles. Whether the proportionality test is to be conducted within or without the new Rules was ultimately a sterile question.⁵ By contrast, the private life rules (paras 276ADE–276DH) and Appendix FM are not a 'complete code' so far as Article 8 compatibility is concerned.⁶ In such cases, the Court of Appeal has approved the notion that it is necessary to find 'compelling circumstances' to justify an assessment of Article 8 outside the Rules,⁷ however, a differently constituted court of appeal found that there was little utility in imposing an intermediary test as a preliminary to consideration of Article 8 outside the Rules for a person who fails under the Rules.⁸

¹ *MF (Nigeria) v Secretary of State for the Home Department* [2013] EWCA Civ 1192, [2014] 1 WLR 544. See CHAPTER **16** for a full analysis of the new deportation provisions.

² HC 395, para 398, as amended by HC 532 with effect from 28.7.2014. Prior to that the rule required 'exceptional circumstances' rather than 'very compelling circumstances' if the public interest in deportation was to be displaced.

³ *R (on the application of MM (Lebanon)) v Secretary of State for the Home Department* [2014] EWCA Civ 985 at 135.

⁴ *Maslov v Austria* [2009] INLR 47.

⁵ *MF (Nigeria)*, para 45.

⁶ *R (on the application of Amin) v Secretary of State for the Home Department* [2014] EWHC 2322 (Admin), para 14, 34; *R (on the application of Ganesabalan) v Secretary of State for the Home Department* [2014] EWHC 2712 (Admin), paras 10–13; *Shahzad (Art 8: legitimate aim) Pakistan* [2014] UKUT 85 (IAC).

⁷ *Haleemudeen v Secretary of State for the Home Department* [2014] EWCA Civ 558, paras 44 and 47, acknowledging the approach of Sales J in *R (on the application of Nagre) v Secretary of State for the Home Department* [2013] EWHC 720 (Admin) at para 29:

> 'in many cases the main points for consideration in relation to Article 8 will be addressed by decision-makers applying the new rules. It is only if, after doing that, there remains an arguable case that there may be good grounds for granting leave to remain outside the Rules by reference to Article 8 that it will be necessary for Article 8 purposes to go on to consider whether there are compelling circumstances not sufficiently recognised under the new rules to require the grant of such leave'.

This aspect of *Nagre* was adopted in an oft-cited decision of Cranston J in the Upper Tribunal *Gulshan (Article 8 – new Rules – correct approach) Pakistan* [2013] UKUT 640 (IAC), however, it must now be seen in the light of Aikens LJ's observations in *MM (Lebanon)*, fn 8 below.

⁸ *MM (Lebanon) v Secretary of State for the Home Department* [2014] EWCA Civ 985 per Aikens LJ at 129, although it should be noted that *Haleemudeen* was not cited by the Court in *MM(Lebanon)*. In *Ganesabalan* Michael Fordham QC (sitting as a Deputy High Court Judge) considered both *Haleemudeen* and *MM (Lebanon)* and said in respect of the exercise of discretion to grant leave to remain outside the Rules on Article 8 grounds:

> 'There is no prior threshold which dictates whether the exercise of discretion should be

considered; rather the nature of the assessment and the reasoning which are called for are informed by threshold considerations, those threshold circumstances include (a) whether an arguable basis for the exercise of the discretion has been put forward; (b) whether the relevant factors have already been assessed; (c) whether a repeat evaluation is unnecessary.'

7.102 As noted above, the 'ultimate question' arises when the life of the family cannot reasonably be expected to be enjoyed elsewhere and, following the decisions in *Huang* and *EB(Kosovo)* this has been elucidated further by the Court of Appeal. Whilst the phrase 'insurmountable obstacles' has been used in Strasbourg judgments and most notably in *R (on the application of Mahmood) v Secretary of State for the Home Department*[1] as a matter of domestic law '*EB (Kosovo)* now confirms that the material question in gauging the proportionality of a removal or deportation which will or may break up a family unless the family itself decamps is not whether there is an insuperable obstacle to this happening but whether it is reasonable to expect the family to leave with the appellant.'[2] Nor is there a requirement that it must be 'impossible or exceptionally difficult' for a deportee's family to relocate with him or her to the country of removal, although that is another phrase that has been used by the Strasbourg Court when assessing the seriousness of the difficulties that relocation would entail.[3] The issue is whether the decision gives rise to hardship far enough beyond matters of mere hardship, mere difficulty, mere obstacle or mere inconvenience.[4] The impact of proposed relocation on the rights attaching to the British citizenship of any family member would weigh heavily.[5] In many cases, a decision-maker cannot be expected to determine whether in fact future removal would break up a family; in such cases, the hardship of the dilemma facing family members confronted with having to decide between staying together and staying in the country would have to be evaluated.[6] As a result of the Court of Justice of the European Union decisions in *Zambrano*[7] and *Dereci*,[8] the Secretary of State has confirmed that as citizens of the European Union, it is not possible to require a British citizen child (and an accompanying British parent), to relocate outside of the Union, or to submit that it would be reasonable for them to do so, as a means of avoiding an interference with family life rights.[9] The phrase 'insurmountable obstacles to family life . . . continuing outside the UK' has resurfaced in the post-9 July 2012 Immigration Rules.[10] In applying such a test within the Rules, the Court of Appeal in *MF(Nigeria)* has observed *obiter* that 'if "insurmountable" obstacles are literally obstacles which it is impossible to surmount, their scope is very limited indeed.'[11] Further the Court in *MF(Nigeria)* expressly approved the Upper Tribunal's reasoning in *Izuazu*[12] that to reject a claim under Article 8 because the test of 'insurmountable obstacles' is not met would be contrary to established law. However, in cases where family life has been established whilst the immigration status of a migrant was precarious, it was well established in the Strasbourg case law that it is likely only to be in exceptional circumstances that removal of the non-national family member will violate Article 8.[13] This approach in 'precarious' cases has been reconfirmed by the Grand Chamber of the European Court of Human Rights in *Jeunesse v The Netherlands*.[14]

[1] *R (on the application of Mahmood) v Secretary of State for the Home Department* [2001] 1 WLR 840.
[2] Sedley LJ in *VW (Uganda) v Secretary of State for the Home Department* [2009] EWCA Civ 5, [2009] All ER (D) 92 (Jan), *following LM (Democratic Republic of Congo) v Secretary*

of State for the Home Department [2008] EWCA Civ 325, [2008] All ER (D) 226 (Mar). See also YO *(Togo) v Secretary of State for the Home Department* [2010] EWCA Civ 214, [2010] All ER (D) 97 (Feb).

3 *JO (Uganda) and JT (Ivory Coast) v Secretary of State for the Home Department* [2010] EWCA Civ 10.

4 *VW (Uganda)*, fn 2 above.

5 *AB (Jamaica) v Secretary of State for the Home Department* [2007] EWCA Civ 1302, [2008] 1 WLR 1893.

6 *VW (Uganda)*, fn 2 above.

7 *Ruiz Zambrano v Office National de l'Emploi (ONEm)*: C-34/09; [2012] QB 265.

8 *Dereci v Bundesministerium für Inneres*: C-256/11.

9 This came by way of a written concession made by the Secretary of State in *Sanade and others (British children – Zambrano – Dereci) India* [2012] UKUT 48 (IAC), and clarified in *Secretary of State for the Home Department v Izuazu* [2013] UKUT 45 (IAC).

10 HC 395, para EX.1. of Appendix FM and for a period of time in para 399.

11 *MF (Nigeria) v Secretary of State for the Home Department* [2013] EWCA Civ 1192, [2014] 1 WLR 544 at para 49.

12 *Izuazu*, paras 53–59. Importantly the Tribunal dismissed any suggestion that the decisions of the UK courts in *Huang* ,*EB (Kosovo)* and *VW (Uganda)*, rejecting 'insurmountable obstacles' as a test, were contrary to the Strasbourg jurisprudence on the basis that the European Court of Human Rights applied minimum standards rather than a uniform approach binding on every contracting state. The principle of subsidiarity afforded a margin of appreciation to the institutions of the contracting state and the national courts and tribunals are better placed than the international court to conduct a primary examination of the competing considerations (paras 60–64).

13 *MF (Nigeria)*, para 42 approving Sales J's analysis of this aspect of the Strasbourg case law in *R (on the application of Nagre) v Secretary of State for the Home Department* [2013] EWHC 720 (Admin) at paras 40–42.

14 12738/10-*Grand Chamber Judgment* [2014] ECHR 1036, para 108. It is of note that on the facts of the case, the Grand Chamber concluded that despite the absence of insurmountable obstacles to family life taking place in Suriname (para 117), the applicant's case was exceptional and her removal would violate her rights under Article 8 (para 122).

7.103 The suggestion that there would be no interference with the family life shared by members of an interdependent household if one of them was removed because they could maintain communication by means of telephone calls and video conferences was mistaken.[1] As Mr Justice Ouseley has said:

'The essence of family life, which makes it possible that the ECHR extends to some non-nationals outside of the territorial jurisdiction who seek respect for their family life with someone settled here, is the need for physical proximity between those persons'.[2]

When assessing the importance to be given to an individual's family or private life 'particular weight' must be given to the mental state of a victim of trafficking.[3]

1 *R (on the application of Mansoor) v Secretary of State for the Home Department* [2011] EWHC 832 (Admin), [2011] All ER (D) 136 (Apr).

2 *Moon v Secretary of State for the Home Department* [2005] UKIAT 00112, para 68.

3 *AM and BM (Trafficked women) Albania CG* [2010] UKUT 80 (IAC).

7.104 A new Part 5A of the Nationality, Immigration and Asylum Act 2002, comprising new sections 117A–117B,[1] represents an unprecedented legislative mechanism by which courts and tribunals are required to assess the public interest in Article 8 cases with reference to Parliament's view as expressed in the legislation. Part 5A applies where a court or tribunal is required to determine whether a decision made under the Immigration Acts breaches a person's rights under Article 8 such that it would be unlawful under section 6 of the Human Rights Act 1998.[2] The 'public interest question' is defined as the question of 'whether an interference with a person's right to respect for private and family life is justified under Article 8(2)'.[3] In considering the public interest question 'the court or tribunal must (in particular) have regard':

(a)　　in all cases, to the considerations listed in section 117B; and

(b)　　in cases concerning the deportation of foreign criminals, to the considerations listed in section 117C.[4]

Within Part 5A, a 'qualifying child' is defined as a person who is under the age of 18 and who:

(a)　　is a British citizen, or

(b)　　has lived in the UK for a continuous period of seven years or more.[5]

A 'qualifying partner' is a partner who:

(a)　　is a British citizen, or

(b)　　who is settled in the UK.[6]

A 'foreign criminal' is defined as a person:

(a)　　who is not a British citizen,

(b)　　who has been convicted in the UK of an offence, and

(c)　　who:

　　　(i)　　has been sentenced to a period of imprisonment of at least 12 months,

　　　(ii)　　has been convicted of an offence that has caused serious harm, or

　　　(iii)　　is a persistent offender.[7]

References in Part 5A to persons sentenced to a particular period of imprisonment do not include those who have received a suspended sentence, or those for whom the period of imprisonment is only as a result of aggregating consecutive sentences,[8] but they do include those sentenced, ordered or directed to be detained in places other than a prison such as a hospital or young offenders institute.[9] They also include a person who is sentenced to imprisonment or detention for an indeterminate period.[10]

[1]　Inserted by the Immigration Act 2014, s 19 of and brought into force on 28 July 2014 by art 3(o) of Immigration Act 2014 (Commencement No 1, Transitory and Saving Provisions) Order 2014, SI 2014/1820. There are no specific transitional provisions governing the commencement of section 19, which took immediate effect upon all courts and tribunals to which it applies.

[2]　NIAA 2002, s 117A(1)(a),(b). In *YM (Uganda) v Secretary of State for the Home Department* [2014] EWCA Civ 1292, the Court of Appeal held that where, after 28 July 2014, a court or tribunal is deciding whether a lower court has, before 28 July 2014, perpetrated an error of law in respect of Article 8, Part 5A NIAA 2002 will be irrelevant to that task, but if the court or tribunal does re-make the Article 8 decision for itself then Part 5A will apply.

[3]　NIAA 2002, s 117A(3).

[4]　NIAA 2002, s 117A(2)(a),(b).

[5]　NIAA 2002, s 117D(1). See para **7.113**, fn 4 below, setting out the Secretary of State's view of the relevance of seven years residence in the UK by a child.

[6]　NIAA 2002, s 117D(1).

[7]　NIAA 2002, s 117D(2).

[8]　NIAA 2002, s 117D(4)(a),(b).

[9]　NIAA 2002, s 117D(4)(c).

[10]　NIAA 2002, s 117D(4)(d).

7.105 Section 117B of the NIAA 2002 describes six public interest considerations applicable in all cases. The first three are statements of what is in the
public interest, namely:

(1)   the maintenance of effective immigration control;[1]
(2)   that persons seeking to enter or remain in the UK speak English,
       because such persons are less of a burden on taxpayers and are better
       able to integrate into society;[2] and
(3)   that persons who seek to enter or remain in the UK are financially
       independent, again because such persons are less of a burden on
       taxpayers and are better able to integrate into society.[3]

The fourth and fifth are instructions are that little weight should be given to a
private life or a relationship formed with a qualifying partner at a time when
a person is in the UK unlawfully,[4] and that little weight should be given to a
private life established by a person at a time when the person's immigration
status is precarious.[5]

[1]   NIAA 2002, s 117B(1).
[2]   NIAA 2002, s 117B(2)(a), (b).
[3]   NIAA 2002, s 117B(3)(a), (b).
[4]   NIAA 2002, s 117B(4)(a), (b).
[5]   NIAA 2002, s 117B(5).

7.106 The sixth consideration to which section 117B of the NIAA 2002 refers
is different to the others in that it provides an answer to 'the public interest
question' rather than just indicating matters that are relevant for the purpose
of answering the question. It applies, and the public interest does not require
a person's removal, where:

(a)   a person has a genuine and subsisting relationship with a qualifying
       child; and
(b)   the person is not liable to deportation; and
(c)   it would not be reasonable to expect the child to leave the UK.[1]

If those circumstances exist then as far as the legislation is concerned there can
be no justification for the interference with family life under Article 8(2). This
appears to have been the Secretary of State's intention in proposing the
legislation.[2] Where Parliament has unambiguously and expressly declared
what the public interest requires, 'the respondent's view of the public interest
has no relevance'[3] which means that the Secretary of State's view should be
disregarded if she contends that a person should be expelled notwithstanding
that those circumstances are present. The reference to 'reasonable to expect the
child to leave the UK' is, we think, reference to the best interests of the child[4]
only and not to all considerations that might have a bearing on proportionality. Part 5A raises important constitutional questions about the respective
roles of Parliament and the courts in the adjudication of human rights, and the
precise extent of Part 5A's impact on judicial decision-making in Article 8 cases
remains to be seen.

[1]   NIAA 2002, s 117B(6)(a),(b).
[2]   In the document *Immigration Bill: European Convention on Human Rights: Memorandum by
       the Home Office* (October 2013) which was produced by the Secretary of State when the
       Immigration Bill was introduced to Parliament, paragraph 74 says in respect of the 'new
       Section 117B(6)': 'This is self-explanatory and is intended to broadly reflect case law. It

provides that certain countervailing factors will not justify removal in an immigration case (it does not apply to criminals or other non-conducive deportations).'

3 Per Sedley LJ in *MK (deportation foreign criminal public interest) Gambia* [2010] UKUT 281 (IAC), [2011] Imm AR 60, in the context of the automatic deportation regime in the UK Borders Act 2007, and approved in by Laws LJ in *Richards v Secretary of State for the Home Department* [2013] EWCA Civ 244. In *SS (Nigeria) v Secretary of State for the Home Department* [2013] EWCA Civ 550, [2014] 1 WLR 998, also concerning automatic deportation, Laws LJ acknowledged:

'the free-standing importance of the legislative source of the policy as a driver of the decision-maker's margin of discretion when the proportionality of its application in the particular case is being considered' (para 51)

and said that:

'The width of the primary legislator's discretionary area of judgment . . . is lent added force where, as here, the subject-matter of the legislature's policy lies in the field of moral and political judgment, as to which the first and natural arbiter of the extent to which it represents a "pressing social need" is what I have called the elected arm of government: and especially the primary legislature, whose Acts are the primary democratic voice' (para 52).

4 In a letter to the Joint Committee on Human Rights of 12 November 2013, Mark Harper the Immigration Minister said 'The new section 117B . . . includes subsection (6), which sets out that the public interest does not require the removal of a person who has a qualifying child where it would not be reasonable to expect the child to leave the UK. This provision is a proper reflection of the best interests of children in the UK – both British and foreign – which the law requires to be a primary consideration in immigration decisions'. This accords with the House of Lords' equation of 'best interests' with the question of whether it is 'reasonable to expect the child to leave the UK' in *ZH(Tanzania) v Secretary of State for the Home Department* [2011] UKSC 4 ; [2011] 2 AC 166, where Lady Hale says at para 29: 'Applying, therefore, the approach in *Wan* to the assessment of proportionality under article 8(2), together with the factors identified in Strasbourg, what is encompassed in the 'best interests of the child'? As the UNHCR says, it broadly means the well-being of the child. Specifically, as Lord Bingham indicated in *EB (Kosovo)*, it will involve asking whether it is reasonable to expect the child to live in another country. Relevant to this will be the level of the child's integration in this country and the length of absence from the other country; where and with whom the child is to live and the arrangements for looking after the child in the other country; and the strength of the child's relationships with parents or other family members which will be severed if the child has to move away'.

7.107 Section 117C describes the additional public interest considerations applicable in cases involving foreign criminals. The first is a statement that the deportation of foreign criminals is in the public interest.[1] and the second that the more serious the offence committed by a foreign criminal, the greater is the public interest in deportation of the criminal.[2] For foreign criminals who have been sentenced to a period of imprisonment of less than four years, the public interest requires their deportation unless one of two exceptions applies.[3] The first exception applies where the foreign criminal has been lawfully resident in the UK for most of his or her life, is socially and culturally integrated into the UK, and there would be very significant obstacles to his or her integration into the proposed country of deportation.[4] The second exception applies where the foreign criminal has a genuine and subsisting relationship with a qualifying partner, or a genuine and subsisting parental relationship with a qualifying child, and the effect of his or her deportation on the partner or child would be unduly harsh.[5] As with section 117B(6) of the NIAA 2002, if the conditions in the exceptions are satisfied the public interest does not require deportation, and therefore there is no justification for the interference under Article 8(2). The 'unduly harsh' test would seem to connote a balancing exercise in which relevant proportionality considerations, such as reasonableness of expecting family life to take place elsewhere, best interests of the child, and the seriousness of the offence, will be weighed. For foreign criminals who have been sentenced to at least four years imprisonment, the public interest will require their deportation unless there are very compelling circumstances over and above those described in Exceptions 1 and 2.[6] Section 117D and paragraphs 398–399A of the Immigration Rules broadly reflect similar considerations, although the equivalent exceptions in paragraph 399 appear to erect greater hurdles for deportees. In the event of any conflict, Parliament's view of what is in the public interest should prevail over the Secretary of State's.

[1] NIAA 2002, s 117D(1).
[2] NIAA 2002, s 117D(2).
[3] NIAA 2002, s 117D(3).
[4] NIAA 2002, s 117D(4)(a), (b), (c).
[5] NIAA 2002, s.117D(5).
[6] NIAA 2002, s 117D(6).

7.108 In *R (on the application of Chikwamba) v Secretary of State for the Home Department*[1] the House of Lords addressed the question of whether the policy of insisting on departure from the UK and the making of an application for entry clearance by a person wishing to stay in the UK to enjoy Article 8 rights but unable to do so in accordance with the rules was legitimate and proportionate.[2] The answer was that 'only comparatively rarely, certainly in family cases involving children, should an Article 8 appeal be dismissed on the basis that it would be proportionate and more appropriate for the appellant to apply for leave from abroad'.[3] In 'most cases' it was better that the Article 8 claim should be decided once and for all, not deferred to be decided out of country by an entry clearance officer and then on appeal by the Tribunal.[4] Considerations relevant to determining whether the entry clearance requirement should be enforced in a particular case included: the individual's immigration history and whether he or she had entered the country illegally and if the person had, whether it was for a good reason (eg to advance a genuine asylum claim) or a bad reason (eg to enrol as a student); whether and if so for how long the Secretary of State had delayed in dealing with the case; the length and degree of family disruption involved in going abroad for entry clearance would always be 'highly relevant'; whether the ECO would be better placed to investigate the claim (eg as to the genuineness of a marriage or other relationship) in which case there might be good reason to enforce the entry clearance requirement; whether it was likely that there would be an appeal against a refusal of entry clearance at which the appellant would be unable to give live evidence. The Court of Appeal has confirmed that *Chikwamba* applies to family cases generally, not just those involving children, and further, that where Article 8 is engaged, it will be a disproportionate interference with Article 8 rights to enforce an entry clearance requirement unless there is a 'sensible reason' for doing so.[5] The blanket bar in the Immigration Rules which prevented the partners of Points Based System Migrants from switching in-country into the PBS dependant category from another immigration category was, in the vast majority of cases which engaged family life rights, unsustainable in the light of the ratio of *Chikwamba*.[6]

[1] [2008] UKHL 40;[2009] 1 All ER 363 ; [2008] 1 WLR 1420.
[2] Paragraph 39.
[3] Lord Brown, para 44; Lord Bingham (para 1); Lord Hope (para 2) Lord Scott (para 3) and Baroness Hale (para 7) agreeing.
[4] Paragraph 44.

⁵   *MA (Pakistan) v Secretary of State for the Home Department* [2009] EWCA Civ 953, and restated in *Hayat (Pakistan) v Secretary of State for the Home Department* [2012] EWCA Civ 1054.
⁶   *R (on the application of Zhang) v Secretary of State for the Home Department* [2013] EWHC 891 (Admin). This decision resulted in changes to paras 319C(h) and 319H(h) from 1 October 2013, by virtue of HC 628, which permitted in-country switching into PBS dependant from all immigration categories save for visitors.

7.109 In *EB (Kosovo)*[1] the House of Lords held that delay in the decision-making process could be relevant to a claim to stay in the UK relying on Article 8 in three ways. Firstly, it could result in the applicant developing closer personal and social ties and establishing deeper roots in the community thereby strengthening any Article 8 claim. Secondly, the precarious immigration status of one party to a relationship may imbue it with a sense of impermanence and so counts against the immigrant in the assessment of proportionality. However, the passage of time without a decision being made reduces that sense of impermanence and thereby affects the proportionality of removal. Thirdly, 'if the delay is shown to be the result of a dysfunctional system which yields unpredictable, inconsistent and unfair outcomes' then it may reduce the weight to be given in the assessment of proportionality to the requirements of immigration control.[2]

¹   *EB (Kosovo) v Secretary of State for the Home Department* [2008] UKHL 41;[2008] 4 All ER 28.
²   Lord Bingham, para 16. Lord Brown dissented in respect of this third way in which delay could be relevant.

7.110 In *ZH (Tanzania) v Secretary of State for the Home Department*[1] the Supreme Court made an important decision about the relationships between Article 8 of the ECHR, the UN Convention on the Rights of the Child and the domestic law obligation in section 55 of the Borders, Citizenship and Immigration Act 2009. It was already established that consideration of whether a decision to remove an individual breaches Article 8 necessitates assessment of the impact of the removal on all members of the family.[2] Of particular importance in conducting that assessment is whether a child can reasonably be expected to follow the removed parent to the country of removal.[3] Recent decisions from the European Court of Human Rights had highlighted the importance of considering 'the best interests and well-being' of children affected by an expulsion decision[4] or an ordinary removal decision.[5] Such decisions reiterated principles consistently stated by the Court in immigration cases, for example that Article 8 does not entail a general obligation to respect immigrants' choices as to the countries in which to enjoy family life; whether a state is obliged to admit family members to its territory depends on the particular circumstances of the person involved and the general interest, taking into account factors such as whether the family can reasonably live elsewhere; whether family life was established when they knew the immigration status of one of them to be precarious and so on. However, in the Court's recent decisions that approach 'is tempered by a much clearer acknowledgment of the importance of the best interests of a child caught up in a dilemma which is of the parents' and not of her own making'.[6] The source of that was 'the broad consensus – including in international law, in support of the idea that in all decisions concerning children, their best interests must be paramount'.[7] In this context, the most significant obligation is that contained in Article 3(1) of the UN Convention on the Rights of the Child.

1   [2011] UKSC 4, [2011] 2 All ER 783, [2011] 2 WLR 148.
2   By *Beoku-Betts v Secretary of State for the Home Department* [2008] UKHL 39, [2009] AC 115, [2008] 4 All ER 1146.
3   Baroness Hale, *ZH (Tanzania)* para 15.
4   *Uner v Netherlands* (Application No 46410/99) (2006) 45 EHRR 421, [2006] 3 FCR 340, ECtHR and *Maslov v Austria* [2009] INLR 47.
5   *Da Silva and Hoogkamer v Netherlands* (Application 50435/99) (2006) 44 EHRR 729, [2006] 1 FCR 229, ECtHR. In *Nunez v Norway* (Application No 55597/09) (28 June 2011, unreported) which was decided after *ZH (Tanzania)*, the Court held that removing a mother who had never been lawfully resident; who never had a reasonable expectation of being able to stay; whose history of breaching immigration laws was such as to have an 'aggravated character' so that heavy weight had to be given to the public interest in removing her would nevertheless breach article 8 because detrimental to the best interests of her children.
6   Baroness Hale, *ZH (Tanzania)* para 20.
7   Baroness Hale, *ZH (Tanzania)* para 21, citing *Neulinger v Switzerland* (Application 41615/07) [2011] 2 FCR 110, [2011] 1 FLR 122, ECtHR.

7.111 Article 3(1) of the UN Convention on the Rights of the Child provides: 'In all actions concerning children, whether undertaken by public or private social welfare institutions, courts of law, administrative authorities or legislative bodies, the best interests of the child shall be a primary consideration'. It is 'a binding obligation in international law, and the spirit, if not the precise language has also been translated into our national law' by section 11 of the Children Act 2004 and, after the UK lifted its reservation to the Convention on the Rights of the Child concerning immigration matters, by section 55 of the Borders, Citizenship and Immigration Act 2009.[1] That requires the Secretary of State to make arrangements for immigration, asylum and nationality functions to be discharged having regard to the need to safeguard and promote the welfare of children who are in the UK. Leading counsel for the Secretary of State acknowledged that that duty applied 'not only to how children are looked after in this country while decisions about immigration, asylum, deportation or removal are being made, but also to the decisions themselves'.[2] Consequently, a decision taken without regard to the need to safeguard and promote the welfare of any children involved would not be 'in accordance with the law' for the purposes of Article 8(2).[3] Although section 55 of the Borders Citizenship and Immigration Act 2009 does not apply in respect of a child outside the UK applying for entry clearance, his or her best interests are a primary consideration for the purpose of deciding whether refusal of entry clearance would breach Article 8.[4]

1   Baroness Hale, *ZH (Tanzania)* para 23.
2   *ZH (Tanzania)* para 24.
3   Baroness Hale, *ZH (Tanzania)* para 24.
4   This derives from the broader duty imposed by Article 3 of the UN Convention on the Rights of the Child in respect of all administrative decision making: *Entry Clearance Officer-Kingston v T* [2011] UKUT 00483 (IAC) and *Mundeba (s 55 and para 297(i) (f)) Democratic Republic of Congo* [2013] UKUT 88.

7.112 Requiring that the best interests of the child 'must be a primary consideration' means that a decision maker had to identify what the child's best interests required are, and then decide whether they were outweighed by any other considerations. The decision did not necessarily have to be in conformity with those interests so long as the decision maker considered the child's interests first and did not regard any other consideration as inherently more significant.[1] Whilst 'what is determined to be in a child's best interests should customarily dictate the outcome of cases such as the present, therefore, and it will require considerations of substantial moment to permit a different result',[2] a child's best interests can be outweighed by the cumulative effect of other considerations, such as the maintenance of immigration control, precarious immigration status and criminality.[3] Assessment of the best interests of the child 'will involve asking whether it is reasonable to expect the child to live in another country. Relevant to this will be the level of the child's integration in this country and the length of absence from the other country;[4] where and with whom the child is to live and the arrangements for looking after the child in the other country; and the strength of the child's relationships with parents or other family members which will be severed if the child has to move away'.[5] The child's own views of what is in his or her best interests should be ascertained to the extent possible which may entail the child having separate representation[6] or directions being made by the tribunal that the child should be interviewed.[7] The child's nationality is of particular importance and if the child is British 'the intrinsic importance of citizenship' must be given proper recognition because British children 'have rights which they will not be able to exercise if they move to another country. They will lose the advantages of growing up and being educated in their own country, their own culture and their own language'.[8] Accordingly, whilst a child's British citizenship 'does not trump everything else' it will 'hardly ever be less than a very significant and weighty factor against moving children' with a parent who has no right to be in the UK.[9] The fact that the parent's immigration status may have been precarious when the child was conceived or even that having the child may have been seen as a means to strengthen the parent's immigration case cannot be held against the child: 'it would be wrong in principle to devalue what was in their best interests by something for which they could in no way be held responsible'.[10] Thus, the view of the Home Office and the Office of the Children's Champion that because a British citizen child could accompany his family upon removal, his British citizenship was irrelevant to consideration of the child's welfare and of proportionality was unlawful.[11]

1   Baroness Hale, *ZH (Tanzania)* para 26. The Court of Appeal has subsequently held that the decision maker was not necessarily required to consider the child's interests first but could ask whether the interests served by deportation were outweighed by the best interests of the child. What mattered was substance rather than form and that there was a properly structured appraisal of the evidence and a correct understanding of the child's interests: *AJ (India) v Secretary of State for the Home Department* [2011] EWCA Civ 1191, [2011] All ER (D) 222 (Oct). There is a general duty on the tribunal to consider, of its own motion if necessary, the best interests of any children: *DS (Afghanistan) v Secretary of State for the Home Department* [2011] EWCA Civ 305, [2011] INLR 389, *SS (Sri Lanka) v Secretary of State for the Home Department* [2012] EWCA Civ 945.

2   This is how Lord Kerr explained the meaning of the child's interests being a primary consideration and in so doing, was said by the Court of Appeal to be expressing 'the same view as Lady Hale': *Lee v Secretary of State for the Home Department* [2011] EWCA Civ 348, [2011] All ER (D) 313 (Mar).

3   Baroness Hale, *ZH (Tanzania)* para 33.

4   The tribunal has held that for the purpose of assessing proportionality, in the absence of any other policy guidance from the Secretary of State following the withdrawal of DP5/96 it remains legitimate for immigration judges to give some regard to the previous policy that seven years residence by a child under 18 would afford a basis for regularizing the position of children and parents: *EM (Zimbabwe) (Returnees) v Secretary of State for the Home Department* [2011] UKUT 98 (IAC).

5   Baroness Hale, *ZH (Tanzania)*, para 29. Although *ZH (Tanzania)* was concerned with a child who would accompany the parent who was to be removed, the same approach applies where

the parent removed would leave the child behind: *Lee v Secretary of State for the Home Department* [2011] EWCA Civ 348 and *R (on the application of Nkhoma) v Secretary of State for the Home Department* [2011] EWHC 2367 (Admin) para 123, [2011] All ER (D) 73 (Sep).

6   Baroness Hale, *ZH (Tanzania)* para 34ff, citing *EM (Lebanon) v Secretary of State for the Home Department* [2008] UKHL 64, [2009] AC 1198, [2009] 1 All ER 559, para 49.

7   *Entry Clearance Officer-Kingston v T* [2011] UKUT 00483 (IAC).

8   Baroness Hale, *ZH (Tanzania)* para 32.

9   Lord Hope, *ZH (Tanzania)* para 41.

10   Lord Hope, para 44. Applied in *R (on the application of Reece-Davis) v Secretary of State for the Home Department* [2011] EWHC 561 (Admin).

11   *R (on the application of SM) v Secretary of State for the Home Department* [2011] EWHC 338 (Admin), [2011] All ER (D) 53 (Mar). *DS (Afghanistan) v Secretary of State for the Home Department* [2011] EWCA Civ 305. Although s 55 of the Borders, Citizenship and Immigration Act 2009 does not apply in respect of a child outside the UK applying for entry clearance, his or her best interests are a primary consideration for the purpose of deciding whether refusal of entry clearance would breach art 8.

7.113 When considering the welfare and best interests of a young child, the starting point is that it is in the best interests of a child to live with and be brought up by his or her parents, subject to any strong contra-indication.[1] It is generally in the interests of children to have both stability and continuity of social and educational provision and the benefit of growing up in the cultural norms of the society to which they belong.[2] Lengthy residence in a country other than the state of origin can lead to development of social cultural and educational ties that it would be inappropriate to disrupt, in the absence of compelling reasons to the contrary.[3] What amounts to lengthy residence is not clear cut but past and present policies have identified seven years as a relevant period.[4] When considering a child's education it is important to have regard not just to the evidence relating to any short-term disruption of current schooling that will be caused by any removal but also to that relating to the impact on a child's educational development, progress and opportunities in the broader sense.[5] The best interests of the child must be addressed 'first and as a distinct stage of the inquiry' and without reference to extraneous factors such as the parents' poor immigration history or criminality.[6] Further, the best interests of the child are to be determined without reference to the immigration status of either parent.[7] As well as having regard to the best interests of the child for the purpose of making substantive decisions, the Secretary of State is obliged to make arrangements for dealing with applications, eg for leave to remain, in such a way that safeguards and promotes the welfare of any affected child.[8]

1   *E-A (Article 8-best interests of child) Nigeria* [2011] UKUT 315, para 35.

2   *Azimi-Moayed and Others (Decisions Affecting Children; Onward Appeals) Iran* [2013] UKUT 197 (IAC), para 13(ii).

3   *Azimi-Moayed*, para 13(iii).

4   *Azimi-Moayed*, para 13(iv). In a letter dated 12 November 2013, Mark Harper, the Immigration Minister, in response to a letter from the Joint Committee on Human Rights during the passage of the Immigration Act 2014, said: 'We have acknowledged that, if a child has reached the age of 7, the child will have moved beyond simply having his or her needs met by the parents. The child will be part of the education system and may be developing social networks and connections beyond their parents and the home.'

5   *MK (best interests of child) India* [2011] UKUT 475 (IAC), para 41.

6   *MK*, para 19, approved in *JW (China) v Secretary of State for the Home Department* [2013] EWCA Civ 1526.

7   *EV (Philippines) v Secretary of State for the Home Department* [2014] EWCA Civ 874 at para 33 per Christopher Clarke LJ, giving the lead judgment. However, the concurring judgment of Lewison LJ appears to suggest that the evaluation of the best interests should be

evaluated based on 'real world facts', namely the immigration status of the parents. In cases where the central issue is whether the parents are to be removed, we respectfully suggest that to assess the best interests of the child on the assumption that the parents will be removed is to pre-judge the outcome of the inquiry into that central issue.

8   *R (on the application of Shah) v Secretary of State for the Home Department* [2014] EWHC 2192 (Admin).

7.114 The existence of a policy apart from the Immigration Rules may be relevant to the assessment of proportionality. When 'exceptionality' was thought to be the applicable test for deciding whether an interference with an Article 8 protected right was proportionate, the Court of Appeal held in a number of cases that if a person fell within the terms of a policy that might justify a conclusion that his or her case was 'truly exceptional'.[1] A better analysis (following *Huang* in the House of Lords) is that whether a person falls within a policy is relevant for the purpose of determining what weight (if any) should be attached to the interests of immigration control in removing or excluding a person.[2] If such an issue arises in an appeal, the tribunal would have to decide for itself whether the policy applies to the appellant, even if the original decision maker has not applied the policy[3] because doing so is necessary in order to determine whether the decision is incompatible with the appellant's human rights; that is quite a different exercise from what would be an impermissible determination by the tribunal of how, in the light of the policy, discretion to depart from the rules should be exercised.[4] Even if a person does not satisfy all of the requirements of a policy, it would be relevant to the assessment of proportionality that he or she met its substantive requirements.[5] A decision maker would have to determine whether a person fell within any discernible rationale[6] or spirit of the rules or policy even if the person fell outwith the letter[7] and would have to make an evaluation of the significance of any non-compliance with the rule or policy.[8] That would have to be done not in order to extend the scope of a policy[9] but in order to inform the assessment of what weight should be given to the interests of immigration control when making a judgment on proportionality. Despite the earlier Court of Appeal decision in *Pankina*, there is no 'near-miss' principle applicable to the Immigration Rules which requires, in the assessment of proportionality under Article 8, an evaluation of the degree of non-compliance with particular criteria in the Rules, nor of their significance.[10] The Supreme Court has endorsed the lack of a 'near-miss' penumbra, but has held that the context of the Rules, for example the 'family values' which underlie a particular Rule under which an applicant has failed, may nevertheless be relevant to the consideration of proportionality.[11] Article 8 is not a general dispensing power, and must be distinguished from the Secretary of State's discretion to allow leave to remain outside the Rules, which may be unrelated to any protected human right.[12]

1   *Shkembi v Secretary of State for the Home Department* [2005] EWCA Civ 1592; *R (on the application of Tozlukaya) v Secretary of State for the Home Department* [2006] EWCA Civ 379.
2   *AG (Kosovo)* [2007] UKAIT 00082.
3   *R (Tozlukaya)*, fn 1 above.
4   Impermissible because of the Nationality, Immigration and Asylum Act 2002, s 86(6). Outside the context of assessing proportionality, and where the appellant does not qualify under the rules the Tribunal may only determine whether the decision maker has given effect to a relevant policy and if the Tribunal finds that he or she has not, may allow the appeal on the ground that the decision is 'not in accordance with the law'. The Tribunal may not apply the

policy for itself but is restricted to requiring the decision maker to do so. See *Abdi (Dhudi Saleban) v Secretary of State for the Home Department* [1996] Imm AR 148. If an appellant challenges a decision on the ground that it is not in accordance with the law owing to failure to give effect to a policy and on the ground that because he was capable of qualifying under the policy, the decision was a disproportionate interference with an Article 8 right, the Tribunal would be bound to determine both grounds because of the Nationality, Immigration and Asylum Act 2002, s 86(2)(a). The change in the statutory regime would prevent a Tribunal from allowing the appeal on the first ground and therefore declining to deal with the human rights ground as in *H (Somalia)* [2004] UKIAT 27.

5   *Miao v Secretary of State for the Home Department* [2006] EWCA Civ 75. The refugee family reunion policy required those relying on it to be outside the country and applying for entry clearance. The Court of Appeal held that the proportionality of removing the appellant had to be assessed on the basis that but for his presence in the UK he would fall within its terms.

6   *Shkembi v Secretary of State for the Home Department* [2005] EWCA Civ 1592.

7   *R (on the application of Lekstaka) v Immigration Appeal Tribunal* [2005] EWHC 745 (Admin), [2005] All ER (D) 222 (Apr) approved in *SB (Bangladesh) v Secretary of State for the Home Department* [2007] EWCA Civ 28, [2007] 1 FLR 2153.

8   *Secretary of State for the Home Department v Pankina* [2010] EWCA Civ 719, [2010] All ER (D) 196 (Jun), (2010) Times, 20 July.

9   Which the Court held in *Mongoto v Secretary of State for the Home Department* [2005] EWCA Civ 751 would have been an impermissible exercise by the Court of creating enforceable rights for the benefit of those falling outside the terms of the policy. Policies are not to be extended by a 'near miss penumbra' – *R (on the application of Rudi) v Secretary of State for the Home Department* [2007] EWHC 60 (Admin), [2007] All ER (D) 225 (Jan).

10 *Miah v Secretary of State for the Home Department* [2012] EWCA Civ 261, [2013] QB 35.

11 *Patel v Secretary of State for the Home Department* [2013] UKSC 72, [2014] AC 651.

12 *Patel and others v Secretary of State for the Home Department* [2013] UKSC 72, [2014] AC 651, para 57 in which Lord Carnwath said that 'The opportunity for a promising student to complete his course in this country, however desirable in general terms, is not in itself a right protected under Article 8'. In *Nasim and others (Article 8)* [2014] UKUT 00025 (IAC) the Upper Tribunal was concerned with the rights of former students to undertake a period of post-study work in the UK. The Tribunal held that the Supreme Court's decision in *Patel* served to 'to re-focus attention on the nature and purpose of Article 8 of the ECHR and, in particular, to recognise that Article's limited utility in private life cases that are far removed from the protection of an individual's moral and physical integrity.'

7.115 It may be relevant to the assessment of proportionality that a cause of family separation was the historical operation of legislation and legislative powers now acknowledged to be unjust and but for which, family reunification could have been achieved long before.[1] Conversely, the fact that an individual previously had the benefit of a policy, now withdrawn, under which she was granted periods of limited leave to remain in order to receive treatment for HIV and which thereby expressed compassion and a sense of moral commitment to her was relevant for the purpose of deciding whether refusing further leave to remain was proportionate.[2] While a 'health care' removal case could in principle succeed under Article 8 despite failing under Article 33, the absence of medical treatment in the country of removal will be relevant to Article 8 where it is an additional factor combined with others which by themselves engage Article 8, such as family life.[3] The consequences of removal for the health of a claimant who cannot access equivalent health care in their country of nationality is relevant to the question of proportionality, although resource considerations for the UK's health service will usually weigh heavily in favour of removal.[4] In the case of a child whose health would be affected by removal, Article 8 has a greater protective scope, particularly as the child's best interests have to be a primary consideration in the assessment of proportionality.[5]

1   *NH (India) v Entry Clearance Officer* [2007] EWCA Civ 1330, [2007] All ER (D) 199 (Dec).

2   *JA (Ivory Coast) v Secretary of State for the Home Department* [2009] EWCA Civ 1353,
     (2010) Times, 2 February. Following remittal by the Court of Appeal, JA's appeal was allowed
     by the Upper Tribunal on Article 8 grounds: HR/00204/2008, 31 May 2011.
3   *MM (Zimbabwe) v Secretary of State for the Home Department* [2012] EWCA Civ 279,
     para 23.
4   *Akhalu (health claim: ECHR Article 8) Nigeria* [2013] UKUT 400 (IAC).
5   *R (on the application of SQ (Pakistan)) v Upper Tribunal Immigration and Asylum Chamber*
     [2013] EWCA Civ 1251 and *AE (Algeria) v Secretary of State for the Home Department*
     [2014] EWCA Civ 653.

7.116 The domestic courts have been slower to find in applicants' favour where removal is said to interfere with physical or moral integrity as an aspect of private life. However, in *Razgar*[1] the House of Lords accepted that in an Article 8 claim reliance may in principle be placed on the consequences for a person's mental health of removal to the receiving country. 'Private life' in Article 8 extended to those features which are integral to a person's identity or ability to function socially as a person. This must be taken as a more definitive statement of the ambit of and meaning of 'private life' than that of the Court of Appeal which considered that 'there must be a sufficiently adverse effect on physical and mental integrity and not merely on health' for Article 8 to be engaged. The House of Lords judgment must also call into question the decision in *Djali*,[2] where the Court of Appeal found that the removal of a woman with severe post-traumatic stress disorder suffered as a result of her ill-treatment in Kosovo would not engage Article 8, since at worst it would merely imperil her prospects of a better recovery,[3] and added that even if Article 8(1) had been engaged, the decision-maker would inevitably regard the interests of immigration control, as the imperative and overriding factor, given the grave problems of asylum overload.[4] More recently, and in the light of *Huang and AG (Eritrea)*[5] the Court of Appeal confirmed that once the existence of private life in the UK has been established, its character and intensity affect the proportionality of the interference, not whether there is an interference at all.[6] In *Jegatheeswaran*,[7] the High Court held that removal of a child with severe hearing loss and learning difficulties to Germany could breach Article 8, since he would be unable to communicate in any spoken language. Having to live with a constant fear for one's own safety might also breach the right to respect for private life.[8] The Tribunal dismissed the risk to physical integrity from depleted uranium in Kosovo as 'remote' in *FZ*.[9] The Court of Appeal has acknowledged, consistently with the Strasbourg jurisprudence, that the right to respect for private life includes the right to conduct ordinary activities, including the right to work.[10] The extent of an individual's contribution (or lack of contribution) to the community is not a freestanding matter to be taken into account when making a decision on proportionality, but may be of relevance if it forms part of the individual's private life.[11] Whilst the decision of the House of Lords in *Huang* was concerned with interference with the right to respect for family life, its reasoning applies equally to cases concerned with private life.[12] The Court of Appeal declined to determine whether delay by the Secretary of State in issuing papers relating to the appellant's refugee status breached the appellant's right to respect for private life because to have done so would have been of merely academic significance, the papers having been issued by the time of the appeal to the Court of Appeal; the Secretary of State having apologised and the Home Office complaints procedure having been set in motion with a view to compensating the appellant.[13]

1   *R (on the application of Razgar) v Secretary of State for the Home Department* [2004] UKHL
      27, [2004] 2 AC 368, at para 9, quoting with approval an Article by Professor Feldman 'The
      Developing Scope of Article 8 of the European Convention on Human Rights' (1997) EHRLR
      265, at 270.
2   *Djali v Immigration Appeal Tribunal* [2003] EWCA Civ 1371, [2004] 1 FCR 42.
3   *Djali* above, para 17.
4   *Djali* above, para 26, per Simon Brown LJ. One has to ask whether the 'interests of
      immigration control', which is not one of the factors listed in art 8(2), is factored into the 'fair
      balance' not by virtue of its connection to any of these factors, but because of the international
      law rule that States have a right to control the entry and expulsion of aliens. It is certainly the
      darling concept of some sections of the judiciary, but like any unruly pet, it needs to kept in
      its proper place: see in particular Lord Bingham in *European Roma Rights Centre v
      Immigration Officer at Prague Airport* [2004] UKHL 55, [2005] 1 All ER 527, para 11 ff. See
      also *R v Secretary of State for the Home Department, ex p Ay Yurdugal* [2003] EWCA Civ 1,
      where the Court of Appeal considered that the harm suffered by children on removal to
      Germany had to be weighed against the interests of the public and the consequences flowing
      from the fact that the children might benefit from the unlawful actions of their parents who
      had remained in the UK in breach of immigration controls and evaded return to Germany.
5   *AG (Eritrea) v Secretary of State for the Home Department* [2007] EWCA Civ 801.
6   *DM (Zambia) v Secretary of State for the Home Department* [2009] EWCA Civ 474.
7   *R (on the application of Jegatheeswaran) v Secretary of State for the Home Department* [2005]
      EWHC 1131 (Admin), [2005] All ER (D) 178 (Apr).
8   *R (on the application of Sivapalan) v Secretary of State for the Home Department* [2008]
      EWHC 2955 (Admin), [2008] All ER (D) 01 (Dec).
9   [2003] UKIAT 315, [2003] Imm AR 633.
10   *MA (Afghanistan) v Secretary of State for the Home Department* [2006] EWCA Civ 1440, 150
      Sol Jo LB 1330.
11   *RU (Sri Lanka) v Secretary of State for the Home Department* [2008] EWCA Civ 753,
      [2008] All ER (D) 21 (Jul).
12   *JN (Uganda) v Secretary of State for the Home Department* [2007] EWCA Civ 802,
      [2007] All ER (D) 502 (Jul).
13   *R (on the application of MD (China)) v Secretary of State for the Home Department* [2011]
      EWCA Civ 453, [2011] All ER (D) 175 (Apr).

7.117 The rights to respect for private life, home and correspondence are
engaged by searches of premises,[1] which must be a proportionate measure in
all the circumstances,[2] justified by relevant and sufficient reasons and accompanied by adequate and effective safeguards.[3] The ECtHR has given a broad
interpretation to 'home', requiring no legal right of occupation but constituting a haven against intervention by public authorities.[4] The right to respect for
home may be engaged by a refusal of readmission after a long absence, where
the applicant has no other home.[5]

1   *Funke v France* (1993) 16 EHRR 297; *Miailhe v France* (1993) 16 EHRR 332; *Niemietz v
      Germany* (1992) 16 EHRR 97; *Chappell v United Kingdom* (1989) 12 EHRR 1.
2   *McLeod v United Kingdom* (1998) 27 EHRR 493.
3   *Camenzind v Switzerland* (1997) 28 EHRR 458, para 45.
4   *Wiggins v United Kingdom* (1978) 13 DR 40; *Buckley v United Kingdom* (1996) 23 EHRR
      101.
5   *Gillow v United Kingdom* (1986) 11 EHRR 335 where refusal of a resident's licence to live in
      a house in Guernsey built by the applicant after 18 years' absence was held to breach
      art 8 ECHR.

Freedom of thought, conscience and religion

7.118 Article 9 of the ECHR provides that:

'1   Everyone has the right to freedom of thought, conscience and religion; this right includes freedom to change his religion or belief and freedom, either alone or in community with others and in public or private, to manifest his religion or belief, in worship, teaching, practice and observance.

2   Freedom to manifest one's religion or beliefs shall be subject only to such limitations as are prescribed by law and are necessary in a democratic society in the interests of public safety, for the protection of public order, health or morals, or for the protection of the rights and freedoms of others.'

The right in paragraph 1 includes the absolute and non-derogable right to freedom of thought, conscience and religion, reflecting the ECtHR's general understanding that it is 'one of the foundations of a "democratic society"'.[1] Although the manifestation of beliefs (paragraph 2) is a qualified right, the importance of religious freedom means that States' margin of appreciation is limited.[2] The obligation to ensure the peaceful enjoyment of religious rights[3] may in certain circumstances require an exception to laws of general application.[4] The communal aspect of religious worship has also been recognised.[5] The House of Lords held in *Ullah* that interference with religious freedoms in a receiving State will ground a challenge to expulsion, if there is a real risk of a flagrant denial or gross violation, where the very essence of the right will be completely denied or nullified in the receiving country.[6] The Court of Appeal rejected the Secretary of State's contention that the UK's courts could not scrutinise the legislation of another EU member state to assess its compatibility with the ECHR and to assess whether the operation of that legislation would breach the Article 9 rights of a person removed to that country.[7] Article 9 may be engaged if it can be shown that an expulsion was designed to repress the exercise of the right and to stifle the spreading of the philosophy or religion, as in the case of a re-entry ban imposed against a member of the Unification Church in Russia.[8] An unsuccessful attempt was made by Reverend Sun Myung Moon to rely on Article 9 (together with Articles 10 and 11) in an appeal against refusal of entry clearance on grounds that his presence was not conducive to the public good.[9] His appeal failed because the tribunal held that he was outside the territorial jurisdiction of the Convention and therefore could not rely on Convention rights in his appeal. However, had he been able to do so the tribunal would have found that preventing him, a religious leader, from being physically present in the UK amongst his followers interfered with his right to manifest his religion (as well as his rights of freedom of expression and association) and that the Secretary of State had failed to justify the interference as being necessary to prevent the Unification Church returning to coercive methods of recruiting followers.

1   *Kokkinakis v Greece* (1993) 17 EHRR 397, para 31.
2   *Sidiropoulos v Greece* (1998) 27 EHRR 633.
3   *Otto-Preminger Institute v Austria* (1994) 19 EHRR 34.
4   *Thlimmenos v Greece* (2000) 9 BHRC 12, para 44.
5   Restrictions placed on freedom of movement which impair a population's ability to observe their religious beliefs, and in particular, their access to places of worship outside their own area and their participation in other aspects of religious life were held to violate Article 9 rights in *Cyprus v Turkey* (25781/94) (2001) 11 BHRC 45. See also *Wang v MIMA* [2000] FCA 1599) Fed Ct Aust).
6   *R (on the application of Ullah) v Special Adjudicator* [2004] UKHL 26, [2004] INLR 381.
7   *R (on the application of B) v Secretary of State for the Home Department* [2014] EWCA Civ 854. The case concerned a Muslim woman resisting removal to France on the ground that French law would breach her Article 9 rights by prohibiting her from covering her head whilst at school. The Court held that any breach would not satisfy the flagrancy requirement applicable in what was a foreign case.

8   *Nolan and K v Russia* [2009] ECHR 262
9   *Moon (USA)* [2005] UKIAT 00112.

7.119 One of the significant areas of application of Article 9 in the ECtHR jurisprudence has been in relation to conscientious objection to military service, in conjunction with ECHR, Article 4, which leaves open the possibility that failure to take account of the individual's beliefs may violate his or her human rights.[1] There is growing support in international human rights law for the proposition that there is a human right of conscientious objection to military service, although no international human rights instrument as yet expressly recognises such a right.[2] In 1973, the Commission found that Article 9, as qualified by Article 4(3)(b), 'does not impose on a State the obligation to recognise conscientious objectors and . . . does not prevent a State . . . from punishing those who refuse to do military service'.[3] But this case law is now thought to be out of date. All countries in the Council of Europe, except three, now recognise such a right in their domestic law. Such recognition is now required before new members are admitted to the Council, and in *Thlimmenos v Greece*[4] the Commission members accepted (without deciding) that punishment for refusal to perform military service which is motivated by religious beliefs may breach Article 9 (freedom of conscience and religion).[5] By 1979, the UNHCR's position was that 'it would be open to contracting States to grant refugee status to persons who object to performing military service for genuine reasons of conscience'.[6] In *Sepet and Bulbul*[7] the Court of Appeal, by a majority, held that the right to conscientious objection was not so established that denial of it constituted persecution for the purposes of the Refugee Convention, while acknowledging that Article 9 might in future lay the foundations for a general right of conscientious objection. The majority's conclusion was upheld by the House of Lords. Developments in European law may now put conscientious objection back on the menu, despite the ruling in the House of Lords. The European Charter of Fundamental Rights refers to conscientious objection. Article 10.2 reads 'The right to conscientious objection is recognised, in accordance with the national laws governing the exercise of this right.' The Qualification Directive, as adopted by the Council, refers to its compatibility with the Charter and in particular, it states that it seeks to ensure full respect for the right to asylum.[8] The Reform Treaty of Lisbon would make the Charter legally binding, thereby becoming part of the obligation for EC law to comply with human rights as general principles of Community law. As such its application in the UK would not be prevented by the legally binding Protocol, which the UK government has negotiated for itself, which says that no court can rule that the 'laws, regulations or administrative provisions, practices or action' of the UK are inconsistent with the principles laid down in the charter. It adds 'for the avoidance of doubt' that the charter creates no new rights enforceable in the UK, over and above those already provided for in national law.

1   See Goodwin-Gill, Guy, report in *Sepet and Bulbul*, para 48.
2   See Asbjørn Eide and Chama Mubanga-Chipoya 'Conscientious Objection to Military Service,' UN document E/CN/4/Sub/2/1983/30/Rev.1; Commission on Human Rights Resolution 1998/77, 22 April 1998: 'Conscientious Objection to Military Service', recalled in Resolution 2000/34, 20 April 2000. See also judgment of Waller LJ in *Sepet v Secretary of State for the Home Department* [2001] EWCA Civ 681, [2001] Imm AR 452.
3   *X v Austria* (1973) 43 CD 161.
4   (Application 34369/97) (2000) 31 EHRR 411, ECtHR.

5   *Thlimmenos v Greece*, Commission opinion above at para 44–45. The court based its judgment on ECHR, art 14, and did not deal with this aspect of the case.
6   *Handbook*, para 173.
7   *Sepet v Secretary of State for the Home Department* [2001] EWCA Civ 681, [2003] UKHL 15, [2003] 3 All ER 304; see CHAPTER 12 below.
8   Preamble, Recital 10.

Freedom of expression

7.120 Article 10 of the ECHR provides that:

(1)   Everyone has the right to freedom of expression. This right shall include freedom to hold opinions and to receive and impart information and ideas without interference by public authority and regardless of frontiers . . .

(2)   The exercise of these freedoms, since it carries with it duties and responsibilities, may be subject to such formalities, conditions, restrictions or penalties as are prescribed by law and and are necessary in a democratic society, in the interests of national security, territorial integrity or public safety, for the prevention of disorder or crime, for the protection of health or morals, for the protection of the reputation or rights of others, for preventing the disclosure of information received in confidence, or for maintaining the authority and impartiality of the judiciary.

Article 10 is rarely engaged in the immigration context, but was litigated in *Farrakhan*,[1] in which the Court of Appeal, reversing the High Court, held exclusion proportionate to the legitimate aim of prevention of disorder. The court held that Article 10 was engaged by an exclusion imposed largely to prevent the exercise of freedom of expression in the UK, but not by the exercise of control not directed at those rights, which prevents their exercise. In *A*, it was held that there was no breach of Article 10 arising from arrangements for monitoring journalists' interviews with asylum seekers detained as suspected terrorists.[2] Article 10 was also relied on in *Moon*.[3]

1   *R (on the application of Farrakhan) v Secretary of State for the Home Department* [2002] EWCA Civ 606, [2002] 3 WLR 481.
2   *R (on the application of A) v Secretary of State for the Home Department* [2003] EWHC 2846 (Admin), [2003] All ER (D) 402 (Nov).
3   See **7.118** above.

The right to marry and found a family

7.121 Article 12 of the ECHR provides that:

'Men and women of marriageable age have the right to marry and found a family according to the national laws governing the exercise of his right.'

The right to marry and found a family is one right, not two, and it is at least questionable whether it applies only to persons of opposite biological sex.[1] The right to marry 'is a strong right' which, by contrast to Articles 8, 9, 10 and 11 has no second paragraph permitting interferences or limitations.[2] It is subject only to 'national laws' which may interfere with the right in relation to procedural matters and in order to protect the institution of marriage[3] but also to promote other social goals such as the prevention of marriages of convenience for immigration purposes[4] and to that end the authorities may delay a proposed marriage for a reasonable period in order to investigate whether it is one of convenience.[5] However, the article does not authorise a scheme such as that operated under Asylum and Immigration (Treatment of Claimants, etc) Act 2004, s 19 whereby permission to marry would be withheld not as a result of individualised assessment of whether the proposed marriage was a sham but on the basis of immigration status.[6] Moreover, national laws regulating the exercise of the right to marry may not injure or impair the substance of the right eg by charging of a fee for applications for permission to marry which needy applicants could not afford.[7] Article 12 does not confer a right to choose a particular country in which to marry, even the country in which both parties currently reside[8] but that by itself is not sufficient to justify preventing marriage in that country.[9] The refusal of a marriage registrar to marry a couple could engage Article 12.[10] The ECtHR has held that the arrest of an illegal entrant immediately before his or her marriage could found an Article 12 claim if it had the effect of preventing or substantially delaying it.[11]

[1] The right of 'a man and a woman' to marry does not assume that these terms must refer to a determination of gender by purely biological criteria: *Goodwin v United Kingdom* (28957/95), 11 July 2002, departing from its earlier decisions in *Rees v United Kingdom* (1986) 9 EHRR 56, para 49 and *Cossey v United Kingdom* (1990) 13 EHRR 622 para 43. The House of Lords refused to follow *Goodwin* in *Bellinger v Bellinger* [2003] UKHL 21, [2003] 2 AC 467, holding it was for Parliament to remedy the incompatibility of the Matrimonial Causes Act 1973.

[2] *R (on the application of Baiai) v Secretary of State for the Home Department* [2008] UKHL 53, [2008] 3 All ER 1094.

[3] In relation to matters such as capacity, consent, prohibited degrees of consanguinity or the prevention of bigamy – see, for example, *Hamer v United Kingdom* (1979) 4 EHRR 139 and *F v Switzerland* (1987) 10 EHRR 411.

[4] *Klip and Kruger v Netherlands* (1997) 91-A DR 66.

[5] *R (on the application of Baiai) v Secretary of State for the Home Department* [2008] UKHL 53, [2008] 3 All ER 1094.

[6] *R (on the application of Baiai) v Secretary of State for the Home Department* [2008] UKHL 53, [2008] 3 All ER 1094.

[7] *R (on the application of Baiai) v Secretary of State for the Home Department* [2008] UKHL 53, [2008] 3 All ER 1094. The fixed fee of £295 or £590 if both of a couple were subject to immigration control imposed by the Immigration (Procedure for Marriage) Regulations 2005, SI 2005/15 would be likely to have such an effect.

[8] *Application 9773/82 v United Kingdom* (1982) 5 EHRR 296 and *Application 10914/84 v Netherlands* (1986) 8 EHRR 308.

[9] *Secretary of State for the Home Department v Baiai.*

[10] But registrars are merely giving effect to primary legislation, Immigration and Asylum Act 1999, s 24(5) and so would not be liable under the Human Rights Act 1998. For discrimination in pre-marriage checks see *Tejani v Superintendent Registrar for the District of Peterborough* [1986] IRLR 502, CA. Article 12 ECHR should be read with art 14.

[11] *Shahara and Rinea v Netherlands* (Application 10915/85), held inadmissible because the marriage was only deferred for nine days.

Protection of property

7.122 The right to enjoyment of private property is protected by Article 1 of the first protocol to the Convention[1] which begins 'every natural or legal person is entitled to the peaceful enjoyment of his possessions. No one shall be deprived of his possessions except in the general public interest and subject to conditions provided for by law and by the general principles of international law'. Exclusion from the UK may be challenged on the ground that it interferes with a person's peaceful enjoyment of his possessions in circumstances where the applicant is outside the UK and his property can only be enjoyed in the UK.[2]

[1] Which is one of the 'Convention rights' protected by the Human Rights Act 1998 – see s 1(1)(b) of that Act.

[2] *R (on the application of Murungaru) v Secretary of State for the Home Department* [2006] EWHC 2416 (Admin). The property concerned here was a contract for the provision of medical treatment to the applicant. However, the Court of Appeal held that whilst possessions could include contracts, the contract in this case was not a possession so that on the facts, no Convention claim arose – *M (Kenya) v Secretary of State for the Home Department* [2008] EWCA Civ 1015, [2008] All ER (D) 66 (Sep).

Non-discrimination

7.123 Article 14 of the ECHR prevents discrimination in the enjoyment of the Convention rights on grounds of sex, race, colour, language, religion, political or other opinion, national or social origin, association with a national minority, property, birth or other status.[1] The Article does not create a free-standing right not to be discriminated against,[2] but one linked to enjoyment of Convention rights.[3] It is not necessary to show a breach of a substantive right, however, to establish a breach of Article 14.[4] The questions which arise in relation to a claim engaging Article 14 are similar to those arising in respect of a qualified right: has there been a difference in treatment in an area within the ambit of the Convention;[5] if so, was it on a 'status' ground such as race, sex etc,[6] did the differential treatment have a legitimate aim, and an objective and reasonable justification, ie was there a reasonable relationship of proportionality between the means employed and the aim sought to be realised?[7] Discrimination on 'suspect' grounds[8] such as race,[9] sex,[10] sexual orientation,[11] nationality,[12] religion[13] or legitimacy,[14] is identified as particularly serious. If a restriction on a fundamental right applies to a particularly vulnerable group in society that has suffered considerable discrimination in the past then the state's margin of appreciation is substantially narrower and it must have 'very weighty reasons' for the restriction; one such group is people with HIV who have an 'other status' within the meaning of Article 14.[15] Immigration status may also be an 'other status' albeit not one of the kind requiring 'very weighty reasons' to justify basing differential treatment upon it.[16] There is a consensus in the Member States to eliminate discrimination on such grounds, backed by international instruments.[17] In such cases the court will subject the alleged discrimination to 'severe scrutiny'[18] and a heavier burden is placed upon the State to justify the difference in treatment[19] by giving 'very weighty reasons'.[20] By contrast, a difference in treatment on grounds other than suspect grounds would not be subject to such intense scrutiny by the court and a rational justification for the distinction would be sufficient.[21] Differences of treatment in such cases are said to be underpinned by decisions about the general public interest which are properly for the elected branches of government rather than the court[22] but this does not mean that the issue can be left entirely to Parliament and the executive;[23] the difference in treatment still has to be justified.[24] There are borderline cases in which it is not easy to allocate the ground of discrimination to one category or another[25] and it may be that there is a spectrum rather than a clear demarcation of categories.[26] An unjustifiable difference in treatment in the operation of the Immigration Rules regarding admission of spouses on grounds of gender was held to constitute a breach of the anti-discrimination provision of ECHR, Article 14 in conjunction with Article 8 in *Abdulaziz*.[27] However, in the same case the ECtHR rejected the argument that the Rules also discriminated on grounds of race, an argument which relied on the disproportionate impact the Rules had on immigrants from the Indian sub-continent as constituting indirect discrimination. The broad margin of appreciation which the court gave there to the domestic authorities meant it could not establish any ulterior discriminatory purpose behind government policy. This approach can of course be avoided by looking at the discriminatory *effect* of policy rather than seeking a discriminatory *purpose*, the approach of the European Court of Justice and of the UK courts under the Equal Treatment Directive[28] and the Sex Discrimination and Race Relations Acts.[29] The Strasbourg Court has now accepted that that there is no need to establish a discriminatory intent to show a breach of Article 14 and that a general policy or measure that has a disproportionately prejudicial effect on a particular group may be considered discriminatory even if not aimed at that group.[30] In such circumstances, the government would have to show that the differential impact of the measure was a consequence of objective factors, unrelated to the ground on which discrimination was alleged.[31] The House of Lords rejected the claim that the 'family amnesty' breached Article 14 owing to the difference in treatment between individuals who were or had been part of a family unit in the UK with their parents and individuals who were in the UK without their parents, their parents being dead or missing.[32]

[1] 'Status' has been interpreted by the Strasbourg Court as 'a personal characteristic . . . by which persons or groups of persons are distinguishable from each other' – *Kjeldsen, Busk Madsen and Pedersen v Denmark* (1976) 1 EHRR 711, applied in *R (on the application of S) v Chief Constable of South Yorkshire* [2004] 1 WLR 2196. 'Immigration status' (in *R (on the application of Morris) v Westminster City Council* [2004] UKHL 39, [2005] EWCA Civ 1184) and being an unaccompanied asylum seeking child or not being a member of a family (*AL (Serbia) v Secretary of State for the Home Department* [2006] EWCA Civ 1619, [2008] 4 All ER 1127) have been accepted as falling within 'other status'

[2] Such a free-standing right is created by ECHR, Protocol 12, adopted by the Committee of Ministers in June 2000 and opened for signature in November 2000. The UK has not signed or ratified it, and by March 2004 there were only six ratifications. It requires ten Council of Europe States to ratify it to come into force.

[3] The Secretary of State's refusal to register as a British citizen an illegitimate child of a British father was held not to violate art 14 ECHR together with art 8 in *R (on the application of Montana) v Secretary of State for the Home Department* [2001] 1 WLR 552, CA, as the right to nationality is not within the ambit of the Convention, and the discrimination did not in fact impact on family life.

[4] In *R (on the application of Morris) v Westminster City Council* [2005] EWCA Civ 1184 Sedley LJ said 'Convention rights have a penumbra within which unjustifiable discrimination is forbidden even in the absence of a violation of the right'. The Strasbourg court has also recognised that the right not to be discriminated against is also violated when States without objective and reasonable justification fail to treat differently persons whose situations are significantly different: *Thlimmenos v Greece* (2000) 31 EHRR 411 (ban on civil service employment for those with criminal convictions caught an applicant with a conviction for conscientious objection, and thus discriminated in the enjoyment of rights of conscience).

[5] *Inze v Austria* (1987) 10 EHRR 394.

[6] The prohibited grounds set out in art 14 are illustrative, not exhaustive. In *R (on the application of T) v Secretary of State for Health* [2002] EWHC 1887 (Admin), (2002) Times, 5 September, the status of 'asylum seeker' was held to be a status within art 14 such that discriminatory denial of fundamental rights of asylum seekers could breach the ECHR.

7   *Belgian Linguistics Case (No 2)* (1968) 1 EHRR 252; *Marckx v Belgium* (1979) 2 EHRR 330; *Rasmussen v Denmark* (1984) 7 EHRR 371; *Abdulaziz, Cabales and Balkandali v United Kingdom* (1985) 7 EHRR 471. The Court of Appeal has set out the 'structured task' it faces in assessing an art 14 claim: has there been (i) a difference in treatment (ii) in an area within the ambit of the Convention; (iii) is the chosen comparator analogous; (iv) is there an objective or reasonable justification for the differential treatment: *Wandsworth London Borough Council v Michalak* [2002] EWCA Civ 271, [2003] 1 WLR 617, para 20. However, the *Michalak* approach has been 'superseded' by *R (on the application of Carson) v Secretary of State for Work and Pensions* [2005] UKHL 37, [2006] 1 AC 173 in which Lord Nicholls 'sounded a new keynote' (to use Sedley LJ's phrase in *Morris* fn 1 above) saying: 'Article 14 does not apply unless the alleged discrimination is in connection with a Convention right and on a ground stated in Article 14. If this prerequisite is satisfied, the essential question for the courts is whether the alleged discrimination, that is, the difference in treatment of which complaint is made, can withstand scrutiny. Sometimes the answer to this question will be plain. There may be such an obvious, relevant difference between the claimant and those with whom he seeks to compare himself that their situations cannot be regarded as analogous. Sometimes, where the position is not so clear, a different approach is called for. Then the Court's scrutiny may best be directed at considering whether the differentiation has a legitimate aim and whether the means chosen to achieve the aim is appropriate and not disproportionate in its adverse impact'.

8   Ie 'those grounds of discrimination which prima facie appear to offend our notions of the respect due to the individual', Lord Hoffmann in paragraph 15 of *R (Carson)*.

9   *East African Asians v United Kingdom* (1973) 3 EHRR 76. The court held differential entitlement to emergency social security assistance as between nationals and non-nationals to violate Article 14 with Protocol 1 Article 1, as not based on any objective and reasonable justification, in *Gaysusuz v Austria* (1997) 23 EHRR 364.

10 *Abdulaziz*, fn 7, above. It is no longer appropriate for the State to discriminate against transsexuals in the enjoyment of family and private life: *Goodwin v United Kingdom* (2002) 35 EHRR 18.

11 Differences in treatment based on sexual orientation require particularly serious reasons by way of justification: *Smith and Grady v United Kingdom* (1999) 29 EHRR 493; *SL v Austria* (Application 45330/99) (2003) 37 EHRR 799; *L v Austria* (39392/98, 39829/98) (2003) 13 BHRC 594, para 37; *Karner v Austria* (40016/98) [2004] 2 FCR 563. See also *Ghaidan v Godin Mendoza* [2004] UKHL 30, [2004] 2 AC 557 and *LD S(Brazil)* [2006] UKIAT 00075.

12 *R (on the application of Baiai) v Secretary of State for the Home Department* [2006] EWHC 823 (Admin), [2006] 3 All ER 608, Silber J, relying in part on *Gaysusuz v Austria* (1997) 23 EHRR 364 and *Morris* as in fn 1 above.

13 *R (on the application of Baiai) v Secretary of State for the Home Department* [2006] EWHC 823 (Admin), [2006] 3 All ER 608 holding that the Asylum and Immigration (Treatment of Claimants, etc) Act 2004, s 19 discriminated on grounds of religion and nationality because the requirement that it imposed to obtain the Secretary of State's permission to marry did not apply to those marrying by an Anglican ceremony but did apply to those marrying by any other religious ceremony.

14 *Marckx* fn 7 above.

15 *Kiyutin v Russia* (Application 2700/10).

16 *Bah v United Kingdom* (Application No 56328/07) [2011] 39 LS Gaz R 19, (2011) Times, 15 November, ECtHR.

17 Convention for the Elimination of All forms of Discrimination Against Women 1978 (CEDAW); Convention for the Elimination of all forms of Racial Discrimination (CERD).

18 Lord Walker's phrase in *R (on the application of Carson) v Secretary of State for Work and Pensions* [2005] UKHL 37, [2006] 1 AC 173.

19 *Abdulaziz* above.

20 'In its judgments the European Court of Human Rights often refers to "very weighty reasons" being required to justify discrimination on these particularly sensitive grounds', Lord Walker in *R (on the application of Carson)* above.

21 *R (on the application of Carson)*, Lord Walker, paras 56, 58.

22 *R (on the application of Carson)*, Lord Hoffmann, para 16.

23 As the tribunal said it could in *HK (Somalia)* [2006] UKAIT 00021 (where it was argued that the refugee family reunion rules discriminated against a refugee child who could not bring a

parent whereas a refugee parent could bring her child) and in *KP (India)* [2006] UKAIT 00093
(where it was argued that paragraph 317 of the rules discriminated against mothers in law
compared with mothers).

24 *AL (Serbia) v R (on the application of Morris) v Westminster City Council* [2006] EWCA Civ
    1619.
25 *R (on the application of Carson).*
26 *AL (Serbia) v R (on the application of Morris) v Westminster City Council* [2006] EWCA Civ
    1619 where the Court of Appeal had difficulty deciding whether being an unaccompanied
    asylum seeking child was a suspect category.
27 *Abdulaziz* above, where the court rejected the government's attempt to justify on economic
    grounds and grounds of 'public tranquillity' the rules which made it more difficult for foreign
    husbands to join wives in the UK than vice versa.
28 ETD 76/207.
29 Sex Discrimination Act 1975; Race Relations Act 1976. See the House of Lords' application
    of the proportionality test to a situation of indirect discrimination in *R v Secretary of State for
    Employment, ex p Equal Opportunities Commission* [1995] 1 AC 1.
30 *DH v Czech Republic* (2007) App No 57325/00 (Grand Chamber).
31 *DH v Czech Republic.*
32 *AL (Serbia) v Secretary of State for the Home Department* [2008] UKHL 42.

7.124 The common law has long held that in the field of administrative
decisions unjustified discrimination on grounds of race, colour, gender, religion
or any other irrational ground is unlawful,[1] and the constitutional principle of
equality developed domestically by the English courts is wider than that
protected by the ECHR, since it does not depend on showing an impact on
another fundamental right.[2] In *Ali (Arman)*[3] Collins J held that the Immigration Rules requiring spouses to support and accommodate themselves and
their dependants without recourse to public funds as a prerequisite of
admission must be read so as to include the possibility that they could be
maintained indefinitely by third parties or by their nominal dependants, so as
to ensure compatibility with ECHR, Article 8 rights. Otherwise the Rule could
discriminate on grounds of disability or age against couples too old or ill to
work but with family support. The decision led to a change in the rules regarding recourse to public funds,[4] and has been applied by the Tribunal in
analogous situations.[5] In the *Roma Rights* case[6] the House of Lords held that
the fact that Roma passengers were questioned more intensively, sceptically
and for longer, and refused boarding more often than non-Roma passengers at
Prague airport, amounted to unlawful discrimination under domestic[7] and
international law.[8] Although there was an authorisation, which might have
exempted the immigration service, the Prague operation was not in fact
operating under it. The government's case was that there was no discrimination at all. The House came to the inevitable conclusion that the operation was
inherently and systemically discriminatory and unlawful. In *A v Secretary
of State for the Home Department; X v Secretary of State for the Home
Department*[9] the detention of foreign terrorist suspects was held incompatible
with Article 14 read with Article 5 in the derogation case, on the grounds that
it applied only to foreign nationals and not to British citizens who were also
part of the threat. Discrimination against homosexuals in an immigration
context, which was formerly accepted as legitimate by the ECtHR,[10] would no
longer be upheld.[11]

1 *Kruse v Johnson* [1898] 2 QB 91; *Matadeen v Pointu* [1999] 1 AC 98 (PC). Discrimination on
   grounds of race, gender or disability is prohibited by statute (Race Relations Act 1976 (as
   amended by the Race Relations Amendment Act 2000), Sex Discrimination Acts 1975 and
   1986, Disability Discrimination Act 1995). But discrimination on grounds of nationality,
   national or ethnic origin is not unlawful if carried out by a 'relevant person' in carrying out

immigration and nationality functions (Race Relations Act as amended, s 19D), although it remains unlawful to discriminate on grounds of race or colour. The distinction between 'race' and 'ethnic origin' is problematic. In *R (on the application of the Tamil Information Centre) v Secretary of State for the Home Department* [2002] EWHC 2155 (Admin), the court interpreted the exceptions very narrowly.

2   See lecture of 18 September 2002 in honour of Lord Cooke of Thoronden, quoted in *Gurung v Ministry of Defence* [2002] EWHC 2463 (Admin), [2003] 06 LS Gaz R 25, in which Lord Steyn emphasised the importance of the principle of equality: 'Individuals are . . . comprehensively protected from discrimination by the principle of equality. This constitutional right has a continuing role to play. The organic development of constitutional rights is therefore a complementary and parallel process to the application of human rights legislation.'

3   *R v Secretary of State for the Home Department, ex p Ali (Arman)* [2000] INLR 89.

4   HC 395 para 6A was inserted on 2 October 2000, providing that the 'no recourse to public funds' rule for spouses did not prevent a British spouse enjoying public funds in his or her own right, provided that the arrival of the partner did not result in additional recourse.

5   See eg *Abdulla (Intekab)* [2002] UKIAT 07516, where the Tribunal accepted that savings made by a sponsor from public funds could satisfy the 'no recourse' requirements and that a generous interpretation of the rules was required to attain compatibility with art 8 read with art 14, particularly where disability prevented a spouse from working.

6   *European Roma Rights Centre v Immigration Officer at Prague Airport* [2004] UKHL 55, [2005] 1 All ER 527.

7   Section 19B of the Race Relations Act 1976 as amended by the Race Relations (Amendment) Act 2000, which came into force on 2 April 2001.

8   *Roma Rights* case, above, per Lady Hale at para 98: 'In this respect it was not only unlawful in domestic law but also contrary to our obligations under customary international law and under international treaties to which the United Kingdom is a party.' At para 103 she also noted that the General Assembly of the UN has 'urged all States to review and where necessary revise their immigration laws, policies and practices so that they are free of racial discrimination and compatible with their obligations under international human rights instruments' (UNGA Resolution 57/195, para I.6, adopted 18 December 2002; see also UNGA Resolution 58/160 adopted on 22 December 2003). The UN Committee on the Elimination of Racial Discrimination has expressed its concern at the application of section 19D, which it considers 'incompatible with the very principle of non-discrimination' (UN doc CERD/C/63/CO/11, para 16, 10 December 2003).

9   *A v Secretary of State for the Home Department; X v Secretary of State for the Home Department* [2004] UKHL 56, [2005] 2 WLR 87.

10   *S v United Kingdom* (1986) 47 D & R 274, para 7; *B v United Kingdom* (1990) 64 DR 278, para 2.

11   There has been no recent ECHR jurisprudence on homosexual partners' family or private life rights in the immigration context, but see ECtHR's observations in *Smith and Grady v United Kingdom* (1999) 29 EHRR 493; *Goodwin v United Kingdom* (2002) 35 EHRR 18. The UK Immigration Rules were amended to admit same-sex partners on 2 October 2000 (HC 395 para 295A, see **11.48** below. In another context, a same-sex partner was held equivalent to a spouse, reading the interpretation of the phrase 'wife or husband' in the Rent Acts (for succession to a tenancy) compatibly with art 14 with art 8, in *Ghaidan v Mendoza* [2004] UKHL 30, [2004] 3 All ER 411, HL.

Effective remedy

7.125 Article 13 of the ECHR provides that:

'Everyone whose rights and freedoms as set forth in this Convention are violated shall have an effective remedy before the national authority notwithstanding that the violation has been committed by persons acting in an official capacity.'

Article 13 requires a remedy at national level to enforce the substance of Convention rights and freedoms in whatever form they have to be secured in the domestic legal order.[1] It does not stand alone, but has to be considered in conjunction with other Convention rights. The 'remedy' must consider the substance of an arguable complaint under the Convention, and grant appropriate relief. It must be effective in practice and in law,[2] and its exercise must not be unjustifiably hindered by the acts or omissions of the respondent State authorities.[3] Article 13 is not among the Convention rights listed in the Human Rights Act 1998, because the Lord Chancellor believes that section 8 of the Act meets the UK's obligations under Article 13.[4] Judicial review has been held to constitute an effective remedy in expulsion cases raising Article 3 issues in *Soering v United Kingdom*,[5] and subsequent cases, on the basis that the courts could effectively control the legality of executive discretion on substantive and procedural grounds and quash decisions.[6] In *Chahal v United Kingdom*[7] the court found the scope of review, and so the effectiveness of the remedy, restricted because of the national security element. That has now been remedied by the Special Immigration Appeals Commission mechanism.[8] However, in *Smith and Grady v United Kingdom*[9] it was held that judicial review was ineffective to comply with the requirements of Article 8(2) in a case in which homosexuals were banned from the armed forces. The ECtHR held that the domestic court placed the threshold of irrationality 'so high that it effectively excluded any consideration by the domestic courts of the question whether the interference with the applicants' rights answered a pressing social need or was proportionate to the national security and public order aims pursued'.[10] In *Daly*[11] the House of Lords affirmed that the courts' intensity of review in human rights cases had to be more rigorous than before. The government's proposal in late 2003 to oust the jurisdiction of the higher courts over decisions of the appellate authority which may be flawed by errors of law or procedural unfairness, contained in the Asylum and Immigration (Treatment of Claimants) Bill,[12] which was withdrawn after being greeted with outrage by (among others) senior judges, would have meant the loss of an effective remedy for significant numbers alleging that their removal would breach fundamental human rights.

[1]   *Boyle and Rice v United Kingdom* (1988) 10 EHRR 425, para 52.

[2]   There must be a rigorous and independent scrutiny of the claim and (in the context of removal to potential art 3 ill-treatment) the possibility of suspending the implementation of the measure impugned: *Jabari v Turkey* [2001] INLR 136. A discretionary stay on expulsion is not sufficiently effective, since the implementation of the remedy is too uncertain to enable the requirements of art 13 to be satisfied: *Conka v Belgium* (51564/99) 5 February 2002. The lack of an expeditious avenue of complaint for a prisoner, capable of quashing a punishment before its execution, and the lack of an effective remedy for bereaved persons to establish responsibility for a death in prison and obtain compensation, were held to breach art 13 in *Keenan v United Kingdom* (2001) 33 EHRR 38.

[3]   *Aksoy v Turkey* (1996) 23 EHRR 553; *Aydin v Turkey* (1997) 25 EHRR 251; *Hilal v United Kingdom* (2001) 33 EHRR 31 (para 75); *Kaya v Turkey* (1999) 28 EHRR 1 (para 106). An extradition despite an interim measure under rule 39 (request for a stay) was held to preclude the effective examination of complaints and to render nugatory the right to individual application in *Mamatkulov and Abdurasulovic v Turkey* (Applications 46827/99 and 46951/99) (2003) Times, 13 March.

[4]   HL Official Report (5th series) cols 476–477, 18 November 1997. Article 13 'reflects the long-standing principle of our law that where there is a right there should be a remedy. Parliament's intention was, of course, that the Human Rights Act itself should constitute the UK's compliance with Article 13, but this makes it if anything more important that the courts . . . should satisfy themselves so far as possible that the common law affords adequate control . . . of the legality of official measures which interfere with personal autonomy': *R (on the application of K) v Camden and Islington Health Authority* [2001] EWCA Civ 240, [2002] QB 198.

[5]   (1989) 11 EHRR 439; *Vilvarajah v United Kingdom* (1991) 14 EHRR 248; *Hilal v United Kingdom* (fn 3 above). The increasing breadth and depth of judicial review was noted in *R (on the application of Q) v Secretary of State for the Home Department* [2003] EWCA Civ 364, [2003] 2 All ER 905.

6   *Hilal v United Kingdom* above, paras 77–78.
7   (1996) 23 EHRR 413.
8   Special Immigration Appeals Commission Act 1997; see CHAPTER **22**. Whether proceedings before SIAC are capable of constituting an effective remedy for breaches of arts 3 and 8 arising from indefinite detention and/or conditions of detention is currently being litigated in *G v Secretary of State for the Home Department* [2004] EWCA Civ 265.
9   (1999) 29 EHRR 493.
10 (1999) 29 EHRR 493, paras 136–139.
11 *R (on the application of Daly) v Secretary of State for the Home Department* [2001] UKHL 26, [2001] 2 AC 532.
12 Clause 11 of the Bill.

HUMAN RIGHTS APPEALS

7.126 The issue of whether an immigration decision breaches or would breach a person's human rights may be raised in an appeal to the First-tier Tribunal and thereafter to the Upper Tribunal and the Court of Appeal. Such appeals are discussed in CHAPTERS **21** and **22**.

GOING TO EUROPE

ECtHR

7.127 For those cases where the applicant has exhausted all domestic remedies from the Tribunal or the courts in the UK, there remains the possibility of applying to the ECtHR. Article 34 of the Convention enables any person, non-governmental organisation or group of individuals claiming to be the victim of a violation by one of the parties to the Convention to make an application to the Court. A detailed exposition of the procedures of the court is beyond the scope of this work, but a brief summary follows.[1] The Court became full-time and took over the functions of the Commission in November 1998. A variety of measures have been taken to streamline the operation of the Court and reduce the backlogs including most recently Protocols 14, 15 and 16 to the Convention.[2] The Court consists of a number of judges equal to the number of parties to the Convention.[3] The Court may sit as a single judge, in a committee of three judges, in chambers of five or seven judges and in a Grand Chamber of 17 judges.[4] Single judges may be assisted by non-judicial rapporteurs appointed by the President of the Court.[5] Single judges and committees may decide on the admissibility of applications to the Court[6] and a committee may give a judgment on the merits if the underlying question in the case is already the subject of well-established case law of the Court.[7] Decisions of single judges and committees as to admissibility and judgments given by a committee are final.[8] Alternatively, the single judge or committee may forward the application to a chamber for decisions as to admissibility and on the merits.[9] A chamber may refer a case pending before it to the Grand Chamber, unless one of the parties objects, if it raises a serious question affecting the interpretation of the Convention or the Protocols or where the outcome of the case before the chamber may have a result inconsistent with a judgment previously delivered by the Court.[10] In addition, within three months of a chamber giving judgment, any party to the case may 'in exceptional cases' request that the case be referred to the Grand Chamber.[11] A panel of five judges of the Grand Chamber will accept such a request 'if the case raises a serious question affecting the interpretation or application of the Convention or the Protocols thereto, or a serious issue of general importance'.[12]

1   The reader is referred to Philip Leach, *Taking a Case to the European Court of Human Rights*, third edition (2011), Oxford.
2   Protocol 14 came into force on 1 June 2010, Protocols 15 and 16 are not yet in force as they do not yet have the requisite number of ratifications. Protocol 15 amends the Convention to introduce a reference to the principle of subsidiarity and the doctrine of the margin of appreciation. It also reduces from six to four months the time-limit within which an application may be made to the Court following the date of a final domestic decision. Protocol 16 will allow the courts of State Parties to request the Court to give advisory opinions on questions of principle relating to the interpretation or application of the Convention.
3   ECHR, art 20.
4   ECHR, art 26.
5   ECHR, art 24(2).
6   ECHR, arts 27 and 28.
7   ECHR, art 28(1)(b).
8   ECHR, art 27(2) and 28(2).
9   ECHR, arts 27(2) and 29.
10 ECHR, art 30.
11 ECHR, art 43(1).
12 ECHR, art 43(2). In 2013 the Grand Chamber gave only 13 judgments.

Procedure

7.128 An application to the Court must be made within 6 months of the date of the final decision by the domestic courts.[1] The Court's Registrar is the channel for all communications to and from the Court.[2] In a further attempt to streamline it's demanding caseload the Court has become much stricter on application requirements.[3] Applications to the Court can now only be made on the specified application form, must contain all the specified information and documentation set out in Rule 47 of the Rules of Court. Failure to comply with the requirements will usually result in the application not being examined by the Court.[4] The date of introduction of the case to the Court for the purposes of the six months time-limit will be the date on which an application form satisfying all the requirements is sent to the Court. The relevant date is the date on the postmark of the application not the date of receipt by the Court.[5] Following receipt of the application it may be declared inadmissible or struck out of the list by a single judge if or assigned to a judge as judge rapporteur to examine the application, request further information, decide whether to refer the case to a committee or to a chamber and prepare a report to that body.[6] A chamber has broad powers to request or take evidence, including to ask any person or institution to express an opinion or make a written report and may carry out its own investigations.[7] In cases which are not obviously inadmissible, the case may be communicated to the respondent government whereby they are given written notice of the application and asked to submit observations on an application.[8] There may be an oral hearing on admissibility.[9] A Committee may decide, by unanimous vote, to declare inadmissible or strike out an application where it can do so without further examination. If an application is declared admissible its merits will be considered by a chamber. The chamber may attempt a friendly settlement[10] while pursuing the merits of the case. A hearing on the merits may be requested if there was no hearing at admissibility stage, otherwise it is at the chamber's discretion.[11] Individuals may submit applications themselves but legal representation is recommended and is required for hearings or once an application has been communicated to the Government.[12] There is a legal aid scheme for applicants but legal aid is not available until after the first set of observations from the Government are received following communication of the case.[13]

[1] Article 35(1) ECHR, note if Protocol 15 to the ECHR is brought into force by a sufficient number of ratifications the time limit to bring an application will be reduced to four months.

[2] ECHR, art 24(1) and Rules of the European Court of Human Rights, r 17(2).

[3] Amendments made to Rule 47 on 6 May 2013 came into force on 1 January 2014. See also Practice Direction: Institution of Proceedings, 1 January 2014.

[4] Unless (a) the applicant has provided an adequate explanation for the failure to comply; (b) the application concerns a request for an interim measure; or (c) the Court otherwise directs of its own motion or at the request of an applicant, r 47(5.1). See *Abdulrahman v the Netherlands* (Application 66994/12 Decision (5 February 2013, unreported), ECtHR; *Yartsev v Russia* (Application 13776/11) (26 March 2013, unreported) and *Ngendakumana v Netherlands* (Application 16380/11) (5 February 2013, unreported) illustrate the Court's more rigorous recent approach to the interpretation of Article 35 § 1 of the Convention, taken together with the relevant Practice Direction: Institution of Proceedings, in determining the date of introduction of an application although both cases were decided under the previous version of r 47.

[5] Rule 47 (6)(a). Where it finds it justified, the Court may nevertheless decide that a different date shall be considered to be the date of introduction under r 47(6)(b).

[6] Rules of the European Court of Human Rights, r 49.

[7] Annex to the Rules of the Court concerning Investigations. These powers have been used under ECHR, arts 2 and 3 against Turkey, where the government disputes the facts. See eg *Akdivar v Turkey* (1996) 23 EHRR 143.

[8] Rules of the European Court of Human Rights, r 54(2). In 2012 and 2013 around 65,000 cases were allocated each year. In 2012 only 5,236 were communicated to the Respondent Government and in 2013 7,931 were communicated. Figures taken from the Court's Annual Report 2013.

[9] Rules of the European Court of Human Rights, r 54(3).

[10] Rules of the European Court of Human Rights, r 62.

[11] Rules of the European Court of Human Rights, r 59.

[12] Rules of the European Court of Human Rights, r 36.

[13] Rules of the European Court of Human Rights, r 100. Legal aid rates are not comparable with those in the UK and do not reflect the amount of work that an application usually entails.

Interim measures

7.129 The court has no power to make an order in the form of an injunction against the respondent State, but if the applicant is about to be expelled or deported, the application may contain a request for an interim measure under Rule 39 of the Rules of the court which the court considers to be binding on the parties. Rule 39 provides that the Chamber or, where appropriate, its President may 'indicate to the parties any interim measure which it considers should be adopted in the interests of the parties or of the proper conduct of the proceedings before it'. This would include a request not to proceed with a removal.[1] In accordance with the established practice of the court interim measures are urgent measures that apply only where there is an imminent risk of irreparable damage.[2] The power to issue a Rule 39 indication is used very sparingly.[3] Initially a Rule 39 Indication was not considered binding on State Parties.[4] However, subsequent case law of the court makes it clear that the failure to comply with a Rule 39 indication may constitute an interference with the right of individual petition protected by Article 34 ECHR.[5] An application under Rule 39, like any other application to the court, can be made only once all possible domestic remedies have been exhausted.[6] The Court's practice is to examine each request on an individual and priority basis through a written procedure. Applicants and governments are informed of the Court's decisions on interim measures. Refusals to apply Rule 39 cannot be appealed against. The length of an interim measure is generally set to cover the duration of the proceedings before the Court or for a shorter period. The application of Rule 39 may be discontinued at any time by a decision of the Court. In particular, as such measures are related to the proceedings before the Court, they may be lifted if the application is not maintained.[7] In the context of an imminent risk of irreparable harm caused by removal from the UK Rule 39 has been applied most frequently in cases engaging Article 3 and Asylum grounds.[8] It has been applied only exceptionally in cases that engage Article 8 ECHR[9] but has been applied in the contexts of Article 5 and 6 ECHR.[10] The Court has issued a Practice Direction relating to requests for interim measures. A request should be sent by fax or by post and should be marked, in bold in the face of the request: 'Rule 39 – Urgent: Person to contact (name and contact details); Date and time of removal and destination' (in removal or extradition cases).[11] The request, as well as stating the reasons for the request must be accompanied by all necessary supporting documents including any domestic court, tribunal or other decisions and any material substantiating the reasons given for the request. In removal cases, the date and time of the expected removal, the applicant's address or place of detention and the domestic case reference number must be provided.

[1] See eg *Hilal v United Kingdom* (2001) 33 EHRR 31, para 5.

[2] See *Mamatkulov and Askarov v Turkey [GC]*, nos 46827/99 and 46951/99, § 104, 4 February 2005 and *Paladi v Moldova* [GC], no 39806/05, §§ 86–90, 10 March 2009).

[3] In 2013 there were 1,588 requests for interim measures. 108 were granted. European Court of Human Rights: Thematical Statistics, Interim Measures 2010–2013.

[4] See eg *Cruz Varas v Sweden* (1991) 14 EHRR 1.

[5] *Mamatkulov and Abdurasulovic v Turkey* (46827/99 and 46951/99) (2003) Times, 13 March, in which two nationals of Uzbekistan were extradited from Turkey despite a Rule 39 indication having been made by the President of the Court.

[6] Article 35(1) ECHR.

[7] Information here taken verbatim from the Court's Factsheet on Interim Measures.

[8] Examples of cases where Rule 39 indications have been made include: *Lunguli (Abraham) v Sweden* (Application 33692/02) (1 July 2003, unreported); *FH v Sweden* (no 32621/06) 20.01.2009 (religion); *KN v France* (no 47129/09) 19.06.2012 (sexual orientation) *Einhorn v France* (no 71555/01) 19.07.2001 (suicide risk); *M v the United Kingdom* (no 16081/08) 01.12.2009 (trafficking).

[9] *Amrollahi v Denmark* (no 56811/00) 11.07.2002; *Eskinazi and Chelouche v Turkey* (no 14600/05) 06.12.2005.

[10] *Othman (Abu Qatada) v the United Kingdom* (no 8139/09) 17.01.2012, *Soering v United Kingdom* (no 14038/88).

[11] Practice Direction: Requests for Interim Measures, issued on 5 March 2003 and amended on 16 October 2009, 7 July 2011, the current version is dated 1 July 2014. See also the court's *Factsheet on Interim Measures* which gives a very detailed analysis of relevant case law and is updated from time to time.

Admissibility

7.130 Most cases fail at admissibility stage, and therefore if an application is to have a chance of proceeding to consideration on its merits, careful attention must be paid to the admissibility criteria. An application will be declared inadmissible if it fails to comply with the requirements of Article 35 of the ECHR. The Rules set out there are:

(i)   the six-month rule: the application must be communicated within six months of the last domestic decision.[1] This is strict and cannot be waived. The time limit may not be relevant in the case of complaints of continuing breaches, although these are strictly interpreted;[2]

(ii)   exhaustion of domestic remedies: the application will be inadmissible if available remedies were not pursued,[3] whether this was because of an adviser's failure or for other reason, unless the failure was due to the respondent State's obstruction.[4] But this rule only requires potentially effective remedies to be exhausted; where a binding authority meant certain failure, a domestic remedy need not be pursued. In such a case the opinion of a senior lawyer should be provided to the court. But a remedy may be effective even if success is not guaranteed. Where the potential remedy does not have suspensive effect and would not operate as a bar to removal it does not have to be exhausted;[5]

(iii)   manifestly ill-founded applications, ie those disclosing no prima facie breach of a Convention right, or where the complaint is unsubstantiated or the applicant has ceased to be a victim,[6] and applications considered an abuse of the right of application,[7] will be rejected as inadmissible. The 'manifestly ill-founded' provision is very broadly interpreted by the court, which may declare an application to be manifestly ill-founded after examining it in considerable detail;[8]

(iv)   anonymous complaints are inadmissible.[9] An applicant must disclose his or her identity when applying, although there is provision for non-disclosure of identity to the public;

(v)   repetitive applications are inadmissible, although if the complaint is based on new factual information it will not be disqualified;[10]

(vi)   applications which fall outside the jurisdiction of the Convention are inadmissible. This could be in terms of time – *ratione temporis* (eg a claim based on a Protocol not ratified by the respondent State at the time of the alleged violation), or place – *ratione loci* (ie there is no territorial link with the respondent State), or because it covers matters not within the terms of the Convention at all – *ratione materiae*, such as a right to work in a particular occupation,[11] or matters covered by a derogation.[12] Inadmissability by reason of *ratione personae* applies where the State is not responsible for the alleged breach or the applicant does not have standing or is not a victim;

(vii)   the applicant has not suffered a significant disadvantage, unless respect for human rights as defined in the Convention and Protocols requires an examination of the application on its merits and provided the case has been duly considered by a domestic court or tribunal.[13] The obligation to respect human rights must mean that where a significant disadvantage is anticipated rather than already suffered, as in the case of threatened removal, examination on the merits may be required.

---

[1]   ECHR, art 35(1). See the Court's Practical Guide on Admissibility Criteria published first in 2009, then in 2011 and most recently in January 2014, available on www.echr.coe.int.

[2]   Application 9852 *United Kingdom and Ireland, Re* (1985) 8 EHRR 49. See also *Yavuz (Bulut and Hatice) v Turkey* (73965/01) (28 May 2002, unreported), where the court considered that

even in the case of an alleged continuing violation of the Convention, applicants should make their applications under art 34 ECHR once they become aware that domestic remedies will be ineffective.

3   ECHR, art 35(1).
4   See eg *Hilton v United Kingdom* (1978) 3 EHRR 104.
5   See *Soering v United Kingdom* (1989) 11 EHRR 439. (*Jabari v Turkey* (dec.), No 40035/98, 28 October 1999). (*Bahaddar v Netherlands* (Application 25894/94) (1998) 26 EHRR 278 applied in *NA v United Kingdom* (Application 25904/07) (2008) 48 EHRR 337, [2008] ECHR 616.
6   Eg by accepting damages in settlement of a civil claim: see *Hay v United Kingdom* (41894/98) (17 October 2000, unreported). This could also be inadmissible *ratione persone*.
7   Eg with no legal foundation, to make a political or other point.
8   *TI v United Kingdom* [2000] INLR 101.
9   ECHR, art 35(2)(a).
10   ECHR, art 35(2)(b).
11   *X v Germany* (Application 6742/74) (1975) 3 DR 98.
12   *Brannigan and McBride v United Kingdom* (1993) 17 EHRR 539.
13   ECHR, art 35(4).

Chapter 8
VISITS, STUDY AND TEMPORARY PURPOSES

INTRODUCTION

8.1 In this chapter we deal with the formal requirements of the Immigration Rules relating to visits. It should be noted, however, that compliance with these Rules may not be sufficient to gain entry and the general requirements for refusal of entry may apply. Passengers who qualify formally for admission may be refused entry because of their restricted returnability, their past immigration or criminal record, for medical reasons or for the other general reasons already referred to.[1] Similarly, extensions of leave may be refused on any of the general grounds contained in the Immigration Rules, even though the formal requirements for an extension are satisfied.[2] In addition, section 8B of the Immigration Act 1971[3] provides for Designated Travel Ban Orders requiring the mandatory exclusion of 'excluded persons' named or described in a designated UN Security Council Resolution or an instrument of the EU Council.[4] The effect of including these travel bans in the Order is that, unless subject to one of the exemptions set out in Article 3 of the Immigration (Designation of Travel Bans) Order 2000, a person named by or described in a designated travel ban is an excluded person and must be refused leave to enter or remain in the UK, including transit through the UK. Any existing leave is automatically cancelled, and any exemption from immigration control, for example, as a diplomat, ceases.

[1] HC 395, para 320. Grounds (1) to (7D) specify circumstances in which entry clearance or leave to enter *is* to be refused and (8) to (22) where it *should normally* be refused. See **3.136** ff above.

[2] HC 395, para 322(1)–(1A) where leave *is to* be refused, and (2)–(12) where leave *should normally* be refused. See **3.92** ff above.

[3] Inserted by Immigration and Asylum Act 1999, s 8.

[4] The Schedule to the Immigration (Designation of Travel Bans) Order 2000, SI 2000/2724 has been regularly updated and is currently replaced by Schedule 1 to the Immigration (Designation of Travel Bans) (Amendment) Order 2014/1849, which came into force on 21 July 2014. Part 1 of Schedule 1 specifies various UN Resolutions, and Part 2 of Schedule 1 specifies Common EU Positions and/or Council Decisions; they are now too numerous to set out here.

8.2 Non-visa nationals coming for a period of less than six months for a visit or other purpose, for which an entry clearance is not needed, do not need prior entry clearance.[1] On the other hand, all visa nationals require a visa for a visit or any of the purposes set out in this and other chapters.[2] Although entry clearance is not essential for non-visa nationals coming for many of these purposes, those coming for more than six months must now obtain an entry clearance before they come, as this operates as a grant of leave to enter.[3] Whether entry clearance is required for particular categories of entrant is dealt with in the relevant Chapter. Refusal of entry clearance attracts no right of appeal in the case of short-term and prospective students and non-family visitors. The Asylum and Immigration Appeals Act 1993 abolished rights of appeal against refusal of entry clearance for all visitors, short-term and prospective students. The Immigration and Asylum Act 1999 re-introduced appeal rights for family visitors and its 2002 successor continued these. However on 25 June 2013 family visit appeals were abolished.[4] See further **8.40** below. Appeals can only be brought on human rights or race discrimination grounds.

[1] HC 395, para 23A, inserted by HC 645. So far as Canada and the USA are concerned there are mutual visa waiver requirements for visitors under the visa waiver programme (VWP). The EU allows citizens of both these countries free travel throughout the EU, but this right is not reciprocated for Bulgaria, Cyprus, Poland and Romania.

[2] HC 395, paras 24 and 25. For the list of visa countries, see HC 395, App 1.

[3] Immigration (Leave to Enter and Remain) Order 2000, SI 2000/1161, art 2, and HC 395 para 24 (amended by HC 645, which came into force on 13 November 2005) and para 25A (inserted by HC 704). The requirement for prior entry clearance now applies to all non-visa nationals who do not have a right of abode. These are, British Nationals (Overseas) (BN(O)s), British Overseas Territories citizens (BOTCs), British Overseas citizens (BOCs), British Protected Persons (BPPs) and persons who under the British Nationality Act 1981 are British subjects: HC 395, para 24(2), as inserted by HC 645.

[4] See the Nationality, Immigration and Asylum Act 2002, 88A, as amended by the Crime and Courts Act 2013, s 52, and the Crime and Courts Act 2013 (Commencement No 1 and Transitional and Saving Provision) Order 2013, SI 2013/1042.

8.3 Section 55 of the Borders, Citizenship and Immigration Act 2009[1] requires the UK Border Agency to carry out its existing functions in a way that takes into account the need to safeguard and promote the welfare of children in the UK. It does not impose any new functions, or override existing functions. Entry Clearance and Immigration Officers considering applications for entry clearance/leave to enter must make decisions affecting children with due regard to section 55.

There has been a wealth of decided cases on the best interests of children and the extent of the Secretary of State's duties under section 55 of the 2009 Act, following the Supreme Court decision in *ZH (Tanzania) v Secretary of State for the Home Department*[2], see for example *Omotunde (best interests – Zambrano applied – Razgar) Nigeria*[3], *Mundeba* (s 55 and para 297(i)(f))[4] and, *R (on the application of T) v Secretary of State for the Home Department.*[5] These are dealt with in more detail in CHAPTER 11 below.

[1] In force from 2 November 2009; Borders, Citizenship and Immigration Act 2009 (Commencement No 1) Order 2009, SI 2009/2731.
[2] [2011] UKSC 4, [2011] 2 All ER 783, [2011] 2 WLR 148.
[3] [2011] UKUT 247 (IAC).
[4] [2013] UKUT 88(IAC).
[5] [2011] EWHC 1850 (Admin), [2011] All ER (D) 224 (Oct).

CATEGORIES OF VISITOR

8.4 Visitors to the UK constitute by far the largest single category of passenger passing through the immigration control and the majority leave within the period of their leave to enter.[1] Save for visitors in transit, medical visitors, some of the special visitors like academics and subject to the additional requirements for marriage and civil partnership visitors, the same considerations apply whatever the purpose of the visit, although the purpose may influence the decision whether or not to admit. Independent tourists are likely to receive less attention from immigration officers than persons coming to visit relatives and friends who have themselves come from overseas and settled in the country. Another factor influencing the immigration officer's assessment of whether a person is a genuine visitor or not is the country from which a visitor comes and the general standard of living there. The IDI advise that the proposed purpose of the visit must bear some reasonable relationship to the financial means of the passenger and his or her family, social and economic background and that ties to the home country and previous immigration history and visits to the UK, are also matters to be taken into account.[2] From the immigration statistics it used to be possible to calculate the ratio of admissions to refusals for nationals of different countries.[3] They invariably showed a much higher refusal rate from countries such as Ghana, Nigeria, Pakistan, Bangladesh and Jamaica (whose nationals all require visas)[4] compared with the US, Canada, Australia or New Zealand (whose nationals do not). Nowadays, the Home Office publishes 'selected' statistics, which makes this information less easy to find.

[1] Former IDI (Mar 10), Ch 2, s 1, para 1 – UKBA archive website.
[2] IDI Modernised Guidance, General Visitors, 14 July 2014: 'Establishing credibility and intentions'. See also **8.12** below.
[3] See eg *Control of Immigration Statistics* – UK, published annually by HMSO.
[4] The refusal rate for Jamaican nationals drastically increased from 1 in 650 in 1984 to 1 in 67 in 1991 to 1 in 23 in 1999, which compared with a 1 in 2,014 refusal rate for US nationals in 1991, falling to 1 in 4,390 in 1999: *Control of Immigration Statistics*: UK (Cm 4876, October 2000) Table 3.2. Recent statistics (Cm 6053 Nov 2003) reveal a 500% increase in

refusal of entry clearance for Jamaican nationals, from 425 Jamaicans refused entry in 2001 compared with 2635 refused the following year. Similar increases have occurred for nationals from Zimbabwe, Kenya and the DRC. See further *Report of the Independent Monitor* June 2004 (the annual report of the independent monitor of entry clearance refusals); Target Caribbean: *The rise in visitor refusals from the Caribbean* (JCWI, 1990); S Leigh *An Analysis of Racial Discrimination in Law and Practice of Immigration Control*; also CRE 'Immigration Control Procedures; Report of a Formal Investigation' (1985) p 78. Discrimination on the basis of nationality and ethnic origin is expressly authorised by ministerial authorisations under the Race Relations Act 1976, s 19D inserted by the Race Relations (Amendment) Act 2000; these are set out in IDI Ch 1, s 11, Annexes EE1 and EE3. Section 19D still operates despite the passing of the Equality Act 2010. See CHAPTER 1, above.

8.5 The high refusal rates from West Africa and the Indian subcontinent were institutionalised by the late 1980s by making citizens of Bangladesh, Ghana, India, Nigeria, Pakistan, Sri Lanka, and Uganda, amongst others,[1] by requiring them to obtain a prior entry clearance even if they only wish to come for a visit, although they are Commonwealth countries with allegiance to the Crown, whose nationals are not aliens, nor 'foreign nationals' for the purpose of registration with the police.[2] The list of countries whose nationals require a visa now includes Jamaica, and all the refugee producing countries including Afghanistan, Iran, Iraq, Sudan and Zimbabwe. There is a common list of countries, whose nationals must have a visa to enter the European Union (known as the European common visa list), but the UK or Ireland have not signed up to these measures and they do not apply to either country.[3] Special arrangements are in force for tourist groups from the People's Republic of China, pursuant to the Approved Destination Status agreement signed in January 2005.[4]

[1] HC 395, Appendix 1. The imposition of a visa requirement on Commonwealth citizens is not *ultra vires*: *R v Secretary of State for the Home Department, ex p Suresh Kumar* [1986] Imm AR 420. Now the whole of the Commonwealth, except a few Caribbean countries (not including Jamaica or Guyana), Australia, Canada, New Zealand, and South Africa are included as visa countries.
[2] HC 395, paras 325–326 (substituted by HC 194 from 1 February 2005).
[3] Council Regulation (EC) 539/01 (OJ 2001 L 81/1), as amended by Regulation 453/03 (OJ 2003 L 69/10). See CHAPTER 6 above.
[4] See HC 486, amending HC 395 with effect from 5 April 2005. See HC 395, para 56G.

8.6 People may visit this country for a variety of reasons – as tourists, to see relatives or friends, to transact business, to take part in a conference or in some sporting competition or to seek medical treatment. A visit is any temporary stay in the UK for a purpose which does not place the person in a different category of the Immigration Rules[1]. It is perfectly proper for a person to seek entry as a visitor in order to give evidence at his or her own appeal,[2] to take over domestic responsibilities temporarily or to care for a sick relative,[3] to be a temporary child minder for a relative,[4] to visit a spouse who is a student[5] or a working holidaymaker,[6] or for the purpose of marriage or entering into a civil partnership[7]. Overseas doctors coming to take the Professional and Linguistic Assessment Board (PLAB) test to demonstrate their knowledge of English and their medical expertise used to come in as visitors, but since 15 March 2005 a specific category was created within the Immigration Rules for them.[8]

[1] *Secretary of State for the Home Department v Yi* [1993] Imm AR 519; *Kelada v Secretary of State for the Home Department* [1991] Imm AR 400.

[2] *Patel (Chhaganbhai Chhitaram) v Visa Officer, Bombay* [1991] Imm AR 97; *Patel v Entry Clearance Officer, Bombay* [1991] Imm AR 273. In Gaud (16386) 1999 2 IAS No 6, the Tribunal held that visitor was the correct category for someone in the UK awaiting trial for a criminal offence. The IDI 'Modernised Guidance': General Visitors, 14 July 2014 provides in the section 'Arrivals at UK ports with an appeal outstanding' that persons must not be granted leave to enter at a UK port for the sole purpose of attending their hearing if they are appealing against refusal of entry clearance, or appealing from abroad against a previous refusal of leave to enter at a UK port. Oddly, the guidance continues: 'A person arriving at a UK port with an outstanding appeal still has the right to seek entry as a visitor.' In any event, the guidance would not seem to preclude a person seeking entry clearance as a visitor in advance of their arrival, such entry clearance acting as leave to enter upon arrival.

[3] IDI, Ch 17 (employment outside the rules), s 2 (carers).

[4] *Entry Clearance Officer, Manilla v Magalso* [1993] Imm AR 293; IDI (Feb/06), Ch 2, s 1, Annex B, para 7.

[5] *Secretary of State for the Home Department v Xi* [1993] Imm AR 519.

[6] *Deen (9563)* unreported; referred to in [1993] INLP 73.

[7] Visits for marriage and civil partnership (HC 395, paras 56D–56F) are dealt with below.

[8] Doctors who qualify overseas and wish to come to the UK to sit their PLAB test are now dealt with by HC 395, paras 75A–75F. See also **9.69** below. Further opportunities for foreign national doctors educated abroad to practice in the UK have been limited by change of Immigration Rules HC1016 from 3 April 2006; see *Odelola v Secretary of State for the Home Department* [2009] UKHL 25, [2009] 3 All ER 1061, [2009] 1 WLR 1230 (20 May 2009).

8.7 The varieties of visitor who can enter the UK are wide, and Rule 6 of the Immigration Rules[1] defines different types of visitor including business visitor,[2] academic visitor,[3] visiting professor,[4] sports visitor,[5] entertainer visitor,[6] and special visitor.[7] There are other categories not having a specific definition within Rule 6, HC 395, but which are provided for in the body of the Rules, or are otherwise discussed in the IDI.[8] These include visitors under the Approved Destination Status (ADS) agreement with China,[9] persons seeking leave to enter the UK to attend an appeal against refusal of leave to enter,[10] visiting archaeologists,[11] carers,[12] child minders for relatives,[13] visitors from country A entering the UK to seek entry to country B,[14] including settlement visas in a third county.[15]

We deal with some of these categories below. Previously, visits organised through the British Universities North America Club (BUNAC), or visits by unpaid volunteers for certain charitable organisations and registered charities were dealt with by the IDI's, but are now dealt with under Tier 5 (Youth Mobility Scheme) and Tier 5 (Temporary Worker – Charity Worker) respectively.

[1] Following amendment by HC 1113 from 27 November 2008.

[2] A person granted leave to enter or remain under HC 395, paras 46G–L, 75A–F, or 75G–M; and see IDI 'Modernised Guidance, Business Visitors, 1 October 2013.

[3] A person from an overseas academic institution or who is highly qualified in his own field of expertise seeking leave to enter the UK to carry out research and associated activities for his own purposes; and see IDI 'Modernised Guidance', Business Visitors, 1 October 2013, section on Academic Visitors.

[4] A person who is seeking leave to enter the UK as an academic professor to accompany students who are studying here on Study Abroad Programmes; and see IDI 'Modernised Guidance', Business Visitors, 1 October 2013, section on Visiting professors and teachers accompanying student.

[5] A person granted leave to enter or remain under HC 395, paras 46M–R; and see IDI Modernised Guidance, Sports Visitors, 23 September 2013.

[6] A person granted leave to enter or remain under HC 395, paras 46S–X; and see IDI Modernised Guidance, Entertainer Visitors, 16 June 2014.

[7] A person granted leave to a short-term visit in a variety of categories set out within Rule 6 of HC 395, and discussed further at **8.18** below.

8   IDI 'Modernised Guidance', General Visitors, 14 July 2014.
9   HC 395, para 56G–J; and see IDI Modernised Guidance, Visitor under the Approved Destination Status (ADS) agreement with China, 26 September 2013.
10 Although appellants coming to the UK to attend their appeals have no right to enter for the sole purpose of attending the appeal, appellants can be admitted as visitors if they can satisfy the immigration officer that only a visit is intended, that they will leave the UK regardless of the outcome of their appeal and that they otherwise qualify for entry under the rules – see footnote 2 to para **8.6** above.
11 IDI Modernised Guidance, General Visitors, section on 'Archaeological excavations'
12 IDI Ch 17 (employment outside the rules), 4 December 2013, s 2 carers.
13 IDI Modernised Guidance, General Visitors, 14 July 2014, section on Child minders for relatives. See also Entry Clearance Guidance, Visit and Transit, VAT 24 – Child Minders for Relatives, 11 December 2013.
14 IDI Modernised Guidance, Transit Visitors, 3 July 2014, and Entry Clearance Guidance, Visit and Transit, VAT 25 – Visitors seeking visas to settlement for other countries, 11 December 2013.
15 IDI Modernised Guidance, Transit Visitors, 3 July 2014, and Entry Clearance Guidance, Visit and Transit, VAT 25 – Visitors seeking visas to settlement for other countries, 11 December 2013.

GENERAL RULES ON ADMISSION

8.8 The rules relating to the admission of visitors are contained in HC 395, paragraphs 40–46. The Home Office's IDI and Modernised Guidance and the UKBA's visa services website Entry Clearance Guidance give further guidance.[1] Under paragraph 41 a passenger seeking entry as a general visitor must satisfy the immigration authority that he:

(i)   is genuinely seeking entry as a general visitor for a limited period as stated by him, not exceeding 6 months, or not exceeding 12 months in the case of a person seeking entry to accompany an academic visitor, provided in the latter case the visitor accompanying the academic visitor has entry clearance; and

(ii)   intends to leave the UK at the end of the period of the visit as stated by him; and does not intend to live for extended periods in the United Kingdom through frequent or successive visits; and

(iii)   does not intend to take employment in the UK; and

(iv)   does not intend to produce goods or provide services within the UK, including the selling of goods or services direct to members of the public; and

(v)   save to the extent provided by paragraph 43A, does not intend to undertake a course of study; and

(vi)   will maintain and accommodate himself and any dependants adequately out of resources available to him without recourse to public funds or taking employment, or will, with any dependants, be maintained and accommodated adequately by relatives or friends who can demonstrate they are able and intend to do so, and are legally present in the United Kingdom, or will be at the time of the visit; and

(vii)   can meet the cost of the return or onward journey; and

(viii) is not a child under the age of 18.[2]

Leave to enter is discretionary and the immigration officer must be satisfied that each of the requirements of paragraph 41 is met;[3] otherwise, leave will be refused.[4]

HC 1113 has added the following four requirements for entry to the existing list set out in HC 395, para 41. The visitor:

(ix)   does not intend to do any of the activities covered by the new rules for business visitors, sports visitors or entertainer visitors;

(x)   does not, during his or her visit, intend to marry or form a civil partnership, or to give notice of marriage or civil partnership;

(xi)   does not intend to receive private medical treatment during the visit; and

(xii)   is not in transit to a country outside the common travel area.

A feature of the changes is that other types of visitor cannot switch half way through their visit into the general visitor category except child visitors (see paragraph 44(iii)) and a general visitor cannot generally switch into any of those other categories other than a medical visit.

On 25 June 2008, the government announced proposals to introduce a requirement of sponsorship licences for sponsors in the UK to sponsor family visitors. This has not yet happened.

¹   Modernised Guidance 'Visiting' and Entry Clearance Guidance (ECG) (formerly DSPs), Visit and Transit section. See the government website: www.gov.uk/government/collections/visiting -modernised-guidance and the ECGs: www.gov.uk/government/collections/visit-and-transit-e ntry-clearance-guidance.
²   HC 395, para 41(viii) as inserted by HC 819.
³   HC 395, para 42.
⁴   HC 395, para 43.

Time limits and other conditions on stay

8.9   The immigration authority will always impose a time limit on the period of the visitor's stay and of any dependants. A period of six months will normally be appropriate[1] unless there are particular circumstances, such as restricted returnability, or if the passenger is booked out on a particular charter flight, or the visitor's case ought to be subject to early review by the Home Office.[2] The courts have said that it is the job of immigration officers to consider what period would be suitable given the visitor's financial and other circumstances.[3] Persons who are extremely vague about their length of stay may fail to satisfy the immigration authorities that they could support themselves without working for the period of visit as stated by them,[4] or the length of the proposed visit may be too vague.[5] On the other hand, where, in the nature of the visit, it is not possible to give an exact date for leaving, leave should still be given if the visit is for an ascertainable period of less than six months and the visitors can show that they would leave when the purpose of the visit had been achieved.[6] Old cases are not necessarily a good guide to the current practice and the most recent versions of the IDI, Modernised Guidance and Entry Clearance Guidance are usually more reliable guides.

In *Oppong (visitor: length of stay) Ghana*[7], the UT held that whilst Paragraph 41(i) of HC 395 requires a person seeking leave to enter the United Kingdom as a general visitor (other than to accompany an academic visitor) to show that he or she 'is genuinely seeking entry as a general visitor for a limited period as stated by him, not exceeding 6 months', an application for a visit visa which, if granted, could result in permission to spend more than six of twelve months in the United Kingdom is likely to be scrutinised rigorously but it is wrong to refuse someone entry clearance as a general visitor just because they have spent more than six of the last twelve months in the United Kingdom. In certain circumstances a person can utilise paragraph 41 in order to visit the United Kingdom to provide temporary care for a person present here.

Under the Immigration (Leave to Enter and Remain) Order 2000[8] visit visas now act as multiple entry visas for the period of the visa's validity.[9] On each entry, a holder is treated as being granted six months' leave to enter if six months or more remain on the visa's period of validity, or for the visa's remaining period of validity, if less than six months.[10] The current IDI on visitors provides that passengers granted leave to enter as general visitors should normally be admitted on either Code 5N or on Code 3 for six months. Leave to enter as a visitor lapses upon leaving the common travel area.[11]

[1] HC 395, paras 42 and 44 and see IDI Modernised Guidance, General Visitors, 14 July 2014. For visitors entering the UK under the Approved Destination Status (ADS) Agreement with the People's Republic of China the maximum period is 30 days: HC 395, para 56G–H, inserted by HC 486 from 5 April 2005, but academic visitors and other 'special' categories may be granted up to 12 months: IDI Modernised Guidance, General Visitor, 14 July 2014.

[2] *Visa Officer, Aden v Thabet* [1977] Imm AR 75.

[3] *R v Secretary of State for Home Affairs, ex p Singh (Harnaik)* [1969] 2 All ER 867, [1969] 1 WLR 835, DC; *Khan* (18 April 1969, unreported), CA, referred to in *Immigration Officer, London (Heathrow Airport) v Schönenburger* [1975] Imm AR 7 at 9.

[4] *Immigration Officer, London (Heathrow Airport) v Schönenburger* [1975] Imm AR 7.

[5] *Hashim v Secretary of State for the Home Department* [1982] Imm AR 113 – a vague period of medical treatment.

[6] *R v Secretary of State for the Home Department, ex p Arjumand* [1983] Imm AR 123, QBD (a period depended on father's health and winding up of his business); *Patel v Entry Clearance Officer, Bombay* [1991] Imm AR 273 (entry clearance sought for visit to give evidence at entry clearance appeal, no date for the appeal having been fixed). The IDI state that the likely timescale for the appeal should be considered before leave is granted: IDI (Mar 10), Ch 2, s 2.18.

[7] [2011] UKUT 431 (IAC).

[8] SI 2000/1161.

[9] IDI Modernised Guidance; General Visitor, 14 July 2014, section on 'Multi-entry visa'.

[10] Ibid.

[11] See Immigration Act 1971, s 3(4), which provides that all leave lapses upon leaving the CTA, However, the effect of that provision is now much restricted by the insertion of ss 3A and 3B into the 1971 Act by the Immigration and Asylum Act 1999, and the Immigration (Leave to Enter and Remain) Order 2000, SI 2000/1161. However, art 13(2)(a) of that Order provides that leave to enter as a visitor does still lapse upon leaving the CTA.

Frequency of visits

8.10 In *Powell*[1] it was held that as long as the appellant was a genuine visitor who intended to leave the country within the period stated by her, the immigration officer should not have been concerned with the number of visits that had been made. The Entry Clearance Guidance points out that there is no restriction on the number of visits a person may make to the UK nor any requirement that a specified time must elapse between successive visits, and the fact that a person has made a series of visits with only brief intervals between them would not, in the absence of any other relevant factors, constitute a sufficient ground for refusal.[2] But a visitor should not normally spend more than six out of any 12 months in this country.[3] A change of circumstances after a visitor's visa was issued is not necessarily a ground for cancellation, if the passenger is seeking a limited period of stay.[4] However the Modernised Guidance also provides that Visitors must not be living in the UK for extended periods because of frequent, successive visits.[5]

Visitors are normally prohibited from taking employment,[6] and are required to maintain and accommodate themselves and any dependants without recourse to public funds.[7] They may also be subject to other conditions to register with the police, to report to an immigration officer or the Secretary of State and to a condition about residence.[8] The power to impose these last two conditions was created by section 16 of the UK Borders Act 2007, in force from 31 January 2008.[9] Registration with the police goes a long way back. Visitors from the Commonwealth never have to register with the police, and foreign nationals may only be required to do so in exceptional cases.[10] The new conditions look as if they are intended to replace registration with the police.

[1]   (3129) unreported.
[2]   ECG VAT 1.5.
[3]   ECG VAT 1.5. But exceptions may be made in the case of visitors for private medical treatment and occasionally a business visitor (eg where machinery is being installed or faults being diagnosed and corrected). See also *Oppong (visitor: length of stay) Ghana* [2011] UKUT 431 (IAC), discussed in para **8.9** above.
[4]   *Corte* (12708) (1996) 10 INLP.
[5]   See Modernised Guidance, General Visitors, section on Frequency and duration of visits, 14 July 2014. The same section also provides that this is not a hard and fast rule and you must consider the circumstances of each case on an individual basis and gives guidance on assessing residence through successive visits.
[6]   HC 395, para 42.
[7]   HC 395, para 41(vi).
[8]   Immigration Act 1971, s 3(1)(c), as amended by the UK Borders Act 2007, s 16.
[9]   By operation of SI 2008/99.
[10] HC 395, para 325. See further 3.50.

Genuine visit

8.11 Before granting admission the immigration authority has to be satisfied that the applicant is genuinely seeking entry for the period of the visit as stated by him or her and does not intend to overstay or take employment. An application should not be refused on the basis of one ambiguous answer in interview, particularly by someone who has previously complied with visit requirements.[1] If the immigration authority is satisfied that the applicant will leave, but not within the period stated, this does not necessarily mean it is not a genuine visit.[2] For reasons we have discussed, the exact length of stay may be difficult to ascertain, and it is quite wrong for the immigration officer to refuse leave, merely because he or she thinks the passenger may seek an extension of stay.[3] Most disputed cases, however, are concerned with visitors who, according to the immigration authorities, intend to stay on at the end of their leave. In considering these cases the person's incentives to stay or leave are clearly of great importance. In one case the evidence was that a widower, whose two sons lived in England, had money of his own and property in India and could not live in a cold climate because of his rheumatoid arthritis. This showed a clear incentive to leave at the end of the stated period of visit and persuaded a tribunal to reverse earlier decisions to refuse entry.[4] Employment to return to in another country may well be a material consideration, and evidence confirmatory of such employment and a period of leave is frequently helpful.[5]

But loss of such employment between issue of entry clearance and arrival here might amount to a change of circumstances that enables the immigration officer to go behind the entry clearance and cancel the deemed leave to enter.[6]

[1]   *R v Entry Clearance Officer, Chennai, ex p Sundamoorthy* (CO 4896/99) (20 June 2000, unreported).

[2]   *Visa Officer, Cairo v Malek* [1979–80] Imm AR 111.

[3]   *R v Secretary of State for the Home Department, ex p Arjumand* [1983] Imm AR 123, QBD.

[4]   *Singh (Bhagat) v Entry Clearance Officer, New Delhi* [1978] Imm AR 134. See also *Afzal v Entry Clearance Officer, Islamabad* [2002] UKIAT 02732, where a Pakistani farmer's proposed visit to his Birmingham-based cousin to explore UK farming methods was upheld as genuine. Conversely, a lack of apparent incentive to return from a family visit might be fatal to an application: see eg *R v Entry Clearance Officer, ex p Abu-Gidary* (CO 965/1999) (8 March 2000, unreported).

[5]   *Huda v Entry Clearance Officer, Dacca* [1976] Imm AR 109; see also *Visa Officer, Cairo v Ashraf* [1979–80] Imm AR 45. The onus is on the applicant to prove her case, not on the ECO to undertake investigations about claimed employment: *E (Cameroon)* [2004] UKIAT 00077 'Reported'.

[6]   Under HC 395, para 321A(ii). See further **3.50**.

8.12 Other factors which may be taken into account in deciding whether a person genuinely seeks entry as a visitor include the family's immigration history,[1] the length and purpose of the visit and their means and position in their own country.[2] Previous immigration history and evidence of a pattern of family migration, both here and abroad, may be taken into account. The Modernised Guidance state that the decision maker must consider if a visitor's proposed purpose in coming to the UK is reasonable taking into account their and their family's financial means and social and economic background.[3] Sometimes the Tribunal is not clear about what is or is not a relevant factor. For example, whether possession of a UK passport is relevant or not is the subject of contradictory decisions. In *Mohamed Din*[4] the fact that the applicant was a non-patrial UK passport holder, and therefore unlikely to be removed from the UK if he overstayed, was held not of itself to be a relevant consideration when determining whether the applicant intended more than a visit, unless there were indications of bad faith. His appeal was allowed. But in *Patel*[5] a differently constituted Tribunal held that the possession of a UK passport was a matter which the immigration authority must take into account, and this together with other factors, meant that the applicant had been properly refused a visit. The position probably no longer needs resolving, because of the new nationality provisions, giving automatic British citizenship to some of these visitors and a right to register as British citizens to others.[6]

[1]   *R v Secretary of State for the Home Department, ex p Kurumoorthy* [1998] Imm AR 401; *R v Entry Clearance Officer, ex p Abu-Gidary* (CO 965/1999) (8 March 2000, unreported), distinguishing *R v Entry Clearance Officer, ex p Edebali* (CO 3237/97) (21 October 1997, unreported), where Sedley J disapproved the adverse inferences drawn from previous family migration. See also *Dalvi* [2002] UKIAT 07201, where the Tribunal relied on a family pattern of migration, as well as evasion and embellishment by the applicant and her sponsor, to uphold a refusal of entry clearance for a family visit.

[2]   Persons of means and position in their own country might well be accepted as genuine visitors even if their declared intention was 'only to visit the maze at Hampton Court', but where it was proposed that a considerable sum of money should be expended by a family with limited resources, the immigration authorities were entitled to consider carefully the reasons for the expenditure: *Manmohan Singh v Entry Clearance Officer, New Delhi* [1975] Imm AR 118, IAT.

[3]   See Modernised Guidance, General Visitors, section on Credibility and Intentions, 14 July 2014. Ties to their home country and previous immigration history and visits to the UK are also relevant to the genuineness of a visit. However, the mere fact that parents on whom a

young person finishing education was financially dependent lived in the UK did not justify refusal of entry clearance for a visit to them: *R v Entry Clearance Officer, Chennai, ex p Sundamoorthy* (CO 4896/99) (20 June 2000, unreported).

4   *Mohamed Din v Entry Clearance Officer, Karachi* [1978] Imm AR 56.
5   *Patel v Entry Clearance Officer, Bombay* [1978] Imm AR 154.
6   See **2.16–2.22**, above.

8.13 In considering an applicant's intentions, a distinction has to be drawn between a wish and an intention. The distinction was drawn in another context in *Masood v Immigration Appeal Tribunal*,[1] where Glidewell LJ said that a wish is not an intention, unless there is some reasonable prospect of its being fulfilled. The previous expression of a wish to settle or study in the UK is not necessarily prejudicial to a subsequent application for a visit.[2] Otherwise, someone who discloses an earlier wish to settle could never subsequently qualify as a *bona fide* visitor.[3] On the other hand, the distinction between a wish and an intention will disappear if, taking that and the other circumstances of the case into consideration, there is a strong inference of an intention not just to visit but to stay for study or work.[4] Previous exceptions to this rule, for instance, allowing doctors present in the UK to undertake a Professional and Linguistic Assessment Board (PLAB) test to switch to employment in the UK thereafter, no longer exist.[5] A person coming to look after children and learn English may qualify as a visitor, although the application may look like an 'au pair' application, so long as the intention is to leave at the end of the visit and what is sought is not employment,[6] but if the purpose is quite different from a visit, for example, to claim asylum, seeking entry as a visitor will make the person an illegal entrant.[7]

1   [1992] Imm AR 69, CA at 78. See also *R v Immigration Appeal Tribunal, ex p Shaikh* [1981] 3 All ER 29, [1981] 1 WLR 1107, QBD.
2   *Patel v Immigration Appeal Tribunal* [1983] Imm AR 76, CA, per Dillon LJ at 80, CA; *Ex p Arjumand*, above.
3   *Entry Clearance Officer, Hong Kong v Lai* [1974] Imm AR 98; *El Atrash* (3209) and *Ghailane* (3648) where the appellant had made an application in the alternative either for settlement to join his wife and children or to visit them; see also *Karachiwalla* (4726) where the appellant was held to be a genuine visitor despite a wish to settle in the UK with her family.
4   *R v Secretary of State for the Home Department, ex p Brakwah* [1989] Imm AR 366, DC; see further *Adesina v Secretary of State for the Home Department* [1988] Imm AR 442, CA (both illegal entry cases).
5   Having been deleted by HC 1113 with effect from 28 November 2008.
6   *Gusakov* (11672). *Entry Clearance Officer, Bombay v Shaikh (Salmaben)* [2002] UKIAT 02732.
7   *Bugdaycay v Secretary of State for the Home Department* [1987] AC 514; *Al-Zahrany (Rasmish) v Secretary of State for the Home Department* [1995] Imm AR 510, CA. See also *R (on the application of Montezano) v Secretary of State for the Home Department* [2001] EWHC Admin 255 (Admin), [2001] 1 WLR 1673 where the Administrative Court held that, where an entrant's answers to the immigration officer admit two possible bases for entry (visit or study) the IO does not act reasonably or lawfully if he or she considers only one of the activities.

8.14 It is always the applicant's intentions which count rather than those of the sponsoring relative or friend in this country.[1] It is the intention on the present visit that is critical but if there has been a previous deception the visit will fall to be refused on general grounds.[2] The fact that the sponsor is likely to ensure the applicant's departure is a relevant factor to be taken into account, since it tends to show an intention to depart.[3] The Modernised Guidance states that it may be appropriate and acceptable to take into account promises of maintenance and/or accommodation made by a sponsor.[4]

1 *Ragavan* (3418) and cases cited therein.
2 See general grounds for refusal of entry clearance in HC 395, eg para 320(7A) (mandatory) where false representations have been made or false documents or information have been submitted (whether or not material to the application, and whether or not to the applicant's knowledge), or material facts have not been disclosed, in relation to the application, and para 320(15) (discretionary) whether or not to the holder's knowledge, the making of false representations or the failure to disclose any material fact for the purpose of obtaining an immigration employment document. See above CHAPTER 3.
3 *Entry Clearance Officer, New Delhi v Kumar* [1978] Imm AR 185; *Chaudhury* (3157).
4 See Modernised Guidance, General Visitors, section on Undertakings and Guarantees, 14 July 2014. Paragraph 35 of the Immigration Rules allows immigration officers to ask a sponsor to give an undertaking in writing that they will be responsible for the applicant's maintenance and accommodation for the duration of their stay. Paragraph 320(14) allows a person to be refused entry on the grounds that their sponsor has refused to give such an undertaking when requested to do so.

Maintenance and accommodation

8.15 The ability of visitors to maintain and accommodate themselves using resources available to them without taking employment or becoming a charge on public funds is always an important factor.[1] Obviously, ordinary tourists will need to have their own funds. The Modernised Guidance invite the decision maker to consider:

(a)   the level of funds available to them and anyone with them and if this is enough to cover their expenses for the duration of the visit;

(b)   what their plans are in the UK and the duration of their stay; and

(c)   what arrangements have already been made for their accommodation.[2]

In the case of persons staying with relatives or friends, it does not matter whether they maintain themselves or are maintained by their relatives. The Immigration Rules now allow indirect reliance on public funds provided to the sponsor, so long as the passenger's presence does not result in entitlement to an increased amount.[3] But notwithstanding this relaxation, the provisions regarding visitors make it much more difficult for poor people to be allowed to visit this country than the well-off. As well as being less likely to be accepted as genuine visitors, they have a much greater chance of being rejected on maintenance and accommodation grounds, even though, as 'persons from abroad' for the purposes of social security and homelessness legislation, they are ineligible to claim any assistance.[4] Since 1994 the Immigration Rules have provided that a sponsor may be asked to give an undertaking in writing to be responsible for the visitor's maintenance and accommodation for the period of any leave granted, including any further variation, and according to the current Modernised Guidance this includes visitors.[5]

1 HC 395, para 41(vi).
2 See Modernised Guidance, General Visitors, section on Maintenance and Accommodation, 14 July 2014. If a visitor is dependent on a sponsor (family or friend) to provide accommodation or financial support during their visit, the ECO must be satisfied the sponsor is: Legally present in the UK, or legally present at the time of their visit (if they are a visitor themselves); Able and intending to provide this support for the duration of the visitor's stay. In particular they must consider if the sponsor and visitor have a genuine relationship; where they met; how they maintain communication and how often they communicate, and the

sponsor's previous history of sponsoring visitors. According to the guidance previous failure to support visitors may call into question their intention and ability to do so for this application.

3   HC 395, para 6A.
4   See eg Income Support (General) Regulations 1987, SI 1987/1967, reg 21(3)(a), Sch 7; Housing Benefit Regulations 2006, SI 2006/213, reg 10; Asylum and Immigration Act 1996, s 11; Immigration and Asylum Act 1999, s 115; Social Security (Immigration and Asylum) (Consequential Amendments) Regulations 2000, SI 2000/636; see CHAPTER 14 below.
5   HC 395, para 35. See **8.14**, fn 4, above.

EXTENSION OF STAY AS A VISITOR

8.16 Six months is, as a general rule, the maximum permitted leave which may be granted to a visitor.[1] A visitor who has been given less than six months on entry may, however, extend his or her visit up to the six-month period.[2] To obtain such an extension a visitor must continue to meet the requirements for a visit, in particular the maintenance and accommodation provisions and the ability to meet the cost of the return or onward journey. The Rules now provides that a period of overstaying of 28 days or less will be disregarded.[3] If these requirements continue to be met an extension may be granted,[4] but otherwise refusal is mandatory.[5] In *YT (HC 395 paragraph 44 – extension of stay) Belarus*,[6] the AIT held that, prior to its amendment by HC 1113 with effect from 27 November 2008, para 44 of HC 395 (requirements for an extension of stay as a visitor) was not limited in its application to persons in the UK on a visitor's visa and there was no legal impediment to someone switching from leave under the sector-based scheme to leave as a visitor. However, the new wording of para 44(iii) reverses this decision. Visitors under the Approved Destination Status Agreement with China are not allowed to extend the length of their stay.[7] The Modernised Guidance specifically consider organ donors providing that applicants coming to donate an organ to private patients are assessed under the 'visitor for private medical treatment' Rules and applicants coming to the UK to donate an organ to an NHS patient or to be assessed as a suitable donor are considered outside of the Immigration Rules.[8] Where child visitors wish to have an extension of stay, within the maximum six-month period allowed for visits, they will have to be able meet the cost of their return or onward journey, be under the age of 18, can demonstrate that there are suitable arrangements for their care in the UK and that they have a parent or guardian in their home country or country of habitual residence who is responsible for their care.[9]

1   HC 395, para 44. A person accompanying an academic visitor as a general visitor may be granted up to 12 months. Also the Modernised Guidance, General Visitors, 14 July 2014
2   HC 395, para 44(ii). Visitors under the ADS Agreement with China may not extend their leave and are only granted a maximum of 30 days: HC 395, para 56G – J, and see Modernised Guidance, Visitor under the Approved Destination Status (ADS) agreement with China, 26 September 2013.
3   HC 395, para 44 (iv).
4   HC 395, para 45.
5   HC 395, para 46.
6   [2009] UKAIT 00003.
7   HC 395, para 56G – J, and see Modernised Guidance, Visitor under the Approved Destination Status (ADS) agreement with China, 26 September 2013.
8   See Modernised Guidance, General Visitors, section on Organ Donors, 14 July 2014.

[9] HC 395, para 46D, inserted by HC 819 with effect from 12 February 2006, and See Modernised Guidance, Child Visitors, 27 September 2013.

Departure and return

8.17 A visit visa operates as leave to enter on each occasion on which the holder enters the UK during the period of its validity. The holder will be treated as having been granted six months' leave to enter beginning on the date of arrival in the UK, where six months or more remain of the period of the visa's validity, but less if the period left on the visa is less than six months.[1] To operate as leave to enter, the entry clearance must be endorsed with any conditions to which it is subject.[2]

[1] Immigration (Leave to Enter and Remain) Order 2000, SI 2000/1161, art 4(1), (2). See the problems posed by this in relation to the six-month period for fiancé(e) s in rule 284(i) in *FB (HC 395 para 284(i)) Bangladesh* [2006] UKAIT 00030.

[2] SI 2000/1161, art 3(3)(a).

Particular visits

8.18 As well as General Visitors the Rules now provide for particular categories of visits or Special Visitors including as follows:

(a)   a person granted leave as a child visitor under paras 46A–F;

(b)   a person granted leave to enter as a business visitor under paras 46G – L;

(c)   a person granted leave to enter as a sports visitor under paras 46M-R;

(d)   a person granted leave to enter as an entertainer visitor under paras 46S–46X;

(e)   a person granted leave as a visitor in transit under paras 47–50;

(f)   a visitor granted leave for private medical treatment under paras 51–56;a person granted leave as a parent of a child at school under paras 56A–C;

(g)   a person granted leave for the purpose of marriage or civil partnership under para 56D–F;

(h)   a person granted leave to enter under the Approved Destinations Status (ADS) agreement with China under paras 56G–56J;

(i)   a person granted leave to enter as a student visitor under paras 56K–M;

(j)   a person granted leave as a prospective student under paras 82A–87;

(k)   a person granted leave to enter as a Prospective entrepreneur under paragraphs 56N–56Q of these rules. See para **8.37** below;

(l)   a person granted leave to enter as a visitor undertaking permitted paid engagements under paras 56X–56Z.

CHILD VISITORS

8.19 The category of child visitors set out in HC 395, para 46A, first introduced by HC 819 with effect from 12 February 2006, has been the subject of amendment and complete substitution, The latest version of the rule requires that the applicant:

(i) is genuinely seeking entry as a child visitor for a limited period as stated, not exceeding six months, or not exceeding 12 months to accompany an academic visitor, provided in the latter case the applicant has entry clearance; and

(ii) meets the requirements of para 41 (ii)–(iv), (vi)–(vii) and (x)–(xii); and

(iii) is under the age of 18; and

(iv) can demonstrate that suitable arrangements have been made for their travel to,[1] and reception and care in the United Kingdom; and

(v) has a parent or guardian in their home country or country of habitual residence who is responsible for their care and who confirms that they consent to the arrangements for the applicant's travel, reception and care in the United Kingdom; and

(vi) if a visa national:

    (a) the applicant holds a valid United Kingdom entry clearance for entry as an accompanied child visitor and is travelling in the company of the adult identified on the entry clearance, who is on the same occasion being admitted to the United Kingdom;[2] or

    (b) the applicant holds a valid United Kingdom entry clearance for entry as an unaccompanied child visitor; and

(via) except to the extent limited by sub-paragraph (viii), does not intend to study at a maintained school; and

(vii) if the applicant has been accepted for or intends to follow a course of study, this is to be provided by an institution which is outside the maintained sector and is:

    (a) the holder of a Sponsor Licence for Tier 4 of the Points Based System; or

    (b) the holder of valid accreditation from Accreditation UK; the Accreditation Body for Language Services (ABLS); the British Accreditation Council (BAC) or the Accreditation Service for International Colleges (ASIC), or

    (c) the holder of a valid and satisfactory full institutional inspection, review or audit by one of the following bodies: the Bridge Schools Inspectorate; the Education and Training Inspectorate; Estyn; Education Scotland; the Independent Schools Inspectorate; Office for Standards in Education; the Schools Inspection Service or the Education and Training Inspectorate Northern Ireland.

(viii) if the applicant is undertaking an exchange or educational visit only, this is to be provided by one of the following schools:

    (a) For England and Wales, maintained schools as defined under section 20(7) of the School Standards and Framework Act 1998; non-maintained special schools approved under section 342 of the Education Act 1996; independent schools as defined under section 463 of the Education Act 1996 and registered independent schools entered on the register of independent schools maintained under section 158 of the Education Act 2002; academies as defined in section 1(10) of the Academies Act 2010; city technology colleges and city colleges for technology of the arts as established under the Education Act 1996 and treated as academies under section 15(4) of the Academies Act.

    (b) For Scotland, public schools, grant-aided schools and independent fee paying schools as defined under Section 135 of the Education (Scotland) Act 1980.

    (c) For Northern Ireland, grant-aided schools as defined under Articles 10 and 11 of and Schedules 4 to 7 to the Education and Libraries (NI) Order in Council 1986; grant maintained integrated schools as defined under Article 69 of and Schedule 5 to the Education Reform

(NI) Order 1989; independent fee paying schools as defined under Article 38 of the Education and Libraries (NI) Order 1986.

The intention of these rules is that in the case of a child, who subsequently comes to the attention of the caring or educational services, there will be a record of their family or carers, both prior to, and immediately after, their arrival. If the provision of these gives cause for concern, then entry to the UK may be refused or further investigation will need to take place. Children who are accompanied by an adult, whether a family member or not, and seeking entry as visitors, will have to give details of the accompanying adult so that the nature of the journey and the relationship can be established. If the provisions of this information or the information itself gives cause for concern, either when provided or at the point of entry, then entry to the UK may be refused and further investigation may have to take place. The information and identities provided will be a record that may be assessed, if the child subsequently comes to the attention of the caring or educational services.

The concern which has prompted these rules is the concern that minors are brought to the UK for trafficking purposes or that the accompanying adult disappears and the children then claim asylum.

The effect of the most recent version of the rule is to amend the provisions as to what sort of studies a child visitor may engage in and limits the institutions at which a child visitor can study.

1   Entry Clearance Officers need to establish and record that the parent/guardian is in the home country and agrees to the child travelling. A letter of consent from the parent or guardian and a letter from the school where applicable should be provided. The guidance provides that ECO should refuse the application if they have doubts about whether consent has been given, or where there is nothing from the parent or guardian and no reasonable explanation as to why this is so. See Entry Clearance Guidance Visitors and Transit, Special Visitors, Child Visitors: VAT 03, 5 July 2013, at Section 4.

2   Entry Clearance Guidance Visitors and Transit, Special Visitors, Child Visitors: VAT 03, 5 July 2013, at Section 7.7. advises if the child obtains a multi-entry visa and does not always intend to travel with the same adult and it may be better for them to be issued with an 'unaccompanied' visa even though they may not be travelling alone. A child with an 'Unaccompanied' Child Visitor visa is able to travel with or without any other person.

STUDENT VISITORS

8.20 Previously, visitors could study during their stay provided it was not at a maintained school. However now visitors cannot study at any institution, unless they seek entry either in the new student visitor category or under the student route.[1] A general visitor can study on a permissible course which does not exceed 30 days in duration and is a recreational course and not an English language course.[2] A longer course will require a student visit visa. Under HC 395, para 56K the requirements to be met by a person seeking leave to enter the UK as a student visitor are that he or she:

(i)   is genuinely seeking entry as a student visitor for a limited period as stated by him, not exceeding six months; and

(ii)   has been accepted on a course of study which is to be provided by an institution which is:

(a)   the holder of a Sponsor licence for Tier 4 of the Points Based System, or

(b)   the holder of valid accreditation from Accreditation UK, the Accreditation Body for Language Services (ABLS), the British Accreditation Council (BAC) or the Accreditation Service for International Colleges (ASIC), or

(c)   the holder of a valid and satisfactory full institutional inspection, review or audit by one of the following bodies: Bridge Schools Inspectorate; the Education and Training Inspectorate; Estyn; Education Scotland; the Independent Schools Inspectorate; Office for Standards in Education; the Quality Assurance Agency for Higher Education; the Schools Inspection Service or the Education and Training Inspectorate Northern Ireland, or

(d)   an overseas Higher Education Institution offering only part of their programmes in the United Kingdom, holding its own national accreditation and offering programmes that are an equivalent level to a United Kingdom degree, or

(iia)   -

(a)   is enrolled on a course of study abroad equivalent to at least UK degree level study, and

(b)   has been accepted by a UK recognised body or a body in receipt of public funding as a higher education institution from the Department for Employment and Learning in Northern Ireland, the Higher Education Funding Council for England, the Higher Education Funding Council for Wales or the Scottish Funding Council to undertake research or research tuition at the UK institution, providing that-

(c)   the overseas course provider confirms that the research or research tuition is part of or relevant to the course of study mentioned in sub-paragraph (a) above, and

(d)   the student is not to be employed as a sponsored researcher under the relevant Tier 5 Government Authorised Exchange scheme, or under Tier 2 of the Points-Based System, at the UK institution; and

(iii)   intends to leave the UK at the end of his visit as stated by him; and

(iv)   does not intend to take employment in the UK;

(v)   does not intend to engage in business, to produce goods or provide services within the UK, including the selling of goods or services direct to members of the public; and

(vi)   does not intend to study at a maintained school;

(vii)   will maintain and accommodate himself and any dependants adequately out of resources available to him without recourse to public funds or taking employment; or will, with any dependants, be maintained and accommodated adequately by relatives or friends; and

(viii)   can meet the cost of the return or onward journey;

(ix)   is not a child under the age of 18; and

(x)   meets the requirements set out in para 41 (ix)–(xii).

If each of these requirements is met the student visitor may be admitted for up to six months, subject to a condition prohibiting employment and recourse to public funds.[3]

In *RS (Pakistan) v Secretary of State for the Home Department*[4] the Court of Appeal considered the situation of an appellant seeking to return to the UK to re-sit examinations, and commented that at first blush it was not clear that para 56K automatically permitted a student to return, but observed the position taken on behalf of Counsel for the Secretary of State, who confirmed in submissions that 'the Department's position that re-entry for the purpose of a re-sit is not only acceptable but is customarily accepted under the terms of Rule 56K. The Court sees no reason to question that statement of practice, which rightly acknowledges the need for provision to deal with this issue'.

1 Changes introduced on 1 September 2007. See Explanatory Memorandum to Cm 7074, para 7. In *CT (Rule 60(i), student entry clearance?) Cameroon* [2008] UKAIT 00010 (12 February 2008): the Tribunal held that a person who entered the United Kingdom with entry clearance as a short-term student prior to 1 September 2007, although subject to a condition prohibiting work, was admitted to the UK in possession of a valid entry clearance in accordance with para 57 of HC 395 and as a student not as a visitor.
2 HC 395, para 43A. See also Modernised Guidance, General Visitors, 14 July 2014, section on 'Permissible Study'.
3 HC 395, para 56L.
4 [2011] EWCA Civ 434, [2011] All ER (D) 172 (Apr).

BUSINESS VISITS

8.21 The ambit of a business visit has not always been easy to define. Under the changes made by HC 1113, which came into force on 27 November 2008, the old formula of coming 'to transact business (such as . . .)' has gone. The current Rules provide a lengthy list of who and what activities are included in the category of Business Visitor, which includes Academic Visitors[1], Visiting Professors[2], film crews and religious workers. The new requirements, set out in HC 395, para 46G (as amended by HC693 which took effect on 6 November 2014), are that the business visitor:

(i)   is genuinely seeking entry as a business visitor for not more than:
        (a)   six months; or
        (b)   twelve months if seeking entry as an academic visitor;
(ii)   meets the requirements of the general visitor sub-paras 41(ii)–(iv), subject to paragraph 46HA, (v), (vi)–(viii) and (x)–(xii); and (iii) intends to do one or more of the following during his visit:

    (a)   to carry out one of the following activities;
        (i)   to attend meetings, conferences and interviews, provided they were arranged before arrival in the UK and, if the applicant is a board-level director attending board meetings in the UK, provided they are not employed by a UK company (although they may be paid a fee for attending the meeting);
        (ii)   to attend trade fairs for promotional work only, provided they are not directly selling;
        (iii)   to arrange deals, or negotiating or signing trade agreements or contracts;
        (iv)   to carry out fact-finding missions;
        (v)   to conduct site visits;
        (vi)   to work as a driver on a genuine international route delivering goods or passengers from abroad;[3]
        (vii)   to work as a tour group courier, providing the applicant is contracted to a firm with headquarters outside the UK, is seeking entry to accompany a tour group, and will depart with that tour, or another tour organised by the same company;
        (viii)   to speak at a one-off conference which is not organised as a commercial concern, and is not making a profit for the organiser;
        (ix)   to represent a foreign manufacturer by:

(I)   carrying out installing, debugging or enhancing work for computer software companies,

(II)   servicing or repairing the manufacturer's products within the initial guarantee period, or

(III)   being briefed on the requirements of a UK customer, provided this is limited to briefing and does not include work involving use of the applicant's expertise to make a detailed assessment of a potential customer's requirements;

(x)   to represent a foreign machine manufacturer, as part of the contract of purchase and supply, in erecting and installing machinery too heavy to be delivered in one piece;

(xi)   to act as an interpreter or translator for visiting business people, provided they are all employed by, and doing the business of, the same overseas company;

(xii)   to erect, dismantle, install, service, repair or advise on the development of foreign-made machinery, provided they will only do so in the UK for up to six months;

(b)   to take part in a location shoot as a member of a film crew meaning he is a film actor, producer, director or technician paid or employed by an overseas firm other than one established in the UK and is coming to the UK for location sequences only for an overseas film;

(c)   to represent overseas news media including as a journalist, correspondent, producer or cameraman provided he is employed or paid by an overseas company and is gathering information for an overseas publication;

(d)   to act as an Academic Visitor but only if

(1)   he is an academic who is:

(A)   on sabbatical leave from an overseas academic institution to carry out research;

(B)   taking part in formal exchange arrangements with UK counterparts (including doctors);

(C)   coming to share knowledge or experience, or to hold informal discussions with their UK counterparts, or

(D)   taking part in a single conference or seminar that is not a commercial or non-profit venture;

(E)   an eminent senior doctor or dentist taking part in research, teaching or clinical practice; and

(2)   he has been working as an academic in an institution of higher education overseas or in the field of their academic expertise immediately prior to seeking entry;

(e)   to act as a Visiting Professor; subject to undertaking only a small amount of teaching for the institution hosting the students he is supervising, being employed and paid by the overseas academic institution and not intending to base himself or seek employment in the UK.

(f)   to be a secondee to a UK company which is directly contracted with the visitor's overseas company, with which it has no corporate relationship, to provide goods or services, provided the secondee remains employed and paid by the overseas company throughout the secondee's visit;

(g)   to undertake some preaching or pastoral work as a religious worker, provided his base is abroad and he is not taking up an office, post or appointment;

(h)   To act as an adviser, consultant, trainer, internal auditor or trouble shooter, to the UK branch of the same group of companies as the visitor's overseas company, provided the visitor remains employed and paid by the overseas company and does not undertake work, paid or unpaid with the UK company's clients;

   (i)   To receive specific, one-off training on techniques and work practices used in the UK where:

      (A)   the training is to be delivered by the UK branch of the same group of companies to which the individual's employer belongs; or

      (B)   the training is to be provided by a UK company contracted to provide goods or services to the overseas company; or

      (C)   a UK company is contracted to provide training facilities only, to an overseas company; or

      (D)   the training is corporate training which is being delivered by an outside provider to overseas and UK employees of the same group of companies; or

      (E)   the training is corporate training provided for the purposes of the person's employment overseas and delivered by a UK company that is neither part of the person's employer's corporate group nor whose main activity is the provision of training.

   (j)   To share knowledge or experience relevant to, or advise on, an international project that is being led from the UK as an overseas scientist or researcher, provided the visitor remains paid and employed overseas and is not carrying out research in the United Kingdom;

   (k)   To advise a UK client on litigation and/or international transactions as an employee of an international law firm which has offices in the UK, provided the visitor remains paid and employed overseas.

This is a much clearer list than existed before and although not exhaustive there is a lot less room for concessions outside the Rules as was the practice previously. On arrival, a business visitor who meets the requirements of the Rules will usually be admitted for six months. All business or academic visitors are subject to a condition prohibiting employment and recourse to public funds.[4] An academic visitor with entry clearance can get up to twelve months; those without one, six months. Twelve months is the maximum permitted leave which may be granted to an academic visitor and six months is the maximum that may be granted to any other form of business visitor.[5] The 'Business Visitor' category is a self-contained one and a business visitor cannot generally switch to any other category during their visit other than a medical visit should the need arise (see para 46J(iv)). Under the rules a 'Business Visitor' is defined to include two additional classes of visitor: (i) medical graduates coming to the UK to take the PLAB test under paras 75A–F, and (ii) medical and dental graduates coming to undertake a clinical attachment or dental observer post in the UK under paras 75G–M of these Rules. These are quite separate rules and are discussed at **9.57** and **9.69**.

[1]   HC 395, para 46G(iii)(d). Academic visitors can stay up to 12 months: para 46G(i)(b).An 'Academic Visitor' is a person who is from an overseas academic institution or who is highly qualified within his own field of expertise seeking leave to enter the UK to carry out research and associated activities for his own purposes,: HC 395, para 6.

[2]   HC 395, para 46G(iii)(e) A 'Visiting Professor' is a person who is seeking leave to enter the UK as an academic professor to accompany students who are studying here on Study Abroad Programmes: HC 395, para 6.

[3]   The majority of long-distance lorry drivers come from the EEA and Switzerland in any event, or are employed by an EEA-established company; in either case they are covered by the EC free movement provision: *Rush Portuguesa Lda v Office National d'Immigration* [1990] ECR I-1417, [1991] 2 CMLR 818, ECJ; see CHAPTER 6 above. The same would apply to coach drivers from the EEA and Switzerland.

[4]   HC 395, para 46H.

[5]   HC 395, para 46J.

8.22 Passengers do not qualify as visitors if they intend to take employment or to produce goods or provide services in the UK, including selling goods and services direct to the public.[1] They are normally prohibited from taking employment by a condition stamped in their passport,[2] and sometimes the stamp also prohibits them from entering any business or profession, although there is no provision for this condition in the Acts or the Immigration Rules. 'Business Visitors' will of course be permitted to undertake the activities specified at paragraph 46G(iii)(a). The immigration officer must be satisfied that he or she works abroad and has no intention of transferring his or her base to the UK even temporarily. Business visitors are expected to receive their salary from abroad but may receive reasonable expenses to cover the costs of their travel and subsistence. They must not receive a salary or fee from a UK source, unless they work for a multinational company which, for administrative reasons, handles payment of worldwide salaries from the UK[3].

The Rules were amended on 20 October 2014 to align the Immigration Rules with UK Visas and Immigration's practice to confirm that a child, spouse or partner of an Academic Visitor can accompany them to the UK as General Visitors (HC693).

[1] HC 395, para 41(iii) and (iv). For special dispensation to enter as a visitor for recognised festivals and charity concerts, which would normally require a work permit, see now the category of Entertainer Visitors at **8.25** below, and the associated IDI Modernised Guidance, Entertainer Visitors, 16 June 2014; the Entry Clearance Guidance, Visit and Transit, VAT 18 Entertainer Visitor; and Appendix R to the Immigration Rules, List of recognised festivals for which entry by amateur and professional entertainer visitors is permitted.
[2] HC 395, para 42.
[3] IDI Modernised Guidance, Business Visitors, 19 March 2014, Section on 'Business visitor's pay'.

ACADEMIC VISITORS

8.23 The academic visitor category was previously a concession outside the Immigration Rules allowing academics to visit the UK for 12 months to undertake certain academic activities. However, the category is now[1] a subcategory of business visitor as set out in HC 395, paragraph 46G (see **8.21** above) which provides that an academic visitor may be granted leave to enter for a period not exceeding 12 months. The term 'academic visitor' is itself defined in HC 395, paragraph 6 as being a person who is from an overseas academic institution or who is highly qualified within his own field of expertise seeking leave to enter the UK to carry out research and associated activities for his own purposes.

In addition to meeting all the requirements of the business visitor category at 46G(i)–(ii) the Academic Visitor must also meet the requirements at paragraph 46G (iii)(d)(1) as follows:

• be an academic who is:
  – on sabbatical leave from an overseas academic institution to carry out research;
  – taking part in formal exchange arrangements with UK counterparts (including doctors);
  – coming to share knowledge or experience or to hold informal discussions with their UK counterparts; or

> – taking part in a single conference or seminar that is not a
> commercial or non-profit venture;
> – an eminent senior doctor or dentist taking part in research,
> teaching or clinical practice.

An academic visitor must also be able to produce evidence that they have been working as an academic in an institution of higher education overseas, or in the field of their academic expertise immediately prior to seeking entry clearance.

The Modernised Guidance[2] provides that applicants are unlikely to qualify as academic visitors if they are:

- recent graduates, including those with UK degrees (their level of relevant expertise as an academic is likely to be insufficient);
- people on sabbatical leave from private research companies;
- post-graduate researchers who are undertaking studies leading to an accredited UK academic qualification;
- named researchers undertaking grant funded research. They must apply under Tier 2 of the points-based system;
- lecturers undertaking a series of fee-paid lectures. They must seek entry under Tier 2 of the points-based system;
- sponsored researchers. They must enter the UK under Tier 5 (government authorised exchange) of the points-based system.

[1] Since 27 November 2008, introduced by HC 1113.
[2] IDI Modernised Guidance, Business Visitors, 19 March 2014, Section on Academic Visitors.

ENTERTAINERS AND SPORTSPERSONS

8.24 Professional entertainers and sportspersons, players and coaches, who wished to come and work in the UK previously required work permits unless they were EEA citizens or Swiss nationals. Such persons would now need to apply under the points based scheme. However, the position was much less clear cut, where someone sought entry for a single event such as a concert, a golf tournament or a football match. The Immigration Rules and the DSP were previously silent on this issue, and we had to rely on the Home Office IDI to find out who could come in as a visitor and who required a work permit. Readers are referred to the Seventh edition of this work at 8.21 for further details of the relevant concession.

However, from 28 November 2008, the categories of sports visitor[1] and entertainer visitor[2] were inserted in the Immigration Rules, and are considered below.

[1] HC 395, paras 46M–46R. See IDI Modernised Guidance, Sports Visitors, 23 September 2013 and Entry Clearance Guidance, Visitors And Transit, Sports Visitors: VAT17, 10 December 2013.
[2] HC 395, para 46S–46X. See IDI Modernised Guidance, Entertainer Visitors, 16 June 2014 and Entry Clearance Guidance, Visitors And Transit, Entertainer Visitors: VAT18, 10 December 2013.

Entertainer visitors

8.25 'Entertainer Visitor' was a new category of visit introduced by HC 1113 as from 27 November 2008. The requirements to be met by a person seeking entry under this category, set out in HC 395, paragraph 46S, are that he or she:

(i)   is genuinely seeking entry for not more than six months;

(ii)   meets the requirements of the General Visitor rules contained in sub-paras 41(ii)–(viii) and (x)–(xii) and (iii) (except that the requirement in paragraph 41(v) is to be read as if it were not qualified by paragraph 43A) and intends to do one or more of the following during his or her visit:

(a)   to take part as a professional entertainer in one or more music competitions; and/or

(b)   to fulfil one or more specific engagements as either an individual Amateur entertainer or as an Amateur group; and/or

(c)   to take part, as an amateur or professional entertainer, in one or more cultural events or festivals on the list of permit free festivals at Appendix R to these Rules.

(d)   serve as a member of the technical or personal staff, or of the production team, of an entertainer coming for one or more of the purposes listed in (a), (b), or (c), or attending the same event as an entertainer carrying out permitted paid engagements as a visitor

If the person satisfies each of the above requirements, leave to enter as an entertainer visitor may be granted for a period not exceeding six months, subject to a condition prohibiting employment and recourse to public funds.[1] Six months is the maximum permitted leave which may be granted to an entertainer visitor.[2] Entertainer visitors cannot generally switch to any other class of visit during their stay (see para 46V(iii)). The Modernised Guidance includes examples of work that qualifies under this category.[3] It includes professional entertainers taking part in music competitions, charity concerts or shows where the organisers are not making a profit and the entertainer receives no fee. It also covers internationally famous people taking part in broadcasts or public appearances provided they are not performing and are not being paid. Those undertaking an audition provided this is not performed in front of an audience, either paying or non-paying, can qualify as Entertainer Visitors. As can amateur entertainers here as individuals, or as a group such as a choir or youth orchestra, for a specific engagement. Amateur entertainers should not be paid but may receive reasonable expenses and be provided with board and lodgings.

[1]   HC 395, para 46T.
[2]   HC 395, para 46V.
[3]   See IDI Modernised Guidance, Entertainer Visitors, 16 June 2014, section on permissible activities for entertainer visitors.

Sports visitors

8.26 The 'Sports Visitor' category of visit was introduced by HC 1113 as from 27 November 2008. The requirements to be met by a person seeking leave to enter the United Kingdom as a Sports Visitor, set out in para 46M of HC 395, are that he or she:

(i) is genuinely seeking entry as a sports visitor for up to six months;

(ii) meets the requirements of the General Visitor rules contained in sub-paras 41(ii)–(viii) and (x)–(xii) (except that the requirement in paragraph 41(v) is to be read as if it were not qualified by paragraph 43A); and

(iii) intends to do one or more of the following during his or her visit:

(a) to take part in a sports tournament, a particular sporting event or series of sporting events[1] in which the applicant is either:

(i) taking part, either as an individual or as part of a team;

(ii) making personal appearances and promotions, such as book signings, television interviews, guest commentaries, negotiating contracts, or to discuss sponsorship deals;

(iii) taking part in 'trials', providing it is not in front of an audience, either paying or non-paying;

(iv) undertaking short periods of training, either as an individual or as part of a team, providing the applicant is not intending to settle in the UK, being paid by a UK sporting body, or joining a UK team where they are involved in friendly or exhibition matches.

(b) To take part in a specific one off charity sporting event, provided no payment is received other than for travelling and other expenses;

(c) To join, as an Amateur[2], a wholly or predominantly amateur team provided no payment is received other than for board and lodging and reasonable expenses;

(d) To serve as a member of the technical or personal staff, or as an official, attending the same event as a visiting sportsperson coming for one or more of the purposes listed in (a), (b) or (c) or attending the same event as a sports-person carrying out permitted paid engagements as a visitor.

If the person satisfies the above requirements leave to enter as a sports visitor may be granted for a period not exceeding six months, subject to a condition prohibiting employment and recourse to public funds.[3] Six months is the maximum permitted leave which may be granted to a sports visitor.[4] Sports visitors cannot generally switch to any other class of visit during their stay (see para 46P(iii)). Although the rules do not define what they consider a sport the Modernised Guidance warns that a person applying to come to the UK as a sports visitor might not be participating in a genuine sport.[5]

---

1 A 'series of events' is two or more linked events, such as a tour, or rounds of a competition, which do not add up to a league or a season: HC 395, para 6.

2 An 'amateur' is a person who engages in a sport or creative activity solely for personal enjoyment and who is not seeking to derive a living from the activity: HC 395, para 6.

3 HC 395, para 46N.

4 HC 395, para 46P.

5 See IDI Modernised Guidance, Sports Visitors, 23 September 2013, section on Taking part in a particular sporting event.

MEDICAL TREATMENT

8.27 Under the Immigration Rules visitors may be admitted for private medical treatment at their own expense, provided that they meet the ordinary requirements of the visitor rule (no work or provision of services, no study at a maintained school, maintenance and accommodation and ability to meet the costs of the return or onward journey).[1] In the case of a passenger suffering from a communicable disease, the medical inspector must be satisfied that there is no danger to public health.[2] If required to do so, the passenger must be able to show that any proposed course of treatment is of finite duration and that he or she intends to leave the UK at the end of it,[3] but the passenger is not required to be precise about the length of it.[4] Before being admitted for medical treatment a passenger may be required to produce evidence of his or her medical condition requiring consultation and treatment, of the arrangements for consultation and treatment at his own expense, the estimated costs, the likely duration and the availability of sufficient funds in the UK to meet the cost, and may be required to give an undertaking to this effect.[5] The reference in the Rules to consultation or treatment 'at his own expense' does not mean that the visitor must necessarily pay personally.[6] Nor is the availability of treatment in the passenger's own country a ground for refusing admission.[7] Where leave is granted it will normally be for a period not exceeding six months, subject to a condition prohibiting employment, study and recourse to public funds.[8] If the passenger cannot meet all the requirements of the Rules, leave is to be refused.[9] Certain types of medical treatment last for longer than six months and following changes made to paragraph 51 on 20 October 2014 visitors may now apply for a visa for up to 11 months. Evidence from a medical practitioner of the likely duration of the treatment is required. Also the Rules were amended to clarify that Private Medical visitors can extend their leave for a period of up to six months where there is an on-going need to receive private medical treatment in the UK.

HC 1113 has added the following additional requirement for entry to the existing list, set out in HC 395, paragraph 51: (i) the person seeking entry for medical treatment meets the requirements of the General Visitor rules contained in sub-paragraph 41(iii)–(vii), (ix)–(x) and (xii) of HC 395. Paragraph 54 contains a similar requirement when the person is applying for an extension of leave. Visitors under the Approved Destination Status (ADS) with China cannot switch to a medical visit during their stay (paragraph 54(v)).

1   HC 395, para 51(i), referring to para 41(iii)–(vii).
2   HC 395, para 51(ii).
3   HC 395, para 51(iii) and (iv).
4   See *Foon v Secretary of State for the Home Department* [1983] Imm AR 29 and *Onofriou* (2704).
5   HC 395, para 51(v).
6   See *Foon v Secretary of State for the Home Department* [1983] Imm AR 29.
7   *Mohan v Entry Clearance Officer, Lahore* [1973] Imm AR 9.
8   HC 395, para 52.
9   HC 395, para 53.

8.28 An extension of stay for a medical visit can only be granted if the requirements for entry continue to be met.[1] Paragraphs 54 and 55 do not prevent switching into the private medical treatment category except where the last grant of leave was under the Approved Destination Status Agreement with

China route. In addition, evidence must be produced in the form of a letter on headed notepaper from a registered medical practitioner, who holds an NHS consultant post or who appears in the Specialist Registrar of the General Medical Council that provides full details of the:[2]

(a)   nature of the illness;

(b)   proposed or continuing treatment;

(c)   frequency of consultations;

(d)   probable duration of the treatment;

(e)   details of the cost of treatment and confirmation that all expenses are being met; and

(f)   where treatment amounts to private visits to a consultant for a relatively minor ailment, details of the progress being made.

Patients must also be able to show that they have met any costs and expenses incurred in relation to their treatment in the UK out of the resources available to them,[3] and that they have sufficient funds available in the UK or if relying on funds from abroad has provided evidence that those funds are fully transferable to the UK to meet the likely costs of his treatment and intend to do so.[4] If sufficient evidence of these matters is produced, an extension of stay will normally be given.[5] If there is reason to believe the treatment will be at public expense or that the applicant does not intend to leave the UK at the end of the treatment,[6] or if insufficient evidence of the other matters is available, leave will be refused[7]. There is no provision in the Immigration Rules for the dependant of a person admitted for private medical treatment to be granted an extension of stay beyond the six-month period given for a visitor, but one may be given where, for example, someone is having fertility treatment.[8]

[1]   HC 395, para 54(i). A passenger admitted under the ADS Agreement with China (see **8.7** fn 9 above) may not be granted an extension of leave for medical treatment: para 54(v), inserted by HC 486 from 5 April 2005.

[2]   HC 395, para 54(ii).

[3]   HC 395, para 54(iii).

[4]   HC 395, para 54(iv).

[5]   HC 395, para 55.

[6]   See *Foon v Secretary of State for the Home Department* [1983] Imm AR 29 and *Onofriou* (2704).

[7]   HC 395, para 56.

[8]   IDI Modernised Guidance, Visitor for private medical treatment, 11 July 2014, section on 'Dependants'.

NHS treatment

8.29 The Immigration Rules do not provide for persons to be granted leave for the sole purpose of receiving free treatment under the NHS, and normally entry clearance or leave to enter for this purpose will be refused on the basis that it is being sought for a purpose not covered by the Immigration Rules.[1] There are exceptional arrangements for the admission of a handful of people each year from countries with which the UK has reciprocal arrangements.[2] Additionally, applications for leave to remain to complete a course of NHS treatment which has already begun will not be refused if it would clearly be unreasonable to require the applicant to leave the UK (eg because he or she was in hospital following an accident).[3]

1   IDI Modernised Guidance, Visitor for private medical treatment, 11 July 2013, section on 'NHS treatment as sole purpose for visiting UK', which provides that entry clearance or leave to enter for this purpose should be refused or cancelled under para 320(1) or para 321(A) respectively and leave to remain under para 322(1).
2   See The National Health Service (Charges to Overseas Visitors) Regulations 2011, SI 2011/1556, in force from 1 Aug 2011, revoking and replacing the equivalent set of regulations from 1989, SI 1989/306. Regulation 10 provides that no charge may be made or recovered in respect of any relevant services provided to an overseas visitor where those services are provided in circumstances covered by a reciprocal agreement with a country or territory specified in Schedule 2. The countries set out in that Schedule are Anguilla, Armenia, Australia, Azerbaijan, Barbados, Belarus, Bosnia, British Virgin Islands, Croatia, Falkland Islands, Georgia, Gibraltar, Isle of Man, Israel, Jersey, Kazakhstan, Kyrgyzstan, Macedonia, Moldova, Montenegro, Montserrat, New Zealand, Russia, Serbia, St Helena, Tajikistan, Turkmenistan, Turks and Caicos Islands, Ukraine, and Uzbekistan.
3   IDI Modernised Guidance, Visiting, Visitor for private medical treatment, 11 July 2014, section on 'NHS treatment as sole purpose for visiting UK'.

8.30 The General Grounds for Refusal of the Immigration Rules now include at paragraph 320(22) for discretionary grounds for refusal of entry clearance and at paragraph 322(12) for refusal of leave to remain, variation of leave to enter or remain or curtailment of leave on the grounds that where one or more relevant NHS body has notified the Secretary of State that the person seeking (entry, leave to enter, leave to remain or a variation of leave to enter or remain, as the case may be) has failed to pay a charge or charges with a total value of at least £1000 in accordance with the relevant NHS regulations on charges to overseas visitors.

Previously, visitors acting as organ donors to recipients in the UK with private healthcare entered as Private Medical Visitors, and visitors acting as organ donors to recipients who are receiving treatment on the National Health Service were assessed outside the Immigration Rules. A new provision within the General Visitor route at paragraph 41A brought in by HC693 and which took effect from 6 November 2014 is to accommodate visitors who are coming to the UK to act as an organ donor, or to be assessed as a suitable organ donor, to an identified recipient in the UK.

PARENT OF A CHILD AT SCHOOL

8.31 Under early Immigration Rules, visits for family purposes for quite long periods at a time were allowed.[1] In *Hamilton v Entry Clearance Officer, Kingston, Jamaica*[2] a three-year visit by a mother, while her daughter did a teachers' training course, was allowed. Family visits to be with older children have long been impossible, because of the six-month time limit,[3] but since September 2000 there has been specific provision in the rules for the parents of young children (under 12) at independent fee-paying schools.[4] Under the rule, as it currently reads at paragraphs 56A–56C, the requirements to be met by a person seeking leave to enter or remain in the United Kingdom as the parent of a child at school are that:

(i)   the parent meets the requirements set out in paragraph 41(ii)–(xii) (except that the requirement in paragraph 41(v) is to be read as if it were not qualified by paragraph 43A which relates to permitted study as a general visitor); and

(ii)   if the child:

      (1)   has leave under paras 57 to 62 of these Rules, the child is attending an independent fee-paying day school and meets the requirements set out in para 57(i)–(ix); or

      (2)   is a Tier 4 (Child) Student, the child is attending an independent fee-paying day school and meets the requirements set out in para 245ZZA (if seeking leave to enter) or 245ZZC (if seeking leave to remain); and

(iii)   the child is under 12 years of age; and

(iv)   the parent can provide satisfactory evidence of adequate and reliable funds for maintaining a second home in the United Kingdom; and

(v)   the parent is not seeking to make the United Kingdom his or her main home; and

(vi)   the parent was not last admitted to the United Kingdom under the Approved Destination Status Agreement with China.

The child must meet all the rules relating to students who have their main home outside the UK, to be given leave to remain for up to 12 months at a time.[5]

The 7th edition of this work suggested (at 8.25) that a parent who wishes to remain continuously in the UK with a child during his or her primary education may do so, provided they are not seeking to make the UK their main home. Former IDI (Mar) 10 suggested that leave to enter to the parent may be granted up to a maximum of 12 months in this category. The current Modernised Guidance provides that applicants under this route are able to extend their leave for periods of up to 12 months until their child reaches the age of 12. This means applicants must not be considered as living in the UK through successive periods as long as they continue to maintain their permanent home outside the UK.[6]

---

[1] See Cmnd 4298 (pre-1973 Rules), para 12; *Afoakwah v Secretary of State for the Home Department* [1972] Imm AR 17.

[2] [1974] Imm AR 43. See *Nourai v Secretary of State for the Home Department* [1978] Imm AR 200; *Obeyesekere v Secretary of State for the Home Department* [1976] Imm AR 16.

[3] *Kelada v Secretary of State for the Home Department* [1991] Imm AR 400.

[4] HC 395, paras 56A–56C.

[5] HC 395, para 56A–C, inserted by Cm 4851 in Sep 2000. The Rule requires satisfactory evidence of adequate and reliable funds for maintaining a second home in the UK and compliance with all the visitor requirements save the six-month time limit. See also Modernised Guidance, Visiting, Parent of a child at school, 27 September 2013.

[6] IDI Modernised Guidance, Visiting, Parent of a Child at School, 27 September 2013, section on 'Successive periods of leave' and 'Grant or refuse extension of stay in the UK'. See also Entry Clearance Guidance, Visitors And Transit, Special visitor, parents with children under 12 at school in UK: VAT05, 9 June 2013.

CARERS

8.32 The rules make no express provision for applications from persons here as visitors or in another temporary capacity seeking leave to remain to care for a sick relative or a friend who is suffering from a terminal illness, and although previously referred to in the IDIs under compassionate circumstances warranting the grant of leave to remain outside the rules for a longer period than six months the current IDIs are silent on this. Where an applicant wishes to care for a friend or relative for a short period, the application may be considered under the requirements of the rules relating to visitors. Applications for leave to remain in order to care for a sick or disabled friend are likely to be refused.

Under a further special category not mentioned in the rules but contained in the Modernised Guidance[1] it is acceptable for visitors to act as temporary child minders for relatives where:

(i)   the visitor is a close relative of the parent (eg parent, sibling, in-law). More distant relatives are only acceptable if they have formed part of the family unit or are the closest surviving relatives of the parents;

(ii)   neither parent is able to supervise the daytime care of the child;

(iii)   it is not simply an arrangement to enable both parents to take gainful employment or to study;

(iv)   neither parent is in a category leading to settlement;

(v)   the visitor will not receive a salary (disregarding provision of board, accommodation and pocket money);

(vi)   the visitor intends to remain in the UK for not more than six months.

The minder retains the status of visitor, provided they do not receive pay.[2] If the parent or parents are EEA nationals they may be able to rely on European Law. Under the Citizens' Directive:[3]

'the host member State shall, in accordance with its national law, facilitate entry and residence for . . . family members . . . where serious health grounds strictly require the personal care of the family member of the Union citizen.'

In *TR (reg 8(3) EEA Regs 2006)*[4] the Tribunal examined the right of family members to act as carers under the EEA Regulations. They held that the use of the word 'serious' requires the 'health grounds' to be well beyond ordinary ill health and as a matter of practice to require detailed medical evidence in support of any claim. The Regulation of Care (Scotland) Act 2001 provided a useful definition of 'Personal care'. The word 'strictly' is a restrictive or limiting requirement and imports a need for complete compliance or exact performance and reinforces the need for personal care to be provided on a day-to-day basis.

1   IDI Modernised Guidance, Visiting, General Visitors, 14 July 2014, section on 'childminder for relatives'.
2   See *Goodluck* (4244) (undertaking child-minding duties for a young mother and her baby for payment was employment, not just a visit); *Tan (Swee Hong)* (5212) (looking after a sister's baby for payment was employment).
3   Directive 2004/38/EC. This has been transcribed into domestic law by reg 8(3) of the Immigration (European Economic Area) Regulations 2006, SI 2006/1003.
4   [2008] UKAIT 00004 (28 December 2007).

VISITS FOR MARRIAGE AND CIVIL PARTNERSHIP

8.33 A visitor seeking entry for the purpose of marriage or civil partnership ceremonies must show that he or she:

(i)   meets the requirements set out in paragraph 41(i)–(ix) and (xi)–(xii) (except that the requirement in paragraph 41(v) is to be read as if it were not qualified by paragraph 43A which relates to permitted study as a general visitor); and

(ii)   can show that he or she intends to give notice of marriage or civil partnership, or marry or form a civil partnership, in the United Kingdom within the period for which entry is sought; and

(iii)   can produce satisfactory evidence, if required to do so, of the arrangements for giving notice of marriage or civil partnership, or for his or her wedding or civil partnership to take place, in the United Kingdom during the period for which entry is sought; and

(iv)   holds a valid United Kingdom entry clearance for entry in this capacity.[1]

A couple seeking to marry or enter into a civil partnership in the UK need not have any connection with the country, and neither spouse needs to be British or settled here. But even if one prospective spouse is British or settled, entry as a visitor for the purpose of marriage does not entitle a person to remain in the UK as a spouse after the marriage; for that, a fiancé(e) visa would be required. Following changes to the Rules on 20 October 2014, paragraph 56D(iv) now prohibits a person coming to the UK for the purpose of entering into a sham marriage or sham civil partnership.

---

[1]   HC 395, para 56D–F, inserted by HC 346 from 15 March 2005, as subsequently amended. This requires the marriage or civil partnership ceremony visitor to satisfy all the requirements of the visit rules, including an intention to leave at the end of the visit. Visitors who have not entered with the right visit visa may not be allowed to marry or enter into a civil partnership without Home Office permission: see CHAPTER 11 below.

VISITING RELIGIOUS WORKERS

8.34 It has long been recognised that religious communities in the UK face difficulties in recruiting sufficient numbers of priests and other religious workers from within the UK. New categories of visiting religious worker or religious worker in a non-pastoral role were created by rule changes in HC 769, which took effect from 9 January 2006.[1] It is debatable whether these applicants were truly visitors or were employees who do not need a work permit. However, their stay was temporary, in one of the two categories being no more than six months and in the other no more than 24 months and they were not to be confused with the separate category of Ministers of religion, dealt with in CHAPTER 10. However, from 29 November 2008,[2] these categories were deleted from the rules, and a new category of business visitor was created. This category is now contained as a sub-section of business visitor at HC 395, para 46G(iii)(g), providing for six months entry for persons seeking to enter to undertake some preaching or pastoral work as a religious worker, provided his base is abroad and he is not taking up an office, post or appointment.[3] As explained in the IDI,[4] people coming to the United Kingdom to fill a vacancy as a religious worker for a recognised religion, who will be undertaking preaching and pastoral work will now need to qualify under Tier 2 – Ministers of Religion – of the Points Based System, and people coming to work temporarily as a religious worker for a recognised religion will need to qualify under Tier 5 – Religious Workers – of the Points Based System.

---

[1]   Creating HC 395, paras 177A-G.
[2]   By operation of HC 1113.
[3]   IDI Modernised Guidance, Business Visitors, 19 March 2014, Section on 'religious workers'.
[4]   IDI Modernised Guidance, Business Visitors, 19 March 2014, Section on 'religious workers'.

VISITORS FROM CHINA

8.35 HC 486 created a new category of 'ADS visitor'[1] or those seeking to enter the UK under the terms of the Memorandum of Understanding (MoU) on visa and related issues concerning tourist groups from the People's Republic of China to the UK. The requirements are now contained at HC 395, paragraphs 56G–56J.

The rule is intended to regulate outward tourism from China to the UK by providing a mechanism for issuing visas for groups of Chinese tourists to authorised travel agents. The category is necessary because the terms of the MoU differ from the existing requirements for visitors under the Immigration Rules. ADS visitors will have to meet the requirements for ordinary visitors at para 41(ii)–(vii) of HC 395, but in addition, applicants must be Chinese nationals; must be genuinely seeking entry as a visitor for a maximum period of 30 days; must intend to enter, travel and leave the UK as part of a group and will not be permitted to extend their stay beyond the maximum 30-day period.[2] In conjunction with these rules changes, the Immigration (Leave to Enter and Remain) (Amendment) Order 2005, which came into force on 5 April 2005, provides that visas issued pursuant to the MoU shall have effect as single entry visas and have effect as leave to enter on one occasion unless endorsed as dual entry visas; in which case they shall have effect as leave to enter on two occasions.[3] From 27 November 2008, HC 1113 added the following additional requirement for entry to the existing list, set out in HC 395, para 56G: the visitor must meet the requirements of the General Visitor rules contained in sub-paras 41(ii)–(xii).

[1]   Approved Destination Status, created by The UK/China ADS Memorandum of Understanding which was signed on 21 January 2005.
[2]   In order to prevent ADS tourists being able to extend their stay by applying for an extension in another visitor category, visitors under the ADS with China cannot switch to a general visit or a medical visit during their stay (paras 44(iii) and 54(v)).
[3]   SI 2005/1159.

VISITORS IN TRANSIT

8.36 Visitors who arrive in the UK in transit to another country are dealt with separately under the Immigration Rules and the IDI.[1] First, they must be in transit to a country outside the common travel area; secondly, they must have both the means and the intention of proceeding there at once; thirdly, they must be assured of entry there; and fourthly, they must intend and be able to leave the UK within 48 hours.[2] Passengers meeting these conditions will be given a leave not exceeding 48 hours with a prohibition on employment, study and recourse to public funds.[3] Otherwise leave is to be refused.[4] Forty-eight hours is the maximum permitted leave and any application for an extension beyond this period is to be refused.[5] Where a woman on a tour party was given 48 hours by an immigration officer who wished to treat her as a transit passenger, but did not make this clear in the leave stamp, the Tribunal held that she was to be treated as an ordinary visitor with a right to apply for an extension and, if necessary, to appeal against a refusal.[6] The IDI provide that visa requirements may be waived for air travellers with a confirmed flight within 24 hours of arrival, and for cruise passengers and others arriving by ship and leaving on the same ship within 24 hours.[7] The Rules were amended with effect from 1 December 2014 to allow visa nationals to transit landside through the UK provided they hold a valid exemption document under the transit without visa scheme. This change replaces a concessionary arrangement which operated outside the Immigration Rules and which allowed some visa nationals to enter the UK without a visa whilst in transit purely on the basis of a confirmed onward ticket (and no exemption document) and required others to hold an exemption document. While most of the documents referred to in the transit without visa scheme were part of the previous concession, Irish biometric visas and Australian and New Zealand residence permits have been added. The visa waiver concession does not apply to nationals of the countries specified in the Immigration (Passenger Transit Visa) Order 2003.[8] These nationals require a UK Direct Airside Transit Visa (DATV) even when transiting airside without passing through the immigration control.[9]

[1]   HC 395, paras 47–50; IDI Modernised Guidance, Transit Visitors, 3 July 2014.
[2]   HC 395, para 47.
[3]   HC 395, para 48.
[4]   HC 395, para 49.
[5]   HC 395, para 50.
[6]   *Low v Secretary of State for the Home Department* [1995] Imm AR 435.
[7]   IDI Modernised Guidance, Visitors in Transit, 3 July 2014, section on 'Visitors in transit without visa (TWOV) concession'.
[8]   SI 2003/1185, as variously amended, most recently by SI 2011/1553, inserting Yemen from 14 July 2011. The full list is Afghanistan, Albania, Algeria, Angola, Bangladesh, Belarus, Bolivia, Burma, Burundi, Cameroon, Congo, Democratic Republic of the Congo, Ecuador, Egypt, Eritrea, Ethiopia, Former Yugoslav Republic of Macedonia, Gambia, Ghana, Guinea, Guinea-Bissau, India, Iran, Iraq, Ivory Coast, Jamaica, Kenya, Lebanon, Lesotho, Liberia, Libya, Malawi, Moldova, Mongolia, Nepal, Nigeria, Pakistan, Palestinian Territories, People's Republic of China, Rwanda, Senegal, Serbia and Montenegro, Sierra Leone, Somalia, South Africa, Sri Lanka, Sudan, Swaziland, Syria, Tanzania, Turkey, Uganda, Vietnam, Yemen, Zimbabwe. See also Chapter 3 above.
[9]   IDI Modernised Guidance, Visitors in Transit, 3 July 2014, section on 'Direct Airside Transit Visa (DATV)'.

PROSPECTIVE ENTREPRENUERS

8.37 'Prospective entrepreneurs' were introduced at paragraphs 56N–56Q of HC 395 as a new category of 'Special Visitor' (as defined by HC 395 paragraph 6) on 6 April 2011 by Statement of Changes HC 863. The explanatory memorandum of HC 863 explains the rationale: 'A new form of visitor category is being created to allow prospective entrepreneurs to enter the UK in order to obtain funding and build their teams, if they are not yet ready to establish their business and cannot therefore qualify under the Tier 1 (Entrepreneur) category.' Paragraph 56N provides that this category is to enable individuals who are at the time of applying for leave under this route in discussions with:

(i)   one or more registered venture capitalist firms regulated by the Financial Conduct Authority, and/or

(ii)   one or more UK entrepreneurial seed funding competitions which is listed as endorsed on the UK Trade & Investment website, and/or

(iii)   one or more UK Government Departments, to secure funding in order to join, set up or take over, and be actively involved in the running of, a business in the UK.

The requirements are set out at paragraph 56O and include that the applicant's primary intention in applying as a Prospective Entrepreneur is to secure funding in order to join, set up or take over, and be actively involved in the running of a business in the UK.[1] Prospective entrepreneur visitors must have obtained an entry clearance before travelling and must not be under the age of 18 nor in transit to a country outside the common travel area. Paragraph 56P provides that leave to enter is to be granted for a maximum of six months, employment, study and recourse to public funds prohibited. There are no provisions to allow for such leave to be extended, but the Prospective entrepreneur may switch to leave to remain as a Tier 1 (entrepreneur) Migrant before the end of the period of their visit.[2] The associated IDI Modernised Guidance, Visiting, Prospective Entrepreneurs, 21 March 2014. A more detailed account is to be found in CHAPTER 10.

[1]   HC 395, para 56O(c). See also the associated IDI Modernised Guidance, Visiting, Prospective Entrepreneurs, 21 March 2014.
[2]   HC 395, para 56O(e).

VISITORS – SWITCHING CATEGORIES

8.38 The rules as to whether a migrant may switch from visitor to another form of leave to remain, without having to leave the UK and return, has been the subject of regular change. Visitors who wish to remain in the UK in order to do something else have quite limited options. Readers are referred to the 7th edition of this work for an historical perspective. The scenario most likely to arise is visitors wishing to switch to student status. From 31 March 2009, HC 314 deleted most of the existing provisions relating to leave to enter and remain as a student, and brought the rules relating to Tier 4 (General) Students and Tier 4 (Child) Students[1] into effect. The categories of person who may switch from one form of leave to enter or remain to Tier 4 (General) Student are set out at paragraph 245ZX(b), HC 395, or to switch to leave to remain as a Tier 4 (Child) Student, at paragraph 245ZZC(b), HC 395. They do not permit switching from leave to enter as a visitor. People who wish to visit with a view to enrolling on a course or going to college need to obtain a prospective student visa before leaving home.[2] A non-visa national who obtains entry as a visitor while harbouring an intention to study risks summary removal as an illegal entrant.

General visitors cannot generally switch to other categories of visitor, except medical visitor under HC 395, paragraphs 54 and 55;[3] but Child Visitors can become General Visitors (see **8.19**, above).[4] However, visitors can apply for indefinite leave, if they are Gurkhas, or foreign or Commonwealth citizens, who have seen service in the British armed forces.[5] Doctors having entered the UK under HC 395, paragraph 75A to take the PLAB test may apply to extend leave to undertake a clinical attachment or dental observer post.[6]

Otherwise the IDI[7] confirm that visitors may not switch to employment under the Points Based System.[8] Switching to a purpose covered in the Points Based System after entry to the United Kingdom as a sports visitor is not permissible. However, if a person has been issued with a Certificate of Sponsorship for Tier 5 – (temporary worker – Creative and Sporting) – before they come to the UK, they may use this to apply for leave to remain to continue with the Tier 5 work without leaving the UK.[9]

The position of visitors who are EEA, Swiss or Turkish nationals under community law is dealt with in CHAPTER 6.

1   HC 395, paras 245ZT–ZZD.
2   HC 395, paras 82–87.
3   Transfer from a visitor under the Approved Destination Status Agreement with China to medical visitor is not permitted – see HC 395, para 54(v).
4   HC 395, para 44 (iii).
5   HC 395, paras 276I (Gurkhas) and 276O (foreign and Commonwealth citizens discharged from HM Forces), as inserted by HC 1112, as from 18 October 2004.
6   See HC 395, para 75K(i)(a) and ECG, Business visitor, doctors and dentists: VAT16.
7   See for example the Modernised Guidance, Tier 4 (General) student visa, Switch to this visa. An applicant cannot switch from any of the visitor categories to a student visa, but can switch from prospective student to student.
8   For example the Modernised Guidance, Tier 1 (Graduate Entrepreneur) sets out from which categories you can switch into this category and visitor is not permitted.
9   IDI Modernised Guidance, Sports Visitors, 13 September 2013, 'Switching'.

8.39 A previous exception to the no-switching rule was that a visitor could apply for leave to remain as the unmarried partner of someone in the UK,[1] whereas they could not do so for leave as a civil partner or a married partner.[2] However, from 31 October 2011, no such distinction is made and the previous exception is unlikely to be a practical possibility. The effect of the HC 1511 amendments to the rules is to prevent an extension of leave being granted to a visitor, 'other than where as a result of that leave he would not have been in the United Kingdom beyond six months from the date on which he was admitted to the United Kingdom on this occasion in accordance with these rules'. For the most part this precludes visitors, who will have been granted only six months leave to enter from any kind of switching. Persons with visit leave may apply at any time for asylum[3] or for Humanitarian Protection or Discretionary Leave on human rights grounds.[4]

1   HC 395, para 295D(i) inserted by Cm 4851. The couple must already have been living together in a relationship akin to marriage for two years.
2   HC 395, para 284(i) as amended by Cm 5949 from 25 August 2003.
3   See CHAPTER 12 below.
4   See CHAPTER 7 above.

APPEALS BY VISITORS

8.40 On 25 June 2013 all appeals for visitors including family visitors, were abolished (except on race discrimination or human rights).[1] There may be circumstances in which refusal of a visa to visit family engages Article 8.[2] Race discrimination is rarely argued in the immigration tribunal. Those refused a visit visa will need to make a fresh application which according to the Modernised Guidance will be considered on the merits.[3] Refusals to extend leave in-country do attract a right of appeal but as already discussed extensions are limited and switching from visitor into another category is generally not permissible. Refusal or cancellation of leave on conducive grounds by the Secretary of State in person or on his or her direction attracts rights of appeal as above, but to the Special Immigration Appeals Commission rather than to the First Tier Tribunal, Immigration and Asylum Chamber.[4]

1 See the Nationality, Immigration and Asylum Act 2002, s 88A, as amended by the Crime and Courts Act 2013, s 52, and the Crime and Courts Act 2013 (Commencement No 1 and Transitional and Saving Provision) Order 2013, SI 2013/1042.

2 For example in *Ramsew (Anand) v Entry Clearance Officer, Georgetown* (01/TH/2505) (24 October 2001, unreported), the Tribunal emphasised that family visit appeals involved elements of Article 8 and that care should be taken in determining such appeals.

3 IDI Modernised Guidance, General Visitors, 14 July 2014, section on 'Visiting family in the UK – family visitors'.

4 Nationality, Immigration and Asylum Act 2002, ss 97–98; Special Immigration Appeals Commission Act 1997, s 2(1).

8.41 Visitors who have no right of appeal against refusal of entry clearance or refusal of leave to enter or remain may apply for judicial review if they can show unfairness or an error of law by the immigration officer,[1] but those with a right of appeal should exercise it rather than seek judicial review.[2] Judicial review of refusal of leave to enter as a visitor may be pursued after an applicant has left the UK,[3] if it is not purely academic (ie because refusal might affect future plans to visit). Judicial review is not a time or cost effective solution, but where re-applying has been tried it may be the only way for some individuals to challenge a visa refusal.

1 *R v Secretary of State for the Home Department, ex p Arjumand* [1983] Imm AR 123, QBD. Where there is no appeal judicial review may be ineffective: see, for example, *R (on the application of Khawaja) v UK Border Agency* [2011] EWHC 2537 (Admin) (Stadlen J) (ECO reached his conclusion about genuineness of K's visit to a high degree of probability; so no Wednesbury unreasonableness; so evidence not available to the ECO, including audited accounts which showed that K's bank statements were genuine and that K was in business as he had represented, did not help K as they might have on an appeal).

2 *R v Secretary of State for the Home Department, ex p Swati* [1986] 1 All ER 717, [1986] Imm AR 88, CA. This is so even if the appeal can only be exercised after departure.

3 In *R v Secretary of State for the Home Department, ex p Kekana* [1998] Imm AR 136 Potts J held that it was academic to pursue such an action where the applicant had already left the UK; in *R v Secretary of State for the Home Department, ex p Honegan* (10 April 1995, unreported), Tucker J held that it was not, and an application to set aside leave in *R v Secretary of State for the Home Department, ex p Dombaj* (CO 3150/1997) was dismissed by Owen J on 25 March 1998 (reported in *Legal Action* November 1998; the immigration officer's decision was quashed on 1 December 1998).

Chapter 9
STUDENTS

INTRODUCTION

9.1 All the old familiar rules contained in HC 395, paragraphs 57 to 70 have gone. Students who entered under the old rules before Tier 4 came into force in March 2009 , if there are any left, will now need to switch to Tier 4 if they need an extension of leave. The only remnants of the old rules which might still be relevant are: (1) those for an overseas qualified nurse or midwife, seeking an extension of stay,[1] who has previously been granted leave (a) as an overseas qualified nurse or midwife under HC 395, paras 69M–69R or (b) to undertake an adaptation course as a student nurse under HC 395, paras 63–69 of these Rules; (2) those for a graduate from a medical school who intends to take the PLAB Test in the United Kingdom or for graduates from medical or dental schools seeking leave to enter the United Kingdom to undertake a clinical attachment or dental observer post;[2] (3) those dealing with prospective students, but only if they are coming to do a course of study which would meet the requirements for an extension of stay as a student under paragraph 245ZX or paragraph 245ZZC;[3] and (4) those dealing with spouses or civil partners of students or prospective students granted leave under part 3 of the Rules.[4] Those needing to know the details of these rules should consult Chapter 9 of the 7th edition.

---

[1] HC 395 69P–69R still apply. An extension of stay in this category which, when amalgamated with those previous periods of leave, must not total more than 18 months: HC 395, para 69P.
[2] HC 395, paras 75A–75M still apply.
[3] HC 395, paras 82–87.
[4] HC 395, paras 76–81.

OVERVIEW OF THE POINTS-BASED SYSTEM

9.2 Tier 4 of the Points-Based System (PBS) entered into force on 31 March 2009[1] as a route for migrants wishing to study in the UK. Paragraphs 245ZT–245ZZD replace former paragraphs 57–70 of HC 395[2] and apply to all new applications for those wishing to study in the UK from the date of entry into force. It consists of two general sub-categories: (i) Tier 4 (General) Students aged 16 and over and (ii) Tier 4 (Child) Students aged between 4 and 17 years old (inclusive). Policy Guidance[3] sets out in considerable detail the requirements to be met for entry clearance and leave to remain under the Immigration Rules, in particular, the limited and specific way in which such applications must be evidenced, thus minimising a caseworker's discretion in deciding student applications. The Policy Guidance is subject to frequent changes uploaded to the UKVI website; the guidance in force at the date of decision will be applicable.[4] In *NA and Ors*[5] the Tribunal described these *new style* Immigration Rules and the closely connected Policy Guidance to be a 'hybrid rule of a new kind', being guidance written expressly for applicants and containing some provisions integral to the understanding and operation of the relevant Immigration Rules. However, the Court of Appeal in Pankina,[6] entirely rejected this approach, holding that substantive requirements which a student had to meet in order to get leave to study, which were set out in Policy Guidance, were ultra vires the Immigration Act 1971 sections 1(4) and 3(2), since they were not laid before Parliament. The effect was that 'a discrete element of the rules is placed beyond Parliament's scrutiny and left to the unfettered judgment of the rule-maker', undermining a constitutional principle standing as a pillar of the separation of powers for over four centuries. Whilst there was nothing inherently objectionable in an Immigration Rule which 'derives part of its content from an extant and accessible outside source', what was impermissible was to create 'rules which purport to supplement themselves by further rules derived from an extraneous source'. Applying this rationale, the court refused to apply substantive requirements set out only in the accompanying Policy Guidance. The result of this judgment was the publication of revised Immigration Rules that include the substantive requirements previously only set out in the Policy Guidance.

This approach was subsequently upheld on this point by the Supreme Court in *Alvi*,[7] which held that section 3(2) of the Immigration Act 1971[8] applied to any requirement which a migrant had to satisfy as a condition of being given leave to enter or remain in the United Kingdom, as well as any provision as to the period for which leave was given and any conditions attached to it in different circumstances. In consequence, the Immigration Rules should include all provisions which set out in an extraneous document criteria which were or might be determinative of an application for leave to enter or remain. In a series of subsequent decisions the courts have applied the *Pankina* principle in a variety of contexts,[9] dis-applying substantive criteria for admission or leave to remain which are not found in the Immigration Rules.[10] The Secretary of State's response to these decisions has been to revise the Immigration Rules so as to include substantive requirements previously found only in the Policy Guidance.

However, these are not the rules which apply to educational institutions which require a sponsor licence in order to recruit overseas students. Sponsor licences are almost wholly regulated by Guidance. This practice was upheld by the Supreme Court in the *New London College* case, where the majority of the Court agreed with the judgment of Lord Sumption, who held that the statutory power of the Secretary of State to administer the system of immigration control must necessarily extend to a range of ancillary and incidental administrative powers not expressly spelt out in the Act, including the vetting of sponsors (para 29). Lord Carnwath took issue with the width of

691

this power (paras 35–38), preferring to treat the licensing process as linked to the specific provisions for regulating entry under section 1(4) of the 1971 Act but not to the general system of immigration control under the Act.

¹ HC 341, 9 March 2009.

² Ibid at para 27(a). For the jurisprudence on former paras 57–62, see the previous editions of *Macdonald's Immigration Law and Practice*.

³ All references to the Tier 4 Policy Guidance refer to the Guidance dated 6 November 2014, in force at the time of writing. Guidance for Tier 4 Students, referred to below as 'Tier 4 Policy Guidance' is available at: www.gov.uk/government/uploads/system/uploads/attachment_data/file/370866/T4_Guidance_11-14.pdf. Guidance for the dependants of Tier 4 students, referred to below as 'Dependent Policy Guidance' may be found at: www.gov.uk/government/upload s/system/uploads/attachment_data/file/324611/DEP_guidance_07-14.pdf. Guidance for Sponsors, in three parts and referred to below as 'Tier 4 Sponsor Guidance' is available at www.gov.uk/government/publications/sponsor-a-tier-4-student-guidance-for-educators. Guidance on Highly Trusted Sponsors, referred to below as 'Highly Trusted Policy Guidance' may be found at: www.gov.uk/government/publications/points-based-system-licensing-highly-truste d-sponsors

⁴ *Odelola v Secretary of State for the Home Department* [2009] UKHL 25, [2009] 3 All ER 1061, [2009] 1 WLR 1230.

⁵ [2009] UKAIT 00025, paras 46–53.

⁶ *Secretary of State for the Home Department v Pankina* [2010] EWCA Civ 719, [2011] QB 376. This principle was applied in *R (on the application of English UK Ltd) v Secretary of State for the Home Department* [2010] EWHC 1726 (Admin), [2010] All ER (D) 86 (Jul) as the basis for finding that raising the level at which a student may study English in the UK from level A2 to B2 of the Common European Framework of Reference for Languages (CEFR) in Policy Guidance, was unlawful. For further consideration of the status of policy guidance, see *R (on the application of BAPIO Action Ltd) v Secretary of State for the Home Department* [2007] EWCA Civ 1139 at [29], [2007] All ER (D) 172 (Nov); *Wilson v First Country Trust Ltd (No 2)* [2003] UKHL 40, [2004] 1 AC 816 at [139], [2003] 4 All ER 97; *Huang v Secretary of State for the Home Department* [2007] UKHL 11, [2007] 2 AC 167, [2007] 4 All ER 15 per Lord Bingham; and *ZH (Bangladesh) v Secretary of State for the Home Department* [2009] EWCA Civ 8.

⁷ Section 1(4) of the Immigration Act 1971 requires the immigration rules to include provision for admitting (in such cases and subject to such restrictions as may be provided by the rules, and subject or not to conditions as to length of stay or otherwise) persons coming for the purpose of taking employment, or for purposes of study, or as visitors, or as dependants of persons lawfully in or entering the UK. Section 3(2) requires to be laid before Parliament statements of the rules and of any changes to the rules as to the practice to be followed in the administration of the Act for regulating the control of entry into and stay in the United Kingdom of persons who required leave to enter.

⁸ *R (on the application of Alvi) v Secretary of State for the Home Department (Joint Council for the Welfare of Migrants intervening)* [2012] UKSC 33, [2012] 1 WLR 2208.

⁹ See *FA and AA (PBS: effect of Pankina) Nigeria* [2010] UKUT 00304 (IAC), in which the Tribunal noted that decision of the Court of Appeal in *Pankina* was 'not limited to the "three-month rule" in relation to evidence of funds' and construed the word 'available' in the Policy Guidance as extending to funds provided by the applicant's spouse. The same approach was taken in *CDS (PBS: 'available': Article 8) Brazil* [2010] UKUT 00305 (IAC) in concluding that funds were 'available' if they were provided by third parties. Attempts to impose interim limits on the numbers of Tier 1 (General) applications that would be granted and a cap on Tier 2 employers issuing Certificates of Sponsorship were successfully challenged in *R (on the application of the Joint Council for the Welfare of Immigrants) v Secretary of State for the Home Department* [2010] EWHC 3524 (Admin), [2010] All ER (D) 244 (Dec). Applying the *Pankina* principle, Sullivan LJ found that the failure to lay such important changes to the Immigration Rules before Parliament and instead uploading them onto the UKBA website frustrated and deliberately evaded that purpose and placed the interim limits beyond the bounds of ministerial scrutiny. See also *Owolabi (Tier 2 – skilled occupations) Nigeria* [2011] UKUT 313 (IAC). In *Aleem (Pankina – Uplift for overseas earnings) Sri Lanka* [2011] UKUT 120 (IAC), the Tribunal found that the Rules were silent on whether an uplift for overseas earnings in a Tier 1 (General) application could be used to acquire the relevant points; only the Policy Guidance imposed a limitation on the place where the work was carried out and for that reason fell to be dis-applied. However, in *R (on the application of English Speaking Board*

(International) Ltd) v Secretary of State for the Home Department [2011] EWHC 1788 (Admin), [2011] All ER (D) 119 (Jul), whilst it was conceded that the changes to the Immigration Rules bringing these provisions into force were undertaken without proper consultation, that failure did not result in a quashing order, given that all those involved in the litigation accepted the aim behind the change was properly formulated and the impact on accreditation bodies had been limited.

10 By contrast, the means of proving such eligibility which appear in published guidance need not be subject to Parliamentary scrutiny: *Secretary of State for the Home Department v Pankina* [2010] EWCA Civ 719, [2011] QB 376, [2010] All ER (D) 196 (Jun) at [6] and [24]–[26]. See also *R (on the application of the Joint Council for the Welfare of Immigrants) v Secretary of State for the Home Department* [2010] EWHC 3524 (Admin), [2010] All ER (D) 244 (Dec) at [43]; *R (on the application of Ahmed (Abdullah Bashir)) v Secretary of State for the Home Department* [2011] EWHC 2855 (Admin), [2011] All ER (D) 112 (Nov). Equally, Wyn Williams J in *R (on the application of New London College Ltd) v Secretary of State for the Home Department* [2011] EWHC 856 (Admin), [2011] All ER (D) 60 (Apr) held that the absence of specific provision in the Rules for the Sponsor licences and the ability of the Secretary of State to vary the policy guidance detailing sponsor's obligations did not fall foul of the *Pankina* principle.

9.3 All colleges and universities that wish to recruit foreign students require a Sponsorship Licence and are required to take on a policing role over their international students, helping the government crack down on those who abuse the rules. The licence acts as a pledge from the college or university that they accept responsibility for the student while they are in the UK. They face losing their licence and being barred from recruiting any more international students, if they fail to (i) keep copies of all their foreign students' passports; (ii) keep and update their students' contact details; (iii) alert the UKVI to any students who fail to enrol on their course; (iv) report unauthorised absences to the UKVI; and (v) inform the UKVI if any students stop their studies.[1] The Policy Guidance sets out rigorous provisions that must be complied with by the Tier 4 sponsor in order to obtain such a licence and to retain it. Tier 4 sponsors must issue students that wish to study with them a Certificate of Acceptance for Studies (CAS) containing a unique reference number and course details. In the past several years further sets of measures were announced as follows. We now take a closer look at the legal underpinning of the Guidance, as decided by the Supreme Court in the *New London College* case.

The legal underpinning is not the Prerogative power: the provisions and powers contained in the Guidance have been put there by statute (except for the fees which Sponsors must pay). Nor is it the immigration rules, because they only deal with students who need leave to enter and remain in order to study, and not their university or college, because they are not migrants and do not need leave to enter or remain. Instead, the Guidance is now based on a concept both new and controversial. To be precise, it is not exactly new, because the 'Ram doctrine' had come into existence in an internal government memorandum in 1945,[2] when a newly elected Labour government rather sheepishly asked Sir Grenville Ram, a senior civil servant, to tell them when they had to pass statutes and when they could just rely on some kind of administrative power. The memo setting out Sir Grenville's advice lay unknown to the public for many years within the echelons of government and their bureaucracy. It was known as the 'Ram doctrine' and was regularly applied, so we have been told. Then all of a sudden on 23 January 2003 the cat was let out of the bag by Lady Scotland, the Parliamentary Secretary to the Lord Chancellor. In a later written answer she breezily announced that this wholly secret document was a well-established part of our constitution. That was a surprise. She then came up with a particularly dotty solution – that ministers and their departments have common law powers which derive from 'the Crown's status as a Corporation Sole.'[3] This, we understand, was not part of the original Ram advice.[4] However, calling it a corporation sole was a means which would enable the Crown to do anything that an ordinary person could do unless it had been banned by statute or otherwise declared unlawful. That would give any government great leeway to take measures, like the sponsor guidance, bypassing Parliament and the need to go through the cumbersome process of legislating. Before the 'Ram doctrine' came into the public arena, something similar began to emerge from New Zealand.[5] A hint of what was to come had already been expressed in 1979 in the phone-tapping case of *Malone v the Metropolitan Police Comr*[6]. The case concerned the legality of recordings of telephone conversations by the Post Office for use by the police in the prevention or detection of crime. What gave the case notoriety was one of the reasons given by Megarry J for his conclusion that the telephone tapping was not unlawful. He said:

> 'The underlying assumption of this contention [of the plaintiff], of course, is that nothing is lawful that is not positively authorised by law. As I have indicated, England is not a country where everything is forbidden except what is expressly permitted. . . . If the tapping of telephones by the Post Office at the request of the police can be carried out without any breach of the law, it does not require any statutory or common law power to justify it: it can lawfully be done simply because there is nothing to make it unlawful.'

Malone was then taken to the Strasbourg Court[7] where the finding of the English Court was overturned on ECHR Article 8 private life grounds that the system of intercepting communications was not 'in accordance with the law' because of a lack of reasonable clarity and foreseeability as to the manner of its use. No argument was made in the *New London College* case about a lack of precision, clarity or foreseeability in a system of bewildering changes in sponsor Guidance at the whim of the executive as regards a college's rights under Article 1 of Protocol 1 of the ECHR. So the point may still be open.

In contrast to *Malone* are the remarks of Laws J in *R v Somerset County Council, ex p Fewings*[8]. Laws J said that whereas individuals 'may do anything . . . which the law does not prohibit', the 'opposite' rule applies to public bodies: anything that they do 'must be justified by positive law'. This suggests that for a 'public body' (whatever that means) to do anything, it must be able to point to legal authority if it is to act lawfully.

Two more recent cases were cited by Lord Sumption in his judgment in the *New London College* case. He stated that in *R v Secretary of State for Health, ex p C*[9] and *R (on the application of Shrewsbury and Atcham Borough Council) v Secretary of State for Communities and Local Government*[10] the Court of Appeal held that the basis of the power was the Crown's status as a common law corporation sole, with all the capacities and powers of a natural person subject only to such particular limitations as were imposed by law. However, he accepted that this was a controversial area and did not base his judgment on any notions of 'corporation sole'. Instead, he justified the use of Guidance to regulate sponsors on a very broad basis – the necessities of immigration control – without anchoring it to any specific statutory provision of the immigration laws, such as the Immigration Act 1971 section 1(4). He said:

'If the Secretary of State is entitled (as she plainly is) to prescribe and lay before Parliament rules for the grant of leave to enter or remain in the United Kingdom which depend upon the migrant having a suitable sponsor, then she must be also be [sic] entitled to take administrative measures for identifying sponsors who are and remain suitable, even if these measures do not themselves fall within section 3(2) of the Act.'

This is muddled thinking. The reasoning is unclear.

- The competence for laying immigration rules before Parliament is statutory, derived from the Immigration Act 1971 sections 1(4) and 3(2). The fact that statute permits making and laying immigration rules before Parliament which depend on the migrant having a suitable sponsor does not tell us why and how far Guidance can, not only identify who is a sponsor. but also create a vast number of rules and regulations for the regulation of those same sponsors.
- In his judgment Lord Sumption identifies two categories of sponsor rules: (i) those in which the Secretary of State has a free hand; and (ii) those which must be consistent with the immigration rules. He argues (at [25]) that, since the Guidance is liable to be changed without parliamentary scrutiny at the discretion of the Secretary of State, the Rules cannot lawfully incorporate by reference from the Guidance anything which constitutes a rule that if not satisfied will lead to the migrant being refused leave to enter or remain: see *R (Alvi) v Secretary of State for the Home Department* at [39] (per Lord Hope). This means that none of the sections of the Guidance incorporated by reference in the Rules cannot raise the bar against migrants any higher than the Rules themselves do. The effect of this is that the legal underpinning of the Guidance is derived in part from very specific statutory provisions. So what about the rest of the Guidance? Why should it not be linked to specific statutory provisions, so that it can be determined whether things like the sponsor guidance are truly necessary and ancillary to the particular legislation?[11]
- Under the rules a student must have a CAS to qualify for leave to enter or remain. The student's leave is conditional on having a current CAS. If the sponsor's licence is suspended, a CAS already issued to a student cannot be used and entry clearance will be refused during the period of suspension. If the licence is revoked, the same will happen to those seeking leave to enter and leave to remain for students already in the UK will reduced to a 60 day period or revoked. Is this not incorporating sections of the Guidance by reference in the Rules?
- If making rules for sponsors is an ancillary administrative measure sanctioned by statute, then presumably that sanction would extend to taking coercive measures; so why is that forbidden (at [29])?
- The sponsor guidance makes provision for imposing penal sanctions on sponsors by suspending and revoking their ability to issue CAS to students. If that is impliedly permitted as necessary ancillary measures sanctioned by the needs of immigration control, then what is it that distinguishes these from the category of coercive measures, which are not permitted but which in sponsor cases did not exist?
- Is there a crossover or blurring of the distinction between necessary and ancillary administrative measures on the one hand and authority derived from some form of third way? It is not clear.

9.3 *Students*

The decision in *New London College* may solve for the time being the underlying legality of the regulation of sponsor licences, but what other measures may the Secretary of State feel free to introduce without any parliamentary scrutiny. The decision leaves a great democratic deficit.

[1] In a letter to the *Guardian*, organised by Ian Grigg-Spall, academic chair of the National Critical Lawyers Group and signed by leading academic lawyers and the head of the lecturers' union, it is said that the proposed new rules for students go far beyond the present monitoring of student progress systems in universities, which has as its basic purpose assisting students to reach their full potential: 'In our view it is hard to justify such detailed monitoring of overseas students, even for immigration control purposes. Surely the Border Agency just needs to know students have registered and are at the university? It does not need to have this constant monitoring. This police-like surveillance is not the function of universities, and alters the educational relationship between students and their teachers in a very harmful manner'.

[2] The memorandum was dated 22 January 2003.

[3] For a more realistic evaluation and critique of the 'corporation sole' justification, see John Howells, 'What the Crown may do', 25 Jul 2009, pp 6-16 at www.blackstonechambers.com /news. The origin of the corporation sole was discussed by F.W Maitland. He did not disguise his contempt of the notion. He called it 'a curious freak of English law' and treated the doctrine as the 'parsonification' of the Crown (F W Maitland, 'The crown as Corporation' (1901) 17 LQR 131–146). In an earlier article (1900) LQR at p 335) Maitland noted that a corporation sole is anomalous for two reasons: (1) it is not a fully independent legal person, which has an existence independent of its members; (2) a corporation sole comprises only one physical person, not a group. According to Maitland, the notion of the incumbent as a corporation sole was largely Sir Edward Coke's idea: see *Sutton's Hospital Case* (1612) 77 ER 937, 10 Co Rep 1a at 29b. For the development of 'corporation sole' as an essentially ecclesiastic conception in feudal times, see Philip Jones, 'Posts about Corporation sole' (28 August 2012), at https://ecclesiasticallaw.wordpress.com/tag/corporation-sole/

[4] Lord Lester, 'The use of ministerial powers without parliamentary authority' [2003] Pub L at p 420. Sir Grenville Ram did not rely on the Crown's status as a corporation sole as the legal justification for his advice.

[5] B V Harris, 'The "Third Source" of Authority for Government Action' (1992) 108 *Law Quarterly Review* 626. See further BV Harris, 'The "Third Source" . . . Revisited' (2007) 123 LQR 225. In the latter article he argues at pp 246–248 that when reviewing the legality of non-statutory executive action, courts should first search for positive authorisation: ' . . . [O]ne would expect the courts on judicial review of all executive action to adopt the intuitive approach of inquiring first whether there is authority in positive law for the action, rather than inquiring . . . whether there is any positive law to prevent the government taking the action which it wishes to take.' This approach, argues Harris, would be 'consistent with the expectation and convention that authority should normally be provided in positive law in advance for all action of the government' (p 248).

[6] [1979] Ch 344, at 367.

[7] (1985) 7 EHRR 14.

[8] [1995] 1 All ER 513, 524.

[9] [2000] 1 FLR 627.

[10] [2008] EWCA Civ 148, [2008] 3 All ER 548.

[11] This was the main basis of Lord Carnwath's disagreement with Lord Sumption's analysis (at [35]–[36]). At [36] he referred to *Hazell v Hammersmith London Borough Council* [1992] 2 AC 1, [1991] 1 All ER 545, which considered the analogous principle in section 111 of the Local Government Act 1972. There, Lord Templeman extracted from the authorities '... the general proposition that when a power is claimed to be incidental, the provisions of the statute which confer and limit functions must be considered and construed.' (at p 31D). In that case the alleged power to enter into swap transactions had to be considered in the context of the specific provisions governing local authority borrowing. Similarly, in *R (on the application of Barry) v Liverpool City; Council* [2001] EWCA Civ 384, [2001] LGR 361, the scheme for vetting door-staff was incidental, not to the council's regulatory powers in general, but to the particular power for licensing places for public entertainment. In each case the source of the incidental power was found in a specific provision conferring specific functions.

9.4 All non-British and non-EEA students, whether General or Child Students, are required to demonstrate they have acquired 30 points for Attributes[1]

and 10 points for Maintenance[2] to study at an educational institute maintained by a Tier 4 sponsor. We set out the requirements to attain these points below. The previous Immigration Rules in HC 395, paras 57–70 have been replaced by the Tier 4 (General) Student category. They are no longer operative and are of mainly historic interest, cropping up, for example, in long residence cases. The commentary on the rules is to be found in earlier editions of this work.

1   HC 395, Appendix A.
2   HC 395, Appendix C.

ATTRIBUTES – 30 POINTS

9.5 To establish they have the necessary 30 points, students must show that their Tier 4 sponsor has issued them with a Confirmation of Acceptance for Studies (CAS).[1] All Tier 4 sponsors are now required to use the Sponsoring Management System, which is a computer program, with a password which is unique to the sponsor but also accessible by UKVI, to issue a CAS.

1   HC 395, Appendix A, paras 115A–120A.

Certificate of Acceptance for Studies (CAS)

9.6 A CAS is not an actual certificate or paper document, but a virtual document, similar to a database record, with a unique reference number. It contains details about the identity of the student and the course for which they have been accepted or upon which they are enrolled, the start and end dates for the course, the number of hours per week the course is taught and the evidence which the Tier 4 sponsor uses to assess the student's academic abilities, including their proficiency in English, and their suitability for the course. A CAS also contains details of the full costs of the course, including any boarding or accommodation fees, and sets out the amounts of money that have been paid by the student as well as any outstanding sums.[1] The Immigration Rules have been amended since the decision in *Pankina* so as to include the requirements for a valid CAS. A failure to provide a valid CAS in virtual form will defeat an application.[2]

The CAS is issued by the Tier 4 sponsor where they are satisfied that the student meets the requirements of the course, ending the problems created by the previous rules which required immigration officers and courts to determine a student's ability and intention to do so.[3] The CAS is accessible to the UKVI and Entry Clearance Officers through the CAS Checking Service[4] allowing verification checks to be made on applications for leave or entry clearance more easily. A CAS must be properly completed by the Tier 4 sponsor to be considered valid.[5] It must be issued by the Tier 4 sponsor no more than six months before the application is made; the CAS will expire unless used for the purposes of an application within this six-month time limit and students will have to obtain a new CAS if they do not submit an application during this time.[6] Equally, the Tier 4 sponsor must not have withdrawn the offer of study since the CAS was issued, and the sponsor must continue to hold a valid Tier 4 (General) Student Sponsorship at the date of decision.[7] Whilst there is nothing to prevent a student from making multiple applications for a CAS from different Tier 4 sponsors, they are permitted to use only one CAS in an application for entry clearance or leave to remain.

1   Detailed guidance on the various fields contained in the CAS and how they must be completed can be found at: https://www.gov.uk/government/collections/sponsorship-information-for-em ployers-and-educators.
2   *R (on the application of Ahmed (Abdullah Bashir)) v Secretary of State for the Home Department* [2011] EWHC 2855 (Admin).
3   In *R (on the application of Pokhriyal) v Secretary of State for the Home Department* [2013] EWCA Civ 1568 Jackson LJ concluded that para 120B of Appendix A, HC 395, makes clear that it is for the college and not the Secretary of State to carry out the assessment of whether a particular course constitutes 'academic progress' for an applicant.
4   HC 395, Appendix A, para 117.
5   It is an express requirement of the Rules that a CAS must be properly completed by the Tier 4 sponsor to be considered valid: HC 395, Appendix A, para 116(f). UKVI may cancel a CAS if they find that a sponsor was not entitled to assign it: Tier 4 Sponsor Policy Guidance, Document 2, para 427.
6   HC 395, Appendix A, para 116(a); Tier 4 Policy Guidance, para 31. See *Bhanushali (re-using same CAS: new rules) India* [2011] UKUT 411 (IAC). There is no restriction in s 3C(5) Immigration Act 1971 on the number of times that a person may seek to vary the original application, provided the notice of variation is given prior to UKVI's decision; the date UKVI is required to take into account for the purposes of determining the points to be awarded under Appendix C, where there has been a variation substituting a new college, is the date of the most recent variation request: *Qureshi (Tier 4 – effect of variation – App C) Pakistan* [2011] UKUT 412 (IAC).
7   HC 395, Appendix A, para 116(e). The list of up-to-date licence holders is set out at: www.g ov.uk/government/publications/register-of-licensed-sponsors-students

9.7 Since the Rules require the institution which issues the CAS to hold a valid Sponsorship Licence at the date of decision,[1] problems may arise for students where the sponsor's licence has been suspended or revoked or where the sponsor withdraws the CAS[2] after a student has submitted an application for entry clearance or leave to remain. Where the licence is *revoked*, any CAS issued by the sponsor will be regarded as invalid, and any application using such a CAS will result in an automatic refusal. All that a student can do in such a situation is try to find an alternate sponsor and re-apply for entry clearance or leave.[3] A student with existing leave will have the leave curtailed to 60 calendar days in order to provide him or her with the opportunity to find a new sponsor.[4] If, however, the student is found to be actively involved in the CAS being assigned improperly their leave will be immediately curtailed.[5] Where a sponsor's Tier 4 licence is *suspended*, the Policy Guidance Annex II, para 10 says applications will go on hold. Since sponsors are not permitted to issue a CAS to a student at a time when it is suspended, any application based upon it will be automatically refused.[6] The Guidance explains that students who are being sponsored at the time of the suspension 'will not be affected', unless UKVI subsequently decide to revoke the licence.[7] Where a student has already been granted entry clearance but has not travelled to the UK when the Tier 4 licence is suspended they are still permitted to travel to the UK and study,[8] although they may be caught by the General Grounds of refusal, if the revocation of the sponsor's licence is treated as a material change of circumstances.[9] The unfair results to students produced by the timings of suspension or revocation would appear to be less important than the government's need to ensure that Tier 4 licence holders strictly comply with their sponsorship duties. A CAS document can only be used once; where a student's application is refused, the student is required to obtain a fresh CAS from the Tier 4 sponsor.[10] The Tribunal has however, to a limited extent, recognised the extent of the unfairness that can be caused upon revocation of sponsor licences where students become aware of revocation only at the time they receive a decision.[11] Sponsors must generally assign a CAS for each separate course of study that is undertaken by the student.[12]

1   HC 395, Appendix A, para 116(e).
2   Tier 4 Sponsor Guidance, Document 2, para 172 explains that sponsors may withdraw a CAS not yet used to support an application for leave to remain in the UK, using the Sponsorship Management System.
3   Tier 4 Sponsor Guidance, Document 3, para 160 and Tier 4 Policy Guidance, Annex 2, para 10. If the Tier 4 licence is withdrawn before application, the CAS will be invalid and result in refusal of entry clearance: HC 395, Appendix A, para 116(c). If the Tier 4 licence has been withdrawn following the grant of entry clearance, but where they have not travelled to the UK, they will be refused leave to enter. If the student is in the UK when the licence is revoked, the student's leave will be curtailed to 60 days, in order to give him/her time to find an alternate sponsor or have his/her leave withdrawn if he/she is considered to be involved in the reasons why the Tier 4 licence was suspended. If the student has an in-country application pending with UKVI at the time of revocation, his/her application will be refused and the student must submit a new application with a new Tier 4 sponsor or leave the UK.
4   Tier 4 Sponsor Guidance, Document 3, paras 160 and 166.
5   Tier 4 Sponsor Guidance, Document 3, paras 165, 168, 170 and Tier 4 Policy Guidance, Annex 2, para 11. If the suspension comes into force whilst the student has an out of country application pending, applications will not be considered. If a student has been granted entry clearance, but has not yet travelled to the UK, students are advised not to travel whilst the suspension is in force, but if they do travel they will be permitted to commence their course. If the student is already in the UK and studying with the Tier 4 sponsor at the time of suspension, no action is taken, unless the licence is subsequently revoked. If an application is pending with UKVI at the time of suspension, the application will not be considered until the suspension is lifted or refused if the licence is subsequently revoked. However, a student is permitted to rely upon a different Tier 4 sponsor using a fresh CAS, where a decision has not been taken by UKVI: *Qureshi (Tier 4 – effect of variation – App C) Pakistan* [2011] UKUT 412 (IAC).
6   Tier 4 Sponsor Guidance, Document 3, para 140 and Tier 4 Policy Guidance, Annex 2, para 10.
7   Tier 4 Sponsor Guidance, Document 3, para 144. Upon revocation students will be permitted 60 calendar days to find a new sponsor unless they were complicit in the CAS being improperly issued.
8   Tier 4 Sponsor Guidance, Document 3, para 149, and Tier 4 Policy Guidance, Annex 2, para 10.
9   HC 395, para 321(ii) or 321A(1).
10   HC 395, Appendix A, para 116(ea)
11   Where a student's leave had already expired at the time of making an application for leave to remain, the Tribunal initially found that there was no legitimate expectation that UKVI will grant a period of 60 days to find a new course provider: *JA (revocation of registration – Secretary of State's policy) India* [2011] UKUT 52 (IAC); *MM and SA (Pankina: near miss) Pakistan* [2010] UKUT 481 (IAC); and *Patel (Tier 4 – no '60-day extension') India* [2011] UKUT 187 (IAC). Where, however, a student had an outstanding in-country application and found out about revocation only when his college closed, it was, in public law terms, unfair to curtail his leave, since this denied him the opportunity to find an alternate Tier 4 Sponsor: *Thakur (PBS – common law fairness) Bangladesh* [2011] UKUT 151 (IAC). The Tribunal recognised the harsh results that can occur when Sponsor licences are revoked and found that UKVI had a duty to act fairly in considering such applications; a failure to notify students of the revocation of licences shortly before making a decision on an outstanding application did not comply with that duty: *Patel (revocation of sponsor licence – fairness) India* [2011] UKUT 211 (IAC). The Tribunal gave guidance to the FTT that where UKVI have failed to act fairly, they may allow an appeal against such a decision as 'not in accordance with the law' with a direction to specify the time needed before the application should be re-determined to allow a fair opportunity to make representations, so as to allow the student to obtain fresh sponsorship. See also *R (on the application of Basharat) v Secretary of State for the Home Department* [2011] EWHC 195 (Admin) and *Kaur (Patel fairness: respondent's policy)* [2013] UKUT 344 (IAC). On the issue of fairness more generally in the context of Points-Based

System applications, see *Naved (Student – fairness – notice of points)* [2012] UKUT 14 (IAC), *R (on the application of Sapkota) v Secretary of State for the Home Department* [2011] EWCA Civ 1320 and *Kabaghe (appeal from outside UK – fairness) Malawi* [2011] UKUT 00473 (IAC).

12 Tier 4 Sponsor Policy Guidance, Document 2, para 126. Tier 4 Sponsors may assign a single CAS to cover both a pre-sessional course and the main course of study in limited circumstances.

PERMISSIBLE COURSES

Courses for Tier 4 (General) Students

9.8 Courses must meet the UKVI's minimum academic requirements set out in the Immigration Rules and the level of course that a sponsor may offer will depend on whether the sponsor is a standard or a Highly Trusted Sponsor.[1] Except in the case of pre-sessional courses, the course offered must lead to an 'approved qualification'.[2] For Tier 4 (General) Students, the course must meet one of the following requirements:

(a) a full-time course of degree level study that leads to an approved qualification;

(b) an overseas course of degree level study that is recognised as being equivalent to a UK Higher Education course and is being provided by an overseas Higher Education Institution;

(c) a full-time course of study involving a minimum of 15 hours per week organised daytime[3] study and, except in the case of a pre-sessional course, leading to a qualification below degree level.[4]

This sensible change in policy emphasis means that it is now educational institutions, not immigration officers, who are responsible for ensuring that the courses offered meet the minimum requirements of the rules and that students have the ability and intention to undertake and complete the course. Where the sponsor holds a Highly Trusted Sponsor Licence and is assigned a CAS on or after 21 April 2011, students may undertake courses approved at the National Qualifications Framework (NQF) level 3, Scottish Credit and Qualifications Framework (SCQF) level 6. Highly Trusted Sponsors may also offer short-term study abroad programme courses undertaken as part of the student's qualification at an overseas higher education institution (HEI) where UK NARIC confirm that the overseas course is equivalent to a UK degree, and English language courses at or above level B2 of the Common European Framework of Reference for Languages (CEFR). In addition, Highly Trusted Sponsors can offer courses which include work placements, which must be an assessed part of the course and must not exceed 50 per cent of the length of the course in the UK.[5] Where, however, the sponsor holds a Standard-rated licence, the level at which it may offer courses is higher. Standard sponsors assigning a CAS on or after 21 April 2011 may only do so where they offer courses at NQF level 4 or above, Qualifications and Credits Framework (QCF) level 4 or above, level 7 SCQF or above. They may also offer short-term study abroad programme courses undertaken as part of the student's qualification at an overseas HEI where UK NARIC confirm that the overseas course is equivalent to a UK degree, and English language courses at, or above, level B2 of the Common European Framework of Reference for Languages

(CEFR). Standard sponsors are not permitted to offer courses below degree level (excluding Foundation degrees) that contain work placements.[6] Except where the student is on a work placement, the rules require that all study must take place on the premises of the Tier 4 sponsor.[7] Tier 4 students are permitted to undertake additional courses as well as their main studies without permission from either the UKVI or their Tier 4 sponsor. The course can be on any subject, and does not have to relate to the main course of study.[8]

[1] HC 395, Appendix A, para 120(a).

[2] HC 395, Appendix A, para 120(b). An approved qualification is one which is either validated by Royal Charter, awarded by a recognised body on the recognised bodies list operated by the Department for Business Immigration and Skills: www.bis.gov.uk/policies/higher-education/r ecognised-uk-degrees/recognised-bodies; or recognised by one or more recognised bodies via a formal articulation agreement with the awarding body, in England, Wales and Northern Ireland, on the Register of Accredited Qualifications (register.ofqual.gov.uk) at National Qualifications Framework (NQF) level 3 or above, in Scotland, accredited at level 6 or above in the Scottish Credit and Qualifications Framework (SCQF) by the Scottish Qualifications Authority, an overseas qualification, on which UK NARIC is able to advise on its validity, with a level equivalent to level 3 or above on the National Qualifications Framework or covered by a formal legal agreement between a United Kingdom recognised body and another education provider or awarding body, which must be signed off by an authorised signatory for institutional agreements within the recognised body: see Tier 4 Sponsor Guidance, Document 2, paras 38–39. Document 2, paras 38–39. Distance learning courses are specifically excluded: see Tier 4 Sponsor Guidance, Document 2, para 40.

[3] Tier 4 Policy Guidance, para 65, Tier 4 Sponsor Guidance, Document 2, para 37 defined as study between 8am–6pm, Monday to Friday.

[4] HC 395, Appendix A, paras 120 and 120A.

[5] HC 395, Appendix A, para 120A relating to all CAS assigned by a HTS on or after 21 April 2011; see also Tier 4 Policy Guidance, para 66. For a CAS issued prior to 21 April 2011, slightly different provisions apply: see HC 395, Appendix A, para 120 and Tier 4 Policy Guidance, para 59 which permitted, in addition to the courses set out above, English language courses at any level for government-sponsored students, or for pre-sessional courses undertaken prior to the commencement of a degree course. For work placements, see HC 395, Appendix A, para 120A(f).

[6] HC 395, Appendix A, para 120A, again relating to all CAS assigned by a standard sponsor on or after 21 April 2011; see also Tier 4 Policy Guidance at para 67. For a CAS issued prior to 21 April 2011, again slightly different provisions apply: see HC 395, Appendix A, para 120 and Tier 4 Policy Guidance, para 60 which permitted, in addition to the courses set out above, English language courses at any level for government-sponsored students, or for pre-sessional courses undertaken prior to the commencement of a degree course

[7] HC 395, Appendix A, para 120(d). Where courses involve periods of study outside the UK and the student intends to return to the UK after that section of the course is completed, the Tier 4 sponsor may either continue to sponsor the student whilst he or she is out of the country (requiring the Sponsor to continue to meet their reporting duties for the student) with the result that the student will be allowed to return to the UK without further application, or end the sponsorship at the point of overseas travel and require the student to re-apply to complete the remainder of the course in the UK: Tier 4 Sponsor Guidance, Document 2, paras 108–110.

[8] HC 395 para 245ZW(c)(iv)(3); Tier 4 Policy Guidance, para 338.

Academic progress

9.9 Where a Tier 4 (General) student is applying for further leave to remain for a new course in the UK and is assigned a CAS on or after 4 July 2011, the Rules have been amended so that a Tier 4 Sponsor may only do so where the new course represents 'academic progress' from their previous course of study. This important new limitation is designed to preclude students from undertaking courses unless they are above the level of or complement 'the previous course for which the applicant was granted leave as a Tier 4 (General) Student or as a Student'[1] and is likely to cause difficulties to students who fail examinations and seek to undertake a new course with a different Tier 4 Sponsor; that route is now effectively closed. Academic progress is not required where it is the student's first course of study in the UK.[2] Generally, the new course should be above the level of the previous course for which leave to remain was previously granted, although the policy guidance recognises that it may be at the same level and in 'rare' instances, at a lower level. The rules now confirm that the course for which further leave is sought can 'complement' the applicant's previous course for which leave was first granted.[3] It will be for the Tier 4 sponsor to demonstrate that the course genuinely represents academic progress.[4] UKVI will closely monitor the student (and the sponsor) where such applications are approved. The only exceptions are where the student has made a first application to move to a new institution to complete a course commenced elsewhere, where the student is re-sitting examinations or repeating modules, or where the student is a Tier 4 (Child) Student.[5]

[1] HC 395, Appendix A, Para 120A prevents the acquisition of points under paras 113–120 of Appendix A: see *Naeem* (Para 120A of Appendix A) [2013] UKUT 465 (IAC).

[2] Note that the requirement in para 120A of Appendix A, HC 395, for the Sponsor to confirm that a proposed course of study must be above the level of or complement 'the previous course for which the applicant was granted leave as a Tier 4 (General) Student or as a Student' is not displaced where the last period of leave granted to the applicant has been for some other reason than as such a student. The benchmark for assessing academic progress is the last course of study. See *Mushtaq (s 85A(3) (a): scope; academic progress) Pakistan* [2013] UKUT 61 (IAC).

[3] HC 395, Appendix A, para 120A(b)(ii).

[4] See *R (on the application of Pokhriyal) v Secretary of State for the Home Department* [2013] EWCA Civ 1568, in which Jackson LJ concluded that para 120B of Appendix A, HC 395, made clear that it was for the college and not the Secretary of State to carry out the assessment of whether a particular course constitutes 'academic progress' for an applicant. The mere issue of a CAS creates a presumption or expectation that the proposed course represents academic progress. Ordinarily, the Secretary of State will not be entitled to go behind the college's assessment of academic progress, save perhaps where there is the presence of fraud or the college has made an assessment which was 'plainly inappropriate on the face of the documents'. The confirmation that a course constitutes academic progress can be contained either in the CAS or a separate document. Para 120B has now been removed from Appendix A. However, the same language (the college must 'confirm') suggests that the same conclusions would apply to para 120A. See too, the Tier 4 Sponsor Guidance, Document 2, paras 100–107. Thus, for example, if a student's previous course was at QCF or NQF6 (and equivalents), the policy guidance asserts that it would expect the next course to be at least level QCF or NQF7. For courses on the same level, the guidance accepts that moving from a taught masters to an MBA or a research-based masters degree or taking a course to develop a deeper specialisation in a particular field will suffice. In VB (Student – attendance and progress not equated) Jamaica [2011] UKUT 119 (IAC) the Tribunal considered that mere attendance on a course could not without more be considered as progress.

[5] Tier 4 Policy Guidance, para 68, Tier 4 Sponsor Guidance, Document 2, para 101.

Courses for Tier 4 (Child Students)

9.10 Tier 4 (Child) Students may study only at independent fee paying schools holding a Tier 4 (Child) Student Sponsor Licence[1] at courses which are taught in line with the National Curriculum or NQF, courses accepted as being the same academic level as the National Curriculum or NQF by Ofsted, the Education and Training Inspectorate (Northern Ireland), Her Majesty's Inspectorate of Education (Scotland) or Estyn (Wales), or courses which are taught in line with existing independent school inspection standards or pre-sessional courses designed to prepare the child student for his or her main course of study.[2]

[1] HC 395, Appendix A, para 124(a) and (e). Children aged between 4–15 years old must be educated at independent fee-paying schools. They are not permitted to be educated at publicly funded schools. Child students may be educated at Further Education Colleges if the College is able to charge for international students. Students must apply in the child student category where they will study at NQF level 2 or below: where the child is 16–17 years old and will be studying a course at or above NQF level 2, the student and sponsor can agree whether to apply as a Tier 4 (General) or Tier 4 (Child) Tier 4 Policy Guidance, paras 215–218.

[2] HC 395, Appendix A, para 126 and Tier 4 Policy Guidance, para 219.

Pre-sessional courses

9.11 Students may be required to complete a pre-sessional course immediately before starting their full-time course of study in the UK, including intensive English language courses or other course aimed at preparing students for their main course of study. Pre-sessional courses must meet the Tier 4 requirements, but unlike main courses, it is not necessary that they lead to a recognised qualification[1] and may be at any level.[2] The pre-sessional provider may be the student's prospective main course sponsor, a 'partner' institution to that sponsor, or one which operates independently of the prospective sponsor.[3] If students: (a) the sponsor is an independent school who has made an unconditional offer for a main course of study and the pre-sessional course plus main course of study is not more than the maximum time for which the applicant may stay in the UK as a Tier 4 student; (b) the sponsor is a HEI who has made an unconditional offer for a main course of study at degree level and the pre-sessional course with the sponsor or partner institution is no more than three-months long and ends no more than one month before the main degree course; or (c) the pre-sessional course is an English language course that is no more than three-months long and ends no more than one month before the main degree course and the student is at B1 level of the Common European Framework of Reference for Languages (CEFR) and will reach B2 level by the end of the pre-sessional course. In all other circumstances the student will have to make two separate applications for two separate CAS.[4]

[1] HC 395, para 245ZW(b)(ii), Tier 4 Sponsor Guidance, Document 2, para 41. Tier 4 (General) Students applying to study on pre-sessional courses are still required to pass an English Language test but the proficiency level may be either B1 or B2 CEFR depending on the academic level of the pre-sessional course: Tier 4 Sponsor Guidance, Document 2, para 46.

[2] HC 395, Appendix A, para 120A(c).

[3] Tier 4 Sponsor Guidance, Document 2, paras 44–47. Pre-sessional course providers can be named as a 'branch' on the prospective if they are a 'partner' institution, even if they are already a licensed sponsor in their own right. If the partner institution is not a licensed sponsor in its own right, it may only offer the pre-sessional courses defined in para 134 of the Tier 4 Sponsor Guidance, Document 2. If the pre-sessional provider is not a 'partner' institution, it must be a licensed sponsor under Tier 4 in its own right

[4] Tier 4 Sponsor Policy Guidance, Document 2, paras 134–135.

Work placements

9.12 Tier 4 students are allowed to undertake work placements as part of their course of study as long as the work placement is an integral and assessed part of the course.[1] Since 6 April 2010, only Highly Trusted Sponsors may offer courses to Tier 4 (General) Students which are below NQF level 6, and include a work placement.[2] Work placements should normally not be more than 33 per cent of the total length of the course. The exceptions to this, where the placements can be up to 50 per cent of the length of the course are where the course is at NQF/QCF 6/SCQF 9 or above and is studied at an HEI or forms part of a study abroad programme, or where the student is a Tier 4 (Child) Student who is aged 16 or above.[3] A further exception is where it is a statutory requirement as to the period of the placement which means it exceeds 33 per cent.[4] The Tier 4 sponsor will remain responsible for them throughout the work placement, notwithstanding the fact that the work placement may take place outside of the sponsor's premises.[5]

[1] HC 395, Appendix A, para 120A(f), Tier 4 Policy Guidance 328–333, Tier 4 Sponsor Guidance, Document 2, paras 85–90.). Work placements are defined as 'employment' for the purposes of HC 395, para 6 but are exempt as a restriction on the conditions attached to student leave: paras 245ZY(c)(iii)(iv), 245ZZB(c)(iv)(3) and 245ZZB(c)(iv)(3).
[2] HC 385, Appendix A, para 120A(f)(ii), Tier 4 Policy Guidance, para 328, Tier 4 Sponsor Guidance, Document 2, para 85. Students enrolled on a higher education course at an overseas higher education institution coming to the United Kingdom to do part of their course may also do a work placement as part of their course as long as it is no more than 50 per cent of their study in the United Kingdom. Child students under 16 are not permitted to undertake work placements: Tier 4 Policy Guidance, para 307.
[3] HC 395, Appendix A, para 120A(f)(i), Tier 4 Sponsor Guidance, Document 2, para 85(a)–(c).
[4] Tier 4 Sponsor Guidance, Document 2, para 85(d).
[5] Tier 4 Policy Guidance, para 333, Tier 4 Sponsor Guidance, Document 2, para 89.

ENGLISH LANGUAGE REQUIREMENTS

Proficiency in English language for Tier 4 (General) Students

9.13 All students wishing to study in the United Kingdom must demonstrate proficiency in the English language. Sponsors. Because the rules and policy guidance have been amended over time, the way in which Tier 4 sponsors determine a student's proficiency in English will depend upon when they assigned the CAS.

The Rules now provide that where a CAS was assigned on or after 21 April 2011, the applicant must meet one of the requirements below:[1]

(1) *For degree level courses* where the CAS has been assigned by a Sponsor which is a Recognised Body or a body in receipt of funding as a HEI from the Department for Employment and Learning in Northern Ireland, the Higher Education Funding Council for England, the Higher Education Funding Council for Wales, or the Scottish Funding Council, and:

    (a) the applicant is a national of Antigua and Barbuda, Australia, The Bahamas, Barbados, Belize, Canada, Dominica, Grenada, Guyana, Jamaica, New Zealand, St Kitts and Nevis, St Lucia, St Vincent and the Grenadines, Trinidad and Tobago or United States of America; or

(b) the applicant has obtained an academic qualification (not a professional or vocational qualification), deemed by UK NARIC to meet or exceed a Bachelor's or Master's degree, or a PhD in the UK, from an educational establishment in one of the aforementioned countries or the UK; or

(c) the applicant has successfully completed a course as a Tier 4 (Child) Student (or under the student rules that were in force before 31 March 2009, where the student was granted permission to stay whilst under 18-years-old) which was at least six months in length and ended within two years of the date the sponsor assigned the CAS; or

(d) the CAS confirms that the applicant has a knowledge of English equivalent to level B2 of the CEFR in all four components (reading, writing, speaking and listening), or above.

(2) *For degree level courses* where the CAS has been assigned by a Sponsor which is not a Recognised Body or is not a body in receipt of public funding as a HEI:

(a) the applicant is a national of Antigua and Barbuda, Australia, The Bahamas, Barbados, Belize, Canada, Dominica, Grenada, Guyana, Jamaica, New Zealand, St Kitts and Nevis, St Lucia, St Vincent and the Grenadines, Trinidad and Tobago or United States of America; or

(b) has obtained an academic qualification (not a professional or vocational qualification), deemed by UK NARIC to meet or exceed a Bachelor's or Master's degree, or a PhD in the UK, from an educational establishment in one of the aforementioned countries; or

(c) the applicant successfully completed a course as a Tier 4 (Child) Student (or under the student rules that were in force before 31 March 2009, where the student was granted permission to stay whilst he was under 18-years-old) which was at least six months in length, and ended within two years of the date the sponsor assigned the CAS; or

(d) the applicant provides an original English language test certificate from an English language test provider approved by the Secretary of State which is within its validity date, stating the applicant's name, that the applicant has achieved or exceeded level B2 of the CEFR in all four components (reading, writing, speaking and listening) unless exempted from sitting a component on the basis of the applicant's disability, and the date of the award.

(3) For courses *below degree level* an applicant must demonstrate that:

(a) they are a national of Antigua and Barbuda, Australia, The Bahamas, Barbados, Belize, Canada, Dominica, Grenada, Guyana, Jamaica, New Zealand, St Kitts and Nevis, St Lucia, St Vincent and the Grenadines, Trinidad and Tobago or United States of America; or

    (b)   obtained an academic qualification (not a professional or vocational qualification), deemed by UK NARIC to meet or exceed a Bachelor's or Master's degree or a PhD in the UK, from an educational establishment in one of the aforementioned countries; or

    (c)   they successfully completed a course as a Tier 4 (Child) student (or under the student rules that were in force before 31 March 2009, where the student was granted permission to stay whilst he was under 18-years-old) which was at least six months in length, and ended within two years of the date the sponsor assigned the CAS; or

    (d)   provides an original English language test certificate from an English language test provider approved by the Secretary of State which is within its validity date, and shows the applicant's name, that they achieved or exceeded level B1 of the CEFR in all four components (reading, writing, speaking and listening), unless exempted from sitting a component on the basis of the applicant's disability, and the date of the award.

Approved English language tests are set out in Appendix O, along with the evidence required to demonstrate their completion.[2] The requirements also apply to students undertaking pre-sessional courses prior to a degree course, Foundation courses or English as a foreign language under Tier 4 at CEFR level B2 or above. Where a Tier 4 (General) student intends to follow a course at NQF 6/QCF 6/SCQF 9 and above at a HEI,[3] the Tier 4 sponsor must check that the student's English language proficiency is at B2 CEFR ensuring that they meet the requirements of the rules set out above which permit it to choose its own method of assessment.[4] Where the course is below degree level or the sponsor is not a HEI, the sponsor must ensure that the student meets the requirements of the rules set out above which require the student to have passed an English language test from the list of approved tests for Tier 4.[5] Where an approved secure English language test has been used to check the student's competence in English language, the sponsor is obliged to include information about any test, including the result for each component in the CAS, unless they are an HEI dealing with an applicant to study at degree level in which case the sponsor just needs to have seen scores equivalent to B2 in each of the four components.[6] Similarly, where studies have been previously completed by a child, the sponsor must include information about the course the child undertook on the CAS. The Rules expressly refer to the fact that applicants must, if required to do so on examination or interview, be able to demonstrate without the assistance of an interpreter English language proficiency (although they will not be subject to formal testing); the policy guidance warns that students may be interviewed to see whether they can hold a simple conversation without an interpreter, and where they cannot, their application will be refused, or they will be refused leave to enter.[7]

[1]   HC 395, Appendix A, para 118(b); Tier 4 Policy Guidance, paras 122–124, 126–133; and Tier 4 Sponsor Guidance, Document 2, paras 92–95. For the previous requirements of the Rules relating to English language requirements, see the previous edition of this work. A HEI sponsor may waive the English language requirement for a Tier 4 (General) Student who is considered to be a 'gifted student'. The Academic Registrar (or equivalent) of the HEI will personally need to assign the CAS which must confirm that the student is being treated as gifted and explain the reasons why: Tier 4 Policy Guidance, paras 125 and 134 and Tier 4 Sponsor Guidance, Document 2, paras 68–74.

[2] Tier 4 Sponsor Guidance, Document 2, para 95. Following allegations of widespread use of proxies to stand in for applicants in tests provided by ETS, the Home Office have published 'Transitional arrangements for applications relying on English language tests which have been removed from Appendix O in 2014.' These are to be found alongside Appendix O on the Home Office website.

[3] An HEI is defined as a recognised body or a body that receives public funding as a HEI from the Department for Employment and Learning in Northern Ireland, the Higher Education Funding Council for England, the Higher Education Funding Council for Wales or the Scottish Funding Council. It includes Richmond, the American International University in London, the UK Foundation Programme Office, and the Yorkshire and Humber Strategic Health Authority: Tier 4 Sponsor Guidance, Document 2, Glossary.

[4] Tier 4 Sponsor Guidance, Document 2, para 92.

[5] Tier 4 Sponsor Guidance, Document 2, paras 92–94. A list of the approved secure English language tests for Tier 4 students, including the time-period the tests are valid for and the scores a Tier 4 (General) must achieve to meet CEFR level B1 or B2 in all four components (reading, writing, speaking and listening), is contained in HC 395, Appendix O, at: https://www.gov.uk/government/publications/immigration-rules-appendix-o.

[6] Tier 4 Sponsor Guidance, Document 2, para 124 and paras 129–131, para 124.

[7] HC 395, para 245ZV(ca) and para 245ZW(da) and Tier 4 Policy Guidance, para 91.

English language courses

9.14 Those wishing to study English language courses in the UK can now only do so at level B2[1] or above of the Common European Framework of Reference for Languages (CEFRL),[2] broadly equivalent to A-level standard, save for students receiving official government sponsorship or where English language is an element of a pre-sessional course. Students are no longer permitted to study English language courses below level B2 CEFR, a rule change which impacts significantly upon a large number of colleges and academic institutions.[3] If a Tier 4 (General) student wishes to undertake another English language course after their first course, they will need to show the formal assessment of the English language level they have achieved from the first course.[4] We consider that a policy requiring such a high level of proficiency in English in order to study in the UK is a blunt and expensive instrument for preventing abuse of immigration control, considering the number of genuine students wishing to learn English in the UK or to enrol on courses in which language skills are not a priority.

[1] Previous rules permitted study at level A2 CEFR.

[2] Tier 4 Policy Guidance, para 71.

[3] See the comments of Foskett J in R (on the application of English UK Ltd) v Secretary of State for the Home Department [2010] EWHC 1726 (Admin), [2010] All ER (D) 86 (Jul) commenting on the evidence of 520,000–600,000 students who had studied on English language courses since 2000 and made a direct contribution of £1.5 billion and stated that the provision of language courses was 'on any view . . . a significant source of revenue for the UK economy' (paras 19–21).

[4] Tier 4 Policy Guidance, para 73.

Documents to be submitted in support of a Confirmation of Acceptance for Studies (CAS)

9.15 Applicants are required, as evidence of previous qualifications, the specified documents that they used to obtain the offer of a place on a course from the sponsor unless the applicant is applying to study with a HTS and is from a specified 'low risk' country, although the UKVI reserves the right to request those documents from the latter class of applicant.[1] The specified documents in the Rules are: (a) the original certificate of qualification or the original transcript of results or, where they have been used, the original copy of references, and (b) the applicant's current valid original passport or travel document.[2] The academic certificates supplied by the student must coincide with those listed by the Tier 4 sponsor on the CAS; students are expected to obtain the list of documents used by their Tier 4 sponsor to grant them a place on a course and to submit them in their original form in support of their application for entry clearance or leave to remain.[3] Where the document is not in English or Welsh, the original must be accompanied by a fully certified translation including the professional translator's credentials and contact details.[4] The Tier 4 Policy Guidance states that applicants must also send the original of any references used by the Tier 4 sponsor to assess the student. Students must also provide evidence they have met the English language requirements. Where this is being demonstrated by the student being a national of a specified country or undertaking a degree in a majority English-speaking country, the evidence required is the applicant's passport or course certificate, respectively.[5] Students following a course below degree level or a course above degree level with a sponsor who is not a UK HEI must include the evidence specified in Appendix.[6] Where the student wishes to undertake undergraduate or postgraduate studies leading to a doctorate or where the sponsor has used a course that the student successfully completed as a Tier 4 (Child) Student to prove English language competence, the applicant must include the course certificate.[7] If the applicant is considered to be a gifted student and the English language requirement is waived, the requisite letter from the Academic Registrar does not have to be submitted with the applicant but should be carried by the student when entering the UK.[8] Masters degree, undergraduate or postgraduate studies leading to a taught Masters degree or other postgraduate qualification or a period of study or research in excess of six months in one of the disciplines listed in paragraphs 1 or 2 of Appendix 6 of the Rules; at an institution of higher education where this forms part of an overseas postgraduate qualification they will require security clearance in the form of a valid Academic Technology Approval Scheme (ATAS) clearance certificate, issued by the Foreign and Commonwealth Office (FCO) a copy of which must be submitted with the application.[9]

---

[1] HC 395, para 244AA and Appendix A, para 118(a) and Appendix C, para 11. Students who qualify for these differential arrangements are nationals of Argentina, Australia, Brunei, Canada, Chile, Croatia, Hong Kong, Japan, New Zealand, Singapore, South Korea, Taiwan (where the passport issued includes the number of the identification card issued by the competent authority) Trinidad and Tobago, United States of America, or a British National Overseas. The list is reviewed annually.

[2] HC 395, Appendix A, para 120–SD. This is substantially less onerous than previous requirements that applicants provide all document submitted by the sponsor and the sponsor list them all in the CAS. Further guidance is provided in the Tier 4 Policy Guidance, paras 136–144.

[3] Tier 4 Policy Guidance, paras 155–156.

[4] Tier 4 Policy Guidance, paras 16–17.

[5] Tier 4 Policy Guidance, paras 128–130.

[6] HC 395, Appendix O, paras 1–2. Where the test was taken with Cambridge English on or after 6 April 2013 no documents will be required as the test scores can be verified on the Cambridge English online system.

[7] Tier 4 Policy Guidance, para 133.

[8] Tier 4 Policy Guidance, para 134.

⁹ HC 395, paras 245ZV(da) and 245ZX(ea), Tier 4 Policy Guidance, paras 145–151.

MAINTENANCE – 10 POINTS

9.16 Previous provisions relating to the adequacy of funds have been revoked in favour of what is asserted to be a transparent and objective mechanism to determine the adequacy of funds and to ensure that students can afford to live in the UK for the duration of their studies.

Maintenance requirements for Tier 4 (General) Students

9.17 To attain the 10 points specified for Tier 4 (General) Students[1] or Tier 4 (Child) Students living independently and aged 16 or 17,[2] applicants must demonstrate that they have the funds required to meet both the costs of the course and their living expenses for the duration of the course.[3] Students must have held these funds for 28 consecutive days, a condition which is strictly applied.[4] The Rules have been amended further to require the student to confirm the money will remain available unless used to pay for course fees or living costs.[5] The amount of money required will depend upon the length of the course upon which a student is enrolled.

(1)   Where the applicant has no 'established presence'[6] of study in the UK and the application is (a) a first application for entry clearance under Tier 4, (b) an application to switch from another category under the Rules into Tier 4, or (c) following completion of a single course of six months or less, the student must demonstrate that he or she has the full course fees (only the first year if the course is longer) together with £1,020 for each month of the course up to a maximum of nine months (ie course fees plus £9,180), if the applicant is studying in a specified London Borough. Where the course is to take place outside the specified London Boroughs, the living expenses drop to £600 per month (ie course fees plus £7,380).[7]

(2)   Where the applicant has an 'established presence' in the UK a lower sum of maintenance is required. If the application is either a second entry clearance application or an application for further leave as a Tier 4 student, as long as the course was completed within the previous four months,[8] a student must demonstrate that he or she has the first year course fees and £1,020 for two months if the course is in a specified London Borough; (ie course fees plus £2,040) and £820 per month where the course is outside the specified London Borough (ie course fees plus £1,640).[9]

Where students have been sponsored by an official financial sponsor[10] within the last 12 months these students must provide UKVI with confirmation from their financial sponsor of their unconditional consent in writing, confirming that the sponsor has no objection to the students continuing their studies in the United Kingdom; otherwise their application will be refused.[11] A Tier 4 sponsor may include details of money already paid by an applicant on the CAS, in which case no further evidence of that payment is required; if not, original paper receipts must be submitted.[12]

¹ HC 395, Appendix C, paras 10–14.

2   HC 395, Appendix C, para 15–22.

3   Tier 4 Policy Guidance (Adult Students), paras 160–213; Tier 4 Policy Guidance (Child students), paras 263–298. For students who are continuing on an existing course and are applying for an extension of leave, the CAS must list the outstanding fees for the remainder of the year or the fees payable for the next academic year: Tier 4 Policy Guidance, para 46.

4   HC 395, Appendix C, para 1A(c). In *NA and Ors v Secretary for State for the Home Department* [2009] UKAIT 00025, at para 103, the Tribunal were of the view that where funds fell below the required sums, 'even for one day' the application would fall to be refused. Whilst the Court of Appeal in *Secretary of State for the Home Department v Pankina* [2010] EWCA Civ 719, [2010] All ER (D) 196 (Jun) found that this requirement was contained in Policy Guidance not laid before Parliament, was ultra vires section 1(4) and 3(2) of the Immigration Act 1971 and should not be applied, following the judgment the Immigration Rules were revised to include an express requirement in the Rules that the amounts specified must be held for 28 days (HC 382): HC 395, Appendix C, see para 1A(c). It should be noted, however, that the Secretary of State has conceded a number of claims for judicial review in cases where an applicant's bank balance dipped below the threshold for very short periods: see *SE and CJ v Secretary of State for the Home Department* CO/2093/09; *R R (on the application of Yokunnu Ebelechukwu Adeyemi-Doro) v Secretary of State for the Home Department* [2009] EWHC 2570 (Admin), per Blake J, at paras 10–11. Where the funds relied upon were obtained whilst a student was in the UK, the funds will be disregarded unless a student had valid leave and was not acting in breach of any conditions attached to that leave: HC 395, Appendix C, para 1A(d).

5   HC 395, Appendix C, para 1A(ca).

6   An 'established presence' is defined by the Rules as that of an applicant who has finished a course at least six months' long within their last period of leave under Tier 4, as a student or as a post-graduate doctor or dentist and the course finished within the last four months, or that of a student who is applying to continue studying on a course, having completed at least six months of the course, which they have been studying in the last four months: HC 395, Appendix C, para 14. In *DN (student – course 'completed' – established presence) Kenya* [2010] UKUT 443 (IAC), the tribunal considered that the meaning of established presence did not require that an applicant had successfully completed a course of more than six months in duration within four months of the date of application, simply that they had been studying on the course; in such circumstances, the applicant was required only to show that they possessed two months worth of funds and course fees to show they met the requirements of the maintenance provisions of the immigration rules; see also *OR (Student: ability to follow course) Bangladesh* [2011] UKUT 166 (IAC). In *Molla (established presence – date of application) Bangladesh* [2011] UKUT 161 (IAC), the Tribunal considered that unless an applicant had studied on a course of more than six months in duration, within a period of four months or less, he could not demonstrate an established presence in the UK. See also the facts of *Qureshi (Tier 4 – effect of variation – App C) Pakistan* [2011] UKUT 412 (IAC). In *Adubiri-Gyimah (Post-study work – Listed institution) Ghana* [2011] UKUT 123 (IAC), the Tribunal considered that the academic institution at which an applicant had studied and gained his qualification, but which subsequently lost its licence, did not defeat a post-study work application.

7   An 'established presence' is defined by the Rules as that of an applicant who has completed a course at least six months' long within their last period of leave under Tier 4, as a student or as a post-graduate doctor or dentist and the course finished within the last four months, or that of a student who is applying to continue studying on a course, having completed at least six months of the course, which they have been studying in the last four months: HC 395, Appendix C, para 14.

8   HC 395, Appendix C, paras 11–12. Para 12 defines the London Boroughs as Camden, Islington, Southwark, City of London, Kensington and Chelsea, Tower Hamlets, Hackney, Lambeth, Wandsworth, Hammersmith and Fulham, Lewisham, Westminster, Haringey and Newham. Where a course is taught at different sites, some in London and others outside, UKVI will look to see whether the CAS states that 50 per cent or more of time is spent in a specified London Borough.

9   HC 395, Appendix C, paras 11–12.

10   An official financial sponsor is defined as the UK government, the student's home government, the British Council or any international organisation, international company, university or United Kingdom independent school: Tier 4 Policy Guidance, para 51. 'Sponsored' means wholly supported by an award which covers both fees and living costs: Tier 4 Policy Guidance, para 53.

11 Tier 4 Sponsor Guidance, Document 2, para 10.
12 Tier 4 Policy Guidance, paras 195–196.

Requirements for Tier 4 (Child) Student

9.18 How the 10 points required for Child Students are gained will depend on the age of the children and whether they will be living at a residential (boarding) school, in private foster care arrangements or being cared for by a close relative:

(a) If the child is studying at a residential independent school, they must demonstrate that they have available to them boarding fees (course fees plus lodging fees) for a full school year for the entire course if it is less than a year long.[1]

(b) If the child is studying at a non-residential independent school and is in a private foster care arrangement[2] or staying with and cared for by a close relative,[3] they must establish they have the full course fees for one year plus £560 per month for up to a maximum of nine months' residence (ie course fees plus £5,040).[4]

(c) If the child is aged under 12 and is or will be studying at a non-residential school and is or will be accompanied by a parent, they must demonstrate that they and their parent have one year of school fees, plus £1,535 per month for a maximum of nine months' residence. If they are accompanied by other children, they must additionally demonstrate £615 per child per month for up to nine months' residence per child.[5]

(d) A child student aged 16 or 17 and living independently who has no 'established presence' studying in the UK must demonstrate that he or she has the full course fees (only the first year if the course is longer) together with £920 for each month of the course up to a maximum of nine months (ie course fees plus £8,280) if the applicant is studying in Inner London or, if in Outer London or anywhere else in the UK, £715 per month (ie course fees plus £6,435).[6]

(e) A child student aged 16 or 17 and living independently who has an 'established presence' in the UK need only demonstrate having the above living costs for two months.[7]

Money already paid to the Tier 4 sponsor, including money paid for accommodation fees, can be taken away from the total amount the applicant needs to show, although the amount deducted from living costs cannot exceed £1,020 even if more has been paid. This information can be included on the CAS and if so no further evidence is required to show that money has been paid.

1 HC 395, Appendix C, para 16 and Tier 4 Policy Guidance, paras 236–242.
2 HC 395, Appendix C, para 17 defines a child student as privately fostered where they are cared for on a full-time basis by a person or persons over 18 who is neither a parent or close relative, for a period of 28 days or more. See also Tier 4 Policy Guidance, paras 232–237.
3 Close relatives are defined as a grandparent, brother, sister, step-parent, uncle (brother or half brother of the child's parent) or aunt (sister or half sister of the child's parent) aged over 18: HC 395, Appendix C, para 18.
4 HC 395, Appendix C, para 16 and Tier 4 Policy Guidance, paras 251–252.
5 As fn 4; see also Tier 4 Policy Guidance, paras 253–256.
6 As fn 4. See also Tier 4 Policy Guidance, para 269.

[7] Tier 4 Policy Guidance, paras 280–281 and 287; where the money paid is not included on the CAS, original paper receipts issued by the Tier 4 sponsor, confirming that the student has paid some or all of the course fees must be provided. Tier 4 Policy Guidance, para 288. Tier 4 (Child) Students also benefit from the relaxed requirements for the production of documentation where they are 'low risk': Tier Policy Guidance, paras 286 and 292.

Documents to prove maintenance is available

9.19 The Rules require that students provide 'specified documents' to prove that they have the funds to meet the requirements of the rule.[1] Students must demonstrate that they hold this money themselves or that it is held in a bank account belonging to their parent or parents and has been so held for a period of 28 consecutive days. To do this they must produce bank statements issued no later than one month prior to the date of application. Joint[2] and multiple accounts[3] can be relied on, provided the combined closing balance meets the financial threshold set in the Rules. UKVI uses the closing balance on the 28-day period that 'most favours the student'.[4] Where a parent's funds are relied upon, the student must also provide evidence that he or she and the parent are related, by producing an original birth certificate, an original certificate of adoption or an original court document naming the 'parent' as the student's legal guardian,[5] together with original translations of those documents if they are not written in English.[6] They must also produce a letter of support written by their parent or guardian, confirming the relationship between them and giving consent for the use of this money.[7]

[1] HC 395, Appendix C, para 1(A)(e). These provisions are subject to 'low risk' nationals who are not required to produce in full documentation to confirm they meet the requirements of Appendix C: see Tier 4 Policy Guidance, paras 194 and 200.

[2] HC 395, Appendix C, para 13 provides that only where the funds are held or provided by (i) the applicant (whether as a sole or joint account holder); (ii) the applicant's parents or legal guardians, who have provided written consent; or (iii) an official financial sponsor which must be Her Majesty's Government, the applicant's home government, the British Council, or any international organisation, international company, university or independent school. As long as the student is named on the account, joint accounts will suffice: Appendix A, para 1A(k). See also *AM and SS (PBS – Tier 1 – joint accounts) Pakistan* [2010] UKUT 169 (IAC): 'A joint account bearing the name of the applicant meets the relevant evidential requirements of paras 93–96 of the Tier 1 Guidance, so further evidence of the ownership of the funds in the account is not required. . . . Provided the money is in the account, it does not appear to matter who it belongs to. It may, for example, have been borrowed simply for the purpose of having bank statements meeting the requirements of the Guidance'. In *CDS (PBS 'available' Article 8) Brazil* [2010] UKUT 305 (IAC) (25 August 2010), the Tribunal concluded that the funds are 'available' to a claimant at the material time if they belong to a third party but that party is shown to be willing to deploy them to support the claimant for the purpose contemplated. In *FA and AA (PBS: effect of Pankina) Nigeria* [2010] UKUT 304 (IAC) (25 August 2010) the Tribunal considered that a bank account held by husband could be used to demonstrate funds were 'available' for a wife. In *HM (PBS – legitimate expectation – paragraph 245ZX(l)) Malawi* [2010] 446 UKUT (IAC), the Tribunal found that where an applicant could show that they held funds in an overseas account, such funds were 'available' to the applicant within the meaning of the rules, even where there were in fact difficulties in withdrawing the sums from the country. However, since these decisions, HC 395, Appendix C, para 13 has been amended to state that funds will be available only where the specified documents show that the funds are 'held or provided by' the applicant, his parents, or an official sponsor.

[3] Tier 4 Policy Guidance, paras 203–204.

[4] Tier 4 Policy Guidance, para 205.

[5] Tier 4 Policy Guidance, para 209.

[6] Tier 4 Policy Guidance, paras 16–17.

9.20 Only cash funds held in a bank or building society will be accepted, but these may include current or savings accounts, even where a notice of withdrawal needs to be given to the bank or building society, and the maintenance requirement will also be satisfied in a loan letter in the case of official financial or government sponsorship. Other financial instruments, such as shares, bonds, overdrafts, credit cards and pension funds are not acceptable, regardless of whether the fund are immediately accessible.[1]

Whilst the Tribunal's view initially was that authorised credit of overdraft facilities could not be used to support the requirements of Appendix C, it is now accepted that they can.[2] Whilst the Tribunal's view initially was that authorised credit of overdraft facilities could not be used to support the requirements of Appendix C, it was later accepted that they could, and the case law cited below[3] did interpret the rules so that students could rely on overdraft facilities, this can no longer be allowed, due to a change to Appendices C and E brought in by HC1039, which expressly prevents reliance on overdraft facilities. It came into force with effect for applications made on or after 6 April 2013. Applications prior to that date, however, are decided by reference to the previous case law and rules. Where foreign currencies are held, the amount in pounds sterling must be included on the application form by specific reference to the exchange rates listed on the OANDA website.[4] Funds must be evidenced in the form of a bank or building society statements, building society or bank passbook, or a letter from the bank, a financial institution regulated by the Financial Services Authority (FSA) in the UK or the official regulatory body of the financial institution in the name of the student or their parent/guardian, confirming that the funds have been in the account for 28 consecutive days and must include the account number, the date of the statement, the financial institution's name and logo and set out the credit balances available.[5] In addition, UKVI is more likely to refuse applications which rely upon documents supplied by certain financial institutions where UKVI considers it is unable to make satisfactory checks.[6] Loans must be evidenced in the form of a letter from a financial institution regulated by the FSA in the UK or the official regulatory body for the country in which the financial institution offering the loan is located, confirming the loan has been granted; such letters must be issued no more than six months before the date of application.[7] Where students are sponsored by financial or government sponsors (eg their own government, British Council or other international organisation, a university or independent school), they may rely upon such sums, but will need confirmation in the form set out in the Rules of the amounts awarded if this is not already included on the CAS.[8] Students must demonstrate that they (or their parents) have held the correct amount of funds for 28 consecutive days in a statement, passbook or letter the period covered being no more than 31 days before the date of application.

[1] HC 395, Appendix C, para 1A(1). Sums earned during the time when the student or his parents were in the UK without leave will not be considered: HC 395, Appendix C, para 1A(d).
[2] See *PO (Points based scheme: maintenance: loans) Nigeria* [2009] UKAIT 00047 and IK (Immigration Rules, construction – purpose) *Pakistan* [2010] UKAIT 00002. However, in *Rana* (PBS – Appendix C – overdraft facility) *India* [2011] UKUT 245 (IAC), the Tribunal considered that such a facility could be used to meet the maintenance requirements of the

713

Rules. Similarly, in *Ejifugha (Tier 4 – funds – credit) Nigeria* [2011] UKUT 244 (IAC), the Tribunal considered that a credit card account which permitted an applicant to draw funds up to an agreed limit, could be used to meet the requirements of Appendix C.

3   HC 395, Appendix C, para 1A(e). The currency converter is available at: www.oanda.com.

4   HC 395, Appendix C, para 1B. See also *CS (Tier 1 – home regulator) USA* [2010] UKUT 163 (IAC), in which the Tribunal confirmed that the ways in which funds could be evidenced were not cumulative and did not require a letter from the home regulator in the USA where bank statements and/or a letter from the bank was available. Ad hoc bank statements are permissible evidence of funds (excluding mini-bank statements issued by cash machines) as are statements printed from on-line accounts, where supported by a letter from the bank (on the bank's headed paper) confirming the authenticity of the statement or where alternatively, the ad hoc statement or on-line print-out is stamped on each page with the bank's official stamp. Bank statements simply showing a balance on a particular day (ie the date of application) will not be accepted, since they do not demonstrate funds held for the 28-day period.

5   HC 395, Appendix C, para 13. A list of financial institutions which do not satisfactorily verify financial statements is contained in HC 395, Appendix P, at https://www.gov.uk/government/publications/immigration-rules-appendix-p.

6   See HC 395, Appendix C, para 1B(d) for the specific details that such letters and statements must include.

7   HC 395, Appendix C, para 13D. If only part of the funding is available, the student will be expected to demonstrate that they have the remaining sums available. Where the course fees and living expenses are met by the Tier 4 sponsor, a matter set out on the CAS, there would appear to be no requirement to provide any additional evidence that the funds are available. If a student is financially sponsored by a government or an international scholarship agency at the date of application, or sponsorship ended within the preceding 12 months, permission from the sponsor in writing will be required giving unconditional consent to the student continuing his or her studies in the UK: Tier 4 Policy Guidance, para 47.

8   HC 395, Appendix C, para 1B. Where the balance drops below the required amount after the date of the statement, passbook or letter, this should not be grounds for refusal since the Policy Guidance is not explicit in requiring any particular 28-day period relied upon.

GENUINENESS

9.21 It is now a requirement for both applications for entry clearance, and for further leave to remain that an applicant be a 'genuine student'.[1] It seems to us that this represents a significant departure from the animating purpose behind the Points-Based System, namely simplification. The Secretary of State's guidance lets applicants know that they may be invited for interview as part of a process of 'credibility testing'. If as a result of the interview, the Secretary of State is not satisfied that the applicant is a genuine student, and/or cannot speak English to the required standard, the application will be refused.[2] Helpfully, the Secretary of State commits not to refuse an application on the basis of paragraph 245ZV(k) (entry clearance) without giving the applicant the chance to respond to questions at interview.[3]

1   Para 245ZV(k) was inserted into the rules relating to entry clearance by HC 514 with effect from 30 July 2012. In relation to applications for leave to remain, para 245ZX(o) was inserted into the rules by HC 628 with application to all decisions made on or after 1 October 2013.

2   Tier 4 Policy Guidance, para 20.

3   Tier 4 Policy Guidance, para 22.

ENTRY CLEARANCE AND LEAVE TO ENTER

Entry clearance for Tier 4 (General) Students

9.22 General students, ie non-EEA nationals over the age of 16,[1] seeking entry clearance as students must comply with the requirements of HC 395, paras 245ZT–245ZV. A student arriving in the UK without prior entry clearance will be refused entry.[2] It is now an express requirement of the Rules that students must not fall foul of the General Grounds for Refusal.[3] General Students need the minimum of 30 points under paras 113–120 of Appendix A of the Rules[4] (Attributes) and 10 points under paras 10–13 of Appendix A (Maintenance). They are only permitted to study at the institution listed on the CAS,[5] save for those who benefit from being a national of a 'low risk' country where the requirements are relaxed. In making the application, they must provide originals of all the documents upon which the CAS was awarded as well as the necessary financial information confirming that they have the required level of funds. There are additional requirements for those intending to study in certain sensitive postgraduate courses. These courses require a valid Academic Technology Approval Scheme clearance certificate from the Counter-proliferation Department of the Foreign and Commonwealth Office relating to their course or area of research.[6] Government sponsored students, those with sponsorship from an international scholarship agency, or whose period of sponsorship has ended in the previous 12 months are additionally required to provide written consent to travel to the UK to undertake a course of study in the UK.[7] There is a three-year limitation on the time spent in the UK by students aged 18 or more, studying courses below degree level; the three-year ceiling, as we have seen, does not include:

- time spent in the UK under the rules in force prior to 31 March 2009;
- time when a Tier 4 (General) child was aged 16–17;
- time spent as a Tier 4 (Child) aged 17 or under; and
- time in any other non-Tier 4 category permitting study.[8]

If the student is 16 or 17 and studying at or above NVQ level 3 (except English language courses), the student and their Tier 4 sponsor may agree that the student applies as either a general student or child student. Students aged 16 or 17 must, however, apply as general students if they wish to study English as a foreign language.[9] General students under 18 must support their application with a letter from their appropriate parents or legal guardian, confirming their consent to the application.[10] As part of the increasing move toward greater checks, students who apply for leave to remain are additionally required to obtain a Biometric Residence Permit requiring them to provide fingerprints and facial image, have their identity confirmed and demonstrate their application to enrol has been successful.

---

1   HC 395, para 245ZV(h).
2   HC 395, para 245ZU.
3   HC 395, para 245ZV(a). See Chapter 3 for a detailed discussion on General Grounds of Refusal. Where an applicant is deemed to have studied at a 'bogus' college, they will be refused further leave to remain on the basis of HC 395, para 322(1A): *NA (Cambridge College of Learning) Pakistan* [2009] UKAIT 00031; *Kulasekara (Sidath Don) v Secretary of State for the Home Department* [2011] EWCA Civ 134, [2011] All ER (D) 208 (Feb); *VVT (LCPS: no post graduate diplomas) India* [2011] UKUT 162 (IAC); *Khalid (Ealing, West London and Hammersmith College) Pakistan* [2011] UKUT 295 (IAC); *Khan and Tabassum (CCOL: Postgraduate certificates) Bangladesh* [2011] UKUT 249 (IAC); and *TR (CCOL cases)*

Pakistan [2011] UKUT 33 (IAC). When a student was interviewed by an Immigration Officer on arrival and found to have difficulty in conversing in English, resulting in his college being contacted and cancelling the CAS, the Administrative Court upheld the decision to cancel entry clearance on the basis of HC 395, para 321A(1): *R (on the application of Kose (Hazret)) v Secretary of State for the Home Department* [2011] EWHC 2594 (Admin). In *Khaliq (entry clearance – para 321) Pakistan* [2011] UKUT 350 (IAC), the Tribunal formed the view with no enthusiasm that cancellation of entry clearance on arrival could only be undertaken in accordance with HC 395, para 321A.

4   HC 395, para 245ZV(b).
5   HC 395, para 245ZW(c)(iv).
6   HC 395, para 245ZV. The list of subjects is set out in Appendix 6 of HC 395. A number of cases involving Syrian students studying what might be considered to be sensitive subjects came before the Special Immigration Appeal Tribunal in 2004. The Academic Technology Approval Scheme (ATAS), (which replaces the Voluntary Vetting Scheme), is designed to help prevent individuals from acquiring or developing knowledge and skills that could be used in the proliferation of weapons of mass destruction. Under the ATAS, this responsibility has been primarily transferred to government. With its mandatory status, the ATAS substantially increases the number of individuals who are subject to clearance procedures and aims to identify a higher number who are of proliferation concern.
7   HC 395, para 245ZV(f).
8   Tier 4 Policy Guidance, para 105.
9   Tier 4 Policy Guidance, para 63.
10   HC 395, para 245ZV(i). Tier 4 Policy Guidance, paras 212 and 280 set out the required content of such a letter from the parents or guardian of a student aged 16 or 17.

Entry clearance for Child Students

9.23 Child students[1] are required to comply with the requirements of para 245ZZA for entry clearance. In addition to demonstrating that they have attained 30 points for attributes in accordance with paras 121–126 of Appendix A and 10 points for maintenance under paras 14–20 of Appendix C. Child students are also required to show if they are going to travel to the UK unaccompanied, that they have the support and consent of their appropriate parent or legal guardian with regard to any arrangements made for the child's travel to, reception and care in, the UK.[2] Child students who are planning to stay with a relative or foster carer need to show that any arrangements made meet the requirements of the Policy Guidance,[3] in particular, the requirement for a written letter in the form of a signed undertaking from the intended carer confirming the arrangements[4] and a letter of consent from their parent(s) or legal guardian also confirming the care arrangements.[5] Where the child student will be staying in a private foster care arrangement, written permission from the local authority is needed.[6] These safeguards must be in step with section 55 of the Borders, Citizenship and Immigration Act 2009 which places UKVI under an obligation to ensure that all children under the age of 18 studying in the UK have suitable care arrangements in place for their travel, for their reception on arrival in the UK and for their living arrangements while in the UK. Tier 4 sponsors are obliged to notify the local authority in whose area the child will be living with the name of the foster carer and the address at which the child student will be living.[7] Child students who are being sponsored by a government or international scholarship agency, or have been within the last 12 months, must provide the written consent of their sponsor to their studies continuing and must produce the documents specified in the Policy Guidance which are needed to meet that the requirements for entry to the UK.[8]

1 Those aged between 4 and 18 and without children: HC 395, para 245ZZA(d) and (e). Child students aged between 4 to 15 must be educated at independent fee paying schools or publically funded education colleges which are able to charge for international students; they are not permitted to study at publically funded schools: Tier 4 Policy Guidance, paras 196–197.
2 HC 395, para 245ZZA(g) and (h).
3 HC 395, para 245 ZZA(f); for the detailed requirements to establish parental consent and written undertakings from intended carers, see Tier 4 Policy Guidance, paras 299–305. For guidance on accommodation arrangements for students under the age of 18 by further education colleges, boarding schools and residential special schools, see the Department of Health websites referred to at para 44 of the Tier 4 Policy Guidance.
4 Providing the current address of the intended carer, the address where the carer and the child will be living in the United Kingdom if different from the intended carer's current address, confirmation that the accommodation offered to the child is a private address, and not operated as a commercial enterprise, (such as a hotel or a youth hostel), the nature of the relationship between the child's parent(s) or legal guardian and the intended carer, that the intended carer agrees to the care arrangements for the child, they have at least £560 per month (up to a maximum of nine months) available to look after and accommodate the child for the length of the course and a list of any other people that the intended carer has offered support to, together with proof that the carer is permitted to reside in the UK (UK passport, EU passport, certificate of naturalisation or a passport confirming their lawful residence in the UK): Tier 4 Policy Guidance, para 302.
5 Parents must explain the nature of their relationship with the intended carer, the address in the United Kingdom where the child and the child's intended carer will be living, that they support the application, and authorise the intended carer to take responsibility for the care of the child during his or her stay in the United Kingdom: Tier 4 Policy Guidance, para 299.
6 Tier 4 Policy Guidance, para 285. Permission will be required from the private foster carer's UK local authority: Children (Private Arrangements for Fostering) Regulations 2005, SI 2005/1533. Children under 16 in private foster care must provide both a copy of the letter of notification from the child's parent(s), legal guardian or intended carer to the UK local authority confirming the arrangements together with the UK local authority's confirmation of receipt of notification of the foster care arrangement.
7 Tier 4 Policy Guidance, paras 51–53 and 286.
8 HC 395, para 245ZZA(i).

DURATION OF LEAVE ON ENTRY

9.24 Specific time limits are now set out under the Rules stating:

(i) that a student cannot apply for leave under Tier 4 more than three months in advance of the course start date;[1]
(ii) when students are permitted to travel to the UK;
(iii) the duration of their leave; and
(iv) the additional period of leave allowed at the end of their course.

The aim of (iii) and (iv) is to give sufficient leave to cover the duration of the course[2] thereby ending previous inconsistencies in the duration of leave given and to avoid the need for repeat in-country applications which used to happen under the previous rules where periods of leave shorter than the duration of the course were granted. For courses lasting 12 months or more[3] students will be granted entry clearance up to one month prior to the course start date listed on the CAS and entry clearance will be granted for the duration of the course plus four additional months at the end of the course. For courses of between 6–12 months, students are granted entry clearance for up to one month prior to the start of the course with an additional two months after completion. For courses of less than six months, students are granted entry clearance to enter no more than seven days prior to the course start date and up to seven days upon completion.[4] For pre-sessional courses[5] lasting more than 12 months, students may enter the UK up to one month prior to the start date of the course and leave is granted for an additional four months at the end. For pre-sessional courses lasting between 6–12 months, students are granted entry clearance for up to one month prior to the start date until two months after the course end date. For pre-sessional courses of less than six months duration, students are granted entry clearance for up one month prior to the start of the course until one month after the course end date.

[1] HC 395, paras 245ZW, 245ZY, 245ZZB and 245ZZD.
[2] HC 395, para 245ZW(a) and (b) and Tier 4 Policy Guidance, para 100. The start and end dates for the course will be listed on the CAS.
[3] A course will be considered to be 12-months' long if it lasts a full calendar year: eg 1 January 2010 to 1 January 2011: Tier 4 Policy Guidance, para 102. September to June courses are considered as 6–12 month courses.
[4] HC 395, para 245ZW(b) and Tier 4 Policy Guidance, paras 99–100.
[5] Defined by the Rules as a course which prepares a student for the student's main course of study in the UK: HC 395, Para 245ZW, Note (ii).

9.25 Doctors and dentists on a recognised foundation programme are granted entry clearance for the duration of the course, up to a maximum of three years, and entry clearance will be granted for an additional one month upon completion.[1] Where a student is in receipt of official financial sponsorship and the official sponsor places a time limit on the duration of the student's stay in the UK, the grant of leave will be limited in line with the official sponsor's requirements.[2] A limitation of three years is placed upon those aged over 18 who come to the UK to study courses below degree level.[3] Tier 4 (Child) students under 16 are granted entry clearance for up to one month prior to the start of the course date listed on the CAS and for such the period as is requested, equal to the length of the programme or six years (whichever is shorter) plus four months at the end.[4] Tier 4 (Child) students over 16 are granted entry clearance for up to one month prior to the start of their course and for such period of time as is requested, equal to the length of the programme being followed or three years, whichever is the shortest, plus an additional four months at the end.[5] Where child students turn 18 during their course, they are permitted to continue studying until the expiry of their leave, but will need to apply as a Tier 4 (General) student if they wish to continue studying thereafter.[6]

[1] HC 395, para 245ZW(b).
[2] Tier 4 Policy Guidance, para 106.
[3] HC 395, para 245ZV(g).
[4] HC 395, para 245ZZB(a).
[5] HC 395, para 245ZZB(b).
[6] Tier 4 Policy Guidance, para 225.

9.26 As with the previous student Rules, entry clearance is granted subject to a prohibition on public funds and registration with the police.[1] Commonwealth students are not required to register with the police, but foreign students over 16, who are nationals of countries listed in Appendix 2 of HC 395, admitted for more than six months, including the foreign spouse or child over 16 of such a student, will be required to register.[2] Within the class of relevant foreign nationals, HC 395, para 326 contains a list of people who are normally exempted. This includes where leave is given as the spouse, civil partner or unmarried or same sex partner of someone settled in the UK,[3] as well as a parent of a child at school. Students may only study at the institution which issued and is listed upon the CAS, although supplementary study, without permission, is permitted.[4]

1   HC 395, paras 245ZW(c)(i) and, (ii) and paras 325–326.
2   HC 395, para 325(ii)–(iii).
3   HC 395, para 326(iv), as amended by HC 40, as from 30 November 2007.
4   HC 395, para 245ZW(c)(iv).

WORKING AS A STUDENT

9.27 Permission to work is regulated by the Rules[1] and, since 4 July 2011, has been limited to students studying at HEIs or other publicly funded further education colleges as a measure designed to crack down on the perceived abuse of students attending private colleges. The general rule for all students is that students are not permitted to work, save for:

(a)   Employment during term time of no more than 20 hours per week and employment of any duration during vacations where the student is following a course of degree level study at (NQF 6/QFC 6/SCQF 9 or above) and is either: (a) sponsored by a sponsor that is a Recognised Body[2] or in receipt of public funding as a higher education institution from the Department of Employment and Learning in Northern Ireland, the Higher Education Funding Council for England, the Higher Education Funding Council for Wales or the Scottish Funding Council; or (b) sponsored by an overseas higher education institution to undertake a short-term Study Abroad Programme in the UK.

(b)   Employment during term time of no more than ten hours per week and employment of any duration during vacations, where the student is following a course of below degree level study (NQF 3, 4 or 5/QCF 3, 4 or 5/SCQF 6, 7 or 8) with a Recognised Body or a public-funded HEI.

(c)   Employment during term time of no more than ten hours per week and employment of any duration during vacations where the student is following a course of study at any academic level and is sponsored by a sponsor that it a public-funded further education college.

(d)   Employment as part of a course-related work placement which forms an assessed part of the applicant's course and provided that any period spent on the placement does not exceed one-third of the total length of the course, except where: (a) it is a UK statutory requirement that the placement exceed one-third of the total course length; or (b) the placement does not exceed one-half of the total course length, the student is undertaking a course of degree level study and the student is either:

(i)   sponsored by a sponsor that is a Recognised Body or a public-funded HEI; or

(ii)   sponsored by an overseas higher education institution to undertake a short-term Study Abroad Programme in the UK.

(e)   Employment as a Student Union Sabbatical Officer for up to two years, provided that the post is elective and is at the institution which is the applicant's sponsor (or they must be elected to a national post with the National Union of Students).

(f)   Employment as a postgraduate doctor or dentist on a recognised Foundation Programme.

(g)   Employment with the Tier 2 sponsor in the role for which the applicant has been assigned a Certificate of Sponsorship (CoS) where an application for leave to remain as a Tier 2 migrant (supported by a CoS) is pending, the application was made following successful completion of a course at degree level or above with a Recognised Body or a public-funded HEI and the applicant has extant leave to remain, until such time as the application is finally determined.

(h)   Self-employment provided the migrant has made an application for leave to remain as a Tier 1 (Graduate Entrepreneur) Migrant which: (a) is supported by a qualifying HEI; (b) is made following successful completion of a UK-recognised degree undertaken in the UK with a sponsor that is a Recognised Body or public-funded HEI; and (c) is made while the applicant has extant leave to remain, until such time as the application is finally determined.

The rules, thus, prevent all students who do not fall into any of the preceding categories from working at all.[3] The rules also expressly prohibit students from becoming self-employed, from working as a doctor or dentist in training (other than on a recognised Foundation Programme), from employment as a professional sportsperson, or as an entertainer, or from employment which fills a permanent full-time vacancy (other than a vacancy on a recognised Foundation Programme, or as a sabbatical officer).[4] A child student under 16-years-old cannot work at all during their time in the UK, but those aged 16 or older may work up to ten hours during term time, full time during vacations, on a work placement or as a student union sabbatical officer.[5]

[1]   HC 395, para 245ZW(c)(iii). Para 245ZY(c)(iii), in relation to further leave to remain, it is in the same terms, save that it also permits a student to work who has applied under the Doctorate Extension Scheme but not yet received a decision.

[2]   Defined in para 6, HC 395, as an institution that has been granted degree awarding powers by either a Royal Charter, an Act of Parliament or the Privy Council. For the purposes of the rules the UKVI consider the Foundation Programme Office, South London Local Education and Training Board, and the Yorkshire and Humber Strategic Health Authority as equivalent to UK Recognised Bodies.

[3]   HC 395, para 245ZW(c)(iii)(1)–(8) and Tier 4 Policy Guidance, para 318.

[4]   HC 395, para 245ZW(c)(iii) and (v).

[5]   HC 395, para 245ZZB(c)(iii) and (iv); and Tier 4 Policy Guidance, paras 125–323.

EXTENSION OF LEAVE AS A TIER 4 STUDENT

Leave to remain for Tier 4 (General) students

9.28 General students applying for an extension of leave to remain must comply with the requirements of para 245ZX. It is again an explicit requirement of the grant of leave to remain that the applicant must not be refused under the General Grounds of Refusal contained in Part 9 of the Rules. The rule requires an applicant to 'have, or have last been granted' entry clearance, leave to enter or leave to remain in various categories, including Tier 4 students, students under the previous provisions of the rules and also Tier 1 and Tier 2 migrants and former work permit holders who wish to cease employment and undertake study.[1] Significantly, the wording of the rule does *not* require a student seeking leave to remain to have *current* leave[2] at the time of making an application. However, the Rules expressly require that where students seek to continue their studies in the UK, there is no more than a 28-day gap between the expiry of their leave and the commencement of the next course.[3] Where there is a gap of more than 28 days,[4] the student will be expected to return to their country of origin to make an out-of-country application and any in-country application will be refused.[5] As with the conditions of entry clearance, general students are required to demonstrate that they score the minimum of 30 points under paras 113–120 of Appendix A of the Rules (Attributes) and 10 points under paras 10–14 of Appendix C of the Rules (Maintenance).[6] The Rules require that a student meets the requirements of the rules at the date of application.[7] Problems may arise where a student has completed a course but not received the results, is not in possession of a transcript of studies, and has no certificate of qualification at the time his or her leave expires. The Tribunal, interpreting the Rules very narrowly, has stated that to claim points in an application as a Tier 1 (Post Study Worker), a former student must have been awarded the degree for which he or she claims points at the date of application[8] since the Rules require submission of either the original certificate of qualification or an original transcript of results at the date of application (although there is the option of relying on references where that is the method by which the sponsor has assessed the applicant)[9]. Where the student wishes to undertake postgraduate studies leading to a Doctorate or Masters by research, postgraduate studies leading to a taught Masters or study or research in excess of six months in one of the disciplines listed in paras 1 or 2 of Appendix 6 to the Rules, they will require a valid Academic Technology Approval Scheme (ATAS) clearance certificate, issued by the Counter-Proliferation Department of the Foreign and Commonwealth Office.[10] As with the provisions for the grant of entry clearance, sponsored students must obtain written permission from the government or scholarship agency to continue their studies in the UK.[11] In addition, the Rules preclude a student from being granted entry clearance or further leave to remain where:

(a) The grant of entry clearance or leave to remain would lead to the applicant having spent more than three years in the UK as a Tier 4 migrant since the age of 18 studying courses that did not consist of degree level study.[12]

(b) The grant of entry clearance or leave to remain would lead to the applicant having spent more than five years in the UK as a Tier 4 migrant, or as a student, studying courses at degree level or above, subject to a number of exceptions set out in the body of the rule.[13]

(c) The applicant has completed a course leading to the award of a PhD in the UK and the grant of entry clearance or leave to remain he or she is seeking would lead to the applicant having spent more than eight years in the UK as a Tier 4 (General) Migrant, or as a Student.[14]

The restrictions set out in paragraph 245ZX(hb) of the Rules do not apply to a Tier 4 (General) Student on the doctorate extension scheme.[15] In relation to the doctorate extension scheme, leave to remain can be granted where:[16]

(a)   the applicant has not previously been granted leave to remain as a Tier 4 (General) Student on the doctorate extension scheme;

(b)   the applicant must be following a course leading to the award of a PhD;

(c)   the applicant must be sponsored by a Sponsor that is a Recognised Body or a public-funded HEI and that sponsor will be the sponsor awarding the PhD;[17] and

(d)   the date of the application must be within 60 days of the expected end date of a course leading to the award of a PhD.

Leave to remain on the doctorate extension scheme will be granted for up to 12 months, beginning on the anticipated end date of the course.[18]

---

[1] HC 395, para 245ZX(b) provides an exhaustive list of persons who may switch from another category of leave and seek leave to remain as a Tier 4 student: Tier 4 (General) Student, Tier 4 (Child) Student, Tier 1 (Post-study Work) Migrant, Tier 2 Migrant, Participant in the International Graduates Scheme (or its predecessor, the Science and Engineering Graduates Scheme), Participant in the Fresh Talent: Working in Scotland Scheme, Post-graduate Doctor or Dentist, Prospective Student, Student, Student Nurse, Student Re-sitting an Examination, Student Writing-Up a Thesis, Student Union Sabbatical Officer, Work Permit Holder. Thus spouses or dependants will not be able to seek leave to remain as a student and will require entry clearance. In addition, those granted leave to remain on Article 8 ECHR, for example, following a successful student appeal, are not included. Whilst the point has yet to be tested, it is arguable that if the basis of granting leave under Article 8 was on account of the fact that the applicant fell foul of the requirements of Tier 4, by a small margin, it would be wrong to expect them to return home to make an entry clearance application. It should be noted that the point has been tested in the context of a person wishing to switch from 'general' to 'partner' visa category but required to leave the country to do so by reason of HC 395, para 319C (h)(i): see *R (on the application of Zhang) v Secretary of State for the Home Department* [2013] EWHC 891 (Admin), [2014] 2 All ER 560 and para **9.35** below.

[2] HC 395, para 245ZX(b); this interpretation was confirmed by UKBA in an email exchange between Judith Walker and Tracey Cook, Immigration Group, UKBA, dated 7 August 2009.

[3] HC 395, para 245ZX(l). See also HC 395, para 320(7B)(i): departure within 90 days of the expiry of leave will not render a person an overstayer resulting in a 12-month ban on re-application and entry (Previous versions of the rules and Immigration Directorate Instructions permitted a gap of four months between the expiry of leave and the commencement of a new course.)

[4] The Policy Guidance suggests that students should apply three months prior to the expiry of leave, since as soon as permission is granted the student's new Tier 4 sponsor becomes responsible for them: para 115. However, given the new fixed-time limits for the grant of student leave, students studying a year course from September to June would be granted leave until August (ie length of course plus two months) and are generally unlikely to be required to return to their country and make a further application for a course commencing in September.

[5] In *QI (Pakistan) v Secretary of State for the Home Department* [2011] EWCA Civ 614, the Court of Appeal accepted that where an applicant has appealed against a refusal to grant further leave to remain in reliance upon s 3C, Immigration Act 1971, he is not in fact without leave and did not fall foul of the provisions of para 245ZX(l). See also *Kishver and others ('limited leave': meaning) Pakistan* [2011] UKUT 410 (IAC) and *Patel (revocation of sponsor licence – fairness) India* [2011] UKUT 211 (IAC).

[6] HC 395, para 245ZX(c)–(d).

[7] In *Secretary of State for the Home Department v Pankina* [2010] EWCA Civ 719 at [39], [2011] QB 376, [2011] 1 All ER 1043, the Court of Appeal considered that the requirements of the Rules were clear and required an applicant to meet the specified criteria at the date of application. Note, however, that for a CAS to be considered to be valid, the rules require that it has been issued by a Tier 4 sponsor which still holds such a licence at the time the application for entry clearance or leave to remain is decided; ie the date of decision: HC 395, Appendix A, para 116(d) and *MM and SA (Pankina: near-miss) Pakistan* [2010] UKUT 481 (IAC) in which the Tribunal found that an IJ had erred in allowing an appeal in which the

appellant's college held a licence at the date of the appellant's application, but was revoked by the date of decision, given the clear wording of the rule. The effect of this decision has been mitigated by the Tribunal which has recognised the harsh and unfair results that ensue: see *Thakur (PBS decision – common law fairness) Bangladesh* [2011] UKUT 151 (IAC); *Patel (revocation of sponsor licence – fairness) India* [2011] UKUT 211 (IAC); *R (on the application of Basharat) v Secretary of State for the Home Department* [2011] EWHC 195 (Admin); *Naved (Student – fairness – notice of points)* [2012] UKUT 14 (IAC); and *Sapkota (Ramesh) v Secretary of State for the Home Department* [2011] EWCA Civ 1320, [2011] All ER (D) 141 (Nov).

8   *Kan (Post-Study Work – degree award required) India* [2009] UKAIT 00022; *NO (Post-Study Work – award needed by date of application) Nigeria* [2009] UKAIT 00054. *AQ (Pakistan) v Secretary of State for the Home Department* [2011] EWCA Civ 833, [2011] All ER (D) 182 (Jul). The same strict approach has been taken recently by the Court of Appeal in refusing a number of appellants permission to appeal in relation to the now-closed Tier 1 (Post Study Work) route: see *Rasheed v Secretary of State for the Home Department* [2014] EWCA Civ 1493, affirming *Nasim and others: (Raju: reasons not to follow?)* [2013] UKUT 610 (IAC).

9   HC 395, Appendix A, paras 118(a) and 120–SD(a). However, where a student has been offered a place by a Tier 4 sponsor because of progress he/she has made on an existing course, the Tier 4 sponsor must include this information on the CAS and no documents need be sent if this is how he/she was assessed: Tier 4 Policy Guidance, para 140.

10   HC 395, para 245ZX(e).

11   HC 395, para 245ZX(g).

12   HC 395, paras 245ZV(g) (entry clearance) and 245ZX(h) (leave to remain).

13   HC 395, paras 245ZV(ga) (entry clearance) and 245ZX(ha) (leave to remain). These paragraphs must be read as requiring the calculation of five years spent in the UK as a Tier 4 migrant or student to include time spent as a student before the introduction of Tier 4: see *Islam (Para 245X(ha): five years' study)* [2013] UKUT 608 (IAC).

14   HC 395, paras 245ZV(gb) (entry clearance) and 245ZX(hb) (leave to remain).

15   HC 395, para 245ZY(bb).

16   HC 395, para 245ZX(n). PhD is defined in Annex 6 of the Tier 4 Policy Guidance.

17   The sponsor is expected to maintain contact with the applicant whom the College is sponsoring. As a minimum, the UKVI expects at least two contact points while a person is on the scheme. The sponsor should withdraw their sponsorship if the applicant misses these contacts without reasonable explanation: para 93, Tier 4 Policy Guidance.

18   HC 395, para 245ZY(ba). The purpose of the scheme is to put in place fewer restrictions on the work applicants can do and to permit them to use the 12 months to gain further experience in their chosen field, seek skilled work, or develop plans to set up as an entrepreneur: para 87, Tier 4 Policy Guidance.

Leave to remain for Tier 4 (Child) students

9.29 Similarly, child students must meet the requirements of paragraph 245ZZC in order to obtain leave to remain. The provisions are identical to those for entry clearance, save for the fact that, as with general students, the proposed course must start no more than 28 days after the expiry of the applicant's leave to enter or remain.[1] In April 2010, the rules were amended to allow a Tier 4 (Child) Student to extend the maximum period of time that a 16- or 17-year-old could remain in the UK from two to three years.[2]

1   HC 395, para 245ZZC(j).

2   See Tier 4 Policy Guidance, para 224; and HC 395, para 245ZZD(b).

Sabbatical officers

9.30 Students are permitted to take up a full-time, salaried, elected executive union position as a sabbatical officer, either during their studies or in the academic year immediately after they graduate. Where their leave expires, they will need to submit a further Tier 4 (General) student application. Leave will be granted for one year but may be extended where the officer is re-elected by further application to UKVI.[1]

1   See Tier 4 Policy Guidance, paras 80–86; Tier 4 Sponsor Policy Guidance, Document 2, paras 68–72. The Tier 4 sponsor is required to notify UKVI of the change of circumstances either by email where leave was granted by visa letter or using the sponsorship management system if leave was granted by CAS. A student wishing to take up a post as a sabbatical officer at the end of his or her course and who has no further leave, will need to submit a new application supported with a CAS issued by the Tier 4 sponsor: Tier 4 Sponsor Policy Guidance, Document 2, para 70.

Re-sitting examinations, repeating study and writing up thesis

9.31 Students sponsored by standard Tier 4 sponsors are permitted to re-sit examinations or repeat any part of their course twice for each examination or modules. Where, however, the Tier 4 sponsor holds a Highly Trusted Sponsor Licence, they may 'in exceptional circumstances', allow further re-sits or repeats of study.[1] If a student has failed more than once then no points at all will be awarded for attributes in any application to extend their student leave, unless the sponsor is a Highly Trusted Sponsor.[2] If a student's leave expires before they have finished taking the re-sit or repeated course, they must make an application for further leave to remain, but Tier 4 sponsors are required for themselves to determine whether they are likely to pass the examination or course and whether to continue to sponsor the student.[3] The Sponsor Guidance explains that a Tier 4 sponsor must also determine whether to continue its sponsorship of a student throughout the re-sit or repeat period, whether the sponsor requires the student's 'continued participation' to re-sit examinations or repeat of study and whether the sponsor is confident that it will be able to meet its sponsor duties during this time; where a student does not need to be in the UK to re-sit the examination or re-take the course, the guidance requires sponsors to advise the student to return to his or her country of origin until he or she needs to be present in the UK.[4]

Similarly, postgraduate students whose leave expires whilst they are writing up their thesis or dissertation, including any oral examination, are required to obtain further leave to remain, but, again, Tier 4 sponsors may do so where they consider that a student's continued participation for this period is required and where they are confident that they can meet their sponsorship duties during this time.[5]

1   HC 395, Appendix A, para 119 and Tier 4 Sponsor Policy Guidance, Document 2, paras 174–177. No guidance is provided on this phrase and given that Highly Trusted Sponsors are given greater flexibility by virtue of holding such a licence, they alone may determine whether in the circumstances a student should be permitted to undertake more than two re-sits. A Standard Tier 4 Sponsor who issues a CAS to a student who has already failed a re-sit or repeat twice, may have its licence downgraded or withdrawn: Tier 4 Sponsor Policy Guidance, para 167.
2   HC 395, Appendix A, para 119. Equally and logically no points will be awarded for this qualification in an application in any other Tier.
3   Tier 4 Sponsor Policy Guidance, Document 2, para 176.
4   Tier 4 Sponsor Guidance, Document 2, paras 178. If the Tier 4 sponsor does not require the student's continued participation within 60 days of the start of the next academic period (with the exception of recognised institutional vacation periods), Tier 4 sponsors are encouraged by the Guidance not to continue to sponsor the student and if the student has continuing leave, but his or her presence is not required during this 60-day period, the Tier 4 sponsor should

notify the UKVI and advise the student to leave the United Kingdom. Where a student's leave is about to expire, and the Tier 4 sponsor does not require continuing participation within 60 days of the start of the next academic period, the Tier 4 sponsor is encouraged to not assign a CAS, and to advise the student to leave the UK; the sponsor can then, at a later stage, assign a CAS to be used in support of an application for entry clearance. In *RS (Pakistan) v Secretary of State for the Home Department* [2011] EWCA Civ 434, [2011] All ER (D) 172 (Apr), the Court of Appeal rejected an appeal brought by a law student who had failed his exam, having been ill for the re-sit and required leave prior to sitting further re-sits. Since he was required under the Rules to be in attendance at a course of full-time study and BPP Law School confirmed that the applicant was not required to attend further classes, the court considered that the Rules did not permit residence in the UK whilst waiting to re-sit the exam.

5 Tier 4 Sponsor Policy Guidance, Document 2, paras 66–67.

CHANGING SPONSORS AND COURSES

Current leave granted before and after 5 October 2009

9.32 It is mandatory to obtain permission from UKVI to change a Tier 4 sponsor and student leave will be curtailed where no permission is sought.[1] A student whose current leave is based on an application made on or after 5 October 2009 and who subsequently wants to switch to a different standard Tier 4 sponsor, must make a fresh application for leave to remain under Tier 4, supported by a new CAS issued by the new Tier 4 sponsor.[2] They are not permitted to start their new course until UKVI has granted them permission to change sponsors. If, however, the student's current leave is based on an application made on or after 5 October 2009 and the sponsor he/she is joining is a Highly Trusted Sponsor who has issued him/her with a CAS and the student has made an in-time application for further leave, the student is entitled to start the new course, but, since he/she will not be able to return to his/her original sponsor, he/she ceases studying at his/her own risk if the new application is refused.[3] Where the CAS was issued by a standard (A or B) sponsor, he/she cannot commence his/her new course until permission from UKVI has been granted.[4] With regard to students granted leave before 5 October 2009, it is difficult to see how many students still exist who might be affected by these old provisions, given that degree level study has a maximum of five years and PhDs a maximum of eight years, but it is quite rare for a PhD to last over five years. For those to whom these provisions are relevant, the previous edition of this work should be consulted.[5]

1 HC 395, para 323A(ii).
2 See *Bhimani (Student: Switching Institution: Requirements)* [2014] UKUT 516 (IAC).
3 Tier 4 Policy Guidance, paras 341 and 344.
4 Tier 4 Policy Guidance, paras 342–343.
5 The position in relation to those applicants who have leave to remain based on an application made before 5 October 2009 is discussed in a previous edition of this work (see the eighth edition at para 9A.31).

Switching course

9.33 Students wishing to switch to a different course with the same Tier 4 sponsor, do not need permission from UKVI to do so, but the Tier 4 sponsor will be required to notify UKVI of the change by updating their records on the Sponsorship Management System. Where the course is shorter, the student is required to email UKVI who may in turn limit the student's current leave to coincide with the course length; where it is longer, the student will need to make an application for further Tier 4 leave either at the point of switching course or at any stage prior to the expiry of their leave.[1]

[1]   Tier 4 Policy Guidance, paras 350–352.

SWITCHING TO EMPLOYMENT AND OTHER CATEGORIES OUTSIDE TIER 4

9.34 Students are permitted, upon completion of their course of study, to apply for an extension of stay in another Tier category (or any other provision of the Rules), where they can demonstrate that they meet the requirements of the Immigration Rules. Express provision is made in the Rules for students to switch to a Tier 1 (Entrepreneur) Migrants,[1] Tier 1 (Graduate Entrepreneur) Migrants,[2] Tier 1 (Investor) Migrants,[3] and Tier 2 (General), Tier 2 (Minister Religion), Tier 2 (Sportsperson) Migrants[4] As was the case under the previous rules, leave as a Tier 4 migrant will not lead to indefinite leave to remain but may well be a stepping stone to another category, where he or she can qualify for indefinite leave. The previously accessible routes of Tier 1 (General) and Tier 1 (Post-Study Work) are now closed to new applicants.

[1]   HC 395, para 245DD(e)(xxi).
[2]   HC 395, para 245FB(e)(i).
[3]   HC 395, para 245ED(c)(xvi).
[4]   HC 395, para 245HD(b)(ii)(1). It is not possible for a Tier 4 (General) migrant to switch in-country into the Tier 2 (Intra Company Transfer) route: see para 245GD.

DEPENDANTS OF STUDENTS

Spouses and children of Tier 4 students

9.35 Paragraphs 319AA–319J of HC 395 make specific provision for entry clearance, limited and indefinite leave to remain for dependants of PBS migrants; inevitably, separate Policy Guidance has been issued.[1] Since 4 July 2011, only students studying certain courses are permitted to sponsor their spouse, civil partner, unmarried partners, same sex partners and children to come to the UK: only new students sponsored by a HEI on a course at NQF level 7 or above lasting 12 months or more, and new Government sponsored students following a course that is longer than six months, will be able to bring their partners and/or children to the UK with them. Dependants with existing permission wishing to extend their stay in the UK are permitted to do so provided they apply at the same time as the Tier 4 (General) Student applies to undertake a course of study that is longer than six months in duration.[2] Dependants are required to have prior entry clearance and will be refused entry on arrival if they do not.[3] As with Tier 4 (General) students, the rules expressly provide that dependants may be refused on general grounds of refusal or because they are illegal entrants.[4] Entry clearance or leave to remain will be granted only where the Tier 4 (General) student upon whom the dependant relies has valid leave to remain or is being admitted to the UK at the same time.[5] In common with other provisions of the Immigration Rules, the relationship between the PBS migrant and their spouse, civil partner, unmarried or same sex partner[6] must be subsisting at the date of application,[7] they must intend to live together in their relationship[8] and they must not intend to stay beyond the period of leave granted to the PBS migrant.[9] Dependent children must be under 18 at the date of application or, if the child is over 18, must have or last have been granted leave as the family member of a PBS migrant or be applying at the same time as the PBS migrant; where they are over 18 and have not previously been granted leave as the family member of the PBS migrant they cannot be granted leave as a dependant.[10] They will be required to show that they are not married or in a civil partnership, have not formed an independent family unit and are not living an independent life.[11] The child dependant must not intend to stay in the UK beyond any period of leave that is granted.[12] Consistent with para 297 of HC 395, children must show that both parents are lawfully present in the UK, or being admitted at the same time, save where the PBS migrant is the sole surviving parent, the PBS migrant has sole responsibility for the child's upbringing or there are serious family or other considerations which would make it desirable not to refuse the application and suitable arrangements have been made for the child's care.[13] The provisions on the circumstances in which a person can follow the dependant route in-country have now been substantially liberalised and brought into line with the comparable provisions in Appendix FM. A person is, thus, able to switch from a 'general' to a 'dependant' route in-country so long as they were not granted entry clearance or leave to enter as a visitor (unless the main applicant has, or is being granted, leave to remain as a Tier 5 (Temporary Worker) Migrant in the creative and sporting subcategory, having met the requirement in paragraph 245ZQ(b)(ii) of the Rules) and is not on temporary admission or release.[14]

---

1   The document can be found at: www.gov.uk/government/uploads/system/uploads/attachmen t_data/file/324611/DEP_guidance_07-14.pdf.

2   HC 395, paras 319C(i) and 319H(i). See also Tier 4 Policy Guidance, paras 309–313. The dependant route is not available for a family member of a Tier 4 (Child) student migrant: PBS Dependant Policy Guidance, paras 33–35.

3   HC 395, paras 319B(a) and 319G(a).

4   HC 395, para 319C(a).

5   HC 395, para 319C(b).

6   Unmarried or same sex partners must additionally show that any previous relationship has broken down permanently, that they are not so closely related that they would be prohibited from marrying and that they have been living together in a relationship similar to marriage or civil partnership for a period of at least two years: see HC 395, para 319C(c).

7   HC 395, para 319C(d).

8   HC 395, para 319C(e).

9   HC 395, para 319C(f).

10 HC 395, para 319H(c) and PBS Dependant Policy Guidance, paras 100 and 102.

11 HC 395, para 319H(d) and PBS Dependant Policy Guidance, paras 102–104.

12 HC 395, para 319H(e).

13 HC 395, para 319H(f).

14 HC 395, paras 319C(h) and 319H(h). See *R (on the application of Zhang) v Secretary of State for the Home Department* [2013] EWHC 891 (Admin), [2014] 2 All ER 560 above at **9.28** following which the immigration rules were amended to take into account this judgment: see HC 628. The amended rules took effect from 1 October 2013.

9.36 Dependants must also establish that they have sufficient funds:[1] dependant spouses, civil partners, unmarried or same-sex partners of Tier 4 (General) students studying in London and *without* an established presence in the UK,[2] must show £615 for each month of the Tier 4 student's leave up to nine months, ie £5,535. If there are children who are dependants they must *additionally* show this same amount for each child.[3] For dependants of those studying outside the London Boroughs, they must show £460 per month up to a maximum of nine months, ie £4,140 for each dependant.[4] Where, however, the Tier 4 student has an established presence in the UK they are required to show only two months maintenance for each dependant: if they are studying in London, they must show £1,230 for each dependant and outside the London Boroughs £920 for each dependant.[5] Dependants must show that they have held the funds for 28 days and any evidence relied upon must pre-date the application by no more than 31 days.[6] The applicant must be able to prove the relevant maintenance threshold by supplying the specified evidence.[7] Entry clearance and leave to remain will be granted on condition of no recourse to public funds[8] and, where required, registration with the police.[9] The ability of the spouse or civil partner to work is a very important factor and may be crucial to the student's continued ability to study and to fulfil the maintenance provisions. However, since April 2010, again as part of the government's crack down on perceived abuse of the student rules, where the Tier 4 student has been granted leave for less than 12 months or has enrolled on a course which is below degree level, his or her dependants are prohibited from working *at all*.[10] The Rules also permit dependants to be granted indefinite leave to remain in line with the Tier 4 (General) student.[11]

[1]   HC 395, para 319C(g) and Appendix E, para (ba)(i)(1) and (2).
[2]   Ie where they have studied in the UK for at least six months: see PBS Dependant Policy Guidance, para 68–69.
[3]   HC 395, para 319C(g) and Appendix E, paras (ba)(i)(1) and (2). Dependant Policy Guidance, paras 74–75: thus a student paying course fees of £12,000 for a three-year course will need to establish in an entry clearance application £12,000 course fees, £9,120 maintenance, £4,535 for their wife and £5,535 for each of their children.
[4]   HC 395, para 319C(g) and Appendix E, paras (ba)(i)(1) and (2). See also paras 76–77 of the PBS Dependant Policy Guidance.
[5]   HC 395, para 319C(g) and Appendix E, paras (ba)(i)(1) and (2). See also paras 78–81 of the Dependant Policy Guidance.
[6]   HC 395, Appendix E, paras (g)(ii) and (m). Again, where the dependants are deemed to be 'low risk', they are not required to produce all the documents to support the application: PBS Dependant Guidance, para 96. The previous concession to those dependants already in the UK on an application made before 1 February 2010, who were required only to establish that they have the funds at the date of application, has been removed from the Dependant Policy Guidance.
[7]   HC 395, para 1B, Appendix C; and para (j), Appendix E. See too the PBS Dependant Policy Guidance, paras 97–99.
[8]   As a general rule, individuals subject to immigration control are not entitled to certain benefits, tax credits, or housing and homelessness support. This is provided for by ss 115, 118 and 119 of the Immigration and Asylum Act 1999, and by section 42 of the Tax Credit Act 2002. Treatment under the National Health Service, or education funded by a local education authority (LEA), does not count as recourse to public funds. Further details can be found in the Secretary of State modernised guidance on public funds (available at www.gov.uk/govern ment/uploads/system/uploads/attachment_data/file/284160/Public_funds_v12_0EXT.pdf) (see page 11 in particular). Child dependants will not, therefore, be eligible for Child Benefit.
[9]   HC 395, paras 319D(b)(i)–(ii) and 319I(b)(i)–(ii); and Appendix 2.
[10] HC 395, para 319D(b)(v).
[11] HC 395, paras 319E and 319J.

Dependants under the old rules

9.37 For students who still have a leave granted under the old rules in HC 395, Part 3, provision is still made under paras 76–81 for the entry and stay of their dependants, spouse or civil partner and dependant children under 18. The main benefit is that the maintenance and accommodation provisions under para 76 are less rigorous than under the PBS. For more details, see Chapter 9A of the eighth edition of this work.

CHALLENGING REFUSALS OF LEAVE AND APPEALS

Strict compliance

9.38 All student applicants are required to use the application form current at the date of application and, given that the forms are subject to change, to check that they are using the correct form and most up-to-date Policy Guidance on the UKVI website. Where they do not use the correct form, the Rules provide that such an application will be ordinarily refused[1] without a right of appeal. Similarly, the Rules require that an application form must be accompanied by the correct application fee,[2] any part of the form specified as mandatory must be completed[3] and photographs accompanying the application must be in a form specified in the policy guidance;[4] any failure to comply with these requirements is likely to result in the rejection of the application as invalid, without substantive consideration and without a right of appeal.[5] A similar set of rules govern applications made by way of the relevant online application process.[6] Given that there is no requirement to have current leave at the date of application,[7] there is nothing to prevent an applicant re-submitting an application form in the correct manner if their application is rejected.[8] UKVI and entry clearance posts will only accept those documents specified in the Rules.[9]

---

[1]   HC 395, paras 34A and 34C(a).

[2]   HC 395, paras A34A(iii)(a) and 34A(ii).

[3]   HC 395, para 34A(iii). See also *R (on the application of Mombeshora) v Secretary of State for Home Department* [2013] EWHC 1252 (Admin), in which Clive Lewis QC, sitting as a High Court judge, quashed a decision to find a Tier 4 application invalid on the basis of a failure to fill in mandatory sections of the form. The essential basis for the judge's decision was that care should be taken in construing the wording of mandatory sections of the application form. The words used should be given their ordinary meaning.

[4]   HC 395, para 34A (vi)(a) and (vii)(a). In *R (Penjilang Fu) v Secretary of State for the Home Department* [2010] EWHC 2473, in which Mitting J found that an applicant had not in fact submitted any photographs at all in his application, and rejected an argument that discretion should have been exercised to permit their subsequent submission given the mandatory requirements of the rules. The same conclusion was reached by HHJ Belcher in *R (on the application of Ajayi) v First Tier Tribunal* [2011] EWHC 1793 (Admin), [2011] All ER (D) 209 (Jul). See also *R (on the application of Kisuule) v Secretary of State for the Home Department* [2011] EWHC 2966 (Admin), [2011] All ER (D) 162 (Nov) in which Edwards-Stuart J found on the facts that photographs had in all likelihood been submitted.

[5]   See para 34C(b) which confers a discretion on the Secretary of State to contact an applicant to permit him or her to correct any error or omission which renders the application invalid. The Secretary of State noting that the decision to reject an application as invalid involves the exercise of discretion. See the current modernised guidance on specified application forms and procedures (available at www.gov.uk/government/uploads/system/uploads/attachment_data/file/371599/Specified_application_forms_v15.0_EXT.pdf). Discretion may be challenged by way of judicial review in appropriate cases. For an example of a case concerning repeated applications to UKVI, highlighting the problems that can arise, see *R (on the application of*

Kobir) v Secretary of State for the Home Department [2011] EWHC 2515 (Admin). For refusals based on general grounds of refusal, see CHAPTER 3. See also *Ahmed (general grounds of refusal – material non-disclosure) Pakistan* [2011] UKUT 351 (IAC) and *Daby (Forgery; appeal allowed; subsequent applications) Mauritius* [2011] UKUT 00485 (IAC). para 34C(b), HC 395, was brought into force in relation to applications made on or after 6 November 2014: see HC 693. With the advent of that provision there is likely to be more scope for challenges based on a failure to exercise, or consider exercising, the discretion contained within the rules.

6   HC 395, para A34. Note, that an online application is only mandatory for applications for Tier 2, Tier 4 or Tier 5 (Temporary Worker) sponsorship licences.
7   See para **9.28** above
8   Given that the Rules do not provide a specific timeframe (save for HC 395 para 320 (7B)(i)) in which invalid applications may be rejected and it may take some months for UKVI to reject an application, it will be necessary to update the financial information in re-submitting the application.
9   HC 395, para 120–SD, Appendix A; paras 1B and 13B–13D, Appendix C.

Administrative review of entry clearance decisions

9.39 Tier 4 applicants wishing to challenge a refusal of entry clearance are not entitled to appeal to the Immigration and Asylum Chamber[1] except on race discrimination and human rights grounds.[2] In theory, because the Points-Based System entails no more than a simple application and the submission of documentation, a Tier 4 application will only be refused when the documents submitted fail to meet the requirements of the Rules and the Policy Guidance. To obtain entry clearance, an applicant should re-apply, paying the application fee again, with the correct documentary evidence. It is for this reason that the right of appeal has been removed. In practice, however, documents are not accepted or improperly considered and applications are refused for a wide variety of reasons. Recognising that Entry Clearance posts do not always reach the correct decision, the government has instead provided an alternative review mechanism; applicants who consider that 'an error has been made in the decision' are entitled to apply for Administrative Review of a Notice of Refusal of Entry Clearance. The review is not governed by the Rules or by statute; it is set out as an Annex to the Policy Guidance.[3] A request for Administrative Review must be made within 28 days from the date the refusal notice is received by the applicant and only considered outside this deadline in exceptional circumstances. A Request Notice will be served with the Notice of Decision. The Review is conducted independently by an Entry Clearance Manager, sometimes from another Post. Applicants are not permitted to send any additional documents since the mechanism is simply a review of the decision on the evidence already supplied. Applicants may request only one Administrative Review per refusal decision.[4]

1   Nationality, Immigration and Asylum Act 2002 (NIAA 2002), s 88A, inserted by the Immigration, Asylum and Nationality Act 2006, s 4(1), with effect from 1 April 2008 in relation to decisions made under Part 6A of the Immigration Rules relating to the Points-Based System: SI 2008/310, art 4.
2   NIAA 2002, s 84(1)(b) and (c).
3   See Annex 4 of the Tier 4 Policy Guidance.
4   Where, however, the Administrative Review upholds a refusal but with different refusal grounds, the applicant may request an administrative review of these new refusal grounds.

9.40 If the applicant has new or further information, documents or other paperwork that were not submitted with their original application, they will need to make a new application and pay the appropriate fee unless the applicant was refused under para 320(7A) or 320(7B) of the Immigration Rules on General Grounds for Refusal; where this is the case, they are permitted to adduce additional evidence to show they did not commit a deception or knowingly made false representations. Reviews are completed, in most cases, within 28 days from the date of receipt of the Request Notice. There are three possible outcomes for a review: the administrative reviewer can uphold decision in its entirety, uphold decision but with revised reasons for refusal or overturn decision and issue entry clearance. The administrative reviewer is obliged to review all aspects of the refusal not just the part of the refusal which the applicant has asked to be reviewed, checking that points have been correctly awarded, documents have been correctly assessed and verification checks have been properly carried out. They may recommend that the reason for refusal should be overturned, if they find that the Entry Clearance Officer failed to properly consider evidence submitted with the original application, failed to apply the Immigration Rules correctly, made a mistake in processing the application or failed to give adequate reasons for refusing entry clearance. Where reasons are found to be defective, the administrative reviewer will recommend that the Entry Clearance Officer revoke the original refusal and serve a new refusal notice giving a full explanation for the refusal. Such decisions remain amenable to judicial review on the grounds of illegality, irrationality or procedural impropriety.

Appeal rights

9.41 Tier 4 applicants wishing to challenge a refusal of entry clearance are not entitled to appeal to the Immigration and Asylum Chamber, as we have seen. So appeal rights are very limited in the new PBS world for students. However, those who arrive in the UK with a visa or entry clearance endorsed with its purpose and conditions are deemed to have leave to enter,[1] and if the leave is cancelled they have a right of appeal under section 82 of the NIAA 2002 and can remain here for the hearing of their appeal unless leave was cancelled or refused because they are seeking to enter for a different purpose.[2] A student who arrives in the UK without a visa or entry clearance and is refused leave to enter has no right of appeal (save on discrimination, human rights or asylum grounds).[3] Depending on the point at which the application was made, in-country applicants refused leave to remain under Tier 4 enjoy a right of appeal to the Immigration and Asylum Chamber.[4] All decisions are based upon whether an applicant meets the requirements of the Rules at the date of application.[5] Whilst the Tribunal in *NA and Ors* found that section 85(4) of the NIAA 2002 permitted an applicant on appeal to adduce evidence in existence at the date of application, even where it was not submitted to UKVI with the application, the position has changed since 23 May 2011, with the entry into force of s 85A, Nationality, Immigration and Asylum Act 2002. Section 85A expressly precludes the Tribunal on appeal from considering documents which were not submitted 'in support of, and at the time of making', a Points-Based System application, save for evidence which is adduced to prove that a document submitted with that application is genuine or valid or is adduced to counter a refusal by the Secretary of State to exercise discretion in an applicant's points.[6] The courts have rejected arguments that an applicant is allowed to rely upon evidence to demonstrate that they meet the requirements of the Points-Based System at the date of hearing.[7]

[1] Immigration (Leave to Enter and Remain) Order 2000, SI 2000/1161, arts 3, 4(3).

[2] NIAA 2002, s 92(3)–(3C), as substituted and inserted by the Asylum and Immigration (Treatment of Claimants, etc) Act 2004, s 28 (from 1 October 2004); Immigration Act 1971, Sch 2, para 2A(9), inserted by the Immigration and Asylum Act 1999, Sch 14, para 57, amended by NIAA 2002, s 114(3), Sch 7, para 2.

[3] NIAA 2002, s 88(2)(b) and (4).

[4] NIAA 2002, s 88(2)(d), (e) and (f).

[5] The date of application is defined as the day when the application was posted, or delivered by courier to UKVI: see para 34G, HC 395. In entry clearance cases, the date of application, is the date on which the application fee is paid: see *Kaur (Entry Clearance – date of application)* [2013] UKUT 381 (IAC). [AQ?] (The day the application is paid in entry clearance cases.)

[6] *NA & Others (Tier 1 Post-Study Work-funds)* [2009] UKAIT 00025, paras 74–75. Section 85A was introduced by the UK Borders Act 2007, s 19; see SI 2011/1293, art 2. The provisions do not apply to an appeal in respect of which a hearing before the First-Tier Tribunal of the IAC has taken place before the 23 May 2011. An oral hearing adjourning a case was a 'hearing' for the purposes of the Order: *Mumtaz (s. 85A – commencement order – adjournment hearing) Pakistan* [2011] UKUT 00472 (IAC); by contrast the service of a Notice of Hearing by the Tribunal prior to the 23 May 2011 was not: *Alam (s 85A commencement – Article 8) Bangladesh* [2011] UKUT 424 (IAC). Thus applicants are no longer able to rely upon evidence not submitted with the application when the provision enters into force to demonstrate that they met the requirements of the Rules at the date of application. See also *Butt (para 245AA(b) – "specified documents" – judicial verification) Pakistan* [2011] UKUT 353 (IAC). Note that s 85A has no application to a refusal to grant ILR following five years lawful residence since such an application is not 'a points based system application': *Philipson (ILR – not PBS: evidence) India* [2012] UKUT 00039 (IAC). However, note the presence of a discretion within para 245AA, HC 395, under which a case owner can write to an applicant to ask for the submission of missing or defective specified documents in certain circumstances. That discretion is referred to in the Secretary of State's modernised guidance on evidential flexibility (available at www.gov.uk/government/uploads/system/uploads/attachment_data/file /299005/Evidential_flexibility_v6.0EXT.pdf). The circumstances in which an applicant could successfully argue that the Secretary of State should have considered exercising her discretion are now fairly limited following the decision of the Court of Appeal in *Rodriguez v Secretary of State for the Home Department* [2014] EWCA Civ 2. See too *Gu v Secretary of State for the Home Department* [2014] EWHC 1634 (Admin), *Akhter & Anr (paragraph 245AA: wrong format)* [2014] UKUT 297 (IAC) and *Durrani (Entrepreneurs: bank letters; evidential flexibility)* [2014] UKUT 295 (IAC). It is likely that the circumstances in which an applicant might succeed on that point will be limited to those cases that are fairly closely analogous to the grounds set out in the rule itself, subject of course to the rule that the Secretary of State must not unlawfully fetter her discretion by over-strict adherence to a policy. In addition, section 85A does not preclude the Tribunal from considering such new documentation on appeal by the Tribunal in support of a claim that denial of further leave would be contrary to Art 8, ECHR. Since an adjournment is not required for the Respondent to consider such documents where they are served late, the same principle would apply where such documents are adduced to support an Art 8 claim: *Butt (para 245AA(b) – "specified documents" – judicial verification) Pakistan* [2011] UKUT 353 (IAC). Blake J in *Naved (Student – fairness – notice of points)* [2012] UKUT 14 (IAC) at [12]–[15] noted both the mischief s 85A was designed to cure and the unfairness created by its operation. The Court of Appeal in *Sapkota (Ramesh) v Secretary of State for the Home Department* [2011] EWCA Civ 1320 has indicated that UKVI should serve removal directions alongside or shortly after service of the notice of decision, in accordance with section 10 of the Immigration and Asylum Act 1999 or under section 47 of the Immigration, Asylum and Nationality 2006 Act; prompting the UKVI to give consideration to paragraph 395C and that a failure to do will render a decision 'not in accordance with the law'. However, in *Patel (consideration of Sapkota – unfairness) India* [2011] UKUT 484 (IAC), the Tribunal characterised the legitimacy of segregating decisions on extensions of leave to remain with decisions on removal as a question of the fair exercise of public law powers rather than a matter of statutory construction turning a power to refuse leave at or shortly after a variation decision into an invariable duty to do so. Where both the Secretary of State in her decision and the Tribunal on appeal had considered paragraph 395C, there was no

requirement to have issued such removal directions alongside the notice of decision. Note, however, that para 395C was abolished as from 13 February 2012 by HC 1733.

[7] The Tribunal's view is that an applicant must meet the requirements of the Rules at the date of application, 'an historic test, fixed to that specified date': *KAN (Post-Study Work – degree award required) India* [2009] UKAIT 00022, *NA and Ors (Tier 1 Post-Study Work-funds)* [2009] UKAIT 0002; *NO (Post-Study Work – award needed by date of application) Nigeria* [2009] UKAIT 00054. In *Pankina and Ors* [2010] EWCA Civ 719, Sedley LJ (paras 38–39) rejected the argument that where an appellant met the requirements at the date of hearing, the Tribunal could allow an appeal concluding that such an interpretation was precluded by the clear wording of the rule itself. The Tribunal in *MS (AS & NV considered) Pakistan* [2010] UKUT 117 (IAC) considered that it was impermissible for an applicant on appeal to raise the fact that he meets the requirements of the rules by a NIAA 2002, section 120 notice. In *AQ (Pakistan) v Secretary of State for the Home Department* [2011] EWCA Civ 833, [2011] All ER (D) 182 (Jul), Pill LJ rejected an argument that a section 120 notice was intended, or had the effect, of allowing a fresh application to be made to the Tribunal, under the Rule, relying on events since the Secretary of State's decision; any other construction was contrary to the intention of the section in the statutory scheme. See too *Ahmed & Anr (PBS: admissible evidence)* [2014] UKUT 365 (IAC), in which the tribunal held that where a provision of the Rules (such as that in para 245DD(k)) provides that points will not be awarded if the decision-maker is not satisfied as to another (non-points-scoring) aspect of the Rule, the non-points-scoring aspect and the requirement for points are inextricably linked. As a result, the prohibition on new evidence in s 85A(4) of the Nationality, Immigration and Asylum Act 2002 applies to the non-points-scoring aspect of the rule: the prohibition is in relation to new evidence that goes to the scoring of points. *Ahmed* is a decision in relation to the genuineness test for Tier 1 (Entrepreneurs). We take the view that it has no direct applicability to applications under Tier 4 due to the very obvious differences in language between para 245DD(k) and paras 245ZV(k) 245ZX(o), in particular the absence of any direct link under the Tier 4 genuineness test to depriving the applicant of points. The 'inextricable link', present in connection with para 245DD(k), is not present under the Tier 4 rules and *Ahmed* should not apply.

9.42 Applicants for entry clearance under the PBS have long been unable to bring appeals against refusals, save on limited grounds.[1] The alternative remedy put in place for those applicants was a system of administrative review, administered internally by the Home Office. A similar process has been put into motion following the entry into force and partial commencement of the Immigration Act 2014. Section 15 of that Act proposed to restrict rights of appeal by amending Part 5 of the Nationality, Immigration and Asylum Act 2002. The Act proposed to allow just three types of decision to attract rights of appeal under an amended section 82 of the 2002 Act:

(a) the refusal of a protection claim;
(b) the refusal of a human rights claim; and
(c) the revocation of a person's protection status.

Section 15 of the Act was not brought into force immediately. It was partially brought into force on 20 October 2014 by the Immigration Act 2014 (Commencement No. 3, Transitional and Saving Provisions) Order 2014 in relation to two specified classes of person:

(a) A person (P1) who becomes a 'foreign criminal' within the definition in section 117D(2) of the 2002 Act[2] on or after 20 October 2014; and a person who is liable to deportation from the UK under section 3(5)(b) of the Immigration Act 1971 because they belong to the family of P1.[3]
(b) A person (P2) who makes an application on or after 20 October 2014 for leave to remain: (a) as a Tier 4 Migrant; (b) as the partner of a Tier 4 Migrant under paragraph 319C, HC 395; or (c) as the child of a Tier 4 Migrant under paragraph 319H, HC 395.[4]

The outcome is that P1, the family of P1 and P2 will not have a right of appeal, whether full or limited, save on the three bases set out in the amended section 82 of the 2002 Act. Thus, where a Tier 4 applicant does not make a human rights claim (which is refused) as part of his application, or at any time after its refusal, he will not acquire a right of appeal. His only remedy will be by way of an administrative review under paragraphs 34L and Appendix AR to HC 395.[5] A right of appeal will be available under the unamended section 82 in circumstances where P2 makes a further application for leave to enter or remain that is not a Tier 4 or Tier 4 dependent application.[6]

[1] See paragraph 9.41 above.
[2] See further 19.12, below.
[3] See articles 2, 9 and 10 of the Immigration Act 2014 (Commencement No 3, Transitional and Saving Provisions) Order 2014, SI 2014/2771.
[4] See articles 2, 9 and 11 of the Immigration Act 2014 (Commencement No. 3, Transitional and Saving Provisions) Order 2014, SI 2014/2771.
[5] Under Appendix AR, para AR.2.4. an applicant can put before the reviewer material that was not before the initial decision-maker in circumstances where he is seeking, inter alia, to demonstrate that a decision in relation to his or her credibility was unreasonable. This is line with our remarks above relating to the case of *Ahmed & Anr (PBS: admissible evidence)* [2014] UKUT 365 (IAC).
[6] See article 11(2) of the Immigration Act 2014 (Commencement No 3, Transitional and Saving Provisions) Order 2014, SI 2014/2771.

9.43 Where Tier 4 applicants fail to meet the requirements of the Rules, for example, where their funds dip below the required threshold even for short periods of time, the Tribunal in *NA and Ors* held that the application automatically fell to be refused. In *Pankina and Ors* the Court of Appeal concluded the rules were more than policy, having on appeal acquired the force of law[1] and left little if any room for discretion outside the rules.[2] Appellants may, however, rely upon human rights grounds on appeal, including most commonly that removal will result in a disproportionate interference with any private and family life rights acquired. This, of course, has more significance, given that study, at least at degree level, is now a stepping stone to the world of work, self employment and establishment in business. Whilst the Tribunal has taken the view that students 'are persons who have come to the UK for a limited purpose and with no expectation of being able to stay except by meeting the requirements of the Immigration Rules',[3] the Court of Appeal has taken the view that the Secretary of State is obliged to give effect to Convention rights including an evaluation of the extent and quality of their family and private life in the United Kingdom and the implications, both for them and for the United Kingdom, of truncating their careers here. The court in *Pankina and Ors* held:

'It is one thing to expect an applicant to have the necessary academic and linguistic qualifications: here a miss is likely to be as good as a mile. It is another for an applicant to fall marginally or momentarily short of a financial criterion which in itself has no meaning: its significance is as a rough and ready measure of the applicant's ability to continue to live without reliance on public funds . . . The Home Office has to exercise some common sense . . . if it is not to make decisions which disproportionately deny respect to the private and family lives of graduates who by definition have been settled here for some years and are otherwise eligible for Tier 1 entry.'[4]

[1] [2010] EWCA Civ 719 at para 16.

²   The Tribunal in *NA and Ors* [2009] UKAIT 00025 at para 103 noted, however, that the
    Secretary of State will always retain a residual discretion in near miss cases.
³   NA and Ors [2009] UKAIT 00025, para 105. See also *MM (Tier 1 PSW; Art 8; private life)
    Zimbabwe* [2009] UKAIT 00037, para 66 and *BN (Article 8 – Post Study Work) Kenya*
    [2010] UKUT 162 (IAC).
⁴   [2010] EWCA Civ 719 at paras 45–6.

BECOMING A SPONSOR

Tier 4 sponsors and policy guidance

9.44 All colleges and universities wishing to offer courses to (non-EEA)
foreign students require a 'Sponsor Licence'.[1] Separate policy guidance for
sponsors has been issued on the procedures for obtaining a Tier 4 Sponsor
Licence. The guidance now takes the form of three separate documents (having
previously been comprised of one consolidated document for sponsors). These
guidance documents are titled:

*   'Document 1: applying for or renewing a Tier 4 sponsor licence and
    highly trusted sponsor status';
*   'Document 2: assigning confirmation of acceptance for studies and
    sponsoring students'; and
*   'Document 3: sponsors' duties and compliance'.[2]

As Lord Sumption observed in *R (on the application of The London
Reading College Ltd) v Secretary of State for the Home Department*, the
system for licensing sponsors is wholly governed by the guidance. Yet the
guidance can be amended at any time and has been amended with 'bewildering
frequency'.[3] The guidance lays down mandatory requirements governing: (i)
the criteria for the award of a sponsor's licence; (ii) the criteria to be applied
by a licensed sponsor in issuing a CAS; (iii) the obligations of those to whom
a licence has been awarded; and (iv) the procedure and criteria for suspending,
downgrading or withdrawing a sponsor's licence.

¹   Defined in paragraph 6 of the Immigration Rules as 'a licence granted by the Secretary of State
    to a person who, by virtue of such a grant, is licensed as a Sponsor under Tiers 2, 4 or 5 of the
    Points-Based System'.
²   Found at: www.gov.uk/government/publications/sponsor-a-tier-4-student-guidance-for-educat
    ors.
³   [2013] UKSC 51, [2013] 1 WLR 2358, paras 15 and 20.

9.45 In the previous edition we suggested that the sponsorship system is
premised upon a psychology of fear designed to ensure compliance from
sponsors under continuous threat of suspension or revocation. This continues
to be our view.[1] Although the Courts have recognised the very substantial
losses that sponsors will suffer if their licence is ultimately revoked,[2] the Courts
have repeatedly emphasised (and, in our view, over-emphasised) the 'considerable' trust that is said to be 'reposed' in sponsors.[3] Sponsorship is said to
involve a pledge from the education provider that they will accept their duties
of sponsoring the Tier 4 student. It is based on three fundamental principles,
two put forward by the government and one by ourselves:

(1)   that those who benefit directly from migration should help to prevent
      the system from being abused;[4]

(2)   those applying to come to the UK to work or study are eligible to do so and a reputable education provider genuinely wishes to take them on; and

(3)   that the UKVI has ultimate and almost unfettered control over the whole process.

There are two ratings for a sponsor licence. An establishment is first given an 'A-rating' following a successful application for a Tier 4 sponsor licence. This is described as a 'transitional rating for 12 months' following which the sponsor must apply for Highly Trusted Status (HTS) no later than 12 months from the date that they were granted their licence.[5] The effect of being granted a Sponsor Licence is that education providers are permitted by UKVI to issue a specified number of Confirmation of Acceptance for Studies (CAS)[6] to students who wish to undertake courses with them (without a Sponsor Licence, or where the licence has been suspended or revoked by UKVI, they may not). The consequential financial implications to education providers following suspension or revocation are self-evidently significant.

[1]   In a statement from the Prime Minister, David Cameron, on 30 July 2014, he stated that: '[w]e are also doing more today to close down bogus student colleges. We've already closed many of them and we will close down more.'

[2]   See, for example, *The London Reading College Ltd v Secretary of State for the Home Department* [2010] EWHC 2561 (Admin), para 9: '[t]he loss of a licence would have the most serious professional and financial consequence for the college and its proprietors. It would also have a serious impact upon both its students and its prospective students'. In *New London College Ltd*, para 1, Lord Sumption similarly recognised that for institutions with a high proportion of non-EEA students, the status of being a licensed sponsor may be 'essential' to enable them to operate as functioning businesses.

[3]   See, for example, *R (on the application of WGGS Ltd (t/a Western Governors Graduate School)) v Secretary of State for the Home Department* [2013] EWCA Civ 177, para 10.

[4]   It is questionable, however, whether requiring sponsors to act as de facto immigration officers is a proper mechanism by which the State enforces immigration control.

[5]   Document 1, para 9.

[6]   Defined in paragraph 6 of the Immigration Rules as: 'a unique reference number electronically issued by a sponsor via the Sponsor Management System to an applicant for entry clearance, leave to enter or remain as a Tier 4 Migrant in accordance with these Rules'. As Lord Sumption explained in *New London College*, para 12: '[a] CAS is not a physical document. It is an entry made by the sponsor in an electronic database to which the sponsor and the UK Border Agency's staff both have access. What the migrant receives is a unique reference number, which he supplies to the Border Agency on applying for leave to enter or remain in the United Kingdom, and which enables the agency to access the electronic file relating to him.'

Applying for a Sponsor Licence

9.46 Each education provider wishing to register as a Tier 4 sponsor must complete an online application and will need to pay the requisite fee at the same time.[1] This is followed by sending in the 'original submission sheet' and all of the mandatory documents listed (originals or certified copies) within five working days.[2] UKVI will undertake checks to determine that the documents submitted with the application are genuine. They may also undertake site visits.[3] The application may only be submitted by the prospective sponsor; applications made by representatives will be refused, although they may assist with the application.[4] In terms of 'educational oversight', Tier 4 sponsors are required to show that they have a current and satisfactory full inspection, review or audit from one of the specified education accreditation bodies.[5]

There are different accreditation bodies depending on whether the education provider is subject to public review,[6] is a private provider,[7] or is a higher education provider based overseas.[8] Any sponsor that ceases to hold educational oversight will become a 'legacy sponsor'.[9] Sponsors with a number of different branches can apply either for a single licence for the head office and all branches, group some of the branches with a separate licence, or apply for a separate licence for each branch.[10] Equally, sponsors operating as franchises may apply for a single licence for the head office and all UK branches, or make a separate application for each franchise, but where the franchise is a separate business entity, an individual licence will be required for each franchise.[11] Tier 4 sponsors may also add more tiers, categories and sub-categories after a Tier 4 Sponsor Licence has been issued, as long as they meet the relevant criteria.[12]

[1] Document 1, paras 32 and 41–42.

[2] Document 1, paras 37 and 150–160. The specified supporting documents are also set out in an 'Appendix A': see www.gov.uk/government/uploads/system/uploads/attachment_data/file/317720/Sponsor_Appendix_A_04-14.pdf. See also paras 38–39 of Document 1 in relation to the absence of mandatory documents rendering applications invalid and how the UKVI will contact the education provider where other documents are missing, or if they require further information, requiring a response within five working days. Failure to respond will lead to the application being refused.

[3] Document 1, paras 162–170. The visits may be announced or unannounced, although the guidance explains that an unannounced visit does not mean that the UKVI has doubts in the sponsor.

[4] Document 1, paras 34 and 45. Tier 4 sponsors may be assisted by a representative in completing the form where they are qualified to provide immigration advice and services in accordance with the Immigration and Asylum Act 1999, s 84 or they are a regulated member of a designated professional body: Document 1, paras 45–51. If after receiving the licence the sponsor wishes to the use the services of a legal representative, they must formally appoint them using the Sponsorship Management System (SMS): Document 1, para 52.

[5] Document 1, paras 119–120.

[6] Education providers subject to public review must show that they have been inspected and audited by one of the following bodies: Quality Assurance Agency for Higher Education, Ofsted, the Bridge Schools Inspectorate, Schools Inspectorate Service, Education Scotland, Estyn (Wales), Education and Training Inspectorate (Northern Ireland) or the Independent Schools Inspectorate: Document 1, paras 121–125.

[7] Document 1, paras 126–128. For higher education private providers the necessary full inspection, review or audit must have been provided by Quality Assurance Agency for Higher Education. For private further education providers or English Language Colleges the necessary full inspection, review or audit must be from Education Scotland, the Education and Training Inspectorate, the Independent Schools Inspectorate, the Bridge Schools Inspectorate or the Schools Inspectorate Service. New private independent schools must provide evidence that they have been formally registered with the relevant government authority.

[8] Overseas higher education institutions offering short-term 'study abroad' programmes in their own premises in the UK are exempt from the educational oversight requirements where students are enrolled at an institution in their home State, they are coming to the UK for no more than 50 per cent of the length of their degree course, and will return to their home State to complete the course which must be equivalent to a UK degree. Instead, such providers must provide evidence of: (a) overseas accreditation that can be confirmed by UK NARIC; (b) that only part of the programme is taught in the UK; and that, (c) where the education provider is using their own premises in the UK they have full legal control over the premises (where classroom space is rented from a third-party, the space must be at a Tier 4 sponsor institution, and the applicant education provider must provide evidence of the facilities to be used, and that they have full legal control of the premises). See generally Document 1, paras 134–138.

[9] See generally Document 3, paras 105–115 in relation to maintaining educational oversight and paras 122–129 in relation to legacy sponsors.

[10] Document 1, paras 57–58. 'Branches' are two or more separate legal entities that are linked by common ownership or control.

[11] Document 1, paras 74–75.

Key personnel

9.47 The application process requires the potential sponsor to identify certain key personnel for four roles which must be filled for the duration of the sponsorship licence:[1]

(a)　　an authorising officer within the sponsor organisation with responsibility for the activities of all users of the sponsorship management system;[2]

(b)　　a key contact, who acts as the main point of contact between UKVI and the Tier 4 sponsor;[3]

(c)　　a level 1 user who undertakes the sponsor's day-to-day activities using the sponsorship management system and who may perform certain activities, including assigning or withdrawing a Confirmation of Acceptance for Studies (CAS), requesting from UKVI an increase in the number of CAS that may be assigned and reporting student absences;[4] and

(d)　　a level 2 user who may also assign CAS and report student activity but who has a more restricted range of permissions than level 1 users.[5]

The roles can be filled by the same person or a combination of different people on condition that they are staff members or office holders permanently based in the UK. Once appointed, these individuals are responsible for ensuring compliance with the licence reporting duties and the Sponsor Management System (SMS).

[1]　Document 1, para 76. See paras 78–79 for general requirements in relation to key personnel, including their being permanently based in the UK for the duration of their role. See paras 86–88 in relation to checks that the UKVI carries out on key personnel against UKVI records, and the police national computer. A failed check may lead to refusal of an application.

[2]　Authorising officers are described as the 'most senior person' responsible for the recruitment of students, and ensuring that all sponsorship duties are met. They are not permitted to be representatives, contractors, consultants, temporary staff members supplied by an agency or undischarged bankrupts. Authorising officers do not have automatic access to the SMS but may additionally be designated as level 1 or 2 users. See Document 1, paras 89–95.

[3]　A key contact must not be a contractor, consultant, or an employee of a third-party organisation engaged to deliver all or part of the provider's HR function or a temporary staff member supplied by an agency. Organisations with overseas branches may only appoint a key contact based in the UK branch of the organisation. An authorising officer may also hold the position of key contact, or the position may be held by different staff members, or office holders. Again, a key contact does not have automatic access to the SMS but may additionally be designated as a level 1 or 2 user. See Document 1, paras 96–99.

[4]　Only one level 1 user may be appointed on application, although further level 1 users may be nominated after the licence has been issued, and may be UK-based representatives. A sponsor must always have a minimum of one level 1 user who is a 'settled worker', unless limited exceptions apply. The sponsor must have at least one level 1 user in place and the UKVI will take action against a sponsor without one. A level 1 user cannot be a contractor, consultant, or a temporary staff member supplied by an agency. See paras 100–107 and 112 of Document 1.

[5]　Document 1, paras 108–112.

Sponsor ratings

9.48 The policy guidance explains that three main questions are used to consider Tier 4 Sponsor Licence applications:[1]

— Are you a genuine organisation operating lawfully in the UK and complying with all appropriate local planning authority regulations?
— Are you dependable and reliable?
— Are you capable of carrying out your duties as a sponsor?

A sponsor licence can have two possible ratings: an A rating, and Highly Trusted Sponsor status rating (HTS status). A sponsor who is first granted a licence is issued with an A-rated licence, a transitional rating that will last for 12 months from the date the licence is granted. A HTS licence can only be issued after a period of 12 months and when the sponsor has demonstrated a good record of performance. After 12 months, A-rated sponsors must apply for HTS.[2] The current guidance indicates that there remains provision for sponsors to become 'legacy sponsors' where they have failed to meet the educational oversight requirements.[3] Legacy sponsors have their CAS allocation set to zero. They will not be able to sponsor new students but can continue to sponsor existing students until they either finish their course, or the sponsor licence expires (whichever happens first).[4] Sponsors will be able to apply for a CAS in order for a student to finish their course.

[1] Document 1, para 161.
[2] Document 3, para 122.
[3] Document 1, para 238.
[4] Document 3, paras 123–124.

Applications and A-rated sponsors

9.49 All new sponsors are granted an A-rated licence, which they must have held for 12 consecutive months, as a stepping-stone to becoming a Highly Trusted Sponsor. The point behind the interim A-rating is to demonstrate 12 months of compliance with the sponsorship duties, a gateway to HTS. Applications are refused in a variety of circumstances,[1] for example, where false documents are relied upon, a sponsor licence (under any Tier) was previously held and the application is made within six months of that licence being revoked, or civil penalties for specified offences have been issued against the sponsor in the last five years. Where, for example, a sponsor has a poor record of compliance with their duties, a licence has been revoked in the past, or the OISC has removed authorisation for the sponsor to provide immigration advice, UKVI will *consider* refusing a sponsor licence application.[2] Sponsors will have provided an estimate of the number of Confirmation of Acceptance for Studies (CAS) they expect to assign in their first year. UKVI will grant a CAS allocation up to a maximum of 50 per cent of the sponsor's total student body, based on information from their compliance officers and contained in the educational oversight inspection report. They will consider whether the number of CAS requested by the sponsor is reasonable, taking into account, for example, the length of time the sponsor has been operating, the number, type and level of courses provided by the organisation, and the student-teacher ratio.[3] UKVI can limit the CAS allocation to zero where appropriate.[4] Sponsors may ask UKVI to increase their CAS allocation if the limit is reached, using the

SMS, unless they have already been allocated 50 per cent of their total student body.[5] The CAS allocation must be used within 12 months, failing which they will expire.[6]

[1] Document 1, para 179.
[2] Ibid, para 177: this is said to depend on the seriousness of the past conduct, how long it has been since the conduct took place and any mitigating circumstances.
[3] Ibid, paras 192–193.
[4] Ibid, para 197.
[5] Ibid, para 195.
[6] Ibid, para 194.

Highly Trusted Sponsors

9.50 In April 2010, Highly Trusted Sponsor (HTS) status was first introduced for Tier 4 sponsors: 'to identify those sponsors who are achieving the highest levels of compliance and whose students are showing the greatest compliance with the terms of their visa or leave,' thereby allowing the then UKBA to 'target . . . resources elsewhere on areas of higher risk'. In *New London College,* Lord Sumption recorded how following a review in summer 2011 of the Tier 4 scheme, which apparently revealed substantial evidence of abuse, HTS status became mandatory from April 2012.[1] HTS status is valid for 12 months and must be renewed every year using the SMS account.[2] Highly Trusted Sponsors may offer courses at QCF or NQF level 3 (and their equivalent) and offer courses below degree level which include a work placement.[3] They benefit from (*inter alia*) a more flexible approach to reporting student non-attendance.[4]

[1] Para 3.
[2] See Document 1, para 287 *et seq*. An application to renew must be made before HTS status expires and sponsors must pay the appropriate fee (unless they are a 'premium sponsor').
[3] Document 1, para 191.
[4] Document 3, table at para 75.

9.51 Sponsors must apply for HTS status no more than 12 months from the date that they became A-rated, and can apply up to one month in advance. The current guidance indicates that sponsors 'must first establish a good record of performance with us . . . the period that you are A-rated will give you the chance to . . . prove that you can meet all of your sponsor duties'.[1] Applicant sponsors will need to satisfy a number of specified requirements in order to attain HTS status.[2] Significantly, the requirements will 'substantially' change and become stricter for applications made on or after 1 November 2014. Transitional arrangements will apply between 1 November 2014 and 31 July 2015. The changes include the following:[3]

— the 'refusal rate' has been reduced from less than 20 per cent to less than 10 per cent;[4]
— the 'scoring aspect' of the consideration has been removed; and
— the 'near miss' outcome and associated processes have also been removed.[5]

Where the application is successful, sponsors are designated as Highly Trusted Sponsors (HTS) on the sponsor register maintained by UKVI. There is no right of appeal against a refusal to award HTS status.[6] If UKVI refuses a sponsor's application for HTS status, their licence will be suspended and they will have 20 working days from the date stated on the notification to submit further representations. If following consideration of any representations received during this period UKVI still considers that the HTS criteria are not met, the sponsor's licence will be revoked.[7]

1   Document 1, para 190.
2   Document 1, paras 245–257.
3   Document 1, para 244 and see paras 265–282 for the new requirements. The 'transitional arrangements' amount to little more than the UKVI stating that for applications made on or after 1 November 2014, they will measure the refusal rate from CAS-used data from 1 August 2014 onwards (when the changes were announced): Document 1, para 269.
4   See section below on 'Challenging UKVI decisions on Sponsor Licences' under the sub-heading 'Refusal rate'.
5   Under the pre-1 November 2014 criteria, sponsors scoring a 'near miss' are allowed to remain on the sponsor register as A-rated sponsors: Document 1, paras 260–263.
6   Decisions may, however, be challenged by way of judicial review (see below).
7   Document 1, paras 258 and 284.

SPONSORSHIP DUTIES

9.52 Level 1 users (and also level 2 users, albeit they are unable to withdraw a CAS)[1] appointed by the Tier 4 sponsor must use the password-protected Sponsor Management System (SMS) an online database to which UKVI staff have access, to record student activity, issue a CAS up to the number allocated by UKVI, cancel a CAS and to carry out their functions as Tier 4 sponsor. The objectives of the duties are claimed to be the prevention of abuse of the assessment procedures, to capture early any patterns of student behaviour that may cause concern and address weaknesses that may cause those patterns and to monitor compliance with the Immigration Rules.[2] The Tier 4 sponsor's duties in relation to their monitoring of a student; commence when they assign the student a CAS. They cease only at the moment when the student prematurely ends their course, and the sponsor has provided details of their future plans, the student leaves the UK, or their permission to stay expires, the student switches to a different Tier 4 sponsor, or when the sponsor's Tier 4 licence is surrendered or revoked by UKVI.[3] The UKVI policy guidance, which can be changed by UKVI at any time without parliamentary, or any other scrutiny, sets out in considerable detail these duties.[4] The following is a non-exhaustive summary of some of the main requirements. It is of note, that the guidance indicates that sponsors must additionally take 'reasonable steps to ensure that every student at your institution has permission to be in the UK. Failure to do this may lead to the revocation of your licence.'[5]

First, Tier 4 sponsors are required to retain accurate records of all students at their institution, retaining paper copies or electronic copies which sponsors must be able to provide to UKVI if so requested:[6]

- each sponsored student's current passport pages showing all personal identity details (including biometric details), leave stamps, or UK immigration status document including the page containing the entitlement to study in the UK;
- a copy of the student's biometric card;
- record of the migrant's absence/attendance (this may be kept either electronically or manually);

- each sponsored student's up-to-date contact details (UK address, telephone number, and mobile telephone number, including email address if the sponsor has one);
- where necessary a copy of the student's Academic Technology Approval Scheme (ATAS) clearance certificate, or the electronic approval notice received by the sponsor;
- any documents UKVI considers relevant (for example, details of the sponsor's practices in making offers to, and enrolling, students); and
- copies (or originals where possible) of any evidence assessed by the sponsor as part of the process of making an offer to the migrants.

Second, on the happening of certain events sponsors must report them to UKVI using the SMS. Sponsors must report within ten working days:[7]

- (running from the end of the enrolment period) the failure of any student to enrol on their course and the reasons for their failure to do so;
- (running from the date the sponsor knew) any student's withdrawal from the course before they travel to the UK (the sponsor should provide details of the institution/course that the student has enrolled on instead);
- (running from the date of the last expected contact) where a student misses ten 'expected contacts';[8]
- (running from the date the sponsor knew) where a student defers their studies and is no longer actively studying;
- (running from the date the sponsor knew about the issue) the sponsor stops sponsoring the student or withdraws a student from the course;
- (running from the date the sponsor knew) if there are any significant changes in the sponsored student's circumstances (eg a change of the place where the student is studying or if the duration of a course of study shortens); and
- any information which suggests that a sponsored student is breaching the conditions of his or her leave.

Sponsors are also required to furnish the police with any information that suggests that the student may be engaging in terrorism or other criminal activity. Sponsors must also report:[9]

- significant changes in the sponsor's circumstances, eg the sponsor ceases trading or becomes insolvent, substantially changes the nature of its business or is involved in a merger or is taken over; or
- the name of the new principal if a private further education institution or higher education institution appoints a new principal or changes owners.

---

[1] See Document 1, para 112 for details of the different functions level 1 and level 2 users can perform in the SMS.
[2] Document 3, para 1.
[3] Document 3, paras 3–5.
[4] Document 3, section 2.
[5] Document 3, para 13.
[6] Document 3, paras 14–20.
[7] Document 3, see para 75 and accompanying table.
[8] For examples of expected contacts see Document 3, table at para 75, rows d and e, and also row j in relation to Tier 1 (Graduate Entrepreneur). Highly Trusted Sponsors are given more flexibility in reporting absences.

⁹   See generally Document 3, paras 21–69.

9.53 *Third,* sponsors must comply with Immigration Rules and statute. In particular, they should assign CAS to students who will meet the requirements of the Tier 4 category and are likely to comply with the conditions of their leave.

Fourth sponsors may only assign a CAS if satisfied that the student both intends to, and is able to, follow the course of study concerned.[1]

Fifth, sponsors must 'do all they can' to ensure the students they sponsor arrive to take up the course and complete it.

Sixth, sponsors must assess a student's ability to follow a course and provide details of the evidence they have used to make this assessment on the student's CAS.[2]

Seventh, sponsors must confirm the student's English language competence where they have not previously completed an academic qualification equivalent to a UK degree which was taught in a (listed) majority English-speaking country, by requiring them to provide a recent secure English language test (SELT) which confirms they have achieved the requisite level of English[3] Sponsors must complete the CAS including details of the test and the student's results/language ability.

Eighth, sponsors owe a duty of co-operation with UKVI: (i) allowing UKVI staff access to any of its premises on demand on prearranged or unannounced visits; (ii) minimising the risk of immigration abuse by complying with any good practice guidance issued by UKVI, or which a regulatory body produces for sponsors; and (iii) complying with any requests for information from the Home Office in connection with the prevention or detection of crime, the administration of illegal working civil penalties; and/or the apprehension or prosecution of immigration offenders.

Ninth, sponsors must ensure their accreditation from the recognised body for the courses they offer is not withdrawn, offer only courses which comply with the policy guidance,[4] ensure that students only work where this is permitted, and for the hours allowed,[5] and where it sponsors Tier 4 (Child) students, provide the name and address where the carer or foster parent and the student will be living, to the local authority in whose area the child will be living.

Tenth, sponsors must hold the appropriate planning permission or local authority planning consent.

1   Document 2, para 125.
2   Document 2, para 124; for example, by confirming any qualifications that the student already holds which make them suitable for the course the sponsor is offering, such as checking and/or verifying a Masters degree where the student is going to undertake a PhD programme; or basing the assessment on the student's progress on their existing course or a recently completed course. Note that UKVI has produced a document to assist sponsors with completing a CAS: see https://www.gov.uk/government/collections/sponsorship-information-for-employers-and-e ducators.
3   Document 2, paras 91–99; see para 92 for students studying at degree level, where CEFR the Common European Framework of Reference (CEFR) level B2 is required; and see paras 93–96 for students studying below degree level, where CEFR level B1 is required.
4   Document 2, para 35.
5   Document 2, paras 78–84.

UKVI SANCTIONS

Suspension and revocation

9.54 A failure to comply with any of the long list of sponsorship duties is likely to result in suspension or revocation of a Sponsor Licence. UKVI may review a sponsor's rating at any time, including, upon receipt of information, upon renewal of the Sponsor Licence, following a visit by UKVI staff, where the sponsor receives a civil penalty, or upon an unsuccessful application as a Highly Trusted Sponsorship Licence. Where the UKVI discovers non-compliance with the sponsorship duties, it may choose to take action. UKVI has indicated that it will usually give a sponsor an opportunity to explain its case, albeit its current policy guidance appears to indicate that action will be taken first, after which it will write to the sponsor.[1]

---

[1] Document 3, para 132. However, as Wyn Williams J observed in *R (on the application of New London College Ltd) v Secretary of State for the Home Department* [2011] EWHC 856 (Admin) at para 60, the duty to act fairly is not to be determined by the contents of UKVI policy. Thus, in certain circumstances, the Respondent will be required to provide *prior* notice to the sponsor of its intention to take action, with sufficiently detailed reasons so that the sponsor can provide a meaningful response: ibid and *R (on the application of The London Reading College Ltd) v Secretary of State for the Home Department* [2010] EWHC 2561 (Admin) at para 37. An obvious (and real-life) example is where the UKVI discovers apparent breaches of the sponsor's duties during a site visit but then delays in taking any action for a number of months. In such circumstances there is no reason why an explanation should not be sought prior to any action being taken; given that the UKVI itself delayed in taking action despite its knowledge of the purported breaches.

Suspension

9.55 Where UKVI has reason to believe that a sponsor is breaching its duties and/or poses a threat to immigration control (for example, assigning confirmations of acceptance for studies (CAS) to students who do not enrol, or fail to complete their course) they may suspend in all the Tiers for which the licence is held whilst further enquiries are made. Following the investigation UKVI may revoke the sponsor's licence, or reinstate the licence.[1] There are two ways in which UKVI will suspend a sponsorship licence, as follows:

(1)   If UKVI has sufficient evidence to suspend the sponsor's licence immediately and without the need for further investigation, they will write to the sponsor giving detailed reasons for the suspension; the sponsor is given 20 working days from the date of the written notification to respond in writing. UKVI will notify the sponsor of the final decision within 20 working days of receiving its response.[2]

(2)   If the UKVI has evidence to warrant a sponsor's licence being suspended pending a full investigation, UKVI will write to the sponsor giving 'initial reasons' for the suspension and informing the sponsor that an investigation will take place. UKVI will 'update' the sponsor on its progress at 'regular intervals'. Sponsors are entitled to make written representations and serve evidence as part of the investigation, and these will be taken into account. In our view, however, sponsors will

only be able to do so, in a meaningful manner, where they have been provided with sufficient information in the 'initial reasons' provided by UKVI.

If the decision goes against it, the sponsor is notified upon completion of the investigation and given 'detailed reasons' for the suspension of their licence. Again, the sponsor is afforded 20 working days to respond in writing and a decision is provided by UKVI 20 working days thereafter.[3] Sponsors are not permitted to assign any confirmations of acceptance for studies during a period of suspension, but must continue with their sponsor duties. Enrolled students are not affected, during the period of suspension, although the sponsor will not be able to assign them a further CAS when their leave expires. Those who have applications for entry clearance or leave to remain will not have their case decided until the suspension is resolved.[4]

[1] See generally Document 3, paras 139–163.
[2] Document 3, paras 150–153. If during the 20 working days the UKVI identifies any further reasons for suspending the sponsor, it will write to the sponsor again, providing another 20 working days to respond to the additional reasons.
[3] Ibid.
[4] Document 3, paras 140–141 and 144–145.

Withdrawal of the licence

9.56 A Tier 4 Sponsor Licence may be revoked by UKVI at any stage. Certain events lead to *mandatory* revocation, for example, where the sponsor ceases operating as an education provider, accreditation from a UKVI approved body is withdrawn, a specified civil penalty is imposed or the sponsor does not hold or ceases to hold the requisite planning permission or consent.[1] UKVI will *consider* revoking a licence where, for example, the sponsor or relevant person has been 'dishonest in any dealings with' UKVI or becomes prohibited from acting as a company director or the organisation fails to keep the specified documents required as part of its duties, or provide these to UKVI when requested.[2] If UKVI decides to revoke the Sponsor Licence, students considered to be 'actively involved' ('complicit') in the sponsor's breach will have their leave curtailed immediately, but those not involved will have their leave curtailed to 60 calendar days to allow them to find an alternative sponsor.[3] The sponsor may apply to rejoin the register following withdrawal, but must re-apply for a new licence and can only do so after a period of six months has elapsed from the date of revocation.[4]

[1] Document 3, paras 158–161.
[2] Document 3, paras 162–163. The guidance indicates that in determining whether to revoke the UKVI will consider the 'number of breaches, previous history and the efforts you have made to address these issues' and will look for evidence that 'you were either not responsible for what happened or, if you were, you took prompt and effective action to remedy the situation when it came to light'.
[3] Document 3, paras 164–165.
[4] Document 3, paras 173–174.

CHALLENGING UKVI DECISIONS ON SPONSOR LICENCES

9.57 There is no right of appeal against a decision by UKVI to downgrade, suspend or withdraw a licence and such decision may only be challenged by way of judicial review. Such claims continue to be heard in the Administrative Court as opposed to the Upper Tribunal. Since the inception of the sponsorship system there have been many such claims for judicial review against the UKVI, with varying degrees of success. Any judicial review challenge will, for example, require consideration of whether UKVI has followed the terms of its policy guidance, has given the sponsor an 'opportunity to explain its case', considered any representations made and/or considered whether the course of action is proportionate and commensurate with the failing identified. A challenge to the ability of the Secretary of State to suspend or revoke licences on the basis of policy guidance, not contained within the Immigration Rules, was rejected by the Supreme Court in *R (on the application of New London College Ltd) v Secretary of State for the Home Department.*[1]

[1]   [2013] UKSC 51, [2013] 1 WLR 2358.

Interim relief

9.58 The Administrative Court has been prepared to grant interim relief against UKVI actions.[1] In *R (on the application of Leeds Unique Education) v Secretary Of State For The Home* Department,[2] Nicol J noted the Secretary of State's concerns about the high numbers of students who had enrolled at a college but then not attended, but considered it arguable that the duty to ensure the percentages set out in the guidance were adhered to was not a compulsory feature of the policy guidance in force at the time. He also considered it arguable that the Secretary of State's decision in another college's case was unlawful given the 'paucity' of the information provided for the Secretary of State's action.[3] Where the claims were at least reasonably arguable, the colleges had suffered and would suffer very significant losses in the absence of interim relief, and the Secretary of State would continue to exercise a supervisory function, he held that the balance of convenience favoured the restoring of the colleges' licences.[4] In *R (on the application of Guildhall College Ltd) v Secretary of State for the Home Department,*[5] Black J, in granting permission, considered it was arguable that there had been a 'material departure from the guidance' in the Secretary of State's failure to adhere to the requirements to provide the sponsor with reasons before revoking the licence. In assessing the application for interim relief, the judge noted that such a decision had 'the capacity to affect [the sponsor's] reputation . . . that students do not wish to sign up for it, and has the potential to have a significant impact upon its finances, particularly because it worries students who are at the College who may seek . . . to recover fees from the College and to go elsewhere, and for the future has an impact upon the ones who may otherwise have wished to have come to this College and go elsewhere . . . ' but found on balance that this was 'a relatively limited impact and one which was justified' on the facts of that case.[6] In *R (on the application of Global Vision College Ltd) v Secretary of State for the Home Department ,*[7] where permission for judicial review had already been granted (albeit by a different judge) Cranston J noted the college's submissions that the Secretary of State's decision to suspend it pending an investigation into various alleged breaches of the sponsorship duties had significant financial consequences, including making staff redundant; the effect on suppliers of printing and cleaning services to the college; as well as the effect on students, unable to extend their leave because they were no longer studying at a licensed college; and that unless interim relief was granted, the college was likely to close for business. He nevertheless refused interim relief giving heavy weight to the public interest in maintaining immigration control[8] and given the claimed serious deficiencies of the college in that particular case, which had apparently continued to be non-compliant even after the Secretary of State's action. In *Global Vision College Ltd v Secretary of State for the Home Department*[9] the Secretary of State's appeal against a judge's grant of additional CAS pending an appeal to the Court of Appeal was allowed by consent, albeit the college was permitted to remain on the sponsor register.[10]

[1]   A judicial review application may also include an application for interim relief. Broadly, interim relief will only be granted where there is a *prima facie* case for judicial review and consideration is given to the 'balance of convenience': *American Cyanamid Co v Ethicon Ltd* [1975] AC 396, [1975] 1 All ER 504, HL, in particular, to identify the course which, in all the circumstances, appears to offer the best prospect that an eventual injustice will be avoided or minimised: *R v Secretary of State for Transport, ex p Factortame Ltd* [1990] 2 AC 85, [1989] 2 WLR 997, including an assessment of the wider public interest (ie immigration control and the prevention of abuse): *Smith v Inner London Education Authority* [1978] I All ER 411 at 422, 142 JP 136, CA. A complaint may also be submitted to UKVI.

[2]   A (repeated) application for interim relief, heard along with the application for permission: *R (on the application of Leeds Unique Education Ltd t/a Leeds Professional College) v Secretary of State for the Home Department; sub nom R (on the application of AA Hamilton College Ltd t/a AA Hamilton College London) v Secretary of State for the Home Department* [2010] EWHC 1030 (Admin), [2010] All ER (D) 145 (May), paras 19–25.

[3]   Ibid, para 32. See further para 36.

[4]   Ibid, paras 29–30 and 39–40. Nicol J did not consider it necessary or appropriate to require an undertaking from either college that they issue CAS only to existing students, despite the preparedness of one college to give such an undertaking: see para 40. However, such an undertaking would address the concern that has been expressed by one judge about new students unknowingly enrolling at a college that may ultimately lose its licence in the event of the claim failing; ie where current students would at least be aware of the ongoing UKVI action (unreported interim relief judgment in the case of *R (on the Application of Global Vision College Ltd) v Secretary of State for the Home Department* [2014] EWHC 205 (Admin)).

[5]   [2010] EWHC 874 (Admin).

[6]   See also *R (on the application of Bhatti) v Croydon Magistrates Court* [2009] EWHC 2772 (Admin), Calvert-Smith J.

[7]   [2010] EWHC 2701 (Admin). See para 11 for Cranston J's decision on the interim relief.

[8]   For further views on the importance attached by the Administrative Court to the public interest in preventing abuse of immigration control, see the views of Silber J in *R (on the application of Westech College) v Secretary of State for the Home Department* [2011] EWHC 1484 (Admin).

[9]   [2014] EWCA Civ 659.

[10]   For further caselaw on stays of execution see: *Department for Environment, Food and Rural Affairs v Downs* [2009] EWCA Civ 257 and *Hammond Suddard Solicitors v Agrichem International Holdings Ltd* [2001] EWCA Civ 2065.

Refusal rate

9.59 The Courts have routinely[1] defended the Secretary of State's use of a 20 per cent refusal rate criterion to determine whether an education provider should be granted HTS.[2] In *R (on the application of London College of*

Management Ltd) v Secretary of State for the Home Department,[3] HHJ Alice Robinson held that it had been lawful for the college to be refused HTS on the basis of its failure to meet the 20 per cent refusal rate, even though that fixed percentage threshold had not existed during the time period being considered by the Secretary of State in assessing the refusal rate. It was sufficient that the Secretary of State had already required sponsors to minimise their refusal rate, and her guidance had foreshadowed the introduction of a threshold.[4] In terms of the refusal rate calculation, the judge held that this could only sensibly be done by reference to CAS that had been used by students, and whose applications had been determined.[5] Following a concession as to the rationality of the use of a percentage threshold, the judge rejected the argument that the Secretary of State should examine the reasons for the refusals relied on, pointing to the 'administrative advantages' to having a fixed threshold.[6] Nevertheless, the judge did recognise that there would be cases where exceptions should be considered and made; to be decided on a 'case by case' basis.[7] In *R (on the application of WGGS Ltd) v Secretary of State for the Home Department,*[8] Thirwall J rejected the argument that the use of a refusal rate was irrational. The Divisional Court expressly agreed with her observations in this regard in the case of *R (West London Vocational Training College Limited) v Secretary of State for the Home Department.*[9] In rejecting the argument that the UKBA had fettered its discretion through its use of the refusal rate, it relied on the UKBA's evidence that it recognised 'that there may be instances when the circumstances of a case are so compelling that rigid application of a mandatory requirement may be disproportionate to the overall aim. In such cases UKBA would consider applying some form of discretion.'[10] In *R (WGGS Ltd) v Secretary of State for the Home Department,*[11] the Court of Appeal also found the use of the refusal rate to be lawful. In *Global Vision College Ltd v Secretary of State for the Home Department*[12], not in itself a challenge to the 20 per cent refusal rate, the Court of Appeal rejected the college's arguments that a significant number of the refusals relied on by UKVI had been unlawful; ie where CAS had been 'invalidated' and deemed to attract no points on a basis not contained within the Rules, such that they should not form part of the refusal rate calculation. In the High Court King J noted the Secretary of State's acceptance that she would 'discount' any 'factually incorrect' refusal by an entry clearance officer/caseworker, and that she had done so in one instance in that case.[13]

---

[1] See most recently the judgment of Hamblen J (9 April 2014) in *R (on the application of Stanley College London UK Ltd) v Secretary of State for the Home Department* [2014] EWHC 1038 (Admin), paras 20–21, where the judge provided an overview of the case law to date.

[2] See above, in relation to the use of the refusal rate for HTS. At the time of writing, the existing case law has concerned challenges in relation to the use of a 20 per cent refusal rate. As stated above, this will be reduced to 10 per cent on 1 November 2014. It remains to be seen whether this rate will be held to be justifiable and lawful, given that the Secretary of State was able to defend the 20 per cent refusal rate on the basis that this was higher than the average refusal rate of 15.3 per cent, thereby giving sponsors 'some further, reasonable, leeway which allowed for refused applications' that they could not reasonably anticipate: see *R (on the application of London College of Management Ltd) v Secretary of State for the Home Department* [2013] EWHC 31 (Admin), paras 38–41.

[3] [2012] EWHC 1029 (Admin).

[4] Paras 21 and 34.

[5] Para 30. In an unreported *ex tempore* permission judgment given on 26 April 2013, this was questioned by HHJ Davies in *Community College Birmingham Ltd v Secretary of State for the Home Department (CO/3392/2013).*

6 Para 37.
7 Para 39.
8 [2012] EWHC 2076 (Admin), para 34
9 [2013] EWHC 31 (Admin), para 40. It indicated that (ibid): 'If a particular sponsor's refusal
   rate is significantly higher than average, it may not prove but it does tend to suggest that there
   has been a less rigorous approach to selection. The policy adopted by the defendant is a strong
   incentive to strict scrutiny.'
10 Para 42.
11 [2013] EWCA Civ 177, para 60, per Jackson LJ: 'Although UKBA's method of assessing
   refusals may be capable of improvement, I do not accept that it is unlawful. It would be quite
   impracticable for UKBA to examine the circumstances of each applicant who is refused entry
   clearance or leave to remain and then to determine whether the college was at fault through
   failing to foresee the problems; and para 62: 'I readily accept that even if a college operates
   proper and rigorous selection procedures, from time to time bogus applicants or unsuitable
   candidates will slip through the net . . . sometimes there will be an unforeseen change in the
   financial circumstances of a genuine candidate . . . . A refusal rate of 20% makes proper
   allowance for those applicants who are unsuitable to come here as students, but cannot
   reasonably be weeded out by the colleges' admissions staff.'
12 [2014] EWCA Civ 659, per Beatson LJ. We consider, however, that this decision is
   inconsistent with the decisions of the Supreme Court in *R (on the application of Alvi) v
   Secretary of State for the Home Department (Joint Council for the Welfare of Migrants
   intervening)* [2012] UKSC 33; [2012] 1 WLR 2208 and *R (on the application of New
   London College Ltd) v Secretary of State for the Home Department* [2013] UKSC 51; [2013]
   1 WLR 2358; and accordingly should not be followed. The Supreme Court was clear in those
   cases that any 'requirement' giving rise to the failure of an individual's application should be
   contained within the Rules; including, for example, checks carried out by the sponsor on the
   resident labour market test: *Alvi* at paras 104–106, 124 and 131. The Court of Appeal's reliance on 'common sense checks' and 'evidential weight' viz. CAS permits the
   Secretary of State to rely on requirements not contained within the Rules, and is thus contrary
   to the Supreme Court judgments.
13 [2014] EWHC 205 (Admin), paras 40–42 and para 54. In *R (on the application of CNM
   (the College of Naturopathic Medicine) Ltd v Secretary of State for the Home Department*
   [2012] EWHC 1851 (Admin), paras 32–33, another challenge relating to a refusal of HTS on
   the basis of the refusal rate, Supperstone J noted the defendant had discounted a refusal and
   had lawfully applied her policy guidance.

Failure to report students who fail to enrol

9.60 Sponsors' arguments that they have not breached their sponsorship
duties by failing to report students who did not gain entry clearance have been
rejected by the Courts: most recently by the Court of Appeal in *WWGS (ante)*.[1]

1 At para 36 the Court held that: 'Colleges are obliged to report every student who fails to enrol.
   There is no express or implied exception from this obligation.' It cited and agreed with case
   law from the High Court in relation to a sponsor's reporting duties: para 38.

Fairness and relevant considerations

9.61 In *San Michael College Ltd v Secretary of State for the Home Department*,[1] Pill LJ considered that the procedure followed by the UKBA was 'so
unfair' and the decision making 'so obscure' that the decision to suspend and
subsequently revoke the college's licence was quashed. In *R (on the application
of Burnley Trading Company Ltd) v Secretary of State for the Home
Department*[2] HHJ Kaye QC considered that given the high degree of trust
demanded by the UKBA from sponsors, sponsors in turn could expect a degree
of fairness from UKBA in its dealings with sponsors and that applications for
a licence would be considered 'seriously, carefully, properly and, above all,

fairly'. In *R (on the application of The London Reading College Ltd) v Secretary of State for the Home Department*[3] Neil Garnham QC found that a failure by the UKBA to provide the college with an opportunity to address additional concerns raised by it, rendered the decision to revoke the licence procedurally unfair and unlawful. In *R (on the application of New London College Ltd) v Secretary of State for the Home Department*,[4] Wyn Williams J found the UKBA had acted unfairly in deciding to suspend a licence, without first giving the college an opportunity to deal with the circumstances said to justify the suspension, and make representations as to whether that should happen. This was despite the fact that the policy guidance in force did not provide for such an opportunity: 'policy or guidance published by UKBA cannot by itself resolve what constitutes the duty [to act fairly]'. In any case the UKBA had not followed its own policy. However, since the UKBA had sought further representations from the college after the suspension decision was made, by the time the revocation decision was taken, the procedural unfairness that vitiated the suspension decision was cured.[5] In *R (on the application of Central College of London Ltd) v Secretary of State for the Home Department Department*,[6] Hickinbottom J rejected the college's argument that it should have been given the opportunity to make representations, particularly about the sanction to be imposed by UKBA, following a change in the policy guidance in this regard; the judge pointed out that the college ought to have been aware of the change and could, if it had wanted, made such representations, but had failed to do so. In *R (on the application of Manchester College of Accountancy & Management) v Secretary of State for the Home Department*,[7] Supperstone J rejected a procedural fairness challenge where the college had been given an opportunity to make representations following a suspension decision but prior to revocation. In *R (on the application of Lords College of Higher Education) v Secretary of State for the Home Department*,[8] Supperstone J granted a claim for judicial review on the sole ground that the UKBA had failed to act in compliance with its published policy, and have regard to relevant 'mitigating factors'.

[1] [2011] EWCA Civ 1336. The college had been penalised for taking the action required by a UKBA Action Plan, and the progress made had not been properly taken into account: paras 42(c), (j) and (g). Pill LJ was clear that, para 44: 'Notwithstanding its serious defaults, the College was entitled to a fair and adequate consideration by UKBA of its case'. The UKBA was also criticised for its failure to provide the necessary evidence to substantiate its assertions that the college had issued more visa letters (which were replaced by CAS) than it had declared, para 34: 'I find it disturbing that the Agency, when challenged to produce the evidence relied on to substantiate the charge, has made such a poor fist of doing so. The importance of immigration control is such that I would have expected records to be kept, and to be kept in a form which could be disclosed if the Agency took action against a sponsor . . . '.

[2] [2011] EWHC 2928 (Admin).

[3] [2010] EWHC 2561 (Admin), paras 38–48. He explained, at para 38: 'if a college is to be able to deal properly with perceived criticism it needs to know a little detail of the nature of the alleged failure'.

[4] [2011] EWHC 856 (Admin), [2011] All ER (D) 60 (Apr).

[5] See paras 56–63 and 76.

[6] [2012] EWHC 1273 (Admin), para 66.

[7] [2013] EWHC 409 (Admin), para 56.

[8] [2013] EWHC 2027 (Admin), paras 38–39.

Damages

9.62 Section 8 of the Human Rights Act deals with the power to award damages under the ECHR provisions. It provides that HRA damages may be awarded only by a court that has power to do so.[1] Under CPR 54.3(2) a claimant in judicial review proceedings can specifically claim damages as part of its application, including damages for breach of the HRA. Under section 8, two of the preconditions of a damage award are that the court should be satisfied, taking account of all the circumstances of the particular case: (i) that an award of damages is *necessary* to afford *just satisfaction* to the person in whose favour it is made; and (ii) that the court should consider an award of damages to be *just and appropriate*.[2] The Strasbourg Court has recognised the principle of *restitutio in integrum*.[3]

[1] Under CPR 54.3(2) a claimant in judicial review proceedings can specifically claim damages as part of its application, including damages for breach of the HRA.
[2] In *R (on the application of Greenfield) v Secretary of State for the Home Department* [2005] UKHL 14, [2005] 1 WLR 673, Lord Bingam stated: 'In deciding whether to award damages, and if so how much, the court is *not strictly bound* by the principles applied by the European Court in awarding compensation under article 41 of the Convention, but it *must take those principles into account*. It is, therefore, to Strasbourg that British courts must look for guidance on the award of damages [6].'
[3] See *Piersack v Belgium* (1984) 7 EHRR 251, para 11; *De Cubber v Belgium* (1987) 13 EHRR 422, para 21) namely, the principle of putting claimants in the position they would have been in, had the public authority not breached their rights. The principle was authoritatively expressed in an Article 6 claim by the Grand Chamber in *Kingsley v United Kingdom* (2002) 35 EHRR 177, at para 40.

9.63 Where losses are incurred by the sponsor flowing from an unlawful decision to suspend or withdraw a licence, there may be grounds to seek damages.[1] In *London Reading College Ltd (ante)* having heard 'the barest of argument' and following a concession that a licence amounted to a possession within the meaning of Article 1 of the First Protocol to the ECHR (A1P1)[2] the judge held that following his finding that the UKBA's decision had been unlawful domestically, the revocation had not been 'subject to the conditions provided for by law' for the purposes of the ECHR, such that there had been a breach of A1P1. However, in *R (on the application of New London College Ltd) v Secretary of State for the Home Department*[3] the Court of Appeal held that a sponsor licence is not a possession within A1P1 and that, on the evidence before the Court, the college had not demonstrated that the 'goodwill' of the business had been adversely affected by the UKBA actions; so as to demonstrate the necessary interference with the economic interests connected with the running of the college. The *New London College* case should be viewed, therefore, as a decision based on there being absent the necessary 'concrete evidential basis' to show an interference with goodwill. We note, that in that case there appears to have been no argument as to the meaning of goodwill and, in particular, the correctness of the definition relied on by Mr Kenneth Parker QC in *R (on the application of Nicholds) v Security Industry Authority*.[4] What then is goodwill?

[1] Note, that there is no right to damages for a public law wrong or an act of maladministration: *R (on the application of Quark Fishing Ltd) v Secretary of State for Foreign and Commonwealth Affairs* [2005] UKHL 57, [2006] 1 AC 529, [2006] 3 All ER 11, per Baroness Hale; *R v Secretary of State for Transport ex p Factortame (No 2)* [1991] 1 AC 603 at 672H, per Lord Goff; *R v Ealing London Borough Council, ex p Parkinson* (1995) 29 HLR 179, (1996) 8 Admin LR 281 at 285C–F, per Laws J (as he then was): it is a 'general principle of

administrative law, namely that the law recognises no right of compensation for an administrative tort'; *R (on the application of Banks) v Secretary of State for Environment, Food and Rural Affairs* [2004] EWHC 416 (Admin), The Times, 19 April 2004, concerning restriction orders on herds, found to be unfair, in which the court considered that it was 'not . . . able to award damages in these proceedings to the claimants even though they have suffered substantial financial loss', despite comments from higher courts that such remedy should be developed: *Somerville v Scottish Ministers* [2007] UKHL 44 at para 77, [2007] 1 WLR 2734, 2008 SC (HL) 45, per Lord Scott; *Stovin v Wise* [1996] AC 923 at 931F–G [1996] 3 All ER 801, HL Equally damages are unlikely to be available in negligence: *W v Home Office* [1997] Imm AR 302, CA, or, in the absence of proof of bad faith or malice, misfeasance in a public office: *Three Rivers District Council v Bank of England (No 3)* [2003] 2 AC 1, [2000] 3 All ER 1, HL; *Thomas v Chief Constable of Cleveland Police* [2001] EWCA Civ 1552, [2001] All ER (D) 29 (Oct).

2   This provides, so far as relevant: 'Every natural or legal person is entitled to the peaceful enjoyment of his possessions. No one shall be deprived of his possessions except in the public interest and subject to the conditions provided for by law and by the general principles of international law.'

3   [2012] EWCA Civ 51, per Richards LJ, paras 96–98.

4   [2007] 1 WLR 2067. See further below.

The definition of goodwill for tax purposes

9.64 A good definition and explanation of the meaning of goodwill is to be found in the *Guidance* and case law extracts produced by HMRC in its capital gains guidance on businesses.[1] It states that 'Goodwill is an *asset* within the meaning of TCGA92/S21(1)' (our emphasis). The term is not defined for the purposes of the Capital Gains legislation in the Taxation and Capital Gains Act 1992. The leading legal authority on its meaning is found in *IRC v Muller & Co's Margarine Ltd*,[2] a stamp duty case, where in answer to the question 'What is goodwill?' Lord Macnaghten said: 'It is a thing very easy to describe, very difficult to define. It is the benefit and advantage of the good name, reputation and connection of a business. It is the attractive force that brings in custom. It is the one thing that distinguishes an old-established business from a new business at its first start'. Lord Lindley said at p 235: 'Goodwill regarded as property has no meaning except in connection with some trade, business or calling.[3] In that connection, I understand the term to include whatever adds value to a business by reason of situation, name and reputation, connection, introduction to old customers, and agreed absence from competition'. Lord Macnaghten indicated that 'Goodwill is composed of a variety of elements. It differs in its composition in different trades and in different businesses in the same trade. One element may preponderate here; and another there'. It should be construed in accordance with legal rather than accountancy principles.[4] When a business is disposed of as a going concern any goodwill attributable to the business will be transferred to the new proprietor. In the *HMRC Manual*, p 68020 goodwill is being clearly described as a distinct asset or property of the business.

1   A section of *HMRC Guidance on Capital Gains Tax*, reference CG68010, entitled *Goodwill: meaning of goodwill*. The full text can be found at www.hmrc.gov.uk/manuals Go to Capital Gains manuals, then click 'businesses' and go to reference CG68010.

2   [1901] AC 217.

3   A number of authorities are cited in *Halsbury* in support of this proposition including the *Muller* case. Of particular relevance are *Wedderburn v Wedderburn (No 4)* (1856) 22 Beav 84 at 104(goodwill is an *appreciable part of the assets* of a concern); also, *Robertson v Quiddington* (1860) 28 Beav.529, at 535 (goodwill is a valuable and tangible asset provided

that it is connected with the business itself); *Star Industrial Company Ltd v Yap Kwee Kor* (1976) FSR 256, at 269, PC (*proprietary right* incapable of existence apart from the business to which it is attached).

[4] *Balloon Promotions Ltd v Wilson (Inspector of Taxes) SpC 524*, [2006], STC (SCD) 167.

Some case law on A1P1

9.65 A key question in determining what are and what are not possessions for the purposes of A1P1 is: (i) to analyse the distinction drawn by both Strasbourg and British courts between 'goodwill' and the loss of future profits; and (ii) to determine how the value of 'goodwill' is properly to be determined. Valuation of assets is essentially the task of accountants but their task is to do so within the ambits of the Strasbourg and domestic court case law, which is not always a clear-cut task. We have already dealt with the *New London College* case and say no more about it.

R (on the application of Malik) v Waltham Forest NHS Primary Care Trust (Secretary of State for Health, interested party)[1] (the removal of a doctor's name from a list of those qualified to work locally for the NHS) the Court of Appeal indicated: (a) that although the licence not be a possession, economic benefits that flow from the licence may be; (b) that goodwill is 'undoubtedly a possession, notwithstanding that its present-day value reflects a capacity to earn profits in the future'; and (c) that the distinction between goodwill and the present value of anticipated future income 'has never had to be determined on the facts'. The case then went to Strasbourg.[2] The ECtHR observed how goodwill for the purposes of A1P1 might be impaired by the removal of a licence, or its equivalent without any need to determine whether the licence is or is not a possession *per se*.

Tre Traktorer Aktiebolag v Sweden[3] (withdrawal of a restaurant's non-transferable liquor licence) the European Court held that the economic interests connected with the running of the business were possessions for the purposes of A1P1, and that the withdrawal of a liquor licence had an adverse effect on the goodwill and the value of the restaurant, and that the action taken to remove the licence amounted to interference with possessions.

Denimark Ltd v United Kingdom[4] the ECtHR drew a distinction between the loss of goodwill and the loss of future income and held that the element of the complaint that related to a diminution in value of the business assessed by reference to the loss of future income, which amounts in effect to a claim for loss of future income, falls outside the scope of A1P1.

R (on the application of Nicholds) v Security Industry Authority[5] (whether the licences given to door supervisors in the security industry amounted to possessions for the purposes of A1P1). Kenneth Parker QC drew a distinction between accounting goodwill and economic goodwill: 'It appears that "goodwill" is being used rather in the economic sense of *the capitalised value of a business or part of a business as a going concern* which, according to modern theory of corporate finance, is best understood as the expected free future cash flows of the business *discounted to a present value at an appropriate after tax weighted average cost of funds*. He noted that it 'is clear on Strasbourg jurisprudence, now confirmed by high domestic authority, that A1P1 protects only "goodwill", as a form of asset with monetary value, and does not protect an expected stream of future income which, for mainly organisational reasons, cannot be or is not capitalised.'

R (on the application of the Countryside Alliance) v A-G[6] (prohibition on the hunting of wild mammals with dogs and or hare coursing) Lord Bingham referred to the clear distinction that had been made between 'goodwill which may be a possession for the purposes of [A1P1] and future income, not yet earned and to which no enforceable claim exists, which may not' be a possession for the purposes of A1P1.

[1] [2007] EWCA Civ 265, [2007] 1 WLR 2092.
[2] *Malik v United Kingdom, (Application 23780/08)* (13 March 2012, unreported), ECtHRSection IV (ECtHR).
[3] (1989) 13 EHRR 309.
[4] (2000) 30 EHRR CD 144.
[5] [2007] 1 WLR 2067.
[6] [2007] UKHL 52, [2007] 1 AC 719.

The upshot

9.66 The meaning of goodwill on the basis of the case law on A1P1 and on capital gains tax (CGT) is that:

(a) Goodwill is composed of a variety of elements. It differs in its composition in different trades and in different businesses in the same trade. The goodwill of a business is the whole advantage of its reputation and connection with customers.

(b) It is the benefit and advantage of the good name, reputation and connection of a business. It is the attractive force that brings in custom.

(c) It represents in connection with any business or business product *the value of the attraction* to the customers that the name and reputation possesses. *Halsbury's Laws of England*, 4th edn, Vol 35, at p 1206.

(d) From the commencement of its activities it will begin to generate goodwill so that on a subsequent disposal of the business as a going concern: *one of the assets* comprised in the disposal *will consist of goodwill*. It includes whatever *adds value* to a business by reason of situation, name and reputation, connection.

(e) In the context of A1P1 the key distinction is between goodwill as an asset that is a possession and some other 'thing' which is merely a present day reflection of anticipated future income, which is not to be considered a possession.

(f) There is a distinction between 'accounting goodwill' and 'economic goodwill', and that for A1P1 purposes it is economic goodwill that counts.

(g) The fact that goodwill may not be reflected in the balance sheet of a business does not mean that it does not exist.

(h) 'Goodwill' in the economic sense is the capitalised value of a business or part of a business as a going concern discounted to a present value.

(i) Where carrying on with the business is dependent on the possession of a licence, the licence itself may not be a possession within A1P1, but the economic benefits that flow from the licence may be a possession. If the withdrawal of the licence has an adverse effect on the goodwill and the value of the business, the removal of the licence will amount to interference with possessions.

(j) However, in the case of doctors or other professional persons, who have enjoyed 'goodwill' in their practices, for example, the advantage that has arisen over 30 years of practice from their own reputation and connections. (The fact that they are prevented by the rules or practices of their profession from selling the goodwill in their practices, means that any decrease in its marketable value would be of no consequence to them.)

The essential characteristics of goodwill for the purposes of A1P1 are:

(a) that it is separate from just future profits;
(b) that its value can be measured from the present day capitalised value of the business reflecting future cash flows, discounted to present day value;
(c) that it is a marketable asset (even if this is a bit of a grey area); and
(d) that goodwill for the purposes of A1P1 is different from goodwill in the technical accounting sense which relates solely to 'goodwill' acquired on the purchase of a business rather than internally generated goodwill in the economic sense of the capitalised value of a business (see Kenneth Parker QC in *Nicholds* at para 72).

A1P1 – Justification

9.67 Once an interference with possessions has been established the court now considers justification under three principles:

(a) *The principle of lawfulness*. The interference must be lawful[1] and any applicable provisions of domestic law must be 'sufficiently accessible, precise and foreseeable in their application'.[2]
(b) The principle of legitimate aim in the general interest.[3]
(c) Not disproportionate but striking a fair balance between the general interest of the community and the individual person or corporation's fundamental rights.[4]

[1] *Hutten-Czapska v Poland* (2005) 45 EHRR 276 (Grand Chamber) para 163; *Jahn v Germany* (2005) 42 EHRR 1084 (Grand Chamber), at para 81.
[2] *Broniowski v Poland* (2004) 40 EHRR 495 (Grand Chamber), para 147.
[3] *Hutten-Czapska*, at para 164; *Jahn v Germany*, at para 89.
[4] *Hutten-Czapska*, at para 167; *Broniowski v Poland*, at paras 150–151.

PROSPECTIVE STUDENTS

9.68 Students who are not yet enrolled on a course can still obtain entry clearance and admission as prospective students outside the PBS.[1] To obtain leave in this capacity, prospective students must be able to demonstrate (i) a genuine and realistic intention of undertaking, within six months of their date of entry, a course of study which would meet the requirements for an extension of stay as a student under para 245ZX or para 245ZZC and (ii) that they intend to leave the UK on completion of their studies or on the expiry of their leave to enter if they are not able to meet the requirements for an extension of stay as a student in accordance with para 245ZX or para 245ZZC. They may then be admitted for a period not exceeding six months. If less than six months' leave is given, prospective students can obtain an extension to give them more time to find a college or school place, but six months is the maximum leave in this category and they cannot extend it beyond this time.[2]

[1]   HC 395, para 82 as amended by HC 314, as from 9 March 2009, at the same time as Tier 4 (Students) came into force.
[2]   See HC 395, paras 85–87.

PLAB TESTS AND CLINICAL ATTACHMENTS

9.69 The test of the Professional and Linguistic Assessment Board (PLAB) is to enable overseas doctors to demonstrate their knowledge of English and their medical expertise. The PLAB test has two parts – part one can be taken in the UK or abroad, but part two can only be taken in the UK. Clinical attachments are available to graduate doctors and dentists and involve observation only and not treatment of patients. The posts are unpaid. Notwithstanding the replacement of most of the pre-March 2009 student rules, the rules on entry to do a PLABS test or undertake a period of clinical attachments are still operative under HC 395, paras 75A–75H for PLABS and under 75J–75M for clinical attachments. Although they are part of medical training, the rules have incorporated important requirements of the visitor rules. So leave is for six months only in both cases and of themselves they are not stepping stones to further leave in a different category, except successful PLABs examinees can then qualify to do a clinical attachment.

Chapter 10

WORKING, BUSINESS, INVESTMENT AND RETIREMENT IN THE UK

INTRODUCTION

10.1 This chapter deals with admission to the UK for all non-EEA nationals[1] who wish to work, conduct business, invest or retire in the UK.[2] The rules and policies for the admission of economic migrants are collectively referred to as 'commercial immigration law'. The whole scheme for admission for work, business and investor purposes has been significantly overhauled over the last six years as part of the previous government's five-year strategy for asylum and immigration.[3] The intention was to introduce a 'transparent points system for all those who come to the UK to work', divided into five tiers. The chapter is divided into three sections. Firstly, applications under Tiers 1, 2 and 5 of the new points based system. Secondly, guidance for companies and other organisations wanting to sponsor applicants under the new points based system. The last part deals with pre-existing categories of entry and leave that have survived the recent changes. In respect of each category, we give some indication whether an applicant may switch in-country to the category concerned. We also identify any provision regarding the admission of family members.

[1] The law governing admission to the UK for employment by EEA nationals and their families, is dealt with in CHAPTER 6 above, as is the establishment of businesses by nationals of Turkey, with whom the EU has concluded an Association Agreement.
[2] For business visitors, au pairs and working holidaymakers, see **10.103** below.
[3] 'Controlling our borders: Making migration work for Britain. Five year strategy for asylum and immigration', Cm 6472, Feb 05, paras 18–22. See further update published by the then BIA on 5 December 2007, 'Highly skilled migrants under the points based system – Statement of Intent'. Available via the UKBA website at: www.talentscotland.com/Students.aspx.

Managed migration and rules versus schemes

10.2 The Points Based System (PBS) was introduced in 2008. Tier 1 of the PBS was designed to allow 'high value' migrants to enter or remain in the UK. This migration route is of importance to the UK, as attracting foreign entrepreneurs, investors and individuals of exceptional talent is seen as a way of promoting economic growth. Tier 2 deals with three categories of worker and Tier 5 with those coming to the UK for short-term work or training. People who are overseas and wish to enter the UK under any of these Tiers can apply for leave to enter (LTE); these applications are considered by Home Office staff working overseas. People already in the UK can apply for leave to remain (LTR); these are normally considered by Home Office staff in Sheffield. In all these tiers, there have been changes to the Tier, with some of the original subcategories being closed and others being opened, especially in Tiers 1 and 5. In November 2010, the Home Secretary said: 'Operating effectively, tier one should only be used by investors, entrepreneurs and people of exceptional talent; in short, the genuinely highly skilled.' See https://www.gov.uk/govern ment/speeches/immigration-home-secretarys-speech-of-5-november-2010.

10.3 Certain of the Tier 1 and 2 categories highlight the difference between two distinct approaches to the formulation of commercial immigration law. Historically, categories such as business persons, together with certain employment categories, have been contained within the Immigration Rules, administered by Home Office officials based in the IND/BIA, and later UKBA at Croydon and subject to the statutory immigration appeals regime. By contrast, the work permit category was a 'scheme' whose requirements were set out in easily amended guidance notes and administered, not by the Home Office, but by the department of state responsible for employment matters. Refusals were not justiciable before the statutory immigration appellate authorities.[1] Responsibility for the work permit scheme, and for processing work permit applications, shifted in 2001 from the Overseas Labour Section of the then Department for Education and Employment to a new Home Office Department, Work Permits (UK). The distinction between categories wholly within the Immigration Rules and 'scheme'-based categories was reinforced by the addition of new scheme-based categories, such as the International Graduates Scheme (IGS) and Science and Engineering Graduate Scheme (SEGS), both of which have now largely disappeared.

[1]   See *Pearson v Immigration Appeal Tribunal* [1978] Imm AR 212, CA.

10.4 The ad hoc development of the rules was largely to blame for the multiplicity of schemes and the lack of coherence among them. However, it is not hard to see why the Home Office preferred schemes to traditional immigration rules-based categories. Schemes are more flexible and refusals can be reviewed in-house as they fall beyond the reach of the statutory immigration appeals regime. Overall, following the transfer of the Sheffield work permits bureaucracy to the BIA and then to the UKBA, there was less and less cause to distinguish between Croydon and Sheffield – they both became part of the then BIA and their acts were the acts of the Secretary of State for the Home Department. But the distinction between Immigration Rules categories and the scheme-based categories – originally defined in terms of the two separate bureaucracies which administered them – became more sharp and significant than ever in the period immediately preceding the introduction of the points based system. The then Home Secretary, Charles Clarke, when introducing the new points based system stated that:

'The system we have at present is complex and difficult to understand. We will bring all our current work schemes and students into a simple points based system designed to ensure that we are only taking migrants for jobs that cannot be filled from our own workforce and focussing on the skilled workers we need most like doctors, engineers, finance experts, nurses and teachers.'[1]

As we shall see the points system cuts a swathe through the previous distinctions. Firstly, the points-based system adopts the single application of the old permit free categories of employment. It is based on what the Home Office calls the concept of one decision. Secondly, although every application is regulated by the Immigration Rules and subject to the normal appeal procedure where applications are made in the UK, where they are made from abroad, like the decision to issue work permits, the substantive basis of the decision cannot be challenged on an appeal to the AIT but is only subject to a rather formal and restrictive administrative review. And, since the question whether an applicant has achieved the right score is largely a question of being able to tick enough boxes, the emphasis of the scheme is based on a need to achieve formal compliance, the assumption being that substantial compliance will already have been achieved by the prior calculation of the correct way in which the points are to be awarded. In the post Immigration Act 2014 world, recent immigration rules (HC 693) make administrative review available for persons refused leave to remain where they do not have a right of appeal. See further Chapter **19**.

[1] Home Office, 'Controlling our borders: Making migration work for Britain. Five year strategy for Asylum and Immigration', Cm 6472, February 2005, p 7.

POINTS BASED SYSTEM (PBS)

10.5 In March 2006, 'A Points-Based System: Making Migration Work for Britain' (CM 6741) was published. This set out proposals to bring in an Australian-style points system comprising of five tiers:

- Tier 1: highly skilled individuals to contribute to growth and productivity;
- Tier 2: skilled workers with a job offer to fill gaps in the UK labour force;
- Tier 3: low skilled workers to fill specific temporary labour shortages (never implemented);
- Tier 4: students;
- Tier 5: youth mobility and temporary workers: people coming to the UK to fulfil primarily non-economic objectives.

In its statement of intent published in December 2007, the government called this the biggest shake-up of the immigration system in its history.[1] The promised changes included implementing the Australian-style points system. The system was launched in the first quarter of 2008, beginning with highly skilled migrants and sponsor registration. This was followed in November 2008, with Tier 2 and Tier 5. The introduction of Tier 3 appears to be on indefinite hold as the UKBA expects that all likely vacancies under this tier can be met by workers from the EU. Sectors effected by the non introduction of Tier 3, primarily agriculture, contest this assumption and have complained of difficulties in sourcing sufficient quantities of seasonal workers. Central to the coalition government's new immigration strategy has been a cap on economic migration from the applicants outside the EU. On 28 June 2010, the Home Secretary announced to Parliament that the government intended to introduce an annual immigration limit in April 2011. At the same time, she announced a number of interim measures. Firstly, from 19 July 2010, there was a temporary limit on the number of applications for entry clearance and leave to enter in certain categories. Secondly, the criteria for all applications for leave to enter and entry clearance and for leave to remain under Tier 1 (General) were toughened up. Finally, there was to be a reduction in the number of certificates of sponsorship which will be granted to licensed employers permitted to sponsor migrant workers to come to the UK under Tier 2. Since then a cap has been maintained on Tier 2 (General).

[1] 'Highly skilled migrants under the points based system – Statement of Intent', see 10.1 fn 3.

10.6 One of the selling points of the points based system is that the need for two applications have been replaced by a single application process, whether in or outside the UK. For example, under the highly skilled migrant programme (HSMP) applicants were required to obtain an approval letter from the Home Office and to then make a separate application under the Immigration Rules for entry clearance or leave to remain. The same need for a double application applied to work permits. Under the points based system, applicants make one application in which all the requirements will be considered. The Home Office call this the concept of one decision.[1] Giving applicants the opportunity of making online applications has also speeded up the application process. As from January 2010 a rule change under HC 1733 gave migrants applying in the UK under Tier 2 or 5 of the Points Based System the opportunity to complete and submit their application online. This has since been extended, as described in CHAPTER 3, above.

[1] Explanatory Memorandum to HC 321, para 7.5.

10.7 The structure of the Immigration Rules governing applications under the new points based system (PBS) are significantly different from other sections of the rules. Applications are in effect, required to meet three rounds of criteria. Firstly, the requirement of the specific rule itself. These follow a similar template to the remainder of the Immigration Rules in that they set out the requirements for entry clearance, leave to enter and leave to remain and the total number of points necessary for a successful application. Secondly, the rules expect the applicant to meet the requirements of specific Appendices to the rules. These Appendices set out how an applicant can achieve the requisite points necessary to qualify under each application. Appendix A details the general attributes needed to qualify under each tier. Appendix B details the English language requirements and Appendix C details the required sums necessary to show that the applicant will be able to maintain themselves without recourse to public funds. The maintenance provisions consist of a requirement to demonstrate a minimum level of savings for a proscribed period of time at the date of application.[1] It would appear to be entirely legitimate for an applicant under the points based system to borrow the required sum, keep it in an account for the requisite period and pay it back after the application has been made![2]

[1] HC 395, Appendix C.
[2] *PO (Points based scheme: maintenance: loans) Nigeria* [2009] UKAIT 00047.

10.8 The third round of criteria is that Appendices A, B and C to the rules rely to a greater or lesser extent, depending on the particular Tier, on outside sources for evidence of compliance, which were initially contained in published guidance, but since the decisions of the Court of Appeal in *Pankina*[1] and the Supreme Court in *Alvi*[2] have been made part of the Immigration Rules. The result has meant that the Immigration Rules have bulked up in a sometimes spectacular fashion and require frequent change.[3]

[1] *Secretary of State for the Home Department v Pankina.* [2010] EWCA Civ 71, (2010) Times, 20 July. Following *Pankina* the Secretary of State has in fact chosen not to appeal (but has kept her options open) and has 'for the avoidance of doubt' brought various existing PBS requirements from Guidance into the Immigration Rules. These first batch were set out in the amendments in HC 863. It is a long, thorough and overdue list. Further transfers into the rules have followed in successive rule changes, following the revised test set out in *Alvi*.
[2] *R (on the application of Alvi) v Secretary of State for the Home Department* [2012] UKSC 33.
[3] See for example Appendix J and P.

Cross cutting measures

Imposing a cap on numbers

10.9 From 23 November 2010 until 17 December 2010, UKBA operated Tier 1 (General) on the basis that an interim limit on the number of permitted out of country applications was in force. Earlier on 28 June 2010 the Home Secretary had announced the imposition of an interim limit on Tier 2 (General). The legality of these limits was contested in the Divisional Court in the *JCWI* case.[1] The court held that the Secretary of State had acted unlawfully in purporting to impose an interim cap. Specifically, the Secretary of State had failed to lay the numerical limits for Tier 1 (General) and for Tier 2 (General) before Parliament as required by the Immigration Act 1971. In order for the Government's interim limit policy to have legal effect, the level of the limit should be specified in the Immigration Rules, as opposed to UK Border Agency guidance. As a result of the judgment, new rules were quickly laid before Parliament to remedy the situation.[2] The effect of these changes was:

- To close Tier 1 (General) with effect from the 23 December 2010 in respect of applications for entry clearance only. It made no changes at that time affecting applications for leave to remain; and
- To specify in the Immigration Rules the level of the Government's interim limit for Tier 2 (General) of the Points Based System between 21 December 2010 and 5 April 2011. For further details, see **10.65**, below.
- The Tier 1 (General) category did not involve a sponsoring employer. The rule changes therefore affected potential migrants only and did not apply to small businesses.

[1] *R (on the application of the Joint Council for the Welfare of Immigrants) v Secretary of State for the Home Department* [2010] EWHC 3524 (Admin), [2010] All ER (D) 244 (Dec).
[2] HC 698, laid on 21 December 2010.

Indefinite leave – some general measures

10.10 In addition to the changes relevant only to particular applications for indefinite leave to remain by Tier 1 and Tier 2 Migrants, such as the accelerated route to settlement for entrepreneurs and investors, which we deal with below, the following general changes are applicable to migrants under PBS, non-PBS and predecessor categories of the PBS. They are:[1]

- A new criminality threshold has been introduced requiring applicants applying for indefinite leave to remain to be clear of unspent convictions.[2] However, it does not apply to HSMP migrants with leave to remain under the terms of the HSMP ILR Judicial Review Policy Document.[3]
- Skilled and highly skilled migrants will be required to pass the 'Life in the UK' test prior to gaining indefinite leave to remain.[4] This applies to the following categories, except where transitional arrangements apply: Work Permit Holders; Highly Skilled Migrant Programme (other than those covered by the HSMP ILR Judicial Review Policy Document); Representatives of overseas newspapers, news agencies or broadcasting organisations; Representatives of overseas businesses; Overseas govern-

ment employees; Ministers of religion, missionaries or members of religious orders; Airport-based operational ground staff of overseas-owned airlines; Persons intending to establish themselves in business; Innovators; Persons intending to establish themselves in business under provisions of EC Association Agreements; Investors; Writers, Composers and Artists; Tier 1 Migrants (Exceptional talent), Tier 1 (General) Migrants, Tier 1 (Entrepreneur) Migrants, Tier 1 (Investor) Migrants; Tier 2 (Intra-Company Transfers) Migrants, Tier 2 (General) Migrants, Tier 2 (Minister of Religion) Migrants, Tier 2 (Sportsperson) Migrant.

- Transitional arrangements are set out with regards to the requirement to pass the Life in the UK Test for those people applying for indefinite leave to remain in one of the categories listed above. The effect of these is that where an applicant has enrolled on an ESOL course or gained an ESOL qualification prior to 23 November 2010 (the date of the relevant rule change), that applicant can still rely on an ESOL qualification to demonstrate sufficient knowledge of the English language and sufficient knowledge about life in the UK for any future application for indefinite leave to remain under one of the categories listed in the amended HC 395, paragraph 33BA.
- An applicant who enrolled on an ESOL course after 23 November 2010 and applies for indefinite leave to remain in one of the categories listed above after 6 April 2011 must now pass the Life in the UK Test.
- An applicant who enrolled on an ESOL course after 23 November 2010 and who gains an ESOL qualification can continue to use that qualification in an application for indefinite leave to remain in one of the categories listed above if that application was made before 6 April 2011.
- Changes, described in the Explanatory Memorandum as technical, have been made to the provisions for indefinite leave to remain applications by the spouse or civil partner of a person who is present and settled here. These amendments add other relevant Tiers of the Points-Based System into the rules (the pre-existing rules referred only to dependants of Tier 1 Migrants).[5]

[1] See HC 863 and the Explanatory Memorandum at para 7.13. The changes which affect work permit holders applying for settlement are dealt with at **10.113**, below.
[2] See HC 395 so far as relevant to PBS and PBS family members, paras 245BF(a), 245CD(a), 245DF(a), 245EF(a), 245GF(a), 245HF(a), 245ZS(aa), 319E(g) and 319J(f). See HC 908, which came into force on 21 April 2011.
[3] See the changes in HC 908, which came into force on 21 April 2011.
[4] HC 395, para 33BA applies.
[5] See HC 395, para 287(a)(i)(d) and (a)(i)(e).

10.11 HC 395, paragraph 245AAA provides some general rules as regards potential impediments to achieving the continuous period five years lawful presence in the UK needed to qualify for indefinite leave, except for those migrants in the categories Tier 1 (Exceptional Talent) (para 245BF), Tier 1 (Entrepreneur) (245DF) and Tier 1 (Investor) (245EF):

(a) 'continuous period of 5 years lawfully in the UK' means residence in the United Kingdom for an unbroken period with valid leave,[1] and for these purposes a period shall not be considered to have been broken where:

(i)   the applicant has been absent from the UK for a period of 180 days or less in any of the five consecutive 12 month periods preceding the date of the application for leave to remain;

(ii)   the applicant has existing limited leave to enter or remain upon their departure and return except that where that leave expired no more than 28 days prior to a further application for entry clearance, that period and any period pending the determination of an application made within that 28 day period shall be disregarded; and

(iii)   the applicant has any period of overstaying between periods of entry clearance, leave to enter or leave to remain of up to 28 days and any period of overstaying pending the determination of an application made within that 28 day period disregarded;

(b)   the applicant must have been employed in the UK continuously throughout the five years, except for periods when the applicant had leave as a Tier 1 (General) Migrant, a Tier 1 (Investor) Migrant, a Tier 1 (Entrepreneur) Migrant, a Tier 1 (Exceptional Talent) Migrant, a highly skilled migrant, a Businessperson, an Innovator, an Investor, a self-employed lawyer or a writer, composer or artist. The employment must have been under the terms of their Certificate of Sponsorship, work permit or in the employment for which they were given leave to enter or remain. The employment must have been continuous, except that certain breaks in employment must be disregarded, if they have been caused by gaps between jobs where they have applied for leave to work for a new employer as a Tier 2 Migrant, or, under Tier 5 Temporary Worker (International Agreement) Migrant as a private servant in a diplomatic household, where in the latter case they applied to enter the UK before 6 April 2012. The gap will be disregarded if it is less than 60 days from the end of their employment with their previous employer or Sponsor.

(c)   Except for periods where the applicant had leave as a Tier 1 (Investor) Migrant, a Tier 1 (Entrepreneur) Migrant, a Tier 1 (Exceptional Talent) Migrant or a highly skilled migrant, any absences from the UK during the five years must have been for a purpose that is consistent with the applicant's basis of stay here, including paid annual leave, or for serious or compelling reasons.

[1]   This is made subject to paragraphs 245CD [Tier 1 (General)) (Tier 1 (General), 245GF ((Tier 2 (Intra-Company Transfer)] and 245HF ([Tier 2 (General), Tier 2 (Minister of Religion) or Tier 2 (Sportsperson))].

Appendix B – English language requirements

10.12 The general rule is that all applicants applying as a Tier 1 Migrant or Tier 2 Migrant must have 10 points for English language. But there are exceptions for applicants seeking:

(i)   entry clearance or leave to remain as a Tier 1 (Exceptional Talent) Migrant, except where the application is for leave to remain and the applicant has, or who was last granted entry clearance or leave to remain as a Tier 1 (Exceptional Talent) migrant;

(ii)   entry clearance or leave to remain as a Tier 1 (Investor) Migrant; and

(iii)   entry clearance or leave to remain as a Tier 2 (Intra-Company Transfer) Migrant.

The levels of English language required are shown in Table 1 of Appendix B. They start at level C1[1] or above for Tier 1 (General) migrants, B1 or above for Tier 1 (Entrepreneur), Tier 1 (Graduate Entrepreneur), Tier 1 (Exceptional Talent) migrants and Tier 2 (Sportsperson). For Tier 2 (Minister of Religion) it is at level B2 or above. Depending on past experience the required level can go up to A1 for Tier 2 (General) and Tier 2 (Sportsperson).

Available points for English language are shown in Table 2. The number of points awarded is 10. For some there may need to be a test. But there are complete exemptions and an automatic 10 points for nationals from English speaking countries, as listed in the Appendix, for those who have a Degree taught in English, or who have met the language requirement in a previous grant of leave. Further details and the documents required to show the person is in an exempted group and need not do a test are set out in the Appendix.

The approved tests, and the levels of English that they are accepted for, are set out in Appendix O to the Immigration Rules. Under HC 532 which took effect on July 11 2014 changes are being made to remove all tests provided by Cambridge International Examinations (CIE) from the list of approved English language tests on 1 August 2014. This is a scheduled withdrawal at this provider's request. Changes are also being made to remove specific tests provided by Cambridge English (the BULATS Online test) and Trinity College London (ESOL Skills for Life tests) from the list of approved English language tests on 1 August 2014. These changes are being made at the providers' requests. Other listed tests from these two providers will continue to be accepted.

[1]   A1, B1 and C1 are grades of the Council of Europe's Common European Framework for Language Learning. These are approximately equivalent to a GCSE pass at grades A–C.

Appendix C – Maintenance (funds)

10.13 In all cases where an applicant is required to obtain points under Appendix C, the applicant under Tiers 1, 2 and 5 must meet the requirements listed below:[1]

(a)   The applicant must have the funds specified in the relevant part of Appendix C at the date of the application;

(b)   If the applicant is applying as a Tier 1 Migrant, a Tier 2 Migrant or a Tier 5 (Temporary Worker) Migrant, the applicant must have had the funds referred to in (a) above for a consecutive 90-day period of time, unless applying as a Tier 1 (Exceptional Talent) Migrant or a Tier 1 (Investor) Migrant;

(c)   If the funds were obtained when the applicant was in the UK, the funds must have been obtained while the applicant had valid leave and was not acting in breach of any conditions attached to that leave;

(d)   Where the funds are in one or more foreign currencies, the applicant must have the specified level of funds when converted to pound sterling (£) using the spot exchange rate which appears on www.oanda.com for the date of the application;

(e)   Where the applicant is applying as a Tier 1 Migrant, a Tier 2 Migrant or a Tier 5 Migrant, the funds must have been under his own control on the date of the application and for the period specified in (b) above;

(f)   Where the application is made at the same time as applications by the partner or child of the applicant (such that the applicant is a Relevant Points Based System Migrant for the purposes of paragraph 319AA), each applicant must have the total requisite funds specified in the relevant parts of appendices C and E.

(g)   The end date of the 90-day period referred to in (b) above will be taken as the date of the closing balance on the most recent of the specified documents (where specified documents from two or more accounts are submitted, this will be the end date for the account that most favours the applicant), and must be no earlier than 31 days before the date of application.

(h)   No points will be awarded where the specified documents show that the funds are held in a financial institution listed in Appendix P as being an institution with which the UK Border Agency is unable to make satisfactory verification checks.

(i)   Maintenance must be in the form of cash funds. Other accounts or financial instruments such as shares, bonds, credit cards, pension funds etc, regardless of notice period are not acceptable.

(j)   If the applicant wishes to rely on a joint account as evidence of available funds, the applicant (or for children under 18 years of age, the applicant's parent or legal guardian who is legally present in the United Kingdom) must be named on the account as one of the account holders.

(k)   Overdraft facilities will not be considered towards funds that are available or under an applicant's own control.

In all cases where Appendix C or Appendix E states that an applicant is required to provide specified documents, the specified documents are:

(a)   Personal bank or building society statements;[2]

(b)   A building society pass book or (c) a letter from a regulated financial institution. Each of these must inter alia show that the necessary funds have been held for a consecutive 90-day period of time, if the applicant is applying as a Tier 1 Migrant, a Tier 2 Migrant a Tier 5 (Temporary Worker) Migrant, or the Partner or Child of a Relevant Points Based System Migrant in any of these categories and a single date within 31 days of the date of the application, if the applicant is applying as a Tier 5 (Youth Mobility Scheme) Migrant.

---

[1]   HC 395 Appendix C, para 1A.

[2]   The statements must not be mini-statements from automatic teller machines (ATMs): Appendix C, para 1B(a)(v).

10.14 An applicant applying for entry clearance or leave to remain as a Tier 1 Migrant must score 10 points for funds, unless applying as a Tier 1 (Exceptional Talent) Migrant or a Tier 1 (Investor) Migrant. The current level of funds needed to obtain an entry clearance is £3,310 for a Tier 1 (Entrepreneur) and £1,890 for a Tier 1 (Graduate Entrepreneur). When seeking leave to remain the level of funds required is £945. However, it is 10 points if the person applying as a Tier 1 (Graduate Entrepreneur) Migrant scores points from Appendix A for an endorsement from UK Trade and

Investment, and UK Trade and Investment has confirmed in the endorsement letter that it has awarded funding of at least £1,890 (for entry clearance applications) or £945 (for leave to remain applications) to the applicant.

Where the applicant is applying as a Tier 1 (Entrepreneur) Migrant, he cannot use the same funds to score points for attributes under Appendix A and to score points for maintenance funds for himself or his dependants under this Appendix or Appendix E.

10.15 An applicant applying for entry clearance or leave to remain as a Tier 2 Migrant will only be awarded 10 points if:

(a)   the applicant has the level of funds shown in the table, viz £945, and provides the specified documents listed in the Appendix; or

(b)   the applicant has entry clearance, leave to enter or leave to remain as:

(i)   a Tier 2 Migrant

(ii)   a Jewish Agency Employee

(iii)   A member of the Operational Ground Staff of an Overseas-owned Airline,

(iv)   a Minister of Religion, Missionary or Member of a Religious Order,

(v)   a Representative of an Overseas Newspaper, News Agency or Broadcasting Organisation, or

(vi)   a Work Permit Holder or

(c)   the Sponsor is an A rated Sponsor and has certified on the Certificate of Sponsorship that, should it become necessary, it will maintain and accommodate the migrant up to the end of the first month of his employment up to an amount of at least £945.

10.16 A Tier 5 (Youth Mobility) Temporary Migrant will only get 10 points if he or she has the level of funds shown in the table, viz £1890. Tier 5 (Temporary Worker) Migrants must score 10 points for funds but these points will only be awarded if an applicant meets the criteria set out in the Table, namely, that he or she has £945; or the Sponsor is an A rated Sponsor and the Certificate of Sponsorship Checking Service confirms that the Sponsor has certified that the applicant will not claim public funds during his period of leave as a Tier 5 (Temporary Worker) Migrant. Points will only be awarded if the applicant provides a valid Certificate of Sponsorship reference number with his or her application.

10.17 Appeal rights under the PBS system have also been curtailed. Section 4 of the Immigration, Asylum and Nationality Act 2006 already sets the scene, by removing the full right of appeal for those applying from abroad to come to the UK under the points system. These restricted rights have been put in place as each points system tier has been implemented, with transitional arrangements to ensure that applicants do not lose the right of appeal until each tier has become fully operational. This has meant that appeal rights on overseas applications have been abolished in all points based sub-categories, except where the appeal is brought on human rights or race discrimination grounds. In-country applicants have had their rights greatly curtailed by the rule on post-decision evidence.[1] The final nail in the appeal rights coffin will occur when the IA 2014 is fully implemented. See CHAPTER **20**, below.

[1] Previously, an applicant could provide evidence after the decision that demonstrated that at the date of application they met the requirements of the rules: *NA (Tier 1 Post-Study Work-funds)* [2009] UKAIT 00025.

TIER 1 (GENERAL)

10.18 This route replaced the old highly skilled migrant programme (HSMP).[1] The rule changes in HC 321 deleted the existing Immigration Rules for leave to remain as a highly skilled migrant from 29 February 2008 for in-country applications, from 1 April 2008 for applicants applying in India and from 30 June 2008 for everyone else. There were transitional arrangements for migrants who were already in the process of applying to become a highly skilled migrant at the date of these rule changes. The transitional provisions catered for migrants who had already applied for entry clearance or leave to remain as a highly skilled migrant before the date of the rules change, as well as migrants who had obtained a HSMP Approval Letter from the Home Office, but had not yet applied for entry clearance or leave to remain.[2]

[1] The aim of the Tier, according to the government, is to boost the UK's economy by attracting and retaining the 'brightest and best' as workers or businesspeople. The requirements for both entry to and staying on in the UK are set at levels commensurate with that objective: Explanatory Memorandum to HC 607, para 7. The now replaced rules are still printed as part of HC 395 and are set out in Appendix D.
[2] See **10.21** below.

10.19 The rule amendments in HC 863 closed the Tier 1 (General) category in-country as from April 6 2011, other than for extension applications from migrants who are already in the UK in this category, or one of the categories, now closed, which preceded it before the introduction of the Points-Based System. The details are:

- The category was closed to in-country switching applications. Tier 1 (General) was already closed to overseas applicants, with effect from the 23 December 2010, as set out in HC 698, laid on 21 December 2010.
- The category remains open to enable migrants in the UK with existing leave under Tier 1 (General), or one of its pre-Points Based System predecessor categories, to extend their leave. The predecessor categories in question are the Highly Skilled Migrant Programme (HSMP); Writers, Composers and Artists; and Self-Employed Lawyers.

Leave to remain

10.20 To qualify for leave to remain as a Tier 1 (General) Migrant,- an applicant:

- must not fall for refusal under the general grounds for refusal,[1] must not be an illegal entrant and must not be in the UK in breach of immigration laws except that any period of overstaying for a period of 28 days or less will be disregarded;

- must have 75 points under paragraphs 7 to 34 of Appendix A, if the applicant has, or has had, leave as a Highly Skilled Migrant, as a Writer, Composer or Artist, Self-Employed Lawyer, or as a Tier 1 (General) Migrant under the Rules in place before 19 July 2010, and has never since that date had any other category of leave;
- must have 80 points under paragraphs 7 to 34 of Appendix A in all cases other than those referred to in the above paragraph;
- must have 10 points under paragraphs 1 to 15 of Appendix B for proficiency in English language;
- must have 10 points under paragraphs 1 to 3 of appendix C;
- must have, or have last been granted, entry clearance, leave to enter or remain:
  - (i) as a Tier 1 (General) Migrant;
  - (ii) as a Highly Skilled Migrant;
  - (iii) as a Writer, Composer or Artist; or
  - (iv) as a self-employed lawyer;
- must have made the application for leave to remain before 6 April 2015, the proposed date when Tier 1 (General) finally closes down.

1   HC 395, para 245C (a)–(h).

10.21 Successful applicants will be granted two years' leave to remain, if their last leave was as a Tier 1 (General) migrant under the rules in place before 6 April 2010; and three years in all other cases.[1] Leave to remain is made subject to the following conditions:[2]

(i)   no recourse to public funds,
(ii)   registration with the police, if this is required,[3] and
(iii) Restricted employment as a Doctor or Dentist in Training, subject to qualifications and exceptions[4]
(iv)   no employment as a professional sportsperson (including as a sports coach).

Successful applicants will be given free access to the labour market and will be able to work for an employer, or be self-employed, subject to two exceptions. They cannot take employment as a professional sportsperson or coach, as we have seen. They will not also, in general, be able to take a post as a doctor or dentist in training, unless they are currently working as such or have obtained a medical or dentistry degree from a UK recognised institution and can meet other conditions set out in the rule.[5] HC 1039 7.29 Amendments are being made to the continuous residence requirement for indefinite leave to remain for Tier 1 (General), to clarify that absences from the UK must be for a specific reason.

1   HC 395, para 245CB (a)–(b).
2   HC 359, para 245CB (c).
3   For requirements to register with the police see HC 359, par 326, above CHAPTER 3.
4   These are set out in subparas (1)-(3) of 245CB(c)(iii).
5   See Fn 4, above. These provisions were introduced at the request of the Department of Health in order to support doctors who received their medical training in the UK in accessing taxpayer-funded NHS training posts. It was at that time the Department of Health's view that this provision would help to maximise the return on the significant investment in post-graduate medical training and to secure the future supply of trained specialists: Explanatory Memorandum to HC 321, para 7.13.

Scoring the points

10.22 In Appendix A an applicant for leave to remain must obtain a total of 75 points or more if they were previously granted leave to remain under either Tier 1 (General), or as a highly skilled migrant, writer, composer or artist, or as a self-employed lawyer (para 7). All other applicants for leave to remain or indefinite leave, will need 80 points or more (para 8). However, someone applying for indefinite leave is not required to score any points for attributes, if he or she has been in the Highly Skilled Migrant JR Programme having made an application prior to 7 November 2006,[1] and has never since been granted entry clearance or leave to remain in any category other than as a Highly Skilled Migrant or Tier 1 (General) Migrant, the must be economically active in the UK in employment or self-employment or both.

Points are scored under three heads: academic qualifications, with a maximum score for obtaining a PHD; previous earnings together with UK experience; and age. Evidence of previous earnings must cover a 12-month period and fall within the 15 months immediately preceding the application. Appendix A states what can and cannot be considered as income for the purpose of calculating previous earnings and lays down what documents are required and in what form.

[1] Appplicants who were issued with an approval letter under the HSMP before 7 November 2006, and who had leave on that basis, only require four years' qualifying leave. There is no need for points for attributes under Appendix A. They also do not need the final period of leave to have been under Tier 1 (General). Leave under either the HSMP; as a work permit holder or as an innovator will be sufficient. HC 395, as amended, para 245E. UKBA's HSMP Forum Ltd Judicial Review: Policy Document. For more details, see the Supplement to the 7th edition at 10.115A, 10.120 and 10.120A.

Indefinite leave to remain

10.23 To qualify for indefinite leave to remain, the applicant:

- must not fall for refusal under the general grounds for refusal[1], be an illegal entrant or be in the UK in breach of immigration laws except that any period of overstaying for a period of 28 days or less will be disregarded, unless the applicant meets the conditions of subpara (f)(i)–(iii), below;
- must have spent a continuous period of four or five years in the UK. Tier 1 (General) migrants will be able to apply for settlement after four years in the UK, if they have been the beneficiaries under the HSMP category, where they received a Highly Skilled Migrant Programme approval letter issued on the basis of an application made before 3 April 2006, and in five years in all other cases;[2]
- must have spent the a continuous period lawfully in the UK[3], of which the most recent period must have been spent with leave as a Tier 1 (General) Migrant, in any combination of the following categories:
  - (i) as a Tier 1 (General) Migrant,
  - (ii) as a Highly Skilled Migrant,
  - (iii) as a Work Permit Holder,
  - (iv) as an innovator,
  - (v) as a Self-Employed Lawyer,

(vi)   as a Writer, Composer or Artist,

(vii)   as a Tier 2 (General) Migrant, a Tier 2 (Minister of Religion) Migrant or a Tier 2 (Sportsperson) Migrant, or

(viii)   as a Tier 2 (Intra-Company Transfer) Migrant[4] provided the continuous period of five years spent lawfully in the UK includes a period of leave as a Tier 2 (Intra-Company Transfer) Migrant granted under the Rules in place before 6 April 2010, or as a Work Permit Holder where the work permit was granted because the applicant was the subject of an Intra-Company Transfer.

- must have 75 points under paragraphs 7 to 34 of Appendix A, if he or she has or has had leave as a Highly Skilled Migrant, a Writer, Composer or artist, a self-employed lawyer or as a Tier 1 (General) Migrant under the Rules in place before 19 July 2010, and has not been granted leave in any categories other than these under the Rules in place since 19 July 2010, the applicant (subpara (e));[5]

- must be economically active in the UK, in employment or self-employment or both, but needs no attribute points under Appendix A, if he or she (i) received a Highly Skilled Migrant Programme approval letter issued on the basis of an application made before 7 November 2006,(ii) was subsequently granted entry clearance or leave to remain on the basis of that letter, and (iii) has not since been granted entry clearance or leave to remain in any category other than as a Highly Skilled Migrant or Tier 1 (General) Migrant (subpara f (i)–(iii));

- must have 80 points under paragraphs 7 to 34 of Appendix A in all cases other than those referred to in the last two subparas (e) or (f) above;

- must have sufficient knowledge of the English language and sufficient knowledge about life in the United Kingdom, in accordance with Appendix KoLL of these Rules, unless the applicant meets the conditions in (f)(i)–(iii) above;

- must provide the specified documents in paragraph 245CD-SD to evidence the reason for the absences set out in paragraph 245AAA, unless the applicant meets the conditions in (f)(i)–(iii) above.

---

[1]   HC 395, para 245CD(b).

[2]   HC 359, para 245CD(f)(i)–(iii).

[3]   In calculating the continuous period, time spent with valid leave in the Bailiwick of Guernsey, the Bailiwick of Jersey or the Isle of Man in a category equivalent to those set out in (c)(i) to (viii) may be included in the continuous period of five years lawful residence in the UK, subject to the provisos to HC 245CD(k).

[4]   HC 395, para 245CD(c).

[5]   For the purposes of paragraph (e), time spent with valid leave in the Bailiwick of Guernsey, the Bailiwick of Jersey and the Isle of Man in a category equivalent to those set out in (e)(i) to (iv) may be included in the continuous period of five years (or four years as the case may be) lawful residence in the UK, subject to the provisos to HC 245CD subpara (l).

10.24 HC 1138 has made further changes with regard to Tier 1. First it is the intention to close the category for extension applications on 6 April 2015, and for settlement applications on 6 April 2018. Secondly provisions for settlement for those affected by the HSMP Forum judgments, previously set out in Appendix S, are being incorporated into the relevant sections in the main body of the Immigration Rules.

TIER 1 (ENTREPRENEUR)

10.25 This sub-tier is for use by business investors who wish to set up, take over, or be actively involved in, the running of a business. For these purposes a business An applicant must be at least 16 years old.[1] For entry clearance an applicant must have a minimum of 75 points under paragraphs 35 to 53 of Appendix A, a minimum of 10 points under paragraphs 1 to 15 of Appendix B and a minimum of 10 points under paragraphs 1 to 2 of Appendix C. In addition to dealing with the attributes in Appendix A and the issues of language ability in Appendix B and maintenance in Appendix C an entry clearance officer must also conduct a genuineness test where he or she examines the viability and credibility of the whole application.[2] However, this exercise cannot take place in a case where the applicant has had entry clearance, leave to enter or leave to remain as a Tier 1 (Entrepreneur) Migrant, a Businessperson or an Innovator in the 12 months immediately before the date of application and is being assessed under Table 5 of Appendix A.[3]

[1]   Where an applicant is under 18 the application must be supported by the applicant's parents or legal guardian or by one parent if that parent has sole legal responsibility for the child and must confirm that they consent to the arrangements for the applicant's care in the UK.
[2]   HC 359, para 245DB (g)–(j).
[3]   Ibid, para 245DB (k)–(m).

10.26 An application for leave to remain can only be made by an applicant who has previously been granted entry clearance or leave in one of the prescribed categories in the rules.[1] Students, post graduate doctors and dentists who were previously sponsored by a government or international scholarship agency, must provide written consent from the sponsoring body in support of the application.[2] HC 395, para 245DD deals with requirements for leave to remain. As with entry clearance the applicant must have a minimum of 75 points under Appendix A, 10 points under Appendix B and 10 points under Appendix C.[3] Then there is similar provision to test the genuineness of the application and the applicant's intentions.[4] If the Secretary of State is not satisfied with the genuineness of the application in relation to a points-scoring requirement in Appendix A, those points will not be awarded.[5] However, the Secretary of State may decide not to carry out the assessment of genuineness if the application already falls for refusal on other grounds, but reserves the right to carry it out in any reconsideration of the decision.[6]

[1]   HC 359, para 245DD(e).
[2]   Ibid, para 245DD(f).
[3]   Ibid, para 245DD (b),(c) and (d).
[4]   Ibid.
[5]   Ibid, para 245DD(k).
[6]   Ibid, para 245DD(l)

10.27 Successful applicants, after seeking entry or leave to remain, will be granted three years and four months on entry clearance and two years' leave, if previously granted leave as a Tier 1 (Entrepreneur) or three years in all other circumstances.[1] Migrants in this sub-tier will not be able to take employment outside the business or businesses they have established, joined or have taken over, cannot be employed as a professional sportsperson or a sports coach and will not be able to claim public funds.[2] They may have to register with the police if required to do so under HC 359, para 326. Leave maybe curtailed if the Tier 1 (Entrepreneur) migrant has failed to meet the six month deadline set out in HC 245DE(c), (d) and (e).

1   HC 395, paras 245DC (a) and 245DE(a).
2   HC 395, paras 245 DC (a) and 245DE (b).

The attributes – Appendix A

10.28 An applicant applying for entry clearance, leave to remain or indefinite leave to remain as a Tier 1 (Entrepreneur) Migrant must score 75 points for attributes (para 35). Available points for applications for entry clearance or leave to remain are shown in Table 4 (para 36). An applicant who is applying for leave to remain and has, or was last granted, entry clearance, leave to enter or leave to remain as (i) a Tier 4 Migrant, (ii) a Student, (iii) a Student Nurse, (iv) a Student Re-sitting an Examination, or (v) a Student Writing Up a Thesis, will only be awarded points under the provisions in (b)(ii) or (b)(iii) in Table 4 (para 36A). The same provisions in (b)(ii) or (b)(iii) apply to an applicant who has come through the Tier 1 (Post-Study Work) route, but the provisions in (d) also apply to this category of migrant, which we deal with below.

10.29 Table 5 applies to an applicant who (a) has had entry clearance, leave to enter or leave to remain as a Tier 1 (Entrepreneur) Migrant, a Businessperson or an Innovator in the 12 months immediately before the date of application, or (b) is applying for leave to remain and has, or was last granted, entry clearance, leave to enter or leave to remain as a Tier 1 (Entrepreneur) Migrant, a Businessperson or an Innovator (Appendix A, para 37). Available points for applications for indefinite leave to remain are shown in Table 6 (para 38).

10.30 Under Table 4 there are two required levels of funds to which the applicant must have access. Not less than £200,000 is the normal requirement.[1]The funds may be entirely the applicants own funds or funds shared with a business partner or supplied by another third party, such as a bank, parent of other family member. But £50,000 is sufficient for someone who has, or was last granted, leave as a Tier 1 (Graduate Entrepreneur) Migrant and someone who has, or was last granted, leave as a Tier 1 (Post-Study Work) Migrant, if they can meet the quite stringent requirements of Appendix A. In the two cases where £50,000 is sufficient, some of the requirements are the same but others differ. First, as regards both categories of applicant the £50,000 must either come from:

- one or more registered venture capitalist firms regulated by the Financial Conduct Authority (FCA),
- one or more UK Entrepreneurial seed funding competitions which is listed as endorsed on the UK Trade & Investment website,
- one or more UK Government Departments, or Devolved Government Departments in Scotland, Wales or Northern Ireland, and made available by the Department(s) for the specific purpose of establishing or expanding a UK business, or

- funds of £50,000 to which the applicant has access. These may be entirely his or her own funds or funds shared with a business partner or supplied by another third party, such as a bank, parent of other family member.

Hereafter the requirements differ. As regards the applicant who has, or was last granted, leave in the Tier 1 (Post-Study Work) category, he or she must either:

- since before 11 July 2014 and up to the date of their application, have been continuously engaged in business activity which was not, or did not amount to, activity pursuant to a contract of service with a business other than his own, and
- during such period, have been continuously: (1) registered with HM Revenue & Customs as self-employed, or (2) registered with Companies House as a director of a new or an existing business,[2] or
- since before 11 July 2014 and up to the date of his application, have continuously been working.[3] 'Working' in this context means that the core service his business provides to its customers or clients involves the business delivering a service in an occupation at this level. It excludes any work involved in administration, marketing or website functions for the business. in an occupation which appears on the list of occupations skilled to National Qualifications Framework level 4 or above, as stated in the Codes of Practice in Appendix J, and
- provide the specified evidence in paragraph 41-SD.

[1] The funds may be entirely the applicants own funds or funds shared with a business partner or supplied by another third party, such as a bank, parent of other family member.

[2] Directors who are on the list of disqualified directors provided by Companies House will not be awarded points.

[3] 'Working' in this context means that the core service his business provides to its customers or clients involves the business delivering a service in an occupation at this level. It excludes any work involved in administration, marketing or website functions for the business.

Entrepreneurial teams

10.31 Two applicants, and no more than two applicants, may claim points for the same investment and business activity in Tables 4, 5 or 6 providing that (a) the applicants have equal level of control over the funds and/or the business or businesses in question; (b) they are both shown by name in each other's applications and in the specified evidence required in the relevant table; and (c) neither applicant has previously been granted leave as a Tier 1 (Entrepreneur) Migrant in reliance on the same funds but with a different partner (Appendix A, para 52). No points will be awarded for funds that are made available to any individual other than the applicant, except:(i) under the terms of paragraph 52 above; or (ii) where the money is held in a joint account with the applicant's spouse, civil partner or partner.[1] No points will be awarded for investment and business activity shared with another Tier 1 (Entrepreneur) applicant, except under the terms of paragraph 52 above.[2]

[1] HC 359, Appendix A, para 53(a). A spouse or partner is defined as a person who has been living together with the applicant in a relationship akin to a marriage or civil partnership for at least two years prior to the date of application, and that spouse or partner is not (or is not applying to be) another Tier 1 (Entrepreneur) Migrant.

10.32 According to Appendix A, para 41, an applicant will only be considered to have access to funds if: (a) The specified documents in paragraph 41-SD are provided to show cash money to the amount required (this must not be in the form of assets); (b) The specified documents in paragraph 41-SD are provided to show that the applicant has permission to use the money to invest in a business in the UK; (c) The money is either held in a UK regulated financial institution or is transferable to the UK; and (d) The money will remain available to the applicant until such time as it is spent for the purposes of the applicant's business or businesses. The Secretary of State reserves the right to request further evidence or otherwise verify that the money will remain available, and to refuse the application if this evidence is not provided or it is unable to satisfactorily verify.

10.33 Problems have arisen with the requirements of para 41-SD where funds are being supplied jointly by an applicant and his or her business partner or some other third party and these funds, though available, are held in a separate bank account. Banks in the UK and in some other countries will not, because of bank confidentiality issues, provide letters to applicants, as required by UKBA (now UKVI) in para 41-SD, referring to funds held by a third party (including a partner) in a different account from that of an applicant. There have been conflicting decisions in appeals in the FT, there is an important decision in the Upper Tribunal and there are (at October 1 2014) several appeals awaiting hearings in the Court of appeal. Further decisions are awaited.

Indefinite leave – Tier 1(entrepreneurs)

10.34 An entrepreneur will be able to apply for settlement after five years in the UK,[1] but there is also the possibility of an accelerated grant of indefinite leave. This is dealt with in Table 6 of Appendix A. The period will be shortened to 3 years if the applicant has either:

(a)   established a new UK business or businesses that has or have created the equivalent of at least 10 new full time jobs for persons settled in the UK, or

(b)   taken over or invested in an existing UK business or businesses and his services or investment have resulted in a net increase in the employment provided by the business or businesses for persons settled in the UK by creating the equivalent of 10 new full time jobs.[2]

Where the applicant's last grant of entry clearance or leave to enter or remain was as a Tier 1 (Entrepreneur) Migrant, these jobs must have existed for at least 12 months of the period for which the previous leave was granted.[3] During the three or five year specified period of continuous lawful presence in the UK the applicant is allowed to be absent from the UK for no more than 180 days in any 12 calendar months.[4] The specified period must also have been spent with leave as a Tier 1 (Entrepreneur) Migrant, as a Businessperson and/or as an Innovator, of which the most recent period must have been spent with leave as a Tier (1) (Entrepreneur) Migrant. On a date no earlier than three months prior to the date of application, the applicant must also have been:

(a)   registered with HM Revenue and Customs as self-employed, or
(b)   registered with Companies House as a director of a new or an existing business. Directors who are on the list of disqualified directors provided by Companies House will not be awarded points.[5]

He or she must also have a minimum of 75 points under paragraphs 35 to 53 of Appendix A;[6] not fall for refusal under the general grounds for refusal nor be an illegal entrant or in breach of immigration laws except that any period of overstaying for a period of 28 days or less will be disregarded;[7] and must have demonstrated sufficient knowledge of the English language and sufficient knowledge about life in the United Kingdom, in accordance with Appendix KoLL.[8]

[1]   Appendix A, Table 6 Row 3.
[2]   Appendix A table 6 Row 2.
[3]   Ibid.
[4]   Time spent with valid leave in the Bailiwick of Guernsey, the Bailiwick of Jersey or the Isle of Man in a category equivalent to the categories set out above may be included in the continuous period of lawful residence, provided the most recent period of leave was as a Tier 1 (Entrepreneur) Migrant in the UK. In any such case, the applicant must have absences from the Bailiwick of Guernsey, the Bailiwick of Jersey or the Isle of Man (as the case may be) of no more than 180 days in any 12 calendar months during the specified continuous period.
[5]   Appendix A, Table 6 Row 1.
[6]   HC 395, para 245DF (c).
[7]   HC 395, para 245DF (b) and (e).
[8]   HC 395, par 245DF (b)–(e)

Prospective entrepreneurs

10.35 'Prospective entrepreneurs' were introduced at paragraphs 56N–56Q of HC 395 as a new category of 'Special Visitor' (as defined by HC 395, para 6) on 6 April 2011 by Statement of Changes HC 863. It is briefly described in CHAPTER 8 at 8.36. The explanatory memorandum of HC 863 explains the rationale: 'A new form of visitor category is being created to allow prospective entrepreneurs to enter the UK in order to seek funding or create a team for a new business idea, if they are not yet ready to establish their business and cannot therefore qualify under the Tier 1 (Entrepreneur) category. Before coming to the UK the prospective entrepreneur must already be in touch with potential funders and already have a business plan in mind. He or she should already be in discussions with any assortment of (i) registered venture capitalist firms and/or (ii) UK entrepreneurial seed funding competitions, and/or (iii) one or more UK Government departments, to secure funding in order to join, set up or take over, and be actively involved in the running of, a business in the UK.'[1]

To get entry clearance it will be necessary for the applicant to provide an original, letter on headed paper signed by an authorised official of the institution supporting the application, dated no earlier than three months before the date of the application. Among the matters the letter should contain are a description of the background and nature of the proposed business, a description of the applicant's suitability to be involved with the proposed venture, and a commitment by the individual(s) and/or organisation(s) supporting the applicant to make a decision to provide a minimum of £50,000 funding within six months of the applicant entering the UK.

Once in the UK there is a list of do's and don'ts. Permissible activities are set out in paragraph 56O(d)(i) of the Immigration Rules (HC 395). These include: attending meetings, including meetings arranged while in the UK; conferences; trade fairs provided this is restricted to promotional work and does not involve selling directly to members of the public; doing deals, negotiating and signing trade agreements and contracts; and recruiting staff for the proposed business. The 'don't' list is a bit more general. The prospective entrepreneur cannot undertake a course of study, marry or form a civil partnership or receive private medical treatment. The primary aim in applying as a prospective entrepreneur is to secure funding within six months of arriving in the UK. At least £50,000 is needed and can be split between a number of supporting organisations.[2]

[1]   HC 395, para 56N, as inserted by HC 863.
[2]   See HC 395, para 56O which deals with the formalities and other requirements needed to qualify. One of these is that the applicant must intend to carry out one of the activities listed in guidance published by the UK Border agency, specifying the activities that a Prospective entrepreneur may undertake during a visit to the UK.

TIER 1 (INVESTOR)

10.36   The government policy is to encourage high worth foreign investors to come to Britain and commit themselves to making substantial investments in British enterprises.[1] Recent changes in the rules are meant as incentives to such investors. HC 863 made the following changes to the Tier 1 (Investor) category:

*   The rules on the granting of indefinite leave to remain have been amended so as to enable Tier 1 (Investor) Migrants to qualify for accelerated settlement if they have invested a sum of at least £10m in UK investments for two years, in which case they qualify for settlement after two years or a sum of £5m or more for three years, in which case they qualify for settlement after three years. If they have stuck to the minimum investment of £1m in the UK investments, they continue to qualify for indefinite leave to remain after five years.[2] The settlement incentive has not proved very successful Investors are more interested in qualifying for British citizenship and this only happens after five years.[3] £1 million is enough to achieve this. An investment of at least £750,000 must be made within a specified three-month period or else the investor faces the risk of having his or her leave curtailed.[4]
*   As with Tier 1 (Entrepreneur), to reduce the likelihood of applicants needing to apply for additional extensions in order to reach the qualifying period for settlement, the period of entry clearance in this category is being increased from three years to three years and four months.[5]
*   Also as with Tier 1 (Entrepreneur), Tier 1 (Investor) Migrants will be permitted to be absent from the UK for up to 180 days in any 12 months, without jeopardising their applications for settlement.[6]
*   This category is not being made subject to an annual limit.
*   It is open to anyone over 16 years of age.

[1]   See James Brokenshire MP, Minister of State for Security and Immigration, 18 March 2014: 'Our emphasis is on attracting the brightest and the best, on ensuring that those who are

skilled and can contribute to our society – of all different creeds, colours, backgrounds, and whichever part of the world they come from – can contribute to our society.'

² HC 395, Appendix A, Table 9.
³ See British Nationality Act 1981 s 6(1) and Sch 1.
⁴ HC 395, para 245EE(c).
⁵ HC 395, para 245EB, 'Period for leave to remain', para (a).
⁶ HC 395, Appendix A, Table 9, Row 2.

10.37 A person can become a Tier 1 (Investor) by switching from 14 different categories of leave as set out in HC359 para 245ED(c). So entry into Tier 1 can either be by way of an entry clearance from abroad or by leave to remain. Entry clearance is granted for a period of three years and four months.[1]. Leave to remain is for three years except in the case of someone last granted leave as a Tier 1 (Investor) (who will already have had three years leave), where leave is for two years,[2] taking the Investor up to the magic five year period, when the investor whose investment remains at £1million can qualify for indefinite leave to remain (ILR). Whether an Investor enters into Tier 1 (Investor) category by entry clearance or by leave to remain, each one has to qualify by obtaining 75 points for attributes,[3] which include the very important Tables 7 and 8 for entry clearance,[4] for leave to remain[5] and Table 9 for indefinite leave to remain. Tables 7 and 8 set out the available points for applications for entry clearance or leave to remain. Table 7 is for those entering into Tier 1 (Investor) for the first time and Tier 8 is dealing with repeat applications by Tier 1 Investor Migrants. The 2 Investment principles used throughout are that:

(i)   The Investor has a minimum of £ 1 million of his or her own money under that persons control; or
(ii)   The Investor uses loan money of £1million minimum under his or her control and owns net personal assets of a value of not less than £2million.[6] If the investment is £5million borrowed money assets of £10million will be needed; if £10million is borrowed, assets of £20million need to be shown).

These are alternatives. To get admitted into the Tier 1 (Investor) category the investor has to use one or the other and on a strict reading of the rules cannot mix and match. Under Table 7 new Investors have to be able to show either:

(i)   That their own money is held in a regulated financial institution and disposable in the UK; or
(ii)   That the money lent to them is held in a registered financial institution and disposable in the UK and they have the required assets. If these conditions are fulfilled by an Investor the full 75 points will be awarded for attributes under Appendix A of the Immigration Rules.

By the time Investors come to make an application for an extension of their leave, Table 8 applies. This applies where the investor has had entry clearance, leave to enter or leave to remain as a Tier 1 (Investor) in the 12 months immediately before the date of application, or is applying for leave to remain and has, or was last granted, entry clearance, leave to enter or leave to remain as a Tier 1 (Investor)[7] (Appendix A, para 56).

¹   HC 359, para 245EC.
²   bid, para 245EE(a).
³   See HC 359 Appendix A, paragraphs 54 to 65-SD.
⁴   HC 359, para 245EB (b) and Appendix A.

5   Ibid, para 245ED(b).
6   HC 395, Appendix A, Table 9 Row 1.
7   Appendix A, para 56.

10.38 Under Table 8 nothing changes as regards the initial financial qualifications, the use of the Investors own money or the use of loan money backed up by personal assets of £2million. That gets 30 points. The second requirement is that investors have to show that they have made the specific investments set out in Table 8, ie a minimum of £750,000 in UK government bonds, share capital or loan capital to actively trading UK registered companies other than property companies and the balance of the £1million by purchase of assets or maintaining money on deposit in a UK registered financial institution. That gets another 30 points. Thirdly, Investors must show that the investment just referred to was made within three months of the date of their entry into the UK or of the date of the grant of entry clearance or of leave to remain as a Tier 1 (Investor) or no earlier than 12 months before the date of the application which led to the grant of Tier 1 (Investor leave. There then follows the quite crucial requirement that in each case the specified investment has not only been put in place within the three or 12 month time frame but has also been maintained for the whole of the remaining period of that leave.[1] That gets the 15 points needed to get up to the overall total of 75 points needed for attributes under the rules.

1   Little excuse is accepted for lateness in making the investments. There must be 'exceptionally compelling reasons for the delay in investing'; this warning is underlined a few lines later; 'Reasons for delay in investing must be unforeseeable and outside of the applicant's control. Delays caused by the applicant failing to take timely action will not be accepted.'

10.39 It is also clear that, irrespective of the requirement to maintain the investment, the possession of a specified minimum of net assets is also a distinct but separate requirement of the acquisition of points. Clearly a failure to maintain the specified minimum could amount to a breach of the conditions attaching to leave to enter or remain. The situation envisaged by the rules is a pragmatic approach. So at the time for renewal of leave the investor must be able to show that his or her assets retain a value above the specified amount. If the Investor cannot maintain the minimum net value of his or her assets or investment at the time of making a fresh application, he or she will fail to get the necessary points and would fail to obtain further leave, even although the specified investment was still in place.

10.40 The upshot is that applicants seeking to switch into the Investor Tier can only do so if previously granted leave in a prescribed category.[1] Students, post graduate doctors and dentists who were previously sponsored by a government or international scholarship agency must provide written consent from the sponsoring body to support the application.[2] If the investor is between the ages of 16 and 18, the assets and investment he or she is claiming points for must be wholly under his control and the application must be supported by the applicant's parent, parents or legal guardian, who must also confirm the arrangements for the applicant's care in the UK.[3] Unlike the other categories of Tier 1 migrants, investors will not need a specific knowledge of English under Appendix B,[4] nor do they have to meet a maintenance requirement under Appendix C. Successful Tier 1 (Investor) migrants will be able to work if they wish to, except that they will not be able to take employment as a doctor or dentist in training unless previously qualified as such in the UK or a professional sportsperson or sports coach.[5] They will be granted three years and four months leave on entry clearance followed by two years' leave if previously granted leave as a Tier 1 (Investor), and three years in all other circumstances.[6] Leave can be curtailed if the applicant fails to invest the required amount within three months of entry into the UK or grant of leave to remain or within a 12 month period after making the application. The risk of curtailment does not apply to an investor who already has a Tier 1 (Investor) leave and is applying for a repeat leave.[7] Settlement will be granted after the specified period of three or five years continuous lawful presence in the UK has been spent with leave as a Tier 1 (Investor) Migrant and/or as an Investor, of which the most recent period must have been spent with leave as a Tier 1 (Investor) Migrant.[8]

[1] HC 395, para 245ED (c).
[2] HC 395, para 245ED(d).
[3] HC 395, para 245(e) and (f).
[4] They will still need to show that they have sufficient knowledge of the English language and knowledge about life in the United Kingdom when applying for settlement. HC 395, as amended, para 245EF (d).
[5] HC 395, paras 245EC(a) and 245EE (iii) and (iv).
[6] HC 395, as amended, paras 245EC(a) and 245EE(a).
[7] HC 395, para 245EE (c)–(e).
[8] HC 395, Appendix A, table 9 Row 3.

TIER 1 (POST-STUDY WORK)

10.41 This sub-tier was intended to encourage international graduates who have previously graduated in the UK to stay and work. It was bridge between study and the world of work and business and had a possible two year stay. The category was closed by HC 1888 which took effect as from 14 June 2012. The Rules for this category (including the Rules for Attributes set out in Appendix A were then added to the archive of historical Immigration Rules in Appendix F. all existing Tier 1 (Post-Study Work) leaves to remain will have run out and no further applications can be made. However, there will almost certainly be cases which have not yet been decided or are under appeal. So for completeness we maintain a brief account of the workings of this category. Anyone needing to know more should consult the 8th edition of this work at **10.18** ff.

10.42 Once admitted to the UK, a Tier 1 (Post-Study Work) applicant would have the same entitlement to enter Tier 1 (Entrepreneur) category[1] or seek employment in Tier 2 (General).[2] Leave was granted for two years, except for applicants who were previously granted leave under either the international graduate or the Fresh Talent: Working in Scotland Schemes who would have that period of leave deducted from their overall entitlement of leave.[3] A Tier 1 (Post-Study Work) could only qualify for settlement by transferring into Tier 1 or 2 and any period spent under this sub-tier would not count towards the necessary five years' leave.

[1] HC 359, para 245DD (e)(v).
[2] HC 395, para 245HD (b)(i).
[3] HC 395, para 245FE (a)(i), archived in Appendix F.

10.43 Before April 2012 existing Tier 1 (Post-Study Work) Migrants could switch into Tier 2 (General) without their sponsoring employer needing to satisfy the Resident Labour Market Test, but only where they had worked for that employer for at least six months (or the job was otherwise exempt because, for example, it was in a shortage occupation). The HC 1888 changes removed the six month requirement for existing Tier 1 (Post-Study Work) Migrants from 6 April 2012. A further change was made so that no other migrants in student routes (including those who have studied the qualifications above but have not graduated) would be able to switch into Tier 2 from within the UK.[1] However, another change was made, due to the closure of Tier 1 (Post-Study Work), to enable Tier 4 (General) Students to switch into Tier 5 (Temporary Worker) if they were applying under a Government Authorised Exchange scheme to undertake a period of professional training or work experience, required to obtain a professional qualification or professional registration in the same professional field as their qualification, after graduation and before returning overseas.[2]

[1]   This change was in line with the Government's view that student routes should not be seen as routes to working or settling in the UK. If such students wish to apply under Tier 2 they would in future have to make an entry clearance application and will be required to meet the full criteria, including the Resident Labour Market Test.
[2]   Explanatory Memorandum, para 7.27.

Tier 1 (Graduate Entrepreneur) Migrants

Purpose of the route

10.44 This route is for (i) UK graduates who have been identified by Higher Education Institutions as having developed genuine and credible business ideas and entrepreneurial skills to extend their stay in the UK after graduation to establish one or more businesses in the UK; and (ii) Graduates who have been identified by UK Trade and Investment as elite global graduate entrepreneurs to establish one or more businesses in the UK.[1] It is a one year stay, but one repeat application is allowed, but no more than one.[2] It is clearly a stepping stone to great things for the successful applicant. Entry into the category is subject to an annual limit of 2,000 places per year (beginning on 6 April and ending on 5 April).[3] 1,900 places will be allocated to qualifying Higher Education Institutions (HEIs) and 100 places to UK Trade and Investment. The allocation to the HEIs is carried out in accordance with a very precise system, set out in Appendix A, para 69(c). Endorsements which have not been used by endorsing bodies cannot be carried over from one year (beginning on 6 April and ending on 5 April) to the next.[4]

[1]   For the purpose of this route 'business' means an enterprise as (i) a sole trader, (ii) a partnership, or (iii) a company registered in the UK: HC 359, para 245F.
[2]   Ibid, para 245FB(h).
[3]   The limit will not apply to applications for leave to remain where the applicant has, or last had, leave to remain as a Tier 1 (Graduate Entrepreneur): ibid, para 69(e).
[4]   Appendix A, para 69(f).

Entry and stay in the UK

10.45 Tier 1 (Graduate Entrepreneur) Migrants must have a valid entry clearance for entry under this route; otherwise they will be refused entry[1]. The main requirements needed to qualify for entry clearance or leave to remain are that an applicant must have a minimum of 75 points for attributes under Appendix A; 10 points for English language under Appendix B and 10 points for maintenance under Appendix C.[2]. If applying for leave to remain he or she must have, or have last been granted, entry clearance or leave to enter or remain in one of the eight prescribed categories in para 245FB(e).[3] A new applicant to this category who is being sponsored by a government or international scholarship agency, or has been in the last 12 months, must provide the unconditional written consent of his or her sponsors, using the correct documents[4], to show that this requirement has been met.[5] Overstaying up to 28 days is disregarded but otherwise illegal entry or stay is a disqualifying factor and as in all other categories under Tier 1 the applicant must not fall for refusal on general grounds.[6]

[1] Ibid, para 245FA.
[2] HC 359, para 245FB.
[3] In the case of a Tier 2 (General) Migrant where leave was given to work as a post-doctoral researcher, the work must have been with the same institution which is endorsing his or her application as a Tier 1 (Graduate Entrepreneur) Migrant: para 245FB(f). Previous leave in the now deleted categories as a Tier 1 (Post-Study Work) Migrant, a Participant in the Fresh Talent: Working in Scotland Scheme, or a Participant in the International Graduates Scheme (or its predecessor, the Science and Engineering Graduates Scheme is not a qualification for the Graduate Entrepreneur route: para 245FB(g).
[4] these are specified in in HC 359, para 245A.
[5] Ibid, para 245FB(i).
[6] Ibid 245FB(a) and (j).

10.46 Under Appendix A endorsement of the applicant – one of the key ingredients of this category – is identified and explained in Table 10. There are two alternatives. Either (a) the applicant has to have the endorsement of a UK Higher Education Institution which has the necessary sponsorship status under Tier 4, Tier 2 or Tier 5, has degree-awarding powers, and has established processes and competence for identifying, nurturing and developing entrepreneurs among its undergraduate and postgraduate population, or (b) the applicant has been endorsed by UK Trade and Investment. This gains 25 points. A degree qualification earns another 25 points. It must be a proper degree (not a qualification of equivalent level which is not a degree) and it must meet or exceed the recognised standard of a Bachelor's degree in the UK. For overseas qualifications, the standard must be confirmed by UK NARIC. A further 25 points are awarded for an endorsement from the endorsing body confirming that they have assessed the applicant and consider that: (a) he or she has a genuine and credible business idea, (b) will spend the majority of his or her working time on developing business ventures, and (c) if the applicant is applying for leave to remain and if his or her last grant of leave was as a Tier 1 (Graduate Entrepreneur), he or she has made satisfactory progress in developing his or his or her business since that leave was granted. It should be noted that if applicants do not make a valid application within three months of the date of their endorsement the endorsement used in that application will be cancelled.[1]

[1] HC 395, Appendix A, para 69(d)(i).

Tier 1 (Exceptional Talent) Migrants

10.47 The HC 863 changes to the Immigration Rules, which came into force on 6 April 2011, introduced a fifth Tier 1 category, Tier 1 (Exceptional Talent), which caters for those who have achieved international recognition, or who have demonstrated exceptional promise to do so, in the fields of science, humanities, engineering and the arts. According to the Immigration Rules they those who are already 'recognised at the highest level as world leaders in their particular field, or who have already demonstrated exceptional promise and are likely to become world leaders in their particular area.'[1] The Tier is subject to a limit of 1,000 places. It is designed to operate in conjunction with a group of Designated Competent Bodies who have agreed with the Home Office the criteria they will use to select those who will qualify for endorsement.[2] These are dealt with these in more detail below.

[1] HC 359, para 245B.
[2] See HC 395, paras 245B–245BF, Appendix A, paras 1–6A, Appendix B, paras 1 and 5, Appendix C, paras 1A(b) and 1 and Appendix L.

10.48 All migrants arriving in the UK and wishing to enter as a Tier 1 (Exceptional Talent) Migrant must have a valid entry clearance for entry under this route. If they do not have a valid entry clearance, entry will be refused.[1] To qualify for entry clearance, an applicant must meet the following requirements[2]:

- must not fall for refusal under the general grounds for refusal;
- must have a minimum of 75 points under Appendix A; and
- if a sponsored student, must provide the unconditional written consent of the sponsoring Government or agency to the application.[3]

Entry clearance will be granted for a period of three years and four months, or two years if the applicant was last granted leave as a Tier 1 (Exceptional Talent) Migrant, and will be subject to the following conditions: no recourse to public funds; registration with the police, if required; and no employment as a Doctor or Dentist in Training, or as a professional sportsperson (including as a sports coach).[4]

To qualify for leave to remain as a Tier 1 (Exceptional Talent) Migrant an applicant[5]:

- must not fall for refusal under the general grounds for refusal, and or be an illegal entrant; (e) must not be in the UK in breach of immigration laws except that any period of overstaying for a period of up to 28 days will be disregarded;
- must have a minimum of 75 points under Appendix A;
- must have a minimum of 10 points under Appendix B, if he or she has or last had leave as a Tier 1 (Exceptional Talent) Migrant;
- must have or last had entry clearance, leave to enter or remain as:
  (i)   a Tier 1 Migrant,
  (ii) a Tier 2 Migrant, or

> (iii) as a Tier 5 (Temporary Worker) Migrant, sponsored in the Government Authorised Exchange sub-category in an exchange scheme for sponsored researchers.

- Leave to remain will be granted for two years to an applicant who has, or was last granted, leave as a Tier 1 (Exceptional Talent) Migrant or for three years, to any other applicant. It will be subject to the same conditions as on leave to enter.[6]

1 HC 395, para 245BA.
2 HC 395, para 245BB.
3 The sponsored student must provide the specified documents as set out in HC 395, para 245BB(d) to show that this requirement has been met.
4 HC 395, para 245BC. On police registration see the requirements set out in HC 395, para 326.
5 HC 395, para 245BD.
6 HC 395, para 245BE.

10.49 To qualify for indefinite leave to remain, a Tier 1 (Exceptional Talent) Migrant[1]:

- must not fall for refusal under the general grounds for refusal, not be an illegal entrant and must not be in the UK in breach of immigration laws except that any period of overstaying for a period of 28 days or less will be disregarded;
- must have spent a continuous period of five years lawfully in the UK. The last grant of leave must have been as a Tier 1 (Exceptional Talent) Migrant; but earlier leaves under Tier 1 or 2 count, except Tier 1 (Graduate Entrepreneur) or Tier 1 (Post-Study Work) or Tier 2 (Intra-Company Transfer);
- must have been absent from the UK of no more than 180 days in any 12 calendar months during the five years;
- must have a minimum of 75 points under Appendix A;
- must have demonstrated sufficient knowledge of the English language and sufficient knowledge about life in the United Kingdom, in accordance with Appendix KoLL.

1 HC 395, para 245BF.

10.50 This category currently operates as follows:

- Applicants who do not have, or have not last had, leave as a Tier 1 Exceptional Talent) Migrant need to be endorsed by a Designated Competent Body according to that Body's criteria as set out in Appendix L.[1]
- All other applications for entry clearance and leave to remain and applications for indefinite leave to remain need to show that the applicant has earned money in the UK as a result of employment or self-employment in his or her expert field as previously endorsed by a Designated Competent Body; and that Body has not withdrawn its endorsement. Appendix A also deals with how the money can be earned and what documents are needed to show earnings.[2]
- The Competent Designated Bodies are The Arts Council, The Royal Society, The Royal Academy of Engineering, The British Academy, and Tech City UK.[3] When assessing applicants they must take into consid-

eration the factors set out in Appendix L para 4. The Arts Council (paras 5-9) and Tech City UK (paras 10-13) have set out their own criteria.

- Applicants must satisfy (a) all of the mandatory 'Exceptional Talent (world leader) criteria', and at least one of the qualifying criteria, or (b) satisfy all of the 'Exceptional Promise (potential world leader)' criteria in the table below para 1 of Appendix L and must supply the documents in Appendix L, paras 2 and 3.
- Applications must be made to UKVI using a specified form, stating which Designated Competent Body the applicant wants to endorse his or her application and providing the specified evidence set out in Appendix L.[4]
- When the route was new, there was a limit of 1,000 grants of entry clearance in the first year of operation from 9 August 2011 to 5 April 2012, and no provision for switching from other categories by in-country applicants. This has now changed and there is limited switching as we have seen, and the limit is now fixed at 1,000 endorsements annually starting on 6 April each year.[5]
- The endorsements are divided up and allocated to each of the Bodies as set out in Appendix A, para 4(b). But there is one minor snag. The number of available endorsements for each Body to endorse will be reduced by one for each Croatian national that body endorses in that period for the purposes of applying to be deemed a highly skilled person under the Accession of Croatia (Immigration and Worker Authorisation) Regulations 2013.[6]
- Migrants seeking entry under the Tier 1 (Exceptional Talent) category will not need sponsorship by an employer and will not therefore need to have a specific job offer. The issue of the Unique Reference Number by the UKBA will be enough.
- Applicants for entry clearance will not need to demonstrate competence in the English language[7] and are excused from having to score ten points for maintenance funds.[8] They will, however, need 10 points under Appendix B paras 1-15 when renewing their leave under this category.[9]

By the summer of 2011, no endorsements had been issued as it was still necessary to finalise the manner in which the route would operate in conjunction with the four Designated Competent Bodies. This work was completed and current Immigration Rules set out the allocated endorsements within the 1,000 limit as 250 for the Arts Council (for arts and culture); 250 for the Royal Society (for natural sciences and medical science research); 150 for the Royal Academy of Engineering (for engineering); and 200 places for the British Academy (for humanities and social sciences). These limits run from 6 April to 5 April for each year unless and until amended by the rules.[10] Applicants are not subject to a maintenance requirement but must provide evidence of their English language skills when they apply to extend their stay.[11]

1   HC 395, Appendix A Table 1.
2   HC 395, Appendix A Table 1 and para 6A.
3   HC 395, Appendix A, para 4(b).
4   HC 395, Appendix A, para 5(a).
5   HC 395, Appendix A paras 4(a) and (b).
6   HC 395, Appendix A, para 5(f).

7   HC 395, Appendix B, para 1.
8   HC 395, Appendix C, paras 1A(b) and 1, as substituted by HC 1148 in July 2011.
9   HC 359, para 245BD(c).
10 HC 395, Appendix A, para 4.
11 HC 395, para 245BD(c) and Appendix B, para 5.

TIER 1 – TRANSITIONAL ARRANGEMENTS

10.51 HC 607 deleted the following categories from the Immigration Rules as from 29 June 2008 and they are now to be found archived in Appendix F of the rules:

- the Highly Skilled Migrant Programme, including earlier deletions under HC 321 of applications made in-country and in India, taking effect in February 2008 under the HC 321 changes;
- International Graduates Scheme;
- Fresh Talent: Working in Scotland;
- business persons;
- innovators;
- investors;
- writers, composers and artists.

Further deletions took place. In addition, the provision for self-employed lawyers, which existed as a concession outside the Immigration Rules, were also deleted.[1]

1   Explanatory Memorandum to HC 607, para 7.29.

10.52 Transitional arrangements were made with the intention of minimising the degree to which these changes disadvantage people with leave in a category that has been deleted. There are firstly a number of provisions in the Explanatory Memorandum to the change in the Immigration Rules introducing Tier 1.[1] Under these provisions, migrants with leave in any of the deleted categories will be able to stay in the UK until their leave expires, provided they continue to meet the conditions under which the leave was originally granted. The UKBA also decided to allow people with leave as a self-employed lawyer, writer, composer or artist, or innovator to apply for further leave in that category at any time before HC 607 came into force on 30 June 2008. If they were successful, they would have been granted enough extra leave to take them up to the threshold for being eligible to apply for settlement.[2] People with leave in the International Graduates Scheme, or its predecessor the Science and Engineering Graduates Scheme, would have been able to apply for a one-off extension in order to take their leave up to a total of two years.[3] The amended rules also made arrangements for a small number of people granted six months' leave to enter under the Fresh Talent: Working in Scotland Scheme to be granted an additional period of leave so they can spend a total of two years in the UK under this scheme and post-study work combined.[4]

1   Explanatory Memorandum to HC 607.
2   Explanatory Memorandum to HC 607, para 7.34.
3   Explanatory Memorandum to HC 607, para 7.35.
4   Explanatory Memorandum to HC 607, para 7.36.

10.53 There were further arrangements under the points based section of the Immigration Rules.[1] Applicants who were in the UK on 29 February 2008, or were in India on 1 April 2008, and had not had their application decided before that date, would have it decided in accordance with the rules in force on 31 March 2008. Similarly, if an applicant made an application for limited leave to remain as a highly skilled migrant before 29 February 2008, and the application had not been decided before that date, it would be decided in accordance with the rules in force on 28 February 2008. If an applicant made an application in India for entry clearance on or after 1 April 2008, or made an application in the UK for limited leave to remain on or after 29 February 2008, or if an applicant made an application other than in India for entry clearance on or after 30 June 2008; and submitted with that application a valid Highly Skilled Migrant Programme approval letter, the applicant would be automatically awarded 75 points under Appendix A and 10 points under Appendix B.[2] Applicants who were last granted entry clearance, leave to enter, or remain as a highly skilled migrant, which was granted in accordance with the rules in force on or before 8 November 2006 and who was working in a self-employed capacity for at least four months prior to application and had ongoing business commitments for at least six months after that date, would be granted three years' leave as a Tier 1 (General) Migrant.[3] No transitional arrangements were made for people with leave in the existing investor and business person routes, as the extension tests for Tier 1 (Investor) and Tier 1 (Entrepreneur) respectively were broadly the same as those that existed in the categories that have been deleted.[4]

[1]   HC 395, as amended, para 245F.
[2]   HC 395, as amended, para 245F(a)–(ca). Para 245 F was renumbered 245CE by HC 863, para 43, as from 6 April 2011. For full detail of further amendments and deletions, see Vol 2, app 3, p 128.
[3]   HC 395, as amended, para 245F(i)–(vii). For the history of this para see fn 2, above.
[4]   Explanatory Memorandum to HC 607, para 7.36.

TIER 2 – EMPLOYEES

10.54 The Skilled Migrant Tier (Tier 2) is aimed at enabling UK employers to recruit individuals from outside the European Economic Area (EEA) to fill a particular job that cannot be filled by a British or EEA worker. It replaced the existing work permit system, and includes the provisions that govern intra-company transfers and the employment of ministers of religion and sportspeople. However, the rules for Tier 2 (General) and Tier 2 (Intra-Company Transfer) have included transitional arrangements to minimise their impact on existing work permit holders. Provided they are working for the same employer, their job meets the Tier 2 skill level requirements, and their employer has obtained a sponsor licence, these migrants will be able to extend their stay in the UK up to a total of five years without having to meet the specific Tier 2 criteria for qualifications, prospective earnings and English language.[1] Time, however, has passed since these changes were made, the old work permit rules have been consigned to the archival Appendix F, and the main relevance of the transitional provisions will be in tracing people's immigration history.

¹   Explanatory Memorandum to HC 113, para 6.13.

10.55 The main players are the UKBA (now UKVI); sponsors, who are employers and other organisations who want to sponsor applicants under Tier 2 and Tier 5, and the Migration Advisory Committee (MAC) which provides advice to the government on where labour market shortages exist that can sensibly be filled by migration and which occupations should be designated as shortage occupations. Possession of a sponsorship licence is crucial. It is only once employers have a sponsorship licence, that they will be able to sponsor skilled migrants from outside the EEA to work in the UK in four sub-categories:

- Tier 2 (Intra Company Transfer) – for skilled workers moving from an overseas branch of a company to a UK branch;
- Tier 2 (General) – for skilled workers coming to do jobs in shortage occupations and jobs that cannot be filled from the resident labour market;
- Tier 2 (Minister of Religion) – for those coming to fill vacancies as religious workers with recognised religions, including preachers or pastoral workers;
- Tier 2 (Sportsperson) – for elite sportspeople or coaches other than EEA nationals who are internationally established at the highest level.

Widespread changes to Tier 2 were introduced by HC 863 as from 6 April 2011. Previously all four Tier 2 categories were dealt with together under the old rules in HC 395, paragraphs 245ZB–245ZH. These have now been deleted and replaced by two distinct set of rules – 245G–245GF-SD for Tier 2 (Intra company transfer) and 245H–245HF-SD for Tier 2 (General), Tier 2 (Minister of Religion) and Tier 2 (Sportsperson). Similarly, the Attributes requirements in Appendix A for Tier 2 (Intra-Company Transfer) and Tier 2 (General) migrants have been reorganised and amended. Old paragraphs 58A–84 and Tables 10 and 11 have been removed and replaced by new paragraphs 73–84A and 5 new Tables 11 to 11D. As we come to each of these subcategories in this chapter we set out the relevant on rules dealing with entry, stay and attributes.

Tier 2 (Intra company transfer)

10.56 Important changes were made to the Tier 2 (Intra company transfer) category by HC 863, which took effect on 6 April 2011. It set the outline of the current rules, which are to be found at HC 359, paras 245G–245GF-SD and Appendix A Table 11 and Notes at paras 73 to 75E. This category caters for skilled workers moving from an overseas branch of a company to a UK branch but it no longer leads to indefinite leave. To qualify for entry clearance they need 50 points under Attributes in Appendix A and ten points under paragraphs 4 and 5 of Appendix C. Applicants for entry clearance or leave to remain under this sub-tier, who were previously sponsored by their government or an international scholarship agency, must provide the written consent of the sponsorship body.¹ They also must be at least 16 years old, with applicants under the age of 18 requiring the support of their parents or guardians who approve of the travel, care and reception arrangements in the

UK.[2]

[1]   HC 395, as amended by HC 983 as from 6 April 2011, paras 245GB(f).
[2]   HC 395, as amended by HC 983 as from 6 April 2011, paras 245GB(g)–(i); and 245GD(i)–(k).

10.57 There are now four sub-categories in this route:[1]

(i)   *Short Term staff.* These are established employees of multi-national companies who are being transferred to a skilled job in the UK for 12 months or less that could not be carried out by a new recruit from the resident workforce;[2]

(ii)   *Long Term staff.* These are established employees of multi-national companies who are being transferred to a skilled job in the UK which will, or may, last for more than 12 months and could not be carried out by a new recruit from the resident workforce;[3]

(iii)   *Graduate Trainees.* These are recent graduate recruits of multi-national companies who are being transferred to the UK branch of the same organisation as part of a structured graduate training programme, which clearly defines progression towards a managerial or specialist role;[4]

(iv)   *Skills Transfer staff.* These are overseas employees of multi-national companies who are being transferred to the UK branch of the same organisation in a graduate occupation to learn the skills and knowledge they will need to perform their jobs overseas, or to impart their specialist skills to the UK workforce.[5]

The following changes were made: pre-April 2010 Established Staff sub-category was the staff sub-category. One reason why it was split into two – Short Term Staff and Long Term Staff – was to enable differing lengths of stay in the UK to be imposed on transferees depending on whether they are to be in the UK for more or less than 12 months.

[1]   HC 395, para 245G.
[2]   HC 395, para 245G(i).
[3]   HC 395, para 245G(ii).
[4]   HC 395, para 245G(iii).
[5]   HC 395, para 245G(iv).

Getting the points

10.58 An employee transferring to the UK in this category requires 50 points under Table 11 of Appendix A – 30 points for a certificate of Sponsorship (CoS) and 20 points for the appropriate salary and 10 points under Appendix C for maintenance.[1] No English language points under Appendix B are needed, until the transferee is one of those lucky people who can still qualify for indefinite leave under this category.[2] In order to obtain points for a CoS, the applicant must provide a valid CoS reference number which must link to a Certificate of Sponsorship Checking Service[3] entry at UKVI that names the applicant, confirms that the Sponsor is Sponsoring him or her as a Tier 2 (Intra-Company Transfer) Migrant and specifies the sub-category under which the employee is applying.[4] Employees seeking to come as Short Term Staff or Long Term Staff must have been working for the sponsor for at least 12 months outside the UK before they can get entry clearance, but there are situations, specified in the rules, where they can get leave to remain if they have had 12 months working for the sponsor in the UK in five listed situations.[5] The 12 month period must usually be a continuous one, but it may be an aggregated period within a 24 month span, working backwards from the date of application, where there have been absences due to maternity, paternity or adoption leave, long-term sick leave, or a spell working for the sponsor in a Graduate Trainee or Skills transfer capacity or lawfully in some other category of the Immigration Rules.[6]

[1] HC 395, para 245GB(b) and (c) (for entry clearance) and 245GD(f) and (h) (for leave to remain).

[2] HC 395, para 245GF(g).This is not a requirement under Appendix B but under Appendix KoLL, which requires a sufficient knowledge of the English language and about life in the UK.

[3] 'Certificate of Sponsorship Checking Service' means a computerised interface with the Points Based System computer database which allows a United Kingdom Border Agency caseworker or entry clearance officer assessing a migrant's application for entry clearance, leave to enter or leave to remain to access and review details of the migrant's Certificate of Sponsorship, including details of the migrant's Sponsor, together with details of the job and other details associated with the circumstances in which the Certificate of Sponsorship was issued. See HC 359, para 6.

[4] HC 359, Appendix A, paras 74 and 74A.

[5] These are (1) a Tier 2 (Intra-Company Transfer) Migrant in either of the Short Term Staff or Long Term Staff sub-categories, (2) a Tier 2 (Intra-Company Transfer) Migrant in the established staff sub-category under the rules in place before 6 April 2011, (3) a Tier 2 (Intra-Company Transfer) Migrant under the rules in place before 6 April 2010, (4) a Qualifying Work Permit Holder (provided that the work permit was granted because the holder was the subject of an Intra-Company Transfer), and/or (5) a representative of an Overseas Business. See HC 359 para 74B(b)(ii).

[6] HC 395, Appendix A, para 74A(c). If requested to do so UKVI, the applicant must supply specified documents as set out in para 74C-SD(a).

Skill levels

10.59 The minimum skill threshold of jobs which may be sponsored under this category and under Tier 2 (General) (see below) has been raised since 2011 from jobs at NQF level 3 (roughly equivalent to A-level) to jobs at level 6 (roughly equivalent to graduate level).[1] However, there is still room for transferees at NQF level 4 or even level 3. Broadly speaking, there are transitional arrangements, by which Tier 2 (Intra-Company Transfer) Migrants who are already in the UK under the Rules in place before 13 June 2012 or 6 April 2011 and will be able to apply to extend their stay without being subject to the higher graduate level job requirement or the higher salary thresholds that go with them. Under the latest version of these arrangements, Level 4 or above will apply, if the employee is in one of the specified creative sector occupations[2] or is applying for his or her first leave to remain since being given leave as a Tier 2 (Intra-Company Transfer) Migrant under the Rules in place between 6 April 2011 and 13 June 2012 and the job is listed in Appendix J as at NQF level 4 or above.[3] Those applying in the Long Term Staff sub-category for their first leave as a Tier 2 (Intra-Company Transfer) Migrant since being given an earlier leave under the rules in place before 6 April 2011 or in this category or as a Qualifying Work Permit Holder can qualify for jobs at NQF level 3, as set out in Appendix J.[4] Further provision is made for the employee who is coming to work in the same job and for the same sponsor but cannot meet the required skill level only because of the reclassification from the

Period and conditions of leave to remain

10.63 Calculating the length of any leave to remain in this category is a ridiculously wordy process and is more fit for a Finance Act than a piece of employment law. It involves four essential steps. First, have the data for calculating three possible alternative candidates for a minimum period of leave. Second, work out the maximum permissible length. Para 245GE (a) and (b) of the rules contains the necessary information. Third, calculate the difference between maximum permissible length and the period of continuous leave the applicant has already had with the company in the UK. In calculating the continuous period of leave ignore any breaks between periods of leave of up to 28 days. Fourth, jot down the lowest period on a piece of paper and, if it above zero, that will be the proper length of leave that should be granted. Here are the three choices of period:

(i)   the length of the period of engagement plus 14 days,

(ii)   five years, or

(iii)   the difference between the continuous period of leave that the applicant has already been granted (notwithstanding any breaks between periods of leave of up to 28 days) as a Tier 2 (Intra-Company Transfer) Migrant, and the maximum time permitted in subpara (b).

If the calculation of the period of leave comes to zero or a negative number, leave to remain will be refused.[1] The maximum permissible time an intra-company employee is permitted to spend in the UK at any one time is six months, if the applicant is applying in the Skills Transfer subcategory, 12 months in either of the Graduate Trainee or Short Term Staff sub-categories,[2] but is more extensive if the applicant is applying in the Long Term Staff subcategory. The maximum period permitted will be five years, if the gross annual salary to be paid is less than £153,500 or £152,100 if the CoS was assigned before 6 April 2014.[3] In either case the CoS Sponsorship Checking Service entry records must show the gross salary figures (including such allowances as are specified as acceptable for this purpose in paragraph 75 of Appendix A). The period will be nine years, if the gross annual salary is £153,500, or higher,[4] and no limit, if the applicant previously had leave as a Tier 2 (Intra-Company Transfer) Migrant under the Rules in place before 6 April 2011 or as a Qualifying Work Permit Holder, and has not been granted entry clearance in this or any other route since the grant of the pre-April 2011 leave. Leave to remain will be granted subject to the following conditions: (i) no recourse to public funds, (ii) registration with the police, if this is required by HC 395, para 326, and (iii)employment restricted to doing the job for which the CoS was granted including any changes in employment notified to UKVI; supplementary employment, and voluntary work.[5]

[1]   Under HC 395, para 245GE(c) an additional period of leave to remain will be granted for the period between the date that the application is decided and the date that the CoS Checking Service records as the start date of employment in the UK, provided this is not a negative value.
[2]   HC 359, para 245GE(a) and (b).
[3]   Ibid, para 245GE(b)(iii).
[4]   Or £152,100 if the CoS used in support of the application was assigned before 6 April 2014, as above footnote.
[5]   HC 395, para 245GE(d).

Indefinite leave to remain – Tier 2 (Intra-Company Transfers)

10.64 Indefinite leave is not available to migrants under the current rules applying to intra-company transfers, but is still available in those transitional cases where Tier 2 (Intra-Company Transfer) Migrants can still qualify for indefinite leave to remain. This happens first, where the applicant has spent a continuous period of five years lawfully in the UK, of which the most recent period has been as a Tier 2 (Intra-Company Transfer) Migrant, in any combination of the following categories: (i) as a Tier 2 (Intra-Company Transfer) Migrant, (ii) as a Qualifying Work Permit Holder, or (iii) as a representative of an overseas Business.[1] Secondly, part of that period must have been spent as a Tier 2 (Intra-Company Transfer) Migrant granted under the rules in operation prior to 6 April 2011 or as a qualifying work permit holder where that applicant was the subject of an intra-company transfer.[2] In addition the applicant's sponsor must still hold a sponsor licence and certify that the applicant is still required for the employment in question and is paid at or above the rate for the job as set out in the Codes of Practice in Appendix J.[3] Periods of employment served in Guernsey, Jersey and the Isle of Man may be counted if the provisions of para 245GF (i) are satisfied.

[1]   HC 395, para 245GF(c).
[2]   HC 395, para 245GF(d).
[3]   See HC 395, para 245GF(e) which also deals with absences due to maternity, paternity and adoption leave and (f) which deals with the specified documents required under paras 245GF(f) and 245AAA.

Tier 2 (General) Migrants, Tier 2 (Minister of Religion) Migrants and Tier 2 (Sportsperson) Migrants

245HA. Entry clearance Requirements

10.65 These routes enable UK employers to recruit workers from outside the EEA to fill a particular vacancy that cannot be filled by a British or EEA worker (245H).all migrants wishing to to come to the UK under any of the above routes must have an entry clearance (245HA) If applying as a Tier 2 (General) Migrant, the applicant must have a minimum of 50 points under paragraphs 76 to 84A of Appendix A; a Tier 2 (Minister of religion) Migrant, a minimum of 50 points under paragraphs 85 to 92A of Appendix A and as Tier 2 (sportsperson) Migrant a minimum of 50 points under paragraphs 93 to 100 of Appendix A. Each group must also have a minimum of 10 points under paragraphs 1 to 18 of Appendix B and (f) a minimum of 10 points under paragraphs 4 to 5 of Appendix C for maintenance.[1] There is now a cooling off period in this category as with Intra-Company transfers. Entry clearance will not be granted if the applicant has had entry clearance or leave to remain as a Tier 2 Migrant at any time during the 12 months immediately before the date of the application, unless the applicant was not in the UK as a Tier 2 Migrant at all during this period, and can provide evidence to show this, or he or she will be paid a gross annual salary of £153,500 or higher.[2] Then there is a genuineness requirement for the Minister of Religion category, which we deal with below plus a further batch of requirements similar to those in other PBS categories as follows:

- As with all the PBS routes the incoming worker must not fall for refusal under the general grounds for refusal.[3] See further CHAPTER **3**.
- Students and Post Graduate Doctors and Dentists being sponsored by a government or international scholarship agency, currently or in the last 12 months must provide the unconditional written consent of the sponsoring Government or agency.[4]
- The applicant must be at least 16 years old and if he or she is between 16 and 18, the application must be supported by the applicant's parent, parents or legal guardian, who must also confirm that they consent to the arrangements for the applicant's travel to, and reception and care in, the UK.[5]
- If the Sponsor is a limited company, the applicant must not own more than 10% of its shares, unless the gross annual salary is £153,500 or higher.[6]

---

[1] HC 395, para 245HB(b) to (d), (e) and (f).
[2] See HC 395, para 245HB(g). The salary including such allowances as are specified as acceptable for this purpose in paragraph 79 of Appendix A must have been entered on the CoS Checking Service files.).
[3] HC 395, para 245HC(a).
[4] HC 395, para 245HB(h).
[5] HC 395, para 245HB, paras (i), (j) and (k).
[6] HC 395, para 245HB(l). The annual salary must be as recorded by the CoS Checking Service entry, including such allowances as are specified as acceptable for this purpose in paragraph 79 of Appendix A).

245HD. Requirements for leave to remain

10.66 Applicants for leave to remain must have the same number of points as set out in the requirements for entry clearance (HC 395, para, 245HD(f)–(h)) and other requirements are repetitive – for those sponsored by a government or international scholarship agency, child applicants between 16 and 18, and ownership of shares in the Sponsor company. The refusal on general grounds is bolstered by another general requirement in the PBS rules, not to be an illegal entrant or in breach of the Immigration Rules other than overstaying for up to 28 days (245HD(p)).

To qualify for leave to remain many applicants will be seeking to switch from other categories in which they have already had leave. These come from employment business or student categories. To qualify an applicant must have, or have last been granted, entry clearance, leave to enter or leave to remain in one of 14 employment and business categories listed in para 245HD(b)(i) or in a list of applicants in eight student and medical categories (para 245HD(b)(ii)), who have already obtained a bachelor's or master's degree, specified post graduate or Professional education qualifications or completed a minimum of 12 months study towards a UK PhD. These courses must have been taken and obtained at a UK Institution holding a Tier 4 Sponsorship licence and the student must have studied the course either during his or her last grant of leave or a period of continuous leave,[1] which included the student's last grant of leave (para 245HD(d)(i) to (v)). In all these cases the applicant must provide the documents specified in subpara (d)(vii).

Two special provisions are made for applicants seeking to switch from different employment categories:

(1)   An applicant who has, or was last granted leave as a Tier 2 (Intra-Company Transfer) can switch into Tier 1 (General) if applying to work for a different sponsor if (i) they have previously had leave under the Tier 2 (Intra-Company Transfer) Rules in place before 6 April 2010, or in the Established Staff sub-category under the Rules in place before 6 April 2011, and (ii) have not have been granted entry clearance in this or any other route since the grant of leave referred to in (i) above (para 245HD(c)).

(2)   Applicant who were last granted leave as a Tier 5 (Temporary Worker) Migrants can switch into the Tier 2 (Sportsperson) category to work as professional footballers, if their leave was previously granted in the Creative and Sporting sub-category of Tier 5 (para 245HD(e)).

[1]   For these purposes continuous leave will not be considered to have been broken if any of the circumstances set out in paragraphs 245AAA(a)(i) to (iii) of the Rules apply.

Tier 2 (General) Migrants – attributes

10.67 Table 11A applies to Tier 2 (General) Migrants only (77F). Paragraph numbers in square brackets are references to paragraphs in Appendix A. There are different Tables for the Minister of Religion and Sportsperson categories. Points under Table 11A are:

(i)   30 points for one of three alternatives:
  •   Job offer passes Resident Labour Market Test;
  •   Resident Labour Market Test exemption applies; or
  •   Continuing to work in the same occupation for the same Sponsor and

(ii)   20 points for appropriate salary.

To obtain points for a CoS the applicant must provide a valid Certificate of Sponsorship reference number (77A) which tallies with the details held by the CoS Checking Service and has been issued by the Sponsor within the time limits set out in the rules (77C). The Sponsor should normally be an A-rated Sponsor, unless the application is a repeat application for leave to remain by someone who previously had leave in one of the categories set out in para 77C(g).There is a cap on the number of CoS that can be allocated to Sponsors (80–84A) (see below). Unless a job is on the list of occupation shortages in Appendix K, sponsors will need to pass the Resident Labour Market test by carrying out the required advertisement, the aim of which is aimed at seeing whether the job can be done by settled workers in the UK or EEA. Recruitment can still take place outside the cap allocation and without having to pass the Resident Labour Market test, where the incoming employee is to be paid a salary of £153,500 (or £152,100, if the recruitment took place before 6 April 2014) or higher. (77B(c) and 78C(a)).

Resident labour market test-Tier 2 (General)

10.68 The resident labour market test is old hat.[1] Under the work permit scheme it was there to protect the local labour market. Now it is described as being there to protect the settled workforce. The idea is that by suitable advertising the prospective employer will be able to show that no suitable settled worker is available to fill the job. To achieve this, it is mandatory for prospective employers to follow the advertising methods set out in Appendix A at Tables 11B and 11C and the Notes thereto. The advertising requirements are also set out in great detail the Tier 2 and 5 Guidance.[2] The exemptions cover:

- Those already working for the employer who wish to extend their leave;[3]
- Filling a job in a shortage occupation for a minimum of 30 hours a week;[4]
- someone whose last leave was in Tier 1 (Post-study work);[5]
- someone whose last leave was in Tier 1 (Graduate Entrepreneur);
- someone whose last leave was in the Fresh Talent Working in Scotland Scheme;
- Students who have got a degree, post graduate education certificate or diploma or completed 12 months doing a PhD thesis;[6]
- High earners with a salary over £ 153,500;[7]
- Academics returning to Higher Education Institution after academic leave;[8]
- Recruits for Supernumerary research positions;[9]
- Postgraduate doctors and dentists in speciality training.[10]

[1] Tier 2 and 5 Guidance for Sponsors, version 09/14 ('Guidance'), para 28.1.
[2] Guidance pp 86–89. However, it is not always necessary to advertise in this way.
[3] See Appendix A, Table 11A and para 78D. This situation earns points separate from and instead of the resident Labour Market or the exemptions of the Resident Labour Market: see Table 11A.
[4] The shortage lists are reviewed regularly. The current version is contained the shortage occupation list in Appendix K: see HC 395, Appendix A, para 78A. The list is also available on the GOV.UK website at: www.gov.uk/government/publications/tier-2-shortage-occupation -list-from-6-april-2013. This document, updated to 6 April 2014, includes a separate list of shortage occupations for Scotland. Filling a vacancy from the Scottish list means the vacancy must be in Scotland.
[5] Appendix A, para 78B; see also Guidance para 28.8. Para 78B also covers the next 3 categories.
[6] Appendix A, para 78B(b)(5–12). All these students must also fulfil the higher Education qualification requirements set out in HC 395, para 245(d).
[7] Appendix A, para 78C (a); Guidance para 28.9.
[8] Appendix A, para 78C (e); Guidance para 28.10.
[9] Appendix A, para 78C (b); Guidance para 28.11.
[10] Appendix A, para 78C (d); Guidance para 28.12.

Tier 2 (General) skills and appropriate salary

10.69 The skill requirement for Tier 2 (General) is the same as or very similar to that for Tier 2 (Intra-Company Transfer) (see **10.25CA**, above). Apart from the exceptions listed below, migrants sponsored under either of these categories can only work in a skilled occupation at or above National Qualifications Framework (NQF) level 6 (or the equivalent in Scotland). This does not mean that the person employed to fill the job must be educated to that level, it means that the work that person will do is pitched at that level.[1] The exceptions can be summarised as follows:[2]

- A worker filling a job on the current list of shortage occupations[3].

- A worker with previous leave as a Tier 2 (General) Migrant or as a Qualifying Work.
- A Permit Holder, *who* has not since been granted leave in any other route *and was the filling* a job on the *then* list of shortage occupations.[4]
- someone coming to work in an occupation within the creative sector Standard *Occupational Classification (SOC) codes.*[5]
- A Croatian national who needs to apply for worker authorisation.[6]
- A worker already working in the UK at or above NQF level 4 or the equivalent level in Scotland, who obtained leave under Tier 2 (General) or Tier 2 (*Intra-Company Transfer*) under the rules in place between 6 April 2011 and 13 June 2012.[7]
- A worker who obtained leave at or above NQF level 3 or the equivalent level in Scotland under Tier 2 (General), or *in one of the predecessor categories available* before 6 April 2011 *and listed in Appendix A, para 77E(e).*

The minimum salary which applies to Tier 2 (General) is £20,500 per annum, or the minimum appropriate rate for the job as set out in the codes of practice, whichever is higher.[8] No points will be awarded if the salary is less than £20,500. However, where migrants have already applied in the UK and their previous leave was granted under the rules in place before 6 April 2011, in the same category or one of the predecessor categories listed in Appendix A, para 79A (a) or as a sponsored nurse or midwife awaiting registration as set out in para 79A(b). In these exceptional cases the minimum salary is the minimum appropriate rate for the job as set out in the codes of practice in Appendix J.[9] When an employer assigns a CoS they must choose the SOC code which contains the job description that best matches the role they want to recruit for. The Codes of Practice contain information about each SOC code and sample job titles and duties that fit within each code. Sometimes it can be difficult finding the SOC code, which contains the correct job title. This is because different employers use the same job title to describe different jobs, or use generic job titles that cover several different jobs. The Guidance has a simple message; 'keep looking'.[10]

[1] See Appendix A, para 78(e); Tier 2 and 5 Guidance for Sponsors, version 09/14, para 24.7.
[2] Appendix A 77E(a)(ii) to 77E(f); Guidance para 24.8.
[3] Appendix A, para 77E(b).
[4] Appendix A, para 77E(c).
[5] Appendix A, para 77E(a)(ii). They are 3411 – Artists; 3412 – Authors, writers and translators; 3413 – Actors, entertainers and presenters; 3414 – Dancers and choreographers; and 3422 – Product, clothing and related designers.
[6] These are exempt because of the worker authorisation scheme. For details of that scheme see CHAPTER 6, above.
[7] Appendix A, para 77E(d).
[8] Appendix A, paras 79A and 79B.
[9] Appendix A, para 79A. See Guidance para 24.12 and Table 1 which shows the current minimum salaries which apply.
[10] Guidance para 25.1.

The cap

10.70 The most important change to Tier 1 (General) since the last edition is the imposition of an annual cap, now regulated under the Immigration Rules and not contained in UKBA Guidance.[1] This change was effected by the HC

863 rule changes, which came into effect on 6 April 2011. Under the rules an annual cap is imposed on the number of overseas applicants who may be sponsored under this category. There is an annual limit of 20,700 which runs from April 6 to April 5 in the following year[2], unless and until the number is changed. The cap mainly affects applications from outside the UK. In-country applications for leave to remain are excluded from the cap, subject to the exceptions.[3]

[1]   Details of the cap are contained in HC 395, Appendix A, paras 80–84A.
[2]   HC 395, Appendix A, para 80A.
[3]   HC 395, Appendix A, para 77B and 77D(b).

10.71   There is an annual limit of 20,700 CoS available to sponsors under Tier 2 (General). The limit runs from 6 April each year to 5 April the following year. It applies to:

- CoS for new hires earning under £153,500 per year coming work in the UK from overseas;[1]
- CoS for the dependant of a migrant who was last granted leave under Tier 4, where that dependant is already in the UK and wishes to switch into Tier 2 (General) and will be paid less than £153,500;[2] and
- CoS for Croatian nationals.[3]

The jobs listed above, except for those done by Croatian workers, are called 'restricted' jobs, for which a 'restricted' CoS is needed.[4] Jobs which are exempt from the limit are called 'unrestricted' jobs, for which an 'unrestricted' CoS is needed. They include:

(a)   Newly hired recruits whose annual salary for the job is £153,500 or more; and

(b)   Migrants who are applying from within the UK, including those extending their stay in Tier 2, changing employer, or switching immigration category.

The only exception is where the migrant switching into Tier 2 (General) is in the UK as a dependant of another migrant whose last leave was as a student under Tier 4 and who will be paid less than £153,500. These dependants do count towards the limit and the employer must apply for a restricted CoS for them.[5]

[1]   HC 395, Appendix A, para 77B(a) and (c).
[2]   HC 395, Appendix A, para 77D (b)(i) and (ii).
[3]   HC 395, Appendix A, para 83(b) and (c). Although a CoS assigned to a Croatian national counts towards the limit, they are entitled to be an unrestricted CoS: Tier 2 and 5 Guidance for Sponsors, version 09/14 Para 27.8. This is because Croatian nationals can work at or above NQF level 4 and the employer is able to choose from the full range of NQF level 4 SOC codes. Ibid, para 27.5
[4]   Tier 2 and 5 *Guidance for Sponsors*, version 09/14 Para 27.6
[5]   *Guidance for Sponsors*, para 27.7.

10.72   The size of the limit imposed by the cap was established following advice from the Migration Advisory Committee (MAC) and is periodically reviewed. Each month, requests by sponsoring employers to sponsor Tier 2 (General) applicants are scored using the criteria in the points Table 11D in Appendix A, with the available allocation going to the highest-scoring requests. The aim in using this scoring system is to prioritise shortage occupations, and give preference to occupations requiring higher academic qualifications, and jobs with high salaries. Under Table 11D where a Sponsor applies for a CoS under the Tier 2 (General) limit, available points are shown in Table 11D[1]. No application will be granted unless it scores a minimum of 30 points under the heading 'Type of Job' and a minimum of two points under the heading 'Salary on Offer'[2]. There are three choices under the 'type of job' heading and 13 'salary on offer' levels which get from two points at the lowest salary level and 30 points at the ceiling level. The 'type of job' with points is as follows:

- Shortage Occupation – 75 points.
- PhD- level occupation code and job passes Resident Labour Market Test – 50 points.
- Job passes Resident Labour Market Test or an exemption applies as set out in paragraphs 78B or 78C – 30 points.

The 'salary on offer' starts at £20,500–£20,999.99 which gets two points and ends at the ceiling salary level, £100,000–£153,499.99, which gets 30 points. 32 points is the minimum needed to get a CoS. Points may only be scored for one entry in each heading. The purpose of all these points is to prioritise shortage occupations, and give preference to occupations requiring higher academic qualifications, and jobs with high salaries. The points gained under Table 11D and the selection those who will get CoS is intended to achieve this result, in a situation where the monthly demand for CoS exceeds their availability on the monthly allocation under the cap.[3] The details are in Appendix A, paras 81A to 84A.

[1]   HC 395, Appendix A, para 80D.
[2]   HC 395, Appendix A, para 80D.
[3]   The annual total is 20,700 Certificates and the provisional monthly allocation is 1,725: HC 395, Appendix A, para 80A and 82A.

Tier 2 (Minister of Religion) or Tier 2 (Sportsperson) categories

10.73 Applicants for leave to enter and leave to remain under Tier 2 (Minister of Religion) or Tier 2 (Sportsperson) need to meet the same requirements under the Immigration Rules as an applicant under Tier 2 (General) Applicants under the Minister of Religion category require a minimum of 50 points under paragraphs 85–92 of Appendix A of the Immigration Rules, and applicants under the Sportsperson category require a minimum of 50 points under paragraphs 93–100 of Appendix A. Both require a minimum of 10 points under paragraphs 5–10 of Appendix B and 10 points under paragraphs 4–5 of Appendix C.[1]

[1]   See HC 395, para 245HB, as renumbered by HC 863 as from 6 April 2011.

Religious workers under Tier 2 and Tier 5 – Attributes

10.74 This category is linked to Tier 5 (Temporary worker) which deals with religious workers seeking to come to the UK to perform religious duties who may get temporary leave of up to two years.[1] Many of the requirements are the same or similar to those applying to Tier 2 (Ministers of Religion). Temporary religious workers' duties must be work which is within the Sponsor's organisation, or directed by them and, may include preaching, pastoral work and non-pastoral work. If the Sponsor is a religious order, the applicant must be a member of that order. Pay and conditions must be at least equal to those given to settled workers in the same role, and pay must comply with or be exempt from National Minimum Wage regulations. As regards the resident labour market test paragraph 92A of Appendix A applies in the same way as it applies to the Tier 2 (Minister of Religion) category.[2]

1   HC 395, para 245ZP(d) and 245ZR(b)(2).
2   HC 395, Appendix A, para 111(d).

10.75 To obtain leave to enter or remain in the Tier 2 category the applicant's duties may include preaching, pastoral work and non-pastoral work, but the main focus should not be on pastoral duties, such as school teaching, media production, domestic work, or administrative or clerical work, unless the role is a senior position in the Sponsor's organisation.[1] The Tier 2 and 5 Sponsor Guidance describes the work involving preaching and pastoral work. Pastoral duties, they say, include:

(a)   leading worship regularly and on special occasions,
(b)   providing religious education for children and adults by preaching or teaching,
(c)   leading at marriages, funerals and other special services,
(d)   offering counselling and welfare support to members of the congregation, and
(e)   recruiting, training and co-ordinating the work of local volunteers and lay preachers.

A wider range of other duties may also be undertaken. The category covers those coming to fill vacancies as religious workers in bona fide religious organisations and is also open to migrants coming to the UK as missionaries or as members of religious orders, for example a monastic community of monks or nuns, or a similar religious community involving a permanent commitment.[2]

1   HC 395, Appendix A, para 92.
2   The tier 2 and 5 Sponsor Guidance, version 09/2014, para 31.4.

10.76 Pay and conditions must be at least equal to those given to settled workers in the same role, and pay must comply with or be exempt from National Minimum Wage regulations. The requirements of the resident labour market test, as set out in paragraph 92A of Appendix A in respect of the job, should also be complied with, unless the applicant is applying for repeat leave to remain with the same Sponsor and meeting the test is not required where:

(a)   the applicant's role is supernumerary, meaning that it is over and above normal requirements of the Sponsor and if the person filling the role was not there, it would not be filled by anyone else; and
(b)   The migrant will mainly live within and be a member of a religious order, for example an order of nuns or monks. The CoS can then be allocated once it is confirmed that the migrant:
    (i)   is qualified to do the job;
    (ii)   intends to be based in the UK;

(iii)   will comply with the conditions of his or her leave, and it is confirmed that the Sponsor will maintain or accommodate the migrant.[1]

[1]   HC 395, appendix A, para 92(a) to (g).

10.77 In the case of Ministers of Religion seeking leave to remain, there is now a genuineness test in HC 395, para 245HD(q)–(t). If the applicant is applying as a Tier 2 (Minister of Religion) Migrant, the Secretary of State must be satisfied that the applicant: (i) genuinely intends to undertake, and is capable of undertaking, the religious role recorded by the CoS; and (ii) will work only for their sponsor but may carry out supplementary employment or voluntary work.[1] The Secretary of State may request additional information to be supplied within 28 working days of the date of the request or may request the applicant attends an interview. If the applicant fails to supply the information within the time limit or attend the interview without giving a reasonable explanation, the application may be refused. This will also be the case if the Secretary of State is not satisfied following the assessment.[2]

[1]   In para HD(q)(ii) reference is made to the terms of paragraph 245HE(g)(iii). This does not exist and the reference must be to para HE(d)(iii). The text is based on the assumption that this is right.
[2]   HC 395, para 245HD(q) to (t).

Sportsperson under Tier 2 and Tier 5 – Attributes

10.78 The Tier 2 (Sportsperson) category is linked to Tier 5 (Temporary worker) creative and sporting subcategory which deals with sportspersons, who can get up to 12 months if they have entry clearance and up to three months if they are non-visa nationals who can come to the UK without an entry clearance to fulfil a single or two successive sporting engagements lasting up to three months.[1]. Many of the requirements for entry or leave to remain are the same or similar to those applying to Tier 2 (Sportspersons). Both categories apply to players and coaches. In the case of the Tier 5 sportsperson, where the CoS has been issued in the Creative and Sporting subcategory to enable the applicant to work as a sportsperson, he or she must: (i) have been endorsed by the Governing Body for their sport (that is, the organisation which is specified in Appendix M as being the Governing Body for the sport in question), and (ii) the endorsement confirms that the player or coach is internationally established at the highest level and/or will make a significant contribution to the development of his sport at the highest level in the UK, and that the post could not be filled by a suitable settled worker.[2] This is exactly the same as the requirement under the Tier 2 sportsperson category.

[1]   HC 395, para 245ZN(b) and 245ZP(a)–(c).
[2]   HC 395, Appendix A, para 111(a).

10.79 In the case of Tier 2 Sportspersons, paragraph 100 of the attributes in Appendix A has one added requirement. Prior to April 2011 it was a requirement that the sportsperson had been endorsed by the Governing Body for his or her Sport (that is, the organisation which is specified in HC 395, Appendix M: sports governing bodies as being the Governing Body for the sport in question) and it is now a rule requirement that this endorsement must confirm that the player or coach is internationally established at the highest level and/or that their employment will make a significant contribution to the development of their sport at the highest level in the UK, and that the post could not be filled by a suitable settled worker.[1] A player who is employed by a club is permitted to take employment outside of the club, when he or she is playing for their national team in the UK.[2] Where a professional footballer has come to the UK under Tier 5 (Temporary worker) in the creative and sporting subcategory, and wishes to remain in the UK he or she can only do so by applying for leave to remain under Tier 2.[3] Professional sportspersons are barred from entering or remaining in the UK under the Tier 1 (Entrepreneur) route, the Tier 1 (investor) route or under the Tier 5 (Youth Mobility Scheme).[4]

[1]   HC 395, Appendix A, para 100(c).
[2]   HC 395, para 245HE(d)(5).
[3]   HC 395, para 245HD(e).
[4]   See HC 395, paras 245DE(b)(iv), 245EE(b)(iv), 245ZL(c).

English and maintenance requirements

10.80 The level of English Language requirements for the different categories of Tier 2 is set out in Table 1 of Appendix B and explained further in para 5. The availability of the necessary ten points needed for an award of CoS is contained in Table 2. The rest of Appendix B deals with the people who get 10 points because of the nationality or education and deals with those who met the English language requirements in a previous application. Applicants, not otherwise exempted, under all classes of Tier 2, with the exception of Tier 2 (Intra-Company Transfer), will need to demonstrate English language competence to the level set out in Table 1. Tier 2 (Minister of Religion) applicants will need to demonstrate that they have at least a level of English equivalent to level B2 of the Council of Europe's Common European Framework for Language Learning. A Tier 2 (General) applicant seeking entry clearance and leave to remain, other than the cases in paragraph 5 below have to be able to demonstrate a knowledge of English equivalent to level B1 or above. Tier 2 (General) applicants need to reach a knowledge of English equivalent to level A1 or above, if he or she is applying for leave to remain as a Tier 2 (General) Migrant and (i) previously had leave as a Tier 2 (General) Migrant under the rules in place before 6 April 2011, a Qualifying Work Permit Holder, a representative of an overseas newspaper, news agency or Broadcasting organisation, a Member of the Operational Ground Staff of an Overseas-owned Airline, or a Jewish Agency Employee, and he or she has not since been granted leave in any other routes [para 5]. Those who have previously met the English language requirement in a previous grant of leave or as a result of transitional arrangements may gain the necessary points if they meet the requirements of Appendix B, paras 11-15 (previous grant) or 16-18 (transitional arrangements).

10.81 A Tier 2 Migrant will meet the requirements of Appendix C, if he or she either:

(a)   has the level of funds shown in the Table at para 5 of Appendix C and provides the specified documents in Appendix C, para 1B.[1] This amounts to £945.

(b) has an entry clearance, leave to enter or leave to remain as:
- (i) a Tier 2 Migrant
- (ii) a Jewish Agency Employee
- (iii) A member of the Operational Ground Staff of an Overseas-owned Airline,
- (iv) a Minister of Religion, Missionary or Member of a Religious Order,
- (v) a Representative of an Overseas Newspaper, News Agency or Broadcasting Organisation,
- (vi) a Work Permit Holder, or

(c) the Sponsor has certified on the CoS that, should it become necessary, it will maintain and accommodate the migrant up to the end of the first month's employment to the amount of at least £945.[2]

---

[1] These include personal bank or building society statements, building society pass books, or letters from the applicant's bank or building society. more details are set out in the paragraph.
[2] Appendix C, para 5 (a)–(c).

Conditions and length of leave

10.82 On 6 April 2011, the Immigration Rules were amended, as we have seen, and the rules for Tier 2 (Intra-Company Transfer) were separated from the rules for Tier 2 (General), Tier 2 (Minister of Religion) and Tier 2 (Sportsperson). The conditions and length of leave referred to here do not refer any more to the length of leave applying to Tier 2 (Intra-Company Transfer), which we have dealt with at **10.56**, above, but do refer to conditions of leave applying to the three other sub-categories of Tier 2.

Entry clearance

10.83 All successful applicants for leave to enter under Tier 2 will be granted either leave for the length of the employment they are sponsored to undertake plus one month or alternatively, five years plus a month for Tier 2 (General) and three years plus a month for Tier 2 (Minister of Religion) or a Tier 2 (Sportsperson), dependent upon which proves to be the shorter.[1] Entry clearance will be granted with effect from 14 days before the recorded start date for the applicant's employment or with immediate effect if it is due to start earlier.[2]

---

[1] HC 395, para 245HC(a) and (b).
[2] HC 395, para 245 HC(c).

Leave to remain

10.84 In the case of leave to remain the calculation is more complicated. The key calculation involves calculating the difference between the continuous period of leave that the applicant has already been granted[1] as a Tier 2 Migrant, and six years. If this results in zero or a negative number, leave to remain will be refused.

(a) If the result is positive, leave to remain will be granted for whichever of the following is the shortest;

(i)   the length of the period of engagement plus 14 days,

(ii)   five years if the applicant is applying as a Tier 2 (General) Migrant, or

(iii) three years if the applicant is applying as a Tier 2 (Minister of Religion) Migrant or a Tier 2 (Sportsperson) Migrant, or

(iv) the result of the calculation above.[2]

(b)   The six year restriction set out in (iv) above will not apply if the applicant:

     (i)   previously had leave under the Rules in place before 6 April 2011 as (1) a Tier 2 (General) Migrant, (2) a Tier 2 (Minister of Religion) Migrant, (3) a Tier 2 (Sportsperson) Migrant, (4) a Jewish Agency Employee, (5) a Member of the Operational Ground Staff of an Overseas-owned Airline, (6) a Minister of Religion, Missionary or Member of a Religious Order, (7) a Qualifying Work Permit Holder, or (8) a Representative of an Overseas Newspaper, News Agency or Broadcasting Organisation, and

     (ii)   has not been granted entry clearance as a Tier 2 (General) Migrant, Tier 2 (Minister of Religion) Migrant or Tier 2 (Sportsperson) Migrant under the Rules in place from 6 April 2011, and

     (iii) has not been granted entry clearance, leave to enter or leave to remain in any other category since the grant of leave referred to in (i) above.

(c)   In addition to the period in (a), leave to remain will be granted for the period between the date that the application is decided and the date that the Certificate of Sponsorship Checking Service records as the start date of employment in the UK, provided this is not a negative value.[3]

Where leave to enter or remain is granted it is on the condition of no recourse to public funds, registration with the police, as necessary and working only for their sponsor[4] unless they are Tier 2 sportspersons employed by a club who are selected to play for their national team in the UK.[5]

---

[1] HC 395, para 245HE(a)(iv). Any breaks between periods of leave of up to 28 days will be disregarded.

[2] HC 395, para 245HE(a).

[3] HC 395, para 245HE(c).

[4] HC 395, paras 245HC (d) and 245HE (d). The requirement that the employee must only work for the sponsor is subject to (1) any notification of a permissible change to the details of that employment other than prohibited changes as defined in para 323AA, (2) supplementary employment and (3) voluntary work. Supplementary employment means that In addition to the job specified on the certificate of sponsorship (CoS), the applicant can do extra work if it is in either a job on the shortage occupation list or a job in the same sector and at the same professional level as the work for which the CoS was assigned. It must be no more than 20 hours a week, and outside the working hours covered by the CoS. If they meet the above requirements the applicant does not need to inform the Home Office. Modern Guidance, Tier 2: supplementary, voluntary and secondary employment, at p103. The applicant can also do voluntary work in any sector. They must not be paid or receive other money for the voluntary work, except reasonable expenses as described in s 44 of the National Minimum Wage Act 1998.

[5] HC 395, Paras 245HC (d) (4) and 245HE (d)(4).

245HF. Requirements for indefinite leave to remain

10.85 In addition to any general points about indefinite leave set out at **10.10** the requirements for indefinite leave to remain are:

- The applicant must not fall for refusal under the general grounds for refusal, must not be an illegal entrant and must not be in the UK in breach of immigration laws except that any period of overstaying for a period of 28 days or less will be disregarded.[1]
- The applicant must have spent a continuous period of five years lawfully in the UK, of which the most recent period must have been spent with leave as a Tier 2 Migrant, in any combination of the categories listed in para 245HF(c)(i) to (x).[2]
- The applicant's last Sponsor must certify in writing that the applicant is still required for the employment in question, and that in the case of a Tier 2 (General) Migrant applying for settlement, the employee is paid at or above the appropriate rate for the job as stated in the Codes of Practice in Appendix J.[3]
- The applicant provides the specified documents in paragraph 245HF-SD to evidence the sponsor's certification in subsection (d)(ii) and to evidence the reason for any absences as set out in paragraph 245AAA.[4]
- The applicant must have sufficient knowledge of the English language and sufficient knowledge about life in the United Kingdom, in accordance with Appendix KoLL.[5]

[1] HC 395,para 245HF(b) and (g).
[2] Time spent with valid leave in the Bailiwick of Guernsey, the Bailiwick of Jersey or the Isle of Man in a category equivalent to any of the categories set out in (c)(i) to (x), may be included in the continuous period of 5 years lawful residence, provided that the provisions of para 245HF(h) are satisfied.
[3] HC 395, para 245HF(d). Where the applicant is not paid at the appropriate rate only due to maternity, paternity or adoption leave, he or she must have been paid at the appropriate rate operative immediately before that leave started.
[4] Ibid, para 245HF(e).
[5] Ibid, para 245HF(f).

TIER 5

10.86 Tier 5 of the Points-Based System caters for youth mobility and temporary workers coming for primarily non-economic purposes, and consists of two categories: Tier 5 (Youth Mobility Scheme) and Tier 5 (Temporary Workers). The Temporary Workers category consists of five sub-categories: Creative and Sporting, Charity Workers, Religious Workers, Government Authorised Exchange, and International Agreement. Applicants must have a Tier 5 Sponsor, which is usually their UK employer.

Tier 5 (Youth Mobility Scheme)

10.87 The Tier 5 (Youth Mobility Scheme) has replaced the old working holiday-maker category, but is a much more limited and controlled scheme. It applies to sponsored young people from participating countries who wish to work in the UK for a temporary period. Each participating country is entitled to a fixed quota of applicants per year. An applicant must either be a non-citizen British national or from one the participating countries, must not have any dependent children under 18, and not have previously had leave under this sub-tier or the previous working holidaymaker scheme.[1] Partners can only join the applicant if they qualify in their own right.[2] Points under Appendix A are granted for being the correct age and coming from one of the participating countries.[3] A successful applicant will be granted two years' leave during which he or she will be able to take up employment or a limited form of self employment.[4] Applicant will need to have £1,890, not including any overdraft facility, in their personal bank account on the date of application for entry clearance,[5] to qualify for 10 points under Appendix C.[6] HC 1693 (in force in December 2011) has extended the Tier 5 Youth Mobility Scheme to qualifying territories as well as countries, so as to include Taiwan to be added as a participant of the Scheme from 2012. Those coming from Taiwan will still need to have a certificate of sponsorship status, but those from all the other participating countries and territories now have a 'deemed sponsorship status'[7] which means that the country or territory is not required to issue its nationals or passport holders with a Certificate of Sponsorship in order to enable a successful application under the Tier 5 Youth Mobility Scheme.[8]

[1] HC 395, as amended, para 245ZK.
[2] Modernised Guidance-Tier 5 (Youth mobility scheme), p3.
[3] HC 395, Appendix A, paras 101–104.
[4] HC 395, para 245ZL. The applicant will not be able to work, however, as professional sportsperson or coach at all or as a doctor or dentist, unless they qualified as such in the UK.
[5] Modernised Guidance-Tier 5 (Youth mobility scheme), p3.
[6] HC 395, Appendix C, paras 6 to 7. They will also need to provide the specified documents in para 1B of the Appendix.
[7] This is defined in HC 395, para 6, as amended by HC 1693 in December 2011.
[8] The list of participating countries and territories and their allocation of places for 2012 is set out in Appendix G of HC 395 as follows: Countries and Territories with Deemed Sponsorship Status: Australia – 32,500 places; Canada – 5,000 places; Japan – 1,000 places; New Zealand – 10,000 places; Monaco – 1,000 places: Countries and Territories without Deemed Sponsorship Status: Taiwan – 1,000 places.

Tier 5 (Temporary workers)

10.88 Tier 5 (Temporary Workers) allows certain types of temporary worker to come to the UK for cultural, charitable, religious or international objectives. Despite the temporary nature of much of this Tier, no-one will qualify for the necessary points under the attributes requirements in Appendix A, unless he or she holds a Tier 5 (Temporary Worker) Certificate of Sponsorship. This Tier covers the following subcategories:

- Creative and Sporting: for people coming to work or perform as sportspeople, entertainers or creative artists;
- Charity workers: for people coming to do temporary and voluntary work for a charity;
- Religious: for people coming to work temporarily in a religious role;
- Government Authorised Exchange: for migrants coming through schemes aimed at sharing knowledge, experience and best practice. All such schemes must be approved by a government department;

- International Agreement: for migrants coming to the UK to provide a service in circumstances covered by an international treaty to which the UK is party.[1] This includes private servants in diplomatic households.

Tier 5 has subsumed a number of immigration rule and policy categories, including:

- some work permits in the creative and sporting sector;
- exchange teachers and language assistants;
- General Agreement on Trades in Services (GATS);
- International Association for the Exchange of Students of Technical Experience (IAETE);
- International Fire Fighter Fellowship;
- EU Leonardo da Vinci Programme;
- Government Authorised Exchange;
- Rudolf Steiner;
- Training and Work Experience Scheme;
- China Graduate Work Experience Programme;
- Vander Elst;
- non-pastoral religious workers;
- visiting religious workers.

[1] The International Agreement subcategory includes migrants under contract to do work that is covered under international law, including the General Agreement on Trade in Services (GATS); similar agreements between the United Kingdom and another country; employees of overseas governments and international organisations; and private servants in diplomatic households. Those already in the UK under the international agreement category can extend their stay if they have been in the UK for less than 24 months, which is the maximum time they are allowed to stay. The one exception is private servants in diplomatic households and employees of overseas governments and international organisations only, who can apply for an extension for a maximum of 12 months at a time, up to a total of six years

10.89 Applicants cannot switch between the different sub-categories of Tier 5 (Temporary worker). They can apply for extensions in the same Tier 5 sub-category, however, if they have not exceeded the maximum grant of leave allowed in that category. Normally switching into Tier 5 is not allowed, but exceptions apply for some students, work permit holders, sports visitors, entertainer visitors and overseas government employees. The only exceptions are:

- Overseas government employees (previously granted leave to enter under the now deleted paragraphs 160–162 and 164–165 of the old Immigration Rules[1] who are applying to switch into the Tier 5 (Temporary Worker) International agreement sub-category;
- Work permit holders who are applying to switch into the Tier 5 (Temporary worker) International agreement sub-category, and hold a CoS which shows they are being sponsored as an overseas government employee in the International agreement sub-category, and will be continuing in employment with the same organisation.
- Work permit holders who are applying to switch into the Tier 5 (Temporary worker) Government authorised exchange sub-category, who were previously issued with a work permit for the purpose of employment as a sponsored researcher, and have been granted a CoS to continue their employment.

- Students (paragraphs 57–62 of the Immigration Rules), students re-
  sitting an examination (69A–69F), student nurse (63–67), student
  union sabbatical officers (87A–87F), people writing up a thesis, postgraduate doctors and dentists, or Tier 4 (General) migrants
  (245ZT–245ZY) can apply to switch into the Tier 5 (Temporary
  worker) government authorised exchange sub-category:
  - (i) provided they have lawfully obtained a UK bachelors or masters
    degree, post graduate certificate in education (PGCE) or post
    graduate diploma in education (PGDE) and
  - (ii) intend to pursue a career overseas at the end of the period of
    work experience or training, and
  - (iii) are being sponsored to undertake postgraduate professional
    training or work experience required to obtain a professional
    qualification or registration in the same professional field as
    their qualification described above, or
  - (iv) are being sponsored to undertake an internship for up to
    12 months which is directly related to the qualification described
    above.

[1]   Paras 160–162 of the Immigration Rules are now in Appendix F.

10.90 Under the Tier 5 (Temporary Worker) route all migrants will need entry
clearance, unless they are coming for three months or less in the creative and
sporting sub-tiers and are not visa nationals.[1] Applications for leave by
applicants under the age of 18 must be supported by their parents or guardians
who approve of the travel, care and reception arrangements in the UK.[2]
Applicants for leave to remain will need to have leave in one of the prescribed
categories set out in the rules and will need a total of 40 points to qualify for
an entry clearance or leave to remain.[3] The 30 available points under the
attributes section of Appendix A will be granted if the applicant has a
certificate of sponsorship from their Sponsor.[4] There are no English language
requirements under Appendix B for Tier 5 applicants. Applicants under Tier 5
(Temporary Worker) will qualify for 10 points under Appendix C if either (i)
they can demonstrate (using the specified documents in paragraph 1B) funds of
at least £945 held in their personal bank or building society for 90 consecutive
days immediately prior to application, or (ii) the applicant's sponsor has
certified that the applicant will not claim public funds during his period of
leave.[5] All applicants will have to meet the requirements for their particular
subcategory in Appendix A paras 101–112 and in particular 111(a)–(g). It
should also be noted that on 1 October 2013 the Immigration Rules changed
to tackle abuse on all Tier 5 (Temporary worker) routes. Genuineness tests
were introduced.[6] When applying for entry clearance, leave to enter or leave to
remain, applicants must genuinely intend to undertake the role described on
the (CoS); be capable of undertaking that role and will not undertake
employment in the UK other than permitted by the entry clearance, leave to
enter or leave to remain, should it be granted.[7]

[1]   HC 395, as amended, para 245ZN.
[2]   HC 395, as amended, para 245ZO(d) and (e) and para 245ZQ(f) and (g).
[3]   HC 395, as amended, para 245ZQ(b).
[4]   HC 395, as amended, Appendix A, paras 105–112.
[5]   See HC 395, Appendix C, paras 1B and 9.
[6]   HC 395, para 245O(i) to (j).

10.91 Migrants who do not have entry clearance, who are in the creative and sporting sub-tier and are not visa nationals will be granted a maximum of three months' leave to cover their engagements in the UK.[1] Otherwise the length of further leave will vary from six to twelve to a maximum of two years with a longer period in two cases. The maximum leave according to the will generally be twelve months. The Modernised Guidance has summarised the maximum periods as follows:[2]

Maximum of 6 months in any 12 month period for the international agreement subcategory for those providing a service under contract as set out in the General Agreement on Trade In Services (GATS) and other similar trade agreements.[3]

Maximum of 12 months for charity, creative and sporting workers and government authorised exchange migrants, where applicants were granted entry clearance in a work experience programme under the Immigration Rules in place on or after 6 April 2012. Creative workers can apply for an additional 12 months leave to remain to take them to maximum 24 months.[4]

Maximum of 24 months for international agreement workers, except for those providing a service under contract as set out in the General Agreement on Trade In Services (GATS) and other similar trade agreements; for religious workers; for government authorised exchange for those who were granted entry clearance in that capacity under the Immigration Rules in place before 6 April 2012 or were granted entry clearance in a research programme, training programme or overseas government language programme under the Immigration Rules in place on or after 6 April 2012. Overseas government employees and employees of international organisations can extend up to two years at a time up to a maximum of six years.[5]

Private servants in diplomatic households can extend up to two years at a time up to a maximum of six years if their entry clearance was granted under the Immigration Rules in place before 6 April 2012, or up to two years at a time up to a maximum of five years if their entry clearance was granted under the Immigration Rules in place on or after 6 April 2012.[6]

Because this is a temporary worker category, indefinite leave is not available, except for one category-for applicants in the Tier 5 – International agreement category who are private servants in diplomatic households if their last grant of entry clearance was made before 6 April 2012.[7]

[1] HC 395, para 245ZP(a) and (b).
[2] Modernised guidance Points-based system: Tier 5 (Temporary Worker) 9 July 2014 p 4.
[3] HC 395, para 245ZP(e).
[4] HC 395, para 245ZP(c).
[5] HC 395, para 245ZR(b)(2) and 245ZR (e)
[6] HC 395, para 245ZR(d) and (e).
[7] HC 395, para 245ZS(b).

10.92 Private servants in diplomatic households if their last grant of entry clearance was made before 6 April 2012 may qualify for indefinite leave under this category. The applicant must meet the requirements of paragraph 245ZS of the Immigration Rules:

- None of the general grounds for refusal in paragraphs 320 to 324 of the Immigration Rules apply and the applicant is not in breach of immigration laws, except that any period of overstaying for a 28 day period or less shall be disregarded.
- The applicant has spent a continuous period of five years in the UK lawfully with leave in the Tier 5 (International agreement) category, working as a private servant in a diplomatic household.
- The applicant has sufficient knowledge of the English language and about life in the UK, with reference to Appendix KoLL (knowledge of language and life) This is unless the applicant is under the age of 18, or aged 65 or over at the time the application is made.
- The applicant provides a letter from the employer detailing any absences from employment, including periods of annual leave. Where the absence was due to a serious or compelling reason, the applicant must provide a personal letter which includes full details of the reason for the absences with all original supporting documents, such as medical certificates, birth or death certificates, and the reasons which led to the absence from the UK.

FAMILY MEMBERS OF PBS MIGRANTS

10.93 The spouse, civil partner, unmarried or same-sex partner, or child under the age of 18 can apply for leave in line along with a successful points based system applicant.[1] The general Immigration Rules for applications by spouses, partners and children apply to an applicant's family members under the points based system.[2] In addition, all applicants for leave to enter will require valid entry clearance, with the exception of family members of a Tier 5 (Temporary Worker) migrant who has been sponsored under the creative or sporting sub-tiers, who are seeking leave for three months or less, and are non visa nationals.[3] There is also an additional maintenance requirement for the spouse, civil partner, unmarried or same-sex partner and for each child. Where the application is connected to a Tier 1 (Migrant) (other than a Tier 1 (Investor) Migrant or a Tier 1 (Exceptional Talent) Migrant) where the Tier 1 Migrant is either outside the UK or has been in the UK for less than 12 months, there needs to be (i) £1,260 in funds, where the application is connected to a Tier 1 (Graduate Entrepreneur) Migrant; and (ii) £1,890 in funds in other cases per additional family member.[4] All other applicants, except Tier 1 (Investor) Migrant and a Tier 1 (Exceptional Talent) Migrant are required to have £630 per family member.[5] Leave will be granted for the same length of time as the points based system migrant with a right to take up employment for the spouse, civil partner, unmarried or same-sex partner.[6] If the PBS Migrant has indefinite leave to remain in a PBS category, or is, at the same time, being granted indefinite leave, or has since become a British Citizen, leave to remain will be granted to the applicant for a period of three years.[7]

The family member is entitled to apply for indefinite leave to remain at the same time as the relevant PBS migrant after two years if they were last granted leave as the family member of a PBS migrant under the Rules in place before 9 July 2012, and after five years, in any other case, provided they fulfil all the requirements of paragraph 319E. In particular the spouse or partner will need to demonstrate that they have been living together for at least the two or five year period, the relationship is subsisting and it is their intention to live together permanently[8] and that they demonstrated sufficient knowledge of the English language and sufficient knowledge about life in the UK, in accordance with Appendix KoLL unless exempted by age.[9] The child of a points based system migrant will need to show that they have not formed their own family unit or are leading an independent life. Both of their parents will either need to be residing lawfully in the UK or one of the parents is seeking entry clearance at the same time as the applicant.[10]

[1] HC 395, para 319AA makes clear who is included in these provisions. In paragraphs 319A to 319K and Appendix E, 'Relevant Points Based System Migrant' means a migrant granted to leave as a Tier 1 Migrant, a Tier 2 Migrant, a Tier 4 (General) Student or a Tier 5 (Temporary Worker) Migrant. The one sub-category under the points based system that does not allow applications for leave by family members is Tier 5 (Youth Mobility Scheme).

[2] HC 395, para 319A. The route is for the spouse, civil partner, unmarried or same-sex partner of a Relevant Points Based System Migrant (Partner of a Relevant Points Based System Migrant). Paras 277 to 280 and 295AA apply. See further CHAPTER 11.

[3] HC 395, para 319B.

[4] HC 395, Appendix E(a). Family members of Tier 1 (Investor) applicants are also exempt from the maintenance requirement.

[5] HC 395, Appendix E(b). Family members of a Tier 2 applicant who is sponsored by an A rated sponsor who provides a written undertaking to accommodate and maintain the applicant and family members for the first month of employment are also exempt. HC 395, as amended, Appendix E(i).

[6] HC 395, para 319D (a)(i). There are no restrictions on the work the spouse, civil partner, unmarried or same-sex partner member can do with the exception of: (a) working as a doctor or dentist in training, unless they qualified as such at a UK recognised institution or are already lawfully working as such in the UK; and (b) employment as a professional sportsperson (including as a sports coach): see HC 395D, para (b)(iii) and (v).

[7] HC 395, para 319D (a)(ii).

[8] HC 395, para 319E. They will also need to provide specified documents together with their application under para 319H-SD and Appendix C para 1B.

[9] HC 395, as amended, para 319E(g). Under Appendix KoLL, para 3.1 the tests do not apply to those under 18 or over 65 or where it would be unreasonable because of the applicant's mental or physical condition.

[10] HC 395, as amended, para 319H. The exceptions to the 'both parents' requirements are that the points based system migrant is the sole surviving parent; he or she has and has had sole responsibility for the child's upbringing or there are serious and compelling reasons to allow the application; para 319H(f).

SPONSORSHIP

Introduction

10.94 Central to the new points based system is the philosophy that those who benefit most directly from migration should play their part in ensuring the system is not abused. The UKBA, through the sponsorship system directly transfers responsibility for monitoring of immigration control from themselves to those who would seek to sponsor migrants. The system introduces a process of sponsorship whereby all migrants, with the exception of those under Tier 1, must be sponsored by an employer, educational institute or certain other bodies. Sponsors take on compliance responsibilities for migrants, including duties to: keep accurate and up-to-date records, report changes in circumstances, comply with the law, co-operate with the UKBA, and meet any additional tier-specific duties.[1] The main text refers to the Sponsorship Guidance Version 09/14. There have been a number of earlier editions of the

Guidance since version 04/10, used in our last edition. The Appendices containing documents to be provided have been changed separately from the main Guidance. For example Version 10/11 had an updated Appendix A on supplying evidence, valid from 5 January 2012, and an updated Appendix D on keeping documents, valid from 6 December 2011. In this section we give website addresses and it is essential that they are consulted. Sending the wrong documents or failing to keep to timetables can result in refusal and we cannot guarantee that our information is up to date.

- Sponsorship Guidance is at:
  www.gov.uk/government/publications/sponsor-a-tier-2-or-5-worker-guidance-for-employers
- The appendices to the Guidance are available at:
  www.gov.uk/government/collections/sponsorship-information-for-employers-and-Educators
- Guidance on applications under Tier 2 and 5 are:
  Tier 2-www.gov.uk/government/publications/application-to-extend-stay-in-the-uk-form-tier-2
  Tier 5 – www.gov.uk/government/publications/guidance-on-application-for-uk-visa-under-tier-5-temporary-worker

¹   Home Affairs Committee – 'Managing Migration: The Points Based System', 15 July 2009.

Applying for a licence

10.95 The initial application for a licence will need to be made online using the online sponsor application at: www.gov.uk/apply-sponsor-licence.¹ The sponsorship applicant must make the application itself. A representative can help fill in the application, but must not send it on the sponsor's behalf. If UKVI find this has happened, they will refuse the application and will not refund the fee.² the sponsor must send the following to validate the application:

(a)   the original submission sheet (not a certified copy), signed and dated by the authorising officer (all pages must be sent);

(b)   all of the mandatory documents listed on the submission sheet (originals or certified copies).

These must all be sent in together within five working days of the date the sponsor submits its online application. If any items are missing or incorrect, the application will be invalid and rejected by UKVI but they will refund the application fee.³ The guidance sets out the mandatorily required documents needed to support the application which should be either in the original form or as certified copies.⁴ As part of the application, the prospective sponsor is asked to indicate under which tiers and/or sub-tiers it wishes to obtain a licence. Prospective sponsors can select as many tiers and sub-tiers as they need and the sponsorship licence will be limited to granting certificates of sponsorship in the applied for categories. The application will be assessed under three guiding principles:

- Is the applicant a genuine organisation operating lawfully in the United Kingdom? 'The eligibility criteria'.

- Is the applicant dependable and reliable? Is the applicant capable of carrying out its duties as a sponsor? 'The suitability criteria'.

The 'eligibility' criteria should be met by providing the required documents in the proscribed form. Suitability will be assessed by history and background of the organisation, its key personnel and of the people who control it. A history of dishonest conduct or immigration crime is likely to lead to a potential sponsor being deemed unsuitable. Suitability may also be judged by evidence of past non-compliance and by visiting the sponsors premises and carrying out an inspection.[5] This may be done either before or after the sponsor licence is granted.

A potential sponsor should be granted an 'A' rating, if they meet the eligibility requirement and suitability requirements.

[1] Tier 2 and 5 Sponsor Guidance Version 04/10 para 3.1.
[2] Ibid, para 3.3.
[3] ibid, para 3.5.
[4] Ibid, Appendix A lists the documents which must be sent to support a licence application and most applications will need to be supported by a minimum of four documents from the list. Certain documents are always required (mandatory). These are shown in list A. The documents in list B are only mandatory for certain types of organisation in certain sectors. The documents in list C can be provided in addition to the mandatory documents but cannot replace the mandatory documents.
[5] Ibid, para 7.5

10.96 The sponsorship applicant is required to allocate certain responsibilities to one or more members of its staff, who are designated as 'key personnel'. They will be an authorising officer; key contact; one or more level 1 users; and one or more level 2 users. The key personnel will need to be permanently based in the United Kingdom and the sponsor will be responsible for the actions of the key personnel. The authorising officer is responsible for the overall management of the sponsor's access to the sponsorship management system. He or she should be the most senior person responsible for the recruitment of all migrant workers and ensuring that all sponsor duties are met. The key contact is the point of contact for the UKVI at the sponsor. Neither will have an automatic right of access to the sponsorship management system (SMS) without an additional designation as a level 1 or level 2 user. Only level 1 and 2 users will have access to the SMS. The level 1 user is responsible for the day-to-day management of the system and will be able to make requests for additional users; assign certificates of sponsorship to migrants; apply for an increase in the number of certificates of sponsorship that can be issued; to inform the UKVI of changes with the sponsor and to monitor and report if necessary on the compliance of the migrants they have granted certificates to. When making an initial application, the sponsor can only nominate one level 1 user. However, once a licence has been granted, the sponsor can nominate additional level 1 users. A level 2 user is entitled to issue certificates of sponsorship or report migrant activity to the UKBA.[1] The sponsor can only apply for level 2 users after they have been granted a licence. The SMS is an online tool to which UKVI have access. It allows the level 1 and 2 users to manage their sponsorship of migrants under the points based system. It allows the sponsor to report changes of circumstances, complying with their reporting duties,[2] and to issue or request additional certificates of sponsorships.[3]

[1] See Tier 2 and 5 Sponsor Guidance Version 09/14, para 6 at pp 20–25 for the key provisions relating to the key personnel.
[2] See Tier 2 and 5 Sponsor Guidance Version 09/14, para 11 at pp 34–35.
[3] Tier 2 and 5 Sponsor Guidance Version 04/10, p 19.

10.97 A licence will be issued for four years and any additional licences applied for by the same sponsor during this period, will have the same lifespan as the original licence.[1] Upon being granted a licence, a sponsor will be issued with a licence number and will be told the maximum number of certificates of sponsorship they are entitled to issue. A sponsor can request additional certificates through the SMS and the UKVI reserves the right to reduce the number of certificates issued to any individual sponsor.[2] Each individual certificate can be used to support one application for leave.[3] Sponsors are also entitled to access the UKVI SMS.[4] A 'B' rated sponsor will initially not be entitled to issue any certificates of sponsorship. However, a 'B' rating for a sponsor is only intended to be transitory and the sponsor will be subject to an action plan by the UKVI, to assist them in achieving an 'A' rating. A 'B' rated sponsor will only be allowed to assign certificates when it has demonstrated its commitment to make improvements by signing up to the measures set out in the action plan and has paid the action plan fee.[5] Failure to comply with the plan will lead to the licence being withdrawn.[6]

[1] Tier 2 and 5 Sponsor Guidance Version 09/14, paras 2.1 at p 7 and 22.2 at p 65.
[2] Ibid, para 23.19 at p 72, p 22.
[3] A CoS can normally only be used once: Guidance 09/14, para 23.4 at p 70 and will only cover one person, but under Tier 5 (Creative and Sporting) a sponsor can assign a 'group CoS' to all members of a group: ibid, para 23.7, at p 70 Another exception is where the certificate has been assigned to and used by a migrant who is a non-visa national and who is entering the United Kingdom under the Tier 5 (Creative and Sporting) route, for less than three months.
[4] Tier 2 and 5 Sponsor Guidance Version 09/14, para 11 at p 34. It can be accessed online at: www.points.homeoffice.gov.uk/gui-sms-jsf/home/SMS-003-Home.faces
[5] Tier 2 and 5 Sponsor Guidance Version 09/14, para 18.11 at p 56.
[6] Ibid, para 18.16 at p 57. An action plan will usually cover a period of three months but could be longer or shorter in appropriate circumstances. At the end of this period, a decision should be made on whether the sponsor should be upgraded to an 'A' rating, or whether a licence should be withdrawn. In exceptional circumstances, where significant progress has been made, The UKVI may decide to keep the sponsor on a 'B' rating but extend the period of the existing action plan. Additionally, the UKVI can decide to revise or issue a new action plan with the cost of the new plan to be borne by the sponsor. A sponsor that has failed to successfully complete an action plan in 12 months will automatically lose its licence.

Certificates of sponsorship

10.98 The certificate is a virtual record that allows the sponsor to issue a reference number to an applicant under Tier 2 or Tier 5. The number of certificates issued to a sponsor will depend upon the number requested in the sponsorship application. The sponsor will be asked to justify why they need the particular number of certificates requested in their application. That will be set against the sponsor's previous history at managing certificates and previously, work permits and the size and nature of the business.[1] The sponsor, through the SMS, is entitled to request further certificates and the UKBA maintain the right to reduce the number allocated. The certificates will need to be allocated within 12 months and any unallocated certificates will be lost.

Upon being allocated to an applicant the certificate is valid for three months whilst an application for leave is made. If the application is unsuccessful and the sponsor wants to continue to sponsor the same applicant, they will need to issue a new certificate.[2]

1   Tier 2 and 5 Sponsor Guidance Version 04/10, para 159.
2   There is one exception to the one certificate per applicant rule. Under Tier 5 (Creative and Sporting) a sponsor can issue a group certificate of sponsorship. The group will need to be seeking entry clearance for three months or less and be non-visa nationals. Each member of the group will be assigned an individual certificate of sponsorship confirming that he or she is a member of the named group, but there will only be one certificate of sponsorship fee payable which will cover the entire group. Tier 2 and 5 Sponsor Guidance Version 09/14 para 23.7, at p 70.

10.99 Each tier and each sub-tier has additional specific requirements for would-be sponsors to meet before they can issue a certificate of sponsorship. The requirements for sponsoring the different categories under Tier 2 and 5 are set out in broad terms in the Sponsor's Guidance.[1]

1   Tier 2 and 5 Sponsor Guidance Version 09/14, paras 4.104.45 at pp 10–17 and paras 29-37 at pp 29–125.

SPONSORSHIP DUTIES

10.100 One of the primary rationales behind the new sponsorship system is that those who benefit most directly from immigration should play their part in making sure the system is not abused. In accordance with this philosophy, the UKBA imposes a series of 'duties' upon sponsors to assist in policing the compliance of migrants under the points based system. These duties commence at the issuing of a sponsorship licence and will apply to each individual sponsored migrant until the licence is either withdrawn or surrendered; the migrant leaves the UK and his or her leave lapses; or he or she leaves the employment of the sponsor and the sponsor has informed the UKBA of this change of circumstances.[1] The duties fall under four distinctive heads: recording keeping duties;[2] reporting duties;[3] complying with the law[4] and co-operating with the UKBA.[5] In addition there are also specific duties for individual tiers and sub-tiers that correspond to the sponsorship requirements for those categories, particularly Tier 2 (General) and Tier 2 (Intra-Company Transfers).[6] Failure to comply with the duties can lead to the sponsor being issued with a written warning; having their sponsorship rating downgraded; the number of certificates they are able to issue reduced; or their licence revoked.[7]

1   Tier 2 and 5 Sponsor Guidance Version 09/14, para 14 at p 45.
2   There is a full list of all documents a sponsor is required to keep a record of at Appendix D of the Tier 2 and 5 Sponsor Guidance Version 09/14 para 15 at p 46.
3   The sponsor is required to report acts of non-compliance by the sponsored migrant or if they cease the sponsorship. All of these actions must be completed within a time frame set out in the UKBA's guidance. Tier 2 and 5 Sponsor Guidance Version 09/14, para 15 at pp 46-47.
4   To ensure that the sponsored migrant complies with immigration laws; to ensure that a migrant who is coming to work is legally entitled to do the job in question and has the appropriate registration and/or professional accreditation where this is legally required. Tier 2 and 5 Sponsor Guidance Version 09/14, para 15 at p 48.

5   Co-operating with any visits by UKBA staff, carrying out the requirements of any action plans
    set and compl ying with established good practice. Tier 2 and 5 Sponsor Guidance Version 0
    9/14, para 15 at p 48.
6   Tier 2 and 5 Sponsor Guidance Version 0 9/14, para 15 at pp 49–50.
7   Tier 2 and 5 Sponsor Guidance Version 09/14, paras 17.8-17.20 at pp 53–54.

NON-PBS CATEGORIES

10.101 Many of the categories in this part of the chapter have now either
become redundant and have been moved to Appendix F, the archive Appendix,
or they have retained the possibility of indefinite leave to remain. Some,
however, still survive as separate non-PBS employment categories and we deal
with them below. In other cases they have been absorbed into the PBS and have
been referred to already under Tier 2 or 5. Readers needing to know the
provisions of redundant categories should go to Appendix F and refer to the
7th edition of this book.

DEFUNCT CATEGORIES

10.102 With the introduction of the PBS in 2008, the following categories
were replaced by the points based system.[1] Applications for leave to enter or
remain as businessman, self-employed person, investor, writer, composer,
artists, innovators, investor,[2] highly skilled migrants,[3] international graduates,
and participants on the Fresh Talent in Scotland Scheme.

1   A full consideration of these former categories can be found in the 7th Edition of this work.
2   The relevant rules for all these categories were deleted on 30 June 2008 by para 17 of
    the Statement of Changes HC 607. The rules as they existed at that date are still contained at
    Annex F of the current Immigration Rules.
3   Under the previously mentioned UKBA HSMP Forum Ltd judicial review policy document (see
    10.21 fn 5 above), an HSMP migrant granted leave before 7 November 2006, can apply for
    an extension of leave on the same basis as previously, in order that he or she can qualify for
    settlement. Applicants who were previously refused an extension of leave because of the
    change in the Immigration Rules on 5 December 2006 can require the UKBA to reconsider that
    decision in line with the rules that existed before the change. Whilst a migrant who had
    previously been granted leave under HSMP and had switched to a new category after
    7 November 2006 can apply to either become a Tier 1 (General) migrant or, if they would have
    qualified under the pre-7 November 2006 Immigration Rules, an HSMP migrant; and thus
    they can qualify for settlement.

10.103 Further deletions came later in 2008 in the statement of changes HC
1113, laid on 4 November 2008. They affected: Overseas Qualified Nurses
and Midwives; Au pairs; Working Holidaymakers; Children of Working
Holidaymakers; Representatives of overseas newspapers etc; Ministers of
Religion; Operational Ground Staff of overseas-owned airlines; Exchange
Teachers and Language Assistants; Private Servants in Diplomatic Households;
Overseas Government Employees; Non-pastoral Religious Workers/visiting
Religious Worker; and Retired Persons of Independent Means.

The following provisions, which existed as concessions outside the Immigration Rules, were also deleted:

* British Universities North America Club (BUNAC);
* Gap Year Entrants;

- Japan: Youth Exchange Scheme;
- Research Assistants to Members of Parliament (under the Points Based System, these will be able to come in either under the Youth Mobility Scheme – if otherwise eligible – or as students provided at least 50% of their time in the UK is taken up by study);
- General Agreement on Trade in Services concession;
- International Association for the Exchange of Students of Technical Experience;
- International Fire Fighter Fellowship Programme;
- EU Leonardo da Vinci Programme;
- Rudolf Steiner;
- Medical Training Initiative;
- China Graduate Work Experience Programme;
- Voluntary workers;
- Named Researchers;
- Jewish Agency Employees.

Transitional arrangements were made. Any application made in these categories before this Statement of Changes came into operation on 27 November 2008 were to be considered under the Rules in force on 26 November 2008.

- Migrants who were currently in the UK as retired persons of independent means would be able to remain in that route and apply for extensions of stay or settlement as appropriate.
- Migrants in some of these categories were subsumed in Tier 2 of the PBS (eg Ministers of Religion and Working Holidaymakers. Representatives of overseas media later became merged with sole representatives of an overseas business and still exists as a non-PBS category (see below).
- In some cases Migrants in the concessionary list have since become part of the tier 2 (Temporary worker) category or are able to enter as visitors.
- Migrants with leave in any of the other categories listed above would be able to stay in the UK until their leave expired, provided they continued to meet the conditions under which it was granted. After that, unless they qualified for settlement, they would need to apply for further leave either under the Points Based System or in another category.
- Some migrants with leave in the categories listed above could at that time apply for settlement (Private Servants in Diplomatic Households, Overseas Government Employees, and Rudolf Steiner). So people with valid leave in these categories would be allowed to apply for an extension before 27 November 2008.
- Successful applicants under these transitional arrangements would be granted a period of leave to take them up to the threshold for being eligible to apply for settlement. They would then have to satisfy the settlement requirements in place at that time.

It is more likely than not that the passage of time will have made the transitional measures well past their sell-by-date, except, possibly, those for retired persons of independent means. But other solutions for their migration to the UK have been found.

10.104 Under the statement of changes (HC 1888) which took effect on 14 June 2012 the following redundant provisions were deleted from the Rules and were added to the archive of historical Immigration Rules in Appendix F:

- Work permit employment and Multiple Entry work permit employment – Work permits and Multiple Entry work permits ceased to be issued to non-EEA nationals following the introduction of Tier 2 on 27 November 2008. The existing settlement provisions were, however, being maintained for those workers who currently had leave as work permit holders.
- Extension provisions in the category for Overseas Qualified Nurses and Midwives. This category closed to new applicants on 27 November 2008 and permitted a total maximum stay of 18 months. By 2012 there would be no remaining applicants who could qualify for extensions.
- The Seasonal Agricultural Workers Scheme (SAWS) – Since 1 January 2007, SAWS work cards were only issued to Bulgarian and Romanian nationals who, as European Union nationals, are now outside the scope of the PBS Rules.

Fully operational categories

Representatives of overseas businesses

10.105 This category now merges two previously separate categories;[1] (i) sole representatives of overseas firms and (ii) employees of overseas newspapers, news agencies or broadcasting organisations. The sole rep category allows a senior employee of an overseas business which has no branch, subsidiary or other representative in the UK with full authority to take operational decisions on behalf of the overseas business for the purpose of representing it in the UK by establishing and operating a registered branch or wholly owned subsidiary which will be concerned with same type of business activity as the overseas business. He or she must be working full time and should not be a majority shareholder in that overseas business. The foreign journalist category enables an employee of an overseas newspaper, news agency or broadcasting organisation to be posted to the UK on a long-term assignment as a representative of their overseas employer, working full time and having suitable qualifications and an appropriate knowledge of the English language, as set out in the rules.

[1] HC 395, para 144.

10.106 There must be an operating overseas business in existence, which must remain centred abroad. Moreover, the application will fail if an overseas business is a one-person business and there will be no one left to run it when the applicant arrives in the UK. The overseas business needs to be an active trading concern overseas, distinct from its proposed activities in the UK[1] and a business which has been trading for less than 12 months will be required to justify the need to establish an overseas presence in the UK. But the fact that the UK branch outgrows its parent, does not mean that the application ceases to be valid.[2]

[1] *Lokko v Secretary of State for the Home Department* [1990] Imm AR 539, QBD affirming the IAT decision at [1990] Imm AR 111.

[2] IDI (Feb 07), Employment, Ch 5, Annex J, para 1.

10.107 The position of sole representatives who are owners of the overseas business, either as shareholders or partners, has in the past caused difficulties. In *Lokko*[1] the Tribunal said that in principle there was nothing wrong with a majority shareholder or director becoming an overseas representative. However, majority shareholders are now expressly barred from qualifying as sole representatives under the current Immigration Rules.[2] The Modernised Guidance merely states 'You must refuse an application when an applicant's shareholding is over 50%.[3] It seems that the older view in deleted IDI that where an applicant owns more than 30% of the overseas business, the application should attract detailed scrutiny, is no longer applicable.[4] Although sole representatives must have been recruited and taken on as employees outside the UK,[5] there is no requirement that they should have to have been employed by the overseas company for any minimum period. If the overseas business already has representation in the UK, the application will need to be sponsored under Tier 2 rather than under this category of the rules.

[1] *Lokko v Secretary of State for the Home Department* [1990] Imm AR 111, IAT.
[2] HC 395, as amended, para 144(iii)(c)
[3] Modernised Guidance Representatives of overseas businesses- version 12.0, Valid from 27 January 2014, p 15
[4] See discontinued IDI (Feb 07), Employment, Ch 5, Annex J, para 2.2.
[5] HC 395, para 144(i); Baydur (5442); Kongar (5501); Hope (832).

10.108 Leave will be granted for two years, if the person was granted leave on or after 1 October 2009, or three years, if last leave granted before 1 October 2009,[1] After five years' continuous leave in this capacity the applicant will qualify for indefinite leave to remain if he or she has met the sole representative requirements throughout the five-year period and is still needed for the employment in question.[2]

[1] HC 395, as paras 145 and 148.
[2] HC 395, para 150.

Domestic workers in private households

10.109 This category has not so far been merged into the points-based system. There are two brands; (i) domestic servants who can get repeated 12 month leaves and can proceed to settlement and (ii) those who only get 6 months without further leave. This category of leave was preceded by a concession outside the rules until 18 September 2002.[1] Under the former concession, domestic workers were permitted entry with their employer provided they had worked for that employer for 12 months before arrival and would be undertaking specific work that exceeded the requirements set out in the International Standard Classification of Occupations.[2] Between 23 July 1998 and 23 October 1999, the Home Office operated a regularisation scheme for overstaying domestic workers, who had an initial entry clearance as a domestic worker and had been forced to leave their original employer due to abuse or exploitation. Subsequently, the Home Office confirmed that it would consider any application not made within the regularisation scheme deadline on a case-by-case basis. They also indicated that a domestic worker who was granted an initial 12 months' leave under the regularisation programme and who subsequently applied for indefinite leave to remain, could count his or her continuous domestic employment prior to the date of regularisation as part of the four-year qualifying period for settlement then in operation.[3] Furthermore, within the regularisation process, where the worker had fled from a domestic household as a result of abuse or exploitation and had gone into other domestic work, but not in a private household, that other work could count towards the four years needed for indefinite leave, but only where the initial regularisation was on that basis.[4] Domestic workers may include cleaners, chauffeurs, gardeners, cooks, those carrying out personal care for their employers or a member of their family, and nannies if they are providing a personal service relating to the running of the employer's household.[4]

[1] For a potted history of the early scheme and the changes made to it in 1998 and 2001, see deleted IDI (Dec 06), Employment, Ch 5, s 12, para 1.1.
[2] Deleted IDI (Dec 06), Employment, Ch 5, s 12, Annex BB. For further details, see 5th edition at 10.14.
[3] The qualification period for settlement is now five, not four years: HC 395, as amended, para 159G.
[4] IDI (Dec 02), Employment, Ch 5, s 12, Annex BB.

10.110 The position is now regulated HC 395, paras 159A–159H. The applicant hast to be aged between 18 and 65 and must have worked for the employer for one year or more immediately prior to the application for entry clearance,[1] either under the same roof as the employer or in a household that the employer uses on a regular basis and where there is evidence that there is a connection between the employer and the domestic worker.[2] HC 395 para 159A now provides a set of safeguards to ensure that the servant has not previously been exploited. There needs to be:

(a)   a written letter from the employer confirming that the domestic worker has been employed by them in that capacity for the twelve months immediately prior to the date of application; and
(b)   one of the following documents covering the same period of employment must be produced by the employer:
        (i)   pay slips or bank statements showing payment of salary;
        (ii)   confirmation of tax paid;
        (iii)   confirmation of health insurance paid;
        (iv)   contract of employment;
        (v)   work visa, residence permit or equivalent passport endorsement for the country in which the domestic worker has been employed by that employer; or
        (vi)   visas or equivalent passport endorsement to confirm that the domestic worker has travelled with the employer.

Other conditions of leave include an intention to work for the employer whilst the employer is in the United Kingdom; and to leave the UK at the end of six months in the UK. She or he and the employer must have agreed in writing terms and conditions of employment in the UK, including specifically that the applicant will be paid in accordance with the National Minimum Wage Act 1998 and any Regulations made under it., and provides evidence of this in the form set out in Appendix 7 with the entry clearance application.[1] If successful leave to enter for that purpose may be given for a period not exceeding

6 months.[2] An extension of stay as a domestic worker in a private household may be granted for a period of six months less the period already spent in the UK.[3]

1   HC 395 para 159A.
2   HC 395 paras 159B.
3   HC 395 para 159E.

10.111 Applicants who last entered the United Kingdom with a valid entry clearance as a domestic worker in a private household under Rules in place before 6 April 2012; and has continued to be employed for the duration of leave granted as a domestic worker in a private household and continues to be required for this employment under the same roof as the employer or in the same household that the employer has lived in and where evidence of this in the form of written terms and conditions of employment in the UK as set out in Appendix 7 are eligible for an extension of stay for a period not exceeding 12 months at a time provided the Secretary of State is satisfied that each of the requirements of paragraph 159EA are met. He or she is the eligible for indefinite leave to remain:

- if he or she has spent a continuous period of five years lawfully in the United Kingdom employed in this capacity;
- continues to be required for employment as a domestic worker in a private household as certified by the current employer;
- has demonstrated sufficient knowledge of the English language and sufficient knowledge about life in the United Kingdom, in accordance with Appendix KoLL; and
- has satisfied the other requirements in para 159EB.

Persons with UK ancestry

10.112 This category entitles a Commonwealth citizen, one of whose grand-parents was born in the UK, to apply for leave with a view to settlement.[1] Upon proof that one of his or her grandparents was born in the UK,[2] a Common-wealth citizen aged 17 or over who wishes to seek or take employment in the UK and can satisfy the maintenance and accommodation requirements will be granted an entry clearance for that purpose. An applicant may be required to demonstrate that they are both willing and able to seek employment. To prove UK ancestry, it will usually be necessary to obtain a certified copy of the grandparent's birth certificate and all necessary marriage and birth certificates to show the connection.[3] An adoptive relationship qualifies under the rule. The word 'grandparents' in HC 395, para 186 refers to both maternal and paternal grandparents. The Immigration Rules expressly provide that the 'parent' of an illegitimate child is not just the mother but includes the father where he is proved to be the father, reversing the practice that resulted from Tribunal and Court of Appeal authority to the contrary.[4] Under previous UKBA guidance, an adoptive relationship also qualified under the rule.[5] Earlier rules provided for immediate settlement on arrival, but now a continuous period of five years in the UK in this capacity is required.[6] Continuous employment is not required, but a Commonwealth citizen with a poor or non-existent employment record is likely to be refused indefinite leave in the absence of a good reason.

1   HC 395, as amended, paras 186–193. The requirement of Commonwealth citizenship only
    needs to be satisfied as of the date of application under the UK ancestry category;
    compare Commonwealth citizens claiming the right of abode in the UK: see CHAPTER 2 above.
2   Including the Channel Islands and the Isle of Man, or a grandparent who was born before
    31 March 1922 in what is now the Republic of Ireland.
3   The word 'usually' permits an entry clearance officer to accept alternate evidence of the
    grandparent's birth in the UK, such as a baptismal certificate or other official records.
4   *C (an infant) v Entry Clearance Officer, Hong Kong* [1976] Imm AR 165, IAT; *R v Secretary
    of State for the Home Department, ex p Crew* [1982] Imm AR 94, CA.
5   IDI (Dec 04), Ch 5, s 8, para 3.3.
6   HC 395, as amended, para 192.

WORK PERMITS

10.113 The work permit scheme has been replaced by Tier 2 (General) and
Tier 2 (Intra-Company Transfers). This means that from 27 November 2008,
no further applications for work permits have been accepted.[1] The original
version of the rules for Tier 2 (General) and Tier 2 (Intra-Company Transfers)
include transitional arrangements to minimise their impact on existing work
permit holders. Provided they are working for the same employer, their job
meets the UKBA skill level requirements and their employer has obtained a
sponsor's licence, these workers will be able to extend their stay in the UK for
up to a total of five years without having to meet the specific Tier 2 criteria for
qualifications, prospective earnings, English language and knowledge of life in
the UK.

1   HC 395, as amended, paras 128–135.

10.114 It should be noted that as a transitional arrangement, Work Permit
Holders who are already in the UK under the Immigration Rules in place
before 6 April 2011 will be able to apply to extend their stay without being
subject to the annual limit, the new graduate level job requirement, the new
salary threshold, or the new English language level.[1]

Once a Work Permit Holder has reached the five-year period, the requirements
needed to qualify contained in HC 395, paragraph 134, were amended by
rule changes taking effect in April and October 2011 and the issue of absences
from the UK has been clarified by a determination of the UT.

- As with Tier 2 (General) Migrants, Work Permit Holders applying for
  indefinite leave to remain will need to provide confirmation by a
  certificate from their employer that they continue to earn at least the UK
  appropriate rate for the job they are doing, as stated in the codes of
  practice for Tier 2 sponsors published by the UKBA.[2]
- They will need to have sufficient knowledge of the English language and
  sufficient knowledge about life in the UK, in accordance with
  para 33BA of the rules, unless they are either under 18 or over 65.[3] For
  transitional arrangements with regards to the requirement to pass the
  Life in the UK Test for Work Permit Holders and others applying for
  indefinite leave to remain, see **10.85**, above.

- A new criminality threshold was introduced requiring applicants applying for indefinite leave to remain to be clear of unspent convictions.[4]
- In the cases of the need to have spent 'a continuous period of 5 years lawfully in the UK',[5] unlike the 'long residence rule' at paras 276A–D, no definition of this requirement is given in HC 395, and there is currently no guidance to be had from the IDIs. However, in *BD Nigeria*[6] it was held that 'a continuous period' must be construed sensibly, so as to allow periods of absence abroad. Where, as in the case of BD, such absence has been required by the appellant's employer in the course of his work permit employment, it need not impair the strength of connexion to the UK which is normally established by five years' residence. The Upper Tribunal held that the rule clearly imports a discretion – a discretion which can be exercised by the Tribunal – as to how much absence can be disregarded in the calculation of a 'continuous period' of five years. Of relevance will be the reason for the absence, and the strength of the person's ties to the UK, as shown in other ways. In the instant case, the appellant's absences had been required of him by his employer, a British company, and he had at all times retained his base in the UK. He was domiciled here for tax purposes, and would seem to have established a domicile of choice for other purposes.

[1] See HC 395, para 33BA(b). This applies whether they are extending with the same employer or changing employers.

[2] HC 395, para 134(iv), as substituted by HC 863. By para 134(v) inserted by HC 1511, they must also produce specified documents set out in the application form.

[3] HC 395, para 134(vi), as substituted by HC 863. Para 33BA was inserted by HC 863.

[4] HC 395, para 134(vii), as substituted by HC 1511.

[5] Of the time spent the most recent period must have been spent with leave as a Work Permit Holder (under paragraphs 128–133 of HC 395), and the remainder in any combination of leave as a Work Permit Holder or leave as a Highly Skilled Migrant (under paragraphs 135A–135F of the Rules) or leave as a self-employed lawyer (under the concession that appeared in Chapter 6, Section 1, Annex D of the Immigration Directorate Instructions), or leave as a writer, composer or artist (under paragraphs 232–237 of the Rules).

[6] *BD (work permit – 'continuous period') Nigeria* [2010] UKUT 418 (IAC).

10.115 There is a further concession granting leave to enter to crew members of ships, aircraft, hovercraft, hydrofoils or international train services to enable them to join their vessel, receive hospital treatment, aid repatriation, or transfer to another vessel.[1] If the crew members concerned are not eligible for entry without leave, the period of leave given will only be sufficient for the specific purpose and there is a presumption against extension,[2] unless the crew member is married to a person present and settled in the UK and meets the requirements for an extension of stay as a spouse under the Immigration Rules.[3]

[1] IDI (Oct 03), Ch 16, s 1 (seamen); IDI (Sep 04), Ch 16, s 2 (aircrews).

[2] IDI (Oct 03), Ch 16, s 1 (seamen); IDI (Sep 04), Ch 16, s 2 (aircrews).

[3] HC 395, as amended, para 324.

RETIRED PERSONS OF INDEPENDENT MEANS

10.116 The category of retired persons of independent means was deleted from the Immigration Rules by HC 1113 in November 2008. However, there may still be those who obtained leave prior to the abolition of this category, who have not yet obtained settlement. So the category remains open for extensions of stay under HC 395 for someone who can meet the requirements of paragraph 266; namely, an income of not less than £25,000 per annum under his or her control and disposable in the UK, adequate maintenance and accommodation and can demonstrate a close connection to the UK. A person in this category can qualify for indefinite leave to remain after a continuous period of five years in the UK under this capacity, provided they have met the requirements of paragraph 266 throughout the five-year period and do not have one or more unspent convictions.

Chapter 11

FAMILIES, PARTNERS AND CHILDREN

INTRODUCTION

11.1 This chapter examines how legislation, the Immigration Rules and current concessions and policies apply to families, partners and children. It will deal with immigration law related to marriage and civil partnership, engagement, unmarried partners and same-sex relationships, family reunion, adoption, surrogacy and unaccompanied (or separated) children. It will also consider the interaction between family and immigration law and the relevant, applicable family law provisions on domicile and habitual residence, the validity of marriage, on overseas divorce, adoption and international surrogacy.

There have been a number of changes in the relevant law and practice since the last edition and its supplement. The most significant of these changes has been the change to the rules for family entry and stay, in effect from 9 July 2012 and set out in Appendices FM and FM-SE to the Rules. Transitional arrangements in HC 395, Para A280 preserve the pre-9 July 2012 Rules for many of the applicants granted entry clearance or limited leave to enter or remain under Part 8 before 9 July 2012 and to those who made Part 8 applications before that date and who are awaiting decisions under the old rules or who, having been granted limited leave to enter/remain, have not yet applied for indefinite leave to remain. In consequence this chapter contains commentary on both the old and the new family rules.

The chapter begins with a consideration of the family law provisions which have application to or are relevant for the Immigration Rules. There have also been a number of important changes in these family law arrangements – and the Immigration Act 2014 enacts additional changes to the marriage and civil partnership procedures which are expected to commence in March 2015.

CHANGES CONCERNING CHILDREN

11.2 Over the past years, there have been a number of important developments giving effect to the UK's obligations to children. It can be important in immigration litigation to know the history of these changes. Thus on 22 September 2008, just prior to the UK government's appearance before the UN Committee on the Rights of the Child, the UK government announced that it would lift the immigration and children in custody reservations to the UN Convention on the Rights of the Child – thus increasing the value of the Convention as an aid to interpretation in children's cases.[1] Section 21 of the UK Borders Act 2007 (which came into force on 6 January 2009) introduced a statutory Code of Practice to ensure that UKBA take appropriate steps to ensure that while children are in the UK they are safe from harm.[2] The section 21 Code of Practice was replaced from 2 November 2009.[3] During the passage of the Children and Young Persons Act 2008, the House of Lords voted in favour of the UKBA being subject to a duty equivalent to that in section 11 of the Children Act 2004 and section 55 of the BCIA 2009 (replacing section 21 of the 2007 Act from 2 November 2009) giving effect to this new duty. Minister of State Phil Woolas MP stated 'It is right that the UK Border Agency is judged by the same standards as every other authority that deals with children'.[4] *Every Child Matters: Change For Children*, now provides the statutory guidance to the UK Border Agency on making arrangements to safeguard and promote the welfare of children.[5] The guidance is issued under section 55 of the BCIA 2009 and, from 2 November 2009, any person exercising immigration, asylum, nationality and customs functions must have regard to this guidance given to them for the purpose by the Secretary of State.[6] As the *Every Child Matters* statement makes clear, 'This means they must take this guidance into account and, if they decide to depart from it, have clear reasons for doing so'.[7] There have been a number of important cases dealing with children's interests and welfare as these issues arise in immigration decision-making.

[1] The reservations were to Arts 22 and 37 of UNCRC. See Press Release Department of Children, Schools and Families, 22 September 2008 at www.dcsf.gov.uk. The reservation was lifted in November 2008 (www2.ohchr.org/emglish/bodies/ratification/docs/UK2008-Eng.pdf). The Children's Convention has clear application in immigration cases. UNICEF summarised: 'The four core principles of the Convention are non-discrimination; devotion to the best interests of the child; the right to life, survival and development; and respect for the views of the child. Every right spelled out in the Convention is inherent to the human dignity and harmonious development of every child' (www.unicef.org/crc/).

[2] Section 21(1) stated: 'The Secretary of State shall issue a code of practice designed to ensure that in exercising functions in the United Kingdom the Border and Immigration Agency takes appropriate steps to ensure that while children are in the United Kingdom they are safe from harm.' Under s 21(2) the Agency shall have regard to the code in the exercise of its functions, and take appropriate steps to ensure that persons with whom it makes arrangements for the provision of services have regard to the code. Under s 21(5) the Agency means immigration officers and other officials of the Secretary of State, and the Secretary of State, in respect of functions relating to immigration, asylum or nationality.

3   The UK Borders Act 2007 (Code of Practice on Children) Order 2008, SI 2008/3158, UK
    Borders Act 2007 (Commencement No 5) Order 2008, SI 2008/3136, art 2(a). For a helpful
    critique of the section 21 Code, see the ILPA Submission to Joint Committee on Human
    Rights: Inquiry on Children's Rights, February 2009 and the UKBA Consultation on the Code
    (April 2008).
4   Hansard, Public Bill Committee, 6th Sitting, 16 June 2009, col 192. See also: UK Border
    Agency commits to keep children safe from harm, UK Border Agency www.ukba.homeoffic
    e.gov.uk/sitecontent/keepingchildrensafefromharm, *Press Release, 6 January 2009*.
5   *Every Child Matters: Change for Children*: Statutory guidance to the UK Border Agency on
    making arrangements to safeguard and promote the welfare of children, Issued under
    section 55 of the Borders, Citizenship and Immigration Act 2009, November 2009. See: ILPA
    response to the draft section 55 guidance, 31 July 2009 – on the ILPA website www.ilpa.or
    g.uk/.
6   Section 55 obliges those exercising immigration functions to safeguard and promote the
    welfare of children This obligation is defined in the guidance to s 11 of the 2004 Act (s 28 in
    Wales) and in Working Together to Safeguard Children as: (i) protecting children from
    maltreatment; preventing impairment of children's health or development (where health
    means 'physical or mental health' and development means 'physical, intellectual, emotional,
    social or behavioural development'); (ii) ensuring that children are growing up in circum-
    stances consistent with the provision of safe and effective care; and (iii) undertaking that role
    so as to enable those children to have optimum life chances and to enter adulthood
    successfully. In the UKBA guidance *Every Child Matters* and in the Hansard debates on
    section 55, it is made clear that UKBA's safeguarding duty to children 'is to mirror as closely
    as possible the effect of Section 11 of the Children Act 2004': Lord West of Spithead, Hansard,
    HL Report 4 March 2009, cols 832–4 (HL Committee stage of the Borders Citizenship and
    Immigration Bill).
7   *Every Child Matters: Change For Children*, para 6, p 5.

11.3 It will be necessary to cross-refer to other chapters in this book for
further information on how the law applies in certain specific family circumstances. For example, the law relating to family reunion for refugees is dealt
with in CHAPTER 12, the law concerning Article 8 family life claims is dealt with
in CHAPTER 7 and the law relating to family members of EEA nationals is
considered in CHAPTER 6 ff.

FAMILY AND IMMIGRATION LITIGATION – THE COMMON AND DIVERGING ISSUES

11.4 Before considering the Immigration Rules concerning families, partners
and children, it is useful to mention the significant interplay between family
and immigration legislative arrangements and case loads. Questions which
arise in an immigration context, over the admission, for example, of a child
who has been adopted overseas, could equally arise in a family law context.
Family and immigration law both concern State and parental decisions
concerning children's travel and the international movements of families.
Immigration and nationality law confer certain entitlements on the spouse and
children of British citizens/residents, and immigration lawyers therefore need a
working knowledge of private international law on the validity of marriage,
adoption and divorce so as to ascertain whether parties are lawful spouse or
the 'parents' of their children.

The UK population includes a core of foreign-born residents[1] who have
contributed to significant changes in the social and religious life of the UK and
to profound changes in family life in recent decades. These changes and the
great variety of forms taken by the family in a multicultural and pluralistic
Britain, have been eloquently sketched out in the Court of Appeal in *Singh v*

Entry Clearance Officer, New Delhi by Munby J, who stressed the need for the law in the combined context of family, human rights and immigration to adapt itself to these new realities.[2] Caseloads in the family courts reflect both this social diversity and the general increase in family mobility. Parents or children in family cases may be British or foreign nationals, permanent or temporary residents, overstayers, claimants for asylum or the victims of trafficking or of domestic violence in their home countries. In certain cases the Home Office, immigration appellate authorities and family courts are simultaneously engaged with the same family, determining questions associated with parental/child contact, care and protection or residence.[3]

The Upper Tribunal and Court of Appeal have given guidance on managing such intersecting cases where a parent is subject to removal or deportation.[4] The guidance can also have relevance in other immigration appeals where family proceedings are material to the immigration or human rights decision.

The guidance approved by the Tribunal and Court is that where appellants appeal to the Tribunal against a removal or deportation decision and there are outstanding family proceedings relating to their children, the judge of the Immigration and Asylum Chamber should first consider the following questions:

(1)   Is the outcome of the contemplated family proceedings likely to be material to the immigration decision?

(2)   Are there compelling public interest reasons to exclude the claimant from the United Kingdom irrespective of the outcome of the family proceedings or the best interest of the child?

(3)   In the case of contact proceedings initiated by an appellant in an immigration appeal, is there any reason to believe that the family proceedings have been instituted to delay or frustrate removal and not to promote the child's welfare?

In addressing the above questions, the judge will normally also want to consider:

(1)   the degree of the claimant's previous interest in and contact with the child;

(2)   the timing of contact proceedings and the commitment with which they have been progressed;

(3)   when a decision is likely to be reached; and

(4)   what materials (if any) are already available or can be made available to identify pointers to where the child's welfare lies.

Having considered these matters the judge will then have to decide:

(1)   Does the claimant have at least an Article 8 right to remain until the conclusion of the family proceedings?

(2)   If so, should the appeal be allowed to a limited extent and a discretionary leave be directed as per the decision on *MS (Ivory Coast)*?[5]

(3)   Alternatively, is it more appropriate for a short period of an adjournment to be granted to enable the core decision to be made in the family proceedings?

(4)   Is it likely that the family court would be assisted by a view on the
        present state of knowledge of whether the appellant would be allowed
        to remain in the event that the outcome of the family proceedings is the
        maintenance of family contact between him or her and a child resident
        here?

The guidance cases make clear that the core question for the Tribunal is
whether an appellant could succeed in his/her family proceedings – not as the
Home Office often asks whether he/she will succeed. The guidance allows for
the family proceedings to take precedence where there is a real contest between
estranged parents and the family court could grant a child arrangement order[6]
identifying with whom and when a child is to live, spend time or have contact
with any person, pronounce on the validity of a divorce or marriage or the
return and relocation of children – issues which are material to the immigration decision.[7]

[1]   See House of Commons Library, Oliver Hawkins, Migration Statistics, 17 June 2014,
        SN/SG/6077.
[2]   See per Munby J in *Singh v Entry Clearance Officer, New Delhi* [2004] EWCA Civ 1075,
        [2004] INLR 515 at paras 61–65, and note his emphasis at para 67 on the secularity and even
        handedness of the law: 'the starting point of the law is a tolerant indulgence to cultural and
        religious diversity and an essentially agnostic view of religious beliefs. A secular judge must be
        wary of straying across the well-recognised divide between church and state.'
[3]   See *Re S (children) (abduction: asylum appeal)* [2002] EWCA Civ 843, [2002] 1 WLR 2548,
        [2002] 2 FCR 642.
[4]   The guidance is given by Lord Justice McFarlane and Mr Justice Blake in *RS (immigration and
        family court proceedings) India* [2012] UKUT 218 (IAC) (04 July 2012); *Nimako-Boateng
        (residence orders – Anton considered)* [2012] UKUT 00216 (IAC) The guidance was endorsed
        by the Court of Appeal in *Mohan v Secretary of State for the Home Department* [2012] EWCA
        Civ 1363, [2013] 1 WLR 922.
[5]   In *MS Ivory Coast* [2007] EWCA Civ 133 the Court held concerning a mother subject to
        removal who had an outstanding family application for contact with her children that she was
        entitled to have determined whether removal from the United Kingdom with an outstanding
        contact application would breach s 6 of the Human Rights Act 1998. That question was
        capable of resolution one way or the other. The Court held: 'What was not appropriate was
        to leave her in this country in limbo with temporary admission and the promise not to remove
        her until her contact application has been concluded. Temporary admission is, as we have
        explained, a status given to someone liable to be detained pending removal. If the appellant
        had a valid human rights claim she is not liable to be detained pending removal. And if she has
        not, she ought to be removed. If she is entitled to discretionary leave to remain she ought to
        have it for the period the Secretary of State thinks appropriate, together with the advantages
        that it conveys; and if not she ought not to.'
[6]   The Children and Families Act 2014, amended s 8 of the Children Act 1989, changing
        terminology and procedure and replacing residence and contact orders with child arrangement
        orders. A child arrangement order means an order regulating arrangements relating to any of
        the following:
        (a)   With whom a child is to live, spend time or otherwise have contact;
        (b)   When a child is to live, spend time or otherwise have contact with any person.
        These provisions also came into force on 22 April 2014. The Child Arrangements Programme
        is contained in Family Procedure Rules 2010, SI 2010/2955, Practice Direction 12(B).
[7]   See on application of the guidance for intersecting family and immigration proceedings:
        Mohammed (Family Court proceedings-outcome) [2014] UKUT 419 (IAC) – the mere
        possibility of a child contact application being made (or pursued) is not a relevant criterion in
        the case of an immigration appeal when deciding whether to adjourn an appeal or to direct a
        grant of discretionary leave in order for such proceedings to be pursued – and on the
        application of this guidance – see the unreported Upper Tribunal determination
        DA/01526/2013, dated 13 January 2014 tribunalsdecisions.service.gov.uk/utiac/da
        -01526-2013

11.5 There are reported cases dealing with intersecting family and immigration issues.[1] Family case practice exemplifies a wide variety of family situations where immigration issues are relevant. Such issues can arise from status questions. If the parties in family litigation have different nationalities, it can be important to consider the nationality or potential nationalities of their children, in order to facilitate family contact in a home country or to guard against the child's abduction.[2] Family litigation can concern children's contacts with parents in or outside the UK, their residence, care or protection or their removal or retention by parents in the UK or may involve a claim for recognition of a foreign adoption. Manifestly such decisions are relevant to whether spouse, parents and children qualify for entry or leave to remain under the Immigration Rules.[3]

Family courts are also on occasions directly involved in immigration processes – for example confirming for an entry clearance officer the necessity for a party in litigation to be permitted entry to participate in family proceedings. Additionally family courts quite often communicate their findings to the Home Office where this is relevant to the entry or stay of a party. Thus family courts may be concerned with difficult financial and child arrangement issues which arise when wives and mothers are taken back to their home countries and 'stranded' there by their British spouse (their passports withheld or their immigration leave deliberately allowed to expire).[4] As Mr Justice Peter Jackson noted of such 'stranded partner' cases:

'Where one party to a failing marriage has secure immigration status and the other does not, the opportunity arises for the former to exploit the latter's weakness by taking advantage of immigration controls.' Where the British partner has contrived to separate mother and child, the Courts have ruled that this 'is a wholesale breach of their right to respect for their family life under Article 8 of the European Convention on Human Rights'

In *ZM* Peter Jackson J held and communicated to the Home Office to enable it to reconsider its refusal of an entry visa – 'the only way in which this breach can be remedied is by the mother regaining the ability to enter this country'.[5]

---

[1] See *J (a minor) (adoption: non-patrial)*, *Re* [1998] 1 FLR 225, CA, *Re S (children) (abduction: asylum appeal)* [2002] EWCA Civ 843, [2002] 1 WLR 2548, [2002] 2 FCR 642, *Re A (children) (care proceedings: asylum seekers)* [2003] EWHC 1086 (Fam), [2003] 2 FLR 921, [2003] Fam Law 806, *G (children) (Adoption proceedings)*, *Re* [2014] EWHC 2605 (Fam).

[2] Practitioners advising on nationality issues need to consider whether the acquisition of British nationality by a child can mean that the child's existing citizenship is lost or jeopardised because the home country does not allow dual nationality.

[3] *Re ND (Children) (Recognition of foreign adoption orders)* [2008] EWHC 403 (Fam), [2008] 1 FLR 1475, [2008] Fam Law 501, *G (children) (Adoption proceedings)*, *Re* [2014] EWHC 2605 (Fam).

[4] *S (A Child)*, *Re (Guidance in cases of stranded spouses)* [2010] EWHC 1669 (Fam), [2011] 1 FLR 305, [2010] Fam Law 1074. Mrs Justice Hogg noted at [60]:

'Sadly, this is not the first case where I have encountered allegations of deliberate separation of child and mother by the paternal family. I know that other judges of this division have encountered similar cases and made similar findings as I have done in this judgment. To separate a mother and child in this way is emotionally harmful to the child and remains so for so long as the child is deprived of the mother. It is something which is abhorrent and unfeeling towards a child and mother. It is selfish and cruel by those who do it.'
See also *H (A Child)* [2014] EWHC 1254 (Fam). In *ZM v AM* [2014] EWHC 2110 (Fam) the Court notes of the husband's regarding the 'stranding' – '43 The father's failure to secure the mother's immigration status was a gross dereliction of his responsibility towards her and towards S. In his evidence, he claims that he was unaware of her precarious position, having left matters of that kind to his own father. He says that when she left the country in July 2011

833

he did not know what the position was. I found the father's evidence incredible and I reject it. He knew perfectly well that if the mother left, she could not return. The reason why the father and his family were so careless of the mother's position was because it suited them.'

5   *ZM v AM* [2014] EWHC 2110 (Fam).

11.6 Immigration and nationality issues also arise in care and wardship cases. Some of these cases involve children privately fostered in the UK in arrangements which have exposed them to risk and exploitation, including as domestic or sex workers.[1] Again the findings in family proceedings may be relevant to whether such children should be granted a term of residence as a trafficking victim.[2] Other care cases concern asylum seekers. Many such applicants have suffered severe trauma, affecting their parenting capacities. Their children too may have been traumatised, and may suffer severe disturbance and prove difficult to manage or to protect. Sometimes asylum claimants or failed asylum seekers participate in care or family proceedings and apply to assume parental responsibility and care for their children who might otherwise be fostered or adopted.[3] Additionally unaccompanied children and young people may be at particular risk of harm, or if they are young, single parents, may need assistance caring for their babies. Their babies may be the focus of local authority concern both in the UK, and in the home country if the young person is to be removed without the requisite parenting skills or protective supports. Local authorities may have protection concerns in particular cases if the Secretary of State seeks to remove unaccompanied children before they become 18. Social services departments are increasingly involved in age assessments, in the care or support of unaccompanied children and they have statutory responsibilities to such children.[4]

1   *West Sussex County Council v H* [2014] EWHC 2550 (Fam), *Barking & Dagenham London Borough Council v SS* [2014] EWHC 3338 (Fam). See Council of Europe, Reply from the Committee of Ministers, adopted at the 1017th meeting of the Ministers' Deputies (6 February 2008) Doc 11554, 3 April 2008, 'Child victims: stamping out all forms of violence, exploitation and abuse', Recommendation 1778 (2007).
2   See CHAPTER 13.
3   In *Moser v Austria (Application No 12643/02)* [2006] 3 FCR 107, ECtHR, the ECHR found that there had been a breach of Arts 6(1) and 8 where in private proceedings a child was removed from the care of her Serbian mother at birth, not because of any parental failings but because the mother could not provide suitable accommodation for the child because the mother's residence status in Austria was uncertain. The Court held that the authorities should have explored arrangements which would have allowed the mother and child to remain in close contact while any family proceedings were pending.
4   Children Act 1989, ss 17, 20, 22–22D, 23A–23E. See: *JS (Former unaccompanied child – durable solution) (Afghanistan)* [2013] UKUT 568 (IAC).

11.7 The intersection of family and immigration jurisdictions and the risk of conflicting outcomes in overlapping cases have persuaded family courts and the Tribunal of their need to share information in cases featured in both jurisdictions.[1] The arrangements for this information sharing are now set out in a Protocol issued by the President of the Family Division and the Senior President of Tribunals entitled 'Protocol on communications between judges of the Family Court and Immigration and Asylum Chambers of the First Tier Tribunal and Upper Tribunal'.[2] The protocols apply where an immigration appeal is pending before the Tribunal and the welfare of a child in the UK is likely to be affected by the decision in those proceedings and there are family proceedings in existence relating to that child.[3] The Protocol allows for judges in each jurisdiction to disclose information and documents about proceedings 'which may affect the outcome of the proceedings before them and to make better decisions'. This information may include – from a family court – interim or fact finding judgments, a care plan, guardian's report, the timetable of hearings and other specified documents and from the tribunal – a determination, Home Office decision letter, witness statements or skeleton arguments filed in immigration proceedings, case management directions or specified documentation.

These arrangements concern communications between family and immigration judges. The Family Procedure Rules also provide for the parties to seek disclosure of family court documents for use in immigration proceedings. Statements filed in Children Act proceedings are confidential to those proceedings[4] but if such statements and reports are relevant to immigration or asylum proceedings, the parties can apply to a court for an order permitting their disclosure to the Home Office and tribunal for those purposes.[5]

In addition there is also an arrangement allowing family courts or parties in family proceedings to obtain information direct from the Home Office concerning the immigration status of parents, carers or affected children. Exchanges of information between family courts and the Home Office are facilitated by a Protocol arrangement issued by the President of the Family Division. The protocol, *Communicating with the Home Office In Family Proceedings* (Re-issued March 2013) sets down the arrangements for information requests or orders directed to the Home Office in family proceedings. A family court request for immigration information is made on form EX660 to the Home Office Liaison Office.[6] Such protocol interventions can be very helpful in securing information on the entry or status of parties, on pending immigration applications or to seek Home Office co-operation in family cases where the immigration status of the child or carers are relevant factors.

1   See *Re S (children) (abduction: asylum appeal)* [2002] EWCA Civ 843, [2002] 1 WLR 2548, [2002] 2 FCR 642, per Thorpe J at para 40. In *BE (Care Proceedings) Jamaica* [2005] UKIAT 00098 (28 February 2005) Ouseley J held that 'the care and the immigration proceedings should be treated as concurrent and independent. Some of the considerations or evidence may overlap, but they are viewed from different perspectives. Each must proceed at its own timetable. If Care Orders override immigration decisions, then they can be invoked to prevent removal; and if not, not.' This guidance is now almost certainly displaced by that in *RS (immigration and family court proceedings) India* [2012] UKUT 218 (IAC); *Nimako-Boateng (residence orders – Anton considered)* [2012] UKUT 00216 (IAC) and *Mohan v Secretary of State for the Home Department* [2012] EWCA Civ 1363, [2013] 1 WLR 922.

2   www.judiciary.gov.uk/wp-content/uploads/2013/03/protocol-communications-between-famil y-court-and-immigration-asylum-tribunals.pdf

3   See the guidance given by Lord Justice McFarlane and Mr Justice Blake in *RS (immigration and family court proceedings) India* [2012] UKUT 218 (IAC) (04 July 2012; *Nimako-Boateng (residence orders – Anton considered)* [2012] UKUT 00216 (IAC). The guidance was endorsed by the Court of Appeal in *Mohan v Secretary of State for the Home Department* [2012] EWCA Civ 1363, [2013] 1 WLR 922.

4   Children Act 1989, s 97.

5   The rules concerning the communication of information relating to children's proceedings are set down in the Family Procedure Rules 2010, Part 12, Chapter 7 para 12.73 and Practice Direction 12G. See: *Re C (A Minor) (Care Proceedings: Disclosure)* [1997] Fam 76, [1997] 2 WLR 322, *sub nom Re EC (Disclosure of Material)* [1996] 2 FLR 725, CA; *Re N (Family Proceedings: Disclosure)* [2009] EWHC 1663 (Fam), [2009] 2 FLR 1152; *Lewisham London Borough Council v D (Disclosure of DNA Samples to Police)* [2010] EWHC 1238 (Fam), [2011] 1 FLR 895.

6   See: www.judiciary.gov.uk/wp-content/uploads/JCO/Documents/Guidance/Communicating-w ith-the-HO-in-family+proceedings-+Revised-amalgamated+guidance-March-2013+.pdf.

11.8 Not only do family and immigration jurisdictions frequently deal with the same families, they are also linked by their shared association with bilateral European and international instruments governing the international movement of children and the recognition of transnational adoptions, abductions and cross-jurisdictional family orders and contacts.[1] In the same way that states have sought to harmonise their immigration control arrangements, states have also made agreements for comity and mutual recognition and enforcement of family orders.[2] Examples include the Immigration Rules for adopted or adoptive children, which incorporate the Hague Convention protections for intercountry adoptions.[3] The arrangements for issuing passports to British children, and the Immigration Rules requiring appropriate parental or other consent for children's applications for entry clearance or for variation of leave, are framed to protect children and to prevent child abduction.[4] In order to achieve consistency with family and human rights provisions favouring contact between children and their parents, the Immigration Rules make provision for parents to enter or remain in the UK for the purpose of contact with their children and to continue an active role in the children's upbringing.[5]

---

[1] For example: The revised Brussels II (variously referred to as BIIR, Brussels IIA or Brussels II Bis). (Council Regulation (EC) No 2201/2003 of 27 November 2003 concerning jurisdiction and the recognition and enforcement of judgments in matrimonial matters and in matters of parental responsibility, repealing Regulation (EC) No 1347/2000) provides exclusive and separate rules of jurisdiction in relation to matrimonial proceedings (ie for divorce, annulment of marriage and separation but not directly for other issues such as for financial relief after divorce) and in respect of matters of parental responsibility for children and for a consequent scheme of recognition and enforcement of family orders. It applies to all EU States save Denmark. In addition the 1996 Hague Child Protection Convention came into force in the United Kingdom on 1 November 2012, following its ratification on 27 July 2012. It is directly effective pursuant to the European Communities Act 1972, s 2 and The European Communities (Definition of Treaties) (1996 Hague Convention on Protection of Children etc) Order 2010, SI 2010/232. Additional provisions, dealing with the manner in which the 1996 Convention has been implemented and to assist with its operation in the jurisdiction, have been made by the Parental Responsibility and Measures for the Protection of Children (International Obligations)(England and Wales and Northern Ireland) Regulations 2010, SI 2010/1898.The 1996 Convention has some 41 signatory states (listed at www.hcch.net/inde x_en.php?act=conventions.status&cid=70). See on the recognition and enforcement of family orders made by courts in Hague member states: *P, Re (Recognition And Registration of Orders Under the 1996 Hague Child Protection Convention)* [2014] EWHC 2845 (Fam) and the recognition and registration of orders from Brussels II member States – *Re S (Foreign Contact Order)* [2010] 1 FLR 982. The IDI entitled 'Children' Chapter 8 Section FM 3.2 does not include a full summary of the international instruments allowing recognition of overseas children's orders. It simply refers to the Child Abduction and Custody Act 1985 which makes provision for certain overseas child custody orders to be recognised and registered with a UK Court. The recognition of overseas custody orders may have some relevance to the question whether the parent has 'sole responsibility' for his/her child.

[2] See note 1 above.

[3] The Hague Convention on Protection of Children and Co-operation in Respect of Intercountry Adoption 1993 is incorporated in The Adoption (Intercountry Aspects) Act 1999. The arrangements for bringing recently adopted or adoptive children into the UK or removing them from the UK for the purpose of adoption abroad are set down in the Adoption and Children Act 2002 and the Adoptions with a Foreign Element Regulations 2005, SI 2005/392. The Immigration Rules HC 395, paras 309A–B, 310–316F seek to reflect certain of these provisions.

[4] See for example HC 395, paras 46A (requirements to be met by a person seeking leave to enter the United Kingdom as a child visitor); Para 245ZZA(f)–(h) (Tier 4 Child Student); Para 320(16), 322(11) (general grounds for refusal). See also: *OM (Children: settlement – cross border movement)* [2005] UKAIT 177 regarding the entry of children under para 322(9) of HC 395, and *FO (Children: settlement, OM distinguished) Nigeria* [2006] UKAIT 00089

(4 December 2006) which held that *OM* has no general application to HC 395, paras 296–316 concerning settlement applications by children. See also Foreign & Commonwealth Office, Guidance on Passports, 21 March 2013, Application for United Kingdom Passport for applicants under 16 Notes for Form C2; *Hamilton Jones v David & Snape (A firm)* [2003] EWHC 3147 (Ch), [2004] 1 All ER 657, a claim for damages against a solicitor's firm which negligently failed to re-register a child at risk of removal with the UK Passport Agency.

⁵ HC 395, paras 246–248F; Appendix FM Sections EC-PT, R-LTR-PT, R-ILR- PT (entry clearance, limited leave to remain and ILR for parents of a child in the UK).

11.9 Further, as a result of the 2008 withdrawal of the UK reservation to the UN Convention on the Rights of the Child, this Convention applies in the family and immigration jurisdictions.[1] Section 55 of the Borders, Citizenship and Immigration Act 2009 (BCIA 2009) provides that from 2 November 2009 the UK Border Agency is to be judged 'by the same standards as every other authority that deals with children' and thus the Secretary of State's functions in relation to immigration, asylum or nationality, any function conferred on an immigration officer or designated customs official and any services provided by another person pursuant to arrangements made by the Secretary of State which relate to the discharge of the said functions – are required to be discharged having regard to the need to safeguard and promote the welfare of children who are in the UK.[2] The Guidance, *Every Child Matters: Change For Children* is issued by the Secretary of State under section 55 of the BCIA 2009 and any person exercising any immigration, asylum, nationality and customs functions must have regard to this guidance given to them for the purpose by the Secretary of State. As the *Every Child Matters* statement makes clear, 'This means they must take this guidance into account and, if they decide to depart from it, have clear reasons for doing so'.[3]

¹ On 22 September 2008, just prior to the UK government's appearance before the UN Committee on the Rights of the Child, the UK government announced that it would lift the immigration and children in custody reservations to the UN Convention on the Rights of the Child. The reservations were to Articles 22 and 37 of UNCRC. See Press Release Department of Children, Schools and Families, 22 September 2008, www.dcsf.gov.uk.

² Then Minister of State Phil Woolas MP stated 'It is right that the UK Border Agency is judged by the same standards as every other authority that deals with children'. Hansard, Public Bill Committee, 6th Sitting, 16 June 2009, col 192. See also: UK Border Agency commits to keep children safe from harm, UK Border Agency. www.ukba.homeoffice.gov.uk/sitecontent/ keepingchildrensafefromharm, Press Release, 6 January 2009. The section 55 obligation to safeguard and promote the welfare of children is not defined. However this same obligation is defined in the guidance to section 11 of the Children Act 2004 Act (section 28 in Wales) and in the Guidance Working Together to Safeguard Children as: (i) protecting children from maltreatment; preventing impairment of children's health or development (where health means 'physical or mental health' and development means 'physical, intellectual, emotional, social or behavioural development'); (ii) ensuring that children are growing up in circumstances consistent with the provision of safe and effective care; and (iii) undertaking that role so as to enable those children to have optimum life chances and to enter adulthood successfully. In the Home Office guidance *Every Child Matters* and in the Hansard debates on section 55, it is made clear that this safeguarding duty to children 'is to mirror as closely as possible the effect of Section 11 of the Children Act 2004': Lord West of Spithead, Hansard, HL Report, 4 March 2009, cols 832-4 (HL Committee stage of the Borders Citizenship and Immigration Bill).

³ *Every Child Matters: Change For Children*, para 6, p 5.

11.10 In these intersecting family and immigration cases, courts and immigration authorities are required to evaluate varied family customs and arrangements when deciding on the validity of marriages, divorces or adoptions as well as whether there is family life between the parties and the effect of removal or relocation on a child's welfare. These judgements are made by reference to 'the diversity of forms' that the family takes in 'our multi-cultural and pluralistic society'.[1] In *Singh v Entry Clearance Officer, New Delhi*[2] the issue was whether there was a 'family life' between parents and their adoptive child where the adoption was valid under Indian law but not recognised in English law, the Court of Appeal noted:[3]

'it is important in this type of case, even if the adoption is not one that our law recognises, to have regard not merely to the fact of the adoption but also to all the personal, emotional and psychological, as well as the social, cultural and religious, consequences that flow from it.'

In an immigration context, the House of Lords considered whether the removal of a mother and child to Lebanon where she would automatically lose custody of her child and her prospects of maintaining contact with her child were limited, the removal was a flagrant denial of rights to equal treatment in the enjoyment of the 'elementary' right to care for one's own child and corresponding right of the child to be cared for by his mother. The House of Lords held that the effect of removal to Lebanon was that the mother and child's rights to respect for their family life would not only be flagrantly violated but would also be completely denied and nullified. In no meaningful sense could occasional supervised visits by the mother even if ordered (and there is no guarantee that they would be ordered), be described as family life. The effect of return would be to destroy the family life of the mother and child as it is now lived. Their Lordships differed concerning whether the flagrancy was established because of Lebanon's discriminatory custody regime or simply the exceptional nature of the case facts.[4]

---

[1] In *Singh v Entry Clearance Officer, New Delhi* [2004] EWCA Civ 1075, [2004] INLR 515 Munby J noted that 'the Strasbourg court has never sought to identify any minimum requirements that must be shown if family life is to be held to exist. That is because there are none. In my judgment there is no single factor whose existence is crucial to the existence of family life, either in the abstract or even in the context of any particular type of family relationship' (at para 72). In *EM (Lebanon) v Secretary of State for the Home Department* [2008] UKHL 64, [2009] 1 All ER 559, [2008] 3 WLR 931, Lord Bingham stated concerning family life at para 37 that:

'Families differ widely, in their composition and in the mutual relations which exist between the members, and marked changes are likely to occur over time within the same family. Thus there is no pre-determined model of family or family life to which article 8 must be applied. The article requires respect to be shown for the right to such family life as is or may be enjoyed by the particular applicant or applicants before the court, always bearing in mind (since any family must have at least two members, and may have many more) the participation of other members who share in the life of that family. In this context, as in most Convention contexts, the facts of the particular case are crucial.'

[2] [2004] EWCA Civ 1075, [2004] INLR 615.

[3] At para 86 per Munby J.

[4] *EM (Lebanon) v Secretary of State For The Home Department* [2008] UKHL 64, 2009] AC 1198, [2009] 1 All ER 559.

11.11 These intersecting family and immigration cases have additional relevance because of the legal consequences of family law restrictions applicable to certain child removals or relocations. These restrictions are not binding on the Secretary of State, but they do have consequences for parents and carers, who may have to decide whether they can voluntarily leave the UK to establish family life elsewhere and for immigration decision-makers deciding whether it is reasonable for partners and children to do so.[1] These issues are most likely to arise where a partner of the person being removed has children from another relationship and the Home Office or immigration authority is considering whether the resident partner can be expected to leave the jurisdiction with his or her excluded partner. The removal of a habitually resident[2] child from the UK without the consent of a parent or carer, or permission of a court, can constitute a wrongful removal or abduction.[3] The Hague Convention on the Civil Aspects of International Child Abduction applies to a child under 16 who, immediately before the retention or removal, was habitually resident in the UK and whose removal is in breach of rights of custody attributed to a person, institution or any other body, either jointly or alone.[4] Section 1 of the Child Abduction Act 1984 which gives the Convention the force of law in the UK thus makes it an offence for a parent to take or send a child out of the UK without the consent of all those with parental responsibility.[5] Section 13 of the Children Act 1989 imposes a restraint on the international movement of children if there is a child arrangement order in force and there is more than one holder of parental responsibility, except that the holder of a child arrangement order can take the child out of the jurisdiction for periods up to a month at a time.[6]

---

[1] See: NIAA 2002, ss 117A(6), 117D(1); *VW (Uganda) v Secretary of State for the Home Department* [2009] EWCA Civ 5, [2009] INLR 295, [2009] Imm AR 436.

[2] In European law dealing with the jurisdiction and the recognition and enforcement of judgments in matrimonial matters and matters of parental responsibility Regulation (EC) No 2201/2003 the ECJ held that the autonomous definition in the Directive placed a child's habitual residence as 'corresponding to the actual centre of interests of the child': *A (Area of Freedom, Security and Justice)* C-523/07, [2010] Fam 42, [2009] 2 FLR 1; *Butt v Butt* [2010] EWHC 1989 (Fam), [2010] All ER (D) 31 (Aug); *Re I (A Child) (jurisdiction: habitual residence outside European Union)* [2009] UKSC 10, [2010] AC 319, [2010] 1 All ER 445. The Supreme Court in *A (children) (jurisdiction: return of child), Re* [2013] UKSC 60 determined that habitual residence, in the context of Brussels IIR, is: 'the place which reflects some degree of integration by the child in a social and family environment.' Baroness Hale [35] said that where the other jurisdiction is not an EU Member State, it is nevertheless: 'highly desirable that the same test be adopted and that, if there is any difference, it is that adopted by the Court of Justice.' In paragraph 54 Baroness Hale summarised the principles to be drawn from the domestic and European jurisprudence (eg *A, Proceedings brought by A* Case (C-523/07) [2010] Fam 42, [2009] 2 FLR 1; *Mercredi v Chaffe* [2012] Fam 22) as follows:

    i)   All are agreed that habitual residence is a question of fact and not a legal concept such as domicile. There is no legal rule akin to that whereby a child automatically takes the domicile of his parents.

    ii)   It was the purpose of the 1986 Act to adopt a concept which was the same as that adopted in the Hague and European Conventions. The Regulation must also be interpreted consistently with those Conventions.

    iii)   The test adopted by the European Court is "the place which reflects some degree of integration by the child in a social and family environment" in the country concerned. This depends upon numerous factors, including the reasons for the family's stay in the country in question.

    iv)   It is now unlikely that that test would produce any different results from that hitherto adopted in the English courts under the 1986 Act and the Hague Child Abduction Convention.

    v)   In my view, the test adopted by the European Court is preferable to that earlier adopted by the English courts, being focussed on the situation of the child, with the purposes and intentions of the parents being merely one of the relevant factors. The test derived from *R v Barnet London Borough Council, ex p Shah* should be abandoned when deciding the habitual residence of a child.

    vi)   The social and family environment of an infant or young child is shared with those (whether parents or others) upon whom he is dependent. Hence it is necessary to assess the integration of that person or persons in the social and family environment of the country concerned.

vii) The essentially factual and individual nature of the inquiry should not be glossed with legal concepts which would produce a different result from that which the factual inquiry would produce.

viii) As the Advocate General pointed out in para AG45 and the court confirmed in para 43 of *Proceedings brought by A*, it is possible that a child may have no country of habitual residence at a particular point in time.'

3   See Council Regulation (EC) No 2201/2003 ('Brussels II Revised') concerning jurisdiction and the recognition and enforcement of judgments in matrimonial matters and the matters of parental responsibility; L (Judgment) [2014] EUECJ C-656/13. According to recital 17 in the preamble to Council Regulation (EC) No 2201/2003:

'In cases of wrongful removal or retention of a child, the return of the child should be obtained without delay, and to this end the Hague Convention of 25 October 1980 would continue to apply as complemented by the provisions of this Regulation, in particular Article 11.'

Article 11 and other Articles of Regulation No 2201/2003 concerning the return of wrongfully removed children have the same scope as the Hague Convention. They may be applied only in conjunction with the corresponding provisions of the Convention. See: Article 218(11) TFEU – Convention on the civil aspects of international child abduction (Opinions of the Court) [2014] EUECJ Avis-1/13.

4   Articles 3, 4, 5. The Convention is incorporated via the Child Abduction and Custody Act 1985, s 1 and Sch 1. Under Article 1 of the 1980 Hague Convention, the objects of the present Convention are:

(a)   to secure the prompt return of children wrongfully removed to or retained in any Contracting State; and;

(b)   to ensure that rights of custody and of access under the law of one Contracting State are effectively respected in the other Contracting States.'

Pursuant to Article 3 of the Convention '(t)he removal or the retention of a child is to be considered wrongful where – a) it is in breach of rights of custody attributed to a person, an institution or any other body, either jointly or alone, under the law of the State in which the child was habitually resident immediately before the removal or retention; and b) at the time of removal or retention those rights were actually exercised, either jointly or alone, or would have been so exercised but for the removal or retention.' Article 12 provides that '(w)here a child has been wrongfully removed or retained in terms of Article 3 and . . . . a period of less than one year has elapsed from the date of the wrongful removal or retention, the authority concerned shall order the return of the child forthwith.' Article 13 describes exceptions to the mandatory return provision created by Article 12.

5   Under the Children Act 1989, s 3(1) 'parental responsibility' is defined as 'all the rights, duties, powers, responsibilities and authority which by law a parent of a child has in relation to the child and his property'. Note that an unmarried father does not automatically have parental responsibility for his child: Children Act 1989, s 2(2). Where the parents of a child are not married to each other, the father acquires parental responsibility for the child if he is registered as the father on the child's UK birth certificate, he and the mother make a parental responsibility agreement providing him with parental responsibility or the court on application orders this (Children Act 1989, s 4). Some aspects of parental responsibility acknowledged by the courts include: determining a child's religion and education, consenting to their medical treatment, having physical possession or contact with the child, consenting to or arranging the child's emigration and protecting and maintaining the child.

6   Where a residence order (now termed a child arrangement order) is in force with respect to a child, no person may remove the child from the UK without either the written consent of every person who has parental responsibility for the child or leave of the court: Children Act 1989, s 13(1). An unmarried father may not have parental responsibility if not on the child's birth certificate or in the absence of a parental responsibility agreement or a court order: Children Act 1989, s 4, but see C *(child abduction: rights of custody), Re* [2002] EWHC 2219 (Fam), [2003] 1 WLR 493, [2002] 1 FLR 252. Note also the prohibition on removal of wards and children in care. It is prohibited to remove a ward from the jurisdiction without leave of the court: Family Law Act 1986, s 38. It is also an offence to remove a child in care from a place of safety or from the responsible person (Children Act 1989, s 49; Children and Young Persons Act 1969, s 32(3)) and an arrangement to assist a child in care to live outside England and Wales requires leave from the Court, even if all persons with parental responsibility for the child have consented: Children Act 1989, Sch 2, para 19. It can also be a criminal offence for a person to remove from the UK a habitually resident or Commonwealth citizen child for the purposes of adopting that child abroad. Such prospective adopters must first get an order from

the High Court giving them parental responsibility for the purposes of adopting abroad. In order to be eligible to apply for parental responsibility for this purpose the child must have had his/her home with the proposed adopter/adopters at all times during the preceding ten weeks. (Adoption and Children Act 2002, ss 84, 85). See *A (a child) (adoption: removal), Re* [2009] EWCA Civ 41, [2009] 3 All ER 479, [2009] 3 WLR 1169, re placement in the USA.

11.12 Although the family and immigration jurisdictions overlap, courts have emphasised that the functions of the court under the Children Act 1989 and related legislation and of the Secretary of State under immigration legislation, are 'by and large separate and distinct'.[1] When exercising their powers under family legislation, courts cannot in the exercise of that jurisdiction interfere with the exercise by the Secretary of State for the Home Department of her powers in relation to matters of immigration and asylum.[2] Family courts must be guided by the interests of the child, and the interests of children are paramount. In the exercise of immigration functions the child's best interests are a primary consideration.[3] As stated above (at **11.7**) while family and immigration functions are separate and distinct there is increased co-operation and information sharing between the two jurisdictions and a recognition that the outcome in a family case may be material to the immigration decision.[4]

[1] *Arif (Mohamed) (an infant), Re* [1968] Ch 643 at 662D per Russell LJ; *Re F (A Minor) (Immigration: Wardship)* [1990] Fam 125, [1989] 1 FLR 233; *Re A (A Minor) (Wardship: Immigration)* [1992] 1 FLR 427; *K and S (minors), Re* [1992] 1 FLR 432; and *Re Matondo* [1993] 1 AC 541. See *BE (Care Proceedings) Jamaica* [2005] UKIAT 00098 (28 February 2005), where Ouseley J held that 'the care and the immigration proceedings should be treated as concurrent and independent.'

[2] *Re A (children) (care proceedings: asylum seekers)* [2003] EWHC 1086 (Fam), [2003] 2 FLR 921, (case also reported as *Rotherham Borough Council v M* [2003] EWHC 1086 (Fam) (16 May 2003)) where the continuation of care proceedings was held abusive in respect of children whose failed asylum seeker parents were to be removed but where the father (in a crisis response later disavowed) threatened to kill the family if removal were to occur. There were no protection concerns for the children at the date of the hearing: *S v S* [2008] EWHC 2288 (Fam), [2009] 2 FCR 415, [2009] 1 FLR 241.

[3] BCIA 2009, s 55. The Home Office Immigration Directorate Instructions Chapter 8 section 4A states:

   'Section 55 of the Borders, Citizenship and Immigration Act 2009 requires the UK Border Agency to carry out its existing functions in a way that takes into account the need to safeguard and promote the welfare of children in the UK. It does not impose any new functions, or override existing functions . . . . Our statutory duty to children includes the need to demonstrate:

   •   fair treatment which meets the same standard a British child would receive;
   •   the child's interests being made a primary, although not the only consideration;
   •   no discrimination of any kind;
   •   asylum applications are dealt with in a timely fashion;
   •   identification of those that might be at risk from harm.'

   See also: *Re A (children) (care proceedings: asylum seekers)* [2003] EWHC 1086 (Fam), [2003] 2 FLR 921; *R (on the application of Anton (Family)) v Secretary of State for the Home Department* [2005] EWHC 2730 (Admin), [2005] EWHC 2731 (Fam), [2005] 2 FLR 818; *R v Secretary of State for the Home Department, ex p Teame* [1995] 1 FLR 293.

[4] See the guidance given by Lord Justice McFarlane and Mr Justice Blake in *RS (immigration and family court proceedings) India* [2012] UKUT 218 (IAC) (04 July 2012; *Nimako-Boateng (residence orders – Anton considered)* [2012] UKUT 00216 (IAC). The guidance was endorsed by the Court of Appeal in *Mohan v Secretary of State for the Home Department* [2012] EWCA Civ 1363, [2013] 1 WLR 922.

11.13 Family courts have stated that if, apart from immigration questions, there is no genuine dispute concerning the child, the court should not allow itself to be used as a means of influencing the decision of the Secretary of State.

The question for the family court is whether there is some 'solid advantage' to the child in the family proceedings.[1] The use of the court's jurisdiction merely to attempt to influence the Secretary of State is an abuse of process. This does not mean that the family court cannot make a residence (now child arrangement) order in respect of a child who is subject to immigration control or cannot make such a child a ward of court. Nor does it mean that the family court cannot make a care order in respect of such a child or invite an entry clearance officer to permit a family litigant to visit the UK for that purpose. What it does mean is that neither the existence of a care order, nor the existence of a residence order, nor even the fact that the child is a ward of court, can limit or confine the exercise by the Secretary of State of his/her powers in relation to a child who is subject to immigration control.[2] In exercising powers of removal or exclusion in such cases, the Secretary of State should have regard to any relevant family court order or finding.[3] The associated principle is that family courts should not deny or limit family rights to persons solely on the basis of their uncertain or irregular immigration status. The ECHR found a breach of Article 8 where a baby was removed from the care of her Serbian mother not because of any parental failings but because the mother could not provide suitable accommodation for the child because the mother's residence status in Austria was uncertain. The Court held that the authorities should have explored arrangements which would have allowed the mother and child to remain in close contact while any family proceedings were pending.[4]

[1] *Re A (children) (care proceedings: asylum seekers)* [2003] EWHC 1086 (Fam), [2003] 2 FLR 921, *R (on the application of Anton (Family)) v Secretary of State for the Home Department* [2005] EWHC 2730 (Admin), [2005] EWHC 2731 (Fam), [2005] 2 FLR 818. See on the meaning of 'solid advantage,' Waite LJ in *Southwark London Borough Council v B* [1993] 2 FLR 559 at p 573, *S v S and Ors* [2008] EWHC 2288 (Fam), [2009] 2 FCR 415.

[2] *Re A (children) (care proceedings: asylum seekers)* [2003] EWHC 1086 (Fam), [2003] 2 FLR 921, *R (on the application of Anton (Family)) v Secretary of State for the Home Department* [2005] EWHC 2730 (Admin), [2005] EWHC 2731 (Fam), [2005] 2 FLR 818, *S v S and Ors* [2008] EWHC 2288 (Fam), [2009] 2 FCR 415.

[3] See comments Hoffmann LJ in *R v Secretary of State for the Home Department, ex p T* [1995] 1 FLR 293 at p 297. For the analogous case concerning the Secretary of State's obligations to consider criminal court findings on Article 8, see *M v Secretary of State for the Home Department* [2003] EWCA Civ 146, [2003] 1 WLR 1980.

[4] *Moser v Austria* (Application 12643/02) [2006] 3 FCR 107 (21 September 2006).

11.14 UK family courts generally have jurisdiction to determine applications in relation to any child who is habitually resident[1] or present within its geographical jurisdiction.[2] This is true even if the child in question is liable to removal or deportation as a family member.[3]

Similarly, family courts can decide on applications for family court orders[4] from adults (parents or carers) who are liable to removal or deportation.[5] These family orders define the rights and obligations of parents in relation to their children in private law cases,[6] or, in the case of public law orders[7] or wardship,[8] operate to protect the child from significant harm at the hands of his or her parents or carers or resolve particular issues concerning children.

[1] See *I (a child) (jurisdiction: habitual residence outside European Union)*, [2009] UKSC 10 [2010] AC 319 *Lambeth London Borough Council v JO* [2014] EWHC 3597 (Fam), In European law dealing with the jurisdiction and the recognition and enforcement of judgments in matrimonial matters and matters of parental responsibility Regulation (EC) No 2201/2003 the ECJ held that the autonomous definition in the Directive placed a child's habitual residence

as 'corresponding to the actual centre of interests of the child': *A (Area of Freedom, Security and Justice)* [2009] EUECJ C-523/07_O (29 January 2009), *Butt v Butt* [2010] EWHC 1989 (Fam), *Re I (A Child)* [2009] UKSC 10, [2009] 3 WLR 1299.

2 Family Law Act 1986, ss 2(3), 2A, 3(1), *R (care orders: jurisdiction), Re* [1995] 3 FCR 305, *Re M (A Minor) (Immigration: Residence Order)* [1993] 2 FLR 858, *Nottingham City Council v LM* [2014] EWCA Civ 152. See for adoption jurisdiction, Adoption and Children Act 2002, s 49. See concerning children born to a surrogate British mother for Turkish domiciled parents: *G (surrogacy: foreign domicile), Re* [2007] EWHC 2814 (Fam), [2008] Fam Law 95 (28 November 2007). Council Regulation 2201/2003 applies in respect of the jurisdiction in public law cases in England and Wales. Following the Supreme Court decisions of *Re I (A Child) (Contact Application: Jurisdiction)* [2009] UKSC 10, [2010] AC 319 and *A (children) (jurisdiction: return of child), Re* [2013] UKSC 60, and by virtue of the amendments to the Family Law Act 1986, the Regulation applies to jurisdictional issues between England and Wales and non-Member State.

3 *R v Secretary of State for the Home Department, ex p T* [1994] Imm AR 368, [1995] 1 FLR 293; *Re A (children) (care proceedings: asylum seekers)* [2003] EWHC 1086 (Fam), [2003] 2 FLR 921, *West Sussex County Council v H* [2014] EWHC 2550 (Fam), *Barking & Dagenham London Borough Council v SS* [2014] EWHC 3338 (Fam).

4 For example, child arrangement orders, contact, specific issues and prohibited steps orders under s 8 of the Children Act 1989 or care or supervision orders under s 31 of the Children Act 1989 or wardship under the High Court's inherent jurisdiction.

5 *R v Secretary of State for the Home Department, ex p T* [1994] Imm AR 368, [1995] 1 FLE 293; *Re A (children) (care proceedings: asylum seekers)* [2003] EWHC 1086 (Fam), [2003] 2 FLR 921.

6 Cases when there is a dispute between parents or other carers about whom the child should live with (child arrangement order) or what contact the child should have with them (contact order) or whether the child should be removed from the jurisdiction (prohibited steps order) or, for example, enrolled at a certain type of school (specific issue order).

7 Care orders which vest parental responsibility in the local authority and supervision orders which place the child under the supervision of a local authority whilst continuing to live with the carers.

8 The inherent jurisdiction developed by the High Court deriving from what Lord Denning in *Re L (An Infant)* [1968] 1 All ER 20 at 24G termed the 'right and duty of the Crown as parens patriae to take care of those who are not able to take care of themselves.'

11.15 These family orders have no necessary or direct effect on the immigration status of any party to the application. The fact that an overstayer parent is granted contact to a British child or that a family court order prevents a parent removing a child from the jurisdiction does not deprive the Secretary of State of the power conferred by the immigration laws to remove the adult or child in question from the UK or deny them entry to the UK.[1] Family courts, whether exercising their private law powers under Part II of the 1989 Act, their public law powers under Part IV of the 1989 Act, the wardship jurisdiction, or the inherent jurisdiction in relation to children recognised and to an extent regulated by section 100 of the 1989 Act, cannot constrain or undercut the immigration powers of the Secretary of State.[2] Adoption proceedings apart,[3] whatever jurisdiction a judge of the Family Court may be exercising, such judge cannot make an order which has the effect of depriving the Secretary of State of the power under immigration law to remove a child or any other party to the proceedings.

1 See on Secretary of State's power to remove a ward, *Arif (Mohamed) (an infant), Re* [1968] Ch 643 at 662D per Russell LJ, *Re F (A Minor) (Immigration: Wardship)* [1990] Fam 125, [1989] 1 FLR 233, *Re A (A Minor) (Wardship: Immigration)* [1992] 1 FLR 427, *K and S (minors), Re* [1992] 1 FLR 432 and *Re M (A Minor) (Immigration: Residence Order)* [1993] 2 FLR 858

2 *Re A (children) (care proceedings: asylum seekers)* [2003] 2 FLR 921 per Munby J at para 48. See also *R (on the application of Family Anton) v Secretary of State for the Home Department* [2004] EWHC 2730/2731 (Admin/Fam), [2005] 2 FLR 818.

[3] Adoption proceedings are distinguished because under the British Nationality Act 1981 where a court in the UK makes an order authorising the adoption of a minor child who is not a British citizen, by an adopter or adopters, one of whom is a British citizen on that date, the child is a British citizen from the date of the adoption. This change in the child's nationality status resolves any irregularity in his/her previous immigration status and prevents the child's deportation or removal: *W (Adoption: Non-Patrial), Re* [1986] Fam 54, [1986] 1 FLR 179. There is no such analogy with Children Act orders, which do not affect the child's nationality status: *R v Secretary of State for the Home Department, ex p T* [1995] 1 FLR 293 per Hoffmann LJ at 297E.

11.16 The Court of Appeal held that it was not a contempt of court for the Secretary of State to remove a person with whom a child had been ordered to live or even to remove the child before family proceedings had been completed.[1] However, as a matter of practice, and consistently with the Human Rights Act 1998, the Secretary of State does not remove or deport children or parents when family or other court proceedings are current and is usually prepared to grant short periods of discretionary leave or to extend temporary admission or release to await the outcome of family litigation.[2] Indeed the Tribunal has recognised that in intersecting family and immigration cases the family court is best placed to evaluate the best interests of the child and the reasons for a family law outcome will be material to the consideration of and may be a decisive consideration in an Article 8 evaluation. In *Nimako-Boateng* the Upper Tribunal noted that the problem facing immigration judges is that, although they must attach weight to the best interests of the child, in many cases they will often not be able to assess what those interests are without the assistance of a decision of the family court. The family court has, amongst other things, procedural advantages in investigating what the child's best interests are, independent of the interests of the parent, as well as the necessary expertise in evaluating them. An informed decision of the family judge on issues concerning a child and, in some cases, the material underlying that decision, is likely to be of value to the immigration judge.[3] In *MS (Ivory Coast) v Secretary of State for the Home Department*,[4] the Court of Appeal noted that the Secretary of State's practice to grant assurances or undertakings not to remove in cases where a person is a party in pending family proceedings is not based on any published statement of policy. The case concerned a failed asylum seeker who was seeking an order for contact to her children, who had been placed in the care of their father.[5] The Court held concerning the particular applicant, that, when the AIT considered her appeal against a removal decision, they did not decide the hypothetical question it was incumbent upon them to decide, namely whether the appellant's Article 8 rights would be violated by a removal when the family contact application was outstanding before a family court:

'The appellant was entitled to have determined whether removal from the United Kingdom with an outstanding contact application would breach s 6 of the Human Rights Act 1998. That question was capable of resolution one way or the other. What was not appropriate was to leave her in this country in limbo with temporary admission and the promise not to remove her until her contact application has been concluded. Temporary admission is, as we have explained, a status given to someone liable to be detained pending removal. If the appellant had a valid human rights claim she is not liable to be detained pending removal. And if she has not, she ought to be removed. If she is entitled to discretionary leave to remain she ought to have it for the period the Secretary of State thinks appropriate, together with the advantages that it conveys; and if not she ought not to.'

In the course of argument the point was made that circumstances could arise where a contact hearing was likely to be resolved in, for example, a matter of days. It would in those circumstances be impractical to expect a human rights decision without knowing the outcome of that application. In the court's judgment that is the kind of situation that can be dealt with by appropriate case management.'

1   *Re T* [1994] Imm AR 368, CA.
2   *R v Secretary of State for Home Department, ex p Kebbeh (CO/1269/98)* (22 April 1999), *Re A (children) (care proceedings: asylum seekers)* [2003] EWHC 1086 (Fam). The fair trial rights protected by Article 6, and the procedural requirements of Article 8, are relevant in such cases: see eg *Ciliz v Netherlands* [2000] 2 FLR 469.
3   *Nimako-Boateng (residence orders – Anton considered)* [2012] UKUT 00216 (IAC); *RS (immigration and family court proceedings) India* [2012] UKUT 218 (IAC) and *Mohan v Secretary of State for the Home Department* [2012] EWCA Civ 1363, [2013] 1 WLR 922.
4   *MS (Ivory Coast) v Secretary of State for the Home Department* [2007] EWCA Civ 133 (22 February 2007).
5   *MS (Ivory Coast) v Secretary of State for the Home Department* at paras 72–73.

11.17 Just as a family court order does not bind the Secretary of State, the Family Court may also make its orders independent of any immigration consideration. As *Re S*[1] shows, the High Court can order the removal of a child, pursuant to its Hague Convention obligations concerning abducted or wrongfully retained children even though the Secretary of State's removal powers are constrained by sections 77, 78 and 78A of the NIAA 2002 (preventing removal of persons awaiting an asylum decision or appeal determination or the immediate removal when appeal rights are exhausted of certain parents and children). The Court of Appeal held that a statutory constraint on removal of this kind is directed to immigration authorities but was not intended 'to occupy any wider canvas', creating an exception to a family court's obligations arising under Article 12 of the Hague Convention or the duty and discretion of a judge exercising the wardship jurisdiction to order the speedy return of an abducted child to his/her country of habitual residence.

1   *Re S (children) (abduction: asylum appeal)* [2002] EWCA Civ 843, [2002] All ER (D) 424 (May) (on the predecessor provisions to Nationality, Immigration and Asylum Act 2002, s 77).

11.18 In certain family cases where the immigration issues are contentious, the Secretary of State may seek to be joined as a party and make representations on the appropriate family orders to be made.[1] The Family Court protocol arrangements help to ensure that the Home Office is alerted where there are immigration issues in family cases and through the protocol arrangements family courts frequently seek relevant evidence from the Home Office concerning the immigration status of the parties or their children or the prospects of the parties or children remaining in or returning to the UK.[2]

1   For example: *Re A (children) (care proceedings: asylum seekers)* [2003] EWHC 1086 (Fam), [2003] 2 FLR 921.
2   See **11.11**, fn 2 and **11.14**, fn 1 above.

11.19 Where a family court has made a child arrangement or contact or care order, the family court judgement concerning care, residence or contact can persuade the Secretary of State that removal or deportation of the child or carer is not appropriate. The Home Office instructions reflect this outcome.

Officers are advised that particularly for younger children, welfare consider-ations may outweigh the immigration considerations and that: 'Decisions about the future of children in the care of the local authority should be left primarily in the hands of their social services department as they will be best placed to act in the child's best interests. . . . If the social services advise that it would be appropriate for the child to remain in the United Kingdom, consideration should be given to granting the child leave to remain.'[1]

[1] IDI, Chapter 8, s 5A, 'Children', Annex M, July 2012, para 7–8. The instructions distinguish between children in care, whose welfare is primarily decided by social services, and those children where the social services are merely 'involved'. In the latter cases, social services' views 'should be taken into account'. However, the instructions state 'it will not always be right to act on their recommendation, particularly if there is independent evidence to justify proceeding with refusal and removal'. The term of stay to be granted to unaccompanied children is not mentioned (except for children born in the UK, who, under the Rules, are to be granted settlement under HC 395, paras 305(i)(c) and 308, if subject to a full care order). The Home Office now limits discretionary leave to end before the child's 18th birthday. Social services or a children's guardian may wish to make representations on the term of leave to be granted in appropriate cases. They may have a welfare interest in and obligations towards a young adult under leaving care arrangements. Under the Children Act 1989, ss 22–24D, Sch 2, Part II, paras 19A–19C, as amended by the Children (Leaving Care) Act 2000, local authorities are required to advise, assist and befriend 'relevant' and 'former relevant children', to take reasonable steps to stay in touch, continue the appointment of a personal adviser and provide and review a 'pathway' plan for their transition out of care. 'Relevant' and 'former relevant' children are those aged 16 and over who have been 'looked after' for at least 13 weeks since they reached the age of 14 and who were being looked after by a responsible authority when he/she turned 16 or 18 (Children Act 1989, ss 23A,23C). See also: *R (on the application of A) v Lambeth London Borough Council* [2010] EWHC 1652 (Admin), [2010] 2 FCR 539, [2010] NLJR 1013. *JS (Former unaccompanied child – durable solution) (Afghanistan)* [2013] UKUT 568 (IAC).

RELEVANT PRINCIPLES OF PRIVATE INTERNATIONAL LAW

11.20 The intersection between family and immigration law is also manifest in private international and domestic family law provisions concerning the validity of marriages, divorces and adoptions. These private international and domestic provisions can establish whether a child is able to establish entitle-ment to citizenship by descent, or whether a person qualifies for entry as a spouse or child of the sponsor. The previous text has shown the importance of a parent's or child's habitual residence in international family cases; the other key concept utilised in immigration and family status questions is domicile.

DOMICILE

11.21 Domicile is an important concept in English law. It is a neutral rule for determining the system of personal law with which the individual has the appropriate connection, so that it shall govern his or her personal status and questions relating to personal transactions – marriage, divorce, the legitimacy of his or her children, adoptions, and rights of inheritance.[1] A person may need to show that he or she has a domicile in 'a part of the United Kingdom or in the Channel Islands or the Isle of Man' in order to have standing to seek a family order.[2] A domicile may be acquired in England and Wales, Scotland or Northern Ireland, but not in the UK or Great Britain. A person's domiciliary law governs capacity to marry, the legitimacy of children, and succession after death to moveable property and the validity of a will.[3] Questions of domicile arise in immigration and nationality cases where it is disputed that an applicant is a spouse, is free to marry, has consented to a marriage, is divorced or that children are legitimate or that the person has standing to seek a parental or adoption order.[4] These can be decisive questions for entry or nationality.

[1] See Dicey, Morris and Collins on *The Conflict of Law*, Vol 1, Chapter 6 (fifteenth edn, 2012, Sweet and Maxwell.

[2] Baroness Hale observed in *Mark v Mark* [2005] UKHL 42 at para 44-47 that 'English law requires only that the intention [of the person claiming to be domiciled by reason of their intention to reside permanently in the UK] be bona fide, in the sense of being genuine and not pretended for some other purpose, such as getting a divorce to which one would not be entitled by the law of the true domicile'.

[3] See *Mark v Mark* 2005] UKHL 42, [2005] INLR 614; *Cyganik v Agulian* [2006] EWCA Civ 129 (24 February 2006).

[4] See *Baig v Entry Clearance Officer, Islamabad* [2003] INLR 117; *Kaur v Singh* [2005] CSOH_96, *Asaad v Kurter* [2013] EWHC 3852 (Fam), [2014] 2 FLR 833.

11.22 Domicile is to be distinguished from other connecting or identifying status factors, such as nationality, or habitual residence. Domicile and nationality are distinct and separate concepts. Nationality identifies the person's political status; domicile shows a person's civil status and connects him or her with a system of law for the purposes of determining a range of matters principally related to status or property.[1] A person may have citizenship of one country and domicile in another as it is possible to acquire a domicile of choice irrespective of nationality.[2] A person also may change nationality without this necessarily affecting domicile,[3] although naturalisation in accordance with the requirements of the BNA 1981, Schedule 1, paragraph 1(1)(d)(i) (an intention that his or her principal home will be in the UK) may evidence a change in domicile. A person may have dual nationality but only has one domicile at a time. A person may be habitually resident in more than one place at a time, or may have no habitual residence at all. By contrast a person must always have a domicile but can only have one domicile at a time. If a new domicile is obtained by choice, the previous domicile is no longer applicable.[4]

[1] *Udny v Udny* (1869) LR 1 Sc & Div 441, 1869 WL 7841. See also *Mark v Mark* [2005] UKHL 42, [2005] INLR 614 at paragraph 38.

[2] *Boldrini v Boldrini and Martini* [1932] P 9, 1931 WL 7870, *Z v C* [2011] EWHC 3181 (Fam).

[3] *Wahl v A-G* (1932) 147 LT 382: a German national lived in England and became a naturalised British subject, and later returned to Germany to look after his father's estate. Held: although he changed his nationality he had retained his domicile of origin in Germany.

[4] *Moorhouse Ltd v Lord* (1863) 10 HL Cas 272 at 285 per Lord Chelmsford, *Barlow Clowes International Ltd v Henwood* [2008] EWCA Civ 577. See also discussion in *Mark v Mark* at para 37.

11.23 Domicile can be acquired by origin, by choice or by dependence.[1] In *Udny* Lord Westbury stated:

'Domicile of choice is a conclusion or inference which the law derives from the fact of a man fixing voluntarily his sole or chief residence in a particular place with an intention of continuing to reside there for an unlimited time . . . it must be a residence not for a limited period or particular purpose, but general and indefinite in its contemplation.'[2]

Where the intended residence is for a limited period, it is immaterial whether that limitation is expressed in terms of time or is made dependent on the happening of some event or the achievement of a particular task during the person's lifetime. The position was spelt out more clearly by Scarman J in *Re Fuld's Estate (No 3)*:[3]

> 'If a man intends to return to the land of his birth upon a clearly foreseen and reasonably anticipated contingency, the end of his job, the intention required by law is lacking; but, if he has in mind only a vague possibility, such as making a fortune (a modern example might be winning a football pool) . . . such a state of mind is consistent with the intention required by law.'

[1]   See now Domicile and Matrimonial Proceedings Act 1973, ss 1–4. A child acquires his/her dependent domicile from a parent and becomes capable of having an independent domicile from the age of 16 (s 3).

[2]   (1869) LR 1 Sc & Div 441 at 458.

[3]   [1968] P 675 at 684–685. See also *Cyganik v Agulian* [2006] EWCA Civ 129, *Sekhri v Ray* [2014] EWCA Civ 119; *Lawrence v Lawrence* [1985] Fam 106, [1985] 2 All ER 733, CA; *R v Immigration Appeal Tribunal, ex p Bibi (Rafika)* [1989] Imm AR 1, QBD. See *also* [2005] UKSSCSC CP_3108_2004 (25 April 2005), a case about entitlement to widow's pension.

11.24 There is a link between habitual residence and domicile, but residence in a particular place does not necessarily establish domicile there.[1] The requirement of an intention to remain permanently in the country/region of domicile distinguishes domicile from mere residence and in particular from the common law definition of ordinary residence.[2] Although for immigration purposes a person is not to be treated as ordinarily resident in the UK at a time when he or she is there in breach of the immigrations laws,[3] a person can be treated as having acquired a British domicile even if residing here unlawfully.[4] The concept of domicile is a neutral rule of law for determining that system of personal law with which the individual has the appropriate connection, so that it shall govern his personal status and questions relating to him and his affairs. As Baroness Hale noted in *Mark v Mark*: 'Unlike some of the purposes for which habitual residence may be important, the State has no particular interest one way or another [in a person's domicile]. Indeed, insofar as it does have an interest, this will probably lie in accepting that those who intend to remain here permanently have acquired a domicile here, whatever their immigration status.'[5]

The legality of a person's presence here is not completely irrelevant as it may well be relevant to whether or not she had formed the required *animus manendi*. But this is a question of fact and not a question of law.[6]

[1]   See Domicile and Matrimonial Proceedings Act 1973, s 5(2).

[2]   On 'ordinary residence' see *Shah v Barnet London Borough Council* [1983] 2 AC 309; see **11.11**, fn 2 and **11.14**, fn 1 above. See note 1 concerning the definition of habitual residence in European law dealing with the jurisdiction and the recognition and enforcement of judgments in matrimonial matters and matters of parental responsibility Regulation (EC) No 2201/2003. The ECJ held that the autonomous definition in the Directive placed a child's habitual residence as 'corresponding to the actual centre of interests of the child': *A (Area of Freedom, Security and Justice)* C-523/07, [2010] Fam 42, [2009] 2 FLR 1. This definition is closer to the common law definition of domicile than to the common law definition of habitual residence.

[3]   Immigration Act 1971, s 33(2).

[4]   *Mark v Mark* [2004] EWCA Civ 168, [2005] Fam 267; affd [2005] UKHL 42, [2005] INLR 614. The case held that illegal residence is not a bar to establishing habitual residence for the purposes of section 5(2) of the Domicile and Matrimonial Proceedings Act 1973.

5   *Mark v Mark*, per Baroness Hale at para 45.
6   *Mark v Mark* at para 50.

11.25 The distinction between a domicile of origin and domicile of choice is important. The domicile of origin is the domicile that everyone acquires at birth and this will equate to the country in which their parent (or if the parents are not married, the mother) is domiciled at the date of the birth.[1] A domicile of origin is never lost. It may be displaced by a domicile of choice but will revive if the domicile of choice is abandoned.[2] A person's capacity to acquire a domicile of choice arises at the age of 16, or if already married, at the date of marriage.[3] Until a child has this capacity, his/her domicile is dependent upon that of the parents and will change when the parent's domicile changes and may depend upon the parent with whom he/she has a home, if the parents are separated.[4]

1   The Domicile and Matrimonial Proceedings Act 1973 abolished the domicile of dependence of married women. If the parents are separated the child will have the domicile of the parent with whom she or he lives.
2   *Udny v Udny* (1869) LR 1 Sc & Div 441, 1869 WL 7841, *Barlow Clowes International Ltd v Henwood* [2008] EWCA Civ 577.
3   Domicile and Matrimonial Proceedings Act 1973, s 3.
4   Domicile and Matrimonial Proceedings Act 1973, s 4.

11.26 The legal principles relevant to the acquisition and retention of a domicile of choice[1] may be summarised as follows:

(i)   'There is a strong presumption in favour of the continuance of the domicile of origin. As contrasted with the domicile of choice, "its character is more enduring, its hold stronger and less easily shaken off".'[2]

(ii)   What has to be proved is an intention freely formed to reside in a certain territory indefinitely. All the elements of the intention must be shown to exist if the change is to be established: if any one element is not proved, the case for a change fails.[3] Statements as to domicile by a testator in a will, by a taxpayer on an Inland Revenue form, or in an application for registration or naturalisation as a British citizen are not necessarily reliable.[4]

(iii)   The burden of proving that a domicile of choice has been acquired rests on the person who asserts that the domicile of origin has been lost.[5] If the burden of proving a change has not been discharged, the domicile of origin will remain.[6]

(iv)   The abandonment of a domicile of choice may be more easily established than its acquisition, although there must be unequivocal evidence of abandonment.[7] A domicile of choice is lost when the subject both ceases to reside in the relevant country and gives up the intention permanently or indefinitely to reside there. If on abandonment of the domicile of choice the person does not acquire a new domicile (of choice), the person's domicile of origin revives.

1   See summary of principles in *Barlow Clowes International Ltd v Henwood* [2008] EWCA Civ 577, (2008) Times, 18 June, [2008] BPIR 778.
2   Per Lord MacNaughten in *Winans v A-G* [1904] AC 287 at 290. For modern examples see *Cyganik v Agulian* [2006] EWCA Civ 129, *Cramer v Cramer* [1986] Fam Law 333, CA; [2005] UKSSCSC CP_3108_2004 (25 April 2005) a case about entitlement to widow's pension; *SM (Domicile of choice, Scots law) Pakistan* [2008] UKAIT 00092 (26 November 2008).

3   In *Fuld's Estate (No 3), Re, Hartley v Fuld* [1968] P 675 per Scarman J at 684, 685, *Buswell v IRC* [1974] 2 All ER 520, [1974] 1 WLR 1631. Every fact, however trivial, is admissible for the purpose of proving an intention to acquire or discard a domicile: *Flynn, Re, Flynn v Flynn* [1968] 1 All ER 49.

4   *Begum (Rokeya) v Entry Clearance Officer* [1983] Imm AR 163; *Khatun (Hamida) v Entry Clearance Officer, Dhaka* [1988] Imm AR 138, IAT; *SM (Domicile of choice, Scots law) Pakistan* [2008] UKAIT 00092 (26 November 2008) – a person who evinces a desire to retain the laws of his original home (as distinct from the rules of UK or Scots law) for a continuing part of his life does not show the intention relevant to a change of domicile.

5   *Winans v A-G* [1904] AC 287 at 290 and 291. See also *R v Entry Clearance Officer, Islamabad, ex p Ali CO* (3585/97) (20 January 1999, unreported) per Turner J, concerning ambiguities and inferences from the questionnaire used by the Home Office to test domicile.

6   *Agulian v Cyganik* [2006] EWCA Civ 129, [2006] 1 FCR 406 (24 February 2006), *Scappaticci v A-G* [1955] P 47, [1955] 1 All ER 193. See also *Ahktar (Ali)* [2002] UKIAT 02135. The Court (per Arden LJ) in *Barlow Clowes International Ltd (In Liquidation) and Ors v Henwood* [2008] EWCA Civ 577 at paras 14–15 stated: 'Given that a person can only have one domicile at any one time for the same purpose, he must in my judgment have a singular and distinctive relationship with the country of supposed domicile of choice. That means it must be his ultimate home or, as it has been put, the place where he would wish to spend his last days'.

7   *Re Lloyd Evans, National Provincial Bank v Evans* [1947] Ch 695 at 703; *Re Raffenel's Goods* (1863) 3 Sw & Tr 49. However, in *Barlow Clowes International Ltd (In Liquidation) and Ors v Henwood* [2008] EWCA Civ 577, Arden LJ at 94–96 disagreed with the dictum that it is easier to show a change from one domicile of choice to another domicile of choice than it is to show a change to a domicile of choice from a domicile of origin in so far as it lays down any general rule of law, stating: '94. It seems to me that as a general proposition the acquisition of any new domicile should in general always be treated as a serious allegation because of its serious consequences'.

11.27 The Immigration Directorate Instructions (IDI)[1] set out the factors which will be taken into account in assessing whether someone has acquired a domicile of choice in the UK. They point out that length of residence is not conclusive, and neither is acquisition of nationality, although it is more important if the person has given up his or her former nationality. A statutory declaration made for naturalisation purposes, that an applicant intends to reside permanently in the UK, may be taken into account, as may possession of property, in particular the purchase of a burial plot. The nature and length of the person's employment in this country, registration as an elector, residence of other family members in the UK and the education of children in the UK are all relevant. The issue of domicile is particularly important in cases concerning the validity of marriages or divorce – especially polygamous marriages. A polygamous marriage entered into outside the United Kingdom is void under English law if either of the parties to the marriage was domiciled in England and Wales at the time of the marriage. That is the effect of the Matrimonial Causes Act 1973, s 11, in particular at paragraph (d). The IDI on domicile and its relevance to polygamous marriages also points out that the burden is on the Secretary of State to show that a polygamous marriage which took place abroad is invalid.[2] A domicile questionnaire to be completed by a sponsor who entered a polygamous marriage abroad is attached to the IDI. In *Ex p Ali*[3] the problems of domicile questionnaires were exposed. The sponsor, not understanding its purpose, had omitted all information which suggested continuing links with Pakistan, which he had left in the late 1960s to work in the UK. Only on the eve of an application for judicial review of the entry clearance officer's refusal of a certificate of entitlement to the children of his second (polygamous) marriage did the sponsor reveal evidence of land purchases, a bank account, frequent long visits and the procreation of more children with his first wife, all of which together negatived the impression given by his answers in the questionnaire that he had lost his domicile of origin in Pakistan and acquired a domicile of choice in the UK by the time of the second marriage. So long as sponsors believe that domicile questionnaires exist to test the sincerity of their desire to live in the UK rather than their domicile and therefore the validity of their second marriage, similar problems are likely to persist.

1 IDI, Chapter 8, Partners Section 1.5, July 2012, para 5.
2 IDI, Chapter 8, Partners Section 1.5, July 2012, para 1. See: *MB (Bangladesh) (by her mother and litigation friend JB) v Secretary of State for the Home Department* [2013] EWCA Civ 220, *MO v RO, RIG Ltd* [2013] EWHC 392 (Fam).
3 *R v Entry Clearance Officer Islamabad, ex p Ali* (CO/3585/97) (20 January 1999, unreported), QBD.

MARRIAGE AND CIVIL PARTNERSHIP ISSUES CONCERNING VALIDITY AND RECOGNITION

Validity of marriage or civil partnerships

11.28 In order to obtain admission as a spouse or civil partner, the applicant must satisfy the entry clearance officer that the marriage or civil partnership is valid and complies with the requirements of the Immigration Rules.[1] Where the marriage is relied upon to show that the person is the spouse of a qualified EEA national the Tribunal held (in the absence of a common definition of marital relationships in EEA States) that the question whether a person is a spouse is governed by and falls within the legal competence of the individual Member state.[2]

A valid marriage requires that both parties had the necessary capacity to marry, and that the celebration was in a valid form. Capacity to marry is normally determined by the ante-nuptial domiciliary law of each party.[3] A valid civil partnership requires that the partners are of the same sex, that neither of them is already a civil partner or lawfully married, both are over 16, and neither are within prohibited degrees of relationship.[4] The formal validity of the marriage or civil partnership is determined by the law of the place of celebration.[5] In general a marriage which is valid by the *lex loci celebrationis* is valid everywhere even though the proceedings if conducted in the place of the parties' domicile it would not be a valid marriage. Additionally if the proceedings is not a marriage in the place where it is celebrated there is not marriage anywhere.[6]

The Civil Partnership Act 2004 gives legal effect to 'overseas relationships' which are either relationships specified in Schedule 20 of the Act (which lists the recognised overseas partnerships[7]) or relationships which meet the general criteria for UK civil partnerships and these relationships are registered with a responsible authority outside the UK by two people who under the relevant law are the same sex at the time of registration, and neither of whom is already a civil partner or lawfully married.[8] The parties can apply to the courts for a declaration that a marriage or civil partnership[9] was at its inception a valid marriage/civil partnership, or that it subsisted or did not subsist at a particular date if one of the parties to the marriage/civil partnership is domiciled in the UK or on the date of application had been habitually resident in England and

Wales for one year preceding the date of the application.[10] The only route to a judicial conclusion that a marriage was void at its inception is a petition for nullity. An alternative route, namely an application for a declaration is proscribed.[11]

A detailed review of private international law relating to the validity of marriages and divorces and civil partnerships is beyond the scope of this work,[12] but we focus on the particular problems likely to be encountered in immigration cases, in particular the rules relating to polygamous marriages and the recognition of *talaq* divorces.

[1]   In *NA (Customary marriage and divorce – evidence) Ghana* [2009] UKAIT 00009, the Tribunal noted the difficulties of establishing a customary marriage or divorce because of the lack of formal procedures but noted the onus of proving either a customary marriage or dissolution rests on the party making the assertion, that it is reasonable to expect the appellant to produce the best available evidence to support this assertion and that this could comprise evidence in the form of a statutory declaration or an affidavit produced by family members or other people able to confirm the dissolution of the customary tribal marriage. See concerning the treatment of contested evidence of a customary marriage *MO v RO, RIG Ltd* [2013] EWHC 392 (Fam).

[2]   *Kareem (Proxy marriages – EU law) Nigeria* [2014] UKUT 24 (IAC). The validity of the marriage in Nigerian law marriage in question was not established to the satisfaction of the tribunal – the Tribunal stating: 'It should be assumed that, without independent and reliable evidence about the recognition of the marriage under the laws of the EEA country, and/or the country where the marriage took place, the Tribunal is likely to be unable to find that sufficient evidence has been provided to discharge the burden of proof. Mere production of legal materials from the EEA country or country where the marriage took place will be insufficient evidence because they will rarely show how such law is understood or applied in those countries. Mere assertions as to the effect of such laws will, for similar reasons, carry no weight.' See also *TA (Kareem explained)* [2014] UKUT 316 (IAC).

[3]   Family Law Act 1986, s 55. See: *X City Council v MB* [2006] EWHC 168 (Fam) (13 February 2006); *SM (Domicile of choice, Scots law) Pakistan* [2008] UKAIT 00092 (26 November 2008). See concerning a marriage valid under Sharia and Bangladeshi law and voidable in English law where the very vulnerable adult lacked the capacity to consent to a *marriage – the Court held that on public policy grounds the marriage was not to be recognised here*: City of Westminster Social and Community Services Department v C [2008] EWCA Civ 198, [2009] 2 WLR 185, [2008] Fam Law 517. In a similar case involving a severely disabled British husband the Tribunal held the marriage celebrated in Pakistan to be valid but in the special circumstances arising from the husband's incapacity to consent it too was not entitled to recognition – noting at para 21 – 'the appellants have not established that the marriage between the sponsor and the first appellant is, albeit valid, entitled to recognition in this country. It is contrary to public policy to recognise as valid a marriage which is voidable for lack of mental capacity of one of the parties, and in which the normal incidents of marriage would amount to the commission of a criminal offence by one of them': *ZB & HB (Validity and recognition of marriage) Pakistan* [2009] UKAIT 00040.

[4]   Civil Partnership Act 2004, s 3. Parental consent is required if a proposed civil partner is under 18 (Civil Partnership Act 2004, s 4).

[5]   *CB (Validity of marriage: proxy marriage) Brazil* [2008] UKAIT 00080 (10 October 2008). The AIT upheld the validity of a proxy marriage celebrated in Brazil between two parties domiciled in the UK because such marriages were valid according to Brazilian law.

[6]   See: Lord Collins of Mapesbury (ed), Dicey, Morris and Collins: *The Conflict of Laws* (15th edn, 2012, at 17.004, p 919. The courts distinguish between a void marriage which may be the subject of a nullity decree and non-marriages where no decree will be granted. See *Asaad v Kurter* [2013] EWHC 3852 (Fam); [2014] 2 FLR 833. Where the marriage ceremony may not have complied with legal procedures in the country of celebration, the courts will assess whether the ceremony of event purported to be a lawful marriage, whether key participants including those officiating intended and understood the ceremony to give rise to a lawful marriage. See Dicey, Morris and Collins: *The Conflict of Laws*, op cit at 17-006, p 919.

[7]   Schedule 20 to the Civil Partnership Act 2004 is updated by The Civil Partnership Act 2004 (Overseas Relationships) Order 2012, SI 2012/2976 which came into effect on 31 January 2013.

8   Civil Partnership Act 2004, ss 212–218. As with marriages the general conditions deal with the capacity of the parties, their intention and compliance with the required formalities. And again congruent with the marriage rules there is a public policy exception which denies recognition if one or both of the partners do not have the capacity to consent to such relationship.
9   Civil Partnership Act 2004, ss 58–61.
10 Family Law Act 1986, s 55. If it is asserted that the marriage was void ab initio, the remedy lies in a petition of nullity. In deciding whether to grant recognition to a foreign marriage, the court will exercise 'common sense, good manners and reasonable tolerance': *Cheni (otherwise Rodriguez) v Cheni* [1965] P 85, recognising the marriage of an uncle and niece as valid under the law of their domicile, but noting that an overseas marriage that would be 'offensive to the conscience of the English Court' may not be recognised even if it is valid under the foreign law. (See fn 2 above.) See on the presumption of validity of marriage: *FI (Bangladesh presumption marriage legitimacy)* [2005] UKIAT 00016 (and of civil partnerships – Civil Partnership Act 2004, ss 58, 224).
11 Family Law Act 1986, ss 55(1); 58(5).
12 IDI, Chapter 8, Partners Section, FM 1.3, July 2012. 'Recognition of Marriage and Divorce', deals with several of the most common validity issues, namely polygamous, proxy and telephone marriages, child spouses, as well as *talaq* and customary divorces, and divorce in the Philippines. See on proxy phone marriage for the purpose of the ECHR, Art 8. *J (Pakistan)* [2003] UKIAT 00167, *SB v Secretary of State for Work and Pensions (BB) (Bereavement and death benefits : bereavement payments)* [2014] UKUT 495 (AAC); *Kareem (Proxy marriages – EU law) Nigeria* [2014] UKUT 24 (IAC) and on the validity of a proxy Brazilian marriage: *CB (Validity of marriage: proxy marriage) Brazil* [2008] UKAIT 00080 (10 October 2008). See on the Islamic institution of muta or sighe which the Tribunal stated is not marriage within the meaning of the Immigration Rules, as its existence does not imply a relationship continuing or intended to continue beyond its termination (*LS (Mut'a or sighe) Iran* [2007] UKAIT 00072 (30 July 2007)). IDI, Chapter 8, Section 2, Annex H 'Civil Partnerships', Jan 2013 deals with the eligibility, registration and dissolution of civil partnerships and lists the foreign civil partnerships recognised in the UK. See on customary marriages and divorce *NA (Customary marriage and divorce, evidence) Ghana* [2009] UKAIT 00009 (12 January 2009), *MO v RO, RIG Ltd* [2013] EWHC 392 (Fam).

POLYGAMOUS MARRIAGES

11.29 Polygamous marriages are those where under the law of the place of the celebration of the marriage (*lex loci celebrationis*) the husband is permitted to marry more than one wife during the subsistence of the marriage, or the wife is permitted to take another husband.[1] A man or woman whose personal law does not allow polygamous marriage has no capacity to contract a valid polygamous marriage.[2] A marriage contracted in a place which permits polygamy may be actually or potentially polygamous. It is actually polygamous where either partner has more than one spouse, and potentially so if the couple have no other spouse but the husband or wife is entitled to take more than one spouse under the local law. A polygamous marriage entered into in England is always invalid.[3] The common law rule was that all marriages celebrated in the UK must be monogamous, whatever the form used.[4] A person with a domicile in England and Wales is not permitted to marry polygamously.[5] For marriages taking place after 31 July 1971, validity is dealt with by statute. The Matrimonial Causes Act 1973, section 11(d) provides that:

'A marriage celebrated after 31 July 1971 shall be void on the following grounds only, that is to say . . .
(d)   in the case of a polygamous marriage entered into outside England and Wales, that either party was at the time of the marriage domiciled in England and Wales.

> For the purposes of paragraph (d) of this subsection a marriage *is not* polygamous if at its inception neither party has any spouse additional to the other.[6]

Thus under the Matrimonial Causes Act 1973, so long as neither party is already married, a couple, either of whom may be domiciled in England and Wales, may marry under a law where polygamy is permitted and will have that marriage accepted as valid under English law.[7] The effect of this provision is that if neither party is married to another at the time the marriage is celebrated then the marriage is not void on the ground that it is potentially polygamous.[8] As noted above, a civil partnership registered in England and Wales will also be void if either of the partners is not eligible to register as civil partners because he/she is already a civil partner or lawfully married, and an overseas relationship is not recognised if these same circumstances apply.[9]

1. The system of marriage where the wife can take a second husband is polyandry. However the amended paragraph 278 of HC 395 uses the word 'polygamous' in a gender-neutral way. Note that paragraph 278 concerns polygamous marriages and civil partnerships.
2. *Re Bethell, Bethell v Hildyard* (1888) 38 Ch D 220; *Ali v Ali* [1968] P 564, [1966] 1 All ER 664. Note, that marriages which start off as polygamous may be converted into monogamous marriages by subsequent events: the spouses may change their religion; may subsequently marry in an English registry office; may obtain a domicile where polygamous marriage is not allowed; or the local law may change and prohibit polygamy: *Chetti v Chetti* [1909] P 67; *Mehta (otherwise Kohn) v Mehta* [1945] 2 All ER 690; *Sinha Peerage Claim* [1946] 1 All ER 348n, *Ohochuku v Ohochuku* [1960] 1 All ER 253, [1960] 1 WLR 183, *Parkasho v Singh* [1968] P 233, [1967] 1 All ER 737.
3. *R v Bham* [1966] 1 QB 159, [1965] 3 All ER 124, CCA; *R v Ali Mohamed* [1964] 2 QB 350n.
4. *Chetti v Chetti* [1909] P 67.
5. Matrimonial Causes Act 1973, s 11(d).
6. The words in italics were inserted by the Private International Law (Miscellaneous Provisions) Act 1995, s 8(2), Sch, para 2(1)–(2) (in force January 1996). Prior to this, the subsection provided that a marriage was polygamous even though at its inception neither party had any additional spouse.
7. Matrimonial Causes Act 1973, s 11(d). However, whilst section 11(d) of the Matrimonial Causes Act 1973 applies so that a potentially polygamous marriage would not be void if either party was at the time of the marriage domiciled in England and Wales, it did not alter the position regarding actually polygamous marriages. Under section 11(d) of the 1973 Act, a polygamous marriage entered into outside England and Wales shall still be void if either party at the time of the marriage was domiciled in England and Wales. *Abdin (domicile – actually polygamous marriages) Bangladesh* [2012] UKUT 309 (IAC).
8. This modification inserted into the Matrimonial Causes Act 1973, s 11(d) by the Private International Law (Miscellaneous Provisions) Act 1995 is generally retrospective. Private International Law (Miscellaneous Provisions) Act 1995, s 6. This resolves the anomaly exposed by *Hussain v Hussain* [1983] Fam 26. The husband in that case had an English domicile and was married in Pakistan which did not permit women to have more than one spouse. The marriage was therefore valid. Had the woman been domiciled in England and the husband domiciled in Pakistan, under the law then applying, the marriage would have been void in English law as potentially polygamous. The change resolved such problems. See also IDI, Chapter 8, Partners, Section FM1.4: Polygamous and potentially polygamous marriages.
9. Civil Partnership Act 2004, ss 3, 49, 212.

11.30 Children born to parents in valid or invalid polygamous marriages under English rules may still be legitimate – the latter where the marriage is valid under the conflict rules of the country in which the parents are domiciled when the child is born. Their legitimate status has been relevant to whether a child takes citizenship from his/her father.[1] Illegitimacy is no bar to admission to join a father under the Immigration Rules.[2] For children born before 1 July 2006, citizenship by descent and acquisition of the right of abode through the father depends on legitimacy – although this restriction will cease to apply when the new citizenship provisions set down in section 65 of the Immigration Act 2014 come into force.[3] Illegitimate children born on or after 1 July 2006, can take their citizenship from their father.[4] A child of a polygamous marriage who has the right of abode is not prevented from entry to the UK in the same way as a spouse, but where the child is not a British citizen and his/her parent would be refused entry or leave to remain pursuant to paragraphs 278 or 278A on the ground of polygamy, Rule 296 does not permit the child to be granted entry clearance, leave to enter, or leave to remain. The Upper Tribunal in *SG (child of polygamous marriage) Nepal*[5] observed that the meaning of this rule is not entirely clear – stating: 'is this provision designed to prevent such a child entering in accordance with any of the rules relating to children or only those rules that give the child a contingent right if being joined by both parents?' The Tribunal concluded the rule did not operate as 'an absolute bar of or child's admission.' It indicates that the mother's presence in the country child and her ability to care for the child mean that it is unlikely that the responsibility eligible for admission to the United Kingdom under the sole

noting:

'There is a legit... woman who is a p... aim in excluding from admission to the United Kingdom a indirect effect of that... an actually polygamous marriage and that aim justifies the more difficult for the ch... usion on the child of such a marriage, in that it will be responsibility and circumstan... to satisfy the Immigration Rules relating to sole ... making exclusion of the child undesirable'.

Paragraph 296 of HC 395, as ... resently applied, does not prevent the admission of such children and wou... probably be contrary to Articles 8 and 14 of the ECHR if it did.[6]

---

[1] See Legitimacy Act 1976, s 1.

> '(1) The child of a void marriage, whenever born, shall, subject to subsection (2) below and Schedule 1 to this Act, be treated as the legitimate child of his parents if at the time of the insemination resulting in the birth or, where there was no such insemination, the child's conception (or at the time of the celebration of the marriage if later) both or either of the parties reasonably believed that the marriage was valid.
>
> (2) This section only applies where the father of the child was domiciled in England and Wales at the time of the birth or, if he died before the birth, was so domiciled immediately before his death.
>
> (3) It is hereby declared for the avoidance of doubt that subsection (1) above applies notwithstanding that the belief that the marriage was valid was due to a mistake as to law.'

See: *Azad v Entry Clearance Officer, Dhaka* [2001] INLR 109, [2001] Imm AR 318, CA; *MB (Bangladesh) (by her mother and litigation friend JB) v Secretary of State for the Home Department* [2013] EWCA Civ 220.

[2] HC 395, para 6 (definition of 'parent' for immigration purposes). The rule at (c) states that a parent includes 'the father as well as the mother of an illegitimate child where he is proved to be the father'.

[3] The Secretary of State may register as a British citizen the illegitimate child of a British citizen father under general registration powers: British Nationality Act 1981, s 3(1). See Nationality Instructions, Chapter 9: Registration of minors at discretion. The 2014 Act inserts sections 4E–4J into the 1981 Act.

[4] BNA 1981, ss 50(9), (9A), (9C). The NIAA 2002, s 9 substituted a new s 50(9) into BNA 1981, which provides that the father of a child is the husband at the time of the child's birth of the woman who gives birth to the child or any person who satisfies prescribed requirements as to proof of paternity. The requirements to be satisfied are those under the British Nationality (Proof of Paternity) Regulations 2006, SI 2006/1496, made under s 50(9B) of BNA 1981, illegitimacy is no longer to be a bar to tracing nationality through the father, who, for nationality purposes, is either (a) the father named in a birth certificate issued within one

year of the birth of the child, or (b) identified as such by s 28 of the Human Fertilisation and Embryology Act 1990, or (c) able to satisfy prescribed requirements as to proof of paternity under the regulations.

5   [2012] UKUT 265 (IAC)
6   *SG (child of polygamous marriage) Nepal* [2012] UKUT 265 (IAC).

RECOGNITION OF *TALAQ* AND OTHER OVERSEAS DIVORCES

11.31 The rules relating to recognition of foreign divorces and judicial separations are found in sections 44 to 54 of the Family Law Act 1986[1] and are not set out comprehensively here. The recognition of Islamic *talaq* divorces is an issue which usually arises in the immigration context when considering whether the parties are married and a claimant can enter the UK as a spouse Under Islamic sharia law, a husband is permitted to divorce a wife wition recourse to court proceedings simply by declaring unequivocally his *talaq* and to repudiate the marriage in the presence of witnesses. This is a bad religious involves no proceedings at all. Most Islamic countries have maq with a court law by requiring some additional formal registration of the conciliation proceedor administrative body and/or that the parties undertake requires registration ings. Thus in Pakistan the Muslim Family Law Ordiact Council, and the *talaq* of the *talaq* with the Chairman of the Union Dict period for reconciliation.[2] A does not become effective until the elapse of enders the husband liable to a failure to comply with these formalities Muslim Family Law Ordinance does penalty.[3] In Azad Kashmir, however, th not apply.[4]

1   In force 4 April 1988. If divorce fails to be recognised under the provisions of the 1986 Act, s 52(4)–(5) of that Act allows 'stepping back' to the previous legislation, the Recognition of Divorce and Legal Separations Act 1971 (in force 1 January 1972), including amendments to that Act by the Domicile and Matrimonial Proceedings Act 1973 (the amendments commenced on 1 January 1974). See IDI, Chapter 8, Section FM 1.3: on the recognition of marriage and divorce.
2   Muslim Family Law Ordinance 1961. See discussion of *Pakistani talaq requirements in Baig v Entry Clearance Officer, Islamabad* [2003] INLR 117, aka *B v Entry Clearance Officer, Islamabad (Pakistan)* [2002] UKIAT 04229 (13 September 2002) (starred).
3   It may be that a divorce that fails to comply with these provisions is still a valid divorce recognised in Pakistan, and may therefore be recognised in the UK under the Immigration Rules where no proceedings have taken place; see below.
4   Azad Kashmir has its separate legal system. See *Khan (Sakhi Daler) v The State of Pakistan* PLD 1957 Lahore 813 and the Azad Jammu and Kashmir Interim Constitution Act 1974. The Tribunal recognised the validity of bare *talaq* divorces arranged in India and Azad Kashmir which were lawful in those states: *NC (bare talaq, Indian Muslims, recognition) Pakistan* [2009] UKAIT 00016.

11.32 Formerly, English common law could give recognition to such a divorce if it were recognised by the law of the parties' domicile, even if the *talaq* had been pronounced in the UK.[1] The position is now governed by statute, which applies to any divorce, whether obtained before or after 5 April 1988.[2] No *talaq* pronounced in the UK will be a valid divorce, even if followed by proceedings overseas, because no divorce obtained in the UK is effective unless it is granted by a court of civil jurisdiction.[3] This rule cannot be evaded by divorcing in a foreign embassy, which is considered to be in the UK.[4] Nor can it be evaded by obtaining a foreign court's recognition of the extra-judicial

English divorce and seeking to recognise the foreign judgment.[5]

1   *Qureshi v Qureshi* [1972] Fam 173, [1971] 1 All ER 325. See also [2005] UKSSCSC CP_3108_2004 (25 April 2005), a case about entitlement to widow's pension.
2   Family Law Act 1986, ss 45 and 52; but the Act preserves, inter alia, s 6 of the Recognition of Divorces and Legal Separations Act 1971, for the survival of some common law rules on recognition.
3   Family Law Act 1986, Pt II s 44(1); *Re Fatima* [1986] AC 527, [1986] 2 All ER 32, HL; *Hamid* (14314) IAS 1996, Vol 4, No 1, *Sulaiman v Juffali* [2002] 1 FLR 479, [2002] 2 FCR 427, [2002] Fam Law 97. See also on a transnational Israeli divorce, *Berkovits v Grinberg (A-G intervening)* [1995] Fam 142 (Fam Div).
4   *Radwan v Radwan* [1972] 3 All ER 967; IDI (Dec/00), Chapter 8, s 1, Annex B.
5   *Maples (formerly Melamud) v Maples* [1988] Fam 14, [1987] 3 All ER 188.

11.33 Section 46 of the Family Law Act 1986 draws a distinction between a divorce 'obtained by means of proceedings' and a divorce 'obtained otherwise than by means of proceedings'.[1] A divorce 'obtained otherwise than by means of proceedings' cannot be valid if either party to the marriage was habitually resident in the UK during the period of one year immediately preceding the date the divorce was obtained.[2] This particular provision is of importance in immigration cases, because, in an immigration context, it frequently happens that one of the parties to the claimed divorce was so resident in the UK. Where the sponsor has at all material times been habitually resident in the UK, the divorce is entitled to recognition in English law only if it was 'obtained by means of proceedings'.[3] In the starred determination *Baig v Entry Clearance Officer, Islamabad*, the Tribunal held that an effective divorce must have been obtained under the law of the country in which it was obtained and that the divorce be 'obtained by means of' the proceedings – one must be able to say that if the proceedings had not taken place, the divorce would not have been obtained.[4] Registration of a *talaq* under the Muslim Family Law Ordinance amounts to proceedings,[5] but a bare *talaq* does not,[6] nor does a *talaq al-hasan*, obtained by the required pronouncements, if it is not notified to the Chairman of the Union Council under the Muslim Family Law Ordinance.[7]

1   Family Law Act 1986, s 46(1) and (2)
2   Family Law Act 1986, s 46(2). On the meaning of 'habitual residence' see **11.11**, fn 2 and **11.14**, fn 1, above.
3   Family Law Act 1986, s 46(1), *Baig v Entry Clearance Officer, Islamabad* [2002] UKIAT 04229, [2003] INLR 117 (starred); *B v Entry Clearance Officer, Islamabad (Pakistan)* [2002] UKIAT 04229 (13 September 2002) (starred). See also *NC (bare talaq, Indian Muslims, recognition) Pakistan* [2009] UKAIT 00016 (19 March 2009) in which the AIT upheld the validity of bare *talaqs* which took place in Kashmir and India. The AIT noted evidence that Indian Muslim husbands may lawfully divorce their wives by bare *talaq*, as may Pakistani Muslim husbands in that part of Kashmir which is in Pakistan. Such divorces are recognised by the United Kingdom (subject to the rules on domicile and habitual residence) pursuant to s 46(2) of the Family Law Act 1986.
4   [2002] UKIAT 04229, [2003] INLR 117. See also Family Law Act 1986, s 46(1); *Qureshi v Qureshi* [1972] Fam 173, [1971] 1 All ER 325; *R v Registrar General of Births, Deaths and Marriages, ex p Minhas* [1977] QB 1, [1976] 2 All ER 246.
5   *Quazi v Quazi* [1980] AC 744, [1979] 3 All ER 897, HL.
6   *Bi (Maqsood)* (10144); *Nadeem* (00TH 00100) IAS 2000, Vol 3, No 8.
7   *Baig v Entry Clearance Officer, Islamabad* [2003] INLR 117, *B v Entry Clearance Officer, Islamabad (Pakistan)* [2002] UKIAT 04229 (13 September 2002) (starred).

11.34 As stated, some provision is made in UK law for recognising overseas divorces which are obtained without any proceedings at all.[1] The requirements are that the divorce is effective under the law of the country in which it was obtained; that either the two parties were domiciled in the country where the divorce was obtained at the time or one party was so domiciled and the divorce is recognised as valid in the law of the other party's domicile; and that neither party was habitually resident in the UK in the year before the divorce.[2] Thus a West African customary divorce may be recognised if evidence of either dissolution by a customary court or agreement by the heads of the parties' families is available by affidavit, accompanied by a document registering the divorce and a certificate of the Minister for Foreign Affairs.[3]

[1] Family Law Act 1986, s 46. The IDI (Chapter 8, Annex B) deal with Filipino divorces, which pose a particular problem for those who retain a Philippines domicile as at present it is only possible to obtain a divorce permitting remarriage in the Philippines if both parties are Muslims. See also *NA (Customary marriage and divorce, evidence) Ghana* [2009] UKAIT 00009 (12 January 2009).

[2] Family Law Act 1986, s 46(2).

[3] See for example *Wicken v Wicken* [1999] Fam 224. In *NA (Customary marriage and divorce – evidence) Ghana* [2009] UKAIT 00009, the Tribunal noted the difficulties of establishing a customary marriage or divorce and stated that it is reasonable to expect the appellant to produce the best available evidence to support this assertion and that this could comprise evidence in the form of a statutory declaration or an affidavit produced by family members or other people able to confirm the dissolution of the customary tribal marriage. See also discussion of evidence required to show a customary marriage in *Kareem (Proxy marriages – EU law) Nigeria* [2014] UKUT 24.

11.35 The above summary of the legal rules suffices for consideration of the validity of divorces for immigration purposes. It should be noted that where there is a dispute between parties, an overseas divorce, whether obtained by proceedings or not, may be refused recognition by the English courts in circumstances: (a) where notice of proceedings was not reasonably given or where a party to the marriage has not been given a reasonable opportunity to take part in the proceedings; (b) where, for divorces obtained otherwise than by means of proceedings, there is no official certificate or document certifying that the divorce is effective under the law of that country; or (c) where recognition would be manifestly contrary to public policy.[1] In *Chaudhary v Chaudhary*[2] an alternative ground for non-recognition of a bare *talaq* was that recognition would be contrary to public policy because the husband pronounced it to defeat the wife's claim to ancillary relief in the UK. Recognition will also be withheld if the foreign divorce conflicts with the judgment on the subsistence or validity of the marriage by a British court or a court whose judgment is entitled to be recognised in the UK.[3] Note that the provisions for the dissolution and nullity of civil partnerships are provided for in Chapter 2 of the Civil Partnership Act 2004. In time, there may be similar legal complexity concerning the recognition of overseas dissolutions of civil partnerships.[4]

[1] Family Law Act 1986, s 51(3).

[2] [1985] Fam 19.

[3] Family Law Act 1986, s 51(1)(b). See also *Tahir v Tahir* 1993 SLT 194, 1992 WL 1349617.

[4] Civil Partnership Act 2004, Pt 5. See also Civil Partnership Act 2004 (Amendments to Subordinate Legislation) Order 2005, SI 2005/2114 and the Civil Partnership (Treatment of Overseas Relationships) Order 2005, SI 2005/3042.

SPOUSE/CIVIL PARTNER UNDER 16

11.36 The age at which a person can contract a valid marriage/civil partnership varies from country to country. An age requirement will usually be classified as a matter of capacity affecting the essential validity of the marriage. It will therefore fall, under English law, to be dealt with according to the law of the domicile of the particular person. A marriage/civil partnership contracted by a spouse/partner domiciled in the UK is not valid if he or she is under 16.[1] However, in a number of countries marriage under the age of 16 is permitted and marriages in such countries by spouse under this age, domiciled there, are regarded as valid. The Immigration Rules concerning young spouses/civil partners are contained in HC 395, para 277. The Rules do not permit entry for settlement or leave to remain as a spouse/civil partner if either the applicant or sponsor is under 18 at the date of arrival or grant of leave.[2]

[1] Matrimonial Causes Act 1973, s 11(a)(ii). Civil Partnership Act 2004, ss 3–4.
[2] On 27 November 2008 the government raised the age for spouse leave from 18 to 21: 'to prevent forced marriages': *Controlling our Borders: Making Migration Work for Britain: The Five year Strategy for Asylum and Immigration*, Cm 6472, February 2005, p 22. In *R (on the application of Aguilar Quila) v Secretary of State for the Home Department* [2011] UKSC 45 a majority of the Supreme Court struck down the rule as the SSHD failed to establish that the interference with the rights of the respondents under Article 8 was justified.

MARRIAGE/CIVIL PARTNERSHIP — THE FORMALITIES AND PROCEDURES

11.37 Apart from the requirement of monogamy, marriages celebrated in the UK must comply with the requirements of the Marriage Act 1949 and subordinate regulations, and are void if they do not comply. Civil partnerships must comply with the requirements in the Civil Partnership Act 2004. The formalities for marriages and civil partnerships are similar. The marriage/civil partnership should have been celebrated in a building approved for civil marriage by the Marriage Act 1994,[1] or Civil Partnership Act 2004 and there should be a marriage/civil partnership certificate issued by a registrar or superintendent registrar.[2] Marriage certificates can also be issued by a clergyman of the Church of England or Wales, a synagogue, a non-conforming church or the Society of Friends.[3] An irregular ceremony *bona fide* entered into may benefit from the presumption of validity of marriage: thus in *Bath*[4] the Court of Appeal relied on the presumption to find that a long marriage preceded by an irregular ceremony in an unregistered Sikh temple was valid; but if there is deliberate or wilful disregard of the requirements the marriage is void.[5] The Immigration Act 2014, Part 4 introduces significant changes to the requirements for marriage and civil partnerships.[6] The requirement to give notice of an impending marriage or civil partnership will be increased from 15 days to 28 days by the Act. This applies to everyone in England and Wales, regardless of their nationality. Notice must be given to a registrar by both parties in person, and they will be required to provide specified evidence of nationality, rather than the current position whereby the registrar/registration authority just needs to be satisfied of nationality. People who do not have the correct documents face being prevented from getting married, or forming a civil partnership, as they will be unable to comply with the new notice requirements. – If one party to the proposed marriage/civil partnership is a non-EEA national (save where the non-EEA national is exempt from immigration control, someone with settled status, permanent residence, or a person who has entry clearance as a fiancé or proposed civil partner) the registrar/registration authority is required to inform the Home Office of the proposed marriage or civil partnership. Once the Secretary of State has been notified, she has 28 days to decide whether or not to mount an investigation into the proposed union. If she does not investigate further, she will notify the registrar/registration authority, and the couple, who may then proceed to marry or form a civil partnership. However, if the Secretary of State has 'reasonable grounds for suspecting that the proposed marriage or civil partnership is a sham' then she can mount an investigation, which extends the notice period to 70 days. The decision whether or not to investigate is stated to be made on the basis of 'intelligence-based risk profiles' and other factors as the Secretary of State deems relevant. The Home Office fact sheet suggests that investigations may be triggered if one of the parties is of a nationality at high risk of involvement in a sham; has a visa of a category which is linked to sham cases; has no immigration status, or leave which is due to expire shortly, or has previously sponsored another partner to enter or remain in the UK. If the couple are deemed by the Secretary of State to have failed to comply with the investigation; the registrar cannot proceed to marry the couple. If the couple have complied with the investigation, but the marriage is deemed a sham, they will be able to marry, but the Secretary of State can decline to grant leave to the spouse/partner, make a decision to remove the person or refer the case for prosecution. A 'sham' marriage or partnership is one where the Secretary of State concludes that there is no genuine relationship between the parties. In summary, the IA 2014 changes to marriage and civil partnership procedures affecting immigration applications include:

— New powers of disclosure of information between: registrars and the Home Office.
— The ending of the exemption from civil preliminaries for non-EEA nationals who are marrying in the Church of England (not yet in force).
— An extension of the duty on registrars to report suspicions of a possible sham marriage – this duty now attaches at an earlier stage, before notice has been formally given (eg where a person is making enquiries) (in force).
— The couple will face increased oversight and scrutiny of their union in future.

If the marriage/civil partnership took place abroad, entry clearance officers are instructed to consider whether the marriage/civil partnership is one recognised in the country in which it took place and properly executed so as to satisfy the requirements of the law in the country in which it took place. If these conditions are satisfied and there is no impediment in the law of either party's country of domicile restricting the person's freedom to enter the marriage, then the marriage should be taken to be valid.[7] The onus is on the parties to prove the relationship as claimed but evidence of a marriage certificate and post-nuptial correspondence may shift the burden of persuasion to the Home Office to disprove the relationship.

[1] Many buildings, including hotels and foreign embassies may be registered for the purpose: Marriage Act 1949, ss 46, 69–73 (as amended); IDI (Feb 10), Chapter 8, s 1, Annex B. Note the requirement from 1 February 2005 for persons who are not EEA nationals and require

leave to enter or remain (whether or not leave has been given) to register for their marriage at a designated registration centre: Asylum and Immigration (Treatment of Claimants, etc) Act 2004, s 19(2); The Immigration (Procedure for Marriage) Regulations 2005, SI 2005/15, Sch 1, and a marriage registered elsewhere may be void: s 20.

2   Marriage Act 1949, s 53; Civil Partnership Act 2004, ss 28–36.

3   Marriage Act 1949, s 53.

4   *Chief Adjudication Officer v Bath* [2000] 1 FCR 419, CA, [1999] UKSSCSC CG_11331_1995 (21 October 1999) a case about entitlement to widow's pension. In paragraph 21 of the Judgment of Evans LJ in *Chief Adjudication Officer v Bath*, [2000] 1 FLR 8, having considered various authorities, he said:

> 'in my judgment, these authorities show that the common law presumed from the fact of extended cohabitation as man and wife that the parties had each agreed to cohabit on that basis, and the presumption was extended to include an inference that the statutory requirements first introduced by Lord Hardwicke's Marriage Act 1753 had been duly complied with; but in each case the presumption was capable of being rebutted by clear and convincing evidence'.

See also *FI (Bangladesh, presumptions – marriage – legitimacy) Bangladesh* [2005] UKIAT 00016 (24 January 2005)

5   *Gereis v Yagoub* [1997] 1 FLR 854. See whether the ceremony was intended to create a marriage or to have a religious ceremony with 'marrriage–like characteristics'. *AM v AM (Divorce: Jurisdiction: validity of marriage)* 2001 2 FLR 6; *Hudson v Leigh* [2009] EWHC 1306 (Fam), 2009 2 FLR 1129; *Al-Saedy v Musawi* [2010] EWHC 3293 (Fam).

6   Many of these changes are to commence on 2.3.2015. See Home Office Fact Sheet on Marriage and Civil partnership changes:www.gov.uk/government/uploads/system/uploads/attachment_d ata/file/377482/Marriage_notice.pdf

7   IDI (July 2012), Chapter 8, Section FM1.3. See IDI, Chapter 8, Section 2, Annex H for civil partnerships.

11.38 Normally, the best proof of a marriage is a marriage certificate, but this is not always available or there may be doubts as to its authenticity or accuracy and the general credibility of the parties,[1] and the existence of the marriage may have to be proved in other ways. The Immigration Appeal Tribunal has accepted presumptions which go to establish the existence of a marriage in the parties' country of origin. Thus in *Begum (Nazir)*[2] the Tribunal accepted the presumption that:

> 'Marriage will be presumed in the absence of direct proof, from:
>
> (a)   prolonged and continued cohabitation as husband and wife; or
>
> (b)   the fact of the acknowledgment by the man of the child born to the woman, provided all the conditions of a valid acknowledgement . . . are fulfilled; or
>
> (c)   the fact of the acknowledgment by the man of the woman as his wife.'[3]

1   In *Kareem (Proxy marriages – EU law) Nigeria* [2014] UKUT 24 (IAC), the UT noted: 'A document which calls itself a marriage certificate will not raise a presumption of the marriage it purports to record unless it has been issued by an authority with legal power to create or confirm the facts it attests. In appeals where there is no such marriage certificate or where there is doubt that a marriage certificate has been issued by a competent authority, then the marital relationship may be proved by other evidence. This will require the Tribunal to determine whether a marriage was contracted'. See also, on the validity of marriage where parties had a false tax family, *R v Immigration Appeal Tribunal, ex p Kaur (Kulbander)* [1991] Imm AR 107; *R v Immigration Appeal Tribunal, ex p Gondalia* [1991] Imm AR 519.

2   [1976] Imm AR 31. See *LS (Mut'a or sighe) Iran* [2007] UKAIT 00072 (30 July 2007) concerning 'temporary marriages' recognised by Ashari Shi'ites.

3   *Chief Adjudication Officer v Bath* [2000] 1 FCR 419, CA, [1999] UKSSCSC CG_11331_1995 (21 October 1999), the Court of Appeal held: 'Where there is an irregular ceremony which is followed by long cohabitation, it would be contrary to the general policy of the law to refuse to extend to the parties the benefit of a presumption [that the marriage was valid] which would apply to them if there were no evidence of any ceremony at all'. See also: *Mulla's Principles*

of Mohamedan Law (nineteenth edn, 1990), s 268 and, *FI (Bangladesh, presumptions; marriage– legitimacy) Bangladesh* [2005] UKIAT 00016 (24 January 2005, unreported).

11.39 In *Akhtar*[1] the Tribunal accepted the view of experts on Islamic law that in that tradition the parties need not have met, and so a telephone marriage was valid even though the husband was not present at the marriage ceremony. In *Ur Rehman* the Tribunal held that if both parties are domiciled in a country where a telephone marriage is valid, the marriage is recognised under English law even if one of the parties was resident in the UK on the date of the marriage.[2] However, the weight of guidance and dictum now suggests that such telephone proxy marriage where one of the parties is in the UK would not be valid.[3] The IDI states that proxy marriages are valid, provided they are recognised in the country where they are celebrated and the marriage is contracted in that country.[4] The fact that a proxy may be appointed by telephone from England would not detract from recognition of the marriage celebrated elsewhere. However, by the time the application for entry clearance is determined, the couple must have met in order to comply with a specific requirement of the Immigration Rules aimed at arranged marriages.[5] A Pakistan Islamic marriage is complete even if the attendant traditional ceremonial such as the departure of the bride (ruksati) is dispensed with.[6]

---

[1] (2166).

[2] *Ur Rehman* (TH 5885/99) IAS 2000, Vol 3, No 15. The IDI however, say that a telephone marriage is not valid if one party is in the UK at the time: IDI (May 2003), Chapter 8, s 1, Annex B, para 3.1. See CB *(Validity of marriage: proxy marriage) Brazil* [2008] UKAIT 00080 (10 October 2008).

[3] *SB v Secretary of State for Work and Pensions (BB) (Bereavement and death benefits: bereavement payments)* [2014] UKUT 495 (AAC). In *City of Westminster Social and Community Services Department v C (reported sub nom. Westminster City Council v C* [2009] Fam 11), but Thorpe LJ said:

'40. In the case of marriages contracted by a transnational telephone call the ascertaining of the place of celebration is likely to involve difficult problems of great legal significance. There are public policy issues'.

'41. One obvious reason why the place of celebration may be legally significant is that one contracting party may escape the rules as to the formation of marriage applicable in that jurisdiction. More than 60 years ago it was decided that recognition of a marriage by proxy in a foreign country was not contrary to English public policy: *Apt v Apt* [1948] P 83. But these courts have not had to consider a marriage by telephone with one spouse in country A and the other in country B. It is for English law to determine *where* – is the place of celebration. It may be in country A, or in country B. Some foreign authors suggest, in the case of proxy marriages, that it should be regarded as celebrated in both countries, thus requiring compliance with the formalities of each: *Rabel, Conflict of Laws* (second edn (1958), vol 1, pp 243–244).

42. In this court there was no investigation nor any argument as to the place of celebration. I would not wish to be taken to endorse whatever consensus was reached between the parties to the effect that the marriage was celebrated in Bangladesh. The important questions of law and public policy which arise must be left for decision in a case in which they arise and in which there is adequate evidence of the foreign law relating to the incidents of the marriage ceremony.

[4] IDI (July 2012), Chapter 8, section FM 1.3, para 3.1.

[5] HC 395, para 281(iii).

[6] *Hussain (Basharat) v Visa Officer, Islamabad* [1991] Imm AR 182.

11.40 If the evidence shows that the parties were indeed married or in a civil partnership it is not necessary to pinpoint the actual date of marriage/partnership.[1] But the date of the marriage may be relevant to questions concerning the age and nationality status of children. A marriage/partnership that is held to be invalid may nevertheless qualify the applicant for admission as a fiancé(e)/proposed civil partner if it is demonstrated that the applicant was willing and able to remarry/enter a civil partnership at the date of the decision,[2] or as an unmarried partner.[3] When in doubt, therefore, simultaneous applications as a spouse/civil partner or as a fiancé(e) or an unmarried partner may need to be made in the alternative.[4]

[1] *Khanom v Entry Clearance Officer, Dacca* [1979] Imm AR 182.
[2] *Ach-Charki v Entry Clearance Officer, Rabat* [1991] Imm AR 162.
[3] HC 395, para 295A(iii). But parties legally unable to marry on grounds of consanguineous relationships or age may not seek admission as unmarried partners: HC 395, para 295A(ii) and see *R v Secretary of State for the Home Department*, ex p Ozminnos [1994] Imm AR 287, QBD; HC 395, para 295AA, amended by HC 164.
[4] The application forms for spouse, civil and unmarried partners and fiancés or proposed civil partners are the same – the Settlement Form (VAF4A Dec 2008) which should allow consideration of the application under both sets of rules. See *SZ (Applicable Immigration Rules) Bangladesh* [2007] UKAIT 00037 (30 March 2007) where the tribunal held: There is no general duty on the Tribunal to consider whether a claimant's case if differently presented or if made the subject of a different application might have succeeded on a different basis from that on which the application or claim was made. Although individual claimants cannot be expected to know the Immigration Rules, there can be no complaint if they receive a judgment on the application or claim as they put it. Exceptionally, however, the facts of a case or, in particular, the terms of a notice of decision may require the Tribunal to consider the appeal on a number of alternative bases.

MARRIAGE AND PARTNERSHIPS IN PART 8 AND THE IMMIGRATION RULES

The Arrangement and Transitional Operation of the Rules

11.41 From the 9 July 2012, the Immigration Rules concerning family members are to be found in HC 395, Part 8, Appendices FM and FM-SE. The organisation, intersection and numbering of these old and new Rules is often unclear and unnecessarily complex. Rules A277–A281 set out the transitional provisions and the interaction between Part 8 and the FM and FM-SE appendices. The transitional rules can be in play depending on the date of the family member's application. The date of an application is established by reference to HC 395, paras 30, 34G. The core arrangements made under rules A277–A281 comprise:

(i) From 9 July 2012 the Appendix FM rules apply to all applications by spouse and partners, by the parents of a British citizen, or settled children in the UK, by the children of persons with limited leave, as a partner, or parent and by adult dependent relatives (HC 395, para A277).

(ii) From 9 July 2012 the Part 8 rules continue to apply to most children's applications for leave to enter or remain whether made before or after 9 July 2012 – in particular, those child applications under rules 297–316F, and to the family members (spouse/partners and children) of relevant Points-Based System (PBS) migrants[1] and to the family members (spouse/partners and children) of refugees and beneficiaries of humanitarian protection (HC 395, para A280 (b), (f)).

(iii)   Part 8 rules also apply to children applying on or after 9 July 2012 for limited leave as the child of a parent with limited leave – if their parent was granted their limited leave to enter or remain following an application made before 9 July 2012.

(iv)   The child applications which are covered by Appendix FM rather than the Part 8 rules include leave applications made after 9 July 2012 by children, including adopted children of parents with limited leave to enter or remain with a view to settlement – where the parent's application for limited leave in these capacities was made on or after 9 July 2012 (paras 314(i)(a),(d) and 316A(i)(d) or (e)). In addition the adopted and adoptive children of a parent with limited leave have to satisfy the financial requirements in Appendix FM E-ECC 2.1–2.3 or E-LTR 2.1–2.3 (HC 395, para 280A(b)).

(v)   Specific Part 8 rules (those dealing with general relationship criteria) apply to all applications made under Part 8 and Appendix FM irrespective of the date of the application or decision (HC 395, para A280A). These include paragraphs 277 (the under 18 age restriction for spouse and partners); 278–280 (concerning polygamous marriages and civil partnerships) 289AA, 295AA (the under 18 age restriction for fiancé(e), proposed civil partners and unmarried partners) and 296 (the restriction on the entry or stay of children whose parent is a party to a polygamous marriage and would be refused admission or leave to remain on that basis).

(vi)   Under transitional arrangements the Part 8 rules generally continue to apply to persons who have made an application before 9 July 2012 under Part 8 which was not decided, as at 9 July 2012; and to applications made by persons in the UK who have been granted entry clearance, or limited leave to enter, or remain under Part 8 before 9 July 2012, and where this is a requirement of Part 8, this leave to enter or limited leave to remain is extant[2]. With some exceptions the Part 8 rules continue to apply to applications for further limited and indefinite leave to remain by such applicants[3] (para A280(b)–(c) and (e)).

(vii)   Under transitional arrangements the Part 8 rules continue to apply to the family members of a British citizen or settled person who is a full-time member of HM Forces (para A280(d))

(viii)   The rules note that in Part 8 the term 'specified' means specified in Appendix FM-SE unless otherwise stated (para A281).
The transitional rules also make provision for the further grants of limited leave to Part 8 claimants who do not meet all the requirements for the grant of ILR, and for the considerations of the family and private life rights of persons refused under the Part 8 rules (para A277B–C).

---

[1]   HC 395, para A280(g). Note the transitional arrangements for preserved Part 8 family members of relevant PBS migrants who do not meet the Part 8 requirements for indefinite leave to remain, but continue to meet the requirements for limited leave to remain (HC 395, paras A277A–277B).

[2]   The IDI, Chapter 8, Transitional Provisions (November 2014) para 3.1.2 states that while Part 8 requires extant leave, the applicant will be considered under Part 8 if their leave has expired by 28 days or less. If the leave has expired for more than 28 days; they no longer qualify for consideration under the Part 8 transitional provisions.

[3]   See paras A277A–A297 for limited application of Appendix FM rules to these preserved Part 8 cases. The persons granted leave in one of the following categories stand to be considered under Part 8 through to their claims for indefinite leave to remain: person exercising rights of

access to a child resident in the UK; fiancé(e); proposed civil partner; spouse/partners; child; adult dependent relative; post-flight family member (of a person granted refugee leave or humanitarian protection in the UK); or 14-year long residence. Note, that persons living outside the UK when their Part 8 leave expired or persons seeking to be sponsored by a spouse/partner who was not their original sponsor under Part 8 must apply under Appendix FM.

11.42 The text immediately below deals with common definitions and requirements which apply to all applications – the post-July 2012 Appendix FM applications as well as to those claimants whose applications are to be dealt with under the pre-July 2012 Part 8 rules.

Relationship Requirements for Transitional and Appendix FM Spouse and Partners

11.43 In order to obtain admission as a spouse, an applicant must satisfy the entry clearance officer that the marriage/civil partnership is lawful or valid. The following sections detail additional strictures or requirements for relationships imposed by the Immigration Rules. These restrictions may deny entry or leave to remain to spouse/civil partners even if the marriage/civil partnership is valid.

Spouse/civil and unmarried or same sex partners under 18

11.44 Marriages/civil partnerships conducted in the UK where spouses/civil partners are under 16 are void,[1] but in some countries marriages/under the age of 16 are permitted and marriages in such countries/by spouse under 16 and domiciled there, can be valid in English law. In the past, wives or husbands under 16 qualified for admission to the UK under the Immigration Rules. An amendment to the rules in 1986 required both parties to a marriage to be aged 16 or above on arrival in the UK before an entry certificate or leave to enter or remain was granted. From 21 December 2004, the rules were amended, to prevent the grant of entry clearance or leave to enter or remain if either the sponsor or the applicant spouse/civil partner was aged under 18 at the date of arrival or grant of leave in the UK.[2] By a further Rules amendment having effect after 27 November 2008 an applicant was to be refused entry clearance, leave to enter, leave to remain or variation of leave as a spouse or civil partner if either the applicant or the sponsor was or would be aged under 21 on the date of arrival in the UK or on the date on which the leave to remain or variation of leave would be granted.[3] The rule change was said to prevent 'forced marriages'.[4] In *Quila & Anor, R (on the application of) v Secretary of State for the Home Department*[5] a majority of the Supreme Court struck down the rule on the ground that while this amendment was rationally connected to the objective of deterring forced marriages what seems clear is that the number of unforced marriages which it obstructs through the exclusionary rule vastly exceeds the number of forced marriages which it deters, and the Secretary of State has thus failed to show that the amendment is no more than is necessary to accomplish her stated objective and strikes a fair balance between the rights of the parties to unforced marriages and the interests of the community in preventing forced marriages. The SSHD failed to establish that the interference with the rights of the respondents under the ECHR, Article 8 was justified. The rule was re-amended from 28 November 2011 to bring the age for spouse and civil partners seeking entry clearance or leave to remain back to 18.[6]

1   Matrimonial Causes Act 1973, s 11(a)(ii); Civil Partnership Act 2004, ss 3-4.

2   HC 395, para 277, as amended by HC 164. Between 31 March 2003 and 20 December 2004, the rule required the sponsor to have reached 18, and the applicant to have reached 16: para 277 as amended by HC 538. The minimum age requirements applied equally to fiancé(e)s, proposed civil,and unmarried, or same-sex partners: HC 395, paras 289AA, 295AA, inserted by HC 164.

3   HC 395, para 277 inserted by HC 1113. Additional changes from 6 April 2010 meant that the minimum age at which a person may be granted leave to enter or remain in the UK as the spouse, civil partner, fiancé(e), proposed civil partner, unmarried partner, or same sex partner of a serving member of the armed forces was 18-years-old. The age in which a serving member of the HM Forces can sponsor such a leave to enter/remain application was also reduced from 21 years of age to 18 years of age. The rule change for the Armed Forces was said to recognise the partner's role in supporting those on the front line.

4   See the Forced Marriage (Civil Protection) Act 2007 (in force from 25 November 2008); IDI, Chapter 8, s 1, Annex A2, Forced Marriage. See research at www.bristol.ac.uk/vawrg 'Forced marriage: the risk factors and the effect of raising the minimum age for sponsor, and of leave to enter the UK as a spouse or fiance(e). The current IDI, Chapter 8, section FM1.2, July 2012 gives guidance on how the Home Office will approach forced marriage cases.

5   [2011] UKSC 45

6   HC 395, para 277. The 2001 amendment was effected by HC 1622.

Polygamous marriages/civil partnerships

11.45 Under immigration law a polygamous spouse/civil partner can in certain circumstances qualify for leave to enter or remain as spouse/civil partners. The rules state as a general proposition that 'nothing in these Rules shall be construed as allowing a person to be granted entry clearance, leave to enter, leave to remain, or variation of leave as the spouse or civil partner of a British citizen of a settled sponsor if his or her marriage or civil partnership to the sponsor is polygamous; and there is another person living who is the husband or wife of the sponsor and who is, or at any time since his or her marriage or civil partnership to the sponsor has been, in the United Kingdom; or has been granted a certificate of entitlement in respect of the right of abode or an entry clearance to enter the UK as the husband or wife of the sponsor.'[1] The rules outline certain exceptions to this general restriction on entry as a spouse/civil partner: if the person who seeks entry clearance, leave to enter, leave to remain, or variation of leave has been in the UK before 1 August 1988 having been admitted for the purpose of settlement as the husband or wife of the sponsor; or has, since their marriage or civil partnership to the sponsor, been in the UK at any time when there was no such other spouse or civil partner living.[2] The rules also make clear that the presence of any wife or husband in the UK as a visitor, an illegal entrant or deemed non-entrant (under s 11(1) of the Immigration Act 1971) is to be disregarded when considering the polygamous spouse restrictions.[3] The person claiming to be permitted entry within these exceptions is required to prove the facts showing the exception.[4] The first marriage must be a valid one in order to disqualify the second wife. The disqualification only applies if the right of abode was obtained as a wife, and will not apply to women who are British citizens.[5] The IDI provides that entry clearance may not be withheld from a second wife where the husband has divorced the previous wife or the previous wife has died.[6] The Immigration Rules have now been amended to preclude the admission of a (so-called) polygamous (polyandrous) husband of a woman in the same terms as the rules for men.[7] The rules apply to all applications made after 2 October 2000, regardless of the date of the marriage. The provisions do not prevent polygamous spouses entering the UK in any other capacity. The Tribunal upheld the refusal of entry for settlement to the husband of a British citizen's second polygamous wife, on the grounds that the husband did not intend to live permanently with the sponsor, as he intended to remain in the UK with the wife for only six months each year, and spend the remaining months with his other wife and family in Bangladesh.[8] Where the child of a polygamous marriage is not a British citizen and his/her parent would be refused entry, or leave to remain pursuant to paragraphs 278 or 278A (on the ground of the polygamy restrictions), paragraph 296 of the Rules does not permit the child to be granted entry clearance, leave to enter or leave to remain – a provision the Upper Tribunal in *SG (child of polygamous marriage) Nepal* [2012] UKUT 265 (IAC) held did not operate as 'an absolute bar on the child's admission . . . *and would probably be contrary to Articles 8 and 14 ECHR if it did*'. The Tribunal noted that the mother's presence in the country of origin, and her ability to care for the child mean that it is unlikely that the child will be eligible for admission to the United Kingdom under the sole responsibility test.

1   Immigration Act 1988, s 2; HC 395, para 278. *Entry Clearance Officer, Dhaka v Begum (Ranu)* [1986] Imm AR 461. The order in which polygamous spouses marry is not important but the order in which they come to the UK for settlement is. It is the spouse who applies for settlement second, rather than the one who marries second, who will be refused: IDI (July 2012), Chapter 8, section FM 1.4. The rules refer to polygamous civil partnerships as well as marriages. See IDI (December 2009), Chapter 8, s 2, Annex H for the list of foreign civil partnerships. See also *SM (Domicile of choice, Scots law) Pakistan* [2008] UKAIT 00092 (26 November 2008).

2   IA 1988, s 2(4); HC 395, para 279.

3   IA 1988, s 2(7); HC 395, para 280.

4   IA 1988, s 2(5); HC 395, para 279.

5   IA 1988, s 2(1).

6   IDI (July 2012) Chapter 8, section FM 1.4, para 8. Caseworkers are instructed to be wary of death or divorce certificates 'especially where talaq or customary laws are involved'. Where there is evidence of a 'divorce of convenience' the case should be referred to a senior caseworker for advice. In respect of a recognised 'bare talaq' divorce see *NC (Bare Talaq-Indian Muslims – recognition)* Pakistan [2009] UKAIT 00016.

7   HC 395, as amended by Cm 4851, para 278. Polyandry is in fact extremely rare.

8   *AB (Settlement – six months in UK) Bangladesh* [2004] UKIAT 00314.

'Genuine' marriages and partnerships

11.46 A marriage/civil partnership is not invalid under the general law of England simply because it is entered for a purpose other than mutual cohabitation.[1] The Immigration Rules require not only that a marriage/civil partnership is valid but that the applicant, and spouse/partner have met,[2] have a genuine and subsisting relationship, and intend to live together permanently in the UK.[3] Appendix FM's 'relationship requirements' for leave to remain as a spouse/partner state that in any application for limited or indefinite leave to remain the applicant must provide evidence that since the grant of entry clearance or the last grant of limited leave to remain as a partner they have lived together in the UK or there is good reason, consistent with a continuing intention to live together permanently in the the UK, for any period in which they have not done so.[4] The Part 8 spouse and partnership rules do not carry this explicit evidential requirement.[5]

[1] In *Vervaeke v Smith* [1983] 1 AC 145, [1982] 2 All ER 144, HL the House of Lords upheld the validity of an English marriage that the wife had contracted in 1954 solely in order to obtain British nationality, and a British passport and to escape the possibility of deportation for being a prostitute. The validity of a marriage has also been upheld in other cases where it has been contracted with the object of evading immigration control: *Silver (otherwise Kraft) v Silver* [1955] 2 All ER 614, [1955] 1 WLR 728; see also *Martens v Martens* (1952) 3 SA 771, approved by Karminski J in *H v H* [1954] P 258, [1953] 2 All ER 1229. See further *Szechter (otherwise Karsov) v Szechter* [1971] P 286, [1970] 3 All ER 905. But see *R v Secretary of State for the Home Department, ex p Puttick* [1981] QB 767, [1981] 1 All ER 776.

[2] The rule that the parties must have met, appears to have been directed principally at arranged marriages. The Tribunal has interpreted the paragraph to exclude casual meetings when the parties were very young. There must be a meeting to the extent that the parties recognise and know each other, but it does not have to be a meeting in the context of marriage. It may be sufficient for the parties to have seen each other and there does not have to have been a conversation between them. *Raj (Rewal) v Entry Clearance Officer, New Delhi* [1985] Imm AR 151, *Meharban (Mohd) v Entry Clearance Officer, Islamabad* [1989] Imm AR 57. See also IDI (July 2014), Appendix FM, Section 1.0a: 'if the parties had been childhood friends, it could be acceptable, although the meeting of two infants would not . . . the parties should have had a face-to-face meeting itself resulting in the making of mutual acquaintance'.

[3] HC 395, para 281(iii), 295A, 295D; Appendix FM, E-ECP 2.6, 2.10; E-LTRP 1.7, 1.10. In *GA ('Subsisting' marriage) Ghana* [2006] UKAIT 00046 a starred decision, the Tribunal held that the requirement in HC395, para 281(iii) that a marriage be 'subsisting' is not limited to considering whether there has been a valid marriage which formally continues. The word requires an assessment of the substance of the current relationship between the parties, rather than to its legal formality, and a decision as to whether in the broadest sense it comprises a marriage properly described as 'subsisting'. This is inconsistent with *BK and ors (Spouses: Marriage – meaning of 'subsisting') Turkey* [2005] UKAIT 00174 in which having heard full argument on the issue the Tribunal concluded: 'A marriage is subsisting for the purposes of these Rules if it has been lawfully entered into and has not thereafter been lawfully dissolved or annulled'. The authors view is that the decision of the Tribunal in *BK* is to be preferred as support for this approach to the meaning of a 'subsisting marriage' is to be found in family law, tax law and pensions law where a marriage is considered to be 'subsisting' until a decree absolute. In *GA* the tribunal did not hear full argument on this issue. See also: *AB (Settlement – six months in UK) Bangladesh* [2004] UKIAT 00314, *Patel (Yanus) v Immigration Appeal Tribunal* [1989] Imm AR 416, CA. See also *VK (marriage of Convenience) Kenya* [2004] UKIAT 00305.

[4] Appendix FM, para E-LTRP 1.10.

[5] HC 395, para 284(vi); 295D(x); HC 395, para 281(iii). A husband in a polygamous marriage who intended dividing his time between his British and Bangladeshi wives was held not to have an intention to live with the British wife permanently in *AB (Settlement six months in UK) Bangladesh* [2004] UKIAT 00314. The Tribunal's interpretation of 'intention to live together permanently' involves the additional requirement that cohabitation should be full-time, which we suggest is wrong. See also *SB v Entry Clearance Officer, Islamabad (Pakistan)* [2002] UKIAT 06623 (19 February 2003) where the appellant's husband was detained in prison. The Tribunal found that in such circumstances the parties did not intend to live together permanently as husband and wife.

'Sham' Marriages/Partnerships and 'Marriages of Convenience'

11.47 There has long been considerable publicity given to the problem of 'sham' marriages/ partnerships, and the text below deals with government's efforts to deter, and punish those who advance a false relationship to gain an immigration benefit. The Immigration Rules simply require spouse and partners to be in genuine relationships. The detailed provisions aimed at detecting and preventing 'sham' marriages are confusingly spread across the Immigration and Asylum Act 1999 (ss 24, 24A), the Civil Partnership Act 2004 (Schedule 23), the Asylum and Immigration (Treatment of Claimants, etc) Act 2004 (ss 19–24) and the Immigration Act 2014 (Part 4 and Schedule 6). A 'sham' marriage/civil partnership is defined in the Immigration and Asylum Act 1999[1] as:

> 'a marriage/civil partnership (whether or not void)
>
> (a)   entered into between a person ('A') who is neither a British citizen nor a national of an EEA State other than the United Kingdom and another person (whether or not such a citizen or such a national); and
>
> (b)   entered into by A for the purpose of avoiding the effect of one or more provisions of the United Kingdom immigration law or the Immigration Rules.'

This definition has been amended by the Immigration Act 2014 in terms which at the time of writing are yet to come into force.[2] The Immigration (European Economic Area) Regulations 2006, reg 2(1) (like the predecessor of the 2000 Regulations and the Immigration (EEA) Order 1994) states that the term: 'spouse does not include a party to a marriage of convenience.'[3] In *R (on the application of Baiai) v Secretary of State for the Home Department*[4] Lord Bingham (and the parties) approved the definition of a 'marriage of convenience' in Article 1 of the EC Council Resolution 97/C382/01 of 4 December 1997 on measures to be adopted on the combating of marriages of convenience, which defined a marriage of convenience as 'a marriage . . . with the *sole* aim of circumventing the rules on entry and residence . . . and obtaining . . . a residence permit or authority to reside in a Member State'. In *Papajorgji (EEA Spouse – Marriage of Convenience) Greece* [2012] UKUT 38 (IAC) the Upper Tribunal held that there is no initial burden on a claimant to demonstrate that a marriage to an EEA national is not one of convenience. However, there is an evidential burden on the claimant to address evidence justifying reasonable suspicion that the marriage in question was undertaken for the predominant purpose of securing residence rights. In *Miah (interviewer's comments: disclosure: fairness)* [2014] UKUT 515 (IAC) the Tribunal emphasised the need for the Secretary of State to disclose 'as a matter of course' the document enshrining an interviewer's comments concerning the genuineness of a relationship (Form ICV.4605) because an appellant's right to a fair hearing dictates this course. Governments have made various changes to marriage and civil partnership formalities with the stated aim of identifying and preventing 'sham marriages'. These arrangements are detailed below.

[1]   Immigration and Asylum Act 1999, s 24(5).

[2]   The Immigration Act 2014, s 55 amends sections 24 and 24A to insert the following (composite) text:

> 'A marriage/civil partnership (whether or not it is void) is a "sham marriage/civil partnership" if—
>
> (a)   either, or both, of the parties to the marriage is not (a) a British citizen, (b) a national of an EEA State other than the United Kingdom, or (c) a national of Switzerland;
>
> (b)   there is no genuine relationship between the parties to the marriage, and
>
> (c)   either, or both, of the parties to the marriage/civil partnership enter into the marriage/civil partnership for one or more of these purposes—
>
> (i)   avoiding the effect of one or more provisions of United Kingdom immigration law (includes any subordinate legislation concerning the right of relevant nationals to move between and reside in member States) or the Immigration Rules;

(ii)   enabling a party to the marriage to obtain a right conferred by that law or those rules to reside in the United Kingdom.

[3] SI 2006/1003, reg 2, definitions of 'spouse' and 'civil partner'. See analysis of the case law in *VK (Marriage of Convenience) Kenya* [2004] UKIAT 00305 (24 November 2004); *IS (marriages of convenience) Serbia* [2008] UKAIT 00031 (11 April 2008);

[4] [2008] UKHL 53, [2008] 3 WLR 549, [2008] 3 All ER 1094.

PERMISSION TO MARRY OR ENTER INTO CIVIL PARTNERSHIPS

Permission to marry/civil partnership

11.48 The government has invoked public concern at the problem of sham immigration marriages as justification for a number of strictures which prevent or limit the rights of persons subject to immigration control and their partners marrying or entering civil partnerships in the UK or switching their short-term leave to remain to leave on spouse or civil partnership grounds.[1] These restrictions impact on the genuine as well as the sham marriage or civil partnership. The 'certificate of approval' scheme – now abolished – had previously been the centrepiece of this marriage/partnership regulatory system. The certificate of approval scheme was set out in the Asylum and Immigration (Treatment of Claimants) Act 2004, ss 19–24 and Schedule 23 to the Civil Partnership Act 2004 which required 'persons who are subject to immigration control'[2] who wished to marry or form a civil partnership in the UK[3] before a registrar[4] to meet an additional qualifying condition before the registrar could enter notice of their proposed marriage, or civil partnership in the notice book.[5] From 1 February 2005, until its abolition in May 2011, such a prospective spouse/civil partner had to satisfy the registrar that he or she has entry clearance as a fiancé(e) or prospective civil partner, or marriage or civil partner visitor,[6] or was 'settled' in the UK (as defined in the Immigration Rules, para 6) or had the written permission of the Secretary of State to marry in the UK (this was evidenced by a Home Office certificate of approval for the marriage or civil partnership). Following the successful challenges to the scheme in the High Court, Court of Appeal and House of Lords, the government acknowledged the scheme's essential incompatibility with Article 14 of the ECHR (read with Article 12).[7] The House of Lords held that section 19(3)(b) of the 2004 Act – dealing with the requirement for written permission from the Secretary of State – should be read as meaning: 'has the written permission of the Secretary of State to marry in the United Kingdom, such permission not to be withheld in the case of a qualified applicant seeking to enter into a marriage which is not one of convenience and the application for, and grant of, such permission is not to be subject to conditions which unreasonably inhibit the exercise of the applicant's right under Article 12 of the European Convention'.[8] Notwithstanding, the abolition of the certificate of approval scheme, there were several components of the 1999 and 2004 Act marriage regulation scheme left intact. These related to the requirement to give notice of the intended marriage to designated registrars, and the duty on registrars to report suspicious marriages/civil partnerships. The IA 2014 has modified and extended these features of the 2004 scheme into an elaborate regulatory system set to commence in March 2015. The new (and at the time of writing, partially implemented) scheme applies to persons intending marriage or civil partnership who are not 'exempt' by reason of their nationality or immigration status. Those exempted from the particular registration strictures comprise British citizens, EEA citizens, and Swiss nationals; those with a right of permanent residence by virtue of an enforceable EU right, or of any provision made under section 2(2) of the European Communities Act 1972, those exempt from immigration control or settled in the United Kingdom (within the meaning of the Immigration Act 1971, s 33(2A)).[9] Thus, where a marriage is to be solemnised on the authority of certificates issued by a superintendent registrar under the Marriage Act 1949[10] and one party to the marriage is not 'exempt' (as defined above)[11] the notice of intention to marry is to be delivered to specified registrars by both parties to the marriage in person.[12] The requirements extend to marriages solemnized according to the rites of the Church of England. At the time of writing, IA 2014, s 57 implementing this arrangement is not yet in force. The section 57 provision will mean that before clergy publish marriage banns or issue a common licence, the persons intending marriage must provide the clergy with specified evidence of their nationality. Where one or both of the persons is not an exempt nationality the banns and common licence process will not be available. In order to be married in the church they will have to obtain a superintendent registrar certificate (subject to the Home Office referral and investigation scheme) unless the Archbishop of Canterbury's special licence applies. The requirement to give notice of an impending marriage or civil partnership will be increased from 15 days to 28 days by the Act. This applies to everyone in England and Wales, regardless of their nationality. From 14 July 2014 the Immigration and Asylum Act 1999, ss 24, 24A (as amended) impose a duty on marriage registrars to report to the Secretary of State without delay where he/she has reasonable grounds for suspecting a marriage or civil partnership will be a sham marriage or partnership. The duty is imposed on registrars to whom a notice of marriage, or proposed civil partnership has been given, or who receive information in advance of a person giving such notice.[13] Once the Secretary of State has been notified – under provisions partially in force at the time of writing – she has 28 days to decide whether or not to investigate whether the proposed marriage/civil partnership in which the two parties are not exempted is a 'sham'.[14] The Secretary of State must notify the registrar and the couple concerning the decision whether or not to investigate, and whether the parties have complied with any investigation.[15] If the Secretary of State does not investigate further, she will notify the registrar/registration authority and the couple, who may then marry/contract a civil partnership. However, if the Secretary of State has 'reasonable grounds for suspecting that the proposed marriage or civil partnership is a sham' then she can conduct an investigation (in accordance with guidance and any regulations) which extends the notice period to 70 days.[16] The relevant parties must comply with the investigation.[17] The Secretary of State's decision whether or not to investigate is stated to be made on the basis of 'intelligence-based risk profiles' and other factors as the Secretary of State deems relevant. The Home Office Fact Sheet suggests that investigations may be triggered if one of the parties is of a nationality at high risk of involvement in a sham; has a visa of a category which is linked to sham cases; has no immigration status or leave which is due to expire shortly, or has previously sponsored another partner to enter or remain in the UK.[18] The consequences of non-compliance with an investigation or of a finding that the marriage/civil partnership is a 'sham' is not spelt out in the legislation but is to be included in regulations (not published at the time of writing). It is expected that if the Secretary of State decides that one or both of the parties have failed to comply with the investigation the registrar cannot proceed to marry the couple. If the couple have complied with the investigation, but the marriage is deemed a sham, they will be able to marry, but the Secretary of State can decline to grant leave to the spouse/partner, make a decision to remove the person, or refer the case for prosecution.[19] A 'sham' marriage or partnership is one where the Secretary of State concludes that there is no genuine relationship between the parties, and that either or both of the parties to the marriage/civil partnership seek to enter into the civil partnership for one or more of the following purposes: (i) avoiding the effect of one or more provisions of United Kingdom immigration law or the Immigration Rules; or (ii) enabling a party to the civil partnership to obtain a right conferred by that law or those rules to reside in the United Kingdom.[20] The IA 2014, Schedule 6 – from 14 July 2014 – also gives the Secretary of State and registration officials enhanced authority to disclose and exchange information – for immigration and 'crime fighting' purposes.

[1] The 'no switching' provision prevents persons from qualifying to vary their leave to remain as the spouse/civil partner of a British citizen or resident if they have not been in the UK beyond six months from the date of last admission, unless admitted as a fiancé/proposed civil partner. (HC 395, para 284 as amended, applying to marriage applications from 1 April 2003). If applying as a partner under Appendix FM – the applicant must not be in the UK as a visitor, with leave for a period of six months or less unless that leave is as a fiancé/ee, or proposed civil partner, or granted pending the outcome of family court or divorce proceedings – or on temporary admission, or in breach of immigration laws (disregarding any overstay of 28 days or less) – unless in respect of the latter applicants the exceptions in Appendix FM, EX1 apply.

[2] A person is 'subject to immigration control' for these purposes if he or she is not an EEA/EU national and requires leave to enter or remain in the UK under the Immigration Act 1971 (whether or not leave has been given): Asylum and Immigration (Treatment of Claimants etc) Act 2004, s 19(4). See below for amended definition substituted by the IA 2014, ss 49, 58(4) – which at the time of writing, has been partially implemented.

[3] AI(TC)A 2004, ss 19–20 (England and Wales), ss 21–22 (Scotland), ss 23–24 (Northern Ireland). These marriage provisions commenced on 1 February 2005. The Civil Partnership Act 2004, Sch 23: the civil partnership provisions commenced on 5 December 2005; and the Immigration (Procedure for Formation of Civil Partnerships) Regulations 2005, SI 2005/2917 on 14 November 2005. The 'permission to marry' scheme was adapted to apply to civil partnerships. Immigration (Procedure for Formation of Civil Partnerships) Regulations 2005, SI 2005/2917, reg 4.

[4] The provisions in the AI(TC)A 2004, s 19(1) apply to marriages solemnised on the authority of certificates issued by a superintendent registrar under Part III of the Marriage Act 1949 (ss 27, 31). This meant that marriages according to the rites of the Church of England solemnised after the publication of banns. or on the authority of special or common licences were not affected by the 2004 provision. The Joint Committee on Human Rights held that the provisions would lead to a significant risk of discrimination on the grounds of religion or belief without necessary objective and reasonable justification (Fourteenth Report Session, 2003–2004). See *R (on the application of Baiai) v Secretary of State for the Home Department* [2006] EWHC 823 (Admin), [2006] 3 All ER 608, [2006] 2 FCR 131, [2006] Fam Law 535 in which Silber J found the scheme discriminatory as the regime: (i) regards all marriages by a person who requires a certificate of approval for marriage (COA) as automatically actually or potentially marriages of convenience; (ii) discriminates irrationally in favour of Anglican marriages conducted under Part II of the 1949 Act; (iii) fails to take account of evidence, if available, that a particular marriage is not a sham; (iv) makes immigration status the only factor affecting whether a non-EEA national can marry in this country; (v) does not allow representations by persons affected by the scheme (paras 74–89). In a second application in the same case, *R (on the application of Baiai) v Secretary of State for the Home Department* [2006] EWHC 1454 (Admin), [2006] 4 All ER 555, the Secretary of State raised the issue of legality but did not challenge the findings on discrimination. The Court of Appeal held that: (i) Article 12, which deals with the right to marry, is regarded in the jurisprudence as a significant and fundamental right, of the sort that the courts must be vigilant to protect

(para 32); (ii) the Secretary of State can only interfere with the exercise of Article 12 rights in cases that involve, or very likely involve, sham marriages; (iii) to be proportionate, a scheme to achieve that end must either properly investigate individual cases, or at least show that it has come close to isolating cases that are very likely to fall into the target category; and (iv) it must also show that the marriages targeted do indeed make substantial inroads into the enforcement of immigration control. The court held that the scheme in issue in this case did not pass that test. The House of Lords was asked to consider the fees charged for marriage approval – then at £590 if both parties required certificates of approval. The House of Lords in *R (on the application of Baiai) v Secretary of State for the Home Department* [2008] UKHL 53, [2008] 3 WLR 549, [2008] 3 All ER 1094 broadly agreed with the Court of Appeal although it set aside the declaration of incompatibility with the ECHR except on the discrimination arising from the different treatment of marriages solemnised in the Anglican church. Rather than finding the whole scheme incompatible the Lords held that permission to marry should not be withheld if the marriage was not one of convenience and that conditions such as a fee should not unreasonably inhibit the right to marry under Article 12 of the ECHR. The IA 2014, s 57 (which at the time of writing was not yet in force) has included Anglican church marriages in the referral and investigation scheme for civil marriages (see below).

5   The entry in the marriage notice book enables the persons to marry in the UK before a registrar. The relevant prospective spouse must give their notice (see on form of prescribed notice the Registration of Marriages (Amendment) Regulations 2005, SI 2005/155) to designated registrars (listed in the Immigration (Procedure for Marriage) Regulations 2005, SI 2005/15) even if they intend marrying in a different registry office. Similar notice provisions apply for civil partnerships: Civil Partnership Act 2004, Sch 23, para 4. Note, that the regulations specify the registration districts in England and Wales at which persons subject to immigration control may give notice of a marriage/civil partnership: SI 2005/2917, reg 5 and Sch 2. According to the Explanatory Notes, the restricted number of locations will enable the Immigration Service to target their intelligence and enforcement effort in order to tackle abuse of the immigration system via sham civil partnerships in England and Wales.

6   See HC 395, paras 56D–F, inserted by HC 346 from 15 March 2005.

7   *R (on the application of Baiai) v Secretary of State for the Home Department* [2006] EWHC 823 (Admin), [2006] 3 All ER 608, [2006] 2 FCR 131, [2006] Fam Law 535; *R (on the application of Baiai) v Secretary of State for the Home Department* [2006] EWHC 1454 (Admin), [2006] 4 All ER 555.

8   *R (on the application of Baiai) v Secretary of State for the Home Department* [2008] UKHL 53, [2008] 3 All ER 1094 at para 32. See House of Common's Library Paper, by Melanie Gower, 'Immigration: Abolition of the certificate of approval to marry requirement', SN/HA/3780, 13 April 2011.

9   IA 2014, ss 49, 55 See also Marriage Act 1949, ss 27E, 28C–28H, 31

10 The referral and investigation of proposed marriages and civil partnerships is extended to Scotland and Northern Ireland. IA 2014, ss 53,54 (partially in force from 20 October 2014).

11 IA 2014, s 58 amending AITCA 2004, s 19(1B)(b) and the Civil Partnership Act 2004, Sch 23, Part 1, paras A1(3)(b) – on a date to be appointed, paras 1, 4 – requires that those claiming to be 'exempt' provide specified evidence of this status. See also Marriage Act 1949, ss 27E, 28C–28H

12 AITCA 2004, s 19(2)(b)

13 IAA 1999, ss 24,24A. (Note – certain of these arrangements in the Immigration and Asylum Act 1999, s 24 were in force from 1 January 2001 and section 24A were in force from 15 April 2005). Thus, the registrars (including district or deputy registrars) concerned were required to report their suspicions to the Secretary of State without delay and in such form and manner as may be prescribed by regulations: section 24(3). See also Reporting of Suspicious Marriages and Registration of Marriages (Miscellaneous Amendments) Regulations 2000, SI 2000/3164, 2000/3233, 2000/3232. Reporting of Suspicious Civil Partnerships Regulations 2005, SI 2005/3174. Reporting of Suspicious Marriages and Civil Partnerships (Amendment) Regulations 2014, SI 2014/1660.

14 IA 2014, s 48(1)–(5).

15 IA 2014, ss 48(7), 51.

16 IA 2014, s 50(1)–(2), (6)–(7).

17 IA 2014, s 50(3)–(6). The regulations can specify any of the following requirements to comply with the investigation: a requirement to make contact with a particular person or description of persons in a particular way (including by telephoning a particular number) within a particular time period; a requirement to be present at a particular place at a particular time; a requirement to be visited at home; a requirement to be interviewed; a requirement to provide

information (whether orally or in writing); a requirement to provide photographs or evidence. In the Public Bill Committee on the Bill for this Act in the House of Commons the Minister stated that the regulations will ensure that the Home Office, in deciding whether a couple have complied with an investigation of their proposed marriage or civil partnership, takes reasonable account of the couple's family, work and other relevant circumstances including child care, carer responsibilities, and any other arrangements they have.

18 Home Office, Immigration Bill Fact Sheet, Sham Marriages and Civil Partnerships.
19 Home Office, Immigration Bill Fact Sheet, Sham Marriages and Civil Partnerships.
20 IA 2014, s 55.

SPONSORSHIP REQUIREMENTS FOR TRANSITIONAL AND APPENDIX FM SPOUSE AND PARTNER APPLICANTS

11.49 In order for family members and unmarried or civil partners to be admitted for entry or permitted to stay in the UK they must have a sponsor who is in the UK and who wants to bring in the family member or partner. The sponsor may be a person with limited leave such as those admitted under the PBS (Tier 1–4) or a British citizen or person settled in the UK. Persons admitted as spouse, or partners, or children are generally granted leave or will be refused leave in line with their sponsors and in immigration terms are only treated as independent of the sponsor when they have been granted settlement.[1]

1 Note, that the spouse and unmarried partner rules do permit the grant of indefinite leave to remain in circumstances where the sponsorship no longer exists, either because the spouse or partner has died or the relationship ended through domestic violence. These concessions are the exception to the ongoing sponsorship requirement.

PRESENCE OF SPONSOR

11.50 For the purpose of the family Immigration Rules, those persons eligible to sponsor defined family members for entry or stay in the UK include British citizens and residents, foreign nationals with limited leave to enter or remain as 'Relevant Points Based System Migrants',[1] refugees and the beneficiaries of humanitarian protection,[2] certain members of HM Forces,[3] and (under transitional arrangements) those previously admitted as work permit holders, the highly skilled, retired persons of independent means, those with UK ancestry, domestic servants, those persons previously admitted for business, or as innovators, investors, or in EC Association categories.[4] Minor children are permitted entry or stay for settlement or with a view to settlement where one parent is a British citizen or settled in the UK, both parents are in the UK, the sponsor is the sole parent, or has sole responsibility for the child, or there are serious, or compelling family considerations which make the child's exclusion undesirable.[5]

1 'Relevant PBS Migrant' means a migrant granted to leave as a Tier 1 Migrant, a Tier 2 Migrant, a Tier 4 (General) Student, or a Tier 5 (Temporary Worker) Migrant.
2 HC 395, as amended, paras 352A–F, 356. Refugee and temporary protection family reunion is open to their spouse, civil, unmarried, and same sex partners, and minor children who are not married, or in a civil partnership, and has not formed an independent family unit. See also *NM ('leading an independent life') Zimbabwe* [2007] UKAIT 00051 (24 May 2007), *MI (Paragraph 298(iii): 'independent life') Pakistan* [2007] UKAIT 00052 (5 June 2006) family members and close relatives of those granted temporary protection under the Temporary Protection Directive EC/2001/55).

3   Those members of HM Forces eligible to sponsor their immediate family member are those who are exempt from immigration control under section 8(4)(a) of the Immigration Act and to sponsor the same family members for settlement the HM forces sponsor must additionally have had at least five years continuous service – HC 395, paras 276AD–AI and 276S–AC.

4   There are certain categories of temporary entrant permitted to sponsor their spouse, civil partners, children or unmarried or same sex partners. These include: those admitted under the PBS (Tiers 1–5) those previously admitted as work permit holders, highly-skilled migrants, international graduates scheme members, representatives of overseas newspapers, news agencies and broadcasting organisations, sole representatives, private servants in diplomatic households, domestic workers in private households, overseas government employees, those previously admitted as ministers of religion, missionaries, members of religious orders, visiting religious workers and religious workers in non-pastoral roles, airport-based operational ground staff of overseas owned airlines, persons with UK ancestry (HC 395, para 194–199, 295J), those previously admitted as persons intending to establish themselves in business, persons intending to establish themselves in business under the provisions of EC Association Agreements, investors, writers, composers and artists (HC 395, paras 240–245, 295J), retirees (HC 395, paras 263–270, 295J), Tier 1, 2, 4 and 5 holders (HC 395, para 319A–319K).

5   HC 395, Appendix FM E–ECC 1.6; paras 125, 197, 274, 319J.

11.51 With the exception of bereaved or domestic violence victim partners, family members seeking entry clearance, leave to enter, or to remain for settlement, or with a view to settlement require a sponsor[1] who is either present and settled in the UK[2] or being admitted for settlement at the same time.[3] These conditions are generally deemed to be satisfied for spouse or civil partners in the case of a sponsor who is a member of the Armed Forces serving abroad but based in the UK, or a permanent member of the diplomatic service or a comparable UK-based staff member of the British Council, or a British staff member of the Department for International Development on a tour of duty abroad.[4] 'Settled' generally means ordinarily resident in the UK without being subject to any restrictions on stay under the immigration laws.[5] A fleeting visit will not be sufficient to establish ordinary residence in the UK,[6] but an intention to live here permanently is not required[7] and one can be ordinarily resident in two places at the same time.[8]

1   Sponsor is defined in HC 395, para 6 as: 'sponsor' means the person in relation to whom an applicant is seeking leave to enter or remain as their spouse, fiance, civil partner, proposed civil partner, unmarried partner, same-sex partner, or dependent relative, as the case may be, under paragraphs 277–295O or 317–319 or the person in relation to whom an applicant is seeking entry clearance, or leave as their partner or dependent relative under Appendix FM.

2   'Present and settled' or 'present and settled in the UK' is defined in HC 395, para 6 as: meaning that the person concerned is settled in the United Kingdom and, at the time that an application under these Rules is made, is physically present here or is coming here with or to join the applicant and intends to make the UK their home with the applicant if the application is successful. The definition notes exceptions where the requirement is to be regarded – namely, British citizens or settled in the UK who are:
    (i)   a member of HM Forces serving overseas; or
    (ii)   a permanent member of HM Diplomatic Service, or a comparable UK-based staff member of the British Council, the Department for International Development, or the Home Office on a tour of duty outside the UK, and the applicant has provided the evidence specified in paragraph 26A of Appendix FM-SE.
    In such cases, for the purposes of Appendix FM the person is to be regarded as present and settled in the UK, and in paragraphs R-LTRP.1.1.(a) and R-ILRP.1.1.(a) of Appendix FM the words 'and their partner must be in the UK' are to be disregarded. For the purposes of an application as a fiancé(e) or proposed civil partner under paragraphs 289AA–295 or Appendix FM, an EEA national who holds a document certifying permanent residence issued under the 2006 EEA Regulations is to be regarded as present, and settled in the UK.

3   HC 395, Appendix FM paras GEN1.3, E-ECP2.1; ELTRP 1.2; E-LTRC 1.6; E-ECPT 2.3; E-LTRPT 2.2; E-ECDR 2.3, and the transitional Part 8 Rules See for example: paras: 281 (spouses, civil partners), 290(i) (fiancé(e)s, proposed civil partners); 295A(i) (unmarried, same

sex partners), 297(i), 301(i), 305(i), 310(i), 311(i), 314(i) (children), 317(i) (other dependants) and 276R(i), 276X, 276AA(i), 276AD(i), 276AG(i), 276U(i) 319C, 319F.

4 HC 395, Para 6, para 281 as amended by Cm 5597.

5 Immigration Act 1971, s 33(2A), as amended; HC 395, para 6 defines 'settled' as meaning 'that the person concerned:

(a) is free from any restriction on the period for which he may remain, save that a person entitled to an exemption under the Immigration Act 1971, s 8 (otherwise than as a member of the Home Forces) is not to be regarded as settled in the United Kingdom except insofar as section 8(5A) so provides; and

(b) is either:

(i) ordinarily resident in the United Kingdom without having entered or remained in breach of the immigration laws; or

(ii) despite having entered or remained in breach of the immigration laws, has subsequently entered lawfully, or has been granted leave to remain and is ordinarily resident.

See also: *TB (Bangladesh) v Entry Clearance Officer* [2007] EWCA Civ 740 (18 July 2007), [2007] All ER (D) 267 (Jul). An entitlement to reside without actual residence will not suffice: *Secretary of State for the Home Department v Wong* [1992] Imm AR 180.

6 *Bibi (Rashida) v Immigration Appeal Tribunal* [1988] Imm AR 298, CA.

7 *Mark v Mark* [2005] UKHL 42 (30 June 2005), *R v Immigration Appeal Tribunal, ex p Rafique (Najma)* [1990] Imm AR 235.

8 *Mark v Mark* [2005] UKHL 42, [2006] 1 AC 98, [2005] 3 All ER 912, *Shah v Barnet London Borough Council* [1983] 2 AC 309, [1983] 1 All ER 226, HL; *R v Secretary of State for the Home Department, ex p Chugtai* [1995] Imm AR 559.

ENTRY CLEARANCE FOR PARTNERS AND SPOUSES UNDER THE PART 8 TRANSITIONAL RULES

11.52 Under the transitional Immigration Rules from the 9 July 2012 the Part 8 rules continue to apply to persons who have made an application before 9 July 2012 under Part 8 which was not decided as at 9 July 2012; and to applications made by persons in the UK who have been granted entry clearance or limited leave to enter or remain under Part 8 before 9 July 2012 and where this is a requirement of Part 8, this leave to enter or limited leave to remain is extant. With some exceptions the Part 8 rules continue to apply to applications for further limited and indefinite leave to remain by such applicants (3) (Para A280(b)–(c) and (e)). In these circumstances – the Part 8 rules for spouse and partners are considered below. There are unlikely to be many spouse, or civil, or unmarried, or same sex partner, still seeking entry clearance under the Part 8 rules. Therefore, it is enough to note the requirements of the Immigration Rules detailed above applying to such cases – presence of sponsor; intention to live together; that the parties have met; and satisfy maintenance and accommodation requirements. In *R (on the application of Chikwamba) v Secretary of State for the Home Department*[1] – an Article 8 challenge to removal – the House of Lords considered whether the policy of insisting on departure from the UK to satisfy entry clearance requirements 'as a whole was legitimate and proportionate'. The Lords doubted whether the policy requiring removal 'should routinely apply . . . in all but exceptional cases', holding that it was 'only comparatively rarely, certainly in family cases involving children, should an article 8 appeal be dismissed on the basis that it would be proportionate and more appropriate for the appellant to apply for leave abroad'.[2] The Court of Appeal in *MA (Pakistan) v Secretary of State for the Home Department*[3] concluded that the principle enunciated in *Chik-*

wamba was not confined to families where children were involved.

1 [2008] UKHL 40, [2009] 1 All ER 363.
2 Lord Brown, para 44; Lord Bingham (para 1); Lord Hope (para 2); Lord Scott (para 3) and Baroness Hale (para 7) agreeing.
3 [2009] EWCA Civ 953. See para 7 of the judgment.

THE PART 8 TRANSITIONAL RULES — LIMITED AND INDEFINITE LEAVE TO ENTER AND REMAIN FOR SPOUSE/PARTNERS

11.53 Under the Part 8 rules for spouse and partners, fiancé(e)s, proposed civil partners and spouses/civil, unmarried and same-sex partners seeking to enter the UK must normally have entry clearance.[1] Fiancé(e)s, proposed civil partners were given up to six months leave to enter, with a prohibition on taking employment,[2] and spouses or civil, unmarried and same-sex partners were given an initial period, which is often referred to as a probationary period, not exceeding 27 months, with no employment prohibition. Spouses or partners could be granted indefinite leave to enter if they have been married or in a civil, same-sex, or unmarried partnership, and have been living together outside the UK for at least four years prior to the application).[3] If a fiancé(e) or proposed civil partner failed to marry during the initial period of leave, an explanation will have had to be given to the Home Office, and an extension of leave for an appropriate period given if the explanation was acceptable and there was evidence that the marriage or civil partnership would take place soon.[4] Once the fiancé(e) or proposed civil partner married and had obtained the initial probationary leave to remain as a spouse or civil partner, the employment prohibition was lifted. A person admitted in another capacity (for a period greater than six months) who married or entered a civil partnership during his or her stay here[5] could apply for leave to remain as the spouse or civil partner if, in addition to fulfilling the requirements for entry in that capacity (except for entry clearance) he or she had not remained in breach of the immigration laws, and neither the marriage nor the civil partnership took place after a decision to deport or a recommendation for deportation had been made, or a preparatory notice served.[6] Rule 284 – in addition to status, language and financial criteria – states that the requirements for an extension of stay as the spouse or civil partner of a person present and settled in the UK are that: applicants are married to or the civil partner of a person present and settled in the United Kingdom, have limited leave to enter or remain given in accordance with any of the provisions of these Rules and the leave was granted for a period of six months or more, unless it was granted as a fiancé(e) or proposed civil partner; and the leave was not as the spouse, civil partner, unmarried or same-sex partner of a Relevant PBS Migrant.[7] In addition to these restrictions on those eligible to seek extensions of stay as spouse or partners, the Part 8 rules also restrict applicants switching.

1 See HC 395, paras 281(vi) (spouses/civil partners) and 290(viii) (fiancé(e)s)/proposed civil partners), 295A(viii) (unmarried and same-sex partners).
2 HC 395, para 291.
3 HC 395, para 282, 295B. Note, that to qualify for indefinite leave to remain applicants (except those aged under 18 or over 65 at the time of the application) must show that they have a sufficient knowledge of the English language, and about life in the UK. HC 395, paras 282(c), 287(a)(vi), 295B(c), 295F(vi). The 27-month term is to give applicants time to arrange their travel to the UK and complete their period of two years as the spouse or civil partner of a

person present and settled in the United Kingdom – the probationary term necessary to qualify for settlement (inserted into the Rules by HC 971, July 2008).

4   HC 395, paras 293–294.
5   See above on restrictions on the right to marry in the UK.
6   HC 395, para 284(i) and (iv)–(v). FB (HC 395 para 284: 'six months') *Bangladesh* [2006] UKAIT 00030, [2006] Imm AR 400, the Tribunal considered the terms of para 284(i) of the Immigration Rules, HC 395.
7   HC 395, para 284.

The Part 8 Transitional Rules – indefinite leave for spouse and partners

11.54 After what was a 12 months' and for transitional Part 8 spouse and partners is now a two years' probationary leave as a spouse, or civil, same-sex or unmarried partner, an application can be made for indefinite leave to remain, which should be granted provided the maintenance and accommodation conditions are still met, the marriage or partnership is subsisting, each of the parties intends to live permanently with the other as his or her spouse or partner and the applicant has sufficient knowledge of the English language and about life in the UK (save for certain exempt applicants and those over 65).[1] Under earlier transitional arrangements, HC 395, paras 33E and 33F stated that until 31 January 2008, applications for ILR from those who did not satisfy the English language and knowledge of UK life tests will be considered instead as an application to extend temporary stay in the UK. Since 1 February 2008, such applications are to be refused.[2] It follows that applicants will have to have evidence of their language and life in the UK knowledge and skills before making an application for indefinite leave to remain. Those without such skills can apply for and be granted repeat terms of temporary leave as spouse/partners.[3]

1   Relevant to this chapter, the exempted candidates include: those qualifying for permanent residence under the domestic violence rules, are the husband, wife or civil partner of the citizen of another country on discharge from HM Forces (including Gurkhas); are a bereaved husband, wife, civil partner or unmarried partner, are the husband, wife, civil partner, or unmarried or same-sex partner of a British citizen or of a permanent resident of the UK who is a permanent member of HM Diplomatic Service, a staff member of the British Council on a tour of duty abroad, or staff member of the Department for International Development or can show medical evidence of a 'long-standing, permanent disability that prevents you from learning English'. See IDI Annex FM 1.21, English Language Speaking and Listening Requirement – Family Members under Part 8, Appendix FM (July 2014).
2   HC 395, paras 33E–33F were deleted by HC 314 from 31 March 2009. The Explanatory Memorandum states that: 'A person who is unable to satisfy the requirement to demonstrate knowledge of language and life in the UK can still be considered for an extension of stay but will need to ensure that they apply specifically for further leave to remain in the UK rather than for indefinite leave to remain. Applications for indefinite leave to remain that do not meet the requirement to demonstrate knowledge of language and life in the UK where it is required will be refused'.
3   See HC 395, paras A277A–B.

11.55 Extensions of stay as spouse or partner, including the grant of indefinite leave are subject to the general discretion to refuse on the ground of undesirable conduct.[1] Save in the cases of bereavement or where the marriage/partnership was caused to break down permanently as a result of domestic violence there is no discretion to grant leave to remain under the Immigration Rules in the case of marriage or civil partnership breakdown.[2] However, if such spouse or partners have children resident in the UK they may qualify for leave to remain as parent carers or parents exercising contact rights concerning their children. Where a person leaves the UK during the currency of temporary spouse/partner leave, that person may be re-examined on their return as to the fulfilment of the partnership requirements, and notwithstanding that the person has extant leave – their leave may be cancelled if the marriage has broken down,[3] Spouse or partnership leave can be curtailed if the person ceases to meet the requirements of the Rules under which that leave was granted.[4] Previous IDI instructions on curtailment emphasised that the curtailment provisions are 'discretionary and careful consideration should accordingly be given to all the person's circumstances'[5] – an appropriate admonition in spouse/partnership cases where the relationship may have broken down due to domestic violence, or where the person has contact with a child, or where divorce or other family proceedings are pending.[6] However, the current modernised guidance on curtailment while acknowledging officers must not automatically curtail leave where marriage or partnerships have broken down, advise that curtailment must be considered.[7] Where the settled spouse/civil/same-sex or unmarried partner has died during the probationary period, indefinite leave will be granted provided that the marriage/partnership was subsisting at the time of the death and the parties intended to continue cohabitation.[8]

1   HC 395, paras 322–323. See on general grounds for refusal, JC (Part 9, HC 395, burden of proof) *China* [2007] UKAIT 00027 (8 March 2007); *RM (Kwok On Tong: HC 395, para 320) India* [2006] UKAIT 00039 (18 April 2006); *R (on the application of Mirza) v Secretary of State for the Home Department* [2010] EWHC 2002 (Admin), [2010] All ER (D) 353 (Jul); *AA (Nigeria) v Secretary of State for the Home Department* [2010] EWCA Civ 773; *R (on the application of Boahen) v Secretary of State for the Home Department* [2010] EWCA Civ 585, [2010] All ER (D) 14 (Jun); *KB (para: 320(7A): 'false representations') Albania* [2009] UKAIT 00043; *Shen (Paper appeals; proving dishonesty)* [2014] UKUT 236 (IAC), *Mumu (para 320; Article 8; scope) Bangladesh* [2012] UKUT 143 (IAC), *Singh (para 320 (7A) – IS151A forms – proof) India* [2012] UKUT 162 (IAC), *Singh (para 320 (7A) – IS151A forms – proof) India* [2012] UKUT 162 (IAC), *Ahmed (general grounds of refusal – material non-disclosure) Pakistan* [2011] UKUT 351 (IAC), *PS (para 320(11) discretion: care needed) India* [2010] UKUT 440 (IAC).
2   *Patel (Ilyas Yakub) v Secretary of State for the Home Department* [1986] Imm AR 440.
3   HC 395, para 321A, *R v Immigration Appeal Tribunal, ex p Chaudhry* [1983] Imm AR 208, QBD.
4   See the Immigration Act 1971, s 3(3)(a); HC 395, para 323.
5   IDI (Aug 09), Chapter 9, s 5, para 3.5.
6   See *MS (Ivory Coast) v Secretary of State for the Home Department* [2007] EWCA Civ 133 (22 February 2007) on the government practice not to remove persons engaged in family litigation and the Court finding concerning the grant of discretionary leave to certain such applicants.
7   Home Office, *Modernised Guidance, Curtailment of Leave*, July 2014, pp 67–68.
8   HC 395, para 287(b), inserted by Cm 4851.

PART 8 TRANSITIONAL RULES AND VICTIMS OF DOMESTIC VIOLENCE

11.56 A spouse/civil or unmarried/same-sex partner may be granted indefinite leave to remain provided such applicants have been granted probationary leave as a spouse, civil or unmarried partner, and his/her relationship was subsisting at the beginning of that probationary period[1] and they are able to produce evidence to establish that a permanent breakdown of the relationship was caused[2] before the end of that period as a result of domestic violence.[3] The rule (formerly a concession outside the Rules) does not apply to persons admitted to the UK as the spouse or unmarried partner of a sponsor who had only limited leave to remain, or to fiancé(e)s or proposed civil partners. The EEA regulations also make provision for a family member to retain rights of residence where the partner's continued right of residence is warranted by particularly difficult circumstances such as the person having been a victim of domestic violence while the marriage or partnership was subsisting.[4] The Part 8, para 289A rule requires that the applicant 'is able to produce evidence to establish that the relationship was caused to permanently break down before the end of that period as a result of domestic violence'. The *Modernised Guidance* suggest the following:[5]

(i)   an injunction, non-molestation order or other protection order made against the sponsor;
(ii)   a relevant court conviction against the sponsor;
(iii)   full details of a relevant police caution issued against the sponsor; or
(iv)   a multi-agency risk assessment conference (MARAC).

In recognition of the fact that it is difficult for victims of domestic violence to produce such documentary evidence, the *Guidance* also suggests evidence that might be available and would help prove domestic violence:

(i)   a medical report from a hospital doctor confirming that the applicant has injuries consistent with being a victim of domestic violence;
(ii)   a letter from a family practitioner who has examined the applicant, and is satisfied that the injuries are consistent with being a victim of domestic violence;
(iii)   an undertaking given to a court that the perpetrator of the violence will not approach the victim;
(iv)   a police report confirming attendance at the home of the applicant as a result of a domestic violence incident;
(v)   a letter from a social services department confirming its involvement in connection with domestic violence; or
(vi)   a letter of support or report from an identified women's refuge.[6]

In the past the Secretary of State contended that evidential requirements in the then IDI were prescriptive and domestic violence could only be proved to the Secretary of State's satisfaction via such documentation. In *Ishtiaq*[7] the Court of Appeal disagreed as evidenced in the judgment given by Dyson LJ who said that:

> 'para 289A(iv) should be construed so as to further the policy of enabling persons whose relationships have permanently broken down as a result of domestic violence before the end of the probationary period to be granted indefinite leave to remain. A construction which precludes an applicant, whose relationship has in fact broken down as a result of domestic violence, from proving her case by producing cogent relevant evidence would defeat the evident purpose of the rule. The purpose of para 289A(iv) is to specify what an applicant has to prove in order to qualify for indefinite leave to remain during the probationary period: viz. that the relationship has been caused to break down permanently as a result of domestic violence. It is not the purpose of para 289A(iv) to deny indefinite leave to remain to victims of domestic violence who can prove their case, but cannot do so in one of the ways that have been prescribed by the Secretary of State in his instructions to caseworkers . . . . I would hold that para 289A(iv) gives the caseworker a discretion to decide what evidence to require the applicant to produce in the individual case. In

exercising that discretion, I would expect the caseworker usually to start by applying the guidance given in section 4 of chapter 8 of the IDIs. But if the applicant is unable to produce evidence in accordance with that guidance, it would seem to me that the caseworker should seek an explanation for his or her inability to do so. If the applicant provides a reasonable explanation for her inability to produce such evidence, then the caseworker should give the applicant the opportunity to produce such other relevant evidence as she wishes to produce.'

The *Modernised Guidance* seeks to comply with this dictum. Where an applicant submits evidence to show that he or she has been subjected to domestic violence from persons other than the sponsor, he/she may still qualify under the Rule if it is clear that this has been the reason for the marriage/partnership/relationship breakdown, for example, where those abusing the applicant are members of the sponsor's family against whom the sponsor offers no protection.[8] The application for indefinite leave to remain is not required to be made while the applicant still has leave to remain as a spouse or partner.[9] The Home Office Guidance contains details of the destitution domestic violence (DDV) concession effective from 1 April 2012. Under this concession a person who flees domestic violence and intends to make a claim for settlement (indefinite leave to remain) under paragraph 289A or section DVILR of the Immigration Rules who is: the migrant spouse, or partner of a person present and settled in the UK – can notify the Home Office they wish to be considered for limited leave under the DDV concession on the basis that they claim to be destitute. They can be granted three months limited leave to remain outside the rules with a visa condition permitting recourse to public funds. It is expected such applicants will be eligible to apply for public funds or housing assistance and will make their application for ILR within the term of the concessionary leave.[10]

---

[1] HC 395, para 289A.

[2] HC 395, para 289A. See, on whether the proven domestic violence was the cause of the breakdown of the relationship, *R (on the application of Butler) v Secretary of State for the Home Department* [2002] EWHC 854 (Admin), [2002] All ER (D) 259 (Apr); *R (on the application of B) v Secretary Of State For Home Department* [2002] EWCA Civ 1797, where the Court of Appeal quashed a decision of the SSHD that a relationship had not broken down as a result of domestic violence when the wife secured a non-molestation order after the parties had separated. The Court (per Judge J and Hale LJ at paras 21–26, 30–33) held that the domestic violence caused the breakdown of the relationship as it was 'a significant contributory factor to what happened' and part of a 'stormy' relationship prior to their separation. See also *LA (para 289A: causes of breakdown) Pakistan v Secretary of State for the Home Department* [2009] UKAIT 00019 where the Tribunal observed 'that whenever a relationship breaks down one or both parties to that relationship are likely to announce an intention to leave and/or in fact leave the matrimonial home. Whilst that might define when a relationship broke down it does not explain the cause. In order to assess the cause of the breakdown it is also necessary to look at the relationship as a whole' [para 41].

[3] Home Office, *Modernised Guidance, Victims of Domestic Violence*, Jan 2014, p 9 defines domestic violence as a 'Any incident or pattern of incidents controlling, coercive or threatening behaviour, violence or abuse between those aged 16 or over who are or have been intimate partners or family members regardless of gender or sexuality. This can include, but is not limited to, the following types of abuse: psychological; physical; sexual; financial; emotional. 'Controlling behaviour' is a range of acts designed to make a person subordinate and/or dependent by: isolating them from sources of support; exploiting their resources and capacities for personal gain; depriving them of the means needed for independence; resistance and escape, and regulating their everyday behaviour.'
'Coercive behaviour' is: an act or a pattern of acts of assault, threats, humiliation and intimidation, or other abuse that is used to harm, punish, or frighten their victim.
In *AN (Pakistan) v Secretary of State for the Home Department* [2010] EWCA Civ 757, [2010] All ER (D) 52 (Jul) in which counsel for the appellant accepted that for conduct to

constitute domestic violence it must reach some minimum level of seriousness, which will depend upon context and particular circumstances, the court observed at para 24: 'That is inherent . . . in the very concept of "violence" or "abuse". It is also consistent with the underlying policy as indicated by the categories of documentary evidence listed in the guidance (medical reports confirming injuries, police reports of attendance at domestic violence incidents, non-molestation orders and the like). Though, *AI (Pakistan) v Secretary of State for the Home Department* [2007] EWCA Civ 386, (2007) Times, 22 May establishes that an applicant is not limited to evidence within those categories. 'The definitions used by the United Nations and by the Family Division practice direction point in the same direction by their references to harm or the likelihood or risk of harm.'

4 The Immigration (European Economic Area) Regulations 2006, reg 10(5)(d)(iv). See ECI, Chapter 5, para 5.4.8.9.

5 *Modernised Guidance, Victims of Domestic Violence*, Jan 2014, pp 23.

6 *Modernised Guidance, Victims of Domestic Violence*, Jan 2014, pp 26–27.

7 *Ishtiaq v Secretary of State for the Home Department* [2007] EWCA Civ 386, per Dyson LJ at paras 31 and 38. The Court held that the Tribunal determination in *RH (HC 395, para 289A: no discretion) Bangladesh* [2006] UKAIT 43 was wrong and rejected the reasoning adopted by the Tribunal in *JL (Domestic Violence: evidence and procedure) India* [2006] UKAIT 58.

8 *Modernised Guidance, Victims of Domestic Violence*, Jan 2014, p 28.

9 HC 395, para 289A. The Rules only require a person to have been previously admitted or granted as a spouse/civil partner/unmarried partner/same-sex partner. The rule will also apply to those spouses still on temporary leave because they are unable to meet the knowledge of life and language tests for ILR.

10 *Modernised Guidance, Victims of Domestic Violence*, Jan 2014, pp 40–42.

PART 8 TRANSITIONAL RULES – UNMARRIED AND SAME SEX PARTNERS

11.57 The Immigration Rules, Part 8 also make provision for the admission of people who are not married but have a permanent relationship.[1] The Rules replaced hard-won concessions concerning the admission of heterosexual cohabitees and same-sex partners, and were added in October 2000 to give effect to the right to family, or private life under Article 8 of the ECHR. The Rules allow for the admission of men and women aged 18 or over to join partners of the same or opposite sex aged 18 or over,[2] who are present and settled, or being admitted for settlement in the UK,[3] and with whom they have been living in a relationship akin to marriage for two years.[4] The intention of the rules relating to unmarried and same-sex partners is to allow genuine long-term relationships to continue. Any previous marriage or similar relationship must have permanently broken down.[5] There is no longer any requirement that the parties are unable to marry, but they must not be involved in a consanguineous relationship.[6] They must intend to live together permanently[7] and be able to satisfy the maintenance and accommodation criteria.[8]

1 HC 395, paras 295A–295O, inserted by Cm 4851 on 2 October 2000.

2 HC 395, para 295AA;

3 HC 395, para 295A(i). A member of HM forces serving overseas, a permanent member of the diplomatic service or a UK-based staff member of the British Council on a tour of duty abroad, or a staff member of the Department for International Development who is a British citizen or settled in the UK, is to be regarded as 'present and settled' for this purpose: para 295A as amended by Cm 5597. There is provision for the entry, stay and settlement of the spouse, civil partners, and children of discharged Gurkhas or Commonwealth soldiers in HM Forces who are settled or admitted for settlement under HC 395, paras 276S–W, 281 and para 295A of HC 395 make provision for the entry/stay and settlement of spouse, civil partners, same-sex, or unmarried partners of members of HM Forces, permanent members of the Diplomatic

Service, comparable UK-based staff members of the British Council on a tour of duty overseas, or staff members of the Department for International Development who are British citizens or UK-settled.

4   HC 395, para 295A(i). The policy formulated in October 1997 required four years' cohabitation as a threshold period, which made it very difficult for someone who began a relationship with a British citizen while here in a temporary capacity, eg as a student, to qualify. The minimum cohabitation period was reduced to two years as from 16 June 1999.
5   HC 395, paras 295A(ii), 295D(ii) and 295J(ii).
6   HC 395, paras 295A(iii), 295D(v), 295J(iii), inserted by Cm 5949. Paragraph 295A(iv), which required inability to marry, was deleted by HC 538. The Rule gives statutory effect to the decision in *R v Secretary of State for the Home Department, ex p Ozminnos* [1994] Imm AR 287, QBD.
7   HC 395, paras 295A(vii), 295D(x): for those joining partners with limited leave to remain they must intend to live together during the partner's stay: para 295J(v).
8   HC 395, paras 295A(v)–(vi); 295D(viii)–(ix); and 295J(vi)–(vii).

11.58 Under the Part 8 rules on-entry unmarried partner applicants need entry clearance, just as spouses/civil partners do.[1] Normally, leave will have been granted for an initial period not exceeding 27 months (allowing a two-year probationary period) followed by settlement, if the relationship still subsists, and the English language and knowledge of life tests are satisfied. However, where an unmarried partner has lived abroad with their British citizen or settled partner for a period of four years, indefinite leave to enter could have been granted on entry – again subject to the language and knowledge of life criteria.[2] Applicants seeking to enter or remain as the partner of a person with limited leave for such purposes as the PBS must not intend to remain beyond the period of leave granted to their partner.[3] After-entry applicants (those who switched from another category such as student) must not have remained in breach of the immigration laws, and the relationship must have pre-dated any enforcement action (decision to deport, recommendation for deportation or service of notice preparatory to recommendation, or directions for removal as an overstayer under section 10 of the IAA 1999).[4]

1   HC 395, paras 295A(viii) and 295J(ix).
2   HC 395, para 295B as amended by HC 538 on 31 March 2003, 295A(b)(i)–(ii).
3   HC 395, para 319D.
4   HC 395, para 295D(i), (iv) and (vii).

11.59 Under the Part 8 transitional rules leave to enter to join or accompany an unmarried partner settled in the UK, or leave to remain with such a partner, will normally have been granted for 27 months in the first instance,[1] and indefinite leave may be granted at the end of the two-year probationary period, provided the relationship is still subsisting, each of the parties intends to live permanently with the other as his or her partner, the maintenance and accommodation criteria are still met and the applicant (unless over 65 or exempted) has sufficient knowledge of the English language and about life in the UK.[2] Indefinite leave may also be granted if the UK-settled partner dies during the probationary period, and at the time of the death the relationship was subsisting and the parties intended to live together permanently.[3] The Rules as amended make it clear that for the purposes of admission of unmarried partners, a member of HM Forces serving overseas, a permanent member of HM Diplomatic Service or a comparable UK-based member of staff of the British Council on a tour of duty abroad or a staff member of the Department for International Development who is a British Citizen, or is settled in the UK is to be regarded as present and settled in the UK. Unmarried partners might also have benefitted from the provisions of the rules relating to access to children,[4] and from the domestic violence rule, in the same way as parties to a marriage.[5]

[1] HC 395, paras 295B, 295E, 295G (save for those above, who have been living together in a relationship outside the UK for four years or more, who could have been granted indefinite leave to enter).
[2] HC 395, paras 295G–295H.
[3] HC 395, paras 287(b) and 295M–295O, putting unmarried partners on a par with married couples. Note, bereaved partners, as with bereaved spouses and civil partners are not required to satisfy the English language and life in the UK tests.
[4] HC 395, paras 246–248F, as amended by Cm 4851.
[5] HC 395, para 289A.

PART 8 TRANSITIONAL RULES – UNMARRIED AND SAME SEX BEREAVED PARTNERS

11.60 Under the Part 8 transitional rules paras 287 and 295M of HC 395 provision is made to grant indefinite leave to spouses, civil partners, and unmarried and same-sex couples, if they had been admitted to the UK as probationary spouse/partners of a person present and settled in the UK in accordance with paras 281–286 or 295AA–295F, they intended to live permanently with each other as spouse/partners but their spouse or partner died during their probationary period of leave, providing the marriage or partnership was subsisting at the time of the death.

PART 8 TRANSITIONAL RULES – MAINTENANCE AND ACCOMMODATION FOR SPOUSE AND CIVIL PARTNER

11.61 Before granting entry clearance to family members to join a sponsor, the entry clearance officer will have had to be satisfied that there was adequate maintenance and accommodation for them in the UK without recourse to public funds.[1] The rules refer to both accommodation and maintenance. The spouses, civil partners, unmarried and same-sex partners and children of refugees, of persons granted humanitarian protection, or of persons granted temporary protection and the spouse, civil partners and children of Gurkhas and foreign and Commonwealth soldiers discharged from the British army are not subject to the maintenance and accommodation requirements.[2] In the past, the Home Office has also waived the maintenance and accommodation requirement in particular cases for family members of those with exceptional leave to remain (now humanitarian protection or discretionary leave) and the UK's responsibilities under Article 8 may necessitate waiver to ensure compliance with the Human Rights Convention.[3] 'Public funds' are defined[4] as:

(a)   Housing under Part VI or VII of the Housing Act 1996 and under Part II of the Housing Act 1985, Part I or II of the Housing (Scotland) Act 1987, Part II of the Housing (Northern Ireland) Order 1981 or Part II of the Housing (Northern Ireland) Order 1988.[5]

(b)   In England, Scotland and Wales, attendance allowance, severe disablement allowance, carer's allowance and disability living allowance under Part III of the Social Security Contribution and Benefits Act 1992;[6] income support, council tax benefit and housing benefit under Part VII of that Act; a social fund payment under Part VIII of that Act; child benefit under Part IX of that Act;[7] income based jobseeker's allowance under the Jobseekers Act 1995, income related allowance under Part 1 of the Welfare Reform Act 2007 (employment and support allowance) state pension credit (SPC) under the State Pension Credit Act 2002; or child tax credit and working tax credit under Part 1 of the Tax Credits Act 2002.[8]

(c) In Northern Ireland, attendance allowance, severe disablement allowance, carer's allowance and disability living allowance under Part III of the Social Security Contribution and Benefits (Northern Ireland) Act 1992; income support, council tax benefit, housing benefit under Part VII of that Act; a social fund payment under Part VIII of that Act; child benefit under Part IX of that Act; or income based jobseeker's allowance under the Jobseekers (Northern Ireland) Order 1995 or income related allowance under Part 1 of the Welfare Reform Act (Northern Ireland) 2007.

(d) Universal Credit under Part 1 of the Welfare Reform Act 2012, or Personal Independence Payment under Part 4 of that Act.

(e) Universal Credit, Personal Independence Payment or any domestic rate relief under the Northern Ireland Welfare Reform Act 2010.

(f) A council tax reduction under a council tax reduction scheme made under section 13A of the Local Government Finance Act 1992 in relation to England or Wales, or a council tax reduction pursuant to the Council Tax Reduction (Scotland) Regulations 2012, or the Council Tax Reduction (State Pension Credit) (Scotland) Regulations 2012.

Neither NHS treatment nor State education counts as recourse to public funds for the purpose of the Rule.[9] There are a number of precise exceptions which qualify the scope of the public funds prohibition list, set out in the relevant instructions.[10] For example, working tax credit can be claimed by a foreign spouse, civil or unmarried partner and it is not considered recourse to public funds for the purposes of the rule.[11] A common question was whether the receipt of public funds by sponsors in their own right could disqualify partners/relatives from joining them in circumstances where there would be no additional recourse to public funds, but where the partners or relatives benefited indirectly. This was known as 'indirect reliance on public funds'. After years of divergence between Home Office policy as set out in correspondence[12] and the wording of the rules, and of conflicting Tribunal and High Court decisions,[13] this issue was put to rest in 2000 by an Immigration Rule amendment stating that 'a person is not to be regarded as having (or potentially having) recourse to public funds merely because he is (or will be) reliant in whole or in part on public funds provided to his sponsor, unless, as a result of his presence in the UK, the sponsor is (or would be) entitled to increased or additional public funds'.[14]

---

[1] See **11.61**, above.

[2] HC 395, as amended, paras 276R, 276X, 352A, AA, D, FA, FD, FG, 356.

[3] See: *R (on the application of MM (Lebanon)) v Secretary of State for the Home Department* [2014] EWCA Civ 985. See on the necessity for discretionary decisions outside the Rules to be made within a Convention-compliant policy framework: *AB (Jamaica) v Secretary of State for the Home Department* [2007] EWCA Civ 1302, [2007] All ER (D) 97 (Dec).

[4] HC 395, paras 6, 6A–6C. Amendments to 6A and the insertion of 6C deal with claims for tax credits as a couple. This is permissible and may not count as recourse to public funds but applicants from outside the UK seeking entry clearance cannot count any future entitlement to

tax credits as a couple to show that they have adequate maintenance under the Rules. See also: Tax Credits (Immigration) Regulations 2003, SI 2003/653.

5   See: *KA (Public funds: housing) Iraq* [2007] UKAIT 00081 (14 August 2007) in which the Tribunal held that the provision of larger Council accommodation to house the sponsor's family was housing made available under the statutory provisions mentioned in sub-para (a) of the definition of 'public funds' in para 6 of the Immigration Rules, whether or not in fulfilment of a duty to house homeless persons, and therefore is recourse to public funds, even where the tenure of the housing is governed by some other statute. In our view this decision, premised on grounds which the Tribunal itself appears to have identified at the reconsideration, is flawed in its reasoning. The Tribunal rejected the City of Edinburgh Council evidence that the secure tenancy in issue would be granted pursuant to the Housing (Scotland) Act 2001, Part 2 and held that there could be no tenancy unless the council was enabled by the Part I or II of the Housing (Scotland) Act 1987 to have a house to let to the appellant. The Tribunal gave no consideration to para 6A of the Rules or to a consideration of Article 8 of the ECHR.

6   In a series of cases the Tribunal has assumed that sponsors on disability benefits required the whole of those benefits for his/her own adequate maintenance and the sponsor's savings from such benefits could not be relied upon to show that there was adequate maintenance for the spouse, partner or child. *Nisa (Munibun) v Entry Clearance Officer, Islamabad* [2002] UKIAT 01369; *KA (Adequacy of maintenance) Pakistan* [2006] UKAIT 00065; *MK (Adequacy of maintenance, disabled sponsor) Somalia* [2007] UKAIT 00028 (13 March 2007). However, a majority of the Court of Appeal in *MK (Somalia) v Entry Clearance Officer* [2007] All ER (D) 443 (Nov) on 28 November 2007 accepted that as it was for the sponsor to spend her disability allowance as she wished as there was nothing in the Social Security Contributions and Benefits Act 1992 that required it to be spent on assistance. If the sponsor chose to spend that money on the claimant, and it was adequate for his maintenance, then there would be no recourse to public funds, and it could not be said that she was doing anything improper. See also *HI HI (Uganda) v ECO* [2007] All ER (D) 419 (Oct); *NM (Disability discrimination) Iraq* [2008] UKAIT 00026 (25 March 2008).

7   The British/settled spouse or civil partner may claim child benefit for his or her family if the spouse/civil partner is entitled to this under DWP legislation.

8   UK-settled sponsors may claim working credit and child benefit for his or her family if they are entitled to it under social security legislation. Under the tax credit arrangements the benefit claim is made as a couple. The rule therefore makes clear that tax credits paid in respect of a spouse/ partner subject to immigration control are not recourse to public funds. However, when such spouse/partner is making his/her application for entry clearance, his/her expectation of obtaining tax credits through his/her spouse/partner cannot be counted to show he/she meets the adequate maintenance criteria: IDI (Mar 06), Chapter 8, ss 1–2, Annex F, para 2. See Chapter 14 below. In *GS (public funds – tax credits) India* [2010] UKUT 419 (IAC) the Tribunal noted paragraph 6C of the Immigration Rules specifies that an applicant for entry clearance whose arrival would cause an increase in the tax credits which his sponsor is already receiving will (in contrast to in-country applicants under paragraph 6B) be regarded as having recourse to public funds. But where the applicant will be joining a spouse or partner who is both working and bringing up children, the amount of working tax credit payable will actually be reduced. That is because the sponsor will lose the lone parent supplement that forms part of the working tax credit.

9   HC 395, para 6, 6A–C.

10 See HC 395, para 6B, inserted by HC 3546 in February 2005, which provides for exceptions by way of regulations under the IAA 1999, s 115 and Tax Credits Act 2002, s 42. The paragraph states: 'A person shall not be regarded as having recourse to public funds if he is a person who is not excluded from specified benefits under s 115 of the IAA 1999 by virtue of regulations made under sub-ss (3)–(4) of that section or s 42 of the Tax Credits Act 2002.'

11 The Tax Credits (Immigration) Regulations 2003, SI 2003/653 provide that where one member of a couple is a person subject to immigration control and the other is not, or is in one of the excepted categories set out in the regulations, their entitlement to tax credit is determined as if neither is subject to control. See also HC 395, paras 6B–6C.

12 See eg letter from Nicholas Baker to Sir Giles Shaw MP, October 1994, (1995) Legal Action (July) at 21; Nicholas Baker to Max Madden MP, set out in *Kausar v Entry Clearance Officer (Islamabad)* [1998] INLR 141 at 144.

13 *R v Immigration Appeal Tribunal, ex p Singh* [1989] Imm AR 69; *R v Secretary of State for the Home Department, ex p Bibi (Islam)* [1995] Imm AR 157; *Entry Clearance Officer v*

Ahmed (Bashir) [1991] Imm AR 130; *Kausar v Entry Clearance Officer (Islamabad)* [1998] INLR 141.

14 HC 395, para 6A, inserted by Cm 4851 from 2 October 2000. For applications lodged after the 30 March 2009, the rules on this issue, as amended by HC 314, apply. These changes amend the definition of public funds in the Immigration Rules to make it clear that where a sponsor's increased entitlement to public funds is due only to an increase that he and the dependant are jointly entitled to receive by virtue of the relevant regulations, this will not be treated as recourse to public funds. The new Rule at para 6C makes it clear that anticipated entitlement to public funds payable either to the person or to the sponsor as a result of the dependant's presence in the UK cannot be relied upon to satisfy the maintenance and accommodation requirements of an Entry Clearance application.

Part 8 Transitional Rules and third-party support

11.62 The Part 8 maintenance rules are significantly different to those applying to family applicants under Appendix FM. It is this difference which makes it important to ascertain if clients fall within the transitional Part 8 or the Appendix FM rules. The maintenance and accommodation rules for the admission for settlement of spouses, civil and unmarried or same-sex partners, for children and other relatives are different. Spouses, civil and unmarried/same-sex partners need to show that there will be adequate accommodation for themselves and any dependants, without recourse to public funds, in accommodation which they own or occupy exclusively, and that they (the parties) will be able to maintain themselves and any dependants adequately, without recourse to public funds.[1] Children must show that they can and will be accommodated adequately by the parent, parents or relative sponsoring the child, without recourse to public funds, in accommodation owned or occupied exclusively by the parent, parents or relative, and that they can and will be maintained adequately by the parent, parents or relative, without recourse to public funds.[2] Other dependent relatives must show that they can and will be accommodated adequately together with any dependants, without recourse to public funds, in accommodation owned or occupied exclusively by the sponsor, and that they can and will be maintained adequately, together with any dependants, without recourse to public funds.[3] The different wording reflects the Home Office view as to who should be responsible for maintaining and accommodating the particular relatives. In the case of spouses, the Rule was taken to require that the spouses will provide for

... as '297(iv)– ... partners may not work before the marriage/civil partner-
HC 395, partner) 310(iv), 311(iv), 298(iv)–(v), those for spouses/civil partners: HC 395, para 290(iv)–(vi).
HC 395, para 317(iv)–(iva), as amended by Cm 4851 in October 2000.

11.63 The Supreme Court in *Mahad/AM (Ethiopia and Ors)*[1] held that HC 395, paras 281, 297 and 317 should be interpreted as permitting reliance on third-party support and joint sponsorship both in respect of maintenance and accommodation. The Court noted that financial assistance provided by large supportive immigration communities should not be ignored although the part played by the sponsor (or the parent in the case of para 297) is of the first importance. The Court rejected the view of the court below that third-party arrangements are invariably more precarious than sponsor generated income. The Supreme Court also noted that provided the relative abroad is getting funds which he would not have received had he not had a relative present and settled in the UK, it is not necessary for the funds to have ever been part of the settled relative's own personal resources. This would therefore provide for a situation where the settled relative is a conduit for funds provided by third party support. The Court noted in regard to the different wording in HC 395, para 297 that this was a child protection measure designed to ensure that children came to live with relative(s) they are supposed to be joining and not somebody else.

1   *Mahad (previously referred to as AM) (Ethiopia) v Entry Clearance Officer* [2009] UKSC 16, [2010] 1 WLR 48, [2010] 2 All ER 535.

11.64 The Part 8 Immigration Rules do not require that adequate maintenance and accommodation are available at the date of the decision (which would preclude the entry of spouses and partners and other economically active family members whose own earning power in the UK is relied on to satisfy the rule), but on the person's arrival in the UK. A written undertaking of support may be required, although rarely in the case of admission of spouses, civil partners and children under 16, where the condition preventing access to public funds prevents access to benefits anyway.[1] A refusal to provide such an undertaking may lead to a refusal of the application for entry clearance.[2]

1   See National Assistance Act 1948, s 43, as amended by Family Law Reform Act 1987, Sch 2; Social Security Administration Act 1992, s 78 (liability to maintain as a result of an undertaking under the Immigration Act 1971). See: *R (on the application of Begum) v Social Security Comrs* [2003] EWHC 3380 (Admin), [2003] 48 LS Gaz R 18, (2003) Times, 4 December; *Ahmed v Secretary of State for Work and Pensions* [2005] EWCA Civ 535, (2005) Times, 19 May where the Court held that, in determining whether a declaration constituted a maintenance undertaking, the Court had to look to the substance of the declaration rather than the form. A maintenance undertaking had to express in reasonably clear language some future promise or agreement as to the maintenance of a sponsored immigrant. In the instant case, the use of the phrase 'I am able and willing' by R's nephew was insufficient as it was a reference to his current ability rather than a promise to the future.
2   ~~~ para 320(14).

11.65 In de ~~~ from third partie ~~~ information is obtaine ~~~ or the income and committm ~~~ whether the money available wi ~~~ cerned.[1] Fiancé(e)s/proposed civil par ~~~ ers (with or without assistance their leave has been extended after marriage.[3] The ~~~ dependants, can take into account their own earnings. ~~~ do not count when ~~~ partner's prospective earnings ~~~ Income support has been held available to the sponsor and ~~~ maintenance is 'adequate'.[4] ~~~ benefits: proof of receipt; evid ~~~ stick to assess whether the income available to the sponsor ~~~ family would be adequate.[5] In *Ahmed* (benefits: proof of receipt; evid ~~~ *Bangladesh* [2013] UKUT 84 (IAC) the Upper Tribunal stated that proper evidence of the couple's combined projected income and its comparison with benefit rates at the particular time should be provided by parties including the ECO. Where the likely income of a family falls below the established (income support) level; the shortfall can be met where there are sufficient savings. The assessment of the appropriate level of savings is not an arbitrary calculation, and the proper reference is to the length of the initial visa. If an appellant is able to meet the requirements of adequacy for the period of the initial visa, and there is no reason to believe that he will not be able to meet the maintenance requirements in the longer term, then he is entitled to entry clearance.[6] While the Tribunal has stated that it doubts whether it would ever be right to say that children could be maintained 'adequately' at less than the level which would be available to the family on income support, merely because one of their parents asserts that the family will live frugally,[7] the Court of Appeal held that although the disability living allowance was calculated according to the sponsor's need for care and mobility, once the disability living allowance was in her hands, it was for her to spend as she chose, as there was nothing in sections 72 and 73 of the 1992 Act that required it to be spent on assistance. If the sponsor chose to spend that money on the claimant, and it was adequate for his maintenance, then there would be no recourse to public funds, and it could not be said that she was doing anything improper.[8]

1   *Mahad (previously referred to as AM) (Ethiopia) v Entry Clearance Officer* [2009] UKSC 16, [2010] 1 WLR 48, [2010] 2 All ER 535; *MW (Liberia) v Secretary of State for the Home Department* [2007] EWCA Civ 1376, [2008] 1 WLR 1068.
2   HC 395, para 291.
3   The IDI (April 2013), Maintenance, Chapter 8, Section FM 1.7A.
4   IDI (April 2013), Maintenance, Chapter 8, Section FM 1.7A.
5   *KA (Adequacy of maintenance) Pakistan* [2006] UKAIT 00065 (4 September 2006); *MK (Adequacy of maintenance, disabled sponsor) Somalia* [2007] UKAIT 00028 (13 March 2007). See *RB (Maintenance income support schedules) Morocco* [2004] UKIAT 00142, where voluntary payments from family members reduced the level of income support. *Yarce (adequate maintenance: benefits) Colombia* [2012] UKUT 425 (IAC). The IDI (April 2013) Maintenance, Chapter 8, Section FM 1.9A states that in calculating whether the applicant can be adequately maintained, the decision-maker should follow the following steps:
    (a)   Establish the sponsor's and/or applicant's (if they are in the UK with permission to work) current net income. The net income should be established, and if the income varies, an average should be calculated. Income from benefits can be included as income.
    (b)   Establish the sponsor's current housing costs from the evidence provided.
    (c)   Deduct the housing costs from the net income.
    (d)   Calculate how much the sponsor and his family would receive if they were on Income Support.
6   *Jahangara Begum & others (maintenance: savings) Bangladesh* [2011] UKUT 246 (IAC).
7   *KA (Adequacy of maintenance) Pakistan* [2006] UKAIT 00065 (4 September 2006), *MK (Adequacy of maintenance, disabled sponsor) Somalia.*
8   *MW (Liberia) v Secretary of State for the Home Department* [2007] EWCA Civ 1376, [2007] All ER (D) 340 (Dec).

11.66 The Rules do not prohibit the provision of accommodation by a third party.[1] However, the accommodation available for the family member must either be owned or occupied exclusively by the parties or the sponsor – these requirements being alternatives. Occupation of premises may be as a licensee or lodger. It is doubtful whether boarding children with a neighbour will suffice,[2] but there is no requirement that the accommodation should be the sponsor's sole or main residence. The requirement that a person does 'own or occupy exclusively' property does not carry any technical legal meaning of exclusive occupation. It is sufficient if there is a defined place where the person lives and which he has as his home, with the implication of stability that that implies.[3] Exclusive occupation does not have to extend to the whole of premises; exclusive occupation of a bedroom will suffice, with shared use of the remainder of the premises.[4] Accommodation can be shared with other members of a family provided that at least part of the accommodation is for the exclusive use of the sponsor and his dependants. The unit of accommodation may be as small as a separate bedroom but it must be owned or legally occupied by the sponsor; its occupation must not contravene public health regulations; and its occupation must not cause overcrowding as defined in the Housing Act 1985.

[1] *AB (Third-party provision of accommodation)* [2008] UKAIT 00018 (06 March 2008), *Mahad (previously referred to as AM) (Ethiopia) v Entry Clearance Officer* [2009] UKSC 16, [2010] 1 WLR 48, [2010] 2 All ER 535.
[2] *Entry Clearance Officer, New Delhi v Baidwan* [1975] Imm AR 126; *Mahad (previously referred to as AM) Ethiopia v Entry Clearance Officer* [2009] UKSC 16, [2010] 1 WLR 48, [2010] 2 All ER 535.
[3] *KJ ('Own or occupy exclusively') Jamaica* [2008] UKAIT 00006 (16 January 2008).
[4] *Zia v Secretary of State for the Home Department* [1993] Imm AR 404 at 412; *Kasuji v Entry Clearance Officer, Bombay* [1988] Imm AR 587.

11.67 Like maintenance, accommodation does not have to be available at the time of the application or decision, but only when the family member arrives in the UK.[1] The standard of adequacy of the accommodation is that the applicant may live there without breach of the public health laws or statutory overcrowding.[2] An applicant should not, however, be required to produce a report from a local authority as to the fitness of accommodation in every case, since in most cases the issue is not adequacy but availability of accommodation.[3] Accommodation is not 'adequate' if it is to be shared with someone who has abused the child applicant.[4]

[1] Note, *KA (Public funds: housing) Iraq* [2007] UKAIT 00081 (14 August 2007) concerning whether the provision of larger Council accommodation for applicants under any of the statutory provisions mentioned in sub-para (a) of the definition of 'public funds' in para 6 of the Immigration Rules is recourse to public funds, even where the tenure of the housing is governed by some other statute.
[2] See *S (Pakistan)* [2004] UKIAT 00006 where a surveyor confirmed adequacy of accommodation in terms of the Housing Act 1985, although accepting that the accommodation would be congested and the IAT held that on a 'practical' view it would not be adequate.
[3] *Rehman v Entry Clearance Officer* [1998] INLR 500.
[4] See *M and A v Secretary of State for the Home Department* [2003] EWCA Civ 263, [2003] Imm AR 4, where the Court of Appeal held that it is not a misuse of the language to describe accommodation as inadequate for a child because it is occupied by a parent who has physically or sexually abused the child in the past, and is likely to do so in the future. In such a case, the accommodation is patently unsafe and therefore inadequate.

APPENDIX FM AND FM-SE – THE RULES FOR SPOUSES, PARTNERS AND PARENTS

Appendix FM rules

11.68 Appendix FM came into force on 9 July 2012, replacing the majority of Part 8 of the Immigration Rules. It was a significant change to family migration into the UK. The Appendix FM rules were said to be intended to 'unify consideration under the rules and Article 8, by defining the basis on which a person can enter or remain in the UK on the basis of their family or private life.'[1]

In general the policy of the Rules is to utilise the Appendix FM criteria as a surrogate for Article 8 consideration – with asylum, humanitarian protection and removal decisions all to be considered by reference to the applicability of the Appendix FM rules.[2] Appendix FM GEN.1.9 facilitates that consideration by providing that in this Appendix the requirement to make a valid application will not apply when the Article 8 claim is raised:

'(i)   as part of an asylum claim, or as part of a further submission in person after an asylum claim has been refused;
(ii)   where a migrant is in immigration detention;
(iii)   where removal directions have been set pending an imminent removal;
(iv)   in an appeal; or
(v)   in response to a (one stop) notice issued under section 120 of the Nationality, Immigration and Asylum Act 2002'.

This chapter does not deal with the intersection between these new rules and Article 8. This is dealt with in CHAPTER 7. The following paragraphs deal with the Appendix FM and FM-SE Immigration Rules simply as family rules pertaining to entry, stay and settlement.

[1]   See The General Purpose section of Appendix FM, GEN.1.1. and Overview Of Rule Changes Coming Into Effect In July 2012, the Statement of Intent available at: www.gov.uk/g overnment/uploads/system/uploads/attachment_data/file/257359/soi-fam-mig.pdf
[2]   See for example:

'326A. The procedures set out in these Rules shall apply to the consideration of asylum and humanitarian protection.
326B.   Where the Secretary of State is considering a claim for asylum or humanitarian protection under this Part, she will consider any Article 8 elements of that claim in line with the provisions of Appendix FM (family life) and paragraphs 276ADE to 276DH (private life) of these Rules.

. . .

400.   Where a person claims that their removal under paragraphs 8 to 10 of Schedule 2 to the Immigration Act 1971, section 10 of the Immigration and Asylum Act 1999 or section 47 of the Immigration, Asylum and Nationality Act 2006 would be contrary to the UK's obligations under Article 8 of the Human Rights Convention, the Secretary of State may require an application under paragraph 276ADE (private life) or Appendix FM (family life) of these rules. Where an application is not required, in assessing that claim the Secretary of State or an immigration officer will, subject to paragraph 353, consider that claim against the requirements to be met under paragraph 276ADE or Appendix FM and if appropriate the removal decision will be cancelled.'

11.69 Appendix FM provides certain distinct 'routes' to a grant of leave to enter or remain. Terms used in the particular visa categories are defined (Section GEN and Para 6). Each category follows a similar format – a 'requirements' section, which provides an overview of what must be shown in order to qualify under the route and the 'suitability' and eligibility requirements which delineate those requirements. The eligibility requirements are commonly subdivided into 'relationship', 'immigration status', 'financial' and 'English language' criteria. The 'decisions' section sets out the term of leave which an applicant should be granted and the conditions attached to that leave. The routes/visa categories comprise:

(i)   family life as a partner;

(ii)   bereaved partners;

(iii)   victims of domestic violence;

(iv)   family life as a child of a person with limited leave as a partner or parent;

(v)   family life as a parent of a child in the UK; and

(vi)   adult dependent relatives.

In respect of the 'Family life as a partner' and 'Family life as a parent of a child in the UK' rules certain criteria can be waived – via an exception detailed in Section EX1.[1] The exception is not free standing but allows the waiver of specific criterion.[2] At least as pertains to entry clearance decisions, the current policy guidance also advises that the Entry Clearance Officers must in every case consider whether there may be exceptional circumstances raised in the application which make refusal of entry clearance a breach of Article 8 of the ECHR (the right to respect for family life) because refusal would result in unjustifiably harsh consequences for the applicant or their family and whether there are any compassionate factors — that is compelling compassionate reasons —which might justify a grant of entry clearance outside the rules.[3]

[1]   Exception within the Rules at Ex.1 (here showing Rules of 28 July 2014 consistent with statutory changes introduced by 2014 Act):

> *"Section EX: Exception*
>   **EX.1.** This paragraph applies if
>   (a)(i)   the applicant has a genuine and subsisting parental relationship with a child who:
>   (aa)   is under the age of 18 years, or was under the age of 18 years when the applicant was first granted leave on the basis that this paragraph applied;
>   (bb)   is in the UK;
>   (cc)   is a British Citizen or has lived in the UK continuously for at least the 7 years immediately preceding the date of application; and
>   (ii)   it would not be reasonable to expect the child to leave the UK; or
>   (b)   the applicant has a genuine and subsisting relationship with a partner who is in the UK and is a British Citizen, settled in the UK or in the UK with refugee leave or humanitarian protection, and there are insurmountable obstacles to family life with that partner continuing outside the UK.
>   **EX.2.** For the purposes of paragraph EX.1.(b) "insurmountable obstacles" means the very significant difficulties which would be faced by the applicant or their partner in continuing their family life together outside the UK and which could not be overcome or would entail very serious hardship for the applicant or their partner.'

On subsisting relationships see for example *Goudey (subsisting marriage – evidence) Sudan* [2012] UKUT 41 (IAC), *Naz (subsisting marriage – standard of proof) Pakistan* [2012] UKUT 40 (IAC), *GA (Subsisting marriage) Ghana** [2006] UKAIT 46.

[2]   *Sabir (Appendix FM – EX.1 not free standing)* [2014] UKUT 63 (IAC). In *Sabir (Appendix FM – EX.1 not free standing)* [2014] UKUT 63 (IAC). The UTIAC found that it is plain from the architecture of the Rules as regards partners that EX.1 is 'parasitic' on the relevant Rule within Appendix FM that otherwise grants leave to remain. If EX.1 was intended to be a free-standing element some mechanism of identification would have been used. The structure of the Rules as presently drafted requires it to be a component part of the leave granting Rule.

[3]   IDI Family Migration, Appendix FM, Section 1.0a Family Life as a partner or parent – five year routes P45 which states:

> 'Where an entry clearance application does not meet the requirements of the Immigration Rules, the Entry Clearance Officer must consider whether there are exceptional circumstances or compassionate factors which mean the Home Office should consider granting entry clearance outside the rules . . . . Compassionate factors are, broadly speaking, exceptional circumstances, e.g. relating to serious ill health, which might mean that a refusal of entry clearance would result in unjustifiably harsh consequences for the applicant or their family but might not constitute a breach of Article 8. Where an application does not meet the requirements of the Rules under Appendix FM and/or Appendix FM-SE, the Entry Clearance Officer must in every case go on to consider whether there may be exceptional

circumstances which warrant a grant of entry clearance outside the Rules on Article 8 grounds. If the Entry Clearance Officer is of the view that there may be exceptional circumstances in line with this guidance, they must refer the application to RCU.'

11.70 Section GEN not only outlines the General Purpose of the Appendix FM family provisions but also defines and clarifies the application of the rules concerning:

— The meaning of 'partner'[1] and other terms such as 'application for leave to remain' and references to a British citizen in the UK (GEN 1.2–1.3).
— Following on from the approach taken in the PBS, where evidence was specified as necessary in all applications in supporting appendices to the Immigration Rules, GEN.1.4. makes clear that where a document is 'specified' in Appendix FM, it means 'specified in Appendix FM-SE' unless the context requires otherwise.
— That documents will be discounted if an entry clearance officer or the Secretary of State has reasonable cause to doubt the genuineness of any document submitted and having taken steps to verify it is unable to verify that it is genuine (GEN 1.5).
— Lists the countries whose nationals are taken to be English language speakers who meet the English language requirement (GEN 1.6).
— Lists the Part 8 rules (paras 277–280, 289AA, 295AA, and 296) which apply to the Appendix and (as noted above).
— Outlines the circumstances when the requirement to make a valid application for leave under Appendix FM will not apply (GEN 1.9).
— Sets out the normal expectation that where an applicant is granted leave to enter or remain outside the Rules on Article 8 grounds, they will normally be granted entry clearance for a term not exceeding 33 months or leave to enter or remain for a term not exceeding 30 months. Ordinarily the grant of leave will be subject to a condition of no recourse to public funds unless it is considered that the applicant should not be subject to such a condition (GEN 1.10). GEN.1.11. grants the decision-maker a residual discretion to make leave granted outside the Rules on Article 8 grounds subject to such conditions as are considered appropriate.

As a further general consideration, the grounds for refusal contained in Part 9 of the Immigration Rules do not all apply to Appendix FM, which has its own set of suitability criteria.[2] The exceptions are paragraph 320(3), (10) and (11) and paragraphs 321 (refusal of leave to enter to a person with an entry clearance) and 321A (cancellation of leave to enter or remain at port or while holder outside the UK). The standard grounds on which leave to enter or remain can be curtailed, set out in paragraph 323, continue to apply to Appendix FM.

[1] Within Appendix FM, 'partner' is defined as:
   (i)   an applicant's spouse;
   (ii)   an applicant's civil partner;
   (iii)   an applicant's fiancé(e) or proposed civil partner;
   (iv)   a person with whom the applicant has been living in a relationship akin to marriage or civil partnership for at least two years prior to the date of application subject to the caveat that the context can require otherwise (see GEN.1.2).
In *Fetle (Partners: two year requirement)* [2014] UKUT 00267 (IAC) the UTIAC held, in contrast to the requirement of para GEN 1.2(iv) of Appendix FM, a requirement (such as in paragraph 352AA of the Immigration Rules) that 'parties have been living together in a relationship akin to either a marriage or a civil partnership which has subsisted for two years

or more' does not require two years cohabitation, but two years subsistence of the relationship. Whether the relationship still subsists, as required by the tense of that requirement and as may be separately required, is a different issue.

2   See HC 395 paragraph A320.

RELATIONSHIP REQUIREMENTS — PARTNERS

Family life with a partner

11.71 The family life with a partner route replaces the family migration routes previously available under Part 8 of HC 395. Provision is made within the route for entry clearance, leave to remain and indefinite leave to remain as the partner of a British citizen, a person present and settled in the UK, or a person with leave to remain as a refugee or with humanitarian protection. The principle requirements (with variations for entry in which route – amongst other matters the EC1 exception does not apply/leave to remain and settlement) are that:

(a)   the applicant and their partner must be in the UK;

(b)   the applicant must have made a valid application for limited or indefinite leave to remain as a partner; and either;

(c)   the applicant must not fall for refusal under the suitability rules (Section S-LTR)

(d)   the applicant must meet relationship criteria with a British citizen or settled partner with whom they have a genuine and subsisting relationship and intend to live together permanently in the UK

(e)   the applicant must meet immigration status requirements (subject to the exception clause)

(f)   The applicant must provide specified evidence, from prescribed sources of
       –a specified gross annual income of at least –
       (i)   £18,600;
       (ii)   an additional £3,800 for the first child; and;
       (iii) an additional £2,400 for each additional child; alone or in combination with specified savings of £16,000 and additional prescribed savings[1] 1

(g)   the applicant must provide evidence that there will be adequate accommodation, without recourse to public funds, for the family, including other family members who are not included in the application but who live in the same household, which the family own or occupy exclusively, unless paragraph EX.1. applies

(h)   the applicant must meet English language skill requirements[2]

---

1   IDI, Chapter 8, Financial Requirements Annex FM Section FM 1.7 Paragraphs 6A and 6C of HC 395. See *Ahmed (benefits: proof of receipt; evidence)* [2013] UKUT 84 (IAC).

2   The language testing providers that are approved are set out in HC 395 Appendix O. See *Akhtar (CEFR; UKBA Guidance and IELTS)* [2013] UKUT 306 (IAC). IDI, Annex FM 1.21, English Language Speaking and Listening Requirement – Family Members under Part 8, Appendix FM and Appendix Armed Forces of the Immigration Rules at section 7.1. In *R (on the application of Bibi) v Secretary of State for the Home Department (Liberty and Joint Council for the Welfare of Immigrants, intervening)* [2013] EWCA Civ 322, [2014] 1 WLR 208. the Court of Appeal held that the pre-entry English language requirement is compatible with Article 8 of the ECHR. As part of its analysis, the Court looked at the exceptional circumstances provision, and considered that the provision for exempt and exceptional cases supported the lawfulness of the requirement. Sir David Keene, dissenting, concluded that the requirement was incompatible with Article 8. The Court had been told that the exceptional cases provision would apply to those countries in which there was no test

centre (though note, that rationale has now disappeared). Sir David took the view that this was insufficient because it would not apply to countries such as India and Pakistan where there are test centres but the distances involves may make it extremely difficult for an applicant to obtain access to the necessary testing, let alone adequate tuition. The claimants were granted permission to appeal to the Supreme Court on 7 April 2014.

11.72 Many of the difficulties arising in Appendix FM family claims concern the prescriptive evidential and calculation requirements, particularly those intended to show that the applicants meets the Rules' maintenance requirements. Appendix FM-SE provides detailed rules regarding the type of evidence necessary to demonstrate compliance with the financial requirements in Appendix FM for those applicants applying for leave to enter or remain or indefinite leave to remain in the UK as a non-EEA national partner or dependent child of a person who is a British citizen, settled in the UK, or in the UK with refugee leave, or humanitarian protection as well as binding guidance on how to calculate gross annual income under Appendix FM. FM-SE must be read in conjunction with the relevant substantive rule in Appendix FM. Notably, FM-SE states at para B that 'Where evidence is not specified by Appendix FM, but is of a type covered by this Appendix, the requirements of this Appendix shall apply.' There are countless examples of situations where applicants meet the substantive requirement of the rule under Appendix FM and can indeed demonstrate through some form of evidence that they meet the minimum financial requirements of the rules, but their application fails under the Immigration Rules because they cannot provide the prescribed evidence in FM-SE. These refusals can be particularly frustrating to applicants and families.

As set out in Appendix FM-SE and the IDI, the financial requirement can be met in one of five ways:

(1) Income from salaried (in the IDI termed Category A) or non-salaried (termed Category B) employment of the partner (and/or applicant if they are in the UK with permission to work). Non-salaried refers to employment that is paid at an hourly or other rate and the number of hours may vary or paid an amount which varies according to the work undertaken.

(2) Non-employment income, for example, from property rental or dividends from shares (termed Category C).

(3) Cash savings of the applicant's partner and/or the applicant above £16,000, held by the partner and/or the applicant for at least 6 months and under their control (termed Category D). The amount above £16,000 must be divided by 2.5 (to reflect the 2.5 year or 30-month period before the applicant will have to make a further application). This calculation gives the amount which can be added to income. At the indefinite leave to remain stage the whole amount above £16,000 can be added.

(4) State (UK or foreign) or private pension of the applicant's partner and/or the applicant (termed Category E).

(5) Income from self-employment (termed Category F), and income as a director of a specified limited company in the UK (termed Category G), of the partner (and/or the applicant if they are in the UK with permission to work).

In calculating whether an applicant meets the financial requirements in Appendix FM – income under Category A can be combined with Category C, D and E if necessary, but not Category B. A detailed chart in the IDI, Annex FM, Section FM 1.7, July 2014 at p15 shows which categories of income can be combined. Within each of the above categories there are detailed rules on calculating the income and what specifically is required for that income to be counted. So for example, in cases where evidence is being provided of salaried employment of at least six months duration, the applicant must have been paid throughout that period at a level of gross annual salary or income which equals or exceeds the level relied upon in the application. If the applicant has been paid at different amounts then the lower amount will be used. So, if for example an individual was paid £16,000 for three months and then received a promotion and was paid £22,000 for three months it would not be the average salary which is used (and which would be £19,000, sufficient to meet the requirement for a partner) but rather the lower amount of £16,000 which would preclude the applicant from succeeding. In those cases it would, of course, be advisable for the applicant to wait until they have been paid at the higher level for six months before making the application. The income calculation is further prescribed by Appendix FM-SE via its dictation of the financial year to be used. In *Hameed (Appendix FM – financial year)* [2014] UKUT 266 (IAC) (4 April 2014) the UTIAC held that the financial year for the purposes of Appendix FM is the tax year (ie the year from 6 April one year to 5 April the next) not the year which the sponsor selected for accounting purposes.

Appendix FM-SE also details the way in which the required level of income can be demonstrated or evidenced. The *Guidance* in Appendix FM-SE runs to some 26 pages – and only the core matters are set out herein as follows:

(1)   FM-SE sets out, amongst other things, the permitted sources of income/savings, the time periods and permitted combinations of sources applicable to each permitted source relied upon and the evidence required for each permitted source relied upon (see Appendix FM-SE, para A1(b)).

(2)   FM-SE also explains what to do when copies, not originals are available; when documents are not in English or Welsh; what alternatives to a bank statement will be accepted; what foreign currency conversion tool is to be used; how income from employment or self-employment outside the UK can be evidenced, what proof is needed to demonstrate exemption from the rules and so on.

(3)   For those applicants who are exempt from meeting the minimum financial requirement in Appendix FM (see para A1(12) of FM-SE) FM-SE details the evidence which must be provided for the exemption to apply (see paras A1(12) which includes official documentation from DWP or the Veterans Agency confirming the person's entitlement and the amount received and at least one personal bank statement in the 12-month period prior to the date of the application showing payment of the benefit or allowance into the person's account).

(4)   As a general note, all income and cash savings relied upon under FM-SE must be in the name of the applicant, their partner or their joint names. Income can be paid into, or cash savings held in, any bank or savings account in the name of the applicant, the applicant's partner or

both, provided that the account is held in a financial institution that is regulated by the Financial Services Authority (FSA) or the appropriate regulatory body for the country in which that institution is operating; and the financial institution does not appear on the list of excluded institutions under Appendix P of the Immigration Rules.

(5)   Bank statements must be on official bank stationary or if electronic they must be either accompanied by a letter from the bank on its headed stationary confirming they are authentic, or bear the official stamp of the issuing bank on every page.

(6)   All income and savings must be lawfully derived which means that employment income can only be relied upon if the individual is working legally.

(7)   Promises of third-party support cannot be counted towards the financial requirement (see para A1(1)(b)). The applicant and their partner must have the required resources under their own control, not somebody else's. In the accompanying IDI this is said to be because 'Promises of support from a third party are vulnerable to a change in that person's circumstances or in the applicant's or partner's relationship with them' (IDI: Family Members under Appendix FM and Appendix Armed Forces of the Immigration Rules, Annex FM Section FM 1.7: Financial Requirement, July 2014, para 3.3.2). The exceptions to this rule include payments from a former partner for child maintenance or maintenance of the partner, income from a dependent child who has turned 18, a gift of cash savings provided it has been held for at least six months and is under the applicant's control and a maintenance grant or stipend for undergraduate or postgraduate study or research (para A1(1)(b)).

(8)   Other sources of income which cannot count toward the minimum income requirement include income from others living in the same household except the dependent child of the applicant who has turned 18, loans and credit facilities, means-tested benefits, some contributory benefits, child benefit, working and child tax credits, and generally speaking any source of income *not* specified in FM-SE.

There is some limited 'evidential flexibility' provided to decision-makers in FM-SE paragraph D. Thus decision-makers can contact applicants and inform them of a missing document in a sequence, a document in the wrong format, a document which is copy (and not an original) or a document that doesn't contain specified information – providing them with the opportunity to rectify the error. (A decision-maker can grant leave exceptionally where a document does not contain specified information but this can be verified through other documents, the website of the issuing body or the website of the appropriate regulatory body.) The decision-maker can overlook a lack of evidence where it is not available because, for example, it is not issued in a particular country or is permanently lost.

Appendix FM-SE itself has not been subjected to detailed analysis by the courts. In the case of *R (on the application of MM (Lebanon)) v Secretary of State for the Home Department*[1] the Court of Appeal was solely concerned with a challenge to the lawfulness of the substantive minimum financial requirement within the Immigration Rules, not with the lawfulness of the evidential requirements. However, in *MM v The Secretary of State for the*

Home Department[2] Blake J in the Administrative Court found the following, which arguably was not doubted by the Court of Appeal and which may be used to demonstrate that Appendix FM-SE requirements focus unduly on form not substance:

'140. In my judgment, the aim of transparency cannot justify an agglomeration of measures that cumulatively very severely restrict the ability of many law abiding and decent citizens of this nation who happen not to earn substantial incomes in their employment from living with their spouses in the land of their nationality. Transparency can be best achieved by clarity as to the kinds of documents required to demonstrate the relevant facts rather than a blanket rule preventing receipt of data that may well be sufficient and reliable . . . .

141. Moreover, both past practice in the administration of the rules and the survival of a number of instances in the new rules where the additional recourse to public funds approach is retained, belies the alleged difficulty or complexity in making an assessment of future economic prospects based on data before the Entry Clearance Officer. The experience of the Tribunal judiciary suggests that these are not inherently complex and imponderable questions; having a minimum income significantly above subsistence level identifies clearly what is to be achieved but the denial of legitimate means of being able to demonstrate that a couple will meet the minimum and be self-sufficient, is to require the means of proof to predominate over the right itself, and results in a disconnection from the legitimate aim of economic self-sufficiency and the promotion of integration.'

[1] [2014] EWCA Civ 985
[2] [2013] EWHC 1900 (Admin)

Appendix FM – Bereaved partners and victims of domestic violence

11.73 Under these routes – in terms similar to the equivalent Part 8 rules – applicants can apply for indefinite leave to remain as the bereaved partner of a person of a British citizen or a person present and settled in the UK or as an estranged partner of such person whose relationship with their partner broke down permanently as a result of domestic violence (see **11.56**). While it is required that applicants under these rules provide evidence to show that they were last granted leave as a partner of a British citizen or person settled in the UK (E-BLILR 1.2; E-DVILR 1.2) these rules do not require that bereaved or victim applicants must have current leave. The Home Office *Guidance* notes that in most bereavement cases, provided that the other criteria are satisfied, it will be appropriate to grant indefinite leave to remain on sight of the partner's death certificate and without further inquiry. It will not normally be appropriate to make detailed enquiries as to the subsistence of the marriage, civil partnership or relationship unless there are doubts about this.[1] In domestic violence claims – as with transitional Part 8 cases seeking ILR in such circumstances, there are more searching inquiries clear guidance concerning the type of evidence to be provided to show that the partnership ended through domestic violence.

[1] IDI, Appendix FM, Section 1.0a, Family Life (as a Partner or Parent): 5-Year Routes (July 2014), section 16.4.

Appendix FM – Family life as a parent of a child in the UK

11.74 In 1994, the Immigration Rules made provision for the first time for parents to come to the UK so as to have contact visits with their UK-resident children. The rules were substantially amended in October 2000 in order to ensure compliance with ECHR, Article 8 obligations of respect for family life. Under the old Part 7 rules (preserved in transitional arrangements for those who applied for leave as a contact parent before 9 July 2014 and whose claim is pending) the parent could qualify for leave to remain for 12 months and thereafter be granted ILR. (HC 395, paras 246–248, amended by Cm 4851 on 2 October 2000.)

The Appendix FM provision replaces the Part 7 rule. The Secretary of State's *Guidance* suggests that the Appendix FM provision is a route intended for a parent who has responsibility for or access to their child following the breakdown of their relationship with the child's other parent.[1] The principal criteria for an Appendix FM parent case comprise requirements for a valid application, that the applicant does not fall for refusal on suitability grounds, meets relationship, immigration status, financial and English language criteria. As to the parental relationship the Appendix FM rule requires that the child of the applicant must be:

(a)   under the age of 18 years at the date of application, or where the child has turned 18 years of age since the applicant was first granted entry clearance or leave to remain as a parent under this Appendix, must not have formed an independent family unit or be leading an independent life;

(b)   living in the UK; and

(c)   a British Citizen or settled in the UK; or

(d)   has lived in the UK continuously for at least the seven years immediately preceding the date of the application (though paragraph EX1 applies).

The applicant parent:

(a)   must have sole parental responsibility for the child or the child normally lives with the applicant and not their other parent (who is a British Citizen or settled in the UK); or

(b)   the parent or carer with whom the child normally lives1 must be –
  (i)   a British Citizen in the UK or settled in the UK;
  (ii)   not the partner of the applicant (which here includes a person who has been in a relationship with the applicant for less than two years prior to the date of application); and
  (iii)   the applicant must not be eligible to apply for leave to remain as a partner under this Appendix; or

(c)   The applicant must provide evidence that they have either –
  (i)   sole parental responsibility for the child, or that the child normally lives with them; or
  (ii)   access rights to the child;[2] and that they are taking, and intend to continue to take, an active role in the child's upbringing.

[1]   IDI, Appendix FM 1.0 Family Life (as a Partner or Parent): 5-Year Routes (July 2014) at p 14. The Guidance suggests that the 'normally lives with' requirement is not intended to cover a parent with whom the child occasionally lives (for example , at the weekend, during holidays or a single weekly overnight stay or who can qualify under Appendix FM as a partner (in

which case that is the route under which the applicant should apply): IDI Appendix FM1.0 Family Life as a Partner or Parent 5 Year Routes, July 2014 at p 33.

2   In order to prove access rights, the Secretary of State's guidance requires applicants to provide either a residence or contact (now a child arrangement) order made by a court in the UK or a sworn affidavit from the UK resident parent, or carer of the child confirming that the applicant parent can have access to the child, describe 'in detail' the arrangements for this and if the contact is supervised any supervisor must endorse the statement: IDI, Appendix FM 1.0, Family Life (as a Partner or Parent): 5-Year Routes (July 2014) at pp 33–34.

ADMISSION OF CHILDREN UNDER 18

11.75–11.76 In this section we examine the rules relating to children under the age of 18 at the time of the application. A child who has the right of abode has a right of entry but must be in a position to prove it by production of either a British passport or a certificate of entitlement.[1] On proof of the right of abode, the child does not require leave to enter and is dealt with in the same way as a British citizen. A child will acquire the right of abode if, after 1 January 1983, he or she has been registered as a British citizen, or was born in the UK to a parent who was settled in the UK at the time of birth; or was born abroad to a parent who was a British citizen otherwise than by descent, at the time of birth.[2] For other children their entry and stay is provided for in the Immigration Rules dealing with dependent relatives.[3] We examine in turn:

(i)   the rules relating to children born in the UK who are not British citizens;

(ii)   the rules for admission of children born abroad who have at least one parent settled or intending to settle here;

(iii) the sole responsibility and 'exclusion undesirable' rules;

(iv)   inter-country adoptions and surrogacy arrangements.

(v)   unaccompanied minors

(vi)   removal of children.

1   Immigration Act 1971, s 3(9). Without such documents the child may be unable to board an airline to get to the UK, or (if refused leave to enter on arrival) appeal before removal save on human rights grounds: see Nationality, Immigration and Asylum Act 2002, s 88(2), (6). *See* also *R v Secretary of State for the Home Department, ex p Bibi (Shorzan)* [1987] Imm AR 213. There is a right of appeal against a refusal of a certificate of entitlement: Nationality, Immigration and Asylum Act 2002, s 82(1), (2)(c).

2   See *TB (Bangladesh) v Entry Clearance Officer* [2007] EWCA Civ 740 (18 July 2007), [2007] All ER (D) 267 (Jul) which considered whether a widow and children, who remained abroad, have a right of abode in the UK whether the husband/father, a Commonwealth citizen, now deceased, gained admission to the UK by assuming another person's identity and obtained registration in that assumed identity as a citizen of the UK and Colonies. The Court held that because he applied in a false identity the husband/father never had citizenship of the UK and Colonies. (See further Chapter 2.)

3   HC 395, para 317. Until 1994, unmarried dependent daughters between 18 and 21 could be admitted to join parents in the UK if they had been living as part of the family unit: HC 251, para 55. More generous age limits for children applied under the special voucher scheme, which has now been abolished. For details of the scheme, see the fifth edition at **8.83**, and *Patel v Entry Clearance Officer (Mumbai)* [2010] EWCA Civ 17; *JB (India) v Entry Clearance Officer* [2009] EWCA Civ 234, *HG & RG* [2005] UKIAT 00062; *RM (Special Vouchers – representation) India* [2005] UKIAT 00067 'Reported'; *HT (Special Voucher Holder, dependants) India* [2007] UKAIT 00031 (5 March 2007). For applicants benefiting from the under 12s concession withdrawn on 29 March 2003, see *KK (under 12 policy in-country) Jamaica* [2004] UKIAT 00268.

Meaning of 'parent'

11.77 Under the Immigration Rules, a parent is defined to include:

(a) the stepfather of a child whose father is dead and the reference to stepfather includes a relationship arising through civil partnership;

(b) the stepmother of a child whose mother is dead and the reference to stepmother includes a relationship arising through civil partnership;

(c) the father as well as the mother of an illegitimate child where he is proved to be the father;

(d) an adoptive parent in a recognised or de facto adoption;

(e) in the case of a child born in the UK who is not a British citizen, a person to whom there has been a genuine transfer of parental responsibility on the ground of the original parent(s)' inability to care for the child.[1]

The Instructions to entry clearance officers, the Entry Clearance Guidance notes that the commissioning British parent in the surrogacy arrangement may also be a parent under the rules.[2]

The Immigration Rules recognises as 'parent' both the mother and father of an illegitimate child if paternity is proved.[3] This contrasted with the position in British nationality law, where (until 1 July 2006 which saw the commencement of section 9 of the Nationality Immigration and Asylum Act 2002), the father of an illegitimate child was not able to pass on citizenship.[4] Illegitimate children are treated the same as others for the purposes of all of the Immigration Rules, and for those born after the 1 July 2006 are treated the same as others for the purposes of nationality, subject to proof of the relationship.

1   HC 395, para 6.
2   *UK Visas Entry Clearance Guidance*, Vol 1, Chapter 14, para 14.22. See also UKBA 'International Surrogacy and the Immigration Rules', 1 June 2009, on UKBA website. The Human Fertilisation and Embryology Act 2008 defines both mother and father of a surrogate child. The Act came into force in April 2009.
3   HC 395, para 6. See CHAPTER 2, above for more details. See on DNA testing of children, IDI (Nov 09), Chapter 8, s 5A, Annex N.
4   BNA 1981, s 50(9) provides that a child's mother is the woman who gives birth to the child; a child's father is the husband, at the time of the child's birth, of the woman who gives birth to the child, the father under section 35 of HFEA 2008 or if neither of these apply is any person who satisfies prescribed requirements as to proof of paternity. Under the British Nationality (Proof of Paternity) Regulations 2006, SI 2006/1498 the father is taken to be the person named as such in a birth certificate issued within one year of the child's birth or a person who satisfies the Secretary of State he is the father (generally by DNA) (reg 2). See, on birth registration of a child born to an unmarried father, Children Act 1989, s 4. The nationality provision came into force on 1 July 2006 and applies to children born after that date. The Immigration and Nationality Directorate has a policy of discretionary registration of illegitimate children born before that date where there are no doubts as to paternity, no reasonable objection from either parent and no character objections: NI, Chapter 9, s 9.

11.78 Certain aspects of the Immigration Rule definition of parent are particular to immigration law and inconsistent with family law provisions. First, a step-parent will only qualify as a parent when the natural parent whom the step-parent replaces is dead.[1] Second, in the case of children born in the UK who are not British, 'parent' is extended to mean a person to whom there has been a genuine transfer of parental responsibility on the ground of the original parent or parents' inability to care for the child.[2] This could include guardians, the local authority where a care order is in force, foster parents with whom the child has lived for at least a year, or any person or relative granted a residence or special guardianship order in respect of the child.[3] For the purposes of all the rules, except those (paras 297–303) relating to children joining parents for settlement, 'parent' includes an adoptive parent, but only where a child was adopted in accordance with a decision taken by the competent administrative authority or court in a country whose adoption orders are recognised by the UK or is the subject of a de facto adoption which meets the requirements of the relevant rule.[4] There are different hurdles to overcome to join adoptive parents in the UK for settlement.[5] The rules have been amended to include de facto adoptions in certain circumstances.[6] There is no concept of de facto adoption in family law. The rules also provide for a child to come to the UK for the purpose of adoption but not for special guardianship orders – the family order designed in part to accommodate ethnic communities who have 'religious and cultural difficulties with adoption'.[7]

[1] HC 395, para 6.
[2] HC 395, para 6. Parental responsibility is defined in section 3 of the Children Act 1989 as 'all the rights, duties, powers, responsibilities and authority which by law a parent of a child has in relation to the child and his property. More than one person may have parental responsibility for the same child at the same time (Children Act 1989, s 2(5)).
[3] See Children Act 1989, ss 3–5, 10, 14A, 33.
[4] HC 395, para 6, as amended by HC 538. The requirements for recognition of a de facto adoption are dealt with at para 309A, as inserted.
[5] HC 395, para 310(i)(a)–(g).
[6] HC 395, paras 309A, 310(vi)(b).
[7] HC 395, paras 316A–F. On special guardianship orders, see the Children Act 1989, ss 14A–14F.

Proving the relationship of parent and child

11.79 The difficulties in establishing the relationship of parent and child have been largely resolved by DNA testing,[1] although problems remain where the parents are dead or a full blood comparison is not possible. Past disputed relationships gave rise to the problem of re-applications by adult children who were refused as minors, but later recognised as related as claimed to the parent settled in the UK. The Immigration Rules made no provision for such cases, and the policy outside the Rules is restrictive, requiring strong compassionate circumstances and that the over-age child remained unmarried and fully dependent on the UK parent.[2] The High Court held that the policy was not unreasonable.[3] Other over-age applicants must comply with the dependent relatives rules.[4] Problems can arise if the children who are claimed as the child of both parents after DNA analysis are discovered to be the child of only one of them. In such cases admission may be possible under either the 'exclusion undesirable' or 'de facto adoption' rules, particularly if the child has been brought up as a child of both parents. Evidence of age or relationship which was not available to the entry clearance officer has always been admissible on appeal, as it is not evidence of post-decision facts (which remains inadmissible in entry clearance appeals despite the liberalisation of the evidence require-ments in relation to all other appeals),[5] but post-decision evidence of already existing facts.[6]

1   IDI (Nov 08), Chapter 8, s 5A Annex N, 'DNA Testing Children'.
2   Ministerial statement, 14 June 1989. See *AA & NA (Concession on DNA testing) Bangladesh* [2004] UKIAT 00180.
3   *R v Immigration Appeal Tribunal, ex p Ali (Jaifor)* [1990] Imm AR 531; *Miah (Hassan) v Secretary of State for the Home Department* [1991] Imm AR 437, CA. However, depending on the circumstances, refusal of admission to an over-age child might be a breach of ECHR, Art 8. See discussion on relevant family issues in *Patel v Entry Clearance Officer (Mumbai)* [2010] EWCA Civ 17; *JB (India) v Entry Clearance Officer* [2009] EWCA Civ 234; *HT (Special Voucher Holder, dependants) India* [2007] UKAIT 00031 (5 March 2007); *NH (India) v Entry Clearance Officer* [2007] EWCA Civ 1330 (13 December 2007); *NH (Female BOCs, exceptionality, Art 8, para 317) British Overseas Citizens* [2006] UKAIT 00085 (26 October 2006).
4   HC 395, paras 317–319.
5   Nationality Immigration and Asylum Act 2002, s 85(4)–(5). For the admission of evidence of post-decision facts in 2002 Act appeals see *DR (Entry Clearance Officer post decision evidence) Morocco* [2005] UKIAT 00038, *LS (post-decision evidence; direction; appealability) Gambia* [2005] UKAIT 00085 (19 April 2005, unreported). Evidence of post-decision facts is relevant only for the light it sheds on the position at the date of decision: *R v Immigration Appeal Tribunal, ex p Hoque and Singh* [1988] Imm AR 216, CA; *AS (Somalia) v Secretary of State for the Home Department* [2009] UKHL 32, [2009] 1 WLR 1385, [2009] 4 All ER 711.
6   *R v Immigration Appeal Tribunal, ex p Hassanin* [1987] 1 All ER 74, [1986] 1 WLR 1448, [1986] Imm AR 502; *R v Immigration Appeal Tribunal, ex p Nathwani* [1979–80] Imm AR 9; *R v Immigration Appeal Tribunal, ex p Kotecha* [1983] 1 WLR 487, [1982] Imm AR 88. See also *R v Immigration Appeal Tribunal, ex p Secretary of State for the Home Department* [1993] Imm AR 298, QBD, affirmed in the Court of Appeal under the name *Hussain (Dilowar and Iqbal) v Secretary of State for the Home Department* [1993] Imm AR 590.

11.80 Children will have to establish their age. The relevant age for the settlement rules is the age of the child when the application is made, rather than at the date of decision,[1] and entry clearance or leave to enter will not be refused merely because the child has become over-age since the application was made.[2] The child's date of birth will have to be established by reference to birth certificates, or by reference to contemporaneous declarations, the date of marriage if applicable and return visits by parent sponsors or other credible testimony. On the contentious issue of age dispute questions in the context of unaccompanied child asylum seekers.

1   HC 395, paras 27 and 321(ii). Equally a child who becomes over-age while the UKBA or the appellate authority is considering the application is not disadvantaged: para 298(i)–(ii); *Mahmood (Fazal)* [1979–80] Imm AR 71n. A person admitted with a view to settlement may still be able to obtain indefinite leave to remain after entry despite becoming over age: see para 298(ii)(a), (b); but a child who enters in some other capacity and then seeks indefinite leave to remain as a dependent child must apply before his or her 18th birthday in order to comply with the Immigration Rules and may be refused if at the time of the appeal decision he/she is over 18: *SO (Nigeria) v Secretary of State for the Home Department* [2007] EWCA Civ 76 (30 January 2006). Note that the relevant age for children accompanying or joining parents for purposes other than settlement is the age at the date of the decision: para 27. (See also IDI (Nov 09), Chapter 8, s 5A, Annex M, para 2.)
2   HC 395, paras 27, 321(ii). An application for entry clearance is not made until any fee payable in respect of a specific application is paid: HC 395, para 30, reversing *Entry Clearance Officer, Port Louis v Ross* [1992] Imm AR 493. For the previous decisions on what is an application see also *Brown v Entry Clearance Officer, Kingston* [1976] Imm AR 119; *Prajapati v Immigration Appeal Tribunal* [1981] Imm AR 199, QBD; affd [1982] Imm AR 56, CA; *Soyemi v Secretary of State for the Home Department* [1990] Imm AR 564, IAT.

PART 8 AND APPENDIX FM RULES – ADMISSION AND STAY OF CHILDREN

Non-British children born in the UK

11.81 It has already been noted that children born in the UK after 1 January 1983 do not become British citizens by birth in the UK if neither parent was a British citizen or settled in the UK.[1] A child who remains in the UK continuously for the first ten years of his or her life (with limited provisions for short absences abroad) is entitled to registration as a British citizen.[2] A child born in the UK, will also be entitled to register as a British citizen if while he/she is a minor his father or mother becomes a British citizen or settled in the UK.[3] Special Immigration Rules apply to children born in the UK after 1 January 1983 who do not become British citizens.[4] While they remain in the UK, they are not required to obtain leave to remain. Obtaining leave to remain is advisable and will be necessary if it is expected that the child will travel and seek re-admission, when leave to enter will be required.[5]

[1] BNA 1981, s 1(1).
[2] BNA 1981, s 1(4). If the child's parents are British Overseas Territories citizens, the child will be eligible for registration as a British citizen after five years in the UK (s 4).
[3] BNA 1981, s 1(3).
[4] HC 395, paras 304–309.
[5] HC 395, para 304.

11.82 The Part 8 Immigration Rules lay down requirements for non-British children born in the UK seeking leave to enter and leave to remain. Such children seeking leave to enter or remain as the child of a parent/parents given leave to enter or remain in the UK must be accompanying or joining such parents or a child in respect of whom parental rights and duties are vested solely in a local authority and must be under 18, unmarried, or not a civil partner, not leading an independent life or having formed an independent family unit, and (for those seeking leave to enter) must not have been away from the UK for more than two years.[1] If the child is accompanied by or seeking to join a parent with limited leave, leave to enter is given for the same period as that of the parents, or the longer of the two periods if each parent has a different period of leave, save where the parents are separated, in which case leave is given for the same period as the parent who has day-to-day control.[2] If neither of the parents has a current leave, leave to enter or remain will normally be refused, unless it is unlikely that the parents will be removed in the immediate future and there is no other person outside the UK who could reasonably be expected to care for the child.[3] In such cases, three months' leave to enter may be given. If one of the parents is a British citizen or if the parental rights and duties in respect of the child are vested in a local authority, indefinite leave to enter or remain may be given.[4] Children born in the UK who are not British citizens are not removable in their own right, as they are neither overstayers nor illegal entrants but can be removed as a member of the family of an overstayer or illegal entrant parent.[5]

[1] HC 395, para 305(i)–(v).
[2] HC 395, paras 305(i)(a) and 306.
[3] HC 395, para 307.
[4] HC 395, paras 305(i)(b) and (c) and 308. The guidance for dealing with children in local authority care is contained in IDI (Nov 09), Chapter 8, s 5A, Annex M, para 8. See also IDI (Nov 09), Chapter 8, s 4A Children Born in the UK not British Citizens. A parent may retain

parental responsibility for their child even where the child is subject to a care order to a local authority. It can be assumed that para 305(1)(c) which does not reflect family law provisions concerning the sole vesting of parental rights and duties, should be taken to apply when a full as opposed to an interim care order is made.

5 Immigration Act 1971, Sch 2, para 10A (inserted by the Nationality Immigration and Asylum Act 2002 from 10 February 2003); HC 395, para 395C. The Secretary of State will not normally remove the person if she/he ceases to be a member of the family of the person to be removed. Care should be taken to ascertain whether such child might have a claim to British citizenship because he/she has lived here for ten years or has an expectation of being permitted to remain because of seven years residence. NIAA 2002, s 117B (6).

11.83 The distinguishing feature of the Immigration Rules for these children compared with those applying to other children is that, provided they return to the UK within two years of leaving, they do not have to satisfy the requirements in para 297 as regards adequate maintenance, accommodation or the presence in the UK of both parents.[1] They can obtain prior entry clearance, but do not have to do so, unless they are visa nationals. Children born in the UK who return after an absence of over two years have to qualify under the ordinary rules, either as dependent children or in some other capacity, such as students.

1 HC 395, paras 305-8.

Children under 18 with UK-settled parent, parents or relative

11.84 The Part 8 Immigration Rules limit family reunion rights. Children who have no right of abode and were not born in the UK, who are seeking to enter or remain with a UK-settled parent, parents or a relative, must be under 18 at the date of application, unmarried, not a civil partner, not leading an independent life[1] or have formed an independent family unit,[2] and can and will be maintained and accommodated adequately by the parent/parents or relative without recourse to public funds and in accommodation which the parents/relatives own or occupy or will occupy exclusively.[3] Under the Part 8 Rules a distinction is drawn between children both of whose parents (or in the case of death, the surviving parent) live or are to be settled in the UK, and those children who seek entry or stay to accompany or join only one of their parents or are seeking to join a relative other than a parent. From 9 July 2012 a further distinction is made as between children joining settled parents, and children who after that date apply for leave to enter and remain as a child of a parent or parents with limited leave to enter or remain with a view to settlement. The applications of the latter cohort of children are dealt with in accordance with the Appendix FM rules (family Life as a child of a person with limited leave as a partner or parent) while children with settled parents continue to have their applications dealt with under the Part 8 rules.

1 HC 395, paras 6 and 297iii. The paragraph 6 definition interprets 'not leading an independent life' as not having a partner (as defined in Appendix FM), living with parents (except where at boarding school, college or university), not in full time employment (unless aged 18 and over) and wholly or mainly dependent upon parents for financial and emotional support. In *Luchow* (2004 unreported) the Tribunal accepted that a 17-year-old who had moved away from the family home to study, was staying with relatives and remained financially dependent on the sponsor, was not leading an independent life. In *NM ('leading an independent life') Zimbabwe* [2007] UKAIT 00051 (24 May 2007) the Tribunal held that in order to establish that the child is not 'leading an independent life', he or she must not have formed through choice a separate (and therefore independent) social unit from the parents' family unit whether alone or with

others. A child who, for example, chooses to live away from home may be 'leading an independent life' despite some continuing financial and/or emotional dependence upon his or her parents. In this case, the Tribunal accepted the appellant was not leading an independent life, notwithstanding that she had been employed and had moved temporarily out of her parent's home due to overcrowding. The relevant issue is not an individual's capacity to lead an independent life but rather whether she is leading such a life. The Rule is concerned with whether the child applicant has formed an independent family unit. It is not enough to show the child is living with another family, or that his/her parents may have new families/partners. The child is disqualified under the Rules only if he/she has formed an independent family unit. Further, in context, the term 'independent family unit' should be taken to have a similar character and the settled status associated with a marriage or civil partnership and for a child applicant to have formed such unit, he/she would have to be shown to have a settled family and an attachment with, and a commitment to and from, the new family. See also *BM and AL* (352D(iv); meaning of 'family unit') *Colombia* [2007] UKAIT 00055 and *MI* (para 298(iii): 'independent life') Pakistan [2007] UKAIT 00052 (5 June 2006) in which the Tribunal held there is no requirement that the dependency must be one of necessity. The fact that the child lives with his/her parents as a matter of custom is irrelevant: all one need show is that he/she is not leading an independent life, not why.

2 In *Tabassum v Entry Clearance Officer, Karachi* [2002] UKIAT 03749, siblings some of whom worked to support the others were held to be in an 'independent family unit'. See also *BM and AL* (352D(iv); meaning of 'family unit') *Colombia* [2007] UKAIT 00055 (13 June 2006), *Tuquabo-Tekle v Netherlands* (Application 60665/00) [2005] 3 FCR 649.

3 HC 395, para 297(ii)–(vi). Adequate maintenance is is defined in Para 6 of the Immigration Rules to mean that after tax (national insurance) and housing costs have been deducted there must be available to the family the level of income that could have been available if the family were in receipt of income support.

11.85 Children who have both their parents settled or entering for settlement in the UK, and who satisfy the general Rule 297 criteria, qualify for entry clearance, which will operate as indefinite leave to enter[1]. Children can also qualify for indefinite leave to enter/remain if both parents are being admitted for or qualify for settlement in the UK at the same time as the child,[3] or one is settled and the other parent is being admitted on the same occasion for settlement,[4] or one parent is settled or will be admitted for settlement and the other parent (including a parent of an illegitimate child) is dead.[5] Where one parent has died and the other parent has remarried, then the step-parent (who in these circumstances is treated as a 'parent' under Paragraph 6 of the Rules) must be settled or admitted for settlement as well as the natural parent,[6] although the relationship of step-parent would terminate on divorce of the parties. Where the child is an adoptive child the parents in question are the adoptive parents in a recognised or de facto adoption.[7] A child who enters in some other capacity, for example as a visitor or student, may qualify for the grant of indefinite leave to remain if the same conditions are met after entry.[8]

1 HC 395, paras 297(i)(a) and 299; Immigration (Leave to Enter and Remain) Order 2000, SI 2000/1161, Arts 2 and 3.
3 HC 395, para 297(i)(b).
4 HC 395, para 297(i)(c).
5 HC 395, para 297(i)(d).
6 HC 395, para 6 (definition of parent); see also *Alam (Manzar) v Entry Clearance Officer, Lahore* [1973] Imm AR 79 and *McGillivary v Secretary of State for the Home Department* [1972] Imm AR 63.
7 HC 395, para 6 (definition of parent) Adoption and Children Act 2002, ss 66 and 67 The recognised adoptions will be 'overseas adoptions'.
8 HC 395, para 298.

11.86 Where one parent is settled and the other parent is given a limited leave to enter with a view to subsequent settlement, the child is given the same leave as the non-settled parent and where such application is made after 9 July 2012 the relevant Appendix FM rules apply.[1] The Appendix FM provision for such children is headed 'Family Life as a Child of Parents with Limited Leave as a Partner or Parent'. Where the application is for entry clearance such child applicants must be outside the UK; or for leave to remain must be in the UK and must have made a valid application for entry clearance as a child, must meet the suitability requirements contained in Section S-EC and all the eligibility requirements of Section E-ECC or R-LTRC. The eligibility criteria include:

(i) Relationship requirements. (These replicate the Part 8 relationship criteria – see: HC 395, paragraph 297(i) and (iii).[2]

(ii) Financial requirements.[3]

(iii) Evidence that there will be adequate accommodation available for the family without recourse to public funds which they own or occupy exclusively.[4]

The fact that a child has become over 18 since arrival in the UK does not matter if the child was previously admitted by the immigration service with a view to settlement.[5]

---

[1] If the child applied before 9 July 2012 the application will have been decided under HC 395, paras 302–303FF. Applications by children in these circumstances after 9 July 2012, Appendix FM applies.

[2] See Immigration Directorate Instruction, Chapter 8, Section 5A, Annex M, Children (July 2011) at Section 3; and Immigration Directorate Instruction, Chapter 8, Section FM 3.2, Children (July 2012) at Section 3. The relationship requirements for leave to remain are the same as the requirements imposed for entry clearance applications under Section EC-C save that for leave to remain the applicant's parent must be in the UK and have leave to enter or remain or indefinite leave to remain, or will be granted any one of those things, in accordance with Appendix FM. Any such parent leave cannot be as an adult dependent relative (E-LTRC.1.6.).

[3] The starting point for a child applicant is that he or she (via the parents) must provide specified evidence from the sources set out in E-ECC.2.2. currently of either:
   (i) a specified gross annual income of at least £18,600 (E-ECC.2.1.(a))
   (ii) specified savings of £16,000 and additional savings of an amount equivalent to 2.5 times the amount of the difference between (a) the gross annual income of the applicant from the sources set out in E-ECC.2.2.(a)-(f) and (b) the total amount required under E-ECC.2.1.(a) (E-ECC.2.1.(b))
   The Rules permit an applicant to mix a specified gross annual income with specified savings. However income from only a very limited number of sources can be used in support of an application:
   (i) income of the applicant's parent's partner (i.e. the British citizen or settled person) from specified employment or self-employment, which, in respect of a partner returning to the UK with the applicant, can include specified employment or self-employment overseas as well as in the UK (E-ECC.2.2.(a));
   (ii) income of the applicant's parent (i.e. the partner with leave to enter or remain under Appendix FM) from specified employment or self-employment in the UK, unless they are working illegally (E-ECC.2.2.(b));
   (iii) specified pension income of the applicant's parent and that parent's partner (E-ECC.2.2.(c));
   (iv) any specified maternity allowance or bereavement benefit received by the applicant's parent and that parent's partner in the UK or any specified payment relating to service in HM Forces received by the applicant's parent and that parent's partner (E-ECC.2.2.(d));
   (v) other specified income of the applicant's parent and that parent's partner (E-ECC.2.2.(e));
   (vi) specified savings of the applicant's parent, that parent's partner and a dependent child of the applicant's parent within the meaning of E-ECC.2.1. who is aged 18 years or older (E-ECC.2.2.(f)).

The exception to the new financial requirements is for those applicants whose parent's partner receives one or more of a list of state benefits set out in E-ECC.2.3(a). In those cases, an applicant must provide evidence that their parent's partner is able to maintain and accommodate themselves, the applicant's parent, the applicant and any dependents adequately in the UK without recourse to public funds (E-ECC.2.3.(b)). This is the same formula as was used in respect of the Part 8 Rules. On that basis, the pre-existing case-law on adequate maintenance will remain relevant.

The financial requirements for leave to remain are the same as the requirements imposed for entry clearance applications under Section EC-C. The only salient difference is that where the applicant's parent is applying for indefinite leave to remain, the specified savings that an applicant must show is reduced from 2.5 times to simply the difference between (a) the gross annual income of the applicant from the sources set out in E-LTRC.2.2.(a)-(f) and (b) the total amount required under E-LTRC.2.1.(a) (E-LTRC.2.1.(b)(ii)).

4   This criterion is the same as for the partner routes.
5   HC 395, para 298(ii)(b). See also Appendix FM Family life as the child of a parent with limited leave at E-LTRC 1.2 which requires applicants to be under 18 at the date of the application or when first granted leave as a child under this route.

The sole responsibility rule

11.87 Where one parent (including a step-parent where a natural parent is dead) is settled in the UK and the other parent is not coming to the UK for settlement, their child applicant seeking entry clearance for settlement, entry clearance/limited leave to enter or remain (with a view to settlement) under Appendix FM or indefinite leave to remain under the Part 8 rules must satisfy the entry clearance officer either that the parent in the UK has had sole responsibility for the child or that there are serious and compelling family or other considerations which make exclusion of the child undesirable and suitable arrangements have been made of the child's care.[1] The phrase 'sole responsibility' is intended to reflect a situation where the primary parental responsibility for the child's upbringing rests with one parent. The parent claiming sole responsibility must satisfactorily demonstrate that he or she has been the person exercising primary decision-making concerning the child's upbringing.[2] Sole responsibility' is a factual matter to be decided upon all the evidence. Where one parent is not involved in the child's upbringing because he (or she) had not assumed any responsibility for the child, the issue may arise between the remaining parent and others who have day-to-day care of the child abroad. The test is whether the parent has continuing control and direction over the child's upbringing, including making all the important decisions in the child's life. Where both parents are involved in a child's upbringing, the assessment of sole responsibility is more difficult. In *TD (Paragraph 297(i)(e); sole responsibility) Yemen*, the Tribunal noted of such cases: 'Wherever the parents are, if both parents are involved in the upbringing of the child, it will be exceptional that one of them will have sole responsibility.' The Court in *Buydov v Entry Clearance Officer, Moscow* [2012] EWCA Civ 1739 at [19] observed concerning this *TD* guidance:

'It is . . . important to remember that the [sole responsibility] question remains one of fact in each case, and not to elevate the distinction into a presumption of law. There might be some risk of misreading the distinction as such a presumption, or as importing some independent legal test of exceptionality, if one were to take out of context [the above] summary contained at [52] of TD.

The IAT clearly did not mean to impose a legal test. Its review of the cases is predicated on the fundamental proposition that the issue of sole responsibility is one of fact. It was doing no more than identifying where the necessary factual enquiry is likely in most two-parent cases to lead, and as such the proposition is accurate.'

Financial support, even exclusive financial support, will not necessarily mean that the person providing it has 'sole responsibility' for the child. It is a factor but no more than that.[3] Where the sole responsibility test is not met, then the child may still qualify under the 'exclusion undesirable' rule considered below.[4]

[1] HC 395, paras 297(i)(e), 298(i)(c-d); 310 (i)(e-f); 319H(b)(i)(b-c); Appendix FM E- E- ECC 1.6 (b-c); E-LTRC 1.6 (b-c).

[2] See *TD (Paragraph 297(i)(e); sole responsibility) Yemen* [2006] UKAIT 49 and *Buydov v Entry Clearance Officer, Moscow* [2012] EWCA Civ 1739. The Home Office guidance defines 'sole responsibility' as meaning that 'one parent has abdicated or abandoned parental responsibility and the remaining parent is exercising sole control in setting and providing the day to day direction for the child's welfare': Immigration Directorate Instruction, Appendix FM 1.0 Family Life (as a Partner or Parent): 5-Year Routes (July 2014) at page 31. In *Buydov* the Court cautioned against the use of the term 'abdication of responsibility' insofar as this implies a more stringent test of sole responsibility. It is said in the IDI guidance that it will be rare where both parents are involved in a child's upbringing for a person to establish sole responsibility. See too Section 4 of the Immigration Directorate Instruction, Chapter 8, Section 5A, Annex M, Children (July 2011) and the Immigration Directorate Instruction, Chapter 8, Section FM 3.2, Children (July 2012). See also: *Nmaju v Immigration Appeal Tribunal* [2001] INLR 26, CA; *Ramos v Immigration Appeal Tribunal* [1989] Imm AR 148, *Cenir v Entry Clearance Officer* [2003] EWCA Civ 572. See also *NA (Bangladesh) v Secretary of State for the Home Department* [2007] EWCA Civ 128 (24 January 2007) in which the Court of Appeal accepted that a parent can have sole responsibility, notwithstanding the fact that the financial responsibility component was shared as between the father and his sons.

[3] *TD (Paragraph 297(i)(e): 'sole responsibility') Yemen* [2006] UKAIT 00049 (24 May 2006).

[4] HC 395, paras 297(i)(f), 298(i)(d).

11.88 If the child's application is to join both parents, who are themselves settled or settling, there is no investigation required of the parent's responsibility for the child's upbringing. In effect, the rules assume that between them the parents have full responsibility. The condition of sole responsibility exists only where there is but a single sponsoring parent in the UK whom the applicant seeks to join. In any case where a parent comes to the UK and leaves the child behind, the person who is looking after the child clearly has some responsibility for the child's upbringing. A literal interpretation of 'sole responsibility' would defeat all claims. This was recognised in *Emmanuel v Secretary of State for the Home Department*[1] where the Tribunal found that literal or absolute sole responsibility of the parent in the UK could never be established and there must be, in nearly all such cases, some form of responsibility with the relative with whom the child lives. This does not prevent the parent in the UK having 'sole responsibility'. Sole responsibility is not the same as legal custody. In *Nmaju*[2] the Court of Appeal stated that a parent's legal responsibility for the child under the appropriate legal system would be a relevant consideration in deciding sole responsibility, but would not be conclusive. It is necessary to look at what actually was done in relation to the child's upbringing, by whom and whether it had been done under the direction of the parent settled here. In *Sloley v Entry Clearance Officer, Kingston Jamaica*[3] the mother left her son with her mother but had sole financial responsibility and had been continuously consulted about the child's schooling, upbringing and activities. In holding that she had had sole responsibility, the Tribunal considered as relevant, inter alia, the source and degree of financial support of the child and whether there was cogent evidence of genuine interest in and affection for the child by the sponsoring parent in the

UK. In *Buydov* where the child was living with his mother and stepfather in the UK but having contact with his father in Russia the Court upheld the Tribunal assessment that the mother did not have sole responsibility. The Court confirmed that it was not necessary to show the other parent had entirely abandoned or abdicated interest in the child in order to show sole responsibility. The question was one of fact. It rejected the submission that a parent who is the primary carer and home-provider will ordinarily have sole responsibility – noting: 'When parents split up, the children will ordinarily live either wholly or principally with one of them, but the range of possible ways of sharing responsibility for their upbringing is nevertheless almost infinite. Family courts increasingly encourage the acknowledgement that responsibility is shared, whatever the form of order or of agreement without order. A non-resident parent may easily have important responsibilities for the child, financial, educational, recreational and decision-making amongst them.'[4]

1 [1972] Imm AR 69.
2 *Nmaju v Immigration Appeal Tribunal* [2001] INLR 26, CA. See also *TD (Paragraph 297(i)(e): 'sole responsibility') Yemen* [2006] UKAIT 00049 (24 May 2006).
3 [1973] Imm AR 54. See also: *Martin v Secretary of State for the Home Department* [1972] Imm AR 71; *McGillivary v Secretary of State for the Home Department* [1972] Imm AR 63. In *Cenir v Entry Clearance Officer* [2003] EWCA Civ 572, [2003] All ER (D) 286 (Mar), the court stressed the importance of the parent with responsibility, albeit at a distance, having direction over or control of important decisions in the child's life.
4 *Buydov v Entry Clearance Officer, Moscow* [2012] EWCA Civ 1739 at [23–24] per Hughes LJ for the Court; See *Alagon v ECO, Manilla* [1993] Imm AR 336; *TD (Paragraph 297(i)(e): 'sole responsibility') Yemen*.

11.89 The IDI[1] suggest that the following factors should be considered where the issue is not clear:

(i)   the period for which the parent in the UK has been separated from the child;

(ii)   what the arrangements were for the care of the child before that parent migrated to the UK;

(iii)   who has been entrusted with day-to-day care and control of the child since the sponsor migrated here;

(iv)   who provides the financial support for the child's care and upbringing and in what proportion;

(v)   who takes the important decisions about the child's upbringing, such as where and with whom the child lives, the choice of school, religious practice, etc;

(vi)   the degree of contact that has been maintained between the child and the parent claiming responsibility; and

(vii)   what part in the child's care and upbringing is played by the parent not in the UK and relatives.

The family courts have acknowledged as aspects of parental responsibility: determining and fostering the child's religion; determining and encouraging the child's education; consenting to the child's medical treatment; representing and assisting the child with respect to legal proceedings and agreeing to their interview; lawfully correcting a child; arranging the child's residence and emigration; protecting and maintaining and having contact with a child.[2]

1 IDI (July 2012), Chapter 8, Section FM 3.2, para 4.3.

² Children Act 1989, s 3

11.90 In *Uddin*[1] the High Court stated that the sponsor did not need to have had responsibility for the upbringing of the child for the whole of his or her life, but for a 'not insubstantial period'. In *Nmaju*[2] the Court of Appeal deprecated the Tribunal's attempt to treat the phrase 'a not insubstantial period' as though it were incorporated into the Immigration Rules; time was a relevant, but not conclusive, factor. In that case it upheld the claim of a mother who had had the sole responsibility for her child for two-and-a-half months.

1   *R v Immigration Appeal Tribunal, ex p Uddin (Fojor) and Uddin (Nur)* [1986] Imm AR 203, QBD.
2   *Nmaju v Immigration Appeal Tribunal* [2001] INLR 26, CA.

11.91 Construing the meaning of sole responsibility in the context of the Immigration Rules as a whole, it might be thought that the word 'sole' refers only to responsibility as between the two parents. It is irrelevant if a child has been left with grandparents during its formative years, if both parents are settled in the UK, so why should a child be disqualified merely because only one parent is so settled? The sole responsibility criteria can be particularly inapt in cases of adoption where the children are required to be left with carers while their entry in accordance with family and immigration laws is arranged. But the Tribunal, the High Court and the Court of Appeal have endorsed the practice in sole responsibility cases of having regard to persons other than parents with whom responsibility could be shared.[1] However, as stated, if the child has been living abroad with the other parent, or that parent's relatives, it can be more difficult to establish that the UK-settled parent had sole responsibility than if the child has been living with a relative of the UK-settled parent.[2] In earlier decisions it had been held that daily attention and care by the other natural parent would be fatal to the application of this rule, even though it may have been intermittent and insubstantial.[3] However, this is no longer the case. To disqualify a child for admission, the other parent's involvement should be more than simple contact and should be assessed to ascertain whether the other parent has independently exercised responsibility for the child.[4] Certainly, distant past responsibility by the other parent should not mean the sponsoring parent does not currently have sole responsibility.[5]

1   *R v Immigration Appeal Tribunal, ex p Mahmood* [1988] Imm AR 121, QBD; *Ramos (Suzara) v Immigration Appeal Tribunal* [1989] Imm AR 148, CA.
2   IDI (July 2012), Chapter 8, Section FM 3.2, para 4.1 and 4.2 states that where two foreign nationals separate and the child remains with the parent abroad for several years and then wishes to join the UK parent to take advantage of the educational system, there is no reason why the child should not remain with the parent abroad, and the UK parent would not be considered to have sole responsibility.
3   *Secretary of State for the Home Department v Pusey* [1972] Imm AR 240; see also *Eugene v Entry Clearance Officer* [1975] Imm AR 111.
4   *Buydov v Entry Clearance Officer, Moscow* [2012] EWCA Civ 1739; *Nmaju v Immigration Appeal Tribunal* [2001] INLR 26, CA. *Entry Clearance Officer, Manila v Acheampong* [2002] UKIAT 06687; *Qui Zou* [2002] UKIAT 07463. See also *Alagon v Entry Clearance Officer, Manila* [1993] Imm AR 336 CS, Lord Prosser. These are issues of fact. The Tribunal observation in *TD (Paragraph 297(i)(e): 'sole responsibility') Yemen* [2006] UKAIT 00049 (24 May 2006) that where both parents are involved in a child's upbringing, it will be exceptional that one of them will have 'sole responsibility' should not be applied as a new test. The issue to be resolved concerns an evaluation of the exercise of responsibility by both parents.

The rule that family or other considerations make exclusion undesirable

11.92 Children who fail to qualify under the sole responsibility rule may qualify on the grounds that there are serious and compelling family or other reasons which make their exclusion from the UK undesirable and arrangements have been made for their care.[1] This rule permits such children to join either a parent or a relative other than a parent. 'Relative' is not defined and may be given a broad definition to include those related by blood or marriage, including fairly distant relatives.

1 HC 395, paras 297(i)(f) and 298(i)(d). Where a child is shown by DNA tests to be the child of only one of its claimed parents, he or she may nevertheless qualify under this paragraph: *R v Immigration Appeal Tribunal, ex p Ali (Iqbal)* [1994] Imm AR 295, CA. For the jurisdiction of the Tribunal to entertain a child's application under a different rule than first identified see *Hussain (Shabir) v Entry Clearance Officer, Islamabad* [1991] Imm AR 483. *SZ (Applicable immigration rules) Bangladesh* [2007] UKAIT 00037.

11.93 The Immigration Rules – including Appendix FM – make it clear that if family or other considerations are to make exclusion undesirable, they must be of a serious and compelling nature. The Rules do not amplify this expression, unlike earlier rules, which gave the example of the other parent's incapacity (physical or mental) to care for the child.[1] In *Mundeba (s 55 and para 297(i) (f)) Democratic Republic of Congo* [2013] UKUT 88 (IAC) the UT held:

'The exercise of the duty by the Entry Clearance Officer to assess an application under the Immigration Rules as to whether there are family or other considerations making the child's exclusion undesirable inevitably involves an assessment of what the child's welfare and best interests require.

Where an immigration decision engages Article 8 rights, due regard must be had to the UN Convention on the Rights of the Child. An entry clearance decision for the admission of a child under 18 is "an action concerning children...undertaken by . . . administrative authorities" and so by Article 3 "the best interests of the child shall be a primary consideration".

Family considerations require an evaluation of the child's welfare including emotional needs. "Other considerations" come in to play where there are other aspects of a child's life that are serious and compelling for example where an applicant is living in an unacceptable social and economic environment. The focus needs to be on the circumstances of the child in the light of his or her age, social backgrounds and developmental history and will involve inquiry as to whether:
   a.   there is evidence of neglect or abuse;
   b.   there are unmet needs that should be catered for;
   c.   there are stable arrangements for the child's physical care;

The assessment involves consideration as to whether the combination of circumstances are sufficiently serious and compelling to require admission.'

The IDI state that where the UK sponsor is a UK-settled parent, the circumstances may relate to the child or the parent, but where the sponsor is not settled or is not a parent, the factors to be considered must relate only to the child.[2] This test is inconsistent with the Rule which makes no distinction between parents and relatives in considering the family circumstances and is concerned with serious and compelling family *or other* considerations which make exclusion of the child undesirable. The phrase 'compelling, compassionate reasons' in the refugee family reunion policy has been interpreted by the Court of Appeal to mean reasons 'which would compel, not merely invite, an objective decision-maker to feel compassion'.[3] This interpretation has application to the 'serious and compelling considerations' requirement in the rules.

[1]   HC 251, para 53(f). In *Mundeba (s 55 and para 297(i) (f)) Democratic Republic of Congo* [2013] UKUT 88 (IAC) the Tribunal stated: 'In our view, "serious" means that there needs to be more than the parties simply desiring a state of affairs to obtain. "Compelling" in the context of paragraph 297(i)(f) indicates that considerations that are persuasive and powerful. . . . The analysis is one of degree and kind. Such an interpretation sets a high threshold that excludes cases where, without more, it is simply the wish of parties to be together however natural that ambition that may be.' See *TM (Jamaica) v Secretary of State for the Home Department* [2007] EWCA Civ 178 (6 February 2007) where the facts – the adolescent daughters exposure to the risk of non-consensual sexual activity – were capable of constituting exceptional circumstances, but the actual evidence on this issue before the Tribunal was inadequate; and *SO (Nigeria) v Secretary of State for the Home Department* [2007] EWCA Civ 76 (30 January 2006) where the age, growing maturity and independence of an applicant were accepted as relevant to the substance of a decision concerned with 'serious and compelling reasons'. The IDI (July 12), Chapter 8, Section FM 3.2 M, para 1, states that when assessing serious and compelling family or other considerations, officers must have regard to their duties under s 55 of the Borders, Citizenship and Immigration Act 2009 – it states: 'Our statutory duty to children includes the need to demonstrate: fair treatment which meets the same standard a British child would receive; the child's interests being made a primary, although not the only consideration; no discrimination of any kind; asylum applications are dealt with in a timely fashion and identification of those that might be at risk from harm. This paragraph relates to considerations referred to in paragraphs 297(i)(f), 298(i)(d), 301(i)(c), 310(i)(f), 311(i)(d) and 314(i)(c) of HC 395'.

[2]   IDI (July 12), Chapter 8, Section FM, paras 1.2–1.3. The authors consider this guidance to be incorrect, imposing additional obligations for certain child applicants.

[3]   *Miao v Secretary of State for the Home Department* [2006] EWCA Civ 75 (16 February 2006) at paragraph 15 per Sedley LJ. See also *Senanayake v Secretary of State for the Home Department* [2005] EWCA Civ 1530 (16 November 2005) at paragraph 21 per Chadwick LJ

11.94–11.98 In *Secretary of State for the Home Department v Campbell*[1] it was said that when considering family or other considerations, the conditions under which the child is living in the home country are not to be weighed against the conditions available for the child in the UK. Conditions in this country are only to be considered if conditions in the overseas country show that exclusion is undesirable. This dictum requires to be reconsidered by reference to the *Mundeba* guidance – which included consideration of the children's best interests. In *Entry Clearance Officer, Kingston v Holmes*[2] the test was satisfied where the child was living in poverty and overcrowded conditions and, importantly, her mother who had been looking after her was about to emigrate to Canada and would not be able to take the child with her. The Tribunal has also considered the death of the carer as being capable of amounting to a compelling and compassionate circumstance. The fact that there are far worse conditions elsewhere in the country is not relevant. Bad conditions are not made better by the existence of worse ones. However, it has also been held that if there is overcrowding it must be shown to be unavoidable.[3] Initially, the Tribunal set a high standard of 'intolerable' conditions[4] but in *Rudolph (Dilkish Antoinette Hayley) v Entry Clearance Officer, Colombo*[5] the Tribunal rejected the 'intolerable conditions' test, pointing out that the underlying purpose of the Immigration Rules is to unite families and not divide them and holding that where a father was incapable of caring for a child, that in itself would be grounds for deeming exclusion undesirable. Voluntary abandonment may make the circumstances compelling.[6] Relevant factors to be weighed may include the willingness and ability of the overseas adult to look after the child; the living conditions available for the child; the greater vulnerability of small children; and the importance of family unity.

[1]   [1972] Imm AR 115.
[2]   [1975] Imm AR 20. See also *AQ (Kenya) v Entry Clearance Officer* [2007] EWCA Civ 1279 (5 December 2007).
[3]   *Pinnock v Entry Clearance Officer, Kingston, Jamaica* [1974] Imm AR 22.
[4]   *Howard v Secretary of State for the Home Department* [1972] Imm AR 93.
[5]   [1984] Imm AR 84.
[6]   This rule, unlike certain of the adoption rules, does not require inability to care for the child on the part of the parent or carer abroad, cf *Sharma v Entry Clearance Officer, New Delhi* [2005] EWCA Civ 89.

INTER-COUNTRY ADOPTION AND SURROGACY ARRANGEMENTS

11.99 Inter-country adoption and inter-country surrogacy arrangements are increasingly common and are sought to be regulated so as to protect children and women from exploitative and commercial trafficking and 'baby buying' or 'baby farming' practices.

An inter-country adoption is one in which the prospective adoptive parent does not have the same nationality and/or country of residence as the child he or she wishes to adopt and it is intended to move the child to the adopter's country of habitual residence or nationality.[1] In inter-country surrogacy arrangements the parent providing the genetic material for his/her child's conception, has a different nationality or country of residence from the surrogate/ birth mother and/or child conceived as a result of the surrogacy arrangement.[2] Again these surrogacy arrangements become international/inter-country surrogacies where the commissioning parents having arranged an overseas surrogacy then seeks to travel with and /or reside with their child in the UK.

These inter-country arrangements may be undertaken in and outside the UK. Certain British citizens and residents travel abroad to adopt children or enter into surrogacy arrangements through clinics based abroad. In a similar fashion overseas nationals enter the UK to arrange the removal of children for adoption in their home country or to arrange a non-commercial surrogacy arrangement through British clinics.[3] These arrangements often involve relatives of the persons seeking adoption or surrogacy. Inter-country adoptions from the UK often involve local authorities and generally occur when local authorities are seeking to place a British child with overseas relatives because of the death or incapacity of the child's British parents.

[1]   Adoption and Children Act 2002 (ACA), ss 66, 87 and 97.
[2]   Surrogacy arrangements are regulated under the Surrogacy Arrangements Act 1985 and Human Fertilisation and Embryology Act 2008.
[3]   On the legal issues associated with surrogacy arrangements undertaken in the UK involving commissioning parents who were not domiciled in the UK, see: *G (surrogacy: foreign*

domicile), Re [2007] EWHC 2814 (Fam), [2008] Fam Law 95. The case concerned a non-commercial surrogacy arranged by a Turkish couple in the UK.

11.100 Until relatively recently inter-country adoptions were not subject to internationally agreed standards or procedures, and the children being adopted were vulnerable to exploitation and even trafficking for gain. The Hague Convention on Protection of Children and Co-operation in Respect of Intercountry Adoption (the Convention) was drafted to deal with these problems.[1] The UK ratified the Convention on 1 June 2003 and its provisions were extended to the Isle of Man on 1 November 2003. As on 6 January 2014 there were 93 contracting states to this Convention.[2] The Russian Federation has signed but not yet ratified it.[3]

The Convention has three important objectives. It seeks to establish internationally agreed safeguards to ensure that inter-country adoptions take place in the best interests of the child and with respect for his or her fundamental rights. It aims to establish a system of co-operation amongst Contracting States to ensure that those safeguards are respected and the abduction, sale or trafficking of children for adoption prevented. Finally, it enables Contracting States to recognise adoptions made in other Contracting States, so preventing the need for children to be adopted for a second time in the receiving state.[4] Adoptions made in Convention States in accordance with Convention requirements and certified as Convention compliant adoptions are termed Hague Convention or Convention adoptions.[5]

Inter-country adoptions involve the consideration of domestic and private international family law as well as immigration law. These principles and the associated arrangements to enforce them have become a feature of Convention and non-Convention inter-country adoptions in the UK.[6] There are no concluded international agreements concerning transnational surrogacy agreements. In the absence of such international standards, the Home Office *Guidance* stress that such arrangements should be in harmony with the Human Fertilisation and Embryology Act 2008.[7]

[1]   The Convention was concluded on 29 May 1993 and its text can be found in Schedule 1 to the Adoption (Intercountry Aspects) Act 1999.
[2]   The Hague Convention website: www.hcch.net/index regularly updates the list of states which have ratified the Convention.
[3]   See the status table: www.hcch.net/index_en.php?act=conventions.status&cid=69
[4]   Adoption (Intercountry Aspects) Act 1999, Sch 1; The Convention, Article 1.
[5]   The Convention, Article 23(1); ACA 2002, s 66(1).
[6]   For guidance on intercountry adoptions see: Home Office Guidance 'Adopted Children' Jan 2014; Department for Education, 'Statutory Guidance on Adoption' July 2013 and Annex C 'Adoptions with a Foreign Element' (2013); See also 'Statutory Guidance on Placing a Child in Care with Relatives Abroad Prior to a Possible Adoption' – Guidance issued by the Secretary of State for Children, Schools and Families under the Local Authority Social Services Act 1970, s 7.
[7]   For definitions of 'parent', see the Human Fertilisation and Embryology Act 2008, ss 33 and 35–41. In the UK, surrogacy agreements are unenforceable and it is illegal to negotiate a commercial surrogacy arrangement: Surrogacy Arrangements Act 1985, ss 1–2. Commercial surrogacy arrangements are permitted (sometimes with restrictions) in other jurisdictions, for example, Ukraine, India and some states in the United States. Inter-country surrogacy cases can produce complex issues in private international law – see *X (children) (parental order: foreign surrogacy), Re* [2008] EWHC 3030 (Fam), [2009] Fam 71, [2009] 2 WLR 1274; *IJ (a child) (overseas surrogacy: parental order), Re* [2011] EWHC 921 (Fam); *X and Y (children-*

foreign surrogacy), Re [2011] EWHC 3147 (Fam); *WT (a Child: foreign surrogacy arrangements), Re* [2014] EWHC 1303 (Fam), *Z v C* [2011] EWHC 3181 (Fam).

11.101 The Adoption (Intercountry Aspects) Act 1999, which came into force on 1 June 2003, was passed in order to give effect to the Hague Convention on intercountry adoptions in domestic law. The Adoption and Children Act 2002 (the 2002 Act) which came into force on 30 December 2005 replaced the 1999 Act and the Adoption Act 1976. Together with the Adoptions with a Foreign Element Regulations 2005, the 2002 Act sets down many of the arrangements for inter-country adoptions.[1]

The Children and Adoption Act 2006 includes a statutory framework, (in effect from 2 August 2007), for the suspension of inter-country adoption from specified countries where there are concerns about their adoption practices.[2] Relevant to the entry into the UK and removal from the UK of children for the purposes of adoption, these legislative provisions collectively set out the requirements and conditions that must be met for adoptions with a foreign element (which might be Convention or non-Convention adoptions) ordered by courts in or outside the UK. In particular there are provisions dealing with:

- persons habitually resident in the UK who wish to bring into the UK children whose habitual residence is outside the UK, such children being either recently adopted under an external adoption or proposed for adoption by the British resident in the UK. These arrangements cover children habitually resident in Convention States and non-Convention States;[3]

- a person or couple who wish to remove a child for the purposes of adoption under the law of a country or territory outside the British Islands – these removal arrangements can be for a non-Convention adoption abroad or where the adoptive parents are from a Convention State and wish to obtain a Convention adoption in the UK.[4]

[1] The 2002 Act replaced the Adoption Act 1976 (1976 Act) and also incorporates most of the provisions of the 1999 Act. The relevant sections of the 1999 Act which remain in force include s 1 and part of s 2, which enabled the UK to implement the Hague Convention, s 7 which amended the BNA 1981, and Sch 1, which contains the text of the Convention. Inter-country adoptions in England and Wales have been regulated between 2003 and 30 December 2005 by the Intercountry Adoption (Hague Convention) Regulations 2003, SI 2003/118, and the Adoption (Bringing Children into the United Kingdom) Regulations 2003, SI 2003/1173, made under the transitional provisions in the 2002 Act which amended the 1976 Act. SI 2003/1173 applied to adoptions from non-Hague Convention countries. The 2003 regulations have now been repealed and replaced by the Adoptions with a Foreign Element Regulations 2005, SI 2005/392 (the AFE Regulations 2005). The AFE Regulations 2005 apply to bringing certain adopted or adoptive children into the UK and to removing children from the UK for the purposes of adoption.

[2] On the 27 September 2007, there was a temporary suspension of adoptions from Cambodia, on 6 December 2007 adoptions from Guatemala were suspended due to concerns at their adoption practices, and on 3 May 2010 adoptions from Nepal were suspended. The Adoptions with a Foreign Element (Special Restrictions on Adoptions from Abroad) Regulations 2008, SI 2008/1807 now apply to adoptions from Cambodia and Guatemala (see SSI 2008/304, 2008/305 for Scotland) and Nepal (see Special Restrictions on Adoptions from Abroad (Nepal) Order 2010, SI 2010/951) and Haiti Restrictions on Adoptions from Abroad (Haiti) Order 2010, SI 2010/2265. See also The Adoption (Recognition of Overseas Adoptions) (Scotland) Regulations 2013 (Scottish SI 2013/310) and The Adoptions with a Foreign Element (Special Restrictions on Adoptions from Abroad) (Scotland) Regulations 2008, Scottish SI 2008/303. The effect of these restrictions is that the Minister cannot take any steps to assist a person habitually resident in the UK to bring into the UK a child from a restricted

country who has been recently adopted or for the purpose of adoption unless he/she is satisfied following a request for special exception from the prospective adopter that such steps should be taken.

3   Adoption and Children Act 2002, ss 83–86; AFE Regulations 2005, Pt 2, Ch 1, regs 3–11. On habitual residence.

4   Adoption and Children Act 2002, ss 84–86; AFE Regulations 2005, Pt 2, Ch 2 for removal for a Non-Convention adoption abroad, and Pt 3, Ch 2 where the adoption is in the UK, but the adopters are from a Convention State.

The assessment and approval of adoptive parents

11.102 The key safeguards agreed under the Convention for adopted and prospective adoptive children are set down in the 2002 and 2006 Acts and the AFE Regulations 2005. These agreed international protections for adoptions now apply to our domestic adoptions and to other adoptions with a foreign element. The requirements and restrictions in the 2002 Act and AFE Regulations do not apply to Convention adoptions because Convention adoptions have their own protective arrangements to ensure adopters are suitable, the birth parents have given their full consent and the adoption is in the child's best interests.[1]

The 2002 Act and the AFE Regulations set down the arrangements which must be complied with by persons habitually resident in the UK who wish to bring into the UK either a child adopted by a British resident under an external adoption effected within 12 months of entry[2] or a child intended to be adopted in the UK by the British resident.[3] Section 83 of the 2002 Act makes it an offence for a person habitually resident in the UK to bring in such children, except in compliance with the regulatory arrangements.[4] Where the child is being brought into the UK or their entry arranged by a parent/carer who is habitually resident in the UK, the restriction is set to prevent the entry for any purpose (even a family visit) by the recently (within 12 months) adopted child and the entry of any adoptive children for the purpose of adoption. A key safeguard in the regulatory arrangements is the requirement for prospective adoptive or recent adoptive parents to be assessed and approved as suitable adoptive parents by an approved adoption agency – often inaptly termed a 'home study' report.[5] If this approval of the adopters is given and certified by the central authority, the child's entry immediately after the external adoption or for adoption is lawful.

The adoption agency which receives the application for assessment of suitability by prospective adopters is obliged to consider, report on and decide the persons' suitability as adoptive parents.[6] It is a criminal offence for anyone but a prescribed Adoption Agency to provide a report on the suitability of prospective adopters for an inter-country adoption.[7] If the prospective adopters are approved as suitable adopters by the adoption agency, the report and case papers are then sent to the Intercountry Adoption Casework Team at the Department for Education for the issue of a Certificate of Eligibility and Suitability from the Secretary of State for Education.[8] When the child arrives in the UK, the prospective adopter must inform his or her local authority within 14 days of the child's arrival and of his/her intentions concerning adoption.[9]

From 6 September 2012, para 309B of the Immigration Rules has purported to incorporate the section 83 and AFE Regulation strictures into the rules for all entry clearance applications under the child adoption Rules in paras 310–316F.[10] There are a number of problems with the drafting of Rule 309B.

Rule 309B states:

> '309B. Inter-country adoptions which are not a de facto adoption under paragraph 309A are subject to the Adoption and Children Act 2002 and the Adoptions with a Foreign Element Regulations 2005. As such all prospective adopters must be assessed as suitable to adopt by a competent authority in the UK, and obtain a Certificate of Eligibility from the Department for Education, before travelling abroad to identify a child for adoption. This Certificate of Eligibility must be provided with all entry clearance adoption applications under paragraphs 310–316F.'

First, the Rule – through the linking phrase 'as such' – clearly intends to incorporate and apply the section 83 and the AFE Regulations. However, the opening sentence is an incorrect statement of those laws. Not all intercountry adoptions which are not de facto adoptions are subject to the 2002 Act and the AFE Regulations. Section 83 explicitly applies only where a person habitually resident in the British Islands brings or causes another to bring in a child habitually resident outside the British Islands, and the child has been adopted abroad by the British resident in the last 12 months, or is being brought here for the purpose of adoption by the British resident. British ex-patriates who have lived abroad for some time and who may have recently adopted a child via an external adoption or who may be bringing an infant child into the UK for adoption are unlikely to be within the scope of section 83 of the 2002 Act because they are unlikely to be habitually resident here. If they are not habitually resident in the British Islands they are not within the scope of section 83, and, despite the broad opening sentence in paragraph 309B there is no requirement for the child applying for entry clearance to show their adopted or adoptive parent has been assessed, approved and certified by a competent authority in the UK.

In addition, Rule 309B purports to summarise the effects of section 83 and the AFE Regulations yet:

(i)   It fails to note that section 83(2) and (3) states that its terms do not apply to Convention adoptions. Children applying for entry clearance under paragraph 310 may have been adopted under a Convention adoption. Paragraph 309B applies the section 83 and AFE regulation restrictions to all entry clearance applications under paragraph 310. Its term thus wrongly expands the scope and application of the 2002 Act.

(ii)   In its terms paragraph 309B deals only with prospective adopters and neglects to make mention of section 83's additional restriction on the bringing in of an externally adopted child within 12 months of their adoption. Section 83 and the AFE regulations apply so that where children adopted abroad except via a Convention adoption are brought into the UK by an adoptive parent who is habitually resident in the British islands within 12 months of the adoption, their entry (even for a visit) is unlawful unless the British resident parent has first been assessed, approved and certified as a suitable adopter by an accredited adoption agency and the Department for Education. A proper incorporation of the adoption restrictions in the 2002 Act and AFE regulation would include this 12-month post-adoption bar.

(iii) Finally Rule 309B wrongly states that prospective adopters must be approved and certified before travelling abroad to identify a child for adoption. This is not a requirement in section 83 or the AFE Regulations. And paragraph 309B assumes that applications for entry clearance under paragraph 310 of the Rules are applications by prospective adopters. However, paragraph 310 concerns the entry for settlement of adopted children whose external adoptions or Convention adoptions have been recognised in the UK. The children applying under paragraph 310 whose adoptions are recognised in the UK are not adoptive children because under English law their overseas adoption has the legal effect that they are treated as if they were born to their adoptive parents.

Given these drafting errors many adopted children are being wrongly refused under paragraph 309B when the 2002 Act and AFE Regulations have no application to their entry clearance applications. It cannot have been Parliament's intention to enlarge the reach of the 2002 Act and the AFE Regulations via the Immigration Rules. Rule 309B should be read to be compatible and congruent with the 2002 Act.[11]

Section 83, ACA creates a criminal offence. Its terms therefore are required to be strictly interpreted. If Rule 309B is applied incompatibly with section 83, this would offend the principles of legal certainty and against 'doubtful penalisation'. The principle that statutes *in pari materia* should be construed as one, requires the Rule to be construed compatibly with the ACA.[12]

---

[1] The Adoption and Children Act 2002, s 83(2).

[2] The Adoption and Children Act 2002, s 83(1)(b) placed a restriction on entry where the child had been adopted within the six months immediately prior to entry. This provision has been amended by the Children and Adoption Act 2006, s 1 and from 1 October 2007 the restriction on entry now covers children adopted in the previous 12 months. An external adoption is an adoption other than a Convention adoption of a child effected under the law of any country or territory outside the British islands whether or not it is a full adoption – that is one in which the child is treated in law as the child of no person other than the adopters: Adoption and Children Act 2002, ss 83(3), 88(3). The Scottish provisions are in the Adoption and Children (Scotland) Act 2007, s 58.

[3] The Adoption and Children Act 2002, s 83; The Adoption and Children (Scotland) Act 2007, ss 58 and 61.

[4] The Adoption and Children Act 2002, s 83(7). Adoption and Children (Scotland) Act 2007, ss 58, 61(1). Section 83 and the Scottish provision s 58(3) does not apply if the child is intended to be adopted or has recently been adopted under a Convention adoption order: s 83(2).

[5] AFE Regulations 2005, regs 3–5. An adoption agency is defined in the Adoption and Children Act 2002, s 2(1) as either a local authority or registered adoption society. On registered adoption society, see the Care Standards Act 2000, Pt 2; SI 2004/3203, art 2(1)(a). See also the Suitability of Adopters Regulations 2005, SI 2005/1712. See for Wales, the Local Authority Adoption Services (Wales) Regulations 2007, SI 2007/1357, the Adoption Agencies (Wales) Regulations 2005, SI 2005/1313, and for Scotland, the Adoption and Children (Scotland) Act 2007, which received Royal Assent on the 15 January 2007 and came into force on 20 April 2009 and Adoptions with a Foreign Element (Scotland) Regulation, Scottish SI 2009/182. For a full list of all Voluntary Adoption Agencies, see the government adoption site and for up-to-date information on inter-country adoptions, see: www.gov.uk/childrens-services/adoption.

[6] AFE Regulations 2005, reg 3; the Adoption Agencies Regulations 2005, SI 2005/389, regs 21–30. The AFE Regulations 2005 need to be read with the Adoption Agencies

Regulations 2005, SI 2005/389. The Adoption Agencies Regulations set out the procedure to be followed in respect of the assessment of prospective adopters including obtaining information and various reports from police and medical practitioners concerning the adopters (regs 23, 25). See also Adoptions with a Foreign Element (Scotland) Regulation, Scottish SI 2009/182. Under s 91A of the Adoption and Children Act 2002 (as amended), from 2 April 2007 the Secretary of State can charge a fee to adopters seeking services for adoption for foreign element adoptions or those to which s 83 of the 2002 Act applies. The Adoption and Children (Scotland) Act 2007, s 66 also allows for the charging of fees to prospective adopters.

7   Adoption and Children Act 2002, s 94. See also the Restriction on the Preparation of Adoption Reports Regulations 2005, SI 2005/1711. See *Re M (Adoption: international adoption trade)* [2003] EWHC 219 (Fam), [2003] 3 FCR 193 in which a private home study report did not reflect the true reality of the family into which the child was to be adopted or the fact that a child already in the family had been on the Child Protection Register and the mother had not been found suitable to be an adopter by either her local authority or Barnardos. See also Adoption and Children (Scotland) Act 2007, ss 72 and 75.

8   See the Adoption Agencies Regulations 2005, regs 21–30; AFE Regulations 2005, regs 18–19. In Wales, certification of suitability is undertaken by the Children's Health and Social Care Directorate National Assembly of Wales – Adoptions with a Foreign Element, in Scotland by the Children and Young People's Group Scottish Executive – Intercountry Adoption, and in Northern Ireland by the Childcare Policy Directorate, Department of Health, Social Services and Public Safety. The Certificate of Eligibility and Suitability confirms that the prospective adopter has been assessed, approved as suitable to be an adoptive parent, is eligible to adopt, and that the child will be authorised to enter and reside permanently in the UK if entry clearance and leave to enter or remain is granted and not revoked or curtailed.

9   AFE Regulations 2005, reg 24. Thereafter, until the adoption the local authority has obligations to visit, review and report on the child's placement: reg 5. See also, Scottish SI 2009/182, reg 5.

10   See Statement of Changes in the Immigration Rules, HC 565.

11   See: *R (on the application of Zenovics) v Secretary of State for the Home Department* [2002] EWCA Civ 273.

12   See *A-G v HRH Prince Ernest Augustus of Hanover* [1957] AC 436 at 461; *Chief Adjudication Officer v Foster* [1993] AC 754 at 769.

11.103 There are several different types of adoption. The Adoption and Children Act 2002, s 66 defines adoptions to include an English, Scottish, Northern Ireland, Isle of Man or Channel Islands adoption order[1] (s 66(1)(a)–(b), an adoption effected under the law of a Convention country outside the British Islands and certified under Article 23(1) of the Convention as a Convention adoption (s 66(1)(c), an 'overseas adoption' (s 66(1)(d) and an adoption recognised by the law of England and Wales and effected under the law of any other country (s 66(1)(e)). These adoptions — domestic and inter-country or foreign element adoptions – have effect in law so that the adopted person is to be treated in law as if born legitimately as the child of the adopters or adopter and as not the child of any person other than the adopter or adopters.[2]

The recognised intercountry and foreign element adoptions which are relevant in immigration proceedings are:

- Convention adoptions made in a court in the UK or by the relevant court or authority in another Convention State. A Convention adoption order made by a UK court can be to enable a habitually resident child to be adopted here and taken from the UK to reside with the adoptive parents in the Hague Convention Member State in which they are habitually resident or made in respect of a child formerly habitually resident in a Convention State who is brought to the UK by a UK prospective adopter for the purposes of obtaining a Convention adoption order in a UK court. A Convention adoption is one which is certified by the competent authority in the State where the adoption order was made confirming that the adoption was made in accordance with Convention procedures.[3]

- Overseas adoptions[4] effected under statute law in a country designated by the Secretary of State for the Home Department and listed in the Adoptions (Designation of Overseas Adoptions) Order 1973, SI 1973/19 if the adoption order was made before 3 January 2014 or for adoption orders made after that date – in a country listed in The Adoption (Recognition of Overseas Adoptions) Order 2013, SI 2013/1801 or The Adoption (Recognition of Overseas Adoptions) (Scotland) Regulations 2013, SSI 2013/310; whose adoption orders are recognised. The countries listed in SI 2013/1801 are all Hague Convention States. It follows that if the adoption was made in Hague State under its domestic adoption law, these orders will now be 'overseas adoptions'. Such Hague country adoptions are only Convention adoptions if certified under Article 23 as Convention compliant.

- Other foreign element adoptions: legal (non-Convention) adoptions in the child's home State but an external adoption which is not automatically recognised in UK law. An external adoption which is a legal adoption in the child's home state may secure recognition at common law, by application in the High Court.[5]

- These adoptions have differing legal effect in family law and in immigration law. In family law, the issue concerns whether the adoption creates the legal relationship of parent and child and the adoptive parent has parental responsibility for the child.[6] In immigration terms, the issue concerns whether the adoption confers British citizenship on the child, or provides a basis for entry under the rules.

Convention and designated/recognised 'overseas' adoptions[7] and external adoptions recognised by the High Court are recognised and given full legal effect in family and immigration law in the UK.[8] By contrast, de facto adoptions[9] are not recognised in family law as conferring parental responsibility on the 'parent', but such 'adoption' can be effective in immigration law[10] as a basis for entry and stay.[11] Adopters and prospective adopters may need advice concerning the legality and effect of a foreign adoption that they have obtained or on the procedures they must follow in order to adopt a foreign child in the UK or abroad. All such adoptions require consideration of the adopter's capacity to adopt here and/or abroad. Depending on the law in the adopting and reception countries, the adopters may need to establish domicile, habitual or a specified term of residence or to have particular religious beliefs to obtain a legal adoption.[12] Some countries do not have formal adoption laws and any transfer of parental responsibility may be via a guardianship order or informal or 'de facto adoption'.[13] A legal guardianship made in these circumstances may closely approximate to the UK's 'special guardianship orders' and in circumstances where the child's home country does not have adoption arrangements or adoption is contrary to the 'parent's' religious beliefs, the 'parents' may seek entry for the purpose of obtaining a special guardianship order in the UK giving them parental responsibility for the child.[14] Such application requires to be determined outside the rules. The intersection of family and immigration law in international child placements whether by adoption, guardianship or via surrogacy creates legal complexities.

Thus those de facto adopted children who qualify for entry under the Immigration Rules[15] may require a family order after entry to ensure their 'parent' is granted the formal legal parental responsibility necessary to obtain such things as medical consents, arranging travel documentation and dealing with public authorities. In this complex area of law and practice, advisers need to be aware of both family and immigration law requirements.

[1]   Note, the residence and domicile requirements before an adoption order can be made under the Adoption and Children Act 2002, s 42 requires that the child have his/her home with the adopters for varying terms depending on whether the child is formally placed with the adopters or the child of a partner. If the prospective adopter is the parent, or the child was placed for adoption with the applicant by an adoption agency or in pursuance of an order of the High Court, he/she will have to have the child living with him or her for ten weeks before an application for adoption can be made. If the applicant is a step-parent of the child or a partner to the child's parent he/she has to wait for six months before lodging the adoption application. If the applicants are local authority foster parents the child will have to have lived with them for one year preceding the application. All other adopters have to have had the child living with them or with both of them if it is a couple for a period of three years (continuous or not) in the five years preceding the application'. The Court can give leave for certain adoption applications to be issued before expiry of the one-year and three-year residence periods – s 42(6). Section 49 also requires either that the adopter (or one of the couple) be domiciled in the UK or that the adopters (both of the couple) have been habitually resident in the UK for not less than one year ending with the application. See concerning residence for Convention adoptions – AFE Regulations 2005, reg 56.

[2]   Adoption and Children Act 2002, s 67. See also Adoption and Children (Scotland) Act 2007, ss 39–40.

[3]   Adoption (Intercountry Aspects) Act 1999, Sch 1, The Convention, Article 23.

[4]   For the definition of 'overseas adoption' see Adoption and Children Act 2002, s 87; Adoption and Children (Scotland) Act 2007, s 67.

[5]   Concerning High Court orders and declarations recognising an external adoption, see *Re Valentine's Settlement* [1965] Ch 831 at 843A-C per Lord Denning; *ND (Children) (Recognition of foreign adoption orders), Re* [2008] EWHC 403 (Fam), [2008] All ER (D) 398 (Jun), *Re N (Recognition of Foreign Adoption Order)* [2010] 1 FLR 1102 (Bennett J), *R (a child) (adoption abroad), Re* [2012] EWHC 2956 (Fam) (Hedley J), *Z v Z* [2013] EWHC 747 (Fam) *A Council v M* [2013] EWHC 1501 (Fam) (Jackson J), *G (children) (Adoption proceedings), Re* [2014] EWHC 2605 (Fam).

[6]   See the Adoption and Children Act 2002, s 67 – status conferred by adoption.

[7]   Adoption and Children Act 2002, ss 87, 66(1)(d).

[8]   Adoption and Children Act 2002, s 66(1)(e).

[9]   See below on de facto adoptions.

[10]   HC 395, para 6 provides that an adoption generally includes a de facto adoption in accordance with the requirements of para 309A of these rules, and 'adopted' and 'adoptive parent' should be construed accordingly. A parent' includes an adoptive parent, where a child was adopted in accordance with a decision taken by the competent administrative authority or court in a country whose adoption orders are recognised by the UK or where a child is the subject of a de facto adoption in accordance with the requirements of para 309A of these rules (except that an adopted child or a child who is the subject of a de facto adoption may not make an application for leave to enter or remain in order to accompany, join or remain with an adoptive parent under paras 297–303. See SK ('Adoption' not recognised in UK) *India* [2006] UKAIT 00068 (1 September 2006). See criticism of this decision at **11.113**.

[11]   HC 395, paras 6, 297, 309A–316F.

[12]   See **11.11**, fn 2 and **11.14**, fn 1 above on habitual residence, and above on domicile. To take the example of the Hindu Adoptions and Maintenance Act 1956, ss 6–8 this requires adult prospective adopters to be of sound mind and to be Hindu. Married women cannot apply to adopt under the 1956 Act but the adoption order includes both married parties on the adoption order as the child's parents.

[13]   Islamic jurisprudence recognises the concepts of '*kafala*' – the placement of a child with a caring family without changing his lineage. The Protection Of Children (Hague Convention) Act, 2000 incorporates the Hague Convention of 19 October, 1996, on jurisdiction, applicable law, recognition, enforcement and co-operation in respect of parental responsibility

and measures for the protection of children (the Abduction Convention). The Hague Convention, Art 3 recognises *kafala* as an analogous relationship of authority determining the rights, powers and responsibilities of parents.

14 The Adoption and Children Act 2002 created the new relationship of special guardianship under which the special guardian has legal parental responsibility for the child which is expected to last until the child is 18. Unlike adoption orders, a special guardianship order does not remove parental responsibility from the child's birth parents, although their ability to exercise it is limited and the special guardian has enhanced parental responsibility rights *vis a vis* the parents. See the Children Act 1989, ss 14A–F.

15 HC 395, paras 309A, 311, 314.

CONVENTION ADOPTIONS

11.104 The Hague Convention on Protection of Children and Cooperation in respect of Intercountry Adoptions applies where a child habitually resident in one Contracting State has been, is being, or is to be moved, to another Contracting State by adopters or adoptive parents habitually resident in the receiving Contracting State. The child may be moved after his/her adoption in the child's State or for the purpose of adoption in the adopter's State.[1] A British citizen or resident who has the legal capacity (that is, as noted above, the required connecting factor to the child's country which may be domicile or residence) may obtain a Convention adoption abroad. In the same way adopters applying for a Convention adoption in the UK must meet residence and domicile requirements for standing to seek and adoption in the UK.[2] In addition, wherever the adoption order is made the adoption must be made in accordance with Convention requirements. The requirements comprise the assessment, approval, and certification of the proposed adopters, and the approval of the child for an intercountry adoption, as well as confirmation by the competent authority in the receiving State that the child is or will be authorised to enter and reside there permanently.[3] These safeguards are necessary for all Convention adoptions.[4]

A Convention adoption is not simply an adoption made by a court in a country which has ratified the Hague Convention on Intercountry Adoptions. It is an adoption made in a Convention State in accordance with Convention procedures. These adoptions require reciprocal approvals and consents between central authorities (or accredited agencies) and are made by reference to State reciprocities, international comity and the avoidance of conflicts of law in the interests of protecting children adopted across State borders.[5]

Where a child has been adopted overseas by means of an Article 23 certified Convention adoption the certified Convention adoption is recognised in the UK and all Convention States.[6] If in an overseas Convention adoption the adopter or, in the case of a joint adoption, one of the adopters is a British citizen and the adopter, or if joint, both adopters are habitually resident in the UK on the date the adoption order is made or effected under the law of a country outside the UK, the child acquires British citizenship by virtue of the Convention adoption.[7] The adoptive parents can apply for the child to be issued with a British passport at the appropriate post abroad. If neither parent is British but they are settled in the UK or if the parent(s) are British but not habitually resident here, the adopted child will have to qualify for leave to enter as their child under the Immigration Rules.[8]

1 Convention, Article 2.

2   Note, the residence and domicile requirements before an adoption order can be made under the Adoption and Children Act 2002, s 42 requires that the child have his/her home with the adopters for varying terms depending on whether the child is formally placed with the adopters or the child of a partner. If the prospective adopter is the parent, or the child was placed for adoption with the applicant by an adoption agency or in pursuance of an order of the High Court, he/she will have to have the child living with him or her for ten weeks before an application for adoption can be made. If the applicant is a step-parent of the child or a partner to the child's parent he/she has to wait for six months before lodging the adoption application. If the applicants are local authority foster parents the child will have to have lived with them for one year preceding the application. All other adopters have to have had the child living with them or with both of them if it is a couple for a period of three years (continuous or not) in the five years preceding the application'. The Court can give leave for certain adoption applications to be issued before expiry of the one-year and three-year residence periods – s 42(6). Section 49 also requires either that the adopter (or one of the couple) be domiciled in the UK or that that the adopters (both of the couple) have been habitually resident in the UK for not less than one year ending with the application. See concerning residence for Convention adoptions – AFE Regulations 2005, reg 56.

3   Convention, Arts 14–21, 23.

4   Convention, Art 23.

5   Adoption and Children Act 2002, ss 67, 88–91. These provisions embody Articles 23 to 27 of the Convention dealing with the recognition and effects of Convention inter-country adoptions. The provisions deal with the effect of Convention adoptions which are not 'full adoptions' permanently extinguishing the parental rights of the birth parents but 'simple' adoptions which leave the birth parent's parental rights intact. The AFE Regulations 2005, SI 392/2005 implement the required Convention adoption arrangements. The central authority in the UK for Convention adoptions is the Department for Education.

6   The Adoption and Children Act 2002, s 66 defines an adoption as including a Convention adoption. The effect is to enable Convention adoptions to be recognised automatically obviating the need for a domestic adoption. HC 395, para 6 – a 'parent' includes an adoptive parent, where a child was adopted in accordance with a decision taken by the competent administrative authority or court in a country whose adoption orders are recognised by the UK. The Convention, Arts 23–24 provide that certified Convention adoptions are recognised in all Convention States and recognition may only be refused in a contracting State if the adoption is manifestly contrary to its public policy, taking into account the best interests of the child.

7   BNA 1981, s 1(5), (5A), inserted by the Adoption (Intercountry Aspects) Act 1999, s 7, in force from 1 June 2003. Where the child is adopted abroad in a certified Hague Convention adoption and the child does not acquire British citizenship by the adoption, the child can expect to be registered as a British citizen under the Secretary of State's broad discretionary citizenship registration powers for children. BNA 1981, s 3(1). This expectation derives from policy instructions in the Nationality Instructions, chapter 9 which state that where children have been adopted abroad by British citizen parents and the adoption is recognised in UK law, the child's registration as a British citizen under s 3(1) would 'normally' be approved.

8   HC 395, para 6 (definition of 'parent' at (d)), 297, 310.

11.105 As stated above, when a child is adopted overseas via a Convention adoption, and one of the adoptive parents[1] is a British citizen and the sole adopter or both of them is habitually resident in the UK at the time of the making or effecting of the Convention adoption order, the child will have acquired British citizenship, and will not need leave to enter the UK.[2] If the Convention adopted child does not become a British citizen she/he will need leave to enter. Under the Immigration Rules adopted children, even those whose adoption orders are recognised by the UK,[3] will need to qualify for entry under the provisions of HC 395, para 310, which contain more onerous requirements than the carefully thought out safeguards of the Convention regime. One can envisage some children adopted via overseas Convention adoptions failing under these additional strictures, particularly if the adoption followed from a family placement of the child.[4] Paragraph 310 requires that in addition to the requirement for a recognised adoption that the child must have been adopted due to the inability of the original parents, or current carers to care for him/her, and that the child has lost or broken ties with the family of origin.[5]

If the child has been placed with but has not been adopted by his or her British adoptive parents, the child may qualify for limited leave to enter the UK with a view to settlement as a child for adoption. In such cases it will be necessary to show that the child is seeking leave to accompany or join his or her prospective adopter or adopters who are present and settled in the UK and who wish to adopt him or her in the UK under the Hague Convention. In such a case the child will have been entrusted to the prospective parents by the competent administrative authorities of the country from which he or she is coming for adoption under the Hague Convention. Such children are only entrusted under Article 17 when the central authorities in both countries have assessed and approved the adoptive parents, have reported on the child's circumstances, and approved the adoption, and the child's relocation, and confirmed the birth parent's consent to the adoption and the child will be authorised to enter and reside permanently in the receiving State.[6] Rule 316D–F, which apply to children seeking limited leave to enter the UK with a view to settlement as a child for adoption under the Hague Convention requires that the child has been entrusted to adoptive parents habitually resident in the British Islands, is the subject of an Article 17c agreement by both States that the adoption may proceed and that the child can and will be maintained and accommodated adequately without recourse to public funds in accommodation which the prospective parent or parents own or occupy exclusively.[7] Children coming to be adopted by means of a Convention Adoption may be admitted for a period not exceeding 24 months. As this Rule applies to children sponsored by adopters who are habitually resident in the UK, on adoption the child will become a British citizen.[8] The prospective adopters must inform their local authority of the child's arrival within 14 days.[9] Most adopters have to wait for six months before lodging an adoption and twelve months before an adoption order can be made.[10] If an adoption order is subsequently made in the UK and the adopter, or if it is a joint adoption by a married couple, one of them, is a British citizen the child becomes a British citizen automatically.[11] If the adoption order is subsequently annulled, the child's citizenship will not be revoked.[12] However, this is not the case if the Home Office has successfully appealed against the making of the order in the first place.[13]

[1] HC 395, para 6 defines the parents of adopted children whose adoption is recognised in the UK as 'a parent' for the purpose of the Immigration Rules. However, paragraph 6 expressly forbids adopted children from applying for leave in order to accompany or join their parent or parents in the UK under HC 395, paras 297–303 (entry of children joining or accompanying parents). Instead they must apply for leave to enter the UK under para 310 (which by comparison with para 297 has more onerous requirements for the entry of adopted children).

[2] British Nationality Act 1981, s 1(5), (5A), inserted by the Adoption (Intercountry Aspects) Act 1999, s 7.

[3] Convention and overseas designated adoption orders are recognised by the UK. The Adoption and Children Act 2002, s 66 defines an adoption as including a Convention adoption. The effect is to enable Convention adoptions to be recognised automatically by operation of law and the adopted person's status as parent to be effected in law: see ss 67–76.

[4] See **11.113** on adoptions by relatives.

[5] See *VB v Entry Clearance Officer – Ghana* [2002] UKIAT 01323, [2003] INLR 54.

[6] Convention Arts, 15–17.

[7] HC 395, para 316A(i)–(vii), and for Convention adoptions in the UK, para 316D(i)–(vi). Children placed but to be adopted under a Convention adoption do not have to show that they were adopted due to the inability of the original parents but some children adopted abroad under a Convention adoption who are not British citizens as a result of that adoption will have to meet this criteria when seeking entry under para 310.

[8] HC 395, para 316E. There is no provision for the 24 months to be extended. Note, Rule 316D does not require that the child is sponsored by a British citizen adopter. The child only acquires British citizenship by this adoption made in the UK if one of the adopters is a British citizen. British Nationality Act 1981, ss 5, 5A.

[9] AFE Regulations 2005, SI 2005/392, regs 21, 24.

[10] Adoption and Children Act 2002, s 42, AFE Regulations 2005, SI 2005/392, regs 9, 31.

[11] BNA 1981, s 1(5).

[12] BNA 1981, s 1(6).

[13] *Re K (A Minor)* [1994] 3 All ER 553.

DESIGNATED AND RECOGNISED OVERSEAS ADOPTIONS

11.106 Where a child is adopted before 3 January 2014 in a country[1] whose adoption orders made under their statute law have been designated for the purposes of the Adoption (Designation of Overseas Adoptions) Order 1973, SI 1973/19, or after 3 January 2014 have been adopted under statute law in a State listed in the Schedule to The Adoption (Recognition of Overseas Adoptions) Order 2013, SI 2013/1801, the UK recognises that there has been a legal Overseas Adoption.[2] The Adoption and Children Act 2002, s 87 terms these adoptions 'overseas adoptions'. It is not necessary to adopt a child adopted under an overseas adoption to be re-adopted in the UK because pursuant to the Adoption and Children Act 2002, s 67 and the Adoption and Children Act (Scotland) 2007, s 40, such adopted children are treated in law as if they were legitimately born to their adoptive parents and were the children of no other person than their adoptive parents.

However, where the adopters or any one of them are habitually resident[3] in the UK and the overseas adoption has taken place during the previous 12 months, before bringing the adopted child into the UK (even for a visit) the adopters must comply with the requirements and conditions set out in the Adoptions with a Foreign Element Regulations 2005[4] before bringing the child to the UK.[5] These are family law requirements and now find some confirmation in Rule 309B. If the recently adopted child is brought into the UK and the habitually resident adopters have not sought and obtained approval of themselves as adopters, there may be a breach of s 83 of the Adoption and Children Act 2002 and such breach may result in conviction and may render an adopter liable up to six months' imprisonment or a fine on summary conviction or up to 12 months' imprisonment or a fine on conviction on indictment.[6]

An overseas adoption does not change the child's nationality in the way that a Convention Adoption may do, and the child will require leave to enter the UK as the child of his or her adopted parent or parents for settlement[7] and must meet the criteria listed in para 310 of the Immigration Rules, HC 395.

In a number of entry clearance applications lodged under para 310 it became a practice for entry clearance officers to challenge the validity of the overseas adoption as one of the reasons for refusal. Officers would examine the foreign adoption statute and point to omissions or errors in documentation and assert that the adoption was void. In *Buama (inter-country adoption – competent court) Ghana* [2012] UKUT 146 (IAC) the Upper Tribunal deprecated this practice, stating: 'The Immigration Rules do not appear to contemplate a refusal to accept the validity of the order of a competent court. Further, any challenge to the validity of the order had to be by expert evidence in my view. Simply setting out the provisions of a statute is not sufficient.'

1   In January 2008, these were the Commonwealth countries of Anguilla, Australia, Bahamas, Barbados, Belize, Bermuda, Botswana, British Virgin Islands, Canada, Cayman Islands, Cyprus, Dominica, Fiji, Ghana, Gibraltar, Guyana, Hong Kong, Jamaica, Kenya, Lesotho, Malaysia, Malawi, Malta, Mauritius, Montserrat, Namibia, New Zealand, Nigeria, Pitcairn Island, St Christopher and Nevis, St Vincent, Seychelles, Singapore, South Africa, Sri Lanka, Swaziland, Tanzania, Tonga, Trinidad and Tobago, Uganda, Zambia and the non-Commonwealth countries of Austria, Belgium, China (but only where the child was adopted on or after 5 April 1993), Denmark (including Greenland and the Faroes), Finland and France (including Reunion, Martinique, Guadeloupe and French Guyana), Germany, Greece, Iceland, Ireland, Israel, Italy, Luxembourg, The Netherlands (including the Antilles), Norway, Portugal (including the Azores and Madeira), Spain (including the Balearic and Canary Islands), Surinam, Sweden, Switzerland, Turkey, the United States of America, (but none of the states which make up the former Yugoslavia) and Zimbabwe.
2   Adoption and Children Act 2002, s 66(1); Adoption (Designation of Overseas Adoptions) Order 1973. See also The Adoption (Recognition of Overseas Adoptions) (Scotland) Regulations 2013. The countries listed in the new Schedule are all Hague Convention States.
3   See **11.11**, fn 2 and **11.14**, fn 1.
4   AFE Regulations 2005, SI 2005/392.
5   See the Adoption and Children Act 2002, s 83(1)(b), (3).
6   Adoption and Children Act 2002, s 83(7).
7   HC 395, para 310. (See above at **11.102** for discussion of Rule 309B and its application to children adopted via an 'overseas adoption'.)

ENTRY AND STAY FOR ADOPTED CHILDREN

11.107 The preceding text makes clear that different types of adoption have a different status in immigration law. Certain Convention adoptions will have the effect of conferring British citizenship on the adopted child. Such children therefore do not require entry clearance.[1] All other children adopted abroad by British citizens or residents will need entry clearance as adopted children – if coming for settlement. Some adopted children or children intended for adoption are brought in as visitors; the guidance for immigration officers alerts them to identify such children at port, on their arrival.[2] Under the Immigration Rules, the adoptive parent is recognised as a 'parent' where a child was adopted in accordance with a decision taken by the competent administrative authority or court in a country whose adoption orders are recognised by the UK or where a child is the subject of a de facto adoption in accordance with the requirements of para 309A of these Rules (para 6). The Rules do not permit such children to make an application for leave to enter or remain in order to accompany, join or remain with an adoptive parent under paras 297–303.[3] The entry rules for settlement for adopted children impose additional requirements, namely:[4]

- that the child was adopted at a time when (a) both adoptive parents were resident together abroad; or (b) either or both adoptive parents were settled in the UK; and
- has the same rights and obligations as any other child of the adoptive parent's or parents' family; and

- was adopted due to the inability of the original parent(s) or current carer(s) to care for him and there has been a genuine transfer of parental responsibility to the adoptive parents; and
- has lost or broken his ties with his family of origin; and
- was adopted, but the adoption is not one of convenience[5] arranged to facilitate his admission to or remaining in the UK.

[1]   See **11.104** above.

[2]   The Home Office *Guidance* on adoption IDI January/08 Chapter 8, s 6 – Adopted Children – Annex Q states: 'IOs should be extremely vigilant where a parent(s) claims to be bringing a child to the UK solely for a visit, when the actual intention may be to adopt the child once admitted to the UK. If there is any doubt in such circumstances, the DCSF/Devolved Authority or local authority social services should be contacted as appropriate'. This *Guidance* has been withdrawn from the Home Office site and archived and the *Modernised Adoption Guidance* is being rewritten. However, as the author's experience shows the following continues to be Home Office practice, it is reproduced. Concerning parents arriving at port with their 'adopted' child the *Guidance* states:

> 'Difficulties could arise where "parent" present themselves to IOs on entry and state that they wish to adopt "their" child through the UK courts, if an adoption order from a Hague or designated country has not already been obtained. IOs would then be in the difficult situation of having to refuse entry to the child, (the child would not hold prior entry clearance), which may not be in the interests of safeguarding the child and would be presentationally difficult. However, if IOs were to grant entry to the child, the parents would then potentially be liable to prosecution, under the terms of the new regulations for inter-country adoption. The parents are unlikely to have obtained entry clearance or followed the new DCSF procedures, in such cases. The advice to IOs, therefore, is to notify immediately the prospective adoptive parent(s) that they may be in breach of the Adoptions with a Foreign Element Regulations 2005. The prospective adoptive parent(s) should be told to contact their local authority of their intention to adopt the child (within 14 days of arrival with the child in the UK). This should lead to an early decision concerning the welfare of the child and any potential prosecution of the parents. If the prospective adoptive parent(s) still wish to enter the UK with the child once they have learnt of their legal position, the child should be granted temporary admission. If they do enter, the IO should also notify the appropriate local authority and the police, then inform the DCSF that this action has been taken. . . . This will be to the benefit of the child's welfare, always the prime consideration, and the avoidance of media attention, which is unlikely to be in the child's best interest.'

[3]   HC 395, para 6: 'parent'.

[4]   HC 395, paras 310–316. See also IDI, Chapter 8, s 7, Annex Q 'Adoption', Jan 2008 (archived).

[5]   In *VB v Entry Clearance Officer Ghana* [2002] UKIAT 01323 Collins J pointed out that most overseas adoptions took place in order to facilitate entry into the UK and that by itself would not make it an adoption of convenience. The Tribunal approved the approach of an Adjudicator who had directed himself as follows:

> 'An adoption of convenience, rather like a marriage of convenience, is one that exists purely for a particular purpose, there is no real substance to it, save in relation to that purpose'.

'Genuine transfer of parental responsibility . . . '

11.108 The requirement that the transfer of parental responsibility must be due to the original parents' or current carer's inability to care for the child is not a test that is applied in the domestic courts in adoption proceedings.[1] In *SK ('Adoption' not recognised in UK) India* the Tribunal held in respect of a child 'gifted' to relatives who were unable to conceive a child, that the adoption 'arose from choice, not strictly speaking from their "inability" to care for the appellant'.[2] The Court of Appeal held in *Sharma v Entry Clearance Officer*

(New Delhi) that the original parents' rejection of the child because of her gender did not satisfy the requirement that the original parent was 'unable' to care for the child.[3]

As to the further Rules requirement that the child must have 'lost or broken his ties with his family of origin': Collins J held in *Boadi v Entry Clearance Officer, Ghana* that the rule referred to ties of responsibility, not ties of affection.[4] Thus, a child adopted in an intra-family adoption is not required to show that she has severed the ties and relationship with her birth family to qualify for adoption. As good adoption practice can include continuing contact with the birth parents, the *Boadi* approach is to be commended.

[1]   See Adoption and Children Act 2002, s 1.
[2]   *SK ('Adoption' not recognised in UK) India* [2006] UKAIT 00068.
[3]   *Sharma v Entry Clearance Officer, New Delhi* [2005] EWCA Civ 89, (2005) Times, 23 February. The 'inability to care' requirement may, however, be waived where all the other requirements of the rule are met and the child has lived as a member of the adoptive family unit for more than 12 months: DSP 14.11 (Feb 05).
[4]   *Boadi v Entry Clearance Officer, Ghana* (also reported as *VB v Entry Clearance Officer-Ghana)* [2002] UKIAT 01323, [2003] INLR 54. The later case of *MF (Immigration, adoption, genuine transfer of parental responsibility) Philippines* [2004] UKIAT00094 cannot, we submit, stand with the earlier case.

Legal but unrecognised adoptions

11.109 As stated, if a child has been legally adopted abroad in accordance with the law of a country which is not on the designated or recognised lists of countries whose adoption orders are recognised and the adoption is not a Convention adoption – the adoption is not recognised for the purpose of our domestic law.[1] In certain such cases the child's parents have made applications for the High Court for an order recognising the external adoption, and their child has sought a declaration from the Court that he/she is the child of her adoptive parents.[2] This order has the effect that the adopters are taken to be the child's parents.

If none of these arrangements for recognition have been taken, then in UK law the child is not the adopted child of her adoptive parents. In such a case the parents may wish to bring the child to the UK for the purpose of adoption. If such a child is to be brought here to be adopted, and, absent any other basis for entry, if entry is for the purpose of adoption, the child will require entry clearance for that purpose.[3] The prospective adopter – if habitually resident in the British Islands – must comply with the requirements of s 83 of the Adoption and Children Act 2002 and the AFE Regulations 2005.[4] In these circumstances to avoid the commission of an offence under s 83, the habitually resident adoptive parent will have to arrange to be assessed and approved by an accredited adoption agency and panel, and obtain certification from the Secretary of State for Education of this approval and that if an adoption order is made the child will be authorised to enter and reside permanently in the UK.[5] Depending on the family circumstances this assessment and approval may be very difficult to arrange. Most problems occur where the parents 'adopt' the child in advance of or in ignorance of the requirement for their assessment or approval as prospective adopters. The child is placed with the family abroad but the child's entry may breach section 83, and/or the child fails to qualify for entry clearance under the Immigration Rules. The Tribunal has stated that the law and Immigration Rules distinguishing between adoptions in those countries whose adoptions are recognised in the UK and other adoptions have a sound objective basis and are not unlawfully discriminatory under the Race Relations Act 1976 (as amended) or Article 14 of the ECHR.[6] The child will need leave to enter the UK for adoption.[7]

[1]   Adoption and Children Act 2002, ss 66(1) and 67; Adoption and Children (Scotland) Act 2007, ss 39 and 40.
[2]   *G (children) (Adoption proceedings), Re* [2014] EWHC 2605 (Fam).
[3]   The child may have another basis for entry under HC 395, para 297 if a relative of the proposed adopters. If the adoptive parents are in the UK in a temporary capacity, they may wish their child to enter as their dependent. The entry is not for the purposes of adoption. See also *MN (India) v Entry Clearance Officer* [2008] EWCA Civ 38, [2009] 1 FCR 300, [2008] 2 FLR 87.
[4]   The Adoption and Children Act 2002, s 83(1)(b); Adoptions with a Foreign Element Regulations 2005, SI 392/2005, regs 3–4.
[5]   *MN (Non-recognised adoptions: unlawful discrimination?) India* [2007] UKAIT 00015 (12 February 2007). See *Singh v Entry Clearance Officer New Delhi* [2004] EWCA Civ 1075 (30 July 2004) at para 12; *Singh (Pavittar) v United Kingdom* (Application 60148/00) [2006] ECHR 606 (8 June 2006).
[6]   *MN (Non-recognised adoptions: unlawful discrimination?) India* [2007] UKAIT 0015.
[7]   HC 395, para 316A.

Bringing a child into the UK to be adopted

11.110 The Immigration Rules make provision for a child who enters the UK for a domestic and a Convention adoption.[1] Where the entry is for a domestic adoption the strictures for adopted children, namely: that the child will have the same rights and obligations as any other child of the family, is being adopted due to the inability of the original parent(s) or carer(s) to care for him,[2] that there is a genuine transfer of parental responsibility, that the child has lost or broken or intends to lose or break his or her ties with his family of origin and the proposed adoption is not one of convenience arranged to facilitate his or her admission to the UK – these are retained for prospective adoptive children.[3] Where the entry is for a Convention adoption these additional strictures do not apply.[4] Once the child has been admitted to the UK for the purposes of adoption the procedures for making and obtaining an adoption order must be followed.[5]

[1]   HC 395, paras 316A, 316D. *MN (India) v Entry Clearance Officer* [2008] EWCA Civ 38, [2009] 1 FCR 300, [2008] 2 FLR 87.
[2]   HC 395, para 316A(vi). Note, this criterion states: 'is being adopted due to the inability of the original parent(s) or current carer(s) (or those looking after him immediately prior to him being physically transferred to his prospective parent or parents) to care for him'.
[3]   HC 395, para 316A.
[4]   HC 395, para 316D.
[5]   Adoption and Children Act 2002, ss 42–52; Family Procedure Rules 2010, SI 2010/2955, Pt 14; Adoptions with a Foreign Element Regulations 2005, SI 2005/392, regs 5 and 9. Where the requirements for assessment, approval and certification in ACA, s 83 have been complied with the child is to live with the adopters for six months before the adopters can make their adoption application. Where the section 83 requirements have not been complied with, the child is to live with the adopters for 12 months before an adoption application can be made. AFE Regulations, reg 9.

De facto adoptions

11.111 Some countries, for example certain countries with Islamic law systems, have not enacted laws concerning adoption. In such countries, children cannot be formally adopted, although there is general social recognition of changed family relationships equivalent to the UK's special guardianship arrangements. In these arrangements the guardian substitutes for the child's parents and assumes parental responsibility for the child, but the child's lineage and family identity is unaffected. As the Adoption and Children Act 2002, s 67 makes clear, our adoption orders change a child's identity and the law treats the child as if she were born to the adopters.

UK immigration law commendably makes provision for the entry and stay of children integrated in families, but not formally adopted by their carers. In immigration law terms certain of these long-standing guardianship or carer arrangements will qualify as 'de facto adoptions'. It is accepted that these relationships have real significance for the parties involved and should be given some legal effect in immigration law. In certain circumstances, children who are the subject of de facto adoptions may be admitted to the UK for settlement with their adoptive parents[1]. The term 'de facto' adoption has no meaning in family law. The carers may have no formal parental responsibility or rights concerning the children. The term is only used in immigration law.

Immigration Rule, 309A defines the term 'de facto adoption'. This states that for the purpose of adoption in rules 310–316C, a de facto adoption shall be regarded as having taken place if at the time immediately preceding the application for entry clearance under these Rules the adoptive parent (or if it is the joint de facto adoption, both parents) have been living abroad for at least 18 months and have cared for and been living together with the child for at least the 12 months immediately preceding the application for entry clearance. They must have assumed the role of the child's parents since the beginning of the 18-month period, so that there has been a genuine transfer of parental responsibility.[2] Any child who is informally adopted (eg via a religious ceremony) needs to satisfy the requirements of paragraph 309A.[3] De facto adopted children do not have to satisfy the Adoption and Children Act 2002, s 83 requirements for their adoptive parents to be assessed, approved and certified as suitable adopters.[4] Rule 309B which makes this statement is presumably exempting such adoptive parents from these family law requirements on the assumption they are no longer habitually resident in the British Islands because to qualify as the parents of a de facto adopted child they must have lived abroad for 18 months.[5]

The Rules define 'parent' to include the carers of a de facto adopted child, but note that de facto adopted children may not make an application for leave to enter or remain to accompany, join or remain with their adoptive parent under the dependent child rules in paragraphs 297–303.[6]

Where a child, who is the subject of a de facto adoption, arrives in the UK without prior entry clearance, immigration officers have been instructed to inform the appropriate local authority and the police.[7] This is to allow investigation of any possible trafficking and abduction and to allow the arrangement to be treated as a private fostering.[8] Where a child is admitted for settlement on the basis of a de facto adoption the parent can subsequently apply to adopt the child in the UK.

1 HC 395, para 310(vi).
2 HC 395, para 309A, inserted by HC 538 from 31 March 2003.
3 HC 395, paras 6 'a parent', 309A; *R (on the application of Acan) v Immigration Appeal Tribunal* [2004] EWHC 297 (Admin); *MK (Somalia) v Entry Clearance Officer* [2008] EWCA Civ 1453, [2008] All ER (D) 252 (Dec) *Mohamoud (paras 352D and 309A – de facto adoption) Ethiopia* [2011] UKUT 378 (IAC).
4 HC 395, para 309B.
5 See above at **11.102** for a discussion of para 309B and the Adoption and Children Act 2002 requirements for bringing adopted and adoptive children into the UK.
6 HC 395, para 6 'a parent'.
7 IDI (Sept 04), Chapter 8, Annex Q, para 3.3; Annex R. (This policy instruction has been archived and at the time of writing the modernised guidance on adoption is being reviewed.)
8 Carers are under an obligation to inform their local authority within three days of the child's arrival in the UK in accordance with the Children Act 1989 guidance on private fostering arrangements and if the 'parents'/carers do not notify their local authority, they will be committing an offence under section 70(1)(a) of the Children Act 1989 or, in Scotland, under section 15(1)(a) of the Foster Children (Scotland) Act 1984.

Adoptions recognised at common law

11.112 An external adoption can acquire the status of a 'recognised' adoption necessary for the Immigration Rules if the High Court recognises the adoption order and makes a declaration on the application of the child that he/she is the child of the adoptive parents.[1] In any such application the parents seeking recognition of their adoption apply to the High Court for an order recognising their adoption order. The Court considers whether the adoption was obtained wholly lawfully in the foreign jurisdiction, if the concept of adoption in that jurisdiction substantially conforms with the English concept and whether there are any public policy considerations that should mitigate against recognition.[2] If the Court is satisfied on these issues the Court is likely to make an order recognising the foreign adoption. In order for the recognition to be recorded as a declaration, the child applies for a declaration pursuant to section 57 of the Family Law Act 1986 that he/she is the adopted child of the parents.[3]

The High Court recognition of the foreign adoption is generally taken to satisfy the Immigration Rule requirement for the adoption to be recognised by the United Kingdom.[4] The Rule does not properly reflect the varied recognition arrangements in the Adoption and Children Act 2002, s 66, as the text of para 310(vi) refers only to 'overseas adoptions' – that is those made in a country whose adoption orders are recognised by the United Kingdom. In practice entry clearance officers accept English High Court recognition orders and declarations as satisfying this criterion.

1 The recognition procedure is in two stages involving consideration of *recognition* of the foreign adoption (under the High Court's inherent jurisdiction) and then separately, if the adoption is recognised the grant of a *declaration* (pursuant to section 57 Family Law Act 1986).
2 Concerning High Court orders and declarations recognising an external adoption, see *Re Valentine's Settlement* [1965] Ch 831 at 843A-C per Lord Denning; *ND (Children) (Recognition of foreign adoption orders), Re* [2008] EWHC 403 (Fam), [2008] All ER (D) 398 (Jun), *Re N (Recognition of Foreign Adoption Order)* [2010] 1 FLR 1102 (Bennett J), *R (a child) (adoption abroad), Re* [2012] EWHC 2956 (Fam) (Hedley J), *Z v Z* [2013] EWHC 747 (Fam) (Theis J), *A Council v M* [2013] EWHC 1501 (Fam) (Jackson J), *G (children) (Adoption proceedings), Re* [2014] EWHC 2605 (Fam).

³ See *G (children) (Adoption proceedings), Re* [2014] EWHC 2605 (Fam).
⁴ HC 395, para 310(vi).

Adoptions by relatives

11.113 It is quite common for childless couples to adopt the children of close relatives or for relatives to assume the care of young relatives where they have been neglected by their parents or orphaned. These cases generally fall to be decided not only under the adoption rules but also under the dependent relative Immigration Rules.¹

The landmark decision of the Court of Appeal in *Singh v Entry Clearance Officer, Delhi*² focussed attention on the nature and significance of the relationship between the parties in these cases. The appellant was a seven-year-old boy who had been adopted in India by his uncle and aunt who lived in the UK. The adoption had been carried out within the family in accordance with a social, religious and cultural tradition which served a humane purpose. It had legal effect in India. Three things flowed from this: first, although the child was not living with his adoptive parents, there had been a genuine transfer of parental responsibility; secondly, the child had become a member of his adoptive parents' family for the purposes of Article 8 of the ECHR; and third, the failure to grant him entry clearance to come to the UK was a violation of Article 8. The court found there was a family life established between the child and his adoptive parents even though their relationship had no formal recognition and they were not living together and upheld the Adjudicator's finding that his exclusion was disproportionate. In our view, the Tribunal's response to this judgment in *SK ('Adoption' not recognised in UK) India* is wrong. The Tribunal has discounted the significance and application of *Singh* on the ground that the case was concerned 'solely' with whether family life within the meaning of Article 8(1) of the ECHR existed between the child and adoptive parents and 'The case has . . . nothing to say about whether interference with family life would be proportionate'. Second, the Tribunal's starting premise that 'there can be no "human right" to enjoy in any particular State as the consequence of adoption, unless the adoption is one recognised as such in that state', was precisely one of the core issues in contention in *Singh*, which the Court resolved not by focus on the status of the adoption but the parties' family relationship. The Tribunal also proceeded on the premise that the Immigration Rules are consistent and coherent with adoption law, 'because otherwise the person might be treated as a child of the family for immigration law purposes but not otherwise'. The Tribunal omitted to consider that there is in fact only limited congruence between the rules and adoption law. In particular de facto adopted children admitted under the rules are not treated as the children of the family of their sponsoring 'parent' and there is no family law requirement that the birth parents be shown to be unable to care for the child before an adoption order is made. As this criterion is the basis for many relative adoption refusals the tribunal's presumption is inapt.

Numbers of these relative adoptions involve Indian families. Providing one of the adoptive parents has an Indian domicile, they have undertaken a formal court adoption in India (not merely a religious 'gifting' ceremony), and can show it was a 'best interests' adoption (with Indian home study reports and supervision of parental consents), the parents may succeed in getting recognition of their adoption from the High Court.[3]

1   See HC 395, paras 297, 310. See *SZ (Applicable Immigration Rules) Bangladesh* [2007] UKAIT 00037 (30 March 2007) in which the Tribunal held that while there is no general duty on the Tribunal to consider whether a claimant's case might have succeeded under a different Immigration Rule, exceptionally, the facts of a case or the terms of a notice of decision may require the Tribunal to consider the appeal on a number of alternative bases. In this case the child has been 'de facto' adopted but could not succeed under paragraph 310 but should have been determined under paragraph 297 as a dependent relative. See also *SK ('Adoption' not recognised in UK) India* [2006] UKAIT 00068 (1 September 2006) where the Tribunal rejected the broader Article 8 arguments but allowed the Article 8 appeal 'narrowly' by finding the child satisfied para 297(1)(f).

2   *Singh v Entry Clearance Officer, Delhi* [2004] EWCA Civ 1075 [2004] INLR 515. Clearly such cases are fact sensitive. Munby J compared this case favourably with *J (a minor) (adoption: non-patrial), Re* [1998] 1 FLR 225, [1998] INLR 424, CA, but contrasted it with a 'sordid inter-country adoption' in Re M (Adoption: International Adoption Trade) [2003] EWHC 219 (Fam), [2003] 1 FLR 1111.

3   *Re Valentine's Settlement, Valentine v Valentine* [1965] Ch 831; *Re ND (Children) (Recognition of foreign adoption orders)* [2008] EWHC 403 (Fam), [2008] All ER (D) 398 (Jun), *R (a child) (adoption abroad), Re* [2012] EWHC 2956 (Fam) (Hedley J), *Z v Z* [2013] EWHC 747 (Fam) (Theis J), *A Council v M* [2013] EWHC 1501 (Fam) (Jackson J), *G (children) (Adoption proceedings), Re* [2014] EWHC 2605 (Fam).

Adoptions in the UK conferring an immigration benefit

11.114 On occasion British citizens or residents have applied in family courts to adopt foreign children who are in the UK as overstayers, illegal entrants or with temporary leave to remain. The child's adoption in the UK by a British citizen confers British citizenship on the child.[1] The conferral of British citizenship is clearly an immigration benefit, particularly for children with irregular immigration status.

At one time, the family court considering such adoptions conferring immigration benefits on the child gave greater weight to the need to maintain strict immigration controls when considering whether to grant the adoption.[2] Following the House of Lords' decision in *Re B (adoption order: nationality)*[3] the courts now consider whether, 'the adoption will bring about a genuine transfer of parental responsibility and not only be motivated by a wish to assist the child to obtain a right of abode' and, 'taking into account all the child's circumstances, including the benefits of British citizenship' whether the adoption will confer real benefits on the child throughout his or her childhood.' The House stated that although the views of the Home Office should be taken into account, it was very unlikely that general concerns relating to the maintenance of immigration controls would justify the rejection of an order which met both the two tests outlined above. In *Re B*, the child in question was 16 years old and was being adopted by her grandparents. Her mother had returned to Jamaica to a life of destitution and her grandparents wanted to be able to provide the child with a secure home and educational opportunities.

The Secretary of State can apply under rule 23 of the Adoption Rules[4] to be joined as a party to the application. It is her policy[5] to do so unless a child:

(1)   is being adopted by a couple one of whom is a natural parent;

(2)   was admitted in possession of an entry clearance endorsed 'for adoption';

(3)   has been granted or would qualify for indefinite leave to remain or leave in some other capacity where it is accepted that the child's original family is unable to care for him eg as a minor dependent relative or in the absence of parents; or

(4)   has been granted or would qualify for leave to remain for the purpose of adoption.

In *ASB and KSB v MQS (Secretary of State for the Home Department intervening)*[6] where the Secretary of State intervened to oppose the making of the adoption order because of deceptions practised to secure the child, M's entry to the UK, the Court noted that 'it remains the court's obligation . . . to be on its guard in adoption proceedings against misuse of such proceedings. Misuse of adoption proceedings to gain a right of abode (as opposed to exercising parental authority) is most unlikely to be in the child's welfare as well as undermining immigration policies and procedures.' The Court (per Bennett J) made the adoption order – the reasons exemplify the best interests analysis required in such cases:

'42.   . . . M is well and happily settled in England. There is a genuine relationship between M and the applicants of son and parents. M sees them as his father and mother. They see him as their son and the child they have longed for. M fervently wishes to be adopted by them; he is 17 and his wishes and feelings are very important. He is doing well at school and has a network of friends. The applicants can assist him to achieve his educational and career goals and can provide him with continuity of religious and cultural norms. He will be adopted into a family that shares the same background, history, religion and cultural practices as his birth family. He will continue to have meaningful contact with his extended and birth families. I agree with the guardian that there is a real risk of a severe detrimental effect on M if the adoption order is refused thereby leading to his likely return to Pakistan. It would fracture his relationship with the applicants and most likely lead to instability and insecurity in his life now and in the future. In my judgment there is no order other than adoption that I can make that will secure M's best interests throughout his life. So, in conclusion, I have no doubts that adoption by the applicants of M will confer real benefits on him throughout his life.

43.   I do not ignore the fact that M is an overstayer and thus in breach of the Immigration Rules . . . in my judgment immigration considerations cannot, in the circumstances of this case as I have found them to be, justify the refusal of the order the applicants seek. The weight to be given to the breach of Immigration Rules perpetrated by M's parents and/or maternal uncle must be small'.

Some of these 'immigration benefit' adoptions will also concern irregular adoption placements or children who were brought in to the UK in breach of section 83 of the Adoption and Children Act 2002. The Court is not prevented from making an adoption order if such safeguards are breached.[7]

---

[1]   BNA 1981, s 1(5), (5A). If it is a joint adoption, it is enough that one of the adopters is a British citizen. The child does not lose his/her British citizenship if the adoption order ceases to have effect or is annulled (s 1(6)).

[2]   *Re W (A Minor) (Adoption: Non-patrial)* [1986] Fam 54; *Re K (Adoption and Wardship)* [1997] 2 FLR 221.

[3]   *Re B (adoption order: nationality)* [1999] 2 AC 136, HL. See also *Re H (A Minor) (Adoption Non-patrial)* (1982) 12 Fam Law 218, CA; *Re H (a minor) (adoption: non-patrial)* [1996]

4 All ER 600, [1997] 1 WLR 791, [1996] 2 FLR 187, *sub nom Re A (a minor) (adoption: non-patrial)* [1996] 3 FCR 1, CA; *Re Adoption Application* [1992] 1 WLR 596, [1992] 1 FLR 341, [1992] Fam Law 241, *sub nom Re GD* [1992] 1 FCR 433; *Re J (a minor) (adoption: non-patrial)* [1998] 1 FCR 125, [1998] 1 FLR 225, [1998] Fam Law 130, CA; *Re B (adoption order: nationality)* [1999] 2 AC 136, [1999] 2 All ER 576, [1999] 2 WLR 714; *Re R (a minor) (inter-country adoptions: practice)* [1999] 4 All ER 1015, [1999] 1 WLR 1324, [1999] 1 FCR 418, [1999] 1 FLR 1042, [1999] Fam Law 289; *Re C (a minor) (adoption illegality)* [1999] Fam 128, [1999] 2 WLR 202, [1998] 2 FCR 641. See also *X (children) (parental order: foreign surrogacy), Re* [2008] EWHC 3030 (Fam), [2009] Fam Law 115.

4   Family Procedure (Adoption) Rules 2005, SI 2005/2795.
5   IDI (July 01), Chapter 8, Annex S, para 5. It is the practice of family courts to inform the Secretary of State of an adoption application with immigration consequences on the first direction hearing
6   [2009] EWHC 2491 (Fam), [2010] 1 FLR 748
7   Under s 24(2) of the Adoption Act 1976 (now repealed), the court could not make an adoption order if there had been a contravention of the s 57 prohibition on making certain payments for adoption. Section 57, although repealed, has been replicated and expanded in s 95 of the Adoption and Children Act 2002 but the court is not precluded from making an adoption order in the event of contravention. Further, the 2002 Act gives greater emphasis to the paramount consideration of the child's welfare 'throughout his life'. It can be expected that the case law balancing welfare and public, including immigration, policy will continue to be important in such cases: see sixth edition, 11.117.

INTERNATIONAL SURROGACY

11.115 UK law governing surrogacy stems from the 'baby Cotton' case[1] in which Kim Cotton, a surrogate mother was paid £5,000 to bear a child for a commissioning couple. The local authority intervened and the commissioning parents were granted orders in wardship giving them care of the child.

UK law does not permit commercial surrogacy arrangements and no surrogacy agreement is legally enforceable by or against any of those entering into the agreement.[2] Increasingly British citizens and residents are entering into commercial surrogacy arrangements abroad. They can face legal difficulties arranging for their surrogate born child's re-entry to the UK or securing family orders recognising them as the parents of the child. These immigration and family law issues are complex.

There are several different types of surrogacy – the surrogate mother may be the genetic mother of the child and the commissioning father the sperm donor; or the surrogate mother may have no genetic link to the child – with egg and sperm donated by the commissioning couple, by one or neither of the commissioning couple. As described below, these different fertilisation arrangements create different family identities as between the commissioning couple, the surrogate mother, her husband (if she is married) and the child. Further, the overseas surrogacy laws differ. Some states recognise the commissioning couple as the legal parents for all purposes and remove all parental rights from the surrogate mother.[3]

1   *Re C (a minor) (Wardship: Surrogacy)* [1985] FLR 846, [1985] Fam Law 191, [1985] NLJ Rep 106.
2   Surrogacy Arrangements Act 1985, ss 1, 2.
3   See *X (children) (parental order: foreign surrogacy), Re* [2008] EWHC 3030 (Fam). See on legal complications when the US court made an adoption order to the commissioning mother, *CC v DD* [2014] EWHC 1307 (Fam).

11.116 Under UK law[1] the mother of a surrogate born child is the woman who carries and gives birth to the child, regardless of the method of surrogacy. This rule applies whether or not the surrogate mother has any genetic link to the child she is carrying or was in the UK or overseas at the time of the placing in her of the embryo or sperm. English law does not permit the surrogate/birth mother to surrender her parental responsibility of the child to anyone other than in an adoption or parental order proceedings and she only ceases to be the 'mother' if the child is adopted or if a parental order is made.[2] The paternity of a surrogate born child – whether born in the UK or abroad – is more complex. If at the time of her artificial insemination or the placing in the surrogate mother of the embryo, eggs and sperm, the surrogate mother is married, then her husband (or for children born after 6 April 2009 – her civil partner) will be the legal father/parent of the child unless it is shown that he/she did not consent to the insemination.[3] If the surrogate mother was unmarried/not in a civil partnership at the time of insemination or if her husband/civil partner did not consent to the insemination, and the sperm of the commissioning father is used, the commissioning father is treated as the legal father of the child. These provisions in the Human Fertilisation and Embryology Act 2008 also apply to define 'a child's mother' and 'father' for nationality purposes.[4] The BNA 1981 additionally provides in respect of a surrogate born child that where the birth mother's husband is not the father and there is no person treated as the father or parent of the child under the Human Fertilisation and Embryology Act 2008, a person who satisfies prescribed requirements as to proof of paternity is the father.[5]

[1] Parenthood for these purposes is defined in the Human Fertilisation and Embryology Act 2008, and the BNA 1981, s 50(9). The definition of 'parent' in the BNA 1981 was amended by NIAA 2002, s 9(1). These amendments which take effect for children born after 1 July 2006 eliminated the discrimination against illegitimate born children, allowing them to take their citizenship status from fathers who were not married to their mothers and also made provision for the citizenship status of surrogate born children.

[2] Human Fertilisation and Embryology Act 2008, s 33. Note, that where the woman carrying the child conceived by artificial insemination, her female civil partner and in certain circumstances a second woman where it is agreed she will be a parent – will be joint mothers of the child with the birth mother. (See ss 42–44.)

[3] Human Fertilisation and Embryology Act 2008, ss 35, 42, 43.

[4] BNA 1981, s 50(9), (9A).

[5] BNA 1981, s 50(9A)(c). The British Nationality (Proof of Paternity) Regulations 2006, SI 2006/1496 prescribe that paternity is proved where: (a) the person is named as the father of the child in a birth certificate issued within one year of the date of the child's birth; or (b) a person satisfies the Secretary of State that he is the father. The Secretary of State may have regard to any evidence including DNA evidence or an official acknowledgement of paternity, for example, in a court order.

11.117 If the commissioning parents are not the parents of the surrogate born child in UK law, they may be eligible to apply for, and obtain, a parental order – an order recognising them as parents and extinguishing the parental responsibility of the surrogate mother and her husband. Prior to the commencement of section 54 of the Human Fertilisation and Embryology Act (in April 2010), only a married couple could apply for such order.[1] The 2008 Act extends the eligible applicants for parental orders to include married couples, civil partners or two persons in an enduring same-sex partnership not within the prohibited degrees of relationship to each other.[2] The Act does not allow applications by single 'parents'. The Act prescribes specific conditions for the making of a parental order as follows.

- The child must be a surrogate born child and gametes (sperm/eggs) of the commissioning father or mother or both used to bring about the creation of the embryo.
- The application for the parental order must be made within six months of the child's birth[3] or in the case of civil partners or persons living within an enduring relationship who have only been able to apply for a parental order since section 54(2) of the HFEA 2008 came in to force, within six months of the coming in to force of section 54(2) (ie before October 2010).
- At the time of the application for the parental order and at the time of the order being made, the child's home must be with the commissioning parents and one or both must be domiciled in a part of the UK or in the Channel Islands or the Isle of Man.
- At the time the order is made, both commissioning parents must be 18 or over.
- The court must be satisfied that the surrogate mother and, if appropriate, her husband, have consented freely, with full understanding and unconditionally to the making of a parental order. (Agreement can be waived if the persons concerned cannot be found or is/are incapable of giving consent. The agreement of the surrogate mother is ineffective if given when the child is less than six weeks old.[4])
- The court must be satisfied that no money or other benefit (other than for expenses reasonably incurred) has been given or received by the commissioning parents for, or in consideration of, the making of the order, any agreement, the handing over of the child or the making of any arrangements with a view to the making of the order, unless authorised by the court.[5]

In order to return to the UK with their child the commissioning parents will have to arrange travel documents and the entry clearance for the surrogate-born child. As noted above, some surrogate born children may be British citizens or entitled to be registered as British citizens. Others may have the citizenship of their country of birth and require entry clearance in order to settle in the UK. Such children born in the United States (a common source country for surrogate born children) will have US citizenship (by birth in the country) and a right to a US passport – but in some cases the child may be stateless and without travel documents.[6] There is no Immigration Rule permitting the grant of entry clearance for the purpose of obtaining a parental order. Such cases are dealt with outside the Rules.

1 Human Fertilisation and Embryology Act 1990, s 30.
2 Human Fertilisation and Embryology Act 2008, s 54.
3 See *JP v LP (surrogacy arrangement: wardship)* [2014] EWHC 595 (Fam), *X (A Child) (Surrogacy: Time Limit)* [2014] EWHC 3135 (Fam).
4 See concerning the arrangements for evidencing parental consent – Human Fertilisation and Embryology (Parental Orders) Regulations 2010, SI 2010/985, Sch 1, applying ss 104, 144(1) of the Adoption and Children Act 2002; *D and L (children) (surrogacy: parental order), Re* [2012] EWHC 2631 (Fam), [2013] 1 WLR 3135; *WT (a Child: foreign surrogacy arrangements), Re* [2014] EWHC 1303 (Fam).
5 Human Fertilisation and Embryology Act 2008, s 54. On the authorisation of payments in excess of reasonable expenses, see *X (children) (parental order: foreign surrogacy), Re* [2008] EWHC 3030 (Fam), [2009] 2WLR 1274; *L (a child) (surrogacy: parental order), Re* [2010] EWHC 3146 (Fam), [2011] 2 WLR 1006; *IJ (a child) (overseas surrogacy: parental order), Re* [2011] EWHC 921 (Fam), [2011] Fam Law 695; *X and Y (children-foreign surrogacy), Re* [2011] EWHC 3147 (Fam); *P-M (children) (parental order), Re* [2013] EWHC 2328 (Fam), C

(a child) (parental order: surrogacy arrangement), Re [2013] EWHC 2408 (Fam), W *(children: surrogacy, parental orders), Re* [2013] EWHC 3570.
6   See *Re X & Y (Foreign Surrogacy)* [2008] EWHC 3030 (Fam), [2009] 2WLR 1274.

11.118 UKBA's explanatory leaflet, *Intercountry Surrogacy and the Immigration Rules*, published 1 June 2009, set down the guidance for such applications. It begins by dealing with those surrogate born children who are British citizens or who may be entitled to register as British citizens.[1] In such cases the British Embassy may facilitate the citizenship registration of the child or issue the child's British passport. Where the commissioning father is the 'father' (because the surrogate mother was unmarried or her husband did not consent to the surrogacy) but he cannot pass on British citizenship to the child (for example, because he is not a British citizen or is a British citizen by descent and the child has no entitlement to registration under section 3(2) of the British Nationality Act 1981), as he is a 'parent' for Immigration Rule purposes (para 6) the child could qualify for entry clearance for settlement under para 297 of the Immigration Rules as a dependent child of her British citizen parent.[2]

1   BNA 1981, ss 2, 3(2), (3), 50(9), (9A)–(9C). The commissioning father may be treated as the father under the Human Fertilisation and Embryology Act 2008, s 35 or permitted to establish paternity under the British Nationality (Proof of Paternity) Regulations 2006, SI 2006/1496.
2   See Home Office, Intercountry Surrogacy and the Immigration Rules, para 40

11.119 In other cases the commissioning parents are reliant on Home Office discretion – permitting discretionary citizenship registration of the child under section 3(1) of the British Nationality Act 1981 or the grant of entry clearance outside the Rules. The Home Office *Surrogacy Policy Guidance* leaflet and the *Nationality Instructions* state concerning the discretionary citizenship registration options: that where the commissioning male is genetically related to the child, on an application to register the child as a British citizen under section 3(1) of the British Nationality Act 1981, the Secretary of State will normally grant the application if satisfied about the paternity of the child; has the consent of all those with parental responsibility; and is satisfied that, had the child been born to the father legitimately the child would have had an automatic claim to British citizenship under sections 1(1), 2(1) or an entitlement to registration under either sections 1(3), 3(2) or (5) of the Act and there is no reason to refuse on character grounds.[1] If the British commissioning 'father' is not genetically related to the child or the commissioning 'mother' is British (whether she is the child's biological mother or not) such discretionary section 3(1) citizenship registration of the surrogate born child may be approved if:

(i)   the Secretary of State is satisfied that if the commissioning parents had been the father or mother for nationality law purposes the child would have been British or entitled to be registered as a British citizen; and

(ii)   the 'father' or 'mother' has been granted either an order under sections 30 and 54 respectively of the Human Fertilisation and Embryology Acts 1990 and 2008, or an order by a foreign court, within whose jurisdiction the child was born, directing that he/she be treated, in law, as the child's father or mother.[2]

Where the child does not qualify or meet the policy criteria for British citizenship, the *Surrogacy Policy Guidance* states that such children may be granted entry clearance outside the Rules. The *Guidance* indicates that such entry clearance will only be granted on condition that the sponsoring 'parents' apply for a parental order within six months of the child's birth and evidence suggests that such an order is likely to be granted and one of the commissioning parents establishes their genetic link to the child – 'as without this proof, the UK courts will not grant a parental order.[3]

If the 'parents' who commissioned the surrogacy are EU citizens, depending on the nationality laws in their State, the child may be an EU citizen or if a third-country national may be a 'family member' of the 'parent' with entry and residence rights.[4]

[1] Home Office, 'Inter-Country Surrogacy and the Immigration Rules', June 2009, paras 32–39, Nationality Instructions, Chapter 9, Registering Minors at Discretion, paras 9.9 and 9.10.2.
[2] Home Office, 'Inter-Country Surrogacy and the Immigration Rules', June 2009, paras 43–44. *Nationality Instructions*, Chapter 9, Registering Minors at Discretion, paras 9.9, 9.10.2, and 9.10.4.1.
[3] Home Office, 'Inter-Country Surrogacy and the Immigration Rules',at paras 41–42.
[4] A 'family member' is defined as a 'direct descendant' under the age of 21 of the EU citizen, his/her spouse or civil partner or their dependant. Note, that this definition is not concerned with whether the EU citizen is a 'parent' of the child. The Immigration (European Economic Area) Regulations 2006, reg 7(1).

Proposal for British resident child to be adopted abroad

11.120 The Adoption and Children Act 2002 restricts the removal of certain children from the United Kingdom where it is proposed to adopt them abroad. It is a criminal offence to arrange, initiate, take part in negotiations concerning the removal of a Commonwealth citizen child or a child habitually resident in the UK[1] for adoption abroad unless the Court has given parental responsibility for the child to the prospective adopters.[2] A parental responsibility order for this purpose will not be made unless prescribed requirements are met – for example, that the parents of the child or a guardian with parental responsibility have given consent or their consent dispensed with by a court, and at all time during the preceding ten weeks the child's home was with the proposed adopters.[3] These removals are often initiated by a local authority in care proceedings where the local authority may wish to place the child abroad for adoption by his/her relatives. In such cases the local authority is a party in the proceedings seeking permission to remove the child for the purpose of adoption abroad.[4] These arrangements can involve securing entry for the overseas relative so that the relative can be assessed by the local authority as suitable to adopt the child and the placement of the child with the proposed adopter is tested. If the overseas placement is approved the prospective adopters/carers and be granted an order giving them formal parental responsibility for the child.[5] This order may not be made unless the child has had his/her home with the adopters for the ten preceding weeks. In *A (A Child), Re*[6] the Court ruled that in an overseas adoption, a child's 'home' with prospective adopter(s) during the ten-week period can be with the prospective adopters wherever they happen to be living. It is not necessary that the adopters and child live for that ten weeks in a home in the UK. Thus the child may first depart from the UK as a visitor travelling to the adopter's home country.

Providing the adoption is approved, the child will then be placed with the adopters, and permitted to leave the UK for the purpose of adoption abroad.

¹ On the meaning of 'habitual residence' see: *A v A, (Children: Habitual Residence)* [2013] UKSC 60, [2014] AC 1, *KL (a child) (abduction: habitual residence: inherent jurisdiction), Re* [2013] UKSC 75, [2014] 1 All ER 999 and *LC (children) (Reunite International Child Abduction Centre, intervening), Re* [2014] UKSC 1, [2013] 1 All ER 1181.
² Adoption and Children Act 2002, ss 84, 85(1), (3)
³ Adoption and Children Act 2002, s 84.
⁴ Children Act 1989, Sch 2, para 19. See *S (a child) (adoption: procedure), Re* [2002] EWCA Civ 798. See also the Adoption and Children Act 2002, s 85; *G (an infant) (adoption: placement outside jurisdiction), Re* [2008] EWCA Civ 105, [2009] 1 FCR 210. See concerning the residence requirement for such overseas adoptions *A (a child) (adoption: removal), Re* [2009] EWCA Civ 41, [2009] 3 All ER 479, [2009] 3 WLR 1169.
⁵ Adoption and Children Act 2002, s 84. In order to obtain a section 84 order the applicant must have had a home with the child in the UK for the previous ten weeks. See also *Re B (children) (adoption: removal from jurisdiction)* [2004] EWCA Civ 515, [2004] 2 FCR 129, [2004] All ER (D) 305 (Apr), *sub nom Re A (adoption: placement outside jurisdiction)* [2005] Fam 105, [2004] 3 WLR 1207, [2004] 2 FLR 337, *sub nom B v Birmingham City Council* (2004) Times, 10 June. See *A (A Child), Re* [2009] EWCA Civ 41; [2009] 3 WLR 1169, [2010] 1 Fam 9, [2009] Fam Law 380, [2009] 3 All ER 479.
⁶ [2009] EWCA Civ 41; [2009] 3 WLR 1169, [2010] 1 Fam 9, [2009] Fam Law 380, [2009] 3 All ER 479

SEPARATED CHILDREN

11.121 Separated children are those children under 18 years of age who are outside their country of origin and separated from both parents or their previous legal/customary primary caregiver.¹ The core issues associated with separated children relate to age assessments and leaving care arrangements, processing their claims for asylum/humanitarian/subsidiary protection and family tracing, as victims of trafficking, detention and the safe arrangements for their removal. These issues are dealt with in the chapters on asylum, trafficking and support.

¹ The preferred definition of The Separated Children in Europe Programme, a joint initiative of some members of the International Save the Children Alliance in Europe and the UNHCR.

PARENTS, GRANDPARENTS AND OTHER DEPENDENT RELATIVES

The classes of admissible dependent relatives

11.122 One of the significant changes effected in July 2012 was to substitute new, very restrictive Appendix FM Rules concerning the entry of adult dependent relatives. The new adult dependent relative provision replaced the Part 8, paragraph 317 adult dependent relative rule. The change effectively closes down the immigration arrangements for older parents and grandparents and prevents them from settling with their British families.¹ Under the paragraph 317 rules before July 2012 a parent or grandparent could qualify for immediate settlement in the UK, if he or she was over the age of 65, wholly or mainly financially dependent on the sponsoring relative, had no other close relatives in their own country to turn to for financial support and could meet the maintenance and accommodation requirements. The Appendix FM rules in place since July 2012 removed the option for immediate settlement, or of qualifying for leave to remain in this capacity from within the UK and also introduced far more strenuous eligibility criteria, effectively rendering the elderly dependant relative immigration route all but impossible to fulfil in practice. According to Home Office record Freedom of Information request response – 8 April 2014. Only 34 adult dependent relative settlement visas were issued under Appendix FM of the Immigration Rules Between 1 November 2012 to 30 September 2013. The statistic hints at the distress in families unable to live with and care for their separated adult dependent relatives. The Secretary of State's guidance makes plain that the new rules are intended to 'end the routine expectation of settlement' in the UK for parents and grandparents aged 65 or over who are financially dependent on a relative in the UK. Immigration Directorate Instructions, Chapter 8, Section FM 6.0 Adult dependent relatives (13 December 2012) at Section 1.

[1]   HC 395 Appendix FM Adult Dependent Relative Section EC-DR. The restrictive criteria states:

> 'E-ECDR.2.4. The applicant or, if the applicant and their partner are the sponsor's parents or grandparents, the applicant's partner, must as a result of age, illness or disability require long-term personal care to perform everyday tasks.
> E-ECDR.2.5. The applicant or, if the applicant and their partner are the sponsor's parents or grandparents, the applicant's partner, must be unable, even with the practical and financial help of the sponsor, to obtain the required level of care in the country where they are living, because-(a) it is not available and there is no person in that country who can reasonably provide it; or (b) it is not affordable.
> (a)   it is not available and there is no person in that country who can reasonably provide it; or
> (b)   it is not affordable.'

Appendix FM-SE paras 34-37 detailed the prescribed evidence required to show the above criteria are satisfied.

11.123 Under transitional arrangements adult dependent relatives who had applied for entry clearance or leave to remain prior to 9 July 2012 and whose applications had not been determined – were to be considered under the Part 8, Paragraph 317 rule. There may be some such cases still unresolved. For such cases see paragraphs 131-140 in the 8th edition of this work.

Recommendation R (1981) 16 on the Harmonisation of National Procedures Relating to Asylum (Plender **12.1** fn 2 above, pp 140, 147).

[3] With the Asylum and Immigration Appeals Act 1993, s 1 of which (still in force) for the first time defined 'asylum' as meaning refugee status within the meaning of the Convention Relating to the Status of Refugees (Geneva, 1951) and its 1967 Protocol (collectively the Refugee Convention). See also the Immigration Rules HC 395, para 327, defining an asylum applicant as a person who claims that it would be contrary to the UK's obligations under the Refugee Convention for him to be removed from or required to leave the UK. However, for the purposes of 'asylum support' in Pt VI of the 1999 Act, a 'claim for asylum' is defined to include a claim that removal would be contrary to art 3 ECHR: see s 94. A similar definition is used in Part 2 (Accommodation Centres) of the Nationality, Immigration and Asylum Act 2002: see s 18(3).

[4] See Home Office evidence to the House of Commons Home Affairs Committee Sub-Committee on Race and Immigration 1984–85, 72 HC Official Report (6th series) col iv, 17 December 1984. The Education (Mandatory Awards) Regulations 1991, SI 1991/1838 referred to 'refugees or others granted asylum', but the regulations made since 1993 no longer use this terminology.

[5] Nationality, Immigration and Asylum Act 2002, ss 82 and 84(1)(g). This does not preclude other matters, including human rights grounds, from being litigated in the same proceedings: see CHAPTER 19 below.

12.3 However wide the definition of refugee, there will be those deserving protection under other international instruments who may fall outside it. People may be fleeing torture and inhuman or degrading treatment even though such treatment may not be on the grounds of race, religion, nationality, membership of a social group or political opinion.[1] Expulsion of such persons in circumstances where there are substantial grounds to conclude that they face such treatment would be contrary to other international obligations.[2] The distinction is recognised in EU law by the grant of a subsidiary status to those who cannot be expected to return to their country of origin for reasons not qualifying them for refugee status.[3] Although historically such persons have been unrecognised in the Immigration Rules but might have been granted exceptional leave to remain in accordance with extra-Rules policies and discretions, the Rules now provide for the grant of Humanitarian Protection to those falling within the EU law definition of a person in need of 'subsidiary protection'.[4] Those not qualifying for Humanitarian Protection but nevertheless entitled to protection on human rights grounds may be protected by the Home Office policy on Discretionary Leave,[5] and the incompatibility of an immigration decision with rights protected under the Human Rights Convention has since 2 October 2000 been a statutorily recognised ground of appeal.[6] We examined the ECHR in CHAPTER 7 above and will look at the grant of Humanitarian Protection and Discretionary Leave at **12.195** ff and **12.199** ff below.

[1] See *Ameyaw v Secretary of State for the Home Department* [1992] Imm AR 206 (unfair trial); *R v Secretary of State for the Home Department, ex p Zibirila-Alassia* [1991] Imm AR 367, QBD (fear of being selected as victim of ritual sacrifice); *R v Immigration Appeal Tribunal, ex p Hernandez* [1994] Imm AR 506, QBD (retribution from guerilla groups); *Hamieh v Secretary of State for the Home Department* [1993] Imm AR 323 (pressure from extremist groups) for examples of possible persecution for non-Refugee Convention reasons.

[2] Most notably art 3 of the ECHR and art 3 of the UN Convention Against Torture: see *R v Secretary of State for the Home Department, ex p Chahal* [1994] Imm AR 107, [1995] 1 All ER 658, CA; *Chahal v United Kingdom* (1996) 23 EHRR 413. See also *Mutombo v Switzerland* (1994) 15 HRJ 164; *Alan v Switzerland* [1997] INLR 29. See also Gorlick 'Refugee Protection and the Committee Against Torture' (1995) 7 IJRL 504.

[3] In Article 63(2)(a) EC, inserted by Treaty of Amsterdam, signed on 2 October 1997 by 15 Member States, such persons are described as 'other persons in need of international

protection'. See now the Council Directive 2004/83/EC on minimum standards for the qualification and status of third country nationals and stateless persons as refugees or as persons who otherwise need international protection, in force 20 October 2004 (2004 OJ L 304/12) (hereafter the 'Qualification Directive') which is considered below. Note also Council Directive 2001/55/EC of 20 July 2001 regarding the giving of temporary protection by Member States in the event of a mass influx of displaced persons (the 'EC Temporary Protection Directive', dealt with in Part 11A of the Immigration Rules, HC 395).

4   Cm 6918, amending HC 395 with effect from 9 October 2006.

5   Nationality, Immigration and Asylum Act 2002, ss 82 and 84. Decisions before 1 April 2003 attract appeal rights under the Immigration and Asylum Act 1999, s 65. Prior to 2 October 1999, the only remedy for refusal to give effect to ECHR obligations was judicial review. See the judgment of Sedley J in *R v Secretary of State for the Home Department, ex p McQuillan* [1995] 4 All ER 400 for a most coherent exposition of *R v Secretary of State for the Home Department, ex p Brind* [1991] 1 AC 696 and the court's jurisdiction to ensure that domestic standards of rationality do not fall out of line with international obligations.

6   Nationality Immigration and Asylum Act 2002, s 84(1)(c), (g).

12.4 The present UK practice is that all those who are granted asylum in the UK are recognised as refugees and the appropriate Refugee Convention travel document is given in recognition of this status.[1] But refugees present in the UK do not have to be given asylum here if there is a safe third country to which they can be removed.[2] Those who do not qualify as refugees may be granted a period of Humanitarian Protection or Discretionary Leave, which may be renewed on review, and may lead to settlement. They will not receive a Convention travel document, but may apply for a Home Office travel document.[3] Refugees enjoy family reunion rights with their pre-existing spouses and minor children who formed part of the family unit prior to the principal's departure,[4] and the refugee sponsor is not expected to meet the maintenance and accommodation requirements of the Immigration Rules. A person granted humanitarian protection on or after 30 August 2005 is eligible to apply for family reunion[5] but a person with discretionary leave may not do so until he or she has indefinite leave to remain.

1   As required by the Refugee Convention, art 28, Schedule.

2   HC 395, paras 334, 345. We examine the UK's practice on safe third countries at **12.139** below.

3   For humanitarian protection and discretionary leave see **12.204** below. For travel documents see **12.203** below. The provisions have been substantially tightened with effect from 27 March 2003.

4   The position of the spouse, partner and children of refugees is covered by the Immigration Rules (paras 352A–E of HC). The Asylum Policy Instrutions (API) also cover other family members. See **12.204** below.

5   See **12.205** below; prior to the insertion of this provision into the Immigration Rules by HC 28 with effect from 8 November 2007, this was addressed by the API Humanitarian Protection of October 2006.

12.5 The general rule of customary international law is that no individual may assert a right to enter a state of which he or she is not a national, and this rule is normally accepted as applying to refugees as well as ordinary migrants.[1] In accordance with this rule the right of asylum is not a right accorded to an individual refugee (except vis-à-vis the country of origin),[2] but is a discretion-ary right of a state to grant or withhold asylum.[3] The importance of giving states the right to grant asylum was to emphasise that such a grant was not an unfriendly act against the state of which the refugee was a national. These provisions of customary international law are reflected in the international legal instruments that have come into being since 1948. Article 14 of the

Universal Declaration of Human Rights 1948 (UDHR) recognised the fundamental right to 'seek and enjoy asylum', and although the Convention and
Protocol studiously avoid creating any legal right to asylum or any duty to
grant asylum or to give a refugee leave to enter a particular territory, the two
provisions are not incompatible. First, if there is a right to seek asylum (as
posited by Article 14 of UDHR), there is a corresponding duty on the country
where it is sought at least to consider that application and in doing so to act
fairly and consistently as between one asylum seeker and another.[4] Secondly,
this implies a further obligation on that country, which is to offer asylum
seekers at the very least temporary admission until the state has assured itself
that their return to a third country or to their country of origin would not be
in breach of Article 33.[5] Furthermore, it is a matter of contention whether over
50 years of state practice have modified this position in customary international law.[6] European Union law now recognises a right to asylum via the
Charter of Fundamental Rights, Article 18.[7]

[1] Lauterpacht *Oppenheim's International Law* (7th edn, 1952) p 616; R Plender *International Migration Law* (2nd edn, 1988) p 394; see also F Morgenstern 'The Right of Asylum' (1949) 26 BYBIL 327 at 335; P Weis 'Legal Aspects of the Convention Relating to the Status of Refugees' (1953) 30 BYBIL 478 at 481. See also Goodwin-Gill *The Refugee in International Law* (2nd edn, 1996); Goodwin-Gill's editorial comment 'Asylum: The Law and Politics of Change' (1995) 7 IJRL 1; and Roman Boed, 'The state of the right of asylum in international law', (1994) 5 Duke Journal of Comparative International Law 1.

[2] UDHR, art 13(2); International Covenant on Civil and Political Rights, art 12(2).

[3] The position in municipal law might be different: see Immigration Rules, HC 395, para 334; *R v Secretary of State for the Home Department, ex p Mersin (Deniz)* [2000] INLR 511, QBD, at **12.103**, fn 19 below where Elias J held that an asylum seeker who had succeeded on appeal had a right to be granted refugee status and indefinite leave to remain. However, see above **12.2** fn 1.

[4] The duty to consider has given rise to internationally applied practices and procedures, the key element of which can be found in the UNHCR *Handbook* Part 2 (see dicta in Court of Appeal in *Robinson (Anthonypillai Francis) v Secretary of State for the Home Department and Immigration Appeal Tribunal* [1997] Imm AR 568, at para 11, per Brooke LJ.

[5] See UNHCR *Handbook*, para 192 (vii).

[6] UNHCR refers to instances of denial of access to protection through closure of borders and non-admission to the territory or to asylum procedures as 'serious breaches of the interna-tionally recognised rights of refugees and asylum seekers' in its *Note on International Protection*, ExCom 50th session, UN doc A/AC.96/914, 7 July 1999, (1999) 11(3) IJRL 557. The existence of an international law duty which is broader in its terms than the Ge-neva Convention obligation of *non-refoulement* was doubted in *European Roma Rights Centre v Immigration Officer at Prague Airport* [2004] UKHL 55, [2005] 2 WLR 1.

[7] Article 18: 'The right to asylum shall be guaranteed with due respect for the rules of the Geneva Convention of 28 July 1951 and the Protocol of 31 January 1967 relating to the status of refugees and in accordance with the Treaty establishing the European Community' cf *R (on the application of MK) v Secretary of State for the Home Department* [2010] EWCA Civ 115.

The Geneva Convention

12.6 The key international instrument is the Geneva Convention of 1951
Relating to the Status of Refugees, as amended by the Protocol to the Convention 1967 (collectively the Refugee Convention). The original Convention
was concerned with the displacement of people as a result of the Second World
War and its aftermath, and restricted the definition of refugees to those whose
fear of persecution arose from events occurring before 1 January 1951. The
Protocol removed this time limitation, but enabled parties who had imposed a
geographic limitation on the application of the Convention to continue such

limitations to post-1951 refugees. Some states made declarations limiting the application of the Convention to refugees fleeing their countries as a result of events occurring in Europe. In the past this included some European countries, but now all EU countries have ratified both Convention and Protocol without temporal or geographical limitations.[1] The Asylum and Immigration Appeals Act 1993 incorporated the Convention into UK law to the extent of providing that it would be unlawful for the Secretary of State to make Immigration Rules that are inconsistent with the Convention.[2] Since 2006 the Convention's legal bite has been strengthened by the entry into effect of the Qualification Directive, which is in turn given domestic force by the European Communities Act 1972.[3] The courts will read down statutory provisions where they are inconsistent with those provisions of the Refugee Convention that are enshrined in the Directive.[4]

[1] Italy, in particular, used to have a geographical reservation. In 1990 the Member States of the EU formulated the Dublin Convention to prevent asylum seekers making multiple applications within the EU. In order to achieve this, signatory states were required to have ratified the Protocol. This first Dublin Convention, which came into force in September 1997, was substituted with effect from 1 September 2003 by Council Regulation (EC) No 343/2003 of 18 February 2003 establishing the criteria and mechanisms for determining the Member State responsible for examining an asylum application lodged in one of the Member States by a third-country national (known as Dublin II). See further **12.148** below.

[2] Asylum and Immigration Appeals Act 1993, s 2; HC 395, para 334. The House of Lords in *R v Secretary of State for the Home Department, ex p Sivakumaran* [1988] AC 958 took the view that 'the UK having acceded to the Convention and Protocol, their provisions have for all practical purposes been incorporated into UK law', In *R v Uxbridge Magistrates' Court, ex p Adimi* [1999] INLR 490 the Divisional Court held that refugees had a legitimate expectation that the provisions of the Convention would be followed. In *European Roma Rights Centre v Immigration Officer at Prague Airport* [2004] UKHL 55, [2005] 2 WLR 1, the House of Lords confirmed that the Convention was incorporated into domestic law (per Lord Bingham at para 7, Lord Steyn at paras 41–42 and Lord Hope at para 50).

[3] Sedley LJ in the Court of Appeal in *Al-Sirri v Secretary of State for the Home Department (United Nations High Comr for Refugees intervening)* [2009] EWCA Civ 222 (also cited as YS Egypt) at [28], [2009] All ER (D) 220 (Mar).

[4] *EN (Serbia) v Secretary of State for the Home Department* [2009] EWCA Civ 630, [2010] 3 WLR 182, (2009) Times, 24 July Stanley Burnton LJ at [60], citing Diplock LJ in *Post Office v Estuary Radio* [1968] 2 QB 740, at 756, [1967] 3 All ER 663, CA: ' . . . there is a presumption that the Crown did not intend to break an international treaty (see *Salomon v Customs and Excise Comrs* [1967] 2 QB 116), and if there is any ambiguity in the Order in Council, it should be resolved so as to accord with the provisions of the Convention in so far as that is a plausible meaning of the express words of the order'. For inconsistencies in the other direction, between Refugee Convention and the Directive, see **12.22** fn 13.

12.7 In broad terms the Refugee Convention provides a definition of refugees, creates exclusions from the definition and sets out circumstances when a person may cease to be a refugee,[1] and defines the duties owed to and by refugees vis-à-vis their host states. While the principal duty owed to refugees is that of *non-refoulement*,[2] it is clear from the decision in *Saad*[3] that this is not the only duty; as a party to the Refugee Convention the UK must afford all the Convention rights to anyone who is a refugee within the meaning of Article 1A to avoid a breach of the UK's international obligations. Where someone is recognised as a refugee and granted asylum, signatory states are under a duty to secure equal treatment with own nationals, or sometimes with other lawfully resident third country nationals, in respect of religion, personal status, property, freedom of association, gainful occupation, welfare, administrative measures and the issue of special travel documents to be used in place of the refugee's national passport.[4] It is important to note that refugees are recognised by states rather than created by them[5]: an asylum claimant should thus be treated as a potential refugee unless and until a valid determination is made that he or she is not to be so recognised.[6] However this principle does not preclude the construction of the particular Articles of the Convention which refer to refugees 'lawfully on the territory' as referring to recognised refugees who have been granted leave to stay.[7]

[1] Refugee Convention, art 1.
[2] See **12.8** below.
[3] *Diriye v Secretary of State for the Home Department; Osorio v Secretary of State for the Home Department* [2001] EWCA Civ 2008, [2002] Imm AR 471 [2002] INLR 34.
[4] Refugee Convention, arts 4–30.
[5] Their status being determined by the Convention, the provisions of which have autonomous meaning. See, for example, *IH (s 72; 'Particularly Serious Crime') Eritrea* [2009] UKAIT 00012 (09 March 2009).
[6] See UNHCR *Handbook on Procedures and Criteria for Determining Refugee Status* (1979) para 28; *Khaboka (Alimas) v Secretary of State for the Home Department* [1993] Imm AR 484 at 487, CA, per Nolan LJ.
[7] See For the meaning of 'lawfully in the territory' see *Bugdaycay v Secretary of State for the Home Department* [1987] AC 514 at 526, per Lord Bridge. See also *R v Secretary of State for the Home Department, ex p Joint Council for the Welfare of Immigrants* [1996] 4 All ER 385, [1997] 1 WLR 275, where the Court of Appeal assumed that art 23 of the Refugee Convention (the right of refugees lawfully staying on the territory to social security on the same basis as nationals) did not apply to asylum seekers.

12.8 The states that are signatories to the Refugee Convention did not surrender their discretionary power to grant or withhold asylum, but in practice the scope of this discretion is greatly narrowed by duties assumed by states signatory to the Convention and the other instruments, such as the UN Convention Against Torture and the regional human rights Treaties, such as the ECHR.[1] Signatory states agree to abide by Article 33 which prohibits *refoulement* (ie the expulsion or return of refugees in any manner whatsoever to the frontiers of territories where their lives or freedom would be threatened on account of their race, religion, nationality, membership of a particular social group or political opinion). If there is no safe third country to which a person can be sent, the principle of *non-refoulement* effectively requires a state to determine an asylum claim made by someone within its territory (including the border or transit zone at an airport).[2] In the UK, if a person is recognised as a refugee, asylum is granted. The Immigration Rules provide for a grant of limited leave and from 30 August 2005 the former policy of granting indefinite leave to those recognised as refugees was replaced with a policy of giving five years' leave.[3] The Qualification Directive sets out the residence rights which should be granted to recognised refugees and to other persons needing international protection throughout the Community.[4]

[1] *T v Immigration Officer* [1996] AC 742, [1996] 2 WLR 766, [1996] Imm AR 443 at 446, per Lord Mustill. See also Joan Fitzpatrick 'Revitalising the 1951 Refugee Convention' (1996) 9 Harvard Human Rights Journal 229 at 251: 'The most enduring contribution of the Convention is its elevation of *non-refoulement* to the status of an international norm.'
[2] The French attempt to circumvent domestic constraints on detention of asylum seekers by declaring the airport an 'international zone' was thwarted in *Amuur v France* (1996) 22 EHRR 533 where the detention was held to breach Art 5 of the ECHR. The UTIAC in *RR (refugee-safe third country) Syria* [2010] UKUT 422 (IAC) stated that if the Secretary of State has identified an alternative country of proposed removal in the context of asylum appeal proceedings, then an appeal should be allowed only where the Immigration Judge was satisfied not only that a claimant is a refugee from their country of nationality or habitual residence but

also that return to the alternative destination would be contrary to Art 3; however it was not for an Immigration Judge to go beyond the refusal letter if no other candidate country was identified [21]-[22]. However, see the discussion of the Qualification Directive in **12.10** below.

3   See HC 395, para 335; see also *Asylum applications: a brief guide to procedures in the UK* (on Home Office website) p 87. The government proposes to grant refugees temporary leave in the first instance, with a review after five years: see *Controlling our borders: Making migration work for Britain: Five year strategy for asylum and immigration*, Cm 6472, Feb 2005, para 39.

4   Qualification Directive, **12.3** fn 3 above, Arts 20–30.

12.9 An important issue in contemporary refugee law is whether the Refugee Convention has extra-territorial effect. The question has assumed great importance as more and more states employ measures, ranging from carrier sanctions and visa controls to airline liaison officers, to prevent undocumented passengers boarding transport in countries of origin, physical interception and return of asylum seekers on the high seas, and increasingly, agreements with countries of origin and transit to prevent asylum seekers leaving for western countries. UNHCR takes the view that the obligation of *non-refoulement*, which is 'progressively acquiring the character of a peremptory rule of international law', extends to all government agents acting in an official capacity, whether within or outside national territory. 'Given the practice of States to intercept persons at a great distance from their own territory, the international refugee protection regime would be rendered ineffective if States' agents abroad were able to act at variance with their obligations under international refugee law and human rights law.'[1] Similarly, Goodwin-Gill has trenchant criticism of the US Supreme Court's decision in *Sale v Haitian Centers Council*[2] upholding the policy of extra-territorial interception and return of Haitian asylum seekers to Haiti by US coastguards without any determination of their claims,[3] and Lord Bingham expressly distinguished *Sale*, where the asylum seekers were outside the country of their nationality and so *prima facie* entitled to protection under the Convention, from the situation in *European Roma Rights*, where pre-entry controls were carried out in the country of origin of the would-be asylum claimants.[4] Their Lordships did not however expressly state that asylum claimants who were outside their country of nationality but not at the borders of the UK should be allowed to continue their journey, and their judgements make no inroads on the carriers' liability and other provisions which prevent travel to the UK. The interception and forced return of asylum seekers on the seas to a country where they faced a real risk of torture, poor hygiene conditions, lack of appropriate medical care, precarious living conditions and a risk of refoulement has now been found incompatible with the ECHR in *Hirsi v Italy*.[5] Such activities fall within the jurisdiction of a Member State making it a matter for the Member State to ensure that the destination of removal offered sufficient guarantees to prevent the person concerned being refouled, whether or not they asked for asylum or themselves describe the risks faced abroad: such actions could contravene both ECHR, Article 3 and the prohibition on collective expulsion in Article 4 of Protocol No 4. In an earlier case the High Court concluded that, where a Tamil seeking asylum had been detained in Oman for using false documents to board a plane to come to the UK to claim asylum, the international obligation only arose when the claimant reached the territory of the state where asylum was claimed.[6] The courts have recognised the effect that carrier sanctions have on refugees' ability to seek asylum, but have not declared them unlawful.[7]

1 UNHCR ExCom Standing Committee, *Interception of asylum seekers and refugees*, 18th meeting, 9 June 2000, EC/50/SC/CRP.17, paras 21–23. See also UNHCR: *The trafficking and smuggling of refugees: the end game in European asylum policy?* July 2000; UNHCR ExCom 50th session, Note on International Protection, UN doc A/AC.96/914, 7 July 1999, in (1999) 11(3) IJRL 557.

2 113 S Ct 2549 (1993), in which the court by 8–1 held that the US Immigration Service had acted lawfully in intercepting a boatload of Haitian would-be asylum seekers in international waters and returning them to Haiti. Blackmun J, dissenting, found it 'extraordinary . . . that the executive, in disregard of the law, would take to the seas to intercept fleeing refugees and force them back to their persecutors – and that the court would strain to sanction that conduct'. The Inter-American Commission for Human Rights in Report No 51/96 preferred Blackmun J's dissenting judgment but in *European Roma Rights Centre* (fn 4 below) Lord Hope considered that the majority had been correct. For the EU's own interception and return project, Operation Ulysses, see Institute of Race Relations website (www.irr.org.uk).

3 Goodwin-Gill **12.5** fn 1 above, pp 142–144. See also (1994) 6(1) IJRL 68–109.

4 *European Roma Rights Centre v Immigration Officer at Prague Airport (United Nations High Comr for Refugees intervening)* [2004] UKHL 55, [2005] 2 WLR 1. The appellants and UNHCR argued that the pre-entry clearance regime which prevented an asylum seeker from reaching the border was contrary to the good faith obligation interpreted in the light of the object and purpose of the Refugee Convention.

5 *Hirsi Jamaa v Italy* 27765/09 – HEJUD [2012] ECHR 1845.

6 *R v Secretary of State for the Home Department, ex p Sritharan* [1992] Imm AR 184. It was held that there was no arguable case that the UK owed an obligation to issue a visa to enable him to continue his journey, despite the risk that Oman would return him to Sri Lanka without entertaining an asylum claim. For a discussion of diplomatic asylum and public international law see *R (on the application of B) v Secretary of State for Foreign and Commonwealth Affairs* [2004] EWCA Civ 1344, [2005] 2 WLR 618 (a challenge to the return to Australian custody of Afghan children who had escaped from detention in Australia and sought protection in the British embassy, decided with reference to the ECHR, not the Geneva Convention).

7 *European Roma Rights* (fn 4 above); *R v Secretary of State for the Home Department, ex p Yasine (or Yassine)* [1990] Imm AR 354, QBD; *R v Uxbridge Magistrates' Court, ex p Adimi* [1999] INLR 490; *R v Secretary of State for the Home Department, ex p Hoverspeed* [1999] INLR 591, at **15.100** below. On the compatibility of carrier sanctions with international law see Erika Feller 'Carrier Sanctions and International Law' (1989) 1 IJRL 48; A Ruff 'The United Kingdom Immigration (Carriers Liability) Act 1987' (1989) 1 IJRL 481. For the background to the enactment of the first carrier sanctions see Nicholas Blake 'The Road to *Sivakumaran*' in (1989) 3 INLP 1 at 12. For detailed consideration of carrier sanctions see **15.93** ff below.

12.10 Article 32 of the Refugee Convention gives refugees lawfully within the territory of a contracting state a right not to be expelled, save on grounds of national security or public order. Even then, expulsion is only possible following a decision reached in accordance with due process of law, and there must be a right of appeal and of representation before a competent authority. The UK provisions for deportation now give effect to this requirement, although only since 1998 in cases of removal on grounds relating to national security.[1] Article 32 does not apply to asylum seekers who claim asylum on arrival, since they cannot claim to be 'lawfully within the territory' until they have been given leave to enter.[2] It does not, therefore, prevent removal of potential refugees to safe third countries for determination of their claim elsewhere, or guarantee appeal rights to asylum seekers before removal.[3] In this respect, the Qualification Directive[4] provides greater protection than does the Refugee Convention in that a person who satisfies the definition of a refugee contained in the Qualification Directive is thereby entitled to refugee status.[5] The person need not show in addition that his or her removal from or being required to leave the country of asylum[6] would be in breach of the

Directive. So, for example, a woman who, upon claiming asylum on arrival was found to have well-founded fear of being persecuted for a Convention reason in Eritrea, her country of nationality, could be removed without breach of the Refugee Convention to Ethiopia, the country in which she had formerly lived because she was unable to show relevant risk in Ethiopia as well.[7] However, for the purposes of the Qualification Directive, well-founded fear in her country of nationality was sufficient by itself to entitle her to asylum.

1   Following the condemnation of the UK for lack of an effective remedy under Article 13 of the ECHR in *Chahal v United Kingdom* (1996) 23 EHRR 413, the government set up the Special Immigration Appeals Commission (SIAC) (Special Immigration Appeals Commission Act 1997) which hears all appeals, including asylum appeals, in which there is a national security element. See CHAPTER 19 below. See also *Saadi v Italy* (2009) 49 EHRR 730 at paras 117–123, [2008] Crim LR 898, ECtHR for the UK's unsuccessful intervention on the issue of national security.
2   *Bugdaycay v Secretary of State for the Home Department* [1987] AC 514 at 526, per Lord Bridge and *R (on the application of T) v Secretary of State for the Home Department* [2010] EWCA Civ 643.
3   See Nationality, Immigration and Asylum Act 2002, s 94 (and s 115 'transitional' provisions); Directive 2005/85/EC, art 39(3), and **12.165** below.
4   Council Directive 2004/83/EC.
5   Articles 2(c) and 13.
6   Whereas the Immigration Rules, inconsistently with the Qualification Directive, include the requirement that the person be at risk in the country to which he or she would be required to go – para 334(v).
7   *R (on the application of ST (Eritrea)) v Secretary of State for the Home Department* [2012] UKSC 12 where the Supreme Court held that notwithstanding that the appellant was a refugee, owing to having the requisite fear in her country of nationality, Eritrea, removing her would not breach the UK's obligations under the Convention because she had no such fear in Ethiopia, the country to which she was to be removed. The Supreme Court considered whether the fact that she had been granted temporary admission meant that she was lawfully within the territory so that her removal would be prohibited by art 32. Given that Immigration Act 1971, s 11 said that a person with temporary admission was deemed not to have entered the UK it could not be said of an asylum seeker with temporary admission that she was 'lawfully in the territory'. However, Lord Hope highlighted that the Qualification Directive did not apply to the case before the Court and noted that the Qualification Directive 'goes further in some respects than the Refugee Convention because, for example, it requires a residence permit to be issued as soon as possible when an applicant qualifies as a Refugee' [45].

12.11 Article 31(1) of the Refugee Convention precludes a state from imposing penalties on refugees coming directly from territories where they are persecuted on account of their illegal entry and presence, provided they report themselves to the authorities promptly.[1] A refugee is not an illegal entrant simply because he or she arrives without a passport or visa, or may have deceived the carrier in order to travel to the UK,[2] but lies told to the immigration officer on arrival are a different matter.[3] The meaning and application of Article 31(1) was considered by the Divisional Court in *R v Uxbridge Magistrates' Court, ex p Adimi*,[4] which concerned asylum seekers who had used false passports to enter the UK. Mr Adimi had claimed asylum after being refused leave to enter as a visitor on the basis of a false passport. He had come from Algeria via Italy and France (neither of which recognised persecution by non-state agents as giving rise to a Convention claim), and had spent several weeks in transit. He had been charged with a Forgery and Counterfeiting Act offence and sought judicial review of the magistrates' refusal to stay the proceedings because of Article 31(1) of the Refugee Convention. The other two applicants, Sorani and Kaziu, were Albanians who had entered the UK in transit to Canada, where they hoped to claim asylum. They had been apprehended boarding the onward flight with false passports and had been taken off. They had been similarly charged, convicted and sentenced to several months' imprisonment, which they had served. All three applicants were held to be covered by the protection of Article 31(1). The court held that where illegal entry or the use of false documents or delay can be attributed to a bona fide desire to seek asylum, whether here or elsewhere, that conduct should be covered by Article 31(1).[5] As to 'coming directly', some element of choice is, the court held, open to refugees as to where they may properly claim asylum. Any merely short-term stopover en route to such intended sanctuary cannot forfeit the protection of the Article. The main touchstones by which exclusion from protection should be judged are the length of stay in the intermediate country, the reasons for delaying there (even a substantial delay in an unsafe third country would be reasonable where the time was spent trying to acquire the means of travelling on), and whether or not the refugee sought or found there protection de jure or de facto from the persecution they were fleeing.[6] The requirement that the refugee presents himself or herself promptly does not require an asylum seeker to claim on arrival, so long as there is an intention to claim asylum within a short time of arrival having successfully secured entry on false documents.[7] The prohibition on penalties does not prevent the detention of asylum seekers,[8] nor does it prevent their being charged as long as they are not convicted.[9] There is now a statutory defence in section 31 of the Immigration and Asylum Act 1999 to protect asylum seekers against wrongful conviction of possession or use of false documents in breach of the Article: see CHAPTER 15, and in *Pepushi*[10] the Administrative Court, following the reconsideration of *Adimi* by the Court of Appeal in the *European Roma Rights Centre* case,[11] held that the prosecuting authority and the court were bound to apply the narrower provisions of section 31, even if this results in the UK being in breach of the Refugee Convention. We find this reading very difficult to reconcile with the House of Lords' judgment in *European Roma Rights*.[12] Many *bona fide* asylum seekers are now being charged, convicted and imprisoned for the new offence of failing to produce a travel document at a post-arrival interview – in many cases, we suggest, in flagrant breach of Article 31, because of the mis-match between its provisions and the requirements of the statutory defence.[13] Section 31 of the 1999 Act should not be read as limited to offences attributable to a refugee's entry into or presence in this country, but should provide immunity, if the other conditions are fulfilled, from the imposition of criminal penalties for offences attributable to the attempt of a refugee to leave the country in the continuing course of a flight from persecution even after a short stopover in transit.[14] Article 31(2) does not prevent return of asylum seekers to 'safe third countries' or consultation with the authorities in those countries to ensure that asylum will be offered there.[15]

---

1   On Art 31 of the Refugee Convention, see Hathaway and Neve 'Making International Refugee Law Relevant Again: A Proposal for Collectivized and Solution-Orientated Protection' (1997) 10 Harvard Human Rights J 115 at 161; Rodger Haines 'International Law and Refugees in New Zealand' [1999] NZLR 119 at 128–130.

2   *R v Naillie* [1993] AC 674; *Nzamba-Liloneo v Secretary of State for the Home Department* [1993] Imm AR 225, CA. For the offence under the Asylum and Immigration (Treatment of Claimants, etc) Act 2004, s 2 see text and fn 13 below, and see further **15.102**.

3   See illegal entry through deceiving the immigration officer at **17.23** below.

4   *R v Uxbridge Magistrates' Court, ex p Adimi* [1999] INLR 490. In *Qurbani, Re:* C-481/13 (17 July 2014, unreported) the CJEU recognised that, there being no provision in European Union law which makes a *renvoi* to Art 31, it had no jurisdiction to interpret Art 31.

5   *Adimi* above at 496.

6   *Adimi* above at 497.
7   *Adimi* above at 498.
8   See *A-G v E* [2000] 3 NZLR 257; see also A Davidson 'Article 31(2) of the Refugee Convention and its implementation in New Zealand: Is detention defensible?'.
9   See further **15.36** ff below.
10   *R (on the application of Pepushi) v Crown Prosecution Service* [2004] EWHC 798 (Admin), [2004] All ER (D) 129 (May), Thomas LJ and Silber J, who also held that the proper course to follow for unexceptional challenges to decisions to prosecute was to take the point in the criminal courts rather than bringing an application before the High Court. See also *R (on the application of Hussain) v Secretary of State for the Home Department* [2001] EWHC 555 (Admin), holding that Immigration and Asylum Act 1999, s 31 represented the UK's incorporation of art 31 and so should be followed.
11   *European Roma Rights Centre v Immigration Officer at Prague Airport (United Nations' High Comr for Refugees Intervening)* [2003] EWCA Civ 666, [2004] QB 811, [2003] 4 All ER 247, in which Simon Brown LJ doubted his decision in *Adimi* and Laws LJ denounced as constitutionally heretical the basis of the decision, ie incorporation by legitimate expectation of an international treaty.
12   The House of Lords in *European Roma Rights Centre* [2004] UKHL 55, [2005] 2 WLR 1 confirmed that the Convention was incorporated; see **12.6** fn 2 above.
13   Under the Asylum and Immigration (Treatment of Claimants, etc) Act 2004, s 2. See further **15.102** below. See also *Asfaw* in the House of Lords, addressed at **15.46** below.
14   The majority of the House of Lords in *R v Asfaw (UN High Comr for Refugees Intervening)* [2008] UKHL 31, [2008] 1 AC 1061.
15   Immigration and Asylum Act 1999, ss 11, 12; Nationality, Immigration and Asylum Act 2002, s 80; Asylum and Immigration (Treatment of Claimants, etc) Act 2004, s 33, Sch 3; HC 395, para 345.

United Nations High Commissioner for Refugees

12.12 The Office of the UN High Commissioner for Refugees (UNHCR) was established in 1951 pursuant to a UN General Assembly resolution.[1] The High Commissioner is called upon to provide international protection, under the auspices of the UN, to refugees falling within the competence of the Commissioner's office. This mandate covers all those who are outside their country of nationality or habitual residence and have or have had a well-founded fear of persecution for Refugee Convention reasons,[2] whether or not recognised as refugees. In some countries the determination of refugee status is performed by the UNHCR on behalf of the receiving state. This is not the case in the UK, save for a small number of 'quota' refugees,[3] but the views of the UK representative may be taken into account.[4] The Supreme Court has said that a decision by the UNHCR to recognise an individual as a refugee has 'considerable authority' because of 'the unique and matchless experience and expertise of the UNHCR, considerations of comity, legal diplomacy and the need for consistency of approach' so that 'substantial countervailing reasons are required to justify a different conclusion' to that reached by the UNHCR.[5] The Immigration Rules make provision for the UNHCR to have access to applicants for asylum, including those in detention, to have access to information about individual asylum claims and for the UNHCR to make representations to the Secretary of State about individual asylum claims.[6]

1   General Assembly Resolution 428, December 1950; Goodwin-Gill, **12.5** fn 1, p 241; Plender Documents **12.1** fn 2 above, p 81.
2   Statute of the Office of the UNHCR, arts 6A and 6B (Plender above, 82–83). See also the UK government's paper and the UNHCR reply in (1995) 7(1) IJRL 2 and *QD (Iraq) v Secretary of State for the Home Department* [2009] EWCA Civ 620, [2010] 2 All ER 971.

3 Under a scheme started in 2004, like that involving Vietnamese refugees in the 1960s and 70s, accepting for settlement a small number of refugees processed abroad by UNHCR. Although not all these will necessarily be Convention refugees, the government has expressed interest in developing this model in order to reduce the number of 'ad hoc' refugees. See House of Lords, EU Committee, 11th report 2003–4, 'Handling EU asylum claims: new approaches examined' (HL 74) for a critique of similar schemes involving extra-territorial processing.

4 Though see decisions such as the Tribunal in *AA (Exclusion Clause) Palestine* [2005] UKIAT 00104 (18 May 2005) showing the views of UNHCR will not necessarily prevail.

5 *IA v Secretary of State for the Home Department* [2014] UKSC 6, para 44-51. This decision calls into question the earlier decision of the Court of Appeal concerned with the status of UNHCR guidelines about risk in a particular country. The Court of Appeal rejected the argument that such guidelines should be followed unless there are cogent reasons for not doing so, saying instead that the weight to be given to them was a matter for the decision maker based on the 'intrinsic quality' of the guidelines rather than the status of their author: *HF (Iraq) v Secretary of State for the Home Department* [2013] EWCA Civ 1276, para 44.

6 HC 395, para 358C inserted to implement Article 21 of Council Directive 2005/85/EC on minimum standards on procedures in Member States for granting and withdrawing refugee status. See also *MM (Status of recognised mandate refugees) Iran* [2009] UKAIT 00029 (20 July 2009).

12.13 The statute setting up the Office of the High Commissioner for Refugees provides that, in the exercise of his or her functions, the Commissioner shall request the opinion of an advisory committee on refugees in matters of difficulty.[1] The advisory committee is composed of representatives of states selected by the Economic and Social Council of the UN 'on the basis of their demonstrated interest in and devotion to the solution of the refugee problem'.[2] The advisory committee is called the Executive Committee of the Programme of the United Nations High Commissioner for Refugees, and is known as ExCom. Its recommendations, conclusions and reports provide valuable guidance on the interpretation of the Refugee Convention and the procedures to be adopted. The collected conclusions are published by the UNHCR. In 1979, at the request of Ex Com, a *Handbook on Procedures and Criteria for Determining Refugee Status* was produced. The *Handbook* is frequently referred to and approved by the immigration judiciary and the courts,[3] and should form part of the equipment of any lawyer practising in this area of immigration law.[4] In addition, UNHCR periodically produces Guidelines on aspects of international protection which are giving rise to difficulty or controversy. Recent issues have covered internal relocation, religion and gender-based claims, the cessation and exclusion clauses and the meaning of 'particular social group' within the refugee definition.[5] The House of Lords has approved significant parts of the UNHCR *Guidelines on International Protection* relating to internal relocation[6] and membership of a particular social group as a Convention reason for fear of being persecuted.[7]

1 See Statute of the Office of UNHCR, Ch 1, para 1; Plender Documents, **12.1** fn 2 above, p 82.

2 Statute of the Office of the UNHCR, para 4.

3 See eg *T v Immigration Officer* [1996] AC 742, [1996] 2 All ER 865, [1996] 2 WLR 766, [1996] Imm AR 443, HL; *Adan v Secretary of State for the Home Department* [1999] 1 AC 293; *R v Secretary of State for the Home Department, ex p Adan* [2001] INLR 44, HL.

4 The *Handbook* is reproduced in *Butterworths Immigration Law Service*, 2C[73] and is available from the UNHCR (on its website, and see Appendix 2). ExCom's conclusions are published in booklet form; many of them are set out as appendices to Goodwin-Gill **12.5** fn 1 above and all are available on the UNHCR website.

5 Guidelines on international protection No 1: Gender-related persecution within the context of Article 1A(2) of the 1951 Convention and/or the 1967 Protocol relating to the status of refugees (HCR/GIP/02/01) 7 May 2002; No 2: 'Membership of a particular social group' within the context of Article 1A(2) of the 1951 Convention and/or the 1967 Protocol relating

to the status of refugees (HCR/GIP/02/02) 7 May 2002; No 3: Cessation of refugee status under Article 1C(5) and (6) of the 1951 Convention (the 'ceased circumstances' clauses) (HCR/GIP/003/03) 10 February 2003; No 4: 'Internal flight' or the 'internal relocation alternative' within the context of Article 1A(2) of the 1951 Convention and/or the 1967 Protocol relating to the status of refugees (HCR/GIP/03/04) 23 July 2003; No 5: The application of the exclusion clause, Article 1F of the 1951 Convention (HCR/GIP/03/05) 4 September 2003; No 6: Religion-based refugee claims under Article 1A(2) of the 1951 Convention and/or the 1967 Protocol relating to the status of refugees (HCR/GIP/04/06) 28 April 2004. UNHCR also produce important publications from time to time such as 'Beyond Proof – Credibility Assessment in EU Asylum Systems' published as part of the project Towards Improved Asylum Decision-Making in the EU (also known as the CREDO project)

6   *Januzi v Secretary of State for the Home Department; Hamid v Same; Gaafar v Same; Mohammed v Same* [2006] UKHL 5, [2006] 3 All ER 305, [2006] 2 WLR 397.

7   *Fornah v Secretary of State for the Home Department* [2006] UKHL 46, [2007] 1 AC 412, [2007] 1 All ER 671.

12.14 The UNHCR materials do not have the force of law or form part of the Refugee Convention. Neither the ExCom recommendations and conclusions nor the *Handbook* have been incorporated into UK Immigration Rules, and therefore, although they can provide guidance, they will not override express terms of the Immigration Acts or Rules, and will not be the subject of construction and application by the courts.[1] In *Robinson* the Court of Appeal described the *Handbook* as particularly helpful:

'as a guide to what is the international understanding of the Convention obligations, as worked out in practice, based on the knowledge accumulated by the High Commissioner's Office. This knowledge was derived, inter alia, from the practice of states in regard to the determination of refugee status, exchanges of views between the office and the competent authorities of contracting states, and the literature devoted to the subject over the previous quarter of a century.'[2]

The provisions are general rather than specific, and tend to be more exhortatory in tone than directive, although they are nonetheless an authoritative guide to the proper interpretation of the Refugee Convention.[3] The duty of co-operation with the UNHCR imposed by Article 35 of the Convention does not translate into a legally enforceable duty to comply with the recommendations of the High Commissioner and the Executive Committee.[4] The Secretary of State is entitled to have regard to them when deciding whether the UK is an appropriate country of asylum, and it is 'an important source of law, though not having the force of law',[5] but there is no requirement to follow them.[6] In short, the UNHCR materials are useful and authoritative aids to interpretation of the Convention and may be relevant to the exercise of a broad discretion, although not themselves the source of obligations and duties.

1   See *Bugdaycay v Secretary of State for the Home Department* [1987] AC 514 at 524, per Lord Bridge. See also the arguments of the intervener in *R v Secretary of State for the Home Department, ex p Sivakumaran* [1988] AC 958, and at 1000–1001, per Lord Goff, and observations in *T v Immigration Officer* [1996] AC 742; *Adan v Secretary of State for the Home Department* [1999] 1 AC 293; *R v Immigration Appeal Tribunal, ex p Shah* [1999] 2 AC 629; *Danian v Secretary of State for the Home Department* [2000] Imm AR 96 at 120.

2   *Robinson (Anthonypillai Francis) v Secretary of State for the Home Department and Immigration Appeal Tribunal* [1997] Imm AR 568, CA at 11. See also, to similar effect, *R v Secretary of State for the Home Department, ex p Adan; R v Secretary of State for the Home Department, ex p Subaskaran; R v Secretary of State for the Home Department, ex p Aitseguer* [1999] 3 WLR 1274 at 1296.

3   See observations of Purchas LJ in *Alsawaf v Secretary of State for the Home Department* [1988] Imm AR 410 at 419, CA.

⁴ This argument was advanced and rejected in *R v Secretary of State for the Home Department, ex p Mehari* [1994] QB 474, [1994] Imm AR 151.

⁵ *T v Secretary of State for the Home Department* [1996] AC 742; *MM (Status of recognised mandate refugees) Iran* [2009] UKAIT 00029 (20 July 2009).

⁶ See *Miller v Immigration Appeal Tribunal* [1988] Imm AR 358, CA; *R v Secretary of State for the Home Department, ex p Yasine (or Yassine)* [1990] Imm AR 354, QBD. See further *Sepet v Secretary of State for the Home Department* [2001] EWCA Civ 681; [2003] UKHL 15, [2003] 3 All ER 304. In *Golfa v Secretary of State for the Home Department* [2005] EWHC 2282 (Admin), [2005] All ER (D) 348 (Jun), Moses J, citing *Mhute v Secretary of State for the Home Department* [2003] EWCA Civ 1029, [2003] All ER (D) 229 (Jun), held that the decision maker was obliged to have regard to UNHCR recommendations relating to removal to a particular country but was not bound to follow them. See also *NM (Somalia)* [2005] UKIAT 00076 where the Tribunal discussed its approach to UNHCR material.

Determination of status

12.15 The Refugee Convention sets out no procedures for the determination of refugee status. It is left to contracting states to establish appropriate procedures having regard to their particular constitutional and administrative structures.¹ The wide variation in what was believed appropriate by different contracting states led the Executive Committee to formulate basic requirements for a fair procedure:²

(i)   the official (immigration officer or border police) receiving the claim should have clear instructions on how to deal with cases engaging international obligations, must act in accordance with the principle of *non-refoulement* and refer the case to a higher authority;

(ii) the applicant should receive necessary guidance on procedure;

(iii) a clearly identified authority should have responsibility for examining requests and taking first-instance decisions;

(iv) the applicant should be given the necessary facilities, including a competent interpreter, for submitting the case, and should have the right to contact a UNHCR representative (and be informed of it);

(v)   if recognised as a refugee, the applicant should be informed and issued with appropriate documentation;

(vi) if not, there should be a right to appeal either to the same or a different authority (administrative or judicial);

(vii) both the claim (unless established as clearly abusive) and the appeal should be suspensive.

The EU Procedures Directive³ provides for an effective remedy whereby the national court can review the merits of a decision to reject an asylum claim whether for substantive, formal or procedural reasons.⁴ However, the entitlement is to a remedy before a judicial body, not to two or more appellate tiers⁵ and in the absence of a right of appeal to the tribunal, judicial review is said to be an effective and sufficient remedy.⁶

¹ UNHCR *Handbook*, **12.13** fn 4 above, para 189. In Europe that discretion is circumscribed, to some extent, by Council Directive 2005/85/EC on minimum standards on procedures in Member States for granting and withdrawing refugee status: however, it gives a wide discretion as to permissible processes.

² At its 28th session in 1977: see UNHCR *Handbook* above, para 192. It may be that the demands of fairness are more rigorous a quarter of a century on.

³ Council Directive (2005/85/EC) of 1 December 2005 on minimum standards on procedures in Member States for granting and withdrawing refugee status, art 39.

4   Case C-69/10 *Samba Diouf v Ministre du Travail, de l'Emploi et de l'Immigration*
    [2012] 1 CMLR 204 (Second Chamber, CJEU).
5   *Diouf v Minstre du Travail, de l'Emploi et de l'Immigration.*
6   *TN (Afghanistan) v Secretary of State for the Home Department* [2013] EWCA Civ 1609.

Legislation relating to asylum in the UK

12.16 The UK had a long history of affording asylum before the 1951 Convention and its 1967 Protocol, and both the Extradition Act 1870 and the
Aliens Act 1905 contained provisions exempting respectively political offences
from extradition and political and religious refugees from refusal of entry.[1] The
express enactment of these provisions in 1870 and 1905 meant that it was the
UK courts rather than the Secretary of State who decided whether an offence
was political or not. This has remained the practice in extradition cases.[2]
However, when the Aliens Restriction Acts 1914 and 1919 replaced the
1905 Act, the exemption for refugees was not repeated, and subsequent
immigration statutes followed this course until 1993. This omission gave rise
to a body of jurisprudence that refugee status was not a matter for the courts
but only the Secretary of State,[3] an attitude which passed into the modern
decisions under more recent immigration laws.[4] In *Bugdaycay*[5] the House of
Lords made it clear that in judicial review proceedings whether a person was
a 'refugee' was a question for the Secretary of State and not a matter of
jurisdictional fact or law for the courts.[6] However, even before the Asylum and
Immigration Appeals Act 1993 restored the statutory recognition of refugees,
the appellate authorities could review the merits of certain decisions of the
Secretary of State relating to asylum.[7]

1   Extradition Act 1870, s 3(1); Aliens Act 1905, s 1(3); see also Fugitive Offenders Act 1967,
    s 5(1) and Extradition Act 1989, ss 6, 24. For a full history of policy in this respect see
    Dummett and Nicol *Subjects, Citizens, Aliens and Others* (1990), in particular, chapters 6 and
    8.
2   See *Cheng v Governor of Pentonville Prison* [1973] AC 931; *R v Governor of Brixton Prison,
    ex p Kolczynski* [1955] 1 QB 540 and **12.51** below.
3   See eg *R v Chiswick Police Station Superintendent, ex p Sacksteder* [1918] 1 KB 578, CA; *R
    v Secretary of State for Home Affairs, ex p Duke of Chateau Thierry* [1917] 1 KB 922, CA;
    R v Zausmer (1911) 7 Cr App Rep 41; *R v Governor of Brixton Prison, ex p Sarno* [1916]
    2 KB 742.
4   See *Ali (D M) v Immigration Appeal Tribunal* [1973] Imm AR 33 at 35, CA, following *R v
    Governor of Brixton Prison, ex p Soblen* [1963] 2 QB 243, [1962] 3 All ER 641, CA.
5   *Bugdaycay v Secretary of State for the Home Department* [1987] AC 514.
6   cf *R (on the application of Nasseri) v Secretary of State for the Home Department* [2009]
    UKHL 23 where Lord Hoffmann stated at [12]-[14] that, on a judicial review when the
    challenge is based upon an alleged infringement of a Human Rights Convention right, the
    position was different from normal domestic judicial review proceedings (where the court is
    usually concerned with whether the decision-maker reached his decision in the right way
    rather than whether he got what the court might think to be the right answer): in these cases
    there must be a rigorous audit of the correctness of the decision itself.
7   There was an in-country appeal against refusal of leave to enter (ie if the passenger held an
    entry clearance), or a variation or a deportation appeal under ss 13–15 of the Immigration Act
    1971, if the appellant had claimed asylum.

12.17 Since the 1993 Act more legislation has come onto the statute books
addressing asylum. The Asylum and Immigration Act 1996 removed in-
country appeals against decisions to remove asylum seekers to 'safe third
countries', and created a so-called 'white list' of 'safe' countries of origin,
whose nationals had restricted appeal rights.[1] The Immigration and Asylum

Act 1999 introduced human rights appeals and abolished the 'white list', but introduced a presumption of safety in the EU and in designated third countries.[2] The Nationality, Immigration and Asylum Act 2002 re-introduced a 'white list' of safe countries of origin and removed suspensive appeals from applicants whose claims the Secretary of State deemed 'clearly unfounded',[3] which, together with the presumption of safety, removed the possibility of appeal from thousands. The 1999 and 2002 Acts also removed asylum claimants from mainstream welfare benefits and, in many cases, from all support (see CHAPTER 14), a process continued and extended by the Asylum and Immigration (Treatment of Claimants, etc) Act 2004 (AI(TC)A 2004). The 2004 Act also criminalised asylum claimants unable to produce a travel document and those refusing to cooperate with arrangements for their removal, and extended the 'safe third country' provisions to many more countries and parts of countries.[4] The Immigration, Asylum and Nationality Act 2006 (IAN 2006) made further provision about asylum appeals and asylum support; it dictates how Article 1F(c) of the Refugee Convention (exclusion for acts contrary to the principles and purposes of the UN) is to be construed and applied and how issues relating to exclusion from refugee status and expulsion of refugees are to be detemined by the Tribunal.[5] The Criminal Justice and Immigration Act 2008 sets out provisions for 'special immigration status' which make particular provision preventing the grant of leave to remain to those excluded from refugee status or who have been deprived of the benefit of the prohibition on *refoulement* due to their dangerousness.[6] The Borders, Citizenship and Immigration Act 2009 contains various procedural developments, such as the extension of the information sharing duties of government departments.[7]

[1] Asylum and Immigration Act 1996, ss 1, 2, referring to and amending Asylum and Immigration Appeals Act 1993, Sch 2, para 5.
[2] Immigration and Asylum Act 1999, s 11, reproduced in the Nationality, Immigration and Asylum Act 2002, s 80.
[3] Nationality, Immigration and Asylum Act 2002, s 94.
[4] AI(TC)A 2004, ss 2, 35, 33 and Sch 3.
[5] IAN 2006, ss 1, 3, 9, 13, 43–45, 54, 55.
[6] Criminal Justice and Immigration Act 2008, Pt 10: commencement still awaited as at June 2010.
[7] Borders, Citizenship and Immigration Act 2009, s 21.

12.18 During the 1960s the first Immigration Rules were published and, after representations from the UNHCR, these Rules made reference to asylum and refugees, although not to the 1951 Convention. Considerable advance was achieved in 1980 with the first reference in the Rules to the 1951 Convention and 1967 Protocol. But before 1993 there was tension between the provisions of the Rules giving primacy to the 1951 Convention and the Immigration Act 1971, which made no reference to the Convention and whose provisions were in some respects incompatible with it.[1] People who claimed asylum on arrival and who had no entry clearance had only an out-of-country appeal exercisable on return to the place of feared persecution, and so relied on judicial review for their remedy against removal.[2] The Asylum and Immigration Appeals Act 1993 gave statutory effect to the primacy of the Convention in the Immigration Rules,[3] and the rules made since the passing of the AIAA 1993 have attempted to provide a coherent structure in which asylum applications are considered and determined.[4] In addition, since 1998 the Asylum Directorate's instructions to caseworkers (ADI) (now Asylum Policy Instructions or API) and Guidance for Asylum Team Case Owners have been published, providing a yet more detailed framework within which decisions are taken.[5]

[1] See *R v Immigration Appeal Tribunal, ex p Muruganandarajah* [1983] Imm AR 141, QBD, affirmed on appeal [1986] Imm AR 382, CA, for absence of rights of appeal in deportation cases following court recommendations.

[2] See *R v Secretary of State for the Home Department, ex p Sivakumaran* [1988] AC 958 where asylum seekers were unsuccessful in judicial review but succeeded on appeal to an adjudicator after removal to Sri Lanka where a number were tortured: *Secretary of State for the Home Department v Immigration Appeal Tribunal* [1990] Imm AR 492. In *Vilvarajah v United Kingdom* (1991) 14 EHRR 248 the ECtHR held, reversing the Commission, that judicial review was an effective remedy against the refusal of asylum for the purposes of art 13 of the ECHR. The decision surprised the British government, which had decided to concede in-country appeal rights to asylum seekers in anticipation of losing on this point.

[3] Asylum and Immigration Appeals Act 1993, s 2.

[4] HC 395, Parts 11, 11A and 11; Asylum and Immigration Appeals Act 1993. Laws J in *R v Secretary of State for the Home Department, ex p Mehari* [1994] QB 474, [1994] Imm AR 151, QBD had regard to the Immigration Rules and the statutory instruments 'intended to dovetail with the new regime' in interpreting the 1993 Act.

[5] The API, which are regularly updated, and the Guidance for Asylum Team Case Owners are available on the Home Office website (www.ind.homeoffice.gov.uk/) and in hard copy at selected addresses (see Appendix 2).

12.19 People who have had an asylum claim turned down generally have a right of appeal prior to removal on the ground that to remove them would breach the UK's obligations under the Refugee Convention.[1] For third country cases, where the asylum claim is not entertained, see **12.139** ff below. The appeal deals with the question of whether the appellant is a refugee. Where refugee status has been refused but the claimant has been granted leave to enter or remain, an appeal against the refusal of asylum is possible only where the leave granted exceeds one year in total.[2] Time there was when appellants could appeal to an adjudicator and then to the Immigration Appeal Tribunal, but the Asylum and Immigration (Treatment of Claimants etc) Act 2004 abolished the two-tier immigration appellate authority, replacing it with a single-tier Asylum and Immigration Tribunal (AIT);[3] that unitary system reverted to two tiers with the unification of the Tribunal system.[4] Repeated applications for asylum on the same basis will not trigger a fresh right of appeal.[5] But the right of an asylum seeker to make a fresh application for asylum has been recognised by the Court of Appeal in *R v Secretary of State for the Home Department, ex p Onibiyo*[6] and is reflected in paragraph 353 of HC 395. The new rule no longer stipulates that the new material must have been previously unavailable, perhaps because if the material is sufficiently compelling it would clearly breach Convention obligations to refuse to look at it.[7]

[1] Under Nationality, Immigration and Asylum Act 2002, s 82 (in force 1 April 2003) the appeal lies against the immigration decision, and the Refugee Convention provides a ground of appeal. Those with leave to enter or remain in another capacity when they claim asylum will not have a right of appeal if their original leave is still extant at the date of decision: see s 82(2)(d), and will have to await a decision to remove them to have an appeal (under s 82(2)(g). The in-country appeal is provided by s 92(4) (unless the Secretary of State has issued a third country certificate under Sch 3 to the AI(TC)A 2004 (or, more controversially, where the Secretary of State certifies that the claim is clearly unfounded under NIAA 2002, s 94 (as amended by AI(TC)A 2004, s 27): see **12.175** ff below).

[2] Nationality, Immigration and Asylum Act 2002, s 83, see **12.174** below. This will apply where, for example, a person is not recognised as a refugee but granted Humanitarian Protection or Discretionary Leave, see generally the APIs on Humanitarian Protection and on Discretionary Leave. The restriction on the right of appeal is difficult to justify in light of the

importance of recognition of the status of refugee, and the advantages of refugee status over subsidiary protection: see eg *Adan v Secretary of State for the Home Department* [1997] Imm AR 251 at 256, CA per Simon Brown LJ; *Saad v Secretary of State for the Home Department; Diriye v Secretary of State for the Home Department; Osorio v Secretary of State for the Home Department* [2001] EWCA Civ 2008, [2002] INLR 34. See also Qualification Directive, **12.3** fn 3 above, arts 20–30, where the gap between the two kinds of protection is fully exposed.

3   AI(TC)A 2004, s 26.

4   See CHAPTERS **19–21** generally.

5   Nationality, Immigration and Asylum Act 2002, s 96, as amended by AI(TC)A 2004, s 30 from 1 October 2004; see 13.138 below. In *R v Secretary of State for the Home Department, ex p Kazmi* [1995] Imm AR 73, Dyson J held that *Kalunga (Lemba) v Secretary of State for the Home Department* [1994] Imm AR 585, CA bound him to apply a judicial review approach to the Secretary of State's decision as to whether a further decision could be made, generating a further right of appeal. An asylum application made after a prior refusal of leave to enter on some other ground must trigger a fresh refusal of leave to enter, however: HC 395, para 332 and *Kazmi* (above). On the judicial review approach to whether further representations constitute a fresh claim see also *Cakabay v Secretary of State for the Home Department (No 2)* [1999] Imm AR 176, [1998] INLR 623, CA. *Nassir v Secretary of State for the Home Department* [1999] Imm AR 250; *R v Secretary of State for the Home Department, ex p Bell* [2000] Imm AR 396.

6   [1996] Imm AR 370, CA. The test for a fresh application is whether the claim advanced is significantly different from the material previously considered, ie if the content has not already been considered, and taken together with the previously considered material, create a realistic prospect of success: HC 395, para 353 (inserted by HC 1112, 18 October 2004, in place of para 346, which was deleted). The evidence must be apparently credible though not uncontrovertible: *R v Secretary of State for the Home Department v Boybeyi* [1997] Imm AR 491, CA; and see also *R (on the application of BA (Nigeria)) v Secretary of State for the Home Department* [2009] UKSC 7, [2010] AC 444, [2010] 2 All ER 95. See **12.185** below.

7   A failure by advisers to obtain evidence earlier did not make the evidence 'previously unavailable' under the previous provision: *Kabala (Mehmet) v Secretary of State for the Home Department* [1997] Imm AR 517. But 'unavailability' includes psychiatric inability to give evidence: *R v Secretary of State for the Home Department, ex p Ejon (Molly)* [1998] INLR 195. See also *Haile v Immigration Appeal Tribunal* [2001] EWCA Civ 663, [2002] Imm AR 170, [2002] INLR 283, and discussion of fresh evidence in *E v Secretary of State for the Home Department* [2004] EWCA Civ 49, [2004] QB 1044, [2004] 2 WLR 1351.

12.20 There may be an appeal against the decision to remove the appellant to a safe third country without considering the asylum claim,[1] although such appeals have become very rare; in most cases appeal is now precluded by statute.[2] Under the 1999 and 2002 Acts, EU Member States to which it was proposed to send an asylum seeker under standing arrangements benefitted from a statutory presumption that they were safe and would not return the appellant elsewhere save in accordance with the Refugee Convention.[3] These presumptions of safety are extended to other specified states, and to the Human Rights Convention, by the provisions of the 2004 Act, which dramatically reduces the possibilities for appeals (both in-country and out of country) in 'third country' cases.[4]

1   For 'safe third country' removals see **12.139** ff below.

2   AI(TC)A 2004, Sch 3 (in force 1 October 2004 in respect of all claims certified on or after that date, SI 2004/2523 art 3) removes appeal rights on asylum and quasi-asylum human rights grounds in respect of removals to states deemed safe for the purposes of the Refugee and/or Human Rights Conventions, and on non-asylum human rights grounds (eg grounds depending on illness or the presence of family members) where the Secretary of State certifies the claim clearly unfounded, which is the 'default position'; see **12.145** ff.

3   Immigration and Asylum Act 1999, s 11 (as substituted by Nationality, Immigration and Asylum Act 2002, s 80), inserted after the Court of Appeal held, in *R v Secretary of State for the Home Department, ex p Adan; R v Secretary of State for the Home Department, ex p Subaskaran; R v Secretary of State for the Home Department, ex p Aitseguer* [1999] INLR

362, that the French and German interpretation of the Refugee Convention was unlawful in not recognising persecution from non-state agents. The decision has since been upheld by the House of Lords at [2001] INLR 44.

4 AI(TC)A 2004, s 33, Sch 3, repealing and replacing the previous 'third-country' regime as from 1 October 2004. The provisions preclude appeals inconsistent with the presumptions of safety (under the Refugee Convention, the Human Rights Convention or both) which apply to EU Member States, to other States specified by order of the Secretary of State and to states certified by him as safe for individuals. See further **12.147** ff below. See *NS v Secretary of State for the Home Department (Amnesty International Ltd and the AIRE Centre (Advice on Individual Rights in Europe) (UK))*: C-411/10[2013] QB 102, [2012] All ER (EC) 1011, ECJ, however, demonstrating that these deeming provisions contravene European Union law, which 'precludes the application of a conclusive presumption that the Member State which Article 3(1) of Regulation No 343/2003 indicates as responsible observes the fundamental rights of the European Union.'

The European Union Qualification Directive

12.21 Article 63(1) of the Treaty Establishing the European Community required the Council to adopt 'measures on asylum, in accordance with the Geneva Convention . . . and the Protocol . . . relating to the status of refugees and other relevant treaties'. These measures were to include 'minimum standards with respect to the qualification of nationals of third countries as refugees'.[1] Pursuant to that provision, the Council made the 'Qualification Directive'[2] which entered into force on the 20th day following its publication (on 30 September 2004) in the *Official Journal of the European Union*.[3] Article 38(1) of the Directive required Member States to 'bring into force the laws, regulations and administrative provisions necessary to comply with this Directive before 10 October 2006'. The UK has sought to comply with that obligation by means of the Refugee or Person in Need of International Protection (Qualification) Regulations[4] and by amendments to the Immigration Rules.[5] The Regulations apply to any application for asylum and any immigration appeal made or pending on or after 9 October 2006.[6] Although the amended Immigration Rules do not make express provision as to the time from which they apply, the President of the AIT issued a *Practice Direction* on 9 October 2006 saying that the rules would be taken as applying to all applications and appeals pending on 9 October 2006 and thereafter: although given that the Directive is directly effective, this was no more than a reminder of the legal reality.[7] The Practice Direction also provided that the Tribunal would treat the grounds of appeal in appeals pending on 9 October 2006 as including such grounds as are needed to enable consideration of matters under the Regulations and Rules. Some of the specific provisions contained in the Directive and the implementing rules and Regulations are referred to below.

1 Article 63(1)(c) of that Treaty; however, under the Lisbon Treaty, this becomes Article 88, which if anything intensifies the obligation to respect the Refugee Convention: 'This policy must be in accordance with the Geneva Convention of 28 July 1951' (Art 78(1)).

2 Council Directive 2004/83/EC of 29 April 2004 on minimum standards for the qualification and status of third country nationals or stateless persons as refugees or as persons who otherwise need international protection and the content of the protection granted. The literature on the Directive includes: Anja Klug 'Harmonization of Asylum in the European Union – Emergence of an EU Refugee System?' (2004) 47 GYIL; *UNHCR Annotated Comments on the EC Council Directive 2004/83/EC of 29 April 2004* (Jan 2005); Jane McAdam 'The European Union Qualification Directive: The Creation of a Subsidiary Protection Regime' (2005) IJRL 461; Helene Lambert 'The EU Asylum Qualification Directive, its Impact on the Jurisprudence of the United Kingdom and International Law' (2006) 55 ICLQ 161.

[3]   Qualification Directive, art 39. The European Commission in COM(2009) 551 and COM(2009) 554/4 proposes a recast version of Directives 2004/83 and 2005/85; and by letter of 25 January 2010, Chief Executive of the UK Borders Agency, Lin Homer, wrote to the Refugee Council explaining that the UK would not be opting in to the proposed recast measures.

[4]   SI 2006/2525.

[5]   CM 6918, amending HC 395.

[6]   SI 2006/2525, reg 1(2).

[7]   Stanley Bunton LJ in EN (Serbia) v *Secretary of State for the Home Department* [2009] EWCA Civ 630 at [62], [2010] 3 WLR 182, (2009) Times, 24 July.

12.22 Among the issues that are likely to arise in the interpretation and application of the Qualification Directive are the following. First of all there is the issue of the relationship between the criteria for qualification for refugee status contained in the Directive and those contained in the Refugee Convention, as interpreted[1] by the courts in the UK. The Directive acknowledges the Geneva Convention and Protocol as the 'cornerstone of the international legal regime for the protection of refugees'[2] and its substantive provisions quite closely reflect the Geneva Convention. However, the Directive does not purport to interpret refugee status as defined under the Geneva Convention; instead it contains an autonomous definition of a refugee[3] and imposes on Member States an obligation under the Directive rather than the Convention to recognise refugee status.[4] The Directive expressly recognises Member States' other obligations under international law to avoid *refoulement*[5] and confer refugee status.[6] Moreover, the purpose of the Directive is to set minimum standards[7] and it expressly acknowledges that Member States may introduce or retain more favourable standards.[8] It would seem, therefore, that in circumstances where the UK's interpretation of the Geneva Convention would lead to recognition of refugee status, such status would have to be recognised even if the person did not qualify under the Directive. However, many of the provisions in the Directive are expressed in mandatory terms.[9] Article 3 which permits Member States to introduce or retain more favourable standards contains the proviso 'in so far as those standards are compatible with this Directive'. It might be argued that where the UK's interpretation of the Geneva Convention is more generous than any of the mandatory requirements of the Directive, the UK interpretation will have to succumb to the Directive. Resolution of this issue is likely to entail consideration of whether a minimum standards Directive can operate so as to impose maximum standards; whether the proviso, contextually and purposively construed can legitimately limit the protection that would otherwise be provided by the UK and whether the proviso which applies to the standards for qualification for refugee status under the Directive has any application at all to the standards for qualification under the separate Geneva Convention regime. This issue may need to be decided in relation to issues such as the capacity of non-state bodies to provide protection capable of obviating the need for refugee status,[10] whether membership of a particular social group requires *both* a shared, innate characteristic *and* social perception of group membership,[11] and the arguably higher threshold for persecution that the Qualification Directive imposes compared to that accepted as applicable under the Refugee Convention.[12] Decisions of the UK courts on the Refugee Convention that represent the domestic last word on the subject may yet require revisiting if the CJEU reconsiders some of their more controversial findings: for example the approach to the plight of civilians in armed conflicts[13] and the protection test,[14] both of which have been the subject of detailed criticism elsewhere.[15] Only the ECJ, not the domestic court, can adjudicate upon the vires of the Directive[16] but that need not prevent the domestic court from finding that a person is entitled to protection under the Refugee Convention even if not under the Directive.

1　The Convention, has a single, autonomous meaning that is authoritatively determined by the court: *R v Secretary of State for the Home Department, ex p Adan* [2001] 2 AC 477, [2001] 1 All ER 593, [2000] All ER (D) 2357, HL.

2　Qualification Directive, preamble (3).

3　Qualification Directive, art 2(c). The clearest difference between the Geneva Convention definition and the definition in the Directive is that is that the latter applies only to third country, ie non-EU nationals and stateless people. However, Article 9 is expressed as being interpretive of 'persecution within the meaning of Article 1A of the Geneva Convention.

4　Qualification Directive, Article 2(d).

5　Qualification Directive, Article 21(1).

6　Qualification Directive, Article 20(1).

7　Consolidated Version of the Treaty Establishing the European Community, art 63(1)(c).

8　Qualification Directive, preamble (8) and art 3.

9　Eg Qualification Directive, art 7: 'Protection can be provided by . . . '; art 9(1): 'Acts of persecution . . . must'; art 10(1): 'member states shall . . . '; art 12(1) and (2): 'A third country national or a stateless person is excluded . . . '.

10　Qualification Directive, art 7(1)(b) which mandates a lower standard of refugee protection than does the Geneva Convention as interpreted in *Gardi v Secretary of State for the Home Department* [2002] EWCA Civ 750, [2002] 1 WLR 2755, [2003] Imm AR 39 and *Vallaj v Special Adjudicator* [2001] EWCA Civ 782, [2001] INLR 342.

11　As per the Qualification Directive, art 10(1)(d), by contrast to the position under the Geneva Convention as interpreted in the UK where the two are alternative tests. *K v Secretary of State for the Home Department; Fornah v Secretary of State for the Home Department* [2006] UKHL 46, [2007] 1 AC 412, [2007] 1 All ER 671.

12　See *SH (Palestinian Territories) v Secretary of State for the Home Department* [2008] EWCA Civ 1150, [2008] All ER (D) 221 (Oct).

13　*Secretary of State for the Home Department v Adan* [1999] 1 AC 293, [1998] Imm AR 338, [1998] INLR 325, HL.

14　*Horvath v Secretary of State for the Home Department* [2000] INLR 239, HL.

15　In New Zealand, the Refugee Status Appeal Authority declined to follow Horvath, stating 'this interpretation of the Refugee Convention is at odds with the fundamental obligation of non-refoulement' in Refugee Appeal No 71427/99 and at [66] held that the proper approach to the question of state protection is to enquire whether the protection available from the state will reduce the risk of serious harm to below the level of well-foundedness, or, as it is understood in New Zealand, to below the level of a real chance of serious harm; *Adan* has been subjected to a cogent critique in Refugee Appeal No 71462/99 (RSAA, NZ) and the High Court of Australia in *Minister for Immigration and Multicultural Affairs v Ibrahim (Haji)* [2000] HCA 55, see eg *AM & AM (armed conflict: risk categories)* Rev 1 Somalia CG [2008] UKAIT 00091 at [72].

16　*EN (Serbia) v Secretary of State for the Home Department* [2009] EWCA Civ 630, [2010] 3 WLR 182, (2009) Times, 24 July.

THE DEFINITION OF REFUGEE

12.23 The definition of refugee for the purposes of the Refugee Convention is contained in Article 1A(2), as applied by the 1967 Protocol. A refugee is any person who:

'owing to a well-founded fear of being persecuted for reasons of race religion nationality membership of a particular social group or political opinion, is outside his country of nationality and is unable or, owing to such fear, is unwilling to avail himself of the protection of that country; or who, not having a nationality and being outside the country of his former habitual residence . . . is unable or, owing to such fear, is unwilling to return to it."

We will now consider the various elements.[2]

[1] Convention Relating to the Status of Refugees 1951, art 1A(2), as applied by the 1967 Protocol. The New York Protocol of 1967 applies the 1951 Convention, for those (but only for those) countries that are parties to the Protocol (whether or not they also be parties to the Convention), as if the words in art 1A(2) of the Convention, which impose a temporal limitation on refugee claims are omitted: see art 1 of the Protocol. Thus the Protocol does not strictly amend the Convention but rather applies it in such a way as to allow for persons to be refugees as a result of events that have occurred since 1951: see *Minister for Immigration & Multicultural Affairs v Savvin* [2000] FCA 478 per Katz J in the Full Court of the Federal Court of Australia.

[2] In *R v Secretary of State for the Home Department, ex p Adan, R v Secretary of State for the Home Department, ex p Aitseguer* [2001] 2 AC 477, the House of Lords emphasised the importance of attaching an autonomous meaning to each of the terms within the refugee definition, per Lord Slynn at 509: 'The phrase "otherwise than in accordance with the Convention" does not mean "otherwise than in accordance with the relevant state's possible reasonable, permissible or legitimate view of what the Convention means"'.

'Owing to a well-founded fear'

The fear

12.24 A genuine fear of persecution must be behind the asylum seeker's absence from his or her country of residence or nationality. This is referred to as the subjective element.[1] If a person is at risk of being persecuted in his home country as a consequence of being returned there forcibly the risk would not make him or her a refugee if it was possible for the person, by returning voluntarily, to avoid the risk: in such a case it is the unwillingness to return to the country that gives rise to the risk and the consequential fear rather than the fear that results in the unwillingness to return. Therefore the person would not satisfy the refugee definition.[2] Even if objective conditions are such that a reasonable person would have reason to fear persecution, the claimant will not be a refugee unless he or she has such a fear. The use of the term 'fear' was intended to emphasise the forward-looking nature of the test, and not to ground refugee status in an assessment of the refugee claimant's state of mind.[3] The refugee does not have to have left the country because of such a fear, since a person can become a refugee by reason of events after their departure; such a person is referred to as a 'refugee *sur place*'.[4] There is no reason why the fear should not arise from the refugee's activities abroad, even if carried out in bad faith, although a claim based exclusively on such acts will be scrutinised with some scepticism as self-serving and lacking in credibility.[5] The Qualification Directive acknowledges that a need for protection may arise as a result of events occurring after the applicant left the country of origin and that such events may include the applicant's own activities outside the country of origin.[6] However, the Qualification Directive permits refugee status to be withheld where the applicant has deliberately created a risk of persecution,[7] eg by deliberately bringing him or herself to the hostile attention of his/her authorities. The implementing Immigration Rules make provision for 'sur place' claims but do not exclude 'bad faith' claims.[8] The fear must still exist at the date of determination; despite indications in the *travaux préparatoires* of the 1951 Convention which suggested that historic fear may be sufficient to ground refugee status if the refugee is currently unable to return,[9] this interpretation, accepted by the majority in the Court of Appeal,[10] was rejected by the House of Lords in *Adan*,[11] which held that while a historic fear may be relevant in providing evidence to establish a present fear, it is the existence or otherwise of a present fear which is determinative. Where objectively it is shown that there is a serious possibility of persecution, then it may well be difficult to refuse an application on the basis that the applicant does not believe the persecution will occur.[12]

[1] See UNHCR *Handbook*, **12.13** above, paras 37 and 38; *R v Secretary of State for the Home Department, ex p Singh* [1987] Imm AR 489, DC.

[2] *AA v Secretary of State for the Home Department; LK v Secretary of State for the Home Department* [2006] EWCA Civ 401, [2006] NLJR 681, [2007] 1 WLR 3134. This principle appears to have been transported into the humanitarian protection regime because humanitarian protection will be refused if the person could avoid the risk of serious harm by returning voluntarily – see API Humanitarian Protection, October 2006

[3] James Hathaway *The Law of Refugee Status* (1991) pp 68–69. Hathaway gives one of the most authoritative and highly regarded accounts of the Convention, with particular reference to Canadian and US case law, and is regularly cited with approval in the higher courts. See also, on meaning of 'fear', *Asuming* (11530).

[4] UNHCR *Handbook*, **12.13** above, paras 94–96

[5] *Danian v Secretary of State for the Home Department* [2000] Imm AR 96, [1999] INLR 533, CA; HC 395, para 341(vi). The Qualification Directive (30.9.04 OJ L304/12, in force 30 October 2004), art 20(6) provides that within the limits set out by the Refugee Convention, Member States may reduce the benefits granted to a refugee whose refugee status has been obtained on the basis of activities engaged in for the sole or main purpose of creating the necessary conditions for being recognised as a refugee.

[6] Qualification Directive, art 5. In such a case, proper analysis is required of whether such activities create a relevant risk, given the general activities and posture of the feared authorities: *H v Secretary of State for the Home Department* [2006] EWCA Civ 803, [2006] All ER (D) 79 (Nov).

[7] Qualification Directive, art 5(3).

[8] HC 395, para 339P, as inserted by HC 6918.

[9] See UN Doc E/1818 containing Ecosoc Res 319 (X1 B): 'who has had, or has well founded fear . . . and owing to such fear has had to leave, shall leave or remains outside the country of nationality.' The drafting group's explanatory note of the definition was 'that a person has either been actually a victim of persecution or can show good reason why he [or she] fears persecution'.

[10] *Adan v Secretary of State for the Home Department, Nooh v Secretary of State for the Home Department* [1997] Imm AR 251, CA.

[11] *Secretary of State for the Home Department v Adan* [1999] 1 AC 293, [1998] Imm AR 338, [1998] INLR 325, HL.

[12] *Radivojevic* (13372), followed in *Gashi v Secretary of State for the Home Department* [1997] INLR 96, IAT.

Well-founded

12.25 The fear of persecution must not only exist but must be well-founded. In *Sivakumaran*[1] the House of Lords, reversing the Court of Appeal, rejected the advice in paragraph 42 of the *Handbook*:

'In general the applicant's fear should be considered well-founded if he can establish, to a reasonable degree, that his continued stay in his country of origin has become intolerable to him for the reasons stated in the definition, or would for the same reasons be intolerable if he returned there.[2]'

It held that well-foundedness was an objective test, to be ascertained independently of the appellant's state of mind. But this does not mean that there must have been actual persecution in the past. It is sufficient if there is a well-founded fear of it occurring in the future.[3] A person may still be at risk of being persecuted even if his account of past persecution has been rejected as unbelievable.[4] Moreover, where an asylum seeker's claim has been disbelieved, it would be wrong to treat a subsequent, alternative claim as being an abuse of process which should not therefore be considered;[5] 'the fact that a claim is inconsistent with the first claim made does not of itself deprive an applicant of the protection of the Refugee Convention or the European Convention on Human Rights'.[6]

Past persecution will always be of great significance. The *travaux* reveal that the drafting group's explanatory note of the Article 1A definition was that 'a person has either been an actual victim of persecution or can show good reason why he [or she] fears persecution'.[7] The House of Lords' decision in *Adan* means, however, that a refugee must have a current risk, as well as a current fear, of persecution.[8] But past persecution means that future persecution is more likely (and the fear of it more likely to be well-founded) unless there has been a significant change of circumstances.[9] The Qualification Directive provides that the fact that an individual has experienced persecution or serious harm in the past or direct threats of such persecution or harm is a 'serious indication' of current risk unless there are 'good reasons' to consider that such serious harm or persecution will not be repeated.[10]

The past persecution of an individual may be contrasted with a past generalised risk of violence in an area which has been diminished by government measures to prevent abuse. Thus in *Ravichandran*[11] the Court of Appeal distinguished the Canadian case of *Thirunavukkarasu*[12] on the safety of Tamils in Colombo, on the basis that it related to a different time.

[1]   *R v Secretary of State for the Home Department, ex p Sivakumaran* [1988] AC 958 at 996, per Lord Keith.

[2]   UNHCR *Handbook*, **12.13** above, para 195.

[3]   Hathaway, 12.24 fn 3 above, paras 3.1, p 66, 3.2.3, p 87. See *Horvath v Secretary of State for the Home Department* [1999] INLR 7 at 18F, IAT, and Kiani [2002] UKIAT 01328 at para 7. See also *Appellant S395/2002 v Minister for Immigration and Multicultural Affairs; Appellant S396/2002 v Minister for Immigration and Multicultural Affairs* [2003] HCA 71 at para 58 per McHugh and Kirby JJ and at paras 72–77 per Gummow and Hayne JJ in the High Court of Australia for a recent and instructive restatement of some basic principles relating to the application of the refugee definition in respect of fear of future persecution.

[4]   *Daoud v Secretary of State for the Home Department* [2005] EWCA Civ 755, [2005] All ER (D) 259 (May), where Sedley LJ said: 'To claim falsely that you have been persecuted in the past because of your ethnicity does not mean that you may not face risks in future because of it'.

[5]   Which was the approach taken in the tribunal's starred determination *MY (Somalia)** [2004] UKIAT 00174. Ouseley J held in that case that it would be an abuse of process to permit the appellant, whose claim to be Somali had been disbelieved, to advance a claim on the alternative basis, inconsistent with the first, that he would be at risk on return to Somalia for the reason that he was not Somali.

[6]   *Yusuf v Secretary of State for the Home Department* [2005] EWCA Civ 1554, 150 Sol Jo LB 90, [2005] All ER (D) 194 (Dec), the appeal from *MY (Somalia)* per Pill LJ.

[7]   Report of the Ad Hoc Committee, 17 February 1950, p 39. See the argument of the intervener in *R v Secretary of State for the Home Department, ex p Sivakumaran* [1988] AC 958 at 976–989 for the drafting history of art 1 of the Refugee Convention and the admissibility of *travaux préparatoires* as an aid to the construction of international instruments. For the relevance of *travaux* in the construction of an international instrument see Vienna Convention on the Law of Treaties (1969), art 32. And as noted at **12.12** above, UNHCR's jurisdiction extends to those who 'have had' a well-founded fear of persecution. Hathaway suggests that the final definition adopted by the drafters intended persecution to be prospective save for those who had suffered pre-1951 persecution and became refugees by reason of art 1A(1) of the Refugee Convention and whose status is not now a matter of present debate: Hathaway above, para 3.1.1 p 66ff.

[8]   *Adan v Secretary of State for the Home Department* [1999] 1 AC 293, [1998] Imm AR 338, [1998] INLR 325. See also *R (on the application of Hoxha) v Secretary of State for the Home*

Department, R (on the application of B) v Secretary of State for the Home Department [2005] UKHL 19, [2005] 1 WLR 1063, (2005) 149 Sol Jo LB 358.

⁹ See eg *Demirkaya v Secretary of State for the Home Department* [1999] INLR 441 at 449D, CA; *Avci v Secretary of State for the Home Department* [2002] EWCA Civ 977, [2002] All ER (D) 254 (Jul); *S* (01/TH/00632) at para 9. Hathaway, above, concludes that 'individualised past persecution is generally a sufficient, though not a mandatory means of establishing prospective risk' (p 88). The German Constitutional Court goes further, stating that where there has been past persecution the test for the determining authority is whether 'future persecution could be excluded with sufficient certainty': Case No 193 (1994) 6(2) IJRL 282. See also UNHCR *Handbook* at para 45.

¹⁰ Qualification Directive, Art 4(4), implemented by HC 395, para 339K, as inserted by HC 6918.

¹¹ *Ravichandran (Senathirajah) v Secretary of State for the Home Department* [1996] Imm AR 97.

¹² *Thirunavukkarasu v Minister of Employment and Immigration* (1993) 109 DLR (4th) 682.

12.26 Problems can arise where a decision on refugee status has been delayed for several years, during which time the human rights environment has improved without there being some fundamental alteration in the factors giving rise to the fear. In *Arif*¹ the Court of Appeal decided to proceed by analogy with the cessation clause at Article 1C(5) of the Refugee Convention and held that, since the appellant would have qualified for refugee status had his application been dealt with expeditiously, it was now for the Home Office to demonstrate that a significant change of circumstances had removed the basis for the claim.² However, in *Hoxha and B*³ the Court of Appeal held that the cessation clause in Article 1C(5) can itself only be relevant where a person has been formally recognised as a refugee, a conclusion upheld by the House of Lords.⁴

¹ *Arif (Mohammed) v Secretary of State for the Home Department* [1999] INLR 327, where the appellant had been sentenced *in absentia* to a persecutory prison sentence, but by the date of the hearing, his own party had regained power. However, where there is no evidence that the applicant would have so qualified, the shifting evidential burden does not apply: *Salim (Nabil) v Secretary of State for the Home Department* [2000] Imm AR 503, CA. In *S* (01/TH/00632) at paras 8–9 the then President of the IAT, Collins J, criticised reliance on *Arif* as 'unhelpful . . . if . . . there is no significant change in the situation and the appellant was persecuted for a Convention reason before he left, it would be difficult to see how the decision could not be favourable to him.' See also *S v Secretary of State for the Home Department* [2002] EWCA Civ 539, [2002] INLR 416 at paras 13–15.

² See **12.86** below for the cessation clause.

³ *R (on the application of Hoxha) v Secretary of State for the Home Department, R (on the application of B) v Secretary of State for the Home Department* [2002] EWCA Civ 1403, upheld at [2005] UKHL 19, [2005] 1 WLR 1063, (2005) 149 Sol Jo LB 358.

⁴ The Court of Appeal (and the House of Lords) also held that the proviso to art 1C(5) only applies to statutory refugees falling under the definition in art 1A(1) of the Convention – persons recognised as refugees under International Arrangements and Conventions pre-dating the 1951 Convention (and is therefore no longer of practical relevance). See **12.86** below.

The burden and standard of proof

12.27 The burden of establishing a well-founded fear is on the applicant. In *Sivakumaran*¹ the House of Lords held that for a fear to be well-founded, the question was whether there was a 'real and substantial risk' or a 'reasonable degree of likelihood' of persecution for a Refugee Convention reason. It is clear that showing a real likelihood of persecution is a lesser standard than proving that persecution will occur on the balance of probabilities, and the House of Lords approved the words of Lord Diplock in *Fernandez v*

*Government of Singapore*² to this effect. Lord Diplock had suggested that the requisite degree of likelihood could be indicated by words such as 'a reasonable chance', 'substantial grounds for thinking', or 'a serious possibility'. In his speech in *Sivakumaran* Lord Keith³ appeared to approve Stevens J's dictum in the US case of *INS v Cardozo-Fonseca*⁴ that a one in ten chance of being persecuted could amount to a reasonable possibility of persecution.⁵ In those circumstances the addition of the word 'substantial' to 'real' ('a real and substantial possibility . . . of persecution') can only be intended to eliminate minimal or mere possibilities rather than to indicate something in the nature of a probability or a prediction. In *Adjei v Minister of Employment and Immigration*⁶ a Canadian Court of Appeal preferred to follow the language of reasonable possibility rather than some of the alternative formulations mentioned in the speeches in *Sivakumaran*. The Canadian court indicated that use of the word 'would' instead of 'could' in determining the reality of persecution was evidence of a misdirection on burden of proof. This reflects the words of Lord Keith, who had succinctly stated the issue: 'if the examination shows that persecution might indeed take place then the fear is well-founded'. In the case of *Chan Yee Kin v Minister for Immigration and Ethnic Affairs* ⁷ the Australian High Court adopted the test of 'real chance'. To avoid any possibility of confusion in the application of the *Sivakumaran* test, we prefer to state the test in terms of real risk rather than likelihood.⁸ The burden of proof in relation to future events is discharged 'by showing that there is a real as opposed to a fanciful risk that they will happen'.⁹

¹ *R v Secretary of State for the Home Department, ex p Sivakumaran* [1988] AC 958, [1987] 3 WLR 1047, CA.
² [1971] 2 All ER 691, [1971] 1 WLR 987, HL. In *Brown (aka Bajinja) v Government of Rwanda and Secretary of State for the Home Department* [2009] EWHC 770 (Admin), [2009] All ER (D) 98 (Apr), Laws LJ stated at [34]: 'But "real risk" does not mean proof on the balance of probabilities. It means a risk which is substantial and not merely fanciful; and it may be established by something less than proof of a 51% probability. The approach is the same as that taken in refugee cases, where the asylum seeker has to show a real risk that if he is returned to his home State he will be persecuted on any of the grounds set out in the 1951 United Nations Refugee Convention (see *Sivakumaran* [1988] 1 AC 958)'.
³ [1988] AC 958 at 994.
⁴ 94 L Ed 434 (1987).
⁵ Sedley LJ, pointing out the danger of assimilating risk to probability in *Batayav v Secretary of State for the Home Department* [2003] EWCA Civ 1489, [2004] INLR 126, said: 'If a type of car has a defect which causes one vehicle in ten to crash, most people would say that it presents a real risk to anyone who drives it, albeit crashes are not generally or consistently happening' (at paras 38–9).
⁶ (1989) 57 DLR (4th) 153.
⁷ (1989) 63 ALJR 561.
⁸ In *R v Gough* [1993] AC 646 at 670 Lord Goff noted in the context of the appropriate test for bias, 'for the avoidance of doubt I prefer to state the test in terms of real danger rather than real likelihood, to ensure that the court is thinking in terms of possibility rather than probability of bias'. In *Kacaj v Secretary of State for the Home Department* [2001] INLR 354 (starred) at para 12, the Tribunal held that it would now be better in both refugee asylum and human rights cases, for the phrase, 'real risk', to be adopted in preference to those of a 'serious possibility' or a 'reasonable degree of likelihood' – all of which in any case seek to convey the same meaning and are to be distinguished from 'beyond reasonable doubt' or 'on a balance of probabilities'. In *Ahmed (Hussain)* [2002] UKIAT 00841, Professor Jackson's Tribunal warned at paras 36–38 that the 'real risk' test should not be taken as amounting to more than a 'serious possibility' and that the phrase 'substantial grounds for believing' did not import another standard.
⁹ *MH (Iraq) v Secretary of State for the Home Department* [2007] EWCA Civ 852, [2007] All ER (D) 84 (Jul).

12.28 The general human rights background of the country in question is important in assessing the objective foundation for the fear.[1] Background human rights data should be collected from a broad cross-section of official and non-governmental sources in order to supplement the claimant's evidence. The Secretary of State has an obligation under the Immigration Rules to obtain 'reliable and up-to-date information' about the 'general situation prevailing in the countries of origin of applicants for asylum' and to make it available to those deciding asylum claims.[2] The Immigration and Nationality Directorate of the Home Office now has a 'Country of Origin Information Service' which produces sourced country reports on the main refugee-producing countries:[3] the Operational Guidance Notes are, however, policy documents and it should be borne in mind that they may lack independent scrutiny and objectivity.[4] There is also an Independent Advisory Group on Country Information, established under the auspices of the Chief Inspector of the UKBA to consider and make recommendations about the content of country information reports.[5] The existence of a consistent pattern of gross, flagrant or mass violations of human rights in a country can in itself, but does not necessarily (it depends on all of the facts), constitute a sufficient ground for determining that a person would be in danger on return,[6] but where human rights reports substantiate that a real risk of ill-treatment exists, a genuine fear of persecution in a country is likely to be well-founded if it is for a Refugee Convention reason.[7] Where there is a doubt after all the evidence has been placed before the Tribunal of fact, the benefit of it should be given to the applicant.[8] The absence of positive evidence about a particular practice (eg monitoring of expatriate opposition groups by a state's foreign legations and intelligence services) should not necessarily result in an applicant's failure to establish its existence; the objective evidence that there is (eg about the state's suppression of opposition activities) may require the existence of the practice to be inferred.[9] Factors creating or abating risk (such as the existence of reliable diplomatic assurances as to a person's future treatment) must be evaluated by judicial decision makers rather than being left to the discretion of administrative decision makers[10] (including risks arising from the route or method of return)[11] though a person cannot rely on their own failings (as where they do not co-operate in securing valid travel documentation) to obtain international protection.[12]

Country Guidance determinations of the Tribunal should be followed: see the discussion in CHAPTER 20.

[1] UNHCR *Handbook* **12.13** above, paras 196, 204; Hathaway, **12.24** fn 3 above, pp 89–90. See also UN Convention Against Torture, art 3(2); *Mutombo v Switzerland* (1994) 15 HRLJ 164. The principle is now incorporated in the Immigration Rules, HC 395, para 339J(i).
[2] HC 395, para 339JA.
[3] See Home Office website at: www.homeoffice.gov.uk/rds/country_reports.html. See further **12.132**.
[4] *KD (Inattentive Judges) Afghanistan* [2010] UKUT 261 (IAC) (30 July 2010)
[5] Established under UK Borders Act 2007, s 48(2)(j), successor to the Advisory Panel on Country Information established under the now repealed Nationality, Immigration and Asylum Act 2002, s 142. The reports of the Advisory Panel on Country Information are on its website at: www.apci.org.uk whilst the Chief Inspector's website includes the Independent Advisory Group on Country Information.
[6] See *Alan v Switzerland* [1997] INLR 29 (UNCAT); *Hariri v Secretary of State for the Home Department* [2003] EWCA Civ 807, (2003) 147 Sol Jo LB 659, [2003] All ER (D) 340; *Batayav v Secretary of State for the Home Department* [2003] EWCA Civ 1489, [2003] All ER (D) 60 (Nov); *Iqbal (Muzafar)* [2002] UKIAT 02239. The Supreme Court in *R (on the*

application of *EM (Eritrea) v Secretary of State for the Home Department* [2014] UKSC 12 said that the relevant question in an Art 3 case is whether there is a real risk of the minimum level of severity being traversed. Identification of a systemic failure is one route by which this may be demonstrated, but it is by no means a necessity in every case.

7 Hathaway, **12.24** fn 3 above, cites the Federal Court of Appeal in *Attakora (Benjamin) v Minister for Employment and Immigration* (Decision A-1091-87) *(19 May 1989, unreported), at para 3.2.1 (p 80)* that 'persons who flee countries that are known to commit or acquiesce in persecutory behaviour should benefit from a rebuttable presumption that they have a genuine need for protection'. For an example of a situation where an appellant had not suffered persecution and relied wholly on evidence of country conditions see *Drrias v Secretary of State for the Home Department* [1997] Imm AR 346, CA.

8 UNHCR *Handbook* (**12.13** above), paras 196, 203. See also *Kaja v Secretary of State for the Home Department* [1995] Imm AR 1, **12.29** below.

9 *YB (Eritrea) v Secretary of State for the Home Department* [2008] EWCA Civ 360, [2008] All ER (D) 195 (Apr).

10 The Court of Appeal found in *J1 v Secretary of State for the Home Department* [2013] EWCA Civ 279 it is in principle wrong for the court to allow the Secretary of State to determine any element of the asylum claim (such as whether diplomatic assurances were sufficient to ameliorate risks that would otherwise prevail.

11 In *HH (Somalia) v Secretary of State for the Home Department* [2010] EWCA Civ 426 the Court provisionally considered that an asylum seeker was owed, under the Common European Asylum System, a timely decision following their application on every aspect of their case including route of return, rather than having to wait for the setting of removal directions for 'return' issues to be evaluated. At T62]-[63] they accepted that the Tribunal should assess the risks arising from the method of return in so far as it is known as the date of hearing.

12 *HF (Iraq) v Secretary of State for the Home Department* [2013] EWCA Civ 1276.

12.29 The correct approach to assessment of past events was authoritatively set out by the Court of Appeal in *Karanakaran*.[1] The Tribunal had been divided on what standard of proof to apply to evidence of past or present facts before the necessary assessment of future risk is undertaken. In *Kaja*[2] the minority had held that historic events should be proven on the normal civil balance and the reduced burden of 'reasonable likelihood' should apply only in respect of future events, while the majority had concluded that the decision-maker should not omit from the assessment of future risk any evidence of past events to which they were prepared to give some credence. They referred to the 'positive role for doubt' in asylum, given the inability of the asylum seeker to produce witnesses from the country of persecution, and the general lack of documentary or other evidence proving either past or future persecution.[3] The Court of Appeal endorsed this approach, which does not lay down a standard of proof for past events but asks the decision-maker to weigh everything for what it is worth in assessing the risk of persecution. Sedley LJ warned that:

> 'the decision-maker must not, by a process of factual findings on particular elements of the material which is provided, foreclose reasonable speculation on the chances of persecution emerging from a consideration of the whole of the material. Everything capable of having a bearing has to be given the weight, great or little, due to it . . . [The] facts, so far as they can be established, are signposts on the road to a conclusion.'

Brooke LJ, relying on the Australian decision of *Wu Shan Liang*,[4] distinguished between civil litigation, where 'the court has to decide where, on the balance of probabilities, the truth lies as between the evidence the parties to the litigation have thought it in their respective interests to adduce at the trial', and administrative decision-making, where 'a whole range of possible approaches

. . . may be correct' and 'the use of such terms provides little assistance'. He reproduced with approval a number of principles derived from the Australian case law:[5]

'(1)   There may be circumstances in which a decision-maker must take into account the possibility that alleged past events occurred even though it finds that these events probably did not occur. The reason for this is that the ultimate question is whether the applicant has a real substantial basis for his fear of future persecution. The decision-maker must not foreclose reasonable speculation about the chances of the future hypothetical event occurring.

(2)   Although the civil standard of proof is not irrelevant to the fact-finding process, the decision-maker cannot simply apply that standard to all fact-finding. It frequently has to make its assessment on the basis of fragmented, incomplete and confused information. It has to assess the plausibility of accounts given by people who may be understandably bewildered, frightened and, perhaps, desperate, and who often do not understand either the process or the language spoken by the decision-maker/investigator. Even applicants with a genuine fear of persecution may not present as models of consistency or transparent veracity.

(3)   In this context, when the decision-maker is uncertain as to whether an alleged event occurred, or finds that although the probabilities are against it, the event may have occurred, it may be necessary to take into account the possibility that the event took place in deciding the ultimate question (for which see question 1 above) . . .

(4)   Although the "What if I am wrong?" terminology has gained currency, it is more accurate to see this requirement as simply an aspect of the obligation to apply correctly the principles for determining whether an applicant has a 'well-founded fear of being persecuted' for a Convention reason.

(5)   There is no reason in principle to support a general rule that a decision-maker must express findings as to whether alleged past events actually occurred in a manner that makes explicit its degree of conviction or confidence that its findings were correct . . .

(6)   If a fair reading of the decision-maker's reasons as a whole shows that it "had no real doubt" that claimed events did not occur, then there is no warrant for holding that it should have considered the possibility that its findings were wrong.'

[1]   *Karanakaran v Secretary of State for the Home Department* [2000] 3 All ER 449, [2000] INLR 122, [2000] Imm AR 271. The Court of Appeal's evaluative approach to refugee status determination in *Karanakaran* was approved by the House of Lords in *R (on the application of Sivakumar) v Secretary of State for the Home Department* [2003] UKHL 14, [2003] 2 All ER 1097.
[2]   *Kaja v Secretary of State for the Home Department* [1995] Imm AR 1.
[3]   See UNHCR *Handbook* (**12.13** above), paras 196–197.
[4]   *Minister for Immigration and Ethnic Affairs v Wu Shan Liang* (1996) 185 CLR 259.
[5]   *Rajalingam v Minister for Immigration and Multicultural Affairs* [1999] FCA 719, per Sackville J, conveniently summarised and quoted in [2000] Imm AR 271 at 290–292.

12.30 It is, however, for the applicant to establish his or her claim, albeit to a lower than normal civil standard.[1] Thus it is for him or her to establish what his or her nationality is or that he or she is stateless if it forms part of the claim.[2] However, in the context of asylum as elsewhere, where it is the Secretary of State who asserts something, such as that a document produced by an applicant is a forgery, the burden is on him or her to prove it. With regard to documents, the issue is more likely to be whether the document is reliable evidence rather than whether it is false and in that respect it is generally for the asylum seeker to establish the reliability of documents upon which he or she relies, although in exceptional circumstances, eg where a document that is key to the asylum claim could readily be verified by the Secretary of State she may be expected to make inquiries.[3] *Karanakaran*[4] was a case about the 'internal relocation alternative', ie where it is accepted that the applicant faces persecution in part of the country and the issue is whether it would be unduly harsh for him or her to relocate to a safe area.[5] Again, different divisions of the Tribunal had differed on whether the applicant had to show on the balance of probabilities that it would be unduly harsh,[6] or only that it was a 'serious possibility'.[7] The court in *Karanakaran* held that it would be quite impracticable to maintain a regime in which there was one approach to the evidential material relating to historic or existing facts for the purpose of the first part of the definition of 'refugee' in the Convention, and a different approach to such material for the purpose of considering issues of protection and internal relocation.[8] The question was simply 'would it be unduly harsh', but in answering it, only evidence about which there was no doubt that it was not correct should be excluded. The guidance in *Karanakaran* does not, however, disturb the line of jurisprudence to the effect that where there is no real doubt that the whole story of the applicant is unworthy of belief, issues of standard of proof do not arise.[9] Even where an applicant has been disbelieved, it is still necessary, as in every case, to determine whether there is a real risk of being persecuted; 'the Court's duty is to vindicate a good asylum claim even though the applicant may have lied or otherwise acted in bad faith'.[10] However, if success in an asylum claim depends upon the applicant establishing that he or she had done something in the past (illegally departed Eritrea) and the applicant is disbelieved on her evidence then the claim fails; in the face of rejection of her evidence, a reasonable likelihood that she had done the act could not be established on the basis that it was implausible or unlikely that she had not done that act.[11] Nevertheless, the decision maker is bound to have regard to any evidence that might, independently of the claimant's unreliable testimony, shed sufficient light upon his or her circumstances to make good the claim to protection.[12]

[1]   The burden is not different or lower for someone with mental problems: *Bolat v Secretary of State for the Home Department* (99/6206/C) (23 February 2000, unreported), CA; *Singh (Amrik) v Secretary of State for the Home Department* [2000] Imm AR 340, CA.

[2]   Stanley Burnton LJ in the Court of Appeal in *MA (Ethiopia) v Secretary of State for the Home Department* [2009] EWCA Civ 289 at [78]. *Tikhonov* [1998] INLR 737, IAT. In *Smith (Agartha)* (00/TH/02130) the Tribunal suggested that a more flexible approach to proof of nationality should be adopted in asylum cases (as they were not nationality arbitrations – a criticism of the approach in *Tikhonov*) and that in most cases the decision on nationality has to be made on the same basis as decisions on other elements of the refugee definition. 'If there is some valid evidence that can be weighed in the balance, even if meagre, then that may suffice to discharge the burden lying on the appellant to prove nationality (or statelessness)' (paras 54–55). It would be sufficient for an asylum seeker to establish 'a serious possibility' that he or she was of the claimed nationality – *Lucas v Secretary of State for the Home Department* [2002] EWCA Civ 1809. In *Hamza* [2002] UKIAT 05185 (starred) Collins J (the then President) held that in the context of making findings in respect of nationality an adjudicator 'must bear in mind that if he is going to make a positive finding against the appellant, then he must do so not on the asylum standard, but on a higher standard which would be the balance of probabilities' (para 12). If it was part of an applicant's case that she would not be admitted to the country to which she was to be returned then she could be expected to establish that fact by taking all reasonably practicable steps to demonstrate that

she would not be admitted, including applying to the country's embassy for documentation to enable her return – *MA (Ethiopia) v Secretary of State for the Home Department* [2009] EWCA Civ 289.

3 *R v Immigration Appeal Tribunal, ex p Shen* [2000] INLR 389, QBD; *Makozo* (20033) 12 February 1999, IAT; *Escobar* (20553) 26 March 1999, IAT. But see *R v Immigration Appellate Authority, ex p Mohammed (Mukhtar)* [2001] Imm AR 162, QBD. In *Ahmed (Tanveer) v Secretary of State for the Home Department* [2002] UKIAT 00439, [2002] Imm AR 318, [2002] INLR 345, IAT, the IAT held that whether or not a document is a forgery is rarely the real issue and that the real, or indeed only, question is whether the document is one upon which reliance should properly be placed. This approach was approved in *Mungu v Secretary of State for the Home Department* [2003] EWCA Civ 360 at paras 18–19, [2003] All ER (D) 289 (Feb). See also *Zarandy v Secretary of State for the Home Department* [2002] EWCA Civ 153, [2002] All ER (D) 355 (Jan). In *Singh v Belgium (Application 33210/11)* (2 October 2012, unreported), ECtHR the failure by both the initial decision maker and the appeal body to attempt to verify the authenticity of the highly pertinent documents was ruled by the Strasbourg Court to be 'at odds with the close and rigorous scrutiny that the Court would have expected of the domestic authorities, which had thus failed to ensure effective protection against treatment in breach of Article 3.' The Tribunal in *MJ (Singh v Belgium: Tanveer Ahmed unaffected) Afghanistan* [2013] UKUT 253 (IAC) looked at the compatibility of the eponymous doctrine with Singh and Belgium finding that the latter authority was relevant in cases where authentication was realistic. In *PJ (Sri Lanka) v Secretary of State for the Home Department* [2014] EWCA Civ 1011 Gloster LJ stated that the involvement of lawyers abroad does not create a rebuttable presumption that the documents they produce are reliable, though exceptionally such documents may necessitate an element of investigation by the national authorities, in order to provide effective protection against mistreatment under Art 3, ECHR, failing which the Secretary of State will be unable thereafter to mount an argument challenging the authenticity of the relevant documents unless and until the breach is rectified by a proper enquiry.

4 *Karanakaran v Secretary of State for the Home Department* [2000] 3 All ER 449, [2000] INLR 122, [2000] Imm AR 271.

5 *Robinson (Anthonyppillai Francis) v Secretary of State for the Home Department and Immigration Appeal Tribunal* [1997] Imm AR 568; *AE and FE v Secretary of State for the Home Department* [2003] EWCA Civ 1032, [2004] QB 531, [2004] 2 WLR 123. See **12.45** below. Whether 'internal relocation/flight' is in issue at all should depend initially on the applicant's claim, and, just as for other aspects of the refugee claim, the responsibility for putting the factual basis and burden of establishing the case lies on the applicant: see *Aziz v Secretary of State for the Home Department* [2003] EWCA Civ 118; *R v Secretary of State for the Home Department, ex p Salim* [2000] Imm AR 6, [1999] INLR 628, QBD.

6 A school of thought exemplified by *Manoharan* [1998] Imm AR 455.

7 *Sachithananthan* [1999] INLR 205.

8 *Karanakaran v Secretary of State for the Home Department* [2000] Imm AR 271 at 293.

9 *R v Secretary of State for the Home Department, ex p Kingori (aka Mypanguli)* [1994] Imm AR 539, CA; *Bulut (Huseyin) v Secretary of State for the Home Department* [1999] Imm AR 210, CA.

10 *GM (Eritrea) v Secretary of State for the Home Department* [2008] EWCA Civ 833, Laws LJ.

11 *GM (Eritrea)*.

12 *HH (Somalia) v Secretary of State for the Home Department* [2010] EWCA Civ 426. The Supreme Court held in *MA (Somalia) v Secretary of State for the Home Department* [2010] UKSC 49, that the overriding test will be whether the general country evidence 'can counteract the pull of the appellant's lies', making the point that dishonesty might well be explained by factors other than outright dishonesty and were not necessarily evidence that the asylum seeker was not at risk.

Credibility

12.31 The debate about standard of proof is inextricably linked with issues of credibility. The issue of credibility is one which needs to be addressed seriously, in light of the widespread perception that adverse credibility findings are too easily reached, on too little material, both by the Secretary of State for the Home Department and on appeal.[1] For a fuller treatment of credibility in the context of asylum appeals see **12.179** below.

1 See (in a non-asylum context but equally applicable) *R v Immigration Appeal Tribunal, ex p Hussain* (CO 990/1995) (25 April 1996, unreported), QBD where Turner J said that 'Credibility is not in itself a valid end to the function of an adjudicator . . . there is a risk . . . that overemphasis on the issue of credibility may distort the findings of an adjudicator'. See also *Horvath v Secretary of State for the Home Department* [1999] INLR 7, [1999] Imm AR 121, IAT. It has been largely left to organisations such as Asylum Aid to draw attention to the 'culture of disbelief' informing Home Office asylum decisions: see eg Asylum Aid *No reason at all* (1995) and Asylum Aid *Still no reason at all* (1999). 'As an advocate I have seen over the years good and bad judicial practice in immigration and asylum hearings with respect to treatment of appellants and credibility findings': the Speech by The Hon Mr Justice Blake, President of UTIAC to the Upper Tribunal Immigration Judiciary: 'The Arrival of the Upper Tribunal Immigration and Asylum Chamber' (11 February 2010).

12.32 The principle of the benefit of the doubt operates once all the evidence is submitted. In order to benefit from it, the applicant should have co-operated with the investigating authorities and should not attempt to deceive them.[1] Section 8 of the AI(TC)A 2004, and para 341 of the Immigration Rules, HC 395, as substituted by HC 164 from 1 January 2005, list different kinds of behaviour which must be taken into account as potentially[2] damaging the claimant's credibility. Whilst the English courts have so far taken the view that the Sprakab organisation, sometimes employed by the Home Office to analyse speech patterns with a view to determining a person's origin,[3] the Court of Session has been concerned as to the expertise of that body and of undue delegation of ultimately judicial judgments to a third party.[4] See credibility more generally at **12.179** below.

1 UNHCR *Handbook*, para 205;
2 The Court of Appeal has read the word 'potentially' into the statute as being necessary in order to respect the constitutional principle of separation of powers which requires the administrative or judicial decision maker to make its own assessment of the facts: *JT (Cameroon) v Secretary of State for the Home Department* [2008] EWCA Civ 878 [2008] All ER (D) 348 (Jul).
3 *RB (Somalia) v Secretary of State for the Home Department* [2012] EWCA Civ 277.
4 The Court of Session, Inner House, in *MABN v Advocate General for Scotland* [2013] CSIH_68. See further *Secretary of State for the Home Department v MN and KY (Scotland)* [2014] UKSC 30, [2014] 4 All ER 443, [2014] 1 WLR 2064.

Behaviour in the country of asylum

12.33 Issues of credibility are also engaged where a person's claim to asylum is based solely on acts done since leaving the country of feared persecution which are inconsistent with previous beliefs.[1] In *Danian*[2] the Court of Appeal reviewed earlier authorities which had held that unreasonable activities, or activities performed in bad faith, could not be relied on by an asylum seeker in support of his or her claim.[3] It concluded that a refugee *sur place* who has acted in bad faith did not fall outside the protection of the Refugee Convention and could not be removed if the activities gave rise to a genuine and well-founded fear of persecution.[4] Brooke LJ, noting the decision in *Mbanza*[5] that a fraudulent claim could attract protection, emphasised that the credibility of such an application was likely to be low and would be rigorously scrutinised. Buxton LJ pointed out that the Convention had provided specific exceptions to refugee status (in Articles 1D–F) which should not be added to unless required by a clear international consensus or international practice.

Neither criterion was fulfilled in the case of a 'bad faith' claim.[6] Part of the rationale for the decision was the recognition that the applicant would have an irresistible claim to protection under Article 3 of the ECHR.[7] It has been held in other cases that the mere fact of having claimed asylum in another state may put the person at risk for a Convention reason.[8] Activities in the United Kingdom which are consistent with earlier political beliefs are more likely to give rise to a tenable asylum claim, but even those which are not borne of a genuine participation in political protest may nevertheless attract harm from an oppressive regime.[9] The Tribunal has given guidance on the issues arising in assessing harm from involvement in activities in this country.[10]

[1] Directive 2004/83 at Art 4(3)(d) addresses this stating that 'whether the applicant's activities since leaving the country of origin were engaged in for the sole or main purpose of creating the necessary conditions for applying for international protection, so as to assess whether these activities will expose the applicant to persecution or serious harm if returned to that country'; see Immigration Rule 339J(iv).
[2] *Danian v Secretary of State for the Home Department* [2000] Imm AR 96.
[3] *R v Immigration Appeal Tribunal, ex p B* [1989] Imm AR 166; *Gilgham (Mustapha) v Immigration Appeal Tribunal* [1995] Imm AR 129; *Re HB* (1995) 7 IJRL 332 (NZ).
[4] *Danian* fn 1 above, at 122.
[5] *Mbanza v Secretary of State for the Home Department* [1996] Imm AR 136.
[6] *Danian* above, at 130.
[7] *Chahal v United Kingdom* (1996) 23 EHRR 413, paras 79–80, cited at *Danian* above, at 118.
[8] See observations of Laws J in *R v Immigration Appeal Tribunal, ex p Senga* (unreported, 9 March 1994); see also (1992) 4(3) IJRL 261, Case 111 (Polish asylum seeker held to have been prejudiced by information given in a claim made in Germany). The difficulties in establishing a Convention reason were demonstrated in the case of *Senga* itself when remitted to the tribunal (12842) – see comment in [1998] 10(3) INLP 110. See also *L (DRC)* [2004] UKIAT 00007 at paras 32–33. However, in *Mohammed (Baheldin)* (13465) a Sudanese claim based on likely inquiries on return succeeded.
[9] The Court of Appeal in *KS (Burma) v Secretary of State for the Home Department* [2013] EWCA Civ 67 (13 February 2013) stated that activities other than bona fide political protest can create refugee status sur place. It could not be presumed absent evidence that a repressive, arbitrary regime would conduct a rational and careful assessment of the cases of returning failed asylum seekers so as to target only genuine political activists; see further Lord Mackay of Drumadoon in the Court of Session, Outer House in *WKA v Secretary of State for the Home Department* [2013] CSIH_51, and Longmore LJ in *TS (Burma) v Secretary of State for the Home Department* [2011] EWCA Civ 110 at [6] stating that a Tribunal of fact needs to identify an evidential basis for a conclusion that the authorities of a repressive regime would know somebody to be a hanger-on with no real commitment to the oppositionist cause who was demonstrating merely in order to enhance a false claim for asylum.
[10] *BA (Demonstrators in Britain-risk on return) Iran CG* [2011] UKUT 36 (IAC).

Refraining from acts exacerbating risk

12.34 The extent to which refugee status can be founded upon the risks flowing from future engagement in voluntary conduct such as political activity or religious proselytising or in the manifestation of an identity that the individual could conceal, such as his or her sexuality has proved controversial: see paragraphs 12.34-35 of the 8th edition. It had been established that if in fact the individual would engage in the activity or manifest the identity and would be persecuted as a result then refugee status should not be withheld on the ground that the refugee's conduct would be unreasonable.[1] However, the position had been that if the individual would in fact conceal his or her identity (or refrain from the activity giving rise to the risk) then the individual would not be entitled to asylum unless acting 'discretely' would itself cause such suffering as to amount to persecution.[2] Much of the controversy has been resolved by the Supreme Court's landmark decision in *HJ (Iran).*[3] The Supreme Court recognised that the Refugee Convention protects against persecution for reason of the protected characteristics identified in Article 1A(2) so that it is no answer to a refugee claim that the applicant could avoid being persecuted whilst remaining in his or her own country by concealing that protected characteristic and the normal incidents of that identity. The proper approach to claims by gay asylum seekers based on fear of persecution for reason of their sexuality is to determine firstly whether they are indeed gay; if so, does the evidence demonstrate a real risk of persecution for an openly gay person in the relevant country; if so, how will the applicant live on return; and if the decision maker decides that the applicant will conceal his or her sexuality on return, and thereby avoid being persecuted, then the decision maker must consider why the applicant will do this. If a material reason for the applicant concealing his or her sexuality on return would be a fear of persecution which would follow if he or she were to live as openly gay, then the claim for asylum is made out. The principle applies vis-à-vis all Convention reasons, including political opinion[4] and religion.[5]

[1]   *Ahmed (Iftikhar) v Secretary of State for the Home Department* [2000] INLR 1.
[2]   See eg *RG (Colombia) v Secretary of State for the Home Department* [2006] EWCA Civ 57 and *J v Secretary of State for the Home Department* [2006] EWCA Civ 1238.
[3]   *HJ (Iran) v Secretary of State for the Home Department* [2010] UKSC 31, [2011] 1 AC 596, [2011] 2 All ER 591 reversing *J v Secretary of State for the Home Department* [2006] EWCA Civ 1238, [2006] All ER (D) 382 (Jul). The CJEU came to a similar conclusion in *Minister voor Immigratie en Asiel v X, Y and Z:* C-199/12, C-200/12 and C-201/12 [2014] 3 WLR 770, [2014] 2 CMLR 561, ECJ. The principles have been applied in decisions including *LZ (homosexuals) Zimbabwe CG* [2011] UKUT 487 (IAC).
[4]   The Supreme Court in *RT (Zimbabwe) v Secretary of State for the Home Department* [2012] UKSC 38 confirmed that the *HJ Iran* principle applies to asylum claims turning on attributed political opinion: thus it was unattractive and offensive to suggest that a person who would otherwise suffer persecution should be required to take steps to evade it by fabricating a loyalty, which he or she did not hold, to a brutal and despotic regime. It was clear that the right of freedom of thought, conscience and religion extended to those who held no political opinions to the extent that they could not be expected to lie any more than could the committed activist: both would suffer an affront to their human dignity.
[5]   The CJEU in *Bundesrepublik Deutschland v Y; Bundesrepublik Deutschland v Z:* C-71/11 and C-99/11 [2013] All ER (EC) 1144, [2013] 1 CMLR 175, ECJ. In *MN and others (Ahmadis-country conditions-risk) Pakistan CG* [2012] UKUT 389 (IAC) the Tribunal found that an Ahmadi who could show that they would engage in various forms of behaviour would have a viable claim to refugee status given the severity of the sanctions imposed for these forms of conduct: however they would need to demonstrate that engagement in the particular form of behaviour was 'of particular importance' to their own religious identity. In *AMM and others (conflict; humanitarian crisis; returnees; FGM) Somalia CG* [2011] UKUT 445 (IAC) the UTIAC examined the need for returning Somails to 'play the game' of compliance with the religious conduct and mores required by the extremist Al-Shabaab armed group, noting at [194] that 'the more such religiously motivated or inspired laws interfere with the ability of a person to hold and practise his or her religious or other beliefs, the more intense will be the scrutiny and the more important will become the issue of proportionality.' See also *R (on the application of Yameen) v Secretary of State for the Home Department* [2011] EWHC 2250 (Admin).

'Outside the country of nationality . . . residence'

12.35 It is fundamental to the definition of a Convention refugee that the person should be outside his or her country owing to the fear of persecution.[1]

A person sheltered in a foreign embassy in the country of persecution is outside that country's jurisdiction, but not its territory, and cannot be recognised as a Convention refugee.[2]

1   See UNHCR *Handbook* **12.13** above, para 88. For a discussion of this territorial limitation – the principle of 'alienage' – generally see Hathaway **12.24** fn 3 above, pp 29–33. In *European Roma Rights Centre v Immigration Officer at Prague Airport* [2004] UKHL 55, [2005] 2 AC 1, especially per Lord Bingham, the House of Lords held that measures specifically designed to prevent potential asylum seekers ever reaching a state's territory are not contrary to the Convention. Their Lordships also rejected arguments to the effect that measures designed to prevent asylum seekers even being able to reach UK territory in order to make a claim here, were unlawful in terms of customary international law as being contrary to the 'spirit' of the Convention. See also the Australian High Court in *Minister for Immigration and Multicultural Affairs v Ibrahim (Haji)* [2000] HCA 55 and *Minister for Immigration and Multicultural Affairs v Khawar* [2002] HCA 14, and the US Supreme Court in *Sale V, Acting Comr, Immigration and Naturalisation Service v Haitian Centers Council Inc* 509 US 155, and see **12.9** above.
2   UNHCR *Handbook* above, para 88, fn. See the discussion of 'diplomatic asylum' in *R (on the application of B) v Secretary of State for Foreign and Commonwealth Affairs* [2004] EWCA Civ 1344, [2005] 2 WLR 618, (2004) Times, 25 October.

12.36 It may be necessary to determine what the person's true nationality is, since, if it is not that of the country of feared persecution, the claimant can be returned to the country of nationality.[1] Similarly, a person who is a national of more than one country will be expected to satisfy the refugee definition in respect of each country, or seek protection of that country where persecution is not feared.[2] But the second nationality must be effective, not merely formal, before it disqualifies someone from refugee status vis-à-vis the country of persecution.[3] Where there is a dispute as to nationality, the decision of the country of purported nationality will be decisive, rather than the host country's conclusion as to what the nationality should be.[4] Possession of a passport issued by another state may not be evidence of nationality if it was issued as a travel document to enable the bearer to move elsewhere.[5] An asylum seeker may be expected to make such applications as are reasonable in order to determine whether they are a national of a particular country (and it would be unreasonable to expect them to make enquiries that might endanger family members abroad), the question of nationality ultimately being assessed on the balance of probabilities.[6] However, possession of such a travel document may be evidence that the person can be removed to a safe third country.[7] Arbitrary exclusion from the country of nationality, implying cutting off from the enjoyment of all the benefits and rights enjoyed by citizens, can itself amount to persecution;[8] the denial of re-entry to the country of habitual residence for a stateless person lacks that quality, however.[9] The Convention definition applies to stateless persons as well as to those who have a nationality. Stateless persons[10] qualify if they flee from the country of former habitual residence[11] and cannot go back there because of a well-founded fear of persecution,[12] although if they are unable to return to the country of habitual residence, other international law obligations are engaged.[13] Refusal to re-admit a stateless person to the country of his or her former habitual residence is not by itself persecutory because (by contrast to a national) the stateless person does not have a right of admission.[14] Treatment may become persecutory when visited upon the stateless when considered in the overall context of discrimination and mistreatment that they suffer.[15]

1   *R v Special Adjudicator, ex p Abudine* [1995] Imm AR 60, QBD. In *Smith (Agartha)* (00/TH/02130) the IAT held that although a failure to make a positive finding as to nationality may be fatal to a determination of an asylum claim, it need not be in every case so long as a particular country is identified as being the one in which persecution is feared.

2   Refugee Convention, art 1A(2); UNHCR *Handbook* 12.13 above, paras 106–107; *A-G of Canada v Ward* [1997] INLR 42, S Ct Can. In the particular context of cases involving possible Ethiopian and/or Eritrean nationality or neither, leading to statelessness, see *Tecle v Secretary of State for the Home Department* [2002] EWCA Civ 1358 (CA permission refusal); *R (on the application of Tewolde) v Immigration Appeal Tribunal* [2004] EWHC 162 (Admin); and *L (Ethiopia)* [2003] UKIAT 00016, to the effect that a claimant asserting statelessness should prove it, if necessary by applying for the relevant nationality.

3   *R v Immigration Appeal Tribunal, ex p Milisavljevic* [2001] EWHC 203 Admin, [2001] Imm AR 580; and the Australian Federal Court cases of *Jong Kim Koe v Minister for Immigration and Multicultural Affairs* [1997] FCA 306 and *Al-Anezi v Minister for Immigration & Multicultural Affairs* [1999] FCA 355 *(per Lehane J)*. In *KK and others (Nationality: North Korea) Korea CG* [2011] UKUT 92 (IAC) the UTIAC observed that if a person would be returned to a place of persecution from their country of nationality they could nevertheless claim to have a 'valid reason based on well-founded fear' for not returning there. The tribunal held that when deciding whether the person had another nationality and thus a destination where he or she would not be persecuted the proper approach depended on whether they (i) actually possessed the nationality (ie hold the nationality as shown by their passport or unequivocal documentary evidence); (ii) had an undoubted claim to such nationality (because on their account read with the relevant nationality law, they were plainly and undeniably entitled to such citizenship); (iii) were entitled to the nationality only if some discretion was exercised in their favour (as with some aspects of British nationality law, where the Secretary of State is entitled to register children and others on a discretionary basis). It was wrong to treat category (iii) cases, where nationality could be obtained only if a discretion was afforded them, as for the purposes of the Refugee Convention having the nationality in question.

4   See *Oppenheimer v Cattermole* [1976] AC 249, [1975] 1 All ER 538, HL; *Stoeck v Public Trustee* [1921] 2 Ch 67; *Bibi (Mahaboob) v Secretary of State for the Home Department* [1987] Imm AR 340, CA. This also accords with the rule of public international law that in general each state may determine who are its nationals: see R Plender *International Migration Law* (2nd edn, 1998), pp 39ff. But the decision of the purported country of nationality may be ignored if it violates international humanitarian law: *Oppenheimer v Cattermole* [1976] AC 249, HL. UNHCR state in *The 1954 Convention relating to the Status of Stateless Persons: Implementation within the European Union Member States and Recommendations for Harmonisation* (October 2003) at [36] that 'it might be assumed that if a State refuses to indicate that a person is a national, this itself is a form of evidence which could have a bearing on the claim because States normally extend diplomatic services and protection to their nationals.'

5   (1993) 5(3) IJRL 466, Case No 156.

6   *MA (Ethiopia) v Secretary of State for the Home Department* [2009] EWCA Civ 289.

7   *Alsawaf v Secretary of State for the Home Department* [1988] Imm AR 410, CA.

8   See the decision of the Court of Appeal in *Lazarevic v Secretary of State for the Home Department* [1997] Imm AR 251 at 270–272, per Hutchison LJ, CA and *EB (Ethiopia) v Secretary of State for the Home Department* [2007] EWCA Civ 809, [2008] 3 WLR 1188. See also *Stula* (14622), though of course it remains for the applicant to establish a discriminatory Convention reason. See also Elias LJ in the Court of Appeal in *MA (Ethiopia) v Secretary of State for the Home Department* [2009] EWCA Civ 289 (2 April 2009) at [60].

9   *MA (Palestinian Territories) v Secretary of State for the Home Department* [2008] EWCA Civ 304 (9 April 2008) [2008] Imm AR 617, [2009] INLR 163, Maurice Kay LJ at [26]: 'The lot of a stateless person is an unhappy one, but to deny him a right that he has never enjoyed is not, in itself, persecution'.

10   See *Samanter* (14520) for circumstances in which statelessness may arise.

11   A stateless applicant who has lived in more than one country before claiming asylum in yet another should only have to show that he is a refugee in relation to one of the former countries, or at least only in relation to the first of them: see UNHCR *Handbook*, para 104 and *Al-Anezi* (fn 3 above). This is because an applicant with only one nationality is not precluded from refugee status merely by the fact that he has lived in third countries, and as far as possible applicants with and those without nationality should be treated equally under the Convention. For the difference between a country in which a stateless applicant 'most recently lived' and

one of former 'habitual residence', see *Zrilic* (17106). In *Dag* [2001] Imm AR 587 a starred Tribunal held, following the reasoning of *Thje Kwet Koe v Minister for Immigration and Ethnic Affairs* [1997] FCA 912, that the Turkish Republic of Northern Cyprus, which was not a state in international law, is not capable of being the country of a person's nationality (paras 30–33), and 'tentatively', that although the phrase 'country of former habitual residence' was wider, an area which formed part of an unrecognised state could not itself be a country of former habitual residence within the meaning of the Refugee Convention (para 39). On the related issue of 'protection', within the meaning of the refugee definition, in the context of de facto, non-internationally recognised, quasi-state entities, see **12.43** below.

12 *Revenko v Secretary of State for the Home Department* [2000] Imm AR 610, [2000] INLR 646, where the Court of Appeal rejected the argument that a stateless person needed only to show inability to return to qualify as a refugee – again, this conforms with the principle that as far as possible applicants with and those without nationality should be treated equally under the Convention (see fn 9 above).

13 UN Convention on the Status of Stateless Persons 1954: see **7.127** above. See also *Thje Kwet Koe v Minister for Immigration and Ethnic Affairs* [1997] FCA 912.

14 *MA (Palestinian Territories) v Secretary of State for the Home Department* [2008] EWCA Civ 304, [2008] All ER (D) 123 (Apr); *MT (Palestinian Territories) v Secretary of State for the Home Department* [2008] EWCA Civ 1149, [2008] All ER (D) 215 (Oct); *SH (Palestinian Territories) v Secretary of State for the Home Department* [2008] EWCA Civ 1150, [2008] All ER (D) 221 (Oct).

15 *SH v United Kingdom (Application 19956/06)* (2010) 54 EHRR 104, [2010] ECHR 19956/06.

12.37 Before the British Nationality Act 1981 came into force in 1983, it was doubtful whether Commonwealth citizens could be afforded refugee status in the UK, because all were 'British subjects'.[1] As such, they might be said to be British nationals for the purposes of international law and thus under British protection. In the light of the restricted definition of British subject under the 1981 Act, citizens of independent Commonwealth countries ceased to be British subjects and, therefore, British nationals.[2] The problem, however, remained in respect of British Nationals (Overseas) and British Overseas citizens who found themselves persecuted in their country of habitual residence.[3] The problem has been resolved for the future by statutory provision for the grant of full British citizenship, carrying the right of abode, to all categories of British nationals, including British protected persons, who have no other nationality.[4]

1 For British nationality, see CHAPTER 2 above.

2 British Nationality Act 1948 s 1(2) repealed and replaced by British Nationality Act 1981, s 37(4).

3 In *R v Chief Immigration Officer, Gatwick Airport, ex p Singh (Harjendar)* [1987] Imm AR 346, it was held that where a British Protected person had been rejected elsewhere, he or she could be treated as a person without nationality and issues were, therefore, raised under the Refugee Convention – a very practical way of bypassing what otherwise might have been difficult questions of the UK's international obligations.

4 British Nationals (Overseas) with no other nationality may register as British citizens under the British Nationality (Hong Kong) Act 1997. British Overseas citizens, British subjects under the 1981 Act and British protected persons with no other nationality may register under s 4B of the 1981 Act as inserted by Nationality, Immigration and Asylum Act 2002, s 12: see **2.21** above.

Statelessness under the Immigration Rules

12.38 Statelessness without more does not give rise to a viable claim to be Convention refugee; those legal rights and duties that arise in the context of the stateless emanate from the Convention on Statelessness.[1] Nevertheless the

Immigration Rules now give a specific claim to leave to remain to some classes of stateless person, of whom there may be many in the United Kingdom.[2] To be stateless for the purpose of the Rules a person must be present in the United Kingdom, not be considered as a national by any State under the operation of its laws, and not fall for exclusion[3] under clauses modelled on those of the Refugee Convention.[4] However, it is not categorisation as stateless which is the gateway to the true benefits of the Rule, but rather satisfying the requirements for leave to remain as a stateless person; namely having made a valid application to be considered as such (which requires that they have 'obtained and submitted all reasonably available evidence to enable the Secretary of State to determine' the issue) and are not admissible to their country of former habitual residence or any other country.[5] An application may fall for refusal either because these inclusionary considerations are not satisfied or due to the person being a danger to the security or public order of the United Kingdom or under the general grounds for refusal that apply across the Rules.[6] Successful candidates will receive a grant of leave to remain for 30 months which may be curtailed for the reasons of danger to the security or public order of the United Kingdom or under the general grounds for curtailment of leave.[7] This migration category can lead to settlement where a person has lived lawfully in the United Kingdom for five years (up to 28 days' overstaying being disregarded) having previously been granted leave to remain under the Rules on statelessness and continues to meet the eligibility criteria of non-admissibility abroad.[8] Their family members (spouse; civil partner; unmarried or same sex partner with whom they have lived together in a subsisting relationship akin to marriage or a civil partnership for two years or more; unmarried minor children not leading independent lives)[9] may be granted leave (including entry clearance) as their dependents where they make a valid application[10] subject to refusal for either posing the specific dangers that exclude the stateless or the general refusal reasons within the Rules.[11] Grants of leave to remain are for 30 months[12] and may be curtailed on similar grounds to those already set out.[13] Settlement may follow for family members who continue to satisfy the entrance requirements for the Rule.[14]

---

[1]   The 1954 Convention relating to the Status of Stateless Persons. Another key instrument is the 1961 Convention on the Reduction of Statelessness: The United Kingdom has ratified both instruments, as have 37 other States.

[2]   See the publication by Asylum Aid, *Mapping Statelessness in the United Kingdom* (January 2012) which sets out that there might be 12,211 in the United Kingdom as at summer 2011: of whom 66 were labelled 'Officially stateless', though a further 3,530 were recorded as being a 'Stateless person' (Article 1 of 1954 Convention). The UKBA database recorded a great many more people as 'Nationality currently unknown' or of 'Unspecified nationality'.

[3]   Immigration Rules, para 401.

[4]   Immigration Rules, para 402.

[5]   Immigration Rules, para 403.

[6]   Immigration Rules, para 404 referring to the general grounds for refusal under para 322.

[7]   Immigration Rules, para 405, referring to the general grounds for curtailment under para 323.

[8]   Immigration Rules, para 407.

[9]   Immigration Rules, para 410.

[10]   Immigration Rules, para 411.

[11]   Immigration Rules, para 412.

[12]   Immigration Rules, para 413.

[13]   Immigration Rules, para 414.

[14]   Immigration Rules, para 415.

12.39 Although refugees must first leave their own country in order to claim asylum, many of the countries from which refugees are fleeing are visa countries, ie their nationals require visas to enter the UK and other EU countries. While there is nothing in the Refugee Convention that would prevent a contracting state issuing a visa to enable a person to enter as a refugee, nor is there any obligation to do so.[1] UK practice was at one time for entry clearance officers to have discretion to accept applications for entry clearance where applicants meet the requirements of the Convention and had close ties with the UK (family, or time spent there as a student) where the UK was the most appropriate country of long-term refuge. The visa application form would then be sent to the Home Office.[2] However, the applicant is still required to be outside his or her own country. If a visa is refused or not applied for, but the asylum seekers nevertheless reach the UK, the absence of a visa will not prevent their claims to asylum from being considered. However, the corollary to the imposition of a mandatory visa requirement for most refugee-producing countries has been the enactment of measures penalising the carriers of asylum seekers. This began with the Immigration (Carriers' Liability) Act 1987, which provided for the imposition of a penalty on carriers for each passenger brought into the UK without proper documentation.[3] During the parliamentary debate on the passage of the 1987 Act, amendments to exempt carriers from financial penalties in the case of refugees were rejected. Instead, policy guidelines on the exercise of discretion were adopted (making limited provision for the waiver of fines, inter alia, where a passenger was subsequently accepted as a genuine refugee or where the passenger was in 'imminent and self-evident danger of his life').[4] The 1987 Act was repealed by the Immigration and Asylum Act 1999,[5] and re-enacted in amended form in sections 40–43.[6] The 1999 Act also imposes civil penalties on carriers bringing 'clandestine entrants' into the country, whether by design or inadvertently, which force van and lorry drivers and rail freight operators to check their vehicles and containers for stowaways.[7] The Government has rejected demands for a waiver of penalties in respect of clandestine entrants recognised as refugees, although it has a policy of waiving penalties imposed on carriers for inadequately documented passengers.[8]

[1] See *European Roma Rights Centre v Immigration Officer at Prague Airport* [2004] UKHL 55, [2005] 2 WLR 1.

[2] The practice was set out in the API on 'Applications from abroad'. See Judge Birtles sitting as a Deputy High Court judge in *R (on the application of MA (by her litigation FD)) v Secretary of State for the Home Department* [2012] EWHC 2683 (Admin), [2012] All ER (D) 181 (Oct) recording a letter of 19 March 2012 at [27]: 'The previously published policy on asylum application from abroad, which was withdrawn on 21 September 2011 for the purpose of being reviewed, made it clear that consideration would only be given, on a discretionary basis, to an application for asylum from abroad where the individual had very clear protection needs, and had particularly close ties with the UK, and the UK was the most appropriate country for asylum/ long-term refuge'. Subsequently Elias LJ in *R (on the application of MA (Somalia)) v Secretary of State for the Home Department* [2013] EWCA Civ 966, [2013] All ER (D) 214 (Feb) noted that under the policy, whether the applicants were refugees as defined by the Geneva Convention was a quite distinct question from whether they were applicants seeking asylum

[3] For the background to the passage of this Act see Nicholas Blake 'The Road to *Sivakumaran*' in (1989) 3 INLP 1 at 12. From 1991 the level of the fine per undocumented passenger was £2,000 (SI 1991/1497); Immigration and Asylum Act 1999, s 40(2) (as amended by the Nationality, Immigration and Asylum Act 2002) sets the fine at £2,000, or such other sum as may be substituted by order of the Secretary of State: 1999 Act, s 40(10) (as amended). For more detailed discussion of carrier sanctions see **15.97** ff below.

[4] See **15.98** below, where the guidance is set out in full.

5 IAA 1999, Sch 16.
6 The 1999 Act, ss 40–43 were amended by the Nationality, Immigration and Asylum Act 2002, Sch 8 (such that new ss 40A and 40B were added and s 42 repealed). See fn 3 above and CHAPTER 15 below.
7 See **15.93** ff below.
8 326 HC Official Report (6th series) col 1032.

'Unable or . . . unwilling to avail himself of the protection'

12.40 The failure of state protection is at the heart of refugee law. The refugee definition treats those with nationality and those who are stateless differently. To qualify as refugees, the former must be unable or unwilling to avail themselves of the protection of their country; the latter unable or unwilling to return to the country of habitual residence.[1] At the time of drafting the Refugee Convention it was envisaged that stateless persons, and nationals 'refused passport facilities or other protection by their own governments', would be the main categories qualifying through inability (as opposed to unwillingness) to obtain protection or to return.[2] But the category of refugees who have a nationality but are unable to secure the protection of their country is much wider than originally contemplated. It includes those who are unable through circumstances beyond the control of the state (for example, civil war or grave disturbance) as well as circumstances for which the state is directly responsible (for example, the refusal of passport facilities or denial of admission to the territory, which may itself in particular cases amount to persecution).[3] 'Inability' implies circumstances beyond the control of the person concerned, while 'unwillingness' implies his or her refusal to accept protection because of a fear of persecution.[4] For stateless persons, no question of availment of protection arises and the abandonment of the country of former habitual residence may in itself mean that the person is unable to return.[5] But all categories of refugees, including stateless persons, must demonstrate a current well-founded fear of Convention persecution to fulfil the definition requirements.[6]

1 Refugee Convention, art 1A(2): see **12.23** above. The meaning of 'country' in each phrase has been held to be different by the tribunal in *Dag* [2001] Imm AR 587 at **12.37** fn 9 above. See also *Tjhe Kwet Koe v MIEA* [1997] FCA 912 (Aust); *Zalzali v Minister of Employment and Immigration* [1991] 3 CF 605, CA (Can). See also however **12.36**, fnn 9 and 10 above for the principled approach to interpretation of the refugee definition that seeks, as far as possible, to minimise the differences in treatment between nationals and stateless persons.
2 See Goodwin-Gill **12.5** fn 1 above, p 41 citing report of the *Ad Hoc* Committee: UN doc. E/1618, 39. In the High Court of Australia in *Minister for Immigration and Multicultural Affairs v Khawar* [2002] HCA 14, Gleeson CJ stated that the words 'the protection of that country', of which a refugee with nationality must be unable or, owing to his well-founded fear, unwilling to avail himself for the purposes of the art 1A(2) definition, refer to diplomatic or consular protection abroad. Thus, where the country of nationality has a consular post in the country of refuge, a refugee will be unwilling to avail himself of his own country's protection there owing to his well-founded fear of being persecuted. Where there is no such consular post, the refugee will be unable to avail himself of any protection from his own country. McHugh and Gummow JJ agreed with Gleeson CJ on this issue.
3 *Lazarevic v Secretary of State for the Home Department* [1997] Imm AR 251 at 272, per Hutchison LJ. The example in that case was the refusal of the Federal Republic of Yugoslavia to permit the return of its nationals who had fled the conflict in former Yugoslavia and sought asylum abroad. See **12.36**, fn 7 above.
4 UNHCR *Handbook*, **12.13** above, paras 97–100. In *Svazas v Secretary of State for the Home Department* [2002] EWCA Civ 74, [2002] INLR 197 at para 22, Sedley LJ gave as an example of refugees who are unwilling to avail themselves of State protection, German Jews who had

been attacked by Brownshirt thugs in 1938 at a time when the Nazi authorities were pretending that such attacks were beyond their control. Clearly the reality then was that the authorities were in fact able to protect the Jews and so the drafters of the 1951 Convention would have had this in mind when inserting the 'unwilling to avail' clause. The extent to which an applicant may be expected to seek protection from their country of origin may depend on the applicant's sophistication and courage, see Finn J in the Federal Court of Australia in *AZAAR v Minister for Immigration and Citizenship* [2009] FCA 912 (19 August 2009). The more developed the state, the stronger will be the presumption that protection would have been forthcoming had the applicant sought to avail himself of it: Snider J in the Federal Court of Canada in *Alvandi v Canada (Citizenship and Immigration)* 2009 FC 790 (31 July 2009).

5   UNHCR *Handbook* above, para 101; *R v Secretary of State for the Home Department, ex p Adan* [1999] 1 AC 293.
6   *Revenko v Secretary of State for the Home Department* [2000] Imm AR 610, [2000] INLR 646, CA.

12.41 The mere possession of a valid national passport from the country where persecution is feared is not evidence that the person continues to seek protection from that country and is therefore no bar to refugee status; however, refugees who refuse to surrender their national passports to the host country without good reason may throw doubts on their unwillingness to avail themselves of the protection of their own country.[1] Similarly, an application for a national passport may raise such doubts but it would be an error of law to treat such an application as necessarily disentitling the person to refugee status.[2]

1   UNHCR *Handbook*, **12.13** above, paras 48–49, 97–101; *Refugee Appeal No 67/92 Re BR* (10 November 1992, unreported) (NZRSAA). See also *Minister for Immigration and Multicultural Affairs v Khawar* [2002] HCA 14, at **12.40** fn 2 above.
2   *NM (Afghanistan) v Secretary of State for the Home Department* [2007] EWCA Civ 214, [2007] All ER (D) 225 (Mar).

12.42 In *Adan*[1] the House of Lords considered whether a Somali national who had left his own country because of a well-founded fear of persecution, and who was unable to avail himself of the protection of that country because there was no effective state, was a refugee although he no longer had a well-founded fear of persecution. The Court of Appeal had held by a majority that as long as past persecution or fear of it was still a reason for the refugee's presence in the host country, it was unnecessary to show a current well-founded fear of persecution.[2] The House of Lords disagreed. Lord Lloyd, giving the leading judgment,[3] analysed the refugee definition as comprising a 'fear test' and a 'protection' test', both of which had to be satisfied.[4]

1   *R v Secretary of State for the Home Department, ex p Adan* [1999] 1 AC 293, [1998] INLR 325.
2   *Lazarevic v Secretary of State for the Home Department* [1997] 1 WLR 1107 at 1114–1115, [1997] INLR 1 at 8, [1997] Imm AR 251.
3   [1999] 1 AC 293 at 304–305; [1998] INLR 325, at 330–331. Lord Slynn reasoned that the use of the present tense in the definition, '*is* unable or, owing to such fear, unwilling to avail himself of the protection of that country' required a well-founded fear when refugee status was determined. Lords Goff, Nolan and Hope agreed with Lord Lloyd's reasoning. In *Sivakumaran* (18147) the IAT held that the same reasoning must apply to stateless applicants: see also *Revenko v Secretary of State for the Home Department* [2000] Imm AR 610, [2000] INLR 646, CA, at **12.37** above, text and fn 10.
4   Lord Lloyd's formulation was, however, significantly modified by the House of Lords in *Horvath v Secretary of State for the Home Department* [2000] INLR 329, HL, in the context of the meaning of 'persecution': see **12.55** below.

12.43 In *Vallaj*[1] the Administrative Court considered and rejected as 'narrowly linguistic' an argument that the protection available to someone to disqualify him or her from refugee status had necessarily to be provided by the authorities of the country of nationality. The issue arose in relation to ethnic Albanians in the Serbian province of Kosovo, in the Federal Republic of Yugoslavia, who were receiving protection not from the authorities of their own country but from a UN interim administration (known as UNMIK) and by NATO troops (known as KFOR) mandated by a UN security council resolution. An earlier starred Tribunal case, *Dyli*,[2] had held that the phrase 'the protection of the country' in the refugee definition referred to any protection available in the territory of the country of nationality, whatever its source. In *Vallaj* Dyson J held that the Refugee Convention should, as a living instrument, be interpreted in a way which takes account of the realities of the interventionist role that the UN Security Council now adopts when circumstances require it. Protection provided under lawful authority by a body to which all the powers and functions of the state (including the function of protection) have been transferred falls within the definition of 'protection of the country', and a person in receipt of such protection is not, subject to issues of adequacy of protection, a refugee.[3] On the other hand, in *Gardi*[4] the Court of Appeal acknowledged, obiter, the strength of the argument that the appellant – an Iraqi Kurd – could not avail himself of the 'protection of his country', for the purposes of the refugee definition, by seeking the protection of one of the two major Kurdish parties that had de facto control of northern Iraq. Unfortunately, for jurisdictional reasons, the Court of Appeal had to declare its judgment a nullity.[5] However, in *Saber*[6] the Inner House of the Scottish Court of Session (to which the appeal in *Gardi* had properly lain) fully adopted both the ratio and the obiter of the *Gardi* judgment and held that such de facto authorities were not capable of providing protection within the meaning of the refugee definition. However, the Qualification Directive[7] provides that protection 'can be provided by a state or by parties or organisations, including international organisations, controlling the state or a substantial part of the territory of the state' – a formulation which seems at odds with the refugee definition.[8]

1   *R (on the application of Vallaj) v Immigration Appeal Tribunal* [2001] INLR 655, per Dyson J.
2   *Dyli v Secretary of State for the Home Department* [2000] INLR 372, [2000] Imm AR 652.
3   *Vallaj* above, paras 24–35. Leave to appeal was refused by the Court of Appeal on 24 May 2001 in a reasoned judgment fully upholding Dyson J's approach: *Vallaj v Special Adjudicator* [2001] EWCA Civ 782, [2001] INLR 342, CA.
4   *Gardi v Secretary of State for the Home Department* [2002] EWCA Civ 750, [2002] 1 WLR 2755, [2003] Imm AR 39.
5   Because the adjudicator from whom the appeal emanated had sat in Scotland: see *Gardi v Secretary of State for the Home Department* [2002] EWCA Civ 1560, [2002] 1 WLR 3282.
6   *Saber v Secretary of State for the Home Department* (Appeal No XA129/02) 2003 SLT 1409, 2004 SCLR 621. See also *R (on the application of Mahmud) v Secretary of State for the Home Department* [2004] EWHC 148 (Admin), (2004) All ER (D) 102 (Feb) per Sullivan J The dominant judicial trend has been to reject the *Gardi/Saber* approach: see the Tribunal in *SF (Sufficiency of Protection-KAA-Michigan Guidelines) Iraq CG* [2002] UKIAT 07376); *DM (Majority Clan Entities Can Protect) Somalia* [2005] UKAIT 00150 (27 July 2005); *GH (Former KAZ-Country Conditions-Effect) Iraq CG* [2004] UKIAT 00248; Collins J in the Administrative Court in *R (on the application of A) v Secretary of State for the Home Department* [2006] EWHC 526 (Admin), [2006] All ER (D) 322 (Mar); and, earlier, the Tribunal in *Fadil Dyli (Protection, UNMIK, Arif, IFA, Art1D) (Kosovo) CG* (starred) [2000] UKIAT 00001 (30 August 2000) [2000] UKIAT 00001, [2000] INLR 372, [2000] UKIAT 1, [2000] Imm AR 652.

7   Directive 2004/83/EC, **12.3** fn 3 above, art 7.
8   The Tribunal in *GH (Iraq) CG* [2004] UKIAT 00248 referred obiter to a Canadian case, *Zalzali v Minister of Employent and Immigration* [1991] 3 CF 605 in support of the proposition that it was practical protection that was relevant to refugee status rather than the protection of the official government in circumstances of civil war. The status of the Canadian authority is not clear and the judgment cited appears to be one of impression rather than authority.

Internal relocation alternative

12.44 Because the principal concern of refugee law is the provision of international protection to persons unable to receive protection in their own country, a purely localised risk will generally be insufficient to make someone a refugee. International protection is not needed if the person can obtain protection by moving elsewhere in his or her own country.[1] But if, as the UNHCR *Handbook* points out, internal flight or internal relocation, to another part of the country is not reasonable or safe, it is not necessary to prove that persecution for a Convention reason extends to the whole of the country.[2] The Qualification Directive allows Member States to refuse asylum if there is a part of the country of origin where there is no well-founded fear of persecution or real risk of suffering serious harm, and where the applicant can reasonably be expected to stay.[3] These considerations are reflected in the Immigration Rules,[4] which provide that an asylum claim *may* be refused if there is a part of the country to which it would be reasonable to expect the applicant to go, where he or she does not have a well founded fear of persecution. The issue of internal relocation only arises if the asylum seeker has a well-founded fear of persecution in his or her home area, or if he or she cannot return there without a real risk of persecution on the way[5] either at the point of arrival or en route from there to a place of safety. Such travel-related risks, even for a person with a safe home area, can be sufficient to establish a claim to protection and must be considered as part of the process of deciding upon an asylum claim, at least to the extent that the evidence as to where the person would be returned allows. Moreover, it is arguable that if an applicant advances a cogent claim of travel-related risks the authorities have an obligation to produce evidence as to the place of return in the course of status determination; the issue cannot be deferred until such time as removal directions are given.[6] There is academic opinion that internal relocation is ruled out where persecution emanates from the state itself or its own agents;[7] UNHCR's view is that in such a case there should be a (rebuttable) presumption against there being a possible internal relocation alternative.[8] However, that proposition has now been rejected by the House of Lords.[9] In a case of persecution by the state, whether there is an internal flight alternative is a question of fact which requires analysis of the nature of the state's involvement in the persecution. 'The more closely the persecution in question is linked to the State, and the greater the control of the State over those acting or purporting to act on its behalf, the more likely (other things being equal) that a victim of persecution in one place will be similarly vulnerable in another place within the State. The converse may also be true'.[10] Article 8 of the Qualification Directive[11] relating to internal protection has now been implemented by the Immigration Rules.[12] The Directive and the rules both provide for a person to be disqualified from international protection if there is an 'internal flight alternative' but return to the country of origin is prevented by 'technical obstacles'.[13]

1. See eg *R v Secretary of State for the Home Department, ex p Robinson* [1998] QB 929, [1997] INLR 182, [1997] Imm AR 568; *AE and FE v Secretary of State for the Home Department* [2003] EWCA Civ 1032, [2004] QB 531.

2. UNHCR *Handbook* **12.13** above, para 91. The previously preferred term, 'internal flight', is problematic in that it refers to the past (whether the applicant *could have* moved elsewhere) rather than to the crucial issue as to whether now, on return to the country, the applicant could internally relocate within it: see *AE and FE v Secretary of State for the Home Department* [2003] EWCA Civ 1032, [2004] QB 531 at [19]. The preferable concept is 'internal protection': see the Michigan Guidelines on the Internal Protection Alternative, April 1999, given 'outline approval' by the Court of Appeal in *Vallaj v Special Adjudicator* [2001] EWCA Civ 782, [2001] INLR 342 at para 27. See also *Refugee Appeal No 71684/99* [2000] INLR 165, NZRSAA – although the Court of Appeal rejected the ratio of this New Zealand decision in *E v Secretary of State for the Home Department* [2003] EWCA Civ 1032, [2004] QB 531 at paras 47–48.

3. Directive 2004/83/EC, **12.3** fn 3 above, art 8. This affords significantly weaker protection than its predecessor, the EU Joint Position (96/196/JHA) of 4 March 1996 on harmonised application of definition of the term 'refugee' (*Butterworths Immigration Law Service*, 2D[138]), which required 'effective protection' in the 'safe' part of the country in order to disqualify the claimant from international protection. Though there appears to be a procedural safeguard for asylum seekers, in that the Secretary of State should raise internal relocation at the time of original decision or not at all, see Directive 2004/83, art 8(2): 'Member States shall at the time of taking the decision on the application'.

4. HC 395, para 343.

5. *Dyli* [2000] INLR 372, [2000] Imm AR 652, (starred IAT); *R (on the application of Vallaj) v A Special Adjudicator* [2001] INLR 655, QBD, per Dyson J; upheld as *Vallaj v Special Adjudicator* [2001] EWCA Civ 782, [2001] INLR 342 (permission refusal) The alternative area must be reachable on return without the applicant having to land in or travel through an area in which he does have a well-founded fear of Convention persecution: see *Senga (Jouanna)* (11821) (UNITA supporter could not be safely returned to Luanda as she would be at risk of persecution there before she would be able to reach 'safe' UNITA held territory); see also *Ganeshan v Secretary of State for the Home Department* (SLJ 99/6274/3) (27 August 1999, unreported), CA, grant of permission per Schiemann LJ (it is arguably incumbent upon the UK authorities to consider whether a claimant is likely to be persecuted or is at risk of being persecuted in the part of the country to which it is proposed to return him or her). In *EM and others (Returnees) Zimbabwe CG* [2011] UKUT 98 (IAC) the UTIAC at [220] explained that the question of a person's home area must be assessed as a matter of fact (ie it is not necessarily place of birth, but might be the place the asylum seeker habitually lived before fleeing abroad).

6. *HH (Somalia) v Secretary of State for the Home Department* [2010] EWCA Civ 426; *AG (Somalia) v Secretary of State for the Home Department* [2006] EWCA Civ 1342; *GH (Iraq) v Secretary of State for the Home Department* [2005] EWCA Civ 1182.

7. Expressed by a panel of expert specialists in refugee law including Professor Hathaway in the Michigan Colloquium of April 1999: see the Michigan Guidelines on the internal protection alternative, April 1999, available at www:refugee.law.nz.

8. See the UNHCR 'Position Paper on Relocating Internally as Reasonable Alternative to Seeking Asylum', February 1999. See also UNHCR's 'Guidelines on International Protection No 4: Internal Flight or the Internal Relocation Alternative within the context of art 1A(2) of the 1951 Convention and/or the 1967 Protocol relating to the status of refugees (HCR/GIP/03/04) 23 July 2003. This approach is adopted in New Zealand – see eg NZ Court of Appeal decision *(Daniel Martin) v Attorney General and Refugee Status Appeals Authority* (Decision No 181/97) (13 October 1997, unreported), NZ CA. In *R v Immigration Appeal Tribunal, ex p Guang (Chen)* [2000] INLR 80, QBD, Keene J accepted that internal relocation was less likely to be an option where the fear was of state authorities, but disliked elevating this idea into a presumption. The presumption against internal relocation in state agent cases may be rebutted where the fear is of a specific local police force (eg the Punjab police in India: see *Singh (Chinder) v Secretary of State for the Home Department* [1998] Imm AR 551; or the police in Zanzibar, where there is a possibility of relocation to mainland Tanzania: see *R v Secretary of State for the Home Department, ex p Salim* [1999] INLR 628, [2000] Imm AR 6, QBD and *Aziz v Secretary of State for the Home Department* [2003] EWCA Civ 118).

9. *Januzi v Secretary of State for the Home Department; Hamid v Secretary of State for the Home Department; Gaafar v Secretary of State for the Home Department; Mohammed v Secretary of State for the Home Department* [2006] UKHL 5, [2006] 3 All ER 305, [2006] 2 WLR 397.

[10] *Januzi v Secretary of State for the Home Department* per Lord Bingham at para 21.
[11] Council Directive 2004/83/EC.
[12] HC 395, para 339O, as inserted by HC 6918.
[13] Qualification Directive, art 7(3); HC 395, para 339O(iii).

12.45 In *Robinson*[1] the Court of Appeal considered the appellate jurisdiction to decide on the reasonableness of relocation to an area of the country where there was no fear of persecution. The Tribunal had been divided on whether it could consider the issue, with one division holding that its jurisdiction was limited to the issue whether returning the appellant would breach the UK's obligations under the Refugee Convention[2] and that the wording of paragraph 343 of the Immigration Rules reflected an unreviewable discretion,[3] and another that the possibility of internal flight was part of the refugee definition.[4] The Court of Appeal, after reviewing Commonwealth jurisprudence and the views of academics, held that both the safety and the reasonableness of the 'internal flight alternative' went to ability and willingness to avail oneself of the protection of the country of persecution, and thus were within jurisdiction on appeal. As to what would be 'reasonable', the court emphasised that decision-makers must consider 'all relevant circumstances against the backcloth that the issue is whether the claimant is entitled to the status of refugee'. Such circumstances might include whether as a practical matter (for financial, logistical or other good reason) the 'safe' part of the country is reasonably accessible; whether the claimant is required to encounter great physical danger or to undergo undue hardship in travelling there or staying there, whether the claimant would have to go into hiding,[5] and whether the quality of the internal protection fails to meet basic norms of civil, political and socio-economic human rights.[6] The court approved the test by Linden JA in the Canadian Federal Court in *Thirunavukkarasu*:[7] 'Would it be unduly harsh to expect this person to move to another less hostile part of the country?'[8] The comparison is between the refugee's circumstances in his or her home area and the proposed place of relocation, not between conditions in the country of asylum and the internal flight alternative.[9] In *Canaj*[10] the Court of Appeal suggested that *Robinson* should now be read together with the New Zealand decision in *Refugee Appeal No 71684/99*.[11] The New Zealand case[12] had decided that whether there was an internal flight alternative had to be determined according to whether basic norms of civil, political and socio-economic human rights were satisfied in the putatively 'safe area'. That approach has been rejected by the House of Lords.[13] The question is simply whether it would be unreasonable to expect the refugee to relocate within his or her country: or as it is sometimes put, whether this would be 'unduly harsh'.[14]

[1] *R v Secretary of State for the Home Department, ex p Robinson* [1998] QB 929, [1997] INLR 182, [1997] Imm AR 568.
[2] Asylum and Immigration Appeals Act 1993, s 8 (now Nationality, Immigration and Asylum Act 2002, s 84(1)(g), (3)); *R v Secretary of State for the Home Department, ex p Mehari* [1994] QB 474.
[3] *Dupovac* (11846); *Ahmed* (13371); *Nirmalan* (14361).
[4] *Ikhlaq* (13679).
[5] Kelen J in the Federal Court of Canada summarising the Canadian approach to internal relocation at [34] in *Gallo Farias v Canada (Citizenship and Immigration)* 2008 FC 1035 (16 September 2009): 'Claimants are not compelled to hide out in an isolated region like a cave or a desert or a jungle'.
[6] *Robinson* **12.45** above, para 18, referring to the Preamble to the Refugee Convention.

7   *Thirunavukkarasu v Minister of Employment and Immigration* (1993) 109 DLR (4th) 682 per Linden JA at 687 (Can Fed Ct).
8   *Robinson* above, para 29.
9   *AE and FE v Secretary of State for the Home Department* [2003] EWCA Civ 1032, [2004] QB 531, [2004] 2 WLR 123.
10 *Vallaj v Special Adjudicator* [2001] EWCA Civ 782, [2001] INLR 342 (but see **12.43**, above).
11 [2000] INLR 165.
12 *Refugee Appeal No 71684/99* [2000] INLR 165, approved in *Canaj v Secretary of State for the Home Department*; *Vallaj v Special Adjudicator* [2001] EWCA Civ 782, [2001] All ER (D) 322 (May), [2001] INLR 342.
13 *Januzi v Secretary of State for the Home Department*; *Hamid v Secretary of State for the Home Department*; *Gaafar v Secretary of State for the Home Department Mohammed v Secretary of State for the Home Department* [2006] UKHL 5, [2006] 3 All ER 305, [2006] 2 WLR 397.
14 *Januzi v Secretary of State for the Home Department* per Lord Bingham at para 15 and Lord Hope at para 47. Directive 2004/83 refers clearly to whether a person 'can reasonably be expected to stay in that part of the country', rather an undue harshness, as being the measure: art 8(1).

12.46 Lord Bingham commended the UNHCR Guidelines on International Protection of 23 July 2003 as providing 'valuable guidance' on the approach to reasonableness and undue harshness in this context.[1] According to that guidance, internal relocation would be unduly harsh if the person would suffer deprivation of human rights that were fundamental to the particular individual and sufficiently harmful to render the area an unreasonable alternative or if the person could not 'sustain a relatively normal life at more than just a minimum subsistence level' or if the person would be denied access to land, resources and protection because he or she does not belong to the dominant clan, tribe, ethnic or religious or cultural group in the area or if the person was required 'to relocate to areas, such as the slums of an urban area, where [he or she] would be required to live in conditions of severe hardship'.[2] The Tribunal[3] was wrong in interpreting this such that nothing less than a breach of Article 2 or 3 of the European Convention on Human Rights would establish that internal flight was 'unduly harsh'.[4] The House of Lords subsequently revisited the issue of internal relocation and held that to adopt such an approach would have been 'an egregious and inexplicable error' on the part of the Tribunal.[5] Whilst the terms in which the Tribunal expressed itself in the case that was before the House of Lords indicated that that was indeed the test that the Tribunal had applied, the House of Lords felt able to infer from the fact of the Tribunal's eminence and expertise that it could not have made such an error. Although the conclusion reached by the House of Lords might appear to result from an application of the principle that, 'the worse the apparent error is, the less ready an appellate court should be to find that it has occurred', the Court of Appeal emphasised, in a judgment that considered the House of Lords decision, that there is no such principle.[6] When assessing the possibility of internal relocation the decision maker is not restricted to comparing conditions for the asylum seeker in his or her home area and the place of relocation (as the Court of Appeal had apparently held in a number of cases[7]) but may have regard to conditions in the country generally. When internal relocation is in issue 'the decision-maker, taking account of all relevant circumstances pertaining to the claimant and his country of origin, must decide whether it is reasonable to expect the claimant to relocate or whether it would be unduly harsh to expect him to do so'[8] and to that end 'the enquiry must be directed to the situation of the particular applicant, whose age, gender, experience, health, skills and family ties may all be very relevant. There is no warrant for excluding, or giving priority to, consideration of the applicant's way of life in the place of persecution. There is no warrant for excluding, or giving priority to consideration of conditions generally prevailing in the home country'.[9] What is required is an 'individualised, holistic assessment' of all relevant factors.[10] Thus, although the Tribunal's country guidance was that in general it was not unduly harsh for persecuted Sudanese to relocate to the appalling conditions of extreme poverty in the IDP camps, that was not a sufficient basis to find that the applicant had an internal relocation alternative. The impact of those conditions on the individual claimant had to be assessed in the light of his particular circumstances which included 'everyday knowledge that those responsible for such conditions are also responsible for the death of his every living relative'.[11] An example of the factual span of the likely inquiries is shown by the Tribunal's consideration of whether a gay Palestinian could relocate within Lebanon taking account of the legal ban on Palestinians owning property; accommodation being too expensive; the legal exclusion of Palestinians from many trades and professions; the difficulty of obtaining a work permit and the difficulties that would be faced by a homosexual living in a Muslim area of the country.[12] A person's economic background is likely to be relevant to their ability to survive in a different economic environment.[13] An internal flight alternative might be unreasonable if it depended upon an individual having to conceal some aspect of his or her identity or history and having to live with the consequent fear of discovery.[14] Internal relocation may pose particular challenges for women: where they need to seek their family's permission to travel or where travelling unaccompanied is dangerous, where social and cultural norms prescribing gender roles promote discrimination that may force a woman into desperate measures such as prostitution, and where there is a proximity to dangerously inactive males.[15] In *AA Afghanistan* the Tribunal highlighted the relevance of child specific issues to internal relocation, stressing that the Convention on the Rights of the Child is relevant to the question of whether internal relocation would be unduly harsh.[16] Humanitarian crises that are the legacy of man-made conditions, such as armed conflict, do not have to reach an especially high threshold before constituting unreasonable internal relocation conditions.[17] There is a high duty on the Secretary of State to raise the issue as a matter of procedural fairness.[18]

---

[1] *Januzi v Secretary of State for the Home Department* [2006] UKHL 5, [2006] 3 All ER 305, [2006] 2 WLR 397 at para 20.

[2] UNHCR Guidelines on International Protection of 23 July 2003, cited in *Januzi v Secretary of State for the Home Department* [2006] UKHL 5, [2006] 3 All ER 305, [2006] 2 WLR 397. Though see Lord Brown in the House of Lords in *AH (Sudan) v Secretary of State for the Home Department* [2007] UKHL 49, [2008] 1 AC 678, [2008] 4 All ER 190 at [48], [2007] 3 WLR 832 for one view on the height of the threshold.

[3] *HGMO (Sudan) CG* [2006] UKAIT 00062 (SIJs Hodge, Storey and Lane), the determination of the Sudanese appeals following their remital to the Tribunal by the House of Lords in *Januzi*. In *AB (Jamaica) CG* [2007] UKAIT 00018 the Tribunal's determination (written by Dr Storey, as was the determination in HGMO) said 'as clarified by the House of Lords in *Januzi*, unreasonableness or undue hardship under the Refugee Convention as well as under Article 3 of the ECHR can only be shown if there is, in the particular circumstances of the individual's case, a real risk of a violation of a basic, non-derogable human right: see *Januzi* [2006] UKHL'.

[4] Lord Bingham in the House of Lords in *Secretary of State for the Home Department v AH (Sudan) and Ors* [2007] UKHL 49, [2008] 4 All ER 190 at [9].

[5] *AH (Sudan) v Secretary of State for the Home Department* [2007] UKHL 49, Lord Bingham in para 11, [2007] 3 WLR 832.

6 *NH (India) v Entry Clearance Officer* [2007] EWCA Civ 1330, [2007] All ER (D) 199 (Dec), Sedley LJ.

7 As the Court of Appeal had approached the issue in the instant case, *AH (Sudan) v Secretary of State for the Home Department* [2007] EWCA Civ 297, [2007] All ER (D) 55 (Apr) consistently with earlier decisions of the Court of Appeal such as *AE and FE v Secretary of State for the Home Department* [2003] EWCA Civ 1032, [2004] QB 531.

8 *Januzi v Secretary of State for the Home Department* [2006] UKHL 5, Lord Bingham in para 21, [2006] 2 AC 426, [2006] 3 All ER 305, cited by Lord Bingham in *Secretary of State for the Home Department v AH (Sudan)* [2007] UKHL 49, para 5

9 *Secretary of State for the Home Department v AH (Sudan)*, para 5.

10 *KH (Sudan) v Secretary of State for the Home Department* [2008] EWCA Civ 887, [2008] All ER (D) 08 (Aug), referring to Baroness Hale's speech in *Secretary of State for the Home Department v AH (Sudan)*.

11 *KH (Sudan) v Secretary of State for the Home Department* [2008] EWCA Civ 887, [2008] All ER (D) 08 (Aug).

12 *HC v Secretary of State for the Home Department* [2005] EWCA Civ 893, [2005] All ER (D) 267 (Jul). Subjective fear may be relevant, see Sedley LJ in the Court of Appeal in *FK (Kenya) v Secretary of State for the Home Department* [2008] EWCA Civ 119 at [29] stating that 'the reasonableness of a particular relocation is not necessarily confined to what is objectively to be feared there . . . There may be cases where the tribunal is satisfied that, objectively, the appellant can be safe on relocation, but the appellant is so traumatised by past events that she remains in genuine terror of being returned there.'

13 *EM and others (Returnees) Zimbabwe CG* [2011] UKUT 98 (IAC) at [223].

14 *Hysi v Secretary of State for the Home Department* [2005] EWCA Civ 711, (2005) Times, 23 June, [2005] All ER (D) 135 (Jun).

15 UN High Commissioner for Refugees, Displacement, Statelessness and Questions of Gender Equality under the Convention on the Elimination of All Forms of Discrimination against Women, August 2009, PPLAS/2009/02.

16 *AA (unattended children) Afghanistan CG* [2012] UKUT 16 (IAC).

17 *Sufi and Elmi v United Kingdom* [2011] ECHR 1045;*AMM and others (conflict; humanitarian crisis; returnees; FGM) Somalia CG* [2011] UKUT 445 (IAC); *SHH v United Kingdom* 60367/10-HEJUD [2013] ECHR 102.

18 *AMM and others (conflict; humanitarian crisis; returnees; FGM) Somalia CG* [2011] UKUT 445 (IAC) at [225]-[227].

12.47 A further question with internal relocation related to the burden and standard of proving whether internal relocation was reasonable or 'unduly harsh'. Who had to prove what, to which standard? In *Manoharan*[1] a Tribunal had held that the burden was on the applicant to show on balance of probabilities that it would be unduly harsh to return him; in *Sachithananthan*[2] a Tribunal held (following *Thirunavukkarasu*)[3] that the test was whether there was a serious possibility that it would be unduly harsh. The issue was resolved in *Karanakaran*[4] where the Court of Appeal decided that no 'standard of proof' as such applied; the question was simply whether, taking all relevant[5] matters into account, return of the claimant would be unduly harsh. This was a matter of evaluation and conscientious judgment.[6] Everything capable of having a bearing on the question was to be taken into account (which might include the need to consider the cumulative effect of a whole range of disparate considerations).[7] The court commended the methodology of the Tribunal in the case of *Sayandan* where, in considering whether return would be unduly harsh, it had set out some eleven disparate risks as matters worthy of attention and had evaluated both the likelihood of a risk eventuating and the seriousness of the consequences.[8] The burden remains on the applicant to demonstrate that it would not be reasonable to expect him to relocate internally within his country of origin.[9] However, internal flight is only a legitimate issue in an appeal if proper notice that it is to be raised is given.[10] Moreover, notwithstanding that there is no formal burden of proof on the Home Office in relation to internal flight, an otherwise well-founded claim may only be rejected if the evidence satisfies the judge of fact that internal relocation is a safe and reasonable option.[11]

1 *Manoharan v Secretary of State for the Home Department* [1998] INLR 519.
2 *Secretary of State for the Home Department v Sachithananthan* [1999] INLR 205.
3 *Thirunavukkarasu v Minister of Employment and Immigration* (1993) 109 DLR (4th) 682.
4 *Karanakaran v Secretary of State for the Home Department* [2000] 3 All ER 449, [2000] INLR 122, CA.
5 In *Gnanam v Secretary of State for the Home Department* [1999] INLR 219, CA Tuckey LJ emphasised that what may be relevant factors in one case would not necessarily be so in another, whether considered individually or cumulatively.
6 *Karanakaran v Secretary of State for the Home Department* above [2000] 3 All ER 449 at 477and 479, [2000] INLR 122 at 152 and 154, CA. This approach was expressly approved by Lord Steyn in *R (on the application of Sivakumar) v Secretary of State for the Home Department* [2003] UKHL 14, [2003] INLR 457, at para 19, HL. On this approach presumably it would be open to different countries to take different views about what was reasonable: see *R (on the application of Yogathas) v Secretary of State for the Home Department; R (on the application of Thangarasa) v Secretary of State for the Home Department* [2002] UKHL 36, [2003] 1 AC 920, [2002] INLR 620, at para 115, per Lord Scott.
7 *Gnanam* (above) and *Karanakaran* at INLR 145, per Brooke LJ. Sedley LJ observed at INLR 154–155 that the correct approach coincided with that advocated by Simon Brown LJ in *Ravichandran (Senathirajah) v Secretary of State for the Home Department* [1996] Imm AR 97 at 109, ie consideration of the 'single composite question' whether a person has a 'well-founded fear of being persecuted for Convention reasons' in the round and with all relevant circumstances brought into account. In Australia a similar wide-ranging approach to internal flight has been adopted: see eg *Randhawa v MILGEA* (1994) 52 FCR 437; *Franco-Buitrago v Minister for Immigration and Multicultural Affairs* [2000] FCA 1525.
8 *Sayandan* (16312) 5 March 1998. The risks identified in returning a Tamil to Colombo were arrest and return to the North East because of lack of documents; repeated arrest in round-ups; being subject to extortion; unduly harsh treatment before accessing judicial process; dreadful prison conditions if detained; not being able to find or retain accommodation; not being able to find employment because of discrimination; where the appellant could not speak Sinhalese; being subjected to a regime where racial discrimination was part of everyday life; having no real contacts or ties in Colombo; and previous ill-treatment in Sri Lanka by both the LTTE and the security forces.
9 See *Aziz v Secretary of State for the Home Department* [2003] EWCA Civ 118; *R v Secretary of State for the Home Department, ex p Salim* [1999] INLR 628, [2000] Imm AR 6, QBD.
10 *Daoud v Secretary of State for the Home Department* [2005] EWCA Civ 755, [2005] All ER (D) 259 (May).
11 Sedley LJ's dissenting judgment in *Jasim v Secretary of State for the Home Department* [2006] EWCA Civ 342, (2006) Times, 17 May. The majority dismissed the appeal on the basis that the immigration judge had been entitled to find on the evidence that internal relocation was safe and reasonable. See also *AA (Uganda) v Secretary of State for the Home Department* [2008] EWCA Civ 579, [2008] All ER (D) 300 (May): the Tribunal had been wrong to find the appellant had an internal relocation alternative on the basis that there was no evidence that she would be unable to obtain support from her church in that location. The question it should have addressed was whether, on the evidence, such support would be available to her so as to establish an internal relocation alternative.

Persecution for Convention reasons

Persecution

12.48 The Refugee Convention does not define persecution[1] and, although the term, like the entire refugee definition, has an autonomous meaning,[2] there is no universally accepted definition.[3] As we shall see in relation to persecution by non-state agents, its meaning is linked to the availability of state protection, at least so far as the UK is concerned.[4] The *Handbook* indicates that, while a threat to life or freedom for the relevant reason will always amount to persecution,[5] persecution does not have to involve threats to life or freedom; other serious violations of human rights will also qualify.[6] In *Jonah*[7] Nolan J ruled that the word must be given its ordinary dictionary definition 'to pursue with malignancy or injurious action, especially to oppress for holding a heretical opinion or belief'. The case law reveals a tension between (i) the approach which sees the issue solely as one of fact for the decision maker and the immigration judge, subject to challenge in the Administrative Court solely on *Wednesbury* principles,[8] and (ii) attempts to provide a coherent framework for persecution based on human rights law. Whether a particular act constitutes persecution is a mixed question of fact and law.[9] The human rights approach dictated by the preamble of the Refugee Convention has been propounded by James Hathaway, who in his seminal book *The Law of Refugee Status* defined persecution as 'the sustained or systemic failure of state protection in relation to one of the core entitlements which has been recognised by the international community',[10] a definition endorsed by Lord Steyn in *Ullah*.[11] In the influential case of *Gashi*,[12] the Tribunal adopted UNHCR's analysis of persecution,[13] which drew heavily on Hathaway's definition,[14] in relation to three categories of human rights. Breaches of inviolable human rights such as the right to life and the prohibition against torture, cruel, inhuman or degrading treatment would always be persecution. Violation of rights whose limited derogation or curtailment by the state could be justified only in time of public emergency (freedom from arbitrary arrest and detention and freedom of expression) would be persecution if unjustified. The denial of rights reflecting goals for social, economic or cultural development, such as the right to a livelihood, could amount to persecution if it was systematic and discriminatory. More recently, Goodwin-Gill[15] has stated that the 'core meaning' of persecution 'readily includes the threat of deprivation of life or physical freedom' although 'less overt measures may suffice, such as the imposition of serious economic disadvantage, denial of access to employment, to the professions, or to education, or other restrictions on the freedoms traditionally guaranteed in a democratic society'.[16] In *Appellant S*[17] in the Australian High Court McHugh and Kirby JJ made the point that a *threat* of serious harm, with its 'menacing implications', can constitute persecution, especially when it causes a person to alter his or her behaviour.[18] Although mere discrimination is probably not enough, evidence of discrimination will make it easier to demonstrate persecution. And where discrimination is so severe, frequent or protracted that it inhibits freedom to exercise basic human rights such as the right to a livelihood or to practice a religion, it may amount to persecution.[19] Being forced to live in dire social and economic conditions may amount to being persecuted.[20] Arbitrary deprivation of citizenship amounts to persecution without the need further to demonstrate that the loss of citizenship has consequences of sufficient severity to amount to persecution[21] although denial to a stateless person of re-entry to the country of his or her former habitual residence would not by itself be persecutory.[22] The disadvantage of linking the definition of persecution to core human rights is that if the asylum seeker cannot establish the existence of the core right, there will be no persecution.[23] The Qualification Directive sets out a definition of 'acts of persecution'[24] in mandatory terms in art 9(1) by which they must be '(a) sufficiently serious by their nature or repetition as to constitute a severe violation of basic human rights, in particular the rights from which derogation cannot be made under art 15(2) of the European Convention for the Protection of Human Rights'[25] or '(b) be an accumulation of various measures, including violations of human rights which is sufficiently severe as to affect an individual in a similar manner as mentioned in (a)'. It lists various forms that acts of persecution may take (eg acts of physical or mental violence, legal, administrative, police or judicial measures which are discriminatory) but it is important to note that the list is illustrative, not exhaustive.[26] The individual's particular characteristics and circumstances including background, gender and age must be taken into account in order to determine whether the acts feared would amount to persecution or serious harm.[27] The Court of Appeal has held that the threshold for persecution imposed by the Directive is higher than under the Refugee Convention as interpreted in the authorities.[28] Article 9(1)(a) contains an exhaustive, not an illustrative definition of the 'basic human rights', which have to be violated for there to be persecution. They are the non-derogable rights contained in arts 2 (right to life), 3 (freedom from inhuman and degrading treatment and torture), 4(1) (prohibition of slavery) and 7 (prohibition of retrospective penalisation) of the ECHR. Moreover, the violation must be 'severe' in order to amount to persecution under the Directive.[29] However, if 'basic human rights' are limited to the non-derogable rights in that way it would mean that the Directive contemplates the possibility of violations of those rights which are not severe and therefore are not persecutory. It is difficult to imagine how there can be a violation of, for example, the right not to be tortured or enslaved or unlawfully killed which would be anything other than severe.

1   This section considers the meaning of 'persecution' at the hands of the state – the classic or paradigm case of persecution that would have been foremost in the minds of the drafters of the Refugee Convention in the aftermath of the Second World War and the defeat of the Nazi regime. Following *Horvath v Secretary of State for the Home Department* [2001] 1 AC 489, [2000] INLR 239, a modified meaning is required where the allegation relates to persecution by non-state agents: see *Persecution by non-state actors* at **12.40** ff above. See also **12.44** above on the differing relevance of the 'internal relocation alternative' depending on whether the persecutor is a state or non-state actor.

2   See *R v Secretary of State for the Home Department, ex p Adan, R v Secretary of State for the Home Department, ex p Aitseguer* [2001] 2 AC 477, [2001] INLR 44.

3   In *Appellant S395/2002 v Minister for Immigration and Multicultural Affairs* [2003] HCA 71 at para 66, Aust High Ct, Gummow and Hayne JJ (in a joint judgment forming part of the majority) pointed out that 'It is not of great assistance and is apt to mislead to approach the matter by saying, as did an English court, that "persecution" is a "strong word".' The English case was *R v Secretary of State for the Home Department, ex p Binbasi* [1989] Imm AR 595 at 599 per Kennedy J See also **12.47**, fn 13 below.

4   *Horvath* fn 1 above, and below at **12.53** ff.

5   This is clear from the *'non-refoulement'* provision in art 33, which prohibits the return of a refugee to the frontiers of territories where 'life or freedom would be threatened' for a Refugee Convention reason.

6   UNHCR *Handbook* **12.13** above, para 51; *R v Secretary of State for the Home Department, ex p Sivakumaran* [1988] AC 958, per Lord Goff; *Horvath* above, at 215H, per Lord Lloyd.

7   *R v Immigration Appeal Tribunal, ex p Jonah* [1985] Imm AR 7.

8   See *Kagema v Secretary of State for the Home Department* [1997] Imm AR 137; *Faraj v Secretary of State for the Home Department* [1999] INLR 451. In *Horvath* above Lord Lloyd described the proposition that persecution should be given its ordinary dictionary meaning as 'settled law' (at 251).

9   Stanley Burnton LJ in the Court of Appeal in *MA (Ethiopia) v Secretary of State for the Home Department* [2009] EWCA Civ 289 (02 April 2009) at [62].

10   See **12.24** fn 3 above.

11 *R (on the application of Ullah) v Special Adjudicator* [2004] UKHL 26, [2004] 3 WLR 23, at para 32. See also Lord Hope in *Horvath v Secretary of State for the Home Department* [2000] 3 All ER 577, [2000] 3 WLR 379, HL; Lord Bingham in *Sepet v Secretary of State for the Home Department* [2003] 1 WLR 856 (para 7). But see *Amare v Secretary of State for the Home Department* [2005] EWCA Civ 1600, [2005] All ER (D) 300 (Dec) where the Court of Appeal said that Professor Hathaway's definition had to be 'treated with a degree of caution' because it did not give a clear place to the requirement that the human rights violation had to be sufficiently serious by reference either to its intensity or duration. See also *RG (Colombia) v Secretary of State for the Home Department* [2006] EWCA Civ 57 applying what had been said obiter in *Amare*; see further *MI (Pakistan) v Secretary of State for the Home Department* [2014] EWCA Civ 826.

12 *Gashi v Secretary of State for the Home Department* [1997] INLR 96. See also Schiemann LJ in *Blanusa v Secretary of State for the Home Department* (IATRF 98/1495/4) (18 May 1998, unreported), CA.

13 UNHCR appeared as intervener in the case.

14 In Hathaway's formulation, the types of harm to be protected against include the breach of any right within the first category, a discriminatory or non-emergency abrogation of a right within the second category, or the failure to implement a right within the third category which is either discriminatory or not grounded in the absolute lack of resources: see *The Law of Refugee Status* (n 9 above) pp 101–116.

15 *The Refugee in International Law*, **12.5** fn 1 above, pp 66–68.

16 Whether such restrictions amount to persecution requires assessment of a complex of factors, including (1) the nature of the freedom threatened, (2) the nature and severity of the restriction, and (3) the likelihood of the restriction eventuating in the individual case: Goodwin-Gill fn 14 above. See *Chen Shi Hai v Minister for Immigration* [2000] INLR 455, Aust HC: adverse treatment which a 'black child' (one born in contravention of the 'one child' policy) is likely to receive in China – denial of access to food, education and health care – could amount to persecution. In *Chan Yee Kin v Minister for Immigration and Ethnic Affairs* (1989) 169 CLR 379, Aust HC, McHugh J considered that measures in disregard of human dignity may, in appropriate cases, constitute persecution (a proposition approved in the joint judgment of six members of the High Court in *Minister for Immigration and Ethnic Affairs v Guo* (1997) 191 CLR 559). See the judgment of Lady Hale in *R (on the application of Hoxha) v Secretary of State for the Home Department, R (on the application of B) v Secretary of State for the Home Department* [2005] UKHL 19, [2005] 1 WLR 1063, (2005) 149 Sol Jo LB 358.

17 See fn 3 above: Gummow and Hayne JJ and McHugh and Kirby JJ, each giving joint judgments, formed the majority.

18 Conversely however, in *R (on the application of Hoxha) v Secretary of State for the Home Department* [2002] EWCA Civ 1403, [2003] 1 WLR 241 the Court of Appeal rejected an argument that the *sequelae* of past persecution can amount to persecution. However, the House of Lords did not rule this out; Lady Hale dealt in particular with the continuing punishment of stigma and ostracism likely to result from a public rape in the context of a deeply patriarchal society; see [2005] UKHL 19 at paras 30 ff. She referred to this again in her judgment in *N v Secretary of State for the Home Department* [2005] UKHL 31, para 58, [2005] 2 AC 296, [2005] 4 All ER 1017.

19 UNHCR *Handbook*, at **12.13** above, paras 54–55; *Chen* above, at 24; *Ahmad v Secretary of State for the Home Department* [1990] Imm AR 61 at 66, per Farquarson LJ. Tribunal determinations in which findings of persecution have been made in 'third category' cases include *Padhu* (12318) (inability to work and deprivation of state benefits) and *Lucreteanu* (12126) (threatening phone calls in Romania). In *Kadham v Canada* IMM-652–97 (8 January 1998, unreported), FC Moulden J observed that harassment could constitute persecution if it was sufficiently serious or long-lasting as to threaten the claimant's physical or moral integrity. See Pill LJ's judgment in *EB (Ethiopia) v Secretary of State for the Home Department* [2007] EWCA Civ 809 in which, with reference to the Qualification Directive, art 9(2)(b) he said that 'persecution may take the form of administrative and other measures which are discriminatory or are implemented in a discriminatory manner. Measures which deprive a national of the opportunity to conduct a business, follow employment and retain documentation on which the conduct of ordinary life depends' may amount to or contribute to a finding of persecution.

20 *HH (Somalia) CG* [2008] UKAIT 00022 and *AM and AM (Somalia) CG* [2008] UKAIT 00091.

21 So the majority of the Court of Appeal held in *EB (Ethiopia) v Secretary of State for the Home Department* (Longmore and Jacob LJJ; Pill LJ dissenting), disapproving *MA* [2004] UKIAT 00324 and applying the US Supreme Court judgment in *Trop v Dulles* 356 US 86 (1957)

which held that deprivation of citizenship was 'the loss of the right to have rights' and also *Lazarevic v Secretary of State for the Home Department* [1997] 1 WLR 1107.

22   *MA (Palestinian Territories) v Secretary of State for the Home Department* [2008] EWCA Civ 304, [2008] All ER (D) 123 (Apr); *MT (Palestinian Territories) v Secretary of State for the Home Department* [2008] EWCA Civ 1149, [2008] All ER (D) 215 (Oct) and *SH (Palestinian Territories) v Secretary of State for the Home Department* [2008] EWCA Civ 1150, [2008] All ER (D) 221 (Oct). In *ST (Ethnic Eritrean- nationality- return) Ethiopia CG* [2011] UKUT 00252 (IAC) the UTIAC demonstrated that a person who is found to have suffered arbitrary deprivation of citizenship may find it relatively easy to show that present bureaucratic problems are, in reality, part of a continuing pattern of hostility towards that person and that the deprivation of nationality for Convention reasons is ongoing.

23   *Sepet v Secretary of State for the Home Department* [2003] UKHL 15, [2003] 3 All ER 304, [2003] 1 WLR 856, [2003] Imm AR 428 (no right of conscientious objection to military service).

24   Qualification Directive, art 9(1), implemented by the Refugee or Person in Need of International Protection (Qualification) Regulations 2006, SI 2006/2525, reg 5(1).

25   ie ECHR, arts 2, 3, 4 and 7.

26   Qualification Directive, art 9(2) and the Refugee or Person in Need of International Protection (Qualification) Regulations 2006, reg 5(2).

27   Qualification Directive, art 4(3)(C), implemented by HC 395, para 339J(iii), as inserted by HC 6918.

28   *SH (Palestinian Territories) v Secretary of State for the Home Department* [2008] EWCA Civ 1150. This ruling, however, overlooked the approach taken to the text at European level: see the contribution of the legal service to the Asylum Working Party (Brussels, 15 November 2002; 14348/02): '9. The words "in particular", "inter alia" or similar indicate that the listing of criteria or elements in a provision is not exhaustive (see, for instance, Article 12 of the draft directive), thus allowing Member States to take into account other aspects than those mentioned in the provision in question'.

29   In *SS (Malaysia) v Secretary of State for the Home Department* [2013] EWCA Civ 888, [2013] All ER (D) 215 (Jul) found that an inability to bring up one's child as a Christian and the possibility that he would face circumcision, was, in the context of a case involving legitimate national laws addressing the consequences of domestic violence and family breakdown, was not a case where it could be said that the decision in question would 'destroy or nullity the family life that they currently share'.

12.49 In *Ravichandran*[1] the Court of Appeal found Hathaway's human rights-based analysis of persecution instructive. In *Adan*[2] Hutchinson LJ saw no reason not to accept it. And in *Horvath*[3] it received the seal of approval from Lord Hope. *Ravichandran* held that the arbitrary detention of young Tamils for periods of a few days following terrorist atrocities did not amount to persecution, although long-term detention, or detention accompanied by ill-treatment, would have been a different matter.[4] The court held that the question whether an individual's fear is one of persecution for a Convention reason is a single composite question to be determined in the round with all relevant circumstances being taken into account.[5] Breaches of rights other than absolute rights probably require an element of persistence to constitute 'persecution'.[6] But the question of whether persistence is a necessary element of physical ill-treatment has been the subject of conflicting decisions. While the reference in Hathaway to 'sustained or systemic denial of core human rights' is meant to refer to country practices underlying individual claims, it was adopted in *Ravichandran*[7] as an individual requirement by Staughton LJ, who observed that 'persecution must at least be persistent and serious ill-treatment without just cause by the state, or from which the state can provide protection but chooses not to'. His remarks have become detached from their context (short-term but arbitrary and unlawful detention of Tamils as terrorist suspects) and wrongly applied as a rigid legal criterion regardless of the nature of the feared persecution.[8] There may be cases in which a single incident could found a case for asylum.[9] It would be absurd to deny refugee status to someone with a well-founded fear of life-threatening torture on the ground that the torture would not be repeated. Freedom from torture is an absolute right which can never be balanced or qualified, and its violation must always constitute persecution.[10] This was accepted by the Court of Appeal in *Demirkaya*,[11] although apparently not by a different division of the court in *Faraj*.[12] The Australian and New Zealand courts regard any requirement of systematic conduct aimed at the claimant as a misdirection.[13] In the UK, the higher courts have held that the threshold of 'serious harm' is a high one,[14] although regard should be had to the individual's characteristics and expectations in deciding what the refugee from a troubled part of the world ought to be able to put up with.[15] There is no requirement that a person be 'singled out' for persecution to be a refugee.[16] In *Katrinak*[17] Schiemann LJ considered that it is possible to persecute an individual by persecuting a close member of his or her family.

[1] *Ravichandran (Senathirajah) v Secretary of State for the Home Department* [1996] Imm AR 97 at 107. It had already been accepted by La Forest J in the leading Canadian case of *A-G of Canada v Ward* [1993] 2 SCR 689 at 709.

[2] *Adan v Secretary of State for the Home Department* [1997] 1 WLR 1107 at 1126E.

[3] *Horvath v Secretary of State for the Home Department* [2001] 1 AC 489 at 498E–G.

[4] 'If there remained a practice of torturing those detained, I very much doubt whether a finding of persecution on Convention grounds would be precluded merely because the torture was intended to discourage terrorism or to persuade detainees to inform on their associates rather than inflicted for purposes of oppression': Simon Brown LJ at 109. See also *R (on the application of Sivakumar) v Secretary of State for the Home Department* [2003] UKHL 14, [2003] 2 All ER 1097, see **12.67** fn 4, below.

[5] *Ravichandran* above; see also *Karanakaran v Secretary of State for the Home Department* [2000] INLR 122, CA.

[6] See the reference to 'cumulative grounds' in UNHCR *Handbook* **12.13** above, para 53.

[7] *Ravichandran (Senathirajah) v Secretary of State for the Home Department* [1996] Imm AR 97 at 114.

[8] Simon Brown LJ understood this distinction; see his reference in *Ravichandran* above to a 'practice of torturing those detained' as opposed to an individual requirement of repetitive ill-treatment.

[9] Keene LJ in the Court of Appeal in *BA (Pakistan) v Secretary of State for the Home Department* [2009] EWCA Civ 1072 (6 February 2009), citing Article 9 of Directive 2004/83: '[21] That phrase "by their nature or repetition" is disjunctive. It emphasises that there need not be repeated acts if an act is sufficiently serious.'

[10] See UNHCR *Handbook* above, para 51. In *Sepet v Secretary of State for the Home Department* [2001] EWCA Civ 681, [2001] INLR 33, 403, Laws LJ stated at [63] that: 'There are some classes of case in which threatened conduct is of such a kind that it is universally condemned, by national and international law, and always constitutes persecution: torture, rape (though of course it is not necessarily persecution for a Convention reason) . . . Torture is absolutely persecutory; imprisonment only conditionally so.'

[11] *Demirkaya v Secretary of State for the Home Department* [1999] INLR 441. This accords with the Qualification Directive, **12.3** fn 3 above, art 9(1)(a) which states that acts of persecution '. . . must be sufficiently serious, by their nature or their repetition' (our emphasis).

[12] *Faraj v Secretary of State for the Home Department* [1999] INLR 451, CA. But on the analysis of Peter Gibson LJ, a claimant might be a refugee based on a single incident 'if there are other incidents affecting a group of which that person is a member' (at 456E). See also the obiter remark of Lord Clyde in *Horvath v Secretary of State for the Home Department* [2000] INLR 239, HL quoting Hathaway ('sustained or systemic') when stating that persecution appeared to carry with it 'some element of persistence' (at 261F).

[13] See *Appellant S395/2002 v Minister for Immigration and Multicultural Affairs* [2003] HCA 71 at para 66; *Minister for Immigration and Multicultural Affairs v Ibrahim (Haji)* (2000) 204 CLR 1, [2001] INLR 228; *Chan Yee Kin v Minister for Immigration and Ethnic Affairs* (1989) 169 CLR 379, 430; *Abdalla v Minister for Immigration and Multicultural Affairs* (1998) 51 ALD 666 at 671–673; *Anjum v Minister for Immigration and Multicultural Affairs* (1998) 52

ALD 225 at 230–232; *Refugee Appeal No 71462/99* [2000] INLR 311, para 78 (NZRSAA). See also *Doymus* (00 TH 01748) (19 July 2000, unreported), IAT: 'persistence is usual but not universal'; *Foughali* (00 TH 01514) (2 June 2000, unreported), IAT.

14 See *Horvath v Secretary of State for the Home Department* [2000] INLR 15, CA, at 50, per Ward LJ: 'anything short of a really serious flouting of the citizen's human rights and dignities will not do'.

15 UNHCR *Handbook* above, para 52.

16 *R v Secretary of State for the Home Department, ex p Jeyakumaran* [1994] Imm AR 45.

17 *Katrinak v Secretary of State for the Home Department* [2001] EWCA Civ 832, [2001] INLR 499 at para 23 per Schiemann LJ: 'It is possible to persecute a husband or a member of a family by what you do to other members of his immediate family. The essential task for the decision taker . . . . . is to consider what is reasonably likely to happen to the wife and whether that is reasonably likely to affect the husband in such a way as to amount to persecution of him'.

Prosecution

12.50 Persecution must be distinguished from prosecution, and the *Handbook* points out that fugitives from common law offences are unlikely to be refugees.[1] But prosecution is not always inconsistent with persecution and may be good evidence of it. The nature of the allegations against the applicant and procedural safeguards to ensure a fair trial will have to be examined with care. The conclusion of persecution may be drawn where a fair trial would be denied;[2] where punishment is excessive; where a particular political viewpoint or religion is expressly prohibited or the state's laws prohibit other normal and reasonable human activity guaranteed by fundamental human rights; or where there is other reason to suspect that the prosecution is being conducted for political reasons.[3] In deciding whether arrangements in the country of origin breach the Refugee Convention, the principles of comity between nations have no place.[4] Of course, a persecutory prosecution must also relate to a Convention reason to found refugee status.[5] In *Iqbal*[6] the Tribunal summarised how asylum claims, based on a fear of prosecution amounting to persecution, should be dealt with: (1) although it is not the purpose of the asylum determination process to judge guilt or innocence, nonetheless a factual evaluation as to whether there is a real risk that the claimant faces injustice rather than justice must be made; (2) whether prosecution amounts to persecution is a question of fact, and all relevant circumstances must be considered on a case by case basis; (3) the criminal justice process in the county of origin must be looked at as a whole, with possible harms considered cumulatively and not separately; (4) whether prosecution amounts to persecution must be analysed by reference to international human rights norms; (5) prosecution does not amount to persecution unless likely failures in the fair trial process go beyond shortcomings and pose a threat to the very existence of the right to a fair trial; (6) when considering whether there is a general risk of persecution to any person subjected to the criminal law process in a given country, it is important to establish the scale of relevant human rights violations, particularly in relation to mistreatment in detention and the right to a fair trial, and, using Article 3 ECHR as a benchmark, it is useful to ask whether the level of human rights abuse rises to the level of a 'consistent pattern of gross, flagrant or mass violations of human rights'.[7] This approach of the Tribunal in *Iqbal* was approved by the Court of Appeal in *Hariri*[8] and again in *Batayav*[9] (with Sedley LJ sounding a note of caution to the effect that the need to show a 'consistent pattern' of human rights violations was 'intended to elucidate the jurisprudential concept of real risk, not to replace it.')[10] As examples of 'acts of persecution' the Qualification Directive refers to prosecution or punishment which is disproportionate or discriminatory,[11] denial of judicial redress resulting in a disproportionate or discriminatory punishment[12] and prosecution or punishment for refusal to perform military service in a conflict, where performing military service would include acts constituting crimes against peace, war crimes, crimes against humanity, serious non-political crime or acts contrary to the purposes and principles of the UN.[13] A refusal to pay unjust 'taxes' levied by a criminal organisation, where motivated by principle and resulting in a real risk of serious harm, may give rise to a viable asylum claim.[14]

1   UNHCR *Handbook* **12.13** above, paras 56–60; *R v Secretary of State for the Home Department, ex p Singh (Bilged)* [1994] Imm AR 42. See also Goodwin-Gill **12.5** fn 1 above, at 4.3.2.

2   For example, where evidence obtained by torture will be used in a trial: Lord Phillips in *RB (Algeria) v Secretary of State for the Home Department* [2009] UKHL 10 (18 February 2009), [2009] 2 WLR 512 stated at [153] that the question was 'whether there were reasonable grounds for believing that . . . the . . . trial that he would there face would have defects of such significance as fundamentally to destroy the fairness of his trial', rather than, at [154], requiring 'a high degree of assurance that evidence obtained by torture would not be used in the proceedings'. Ascribing little or even 'no significant weight' to such material will be impermissible, see Sedley LJ in the Court of Appeal in *Al-Sirri v Secretary of State for the Home Department & Anor* [2009] EWCA Civ 222 (18 March 2009) (also cited as *YS Egypt*), paras [40], [42], [44].

3   Hathaway **12.24** fn 3 above, para 5.6.1, p 169. The Qualification Directive, **12.3** fn 3 above, art 9(2) states that acts of persecution may include discriminatory legal or judicial measures (or measures implemented in a discriminatory way), discriminatory or disproportionate prosecution or punishment or denial of judicial redress. Prosecution for participation in a protest march is likely to be persecution: *R (on the application of Tientchu) v Immigration Appeal Tribunal* (C/00/6288) (18 October 2000, unreported), CA.

4   *Krotov v Secretary of State for the Home Department* [2004] EWCA Civ 69, [2004] 1 WLR 1825 at paras 43–51 per Potter LJ; *Zaitz v Secretary of State for the Home Department* [2000] INLR 346 at paras 39–41, per Buxton LJ; *Islam v Secretary of State for the Home Department* [1999] INLR 144 at 166B–C, per Lord Hoffmann.

5   Trials of smugglers before a Tribunal condemned as unfair did not give rise to a Refugee Convention claim in *Ameyaw v Secretary of State for the Home Department* [1992] Imm AR 206; but contrast 4(3) IJRL 261, Case 111 where the risk of prosecution for revealing state secrets was held to be Convention persecution.

6   *Iqbal (Muzafar)* [2002] UKIAT 02239. See also *Fazilat* [2002] UKIAT 00973 and *HD (Iran)* [2004] UKIAT 00209.

7   See *Drozd and Janousek v France and Spain* (Application 12747/87) (1992) 14 EHRR 745, ECtHR and *Devaseelan* [2002] UKIAT 00702 (starred). The European Court of Human Rights in *Harkins and Edwards v United Kingdom* 9146/07 [2012] ECHR 45 highlights relevant considerations as to when poor prison conditions may cross the Rubicon into Art 3 incompatibilty: eg that measures are implemented in a manner which nonetheless caused feelings of fear, anguish or inferiority, the absence of any specific justification for the measure imposed, the arbitrary punitive nature of the measure, the length of time for which the measure was imposed, and the fact that there has been a degree of distress or hardship of an intensity exceeding the unavoidable level of suffering inherent in detention, the fact that the measure was implemented in a manner which nonetheless caused feelings of fear, anguish or inferiority, the absence of any specific justification for the measure imposed, the arbitrary punitive nature of the measure, the length of time for which the measure was imposed, and the fact that there has been a degree of distress or hardship of an intensity exceeding the unavoidable level of suffering inherent in detention.

8   *Hariri v Secretary of State for the Home Department* [2003] EWCA Civ 807, (2003) 147 Sol Jo LB 659.

9   *Batayav v Secretary of State for the Home Department* [2003] EWCA Civ 1489, [2003] All ER (D) 60 (Nov), CA. See *R (on the application of EM (Eritrea) v Secretary of State for the Home Department* [2014] UKSC 12 for a rejection of any threshold for Art 3 breaches other than the *Soering* standard.

10   *Batayav* at para 38: see also **12.27** fn 5 above.

11 Qualification Directive, art 9(2)(c), implemented by the Refugee or Person in Need of International Protection (Qualification) Regulations 2006, SI 2006/2525, reg 5(2)(c).
12 Qualification Directive, art 9(2)(d), implemented by the Refugee or Person in Need of International Protection (Qualification) Regulations 2006, reg 5(2)(d).
13 Qualification Directive, art 9(2)(e), implemented by the Refugee or Person in Need of International Protection (Qualification) Regulations 2006, reg 5(2)(e). The list of acts which performing military service would include comes from Article 12(2).
14 *AMM and others (conflict; humanitarian crisis; returnees; FGM) Somalia CG* [2011] UKUT 445 (IAC) at [205]-[206].

12.51 The distinction between prosecution and persecution is also relevant to a consideration of the exclusion from protection of refugees who have committed serious non-political offences.[1] UK practice on extradition gave a generous interpretation to the political offence exemptions in the Extradition Act 1870 and Fugitive Offenders Act 1967, and the Extradition Act 2003 still enables a fugitive to demonstrate that 'the request for his extradition (though purporting to be made on account of the extradition offence) is in fact made for the purpose of prosecuting or punishing him on account of his race, religion, nationality, gender, sexual orientation or political opinions; or if extradited he might be prejudiced at his trial or punished, detained or restricted in his personal liberty by reason of his race, religion, nationality, gender, sexual orientation or political opinions'.[2] These considerations are equally relevant to the determination of refugee status.[3]

1 See *Re Castioni* [1891] 1 QB 149; *Re Meunier* [1894] 2 QB 415; *R v Governor of Brixton Prison, ex p Kolczynski* [1955] 1 QB 540; *Schtraks v Government of Israel* [1964] AC 556, [1962] 3 All ER 529, HL; *Re Gross* [1968] 3 All ER 804, [1969] 1 WLR 12; *Fernandez v Government of Singapore* [1971] 2 All ER 691, [1971] 1 WLR 987; *Cheng v Governor of Pentonville Prison* [1973] AC 931, [1973] 2 All ER 204, HL; *R v Governor of Winson Green Prison, ex p Littlejohn* [1975] 3 All ER 208, [1975] 1 WLR 893. But see *T v Immigration Officer* [1996] AC 742; see also **12.96** below.
2 Extradition Act 2003, ss 13 and 81.
3 Note that although the references to 'gender and sexual orientation' are not included in the refugee definition in art 1A(2) of the Refugee Convention, they will often in practice be encompassed by 'membership of a particular social group': see **12.80** ff below.

12.52 Prosecution for an offence which is political in itself (such as sedition) or for contravention of laws which themselves infringe human rights[1], will give rise to an inference of persecution more easily than common law offences which are committed for a relevant political purpose,[2] unless in the latter case the accused is likely to be prejudiced in the trial or during lawful punishment[3] for a Convention reason.[4] Even where there is such a risk, the decision of the House of Lords in *T v Immigration Officer*[5] means that Convention protection can be lost if the crime is an atrocious one or the violence inflicted is considered too remote from an effective political objective to be said to be political, although the offender could be exempted from extradition because of the prohibition on extradition for a political offence. In these circumstances, the broader protection against torture and inhuman and degrading treatment offered by the ECHR and other international instruments will be very relevant.[6] A number of cases raise the question whether a prosecution under a law of general application amounts to persecution for a Convention reason. The question is posed in an acute way in cases of conscientious objection to military service. Why is a prosecution persecution? Is the person being prosecuted for merely breaking the law, or being persecuted for a Convention reason? The House of Lords held in *Sepet v Secretary of State for the Home*

Department[7] that unless and until the right to conscientious objection to military service becomes a recognised human right, prosecution for refusing to bear arms does not amount to persecution. In Canada, the courts have adopted a test of looking at the intent of the law of general application to see whether it is 'neutral' or 'persecutory'.[8] For discussion of the problems raised by evasion of military service see **12.77** below.

1   *Jain v Secretary of State for the Home Department* [2000] Imm AR 76 at 84 per Evans LJ: 'If a state imposes or threatens punishment for what is regarded for the purposes of the Convention as legitimate sexual activity, then I wonder whether the actual or threatened loss of liberty is not the relevant form of persecution . . . It seems to me that under the Convention the individual enjoys the right not to be persecuted for his private legitimate behaviour.'
2   *O v Immigration Appeal Tribunal* [1995] Imm AR 494, where the Court of Appeal rejected a submission that prosecution for the offence of stockpiling arms to foment a tribal insurrection was in itself persecution for a political reason. But the court's reference to a latter-day Guy Fawkes confuses the issue, since a member of a persecuted religious minority who tried to end the persecution by eliminating the government would have a case for Convention status if he or she faced torture and execution in a prosecution for high treason.
3   *Saadi v Italy* (2008) 49 EHRR 730 at para 135, [2008] Crim LR 898, ECtHR: 'In order for a punishment or treatment associated with it to be "inhuman" or "degrading", the suffering or humiliation involved must in any event go beyond that inevitable element of suffering or humiliation connected with a given form of legitimate treatment or punishment'.
4   Goodwin-Gill **12.5** fn 1 above, p 52; Qualification Directive (**12.3** fn 3 above) art 11(2).
5   [1996] AC 742, [1996] 2 WLR 766, sub nom *T v Secretary of State for the Home Department* [1996] Imm AR 443.
6   *Chahal v United Kingdom* (1996) 23 EHRR 413; see Chapter 7 above.
7   *Sepet v Secretary of State for the Home Department* [2003] UKHL 15, [2003] 3 All ER 304, [2003] 1 WLR 856, [2003] Imm AR 428, affirming *Sepet v Secretary of State for the Home Department (UNHCR intervening)* [2001] EWCA Civ 681, [2001] INLR 33.
8   *Zolfagharkani v Canada* [1993] 3 FC 540 at 552, per MacGuigan JA; *Ciric v Canada* [1994] 2 CF 65.

Persecution by non-state actors

12.53 The *Handbook* states that although:

> 'persecution is normally related to action by the authorities of a country [it] may also emanate from sections of the population that do not respect the standards established by the laws of the country concerned . . . where serious discriminatory or other offensive acts are committed by the local populace, they can be considered as persecution if they are knowingly tolerated by the authorities, or if the authorities refuse, or prove unable, to offer effective protection'.[1]

The authorities of a country here include regional or local government, or parties which in practice control the state.[2] Where legal authority is breaking down, anyone purporting to exercise government authority may be an agent of persecution, whether the state is legally recognised internationally or not. The security forces of a country do not cease to be agents of official persecution merely because it is not the policy of central government to persecute the victims in question.[3] It is equally persecution when the authorities condone, tolerate or fail to protect against persecution by one section of the population against another. In *Jeyakumaran*[4] Tamils resident in Colombo were the victims of reprisal by the local Sinhalese population and received no protection from the state. The High Court held it irrelevant to the merits of the claim that the victims were not 'singled out' for persecution by the government. The House of Lords in *Adan and Aitseguer*[5] affirmed the principle established in *Ward*[6] and *Adan v Secretary of State for the Home Department*[7] that the autonomous meaning of 'persecution' does not limit the concept to conduct which can be attributed to a state, but includes circumstances where the state is not complicit in the persecution, whether this is because it is unwilling or unable to afford protection.[8] The Qualification Directive identifies as 'actors of persecution' the state, parties or organisations controlling the state or a substantial part of the territory of the state and non-state actors. In the case of non-state actors, there must be a want of protection provided by the state or party before they can be treated as 'actors of persecution'.[9]

[1] UNHCR *Handbook* **12.13** above, para 65.
[2] Contrast the authorities able to provide the 'protection of the country' within the meaning of the refugee definition: see **12.43** above. (But note that the Qualification Directive (**12.3** fn 3 above) art 7 provides that parties or organisations controlling the state or a substantial part of its territory may be providers of protection so as to disqualify those who can access such 'protection' from refugee status.)
[3] Hathaway **12.24** fn 3 above, para 4.5.1; *R v Secretary of State for the Home Department, ex p Chahal* [1995] 1 WLR 526 at 536, per Staughton LJ.
[4] *R v Secretary of State for the Home Department, ex p Jeyakumaran* [1994] Imm AR 45.
[5] *R v Secretary of State for the Home Department, ex p Adan, R v Secretary of State for the Home Department, ex p Aitseguer* [2001] INLR 44, HL.
[6] *A-G of Canada v Ward* (1993) 103 DLR (4th) 1, [1993] 2 SCR 689, [1997] INLR 42, Canada Sup Ct.
[7] *Adan v Secretary of State for the Home Department* [1999] 1 AC 293 at 305–306: 'if for whatever reason the state is unable to afford protection against factions within the state, the qualifications for refugee status are complete'.
[8] Traditionally there have been two approaches to the situation where the feared harm emanates not from the state itself but from individuals or groups within it – the 'attribution theory', in which a degree of state complicity in the persecution is required to ground refugee status, and the 'protection theory', where refugee status will be granted unless the state is both able and willing to protect against the persecutory acts of others. German and French adherence to the attribution theory caused the HL in *Adan and Aitseguer* to hold that the Secretary of State was wrong in law to certify that the applicants could be returned compatibly with Article 33 of the Convention to Germany (where a person cannot be a refugee from a country where there is no state authority) and France (where a person cannot be a refugee if the state is merely unable, as distinct from unwilling, to protect him) respectively. The Qualification Directive (**12.3** fn 3 above) art 6(c) adopts the 'protection theory', in line with UK practice.
[9] Qualification Directive, art 6, implemented by the Refugee or Person in Need of International Protection (Qualification) Regulations 2006, SI 2006/2525, reg 3.

12.54 The appellant in *Horvath*[1] was a Roma from Slovakia who feared persecution by skinheads against whom, he said, the Slovak police were unable to provide protection. He also alleged discrimination in the field of employment, the right to marry and education. The principal focus of the opinions in the House of Lords was on whether the word 'persecution' denotes merely sufficiently serious ill-treatment, or sufficiently severe ill-treatment against which the state fails to afford protection. The House of Lords upheld the Tribunal's conclusion that the fear of violence at the hands of non-state agents was not a fear of 'persecution', since the authorities were neither involved nor failed to provide a 'sufficiency of protection'.[2] In the leading judgment, Lord Hope pointed out that:

'the obligation to afford refugee status arises only if the person's own state is unable or unwilling to discharge its own duty to protect its own nationals . . . to satisfy the 'fear' test in a non-state agent case, the applicant must show that the persecution which he fears consists of acts of violence or ill-treatment against which the state is unable or unwilling to provide protection. The applicant may have a well-founded fear of threats to his life due to famine or civil war or of isolated acts of violence *or of ill-treatment for a Convention reason which may be perpetrated against him.* But the risk, however severe, and the fear, however well-founded, do not entitle him to the status of refugee. The Convention has a more limited objective, the limits of which are identified by the list of Convention reasons and by the principle of surrogacy.'[3]

He thus assimilated ill-treatment for a Refugee Convention reason with famine and civil war, and concluded that ill-treatment for a Convention reason does not amount to persecution unless there is a failure of state protection. This was the majority view. Lord Lloyd disagreed with this approach, holding that the ordinary meaning of the word 'persecution' does not involve a failure of state protection. 'The text of the Convention does not suggest that anything other than the ordinary meaning should be used, nor is there any hint that the failure of state protection is an ingredient in the meaning of the word.'[4] We agree, and so in effect did the Australian High Court in *Khawar*,[5] in which, in a joint judgment, McHugh and Gummow JJ criticised the House of Lords' approach to the issue of protection in *Horvath*, taking the view that the 'internal' protection and 'surrogacy' protection theories as a foundation for the construction of the Convention 'add a layer of complexity . . . which is an unnecessary distraction'.[6] The court preferred the approach of the UNHCR.[7]

[1] *Horvath v Secretary of State for the Home Department* [2000] INLR 239, HL.
[2] [1999] INLR 7. There had been a line of Tribunal decisions on what was a 'sufficiency of protection' which would disqualify the victim of non-state persecution from international protection, eg *Jaworski* (17152); *Debrah v Secretary of State for the Home Department* [1998] INLR 383; *Singh (Chinder)* [1998] Imm AR 551; *Mojka* (18265); *Dymiter* (18467).
[3] *Horvath* above, at 247–248. Our emphasis.
[4] *Horvath* above at 251–252. On this analysis, the availability and efficacy of protection is relevant to the well-foundedness of the fear.
[5] *Minister for Immigration and Multicultural Affairs v Khawar* [2002] HCA 14.
[6] They identified the source as being the 'writings of a Canadian scholar, Professor Hathaway concerning "surrogate" or "substitute" protection': *Khawar* above, paras 66–73.
[7] See Fortin, 'The Meaning of 'Protection' in the Refugee Definition', (2001) 12 IJRL 548 and 'Interpreting Article 1 of the 1951 Convention Relating to the Status of Refugees' (UNHCR, April 2001).

12.55 According to the majority in *Horvath*, the standard of protection which disqualifies victims of non-state violence from international protection is not one which would eliminate all risk; rather, it is a 'practical standard' taking proper account of the duty owed by the state to all its own nationals. Lord Clyde cited the ECHR case of *Osman*[1] to the effect that the obligation to protect must not be so interpreted as to impose an impossible or disproportionate burden on the authorities. For him, what was required was 'a system of domestic protection and machinery for the detection, prosecution and punishment of actings contrary to the purposes which the Convention requires to have protected', and 'more importantly . . . an ability and a readiness to operate that machinery'.[2] He approved Stuart Smith LJ's formulation in the Court of Appeal:[3]

'There must be in force in the country in question a criminal law which makes the violent attacks by the persecutors punishable by sentences commensurate with the gravity of the crimes. The victims as a class must not be exempt from the protection of the law. There must be a reasonable willingness by the law enforcement agencies, that is to say the police and courts, to detect, prosecute and punish offenders . . . .'

Further, inefficiency and incompetence is not the same as unwillingness, there may be various sound reasons why criminals may not be brought to justice, and the corruption, sympathy or weakness of some individuals in the system of justice does not mean that the state is unwilling to afford protection. It will require cogent evidence that the state which is able to afford protection is unwilling to do so, especially in the case of a democracy.[4] Under the Refugee Convention only the state or an international body to which the functions and powers of the state have been transferred as a matter of international law is capable of providing 'protection' of a kind that obviates the need for international protection.[5] The Qualification Directive allows for such protection to be provided not only by the state but by parties or organisations, including international organisations, controlling the state or a substantial part of the territory of the state.[6] As for the quality of protection, the 'actors of protection' have to take 'reasonable steps' to prevent the persecution or serious harm, 'inter alia by operating an effective legal system for the detection, prosecution and punishment of acts constituting persecution or serious harm and the applicant must have access to such protection'.[7] The implementing Regulations are materially different in that they do not reproduce the phrase 'inter alia' used in the Directive.[8] The effect of that is that operation of an effective legal system becomes in the Regulation a sufficient rather than (as in the Directive) a necessary but not necessarily sufficient condition for the provision of protection. An example might be that a reasonable step that should be taken by an actor of protection to prevent a woman suffering domestic violence is the provision of women's refuges[9]. The absence of such refuges might, under the Directive, establish that there is not sufficient domestic protection. However, under the Regulation, the provision of an effective legal system would be all that could be required of the asylum seeker's home country in order to establish sufficient protection there.

[1] *Osman v United Kingdom* (1998) 29 EHRR 245.
[2] *Horvath* **12.54** fn 1 above, at 259.
[3] [2000] INLR 15, para 22.
[4] *Horvath* above, at 260A–D.
[5] *Vallaj v Special Adjudicator* [2001] EWCA Civ 782, [2001] INLR 342; *Gardi v Secretary of State for the Home Department* [2002] EWCA Civ 750, [2002] 1 WLR 2755, [2003] Imm AR 39.
[6] Qualification Directive, art 7(1), implemented by the Refugee or Person in Need of International Protection (Qualification) Regulations 2006, SI 2006/2525, reg 4(1).
[7] Qualification Directive, art 7(2).
[8] The Refugee or Person in Need of International Protection (Qualification) Regulations 2006, reg 4(2).
[9] There is a duty on a state to prevent gender based violence; European Court of Human Rights in *Opuz v Turkey* (Application No 33401/02; 9 June 2009), which indicated a need for a gender-sensitive operation of laws in order to fulfil the duty. Where incidence of domestic violence is increasing the court may infer that sufficient protection is lacking; Mactavish J in the Federal Court of Canada in *Lee v Canada (Citizenship and Immigration)* 2009 FC 782 (29 July 2009)

12.56 A further question considered in *Horvath* concerned the phrase 'unwilling, owing to such fear, to avail himself of the protection' of the country of nationality, and its application to non-state cases. Lord Hope considered that the fear which prevented recourse to state protection in such cases had to be fear of reprisals from the persecutors. In other words, the fear had to be a well-founded fear of being persecuted *because* the claimant had sought the state's protection.[1] We believe a more realistic analysis was given in *Svazas*,[2] where Sedley LJ used, as an example of unwillingness, the situation of German Jews who had been attacked by Brownshirt thugs in 1938 at a time when the Nazi authorities were pretending that such attacks were beyond their control – an example the drafters of the 1951 Convention would have had in mind when inserting the 'unwilling to avail' clause. On this reading, unwillingness might be caused by a perception of collusion by the state with the perpetrators.

1   *Horvath* **12.54** fn 1 above. Lord Hope and Lord Clyde delivered the two main judgments. Lord Hobhouse agreed with Lord Hope (266G); Lord Browne-Wilkinson (249G) agreed with Lords Hope and Clyde. Lord Lloyd (249H–256D) disagreed with the majority on the first question.
2   *Svazas v Secretary of State for the Home Department* [2002] EWCA Civ 74, [2002] 1 WLR 1891 at para 22.

12.57 The majority in *Horvath* have, we believe, adopted a strained and difficult definition of 'persecution' in non-state cases which could lead to the rejection of cases deserving of international protection.[1] The test for sufficiency of protection has moved perilously close to the 'attribution' test rejected by the Lords in *Adan and Aitseguer*.[2] New Zealand's Refugee Status Appeals Authority has suggested that the House of Lords' decision in *Horvath* enables an individual to be returned to his or her country of origin notwithstanding a well-founded fear of persecution for a Convention reason, and has commented that:

'[T]his interpretation of the Refugee Convention is at odds with the fundamental obligation of non-refoulement . . . [which] cannot be avoided by a process of interpretation which measures the sufficiency of state protection not against the absence of a real risk of persecution, but against the availability of a system for the protection of the citizen and a reasonable willingness by the state to operate that system. The point which emerges from *Ward* is that the refugee inquiry is not an inquiry into blame. Rather the purpose of refugee law is to identify those who have a well-founded fear of persecution for a Convention reason. If the net result of a state's 'reasonable willingness' to operate a system for the protection of the citizen is that it is incapable of preventing a real chance of persecution of a particular individual, refugee status cannot be denied that individual. The persecuted clearly do not enjoy the protection of their country of origin.'[3]

1   The House of Lords accepted that persons with a well-founded fear of serious harm for a Convention reason – like the Slovakian Roma family in the case before them – would not, on their formulation, be entitled to protection, because the state is 'reasonably willing' to operate the machinery of protection: see below; so what the family fears is not 'persecution'. The European Commission in its proposal for a recast Qualification Directive states (COM(2009) 551): ' . . . even actors who are willing and able *in principle* to provide protection but *not providing it in reality* or who can provide protection *only on a transitional or temporary basis* are excluded from the scope of the concept'.
2   The attribution or accountability test confines persecution to conduct which can be attributed to a state. *R v Secretary of State for the Home Department, ex p Adan, R v Secretary of State for the Home Department, ex p Aitseguer* [2001] INLR 44, HL, see **12.53** above.
3   Refugee Appeal No 71427/99, [2000] INLR 608 (R P G Haines QC and L Tremewan), NZRSAA. See also the IAT's obiter view in *Kovac* (00/TH/00026).

12.58 The criticism of *Horvath* from New Zealand was specifically rejected by Auld LJ sitting in the Divisional court in *Dhima*,[1] and in *Bagdanavicius*[2] the Court of Appeal reviewed the jurisprudence on the question of state protection from feared harm at the hands of non-state agents, rejected all criticisms of the *Horvath* approach and concluded, in a summary set out at the beginning of the judgment, that:

'(1)   The threshold of risk is the same in both asylum and Article 3 ECHR claims; the main reason for introducing a human rights appeal was not to provide an alternative, lower threshold of risk and/or a higher level of protection, but to widen the reach of protection regardless of the motive giving rise to the persecution;

(2)   An asylum claimant is entitled to asylum if he or she can show a well-founded fear of persecution for a Refugee Convention reason *and* that there would be insufficiency of state protection to meet it: *Horvath;*

(3)   Fear of persecution is well-founded if there is a 'reasonable degree of likelihood' that it will materialise: *Sivakumaran;*

(4)   Sufficiency of state protection (whether from acts of state agents or of non-state actors) means a willingness *and* ability by the state to provide through its legal system a reasonable level of protection from ill-treatment of which the claimant for asylum has a well-founded fear: *Osman,*[3] *Horvath, Dhima;*

(5)   The effectiveness of the system is normally to be judged by its systemic ability to deter and/or prevent the form of persecution of which there is a risk, not just punishment of it after the event: *Horvath, Banomova,*[4] *McPherson*[5] and *Kinuthia;*[6]

(6)   Notwithstanding systemic sufficiency of state protection, a claimant may still have a well-founded fear of persecution if its authorities know or ought to know of circumstances particular to his or her case giving rise to the fear, but are unlikely to provide the additional protection the particular circumstances reasonably require: *Osman.'*

When *Bagdanavicius* went to the House of Lords[7] Lord Brown (giving the single judgment) neither approved nor disapproved that summary but the Tribunal has held that it may still be taken as a summary of established principles.[8]

---

[1]   *Dhima v Immigration Appeal Tribunal* [2002] EWHC 80 (Admin), [2002] Imm AR 394, [2002] INLR 243. Auld LJ stated at [35] that the NZRSAA had misunderstood the ratio of the Lords' judgment in *Horvath*, which was that 'what is critical is a combination of a willingness and ability to provide protection to the level *that can reasonably be expected to meet and overcome the real risk of harm from non-state agents.* What is reasonable protection in any case depends, therefore, on the level of the risk, without that protection, for which it has to provide'. (Our emphasis)

[2]   *R (on the application of Bagdanavicius) v Secretary of State for the Home Department* [2003] EWCA Civ 1605, [2004] 1 WLR 1207 (leave to appeal to the HL granted: [2004] 1 WLR 2449).

[3]   *Osman v United Kingdom* (1998) 29 EHRR 245.

[4]   *Banomova v Secretary of State for the Home Department* [2001] EWCA Civ 807, [2001] All ER (D) 344 (May).

[5]   *McPherson v Secretary of State for the Home Department* [2001] EWCA Civ 1955, [2002] INLR 139.

[6]   *Kinuthia v Secretary of State for the Home Department* [2001] EWCA Civ 2100, [2002] INLR 133.

[7]   *R v Secretary of State for the Home Department ex p Bagdanavicius* [2005] UKHL 38, [2005] 2 AC 668, [2005] 4 All ER 263.

[8]   *IM (Malawi)* [2007] UKAIT 00071. *SA (Pakistan)* [2011] UKUT 30 (IAC) and *AW (sufficiency of protection) Pakistan* [2011] UKUT 31 (IAC) both emphasise that not only must the question of general sufficiency of protection be addressed, but also whether the individual's particular circumstances are such that he or she would receive adequate protection.

12.59 Thus, in post-*Horvath* cases, the courts and the tribunal have made it clear that, while it will always be relevant to ask whether or not there is in general sufficiency of protection in a country, the crucial question remains whether there is a reasonable likelihood of Convention persecution in the individual case.[1] The axiom of refugee determination, that one examines both the general situation and the situation of the individual claimant, does not lose force simply because the focus of the examination is the protection issue.[2] In *Noune* the Court of Appeal held that if a decision-maker interpreted *Horvath* to mean that where the law enforcement agencies are doing their best and are not being either generally inefficient or incompetent, this was enough to disqualify a potential victim from being a refugee, this interpretation would be an error of law.[3] The issue is not whether the authorities are willing to provide protection but whether they are capable of providing the particular individual with adequate protection.[4] The Qualification Directive similarly requires individualised assessment of whether there is sufficient protection, saying that protection is 'generally' provided where actors of protection 'take reasonable steps to prevent the persecution or suffering of serious harm, inter alia, by operating an effective legal system for the detection, prosecution and punishment of acts constituting persecution or serious harm, and the applicant has access to such protection'.[5] It does not say that such provision amounts to adequate protection in every case.[6] By way of example, whilst in Jamaica the authorities are said to be able generally to provide sufficient protection, they are not able to do so for those targeted by criminal gangs.[7] In *Kinuthia*[8] the Court of Appeal held that the possibility of recourse to remedies after ill-treatment has been suffered does not in itself provide adequate protection against such ill-treatment. The Tribunal has held that the crucial part of any case involving non-state agents is precisely where the general system of protection in force is tested against how it actually worked in the individual case.[9] Jews targeted by anti-Semites in Russia and Roma from the Czech and Slovak Republics and some areas of Poland have been held to be refugees.[10]

[1]   *Noune (Souad) v Secretary of State for the Home Department* [2001] INLR 526, CA (Algerian civil servant targeted by Islamists); *Koudriachov* (00TH02254) (Jews and their families in Russia). Auld LJ in *Skenderaj v Secretary of State for the Home Department* [2002] EWCA Civ 567: '[42] . . . Thus, if the state cannot or will not provide a sufficiency of protection, if sought, the failure to seek it is irrelevant. And that is so whether the failure results from a fear of persecution or simply an acceptance that to do so would be futile.' In *A W (sufficiency of protection) Pakistan* [2011] UKUT 31 (IAC) the Tribunal considered the test for when state protection was adequate noting that there will be cases where the authorities need to provide additional protection because of the particular circumstances of an individual, and that past persecution is highly relevant to any judgment as to the efficacy of protection.

[2]   Refugee Appeal No 71427/99, [2000] INLR 608, **12.57** fn 3, above.

[3]   *Noune (Souad)* above, at para 28, per Schiemann LJ. Similarly, in the context of obviating a real risk of mistreatment violating art 3 ECHR (see CHAPTER 7 above), in *McPherson v Secretary of State for the Home Department* [2002] INLR 139 at 147 (para 21) Sedley LJ stated that: 'What matters is that protection should be practical and effective, not that it should take a particular form.' Arden LJ at paras 31, 36, 37, 38 and 39 also made clear that in terms of domestic protection 'measures for the purposes of art 3 must be those which attain an adequate degree of efficacy in practice as well as exist in theory' (see para 38 at 151).

[4]   *DK v Secretary of State for the Home Department* [2006] EWCA Civ 682.

[5]   Qualification Directive, art 7, implemented by the Refugee or Person in Need of International Protection (Qualification) Regulations 2006, SI 2006/2525, reg 4(2). See *IM (Malawi)* [2007] UKAIT 00071.

[6]   *IM (Malawi)*.

[7]   Unless admitted to a witness protection scheme: *AB (Jamaica) CG* [2007] UKAIT 00018.

[8]   *Kinuthia v Secretary of State for the Home Department* [2001] EWCA Civ 2100, [2002] INLR 133.

[9]   *Harangova* (00TH01325) (8 November 2000, unreported).

[10] *Doudetski* (00TH01768); *Koudriachov* above; *Hinar* (00/TH/02407), *Franczak* (00TH02394), *Ferenc* [2002] UKIAT 00343 and *Havlicek* (00TH01448).

12.60 Of importance in this context is the degree to which an asylum claimant needs to have made efforts to avail him or herself of domestic protection before seeking 'surrogate' protection abroad. In *Canada v Ward* La Forest J stated:[1]

'Only in situations in which State protection "might reasonably have been forthcoming", will the claimant's failure to approach the State for protection defeat his claim . . . the claimant will not meet the definition of 'Convention refugee' where it is objectively unreasonable for the claimant not to have sought the protection of his home authorities; otherwise, the claimant need not literally approach the State.

. . . . clear and convincing confirmation of a State's inability to protect must be provided. For example, a claimant might advance testimony of similarly situated individuals let down by the State protection arrangement or the claimant's testimony of past personal incidents in which State protection did not materialise. Absent some evidence, the claim should fail, as nations should be presumed capable of protecting their citizens.'

In *Harakal*,[2] the Court of Appeal in the case of a Czech Roma, held that, on the particular facts, it was not necessary for the applicant to have exhausted all possible domestic remedies to demonstrate a failure of protection.[3]

[1] *Canada v Ward* [1993] 2 SCR 689, [1997] INLR 42, Supreme Court of Canada (30 June 1993). La Forest J's judgment (giving the judgment of the court) on this point at 60–61 was effectively adopted by the IAT in *Horvath* [1999] INLR 7 at 33.
[2] *R (on the application of Harakal) v Secretary of State for the Home Department* [2001] All ER (D) 139 (May), CA.
[3] See also *R (on the application of Bagdanavicius) v Secretary of State for the Home Department* [2003] EWCA Civ 1605, [2004] 1 WLR 1207, proposition 6 (at **12.58** above).

12.61 What of the situation where the feared harm emanates from state agents acting 'unofficially' rather than from 'sections of the population'?[1] It might seem that where mistreatment emanates from police officers, or other state agents, the *Horvath* principle has no application and the very fact of the mistreatment illustrates the lack of protection. After all, governments rarely if ever formally sanction the use of torture or other serious harm by their 'agents' and no state is capable of persecuting anyone other than through the actions of its agents. However, the Court of Appeal in *Svazas*[2] rejected the argument that the *Horvath* principle had no part to play in this situation, and the majority (Simon Brown LJ and Sir Murray Stuart-Smith) effectively held that it was simply a question of degree.[3] Sedley LJ, on the other hand, demanded a different and higher standard of domestic protection where the feared mistreatment emanates from state agents misbehaving themselves, holding that evidence of 'timely and effective rectification of the situation which is allowing the misconduct to happen' would be necessary to disqualify the victim from international protection.[4] It was an error of law for the Tribunal to have held that repeated rape by government soldiers was no different from the conduct of civilian rapists where the evidence showed that the soldiers were in a position to commit and repeat their crime with no apparent prospect of detection or punishment.[5]

[1] UNHCR *Handbook* **12.13** above, para 65 and **12.53** above.

[2] *Svazas v Secretary of State for the Home Department* [2002] EWCA Civ 74, [2002] 1 WLR 1891, which involved police officers in Lithuania physically mistreating detainees who were Communist Party members.

[3] *Svazas* at paras 44–46 per Sir Murray Stuart-Smith and at [51]–[53] per Simon Brown LJ, who also held at para 54 that, in cases such as this, the seniority of the police officers involved in the misconduct is relevant to determining whether the system of protection is sufficient.

[4] *Svazas* at para 37.

[5] *PS (Sri Lanka) v Secretary of State for the Home Department* [2008] EWCA Civ 1213, [2008] All ER (D) 64 (Nov.

12.62 In *Fadli*[1] the Court of Appeal held that the risk to a soldier or ex-soldier of being killed by a terrorist group was not a risk of persecution for a Refugee Convention reason. The reasoning of the court was that the Convention does not distinguish between soldiers engaged on the battlefield in combat against others observing the rules of war and those engaged on internal security duties against terrorists who breach the laws of war. It held that to allow soldiers' claims for asylum based on the failure of the state to provide practical protection to the soldiers would strengthen the terrorists' hand and 'hinder the home state in providing the very protection for the generality of its citizens which the definition of refugee in the Convention assumes that the home state should provide'. However, where soldiers face systemic violations of international humanitarian law, they may have viable asylum claims.[2] Claims from military service evaders are not restricted to those serving in war time: for 'elementary considerations of humanity' can be 'even more exacting in peace than in war': thus sowing anti-personnel mines in unmarked terrain from which civilians were not excluded was compelling evidence of either intent to kill and maim at random or, at lowest, of recklessness towards the taking of human life.[3] However soldiers who can show that their state fails to offer adequate protection against systemic violations of international humanitarian law may be able to establish that they face persecution against which state protection is inadequate.[4] The existence of a state of emergency in the country of origin may be relevant to the assessment of the availability of protection.[5]

[1] *R (on the application of Fadli) v Secretary of State for the Home Department*, [2001] 02 LS Gaz R 40, CA. The decision in *Fadli* was applied to both the asylum and human rights claims of a Sri Lankan intelligence officer fearing assassination by the LTTE. Newman J in *R (on the application of Gedara) v Secretary of State for the Home Department* [2006] EWHC 1690 (Admin) held that the state did not have a duty to protect him from the risk of harm resulting from his own actions in providing protection to fellow citizens so that that risk could not establish a claim to refugee status or under the ECHR.

[2] The Tribunal in *ZQ (serving soldier) Iraq CG* [2009] UKAIT 00048.

[3] The Court of Appeal in *BE (Iran) v Secretary of State for the Home Department* [2008] EWCA Civ 540 at [31], [35].

[4] The Tribunal in *ZQ (serving soldier) Iraq CG* [2009] UKAIT 00048.

[5] In *MS (Coptic Christians: Egypt) CG* [2013] UKUT 611 (IAC) (3 December 2013) the Tribunal looked at the impact of a state of emergency on the assessment of persecution and protection, leading to a conclusion that 'In relation to a country which is in a state of emergency affecting the life of the nation and which takes measures strictly required by the exigencies of the situation, its ability to afford adequacy of protection under Directive 2004/83/EC (the Qualification Directive) is to be assessed by reference to its general securement of non-derogable rights as set out in the ECHR.'

Civil war

12.63 The House of Lords held in *Adan and Aitseguer*[1] that for someone to qualify for refugee status, there need be no effective state authority and that the state does not have to encourage or tolerate the feared persecution.[2] The inability of the state to provide protection against Convention persecution, for any reason, including civil war or internal armed conflict, founds refugee status. But in an earlier *Adan* case,[3] the House of Lords, reversing the Court of Appeal, held that:

> 'the language of the Convention did not apply to those caught up in a civil war where law and order had broken down and every group was fighting some other group or groups in an endeavour to gain power. What the members of each group may have is a well-founded fear not so much of persecution by other groups as of death or injury or loss of freedom due to the fighting between the groups. In such a situation the individual or group has to show a well-founded fear of persecution over and above the risk to life and liberty inherent in the civil war'.[4]

Lord Lloyd referred to it as 'differential impact'.[5]

[1] *R v Secretary of State for the Home Department, ex p Adan, ex p Aitseguer* [2001] INLR 44, HL.
[2] The former was the situation in Somalia in *Adan*, the latter in Algeria in *Aitseguer*: see **12.53** above.
[3] *Secretary of State for the Home Department v Adan* [1999] 1 AC 293, [1998] Imm AR 338, [1998] INLR 325, HL.
[4] *Adan* above [1998] INLR 325 at 327, per Lord Slynn.
[5] *Adan* above [1998] INLR 325 at 336.

12.64 The decision in *Adan* is hard to comprehend where the civil war (and therefore the risk of persecution) is itself motivated by factors which are themselves Convention reasons. In the Court of Appeal Simon Brown LJ appreciated the 'floodgates' consequences of holding that all who may be identified with the interests of either side are potential refugees, but considered that his conclusion more faithfully reflected the Convention and gave better effect to its broad humanitarian instincts.[1] We agree. If a refugee claimant from a civil war is at risk of persecution because of his or her race, it is not legitimate to ignore that fact simply because the source of the risk is a civil war, and to require a fear of something over and above 'the ordinary risks of clan warfare'. Once the claimant has shown a real risk of persecution for reasons of one of the five Convention reasons he or she is a refugee and nothing more can be required.[2] The danger inherent in the House of Lords' approach is that it reintroduces in a civil war situation the requirement of being 'singled out'.[3] The Canadian case of *Salibian* on which Lord Lloyd relied[4] shows that the Convention may provide protection against a fear shared with a group or even with every citizen of the refugee's country. If that is so, there can be no warrant for requiring an individual to demonstrate a fear that can be differentiated from that experienced by others.

[1] [1997] Imm AR 251 at 264–265.
[2] See decision of New Zealand Refugee Status Appeals Authority in Refugee Appeal No 71462/99 [2000] INLR 311, declining to follow *Adan* for these reasons (paras 67–86 at 328).
[3] What the NZRSAA calls 'the old heresy ([2000] INLR 311, para 69), following Crawford and Hyndman 'Three heresies in the application of the Geneva Convention' (1989) 1 IJRL 155. The reasoning in *Adan* was also rejected by the full court of the Australian FCA in *Minister for Immigration and Multicultural Affairs v Abdi* (1999) 162 ALR 105; see also *Minister for Immigration and Multicultural Affairs v Ibrahim* [2000] HCA 55.

Salibian v Minister of Employment and Immigration [1990] 73 DLR (4th) 551.

12.65 It is important, however, to realise how limited the application of *Adan* is. Their Lordships were not concerned to exclude from the refugee definition those at risk of death, torture or imprisonment on suspicion of siding with one party in territory under the effective control of the other. They are concerned only with a situation where 'the fear is felt indiscriminately by all citizens as a consequence of the civil war', or where law and order have completely broken down[1] and state authority has ceased to exist, as in Somalia in the circumstances of that case.[2] Lord Lloyd, citing Goodwin-Gill,[3] contrasted the civil war in Somalia with that in Liberia 'on the ground that in the former country none of the competing clans has yet emerged as an authority in fact, controlling territory and possessing a minimum of organisation'.[4] The distinction reflects the rules of international law on the recognition of a government of a state.[5] *Adan* does not apply, for example, to Sri Lanka, Algeria or Angola, where, although engaged against insurrectionary movements, fully functioning states continue to exist.[6] Even where *Adan* does apply, however, the applicant will very likely be entitled to humanitarian protection.[7] Civilians who face a real risk of serious violations of peremptory norms of international humanitarian law and human rights law may still be entitled to refugee status.[8]

[1]   *Adan* above, at 327H–328A, per Lord Slynn (12.63 above).
[2]   In *R v Secretary of State for the Home Department, ex p Aitsegeur* at first instance, 18 December 1998, Sullivan J held *Adan* applicable in civil war situations 'where state authority had ceased to exist', and in *R v Secretary of State for the Home Department, ex p Adan (Lul)* [1999] INLR 84, the Secretary of State for the Home Department accepted that it applied to situations 'where civil war has destroyed state authority'.
[3]   Goodwin-Gill **12.5** fn 1 above, p 76.
[4]   *Adan* above at 336.
[5]   See *Somalia (Republic of) v Woodhouse, Drake & Carey (Suisse) SA* [1993] QB 54 where Hobhouse J held (at 67–68) that factors to be taken into account in recognition were (a) whether it is the constitutional government of the state; (b) the degree, nature and stability of administrative control, if any, that it exercises over the territory of the state; (c) whether Her Majesty's Government has any dealings with it and if so the nature of those dealings; and (d) in marginal cases, the extent of international recognition that it has as the government of the state.
[6]   See, for example, *Matondo v Secretary of State for the Home Department* (15 March 1999, unreported), where leave to appeal was granted against a Tribunal decision purporting to apply *Adan* to the situation in Angola, and the appeal was allowed by consent on the appellant being recognised as a refugee. See also *Yogarajah v Secretary of State for the Home Department* (14 January 1999, unreported), CA, where in a consent order, the Secretary of State accepted that the situation in Sri Lanka was not analogous to that in Somalia, where there had been a total breakdown of society, and that the test in *Adan* applied only to 'this type of extreme and widespread form of civil war'. In *SS (Burundi) CG* [2004] UKIAT 00290 the IAT held that *Adan* could not apply in Burundi because the civil war there had ended. But see *Kibiti v Secretary of State for the Home Department* [2000] Imm AR 594, CA, where the Immigration Appeal Tribunal's application of *Adan* to Congo was upheld. See also Theodor Meron *Human Rights in Internal Strife* (1987); von Sternberg 'Political Asylum and the Law of Internal Armed Conflict' (1993) 5(2) IJRL 153; UNHCR Executive Committee Conclusion (October 1994) (1995) 7(1) IJRL 142; and the decision of the German Constitutional Court in a Bosnian case: (1995) 7 IJRL 140 Case 226.
[7]   See **12.3** above. The applicant Adan himself had been granted exceptional leave.
[8]   *AM & AM (armed conflict: risk categories) Rev 1 Somalia CG* [2008] UKAIT 00091 (27 January 2009) at [76].

'For reasons of'

12.66 The definition of a refugee requires consideration of the reasons for the persecution. It is not enough to face persecution; it must be connected to one of the reasons assigned by the Refugee Convention.[1] In non-state agent cases (see above), the Convention reason may be the reason for the non-state agents' actions, with the state simply unable to protect the applicant, or it may be the reason for the state's unwillingness to protect the applicant against non-state agents however motivated; it need not be both.[2] Moreover, the only Convention reason requiring 'membership' on the part of the refugee is 'particular social group'; in respect of the other reasons, the Convention does not specify whether the religion or other Convention reason is that of the persecutor or that of the refugee so that a claim for refugee status may be based on fear of persecution for reasons of the persecutor's religion[3] or nationality or race or political opinion. Nonetheless, the issue of causation raises difficult questions. Should the proper focus of attention be the fear of the applicant or the motives of the persecutor? To what extent does the motivation of the persecutor need to be established? Persecutory conduct may have more than one motive, and it is established that so long as one motive is a Convention ground, the requirement is satisfied.[4] It is not necessary that the Convention ground is the sole reason for the fear.[5] The question of causation must be considered principally on the particular facts of the individual case, rather than on a 'group basis'.[6] The causal nexus between the feared persecution and the 'convention reason' required by the Qualification Directive is merely that there be 'a connection' between them[7] but the connection required is that the reason entertained by the persecutor for the actual or apprehended persecution is the Convention characteristic.[8] Moreover, it is immaterial whether the applicant actually possesses the characteristic which attracts the persecution so long as the characteristic is attributed to the applicant by the actor of persecution.[9]

[1]   In recent years there has been a tendency for the courts to require discrimination on Convention grounds (as well as lack of sufficient protection: see **12.53** ff above) before 'serious harm' can be held to constitute 'persecution' at all: see *R v Immigration Appeal Tribunal, ex p Shah (United Nations High Comr for Refugees intervening); Islam v Secretary of State for the Home Department (United Nations High Comr for Refugees intervening)* [1999] 2 AC 629, [1999] INLR 144 (see **12.69** below); *Horvath v Secretary of State for the Home Department* [2001] 1 AC 489, [2000] INLR 239; *Ravichandran (Senathirajah) v Secretary of State for the Home Department* [1996] Imm AR 97, CA; *R (on the application of Pedro) v Immigration Appeal Tribunal* [2000] Imm AR 489, CA.

[2]   See *Shah and Islam* (above) and *Horvath v Secretary of State for the Home Department* [2000] Imm AR 205, CA, per Hale LJ. See also *Refugee Appeal No 71427/99* [2000] INLR 608 (NZRSAA) and *Minister for Immigration and Multicultural Affairs v Khawar* [2002] HCA 14 (Aust HC).

[3]   Lord Brown in *Fornah v Secretary of State for the Home Department* [2006] UKHL 46, [2007] 1 AC 412.

[4]   *Suarez v Secretary of State for the Home Department* [2002] EWCA Civ 722, [2002] 1 WLR 2663 per Potter LJ, approved in *R (on the application of Sivakumar) v Secretary of State for the Home Department* [2003] UKHL 14, [2003] 2 All ER 1097, by Lord Rodger, with whom Lord Hoffmann agreed. See also *Singh (Harpinder) v Ilchert* 63 F 3d 1501 (US Ct of Apps (9th Cir), 1995).

[5]   *Jahazi v Minister for Immigration and Ethnic Affairs* (1995) 133 ALR 437, 443 (French J); approved in *Minister for Immigration and Multicultural Affairs v Abdi* (1999) 162 ALR 105, 112 (FC). *Sivakumar*, *Suarez* (above).

[6]   See *Appellant S395/2002 v Minister for Immigration and Multicultural Affairs* [2003] HCA 71 per McHugh and Kirby JJ at para 58; the UNHCR *Guidelines on International Protection: 'Membership of a particular social group'* (7 May 2002) (HCR/GIP/02/02) point out at para 17 that not all members of a group must be at risk of being persecuted; see also *R v*

Immigration Appeal Tribunal, ex p Shah; Islam v Secretary of State for the Home Department
[1999] 2 AC 629, [1999] INLR 144, per Lords Steyn and Hoffmann.
[7]   Qualification Directive, art 9(3). The language of the implementing legislation is different. It
provides that 'an act of persecution must be committed for at least one of' the Convention
reasons: the Refugee or Person in Need of International Protection (Qualification) Regulations
2006, SI 2006/2525, reg 5(3).
[8]   *IR (Morocco) v Secretary of State for the Home Department* [2014] EWCA Civ 966.
[9]   Qualification Directive, art 10(2) and the Refugee or Person in Need of International
Protection (Qualification) Regulations 2006, reg 6(2).

12.67 The humanitarian obligation is to be interpreted broadly: a refugee may
well not be aware of the reasons for the persecution, and it is not his or her
duty to identify or analyse the reasons in detail.[1] The focus therefore is on the
acts of the persecutors. Thus a person who is not in fact involved in any
political opposition to the government may nevertheless be persecuted by the
government for perceived or imputed opinions.[2] The Convention ground does
not have to be the sole cause of the persecution,[3] and the fact that the
persecutor may have some ulterior motive, such as suppression of disorder or
terrorism, does not necessarily remove it from the realm of Convention
persecution if acts of sufficient gravity are done against a person or group
identified by race, religion, nationality, social group or political opinion.[4] The
test of Canadian law is whether the applicant's personal status exposes him or
her to heightened risk so that persecution would not arise *but for* race, religion
or another Convention ground. Other international cases adopt the approach
of whether the persecution is 'related' to Convention reasons.[5]

[1]   UNHCR *Handbook* **12.13** above, para 66.
[2]   In *Danian v Secretary of State for the Home Department* [1999] INLR 533 at 557H,
Buxton LJ stated as being an elementary proposition that 'a political opinion may be one
imputed to him by the authorities of the country in question, even if it is not in fact held by
him.' See also *Asante* [1991] Imm AR 78; *R v Secretary of State for the Home Department and
Special Adjudicators, ex p Stefan, Chiper and Ionel* [1995] Imm AR 410 at 413; *A-G of
Canada v Ward* [1993] 2 SCR 689, [1997] INLR 42.
[3]   See **12.66**, fns 4 and 5 above and see Hathaway **12.24** fn 3 above, p 140.
[4]   *Ravichandran (Senathirajah) v Secretary of State for the Home Department* [1996] Imm AR
97 at 109. See also (1993) 5(2) IJRL 154 (sexual abuse linked to political opinion or other
characteristics); (1993) 5(3) IJRL, Case 161 *Veeravagu v Canada* (1992) FCJ No 468 where
the Canadian Court of Appeal held that, irrespective of whether young Tamils constituted a
social group, there was racial persecution if a person faced real risk of oppression because he
belonged to a group one of whose defining characteristics was race. However in *R (on the
application of Sivakumar) v Secretary of State for the Home Department* [2003] UKHL 14,
[2003] 2 All ER 1097 the House of Lords rejected both the Secretary of State's argument that
persecutory harm by state agents in the process of investigating suspected terrorism necessarily
falls outside the protective net of art 1A of the Refugee Convention, and the applicant's argument that it necessarily falls within art 1A since terrorism involves matters of
political opinion. They held that there could be no legal inference or presumption that severe
mistreatment of someone of a particular social group, race or likely political opinion
amounted to persecution for a Convention reason; the cumulative effect of all the relevant
factors in the case had to be evaluated.
[5]   See (1992) 4(2) IJRL 259, Case 109, Case 110; (1993) 5(2) IJRL 275, Case 154.

12.68 The issue of causation had earlier been considered by the House of
Lords in *Shah and Islam*[1] where Lord Hoffmann rejected the Canadian 'but
for' test[2] as too simplistic and noted that the meaning of any statutory notion
of causation depends on the context. He gave the example of women
vulnerable to sexually motivated attacks by marauding men during a time of
civil unrest. While the *but for* test would be satisfied (the women would not be

subject to rape but for their gender), in a context where attacks and failure of protection alike were indiscriminate, their treatment was not *for reasons of their gender.* By contrast, a Jew in Germany in 1935 who was punished for contravening racial laws (by failing to wear a yellow star) was persecuted on ground of race; so was a Jewish shopkeeper attacked for reasons of commercial rivalry in a climate of impunity, because the authorities' failure to provide protection was based on race.[3]

[1] *R v Immigration Appeal Tribunal, ex p Shah; Islam v Secretary of State for the Home Department* [1999] 2 AC 629, [1999] INLR 144. Such an analysis may well underestimate the use of rape as a weapon as war: see Lady Hale in *R (on the application of Hoxha) v Secretary of State for the Home Department; R (on the application of B) v Secretary of State for the Home Department* [2005] UKHL 19, [2005] 1 WLR 1063, (2005) 149 Sol Jo LB 358, at paras 30 ff, and in *N v Secretary of State for the Home Department* [2005] UKHL 31 at para 58. See **12.82** below.

[2] Ie the women would not have feared persecution *but for* their gender: see above.

[3] See further **12.66** fn 2 above.

12.69 In *Shah and Islam* the House of Lords used the touchstone of discrimination in deciding that the persecution was for reasons of membership of a particular social group (Pakistani women). The House concluded that a fundamental purpose of the Refugee Convention was counteracting discrimination[1] and that the concept of discrimination was central to an understanding of the Convention.[2] It was concerned with persecution based on discrimination, or with making distinctions inconsistent with the right of every human being to equal treatment and respect. All Convention reasons are grounds upon which a person may be discriminated against by society.[3] Persecution must be discriminatory.[4] In the light of this formidable authority it is difficult to assert that discrimination is not usually necessary in establishing causation.[5] Where there is evidence of discrimination, it will not be difficult to establish the necessary causal link between the fear and the Convention reason. But it will not always be necessary to prove conscious discrimination by the persecutor. In *Omoruyi*[6] Simon Brown LJ suggested that some element of conscious discrimination, based on a Convention reason, is a necessary ingredient of Convention persecution. On the facts of the case, concerning the motives of a criminal gang, this was correct. But in cases of state persecution, conscious discrimination is not a prerequisite of Convention persecution, as his judgment went on to acknowledge.[7] An objective approach which looks at the discriminatory *impact* of persecutory laws or practices, is in line with UK domestic law in the context of the Race Relations and Sex Discrimination Acts.[8] In *Sepet*[9] the Court of Appeal held that conscious discrimination was not a necessary element of persecution for a Convention reason, although it would be strong evidence of it. In the House of Lords, Lord Hoffmann was inclined to agree,[10] while Lord Bingham accepted that in most cases decision makers were not concerned to explore the motives or purposes of the persecutors and that the application of the causation test called for the exercise of an objective judgment.[11] In *Sivakumar*, heard by the same constitution of the House, Lord Rodger noted that 'the law is concerned with the reasons of the persecution and not with the motives of the persecutor'.[12]

[1] [1999] INLR 144 at 150E, per Lord Steyn.

[2] [1999] INLR 144 at 161G–H, per Lord Hoffmann.

[3] [1999] INLR 144, per Lord Hope.

[4] [1999] INLR 144 at 170A, per Lord Millett.

5 See Goodwin-Gill, in his commentary on *Shah and Islam* in (1999) 11 IJRL. In *Skenderaj v Secretary of State for the Home Department* [2002] EWCA Civ 567, [2002] 4 All ER 555, [2002] Imm AR 519 the CA doubted that discrimination plays a determinative role in defining a particular social group where the feared persecution emanates from non-state actors or agents. But see Lady Hale's judgment in *R (on the application of Hoxha) v Secretary of State for the Home Department, R (on the application of B) v Secretary of State for the Home Department* [2005] UKHL 19, [2005] 1 WLR 1063, (2005) 149 Sol Jo LB 358. See further **12.53** text and fn 2 above, **12.80** ff below.

6 *Omoruyi v Secretary of State for the Home Department* [2001] Imm AR 175, CA.

7 'Discrimination, *at least in the sense that the substantive law or its enforcement in practice bears unequally upon different people or different groups*, is essential to the concept of persecution under the Convention' (Our emphasis).

8 These laws recognise direct and indirect discrimination, and the case law makes it clear that direct discrimination does not need to be conscious or intentional: *Nagarajan v London Regional Transport* [1999] IRLR 572, HL; *Birmingham City Council v Equal Opportunities Commission* [1989] IRLR 173, HL; *James v Eastleigh Borough Council* [1990] IRLR 288, HL; *European Roma Rights Centre v Immigration Officer at Prague Airport (United Nations High Comr for Refugees intervening)* [2003] EWCA Civ 666, CA per Laws LJ, [2004] UKHL 55, [2005] 2 WLR 1, per Lord Steyn and Baroness Hale; *Perera v Civil Service Commission* [1982] IRLR 147, EAT.

9 *Sepet v Secretary of State for the Home Department* [2001] EWCA Civ 681 per Laws LJ at para 93: 'The question is always whether the asylum claimant faces discrimination on a Convention ground. There will be, are, cases where that is made out by reference to the persecutor's motives. There will be, are, others where his motive matters not.'

10 *Sepet v Secretary of State for the Home Department* [2003] UKHL 15, [2003] 1 WLR 856, para 54.

11 [2003] UKHL 15, para 55. Lords Steyn and Hutton agreed with Lord Bingham, and Lord Rodger agreed with him about how a decision-maker should determine the reasons for the persecution feared.

12 *R (on the application of Sivakumar) v Secretary of State for the Home Department* [2003] UKHL 14, [2003] 2 All ER 1097 at para 41.

12.70 The House of Lords in *Sivakumar* and *Sepet* noted the Australian High Court case of *Chen Shi Hai*,[1] which also held that proof of the persecutor's motives is unnecessary. The case concerned a Chinese child born in contravention of the one-child policy and likely to be denied access to food, shelter, medical treatment and education under Chinese law. The Court decisively rejected any requirement of personal animus, enmity or malignancy to the Refugee Convention attribute as a necessary ingredient of causation.[2] Such attribution, it held, 'risks a fictitious personification of the abstract and the impersonal'. The court also took into account the extreme difficulty or impossibility of an inquiry into the motives and feelings of the alleged persecutors in a foreign country.[3] It rejected any formula, rule or principle which could be substituted for the Convention language. As Kirby J said, 'In the end it is necessary . . . to return to the broad expression of the Convention . . . the decision-maker must evaluate the postulated connection between the asserted fear of persecution and the ground suggested to give rise to the fear.'

1 *Chen Shi Hai v Minister for Immigration and Multicultural Affairs* [2000] INLR 455, Aust HC.

2 Goodwin-Gill does not accept that motivation is a necessary condition of persecution: *The Refugee in International Law* (2nd edn, 1996) pp 50–51.

3 *Chen Shi Hai v Minister for Immigration and Multicultural Affairs* [2000] INLR 455, Aust HC, para 64.

Race

12.71 A broad definition of race that includes membership of ethnic groups is to be adopted.[1] The EC Qualification Directive includes colour, descent and membership of an ethnic group in the Convention meaning of race.[2] Article 1 of the Convention on the Elimination of All Forms of Racial Discrimination 1965 (CERD) defines 'racial discrimination' as 'any distinction, exclusion, restriction or preference based on race, colour, descent, or national or ethnic origin'. The House of Lords in *Shah and Islam*[3] emphasised that counteracting discrimination was a fundamental purpose of the Convention. Racial discrimination represents an important element in determining the existence of racial persecution, and may be a sufficient foundation for recognition if it affects human dignity to the extent of incompatibility with inalienable or elementary rights.[4]

[1] *King-Ansell v Police* [1979] 2 NZLR 531, 533; *Mandla (Sewa Singh) v Dowell Lee* [1983] 2 AC 548 at 563–564.
[2] Qualification Directive, **12.3** fn 3 above, art 10(1)(a). This supersedes the EU Joint Position (96/196/JHA), 4 March 1996, para 7.1, which stated that 'persecution should be deemed to be founded on racial grounds where the persecutor regards the victim of his persecution as belonging to a racial group other than his own, by reason of a real or supposed difference, and this forms the grounds for his action.'
[3] *R v Immigration Appeal Tribunal, ex p Shah; Islam v Secretary of State for the Home Department* [1999] 2 AC 629, [1999] INLR 144 at 150, per Lord Steyn.
[4] UNHCR *Handbook* **12.13** above, paras 68–69.

Religion

12.72 Persecution may take the form of a total ban on worship and religious instruction, or severe discrimination in the profession of a religion which renders life unbearable.[1] Apostate Muslims who convert to Christianity have in some cases been held to have a well-founded fear of persecution on account of the severity of the penalties for conversion.[2] Punishment for proselytising has created difficulties. The Universal Declaration of Human Rights proclaims the right to manifest a religion in public, but a state has some margin of appreciation that would preclude causing offence to others.[3] A number of cases concern the Ahmadi sect, regarded as heretical by orthodox Pakistani Muslims, whose members are subjected to severe punishments for proselytising.[4] In *Ahmed (Iftikhar)* the Court of Appeal held that if an Ahmadi would proselytise on return and would therefore be at risk of persecution, a claim for refugee status would not be defeated on the basis that the claimant is inviting persecution and should refrain.[5] In so holding, the court put to rest the suggestion found in *Mendis*[6] and *Ahmad*,[7] that a claim could not be founded on deliberate conduct inviting persecution (at least where the conduct is an exercise of fundamental rights of freedom of conscience).[8] Discriminatory punishment for conscientious objection to military service based on religious conviction could be Refugee Convention persecution.[9] Apostasy, without the adoption of another religion, has been accepted as founding a claim on the basis of fear of persecution for reason of religion,[10] and in *Omoruyi*[11] Simon Brown LJ held that:

> 'It is, therefore, plain (and hardly surprising) that, whether the harm is perpetrated by the religious upon the non-religious or vice versa (or indeed by one religious body upon another), and whether because of adherence (or a refusal to adhere) to a belief

or because of behaviour, there will be persecution for reasons of religion provided always that the other ingredients are satisfied.'[12]

The Qualification Directive requires a broad interpretation of religion to include the holding of theistic, non-theistic and atheistic beliefs, the participation in or abstention from formal worship in private or in public, alone or in community with others, other religious acts or expressions of view or forms of personal or communal conduct based on or mandated by any religious belief.[13]

[1] UNHCR *Handbook* **12.13** above, paras 71–73. In its *Guidelines on International Protection No 6:* Religion-based refugee claims under art 1A(2) of the 1951 Convention and/or the 1967 Protocol relating to the status of refugees (HCR/GIP/04/06), 28 April 2004, UNHCR divides religion-based claims into those involving religion as belief (or non-belief); religion as identity; and religion as a way of life (para 5). Qualification Directive (**12.3** fn 3 above), art 10(1)(b) defines 'religion' as including beliefs (theistic, non-theistic or atheistic); participation in or abstention from worship (private or public), or communal conduct based on or mandated by religious belief. Two German cases show that the link to religions need not be direct: in one, membership of a Christian social club was viewed with suspicion by the authorities (1993) 5 IJRL 474 Case 164; in another, an Iranian Muslim would face measures for having married a Catholic Polish woman: (1993) 5 IJRL 475 Case 165.

[2] *R v Secretary of State for the Home Department, ex p Kazmi* [1994] Imm AR 94, QBD. More recently see *FS (Iran – Christian converts) CG* [2004] UKIAT 00303 for lengthy IAT guidance on the risk faced by Iranian converts from Islam to Christianity. See also *Bastanipour v INS* 980 F 2d 1129 (US Ct of Apps (7th Cir), 1992), a US decision that an Iranian convicted drug smuggler who converted to Christianity in prison had a well-founded fear. UK cases involving Iranian converts to Christianity have focussed on the 'genuineness' of the claimant's new-found faith (see eg *J (Iran)* [2004] UKIAT 00158 and *Ghodratzadeh* [2002] UKIAT 01867), a focus approved in relation to post-departure conversion cases in UNHCR's *Guidelines on International Protection:* Religion-based refugee claims (fn 1 above) para 34, whereas in Canada, the emphasis has been on the attitude of the authorities to the fact of conversion; see Rouleau J in the Federal Court in *Sadeghi v Minister of Citizenship and Immigration* [2002] FCT 1083 at para 18.

[3] See the discussion of prosecution and persecution at **12.50** above. Religions which have proselytising as the essence of their witness will more easily lead to recognition *Ahmad v Secretary of State for the Home Department* [1990] Imm AR 61, CA, per Farquarson LJ. See also *Ahmed (Iftikhar)* below.

[4] See inter alia *Khan* (18982); *R v Secretary of State for the Home Department, ex p Arshad* (C/2000/5154) (14 July 2000, unreported), QBD.

[5] *Ahmed (Iftikhar) v Secretary of State for the Home Department* [2000] INLR 1, reinstating the decision of a Special Adjudicator, which had been reversed on appeal by the Tribunal on the grounds that the claimant should 'make some allowances for the situation in Pakistan and . . . . exercise a measure of discretion in his conduct and in the profession of his faith'. UNHCR's *Guidelines on International Protection:* Religion-based refugee claims (fn 1 above) also indicate that religion 'can be seen as so fundamental to human identity that the individual should not be compelled to hide, change or renounce it in order to avoid persecution' (para 13).

[6] *Mendis v Immigration Appeal Tribunal* [1989] Imm AR 6, CA.

[7] *Ahmad* [1990] Imm AR 61.

[8] See also *Danian v Secretary of State for the Home Department* [1999] INLR 533, CA.

[9] *Kokkinakis v Greece* (1993) 17 EHRR 397; *Thlimmenos v Greece (Application 34369/97)* (2000) 31 EHRR 411, 9 BHRC 12, see **7.70** fn 6 above. Cf *Sepet v Secretary of State for the Home Department* [2001] EWCA Civ 681, [2001] Imm AR 452, [2003] UKHL 15, [2003] 3 All ER 304.

[10] *Yaqub* (19569) – applicant from Pakistan lost his faith whilst in the UK and became an atheist.

[11] *Omoruyi v Secretary of State for the Home Department* [2001] Imm AR 175.

[12] See also *Hellman v Minister for Immigration and Multicultural Affairs* [2000] FCA 645; *Dehlaghijadid* [2002] UKIAT 06165: 'In the context of a state which persecutes many of those who reject the state religion, being perceived as against a religion can be as much a basis for persecution on account of religion as can being perceived as in favour of a different religion.' Whether harm arising from disapproval of the applicant's conduct by religious people can be said to be persecution for reasons of religion has received different answers in *Ameen* [2003]

INLR 595 and *A (Iran)* [2003] UKIAT 00095. UNHCR's Guidelines on Religion-based refugee claims and the Qualification Directive (both at fn 1 above) agree that it can.

13 Qualification Directive, art 10(1)(b), implemented by the Refugee or Person in Need of International Protection (Qualification) Regulations 2006, SI 2006/2525, reg 6(1)(b). The CJEU in *Bundesrepublik Deutschland v Y; Bundesrepublik Deutschland v Z*: C-71/11 and C-99/11 [2013] All ER (EC) 1144, [2013] 1 CMLR 175, ECJ emphasised that religion for the purposes of the Directive 2004/83 should be given a broad definition [63], and the protection given to religious faiths extended not only to the freedom to practice one's faith in private, but also to live that faith publicly [64] so that a risk of ill treatment arising because of public expression of one's faith can constitute persecution [69] – and this is so whether the observation of the particular practice constitutes a core element of the religious beliefs or not, so long as it is part of the religious identity of the asylum seeker [70].

Nationality

12.73 Like race, 'nationality' should be interpreted broadly to include a specific cultural or linguistic minority identifying itself as such.[1] The persecution of Gypsies or the Roma community may be on grounds of race or nationality.[2] Denial of full citizenship in a person's own country may ground refugee status if this puts him or her at risk of persecution.[3] The right to return is one of the normal incidents of 'nationality' and where citizens are arbitrarily deprived of their right to return this can amount to persecution (although there may be overlap with other Convention reasons in such cases).[4] The Qualification Directive also requires a broad interpretation of nationality so as to include membership of a group determined by its cultural, ethnic, or linguistic identity, common geographical or political origins or its relationship with the population of another state.[5]

1 UNHCR *Handbook* **12.13** above, paras 74–76; Qualification Directive (**12.3** fn 3 above) art 10(1)(c), which defines 'nationality' as including membership of a cultural, ethnic or linguistic group, geographical or political origins, and relationship with the population of another state.

2 Nowadays it is more likely to be described as persecution on grounds of race or ethnicity. See eg *Harangova* (00TH 01325) (8 November 2000, unreported); *Franczak* CC-10255-00. See *Commission for Racial Equality v Dutton* [1989] QB 783, CA (Gypsies are an ethnic group for the purposes of the Race Relations Act 1976).

3 Hathaway **12.24** fn 3 above, p 144. See the Court of Appeal in *MA (Ethiopia) v Secretary of State for the Home Department* [2009] EWCA Civ 289, discussed above at **12.37**.

4 See *Adan, Lazarevic v Secretary of State for the Home Department* [1997] Imm AR 251, CA where Hutchison LJ stated that 'if a state arbitrarily excludes one of its citizens, thereby cutting him off from enjoyment of all those benefits and rights enjoyed by citizens and duties owed by a state to its citizens, there is in my view no difficulty in accepting that such conduct *can* amount to persecution' (at 272). Certain nationals of the former Yugoslavia have been denied the right to return to the Federal Republic of Yugoslavia (Serbia) since 1994. See eg *Stula* (14622), where a Tribunal found persecution by reason of the Federal Republic of Yugoslavia's deprivation of citizenship and the denial of the refugee claimant's right to return. (The case was quashed by the CA on grounds not affecting the Tribunal's discussion of the principles.)

5 Qualification Directive, art 10(1)(c), implemented by the Refugee or Person in Need of International Protection (Qualification) Regulations 2006, SI 2006/2525, reg 6(1)(c).

Political opinion

12.74 Freedom of expression is a core value of democratic societies,[1] and freedom of thought, conscience, opinion, expression, assembly and association are human rights protected by various international instruments.[2] These considerations, together with the need to adopt a broad purposive construction to all Refugee Convention grounds,[3] provide the context for the construction of the term 'political opinion'. For Goodwin-Gill, 'political opinion' covers 'any opinion on any matter in which the machinery of state, government and policy may be engaged',[4] while Hathaway defines political opinion as 'any action perceived to challenge governmental authority'.[5] The latter definition was approved by a 'starred' Tribunal in *Gomez*,[6] which involved a Colombian citizen who was threatened by guerrillas, after assisting a victim of extortion. At issue was whether, as a differently constituted tribunal had found in *Acero-Garces*,[7] persecution by non-state actors of persons obstructing their aims and activities was for reasons of political opinion.[8] In the Colombian context, this involved scrutiny of the relationship between political and criminal activity. The Tribunal held that this was not necessarily so, in a decision which reviewed international jurisprudence. Looking at the definition of political opinion, the Tribunal in *Gomez* observed that where non-state actors are involved, the phrase had to be given 'a more inclusive, multi-sided definition' than one limited by reference to party politics[9] or to government or governmental authority,[10] but doubted whether it would embrace power relationships at all levels of society. Save in very unusual circumstances political opinion would not be established 'at the purely domestic or interpersonal level'.[11] The Qualification Directive includes within 'political opinion' 'the holding of an opinion, thought or belief on a matter related to the potential actors of persecution . . . and to their policies or methods, whether or not that opinion, thought or belief has been acted upon by the applicant'.[12]

[1] See *Handyside v United Kingdom* (1976) 1 EHRR 737.
[2] See UDHR, arts 18–20; International Covenant on Civil and Political Rights, arts 19, 20, 21, 22; ECHR, arts 9–11.
[3] *R v Immigration Appeal Tribunal, ex p Shah; Islam v Secretary of State for the Home Department* [1999] Imm AR 283 at 293, HL.
[4] Goodwin-Gill **12.5** fn 1 above, p 49. The starred Tribunal in *Gomez (Emila del Socorro Gutierrez)* [2000] INLR 549 doubted whether this definition was wide enough.
[5] Hathaway **12.24** fn 3 above, p 154, approved by the Federal Court of Australia in *V v Minister for Immigration and Multicultural Affairs* [1999] FCA 428 and cited with approval by Waller LJ in *Sepet v Secretary of State for the Home Department* [2001] EWCA Civ 681, [2001] INLR 376 at 433 at para 159.
[6] *Gomez* fn 4 above, endorsed by Keene LJ in *Suarez v Secretary of State for the Home Department* [2002] EWCA Civ 722, [2002] 1 WLR 2663.
[7] *Acero-Garces* [1999] INLR 460.
[8] *Gomez* above, para 4.
[9] As in the 'classical' definition of Lord Diplock in *Cheng v Governor of Pentonville Prison* [1973] AC 931; *Gomez* above, para 28.
[10] *Gomez* above, para 31ff, referring to *V v Minister for Immigration and Multicultural Affairs* [1999] FCA 428, Federal Court of Australia.
[11] To engage the Refugee Convention, power relationships must in some way link up to the major power transactions that take place in government or related sectors such as industry and the media. Politics at the 'micro' level must in some way relate to politics at the 'macro' level: *Gomez* above, para 38.
[12] Qualification Directive, art 10(1)(e) and the Refugee or Person in Need of International Protection (Qualification) Regulations 2006, SI 2006/2525, reg 6(1)(f).

12.75 The Convention ground of political opinion refers both to the holding of the opinion and the expression of it.[1] Having an opinion implies the right to express it and persecution will not usually be alleged on the ground of having the opinion alone;[2] but political *action* or *activity*, although possibly an important indication of political opinion, is not necessary to found a claim.[3]

Political opinion may be express, implied or imputed,[4] and in establishing an imputed political opinion it is not the persecutor's political opinions but those attributed, rightly or wrongly, to the victims which are considered.[5] Thus a civil servant accused of politically motivated sabotage may have been performing functions negligently rather than expressing a political opinion, but the imputation of such an opinion by persecutors would establish the Convention reason.[6] In *Ward*[7] the Supreme Court of Canada held that punishment of a former member of a terrorist political group for failing to execute hostages could amount to persecution for the political opinion that placed humanitarian obligation over the orders of the group.[8] In certain circumstances, as the Tribunal in *Gomez* recognised, neutrality may constitute a political opinion.[9] Trade union activists and those working against the power of organised cartels may have political opinions attributed to them in particular situations.[10] But there is no universal proposition that those on the side of law and order and justice who face persecution from non-state actors, be they guerrilla organisations or political or criminal gangs, will have a political opinion attributed to them.[11] All would depend on the relationship between crime and power in a particular country at a particular time.[12] While non-state actors might have political objectives, persecutors do not always attribute political opinions to victims or opponents,[13] and not all persecution by political groups is for political reasons; sometimes it is simple extortion of money or drugs.[14]

[1]   UNHCR *Handbook* **12.13** above, para 80ff.
[2]   UNHCR *Handbook* above, para 81. On the other hand, in terms of the relevance of the *right* to express a political opinion on return to the country of feared persecution and the effect of the likely exercise of this right on refugee status, see **12.34** ff.
[3]   *Minister for Immigration and Ethnic Affairs v Guo* (1997) 191 CLR 559, High Court of Australia; *Gomez (Emila del Socorro Gutierrez)* [2000] INLR 549, para 24; see also *Orlov* (18505).
[4]   See eg *Adan v Secretary of State for the Home Department, Lazarevic v Secretary of State for the Home Department* [1997] Imm AR 251; *Danian v Secretary of State for the Home Department* [1999] INLR 533; *Sepet v Secretary of State for the Home Department* [2001] EWCA Civ 681, [2001] INLR 376; *Otchere* [1988] Imm AR 21; *Asante* [1991] Imm AR 78; *A-G of Canada v Ward* [1993] 2 SCR 689, [1997] INLR 42.
[5]   *Danian v Secretary of State for the Home Department* [1999] INLR 533 at 557H, where Buxton LJ stated this as an elementary proposition. See also *Sanga v INS* 103 F 3d 1482 (US Ct of Apps (9th Cir), 1997), *Allie* (14814); *Galvis* (22502).
[6]   See *Asante* [1991] Imm AR 78.
[7]   *A-G of Canada v Ward* [1993] 2 SCR 689, [1997] INLR 42.
[8]   Cited, together with *Klinko v Canada (Minister of Citizenship and Immigration)* 22 February 2000, FCA, in *Gomez* above, para 32.
[9]   *Sanga v INS* above.
[10]   *Gomez* **12.74** fn 4 above, paras 48, 51; *R v Secretary of State for the Home Department, ex p Walteros-Castenada* (CO/2383/99) (27 June 2000, unreported), QBD.
[11]   *Gomez* above, para 47. To this extent the starred Tribunal disapproved *Acero-Garces* (above).
[12]   In *Storozhenko v Secretary of State for the Home Department* [2001] EWCA Civ 895, [2001] All ER (D) 160 (Jun) the Court of Appeal upheld the Tribunal's determination (19935) that those on the side of law and order in the Ukraine would not have a political opinion imputed to them.
[13]   *Gomez* above, para 52.
[14]   *Gomez* above, at para 54; *R v Secretary of State for the Home Department, ex p Hernandez* [1994] Imm AR 506; *R v Immigration Appeal Tribunal, ex p Gedrimas* [1999] Imm AR 486; *R v Special Adjudicator, ex p Roznys (Sigitas)* [2000] Imm AR 57; *Quijano* (10699); *Re Jeah* (Refugee Appeal No 2507/95), NZRSAA; *INS v Elias-Zacarias* 112 S Ct 812 (1992) (US).

12.76 Thus the term 'political opinion' needs to be a flexible one, since the boundaries between the political and the non-political will change in historical time and place.[1] What makes an opinion political is the social structure and social context of the asylum seeker's country of origin.[2] There is little doubt that feminism qualifies as a political opinion,[3] and the Home Office APIs recognise that 'if a woman resists gender oppression, her resistance is political'.[4] Transgression of social roles and behaviour,[5] such as violation of dress codes in a fundamentalist Muslim country,[6] seeking exercise of a fundamental human right, as in the case of China's one-child policy, or unauthorised travel abroad, may establish a sufficient link with a political opinion, depending on all the circumstances.[7] Working in local government will not normally provide the basis of itself for the imputation of political opinions, although this may be the case where there is a major armed conflict between the authorities and guerrilla groups.[8] Similarly, there are no fixed distinctions between what is political and what is criminal,[9] nor between what is political and economic,[10] nor between actions motivated by personal interests and by political opinions.[11] A person who has not previously expressed his political dislike of the regime may be exposed by the very fact of flight and claiming asylum.[12] A claim may be based on the future expression of political opinion.[13]

---

1 The Refugee Convention is a living instrument constantly adapting to meet changing times: see Sedley J in *R v Immigration Appeal Tribunal and Secretary of State for the Home Department, ex p Shah* [1997] Imm AR 145 at 152 and Schiemann LJ in *Jain v Secretary of State for the Home Department* [2000] INLR 71 at 77C and *Beganović v Croatia* (Application No 46423/06; 25 June 2009) at para 66.

2 Berkowitz and Jarvis *Immigration Appellate Authority Asylum Gender Guidelines* (Nov 2000) paras 3.18, 3.22ff.

3 *Fatin v INS* 12 F 3d 1233 (US Ct of Apps (3rd Cir), 1993).

4 See the API on 'gender issues in the asylum claim'.

5 *Fathi and Ahmady* (14264).

6 *Re MN*, Refugee Appeal No 2039/93, 12 February 1996 (NZRSAA); *Gomez* **12.72** fn 4 above, para 40.

7 Canada: *Cheung v Minister of Employment and Immigration* (1993) 102 DLR (4th) 214; *Chan v Minister of Employment and Immigration* (1995) 128 DLR (4th) 213 SCJ; Australia: *Minister for Immigration and Ethnic Affairs v A* (24 February 1997, unreported); New Zealand: *Re ZWD Refugee Appeal 3/91* (20 October 1992, unreported). See also Goodwin-Gill **12.5** fn 1 above, pp 52–53, 359. Gender guidelines for the application of the Refugee Convention to women who face compulsory abortions have been established in Canada, US, Australia and New Zealand as well as in the UK, although the ambit of the protection has proved politically controversial in the US and Australia. See *Asylum Gender Guidelines* above, para 2A.17.

8 *Gomez* **12.74** fn 4 above, para 40. See *Doufani* (14798) and *Woldemichael* (17663).

9 *Gomez* above, paras 41–42 and cases there discussed. Participation in a banned demonstration is clearly political rather than criminal: *R (on the application of Tientchu) v Immigration Appeal Tribunal* (18 October 2000, unreported), CA.

10 *Gomez* above, para 43.

11 *Gomez* above, para 44

12 UNHCR *Handbook* **12.13** above, paras 82–83; Hathaway **12.24** fn 3 above, pp 149ff. See *M v Secretary of State for the Home Department* [1996] Imm AR 136, CA: where the act of claiming asylum is perceived by a regime as expressing hostile political opinions towards it, the act of putting forward a baseless claim for asylum (and thereby establishing risk on return) could itself found a claim based on imputed political opinion.

13 *Omar v Minister for Immigration and Multicultural Affairs* [2000] FCA 1430, drawing on *Ahmed (Iftikhar) v Secretary of State for the Home Department* [2000] INLR 1; *Danian v Secretary of State for the Home Department* [2000] Imm AR 96; *Minister for Immigration and Multicultural Affairs v Mohammed* [2000] FCA 576, Fed CA (Aust).

Refusal to perform military service

12.77 The UNHCR *Handbook* makes it clear that those who claim refugee status on the basis of a refusal to perform military service[1] are not refugees per se, since a state may require compulsory military service of its nationals and prosecution and punishment arising from refusal may be seen not as persecution but as prosecution and punishment under a law of general application.[2] However, draft evaders and deserters are not excluded from refugee status either; the state's right to demand military service is not absolute and there are important exceptions to the general rule. According to the *Handbook* it is certainly open to states to regard prosecution and punishment as persecutory if they override a genuine and deeply held conviction on conscientious or other principled grounds,[3] and the UK courts may eventually follow suit, if and when they find that the right of conscientious objection to military service is recognised as a fundamental human right. The list of acts contained in the Qualification Directive and capable of amounting to acts of persecution includes 'prosecution or punishment for refusal to perform military service in a conflict where performing military service would include' crimes against peace, war crimes, crimes against humanity, serious non-political crimes or acts contrary to the purposes and principles of the UN.[4] The list of persecutory acts is illustrative, not exhaustive and the Directive does not pretend to identify all of the circumstances in which refusal to perform military service may result in being persecuted.

[1] See generally UNHCR *Handbook* **12.13** above, paras 167–170; Hathaway **12.24** fn 3 above, pp 179–185; Goodwin-Gill, *The Refugee in International Law* (2nd edn, 1996) pp 54–59.
[2] UNHCR *Handbook* above, para 167.
[3] UNHCR *Handbook* above, paras 168–172.
[4] Qualification Directive, arts 9(2)(e), 12(2) and the Refugee or Person in Need of International Protection (Qualification) Regulations 2006, SI 2006/2525, reg 5(2)(e).

12.78 In *Foughali*[1] the Tribunal analysed the principles and identified four broad exceptions to the general rule that draft evasion or desertion does not ground refugee status:

(i)   persecution due to the conditions of life in the military service in question;

(ii)   persecution due to the repugnant nature of military duty likely to be performed;

(iii)   persecution due solely to genuine political, religious or moral convictions, or to valid reasons of conscience;[2] and

(iv)   persecution due to likely disproportionate punishment.

Paragraphs (i), (ii) and (iv) are not in dispute. The area of contention is (iii), and in *Sepet*[3] the House of Lords upheld the judgment of the majority in the CA to the effect that there is as yet no recognised, codified human right to conscientious objection, so that punishment for draft evasion based on such an objection will not per se amount to persecution.[4] Nonetheless the Court of Appeal in *Sepet*[5] unanimously held that an objection to serve in the military is inherently an implied expression of political opinion, contrary to governmental authority, and that punishment for refusing to serve in circumstances where there was a likelihood of being forced to commit atrocities or gross human rights abuses or participate in a conflict condemned by the international community[6] could amount to persecution for reason of political opinion. This was not disputed in the House of Lords. Accordingly, while the traditional conscientious objector (such as the pacifist Quaker) may not yet have a right to object based on freedom of conscience which takes priority over the state's right to require performance of military service,[7] others who object to fighting on principled grounds may have their fundamental rights violated by the requirement to perform military service. For example, they may object to the use of chemical weapons,[8] or to fighting an oppressed minority or their own people.[9] Punishment for deserting so as to avoid obeying an order to 'commit a grave violation of human rights' in the form of planting anti-personnel land mines would be persecution.[10] Domestically, *Sepet* is the leading case. There may, however, be other circumstances in which soldiers may be persecuted, for example, if they are offered inadequate protection in the context of a consistent pattern of war crimes.[11] It has to be remembered that human rights are developing all the time and should a right to conscientious objection evolve in the meantime, perhaps in other jurisdictions, the domestic position could change. Internationally, there is uncertainty, however, as to whether the holding of a genuine and principled objection to the performance of military service can of itself substantiate a claim.[12] The language of the UNHCR *Handbook* is somewhat cautious, merely stating that it is open to contracting states to grant refugee status to 'persons who object to performing military service for genuine reasons of conscience'.[13] The House of Lords held in *Sepet* that 'there is as yet no authority' to support the contention that there was a right to conscientious objection to military service,[14] clearly thereby acknowledging that such a right might eventually be established. The position may now be different. Firstly, the Charter of Fundamental Rights of the European Union which, by art 10(2), recognises a right to conscientious objection now has a substantial legal status that it did not have when *Sepet* was decided.[15] Secondly, the Grand Chamber of the European Court of Human Rights has revisited and departed from its previous jurisprudence so as to hold that art 9 of the ECHR does confer a right to conscientious objection.[16]

1   (00TH01513), para 9.
2   See UNHCR *Handbook* **12.13** above, para 170. Note in this context that the listing of particular types of conscientious objection has given way to what the Tribunal in *Foughali* described as 'a more flexible "compelling reasons of conscience"' definition. See eg Council of Europe Committee of Ministers Recommendation R(87)8; UN Commission on Human Rights report 2 March 1995, E/CN.4/1995/L.82, noting the general comment No 22(48) of the Human Rights Committee that 'there should be no differentiation between conscientious objectors on the basis of the nature of their particular beliefs'.
3   *Sepet v Secretary of State for the Home Department* [2003] UKHL 15, [2003] 1 WLR 856.
4   In *Sepet v Secretary of State for the Home Department* [2001] EWCA Civ 681, [2001] Imm AR 452 the Court of Appeal held that the apparent acceptance, without argument on the issue, of a human right to conscientious objection by the Court of Appeal in *Zaitz v Secretary of State for the Home Department* [2000] INLR 346 was not in any way authoritative and that the Tribunal in *Foughali* (above) had erred in treating it as such.
5   *Sepet v Secretary of State for the Home Department.*
6   *Sepet v Secretary of State for the Home Department*, Lord Bingham, para 8.
7   See ECHR art 9, and the views of Commission members in *Thlimmenos v Greece* (App 34369/97) (2000) 31 EHRR 411, (2000) 9 BHRC 12, at paras 44–45.
8   *Zolfagharkani v Canada* [1993] 3 FC 540.
9   *Ciric v Canada* [1994] 2 CF 65. Note however that *Sepet* (above) involved Turkish Kurds who objected to performing military service because it was likely to involve fighting fellow Kurds; the Tribunal ([2000] Imm AR 445) had dismissed the appeals on the ground (not upheld by the Court of Appeal or the House of Lords) that the appellants' objection was partial and contained unacceptable discrimination against non-Kurds.

[10] *BE (Iran) v Secretary of State for the Home Department* [2008] EWCA Civ 540, (2008) Times, 18 June.
[11] The Tribunal in *ZQ (serving soldier) Iraq CG* [2009] UKAIT 00048, see **12.62** above.
[12] See the speech of Lord Hoffmann in *Sepet* in the House of Lords (fn 3 above) at paras 39 and 52, and the judgments of Laws and Waller LJJ in the Court of Appeal (fn 5) at paras 20–81, 187–200.
[13] Note however that the *Handbook* was written in 1979. See also Goodwin-Gill *The Refugee in International Law* (2nd edn, 1996) at p 55 ff.
[14] *Sepet v Secretary of State for the Home Department* [2003] UKHL 15 at [17], [2003] 3 All ER 304, [2003] 1 WLR 856.
[15] Joined cases C-411/10 and C-493/10: *NS v Secretary of State for the Home Department*.
[16] *Bayatyan v Armenia* (Application 23459/03) (2011) 54 EHRR 467, 32 BHRC 290.

12.79 In *Adan and Lazarevic*[1] the Court of Appeal held that a person who faces prosecution for a genuine objection to the performance of military service involving action contrary to basic rules of human conduct is expressing a political opinion and is a refugee.[2] Paragraph 171 of the UNHCR *Handbook* refers to military action 'condemned by the international community', and in *Krotov*[3] the Court of Appeal considered conflicting Tribunal decisions on when military action with which an asylum claimant does not wish to be associated, can properly be said to be condemned by the international community as contrary to the basic rules of human conduct, so that punishment for desertion or refusal to serve can itself amount to persecution.[4] Potter LJ held that where acts prohibited by the humanitarian norms expressed in the international law of armed conflict, such as genocide, the deliberate killing and targeting of the civilian population, rape, torture, the execution and ill-treatment of prisoners and the taking of civilian hostages,[5] 'are committed on a systemic basis as an aspect of deliberate policy, or as a result of official indifference to the widespread actions of a brutal military' they 'qualify as acts contrary to the basic rules of human conduct in respect of which punishment for a refusal to participate will constitute persecution within the ambit of the 1951 Convention'.[6] He emphasised that the individual asylum-seeker had to be at real risk of being 'required to participate' in such military actions, rather than merely being 'associated' with them, eg through wearing of the uniform.[7] In *Adan and Lazarevic*,[8] the issue was whether refugee status could be granted to draft evaders from an army engaged in an internationally condemned conflict, regardless of whether their objection to fighting was genuine or (as the adjudicator had found) opportunistic. Hutchison LJ held that the fact that they were opportunists and not genuine objectors was fatal to their claim. It will always be important for asylum seekers who base their claims on a wish to avoid the performance of military service to give detailed and cogent evidence.[9]

[1] *Adan v Secretary of State for the Home Department, Lazarevic v Secretary of State for the Home Department* [1997] 1 WLR 1107 approved by *Sepet v Secretary of State for the Home Department* [2003] UKHL 15 at [8]. See further *Altun v Secretary of State for the Home Department* (1999/0845/C), 28 January 2000, where the Court of Appeal accepted that the interpretation of art 1A(2) of the Refugee Convention required recognition in such circumstances. See also *Sepet*, CA (12.78 above).

[2] UNHCR *Handbook* **12.13** above, para 171. See also (in the context of the *Yugoslavian* conflicts) *Azapovic* (13611) and *Drvis* (13129); *Tallah* [1998] INLR 258 and *Rieda* (14359) (Algeria); *Zolfagarkhani v Canada* [1993] 3 FC 540 (use of chemical weapons in Iran-Iraq war). For an attempt to argue that laying land mines in a civilian area falls within the ambit of repugnant military action, punishment for refusal to perform which gives rise to refugee status, see *BE (Iran)* [2004] UKIAT 00183 (awaiting rehearing following remittal from the Court of Appeal).

3   *Krotov v Secretary of State for the Home Department* [2004] EWCA Civ 69, [2004] 1 WLR 1825.

4   In *Foughali* (00TH01513) and again in *B (Russia)* [2003] Imm AR 591 the IAT held that the correct approach was to consider the nature of the military actions in question (as objectively evidenced by human rights reports on the given conflict) in the context of international human rights law and international law governing armed conflicts and determine whether such actions are contrary to the basic rules of human conduct. International condemnation, especially by the UN General Assembly, would merely be one indicator – albeit a strong one – that the military actions in question were contrary to the basic rules of human conduct. However in *Krotov* [2002] UKIAT 01325 the Tribunal held that some kind of formal condemnation by the international community of the military actions in question was a prerequisite for any asylum claim to succeed on the basis that punishment per se for refusal to serve in an army that committed such actions amounts to persecution. The Court of Appeal in *Krotov* held in favour of the *Foughali* and *B* approach.

5   See Annexes V and VI to the UNHCR *Handbook* for Article 6 of the Charter of the International Military Tribunal established to try and punish Axis war criminals; The Rome Statute of the International Criminal Court 1998, arts 6–8 (defining genocide, war crimes and crimes against humanity); and for a useful summary of the international laws of armed conflict, see Ministry of Defence *Manual of the law of armed conflict* (July 2004, OUP): see also the list in *Krotov* [2004] EWCA Civ 69 (above) at para 30.

6   *Krotov* [2004] EWCA Civ 69 (above) at para 37. He concluded: 'If a court or tribunal is satisfied (a) that the level and nature of the conflict, and the attitude of the relevant governmental authority towards it, has reached a position where combatants are or may be required on a sufficiently widespread basis to act in breach of the basic rules of human conduct generally recognised by the international community, (b) that they will be punished for refusing to do so and (c) that disapproval of such methods and fear of such punishment is the genuine reason motivating the refusal of an asylum seeker to serve in the relevant conflict, then it should find that a Convention ground has been established.' [51].

7   *Krotov* [2004] EWCA Civ 69 (above) at para 40. Rix and Carnwath LJJ agreed. In Canada, the case of *Zolfagarkhani v Canada* [1993] 3 FC 540 is authority for the proposition that the applicant does not have to prove that he or she would be required to participate in acts contrary to Article 1F of the Refugee Convention, only that the army in question performed them.

8   *Adan, Lazarevic v Secretary of State for the Home Department*, fn 1 above.

9   See eg UNHCR *Handbook* **12.13** above, para 174, referring to the need for 'a thorough investigation of . . . personality and background' to establish the genuineness of the objection. Immigration judges tend to draw adverse conclusions on credibility more readily where the appellant's views are not explained in detail. See also *Kulet* (00TH00391).

Membership of a particular social group

12.80 This last category has been the most litigated of all the Refugee Convention reasons and the one where the necessity to see the Convention as a living instrument, constant in motive but mutable in form,[1] is most apparent. The cases have raised controversial issues as to the limits of Convention protection. However, those limits can be stated with a far greater degree of certainty following *Shah and Islam*[2] in which the House of Lords held that women in Pakistan constituted a particular social group. Lord Steyn approved the following passage from the decision of the US Board of Immigration Appeals in *Acosta*:[3]

'We find the well-established doctrine of *ejusdem generis* . . . to be most helpful in construing the phrase . . . Each of [the other grounds] describes persecution aimed at an immutable characteristic: a characteristic that either is beyond the power of an individual to change or is so fundamental to individual identity or conscience that it ought not be required to be changed . . .

Applying the doctrine of *ejusdem generis*, we interpret the phrase . . . to mean persecution that is directed toward an individual who is a member of a group of persons all of whom share a common, immutable characteristic. The shared characteristic might be an innate one such as sex, colour, or kinship ties, or in some circumstances it might be a shared experience such as former military leadership or land ownership . . . By construing [the phrase] in this manner we preserve the concept that refugee status is restricted to individuals who are either unable by their own actions, or as a matter of conscience should not be required, to avoid persecution.'[4]

Whether a number of people sharing particular characteristics constitute a 'particular social group' depends on the factual situation in the particular country. Westernised women may be seen as a distinct social group in some Middle Eastern countries but not in Israel, just as landowners were such a group in pre-revolutionary Russia but would not be in England today.[5] The following underlying principles emerge from the judgments:

(i)   interpretation of the phrase 'particular social group' must be seen in the context of the fundamental purpose of the Refugee Convention of counteracting discrimination;[6]

(ii)   the social group must exist independently of, and not be defined by, the persecution, otherwise anyone persecuted for whatever reason would qualify;[7]

(iii)   however, this does not mean that discrimination against members is irrelevant as a means of identifying the group.[8] On the contrary, women in Pakistan were held to be a particular social group precisely because as a group distinguished by gender, they were discriminated against and unprotected by the state;[9]

(iv)   although cohesiveness may prove the existence of a particular social group, it is not a requirement for the existence of the group.[10]

In an attempt to unify the divergent approaches (referred to as the 'protected characteristics' approach and the 'social perception' approach) to the meaning of the phrase at the international level, the UNHCR gives the following definition:[11]

'A particular social group is a group of persons who share a common characteristic other than their risk of being persecuted, or who are perceived as a group by society. The characteristic will often be one which is innate, unchangeable, or which is otherwise fundamental to identity, conscience or the exercise of one's human rights.

This definition includes characteristics which are historical and therefore cannot be changed, and those which, though it is possible to change them, ought not to be required to be changed because they are so closely linked to the identity of the person or are an expression of fundamental human rights. It follows that sex can properly be within the ambit of the social group category, with women being a clear example of a social subset defined by innate and immutable characteristics, and who are frequently treated differently to men.

If a claimant alleges a social group that is based on a characteristic determined to be neither unalterable nor fundamental, further analysis should be undertaken to determine whether the group is nonetheless perceived as a cognisable group in that society. So, for example, if it were determined that owning a shop or participating in a certain occupation in a particular society is neither unchangeable nor a fundamental aspect of human identity, a shopkeeper or members of a particular profession might nonetheless constitute a particular social group if in the society they are recognised as a group which sets them apart.'

This definition was approved by the House of Lords in *Fornah v Secretary of State for the Home Department*.[12] There, Lord Bingham noted that the Qualification Directive apparently provides that the 'protected characteristics' requirement and the 'social perception' requirement were cumulative, rather than alternative tests, both having to be satisfied in order to establish membership of a particular social group[13] and thereby the Qualification Directive 'propounds a test more stringent than is warranted by international authority'. Lord Hope held that it was not necessary for a particular social group to be recognised as such by the society of which it was a part so long as membership of the group could be identified objectively as the reason for the persecution.[14] Lord Brown commented that any Regulations made under the Directive would have to be interpreted consistently with the UNHCR's definition of particular social group in which 'protected characteristics' and 'social perception' were alternative and not cumulative requirements.[15] Against the weight of this authority, the tribunal has interpreted the Regulation implementing the Qualification Directive[16] as imposing those requirements cumulatively rather than as alternatives.[17] The Directive expressly acknowledges that sexual orientation may be the common characteristic upon which a particular social group is based but excluding acts considered to be criminal in the national law of the Member States from the meaning of sexual orientation.[18] Surprisingly, and plainly at odds with the UK's interpretation of the Refugee Convention, the Directive says that gender may be relevant but is not by itself capable of constituting a particular social group;[19] the implementing Regulations do not give effect to this part of the Directive.[20]

1   *R v Immigration Appeal Tribunal and Secretary of State for the Home Department, ex p Shah* [1997] Imm AR 145 at 152, per Sedley J His formulation was approved by the House of Lords.
2   *R v Immigration Appeal Tribunal, ex p Shah; Islam v Secretary of State for the Home Department* [1999] 2 AC 629, [1999] Imm AR 283, [1999] INLR 144.
3   (1985) 19 I & N 211.
4   See also LA Forest J's (similar) formulation in *A-G of Canada v Ward* (1993) 103 DLR (4th) 1, [1993] 2 SCR 689, [1997] INLR 42.
5   *Shah and Islam* above, per Lord Millett. See also UN High Commissioner for Refugees Amicus Curiae Brief in *Valdiviezo-Galdamez v Holder, Attorney General* (No 08-4564; 14 April 2009): '"Social perception" does not require that the common attribute be visible to the naked eye in a literal sense of the term nor that it be one that is easily recognizable to the general public. Nor is "social perception" meant to suggest a sense of community or group identification as might exist for members of an organization or association; members of a social group may not be visibly recognizable even to each other. Rather, the determination rests on whether a group is "cognizable" or "set apart from society at large" in some way'.
6   [1999] INLR 144 at 150A–F, 161E–162D, 167B–C. In *A v Minister for Immigration and Ethnic Affairs* [1998] INLR 1 at 15, Dawson J said that where a persecutory law or practice applies to all members of society, it cannot create a particular social group consisting of all who bring themselves within its terms (referring to China's one-child policy). Where the feared persecution emanates from non-state actors, it may be their discrimination or that of the state in failing to protect which constitutes the particular social group. But see *Skenderaj v Secretary of State for the Home Department* [2002] EWCA Civ 567, [2002] 4 All ER 555, [2002] Imm AR 519.
7   [1999] INLR 144 at 151A–151C, 156D–G, 167C. See also *Secretary of State for the Home Department v Savchenkov* [1996] Imm AR 28. But this does not mean that the actions of the persecutors cannot 'identify or even cause the creation of a particular social group in society': see Lord Steyn at 156D–G, endorsing McHugh J in *A v Minister for Immigration and Ethnic Affairs* [1998] INLR 1. Forgetting this may give rise to error of law: see *Liu v Secretary of State for the Home Department* [2005] EWCA Civ 249, (2005) All ER (D) 304 (Mar).
8   [1999] INLR 144 at 167E–F.
9   In the words of Lord Hoffmann, 'discrimination was the critical element in the persecution' ([1999] INLR 144 at 164H–165A). See also *R (on the application of Hoxha) v Secretary*

of State for the Home Department, R (on the application of B) v Secretary of State for the Home Department [2005] UKHL 19, [2005] 1 WLR 1063, (2005) 149 Sol Jo LB 358 per Baroness Hale at paras 30ff.

10 Staughton LJ had held that cohesiveness (or interdependence or co-operation) was an essential prerequisite of a 'particular social group' in the Court of Appeal ([1998] INLR 97). Lord Steyn at 151D–154H and Lord Hoffmann at 162E–H rejected this ([1999] INLR 144), approving the decision of La Forest J in *Ward* (social group could include 'such bases as gender, linguistic background and sexual orientation' – none of which implied interdependence or co-operation).

11 UNHCR *Guidelines on International Protection: 'Membership of a particular social group'* (7 May 2002) (HCR/GIP/02/02) at para 11. The UNHCR guidelines, at para 15, also firmly reject any need for the group to be cohesive. See further Qualification Directive (30.9.04 OJ L304/12, in force 20 October 2004), art 10(1)(d).

12 *Fornah v Secretary of State for the Home Department* [2006] UKHL 46, [2007] 1 AC 412, [2007] 1 All ER 671.

13 Qualification Directive, art 10(1)(d) and the Refugee or Person in Need of International Protection (Qualification) Regulations 2006, SI 2006/2525, reg 6(1)(e).

14 Lord Hope, para 46, following McHugh J in *Applicant S v Minister for Immigration and Multicultural Affairs* (2004) 217 CLR 387.

15 Lord Brown, para 118.

16 The Refugee or Person in Need of International Protection (Qualification) Regulations 2006, SI 2006/2525, reg 6(1)(d).

17 *SB (Moldova) CG* [2008] UKAIT 00002, followed by *AZ (Thailand) CG* [2010] UKUT 118 (IAC).

18 Qualification Directive, art 10(1)(d), the Refugee or Person in Need of International Protection (Qualification) Regulations 2006, reg 6(1)(e).

19 Qualification Directive, art 10(1)(d).

20 See the Refugee or Person in Need of International Protection (Qualification) Regulations 2006, reg 6(1)(e) which reproduces that part of the Directive relating to sexual orientation but not the immediately following part about gender.

12.81 Prior to *Shah and Islam* gender[1] had not been accepted in practice as the basis of a particular social group,[2] although it had been cited as one of the immutable characteristics which *could* found such a group in *Acosta* and *Ward*. Particular sub-groups defined partly by gender and partly by another characteristic (such as transgressing social mores) had been recognised.[3] Women who faced compulsory sterilisation or abortion because of China's one-child policy had been held to be refugees on the grounds of social group[4] or political opinion.[5] A divorced Somali woman who had no effective state protection from abuse by her husband and whose daughter might face mutilation was recognised as a refugee.[6] Western-educated Afghani,[7] Algerian[8] and Iranian[9] women had been held to have a well-founded fear of persecution arising from Islamic opposition to their identities and way of life.[10] A number of Canadian decisions had recognised as refugees women fleeing domestic violence,[11] forced marriage[12] or sexual exploitation[13] from which their state would or could not protect them. Rape and severe sexual harassment had been recognised in some cases as constituting Convention persecution,[14] and the Home Office had recognised that rape, forcible abortion, forcible sterilisation, acts involving genital mutilation or allied practices 'probably always' constitute torture.[15] But gender-based social groups had been rejected in a number of cases.[16]

1 See for discussion of gender persecution UNHCR *Guidelines on International Protection: Gender-Related Persecution* (7 May 2002) (HCR/GIP/02/01); Rodger Haines 'Gender-related persecution', in Feller, Turk and Nicholson *Refugee Protection in International Law, UNHCR's Global Consultations on International Protection* (2003); Heaven Crawley,

Refugees and Gender: Law and Process (2001); Berkowitz and Jarvis *Immigration Appellate Authority Asylum Gender Guidelines* (Nov 2000). See also the API on 'Gender issues in the asylum claim'.

2 UNHCR's Executive Committee had issued a recommendation, No 39 of 1985, indicating that states *could* recognise women at risk for transgressing social mores as refugees; see also UNHCR *Guidelines on the Protection of Refugee Women* (1991) paras 54–57; Canadian Immigration and Refugee Board Guidelines above; US INS *Considerations for Asylum Officers Adjudicating Asylum Claims from Women* (May 1995); Australian Dept of Imm and Multicultural Affairs, Refugee and Humanitarian Visa applicants *Guidelines on Gender Issues for Decision Makers* (July 1996).

3 See UNHCR ExCom conclusion 39 (1985) above.

4 *Cheung v Minister of Immigration* (1993) FCJ No 309 digested in (1994) 6(1) 118, IJRL case 184. But contrast *Yu (Chang Zheng)* (15469) where a tribunal held that the one-child policy could not provide the basis of a social group. And see also *A v Minister for Immigration and Ethnic Affairs* (1997) 142 ALR 331, [1998] INLR 1, High Court of Australia: a husband and wife who feared forced sterilisation under the 'one-child policy' were not members of a social group. Lord Steyn in *Shah and Islam* ([1999] INLR 144 at 153B–D) said that the uniform application of the policy meant that there was 'no obvious element of discrimination'. On the other hand, children born in defiance of the one child policy, who then face official as well as societal discrimination for this reason, can constitute a particular social group for the purposes of the refugee definition: see *Chen Shi Hai v Minister for Immigration and Multicultural Affairs* (2000) 170 ALR 553, [2000] INLR 455, Aust HC.

5 *Guo v Carroll* 62 US Law Week 2473.

6 (1994) 6(4) IJRL 662 Case 207.

7 *Shaysta Ameer-Ali v Minister of Citizenship and Immigration* Imm-3404-95, 23 September 1996 (Can).

8 (1994) 6(4) IJRL 666 Case 209.

9 (1993) 5(4) IJRL 611, Case 170.

10 See eg *Fatin v INS* 12 F 3d 1233 (US Ct of Apps (3rd Cir), 1993); *Fisher v INS* 37 F 3d 1371 (US Ct of Apps (9th Cir), 1994).

11 *Mayers v Minister of Employment and Immigration* (1992) 97 DLR (4th) 729; *Narvaez v Canada* [1995] 2 CF 55; *Tahusi*, CRDD T9802494, 7 September 1999 (Georgia).

12 *Vidhani v Canada (Minister of Citizenship and Immigration)* TD Imm-3528-94, 8 June 1995.

13 *Cen v Canada (Minister of Citizenship and Immigration)* TD Imm-1023-95, 1995.

14 (1995) 5(4) IJRL 613 Case 173; (1994) 6(4) IJRL 668 Case 211; *Ransell (Eustaquio)* CRDD T98-04880, 20 October 1999 (Romania). See Laws LJ in *Sepet v Secretary of State for the Home Department* [2001] EWCA Civ 681, [2001] INLR 376 at 403, at para 63.

15 API Jul 98, Ch 3, para 2.1. European Union law now achieves the same result, see Regulation 9(2)(f), Directive 2004/38; not in terms transposed by the Refugee or Person in Need of International Protection (Qualification) Regulations 2006 SI 2006/2525, art 5(2), not that this is material, see *MA (Palestinian Arabs, Occupied Territories, Risk) Palestinian Territories CG* [2007] UKAIT 00017.

16 See eg *Khan (Nafees Parveen)* (15884) (unprotected Pakistani widow); *Safraz (Lubna)* (16179) (Pakistani woman at risk from husband); *Gomez v INS* 947 F 2d 660 (1991) (women previously raped by guerrillas).

12.82 Following *Shah and Islam* the Tribunal and the Court of Appeal upheld a number of gender-based claims, including: an Iranian woman who feared prosecution for adultery after leaving her violent husband;[1] a Pakistani woman whose illegitimate children would be seen as evidence of sexual immorality;[2] a single Pakistani woman without male protection at risk from the Mohajirs;[3] educated Afghan women perceived as pro-western and anti-Islamic;[4] a woman in Ethiopia fearing forced marriage;[5] a Ukrainian woman forced into prostitution[6] and an Albanian woman trafficked for prostitution.[7] In the last two cases there was evidence that the Ukraine and Albania were important source countries of girls and women trafficked for sexual exploitation. The Tribunal has held that in *Moldova*, former victims of trafficking for sexual exploitation constitute a particular social group because of their shared, past experience of having been trafficked and societal recognition of their consequent distinctiveness.[8] On the other hand, attempts to establish Jaffna Tamil women at risk of arrest and rape in Colombo as a social group failed for lack of evidence of 'differential gender victimisation',[9] and a deserted Kurdish wife who feared sexual exploitation and violence by neighbours and in-laws was held not to belong to a particular social group in *Karakas*,[10] because of lack of legal discrimination against women in Turkey. The Tribunal and the Court of Appeal were until recently fairly reluctant to allow gender-based claims. While forced marriage[11] and domestic violence[12] grounded claims in the US,[13] women at risk of rape from soldiers in Uganda were held not to constitute a particular social group in *R (on the application of N) v Secretary of State for the Home Department*,[14] and women and girls from various African countries who risk female genital mutilation were held not to constitute a particular social group, on the basis that a group cannot be defined by its persecution.[15] The Tribunal has repeatedly emphasised the need to show a combination of legal and social discrimination of a particular level of intensity.[16] However, recent cases suggest a more open approach. In *P and M* the Court of Appeal castigated the Tribunal for reversing first instance decisions that Kenyan women constituted a particular social group, and accepted that domestic violence or female genital mutilation, against which police would not provide protection despite central government initiatives, were capable of giving rise to refugee status.[17] In *Fornah v Secretary of State for the Home Department*[18] the House of Lords overturned the decision of the majority in the Court of Appeal that a woman's fear of female genital mutilation, albeit accepted as capable of being a fear of persecution, was not for reason of membership of the particular social group of intact or uninitiated women because the group was thereby and impermissibly defined by reference to the persecution.[19] The House of Lords held that her fear was either for reason of being a woman in Sierra Leone (a group sharing the common characteristic of a position of social inferiority compared with men in Sierra Leone and being perceived by society as inferior[20]); a woman from Sierra Leone belonging to one of the tribes practising FGM[21] or intact or uninitiated woman from Sierra Leone;[22] each of those characteristics would be identifiable quite apart from the persecution. The Tribunal in *NS* held that a first-instance finding that a rape was motivated by attraction was not based on the evidence and constituted an error of law.[23] Lady Hale's discussion of gender persecution in *B and Hoxha* took the analysis further, indicating that stigmatisation and marginalisation of women who have been rape victims, and of their families, through deep-seated prejudices may ground a refugee claim, if the state is unable to afford protection. Her judgment confirms that state complicity, or state-anointed discrimination, is not a prerequisite to a gender-based refugee claim.[24]

[1]   *Fatemeh (Miriam)* (00TH 00921) (for reasons mirroring those in *Shah and Islam*, given the similar position of women in Iran). See also *Hanif* [2002] UKIAT 07617 (Pakistani women). In *Davoodipanah v Secretary of State for the Home Department* [2004] EWCA Civ 106, the Court of Appeal held that the Secretary of State could not withdraw a concession made before the adjudicator that 'adulterous wives in Iran' constitute a particular social group. In *ZH (Iran) CG* [2003] UKIAT 00207, the tribunal held that institutional discrimination against women in Iran did not necessarily constitute them a particular social group, but in *TB (Iran)* [2005] UKIAT 00065, the tribunal held that that case was based on insufficient evidence.

[2]   *Altaf (Robina)* (00TH 01370). Cf *Babalola (Olayinka Adebukola)* (00TH00926) where the social group contended for was divorced women in Nigeria. But since the claimant could establish no well-founded fear of persecution, the tribunal did not consider the evidence on the position of divorced women in Nigeria; see also *SN and HM (Divorced women: risk on return) Pakistan CG* [2004] UKIAT 283 Reported.

3   *Begum (Syeda)* (21257).

4   *Afghan cases 30, 27, 28* [2002] UKIAT 06500. The women in that case were additionally at
    risk for their family political connections.

5   *RG (Ethiopia) v Secretary of State for the Home Department* [2006] EWCA Civ 339, 150 Sol
    Jo LB 473, [2006] All ER (D) 20 (Apr).

6   *Dzhygun* (00TH00728). The particular social group was defined as 'women in the Ukraine
    forced into prostitution against their will', whose defining characteristics included gender and
    lack of state protection.

7   *SK (Albania) v Secretary of State for the Home Department* [2003] UKIAT 00023. The
    particular social group accepted by the tribunal was 'women from the north-east of Albania'.
    In *VD (Albania) v Secretary of State for the Home Department* [2004] UKIAT 00115, the
    tribunal rejected a wider group of 'Albanian women' but implicitly recognised that such
    women who had been sold and had escaped from their trafficker could be at risk of persecution
    (and could constitute a particular social group). But see the tribunal's extraordinarily harsh
    decision in *JO (Nigeria)* [2004] UKIAT 00251, based on internal relocation for a victim of
    trafficking still under 18 at the date of hearing.

8   *SB (Moldova) CG* [2008] UKAIT 00002. The tribunal, applying the Refugee or Person in
    Need of International Protection (Qualification) Regulations, 2006/2525, reg 6(1)(d) held that
    both the shared immutable characteristic and the societal perception were necessary to
    constitute a particular social group. Surprisingly, the tribunal also held that for gender to be
    a particular social group it was necessary to show gender based discrimination as a constituent
    of the group's identity apart from the feared persecution. On the Council of Europe Conven-
    tion against the Trafficking in Human Beings, see CHAPTER 13.

9   See eg *Thangarajah (Vathana)* (16414) where the tribunal held that Tamil women from Jaffna
    were not a social group because it was not established that they were being raped or sexually
    assaulted as such, nor with impunity; *Muralitharali* (B20813).

10 [2002] UKIAT 06406.

11 A76-512-001, Imm Ct Chicago, 18 October 2000. See now *TB (Iran)* [2005] UKIAT 00065
    (starred) for a UK forced marriage case.

12 *Aguirre-Cervantes v INS*, 21 March 2001, US CA (9th Cir). See now *P v Secretary of State for
    the Home Department* [2004] EWCA Civ 1640, [2004] All ER (D) 123 (Dec), discussed
    below.

13 See also the Canadian cases cited at **12.79** fn 11 and 12 above, and see the comprehensive
    treatment of gender issues in H Crawley *Refugees and gender: law and process* (2001).

14 *R (on the application of N) v Secretary of State for the Home Department* [2002] EWCA Civ
    1082, dismissed on the objectionable grounds that what was feared was 'dreadful lust' rather
    than Convention persecution. See also *Castro (Rosa del Carmen)* [2002] UKIAT 00199
    (women in Ecuador).

15 See *RM (Sierra Leone)* [2004] UKIAT 00108, where the tribunal rejected 'Mendi women and
    girls who were intact' as a social group; see also *M (Kenya)* [2004] UKIAT 00022 (reversed by
    the Court of Appeal), disapproving *Yake* (00TH00493) and *Kasinga* (1996) US Bd Imm
    Appeals Int Dec 3278. The Tribunal in *M (Kenya)* also rejected the groups of 'Kenyan women',
    'Kenyan women under 65' and 'Kikuyu women'. In *Hashim* [2002] UKIAT 02691, the
    tribunal rejected the argument that young girls in Sudan constituted a particular social group
    because of their inability to escape FGM (they allowed the appeal on art 3 ECHR grounds).
    The Tribunal's approach was criticised as over-technical in *P v Secretary of State for the Home
    Department* [2004] EWCA Civ 1640, [2004] All ER (D) 123 (Dec) and the appellant M
    granted status.

16 See *JO (Nigeria)* [2004] UKIAT 00251; *HM (Somalia) (CG)* [2005] UKIAT 40; *RA
    (Bangladesh)* [2005] UKIAT 70.

17 *P v Secretary of State for the Home Department* [2004] EWCA Civ 1640, [2004] All ER (D)
    123 (Dec). The judgment, indicates the incorrectness of the tribunal's analysis in *M (Albania)*
    [2004] UKIAT 00059 and *NA (Tajikistan)* [2004] UKIAT 00133, to the effect that clear
    discrimination against women enshrined in the law of the country concerned is an essential
    requirement of gender persecution. See also *RG (Ethiopia) v Secretary of State for the Home
    Department* [2006] EWCA Civ 339, 150 Sol Jo LB 473, [2006] All ER (D) 20 (Apr) and
    the ECtHR in *Opuz v Turkey* (Application no 33401/02; 9 June 2009).

18 *Fornah v Secretary of State for the Home Department* [2006] UKHL 46, [2007] 1 AC 412,
    [2007] 1 All ER 671.

19 *Fornah v Secretary of State for the Home Department* [2005] EWCA Civ 680, [2005] 1 WLR
    3773, Auld and Chadwick LLJ, Arden LJ dissenting.

20 *Fornah v Secretary of State for the Home Department*, Lord Bingham, para 31.

[21] *Fornah v Secretary of State for the Home Department*, Baroness Hale, para 111. See *K and others (FGM) Gambia CG* [2013] UKUT 62 (IAC) for a detailed discussion of the evaluation of such cases. In *AMM and others (conflict; humanitarian crisis; returnees; FGM) Somalia CG* [2011] UKUT 445 (IAC) the UTIAC found that there would be no viable asylum claim for a person who faced a real chance of inflicting FGM on a child unless they could establish duress or similar.

[22] *Fornah v Secretary of State for the Home Department*, Lord Hope, para 58, Lord Roger, para 80, Lord Brown, para 119.

[23] *NS (Social group – women – forced marriage) Afghanistan CG* [2004] UKIAT 00328 'Reported', This analysis finally sets out the obvious truth underlying violence against women, locating sexual violence in power relations.

[24] *R (on the application of Hoxha) v Secretary of State for the Home Department, R (on the application of B) v Secretary of State for the Home Department* [2005] UKHL 19, [2005] 1 WLR 1063, (2005) 149 Sol Jo LB 358, at paras 30 ff. The judgment refers approvingly to the UNHCR *Guidelines on International Protection: Gender-Related Persecution* (7 May 2002) and indicates that the source of the discrimination may be deep-seated patriarchal attitudes against which the state cannot contend. Lady Hale reinforced her observations about rape as a weapon of war in *N v Secretary of State for the Home Department* [2005] UKHL 31 at para 58, [2005] 2 AC 296, [2005] 4 All ER 1017.

12.83 The decision in *Shah and Islam* also made it clear that a particular social group may be constituted on grounds of sexuality or gender preference[1] if, as a group defined by their sexuality or gender preference (an immutable characteristic or one that the individual should not be expected to change), they suffer discrimination.[2] There had been contradictory decisions of differently constituted Tribunals on this question.[3] In *Jain*[4] it was common ground before the Court of Appeal that homosexuals in India constitute a particular social group, since Indian law makes sodomy an offence, thus discriminating against the group on grounds of sexuality. Since *Shah and Islam*, homosexuals in various countries have been held to be members of a particular social group because of the combination of societal and legal discrimination against them.[5]

[1] It is now customary to compendiously describe the groups most commonly at risk as LGBTi, signifying lesbian, gay, bisexual, transsexual and intersexual gender preferences.

[2] [1999] INLR 144 per Lord Steyn at 154D–F; Lord Hoffmann at 162H; Lord Millett at 173F–H. Note Lord Steyn's express endorsement of the decision of the New Zealand Refugee Status Authority in *Re GJ* [1998] INLR 387. The UNHCR *Guidelines on International Protection: Gender-Related Persecution* (7 May 2002) at paras 16–17 and 30 also make clear that severely discriminatory policies or practices directed against homosexuals for reason of their sexuality can amount to persecution for reason of membership of a particular social group.

[3] See for example *Vraciu* (11559); *Golchin* (7623); *Jacques* (11580); *Saddegh* (13124): see also *R v Secretary of State for the Home Department, ex p Binbasi* [1989] Imm AR 595 where the court had assumed, without deciding, that homosexuals could form a social group; the Tribunal in *AJ (Risk to Homosexuals) Afghanistan CG* [2009] UKAIT 00001 (05 January 2009).

[4] *Jain v Secretary of State for the Home Department* [2000] INLR 71. The court however found that there was no real risk of persecution.

[5] See *Beteringhe* (18120), in relation to Romania, where the claim succeeded, and *Dumitru* (00TH00945) where the claim failed on the facts, the Tribunal holding that the evidence fell short of establishing risk to gay asylum seekers of a 'widespread and systematic pattern of abuses of their human rights'. In *Apostolov* (18547) a Tribunal accepted that a Bulgarian homosexual was a member of a social group, although dismissing the appeal on the facts. Ukrainian homosexuals were held to constitute a particular social group in *Bespalko* [2002] UKIAT 00135 (appeal allowed); Pakistani homosexuals in *Ali (Mohammed Asghar)* [2002] UKIAT 02153 (appeal allowed); Eritreans in *F (Eritrea)* [2003] UKIAT 00177, Ugandans in *K (Uganda)* [2004] UKIAT 00021 (appeals dismissed).

12.84 Although *Shah and Islam* resolved many issues of principle on the particular social group, difficulties still occur in areas such as what characteristics are 'immutable', what is included in 'individual identity or conscience' and the relationship between persecution and the existence of the group. Previously, in *Savchenkov*,[1] the Court of Appeal had held that those refusing to join a Russian mafia were not a social group because they did not exist independently of the persecution feared.[2] Attempts since *Shah and Islam* to persuade Tribunals to reach a different conclusion and to identify groups by reference to risks from criminal gangs or corrupt officials have generally failed on the same basis: civic conscience is not, in most cases, enough to constitute a particular social group.[3] Linked to this is the important principle that it is far easier to establish membership of a particular social group on the basis of what one *is*, rather than on the basis of what one has *done*. Thus in *Morato v Minister for Immigration and Ethnic Affairs*[4] a citizen of Bolivia had claimed asylum on the grounds that he had been a police informer and as such a member of a group of police informers in fear of reprisals. The Australian Federal Court rejected the argument on the grounds that the applicant's problems resulted from his actions and not from his membership of any group.[5] In *Montoya*[6] the Tribunal summarised the jurisprudence on particular social groups, in the context of a claim by a landowner targeted by guerrillas in Colombia. In *Ouanes*[7] an Algerian government-employed midwife whose work involved giving advice on contraception (which put her at risk of persecution from fundamentalists) was held not to be employed in an occupation having 'that impact upon individual identities or conscience necessary to constitute employees a particular social group'. The court accepted that certain employments could reflect identity and conscience, citing membership of a religious order.[8] We suggest that this is an overly restrictive approach; many professions engage identity and conscience sufficiently to be capable of constituting a particular social group. Opportunist draft-evaders were held not to constitute a particular social group in *Lazarevic*.[9] Refugees[10] have been held not to constitute a social group, although it is hard to see why not, if they suffer marginalisation and discrimination as a group defined by the shared experience of exile: returning asylum seekers have also had their claims rejected.[11] Children may constitute a particular social group because their youth is immutable at the time their claim is assessed.[12]

---

1   [1996] Imm AR 28, CA.
2   But see *Chun Lan Liu v Secretary of State for the Home Department* [2005] EWCA Civ 249, where the Court of Appeal reminded the Tribunal that actions of the persecutors might serve to identify or even create a particular social group. See also *S v Minister for Immigration and Multicultural Affairs* [2004] HCA 25, where 'able-bodied young men' were accepted as a particular social group under the Taliban regime in Afghanistan.
3   See eg *Storozhenko v Secretary of State for the Home Department* [2001] EWCA Civ 895 (citizens of Ukraine conscientiously fulfilling their civic duty by seeking redress against the illegal actions of agents of the state are not a social group in the absence of discrimination or inability or unwillingness of the state to provide protection); *R v Immigration Appeal Tribunal, ex p Gedrimas* [1999] Imm AR 486 (Lithuanian businessmen at risk from Mafia not arguably a social group); *Jegorovas* (00TH00724) (adjudicator's acceptance as social group 'Lithuanians who challenge the power of the Mafia' reversed on appeal as group identified by persecution – there was no evidence of an identifiable group); *Stankeviciute* (00TH01321) (attempts by embezzling ex-mayor to have Lithuanian claimant killed was a private vendetta); *Kayani* (19646) (informants in Pakistan about suspected crimes and drugs criminals not a social group because such group defined only by persecution). But see eg *Ermakova* [2002] UKIAT 07728 (member of a family of a political activist pursued by the state in collusion with the mafia), and *Gvarjaladze* [2002] UKIAT 07435 (members of a family opposing high-level

corruption) for examples of positive decisions, which appear to depend on the involvement of high-level government figures in the corruption, thus making the persecution of the principal 'political'. See **12.74** above.

4   (1992) 106 ALR 367.

5   Similarly, parents who defy China's one child policy have been held not to be members of a particular social group (*A v MIEA* [1997] 142 ALR 331, [1998] INLR 1, Aust HC) while their children, born of that defiance, have been held to be members of such a group: *Chen Shi Hai v Minister for Immigration and Multicultural Affairs* (2000) 170 ALR 553, [2000] INLR 455, Aust HC): see **12.81** fn 4 above. (For an overview of the jurisprudence on refugee claims based on China's one child policy and membership of a particular social group, see *Chun Lan Liu v Secretary of State for the Home Department* [2005] EWCA Civ 249.) See also *E (Iran)* [2003] UKIAT 00166 (Iranian male adulterer not member of a particular social group); *Britton* [2002] 02514 (family of police informers in Jamaica). Cf *Osorio-Bonilla* (11451) (pre-*Shah and Islam*): those with criminal records *could* establish a social group if, because of their record, they were viewed by society in a particular way.

6   *Montoya v Secretary of State for the Home Department* (00TH00161), upheld and approved by the Court of Appeal at [2002] EWCA Civ 620, [2002] All ER (D) 130 (May). See also *Diallo* (00TH01231) (wealthy educated Sierra Leonean mine owner not member of social group where there were no immutable characteristics and risk was from generalised effects of civil war).

7   *Ouanes v Secretary of State for the Home Department* [1998] Imm AR 76.

8   *Ouanes* above, at 82.

9   *Lazarevic v Secretary of State for the Home Department* [1997] Imm AR 251, CA.

10   *R v Secretary of State for the Home Department, ex p Natando* Immigration Law Digest, Vol 1 no 4.

11   The Tribunal in *AM & AM (armed conflict: risk categories) Rev 1 Somalia CG* [2008] UKAIT 00091 at [205].

12   *LQ (Age: immutable characteristic) Afghanistan* [2008] UKAIT 00005. UN High Commissioner for Refugees' Amicus Curiae Brief in *Valdiviezo-Galdamez v Holder* (Reflex; No 08-4564; 14 April 2009): '"Youth" can be considered an immutable characteristic as one cannot change one's age, except by waiting and letting time pass; thus, the immutable character of "age" or "youth" is gradual, yet, in effect, unchangeable at any given point in time'.

12.85 The family is the social group *par excellence*, and family membership may form the basis of a 'particular social group'.[1] The question which has emerged from the case law but which has now been resolved by *Fornah v Secretary of State for the Home Department*[2] is whether it is enough to be persecuted because of membership of a family regardless of the reason for that family's original persecution, or whether another Convention reason must be behind the initial persecution. In *Ex p De Melo and De Arujo*[3] Laws J adopted the reasoning of the Tribunal in *Hernandez*[4] to the effect that although the murder of the head of the family by drug gangs might not be for a Convention reason, persecution of family members because of their family relationship to the dead man could be. He rejected the Secretary of State's argument that the non-Convention reason advanced against the principal continued to operate against the family, and concluded that membership of a social group was a distinct Convention reason and not a sub-group that had to be qualified by another Convention reason such as political opinion. The Court of Appeal in *Quijano*,[5] however, narrowed the application of the definition to exclude circumstances where ill-treatment of family members by a drug cartel was a fortuitous by-product of criminal activities, as likely to have been directed at employees as family members, and persecution was not therefore for reasons of membership of the family. The House of Lords in *Fornah v Secretary of State for the Home Department* held that *De Melo* had been right and *Quijano* was wrong. Much depends on the reason for the targeting. Thus in *Jaramillo-Aponte*[6] (another case involving Colombian asylum seekers) a tribunal found Convention persecution because the claimants were at risk 'as members of the Escobar family'.[7] Although membership of a family is the basis of 'blood feuds', which specifically target adult male members of the target family, a blood feud was held in *Skenderaj* not to give rise to a refugee claim based on membership of a particular social group, because the family in question was not regarded as a distinct group by the claimant's society, while reliance on the attitude of the other party to the feud would be artificial.[8] It is questionable, in the light of *Fornah* whether this decision is correct; as Lord Hope emphasised, it was not necessary for society to recognise a particular social group as being set apart from the rest of society – 'it is sufficient that the asylum seeker can be seen objectively to have been singled out by the persecutor or persecutors for reasons of his membership of a particular social group whose defining characteristics existed independently of the words or actions of the persecutor'.

[1] A kinship tie plainly is an immutable characteristic: see **12.80** above. A family as a social group was readily accepted by the Court of Appeal in *Quijano* below. See also *Kagedan*, CRDD A99-00215 (*9 September 1999, unreported*).

[2] *Fornah v Secretary of State for the Home Department* [2006] UKHL 46, [2007] 1 AC 412, [2007] 1 All ER 671.

[3] *R v Immigration Appeal Tribunal, ex p De Melo and De Arujo* [1997] Imm AR 43.

[4] *Hernandez* (12773) was not followed by the IAT in *Quijano* (13693).

[5] *Quijano (Fabian Martinez) v Secretary of State for the Home Department* [1997] Imm AR 227, upholding IAT (13693). See also *Obikwelu* (15343) where the claimant's child was at risk of sacrifice not as a member of the husband's family but for random and opportunistic reasons; *K v Secretary of State for the Home Department* [2004] EWCA Civ 986, [2004] All ER (D) 516 (Jul).

[6] *Jaramillo-Aponte and Ayala* (00TH00428).

[7] But the Tribunal allowed appeals in *Gvarjaladze* [2002] UKIAT 07435 (members of a family opposing high-level corruption), and in *Ermakova* [2002] UKIAT 07728 (member of a family of a political activist pursued by the state in collusion with the mafia).

[8] *Skenderaj v Secretary of State for the Home Department* [2002] EWCA Civ 567, [2003] INLR 323.

Cessation

12.86 The starting point is that refugee status, once granted, should not be reviewed or annulled except on the most substantial and clear grounds.[1] Formal recognition as a refugee carries the assurance of a secure future in the host country, and a legitimate expectation that he or she will not be stripped of this save for demonstrably good and sufficient reason.[2] A person who is a refugee may cease to qualify for international recognition if circumstances arise to bring about the operation of the cessation clauses of the Refugee Convention.[3] These are:

(i)   voluntary reavailment of the protection of the country of nationality;

(ii)   voluntary reacquisition of the refugee's old nationality;

(iii)   acquisition of a new nationality and enjoyment of the protection of the country of the new nationality;

(iv)   voluntary reestablishment in the country where persecution was feared;

(v)   change of circumstances giving rise to recognition as a refugee.

The four 'voluntary' cessation clauses[4] are given direct domestic effect in the UK by paragraph 339A (i)–(iv) of the Immigration Rules and the Nationality, Immigration and Asylum Act 2002, section 76(3),[5] under which the Secretary of State may revoke a refugee's indefinite leave to enter or remain in the UK (and that of his or her dependants[6] unless they are refugees in their own right[7]) if the person ceases to be a refugee for any of the relevant four reasons. Furthermore, like anyone else settled in the UK, refugees can lose their indefinite leave if they remain outside the UK for more than two years continuously.[8] A person's refugee status is automatically revoked if he or she acquires British citizenship.[9] But holders of Refugee Convention travel documents are entitled to readmission at any time, so if the document is valid for more than two years, the holder cannot be denied admission even if absence has been for more than two years.[10] The Qualification Directive[11] effectively reproduces the 'Cessation clauses' in Article 1C of the Refugee Convention except for the proviso whereby a statutory refugee could invoke 'compelling reasons arising out of previous persecution' to avoid the application of the Cessation clause. For refugee status to cease owing to a change of the circumstances in connection with which the person became a refugee, the change of circumstances must be of such a significant and non-temporary nature that the refugee's fear of persecution can no longer be regarded as well-founded.[12] The Directive obliges the Member State to revoke or refuse to renew refugee status if the person ceases to be a refugee and asylum had been sought after the Directive came into force.[13] In such circumstances, the Member State is required to demonstrate that the person has ceased to be a refugee.[14] In addition, refugee status is to be revoked, ended or not extended if the Member State shows that misrepresentation or omission of facts, including the use of false documents were decisive for the granting of refugee status.[15]

---

1   *Babela* [2002] UKIAT 06124, citing UNHCR. See also *LW (Ethiopia – Cancellation of refugee status)* [2005] UKIAT 00042 and *KK (DRC – Recognition elsewhere as refugee)* [2005] UKIAT 00054.

2   *R (on the application of Hoxha) v Secretary of State for the Home Department, R (on the application of B) v Secretary of State for the Home Department* [2005] UKHL 19, [2005] 1 WLR 1063, (2005) 149 Sol Jo LB 358, per Lord Brown at para 65.

3   Refugee Convention, art 1C. These provisions are 'mirrored' in the Qualification Directive, **12.3** fn 3 above, art 11(1).

4   Ie (i)–(iv) above relating to changes in the refugee's situation brought about voluntarily by the refugee.

5   Nationality, Immigration and Asylum Act 2002, s 76(3) (in force from 10 February 2003: SI 2003/1). art 1C(3) (acquiring a new nationality) is only relevant, in the domestic context, where the new nationality is other than British: see Nationality, Immigration and Asylum Act 2002, s 76(3)(c).

6   A dependant being a spouse or minor child related to the person concerned at the time when it is considered whether indefinite leave should be revoked – API Revocation of Indefinite Leave, under 'Dependants'

7   API on Revocation of Indefinite Leave, under 'Dependants'.

8   See Immigration (Leave to Enter and Remain) Order 2000, SI 2000/1161, art 13(4)(a) and HC 395, para 18; though also see HC 395, para 19, regarding persons who have lived in the UK for most of their lives. This would not necessarily affect their entitlement to refugee status if they remained in danger, depending on whether their stay abroad itself called one of the limbs of cessation into play. Since August 2005, refugees have been granted five years leave to remain, rather than indefinite leave to remain: so until August 2010 it will not be possible to monitor the executive treatment of refugees granted settlement after a limited period of refugee status. Directive 2004/83, Art 24 mandates the grant of a residence permit for at least three years 'As soon as possible after their status has been granted'.

9   HC 395, para 339BA as amended by Cm 7944 from 1 October 2010

10 *R v Secretary of State for the Home Department, ex p Shirreh* (CO 2194/97) (15 August 1997, unreported).

11 Qualification Directive, Art 11(1), implemented in the UK by HC 395, para 339A, as inserted by HC 6918.

12 Qualification Directive, Art 11(2), implemented in the UK by HC 395, para 339A, as inserted by HC 6918. The CJEU in C-175/08: *Abdulla (Salahadin) v Bundesrepublik Deutschland* [2011] QB 46, [2010] ECR I-1493 ruled that in the assessment of whether change was significant and non-temporary, it was necessary to the look at whether there remained a real risk of persecution based on the refugee's individual situation and the ongoing availability of protection.

13 Qualification Directive, Art 14(1) and HC 395, para 339A(i)–(iv). Applicable, according to the Rules, where asylum was sought on or after 21 October 2004.

14 Qualification Directive, art 14(2).

15 Qualification Directive, Art 14(3) and HC 395, para 339A(viii).

12.87 Refugees who apply for and obtain a fresh passport from the authorities from whom they feared persecution may be acting inconsistently with their fear and raise the question of voluntary reavailment. They are entitled to a Refugee Convention travel document with which to travel abroad. If they voluntarily obtain a fresh passport from the country from which they fled, or entry permits with a view to returning there, they will be presumed to intend to avail themselves of their country's protection in the absence of proof to the contrary[1] But renewal of a national passport without more does not automatically give rise to such a presumption.[2] If the country of asylum instructs individuals to apply for a national passport, that will not be counted against them as it would not be a voluntary reavailment of protection.[3] There may be circumstances beyond their control which require them to have recourse to some measure of protection. This may particularly arise when the refugee is awaiting recognition and has not yet received a Convention travel document or any other document issued by the country where asylum is claimed. Obtaining other official documents such as marriage or birth certificates is less likely to give rise to a presumption of voluntary reacquisition of protection.[4] Acquisition of a new nationality means cessation of status.[5] But where the new nationality is lost, depending on the circumstances of the loss, refugee status may be revived.[6]

1 UNHCR *Handbook* **12.13** above, paras 120–124. *RD (Algeria)* [2007] UKAIT 00066 – obtaining a national passport creates a rebuttable presumption that the refugee intends to avail him or herself of the protection of the country. See also *Thi Xuan Mai Phan*, Commission des recours des réfugiés, France, No 57165, 15 Sep 1989 (UNHCR Refworld) (obtaining national passport and using it for tourist visit was inconsistent with refugee status). The API *Revocation of Indefinite Leave* at 'An Explanation of S.76(3) (a)–(d)' gives as an example of voluntary re-availment of protection, a refugee 'seek[ing] to obtain or renew a national passport *and us[ing] it in preference* to a refugee travel document.' (emphasis added) and also makes the point that a person granted asylum on grounds fearing non-state agents would not necessarily be reavailing him or herself of the country's protection by obtaining a national passport.

2 *Thevarayan*, Conseil d'Etat, France, No 78.055, 13 Jan 1989 (UNHCR Refworld). The API (see fn 1 above) points out that: 'Where refugee status was granted on the grounds of non-state agent persecution, a person who seeks to obtain or renew a national passport would not necessarily be re-availing themselves of the protection of their country. It would depend on the circumstances of the case'.

3 UNHCR *Handbook* above, para 120.

4 UNHCR *Handbook* above, para 121; *Paramanathan (Sellathurai)*, Commission des recours des réfugiés No 247916, 7 July 1995 (going to Sri Lankan consulate in Singapore for documents in order to marry did not constitute 'reavailment of protection').

5 See Nationality, Immigration and Asylum Act 2002, s 76(3)(c), **12.86** fn 4 above.

6 UNHCR *Handbook* above, para 132.

12.88 Questions of voluntary re-establishment may arise if refugees visit their country of nationality on their Refugee Convention travel document.[1] Where humanitarian protection (previously exceptional leave to remain for protection reasons) has been granted, holders of such a status are also vulnerable to a cancellation of such leave and refusal of readmission to the UK.[2] A temporary visit, however, usually falls far short of reestablishment,[3] and before any inference of voluntary re-acquisition of protection is drawn, regard should be had to the particular circumstances, such as the need to visit sick relatives or business associates.[4] The API allows for certain refugees to return 'home' for a brief visit, with prior approval from the Home Office, without risking their refugee status or indefinite leave to enter or remain in the UK.[5]

1   The API 'Cessation, cancellation and revocation of refugee status' October 2006 says that '"Voluntary re-establishment" means a return to the country from which protection as sought, with a view to taking up permanent residence. A lengthy stay would normally be involved. A short visit to the country in question is not likely to constitute "re-establishment".' The API on 'Revocation of Indefinite Leave', January 2006 at para 3 states: 'The key question is whether the person has "re-established" themselves in that country and the purpose of the return to the country from which protection was sought will be relevant. Each case must be considered on its own facts.'
2   See *R v Secretary of State for the Home Department, ex p Zib* [1993] Imm AR 350; and see the API on 'humanitarian protection', para 7.1.
3   UNHCR *Handbook* **12.13** above, para 134; see also Decision A 1008308-479, 20 March 1992, Bundesamt für die Anerkennung ausländischer Flüchtlinge (brief visit to country of origin without notifying local authorities did not constitute reestablishment).'
4   UNHCR *Handbook* above, para 125. See also Goodwin-Gill **12.5** fn 1 above, para 3.1, pp 80–83; API on 'Revocation of Indefinite Leave' January 2006, para 3.
5   Exploratory visits to consider return, whether through an official 'Explore and Prepare' Programme or otherwise, are encouraged as an aid to resettlement, but the API Revocation of Indefinite Leave, January 2006 envisages approval for other visits, for 'exceptional reasons': para 3(d). See also the API *Cessation, cancellation and revocation of refugee status* (version 3.0; 18 December 2008), section 4.2.4 – any refugee who contacts the IND before travelling and produces evidence of 'exceptional reasons' which are then approved should be allowed to do so without fear of losing refugee status.

12.89 If the circumstances in the country of nationality or, in the case of stateless persons, former habitual residence, have so changed that refugees can no longer refuse to avail themselves of the protection of that country, Refugee Convention refugee status will cease.[1] This rule is subject to an exception in the case of what the Convention terms 'statutory refugees' (essentially, pre-1939 refugees still recognised as such under Article 1A(1) of the Convention), who do not lose refugee status 'where there are compelling reasons arising out of previous persecution for refusing to avail themselves' of such protection.[2] The UNHCR *Handbook* suggests that similar considerations could also apply to post-1951 refugees on the general humanitarian principle that those who have suffered particularly atrocious forms of persecution should never be expected to repatriate.[3] However in *Hoxha*[4] the House of Lords, after reviewing the language of the proviso, the *travaux* and current State practice, held that the proviso to Article 1C(5) only applies to statutory refugees falling under the definition in Article 1A(1) of the Convention (and is therefore of no practical significance at all anymore). A cessation of circumstances refers to fundamental changes rather than merely transitory ones[5] and the UNHCR is of the view that refugee status should not be *lost* on the basis of a fundamental change of circumstances in part of the country of origin only, to which internal relocation would be possible such as would be enough to defeat an initial application.[6] A refugee's status should not be subject to frequent review since this would jeopardise a sense of security which the Convention was designed to provide.[7] Proof that the circumstances of persecution have ceased to exist would fall upon the receiving state.[8] In *Hoxha* the Court of Appeal held that the cessation clause in Article 1C(5) can only be relevant where a person has been formally recognised as a refugee, and this holding was upheld by the Lords.[9] However when an authority takes a long time to determine the claim of someone who would have been accepted as a refugee if the claim had been dealt with promptly, and circumstances change in the meantime, the Court of Appeal has also held that the situation is *analogous* to Refugee Convention, Article 1C(5) cessation such that the state bears an evidential burden to show that the change is sufficiently fundamental to deny status.[10] UNHCR and states parties to the Convention may issue formal declarations of general cessation of refugee status in respect of refugees from particular countries.[11] However, cessation of refugee status, whether on an individual or group basis, will not automatically mean repatriation, since many refugees will have acquired settlement rights in their country of refuge.[12] The legislation giving effect to the cessation provisions as grounds for revocation of indefinite leave to remain (see **12.86** above) does not include change of circumstances in the country of origin as a statutory ground for revocation, and Home Office policy is generally not to revoke refugee status on this ground.[13]

[1]   Refugee Convention, art 1C(5) and, for stateless persons, art 1C(6). See generally the UNHCR *Guidelines on International Protection No 3: Cessation of Refugee Status under Article 1C(5) and (6)* (10 February 2003) (HCR/GIP/03/03). For a criticism of these UNHCR guidelines, on the grounds that they 'appear to go considerably beyond the Convention' in pursuit of wider humanitarian concerns, see *SB (Haiti – cessation and exclusion)* [2005] UKIAT 00036.

[2]   Refugee Convention, art 1C(5) and (6), second paras.

[3]   UNHCR *Handbook* **12.13** above, para 136 and see UNHCR Guidelines (fn 1 above) at paras 20 and 21. The Refugee Status Appeals Authority in New Zealand in *Re RS* (135/92, 18 June 1993, unreported) held that although the strict wording of the proviso in art 1C(5) refers only to those refugees falling within art 1A(1), 'the validity of the underlying humanitarian principles do not depend upon their inclusion in any particular one Article.' However there was a certain degree of retraction from that earlier position by the same authority in *Refugee Appeal No 71684/94* [2000] INLR 165 and see now *Hoxha and B*, fn 4 below.

[4]   *R (on the application of Hoxha) v Secretary of State for the Home Department, R (on the application of B) v Secretary of State for the Home Department* [2005] UKHL 19, [2005] 1 WLR 1063, (2005) 149 Sol Jo LB 358.

[5]   UNHCR *Handbook* above, para 135 and UNHCR Guidelines (fn 1 above) paras 10–16. See eg *SB (Haiti)* (fn 1 above) and Decision V97/07790, 31 March 1998, Refugee Review Tribunal (Aus) (Austlii website: see Appendix 3). According to art 11(2) of the Qualification Directive, **12.3** fn 3 above, a change of circumstances should be 'of a significant and non-temporary nature'. The Immigration Rules HC 395, para 339A impose a similar requirement. Stanley Burnton LJ in the Court of Appeal in *EN (Serbia) v Secretary of State for the Home Department* [2009] EWCA Civ 630, [2010] 3 WLR 182, (2009) Times, 24 July: '. . . what may fairly be considered to be a durable change in conditions in a country of nationality that results in a refugee having no genuine fear of persecution on his return may fairly be regarded as fundamental'. The ECJ in *Abdulla (Salahadin) v Bundesrepublik Deutschland* C-175/08 [2010] All ER (EC) 799, ECJ at [72] held: 'The change of circumstances will be of a 'significant and non-temporary' nature, within the terms of Article 11(2) of the Directive, when the factors which formed the basis of the refugee's fear of persecution may be regarded as having been permanently eradicated'. It will be necessary to determine whether there is 'effective' protection in place: *Abdulla* at [76]; and the whole enquiry must 'be carried out with vigilance and care, since what are at issue are issues relating to the integrity

of the person and to individual liberties, issues which relate to the fundamental values of the Union' [90]. Immigration Rule 339K may be relevant (transposing, as it does, Article 4(4) of Directive 2004/83: *Abdulla* at [100].

6   UNHCR Guidelines (fn 1 above) para 17 (and see **12.42** above).

7   UNHCR *Handbook* above, para 135 and UNHCR Guidelines (fn 1 above) para 18.

8   UNHCR Guidelines (fn 1 above) para 25(ii); Hathaway **12.24** fn 3 above, p 199. 'In the absence of compelling evidence to the contrary it should not be inferred that the grounds for fear had dissipated . . . In the absence of facts indicating a material change in the state of affairs in the country of nationality, an applicant should not be compelled to provide justification for his continuing to possess a fear which he has established was well-founded at the time when he left the country of his nationality': *Chan Yee Kin v Minister for Immigration and Ethnic Affairs* (1989) 169 CLR 379 (Aus). In *SB (Haiti)* (fn 1 above) the Secretary of State conceded that he bore the burden of showing that art 1C(5) applies.

9   See fn 4 above. In *N (Kenya)* [2004] UKIAT 00009 the IAT had held that art 1C(5) can be applied to a person who had previously been recognised as a refugee by an earlier Tribunal but never granted a status letter or ILR.

10 *Arif v Secretary of State for the Home Department* [1999] INLR 327, CA. But see *Salim (Nabil) v Secretary of State for the Home Department* [2000] Imm AR 503, CA and *S v Secretary of State for the Home Department* [2002] EWCA Civ 539, [2002] INLR 416 at paras 13–15: this *only* applies where it is accepted (by the Secretary of State) that the applicant would have qualified as a refugee; see also *Hoxha and B* (above) and *Dyli* [2000] Imm AR 652, IAT. See the discussion in Goodwin-Gill **12.5** fn 1 above, pp 86–87 and *Yusuf v Canada* [1995] FCJ No 35: the issue of changed circumstances is in danger of being elevated in a question of law, when at bottom it is simply one of fact; the fundamental issue is the possibility or risk of persecution. In *AMM and others (conflict; humanitarian crisis; returnees; FGM) Somalia CG* [2011] UKUT 445 (IAC) at [345] the UTIAC found that 'any assessment that material circumstances have changed, will need to demonstrate that such changes are well established evidentially and durable'.

11 UNHCR has such competence under art 6A of the Statute of the Office of the High Commissioner for Refugees (see **12.12** and **12.13** above) in conjunction with art 1C of the Refugee Convention: see UNHCR Guidelines (fn 1 above) at para 3. See below as to 'Ministerial Statements' on relevant changes of circumstances.

12 See two German cases reported in (1995) 7(1) IJRL 668, Case 218 and (1994) 7 IJRL 138 Case 224. In the latter case the change of regime in Ethiopia removed the claim to Convention persecution but expulsion was not permitted because there was still fighting that made a compulsory return contrary to art 3 ECHR. However, the applicant Thangarasa in the House of Lords 'third country case' of *R (on the application of Yogathas) v Secretary of State for the Home Department; R (on the application of Thangarasa) v Secretary of State for the Home Department* [2002] UKHL 36, [2003] 1 AC 920, [2002] INLR 620 (see **12.145** below) had had refugee status in Germany but appears to have lost it on art 1C(5) cessation grounds.

13 See Lord Bassam of Brighton, *Hansard* HL 17.7.02, col 1331. However, the Qualification Directive (**12.3** fn 3 above), art 14(1) states that in respect of applications for international protection filed after the entry into force of the Directive, Member States *shall* revoke, end or refuse to renew the refugee status of a person who has ceased to be a refugee as per the cessation provisions in art 11 (see **12.86** fn 12 above). This is mandatory in tone and implies that the UK will have to revoke the refugee status (albeit not necessarily the indefinite leave, since the Directive is designed to impose *minimum* standards of protection) of persons who have ceased to be refugees in accordance with cessation clauses. The change of policy to grant refugees temporary leave in the first instance, with a review after five years: was announced in *Controlling our borders: Making migration work for Britain: Five year strategy for asylum and immigration*, Cm 6472, Feb 2005.

Exclusion

12.90 The Refugee Convention will not apply to refugees in circumstances where the protection of another state is unnecessary or the person is not deserving of protection. Article 1D of the Convention provides that refugees who are in receipt of assistance from a branch of the UN other than the UNHCR are outside the terms of the Convention until such assistance ceases.[1]

In *El-Ali*[2] the Court of Appeal had held that Article 1D only applies to those persons who, at the date of the signing of the Refugee Convention on 28 July 1951, were receiving protection from organs or agencies of the UN other than the High Commissioner for Refugees, so that in practice, only Palestinians who were alive and who were registered as receiving assistance from the United Nations Reliefs and Works Agency (UNRWA) at that date fell under the Article.[3] However, the Qualification Directive substantially reproduces[4] Article 1D of the Refugee Convention and in *Bolbol*[5] the CJEU disapproved the narrow approach to the exclusion clause adopted by the Court of Appeal, holding that Article 1D 'merely excludes from the scope of the Convention those persons who are 'at present receiving' protection or assistance from an organ or agency of the United Nations other than UNHCR, implying that the question was whether, as at the present time, assistance was received. This approach has now been fully endorsed by the CJEU in *Karem El Kott*[6] in which the Court held that the ground for exclusion should be construed narrowly, that voluntary departure from UNWRA protection could not be sufficient to end the exclusion from refugee status laid down in the provision but that it was sufficient that a Palestinian refugee be forced by reasons beyond his control, in particular for reasons relating to his personal safety, to leave the area in question and thus prevent him from receiving UNWRA assistance and protection, for the 'inclusion' part of Article 1D to be activated.[7] As regards the phrase 'those persons shall *ipso facto* be entitled to the benefits of this Directive' the Court, in agreement with the approach in *El Ali*[8], held that this meant that such persons were to be recognised as refugees without having to fulfil any further inclusion criteria.[9]

[1]   Refugee Convention, art 1D; UNHCR *Handbook* **12.13** above, paras 142–143.

[2]   El-Ali v Secretary of State for the Home Department [2002] EWCA Civ 1103, [2003] 1 WLR 95; leave to appeal to the House of Lords refused: [2003] 1 WLR 1811.

[3]   Accordingly all other persons, including Palestinians born after that date, even though receiving assistance from UNRWA, need to establish their status as refugees in the normal way under art 1A(2) of the Convention. Laws LJ (with whom Lord Phillips MR and May LJ agreed) also held (obiter) that, for the purposes of the second sentence of art 1D, the phrase 'such protection or assistance has ceased for any reason' refers to UNWRA ceasing to exist or ceasing to provide assistance and not to an individual Palestinian ceasing for whatever reason to be assisted by UNRWA – although the potential difficulty this would present where such a person was prevented from re-availing him- or herself of UNRWA's assistance was acknowledged. The court also acknowledged that the phrase 'these persons shall *ipso facto* be entitled to the benefits of this Convention' means that if UNRWA ceases to provide assistance to those Palestinians who were registered with it on 28 July 1951 without their having been able to return to their original pre-1948 homes, they are automatically to be treated as refugees within the meaning of the 1951 Refugee Convention. See also Asylum Policy Guidance on UNRWA assisted Palestinians, 15 November 2013. Note that Article 1D has been held not to be exhaustive of all the circumstances in which the role of international agencies is relevant for the purposes of the Convention definition: See eg *Vallaj v Special Adjudicator* [2001] EWCA Civ 782, [2001] INLR 342: see further **12.43** above.

[4]   Qualification Directive, art 12(12) and the Refugee or Person in Need of International Protection (Qualification) Regulations 2006, SI 2006/2525, reg 7(1).

[5]   *Nawras Bolbol v Bevandorlasi es Allampolgarsagi Hivatal* (Case C-31/09) [2010] ECR I-5539, [2012] All ER (EC) 469, ECJ. However, as Ms Bolbol had, on the facts, never availed herself of UNRWA assistance, she was not excluded by Article 1D (and thus could not benefit from it either but had to demonstrate that she was a refugee as per art 1A(2) in the normal way). The Tribunal in *Said (Article 1D: meaning) Palestinian Territories* [2012] UKUT 413 (IAC), recognising that this disapproval of the key part of the reasoning of the Court of Appeal in *El-Ali* meant that its overall conclusions were now open to doubt, considered the potential that the inclusion clause within art 1D might become of increased effectiveness and held that

as the appellant had been displaced from his UNRWA refugee camp through circumstances beyond his control he qualified. *ipso facto*, as a refugee.

6   *Abed El Karem El Kott (Mostafa) v Bevandorlasi es Allampolgarsagi Hivatal (ENSZ Menekultugyi Fobiztossaga, intervening)* (Case C-364/11) [2013] All ER (EC) 1176, ECJ.

7   Thus rejecting the approach in *El-Ali* that it was necessary for UNWRA itself to cease to exist or to cease to provide protection (see fn 3 above). The CJEU held that it was for the asylum determining authorities of the relevant Member State to determine on an individual factual basis whether, for reasons beyond his control and independent of his volition, it was no longer possible for the person concerned to benefit from the assistance of which he had availed himself before leaving the UNRWA area of operations.

8   See fn 3 above.

9   Per the CJEU at [73] 'The statement at the end of the second sentence of Article 12(1)(a) of Directive 2004/83, to the effect that the persons concerned "shall ipso facto be entitled to the benefits of [the] Directiv'", would be superfluous and ineffective if its only purpose was to point out that the persons who are no longer excluded from refugee status by virtue of the first sentence of that provision may rely on the directive to ensure that their application for refugee status will be considered in accordance with Article 2(c) of the directive.' The Court was at pains to point out that such a Palestinian claimant would still be subject to consideration of exclusion under Articles 1E and 1F of the Refugee Convention as per Qualification Directive, art 12(1)(b) and (2) and (3): see below.

12.91 People are not entitled to Refugee Convention protection if they do not need it because the authorities of the territory in which they have taken up residence recognise them as having the rights and obligations attached to the possession of nationality of that country.[1] This exception is of limited application. The person's status must be largely assimilated to that of a national of the receiving country for the exclusion to apply; for example, he or she must be fully protected against deportation or expulsion.[2] The UNHCR *Handbook* suggests that the drafters had in mind refugees of German extraction settling in Germany and recognised there as having the rights and obligations of Germans.[3] In UK terms this would suggest that a grant of settlement or of a subsidiary British nationality which did not confer full citizenship rights would not be enough to bring a person within the exception.[4]

1   Refugee Convention,Art 1E; Qualification Directive, Art 12(1)(b): this adds the phrase: 'or rights and obligations equivalent to those.' UNHCR *Handbook* **12.13** above, paras 144–146.

2   In *Seare* (3853) unreported, refugee status in Sudan afforded to an Ethiopian national did not exclude the person from the Refugee Convention when he travelled to the UK. See also, in terms of the effect of a grant of asylum abroad on refugee status determination in the UK, *LW (Ethiopia – Cancellation of refugee status)* [2005] UKIAT 00042 (Ethiopian granted asylum in Uganda – burden on Secretary of State to show 'the most substantial and clear grounds' for revisiting the earlier grant of asylum); *KK (DRC – Recognition elsewhere as refugee)* [2005] UKIAT 00054 (DRC citizen granted asylum in Zimbabwe under OAU Convention on refugees in Africa – not determinative of Geneva Convention refugee status); and *Babela* [2002] UKIAT 06124 (Congolese national with refugee status in South Africa – earlier grant of status should not be questioned unless there is a very good reason for doing so); Hathaway **12.24** fn 3 above, para 6.2.3.

3   UNHCR *Handbook* **12.13** above, para 144.

4   Interesting issues could arise where a former refugee is deprived of British citizenship underBNA 1981, s 40 (as substituted by NIAA 2002, s 4).

Exclusion for criminal activity

12.92 Article 1F of the Refugee Convention provides that the protection of the Convention does not apply where there are serious reasons for considering that a refugee has committed:

(a)   a war crime or a crime against humanity as defined in the relevant international instruments;[1]

(b)   a serious non-political crime committed outside the country of refuge prior to admission to that country as a refugee; or

(c)   an act contrary to the purposes and principles of the UN.[2]

The terms of Article 1F of the Convention are mandatory; the protective provisions of the Convention 'shall not' apply in these cases.[3] Whereas (b) has a geographical and temporal limit in respect of where and when the crime in question must have been committed, no such limits apply to the crimes and acts covered by Article 1F (a) and (c).[4] The intense focus of governments and international organisations on terrorism since September 2001 has brought wide discussion of these exclusion provisions in the Convention, but in the rush to judgment little notice has been taken of careful analysis in a growing body of literature.[5] In particular our own government has rushed into legislation which thrusts on to our courts and tribunals an order of working and a set of presumptions, which flout the spirit and aim of the Convention. We deal with these below. The Qualification Directive reproduces the exclusion clause in Article 1F of the Refugee Convention (exclusion for war crimes, crimes against peace, crimes against humanity, serious non-political crimes and acts contrary to the purposes and principles of the UN) but with a number of substantial alterations and additions that impact on the scope of the provisions.[6] Firstly, Article 1F(b) of the Refugee Convention excludes a person who 'has committed a serious non-political crime outside the country of refuge prior to his admission to that country as a refugee'. The Directive defines the phrase 'prior to his or her admission as a refugee' as meaning prior to the time of being issued with a residence permit based on the granting of refugee status.[7] Secondly, the Directive also provides that 'particularly cruel actions, even if committed with an allegedly political objective, may be classified as serious non-political crimes' for the purpose of the exclusion clause.[8] UNHCR's understanding of 'particularly cruel actions' is 'criminal acts which are particularly egregious'.[9] Thirdly, the Directive defines 'acts contrary to the purposes and principles of the United Nations' as being acts contrary to the Preamble and Articles 1 and 2 of the Charter of the United Nations.[10] The implementing Regulation does not reproduce that part of the Directive defining 'acts contrary to the purposes and principles of the United Nations'. Fourthly, the Directive expressly provides that each of the three exclusion clauses ((a), (b) and (c) above) shall apply to persons who instigate or otherwise participate in the commission of the crimes or acts mentioned therein.[11] Oddly, the implementing Regulation provides that only the exclusion clauses in (a) and (b) of Article 1F of the Refugee Convention shall apply to a person who instigates or otherwise participates in the commission of the crimes or acts specified in those provisions.[12] The Directive obliges the Member State to revoke, end or refuse to renew the refugee status of a person who is or should have been excluded from being a refugee.[13]

---

[1]   These are listed in the UNHCR *Handbook* (12.13 above) at Annex VI and include the London Agreement 1945, the charter of the Nuremberg International Military Tribunal (extract in Annex V of the UNHCR *Handbook*), and the Geneva Conventions and additional Protocol relating to the protection of victims of war and international armed conflicts. The Rome Statute of the International Criminal Court 1998, arts 7 and 8, provides updated definitions of war crimes and crimes against humanity.

[2]   Refugee Convention, art 1F.

3 See *Gurung* [2002] UKIAT 04870 (starred) and *KK (Turkey)* [2004] UKIAT 00101. In *A (Iraq) v Secretary of State for the Home Department* [2005] EWCA Civ 1438, 149 Sol Jo LB 1492, [2005] All ER (D) 22 (Dec), the Court of Appeal held that a tribunal erred in law by failing to consider whether an asylum seeker from Iraq should be excluded for 'serious non-political crimes' on account of his admitted involvement in detaining and torturing opponents of the Saddam Hussein regime even though the Secretary of State had not raised the possibility of exclusion; were he to be recognised as a refugee in circumstances where he should have been excluded, there would be a breach of the Convention. In *AA (Palestine)* [2005] UKIAT 00104, the tribunal found a similar error where an adjudicator failed to consider whether art 1F applied to a member of the Jihad Islamic Movement who had been involved in its armed activities in Gaza, including a (failed) suicide bombing.

4 See *RB (Algeria) v Secretary of State for the Home Department* [2009] UKHL 10, [2010] 2 AC 110. In *KK* (above) the act relied on as contrary to the purposes and principles of the UN (arson attacks on Turkish businesses), occurred in the UK after the claimant had claimed asylum here: see **12.95** fn 13 below.

5 See, for instance, Background Note on the Application of the Exclusion Clauses: Article 1F of the 1951 Convention relating to the Status of Refugees, UNHCR 2003 (hereinafter: UNHCR Background Note), UNHCR Executive Committee, Standing Committee sessions of 1997 (8th meeting) and 1998 (10th meeting); UNHCR Global Consultations on International Protection, Lisbon Expert Roundtable (May 2001), Summary Conclusions – Exclusion from Refugee Status, UNHCR Doc. EC/GC/01/2Track/1 (hereinafter UNHCR Lisbon Roundtable); UNHCR *Guidelines on International Protection No 5*: Application of the exclusion clauses: Article 1F (HCR/GIP/03/05) 4 September 2003; Lawyers Committee for Human Rights, Research and Advocacy Project *Safeguarding the Rights of Refugees under the Exclusion Clauses* in IJRL Vol 12 Special Supplementary Issue 2000 Exclusion from Protection; and *Refugees, Rebels and the quest for justice, 2002;* PJ van Krieken (ed) *Refugee Law in Context: The Exclusion Clause* (The Hague 1999); ECRE, Position on the Interpretation of Article 1 of the Refugee Convention (September 2000); ECRE, Position on Exclusion from Refugee Status (March 2004).

6 Qualification Directive, art 12(2).

7 Qualification Directive, art 12(2)(b) and the Refugee or Person in Need of International Protection (Qualification) Regulations 2006, SI 2006/2525, reg 7(2)(b).

8 Qualification Directive, art 12(2)(b) and the Refugee or Person in Need of International Protection (Qualification) Regulations 2006, reg 7(2)(a).

9 UNHCR Annotated Comments on the EC Council Directive 2004/83/EC (January 2005).

10 Qualification Directive, art 12(2)(c).

11 Qualification Directive, art 12(3).

12 Refugee or Person in Need of International Protection (Qualification) Regulations 2006, SI 2006/2525, reg 7(3).

13 Qualification Directive, art 14(3) and HC 395, para 339A(vii), as inserted by HC 6918.

12.93 The UNHCR *Handbook* points out that in view of the serious consequences of a decision to exclude from protection Article 1F must be interpreted restrictively.[1] The same point was made by the 1996 EU Joint Position, which stressed that the exclusion clause was to be applied only in very exceptional cases after thorough and careful consideration;[2] however the Qualification Directive makes no reference to a restrictive interpretation.[3] In asylum appeals the Secretary of State may certify that the appellant is not entitled to the protection of the Convention because Article 1F applies or because Article 33(2) applies on national security grounds. If such a certificate is issued (which should not occur if the Secretary of State rejects the credibility of the relevant assertions: in such cases exclusion should simply be raised in the refusal letter in the alternative[4]), the Tribunal or the SIAC hearing an appeal which raises Refugee Convention grounds is required to decide first whether it agrees with the certificate and if it does, is required to dismiss that part of the appeal which relates to the asylum claim without considering any other aspect of the case.[5] 'Serious reasons for considering' are not the same as proof of guilt beyond doubt. In *Al-Sirri*[6] the Supreme Court, on consideration of wide ranging domestic and international jurisprudence on the meaning of the phrase, drew the following conclusions: '(1) "Serious reasons" is stronger than "reasonable grounds". (2) The evidence from which those reasons are derived must be "clear and credible" or "strong". (3) "Considering" is stronger than "suspecting". In our view it is also stronger than "believing". It requires the considered judgment of the decision-maker. (4) The decision-maker need not be satisfied beyond reasonable doubt or to the standard required in criminal law. (5) It is unnecessary to import our domestic standards of proof into the question. The circumstances of refugee claims, and the nature of the evidence available, are so variable. However, if the decision-maker is satisfied that it is more likely than not that the applicant has not committed the crimes in question or has not been guilty of acts contrary to the purposes and principles of the United Nations, it is difficult to see how there could be serious reasons for considering that he had done so. The reality is that there are unlikely to be sufficiently serious reasons for considering the applicant to be guilty unless the decision-maker can be satisfied on the balance of probabilities that he is. But the task of the decision-maker is to apply the words of the Convention (and the Directive) in the particular case.' Legislation and the authorities are against applying any principle of proportionality (ie balancing the harm that the claimant may suffer if denied protection against the harm that he or she has committed).[7] Furthermore, the European Court of Justice held in *Germany v B and D*[8] that exclusion from refugee status pursuant to Article 1F (as applied through Article 12(2) of the Qualification Directive) is not conditional on the person concerned representing a present danger to the host member state. Where there is a real risk of severe harm, removal is in any case prohibited by virtue of Article 3 of the EHCR.[9]

1   UNHCR *Handbook* **12.13** above, para 149 and see UNHCR *Guidelines on International Protection: Application of the Exclusion Clauses: Article 1F* (4 September 2003) (HCR/GIP/03/05) para 2. See also the Netherlands Council of State decision of *JMS v Staatsecretaris van Justitie* (17 December 1992) (NAV 1993, 1), digested in (1995) 7(1) IJRL 129. See also Lord Brown in *R (on the application of JS (Sri Lanka)) v Secretary of State for the Home Department* [2010] UKSC 15; [2011] 1 AC 184 at [2] summarising 'common ground' between the parties as regards Art 1F(a); the jointly given judgment of the Supreme Court in *Al-Sirri v Secretary of State for the Home Department (United Nations High Commissioner for Refugees intervening)* [2012] UKSC 54; [2013] 1 AC 745 at [16] with specific respect to Art 1F(c), and at [75] with more general regard to the the autonomous meaning of the words 'serious reasons for considering'; and Stanley Burnton LJ in the Court of Appeal in *KJ (Sri Lanka) v Secretary of State for the Home Department* [2009] EWCA Civ 292 at [35].
2   Joint Position of 4 March 1996, para 13; see also Minister for Immigration and Multicultural Affairs v Singh [2002] HCA 7 (Aust HC).
3   Qualification Directive, **12.3** fn 3 above, art 12.
4   Para 3.8 of Asylum Instruction on Exclusion: Article 1F of the Refugee Convention (30 May 2012).
5   IAN 2006, s 55. Formerly this approach applied only in appeals to SIAC by virtue of the Anti-terrorism, Crime and Security Act 2001 s 33(3), (4), repealed by the IAN 2006, s 55(6). The Tribunal had already concluded (in *Gurung*) that it should follow that approach, considering the issue of exclusion first and not determining the question of inclusion if it found that the exclusion clause applied, save in borderline cases: *Gurung* [2002] UKIAT 04870 (starred). For the previous contrary view see Singh (10860) and see also *JMS v Staatsecretaris van Justitie* fn 1 above. However the Canadian Federal Court of Appeal held it was not an error for the Tribunal to apply the exclusion clause without making any explicit finding on inclusion, in *Gonzalez v Minister of Employment and Immigration* (1994) FCJ 765. See Goodwin-Gill **12.5** fn 1 above, para 4.1.2, p 97.
6   *Al-Sirri (FC) v Secretary of State for the Home Department* [2012] UKSC 54; [2013] 1 AC 745 at [75]. See *Dhayakpa v Minister for Immigration and Ethnic Affairs* (1995) 62 FCR 556

(Aus): 'Serious reasons for considering' means it is unnecessary for the state to make a positive or concluded finding about the commission of the crime or the act of the class referred to.' See also Robinson 'Convention relating to the Status of Refugees' (1953) cited in Hathaway **12.24** fn 3 above, para 6.3, p 215. But the UNHCR Guidelines (fn 1 above) call for 'clear and credible evidence' which should be available to the individual concerned so that it can be challenged: paras 35, 36. Contrast the approach to evidence of the SIAC (see CHAPTER **22**): see *Singh (Mukhtiar) and Singh (Paramjit) v Secretary of State for the Home Department* (SIAC, 31 July 2000).

7 Anti-terrorism, Crime and Security Act 2001, s 34; *T v Immigration Officer* [1996] AC 742, [1996] 2 WLR 766; Cases C-57/09 and C-101/09: *Bundesrepublik Deutschland v B and D (Vertreter des Bundesinteresses beim Bundesverwaltungsgericht intervening)* [2010] ECR I-10979, [2012] 1 WLR 1076, ECJ; *Singh (Mukhtiar) and Singh (Paramjit) v Secretary of State for the Home Department* (SIAC, 31 July 2000); *Gurung* [2002] UKIAT 04870 (starred) and *KK (Turkey)* [2004] UKIAT 00101. Contrast the UNHCR *Guidelines* (fn 1 above) para 24 which, whilst acknowledging that a proportionality analysis would 'not normally be required in the case of crimes against peace, crimes against humanity, and acts falling under Art 1F(c), as the acts covered are so heinous', considers that proportionality is relevant to Art 1F(b) crimes and to less serious war crimes under Art 1F(a).

8 *Bundesrepublik Deutschland v B and D (Vertreter des Bundesinteresses beim Bundesverwaltungsgericht intervening)* [2010] ECR I-10979, [2012] 1 WLR 1076, ECJ: the grounds for exclusion (here specifically under art 12(2)(b) and (c) of the Directive – but there can be no clear reason why this would not apply equally to art 12(2)(a)) were intended as a penalty for acts committed in the past and were introduced with the aim of excluding from refugee status persons who are deemed undeserving of the protection which that status entails and of preventing that status from enabling those who have committed certain serious crimes to escape criminal liability.

9 *Chahal v United Kingdom* (1996) 23 EHRR 413. Note that the Qualification Directive (**12.3** fn 3 above) art 17 contains identical exclusion clauses for subsidiary protection. See also *Saadi v Italy* (2009) 49 EHRR 730, [2008] Crim LR 898, ECtHR.

12.94 The burden of establishing that the exclusion clause applies rests on the state seeking to deny protection.[1] In practical terms, the decision maker must be satisfied that it is at least probable that the applicant is guilty of the relevant crimes or acts.[2] 'Serious reasons for considering' do not require that there has been a successful prosecution for a crime.[3] The presumption of innocence in criminal proceedings does not carry over to refugee status determination.[4] The extent of participation required for exclusion requires some personal activity, whether as a leader, organiser or accomplice participating in the planning, financing or the execution of the crime; mere membership of a group which from time to time commits international offences is not normally sufficient for exclusion from refugee status.[5] Where international crimes are in play, the Rome Statute will be the starting point for determining complicity.[6] In general, cases will be determined on the evidence, absent presumption:[7] even where an organisation is principally directed to a limited, brutal purpose, such as a secret police activity, mere membership does not necessarily involve personal and knowing participation in persecutory acts.[8] An accused will be disqualified under Article 1F if there are serious reasons for considering him voluntarily to have contributed in a significant way to the organisation's ability to pursue its purpose of committing war crimes, aware that his assistance will in fact further that purpose:[9] the making of a 'substantial contribution' may capture the concept,[10] this being a participation exceeding mere passivity or continued involvement in the organisation after acquiring knowledge of the war crimes or crimes against humanity.[11] It is not only those deploying state powers who may fall for exclusion.[12]

1 Sedley LJ in the Court of Appeal in *Al-Sirri v Secretary of State for the Home Department (United Nations High Commissioner for Refugees intervening)* [2009] EWCA Civ 222 at [27],

[2009] All ER (D) 220 (Mar); see also Arden LJ at [77]. *Ramirez v Minister of Employment and Immigration* (1992) FCJ 109. See also UNHCR Guidelines on International Protection: Application of the Exclusion Clauses: Article 1F (4 September 2003) (HCR/GIP/03/05) para 34. Lord Brown in the Supreme Court in *R (on the application of JS (Sri Lanka)) v Secretary of State for the Home Department* [2010] UKSC 15 at [39], [2010] 3 All ER 881, [2010] 2 WLR 766: '"serious reasons for considering" obviously imports a higher test for exclusion than would, say, an expression like "reasonable grounds for suspecting". "Considering" approximates rather to "believing" than to "suspecting"'.

2   *Al-Sirri (FC) v Secretary of State for the Home Department* [2012] UKSC 54; [2013] 1 AC 745 – see **12.93** above.

3   See Toulson LJ in the Court of Appeal in R (on the application of *JS (Sri Lanka)) v Secretary of State for the Home Department* [2009] EWCA Civ 364 at [28]; Stanley Burnton LJ in the Court of Appeal in *KJ (Sri Lanka) v Secretary of State for the Home Department* [2009] EWCA Civ 292 at [35]; Sedley LJ in the Court of Appeal in *YS (Egypt) v Secretary of State for the Home Department & Anor* [2009] EWCA Civ 222 at [35]. Refugee Status Appeals Authority of New Zealand in Refugee Appeal No 74796 (RPG Haines QC (Chairperson); 19 April 2006) at [87]. A conviction will, of course, be sufficient, see eg *KK (Article 1F(c), Turkey)* [2004] UKIAT 00101 (07 May 2004), [2005] INLR 124, [2004] UKIAT 00101, [2004] Imm AR 284 at [10] – subject to the conviction being for a sufficiently serious crime: see *AH (Algeria) v Secretary of State for the Home Department* [2012] EWCA Civ 395; [2012] 1 WLR 3469 and see **12.97** below.

4   Sedley LJ in the Court of Appeal in *Al-Sirri v Secretary of State for the Home Department & Anor* [2009] EWCA Civ 222 at [25].

5   See *Bundesrepublik Deutschland v B and D (Vertreter des Bundesinteresses beim Bundesverwaltungsgericht intervening)* [2010] ECR I-10979, [2012] 1 WLR 1076, ECJ. This is highly relevant in the light of the proscription of several organisations to which exiles might belong, including the LTTE and the PKK, under the provisions of the Terrorism Act 2000. The Qualification Directive, **12.3** fn 3 above states that the exclusion clauses apply to persons who 'instigate or otherwise participate in the commission of the crimes or acts mentioned therein' (Art 12(3) – see **12.92** above).

6   Lord Brown in the Supreme Court in *R (on the application of JS (Sri Lanka)) v Secretary of State for the Home Department (Rev 1)* [2010] UKSC 15 at [8].

7   Thus it was noted in *KJ (Sri Lanka) v Secretary of State for the Home Department* [2009] EWCA Civ 292 that the Liberation Tigers of Tamil Eelam (LTTE) pursued its political ends in part by acts of terrorism and in part by military action directed against the armed forces of the government of Sri Lanka: a foot soldier in such paramilitary forces who had not personally participated in excludable acts was innocent of acts contrary to the purposes and principles of the United Nations.

8   Lord Hope in the Supreme Court in *R (on the application of JS (Sri Lanka)) v Secretary of State for the Home Department (Rev 1)* [2010] UKSC 15 at [44], thus qualifying the approach of *Ramirez* (fn 1 above).

9   Lord Brown in the Supreme Court in *JS (Sri Lanka)* (fn 8 above) at [38].

10 Lord Hope in the Supreme Court in *JS (Sri Lanka)* (fn 8 above) at [48].

11 Lord Kerr in the Supreme Court *in JS (Sri Lanka)* (fn 8 above), at [56]. See also *Bundesrepublik Deutschland v B and D (Vertreter des Bundesinteresses beim Bundesverwaltungsgericht intervening)* [2010] ECR I-10979, [2012] 1 WLR 1076, ECJ and *Al-Sirri v Secretary of State for the Home Department (United Nations High Commissioner for Refugees intervening)* [2012] UKSC 54; [2013] 1 AC 745.See also *MT (Article 1F (a) – aiding and abetting) Zimbabwe* [2012] UKUT 00015 (IAC).

12 *Bundesrepublik Deutschland v B and D (Vertreter des Bundesinteresses beim Bundesverwaltungsgericht intervening)* [2010] ECR I-10979, [2012] 1 WLR 1076, ECJ makes it clear that Art 1F is not limited to cases where the asylum-seeker was deploying state powers.

War crimes, crimes against humanity and crimes against the purposes and principles of the UN

12.95 The drought of cases from the higher courts addressing war crimes, crimes against humanity[1] and crimes against the purposes and principles of the UN[2] broke with a wave of decisions in 2009.[3] Earlier in the law's development, the Tribunal in *Amberber* had allowed an appeal of an Ethiopian accused of 'wars of aggression' for participation in internal attacks, ruling that Article 1F(a) of the Refugee Convention only applied to waging war across international boundaries;[4] this holds good too for Article 1F(c), 'terrorist crimes' needing an international dimension if they are to be said truly to contravene the purposes of the United Nations.[5] The Statute of the International Criminal Court contains the relevant definitions of war crimes and crimes against humanity.[6] As regards 'acts contrary to the purposes and principles of the UN', the proper approach is that laid down in the UNHCR Guidelines.[7] Former government officials who have resorted to barbaric methods against civilians in the repression of disorder are liable to exclusion.[8] The killing of civilians in the course of internal conflict has been held not to engage the clauses[9] (unless deliberate)[10] but torture, genocide, and arbitrary reprisals do.[11] It is not sufficient that the act alleged *could* be a crime against humanity; it must be established that it *would* be.[12] In *Pushpanathan*[13] the Canadian Supreme Court held that narcotics trafficking was not an act 'contrary to the purposes and principles of the UN'. It reasoned that the rationale of Article 1F was that those responsible for the persecution which creates refugees should not enjoy the benefits of the Convention designed to protect those refugees. The purpose of Article 1F(c) was 'to exclude those individuals responsible for serious, sustained or systemic violations of fundamental human rights which amount to persecution in a non-war setting'. In *Singh and Singh*[14] the Special Immigration Appeals Commission (SIAC) rejected the appellants' contentions that (1) Article 1F(c) applied only to those holding a position of authority in a state or acting on behalf of a state and (2) acts could only fall within Article 1F(c) if they were committed other than for political reasons or in pursuance of a right of self-determination.[15] Acts of terrorism are contrary to the purposes and principles of the UN and accordingly come within the ambit of Article 1F(c) wherever and whenever committed, considering not only Articles 1 and 2 of the 1945 Charter of the United Nations (which set out the purposes and principles of the UN),[16] but also, in the light of Article 31 of the Vienna Convention on the Law of Treaties (which sets out general rules of interpretation of treaties), subsequent Security Council and General Assembly resolutions that unequivocally condemn terrorism and terrorist acts.[17] In interpreting the ambit of these decisions, some care is needed, first, because of the very divergent definitions of terrorism; and, secondly, because the exclusive focus of the UN Security Council Resolutions after 11 September 2001 has been on Al Qaeda and a long list of named organisations and individuals allegedly associated with it, rather than on Turkish Kurds fighting for self-determination or Muslims in Gujerat, India, fighting against extremist communalism, but who have nevertheless been labelled as terrorists by the EU or under Indian anti-terrorist legislation: military action against government forces is not to be regarded as a war crime.[18] Although military actions against a government are not necessarily contrary to the purposes and principles of the UN, attacks on UN mandated forces acting in accordance with a Security Council Resolution would be.[19] Section 54 of the IAN 2006[20] imposes a statutory interpretation of Article 1(F)(c) of the Convention[21] according to which acts contrary to the purposes and principles of the UN includes acts of committing, preparing or instigating terrorism and of encouraging or inducing others to commit, prepare or instigate terrorism: though this must be read down to achieve consistency with the European law framework.[22] The acts include inchoate offences and terrorism has the meaning given by section 1 of the Terrorism Act 2000.[23] Membership of and intentional participation in the activities of a terrorist group is not by itself sufficient to justify exclusion from refugee status; there have to be serious reasons for considering the individual guilty of terrorist acts which can only be established by an individualised assessment of the person's role in the perpetration of the crimes or acts attributed to the organisation; his or her position within the organisation; the person's knowledge of the activities of the organisation and any pressure to which the person was exposed.[24] The Qualification Directive defines the principles and purposes of the UN as being those set out in the preamble and Articles 1 and 2 of the Charter of the United Nations.[25] The provision refers to 'acts' rather than 'crimes', and thus its assessment may go beyond a determination of criminal liability.[26] In the ordinary course the provision of medical or nursing services would not bring a person within Article 1F(c) on the basis that they form part of the infrastructure of support for a terrorist organisation; but in each case the point will have to be taken into account with other relevant factors in reaching an overall assessment. The humanitarian nature of nursing injured fighters, might well, in context, weigh against rather than in favour of a finding of complicity in the terrorist acts.[27] In determining complicity in war crimes, it is preferable to focus from the outset on what ultimately must prove to be the determining factors in any case, principally: (i) the nature and (potentially of some importance) the size of the organisation and particularly that part of it with which the asylum-seeker was himself most directly concerned; (ii) whether and, if so, by whom the organisation was proscribed; (iii) how the asylum-seeker came to be recruited; (iv) the length of time he remained in the organisation and what, if any, opportunities he had to leave it; (v) his position, rank, standing and influence in the organisation; (vi) his knowledge of the organisation's war crimes activities; and (vii) his own personal involvement and role in the organisation including particularly whatever contribution he made towards the commission of war crimes.[28]

1   Refugee Convention, Art 1F(a); Qualification Directive, art 12(2)(a).
2   Refugee Convention, Art 1F(c); Qualification Directive, art 12(2)(c).
3   *YS Egypt v Secretary of State for the Home Department & Anor* [2009] EWCA Civ 222; *KJ (Sri Lanka) v Secretary of State for the Home Department* [2009] EWCA Civ 292; *R (on the application of JS (Sri Lanka)) v Secretary of State for the Home Department* [2009] EWCA Civ 364; *MH (Syria) v Secretary of State for the Home Department* [2009] EWCA Civ 226, [2009] 3 All ER 564. Also *DD (Afghanistan) v Secretary of State for the Home Department* [2010] EWCA Civ 1407. Note that appeals in *YS Egypt and DD (Afghanistan)* were heard jointly by the Supreme Court: *Al-Sirri v Secretary of State for the Home Department (United Nations High Commissioner for Refugees intervening)* [2012] UKSC 54; [2013] 1 AC 745.
4   *Amberber* (00TH 01570) (13 June 2000, unreported), IAT. The European jurisprudence on art 1F(a) of the Refugee Convention is set out in Jean-Yves Carlier et al (eds) *Who is a Refugee?* (1997). In *PK (Sri Lanka)* [2004] UKIAT 00089 the Tribunal held that the adjudicator had erred in law in applying art 1F(a) to a member of the LTTE who had admitted to having killed Sri Lankan soldiers in battle; the adjudicator had mistakenly assumed that the claimant had admitted to killing injured soldiers other than in the course of the battle itself. On the other hand, a member of the LTTE who voluntarily drove an assassination squad to and from the places where they killed civilians, knowing what the assassins were doing was excluded: *AN and SS (Sri Lanka) CG* [2008] UKAIT 00063.
5   *Al-Sirri v Secretary of State for the Home Department (United Nations High Commissioner for Refugees intervening)* [2012] UKSC 54; [2013] 1 AC 745. See fn 19 below.
6   Asylum Instruction on Exclusion: Article 1F of the Refugee Convention (30 May 2012), Part 4. See *MT (Article 1F (a) – aiding and abetting) Zimbabwe* [2012] UKUT 00015 (IAC).
7   UNHCR *Guidelines on International Protection: Application of the Exclusion Clauses: Article 1F* (4 September 2003) (HCR/GIP/03/05) para 17: 'Article 1F(c) is only triggered in extreme circumstances by activity which attacks the very basis of the international communi-

ty's coexistence. Such activity must have an international dimension. Crimes capable of affecting international peace, security and peaceful relations between states, as well as serious and sustained violations of human rights would fall under this category.' See *Al-Sirri v Secretary of State for the Home Department (United Nations High Commissioner for Refugees intervening)* [2012] UKSC 54; [2013] 1 AC 745 at [38].

8 See Article by Feisman (1996) 8 IJRL 111. Goodwin-Gill **12.5** fn 1 above, pp 95–100 suggests a somewhat narrower basis for exclusion under this head relying on the *travaux* and their reference to the principles established by the London Charter of the International Military Tribunal.

9 *Polyukhovich v Commonwealth of Australia* (1991) 172 CLR 501 at 669, per Toohey J.

10 *KJ (Sri Lanka) v Secretary of State for the Home Department* [2009] EWCA Civ 292.

11 *Gonzalez v Minister of Employment and Immigration* (1994) FCJ 765.

12 *Moreno v Minister of Employment and Immigration* (1993) 159 NR 210.

13 *Pushpanathan v MCI* [1998] 1 SCR 982, [1999] INLR 36. The refugee could not be excluded under art 1F(b) of the Refugee Convention ('serious non-political crime') because the acts were committed inside Canada after recognition.

14 *Singh (Mukhtiar) and Singh (Paramjit) v Secretary of State for the Home Department* (SIAC, 31 July 2000).

15 As the SIAC rightly pointed out at para 65(b), there are no such caveats expressed in art 1F(c), as distinct from the specified requirement that the 'serious crime' be 'non-political' in art 1F(b) (below). The ECJ in *Bundesrepublik Deutschland v B and D (Vertreter des Bundesinteresses beim Bundesverwaltungsgericht intervening)* [2010] ECR I-10979, [2012] 1 WLR 1076, ECJ makes it clear that Art 1F(c) is not limited to cases where the asylum-seeker was deploying state powers. Thus, art 1F(c) is highly relevant to separatist groups who use violence in pursuit of their aims.

16 *Al-Sirri v Secretary of State for the Home Department (United Nations High Commissioner for Refugees intervening)* [2012] UKSC 54; [2013] 1 AC 745 at [39]: 'It is, it seems to us, very likely that inducing terror in the civilian population or putting such extreme pressures upon a government will also have the international repercussions referred to by the UNHCR.' See fn 7 above re UNHR Guidelines. See also *Germany v B and D* [2012] 1 WLR 1076; [2011] Imm AR 190; [2011] INLR 13 (ECJ); *Singh (Mukhtiar) and Singh (Paramjit) v Secretary of State for the Home Department* (SIAC, 31 July 2000); *KK (Turkey)* [2004] UKIAT 00101.

17 Particularly SC Resolutions 1269 (1999) and 1373 (2001); and GA Resolutions 49/60 (1994), 51/210 (1996) and 54/164 (2000).

18 Lord Brown in the Supreme Court in *R (on the application of JS (Sri Lanka)) v Secretary of State for the Home Department (Rev 1)* [2010] UKSC 15 at [27]. Thus the LTTE of Sri Lanka could not be said to be 'predominantly terrorist in character'. But see regarding actions against the ISAF in Afghanistan: fn 5 above.

19 *Secretary of State for the Home Department v DD Afghanistan* [2010] EWCA Civ 1407: affd *Al-Sirri v Secretary of State for the Home Department (United Nations High Commissioner for Refugees intervening)* [2012] UKSC 54; [2013] 1 AC 745. An attack, within Afghanistan, against the International Security Assistance Force (ISAF), was in principle capable of being an act contrary to the purposes and principles of the United Nations because the fundamental aims and objectives of ISAF accord with the first purpose stated in art 1 of the United Nations Charter and by attacking ISAF, the appellant was seeking to frustrate that purpose: see *Al-Sirri* at [68]. See also per Hogan J in the High Court of Ireland in *B v Refugee Appeals Tribunal and others* [2011] IEHC 198 at [56].

20 Which came into force on 31 August 2006, but applies to acts that took place before the provision was enacted: see *Secretary of State for the Home Department v DD Afghanistan* (above).

21 Contrary to the principle that 'the Convention must be interpreted as an international instrument, not a domestic statute, in accordance with the rules prescribed by the Vienna Convention on the Law of Treaties' (*Januzi v Secretary of State for the Home Department; Hamid v Same; Gaafar v Same; Mohammed v Same* [2006] UKHL 5, [2006] 3 All ER 305, [2006] 2 WLR 397, per Lord Bingham, para 4).

22 Sedley LJ in *YS (Egypt) v Secretary of State for the Home Department* [2009] EWCA Civ 222: approved in the Supreme Court in *Al-Sirri v Secretary of State for the Home Department (United Nations High Commissioner for Refugees intervening)* [2012] UKSC 54; [2013] 1 AC 745 at [36].

23 But see *Al-Sirri v Secretary of State for the Home Department (United Nations High Commissioner for Refugees intervening)* [2012] UKSC 54; [2013] 1 AC 745 at [36]: fn 22 above.

[24] See Cases C-57/09 and C-101/09: *Bundesrepublik Deutschland v B and D (Vertreter des Bundesinteresses beim Bundesverwaltungsgericht intervening)* [2010] ECR I-10979, [2012] 1 WLR 1076, ECJ; and *R (on the application of JS (Sri Lanka)) v Secretary of State for the Home Department (Rev 1)* [2010] UKSC 15; [2011] 1 AC 184. See also Richards LJ in the Court of Appeal in *MH (Syria) v Secretary of State for the Home Department* [2009] EWCA Civ 226 (24 March 2009) at [36]; and *Asylum Instruction on Exclusion: Article 1F of the Refugee Convention*, (30 May 2012), section 3.3.

[25] Qualification Directive, Art 17(1)(c).

[26] Richards LJ in the Court of Appeal in *MH (Syria)* (fn 24 above) at [30].

[27] As above, at [31].

[28] Lord Brown in the Supreme Court in *R (on the application of JS (Sri Lanka)) v Secretary of State for the Home Department (Rev 1)* [2010] UKSC 15; [2011] 1 AC 184 at [30].

Serious non-political crime

12.96 It is only serious[1] offences that will bring this limb of the exclusion clause (ie serious reasons for considering that he or she 'has committed a serious non-political crime outside the country of refugee prior to his admission to that country as a refugee') into operation. The UNHCR *Handbook* suggests that they will have to be capital crimes or very grave punishable acts.[2] However, the Secretary of State applies a far lower threshold for the purpose of identifying what is a 'serious non-political crime', drawing by analogy from the definition of 'particularly serious crime' in the NIAA 2002, s 72 (as to which see **12.100** below). The Asylum Instruction[3] equates 'serious crime' with any one which, if committed in the UK, a custodial sentence of two years could be expected: see the Order made under the NIAA, s 72(4) (though the Order that was in fact made was declared void: given it purported to specify 'particularly serious' crimes, it was in any event an unsuitable guide to what was merely a 'serious' one).[4] The Tribunal has held that a serious crime, for the purposes of Article 1F(b), cannot be defined purely by national law or the length of sentence; rather the required level of seriousness was indicated by Articles 1F(a) and 1F(c) (see above).[5] What constitutes a 'non-political offence' has given rise to difficulty. The drafters of the Refugee Convention intended a link with the international principles of extradition, and the extradition case law is likely to be relevant.[6] The fact that violence is used in support of a political objective does not render the case outside the political offence exception.[7] In the case of *T v Immigration Officer*[8] the House of Lords had to consider the exclusion clause in relation to someone who had been an organiser of a group which had planted a bomb at a civilian airport, killing a number of innocent people. Lord Lloyd, delivering the principal judgment, held that a crime is a political crime for the purposes of Article 1F(b) of the Refugee Convention if, and only if, it is committed for a political purpose (ie with the object of overthrowing or subverting or changing the government of a state or inducing it to change its policy),[9] and there is a sufficiently close and direct link between the crime and the alleged political purpose. In determining whether such a link exists, the court will bear in mind the means used to achieve the political end, the target (whether civilian or military) and whether it involved indiscriminate killing. The House disapproved the *Handbook's*[10] suggestion that the impugned acts should be balanced against the consequences to the applicant in deciding whether the acts constituted serious non-political crimes.[11] Statute dictates that a particularly cruel action even if committed with an allegedly political objective is non-political.[12] Article 1F(b) of the Refugee Convention applies to a crime committed by a person 'outside the country of refuge prior to his admission to that country as a refugee'. Legislation transposing the Qualification Directive now requires that to be construed as meaning 'the time up to and including the day on which a residence permit is issued'.[13] The legislation thereby imposes only a construction of the reference to the time when the commission of a crime may result in exclusion under Article 1F(b). It says nothing that affects the clear and unambiguous language of Article 1F(b) which limits application of the Article to crimes committed 'outside the country of refuge'. We think, therefore, that the Asylum Instruction is plainly wrong in saying that reliance on the statutory interpretation of Article 1F(b) means that it may apply to crimes committed in the UK prior to the issue of a residence permit.[14]

[1] The Tribunal noted in *IH (s 72; 'Particularly Serious Crime') Eritrea* [2009] UKAIT 00012 at [67] that the addition of the word 'particularly' in Article 33(2) suggests a higher threshold than is required for exclusion under Article 1F(b). See Henry LJ in the New Zealand Court of Appeal in *S v Refugee Status Appeals Authority* [1998] NZLR 91; and the Tribunal in *KK (Turkey)* [2004] UKIAT 00101 on the role for judgment at [80].

[2] UNHCR *Handbook* **12.13** above, para 155. See also Hathaway **12.24** fn 3 above, p 224; Goodwin-Gill **12.5** fn 1 above, para 4.2.1, pp 101–108. For a consideration of the application of the sub-paragraph to drugs offences see Martin Gottwald 'Asylum claims and drug offences: the seriousness threshold of art 1F(b) of the 1951 Convention relating to the status of refugees and the UN Drug Conventions', UNHCR, 2004.

[3] *Asylum Instruction on Exclusion: Article 1F of the Refugee Convention*, (30 May 2012), section 5.2.

[4] The NIAA 2002 (Specification of Particularly Serious Crimes) Order 2004, SI 2004/1910. However that Order was struck down for invalidity, see Stanley Burnton LJ in the Court of Appeal in *EN (Serbia) v Secretary of State for the Home Department* [2009] EWCA Civ 630 at [68] and *IH (s 72; 'Particularly Serious Crime') Eritrea* [2009] UKAIT 00012 (9 March 2009) at [77].

[5] *AH (Article 1F(b): Serious: Algeria)* [2013] UKUT 382 (IAC); [2013] Imm AR 1169 (on remittal from the Court of Appeal in *AH (Algeria) v Secretary of State for the Home Department* [2012] EWCA Civ 395). The appellant had been convicted in France of participation in a criminal association with a terrorist enterprise and sentenced to two years' imprisonment. The Tribunal considered that in the absence of some strikingly unfair procedural defect, United Kingdom courts and tribunals should accord a significant degree of respect to the decision of senior sister Courts in European Union legal systems; there is a particular degree of mutual confidence and trust between legal systems that form part of the same legal order within the European Union.

[6] Hathaway above, pp 221–222. It was drawn on extensively in *T v Immigration Officer*; see below.

[7] *Handbook* above, para 152. A hijacking was held not to fall under the exclusion clause in the Dutch case of *YYA v Staatsecretaris van Justitie* (R 02880417) (8 April 1991) (Council of State). On the other hand, rioting in which buses were burned, stones thrown and stores looted was held capable of doing so in the US SC case of *INS v Aguirre-Aguirre* [2000] INLR 60, on the basis that the criminal outweighed the political aspect of the offence. The decision of the Board of Immigration Appeals (BIA), which had held the acts disproportionate to the aim (protest against government failure to investigate disappearances and rise in bus fares), was approved, and the court said it was not necessary for the acts to be atrocities for them to be disproportionate and so lose their political character.

[8] [1996] AC 742, [1996] 2 WLR 766.

[9] Notwithstanding the 'if and *only* if' formulation of Lord Lloyd, the House in *T* did not consider or reject Lord Diplock's conclusion in *R v Governor of Pentonville Prison, ex p Cheng* [1973] AC 931 (an extradition case) that an offence might be political if committed to 'enable [the offender] to escape from the jurisdiction of a government of whose political policies the offender disapproved but despaired of altering so long as he was there' (emphasis added). See also *R v Governor of Brixton Prison, ex p Kolczynski* [1955] 1 QB 540 at 550 per Lord Goddard CJ: 'The revolt of the crew was to prevent themselves being prosecuted for a political offence and in my opinion, therefore, the offence had a political character.'

10 UNHCR *Handbook* above, para 156 and see UNHCR *Guidelines on International Protection: Application of the Exclusion Clauses: Article 1F* (4 September 2003) (HCR/GIP/03/05) para 24; see also Hathaway above, p 224; *SAM v BFF* (1994) 6(4) IJRL 672 Case 215.

11 [1996] 2 All ER 865 at 882. See **12.93**, fn 7 above.

12 The Refugee or Person in Need of International Protection (Qualification) Regulations 2006, SI 2006/2525, reg 7(2)(a) applying the Qualification Directive, art 12(2)(b), although the Directive provides only that particularly cruel actions 'may' be classified as non-political whereas the Regulation adopts a mandatory classification.

13 SI 2006/2525, reg 7(2)(b), following the Qualification Directive, art 12(2)(b): incompatibility between the Directive and the Refugee Convention can be resolved only by the European Court of Justice, according to Stanley Burnton LJ in *EN (Serbia) v Secretary of State for the Home Department* [2009] EWCA Civ 630, [2010] 3 WLR 182, (2009) Times, 24 July citing *Foto-Frost v Hauptzollamt Lubeck-Ost* 314/85[1987] ECR 4199, [1988] 3 CMLR 57, ECJ. See also *R (on the application of International Air Transport Association) v Department for Transport* (C-344/04) [2006] ECR I-00403, [2006] NLJR 113, ECJ.

14 *Asylum Instruction on Exclusion: Article 1F of the Refugee Convention*, (30 May 2012), section 5.4.

12.97 There has been little judicial enthusiasm for limiting application of the exclusion clauses where the offence has been the subject of an amnesty or is no longer capable of prosecution (other than because the claimant has already been convicted and served his sentence).[1] It can only apply to conduct committed before entry to the country of asylum.[2] Conduct arising after admission to the country of asylum should properly be confined to the loss of the benefit of the prohibition on *refoulement*, and is considered in the following paragraphs.

1   For a view that it should not see Hathaway **12.24** fn 3 above, pp 222–223; see also *JMS v Staatsecretaris van Justitie* **12.93** fn 1 above. As to 'expiation', where the individual has already been punished for his crime, UNHCR suggest that the exclusion clause should not apply; see *Guidelines on International Protection: Application of the Exclusion Clauses: Article 1F* (4 September 2003) (HCR/GIP/03/05) para 23, but the Tribunal in *KK (Turkey)* [2004] UKIAT 00101 rejected the argument (at para 91) as did the ECJ in Cases C-57/09 and C-101/09: *Bundesrepublik Deutschland v B and D (Vertreter des Bundesinteresses beim Bundesverwaltungsgericht intervening)* [2010] ECR I-10979, [2012] 1 WLR 1076, ECJ. In *AH (Article 1F(b) – 'Serious') Algeria* [2013] UKUT 382 (IAC) the Tribunal considered that the examination of seriousness should be directed at the criminal acts when they were committed, although events in the supervening passage of time may be relevant to whether exclusion is justified: a formal pardon, or subsequent acquittal, or other event illuminating the nature of the activity may be relevant to this assessment. But, despite suggestions to the contrary by respected commentators, it did not appear to be the case that service of the sentence, or indeed a final acquittal, brings the application of the exclusion clause to an end.

2   *Pushpanathan v MCI* [1998] 1 SCR 982, [1999] INLR 36 – see **12.95** fn 13. Subject to the statutory regime discussed above.

EXPULSION OF REFUGEES

12.98 Article 33 of the Refugee Convention imposes an express duty on receiving states that may result in the grant of asylum. It provides:

'1.   No Contracting State shall expel or return (*"refouler"*) a refugee in any manner whatsoever to the frontiers of territories where his life or freedom would be threatened on account of his race, religion, nationality, membership of a particular social group or political opinion.

2.   The benefit of the present provision may not, however, be claimed by a refugee whom there are reasonable grounds for regarding as a danger to the

security of the country in which he is, or who, having been convicted by a final judgment of a particularly serious crime, constitutes a danger to the community of that country.'

As far as the courts in the UK are concerned, the reference to 'would be threatened' does not import a higher standard of proof than under Article 1 of the Convention.[1] This is consistent with the purpose of the Convention, which is to prevent the removal of potential refugees to the place where they fear persecution. Unless there is a prior proper determination that a person is not a refugee, he or she may be one, and so removal without determination of refugee status can only be effected to a country where there is no risk of persecution or of onward removal to the country of persecution.[2]

1 See *R v Secretary of State for the Home Department, ex p Sivakumaran* [1988] AC 958, HL where Lord Keith distinguished *INS v Cardozo-Fonseca*, 480 US 421, a US case where the different standard of proof arose from the terms of the US statute.
2 Re Musisi [1987] AC 514 at 526.

12.99 The only exceptions to the prohibition on *refoulement* under the Refugee Convention[1] are (i) where there are reasonable grounds for regarding the refugee as a danger to the security of the country in which he or she is,[2] or (ii) the refugee constitutes a danger to the community in that country having been convicted of a particularly serious crime.[3] The weight of international opinion is that these are two separate requirements, ie that the conviction of a particularly serious crime is not conclusive, and whether the commission of such a crime makes the refugee a danger to the community is a question of fact. The application of Article 33(2) of the Convention is not mechanistic, and will always involve a question of proportionality, with account taken of the consequences likely to befall the refugee on return.[4] The Canadian approach is to look both to the context of the crime and to the degree of persecution faced in the home country.[5] In *A v Minister for Immigration and Multicultural Affairs*[6] the Australian Federal Court of Appeal held that the provision was concerned with the perils represented by the refugee, and thus the nature of the crime committed was not conclusive.[7] Article 33(2) applies both to recognised refugees and to asylum seekers, but while the provisions of Article 1F above are mandatory, this is discretionary.

1 But even if art 33(2) of the Refugee Convention applies, art 3 of the ECHR prevents removal to torture or inhuman or degrading treatment or punishment, whatever the person has done and whatever threat he or she represents: *Chahal v United Kingdom* (1996) 23 EHRR 413; *Saadi v Italy* (2009) 49 EHRR 730. Also, as the Tribunal in *SB (cessation and exclusion) Haiti* [2005] UKIAT 00036 point out, a refugee (within the meaning of Art 1 of the Convention) who has lost the benefit of *non-refoulement* in terms of Art 33(2), but who cannot be removed due to ECHR Art 3 considerations, remains a refugee.
2 See **12.102** below.
3 The Tribunal in *IH (s 72; 'Particularly Serious Crime') Eritrea* [2009] UKAIT 00012 at [14]: 'it must be established that the individual was *in fact* convicted of the "particularly serious crime" and that he is *in fact* a "danger to the community"; reasonable grounds alone for so concluding will not suffice'.
4 *R v Secretary of State for the Home Department, ex p Chahal* [1994] Imm AR 107 at 113; *Raziastaraie v Secretary of State for the Home Department* [1995] Imm AR 459 at 464. See Goodwin-Gill at **12.5** fn 1 above, para 3.2, p 140. However in *SB (Haiti - cessation and exclusion)* [2005] UKIAT 00036 at para 81, a Tribunal chaired by the then President rejected the contention that a balance must be struck under Art 33(2) between the risk to the refugee on refoulement and the danger which his continued presence poses to the community. This meant that that the threshold for 'a particularly serious crime' and 'danger' must be higher than if there were a balance to be struck.

5   *Re Chu and MCI* (1998) 161 DLR (4th) 499.
6   [1999] FCA 227, 16 March 1999, Australian Federal Court of Appeals.
7   See also *Betkoshabeh v Minister for Immigration and Multicultural Affairs* (1998) 157 ALR
    95. This appears analogous to the EC provisions on deportation, where the criminal offences
    committed are not conclusive of deportation: see **6.176** above.

12.100 In the UK, conviction of an offence followed by a sentence of at least
two years[1] (and, until its illegality was identified, conviction of an offence
specified by Order),[2] (whether in the UK or abroad)[3] carries a statutory
presumption[4] that the person has been convicted by final judgment of a
particularly serious crime and constitutes a danger to the community of the
UK.[5] The presumption that the crime is particularly serious might seem
irrebuttable on the face of the statute, but to so treat it would defeat the
fact-sensitive enquiry that the autonomous meaning of the Refugee Convention demands;[6] there is express provision to rebut dangerousness.[7] In considering whether the presumption has been rebutted, no account is to be taken of
the gravity or likelihood of risk of persecution.[8] On refusing a person asylum
as a refugee, the Secretary of State may issue a certificate that a presumption
under this provision applies to him or her[9] and on appeal, the appellate body
must begin its substantive deliberation on the appeal by considering the
certificate and, if accepting that the presumption applies, having given the
appellant an opportunity for rebuttal, must dismiss the appeal insofar as it
relies on refugee asylum grounds.[10] However, the issue by the Secretary of State
of a certificate is not a precondition for the statutory presumptions contained
in the provision to apply; rather they apply once the facts giving rise to the
presumptions have been established so that a tribunal would be obliged to
consider them whether a certificate had been issued or not.[11] Under the
Refugee Convention the Secretary of State bears the burden of proof[12] but this
is effectively limited to establishing the fact of conviction, from which point the
onus is on the asylum seeker.[13] It seems unlikely that the drafters of the
Refugee Convention envisaged two-year sentences marking a crime as particularly serious and the offender as a danger to the community so that the
protection of the Refugee Convention may be withdrawn.[14] The Qualification
Directive enables Member States to revoke, end or refuse to renew refugee
status if there are reasonable grounds for regarding the person to be a danger
to the security of the state or, having been convicted of a particularly serious
crime he or she constitutes a danger to the community.[15]

1   Nationality, Immigration and Asylum Act 2002, s 72(2). The reference to a sentence of
    imprisonment of at least two years does not include reference to suspended sentences but does
    include references to sentences of detention in institutions other than prisons (in particular a
    hospital or a young offenders institution) and does include references to sentences of detention
    for indeterminate periods (provided that they may last for two years): 2002 Act, s 72(11). It
    is important to note that the presumption only applies if the sentence actually passed is two
    years or more, not merely on conviction of an offence carrying such a sentence.
2   NIAA 2002, s 72(4)(a). Such an order must be made by statutory instrument and shall be
    subject to annulment in pursuance of a resolution of either House of Parliament: NIAA 2002,
    s 72(5). The offences listed in the Nationality, Immigration and Asylum Act 2002 (Specifica-
    tion of Particularly Serious Crimes) Order 2004, SI 2004/1910, made under the section range
    from undoubtedly serious crimes of violence or related to violence including manslaughter,
    kidnapping, possession of firearms with intent to endanger life or injure property; rape,
    indecent assault, importation, production or supply of Class A or Class B drugs; terrorism
    related offences including directing terrorism, terrorist fundraising, terrorist weapons training
    or membership of a proscribed organisation; other offences such as trafficking in prostitution,
    to minor offences of theft, criminal damage and public order offences. The inclusion of minor

offences in the list caused the Court of Appeal in *EN (Serbia) v Secretary of State for the Home Department* [2009] EWCA Civ 630 to hold that the order was ultra vires: Stanley Burnton LJ at [82].

3 Where a person is convicted outside the UK, the rebuttable presumption applies if the offender could have been sentenced to two years on conviction in the UK: s 72(3), or the Secretary of State certifies that in his opinion the offence is similar to an offence specified in the order: s 72(4)(b). Whether or not the use of art 33(2) is appropriate in the case of crimes committed abroad (and art 1F(b) applies to offences committed abroad before arrival in the country of refuge), the person cannot be removed in any event by virtue of art 3 of the ECHR.

4 NIAA 2002, s 72 (in force since 1 April 2003: SI 2003/754). Section 72(1) states that the section applies 'for the purpose of the construction and application of Article 33(2) of the Refugee Convention (exclusion from protection)'. In *N (Kenya)* [2004] UKIAT 00009 at para 21 the IAT was in no doubt (although their view was *obiter*) that, as an interpretative provision, the section has retrospective effect and can therefore apply to a person whose conviction and sentence occurred before the provision came into force. The Tribunal recognised that there are difficulties in interpreting the provision, especially with how the presumption is to be rebutted by evidence from the claimant. In *SB (Haiti - cessation and exclusion)* [2005] UKIAT 00036 a Tribunal chaired by the President, sitting with the Deputy President (who had chaired in *N (Kenya)*), concluded that s 72 can only apply to *appeals* brought under the 2002 Act itself – and therefore only in respect of immigration decisions taken on or after 1 April 2003 (though clearly an immigration decision can be taken on the basis of a conviction that pre-dates it).

5 NIAA 2002, s 72(2), (3) and (4). The presumption does not apply while an appeal against conviction or sentence is pending or could be brought in time: NIAA 2002, s 72(7).

6 Stanley Burnton LJ in the Court of Appeal in EN (Serbia) v Secretary of State for the Home Department [2009] EWCA Civ 630 at [66], [68].

7 NIAA 2002, s 72(6); see the Tribunal in *IH Eritrea* at [75] and [80]. Stanley Burnton LJ in the Court of Appeal in *EN (Serbia) v Secretary of State for the Home Department* [2009] EWCA Civ 630 at [46].

8 NIAA 2002, s 72(8) (by applying Anti-terrorism, Crime and Security Act 2001, s 34: see **12.93** fn 7).

9 NIAA 2002, s 72(9)(b).

10 NIAA 2002, s 72(9) and (10). If the appellate body agrees with the Secretary of State's certificate to the effect that art 33(2) applies, it does not go on to consider whether or not the appellant is a refugee under art 1A(2) of the Refugee Convention.

11 *AQ (Somalia) v Secretary of State for the Home Department* [2011] EWCA Civ 695, and *TB (Jamaica) v Secretary of State for the Home Department* [2008] EWCA Civ 977, (2008) Times, 9 September.

12 IH (s 72; 'Particularly Serious Crime') Eritrea [2009] UKAIT 00012 (9 March 2009) at [13]; Stanley Burnton LJ in the Court of Appeal in EN (Serbia) v Secretary of State for the Home Department [2009] EWCA Civ 630 at [66].

13 *IH Eritrea* (fn 11 above) at [78].

14 UNHCR expressed concern that section 72 'suggests an approach to Article 33(2) of the 1951 Convention which is at odds with the Convention's objects and purposes' (Briefing on the Nationality, Immigration and Asylum Bill, see *Butterworths Immigration Law Service* at A[2671]). See *Betkoshabeh* at **12.99** fn 6 for a model application of the true autonomous approach; a domestic reference point is permissible, see *EN Serbia* (fn 6 above) at [40].

15 Qualification Directive, art 14(4) and HC 395, para 339A(ix) and (x).

12.101 A refugee who has already been recognised and granted admission to the UK can only be expelled to a country or territory other than that in which persecution is feared,[1] in accordance with the provisions of Article 32 of the Refugee Convention.[2] First, this means that the only legitimate grounds of expulsion are national security or public order. Secondly, except where compelling reasons of national security otherwise require, 'the refugee shall be allowed to submit evidence to clear himself, and to appeal to and be represented before competent authority'. Previous UK practice provided an appeal only where the person was lawfully in the country at the date of the decision,[3] but following *Chahal*[4] there is always an appeal before expulsion, at least where asylum or human rights issues are raised, whether to the Tribunal under section 82 of the Nationality, Immigration and Asylum Act 2002 as amended, or by virtue of section 2 of the Special Immigration Appeals Commission Act 1997. Where a receiving country intends to remove a refugee lawfully, an opportunity should be afforded for an alternative country of refuge to be found.[5]

1 As to which see art 33 at **12.97** ff above.
2 In *R (on the application of ST (Eritrea)) v Secretary of State for the Home Department* [2012] UKSC 12, [2012] 2 AC 135, the Supreme Court held that a refugee was not entitled to the protection of art 32 unless he or she had been granted the right of lawful presence in the state in question according to the domestic law of that state; and that temporary admission for the purpose of the determination of a claim for asylum did not render a stay lawful for the purposes of Art 32.
3 *NSH v Secretary of State for the Home Department* [1988] Imm AR 389, CA.
4 *Chahal v United Kingdom* (1996) 23 EHRR 413, see **12.102** below.
5 Refugee Convention, art 32(3). An attempt to expel a leading Saudi dissident, Mohammed al-Masari, to Dominica failed in March 1996 when the appellate authority held that Dominica was not safe. The attempt was notorious for the exposure of the close links between diplomatic staff and arms salesmen (sometimes the same people), and by ministers' admission that the proposed expulsion was demanded by the Saudi authorities, and that the motivation for acceding to the demand was fear that billions of pounds' worth of arms contracts would be lost by Mr al-Masari's continued presence in the UK.

National security

12.102 National security can thus ground expulsion of asylum seekers and of recognised refugees by virtue of Articles 33(2) and 32 of the Refugee Convention. But the phrase is not defined in the Convention. In *Rehman*[1] the House of Lords gave an extremely broad meaning to the phrase 'national security' in the context of a non-asylum deportation; see CHAPTER **16** below. However, the ECHR in *Chahal v United Kingdom*[2] confirmed that even where there are national security grounds to expel an asylum claimant, Article 3 of the EHCR prohibits expulsion to a territory where there is a real risk of torture. And it is to *Chahal* that the edifice of the SIAC is owed; the Strasbourg court roundly condemned the 'advisory panel' procedure in national security expulsions as not providing the necessary safeguards to the appellant – legal representation, information about the grounds for the expulsion decision, and not sufficiently independent or open, to constitute a court or an effective remedy for a potential breach of Article 3.[3] Now, section 2 of the Special Immigration Appeals Commission Act 1997 provides an appeal against expulsion, including on asylum and human rights grounds. The special procedure adopted there means that the refugee or asylum seeker does not hear all the evidence but his or her interests are represented in closed sessions by a special advocate. The system is certainly a vast improvement on the discredited advisory procedure, but still falls far short of the minimum requirements of fair trials set out in Article 6 ECHR.[4]

1 *Secretary of State for the Home Department v Rehman* [2001] UKHL 47, [2003] 1 AC 153, [2001] 3 WLR 877.
2 (1996) 23 EHRR 413. See also *Saadi v Italy* (2009) 49 EHRR 730, [2008] Crim LR 898, ECtHR which confirms *Chahal* at [127], [139].
3 (1996) 23 EHRR 413, para 130.
4 See CHAPTER **7** 'Fair Trial' above.

CONSEQUENCES OF RECOGNITION

12.103 Where the authorities recognise someone within their territory as a Convention refugee, they must issue identity papers or a travel document to enable the refugee to travel outside the country of asylum.[1] The charge for its issue must not exceed the lowest scale of fees for national passports.[2] Refugees must be readmitted to the state which issued the document at any time during its validity.[3] The Convention requires that refugees are granted the 'most favourable treatment accorded to nationals of a foreign country' as regards trade union membership (Article 15), entry to wage-earning employment (Article 17), self-employment (Article 18) and membership of the liberal professions (Article 19). They should be given 'treatment as favourable as possible' as regards housing (Article 21) and education (Article 22) and approximately the same treatment as nationals with respect to public relief and assistance (Article 23), labour legislation and social security (Article 24).[4] Their freedom of movement within the country of asylum is guaranteed by Article 26 and any state may, at the time of signing, ratifying or acceding to the Convention, declare that it shall extend to all or any territories for the international relations of which it is responsible (Article 40).[5] The policy of the Convention is that after asylum has been given, refugees shall as far as possible be integrated into their country of asylum and to that end contracting states are urged to expedite naturalisation procedures.[6] However, a person's recognition as a refugee does not entitle him to the diplomatic protection of the country that has granted asylum.[7]

There has been a debate in the UK appellate authorities as to whether refugee status can be backdated on an appeal against refusal of asylum being allowed.[8] But the Divisional Court has condemned the delays in the grant of status following a successful appeal, which can be severely prejudicial to refugees.[9]

[1] Refugee Convention, Art 28.
[2] Refugee Convention, Sch, para 3.
[3] Refugee Convention, Sch, para 13. Thus a Somali refugee with indefinite leave to remain who had stayed in Ethiopia for over two years caring for a sick relative was wrongly refused re-entry as a returning resident since his refugee travel document was still valid: *R v Secretary of State for the Home Department, ex p Shirreh* (CO 2194/1997) (15 August 1997, unreported), QBD (permission; the case was conceded by the Home Office).
[4] In UK practice community support, housing, education (including language learning) access to health services, social security benefits and employment are perceived as the essential elements of refugee integration: Home Office Immigration and Nationality Directorate *The Integration of Recognised Refugees in the UK* (1999). See also the 'Home Office Research Report 37': presenting 'findings from the Survey of New Refugees, a longitudinal study of refugee integration in the UK' (on the Home Office website). Refugees are treated as own nationals for the purpose of health care, social security and housing, and as home students for education fees and grants purposes. There are no employment restrictions on recognised refugees.
[5] Under art 40(2) extensions can be made after the Convention is in force by notifying the Secretary-General of the UN. The UK currently extends the Convention to the Channel Islands and the Isle of Man and to the Falkland Islands, St Helena and Montserrat (though a refugee recognised in the UK will be subject to the same restrictions on travelling to and staying in the Overseas Territories as would a British citizen – see Fransman *British Nationality Law*).
[6] Refugee Convention, art 34.
[7] R (on the application of *Al Rawi*) *v Secretary of State for Foreign and Commonwealth Affairs* [2006] EWHC 972 (Admin), [2006] NLJR 797, (2006) Times, 19 May. Thus there was no obligation on the UK government even to consider making representations to the government of the USA on behalf of claimants recognised in the UK as refugees and detained in Guantanamo Bay; there was an obligation to consider making representations in respect of British citizens: *R (on the application of Abbasi) v Secretary of State for Foreign and Commonwealth Affairs* [2002] EWCA Civ 1598, (2002) Times, 8 November.

8   The Tribunal in *Haibe* [1997] INLR 119 held that because refugee status is not granted but recognised, in an appropriate case it is open to the appellate authority to declare that the status of refugee existed at the date of the decision or other appropriate date, and a direction can be given to that effect. Another Tribunal in *Merzouk* [1999] INLR 468 disapproved *Haibe*, saying that nothing in the Immigration Act 1971 allows directions of a retrospective nature and that it is no part of the appellate authorities' function, nor does the Refugee Convention require them to determine exactly when a person became a refugee. See also *Altun* (16628) *17 July 1998*, in line with *Merzouk*. Any direction given by the Tribunal on allowing an appeal counts as part of its determination for appeal or review purposes: Nationality, Immigration and Asylum Act 2002, s 87(4).

9   'It would wholly undermine the rule of law if the Secretary of State could simply ignore a ruling without appealing it, nor could he deliberately delay giving effect to it': Elias J in *R v Secretary of State for the Home Department, ex p Mersin* [2000] INLR 511, QBD. A successful appellant has a right to be granted refugee status unless or until there was a change in the position. See also *R (on the application of Saribal) v Secretary of State for the Home Department* [2002] EWHC 1542 (Admin); *R (on the application of Boafo) v Secretary of State for the Home Department* [2002] EWCA Civ 44, [2002] 1 WLR 1919, [2002] Imm AR 383; and *TB (Jamaica) v Secretary of State for the Home Department* [2008] EWCA Civ 977, (2008) Times, 9 September.

12.104 Where a refugee has left the country of refuge and entered another territory and lived there lawfully for a period of time, the Refugee Convention envisages that the responsibility for the issue of a further travel document may become that of the second country of residence.[1] The circumstances when this might happen are uncertain; a refugee has no right to have asylum transferred to a country in which he or she has temporary residence. In order to eliminate ambiguity, Member States of the Council of Europe drew up the European Agreement on Transfer of Responsibility for Refugees (EATRR)[2] which provides for the transfer of responsibility after two years' continuous lawful residence other than for the purposes of study, training, medical visit, or a period of imprisonment,[3] or if the refugee has been permitted to stay beyond the validity of his or her travel document from the first state (unless the extension beyond validity was for study or training, or the refugee is still re-admissible to the first state). The Agreement does not, however, assist in cases of unlawful residence, nor does it provide any mechanism or criteria for transfer of lawful residence.[4] Home Office policy was to consider cases falling outside the European Agreement on a case-by-case basis, accepting responsibility only where the UK clearly is the most appropriate place of long-term refuge.[5] For short-term visa-free travel, the European Agreement on the Abolition of Visas for Refugees 1959[6] enables refugees resident in a contracting state and possessing a valid travel document issued under the Refugee Convention to travel without a visa to any other contracting state[7] for visits of up to three months.[8] The UK has suspended its obligations under the Agreement, and refugees living in contracting states now need visas to enter.[9]

1   Refugee Convention, Sch, para 11.
2   16 October 1980, European Treaty Series (ETS) 107, Cmnd 8127. Currently in force for: Denmark, Finland, Germany, Italy, Netherlands, Norway, Poland, Portugal, Romania, Spain, Sweden, Switzerland and UK. (The following Council of Europe Member States have signed but not yet ratified the Agreement: Belgium, Czech Republic, Greece and Luxembourg.)
3   European Agreement on Transfer of Responsibility for Refugees 1980 above, art 2.
4   See *Rahman* [1989] Imm AR 325 for a case where the appellate authority exercised a broad discretion on a transfer of status case. An appeal on human rights grounds would be available where an immigration decision involved a refusal to transfer status and meant continued separation from close family members.
5   The API on 'transfer of refugee status' has been withdrawn and replaced with an 'interim notice' on 'transfer of refugee status'. The 'interim notice' is dated 5 February 2013 and states:

'The UK's obligations do not extend to the consideration of applications to transfer refugee status where the country which recognised the refugee is not a signatory to the EATRR. Neither do they extend to the consideration of applications made abroad and, with immediate effect, no application made abroad will be accepted by a UK visa-issuing post or by the UK Border Agency pending a review of the policy and guidance.'

6   20 April 1959, UNTS 85, ETS 31, reproduced in Butterworths Immigration Law Service, 2D[1].

7   Belgium, Czech Republic, Denmark, Finland, France, Germany, Hungary, Iceland, Ireland, Italy, Liechtenstein, Luxembourg, Malta, the Netherlands, Norway, Poland, Portugal, Romania, Slovakia, Spain, Sweden, Switzerland and the UK. Armenia and Cyprus have signed but not yet ratified the Agreement.

8   See also *Shramir v Secretary of State for the Home Department* [1992] Imm AR 542, IAT.

9   France suspended its obligations under the Agreement (in accordance with art 7) in 1986, and the UK followed suit in February 2003. See Declaration of suspension contained in a letter from the Permanent Representative of the United Kingdom, dated 7 February 2003, registered at the Secretariat General of the Council of Europe on 7 February 2003 and with effect from 11 February 2003. For the Secretary of State's justification for suspension see *Hansard* HC 7 February 2003, Col 31WS.

Refugees in the EU

12.105 Until refugees obtain the nationality of the country of refuge, they will not be entitled to freedom of movement rights as EU nationals. Article 45 of the Treaty on the Functioning of the European Union (ex art 39 of the EC Treaty) dealing with the freedom of movement of workers does not apply to refugees. Apart from the European Agreements noted above, adopted within the framework of the Council of Europe in 1959 and 1980, the only other measure designed to give refugees rights within Europe was the 1964 EEC Council of Ministers' declaration that:

'the entry to their territories for the purpose of engaging in a paid activity there, of refugees recognised as such within the meaning of the Convention of 1951 and established in the territory of another Member State of the community should be examined with particular favour, particularly so as to afford to such refugees within their territories the most favourable treatment possible.'

Further to this declaration, Council Regulation (EEC) 1408/71[1] provided that refugees resident in the territory of a Member State are entitled to the same social security benefits as nationals of that state, a measure which did no more than Europeanise Article 24 of the Refugee Convention.

1   Article 2(3).

12.106 From the mid-1980s EU Member States' asylum policy was restricted to trying to stop 'irregular movements' – in practice, all movement of refugees into EU territory, by treating asylum seekers as essentially a policing problem. The early products of the work of the Ad Hoc Working Group in this field are described in the fifth edition of this work at **12.102**. After 1993, when the Treaty on European Union institutionalised the inter-governmental character of immigration and asylum issues (apart from visa policy) in the Third Pillar of the Treaty, there was an attempt to harmonise criteria, procedures,[1] reception conditions[2] and refugees' rights[3] within the EU. The non-binding Joint Position of March 1996[4] was the main fruit of this process. It was the first attempt to reconcile the varying interpretations of the Convention by the

Member States. Although welcomed in *Robinson*,[5] the Joint Position was dismissed in *Adan*[6] as no more than a political agreement which was not particularly useful.

1   See eg Resolution on minimum guarantees for asylum seekers and refugees, 21 June 1995, OJ 1996 C 274, 19 September 1996.
2   Draft Joint Action on the minimum conditions for the reception of asylum seekers, 17 August 1995, ASIM 223.
3   Draft Council Act adopting a common action on certain aspects on the status of refugees recognised by the Member States of the EU, 6784/95.
4   Joint Position of 4 March 1996 defined by the Council on the basis of Art K3 of the Treaty on European Union on the harmonised application of the term 'refugee' of art 1 of the Convention relating to the status of refugees (Geneva, 28 July 1951), 96/196/JHA, reproduced in *Butterworths Immigration Law Service*, 2D[138].
5   *Robinson (Anthonypillai Francis) v Secretary of State for the Home Department and Immigration Appeal Tribunal* [1997] Imm AR 568.
6   On the issue of agents of persecution: *R v Secretary of State for the Home Department, ex p Adan* [1999] Imm AR 521, [1999] INLR 362, CA. See also Lord Steyn [2001] INLR 44 at 57, HL.

12.107 In 1997 the Treaty of Amsterdam[1] resulted in immigration and asylum policy as a whole being taken into Community competence. Title IV inserted visas, asylum, immigration and other policies related to free movement of persons into the EC Treaty. Now see Title V of the Treaty on the Functioning of the European Union. In accordance with the Treaty of Amsterdam, the European Commission has drawn up proposals for new Regulations and Directives for approval by the Council of Ministers (thereby giving them legislative effect). The Council of Ministers has approved a Directive on Family Reunion;[2] a Directive laying down minimum standards for the reception of asylum seekers;[3] a Directive on temporary protection;[4] a Directive setting out the minimum standards for the qualification and status of third country nationals and stateless persons as refugees or as persons who otherwise need international protection (the 'Qualification Directive');[5] and a Directive on minimum standards on procedures in Member States for granting and withdrawing refugee status (the Procedures Directive)[6]; Regulations on Eurodac, the European fingerprint data and exchange system,[7] and sequential Council Regulations 'establishing the criteria and mechanisms for determining the Member State responsible for examining an application for international protection lodged in one of the Member States by a third-country national or a stateless person (recast)'.[8]

1   Signed on 2 October 1997 by the then 15 Member States.
2   Council Directive 2003/86/EC of 22 September 2003. The UK and Ireland and Denmark however have opted out.
3   Council Directive 2003/9/EC of 27 January 2003. Ireland and Denmark have opted out The UK government has amended the Immigration Rules to take account of this Directive, particularly the right of asylum seekers whose claim has not been dealt with to request permission to seek employment after a year: see HC 395, paras 357–361, making up Part 11B (as inserted by HC 194 from 4 February 2005). The EU Parliament and Council have adopted, on 26 June 2013, a 'recast' Reception Conditions Directive, 2013/33/EU, with a transposition date of 20 July 2015. The UK, along with Denmark and Ireland have opted out of this recast directive.
4   Council Directive 2001/55 (OJ 2001 L212/12). See **12.181** below.
5   Council Directive 2004/83/EC of 29 April 2004: the 'Qualification Directive' (30.9.04 OJ L304/12), which came into force on 20 October 2004 and in accordance with Article 38 had to be implemented by Member States in national measures by 10 October 2006. The UK has domestically implemented the Directive, from 9 October 2006, by way of the Refugee or Person in Need of International Protection (Qualification) Regulations 2006, SI 2006/2525

and by inserting provisions into the Immigration Rules by Cm 6918. The EU Parliament and Council have adopted, on 13 December 2011, a 'recast' Qualification Directive, 2011/95/EU, with a transposition date of 21 December 2013. The UK, along with Denmark and Ireland have opted out of this recast directive.

6   Council Directive 2005/85/EC of 1 December 2005. The Directive entered into force on 2 January 2006 and it required that Member States shall bring into force the laws, regulations and administrative provisions necessary to comply with the Directive by 1 December 2007, to be applied to all applications for asylum lodged after that date (but also only to applications for asylum lodged after that date) and to procedures for the withdrawal of refugee status commenced after that date. The UK has domestically implemented the Directive, from 1 December 2007, principally by inserting provisions into the Immigration Rules by HC 82. See also the Asylum (Procedures) Regulations 2007, SI 2007/3187. The EU Parliament and Council have adopted, on 26 June 2013, a 'recast' Procedures Directive, 2013/32/EU, with a transposition date of 20 July 2015. The UK, along with Denmark and Ireland have opted out of this recast directive.

7   Now 'recast' Regulation (EU) 603/2013 of 26 June 2013 (OJ 2013 L 180/1); previously Council Regulation 2725/2000; and Council Regulation 407/2002 implementing the Eurodac Regulation (OJ 2002 L 62/1).

8   Regulation (EU) No 604/2013 of 26 June 2013, the 'Dublin III Regulation' replacing the Dublin II Regulation (343/2003 of 18 February 2003) which in turn replaced the Dublin Convention. Denmark however opted out of both Regulations (Dublin III Regulation preamble, para 42) See further **12.149** ff.

12.108 EU nationals are not prevented from applying for asylum in another Member State,[1] but their claims must be assessed against the presumption contained in the 1997 Protocol to the EC Treaty[2] that 'given the level of protection of fundamental rights and freedoms, Member States shall be regarded as constituting safe countries of origin in respect of each other for all legal and practical purposes in relation to asylum matters'. Applications may be considered or declared admissible only if the applicant's Member State has taken measures derogating from the ECHR, or the Council determines that the Member State in question is in serious and persistent breach of principles of liberty, democracy, respect for human rights and fundamental freedoms,[3] or if the procedure for such a determination has been initiated. If a Member State unilaterally decides to consider an asylum claim and none of these conditions apply, the Council must be immediately informed, and the application will be dealt with as manifestly unfounded. The presumption in Protocol 24 therefore applies to asylum claims made by nationals of all EU states and in practice, in the UK, such asylum claims will be refused and certified as 'clearly unfounded'.[4]

1   However, the 'Qualification Directive' (see **12.107** fn 3 above) does not apply to EU nationals as it applies only to the qualification and status of third country nationals or stateless persons as refugees or as persons who otherwise need international protection. See also HC 395, para 357 (as inserted by HC 194 from 4 February 2005) which declares that Part 11B of the Immigration Rules, dealing with 'reception conditions for non-EU asylum applicants' only applies to asylum applicants who are not nationals of a Member State.

2   Protocol No 24 to the Treaty on the European Union and to the Treaty on the Functioning of the European Union on asylum for nationals of Member States of the European Union, (originally Protocol No 29 to the TEU added by the Treaty of Amsterdam in 1997).

3   Treaty on European Union, arts 6 and 7.

4   Currently under the Immigration (European Economic Area) Regulations 2006, SI 2006/1003, Sch 2, para 4(4) and (5).

UK PRACTICE ON ASYLUM

The application

12.109 One of the few provisions of the Asylum and Immigration Appeals Act 1993 that remains in force defines an asylum claim as a claim that it would be contrary to the UK's obligations under the Refugee Convention for the person to be removed from or required to leave the UK.[1] Under the Immigration Rules, an asylum applicant is a person who makes a request to be recognised as a refugee under the Geneva Convention on the basis that it would be contrary to the UK's obligations to remove or require the person to leave the UK or otherwise makes a request for international protection.[2] The Immigration Rules have been substantially amended[3] in order to implement the EU Council Directive on minimum standards on procedures in Member States for granting and withdrawing refugee status.[4] The Rules now contain detailed procedural provisions which apply to the consideration of applications for asylum and humanitarian protection.[5] The asylum application will be determined in accordance with the UK's obligations under the Convention and will be granted if the applicant is in the UK or has arrived at a port of entry in the UK, is a refugee as defined in the Refugee Qualification Regulations[6], there are no reasonable grounds for regarding the person as a danger to the security of the UK, the person does not constitute a danger to the community of the UK, and refusing his or her application would result (whether immediately or after the expiry of leave) in *refoulement* contrary to the Convention.[7] An application which does not meet those criteria will be refused.[8] A person who has claimed asylum may not be removed from the UK whilst the claim is pending, ie until he or she is given notice of the Secretary of State's decision on the claim,[9] unless the application is certified on safe third country grounds (as to which see below under 'Removal to Safe Third Countries'). Nor may the person be removed whilst an appeal against an immigration decision, brought within the UK is pending[10] or whilst the Secretary of State decides whether to treat representations made by a failed asylum seeker as a fresh claim for asylum.[11] If an asylum applicant requests the return of his or her passport from the Home Office for the purpose of leaving the UK, the passport will only be returned if the person signs a declaration acknowledging that the asylum claim will be treated as withdrawn upon return of the passport.[12] If an applicant withdraws a claim for asylum or is treated as having done so, consideration of the claim will be discontinued.[13] Prior to September 2011, entry clearance officers had a discretion to accept an application for entry clearance to come to the UK as a refugee, albeit there was no provision in the rules for such an application. However, since 20 September 2011 the policy guidance on the discretionary referral to the UK Border Agency of applications for asylum by individuals in a third country who have not been recognised as refugees by another country or by the UNHCR under its mandate, has been withdrawn.[14]

---

[1] Asylum and Immigration Appeals Act 1993, s 1;

[2] HC 395, para 327. There is no specific definition of 'international protection' in the rules. Other definitions of 'asylum claim' appear in other statutory contexts. Eg for the purpose of the appeals provisions of the NIAA 2002, s 113(1) defines an asylum claim as a claim made by a person to the Secretary of State at a place designated by him that to remove the person from the UK would breach the UK's obligations under the Refugee Convention. Other definitions of 'asylum seeker' are provided by NIAA 2002, s 18 relating to the statutory provisions concerned with 'accommodation centres' and IAA 1999, s 94(1) in relation to support for asylum seekers.

3   By HC 82, laid before Parliament on 19 November 2007.
4   Council Directive 2005/85/EC of 1 December 2005.
5   HC 396, para 326A.
6   The Refugee or Person in Need of International Protection (Qualification) Regulations 2006, SI 2006/2525, reg 2.
7   HC 395, para 334.
8   HC 395 para 336
9   NIAA 2002, s 77 and HC 395, para 329.
10 NIAA 2002, s 78. In *R (on the application of Kagabo) v Secretary of State for the Home Department* [2009] EWHC 153 (Admin), Pitchford J held that section 78 of the 2002 Act does not protect a person from being removed from the UK during the period in which she has sought to institute a first instance appeal to the Tribunal by lodging notice of appeal out of time but before a preliminary decision has been made by the Tribunal on whether to extend time. However, a decision to remove while an extension of time application is awaiting decision is reviewable by the High Court in proceedings for judicial review.
11 HC 395, para 353A.
12 API 'Travel abroad'.
13 HC 395, para 333C, as amended. An application may be treated as impliedly withdrawn if the applicant fails to attend for interview and fails to demonstrate within a reasonable time that the non-attendance was due to circumstances beyond his or her control. A subsequent application would be considered under para 353 of the Rules, ie as to whether it constitutes a fresh claim for asylum. See also API 'Withdrawal of Applications'.
14 See UK Visas and Immigration 'Applications from abroad' Policy (20 September 2011).

Dependants of asylum applicants

12.110 A spouse, civil partner, unmarried or same sex partner or minor child accompanying a principal applicant may be included in his or her application for asylum as a dependant, subject to the consent of each adult dependant[1] or may make an asylum claim in his or her own right, which will be considered individually, and which should be made as soon as possible.[2] If the principal applicant is granted asylum and leave to enter or remain, dependants will be granted leave to enter or remain for the same duration.[3] The parents of an asylum seeking child cannot be treated as his or her dependant, nor can a child normally be treated as the dependant of another child (eg a sibling) other than where the children are married to each other or are in a civil, same-sex or unmarried partnership.[4] A person who has been treated as a dependant may claim asylum in his or her own right[5] at any time, including after refusal of the principal applicant's claim and exhaustion of any rights of appeal that the principal applicant had[6] and such a claim will be given individual consideration.[7] This applies equally to the dependants of a person whose asylum claim is refused on exclusion grounds or in reliance on Article 33(2) of the ECHR; their claims must be considered on their own merits and they cannot simply be excluded because of the actions of the principal applicant.[8] However, adverse inferences as to credibility may be drawn from failure to claim asylum at the earliest opportunity, absent a reasonable explanation for the failure.[9] Moreover, a former dependant who claims asylum may previously have been given a one-stop notice[10] and if he or she failed to raise asylum in a statement of additional grounds, the Secretary of State will consider certification of the claim under the NIAA 2002, s 96[11] and the making of a certificate under section 96 will prevent the person from appealing (see further under 'Procedure on Asylum Appeals' as to certification). The application has to be made by personal attendance at the Liverpool or Croydon screening unit.[12] Where a principal applicant's claim has been refused and certified as clearly unfounded and his or her dependants then claimed asylum, the erstwhile principal applicant 'would not normally' be removed pending a decision on the dependant's claim and pending the determination of any appeal that the dependant may have[13] although removal would normally be appropriate if the family had chosen to live separately.[14] Moreover, the Qualification Directive now obliges the UK to ensure that family unity can be maintained[15] and the removal of a family member of a person whose entitlement to refugee status is yet to be determined by the Tribunal would be inconsistent with that obligation.

[1] HC 395, para 349.
[2] HC 395, para 349.
[3] HC 395, para 349.
[4] Asylum Process Guidance: processing an asylum application from a child: policy relating to dependent children.
[5] HC 395, para 349.
[6] API: Dependants and former dependants (May 2014).
[7] HC 395, para 349.
[8] Asylum Instruction, Exclusion: Article 1F of the Refugee Convention, 30 May 2012, section 3.12, and the general principle, acknowledged in the rules that asylum, humanitarian protection and human rights claims will be assessed on an individual basis – HC 395, para 339J.
[9] HC 395, para 349.
[10] NIAA, s 120.
[11] See CHAPTER 19 on appeals.
[12] Asylum Process Guidance: Handling Claims.
[13] Asylum Process Guidance: 'Non Suspensive Appeals (NSA) Certification under Section 94 of the NIA Act 2002', section 7.4.
[14] As in fn 16 above.
[15] Qualification Directive, art 23(1).

Applications at the port

12.111 A person arriving at a port of entry who intends to seek asylum will normally ask for it from an immigration officer on arrival; this is the approved method of seeking asylum in the UK[1]. No particular form of words is required, and if a person expresses unwillingness to return to their country of nationality or habitual residence because they believe they would be in danger, it should be assumed that they are making an asylum application.[2] Arrangements whereby passengers without visas are prevented from leaving the aircraft and making a claim to an immigration officer are contrary to the UK's obligations under the Refugee Convention,[3] although the operation of pre-entry immigration controls by UK immigration officers abroad which prevent passengers embarking for the UK has been held not to violate the UK's obligations under the Refugee Convention.[4] Facilities at the port of entry must include an interpreter so that an applicant can make a claim. In the rare case where an entry clearance has been granted in order for a claim for asylum to be made, the immigration officer may grant leave to enter.[5] In all other cases, the claim will be referred to the UKBA for determination.[6] Current practice in port cases is to conduct screening immediately (this will include taking identity details, fingerprinting[7] and, if the applicant is potentially returnable to a safe third country, questioning about the route of travel and any periods of stay in third countries).[8] The EU Reception Directive requires third-country and stateless asylum claimants to be given information and documentation reflecting their status and their right to remain in the country pending determination of their claim, and these requirements are reflected in the Immigration Rules.[9]

1   In an announcement of 13 October 2009, the Minister of State for Borders and Immigration stated that: 'We expect individuals to make their claim at a port of entry . . . ' (see the Home Office website).
2   See API Handling Claims, under the heading 'identifying asylum claims' (emphasising also that 'not all applicants know about the UN Convention so might not use the words "asylum" or "refugee"'). See also *R v Uxbridge Magistrates' Court, ex p Adimi* [1999] INLR 490 at 499, 506, *and* Article 2 of Council Directive 2005/85/EC on minimum standards on procedures in Member States for granting and withdrawing refugee status.
3   A number of cases of such practices came to light in 1990; judicial review proceedings were settled after the grant of permission. Similarly, cases have come to light of stowaways being removed without being able to make contact with an immigration officer.
4   European Roma Rights Centre v Immigration Officer at Prague Airport [2004] UKHL 55, [2005] 2 WLR 1. See **12.9** above.
5   See **12.114** below.
6   HC 395, para 328.
7   IAA 1999, s 141 gives power to fingerprint inter alia asylum seekers: s 141(7)(e); their dependants: s 141(7)(f) and 141(14); and anyone else without a valid passport or a reasonable excuse: s 141(7)(a), (10). Home Office policy is to fingerprint all asylum seekers and their dependants who are over five: see Asylum screening and routing guidance: Fingerprinting (15 November 2013). Children must be fingerprinted in the presence of a responsible adult: ibid. The High Court has held that a policy of fingerprinting unaccompanied children whose identity is in doubt is lawful: *R v Secretary of State for the Home Department, ex p Tabed (Ahmed)* [1994] Imm AR 468. See **12.118** below.
8   The purpose of screening is firstly, at stage one, to establish the claimant's 'bio-data' (identity, nationality etc), travel history and documentation, health, basis of claim summary and security screening; and secondly, at stage two, to establish family background: see the API on Registering an Asylum Application in the United Kingdom, 12 October 2009, at section 6.
9   EU Directive 2003/9 on reception conditions for asylum seekers (OJ 2003 L31/18); see HC 395, Part 11B (paras 357–361), inserted by HC 194, in effect from 4 February 2005, requiring the Secretary of State to provide information about the asylum procedure within 15 days of the claim, and a document indicating the asylum claimant's status within three days if possible.

12.112 After screening there are different procedures that may be followed.[1] Applicants[2] who are liable to immigration detention[3] who are thought to have straightforward claims[4] may be sent to Harmondsworth or another Removal Centre and subjected to super 'fast-track' procedures (the Detained Fast Track (DFT) with induction on the day of arrival, a full asylum interview the next day, a decision the day or so after and an appeal within three days).[5] The fast-track procedure is used for 'in-country' as well as port cases. A challenge to the inherent unfairness of these procedures was dismissed by the Administrative Court in *R (on the application of the Refugee Legal Centre) v Secretary of State for the Home Department*.[6] Whilst Collins J recognised the real concerns of those working under the scheme that it had the potential for unfairness and that anything faster would be impossible to justify, he was satisfied that the scheme was flexible enough to cater for individual difficulties, and was not unlawful. The Court of Appeal upheld the decision, but told the Home Office it must formulate a policy setting out the criteria for departing from the three-day timetable, to ensure that the timetable was in truth 'guidance and not a straitjacket'.[7] More recently, Ouseley J found that although the 'DFT' policy is not unlawful in its terms, the process is not as focussed on the fair presentation of the claim as it should be throughout and that the shortcomings at various stages require the early instruction of lawyers to advise and prepare the claim, and to seek referrals for those who may need them, with sufficient time before the substantive interview. He concluded that this is the crucial failing in the process as operated and that it is sufficiently significant that the DFT as operated carries with it too high a risk of unfair determinations for those who may be vulnerable applicants.[8] Applicants who are not subject to the DFT may simply be given a Statement of Evidence form to complete and return within 10 working days.[9] On return of the form, if asylum is not granted an interview will be fixed for five days ahead, and a decision will be taken immediately after that.

[1] Procedures are subject to fairly regular change, as the UKBA frequently devises and runs pilot schemes.

[2] Originally the fast track was used only for single males. However, the description 'single males' did not preclude the use of the procedure to process those with family ties in the UK, although as a matter of policy, those with family members dependent on the claim would not be so processed: *R (on the application of Kpandang) v Secretary of State for the Home Department* [2004] EWHC 2130 (Admin), [2004] All ER (D) 555 (Jul). However, accommodation for asylum claimants must have regard to family unity, and to the special needs of vulnerable people: see the Asylum Seekers (Reception Conditions) Regulations 2005, SI 2005/7, made to comply with the EU Reception Directive 2003/9/EC. From May 2005, the fast track was extended to include women who could be detained at Yarls Wood.

[3] See CHAPTER 18 on immigration detention. Port applicants and illegal entrants are liable to be detained under immigration powers.

[4] Asylum Process Guidance: Detained Fast Track Processes, 11 June 2013 (formerly titled: 'DFT [Detained Fast Track] & DNSA [Detained Non-Suspensive Appeal] – Intake Selection (AIU Instruction)'). 'An applicant may enter into or remain in DFT/DNSA processes only if there is a power in immigration law to detain, and only if on consideration of the known facts relating to the applicant and their case obtained at asylum screening (and, where relevant, subsequently), it appears that a quick decision is possible, and none of the Detained Fast Track Suitability Exclusion Criteria apply.' The suitability exclusion criteria are listed at section 2.3 and include, pregnant (24 weeks) women; family cases (with caveats); applicants with certain physical and or mental disabilities that render them unsuitable; applicants in respect to whom there has been a reasonable grounds decision taken (and maintained) by a competent authority stating that the applicant is a potential victim of trafficking or where there has been a conclusive decision taken by a competent authority stating that the applicant is a victim of trafficking; applicants in respect of whom there is independent evidence of torture. Assignment to the fast track should not be a once and for all decision; the Home Office is bound to maintain a continuous assessment of suitability for the fast track and to remove a person from the fast track if evidence suggests he or she is no longer suitable. See also the Asylum Instruction on Detained Fast Track Processes Timetable Flexibility.

[5] See Asylum and Immigration Tribunal (Fast Track Procedure) Rules 2005, SI 2005/560. The list of removal centres to which claimants assigned to the fast track may be sent is at Sch 2. Note that in DNSA (see fn 4 above) there is no suspensive or in-country right of appeal (see 12.167 below). For DNSA cases, the indicative timescale from entry to the process in the appropriate Immigration Removal Centre (IRC) to decision service will be around 10-14 days: see *Asylum Process Guidance: Detained Fast Track Processes*, 11 June 2013, section 2.2.2.

[6] [2004] EWHC 684 (Admin), [2004] All ER (D) 580 (Mar).

[7] [2004] EWCA Civ 1481, [2004] All ER (D) 201 (Nov). Accordingly, the Home Office produced 'Detained Fast Track Processes Operational Instruction', 26 April 2005. Now see fn 4 above.

[8] *Detention Action v Secretary of State for the Home Department (Equality Human Rights Commission intervening)* [2014] EWHC 2245 (Admin).

[9] The deadline is impossibly tight given that most asylum seekers who are not detained are dispersed all over the country for asylum support, with inadequate infrastructure of legal, linguistic or medical expertise to assist in completing the Statement of Evidence forms. The Home Office has refused to allow more time, however (although immigration officers have a discretion to extend time), and is adamant that the forms can be completed without legal assistance. They must be completed in full and in English, and returned with translations of all evidence relied on. See further API 'Non-compliance' (15 November 2013).

12.113 Port asylum claimants will either be detained[1] or granted temporary admission[2] pending consideration of the claim. Temporary admission is given by immigration officers at ports to allow applicants physically to enter the UK while their application is being dealt with.[3] The Home Office guidelines on detention[4] stress that this is used only where there is no alternative and there are good grounds for believing that the person will not keep in touch voluntarily. However, in *R (on the application of Saadi) v Secretary of State for the Home Department*,[5] detention for seven to ten days of persons not likely to abscond in order to determine their claims was upheld as lawful by the House of Lords.[6] For those not facing detention at such facilities, factors, which will be considered when deciding whether or not to detain, include whether there is a sponsor, satisfactory evidence of identity and past immigration history, and whether detention is available. For detailed consideration of detention, see CHAPTER 18 below.

[1]   The power to detain is generally exercisable by immigration officers pursuant to Immigration Act 1971, Sch 2, para 16, although the Secretary of State has wide detention powers pursuant to NIAA 2002, s 62 since 10 February 2003 (SI 2003/1). To comply with art 5 of the ECHR (right to liberty) the power must not be exercised arbitrarily and may only be exercised 'to prevent unauthorised entry into the country' or 'pending deportation', with rigorous judicial scrutiny: *Amuur v France* (1996) 22 EHRR 533. But see *R (on the application of Saadi) v Secretary of State for the Home Department* below. See further Blake 'The international principles governing detention of asylum seekers' in Blake and Fransman (eds) *A guide to the Human Rights Act 1998* (1999); see CHAPTER 18 below.

[2]   The power to grant temporary admission as an alternative to detention is governed by Immigration Act 1971, Sch 2, para 21.

[3]   Immigration Act 1971, s 11. This fiction means that a person can be refused 'leave to enter' after living in the UK for years, something which, in the context of EC law, was not acceptable: see *R (on the application of Yiadom) v Secretary of State for the Home Department* Case C-357/98 [2001] All ER (EC) 267, ECJ; see further **6.180** above.

[4]   API 'Handling claims', under the heading 'Use of detention' refers to Chapter 55 of the Enforcement Instructions and Guidance, as to which see CHAPTER 18.

[5]   [2002] UKHL 41, [2002] 4 All ER 785, [2002] 1 WLR 3131. This case emanated from the Oakington process to which previous editions of this book refer. The Oakington Immigration Reception Centre was closed in November 2010.

[6]   The HL decision was upheld by four votes to three as regards Article 5(1)(f) of the ECHR by a chamber of the European Court of Human Rights in *Saadi v United Kingdom* (2007) 44 EHRR 1005 and further upheld by 11 votes to 6 by the Grand Chamber of the European Court of Human Rights in *Saadi v United Kingdom* (2008) 47 EHRR 427.

12.114 Asylum applicants who are not detained at Harmondsworth (or one of the other fast-track processing centres) will be given an application registration card which may be used to access services provided for them as asylum seekers.[1] Temporary admission[2] may be made subject to residence[3] and reporting[4] conditions. Those granted temporary admission will be referred to the National Asylum Support Service (NASS) for assistance if they appear destitute. Home Office policy enabling asylum seekers to work if their claim remained outstanding for more than six months[5] was abolished in July 2002, in the belief that it encouraged economic migrants to come to the UK as asylum seekers.[6] The prohibition on employment was considered in *R (on the application of Q)*.[7] Pursuant to the provisions of Article 11 of the EU Reception Directive,[8] asylum claimants who are not EEA nationals may apply to work if the application is outstanding for more than a year.[9] However, asylum seekers are restricted to taking employment which on the Home Office list of shortage occupations.[10] A person making a subsequent asylum application, in the same Member State in which he or she has been previously refused asylum with appeal rights exhausted, falls within the ambit of the Reception Directive and so can enjoy the benefits of Article 11, even though the subsequent application has not been recognised as such by the Secretary of State.[11] Non-EAA asylum claimants may not work without an application registration card (ARC) endorsed with permission to work.[12]

[1] NIAA 2002, s 70. For the application registration card (ARC) see **12.116** below.

[2] See 2.14 fn 2 above.

[3] Immigration Act 1971, Sch 2, para 21(2), (2B)ff; Asylum Support Regulations 2000, SI 2000/704. Asylum seekers may be prohibited from living in certain areas, as well as being directed to stay in particular accommodation. See further Chapter 14 below.

[4] Immigration Act 1971, Sch 2, para 21(2).

[5] The policy is set out in the decision of the Court of Appeal in *R v Secretary of State for the Home Department, ex p Jammeh* [1998] INLR 701 at 713H–714A.

[6] The policy was abolished on 23 July 2002.

[7] *R (on the application of Q) v Secretary of State for the Home Department* [2003] EWCA Civ 364, [2004] QB 36, [2003] All ER 905. Considering whether denial of support under s 55 of the 2002 Act constituted 'treatment' for art 3 ECHR, the court held at para 57: 'The imposition by the legislature of a regime which prohibits asylum seekers from working and further prohibits the grant to them, when they are destitute, of support amounts to positive action directed against asylum seekers and not to mere inaction'.

[8] Council Directive 2003/9 on minimum standards for the reception of asylum seekers, OJ 2003 L 31/18, art 11.

[9] Transposed domestically by HC 395, para 360, inserted by HC 194 from 4 February 2005 and amended by Cm 7929 from 9 September 2010 (see fn 11 below). Note that following amendment on 9 September 2010 the Rules, now paras 360 to 360B, purport to limit employment only be taken up in a post which is, at the time an offer of employment is accepted, included on the list of shortage occupations published by the UKBA (as that list is amended from time to time) and prohibit both self-employment and engagement in setting up a business.

[10] HC 395, para 360A and Asylum Policy Instruction 'Permission to Work', 1 April 2014. The restrictions on the occupations that asylum seekers' are permitted to engage in were held to be compatible with art 11 of the Reception Directive (Council Directive 2003/9/EC) and art 8 of the ECHR in *R (Negassi and Lutalo) v Secretary of State for the Home Department* [2013] EWCA Civ 151 and *R (on the application of Rostami) v Secretary of State for the Home Department* [2013] EWHC 1494 (Admin).

[11] *R (on the application of ZO (Somalia)) v Secretary of State for the Home Department* [2010] UKSC 36, [2010] 1 WLR 1948, [2010] 4 All ER 649, [2010] INLR 503. See now amendments to the Immigration Rules, HC 395, paras 360C to 360E as inserted by Cm 7929 from 9 September 2010 – see also fn 9 above regarding limitations.

[12] API 'Application Registration Card' para 4.3.

Applications made in-country

12.115 Asylum applications may be made by applying for variation of a leave already granted[1] (eg as a visitor or a student), or on apprehension as an illegal entrant,[2] or by someone facing removal for overstaying or breach of conditions. An in-country application must be made in person at a place designated by the Secretary of State.[3] In-country claims are screened at an ASU, sometimes immediately when the application is submitted.[4] Then, if the claimant is not detained for fast-track determination at Harmondsworth or Yarl's Wood or one of the other Immigration Removal Centres[5] he or she will be given a Statement of Evidence form to complete and return within ten working days.[6] Applicants are normally interviewed before a decision is taken on their application (unless it is refused on non-compliance grounds or unless there is already enough information on file to warrant a grant of refugee status).[7] There was previously no power to detain someone with leave to enter who applied for asylum, but since February 2003, the Secretary of State can impose restrictions on such asylum seekers as if they were on temporary admission, and can detain them for failure to comply with any such restrictions.[8] Moreover, an asylum claim made shortly after entry as a visitor or a student may result in an interview under caution and a decision to treat the applicant as an illegal entrant, who may be detained.[9] The previous provision for curtailment of leave on refusal of an asylum claim has been dropped.[10] The power to detain illegal entrants and those facing removal as overstayers or deportation is not affected by the making of an asylum claim which precludes immediate removal,[11] but must not be exercised capriciously, unreasonably or contrary to policy.[12] Since 1996 there has been a right to apply for bail pending removal.[13]

[1] Such an application to vary existing leave to enter or remain, on the basis of a claim for asylum, is fee exempt: see the Immigration and Nationality (Fees) Regulations 2014, SI 2014/922, which provide in Sch 1, Table 4 that no fee is payable (inter alia) in respect of an art 3 or Refugee Convention application.

[2] Those apprehended as illegal entrants at ports are generally treated as in-country applicants.

[3] Under the NIAA 2002, this is not a requirement so much as part of the definition of an asylum seeker for different purposes: see s 18(1)(c) (accommodation centres), s 44(2) (amending definition in IAA 1999, s 94 (asylum support), 70(3) (induction centres), s 113(1) (appeals). On 13 October 2009, the Minister of State for Borders and Immigration reiterated the expectation that individuals make their claims for asylum at a port of entry and announced that from 14 October 2009 initial asylum claims made in-country have to be made in person at the Asylum Screening Unit in Croydon. Furthermore, persons seeking to make further submissions, in the hope that the same will be treated as a fresh claim for asylum are required from 14 October 2009 to make them by appointment and in person at Liverpool Further Submissions Unit, if they originally claimed asylum before 5 March 2007, or at a specified reporting centre in their region, if they originally claimed asylum on or after 5 March 2007.

[4] See fn 3 above. This involves fingerprinting, giving details for the Application Registration Card, and perhaps being interviewed to establish why the claim was not made earlier, to decide whether support should be withheld, see Ch 13.

[5] See **12.112** above.

[6] See **12.112** fn 13 above.

[7] See API 'Handling Claims' under the heading 'substantive interviews'.

[8] By Nationality, Immigration and Asylum Act 2002, s 71 (in force on 10 February 2003: SI 2003/1).

[9] Immigration Act 1971, Sch 2, para 16. Note the power to detain on suspicion of illegal entry in para 16(2). During the interview of known or suspected illegal entrants, questions will be asked to ascertain whether deception was used: API 'Illegal entry'. There is nothing unfair about the same immigration officer conducting both an illegal entry interview and an asylum interview: *R v Secretary of State for the Home Department, ex p Range* [1991] Imm AR 505, QBD; see also *Odishu (Yousuf) v Secretary of State for the Home Department* [1994] Imm AR 475, CA. But in the Scottish case of *Kim (Sofia) v Secretary of State for the Home Department* 2000 SLT 249, OHCS, an asylum interview which turned into an illegal entry interview without a caution being administered was held inadmissible to prove illegal entry.

[10] Asylum and Immigration Appeals Act 1993, s 7. The power remains to curtail leave by variation (Immigration Act 1971 s 3(3)(a)) where an asylum claim is inconsistent with the purpose for which leave was granted: see HC 395, para 323. See API, 'Curtailment of limited leave in cases where an asylum or human rights application is refused'.

[11] *R v Secretary of State for the Home Department, ex p Khan* [1995] Imm AR 348, [1995] NLJR 216, CA.

[12] *Vilvaraja (Nadarajah) v Secretary of State for the Home Department* (1987) Times, 31 October, [1990] Imm AR 457; see also *R v Governor of Haslar Prison, ex p Egbe* (1991) Times, 4 June. For current detention policy see CHAPTER 18.

[13] Immigration Act 1971, Sch 2, para 22(1)(b), as amended by Asylum and Immigration Act 1996, Sch 2, para 11.

Application registration card

12.116 The EU Reception Directive requires asylum claimants and their dependants (except for those in detention) to be issued within three working days with a document showing their status and identity.[1] Asylum claimants (except for EU nationals),[2] whether port or in-country, and their dependants,[3] are now issued with an application registration card (ARC), an electronic card which carries their personal details,[4] and is used to identify asylum-seekers, for access support, to prove entitlement to work (where applicable) and to facilitate reporting.[5] An ARC is issued after screening, from specified ports and reporting centres.[6] Detained asylum seekers are not issued with an ARC unless they are released.[7] The 2002 Act has created eight new criminal offences connected with forgery or possession of false registration cards.[8]

[1]   Council Directive 2003/9/EC of 27 January 2003 (12.109 fn 8 above), in force February 2005, now implemented by the Immigration Rules, HC 395, paras 359–359C.
[2]   API 'Application registration card', July 2006, para 3.2. The ARC replaces the Standard Acknowledgement Letter (SAL). A SAL may still be used to acknowledge a claim for asylum where it is not possible to issue an ARC within three days of the claim being lodged, although any SAL issued will normally be valid for just two months from date of issue to enable arrangements to be made for the claimant and any dependants to be issued an ARC: see API 'Application registration card', July 2006, para 3.2.
[3]   All dependants have their own ARCs, even children under five. Since they cannot be fingerprinted, their ARC is endorsed 'CUF' (in this context, 'child under five'): API para 3.3.2.
[4]   The ARC fields are set out in Annex A to the API 'Application registration card'. Five fields are 'reserved' for unspecified information.
[5]   See Immigration Act 1971, s 26A (inserted by Nationality, Immigration and Asylum Act 2002, s 148); API 'Application registration card' para 2.1, 4. The API suggest that the ARC will be the only approved means of proving entitlement to support. Production of the ARC may also be a formal requirement for reporting, and from 1 May 2004 the ARC endorsed with permission to work must be shown to prospective employers.
[6]   API 'Application registration card para 3.1. The places of issue are set out in Annex C and include Dover SEPST, Gatwick, Stansted, Heathrow (Terminals 1–4), Croydon (Lunar House), Liverpool (Reliance House), Oakington and the reporting centres at Croydon (Electric House), Glasgow, Leeds, Manchester, North Shields, Solihull and Folkestone.
[7]   API ibid para 3.2.
[8]   See Immigration Act 1971, s 26A(3), as inserted by NIAA 2002, s 148 and see **1.73** below.

Special cases

12.117 We have referred above to the change in policy so as to generally make it not possible to claim asylum from abroad.[1] Nonetheless the 'Gateway Protection Programme' is operated by UK Visas and Immigration in partnership with the UNHCR and its purpose is to allow for the resettlement of the most vulnerable refugees in the UK on an annual quota basis.[2] Mandate refugees (ie refugees recognised by UNHCR abroad) may claim asylum in the UK based upon a fear of persecution in the country of origin, and/or a claim based on a fear of persecution in the country in which they were recognised as refugees under UNHCR's mandate.[3] The prior recognition of refugee status by the UNHCR is not determinative of the asylum claim, nor does it create a presumption or shift the burden of proof; rather UNHCR's suggested approach to reliance upon their own decisions was commended by the Supreme Court: that there should be departure from their view only for cogent reasons previously unavailable or where new information was before the state decision-maker which directly affects the assessment of the claim for refugee status, including where reliable information was available that material

1071

elements of the account were not credible, so long as that a claim should not be rejected unless the person's credibility is undermined by a source other than their own account.[4] Applications for transfer of refugee status have been considered above.[5] Applications made in the UK from persons currently exempt from control (eg diplomats or consular staff) are dealt with as special cases,[6] as are claims by EU nationals.[7]

[1] At 12.110 above.
[2] See Home Office website for guidance on the 'Gateway Protection Programme' (the API is currently not available). Such refugees may have legal or physical protection needs; be a survivor of violence or torture; be a woman at risk; lack local integration prospects; or be elderly and in a situation that makes them particularly vulnerable. The programme provides for up to 750 refugees to settle in the UK each year, and is completely separate from the standard procedure for claiming asylum in the UK. Applications for resettlement under this programme are made to the UNHCR, who refers them to the UKBA.
[3] API 'Mandate Refugees', 1 June 2012. This replaced previous policy that provided for the possibility of mandate refugees being permitted to come to the UK from abroad where they could demonstrate close ties with the UK, usually through close family, but sometimes through historical connections with the UK: see *ST v Secretary of State for the Home Department* [2014] EWCA Civ 188, the preservation of absolute flexibility was a perfectly rational and lawful way in which to express policy, in circumstances where there is no legal obligation to admit any refugees from outside the UK at all.
[4] *IA v Secretary of State for the Home Department (Scotland)* [2014] UKSC 6. See also the API 'Mandate Refugees', 1 June 2012.
[5] See **12.104** above.
[6] API 'Exempt Persons'.
[7] Claims from EU nationals may be entertained, but will be presumed clearly unfounded: see API 'Claims from EU Nationals'; and **12.108** above.

Children

12.118 There are special provisions[1] for dealing with claims by children, both accompanied and unaccompanied.[2] A child is defined as a person who is under 18 or who, in the absence of documentary evidence, appears to be under that age.[3] An unaccompanied asylum seeking child is a child applying for asylum in his or her own right who is separated from both parents and not being cared for by an adult who by law or custom has responsibility to care for the child.[4] When an unaccompanied child comes to the attention of immigration officers at the port or at the asylum unit at the Home Office, or where a child becomes unaccompanied during the asylum process (by being abandoned or taken into care, for example) UKBA staff are required to notify the Refugee Council's non-statutory Panel of Advisers,[5] whose members act as a 'friend' to the child in his or her dealings with the Home Office and other central and local government agencies. The Secretary of State must also take measures to ensure that an unaccompanied asylum seeking child is represented in connection with the asylum claim.[6] It is also UKBA's responsibility to ensure that all unaccompanied children who apply for asylum who are not already in the care of Social Services are referred to the responsible Social Services Department as soon as they have made their claim.[7] The UKBA will also inform the local authority of concerns they may have about the suitability of the child's guardian or about other concerns relating to current or future abuse; the quality of support the child is receiving; where the child is being looked after by someone other than parents; where there are concerns that the family is not meeting the child's developmental needs and trafficking.[8] The Secretary of State has an obligation to endeavour to trace the family members of an unaccompanied asylum seeking child as soon as possible after the asylum claim is made.[9] Discharge of the obligation is a necessary element in the determination of an asylum claim,[10] but the legal consequences of failure by the Secretary of State to discharge the obligation depend on the demonstrable effects of the failure on the asylum claim given the facts of the particular case.[11] Where there are disputes over age, the Panel will be informed without prejudice, even if the application is proceeded with as for an adult.[12] Applications from children (accompanied or not) receive priority at all stages[13] and their claims will be decided by caseworkers trained to deal with asylum claims from children.[14] It will rarely be acceptable to hold an application from an unaccompanied child with no action on it for longer than six months.[15] Accompanied or unaccompanied children over the age of 12 will be interviewed about the substance of their asylum claim or to determine their age and identity unless unfit or unable to be interviewed;[16] discretion should be used on whether to interview in cases where the child is younger especially if the child is mature and, if given the option, is willing to be interviewed.[17] Interviews must be conducted by a specially trained case owner in the presence of an appropriate adult,[18] and the rules provide that interviewers must be sensitive to distress or tiredness, and if necessary stop the interview.[19] The child's legal representative has the right to be present at the interview and to ask questions and make comments in the interview.[20] Interviewing a child in breach of those procedural requirements would not render the interview inadmissible as evidence, but would necessitate the exercise of a considerable degree of caution by the decision maker before relying against the child on any answers that he or she gave.[21] The Guidance to case workers says that the files of family members or guardians who have made asylum claims should be obtained by the caseworker and there should be a check for any visa application on the UKBA's 'Central Reference System'.[22] Particular care is needed in assessing the evidence of minors, taking account of 'child specific factors such as the child's age, maturity and a more liberal application of the benefit of the doubt is called for.[23] In assessing an application from a child (whether accompanied or not) more weight should be given to objective indications of risk than to the child's state of mind. An asylum application from or on behalf of a child should not be refused solely because the child is too young to understand his or her situation or to have formed a fear of persecution.[24] The Administrative Court has emphasised the importance of making special provision for determining asylum claims by children and held that failure by the Secretary of State to apply his own guidelines made the decision on a child's claim unlawful.[25]

[1] The Borders, Citizenship and Immigration Act 2009, s 55 requires that the Secretary of State must make arrangements for ensuring that any of his or her own functions or those of immigration officers in relation to immigration, asylum or nationality are discharged having regard to the need to safeguard and promote the welfare of children who are in the UK. There is presently no API relating to children, nor an API on dependants. Reference should be made to the Asylum Process Guidance – 'Processing an asylum application from a child' and APU Notice 3/2007 'Amendment to Discretionary Leave Policy relating to Asylum Seeking Children' (on the APIs section of the website) For best practice as regards children see Heaven Crawley and others Working with children and young people subject to immigration control – guidelines for best practice, ILPA November 2004. See further CHAPTER 11.

[2] HC 395, paras 349, 350–352; Unaccompanied Minors Best Practice, reflecting the concerns expressed in the UNHCR *Handbook* **12.13** above, paras 213–219.

[3] HC 395, para 349. For assessment of age, see **12.120** below.

[4] Asylum Process Guidance – 'Processing an asylum application from a child'. See also *AA (Afghanistan) v Secretary of State for the Home Department* [2007] EWCA Civ 12.

5   Asylum Process Guidance – 'Processing an asylum application from a child'. Ministers agreed to fund this panel on a non-statutory basis during the passage of the Asylum and Immigration Appeals Act 1993, to reflect the guidance in para 214 of the UNHCR *Handbook*.

6   HC 395, para 352ZA, as inserted from 1 December 2007 by HC 82 to give effect to Article 17(1) of Council Directive 2005/85/EC on minimum standards on procedures in Member States for granting and withdrawing refugee status.

7   Asylum Process Guidance – 'Processing an asylum application from a child'. Unaccompanied children are referred to the Social Services Department covering the area of the address the child gives or if the child has no established connection with the particular local authority area, with the local authority for the port or asylum screening location where the claim is made.

8   Asylum Process Guidance – 'Processing an asylum application from a child'.

9   Council Directive 2003/9/EC laying down minimum standards for the reception of asylum seekers ('the Reception Directive'), art 19, implemented by the Asylum Seekers (Reception Conditions) Regulations 2005, SI 2005/7, reg 6 and *DS (Afghanistan) v Secretary of State for the Home Department* [2011] EWCA Civ 305; *HK (Afghanistan) (by their litigation friend) v Secretary of State for the Home Department* [2012] EWCA Civ 315 and *KA (Afghanistan) v Secretary of State for the Home Department* [2012] EWCA Civ 1014.

10   *HK (Afghanistan) v Secretary of State for the Home Department* [2012] EWCA Civ 315.

11   See for example, *HK (Afghanistan) v Secretary of State for the Home Department* [2012] EWCA Civ 315; *EU (Afghanistan) v Secretary of State for the Home Department* [2013] EWCA Civ 32; *AA (Afghanistan) v Secretary of State for the Home Department* [2013] EWCA Civ 1625.

12   API Aug 00, Ch 2, s 5, para 3.9 (no longer current: see fn 1 above).

13   HC 395, para 350.

14   HC 395, para 352, as amended to give effect to Article 17(4)(b).

15   API Aug 00, Ch 2, s 5, para 3.9 (no longer current). Asylum Process Guidance – 'Processing an asylum application from a child' in its 'process map' envisages decisions being made within 36 days of the date of application.

16   HC 395, para 352 and Asylum Process Guidance – 'Processing an asylum application from a child' at section 13.2. Previously, the rules leant against interviewing children unless it was impossible to obtain sufficient information to determine the claim from other sources; in *Orman* [1998] Imm AR 224 the Tribunal doubted the wisdom of this approach and suggested that a preferable course would be to allow the child to be interviewed with the Panel adviser.

17   Asylum Process Guidance – 'Processing an asylum application from a child' at section 13.2.

18   An adult who is independent of the Secretary of State and who has responsibility for the child: HC 395, para 352 and Asylum Process Guidance – 'Processing an asylum application from a child'. There should be no adverse reliance on interviews conducted in the absence of a responsible adult, either in assessing the claim or on appeal: *Ehalaivan* (00TH01749) (3 August 2000, unreported), IAT; *Omotayo* (00TH00854) (12 April 2000, unreported), IAT.

19   HC 395, para 352. The rules require close attention to be paid to the welfare of the child at all times: ibid para 351.

20   HC 395, para 352ZA (see fn 6 above).

21   *R (on the application of AN (a child) and FA (a child)) v Secretary of State for the Home Department* [2012] EWCA Civ 1636 and *JA (Afghanistan) v Secretary of State for the Home Department* [2014] EWCA Civ 450.

22   Asylum Process Guidance – 'Processing an asylum application from a child' at sections 13.6 and 14.

23   The principle set out in UNHCR *Handbook*, para 219 (see **12.13** above), now incorporated in Asylum Process Guidance – 'Processing an asylum application from a child' in section 15.4.

24   HC 395, para 351 and Asylum Process Guidance – 'Processing an asylum application from a child' at section 15.2.

25   *R (on the application of Mlloja) v Secretary of State for the Home Department* [2005] EWHC 2833 (Admin), [2005] All ER (D) 234 (Nov), Gibbs J.

12.119 No unaccompanied child will be removed from the UK unless there are adequate reception and care arrangements in the country to which he or she is to be removed.[1] The same policy applies where the parent or guardian of an accompanied asylum seeking child cannot be removed with him or her.[2] The Immigration Rules provide for leave to remain to be granted to an unaccompanied child under the age of 171/2 who has been refused asylum and humanitarian protection if there are not adequate reception arrangements in the country to which the child would be returned and the child would not be excluded from a grant of refugee status or humanitarian protection; is not a danger to the security of the UK; has not been convicted of a particularly serious crime and is not subject to deportation proceedings.[3] Leave should be granted to a qualifying child for 30 months or until the child is 171/2, whichever is the shorter period.[4] A child formerly treated as another asylum seeker's dependant may make a claim for asylum at any time. Delay on the part of a child in making a claim for asylum will be taken into account in assessing credibility but in doing so the case worker must be aware that there may be legitimate reasons why the child failed to apply earlier.[5] If an unaccompanied child was granted more than one year's leave, the UKBA caseowner should contact the child and the child's social worker or guardian before expiry of the leave to 'discuss available options'.[6] An application for further leave to remain by a child should be treated as an asylum and human rights application; the 'fresh claims' rule (para 353 of the Immigration Rules) should not be applied and the child's eligibility for asylum, humanitarian protection or discretionary leave should be assessed. However, consideration may be given to certification of the claim as 'clearly unfounded' under the Nationality, Immigration and Asylum Act 2002, s 94. The child should be interviewed if he or she was not interviewed in connection with the original asylum claim or if the caseowner thinks an interview would produce further information that would assist in making a decision.[7]

[1] Asylum Process Guidance – 'Processing an asylum application from a child' in section 17.7. In *AA (Afghanistan) v Secretary of State for the Home Department* [2007] EWCA Civ 12 the Tribunal had erred in law in holding that it was sufficient for there to be a reasonable likelihood that the returned child would be adequately received. It was for the Secretary of State to be satisfied that there would be adequate reception arrangements.

[2] APU Notice 3/2007, Amendment to Discretionary Leave Policy relating to Asylum Seeking Children. For background see *Re Sujon Miah* (CO 3391/1994) (6 December 1994, unreported); API Aug 00, Ch 2, s 5, para 3.5 (not current). See also the recommendation given by the Tribunal in *Afrifa* (18392) (24 March 2000, unreported), that before removal of the appellant whose asylum appeal it had rejected, International Social Services, International Red Cross and the British High Commission be asked to report on reception and care arrangements.

[3] HC 395, para. 352ZC, inserted by HC 1039 with effect from 6.4.2013. Prior to that, similar provision was made for UASCs in APU Notice 3/2007 and Asylum Process Guidance – 'Processing an asylum application from a child' in section 17.7. For the consequences of a breach by the Secretary of State of the policy to grant discretionary leave to such unaccompanied children who have claimed asylum, see *AA (Afghanistan) v Secretary of State for the Home Department* [2007] EWCA Civ 12 and *SL (Vietnam) v Secretary of State for the Home Department* [2010] EWCA Civ 225.

[4] HC 395, para. 352ZE.

[5] Asylum Process Guidance – 'Processing an asylum application from a child'.

[6] 'Active Review of Unaccompanied Asylum Seeking Children Discretionary Leave', 26 October 2009.

[7] See fn 6 above.

12.120 The determination of age is controversial. The Home Office's policy on age assessment is now set out in some detail in the Asylum Process Guidance – 'Assessing Age' which can be found on the UKBA website. In principle the burden is on the applicant to demonstrate that he or she is a minor, but the policy of the Home Office is to dispute the age of an applicant only if the person's 'physical appearance and/or general demeanour very strongly suggests that they are aged 18 or over' and there is no other persuasive evidence to establish the claimed age.[1] In borderline cases, the policy is to give the applicant the benefit of the doubt and treat him or her as a child.[2] The issue of age determination was thoroughly explored in *R (on the application of B) v Merton London Borough Council*[3] and age assessments should now be '*Merton* compliant'.[4] In *Merton* Stanley Burnton J noted that in the light of the five-year margin of error described by paediatricians, objectively verifiable determination of age for those between 16 and 20 was impossible.[5] He considered local authorities' guidelines for age assessment[6] and concluded that in general, in order to assess age it was important to elicit a history from the applicant, including family circumstances, education, activities and ethnic and cultural information. If the history is accepted as true and is consistent with an age below 18, the applicant will be accepted as a child, while an untrue history is not necessarily indicative of lies about age but would be relevant.[7] He held that the burden of proof was not helpful.[8] Reasons would always be required for a decision that an applicant was not a child, because of the consequences.[9] Such reasons would have to explain why the authority disagreed with expert evidence relied on by the applicant.[10] An age assessment may be challenged on procedural grounds such as factual error, lack of expertise of the personnel conducting them, or a failure to achieve *Merton* compliance.[11] Alternatively, challenges may be made on substantive grounds because the decision on real age is ultimately one for the court.[12] It is Home Office policy to give considerable weight to the findings of age made by local authority social workers, recognising their particular expertise through working with children and in cases where the social worker's assessment is the only source of information about the person's age, their assessment will normally be accepted as the decisive evidence of the person's age.[13] An applicant claiming to be under 18 must not be placed in the detained fast track process or allocated to Oakington unless there is credible, clear documentary evidence that the person is over 18 or a Merton compliant age assessment by a local authority establishing that the applicant is over 18 or the applicant's physical appearance or general demeanour very strongly indicates that the person is significantly over 18 and there is no credible evidence to the contrary.[14] Even if the Home Office disputes the applicant's age, his or her asylum claim should be dealt with in accordance with the procedures for considering claims by children until satisfactory evidence establishes that the person is an adult or it is considered that physical appearance or demeanour very strongly suggests the person is significantly over 18.[15]

---

[1]   In cases of dispute the court must decide itself whether a person is a child on the balance of probabilities and is not limited to a *Wednesbury* style review of the Secretary of State's decision on the matter: see *R (on the application of A) v Croydon London Borough Council* [2009] UKSC 8.

[2]   Asylum Process Guidance – 'Assessing Age'. Stanley Burnton J in *R (on the application of B) v Merton London Borough Council* [2003] EWHC 1689 (Admin), [2003] 4 All ER 280 held that except in clear cases, age could not be determined solely on the basis of appearance (para 37). See also **11.122** above. Collins J in the Administrative Court in *R (on the application of A) v Croydon London Borough Council* [2009] EWHC 939 (Admin): '[9] . . . the approach adopted by the Secretary of State that, if the decision maker is left in doubt, the claimant should receive the benefit of that doubt is undoubtedly proper'.

[3]   *R (on the application of B) v Merton London Borough Council* (fn 1 above), at paras 22, 28. See also *R (on the application of T) v Enfield London Borough Council* [2004] EWHC 2297 (Admin), in which the local authority's age assessment was held woefully defective, based as it was largely on the applicant's demeanour and appearance during an 'unfair and unduly hostile' interview.

4   That is to say, compliant with the observations of Stanley Burnton J in *R (on the application of B) v Merton London Borough Council* (fn 1 above). See Collins J *in R (A) v London Borough of Croydon* [2009] EWHC 939 (Admin) at [13].

5   This case, and the evidence cited in it, should sound the death-knell for purely anthropometric assessments of age. There has been widespread concern over the reliability of such assessments, although in some cases it might still be appropriate as a purely voluntary matter, ancillary to the other methods of investigation. X-rays were held 'inappropriate' for use in age determination for immigration purposes only in July 1998 ADI (Ch 2, s 5, para 3.13); previously, 'bone-age testing' by X-ray was sometimes conducted at the behest of the immigration authorities in the context of family reunion applications from the Indian sub-continent.

6   The issue has become relevant for local authorities since they have duties under the Children Act 1989 to under-18s, but not to adults (except those leaving care).

7   *R (on the application of B) v Merton London Borough Council* (fn 1 above), at para 28.

8   *R (on the application of B) v Merton London Borough Council* (fn 1 above) at para 38.

9   *R (on the application of B) v Merton London Borough Council* (fn 1 above) at paras 45 et seq. The consequences vis-à-vis the Home Office might be the grant or withholding of discretionary leave; vis-à-vis the local authority, the grant or withholding of accommodation and support.

10 *R (on the application of C) v Merton London Borough Council* [2005] EWHC 1753 (Admin), [2005] 3 FCR 42, [2005] All ER (D) 221 (Jul).

11 See per Collins J in *R (A) v London Borough of Croydon* [2009] EWHC 939 (Admin) at paras 38 and 81.

12 See fn 1 above.

13 Asylum Process Guidance – 'Assessing Age'.

14 Asylum Process Guidance – 'Assessing Age'.

15 Asylum Process Guidance – 'Assessing Age'.

12.121 Any unaccompanied child who claims asylum must be referred either to the social services department for the area in which he or she lives or, if he or she has no address or local connection, to the department covering the area where the asylum claim was made.[1] The UKBA must also pass the child's details to the Refugee Council's Panel of Advisers within 24 hours of the claim being lodged, even if they are disputing that the person is a minor.[2] Despite what was said in the Government's White Paper *Every Child Matters*,[3] the Panel of Advisers is usually able to do no more than provide the child with the name and address of an immigration solicitor with an LSC contract and a referral to his or her local social services department. In addition, as the White Paper acknowledges, the Panel can only provide support to a minority of unaccompanied asylum seeking children.[4] This means that many unaccompanied minors are having to fend for themselves in relation to both the determination of their asylum or immigration application and their access to support.

1   ADI Unaccompanied Asylum Seeking Children Information Note, para 3.

2   Asylum Process Guidance – 'Processing an asylum application from a child', section 5.3. The Panel is funded by the Home Office to give initial advice to unaccompanied asylum seeking children but has no statutory status and neither central or local government is obliged to follow its recommendations.

3   *Every Child Matters* CM 5860 September 2003, para 2.53.

4   In 2002/2003, of 6,404 such children referred to the Panel only 1,500 were allocated a named adviser: statistics from the Refugee Council 2003.

12.122 UNHCR has recommended that each country which has ratified the Refugee Convention should establish an independent and formally accredited organisation which would provide each unaccompanied child with a guardian, who would ensure that the interests of the child were safeguarded at each stage of the process and that his or her legal, social, medical and psychological needs are appropriately met during the refugee status determination process and until a durable solution for the child has been found and implemented.[1] There is a presumption that unaccompanied children will be accommodated by their local authority under section 20 of the Children Act 1989,[2] which has led to unaccompanied asylum seeking children making up approximately 6% of all children looked after nationally by local authorities, many in London and the south east.[3]

[1] UNHCR *Guidelines on Policies and Procedures in dealing with Unaccompanied Children Seeking Asylum* para 5.7. It also recommends that 'as an unaccompanied asylum seeking child is not legally independent they should be represented by an adult who is familiar with his or her background and whose role it is to protect his or her interests': para 8.3. This is in addition to being provided with a qualified legal representative.
[2] Asylum Process Guidance – 'Processing an asylum application from a child', section 5.1.
[3] In November 2002, there were 4,872 unaccompanied asylum seeking children being supported by London local authorities. This fell to 4,266 by November 2003: Report to Leaders' Committee of the Association of London Government, 10.02.2004. Due to pressure on resources a number of the unaccompanied children being initially accommodated by authorities in London and the south east of England were then being placed outside these areas on an ad-hoc basis, many hundreds of miles from the social workers who were supposed to be responsible for them.

Investigation of asylum claims

12.123 As a result of the particular difficulties experienced by those fleeing persecution, and the likely lack of documentary evidence in support of claims, the UNHCR *Handbook*[1] indicates that the duty to ascertain and evaluate all the relevant facts is shared between the applicant and the examiner. The applicant should tell the truth and assist the examiner to the full in establishing the facts of his or her case, make an effort to support his or her statements by any available evidence, give a satisfactory explanation for any lack of evidence, and if necessary make an effort to procure additional evidence. He or she should supply as much detail as is necessary about him- or herself and should answer any questions put. The examiner should ensure that the applicant presents his or her case as fully as possible, with all available evidence; assess his or her credibility and evaluate the evidence, if necessary giving the applicant the benefit of the doubt, in order to establish the objective and subjective elements of the claim, and relate the elements to the relevant criteria of the Refugee Convention to arrive at a correct conclusion on the applicant's refugee status.[2] This guidance would suggest that all asylum claimants should be interviewed.

[1] 12.13 above, paras 195–205.
[2] UNHCR *Handbook* above, Summary, para 205.

12.124 The White Paper of July 1998[1] contained an undertaking to reduce the time taken on determination of asylum claims to a total of six months: two months for the initial determination and four months for the appeal. The commitment to reduce the time taken to determine asylum claims has been given even greater prominence in recent years by the fast-tracking of claims at the Harmondsworth and other Removal Centres. Previous delays of several years were unjust; they denied refugees the prompt determination of status which they deserved, and created difficulties for those who were ultimately found not to need international protection. But the implementation of the commitment to reduce delays has caused its own problems. The conditions under which asylum determination is now carried out in the UK – in particular, the pernicious combination of an overly ambitious and over-rigid timetable for determining claims and the dispersal or detention of asylum seekers (neither of which is conducive to clarity of recollection or articulation) – make compliance with the duties set out in the *Handbook* extremely difficult, if not impossible, for both the applicant and the examiner. As we have seen above, in many port cases applicants are detained and interviewed within a day or two of arrival,[2] and have no effective opportunity to submit evidence in support of the claim.[3] Many other applicants are sent hundreds of miles to areas where legal, medical, social and linguistic support is scarce and living conditions squalid, and are given 14 days to complete evidence forms in full and in English, obtain all relevant documents and get them translated. The tendency in recent years has been towards greater flexibility with time limits in non-detained cases.[4] The Immigration Rules provide for an asylum applicant or a person whose refugee status may be revoked to be allowed an 'effective opportunity' to consult a lawyer.[5] Notwithstanding all this, delay in the determination of asylum claims remains a significant problem.

[1] *Fairer, faster and firmer: a modern approach to immigration and asylum.*

[2] A wealth of evidence has been presented to the Home Office showing how exhaustion, fear, linguistic difficulties, confusion and unfamiliarity all combine to render on-arrival interviews less than comprehensive or reliable: see **12.172** below. The Home Office does not generally conduct a substantive asylum interview on the day of arrival, but overnight detention compounds the difficulties. The UNHCR *Handbook* **12.13** above, para 198 points out that non-disclosure at a first interview should not be held against the asylum seeker; see further below. Sedley LJ in *R (on the application of the Refugee Legal Centre) v Secretary of State for the Home Department* [2004] EWCA Civ 1481, [2005] 1 WLR 2219 said that, whether or not an asylum claimant was entitled to an appeal, a fair initial hearing and decision must be provided. The question had to be: 'Does the system provide a fair opportunity for the asylum seeker to put his case?' and held that the three-day timetable at Harmondsworth, while not inherently unfair, had to be used as 'guidance, not a straitjacket'. See also per Ouseley J in *Detention Action v Secretary of State for the Home Department (Equality Human Rights Commission intervening)* [2014] EWHC 2245 (Admin) regarding unfairness arising from lack of legal representation from the earliest stages: see 12.113 above.

[3] Non detained applicants are normally given five working days to submit further evidence: see API 'Asylum Interviews', 31 March 2014, at section 5.14. The API 'Medico-Legal Reports from the Helen Bamber Foundation and the Medical Foundation Medico-Legal Report Service', 17 January 2014, provides for greater flexibility where referral has been made for medical reports. See *R (on the application of the Refugee Legal Centre) v Secretary of State for the Home Department* above.

[4] See APIs 'Asylum Interviews', 31 March 2014, and 'Medico-Legal Reports from the Helen Bamber Foundation and the Medical Foundation Medico-Legal Report Service', 17 January 2014, above.

[5] HC 395, para 333B, implementing Article 15(1) of Council Directive 2005/85/EC on minimum standards on procedures in Member States for granting and withdrawing refugee status.

12.125 The Immigration Rules now contain an express requirement that the Secretary of State decides claims for asylum 'as soon as possible' and that where a decision cannot be taken within six months of the claim being recorded, the Secretary of State is to inform the applicant of the delay or, if asked to do so in writing, provide the applicant with information about the timeframe within which a decision can be expected.[1] Even without provision in the Immigration Rules as to the time within which a decision should be made it is implicit in the statute that claims should be dealt with within a reasonable time.[2] However, what is 'a reasonable time' depends on all of the circumstances including the volume of applications, the available resources to deal with them and the different needs and circumstances of different groups of asylum seekers.[3] A particular period cannot be specified as the limit of what is a reasonable time.[4] A rational policy, operated fairly and consistently, for the deployment of limited resources in the determination of asylum claims would make it difficult to establish unlawful delay unless the time taken was manifestly unreasonable or the Home Office failed to take account of a particular prejudice suffered by an applicant.[5] The Home Office policy[6] for dealing with 'the legacy', ie unresolved asylum claims lodged before March 2007 was concluded in July 2011. From 20 July 2011 it has been Home Office policy to grant only limited discretionary leave at best to claimants who made their original asylum claims prior to March 2007.[7]

[1] HC 395, para 333A, implementing Article 23(2) of Council Directive 2005/85/EC on minimum standards on procedures in Member States for granting and withdrawing refugee status. However, the Secretary of State is not obliged to determine the claim within the timeframe.

[2] *R (on the application of S) v Secretary of State for the Home Department* [2007] EWCA Civ 546, 151 Sol Jo LB 858.

[3] *R (on the application of S) v Secretary of State for the Home Department.*

[4] As the Tribunal did in *MM* [2005] UKIAT 00763, specifying a time of 12 months; see *R (on the application of FH) v Secretary of State for the Home Department* [2007] EWHC 1571 (Admin), [2007] All ER (D) 69 (Jul).

[5] *R (on the application of (FH) v Secretary of State for the Home Department* where Collins J was satisfied that there was such a policy so that delays of two or three years in dealing with second claims for asylum, given the overall volume of claims being dealt with, were not so manifestly unreasonable as to be unlawful. A delay of five years, however, was. See also *R (on the application of Ghaleb) v Secretary of State for the Home Department* [2008] EWHC 2685 (Admin), [2008] All ER (D) 80 (Dec); and *R (on the application of Geraldo & Others) v Secretary of State for the Home Department* [2013] EWHC 2763 (Admin). On the other hand, a policy of simply deferring the making of decisions on claims made prior to a particular date in order to comply with a Public Service Agreement made with the Treasury was not a principled, fair and consistent response to the competing demands facing the Home Office making the delay occasioned by that policy unlawful (*R (on the application of S) v Secretary of State for the Home Department (fn 2 above)*).

[6] APU Notice: 'Case Resolution Directorate – Priorities and Exceptional Circumstances'. See the 8th edition of this book at 12.126.

[7] The July 2011 change in policy in this regard has resulted in much litigation based *inter alia* on claims that further delay, beyond the date of the change, by the Home Office in deciding these so called 'legacy cases' has led to detriment and loss of a grant of indefinite leave to the applicants. The courts have been mostly unsympathetic to these claims: see eg *Hakemi v Secretary of State for the Home Department* [2012] EWHC 1967 (Admin); *R (on the application of Geraldo) v Secretary of State for the Home Department* [2013] EWHC 2703 (Admin); *Hamzeh v Secretary of State for the Home Department* [2013] EWHC 4113 (Admin) and [2014] EWCA Civ 956; *R (on the application of Mohamed) v Secretary of State for the Home Department* [2014] EWHC 1405 (Admin); *R (on the application of Jaku) v Secretary of State for the Home Department* [2014] EWHC 605 (Admin); *RN (Sri Lanka) v Secretary of State for the Home Department* [2014] EWCA Civ 938; *R (on the application of Tesfay) v Secretary of State for the Home Department* [2014] EWHC 2109 (Admin).

12.126 The Immigration Rules have been amended[1] to provide various procedural safeguards for asylum seekers. They include provision: that the Secretary of State will ensure that those responsible for examining and deciding asylum claims 'have the knowledge with respect to relevant standards applicable in the field of asylum and refugee law;'[2] for the individual assessment of a person's entitlement to asylum or humanitarian protection;[3] for written notice of decision on an asylum application to be given 'in reasonable time'[4] with reasons for the decision if asylum is refused together with information about how to challenge the decision;[5] for asylum applicants to be informed in a language they may reasonably be supposed to understand of the procedure to be followed; their rights and obligations during the procedure; the possible consequences of their non-compliance; the likely timeframe for consideration of the claim and how they may submit relevant information;[6] for an interpreter to be provided at public expense;[7] for applicants to have the opportunity to be interviewed (unless it is not reasonably practicable, eg because the applicant is unfit or prevented by enduring circumstances beyond his or her control from being interviewed)[8] in conditions ensuring confidentiality[9] and for a written report of the interview to be made and copied for the applicant;[10] for asylum applicants to have an 'effective opportunity' to consult a lawyer (at their own expense);[11] for the UNHCR to have access to individual asylum seekers and information about their cases and for the UNHCR to have the right to make representations about any individual claim.[12]

[1] Largely to give effect to the Qualfication Directive and Council Directive 2005/85/EC on minimum standards on procedures in Member States for granting and withdrawing refugee status.
[2] HC 395, para 339HA.
[3] HC 395, para 339J.
[4] HC 395, para 333.
[5] HC 395, para 336.
[6] HC 395, para 357A.
[7] HC 395, para 339ND.
[8] HC 395, para 339NA.
[9] HC 395, para 339NB(ii).
[10] HC 395, para 339NC.
[11] HC 395, para 333B.
[12] HC 395, 358C.

12.127 Home Office policy is that claims for asylum should be assessed in accordance with what is said in the UNHCR *Handbook on Procedures and Criteria* for determining refugee status about 'establishing the facts'[1] including the principles that the examiner of an asylum claim has an obligation to assist the applicant to ascertain relevant facts and even 'to use all the means at his disposal to produce the necessary evidence in support of the application';[2] to ensure that the applicant presents his or her claim as fully as possible and with all available evidence;[3] should recognise that because of their experiences asylum seekers may be afraid to speak freely and give a full and accurate account;[4] that the examiner may have to find an explanation for any misrepresentation or concealment of material facts[5] and may have to give an asylum seeker the benefit of the doubt.[6] However, the Immigration Rules highlight the obligation on the applicant to establish his or her claim[7] and provide for the Secretary of State to find that a claim has not been made out if the person 'fails, without reasonable explanation, to make a prompt and full disclosure of material facts'.[8] The rules acknowledge that a person's statements need not be corroborated but impose stringent preconditions for the benefit of that principle to be obtained including that the person has made a 'genuine effort' to substantiate his or her claim; that all available evidence has been submitted or a satisfactory explanation for the lack of relevant material is given; the person's statements are found to be coherent, plausible and not counter to other available information about the person's case; that the person claimed at the earliest possible time or demonstrated good reason for not doing so and the person has established his or her general credibility.[9] These are far more demanding criteria than contained in the *Handbook* which requires the applicant to be given the 'benefit of the doubt' if the account appears credible and absent good reasons not to do so.[10]

1   Ie paragraphs 195–215 of the *Handbook*. See API on 'Considering the protection (asylum) claim and assessing credibility', 30 July 2012, which refers frequently to the UNHCR *Handbook*.
2   UNHCR *Handbook*, para 196.
3   UNHCR *Handbook*, para 205(b)(i).
4   UNHCR *Handbook*, para 198.
5   UNHCR *Handbook*, para 199.
6   UNHCR *Handbook*, para 196.
7   HC 395, para 339L.
8   HC 395, para 339M.
9   HC 395, para 339L. Thus an asylum seeker who neither provided a witness statement from his mother who was in Albania, nor an explanation for not doing so was denied the benefit of the principle: *MF (Albania) v Secretary of State for the Home Department* [2014] EWCA Civ 902.
10   UNHCR *Handbook*, para 196. See also per Brooke J in *R v Secretary of State for the Home Department, ex p Akdogan* [1995] Imm AR 176.

Asylum interviews

12.128 The Immigration Rules now provide for applicants to have a personal interview with a representative of the Secretary of State who is legally competent to conduct such an interview[1] at which the claimant should be given every opportunity to put forward the basis of his or her claim and to explain any apparent discrepancies.[2] However, there is a wide range of circumstances in which such an interview need not be conducted including where the person has only raised issues that are not relevant or are only minimally relevant to an asylum claim; the person's claim is 'clearly unconvincing in relation to his having been the object of persecution'; the person has made a fresh asylum claim which does not raise relevant new issues; the application has been made merely to delay or frustrate removal or it is not reasonably practicable owing to 'enduring circumstances' beyond the person's control.[3] The practice of interviewing on or shortly after arrival cuts across the principle that applicants may have access to a lawyer throughout the asylum procedures[4] not to mention the entitlement to 'an effective opportunity to consult' a lawyer now contained in the Immigration Rules.[5] Legal assistance at the asylum interview has been recommended by UNHCR[6] and its importance recognised by (inter alia) the Lord Chancellor's Department and the Legal Services Commission.[7] Moreover, the importance of a representative at the asylum interview was recognised in *Dirshe*, to ensure the requisite standards of fairness by providing 'a real, practical safeguard against faulty interpreting or inadequate or inaccurate record keeping'.[8] Although there is no right to legal representation at interview,[9] the Home Office practice has become more accepting of the importance of representatives attending interviews.[10] However, from 1 April 2004, public funding was generally not available for attending an interview conducted on behalf of the Secretary of State with a view to his reaching a decision on a claim for asylum.[11] Limited exceptions are made in the cases of unaccompanied minors; applicants going through fast-track initial decision processes and those suffering from a recognised and verifiable mental incapacity making it impractical to undergo an interview without support.[12] When funding was available for attendance, Pitchford J had held in *Mapah* that it was not procedurally unfair for the Secretary of State to refuse to allow representatives to tape record interviews.[13] But the Court of Appeal held in *Dirshe* that the absence of a legal representative from the interview, because of the withdrawal of funding for attendance, meant that tape recording of interviews provided the only safeguard for claimants.[14] Current Home Office policy is to record interviews if requested by a claimant who is not entitled to have a publicly funded representative at the interview and is unable to provide his or her own representative.[15]

1   HC 395, para 339NA, giving effect to Council Directive 2005/85/EC on minimum standards on procedures in Member States for granting and withdrawing refugee status.

2   API 'Considering Asylum Claims and Assessing Credibility', 30 July 2012, section 4.3.1. See also the API 'Asylum Interviews', 31 March 2014.

3   HC 395, para 339NA.

4   The philosophy of the Home Office has, in the past, been that lawyers are not needed by asylum seekers at interviews. However, the current API 'Asylum Interviews', 31 March 2014, at section 7.1 now states: 'An asylum claimant has the right to consult a legal representative at his own expense or at public expense in accordance with provision made by the Legal Aid Agency, the Scottish Legal Aid Board, or the Northern Ireland Legal Services Commission. Legal representatives from qualified solicitors or advisers regulated by the Office of the Immigration Services Commissioner are welcome to attend a client's interview. However, the legal aid rules are narrowly framed, and it can be assumed that a representative who is funded to attend the interview will have good reason to do so. If possible, their availability should be accommodated when arranging the interview.' See also per Ouseley J in *Detention Action v Secretary of State for the Home Department (Equality Human Rights Commission intervening)* [2014] EWHC 2245 (Admin) at 12.112 above regarding the vital importance of legal representation throughout in order to render the Detained Fast Track fair.

5   HC 395, para 333B.

6   'The presence of a legal representative or other counsel who is familiar with the refugee criteria, local jurisprudence and the applicant's claim is helpful not only to the applicant but also to the interviewer': UNHCR Guidelines 1995, para 15.

7   ACLEC Improving the quality of immigration advice and representation: A report (1998), para 2.23. See also ILPA Breaking down the barriers: a report on the conduct of asylum interviews at ports (1999).

8   *R (on the application of Dirshe) v Secretary of State for the Home Department* [2005] EWCA Civ 421, a judgment which is very important for its recognition of the difficulties faced by unrepresented applicants at interview.

9   *R v Secretary of State for the Home Department, ex p Lawson* [1994] Imm AR 58.

10   See fn 4 above.

11   Community Legal Service (Scope) Regulations 2004, SI 2004/1055, made under s 6(7) of the Access to Justice Act 1999 and amending Sch 2 to the Act (repealed by Legal Aid, Sentencing and Punishment of Offenders Act 2012, Sch 5(1), para 51(a) from 1 April 2013: repeal has effect subject to saving and transitional provisions as specified in SI 2013/534, regs 6-13). For the government's justification see Lord Filkin *Hansard* HL 31.3.04 Col 1411. There was vehement opposition to these 2004 proposals in the House of Lords, see eg HL EU Committee 11th report 2003–4, HL 74, para 111: 'undue restrictions on legal aid and access to qualified legal representation are likely to lead to unfairness and more poor decisions'. See also to similar effect Second Report of the Constitutional Affairs Committee, 2003/4, on Asylum and Immigration Appeals, HC 211-1, February 2004. Now see Immigration and Asylum Specifications in the Standard Civil Contract under the provisions of the Legal Aid, Sentencing and Punishment of Offenders Act 2012.

12   See Lord Filkin, *Hansard* above; the exception is not reflected in legislation.

13   *Mapah v Secretary of State for the Home Department* [2003] EWHC 306 (Admin), [2003] Imm AR 395.

14   See fn 9 above. The decision gives unrepresented applicants the right to have their asylum interview tape-recorded.

15   API 'Asylum Interviews', 31 March 2014, at section 6. Under that Guidance, applicants who are entitled to publicly funded representation at interview but choose not to have their

representative present and applicants who have a representative at the interview are not entitled to have the interview tape-recorded.

12.129 The APIs contain detailed guidance governing the conduct of substantive interviews and the roles of interviewing officers, representatives and their interpreters.[1] The interviewer has a duty to elicit details of the claim, to enable the applicant to do justice to it.[2] Representatives (if present) are normally invited to add any comments at the end of the interview rather than during questioning, but this should not be rigidly applied. A legal representative can, for example, assist the interview process by drawing attention to a potentially serious misunderstanding.[3] Present policy is that for reasons of confidentiality, a claimant will normally be interviewed alone or in the presence of a legal representative or regulated adviser and only exceptionally a friend or other companion may be admitted to provide emotional or medical support, at the discretion of the caseworker.[4] The APIs contain guidance on the interviewing of applicants who are children, victims of torture, victims of trafficking, traumatised, mentally ill, and pregnant.[5] Previous Asylum Directorate Instructions emphasised the importance of agreeing the transcript of the interview with the applicant at the end of the interview,[6] which is clearly desirable in the interests of fairness and accuracy; in June 2000 however the Home Office announced the end of the 'read-over' procedure[7] except in cases involving illiterate or traumatised applicants, where the immigration officer retains a discretion.[8] The claimant must be given a copy of the record of the interview.[9] The extent to which a failure to mention aspects of the claim at an initial screening interview should be allowed adversely to affect credibility remains controversial.[10]

[1] API 'Asylum Interviews', 31 March 2014.
[2] *R v Secretary of State for the Home Department, ex p Akdogan* [1995] Imm AR 176, QBD (although see *R (on the application of Zaier) v Immigration Appeal Tribunal* [2003] EWCA Civ 937, [2003] All ER (D) 153 (Jul) at **12.117** above).
[3] API 'Asylum Interviews', 31 March 2014, section 7.3. The guidance states that if the interviewer believes an adviser or legal representative is acting unreasonably and disrupting the flow of the interview, this should be discussed with a senior officer and appropriate action taken, though the difficulties should be resolved by agreement if at all possible.
[4] API 'Asylum Interviews', 31 March 2014, section 3.9 See *R v Secretary of State for the Home Department, ex p Bostanci* [1999] Imm AR 411 on unfair exclusion of an interpreter brought by the claimant.
[5] See API 'Asylum Interviews', 31 March 2014.
[6] ADI (July 98), Ch 16, s 3, para 6.4, Annex A, para 4: 'The readback is an essential part of the interview.'
[7] IND letter, 23 June 2000, stating that the SEF form lessens the scope for omissions and misunderstandings at interview, while in non-SEF cases the applicant has five days after interview to make representations. See now Asylum Process Guidance 'Conducting the Asylum Interview' which states that: 'It is Home Office policy to not routinely read out the interview record after the conclusion of a substantive asylum interview. Read overs should only be given in very exceptional circumstances'. A copy of the interview record should be handed to the applicant. The Tribunal in *Bilbil v Secretary of State for the Home Department* (01TH1603) (referred to by Pitchford J in *Mapah v Secretary of State for the Home Department* [2003] EWHC 306 (Admin), [2003] Imm AR 395) described the change of policy as a regrettable step and one which failed implicitly to protect the interests of the interviewee and the interviewer.
[8] Now see API 'Asylum Interviews', 31 March 2014, section 5.16.
[9] HC 395, para 339NC(ii) and see API 'Asylum Interviews', 31 March 2014, section 5.16: 'The interviewer must always provide a photocopy of the interview record for the claimant, who should be asked to sign the original copy of the interview record. This is simply to confirm receipt, not to signify agreement to the contents.'

10 In *Salim* (13202) and *Simsek* (13202) the Tribunal held that great care was needed in weighing discrepancies between the first, unsigned interview, at which 'basic details only' were sought, and the full asylum interview. See also *Mayisokele* (13039); *Vimaleswaran* (15493); *Jeevaponkalan* (17742); *Kasolo* (13190). But failure to mention a central feature of the claim may affect credibility: *R v Secretary of State for the Home Department, ex p Agbonmenio* [1996] Imm AR 69; *Singh (Kulwinder) v Secretary of State for the Home Department* [2000] SC 288 (Outer House, Court of Session). In *R (on the application of the Refugee Legal Centre) v Secretary of State for the Home Department* [2004] EWCA Civ 1481, [2004] All ER (D) 201 (Nov), Sedley LJ pointed out that 'if the record of interview which goes before the adjudicator has been obtained in unacceptably stressful or distressing circumstances so that it contains omissions and inconsistencies when compared with what the applicant later tells the adjudicator, the damage may not be curable' (para 15).

12.130 Since the elaboration of gender guidelines by the Refugee Women's Legal Group in 1998,[1] the Home Office has begun to recognise the importance of gender-sensitive procedures and has elaborated its own gender guidelines for caseworkers.[2] They confirm that every effort will be made to provide same sex interviewing officers and interpreters where requested.[3] They also acknowledge that victims of sexual assault or abuse may need to be interviewed alone, may suffer trauma affecting their confidence, concentration and memory, and may be reluctant to talk in detail about their experiences,[4] a reluctance recognised by the High Court in *Ejon*.[5] If indicators of trafficking first come to light during the asylum interview the caseworker, as the first responder, must complete the National Referral Mechanism (NRM) referral form, providing the potential victim consents to being entered into the NRM process.[6] The policy instructions on interviewing accept that victims of torture and sexual violence generally may face particular difficulties in recounting their experiences.[7] Claimants with scars should be asked for an explanation of how scars or bruising occurred and this account must then be given due weight in the totality of the evidence available.[8] The Home Office recognises the particular expertise of the medico-legal bodies that care for victims of torture and the potential importance of obtaining medico-legal reports on claimants.[9] Guidance on interviewing states that where an account of torture or serious harm is given during the interview, the caseworker should suggest that the applicant may wish to approach one of the Foundations for care and treatment.[10] Medico-legal reports should comply with the 'Istanbul Protocol'[11] and should be given due weight in the asylum determination process.[12]

1   Refugee Women's Legal Group Gender Guidelines for the Determination of Asylum Claims in the United Kingdom (July 1998). The guidelines were referred to with approval by Lord Hoffmann in *Islam v Secretary of State for the Home Department*; *R v Immigration Appeal Tribunal* [1999] 2 AC 629; [1999] INLR 144, HL. See also the Asylum Gender Guidelines issued by the IAA in November 2000, and see also H Crawley Refugees and gender: law and process (Jordans, 2001) chs 1 and 10. The Court of Appeal in *C v Secretary of State for the Home Department* [2006] EWCA Civ 151, [2006] All ER (D) 122 (Feb) approved the statement in para 5.40 of the AIT Guidelines that women may face additional problems in demonstrating that their claims are credible.
2   API, 'Gender issues in the asylum claim', 29 September 2010.
3   API, 'Gender issues' above, under the heading 'interviewing'. Each applicant will have been asked at screening to indicate a preference for a male or female interviewer, and it should normally be possible to comply with a request for a male or female interviewer or interpreter that is made in advance of an interview. Requests made on the day of an interview for a male or female interviewer or interpreter should be met as far as is operationally possible.
4   Ibid. The API acknowledge that feelings of guilt and shame may inhibit full disclosure and that inability to provide information should not affect credibility. They also acknowledge that many forms of abuse do not leave physical signs. The API on gender issues should be read and

re-read by Home Office caseworkers, presenting officers and by AIT members, who are on occasion all too ready to disbelieve women's accounts of sexual abuse.

5   *R v Secretary of State for the Home Department, ex p Ejon (Molly)* [1998] INLR 195, QBD: psychiatric as much as physical injury may prevent early disclosure of evidence.

6   API 'Asylum Interviews', 31 March 2014, section 5.9.

7   API 'Asylum Interviews', 31 March 2014, section 5.7. The API states that, nevertheless it is important to ask for information about when, where, how, and by whom the torture was inflicted, taking care not to cause undue distress. The API continues: 'For victims of rape or other forms of sexual violence, obtaining details of the act itself would be inappropriate, but it is important that information is obtained regarding the events leading up to, and after, the act, together with the surrounding circumstances at the time it took place, as well as the motivation of the perpetrator, if known.'

8   API 'Asylum Interviews', 31 March 2014, section 5.8. The API states that the interviewer may accept an offer to see scars only if they are on a visible part of the body, for example the lower arms or legs. If the interviewer sees the scars, the interview record must be noted as to where the scars or marks are on the body and the approximate shape/size. If the interviewer does not consider that it would be appropriate to look at the scars, this must be recorded. See regarding scars and their possible causes: *RT (Medical reports-causation of scarring) Sri Lanka* [2008] UKAIT 00009; and *KV (scarring-medical evidence) Sri Lanka* [2014] UKUT 230 (IAC).

9   API, 'Medico-Legal Reports from the Helen Bamber Foundation and the Medical Foundation Medico-Legal Report Service', 17 January 2014.

10 Ibid, at section 2.1. The API goes on to state however that it is for the applicant or their representative to decide whether to seek an appointment with one of the Foundations; and that where a caseworker suggests a referral, this does not necessarily mean that the claim of torture has been accepted at this point.

11 'Istanbul Protocol': Manual on the Effective Investigation and Documentation of Torture and Other Cruel, Inhuman or Degrading Treatment or Punishment: from the Office of the United Nations High Commissioner for Human Rights, 2004: see *KV (scarring-medical evidence) Sri Lanka* [2014] UKUT 230 (IAC) at [15]-[20].

12 API, Medico-Legal Reports from the Helen Bamber Foundation and the Medical Foundation Medico-Legal Report Service', 17 January 2014, section 3.3.. See *SA (Somalia) v Secretary of State for the Home Department* [2006] EWCA Civ 1302; also *AJ (Assessment of medical evidence –examination of scars) Cameroon* [2005] UKIAT 00060; *KV (scarring-medical evidence) Sri Lanka* [2014] UKUT 230 (IAC).

12.131 There was previously no reflection in the Immigration Rules or the APIs of the UNHCR *Handbook*'s guidance for investigation of the claims of mentally disturbed persons.[1] The Tribunal has held that it is totally wrong to conduct an interview by asking a series of leading questions, and especially so if the interviewee has a known mental condition; such claimants must be allowed to tell their story in their own way.[2] Current policy instructions now provide that, in 'the interests of fairness to all claimants', interviews should not be cancelled or suspended on the grounds of past or present mental illness unless the claimant is clearly unable to cope with an interview and where the validity of the replies could be called into question.[3]

1   UNHCR *Handbook* **12.13** above, paras 206–212, which point out the necessity for different techniques of examination, with more emphasis on medical and objective evidence, and perhaps requiring a lighter burden of proof (para 210), but calling for a close examination of the applicant's past history and background, using whatever outside sources of information may be available. The Court of Appeal has rejected the idea that a mentally ill applicant enjoyed a lighter burden of proving her claim in *Bolat v Secretary of State for the Home Department* (permission) (99/66206/C) (23 February 2000, unreported); see also *Yesilyurt* (permission) (A99-7352-C) (2 March 2000, unreported). See also *Singh (Amrik) v Secretary of State for the Home Department* [2000] Imm AR 340, CA, regarding the situation where a mentally disturbed applicant's evidence is considered to be unreliable with the consequence that he cannot overcome the burden of proving that he is a refugee. The particular difficulties where clients are unable to give instructions might make it appropriate for representatives to consider appointing a guardian.

2 *Ibrahim v Secretary of State for the Home Department* [1998] INLR 511, IAT. See also *Ermias* (HX00312) (11 August 1999, unreported), where the Tribunal agreed that an interview with an applicant who was not fit to be interviewed had no evidential value.

3 API, 'Asylum Interviews', 31 March 2014, section 5.11. The API acknowledges that this is a sensitive matter and that if possible the interviewing officer should discuss the claimant's capacity with his or her representative before or after the interview. The API states that if a GP's or Consultant's letter is received confirming that the person is unable, for the foreseeable future, to cope with an interview, the personal interview should be omitted and written evidence taken in accordance with HC 395, para 339NA.

12.132 The UNHCR *Handbook*[1] indicates that in the light of the particular evidential and practical difficulties faced by asylum seekers, the duty to ascertain and evaluate all the relevant facts is shared between the applicant and the examiner.[2] The Immigration Rules now require the Secretary of State to ensure that the officials who examine and determine claims for asylum 'have the knowledge with respect to relevant standards applicable to the field of asylum and refugee law'[3] They also oblige the Secretary of State to obtain 'reliable and up to date information' from 'various sources' about the general situations prevailing in the countries from which asylum seekers come and to make the information available to those examining and deciding asylum claims.[4] The Home Office's Country of Origin Information Service produces detailed, sourced and publicly available assessments of the main refugee-producing countries.[5] In March 2004 a War Crimes Unit (now War Crimes Team: WCT) was established in the Home Office for the purpose of identifying individuals who may have committed or been complicit in war crimes. Current policy provides that caseworkers are supposed to refer cases to the WCT if there is any evidence of such involvement and that no further action is to be taken without consulting the WCT.[6]

1 See **12.13** above. Paras195–205 deal with establishing the facts.

2 *Handbook* para 196, which continues that in some cases it might be for the examiner to use all the means at his (sic) disposal to produce the necessary evidence in support of the application. Para 200 requires the examiner to gain the confidence of the applicant to assist the latter in putting forward the case.

3 HC 395, para 339HA, inserted in response to Council Directive 2005/85/EC on minimum standards on procedures in Member States for granting and withdrawing refugee status ('the Procedures Directive').

4 HC 395 para 339JA, inserted in response to the Procedures Directive.

5 The country of origin information service is available in the Home Office website.

6 Asylum Policy Guidance 'Criminality, Adverse Immigration History and Other Information – Migration Casework Actions'.

Reasons for refusal

12.133 A significant development has been the Home Office practice of giving full reasons for rejection of asylum claims.[1] It is now recognised generally in administrative law that even in the absence of statutory obligation, reasons are required for a decision which will have significant effects on the rights of individuals affected.[2] Once the giving of reasons became standard practice it was apparent that in a number of cases adverse inferences were being drawn on matters that were capable of reply and had never been canvassed in interview. In a series of cases the courts held that such an approach was a breach of the duty of fairness.[3] In *Thirukumar*[4] the Court of Appeal held that if an opportunity to make representations was to be meaningful an applicant should be informed of the matters to which his or her attention needed to be directed, and, where time had elapsed since the interview, to be reminded of what had been said. The introduction of a right of appeal in July 1993 put an end to the provisional decision to refuse which invited observations as to why a different course should be adopted. Now, if adverse inferences are wrongly drawn in a refusal letter, the remedy is to address them at the statutory appeal, and failure to do so will mean that they stand.[5] Where the appeal is non-suspensive,[6] there must be an opportunity to correct adverse inferences before implementation of the decision.[7] Now that there is power to serve refusal of leave to enter by post after adjourning examination of an applicant for further inquiries,[8] there is no longer an expectation of a final interview at which the refusal letter will be served and the applicant asked for comments.[9]

[1]   Since the case of *R v Secretary of State for the Home Department, ex p Singh (Gurmeet)* [1987] Imm AR 489 in which the Divisional Court indicated that the giving of reasons was highly desirable in asylum cases. The Immigration Rules now require the 'reasons in fact and law' for refusal of asylum to be stated in the decision – HC 395, para 336, inserted by HC 82.

[2]   *R v Secretary of State for the Home Department, ex p Doody* [1994] 1 AC 531; *Stefan v General Medical Council* [1999] 1 WLR 1293; *R v Secretary of State for the Home Department, ex p Zighem* [1996] Imm AR 194.

[3]   *R v Secretary of State for the Home Department, ex p Yemoh* [1988] Imm AR 595; *Gaima v Secretary of State for the Home Department* [1989] Imm AR 205, CA; *R v Secretary of State for the Home Department, ex p Oran (Ayse)* [1991] Imm AR 290.

[4]   [1989] Imm AR 402, CA, upholding the QBD at [1989] Imm AR 270.

[5]   See CHAPTER 20 below.

[6]   Under NIAA 2002, 94: see **12.163** below.

[7]   *R (on the application of L) v Secretary of State for the Home Department* [2003] EWCA Civ 25, [2003] Imm AR 330, [2003] INLR 224.

[8]   Immigration (Leave to Enter and Remain) Order 2000, SI 2000/1161, art 12. Previously, the provisions of Immigration Act 1971, Sch 2, para 6(1) (six months' leave to enter deemed given where notice of decision not given within 24 hours of final examination) meant that, in port cases, immigration officers had to complete examination by calling the applicant to a final interview where the refusal letter was served. See **3.95** above.

[9]   See CHAPTER 20 for service of refusal decisions.

12.134 Refusal letters usually set out a summary of the applicant's claim and often contain a number of standard paragraphs referring to credibility issues such as failure to claim in a country of transit or on arrival, and to conditions in the country of feared persecution. Following complaints about unsourced assertions and unfair credibility findings in refusal letters, the Immigration and Nationality Directorate promised in May 2000 that paragraphs on country conditions would be sourced by reference to the Country of Origin Information Service country reports, that credibility would not be given disproportionate weight and letters would set out clear findings on what was and was not accepted.[1]

[1]   Asylum Processes Stakeholders' Group meeting, May 2000. In its June 2004 response to the 2nd report of the Constitutional Affairs Committee on Immigration Appeals, the government proposed that UNHCR provide an external assessment of the quality of decisions (Cm 6236, para 3).

Confidentiality

12.135 The Immigration Rules have been amended to make some provision relating to the confidentiality of asylum claims. For the purpose of examining an asylum application neither the fact that an asylum claim has been made nor information provided in support of the claim is to be disclosed to the alleged persecutors.[1] Nor may information be sought from the alleged persecutors that would result in them being directly informed that an asylum claim had been made and would jeopardise the physical integrity of the applicant or the liberty and security of his family living in the country of origin.[2] There are serious concerns about the apparent limits to the protection provided by the rules as framed: the prohibition on disclosing or seeking information to or from the persecutor is expressed to apply only for the purpose of examining the asylum claim and is not expressly applicable to other possible purposes for such communication (eg a criminal investigation or, once the asylum claim has been examined and refused, removing the applicant); the requirement that jeopardy to the applicant's or applicant's family must be shown as a condition for preventing information being sought from the persecutor is far too onerous and would provide little or no protection to a refused asylum seeker. Nevertheless, the UKBA respects the principle of confidentiality in general in asylum claims,[3] and that principle is given added weight by the fact that respect for confidential information is a vital aspect of the right to respect for privacy under Article 8 of the ECHR.[4] The previous API on 'Disclosure and Confidentiality'[5] provided that information given by an asylum claimant may be disclosed to third parties in certain circumstances: if asylum is refused and the person is to be removed, details relating to his or her identity may be provided to the country of origin for the purpose of re-documentation but without reference to the fact that the individual claimed asylum; to the asylum authorities of third countries; to other government departments and local authorities; details of a claimant's immigration status may be given to the police; to international organisations such as the UNHCR and Red Cross; It is not permissible for a decision to refer to information provided in confidence by another applicant, including a spouse, unless that information is already in the public domain. The Home Office considers information to have entered the public domain if it is discussed in court or in the AIT during a public hearing. Details from forgery reports relied on to discredit documents produced by an asylum claimant will not normally be disclosed.[6]

[1] HC 395, para 339IA(i).
[2] HC 395, para 339IA(ii).
[3] See Chapter 24 of the IDI at section 5: Disclosure of information relating to asylum applications, November 2008.
[4] *Z v Finland* (1997) 25 EHRR 371. The IDI Ch 24, Section 5 (above) gives guidance on the circumstances when information about asylum seekers may be disclosed to other government departments or agencies, international organisations and other bodies in the exercise of their functions.
[5] No longer available on the Home Office's new and generally unsatisfactory website.
[6] See NIAA 2002, s 108 and SI 2005/230, r 54(2).

Non-compliance refusal

12.136 HC 395, para 339M provides that a failure without reasonable explanation to make a prompt disclosure of material facts or to assist the Secretary of State in establishing the facts of the case may lead to refusal. It includes failure to comply with a requirement to report for fingerprinting, failure to complete an asylum questionnaire and failure to attend for interview or to report to an immigration officer for examination.[1] The rule that provided for the actions of an agent to be taken into account for these purposes has been deleted.[2] Failure to return Statement of Evidence (SEF) forms in time[3] leads to refusal of the claim for non-compliance, even (in one case) where the asylum seeker concerned was in hospital having a baby when the form was due.[4] Late receipt of the form does not result in cancellation of the refusal decision or to interview on the claim, merely to 'consideration' of the material in the form.[5] Failure to attend a screening interview may also lead to non-compliance refusal depending on the explanation, if any, given by the applicant.[6] Failure to attend a substantive interview, without a good explanation, may lead to the application being treated as withdrawn.[7] To an extent this is a way of evading the decision in *Haddad*, in which a starred Tribunal held that an application may not be refused on non-compliance grounds alone and that in each case the Home Office is obliged to decide the asylum claim, and the appellate authority the appeal, on the material available.[8] Home Office practice, where the application is not just treated as withdrawn, is now to consider all available information and make a substantive decision on the claim instead of or as well as refusing for non-compliance.[9] In *Busuulwa* the Tribunal lamented that the words of the statute forced the appellate authority to exercise original jurisdiction over asylum claims which have never been considered substantively,[10] although it was wrong in principle for the primary decision to be taken other than in accordance with the UNHCR guidelines. It called on the Secretary of State to withdraw non-compliance refusals which failed to review the merits of the asylum claim.[11] In *Nori*[12] the Tribunal reviewed flawed non-compliance refusals, ie, refusals on non-compliance grounds where the Statement of Evidence form was received in time, or where a claimant's failure to attend an interview was occasioned by error on the part of the Home Office.[13] It noted that once an incorrect decision had been withdrawn (which it had to be), there was nothing left to appeal against.[14] After *Nori*, the Home Office reviewed its procedures, and the policy instructions state that where the claim was made in-country, a flawed non-compliance decision will be withdrawn;[15] decisions regarding port claims will be cancelled.[16] Where an appeal has been lodged, the UKBA will additionally notify the Tribunal that the decision to which the appeal relates has now been withdrawn and that a new decision will be made.[17] As noted above, the Immigration Rules have been amended so that failure to attend an asylum interview will result in the asylum claim being treated as withdrawn unless within a reasonable time the person demonstrates that the failure to attend was due to circumstances beyond his or her control.[18] After deemed withdrawal of the claim any further claim (including reinstatement of the original claim) will be considered under the 'fresh claim' rule.[19] It can be anticipated that the Secretary of State will say (wrongly we think) that unless the claim has a 'realistic prospect of success', the person will not be someone who 'has made an asylum claim' so as to be entitled to an in-country right of appeal.[20]

---

[1]   HC 395, para 339M which replaced para 340 from 9 October 2006.

[2]   HC 395, para 342, deleted from 9 October 2006.

[3]   The Statement of Evidence form must be returned within ten working days. Requests to extend the time limit should be considered and discretion exercised reasonably where there are exceptional circumstances, but an extension will not be granted to enable the applicant to instruct a representative to complete the form: API 'Non-compliance' November 2013, under the heading: 'Failure to Submit or Late Submission of the Statement of Evidence Form (SEF) Self Completion'. Even if the SEF is late, the application should only be refused on non-compliance grounds if not received by the time the decision is made – API, as before. Note

that non-compliance may also lead to withdrawal of asylum support: see Asylum Support Regulations 2000, SI 2000/704, reg 20 as amended by SI 2005/11 pursuant to the Reception Directive 2003/9/EC, from 5 February 2005.

4   Judicial review proceedings were lodged but were withdrawn when the Home Office accepted the late Statement of Evidence.

5   See correspondence between ILPA and Barbara Roche, 24 October 2000.

6   API 'Non-compliance', November 2013, under the heading: 'Failure to attend a screening interview'.

7   HC 395, para 333C; and see 'Asylum Interviews', 31 March 2014, section 3.5.

8   *Haddad (Ali) v Secretary of State for the Home Department* [2000] INLR 117. Earlier cases such as *Davies (Sandra)* (17797), holding that the correct course for the appellate authority finding good reason for non-compliance was to allow the appeal and remit to the Secretary of State for substantive consideration of the asylum claim, were not referred to. In *Shreef* (01TH00476) another Tribunal held that the course adopted in *Davies* was correct. But the Court of Appeal approved *Haddad* in R *(on the application of Zaier) v Secretary of State for the Home Department* [2003] EWCA Civ 937, [2003] All ER (D) 153 (Jul) at paras 31 and 37 per Auld LJ. Since *Haddad*, refusal letters relying on non-compliance also refer to the Refugee Convention claim not being made out (HC 395, para 336). However the alternative route is to treat the application as withdrawn pursuant to rule 333C (see fn 7 above and see 12.110).

9   API 'Non-compliance', November 2013, under the heading: 'Refusing asylum or humanitarian protection on non-compliance grounds'.

10 *Busuulwa* (01TH00239). By March 2001, nearly one-third of all claims were refused without consideration of the merits, for alleged non-compliance with time limits. A fair proportion of these were erroneous, eg there was evidence that the Statement of Evidence form had been returned in time.

11 *Busuulwa* above.

12 Nori (Rasheed) [2002] UKIAT 01887.

13 See API 'Non-compliance' under the heading: 'incorrect refusals on non-compliance grounds'.

14 *Nori* above, para 19. The Tribunal pointed out that once the decision to refuse asylum had been withdrawn, the refusal of leave to enter or remain (ie, the immigration decision against which the appeal was brought) could not stand.

15 See fn 13 above.

16 API 'Non-compliance' as per fn 13 above, advising that the refusal of leave to enter will be cancelled and the claimant advised that they are required to attend for further examination (to prevent the deemed six months' leave which would otherwise arise by statute: Sch 2, para 6 of the Immigration Act 1971, see **3.95** above).

17 API 'Non-compliance' as per fn 13 above. The appeal is then treated as withdrawn by the Tribunal in accordance with SI 2005/230, r 17(2).

18 Paragraph 333C of the Rules, as substituted by HC 420 which came into force on 7 April 2008.

19 Paragraph 353 of the Rules, as amended by HC 420.

20 By virtue of the Nationality, Immigration and Asylum Act 2002, s 92(4).

Asylum and the one-stop procedure

12.137 The aim of the one-stop procedure is to make applicants give all their reasons for wanting to enter or remain in the UK as early as possible. This is intended to allow the Home Office to deal with applications quickly, taking into account all the reasons why the person may wish to remain.[1] The 'one-stop' procedures implemented by the Immigration and Asylum Act 1999[2] have been considerably simplified by the Nationality, Immigration and Asylum Act 2002 and the AI(TC)A 2004. Section 120 of the 2002 Act allows[3] the Secretary of State or an immigration officer to require[4] any person who has applied to enter or remain in the UK or in respect of whom an immigration decision[5] has been or may be taken, to state his or her reasons for wishing to enter or remain in the UK, any grounds on which he or she should be permitted to enter or remain and any grounds on which he or she should not be removed from or required to leave the UK.[6] Failure to set out all such grounds in response to a one-stop warning, or to use an earlier right of appeal to litigate them, may result in certification[7] of a later application, which precludes a further appeal.

[1] API 'Appeals: one-stop procedure' para 1 (no longer current).

[2] Immigration and Asylum Act 1999, ss 74–77. There were different procedures for in-country claimants on the one hand and for port claimants, illegal entrants and overstayers on the other. Relevant family members were also included in the procedure. For details see the 5th edition of this work, at 12.123 and 18.53.

[3] There is no statutory obligation on the Secretary of State or the immigration officer to serve a one-stop warning at any particular time or at all (see *Lamichhane v Secretary of State for the Home Department* [2012] EWCA Civ 260). See generally on the one-stop procedure, *AS (Afghanistan) v Secretary of State for the Home Department* [2009] EWCA Civ 1076; approved in *Patel v Secretary of State for the Home Department* [2013] UKSC 72; [2014] AC 651; [2014] 1 All ER 1157; [2014] Imm AR 456; [2014] INLR 205.

[4] By notice in writing: Nationality, Immigration and Asylum Act 2002, s 120(2). In practice this is often done by a paragraph in a notice refusing leave, or in the reasons for refusal letter. There is no time limit within which the applicant must return a statement of additional grounds.

[5] Ie, a decision listed in Nationality, Immigration and Asylum Act 2002, s 82(2) thus attracting a right of appeal under s 82(1). A one-stop notice is not served where the decision is to grant humanitarian protection or discretionary leave because there is then no right of appeal under s 82 and any right of appeal under Nationality, Immigration and Asylum Act 2002, s 83 can be on asylum grounds only (s 84(3)).

[6] Nationality, Immigration and Asylum Act 2002, s 120(2). The response to the one-stop warning need not repeat grounds already set out in the application: s 120(3).

[7] Under NIAA 2002, s 96(1) as substituted by AI(TC)A 2004, s 30 from 1 October 2004, the Secretary of State or an immigration officer may, in refusing an application, certify that the new application relies on a ground which could have been raised on appeal earlier (whether or not the applicant used the earlier right of appeal, and whether or not he or she has been out of the country since); and under s 96(2) (as substituted), an application can be certified if it relates to a ground which the person should have included in a statement he was required to make under s 120 in relation to another immigration decision or application. In each case a reasonable explanation for the failure to raise the matter earlier should preclude certification. Certification prevents an appeal under s 82(1) from being brought. See Chapter 19 below.

Curtailment of limited leave where asylum is refused

12.138 Home Office policy is to consider curtailing any limited leave to enter or remain that a person has following refusal of an asylum or human rights claim.[1] Such leave would normally be curtailed if it was granted for non-protection reasons; the person was warned of his or her liability to curtailment of leave prior to the decision to refuse asylum or the human rights claim; the person no longer meets the requirements of the limited leave (a condition likely to be satisfied where an intention to leave the UK was a requirement and the asylum or human rights claim indicates that intention is absent) and the person does not otherwise qualify for leave. However, limited leave would not be curtailed if the person is the spouse or civil partner of a British citizen or EU citizen exercising community law rights or has leave in a category leading to settlement or is terminally ill with a life expectancy less than six months. Dependants' limited leave should also be curtailed if the same conditions are satisfied.

[1] See Asylum decision making guidance on 'Implementing substantive decisions', 15 November 2013, at section 5 on curtailment (and which refers to the now unavailable API on 'Curtailment').

REMOVAL TO SAFE THIRD COUNTRIES

Introduction

12.139 The Asylum and Immigration Appeals Act 1993 was the first statutory provision[1] incorporating and extending an international practice whereby claims for asylum made in one state could be refused without substantive consideration on the basis that the claimant could be removed to a country other than the country of feared persecution, which would be responsible for determining the asylum claim. The practice was based upon the 'first country of asylum' principle of international law whereby neighbouring countries were expected to take refugees fleeing a persecuting state.[2] In modern times, governments have turned the principle round so as to expect a refugee to find refuge locally wherever possible.[3] Removal to 'safe third countries' is a controversial practice[4] and one that resulted in substantial and protracted litigation during the 1990s, and consequential significant statutory amendment in the Asylum and Immigration Act 1996, the Immigration and Asylum Act 1999, the Nationality, Immigration and Asylum Act 2002 and the AI(TC)A 2004. This section examines briefly the third country regimes under the provisions of the 1993 and the 1996 Acts. The 1999 Act (amended by the 2002 and 2004 Acts) is considered in more detail as it provides the background to and template for the current regime.[5] Thereafter we set out the current regime contained in the 2004 Act.

1 Prior to the Asylum and Immigration Appeals Act 1993, removal of an asylum seeker on third country grounds had been entirely a matter of administrative discretion subject only to the requirement in the Immigration Rules that the rules should lay down no practice which was not in accordance with the Refugee Convention. The landmark and foundation case of *Re Musisi* [1987] AC 514, in which the removal of a Ugandan to Kenya was quashed because of Kenya's practice of returning Ugandans home, had established that art 33 of the Refugee Convention prevented indirect as well as direct *refoulement*: *Musisi* at 532C–E.
2 See references in Goodwin-Gill **12.5** fn 1 above.
3 See eg Preamble to Resolution on a harmonised approach to questions concerning host third countries, approved by EU ministers 30 November 1992 under Third Pillar.
4 See UNHCR 'The "safe third country" policy in the light of the international obligations of countries vis-à-vis refugees and asylum seekers' London, July 1993. See also Amnesty International *Playing human pinball: Home Office practice in 'safe third country' asylum cases* (June 1995); ECRE *Safe third countries: myths and realities* (February 1995). In *R v Uxbridge Magistrates' Court, ex p Adimi* [1999] INLR 490, the Divisional Court held, rejecting the submission of the Home Office to the contrary, that asylum seekers had an element of choice as to where they might claim asylum: per Simon Brown LJ at 496H–497A–C and Newman J at 507C.
5 For a discussion of the relationship between the provisions of the 1999 and 2002 Acts see *ST (Sri Lanka)* [2005] UKIAT 00006.

12.140 A third country removal engages the UK's obligations under the Refugee Convention only if it exposes the claimant (directly or indirectly)[1] to a real risk of *refoulement*;[2] there is no breach if removal may be ineffective in the sense that the third country returns the applicant to the UK.[3] However, repeated ineffective removals would be oppressive and might constitute inhuman treatment;[4] in practice the Home Office normally only operated the third country procedure once, dealing with the claim substantively if the person is returned here. The Immigration Rules now provide that if a person is not admitted to a safe third country (other than one to which he or she has been removed in accordance with the Dublin Regulation[5]), the person will be admitted to the asylum procedure in the UK.[6] If the third state removes the claimant to a fourth state, that in itself would not breach the UK's obligations under the Convention if it were a safe country and a procedure was in place in the third state to assess the safety of the fourth state,[7] but where a removal by the UK instigated a real risk of *refoulement* via a chain of states then the UK's obligation would still be engaged.

[1] *Re Musisi* at **12.139** fn 1 above.

[2] Ie return to the borders of the territory where persecution is feared. See Goodwin-Gill **12.5** fn 1 above, ch 4.

[3] *R v Secretary of State for the Home Department, ex p Dursun* [1991] Imm AR 297; *R v Secretary of State for the Home Department, ex p Mehari* [1994] QB 474, [1994] 2 All ER 494; *Thavathevathasan v Secretary of State for the Home Department* [1994] Imm AR 249; *Jafar v Secretary of State for the Home Department* [1994] Imm AR 497.

[4] *Karali v Secretary of State for the Home Department* [1991] Imm AR 199.

[5] See **12.157ff** below.

[6] HC 395, para 345(2), as inserted to implement Article 27(4) of Council Directive 2005/85/EC on minimum standards on procedures in Member States for granting and withdrawing refugee status.

[7] *Martinas v Special Adjudicator and the Secretary of State for the Home Department* [1995] Imm AR 190, CA.

The 1993 and 1996 Acts

12.141 Section 6 of the Asylum and Immigration Appeals Act 1993[1] prohibited the removal of asylum seekers until their claims were determined, but asylum claims by those deemed removable to a third country[2] were determined by the Secretary of State without consideration of the merits and certified 'without foundation' as not engaging the UK's obligations under the Refugee Convention.[3] An in-country appeal against refusal on third country grounds was provided, with its own special procedures.[4] The procedure was predicated on speedy removals[5] and an underlying assumption that there would be little if any basis for challenging the certificates, since most third-country returns were to European, usually EU, states. But many certificates were overturned on appeal or on judicial review because of unsafe procedures in EU Member States and the risk of chain or direct *refoulement* from them.[6] The Asylum and Immigration Act 1996 removed the in-country right of appeal where the third country was an EU Member State or a designated country.[7] The 1996 Act expressly excluded asylum claimants removable to third countries from the protection from removal provided in section 6 of the Asylum and Immigration Appeals Act 1993[8] and put into statutory form the criteria for certification on 'third country' grounds previously only contained in the Immigration Rules.[9]

[1] Re-enacted as Immigration and Asylum Act 1999, s 15.

[2] Defined under the Immigration Rules, HC 395, para 345 (still in force, though substituted from 25 October 2004 by Cm 1112), as those who had not arrived directly in the UK from the place where persecution is feared and had had an opportunity to make contact with the authorities of another country to seek their protection, or there was clear evidence of their admissibility to a third country, and who could be removed (a) to a country of which they were not a national or citizen, (b) where their life or freedom was not threatened contrary to Article 33 of the Refugee Convention and (c) from where they would not be sent elsewhere in a manner inconsistent with the Convention.

[3] Asylum and Immigration Appeals Act 1993, Sch 2, para 5(2).

[4] Asylum and Immigration Appeals Act 1993 s 8; Asylum Appeals (Procedure) Rules 1993, SI 1993/1661.

5   *R v Secretary of State for the Home Department, ex p Mehari* [1994] Imm AR 151, QBD; *Secretary of State for the Home Department v Abdi and Gawe* [1994] Imm AR 402, CA, [1996] Imm AR 288, HL.

6   Between 1993 and 1996, special adjudicators (designated under Asylum and Immigration Appeals Act 1993, s 8(5) to hear asylum appeals) consistently rejected certificates relating to removals to France and Belgium: see *R v Secretary of State for the Home Department, ex p Canbolat* [1997] Imm AR 442 at 454; *R v Special Adjudicator, ex p Turus, Bostem, Ammen, Folly-Notsron and Ururgul* [1996] Imm AR 388 at 393, and frequently rejected certificates relating to other Member States; and the Secretary of State ceased removing asylum seekers to Italy, Greece and Portugal following adverse decisions on their asylum procedures.

7   Asylum and Immigration Act 1996, s 3(2). The countries designated under s 2(3) as safe third countries were Canada, Norway, Switzerland and the US: Asylum (Designated Countries of Destination and Designated Safe Third Countries) Order 1996, SI 1996/2671, in force 1 October 1996. The same four countries were then designated under the Asylum (Designated Safe Third Countries) Order 2000, SI 2000/2245 (lapsed on the repeal of the enabling authority by the AI(TC)A 2004, s 33(2), 47, Sch 4, as from 1 October 2004). Following the coming into force of the 1996 Act the Secretary of State resumed third country removals to all EU Member States (see fn 6 above).

8   Asylum and Immigration Act 1996, s 2(2).

9   Asylum and Immigration Act 1996, s 2(2).

The 1999 and 2002 Acts

12.142 Sections 11,[1] 12[2] and 15[3] of the Immigration and Asylum Act 1999 replaced the provisions of the 1993 and 1996 Acts in respect of all three categories of third-country cases: removals to EU Member States under standing arrangements,[4] removals to Member States otherwise than under standing arrangements[5] and to designated countries,[6] and removals to non-EU and non-designated countries.[7] The Nationality, Immigration and Asylum Act 2002 amended these provisions, as well as replacing the appeals regime under the IAA 1999.[8] The AI(TC)A 2004 repealed sections 11 and 12 of the 1999 Act with effect from 1 October 2004,[9] subject to transitional provisions.[10]

1   As substituted by NIAA 2002, s 80.

2   As amended by the Nationality, Immigration and Asylum Act 2002 (Consequential and Incidental Provisions) Order 2003, SI 2003/1016, Schedule, para 11, to reflect its legal effect within the new appeals framework in Part 5 of the NIAA 2002.

3   Replaced by NIAA 2002, s 77.

4   Immigration and Asylum Act 1999, s 11 (as substituted).

5   IAA 1999, s 12(1)(a).

6   IAA 1999, s 12(1)(b). The countries designated under the 1999 Act were, as before, Canada, Norway, Switzerland and the US: Asylum (Designated Safe Third Countries) Order 2000, SI 2000/2245 (see **12.141** fn 7 above).

7   Immigration and Asylum Act 1999, s 12(4), (5) (as amended).

8   See Part V of the NIAA 2002 (ss 81–117).

9   Section 33(2) of the AI(TC)A 2004 and Asylum and Immigration (Treatment of Claimants, etc) Act 2004 (Commencement No 1) Order 2004, SI 2004/2523.

10 SI 2004/2523 art 3.

Removals to EU countries under standing arrangements under the 1999 and 2002 Acts

12.143 Section 11 of the Immigration and Asylum Act 1999 (as substituted)[1] allowed asylum seekers to be removed despite the statutory protection against removal[2] if the Secretary of State had certified that: (i) a Member State had accepted responsibility under standing arrangements for the asylum claim[3] and

(ii) in his or her opinion, the claimant was not a national or citizen of the Member State to which he or she was to be sent[4] (unless a human rights claim had been made,[5] which had not been certified clearly unfounded,[6] and an appeal could be brought or was pending).[7] Section 11(1) contained the first statutory presumption of safety, providing that in determining whether the person would be removed under standing arrangements a Member State was to be regarded 'as a place where life and liberty is not threatened for Refugee Convention reasons and from which the person will not be sent to another country otherwise than in accordance with the Refugee Convention'.[8] As the Court of Appeal subsequently held in *Ibrahim*,[9] the statutory presumption of safety worked. Despite the wording of section 11(3) and (4), suggestive of in-country appeal possibilities, in the great majority of cases there was no in-country appeal right. This was because the Secretary of State certified the human rights claim as clearly unfounded in the vast majority of cases, and the issue of the certificate prevented an in-country appeal.[10]

[1] By NIAA 2002, s 80 (with full effect from 1 April 2003 (see Nationality, Immigration and Asylum Act 2002 (Commencement No 4) Order 2003, SI 2003/754). For a discussion of the relationship between the provisions of the 1999 and 2002 Acts see *ST (Sri Lanka)* [2005] UKIAT 00006.

[2] See NIAA 2002, s 77.

[3] Immigration and Asylum Act 1999, s 11(2)(a) (as substituted). Standing arrangements were defined in s 11(5) as arrangements in force between two or more Member States for determining which State was responsible for considering applications for asylum. Although not specifically named, this meant the Dublin II regulation (Council Regulation (EC) No 343/2003 of 18 February 2003 establishing the criteria and mechanisms for determining the Member State responsible for examining an asylum application lodged in one of the Member States by a third-country national), which replaced the 1990 Dublin Convention with effect from 1 September 2003.

[4] IAA 1999, s 11(2)(b) (as substituted).

[5] NIAA 2002, s 113(1) defined a 'human rights claim' as 'a claim made by a person to the Secretary of State at a place designated by the Secretary of State that to remove the person from or require him to leave the UK would be unlawful under section 6 of the Human Rights Act 1998 (c 42) (public authority not to act contrary to Convention) as being incompatible with his Convention rights'.

[6] NIAA 2002, s 93(2). Note the separate power to certify a third country 'safe' in human rights terms, under s 94(7). This human rights certification was developed under the 2004 Act, Sch 3: see **12.147** ff below.

[7] IAA 1999, s 11(4) (as substituted). No in-country appeal could be brought if the Secretary of State certified removability to a third country unless a human rights claim had been made which was not certified. Note that there were potentially two certificates in play here: (i) under IAA 1999, s 11(2) or 12(2) (as amended), allowing removal to the third country; (ii) under NIAA 2002, s 93(2)(b), that a human rights claim was clearly unfounded: see eg *R (on the application of Nadarajah) v Secretary of State for the Home Department; R (on the application of Abdi) v Same* [2005] EWCA Civ 1363, (2005) Times, 14 December, Laws LJ at paras 36–37 regarding separate challenges to each certificate.

[8] IAA 1999, s 11(1)(a) and (b). The presumption was inserted during the passage of the 1999 Act in direct response to the Court of Appeal's decision in *Adan* in order to meet and defeat challenges to removal without investigation by the courts into Member State's interpretation or application of the Convention (see *R v Secretary of State for the Home Department, ex p Adan* [1999] 4 All ER 774, subsequently upheld by the House of Lords in *R v Secretary of State for the Home Department v Adan, R v Secretary of State for the Home Department, ex p Aitseguer* [2001] INLR 44 and see **12.144** below). Announcing the amendment in July 2000, the minister explained that it was based on 'the principle that Member States trust each other to consider asylum claims in accordance with the 1951 Convention'. But the lesson of the litigation since 1993 is that trust alone cannot ensure compliance with the UK's obligations to refugees.

[9] *R v Secretary of State for the Home Department, ex p Ibrahim (Ayman)* [2001] EWCA Civ 519, [2001] Imm AR 430; see also *R v Secretary of State for the Home Department, ex p Hatim* [2001] EWHC574 (Admin), [2001] Imm AR 688. In Simon Brown LJ's words,

'Parliament has, it is clear, in unambiguous terms dictated that henceforth France, amongst other Member States, is to be regarded as a safe third country. Of course the Secretary of State is not bound to certify in every case, but where he chooses to do so, in my judgment that certificate cannot be impugned on grounds that France after all is not properly to be regarded as a safe third country.' Although the only challenge was to the section 11 certification, and no human rights claim had yet been made, both Simon Brown LJ and Tuckey LJ expressed the view that certification of any such claim would be difficult to challenge (at paras 26 and 30). See further **12.147** ff below.

10   IAA 1999, s 11(4)(b) (as substituted).

Other removals under the 1999 and 2002 Acts

12.144 Section 12 of the Immigration and Asylum Act 1999 (as amended)[1] applied to removals to (i) EU Member States (or territories forming part of a Member State) otherwise than in accordance with standing arrangements,[2] (ii) designated countries[3] and (iii) countries which are neither Member States nor designated.[4] The conditions for certification on third-country grounds in such cases were that (a) the claimant was not a national or citizen of the country to which he or she was to be sent; (b) his or her life and liberty would not be threatened there by reason of his or her race, religion, nationality, membership of a particular social group, or political opinion; and (c) the government of that country would not send him or her to another country otherwise than in accordance with the Refugee Convention.[5] Unlike the position where return to the third country was under standing arrangements, there was no statutory presumption of safety of the third state in these cases. Subsections (7A) and (7B) of section 12 replicated the provisions of subsection (3) and (4) of section 11.[6] Shortly stated, the effect was that persons being removed under third-country provisions to countries in categories (i) and (ii) above all had an in-country appeal if they made a human rights claim in the UK, unless the human rights claim was certified as clearly unfounded. In the event of certification the only remedy was judicial review, although without the difficulties caused by the statutory presumption of safety in IAA 1999, section 11(1). In cases involving non-Dublin removals to EU states, and all other removals, the full range of arguments on the third state's interpretation and application of the Convention, and the likelihood of *refoulement* or chain removal from there, were open (whether on appeal or judicial review, depending on whether the human rights claim has been certified). Finally, where removal was to a country falling within category (iii) above (neither EU Member States nor designated countries) there was always a suspensive in-country appeal right, irrespective of whether any human rights claim had been made).[7]

1   By the Nationality, Immigration and Asylum Act 2002 (Consequential and Incidental Provisions) Order 2003, SI 2003/1016, Schedule, para 11. For a discussion of the relationship between the provisions of the 1999 and 2002 Acts see *ST (Sri Lanka)* [2005] UKIAT 00006.
2   IAA 1999, s 12(1)(a).
3   Canada, Norway, Switzerland and the USA: Immigration and Asylum Act 1999, s 12(1)(b); Asylum (Designated Safe Third Countries) Order 2000, SI 2000/2245 (see **12.141** fn 7 above). See *R v Secretary of State for the Home Department, ex p Salas* [2001] Imm AR 105 in which challenge was made to the safety of the USA as a third country, in particular as to that country's interpretation of arts 1A(2) and 33 of the Refugee Convention (leave to appeal to the CA was granted, but the matter settled).
4   IAA 1999, s 12(4).
5   IAA 1999, s 12(7).
6   See **12.143** above.

7   NIAA 2002, s 93(1) prevented in-country appeals where certificates were issued under IAA 1999, ss 11(2) and 12(2). Countries which are neither Member States nor designated were dealt with separately under IAA 1999, s 12(4). One significant change introduced by the appeals regime under the NIAA 2002 for third country appeals was the ability to appeal on the ground that a discretion conferred by the Immigration Rules should have been exercised differently (NIAA 2002, s 84(1)(f)). Under the previous appeals regime, a person facing return to a third country could not argue by reference to any such discretion, because the appeal was limited to consideration of the UK's obligations under the Refugee Convention (see *R v A Special Adjudicator, ex p Mehari* [1994] QB 474, [1994] 2 All ER 494, [1994] Imm AR 151). Since para 345 of the Immigration Rules sets out how the Secretary of State will 'normally' approach third country cases, the rule conferred a reveiwable discretion.

Certification of human rights claims under the 2002 Act

12.145 As pointed out above,[1] the presumption of safety under section 11 of the IAA 1999 applied only as regards the Refugee Convention. A person facing removal to a third country (whether under standing arrangements or otherwise) might have raised various human rights claims against removal.[2] The approach on judicial review to challenges to a 'third country' removal which is likely to lead to suicide or to interfere with the right to respect for family and private life is considered in CHAPTER 7. Here, we consider the scope under the IAA 1999 regime for arguing that removal under standing arrangements to an EU Member State engages Article 3 ECHR because of the risk of *refoulement*. In the fifth edition we pointed out that since the presumption of EU Member States' safety is a statutory one, it could only be overridden by the appellate authority reading in the words 'unless the contrary is proved',[3] in accordance with the interpretative obligation of the Human Rights Act 1998[4] to interpret legislation in a way which gives effect to, rather than defeats, human rights. This would allow the asylum seeker to adduce evidence disproving the presumption in a particular case. Cogent evidence that the statutory presumption of safety was not justified in an individual case or category of case ought to have provided a basis for challenge to a certificate that the human rights claim is clearly unfounded.[5] It might have been thought that the decision in *Adan and Aitsegeur*[6] would provide the basis for such a challenge, in particular in light of the decision of the ECtHR in *TI v United Kingdom*,[7] where the court ruled both that removal through an intermediary country (also a contracting state) did not affect the UK's obligation to ensure that the claimant was not exposed to treatment contrary to Article 3 ECHR, and that the Dublin Convention, as an international agreement for attribution of responsibility between European countries for deciding claims in the related area of asylum, did not absolve the UK from its obligations under the ECHR.[8] In *Thangarasa*,[9] the Secretary of State certified as manifestly unfounded[10] the human rights claim of a Sri Lankan Tamil facing removal to Germany (based on the risk of chain removal to Sri Lanka), and a challenge to the certification of the human rights claim based on the decision of the ECtHR in *TI v United Kingdom* was rejected by the House of Lords.[11] There have to date been no successful challenges to certification on *refoulement* grounds. Thus in practical terms, even though the statutory presumption of safety under section 11(1) applied expressly only to the Refugee Convention, it defeated ECHR-based *refoulement* arguments as well. Nevertheless, as will be seen, under the AI(TC)A 2004, the statutory presumption of safety in repect of *refoulement* under the Refugee Convention is treated separately from any such presumption with reference to the Human Rights Convention, with some countries being deemed 'safe' in respect of both Conventions, while others are deemed safe only in respect of the former Convention.[12]

1   See **12.143** above.
2   See **12.143** above.
3   By analogy with the court's approach to an irrebuttable presumption of service contained in former procedural rules, in *R v Secretary of State for the Home Department, ex p Saleem (Asifa)* [2000] INLR 413, CA; see 5th edition at **12.156**.
4   Human Rights Act 1998, s 3; see **7.15** above. Otherwise, the Divisional Court might have to make a declaration of incompatibility under s 4 of the Human Rights Act 1998, on the basis that preventing an asylum seeker from proving the existence of facts which make his or her removal potentially in breach of art 3 of the ECHR is itself a breach of that Article together with art 13 of the ECHR (the right to an effective remedy): see **7.17** above and see *R (on the application of Nasseri) v Secretary of State for the Home Department* [2009] UKHL 23, [2010] AC 1, [2009] 2 WLR 1190 at **12.147** below.
5   Ie, a certificate under Nationality, Immigration and Asylum Act 2002, s 93(2)(b), referred to in Immigration and Asylum Act 1999, s 11(4)(b) (as substituted by NIAA 2002, s 80). See, however, *Nasseri* (fn 4 above).
6   *R v Secretary of State for the Home Department, ex p Adan, R v Secretary of State for the Home Department, ex p Aitseguer* [2001] INLR 44, HL, upholding the Court of Appeal's judgment in *R v Secretary of State for the Home Department, ex p Adan* [1999] 4 All ER 774 that French and German interpretations of the Refugee Convention were incorrect.
7   *TI v United Kingdom* [2000] INLR 211 (ECtHR).
8   *TI v United Kingdom* above, at 228–229. The ECtHR rejected the application as manifestly ill-founded on the facts, concluding that there was no real risk that Germany would expel the applicant to Sri Lanka in breach of art 3 ECHR.
9   *R (on the application of Thangarasa) v Secretary of State for the Home Department* [2001] EWHC 420 (Admin) *(Collins J)*, upheld by the Court of Appeal at [2001] EWCA Civ 1611, [2001] All ER (D) 121 (Sep) and by the House of Lords at [2002] UKHL 36, [2003] 1 AC 920, [2002] 4 All ER 800, [2002] 3 WLR 1276, [2002] INLR 620.
10 The 1999 Act certification regime was based on claims being 'manifestly unfounded'; the 2002 Act introduced the present formulation, clearly unfounded' (which has the same meaning: see *R (on the application of L) v Secretary of State for the Home Department* [2003] EWCA Civ 25, [2003] Imm AR 330, [2003] INLR 224).
11 The Court of Appeal accepted that in Germany the applicant would have a right of individual petition to the ECtHR, that Germany would scrupulously comply with any request from the court to suspend execution of any deportation order and that it was the universal practice of the German courts and executive to comply with ECtHR judgments (paras 65–66). Lord Hope in the House of Lords found these considerations 'conclusive of the issue as to whether his rights under art 3 would be at risk of being violated if he were to be returned to Germany' (HL para 56). See also *KRS v United Kingdom* (Application No 32733/08); (2009) 48 EHRR SE8) holding inadmissible, as manifestly ill-founded, the Iranian applicant's complaint that his removal from the UK to Greece would violate his art 3 rights.
12 AI(TC)A 2004, Sch 3; see below at **12.147**.

Third country certification under section 94 of the 2002 Act

12.146 We have shown above that the third country regime was based on an interplay between sections 11 and 12 of the 1999 Act (as amended) and the appeals provisions of the NIAA 2002. The hallmarks of the regime were the certification procedures enabling the Secretary of State to effect removal of asylum seekers to third countries without substantive consideration of their claims and, in some cases, without suspensive appeal. Section 94 of the NIAA 2002 controversially extended the non-suspensive appeal regime in a number of ways.[1] First, section 94(7) is a discrete provision enabling any third-country case to be certified on the ground that there is 'no reason to believe that the person's rights under the Human Rights Convention will be breached' in the third country. Certification prevents the bringing of an in-country appeal against removal. Secondly, there is a statutory presumption of safety contained in section 94(8) in respect of countries which are the subject of section 94(7) certificates. This presumption of safety mirrors that contained in section 11(1) of the IAA 1999.[2] But whereas the section 11(1) presumption bit only in respect of removals under standing arrangements to EU Member States, certification and the statutory presumption of safety under section 94(8) can be applied to *any* country. This is reminiscent of the famous 'Humpty Dumpty' speech of Lord Atkin;[3] the Secretary of State can make any country 'safe' simply by certifying it so, and neither you nor I nor the vicar's dog may gainsay him. This is faith, not justice.

1   See NIAA 2002 s 94, and **7.120** above.
2   It provides that in determining whether a person in relation to whom a certificate has been issued under sub-s (7) may be removed from the UK, the country specified in the certificate is to be regarded both as a place where a person's life and liberty is not threatened by reason of his race, religion, nationality, membership of a particular social group, or political opinion, and a place from which a person will not be sent to another country otherwise than in accordance with the Refugee Convention: NIAA 2002, s 94(8). The provision is somewhat curious since the focus of sub-s (8) is on the *Refugee* Convention whereas certification, under sub-s (7), arises in respect of third country removals where there is no reason to believe that the person's righs under the *Human Rights* Convention will be breached.
3   Dissenting in *Liversidge v Anderson* [1942] AC 206.

Asylum and Immigration (Treatment of Claimants, etc) Act 2004

12.147 The third country regime is substantially re-cast (again) by the provisions of the AI(TC)A 2004 which further develop the main ideas of the 1999 and 2002 Acts (a lava flow of presumptions of safety and relentless removal of in-country appeal rights). Sections 11 and 12 of the IAA 1999 (as amended) were repealed with effect from 1 October 2004 and replaced by the provisions in the AI(TC)A 2004, Sch 3, although the previous provisions continued to have effect in relation to those already subject to certificates under the 1999 Act regime.[1] Part 2 of the Schedule contains a list of 29 countries, the 'First List of Safe Countries (Refugee Convention and Human Rights)',which presently comprise 26 other EU Member States (UK excepted and Croatia not yet added) together with Iceland, Norway and Switzerland.[2] For the purposes of the determination by any person, tribunal or court whether an asylum or human rights claimant may be removed from the UK to a state of which he is not a national or citizen the First List countries are to be treated as places:

(i)   where a person's life and liberty are not threatened by reason of his race, religion, nationality, membership of a particular social group or political opinion;

(ii)   from which a person will not be sent to another State in contravention of his [Human Rights] Convention rights; and

(iii) from which a person will not be sent to another State otherwise than in accordance with the Refugee Convention.[3]

One consequence of this provision is that even if the Secretary of State was to be presented with clear and compelling evidence that an asylum seeker's removal to a listed country would result in his or her further removal in breach of the ECHR, the Secretary of State, being a 'person' within the meaning of para 3(1) of Sch 3, would be bound to ignore that evidence in deciding whether to remove the person.[4] That consequence led the Administrative Court in *Nasseri* to make a declaration under section 4 of the Human Rights Act 1998 that para 3 of Sch 3 is incompatible with the obligation under art 3 of the ECHR to investigate a potential breach of Article 3 resulting from the claimant's removal from the UK to a country on the first list of safe countries.[5] However, the Court of Appeal and then the House of Lords reversed the Administrative Court's decision.[6] The Lords held that the irrebutable presumption as to safety is not incompatible with Article 3, firstly, because the presumption only applies for the purpose of determining whether a person may be removed lawfully from the UK to a listed country and does not preclude an inquiry into whether his or her Article 3 rights will be infringed for the different purpose of deciding whether a provision which makes such a removal lawful would be incompatible with Convention rights – such a declaration of incompatibility has no effect on the *lawfulness* of the removal, which is the only purpose for which the 2004 Act precludes an inquiry; secondly, because the judge had been wrong to say that Article 3 creates a procedural obligation to investigate whether there is a risk of a breach by the receiving state, independently of whether or not such a risk actually exists; thirdly, because Members States of the EU were entitled to assume – not conclusively presume, but to start with the assumption – that other Member States would adhere to their treaty obligations, including those under the ECHR, unless the evidence demonstrated otherwise.[7] The prohibition on removal while a claim for asylum is pending under s 77 of the NIAA 2002 does not prevent removal from the UK to one of the First List countries, provided that the Secretary of State certifies that in his opinion the person is not a national or citizen of the destination state.[8] Further, a certificate to the same effect issued by the Secretary of State prevents an in-country appeal being brought even on the basis of a claim that the country is not safe in *refoulement* terms as regards either the Refugee Convention or the Human Rights Act 1998.[9] As regards any other human rights claims, there is no in-country appeal where the Secretary of State certifies the claim 'clearly unfounded'.[10] What is new here is the requirement to certify unless satisfied that the claim is not clearly unfounded, extending the provisions of s 94(3) of the NIAA 2002 to human rights claims in third country cases.[11] Moreover, even where a person appeals after removal, an appeal cannot be brought on any ground that is inconsistent with the presumptions of safety as regards First List countries – either asserting that life or liberty are threatened for Refugee Convention reasons in the country, or asserting a risk of *refoulement* under the Refugee Convention or engaging the Human Rights Act 1998.[12] On the other hand, the question as to whether the applicant would face a real risk of Article 3 violation (in particular in the form of inhuman or degrading living conditions as an asylum seeker there) in the listed 'safe third country' itself, is to be answered according to the 'normal' test in *Soering*[13] and there is no requirement that the applicant need demonstrate 'systemic deficiencies' in the listed country's asylum procedures and reception conditions for removal from the UK to the listed country to be unlawful.[14] Finally, although the position as regards suspensive appeals does not preclude a challenge by judicial review, it would still be necessary to contend with the statutory presumptions of safety and the position adopted by Simon Brown LJ in *Ibrahim*[15] and by the House of Lords in *Nasseri*.[16]

1 AI(TC)A 2004, s 33(2) repeals ss 11 and 12 of the IAA 1999, s 33(3) repeals ss 80 and 93 of the NIAA 2002, and s 33(1) refers to the detailed provisions of Sch 3. For commencement see SI 2004/2523. Article 3 of the Order provides that ss 11 and 12 of the 1999 Act and ss 80 and 93 of the Nationality, Immigration and Asylum Act 2002 continue to have effect in relation to a person who is subject to a certificate under s 11(2) or s 12(2) or (5) of the 1999 Act issued before 1 October 2004. See above at **12.1432–12.145**.

2 The countries are those which are subject or have agreed to be bound by the Dublin arrangements. Additional countries joining the Dublin arrangements may be added by order: see Sch 3, Part 6, providing for amendment by statutory instrument of the Sch 3, para 2 list by addition of states. Bulgaria and Romania were added to the original list of 26 countries by SI 2006/3393 with effect in relation to decisions refusing leave to enter or to remove made on or after 1 January 2007 in response to asylum and human rights claims even if made before 1 January 2007. Switzerland was added by SI 2010/2802 with effect in relation to decisions refusing leave to enter or to remove made on or after 20 November 2010 in response to asylum and human rights claims even if made before 20 November 2010. Unlike the position with the Second and Third Lists in Sch 3, paras 7 and 12, there is no power to remove a State from the First List and there is no legal requirement on the Secretary of State to promote primary legislation to remove a State from the First List: *R (on the application of Nasseri) v Secretary of State for the Home Department* [2009] UKHL 23, [2010] AC 1,, [2009] 2 WLR 1190 per Lord Hoffmann at paras 21–22.

3 AI(TC)A 2004, Sch 3, para 3.

4 See *R (on the application of Nasseri) v Secretary of State for the Home Department* [2009] UKHL 23, [2010] AC 1, [2009] 2 WLR 1190: see text above.

5 *R (on the application of Nasseri) v Secretary of State for the Home Department* [2007] EWHC 1548 (Admin), [2008] 1 All ER 411 – in respect to removals to Greece.

6 *R (on the application of Nasseri) v Secretary of State for the Home Department* [2008] EWCA Civ 464 [2009] 1 All ER 116; [2009] UKHL 23, [2009] 2 WLR 1190, [2010] AC 1.

7 *R (on the application of Nasseri) v Secretary of State for the Home Department* [2009] UKHL 23, [2010] AC 1, [2009] 2 WLR 1190, especially per Lord Hoffmann. The CA and the HL had been influenced by the Strasbourg decision in *KRS v United Kingdom* (Application No 32733/08; 2 December 2008) (2009) 48 EHRR SE8, in concluding that there was an absence of evidence of refoulment from Greece. However in *MSS v Belgium and Greece* (Application No 30696/09) (2011) 53 EHRR 2, the Grand Chamber, as well as finding that the applicant would be at real risk of art 3 violation in Greece itself if removed there from Belgium, also found that there was a real risk of his being refouled in violation of his art 3 rights from Greece to Afghanistan. See also *NS v Secretary of State for the Home Department (Principles of Community law)* [2011] EUECJ C-411/10: see paras **12.161** et seq below. See also regarding Cyprus, *R (on the application of Elayathamby) v Secretary of State for the Home Department* [2011] EWHC 2182 (Admin): see **12.165** below. See also regarding Romania, *VT (Dublin Regulation: Post-removal Appeal: Sri Lanka)* [2012] UKUT 308 (IAC), [2013] Imm AR 45. The litigation relating to third country removals to Italy has concentrated on the asserted risk of violation of art 3 rights for asylum seekers in Italy itself: see *R (on the application of EM (Eritrea) v Secretary of State for the Home Department* [2014] UKSC 12, [2014] 2 WLR 409, [2014] 2 All ER 192, [2014] Imm AR 640: see fn 14 below. See also *R (on the application of Tabrizagh) v Secretary of State for the Home Department* [2014] EWHC 1914 (Admin).

8 AI(TC)A 2004, Sch 3, para 4.

9 AI(TC)A 2004, Sch 3, para 5(2) precludes, any appeal which would otherwise be in-country under NIAA 2002, s 92(2) including a variation appeal, and a deportation appeal, or under NIAA 2002, s 92(3) an appeal against refusal of leave to enter where the person concerned holds an entry clearance: AI(TC)A 2004, Sch 3, para 5(2). Sch 3, para 5(3) precludes an in-country appeal relying on s 84(1)(g) of the 2002 Act.

10 AI(TC)A 2004, Sch 3 para 5(4), (5).

11 See Explanatory Notes to the AI(TC)A 2004 at para 148.

12 AI(TC)A 2004, Sch 3, para 6. See for an example of such an appeal, *VT (Dublin Regulation: Pos-removal Appeal: Sri Lanka)* [2012] UKUT 308 (IAC), [2013] Imm AR 45.

13 *Soering v United Kingdom* (1989) 11 EHRR 439.

14 *R (on the application of EM (Eritrea) v Secretary of State for the Home Department* [2014] UKSC 12, [2014] 2 WLR 409, [2014] 2 All ER 192, [2014] Imm AR 640: the SC reversed the CA on the issue relating to 'systemic deficiencies' and explained the CJEU ruling in *NS v*

Secretary of State for the Home Department (Amnesty International Ltd and the AIRE Centre (Advice on Individual Rights in Europe) (UK)): C-411/10[2013] QB 102, [2012] All ER (EC) 1011, ECJ: see **12.159** below.

15 *R v Secretary of State for the Home Department, ex p Ibrahim (Ayman)* [2001] EWCA Civ 519, [2001] Imm AR 430; see also *R v Secretary of State for the Home Department, ex p Hatim* [2001] EWHC 574 (Admin) 574, [2001] Imm AR 688 and see above at **12.143** fn 9 above.

16 Fns 6 and 7 above.

12.148 We set out below an example of how the provisions of the AI(TC)A 2004 would work in respect of the claim for asylum made by someone arriving in the UK from a First List country:

'A Somali national claims asylum at Dover having arrived by ferry from Calais. As well as claiming asylum based on her fear of return to Somalia, she claims that removal to France would result in France returning her to Somalia in breach of the Refugee Convention (because of France's application or interpretation of the Refugee Convention – thereby also breaching Article 3 ECHR), and that her removal would also breach her right to respect for family life (under Article 8 ECHR) based on the presence in the UK of family members.[1]

(i) France is a First List country. Unlike the position under the previous third country regimes it does not matter whether the French authorities accept that France is the State responsible for determining the asylum claim under Dublin arrangements.[2] The Secretary of State may refuse leave to enter and issue a certificate under Sch 3 paras 3 and 4 of the AI(TC)A 2004 to the effect that removal is to a First List country and that in his opinion the claimant is not a national or citizen of that State.

(ii) The certificate under Schedule 3, paragraph 3 prevents her from bringing an appeal in country by reliance on NIAA, s 92(2) (which provides that specified immigration decisions are normally appealable in-country) or by reliance on section 92(3) (whereby refusal of leave to enter can be appealed in country if the person had entry clearance).[3]

(iii) Moreover, she cannot appeal by virtue of section 92(4)(a) (that is as a person who has made an asylum or human rights claim)[4] in reliance on any assertion that her removal to France would breach the UK's Refugee Convention obligations,[5] nor in reliance on an assertion that her removal to France would breach her human rights 'because of the possibility of removal from [France] to another state'.[6]

(iv) This leaves only the claimant's Article 8 claim based on the presence of family members in the UK, which will give rise to an in-country appeal unless the Secretary of State certifies the claim as clearly unfounded. But the Secretray of State is likely to certify the claim, since he or she is required to do so 'unless satisfied that the claim is not clearly unfounded'.[7]

The only remedy for the claimant is judicial review. We consider the possibility of challenge to the certification of human rights claims below. Finally, as regards any discrete judicial review challenge to the application of Dublin III, see the discussion at **12.158** ff below.

1 *Refoulement* and family life issues are of course not the only possible human rights grounds that might be raised in a third country case. Factors relating to the health of the claimant if the impact of removal is sufficiently severe to engage art 3 ECHR, *R (on the application of Soumahoro) v Secretary of State for the Home Department* [2002] EWHC 2651 (Admin), [2002] All ER (D) 483 (Nov), or the moral and physical integrity of the person as an aspect of their private life protected by art 8 may also be raised: see eg *R (on the application of Razgar) v Secretary of State for the Home Department* [2004] UKHL 27, [2004] 3 WLR 58, **7.95** above. See also regarding possible arguments relating to reception conditions and the treatment of asylum seekers in the listed third country: see **12.146** fns 13 and 14 above.

[2]   Note that although the provisions of AI(TC)A 2004, Sch 3 make no reference to standing arrangements or acceptance of responsibility, the UK is party to Dublin III and judicial review might be available to challenge any irregularity in its appication: see further below at **12.158** ff.

[3]   AI(TC)A 2004, Sch 3, para 5(2) which disapplies the provisions of s 92(2) and (3) Nationality, Immigration and Asylum Act 2002, which provide in-country appeal rights to persons refused a certificate of entitlement, variation (in certain circumstances), revocation of indefinite leave, persons facing deportation and to certain persons refused leave to enter when holding entry clearance or a work permit.

[4]   Generally, those making human rights claims in the UK may appeal in-country: Nationality, Immigration and Asylum Act 2002, s 92(4)(a).

[5]   AI(TC)A 2004, Sch 3, para 5(3)(a).

[6]   AI(TC)A 2004, Sch 3, para 5(3)(b).

[7]   AI(TC)A 2004, Sch 3, para 5(4).

12.149 The 'Second List of Safe Countries (Refugee Convention and Human Rights)', the subject-matter of Part 3 of Schedule 3, are states which may be specified by the Secretary of State by statutory instrument.[1] In third-country proceedings, these specified states are to be treated as places (i) where a person's life and liberty are not threatened by reason of his race, religion, nationality, membership of a particular social group or political opinion; (ii) from which a person will not be sent to another State otherwise than in accordance with the Refugee Convention.[2] As with the First List countries in Part 2 of Schedule 3, the presumption of safety precludes any appeal (in- or out of country) which is inconsistent with it.[3] A certificate that an applicant is not a national or citizen of the state will disapply the statutory protection against removal to a specified state[4] and will prevent an in-country immigration appeal,[5] including one relying on an asylum claim based on *refoulement* arguments.[6] Human rights claims will not attract an in-country appeal if certified as clearly unfounded, and certification is the 'default' position.[7]

[1]   At the time of writing, no statutory instrument has been made, so there are no states in this Part.

[2]   AI(TC)A 2004, Sch 3, para 7.

[3]   AI(TC)A 2004, Sch 3, para 11. Note that on an out-of-country appeal it is still possible to argue that removal to the specified state was likely to lead to a breach of art 3 ECHR, whether direct or by *refoulement* from there to the country of origin, since unlike the limitation in para 6 on grounds which may be raised in relation to First List countries, there is nothing in Sch 3, para 11 to prevent the argument as regards removal contrary to the ECHR.

[4]   AI(TC)A 2004, Sch 3, para 9.

[5]   AI(TC)A 2004, Sch 3, para 10(2); see **12.147** fn 3 above.

[6]   AI(TC)A 2004, Sch 3, para 10(3).

[7]   AI(TC)A 2004, Sch 3, para 10(4). The effect of the two sub-paragraphs taken together is that in-country human rights appeals, whether relying on *refoulement* arguments (see **12.142** above) or not, may be brought but are likely to be prevented by certification that the claim is clearly unfounded. In any event, s 94(7) Nationality, Immigration and Asylum Act 2002 remains in force, enabling the Secretary of State to certify that there is no reason to believe that the person's rights under the Human Rights Convention will be breached in the third country concerned, which also prevents an appeal: see **12.145** above.

12.150 The 'Third list of safe countries (Refugee Convention only)' referred to in Part 4 of the Schedule,[1] are once again countries which are to be specified by order of the Secretary of State. In relation to these countries, the same presumptions apply, with the same effects, as with the 'Second List' countries, save that an in-country human rights appeal may be brought unless the Secretary of State certifies it clearly unfounded, and there is no 'default position' that he or she will so certify.[2]

1   AI(TC)A 2004, Sch 3, paras 12–16. As in relation to the second list, at the time of writing no statutory instrument has been made, so there are no states in this Part.
2   AI(TC)A 2004, Sch 3, para 15(4), cf para 10(4).

12.151 Part 5 of the Schedule deals with 'Countries certified as safe for individuals'. As its title suggests, this Part enables the Secretary of State to certify any other third country as a place (i) where a person's life and liberty will not be threatened by reason of his race, religion, nationality, membership of a particular social group or political opinion; (ii) from which the person will not be sent to another State otherwise than in accordance with the Refugee Convention.[1] As with the Third List countries, certification under this part disapplies the statutory protection against removal,[2] prevents an in-country immigration appeal, including one relying on an asylum claim based on *refoulement* arguments,[3] and prevents out-of-country asylum appeals which challenge the presumption of safety.[4] Human rights claims will not attract an in-country appeal if certified clearly unfounded, but there is no 'default position' that such a claim is clearly unfounded, as with the first two lists.[5] The pernicious aspect of this Part (as with the power under section 94(7) of the 2002 Act, see **12.145** above) is that there is no Parliamentary scrutiny whatever of the Secretary of State's opinion that a particular country is safe for the individual, an opinion which results in a very serious loss of judicial protection for the individual. It is all part of a philosophy of creating a sheltered system of unchallengeable executive decisions which are kept as immune from judicial scrutiny as possible.

1   AI(TC)A 2004, Sch 3, para 17(c).
2   AI(TC)A 2004, Sch 3, para 18.
3   AI(TC)A 2004, Sch 3, para 19(a), (b).
4   AI(TC)A 2004, Sch 3, para 19(d).
5   AI(TC)A 2004, Sch 3, para 19(c).

12.152 Until the introduction of the statutory presumption of safety under the 1999 Act, the principal issue in third country cases was the possibility that the third country would remove the claimant in a manner inconsistent with its Refugee Convention obligations. As we have seen, the presumption was reinforced by the 2002 Act, and the current 2004 Act regime for the first time extends the presumption as regards First List countries so as to preclude the possibility of raising *refoulement* arguments under the ECHR. Nevertheless, and as acknowledged by the House of Lords in *Nasseri*,[1] the presumption of safety cannot be necessarily conclusive, and there may be some cases to which it cannot be applied consistently with the UK's ECHR obligations. The fact that the country has signed the Refugee Convention or other relevant international agreements that reaffirm its Convention obligations, that it co-operates with the UNHCR and has procedures in place to give effect to its obligations, has been held to constitute some evidence on which the Secretary of State could rely to conclude that removal would not be contrary to the UK's obligations.[2] But these factors were held to create a rebuttable presumption of safety which could be displaced by examination of the actual practice and procedures of the country.[3] The difficulty, in the light of the statutory presumption, lies in being able to litigate such matters. However, the possibility of *refoulement* by the third country has been the subject matter of close scrutiny by the courts, and readers are referred for analysis to the fifth edition of this work.[4] Other issues that have arisen in third country cases and have been the subject matter of scrutiny by English courts have included different approaches taken to the Refugee Convention (which culminated in the decision of the House of Lords in *Adan and Aitsegeur*[5] rejecting the Secretary of State's argument that there is a permissible range of interpretations of the Refugee Convention);[6] chain removals; de facto protection;[7] and the relevance of previous refusals.

[1]   See **12.146** above.

[2]   See **12.146** fn 7 above.

[3]   In *R v Secretary of State for the Home Department, ex p Gashi* [1999] INLR 276; revsd [1999] Imm AR 415, the Court of Appeal quashed a certificate in respect of the removal of two Kosovar Albanians to Germany on the basis that the Secretary of State could not demonstrate that adequate inquires had been made which would explain the gross disparity in outcome of claims from ethnic Albanians in the UK, where they were universally recognised as refugees, and Germany, where only a tiny%age were given refugee status and many were returned to ethnic cleansing in the Federal Republic of Yugoslavia. The Secretary of State withdrew an appeal to the House of Lords, and *Gashi* remains good law on the standard of inquires expected of the Secretary of State in such cases. The change in conditions in Kosovo in 1999 after the UN-sanctioned intervention meant that after June 1999 the disparity in treatment as between Germany and the UK disappeared and the Secretary of State could resume the certification of Germany as safe in such cases: *R v Secretary of State for the Home Department, ex p Gjoka and Gashi (Shefki)* (15 June 2000, unreported), Collins J More controversially the Secretary of State sought to re-certify in cases which had been stayed pending the resolution of the litigation in *Gashi*. In *R (on the application of Zeqiri) v Secretary of State for the Home Department* [2001] EWCA Civ 342, the House of Lords held that the decision of the Court of Appeal in *Besnik Gashi* did not create any legitimate expectation for applicants 'stacked up' behind him such as Mr Zeqiri (see [2002] UKHL 3, [2002] Imm AR 296, [2002] All ER (D) 184 (Jan)).

[4]   See 5th edition, 12.131–12.133.

[5]   *R v Secretary of State for the Home Department, ex p Adan, R v Secretary of State for the Home Department, ex p Aitseguer* [2001] INLR 44, HL, holding that the true meaning of art 1A(2) did not require state complicity for harm inflicted by non-state agents to constitute persecution; the protection of the Convention extends to those persecuted by non-state agents where 'for whatever reason the state in question is unable to afford protection against factions within the state'. See also *R (on the application of Kerkeb) v Secretary of State for the Home Department* (22 May 2000, unreported), QBD, upheld in the Court of Appeal at [2001] EWCA Civ 747, [2001] Imm AR 614.

[6]   With the coming into force of the Qualification Directive (**12.3** fn 3 above), great disparities in interpretation among EU Member States, such as formed the basis of the *Adan and Aitseguer* litigation, should have disappeared. It is important to note that the Directive lays down *minimum* standards, necessarily admitting of more favourable interpretation, and cannot override the terms of the Convention itself, which the courts must still be free to determine, although the Directive would be relevant to interpretation of the Convention as evidence of State practice: see Vienna Convention on the Law of Treaties, arts 31, 32.

[7]   In *Adan and Aitsegeur* the House of Lords left open the question of whether the conditions for removal were satisfied by alternative forms of protection in the receiving state despite differences in interpretation which would exclude asylum seekers from recognition as refugees there. In previous editions of this work, we suggested that any such alternative protection would have to be measured against the protection requirements of the Refugee Convention, so that to avoid a breach of art 33, the Secretary of State would have to show that equivalent protection was available in the third country. The House of Lords considered and rejected this suggestion in *R (on the application of Yogathas) v Secretary of State for the Home Department; R (on the application of Thangarasa) v Secretary of State for the Home Department*, holding that 'the Convention is directed to a very important but very simple and very practical end, preventing the return of applicants to places where they will or may suffer persecution. Legal niceties and refinements should not be allowed to obstruct that purpose' ([2002] UKHL 36, [2002] INLR 620, para 9, per Lord Bingham of Cornhill). If in practice

refoulement from the third state is not likely, a lesser status in that state will not prevent removal there from the UK.

Opportunity to claim in the third state

12.153 The Immigration Rules indicate that the Secretary of State will not issue a certificate to remove an asylum claimant to a 'safe' third country in accordance with Schedule 3 to the AI(TC)A 2004 unless the claimant arrived in the UK via another country and had an opportunity at the border of or within that country to claim asylum or there is some other clear evidence of the person's admissibility to the third country.[1] In most cases, certification will proceed on the basis of clear evidence of admissibility (for which see below), but where that evidence is lacking or ambivalent, the issue of opportunity to claim in the third country will assume importance. In considering whether the asylum claimant had the opportunity to claim asylum in the third country or at its borders, opportunity is to be objectively assessed. It does not mean a knowing opportunity in the sense that the claimant was aware of the third country's procedures for receiving refugee applications and could form a judgment as to whether it was appropriate to apply there. The question is whether the claimant could have approached the authorities at the border or internally and could have had an asylum claim received.[2] Of course, opportunity is only relevant if the country is safe. The courts have held that the fact that an agent planned the journey and for all intents and purposes dictated the claimant's actions does not preclude the claimant from having had an opportunity to make a claim *en route*.[3] But there will be no opportunity if the claimant was transported clandestinely through a country in a vehicle, or the method or duration of the transit is such that no immigration officials were met. The Rule does not import the concept of 'constructive opportunity': it must be the claimant who has the opportunity, not some third party over whom he or she has no control.

[1]   HC 395, para 345(2), substituted by HC 1112, 18 October 2004.
[2]   *R v Special Adjudicator, ex p Kandasamy* [1994] Imm AR 333, QBD.
[3]   *Dursun v Secretary of State for the Home Department* [1993] Imm AR 169, CA; *R v Secretary of State for the Home Department, ex p Musa* [1993] Imm AR 210, QBD.

Clear evidence of admissibility

12.154 This is the alternative 'condition precedent' for third country removal, where the Secretary of State cannot prove that the asylum claimant had an opportunity to claim asylum in the third country to which removal is proposed.[1] 'Clear evidence of admissibility' is a higher threshold than 'reason to believe he would be admitted' which is the criterion for selecting removal destination in other refusal of entry cases,[2] but authorities on the latter test have some relevance. In *Alsawaf*[3] the court held that claimants do not have to be admitted for settlement in the third country for the test to be satisfied; it is enough if they are accepted for a temporary period while their asylum claim and other relevant circumstances are considered. This approach was followed and applied in *de Carvalho*.[4] In *Yassine*[5] Lebanese claimants with tourist visas for Brazil, who claimed asylum while in transit in the UK, were refused asylum on the assumption that they could travel on to Brazil; the decision was quashed as the Secretary of State had not demonstrated that the claimants would be admitted to Brazil. The visas had been obtained by misrepresentation: the claimants were refugees, not tourists, and they had no other connection with Brazil apart from the visa. However, in *Shah*[6] Collins J held that a Portuguese visa on a passport which had been obtained by deception and to which the holder was not entitled was a 'valid' visa for the purposes of the Dublin Convention, enabling the applicant to be returned to Portugal. Note that it is not possible for an applicant to resist removal to a safe third country pursuant to AI(TC)A 2004, Schedule 3, with reference to the 'private life' grounds in the immigration rules on the basis of there being very significant obstacles to the applicant's integration into the country to which he would have to go if required to leave the UK.[7]

[1] HC 395, para 345(2)(ii), substituted by HC 1112 from 18 October 2004.
[2] Immigration Act 1971, Sch 2, para 8(1)(c)(iv).
[3] *Alsawaf v Secretary of State for the Home Department* [1988] Imm AR 410, CA, at 422, per Staughton LJ.
[4] *R v Secretary of State for the Home Department, ex p Carvalho* [1996] Imm AR 435.
[5] *R v Secretary of State for the Home Department, ex p Yasine (or Yassine)* [1990] Imm AR 354, QBD.
[6] *R (on the application of Shah) v Secretary of State for the Home Department* [2001] EWHC 197 (Admin), para 31.
[7] See HC 395, paras 276ADE(1)(vi) and 276ADE(2).

12.155 In most cases of removal to the EU, the terms of the Dublin Convention,[1] which came into force in September 1997, and its successors the EC Dublin II and III Regulations,[2] provide sufficient evidence of admissibility to another Member State, and for the most part it is no longer a live issue. Admissibility is relevant to cases of removal to non-designated countries. Other forms of re-admission agreements could provide evidence of admissibility, along with residence permits, a valid visa, or other evidence of a right of entry.[3] Specific provision is made in the Immigration Rules for an applicant, who is not admitted to a safe third country and where the Dublin Regulation does not apply, to be admitted into the UK asylum procedure.[4]

[1] See below **12.156**.
[2] See Council Regulation 2003/343/EC (OJ 2003 L 50/1, in force 1.9.03) and Regulation 2003/1560/EC (OJ 2003 L 222/3, in force 6.9.03), implementing Dublin II; and Regulation (EU) No 604/2013 of 26 June 2013, in force 1.1.14, the 'Dublin III Regulation'. These Regulations establish the criteria and mechanisms for determining the Member State responsible for examining an asylum application, lodged in one of the Member States by a third-country national (at **12.157** below).
[3] *Miller v Immigration Appeal Tribunal* [1988] Imm AR 358, CA. An attempt to avoid removal to Belgium by withdrawing an asylum claim was rejected in *R v Secretary of State for the Home Department, ex p Zajmi* , (15 November 2000, unreported), CA.
[4] HC 395, para 345(2A)(iv) – subject to determining and resolving the reasons for non-admission.

Dublin Convention 1990

12.156 The Dublin Convention[1] was one of the first multilateral agreements between states to delineate responsibility for examining asylum applications. Its main purposes were on the one hand to prevent multiple claims and 'forum-shopping' by asylum seekers,[2] and on the other to prevent the situation of refugees 'in orbit', passed between states with no one state having responsibility for examining the asylum application, by guaranteeing a determination of the asylum claim in one country. The Dublin Convention has been superseded by the Dublin II Regulation and then by the Dublin III Regulation (see below). For discussion of the provisions of the Dublin Convention and the Dublin II Regulation, see respectively the fifth and eighth editions of this work. In this edition however we focus on Dublin III, to which we now turn.

¹ The Convention Determining the State Responsible For Examining Applications For Asylum Lodged in One of the Member States of the European Community [1990] Imm AR 604. It came into force on 1 September 1997. See A Nicol and S Harrison 'The law and practice in the application of the Dublin Convention in the UK' (1999) 1 EJML 465. For detailed consideration of the Dublin Convention see the 5th edition of this work, **12.145–12.150**.

² As has been pointed out repeatedly by non-governmental organisations since the Dublin Convention was signed, when the protection offered by contracting states varies, there is profound injustice if asylum claimants have no choice over their country of asylum. For discussion of this problem see Gregor Noll, 'Formalism vs empiricism: some reflections on the Dublin Convention on the occasion of recent European case law' ECRAN weekly update, 25 January 2001.

The Dublin II and Dublin III Regulations

12.157 Third country returns are now governed by Regulation 604/2013¹ ('Dublin III', to be contrasted with its predecessor Regulation 343/2003, 'Dublin II') which entered force on 1 January 2014² from which date it applies to all asylum applications lodged thereafter, and additionally to all requests to take back or take charge of asylum applications made after that date.³ Its objectives are to guarantee effective access to the status determination procedures⁴ without compromising the need to rapidly process asylum application whilst ensuring higher standards of protection for asylum seekers,⁵ and always bearing in mind that the non-refoulement duty is central to the obligations of State Parties to the Refugee Convention and to the European *acquis*.⁶ There are a number of important differences between Dublin II and Dublin III: in particular the newer instrument applies to all protection seekers and not just those seeking asylum,⁷ and provides strong procedural rights to sufficient information via the provision of a leaflet and an interview to ensure that an asylum seeker is able to understand and effectively make submissions on the presence of family members or relatives on the territory⁸, contains specific controls on the use of detention,⁹ clarifies the circumstances in which Member States will be under a duty to ensure that family members are kept together,¹⁰ and introduces an effective appeal both in relation to the application of the Regulation and relating to conditions in the third country.¹¹ Various implementing acts by the Commission are envisaged in order to provide detailed procedures for the Regulation to be implemented.¹²

¹ Regulation (EU) No 604/2013 of the European Parliament and of the Council of 26 June 2013 establishing the criteria and mechanisms for determining the Member State responsible for examining an application for international protection lodged in one of the Member States by a third-country national or a stateless person (recast). There is a useful website at www.dublin-project.eu which provides details of national procedures and the latest legal authorities from different national courts. See also the two Dublin Regulations' own implementing regime: Regulation No 2003/1560/EC (OJ 2003 L 222/3, in force 6 September 2003), setting out more detailed provisions for the implementation of the Regulations as amended by Implementing Regulation No 118/2014 of 30 January 2014.

² Dublin III, art 49.

³ Dublin III, art 49.

4   In *R (on the application of MA, BT and DA) v Secretary of State for the Home Department (the AIRE Centre (Advice on Individual Rights in Europe) (UK), intervening)*: 648/11 [2014] All ER (EC) 181, [2013] 1 WLR 2961 the CJEU states at [54] that 'the main objective of the regulation . . . is to guarantee effective access to an assessment of the applicant's refugee status.'

5   Recitals (5), (9); Commission Proposal 2008/0243 (COD) (3 December 2008).

6   See eg Art 78(1) of the TFEU: 'The Union shall develop a common policy on asylum, subsidiary protection and temporary protection with a view to offering appropriate status to any third-country national requiring international protection and ensuring compliance with the principle of non-refoulement'; see further Recital (2) to Dublin II and Recital (3) to Dublin III, art 21(1) of Directive 2004/83, and the CJEU in *NS v Secretary of State for the Home Department (Amnesty International Ltd and the AIRE Centre (Advice on Individual Rights in Europe) (UK))*: C-411/10[2013] QB 102, [2012] All ER (EC) 1011, ECJ wrote that 'The Common European Asylum System is based on the full and inclusive application of the Geneva Convention and the guarantee that nobody will be sent back to a place where they again risk being persecuted.' The European Court of Human Rights requires strong guarantees against the prospect of refoulement: see eg *MA v Cyprus* 41872/10-Chamber Judgment [2013] ECHR 717 at [137]: Holman J in the Administrative Court in *Al-Ali, R (on the application of) v Secretary of State for the Home Department* [2012] EWHC 3638 (Admin) concluded at [62] that an asylum seeker who had actually been refouled (but subsequently made their way back to the third country) should not be subject to any further transfer absent investigation and explanation.

7   See art 1 defining the respective scope of each instrument.

8   Dublin III, arts 4-5.

9   Dublin III, art 28.

10   Dublin III, art 16.

11   Dublin III, art 27.

12   Eg vis-à-vis the identification of family members of unaccompanied minors, under art 6(5); reviewing the lists of proof and circumstantial evidence relevant to establishing an asylum seeker's presence under art 24(5); the design of the *laissez-passer* under art 29(1); information exchange regarding transfers under art 29(4); data transfer under art 31(4); for exchanging data and designing the health certificate under art 31; and establishing electronic transmission channels under art 35(4). Commission Implementing Regulation (EU) No 118/2014 of 30 January 2014 amending Regulation (EC) No 1560/2003 laying down detailed rules for the application of Council Regulation (EC) No 343/2003 establishing the criteria and mechanisms for determining the Member State responsible for examining an asylum application lodged in one of the Member States by a third-country national has already been forthcoming.

GENERAL PRINCIPLES

12.158 The Regulations are to be read alongside general principles of European Union law[1] as well as fundamental rights obligations expressed in instruments such as the European Convention on Human Rights, the Charter of Fundamental Rights[2] and the European Convention on Trafficking;[3] thus respect for family life should be a primary consideration when implementing the Regulations[4] (including the desirability of ensuring consistency of decision making amongst family members)[5] as should the best interests of the child, including their well-being and social development, relevant safety and security considerations, and their views in accordance with their age, maturity, and background.[6] Dublin III expressly recognises the limitations of the systems that receive asylum seekers, recognising that their deficiency and collapse may risk fundamental rights violations[7] and adopts the conclusion of the CJEU in *NS v United Kingdom*[8] as to the circumstances in which there can be no removals to a State that the Regulation's criteria would otherwise deem responsible.[9]

1   The CJEU stressed in *NS v Secretary of State for the Home Department (Principles of Community law)* [2011] EUECJ C-411/10 at [77] that it was necessary to interpret

legislation implementing Dublin II consistently 'with the other general principles of European Union law'.

2   Recitals (12) of Dublin II, (32) of Dublin III, comprise a reminder that 'Member States are bound by their obligations under instruments of international law, including the relevant case-law of the European Court of Human Rights'. The CJEU in *R (on the application of MA, BT and DA) v Secretary of State for the Home Department (the AIRE Centre (Advice on Individual Rights in Europe) (UK), intervening)*: 648/11 [2014] All ER (EC) 181, [2013] 1 WLR 2961 had already identified the central importance of Charter rights such as those proclaiming the best interests of the child, and the rights to dignity and asylum. Lord Kerr in *R (on the application of EM (Eritrea) v Secretary of State for the Home Department* [2014] UKSC 12 emphasised the need for the Regulation to be interpreted in conformity with fundamental rights. In *AR (Iran), R (On the Application Of) v Secretary of State for the Home Department* [2013] EWCA Civ 778 the Court of Appeal rejected the argument that art 41 of the Charter of Fundamental Rights of the European Union, which provides, as expanded by jurisprudence, that in matters relating to Community law citizens have a right to be heard 'before any individual measure which would affect him or her adversely is taken', could apply in a Dublin II case: because it is to be assumed that there can be no adverse effect arising from the forum where an application is heard, all being treated equally under the Dublin system.

3   Articles 40(3)-(4) of the Trafficking Convention states that Community and European Union rules should be applied 'governing the particular subject concerned and applicable to the specific case, without prejudice to the object and purpose of the present Convention' and that 'Nothing in this Convention shall affect the rights, obligations and responsibilities of States and individuals under international law, including international humanitarian law and international human rights law'. See Philip Mott QC sitting as a Deputy High Court judge in *R (on the application of E) v Secretary of State for the Home Department* [2012] EWHC 1927 (Admin) (17 July 2012) at [54].

4   Dublin III Recitals (14), (39). Directive 2004/83 (the 'Qualification Directive') at art 23(5) sets out that 'Member States may decide that this Article also applies to other close relatives who lived together as part of the family at the time of leaving the country of origin, and who were wholly or mainly dependent on the beneficiary of refugee or subsidiary protection status at that time.' Article 7 of the Charter of Fundamental Rights proclaims that 'Everyone has the right to respect for his or her private and family life, home and communications'; see also art 9: 'The right to marry and the right to found a family shall be guaranteed in accordance with the national laws governing the exercise of these rights.'

5   Dublin III, Recital (15).

6   Dublin III, Recital (13), art 6: thus a minor should have an appropriate representative with relevant qualifications and expertise who has access to their file including the information leaflet, see para **12.166** below. The CJEU in *MA & Ors v Secretary of State for the Home Department* [2013] EUECJ C-648/11 had already explained, interpreting art 6 of Dublin II, the central attention to be given the Charter of Fundamental Rights and the provisions therein regarding the best interests of the child: stating at [59] that 'the effect of art 24(2) of the Charter, in conjunction with art 51(1) thereof, is that the child's best interests must also be a primary consideration in all decisions adopted by the Member States'. Stephens J in *ALJ and A, B and C, Re Judicial Review* [2013] NIQB 88 found that the reception conditions in Ireland were not adequate to secure a child's best interests.

7   Dublin III, Recital (21).

8   *NS v Secretary of State for the Home Department (Amnesty International Ltd and the AIRE Centre (Advice on Individual Rights in Europe) (UK))*: C-411/10[2013] QB 102, [2012] All ER (EC) 1011, ECJ.

9   Dublin III, art 3(2). Lord Kerr in *EM Eritrea and Others* [2014] UKSC 12 at [45] to [64] explained that systemic failure was only one means by which a removal under Dublin II might be incompatible with Convention rights concluding at [63] that:

> 'Where, therefore, it can be shown that the conditions in which an asylum seeker will be required to live if returned under Dublin II are such that there is a real risk that he will be subjected to inhuman or degrading treatment, his removal to that state is forbidden. When one is in the realm of positive obligations (which is what is involved in the claim that the state has not ensured that satisfactory living conditions are available to the asylum seeker) the evidence is more likely to partake of systemic failings but the search for such failings is by way of a route to establish that there is a real risk of article 3 breach, rather than a hurdle to be surmounted.'

12.159 Reports from credible sources have cast doubt on the operation of various asylum systems across the European Union and this has led to a series of judicial decisions as to the circumstances in which the return of asylum seekers may pose a threat to their fundamental rights. The crisis for asylum seekers in Greece provided the first opportunity for the European courts to consider these questions, initially culminating in the admissibility decision of the Fourth Section of the European Court of Human Rights in *KRS v United Kingdom*,[1] a decision relied upon by various English authorities[2] for the proposition that the destitution of asylum seekers in Greece was not clearly shown to be a matter for which the Greek state was responsible, and certainly not a matter that might engage the responsibility of the United Kingdom. In its landmark decision in *MSS v Belgium and Greece*[3] the Strasbourg Court revisited its earlier thinking and ruled that the duty in the Reception Directive to provide 'material reception conditions' such as to 'ensure a standard of living adequate for the health of applicants and capable of ensuring their subsistence' meant that a failure to so provide was capable of constituting 'treatment' that was inhuman or degrading, and attached considerable importance to the applicant's status as an asylum seeker and, as such, a member of a particularly underprivileged and vulnerable population group in need of special protection[4] (refugees are owed duties that mean their cases should be treated similarly).[5] The Grand Chamber found that where an Applicant spent months living in a state of the most extreme poverty, unable to cater for his most basic needs such as food, hygiene and a place to live, with the ever-present fear of being attacked and robbed and the total lack of any likelihood of his situation improving, and given the feelings of fear, anguish or inferiority capable of inducing desperation likely to result from this, combined with the prolonged uncertainty in their situation and the total lack of any prospect of improvement, there was likely to be a breach of Article 3 ECHR.[6] In these circumstances the removing authorities were under an active duty to enquire into how the responsible country operated its legislation in practice rather than simply relying on its theoretical description.[7] Before a claim could be refused on the basis of a belief that the responsible country had systems available to secure compliance with fundamental rights, any such domestic remedies had to be closely scrutinised as to whether they were available in practice and operated without unjustifiable hindrance and with prompt and suspensive effect.[8]

[1] *KRS v the United Kingdom* 32733/08 [2008] ECHR 1781.
[2] *R (on the application of Nasseri) v Secretary of State for the Home Department* [2009] UKHL 23. Cranston J in *R (on the application of Saeedi) v Secretary of State for the Home Department* [2010] EWHC 705 (Admin) considered that the link between the Secretary of State's removal decision and the conditions abroad would be too attenuated to enliven UK responsibility. See also Hickinbottom J in *R (on the application of EW) v Secretary of State for the Home Department* [2009] EWHC 2957 (Admin), [2009] All ER (D) 194 (Nov).
[3] *MSS v Belgium and Greece* (2011) 53 EHRR 28.
[4] *MSS* at [251] onwards. Mitting J in *MB v Secretary of State for the Home Department* [2013] EWHC 123 (Admin) at [20]-[30] sets outs that 'A person who makes an application for asylum in that member state is not an "applicant for asylum" as defined in Article 2(c), because a final decision has already been made by the responsible member state under the Dublin 2 regulation' and goes on to give his view that in such cases they are not owed the duties set out in the Reception Directive, as there is no duty to make provision for their accommodation and subsistence.
[5] *R (on the application of EM (Eritrea) v Secretary of State for the Home Department* [2014] UKSC 12; though contrast *Hassan v Netherlands and Italy* (ECtHR; Application No 40524/10; 27 August 2013).

6 *MSS* at [263].
7 *MSS* at [354]-[359].
8 *MSS* at [290]-[293].

12.160 The CJEU took up these themes in *NS*,[1] finding that it was necessary to interpret Dublin II consistently with other principles of European law including the Charter of Fundamental Rights and fundamental EU law principles, and that whilst 'it must be assumed that the treatment of asylum seekers in all Member States complies with the requirements of the Charter, the Geneva Convention and the ECHR', nevertheless the Dublin 'system may, in practice, experience major operational problems in a given Member State, meaning that there is a substantial risk that asylum seekers may, when transferred to that Member State, be treated in a manner incompatible with their fundamental rights'. This presumption must not extinguish a fact-sensitive exercise via the presentation and consideration of relevant evidence,[2] and indeed a conclusive presumption against removal would be incompatible with fundamental rights standards.[3] Whilst 'minor infringements' of the Procedures, Reception and Qualification Directives would not suffice to prevent a transfer,[4] if there are substantial grounds for believing that there are systemic flaws in the asylum procedure and reception conditions for asylum applicants in the Member State responsible, resulting in inhuman or degrading treatment, within the meaning of Article 4 of the Charter, of asylum seekers transferred to the territory of that Member State, the transfer would be incompatible with that provision'. Where the Member State assessing responsibility under Dublin procedures finds that dangers to fundamental rights preclude a removal to the country that the criteria otherwise indicate is responsible, it should continue its investigation under those criteria to determine whether there is another responsible Member State, subject to avoiding any undue delay in the case's substantive consideration[5] taking account of the vulnerability of the asylum seeker.[6] Whilst the view of bodies such as UNHCR (whose views are of special importance given the organisation's unique and unrivalled expertise in asylum law) and the European Commission are of particular importance, there is no duty to consult them in a particular case (at least where the documents establish that the country of responsibility is in breach of the European Union law of asylum)[7] and Member States may nevertheless acquire knowledge of the possibility of inhuman and degrading treatment via other sources, and thus evidence from other agencies including NGOs may be adequate.[8] The interpretation afforded *NS* in *EM (Eritrea)* (CA),[9] was that the only way of establishing that Article 3 ECHR breaches might prevent removal in a Dublin case would be to show that they flowed from a systemic failure and that absent that characteristic even powerful evidence of individual risk was irrelevant. That was disapproved by the Supreme Court in *EM (Eritrea)*[10] which held that the central question in these, as all other Article 3 cases, is whether there is a real risk of the minimum level of severity being traversed: identification of a systemic failure is one route by which this may be demonstrated, but it is by no means a necessity in every case. Whereas Greece's asylum reception conditions have been generally recognised as in a state of systemic failure for some time,[11] and UNHCR has issued a similar conclusion vis-à-vis Bulgaria,[12] the ECtHR has found that conditions in Italy[13] and Hungary[14] do not exhibit such failings, and the domestic courts have found that conditions in Cyprus,[15]

Malta[16] and Ireland[17] are not in contravention of Article 3. Beyond challenges based on reception conditions, judges have considered evidence as to whether the low recognition rates in some countries represent a systemic failure of the asylum procedure.[18] Challenges based on interference with qualified and limited rights abroad will have to establish that there is a flagrant breach of the protected interest before a transfer might become unlawful[19]; it would be interesting to see the answer of the CJEU to the question of whether status determination might infringe the right to fair trial if a witness who could give material evidence in another asylum seeker's proceedings faced removal on the basis of the Dublin responsibility criteria in circumstances ruling out their meaningful participation in the latter's asylum proceedings.[20]

[1]   *NS (European Union law)* [2011] EUECJ C-411/10.

[2]   *R (on the application of EM (Eritrea) v Secretary of State for the Home Department* [2014] UKSC 12.

[3]   *NS v Secretary of State for the Home Department (Amnesty International Ltd and the AIRE Centre (Advice on Individual Rights in Europe) (UK)):* C-411/10[2013] QB 102, [2012] All ER (EC) 1011, ECJ. In *Nasseri v United Kingdom* 24239/09-Communicated Case [2013] ECHR 967 (23 September 2013) the ECHR communicated the question '1. Did the application of paragraph 3(2)(b) of Part 2 of Schedule 3 to the Asylum and Immigration (Treatment of Claimants, etc) Act 2004 in the present case breach the applicant's rights under Article 3 of the Convention, either read alone or in conjunction with Article 13 of the Convention?'.

[4]   Lord Kerr in *EM Eritrea and Others* [2014] UKSC 12 emphasised that the obligations under the Reception Directive were the means by which fundamental rights were secured under the Dublin system, at [59]: 'Article 13(1) of Council Directive 2003/9/EC (the Reception Directive) requires that member states provide "material reception conditions' for applicants for asylum. Article 13(2) stipulates that these conditions should be such as 'to ensure a standard of living adequate for the health of applicants and capable of ensuring their subsistence'.

      The scope for other breaches of Charter rights inhibiting transfers has yet to be fully delineated: it is difficult to imagine that prospective breaches of the right to life would not inhibit removal, and as already noted, the right to family life is given especial attention in Dublin III(see 12.158 above, fn 4). However the response of the CJEU to the question of whether infringements of the rights to dignity, asylum and fair trial would prevent transfers was Delphic in *NS (European Union law)* [2011] EUECJ C-411/10 at [109] to [115], the questions having become academic following the Court's finding that evidence of risks of inhuman or degrading treatment would prevent removal which addressed the situation as found by the Strasbourg Court in *MSS v Belgium and Greece*: nevertheless in *R (on the application of Medhanye) v Secretary of State for the Home Department* [2012] EWHC 1799 (Admin), Parker J found that the principle of mutual trust and confidence that European Union Member States can have in one another's compliance with human rights obligations, could be offset only in the precisely delineated and extraordinary circumstances set out in *NS* and applied only to breaches of the right to be free from inhuman and degrading treatment.

[5]   *Federal Republic of Germany v Puid (Kaveh):* C-4/11 [2014] QB 346, [2014] 2 WLR 98, ECJ; now see Dublin III at art 3(2).

[6]   *R (on the application of MA, BT and DA) v Secretary of State for the Home Department (the AIRE Centre (Advice on Individual Rights in Europe) (UK), intervening):* 648/11 [2014] All ER (EC) 181, [2013] 1 WLR 2961 stated that vis-à-vis 'particularly vulnerable persons, it is important not to prolong more than is strictly necessary the procedure for determining the Member State responsible'.

[7]   *Zuheyr Frayeh Halaf v Darzhavna agentsia za bezhantsite pri Ministerskia savet:* C-528/11 [2013] 1 WLR 2832, [2013] All ER (D) 62 (Jun), ECJ.

[8]   *EM Eritrea and Others* [2014] UKSC 12. Sales J in *Elayathamby* considered at [59](vii) that expert reports were not a suitable means to assess these issues as Member States would not have had an adequate opportunity to answer their concerns. Debate continues as to the import of the CJEU's phrase at [94] of *NS* as to the circumstances in which a Member State 'cannot be unaware' of the relevant circumstances abroad; in *MSS v Belgium and Greece* (2011) 53 EHRR 2 at [347]-[349] the ECtHR stated that the Belgium authorities were responsible for the foreseeable consequences of removal to Greece where there were 'numerous

reports and materials [which] . . . all agree[d]' on the state of play there including a UNHCR letter to which the ECtHR paid 'critical importance'.

9 *EM (Eritrea) v Secretary of State for the Home Department* [2012] EWCA Civ 1336 on appeal from *Medhanye, R (on the application of) v Secretary of State for the Home Department* [2012] EWHC 1799 (Admin).

10 *EM Eritrea and Others* [2014] UKSC 12.

11 See generally *MSS v Belgium and Greece* (2011) 53 EHRR 28. Sadly, the Brussels bureau of the news agency European Affairs was able to report, on 5 June 2014, that 'In the first case of its kind, an African refugee has been granted asylum by Belgium despite already having asylum status in Greece. Mamadou Ba, who is from Guinea, was targeted by the far-right group Golden Dawn. He was first physically attacked and that was followed by a campaign of harassment.'

12 On 2 January 2014, in its Observations on the Current Situation of Asylum in Bulgaria, UNHCR called for the suspension of all transfers to Bulgaria under the Dublin Regulation.

13 *Hussein* (Application no 27725/10) and *Daytbegova* (Application No 6198/12); *Hassan v Netherlands and Italy* (Application no 40524/10; 27 August 2013). *EM Eritrea and Others* [2014] UKSC 12 noted the submission of UNHCR before them that notwithstanding that they had not called for a halt of returns to Italy, this did not mean the agency had given Italy 'a clean bill of health'. In *AB (Sudan) v Secretary of State for the Home Department* [2013] EWCA Civ 921 the Court of Appeal considered that in general, judicial review claims of asylum seekers seeking to resist return to Italy because of the reception conditions there should no longer be stayed contingently on the then awaited decision from the Supreme Court decision in *EM* because of the significant and directly relevant Strasbourg decisions. In *Tabrizagh & Ors, R (On the Application Of) v Secretary of State for the Home Department* [2014] EWHC 1914 (Admin). the Administrative Court found that removals to Italy did not infringe art 3 ECHR. Nevertheless the German Administrative Court in Frankfurt Am Main found that there was a systemic failure of Italian reception conditions in Italy in Case Ref No 7 K 560/11 F A. The decision of the Grand Chamber of the ECtHR in *Tarakhel v Switzerland (relinquishment)* (Apn No 29217/12) may resolve the question for now.

14 The Strasbourg Court in *Mohammed v Austria* 2283/12 (Communicated Case) [2012] ECHR 1226 communicated questions to the parties, given that UNHCR had reported that in Hungary judicial review of detention (which for asylum seekers was said to be within a strict prison regime with exercise taken in handcuffs) was merely a formality with no substantive review of the grounds for detention, and that asylum seekers risked frequent police brutality and systematic medication with tranquilisers, and that only 20% of asylum requests led to substantive decisions. However the Chamber Judgment of the First Section in [2013] ECHR 516 (06 June 2013) found that reports of a diminished level of detention and planned changes in the law sufficed to answer these concerns.

15 Sales J in *Elayathamby, R (on the application of) v Secretary of State for the Home Department* [2011] EWHC 2182 (Admin).

16 Mitting J in *MB v Secretary of State for Home Department* [2013] EWHC 123 (Admin).

17 Stephens J in *ALJ and A, B and C, Re Judicial Review* [2013] NIQB 88.

18 Stephens J in *ALJ and A, B and C, Re Judicial Review* [2013] NIQB 88 finding that whilst there was no systemic failure of reception conditions in the Republic of Ireland, the Direct Provision accommodation arrangements there combined with the delay in determining asylum claims 'results in health and psychological problems, isolation and frustration that in certain cases lead to mental illness' which was contrary to the best interests of children, safeguarded by section 55 of the Borders, Citizenship and Immigration Act 2009 and the Convention on the Rights of the Child.

19 Mitting J in *MB v Secretary of State for Home Department* [2013] EWHC 123 (Admin). The circumstances in which returning a mother and child to street homelessness might constitute a flagrant breach of their private lives were considered in *R (on the application of Asefa) v Secretary of State for the Home Department* [2012] EWHC 56 (Admin) and *EM (Eritrea) & Ors v Secretary of State for the Home Department* [2012] EWCA Civ 1336, the latter case determining that their UK connections were too exiguous to warrant detailed scrutiny given that the Court of Appeal was 'required to deem conditions for refugees in Italy (so far as they can enter at all into the article 8(2) exercise) to be compliant with the state's international obligations, whatever the evidence to the contrary': however the foundation for this reasoning was undermined with the reversal of *EM (Eritrea)* in *EM Eritrea and Others* [2014] UKSC 12.

20 In *R (on the application of MK) v Secretary of State for the Home Department* [2010] EWCA Civ 115, Sedley LJ at [75] stated that art 13 of Directive 2004/83 (the Qualification Directive) setting out that 'Member states shall grant refugee status to a third country national or a

1115

stateless person who qualifies as a refugee in accordance with chapters 2 and 3' was 'capable of changing the decided or assumed relationship of article 6 to asylum claims' whilst holding that the consistent approach of the Strasbourg Court to contrary effect presently required the Court of Appeal 'to continue to treat asylum claims as outside the scope of the civil rights protected by article 6.' However this was a pre-Charter case, relating as it did to an asylum claim pursued from September 2004 until August 2008, given that the Charter of Fundamental Rights entered force on 1 December 2009 with the Lisbon Treaty. Recital (7) of Dublin II and Recital (7) of Dublin III stress the importance of achieving consistent decisions on international protection in the cases of family members. Cf Philip Mott QC sitting as a Deputy High Court judge in *R (on the application of Jeyarupan) v Secretary of State for the Home Department* [2014] EWHC 386 (Admin) at [45] considering that it was to be assumed that under the Dublin II process that corroborative evidence would be made available between Member States in such cases.

ASSESSING RESPONSIBILITY

12.161 As at the time of writing the Dublin III Regulation had recently entered force, whilst many extant cases will be subject to treatment under Dublin II[1], for which reason it is convenient to address the provisions of the two instruments together in so far as the criteria and procedures within them are similar. The obligation to examine an asylum application made by any third-country national at the border or in the territory of a Member State belongs to a single Member State which is to be identified by reference to the hierarchy of criteria' set out in Chapter III of the Regulation,[2] although Member States are free to examine any applications whether or not they are their responsibility under Dublin.[3] Member States have the right to send an asylum seeker to a safe third country consistently with Reception Directive standards.[4] The responsibility for examining a claim includes responsibility for minors accompanying a parent or guardian asylum seeker.[5] Where an asylum seeker is present in one Member State but lodges an application with the authorities of a second Member State, the Member State in whose territory the applicant is present identifies the Member State responsible for examination of the claim.[6] Where an asylum seeker is present in a second Member State and lodges an application there after withdrawing his or her application made in a first Member State during the process of determining the responsible Member State, he or she must be taken back by the first Member State to complete the process of determining the responsible Member State: the obligation ceases if the asylum seeker has in the meantime left the EU for at least three months or has obtained a residence document from a Member State.[7]

[1]   Which is repealed: Dublin III, art 48.
[2]   Dublin II, art 3(1); Dublin III, art 3(1). The process of determining the Member State responsible is to commence 'as soon as an application for asylum is first lodged with a Member State' (which is deemed to be once an application form or a report prepared by the authorities has reached the competent authorities: art 4(1), (2)) of Dublin II; art 20(1) of Dublin III.
[3]   Dublin III, art 3(2); see also Preamble para 7, pointing out that Member States should be able to derogate from the responsibility criteria so as to make it possible to bring family members together where this is necessary on humanitarian grounds; art 17(1) of Dublin III. In this case, the Member State should inform the state previously responsible, the one conducting a procedure for determining the Member State responsible or the one which has been requested to take charge of or take back the applicant. Cf *R v Secretary of State for the Home Department, ex p S* [1998] Imm AR 416, where Forbes J held that the UK had not assumed responsibility under art 3(4) of the original Dublin Convention for examination of the claim, even though the claimant had been interviewed about the merits of the claim on two occasions

for a total of nine hours. In the absence of some positive statement that the UK has accepted the unconditional or exclusive right to examine the claim, the actual examination of the claim was not sufficient.

4   Dublin II, art 3(3); Dublin III at art 3(3) holds that such returns must be 'subject to the rules and safeguards laid down in Directive 2013/32/EU', an instrument to which the United Kingdom has not opted in.

5   Dublin II, art 4(3); Dublin III at art 20(3). The same applies to children born after the asylum seeker arrives in the territory of a Member State, although without the need to initiate a new procedure.

6   Dublin II, art 4(4); Dublin III at art 20(4). The latter Member State must be informed without delay by the Member State which received the application and is then regarded as the state with which the application for asylum was lodged.

7   Dublin II, art 4(5). Dublin III at art 20(4). The fact of such absence should be established via proof or circumstantial evidence as described in the two lists mentioned in art 18(3) (Art 22(3) of Dublin II). Article 4 of Regulation 1560/2003, which lays down detailed procedures for the application of the Dublin regime, provides: 'Where a request for taking back is based on data supplied by the Eurodac Central Unit . . . the requested Member State shall acknowledge its responsibility unless the checks carried out reveal that its obligations have ceased under . . . .Article 16(3) of [Dublin II]. The fact that obligations have ceased on the basis of those provisions may be relied on only on the basis of material evidence or substantiated and verifiable statements by the asylum seeker.' In *WKR, Re Judicial Review* [2012] ScotCS CSOH_188 the Court concluded at [16]: 'In English, the phrase is ambiguous: but I am satisfied, first, by the juxtaposition of the two kinds of proof – "material evidence" and "statements" – and, secondly, by the terms of the French text – d'éléments de preuve matériels – that "material evidence" means "physical evidence" including "documentary evidence".' The Administrative Court in *R (on the application of Mota) v Secretary of State for the Home Department* [2006] EWHC 1070 (Admin) found that there was no continuing obligation on the United Kingdom to supply such further information, notwithstanding the duties under art 21 of Dublin II to provide the other country with relevant and up-to-date information regarding topics including identity and travel papers; in a reported permission refusal against that decision in [2006] EWCA Civ 1380, Pill LJ found that in any event the Secretary of State's conclusion that the claimant had not established that she had left the European Union was a reasonable one. See further Silber J in *R (on the application of Chen) v Secretary of State for the Home Department* [2008] EWHC 437 (Admin) holding that there no obligation on the Secretary of State to inform the other country of developments after their acceptance of responsibility for the asylum claim, and Wyn William J's decision to similar effect in *R (on the application of Shayanth) v Secretary of State for the Home Department* [2009] EWHC 1208 (Admin). See further Lewis J in *Habte v Secretary of State for the Home Department & Ors* [2013] EWHC 3295 (Admin) for a case where the detail of the request form provided by the United Kingdom made clear the possibility of departure from the European Union notwithstanding that the standard form tick-boxes had also indicated that there had been no such departure.

THE HIERARCHY OF CRITERIA

12.162 The criteria for determining which Member State is responsible for examining an asylum application are set out in Chapter III of both Regulations. They must be applied in the order in which they are set out and on the basis of the factual situation when the application was first lodged with a Member State.[1] In *AA (Somalia)* Dublin II was interpreted as providing for a single screening process during which the criteria are applied, without requiring or enabling a second screening to be conducted on the basis of newly disclosed facts or newly established circumstances if the claimant applies for asylum in another country.[2] The criteria are as follows:

- *Minors including unaccompanied minors*: the Member State responsible for examining the application is the one where a member of his or her family[3] is legally present, provided that this is in the best interest of the minor (which thus under Dublin III becomes a 'binding responsibility criterion'[4]). Unaccompanied minors without relatives have their claim determined in the State 'where the unaccompanied minor has lodged his or her application':[5] there is no question of their return to a country where they merely transited without claiming asylum under the hierarchy. The CJEU in *MA*,[6] interpreting Dublin II, ruled that in the absence of a family member, the responsible Member State where a child has lodged an asylum claim in more than one of them was that where the most recent application was lodged, because of the likelihood that their best interests require speedy resolution of their situation.[7] The Member State first considering the case must take appropriate action to identify family members, siblings or relatives.[8] Whether a person is a minor is, in domestic law, a matter for judicial assessment rather than being solely a matter of the opinion of the Secretary of State subject to review on public law grounds:[9] however where the focus of challenge is on questions other than age in the context of statutory childcare responsibility, the courts have so far found that this is a matter for public law review rather than being a question of fact for the Court to determine.[10]

- *Family members of refugees*: the Member State responsible for examining the application (provided that the persons concerned so desire) is the one where a family member[11] of an asylum seeker has been allowed to reside as a refugee (regardless of whether the family was previously formed in the country of origin).[12]

- *Family members of asylum/protection seekers*: the Member State responsible for examining the application, provided that the persons concerned so desire, is the one where the asylum seeker has a family member whose asylum application remains undecided.[13]

- *Family members facing separation under Dublin III hierarchy*: where the normal application of the responsibility criteria would separate family members or minor unmarried siblings who have applied at or around the same time, the responsible Member State for them all shall be that which is responsible for the greater number, and if that does not produce a definitive result, that responsible for the oldest of them.[14]

- *Residence documents and visas*: Where the asylum seeker is in possession of a valid residence document the responsible state is the one which issued the document. The situation is the same in relation to a valid visa,[15] unless the visa was issued on behalf of or on the written authorisation of another Member State, in which case that other Member State is responsible.[16] Where the asylum seeker is in possession of more than one valid residence document or visa issued by different Member States, responsibility is assumed in the following order: (a) the Member State which issued the residence document conferring the right to the longest period of residency or, where the periods of validity are identical, the Member State which issued the residence document having the latest expiry date; (b) the Member State which issued the visa having the latest expiry date where the various visas are of the same type; (c) where visas are of different kinds, the Member State which issued the visa having the longest period of validity, or, where the periods are identical, which issued the visa having the latest expiry date.[17] Where the asylum seeker possesses one or more residence documents which have expired less than two years previously, or one or more visas which have expired less than six months previously and which enabled him or her actually to enter the territory of a Member State, then these provisions apply while the applicant remains in the territories of the Member States. But once over two years or six months respectively have elapsed since the expiry of the residence documents or visas, the responsible Member State is the one in which the application is lodged.[18]

- *Asylum seekers irregularly crossing borders*: the Member State into which an asylum seeker irregularly crosses the border by land, sea or air having come from a third country, is responsible for examining an application for asylum made within twelve months.[19] After that time, responsibility will lie with the Member State in which, at the time of lodging the application, the asylum seeker has been previously living for a continuous period of at least five months (or, where there is more than one such state, the one in which the asylum seeker has lived most recently).[20]

- *Waiver of visa requirement*: responsibility lies with the Member State which waived the requirement, although the principle does not apply if the third country national lodges an asylum application in another Member State in which the visa requirement is also waived, when the latter Member State is responsible.[21]

- *International transit areas*: Responsibility for an application made in an international transit area of an airport of a Member State will lie with that Member State.[22]

- *No Member State responsible*: Where these criteria do not identify a responsible Member State, then responsibility lies with the first Member State with which the application for asylum was lodged.[23]

When determining responsibility, the Member State conducting the evaluation must take account of any available evidence regarding family members, relatives and other family relations, providing that it is supplied prior to acceptance of responsibility by a Member State acting on a request to take back or take charge of the application.[24]

1   Dublin II at art 5; Dublin III at art 7(1). Article 7(3) of Dublin III does not include the general discretion at art 17 amongst those provisions as to which evidence must be produced prior to acceptance of a request to take responsibility.

2   *AA (Somalia) v Secretary of State for the Home Department* [2006] EWCA Civ 1540, [2006] All ER (D) 178 (Oct) following Wilson J in *R (on the application of G) v Secretary of State for the Home Department* [2004] EWHC 2848 (Admin), [2004] All ER (D) 289 (Nov).

3   Whereas relevant family members for minors under Dublin II are parents and guardians (Art 2(i)(iii)), under Dublin III they are parents or other responsible adult as a matter of law or practice where the adult is present: art 2(g) of Dublin III. Additionally under Dublin III where there is a relative (uncle, aunt or grandparent whether or not via a legitimate relationship: art 2(h)) who is legally present in another Member State and able to care for them, that Member State should become responsible so long as this is in the best interests of the asylum seeker. In the event there are responsible family members or relatives present in different Member States, there should be an enquiry into who provides an optimal solution vis-à-vis the child's best interests: art 8(3). The Court of Appeal in *AA (Somalia) v Secretary of State for the Home Department* gave a narrow construction to the term 'guardian' in the Regulation as requiring more than that the person has assumed the care of a minor, holding that the guardian must be a person responsible for the minor by law or custom where custom 'denotes a formal assumption of responsibility according to some external rule or practice whether it be traditional, cultural, tribal or other' (Laws LJ).

4   Recital (16) of Dublin III.

[5] Dublin II, art 6; Dublin III at art 8(4).

[6] *R (on the application of MA, BT and DA) v Secretary of State for the Home Department (the AIRE Centre (Advice on Individual Rights in Europe) (UK), intervening)*: 648/11 [2014] All ER (EC) 181, [2013] 1 WLR 2961.

[7] *MA* at [55]: 'Since unaccompanied minors form a category of particularly vulnerable persons, it is important not to prolong more than is strictly necessary the procedure for determining the Member State responsible, which means that, as a rule, unaccompanied minors should not be transferred to another Member State.'

[8] Dublin III at art 6(4): this may include taking actions to facilitate family tracing which may include introducing the minor to the tracing services of international or other relevant organisations. Implementing Regulation No 118/2014 of 30 January 2014 inserts into Regulation 1560/2003 at art 12(3)-(6) further provisions requiring that the Member State shall 'search for and/or take into account any information provided by the minor of coming from any other source familiar with the personal situation or the route followed by the minor or a member of his or her family, sibling or relative.'

[9] *R (on the application of A) v Croydon London Borough Council* [2009] UKSC 8, [2009] 1 WLR 2557.

[10] In *R (on the application of YZ) v Secretary of State for the Home Department* [2011] EWHC 205 (Admin) (10 February 2011) Beatson J in the Administrative Court found that the notion that these were issues to be judicially tried (rather than administratively determined and then challenged by public law principles alone) was contrary to the general scheme of Dublin II which regulated relations between Member States. Cf *R (on the application of AA) v Secretary of State for the Home Department* [2013] UKSC 49 holding that questions arising from s 55 of the Borders, Citizenship and Immigration Act 2009 and the 'best interests of the child' principle were to be assessed on public law grounds in challenges to the lawfulness of detention, albeit that, according to Lord Toulson for the majority at [53], there was sympathy for the argument that in a case where there was no parallel challenge to the local authority's statutory duties to care for children alongside a judicial review claim for unlawful detention, 'the court's habeas corpus jurisdiction in this type of situation should not be confined to determining whether the Secretary of State had acted lawfully in the detention of the claimant, but should extend to enable the court to make a fresh determination of the claimant's age, which would necessarily impact on the lawfulness of his continued detention.'

[11] 'Family member' is defined in art 2(i) of Dublin II and 2(g) of Dublin III (insofar as the family already existed in the country of origin) as (i) the spouse of the asylum seeker or his or her unmarried partner in a stable relationship, where the legislation or practice of the Member State concerned treats unmarried couples in a way comparable to married couples under its law relating to aliens; (ii) the minor children of couples referred to in (i) or of the applicant, on condition that they are unmarried and dependent and regardless of whether they were born in or out of wedlock or adopted as defined under the national law.

[12] Dublin II, art 7; Dublin III at art 9(1).

[13] Dublin II, art 8; Dublin III at art 10(1).

[14] Dublin III at art 11.

[15] The fact that a residence document or visa was issued on the basis of a false or assumed identity, or on submission of forged, counterfeit or invalid documents, does not prevent responsibility being allocated to the Member State which issued it, but if the fraud was committed after the document or visa had been issued, the issuing Member State is not responsible: Article 9(4) of Dublin II; Dublin III at art 12(5). This principle is also reflected in *R (on the application of Shah) v Secretary of State for the Home Department* [2001] EWHC 197 (Admin), where Collins J held that a Portuguese visa on a passport obtained by deception to which the holder was not entitled was still a valid visa under the Dublin Convention.

[16] Dublin II, art 9(1)-(2); Dublin III at art 12(1)-(2). Where however a Member State first consults the central authority of another Member State, in particular for security reasons, the latter's reply to the consultation shall not constitute written authorisation within the meaning of this provision: Dublin III has no equivalent to this provision.

[17] Dublin II, art 9(3); Dublin III at art 12(3).

[18] Dublin II, art 9(4); Dublin III at art 12(4).

[19] Dublin II, art 10. Irregular border crossing is to be established on the basis of proof or circumstantial evidence as described in the two lists mentioned in art 18(3), including the data referred to in Chapter III of Regulation (EC) 2725/2000. The Dublin III equivalent is at art 13(1) with the admissible evidence specified in art 22(3).

[20] Dublin II, art 10(2); Dublin III at art 13(2).

[21] Dublin II, art 11; Dublin III at art 14.

22. Dublin II, art 12, reflecting art 7(3) of the original Dublin Convention. Cf *R v Secretary of State for the Home Department, ex p Behluli* [1998] INLR 594, CA where a dispute arose between the UK and Italian governments as to the application of art 7, when 53 Kosovo Albanians were held in transit in an Italian airport for over 24 hours while officials argued about whether they could travel on to the UK. The dispute centred on whether asylum claims had been made in Italy. The Italian government denied it was responsible under art 7, but agreed to the Kosovans' return as a matter of discretion. The Dublin III equivalent is at art 15.
23. Dublin II, art 13; Dublin III at art 3(2).
24. Article 7(3) of Dublin III, though on one reading the provisions on minors, family member protection seekers and dependent persons appear not to take their usual hierarchic preference where the asylum application has received a first decision on its substance. If there had been a failure to adequately implement the procedural protection in arts 4 and 5 with respect to the collation of relevant family data, consideration would have to be given whether the procedure had operated fairly.

THE HUMANITARIAN CLAUSES

12.163 The prominence afforded family unity in both Dublin Regulations is reflected by the humanitarian clauses Article 15 of Dublin II and Article 16 of Dublin III. The Dublin II provision set out that any Member State, even where not responsible under the criteria, may take on responsibility for examining a claim so as to bring together family members, as well as other dependent relatives, on humanitarian grounds based in particular on family or cultural considerations, and 'shall' do so when requested by another Member State (subject to the consent of the family member concerned).[1] The power should be exercised where the person concerned is dependent on the assistance of another on account of pregnancy or a new-born child, serious illness, severe handicap or old age (provided that family ties existed in the country of origin).[2] Moreover, where the asylum seeker is an unaccompanied minor who has a relative or relatives in another Member State who can take care of him or her, Member States shall if possible unite the minor with his or her relative or relatives, unless this is not in the best interests of the minor.[3] Article 16 of Dublin III is narrower in scope in that the only qualifying family members are legally resident children, siblings or parents (where family ties existed in the country of origin), but where these scenarios arise they call into play a greater intensity of obligation: for now Member States 'shall normally' ensure that that persons so dependent shall be brought or kept together[4] (which thus becomes a 'binding responsibility criterion').[5] Where the child, sibling or parent is legally resident in another Member State to that where the applicant presently resides, it is the former's location which becomes responsible under the Regulation, unless the applicant's health is such as to prevent their travel there for a significant period, in which case the latter's State of residence will take responsibility, without the obligation to bring the relative abroad onto its territory.[6] Whereas the English Court of Appeal considered in *G*[7] that Article 15 of Dublin II did not confer a freestanding substantive right on individual applicants, and that its effect was simply 'to regulate the relationship between two or more Member States', the CJEU took an inconsistent view in *K v Bundesasylamt*,[8] stressing that in a case of dependency (be this of asylum seeker upon relative or vice versa) between individuals bonded by family ties (and not merely between family members as defined in the Regulation) established in the country of origin, a Member State could derogate from the obligation to keep them together only exceptionally; there is no requirement for a request to be made between Member States, contrary to the suggestion in the text of Article 15, as that would 'run counter to the obligation to act speedily, because it would unnecessarily prolong the procedure for determining the Member State responsible'. The scope of the humanitarian clause awaits further delineation: for example given the Regulations necessarily predicate the possibility of dependency of an asylum seeker newly arrived in the European Union on a relative who is already established here, the absence of recent geographical proximity between the two cannot be fatal to a finding that even a brief dependency can constitute a Member State responsible under the Article.[9] Claims based on family life beyond the terms of Article 15 will need to be assessed having regard to the primary status of that consideration,[10] taking account of the fact that any perceived 'precariousness'[11] in a person's situation in the European Union is based upon forced migration[12] in which personal choice will have been limited[13].

[1] Dublin II, art 15(3). The Article makes provision for conciliation mechanisms for settling differences between Member States on the need to unite family members or the place (ie, country) where it should be done. See paragraph on Administrative cooperation and Conciliation at **12.179** below.

[2] Dublin II, art 15(2). Regulation 1560/2003 at art 11(2) provides that that such dependency 'shall be assessed, as far as possible, on the basis of objective criteria such as medical certificates. Where such evidence is not available or cannot be supplied, humanitarian grounds shall be taken as proven only on the basis of convincing information supplied by the persons concerned' and that relevant considerations (Art 11(3)) will be the family situation which existed in the country of origin, the circumstances in which the persons concerned were separated and the status of the various asylum procedures or procedures under the legislation on aliens under way in the Member States. Philip Mott QC sitting as a Deputy High Court judge in *R (on the application of Jeyarupan) v Secretary of State for the Home Department* [2014] EWHC 386 (Admin) at [34] rejected the notion that the discretion in art 3(2) should be construed such as to capture cases akin to, but not expressly falling within, art 15 of Dublin II.

[3] Dublin II, art 15(3).

[4] Dublin III at art 16(1). Where the persons in question reside in different countries, Implementing Regulation No 118/2014 of 30 January 2014 inserts into Regulation 1560/2003 at art 11(6) further provisions on consultation and exchange of information between the two Member States where they respectively reside relating to the proven family and dependency links, care capacity and travel ability.

[5] Recital (16) to Dublin III.

[6] Dublin III at art 16(2).

[7] *R (on the application of G) v Secretary of State for the Home Department* [2005] EWCA Civ 546.

[8] *K v Bundesasylamt*: C-245/11 [2013] 1 WLR 883, ECJ.

[9] One question to be considered is whether 'dependent' within the meaning of art 15 of Dublin II equates to present/historic dependency, or to developing/future dependency, in the context of a victim of torture whose physical and moral integrity is likely to benefit from the care of a relative.

[10] See **12.158** above, fn 4.

[11] Discussed in cases such as *Izuazu (Article 8 – new rules)* [2013] UKUT 45 (IAC) and *Boultif v Switzerland* [2001] ECHR 497. Sedley LJ in *R (on the application of AM (Somalia)) v Secretary of State for the Home Department* [2009] EWCA Civ 114, [2009] All ER (D) 248 (Feb) emphasised that in a Dublin case the imperative of immigration control as a factor in proportionality lay primarily in the future, given that an asylum seeker had a contingent right to be present in the European Union pending determination of their case; and found that separating an asylum seeker from his brothers such that if given status in the responsible country he would face 'a life of isolation and probable relapse' might well represent circumstances where 'the lawful purpose of the Dublin Regulation was not sufficient to justify the damaging effect on this appellant of disrupting what is now his private and family life by compelling him to present his asylum claim [abroad] rather than here'. In the reported permission application of *R (on the application of Juzbasa-Tanackovic) v Secretary of State for the Home Department* [2006] EWHC 1071 (Admin) (which was not a third country case) the Administrative Court considered that where a claimant's spouse had an undecided application

awaiting determination by the Home Office, the right course was to conclude that there was no substantive right to remain in relation to the claimant, but that they possessed a claim to a stay of their judicial review, or an injunction, until the determination of the spouse's claim. Moses LJ in *R (on the application of Fawad Ahmadi) v Secretary of State for the Home Department* [2005] EWCA Civ 1721, [2005] All ER (D) 169 (Dec) found that the pre-existing blood ties of two brothers, coupled with the declared intention of the asylum seeker brother to care for and support his schizophrenic elder brother present in the United Kingdom as a refugee could found a viable art 8 claim; cf Lewis J in *Habte v Secretary of State for the Home Department; R (on the application of RH (Eritrea)) v Secretary of State for the Home Department* [2013] EWHC 3295 (Admin), [2013] All ER (D) 64 (Nov).

12   Directive 2004/83 Recital (1) makes it clear that the Common European Asylum System has as its intended beneficiaries those who "forced by circumstances, legitimately seek protection in the Community".

13   See eg the words of the then President of the Asylum and Immigration Tribunal, Ouseley J in *H (Somalia)* [2004] UKIAT 00027 at [14]: 'it cannot be right to approach the disruption to family life which is caused by someone having to flee persecution as a refugee as if it were of the same nature as someone who voluntarily leaves, or leaves in the normal course of the changes to family life which naturally occur as children grow up'.

RESPONSIBILITY DUE TO OBLIGATION AND DISCRETION

12.164 Article 3(2) is an important provision of the Dublin II Regulation, preserving Member States' sovereign discretion to consider asylum claims for which they are not responsible according to the other criteria.[1] Article 3(2) has been the means through which fundamental rights have been safeguarded, and indeed where a removal would contravene such rights there is no scope for declining to exercise discretion.[2] The operation of that discretion will be driven by considerations that include the larger legal regime of which Dublin III is part, which in some cases may leave no margin for meaningful choice if general principles of European Union law including fundamental rights obligations are to be respected.[3] The ability to depart from the normal practice by reference to factors such as links with a particular country also promotes a subsidiary purpose of the Refugee Convention and the Qualification Directive, which is the integration of refugees into the host community[4] – an aim more likely to be achieved if they have pre-existing connections with it. Dublin III reposes a similar discretion in Member States to take responsibility under Article 17, both on general sovereignty grounds[5] and where humanitarian grounds, particularly family and cultural ones, are identified.[6] Furthermore, where the responsible Member State under the criteria of the hierarchy transpires to be one where there are systemic flaws in the asylum procedure and reception conditions that result in a risk of inhuman or degrading treatment, then the Member State currently determining responsibility must continue to apply those criteria until another Member State is identified as responsible, and itself take responsibility if no alternative candidate is thus forthcoming.[7] It has been suggested that only minimal reasoning is required in declining to exercise discretion under Article 3(2) of Dublin II.[8]

1   In *Zuheyr Frayeh Halaf v Darzhavna agentsia za bezhantsite pri Ministerskia savet*: C-52/11 [2013] 1 WLR 2832, [2013] All ER (D) 62 (Jun), ECJ the CJEU stated that 'exercise of that option is not subject to any particular condition' and went on at [37]: 'That conclusion is also corroborated by the preparatory documents for the Regulation. The Commission proposal that led to the adoption of Dublin II (COM(2001) 447 final)) states that the rule in art 3(2) of the Regulation was introduced in order to allow each Member State to 'sovereignly decide, for political, humanitarian or practical considerations, to agree to examine an application for asylum even if it is not responsible under the criteria in the Regulation.' Cranston J in *R (on the application of Saeedi) v Secretary of State for the Home Department* [2010] EWHC 705

(Admin), [2010] All ER (D) 16 (Apr) noted that there was by then no extant policy for the domestic exercise of discretion other than where an individual's circumstances were sufficiently exceptional to warrant the favourable exercise of discretion. Historically there have been policies, and on 22 July 2002 the policy was restated in *Hansard*, HC Offical Reports, 22 July 2002, col 860W (Beverley Hughes MP) explaining that a claimant would not normally be removed on third-country grounds if (i) they had a spouse (excluding spouses where the marriage took place after arrival in the UK) or unmarried minor children in the UK or (ii) they were an unmarried minor with a parent in the UK; additionally a claimant would have to establish 'substantial links' with the UK.

2   See eg *NS v Secretary of State for the Home Department (Amnesty International Ltd and the AIRE Centre (Advice on Individual Rights in Europe) (UK))*: C-411/10[2013] QB 102, [2012] All ER (EC) 1011, ECJ: 'discretionary power must be exercised in accordance with the other provisions of that regulation' and art 4 of the Charter of Fundamental Rights; see above at **12.158** for the general principles which apply.

3   See above at **12.158**.

4   Dublin III at art 17(1). See above at **12.158** for the overriding objectives of the Dublin III which must inform the exercise of discretion.

5   See Recitals (30) and (36) and art 33, Directive 2004/83; and under the Refugee Convention, the many rights afforded refugees to receive the same treatment as nationals or treatment not less favourable than shown to aliens generally.

6   Dublin III at art 17(2); specifically this is likely to involve bringing together 'family members, relatives or any other family relations . . . even if such examination is not its responsibility under the binding criteria laid down in this Regulation': Recital (17). It should be noted that the restriction on evidence relevant to the exercise of discretion being produced before another Member State accepts responsibility does not apply to art 17 cases: art 7(3).

7   Dublin III at art 3(2).

8   Philip Mott QC sitting as a Deputy High Court judge in *R (on the application of Jeyarupan) v Secretary of State for the Home Department* [2014] EWHC 386 (Admin), [2014] All ER (D) 205 (Feb) at [38].

TAKING CHARGE AND TAKING BACK

12.165 Chapter V of Dublin II and Chapter 6 of Dublin III lay down detailed procedures to be applied between Member States dealing with the 'taking charge and taking back' of asylum seekers ('taking back' refers to cases where an asylum claim has been commenced in the requested Member State, 'taking charge' applies where no asylum claim was previously made there). We have seen that the process of determining the Member State responsible is to commence 'as soon as an application for asylum is first lodged with a Member State'.[1] Where a Member State considers that responsibility for examination of the claim lies with another Member State it has a maximum of three months (two months where a Eurodac hit founds the case for responsibility under Dublin III) within which to call upon the other Member State to take charge of the applicant, failing which responsibility remains with the Member State in which the application was lodged.[2] Once a request is made, the requested state has two months to make the necessary checks and give a decision on the request to take charge, except where urgency has been pleaded,[3] in which case the reply should be given within the time requested, or if this is not possible, in any case within one month.[4] Failure to act within the two-month or one-month period is tantamount to accepting the request.[5] The asylum seeker must be notified of the acceptance of responsibility by the Member State in which the application was lodged.[6] Any appeal or review will not suspend the implementation of the transfer unless the courts or competent bodies of the Member State so decide.[7] The transfer of the asylum applicant must be carried out as soon as practically possible, and at the latest within six months of acceptance of the request (or of the decision on an appeal or review where it is given suspensive effect).[8] Failure to comply with the six-month time limit means that responsibility reverts to the Member State in which the application for asylum was lodged.[9] Provision is made for the taking back of an asylum applicant (i) who is in the territory of another Member State without permission, or (ii) has withdrawn an application and made an application in another Member State or (iii) goes to the territory of another Member State without permission after rejection of an application.[10] Under Dublin III there are similar provisions for taking back asylum seekers as already described in relation to taking charge of cases;[11] additionally, where taking back an asylum seeker, the receiving Member State is to ensure that the examination of the outstanding application is completed, or that a new application may be lodged, without being treated as a 'subsequent application' (with the diminished procedural protection that might result) and that if an adverse first decision has been made, an effective remedy is awarded against it.[12] Where the requested Member State does not accept that its responsibility is established by the information provided, it should provide full and detailed reasons for its refusal, and if the requesting State considers this stance to be based on a misappraisal of the situation, or where it has additional evidence to put forwards, it may request a re-examination of the case.[13]

1   **12.156** above.
2   Dublin II, art 17(1). Article 17(2) enables the requesting state to ask for an 'urgent reply' in cases where the asylum seeker's stay is irregular or where he or she is held in detention. Article 17(3) makes provision for the form in which such requests to take charge are to be made, including the evidence required to enable the requested state to check whether it is responsible. The equivalent provisions are in art 21 of Dublin III. The standard terms for take back requests appear in Annex II of Regulation No 118/2014.
3   Urgency applies in all detained cases: Dublin III, art 28(3).
4   Dublin II, art 18(1); Dublin III at art 22(1). Articles 18(2)–(5) of Dublin II make provision for the elements of proof and circumstantial evidence to be used and these are then specified in detail in Annex II to Regulation 2003/1560/EC (OJ 2003 L 222/3 and Annex II to Implementing Regulation No 118/2014 of 30 January 2014.
5   Dublin II, art 18(7); Dublin III at art 22(7). Stadlen J in *Kheirollahi-Ahmadroghani v Secretary of State for the Home Department* [2013] EWHC 1314 (Admin), [2013] All ER (D) 338 (May) at [134] found that the country of proposed transfer might well be fixed with responsibility under this provision, if it had dragged its heels in acknowledging a request to take responsibility, notwithstanding other arguments as to its responsibility under the hierarchy having been assessed erroneously, in I because of the asylum seeker's arguable possession of a valid unexpired visa.
6   Dublin II, art 19(1); Dublin III at art 22(1).
7   Dublin II, art 19(2); see below for art 27 of Dublin III addressing the contemporary requirements of the suspensive remedy against transfer. In *R (on the application of YZ) v Secretary of State for the Home Department* [2011] EWHC 205 (Admin), [2011] All ER (D) 157 (Feb) Beatson J in the Administrative Court looked at art 20(1)(e) of Dublin II which empowers 'the courts or competent bodies' to suspend the time for implementing a transfer to the Member State which has agreed to take that person back in the context of whether the government authority was a 'competent body' for this purpose. He found that it was competent to suspend transfers, because otherwise it might be necessary for the government to institute legal proceedings itself to create circumstances for a suspension to take place, contrary to the general policy of Dublin II for speedy determination of claims.
8   Dublin II, art 19(3); Dublin III at art 29(1).
9   Dublin II, art 19(4); Dublin III at art 29(2). This time limit may be extended up to a maximum of one year if the transfer could not be carried out due to imprisonment of the asylum seeker or up to a maximum of 18 months if he or she absconds.
10   Dublin II, art 20; Dublin III at art 18(1).
11   Dublin III at arts 23-25.
12   Dublin III, art 18(2).

¹³ Article 5 of Regulation 2003/1560/EC; see further art 4 of Regulation 1560/2003 at **12.16** above, fn 6 for the requirement of 'material evidence or substantiated and verifiable statements by the asylum seeker'.

12.166 The obligations to receive back asylum seekers are terminated by the grant of a residence permit by another Member State, which then takes responsibility under the Regulation,¹ where it is established that the person concerned has left the territory of the European Union for at least three months² or where they departed under a removal order or return decision following the withdrawal or rejection of their application.³ Delays in effecting transfers may impact on whether it is appropriate to continue with a transfer, particularly where a situation involving infringement of fundamental rights may be worsened by delay.⁴ An erroneous transfer (including where an appeal has succeeded subsequent to a transfer decision) should be rectified by prompt acceptance back of the person concerned.⁵ Under Dublin III supervised departures and escorted transfers should be undertaken in a humane manner, in full compliance with fundamental rights and respect for human dignity, as well as with the best interests of the child.⁶ The Regulation no longer applies once an asylum application is withdrawn prior to the acceptance of responsibility.⁷

¹ Dublin III, art 19(1).
² Dublin II, art 16(3); Dublin III, art 19(2).
³ Dublin III, art 19(3).
⁴ In *Bundesrepublik Deutschland v Kaveh Puid*: C-528/11 [2013] 1 WLR 2832, [2013] All ER (D) 62 (Jun), ECJ the CJEU states that the 'Member State in which the asylum seeker is located must, however, ensure that it does not worsen a situation where the fundamental rights of that applicant have been infringed by using a procedure for determining the Member State responsible which takes an unreasonable length of time.' In *R (on the application of Ahmadzai) v Secretary of State for the Home Department* [2006] EWHC 318 (Admin) Bean J held that by reason of a delay some 25 times that permitted by the one month countenanced by art 11(5) of the Dublin Convention and significant prejudice resulting therefrom it would be wholly unreasonable for the Secretary of State to transfer the claimant against his wishes to Austria. The appeal of the Secretary of State against this decision was allowed in *R (on the application of AA (Afghanistan)) v Secretary of State for the Home Department* [2006] EWCA Civ 1550, the Court of Appeal finding that it was not unreasonable in a public law sense for the Secretary of State to decide that the removal should proceed absent any human rights dimension to the case (it seems that there may have been a failure to formally plead art 8 ECHR issues in that case). The CJEU in *R (on the application of MA, BT and DA) v Secretary of State for the Home Department (the AIRE Centre (Advice on Individual Rights in Europe) (UK), intervening)*: 648/11 [2014] All ER (EC) 181, [2013] 1 WLR 2961 stated that vis-à-vis 'particularly vulnerable persons, it is important not to prolong more than is strictly necessary the procedure for determining the Member State responsible'.
⁵ Dublin III, art 29(3).
⁶ Dublin III (Recital (24)), art 29(1); art 1 of the Charter of Fundamental Rights holds that 'Human dignity is inviolable. It must be respected and protected.'
⁷ *Migrationsverket v Kastrati*: C-620/10[2013] 1 WLR 1, ECJ, the CJEU noting that the take back obligations under Dublin II 'presuppose the existence of an asylum application'.

PROCEDURAL SAFEGUARDS

12.167 Whilst under Dublin II¹ there was a requirement to inform asylum seekers in writing and in a language they may reasonably be expected to understand regarding the application of the Regulation, its time limits and its effects, there are significantly stronger safeguards operative under Dublin III: thus it is essential that at the interview stage when the asylum application is first lodged, a proper explanation is given of the operation of the Regulation and an effective opportunity given to explain the presence of family members, relatives or other family relations.[2] Asylum seekers must be provided with information, via the provision of a leaflet drawn up by the Commission,[3] relating to the objectives of the Regulation and the consequences of moving between Member States during the asylum process, the operation of the Dublin hierarchy's criteria including the possibility of responsibility being fixed outside of those criteria, of the interview process by which information regarding family and relatives can be provided, the possibility of a suspensive challenge to a transfer and the implications of data transfer.[4] A personal interview must then be conducted[5] unless the asylum seeker has absconded or has already provided the relevant information:[6] and during this encounter it must be ensured that the asylum seeker understands the contents of the leaflet.[7]

[1] Dublin II Article 3(4).
[2] Recital (18).
[3] Article 4(2). Its terms appear in Annex X of Regulation No 118/2014.
[4] Article 4(1).
[5] Article 5(1) – in a timely manner and before any decision is taken to transfer the asylum seeker, art 5(3), and via appropriate interpretation (Art 5(4)), in confidential conditions (Art 5(5)) and via an appropriately qualified person (Art (5(6)).
[6] Article 5(2).
[7] Article 5(1).

12.168 Decisions not to consider a person's substantive asylum application and to implement a transfer decision are to be notified to their subject[1] or their legal advisor[2] together with information as to the possibility of any challenge thereto, its time limits and potential suspensive effect.[3] Before a transfer takes effect personal data should be communicated to the competent authorities abroad (such as is appropriate, relevant and non-excessive) with the sole purpose of ensuring that they are in a position to provide the transferee with adequate assistance including the provision of immediate health care to protect their vital interests and the continuity of their rights and protection under the Regulation[4]; and also the transferring authority should provide available information regarding their family members, relatives and other family relations in the receiving State, and regarding the education of minors and any age assessment.[5] Information should also be provided on the special needs including physical and mental health of disabled persons, elderly people, pregnant women, minors and persons who have been subject to torture, rape or other serious forms of psychological, physical and sexual violence, via the common health certificate with the necessary documents attached.[6] Domestic decisions have so far indicated that no further procedural safeguards should be implied into Dublin II beyond those already present therein, given the policy of speedy determination of forum that the system envisages.[7]

[1] Dublin Article 19(1); Dublin III, art 26(1).
[2] Dublin III, art 26(1).
[3] Dublin III, art 26(1).
[4] Dublin III, art 31(1).
[5] Dublin III, art 31(2).
[6] Dublin III, art 32(1); consent is required art 32(2) and the data processing is to be carried out only by a health professional subject to duties of personal secrecy and used only for the specified purposes (Art 32(3)-(4)). The terms of the health certificate appear in Annex IX of Regulation No 118/2014.
[7] See eg Lewis J in *Habte v Secretary of State for the Home Department & Ors* [2013] EWHC 3295 (Admin) who considered that there could be few if any circumstances in which domestic

public law principles would add to those available under Dublin II; *R (on the application of AR (Iran)) v Secretary of State for the Home Department* [2013] EWCA Civ 778, followed by Philip Mott QC sitting as a Deputy High Court judge in *R (on the application of Jeyarupan) v Secretary of State for the Home Department* [2014] EWHC 386 (Admin).

APPEAL AND REVIEW

12.169 The appeal provisions that are required under Dublin III must guarantee an effective remedy (within a reasonable time)[1] vis-à-vis transfer decisions permitting challenge to both the examination of the application of the Regulation and of the legal and factual situation prevailing in the state to which removal is proposed[2] which respects the terms of Article 47 of the Charter (and thus must provide a fair and public hearing within a reasonable time by an independent and impartial tribunal previously established by law in which litigants have the possibility of representation, via the provision of legal aid in so far as that is necessary to ensure effective access to justice).[3] The remedy is to have suspensive effect pending a decision by a court or tribunal as to whether the appeal or review proceedings should continue to suspend removal[4] (in any event provision may be made for the administrative authority to suspend the transfer decision of their own motion).[5]

[1] Article 27(2).
[2] Recital (19); art 27(1): 'an effective remedy, in the form of an appeal or a review, in fact and in law, against a transfer decision, before a court or tribunal'.
[3] Article 47 of the Charter of Fundamental Rights. Article 27(5)-(6) of Dublin III requires access to free legal aid (by way of assistance with procedural documents and representation in court, art 27(6)) and linguistic assistance (subject to a merits assessment by a court, tribunal or competent authority as to whether the action has any tangible prospect of success: art 27(6), with any non-judicial decision being open to challenge before a court or tribunal), and as regards fees and other costs, the access to legal assistance of asylum seekers subject to Dublin is not to be more favourable to that generally afforded the Member State's own nationals. In *DEB Deutsche Energiehandels - und Beratungsgesellschaft mbH v Bundesrepublik Deutschland*: C-279/09 [2010] ECR I-13849, [2011] 2 CMLR 529, ECJ the CJEU held that:

'it is for the national court to ascertain whether the conditions for granting legal aid constitute a limitation on the right of access to the courts which undermines the very core of that right; whether they pursue a legitimate aim; and whether there is a reasonable relationship of proportionality between the means employed and the legitimate aim which it is sought to achieve. In making that assessment, the national court must take into consideration the subject matter of the litigation; whether the applicant has a reasonable prospect of success; the importance of what is at stake for the applicant in the proceedings; the complexity of the relevant law and procedure; and the applicant's capacity to represent himself effectively. In order to assess the proportionality, the national court may also take account of the amount of the costs of the proceedings in respect of which advance payment must be made and whether or not those costs might represent an insurmountable obstacle to access to the courts.'

[4] Article 27(3).
[5] Article 27(4).

DETENTION

12.170 Those detained under third country procedures now enjoy distinct protections against arbitrary detention. Detention must be for as short a period as possible (and for no longer than is reasonably necessary to fulfil transfer procedures with due diligence)[1] and subject to the principles of necessity and proportionality, taking account of Article 31 of the Refugee Convention and generally adhering to the standards set out in the Recast Reception Directive:[2] ie that delays in administrative procedures that cannot be attributed to the applicant shall not justify a continuation of detention,[3] there must be 'immediate' provision of written reasons upon detention, release must be 'immediately' on a finding of unlawful detention[4], the health of the vulnerable should be a 'primary concern' of the detaining authority and there shall be 'ensure regular monitoring and adequate support taking into account their particular situation, including their health'[5]: minors shall be detained only as a 'measure of last resort' and 'they shall have the possibility to engage in leisure activities, including play and recreational activities appropriate to their age'.[6] A person may not be detained for the sole purpose of Dublin proceedings[7] and detention is permissible only to prevent a significant risk of absconding[8] where other less coercive measures cannot be applied effectively.[9] The procedures for making and responding to take back and take charge requests are expedited so that the transfer request must be made within one month from the asylum application being lodged with a reply being given within two weeks, on pain of deemed acceptance of the transfer; if the transfer is not made within six weeks of deemed or express acceptance, then detention must end.[10]

---

[1] Dublin III, art 28(3).
[2] Recital (20), Article 28(4), of Dublin III, referencing Directive 2013/33/EU.
[3] Directive 2013/33/EU, art 9(4).
[4] Directive 2013/33/EU, art 9(3).
[5] Directive 2013/33/EU, art 11(1).
[6] Directive 2013/33/EU, art 11(2).
[7] Dublin III, art 28(1).
[8] Article 2(n) of Dublin III: '"risk of absconding" means the existence of reasons in an individual case, which are based on objective criteria defined by law, to believe that an applicant or a third-country national or a stateless person who is subject to a transfer procedure may abscond.'
[9] Dublin III, art 28(2).
[10] Dublin III, art 28(3).

ADMINISTRATIVE COOPERATION AND CONCILIATION

12.171 In Chapter V of Dublin II and Chapter VII of Dublin III, which deal with administrative cooperation, Member States agree (subject to specified limitations) to exchange information for the determination of the Member State responsible for examining the application for asylum, for the examination of the application for asylum and for the implementation of any obligation arising under the Regulation.[1] An asylum seeker has the right to be informed, on request, of any data that is processed concerning him or her.[2] Provision is made also enabling bilateral administrative arrangements to be established between Member States concerning the practical details of the implementation of the Regulation, in order to facilitate its application and increase its effectiveness.[3] There is a conciliation procedure for disputes arising in the context of the application of the Regulation between Member States, by which three Committee[4] members from neutral Member States shall provide a proposed solution within a month of receiving written arguments from the disputing parties which shall be given utmost account by them.[5] The Commission is to report to the European Parliament and Council on the operation of the Regulation by 21 July 2016.[6] Within the field of European Union law obligations, there is a general duty of sincere cooperation between Member States.[7]

1   Dublin II, art 21; Dublin III at art 34(1).
2   Dublin II, art 21(9); Dublin III at art 34(9). If information has been processed in breach of the
    Regulation or of Directive 95/46/EC of the European Parliament and the Council of
    24 October 1995 on the protection of individuals with regard to the processing of personal
    data and on the free movement of such data, in particular because it is incomplete or
    inaccurate, the asylum applicant is entitled to have it corrected, erased or blocked: art 21(8)
    (Art 34(9) of Dublin III). Exchanged data shall be kept for a period not exceeding that which
    is necessary for the purposes for which it is exchanged: art 21(11) (Art 34(11) of Dublin III).
    See further Council Regulation (EC) No 2725/2000 of 11 December 2000 which concerns the
    establishment of Eurodac for the comparison of fingerprints, and sets out at art 18 that there
    is a right of access to data, and a right for incorrect data to be rectified 'without excessive
    delay'. The AIT found in *RZ (Eurodac, fingerprint match, admissible) Eritrea* [2008] UKAIT
    00007 that: 'The safeguards within the Eurodac system are such that in the absence of cogent
    evidence to the contrary, (a) fingerprint images held in the system and data as to where, when
    and why those fingerprints were taken should be accepted as accurate and reliable; and (b)
    evidence of a fingerprint match identified by the system and confirmed by the Immigration
    Fingerprint Bureau should be regarded as determinative of that issue.'
3   These may relate to the exchanges of liaison officers and the simplification of the procedures
    and shortening of the time limits relating to transmission and the examination of requests to
    take charge of or take back asylum seekers: Dublin II, art 23; art 36(1) of Dublin III. The
    arrangements must be communicated to the Commission, which is obliged to check that they
    do not infringe the Regulation. See also the two Dublin Regulations' own implementing
    regime: Regulation 2003/1560/EC (OJ 2003 L 222/3, in force 6 September 2003), setting out
    more detailed provisions for the implementation of the Dublin II regulation; and Implementing
    Regulation No 118/2014 of 30 January 2014.
4   Established under Dublin III at art 34 to assist the Commission.
5   Dublin III at art 37.
6   Dublin III at art 46.
7   Article 4(3) of the Treaty on European Union: 'Pursuant to the principle of sincere
    cooperation, the Union and the Member States shall, in full mutual respect, assist each other
    in carrying out tasks which flow from the Treaties'; see further the CJEU in *Hilmar
    Kellinghusen v Amt für Land- und Wasserwirtschaft Kiel and Ernst-Detlef Ketelsen v Amt
    für Land- und Wasserwirtschaft Husum* (Cases C-36/97 and C-37/97).

APPLICATION OF DUBLIN REGULATIONS BETWEEN MEMBER STATES AND INDIVIDUALS

12.172 The Dublin II Regulation was adopted under Article 63(1)(a) EC
Treaty,[1] and has general application and is binding in its entirety and directly
applicable in all Member States.[2] The Dublin II Regulation thus has *direct
effect*. This should mean that individuals can in principle rely on its provisions
before national courts where these conflict with any national law measures. As
the Advocate General stated in his opinion in *Panayatova*, 'inherent in the
recognition of direct effect is an idea of effectiveness and judicial protection of
the individual rights granted to individuals'.[3] This makes Dublin II very
different to the original Dublin Convention, which did not have direct effect
and whose provisions could not be relied on in the courts.[4] However, Dublin
II at least is primarily aimed at determining responsibility between Member States, rather than conferring rights on individuals (short of cases where
fundamental rights are in play):[5] many decisions of the courts[6] have so found,
particularly where an express acceptance of responsibility by the receiving
country creates an agreement on the 'international plane' which is domestically
unimpeachable,[7] including *Abdullahi*[8] in the CJEU. One of the jurisprudential
questions thrown up by Dublin III is whether the new Regulation intends to
instil directly effective rights of challenge against determinations of state

responsibility, not only with respect to reception conditions that threaten fundamental rights but additionally as to the allocation of responsibility under the hierarchy of criteria including questions of responsibility lapsing,[9] and thus to incidentally undermine the reasoning in the cases decided in relation to Dublin II.[10] In our view it certainly does, bearing in mind that the basic test for identifying when European Union law obligations have direct effect is whether the obligation in question is sufficiently clear, precise and unconditional,[11] a test which the words of Dublin III 'the applicant . . . shall have the right to an effective remedy . . . in fact and in law, against a transfer decision' addressing 'both the examination of the application of this Regulation and of the legal and factual situation in the Member State to which the applicant is transferred'.[12]

[1] Under art 63(1)(a), the Council is to adopt measures on asylum on the criteria and mechanisms for determining which Member State is responsible for considering an application for asylum submitted by a national of a third country in one of the Member States. See further **7.34**.

[2] Article 249, EC Treaty; final sentence Dublin II Regulation.

[3] *Panayotova v Minister voor Vreemdelingenzaken en Integratie* Case C-327/02 [2004] ECR I-11055, ECJ, para 36. See further classic statements of principle to such effect in *Algemene Transport-en Expeditie Onderneming van Gend en Loos NV v Nederlandse* Belastingadministratie: C-26/62 [1963] ECR 1, [1963] CMLR 105 and Case C-253/00 *Muñoz (Antonio) y Cia SA and Superior Fruiticola SA v Frumar Ltd and Redbridge Produce Marketing Ltd* [2002] ECR 1-7289.

[4] See fifth edition of this work at **12.148** and cases cited there including the Court of Appeal in *R (on the application of G) v Secretary of State for the Home Department* [2004] EWHC Admin 2848 and [2005] EWCA Civ 546. See Chadwick LJ at [30] of *Omar v Secretary of State for the Home Department* [2005] EWCA Civ 285.

[5] See **12.158-12.172** addressing the right to be from inhuman and degrading treatment and **12.172** vis-á-vis family life particularly fn 10-12 above, *K v Bundesasylamt*: C-245/11 [2013] 1 WLR 883, ECJ and Philip Mott QC sitting as a Deputy High Court judge in *R (on the application of Jeyarupan) v Secretary of State for the Home Department* [2014] EWHC 386 (Admin) at [35]-[36].

[6] See the cases at **12.165** fn 6 above, and *AA (Afghanistan)* [2006] EWCA Civ 1550; *R (on the application of J) v Secretary of State for the Home Department* [2009] EWHC 1182 (Admin); *MK (Iran), R (on the application of) v Secretary of State for the Home Department* [2010] EWCA Civ 115; Beatson J in *R (on the application of YZ) v Secretary of State for the Home Department* [2011] EWHC 205 (Admin); Lewis J in *Habte v Secretary of State for the Home Department; R (on the application of RH (Eritrea)) v Secretary of State for the Home Department* [2013] EWHC 3295 (Admin); Stadlen J in *Kheirollahi-Ahmadroghani v Secretary of State for the Home Department* [2013] EWHC 1314 (Admin) interpreted the ECJ decision of *Leonesio v Italian Ministry of Agriculture and Forestry* (Case 93/71) [1973] CMLR 343 as demonstrating that that Court 'contemplated that there may be Regulations which, even though they are directly applicable in all Member States and even though they have direct effect do not create individual rights which national courts must protect.' The Court of Appeal held in *Omar (Mohammed Abdi) v Secretary of State for the Home Department* [2005] EWCA 285, upholding the Administrative Court at [2004] EWHC 1427, that the Dublin Regulation drew a clear distinction between criteria and mechanisms, and a breach of procedures did not give rise to a right on the part of the asylum claimant to have his or her claim dealt with in the UK. The Court of Appeal treated the matter as determined beyond peradventure by the time of *R (on the application of AR (Iran)) v Secretary of State for the Home Department* [2013] EWCA Civ 778.

[7] Eg, Laws J in *R (on the application of Simba) v Secretary of State for the Home Department* [1998] EWHC 799 (Admin) saying that 'once it is plain that there has been an agreement for the purposes of dealing with an asylum claim, following application of the provisions of Article 5.2 the approach of the court must be simply to accept that that has been agreed to on the international plane and the matter is thereby closed'. The Court of Appeal's conclusions in *AR (Iran), R (On the Application Of) v Secretary of State for the Home Department* [2013] EWCA Civ 778 at [33]: '5. Full faith and credit between member states, including the courts of those member states, does not permit or encourage further enquiry into or disregard of decisions of fellow member states . . . ' (see further **12.158** above fn 2).

8   *Abdullahi (Judgment of the Court)* [2013] EUECJ C-394/12; see also *Federal Republic of Germany v Puid (Kaveh)*: C-4/11 [2014] QB 346, [2014] 2 WLR 98, ECJ.
9   See above paragraph 12.165.
10   See above paragraph 12.169.
11   See *Algemene Transport-en Expeditie Onderneming van Gend en Loos NV v Nederlandse Belastingadministratie*: C-26/62 [1963] ECR 1, [1963] CMLR 105 relating to 'obligations which the Treaty imposes in a clearly defined way upon . . . . Member States'.
12   Article 27(1) and Recital (19) of Dublin III.

12.173 The Immigration Rules provide for a discretion on the part of the Secretary of State as to whether or not to remove an asylum applicant to a safe third country when the legal conditions for doing so are fulfilled[1] and the Secretary of State's policy on the circumstances in which discretion would be exercised by considering an asylum claim substantively in the UK despite the person's arrival from a 'safe' third country was first set out in a written answer to a parliamentary question dated 25 July 1990. It required evidence of 'substantial links' with the UK making it reasonable for the claim exceptionally to be considered in the UK.[2] A restrictive approach to the exercise of discretion in this area has not always been approved by the courts.[3] In *Ex p Nicholas*[4] a decision to remove a claimant who had married after arrival, pursuant to a policy distinction between pre- and post-arrival marriage, was quashed as unreasonable where there was no issue as to the genuineness of the marriage. On 22 July 2002, the policy was restated.[5] It still required 'substantial links' with the UK and expressly excluded spouses where the marriage took place after arrival in the UK.[6] According to the 2002 policy, a claimant will not normally be removed on third-country grounds if (i) he or she has a spouse or unmarried minor children in the UK or (ii) he or she is an unmarried minor with a parent in the UK. Discretion may be exercised if the minor is married, although this is more likely if the married minor is the applicant with a parent in the UK, than if the applicant is a parent with a married minor child in the UK. Discretion may also be exercised where the applicant is an elderly or otherwise dependent parent. Other family links may qualify but only where there is clear evidence that the applicant is wholly or mainly dependent on the relative in the UK and there is an absence of support elsewhere. Adult claimants with parents and/or siblings in the UK have rarely had discretion exercised in their favour.[7] The 2002 policy also limits the meaning of 'in the UK'.[8] In these and other respects, it is suggested that the Secretary of State 'substantive links' policy does not adequately reflect the considerations set out in Dublin III, and the policy will need to be reassessed generally and in particular cases to ensure conformity with Article 8 of the ECHR.[9]

1   HC 395, para 345(1): the wording of the rule is that where the Secretary of State is satisfied that the conditions in paragraphs 4 and 5(1) . . . . of Schedule 3 to the AI(TC)A 2004 are fulfilled, he will normally decline to examine the asylum application substantively and issue a certificate . . . .'.
2   Written reply by then Minister David Waddington MP, *Hansard*, HC Official Reports, cols. 262–263. The reference to 'substantial links' was explained in a letter dated 21 March 1991 from IND to UKIAS, reproduced in *Butterworths Immigration Law Service*.
3   In *R v Secretary of State for the Home Department, ex p B* (CO 1818/1998) (24 June 1999, unreported), removal of a minor was held 'cruel'. See also *R v Secretary of State for the Home Department, ex p Islam (Asif)* (CO 628/1999) (1 February 2000, unreported).
4   *R v Secretary of State for the Home Department, ex p Nicholas* [2000] Imm AR 334.
5   *Hansard*, HC Offical Reports, 22 July 2002, col 860W (Beverley Hughes MP).
6   The July 2002 policy, depriving those who had married after arrival in the UK from the benefit of the policy, came after the grant of permission in *R (on the application of Nadarajah) v*

Secretary of State for the Home Department, a *Nicholas*-type case (see fn 3 above). Regarding this revision, the CA held in *Nadarajah and Abdi v Secretary of State for the Home Department* [2005] EWCA Civ 1363 that it was not unlawful for the Secretary of State not to apply the revised policy to a claimant whose wife was an asylum *appellant* in the UK in circumstances where he had previously refused to apply the unrevised policy on his understanding of its true meaning (as not applying where the spouse was only in the UK as an appellant) which had been held to be incorrect in the High Court (see *R (on the application of Nadarajah) v Secretary of State for the Home Department* [2002] EWHC 2595 (Admin)).

7   In *R v Secretary of State for the Home Department, ex p Raj (Reena)* (CO 2630/1998) (30 November 1999, unreported) the Secretary of State conceded a challenge to the removal of an Indian woman who, prior to her last entry into the UK, had been continuously resident for nine years in the UK, had been educated, employed and established a substantial network of supportive friends here and was vulnerable to mental illness if deprived of these support networks. However in *R v Secretary of State for the Home Department, ex p Ahmed (Marion)* (1 February 1999, unreported), the Court of Appeal held that the applicant could not rely on connections made during delays caused by her own representations or litigation against removal.

8   'In all cases "in the United Kingdom" is to be taken as meaning with leave to enter or remain or on temporary admission to this country as an asylum seeker prior to an initial decision on their application': *Hansard* (fn 4 above).

9   However, both the 1991 and 2002 policies have been found to be lawful and in conformity with Art 8 ECHR: see eg *R v Secretary of State for the Home Department, ex p Demiroglu* [2001] EWHC 663 (Admin), *(Collins J)*; *R (on the application of Kozany) v Secretary of State for the Home Department* [2002] EWHC 2830 (Admin), [2002] All ER (D) 39 (Dec) *(Gibbs J)*. The 2002 policy makes it clear that cases citing other family ties and not displaying any of the features which engaged the exercise of discretion, would not normally be considered substantively. Thus 'a brother, who was not dependent on his sibling(s), would not normally have his case considered here, no matter how strong his cultural or linguistic links with the United Kingdom'.

ASYLUM APPEALS

12.174 The appeals regime is considered in detail in CHAPTERS **19** to **21** and note must be taken of the wide ranging changes to the appeal system enacted but only partially brought into force, by the Immigration Act 2014. Under the pre-2014 Act provisions, refusal of asylum is not in itself a decision against which an appeal may be brought. However, a person's entitlement to asylum can be raised in an appeal against the following decisions: under section 82 of the NIAA 2002 against an 'immigration decision';[1] in an appeal against refusal of asylum in circumstances where the person has been granted leave for a period exceeding one year;[2] against a variation of leave following a decision that a person who had been granted asylum is not a refugee[3] or in an appeal to the SIAC.[4] There is specific statutory provision for the appellant's claimed entitlement to asylum to be raised as a ground of appeal.[5] The making of an asylum claim whilst in the UK entitles a person to appeal from within the country against a subsequent immigration decision[6] unless he or she is to be removed to a 'safe third country' in accordance with the procedures discussed above or the asylum claim is certified as 'clearly unfounded'. We consider below the certification of asylum claims as 'clearly unfounded'. The making of a human rights claim also entitles a person to appeal from within the UK[7] unless the human rights claim is certified as clearly unfounded.[8] We deal with human rights claims and the certification of human rights claims in CHAPTER 7. It should be noted that there are some immigration decisions against which an appeal may be brought from within the UK unless the person makes an asylum or human rights claim and one or both of those claims is certified clearly unfounded.[9] Certification of an asylum claim as clearly unfounded cannot prevent the bringing of an in-country appeal in respect of two immigration decisions only: revocation of indefinite leave under section 76 of the NIAA 2002, and a decision to make a deportation order.[10] Section 94(6B) of the NIAA 2002 would, if it had ever come into force, have prevented the certification of asylum and human rights claims that relate to variation appeals where the leave was given in circumstances specified by the Secretary of State.[11] The Immigration Act 2014 abolishes the rights of appeal described above, replacing them with rights of appeal against refusal of a protection claim (ie a claim that removal from the UK would breach the UK's obligations under the Refugee Convention or obligations to a person entitled to humanitarian protection); refusal of a human rights claim and revocation of protection status.[12]

[1]   The immigration decisions are set out in Nationality, Immigration and Asylum Act 2002, s 82(2)(a)–(k) and (3A).
[2]   NIAA 2002, s 83. The right of appeal under s 83 arises only in circumstances where the grant of leave to remain post-dates the refusal of asylum, albeit that the grant of leave does not necessarily have to be a direct or immediate consequence of the refusal of asylum: see *AS (Somalia) v Secretary of State for the Home Department* [2011] EWCA Civ 1319; and *MS (Uganda) v Secretary of State for the Home Department* [2014] EWCA Civ 50.
[3]   Nationality, Immigration and Asylum Act 2002, s 83A (as inserted by IAN 2006, s 1).
[4]   Special Immigration Appeals Commission Act 1997, s 2.
[5]   NIAA 2002, s 84(1)(g) (in relation to appeals under s 82, the ground is 'that removal of the appellant from the United Kingdom in consequence of the immigration decision would breach the United Kingdom's obligations under the Refugee Convention'), section 84(3) in relation to appeals under ss 83 and 84(4) in relation to appeals under s 83A, both of which are in the same terms, ie 'that removal of the appellant from the United Kingdom would breach the United Kingdom's obligations under the Refugee Convention'. This ground of appeal has been extended, relying on the EU principle of equivalence, to include a claim that the removal would breach the right to subsidiary protection pursuant to the Qualification Directive (EU Directive 2004/83/EC): see the decision of the Court of Appeal in *FA (Iraq) v Secretary of State for the Home Department* [2010] EWCA Civ 696. By the Special Immigration Appeals Commission Act 1997, s 2(2)(e) provision is made for the same grounds of appeal in relation to an appeal against an immigration decision but no specific similar provision is made in relation to appeals under NIAA 2002, ss 83 and 83A: see Special Immigration Appeals Commission Act 1997, s 2(3).
[6]   NIAA 2002, s 92(4)(a).
[7]   NIAA 2002, s 92(4)(a).
[8]   NIAA 2002, s 94(1A) and (2).
[9]   Those immigration decisions are refusal of a certificate of entitlement to the right of abode; refusal to vary leave; variation of a person's leave or a decision that a person is to be removed upon the expiry of his or her statutorily extended leave. See NIAA 2002, ss 92(2) and 94(1A).
[10] Those decisions are included in NIAA 2002, s 92(2) but not in section 94(1A). However, where a decision to make a deportation order is made in accordance with the 'automatic deportation' provisions in the UK Borders Act 2007, s 32, certification of an asylum claim as clearly unfounded can prevent the bringing of an in-country appeal: this is because such a decision is not an immigration decision as included in s 92(2).
[11] As inserted by IAN 2006, s 13 from a date to be appointed. But note that IAN 2006, s 13 is itself repealed by Immigration Act 2014, Sch 9, para 57(3) from a date to be appointed.
[12] Immigration Act 2014, s 15. These appeal provisions, the extent to which they have come into force and the associated provisions for certification are discussed in CHAPTERS **19-21**.

Clearly unfounded asylum claims

12.175 The Secretary of State is obliged to certify an asylum claim as 'clearly unfounded', unless satisfied that the claim is not clearly unfounded, if the person comes from a safe country of origin.[1] The test as to whether an individual claim is clearly unfounded is an objective one.[2] Countries of origin were first designated 'safe' by provisions of the Asylum and Immigration Act 1996.[3] The countries designated in 1996 – the so-called 'white list' – were Bulgaria, Cyprus, Ghana, India, Pakistan, Poland and Romania.[4] The designation power was very controversial,[5] as was its use, particularly in relation to Pakistan in the light of the difficulties faced there by Christians, Ahmadis and women among others. A certified claim reduced (but did not remove) in-country appeal rights available to nationals of certified countries.[6] The measure was controversial, and was not replicated when the Immigration and Asylum Act 1999 replaced the appeals provisions of the 1993 and 1996 Acts.

---

[1]   NIAA 2002, s 94(3).
[2]   See, for example, *ZT (Kosovo) v Secretary of State for the Home Department* [2009] UKHL 6, [2009] 1 WLR 348 *per Lord Phillips at [23]*, per Lord Brown at [75]–[76] and per Lord Neuberger at [83]: 'The test is an objective one: it depends not on the Home Secretary's view but upon a criterion which a court can readily re-apply once it has the materials which the Home Secretary had. A claim is either clearly unfounded or it is not'. See also *R (on the application of YH) v Secretary of State for the Home Department* [2010] EWCA Civ 116, [2010] All ER (D) 280 (Feb).
[3]   Section 1 of the 1996 Act substituted a new para 5 of Sch 2 to the Asylum and Immigration Appeals Act 1993 which included (in sub-para (2)) the power to designate a country or territory as one in which it appeared to the Secretary of State that there was 'in general no serious risk of persecution'. If the adjudicator accepted that the person was a national of a 'white list' country, the appellant could not appeal to the Immigration Appeal Tribunal (Sch 2, para 5(7)).
[4]   Asylum (Designated Countries of Destination and Designated Safe Third Countries) Order 1996, SI 1996/2671.
[5]   In that it tended to undermine the principle of individual determination of claims required by the Refugee Convention.
[6]   The adjudicator could not discharge the certificate (in the absence of evidence of torture), on the ground that the claim should not have been certified (*R v Special Adjudicator, ex p Zaman (Mohammed)* [2000] Imm AR 68; *Bajwa (Talat) v Secretary of State for the Home Department* [2000] Imm AR 364, CA). Any challenge to designation and to certification had to be by way of judicial review (*R v Special Adjudicator and Secretary of State for the Home Department, ex p Dhanoa* (1999/7535/C) (21 January 2000, unreported), CA). In *R (on the application of Javed) v Secretary of State for the Home Department* [2001] EWCA Civ 789, [2002] QB 129, the Court of Appeal held that the Secretary of State's decision to designate Pakistan as a country in which there was in general no risk of persecution was made on an erroneous view of the facts or the law. However, in *R (on the application of Singh (Balwinder)) v Secretary of State for the Home Department* [2001] EWHC 925 (Admin), [2001] All ER (D) 235 (Nov), Burton J held that India had not been unlawfully designated.

12.176 The use of discredited 'white lists' returned with a vengeance in section 94 of the NIAA 2002, which makes provision for the certification of both refugee and human rights claims. Where a claimant who applied after 7 November 2002[1] is entitled to reside[2] in a listed State,[3] including one (or part of one) designated by order of the Secretary of State as a State in which there is in general no serious risk of persecution and removal to which will not in general contravene the UK's obligations under the Human Rights Convention,[4] then the Secretary of State is obliged to certify such claim as clearly unfounded unless satisfied that it is not.[5] A new section 94A has been inserted into the Act[6] requiring the Secretary of State to make a 'European Common List of Safe Countries of Origin' and to certify as clearly unfounded (unless satisfied that they are not) asylum and human rights claims made by nationals of those states or stateless persons formerly habitually resident there.[7] The difference between the 2002 Act regime and that contained in the 1996 Act however is dramatic. Whereas under the 1996 Act the scope of appeal was limited to appeals to adjudicators without the possibility of further appeal to the Immigration Appeal Tribunal, under the new regime those whose claims are certified as clearly unfounded have no suspensive in-country appeal.[8] The range of states whose nationals may have their asylum or human rights claims certified clearly unfounded was radically increased by section 27 of the AI(TC)A 2004. It provides that a state or part of a state may be added to the list in respect of persons of a particular description (eg, in relation to gender) where in relation to persons of that description there is in general no serious risk of persecution in the state or part of the state and removal would not breach the UK's obligations under the ECHR.[9] The purpose of the provision is said to be 'to provide extra flexibility to identify groups of persons within a State or part for whom conditions are generally safe'.[10] The Secretary of State's policy is to consider including a State in the 'white list' if there are significant numbers of asylum claims made by nationals of the State and returns there can be enforced.[11] If a State is added to the list in respect of a particular description of people, such as 'males', a successful challenge to the inclusion would have to show sufficiently systematic persecution of people of that description; evidence of children or women being persecuted would not suffice.[12] The inclusion of Bangladesh on the list of designated States was successfully challenged in *Zakir Husan*,[12] and Pakistan (whose designation under the 1996 Act was successfully challenged in *Javed*,[13]) has not been included. In *JB (Jamaica)*[14] the Court of Appeal held that the inclusion of Jamaica on the list of designated States was unlawful owing to the serious risk of persecution faced there by the lesbian, gay, bisexual and transgender community.[15] Further amendments to the 2002 Act mean that a claimant who is subject to extradition proceedings who would normally have a *non-suspensive* right of appeal will have a *suspensive* right of appeal against any refusal of an asylum or human rights claim.[16]

[1] Nationality, Immigration and Asylum Act 2002, s 94 did not come into force until 1 April 2003 (SI 2003/754, art 2(1) and Sch 1), but transitional provisions under s 115, in identical terms, came into force on the passing of the Act: s 162(2)(w).

[2] According to the Asylum Decision Making Guidance 'Non Suspensive Appeals (NSA) Certification under Section 94 of the NIA Act 2002', 24 May 2013, section 3.3 those 'entitled to reside' in a state include, as well as citizens, those who are 'normally resident there and have a clear legal basis to reside there'. If a person claims to be from a non-listed state, that claim would have to be accepted absent documentary or other credible evidence that the person was from the state. If a person claims not to be entitled to reside in a listed state, 'case owners should consider whether there is evidence that they are entitled to reside in the state, (passport or travel document issued in the state or other evidence that they had been there for many years). If there is such evidence then the claim should be considered on the basis that they are entitled to reside in a designated state.'

[3] The original version of s 94(4) listed the Accession States (the Republic of Cyprus, the Czech Republic, the Republic of Estonia, the Republic of Hungary, the Republic of Latvia, the Republic of Lithuania, the Republic of Malta, the Republic of Poland, the Slovak Republic, and the Republic of Slovenia) which joined the European Union on 1 May 2004. These states were removed from the list on 1 October 2004 by AI(TC)A 2004, s 27(4): SI 2004/2523. From that date, the appeal rights of asylum claimants from one of those states are governed by the Immigration (European Economic Area) Regulations 2006, SI 2006/1003.

[4] NIAA 2002, s 94(5). The states presently listed are: Albania, Jamaica, Macedonia, Moldova (added to the list from 1 April 2003 by SI 2003/970); Bolivia, Brazil, Ecuador, South Africa, Ukraine (from 23 July 2003, save in relation to asylum or human rights claims before that date: SI 2003/1919); India (from 13 February 2005, save in relation to asylum or human rights claims before that date: SI 2005/330); Mongolia, Ghana (in respect of men), Nigeria (in respect of men) (from 2 December 2005, except in relation to asylum or human rights claims made

before that date: SI 2005/3306); Bosnia-Herzegovina, Gambia (in respect of men), Kenya (in respect of men), Liberia (in respect of men), Malawi (in respect of men), Mali (in respect of men), Mauritius, Montenegro, Peru, Serbia, Sierra Leone (in respect of men) (from 27 July 2007 except in relation to claims made before that date: SI 2007/2221); Kosovo and South Korea (from 3 March 2010 except in relation to claims made before that date: SI 2010/561). Bangladesh was removed by SI 2005/1016 on 22 April 2005, Sri Lanka by SI 2006/3275 on 13 December 2006 and Bulgaria and Romania by SI 2006/3215 from 1 December 2007. The Asylum (Procedures) Regulations 2007, SI 2007/3187 inserted a new section 94(5D) into Nationality, Immigration and Asylum Act 2002, intended to implement Council Directive 2005/85/EC on minimum standards on procedures in members states for granting and withdrawing refugee status ('the Procedures Directive'), whereby the Secretary of State is required to have regard to circumstances in and information about states or parts of states before adding them to the list.

5   NIAA 2002, s 94(3). The Secretary of State may certify any other asylum or human rights claim clearly unfounded, but this is not the 'default' position, as it is in 'safe country of origin' and 'safe third country' cases; see s 94(2).
6   By the Asylum (Procedures) Regulations 2007, SI 2007/3187, reg 4.
7   Giving effect to Article 29 of the Procedures Directive which provides for the Council of the European Union to draw up a list of 'safe countries of origin'.
8   NIAA 2002, ss 92(1), (4) (which provide for in-country appeals if an asylum or human rights claim has been made in the UK); s 94(1A), (2) (which remove it on certification). Where a certificate is issued under s 94, an appeal taking place outside the UK is to be considered as if the applicant had not been removed: s 94(9).
9   NIAA 2002, s 94 (5A)–(5C), added by AI(TC)A 2004, s 27(5) from 1 October 2004: SI 2004/2523. The 'description of person' refers to Refugee Convention attributes and include additionally gender, language, or 'any other attribute or circumstance that the Secretary of State thinks appropriate': s 94(5C). States added to the 'safe list' under these provisions may be removed, or modified: s 94(6), as inserted.
10 AI(TC)A 2004 Explanatory Notes, at para 129. This could apply to majority groups (defined by ethnicity, religion etc) in countries where minorities are persecuted.
11 Evidence filed for the Secretary of State in *R (on the application of MD (Gambia)) v Secretary of State for the Home Department* [2011] EWCA Civ 121.
12 *R (MD (Gambia)) v Secretary of State for the Home Department* [2011] EWCA Civ 121.
13 *R (on the application of Husan) v Secretary of State for the Home Department* [2005] EWHC 189 (Admin), [2005] All ER (D) 371 (Feb), Wilson J, who held that no rational decision-maker could have been satisfied that the statutory presumptions of safety were met. Following the judgment, Bangladesh was removed from the list of safe countries under s 94(5): see fn 4 above.
14 *R (on the application of JB (Jamaica)) v Secretary of State for the Home Department* [2013] EWCA Civ 666, [2014] 1 WLR 836, [2014] 2 All ER 91, [2014] Imm AR 105, by majority (Moore-Bick LJ dissenting on this issue). Per Pill LJ at [57]: 'My conclusion is that a state in which there is a serious risk of persecution for an entire section of the community, defined by sexual orientation and substantial in numbers, is not a state where in general there is no serious risk of persecution.' Pill LJ rejected the argument on behalf of the Secretary of State that it makes no difference whether or not a state is designated because, in either case, the Secretary of State must give anxious scrutiny to a claim (see 12.177 below). Nonetheless Jamaica remains on the list in NIAA 2002, s 94(4).
15 *R (on the application of Javed) v Secretary of State for the Home Department* [2001] EWCA Civ 789, [2002] QB 129. India (whose inclusion in the earlier list was unsuccessfully challenged in *R (on the application of Singh (Balwinder)) v Secretary of State for the Home Department* [2001] EWHC 925 (Admin)) has been added to the current list.
16 NIAA 2002, s 94(6A), inserted by AI(TC)A 2004, s 27(7) from 1 October 2004: SI 2004/2523.

12.177 Even if a person is entitled to reside in a 'white list' country his or her claim for asylum is not to be certified if the Secretary of State is satisfied that the claim is not 'clearly unfounded'. If a person is not entitled to reside in a 'white list' country, his or her asylum claim may nevertheless be certified if the Secretary of State is satisfied that it is 'clearly unfounded'.[1] The meaning of 'clearly unfounded' is considered in CHAPTER 7, at 7.121. If a person makes both an asylum and a human rights claim and only one of them is considered clearly unfounded by the Secretary of State, it would not be appropriate to certify the 'clearly unfounded' claim.[2] The Secretary of State envisages asylum and ECHR, Article 3 claims being certifiable as clearly unfounded in the following circumstances: where no fear of mistreatment is expressed; where it is clear from objective evidence that 'there is no arguable case that the feared mistreatment will arise'; on the basis of the objective evidence it is clear that the feared mistreatment would not amount to persecution or breach of Article 3; the background evidence shows that where non-state agents are feared, it is clear that the state is providing sufficient protection; internal relocation 'is obviously available' which may be the case where the fear is of non-state agents or rogue state agents or the authorities are not in control of the entire country. However, for a claim to be certified on an internal relocation basis, the caseworker must have explored in interview whether there were any factors which would make relocation unduly harsh; in respect of an asylum claim, where there is no convention reason for the fear.[3] Children's claims may be certified but if the child is unaccompanied and the Secretary of State is not satisfied that there are adequate reception arrangements, the child would be granted discretionary leave so that certification would be inappropriate.[4]

---

[1] NIAA 2002, s 94(2).

[2] Asylum Decision Making Guidance 'Non Suspensive Appeals (NSA) Certification under Section 94 of the NIA Act 2002', 24 May 2013, section 6.

[3] Asylum Decision Making Guidance 'Non Suspensive Appeals (NSA) Certification under Section 94 of the NIA Act 2002', 24 May 2013, section 5.

[4] Asylum Decision Making Guidance 'Non Suspensive Appeals (NSA) Certification under Section 94 of the NIA Act 2002', 24 May 2013, section 7.1.

Procedure on asylum appeals

12.178 Details of appeal procedures are to be found at CHAPTER 20 below. Although asylum appeals are subject to the same appeal procedures as other immigration appeals, the fundamental importance of what is at stake means that the courts are particularly concerned that the highest standards of fairness apply and that procedural and evidential requirements are not over-stringently applied. Thus, where a decision has potentially grave consequences for an asylum seeker, it may be proper to grant an adjournment for further evidence to be adduced,[1] and neither the *Ladd v Marshall*[2] principles governing the reception of fresh evidence, nor the rule in *Al-Mehdawi*[3] apply with their full rigour in asylum or human rights appeals.[4] The Tribunal's own obligations to prevent *refoulement* under the Refugee Convention meant that it must be alive to obvious points of Convention law even when these are not adverted to by the appellant.[5] In asylum cases where the most anxious scrutiny is required,[6] it would only be in an extreme case that a procedural error depriving the appellant of an opportunity to present the case in full could be treated as of no practical effect.[7]

---

[1] *SH (Afghanistan) v Secretary of State for the Home Department* [2011] EWCA Civ 1284, [2011] All ER (D) 55 (Nov); *R (on the application of Fanna) v Secretary of State for the Home Department* [2002] EWHC 777 (Admin) 777, [2002] Imm AR 407.

[2] [1954] 3 All ER 745, [1954] 1 WLR 1489 (CA).

[3] *Al-Mehdawi v Secretary of State for the Home Department* [1989] 3 All ER 843, [1990] 1 AC 876, [1989] 3 WLR 1294, HL, which established that a procedural failure caused by an appellant's own representative did not lead to an appeal hearing being in breach of the rules of natural justice so as to found a judicial review.

4   *Haile v Immigration Appeal Tribunal* [2001] EWCA Civ 663, [2002] INLR 283, CA; R (on the application of Azkhosravi) v Immigration Appeal Tribunal [2001] EWCA Civ 977, [2002] INLR 123 (failure to explain late submission of evidence, approving R v Immigration Appeal Tribunal, ex p Aziz [1999] INLR 355); *FP (Iran) and MB (Libya) v Secretary of State for the Home Department* [2007] EWCA Civ 13; *AK (Iran) v Secretary of State for the Home Department* [2008] EWCA Civ 941, [2008] All ER (D) 100 (Jul). The Court of Appeal gave guidance on the admission of evidence demonstrating a mistake of fact and the role of the Tribunal in *E v Secretary of State for the Home Department*; *R v Secretary of State for the Home Department* [2004] EWCA Civ 49, [2004] QB 1044, [2004] 2 WLR 1351. See also *R (on the application of Tofik) v Immigration Appeal Tribunal* [2003] EWCA Civ 1138, [2003] INLR 623 (extension of time).

5   *Robinson (Anthonypillai Francis) v Secretary of State for the Home Department and Immigration Appeal Tribunal* [1997] Imm AR 568, CA, applied in *R (on the application of Naing) v Immigration Appeal Tribunal, R (on the application of Eyaz) v Immigration Appeal Tribunal* [2003] EWHC 771 (Admin), [2003] All ER (D) 337 (Mar). See also *A (Iraq) v Secretary of State for the Home Department* [2005] EWCA Civ 1438 in relation to exclusion: see 12.92, fn 3 above.

6   The 'most anxious scrutiny' is a quotation from Lord Bridge in *Bugdaycay v Secretary of State for the Home Department* [1987] AC 514, HL. See also per Carnwath LJ in *R (on the application of YH) v Secretary of State for the Home Department* [2010] EWCA Civ 116 at paras 22–24.

7   See eg *R (on the application of RQ (Jordan)) v Secretary of State for the Home Department and Another* [2014] EWHC 559 (Admin), [2014] All ER (D) 86 (Mar). However, in *R (on the application of Makke) v Immigration Appeal Tribunal* [2005] EWCA Civ 176 the CA observed that relief should not be granted unless the underlying claim has merit.

Credibility

12.179 English courts have not given the same assistance to appellate authorities dealing with credibility in the context of asylum claims[1] as has been given by the Canadian courts,[2] which have held that 'when an applicant swears to the truth of certain allegations, this creates a presumption that those allegations are true unless there be reason to doubt their truthfulness',[3] and that 'a reasonable margin of appreciation be applied to any perceived flaws in the claimant's testimony'.[4] But decisions based on adverse credibility have been subjected to careful scrutiny by the Tribunal and the Administrative Court to ensure that they are properly reasoned and take account of relevant evidence,[5] and appellate bodies' unsupported assertions that a witness is not credible are no longer acceptable. Questions of credibility are, however, matters for the Tribunal of fact, which should be cautious in rejecting as incredible an account by an anxious and inexperienced asylum seeker, whose reasons for seeking asylum may well be expected to contain inconsistencies and omissions in the course of its revelation to the authorities and investigation on appeal;[6] as Mr Justice Blake observed:

> 'most people who have experience of obtaining a narrative from asylum seekers from a different language or different culture recognise that time, confidence in the interviewer and the interview process and some patience and some specific direction to pertinent questions is needed to adduce a comprehensive and adequate account. This is particularly the case where sexual assaults are alleged and all kind of cultural and gender sensitive issues may be in play as to why the full picture is not disclosed early on'.[7]

The Tribunal has noted that 'It is perfectly possible for an adjudicator to believe that a witness is not telling the truth about some matters, has exaggerated the story to make his case better, or is simply uncertain about matters, but still to be persuaded that the centrepiece of the story stands'.[8] The API go less far but acknowledge the need to sometimes give the benefit of the doubt and states: '

'In assessing the internal credibility of a claim, decision makers should be aware of any mitigating reasons why an applicant is incoherent, inconsistent and unable to provide detail, or delays in providing details of material facts. These reasons should be taken into account when considering the credibility of a claim and must be included in the reasoning given in the subsequent decision. Factors may include the following (the list is not exhaustive): age; gender; mental health issues; mental or emotional trauma; fear and/or mistrust of authorities; feelings of shame; painful memories particularly those of a sexual nature and cultural implications. It is also important to consider whether a particular line of questioning was reasonable.'[9]

A person may be disbelieved entirely about his or her claimed history of persecution but still be found to be at risk of being persecuted in the future.[10]

[1]   See in particular the UNHCR publication *Beyond Proof, Credibility Assessment in EU Asylum Systems*, May 2013. The Refugee Legal Centre produced a useful training document: 'Issues arising from "credibility", procedure and evidence before the appellate authorities' containing references to Canadian, US, New Zealand and Australian case law to supplement that of the UK courts. See further Catriona Jarvis *The Judge as Juror revisited* [2003] Immigration Law Digest (Winter) p 7; Amanda Weston *A Witness of Truth – Credibility Findings in Asylum Appeals* (1998) INLP, vol 12, No 3; Dr Stuart Turner *Discrepancies and Delays in Histories Presented by asylum seekers: Implications for* Assessment, Traumatic Stress Clinic, 18 Dec/1996; Herlihy et al 'Discrepancies in autobiographical memories: implications for assessment of asylum claims', BMJ 2002, 324-7 (available on BMJ website); R Graycar *The Gender of Judgments: An Introduction*, in Feminist Legal debates, ed Margaret Thornton, OUP 1995; Professor Patricia J Williams *The Obliging Shell (An informal Essay on Formal Equal Opportunity)* in After Identity, ed. Danielson and Engle, Routledge 1995; Sir Thomas Bingham *The Judge as Juror: Judicial Determination of Factual Issues 1985 Current Legal problems; The Challenge of Asylum to Legal Systems*, ed Prakash Shah (2005), Cavendish; and the Canadian Guidelines, below.

[2]   The Immigration and Refugee Board has produced a useful guide 'Assessment of Credibility in Claims for Refugee Protection' (January 2004), setting out all relevant Federal Court of Appeal decisions on various aspects of credibility. It is available on the Immigration and Refugee Board website www.irb.gc.ca.

[3]   *Maldonado v Canada (Minister of Employment and Immigration)* [1980] 2 FC 302, CA, cited in Hathaway **12.22** fn 2 above, p 84. See also *RR (challenging evidence) Sri Lanka* [2010] UKUT 000274 (IAC) for the best UK approach on this issue.

[4]   *Attakora (Benjamin) v Minister for Employment and Immigration* (Decision A-1091-87) (19 May 1989, unreported), cited in Hathaway above, p 85. The UN Committee Against Torture has made the same point, saying that 'complete accuracy is not to be expected from victims of torture', in *Alan v Switzerland* [1997] INLR 29. And in *Hrickova* (00TH 02034) (9 August 2000, unreported), IAT, inconsistencies in the account of a Slovak Roma of stabbing and gang rape were 'properly explained by the nature of human recollection, particularly dealing with traumatic incidents'. See the UNHCR publication *Beyond Proof, Credibility Assessment in EU Asylum Systems* (fn 1 above), eg at page 258: 'Those who have suffered traumatic events often display avoidance symptoms; they avoid thinking and talking about the event. They may experience dissociation, at the time of the traumatic event or when recalling it; they cannot remember some or all aspects of the trauma, because (aspects of) the event were not initially encoded.'

[5]   See cases cited in Chapter 20 below on 'making a determination'.

[6]   Hathaway above, pp 84–88; Re SA, NZRSAA 1/92 (NZ); Matter of SMJ Interim Decision 3303 (BIA) 1997 (US); *Kopalapillai v Minister for Immigration and Multicultural Affairs* [1997] FCA 1510 (24 December 1997) (Aus). See the UNHCR publication *Beyond Proof, Credibility Assessment in EU Asylum Systems* (fn 1 above).

[7]   R (on the application of Ngirincuti) v Secretary of State for the Home Department [2008] EWHC 1952 (Admin).

[8]   *Chiver* (10758); see also *Guo v Minister for Immigration and Ethnic Affairs* (1996) 64 FRC 151 at 194, a decision of the full court of the Federal Court of Australia. Elevation of

peripheral matters into matters of determinative weight was held unlawful in *R (on the application of Choudhrey) v Immigration Appeal Tribunal* [2001] EWHC 613 (Admin 613, [2001] All ER (D) 04 (Aug).

[9] API on 'Considering asylum claims and assessing credibility', 30 July 2012. See also the UNHCR publication *Beyond Proof, Credibility Assessment in EU Asylum Systems* (fn 1 above).

[10] *Daoud v Secretary of State for the Home Department* [2005] EWCA Civ 755, [2005] All ER (D) 259 (May).

12.180 Since it is not in the nature of repressive regimes and societies to behave reasonably, the strange or unusual cannot be dismissed as incredible or improbable, particularly if there is supporting material of similar accounts in the relevant human rights literature, and decision-makers should constantly be on their guard to avoid implicitly recharacterising the nature of the risk based on their own perceptions of reasonability.[1] An assessment of credibility can only be made on the basis of a complete understanding of the entire picture.[2] The approach of the UN Committee on Torture emphasises the importance of a consistent pattern of gross, flagrant or mass violations of human rights in the assessment of risk.[3] There are also difficulties in drawing conclusions on credibility from the manner in which evidence is given, usually through an interpreter, by a person from a different society and cultural background.[4] Nonetheless decision-makers are generally encouraged to make definite findings on credibility before concluding on future risk – rather than approaching the matter by firstly determining whether a claim for refugee status could be made out on the basis that all that the applicant says is true before considering whether or not the evidence is credible.[5]

[1] Hathaway **12.22** fn 2 above, p 81. See *HK v Secretary of State for the Home Department* [2006] EWCA Civ 1037; *Y v Secretary of State for the Home Department* [2006] EWCA Civ 1223; *R (on the application of PN (Gambia)) v Secretary of State for the Home Department* [2008] EWHC 3219 (Admin); *Kasolo* (13190); *Mendes* (12183) and cases cited in Chapter **19** below. A number of influential Canadian and Australian cases have held that adverse findings on plausibility should be made only in the clearest of cases: see eg *Divsalar v Canada* [2002] FCT 653, [2002] FCJ 875; *Shenoda v Canada (Minister for Citizenship and Immigration)* (2003) FCT 207; *WAIJ v Minister for Immigration and Multicultural Affairs* [2004] FCAFC 74. But the Tribunal prefers a more robust approach: see *MM (plausibility) (DRC)* [2005] UKIAT 00019 'IAT reported'.

[2] *Horvath v Secretary of State for the Home Department* [1999] INLR 7, [1999] Imm AR 121, IAT; *R v Immigration Appeal Tribunal, ex p Ahmed (Sardar)* [1999] INLR 473. But this only applies where country conditions are relevant: see *R (on the application of Shockrollahy) v Immigration Appellate Authority* [2000] Imm AR 580, QBD; *R v Secretary of State for the Home Department, ex p Befekadu* [1999] Imm AR 467, QBD. The API on 'Considering asylum claims and assessing credibility', 30 July 2012, under the heading 'external credibility', states that where there is objective country information to support the applicant's account of a past or present event, and the applicant's account is internally consistent, the material claimed fact may be accepted by the decision-maker.

[3] *Mutombo v Switzerland* (Communication No 13/93) unreported, UNCAT (cited in *Alan v Switzerland* [1997] INLR 29).

[4] The observations of Webster J in *R v Secretary of State for the Home Department, ex p Patel* [1986] Imm AR 208, QBD are a salutary reminder of the dangers of adverse findings against a person from a different cultural background speaking through an interpreter. See the materials cited above at **12.179** fn 1.

[5] See the approach of the CA in *He (Jin Tao) v Secretary of State for the Home Department* [2002] EWCA Civ 1150, [2002] Imm AR 590 and in *Mishto v Secretary of State for the Home Department* [2003] EWCA Civ 1978: contrast *Guine* (13868).

12.181 Before 1993, in the absence of a right of appeal a judicial approach had evolved of ensuring that conclusions founded on credibility were not made without an opportunity for the asylum seeker to comment on specific issues.[1] The introduction of in-country rights of appeal removed direct scrutiny of adverse findings in decision letters by the High Court. Instead, the appellant is required to deal with adverse findings by evidence on the appeal. The test laid down in *Musisi* of 'anxious scrutiny'[2] is now applied by the Administrative Court not so much to the Secretary of State's original decision as to the appellate process (except in cases where there is no in-country right of appeal).[3] There is a tension between the appellate function[4] and the prospective nature of the question at issue in asylum claims, which makes the appeal hearing part of the determination process.[5] This has surfaced in appeal hearings where credibility is challenged for the first time; if the facts have not been put in issue by the Home Office, the prospective nature of the question should not necessitate a review of those facts.[6] An opportunity to deal with matters of credibility must be given during the appeal hearing, and if fresh issues are to be raised, the appellant will need sufficient time to deal with them, which may require an adjournment.[7]

[1] For the principles of fairness in cases where there was no right of appeal see *R v Secretary of State for the Home Department, ex p Thirukumar* [1989] Imm AR 402, CA; *Gaima v Secretary of State for the Home Department* [1989] Imm AR 205; *R v Secretary of State for the Home Department, ex p Akdogan* [1995] Imm AR 176, per Brooke J.

[2] [1987] AC 514 at 531.

[3] *R v Immigration Appeal Tribunal, ex p Ali (Omar)* [1995] Imm AR 45, QBD. Where there is no suspensive right of appeal, the Administrative Court will be concerned with the Secretary of State's decision that the claim is clearly unfounded, and in that context, must treat the claimant's account as credible, regardless of adverse credibility findings by the Secretary of State, unless no reasonable decision-maker could believe it: *R (on the application of L) v Secretary of State for the Home Department* [2003] EWCA Civ 25, [2003] Imm AR 330, [2003] INLR 224.

[4] The Tribunal is required to decide whether the decision under appeal was in accordance with the law or the rules: NIAA 2002, s 86(3)(a). The 1999 Act contained explicit jurisdiction to review the 'facts on which the decision or action is based': Immigration and Asylum Act 1999, Sch 4, para 21.

[5] *Ravichandran (Senathirajah) v Secretary of State for the Home Department* [1996] Imm AR 97 at 112–113. This applies equally on appeals on human rights grounds: *R (on the application of Razgar) v Secretary of State for the Home Department* [2004] UKHL 27, [2004] 3 WLR 58 at para 20. For this purpose, NIAA 2002, s 85(4) enables the Tribunal to consider any relevant evidence, including evidence about post-decision facts.

[6] *Ad hoc* challenges to credibility also make a nonsense of the power to give pre-hearing directions to identify and limit the issues in the appeal, in r 45 of the Asylum and Immigration Tribunal (Procedure) Rules 2005, SI 2005/230. However, the Tribunal has held that the Secretary of State's representative at a hearing is entitled to cross-examine on issues not specifically raised in the refusal letter: see eg. *D (Iran)* [2003] UKIAT 00087: 'Unless there is a specific concession, the refusal letter does not fetter or limit the scope of the case to be pursued by the Secretary of State'. Where however the facts are agreed, or the Secretary of State makes a concession that an appellant is telling the truth about specific matters or generally, the Tribunal should not go behind it: *R (on the application of Ganidagli) v Immigration Appeal Tribunal*, [2001] EWHC 70 Admin; *Carcabuk and Bla* (00TH01426) (18 May 2000, unreported), IAT. In *Davoodipanah v Secretary of State for the Home Department* [2004] EWCA Civ 106, [2004] INLR 341, [2004] All ER (D) 285 (Jan), the Court of Appeal held that a concession made by either party may be formally withdrawn on appeal if the appeal court considers that there is good reason to take that course, but otherwise, the appeal court should not revisit issues relevant to a concession clearly made to a first instance immigration judge who had relied on it. See also *NR (Jamaica) v Secretary of State for the Home Department* [2009] EWCA Civ 856, [2010] INLR 169, [2009] All ER (D) 43 (Aug); and *CD (Jamaica) v Secretary of State for the Home Department* [2010] EWCA Civ 768, [2010] All ER (D) 34 (Feb).

7 The Privy Council affirmed the principle that new points originating from the court itself should not take the parties by surprise in *Hoecheong Products Co Ltd v Cargill Hong Kong Ltd* [1995] 1 WLR 404.

12.182 Section 8 of the AI(TC)A 2004 lists various behaviours which must be taken into account as potentially[1] damaging the claimant's credibility. These include:

(i) behaviour which the deciding authority[2] thinks is designed or likely[3] to conceal information or to mislead, or to obstruct or delay the handling or resolution of the claim or the taking of a decision in relation to the claimant;[4]

(ii) failure to take advantage of a reasonable opportunity to make an asylum or human rights claim[5] while in a safe country;[6]

(iii) failure to make an asylum or human rights claim before notification of an immigration decision (unless the claim relies wholly on matters arising after the notification);[7]

(iv) failure to make an asylum or human rights claim before arrest under an immigration provision (unless there was no reasonable opportunity to do so or the claim relies wholly on matters arising since the arrest).[8]

Failure without reasonable explanation to produce a passport on request to an immigration officer or to the Secretary of State, the production of a document which is not a valid passport as if it were, the destruction, alteration or disposal, without reasonable explanation, of a passport, ticket or other document connected with travel, and failure without reasonable explanation to answer a question asked by a deciding authority, are to be treated as designed or likely to conceal information or to mislead.[9]

1 *JT (Cameroon) v Secretary of State for the Home Department* [2008] EWCA Civ 878, [2008] All ER (D) 348 (Jul). See also *AJ (Pakistan) v Secretary of State for the Home Secretary* [2011] CSIH 49, 2012 SLT 162, fn 6 below.

2 Ie, an immigration officer, the Secretary of State, the Tribunal or the SIAC: s 8(7). The section came into force on 1 January 2005: SI 2004/3398. A determination which fails to indicate that the Tribunal has had regard to the statutory matters could be vulnerable to setting aside for error of law, although the weight to be attached to them is clearly for the Tribunal to assess: see *SM (Section 8: Judge's process) Iran* [2005] UKAIT 00116; *JT (Cameroon) v Secretary of State for the Home Department (fn 1 above)*.

3 This formulation is on its face objectionable, since behaviour not designed to deceive, mislead or obstruct, but merely having that effect, should not affect the credibility of the actor. We suggest that the section must be read subject to exceptions on reasonable grounds, in order to be compatible with basic requirements of fairness. See fn 1 above.

4 AI(TC)A 2004, s 8(2).

5 As defined by the NIAA 2002, s 113(1): AI(TC)A 2004, s 8(7).

6 Ie, in a country of transit: AI(TC)A 2004, s 8(4). In *Ozmico* [2002] UKIAT 00484, the Tribunal held that failure to claim in any safe country passed through in the back of a lorry was not a realistic credibility point. In *AJ (Pakistan) v Secretary of State for the Home Department* 2011 CSIH 49, (2012) SLT 162, the Court of Session held that the immigration judge had materially erred by failing to give any explanation or justification for regarding the applicant's failure to claim asylum in Greece as a 'serious credibility issue' in the overall context of the case and in isolating this factor as having a special status on its own rather than treating it as one of the relevant factors in determining credibility.

7 AI(TC)A 2004, s 8(5). An 'immigration decision' means refusal or grant of leave to enter or remain in the UK, a decision to remove the claimant under the Immigration and Asylum Act 1999 s 10 (persons unlawfully in the UK) or the Immigration Act 1971, Sch 2, paras 8–12 (persons refused leave to enter, illegal entrants, and their family members), a decision to make a deportation order or an extradition decision: s 8(7). 'Notification' is defined in the Immigration (Claimant's Credibility) Regulations 2004, SI 2004/3263 to include decisions

given orally or by email, by hand or by fax, and provides that notification which would not be valid under the Notices Regulations is valid for the purposes of s 8(5). The Regulations also contain presumptions about receipt of notice which is posted or sent to a representative. It is hard to relate these provisions rationally to claimants' credibility.

[8] AI(TC)A 2004, s 8(6). An 'immigration provision' means the Immigration Act 1971, ss 28A–28CA (immigration offences), Sch 2, para 17 (control of entry), s 14 of the 2004 Act (immigration officers' powers of arrest for offences of fraud etc) and the Extradition Act 1989: AI(TC)A 2004, s 8(7).

[9] AI(TC)A 2004, s 8(3). A passport is valid if it relates to the person producing it, has not been altered except by or with the permission of the issuing authority, and was not obtained by deception: AI(TC)A 2004, s 8(8). In the asylum context, it can be extremely dangerous to treat the production of a passport obtained by deception as damaging the credibility of the person producing it, which reinforces the suggestion that the provision must be read as subject to a general exonerating clause on reasonable grounds.

12.183 The factors set out in section 8 are additional to those set out in the Immigration Rules which may damage an asylum applicant's credibility. These include failure, without reasonable explanation, to make a prompt and full disclosure of material facts, either orally or in writing, or otherwise to assist the Secretary of State in establishing the facts of the case, by, for example, failing to report to a designated place to be fingerprinted, failing to complete an asylum questionnaire or failing to comply with a requirement to report to an immigration officer for examination.[1] The statutory provision is extraordinarily draconian – coupled with the Credibility Regulations, which are almost surreal[2] – and is in mandatory terms. Only in cases of non-production, destruction or disposal of a passport or a travel document is there the possibility of the decision maker having regard to a reasonable explanation.[3] We suggest that a literal reading of section 8 would result in the deciding authority failing to have regard to relevant circumstances, and thus reaching unlawful decisions. For example, failure to claim asylum in a safe country of transit may be for a very good reason, such as the presence in the UK of all the close relatives of a vulnerable and traumatised claimant. The statutory requirement in all cases to take such failure into account as damaging credibility makes no allowance for such good reasons and denies the element of choice held by the Divisional Court in *Adimi*[4] to be properly open to refugees as to where they may claim asylum.

[1] HC 395, para 339N as inserted from 9 October 2006 by Cm 6918.
[2] Immigration (Claimant's Credibility) Regulations 2004, SI 2004/3263.
[3] In *R v Secretary of State for the Home Department, ex p Yasine (or Yassine)* [1990] Imm AR 354, QBD, and *R v Uxbridge Magistrates' Court, ex p Adimi* [1999] INLR 490, the Divisional Court acknowledged that as a result of the carriers' liability legislation, asylum seekers frequently need the assistance of an agent to obtain false papers to smuggle them out of the country (see **12.9** and **12.11** above, and **15.92** ff below), and are obliged to destroy the documents to prevent the escape route being closed down.
[4] *R v Uxbridge Magistrates' Court, ex p Adimi* above.

12.184 Similarly, there are many valid reasons why people do not make their asylum claim immediately on arrival: lack of knowledge of the procedures, arrival in a confused and frightened state, language differences or fear of officialdom may all be insuperable barriers to making any kind of approach to the authorities at the port of entry.[1] Delay in making an application does not necessarily reflect the absence of a fear: asylum seekers who have permission to remain in some other capacity may well not wish to make an asylum claim, which connotes a definitive break with the country where they may have their family and many other loved associations, and with all the uncertainties as to eventual outcome, unless it is apparent that they have no other claim to remain and face removal. Further, a refugee may be acting reasonably when deferring making a claim until obtaining advice from relatives, friends or advice organisations. The UNHCR Handbook notes that untrue statements by themselves are not a reason for refusal of refugee status and that it is the examiner's responsibility to evaluate such statements in the light of all the circumstances of the case.[2] It is often unfair to make adverse credibility findings on the basis of the use of lies or evasion as to the means of escape, false documents or the destruction of documents, or failure to claim promptly.[3] Such actions have nothing to do with the merits of the asylum claim, and should not be used to diminish credibility – at least, not indiscriminately or without a careful assessment in relation to the facts of individual cases and the applicant's explanation. In *JT (Cameroon)*, Pill LJ urged decision-makers to guard against distorting the fact-finding exercise by an undue concentration on minutiae which may arise under section 8 at the expense of, and as a distraction from, an overall assessment – rather it is a global assessment of credibility that is required.[4]

[1] See the UNHCR publication *Beyond Proof, Credibility Assessment in EU Asylum Systems*, May 2013; see 12.171, fn 1 above. See also the Report of Social Services Advisory Committee (Cm 3062, January 1996) para 38. See also UNHCR *Handbook* **12.13** above, para 198; *R v Uxbridge Magistrates' Court, ex p Adimi* [1999] INLR 490 at 497–498; UNHCR's *Guidelines on applicable Criteria and Standards relating to the Detention of Asylum Seekers* (Butterworths Immigration Law Service, 2C[261]); Atle Grahl-Madsen *The Status of Refugees in International Law* Vol II (1972) p 218.

[2] UNHCR *Handbook* above, para 199; and see also UNHCR's *Beyond Proof, Credibility Assessment in EU Asylum* Systems, above.

[3] See *R v Naillie* [1993] AC 674; *R v Secretary of State for the Home Department, ex p Sivakumaran* [1990] Imm AR 80, QBD; *Nzamba-Liloneo v Secretary of State for the Home Department* [1993] Imm AR 225, QBD.

[4] *JT (Cameroon) v Secretary of State for the Home Department* [2008] EWCA Civ 878, [2008] All ER (D) 348 (Jul) at para 19. See also *AJ (Pakistan) v Secretary of State for the Home Department* [2011] CSIH 49, (2012) SLT 162: see **12.182**, fn 6 above

Fresh claims for asylum

12.185 A person who has previously been refused asylum in the UK or has withdrawn his or her claim for asylum[1] and to whom the appeal provisions of the Immigration Act 2014 do not apply will not normally have an appeal against refusal of a second application. Acquisition of such an appeal depends upon the making of an immigration decision to which the NIAA 2002, s 92 applies. There are a number of situations in which that may happen:

(i)   an immigration decision of a kind that attracts an in-country appeal is made against the individual, for example, a refusal to vary leave or a variation of leave having the consequence that the person has no leave or a decision to make a deportation order;

(ii)   under the Immigration Rules, the second application may be accepted as a fresh claim for asylum, as opposed to further representations on the old claim, in order to generate a further right of appeal.[2] Where an asylum applicant has previously been refused asylum in the UK, the Secretary of State will decide whether further representations should result in a grant of asylum or leave in some other capacity and if not, whether they should be treated as a fresh claim for asylum. A person who has made further representations will not be removed from the UK before the Secretary of State has considered whether to accept a fresh claim for asylum.[3] Representations will be treated as a fresh claim if they are significantly different from the material that has previously been considered. The rule indicates that submissions will only be significantly different if the content has not already been considered, and taken together with the previously considered material, it creates a realistic prospect of success, notwithstanding its rejection.[4] A reasons for refusal letter will always be given if asylum is not granted and written reasons for not accepting a fresh claim must be given;[5] if the Secretary of State accepts that a fresh claim has been made, a new, appealable immigration decision will be made.[6] It is for the Secretary of State to decide if a fresh claim has been made, subject to judicial review.[7] On an application for judicial review of a refusal by the Secretary of State to accept a fresh claim, the court will first consider whether the Secretary of State has asked the correct question which is not whether the Secretary of State thinks that the claim should succeed but whether there is a realistic prospect that a Tribunal, giving anxious scrutiny to the claim, might find in the applicant's favour.[8] In addressing that question, the court must be satisfied that the Secretary of State has satisfied the requirement of anxious scrutiny in evaluating the facts and drawing legal conclusions from them.[9] The Court of Appeal had held that the court was entitled to substitute its own view of whether a putative fresh claim had a 'realistic prospect of success' before a tribunal and was not limited to considering the rationality of the Secretary of State's decision.[10] However, it did so *per incuriam*; rather the approach to be taken by the court is that described in *WM (Democratic Republic of Congo) v Secretary of State for the Home Department*.[11] Some authorities suggest that where evidence of a relevant and substantial change in circumstances, or new evidence is advanced which could not reasonably have been advanced earlier, the Secretary of State is obliged to entertain the new claim, whatever the reasons for rejecting the previous one, unless the new evidence is not credible or is not capable of producing a different outcome.[12] Cases under the old fresh claims provisions continue to be relevant. They indicate that the new evidence would need to have an important influence on the result of the case, although it need not be decisive, and it must be apparently credible, although it need not be incontrovertible.[13] The fact that the person making the fresh claim has previously been disbelieved by an immigration judge does not by itself mean that everything put forward thereafter must equally be disbelieved.[14] The requirement that the claim be 'sufficiently different' from the old one does not require a change in the factual basis of the application; convincing fresh evidence of the same persecution previously alleged is capable of giving rise to a fresh claim,[15] since it will amount to 'content which has not already been considered'. The rule, unlike its predecessor, does not specify that the new material should have been previously unavailable.[16] The same criteria have been applied to second human rights claims[17] and is applied to claims for humanitarian protection made after refusal of asylum.[18] The Court of Appeal has said that 'by restricting the remedial route of an appellant both within the AIT and to the Court of Appeal to legal error, Parliament has increased the burden on the Secretary of State to give the most careful consideration to fresh claims'.[19]

(iii) If the decision on the asylum application was taken before 2 October 2000 (when the statutory provisions enabling human rights to be raised in an appeal came into force) the person would not have been able to rely on human rights grounds in any appeal that he or she may have had.[20] The Secretary of State undertook, in such cases, not to apply para 353 of the Immigration Rules and to accept a human rights claim so as to enable the person to bring an appeal on human rights grounds.[21]

(iv) The Secretary of State has a policy as to when fairness requires a subsequent application to trigger further appeal rights even where the application is not regarded as a fresh one. It includes previous loss of appeal rights by error or a serious miscarriage in procedure.[22] The policy may be prayed in aid where there is no change in the nature of the application or the evidence adduced, but where it would be unjust not to give the applicant an opportunity to appeal. A request for the Secretary of State to issue a fresh refusal to give rise to a fresh appeal on *Kazmi* grounds should be made promptly after the claimed miscarriage of procedure.[23] The case law on s 21 of the Immigration Act 1971, now repealed, is also relevant. This allowed the Secretary of State to refer a dismissed appeal back to the appellate authority for an advisory opinion in certain circumstances.[24] If the statutory appeal route had failed because of an adverse decision following a full hearing or because the applicant had taken a calculated risk in not attending, nothing short of potentially decisive evidence, reasonably capable of acceptance, would be required to prompt further consideration of the claim. Where, however, it had or may have failed because of lack of notice for which the applicant bore no personal or imputed blame, that was a relevant, though not a decisive, consideration for the Secretary of State in deciding whether to exercise the power.[25]

(v) where an unaccompanied asylum-seeking child who was refused asylum but granted discretionary leave pursuant to the policy relating to such children, makes an application for further leave to remain on reaching 18, the application will be treated as an asylum and human rights claim without having to satisfy the 'fresh claim' rule;[26]

(vi) a person refused asylum but granted leave in some other capacity will be able to appeal, if at all, on asylum grounds only (under the NIAA 2002, s 83 if the grant was for more than a year). If such a person then makes human rights submissions, the fresh claim rule should not be applied to the human rights submissions:[27]

(vii) Even if the Secretary of State does not accept further representations as amounting to a fresh claim, there are circumstances where she is nevertheless required to make a further immigration decision against which an appeal may be brought. For example, if an asylum seeker leaves the UK after having been refused asylum and then returns to the UK and makes a further asylum claim, para 353 of the Rules cannot be applied to determine whether to accept a fresh claim.[28] This is because, even if such a claim is not accepted, he or she would not be removeable from the UK until after being refused leave to enter or until a decision was made to give directions for the person's removal as an illegal entrant, each of which is an appealable decision.[29] Another example is that a person against whom a deportation order has been made may apply for the deportation order to be revoked (even before deportation has occurred); a refusal to revoke a deportation order is an appealable decision.[30] In such a circumstance, the Supreme Court has held that an asylum or human rights claim need not be accepted by the Secretary of State as being a fresh claim for the appeal against the new immigration decision to be in-country.[31] However, where there is no need for the Secretary of State to make a new immigration decision in order to effect removal (eg where a person who has previously been refused leave to enter remains in the UK and makes further representations) a fresh right of appeal will only arise where the further representations are accepted as a fresh claim.[32]

(viii) The Secretary of State may accept a fresh claim for asylum, in the context of a need to make a fresh immigration decision, but issue a certificate under Nationality, Immigration and Asylum Act 2002, ss 94 and/or 96 on the grounds that the claim is clearly unfounded and/or relates to a matter that could have been raised in a previous appeal.[33] However, where the Secretary of State accepts that a fresh claim for asylum has been made in the context of the same immigration decision, it would not be appropriate to then certify the claim under either provision.[34]

(ix) The Immigration Act 2014 provides for a right of appeal against refusal of a protection claim.[35] It does not restrict an individual to making only one protection claim, nor does it relieve the Secretary of State from having to make an appealable decision in response to a protection claim made by an individual previously refused asylum or humanitarian protection. The fresh claim rule is relevant for the purpose of deciding whether a new, appealable 'immigration decision' has to be made, but where the refusal of a protection claim is appealable by itself without the need for a further 'immigration decision' the question whether the protection claim is a 'fresh claim' is not relevant.

[1] HC 395, para 353 as amended so as to apply 'when a human rights or asylum claim has been refused or withdrawn or treated as withdrawn under paragraph 333C of these Rules'.
[2] Unless and until the Secretary of State accepts the application as a fresh claim, no decision falls within the section and no right of appeal arises: *R v Immigration Appellate Authority, ex p Secretary of State for the Home Department* [1998] Imm AR 52. Nor is NASS support available until it has been accepted as a fresh claim: see Chapter 14. IAN 2006, s 12, when it comes into force will introduce a new definition of 'asylum claim' for the purpose of the appeals provisions. It makes provision for subsequent asylum claims (and human rights claims) to be disregarded in accordance with the Immigration Rules, thereby giving statutory expression to the long established practice. See also *ZT (Kosovo) v Secretary of State for the Home Department* [2009] UKHL 6, [2009] 1 WLR 348: the majority held that where a previous claim had been refused and certified as clearly unfounded and then further submissions are received, in the context of the same immigration decision, the UKBA must apply the fresh claim procedure. Lord Hope dissented at paras 26–48. He considered that where further submissions are received in the context of a certified claim, HC 395, para 353A sufficed to protect the applicant from removal and the issue for the UKBA was to decide whether, in light of the further submissions, the claim remained clearly unfounded; if the view was then taken that the claim should still be refused but that it was not any longer considered clearly unfounded, the certificate could be revoked and a right of appeal would then arise.
[3] HC 395, para 353A.

4 HC 395, para 353, inserted by HC 1112 on 18 October 2004. The rule replaces para 346, deleted by HC 1112. The case of *R v Secretary of State for the Home Department, ex p Onibiyo* [1996] Imm AR 370, CA established that a second asylum claim could be made following the rejection of an earlier one, according to the test of 'a reasonable prospect that a favourable view could be taken of the new claim'. See also *R (on the application of BA (Nigeria)) v Secretary of State for the Home Department* [2009] UKSC 7, [2009] 3 WLR 1253.

5 See generally the API on 'Further submissions', May 2014.

6 See fn 5 above.

7 *R v Secretary of State for the Home Department, ex p Ravichandran (No 3)* [1997] Imm AR 74; *Cakabay v Secretary of State for the Home Department (No 2)* [1999] Imm AR 176, [1998] INLR 623, CA; *R v Secretary of State for the Home Department, ex p Bell* [2000] Imm AR 396; *WM (Democratic Republic of Congo) v Secretary of State for the Home Department* [2006] EWCA Civ 1495. In all of these earlier cases it was clear that the test was one of Wednesbury reasonableness. More recently, in *R (on the application of YH) v Secretary of State for the Home Department* [2010] EWCA Civ 116, Canrwath LJ answered the question of whether, on judicial review of the Secretary of State's decision, should the court apply its own judgment to that question, or is it limited to Wednesbury review, by holding that on the threshold question the court is entitled to exercise its own judgment, but that it remains a process of judicial review, not a de novo hearing, and the issue must be judged on the material available to the Secretary of State. See also *ZT (Kosovo) v Secretary of State for the Home Department* [2009] UKHL 6, [2009] 1 WLR 348; *QY (China) v Secretary of State for the Home Department* [2009] EWCA Civ 680, (2009) Times, 20 October; and *KH (Afghanistan) v Secretary of State for the Home Department* [2009] EWCA Civ 1354. However in *MN (Tanzania) v Secretary of State for the Home Department* [2011] EWCA Civ 193, [2011] 2 All ER 772, [2011] 1 WLR 3200, the CA made clear that the test to be applied by a judge on an application for judicial review of a refusal by the Secretary of State for the Home Department to treat further representations by an asylum seeker as a fresh claim pursuant to rule 353 was indeed the *Wednesbury* test subject to anxious scrutiny.

8 *WM (Democratic Republic of Congo) v Secretary of State for the Home Department* [2006] EWCA Civ 1495, (2006) Times, 1 December. In *AK (Afghanistan) v Secretary of State for the Home Department* [2007] EWCA Civ 535 the Secretary of State made the error of assessing the credibility and potential impact of new evidence from his own point of view only without addressing the question how an immigration judge might assess the evidence. See *R (on the application of TR (Sri Lanka)) v Secretary of State for the Home Department* [2008] EWCA Civ 1549: 'there is in reality not a great deal of room for deference in the judicial exercise. The primary question for the Court is whether, whatever the Secretary of State thinks of it, there is a fresh claim capable of succeeding before an Immigration Judge'. See fn 7 above. In *R (on the application of AK (Sri Lanka)) v Secretary of State for the Home Department* [2009] EWCA Civ 447, [2010] 1 WLR 855, Laws LJ considered that 'further submissions', in para 353 meant merely representations, short or long, reasoned or unreasoned, advanced on asylum or human rights grounds, and that the test for a 'realistic prospect of success' for a fresh claim under rule 353 was whether there was more than a fanciful prospect of success.

9 *WM (Democratic Republic of Congo) v Secretary of State for the Home Department* [2006] EWCA Civ 1495, (2006) Times, 1 December.

10 *KH (Afghanistan) v Secretary of State for the Home Department* [2009] EWCA Civ 1354, (2010) Times, 19 January: see fn 7 above.

11 [2006] EWCA Civ 1495, (2006) Times, 1 December. So held the court in *MN (Tanzania) v Secretary of State for the Home Department* [2011] EWCA Civ 193, [2011] 2 All ER 772, [2011] 1 WLR 3200 because it had not had regard to *R (on the application of TK) v Secretary of State for the Home Department* [2009] EWCA Civ 1550, [2011] All ER (D) 71 (Mar). See fn 7 above.

12 *R v Secretary of State for the Home Department, ex p Habibi* [1997] Imm AR 391, QBD.

13 *R v Secretary of State for the Home Department, ex p Boybeyi* [1997] Imm AR 491, [1997] INLR 130, CA. API on 'Further submissions', May 2014, states that 'Material must never be discounted entirely on the basis it could or should have disclosed earlier. However, caseworkers should challenge late disclosure especially if there is no reason why it could not have been raised sooner. This is of particular relevance to submissions raised at the point of removal.'

14 *R (on the application of Naseer) v Secretary of State for the Home Department* [2006] EWHC 1671 (Admin), [2006] All ER (D) 227 (Jun) *(Collins J)*. This is also recognised in the API on 'Further submissions', May 2014, Asylum Process Guidance on 'Further submissions' under the sub-heading 'The second test – does the material create a realistic prospect of success?'.

15 *R v Secretary of State for the Home Department, ex p Ravichandran (No 2)* [1996] Imm AR 418; *Ward v Secretary of State for the Home Department* [1997] Imm AR 236; *R (on the application of Senkoy) v Secretary of State for the Home Department* [2001] EWCA Civ 328; *MA (Fresh evidence) Sri Lanka* [2004] UKIAT 00161 (starred).

16 See fn 13 above. The courts might imply such a condition, although it would need to be applied carefully, so as not to defeat good claims. Failure to adduce evidence earlier may be relevant in relation to certification of claims under s 96, for which see below. The failure of advisers to obtain evidence earlier does not make that evidence 'previously unavailable'; *Kabala (Mehmet) v Secretary of State for the Home Department* [1997] Imm AR 517, CA, but evidence was not 'available' if the giver of it was physically or psychologically unable to give it: *R v Secretary of State for the Home Department, ex p Ejon (Molly)* [1998] INLR 195 (traumatised rape victim); cf *R v Secretary of State for the Home Department, ex p Khan (Saleem)* (CO 647/1999) (17 May 1999, unreported), QBD (evidence of the applicant's homosexuality was 'previously available' despite the taboo in Muslim society preventing disclosure to family members who were helping him on his first claim); see also *R (on the application of Maci) v Secretary of State for the Home Department* [2003] EWHC 1123 (Admin).

17 Jackson J in *R (on the application of Ratnam) (Savasoba) v Secretary of State* [2003] EWHC 398 (Admin) held that although the relevant rule (then HC 395, para 346) applied only to asylum applications, the same principles should be applied by analogy to a fresh claim based on human rights issues. See also *Djebbar v Secretary of State for the Home Department* [2004] EWCA Civ 804, [2004] 33 LS Gaz R 36; and *AK (Sri Lanka) v Secretary of State for the Home Department* [2009] EWCA Civ 447, [2010] 1 WLR 855 per Laws LJ at para 29: 'There is no suggestion that any less "anxious scrutiny" is required in the case of a human rights claim than in one seeking asylum'.

18 API on 'Humanitarian Protection', May 2013, states that: 'Where further submissions are lodged, decision-makers should give consideration to the reasons given for requesting such leave, in accordance with the Asylum Instruction on Further Submissions.'

19 *Kaydanyuk v Secretary of State for the Home Department* [2006] EWCA Civ 368, [2006] All ER (D) 26 (Apr).

20 *Pardeepan v Secretary of State for the Home Department* [2000] INLR 447

21 API on 'Further submissions', May 2014, under the heading 'when paragraph 353 should not be applied'. Although this would not apply if the human rights issue had in fact been considered in the earlier appeal or if there were findings of 'basic fact' in the asylum appeal against the person and on which the human rights claim depended.

22 Home Office letter, 22 July 1994, cited in *R v Secretary of State for the Home Department, ex p Kazmi* [1995] Imm AR 73 and see API on 'Further submissions', May 2014, under the heading 'When paragraph 353 should not be applied'.

23 *R v Secretary of State for the Home Department, ex p Kone* [1998] Imm AR 291.

24 See *R v Secretary of State for the Home Department, ex p Bello* [1995] Imm AR 537, QBD; *Khaldoun v Secretary of State for the Home Department* [1996] Imm AR 200, CA.

25 *R v Secretary of State for the Home Department, ex p Yousaf, Jamil* [2000] INLR 432, CA.

26 API on 'Active review of unaccompanied asylum seeking children (UASC) discretionary leave (DL)', section 6, "considering an application for further leave' provides that 'case owners should not apply paragraph 353 of the Immigration Rules to any part of the application for an extension of leave.'

27 API on 'Further submissions', May 2014, under the heading 'When paragraph 353 should not be applied'. Inconsistently with the principle animating that part of the policy (that an individual should have at least one opportunity to appeal), the guidance goes on to say that para 353 of the Rules should be applied to further submissions made by a person refused asylum but granted leave to remain for a year or less where the extent that the Secretary of State is satisfied that an appeal would not have a realistic prospect of success.

28 API on 'Further submissions', May 2014, under the heading 'When paragraph 353 should not be applied'.

29 Under the Nationality, Immigration and Asylum Act 2002, s 82(2)(a) in the case of refusal of leave to enter and s 82(2)(h) in respect of a decision to give removal directions in respect of an illegal entrant.

30 Nationality, Immigration and Asylum Act 2002, s 82(2)(k).

31 *BA (Nigeria) and Anor v Secretary of State for the Home Department* [2009] UKSC 7, [2009] 3 WLR 1253. Note, however, that the Secretary of State can certify the subsequent claim on

refusal as clearly unfounded thereby preventing a further suspensive right of appeal: see, eg *R (on the application of YH) v Secretary of State for the Home Department* [2010] EWCA Civ 116. See **12.175** ff above.

32 *R (on the application of ZA (Nigeria)) v Secretary of State for the Home Department* [2010] EWHC 718 (Admin), [2010] All ER (D) 297 (Mar), Divisional Court; affd [2010] EWCA Civ 926; *R (on the application of WJ) v Secretary of State for the Home Department* [2010] EWHC 776 (Admin), [2010] All ER (D) 97 (Apr).

33 See fn 33 above.

34 See *R (on the application of J) v Secretary of State for the Home Department* [2009] EWHC 705 (Admin) and see API on 'Further submissions', May 2014, under the heading, 'discretion in deciding whether to certify under section 96'.

35 Immigration Act 2014, s 15, substituting a new s 82 in to the NIAA 2002.

12.186 Where the Secretary of State decides that no fresh asylum or human rights claim has been made, she will then decide whether there are exceptional circumstances which mean that removal of the applicant from the United Kingdom is no longer appropriate. In so deciding she will have regard to the applicant's character, conduct and associations including any criminal record and the nature of any offence of which the applicant concerned has been convicted; compliance with any conditions attached to any previous grant of leave to enter or remain and compliance with any conditions of temporary admission or immigration bail where applicable; and length of time spent in the United Kingdom spent for reasons beyond the applicant's control after the human rights or asylum claim has been submitted or refused.[1] In essence, the purpose of the rule is to identify specific points which will weigh in the balance *against* the exercise of the discretion not to remove an applicant, or to qualify the effect of factors that might otherwise weigh in its favour.[2]

1 HC 395, para 353B, as inserted by HC 1733 with effect from 13 February 2012 when para 395C was deleted. See also the factors militating against removal in '353B consideration cases' in Chapter 53 of the Enforcement Guidance Instructions. See also the case law on 'legacy cases' at **12.125**, fn 7 above.

2 See *Qongwane v Secretary of State for the Home Department* [2014] EWCA Civ 957 per Underhill LJ at [40]. The CA held that para 353B does not create any duty on the Secretary of State and accordingly an applicant could not appeal to the Tribunal, under the NIAA 2002, s 84(1)(f) on the ground that discretion should have been exercised differently under the rule. See also *Khanum (Paragraph 353B)* [2013] UKUT 311 (IAC).

12.187 As noted above, even if a further asylum claim is made, a further appeal may be prevented by the issue of a certificate from the Secretary of State or an immigration officer under section 96 of the NIAA 2002, as amended.[1] The criteria for certification under section 96(1) are that there was a previous opportunity to raise the matter now relied on in an appeal (whether or not the right of appeal was exercised), and that there is no satisfactory reason for the failure to raise it then. The section 96(2) criteria for certification are that the application relies on a ground which should have been put forward in response to a one-stop warning under section 120 of the 2002 Act.[2] We have considered these provisions at **7.109** above. The API indicates that the Secretary of State first decides whether representations made after the dismissal of an appeal amount to a fresh claim, and then whether the claim should be certified under section 96.[3] But where the Secretary of State has accepted that representations amount to a fresh claim with a realistic prospect of success on appeal, certification under section 96 which would prevent such an appeal would in all probability be challengeable by way of judicial review.[4] However, a certificate under section 96 is a more likely response where an applicant seeks a further appeal on the ground of miscarriage of procedure.[5] If it is clear that the failure was not the fault of the claimant, who has not had a proper opportunity to have a meritorious claim reviewed by the Tribunal, the certificate is unlikely to be upheld.[6]

[1]   By AI(TC)A 2004, s 30.
[2]   The statute refers to 'a matter' which could have been raised earlier. In *R (on the application of Khan) v Secretary of State for the Home Department* [2014] EWCA Civ 88, [2014] 2 All ER 973 the CA held that 'matter' was a broad word meaning little more than 'thing' and could include evidence as well as issues; and that s 96(1) was properly directed to the advancing of new material as a whole, either in grounds of appeal or evidence in support.
[3]   API on 'Further submissions', May 2014, Section 7.
[4]   See **12.185** fn 35 above. But see *R (on the application of Borak) v Secretary of State for the Home Department* [2004] EWHC 1861 (Admin), upheld on very narrow grounds by the Court of Appeal at [2005] EWCA Civ 110, [2005] All ER (D) 163 (Jan) where judicial review on just such a basis was rejected because of the claimant's failure to advert in his previous appeal to information which he did not then have.
[5]   See one-stop appeals at Chapters **19** and **20** below.
[6]   By analogy with cases where the court has re-opened appeals for procedural irregularity not caused either by the appellate authority or by the appellant: see eg *R (on the application of Tataw) v Immigration Appeal Tribunal* [2003] EWCA Civ 925, [2003] INLR 585; *R (on the application of Hasa) v Immigration Appeal Tribunal* [2003] EWHC 396 (Admin), [2003] All ER (D) 232 (Feb).

Refugee leave

12.188 An application for refugee status in the UK is pursued in the context of the statutory provisions for the grant or variation of leave to enter and remain in accordance with the practice laid down in the Immigration Rules.[1] The Immigration Rules provide for the grant of asylum to a person in the UK who is a refugee and in respect of whom there are no reasonable grounds for regarding him or her as a danger to the security of the UK, who is not as a consequence of having been convicted of a particularly serious crime a danger to the community of the UK and who, if refused asylum would be required to go to a country in which his or her life or freedom would be threatened for a Refugee Convention reason.[2] The Rules further provide that where asylum is granted, a person who does not already have leave to enter will be given such leave[3] and for the variation of leave which a person already has or the grant of leave to remain to a person who entered without leave.[4] However, whilst a person who is exempt from immigration control[5] can apply for asylum and be recognised as a refugee, they cannot be granted (or refused) leave to enter or remain for as long as they remain exempt.[6] In all cases, current policy states that the asylum claim should be considered first and asylum granted if the applicant qualifies; if he or she does not, consideration should then be given to humanitarian protection and finally to discretionary leave.[7] Those recognised as refugees on or after 30 August 2005 are normally granted five years' leave to enter or remain rather than indefinite leave as previously.[8] However, 'the specific situation of a vulnerable person with special needs' may result in a grant of a longer period of leave.[9] There is no statutory provision as to how quickly leave should be granted once refugee status is recognised (whether by the Secretary of State or by the Tribunal upon a claimant succeeding in an appeal) but it must be done within a reasonable period which would be 28 days absent complicating factors.[10] The Secretary of State is required to issue a UK Residence Permit, valid for five years and renewable thereafter, as soon as possible following a grant of asylum.[11] At the end of five years, the refugee will be eligible to apply for indefinite leave to remain, subject to any review of his or her status and to any policies then applicable.[12] If a person makes an 'in-time' application for indefinite leave to remain, the Secretary of State would not normally have to determine whether the person is still a refugee as long as a review should not have been triggered because of information about the person's conduct or a ministerial statement relating to a change of circumstances in the country of origin.[13] An 'out of time' application for indefinite leave to remain will lead to a review of whether a cessation clause is applicable.[14]

1   *Saad, Diriye and Osorio v Secretary of State for the Home Department* [2001] EWCA Civ 2008, referring to the Immigration Act 1971, s 3.
2   HC 395, para 334.
3   HC 395, para 330.
4   HC 395, para 335.
5   Under the Immigration Act 1971, s 8(2),(3) and (4) and the Immigration (Exemption from Control) Order 1972, SI 1972/1613.
6   According to the former API 'People who are exempt from immigration control' October 2006, para 3.
7   API on 'Handling claims'. The previous Asylum Process Guidance, 'Processing Hybrid Applications', that provided for consideration of concurrent claims for refugee status and for leave to enter or remain in some other category, is no longer available and it would seem that current policy is now to treat asylum claims in the above way.
8   The change of policy was foreshadowed in the White Paper 'Controlling our Borders: Making migration work for Britain', February 2005 and set out in a written Ministerial Statement by Tony McNulty on 19 July 2005. An IND Guidance Note 'Changes to Refugee Leave and Humanitarian Protection from 30 August 2005' was issued on 25 August 2005. It stated that regardless of when the decision to grant leave was taken, grants made after 30 August 2005 would be for five years, not indefinite save where the Home Office had previously undertaken to grant indefinite leave or there had been significant delay in actioning an appeal which was out of step with other appeals of a similar nature, for reasons attributable to the Home Office and resulted in leave being granted after 30 August 2005. In *R (Rechachi, Kalobi, Fodil and Yusuf) v Secretary of State for the Home Department* [2006] EWHC 3513 Admin)[2001] EWCA Civ 2008 Davies J held that this change of policy was lawful and that claimants who won appeals on asylum grounds before 30 August 2005 did not thereby have a legitimate expectation of being granted indefinite leave in accordance with the then applicable policy.
9   API 'Refugee Leave', October 2009, section 2.2. The aim is to give effect to art 20(3) of the Qualification Directive (Council Directive 2004/83/EC) which requires states to 'take into account the specific situation of vulnerable persons such as minors, unaccompanied minors, disabled people, elderly people, pregnant women, single parents with minor children and persons who have been subjected to torture, rape or other serious forms of psychological, physical or sexual violence'.
10   *R (on the application of Rechachi, Kalobi, Fadil and Yusuf) v Secretary of State for the Home Department* following *R v Secretary of State for the Home Department, ex p Arbab* [2002] EWHC 1249 Admin. See also *R v Secretary of State for the Home Department, ex p Mersin (Deniz)* [2000] INLR 511 and *R (on the application of Mambakasa) v Secretary of State for the Home Department* [2003] EWHC 319 (Admin). As to the necessity of granting refugee leave to an appellant who has succeeded on asylum grounds before the Tribunal, see *TB (Jamaica) v Secretary of State for the Home Department* [2008] EWCA Civ 977; and *R (Saribal) v Secretary of State for the Home Department* [2002] EWHC 1542 Admin.
11   HC 395, para 339Q.
12   API 'Refugee leave', October 2009, section 8.1 which refers to the 'Five Year Strategy' commitment to introduce settlement tests before ILR is granted with the possibility of English language and knowledge of British life tests.
13   API 'Refugee leave', section 7. See also API 'Settlement Protection', October 2013, which provides that applications should be made on the correct application form, SET (Protection Route), available on the Home Office website 'as this provides everything required to consider the application more quickly.'
14   API 'Refugee leave', section 7.1. See also API 'Settlement Protection', October 2013, which provides that where the delay, or period of overstay, is less than a month detailed enquiries

into the reasons for the delay are unlikely to be necessary. Longer periods of delay will require an explanation for the reasons for the delay and caseworkers should conduct a more in-depth case review to consider whether there is a continuing need for protection.

12.189 The UK's policy with regard to the withdrawal of refugee status is described in the Asylum Policy Instruction, 'Cancellation, cessation and revocation of refugee status'.[1] It is worth highlighting one point in the Instruction which says:

'Where a situation arises where a former refugee who has been naturalised is found to have obtained refugee status by deception and thus fall within the cancellation provisions or where they have engaged in conduct which would have brought them within the scope of the exclusion clauses, then UKBA may review that person's continuing entitlement to British Citizenship'.[2]

The grant of asylum may be reviewed during the initial period of five years (in consequence of information about the conduct of the individual or a change of circumstances in the country of origin) or when the person applies for indefinite leave to remain or on the expiry of the five year period.[3] Such a review may result in asylum being revoked or not renewed[4] if the Secretary of State is satisfied that the person's refugee status has ceased[5] or the person should have been[6] or is to be excluded from being a refugee[7] or the use of deception was decisive for the grant of asylum[8] or there are reasonable grounds for regarding the person as a danger to the security of the UK[9] or the person, having been convicted of a particularly serious crime constitutes a danger to the community of the UK.[10] Asylum will not normally be revoked on the 'voluntary cessation grounds' (reavailment of protection; reacquisition of nationality; acquisition of another nationality or re-establishment in the country of feared persecution) if it was granted over five years previously unless there are exceptional circumstances.[11] Revocation of refugee status on the ground of a change of circumstances in the country from which asylum was sought is normally done only when a Ministerial Statement has been issued announcing that significant and non-temporary changes have occurred in the country as a whole, in a particular part of the country or in relation to a specific category of refugees.[12] Prior consultation with UNHCR is necessary before such a statement is made.[13] If a Ministerial Statement is made, the refugee status of all those falling within the scope of the statement and who were granted limited leave five years or less prior to the Statement being made will be reviewed on a case-by-case basis to determine whether the cessation provision applies.[14] A refugee with indefinite leave or who was granted limited leave over five years previously would not normally have refugee status revoked on grounds of a change of circumstances in the country of origin.[15]

[1] Operational Policy and Process Policy, Guidance and Casework Instruction: 'Cancellation, Cessation and Revocation of Refugee Status', 18 December 2008.
[2] See as per fn 1 above at section 2.8 and see eg *R (on the application of Kaziu) v Secretary of State for the Home Department* [2014] EWHC 832 (Admin).
[3] API 'Refugee leave', October 2009, section 4; and see API 'Settlement Protection', October 2013,
[4] HC 395, para 339A. The APIs ('Cancellation, Cessation and Revocation of Refugee Status' and 'Refugee leave') refer to 'cancellation of refugee status' (where circumstances come to light that indicate that the person should not have been recognised as a refugee in the first place), 'cessation of refugee status' (where the individual ceases to be a refugee owing to a change in country conditions or in the individual's own circumstances) and 'revocation of refugee status' (where the seriousness of a refugee's subsequent conduct warrants revocation of status). The rules refer only to asylum being 'revoked' or not renewed, in all of these situations.

5   HC 395, para 339A(i)–(vi) which broadly reflect the cessation clauses in Article 1C(1)–(6) of
    the Refugee Convention. Under these provisions of the rules asylum is to be revoked or not
    renewed if the person voluntarily reavails him or herself of the protection of the country of
    nationality (the API 'Settlement Protection', October 2013, requires caseworkers to conduct
    checks to establish whether the person has travelled back to their country of origin, or the
    country from which they sought protection, without the knowledge of the Home Office);
    voluntarily reacquires a lost nationality; acquires a new nationality and enjoys the protection
    of the country of the new nationality; voluntarily re-establishes him or herself in the country
    of feared persecution or can no longer refuse to avail him or herself of the protection of the
    country of nationality or (in the case of stateless refugees) refuse to return to the country of
    former habitual residence because the circumstances in connection with which the person was
    recognised as a refugee have ceased to exist.
6   The UNHCR *Handbook on Procedures and Criteria for Determining Refugee Status* at
    para 117 and 141 acknowledge that refugee status may be cancelled if information comes to
    light indicating that an individual should have been excluded.
7   HC 395, para 339A(vii) referring to exclusion in accordance with reg 7 of the Refugee or
    Person in Need of International Protection (Qualification) Regulations 2006, SI 2006/2525
    which provides that a person is not a refugee if he or she falls within the scope of Article 1D
    (exclusion of persons receiving protection or assistance from other UN organs or agencies),
    Article 1E (exclusion of persons recognised by the competent authorities of the country in
    which they have taken residence as having the rights and obligations which are attached to
    possession of nationality of that country) or Article 1F (exclusion of persons in respect of
    whom there are serious reasons to consider that they have committed a crime against peace,
    war crimes, crimes against humanity, a serious non-political crime or acts contrary to the
    purposes and principles of the UN) of the Refugee Convention.
8   HC 395, para 339A(viii). The Refugee Convention makes no such provision but the UNHCR
    Handbook on Procedures and Criteria for Determining Refugee Status, para 117 envisages the
    cancellation of refugee status in such circumstances.
9   HC 395, para 339A(ix), reflecting Article 33(2) of the Refugee Convention and Article
    21(2)(a) of the Qualification Directive.
10 HC 395, para 339A(x), reflecting Article 33(2) of the Refugee Convention and Article 21(2)(b)
    of the Qualification Directive. See also API 'Settlement Protection', October 2013, sections 4.3
    and 5 regarding criminality.
11 API 'Cancellation, Cessation and Revocation of Refugee Status', 18 December 2008,
    section 4.3.
12 API 'Cancellation, Cessation and Revocation of Refugee Status', 18 December 2008,
    section 4.5.
13 API 'Refugee leave', section 6.
14 API 'Refugee leave', section 6.
15 API 'Cancellation, Cessation and Revocation of Refugee Status', 18 December 2008,
    section 4.5.1 (cessation under articles 1C(5) and (6) will only normally be considered for those
    with indefinite leave where removal is envisaged or where UKBA would like to remove in light
    of an individual's actions even where removal is not possible at the present time) and API
    'Refugee leave', section 6 for the requirement that limited leave was granted within the five
    years prior to the statement.

12.190 Exceptionally there are circumstances which will trigger a review of
refugee status and possible revocation of asylum even where revocation would
not normally be considered (ie on voluntary cessation grounds where asylum
was granted more than five years previously or on the ground of a change of
circumstances in the country of origin but absent a Ministerial Statement or
where there is a Ministerial Statement but indefinite leave was granted or
limited leave was granted more than five years prior to the statement).[1] Such
circumstances, in consequence of which the government may wish to remove
an individual, include the following:[2] where the person falls within the scope
of Article 33(2) of the Refugee Convention because there are reasonable
grounds for regarding the person as a danger to national security or, having
been convicted of a particularly serious crime as a danger to the community;
where a court has recommended the individual for deportation after convic-

tion; where the individual is on the Sex Offenders Register; where an extradition request is made, including a request from the country of the refugee's origin; or where the Secretary of State considers that the refugee's presence is not conducive to the public good. The Secretary of State will treat a person's presence as not conducive to the public good[3] if the person engages in 'unacceptable behaviours' either in the UK or abroad. 'Unacceptable behaviours' include using any means or medium, including writing, producing, publishing or distributing material; public speaking including preaching; running a website or using a position of responsibility such as teacher, community or youth leader to express views which foment, justify, glorify or incite terrorist violence in furtherance of particular beliefs or foment or incite criminal activity or foster hatred which may lead to inter-community violence in the UK. The Secretary of State will consider whether these exceptional circumstances are sufficient in themselves to justify revocation of refugee status and if they are not, whether there has been such a change of circumstances that the person is no longer a refugee.[4]

[1]   API 'Refugee leave', section 5.4.
[2]   API 'Refugee leave', section 5.4.
[3]   API 'Refugee leave', section 5.4 and API 'Exclusion: Articles 1F and 33(2) of the Refugee Convention', section 2.6 and API 'Cancellation, Cessation and Revocation of Refugee Status', 18 December 2008, section 6.1 and API 'Settlement Protection', October 2013.
[4]   API 'Cancellation, Cessation and Revocation of Refugee Status', 18 December 2008, section 6.1.

12.191 In any case where an individual's refugee status is being actively reviewed, he or she should be informed in writing of the reasons for the reconsideration and be invited to submit reasons in a personal interview or written statement why refugee status should be retained or why the person should otherwise be permitted to remain in the UK.[1] UNHCR should also be consulted on revocation decisions other than cessation cases reviewed pursuant to a Ministerial Statement (although UNHCR may still be consulted in borderline or complex cases) and some exclusion and Article 33(2) cases.[2] An interview may be necessary in a particularly complex case.[3] Where revocation of refugee status on the ground that it was obtained by deception is being considered an interview may be necessary particularly if removal is a likely consequence of revocation, and should be conducted under caution; in any event, the individual should have the opportunity to respond to the allegation of deception.[4] An interview should be conducted if the possible deception comes to light as a result of information given by a family member in the course of an application for family reunion.[5]

[1]   API 'Refugee leave', section 4.2 and HC 395, para 339BA implementing Article 38(1) of Council Directive 2005/85/EC on minimum standards on procedures in Member States for granting and withdrawing refugee status.
[2]   API 'Refugee leave', section 4.2 and API 'Cancellation, Cessation and Revocation of Refugee Status', 18 December 2008, section 2.4 – which also provides that UNHCR should generally be allowed 15 working days within which to respond.
[3]   API 'Refugee leave', section 4.2.
[4]   API 'Refugee leave', section 5.2; and API 'Cancellation, Cessation and Revocation of Refugee Status', 18 December 2008, section 2.1.
[5]   API 'Cancellation, Cessation and Revocation of Refugee Status', 18 December 2008, section 3.4.1. In deciding whether the information does evidence deception, the decision maker must allow for the fact that the two family members may not share full information about relevant events and discrepancies as to dates, lack of exact knowledge of political activities or

mention of economic betterment should not of themselves be considered as sufficient grounds for revocation.

12.192 Revocation of asylum does not by itself bring a person's leave to enter or remain to an end or render the person removeable. If a refugee has limited leave, the leave may be curtailed if asylum is revoked[1] and as a matter of policy, revocation of asylum will normally result in curtailment of any extant limited leave with a view to removing the person concerned.[2] Nevertheless, if a person's refugee status is revoked, consideration should be given to whether he or she qualifies for humanitarian protection or discretionary leave.[3] If asylum was obtained by deception with a consequential grant of leave, in the case of leave to enter (including indefinite leave to enter) the leave may be disregarded and directions can be given for the person's removal[4] or in the case of leave to remain (including indefinite leave to remain), removal directions can be given which invalidate the leave.[5] Nationality, Immigration and Asylum Act 2002, s 76(3) makes provision for a person's indefinite leave (as well as that of his or her dependants[6] unless they are refugees in their own rights[7]) to be revoked if the 'voluntary cessation clauses' apply. This section 76(3) power of revocation can be exercised in respect of leave granted before the provision came into force but only in reliance on any action taken by the refugee after it came into force.[8] However, the Tribunal has held that pre-commencement conduct may be taken into account to assess the significance of the post-commencement conduct relied upon.[9] Where information comes to the Secretary of State's attention suggesting that section 76(3) may be applied (eg at a port when the individual reenters after visiting the country from which asylum was granted or when an application is made for leave to be endorsed in a national passport) the individual should be given an opportunity to explain his or her actions before any decision to revoke refugee status and indefinite leave is made.[10] Indefinite leave should not be revoked if there are compelling reasons such as length of time spent in the UK (five or more years since the grant of indefinite leave normally being a compelling reason) and in the case of dependants, indefinite leave should not be revoked if they are recognised as refugees in their own right.[11]

---

[1]   Which requires the exercise of a discretion under HC 395 para 339B. Curtailment of leave is an exercise of the power under the Immigration Act 1971, s 3(3)(a) to vary a person's limited leave to enter or remain. HC 395, para 323 expressly provides for leave to be curtailed on any of the grounds in para 339A(i)–(vi) described above (ie on cessation grounds).

[2]   API 'Cancellation, Cessation and Revocation of Refugee Status', 18 December 2008, section 2.1.

[3]   API 'Refugee leave', section 8.2.

[4]   Immigration Act 1971, Sch 2, para 9.

[5]   IAA 1999, s 10(1)(b) and (8).

[6]   A dependant being a spouse or minor child related to the person concerned at the time when it is considered whether indefinite leave should be revoked – API 'Revocation of indefinite Leave' under the heading 'dependants'.

[7]   API 'Revocation of indefinite leave', under the heading 'dependants'.

[8]   NIAA 2002, s 76(6). A right of appeal lies against the decision to revoke under section 82(1), (2)(f); if no appeal is lodged, or if it is finally dismissed, a person whose indefinite leave is revoked under this provision can be removed from the UK as an overstayer under the IAA 1999, s 10(1)(ba) (as inserted by the 2002 Act, s 76(7) with effect from 10 February 2003: SI 2003/1). The IAN 2006, s 2 amended the NIAA 2002, s 82(2)(g) with effect from 31 August 2006, SI 2006/2226 so as to make a decision to give removal directions under s 10(1)(ba) of the 1999 Act an appealable immigration decision.

[9]   RD (Algeria) [2007] UKAIT 00066.

[10] API 'Revocation of indefinite leave', 10 June 2013, section 6.2.3 'in cessation cases'.

[11] API 'Revocation of indefinite leave', 10 June 2013, sections 4 and 5.1 respectively.

12.193 The Home Office's policy is that 'every effort should be made' to remove a person to whom Article 1F of the Convention applies[1] but that if such removal is not possible, eg because it would result in a breach of the person's human rights, 'restricted leave' for a maximum of six months should normally be granted.[2] Such leave will be subject to some or all of the following restrictions: on the person's employment or occupation in the UK; on where the person can reside; a requirement to report to an immigration officer or the Secretary of State at regular intervals; and a prohibition on the person studying at an educational institution.[3] Persons to whom Article 33(2) of the Refugee Convention applies, but who cannot be removed for human rights reasons, will normally be granted periods of discretionary leave.[4] The supposedly interim position on 'restricted leave' in Article 1F cases awaits possible implementation of provisions in the Criminal Justice and Immigration Act 2008 which will, create a 'special immigration status' which the Secretary of State may impose on such persons.[5] The Secretary of State may designate a person for 'special immigration status' if the person is a 'foreign criminal' or a member of the family of a 'foreign criminal'.[6] 'Family' includes a person's spouse or civil partner and children under the age of 18.[7] A person may not be designated if he or she has the right of abode in the UK[8] or the effect of such designation would breach the UK's obligations under the Refugee Convention or the person's rights under the Community (now Union) treaties.[9] A 'foreign criminal' is a non-British person who has been convicted of a 'particularly serious crime' within the meaning of Article 33(2) of the Refugee Convention as construed by the Nationality, Immigration and Asylum Act 2002, s 72[10] or a person to whom Article 1F of the Refugee Convention applies.[11] A designated person does not have leave to enter or remain in the UK[12] although, whilst subject to immigration control,[13] is not in the UK in breach of the immigration laws.[14] It is not clear what effect designation is to have on leave to enter or remain that a person has at the time of being designated. If its effect is to bring to an end any such leave, then designation would be an 'immigration decision' (variation of a person's leave to enter or remain in the UK if, when the variation takes effect, the person has no leave to enter or remain)[15] against which the person may appeal to the Tribunal.[16] Time spent in the UK as a designated person cannot be relied on in relation to an application for naturalisation in the UK.[17] Conditions may be imposed on a designated person by the Secretary of State or an immigration officer relating to residence, employment or occupation or reporting to the police, the Secretary of State or an immigration officer[18] and may include electronic monitoring.[19] Non-compliance with a condition is an offence punishable by a fine and imprisonment of up to 51 weeks.[20] It is likely that imposition of any (save perhaps the lightest of) conditions would breach the UK's obligations under the Refugee Convention; a person to whom Article 33(2) applies may not claim the benefit of Article 33 of the Convention (prohibition on *refoulement*) but for as long as he or she remains in the UK is entitled to the benefit of the other provisions of the Convention (relating, for example, to freedom of movement;[21] employment[22] and self-employment[23]). A person subject to 'special immigration status' may be supported by the Secretary of State under a modified asylum support regime.[24] Designation 'lapses' if the person is granted leave to enter or remain, is notified by the Secretary of State or an immigration officer of a right of residence under the Community (now Union) treaties, leaves the UK or is made the subject of a deportation order.[25]

1   API 'Exclusion: Article 1F of the Refugee Convention', 30 May 2012, section 3.11. 'Exclusion: Articles 1F and 33(2) of the Refugee Convention', section 2.14.
2   Interim Asylum Instruction: Restricted Leave, 28 May 2012. The leave is renewable on an active review: see section 9. In *R (on the application of Boroumand) v Secretary of State for the Home Department* [2010] EWHC 225 (Admin), Beatson J held that renewable grants of six months' 'discretionary leave' (prior to the 'restricted leave' policy) did not disproportionately interfere in the claimant's right to respect for his private life, as based on his problems with employment, banking and foreign travel.
3   As per fn 2 above.
4   API 'Discretionary leave', 19 May 2014, section 2.5.
5   Criminal Justice and Immigration Act 2008, Pt 10.
6   Criminal Justice and Immigration Act 2008, s 130.
7   Criminal Justice and Immigration Act 2008, s 137(3).
8   Criminal Justice and Immigration Act 2008, s 130(4).
9   Criminal Justice and Immigration Act 2008, s 130(5).
10 Ie conviction in the UK and sentence to at least two years' imprisonment; conviction outside the UK and sentence to at least two years' imprisonment if the person could have been convicted and sentenced to two or more years in prison for a similar offence if convicted in the UK; conviction in the UK of an offence specified by order of the Secretary of State (though note that the Nationality, Immigration and Asylum Act 2002 (Specification of Particularly Serious Crimes) Order 2004, SI 2004/1910 was held to be *ultra vires* and unlawful by the CA in *EN (Serbia) v Secretary of State for the Home Department* [2009] EWCA Civ 630 at [81]–[83]) or conviction outside the UK for an offence which the Secretary of State certifies as being similar to such an offence.
11 Criminal Justice and Immigration Act 2008, s 131.
12 Criminal Justice and Immigration Act 2008, s 132(1).
13 Criminal Justice and Immigration Act 2008, s 132(2)(a).
14 Criminal Justice and Immigration Act 2008, s 132(2)(c).
15 Nationality, Immigration and Asylum Act 2002, s 82(2)(e).
16 Nationality, Immigration and Asylum Act 2002, s 82(1).
17 Criminal Justice and Immigration Act 2008, s 132(3).
18 Criminal Justice and Immigration Act 2008, s 133.
19 Criminal Justice and Immigration Act 2008, s 133(3) applying the Asylum and Immigration (Treatment of Claimants, etc) Act 2004, s 36.
20 Criminal Justice and Immigration Act 2008, s 133(5) and (6).
21 Article 26.
22 Article 17.
23 Article 18.
24 Criminal Justice and Immigration Act 2008, ss 134, 135.
25 Criminal Justice and Immigration Act 2008, s 136.

TEMPORARY PROTECTION

12.194 The Immigration Rules[1] provide for the grant of temporary protection pursuant to the terms of Council Directive 2001/55/EC,[2] if the Secretary of State is satisfied that the applicant is in the UK or has arrived at a port, is entitled to temporary protection as defined by the Directive and in accordance with it,[3] does not hold an extant grant of it entitling him or her to reside in another EU Member State,[4] and is not excluded under provisions analogous to Article 1F and Article 33(2) of the Refugee Convention.[5] Temporary protection may be granted whatever the immigration status of the person, and it will consist of leave to enter or remain, not subject to a condition prohibiting employment, for up to 12 months, renewable for further periods of six months.[6] The rules provide for the recipient of temporary protection to be allowed to return to the UK from another EEA Member State,[7] to be provided with documentation,[8] to be registered by the Secretary of State[9] and to be accompanied by a wide range of family members[10] – not just the spouse or unmarried partner[11] and minor children who lived with the principal applicant as part of the family unit immediately prior to displacement, but also parents, grandparents, unmarried adult children, unmarried siblings, uncles and aunts who lived with the applicant and were wholly or mainly dependent on him or her, provided that they would face extreme hardship if reunification did not take place.[12] In considering an application by a dependent child, the Secretary of State is required by the rules to take into consideration the best interests of that child.[13] The grant of temporary protection does not prejudice an asylum claim, but the Directive allows Member States to provide that temporary protection may not be enjoyed concurrently with the status of asylum seeker.[14]

[1]   HC 395, Part 11A (paras 354–356B), inserted by HC 164, in effect 1 January 2005.
[2]   Council Directive 2001/55/EC on minimum standards for giving temporary protection in the event of a mass influx of displaced persons and on measures promoting a balance of efforts between Member States in receiving such persons and bearing the consequences thereof (OJ 2001 L 212/12).
[3]   Under the terms of the Directive, the Council, acting on a proposal from the Commission, decides on the existence of a mass influx of displaced persons (defined as third country nationals or stateless persons who have had to leave their country or region of origin, and are unable to return in safe and durable conditions because of the situation prevailing there, who may fall within the scope of the Geneva convention or other instruments giving international protection, including persons fleeing armed confict or endemic violence, or victims or potential victims of systematic and generalised violations of human rights: art 2). The Council decision has the effect of introducing temporary protection for the displaced persons to whom it relates, in all the Member States (Art 5). Temporary protection comes to an end when the maximum duration has been reached (two years, extendable by the Council for a further year: art 4) or on a Council decision that the situation in the country of origin is such as to permit safe and durable return with due respect for human rights and *non-refoulement* obligatons: art 6.
[4]   HC 395, para 355 as inserted.
[5]   HC 395, para 355A as inserted. Consideration of exclusion is to be based solely on the personal conduct of the applicant concerned and exclusion decisions or measures must be based on the principle of proportionality: ibid.
[6]   HC 395, para 355B, 355C as inserted. Articles 12 and 14 of the Directive require Member States to authorise work, self-employment, education etc, and Article 13 requires them to provide suitable accommodation and social and welfare assistance. The Directive limits temporary protection to two years in total, extendable for a further year on a decision of the Council.
[7]   HC 395, para 355D as inserted.
[8]   HC 395, para 355E as inserted.
[9]   HC 395, para 355F as inserted.
[10] HC 395, para 356–356B as inserted, reflecting the provisions of art 15 of the Directive.
[11] Provided that the parties have been living together in a relationship akin to marriage which has subsisted for at least two years: para 356(a)(ii).
[12] HC 395, para 356(b)(ii). We suggest that 'extreme hardship' is a less severe test than 'the most exceptional compassionate circumstances' for the purposes of the pre-July 2012 distressed relative provisions of para 317.
[13] HC 395, para 356B, reflecting art 15(4) of the Directive. See now also Borders, Citizenship and Immigration Act 2009, s 55.
[14] Directive arts 3(1) and 19(1). HC 395, para 355G enables the Secretary of State to defer consideration of an asylum claim made by someone with temporary protection until he or she ceases to be entitled to it.

SUBSIDIARY PROTECTION AND HUMANITARIAN PROTECTION

12.195 The Qualification Directive creates a legal obligation on Member States to provide 'subsidiary protection' to third country nationals and stateless people who do not qualify as refugees but who face a real risk of suffering serious harm, who are not excluded from protection and to whom protection is not available in their home country.[1] Effect is given to this obligation in the UK by means of 'humanitarian protection'.[2] Serious harm consists of: (a) the death penalty or execution; (b) torture or inhuman or degrading treatment or punishment; or (c) serious and individual threat to a civilian's life or person by reason of indiscriminate violence in situations of international or internal armed conflict.[3] The European Court of Justice has sought to give guidance on the interpretation and application of 'serious harm' in form (c) in the case of *Elgafaji*.[4] The Court held that Article 15(c) has a distinct application from Article 3 of the Human Rights Convention (which informs 'serious harm' as per Article 15(b) of the Qualification Directive), that its interpretation must be carried out independently and that it covers a more general risk of harm than that specified in Article 15(a) and (b).[5] The word 'individual', in Article 15(c), must be understood as covering harm to civilians irrespective of their identity, where the degree of indiscriminate violence characterising the armed conflict taking place, as assessed by the competent national authorities, 'reaches such a high level that substantial grounds are shown for believing that a civilian, returned to the relevant country or, as the case may be, to the relevant region, would, solely on account of his presence on the territory of that country or region, face a real risk of being subject to the serious threat referred in Article 15(c) of the Directive.'[6] Accordingly, 'the existence of a serious and individual threat to the life or person of an applicant for subsidiary protection is not subject to the condition that that applicant adduce evidence that he is specifically targeted by reason of factors particular to his personal circumstances.'[7] Nonetheless, 'the more the applicant is able to show that he is specifically affected by reason of factors particular to his personal circumstances, the lower the level of indiscriminate violence required for him to be eligible for subsidiary protection';[8] and in making the requisite individual assessment[9] account may be taken of the geographical scope of the situation of indiscriminate violence and the actual destination of the applicant in the event that he is returned to the relevant country and of any past persecution or serious harm suffered by the applicant.[10] On a proper construction of Article 15(c), an internal armed conflict exists if a State's armed forces confront one or more armed groups or if two or more armed groups confront each other; it is not necessary for that conflict to be categorised as 'armed conflict not of an international character' under international humanitarian law; nor is it necessary to carry out, in addition to an appraisal of the level of violence present in the territory concerned, a separate assessment of the intensity of the armed confrontations, the level of organisation of the armed forces involved or the duration of the conflict.[11] The provisions of the Directive relating to assessment of facts and circumstances,[12] international protection needs arising *sur place*,[13] actors of persecution or serious harm,[14] actors of protection[15] and internal protection[16] which are applicable to determination of refugee status also apply to the determination of entitlement to subsidiary protection. Eligibility for subsidiary protection ceases if there has been a significant, non-temporary change of circumstances of such a degree that protection is no longer required[17] and in such circumstances, the Member State is obliged to revoke, end or refuse to renew the status.[18] A person is excluded from subsidiary protection if he or she has committed a crime against peace, a war crime or a crime against humanity, a serious crime, has been guilty of acts contrary to the purposes and principles of the UN or constitutes a danger to the community or to the security of the Member State.[19] A person may be excluded from subsidiary protection if he or she committed one or more other crimes which would be punishable by imprisonment had they been committed in the Member State and the person left his or her country of origin solely to avoid sanctions resulting from those crimes.[20]

[1] Qualification Directive 2004, arts 2(e) and 18.
[2] HC 395, paras 339C–339Q, as inserted by HC 6918, make provision for applications for subsidiary protection in the form of humanitarian protection.
[3] Qualification Directive 2004, art 15.
[4] *Elgafaji v Staatssecretaris van Justitie* (Case C – 465/07) [2009] All ER (EC) 651, [2009] 1 WLR 2100, ECJ; see also *Diakite (Aboubacar) v Commissaire general aux refugies et aux apatrides*:: Case C-285/12: [2014] 1 WLR 2477, ECJ[2014] All ER (D) 219 (Jan). The Court of Appeal has also considered art 15(c) in *QD (Iraq) v Secretary of State for the Home Department; AH (Iraq) v Secretary of State for the Home Department* [2009] EWCA Civ 620, [2010] 2 All ER 971 and the Tribunal has considered its application in a whole series of 'Country Guidance' determinations relating particularly to Somalia, Iraq and Afghanistan and most recently to Libya in *AT and Others (Article 15c; risk categories) Libya CG* [2014] UKUT 318 (IAC).
[5] *Elgafaji* (fn 4 sbove) at paras 28, 33 and 36. According to the UNHCR, in para 34 of his submissions to the English Court of Appeal in *QD (Iraq) v Secretary of State for the Home Department; AH (Iraq) v Secretary of State for the Home Department* [2009] EWCA Civ 620, [2010] 2 All ER 971, 'Article 15(c) must be regarded as having distinct, and in certain respects a wider, application than both Article 15(b) and Article 3 of the ECHR'.
[6] *Elgafaji* (fn 4 above) at paras 35 and 43. This interpretation is not invalidated by the wording of recital 26 in the preamble to the Directive, according to which '[r]isks to which a population of a country or a section of the population is generally exposed do normally not create in themselves an individual threat which would qualify as serious harm'. The word 'normally' in the recital is key, as it allows for the possibility of an exceptional situation which would be characterised by such a high degree of risk that substantial grounds would be shown for believing that that person would be subject individually to the risk in question. The exceptional nature of such a situation is confirmed by the fact that the protection under Article 15(c) is subsidiary: *Elgafaji* (fn 4 above) at 3638.
[7] *Elgafaji* (fn 4 above) at para 43.
[8] *Elgafaji* (fn 4 above) at para 39.
[9] As required by Qualification Directive, art 4(3).
[10] *Elgafaji* (fn 4 above) at para 40. See Qualification Directive, arts 4 and 8(1) regarding past persecution/serious harm and internal protection/relocation.
[11] *Diakité* (fn 4 above) at para 35.
[12] Qualification Directive 2004, art 4.
[13] Qualification Directive 2004, art 5.
[14] Qualification Directive 2004, art 6.
[15] Qualification Directive 2004, art 7.
[16] Qualification Directive 2004, art 8.
[17] Qualification Directive 2004, art 16.
[18] Qualification Directive 2004, art 19(1).
[19] Qualification Directive 2004, art 17.
[20] Qualification Directive 2004, art 17(3).

12.196 The Home Office abolished 'exceptional leave to remain' with effect from 1 April 2003, and replaced it with 'humanitarian protection' and 'discretionary leave'.[1] From 9 October 2006, the policy relating to 'humanitarian protection' was reformulated and incorporated into the Immigration Rules[2] as the means by which the UK complies with its obligation under European Union law[3] to provide 'subsidiary protection'[4] to certain people who do not qualify for refugee status. If a person does not qualify for refugee status consideration is to be given to whether he or she qualifies for humanitarian protection[5] and if ineligible for humanitarian protection, whether the person may qualify for discretionary leave.[6] Humanitarian protection is leave granted to a person who is in the UK, does not qualify for refugee status and in respect of whom substantial grounds have been shown for believing that he or she would face a real risk of suffering serious harm in the country of return.[7] The person must also be unable or, owing to the risk, unwilling to avail him or herself of the protection of that country.[8] Serious harm is defined as the death penalty or execution,[9] unlawful killing,[10] torture or inhuman or degrading treatment or punishment of a person in the country of return[11] or serious and individual threat to a civilian's life or person by reason of indiscriminate violence in situations of international or internal armed conflict.[12] As regards this last category of serious harm, following *Elgafaji*[13] the Court of Appeal in *QD (Iraq)*[14] disapproved the pre-*Elgafaji* approach of the Asylum and Immigration Tribunal that had sought to apply concepts of international humanitarian law (IHL) to the meaning of serious harm in Article 15(c).[15] In giving the judgment of the court, Sedley LJ held, rejecting the IHL based approach, that the Directive has to stand on its own legs and be treated as autonomous. He identified three particular problems caused by the drafting of Articles 2(e) and 15(c): '(1) the ostensibly cumulative but logically intractable test of "a real risk" of a "threat"; (2) the contradictory postulation of an individual threat" to life or safety from "indiscriminate violence"; (3) the requirement of "armed conflict" when there may well be only one source of indiscriminate violence'.[16] As to the second, this had been answered by the ECJ in *Elgafaji* and Sedley LJ noted that: 'By using the words "exceptional" and "exceptionally" it is simply stressing that it is not every armed conflict or violent situation which will attract the protection of Article 15(c), but only one where the level of violence is such that, without anything to render them a particular target, civilians face real risks to their life or personal safety'. As to the first, 'a risk of a threat', the court was sure that the Directive seeks to cover only real risks and real threats and that when Article 15(c) speaks of a threat to a civilian's life or person it is concerned not with fear alone but with a possibility that may become a reality, such that '"risk" in article 2(e) overlaps with "threat" in article 15(c), so that the latter reiterates but does not qualify or dilute the former'. Article 15(c) is concerned with 'serious threats of real harm'. However, there is no requirement that there be any 'consistent pattern' of mistreatment in order to bring a situation of armed conflict within the purview of Article 15(c) – 'The risk of random injury or death which indiscriminate violence carries is the converse of consistency'.[17] As to the third problem, the court accepted the proposition, agreed by the parties and the UNHCR, 'that the phrase "situations of international or internal armed conflict" in Article 15(c) has an autonomous meaning broad enough to capture any situation of indiscriminate violence, whether caused by one or more armed factions or by a state, which reaches the level described by the ECJ in *Elgafaji*'. Although there is no requirement that the armed conflict itself need be exceptional there does need to be an intensity of indiscriminate violence 'great enough to meet the test spelt out by the ECJ'. The court agreed with the parties 'that "civilian" in Article 15(c) means not simply someone not in uniform – which by itself might include a good many terrorists – but only genuine non-combatants (though UNHCR submitted that former "combatants" should not be excluded)'. The court concluded by remitting the appeals and putting the critical question as: 'Is there in Iraq or a material part of it such a high level of indiscriminate violence that substantial grounds exist for believing that an applicant such as QD or AH would, solely by being present there, face a real risk which threatens his life or person? By "material part" we mean the applicant's home area or, if otherwise appropriate, any potential place of internal relocation'. Following *QD (Iraq)*, the Tribunal in *GS (Afghanistan) CG*[18] held that the Court of Appeal had confirmed that it is possible, for the purposes of Article 15(c), to have an armed conflict in one part of a country, when other parts may be free of it and that: 'even in an area of internal armed conflict, there may be parts where the high levels of indiscriminate violence, needed to obtain protection, are not achieved'. The Tribunal considered that the difference between discriminate and indiscriminate violence is an issue of fact for case-by-case consideration, that in principle there is no reason why criminal acts should not be included in the scope of indiscriminate violence and that subject to there being a sufficient causal link between the threat to life or person and the indiscriminate violence, there is no need for the indiscriminate violence to be caused by one or more armed factions or by the state. As to the causal nexus, the Tribunal considered that there is no significant distinction between the words 'by reason of' and 'for reason of' and that to succeed an applicant must show that the indiscriminate violence is an effective cause of the serious and individual threat – it does not need to be the only cause, but it cannot be only remotely connected. Whether indirect consequences of indiscriminate violence can be sufficient to bring a person within Article 15(c) will be a question of fact in each case based on this approach to the causal nexus. With reference to *Elgafaji* and the question of enhanced personal risk, the Tribunal considered that although there is 'a moving standard in the required level of indiscriminate violence, when a person is at a higher degree of risk' the ultimate test remains one of a 'real risk'. In *AMM (Somalia)*, the Tribunal reiterated the position from *Elgafaji* that Article 15(c) can be satisfied without there being such a level of risk as is required for Article 3, ECHR, in cases of generalised violence.[19] Similar principles in relation to 'sufficiency of protection'[20] and internal relocation[21] and 'sur place' claims[22] apply to humanitarian protection as to Refugee Convention claims. Those granted humanitarian protection are generally given leave to enter or remain for five years in the first instance with an opportunity then to apply for settlement.[23]

[1] See APU Notice 1/4/2003 'Humitarian Protection and Discretionary Leave' and see para 12.187 of the 8th edition of this book.

[2] Cm 6918, inserting new paras 339C–339H into HC 395.

[3] The Qualification Directive, art 38.

[4] Defined in the Qualification Directive, art 2(e).

[5] HC 395, para 339C(ii) and API 'Humanitarian protection', 15 May 2013, 'Introduction'.

[6] See APIs on 'Humanitarian protection', 'Handling Claims' and 'Discretionary Leave'. A person refused asylum but granted humanitarian protection is to be given a 'reasons for refusal letter' explaining why asylum has been refused. The letter should also make clear whether humanitarian protection was granted on grounds of fear of the authorities or of non-state agents because if the latter, the person would be expected to rely on a national passport and would not be issued with a Home Office travel document: API 'Humanitarian protection', 15 May 2013, at section 6.1.

[7] HC 395, para 339C(i)–(iii). The current API 'Humanitarian Protection', 15 May 2013, no longer seeks to define the meaning of 'country of return'. The Qualification Directive defines a person eligible for subsidiary protection by reference to return 'to his or her country of origin, or in the case of a stateless person, to his or her country of former habitual residence' (Art 2(e)) and defines 'country of origin' as the country or countries of nationality or, for stateless persons, of former habitual residence (Art 2(k)). Note that the current API, 15 May 2013, also no longer stipulates that humanitarian protection will not be granted to a person who would face a real risk of serious harm if removed but who can make a voluntary

return without such a risk: compare *AA v Secretary of State for the Home Department* [2006] EWCA Civ 401 in respect to the Refugee Convention context.

8   HC 395, para 339C(iii). The Refugee or Person in Need of International Protection (Qualification) Regulations 2006, SI 2006/2525, reg 4 defines 'actors of protection' in the same way in relation to protection from persecution and serious harm. The discussion of 'protection' above in relation to refugee claims is equally applicable here.

9   HC 395, para 339C(i) reflecting protocols 6 and 13 to the ECHR.

10 HC 395, para 339C(ii) reflecting ECHR, art 2 which is discussed further in Chapter 7. By including 'unlawful killing' in the definition of serious harm the Immigration Rules go further than the Qualification Directive, which defines 'serious harm' in art 15: see per Sedley LJ in *QD (Iraq) and AH (Iraq) v Secretary of State for the Home Department* [2009] EWCA Civ 620 at [13]. The API on Humanitarian Protection says that 'unlawful killing' 'includes a person who would face a real and individual risk of being killed if returned to a situation of great danger' whilst distinguishing this from the protection afforded by art 15(c): see below. In some respects that provides wider protection than the specific provision in the Rules and the Qualification Directive relating to situations of international or internal armed conflict because the killing need not be by reason of 'indiscriminate violence'.

11 HC 395, para 339C(iii). This of course reflects art 3 of ECHR as to which see Chapter 7. The API, 15 May 2013, specifically addresses 'prison conditions'-'prison conditions which are systematically inhuman and life-threatening are always contrary to Article 3, ECHR. However, even if those conditions are not severe enough to meet that threshold automatically, art 3 will still be engaged if, in that individual's personal circumstances, detention would amount to inhuman or degrading treatment. This would depend on the likely length of detention, the type and conditions of detention facilities, and the individual's age, gender, vulnerability, state of physical or mental health, or any other relevant factors' – and, with reference to the Strasbourg judgements in *NA v United Kingdom* (2009) 48 EHRR 337 and *Sufi and Elmi v United Kingdom* (2011) 54 EHRR 209, to art 3 risk arising from general levels of violence and other severe humanitarian conditions. On the other hand, the API states that even if the impact of removal was sufficient to breach art 3 because of its effect on a person's medical condition, the person would not thereby qualify under the rule but might qualify for discretionary leave.

12 HC 395, para 339C(iv).

13 *Elgafaji v Staatssecretaris van Justitie* (Case C-465/07) 17 February 2009, ECJ: see **12.195** above.

14 *QD (Iraq) and AH (Iraq) v Secretary of State for the Home Department* [2009] EWCA Civ 620, [2011] 1 WLR 689, [2010] 2 All ER 971, [2010] Imm AR 132, [2009] INLR 514. The UNHCR intervened and his submissions are appended to the judgment. See also *HH (Somalia) v Secretary of State for the Home Department* [2010] EWCA Civ 426 at [31]–[40].

15 See *KH (Article 15(c) Qualification Directive) Iraq CG* [2008] UKAIT 00023. See also *HH and Ors (Mogadishu: Armed Conflict: Risk) Somalia CG* [2008] UKAIT 00022; and *AM and AM (Armed Conflict: Risk Categories) Somalia CG* [2008] UKAIT 00091. See also *Diakite (Aboubacar) v Commissaire general aux refugies et aux apatrides*:Case C-285/12 [2014] 1 WLR 2477, ECJ, [2014] All ER (D) 219 (Jan), for further rejection of an IHL based approach, see **12.195** above.

16 *QD (Iraq)* (fn 14 above) at [20] in which Sedley LJ continued by stating: 'The first of these has to be coped with pragmatically. The second has now been resolved in principle by the European Court of Justice. The third, albeit troubling, is the subject of agreement before us'.

17 *QD (Iraq)* (fn 14 above) at [32]. The 'consistent pattern' of mistreatment "test", relevant to real risks of persecution and Article 3, ECHR violations, in cases of general risk to a class of applicant, comes from the Tribunal's test as approved by the Court of Appeal in *AA (Zimbabwe) v Secretary of State for the Home Department* [2007] EWCA Civ 149 at [14] and [21]'.

18 *GS (Article 15(c): Indiscriminate Violence) Afghanistan CG* [2009] UKAIT 00044 at [27]. In *AK (Article 15(c)) Afghanistan CG* [2012] UKUT 00163 (IAC) the Tribunal concluded, in 2012 that: 'Despite a rise in the number of civilian deaths and casualties and (particularly in the 2010-2011 period) an expansion of the geographical scope of the armed conflict in Afghanistan, the level of indiscriminate violence in that country taken as a whole is not at such a high level as to mean that, within the meaning of Article 15(c) of the Qualification Directive, a civilian, solely by being present in the country, faces a real risk which threatens his life or person.' See for a similar view as regards Libya, *AT and Others (Article 15c; risk categories) Libya CG* [2014] UKUT 318 (IAC).

[19] *AMM and others (conflict; humanitarian crisis; returnees; FGM) Somalia CG* [2011] UKUT 00445 (IAC). The Strasbourg Court in *Sufi and Elmi v UK* (2012) 54 EHRR 9 (see fn 11 above) had suggested that there is no difference in the scope of, on the one hand, art 3 of the ECHR (and, thus, art 15(b) of the Qualification Directive) and, on the other, Article 15(c) of the Directive. Rejecting this suggestion, the Tribunal in *AMM* held that 'the binding Luxembourg case law of *Elgafaji* [2009] EUECJ C-465/07 (as well as the binding domestic authority of *QD (Iraq)* [2009] EWCA Civ 620) makes it plain that Article 15(c) can be satisfied without there being such a level of risk as is required for Article 3 in cases of generalised violence (having regard to the high threshold identified in *NA v United Kingdom* [2008] ECHR 616). The difference appears to involve the fact that, as the CJEU found at [33] of Elgafaji, Article 15(c) covers a "more general risk of harm" than does Article 3 of the ECHR; that Article 15(c) includes types of harm that are less severe than those encompassed by Article 3; and that the language indicating a requirement of exceptionality is invoked for different purposes in *NA v United Kingdom* and *Elgafaji* respectively.'

[20] SI 2006/2525, reg 4.

[21] HC 395, para 339O.

[22] HC 395, para 339P.

[23] API 'Humanitarian protection', 15 May 2013, at section 6.1 under the heading ' Refusing recognition of refugee status but granting Humanitarian Protection'. As with refugee leave (see **12.188** above) the API provides, with reference to art 20(3) of the Qualification Directive (Council Directive 2004/83/EC) that in 'the most exceptional of circumstances', with reference to specific vulnerabilities (see **12.188**, fn 9 above), a longer period of leave, in effect immediate indefinite leave, may be granted in the first instance.

12.197 A person may be excluded from humanitarian protection on grounds that mirror those for exclusion from refugee status but which are in some respects significantly wider. A person in respect of whom there are serious reasons for considering that he or she committed or otherwise participated in[1] crimes against peace, war crimes, crimes against humanity or any other serious crimes[2] or is guilty of acts contrary to the purposes and principles of the UN or of the preparation or incitement of such acts[3] is excluded from humanitarian protection. In addition, a person in respect of whom there are serious reasons for considering that he or she constitutes a danger to the security of the UK is excluded from humanitarian protection.[4] Where the Immigration Rules follow the Qualification Directive in diverging very significantly from the Refugee Convention is in excluding a person who is considered 'a danger to the community'.[5] The Refugee Convention provides for the expulsion of a refugee who is reasonably regarded as a danger to the community but only if such a person has been convicted of a 'particularly serious crime'.[6] The Secretary of State may regard a person as representing a danger to the community if: he or she is included on the Sex Offenders Register; his or her presence is deemed by the Secretary of State to be not conducive to the public good, for example on national security grounds, because of his or her character, conduct or associations; he or she has engaged in one or more 'unacceptable behaviours' in the UK or abroad which include the use of any means or medium (eg public speaking or preaching or writing or running websites) to express views which foment, justify, glorify or incite terrorist acts in furtherance of particular beliefs or foster hatred which may lead to inter-community violence in the UK or otherwise because of his or her conduct or associations.[7] These criteria appear in relation to revocation of refugee status not as justification by themselves for revocation of status (unless they also bring the refugee within Articles 1F or 33(2) of the Refugee Convention) but as 'triggers' for consideration of whether status can be revoked on cessation or exclusion grounds.[8] A person is also excluded from humanitarian protection if he or she committed a crime which would be punishable by imprisonment if committed in the UK and left his or her country solely in order to avoid sanctions resulting from the crime.[9] Presently, a person excluded from humanitarian protection would normally be granted restricted leave for six months.[10] If the provisions relating to 'special immigration status' in the Criminal Justice and Immigration Act 2008 are enacted, such a person may be designated for special immigration status instead of discretionary leave in the circumstances described above.[11]

[1]   Regarding instigation, encouragement and participation in relevant crimes or acts, see *R (on the application of JS (Sri Lanka)) v Secretary of State for the Home Department* [2010] UKSC 15, [2011] 1 AC 184, in which the appellant had been excluded from humanitarian protection as well as from refugee status under Article 1F(a) of the Refugee Convention.

[2]   HC 395, para 339D(i), reflecting Article 17(1)(a) and (b) of the Qualification Directive and the Refugee Convention, art 1F(a) and (b), but like the Qualification Directive, not reproducing the requirement in the Refugee Convention in respect of 'serious crimes' that they should be non-political and committed outside the country of refugee prior to admission as a refugee. The API 'Humanitarian protection', 15 May 2013, at section 5, under the heading 'exclusion criteria', with reference to *AH (Algeria) v Secretary of State for the Home Department* [2012] EWCA Civ 395; [2012] 1 WLR 3469 (see **12.94**, fn 3 and **12.96** above), states that: 'A "serious crime" for the purpose of exclusion from Humanitarian Protection was previously interpreted to mean one for which a custodial sentence of at least twelve months had been imposed in the United Kingdom, but it is now accepted that a 12 month sentence (or more) should not alone determine the seriousness of the offence for exclusion purposes.' Rather, the sentence must be considered together with the nature of the crime, the actual harm inflicted, and whether most jurisdictions would consider it a serious crime. Examples of 'serious' crimes include murder, rape, arson, and armed robbery. Other offences which might be regarded as 'serious' include those which are accompanied by the use of deadly weapons, involve serious injury to persons, or if there is evidence of serious habitual criminal conduct. Other crimes, though not accompanied by violence, such as large-scale fraud, may also be regarded as "serious" for the purposes of exclusion.

[3]   HC 395, para 339D(ii), reflecting the Qualification Directive, art 17(1)(c). The Qualification Directive does not expressly refer to inchoate or secondary participation in the acts. The Qualification Directive does go on to identify the purposes and principles of the UN as those set out in the Preamble and Articles 1 and 2 of the Charter of the United Nations.

[4]   HC 395, para 339D(iii), reflecting the Qualification Directive, art 17(1)(d) and the Refugee Convention, art 33(2) which permits the *refoulement* of a refugee where there are reasonable grounds for regarding him or her as a danger to the security of the country.

[5]   HC 395, para 339D(iii) reflecting Article 17(1)(d) of the Qualification Directive.

[6]   Refugee Convention, art 33(2).

[7]   API 'Humanitarian protection', 15 May 2013, under the heading 'exclusion criteria'.

[8]   See API 'Refugee leave' and see **12.190** above.

[9]   HC 395, para 339D(iv), reflecting Qualification Directive, art 17(3).

[10] Interim Asylum Instruction: Restricted Leave, 28 May 2012, see **12.184** above.

[11] Criminal Justice and Immigration Act 2008, Pt 10 as discussed at **12.193** above.

Duration, revocation and settlement

12.198 Leave granted on humanitarian protection grounds should normally be for a period of five years.[1] Humanitarian protection will be revoked or will not be renewed if: the circumstances which led to the grant of humanitarian protection have ceased to exist or have changed to such an extent that protection is no longer required.[2] The change of circumstances would have to be of such a significant and non-temporary nature that the person no longer faces a real risk of serious harm.[3] The Secretary of State anticipates that most grants of humanitarian protection will relate to fear of non-state actors and that being the case, it is unlikely that the need for humanitarian protection will cease because the person accepts the protection of the country in some temporary or limited way, eg by obtaining a passport or re-acquiring nationality.[4] If a Ministerial Statement is issued announcing a review of refugee status on the grounds of a significant change of circumstances in a particular country, grants of humanitarian protection falling within the scope of the Statement will also be reviewed.[5] Humanitarian protection will also be revoked or will not be renewed if any of the grounds for exclusion from humanitarian protection apply or should have been applied[6] or if humanitarian protection was obtained by deception.[7] If a person's humanitarian protection is revoked or is not renewed, any leave which the person has may be curtailed.[8] Humanitarian protection is not normally reviewed during its currency unless certain events occur to trigger such a review and these events are those described above.[9] Applications for settlement after five years of humanitarian protection will be treated in the same way as applications by those with refugee leave.[10]

[1]   API 'Humanitarian protection', 15 May 2013, at section 6.1 under the heading ' Refusing recognition of refugee status but granting Humanitarian Protection'. But see 12.188, fn 22 above regarding possible immediate grant of indefinite leave in 'the most exceptional of circumstances'. Leave granted on humanitarian protection grounds prior to 9 October 2006 was usually for three years.
[2]   HC 395, para 339G(i).
[3]   HC 395, para 339G.
[4]   API 'Humanitarian protection', 15 May 2013, under the heading 'Revocation of Humanitarian Protection'. But the API states that each case will need to be considered on its individual merits to see whether the actions of the person and the reasons for returning to the country of origin justify the conclusion that humanitarian protection is no longer needed.
[5]   API 'Humanitarian protection', under the heading 'Revocation of Humanitarian Protection' cross refers to the API 'Cancellation, Cessation and Revocation of Refugee Status', 18 December 2008, with reference to cases involving a fear of state as opposed to non-state agents: see also 12.190 above.
[6]   HC 395, para 339G(ii)–(iv) and (vi).
[7]   HC 395, para 339G(v).
[8]   HC 395, para 339H.
[9]   API 'Humanitarian protection', under the heading 'Revocation of Humanitarian Protection'.
[10] API 'Settlement Protection', October 2013: see 12.179 above.

Discretionary leave

12.199 Discretionary leave is intended to be used sparingly within limited and specified categories of cases.[1] The categories identified in the API on 'Discretionary leave' where discretionary leave should be granted are cases: where return would breach Article 3 of the ECHR based upon the person's medical condition; other cases where return would breach a person's human rights; exceptional cases following consideration of the criteria in immigration rule 353B;[2] where a UK Competent Authority has conclusively identified a person as a victim of trafficking and in certain other circumstances relating to trafficking;[3] other cases where the circumstances are so compelling that some form of leave should be granted; and cases where an applicant would have been granted refugee status or humanitarian protection but is excluded or is removeable under Article 33(2) of the Refugee Convention and does not fall under the restricted leave policy.[4] Discretionary leave may be granted to an asylum seeker refused refugee status and humanitarian protection; such a person should be given written reasons for the refusal of asylum and humanitarian protection and for the grant of discretionary leave.[5] Note that from 9 July 2012, discretionary leave is no longer granted for Article 8 family or private life reasons and that from 6 April 2013 the policy on granting discretionary leave to unaccompanied asylum seeking children was incorporated into the Immigration Rules.[6]

[1]   API 'Discretionary leave', 19 May 2014, at section 1.1 'Key points'.
[2]   Regarding HC 395, para 353B, see **12.186** above.
[3]   API 'Discretionary leave', 19 May 2014, at section 2.4: a grant of DL should be considered where a UK Competent Authority has conclusively identified the person as a victim of trafficking within the meaning of Article 4 of the Council of Europe Convention on Action Against Trafficking in Human Beings and the individual's personal circumstances, although not meeting the criteria of any of the other categories listed, are so compelling that it is considered appropriate to grant some form of leave. A grant of DL should be considered where the victim has lodged a legitimate compensation claim against the trafficker and a grant of leave would help secure justice for the trafficked person and assist in ensuring the trafficker faces the consequences of their actions. The fact that someone is seeking compensation will be relevant to the consideration but does not, in itself, merit a grant of leave. Leave must only be granted where it would be unreasonable for them to pursue that claim from outside of the UK. If an individual is cooperating with an ongoing police investigation in relation to their trafficking case and their presence is required for this purpose it may be appropriate to grant leave.
[4]   See **12.194** above.
[5]   API 'Discretionary leave', 19 May 2014, at section 3.1: the reasons must make clear under which of the specified categories the person qualifies for DL.
[6]   API 'Discretionary leave', 19 May 2014, at sections 1.1 and 2.7. For unaccompanied asylum seeking children (UASCs) see HC 395, paras 352ZC to 352ZF and see **12.118** to **12.122** above.

12.200 The duration of discretionary leave granted will be determined by a consideration of the individual facts of the case but will not normally be granted for more than 30 months at a time; subsequent periods of leave can be granted providing the applicant continues to meet the relevant criteria; and from 9 July 2012 an applicant normally needs to complete at least ten years (normally consisting of four 30 months' periods of leave) before being eligible to apply for indefinite leave.[1] There may also be cases where leave is granted for a shorter period if it is clear from the individual circumstances that the factors justifying discretionary leave are likely to be short-lived.[2] Where the UK Competent Authority has conclusively identified the applicant as a victim of trafficking and the personal circumstances of the case are so compelling that a grant of leave is considered appropriate, discretionary leave will be granted for a minimum period of 12 months and 1 day and normally for no more than 30 months.[3] There may also be cases where a longer period of leave is considered appropriate, either because it is clearly in the best interests of a child and any countervailing considerations do not outweigh those best interests, or because there are other particularly exceptional or compelling reasons to grant leave for a longer period or immediate indefinite leave.[4] Discretionary leave is not normally subjected to active review and consequential curtailment during its currency but may be if an individual has demonstrated by their own actions that the reasons for which they were granted discretionary leave no longer persist: for example if their medical condition improves.[5] Discretionary leave should also be curtailed on any of the exclusion grounds applicable to humanitarian protection.[6] An application for further discretionary leave will be subject to 'active review' to determine whether the person still qualifies for discretionary leave.[7] Applications for settlement after ten years (see above) must be made on the appropriate form and will be subject to active review.[8] Any time spent in prison in connection with a criminal conviction will not count towards the ten years.[9]

1   API 'Discretionary leave', 19 May 2014, section 4, 'duration of grants of discretionary leave'.
2   API 'Discretionary leave', 19 May 2014, section 4.3.
3   API 'Discretionary leave', 19 May 2014, section 4.5. The minimum period is to enable the applicant to appeal under NIAA 2002, s 83 (see 12.166 above).
4   API 'Discretionary leave', 19 May 2014, section 4.4. The API gives examples and then states that in all cases the onus is on the applicant (or their representative) to provide evidence as to why it is in the best interests of the child to be granted a period of leave that is longer than the standard period of DL. See also **12.201** below for rule 353B cases.
5   API 'Discretionary leave', 19 May 2014, section 5.
6   API 'Discretionary leave' 19 May 2014, section 5.2: the API provides that separate action to vary DL will be required only where a decision to remove cannot be made or removal directions set, eg for Article 3, ECHR reasons).
7   API 'Discretionary leave', 19 May 2014, section 6.
8   API 'Discretionary leave', 19 May 2014, section 7.
9   API 'Discretionary leave', 19 May 2014, section 7.

12.201 In previous editions we referred to the general policy to grant leave in cases outstanding for more than seven years, and the backlog clearance policy announced in April 1999;[1] to the family concession of 24 October 2003; and to so called 'legacy cases' – broadly, those in which a claim for asylum was made prior to 5 March 2007 but had not been resolved by July 2011.[2] Following on from the 'legacy', the practice now is that where removal is no longer considered appropriate following consideration of the exceptional factors set out in immigration rule 353B,[3] 30 months discretionary leave should be granted, unless one of the following situations applies: where the UK Border Agency (as it was) made a written commitment that a case would be considered either before 20 July 2011 or before 9 July 2012, but failed to do so, and later decides that a grant is appropriate; or where the UK Border Agency (as it was) made a decision either before 20 July 2011 or before 9 July 2012 that a grant of leave on the grounds then listed in the relevant enforcement guidance[4] was not appropriate, but after that date carried out a reconsideration of that decision and, on the basis of the same evidence, decides that the earlier decision was wrong and leave should have been granted.[5] Where either scenario applies and the relevant date was before 20 July 2011, then indefinite leave to remain outside of the immigration rules should be granted; where the relevant date was on or after 20 July 2011 but before 9 July 2012, three years discretionary leave should be granted, with the person normally becoming eligible to apply for settlement after two periods of three years leave.[6]

1   See fifth edition at **12.189**.
2   See the eighth edition at **12.201** and see **12.125** above.
3   HC 395, para 353B, see **12.186** above. See also the factors militating against removal in '353B consideration cases' in chapter 53 of the Enforcement Instructions and Guidance (EIG).
4   *Ie* in chapter 53 of the EIG.
5   API 'Discretionary leave', 19 May 2014, section 4.2 under the heading 'exceptional circumstances'.
6   API 'Discretionary leave', 19 May 2014, section 4.2: the API explains that this is because prior to 20 July 2011 indefinite leave was normally granted to cases which met the exceptional circumstances in chapter 53 of the EIG and because between 20 July 2011 and 9 July 2012 the UK Border Agency granted three years DL in cases that met the exceptional circumstances in Chapter 53 of the EIG.

12.202 In deciding whether to grant leave to a refused asylum claimant, the Secretary of State is bound by the factual findings made by the tribunal after hearing evidence on the appeal, unless they are perverse or relate solely to country conditions which he or she is in as good a position to judge as the tribunal.[1] Thus in *Danaie*[2] the adjudicator had rejected an Iranian man's asylum appeal but had found the appellant to be an adulterer; this made him vulnerable to execution in Iran and the Court of Appeal held that the Secretary of State was bound by the finding.

[1] For cases on country conditions where the Secretary of State is not bound, see *R v Secretary of State for the Home Department, ex p Alakesan* [1997] Imm AR 315; *Elhasoglu v Secretary of State for the Home Department* [1997] Imm AR 380.
[2] *R v Secretary of State for the Home Department, ex p Danaie* [1998] Imm AR 84, [1998] INLR 124, CA. On the need for the Secretary of State to respect findings made on appeal, see also *R (on the application of Ivanuskiene) v Special Adjudicator* [2001] EWCA Civ 1271, [2002] INLR 1; *R (on the application of Saribal) v Secretary of State for the Home Department* [2002] EWHC 1542 (Admin), [2002] INLR 596; and *TB (Jamaica) v Secretary of State for the Home Department* [2008] EWCA Civ 977.

TRAVEL DOCUMENTS

12.203 A refugee is entitled to a Convention travel document as evidence of his or her status under the Refugee Convention[1] and the Immigration Rules now provide that such a document will be issued if the Secretary of State receives a completed application unless there are compelling reasons of national security or public order for not issuing a travel document.[2] The holder is entitled to re-admission to the country of refuge at any time during the validity of the document, so if the document is valid for more than two years, the two-year rule for returning residents cannot be applied to refuse readmission.[3] A travel document (or a 'Certificate of Travel') will be issued to a person granted humanitarian protection if the person is unable to obtain a national passport or, if the person can obtain a national passport, he or she can show that reasonable attempts have been made to obtain one and there are serious humanitarian reasons for travel.[4] In addition, if humanitarian protection was granted because of the person's fear of his or her national authorities, the person is not expected to obtain a national passport and will be issued with a travel document.[5] A person granted discretionary leave is normally expected to keep their national passport valid but may be issued with a Home Office Certificate of Travel if they show they have been formally and unreasonably refused a national passport or if it was accepted by the Home Office that the person has well-founded fear of their national authorities.[6] Neither a Convention travel document nor a Home Office Certificate of Travel is generally valid for the country of origin.[7]

[1] Refugee Convention, art 28 and Sch: see **12.103** above. The fee payable should not exceed the minimum payable for a national passport. From 6 April 2014, the fee payable for a Convention travel document is £69.00 (£46 for persons under 16): Immigration and Nationality (Cost Recovery Fees) Regulations 2014, SI 2014/581. Children cannot be named as dependants on the travel document of a parent or guardian but must hold their own travel document.
[2] HC 395, para 344A(i).
[3] *R v Secretary of State for the Home Department, ex p Shirreh* (CO 2194/1997) (15 August 1997, unreported), QBD (permission; the case was conceded by the Home Office).
[4] HC 395, para 344A(ii) and (iii). The fee for a certificate of travel, from 6 April 2014, is £246 (£157 for persons under 16): Immigration and Nationality (Cost Recovery Fees) Regulations 2014, SI 2014/581.

5   API 'Humanitarian protection', 15 May 2013, at section 9 under the heading 'Issuing of travel documents'.

6   API 'Discretionary leave', 19 May 2014, section 9 under the heading 'travel documents'. See fn 4 above regarding the fee payable.

7   See UKBA guidance notes accompanying the form for applying for such travel documents (available on the Home Office website).

FAMILY REUNION

12.204 The Refugee Convention does not incorporate family unity in the definition of the refugee, and family unity is not an obligation of the UK under the Convention, but the Final Act of the UN Conference on the Status of Refugees recommended governments to take the necessary measures for the protection of the refugee's family,[1] and the UK, in common with most other signatory states, makes provision for family reunion in its practices.[2] According to the UNHCR *Handbook* 'family' usually means spouse and unmarried dependent children,[3] unless special circumstances exist, such as recognition of a broader family unit in certain societies.[4] Since October 2000 the Immigration Rules have made provision for the admission of the pre-existing spouse and minor children (but not de facto adopted children[5]) of a refugee and that provision has been extended to cover a refugee's civil partner[6] and the unmarried partner or same sex partner of a person granted asylum on or after 9 October 2006.[7] The rules require that the sponsor of the family reunion application currently has refugee status or humanitarian protection.[8] A grant of leave as a dependant of a principal applicant is insufficient to sponsor an application under the refugee family reunion rules.[9] The rules require that the marriage, civil partnership, same sex or unmarried partnership commenced before the refugee left the country of his or her former habitual residence to seek asylum; the Tribunal has held that that requirement in respect of spouses can be satisfied even if the marriage took place in a third country to which the refugee fled from the country of feared persecution as long as the refugee was habitually resident in that third country.[10] The spouses, civil, same sex or unmarried partners must intend to live permanently together.[11] A person with limited leave to enter or remain as a refugee or with humanitarian protection may sponsor his or her post-flight spouse, civil, unmarried or same-sex partner or child on terms similar to those applicable to a non-refugee, settled sponsor.[12] Children under the age of 18 may join or remain with a parent granted asylum as long as the child is not leading an independent life, is unmarried and is not a civil partner and has not formed an independent family unit.[13] The child must have been part of the refugee's family unit before the refugee left the country of former habitual residence to seek asylum.[14] Whether a child was a member of the refugee's family unit is a question of fact and does not necessarily depend upon them ever having lived together.[15] The normal maintenance and accommodation criteria are not applied to them. Family members of refugees will be granted leave in line with the refugee sponsor but are not necessarily themselves recognised or admitted as refugees.[16] The spouse, civil, same-sex or unmarried partner and the child must show that they would not be excluded from protection by virtue of Article 1F of the Convention were they to apply for asylum themselves.[17] The rules provide that leave to enter on family reunion grounds is to be refused if the applicant does not have entry clearance in that capacity.[18]

1   The Final Act of the United Nations Conference of Plenipotentiaries on the Status of Refugees and Stateless Persons (set out in the UNHCR *Handbook*, Annex I). See *Abdi (Dhudi Saleban) v Secretary of State for the Home Department* [1996] Imm AR 148, disapproving *Ali* (10520), where the Tribunal had held that refugee family reunion was an obligation under the Refugee Convention and therefore within the rules (HC 395, para 327). The debate is no longer so important now that refugee family reunion has been brought within the Immigration Rules.

2   API 'Family Reunion', 5 July 2011, states that: The United Kingdom Border Agency recognises that families become fragmented because of the speed and manner in which a person seeking asylum has fled to the United Kingdom (UK), and because of the nature of conflict, war and persecution. Family reunion is intended to allow family members (that is, those who formed part of the family unit prior to the time that the sponsor fled to seek protection) to reunite with their sponsors who are recognised refugees or are benefiting from a grant of humanitarian protection (post 30th August 2005) and rebuild their lives in the UK.' 'Sponsor' means the individual who has been granted refugee status or humanitarian protection in the UK, and accordingly 'sponsors' the applicant to join them.

3   UNHCR *Handbook*, **12.13** above, Annex I.

4   See UNHCR *Handbook* above, para 185; Somali Family Reunion Policy, set out in [1993] Imm AR 40. The UNHCR has formulated a very broad definition including anyone in fact dependent on the principal: see 'Family Protection Issues', ExCom Sub-Committee 15th meeting, para 3, in (1999) 11(3) IJRL 582. See also ExCom Conclusion No 88 (1999) 'The Protection of the Refugee's Family', which calls on states to consider 'liberal criteria in identifying those family members who can be admitted, with a view to promoting a comprehensive reunification of the family'. API 'Family Reunion', 5 July 2011, lists 'eligible applicants' as spouse; civil partner; an unmarried/same sex partner providing that the parties have lived together in a relationship akin to either marriage or civil partnership for two years or more and the sponsor was granted asylum or humanitarian protection on or after 9 October 2006; a child under the age of 18, who is not leading an independent life, is unmarried and is not in a civil partnership and has not formed an independent family unit.

5   *AA (Somalia) v Entry Clearance Officer* [2013] UKSC 81, [2014] 1 WLR 43, [2014] 1 All ER 774, [2014] Imm AR 540; and *MK (Somalia) v Entry Clearance Officer* [2008] EWCA Civ 1453, [2008] All ER (D) 252 (Dec). De facto adopted children have to satisfy para 309A of the Rules which requires, inter alia, that they should have been living with the adoptive parents for at least 12 months immediately prior to making the entry clearance application – a condition that a refugee sponsored child will be unlikely to satisfy. See also API 'Family Reunion', 5 July 2011, under the heading 'ineligible applicants'.

6   HC 395, para 352A.

7   HC 395, para 352AA. The parties have to have been living together in a relationship akin to marriage or a civil partnership which has subsisted for two years or more and which existed before the person granted asylum left the country of former habitual residence in order to seek asylum.

8   The rules having been amended (by Cm 7944 on 1 October 2010) to reverse the effect of *ZN (Afghanistan) v Entry Clearance Officer* [2010] UKSC 21, [2010] 4 All ER 77, [2010] 1 WLR 1275 which had held that the historical fact of having been granted asylum meant that a sponsor who had become a British citizen satisfied the requirement of the rule.

9   *MS (Somalia) v Secretary of State for the Home Department* [2010] EWCA Civ 1236. See also API 'Family Reunion', 5 July 2011, under the heading 'ineligible sponsors'.

10 *A* (Somalia) [2004] UKIAT 00031.

11 HC 395, paras 352A(iv), 352AA(v).

12 By inclusion in HC 395 of paras 319L–319U, following *FH (Post-flight spouses) Iran* [2010] UKUT 275 (IAC).

13 HC 395, para 352D.

14 HC 395, para 352D(iv).

15 *BM (Colombia) (352D(iv); meaning of 'family unit')* [2007] UKAIT 00055 adopting a purposive construction of the rule having regard to the principle of refugee family unity.

16 API 'Family Reunion', 5 July 2011, under the heading 'Family reunion entitlements (leave not status)'. The API acknowledges that as the dependants of a refugee, they are eligible for certain things that the refugee is entitled to, for example access to public funds, and a Convention Travel Document subject to application form criteria and with the proviso that all Convention Travel Documents issued to successful family reunion applicants since 21 February 2011

should contain an endorsement making it clear that the holder cannot sponsor under the family reunion rules in their own right. See fn 9 above.

¹⁷ HC 395, para 352A(iii), 352AA (iv), 352D(v).

¹⁸ HC 395, para 352C, 352CA, 352F.

12.205 The Immigration Rules also make provision for a person granted humanitarian protection on or after 30 August 2005 to be joined by his or her spouse, civil partner or child[1] and to be joined by his or her unmarried or same sex partner if granted humanitarian protection on or after 9 October 2006.[2] The requirements to be satisfied mirror those for refugee family reunion described in the preceding paragraph. Other family members of persons with limited leave as refugees or with humanitarian protection, ie parents, grandparents and children, siblings, uncles and aunts over the age of 18 may be granted entry clearance or leave to enter or remain on similar terms to such family members of settled, non-refugee sponsors.[3] Family reunion for those with discretionary leave must normally await the settlement of the sponsor, which will generally take ten years.[4] All applicants for family reunion who are outside the UK must apply for entry clearance.[5] Refusal of entry clearance is an 'immigration decision' against which an appeal may be brought to the Tribunal.[6] There are legislative provisions which may result in exclusion of the right of appeal if the decision is taken on particular grounds, including that the applicant for entry clearance does not satisfy a requirement of the rules as to age, nationality or citizenship; does not have an immigration document (eg a passport); is seeking to be in the UK for a longer period than permitted by the rules or for a purpose other than one for which entry is permitted in accordance with the rules.[7] However, those provisions do not prevent the bringing of an appeal on human rights or race discrimination grounds.[8] The Immigration Rules also allow for in country applications[9] and if refused whether there is a right of appeal or not will depend on whether the application was made at a time when the applicant had current leave and whether refusal is accompanied by an immigration decision.[10] See further the chapters on appeals and human rights.

[1] HC 395, para 352FA and 352FG (inserted by HC 28, 7 November 2007).

[2] HC 395, para 352FD (inserted by HC 28, 7 November 2007).

[3] HC 395, paras 319V–319Y, as inserted by HC 1148 from 13 June 2011.

[4] See **12.200** above. The dependants of those with discretionary leave to remain may not seek entry as dependants of those in the UK with a view to settlement under Appendix FM or para 301 of the rules; 'settled' in the context of the rules means 'settled under the rules': *R (on the application of Acan) v Immigration Appeal Tribunal* [2004] EWHC 297 (Admin), [2004] All ER (D) 193 (Feb).

[5] API 'Family Reunion', 5 July 2011, section 3.1. The best known concessionary policy, the Somali Family Reunion Policy, enabled sponsors to apply informally to the Home Office in the UK, who would indicate how a formal application would be decided by the ECO. It was withdrawn in 1996. A similar concession allowed Vietnamese nationals who were refugees in the UK to apply direct to the Home Office by letter for relatives in Vietnam to join them. This concession was withdrawn on 1 November 1999. See API Aug 00, Ch 6, s 2, para 4.

[6] NIAA 2002, s 82(1) and (2)(b).

[7] NIAA 2002, s 88.

[8] NIAA 2002, s 88(4).

[9] HC 395, paras 352A-352FJ. See API 'Family Reunion', 5 July 2011, section 3.2. The API explains that these applications are non-charged and how they should be made.

[10] API 'Family Reunion', 5 July 2011, section 3.6.1.

Chapter 13

VICTIMS OF TRAFFICKING IN HUMAN BEINGS

INTRODUCTION

13.1 The Lord Chief Justice said of trafficking that:

'this vile trade in people has different manifestations. Women and children, usually girls, are trafficked into prostitution: others, usually teenage boys, but sometimes young adults, are trafficked into cannabis farming: yet others are trafficked to commit a wide range of further offences. Sometimes they are trafficked into this country from the other side of the world: sometimes they enter into this country unlawfully and are trafficked after their arrival: sometimes they are trafficked within the towns or cities in this country where they live. Whether trafficked from home or overseas, they are all victims of crime. That is how they must be treated'[1].

13.1 Victims of Trafficking in Human Beings

A person may be trafficked within his or her own country; there need be no border crossing. On the other hand, smuggling migrants across borders is not trafficking unless the purpose of doing so is exploitation rather than just obtaining a financial or other benefit[2].

[1] *L v R The Children's Commissioner for England and Equality and Human Rights Commission intervening* [2013] EWCA Crim 991, [2014] 1 All ER 113, [2013] 2 Cr App Rep 247.
[2] *R (on the application of AA (Iraq)) v Secretary of State for the Home Department* [2012] EWCA Civ 23, (2012) Times, 05 March.

13.2 A person's status as a victim of trafficking or a risk that the person may be trafficked in the future are of potential relevance in the context of immigration decision making in ways that include the following:

(i) a risk of being trafficked may give rise to protection obligations under the refugee convention, the Qualification Directive and the ECHR;

(ii) if there are reasonable grounds to believe a person to be a victim of trafficking, there is an obligation not to remove the person until the 'identification process' as a victim of trafficking has been completed[1] and to allow the person a 'recovery and reflection period of at least 30 days' during which he or she will not be removed[2];

(iii) an obligation to issue a residence permit to a victim of trafficking if the competent authority 'considers that their stay is necessary owing to their personal situation'[3] or 'for the purposes of their cooperation in investigation or criminal proceedings'[4];

(iv) removal of a victim of trafficking from the UK is to be done 'with due regard for the rights, safety and dignity' of the victim of trafficking 'and for the status of any legal proceedings related to the fact that the person is a victim.'[5];

(v) the automatic deportation provisions (ie the irrebuttable presumption that deportation of a 'foreign criminal' is conducive to the public good and the statutory obligation to deport a foreign criminal) do not apply if 'the Secretary of State thinks' that they would contravene the UK's obligations under the Council of Europe Convention on Action against Trafficking in Human Beings, 2005[6];

(vi) victims of trafficking are 'normally considered suitable for detention in only very exceptional circumstances'[7].

[1] Council of Europe Convention on Action against Trafficking in Human Beings, 2005, art 10(2), hereafter 'ECAT'.
[2] ECAT, art.13(1) – the UK's present policy is to grant 45 days.
[3] ECAT, art.14(1)(a).
[4] ECAT, art 14 (1)(b).
[5] ECAT, art 16(2).
[6] UK Borders Act 2007, ss 32 and 33 (6A).
[7] UKVI Enforcement Instructions and Guidance, chapter 55.10.

Trafficking Texts

13.3 The international and regional instruments that are relevant to human trafficking include:

- The UN Protocol to Prevent, Suppress and Punish Trafficking in Persons, especially Women and Children ('the Palermo Protocol') to the UN Convention against Transnational Organised Crime. The Palermo Protocol entered into force on 25 December 2003.
- The Council of Europe Convention on Action against Trafficking in Human Beings ('ECAT') which was signed on the 23 March 2008 and ratified on the 17 December 2008 by the UK.
- Directive 2011/36/EU of the European Parliament and of the Council of 5 April 2011 on preventing and combating trafficking in human beings and protecting its victims, and replacing Council Framework Decision 2002/629/ JHA ('the Trafficking Directive'). The UK decided to opt in to the Directive in July 2011. This was accepted by the European Commission in October 2011. The transposition date was 6 April 2013.
- The European Convention on Human Rights, in particular Article 4.
- The Charter of Fundamental Rights of the European Union, Article 5(3) of which provides that 'Trafficking in human beings is prohibited'.
- Various Anti Slavery Conventions and ILO Conventions.

13.4 In respect of the various international and European anti-trafficking instruments the UK's government has made a number of statements to the public at large, to Parliament and in departmental instructions and policy guidance indicating its intention to be bound by ECAT obligations, to implement and apply its provisions intended to make the United Kingdom 'a hostile environment for traffickers' and to protect victims of trafficking.[1] Similar statements have been made in respect of the Modern Slavery Bill currently before the Commons. The status and application of ECAT was altered when the European Court of Human Rights concluded that trafficking itself, within the meaning of Article 3(a) of the Palermo Protocol and Article 4(a) of ECAT, falls within the scope of Article 4 of the Convention.[2]

[1] See for example: written statement to Parliament on 24 March 2009, the Parliamentary Under-Secretary of State, Ministry of Justice (Lord Bach), 24 Mar 2009: Column WS40; The Explanatory Statement to the CAT CM 7465 (at [15–17].
[2] *Rantsev v Cyprus and Russia* (Application 25965/04) [2010] ECHR 22, 51 EHRR 1, para 282, 288, 317.

THE DEFINITION OF TRAFFICKING IN HUMAN BEINGS

Overview of definition

13.5 Trafficking is not defined in UK legislation. 'The accepted international definition of trafficking'[1] is contained in Article 3 of the Palermo Protocol[2]. A materially identical definition appears in the Council of Europe Convention on Action against Trafficking in Human Beings ('ECAT'), Article 4 and a similar definition is contained in the EU Trafficking Directive[3]. The Palermo Protocol and ECAT definition is applied both by public authorities[4] and domestic courts when assessing and determining whether an individual is a victim of trafficking in human beings. The definition distinguishes between adult and child victims of trafficking in recognition of the particular vulnerability of children to the crime of human trafficking[5].

[1] *Hounga v Allen* [2014] UKSC 47, para 47.

² Directive 2011/36/EU of the European Parliament and of the Council of 5 April 2011 on preventing and combating trafficking in human beings and protecting its victims, and replacing Council Framework Decision 2002/629/ JHA ('the Trafficking Directive'), art 2. There are two main differences between the Palermo Protocol and the EU Trafficking Directive's definition. The first is the expansion in the Directive of the non-exhaustive list of what constitutes exploitation so as to include 'the exploitation of criminal activities' and thereby to reflect current known trends of trafficking. The second is that the Directive provides a definition of 'a position of vulnerability'.

³ Protocol to prevent, suppress and punish Trafficking in Persons, especially Women and Children, supplementing the UN Convention against transnational organised Crime.

⁴ Home Office: Victims of human trafficking for frontline staff, 21.1.2013; Home Office: Victims of human trafficking – competent authority guidance, 24.10.2013.

⁵ See for example *L v R, The Children's Commisioner for England and Equality and Human Rights Commission intervening* [2013] EWCA Crim 991, [2014] 1 All ER 113, [2013] 2 Cr App Rep 247, *Hounga v Allen* [2014] UKSC 47; *R (on the application of AA (Iraq)) v Secretary of State for the Home Department* [2012] EWCA Civ 23, (2012) Times, 05 March.

13.6 Children are defined as those under the age of 18 years old: Palermo Protocol, Article 3(d); ECAT, Article 4(d); Trafficking Directive, Article 2(6). The Trafficking Directive refers in the preamble at [8]; [12]; [19]; [22]; [23]; [24]; [25] and in Articles 2, 13, 14, 15 and 16 to the special status of child victims, in particular where the children are separated children. 'An important source of vulnerability for children lies in their lack of full agency – in fact and under law. A lack of agency is often made worse by the absence of a parent or legal guardian who is able to act in the child's best interests. Such absence is typical: Child victims of trafficking are generally 'unaccompanied', with deliberate separation from parents or guardians being a strategy to facilitate exploitation. In some cases, parents or other authority figures are complicit in the trafficking.'[1]

¹ As noted by Anne T Gallagher in *The International Law of Human Trafficking* (2010) Cambridge University Press p 324.

13.7 The definition of trafficking has three constituent elements:

(i)   The Act (what is done) – recruitment, transportation, transfer, harbouring or receipt of persons;

(ii) The Means (how it is done) – threat or use of force, coercion, abduction, fraud, deception, abuse of power or vulnerability, or giving or receiving payments or benefits to a person to achieve the consent of another person with control of the victim;

(iii) The Purpose (why it is done) – for the purpose of exploitation, which includes exploiting the prostitution of others, sexual exploitation, forced labour or services, including slavery or practices similar to slavery, the exploitation of criminal activities, or the removal of organs.

When applying the terms of the definition to a particular case a gender sensitive,[1] human rights, child rights and labour rights perspective is to be adopted.[2] An adult would need to establish that all three components of the definition are present together but a child is only required to establish that an act was undertaken for the purpose of exploitation to meet the requirements of the definition.[3] The consent of a victim to exploitation is always irrelevant where any of the means have been established.[4] An important principle in the trafficking definition is that a child can never consent to his or her own exploitation.[5] A person who is or has been the subject of trafficking as defined, has the status of being a victim of trafficking; there is no further requirement for attainment or retention of that status that the person should continue to be in a situation of trafficking or subject to the influence of traffickers or in need of assistance or protection under the Trafficking Convention and Home Office policy that had distinguished between 'victims of trafficking' and 'historical victims' was unlawful.[6]

1   See Directive 2011/36/EU of the European Parliament and of the Council of 5 April 2011 on preventing and combating trafficking in human beings and protecting its victims, and replacing Council Framework Decision 2002/629/ JHA ('the Trafficking Directive'), Article 1 and the 'Joint UN commentary on the EU Directive – A Human Rights-Based Approach' (2011), p 30.
2   'Joint UN commentary on the EU Directive – A Human Rights-Based Approach' (2011).
3   EU Trafficking Directive at Article 2(5) and ECAT at Art 4(c).
4   ECAT art 4(b), Trafficking Directive art 2(4).
5   EU Trafficking Directive at arts 2(4) and 2(5) and ECAT at Arts 4(b) and (c).
6   *R (on the application of Atamewan) v Secretary of State for the Home Department* [2013] EWHC 2727 (Admin).

The Act

13.8 The acts provided for in the definition are intended to bring within the definition of human trafficking the conduct not just of recruiters, brokers and transporters but also owners and managers, supervisors, and controllers of any place of exploitation such as a brothel, farm, boat, factory, medical facility, or household.

Recruitment is to be understood in a broad sense, meaning any activity leading from the commitment or engagement of another individual to his or her exploitation. It is not confined to the use of certain means. The definition's reference to recruitment, covers recruitment by whatever method (oral, through the press or via the internet). It would include recruitment through a recruitment agency or a middle person.[1]

1   'Council of Europe Convention on Action against Trafficking in Human Beings: Explanatory Report', paragraph 79. Council of Europe and United Nations, 'Trafficking in Organs, Tissues and Cells and Trafficking in Human Beings for the Purpose of the Removal of Organs' (2009). The Office of the Special Representative and Co-ordinator for Combating Trafficking in Human Beings, in its report 'Unprotected Work, Invisible Exploitation: Trafficking for the Purpose of Domestic Servitude' at 17 recognised in its typology of domestic servitude cases that most of the trafficked migrant workers were recruited via placement agencies.

13.9 *Transportation* is also a general term and does not specify any particular means or kinds of transportation. The act of transporting someone from one place to another is sufficient to constitute this element. It is not necessary for the victim to have crossed any borders,[1] nor is it necessary for the victim to be present illegally in a state's territory.[2]

1   Council of Europe and United Nations, 'Trafficking in Organs, Tissues and Cells and Trafficking in Human Beings for the Purpose of the Removal of Organs' (2009). Article 2 of ECAT.
2   Paragraph 80 of ECAT Explanatory Note.

13.10 *Transfer* includes any kind of handing over or transmission of a person to another person. This is particularly important in certain cultural environments where control over individuals (usually family members) may be handed over to other persons. As the term and scope of this element is broad, the explicit or implied offering of a person for transfer is sufficient; the offer does not have to be accepted for this ingredient of the definition to be satisfied.[1]

[1] Council of Europe and United Nations, Trafficking in Organs, Tissues and Cells and Trafficking in Human Beings for the Purpose of the Removal of Organs (2009). *The International Law of Human Trafficking* (2010) Cambridge University Press, Anne T Gallagher, p 30.

13.11 *Harbouring* means accommodating or housing persons in whatever way, whether during their journey to their final destination or at the place of exploitation.[1]

[1] Council of Europe and United Nations, Trafficking in Organs, Tissues and Cells and Trafficking in Human Beings for the Purpose of the Removal of Organs (2009). *The International Law of Human Trafficking* (2010) Cambridge University Press, Anne T Gallagher, p 30.

13.12 *Receipt of persons* is not limited to receiving the persons at the place of exploitation but includes meeting victims at agreed places on their journey to give them further information or instructions as to where to go or what to do.[1]

[1] Council of Europe and United Nations, Trafficking in Organs, Tissues and Cells and Trafficking in Human Beings for the Purpose of the Removal of Organs (2009). The *International Law of Human Trafficking*, Anne T Gallagher, p 30.

The Means

13.13 Where any of the means referred to in the definition have been used to secure the consent of a victim, the victim's consent is deemed irrelevant.[1] The definition may be satisfied if the 'means' element is used to accomplish the 'act' or the exploitation.[2]

[1] The Council of Europe Convention on Action against Trafficking in Human Beings, Article 4(b); Directive 2011/36/EU of the European Parliament and of the Council of 5 April 2011 on preventing and combating trafficking in human beings and protecting its victims, and replacing Council Framework Decision 2002/629/ JHA, Article 1(4).
[2] Anne T Gallagher, *The International Law of Human Trafficking* (2010) Cambridge University Press, at p 45.

13.14 *Coercion* can be physical or psychological coercion. The Home Office's guidance, notes that physical coercion refers to the threat or use of force against the victim of trafficking or against the victim's family members but that it may also entail more subtle measures of control such as withholding travel or immigration documents[1]. The Home Office guidance gives as examples of psychological coercion: blackmail; ritual oaths; forcing someone to pay an excessive amount of money for substandard accommodation; making significant deductions from an individual's 'salary'; threats of rejection from, or disapproval by a peer group or family or anger or displeasure from the person considered by the victim to be his or her partner; grooming and 'Stockholm syndrome where, due to unequal power, victims create a false emotional or psychological attachment to their controller'.[2] It has been argued that severe economic pressures may constitute psychological coercion.[3] In the context of domestic servitude, the European Court of Human Rights has emphasised that 'a complex set of dynamics, involving both overt and more subtle forms of coercion, to force compliance' may be in play and that investigating such conduct 'requires an understanding of the many subtle ways an individual can fall under the control of another'[4]. They can include retention of the victim's passport and wages and manipulation of his or her fears arising from unlawful or insecure immigration status and implicit or explicit threats of denunciation to the police and deportation[5]. Debt bondage also falls within this means element as a form of 'economic coercion' and is a common 'means' and exploitative practice prevalent in labour trafficking in the UK.[6] Debt bondage is when a person's labour is demanded as a means of repayment for a loan and the value of the labour is not reasonably applied toward the debt or the debt is otherwise continuously inflated[7]. It can occur where an excessive amount is charged for substandard accommodation or significant deductions are made from an individual's 'salary'. Even where a set payment schedule is agreed to and repaid by the victim, the imposition of such a debt is illegal.[8] Evidence shows that debt bondage in itself can be strong enough to ensure that people comply with instructions from traffickers without being physically attacked or confined.[9]

1 Home Office: 'Victims of human trafficking – competent authority guidance', 24.10.2013, p 14

2 Home Office: 'Victims of human trafficking – competent authority guidance', 24.10.2013, p 14f.

3 L A Malone, 'Economic Hardship as Coercion Under the Protocol on International Trafficking in Persons by Organised Crime Elements,' (2001) 25 Fordham International Law Journal 54, at 55.

4 *CN v United Kingdom* (2013) 56 EHRR 24, para 80.

5 *CN v United Kingdom* 2013) 56 EHRR 24, para 80; *CN v France* (Application 67724/09, unreported, para 92 and *Siliadin v France* (Application 73316/01)(2005) 43 EHRR 287, 20 BHRC 654. Forms of coercion used in cases of trafficked domestic workers are identified in the Office of the Special Representative and Co-ordinator for Combating Trafficking in Human Beings, 'Trafficking in Human Beings Amounting to Torture and other Forms of ill-treatment', 2013, at page 22.

6 'Trafficking for Forced Labour in the UK' (2006) Anti Slavery International.

7 Working under a debt bond is a 'slavery-like practice' – see Supplementary Convention on the Abolition of Slavery, the Slave Trade and Practices Similar to Slavery, 1956 Article 1(a).

8 Office of the Special Representative and Co-ordinator for Combating Trafficking in Human Beings, 'Trafficking in Human Beings Amounting to Torture and other Forms of ill-treatment', 2013, at page 54. Debt Bondage is a strong indicator of forced labour as well as being a 'means' to bring victims into an exploitative situation. In the *OSCE Resource Police Training Guide: Trafficking in Human Beings, Publication Series Vol.12, at* 66, it states in respect of forced labour, 'When there is a disparity of income and the labour conditions between the country of origin of the potential victim and the country of destination where they are working. Victims of human trafficking cannot consent to exploitation and they must be treated in the same manner as if they were nationals of the State in which they are working.

9 Office of the Special Representative and Co-ordinator for Combating Trafficking in Human Beings, 'Trafficking in Human Beings Amounting to Torture and other Forms of ill-treatment', 2013, at page 55.

13.15 *Deception and fraud* are examples of less direct means and will generally relate to the nature of the promised work or service and the conditions under which an individual is to undertake or perform a service.[1] For example, an individual may be recruited to work in the sex industry but on the basis of false, inaccurate or misleading information about the conditions of her work.[2]

1 UNODC 'Abuse of a position of vulnerability and other "means" within the definition of trafficking in persons', 2012 at 21[2].

[2] Home Office 'Victims of human trafficking – competent authority guidance', 24.10.2013, p 12.

13.16 *Abuse of power or of a position of vulnerability.* The abuse of a position of vulnerability 'may be of any kind, whether physical, psychological, emotional, family-related, social or economic. The situation might, for example, involve insecurity or illegality of the victim's immigration status, economic dependence or fragile health. In short, the situation can be any state of hardship in which a human being is impelled to accept being exploited. Persons abusing such a situation flagrantly infringe human rights and violate human dignity and integrity, which no one can validly renounce.'[1] The Trafficking Directive defines a position of vulnerability as 'a situation in which the person concerned has no real or acceptable alternative but to submit to the abuse involved.'[2] The various indicators of abuse of power or a position of vulnerability identified by international bodies[3] and the European Court of Human Rights[4] focus on the person's precarious financial, psychological, and social situation, illegal or precarious immigration status and on linguistic, physical, and social isolation of the victim.[5] A victim's poverty in his or her country of origin may constitute personal circumstances of which a trafficker may take advantage to secure the victim's consent to being exploited in the UK.[6] In the Netherlands, the Supreme Court gave guidance on the concept of 'abuse of a vulnerable position', concerning six irregular migrants who, desperate for work and afraid of being discovered by authorities, approached a Chinese restaurant owner for work. They were provided with accommodation and work that paid well below the minimum wage. The Supreme Court disagreed with the lower courts that the perpetrator must 'intentionally abuse' the vulnerable position of the victims. The Court held that 'conditional intent' is sufficient: it was enough that the perpetrator was aware of the state of affairs that must be assumed to give rise to power or a vulnerable position.[7]

[1] Council of Europe Convention on Action against Trafficking in Human Beings: Explanatory Report, para 83.

[2] Directive 2011/36/EU of the European Parliament and of the Council of 5 April 2011 on preventing and combating trafficking in human beings and protecting its victims, and replacing Council Framework Decision 2002/629/ JHA, art 2(2). The Trafficking Directive generally reproduces the definition of trafficking set out in the Palermo Protocol. It adopts the language of the Trafficking in Persons Protocol's Interpretative note in defining 'position of vulnerability' as 'a situation in which the person concerned has no real or acceptable alternative but to submit to the abuse involved' (Article 2(2)). However, it is important to note a significant difference. Whereas the Interpretative Note refers to 'real and acceptable alternative' appearing to require that both elements be satisfied the Trafficking Directive requires only that the alternative be 'real' or 'acceptable'.

[3] For example International Labour Office 'Operational Indicators of Trafficking in Human Beings' (revised edition, September 2009).

[4] Eg *Siliadin v France* (2005) 43 EHRR 287, para 118-129.

[5] The UN Office on Drugs and Crime (UNODC) Model Trafficking Law, released in 2009, suggests that a focus on the state of mind of the perpetrator, rather than that of the victim, could be more protective of the victims (see discussion in Anne T Gallagher, *The International Law of Human Trafficking*, (2010) Cambridge University Press, at 33). Further guidance on this term is found in the UNODC Issue Paper: *Abuse of a position of vulnerability and other 'means' within the definition of trafficking in persons* (2013), as drafted by Dr Anne Gallagher.

[6] *A-G's Reference (Nos 37, 38 and 65 of 2010), R v Khan (Raza Ali)* [2010] EWCA Crim 2880, [2011] Crim LR 336, para 18.

[7] Supreme Court, 27 October 2009, LJN: B17099408. See also: L van Krimpen, 'The interpretation and implementation of labour exploitation in Dutch Case Law', in C Rijken (ed), 'Combating Human Trafficking for Labour Exploitation', 2011, p 498.

13.17 *The giving or receiving of payments or benefits to achieve the consent of a person having control over another person*: This term is opaque and there is little guidance on its meaning. It may extend beyond the situation in which legal control is exercised by one individual over another (for example, a parent over a child) to include de facto control (such as that which may be exercised by an employer over an employee). Presumably it is intended to bring within the definition practices such as payments made to parents in the course of child trafficking, but as the means element is redundant in child cases, the scope of this element remains unclear.[1]

[1] Anne T Gallagher, *The International Law of Human Trafficking* (2010) Cambridge University Press, p 33.

For the purpose of exploitation

13.18 This ingredient of the definition does not require that the intended exploitation actually takes place; a situation of trafficking can arise in the case of an adult victim subjected to an act by one of the means for the specified purpose of exploitation[1] and for a child victim that they were subjected to an act for the purpose of exploitation. The intention to exploit can be that of any of the individuals involved in either the act or the means so it may be that of a final exploiter (eg the brothel owner or factory manager) or it may be that of a recruiter or a broker.[2] The trafficking instruments do not define exploitation. Instead they provide an open-ended list which includes as a minimum the following:

(i) *Forced labour or services, slavery or servitude*[3];

(ii) *Exploitation of the prostitution of others*: This has been interpreted to cover any acts to obtain profit from prostitution such as pimping[4] and 'the unlawful obtaining of financial or other material benefit from the prostitution of another person'.[5]

(iii) *Other forms of sexual exploitation*: This term has been defined as 'any actual or attempted abuse of a position of vulnerability, differential power or trust, for sexual purposes, including but not limited to, profiting monetarily, socially or politically from the sexual exploitation of another'[6]. Forced, child and servile marriages have been identified as a form of sexual exploitation[7]. The inclusion of servile marriage as a form of sexual exploitation shows that receiving or intending to receive sexual gratification from an individual constitutes such exploitation where the individual's consent is ineffective because one of the means contained in the trafficking definition has been used.

(iv) *Practices similar to slavery*: This term is adopted from the 1956 Supplementary Convention on the Abolition of Slavery, the Slave Trade and Institutions and Practices similar to Slavery. This Convention defined the following as practices similar to slavery: debt bondage, serfdom, servile or forced marriage[8] and exploitation of children;[9]

(v) Exploitation for criminal activities: This should be understood as the exploitation of a person to commit, inter alia, pick-pocketing, shop-lifting, drug trafficking and other similar activities which are subject to penalties and imply financial gain.[10]

1   Council of Europe, Explanatory Report on the Convention on Action against Trafficking in
    Human Beings, ETS 197, 16.V.2005 at paragraph 87.
2   Anne T Gallagher, *The International Law of Human Trafficking* (2010) Cambridge University
    Press, p 33.
3   The terms 'forced labour', 'slavery' and 'servitude' should be interpreted consistently with
    other international instruments. This assumption is supported by the saving clauses in the
    Palermo Protocol (Article 14) and the Council of Europe Convention on Action against
    Trafficking (Article 40) which affirm their consistency with existing rights, obligations and
    responsibilities under international law and in the case of ECAT, its consistency with the
    Palermo Protocol (Article 39).
4   Working Group on Trafficking in Persons, 'Analysis of Key Concepts of the Trafficking in
    Persons Protocol' (9 December 2009) CTOC/COP/WG.4/2010/2 para 9-12.
5   United Nations Office on Drugs and Crime 'Model Law against Trafficking in Persons', at 13.
6   United Nations Secretary-General's Bulletin: 'Special Measures for Protection from Sexual
    Exploitation and Sexual Abuse,' UN Doc. ST/SGB/2003/13, Oct.9 2003. For further discus-
    sion see Anne T Gallagher, *The International Law of Human Trafficking* (2010) Cambridge
    University Press, at p 39.
7   Forum on Marriage and the Rights of Women and Girls (2001). *Early Marriage: Sexual
    Exploitation and the Human Rights of Girls. UK: Forum on Marriage and the Rights of
    Women and Girls.* ECPAT UK: Stolen Futures: Trafficking for Forced Child Marriage in the
    UK at 20.
8   See Joint UN Commentary on the EU Directive – A Human Rights Based Approach at p 104.
    Forced Marriage is defined in the UK in the Forced Marriage Act 2007 amending the Family
    Law Act 1996 as: 'A person ('A') is forced into a marriage if another person ('B') forces A to
    enter into a marriage (whether with B or another person) without A's free and full consent. It
    does not matter whether the conduct of B which forces A to enter into the marriage is directed
    against A, B or another person.' Force is defined to include coercion by threats or other
    psychological means. These marriages as well as being forms of sexual exploitation are also
    recognised as forms of domestic servitude – ECPAT UK, 'Stolen Futures: Trafficking for
    Forced Child Marriage in the UK' p 20 and OSCE 'Unprotected Work, Invisible Exploitation:
    Trafficking for the Purpose of Domestic Servitude', p 44.
9   'Any institution or practice whereby a child or young person under the age of 18 years, is
    delivered by either or both of his natural parents, or by his guardian, to another person,
    whether for reward or not, *with a view to the exploitation of the child or young person or of
    his labour'.* Supplementary Convention on the Abolition of Slavery, the Slave Trade and
    Institutions and Practices similar to Slavery 1956, Article 1(d), (emphasis added).
10 This was included in the EU Trafficking Directive, art 2(3) and at preamble (11) of the
    Trafficking Directive.

Exploitation of children

13.19 The European Commission has stated that child exploitation includes: procuring or offering a child for illicit or criminal activities (including the trafficking or production of drugs and begging); using children in armed conflict; using children for work that by its nature or the circumstances in which it is carried out is likely to harm the health and safety of children; the employment or use of a child who has not yet reached the applicable working age; other forms of exploitation; and illegal adoption.[1] The UN Convention on the Rights of the Child (CRC) and its Optional Protocol provide a comprehensive framework for the protection of the rights and dignity of children and it should be considered, in its entirety, as a tool for understanding and responding to the trafficking and related exploitation of children. Whilst the CRC does not make express reference to child trafficking the Committee on the Rights of the Child has regularly raised and pronounced on trafficking-related issues in its concluding observations and found trafficking and child prostitution to directly implicate Articles 34 and 35.[2] The Optional Protocol refers to trafficking in its preamble and Article 2 of the Optional Protocol, defines the sale of children sufficiently broadly to encompass most child trafficking situations.

[1] European Commission – DG Justice, Freedom and Security (JLS). Recommendations on Identification and Referral to Services of Victims of Trafficking in Human Beings, Brussels, 2007, p 5. This echoes the definitions found in the ILO's International Programme on the Elimination of Child Labour (IPEC) in its operations, which incorporated The ILO Convention to Eliminate the Worst Forms of Child Labour (June 1999) (ILO Convention No 182), defining (Article 3) the worst forms of child labour to be prohibited as illustrations of exploitation of children in the context of child trafficking. Articles 32 and 33 of the UN Convention on Rights of a Child 1989 also recognise this form of child exploitation.

[2] For further discussion see Anne T Gallagher, *The International Law of Human Trafficking* (2010) Cambridge University Press, p 66.

DETERMINATION OF THE STATUS OF A VICTIM OF TRAFFICKING

A positive obligation to identify a victim of trafficking

13.20 The purposes of the Palermo Protocol, ECAT and the Trafficking Directive are threefold: they are preventing trafficking, protecting victims and promoting international cooperation.[1] The principal obligations in ECAT and the Trafficking Directive in relation to the protection of victims of trafficking are:

(1)   to identify victims of trafficking, providing trained staff to do so and ensuring collaboration between different authorities to facilitate identification[2];

(2)   once a prima facie victim of trafficking has been identified (termed a reasonable grounds decision) the victim is not to be removed from the territory until the identification is complete[3];

(3)   to provide assistance for victims[4];

(4)   to provide a 'reflection and recovery period' during the two stages of the identification process during which the person may not be expelled[5];

(5)   to issue a residence permit to identified victims of trafficking in circumstances where their stay is necessary owing to their personal situation or to cooperate with the authorities in a criminal investigation or prosecution[6];

(6)   to provide legal assistance and access to compensation for victims.[7]

[1] Protocol to Prevent, Suppress and Punish Trafficking in Persons, especially Women and Children, supplementing the United Nations Convention against transnational organised Crime ('the Palermo Protocol'), Article 2; the Council of Europe Convention on Action against Trafficking in Human Beings ('ECAT'), Article 1 and Directive 2011/36/EU of the European Parliament and of the Council of 5 April 2011 on preventing and combating trafficking in human beings and protecting its victims, and replacing Council Framework Decision 2002/629/ JHA, Article 1.

[2] ECAT, Art 10; Trafficking Directive, Article 11(4).

[3] ECAT, Art 10(2).

[4] ECAT, Art 12; art 11(5) of the Trafficking Directive.

[5] ECAT, Art 13.

[6] ECAT, Art 14.

[7] ECAT, art 15; Art 17 of the Trafficking Directive.

13.21 A central principle implicit in the Council of Europe Convention on Action against Trafficking in Human Beings and spelled out in the Trafficking Directive is that there is no obligation on the victim to identify her or himself as a victim of trafficking at any stage in order to trigger the positive obligations or protections of ECAT or the Trafficking Directive.[1] That is consistent with the existence of a procedural obligation under the European Convention on Human Rights, Article 4 which does not depend upon the making of a complaint by the victim, to investigate a situation of potential trafficking.[2] The identification process should be independent of any criminal proceedings against the traffickers and a criminal conviction is not necessary for either starting or completing the identification process.[3] Victims of human trafficking rarely do self-identify either because trafficking is not a concept known to them or they fear that by self-identifying they would put themselves or their families at risk.[4] The Government's own guidance is explicit, that self-identification is neither required nor (in many cases) likely.[5] It recognises that a potential victim of trafficking is a potential victim of crime and requires that all credible allegations must be referred to either the local police force or a Home Office criminal and financial investigations team.[6] It is of note that UKVI continues to struggle with the concept that there is a freestanding duty to investigate under Article 4 ECHR and therefore requires that proactive measures are taken to identify victims irrespective of referral into the NRM.

[1]   Directive 2011/36/EU of the European Parliament and of the Council of 5 April 2011 on preventing and combating trafficking in human beings and protecting its victims, and replacing Council Framework Decision 2002/629/ JHA, 'the Trafficking Directive', art 9(1) and preamble recital (15)

[2]   *Rantsev v Cyprus and Russia* (2010) 51 EHRR 1, para 288 and *OOO v Comr of Police for the Metropolis* [2011] EWHC 1246 (QB), [2011] UKHRR 767.

[3]   Explanatory report to the Council of Europe Convention on Action against Trafficking in Human Beings, para 134.

[4]   Victims of human trafficking – competent authority guidance, 24 October 2013 at pages 66-67. The Home Office Action Plan (March 2007) states (p 48):

   '. . . For many reasons the reporting of these crimes by victims is extremely rare. Some victims may be unwilling to identify themselves because they . . . may fear that they will be penalized for their immigration status . . . [or they] . . . may have a distrust of the authorities due to past negative experiences . . . .'.

[5]   Victims of human trafficking – competent authority guidance, 24 October 2013.

[6]   Ibid page 37. In Scotland, additionally the case can be referred to the National Human Trafficking Unit.

National Referral Mechanism ('NRM')

13.22 The identification mechanism in place in the UK for potential victims of trafficking is the National Referral Mechanism ('NRM').[1] While adults are referred to the NRM process only with their consent, potential child victims of trafficking are referred without the need for the child's consent – in accordance with child protection procedures. Member States are required to adopt an identification process and procedures which are both gender specific and where the potential victim is a child, child specific.[2]

[1]   The UK has the most formalised identification structure of all the Council of Europe countries which have ratified the ECAT; this has led to both positive and negative developments as a consequence.

[2]   The UN Joint Commentary on the EU Trafficking Directive at p 50 notes that most NRM processes are gender neutral and as such lack the ability to develop a gender-sensitive response

capacity as well as gender-specific mechanisms and tools to address effectively what is now acknowledged to be a highly gendered phenomenon. This is apparent in the underdeveloped experience of providing support and assistance to boys and male victims of trafficking.

First Responders

13.23 Consideration of an individual by the NRM for identification as a victim of trafficking depends upon the individual being referred by a 'first responder'. These are (currently):

- Local Authorities Children Services and designated persons within Safeguard Children Boards (for children).
- Health and Social Care Trusts (HSCT) (Northern Ireland).
- Home Office UK Immigration & Visas Directorate (formerly UKBA).
- Border Force.
- Police.
- Serious Organised Crime Agency (SOCA).
- Gangmasters Licensing Authority.
- Barnardo's (for children).
- CTAC (NSPCC Child Trafficking Advice Centre) (for children).
- TARA Project (Scotland).
- Salvation Army.
- Poppy Project.
- Migrant Help.
- Kalayaan.
- Unseen.
- BAWSO.
- New Pathways.
- Refugee Council.
- Medaille Trust.

There are separate referral forms for adults and children. Both forms provide a checklist of indicators of trafficking, although the Home Office recognise in their own guidance that children may provide very few indicators.[1] The Home Office also sets out some of the key indicators of trafficking in its policy guidance.[2] The referral practices adopted by the first responders are not uniform or consistent. There is no requirement that the referral forms should be read back to the potential victim or that an interpreter should be used. The NRM form are not to be used as an interview record.[3] Although legal representatives, judges[4] and other organisations and NGOs are not first responders, experience shows that if sufficiently robust representations are made, UKVI will usually make a referral to the UKVI competent authority.

---

1. *Victims of human trafficking – competent authority guidance*, 24 October 2013 at pages 17 and 30.
2. *Victims of human trafficking: guidance to front line staff*, 21 January 2013; *Victims of human trafficking – competent authority guidance*, 24 October 2013; Human Trafficking practical guidance 2013.
3. NRM referral form (adult).
4. Judges are a public authority and therefore must act in a way compatible with a Convention right (ss 6(1) and 6(3)(b) of the Human Rights Act 1998). Article 4, ECHR requires that where there exists a credible suspicion of trafficking there is a positive obligation to ensure that an investigation into the trafficking takes place (see *Rantsev v Cyprus and Russia* [2010] ECHR 22, 51 EHRR 1).

13.24 Home Office policy is that in all child trafficking cases the police must be alerted either by notifying the police child protection unit or the public protection unit.[1] First responders who are not part of the Children's Services should ensure a referral is immediately made to their Local Authority Children's Services and the police. Only after both bodies have assessed indicators of trafficking and a child has been protected and safeguarded should the child be referred into the NRM.[2] Where a potential victim claims to be a child, unless their appearance very strongly suggests they are significantly over 18 years old and this is verified by a higher executive officer or chief immigration officer, they must be given the benefit of the doubt and treated as a child until an age assessment by the relevant local authority is carried out.[3] A similar presumption is provided by ECAT[4] and the Trafficking Directive.[5] This presumption is particularly necessary in the light of the increasing amount of evidence that trafficked children will travel on false documents indicating that they are adults.[6]

[1] *Victims of human trafficking – competent authority guidance*, 24 October 2013 pages 38-39.
[2] Home Office National Referral Mechanism: guidance for child first responders at 3; Child NRM referral form.
[3] *Victims of human trafficking: guidance to front line staff*, 21 January 2013.
[4] Council of Europe Convention on Action against Trafficking in Human Beings, Art 10(3).
[5] Directive 2011/36/EU of the European Parliament and of the Council of 5 April 2011 on preventing and combating trafficking in human beings and protecting its victims, and replacing Council Framework Decision 2002/629/ JHA, art 13(2).
[6] 'Joint UN Commentary on the EU Directive – A Human Rights Based Approach' (2011), p 72-73.

Decision making by the Competent Authority

13.25 There is a two stage decision making process adopted by the competent authority.[1] The first is to make a 'reasonable grounds' decision as to whether the individual is a victim of trafficking. That is then followed by a 'conclusive grounds' decision. Whether the identification decisions are positive or negative they must be minuted.[2] It has been the practice of the Home Office only to disclose the minutes of a negative decision to the potential victim of trafficking and not the minutes for the positive decision. The minutes for the positive decision will be kept on the victim's file. There is no reasoned basis provided in the Home Office current guidance for not disclosing the positive decision minutes to the potential victim. Any decision reached on identification must be reviewed by a second caseworker and recorded on the file of the potential victim.[3]

[1] Set out in *Victims of human trafficking – competent authority guidance*, 24 October 2013.
[2] *Victims of human trafficking – competent authority guidance*, 24 October 2013 at page 52.
[3] Ibid.

Interviewing

13.26 At the stage of making a reasonable grounds decision, the potential victim of trafficking should only be interviewed to establish identity, nationality and immigration status in the UK. Questions related to the exploitation suffered should not be asked.[1] For the purpose of making a conclusive grounds decision, the decision maker has to balance the anticipated benefits of an interview against the potential consequences in terms of re-traumatising the potential victim; consideration should be given to whether sufficient information from other sources is available to make a decision without having to conduct an interview and consideration may also be given to asking the support provider or the police to put questions on the competent authority's behalf instead of conducting an interview.[2] Interviewing of children who are suspected victims of trafficking must be kept to a minimum; if a child has to be interviewed it should be done by trained specialist child protection police or social work professional and the competent authority should avoid interviewing a child if the trafficking issues have already been addressed in the asylum process or if there are specialists in other agencies able to conduct an interview.[3] However, it appears to be the practice of the Home Office in dealing with NRM referrals in tandem with a child's asylum application to routinely interview these children and explore the allegation of trafficking.[4] Failure by the Home Office to follow its own guidance for dealing with suspected child victims of trafficking may result in a process so flawed that the lawfulness of its decisions may be called into question.[5]

1   Home Office, *Victims of human trafficking – competent authority guidance*, 24 October 2013, p 62.
2   Home Office, *Victims of human trafficking – competent authority guidance*, 24 October 2013, p 78.
3   Home Office, *Victims of human trafficking – competent authority guidance*, 24 October 2013, p 45.
4   Guidelines relevant to the conduct of such interviews are the World Health Organisation 'Guidelines on interviewing trafficking victims', 2003 and UNICEF: 'Guidelines on the Protection of Child Victims and Witnesses of Trafficking', 2006, p19-20.
5   In *R (on the application of Mlloja) v Secretary of State for the Home Department* [2005] EWHC 2833 (Admin), [2005] All ER (D) 234 (Nov) where a child was treated as an adult throughout the decision-making process, the process was held to be so flawed as to invalidate both the Secretary of State's decision and that of the Immigration Judge. Gibbs J asked:

   'What significance, if any, should the court attach to the failure of the defendant to treat the claimant as a child? In my judgement, substantial significance (sic) should be attached to it, both generally and in relation to this particular case. The underlying reasoning which supports the special detailed provisions for children is obvious. A child, by reason of his lack of knowledge, experience and maturity, cannot be expected to comply with procedures in the same way as an adult. Of course, a child may lie as well as tell the truth, but he may also find it more difficult to answer questions with the necessary understanding and insight . . . .' [para 33].

Credibility

13.27 The credibility of a suspected victim's account may play a significant part in deciding whether in fact the person is a victim of trafficking. The Competent Authority guidance recognises that due to the trauma of trafficking a trafficking victim's account may be inconsistent or lacking in detail and that there may be late disclosure of important facts.[1] The tribunal has deprecated reliance being placed on late disclosure of a trafficking history because there are many reasons other than want of credibility that may explain such late disclosure.[2] Examples include: the victim's fear of the traffickers who may be present in the UK or may pose a threat to the victim's family in the home country;[3] the victim may still be subject to a debt bond or to juju or to other means of exercising control over him or her;[4] the victim's distrust of the authorities,[5] particularly bearing in mind that manipulation of such fear is a common method of control used by traffickers.[6] Moreover, holding late disclosure against a victim may be inconsistent with the important principle that the victim is not required to self-identify.[7]

[1] Home Office, *Victims of human trafficking – competent authority guidance*, 24 October 2013, p 51-59, 64-66.
[2] *AZ v Secretary of State for the Home Department AZ (Trafficked women) Thailand CG* [2010] UKUT 118 (IAC), para 170.
[3] *JB (AP), petitioner* [2014] CSOH 126, para 13.
[4] Home Office National Referral Mechanism: guidance for child first responders, p 7.
[5] Home Office, *Victims of human trafficking – competent authority guidance*, 24 October 2013, p 55.
[6] See the discussion of 'forced and compulsory labour' and 'servitude' below.
[7] Directive 2011/36/EU of the European Parliament and of the Council of 5 April 2011 on preventing and combating trafficking in human beings and protecting its victims, and replacing Council Framework Decision 2002/629/ JHA, 'the Trafficking Directive', Article 9(1) and preamble recital (15) and *Rantsev v Cyprus and Russia* (2010) 51 EHRR 1 para 288.

Reasonable grounds decision

13.28 The first stage of the decision-making process[1] following a referral to the NRM requires the Competent Authority to make a 'reasonable grounds decision' which should be done within five days of receipt of the referral.[2] The test that the decision maker has to apply is 'whether the statement "I suspect but cannot prove (the person is a victim of trafficking)" is true'.[3] The decision maker is required 'to make every effort to secure all relevant information that could prove useful in establishing if there are reasonable grounds', including from the police, the local authority and support provider.[4] Before any negative decision is reached, the Competent Authority has to contact the first responder and support providers to discuss the decision and to give them an opportunity to provide further information.[5]

[1] Set out in Home Office, *Victims of human trafficking – competent authority guidance*, 24 October 2013.
[2] Home Office, *Victims of human trafficking – competent authority guidance*, 24 October 2013, p 47.
[3] Home Office, *Victims of human trafficking – competent authority guidance*, 24 October 2013, p 49.
[4] Home Office, *Victims of human trafficking – competent authority guidance*, 24 October 2013, p 58.
[5] Home Office, *Victims of human trafficking – competent authority guidance*, 24 October 2013, p 59.

13.29 If a positive reasonable grounds decision is made, the recipient should be given a 45-day 'recovery and reflection period'. The Secretary of State has discretion to extend this period where the circumstances warrant this and will review the case on day 30.[1] During this period potential victims must be provided with appropriate and secure accommodation, medical treatment, translation and interpreter services, counselling and information about their legal rights and children must be given access to education.[2] Any potential victim served with a positive reasonable grounds decision whilst detained under Immigration Act powers will normally be released from detention unless the detention can be justified on public order grounds.[3] In respect of children, the Government has begun a pilot project in a limited number of locations of providing unaccompanied children an appointed child advocate as soon as the child is identified as a potential victim of trafficking.

1   Home Office, *Victims of human trafficking – competent authority guidance*, 24 October 2013, pp 47 and 92. On day 30, information should be sought from the support provider, first responder, investigating police force and in the case of children, the local authority.

2   In accordance with arts 14(2) and 16(3) of the Trafficking Directive. See *The Government Response to the Report from the Joint Committee on the draft Modern Slavery Bill* Session (HL Paper 166, HC 1019) (2013–14)

3   Home Office, *Victims of human trafficking – competent authority guidance*, 24 October 2013, pp 43–44.

Conclusive grounds decision

13.30 A further, 'conclusive grounds' decision has to be made and the expectation is that it should be served on the 45th day of the 'recovery and reflection period'[1]. The decision maker is required to consult with 'relevant agencies' such as the police, children's services and support providers, particularly bearing in mind that police and intelligence reports can provide objective evidence to strengthen a claim.[2] The conclusive grounds decision is made on the balance of probabilities.[3] The current NRM model of identification of third country nationals by immigration officials has received significant criticism both at a regional and domestic level, including by the Joint Committee on the Draft Modern Slavery Bill.[4] The NRM is currently under review by the Government.

1   Home Office, *Victims of human trafficking – competent authority guidance*, 24 October 2013, p 75.

2   Home Office, *Victims of human trafficking – competent authority guidance*, 24 October 2013, p 77

3   Home Office, *Victims of human trafficking – competent authority guidance*, 24 October 2013, p 83

4   House of Lords, *House of Commons Joint Committee on the Draft Modern Slavery Bill Report* (HL Paper 166, HC 1019) (2013–14) at 60-65. GRETA Report concerning the implementation of the Council of Europe Convention on Action against Trafficking in Human Beings by the United Kingdom, First evaluation round, 12 September 2012 at 51 [218]. The Anti-Trafficking Monitoring Group report 'Hidden in plain sight': Three years on: updated analysis of UK measures to protect trafficked persons, October 2013 at 8, 13 and 33. UNHCR Trafficking in Persons Report for the UK, 19 June 2012.

13.31 When there is a positive conclusive grounds decision but the criteria for granting leave to enter or remain in the protection categories are not met, the policy provides for discretionary leave to be given if the victim's personal circumstances 'are compelling', if he or she is pursuing a claim for compensation against the traffickers or the person is assisting the police with an investigation.[1] Where leave is not granted to the victim then normal immigration procedures apply, although policy requires that such procedures must comply with the UK's obligations under article 16 of the Trafficking Directive.[2] Where the identified victim is a child victim of trafficking and unaccompanied, the UK has an obligation to find a long-term and sustainable durable solution for that child, based on an individual assessment of the best interest of the child.[3]

1   Home Office, *Victims of human trafficking – competent authority guidance*, 24 October 2013, pp 98 and 101 in compliance with Art 14 of ECAT. This discretionary leave can be extended if circumstances warrant it.

2   Article 16 provides, inter alia, (1) The Party of which a victim is a national or in which that
    person had the right of permanent residence at the time of entry into the territory of the
    receiving Party shall, with due regard for his or her rights, safety and dignity, facilitate and
    accept, his or her return without undue or unreasonable delay. (2) When a Party returns a
    victim to another State, such return shall be with due regard for the rights, safety and dignity
    of that person and for the status of any legal proceedings related to the fact that the person is
    a victim, and shall preferably be voluntary. Referred to in Home Office, *Victims of human
    trafficking – competent authority guidance*, 24 October 2013, p 103.
3   Preamble of the Trafficking Directive at (23) and Article 16(2). Joint UN Commentary of the
    Trafficking Directive at 83.

THE REFUGEE CONVENTION AND TRAFFICKING VICTIMS

13.32 The Palermo Protocol[1] and the ECAT[2] both expressly provide that they
do not affect individuals' and states' rights, obligations and responsibilities
under international law and in particular, under the Refugee Convention and
protocol. The EU Trafficking Directive is without prejudice to the principle of
non-refoulement under the Refugee Convention.[3]

1   Protocol to Prevent, Suppress and Punish Trafficking in Persons, especially Women and
    Children, supplementing the United Nations Convention against transnational organised
    Crime 2000, Article 14(1).
2   Council of Europe Convention on Action against Trafficking in Human Beings 2005, Article
    40(4).
3   Directive 2011/36/EU of the European Parliament and of the Council of 5 April 2011 on
    preventing and combating trafficking in human beings and protecting its victims, and
    replacing Council Framework Decision 2002/629/JHA, preamble recital (10).

Persecution

13.33 Undoubtedly many of the acts associated with trafficking such as
'abduction, incarceration, rape, sexual enslavement, enforced prostitution,
forced labour, removal of organs, physical beatings, starvation, the deprivation
of medical treatment . . . constitute serious violations of human rights
which will generally amount to persecution'.[1] However, quite apart from those
associated acts, being trafficked should by itself be regarded as persecution.
The Qualification Directive defines acts of persecution as ones which are
'sufficiently serious by their nature or repetition as to constitute a severe
violation of basic human rights, in particular, the rights from which derogation
cannot be made under Article 15(2) of the European Convention for the
Protection of Human Rights and Fundamental Freedoms'.[2] Trafficking has
those characteristics. It 'constitutes a violation of human rights and an offence
to the dignity and integrity of the human being'[3]; it is 'a gross violation of
fundamental rights and explicitly prohibited by the Charter of Fundamental
Rights of the European Union'[4] and it falls within the scope of Article 4 of
the ECHR[5] which is one of the non-derogable rights identified in Article 15(2).
Trafficking may constitute persecution even if the individual consents to the
trafficking bearing in mind that the individual's consent is irrelevant if one of
the means contained in the trafficking definition is used.[6]

1   UNHCR 'Guidelines on International Protection: The application of Article 1(A)2 of the
    1951 Convention and/or Protocol relating to the status of refugees to victims of trafficking and
    persons at risk of being trafficked' (2006) HCR/GIP/06/07, para 15.

2   Council Directive (2004/83/EC) of 29 April 2004 on minimum standards for the qualification
     and status of third country nationals or stateless persons as refugee or as persons who
     otherwise need international protection and the content of the protection granted, art 9(1)(a).
3   Council of Europe Convention on Action against Trafficking in Human Beings, preamble.
4   Directive 2011/36EU of the European Parliament and of the Council of 5 April 2011 on
     preventing and combating trafficking in human beings and protecting its victims and
     replacing Council Framework Decision 2002/629/JHA, preamble recital (1)
5   *Rantsev v Cyprus and Russia* (2010) 51 EHRR 1, 28 BHRC 313, para 282.
6   Council of Europe Convention on Action against Trafficking in Human Beings, 2005, Article
     4(b); *AM and BM (Trafficked women) Albania CG* [2010] UKUT 80 (IAC).

13.34 Assessment of the risk that an individual will be trafficked necessitates
attention to the prevalence and patterns of trafficking in his or her country of
origin as well as the individual's particular history and circumstances. The
latter includes, inter alia, the individual's age[1], gender, marital status, domestic
circumstances, availability of family support, educational level, qualifications,
work experience, availability of employment and state of mind.[2] An individual
who has already been trafficked may be at risk of being trafficked again
bearing in mind the general principle that past persecution constitutes a serious
indication of a real risk of being persecuted, absent good reason to think that
it will not be repeated.[3] The history of being trafficked is likely to be revealing
of the individual's vulnerability to being trafficked eg in the form of family
complicity in the trafficking or dire economic circumstances.[4] It may also
exacerbate vulnerability and risk if, for example: having escaped a trafficking
situation the individual assisted in the investigation or prosecution of her
traffickers rendering the person at risk of reprisal;[5] stigma attached to having
been trafficked prevents the individual from receiving family or social support;[6] having once been trafficked, the individual may be 'even more vulnerable to re-trafficking' because she has 'been through the business and knows
how to be compliant . . . the "breaking in" period has already taken place;'[7]
being traumatised by the experience of having been trafficked may compromise the individual's capacity to reintegrate;[8] and resorting to government
facilities to assist victims of trafficking may result in the individual's vulnerability being identified to traffickers who target such facilities.[9]

1   'Children are more vulnerable than adults and therefore at greater risk of becoming victims of
     trafficking in human beings': Directive 2011/36EU of the European Parliament and of
     the Council of 5 April 2011 on preventing and combating trafficking in human beings and
     protecting its victims and replacing Council Framework Decision 2002/629/JHA, preamble
     recital, (8). See UNHCR 'Guidelines on International Protection: Child Asylum Claims under
     Articles 1A(2) and 1F of the 1951 Convention and/or 1967 Protocol relating to the Status of
     Refugees (2009) HCR/GIP/09/08, highlighting the need for a 'child sensitive application of the
     refugee definition' and a 'contemporary and child sensitive understanding of persecution' and
     child trafficking in particular.
2   See for example *AM and BM (Trafficked women) Albania CG* [2010] UKUT 80 (IAC) and *AZ
     v Secretary of State for the Home Department AZ (Trafficked women) Thailand CG* [2010]
     UKUT 118 (IAC).
3   Council Directive (2004/83/EC) of 29 April 2004 on minimum standards for the qualification
     and status of third country nationals or stateless persons as refugee or as persons who
     otherwise need international protection and the content of the protection granted, art 4(4)
4   *A-G's Reference (Nos 37, 38 and 65 of 2010), R v Khan (Raza Ali)* [2010] EWCA Crim 2880,
     [2011] Crim LR 336, para 18 and *AZ (Trafficked women) Thailand CG* [2010] UKUT 118
     (IAC) 'their economic conditions have a direct bearing on the extent of risk they are likely to
     face' (para 163).
5   As in *SB (PSG – Protection Regulations – Reg 6) Moldova CG* [2008] UKAIT 0002.
6   *AM and BM (Trafficked women) Albania CG* [2010] UKUT 80 (IAC).
7   *AZ (Trafficked women) Thailand CG* [2010] UKUT 118 (IAC), para 150.

[8]   *AZ (Trafficked women) Thailand CG* [2010] UKUT 118 (IAC), para 144.
[9]   *AZ (Trafficked women) Thailand CG* [2010] UKUT 118 (IAC), para 144.

Convention reason

13.35 The requirement that the fear of persecution be for a Convention reason is discussed in CHAPTER 12. Victims of trafficking may be a 'particular social group' by reason of the immutable characteristic of their shared experience of having been trafficked.[1] For the purpose of the Refugee Qualification Regulations[2] the tribunal insists that the particular social group should also have 'a distinct identity in the relevant country, because it is perceived as being different by the surrounding society' as well as possessing a shared, immutable characteristic[3]. By doing so, it is at odds with the Refugee Convention as authoritatively interpreted by the House of Lords.[4]

[1]   UNHCR 'Guidelines on International Protection: The application of Article 1(A)2 of the 1951 Convention and/or Protocol relating to the status of refugees to victims of trafficking and persons at risk of being trafficked' (2006) HCR/GIP/06/07, para 39, *SB (PSG – Protection Regulations – Reg 6) Moldova CG* [2008] UKAIT 0002, para 56; *AM and BM (Trafficked women) Albania CG* [2010] UKUT 80 (IAC), para 165.
[2]   Refugee or Person in Need of International Protection (Qualification) Regulations 2006, SI 2006/2525, reg 6(1)(d).
[3]   *SB (PSG – Protection Regulations – Reg 6) Moldova CG* [2008] UKAIT 0002, para 56; *AM and BM (Trafficked women) Albania CG* [2010] UKUT 80 (IAC).
[4]   *Fornah v Secretary of State for the Home Department* [2006] UKHL 46, [2007] 1 AC 412.

Sufficiency of protection

13.36 To qualify for refugee status the person's home state has to be unable or unwilling to provide adequate protection. That requirement may be satisfied if, for example, the country's criminal law does not penalise trafficking[1] or the law is ineffectively implemented[2] or there is significant collusion between traffickers and state officials.[3] Whether the state will provide sufficient protection may be assessed by reference to what international law requires the state to do by way of protecting victims of trafficking, including the provision of assistance; the taking of measures to protect the privacy and identity of victims and to provide for the physical, psychological and social recovery of victims of trafficking and a right to compensation from the traffickers.[4] A victim of trafficking may be unable to avail herself of her state's protection if that protection is dependent upon disclosure about her history of being trafficked, particularly if that inability is a result of trauma related to the trafficking or to suspicion of the authorities.[5]

[1]   See for example *HC and RC (Trafficked women) China CG* [2009] UKAIT 00027 where the tribunal found that acts of forced labour, debt bondage, coercion and involuntary servitude were not penalised by the Chinese penal code.
[2]   *HC and RC (Trafficked women) China CG* [2009] UKAIT 00027, *AZ (Trafficked women) Thailand CG* [2010] UKUT 118 (IAC), para 160.
[3]   *AZ (Trafficked women) Thailand CG* [2010] UKUT 118 (IAC), para 159.
[4]   UNHCR 'Guidelines on International Protection: The application of Article 1(A)2 of the 1951 Convention and/or Protocol relating to the status of refugees to victims of trafficking and persons at risk of being trafficked' (2006) HCR/GIP/06/07, para 22, referring to Part II of the Palermo Protocol.

AZ *(Trafficked women) Thailand CG* [2010] UKUT 118 (IAC), para xx.

Internal Relocation

13.37 An individual may be denied protection if there is a viable internal relocation alternative in the person's own country in which there is no real risk of being persecuted and to which the person can reasonably be expected to go. The applicable principles are discussed in the CHAPTER 12.

TRAFFICKING AND THE EUROPEAN CONVENTION ON HUMAN RIGHTS

General

13.38 The preamble to ECAT notes that 'trafficking in human beings constitutes a violation of human rights and an offence to the dignity and integrity of the human being'[1].The explanatory report lists some of the international legal instruments and declarations that have recognised trafficking in human beings as a violation of human rights[2]. The focus of what follows will be on trafficking as a violation of Article 4 of the European Convention on Human Rights.

[1] Council of Europe Convention on Action against Trafficking in Human Beings, 2005.
[2] Council of Europe Convention on Action against Trafficking in Human Beings, Explanatory Report, para 40-49.

Article 4 of the European Convention on Human Rights

13.39 Article 4 says, inter alia:

(1) No one shall be held in slavery or servitude;
(2) No one shall be required to perform forced or compulsory labour.
    Article 5 of the Charter of Fundamental Rights of the European Union is in similar terms but also says:
(3) Trafficking in human beings is prohibited.

According to the European Court of Human Rights, Article 4 of the ECHR, together with Articles 2 and 3 enshrines one of the basic values of the democratic societies making up the Council of Europe.[1] Moreover, Articles 4(1) and 4(2) are, unlike most of the other rights in the ECHR unqualified and no derogation from them is permissible under Article 15(2), even in the event of a public emergency threatening the life of the nation.[2]

[1] *Siliadin v France* (Application 73316/01)(2005) 43 EHRR 287, 20 BHRC 654.
[2] *CN v United Kingdom (App No 4239/08)*(2013) 56 EHRR 24, para 65.

Slavery

13.40 The European Court of Human Rights refers to the definition of slavery contained in the 1926 Slavery Convention which is that slavery is 'the status or condition of a person over whom any or all of the powers attaching to the rights of ownership are exercised'.[1] The Supplementary Convention on the Abolition of Slavery, the Slave Trade and Practices similar to Slavery 1956, Article 1 defined 'institutions and practices similar to slavery' as including the following: debt bondage;[2] serfdom;[3] forced and servile forms of marriage[4] and the delivery of a child by his or her parents or guardians for the exploitation of the child's labour.

[1] *Siliadin v France* (Application 73316/01)(2005) 43 EHRR 287, 20 BHRC 654.

[2] '[T]hat is to say, the status or condition arising from a pledge by a debtor of his personal services or of those of a person under his control as security for a debt, if the value of those services as reasonably assessed is not applied towards the liquidation of the debt or the length and nature of those services are not respectively limited and defined'.

[3] That is to say, the condition or status of a tenant who is by law, custom or agreement bound to live and labour on land belonging to another person and to render some determinate service to such other person, whether for reward or not, and is not free to change his status;

[4] Any institution or practice whereby: (i) a woman without the right to refuse, is promised or given in marriage on payment of a consideration in money or in kind to her parents guardian, family or any other person or group; or (ii) the husband of a woman, his family, or his clan has the right to transfer her to another person for value received or otherwise; or (iii) a woman on the death of her husband is liable to be inherited by another person. See also OSCE Unprotected Work, Invisible Exploitation: Trafficking for the Purposes of Domestic Servitude June 2010 p 44. Payment of money to a woman's parents in respect of a marriage would not necessarily be 'considered to amount to a price attached to the transfer of ownership, which would bring into play the concept of slavery. The Court reiterates that marriage has deep-rooted social and cultural connotations which may differ largely from one society to another. According to the Court, this payment can reasonably be accepted as representing a gift from one family to another, a tradition common to many different cultures in to-day's society': *M v Italy* (2013) 57 EHRR 29, para 161.

Servitude

13.41 'Servitude' is an obligation to provide one's services that is imposed by the use of coercion and is linked with the concept of slavery.[1] The European Court of Human Rights understanding of servitude and forced labour has been informed by the findings of the Parliamentary Assembly of the Council of Europe that 'today's slaves are predominantly female and usually work in private households, starting out as migrant domestic workers'.[2] Domestic servitude involves a complex set of dynamics, involving both overt and more subtle forms of coercion to force compliance, investigation of which requires an understanding of the many subtle ways an individual can fall under the control of another.[3] The ILO's Domestic Workers Convention,[4] recognises that domestic work is 'mainly carried out by women and girls, many of whom are migrants or members of disadvantaged communities and who are particularly vulnerable to discrimination in respect of conditions of employment and of work, and to other abuses of human rights'. It aims to protect them by regulating relations between domestic workers and their employers eg by requiring specified terms and conditions of employment;[5] a contract of employment for a worker recruited in one country to be employed in another;[6] the worker to retain possession of his or her passport and identity card[7] and regular payment of wages.[8] An employer's non-compliance with such requirements may support an inference that there is a situation of servitude or forced labour. A number of recent decisions by the European Court of Human Rights have concerned such workers. In *Siliadin v France* the Court found a young woman to have been held in servitude given the circumstances: that she was brought to France as a child by a relative; her relatives transferred her to her employers; her employers manipulated her fear of being arrested owing to her unlawful immigration status; she was made to work long hours, seven days each week without remuneration; she was not permitted to leave the house in which she worked, save to take the children to school; she had no freedom of movement and no free time; the promise that she would be sent to school was broken and she had no hope of her situation improving.[9] In a subsequent case the Court found the applicant's claimed circumstances to be 'remarkably similar' and to give rise to a credible suspicion that she had been held in domestic servitude.[10]

[1] *Siliadin v France* (Application 73316/01)(2005) 43 EHRR 287, 20 BHRC 654.

[2] *Siliadin v France* [2005] ECHR 545, para 88, noting the Parliamentary Assembly's Recommendation 1663 (2004), adopted on 22 June 2004 cited in para 49.

[3] *CN v UK* 4239/08 [2012] ECHR 1911, para 80. See OSCE 'Unprotected Work, Invisible Exploitation: Trafficking for the Purposes of Domestic Servitude', June 2010 noting as features of domestic servitude subjugation to place the worker in a situation of vulnerability and dependence, low or no salary, no days off, food and sleep deprivation, no access to medical treatment, psychological, sexual and/or physical violence, limited or restricted freedom of movement, threats of denunciation, and the impossibility of a private life. See also OSCE Resource 'Police Training Guide: Trafficking in Human Beings' July 2013, p 71 noting that the following are established indicators of domestic servitude: living with the family, not eating with the rest of the family, having separate sleeping quarters to the rest of the family, never or rarely leaving the house for social reasons, never or rarely leaving the house without the employer, only being given leftover food to eat, subjected to insults, abuse, threats or violence.

[4] C189 – Domestic Workers Convention 2011 (No 189); Convention concerning decent work for domestic workers.

[5] C189 – Domestic Workers Convention 2011 (No 189); Convention concerning decent work for domestic workers, Article 7.

[6] C189 – Domestic Workers Convention 2011 (No 189), Article 8.

[7] C189 – Domestic Workers Convention 2011 (No 189), Article 9.

[8] C189 – Domestic Workers Convention 2011 (No 189), Article 12.

[9] *Siliadin v France* [2005] ECHR 545, para 129.

[10] *CN v UK* 4239/08 [2012] ECHR 1911.

Forced or compulsory labour

13.42 The drafters of the European Convention on Human Rights relied on the definition of 'forced or compulsory labour' contained in the ILO's Forced Labour Convention[1] and the Court has relied on the ILO Conventions which are binding on almost all of the Council of Europe Member States for the purpose of interpreting Article 4.[2] The Forced Labour Convention defines 'forced or compulsory labour' as meaning 'all work or service which is exacted from any person under the menace of any penalty and for which the said person has not offered himself voluntarily'.[3] The Court treats that definition as 'a starting point' for interpreting Article 4 but bearing in mind that the ECHR is a living instrument to be read in the light of currently prevailing notions.[4] It is noteworthy that the ILO definition refers to 'all work or services' and so encompasses all types of work, employment or occupation, irrespective of the nature of the activity performed, its legality or illegality under national law or its recognition as an 'economic activity'; thus it can apply as much to factory work as to prostitution or begging.[5] The ILO has developed indicators of forced labour, described by the Court in *CN v United Kingdom* as 'a valuable benchmark in the identification of forced labour'.[6] As listed by the Court they were: '1. threats or actual physical harm to the worker; 2. Restriction of movement and confinement to the work place or to a limited area; 3. Debt bondage: where the worker works to pay off a debt or loan, and is not paid for his or her services. The employer may provide food and accommodation at such inflated prices that the worker cannot escape the debt; 4. Withholding of wages or excessive wage reductions, that violate previously made agreements; 5. Retention of passports and identity documents, so that the worker cannot leave, or prove his/her identity and status; 6. Threat of denunciation to the authorities, where the worker is in an irregular immigration status'.[7] In *CN v United Kingdom* the Court held the UK's investigation of an allegation of trafficking to have been inadequate because it failed to give any weight to features of the applicant's situation that were among the ILO's indicators of forced labour.[8] The Supreme Court in *Hounga v Allen* applied the ILO's indicators of forced labour to hold that the appellant was (at least for the purposes of that case) a victim of trafficking on the basis that there had been physical harm or threats of physical harm from her employers; there had been withholding of wages and there had been threats of denunciation to the authorities in circumstances where she had irregular immigration status.[9] In *Siliadin* the Court held that the applicant domestic worker was in a situation of forced labour. Whilst not threatened by a 'penalty' she was nevertheless in an equivalent position: 'she was an adolescent girl in a foreign land, unlawfully present on French territory and in fear of arrest by the police. Indeed, [her employers] nurtured that fear and led her to believe that her status would be regularised'.[10] Giving prior consent to undertaking the labour does not by itself establish that the individual offered him or herself voluntarily: account has to be taken of all the circumstances of the case, including whether it imposed a burden which was so excessive or disproportionate to the anticipated rewards or advantages that resulted in the consent being given.[11]

[1]   *Van der Mussele v Belgium (Application 8919/80)* (1983) 6 EHRR 163, [1983] ECHR 8919/80, para 32.
[2]   *Siliadin v France* [2005] ECHR 545, para 115.
[3]   Forced Labour Convention, 1930 (No 29), Article 2(1).
[4]   *Van der Mussele v Belgium (Application 8919/80)* (1983) 6 EHRR 163, [1983] ECHR 8919/80, para 32.
[5]   'Joint UN Commentary on the EU Directive – A Human Rights – Based Approach' (2011), p 102, citing ILO 'The Cost of Coercion' (2009).
[6]   *CN v United Kingdom* Application 4239/08 [2012] ECHR 1911, para 35.
[7]   *CN v United Kingdom* (Application 4239/08) [2012] ECHR 1911, para 35. An ILO publication 'ILO Indicators of Forced Labour' lists 11 indicators that are 'derived from the theoretical and practical experience of the ILO's Special Action Programme to Combat Forced Labour'.
[8]   *CN v United Kingdom* (Application 4239/08) [2012] ECHR 1911, para 80. Those features were 'the applicant's allegations that her passport had been taken from her, that [her employer] had not kept her wages for her as agreed and that she was explicitly and implicitly threatened with denunciation to the authorities'.
[9]   *Hounga v Allen* [2014] UKSC 47, [2014] 1 WLR 2889, [2014] IRLR 811, para 49.
[10] *Siliadin v France* [2005] ECHR 545, para 118.
[11] *Van der Mussele v Belgium*, para. 37. See fn 1.

Child Labour

13.43 The employment of children may constitute servitude or forced labour. Employment of children is prohibited by the Charter of Fundamental Rights of the EU[1]. ILO Conventions reiterate the need for States to set a minimum age for children to work and to prohibit those under 18 from engaging in work likely to jeopardise the health, safety or morals of young persons.[2] Child domestic servitude is an increasingly prevalent form of exploitation often facilitated by socially and culturally accepted practices of placing a child with a wealthier family or household in the belief that doing so will improve the child's access to education and life chances.[3] These practices, rooted in misplaced trust, are prohibited by the Supplementary Convention on the Abolition of Slavery, the Slave Trade and Practices similar to Slavery 1956.[4] Members States of the ILO are obliged to eliminate 'the worst forms of child labour'.[5]

[1] Article 32.

[2] ILO Convention concerning decent work for domestic workers No 189 Article 4 –setting a minimum age for domestic workers that is consistent with the Minimum Age Convention No 138 and the Worst Forms of Child Labour Convention No 182. ILO Domestic Worker Recommendation No 201. The ILO Declaration on Fundamental Principles and Rights at Work, 1998, declares that the effective abolition of child labour is an obligation arising from membership of the ILO

[3] OSCE 'Unprotected Work, Invisible Exploitation: Trafficking for the Purposes of Domestic Servitude' June 2010 p 24. Arrangements are often made as a purported 'private fostering' whereby a child may enter the UK on another child's passport to live with a 'relative' or to join someone claiming asylum or may be left behind in the UK when the parents leave. Although a regulatory system is in place for social services to assess and monitor bone fide private fostering arrangements of which they are notified, those involving trafficked children exploited for domestic servitude or benefit fraud remain hidden: www.ecpat.org.uk/sites/default/files/u nderstanding_papers/understanding_private_fostering.pdf.

[4] Article 1(d) prohibiting 'any institution or practice whereby a child or young person under the age of 18 years, is delivered by either or both of his natural parents or by his guardian to another person, whether for reward or not, with a view to the exploitation of the child or young person or of his labour.'

[5] ILO Convention concerning the prohibition and immediate action for the elimination of the worst forms of child labour No 182 (1999), Article 6(1). The 'worst forms of child labour' are identified in Article 3 as: 'a. all forms of slavery or practices similar to slavery, such as the sale and trafficking of children, debt bondage and serfdom and forced or compulsory labour, including forced of compulsory recruitment of children for use in armed conflict; b. the use, procuring or offering of a child for prostitution, for the production of pornography or pornographic performances; c. the use, procuring or offering of a child for illicit activities, in particular for the production and trafficking of drugs as defined in the relevant international treaties; d. work which, by its nature or the circumstances in which it is carried out, is likely to harm the health, safety or morals of children". Hazardous work may include: work which exposes children to physical, psychological or sexual abuse; work underground, under water, at dangerous heights or in confined spaces; work with dangerous machinery, equipment or tools; work in an unhealthy environment exposing children to hazardous substances, agents or processes; work under particularly difficult conditions such as work for long hours or during the night or whether the child is unreasonably confined to the premises of the employer: 'ILO Worst Forms of Child Labour, Recommendation No 190, paragraph 3 (1999).

Trafficking and Article 4

13.44 In *Rantsev v Cyprus and Russia*[1] the European Court of Human Rights considered on the one hand, evidence about the increasing scale of trafficking in human beings as a global phenomenon and on the other, the proliferation of measures taken to combat it. Whilst noting that Article 4 of the ECHR makes no reference to trafficking, it reminded itself that the Convention is 'a living instrument which must be interpreted in the light of present-day conditions. The increasingly high standards required in the area of protection of human rights and fundamental liberties correspondingly and inevitably require greater firmness in assessing breaches of the fundamental values of democratic societies'.[2] It also reminded itself of the obligation to interpret the Convention in harmony with other rules of international law[3] and cited in particular the definitional provisions in the Palermo Protocol and ECAT ('the Anti-Trafficking Convention').[4] Having done so, it held[5]:

'In view of its obligation to interpret the Convention in light of present-day conditions, the Court considers it unnecessary to identify whether the treatment about which the applicant complains constitutes "slavery", "servitude" or "forced and compulsory labour". Instead, the Court concludes that trafficking itself, within the meaning of Article 3(a) of the Palermo Protocol and Article 4 of the Anti-Trafficking Convention, falls within the scope of Article 4 of the Convention.'

[1]   *Rantsev v Cyprus and Russia* (2010) 51 EHRR 1.
[2]   *Rantsev v Cyprus and Russia*, para 277.
[3]   *Rantsev v Cyprus and Russia*, para 274.
[4]   Protocol to Prevent, Suppress and Punish Trafficking in Persons, Especially Women and Children, supplementing the UN Convention against Transnational Organised Crime ('the Palermo Protocol'), Article 3 and the Council of Europe Convention on Action against Trafficking in Human Beings, 2005 ('ECAT'), Article 4.
[5]   *Rantsev v Cyprus and Russian,* para 282.

Positive Obligations under Article 4 of the ECHR

13.45 Article 4 imposes a range of positive obligations on signatory states. National legislation must contain a spectrum of safeguards 'adequate to ensure the practical and effective protection of victims or potential victims of trafficking'.[1] Both the UK and France have been found in breach of Article 4 for failing to make specific provision in their criminal law to penalise forced labour and servitude.[2] States are also required to ensure that their Immigration Rules do not encourage, facilitate or tolerate trafficking.[3] In *Rantsev* the Court held that the regime of artiste visas in Cyprus failed to provide practical and effective protection against trafficking and thus breached Article 4. One of the reasons for that was that the visas were obtained by the cabaret owners making the artiste dependant on her employer to secure and retain lawful immigration status and thereby increasing the risk of being trafficked.[4] In accordance with its Article 4 obligations, the UK adopted policies from 1990 onwards intended to protect domestic workers coming to the UK from being exploited, including informing visa applicants of their rights in the UK and ensuring that they were provided with an agreed statement of the terms and conditions of their employment; moreover the Immigration Rules were changed to enable domestic workers to change their employers whilst in the UK.[5] More recent changes to the UK's Immigration Rules have been criticised for tying domestic workers to abusive employers.[6] Both the Palermo Protocol[7] and the ECAT[8] refer to the need for a comprehensive approach to combat trafficking which includes measures to prevent trafficking and to protect victims as well as to measures to punish traffickers and it is in this broad context that the extent of the positive obligations under Article 4 must be considered.[9] They include the obligation to take operational measures in respect of an individual where there is a credible suspicion that he or she had been or was at risk of being trafficked.[10] There is also a procedural obligation on the authorities, as under Articles 2 and 3, to investigate situations of potential trafficking that come to their attention, regardless of whether there has been a complaint from the victim and the investigation must be capable of leading to the identification and punishment of individuals responsible.[11] Moreover, there is an obligation on the state responsible for a breach of Article 4 to make reparation to the victim for the consequences of the breach which may extend to an obligation to grant leave to remain in the UK.[12]

[1] *Rantsev v Cyprus and Russia* (2010) 51 EHRR 1, para 283
[2] *Siliadin v France* (2005) 43 EHRR 287; *CN v United Kingdom* (Application 4239/08) [2012] ECHR 1911; *CN v France* (Application 67724/09) (2012), unreported.
[3] *Rantsev v Cyprus and Russia* (2010) 51 EHRR 1, para 283.
[4] *Rantsev v Cyprus and Russia* (2010) 51 EHRR 1, para 291, 293.
[5] *EK (Article 4 ECHR: Anti Trafficking Convention) Tanzania* [2013] UKUT 00313 (IAC).
[6] Houses of Parliament: *Joint Committee on the Draft Modern Slavery Bill Report*, HL 166, CH 1019, para 225.
[7] Protocol to Prevent, Suppress and Punish Trafficking in Persons, Especially Women and Children, supplementing the UN Convention against Transnational Organised Crime ('the Palermo Protocol').
[8] The Council of Europe Convention on Action against Trafficking in Human Beings, 2005 ('ECAT').
[9] *Rantsev v Cyprus and Russia* (2010) 51 EHRR 1, para 285.
[10] *Rantsev v Cyprus and Russia* (2010) 51 EHRR 1, para 286.
[11] *Rantsev v Cyprus and Russia* (2010) 51 EHRR 1, para 288; *OOO v Commissioner of Police for the Metropolis* [2011] EWHC 1246 QB, [2011] All ER (D) 199 (May), para 143-61.
[12] *EK (Article 4 ECHR: Anti-Trafficking Convention) Tanzania* [2013] UKUT 00313 (IAC).

DEPORTATION OF VICTIMS AND POTENTIAL VICTIMS OF TRAFFICKING

13.46 Any non-British citizen, victim of trafficking or not, is liable to deportation if the Secretary of State deems his or her deportation conducive to the public good[1]; another person to whose family the person belongs is or has been ordered to be deported[2] or the person is 17 or more and having been convicted of an imprisonable offence, is recommended for deportation by the court[3]. If the person is a foreign criminal, ie sentenced to a period of at least 12 months imprisonment or any period of imprisonment for a specified offence, then, subject to the application of a statutory exception, he or she must be deported ('automatic deportation')[4]. However, there are a number of ways in which the individual's status as or risk of becoming a victim of trafficking are relevant to the exercise of the power to deport.

[1] Immigration Act 1971, s 3(5)(a).
[2] Immigration Act 1971, s 3(5)(b).
[3] Immigration Act 1971, s 3(6).
[4] UK Borders Act 2007, ss 32 and 33.

13.47 The first is that if the individual's liability to deportation rests upon a criminal offence that he or she committed or upon having received a sentence of a particular length, the person's status as a victim of trafficking may afford grounds to appeal the conviction or the sentence or to apply to the Criminal Cases Review Commission. That would be on the basis that the person's culpability should be extinguished or reduced by the fact that he or she was a victim of trafficking when the offence was committed and had no realistic alternative but to comply with the dominant force of another individual or group of individuals.[1] A successful appeal would be likely to require the issue of liability to deportation to be revisited.

¹   *L v R, The Children's Commissioner for England and Equality and Human Rights Commission intervening* [2013] EWCA Crim 991, para 13.

13.48 Second, the individual's status as, or risk of becoming, a victim of trafficking may mean that deportation would be contrary to the UK's obligations under the Refugee Convention or the European Convention on Human Rights owing to risk of being persecuted or treated in breach of his or her human rights in the destination country. If the individual is subject to 'automatic deportation' the 'exception 1' to the automatic deportation provisions would apply.¹

¹   UK Borders Act 2007, s 33(1) and (2).

13.49 Third, the individual's status as, or risk of becoming a victim of trafficking may be of relevance to the issue of whether his or her deportation is conducive to the public good. It is now very well established that deportation of criminals serves the public good because of what is communicated by the process of deportation: it is intended to ensure that non-British citizens who are in the UK or might come to the UK 'clearly understand that, whatever the circumstances, one of the consequences of serious crime may well be deportation'.¹ On the other hand, there is a significant public interest in the detection and effective investigation and prosecution of trafficking offences, not to mention obligations on the UK to investigate and prosecute under ECHR Article 4 and under ECAT,² the Palermo Protocol³ and the Trafficking Directive.⁴ Whilst the willingness of victims of trafficking to assist in the investigation and prosecution of such offences is critical, cooperation may be withheld if there is a risk of being deported.⁵ The deportation of victims of trafficking who have been convicted of offences plainly sends out a message to victims of trafficking who have been involved in offending and are considering whether to cooperate with a prosecution that they too will be at risk of being deported. Such a message may be prejudicial to the public interest in the prosecution of trafficking offences and must be weighed against any deterrent effect that deportation might achieve when deciding whether deportation is conducive to the public good. In the context of automatic deportation, the effect of such a message may be contrary to the UK's obligations under ECAT and thus gives rise to the operation of 'exception 6' to the automatic deportation provisions.⁶ These considerations about conflicting public interests may also be relevant to whether deportation is justified by a pressing social need in the context of an Article 8 based challenge to deportation.

¹   *R (on the application of N) v Secretary for State for the Home Department* [2004] EWCA Civ 1094 and the line of cases following.
²   Council of Europe Convention on Action against Trafficking in Human Beings 2005.
³   Protocol to Prevent, Suppress and Punish Trafficking in Persons, Especially Women and Children, supplementing the UN Convention against Transnational Organised Crime ('the Palermo Protocol').
⁴   Directive 2011/36EU of the European Parliament and of the Council of 5 April 2011 on preventing and combating trafficking in human beings and protecting its victims and replacing Council Framework Decision 2002/629/JHA.
⁵   See for example, Joint UN Commentary on the EU Directive – A Human Rights Based Approach, (2011) p 41 and Council of Europe Convention on Action Against Trafficking in Human Beings, Explanatory Report, para 181.

⁶   UK Borders Act 2007, s 33(6A).

DETENTION OF TRAFFICKING VICTIMS

13.50 The SSHD's policy is that victims of trafficking and potential victims of trafficking can only be detained under Immigration Act powers if their detention can be justified on the grounds of public order.¹

¹   Home Office, *Victims of human trafficking – competent authorities guidance*, 24 October 2013, p 71.

CHALLENGING DECISIONS RELATED TO TRAFFICKING

13.51 Decisions of the 'competent authority' as to whether there are reasonable or conclusive grounds that an individual is a victim of trafficking are not immigration decisions that can (or could) be appealed to the tribunal.¹ The remedy in respect of such decisions is judicial review. There are appealable immigration decisions in relation to which the issue of whether an individual is or is not a victim of trafficking may be relevant, eg refusal of leave to remain sought on the ground that the individual was a victim of trafficking whose stay was necessary owing to his or her personal situation² or a decision to remove an individual following refusal of asylum sought on the basis of a history and risk of being trafficked. The tribunal decided that where the competent authority had made a conclusive grounds decision that the appellant was not a victim of trafficking, it would not entertain a 'backdoor challenge' to such a decision because it was not an appealable immigration decision; the recipient could have, but did not bring judicial proceedings in respect of the decision and the Council of Europe Convention on Action against Trafficking ('ECAT') was an unincorporated treaty that could not be invoked as a free standing source of rights, obligations and legal effects in domestic law.³ However, the Court of Appeal in *AS (Afghanistan) v Secretary of State for the Home Department* held that decisions of the competent authority as to whether the appellant had been a victim of trafficking were not conclusive; the Secretary of State had a policy that made provision for decision making by the competent authority and assistance to victims of trafficking so that 'if in fact [the appellant] has been trafficked but the Secretary of State ignores that fact she will have failed to apply the relevant policy in relation to victims of trafficking' so that the decision would be not in accordance with the law.⁴ The Court could also have adopted the same approach as the Supreme Court did in *Hounga v Allen*⁵ which was to apply ECAT directly, deciding for itself whether the appellant was a victim of trafficking in accordance with 'the strong presumption in favour of interpreting English law (whether common law or statute) in a way which does not place the United Kingdom in breach of an international obligation'.⁶ Having found in *AS (Afghanistan)* that competent authority trafficking decisions were not conclusive, the Court of Appeal added the surprising *obiter dicta* that 'if a conclusive decision has been reached by the competent authority, First Tier Tribunals will be astute not (save perhaps in rare circumstances) to allow an appellant to re-run a case already decided against him on the facts. But where, as here, it is arguable that, on the facts found or accepted, the competent authority has reached a decision which was not open to it, that argument should be heard and taken into account'.[7] Such restraint on the part of the tribunal would be at odds with its well established jurisdiction to determine issues afresh for itself without first having to be satisfied that there was an error in the original decision: see the further discussion in CHAPTER 19 on appeals to the first-tier tribunal.

[1] *R (on the application of AA (Iraq)) v Secretary of State for the Home Department* [2012] EWCA Civ 23, (2012) Times, 05 March.
[2] Pursuant to Council of Europe Convention on Action against Trafficking in Human Beings, 2005 ('ECAT'), Article 14(1)(a).
[3] *SHL (Tracing obligation/Trafficking)* [2013] UKUT 00312 (IAC).
[4] *AS (Afghanistan) v Secretary of State for the Home Department* [2013] EWCA Civ 1469, [2013] All ER (D) 266 (Nov), para 14.
[5] *Hounga v Allen* [2014] UKSC 47.
[6] Lord Hoffmann in *R v Lyons* [2002] UKHL 44, [2003] 1 AC 976, [2002] 4 All ER 1028, para 27, cited by Lord Wilson in *Hounga v Allen* [2014] UKSC 47, para 50.
[7] *AS (Afghanistan) v Secretary of State for the Home Department* [2013] EWCA Civ 1469, [2013] All ER (D) 266 (Nov), para 18.

13.52 The UK Borders Act 2007, section 33(6A) provides an exception to the application of the 'automatic deportation' provisions if 'the Secretary of State thinks that the application [of the automatic deportation provisions] would contravene the UK's obligations under the Council of Europe Convention on Action against Trafficking in Human Beings'. That gives rise to the issue of whether a court or tribunal may review or decide for itself the question of whether the UK's obligations under the Trafficking convention are engaged or whether they are restricted to determining whether the Secretary of State 'thinks' the requisite thought. The use in a statute of 'subjective language'[1] will not necessarily accomplish the exclusion of the court's jurisdiction to entertain a challenge to the decision maker's judgment; much will depend on the statutory context.[2] The use of subjective language in the context of liability to deportation, the statute apparently giving the Secretary of State exclusive jurisdiction over the issue of whether deportation is conducive to the public good does not prevent the tribunal from deciding the issue for itself.[3] The statutory context within which the tribunal has decided appeals allows or obliges it to function as a primary decision maker.[4] Moreover, there is no 'subjective language' to constrain the tribunal's jurisdiction when it considers the human rights exception in which it would have to traverse almost identical terrain in relation to trafficking. In those circumstances, it would make no sense to exclude the tribunal or the court from engaging with the issue of whether deportation would be incompatible with the UK's obligations under the trafficking Convention.

[1] Wade and Forsyth, *Administrative Law* (2009), p 354.
[2] *Secretary of State for Education and Science v Tameside Metropolitan Borough Council* [1977] AC 1014, [1976] 3 All ER 665.
[3] *Bah (EO (Turkey) – liability to deport)* [2012] UKUT 00196 (IAC).
[4] See for example *DS (Afghanistan) v Secretary of State for the Home Department* [2011] EWCA Civ 305, [2011] All ER (D) 248 (Mar).

Procedural safeguards for victims of trafficking

13.53 Protection of the privacy of a victim of trafficking is particularly important because of the possible dangers of intimidation and retaliation and also because of the humiliation and hurt that may be caused by unwanted disclosure. Protection of the victim's privacy is essential to preserve the victim's chances of recovery and social integration in either the home or receiving country particularly bearing in mind the stigma that may attach to his or her experiences.[1] An anonymity direction for a victim of trafficking is likely to be appropriate.[2] The trafficking instruments provide clear safeguards for victims of trafficking giving evidence in criminal proceedings related to their trafficking.[3] Bearing in mind that victims of trafficking are to be treated as victims of crime[4] and that 'the civil court should cleave to the same policy as the criminal court'[5] there is plainly good reason for the tribunal to apply the principles set out in the trafficking instruments to ensure that evidence given by victims or potential victims is secured in an appropriate fashion. In summary they are:

(i)   Appropriate measures to provide effective and appropriate protection of the victim of trafficking, including of their identity;

(ii)   Appropriate measures to avoid secondary victimization, including avoidance of unnecessary repetition of interviews, giving evidence in open court and unnecessary questioning of the victim about his or her private life.[6]

---

[1]   Explanatory report to ECAT para 138, Anne T Gallagher, *The International Law of Human Trafficking* pp 303-304.

[2]   Article 11 of ECAT.

[3]   Trafficking Directive: Recital 20, Article 12(4) and in respect of child victims, Article 15. For further discussion see UN Joint Commentary on the Trafficking Directive at 67-68.

[4]   *L v R, The Children's Comr for England and Equality and Human Rights Commission intervening* [2013] EWCA Crim 991, [2014] 1 All ER 113, [2013] 2 Cr App Rep 247.

[5]   *Gray v Thames Trains Ltd* [2009] UKHL 33, [2009] AC 1339, Lord Rodger at para 82.

[6]   Article 28(1)(a) and 30 of ECAT.

Chapter 14

WELFARE PROVISION FOR MIGRANTS AND ASYLUM SEEKERS

WELFARE PROVISION FOR IMMIGRANTS, EU MIGRANTS AND ASYLUM SEEKERS

14.1 This chapter describes welfare provision for migrants, including migrants from the European Economic Area, and the support available for asylum seekers. It includes a description of welfare provision by local authorities, as well as describing access to housing, education, health services and employment. The opening section, however, is concerned with access to welfare benefits.

WELFARE BENEFITS

The evolution of the social security system

14.2 The UK's social security system[1] began modestly with the Old-Age Pensions Act 1908 that provided a means-tested benefit for those aged 70 or over – at a time when the average life expectancy was well below 60. A contribution-based scheme was later adopted for the unemployed under the National Insurance Act 1911. By the end of the 1930s, state provision consisted of social insurance covering the major causes of income loss and conferring benefit at a flat-rate level, combined with a residual means-tested assistance scheme for those not covered or who had exhausted their right to insurance benefit. The Beveridge Report of 1942 aimed to devise a system which would be an attack upon 'the five giants on the road of reconstruction' – want, disease, ignorance, squalor, and idleness. Its primary aim was to make the insurance scheme universal and more comprehensive. Included among the laws passed were the National Assistance Act 1948 – which established a new non-contributory means-tested financial safety net, the precursor of Income Support, and the Family Allowance Act 1945 – which introduced universal family benefits – which later became Child Benefit. Since Beveridge, there have been more than 115 Acts of Parliament concerning the social security system and thousands of amending regulations. Significant changes over the last few decades include:

1983 – the introduction of Housing Benefit to replace rent rebates and allowances;

1992 – the introduction of Disability Living Allowance (DLA);

1996 – the introduction of Jobseeker's Allowance (JSA) in place of unemployment benefits;

2002 – the introduction of Pension Credit;

2003 – the introduction of Tax Credits for individuals and households in work.

The relative importance of means-tested support has grown substantially since 1948, thereby eroding the contributory principle. The UK benefit system is, therefore, a residence and means-based system rather than an insurance-based system. Broadly speaking, with the exception of contributory Jobseekers Allowance (JSA) and Employment Support Allowance (ESA), and the State Pension – eligibility to welfare benefits depends on the individual claimant satisfying a residence test (save where that individual is excluded as a person subject to immigration control).

[1] *The Law of Social Security*, N J Wikeley, Anthony I Ogus, E M Barendt, Oxford University Press; fifth edition (Feb 2005), Chapter 1, 'Evolution of Social Security in Britain', pp 1–8. The benefits of Britain; Growth in Social Security spending since WWII – Olympic Britain Social and economic change since the 1908 and 1948 London Games, Gavin Thompson, et al, House of Commons Library (2010).

Austerity and welfare reform

14.3 The Coalition Government of 2010 came into power in the wake of the international financial crisis of 2008. It commenced an austerity programme aimed at reducing the budget deficit, and the reduction in welfare spending was part of that programme.[1] Government ministers argued that a growing culture of 'welfare dependency' was perpetuating welfare spending.[2] There followed a raft of cuts and cost-saving reforms in an attempt to reduce the social security budget. Some of the most significant items on the Government's 'welfare reform'[3] agenda are:

- *Freezing rates* – at which working-aged benefits are awarded.[4]
- *Benefit Indexing* – the indexing of certain benefits to the Consumer Price Index (CPI) rather than to the Retail Price Index (RPI).[5]

- *Benefit Capping* – the restriction in the amount of housing benefit paid in both the private and social sectors. This includes the introduction of the 'bedroom tax'[6] and the overall benefit cap.[7]
- The increased use of conditionality[8] and sanctions[9] by Jobseeker Plus staff.
- The transfer of responsibility for crisis loans and community care grants to local authorities.[10]
- The replacement of council tax benefit by the less generous council tax reduction scheme.[11]

Many regard the dramatic increase in the use of food banks in the UK as being linked to the cumulative impact of the changes introduced by 'welfare reform'.[12]

[1]   *The Coalition: Our Programme for Government Cabinet Office*, HM Government, May 2010.
[2]   *State of the nation report: poverty, worklessness and welfare dependency in the UK*. HM Government. May 2010.
[3]   DWP reform: DWP's welfare reform agenda explained, April 2014, DWP GOV.UK.
[4]   The Welfare Benefits Up-rating Act 2013.
[5]   Rent Officers (Housing Benefit Functions) (Amendment) Order 2012, SI 2012/646.
[6]   Welfare Reform Act 2012, s 69 and the Housing Benefit (Amendment) Regulations 2012, SI 2012/3040.
[7]   Welfare Reform Act 2012, s 96 and the Benefit Cap (Housing Benefit) Regulations 2012, SI 2012/2994.
[8]   Welfare Reform Act 2012, s 44.
[9]   Welfare Reform Act 2012, s 46.
[10]   Welfare Reform Act 2012, ss 70–73 and the 'Settlement Letter' from Steve Webb to Local Authorities Chief Executives, dated 9 August 2012.
[11]   Local Government Finance Act 2012, s 10.
[12]   See *Food Banks and Food Poverty*, House of Commons Library, Standard Note: SN06657 House of Commons Library (9 April 2014).

The history of the eligibility rules for welfare benefits

14.4 Prior to 1988, the eligibility rules for migrants seeking to access welfare benefits were relatively straightforward. In general terms, aliens and immigrants could not access benefits if there were conditions of entry imposed on their stay that debarred them from receiving public funds. Those from the Common Market were entitled to receive benefits on the same basis as UK nationals. Asylum seekers and those whose immigration status was unresolved could claim means-tested benefits, albeit at reduced rates.[1] Over time, a series of legislative changes has been introduced which restrict or exclude migrants from mainstream welfare benefits.[2] Some of the major changes include:

—   From 1988 onwards, the benefit regulations included a definition of 'person from abroad' to exclude claimants from benefits if they fell into the category of someone who did not have leave to enter or remain in the UK or whose leave was conditional upon not having recourse to public funds.
—   In 1994, the definition of 'person from abroad' was widened by the introduction of the 'habitual residence test' within the Income Support scheme. The aim of the test was to stop someone claiming welfare benefits immediately when they entered the Common Travel Area (the

United Kingdom, the Channel Islands, the Isle of Man or the Republic of Ireland). The test was aimed principally at European Economic Area[3] (EEA) nationals but applies to UK citizens as well.[4]

— In 1996, regulations were introduced designed to remove entitlement for most asylum seekers to Income Support, Housing Benefit and Council Tax Benefit, with savings provisions for certain categories of asylum seekers (including those who claimed 'on arrival'). These provisions were ruled to be *ultra vires* but were re-enacted in primary legislation (the Asylum and Immigration Act 1996).

— In 1996, a general exclusion from welfare benefits for immigrants from countries outside of the EEA was introduced by section 115 of the Immigration and Asylum Act 1999.[5]

— In 2000, benefit entitlement for new asylum seekers who claimed 'on arrival' came to an end. The arrangements for supporting asylum seekers were made separate from the main welfare benefits system.

— In 2004, 'the habitual residence test' was supplemented by the introduction of 'the right to reside test'. Under this test, EEA nationals must show that they are exercising a positive EU right (or are a family member of such a person) before they can claim mainstream welfare benefits.[6] In addition, a Worker's Registration Scheme was introduced for nationals from eight of the Accession states joining the EU in May 2004.[7]

— In January 2007, a worker authorisation scheme was introduced for nationals from Bulgaria and Romania (which was later extended to Croatians).[8] In 2014, changes were made to restrict EEA jobseekers' access to welfare benefits, including a statutory presumption that entitlement to income-based Jobseeker's Allowance ends after six months, alongside the removal of any entitlement to Housing Benefit for certain EEA jobseekers.[9]

[1] *National Welfare Benefits Handbook*, tenth edn 1980/81 CPAG, Janet Allbeson, et al, p 22.

[2] *The Law of Social Security*, by N. J. Wikeley, Anthony I. Ogus, E. M. Barendt Oxford University Press; fifth edn (Feb 2005), Chapter 7, Part 4, 'Persons from abroad', p 232. *Social Security Legislation 2013/14 Volume II: Income Support, Jobseeker's Allowance, State Pension Credit and the Social Fund*, by P Wood, et al, Sweet & Maxwell (Sept 2013), commentary at para 2.155, p 299.

[3] The European Economic Area (EEA) provides for the free movement of goods, persons, services and capital through three of four member states of the European Free Trade Association (EFTA) (Iceland, Liechtenstein and Norway) and 27 of 28 member states of the European Union (EU), with Croatia provisionally applying the agreement pending its ratification by all EEA countries. It was established on 1 January 1994 (OJ 1994 L 1, 3.1,p 3) following an agreement between the member states and the European Community, which later became the EU. One EFTA member, Switzerland, has not joined the EEA but has a series of bilateral agreements, including a free trade agreement, with the EU. The 27 member states of the EU who make up the EEA are: Austria, Belgium, Bulgaria, Cyprus, Czech Republic, Denmark, Estonia, Finland, France, Germany, Greece, Hungary, Italy, Latvia, Lithuania, Luxembourg, Malta, Netherlands, Poland, Portugal, Republic of Ireland, Romania, Slovenia, Slovak Republic, Spain, Sweden and the, United Kingdom. Note, all references to the EEA should be read so as to include Switzerland.

[4] See Actual habitual residence at **14.22** below.

[5] See Persons subject to immigration control (PSIC) at **14.9** below.

[6] See EEA nationals and the right to reside test **14.32** below.

[7] See Special rules for accession nationals at **14.74** below.

[8] See Special rules for accession nationals at **14.74** below.

See Extended right of residence – jobseekers at **14.36** and Retained right of residence – jobseekers at **14.53** below.

The main groups affected by the eligibility rules

14.5 When looking at the eligibility rules on welfare benefits for people coming to the UK from abroad, the groups affected can be split into the following broad groups:

Asylum seekers: Persons waiting for a decision on an asylum application – are not entitled to mainstream welfare benefits. Instead, they may be eligible for accommodation and/or financial support ('asylum support') from the Home Office. Cash support for asylum seekers is less generous than social security benefits. Refugees – ie asylum seekers whose application for asylum has been successful – are able to claim social security benefits and tax credits on the same basis as UK nationals.

Non-EEA nationals: For nationals of countries that are not part of the EU, immigration status is the key factor determining what they can claim. Most members of this group face a general exclusion from welfare benefits if there is a 'no recourse to public funds' condition attached to their leave to enter or remain in the UK.[1]

Persons who have recently arrived in the UK from abroad: All migrants, including UK nationals returning from a period abroad, must show that they are actually habitually resident in the Common Travel Area (the UK, the Channel Islands, the Isle of Man or the Republic of Ireland) before they are eligible to claim mainstream welfare benefits.[2]

EEA nationals: While nationals from the EEA[3] do not require leave to enter the UK, they must nevertheless satisfy the right to reside test in order to access mainstream welfare benefits. Only those EEA nationals who can demonstrate that they have a positive EU right to reside in the UK are eligible to claim welfare benefits under this test.[4]

[1]   See: Migrants from non-EEA countries at **14.8**, and person subject to immigration control (PSIC) at **14.9** below.
[2]   See: Actual habitual residence at **14.22** below.
[3]   The European Economic Area (EEA) consists of the European Union states – ie Austria, Belgium, Bulgaria, [AQ] Croatia check this (accession State), Cyprus, Czech Republic, Denmark, Estonia, Finland, France, Germany, Greece, Hungary, Italy, Latvia, Lithuania, Luxembourg, Malta, Netherlands, Poland, Portugal, Republic of Ireland, Romania, Slovenia, Slovak Republic, Spain, Sweden, United Kingdom plus Iceland, Liechtenstein, and Norway. Switzerland has agreements with the EU so that its citizens are generally treated in the same way as EU nationals.
[4]   See footnote 3 to **14.4** above for details of the EU states that make up the European Economic Area (EEA).

Overview of the rules – the key questions

14.6 Under the current scheme, the determination of whether a migrant can access welfare benefits will depend on a number of factors. These include nationality, immigration status (and any conditions attached to it) the circumstances under which the person arrived in the UK and whether they are in work or looking for work. The key questions for immigration practitioners when considering if someone is eligible to claim welfare benefits include:

(i)   Is the individual excluded from any welfare benefits because they are 'a person subject to immigration control' – ie someone whose leave to remain is subject to a 'public funds' condition?[1]

(ii)   Despite being a person 'subject to immigration control' can the individual nevertheless access certain benefits as they belong to one of the categories of claimants who come within one of the exemptions to the general rule on immigration control?[2]

(iii)   If the individual has recently arrived from abroad, can they establish that they are actually habitually resident in the Common Travel Area (the UK, the Channel Islands, the Isle of Man or the Republic of Ireland) or are they treated as exempt from that test?[3]

(iv)   For certain individuals who have recently arrived from abroad who wish to claim benefits as a jobseeker, have they been 'living in' the Common Travel Area for three months before they claim certain out-of-work benefits?[4]

(v)   For EEA nationals, even though they are not 'a person subject to immigration control', do they have a right to reside in the UK in the sense that they are exercising a positive EU right or are they treated as exempt from that requirement?[5]

(vi)   Are there any additional residence conditions that need to be met, such as the need to be ordinarily resident or a need for a past period of presence in the UK?[6]

[1]   See: Persons subject to immigration control (PSIC) at **14.9** below.
[2]   See: Exemptions to the PSIC rules at **14.10** below.
[3]   See: Actual habitual residence at **14.22** below.
[4]   See: The living in the UK for three months residency rule for certain benefits at **14.30** below.
[5]   See: EEA nationals and the right to reside requirement test **14.32** below.
[6]   See: Further residence requirements at **14.78** below.

OVERVIEW OF THE WORKING-AGE BENEFITS

14.7 According to statistics published by the DWP in February 2014, there were 5.3 million working-age benefit claimants.[1] The main working-age benefits in the UK system can be divided into the following categories:

—   *Income-replacement benefits*: These are designed to meet the day-to-day living costs of those who are unemployed or unable to work because they are sick, disabled, parents of young children or pregnant, such as income-based Jobseeker's Allowance (JSA), income-related Employment and Support Allowance (ESA) and Income Support (IS).

—   *Additional income benefits*: These deliver additional income to people in work and with children, such as Tax Credits and Child Benefit (CHB).

—   *Extra costs benefits*: These provide support to alleviate the extra costs associated with disability, for housing costs, carers, the bereaved and those disabled through an injury or disease as a result of work, such as Housing Benefit (HB), Personal Independence Payment (PIP), Carer's Allowance (CA) and Industrial Injuries Disablement (IID) Benefit.

1   *Quarterly National Statistics on benefit claimants* (November 2013 data) published 14 May 2014 by the DWP, GOV.UK. Working-age benefits are defined by the DWP to be: Jobseeker's Allowance, Income Support, Employment & Support Allowance, Incapacity Benefit and Severe Disablement Allowance.

MIGRANTS FROM NON-EEA COUNTRIES

The public funds condition

14.8 Immigrants with leave to enter the UK but who have a 'no recourse to public funds' condition attached to their leave would be in breach of that condition if they claim welfare benefits that are defined as 'public funds' in the Immigration Rules.[1] Public funds are defined in the Immigration Rules as:

—   Attendance Allowance (AA)
—   Carer's Allowance (CA)
—   Child Benefit (CHB)
—   Child Tax Credit (CTC)
—   Council Tax Reduction (CTR)
—   Disability Living Allowance (DLA)
—   Income-related Employment and Support Allowance (ESA(IR))
—   Housing Benefit (HB)
—   Income-based Jobseeker's Allowance (JSA(IB))
—   Income Support (IS)
—   Pension Credit (PC)
—   Personal Independence Payment (PIP)
—   Service Disablement Allowance (SDA)
—   Social Fund Payments
—   Working Tax Credit (WTC)
—   Universal Credit (UC)
—   An allocation of local authority housing
—   Local authority homelessness assistance

The public funds condition will be breached if the sponsor receives *additional* public funds due to the presence of the person subject to immigration control which they would not otherwise have received. On the other hand, the condition will not be breached if the amount of benefit the sponsor receives is not affected by the person who is subject to the public funds condition – eg where the ineligible person is ignored under the benefit rules. This is confirmed by rule 6A of the Immigration Rules that states:

> '6A. For the purpose of these Rules, a person (P) is not to be regarded as having (or potentially having) recourse to public funds merely because P is (or will be) reliant in whole or in part on public funds provided to P's sponsor unless, as a result of P's presence in the United Kingdom, the sponsor is (or would be) entitled to increased or additional public funds (save where such entitlement to increased or additional public funds is by virtue of P and the sponsor's joint entitlement to benefits under the regulations referred to in paragraph 6B).'

Until recently, 'public funds' did not include benefits that are based on National Insurance contributions. Consequently, immigration status did not affect eligibility to contributory benefits ie contribution-based Jobseeker's Allowance, contributory Employment and Support Allowance and the State Pension. Other work-related benefits including Statutory Maternity Pay, Statutory Adoption Pay, Statutory Paternity Pay, Statutory Sick Pay and Industrial Injuries benefits were also payable regardless of immigration status. However, as a result of the measures due to be introduced by sections 61–63 of the Welfare Reform Act 2012, eligibility for these benefits is to be restricted to those who are entitled to work in the UK. When these provisions come into force if someone has been working illegally in the UK, they will not be entitled to receive these benefits, even if they have paid National Insurance Contributions (NICs).

[1]   The Immigration Rules: Introduction – Interpretation, paragraph 6(a)–(f) (last updated 11 July 2014).

Persons subject to immigration control (PSIC)

14.9 In addition, primary legislation contains a general exclusion from most welfare benefits[1] and tax credits[2] if the non-EEA claimant is a 'person subject to immigration control' (PSIC). A person is subject to the PSIC rule if they require leave to enter or remain in the UK but do not have it;[3] are subject to a 'public funds' restriction;[4] or they were given leave to remain as a result of a maintenance undertaking.[5] The main benefits subject to the PSIC rule are set out below:

— Attendance Allowance (AA)
— Carer's Allowance (CA)
— Child Benefit (CHB)
— Child Tax Credit (CTC)
— Council Tax Reduction (CTR)[6]
— Disability Living Allowance (DLA)
— Income-related Employment and Support Allowance (ESA(IR))
— Employment and Support Allowance in Youth (abolished from April 2012)
— Housing Benefit (HB)
— Incapacity Benefit for incapacity in Youth (abolished from January 2011)
— Income-based Jobseeker's Allowance (JSA(IB))
— Income Support (IS)
— State Pension Credit (SPC)
— Personal Independence Payment (PIP)
— Severe Disablement Allowance (SDA)
— Social Fund Payments (SF)
— Universal Credit (UC)
— Working Tax Credit (WTC)

British citizens cannot be excluded from entitlement to benefits under this provision as they are not subject to the PSIC rule. Nor are EEA nationals excluded under this provision.[7]

[1]   IAA 1999, s 115(1).
[2]   Tax Credits Act 2002, s 42.
[3]   IAA 1999, s 115(9)(a).
[4]   IAA 1999, s 115(9)(b).

5   IAA 1999, s 115(9)(c).
6   Council Tax Reduction Schemes (Default Scheme) (England) Regulations 2012, SI 2012/2886, reg 13, Schedule, para 22.
7   IAA 1999, s 115(9).

List of exemptions to the PSIC rule

14.10 Whilst the definition of 'a person subject to immigration control' in section 115 of the 1999 Act forms the starting point for considering eligibility for welfare benefits, the benefit regulations contain a number of exemptions where the individual can claim benefits despite being subject to the PSIC rule:

—   Cases were the person subject to the PSIC rule is admitted to the UK as sponsored immigrants as a result of a written maintenance undertaking who have been resident in the UK for five years or more and those who have been resident for less than five years but whose sponsor has died.[1]

—   Cases where the person subject to the PSIC rule is a national of a country that has ratified the European Convention on Social and Medical Assistance (ECSMA) or the Council of Europe Social Charter (CESC) and who are lawfully present in the UK or a national of a country which has a reciprocal social security agreement with the UK.[2]

—   Cases where the person subject to the PSIC rule is a family member of an EEA national.[3]

—   Cases where Tax Credits are claimed jointly by a couple but only one member is subject to the PSIC rule.[4]

—   Cases where the ineligible person's partner is receiving the funds they are entitled to.[5]

—   Cases where the person subject to the PSIC rule is appealing a refusal to vary previous leave which was not subject to a public funds condition such that the previous discretionary leave should be extended while the appeal is pending.[6]

Note, that the exemption for those who are temporarily without funds from abroad has been repealed.[7]

1   Social Security (Immigration and Asylum) Consequential Amendments Regulations 2000, SI 2000/636, reg 2(1) and Schedule, Pt I, paras 2–3 – see Exemption based on leave subject to a maintenance undertaking at **14.13**.
2   SI 2000/636, reg 2(1)–(2) and Schedule, Pt I, para 4, Pt II, paras 1–2 – see Exemption as a result of the ECSMA or the Social Charter and the Association agreement with the European Union at **14.14** and Exemption as a result of reciprocal social security agreements at **14.18** below.
3   SI 2000/636, reg 2(1) and Schedule, Pt II, para 3 – see Exemption based on living with a family member of an EEA national at **14.17** below.
4   Tax Credits (Immigration) Regulations 2003, SI 2003/653, reg 3(1) – see: Exemptions in respect of tax credits at **14.19** below.
5   Modernised guidance for UK Border Agency staff, Public funds, at p 17 (v.12–24 February 2014) – see: Couples with mixed immigration status at **14.20** below.
6   Whilst s 115 of the Immigration and Asylum Act 1999 continues to exclude those who have leave to enter or remain only as a result of 1999 Act (s 115(9)(d) refers to Sch 4, para 17). As the latter was repealed by Sch 9 para 1 to the Nationality, Immigration and Asylum Act 2002, it is arguable that the reference in s 115 should in fact read as if to s 3C(2) of the Immigration Act 1971, which would extend the previous leave pending an appeal.
7   The provision in SI 2000/636, reg 2(1) Schedule, Pt I, para 1 was repealed from 29 October 2013 by the Social Security (Miscellaneous Amendments) (No 3) Regulations 2013, SI 2013/2536, reg 9.

Exemption to the PSIC rule under the 2000 Regulations

14.11 The primary legislation does not contain any exceptions to the PSIC rule but the Immigration and Asylum Act 1999 contains a power to exempt persons of specified categories or descriptions from the general exclusion in section 115(3)–(4). This is acknowledged in paragraph 6B of the Immigration Rules[1] that reads:

'6B. Subject to paragraph 6C, a person (P) shall not be regarded as having recourse to public funds if P is entitled to benefits specified under section 115 of the Immigration and Asylum Act 1999 by virtue of regulations made under sub-sections (3) and (4) of that section or section 42 of the Tax Credits Act 2002.'

The relevant regulations are the Social Security (Immigration and Asylum) Consequential Amendments Regulations 2000:[2]

[1]   The Immigration Rules: Introduction – Interpretation, para 6(a)–(f) (last updated 11 July 2014).
[2]   Social Security (Immigration and Asylum) Consequential Amendments Regulations 2000, SI 2000/636.

Part 1 – Exemption for certain means-tested benefits

14.12 Under Part 1 of the Schedule to the Consequential Regulations a person who is subject to the PSIC rule is nevertheless eligible to claim the following means-tested benefits under the normal rules: Universal Credit (UB), income-based Jobseeker's Allowance (JSA(IB)), Income Support (IS), income-related Employment and Support Allowance (ESA(IR)), Housing Benefit (HB), and Social Fund Payments.[1] The categories under this exemption are described below.

[1]   SI 2000/636, reg 2(1) Schedule, Pt I, para 2.

Exemption based on leave subject to a maintenance undertaking

14.13 Under the exemption based on leave subject to a maintenance under-taking, any individual who has been resident for more than five years, starting from the date of entry or the date of the undertaking (whichever is the later)[1] or any individual who has been resident for less than five years but whose sponsor has died,[2] will be eligible to claim the following means-tested benefits: UC, JSA(IB), IS, ESA(IR), HB and Social Fund payments – subject to qualifying under the normal benefit rules. Case law has established that an informal or voluntary sponsorship may not count as an undertaking and it is therefore important that the benefit authorities have regard to the approach set out in case law when determining whether it is a formal undertaking:

- an undertaking entails something in the nature of a promise or an agreement which obliges a sponsor to maintain and accommodate the dependent relative;[3]
- whether a document amounts to an undertaking is a question of fact;[4]
- the burden is on the Secretary of State for Work and Pensions to show that leave to remain has been granted 'as a result of' a maintenance undertaking;[5]

- an undertaking ceases to have effect if the sponsored immigrant becomes a British citizen.[6]

An offence will be committed where the sponsor persistently refuses or neglects to maintain a person and, as a result, income-related benefits are paid to the person. Those benefits can be recovered from the sponsor as overpayments.[7] It should be noted that formal undertakings do not affect access to the non-means-tested benefits under Part 11 of the Schedule to the Consequential Regulations (see below).

1 SI 2000/636, reg 2(1) Schedule, Pt I, para 2.
2 SI 2000/636, reg 2(1) and Schedule, Pt I, para 3.
3 For a summary of the case law on sponsors and undertakings, including *Shah v Secretary of State for Social Security* [2002] EWCA Civ 285 (also reported as R(IS) 2/02), *R (on the application of Begum) v Social Security Comrs* [2003] EWHC 3380 (Admin) (also reported as R(IS) 11/04) and *Ahmed v Secretary of State for Work and Pensions* [2005] EWCA Civ 535 (also reported as R(IS) 8/05) see paragraph 6 of the Commissioner's decision in CIS/1697/2004.
4 *R (Begum) v Social Security Commissioner* [2003] EWHC 3380 (Admin) (also reported as R(IS) 11/04), para 31.
5 R(PC) 1/09 (CPC/1872/2007) para 18.
6 R(PC) 2/07 (CPC/4317/2006) para 7.
7 Social Security Administration Act 1992, ss 105 and 106.

Exemption as a result of the ECSMA or the CESC

14.14 Nationals of Turkey and Macedonia subject to the PSIC rules can claim the non-means-tested benefits listed above without being in breach of the Immigration Rules as those two non-European countries have ratified either of the two Treaties of the Council of Europe, the European Convention on Social and Medical Assistance (ECSMA) or the European Social Charter (CESC).[1] Nationals from these two countries, if they are 'lawfully present'[2] in the UK, can claim the non-means-tested benefits listed under Part 1 of the Schedule under the normal rules. However, ECSMA country nationals still have to meet the right to reside requirement.[3] It has been held that asylum seekers who are nationals of these countries who are on temporary admission do not benefit from these arrangements as lawful presence by virtue of domestic law alone does not equate to a right to reside.[4]

1 SI 2000/636, Schedule, Pt I, para 4. See also *Modernised guidance for UK Border Agency staff, Public funds*, at pp 19–22 and 54 (v.12–24 February 2014).
2 See *Szoma v Secretary of State for the Department of Work and Pensions* [2005] UKHL 64 [2006] 1 AC 564, [2006] 1 All ER 1 (also reported as R(IS) 2/06).
3 See: The right to reside requirement test at **14.32** below.
4 See *Yesiloz (formerly known as Gulhanim Aykac) v Camden Borough Council (Secretary of State for Work and Pensions intervening)* [2009] EWCA Civ 415 (also reported as R(H) 7/09) that held that a Turkish national granted temporary admission as an asylum seeker who was exempt from the actual habitual resident test, was held to be still subject to the right to reside test. (See also *CH/2321/2007* and R(IS) 3/08.)

Part II – Exemption for certain non-means-tested benefits

14.15 Under Part 1 of the Schedule to the Immigration and Asylum Regulations 2000, a PSIC is eligible to claim the following means-tested benefits under the normal rules without breaching the Immigration Rules, namely

Attendance Allowance (AA), Severe Disablement Allowance (SDA), Carer's Allowance (CA), Disability Living Allowance (DLA), Personal Independence Payment (PIP), a Social Fund Payment or Child Benefit (CHB).[1]

[1] Social Security (Immigration and Asylum) Consequential Amendments Regulations 2000, SI 2000/636, reg 2(1) Schedule, Pt I.

Exemption as a result of the Association Agreement with the European Union

14.16 Those subject to the PSIC rules can claim the non-means-tested benefits listed above without being in breach of the Immigration Rules as a result of the Association Agreement with the European Union.[1] The following countries have an Association Agreement with the EU that provides for equal treatment in the field of social security: Turkey, Morocco, Algeria, Tunisia and San Marino. Nationals from these countries who are lawfully working in the UK are entitled to claim the non-means-tested benefits listed above.

[1] SI 2000/636, reg 2(1) and Schedule, Pt II, para 2. See also *Modernised guidance for UK Border Agency staff, Public funds*, at pp 19–22 and 54 (v.12–24 February 2014).

Exemption based on living with a family member of an EEA national

14.17 This exemption covers a claimant who is subject to immigration control but who claims an entitlement to the non-means-tested benefits listed above on the basis that they are a member of a family of an EEA national.[1] Applying the plain meaning of the regulations, the provision includes a British child as the UK is a State contracting party to the EEA agreement as, unlike the Immigration (EEA) Regulations 2006 Immigration and Asylum 2000 Regulations do not exclude the UK from its definition of an 'EEA State'.[2] The provision has been the subject of decisions of the Social Security Commissioners in Great Britain and Northern Ireland. The provision was initially considered by *Deputy Commissioner Poynter* in CDLA/708/2007, which involved a claim for Disability Living Allowance made by a sibling of a child with Irish nationality. The Commissioner concluded that the exemption applied only to families of EU workers exercising freedom of movement rights. However, in *JFP v Department for Social Development*[3] the Chief Commissioner of Northern Ireland declined to follow the approach taken in CDLA/708/2007. Instead it was held that given the clear and unambiguous terms of the provision, it applied to a family member who was a UK national who had not exercised an EU right of free movement.[4] Note that the position of non-EEA nationals with a derived right to reside as a primary carer of a British child however, is more problematic given that the habitual residence test was amended to expressly exclude those whose sole right to reside is based on being *Zambrano* carers from access to CHB.[5]

[1] Social Security (Immigration and Asylum) Consequential Amendments Regulations 2000 SI 2000/636, reg 2(1) and Schedule, Pt II, para 1.
[2] *Child Benefit Guidance* issued by HM Revenue & Customs states that the claimant is covered if their family member is an EEA or Swiss national, or UK national: *Child Benefit Technical Manual*, 10140. *CBTM10140 – Residence and immigration: immigration – exceptions to the general exclusion*.
[3] *JFP v Department for Social Development (DLA)* [2012] NICom 267.
[4] *JFP v Department for Social Development*, paras 43–45. While a decision of a Commissioner in Northern Ireland is not formally binding in Great Britain, it should be treated as having

equal authority when it rules on identical provisions, see *CCS/4994/2002*, para 30 and *Secretary of State for Work and Pensions v Deane* [2010] EWCA Civ 699, [2011] 1 WLR 743] para 26.

5   The Child Benefit and Child Tax Credit (Miscellaneous Amendments) Regulations 2012, SI 2012/2612. It is arguable that *Zambrano* carers should still be able to access CHB under this exemption on the basis that the drawing up of the exception in the 2000 Regulations would be a pointless exercise if only EEA nationals who are exercising free movement rights under the EEA Agreement would be entitled to claim those benefits (and therefore have no need to rely on the exception in the 2000 Regulations).

Exemption as a result of reciprocal social security agreements

14.18   There are also exemptions from the PSIC rule in respect of particular benefits as a result of *reciprocal social security agreements*: The following is a list of non-EEA countries which have reciprocal social security agreements with the United Kingdom: Barbados, Mauritius, Bermuda, New Zealand, Canada, the Philippines, Israel, USA (which also covers American Samoa, Guam, the Northern Mariana, Puerto Rico and the US Virgin Islands), Jamaica, Former Yugoslav Republic of Macedonia (which also covers Bosnia-Herzegovina, Kosovo, Montenegro and Serbia).[1]

1   Social Security Administration Act 1992, s 179. See also *Modernised guidance for UK Border Agency staff, Public funds*, at pp 19–22 and 54 (v.12–24 February 2014) or 'Claiming benefits if you live, move or travel abroad' on GOV.UK.

Exemptions in respect of tax credits

14.19   For Tax Credits there is an exemption from the exclusion of the PSIC rule where the claim for Tax Credits is a joint claim by a couple and only one member of the couple is subject to immigration control.[1] The exemption applies to those in the following five types of case:

(1)   persons given leave to enter or remain on the basis of a maintenance undertaking who have been resident in the UK for at least five years;[2]

(2)   persons given leave to enter or remain on the basis of a maintenance undertaking where the person giving the undertaking has died;[3]

The following exemptions, which are specific to Tax Credit, apply differently depending on whether the claim is for Child Tax Credit or for Working Tax Credit:

(3)   where the claim is for Working Tax Credit, the exemption applies to nationals of countries which have ratified the European Convention on Social and Medical Assistance (ECSMA) or the Council of Europe Social Charter (CESC) and who are lawfully present in the UK. Child Tax Credit is also available under this exemption if immediately before the date of the claim the claimant was eligible for additional Income Support or income-related Jobseeker's Allowance in respect of the child;[4] or

(4)   where the claim is for Child Tax Credit, the exemption applies to nationals of those countries which have made an agreement with the EU providing for the equal treatment of workers in the area of social security: Algeria, Morocco, Slovenia, Tunisia and Turkey. However, such claimants must be 'lawfully working' in Great Britain.[5]

In summary, a married or unmarried couple can claim Tax Credits as though both of them were not subject to the PSIC rule, provided that *one* of them is either not a 'PSIC' *or* is within one of the exempt cases in (1)–(5) above.[6] If the eligible claimant is an EEA national, access to Tax Credits is also subject to the habitual residence requirement.[7]

[1]   Tax Credits (Immigration) Regulations 2003, SI 2003/653, reg 3(1).
[2]   SI 2003/653, reg 3(1) – Case 1.
[3]   SI 2003/653, reg 3(1) – Case 2.
[4]   SI 2003/653, reg 3(1) – Case 4. Child Tax Credits became available under the Tax Credits scheme from 6 April 2004 when the scheme first came into force.
[5]   SI 2003/653, reg 3(1) – Case 5. The agreements confer no right to reside or to work in the UK, so to qualify nationals would have to have leave to enter or remain in the UK which permitted them to work.
[6]   SI 2003/653, reg 3(2). The Immigration Rules refer to the exemptions in the Tax Credit legislation (para 6B) and confirm that such persons will not be treated as in breach of the public funds condition. However, the exemption does not apply when the application for leave is made from outside the UK and the applicant seeks to rely on a future entitlement to a joint claim for tax credits (para 6C).
[7]   SI 2003/653, reg 3(4) and the Tax Credits (Residence) Regulations 2003, SI 2003/654, reg 3(4).

Couples with a mixed immigration status

14.20 The public funds condition will only be breached if additional welfare benefits are received due to the presence of an ineligible person (ie someone who is a PSIC) which they would not otherwise have received. Where the same level of benefits is received regardless of the presence of the ineligible person, then the public funds condition will not have been breached.[1] The rules governing claims made by a couple where one is subject to the PSIC rule are set out below:

- *Child Benefit*: This can only be paid to one person at a time, namely the person who is 'responsible for one or more children in any week'.[2] The amount of CHB paid depends on the number of children for whom a claim is made, regardless of whether the claimant is single or a member of a couple. This means that where a couple is made up of both an eligible and ineligible partner, the eligible person can claim CHB without breaching the other member's public funds condition.
- *Income Support, income-related Employment and Support Allowance, and income-based Jobseeker's Allowance*: For these income-related benefits, if the claimant is eligible but the partner is excluded as a PSIC, the claim will be paid at the single person rate.[3]
- *Housing Benefit*: The rules governing HB provide that in the case of a couple, the claim needs to be made by one person on behalf of the other partner[4] and benefit will be calculated based on the applicable amount set for a couple. However, as there is no provision in the HB rules to ignore the ineligible partner, there is a risk that the public funds condition will be breached.[5]
- *Working Tax Credit and Child Tax Credit*: Where a couple make a joint claim for Tax Credits, the member who is a PSIC can be ignored if he or she comes under one of the exemptions for couples with mixed immigration status in the tax credits regulations[6] (see **14.19** below).

- *Personal Independence Payment.* PIP is paid to the eligible disabled person in their own right, regardless of the ineligible person's presence.[7] Moreover, PIP is not counted as income for other means-tested benefits.[8]
- *State Pension Credit*: The rules for SPC make specific provision for the guarantee credit to be paid at the single rate where the other member of the couple is excluded as a PSIC, thereby avoiding any breach of the public funds condition.[9]
- Where an EEA national is *ineligible* to claim benefit in their own right but he or she is the partner of a UK national, the normal rules for couples with a mixed immigration status apply, ie the benefit will be payable at the single rate.
- In the case of an EEA national who is *eligible* – ie as a 'qualified person' exercising EU rights in the UK, his or her spouse or civil partner will have the same benefit rights as EEA nationals.[10]
- Where an Accession national from Croatia is eligible to claim benefit in his or her own right as an authorised worker (see **14.76**), the person's spouse or civil partner will have the same benefit rights as EEA nationals, save that they cannot access Jobseeker's Allowance.[11]
- Where the eligible claimant's partner receives asylum support, benefit is not payable for the partner, but the value of any asylum support is disregarded if it is paid in kind – eg food vouchers, but it will count as income if paid in cash.[12]

[1] *Modernised guidance for UK Border Agency staff, Public funds*, at p17 (v.12–24 February 2014).
[2] Social Security Contributions and Benefits Act 1992, s 141.
[3] Income Support (General) Regulations 1987, SI 1987/1967, Sch 7, para 16A(a); Jobseeker's Allowance Regulations 1996, SI 1996/207, Sch 5, para 13A(a); and Employment and Support Allowance Regulations 2008, SI 2008/794, Sch 5, para 10.
[4] Housing Benefit Regulations 2006, SI 2006/213, reg 82(1).
[5] SI 2006/213, reg 22, Sch 3; SI 2006/215, reg 12, Sch 1. The public funds condition will not be breached if the eligible person is already receiving the maximum amount of benefit payable based on being in receipt of a means-tested benefit that passports them to full Housing Benefit.
[6] Tax Credits (Immigration) Regulations 2003, SI 2003/653, reg 3(1). Tax Credits (Immigration) Regulations 2003, SI 2003/653, reg 3(1).
[7] The Social Security (Personal Independence Payment) Regulations 2013, SI 337/2013, reg 16.
[8] IS (Gen) Regs 1987/1965, Sch 9, para 6 and 9; JSA Regs 1996/207, Sch 7, paras 7 and 10, ESA Regs 2008/794, Sch 8, paras 8 and 11. HB Regs 2006/213, Sch 5, para 6, SPC Regs 2002/1792, reg 15(1)(aa), and UC Regs SI 2013/376, reg 9(3)(f).
[9] State Pension Credit Regulations 2002, SI 2002/1792, reg 5(1)(h).
[10] Immigration (European Economic Area) Regulations 2006, SI 2006/1003, reg 14(2)(3).
[11] The Accession of Croatia (Immigration and Worker Authorisation) Regulations 2013, SI 2013/1460, regs 5(1) and 6(3)(c).
[12] Income Support (General) Regulations 1987, SI 1987/1967, reg 40(2) and Sch 9, para 21.

PERSONS WHO HAVE RECENTLY ARRIVED FROM ABROAD

The habitual residence test – the three elements

14.21 The habitual residence test was introduced in 1994 in response to concerns about 'benefit tourism'. Successive governments have continued to view the habitual residence test as a necessary measure to safeguard against possible abuse of the benefits system by those with 'no real links to the UK'. The test, in its current form, has three aspects or elements.

(1) *The three months residency rule* – For certain out-of-work benefits – ie income-based Jobseeker's Allowance, Child Tax Credit and Child Benefit, a claimant cannot be regarded as habitually resident until they have 'lived in' the Common Travel Area (the UK, the Channel Islands, the Isle of Man or the Republic of Ireland) for a period of three months before they claim any of those benefits.[1]

(2) *The actual habitual residence test* – This provides that anyone arriving in the UK for the first time, including a returning British national, is required to establish that they are habitually resident in the Common Travel Area before they can access certain benefits.[2]

(3) The *right to reside test* – This provides that a person cannot be treated as habitually resident in the Common Travel Area unless they meet the right to reside requirement. This aspect of the habitual residence test is aimed at EEA nationals and makes it a precondition that they are exercising a positive EU right (or are a family member of such a person) before they can claim mainstream welfare benefits.[3]

[1] See: The living in the UK for three months residency rule, for certain benefits at **14.30** below.
[2] See: Actual habitual residence at **14.22** below.
[3] See: EEA nationals and the right to reside requirement test at **14.32** below.

ACTUAL HABITUAL RESIDENCE

14.22 The habitual residence test (HRT) is applied to all migrants, including UK nationals returning from a period abroad, unless someone has only had a short absence abroad. The purpose of the HRT is to stop someone claiming welfare benefits immediately when they enter the UK. Under the test, the person will be prevented from claiming certain benefits within a certain period of arrival in the Common Travel Area (the UK, the Channel Islands, the Isle of Man or the Republic of Ireland) until they have established that their residence is actually habitual. The benefits covered by the habitual residence test are:

— Attendance Allowance (AA)[1]
— Carer's Allowance (CA)[2]
— Council Tax Reduction (CTR)[3]
— Disability Living Allowance (DLA)[4]
— Housing Benefit (HB)[5]
— Income-based Jobseeker's Allowance (JSA(IB))[6]
— Income-related Employment and Support Allowance (ESA(IB))[7]
— Income Support (IS)[8]
— State Pension credit (SPC)[9]
— Personal Independence Payment (PIP)[10]
— Universal Credit (UC).[11]

Where someone is not accepted as actually habitually resident in the Common Travel Area for IS, ESA(IR) JSA(IB) and HB, they will be classed as 'a person from abroad'. For AA, CA, CTR, DLA, SPC, PIP and UC, a person not accepted as habitually resident will be treated as 'not present in Great Britain' and therefore not entitled to any of those benefits.

1   Social Security (Attendance Allowance) Regulations 1991, SI 1991/2740, reg 1(a)(i).
2   Social Security (Invalid Care Allowance) Regulations 1976, SI 1976/409, reg 9(1)(a).
3   The Council Tax Reduction Schemes (Prescribed Requirements) (England) Regulations 2012, SI 2012/2885, reg 12(2) and the Council Tax Reduction Schemes (Prescribed Requirements) (Wales) Regulations 2012, SI 2012/3144, reg 26(2).
4   Social Security (Disability Living Allowance) Regulations 1991 SI 1991/2890, reg 2(1)(i)(a).
5   Housing Benefit Regulations 2006, SI 2006/213, reg 10(2). See also the Housing Benefit (Persons who have attained the qualifying age for state pension credit) Regulations 2006, SI 2006/214, reg 10(2).
6   Jobseeker's Allowance Regulations 1996, SI 1996/207, reg 85A(1).
7   Employment and Support Allowance Regulations 2008, SI 2008/794, reg 70(1).
8   Income Support (General) Regulations 1987, SI 1987/1967, reg 21AA(1).
9   State Pension Credit Regulations 2002, SI 2002/1792, reg 2(1).
10 The Social Security (Personal Independence Payment) Regulations 2013, SI 2013/377, reg 16(c).
11 The Universal Credit Regulations 2013, SI 2013/376, reg 9(1).

Categories of persons who are exempt from the habitual residence test

14.23 Certain categories of persons do not have to show actual habitual residence in the Common Travel Area as they are treated as exempt from the habitual residence test. These are:

—   an EEA national and a worker or self-employed person under EU law;[1] and an EEA national who retains worker or self-employed status under EU law;
—   a family member of one of the above;[2]
—   an EEA national or family member who has acquired a right of permanent residence;[3]
—   an Accession State worker subject to worker authorisation, who is treated as a worker under the Accession regulations relating to Croatia;[4]
—   a refugee;[5] or
—   a person who has been granted leave or who is deemed to have been granted leave outside the rules made under section 3(2) of the Immigration Act 1971 where that leave is:
    (i)   discretionary leave to enter or remain in the United Kingdom;
    (ii) leave to remain under the Destitution Domestic Violence concession; or
    (iii) leave deemed to have been granted by virtue of regulation 3 of the Displaced Persons (Temporary Protection) Regulations 2005, SI 2005/1379;[6] or
—   a person who has humanitarian protection granted under the Immigration Rules;[7] or
—   a person who is not subject to immigration control and who is in the UK as a result of their deportation, expulsion or other removal by compulsion of law from another country to the UK.[8]

1   IS (Gen) Regs 1987/1967, reg 21AA(4)(za); JSA Regs 1996/207, reg 85A(4)(za); ESA Regs 2008/794, reg 70(4)(za); SPC Regs 2002/1792, reg 2(4)(za), UC Regs SI 2013/376, reg 9(4)(a));. HB Regs 2006, SI 2006/13, reg 10A(4A)(a)(b)(c) and CTR Regs 2012, 2012/2885, reg 13(5)(a).

2   IS (Gen) Regs 1987/1967, reg 21AA(4)(zb); JSA Regs 1996/207, reg 85A(4)(zb); ESA Regs 2008/794, reg 70(4)(zb); SPC Regs 2002/1792, reg 2(4)(zb), UC Regs SI 2013/376, reg 9(4)(b)); HB Regs 2006, SI 2006/13, reg 10A(4A)(b) and CTR Regs 2012, SI 2012/2885, reg 13(5)(b).

3   IS (Gen) Regs 1987/1967, reg 21AA(4)(zc); JSA Regs 1996, SI 1996/207, reg 85A(4)(zc); ESA Regs 2008, SI 2008/794, reg 70(4)(zc); SPC Regs 2012, SI 2002/1792, reg 2(4)(zc), UC Regs SI 2013/376, reg 9(4)(c)); HB Regs 2006, SI 2006/13, reg 10A(4A)(c) and CTR Regs 2012, SI 2012/2885, reg 13(5)(c).

4   The Accession of Croatia (Immigration and Worker Authorisation) Regulations 2013, SI 2013/1460, reg 5(2)–(20).

5   IS (Gen) Regs 1987/1967, reg 21AA(4)(g); JSA Regs 1996/207, reg 85A(4)(g); ESA Regs 2008/794, reg 70(4)(g); SPC Regs 2002/1792, reg 2(4)(g), UC Regs SI 2013/376, reg 9(3)(d)); HB Regs 2006, SI 2006/13, reg 10A(4A)(c) and CTR Regs 2012, SI 2012/2885, reg 13(5)(c).

6   IS (Gen) Regs 1987/1967, reg 21AA(4)(h); JSA Regs 1996/207, reg 85A(4)(h); ESA Regs 2008/794, reg 70(4)(h); SPC Regs 2002/1792, reg 2(4)(h), UC Regs SI 2013/376, reg 9(3)(e); HB Regs 2006, SI 2006/13, reg 10A(4A)(e) and CTR Regs 2012, SI 2012/2885, reg 13(5)(h)(i)-(iii).

7   IS (Gen) Regs 1987/1967, reg 21AA(4)(hh); JSA Regs 1996/207, reg 85A(4)(hh); ESA Regs 2008/794, reg 70(4)(hh); SPC Regs 2002/1792, reg 2(4)(hh), UC Regs SI 2013/376, reg 9(3)(f); HB Regs 2006, SI 2006/13, reg 10A(4A)(hh) and CTR Regs 2012, SI 2012/2885, reg 13(5)(f).

8   IS (Gen) Regs 1987/1967, reg 21AA(4)(i); JSA Regs 1996/207, reg 85A(4)(i); ESA Regs 2008/794, reg 70(4)(i); SPC Regs 2002/1792, reg 2(4)(i), UC Regs SI 2013/376, reg 9(1)(g); HB Regs 2006, SI 2006/13, reg 10A(4A)(i) and CTR Regs 2012, SI 2012/2885, reg 13(5)(g).

Establishing habitual residence

14.24 Although it is used in both domestic and European law, there is no statutory definition of the term 'habitual residence'. In *Nessa v CAO*[1] the claimant had arrived in the UK from Bangladesh where she had lived all her life. Her husband had lived and worked in the UK. On arrival, the claimant had a right of abode in the UK and she intended to settle here. Her claim for Income Support was refused under the habitual residence test. An appeal tribunal allowed the claimant's appeal holding that since she had shown evidence that she had come to the UK voluntarily and for the purpose of settling here, she was therefore 'habitually resident' from the date of her arrival. The House of Lords disagreed, holding that a person is not 'habitually resident' in the UK unless they had *in fact* taken up residence and lived there for a period which showed that the residence had become habitual.[2] Most cases concerned with establishing actual habitual residence are assessed by reference to the following factors:

- *Residence* – This needs to be more than a physical presence in the country. To count as resident, a person must be seen to be making a home here, even though it need not be his or her only home, nor need it be intended to be a permanent one, provided that it is genuinely their home for the time being.[3]
- *Voluntary* – To be habitually resident, the individual's residence in the country needs to have been adopted voluntarily.[4]
- *Settled intention* – As well as being resident, the person must have a settled intention to reside. Establishing a settled intention is to be inferred from all the circumstances. *Nessa v CAO* gave a non-exhaustive list of factors which included: bringing possessions, bringing a family member and taking steps to establish residence before coming.[5]

- *Appreciable period of time* – The appropriate period of time is not a fixed period[6] but it need not be lengthy if the facts indicate that a person's residence has become habitual in nature at an early stage. In some circumstances the period can be as little as one month.[7]

The decision about whether or not someone is habitually resident has to be made on the balance of probabilities, and the onus of proof lies with the decision-maker.[8] A person's financial viability may be a relevant factor, but the test for habitual residence should not be applied so as to prevent access to public funds.[9]

[1] *Nessa v Chief Adjudication Officer* [1999] 1 WLR 1937, HL (also reported as *R(IS) 2/00*).
[2] *Nessa v CAO*, p 1942E-G. Though there can be an exception for some returning residents who are resuming a habitual residence previously had (*Nessa v CAO*, p 1943B).
[3] *R(IS) 6/96 (CIS/1067/1995)*, para 19.
[4] *Shah v Barnet London Borough Council* [1983] 2 AC 309, HL at p 342.
[5] *Nessa v CAO*, p 1942H.
[6] *Nessa v CAO*, p 1943A.
[7] *CIS/4474/2003*, paras 15–17.
[8] *CIS/4474/2003*, para 19 and *R(IS) 7/06 (CIS/3280/2003)*, para 15. However, see *CIS/2559/2005* at para 17 where a Tribunal of Commissioners said that: 'The relevant period of residence required to support evidence of intention is not something that can be reduced to a tariff'.
[9] *R(IS) 6/96*, para 15.

Resuming habitual residence

RESIDENCE RETAINED DURING A PERIOD OF ABSENCE

14.25 Habitual residence is not necessarily lost during periods of temporary or occasional absence and there will be cases where the individual does not lose their habitual residence during a period of absence.[1] Examples where this is likely to be the case include: (i) an absence during a short period of employment outside of the UK; (ii) where a young person has been travelling overseas during a gap-year or where someone is volunteering abroad.[2]

[1] *R(IS) 6/96, (CIS/1067/1995)* paras 26 and 32 in which a claimant who returned to Burma, as her husband was thought to be terminally ill, but came back to the UK the following month, was held to be resuming her habitual residence in the UK.
[2] *KS v Secretary of State for Work and Pensions* (SPC) [2010] UKUT 156 (AAC) held that a claimant had not lost his habitual residence status when he left the UK to work as a volunteer with Voluntary Services Overseas in India for a period of over two years.

RESUMING A PREVIOUS RESIDENCE AFTER RETURNING FROM A NON-EEA COUNTRY

14.26 *Nessa v CAO* acknowledged that there will be cases involving retuning residents where the general rule that an appreciable period of time is necessary before habitual residence can be obtained would not apply and for whom habitual residence could be obtained immediately on arrival.[1] It has been held that in this type of case, the decision-maker should conduct a three-stage enquiry into: (i) the reasons why the claimant left the UK and became habitually resident elsewhere; (ii) the ties and contacts the claimant retained with the UK while abroad; (iii) the circumstances of the claimant's return to the UK, in order to establish whether the claimant is resuming a previous residence.[2]

[1]   *Nessa v Chief Adjudication Officer* [1999] 1 WLR 1937, p 1943B.
[2]   *CIS/1304/1997* and *CJSA/5394/1998*. The claimants had left the UK to live for a period in Pakistan and Malaysia respectively. In both cases it was held that the claimants resumed their previous habitual residence in the CTA immediately on their return to the UK.

RESUMING A PREVIOUS RESIDENCE AFTER RETURNING FROM AN EEA COUNTRY

14.27 In *Swaddling v AO*[1] the question arose as to which version of the 'habitual residence test' should apply in a case where the claimant comes within the scope of the EU co-ordination rules. Mr Swaddling had worked in both the UK and France, but latterly in France. He was made redundant and returned to the UK and claimed Income Support. This was refused. The CJEU said that as Income Support was listed as a Special Non-Contributory Benefit under Article 10a of Regulation 1408/71 (in force at the time), the EU version of the habitual residence test applied.[2] Under the EU test, the length of Mr Swaddling's residence in the UK could not be regarded as determinative.[3] *Swaddling* therefore established that an EEA national covered by the coordination rules cannot be denied a special non-contributory benefit – ie income-based Jobseeker's Allowance (JSA(IB)) – solely on the basis that their period of actual residence is too short.[4] When deciding whether a person is resuming a previous residence using the EU test for habitual residence, the following factors are to be taken into account: (i) the person's main centre of interest; (ii) the length and continuity of residence in a particular country; (iii) the length and purpose of the absence from that country; (iv) the nature of the employment found in the other country to which the person moved for a time; and (v) the intention of the claimant.[5] The following example is taken from the DWP's guide for decision-makers.[6]

> 'The claimant, a UK national, lived and worked in UK before moving to Germany where he worked for several years. He was made redundant and having failed to find work in Germany for three months he returned to the UK where he had family and friends. On claiming JSA(IB) he stated that his intention was to find work and remain permanently in the UK. JSA was awarded because he was resuming a previous habitual residence.'

The meaning given to the term 'habitual residence' in *Swaddling* does *not* apply to persons who have returned to the Common Travel Area from a country outside of the EEA.[7] It should also be noted that an EEA national resuming habitual residence will still be required to meet the right to reside requirement in respect of JSA(IB), unless they qualify for contributory-based JSA. Again, the coordination rules may assist with this.[8]

[1]   Case C-90/97, *Swaddling v Adjudication Officer* [1999] 2 CMLR 679, (also reported as *R(IS)* 6/99).
[2]   Now Article 70 of EU Regulation (EC) 883/04. (NB: Income Support is no longer listed as a special non-contributory benefit.)
[3]   *Swaddling v AO*, paras 25 and 28.
[4]   *Swaddling v AO*, para 30.
[5]   *Swaddling v AO*, para 29. See also EC Regulation No 987/2009, art 11.
[6]   DWP's *Decision makers' guide*: DMG Vol 2, Ch 7, Part 3: *Habitual residence and right to reside IS, JSA and SPC* at 071363, Example 1.

7   *Gingi v Secretary of State for Work and Pensions* [2001] EWCA Civ 1685 [2001] 1 CMLR
    587, (also reported as R(IS) 5/02), paras 20–21. See also *R(IS) 11/01 (CIS/ 4727/1999)*,
    para 36.
8   The CJEU has ruled that Member States can place restrictions on special non-contributory
    benefits in the form of a right to reside test: see Case C-140/12: *Pensionsversicherungsanstalt
    v Brey (Peter)* [2014] 1 CMLR 993, paras 57–61.

EEA Jobseekers and actual habitual residence

14.28 EEA nationals who are seeking work in the UK will be subject to the
actual habitual residence test if they have no established link with the UK
employment market. In *Collins v Secretary of State for Work and Pensions*[1]
the CJEU held that it could be legitimate for a Member State to impose such
a residence requirement as a condition of entitlement to income-based JSA, so
long as it was proportionate and did not go beyond what was necessary in
order to attain that objective.[2] The Court of Appeal subsequently confirmed
that a habitual residence test as the sole means of establishing the requisite
'genuine link' between an applicant for JSA(IB) and the UK employment
market is fully compatible with Community law.[3]

1   *Collins v Secretary of State for Work and Pensions* (C-138/02) [2004] 2 CMLR 147 (also
    reported as R(JSA) 3/06).
2   *Collins v SSWP*, paras 67–72.
3   *Collins v SWP*, para 85.

Decision-making and the habitual residence test

14.29 In December 2013, the Government introduced procedural changes to
how the habitual residence test is to be applied. Under these changes, migrants
are required to provide more detailed answers and submit more evidence
before they make the claim for benefit. Also, for the first time, migrants are
questioned about what efforts they have made to find work before coming to
the UK and whether their English language skills will be a barrier to them
finding employment.[1] It should be noted that a decision-maker (and a First-tier
Tribunal on appeal) can only consider the period of residence up to the date of
the decision on the claim.[2] This means that in cases where the claimant fails the
'appreciable period' of time element of the test, they should consider making
a fresh claim for benefit so that the whole of their residence in the UK can be
taken into account. This can be done without prejudice to any appeal in
respect of the decision on the initial claim.[3]

1   DWP Press release 'Improved benefit test for migrants launched', 13 December 2013. See also
    'Migrants quizzed on English skills before benefits', *BBC News*, 13 December 2013.
2   Social Security Act 1998, ss 8(2)(b) and 12(8)(b) and the Child Support, Pensions and Social
    Security Act 2000, s 68, Sch 7, para 2(b).
3   *Bhakta v Secretary of State for Work and Pensions* [2006] EWCA Civ 65 (also reported as
    R(IS) 7/06) held that an appeal tribunal could consider whether an appreciable period had
    elapsed for up to a period of 13 weeks after the date of the decision under the 'advance award
    provisions'. However, this approach was reversed by the Social Security, Housing Benefit
    and Council Tax Benefit (Miscellaneous Amendments) Regulations 2007, SI 2007/1331.

THE LIVING IN THE UK FOR THREE-MONTHS RESIDENCY RULE

Income-based Jobseeker's Allowance

14.30 From 1 January 2014, in addition to needing to satisfy the habitual residence test (both the factual and the right to reside elements), an individual wishing to claim income-based Jobseeker's Allowance (JSA(IB)) needs to have been 'living in' the Common Travel Area for a consecutive period of three months immediately prior to making the claim.[1] Where this condition is not met, the claimant cannot satisfy the habitual residence test for JSA(IB).[2] The three months rule does not apply to those categories of claimants who are exempt from the habitual residence test (including those who retain worker status as jobseekers[3]). As the three months residency rules apply regardless of nationality, British and Irish nationals coming to the Common Travel Area from countries outside the EEA will also be affected by the rule.[4] There are, however, exemptions for returning UK, EEA and non-EEA nationals who originally left the UK as a result of being posted to work abroad.[5] There is no definition of what constitutes 'living' in the UK, and therefore short absences should not mean that someone has stopped living in the UK. It is also arguable that neither should longer temporary absences count where the claimant can demonstrate that the UK remains his or her home – such that the claimant never ceased to be living in the UK. Note, if someone is coming to, or returning to, the UK, to look for work and has been insured in another EEA State, they may be able to get the other Member State's unemployment benefit for up to three months.[6]

[1]   Jobseeker's Allowance Regulations 1996, SI 1996/207, reg 85A(2)(a), inserted by the Jobseeker's Allowance (Habitual Residence) Amendment Regulations 2013, SI 2013/3196, subject to the saving provision in reg 3.
[2]   JSA Regs, reg 85(4)(za).
[3]   See: Extended right of residence – jobseekers at **14.36**.
[4]   The Social Security Advisory Committee has expressed concern about the impact of the new test on returning UK nationals – Letter to the Secretary of State for Work and Pensions dated 3 February 2014, by the Chair of the SSAC, Paul Gray.
[5]   The Jobseeker's Allowance (Habitual Residence) Amendment Regulations 2014 (SI 2735/2014), reg 2 amends reg 85A(2)(a) of the JSA Regs 1996, with effect from 9 November 2014.
[6]   EU Regulation 883/04, art 64 – see **14.78** – Further Residence Requirements.

Child Benefit and Child Tax Credit

14.31 The three-month rule has been added as an additional requirement within the habitual residence test for Child Benefit and Child Tax Credits from 1 July 2014.[1] This means that it is now a condition of entitlement to these benefits that the claimant must have been living in the Common Travel Area for three months before they can gain access to Child Benefit[2] or Child Tax Credit[3] unless they fall within one of following exemptions.[4] Namely, that the claimant:

—   made the claim before the change in the law (1 July 2014);
—   is a worker or self-employed person in the UK;
—   retains the status of a worker or self-employed person in the UK (under the above Directive);
—   is a national of Croatia and has a right to reside in the UK as a worker;

— is a family member of any of the above;

— has been temporarily absent from the UK for a period not exceeding 8 or 12 weeks;

— has been temporarily absent for less than 52 weeks and had been ordinarily resident in the UK for a period of at least 3 months prior to that absence;

— returns to the UK after being abroad and has continued to pay Class 1 or 2 national insurance contributions during their absence (allowing for a break of up to 3 months prior to the absence);

— has UK refugee status;

— has been granted leave to remain in the UK with recourse to public funds (including restricted leave to remain pending an application under the domestic violence concession or humanitarian protection).

Where the three-month requirement has not been met, the claimant will be deemed to be 'not present in Great Britain' (or Northern Ireland) and therefore not entitled to CHB or CTC. As these are 'family benefits' they come within the scope of the EU coordination rules on social security.[5] This means periods of residence in another EEA country need to be taken into account when considering a residence condition in the UK.[6] Those EEA nationals will still need to show actual habitual residence.[7] As the law currently stands, they will also be required to meet the right to reside requirement in respect of CHB and CTC.[8]

[1] The Child Benefit (General) and the Tax Credits (Residence) (Amendment) Regulations 2014, SI 2014/1511.
[2] The Child Benefit (General) Regulations 2006, SI 2006/223, reg 23(4), as amended by SI 2014/1511.
[3] Tax Credits (Residence) Regulations 2003, SI 2003/654, reg 3(4), as amended by SI 2014/1511.
[4] SI 2006/223, reg 23(6) and SI 2003/654, reg 3(6).
[5] Regulation (EC) 883/2004, art 3(1)(j).
[6] Regulation (EC) 883/2004, art 6.
[7] See: Actual habitual residence at **14.22**.
[8] The right to reside test for CHB and CTC are the subject of infraction proceedings brought by the European Commission: Case C-308/14 *European Commission v United Kingdom of Great Britain and Northern Ireland*: see OJ L 166, p1, 27 June 2014. See: Infringement proceedings brought the European Commission at **14.92**.

EEA NATIONALS

The right to reside requirement

14.32 In the past, EEA nationals were potentially entitled to mainstream welfare benefits such as Income Support, and their precise immigration status was unimportant.[1] However, since 1 May 2004, when the UK Government amended the habitual residence test, a person's right to certain mainstream welfare benefits is now dependent upon him or her having a right of residence in the United Kingdom (or the Channel Islands, the Isle of Man or the Republic of Ireland). The following benefits are subject to a right to reside requirement:

— Child Benefit (CHB)[2]
— Child Tax Credit (CTC)[3]
— Council Tax Reduction (CTR)[4]

—   Housing Benefit (HB)[5]
—   Income-based Jobseeker's Allowance (JSA(IB)D)[6]
—   Income-related Employment and Support Allowance (ESA (IR))[7]
—   Income Support (IS)[8]
—   State Pension Credit (SPC)[9]
—   Universal Credit (UC).[10]

The term 'right to reside' is not defined in EU or domestic legislation. However, case law has established that an EEA national's lawful presence in the UK is not equivalent to having a right to reside in the UK for benefit purposes.[11] This means an EEA national must be exercising a right conferred by the Treaty or under the EEA Regulations 2006 (eg as a worker, self-employed person, student or self-sufficient person) before they or their family members can access mainstream welfare benefits.[12] As the law currently stands, a single parent who is not available for work due to child care responsibilities will not be a 'qualified person' within the meaning of the EEA Regulations 2006, and will not be able to access those welfare benefits and tax credits that have a right to reside requirement.[13]

[1]   See *Chief Adjudication Officer v Wolke* [1997] 1 WLR 1640 (also reported as *R(IS) 13/98*).
[2]   The Child Benefit (General) Regulations 2006, SI 2006/223, reg 23(6).
[3]   Tax Credits (Residence) Regulations 2003, SI 2003/654, reg 5(b)(i).
[4]   The Council Tax Reduction Schemes (Prescribed Requirements) (England) Regulations 2012, SI 2012/2885, reg 12(3) and the Council Tax Reduction Schemes (Prescribed Requirements) (Wales) Regulations 2012, SI 2012/3144, reg 26(3).
[5]   Housing Benefit Regulations 2006, SI 2006/213, reg 10(3). See also the Housing Benefit (Persons who have attained the qualifying age for state pension credit) Regulations 2006, SI 2006/214, reg 10(3).
[6]   Jobseeker's Allowance Regulations 1996, SI 1996/207, reg 85A(2)(b).
[7]   Employment and Support Allowance Regulations 2008, SI 2008/794, reg 70(2).
[8]   Income Support (General) Regulations 1987, SI 1987/1967, reg 21AA(2)(b).
[9]   State Pension Credit Regulations 2002, SI 2002/1792, reg 2(1).
[10]   The Universal Credit Regulations 2013, SI 2013/376, reg 9(2).
[11]   *Abdirahman v Secretary of State for Work and Pensions* [2007] EWCA Civ 657, [2008] 1 WLR 254 *(also reported as R(IS) 8/07)*.
[12]   The lawfulness of using a right to reside condition to restrict access to certain welfare benefits for EEA nationals who lack sufficient resources to avoid becoming a burden on the UK's social assistance scheme has been upheld by the Supreme Court in *Patmalniece v Secretary of State for Work and Pensions* [2011] UKSC 11, [2011] 1 WLR 783 and by the Grand Chamber in Case C-333/13 *Dano v Jobcenter Leipzig* ((2014) Times, 18 November).
[13]   CIS/3182/2005 paras 21–22, CIS/4010/2006, para 9, CIS/599/2007 paras 15–17 and *Dias v Secretary of State for Work and Pensions* [2009] EWCA Civ 807, para 20.

Categories of persons who satisfy or are exempt from the right to reside test

14.33   A person has a 'right to reside' if they:

—   are a British Citizen or have the right of abode in the UK; or
—   have leave to remain in the UK under UK Immigration rules; or
—   have a right to reside under EU law.

The social security regulations also provide that certain categories of persons are exempt from the habitual residence test and therefore do not have to show they have a right to reside in the Common Travel Area – See 'Categories of persons who are exempt from the habitual residence test' at **14.22** above.

The Rights of Residence Directive

14.34 The Rights of Residence Directive 2004/38/EC (also commonly known as the Citizenship Directive)[1] introduced four types or stages of residence for EEA nationals. The Directive has been transposed into domestic law by the Immigration (European Economic Area) Regulations 2006, SI 2006/1003 (EEA Regulations). The four stages of residence are:

— *Initial right of residence:*[2] All EEA nationals and their family members have the right to reside in any other Member State for a period of three months but this does not entail any right to social assistance.
— *Extended right of residence:*[3] After three months, EEA nationals will have an extended right to reside if they start or continue to exercise an EU right (eg as a worker or self-employed person and their families, or as a student attending an institution in the host Member State and their family, provided they can support themselves, or as a jobseeker).
— *Retained right of residence:*[4] Where an EEA national has gained a right to reside, this status can be retained if certain circumstances apply.
— *Permanent right to reside:*[5] EEA nationals who have 'resided legally' in the UK for a continuous period of five years (or less in certain circumstances) acquire permanent right of residence. An EEA national with this status is no longer subject to the need to be economically active or self-sufficient and can access welfare benefits on the same basis as UK citizens.

A person may also have a *derived right to reside*[6] based on another person's right to reside. For example, as a primary carer of a worker's child in education.

[1] Directive 2004/38/EC of the European Parliament and of the Council on the right of citizens of the Union and their family members to move and reside freely within the territory of the Member States (OJ L 158, 30.4.2004, p 77) entered into force 29 April 2014 (art 41), and transposed by Member States from 30 April 2006. In the case of UK this was by means of the Immigration (European Economic Area) Regulations 2006, SI 2006/1003.
[2] Directive 2004/38/EC, art 6. EEA Regs 2006, reg 13. See **14.35** below.
[3] Directive 2004/38/EC, arts 7 and 14. EEA Regs 2006, regs 6(1) and 14. See **14.36** below.
[4] Directive 2004/38/EC, arts 16–18. EEA Regs 2006, reg 15. See **14.63** below.
[5] Directive 2004/38/EC, arts 7(3) and 12–14. EEA Regs 2006, regs 6(2) and 14. See **14.53** below.
[6] EEA Regs 2006, reg 15A.

INITIAL RIGHT OF RESIDENCE

14.35 All EEA nationals and their family members have the right to reside in any other Member State for a period of three months.[1] This includes economically inactive people who are not required to be self-sufficient during this period. However, it has been left to Member States to decide whether to grant social assistance during the first three months of residence.[2] The UK benefit regulations specifically exclude persons from receiving benefits who have a right to reside solely on the basis of the initial three-month residence. They will not be treated as habitually resident in the Common Travel Area and will therefore be a 'person from abroad' or a 'person not present in Great Britain' and therefore not able to access out-of-work benefits (eg IS, JSA(IB), ESA, SPC UC, HB, CHB and CTC) during that period. Only those EEA nationals who are exercising an EU right (eg as a worker or someone self-employed) can access benefits during this initial period.[3] It should be noted that the UK previously awarded JSA(IB) to jobseekers during this period but since 1 January 2014 the benefit rules have been amended so that a JSA(IB) claimant cannot be regarded as habitually resident until they have lived in the UK for a period of three months before they claim benefit.[4]

[1] Immigration (European Economic Area) Regulations 2006, SI 2006/1003, reg 13.
[2] Directive 2004/38/EC, recital (21).
[3] The right to reside which exists by virtue of regulation 13 of the EEA Regs 2006 is an excluded right under the habitual residence test: see IS (Gen) Regs 1987/1967, reg 21AA(4)(zc); JSA Regs 1996/207, reg 85A(4)(zc); ESA Regs 2008/794, reg 70(4)(zc); SPC Regs 2002/1792, reg 2(4)(zc), UC Regs SI 2013/376, reg 9(4)(c), HB Regs, reg 10(4), CHB (General) Regs SI 2006/223, regs 23(6) and TC (Residence) Regs SI 2003/654, reg 5(b)(i).
[4] Jobseeker's Allowance Regulations 1996, SI 1996/207, reg 85A(2)(a). See: The living in the UK for three months residency rule at **14.30** below.

EXTENDED RIGHT OF RESIDENCE

14.36 After three months, EEA nationals who start or continue to exercise an EU right will have an extended right to reside in the UK.[1] The EEA Regulations 2006 provide that someone has a right to reside for as long as s/he remains a 'qualified person'. A qualified person is defined as an EEA national in the UK who is:

—   a jobseeker;[2]
—   a worker;[3]
—   a self-employed person;[4]
—   a self-sufficient person;[5]
—   a student;[6]
—   or a family member of a qualified person.[7]

A qualified person has an extended right to reside in the UK for as long as they remain a qualified person.[8] The concept of a 'qualified person' underpins the right to reside test in the benefit regulations. Each category of EEA national who has an extended right of residence is considered in turn below.

[1] Immigration (European Economic Area) Regulations 2006, SI 2006/1003, reg 14.
[2] SI 2006/1003, reg 6(1)(a). See **14.37** below.
[3] SI 2006/1003, reg 6(1)(c). See **14.42** below.
[4] SI 2006/1003, reg 6(1)(d). See **14.46** below.
[5] SI 2006/1003, reg 6(1)(e). See **14.47** below.
[6] SI 2006/1003, reg 7. See **14.49** below.
[7] SI 2006/1003, reg 7. See **14.50** below.
[8] SI 2006/1003, reg 14(1).

Jobseekers

New measures aimed at restricting EEA migrants' access to out-of-work benefits

14.37 On 19 January 2014, Iain Duncan Smith (Minster for Work and Pensions) and Theresa May (Minster for the Home Office) told the *Daily Mail*[1] that Britain's 'generous' welfare system should no longer be a 'magnet' for citizens of other EEA States and that they would be introducing a number of measures aimed at new migrant jobseekers from the EEA. Those changes are now in place and include:

— from 1 January 2014, people coming to the UK from abroad must have been living in the UK for three months before they can claim income-based Jobseeker's Allowance;[2]
— from 1 January 2014, EEA jobseekers (including former workers) will have to show that they have a 'genuine prospect of finding work to continue to get income-based Jobseeker's Allowance, (JSA(IB)) and after six months they will need to show 'compelling evidence' of their chances of obtaining work, otherwise their entitlement to JSA(IB) (and, if applicable, Housing Benefit (HB), Council Tax Reduction (CTR) Child Benefit (CHB) and Child Tax Credit (CTC) will end;[3]
— from 1 March 2014, a minimum earnings threshold was introduced as guidance for decision-makers in order to help determine whether an EEA national is or was in 'genuine and effective' work;[4]
— from 1 April 2014, new EEA jobseekers have been prevented from accessing Housing Benefit, even if they are in receipt of income-based Jobseeker's Allowance, if this is solely on the basis of being a jobseeker (ie rather than someone with retained worker status);[5]
— from 10 November 2014, 'new entry' EEA jobseekers are only entitled to JSA(IB) for a period of 91 days (3 months); and
— in addition, ministers are preparing plans to bar EEA jobseekers from receiving all out-of-work benefits once the universal credit system is completely introduced.[6]

The upshot is that the benefit authorities are applying the following rules to EEA jobseekers who wish to claim JSA(IB).[7]

(a) *New entry jobseekers*
— newly arrived EEA nationals are excluded from claiming JSA(IB) for the initial first three months under the 'living in UK for three months' rule;
— after three months, a new entry jobseeker can access JSA(IB) for three months (91 days) if they produce evidence that they have a genuine chance of finding work – but they are excluded from any entitlement to Housing Benefit;
— an EEA national who prior to claiming JSA(IB) has exercised a right to reside in the UK (eg as a worker) and then becomes a jobseeker can access JSA(IB) for three months; and
— at the end of three months, entitlement to JSA(IB) can only be extended if the jobseeker produces compelling evidence that they have a genuine chance of finding work.

(b) *Jobseekers with retained worker status*
— where someone with retained worker status has been employed in the UK for less than one year, they can access JSA(IB) for a maximum of six months; and
— where the EEA national has been employed in the UK for at least one year, entitlement to JSA(IB) can be extended beyond six months if they provide 'compelling evidence' that they have a 'genuine chance of being engaged'.

These rules are described in more detail at **14.39** and **14.53** below.

[1] 'Jobless migrants to be denied housing benefit: Ministers insist UK's generous welfare system will no longer be a magnet for citizens of other EU states', *Daily Mail*, 19 January 2014.

[2] See **14.30** above.

[3] See **14.39** and **14.56** below.

[4] See **14.43** below.

[5] See **14.40** below.

[6] See *The Guardian*, 6 November 2014: 'Tories plan to deny EU migrants out-of-work benefits under universal credit – Ministers believe unified system will be exempt from rule that labour-market benefits must be available to all EU workers'.

[7] See *Memo DMG 31/14: JSA Right to Reside as a Jobseeker*, November 2014.

JOBSEEKERS AND THE EXTENDED RIGHT TO RESIDE – THE POSITION BEFORE THE 2014 CHANGES

14.38 In *Antonissen*[1] the Court of Justice for the European Union confirmed that EEA jobseekers should be given a reasonable time in which to find work.[2] The Court, however, went on to hold that this right was time limited and that a Member State could require a jobseeker who has not found work after six months to provide evidence that they are continuing to seek employment and have a genuine chance of being engaged.[3] The Upper Tribunal (Administrative Appeals) has held that for 'most' EEA nationals, an entitlement to Jobseeker's Allowance would be sufficient evidence that they met the 'genuine chance of being engaged' requirement.[4]

[1] Case C-292/89 *R v Immigration Appeal Tribunal, ex p Antonissen* [1991] 2 CMLR 373.

[2] Case C-292/89 *Antonissen* [1991] para 13.

[3] Case C-292/89 *Antonissen* [1991] paras 15, 22.

[4] *Secretary of State for Work and Pensions v IR* (CIS/1951/2008) [2009] UKUT 11 (AAC), para 21.

EEA JOBSEEKERS – THE POSITION FOLLOWING THE 2014 CHANGES

14.39 In 2014, the conditions which an EEA jobseeker must fulfill in order to be classified as a 'qualified person' under the EEA Regulations 2006 were altered.[1] These alterations affect an EEA national's right to reside and therefore their entitlement to Jobseeker's Allowance (JSA(IB)).[2] The amendments brought in a number of new conditions that a newly-arrived EEA jobseeker who have never worked in the UK[3] must meet in order to satisfy the 2006 Regulations. (NB: the position of former workers is considered elsewhere):[4]

— First, the condition that EEA jobseekers provide evidence that they have a genuine chance of being engaged must be supplied from the outset;[5].

— Second, the 'relevant period' that a person is entitled to a right to reside in the UK as a jobseeker has been reduced to 91 days (in the case of 'new entry' jobseekers the period of 91 days runs after the initial right of residence).[6]

— Third, after 91 days (3 months) has elapsed the EEA jobseeker is required to provide 'compelling evidence' that they have a genuine chance of being engaged.[7]

After three months unemployment has elapsed and the jobseeker is required to provide compelling evidence of their chances of finding work, the Jobcentre will conduct a 'genuine prospect of work' assessment. If the EEA national fails this assessment then they will lose the right to reside as a jobseeker and will no longer be entitled to receive JSA(IB) (and consequently other out-of-work benefits such as HB, CTR, CHB, CTC). The Regulations do not give any information on what would constitute 'compelling evidence' but the DWP are interpreting it to mean either an actual job offer or something that will realistically result in a job in the very near future; such as a vocational course, or a move to another area where there are job opportunities.[8] It is arguable that the requirement to produce compelling evidence sets too high a threshold such that it is incompatible with general principles of EU law on the rights of workers seeking work in another EEA member[9] and is therefore likely to be the subject of a legal challenge.

1   The Immigration (European Economic Area) (Amendment) (No 2) Regulations 2014, SI 2013/3032, changes to have effect from 1 January 2014, subject to the transitional provisions in Sch 3, para 1. The Immigration (European Economic Area) (Amendment) Regulations 2014, SI 2014/1451, with effect from 1 July 2014, subject to the transitional provisions in reg 4 and the Immigration (European Economic Area) (Amendment) (No 3) Regulations 2014, SI 2014/2761 with effect from 10 November 2014, subject to the transitional provisions in reg 4.
2   Jobseeker's Allowance Regulations 1996, SI 1996/207, reg 85A(2)(b).
3   Immigration (European Economic Area) Regulations 2006, SI 2006/1003, reg 6(5)(a) – someone who has entered the UK in order to seek work – Condition A.
4   See Retained worker status as a jobseeker **14.54**.
5   SI 2006/1003, reg 6(6) – Condition B.
6   SI 2006/1003, reg 6(8)(b) and (9)(b), inserted by the Immigration (EEA) (Amendment) (No 3) Regulations 2014, SI 2014/2761, reg 3, with effect from 1 November 2014 reduces the 'relevant period' from 182 to 91 days subject to transitional provisions in reg 4.
7   SI 2006/1003, reg 6(7).
8   *Memo DMG 15/14 – Habitual Residence and Right to Reside – JSA* (June 2014), para 15.
9   See Case C-292/89 *R v Immigration Appeal Tribunal, ex p Antonissen* [1991] 2 CMLR 373, and the discussion in *Secretary of State for Work and Pensions v Elmi* [2011] EWCA Civ 1403, [2012] PTSR 780, [2012] AACR 22.

Exclusion of certain EEA Jobseekers from Housing Benefit

14.40 The Housing Benefit regulations were amended to exclude EEA job-seekers with effect from 1 April 2014. Prior to this amendment, an entitlement to income-based Jobseeker's Allowance (JSA(IB)) 'passported' EEA nationals through the habitual residence test for Housing Benefit(HB).[1] The amendment specifically excludes those EEA nationals with a right to reside only as a jobseeker under the EEA Regulations (plus their family members). As a result, new-entry EEA jobseekers will not be able to claim HB unless the benefit authorities are satisfied that their previous employment was 'genuine and effective' such that they have retained worker status.[2] The amendments include a savings provision for those already passported to HB by their JSA(IB) entitlement on 31 March 2014. The protection is lost if entitlement to JSA(IB) ceases, or their is a need to make a new claim for HB, whichever occurs first.[3]Note that the Government has announced that in February 2015 it intends to remove transitional protection for all EEA migrants who were claiming JSA(IB) before these changes were introduced.[4]

1   The Housing Benefit (Habitual Residence) Amendment Regulations 2014, SI 2014/539. The definition of a 'person from abroad' was amended so that a claimant is no longer treated as exempt under HB Regs 2006, SI 2006/213, reg 10(3B) based on receipt of JSA(IB). The reference to JSA(IB) in reg 10(3B)(k) has been deleted.
2   Housing Benefit (Habitual Residence) Amendment Regulations 2014, SI 2014/539, reg 3(2).

[3] See **14.43** on the Minimum Income Threshold (MET) below.
[4] The Chancellor of the Exchequer's Autumn Statement, 3 December 2014.

THE RISK OF DESTITUTION FOR EEA MIGRANTS FOLLOWING THE REMOVAL OF HOUSING BENEFIT

14.41 When the Social Security Advisory Committee (SSAC) considered the amendments affecting EEA nationals' access to benefits[1] it decided that it would be beneficial to gather information about the potential impact of the measure. It held a consultation exercise in which it asked for responses from organizations that have evidence relating to a number of issues including: (i) whether EEA migrants are experiencing particular difficulties in establishing whether or not they have retained worker status for benefit purposes; (ii) the impact for *existing* EEA migrants who lose their employment and who do not have the status of a retained worker; and (iii) the extent to which local authorities will be required to make help available under the Children Act 1989 and the National Assistance Act 1948 and the associated costs of doing so.[2] The *SSAC Report* published in November 2014 describes some of the difficulties facing EEA migrants seeking to establish that they have the status of a retained worker after the six-months period of unemployment has ended. First, many migrants are only able to obtain transient work associated with certain industries, for example, agriculture, catering, hospitality, etc. which pay minimal earnings and use zero-hours contracts. Second, that some employers are poor at record-keeping which means that expecting them to produce the required documentation to prove worker status can be problematic. The *SSAC Report* also questions the underlying presumption that all EEA migrants can be expected to leave the UK if their entitlement to JSA(IB) and HB ends after a period of unemployment and simply return to their 'home' country. There are some EEA migrants who, despite having lived in the UK for a significant period of time, have not acquired the right of permanent residence, based on five-years residence, due to the transient nature of their work, or who face problems producing the necessary documentation. In addition, some EEA migrants will have come to the UK at a very young age. For these existing EEA migrants, any connection with their 'home' country may now be very tenuous, and requiring them to return 'home' could present significant difficulties.[3] Against this background of EEA migrants being at risk of destitution, there are likely to be legal challenges to the UK government's decision to remove HB from certain EEA jobseekers. It is arguable that the denial of out-of-work benefits to existing EEA migrants, regardless of how long they have been residing in the UK or on what basis, would be disproportionate as the application of the right to reside condition makes no allowances for the EEA national's individual circumstances (*Brey*[4]).

[1] *Report of the Social Security Advisory Committee on the Housing Benefit* (Habitual Residence) Amendment Regulations 2014 (SI 2014 No 539), November 2014, available on GOV.UK. See also 'Measures to limit migrants' access to benefits' House of Commons Library Standard Note: SN06889: 21 November 2014, Steven Kennedy, p 18.
[2] SSAC Report, para 1.4.
[3] *SSAC Report*, paras 2.5, 2.9 and 2.14.
[4] Case C-140/12 *Pensionsversicherungsanstalt v Brey (Peter)* [2014] 1 CMLR 993, paras 64 and 76–78.

Workers

14.42 There is no definition of a 'worker' in the Treaty or secondary legislation and it has been left to the Court of Justice to the European Union (CJEU) to interpret the term in case law. The official guidance issued to decision-makers contains a list of 12 factors (derived from EU case law) which should be used to determine whether a claimant is a 'worker' within the meaning of EU law.[1] The relevant extract from the guidance is reproduced below:

'1. The term 'worker' has an EU law meaning[2] and may not be interpreted restrictively.[3]

2. The term 'worker' applies to employees rather than the self-employed. In EU law terms the essential characteristic of an employment relationship is that a person performs services for and under the direction of another person in return for which he receives remuneration.[4]

3. In deciding whether a person is a worker account should be taken of all the occupational activities the person has undertaken in the host Member State.

4. A person working part-time can be a 'worker' provided that the work undertaken is genuine and effective, but not where activities are on such a small scale as to be regarded as purely marginal or ancillary.[5]

5. As a 'worker' must receive remuneration, unpaid voluntary activity is not 'work'.[6]

6. The mere fact that there is a legally binding employment relationship is not of itself conclusive of whether the employee is a worker.[7]

7. As long as the work is 'genuine and effective' it is irrelevant whether it yields an income lower that the amount considered the minimum required for subsistence in the host Member State[8] (in the case of the UK, the relevant applicable amount for an income-related benefit).

8. The fact that a person seeks to supplement the remuneration from his work by means of financial assistance drawn from public funds does not preclude him from being regarded as a worker.[9]

9. Once it has been established that the person is genuinely exercising his right of free movement as a worker, the motives which have prompted the worker to work in another Member State are irrelevant[10] provided the work is genuine and effective.

10. A person employed under an 'on-call' or 'zero-hour' contract is not precluded from being a worker provided the work is genuine and effective.[11]

11. An employee undertaking genuine and effective work is a worker even if the person is employed under a contract that is performed illegally.[12]

12. A commissioner has held that a claimant's physical incapacity to do the work she had undertaken and the fact that she had been dismissed from it after a short period were relevant to the issue of whether the work was genuine and effective'[13]

---

[1] *DMG*, Vol 2, Ch 7, Part 3: paras 071204 and 071210-071211.
[2] Case C-75/63 *Hoekstra (née Unger) v Bestuur der Bedrijfsvereniging voor Detailhandel en Ambachten* [1964] ECR 177.
[3] Case C-53/81 *Levin (DM) v Secretary of State for Justice* [1982] ECR 1035; [1982] 2 CMLR 454.
[4] Case C-357/89, *Raulin v Minister van Onderwijs en Wetenschappen* [1992] ECR I-1027, [1994] 1 CMLR 227.
[5] Case C-53/81, *DM Levin v Staatssecretaris van Justitie*; paras 16–18, 21–23.
[6] *CIS/868/08 & CIS/1837/06*; para 6.
[7] Case C-344/87 *Bettray v Staatssecretaris van Justitie* [1989] ECR 1621; [1991] 1 CMLR. 459, para 17.
[8] Case C-53/81 *DM Levin v Staatssecretaris van Justitie*, para 18.

[9] Case C-139/85 *Kempf v Staatssecretaris van Justitie* [1986] ECR 1741; [1987] 1 CMLR 764, para 14.

[10] Case C-53/81, *DM Levin v Staatssecretaris van Justitie*; para 23.

[11] Case C-357/89 *Raulin*.

[12] *JA v Secretary of State for Work and Pensions (ESA)* [2012] UKUT 122 (AAC), [2013] AACR 15, paras 15–18.

[13] CSIS/467/07, para 12.

The Minimum Earnings Threshold (MET)

14.43 The CJEU does not define the terms 'genuine and effective' but case law indicates that this test sets a relatively low threshold, as work undertaken for low pay, and even for very short periods, has been held to qualify.[1] However, in March 2014, the DWP introduced new guidance[2] for decision-makers deciding JSA(IB) claims on how to determine whether work meets the 'genuine and effective' test by reference to a Minimum Earnings Threshold (MET). Initially the MET guidance only applied to claim for JSA(IB), HB, CHB and CTC, but from October it was extended to IS, ESA and SPC.[3] The DWP Press Release issued at the time states[4]:

> 'Migrants from the European Economic Area (EEA) who claim to have been in work or self-employed in order to gain access to a wider range of benefits will face a more robust test from 1 March 2014.
>
> Being defined as a 'worker' under EU law allows people more generous access to in and out-of-work benefits such as Jobseeker's Allowance (JSA), Housing Benefit, Child Benefit and Child Tax Credit. Currently European Union case law means the definition of a 'worker' is very broad, meaning some people may benefit from this even if, in reality, they do very little work.
>
> So in order to help ensure benefits only go to those who are genuinely working a minimum earnings threshold will be introduced as part of the government's long-term plan to cap welfare and reduce immigration so our economy delivers for people who actively contribute and want to work hard and play by the rules.'

[1] Case C-22/08, *Vatsouras v Arbeitsgemeinschaft (ARGE)* Nurnberg [2009] ECR. I-4585; [2009] All ER (EC) 747, paras 27-29, and Case C-14/09, *Genc v Land Berlin* [2010] 2 CMLR 1208; [2010] ICR 1108, para 20.

[2] *Decision makers' guide*: Vol 2: *International subjects: staff guide*: DMG, Vol 2, Ch 7, Part 3: *Habitual residence and right to reside IS*, JSA and SPC and HB Circular A3/2014: *Minimum Earnings Threshold*, 26 February 2014.

[3] DMG 21/14, September 2014.

[4] Minimum earnings threshold for EEA migrants introduced (21 February 2014) DWP, GOV.UK.

14.44 The MET is based on the point at which an employee is required to make Class 1 National Insurance Contributions.[1] At the time it was introduced – tax year 2013/2014 – it was £149 a week[2] which was roughly equivalent to working 24 hours a week at the National Minimum Wage.[3] The MET guidance introduces a two-tier decision-making process. Where the EEA claimant's average earnings over the last three months satisfy the MET (Tier 1), they will automatically be regarded as having acquired worker status in their previous employment or self-employed work.[4] In the remaining cases, where the EEA's gross earnings fall below the MET (Tier 2), the decision-maker will determine whether the EEA national's activity was genuine and effective, and not marginal and ancillary, by reference to the following questions:

— First, is the person exercising their EU freedom of movement rights as a 'worker' – in deciding this question, as a preliminary issue, decision-makers are advised to look at all the circumstances, including the person's primary motivation in taking up employment and whether, during periods when they were not employed the person seriously wished to pursue employment by actively looking for work with a genuine chance of being engaged.[5]

— Second, is the work 'genuine and effective' – in deciding this question, decision-makers should take into account the list of 12 factors from EU case law (reproduced above at **14.42**) and whether the work was regular or intermittent, the period of employment, whether it was intended to be short-term or long-term, the number of hours worked and the level of earnings.[6]

[1]   The Social Security (Contributions) Regulations 2001, SI 2001/1004.
[2]   The rates for the tax year 2014/2015 increased to £153 per week or £7,956 per year: Social Security (Contributions) (Limits and Thresholds) (Amendment) Regulations 2014, SI 2014/569, reg 3.
[3]   From October 2013, the adult rate was £6.31 an hour: National Minimum Wage rates, GOV.UK.
[4]   *Decision makers' guide*: Vol 2: International subjects: staff guide: *DMG*, Vol 2, Ch 7, Part 3: Habitual residence and right to reside IS, JSA and SPC, at 071203.
[5]   *DMG*, Vol 2, Ch 7, Part 3: para 071208. The Guidance cites *MDB v Secretary of State for the Home Department* [2012] EWCA Civ 1015, [2012] 3 CMLR 1020, a case in which the appellant's application for a residence permit based on being a primary carer of an EEA national in education was dismissed. The appellant had been unemployed since his arrival in the UK in 1999 apart from a period in 2007 when he worked eight hours a day for ten weeks. The Upper Tribunal found that at no time had the appellant actively sought work and that the work that he had done in 2007 'seems to have been undertaken to maintain his claim for benefits' (para 66). The Court of Appeal agreed saying that the facts showed that the appellant was not exercising his right to work given to him by EU law and that: 'In deciding whether a person is actually pursuing or seriously wishes to pursue activities as an employed person, a court is entitled to examine his or her motive' (para 65).
[6]   *DMG*, Vol 2, Ch 7, Part 3: paras 071204 and 071210–071211.

Possible legal challenges to the MET

14.45 The primary legal concern over the MET is that it purports to interpret the concept of a 'worker' by reference to the level of earnings needed to make Class 1 National Insurance Contributions. As such, it appears to breach the principle that it is impermissible to define the EU concept of work by reference to national laws (*Levin*[1]). The DWP argues that the MET does not seek to displace EU law; it merely helps the DWP focus on those cases where greater scrutiny is needed. However, the MET remains open to legal challenge in so far as the EU concept of a 'worker' takes its flavour from the MET (*Hoekstra*[2]). Moreover, the fact that the threshold is roughly equivalent to 24 hours work makes it intrinsically more difficult for EEA nationals in part-time work to satisfy decision-makers using the MET guidance that they meet the 'genuine and effective' test.[3]

[1]   Case C-53/81, *Levin (DM) v Secretary of State for Justice* [1982] ECR 1035; [1982] 2 CMLR 454, para 11.

SELF-EMPLOYED PERSONS

14.46 A self-employed person who is a 'qualified person' continues to have a right to reside after three months residence[1] and is therefore entitled to in-work benefits, such as HB, WTC and, if applicable, CHB.[2] In order for a person to be regarded as self-employed for the purposes of the right to reside, the work involved must be 'genuine and effective'.[3] According to the Minimum Earnings Threshold (MET) guidance, if the average profits (before tax and NI) meet or are more than the threshold and have been at that level for a continuous period of three months, then the decision-maker should accept that the claimant was a self-employed person under EU law.[4] Otherwise, the decision-maker is told to 'arrive at a judgement based on all the facts of the case in accordance with the guidance from EU case law.'[5] This will not always be a straightforward task given the variable nature self-employment, as a decision by the Upper Tribunal[6] explains:

'The concept of self-employment encompasses periods of both feast and famine. During the latter, the person may be engaged in a variety of tasks that are properly seen as part of continuing self-employment: administrative work, such as maintaining the accounts; in marketing to generate more work; or developing the business in new directions. Self-employment is not confined to periods of actual work. It includes natural periods of rest and the vicissitudes of business life. This does not mean that self-employment survives regardless of how little work arrives. It does mean that the issue can only be decided in the context of the facts at any particular time.'

Given the above, decision-makers must take the different nature of self-employment into account when applying the EU test:[7]

'DMs should exercise care in applying the guidance on EU case law in DMG 071206 and 071207 (on the meaning of "worker") to the question of whether self-employment is genuine and effective. Account must be taken of the different nature of self-employment: it may include periods of relative inactivity and there will be periods particularly as a business is starting up when the person may be working long hours but not yet receiving much profit.'

The following example of a self-employed person satisfied the EU test is taken from the DWP's official guidance:[8]

'The claimant was a French national. She came to the UK on 6.1.13 and claimed JSA on 17.2.13. It emerged that the claimant had been working on a self-employed basis as an interpreter. Since arriving she had worked for 12 hours per week on average charging a fee of £15 per hour. The DM decided that the claimant's activity as a self-employed person was genuine and effective and that consequently the claimant had a right to reside as a self-employed person and was therefore not a person from abroad.

[1]   Immigration (European Economic Area) Regulations 2006, SI 2006/1003, reg 6(1)(c) and 14(1). A 'self-employed person' is defined as 'a person who establishes himself in order to pursue activity as a self-employed person in accordance with Article 49 of the treaty on the Functioning of the European Union' (reg 2(1)(b).
[2]   HB Regs 2006, SI 2006/213, reg 10(3B(za), CHB (General) Regs 2006, SI 2006/223, reg 23(6)(b).

3   C-268/99, *Jany v Staatssecretaris van Justitie* [2003] All ER (EC) 193, [2003] 2 CMLR 1, para 33; *Bristol City Council v FV (HB)* [2011] UKUT 494 (AAC), para 7.
4   *Decision makers' guide*: Vol 2: International subjects: staff guide: DMG, Vol 2 Ch 7 Part 3: Habitual residence and right to reside IS, JSA and SPC, at 071214 (Amendment 28 June 2014).
5   DMG, Vol 2, Ch 7, Part 3 at 071186.
6   *Secretary of State for Work and Pensions v JS (IS)* [2010] UKUT 240 (AAC), para 5.
7   DMG, Vol 2, Ch 7, Part 3: at 071215.
8   DMG Vol 2 Ch 7 Part 3: at 071215 – Example 2.

SELF-SUFFICIENT PERSONS

14.47 EEA nationals who are economically inactive may have a right to reside as self-sufficient persons.[1] A 'self-sufficient person' is someone who has (i) sufficient resources not to become a burden on the social assistance system of the UK during his or his period of residence; and (ii) comprehensive sickness insurance cover in the UK.[2] The concept of 'sufficient resources' includes cases where the EEA national's resources are greater than the level of resources at or below which a British Citizen would be entitled to social assistance in the UK.[3] But it can also cover cases where the EEA national's resources are less if, taking into account the personal situation of the EEA national concerned, it nevertheless appears to the decision-maker that the EEA national's resources should be regarded as sufficient.[4] An EU national who claims to be self-sufficient is not asserting a right to enter and reside in another EU state on the basis of economic activity in that country. Rather, they must rely upon their own resources which exist independently of any economic activity in the host Member state. According to case law: (i) it is not possible for a claimant to rely on wages earned in the UK to assert self-sufficiency;[5] (ii) a person's resources includes the individual's accommodation.[6]; and (iii) the claimant must show sufficient resources for the intended period of residence.[7] The benefit authorities do not accept that a person has a right to reside for the purpose of acquiring permanent residence if they have avoided making any claim for means-tested benefits and have not used the national health service. The Upper Triunal had upheld this approach. In *VP v Secretary of State for Work and Pensions*[8] Judge Ward said that: 'he did not accept that a person who otherwise did not meet the self-sufficient test could simply lie low for five years and through a combination of luck and an unusually frugal lifestyle avoid being any kind of burden to the social assistance system and then argue that they have retrospectively shown that they had throughout had the resources to be self-sufficient'.[9]

1   Immigration (European Economic Area) Regulations 2006, SI 2006/1003, reg 6(1)(d).
2   SI 2006/1003, reg 4(1)(c), 4(4)(a), (b).
3   SI 2006/1003, reg 4(4)(a).
4   SI 2006/1003, reg 4(4)(b).
5   *MA & Others (EU national; self-sufficiency; lawful employment) Bangladesh* [2006] UKAIT 00090, para 45.
6   *SG v Tameside Metropolitan Borough Council (HB)* [2010] UKUT 243 (AAC), para 46. A claimant may be self-sufficient if their resources are more than the applicable amount for means-tested benefits and they are provided with free and stable accommodation by friends or family.
7   *VP v Secretary of State for Work and Pensions* [2014] UKUT 32 (AAC); [2014] AACR 25, para 84.
8   [2014] UKUT 32 (AAC); [2014] AACR 25.
9   *VP v Secretary of State for Work and Pensions*, para 84.

Comprehensive sickness insurance cover

14.48 According to domestic case law, the requirement for comprehensive sickness insurance is not met by simple access to free treatment under the NHS.[1] This is despite the view expressed by the European Commission that by refusing to accept that NHS cover is the same as comprehensive health insurance the UK is in breach of EU law.[2] EEA nationals will, however, be regarded as having comprehensive sickness insurance where the UK is entitled to reimbursement of NHS healthcare costs from another Member State. This will usually be the case where the claimant is receiving a pension or invalidity benefit from another Member State, but it can arise in other circumstances.[3]

[1] *W(China) v Secretary of State for the Home Department* [2006] EWCA Civ 1494, [2007] 1 WLR 1514, paras 10–11, and 13; *FK (Kenya) v Secretary of state for the Home Department* [2010] EWCA Civ 1302, para 15; and *Ahmad v Secretary of State for the Home Department* [2014] EWCA Civ 988, paras 70–71 and *VP v Secretary of State for Work and Pensions (JSA)* [2014] UKUT 0032 (AAC), paras 98–105.

[2] See Press Release (IP/12/417 of 26 April 2012) – Free movement: Commission asks the UK to uphold EU citizens' rights.

[3] In *SG v Tameside Metropolitan Borough Council (HB)* [2010] UKUT 243 (AAC), the Secretary of State conceded that a claimant in receipt of a Swedish invalidity benefit pension was able to rely on NHS treatment in order to meet the requirement for comprehensive sickness insurance.

STUDENTS

14.49 In order for an EEA national (or a family member[1]) to have a right to reside as a student, a number of conditions need to be satisfied. First, there are conditions concerning the nature of the course and the status of the education institute providing the course.[2] Secondly, the student must sign a declaration at the beginning of the course that he or she is able to support themselves without social assistance at the time of the declaration and for the foreseeable future and that he or she has comprehensive health insurance for the UK.[3] If an EEA student later needs to claim mainstream welfare benefits, he or she may need to show how their circumstances have changed since then. There is EU case law which suggests that social assistance may be provided to an EEA student, at least on a temporary basis, to tide them over an emergency, eg because their funding has run out before the course has been completed.[4] It should be noted that students' access to benefits are restricted under the normal benefit rules – eg student loans are taken into account as income when calculating means-tested benefits.[5]

[1] The definition of family member is narrower for students: Immigration (European Economic Area) Regulations 2006, SI 2006/1003, reg 7(2).

[2] SI 2006/1003, reg 4(1)(d)(i).

[3] SI 2006/1003, reg 4(1)(d)(ii).

[4] Case C-184/99 *Grzelczyk (Rudy) v Centre Public d'Aide Sociale d'Ottignies-Louvain-la-Neuve* [2002] 1 CMLR 543, [2002] ICR 566, paras 44–45.

[5] HB Regs 2006, SI 2006/213, regs 59-69; ESA Regs 2008, SI 2008/794, regs 132-143 and JS Regs1996, SI 1996/207, regs 130-139.

Family Members

FAMILY MEMBERS OF WORKERS AND SELF-EMPLOYED PERSONS

14.50 Family members of persons who are workers or self-employed persons have the same rights of residence as those persons and are entitled to reside in the UK for as long as they remain family members of a worker or self-employed person or someone who retains the status of a worker or self-employed person.[1] The EEA Regulations defines who counts as 'family members'. These include a spouse or civil partner, direct descendants of the EEA national, his spouse or civil partner who are under the age of 21 or dependants of his, his spouse or civil partner, direct ascendant relatives of the EEA national, his spouse or civil partner, who are dependants;[2] as well as extended family members.[3] Family members are deemed not to be a 'person from abroad' for the purposes of IS, JSA(IB) and ESA(IR) and HB.[4] Nor will they be a person treated as 'not present in Great Britain' for the purposes of SPEC, UC, CHB and CTC.[5]

[1]   Immigration (European Economic Area) Regulations 2006, SI 2006/1003, reg 7(1)(a)–(d).
[2]   SI 2006/1003, reg 7.
[3]   SI 2006/1003, reg 8.
[4]   IS(Gen) Regs 1987/1967, reg 21AA(4)(zb); JSA Regs 1996/207, reg 85A(4)(zb) and ESA Regs 2008/794, reg 70(3)(b)(ii).
[5]   SPC Regs 2002/1792, reg 2(3)(b)(ii), UC Regs SI 2013/376, reg 9(4)(b), HB Regs, reg 10(3B)(d) CHB (General) Regs SI 2006/223, reg 23(6)(e) and TC (Residence) Regs SI 2003/654, reg 3(7)(e).

Guidance on the EU concept of dependency

14.51 If a family member of an EEA national intends to access welfare benefits based on a right to reside derived from an eligible or 'qualified person', it is important that the benefit authority applies the EU concept of dependency correctly. Case law[1] provides that:

- dependency is the result of a factual situation characterised by the fact that material support to meet the needs for a family member is provided by an EEA national who has exercised free movement rights;
- the support must be material, although not necessarily financial, and must provide for, or contribute towards, the basic necessities of life;
- there is no need to determine the reasons for recourse to that support or to raise the question whether the person concerned is able to support himself or herself by taking up paid employment. Nor is the status of a dependent family member automatically lost if they receive social assistance; and
- dependency need not have existed in the family member's country of origin, or the Member State in which they previously resided. It can arise in the host state.[2]

[1]   See Case C-316/85 *Centre Public d'Aide Sociale, Courcelles v Lebon* [1987] ECR 2811, [1989] 1 CMLR 337, paras 20–24, Case C-1/05 *Jia v Migrationsverket* [2007] QB 545, [2007] Imm AR 439, [2007] 1 CMLR 41, paras 35–43 and *CIS/2100/2007*, para 44.
[2]   *Pedro v Secretary of State for Work and Pensions* [2009] EWCA Civ 1358, [2010] 2 CMLR 547, para 66, *Metock v Minister for Justice, Equality and Law Reform* [2009] QB 318, [ECJ], [2008] 3 CMLR 1167, ECJ, para 54.

FAMILY MEMBERS OF BRITISH CITIZENS

14.52 Under the EEA Regulations 2006, if certain conditions are met, family members of British citizens have the same EU law rights to reside as they would have if they were a family member of another EEA State.[1] This is sometimes referred to as the 'Surinder Singh' route.[2] Those conditions were amended with effect from 1 January 2014,[3] but there are some transitional provisions.[4] Under the new rules, the British citizen is required to have 'transferred the centre of their life' to another EEA Member State, where they resided as a worker or self-employed person with their spouse or civil partner before returning to the UK. Where the conditions have been satisfied, the British citizen and their family members will not be a 'person from abroad' for the purposes of HB, IS, JSA(IB), ESA(IR) or CTR.[5] Nor will they be a person treated as 'not present in Great Britain' for the purposes of SPC, UC, CHB or CTC.[6] Note, that until 16 July 2012 persons who held British citizenship and who were also nationals of another EEA Member State could rely on that EEA nationality to benefit from the terms of the Directive.[7] Following the decision in C-434/09 *McCarthy v Secretary of State for the Home Department*,[8] the definition of an EEA national in the EEA Regulations 2006 was amended to preclude dual British citizens/EEA nationals from benefitting from the Directive and therefore also to preclude their family members from relying upon free movement rights.[9] If, however, a British national with dual nationality has lived with a right of residence (ie based on free movement rights) in another Member State (other than the one of which he or she is a national) then when returning to the UK s/he may have residence rights, and be able to confer EU rights on others.

[1] Immigration (European Economic Area) Regulations 2006, SI 2006/1003, reg 9.
[2] Case C-370/90, *R v Immigration Appeal Tribunal and Surinder Singh, ex p Secretary of State for the Home Department* [1992] ECR I-4265; [1992] 3 CMLR 358; [1992] Imm. AR 565. In simple terms the 'Surinder Singh route' involves a UK citizen living and working elsewhere in the EEA for a period of three or more months so that upon their return to the UK they can assert the rights associated with EU citizenship and free movement, which includes bringing family members, including nationals who are third country nationals, from outside EEA.
[3] Immigration (European Economic Area) (Amendment) (No 2) Regulations 2013, SI 2013/3032.
[4] Immigration (European Economic Area) Regulations 2006, SI 2006/1003, regs 9(2)(c) and 9(3).
[5] HB Regs, reg 10(3B)(d), IS(Gen) Regs 1987/1967, reg 21AA(4)(zb); JSA Regs 1996/207, reg 85A(4)(zb) and ESA Regs 2008/794, reg 70(3)(b)(ii).
[6] SPC Regs 2002/1792, reg 2(3)(b)(ii), UC Regs SI 2013/376, reg 9(4)(b), CHB (General) Regs SI 2006/223, reg 23(6)(e) and TC (Residence) Regs SI 2003/654, reg 3(7)(e).
[7] *Secretary of State for Work and Pensions v AA* [2009] UKUT 249 (AAC), para 16.
[8] C-434/09 *McCarthy v Secretary of State for the Home Department* [2011] All ER (EC) 729, [2011] 3 CMLR 10, [2011] Imm AR 586.
[9] Immigration (European Economic Area) Regulations 2006, SI 2006/1003, reg 10(2)(d) as amended by SI 2012/1547 Sch 1, para 3, with effect from 16 July 2012, subject to transitional provisions in Sch 1 para 3 for those persons who have acted in reliance on the previous definition.

RETAINED RIGHT OF RESIDENCE

Retaining worker status

14.53 EU case law has established that the status of a worker is not lost immediately on cessation of employment and that a person may retain that status if they are capable of taking on another job and retaining a link to the labour market.[1] The circumstances in which a former worker can retain the status of a worker are that the person:

(1)   is temporarily unable to work as the result of an illness or accident;[2] or

(2)   is registered as involuntarily unemployed (normally with a Jobcentre and having claimed Jobseeker's Allowance) and he or she:

   (i)   has been employed for one year or more before becoming unemployed;[3] or

   (ii)   has been unemployed for no more than six months, is seeking employment in the UK and has a genuine chance of being engaged;[4] or

(3)   is involuntarily unemployed and has embarked on vocational training;[5] or

(4)   has voluntarily ceased working and embarked on vocational training that is related to the person's previous employment.[6]

[1]   Case 75/63 *Hoekstra (nee-Unger) v Bestuur der Bedrijfsvereniging voor Detailhandel en Ambachten* [1964] ECR 177 – the concept of a 'worker' includes someone who has left one job but is capable of taking another one.
[2]   Directive 2004/38/EC, art 7(3)(a). Immigration (European Economic Area) Regulations 2006, SI 2006/1003, reg 6(2)(a).
[3]   Directive 2004/38/EC, art 7(3)(b) and SI 2006/1003, reg 6(2)(b)(i).
[4]   Directive 2004/38/EC, art 7(3)(c) and SI 2006/1003, reg 6(2)(b)(ii)–(iii).
[5]   Directive 2004/38/EC, art 7(3)(d) and SI 2006/1003, reg 6(2)(c).
[6]   Directive 2004/38/EC, art 7(3)(d) and SI 2006/1003, reg 6(2)(d).

Retained worker status as a jobseeker

14.54 If an EEA national has been employed in the UK such that they are a 'worker' but then becomes 'involuntarily unemployed'[1] (eg on being made redundant or a fixed-term contract ends) and has registered as a jobseeker, they may continue to have a right to reside as someone with retained worker status.[2] An EEA national with a right to reside based on retained worker status can access out-of-work benefits such as JSA(IB), HB, CTR, CHB, CTC and UC.[3]

[1]   When deciding whether an EEA national has become 'involuntarily unemployed' case law requires that the inquiry should focus on whether the claimant is still in the labour market, rather than on the precise circumstances in which he or she ceased to be employed; *Secretary of State for Work and Pensions v EM* [2009] UKUT 146 (AAC), para 10.
[2]   Immigration (European Economic Area) Regulations 2006, SI 2006/1003, reg 6(2)(ba).
[3]   JSA Regs 1996/207, reg 85A(4)(zb); HB Regs 2006/213, reg 10(3B)(c) CTR(PR)(E) Regs 2012/2885, reg 12(5)(a), ; CHB (General) Regs SI 2006/223.reg 23(6)(c); TC (Residence) Regs SI 2003/654, reg 3(7)(c) and UC Regs SI 2013/376, reg 9(4)(a).

THE RULES PRIOR TO JANUARY 2014

14.55 Under the law as it stood before January 2014, EEA nationals who were former workers but who had worked in the UK for *less than a year* would have retained worker status for an initial period of six months, after which they would became subject to the requirement that they have a 'genuine chance of being engaged'. For most EEA nationals, an entitlement to Jobseeker's Allowance was held to be sufficient evidence that they met this requirement.[1] For those former workers who had been employed in the UK for *a year or more*, they would retain worker status indefinitely, provided they continued to be registered as a jobseeker.[2] In addition, if there was a gap between becoming involuntarily unemployed and claiming JSA(IB) this did not necessarily mean that the EEA national could not retain the status of a worker, so long as the gap did not show that the EEA national had withdrawn from the labour market.[3]

1. *Secretary of State for Work and Pensions v IR* (CIS/1951/2008) [2009] UKUT 11 (AAC), para 21 and CIS/4304/2007, para 31.
2. *Secretary of State for Work and Pensions v IA* CIS/601/2008 [2009] UKUT 35 (AAC), para 22. The approach taken by the Upper Tribunal (Administrative Appeals) in relation to entitlement to JSA(IB) can be compared with the stricter approach to the time a person could be considered a jobseeker taken by the Upper Tribunal (Immigration and Asylum) in respect of residence permits: see See *AG and Ors* (EEA-jobseeker-self-sufficient person-proof) *German* [2007] UKAIT 00075, para 49 where the criteria of a reasonable period is discussed.
3. *Secretary of State for Work and Pensions v IR* (CIS/1951/2008) [2009] UKUT 11 (AAC), paras 12–14.

THE RULES POST-JANUARY 2014

14.56 The conditions for being a 'qualified person' under the EEA Regulations 2006 were amended in January 2014.[1] There have been three significant changes to the conditions that must be met in order to be a 'qualified person' as a former worker seeking employment who retains worker status:[2]

— First, the jobseeker must provide evidence that they have a 'genuine chance of being engaged' from the outset of their unemployment, instead of after six months).[3]

— Second, those jobseekers who have been employed in the UK for *less than one year*[4] can only retain worker status for a maximum of six months.[5]

— Third, those jobseekers who have been employed in the UK for *at least one year*[6] are required to provide 'compelling evidence' that they have a 'genuine chance of being engaged' after they have been unemployed for six months.[7]

In addition to the time limits imposed on an EEA national's right to reside as a jobseeker or with retained worker status outlined above, a additional condition, requiring a period of absence from the UK of at least 12 months, was added for those who wished to re-establish jobseeker status following a 'relevant period' of three or six months.[8] Note that the Government has announced that in February 2015 it intends to remove transitional protection for all EEA migrants who were claiming JSA(IB) before these changes were introduced.[9] The EEA Regulations 2006 do not give any information on what would constitute 'compelling evidence' but the DWP are interpreting it to mean either an actual job offer or something that will realistically result in a job in the near future such as a vocational course or a move to another area where there are job opportunities.[10] In either circumstances, the time limited period of six months may be extended at the decision-maker's discretion. The guidance on what can be accepted as 'compelling evidence' issued to decision-makers (DM) states:[11]

'14 The DM can extend the claimant's JSA entitlement where the claimant has provided compelling evidence that a change of their circumstances as set out below has now given them a genuine chance of being engaged:

1. where the claimant has provided reliable evidence that they have a genuine offer of a specific job which will be genuine and effective work provided that job is due to start within 3 months starting from the relevant period plus 1 day point. In this case the relevant period can be extended up to the day before the job actually starts or is due to start (whichever is the earlier); *or*
2. where the claimant can provide proof during the relevant period that a change of circumstance has given them genuine prospects of employment (which will be genuine and effective work and as a result they are awaiting the outcome of job interviews. In these cases the relevant period can be extended by up to 2 months. Any extension is backdated to the date of change.'

1   Immigration (European Economic Area) Regulations 2006, SI 2006/1003, reg 6(5)(b) was amended by SI 2013/3032, with effect from 1 January 2014, subject to the transitional provisions in Sch 3, para 1 of the amending regulations by SI 2014/1451, with effect from 1 July 2014, subject to the transitional provisions in reg 4 in the amending regulations.
2   SI 2006/1003, reg 6(5)(b) – Condition A. Instead of saying 'former worker' the legislation refers to someone present in the UK who is seeking employment 'immediately after enjoying a right to reside' as a qualified person, otherwise than as a jobseeker:
3   SI 2006/1003, reg 6 – Condition B.
4   SI 2006/1003, reg 6(2)(ba).
5   SI 2006/1003, reg 6(2A).
6   SI 2006/1003, reg 6(2)(b).
7   SI 2006/1003, reg 6(7).
8   SI 2006/1003, reg 6(9) and (10).
9   The Chancellor of the Exchequer's Autumn Statement, 3 December 2014.
10 SI 2006/1003, reg 6(9) and (10).
11 *DMG memo* 15/14: *Habitual residence and right to reside* – JSA (June 2014) at paras 14–15.

Are the new conditions for jobseekers in the EEA Regulations 2006 compatible with EU law?

14.57 Legal challenges to the new conditions for EEA jobseekers with retained worker status are likely to focus on whether Member States are entitled to refuse benefit to jobseekers who have established a genuine link to the UK's labour market (*Vatsouras*[1]) based solely on the failure to provide 'compelling evidence' given that there is no reference to this condition in the Citizens Directive 2004/38/EC. It is also arguable that the removal of out-of-work benefits to EEA nationals who do not find work within three or six months, regardless of how long they have been residing in the UK, (or their employment history here), is inconsistent with the need to avoid blanket rules that do not make any allowances for a claimant's individual circumstances (*Brey*[2]). See also: The risk of destitution for EEA migrants following the removal of housing benefit at **14.41** above.

1   Case C-22/08, *Vatsouras v Arbeitsgemeinschaft (ARGE) Nurnberg* [2009] ECR. I-4585; [2009] All ER (EC) 747; [2009] CEC 1024, para 40.
2   Case C-140/12 *Pensionsversicherungsanstalt v Brey (Peter)* [2014] 1 CMLR 993, paras 64 and 76–78.

Retaining worker status due to temporary incapacity

14.58 EEA nationals can retain the status of a worker if they need to give up a job due to temporary incapacity and have registered as involuntarily unemployed.[1] A person can come under the provision if they need to give up a job due to a medical problem, so long as it does not permanently incapacitate them from undertaking all types of work.[2] The length of the period of incapacity is not determinative[3] and the question is ultimately an objective one rather than one based on the worker's subjective understanding of his or her position and his or her intentions at the time.[4] Someone with retained worker status due to temporary incapacity can access out-of-work benefits – ie ESA(IR), HB, CTR, and where there are dependent children, CHB and CTC. It should be noted that an EEA national who has 'retained worker status' as a jobseeker can switch categories and retain that status if they subsequently become ill, such that they can claim ESA(IB).[5] This can be contrasted with the position of an EEA national who is in receipt of JSA(IB) based solely on having a right to reside as a 'jobseeker'. If they become ill before finding work, they will not be able to access ESA(IB) despite being unable to work.[6]

1   Directive 2004/38/EC, art 7(3)(a). EEA Regulations 2006, SI 2006/1003, reg 6(2)(a).
2   CIS/3890/2005, para 5.
3   *FMB (Uganda) v Secretary of State for the Home Department* [2010] UKUT 447 (IAC): The facts of the case concerned someone who had remained incapable of work from 2004 until February 2008, at which point he enrolled as a student. There was medical evidence that showed that he had been unable to work until the medication had stabilised and relieved his condition sufficiently to enable him to commence his studies.
4   *De Brito (Aurelio) v Secretary of State for the Home Department* [2012] EWCA Civ 709, para 33.
5   *Secretary of State for Work and Pensions v IR* (CIS/1951/2008) [2009] UKUT 11 (AAC), para 23.
6   CIS/4304/2007, para 30.

Retaining worker status based on vocational training

14.59 EEA nationals who are registered as jobseekers can retain worker status based on undertaking vocational training. Under the test, the vocational training will count in cases where the EEA national becomes *involuntarily* unemployed and then embarks on vocational training that will assist them in obtaining employment.[1] This can include a course leading to a qualification for a particular profession.[2] Under the second part of the test, the EEA national can retain the status of a worker where they *voluntarily* cease work and take up vocational training in order to find work that is reasonably equivalent to their former employment.[3] The provision only applies where a person has to retrain in order to find work reasonably equivalent to his or her former employment.[4]

1   Immigration (European Economic Area) Regulations 2006, SI 2006/1003, reg 6(2)(c).
2   Case C-197/86 *Brown v Secretary of State for Scotland* [1988] ECR 3205.
3   SI 2006/1003, reg 6(2)(d).
4   *Secretary of State for Work and Pensions v EM* [2009] UKUT 146 (AAC). The claimant had worked in a chicken processing factory. At the end of her maternity leave, instead of returning to that job she left to train as a teaching assistant. It was held that the claimant could not come within the provision of SI 2006/1003, reg 6(2)(d) as her training was not related to her previous employment (para 9).

Retaining worker status after ceasing work due to pregnancy

14.60 A woman on maternity leave (including unpaid maternity leave) is still a worker and does not need to rely on the provisions for retaining worker status.[1] However, prior to the decision in *Saint Prix* (C-507/12)[2] if a woman ceased to work due to pregnancy, she could not access Income Support (IS) on the same basis as UK nationals, save where a pregnancy-related illness prevented her from working.[3] Ms Saint Prix was a teaching assistant who gave up work while in the late stages of pregnancy, when the work became too strenuous and lighter work was not available. In March 2007, eleven weeks before her due date, she applied for IS, but this was refused on the basis that she did not have a right to reside. Her baby was born prematurely and she returned to work three months later in August 2008. The Supreme Court made a reference to the CJEU. The UK government argued that as Directive 38/2004/EC was intended to codify the existing law, Article 7(3) contains an exhaustive list of the circumstances when worker status could be retained but makes no mention of pregnancy. The Court rejected this argument. It reiterated that the concept of 'worker' is a matter of primary law and could not be read restrictively[4] and concluded that the definition of a worker could encompass someone in Ms Saint Prix's situation.[5] Retaining worker status in this type of case is, however, conditional upon the individual intending to return to work or finding another job 'within a reasonable period after confinement'. The DWP has issued guidance[6] stating that it will use the 15-week period after childbirth as a yardstick for considering whether an EEA national in Ms Saint Prix's circumstances returned to work within a 'reasonable period'. On the question of whether someone comes within the scope of the *Saint Prix* judgment the *Guidance* states, at paras 9–10:

> 'Where a claimant indicates that they have an intention to return to their previous job or that they will find another job, the DM can award IS for a fixed period until the end of the 15-week period after the expected date of confinement. If the claimant subsequently does not return to work, a recovery of the IS paid will not be required.
> . . . Where the claimant indicates at the outset of the IS claim that they have no intention of returning to any work within the 15 week period after childbirth or they plan to return to work much later (e.g. when the child is one year old), the conditions in the Saint Prix judgment will not be satisfied, the claimant will not retain worker status and IS cannot be awarded.'

1   *CIS/185/2008*, para 8, where it was conceded that the claimant remained a worker for the purpose of the 2000 Regulations for as long as she was on maternity leave and her contract of employment subsisted. *CIS/4237/2007* [2008] UKUT 227 (AAC), para 7, which held that an accession state national who was on maternity leave is still a 'worker' for the purposes of Article 39 of the Treaty. *Secretary of State for Work and Pensions v SL* [2009] UKUT 227 (AAC), para 11, which held that an employee on unpaid maternity leave remains a 'worker' with continuing employment rights and the status of an EU migrant worker, though no longer in 'remunerative' employment.

2   Case C-507/12 *Saint Prix (Jessy) v Secretary of State for Work and Pensions* [2014] All ER (EC) 987.

3   *CIS/3890/2007.*

4   *Saint Prix* C-507/12, para 38.

5   *Saint Prix* C-507/12, para 33.

6   *DMG Memo* 25/14, 13 October 2014, para 6. The *DWP Guidance* also confirms that an award of IS may be made for up to 26 weeks, commencing 11 weeks before the expected date of confinement and ending 15 weeks after.

Retaining the status of a self-employed person

14.61 A self-employed person can retain that status while on maternity leave[1] or if temporarily incapable of work due to an illness or accident.[2] But a former self-employed person cannot retain self-employed status during a period of 'involuntarily unemployment' under this provision.[3] Notwithstanding the lack of any concept of retained self-employed status under the EEA Regulations 2006, an EEA national may be entitled to a claim JSA(IB) as a self-employed person (and not as a jobseeker) during a period where there is no work but the person can properly be regarded as remaining in self-employment (ie during a period when trading is slow).[4] On the other hand, where self-employment has ceased altogether, then the EEA national will need to claim JSA(IB) as a jobseeker (ie not someone with retained worker status).

[1] CIS/1042/2008, para 5, in which the Secretary of State conceded that as the claimant intended to resume her self-employment after her maternity period, she remained a self-employed person.
[2] Directive 2004/38/EC, art 7(3)(a), EEA Regulations 2006, SI 2006/1003, reg 6(3).
[3] *R (on the application of Tilianu) v Secretary of State for Work and Pensions* [2010] EWCA Civ 1397, [2011] 2 CMLR 12, para 21.
[4] *Secretary of State for Work and Pensions v JB* (JSA) [2011] UKUT 96 (AAC) 5–8.

Family members who retain their right to reside

14.62 As a general rule, if someone is a family member of an EEA national who has a right to reside, the family member will lose their right to reside if the EEA national ceases to have a right to reside or ceases to be a family member. There are, however, some exceptions where a family member can retain their right to reside as a family member of a qualified person or a person with a permanent right to reside.[1] The rules for these exemptions are complex and include cases where the EEA national has died or left the UK or the family member's marriage or civil partnership ends: The main provisions are summarised below.

— Where the termination of a marriage or civil partnership that had lasted for at least three years with both partners residing in the UK for at least one year; or the former spouse or civil partner has custody of their child(ren) or a right of access to the child(ren) in the UK, or if a continued right of residence is warranted by particularly difficult circumstances (eg he or she was a victim of domestic violence during the marriage or civil partnership).[2]
— Where the spouse or civil partner or a family member was a direct descendant of a qualified person or an EEA national who has died or who has left the UK and they were attending an education course in the UK immediately before the EEA national died or left the UK.[2] Or where a parent has actual custody of a child who is attending a course in these circumstances.[3]

These provisions are, however, subject to the proviso that the family member must also satisfy the condition that although not an EEA national, he or she is exercising free movement rights or is the family member of such a person.[4] The family member's right to reside on this basis lasts as long as the conditions apply, or until they acquire a permanent right to reside.[5]

[1] Immigration (European Economic Area) Regulations 2006, SI 2006/1003, reg 10.
[2] SI 2006/1003, reg 10(5)(a)–(d)(i)–(iv).
[3] SI 2006/1003, reg 10(4).
[4] SI 2006/1003, reg 10(2)(c), (6)(a)–(b). See *Okafor v Secretary of State for the Home Department* [2011] EWCA Civ 499, [2011] 1 WLR 3071, [2011] NLJR 636, where the court

rejected a submission that a family member could obtain a right of permanent residence following the death of an EU national without any need to show compliance with these conditions.

5   SI 2006/1003, reg 14(3) and 10(8).

PERMANENT RIGHT OF RESIDENCE

Five years residence

14.63 The Residence Directive introduced a permanent right to reside for EU citizens and members of their family who have 'resided legally' in a host Member State of the EU for a continuous period of five years.[1] Someone who has a right to reside permanently in the UK is exempt from the habitual residence test.[2] The CJEU in *Ziolkowski and Szeja*[3] has held that a person does not 'reside lawfully' in a host State for the purposes of the Directive if s/he does not comply with the conditions contained within it, ie unless they are exercising a right under the Directive as a worker, self-employed person, student or self-sufficient person under article 7(1). The five-year qualifying period therefore includes periods during which the EEA national:

— was a jobseeker;[4]
— was a worker or self-employed person in the UK;[5] or
— retained worker status in the UK whilst temporarily incapable of work because of illness or accident or whilst involuntarily unemployed and seeking work;[6] or
— was both self-sufficient and had comprehensive sickness insurance for themselves and their family members;[7] or
— was a student who was both self-sufficient and had comprehensive sickness insurance;[8] or
— was a family member accompanying or joining a person who satisfied the above conditions;[9]
— was a worker or self-employed person who has ceased activity and the family member of such a person;[10]
— and in certain circumstances, family members of workers or self-employed persons who have died;[11]
— and in certain circumstances, people who were formerly 'family members who had retained the right of residence.[12]

Periods of residence completed in accordance with a derivative right to reside, however, do not count towards the acquisition of a permanent right to reside.[13]

1   Directive 2004/38/EC, art 16. Immigration (European Economic Area) Regulations 2006, SI 2006/1003, reg 15.
2   HB Regs, reg 10(3B)(zc), IS(Gen) Regs 1987/1967, reg 21AA(4)(zc); JSA Regs 1996/207, reg 85A(4)(zc) and ESA Regs 2008/794, reg 70(4)(zc), SPC Regs 2002/1792, reg 2(4)(zc), UC Regs SI 2013/376, reg 9(4)(c).
3   *Ziolkowski v Land Berlin*: C-425/10; *Szeja v Land Berlin*:C-425/10 [2013] 3 CMLR 1013; [2012] Imm. AR 421; [2012] INLR. 467 at paras 45–47.
4   SI 2006/1003, reg 15(1)(a)(b).
5   SI 2006/1003, reg 15(1)(a) and 6(1)(a). Note this is more generous than EU law as Directive 2004/38/EC, art 7 does not include 'jobseekers'. Periods of work seeking mixed with periods of work can therefore count for the purposes of considering a permanent right of residence under the EEA Regulations.
6   SI 2006/1003, reg 15(1)(a) and 6(1)(3).
7   SI 2006/1003, regs 15(1)(a), 6(1)(d) and 4(1)(c).

[8] SI 2006/1003, regs 15(1)(a), 6(1)(e) and 4(1)(d).

[9] SI 2006/1003, regs 15(1)(a), 7(a)–(d) and 4(1)(d).

[10] SI 2006/1003, regs 15(1)(c)(d) – relevant to family members who are non-EEA nationals.

[11] SI 2006/1003, regs 15(1)(e)(i)–(iii) – relevant to family members who are non-EEA nationals.

[12] SI 2006/1003, regs 15(1)(f)(i)–(ii) – relevant to family members who are non-EEA nationals.

[13] SI 2006/1003, reg 15(1A), following the decision in C529/11 *Alarape v Secretary of State for the Home Department (AIRE Centre intervening)* [2013] 1 WLR 2883, [2013] 3 CMLR 1042.

Qualifying periods

14.64 The EEA Regulations 2006[1] provide that the following periods of residence can count towards the acquisition of a permanent right to reside.

- *Periods of residence before the EEA Regulations 2006 came into force* – Any period during which an EEA national carried out activities or was resident in the UK in accordance with UK regulations and Directives concerning the right to reside in EU law that were in force before 30 April 2006 is to be treated as a period in which that activity or residence was in accordance with the EEA Regulations 2006.[2]

- *Qualifying periods before accession* – Any period during which a national of a country which has since acceded to the EU was carrying out an activity or was resident in the UK throughout which they (i) had leave to enter or remain in the UK; and (ii) would have been carrying out that activity or residing in the UK in accordance with the EEA Regulations 2000 in force at the time.[3]

- *Periods where residence was not in accordance with the EEA Regulations* – A period during which the conditions above were satisfied will not be regarded as a period of activity or residence completed in accordance with the EEA Regulations where it was followed by a period of more than two consecutive years throughout which: (i) the person was absent from the UK; or (ii) the person's residence in the UK was not in accordance with the EEA Regulations.[4]

In addition, the Upper Tribunal (IAC) has confirmed that a person may acquire qualifying residence for the purposes of exercising Treaty rights in respect of periods of residence arising before the UK became part of the European Community on 1 January 1973.[5]

[1] Immigration (European Economic Area) Regulations 2006, SI 2006/1003.

[2] SI 2006/1003, reg 31(2), Sch 4, para 6. This codifies what was said in C-162/09 *Secretary of State for Work and Pensions v Lassal (Child Poverty Action Group intervening)* [2011] 1 CMLR 972.

[3] SI 2006/1003, Sch 4, para 6(3)(a)(b). This codifies what was said in C-424/10, C-425/10, *Ziolkowski* and *Szeja v Land Berlin* [2013] 3 CMLR 37; [2012] Imm AR 421; [2012] INLR 467.

[4] SI 2006/1003, Sch 4, para 6(4)(a)(b). Note, that where a claimant holds a residence permit this can ensure that a claimant *preserves* a right of permanent residence already acquired before 30 April 2006, so long as the absence from the workforce is less than two years: C-325/09, *Secretary of State for Work and Pensions v Dias (Maria)* [2011] 3 CMLR 1103; [2011] Imm AR 855,[2011] INLR 772, para 66.

[5] *Vassallo (Qualifying residence; pre-UK accession)* [2014] UKUT 313 (IAC), paras 37-38

Effect of absences

14.65 Once acquired on or after 30 April 2006, the right of permanent residence is only lost by absence from the host Member State for a period exceeding two consecutive years.[1] Absences not exceeding six months in a year, absences of more than six months for compulsory military service, one absence of a maximum of twelve consecutive months for important reasons such as pregnancy, childbirth, serious illness, study or vocational training or a posting abroad[2] do not break the continuity of the residence requirement; though they do not count towards the accrual of the five years continuous residence.[3]

[1]   Immigration (European Economic Area) Regulations 2006, SI 2006/1003, reg 15(2).
[2]   SI 2006/1003, reg 3(2)(a)–(c).
[3]   SI 2006/1003, reg 3(3).

Retaining permanent residence where a worker or self-employed person has 'ceased activity'

14.66 Under certain circumstances an EEA national who previously had worker status or who was self-employed and is now retired or permanently incapacitated can retain the rights of a worker in the host State. These include:

—   where the EEA national has reached State pension age or taken early retirement and on that date they had been employed or a self-employed person in the UK for at least twelve months; and they lived in the UK continuously for more than three years prior to ceasing work.[1]

—   where the EEA national ceased activity as a result of permanent incapacity for work; **and** either they resided in the UK continuously for two years before ceasing that activity, **or** their incapacity for work was as the result of an accident at work or an occupational disease that entitles them to a pension in full or in part by an institution of the UK.[2]

These rights can be extended to the EEA national's family members in prescribed circumstances, even after the EEA national's death.[3]

[1]   Immigration (European Economic Area) Regulations 2006, SI 2006/1003, reg 5(2).
[2]   SI 2006/1003, reg 5(3). Note that for the purpose of calculating these times, certain periods of inactivity are disregarded (reg 5(7)).
[3]   SI 2006/1003, reg 10(1)–(3).

Family members who can retain a permanent right of residence

14.67 If someone is a family member of a person with a permanent right of residence, they will have a right to reside so long as they remain a family member.[1] After five years of being a family member of an EEA national with a permanent right of residence, the family member acquires a permanent right of residence in their own right. The circumstances in which a family member can acquire a permanent right of residence and therefore be eligible to claim welfare benefits on the same basis as UK citizens include:

—   a family member of an EEA national who has acquired a permanent right of residence and the family member is not an EEA national but who has resided in accordance with the EEA Regulations 2006 for a continuous period of five years;[2] or

— a family member of a worker or self-employed person who has died where the family member resided with him or her immediately before his or her death and the worker or self-employed person had resided continuously in the UK for at least two years immediately before his death, or their death was the result of an accident at work or an occupational disease.[3]

If the period as a family member of an EEA national with a permanent right to reside is less than five years, it can be added to other periods of residence as a qualified person in order to acquire a permanent right of residence.[4]

[1] Immigration (European Economic Area) Regulations 2006, SI 2006/1003, reg 14(2).
[2] SI 2006/1003, reg 15(1)(f)(i)–(ii).
[3] SI 2006/1003, reg 15(1)(e)(i)–(iii).
[4] SI 2006/1003, reg 15(1)(a)–(b).

DERIVATIVE RIGHT TO RESIDE OF A PRIMARY CARER

Based on being a primary carer of a self-sufficient child

14.68 The EEA Regulations 2006 have been amended to codify the derived right developed under EU case law.[1] In the case of a self-sufficient child (a *Chen*-type case)[2] a person will have a derivative right to reside in the UK where that person is the primary carer of an EEA national and that EEA national: (i) is under the age of 18; and (ii) is residing in the UK as a self-sufficient person; and (iii) would be unable to remain in the UK if the primary carer was required to leave the UK.[3] In this type of case the primary carer is treated as a family member of the child and the family must have sufficient combined resources to ensure that the primary carer does not become a burden on the social assistance system of the UK during their period of residence. Equally both must have comprehensive health insurance cover.[4] A primary carer with this type of derivative right to reside would not normally be entitled to claim IS, JSA(IB), ESA(IR) and SPC.[5] It has been held that a non-EU citizen, who is residing in the UK by reason of a derived right of residence, including as the primary carer of an EU citizen child, cannot thereby acquire a permanent right of residence in this country.[6]

[1] Immigration (European Economic Area) Regulations 2006, SI 2006/1003, reg 15A(1) and (4A).
[2] Case C-200/02, *Chen and Zhu v Secretary of State for the Home Department* [2004] Imm AR 754, [2004] 3 WLR 1453, [2004] 3 CMLR 1060.
[3] Immigration (European Economic Area) Regulations 2006, SI 2006/1003, regs 15A(1)–(2) and 4(5).
[4] SI 2006/1003, reg 4(1)(c).
[5] DMG, Vol 2: *International subjects: staff guide*: DMG, Vol 2, Ch 7, Part 3: *Habitual residence and right to reside IS, JSA and SPC*, at 071273.
[6] *Bee (Malaysia) (permanent/derived rights of residence)* [2013] UKUT 000 83 (IAC), para 46.

Based on a child of a migrant worker being in general education

14.69 The child of an EEA migrant worker who has entered general education in the UK has a right to reside based on equal access to education under Article 10 of Regulation (EU) 492/2011[1] and a primary carer of that child can obtain a derived right to reside.[2] According to the EEA Regulations 2006, the following circumstances must exist in order for this right to arise:

— the child must have one EEA national parent (though the primary carer can be a non-EEA national);
— the EEA national parent must be, or have been, 'employed' in the UK;[3]
— the EEA national parent must have been living in the UK when the child entered the education system[4] – although there is no need to show that the EEA national parent was working on the date the child entered education[5] or during any period when the child was in education;[6]
— the child must have been entered into 'general education' in the UK.

For the purposes of this derived right, 'child' includes 'step-child'[7] and the fact that the child is British does not preclude reliance on the right.[8] Unlike the rights granted under the Citizens' Directive 38/2004/EC, the derived right is not conditional on the child or the primary carer being self-sufficient.[9]

[1] Article 10 of Regulation (EU) 492/2011 of the European Parliament and of the Council dated 5 April 2011 on freedom of movement for workers within the Union, grants the children of an EU migrant worker who is or has been employed in the territory of another Member State a right to reside based on the right to access education in the host State. This came into force on 5th April 2011 (OJ C 44, 11 February 2011, p 170) and replaced article 12 of Regulation EEC/1612/68.
[2] Immigration (European Economic Area) Regulations 2006, SI 2006/1003, reg 15A(1) and (3)–(4) which codifies the effect of Case C-480/08 *Teixeira v Lambeth London Borough Council* [2010] 2 CMLR 50; [2010] Imm AR 487 and Case C-310/08 *Harrow London Borough Council v Ibrahim* [2010] PTSR 1913; [2010] 2 CMLR 51, [2010] Imm AR 474.
[3] The fact that the parents of the children concerned have meanwhile divorced, that only one parent is a EEA national or that the parent had ceased to be a migrant worker in the UK is irrelevant (Case C-480/08, *Teixeira v Lambeth LBC*, para 37, Case-310/08, *Harrow LBC v Ibrahim*, para 29).
[4] This condition does not appear in the EU case law.
[5] Case C-480/08, *Teixeira v Lambeth LBC*, para 74.
[6] Case C-147/11 *Secretary of State for Work and Pensions v Czop* [2013] Imm AR 104; [2013] PTSR 334, para 26.
[7] *Alarape & Anor (Article 12, EC Reg 1612/68) Nigeria* [2011] UKUT 413 (IAC), para 29.
[8] *Secretary of State for Work and Pensions v RR* [2013] UKUT 21 (AAC) at para 76.
[9] Case C-480/08 *Teixeira v Lambeth London Borough Council*, para 4. Case-310/08 *Harrow London Borough Council v Ibrahim*, para 59.

The meaning of 'general education'

14.70 For the purposes of Article 10 of Regulation (EU) 492/2011, general education means compulsory schooling and so begins when the child enters primary school.[1] Compulsory education includes both primary and secondary school and sixth form or non-advanced further education. It can include up to university level or similar courses and vocational courses, but the primary carer's right to reside generally ends when the child reaches the age of majority, which in the UK is 18.[2] However, under EU law the right under Article 10 can continue beyond that age if the child continues to need the presence and care of that parent in order to be able to complete their education.[3]

[1] Immigration (European Economic Area) Regulations 2006, SI 2006/1003, reg 15A(6)(a). See *Secretary of State for Work and Pensions v IM (IS)* [2011] UKUT 231 (AAC). The Secretary of State has conceded that this include reception class education at a primary school: *Shabani (EEA – jobseekers; nursery education)* [2013] UKUT 315 (IAC).
[2] Family Law Reform Act 1969, s 1.

³ Case C-529/11 *Alarape v Secretary of State for the Home Department (AIRE Centre intervening)* [2014] All ER (EC) 470, [2013] 1 WLR 2883, [2013] Imm AR 752, [2013] INLR 542, para 28.

The meaning of 'employed'

14.71 The question of what can count as work in order to trigger the right under Article 10 of Regulation EU 492/2011 has been the subject of some dispute. The current position is that the term 'employed in the UK':

- does not include an EEA parent jobseeker or a person who, on stopping work, retains worker status;¹
- does not include a self-employed parent;²
- does include a A8/A2 national employed in registered work or as an authorised worker;³ and
- can include a A2/A8 national who has not completed twelve months registered or authorised work.⁴

¹ Immigration (European Economic Area) Regulations 2006, SI 2006/1003, reg 15A(6)(b).
² *RM v Secretary of State for Work and Pensions* (IS) (Residence and presence conditions: right to reside) [2014] UKUT 401 (AAC), para 31.
³ *Secretary of State for Work and Pensions v JS* (IS) [2010] UKUT 347 (AAC), para 14.
⁴ *DJ v Secretary of State for Work and Pensions* [2013] UKUT 113 (AAC) in which it was held that even though the A8 national had not registered their work, they were nevertheless 'employed' for the purposes of article 10 as under the Accession Regulations the first month of work was treated as being for an authorised employer (para 10).

The effect of absences

14.72 The right under Article 10 of Regulation (EU) 492/2011 may be lost during a substantial absence. For example, where an EEA national parent has worked in the UK and this is followed by a period when the parent and child are absent from the UK and later return and the parent is not employed here. The question whether an absence from the UK will result in the loss of Article 10 rights is a matter to be determined in the light of all the circumstances of each case.¹ This will involve a consideration of: (i) the reasons why the parent ceased to be resident in the UK; (ii) the activities of the parent in the country to which they went, including economic activity; (iii) the roots the parent put down in the country to which they went; (iv) the contact which the parent maintained with the UK whilst absent and the quality of that contact; and (v) the length of the absence (the longer the absence, the more difficult it will be to maintain that the right can be reasserted).² It should be noted that the CJEU has held that periods of residence completed in accordance with a derivative right to reside of a child in education do not count towards the acquisition of a permanent right to reside.³

¹ *Secretary of State for Work and Pensions v RR* [2013] UKUT 21 (AAC) at para 79.
² *SSWP v RR* at paras 80–81.
³ Immigration (European Economic Area) Regulations 2006, SI 2006/1003, reg 15(1A) which transposes the decision in Case C-529/11 *Alarape v Secretary of State for the Home Department (AIRE Centre intervening)* [2014] All ER (EC) 470, [2013] 1 WLR 2883, [2013] Imm AR 752, [2013] INLR 542, para 35.

Derived right based on being a primary carer of a British citizen child

14.73 In the landmark case *Ruiz Zambrano v Office national de l'emploi (ONEm)* (C-34/09)[1] the CJEU established the principle that in certain circumstances a third country national (ie a non-EEA national who is subject to immigration control) may have a right to reside if to deny that right would mean that an dependant EU citizen would be deprived of their rights as an EU citizen under the Treaty to move and reside freely within the territory of the EU. This has been codified in the EEA Regulations 2006.[2] However, the right to reside under *Zambrano* has been deemed to be an excluded right to reside under the habitual residence test for welfare benefits[3] (and for eligibility to housing assistance[4]). As a result, a non-EEA national carer of a British child who meets the conditions for being a 'Zambrano carer' under the EEA Regulations 2006 will nevertheless be excluded from claiming IS, JSA(IB), ESA(IR) SPC, HB, CTR, CTC or CHB based on the habitual residence test for those benefits. The extent and scope of the right under *Zambrano* is the subject of a joint appeal before the Court of Appeal.[5] In *Sanneh v Secretary of State for Work and Pensions*[6] the claimant challenged the Upper Tribunal's conclusion that a Zambrano carer does not have an enforceable right under EU law unless and until their departure from the UK is 'imminent'. In *R(HC) v Secretary of State for Work and Pensions and others,*[7] the claimant has challenged the discriminatory nature of the amending regulations as incompatible with EU law and/or Human Rights law. However, as the law currently stands, a *Zambrano* carer can only access those benefits which do not contain a right to reside requirement; eg, Attendance Allowance, Disability Living Allowance, Personal Independence Payment and Carer's Allowance and if they are in work, Working Tax Credits.

[1] Case C-34/09, *Ruiz Zambrano v Office National de l'Emploi (ONEm)* [2012] QB 265, [2011] ECR I-1177, [2011] All ER (EC) 491.
[2] Immigration (European Economic Area) Regulations 2006, SI 2006/1003, reg 15A (1) & (4A).
[3] The Social Security (Habitual Residence) (Amendment) Regulations 2012, SI 2012/2587, the Child Benefit and Child Tax Credit (Miscellaneous Amendments) Regulations 2012, SI 2012/2612.
[4] The Allocation of Housing and Homelessness (Eligibility) (England) (Amendment) Regulations 2012, SI 2012/2588.
[5] The hearing took place on 4–7 November, before Arden, Elias and Burnett LJJ. Judgment was reserved.
[6] On appeal from the decision of UT Judge Jacobs in *Secretary of State for Work and Pensions v JS* [2013] UKUT 490 (AAC).
[7] On appeal from the decision of Mr Justice Supperstone in *R (on the application of HC) v Secretary of State for Work and Pensions* [2013] EWHC 3874 (Admin).

SPECIAL RULES FOR ACCESSION NATIONALS

A8 nationals

14.74 From 1 May 2004 until 30 April 2011, nationals from Czech Republic, Estonia, Hungary, Latvia, Lithuania, Poland, Slovakia and Slovenia (A8 nationals) who wanted to work in the UK needed to register under the Worker Registration Scheme (WRS).[1] Under these transitional arrangements A8 nationals' access to welfare benefits was limited. A8 nationals were only classed as a 'worker' if they were in work that was registered under the WRS, and they were excluded from the category of a jobseeker until they had been in registered work for a period of twelve months.[2] Subject to savings provisions, these restrictions ceased to have effect on 1 May 2011.[3] From that date, A8 nationals became subject to the same EU rules with regard to right to reside. For the purposes of acquiring a permanent right to reside, an A8 worker is treated as having resided in accordance with the regulations during any period before 1 May 2011 in which they were working in the UK for an authorised employer.[4]

[1] Accession (Immigration and Worker Registration) Regulations 2004, SI 2004/1219.
[2] See 13.30 of the eighth edition of Macdonald's for further details.
[3] Accession (Immigration and Worker Registration) (Revocation, Savings and Consequential Provisions) Regulations 2011, SI 2011/544.
[4] Immigration (European Economic Area) Regulations 2006, SI 2006/1003, reg 7A(5).

Romanian and Bulgarian nationals

14.75 From 1 January 2007 until 31 December 2013, Romanian and Bulgarian nationals (A2 nationals) who wanted to work in the UK needed the permission of the Home Office in order to do so, unless they qualified under an exemption.[1] A2 nationals' access to welfare benefits was limited under these transitional arrangements. A2 nationals were only classed as a 'worker' if they were in work which was authorised work under the Workers Authorisation Scheme, and they were excluded from the category of a jobseeker until they had been in this type of work for a period of twelve months.[2] The transitional restrictions on A2 nationals were lifted from the end of December 2013, and A2 nationals will now be treated in the same way as all other EEA nationals.[3] For the purposes of acquiring a permanent right to reside, an A2 worker is treated as having resided in accordance with the regulations during any period before 1 May 2011 in which they were working in the UK for an authorised employer.[4]

[1] The Accession (Immigration and Worker Authorisation) Regulations 2006, SI 2006/3317.
[2] See 13.32 of the eighth edition of Macdonald's for further details.
[3] Immigration (European Economic Area) Regulations 2006, SI 2006/1003, reg 7B, inserted by para 4 of the Schedule to SI 2013/3032.
[4] Immigration (European Economic Area) Regulations 2006, SI 2006/1003, reg 7B(6).

Croatian nationals

14.76 The Republic of Croatia became a Member State of the EU on 1 July 2013. Nationals of Croatia are subject to transitional provisions which impose certain restrictions on their rights to freedom of movement within the EEA, and allow EU Member States to apply national measures restricting their access to the labour market of Member States for a limited period, initially for five years from 1 July 2013.[1] Under these transitional arrangements, their access to welfare benefits is limited. Unless they are exempt, those who wish to work as an employee must seek prior authorisation in order to have a right to reside as a worker.[2] Further, those Croatians who are subject to worker authorisation are excluded from the definition of jobseeker or from retaining worker status.[3] Those Croatians who are exempt[4] from the requirement for worker authorisation are treated in the same way as other EEA nationals. It should be noted that the transitional provisions in the Treaty of Accession do not allow limitation of the principle of freedom of movement for self-employed persons within the EEA. This means that all Croatian nationals (regardless of whether or not they are subject to worker authorisation) have a right to reside as a 'qualified person' when they are working as a self-employed person in the UK.

1   Treaty concerning the accession of the Republic of Croatia. (L:2012:112:TOC, 24 April 2012).
2   The Accession of Croatia (Immigration and Worker Authorisation) Regulations 2013, SI 2013/1460, reg 2(1).
3   SI 2013/1460, reg 5.
4   SI 2013/1460, regs 2(2)–(20) contains an exhaustive list of when a Croatian national is not an access State national subject to worker authorisation. See CHAPTER 6 for further details.

TRANSITIONAL PROTECTION

14.77 There are groups of claimants who are currently in receipt of benefits because they were eligible for benefit under previous legislation and that eligibility has continued under a saving provision. These include:

—   *Protection from the 'person subject to immigration control' exclusion* – Some asylum seekers and others are exempt from the 'person subject to immigration control' exclusion due to saving provisions made in February 1996,[1] whereas others are still in receipt of mainstream benefits due to saving provisions in the 2000 amendments.[2]

—   *Protection from the 'right to reside' requirement test* – The saving provisions in respect of the right to reside requirement provide that the right to reside requirement, introduced on 1 May 2004, will not apply to claimants who, on 30 April 2009, were entitled to any of the following specified income-related benefits – IS, JSA(IB), SPC, HB and CTB.[3] The right to reside requirement will not apply to these claimants so long as there is no break in their entitlement to at least one of the five specified benefits. There were no saving provisions when the right to reside requirement was implemented for CTC[4] or when the requirement was later introduced for CHB.[5]

—   *Protection from rules excluding EEA jobseekers from housing benefits* – EEA nationals are exempt from the exclusion from HB for EEA nationals who are jobseekers due to saving provisions.[6] These provide that those in receipt of HB at 31 March 2014 are protected from the change until their entitlement to JSA(IB) ceases or they need to make a new claim for HB, whichever occurs first.[7] Note that the Government has announced that in February 2015 it intends to remove transitional protection for all EEA migrants who were claiming JSA(IB) before these changes were introduced.[8]

1   Social Security (Persons from Abroad) Miscellaneous Amendments Regulations 1996, SI 1996/30. See 13.34 of the eighth edition of *Macdonald's* for further details.
2   Social Security (Immigration and Asylum) Consequential Amendments Regulations 2000, SI 2000/636, reg 12(4)–(5). See 13.34 of the eighth edition of *Macdonald's* for further details.
3   Social Security (Habitual Residence) Amendment Regulations 2004, SI 2004/1232, reg 6.
4   Tax Credits (Residence) (Amendment) Regulations 2004, SI 2004/1243 with effect from 1 May 2004.
5   Child Benefit (General) Regulations 2006, SI 2006/223, with effect from 10 April 2006.
6   Housing Benefit (Habitual Residence) Amendment Regulations 2014, SI 2014/539 reg 3.
7   SI 2014/539, reg 3(2).

8   The Chancellor of the Exchequer's Autumn Statement, 3 December 2014.

FURTHER RESIDENCE REQUIREMENTS

14.78 Some benefits have additional residence requirements as a condition of entitlement. These include a requirement that the claimant be 'ordinarily resident' in Great Britain (Northern Ireland has a separate social security jurisdiction). The concept has not been defined anywhere in the legislation, but the House of Lords in *LB of Barnet, ex p. Shah*[1] said that 'ordinary residence' is established if there is a regular habitual mode of life in a particular place 'for the time being' – though the residence must be voluntary and adopted for 'a settled purpose'.[2] In addition, most welfare benefits require the claimant to be present in Great Britain and some (but not all) require the claimant to have been present for a past period of time. This means that if someone has recently arrived in the UK, they may not qualify for benefit immediately. An EEA national might be exempt from such a residence condition under the coordination rules if they were subject to a social security system in another EEA country prior to their arrival in the UK (see **14.79** below). The main benefits to which these additional requirements apply are listed below:

Child Benefit: The claimant and the child must be ordinarily resident and present in Great Britain at the time of the claim and for at least 26 weeks in the last 52 weeks. There are additional residence conditions if the child lives temporarily abroad.[3]

Guardian's Allowance: At least one of the child's parents must have been born in the UK, or after reaching 16 years of age or at some time after reaching 16 years of age, have spent a total of 52 weeks in any two-year period in the UK.[4]

Attendance Allowance: The person must be present in Great Britain at the time of the claim and for at least 104 weeks in the last 156 weeks (two out of the last three years), subject to exceptions for those who are terminally ill.[5]

Carer's Allowance: The person must be present in Great Britain at the time of the claim and for at least 104 weeks in the last 156 weeks.[6]

Personal Independence Payment: The person must be present in Great Britain at the time of the claim and for at least 104 weeks in the last 156 weeks, subject to exceptions for those who are terminally ill.[7]

Disability Living Allowance: For children claiming disability living allowance the present conditions are: if the child is under six-months-old, then s/he will need to be present in Great Britain for 13 weeks up until they are one-year-old. If the child is aged between 6 and 36 months, they need to have been present for 26 weeks in the last 156 weeks.[8]

Working Tax Credit and Child Tax Credit: A person must be ordinarily resident in the UK and present in Great Britain.[9]

Category B Retirement Pension: The person must be ordinarily resident in Great Britain on their eightieth birthday or the date they make the claim and have been resident in Great Britain for at least 10 years in the last 20 years.[10]

Contribution-based Jobseeker's Allowance: A person must be present in Great Britain. There is no habitual residence test. Note: If someone is covered by the

EU co-ordination rules they can rely, if necessary, on NI contributions paid in another EEA State to gain entitlement to contribution-based JSA in the UK. However, in most cases, the claimant can only aggregate their contributions if their most recent period of paying or being credited with contributions was in the UK.[11] If someone is coming to, or returning to, the UK from another EEA State to look for work and has been insured in another EEA State, they may be able to get the other Member State's unemployment benefit for up to three months.[12]

Contribution-based Employment and Support Allowance: A person must be present in Great Britain. There is no habitual residence test. Note: If someone is covered by the EU co-ordination rules they can rely, if necessary on NI contributions paid in another EEA State to gain entitlement to contribution-based ESA in the UK.[13]

1 *Shah v Barnet London Borough Council* [1982] UKHL 14, [1983] 2 AC 309.
2 *Shah* pp 344G-H and 345B-D.
3 Social Security Contributions and Benefits Act 1992, s 146, and the Child Benefit (General) Regulations 2006, SI 2006/223, reg 23(1).
4 Guardian's Allowance (General) Regulations 2003, SI 2003/495, reg 9.
5 Social Security (Attendance Allowance) Regulations 1991, SI 1991/2740, reg 1(a)(iii), as amended by the Social Security (Disability Living Allowance, Attendance Allowance and Carer's Allowance) (Amendment) Regulations 2013/389, reg 3(3)(c)(ii) from 8 April 2013.
6 Social Security (Invalid Care Allowance) Regulations 1976, SI 1976/409, reg 9(1)(c), as amended by SI 2013/389, reg 2(2)(c)(i) from 8 April 2013. Note, that this condition is discounted if the claimant living in another EEA State can show that the UK is their 'competent state' under reg 9A. See *Secretary of State for Work and Pensions v JG* (IS) [2013] UKUT 298 (AAC) on the need to show a genuine and sufficient connection with Great Britain as at the date of the claim.
7 The Social Security (Personal Independence Payment) Regulations 2013, SI 2013/377, reg 16(b). Note, that this condition is discounted if the claimant living in another EEA State can show that the UK is their 'competent state' under reg 22c.
8 Social Security (Disability Living Allowance) Regulations 1991 SI 1991/2890, reg 2(1), as amended by SI 2013/389, reg 4(3)(c) from 8 April 2013. Note, that this condition is discounted if the claimant living in another EEA State can show that the UK is their 'competent state' under regs 2A and 2B.
9 Tax Credits (Residence) Regulations 2003, SI 2003/654, reg 3(1).
10 Social Security (Widow's Benefit and Retirement Pensions) Regulations 1979, SI 1979/642, reg 10.
11 EU Regulaton 883/04, art 61(2).
12 EU Regulation 883/04, art 64.
13 EU Regulation 883/04, art 64.

ADDITIONAL WELFARE BENEFIT RIGHTS FOR EEA NATIONALS

The social security coordination rules

14.79 EEA nationals and their family members are entitled to the additional legal protections of EU law in relation to access to benefits provided by Regulation 883/2004 on the coordination of social security systems.[1] Under its framework, Member States retain the right to determine the types of benefits and the conditions for granting them. However, EU law imposes certain rules and principles to ensure that the application of the different national systems does not harm or discourage persons who exercise their rights to free movement. In order to achieve this end Regulation 883/2004: (i) prohibits discrimination on grounds of nationality in social security;[2] (ii) clarifies which state is responsible for paying benefits in a particular case;[3] (iii) allows people to count periods of employment, residence and contributions in one EEA State towards entitlement in another;[4] (iv) allows people to take certain benefits abroad to another EEA State.[5] This Regulation applies to all nationals of an EU country who are or who have been covered by the social security legislation of one of those countries, as well as to the members of their family and their survivors. Someone will have been 'subject to the legislation' of an EEA State if they have been employed or self-employed and paid national insurance in an EEA country. It also covers students, civil servants, pensioners and those entitled to the social security benefits covered by Regulation 883/2004.[6]

[1] Regulation (EC) No 883/2004 on the co-ordination of social security systems (OJ L 200, 7 June 2004, p 1), which replaced Council Regulation 1408/71 from May 2010.
[2] Regulation (EC) No 883/2004, art 4.
[3] Regulation (EC) No 883/2004, art 11.
[4] Regulation (EC) No 883/2004, art 6.
[5] Regulation (EC) No 883/2004, art 7.
[6] Regulation (EC) No 883/2004, art 11(3),

14.80 Regulation 883/2004 covers the following 'social security benefits': sickness, maternity, paternity, old age, invalidity, accidents at work and occupational diseases, unemployment, death, and child allowances[1] – which correspond to the general traditional risks of social security and protects those people who pay or have been credited with National Insurance contributions in an EEA State. On the other hand, 'social assistance' does not fall within its scope. This typically consists of benefits paid to cover minimum living expenses or discretionary one-off payments based on need.[2] Social assistance benefits have traditionally been within the competence of the national Member State who can make access to social assistance by EEA nationals who are not economically active conditional upon them meeting the necessary requirements for obtaining a legal right of residence in the host Member State (though it has been held that Member States cannot 'automatically' refuse to grant such benefits to non-active EEA nationals[3]). This is in contrast to the 'social security benefits' for which residence conditions are prohibited or reduced under the coordination rules and where it is possible to export those benefits when moving to another country in the EEA. Finally, there are some hybrid benefits which contain elements of both social security and social assistance. These fall into a category known as 'special non-contributory cash benefits'.[4] These benefits are provided exclusively in the country where the person concerned resides and are not exportable.[5] The CJEU has recently declared that Member States are permitted to make special non-contributory cash benefits conditional on the EEA national having a legal right of residence in the Host State.[6]

[1] Regulation (EC) No 883/2004, art 3.
[2] Case C-140/12 *Pensionsversicherungsanstalt v Brey (Peter)* [2014] 1 CMLR 993, para 48.
[3] Case C-140/12 Brey, paras 75–77.
[4] Regulation (EC) No 883/2004, art 70, Annex X. For case law on when a benefit is to be regarded as a special non-contributory cash benefit see *Skalka* (C-160/02) paras 25 and 28.
[5] Regulation (EC) No 883/2004, art 70(4).
[6] Case C-140/12 *Pensionsversicherungsanstalt v Peter Brey* [2014] 1 WLR 1080; [2014] 1 CMLR 37, paras 44, 60–61; applied in *Dano v Jobcenter Leipzig*, (C-333/13), para 83.

Family benefits

14.81 As a general rule, the country which is responsible for paying family benefits (the competent state) must take into account the periods of insurance or residence completed under the legislation of any other countries of the EEA under the principle of aggregaton.[1] In cases where there is entitlement to a family benefit from more than one state, then priority rules determine which state pays.[2] In some cases, the claimant will receive family benefit from one state with a lower priority but will receive a supplementary payment topping it up to level paid by the priority state.[3]

1 Regulation (EC) No 883/2004, art 6.
2 Regulation (EC) No 883/2004, art 68(1).
3 Regulation (EC) No 883/2004, art 68(2) and (3); see *R(F) 1/88* and *R(F) 1/98*.

14.82 The coordination rules also provide that a migrant worker can claim family benefits for family members who are living elsewhere in the EEA.[1] This means that if an EEA migrant in the UK is covered by the UK social security system (ie as a worker), they can claim Child Benefit and Child Tax Credit for their dependent children even if they are not resident in the UK. The person making a claim must meet all the usual conditions for entitlement to these benefits, but the ordinary residence and presence requirements for the child or children do not apply and they can claim benefit for them on the same basis as if they were living in the UK.[2] In January 2014, the Prime Minister, David Cameron[3] said that he would try to renegotiate the UK's membership of the European Union to allow it to withhold child benefits for children living in other EEA countries or require that the benefit is paid at the equivalent rate paid in the EEA migrant's home country.

1 Regulation (EC) No 883/2004, art 67.
2 *Ruas v Revenue and Customs Comrs* [2010] EWCA Civ 291, [2010] PTSR 1757, held that this applied where the EEA national had ceased to work in the UK on the ground of incapacity before he claimed CHB for his children living in Portugal (para 50), thereby upholding CF/2266/2007.
3 David Cameron speaking on BBC1's *Andrew Marr* show on 5 January 2014. For further details see: '*Child Benefit and Child Tax Credit for children resident in other EEA countries* – Commons Library Standard Note (8 July 2014) Standard note SN06561, author: Steven Kennedy.

THE CROSS-OVER BETWEEN SOCIAL SECURITY AND IMMIGRATION LAW

The jurisdictional divide between social security and immigration law

Non-EEA nationals

14.83 According to social security case law, only the Secretary of State for the Home Department can grant a person leave to enter or remain in the UK or settled status.[1] The situation is different, however, where the claimant's immigration status has been conferred directly on the individual by the relevant legislation. In those cases, the benefit authorities can determine the claimant's eligibility to benefit without the need for a decision by the Home Office.[2] Otherwise, where the benefit regulations define eligibility by reference to the migrant's immigration status, the decision falls to be made by the Secretary of State for Work and Pensions.[3] A grant of leave does not operate retrospectively,[4] and for benefit purposes it can only take effect either from the date shown in the claimant's passport or from the date of the letter notifying the claimant of the decision[5] Consequently, an award of benefit can only be made once the relevant status document has been issued by the Home Office.[6] This includes cases where the claimant has won an immigration appeal and the tribunal has issued a direction that leave be granted.[7] It should be noted that the Secretary of State for Work and Pensions is not bound by a finding of fact made by an official acting on behalf of the Secretary of State for the Home Department. Hence in a case where two immigration adjudicators had decided that the claimant was married to a British citizen, this did not give rise to an issue estoppel binding on the Secretary of State for Work and Pensions whose department had decided that the claimant was not married and so rejected her claim for a widow's pension.[8]

[1] *R(SB) 25/85*, para 20. A decision of the Social Security Commissioners, the predecessors of the Upper Tribunal (Administrative Appeals Chamber).

[2] *R(SB) 11/88*, para 20 where the claimant fulfilled the statutory conditions for a right of abode. See also *R(PC) 2/07* (CPC/4317/2006).

[3] *SG Tameside Metropolitan Borough Council (HB)* [2010] UKUT 243 (AAC), para 48.

[4] *R(IS) 6/08*, para 6. But see *Her Majesty's Revenue & Customs v AA* [2012] UKUT 121 (AAC), para 21, where the claimant was granted ILR retrospectively based on a declaration by the High Court.

[5] *R (on the application of Anufrijeva) v Secretary of State for the Home Department* [2003] UKHL 36, [2004] 1 AC 604.

[6] *Secretary of State for Work and Pensions v IG* [2008] UKUT 5 (AAC), paras 14, and 19.

[7] *MUN v Secretary of State for Work and Pensions (IS)* [2011] UKUT 373 (AAC), para 13.

[8] *R (Nahar) v Social Security Commissioners* [2001] EWHC Admin 1049, [2002] 2 FCR 442, paras 70-77.

EEA NATIONALS

14.84 The general rule for EEA nationals is that they are not under any legal obligation to obtain an immigration status document from the Home Office as any residence document issued by the host Member State merely has a declaratory effect.[1] The linking of benefit entitlement to the right to reside means that the Secretary of State for Work and Pensions is required to decide whether the conditions for that test have been satisfied when an EEA national claims benefit, despite the fact that the same issue/s could arise in an application for a residence permit within an immigration appeal.[2] An important exception to this rule in respect to EEA nationals is whether someone falls to be treated as an 'extended family member' of an EEA national; this is a matter for the Home Department, and not the benefit authorities, to decide.[3]

[1] Case C-325/09 *Secretary of State for Work and Pensions v Dias (Maria)* [2011] Imm AR 855, [2011] 3 CMLR 1103, paras 48-49.

[2] *SG v Tameside Metropolitan Borough Council (HB)* [2010] UKUT 243 (AAC) at [48]. Social security is a specialist jurisdiction which has its own case law. Whilst some cases reach the higher courts, the majority of decisions are made by the Social Security Commissioners, and, since 3 November 2008, the Upper Tribunal (Administrative Appeals Chamber). These are available on a decisions database on the HM Courts and Tribunal website (www.osscsc.gov. uk/Decisions/decisions.htm) as well as on British and Irish Legal Information Institute website (www.bailii.org).

[3] CPC/3588/2006, para 53 and CIS/0612/2008, para 33 and *SS v Secretary of State for Work and Pensions (ESA)* [2011] UKUT 8 (AAC), paras 13–15.

14.85 A non-EEA national who is the spouse or civil partner of an EEA national does not cease to be a family member in the event of marital breakdown or separation as long as the EEA national continues to exercise Treaty rights in the UK. The non-EEA national continues to have a right of residence until such time as a divorce is finalised, (a Decree Absolute is obtained) or the civil partnership is dissolved.[1] However, a non-EEA national spouse or civil partner will lose their right of residence if the EEA national leaves the UK. In an immigration appeal the Home Office is not under any duty to assist an estranged spouse or civil partner to establish that the EEA national is working or even residing in the UK. Rather, the onus is on the appellant to apply for an order for the production of any documents that might be in the possession of HMRC or the social security authorities.[2] This can be contrasted with the situation in a welfare benefits appeal where, given the inquisitorial nature of adjudication in social security cases,[3] the benefit authorities are under a duty to carry out the necessary checks in order to establish whether the estranged EEA national is working or in receipt of benefits as a jobseeker, eg by producing records of the individual's national insurance contributions and receipt of welfare benefits.

[1] *Diatta (Aissatou) v Land Berlin*: 267/83 [1985] ECR 567, 1986] 2 CMLR 164, ECJ.
[2] *Amos v Secretary of State for the Home Department v SSHD* [2011] EWCA Civ 552, para 42.
[3] *Kerr v Department for Social Development* [2004] UKHL 23, [2004] 1 WLR 1372, paras 61–62. Applied in a claim for Income Support by a young person who was estranged from her Polish father in *PM v Secretary of State for Work and Pensions (IS) (Tribunal procedure and practice (including UT) : evidence)* [2014] UKUT 474 (AAC), paras 3-5.

Delay in processing a new claim

14.86 There is provision to provide a short-term advance of benefit (STBA) if there is a delay in the claim being processed.[1] To be eligible for a STBA: (i) the claimant must have made a claim for benefit; (ii) it must appear that the claimant is entitled to that benefit; and (iii) the claimant is in 'financial need' because of the delay.[2] The claimant must also be in a position to repay the advance within three months (though this may be extended to six months in exceptional circumstances).[3] There is no right of appeal against a refusal to offer an STBA, though the claimant can ask for 'reconsideration' on the only that the DWP did not consider the correct infor~~...~~ reconsideration) be remedy is by way of judicial rev~~...~~ being determined.[5] The conditions for on the claim ~~...~~ dvance or interim payments for Child Tax Credits.[6] ... one claim is for Child Benefit, ... ion to make an interim payment on ... Note, however that there

[3] ~~...~~3/383, reg 5. 'Financial need' is defined to mean 'a serious risk of damage to the health or safety to the claimant or any member of their family' (reg 7).
~~...~~ty (Payment on Account of Benefit) Regulations 2013, SI 2013/383.
[4] SI 2013/383, reg 14.
[5] *R v Secretary of State for Social Security, ex parte Grant* [1997] EWHC 754 (Admin) and *R (on the application of Hall) v Chichester District Council* [2007] EWHC 168 (Admin).
[6] Child Benefit and Guardian's Allowance (Administration) Regulations 2003, SI 2003/492. SI 2003/492, reg 22.

The National Insurance number requirement

14.87 A claim for benefit cannot be processed unless the claimant has (or has applied for) a National Insurance number – known as the NINO requirement.[1] In the past, this rule resulted in many awards of benefit being interrupted when the eligible sponsor was joined by a spouse who was subject to a public funds condition.[2] Since April 2009, however, a partner will be exempt from the NINO requirement if he or she is 'a person subject to immigration control'.[3] If a claim for DWP benefit is delayed due to a lack of a NINO it should still be considered for a STBA.[4] In the case of a claim for Child Benefit there is provision for HM Revenue and Customs to make an interim payment of benefit where it is impracticable to satisfy the NI number requirement immediately.[5] In the case of a claim for Tax Credits, the HMRC has a discretion to disapply the NI number requirement where it is considered that the claimant has a reasonable excuse for making a claim without satisfying it.[6] Given the absence of any provision to make interim or advance payments of Tax Credits this provision should assist refugees and other migrants applying for Child Tax Credit during the transition from asylum support to mainstream benefits. If the lack of an NINO results in a negative decision on entitlement then the claimant (subject to applying for a mandatory reconsideration) can appeal against the decision to refuse benefit to a First-tier Tribunal (Social Entitlement) in the usual way.[7] Judicial proceedings may, however, be necessary in cases where: (i) there are doubts over the First-tier Tribunal's jurisdiction to consider a refusal to allocate a NINO; or (ii) to expedite the appeal were the refusal of benefit results in the claimant being left without sufficient resources to support themselves or their family pending the outcome of the statutory appeal.

1   Social Security Administration Act 1992, ss 1(1A) and 1(1B).
2   See *Secretary of State for Work and Pensions v Wilson* [2006] EWCA Civ 882, [2007] 1 All ER 281 (also reported as *R(H) 7/06*).
3   Social Security (National Insurance Number Information: Exemption) Regulations 2009, SI 2009/471.
4   Short Term Benefit Advances for Benefit Processing and Decision Making Teams, para 14.
5   Regulation 22(1A)(b) of the Benefit and Guardian's Allowance (Administration) Regulations 2003, SI 2003/492.
6   Tax Credits (Claims and Notifications) Regulations 2002, SI 2002/2014, reg 5(6).
7   See *CIS/0345/2003*, para 23 *CH/4085/2007*, para 25 and *LCC v Secretary of State for Work ' Pensions* [2009] UKUT 74 (AAC), para 34.

Payment of benefit s~ claimant's immigration s~

14.88 The DWP has the power ~ circumstances – including where an i~ doubts over the for entitlement to a benefit are or remain fu~ may result in benefits being suspended due ant's immigration status include where:

—   the claimant's leave has expired and the Home Office h~ prescribed decision on the application to renew or extend that leave;[3]

—   the claimant has been granted leave for a limited period;[3]

—   the terms of the claimant's leave on the passport stamp or visa vignett~ are ambiguous or unclear;

—   there is a problem with the spelling of names or the order of names in the status document;

—   the claimant has mislaid their original status document.

If benefit is suspended the claimant can make representations for the suspension to be lifted, eg on the basis that: (i) the decision is based on a misunderstanding of the rules governing their immigration status and/or (ii) the suspension is causing financial hardship. As with any exercise of discretion by a public body, the decision to *DWP Guidance* states that when considering whether a claimant will suffer hardship as a consequence of their benefit being suspended, the decision-maker must consider the following factors:[4]

'•   if the customer is elderly, frail or has physical or mental health problems, it might be unreasonable to expect them to wait for payment if the question was settled in their favour

•   if the customer has young children who would be adversely affected if benefit was suspended

•   if the customer has taken on financial commitments based on a reasonable assumption that benefit would be paid to them

•   it is not usually appropriate to suspend a non-income related benefit solely on the grounds that the customer may also be entitled to an income related benefit, eg JSA(IB) or

•   if deductions are being made from the customer's benefit, consider whether the amount of benefit left is enough to prevent hardship.'

In the case of EEA nationals, a situation may arise where a suspension of payment should be lifted in order to ensure that the claimant's EU rights are protected pending the resolution of the substantive issue, eg where the claimant won before a First-tier Tribunal based on EU rights but the DWP decides to suspend payment of the award of benefit pending the outcome of their appeal on a point of law to the Upper Tribunal (Administrative Appeals).[5]

---

1   The Secretary of State has the power to suspend payment of benefit in prescribed circumstances under section 21(3)(b) of the Social Security Act 1998 and the Social Security and Child Support (Decisions and Appeals) Regulations 1999, SI 1999/991, reg 16.

2   If someone has made an in-time application to extend leave and their previous leave was not subject to an 'a no recourse to public funds condition' then it is arguable that they are not subject to immigration control pending the decision on the application – See **14.9** above.

3   For example, Humanitarian Protection is granted for an initial period of five years, but this has no restrictions on that person's leave to remain and they will not therefore be a 'person from abroad' for benefit purposes: IS (General) Regs 1987/1967, reg 21AA(4hh); JSA Regs 1996/207, reg 85A(4hh), HB Regs 2006/213, reg 10(3B)(hh).

4   Suspension and termination of benefits: staff guide – Guidance for DWP staff who suspend or terminate payment of benefit or defer a decision on a benefit claim, at para 2051, DWP, 1 April 2010, GOV.UK.

5   *R (on the application of Sanneh (Jamil)) v Secretary of State for Work and Pensions and Revenue and Customs Comrs* [2013] EWHC 793 (Admin), para 113.

Legal challenges to the right to reside requirement

Arguments based on discrimination

14.89 In *Abdirahman and Ullusow v Secretary of State for Work and Pensions*[1] Ms Abdirahman was a Swedish national who came to the UK with her three children and claimed Income Support. Mr Ullusow was a Norwegian who was of pensionable age and claimed State Pension Credit. Both claims for benefit were rejected on the basis that, as the claimants were neither workers nor otherwise economically self-sufficient, they did not have a right to reside in the UK. The Court held that though the claimants were lawfully present in the UK, this was not equivalent to having a right to reside at the relevant time.[2] The Court also held that the claimants could not rely on the prohibition on discrimination under article 12 (now article 18) of the Treaty as it did not extend to cases where the individual was economically inactive and had no right of residence under either the Treaty or the relevant domestic law. The instant case could, therefore, be distinguished from the position in *Trojani* (C-456/02)[3] where the claimant had been granted a temporary residence permit under Belgian law.[4] The Court added that if there had been any discrimination, then the need to combat the risks of what the Advocate General in *Trojani* described as 'social tourism' was sufficient justification.[5]

[1] *Ullusow v Secretary of State for Work and Pensions; Abdirahman v Secretary of State for Work and Pensions* [2007] EWCA Civ 657, [2008] 1 WLR 254.
[2] *Abdirahman v SSWP*, para 25.
[3] *Abdirahman v SSWP*, paras 43–45.
[4] Case C-456/02 *Trojani v Centre Public d'Aide Sociale de Bruxelles (CPAS)* (CPAS) [2004] All ER (EC) 1065, [2004] 3 CMLR 820.
[5] *Abdirahman v SSWP*, paras 50, citing *Trojani* (C-456/02), AG para 18.

Patmalniece v SSWP

14.90 In *Patmalniece v Secretary of State for Work and Pensions*[1] Mrs Patmalniece was a Latvian pensioner and in receipt of a Latvian retirement pension. She came to the UK in June 2000. Her asylum claim was unsuccessful, but she was not removed from the UK. She had never worked in the UK. Latvia joined the EU on 1 May 2004. In August 2005, Mrs Patmalniece claimed State Pension Credit (SPC) but her claim was refused on the ground that she was treated as 'not in Great Britain' because she did not have a right to reside. The claimant argued that whereas the Citizens' Directive 2004/38/EC does allow Member States to restrict access to social assistance, EU rules on the coordination of social security do not allow restrictions on social security benefits to those who are habitually resident (as this is defined in the Coordination Rules) in the Member State in question. As SPC is a special non-contributory cash benefit (ie it contains elements of both social security and social assistance) she could rely on the anti-discrimination provision in article 3 of Regulation (EC) 1408/71 on the coordination of social security schemes. As no British person could fail the 'right to reside test' it constituted direct discrimination, which could not be justified. The Supreme Court rejected these submissions holding that the habitual residence test was a cumulative one, and as a UK national could fail the actual habitual residence element of the test it was indirectly, as opposed to directly, discriminatory, and was, therefore, capable of justification.[2] The Court when on to hold (Lord Walker dissenting) that the right to reside test was objectively justified because it was a proportionate response to the legitimate aim of seeking to protect the resources of the UK against social tourism by persons who are not economically or socially integrated with this country and that this justification was independent of the claimant's nationality.[3]

[1] *Patmalniece v Secretary of State for Work and Pensions* [2011] UKSC 11, [2011] 1 WLR 783.
[2] *Patmalniece v SSWP*, para 35.

Dano v Jobcentre Leipzig

14.91 In *Dano v Jobcentre Leipzig* (Case C-333/13) the Grand Chamber reaffirmed that a Member State can refuse to grant certain non-contributory social benefits to economically inactive EU citizens who exercise their right to freedom of movement solely in order to access another Member State's social assistance.[1] Ms Dano and her son had been residing in Germany since November 2010, where they lived in the home of Ms Dano's sister. Ms Dano was not seeking employment and had not worked in Germany or Romania. The proceedings arose out of her request for benefits under the German Social Code (SGB II) by way of basic provision for jobseekers. Ms Dano's claim included subsistence benefits for herself and social allowances and a contribution to accommodation and heating costs for her son. The claim was refused on the basis that the Code expressly excludes 'foreign nationals whose right of residence arises solely out of the search for employment and their family members'.[2] The CJEU held that as Ms Dano and her son did not have sufficient resources, and thus could not claim a right of residence in Germany under the Citizens' Directive 38/2004/EC, they could not invoke the principle of non-discrimination laid down by the Directive nor, following the ruling in *Brey* (C-140/12) could they rely on the non-discrimination rule under Regulation EC/883/2004 on the coordination of social security systems.[3] Given its findings on EU law the CJEU went on to reject Ms Dano alternative argument that she could invoke the Charter of Fundamental Rights of the EU in this context. Having ruled that the Member State has sole competence to lay down conditions for the grant of special non-contributory cash benefits at issue in the proceedings, the CJEU ruled that the Charter had no application.[4]

1   Case C-333/13, *Dano v Jobcentre Leipzig* (2014) Times, 18 November.
2   Book II of the German Social Code, para 7(1)2 cited at para 20 of the judgment.
3   Case C-333/13, *Dano v Jobcentre Leipzig*, paras 81 and 83.
4   Case C-333/13, *Dano v Jobcentre Leipzig*, para 91.

Proceedings brought by the European Commission

14.92 The effect of *Dano* is to uphold the Supreme Court's conclusion in *Patmalniece*, albeit by reference to the ruling in *Brey* (C-140/12)[1] in which it was held that a special non-contributory cash benefit within the meaning of Regulation 883/2004 was also covered by the concept of 'social assistance' within the meaning of Directive 2004/38/EC,[2] and that there was nothing objectionable, in principle, in making the granting of those benefits to EU citizens conditional on them having a right of residence in the host Member State.[3] The effect of this new approach to discrimination arguments can be seen in the way in which the EC's proceedings against the UK Government's use of the right to reside test has evolved and changed over time. When the EU Commission announced that it had commenced infraction proceedings against the UK in September 2011, at that stage, the Commission was arguing that the criteria in the habitual residence test under the coordination rules were strict enough to ensure that certain UK social security benefits (ie State Pension

Credit, income-based JSA, income-related Employment and Support Allowance, Child Benefit and Child Tax Credit) are only granted to those genuinely residing habitually within their territory.[4] However, the Commission subsequently altered its position following the ruling in *Brey* (C-140/12) and when the action was eventually issued in June 2014, the proceedings did not include the special non-contributory cash benefits – SPC, JSA(IB) but was instead based on what the Commission regard to be family benefits under the coordination rules – ie Child Benefit and Child Tax Credits:[5]

> 'The Commission maintains that, in requiring a claimant of child benefit and child tax credit to have a right to reside in the UK as a condition of being treated as resident there, the UK has imposed a condition that Regulation (EC) No 883/2004 does not permit.
>
> Alternatively the Commission submits that by imposing a condition of entitlement to social security benefits that is automatically met by its own nationals the UK has created a situation of direct discrimination against nationals of other Member States and thus breached article 4 of Regulation (EC) No 883/2004.'

[1] Case C-140/12 *Pensionsversicherungsanstalt v Brey (Peter)* [2014] 1 WLR 1080, [2014] 1 CMLR 993.
[2] Case C-140/12 *Brey*, paras 61–62.
[3] Case C-140/12 *Brey*, paras 44, 57.
[4] *Social security coordination: Commission requests United Kingdom to end discrimination of EU nationals residing in the UK regarding their rights to specific social benefits* (Press Notice Reference: IP/11/1118, dated 29 September 2011. For further details see *EEA nationals: the right to reside requirement for benefits*: House of Commons Library, Standard Note: SN/SP/5972, 5 December 2011 by Steven Kennedy, at 4.2, p 15.
[5] Announcement of *European Commission v United Kingdom of Great Britain and Northern Ireland* (Case C-308/14), published in the Official Journal on 29 September 2014 (OJ, 2014/C 329/03).

The need for a proportionality assessment

14.93 Domestic case law has consistently held that EU law does not require an individual consideration of a claimant's circumstances in order to decide whether a social security benefit should be payable.[1] This means that where an EEA national has been refused welfare benefit due to their failure to satisfy the right to reside requirement, according to domestic case law their options are limited to:

— seeking emergency relief provided under domestic law, such as the National Assistance Act 1948, Children Act 1989 or the Mental Health Act 1983;[2]

— returning to their own Member State in order to receive social assistance there;[3] or

— applying to the Home Office for leave to remain where arguments based upon the right to family life and/or fundamental rights could be employed.[4]

[1] *Ullusow v Secretary of State for Work and Pensions; Abdirahman v Secretary of State for Work and Pensions* [2007] EWCA Civ 657, [2008] 1 WLR 254, para 48. Whilst it was later acknowledged that the Treaty can, in exceptional circumstances, confer a right of residence, it was held that this was only available as a remedy if there was a lacuna in the secondary legislation which needed to be filled.[2] Given the recent codification of those rights in the Directive 38/2004/EC, the principle has a very limited role: *Kaczmarek (Sylwia) v Secre-*

tary State for Work and Pensions [2008] EWCA Civ 1310, [2009] 2 CMLR 85, para 20, and there has been only one reported case where it has been found that it would be dispropor-tionate to deny a right of residence to a person who has been refused benefit (in R(IS) 4/09).

² *CIS/3891/2007* [2009] UKUT 17 (AAC), para 41.

³ *CIS/3182/2005*, para 17, *RM v Secretary of State for Work and Pensions (IS)* [2010] UKUT 238 (AAC), para 10.

⁴ *R(IS) 6/08*, para 6, and *Secretary of State for Work and Pensions v SW (IS)* [2011] UKUT 508 (AAC), para 15, upheld by the Court of Appeal in *Mirga v Secretary of State for Work and Pensions* [2012] EWCA Civ 1952 at para 26. However, applying to the Home Office will not be a realistic option for most EEA nationals: see observations in *RM v Secretary of State for Work and Pensions (IS)* [2010] UKUT 238 (AAC) at para 15.

BREY (C-140/12)

14.94 In *Brey* C-140/12[1] the CJEU considered whether the correct approach had been taken to an EU citizen who was economically inactive (following retirement) who sought recourse to welfare benefits to supplement his retirement pension, and declared that national legislation which automatically refuses benefit to an EU citizen in those circumstances was unlawful. For while a claim for benefit in these circumstances could be an indication that the national does not have sufficient resources to avoid becoming an unreasonable burden on the social assistance system of the host Member State, the CJEU said on a proper analysis of the objectives of the Residence Directive 2004/38/EC and the principle of proportionality:

'the competent national authorities cannot draw such conclusions without first carrying out an overall assessment of the specific burden which granting that benefit would place on the national social assistance system as a whole, by reference to the personal circumstances characterising the individual situation of the person concerned.'[2]

The considerations which led the CJEU to reach this conclusion include that: (i) any limitations on the right to freedom of movement must be read narrowly;[3] (ii) Member States must not use their power to impose residence conditions in a manner which would compromise the objectives of the Directive;[3] and (iii) the Directive recognises a certain degree of financial solidarity between nationals of a host Member State and nationals of other Member States, particularly if the difficulties are temporary.[4] The importance of assessing the claimant's personal circumstances and the need to have regard to the principle of proportionality is emphasised at several places in the judgment.[5] The use of the right to reside condition as a blanket rule is therefore prohibited. Early references to *Brey* in domestic case law, have either high-lighted those parts of the judgment which confirm that Member States are permitted to make the granting of welfare benefits to EU citizens conditional upon them having a right of residence[6] or have confined the judgment to the facts in Mr Brey's case.[7] The Supreme Court has, granted permission to appeal to consider whether the denial of benefit is disproportionate in the light of recent CJEU case law.[8]

¹ Case C-140/12 *Pensionsversicherungsanstalt v Brey (Peter)* [2014] 1 WLR 1080, [2014] 1 CMLR 993.

² Case C-140/12 *Brey*, paras 64.

³ Case C-140/12 *Brey*, para 70.

⁴ Case C-140/12 *Brey*, para 71.

⁵ Case C-140/12 *Brey*, paras 67–69, and 72.

[6] *VP v Secretary for Works and Pensions (JSA)* [2014] UKUT 32 (AAC), para 79 and *Ahmad v Secretary of State for the Home Department* [2014] EWCA Civ 988, para 28.

[7] *Revenue and Customs Comrs v Spiridonova (Aiga)* [2014] NICA 63, in which the Court of Appeal Northern Ireland drew attention to the fact that when Mr Brey and his wife, German nationals, moved to Austria in March 2011, they were issued with an EEA citizen registration certificate by the immigration authorities around the same time as they received a decision from the pension authorities denying Mr Brey a compensatory supplement to his retirement pension on the basis that he failed the residence test.

[8] *Mirga v Secretary of State for Work and Pensions* (UKSC 22013/0161) and *Samin v Westminster City Council* (UKSC 2013/0225).

SUMMARY OF THE RULES GOVERNING ACCESS TO WELFARE BENEFITS

14.95 The following is a summary of the eligibility rules and residence conditions for the main welfare benefits. For details of the substantive rules on entitlement to welfare benefits and tax credit, readers should consult the relevant specialist texts – eg the *Child Poverty Action Group Welfare Benefits and Tax Credits Handbook*, which is published annually.

- *Income support* (IS)[1] – To be eligible to claim IS, the claimant needs to be present in Great Britain, have a right to reside, be habitually resident in the Common Travel Area and not be a person who is subject to immigration control. IS is defined as 'public funds' under the Immigration Rules.

- *Income-based Jobseeker's Allowance* (JSA(IB))[2] – To be eligible to claim JSA(IB), the claimant needs to be present in Great Britain, have a right to reside, be habitually resident in the Common Travel Area and not be a person who is subject to immigration control. JSA(IB) is defined as 'public funds' under the Immigration Rules. JSA(IB) is due to be replaced by UC.

- *Housing Benefit* (HB)[3] – To be eligible to claim HB, the claimant must have a right to reside, be habitually resident in the Common Travel Area and not be a person who is subject to immigration control. HB is defined as 'public funds' under the Immigration Rules.

- *Council Tax Reduction* (CTR)[4] – To be eligible to claim CTS, the claimant must be present in Great Britain, have a right to reside, be habitually resident in the Common Travel Area and not be a person who is subject to immigration control. CTR is defined as 'public funds' under the Immigration Rules.

- *Income-related Employment and Support Allowance* (ESA(IR))[5] – to be eligible to claim ESA(IR), the claimant must be present in Great Britain, have a right to reside, be habitually resident in the Common Travel Area and not be a person who is subject to immigration control. ESA(IR) is defined as 'public funds' under the Immigration Rules.

- *Child Benefit*: (CHB)[6] – To be eligible for CHB, the claimant and their child must have been present in Great Britain for 26 weeks out of the last 52 weeks. The claimant must be ordinarily resident and have a right to reside in the Common Travel Area. CHB is defined as 'public funds' in the Immigration Rules.

- *Child Tax Credits* (CTC)[7] – To be eligible to claim CTC, the claimant must be present and ordinarily resident in Great Britain, have a right to reside in the UK and not be a person subject to immigration control. CTC are defined as 'public funds' for the purposes of the Immigration Rules.
- *Working Tax Credits* (WTC)[8] – To be eligible to claim Working Tax Credit (WTC) the claimant must be present and ordinarily resident in Great Britain and not be a person subject to immigration control. WTC are defined as 'public funds' for the purposes of the Immigration Rules.
- *Universal Credit*[9] – To be eligible to claim UC, the claimant must be present in Great Britain, have a right to reside and be habitually resident in the Common Travel Area and not subject to immigration control. UC is defined as 'public funds' under the Immigration Rules.
- *State Pension Credit* (SPC)[10] – To be eligible to claim SPC, the claimant must to be present in Great Britain, have a right to reside, be habitually resident in the Common Travel Area and not be a person who is subject to immigration control. ESA(IR) is defined as 'public funds' under the Immigration Rules.
- *Personal Independent Payment*[11] – To be entitled to claim PIP the claimant must be present in Great Britain and have been present for a past period for at least 104 weeks out of the last 156 weeks, as well as habitually resident in the Common Travel Area and not be subject to immigration control. PIP is defined as 'public funds' in the Immigration Rules.
- *Attendance Allowance*[12] –The presence and residence tests are the same as those for PIP. AA is defined as 'public funds' in the Immigration Rules.
- *Carer's Allowance*[13] – The presence and residence tests are the same as those for PIP. CA is defined as 'public funds' in the Immigration Rules.
- *Disability Living Allowance*[14] – To be entitled the child needs to be present in Great Britain and have been present for a past period for at least 104 weeks out of the last 156 weeks (but different rules apply for children under three years of age, as well as habitually resident in the Common Travel Area and not be subject to immigration control). DLA is defined as 'public funds' in the Immigration Rules.

[1] Social Security Contributions and Benefits Act 1992, s 124(1) and the Income Support (General) Regulations 1987, SI 1987/1967, reg 21AA.
[2] Jobseekers Act 1995, s 1(2)(i) and the Jobseeker's Allowance Regulations 1996, SI 1996/207, reg 85.
[3] Housing Benefit Regulations 2006, SI 2006/213, reg 10 and the Housing Benefit (Persons who have attained the qualifying age for state pension credit) Regulations 2006, SI 2006/214, reg 10.
[4] The Council Tax Reduction Schemes (Prescribed Requirements) (England) Regulations 2012, SI 2012/2885, regs 12 and 13.
[5] Welfare Reform Act 2007, s 1(3)(d) and the Employment and Support Allowance Regulations 2008, SI 2008/794, reg 70.
[6] Social Security Contributions and Benefits Act 1992, s 146 and the Child Benefit (General) Regulations 2006, SI 2006/223, reg 23.
[7] Tax Credits Act 2002, s 3(3), the Tax Credits (Immigration) Regulations 2003, SI 2003/653, reg 3 and the Tax Credits (Residence) Regulations 2003, SI 2003/654, reg 3.
[8] Tax Credits Act 2002, s 3(3), the Tax Credits (Immigration) Regulations 2003, SI 2003/653, reg 3 and the Tax Credits (Residence) Regulations 2003, SI 2003/654, reg 3.
[9] Welfare Reform Act 2012, s 4(1)(c), Universal Credit Regulations 2013, SI 2013/376, reg 9

[10] State Pension Credit Act 2002, s 1(2)(a), State Pension Credit Regulations 2002, SI 2002/1792, reg 2(1).
[11] The Social Security (Personal Independence Payment) Regulations 2013, SI 2013/377, reg 16.
[12] Social Security (Attendance Allowance) Regulations 1991, SI 1991/2740, reg 2.
[13] Social Security (Invalid Care Allowance) Regulations 1976, SI 1976/409, reg 9.
[14] Social Security (Disability Living Allowance) Regulations 1991 SI 1991/2890, reg 2.

BACKDATING OF BENEFIT UPON BEING GRANTED REFUGEE STATUS

Backdating for means-tested benefits – abolished

14.96 Before June 2007, people granted refugee status could make a back-dated claim for mainstream welfare benefits[1] to the date of their asylum application (subject to deductions for benefit or subsistence payments already made). This was based on the principle that a Home Office decision to grant asylum recognises the individual's status as a refugee; it does not confer that status.[2] By having special backdating rules which provide that an asylum seeker's ultimate entitlement to social security benefits is not affected by the delay in recognising their status, the UK was honouring its obligation under the Refugee Convention to accord refugees the same treatment as that afforded to UK nationals.[3] However, in June 2007, the UK Government abolished the backdating of these mainstream benefits by virtue of section 12 of the Asylum and Immigration (Treatment of Claimants, etc) Act 2004[4] and replaced it by integration loans which have to be repaid.[5] The justification given by the government for this change in the law is that the previous system 'was considered unfair as the amount that an individual received was related solely to the time that they spent waiting for a decision rather than their integration needs.'[6] A legal challenge to the UK Government's decision to abolish the backdating of income support for refugees has been dismissed by a panel of three Upper Tribunal judges.[7]

[1] From 15 October 1996, Income Support, Housing and Council Tax Benefit and from 2 July 2002 and State Pension Credit.
[2] *Khaboka (Alimas) v Secretary of State for the Home Department* [1993] Imm AR 484 and R(IS) 9/98, para 24.
[3] Convention and Protocol Relating to the Status of Refugees, arts 23 (public relief) and 24 (social security) when read with art 3 (non-discrimination).
[4] Asylum and Immigration (Treatment of Claimants) Act 2004 (Commencement No 7 and Transitional Provisions) Order 2007, SI 2007/1602.
[5] Integration Loans for Refugees and Others Regulations 2007, SI 1598/2007 issued under section 13 of the Asylum and Immigration (Treatment of Claimants, etc) Act 2004.
[6] *Integration Loans Policy Guidance* – 1 Introduction, at 1.1.
[7] *HB v Secretary of State for Work and Pensions (IS)* [2013] UKUT 0433 (AAC). Permission to appeal has been granted by the Court of Appeal and the case is listed to be heard in January 2015.

Backdating family benefits

14.97 It is still open to refugees to make a claim to backdate certain family benefits. If a claimant who is recognised as a refugee and who submits a claim for Child Benefit or Guardian's Allowance within three months of having been notified of their immigration decision will be treated as having made a claim for benefit from the date they made their asylum claim.[1] In the case of Tax Credits, if the claim is made within one month[2] of being recognised as a refugee, the individual will be treated as having made a claim either from the date of their asylum claim or 6 April 2003 (when the Tax Credits scheme came into force), if this is later.[3] Where the one-month deadline has been missed, then the normal rules for backdating will apply.[4] As Tax Credits are income-related, any subsistence payments of Asylum Support paid to the claimant will be taken into account and offset from the total arrears payable to the claimant.[5]

[1] Child Benefit and Guardian's Allowance (Administration) Regulations 2003, SI 2003/492, reg 6(2)(d)(ii).
[2] Tax Credits (Immigration) Regulations 2003, SI 2003/653, reg 3(5)(b). The previous three-month deadline was reduced to one month by SI 2012/848, with effect from 6 April 2012.
[3] Tax Credits (Immigration) Regulations 2003, SI 2003/653, reg 3(6). See also *FK v Revenue and Customs Comrs* [2009] UKUT 134 (AAC), paras 13–14.
[4] See *Revenue and Customs Comrs v AA* [2012] UKUT 121 (AAC) paras 7 and 10.
[5] SI 2003/653, reg 3(9). *MI v Revenue and Customs Comrs* (CTC/3692/2008) [2009] UKUT 73 (AAC) rejected an argument that the asylum support paid in respect of the child should not be taken into account for the purpose of reducing the amount of backdated Tax Credits.

INTEGRATION LOANS SCHEME

14.98 The integration loans scheme is jointly administered by the Home Office/UK Border Agency (now renamed UK Visas and Immigration). Home Office caseworkers decide who is eligible for a loan and the amount to be awarded. The DWP administers payment and recovery of the loan. Someone can apply for a loan if they meet the following criteria:[1]

'a)   i) They have been granted refugee status, or humanitarian protection and leave to enter or remain or ii) They have leave to enter or remain because they are a dependent of a person in i).
b)   They are aged 18 or over.
c)   They have not received an integration loan (including a joint loan with a partner).
d)   They must have been granted leave to enter or remain after 11 June 2007.
e)   They are not insolvent.'

Only one loan payment is allowed per person but there is provision for couples to make a joint application.[2] A person will be regarded as insolvent if they are incapable of making the repayments or, where they are on benefits and these cannot be used to recover the loan because they are already subject to the maximum number of deductions under the third-party deductions scheme[3].

[1] Integration Loans for Refugees and Others Regulations 2007 SI 2007/1598, reg 4. See also Integration Loans Policy Guidance – 2 Eligibility.
[2] SI 2007/1598, reg 11, Guidance – 2 Eligibility at 2.2.
[3] Guidance – 2 Eligibility at 2.1(e).

Factors taken into account

14.99 When deciding whether to make a loan, the following factors are taken into account: (i) the length of time since an applicant was granted leave to enter or remain in the UK; (ii) the applicant's financial position; (iii) the applicant's likely ability to repay the loan; (iv) the information provided by the applicant as to his or her intended use of the integration loan; (v) the available budget for integration loans.[1] If more than twelve months have elapsed, then the application is likely to be refused 'unless there are compelling circumstances as to why an earlier application was not made'.[2] An award will also be refused if the applicant has an income above £15,000 or savings of more than £1,000, 'unless the applicant can demonstrate that the loan will have a positive effect on their integration'.[3] The loan is intended to cover items associated with the applicant's integration into society and should be used for housing, employment and education needs. It can include vocational training, a deposit for accommodation, buying essential items for the home, or the purchase of tools of a trade, (where financial assistance for these items is not available through Jobcentreplus).[4] No award will be made if it is for any of the items excluded by Official Guidance.[5] Where an application for a loan has been refused or a smaller amount is offered than requested, the applicant can ask for the decision to be reconsidered.[6]

[1]   SI 2007/1598, reg 6(1)(a)–(e).
[2]   SI 2007/1598, reg 6(1)(e).
[3]   Guidance – 7 Financial Position at 7.1.
[4]   Guidance – 9 Ability to Repay at: 9.1.
[5]   The list of excluded items includes: non-essential items, general living expenses, medical services, domestic services and respite care and costs associated with cars, unless it is essential to their job, eg taxi driver (Guidance at 9.3).
[6]   Guidance 12 – Reconsideration of the Application.

Recovery of the loan

14.100 If the request for a loan is accepted, repayments will not usually start until at least six weeks after the loan has been paid. Where the recipient or their partner is in receipt of means-tested benefit, the loan can be collected by the DWP through the provisions for third-party deductions.[1] The scheme allows an amount to be deducted from the claimant's Income Support, income-based Jobseeker's Allowance, Income related Employment and Support or Pension Credit in order to pay off the loan. The rate of deduction per week is prescribed[2] but the DWP can only take a maximum of three separate deductions a week, having regard to the priority given to each type of debt under the scheme.[3] If the recipient is not receiving benefits, then the DWP will negotiate a repayment rate with the applicant based on the size of the loan.[4] The terms for repaying the integration loan can be revised or suspended if the applicant falls into hardship. Resort to civil action to recover the loan should only be taken where there is evidence that the applicant is deliberately avoiding repayment.[5]

[1]   Social Security (Claims and Payments) Regulations 1987, SI 1987/1968, Sch 9, para 7D.
[2]   The rates at 2014–2015 were £3.65 p/wk.
[3]   The priority given to each type of debt in descending order is: rent arrears; fuel charges; water charges; council tax; court fines; child support; Integration loans and repayment of certain loans such as credit unions: SI 1987/1968, Sch 9, para 9.
[4]   SI 2007/1598, reg 9. Guidance – 8 Ability to Repay.
[5]   Guidance – 18 Enforcement Action, at 18.1.

CLAIM FOR ASYLUM HAS BEEN 'RECORDED BY THE SECRETARY OF STATE'

14.101 In order for an asylum seeker to be supported by the Secretary of State, his or her claim for asylum must have been 'recorded by the Secretary of State'.[1] All that is necessary for a claim to have been recorded, we suggest, is that there is in the Home Office some note made by an officer of the Secretary of State which identifies the person making the claim and which is sufficient to indicate that a claim to asylum has been made by that person. Again, the case law of the Social Security Commissioners (now replaced by the Upper Tribunal (Administrative Appeals Chamber)) dealing with claims recorded as having been made for benefits purposes may be applicable in this context. In one case, a Commissioner held that there was no specified manner in which the record of the claim had to be made, and relied on a letter from the Secretary of State issued in response to a complaint as to how a person had been treated on entry to the UK as either a sufficient record of the claim in itself or as secondary evidence of a Home Office record.[2] There is no requirement that the asylum seeker be notified of the recording of the claim. From the language of the provision we suggest that it does not matter if the record of the claim is subsequently lost, for example, if the Home Office loses the relevant file, provided that it can be established that the claim was originally made and recorded.[3] The fact that an in-country asylum claim must be made in person at an Asylum Screening Unit or local enforcement office as soon as reasonably practicable[4] is likely to reduce the uncertainty in relation to whether or not a claim has been recorded.

[1]   IAA 1999, s 94(1).
[2]   Commissioner's Decision CIS/4439/98, paras 3, 7–8; however, see also Asylum Process Guidance 'Registering an Asylum Claim in the United Kingdom' and 'Postal Claims' in respect of in-country applications.
[3]   Section 94(1) of the IAA 1999 uses the perfect tense: 'a claim for asylum which has been recorded by the Secretary of State'.
[4]   See NIAA 2002, s 55 (**14.113** below).

CLAIM FOR ASYLUM HAS BEEN DETERMINED

14.102 As a general rule, a person remains an 'asylum seeker' for support purposes until the claim for asylum 'has been determined'.[1] However, if there is a dependent child in the asylum seeker's household, the person does not cease to be an asylum seeker for the purposes of asylum support under section 94 of the IAA 1999 while the child remains under 18 and both remain in the UK (unless the person is granted leave to remain).[2] The legislation is contradictory: under section 94, asylum support continues to be available to families with children after their claims are determined, while they remain in the UK. But the provisions of Schedule 3, paragraph 6 to the NIAA 2002, which remove support from 'failed asylum seekers'[3] who fail to co-operate with removal directions, and their dependants, contain their own definition of 'asylum seeker', removing the special treatment of families with children.[4] Schedule 3, paragraph 7A of the NIAA 2002[5] provides that a failed asylum seeker accompanied by a dependent child will lose entitlement to any support, either from the Secretary of State or a local authority, 14 days after receiving notice that the Secretary of State for the Home Department has certified that in his opinion he or she is a person who has failed without reasonable excuse to take reasonable steps to leave the UK voluntarily or to place himself or herself in a position to be able to leave the UK voluntarily.[6] A failed asylum seeker will be able to appeal against such a certificate to the First-tier Tribunal (Asylum Support) if the Secretary of State is providing asylum support.[7] A local authority will still have the power to provide accommodation for any dependent children (but not their parents) under section 20 of the Children Act 1989.[8] It will also still retain its child protection powers to provide alternative accommodation for the children if they were deemed to be at risk under section 31 of the Children Act 1989.[9]

[1]   IAA 1999, s 94(1). Amendments made by NIAA 2002, s 44 (in force from a date to be appointed) do not materially affect this definition.
[2]   IAA 1999, s 94(5). The section is replaced by a new s 94(3A), to the same effect, by NIAA 2002, s 44 as from a date to be appointed.
[3]   Heading of NIAA 2002, Sch 3, para 6. The Schedule removes various classes of person from eligibility for housing, social services, community care and asylum support: Sch 3, para 1(1).
[4]   See NIAA 2002, Sch 3, para 17 for the definition of 'asylum seeker' for the purpose of the Schedule. It is not clear how these two definitions interact and whether the provisions of the Schedule condition the provision of support under the 1999 Act.
[5]   Inserted by AI(TC)A 2004, s 9 (in force 1 December 2004) (SI 2004/2999).
[6]   New para 7A, 'failed asylum seeker with family', spells out its application to those treated as asylum seekers for the purpose of the IAA 1999, s 94(3A) (see fn 2 above).
[7]   Under IAA 1999, s 103: see AI(TC)A 2004, s 9(3)(b), (4) (in force 1 December 2004) (SI 2004/2999).
[8]   See NIAA 2002, Sch 3, para 2(1)(b).
[9]   NIAA 2002, Sch 3, para 1 does not remove this power.

14.103 In cases where there are no dependent children, and cases to which the provisions of Schedule 3 to the NIAA 2002 apply,[1] a person ceases to be an asylum seeker when the claim for asylum is determined at the end of such period as may be prescribed, beginning on the day on which the Secretary of State notifies him or her in writing[2] of the decision on the claim for asylum or, if there is an appeal against the decision, when the appeal is disposed of.[3] Where the Secretary of State notifies the claimant of his decision to accept the asylum claim; the Secretary of State notifies the claimant of his decision to reject the asylum claim but at the same time notifies him that he is giving him limited leave to enter or remain in the UK; or an appeal has been disposed of by being allowed, the prescribed period is 28 days. In all other cases it is 21 days.[4] Thus a person remains an asylum seeker, for these purposes, throughout the period during which there is no decision on the asylum application and, if the Secretary of State's decision is negative, throughout the entire appeals process. If an asylum seeker fails to appeal within prescribed time limits and then makes an application for permission to appeal out of time, he or she is not an asylum seeker for the purposes of asylum support until permission has been granted to appeal out of time.[5] Refusal of asylum is not, *per se*, an 'immigration decision' against which an appeal may be brought to the First-tier Tribunal (Immigration and Asylum Chamber).[6] Therefore, if a person is refused asylum but no immigration decision against which the person could appeal is taken against him or her, the person ceases to be an asylum seeker and loses any eligibility for support that is contingent upon being an asylum seeker. In addition, it was the case that a person who had appealed against a non-asylum immigration decision on asylum grounds, did not enjoy the status of 'asylum seeker' for support purposes.[7] To alter this section 17 of the UK

Borders Act 2007, in force from 30 October 2007, provides that a person remains or becomes again an asylum seeker, despite the fact that the claim for asylum has been determined, during any time when an in-country appeal may be brought against an immigration decision under section 82 of the NIAA 2002 or section 2 of the Special Immigration Appeals Commission Act 1997, or an appeal under one of these two sections is pending within the meaning of section 104 of the NIAA 2002.

¹ Ie Sch 3, para 7A (as inserted from 1 December 2004) and para 6.
² IAA 1999, s 94(8).
³ IAA 1999, ss 94(4), 167 (s 94(4) amended by NIAA 2002, s 44 (from a date to be appointed) referring to NIAA 2002, s 104.
⁴ IAA 1999, s 93(3)–(4) (s 94(3) amended by NIAA 2002, s 44 from a date to be appointed). The Asylum Support Regulations 2000, SI 2000/704, regs 2, 2A, as substituted by SI 2002/472, reg 3, from 8 April 2002.
⁵ *R (on the application of Erdogan (Sahsenem)) v Secretary of State for the Home Department* [2004] EWCA Civ 1087, [2004] All ER (D) 421 (Jul).
⁶ However, it is not one of the decisions listed in the NIAA 2002, s 82(2) against which an appeal may be brought.
⁷ *R (on the application of M) v Slough Borough Council* [2006] EWCA Civ 655, (2007) LGR 225, (2006) Times 13 June.

14.104 Viewing the determination of an asylum claim as inclusive of the appeal process both accords with the case law[1] and avoids the situation which arose in 1996 where asylum seekers had, in theory, important appeal rights but were, in practice, unable to exercise them because of destitution.[2] Eligibility for social security benefits, tax credits and community care services is restored when asylum seekers are successful on appeal and are recognised as refugees and granted leave to remain by the Home Office accordingly. There have, unfortunately, been very severe delays in the Home Office granting refugee status to successful appellants, which has caused prejudice in terms of access to conventional social security benefits, tax credits and housing; naturalisation; travel documents and entitlement to work. The High Court has declared such delays unlawful,[3] and a duty of care may arise in such a situation so as to found a damages claim.[4] Financial and other loss caused by such delays may be covered by a Home Office *ex gratia* compensation scheme.[5]

¹ Which sees the asylum appellate process as an extension of the original asylum decision-making process: see *Ravichandran (Senathirajah) v Secretary of State for the Home Department* [1996] Imm AR 97, CA.
² See observations in *R v Secretary of State for Social Security, ex p Joint Council for the Welfare of Immigrants* [1996] 4 All ER 385.
³ *R v Secretary of State for the Home Department, ex p Mersin (Deniz)* [2000] INLR 511, Elias J; timely notification of decisions was a further factor identified by the Audit Commission as critical for the proper and efficient functioning of the dispersal system in *Another Country: Implementing dispersal under the IAA 1999* June 2000.
⁴ *R (on the application of Kanidagli) v Secretary of State for the Home Department* [2004] EWHC 1585 (Admin), [2004] NLJR 1141.
⁵ See 'How we will deal with your complaint' (at www.ind.homeoffice.gov.uk/contact/making acomplaint/dealingwithyourcomplaint/).

Dependants of asylum seekers

14.105 The scheme provides for support to be provided not only to asylum seekers but also to the dependants of asylum seekers.[1] The definition of dependants is set out below. A person is the 'dependant of an asylum seeker' if he or she is related or connected to the asylum seeker in one of the following ways:[2]

(a)   Is the spouse or civil partner of the asylum seeker (almost certainly in a marriage or civil partnership recognised by UK law)?[3]

(b)   Is the child of the asylum seeker or of his or her spouse or civil partner, who is (or was at the relevant time, **14.107**) under 18 and dependent on the asylum seeker?

(c)   Is a member of the asylum seeker's or his or her spouse's or civil partner's 'close family'[4] who is (or was at the relevant time, **14.107**) under 18?

(d)   Has been living as part of the asylum seeker's household either for at least 6 of the 12 months before the relevant time, **14.107**, or since birth and, in either case, and is (or was at the relevant time, **14.107**) under 18?

(e)   Is in need of care and attention from the asylum seeker or a member of his or her household by reason of a disability and is either a member of the asylum seeker's or their spouse's close family or has been living as part of the asylum seeker's household for 6 of the 12 months before the date on which the claim to support was made or since birth?

(f)   Has been living with the asylum seeker as a member of an unmarried couple (including a same sex couple) for at least two of the three years before the relevant time?

(g)   Is living with the asylum seeker as part of his or her household and was receiving assistance from a local authority under section 17 of the Children Act 1989 immediately before 6 December 1999?[5]

(h)   Has made a claim for leave to enter or remain in the UK, or to vary such leave, which is being considered on the basis that the person is the dependant of an asylum seeker? (Under the Immigration Rules,[6] only the spouse, civil partner, unmarried or same-sex partner, and minor children of asylum seekers are to be considered as dependants on the asylum claim, but the Secretary of State may, as a matter of discretion, treat other family members as dependent on the asylum seeker for the purposes of the asylum claim.)[7]

(i)   And in relation to all of the above, is an asylum seeker, in circumstances where his or her dependant has claimed support or is being supported?

---

1   IAA 1999, ss 94(1)(a)–(c), 95(1); Asylum Support Regulations 2000, SI 2000/704, reg 3(3).
2   SI 2000/704, reg 2(4).
3   See CHAPTER 11 above.
4   'Close family' remains undefined in the regulations. See Joint Committee on Statutory Instruments Ninth Report, Appendix 1, where a memorandum from the Home Office sets out the reason for deliberately not defining the term 'close family', in order to reflect different types of family group that exist in other cultures around the world (24 January 2003).
5   The date on which the interim regulations (Asylum Support (Interim Provision) Regulations 1999, SI 1999/3056 came into force, and thus the beginning of the 'interim period' for SI 1999/3056, regs 1(1), 2(1)(g), 2(5); ASR, SI 2000/704, reg 2(4)(g).
6   HC 395, para 349.
7   The acceptance of the spouse and minor child is the 'minimum requirement' of the policy on family reunion of the United Nations High Commission for Refugees and the Final Act of the Conference which adopted the Refugee Convention, although other relatives will be admitted in compelling compassionate circumstances: see CHAPTER 12 above.

14.106 In addition to the categories referred to above, a person qualifies as a dependant for asylum support purposes if he or she is living as a part of the asylum seeker's household and, immediately before 3 April 2000, was receiving support from a local authority in Scotland or Northern Ireland, under section 22 of the Children (Scotland) Act 1995 or Article 18 of the Children (Northern Ireland) Order 1995 as the case may be.[1] This category ensures that dependants in Scotland and Northern Ireland are provided for by the Home Office.

[1]   Asylum Support Regulations 2000, SI 2000/704, reg 2(4)(h).

14.107 The regulations for the asylum support scheme expressly provide that, in categories (b), (c) and (d) above, young people count as dependants if they were under 18 at the 'relevant time', that is (i) the time when the application for support was made,[1] or (ii) the time when they joined a supported asylum seeker in the UK where (i) is inapplicable.[2] Such persons will continue to receive support after their eighteenth birthday, provided all the other conditions continue to be met.

[1]   Asylum Support Regulations 2000, SI 2000/704, reg 3(3).
[2]   SI 2000/704, reg 2(4)(b)–(d), (6).

14.108 Those joining a partner in the UK while the latter was being supported, must have lived with him or her as a couple for two of the three previous years.[1] Further, the support regulations define an 'unmarried couple' as a man and woman who, though not married to each other, are living together as if married, and a same-sex couple as two people of the same sex who, though not civil partners of each other, are living together as if they were.[2]

[1]   Asylum Support Regulations 2000, SI 2000/704, reg 2(4)(f) and (fa), (6).
[2]   SI 2000/704, reg 2(1). See also paragraph 13 of ASA/03/06/6653.

THE DETAIL OF THE SCHEME FOR ASYLUM SUPPORT

14.109 The National Asylum Support Service (NASS) was a body established as part of the Home Office to be responsible for providing comprehensive support to destitute asylum seekers. It became operational on 3 April 2000, when it took on responsibility for the support of certain new asylum applicants.[1] The intention was that, eventually, all destitute asylum seekers would have recourse to NASS rather than to the interim support scheme. By the end of August 2000, all new asylum seekers were eligible to apply for NASS support, and on 4 April 2006, when the interim support scheme ended,[2] NASS was responsible for all asylum seekers.[3] NASS had regional offices in Manchester, Leeds, Newcastle, Birmingham, Leicester, Cambridge, Bristol, Cardiff, Glasgow, Dover, Croydon and Belfast as well as its headquarters in Croydon. These regional offices dealt with outreach work, investigations and housing contract management.[4] In April 2006, it was announced that NASS had ceased to exist as a separate part of the Home Office and its role was taken over by the Border and Immigration Agency (BIA). On 7 April 2008, the UK Border Agency (UKBA) was formed, adopting the functions of the Immigration and Nationality department and the support role of the BIA. Following the abolition of the UKBA on 26 March 2013, the Home Office now deals with all asylum support applications. All applications made after 1 April 2007 are dealt with under the New Asylum Model (NAM) which introduced 'end to end' case management of asylum claims. In the new arrangement, one case owner deals with all aspects of the asylum application from the initial interview through to a final positive or negative outcome and the enforcement of that outcome. NAM case owners are expected to make decisions on asylum support for asylum seekers and failed asylum seekers. Until July 2011 older cases were processed by the Case Resolution Directorate and then by the Case Assurance and Audit Unit. The Older Live Cases Unit (Olcu) based in Liverpool, now deals with applications made before 1 April 2007. This department continues to make asylum support decisions, dealing with asylum applications,appeals, further representations and support matters until leave to remain is granted or the individual leaves the UK.

[1] The system of support provided by NASS is set out in the IAA 1999, Pt VI and Sch 8; the key provisions were brought into force from 3 April 2000 (Immigration and Asylum Act 1999 (Commencement No 3) Order 2000, SI 2000/464, art 2 and Schedule) on which date the regulations which set out the detailed machinery of the scheme also came into force: Asylum Support Regulations 2000, SI 2000/704, reg 1 and the now repealed Asylum Support Appeals (Procedure) Rules 2000, SI 2000/541, r 1.

[2] See Asylum Support (Interim Provisions) (Amendment) Regulations 2005, SI 2005/595

[3] Asylum Support (Interim Provisions) Regulations 1999, SI 1999/3056, as amended, regs 1(1) and 2(5). Local authorities retain community care responsibilities for those whose need for care and attention does not arise solely from destitution, however: R *(on the application of Westminster City Council) v Secretary of State for the Home Department* [2001] EWCA Civ 512, 33 HLR 938, [2001] All ER (D) 100 (Apr).

[4] NASS in the Regions, formerly on the Home Office website.

Applications for asylum support

14.110 The asylum support scheme requires an application to the Secretary of State for support.[1] The application must be in the form currently in use, which at the time of writing is ASF1.[2] The application may not be entertained if it is not in the correct form, or if the Secretary of State is not satisfied that the information provided is complete or accurate or that the applicant is co-operating with enquiries.[3] Asylum seekers may receive assistance completing the form from the voluntary sector 'assistants' who help to identify and convey relevant information to the Secretary of State.[4] The application may be for a sole applicant or for the applicant and his or her dependants,[5] and a group application may be made on one application form. A new or newly arrived dependant of a person who is already being supported by the Secretary of State does not need to complete another application, and the Secretary of State will consider providing additional support when notified of his or her existence.[6] The Secretary of State may make further inquiries of the asylum seeker in connection with any of the details contained in the application form.[7] Those who apply for Home Office support are screened to see if they have claimed asylum as soon as reasonably practicable after their arrival in the UK, before their application is considered further.[8] A person in detention who is awaiting the hearing of a bail application may make an application for support in anticipation of release.[9]

[1] Asylum Support Regulations 2000, SI 2000/704, reg 3 as amended by the Asylum Support (Amendment) (No 3) Regulations 2002, SI 2002/3110 and the Asylum Support Regulations

2007, reg; see also www.ukba.homeoffice.gov.uk/asylum/support/apply/ *Policy Bulletin 73, Provision of Initial Accommodation* and Asylum Process Guidance, 'Eligibilityand Assessment'.

2   IAA 1999, Sch 8, para 12, amended by NIAA 2002, s 57; Asylum Support (Amendment) (No 3) Regulations 2002, SI 2002/3110, reg 2. If the Secretary of State makes further enquiries in connection with the application, the applicant has five working days to respond unless he or she has a reasonable excuse for not doing so: ASR 2000, reg 3(5A) and 3(5B), inserted by SI 2005/11, reg 3. If the applicant does not comply, the application will not be entertained, and temporary support under IAA 1999, s 98 will be discontinued: reg 3(5C) as inserted; See also *Policy Bulletin 79*, 'Section 57 (applications for support: false or incomplete information) 2002 Act guidance'.

3   Migrant Helpline, Refugee Action, the Refugee Council, Scottish and Welsh Refugee Councils, the North of England Refugee Service and the Northern Ireland Council for Ethnic Minorities.

4   SI 2000/704, reg 3(2).

5   SI 2000/704, reg 3(6).

6   SI 2000/704, reg 3(5).

7   NIAA 2002, s 55; see also *Policy Bulletin 75*, 'Section 55 of Nationality, Immigration and Asylum Act 2002: process', version 11, 22 July 2014

8   SI 2000/704, Asylum Support Guidance Notes to NASS1 Form: 'Do you live in any other kind of accommodation?' at www.ukba.homeoffice.gov.uk/asylum/support/apply/. See also the *Asylum Support Policy Bulletins* on the Home Office website and the Bail Flowcharts therein at www.ukba.homeoffice.gov.uk/policyandlaw/guidance/asylumsuppbull/

14.111 The Asylum Support Regulations 2000[1] contain no express time limits for making the decision on support, but we may infer that the process should be extremely speedy.[2] There is no requirement in the regulations that decisions must be in writing, but clearly it is intended that a written explanation will be provided of a decision refusing all support, with details of whether an appeal is available and if so, how to appeal.[3] Emergency support is provided if there is a delay in deciding whether an application for asylum was made as soon as reasonably practicable, and full reasons must be given for a decision that it was not and that asylum support will not be provided.[4]

1   SI 2000/704 as amended.

2   See the very strict and short time limits for appealing refusal of asylum support at **14.174B** below.

3   See Home Office Guidance, Asylum Support Application Form (ASF1), 3 April 2013.

4   *R (on the application of Q) v Secretary of State for the Home Department* [2003] EWHC 195 (Admin), [2003] 15 LS Gaz R 26, (2003) Times, 20 February; affd [2003] EWCA Civ 364, [2004] QB 36, [2003] 2 All ER 905. See also in the Administrative Court, [2003] EWHC 1195 (Admin), in the same case, Maurice Kay J's guidance for claimants seeking to challenge negative decisions under section 55 (for which no right of appeal to the First-tier Tribunal (Asylum Support) is available), which indicates that the Secretary of State should reach a decision on asylum support on the day of or the day following the application.

Persons entitled to asylum support

14.112 In order to be entitled to asylum support a person must satisfy the general conditions of entitlement, ie that a person is an asylum seeker or a dependant of an asylum seeker and is destitute or likely to become so. From 8 January 2003, asylum seekers who are not accompanied by minor dependants[1] and are not themselves unaccompanied minors[2] have also had to establish that they claimed asylum 'as soon as reasonably practicable' after their arrival in the UK, under s 55 of the NIAA 2002.[3] That application of that section has led to thousands of asylum seekers having to sleep on the streets or in parks with inadequate clothing and no food. The despair and degradation this has caused has been the subject of a number of reports and considerable litigation.[4] From February 2005, following the entry into force of the EC Reception Conditions Directive, reduction or withdrawal of support for non-compliance with procedural requirements must comply with the principle of proportionality.[5] Section 55 of the NIAA 2002 applies to support and accommodation provided under ss 4, 95 and 98 of the IAA 1999. It is currently Home Office policy to accept that a person claimed asylum as soon as reasonably practicable where he or she claimed within three days of arriving in the UK, subject to the circumstances in a particular case.[6]

[1] NIAA 2002, s 55(5)(c).
[2] See definition of 'asylum seeker' in IAA 1999, s 94 (as amended by NIAA 2002, s 44 from a date to be appointed).
[3] NIAA 2002, s 55(1), (2). The Secretary of State was entitled to withdraw asylum support previously given to an asylum seeker when he discovered that she had altered her documentation to make it appear that she had claimed on arrival, as she had never been entitled to support: *R (Secretary of State for the Home Department) v Chief Asylum Support Adjudicator* [2003] EWHC 269 (Admin), [2003] All ER (D) 116 (Feb), Toulson J.
[4] See eg Inter-Agency Partnership Section 55 Report, February 2004; *Destitution by Design: Withdrawal of Support from In-country Asylum Applicants: An Impact Assessment for London*, Mayor of London, February 2004.
[5] See **14.93** below.
[6] *Policy Bulletin 75*, 'Section 55 of Nationality, Immigration and Asylum Act 2002: process', version 11, 22 July 2014

'As soon as reasonably practicable'

14.113 The leading case of Q established that the test immigration officers should apply is whether 'on the premise that the purpose of coming to this country was to claim asylum and having regard both to the practical opportunity of claiming asylum and to the asylum seeker's personal circumstances, could the asylum seeker reasonably have been expected to claim earlier that he or she did?'[1] The Court of Appeal also accepted that in deciding whether an asylum seeker claimed asylum as soon as reasonably practicable, it was right to have regard to the effect of anything that the asylum seeker may have been told by his or her facilitator.[2] On 17 December 2003, following further litigation on what was 'reasonably practicable', the Secretary of State announced that as a matter of policy, anyone claiming asylum within three days of his or her arrival in the UK would not be refused support under section 55.[3] However, there remain severe evidential difficulties in proving the date of a clandestine arrival.[4]

[1] *R (on the application of Q) v Secretary of State for the Home Department* [2003] EWCA Civ 364, [2004] QB 36, [2003] 2 All ER 905.
[2] *R (on the application of Q)* above at para 43.
[3] Letter to Tim Crowley, Inter-Agency Co-ordination Team, 12 January 2004; see now [AQ] **14.112** fn 7.
[4] See **14.115** below on procedures. *Policy Bulletin 75*, 'Section 55 of Nationality, Immigration and Asylum Act 2002: process', version 11, 22 July 2014, Chapter 5.

Avoiding a breach of a person's Convention rights

14.114 Section 55 should not disqualify an asylum seeker from support where a failure to provide support would give rise to any breach of the European Convention on Human Rights.[1] This provision has given rise to a huge volume of litigation. In *Q*, the Court of Appeal accepted that denial of support to an asylum seeker constituted 'treatment' for the purposes of Article 3 of ECHR,[2] but held that 'destitution' as defined in the asylum support provisions does not necessarily amount to 'inhuman and degrading' treatment for the purposes of the Article.[3] The court declined to provide a simple test for claimants to satisfy in order to show that failing to support them would breach their human rights, but held that it was not unlawful for the Secretary of State to refuse support unless it was clear that charitable support had not been provided and that the individual was incapable of fending for him- or herself.[4] In *T*,[5] the court held that the condition of the destitute asylum seeker must verge on the degree of severity described in *Pretty v United Kingdom*,[6] where it was described as 'ill-treatment that attains a minimum level of severity and involves actual bodily injury or intense physical or mental suffering [or] treatment [which] humiliates or debases an individual showing lack of respect for, or diminishing his or her human dignity or arousing feelings of fear, anguish or inferiority capable of breaking an individual's moral or physical resistance'. Following these cases, Administrative Court judges continued to differ in their interpretation of the point at which an asylum seeker could be said to verge on the degree of severity needed to attract the protection of Article 3 of the ECHR (and thus section 55(5)).[7] The conflict was resolved when the Court of Appeal held in *Limbuela* and others that it was:

'not necessary . . . to show the actual onset of severe illness or suffering. If the evidence establishes clearly that charitable support in practice is not available, and that [the asylum seeker] has no other means of "fending for himself", then the presumption will be that severe suffering will imminently follow. He has done enough to show that he is "verging on" the necessary degree of severity, and that Article 3 is accordingly engaged'.[8]

The House of Lords dismissed the Secretary of State's appeal.[9] Lord Bingham said that the Secretary of State would be under a duty to provide support under section 55(5)(a) of the NIAA 2002:

'when it appears on a fair and objective assessment of all relevant facts and circumstances that an individual applicant faces an imminent prospect of serious suffering caused or materially aggravated by denial of shelter, food or the most basic necessities of life. Many factors may affect that judgment, including age, gender, mental and physical health and condition, any facilities or sources of support available to the applicant, the weather and time of year and the period for which the applicant has already suffered or is likely to continue to suffer privation.

It is not in my opinion possible to formulate any simple test applicable in all cases. But if there were persuasive evidence that a late applicant was obliged to sleep in the street, save perhaps for a short and foreseeably finite period, or was seriously hungry, or unable to satisfy the most basic requirements of hygiene, the threshold would, in the ordinary way, be crossed.'[10]

---

[1]   NIAA 2002, s 55(5)(a); *Policy Bulletin 75*, 'Section 55 of Nationality, Immigration and Asylum Act 2002: process', version 11, 22 July 2014, Chapter 6

[2]   For ECHR, Art 3 see Chapter 7 above.

[3]   *R (on the application of Q) v Secretary of State for the Home Department* [2003] EWCA Civ 364, [2004] QB 36 at para 59.

[4]   *R (on the application of Q)* at paras 61, 63.

[5]   *R (on the application of T) v Secretary of State for the Home Department* [2003] EWCA Civ 1285, [2004] HLR 254, [2003] NLJR 1474. The claimant failed to establish a breach of his

human rights, since although he was living rough at an airport, he had access to shelter, toilets and wash basins and some food.

6   (2002) 35 EHRR 1, [2002] 2 FCR 97.
7   See *R (on the application of Zardasht) v Secretary of State for the Home Department* [2004] EWHC 91 (Admin), [2004] All ER (D) 196 (Jan) (a hard-line decision); cf the first instance decisions in *R (on the application of Limbuela) v Secretary of State for the Home Department* [2004] EWHC 219 (Admin), [2004] All ER (D) 56 (Feb); *R (on the application of Tesema) v Secretary of State for the Home Department* [2004] EWHC 295 (Admin), [2004] All ER (D) 247 (Feb); *Adam v Secretary of State for the Home Department* [2004] EWHC 354 (Admin), [2004] All ER (D) 264 (Feb).
8   *R (on the application of Adam) v Secretary of State for the Home Department; R (on the application of Tesema) v Secretary of State for the Home Department, R (on the application of Limbuela) v Secretary of State for the Home Department* [2004] EWCA Civ 540, [2004] QB 1440.
9   *R (on the application of Limbuela) v Secretary of State for the Home Department* [2005] UKHL 66, [2006] 1 AC 396, [2005] 3 WLR 1014.
10 *R (on the application of Limbuela) v Secretary of State for the Home Department* at paras 8 and 9.

14.115 The decision on whether the asylum claimant is disqualified from support by claiming too late under section 55(1) of the NIAA 2002 is taken after an interview.[1] If a decision cannot be made immediately, the claimant will be given a letter authorising time-limited emergency accommodation under section 98 of the IAA 1999.[2] If the decision is positive, the asylum seeker will then have to complete and submit an ASF1. If the decision is negative, the asylum seeker will have to vacate his or her emergency accommodation within seven days.[3] The claimant can ask the Secretary of State to reconsider a negative decision in the light of any subsequent evidence or a change in his or her circumstances, and the Secretary of State has undertaken to endeavour to complete this reconsideration within 24 hours.[4] In order to obtain emergency accommodation pending reconsideration, the asylum seeker will have to show a seriously arguable case that the provision of support is necessary for the purposes of avoiding a breach of his or her rights under the ECHR, or obtain an injunction.[5] Heavily pregnant women (and others with particular vulnerabilities) are unlikely to be refused under section 55 as the Secretary of State recognises that this is likely to give rise to a breach of Convention rights.[6] As a result of the Court of Appeal decision in Q,[7] which upheld first instance criticism of the system of decision-making on section 55 as unfair, the screening interview forms and the guidance provided to immigration officers undertaking these interviews were significantly revised.[8] There is no right of appeal against disqualification from asylum support under section 55,[9] with the result that the Administrative Court was clogged with applications for judicial review until the revised policy came into effect.[10]

1   *Policy Bulletin 75*, 'Section 55 of Nationality, Immigration and Asylum Act 2002: process', version 11, 22 July 2014, para.4.1; See also Annex A: Late claim for asylum refusal of support.
2   Letter to Tim Crowley, Inter-Agency Co-ordination Team, 18 November 2003; see also *Policy Bulletin 75*, 'Section 55 of Nationality, Immigration and Asylum Act 2002: process', version 11, 22 July 2014, para 4.2
3   Letter to Tim Crowley, above. See however Maurice Kay J's guidance in *R (on the application of Q) v Secretary of State for the Home Department* [2003] EWHC 2507 (Admin), that the Secretary of State ought not to evict so precipitately, particularly when there is likely to be a challenge on human rights grounds.
4   Letter to Tim Crowley, above. See Maurice Kay J in *R (Q)* above; see also *Policy Bulletin 75*, 'Section 55 of Nationality, Immigration and Asylum Act 2002: process', version 11, 22 July 2014, para 5.4.
5   Letter to Tim Crowley, above. See Maurice Kay J in *R (Q)* above.

6   *Policy Bulletin 75*, 'Section 55 of Nationality, Immigration and Asylum Act 2002: process', version 11, 22 July 2014, Chapter 6
7   *R (on the application of Q) v Secretary of State for the Home Department* [2003] EWCA Civ 364, [2004] QB 36, [2003] 2 All ER 905.
8   *Policy Bulletin 75*, 'Section 55 of Nationality, Immigration and Asylum Act 2002: process', version 11, 22 July 2014
9   NIAA 2002, s 55(10).
10   See the figures cited by Maurice Kay J in *R (Q)* above; for the revised policy see **14.112**, fn 7.

14.116 When unaccompanied minor asylum seekers become 18, they will be interviewed to see whether they claimed asylum as soon as reasonably practicable.[1] Similarly, as soon as an asylum seeker no longer has any minor dependants in his or her household, the Secretary of State will consider the timeliness of his or her application for asylum. This late consideration could lead to asylum support being terminated under section 55.[2] A person who makes an in-country application for asylum following a significant change in circumstances in his or her country of origin will be provided with asylum support as long as her or she makes his or her application at the earliest possible opportunity following that change of circumstances.[3]

1   All asylum seekers who claim to be under 18 are referred to the Refugee Council's Panel of Advisers whether the Secretary of State believes their claimed age or not. If a person claims to be under 18, his or her age will be assessed during the screening process, and a physical appearance strongly suggestive of an over 18-year-old is likely to result in the claimant being treated as an adult unless there is credible evidence to substantiate that he or she is not: *Policy Bulletin 33*, 'Age Disputes', 17 October 2000, para 9.1. It is now Home Office policy to accept the views of a qualified social worker in relation to a claimant's age: see *Best Practice: Unaccompanied Asylum and Non-asylum Children*, the UK Immigration Service, version 01.01.04, para 1.3. See also *R (on the application of B) v Merton London Borough Council* [2003] EWHC 1689 (Admin), [2003] 4 All ER 280; *R (on the application of T) v Enfield* [2004] EWHC 2297 (Admin); *R (on the application of C) v Merton London Borough Council* [2005] EWHC 1753 (Admin) and *R (on the application of A) v Liverpool City Council* [2007] EWHC 1477 (Admin) and CHAPTER 12 above. See also *R (on the application of A) v Croydon London Borough Council* [2008] EWHC 2921 (Admin), [2008] All ER (D) 19 (Dec), *R (on the application of A) v Croydon London Borough Council; R (on the application of M) v Lambeth London Borough Council* [2009] UKSC 8, [2009] 1 WLR 2557, [2010] 1 All ER 469, [2010] 1 FLR 959; and *R (on the application of F) v Lewisham London Borough Council* [2009] EWHC 3542 (Admin), [2010] 2 FCR 292, [2010] 1 FLR 1463.
2   Letter to Tim Crowley, 26 February 2004.
3   *Policy Bulletin 75*, 'Section 55 (late claims) 2002 Act Guidance' – revised version, paras 7.22–7.24.

'Destitute' or likely shortly to become 'destitute'

14.117 In order for asylum seekers to obtain support under the asylum support scheme, they must appear to the Secretary of State to be either destitute or likely to become destitute within 14 days.[1] Where the question arises in respect of a person who is already a supported person or in relation to persons including a supported person, the period is 56 days.[2] The Secretary of State has a power to provide support to such persons. That power becomes a duty where the asylum seeker's claim includes a claim under the Refugee Convention (ie is not made solely on Article 3 grounds), the asylum seeker or his or her family member applies for support and the Secretary of State thinks that he or she is eligible for support.[3] A person is destitute if he or she either[4] does not have 'adequate accommodation' or the means to secure it or has adequate accommodation or the means of getting it but cannot meet his or her other 'essential living needs'. Statutory rules set out what may and what may not be taken into account in determining this issue.[5] The needs that are referred to in the asylum support provisions are generally current needs. The concept of 'entitlement' over a particular period, which exists in social security law, does not form part of the scheme of asylum support, so that asylum seekers may face difficulties in seeking to 'backdate' support.[6]

[1]   IAA 1999, s 95(1), Asylum Support Regulations 2000, SI 2000/704, reg 7(a),
[2]   Asylum Support Regulations 2000, SI 2000/704, reg 7(b).
[3]   Asylum Seekers (Reception Conditions) Regulations 2005, SI 2005/7, reg 5(1), see also Directive 2003/9/EC and **14.98**.
[4]   IAA 1999, s 95(2).
[5]   IAA 1999, s 95(5)–(8) and SI 2000/704, regs 6, 8–9.
[6]   *R v Hammersmith London Borough Council, ex p Isik* (19 September 2000, unreported), CA. But see *ASA 01/02/0202*, paras 4 and 14 where an adjudicator held an asylum seeker legally entitled to amounts due from the date of the asylum support application to the date when he was granted indefinite leave to remain and became entitled to social security benefit, subject only to deduction for backdated income support (as to which see **14.96** above). The applicant may still be able to claim backdated support in circumstances when either the Home Office is at fault or the applicant is at fault, but has a genuine reason for requesting a backpayment. For the considerations required to assess applications in both instances, see *Home Office Guidance, Back payment of Asylum Support*, version 4, 15 July 2014.

Deciding whether a person is destitute under the statutory test

14.118 To determine whether an applicant for support and any dependants are 'destitute' or 'likely to become destitute', the Secretary of State must consider whether they have 'adequate accommodation' or any means of obtaining it, and whether or not they can meet their other 'essential living needs'.[1] In relation to both accommodation and essential living needs, the Secretary of State must take into account any of the following in relation to the applicant *or* his or her dependants:[2]

- any income they have or which they may reasonably be expected to have;
- any other support which is available or which may reasonably be expected to be available;[3] and
- any of the following assets, held in the UK or elsewhere, which might reasonably be expected to be available: cash, savings, investments (including income bonds, life assurance policies, pension schemes, stocks and shares, and unit trusts), land, vehicles, goods for trade or business.

This might also include support from friends and relatives in the UK or from voluntary organisations.[4] Assets which do not fall into these categories including items of jewellery, personal clothing, bedding and medical or optical items must be disregarded. Applicants are, however, required to disclose items of jewellery or watches worth over £1,000 and to inform the Secretary of State immediately if they are sold and how much was received for them, so that the level of support may be adjusted accordingly.[5] The Home Office may grant an applicant support on a limited basis to allow them to sell property, for example, six months for a house. The sum received from the sale is treated as cash or savings and taken into account when the Home Office is deciding whether or not to provide support. When deciding whether an applicant is destitute, the Home Office must ignore any assets belonging to the applicant or their dependants that are not listed in the guidance, and any support or temporary support currently provided to the applicant or their dependants, or that they may be provided with.[6] The Secretary of State uses Home Office internal threshold tables, based loosely on what it would provide, a rule of thumb for the different categories of asylum seeker (below) to determine whether they are able to meet their essential living or accommodation requirements.[7] If the application for support relates to more than one person, the Secretary of State will consider whether the group taken as a whole is destitute or likely to become so.[8] The Secretary of State applies the same approach when considering whether to continue to provide support for those already supported, and their dependants who are already being supported or are being added to the application for support.

[1] *Home Office Guidance, Help and Guidance for asylum support manual application form*, version 8, April 2013, chapters 9 and 10.

[2] IAA 1999, s 95(1), (3).

[3] Asylum Support Regulations 2000, SI 2000/704, reg 6(4)–(5).

[4] For example, the asylum support adjudicators have held that 'emergency money' provided by a relative and not returned may be taken into account (*ASA 00/05/0011*), as may money which the asylum seeker has had, if he or she cannot provide a reasonable explanation of its disposal (*ASA 00/06/0017*) (drawing on conventional social security law: Commissioner's Decision *R(SB) 38/85*); *ASA 00/06/0020*).

[5] SI 2000/704, reg 6(3), (6), *Home Office Guidance, Help and Guidance for asylum support manual application form*, version 8, April 2013, chapter 10.

[6] See *Home Office Guidance, Assessing Destitution*, version 2, 3 July 2014, chapter 4 for destitution threshold tables (in section 4 determinations).

[7] IAA 1999, s 95(4); SI 2000/704, reg 5(1).

[8] SI 2000/704, reg 5(2).

Determining whether a person can meet their 'essential living needs'

14.119 For the purposes of deciding whether a person can meet their essential living needs, certain items are treated as not essential. Inability to pay for sending or receiving faxes, photocopying, buying or using computer facilities, travelling expenses, toys and other recreational items, and entertainment expenses are not relevant to determining destitution[1] (although if a person is found to be destitute, these costs may be met by the Secretary of State either as expenses incurred in connection with the asylum claim or 'exceptional' circumstances). The regulations appear to exclude *any* travelling requirements which a person may have[2] except the costs of the initial journey to asylum support accommodation, or to the applicant's notified address if he or she is not going to asylum support accommodation.[3] The fact that any other need that a person may have is not expressly excluded does not automatically convert it into an 'essential living need' so as to oblige the Secretary of State to take into account an inability to meet it in deciding destitution;[4] The Secretary of State will decide for herself whether any claimed need is essential for the person's living. However, in *Ouji*[5] Collins J held that 'essential living needs' were to be considered from the standpoint of an ordinary person without disabilities, and that individual disability was not a matter to be taken into account by the Secretary of State. This suggests a somewhat Procrustean approach to the issue, seemingly at odds with a human rights-based consideration of the legislation.

1   IAA 1999, s 95(8), Asylum Support Regulations 2000, SI 2000/704, reg 9(3)–(4).
2   SI 2000/704, reg 9(4)(d).
3   SI 2000/704, reg 9(4)(d), (5).
4   SI 2000/704, reg 9(6).
5   *R (on the application of Ouji) v Secretary of State for the Home Department* [2002] EWHC 1839 (Admin), [2003] Imm AR 88.

Clothing

14.120 In deciding whether a person can meet their essential living needs as regards clothing, the Secretary of State cannot take into account personal clothing preferences.[1] The rule is designed to prevent applications based on inability to buy clothing that is more expensive than that which is reasonably required, such as fashion items or designer wear. The Secretary of State must, however, take into account individual circumstances, including health or cultural needs and weather and hygiene requirements, in deciding whether a person can meet their clothing needs.[2]

1   IAA 1999, s 95(7)(b); Asylum Support Regulations 2000, SI 2000/704, reg 9(1)–(2).
2   SI 2000/704, reg 9(2).

Determining whether a person has 'adequate' accommodation

14.121 If a person applies for support, including accommodation, but already has accommodation, the Secretary of State must decide whether the existing accommodation is 'adequate'. Similarly, if a person who is already being supported by the Secretary of State without the provision of accommodation, requests it, the Secretary of State will need to decide whether the accommodation available to the applicant is adequate or whether the Secretary of State should be providing accommodation. In deciding either of these questions,[1] the Secretary of State must have regard to whether:[2]

- it is 'reasonable' for the person to continue to occupy the accommodation;
- the person can afford to pay for the accommodation;
- entry to the accommodation may be gained by the asylum seeker;
- if the accommodation is a houseboat, caravan or some other moveable structure or vehicle which may be lived in, there is somewhere where the person is able to place it and reside in it;
- the person may live in the accommodation together with his or her dependants;
- the asylum seeker or a dependant is likely to suffer harassment, threats or domestic violence if he or she continues to live in the accommodation ('domestic violence' means violence from a person who is or has been a close family member, or threats of violence from such a person that are likely to be carried out).

The Secretary of State may ignore any of the above matters, except the affordability of the accommodation and whether it is temporary accommodation or other emergency accommodation, if the asylum seeker wishes to stay there.[3] There are also certain matters which *cannot* be taken into account in determining whether a person has adequate accommodation,[4] namely: the fact that the person does not have an enforceable right to stay in the accommodation; that it is shared or temporary; and its location. However, the word 'adequate' in section 95 of the IAA 1999 should not be interpreted so as to imply that a lower standard of accommodation might be appropriate for a disabled child than accommodation that was suited to a disabled adult under section 21 of the National Assistance Act 1948.[5]

[1]   The regulations apply to either situation: Asylum Support Regulations 2000, SI 2000/704, reg 8(1)(a)–(b).
[2]   IAA 1999, s 95(5)(a); SI 2000/704, reg 8(1)(a)–(b), (3)–(6).
[3]   SI 2000/704, reg 8(2).
[4]   IAA 1999, s 95(5)–(6).
[5]   *R (on the application of A) v National Asylum Support Service* [2003] EWCA Civ 1473, [2004] 1 All ER 15.

Reasonable to continue to occupy

14.122 In deciding whether it is reasonable for an asylum seeker to continue to occupy accommodation,[1] the Secretary of State may have regard to the general housing circumstances which exist in the district[2] of the local government housing authority in which the accommodation is situated.[3]

[1]   Asylum Support Regulations 2000, SI 2000/704, reg 8(3)(a).
[2]   By SI 2000/704, reg 8(6)(b) 'district' for these purposes is given the same meaning as in s 217(3) of the Housing Act 1996.
[3]   SI 2000/704, reg 8(4).

Affordability of the accommodation

14.123 In determining whether the asylum seeker can afford to pay for the accommodation,[1] the Secretary of State must take account any income or assets within a specified class, see **14.118**, which is or are available to him or her or any dependant, otherwise than by way of asylum support or temporary asylum support, or might reasonably be expected to be so available; the costs in respect of the accommodation and the asylum seeker's other reasonable living expenses.[2]

[1]   Asylum Support Regulations 2000, SI 2000/704, reg 8(3)(b).
[2]   SI 2000/704, reg 8(5)(a)–(c).

Domestic violence

14.124 The Home Office in its *Policy Bulletin* on the subject defines domestic violence as including any violence between current and former partners in an intimate relationship, and family members, wherever and whenever the violence occurs. The violence may include physical, sexual, emotional or financial abuse. The threatening individual in question does not have to formally live with the applicant but it is expected that they would normally stay at the same address.[1] Accommodation providers must give paramount importance to the safety of victims of abuse and their children, and ensure that victims and any children are transferred to alternative accommodation that is safe and secure immediately, and no prior consent from the Secretary of State is required if the victim feels unable safely to return to his or her previous address. If this is impracticable or the victim needs accommodation with support, an accommodation provider can refer the victim to a refuge and the Secretary of State will pay for this accommodation or consult with a local authority about the action to take. If a victim flees from asylum support accommodation on account of domestic violence and finds alternative accommodation, the Secretary of State will pay the reasonable costs of such accommodation or a reasonable contribution towards the costs.[2] The Secretary of State will also provide the victim with interim support vouchers. Accommodation providers must warn offenders of the possible consequences of their abuse, which includes prosecution and loss of their accommodation and support.[3] Victims will eventually be re-housed in alternative asylum support accommodation in either the same or another area. Whilst the Secretary of State is not allowed to have regard to a person's preference as to the locality of accommodation, victims will be consulted regarding the safety of the proposed area.[4]

[1] *Home Office Guidance, Asylum support instructions: Policy Bulletins*, version 2, 29 September 2014, para. 23.2 (replacing *Policy Bulletin 70, Domestic Violence* which in turn replaced the references to domestic violence in *NASS Policy Bulletin 18, Dealing with Allegations of Racial Harassment, General Harassment and Domestic Violence*, from 23 January 2004).

[2] *Help and Guidance for Asylum Support Manual Application form* (Version 8) (April 2013), 'Section 22 & 23: Special accommodation and /or circumstances questions'.

[3] Offenders may be evicted:, *Home Office Guidance, Asylum support instructions: Policy Bulletins*, version 2, 29 September 2014, para 23.3. If an asylum seeker reports domestic violence to a one-stop service, or a one-stop service suspects domestic violence is occurring, it should refer the victim to other appropriate agencies, such as the police and social services and, if the victim consents, it should also report the matter to the asylum support investigations team leader and the accommodation provider. (It is preferable that a victim should not have to resort to asylum support initial accommodation, but if no alternative is immediately available, the one-stop agency may admit the victim and any children to such accommodation in its own region.) Voluntary organisations in other regions cannot admit the victim to emergency accommodation: *Policy Bulletin*, para 23.4. The asylum support investigations team leader should also convene a case conference usually within a week to decide on future accommodation and what action to take in relation to the abuser. He or she should also arrange for the victim to have a suitable interpreter at that conference: *Policy Bulletin*, para 23.6.

[4] *Home Office Guidance, Asylum support instructions: Policy Bulletins*, version 2, 29 September 2014, para 23.6.

Racist incidents

14.125 Asylum support policy involving racist incidents and harassment is contained in *Policy Bulletin 81*. The Secretary of State adopts the definition of a racist incident contained in the report of the Stephen Lawrence Inquiry, ie 'any incident which is perceived to be racist by the victim or any other person'.[1] A racist incident may or may not be a crime in policing terms.[2] The safety and security of the victims of racist incidents must be ensured, and accommodation providers (with the agreement of the Secretary of State) must urgently arrange safe temporary housing where they have concerns for the victim's immediate safety.[3] A permanent transfer must be arranged if there is no prospect of a victim's safe return to the former address, or where, following a report to the police, the police support a transfer.[4] Emergency accommodation must be arranged by the Secretary of State's regional staff where no safe temporary or permanent transfer can be arranged.[5] Accommodation which has become unsafe through racial harassment or where the incident has been reported to the police and the police support the relocation of the victim cannot be considered adequate.[6]

1   *Home Office Guidance, Asylum support instructions: Policy Bulletins*, version 2, 29 September 2014, Chapter 17 (replacing *Policy Bulletin 81, Racist Incidents*, which in turn replaced *Policy Bulletin 18, Dealing with Allegations of Racial Harassment, General Harassment and Domestic Violence*. The *Policy Bulletin* requires accommodation providers to be aware of the *Code of Practice for social landlords*: 'Tacking Racial Harassment', published by the Office of the Deputy Prime Minister.
2   *Home Office Guidance, Asylum support instructions: Policy Bulletins*, version 2, 29 September 2014, para.17
3   *Home Office Guidance, Asylum support instructions: Policy Bulletins*, version 2, 29 September 2014, para 17.5
4   *Home Office Guidance, Asylum support instructions: Policy Bulletins*, version 2, 29 September 2014, para 17.5
5   *Home Office Guidance, Asylum support instructions: Policy Bulletins*, version 2, 29 September 2014, para 17.5
6   *Home Office Guidance, Asylum support instructions: Policy Bulletins*, version 2, 29 September 2014, para 17.6;. See, however, *R (on the application of Gezer) v Secretary of State for the Home Department* [2003] EWHC 860 (Admin) (upheld at [2004] EWCA Civ 1730) for an example of 'worst practice' in responding to racist violence affecting a dispersed family. See also **14.137** below.

EXCLUSION FROM SUPPORT

14.126 The following categories of people are excluded from asylum support:[1]

(1)   persons not excluded from obtaining social security benefits by their immigration status;

(2)   persons not treated by the Home Office as having claimed asylum or as the dependants of an asylum seeker;

(3)   persons eligible to obtain interim support (now obsolete);

(4)   persons who have been offered support under another provision of the 1999 or 2002 Act;[2]

(5)   persons who have not claimed asylum as soon as reasonably practicable, where provision of support is not necessary to avoid a breach of their human rights;[3]

(6)   persons who are nationals of other EEA States[4] or who have been granted refugee status[5] in those states;

(7)   failed asylum seekers who fail to co-operate with removal directions;

(8)   a person within the UK in breach of the immigration laws within the meaning of section 50A of the British Nationality Act 1981 who is not an asylum seeker; and

(9)   failed asylum seekers with dependent children who have without reasonable excuse failed to take reasonable steps to leave the UK voluntarily or to place themselves in a position where they can do so.[6]

Categories (1)–(4) are discussed in turn below, and category (5) has been dealt with at **14.113** above. Categories (6)–(9) are dealt with under the rubric of community care provision. All the categories except for category (5) are also excluded from temporary asylum support,[7] as well as from asylum support.[8] It follows, therefore, that since the Secretary of State has no power to provide support for people in these categories, support will be refused or brought to an end as soon as one of the conditions applies. Emergency accommodation may be provided by the Secretary of State for people in category (5) whilst reconsidering a refusal of support, if it is believed that there is a seriously arguable case that a failure to provide asylum support will lead to a breach of the ECHR.[9] Asylum support cannot be provided to a person in categories (6)–(9). The responsibility falls on the relevant local authority to provide temporary accommodation if this is necessary to prevent a breach of Convention rights or EU Treaty rights. The local authority may make travel arrangements to return persons in category (6) to the relevant EEA State and to provide temporary accommodation to a person in category (6) until the travel arrangements have been made and they fail to comply with them.[10] Provision may be made to accommodate persons in category (8) where that person has not failed to co-operate with removal directions.[11] Accommodation under the Withholding and Withdrawal of Support (Travel Assistance and Temporary Accommodation) Regulations 2002, may only be provided if the person has with him a dependent child and may include arrangements for that child.[12] Travel arrangements for those in category (8) may be made under section 2 of the Local Government Act 2000 if necessary to avoid a breach of human rights protected under the ECHR.[13] Provision for persons in categories (7)–(9) may be available under section 4 of the IAA 1999, which is dealt with at **14.174T** below.

[1] IAA 1999, s 95(2); Asylum Support Regulations 2000, SI 2000/704, reg 4; NIAA 2002, ss 51, 55, Sch 3.
[2] NIAA 2002, s 51 (in force from a date to be appointed).
[3] NIAA 2002, s 55. This only applies to asylum seekers without children.
[4] NIAA 2002, Sch 3, para 5.
[5] NIAA 2002, Sch 3 para 4,
[6] NIAA 2002, Sch 3, paras 3–7A (para 7A inserted by AI(TC)A 2004 s 9). Sch 3, para 1(1) amended on 28 March 2012 by Localism Act 2011 (Consequential Amendments) Order 2012, SI 2012/961, Sch 1, para 4, adding para (ka) which excludes support for applicants subject to local authority's general power of competence.
[7] SI 2000/704, reg 4(8)–(9); NIAA 2002, s 51(2)(c) (not yet in force).
[8] By exclusion from the provisions of the IAA 1999 that require the Secretary of State to provide support: see IAA 1999, s 95(1)–(2); Asylum Support Regulations 2000, SI 2000/704, reg 4; but see also Asylum Seekers (Reception Conditions) Regulations 2005, SI 2005/7, reg 5.
[9] Letter to Tim Crowley, Inter-Agency Co-ordination Team, 18 November 2003; see **14.114** above.
[10] NIAA 2002, Sch 3, paras 8–9; Withholding and Withdrawal of Support (Travel Assistance and Temporary Accommodation) Regulations 2002, SI 2002/3078, reg 3. Where a local authority proposes to make travel arrangements for a person and his or her child, they must consider rights arising under the ECHR, Art 8 and the child's welfare in the proposed country of return, see *R (on the application of M) v Islington London Borough Council* [2004] EWCA Civ 235, [2005] 1 WLR 884, [2004] 4 All ER 709, ; and in respect of human rights issues before local authorities generally, see *Clue v Birmingham City Council (Shelter intervening)* [2010] EWCA Civ 460, [2010] 4 All ER 423, [2011] 1 WLR 99, (2010) Times, 7 May. A local authority could decide to pay for the person concerned to return home: *R (on the application of Kimani) v Lambeth London Borough Council* [2003] EWCA Civ 1150, [2004] 1 WLR 272. This option is not available to deal with other excluded categories, however see *R (on the application of Grant) v Lambeth London Borough Council* [2004] EWHC 1524 (Admin) in respect of the use of section 2 of the Local Government Act 2000.
[11] Withholding and Withdrawal of Support (Travel Assistance and Temporary Accommodation) Regulations 2002, SI 2002/3078; reg 3.
[12] SI 2002/3078, reg 3(4).
[13] *R (on the application of Grant) v Lambeth LBC* [2004] EWHC 1524 (Admin).

Exclusions in group applications for support in categories 1–3

14.127 Persons applying for asylum support not for themselves alone but for others as well, or included in a joint application, are only excluded if every person who is included in that application is excluded from asylum support for any of the three reasons in categories (1)–(3).[1] On its face, the purpose of this provision appears to be to ensure that groups containing 'mixed' applicants are brought within the asylum support scheme. However, households should in fact access all other available means of support before asylum support is made available,[2] and so asylum seekers whose spouses may claim social security benefit may apply for asylum support, but deductions will be made reflecting the amount of the benefit.[3] Accommodation will only be provided by the Secretary of State if what is otherwise available is inadequate (see **14.121** above).

[1] Asylum Support Regulations 2000, SI 2000/704, reg 4(3)–(4); in particular because reg 4(3)(c) refers to each person as falling within any of the categories in reg 4(4); this exclusion only applies to applications for support, not once support has been approved: *ASA 00/06/0018*.

[2] *Policy Bulletin 11, Mixed Households.*

[3] This is the approach which has been applied by the asylum support adjudicators: *ASA 00/07/0039; 00/08/0033; 00/09/0054, ASA 01/02/0202*, citing SI 2000/704, reg 6 that requires the Secretary of State to take into account any other support which is available to the principal or any dependant.

Exclusion where applicant is the dependant of a supported asylum seeker in categories 1–3

14.128 A person is not excluded under categories (1)–(3) whether applying for themselves alone or as part of a joint application, if, when the application is made, the person is the dependant of a person already receiving asylum support.[1]

[1] Asylum Support Regulations 2000, SI 2000/704, reg 4(7). 'Dependant' for these purposes bears precisely the same meaning as dependant of asylum seeker: reg 2(4). See **14.105** above.

Persons not excluded from obtaining social security benefits by their immigration status

14.129 An asylum seeker is excluded from support if, as a sole applicant, he or she is not excluded from obtaining income-based jobseeker's allowance, income support, income-related employment and support allowance, or universal credit through his or her immigration status.[1] Those affected by this exclusion are asylum seekers who, for the purpose of these social security benefits, are exempted from the 'subject to immigration control' test. They are set out at **14.9**. The regulations do not exclude from access to asylum support all the possible categories of asylum seekers who might be able to obtain these benefits.[2] For example, they do not exclude persons who, although they have applied for asylum, still have leave to enter or remain in the UK which is not subject to a condition of not having recourse to public funds, nor as the result of an undertaking, nor leave automatically granted by the law while an appeal is pending.[3] Thus, a person who claims asylum while in the UK as a student may be eligible for social security benefits and asylum support. Nor do the regulations exclude EEA nationals, although Schedule 3 to the NIAA 2002 applies to exclude them. The Secretary of State may refuse support to persons who have access to social security benefits. Proof may also be required from the Jobcentre Plus that benefit has been refused before providing support to asylum seekers who were previously entitled.

1   Asylum Support Regulations 2000, SI 2000/704, regs 4(2), reg 4(6)(a) as amended from 27 October 2008 by the Employment and Support Allowance (Consequential Provisions) (No 3) Regulations 2008 SI 2008/1879 and from 29 April 2013 by universal credit (Consequential, Supplementary, Incidental and Miscellaneous Provisions) Regulations SI 2013/630, Pt 3(7), reg 59(b) following the introduction of Universal Credit; and by reg 4(6)(b) as amended by the Employment and Support Allowance (Consequential Provisions No 2) Regulations (Northern Ireland) 2008, SR 2008/412, reg 9(a), this also includes income-based jobseeker's allowance, income support, income-related employment and support allowance, or housing benefit in Northern Ireland provided under the Jobseekers (Northern Ireland) Order 1995, SI 1995/2705, the Social Security Contributions and Benefits (Northern Ireland) Act 1992, and Pt 1 of the Welfare Reform Act (Northern Ireland) 2007.

2   These are persons who may be seeking asylum in the UK but are not excluded from benefit generally by s 115(9) of the IAA 1999. Section 115(9) was amended on 1 April 2013 by the Welfare Reform Act 2012 (Commencement No 8 and Savings and Transitional Provisions) Order 2013, SI 2013/358, Sch 14(1), para 1 subject to savings and transitional provisions specified in SI 2013/358, arts 9–10. Under Section 115(3) persons subject to immigration control are precluded from entitlement to universal credit, income-based jobseekers allowance, state pension credit, income-related allowance, employment and support allowance, personal independence payment, attendance allowance, severe disablement allowance, carers' allowance, disability living allowance, social fund payment, health in pregnancy grant, and child benefit; unless otherwise prescribed conditions are satisfied.

3   See the Immigration Act 1971, ss 3C and 3D (amended and inserted by s 11 of the IAN 2006 from 31 August 2006, SI 2006/2226). Further amended on 20 October 2014 by the Immigration Act 2014 which restricted the terms on which leave to remain is extended while application is being appealed).

Persons not treated by the Home Office as having claimed asylum or as the dependants of an asylum seeker

14.130 Those excluded from asylum support[1] under this provision are sole applicants who are not treated by the Home Office as 'an asylum seeker or dependent on an asylum seeker' for immigration purposes.[2] Since the definition of 'asylum seeker' under the asylum support provisions is wide, no asylum seeker should be excluded from support under this provision. But it might prevent support being provided, potentially, to a large group of persons who are 'dependants' for support purposes[3] but not for immigration purposes. A spouse, civil partner, unmarried or same-sex partner and minor children who accompany an asylum seeker to the UK, or who are mentioned by the asylum seeker in interview or written application, may be considered by the Home Office as dependants of the asylum claim. It has been Home Office policy that a dependent child who reaches 18 before a decision is made on the asylum seeker's application will continue to be treated as a dependant pending the decision and during the appeals process.[4] In addition, it has been Home Office policy that other relatives and those who do not arrive with the principal applicant may be treated as dependants on the asylum claim at the discretion of the Home Office, provided there has been no decision on the asylum application.[5]

1   This exclusion relates to people who have not made a 'claim for leave to enter or remain in the UK or for variation of any such leave' in which they are being considered an asylum seeker or

dependent on one. A claim for asylum or as the dependant of an asylum seeker is simultaneously a claim for leave to enter or remain in that capacity: see HC 395, paras 326A–335, 349.
2   Asylum Support Regulations 2000, SI 2000/704, reg 4(2), (4)(c).
3   SI 2000/704, reg 2(4) and see **14.105** above.
4   Home Office Guidance, *Dependants and former dependants*, 29 May 2014, para 3.8
5   Home Office Guidance, *Dependants and former dependants*, 29 May 2014, para 3.5

Persons offered alternative form of support

14.131 The Secretary of State may refuse to provide support, including asylum support[1] or temporary support,[2] to a person who has been offered another form of support.[3] The section, which comes into force on a date to be appointed, provides that the form of support offered may be dictated by administrative or other matters not relating to a claimant's personal circumstances, and may include the importance of testing the operation of a particular provision. The purpose of the section is to enable the Home Office to try out other forms of support, in particular accommodation centres, which were controversial from the first.

1   Ie, under IAA 1999, s 95.
2   Under IAA 1999, s 98.
3   Ie support under IAA 1999, s 4 (accommodation for persons temporarily admitted or released from detention) or under NIAA 2002, ss 17 or 24 (accommodation centres; provisional accommodation): NIAA 2002, s 51, in force from a date to be appointed.

SUSPENSION OR DISCONTINUATION OF SUPPORT

14.132 The Asylum Support Regulations additionally provide 11 separate grounds for suspension or discontinuation of support, as follows:[1]

(1)   reasonable grounds to believe the supported person or a dependant has committed a serious breach of the rules of collective accommodation;
(2)   reasonable grounds to believe that the supported person or a dependant has committed an act of seriously violent behaviour;
(3)   commission of an offence in relation to asylum support;
(4)   reasonable grounds to believe the supported person or a supported dependant has abandoned the address without notification or permission;
(5)   non-compliance with request for information about eligibility for or receipt of support;
(6)   failure without reasonable excuse to attend an interview about eligibility for or receipt of support;
(7)   non-compliance with request for information about asylum claim;
(8)   reasonable grounds to believe the supported person or a supported dependant has concealed financial resources and has unduly benefited from receipt of support;
(9)   non-compliance with a reporting requirement;
(10)   reasonable grounds to believe that the supported person or a supported dependant has made or sought to make a concurrent asylum claim in the same or a different name;
(11)   failure without reasonable excuse to comply with a relevant condition.

The criteria for suspension or discontinuation of asylum support were substantially amended by the 2005 Amendment Regulations, as a result of the entry into force in February 2005 of the EC Reception Directive[2] that was recast by the introduction of the EC Recast Reception Directive that came into force on 26 June 2013[3] with restricted grounds on which support may be reduced or withdrawn. There must now be an actual breach of conditions, or an actual commission of a criminal offence, to justify suspension or discontinuation of support; reasonable suspicion of these matters is no longer enough. The 'intentional destitution' ground contained in the unamended regulation 20 of the Asylum Support Regulations, has gone. We consider the grounds for suspension and discontinuation of support in more detail in the following paragraphs.

[1] Asylum Support Regulations 2000, SI 2000/704, reg 20, substituted by the Asylum Support (Amendment) Regulations 2005, SI 2005/11, from 5 February 2005. See *Policy Bulletin 83* 'Duty to offer support, family unity, vulnerable persons, withdrawing support' and *Asylum Process Guidance* 'Breach of Conditions' and 'Change of Address'.

[2] Council Directive 2003/9/EC laying down minimum standards for the reception of asylum seekers. See also the Asylum Seekers (Reception Conditions) Regulations 2005, SI 2005/7.

[3] Council Directive 2013/33/EC recasting standards for the reception of applicants for international protection. Provisions of Directive also applicable in connection with Directive 2011/95/EU (13 December 2011) regarding standards of qualification of third party nationals and stateless persons for international protection.

Procedural requirements for discontinuance of support

14.133 Asylum support can only be suspended or discontinued if an individual is already being supported by the Home Office.[1] Suspension is frequently used when the Home Office requires more time or information to decide whether to discontinue support provision completely. If the Home Office is satisfied that there has been a breach of conditions then it must take into account the extent of the breach when deciding whether or not to continue providing support. Some measure of emergency support should be provided following suspension or termination if it can still be shown that the individual is destitute and requires support to avoid a breach of their human rights. The Home Office is entitled to refuse second applications following discontinuance if there has been 'no material change in circumstances' since the original decision to suspend or discontinue support;[2] and there are no exceptional circumstances that justify considering the application, such as new evidence of destitution. If the Home Office does decide to consider an application for support in these circumstances, it is still entitled to refuse support.[3] In this instance, a decision to refuse or stop asylum support can be appealed to the First-tier Tribunal (Asylum Support Chamber) (see **14.174A** below). All the grounds for suspension or discontinuation of support under regulation 20 are discretionary.[4] Any decision to discontinue support must be taken individually, objectively and impartially, and reasons must be given.[5] Decisions must be based on the particular situation of the person concerned, and particular regard must be had to whether he or she is a vulnerable person, as described by Article 17 of the EC Reception Directive.[6] No one's asylum support may be withdrawn before a decision is made in accordance with the provisions.[7] The principle of proportionality must be applied to decisions on suspension or discontinuance of support.[8]

1   Asylum Support Regulations 2000, SI 2000/704, reg 20(1) refers to support for a 'supported person' or their dependants indicating that the asylum seeker has applied for and been granted support by the Home Office.

2   Asylum Support Regulations, reg 21(2) and reg 15, examples of relevant changed circumstances that must be notified to the Home Office include: being joined in the UK by a dependant; becoming employed or unemployed; becoming pregnant or having a child; going into hospital. See also *Home Office Guidance, Asylum support instructions: Policy Bulletins*, version 2, 29 September 2014, Chapter 14 (replacing *Policy Bulletin 84, Entertaining a further application for support*).

3   SI 2000/704, reg 21(3).

4   Asylum Support Regulations 2000, SI 2000/704, reg 20(1) substituted by the Asylum Support (Amendment) Regulations 2005, SI 2005/11, from 5 February 2005.

5   Council Directive 2003/9/EC, Art 16; SI 2004/704, reg 20(3) as substituted.

6   Council Directive 2003/9/EC, in force 5 February 2005; see also Asylum Seekers (Reception Conditions) Regulations 2005, SI 2005/7, reg 4. 'Vulnerable people' include (but are not limited to): minors, unaccompanied minors, disabled and elderly people, pregnant women, single parents with minor children, and persons who have been subjected to torture, rape or other serious forms of psychological, physical or sexual violence. See also *Policy Bulletin 83, Duty to offer support, family unity, vulnerable persons, withdrawing support*, version 5, 1 July 2014.

7   SI 2000/704, reg 20(4). The regulation appears on the face of it not to preclude suspension of support pending a reasoned decision, but the Directive prohibits withdrawal or reduction of support before a negative decision, which would preclude suspension: Council Directive 2003/9/EC, Art 16.5.

8   Council Directive 2003/9/EC, Art 16.4.

Serious breach of rules of accommodation

14.134 Where support is being provided to the supported person or a dependant in collective accommodation, defined as accommodation which is shared with any other supported person,[1] it may be suspended or discontinued if the Secretary of State has reasonable grounds to believe that the supported person or dependant has committed a serious breach of the rules of that accommodation.[2] There is likely to be considerable overlap between this provision and (11) (non-compliance with conditions) (see **14.144** below) but since suspension or discontinuance under this head can be triggered by reasonable belief, the breach of rules would have to be such as to pose a significant risk to the health, safety or comfort of other supported persons, the accommodation provider or the public, to justify withdrawal of support.

1   This can include accommodation in which only facilities (eg kitchen, bathroom) are shared: Asylum Support Regulations 2000, SI 2000/704, reg 20(6) (reg 20 substituted by SI 2005/11 reg 6 from 5 February 2005).

2   SI 2000/704 reg 20(1)(a) as substituted; Council Directive 2003/9/EC, Art 16.3; Council Directive 2013/33/EU, Art 20 (1) and (4).

Seriously violent behaviour

14.135 Asylum support for a supported person and/or any dependants of such a person may be suspended or discontinued if the Secretary of State has reasonable grounds to believe that any of them has committed an act of seriously violent behaviour, whether or not the act occurs in accommodation provided by way of asylum support, at the authorised address[1] or elsewhere.[2] There is as yet no published guidance on what constitutes 'seriously violent' behaviour, but the use of the qualifying adverb, and the power to suspend support on reasonable belief, both support an interpretation which requires at least actual bodily harm and possibly even the use of a weapon. It should certainly exclude violence in lawful self-defence, and would apparently exclude minor brawls and punch-ups.

[1] Defined for the purposes of the regulation as the accommodation provided by way of asylum support or, if none is provided, the address notified by the supported person to the Secretary of State in the application for asylum support, or in any change of address notified under reg 15 or under the Immigration Rules: SI 2000/704, reg 20(6)(a), (reg 20 substituted by SI 2005/11 from 5 February 2005).

[2] SI 2000/704, reg 20(1)(b) as substituted; Council Directive 2003/9/EC, Art 3; Council Directive 2013/33/EU, Art 20(4).

Commission of an offence in relation to asylum support

14.136 Asylum support for a supported person and/or any dependants of such a person may be suspended or discontinued if any of them has committed a criminal offence under Part VI of the IAA 1999, which is connected to the provision of support.[1] This includes matters such as[2] making false representations or producing false documents or false information,[3] or failure to notify a relevant change of circumstances,[4] or obstructing a person administering support,[5] or refusal or failure to answer questions, give information or produce documents.[6] Before amendment by the Asylum Support (Amendment) Regulations 2005,[7] it was not necessary for the supported person or dependant to have been convicted or even charged with an offence for this ground of exclusion to operate, as only 'reasonable grounds' for suspecting that an offence has been committed were required.[8] Now, however, the offence must actually have been committed, so asylum support should only be suspended or discontinued on conviction of a relevant offence.[9]

[1] Asylum Support Regulations 2000, SI 2000/704, reg 20(1)(c) (reg 20 substituted by SI 2005/11 from 5 February 2005).

[2] All the relevant offences are contained in IAA 1999, Pt VI. (See CHAPTER 15 below.)

[3] IAA 1999, ss 105(1)(a)–(b), 106(1)(a)–(b).

[4] IAA 1999, ss 105(1)(c)–(d), 106(1)(c)–(d).

[5] IAA 1999, s 107(1)(a).

[6] IAA 1999, s 107(1); SI 2000/704, reg 3(2)–(3), (5), Schedule, requiring applicants for support to provide the information contained in the prescribed form and authorising the making of further inquiries into any matter 'connected with the application'.

[7] SI 2005/11 (in force 5 February 2005).

[8] See SI 2004/704, reg 20(1)(b) before amendment (see fifth edition at 13.70).

[9] *Home Office Guidance, Breach of conditions instruction*, version 8, 24 October 2014, para. 2.1.

Abandonment of authorised address

14.137 The Secretary of State may suspend or discontinue support on reasonable grounds for believing that the supported person or any dependant being provided with support has abandoned the authorised address without first informing the Secretary of State or, if such a request was made, without permission.[1] The authorised address for these purposes is either the accommodation the Secretary of State is providing or, where accommodation is not provided, the address notified to the Home Office or a change of address given to the Home Office since the person has been provided with support.[2] It is not necessary for the Home Office to have granted temporary admission on the basis that the asylum seeker will live at the notified address, although a notice of temporary admission with the address on it will constitute the clearest evidence of the address notified to the Home Office by the asylum seeker. Where the person is traced, or voluntarily reports to police, to the Secretary of State or to an immigration officer, the regulations require a 'duly motivated' (reasoned) decision to be taken as to reinstatement of support, in whole or part, based on the reasons for the person's disappearance.[3] Support could not, we suggest, lawfully be withheld if a reasonable excuse was forthcoming for the person's disappearance. The provision is couched in terms of 'reasonable belief' of the Secretary of State because of the difficulties inherent in knowing when absence from accommodation amounts to abandonment of it.

[1]   Council Directive 2003/9/EC, Art 16.1(a); Council Directive 2013/33/EC, Art 20 (1)(a); Asylum Support Regulations 2000, SI 2000/704, reg 20(1)(d) (reg 20 substituted by SI 2005/11 from 5 February 2005). The domestic provision replaces two provisions in the unamended regulations; reg 20(1)(d) enabled support to be removed from persons who 'ceased to reside' at the authorised address, while reg 20(1)(e) did the same for absence from the address for more than seven consecutive days and nights, or a total of more than fourteen days and nights in any six-month period, in either case without the permission of the Secretary of State.
[2]   SI 2004/704 reg 20(6) as substituted.
[3]   SI 2004/704 reg 20(5) as substituted.

Non-compliance with request for asylum support information

14.138 Support may be suspended or discontinued for non-compliance within a reasonable period[1] with a request for information by the Secretary of State relating to the eligibility for, or receipt of, asylum support on the part of the supported person or a dependant.[2] The request may relate to a change of circumstances under regulation 15 of the Asylum Support Regulations.[3] There is no 'reasonable excuse' exception, but failure to have regard to a reasonable explanation for the failure would render the removal of support unlawful. This and the following 'procedural non-compliance' provisions are likely to be used for suspension of asylum support to enforce compliance, and total discontinuance of support as punishment for procedural non-compliance would, we suggest, be disproportionate and incompatible with the standards of the EC Reception Directives.[4]

[1]   Defined as at least five working days beginning with the day on which the request was received: Asylum Support Regulations 2000, SI 2000/704, reg 20(1)(e) (reg 20 substituted by SI 2005/11 from 5 February 2005).
[2]   Council Directive 2003/9/EC, Art 16.1(a); Council Directive 2013/33/EC, Art 20 (1) (b); SI 2004/704, reg 20(1)(e) as substituted.
[3]   See regulation 15, below.
[4]   Council Directive 2003/9/EC and Council Directive 2013/33/EC.

Failure to attend asylum support interview

14.139 Support may be suspended or discontinued if the supported person fails without reasonable excuse to attend an interview relating to the supported person's or dependant's eligibility for or receipt of asylum support.[1] See comments in the paragraph above.

1 Council Directive 2003/9/EC, Art 16.1(a); Council Directive 2013/33/EC, Art 20(1)(b); Asylum Support Regulations 2000, SI 2000/704, reg 20(1)(f) (reg 20 substituted by SI 2005/11 from 5 February 2005).

Non-compliance with request for information on asylum claim

14.140 Support may be suspended or discontinued if the supported person (or his or her dependant, if that person is an asylum seeker) has not complied, within a reasonable period,[1] with a request for information by the Secretary of State relating to the asylum claim.[2] The purpose of this provision is not altogether clear. There is provision within the asylum determination procedure for claims to be treated as withdrawn where claimants fail to attend a personal interview.[3] In earlier versions of the Immigration Rules, a person could have had his or her application for asylum determined adversely for non-compliance. Such claimants who then appealed against non-compliance refusals remained asylum seekers for the purposes of asylum support.[4] The support provision in issue here appears to seek to use the asylum support provisions to deny support pending appeal in this situation. Once again, although the provision does not have a 'reasonable excuse' exception, this is implicit in the discretionary nature of the suspension and discontinuance provisions.

1 Defined as at least ten working days beginning with the day on which the request was received: Asylum Support Regulations 2000, SI 2000/704, reg 20(1)(g) (reg 20 substituted by SI 2005/11 from 5 February 2005).
2 Council Directive 2003/9/EC, Art 16.1(a); Council Directive 2013/33/EC, Art 20(1)(b); SI 2004/704, reg 20(1)(g) as substituted.
3 HC 395, para 333C. For non-compliance refusal: see Chapter 12 above.
4 See definition of 'asylum seeker' in IAA 1999, s 94.

Concealment of financial resources

14.141 Asylum support may be suspended or discontinued if the Secretary of State has reasonable grounds to believe that a supported person or a supported dependant has concealed financial resources and has therefore unduly benefited from the receipt of asylum support.[1] This provision could be used to suspend support where a criminal offence is reasonably suspected, or where charges have been brought, pending a criminal trial.[2]

1 Council Directive 2003/9/EC, Art 16.1(b); Council Directive 2013/33/EC, Art 20(1)(b); Asylum Support Regulations 2000, SI 2000/704, reg 20(1)(h) (reg 20 substituted by SI 2005/11 from 5 February 2005).
2 This is because reg 20(1)(c) requires the commission of a criminal offence, rather than reasonable suspicion of one. See IAA 1999, s 105–106 regarding offences for false or dishonest representations.

Non-compliance with a reporting requirement

14.142 Asylum support may be suspended or discontinued where the supported person, or a supported dependant, has failed to comply with a reporting requirement.[1] For these purposes, a reporting requirement is a condition or restriction requiring the person concerned to report to the police, an immigration officer, or the Secretary of Stat;, imposed as a condition of temporary admission[2] or release from detention[3] or as a condition of bail.[4] Where the person is traced, or voluntarily reports to police, to the Secretary of State or to an immigration officer, the regulations require a 'duly motivated' (reasoned) decision to be taken as to reinstatement of support, in whole or part, based on the reasons for the person's non-compliance.[5]

[1]   Council Directive 2013/33/EC, Art 20(1)(b); Asylum Support Regulations 2000, SI 2000/704, reg 20(1)(i) (reg 20 substituted by SI 2005/11 from 5 February 2005).
[2]   Ie, under IA 1971, Sch 2, para 21; see CHAPTER 17 below.
[3]   Under IA 1971, Sch 2, para 21 or Sch 3, para 2; see CHAPTER 18 below.
[4]   Under IA 1971, Sch 2, para 22 (as amended on 28 July 2014 by Immigration Act 2014 c.22, Pt, s 7(2), or Sch 3, para 5, see CHAPTER 18 below: SI 2000/704, reg 20(6) as substituted.
[5]   SI 2004/704, reg 20(5) as substituted.

Further asylum claim

14.143 Asylum support may be suspended or discontinued if the Secretary of State has reasonable grounds to believe that the supported person, or a supported dependant, has made a claim for asylum ('the first claim') and, before the first claim has been determined, makes or seeks to make a further claim for asylum, being part of the first claim, in the same or a different name.[1] This is another provision which uses the asylum support provisions to police the substantive asylum determination regime, but the circumstances in which it is likely to be deployed are unclear. An attempt to make a second claim in a different name (whether or not a first claim is still pending) is a criminal offence for which support may be discontinued in any event. Further, the one-stop provisions in the 2002 Act require asylum claimants to set out, on demand by the Secretary of State, any other reasons they have for seeking to remain in the UK,[2] and they could hardly have asylum support discontinued as a result of a response which raised further asylum or Article 3 issues.

[1]   Asylum Support Regulations 2000, SI 2000/704, reg 20(1)(j) (reg 20 substituted by SI 2005/11 from 5 February 2005).
[2]   For the one-stop procedure: see Chapter 19 below.

FAILURE WITHOUT REASONABLE EXCUSE TO COMPLY WITH A RELEVANT CONDITION

14.144 The Secretary of State may provide support subject to conditions.[1] Any conditions which are made must be set out in writing[2] and given to the person who is being supported.[3] However, relevant conditions whose breach may lead to suspension or discontinuance of support are narrowly defined as conditions which make the provision of asylum support subject to actual residence by the supported person or a dependant for whom support is being provided in a specified place or location.[4] Behaviour which breaches conditions of support will not otherwise lead to suspension or discontinuance of support if it does not fall within one of the categories set out above. For exclusion on grounds of breach of a relevant condition (ie for failure to go to or live at the specified place) the conditions must have been set out in writing, and given to the asylum seeker;[5] even if it were possible in principle to remove from support an asylum seeker not given the conditions in writing, there will almost certainly be a 'reasonable excuse' for failure to comply in these circumstances.

1   IAA 1999, s 95(9). Breaches of conditions imposed under the subsection which relate to the use of the support provided, or to compliance with a restriction imposed under Immigration Act 1971, Sch 2, para 21 or Sch 3, paras 2 or 5 (temporary admission or release) (IAA 1999 s 95(9A) as inserted by NIAA 2002, s 50(1) from 7 November 2002) are dealt with separately above. In *ASA 00/09/0063* the adjudicator found that an allegation of a physical attack on a fellow asylum seeker at the premises gave the Secretary of State 'reasonable grounds to suspect' a breach of conditions before criminal proceedings were resolved. See now SI 2000/704 reg 20(1)(a) and (b), substituted by SI 2005/11.
2   IAA 1999, s 95(1).
3   IAA 1999, s 95(11); *ASA 00/10/1174* at para 14 and *ASA 00/10/0077*.
4   SI 2000/704, regs 19(2), 20(1)(k), as amended and substituted. Note too that, unlike the previous regulations, the provision requires actual breach of a relevant condition, not merely reasonable suspicion of breach; see also *Home Office Guidance, Breach of conditions instruction*, version 8, 24 October 2014.
5   IAA 1999, s 95(1), (11).

FAILURE TO TRAVEL

14.145 The Secretary of State has adopted a policy in relation to the failure to comply with dispersal arrangements, or to return to accommodation which has been left.[1] There have been a considerable number of decisions of asylum support adjudicators (now the First-tier Tribunal (Asylum Support)) on the circumstances which constitute a reasonable excuse for breach of this condition.[2] Many have concerned previous racial harassment. Asylum support adjudicators have held the nature, degree, frequency, persistence and organisation of harassment and its effect on the asylum seeker all relevant,[3] and whether it has been reported to the police and if so, whether police action has been effective.[4] The 'sufficiency of protection' test of refugee status itself[5] has even been applied to deciding whether a refusal to return to the site of previous racist harassment was reasonable in the light of the police response.[6] These decisions suggest that there is such a thing as an acceptable level of racial harassment (or a level of harassment which asylum seekers must accept, which is the same thing). In our view, a 'sufficiency of protection' test has no place in this area of the law. Reasonable excuse may also derive from a combination of factors such as ill-health, single parenthood with young children, language difficulties, and lack of proof that the Secretary of State had notified details of the travel arrangements.[7] Emotional trauma at the prospect of dispersal,[8] lack of awareness of the travel arrangements,[9] insufficient notice of dispersal decision[10] or finding alternative accommodation[11] have been held good reasons for not travelling to asylum support accommodation. Home Office caseworkers have had to minute their decisions and their reasons for reaching these decisions,[12] and failure to note claimants' reasons for not wishing to be dispersed led to appeals being allowed.[13] *Policy Bulletin 31: Dispersal Guidelines*, indicate situations in which asylum seekers should be allocated accommodation in London or the south-east of England, referring in particular to the need to continue medical treatment or be supported by family members.[14] *Policy Bulletin: Healthcare needs and pregnancy dispersal guidance*, provides particular guidance on its subject matter. The availability of specialist support from the Medical Foundation for the Care of Victims of Torture should also be taken into account.[15] The availability of treatment for those who are HIV positive is also a relevant factor.[16] The need to maintain regular contact with a child was also a reason for dispersal not to be reasonable; in the light of Article 8 of the European Convention on Human Rights.[17]

1   See *Policy Bulletin 17, Failure to travel to allocated accommodation: policy*, version 8, 24 May 2012.
2   However, the Court of Appeal held in *R (on the application of Secretary of State for the Home Department) v Chief Asylum Support Adjudicator and Dogan (Ahmet)* [2003] EWCA Civ 1673, (2003) Times, 13 November, that no right of appeal existed against withdrawal of support offered on condition of dispersa.
3   ASA 00/08/0034; 00/08/0036; 00/09/0044. In ASA 00/09/0066 and 00/08/0036, verbal abuse and gesturing was held insufficient. Frequent racist taunts were held sufficient to constitute reasonable excuse in 00/07/0024. See now Policy *Bulletin 81, Racist Incidents*.
4   *ASA 00/09/0044.*
5   See *Horvath v Secretary of State for the Home Department* [2001] 1 AC 489, [2000] 3 All ER 577, [2000] Imm AR 552.
6   *ASA 00/09/0044.*
7   *ASA 00/09/0046.*
8   *ASA 00/09/0057.*
9   *ASA 00/09/0058.*
10 *ASA/01/04/0269.*
11 *ASA 00/09/0067.*
12 *Policy Bulletin 17, Failure to travel to accommodation: policy*, version 8, 24 May 2012, para 2..
13 *ASA/02/02/1776; ASA/04/02/7597.* However, see fn 2 above.
14 See *ASA/02/02/1829; ASA/03/06/6559; ASA/01/06/ 0365; ASA/02/02/2002; ASA/02/07/4305; ASA/03/03/6140; ASA/00/11/0095; ASA/01/08/0714; ASA/00/1/0095; ASA/01/11/1307;* see also *R (on the application of Wanjugu) v National Asylum Support Service* [2003] EWHC 3116 (Admin), [2004] 2 All ER 776.
15 See *ASA/00/09/047.*
16 See *ASA/02/07/4305; ASA/03/10/7085.*
17 See *ASA/01/06/0369; ASA/04/01/7494.*

PROVISION OF SUPPORT

The EC Reception Directive

14.146 Asylum support has since February 2005 been subject to the minimum requirements of Council Directive 2003/9/EC of 27 January 2003 laying down minimum standards for the reception of asylum seekers.[1] We have noted at **14.132–14.133** above the changes to the procedures and criteria for suspension and discontinuance of support necessitated by the coming into force of the Directive. The Directive also required changes in the provision of asylum support. The Asylum Seekers (Reception Conditions) Regulations[2] transposes these requirements into domestic law. The power to provide asylum support to eligible persons becomes a duty.[3] In providing or arranging for the provision of accommodation for an asylum seeker and his or her family members under section 95 or section 98 of the IAA 1999, the Secretary of State must have regard to family unity and ensure, so far as reasonably practicable, that family members (spouse, civil partner, partner in a stable relationship and unmarried dependent minor children of either) are accommodated together (subject to their consent).[4] The special needs of asylum seekers and/or family members who are vulnerable, ie those who are minors, disabled, elderly, pregnant, single parents with minor children, and victims of torture, rape or other forms of psychological, physical or sexual violence,[5] must be taken into account, and there are duties to trace family members of unaccompanied minors so as to protect the minors' best interests.[6]

[1] OJ 2003 L 31/18.
[2] SI 2005/7.
[3] SI 2005/7, reg 5.
[4] SI 2005/7, regs 2–3. The duty does not apply when the Secretary of State is providing or arranging for the provision of accommodation of the child under IAA 1999, s 122: reg 3(3).
[5] SI 2005/7, reg 4(1)–(2). However, a person is only classified as vulnerable under the provision if they have had an individual evaluation of their situation which confirms that they have special needs: reg 4(3), and the Secretary of State is not obliged to carry out such an evaluation: reg 4(4). It will be for applicants' advisers to secure such assessments, whether through local authorities, by reference to their community care duties (see **14.175** below) or otherwise.
[6] SI 2005/7, reg 6.

Initial asylum support and temporary accommodation

14.147 The Secretary of State must provide support or arrange for temporary accommodation and support to be provided to an asylum seeker or the dependant of an asylum seeker who it appears may be destitute.[1] Various voluntary agencies funded by the Secretary of State to provide this support employ 'reception assistants' who are responsible for placing asylum seekers in temporary accommodation. Temporary support is given where it appears to the Secretary of State that an asylum seeker and any dependants may be destitute but no decision about providing asylum support has been made.[2] Where the asylum seeker is not accompanied by minor dependants, temporary support may also be provided while the Secretary of State decides whether the application for support was made as soon as reasonably practicable or is reconsidering a decision to refuse support under section 55 of the NIAA 2002.[3] Such initial accommodation will also be provided under section 95 of the IAA 1999 to those asylum seekers who have left asylum support accommodation alleging domestic violence, a racial incident, racial harassment or in other exceptional circumstances[4] and to those awaiting transportation to their dispersal accommodation.[5] If the Secretary of State refuses support, temporary accommodation ends the next day or exceptionally within seven days.[6] As with full asylum support, temporary accommodation may be provided subject to conditions, which must be given in writing to the recipients of temporary support.[7] There are no rules governing what can and cannot be provided by way of temporary support,[8] but the Secretary of State has adopted a number of policies on eligibility and procedures for new applicants and for those formerly on cash only support or who have previously left accommodation to which they were dispersed.[9]

[1] IAA 1999, s 98(1); Asylum Seekers (Reception Conditions) Regulations 2005, SI 2005/7, reg 5. The same definition of destitution applies as with full asylum support.
[2] IAA 1999, s 98(2). A funded voluntary agency may admit an asylum seeker and any dependants to initial accommodation if they wish to apply for asylum support and present a valid IS96 temporary admission form date-stamped by an Immigration Officer and bearing an 'applied for asylum on arrival' endorsement, or a 'letter authorising access to initial accommodation to a person who did not apply for asylum at a port of entry immediately on arrival into the UK' (NEAT01), see *Home Office Guidance, Asylum support instructions: policy bulletins*, version 2, 29 September 2014, (replacing *Policy Bulletin 73, Provision of Initial Accommodation*), Chapter 1, para 1.1.1
[3] NIAA 2002, s 55(5)(c).

4 See *Home Office Guidance, Asylum support instructions: Policy Bulletins*, version 2, 29 September 2014, Chapter 1, para 1.1.3.
5 See *Home Office Guidance, Eligibility and assessment of asylum support: instruction*, 22 August 2012.
6 *Home Office Guidance, Asylum support instructions: Policy Bulletins*, version 2, 29 September 2014, (replacing *Policy Bulletin 73, Provision of Initial Accommodation*), Chapter 1, para. 1.1.4.
7 IAA 1999, s 98(3), applying s 95(11).
8 IAA 1999, ss 96–97 (as amended on 29 April 2013 by Welfare Reform Act 2012, c.5, Sch 2, para 53); and Asylum Support Regulations 2000, SI 2000/704, deal with support provided under the full asylum support scheme (IAA 1999, s 95) rather than support provided as a temporary measure (IAA 1999, s 98).
9 *Home Office Guidance, Asylum support instructions: Policy Bulletins*, version 2, 29 September 2014, (replacing *Policy Bulletin 73, Provision of Initial Accommodation*), Chapter 1; see also *Home Office Guidance, Eligibility and assessment of asylum support: instruction*, 22 August 2012.

The kinds of asylum support provided

14.148 The Secretary of State may provide the following kinds of support to eligible asylum seekers and their dependants:[1]

- what appears to him to be essential living needs; and/or
- accommodation which appears to him to be adequate; and/or
- expenses, other than legal expenses and other prohibited expenses, in connection with the asylum claim; and/or
- expenses in attending bail hearings where the asylum seeker or their dependants are detained for immigration purposes;
- for the purposes of maintaining good order among supported persons, services in the form of education including English language lessons, and sporting or other developmental activities;[2]
- *if the circumstances of the particular case are exceptional,* any other form of support which the Secretary of State thinks necessary to enable the asylum seeker and their dependants to be supported.[3]

The Secretary of State may by order restrict the provision of support to those asylum seekers who are also being provided with asylum support accommodation.[4] An order may relate to particular geographical locations or to asylum seekers who made an application by or after a certain date.[5] Statistical data suggests that the majority of asylum seekers who are in receipt of support only assistance are in London and the south-east of England. Asylum seekers who decide not to remain in asylum support accommodation must supply the Secretary of State with their new address. Such persons cannot use their initial accommodation address or any other address previously provided by the Secretary of State as the place where they may be contacted.

1 IAA 1999, s 96(1).
2 IAA 1999, Sch 8, para 4; Asylum Support Regulations 2000, SI 2000/704, reg 14.
3 IAA 1999, s 96(2).
4 NIAA 2002, s 43.
5 NIAA 2002, s 43(2).

14.149 The Secretary of State may disregard any preference which an asylum seeker or dependant may have as to the way support is given.[1] In particular, the Secretary of State may in the future decide to provide asylum support by placing an asylum seeker and any dependants in an accommodation centre.[2] In deciding on the level and kind of support to provide to an applicant and his or her dependants or to anyone already being provided with support, the Secretary of State must take into account (other than by way of asylum support), income which they have or might reasonably be expected to have, support which is or might be reasonably expected to be available, and any assets which are or might reasonably be expected to be available (ie cash, savings, investments, land, cars or other vehicles, and goods held for the purpose of a trade or other business).³ The Secretary of State may take into account previous breach of a relevant condition on which the support has been or is being provided,⁴ but must have regard to the seriousness or triviality of the breach in deciding whether to alter the level of support and by how much.⁵ A relevant condition is one which makes the provision of asylum support subject to actual residence by the supported person or a dependant of his or hers for whom support is being provided in a specific place or location.⁶

¹ IAA 1999, s 97(7).
² NIAA 2002, s 22; in force from a date to be appointed.
³ Asylum Support Regulations 2000, SI 2000/704, reg 12(3).
⁴ SI 2000/704, reg 19(1).
⁵ SI 2000/704, reg 19(1) allows the Secretary of State to take into account the extent to which conditions have been complied with.
⁶ SI 2000/704, reg 19(2).

Providing essential living needs

14.150 Where the Secretary of State decides that a person needs support in relation to essential living needs, as a general rule, he or she will be provided with cash payments.¹ An additional single payment of £50, payable after every period of six months, has now been abolished.² A single, one-off 'maternity' payment of £300 may be provided to asylum seekers to assist with the costs of a newborn baby.³ A written application must be lodged by the father or mother close to the date of the birth, and the child must generally have been born to a Home Office supported person. A maternity payment may also be made in respect of a baby under three-months-old who was born outside the UK to an asylum seeker who subsequently qualified for asylum support or in other exceptional circumstances. From 3 March 2003, an additional weekly payment has been provided to pregnant women and to children under the age of three.⁴ There is provision for replacement of lost or stolen payments.⁵

¹ Asylum Support Regulations 2000, SI 2000/704, regs 10(2), 10A.
² SI 2004/1313, revoking reg 11 of the Asylum Support Regulations 2000, SI 2000/704. The single payment acknowledged that the target period of six months for deciding the claim (including any appeal) had not been met, and that after that period the asylum seeker was likely to have needs, which could not be met by the weekly payments.
³ *Policy Bulletin 37, Maternity Payments*, 20 July 2011 and *Home Office Guidance, Maternity payments and additional support*, 24 February 2011.
⁴ Asylum Support Regulations 2000, SI 2000/704, reg 10A; *Home Office Guidance, Maternity payments and additional support*, 24 February 2011. Babies under one currently receive an additional £5 per week, while those under three, and pregnant mothers receive £3.
⁵ See *Policy Bulletin 80, Backpayment of Asylum Support*, version, 11 July 2014.

Amounts provided

14.151 Regulation 3 of the Asylum Support (Amendment) Regulations 2011, SI 2011/907, amends reg 2 of the Asylum Support Regulations 2000, SI 2000/784, and sets out the current levels of support given to asylum seekers.[1] For the purposes of payment, to count as a married couple or civil partners, the couple who are married to or in a civil partnership with each other respectively, must be members of the same household.[2] To count as an unmarried couple or same-sex partners, the couple must be, although not married or in a civil partnership respectively, living together as though they are married or in a civil partnership.[3] A 'lone parent' is a person who is not a part of a married or unmarried couple, a civil partnership or a same-sex couple, who is the parent of a child under 18, and support is being provided for the child;[4] a 'single person' is a person who is neither a member of a married or unmarried couple, a civil partnership or a same-sex couple, nor the parent of a child under 18 for whom support is being provided.[5] The amounts payable will be reduced where the Secretary of State provides accommodation as part of the support which includes some provision for essential living needs, such as bed and breakfast or full board.[6] The standard weekly rates of asylum support were previously fixed each year by regulations which took effect from April every year. This scheme was halted in April 2011 when rates were frozen, leading to a cut in real terms over several years. In 2014 a claim for judicial review was brought by Refugee Action. The court held that the Home Secretary had acted irrationally and failed to take all relevant factors into account in accordance with her duties under the EU Reception Directive and the Immigration and Asylum Act 1999 to provide asylum seekers' essential living needs.[7] On 9 August 2014 the Home Secretary reviewed the level of support in the light of the judgment, but ultimately decided it should remain unchanged. This may be subject to further legal challenge.

[1] SI 2000/784, in force 18 April 2011, under which the rates are as follows:
  – married couple, unmarried couple, civil partners and same-sex couple at least one of whom is 18 or over but where neither is under 16: £72.54;
  – lone parent aged 18 or over: £43.94;
  – single person aged 25 or over (where decision made prior to 5 October 2009 and the person reached age 25 prior to that date): £42.62;
  – any other single person aged 18 or over: £36.62;
  – person aged at least 16 but under 18 (except a member of a qualifying couple): £39.80;
  – single person aged under 16: £52.96.
[2] SI 2000/704, reg 2(1).
[3] SI 2000/704, reg 2(1).
[4] SI 2000/704, reg 10(4)(b) and (d).
[5] SI 2000/704, reg 10(4)(c).
[6] SI 2000/704, reg 10(5).
[7] *R (on the application of Refugee Action) v Secretary of State for the Home Department* [2014] EWHC 1033 (Admin).

14.152 The amounts payable are less than the 'applicable amounts' of income support which similarly situated persons would be entitled to if they qualified, reflecting approximately 70 per cent of the applicable amounts of income support.[1] This is partly in recognition of the fact that the support is to be temporary[2] and does not need to include the cost of service bills, replacement items of clothing and household items which are usually provided.[3] The rules on provision for essential living needs are, however, all rules of thumb[4] which set out what an asylum seeker can generally expect to receive. In appropriate cases, the Secretary of State may provide more, or less, or make provision in a different form. Where an asylum seeker is married to or is the partner of someone who is in receipt of benefits in his or her own right, the Secretary of State must consider whether the asylum seeker's essential needs could properly be met from his or her income as some of this may be unavailable to him or her due to the partner's needs, and the needs of any of their dependants.[5] Similar provision is also made where some members are entitled to housing assistance or accommodation under Part 7 the Housing Act 1996.

1. Applicable amounts for income support are provided pursuant to the Social Security Contributions and Benefits Act 1992, s 124(4).
2. IAA 1999, s 97(5) (as amended by Welfare Reform Act 2012, s 8(1) (29 April 2013 regarding limitations on the award to the supported person.)
3. See para 305 of Explanatory Notes to the IAA 1999.
4. See Asylum Support Regulations 2000, SI 2000/704, regs 10(2).
5. *R (on the application of Secretary of State for the Home Department) (National Asylum Support Service) v Asylum Support Adjudicators* [2001] EWHC Admin 881, [2001] All ER (D) 13 (Nov). See also *Policy Bulletin 11, Mixed Households*, version 3, 3 June 2014.

Providing accommodation

14.153 The system of 'dispersal' was one of the most controversial aspects of the IAA 1999. In deciding upon the location and nature of the accommodation which a person will be given, the Secretary of State must have regard to the fact that support by way of accommodation is only being provided on a temporary basis until the claim to asylum (including any appeal) has been dealt with, and that it is generally desirable to provide accommodation for asylum seekers in those areas where there is a ready supply of accommodation.[1] But the Secretary of State may not have regard to any preferences of the asylum seeker as to the area in which he or she wishes the accommodation to be located, the nature of the accommodation to be provided;[2] or the nature and standard of the fixtures and fittings in the accommodation.[3] It may, however, take into account the asylum seeker's and his or her dependants' individual circumstances as they relate to their accommodation needs.[4] The court has been fairly generous in its approach, holding in *Ex p Mahida* that location close to a mosque was not merely a matter of preference, but was relevant to the applicant's religious and emotional needs and so to his or her welfare, in assessing adequacy of the accommodation.[5] The Secretary of State must also consider whether dispersal would amount to a breach of Article 8 of the European Convention on Human Rights.[6] Provision has also been made for the transportation and storage of the possessions of asylum seekers supported by the UK Border Agency.[7]

1. IAA 1999, s 97(1)(a) with reference to ss 94(3)–(4), 97(1)(b).
2. IAA 1999, s 97(2)(a), Asylum Support Regulations 2000, SI 2000/704, reg 13(2)(a).
3. SI 2000/704, reg 13(2)(b).
4. SI 2000/704, reg 13(2), and see *ASA 00/11/0110* at para 9, enabling consideration of the asylum seeker's family-related concerns.
5. *R v Islington London Borough Council, ex p Mahida* CO 2519/2000 (14 August 2000, unreported), QBD.
6. *R (on the application of Blackwood) v Secretary of State for the Home Department* [2003] EWHC 97 (Admin), [2003] 44 HLR 638, [2003] ACD 33, *(2003) Times.* 10 February.
7. *Home Office Guidance, Asylum support instructions: Policy Bulletins*, version 2, 29 September 2014, (replacing *Policy Bulletin 86, Possessions*).

14.154 Applying the above statutory criteria, Home Office general policy is to seek to disperse asylum seekers away from London and the south-east.[1] In allocating accommodation to someone who seeks to remain in that area, the Secretary of State will consider whether it is reasonable to disperse, whether such an allocation will meet the person's needs and whether the decision is compatible with the HRA 1998.[2] In determining what is reasonable in a particular case, consideration should be given to medical treatment, unaccompanied asylum-seeking children leaving care, family ties, education, ethnic group, religion, employment, legal advice and language.[3] Where an asylum seeker states that he wishes to stay in a particular area and accommodation is allocated elsewhere, the UK Border Agency should give written reasons for its decision.[4] The standard of accommodation provided is often less than adequate. There is no right of appeal to the First-tier Tribunal (Asylum Support) against the decision to disperse; however, it may be possible to bring a claim by way of an application for judicial review. In respect of a person who is already receiving medical treatment, dispersal may not be reasonable on account of the consequences occasioned by an interruption to treatment.[5] Guidance is also given concerning the dispersal of pregnant women.[6]

[1]   *Policy Bulletin 31, Dispersal Guidelines*, version 8, 2 July 2014, para 2. The *Bulletin* refers to section 97 of the IAA 1999, which requires the Secretary of State to have regard, in general, to the desirability of providing accommodation in areas in which there is a ready supply.
[2]   *Policy Bulletin 31, Dispersal Guidelines*, version 8, 2 July 2014, para 2
[3]   SI 2000/704, reg 13(2); see also *R (on the application of Wanjugu) v Secretary of State for the Home Department* [2003] EWHC 3116 (Admin), [2004] 2 All ER 776, where the court quashed a decision to disperse a claimant with post-traumatic stress disorder. See also **14.145** above. In respect of children leaving care, see *Home Office Guidance, Transition at age 18: instruction*, version 29, 16 July 2014.
[4]   *Policy Bulletin 31, Dispersal Guidelines*, version 8, 2 July 2014, para 2.
[5]   *Policy Bulletin 85*, 'Healthcare needs and pregnancy dispersal guidance', (2 August 2012) (replacing *Policy Bulletin 85: Dispersing asylum seekers with healthcare needs*).
[6]   *Policy Bulletin 85, Healthcare needs and pregnancy dispersal guidance*, (2 August 2012) (replacing *Policy Bulletin 61, Pregnancy*)

14.155 Family ties are clearly a key factor in the light of Article 8 of the ECHR. Although the instruction recognises the need to consider each case on its merits, the Secretary of State is of the view that 'in the absence of exceptional circumstances' relating to this factor, dispersal will normally be appropriate.[1] So far as education is concerned, where an asylum seeker has children who are about to take GCSE A or AS level exams, dispersal should be deferred.[2] The existence of an ethnic community in the preferred area is normally insufficient to militate against dispersal, as asylum support accommodation is all supposed to be in areas which boast an established ethnic minority community and are 'able to sustain a new ethnic group and voluntary and community infrastructures'.[3] If there is only one area where an asylum seeker can properly worship, then his or her request may be accommodated having regard to Article 9 of the ECHR (freedom of thought, conscience and religion).[4] In the case of new port and in-country applicants, where a referral[5] is made to the Medical Foundation for the Care of the Victims of Torture, the Secretary of State must give careful consideration to deferring dispersal from the south-east, and where, after initial assessment, the Medical Foundation accepts the applicant for treatment, the Secretary of State must give sympathetic consideration to providing local accommodation. The same applies to those already receiving treatment.[6] Sending a family to an inner city estate where racial abuse and hostility was prevalent did not breach Article 3 of the ECHR without evidence of a specific risk of the necessary ill-treatment.[7] In *Gezer* Moses J concluded that the Secretary of State was: (1) under an obligation to provide protection against a risk of treatment falling within Article 3 if he knew of, or ought to have known about it; (2) the level of protection he was required to provide was that which was reasonably available; (3) that level need not afford a guarantee against the danger but had to be reasonable, as a matter of practicality, common-sense and humanity, taking into account relevant policy considerations; (4) the measures to be taken are those which afford a real prospect of avoiding the danger; and (5) the extent of the risk will inform the extent to which protection should be offered.

[1]   *Policy Bulletin 31, Dispersal Guidelines*, version 8, 2 July 2014 para 2.3
[2]   *Policy Bulletin 31, Dispersal Guidelines*, version 8, 2 July 2014, para 2.4.
[3]   *Policy Bulletin 31, Dispersal Guidelines*, version 8, 2 July 2014, para 2.5.
[4]   *Policy Bulletin 31, Dispersal Guidelines*, version 8, 2 July 2014, para 2.6.
[5]   Normally the referral should be made by the reception assistant using the standard form at Annex A to former *Policy Bulletin 19, The Medical Foundation for the Care of Victims of Torture.*
[6]   *Home Office Guidance, The Medical Foundation for the Care of Victims of Torture*, 1 January 2009.
[7]   *R (on the application of Gezer) v Secretary of State for the Home Department* [2003] EWHC 860 (Admin), [2003] 64 HLR 972, [2003] ACD 80; (upheld by the Court of Appeal at [2004] EWCA Civ 1730).

14.156 If, applying the above factors, a decision is made to disperse an asylum seeker, he or she is likely to be provided with a document providing details, and stating that the support is provided on condition that the asylum seeker travels there in accordance with the enclosed travel instructions. A warning letter advises the person that travel will only be rearranged where there are exceptional reasons for not travelling at the appointed time. Failure to travel to the accommodation where a person does not have a reasonable excuse, will result in the person being required to leave their temporary accommodation, but the offer of support, conditional on travel to and residence in the specified location, will be kept open.[1]

[1]   Asylum Support Regulations 2000, SI 2000/704, regs 19–21, and see *Policy Bulletin 17, Failure to Travel to Allocated Accommodation*, version 8, 24 May 2014, para 2, 5.2 and 6.2 and *Policy Bulletin 28, Providing Travelling Expenses and Reimbursing Essential Travel Costs*, version 4, 2 November 2004. See **14.145** above. Withdrawal of support which was conditional on failure to travel to dispersal accommodation does not generally give rise to a right of appeal: *R (on the application of Secretary of State for the Home Department) v Chief Asylum Support Adjudicator and Dogan (Ahmet)* [2003] EWCA Civ 1673, (2003) Times, 13 November.

Expenses in connection with asylum claim

14.157 The Secretary of State may meet expenses connected with the asylum claim,[1] excluding 'legal' expenses such as the costs of paying a lawyer for preparation or for representation. Included are travel expenses of the asylum seeker (or those of witnesses) in attending the appeal or interviews or examinations in connection with the claim. Expenses in preparing and copying documents[2] and sending letters and faxes in order to obtain further evidence are also included. Travel expenses for a Medical Foundation assessment in connection with the asylum application or where referred by a GP should generally be met.[3] The Secretary of State also has power to pay for travel expenses incurred by an asylum seeker needing to comply with reporting restrictions.[4]

[1] IAA 1999, s 96(1)(c).
[2] See *Explanatory Notes to the IAA 1999*, at para 300.
[3] See Home Office Guidance, *The Medical Foundation for the Care of Victims of Torture*, 1 January 2009; and *Policy Bulletin 28, Providing Travelling Expenses and Reimbursing Essential Travel Costs*, version 4, 2 November 2004.
[4] NIAA 2002, s 69, in force 7 November 2002.

OTHER SERVICES

14.158 The Secretary of State may provide education services (including English language classes) and sporting or other developmental activities to any person who is receiving asylum support.[1] These services are not provided automatically, but may only be provided in order to 'maintain good order' among supported asylum seekers.[2] This does not require that good order has broken down before these services are provided, but that without the stimulation of sport, education and developmental activities, and the access to and integration with the wider community these activities entail, morale and thus 'good order' could be jeopardised.

[1] IAA 1999, Sch 8, para 4; Asylum Support Regulations 2000, SI 2000/704, reg 14.
[2] SI 2000/704, reg 14(1).

Contributions to support

14.159 In deciding what level of support to provide to a destitute asylum seeker, the Secretary of State must take into account the income, support and assets which are available or might reasonably be expected to be available to him or her or any dependant, otherwise than by way of asylum support.[1] The Secretary of State may set the asylum support for that person at a level which does not reflect the income, support or assets, or as an alternative to reducing the level of support, the Secretary of State may require that the asylum seeker makes a contribution from their own income or assets to the support being provided.[2] In these circumstances, the asylum seeker will be required to make payments directly to the Home Office.[3] Where support is provided with a requirement of a contribution by the asylum seeker, the Secretary of State may make it a condition of the provision of support that 'prompt payments' are made.[4]

[1] Asylum Support Regulations 2000, SI 2000/704, reg 12(3).
[2] SI 2000/704, reg 16(2).
[3] SI 2000/704, reg 16(3).
[4] SI 2000/704, reg 16(4).

National Health Service prescriptions/dental treatment/sight tests

14.160 When an application for asylum support is accepted, the Secretary of State will simultaneously issue the individual with an HC2 certificate entitling the holder to free NHS prescriptions, dental treatment, sight tests and wigs.[1] The asylum seeker may also be eligible for vouchers towards the costs of glasses, contact lenses and refunds on the costs of travel to and from hospital for NHS treatment.[2] Asylum seekers are currently entitled to the full range of NHS treatment free of charge.[3]

[1] Information on what asylum seekers may access is set out on NHS Choices: www.nhs.uk/N HSEngland/Healthcosts/Pages/help-with-health-costs.aspx.
[2] See below, **14.216**.
[3] See below, **14.216**.

CONDITIONS OF SUPPORT

14.161 The Secretary of State may provide support subject to conditions. A condition may relate any matter relating to the use of the support provided, or compliance with a restriction imposed under paragraph 21 of Schedule 2 to the 1971 Act (temporary admission or release from detention) or paragraph 2 or 5 of Schedule 3 to that Act (restriction pending deportation).[1] Any conditions must be set out in writing[2] and given to the person who is being supported.[3] Breach of conditions upon which support is provided may be taken into account in deciding whether to provide or continue support and the level or kind of support provided.[4]

[1] IAA 1999, s 95(9)–(9A).
[2] IAA 1999, s 95(10).
[3] IAA 1999, s 95(11).
[4] Asylum Support Regulations 2000, SI 2000/704, reg 19.

Change of circumstances

14.162 Supported persons are required to notify the Secretary of State of relevant changes in their circumstances.[1] The Secretary of State must be notified if the asylum seeker (or any dependant):[2]

- is joined in the UK by a dependant;
- receives or obtains access to any cash or savings, investments, land, cars or other vehicles, or goods for the purposes of trade or other business which have not previously been declared to the Secretary of State;
- becomes employed or unemployed;
- changes his or her name;
- gets married or forms a civil partnership;
- begins living with another person as if married to, or as if a civil partner of that person;
- gets divorced or becomes a former civil partner on the dissolution of his or her civil partnership;
- separates from a spouse or civil partner or from a person with whom they have been living as if married or as if a civil partner of that person;
- becomes pregnant;
- has a child;
- leaves school;
- begins to share accommodation with another person;
- moves to a different address or otherwise leaves accommodation;
- goes into hospital;
- goes to prison or some other form of custody;

- leaves the UK; or
- dies.

Where, as a result of notification of a change in circumstances, the Secretary of State believes that asylum support should be provided for a person for whom it is not currently provided (for example, a new dependant arriving or the birth of a child) or should not be provided for an existing recipient, or that asylum support is otherwise affected, the Secretary of State may make further inquiries of the person who gave the notification to determine what support should now be provided.[3] She may change the nature or level of the existing support or provide or withdraw support.

[1]   Asylum Support Regulations 2000, SI 2000/704, reg 15(1).
[2]   SI 2000/704, reg 15(2).
[3]   SI 2000/704, reg 15(3)–(4).

FURTHER APPLICATIONS FOR SUPPORT

14.163 In most circumstances, there is nothing to prevent repeat claims for support and the Secretary of State must consider the application unless: (i) it is not made in the form currently in use;[1] (ii) the person has previously had his or her support suspended or discontinued, there has been no material change of circumstances since the suspension or discontinuation and the Secretary of State considers that there are no exceptional circumstances which justify it being entertained,[2] (iii) the claim for asylum was not made as soon as reasonably practicable unless a failure to provide the claimant with asylum support would lead to a breach of the European Convention on Human Rights,[3] or (iv) a further application for support is made after an appeal to the First-tier Tribunal's Social Entitlement Chamber sitting as the First-tier Tribunal (Asylum Support) is dismissed,[4] and there has been no 'material change in circumstances'.[5] A material change of circumstances is one which, if the applicant were a supported person, would have to be notified to the Secretary of State.[6]

[1]   Asylum Support Regulations 2000, SI 2000/704, reg 3(3)–(4).
[2]   SI 2000/704, reg 21.
[3]   NIAA 2002, s 55 (as amended by Localism Act 2011 (Consequential Amendments) Order 2012/961 Sch1, para 3(a)–(b) (28 March 2012) regarding local authorities' general power of competence; *R (on the application of Q) v Secretary of State for the Home Department* [2003] EWCA Civ 364, [2004] QB 36.
[4]   IAA 1999, s 103(6).
[5]   SI 2000/704, reg 21; IAA 1999, s 103(6).
[6]   SI 2000/704, reg 21(2); see also *Home Office Guidance, Asylum support instructions: Policy Bulletins*, version 2, 29 September 2014 (replacing *Policy Bulletin 84*, 'Entertaining a further application for support', Chapter 14.

Preventing abuse

14.164 There are various safeguards to prevent abuse of the asylum support scheme. First, there are the grounds on which people, although destitute, may be excluded from obtaining asylum support by their own conduct. Second, criminal charges may be brought against persons who, in relation to asylum support, make false representations or produce false documents or information,[1] fail to notify a required change of circumstances,[2] delay or obstruct a person administering the support scheme,[3] fail to provide required information,[4] seek assistance or accommodation or further repatriation assistance under Schedule 3 to the NIAA 2002 without mentioning a previous claim for assistance or after repatriation by a local authority,[5] or fail, as a sponsor, to maintain a sponsored person who is then provided with asylum support.[6] Third, there are ways to recover asylum support to which asylum seekers were not entitled.

[1] IAA 1999, ss 105(1)(a)–(b), 106(1)(a)–(b). For criminal offences relating to asylum support, see Chapter 15 below; see also *Home Office Guidance, Breach of condition instruction*, 24 October 2014
[2] IAA 1999, ss 105(1)(c)–(d), 106(1)(c)–(d).
[3] IAA 1999, s 107(1)(a).
[4] IAA 1999, s 107(1)(b).
[5] NIAA 2002, Sch 3, para 13(1)–(2).
[6] IAA 1999, s 108(1).

14.165 To detect and act on abuses of the system, the Secretary of State has a number of further powers. He or she may obtain a warrant from a justice of the peace (or in Scotland, a sheriff or a justice of the peace) to enter premises provided as temporary support or asylum support where there is reason to believe that the person/s who are supposed to be supported there are not in fact resident there or the accommodation is being used for other purposes, or other persons are residing there.[1] Reasonable force may be used to enter the accommodation with a warrant.[2] The Secretary of State may also require the owner or manager of property provided by way of asylum support[3] to provide information about the premises and those living there.[4] The power might be used to require landlords to notify the Secretary of State when an asylum seeker has left or is subletting property.[5] The Secretary of State may further require the Royal Mail, or others delivering post, to provide information about redirection requests.[6] Employers may be required to provide information about employees. For further details on the Secretary of State's information-gathering powers, see Chapter 15 below.[7] By section 18 of the UK Borders Act 2007[8] powers of arrest, entry, search and seizure under the Immigration Act 1971 are applied to the offences of dishonestly obtaining asylum support under the IAA 1999. Section 109A is introduced into the 1999 Act giving an immigration officer the power to arrest without warrant a person he has reasonable grounds for suspecting has committed an offence under section 105 of the 1999 Act (false representations) or section 106 of the 1999 Act (dishonest representations) in relation to obtaining asylum support. Section 18 of the 2007 Act also introduces section 109B into the 1999 Act. This provides for powers of entry, search and seizure under sections 28B, 28D–28E and 28G–28L of the Immigration Act 1971, after a person has been arrested, to be applied to an offence under section 105 or section 106 of the 1999 Act.

[1] IAA 1999, s 125. (See Chapter 15 below.)
[2] IAA 1999, s 125(3)(b).
[3] This power does not extend to temporary asylum support because it relates only to accommodation which has been provided for 'supported persons' (IAA 1999, s 126(1)), defined in s 94(1) of the IAA 1999 as asylum seekers or their dependants in receipt of support under s 95.
[4] IAA 1999, s 126. No regulations have been made under this section.
[5] Explanatory Notes to the IAA 1999, para 126.
[6] IAA 1999, s 127.

7   The criminal offences in ss 105–109 relate to support provided 'under Part VI' of the IAA 1999. The provisions relating to recovery, ss 112 and 114 IAA 1999, Sch 8, para 11(1) read with Asylum Support Regulations 2000, SI 2000/704, reg 17, refer to recovery of support under either or both s 95 and s 98 of the 1999 Act and IAA 1999, s 113 refers to recovery of expenditure on support from a sponsor under IAA 1999, s 95. Entry of premises (s 125) is permitted in relation to support provided under s 95 or s 98, information from property owners may be obtained in respect of persons who have been provided with ordinary asylum support (s 126(1) refers to 'supported persons' who are defined in s 94(1) as persons provided with support under s 95) but information about redirection relates to support under Part VI or for 'for any other purpose relating to the provision of support to asylum seekers' (see s 127(1)(c)).

8   In force 31 January 2008; see the UK Borders Act 2007 (Commencement No 1 and Transitional Provisions) Order 2008, SI 2008/99.

EVICTION FROM ACCOMMODATION

14.166 One of the government's aims was to ensure that the asylum support scheme is untrammelled by the procedural safeguards operating in the general law. So when the time comes for asylum support to be terminated, the legislation makes provision for tenancies or licences provided by way of asylum support to come to an end before they would have done in accordance with the general law. Thus, where asylum support is terminated for any reason, any tenancy or licence granted during the period of support is brought to an end at the end of the period specified in the 'notice to quit',[1] 'regardless of when it could otherwise be brought to an end'.[2] Notices to quit must be given in writing.[3] Accommodation under sections 4, 95 and 98 of the Immigration and Asylum 1999 is excluded from the protective provisions of the Protection from Eviction Act 1977.[4]

1   Not less than seven days in the case of any termination of support other than due to the determination of the claim to asylum (Asylum Support Regulations 2000, SI 2000/704, reg 22(3)(a)); or a period at least as long as whichever is the greater of seven days, or the period beginning with date of services of the notice to quit, and ending with the date of determination of the relevant claim for asylum: where the termination of the support is due to the determination of the asylum claim, that period is 21 days unless the Secretary of State notifies the claimant that his decision is to accept the asylum claim, the Secretary of State notifies the claimant that his/her decision is to reject the asylum claim but at the same time notifies him that he/she is giving him limited leave to enter or remain in the United Kingdom, or an appeal by the claimant against the Secretary of State's decision has been disposed of by being allowed, in which case it is 28 days; (reg 22(3)(b)(i)–(ii) read with IAA 1999, s 94(3) –(4) and SI 2000/704, reg 2(2), (2A)); or, in any case, less than seven days, when the 'circumstances of the case are such that that notice period is justified' (SI 2000/704, reg 22(4)).

2   SI 2000/704, reg 22(1).
3   SI 2000/704, reg 22(3)–(4)(a).
4   See Protection from Eviction Act 1977, s 3, 3A(7A).

RECOVERY OF SUPPORT

14.167 There are five circumstances in which support which has been provided may be recovered:

(1)   where a supported person is later able to realise assets held at the time of the support application;[1]

(2)   where a person was overpaid support as a result of an error;[2]

(3)   where a person obtained support as the result of a misrepresentation or failure to disclose a material fact;[3]

(4)   where it transpires that the supported person and any dependants was or were not in fact destitute;[4]

(5)   recovery from a person who sponsored the stay in the UK of a person who subsequently resorted to asylum support.[5]

These circumstances are considered in more detail below,[6] but the following general comments can be made. In the first two cases and the fourth case, the recovery is, at least *initially*, made directly by the Secretary of State, whereas in the third and fifth cases the Secretary of State makes an application to the court (in the third case, to the county court and in the fifth, to the magistrates, or in Scotland, to the sheriff in either case). It should be noted that there is no equivalent process for Section 4 support.

[1]   Asylum Support Regulations 2000, SI 2000/704, reg 17.
[2]   IAA 1999, s 114; SI 2000/704, reg 18.
[3]   IAA 1999, s 112 (as amended by the Crime and Courts Act 2013, Sch 9(3), para 90(c) implemented 22 April 2014 regarding clarification of county in England, Wales and Scotland.)
[4]   SI 2004/704, reg 17A, inserted by SI 2005/11 from 5 February 2005.
[5]   IAA 1999, s 113.
[6]   See also *Policy Bulletin 67, Overpayments*, version 6, 2 July 2014, and *Home Office Guidance, Breach of condition instruction*, 24 October 2014, Chapter 4.

14.168 Overpayments made as a result of an error, misrepresentation or failure to disclose may be recovered under ordinary asylum support and temporary support,[1] while recovery from realised assets or from a sponsor is available only under ordinary asylum support.[2] Where assets becoming realisable or where overpayment has been made in error, recovery may take the form of deductions from asylum support[3] or the sums may be recovered as a 'debt' due to the Secretary of State in ordinary court proceedings.[4] Where a supported person and any dependants was or were not in fact destitute, the Secretary of State may require a refund and where the refund is not paid within a reasonable period, the sums may be recovered as a 'debt' due to the Secretary of State in ordinary court proceedings.[5] Where overpayment resulted from a misrepresentation or a failure to disclose or from a sponsor's default, recovery starts and ends with the courts.[6] The Secretary of State appears to have a discretion as to whether to pursue recovery of an overpayment in all cases.[7] As noted above, provision is made for recovery of asylum support when it transpires that at any time during which asylum support was being provided, the recipient was not destitute. This is a catch-all category, obviating the necessity to apportion blame.[8]

[1]   IAA 1999, ss 112(1)(b), 114(1).
[2]   The former is referred to only in Asylum Support Regulations 2000, SI 2000/704, reg 17(3)(a), which does not refer to temporary support, and the enabling provisions refer solely to s 95: Sch 8, para 11(1); in the latter case, s 113(1)(b) refers only to s 95 (asylum support); cf ss 112(1)(b) and 114(1), which refer to both s 95 and s 98 (temporary asylum support). See also *Policy Bulletin 67, Overpayments*, version 6, 2 July 2014.
[3]   The deductions themselves may only be made from asylum support: IAA 1999, s 114(4), Sch 8, para 11(2)(b), SI 2000/704, regs 17(4) and 18.
[4]   IAA 1999, s 114(2)–(3), Sch 8, para 11(2)(a)–(b); SI 2000/704, regs 17(4), 18.
[5]   SI 2000/704, reg 17A.
[6]   IAA 1999, ss 112–113.
[7]   The discretion is explicit in IAA 1999, ss 113(2), 114(2) and SI 2000/704, regs 17(2), 17A(1)–(2) and (5) but must be inferred in respect of misrepresentation and failure to disclose in s 112.

[8] SI 2000/704, reg 17A, inserted by SI 2005/11 from 5 February 2005, reflecting Council Directive 2003/9/EC OJ L 31, 6 February 2003, pp 18–25, Art 16.1(b).

Convertible assets

14.169 The Secretary of State may require the repayment of the value of any asylum support which has been provided if, at the time when the supported person applied for support, he or she had assets (in the UK or elsewhere) such as savings, investments, property or shares, which could not then be converted into money, but have become realisable since (even if they have not in fact been converted).[1] The Secretary of State may require repayment up to the total money value of the assets concerned or the total money value of all the support provided (whichever is less).[2]

[1] IAA 1999, Sch 8, para 11, Asylum Support Regulations 2000, SI 2000/704, reg 17(1). The Secretary of State has a discretion to recover less than the recoverable amount, see SI 2000/704, reg 17(2): 'a sum not exceeding'. It is unclear whether the Secretary of State can require a person who is no longer being supported to repay the value of the support, since these provisions contain no wording equivalent to s 114(2) (recovery of overpayments made in error from a person who is or has been a supported person).

[2] SI 2000/704, reg 17(2)–(3), (5).

RECOVERY OF OVERPAYMENTS OF SUPPORT AS A RESULT OF ERROR

14.170 The Secretary of State may require the repayment of any temporary support or asylum support which has been provided as a result of her own error,[1] up to the total money value of the overpayment.[2] For recovery of these overpayments (in contrast to the position with most social security benefits), there is no need for the supported person to be responsible for the overpayment or at fault in any way. The overpayment may be recovered even after support ends.[3]

[1] IAA 1999, s 114(1).
[2] IAA 1999, s 114(2).
[3] IAA 1999, s 114(2).

RECOVERY FOLLOWING MISREPRESENTATION OR FAILURE TO DISCLOSE

14.171 If the Secretary of State determines that a person has received support (temporary or ordinary asylum support) as a result of a misrepresentation or failure to disclose a material fact, he or she may apply to a county court (or, in Scotland, the sheriff) for an order that the person who made the misrepresentation or who was responsible for the failure to disclose, repay the amount.[1] Recovery may be made from any person who made the misrepresentation or failed to disclose, not only from the asylum seeker or dependant who received the support. The amount which the court can order repaid is the total money value of the support paid as a result of the misrepresentation or failure to disclose which would not otherwise have been provided.[2]

[1] IAA 1999, s 112.
[2] IAA 1999, s 112(2)–(3).

RECOVERY BY REFUND

14.172 A refund of asylum support may be required by the Secretary of State from a supported person if it transpires that at any time during which asylum support was being provided to the supported person and any dependants, he or she, and where applicable they, was, or were, not destitute. The refund must not exceed the monetary value of the asylum support provided to the supported person and any dependants for the time during which support was provided and during which the supported person and any dependants was, or were, not destitute.[1] The Home Office may apply to a County Court (or in Scotland, the Sheriff Court) for an order to require the person who made the misrepresentation or who was responsible for the failure to disclose to repay the support. This gives the Home Office the right to apply for repayment from people other than those who actually received the asylum support or their dependants.[2]

[1] Asylum Support Regulations 2000, SI 2000/704, reg 17A, inserted by SI 2005/11, from 5 February 2005, reflecting Council Directive 2003/9/EC OJ L 31, 6 February 2003, pp 18–25, Art 16.1(b).
[2] IAA 1999, s112.

RECOVERY FROM SPONSOR

14.173 Support may be recovered from a sponsor of a person in receipt of (ordinary) asylum support,[1] ie the person who gave a written undertaking for the purposes of the Immigration Rules to be responsible for the maintenance and accommodation of that person when he or she sought to enter or remain in the UK.[2] This form of recovery is intended to deal with the situation where a person obtains admission to the UK as a result of a sponsorship undertaking in a non-asylum capacity and then seeks to remain in the UK as a refugee, and becomes entitled to asylum support during the process. The sponsor can only be made liable to make payments covering the period over which the undertaking has effect.[3] Thus, if a person is granted six months' visitor leave on the strength of an undertaking by a sponsor, and claims asylum (and obtains asylum support) after a month, the sponsor could be made liable to repay five months' support. If the same visitor claims asylum after five months, the liability of the sponsor would be limited to a month. If the visitor overstays, and then claims asylum and support a year later, we suggest the sponsor is not liable, since no asylum support payment has been made over the period of the undertaking.

[1] IAA 1999, s 113.
[2] IAA 1999, s 113. For such undertakings see 14.X above.
[3] IAA 1999, s 113(1)(b).

14.174 The procedure for recovery is that the Secretary of State must make a complaint to a magistrates' court (in Scotland, an application to a sheriff) for an order. The court may order the sponsor to make weekly payments (or otherwise) to the Secretary of State of an amount which the court thinks appropriate having regard to all the circumstances of the case and, in particular, to the sponsor's own income.[1] The weekly sum must not be more than the weekly value of the support being provided to the asylum seeker.[2] The court may order repayment of support already paid before the date of the complaint but, if it does so, it must have regard to the sponsor's income during the period concerned rather than their current income.[3] The order can be enforced in the same way as a maintenance order.[4]

1 IAA 1999, s 113(3).
2 IAA 1999, s 113(4).
3 IAA 1999, s 113(5).
4 IAA 1999, s 113(6).

APPEALS UNDER THE ASYLUM SUPPORT SCHEME

Rights of appeal

14.174A There are rights of appeal against certain asylum support decisions to the First-tier Tribunal (Social Entitlement Chamber) sitting as the First-tier Tribunal (Asylum Support).[1] Prior to that appeals were made to the Asylum Support Tribunal (AST) and before that to the Asylum Support Adjudicators. Legally qualified members of the First-tier Tribunal are Judges.[2] Previously, asylum support adjudicators were appointed by the Secretary of State.[3] The circumstances in which an asylum seeker or dependant may appeal are extremely limited. A person may only appeal if the Secretary of State decides that the person is not entitled to any support at all,[4] or terminates all support for reasons other than the person ceasing to be an asylum seeker.[5] The First-tier Tribunal has jurisdiction to hear an appeal from an applicant relating to the factual circumstances and legal framework permitting the grant of support. This extends to considerations of whether or not the person is an asylum seeker.[6] An asylum seeker with minor dependants may also appeal against a decision by the Secretary of State to terminate his or her support following certification by the Secretary of State that he or she has failed to co-operate with steps to remove him or her from the United Kingdom.[7] The asylum support adjudicators, forerunners of the First-tier Tribunal (Social Entitlement Chamber), were at pains to stress that they had no jurisdiction to hear complaints about location of accommodation,[8] and the limited way this issue has come before them has been in appeals against termination of support for breach of conditions, where the breach is failure to attend or return to dispersed accommodation and appellants have argued that features of the location give rise to a reasonable excuse for the breach. In addition, the Court of Appeal has held that as a matter of statutory construction, a right of appeal under s 103(2) of the 1999 Act only arises where the Secretary of State decides to stop providing support to an asylum seeker or his or her dependants, and not where a decision to provide support is conditional on the asylum claimant moving to a particular location, and the condition is not complied with.[9] This decision affects families with children in particular, as the Secretary of State holds offers of accommodation open where there are minor dependants even if the family refuses to relocate to a dispersal area.[10] The Secretary of State has a power to introduce regulations permitting asylum seekers to appeal against a dispersal location,[11] but has not done so. There is no right of appeal against a decision that a person is not entitled to support by virtue of not having claimed asylum as soon as reasonably practicable.[12] The only means of challenging these decisions is by way of an application for judicial review.[13] It has been accepted that in relation to appeals before an asylum support adjudicator the minimum standards of fairness set out in Art 6 ECHR apply[14] and it is suggested that this must also be true in respect of the First-tier Tribunal.

[1] From 3 November 2008 the functions of asylum support adjudicators in the Asylum Support Tribunal were transferred to the First-tier Tribunal by the Transfer of Tribunal Functions Order 2008, SI 2008/2833. Asylum support appeals are now heard in the First-tier Tribunal's Social Entitlement Chamber.

[2] Tribunals, Courts and Enforcement Act 2007, s 4.

[3] Immigration and Asylum Act 1999, s 102. Asylum support adjudicators constituted an independent Tribunal for the purposes of Art 6 ECHR: *R (on the application of Husain) v Asylum Support Adjudicator* [2001] EWHC 852 (Admin), (2001) Times, 15 November; see CHAPTER 7 above. Asylum support adjudicators became housed within the AST when responsibility for their functions was transferred from the Home Secretary to the Lord Chancellor on 2 April 2007 by the Transfer of Functions (Asylum Support Adjudicators) Order 2007, SI 2007/275.

[4] IAA 1999, s 103(1). There is also an appeal against refusal of 'hard cases' support under s 4 (as to which see **14.174T** ff below): s 103(2A), inserted by the AI(TC)A 2004, s 10(4) from 31 March 2005 by SI 2005/372. Once accommodation centres (for which see **14.174O** ff below) are in use for asylum seekers, the appeals provisions will apply to refusal of support in an accommodation centre (NIAA 2002, s 17): s 103(1), (2) as substituted by the NIAA 2002, s 53 and the AI(TC)A 2004, s 10(4) from a date to be appointed.

[5] IAA 1999, s 103(2), which becomes s 103(3) when the NIAA 2002, s 53 comes into force; where a decision is made to stop providing support the appeal may be made before support actually ends. These are referred to as qualification appeals and stoppage appeals respectively: see *Dogan* below.

[6] *R (on the application of the Secretary of State for the Home Department) v Chief Asylum Support Adjudicator (Interested Party: Flutura Malaj)* [2006] EWHC 3059, (Admin), (2006) Times, 26 December.

[7] NIAA 2002, Sch 3, para 7A, inserted by Asylum and Immigration (Treatment of Claimants etc) Act 2004, s 9. None of the other persons categorised in NIAA 2002, Sch 3 as being ineligible for support may appeal if the decision refusing support was made on or after 1 December 2004: AI(TC)A 2004 s 9(3), SI 2004/2999, Art 4 (transitional provisions).

[8] *ASA 00/09/0046; 00/09/0066; 00/10/0087*; although adjudicators have directed the Secretary of State not to return asylum seekers to particular locations: *ASA 00/07/0024*, para 11.

[9] *R (on the application of Secretary of State for the Home Department) v Chief Asylum Support Adjudicator and Dogan (Ahmet)* [2003] EWCA Civ 1673, (2003) Times, 13 December.

[10] Policy Bulletin 17, Failure to Travel, version 5.0, 5 October 2009, para 3.4.

[11] Under the IAA 1999, s 103(7) (which becomes new s 103A, and applies to location of support provided under s 4 ('hard cases support', when the NIAA 2002, s 53 comes into force. Section 53 is still not in force)

[12] NIAA 2002, s 55(10).

[13] The ECHR does not require that a merits appeal on the facts against all administrative decisions in respect of a person's civil rights: *Kaplan v United Kingdom* (1980) 4 EHRR 64 at para 61; *Bryan v United Kingdom* (1995) 21 EHRR 342; *W v United Kingdom* (1987) 10 EHRR 29. Concerns at the lack of appeal rights in s 55 cases were dismissed by the Court of Appeal in *R (on the application of Q) v Secretary of State for the Home Department* [2003] EWCA Civ 364, [2004] QB 36, but the court indicated that the procedures for determining the claims were not Art 6 compliant. Since the judgment, the procedures have been significantly revised; see also *Tsfayo v United Kingdom* (Application No 60860/00) (2006) 48 EHRR 457, [2007] LGR 1, (2006) Times, 23 November, at paras 39–48, [2006] All ER (D) 177 (Nov), ECtHR.

[14] *R (on the application of Husain) v Asylum Support Adjudicator* [2001] EWHC Admin 852, [2001] All ER (D) 107 (Nov); see also *ASA 00/09/0063, ASA 00/10/0087* and *ASA 00/10/0089*. Concerns under Art 6 relate to the lack of legal aid for representation: *Airey v Ireland* (1979) 2 EHRR 305, ECtHR), particularly if appeals where an appellant's personal conduct are at issue are determined in the appellant's absence: *Muyldermans v Belgium* (1991) 15 EHRR 204, ECtHR at para 64.

Appeal procedures

14.174B The procedural rules for the First-tier Tribunal (Social Entitlement Chamber) are the Tribunal Procedure (First-tier Tribunal) (Social Entitlement Chamber) Rules 2008.[1] The main emphasis in the rules on asylum support appeals is speed. The overriding objective is specified as being to enable the Tribunal to deal with cases fairly and justly including, dealing with the case in ways which are proportionate to the importance of the case, the complexity of the issues, the anticipated costs and the resources of the parties; avoiding unnecessary formality and seeking flexibility in the proceedings; ensuring, so far as practicable, that the parties are able to participate fully in the proceedings; using any special expertise of the Tribunal effectively; and avoiding delay, so far as compatible with proper consideration of the issues. Parties to the appeal are enjoined to help the Tribunal to further the overriding objective and co-operate with the Tribunal generally.[2] The appeal procedures set out in the Rules contain some detail but the Tribunal has a general power to give case management directions on matters connected with the appeal and to make directions on the initiative of the Tribunal or an application by a party.[3] In addition, an irregularity resulting from a failure to comply with any requirement of the Rules, a practice direction or a direction, does not of itself render void the proceedings or any step taken in the proceedings although there are powers to deal with non-compliance.[4] The Tribunal may give a direction substituting a party if the wrong person has been named as a party.[5] Appellants may be represented throughout the appeal procedure by any person whom they choose to represent them, whether legally qualified or not,[6] in which case, provided they are notified, relevant documents sent by the Tribunal or the Secretary of State to the appellant must be sent to the representative.[7] Where two or more cases involve common or related issues of fact or law, one or more cases may be designated as a lead case and the other cases stayed.[8] This is unlikely to occur much in practice given the speed with which asylum support cases are listed.

[1]   SI 2008/2685.
[2]   SI 2008/2685, r 2.
[3]   SI 2008/2685, rr 5 and 6. Under the former asylum support adjudicator appeal regime, it was held that an asylum support adjudicator could use the power to give directions on matters connected with the appeal under the Asylum Support Appeals (Procedure) Rules 2000, SI 2000/541, r 14, to direct the Secretary of State to expedite consideration of a second application for asylum support: ASA 00/06/0017.
[4]   SI 2008/2685, r 7. When an asylum seeker arrived too late for a hearing, having taken the specific train directed, the adjudicator, under the former asylum support adjudicator appeal regime used r 19 of SI 2000/541, the interpretative provisions of s 3 of the Human Rights Act 1998 and fair hearing standards of ECHR, Art 6 to set aside the decision and re-list the appeal: ASA 00/11/0106.
[5]   SI 2008/2685, r 9(1).
[6]   SI 2008/2685, r 11(1). The Housing and Immigration Group set up a 'duty solicitor' scheme, staffed by experienced volunteer solicitors and barristers, to assist claimants at hearings. This scheme has been taken over by the Asylum Support Appeals Project so that it now forms an additional part of the duty scheme supplied by the latter's staff; see http://www.asaproject.org/web/index.php.
[7]   SI 2008/2685, r 11(6).
[8]   SI 2008/2685, r 18.

Notice of appeal

14.174C Any decision against which an appeal lies must be communicated by the Secretary of State by letter.[1] Notice of appeal must be sent so that it is received by the Tribunal no later than three days after the day on which the notice of the decision was received.[2] It is given by filling out the standard form which is issued by the Secretary of State or a self-made form that contains all the required information and documents.[3] The Notice of Appeal form is *Form E09 (2008)*.[4] The form must be signed by the appellant.[5] In particular, the form requires an appellant to provide details of the grounds of appeal, whether the appellant requires an oral hearing and if so, whether an interpreter would be required. The form must be completed in full in English or Welsh[6] and must be accompanied by a copy of the decision being appealed against.[7] Any information or evidence, which has not already been submitted, may be sent in with the form.[8]

[1] The former Asylum Support Regulations 2000, SI 2000/704, contained no express requirement that these decisions must be communicated by letter but the new Tribunal Procedure (First-tier Tribunal) (Social Entitlement Chamber) Rules 2008, SI 2008/2685, r 22(2), assume that they will be. See also Policy Bulletin 23, Asylum Support Appeals Process, version 9, 11 September 2009.

[2] SI 2008/2685, r 22(2).

[3] SI 2008/2685, r 22(3)–(5).

[4] Updated 25 September 2009, at http://www.asylum-support-tribunal.gov.uk/formsguidance.htm.

[5] SI 2008/2685, r 22(3).

[6] SI 2008/2685, r 22(3); see also Form.

[7] SI 2008/2685, r 22(4)(ii).

[8] See Form.

14.174D The Tribunal may be asked to extend the time limit for appealing, either before or after its expiry.[1] The strength of the case is relevant to the question of whether it is in the interests of justice to extend time.[2] If time is not extended the Notice of Appeal is not admitted and there is no appeal. If the Tribunal refuses to extend time, the remedies will be either a new application for support or a judicial review of the refusal. It may or may not be possible in these circumstances to obtain judicial review of the Secretary of State's decision.[3]

[1] The Tribunal Procedure (First-tier Tribunal) (Social Entitlement Chamber) Rules 2008, SI 2008/2685, rr 5(3)(a) and 22(6). Under the previous asylum support adjudicator regime time could only be extended if: (i) it was in the interests of justice; and (ii) the asylum seeker or the representative could not comply with the time limit due to circumstances beyond their control, see the Asylum Support Appeals (Procedure) Rules 2000, SI 2000/541, r 3(4). The asylum support adjudicators applied a liberal approach to the extension of time, where an appellant appeared not to have had access to an interpreter (ASA 00/04/0003); where a notice of appeal was submitted with a page missing (ASA 00/06/0017); where NASS was unable to confirm that the decision had been sent by first class post (ASA 00/07/0021); where no reference to the right of appeal was contained in the decision letter, although the explanatory notes to the application forms said this would be the case (ASA 00/07/0030); and where there had been postal delays (ASA 00/08/0037).

[2] See *R v Immigration Appeal Tribunal, ex p Mehta* [1976] Imm AR 38, CA, and Chapter 18 below. In ASA 00/00/0056 no reasons for extending time were given, but the merits appear to have been relevant.

[3] In judicial review proceedings, the court may refuse to interfere with the decision where an applicant has failed to exercise a statutory right of appeal. See Chapter 21 below.

The service of documents, information and reasons

14.174E On the same day that the Tribunal receives the notice of appeal, or, if that is not reasonably practicable, as soon as practicable on the next day, the Tribunal must send a copy of the notice of appeal and any supporting documents to the Secretary of State.[1] On receipt of the notice of appeal, or a copy of it, the Secretary of State must send or deliver a response to the Tribunal so that it is received within three days after the date on which the Tribunal received the notice of appeal. The response must state the name and address of the decision maker (the Secretary of State); the name and address of the Secretary of State's representative if any; an address where documents may be sent or delivered; whether the Secretary of State opposes the appellant's case and, if so, any grounds for such opposition which are not set out in any documents which are before the Tribunal; and any further information or documents required by a practice direction or direction. It may include a submission as to whether it would be appropriate for the case to be disposed of without a hearing. In addition, the Secretary of State must provide a copy of any written record of the decision under challenge, and any statement of reasons for that decision, if they were not sent with the notice of appeal and copies of all documents relevant to the case in the decision maker's possession unless a practice direction or direction states otherwise. The Secretary of State must provide a copy of the response and any accompanying documents to the appellant at the same time as it provides the response to the Tribunal. The appellant and any other respondent may make a written submission and supply further documents in reply to the Secretary of State's response.[2]

1 The Tribunal Procedure (First-tier Tribunal) (Social Entitlement Chamber) Rules 2008, SI 2008/2685, r 22(7).
2 SI 2008/2685, r 24.

Decision of the Tribunal whether to hold a hearing of the appeal

14.174F The Tribunal must hold an oral hearing before making a decision which disposes of the appeal unless each party has consented to, or has not objected to, the matter being decided without a hearing and the Tribunal considers that it is able to decide the matter without a hearing.[1] The Tribunal may dispose of proceedings without a hearing under r 8, by striking out a party's case. This must happen if the appellant has failed to comply with a direction that stated that failure by the appellant to comply with the direction would lead to the striking out of the proceedings or that part of them. It may happen where the appellant has failed to comply with a direction that stated that failure by the appellant to comply with the direction could lead to the striking out of the proceedings or that part of them.[2] The Tribunal must give each party reasonable notice of the time and place of the hearing. The period of notice must be at least one day's and not more than five days' notice. The Tribunal may give shorter notice with the parties' consent or in urgent or exceptional circumstances.[3]

1 The Tribunal Procedure (First-tier Tribunal) (Social Entitlement Chamber) Rules 2008 SI 2008/2685, rr 27(1) and 32.
2 SI 2008/2685, rr 8(1)-(3) and 27(3).
3 SI 2008/2685, r 29.

Further evidence before determination of the appeal

14.174G If there is further evidence in support of the appeal, which was not submitted with the notice of appeal, it may be submitted subsequently for consideration by the Tribunal, within the extremely tight time limits above. The appellant may make written submissions and supply further documents in reply to the Secretary of State's response to the notice of appeal.[1] However, speed is of the essence. Under the former asylum support adjudicator regime, if no oral hearing was to be held, the adjudicator would proceed to determine the appeal, at most, five days after the notice of appeal was received. The Tribunal has broad powers to admit further evidence from either party before and at the appeal hearing. In addition, evidence may be excluded where the evidence was not provided within the time allowed by a direction or a practice direction, the evidence was provided in a manner that did not comply with a direction or a practice direction, or it would be unfair to admit the evidence.[2]

[1] The Tribunal Procedure (First-tier Tribunal) (Social Entitlement Chamber) Rules 2008, SI 2008/2685, r 24(6).
[2] SI 2008/ 2685, rr 5(1), (2) and 15(2).

Oral hearings

14.174H Hearings before the Tribunal must be heard in public, unless it gives a direction that a hearing, or part of it, is to be held in private.[1] Where a hearing, or part of it, is to be held in private, the Tribunal may determine who is permitted to attend the hearing or part of it. The Tribunal may give a direction excluding from any hearing, or part of it any person whose conduct the Tribunal considers is disrupting or is likely to disrupt the hearing; any person whose presence the Tribunal considers is likely to prevent another person from giving evidence or making submissions freely; any person who the Tribunal considers should be excluded in order to give effect to a direction under r 14(2) (withholding information likely to cause harm) or any person where the purpose of the hearing would be defeated by the attendance of that person. The Tribunal may give a direction excluding a witness from a hearing until that witness gives evidence.[2] The appellant's interests or desire for the appeal to be heard in private is not decisive. There are no rules setting out the procedure to be adopted at the oral hearing and the Tribunal has a broad discretion. However, fairness requires that appellants are allowed to give oral evidence, call witnesses in support,[3] question any witnesses relied on by the Secretary of State, and address the Tribunal on the law and the facts (by themselves or through their representatives). If witnesses are called, the Tribunal may consent to a witness giving, or require any witness to give, evidence on oath, and may administer an oath for that purpose.[4] The Secretary of State should meet an appellant's reasonable travelling expenses to attend the oral hearing.[5] Subject to r 30(5) (exclusion of a person from a hearing), each party to proceedings is entitled to attend a hearing.[6] If a party fails to attend a hearing, the Tribunal may proceed with the hearing if it is satisfied that the party has been notified of the hearing or that reasonable steps have been taken to notify the party of the hearing and considers that it is in the interests of justice to proceed with the hearing.[7] The hearing may also proceed where the appellant indicated in the notice of appeal that he or she did not wish to attend or be represented at the hearing and it may proceed in the absence of a Home Office representative. Appellants may obtain a refund of their travel costs for attending an asylum support appeal.[8]

1   The Tribunal Procedure (First-tier Tribunal) (Social Entitlement Chamber) Rules 2008, SI 2008/2685, r 30(1), (3).
2   SI 2008/2685, r 30(5) and (6).
3   SI 2008/2685, r 16, provides for the summoning or citation (Scotland) of witnesses and the ordering of any person to answer questions or produce documents.
4   SI 2008/2685, r 15(3).
5   Immigration and Asylum Act 1999, s 103(9); see also Policy Bulletin 28, Providing travelling expenses and reimbursing essential travel costs, version 3.0, 26 November 2008.
6   SI 2008/2685, r 28.
7   SI 2008/2685, r 31.
8   ASA 00/07/0027, para 3. IAA 1999, s 103B inserted by the NIAA 2002, s 53 in force from a date to be appointed, provides a further statutory foundation for the Secretary of State's obligation to pay reasonable travelling expenses to enable an appellant to attend an asylum support appeal; see also Policy Bulletin 28, Providing travelling expenses and reimbursing essential travel costs, version 3.0, 26 November 2008.

Decision and reasons

14.174I The Tribunal may give a decision orally at a hearing. Subject to r 14(2) (withholding information likely to cause serious harm), it must provide a decision notice stating its decision to each party as soon as reasonably practicable after making a decision which finally disposes of all issues in the proceedings. The decision notice must be provided at the hearing or sent on the day that the decision is made.[1] The Tribunal must send a written statement of reasons for a decision which disposes of proceedings to each party, if the case is decided at a hearing, within three days after the hearing, or if the case is decided without a hearing, on the day that the decision is made.[2] In respect of appeals to the former asylum support adjudicator appeals regime, it was held that asylum support adjudicators were not bound by their own decisions.[3]

1   The Tribunal Procedure (First-tier Tribunal) (Social Entitlement Chamber) Rules 2008, SI 2008/2685, r 33.
2   SI 2008/2685, r 34(1).
3   ASA 00/08/0034, para 14.

Evidence and burden of proof

14.174J In deciding the appeal, the Tribunal may take into account and admit evidence not available to the Secretary of State and evidence that would not be admissible in a civil trial in the United Kingdom.[1] There are no rules on who bears the burden of proof in asylum support appeals but, applying ordinary legal principles, the person who makes a particular assertion must prove it. The burden may, therefore, rest with the person claiming support to establish matters such as destitution, but if the Secretary of State has sought to exclude someone from support despite prima facie entitlement, she should establish the ground of exclusion.[2] The asylum support adjudicators, the predecessors of the Tribunal, generally applied the balance of probabilities as the appropriate standard of proof,[3] although arguably a higher (civil) standard applies where the Secretary of State alleges particularly egregious conduct in breach of conditions, or an offence under Pt VI of the Immigration and Asylum Act 1999, in order to exclude a person from support.[4]

[1] The Tribunal Procedure (First-tier Tribunal) (Social Entitlement Chamber) Rules 2008, SI 2008/2685, r 15(2).
[2] ASA/02/10/4566.
[3] See eg ASA 00/04/0003.
[4] Asylum Support Regulations 2000, SI 2000/704, regs 19, 20.

The Tribunal's powers

14.174K On deciding the appeal, the Tribunal may require the Secretary of State to reconsider the question of whether the appellant should be provided with support, substitute the Secretary of State's decision with its own decision or dismiss the appeal so that the decision of the Secretary of State stands.[1] The extent of the Tribunal's powers is not specified in the 1999 Act, in contrast to ordinary immigration judges, but it is clear that they must apply the provisions of the 1999 Act and the asylum support regulations. The asylum support adjudicators, the predecessors of the newly formed Tribunal, had also shown themselves willing to consider whether decisions are in accordance with the Secretary of State's policy, as set out, inter alia, in the *Policy Bulletins*.[2] Further, the asylum support adjudicators endeavoured to ensure that their decisions did not constitute or adopt a breach of an appellant's human rights, by, for example, considering whether the termination of support following breach of conditions would leave an appellant exposed to levels of suffering which would engage ECHR, Art 3, or breach rights to respect for the home and private life/physical integrity under ECHR, Art 8.[3] In one case an adjudicator allowed an appeal with reference to ECHR, Art 3 (in the context of reasonable excuse for breach of conditions) where an appellant with heart trouble had to go without food if he missed the hostel meals which were provided at rigidly enforced times.[4]

[1] IAA 1999, s 103(3).
[2] ASA 00/09/0044; 00/09/0049; 00/11/0095.
[3] See eg ASA 00/10/0089.
[4] ASA 00/11/0106.

14.174L The Tribunal's decision is effective from the day on which it is made. Therefore, where the parties are notified at the hearing that the appeal has been successful, the Secretary of State must, as far as possible, take immediate steps to implement the decision rather than wait for the written reasons. It is not apparent from the legislation whether the Tribunal should focus on the date of the Secretary of State's decision or the date of hearing. The power to require the Secretary of State to reconsider the decision suggests the latter.[1] There are no express rules as to the backdating of support or for compensating an asylum seeker who has been without support as a result of an erroneous earlier decision.[2] The interim period will be very short but where no temporary support has been provided during that period, the Secretary of State should presumably take into account the effect of being without support for that period in meeting the asylum seeker's current needs.

1   See the IAA 1999, s 103(3)(a). But see ASA 00/10/0071, where an adjudicator dismissed an appeal on destitution although by the time of the decision the appellant's capital would have diminished sufficiently to qualify. See also ASA 00/11/0105, paras 9 and 15.

2   Although an asylum support adjudicator has held that an asylum seeker is legally entitled to amounts due from the date of the asylum application subject to deduction for backdated social security benefit: ASA 01/02/0202, paras 4 and 14; but see also *R v Hammersmith London Borough Council, ex p Isik* (19 September 2000, unreported), CA.

Procedures following an appeal

14.174M There is no further appeal against the decision of the Tribunal.[1] There are powers to correct clerical mistakes and accidental slips or omissions and to set aside a decision which disposes of proceedings.[2] A party, dissatisfied with a decision of the Tribunal, must proceed by way of judicial review.[3] If the judicial review then reaches the Court of Appeal, it may well be covered by the Court of Appeal practice direction on anonymisation in relation to asylum seekers.[4] This provides that asylum seekers should remain anonymous in proceedings before the Court. Although this practice direction is intended for immigration and asylum cases, it appears to be applied to all cases before the Court concerning asylum seekers. An asylum seeker in such a case would fall to be known by his or her initials followed by country of origin. If the asylum support appeal is dismissed by the Tribunal, the Secretary of State may not consider any further application for support from the appellant unless she is satisfied that there has been a 'material' change of circumstances.[5] Relevant changes would include, but are not limited to, those about which a supported asylum seeker must notify the Secretary of State.[6]

1   IAA 1999, s 103(5); see also s 11(1), (5)(f) of the Tribunals, Courts and Enforcement Act 2007 and the Appeals (Excluded Decisions) Order 2009, SI 2009/275, art 2(a), as substituted by SI 2010/41, from 15 February 2010.

2   The Tribunal Procedure (First-tier Tribunal) (Social Entitlement Chamber) Rules 2008, SI 2008/2685, rr 36 and 37.

3   There have been a number of challenges on behalf of the Secretary of State to decisions by asylum support adjudicators: see eg *R (on the application of the Secretary of State for the Home Department) v Chief Asylum Support Adjudicator* [2003] EWHC 269 (Admin), [2003] All ER (D) 116 (Feb); *R (on the application of the Secretary of State for the Home Department (National Asylum Support Service)) v Asylum Support Adjudicator* [2001] EWHC 881 (Admin) , [2001] All ER (D) 13 (Nov); *R (on the application of Secretary of State for the Home Department) v Chief Asylum Support Adjudicator and Dogan (Ahmet)* [2003] EWCA Civ 1673, (2003) Times, 13 November; *R (on the application of the Secretary of State for the Home Department) v Asylum Support Adjudicator, Osman (Mohammedi), Yillah (Zainab), Ahmad (Alhaj Adam) and Musemwa (Maggie)* [2006] EWHC 1248 (Admin) [2006] ACD 103, (2006) Times, July 11; and *R (on the application of the Secretary of State for the Home Department) v Chief Asylum Support Adjudicator (Interested Party: Flutura Malaj)* [2006] EWHC 3059 (Admin), (2006) Times, 26 December.

4   *Practice Note (anonymisation in asylum and immigration cases in the Court of Appeal)* [2006] EWCA Civ 1359.

5   IAA 1999, s 103(6), to become s 103(7) when the Nationality, Immigration and Asylum Act 2002, s 53 comes into force and substitutes a new s 103 into the IAA 1999, (the substituted s 103 IAA 1999 (not yet in force) has itself been amended by the Asylum and Immigration (Treatment of Claimants, etc) Act 2004, s 10(4)(c) so that when in force it includes support in accommodation centres.

6   See the Asylum Support Regulations 2000, SI 2000/704, reg 15. Other relevant changes might include disentitlement to social security benefits by refusal of an asylum claim.

Ending the appeal by withdrawal

14.174N A party may give notice of the withdrawal of its case, or any part of it (i) at any time before a hearing to consider the disposal of the proceedings or, if the Tribunal disposes of the proceedings without a hearing, before that disposal, by sending or delivering to the Tribunal a written notice of withdrawal; or (ii) orally at a hearing. Where notice is given orally at a hearing, a notice of withdrawal will not take effect unless the Tribunal consents to the withdrawal. The Tribunal must notify each party in writing of a withdrawal. A party who has withdrawn their case may apply in writing to the Tribunal for the case to be reinstated. An application must be received by the Tribunal within one month after the date on which the Tribunal received the notice prior to a hearing or disposal, or the date of the hearing at which the case was withdrawn orally.[1] On the face it, if the Secretary of State withdraws her decision, she is required to make a fresh decision on the application for support, which may be the subject of a further appeal. But in one case[2] the adjudicator treated the further decision as an amendment of the earlier one, so avoiding the delay created by the need to lodge a further appeal.[3]

---

[1] The Tribunal Procedure (First-tier Tribunal) (Social Entitlement Chamber) Rules 2008, SI 2008/2685, r 17.
[2] ASA 00/11/0116.
[3] Such delay could deprive the appellant of the right to a hearing within a reasonable time required by ECHR, Art 6, read with in conjunction with the Human Rights Act 1998, s 3.

ACCOMMODATION CENTRES

14.174O Part II of the NIAA 2002[1] provides for the accommodation of destitute asylum seekers in accommodation centres. No such centres have been established. While asylum seekers would not be 'detained' in these centres were they to be established, the Act enables the Secretary of State to control the movements of asylum seekers and to streamline the asylum process.[2] The proposed establishment of the centres was very controversial; the provisions excluding children from mainstream education were widely seen as particularly damaging to their welfare, and supporters and opponents of asylum seekers both saw the centres as dumping grounds for asylum seekers. It did not help that one of the sites proposed had previously been used for the burial of millions of diseased cattle. An avowed intention of the Home Secretary in seeking to create them was to make removal at the end of the process easier by hindering asylum seekers' integration with local communities.[3] The process of establishing the centres, often in the teeth of local resistance, met with varying success in the courts.[4] Planning permission for the Bicester Accommodation Centre was not granted until November 2004. However, in April 2005, the Home Office was advised that the Bicester Project was no longer economically viable and in June 2005 it was announced that the project was cancelled.[5] It appears that the whole scheme for accommodation centres has been scrapped, although the legislation remains in place.

---

[1] Ie, NIAA 2002, ss 16–42. Only section 16 and sections 40–42 (devolutionary obligations) are fully in force; section 18 (definition of asylum seeker) is in force for other purposes (section 55 and Schedule 3 withdrawal of support: see SI 2003/1, art 2, Schedule.)
[2] The government proposed to establish a number of large centres which would house around 3,000 asylum seekers from application through initial decision to any appeal: see White Paper,

Secure Borders, Safe Havens: Integration with Diversity in Modern Britain, CM 5387, para 4.30.
3 See Rt Hon David Blunkett in *Hansard* HC, 24 April 2002, col 353.
4 See eg *R (on the application of Cherwell District Council) v First Secretary of State and Secretary of State for the Home Department* [2004] EWHC 724 (Admin), [2004] 16 EG 111 (CS), [2004] All ER (D) 94 (Apr) Collins J, upheld by the Court of Appeal on 8 July 2004, [2004] EWCA Civ 1420, [2005] 1 WLR 1128, (2004) Times, 4 November, holding that the decision to approve the development of an accommodation centre in Bicester, Oxfordshire was lawful.
5 National Audit Office Value for Money Report: Home Office: The cancellation of Bicester Accommodation Centre

14.174P The Secretary of State has power to arrange for the provision of accommodation[1] for asylum seekers[2] (or their dependants),[3] who the Secretary of State thinks are destitute or likely to be destitute[4] within a prescribed period.[5] Regulations will prescribe the procedure to be followed in relation to the provision of accommodation in accommodation centres;[6] none have yet been made. The Secretary of State may provide facilities for both the immigration service and immigration adjudicators at or near an accommodation centre.[7] The point at which an asylum claim is treated as determined, the requirement to send a notice informing the asylum claimant of the decision, and the definition of a disposed appeal, for the purpose of support in an accommodation centre,[8] are in substance, the same as section 94(3), (4), (8) and (9) of the IAA 1999. Support under section 95 of the IAA 1999 may be provided by accommodation in an accommodation centre,[9] as may 'hard cases' support.[10] Support will not be available in an accommodation centre once any form of leave is granted.[11]

1 NIAA 2002, s 16(1).
2 Defined in NIAA 2002, s 18(1) (in force for the purpose of exclusion from support under s 55 of, and Sch 3 to, the Act: SI 2003/1), which adds to the definition in the IAA 1999, s 94(1) the requirements that the asylum claim is made at a designated place and that the person is in the UK (see **13.76** above). Section 44 of the Act, when in force, will amend IAA 1999, s 94(1) so that its definition of asylum seeker matches that in section 18(1). A person shall continue to be treated as an asylum seeker while his or her household includes a dependent child under 18: s 18(2). This does not prevent the removal of support from failed asylum seekers with dependent children under Sch 3, para 7A, added by the AI(TC)A 2004, s 9 (in force 1 December 2004: SI 2004/2999).
3 Dependants of asylum seekers are those who are present in the UK, and who further, fall within a prescribed class: NIAA 2002, s 20(2). Section 44 of the Act, when in force, will amend IAA 1999, s 94(5) so that its definition of dependants matches that in s 20(2). The Secretary of State may inquire into and determine a person's age, by s 21(2).
4 NIAA 2002, s 19(1). The definition of destitution is similar to that in IAA 1999, s 95. Section 44 of the Act, when in force, will amend IAA 1999, s 95(2) to (8) so that the definition of destitution, the matters to be considered when determining adequacy of accommodation, and regulations relating to destitution, will match exactly the provisions of s 19.
5 NIAA 2002, s 17(1). This section mirrors the powers given to the Secretary of State to provide support under IAA 1999, s 95.
6 NIAA 2002, s 17(2), (3).
7 NIAA 2002, s 16(3) (not amended to take account of the abolition of immigration adjudicators on 4 April 2005). The hearing of appeals in or near the accommodation centre may adversely affect the perception of the fairness and independence of the appellate authority, as has happened in relation to Harmondsworth Removal Centre.
8 NIAA 2002, s 21(3)–(5).
9 NIAA 2002, s 22.
10 NIAA 2002, s 23(5), referring to accommodation under IAA 1999, s 4 (including that section as amended, from 7 November 2002, by NIAA 2002, s 49). For 'hard cases' support see **14.174T** below.

[11] This is because recipients no longer fall within the definition of 'asylum seeker': see NIAA 2002, s 18(2)(b).

14.174Q A person who is granted temporary admission or release from detention by an immigration officer, or who is subject to deportation proceedings and has been granted temporary release by the Secretary of State, may be required to reside at an accommodation centre as a condition of temporary release.[1] If such a person commits one of the offences specified in section 35 of the NIAA 2002,[2] fails to comply with travel arrangements or breaches the conditions imposed on residents of the accommodation centre, and as a consequence is required to leave the centre,[3] then he or she will be treated as having broken his or her residence restriction.[4] A person may not spend more than six months in accommodation centres,[5] unless an agreement is reached between the person and the Secretary of State, however, if the Secretary of State thinks that it is appropriate because of the individual circumstances of an asylum seeker, he or she may extend the period of time from six months to nine months.[6] The Secretary of State may provide accommodation in an accommodation centre or elsewhere (including an arrangement with a local authority), if he or she thinks that an asylum seeker may be eligible for accommodation in an accommodation centre, but has not yet reached a decision on eligibility.[7]

[1] NIAA 2002, s 23(1)–(2).
[2] The section applies the provisions of the IAA 1999 which create criminal offences relating to asylum support (ss 105–109, see **14.164** above and **15.75** below), to obtaining support in an accommodation centre.
[3] NIAA 2002, s 26: see below.
[4] NIAA 2002, ss 23(4). Such a person will then be liable to arrest under para 24 of Sch 2 to the Immigration Act 1971 for breaching a condition of his or her bail or temporary admission or release.
[5] NIAA 2002, s 25(1).
[6] NIAA 2002, s 25(2)(a), (b).
[7] NIAA 2002, s 24(1).

14.174R The Secretary of State may arrange for the provision of (inter alia) food and other essential items, money, transport, certain expenses, health facilities, education and training, facilities for religious observance and legal advice at an accommodation centre.[1] Conditions to be observed by residents of accommodation centres may be imposed, in particular requiring them to remain at the centre during certain hours and to report to an immigration officer.[2] They must be imposed in writing.[3] If a resident, or his or her dependant breaches a condition, they may be required to leave the accommodation centre.[4] Residents may be subject to a condition requiring them to contribute to the accommodation and support they receive at an accommodation centre.[5] The Secretary of State may terminate accommodation at an accommodation centre if a person or a dependant commits one of the offences specified in section 35 of the NIAA 2002 or fails to comply with travel arrangements,[6] subject to a right of appeal under section 103 of the IAA 1999.[7] Residents of an accommodation centre will not acquire a tenancy or any other interest in any part of the accommodation centre, and any licence to occupy which is acquired will not prevent eviction.[8] All the measures contained within Part VI of the IAA 1999 which are designed to enforce compliance with the scheme of support under that Part of the Act, are applicable to support provided by way of accommodation in accommodation centres.[9] Each accommodation centre will have an Advisory Group who will hear residents' complaints,[10] and the Secretary of State will appoint a Monitor of Accommodation Centres who will report on the operation of accommodation centres, at least once a year.[11]

[1] NIAA 2002 s 29.
[2] NIAA 2002, s 30(1)–(3).
[3] NIAA 2002, s 30(6).
[4] NIAA 2002, s 30(4)–(5).
[5] NIAA 2002, s 31.
[6] NIAA 2002, s 26(1).
[7] NIAA 2002, s 26(4).
[8] NIAA 2002, s 32.
[9] NIAA 2002, s 35 (criminal offences, powers of recovery of expenditure and redirection of post).
[10] NIAA 2002, s 33.
[11] NIAA 2002, s 34.

14.174S The most controversial aspect of Part II of the NIAA 2002 is that residents of accommodation centres are not, for the purposes of education, treated as part of the population of a local education authority's area.[1] This means that children who are resident in an accommodation centre may not be admitted to a maintained school or nursery,[2] unless they are subject to a statement of special educational needs, in which case they may be admitted to the school named in the statement.[3] Residents are precluded from a number of rights that parents of children have, such as stating a preference as to where their child is educated; appealing against a refusal to admit a child to a maintained school; having their child educated in an off-site educational facility; having special needs provision in a mainstream school; and stating a preference as to where a child with special educational needs will be educated.[4] Whoever is running the accommodation centre, or the local education authority, must ensure that a resident child with special educational needs receives appropriate support within the education facilities provided within the centre.[5] There is, however, no such responsibility if it is beyond their capability to comply because of the severity of the child's needs, the disruption it causes to the education of other resident children, or the cost of doing so.[6] However, any decision not to provide for a child with special educational needs will be subject to a reasonableness test.[7] The bar on admission into maintained schools and nurseries is not applicable in relation to resident children if education is not provided in the accommodation centre.[8] The provisions excluding children of asylum seekers from education in the community have been the subject of fierce criticism and may be susceptible to challenge under the Human Rights Act 1998 if they discriminate in relation to the right to education guaranteed by Protocol 1, Article 2 of the ECHR.[9]

[1] NIAA 2002, s 36(1).
[2] NIAA 2002, s 36(2). In special cases, an education provider in an accommodation centre can apply to the local education authority under section 37, asserting that it is not able to provide for a child within the accommodation centre due to his or her special circumstances, and the local education authority has a discretion to provide education for the child concerned (s 37(2)). In such a case, the local education authority can require a maintained school to admit the child, unless that admission would breach the statutory limit on infant class sizes: s 37(4), (5).
[3] NIAA 2002, s 36(3).
[4] NIAA 2002, s 36(5).

⁵ NIAA 2002, s 36(7).
⁶ NIAA 2002, s 36(7)(a)–(c).
⁷ NIAA 2002, s 36(8).
⁸ NIAA 2002, s 36(10).
⁹ Article 14 of the ECHR together with Protocol 1, Art 2.

HARD CASES

14.174T Another controversial area of the asylum support system is the complete termination of all support under sections 95 or 98 of the IAA 1999 to those without dependent children under 18, once all appeals have been exhausted,[1] and to failed asylum seekers with dependent children whose appeals have been exhausted and who have been certified as failing without reasonable cause to take reasonable steps to leave the UK voluntarily or to place themselves in a position in which they are able to do so.[2] The Secretary of State has a reserve power under section 4(1) of the IAA 1999 to provide, or arrange for the provision of facilities for the accommodation of anyone who is temporarily admitted to the UK, released from detention by the immigration authorities or released on bail from immigration detention. She has a policy for the provision of accommodation to those released on bail[3] and a policy for those released on temporary admission or otherwise released from detention.[4] Under the latter of those policies, support should be provided to children whose asylum claims have been finally determined; who are destitute and who are not otherwise eligible for support. Otherwise the policy only contemplates support being provided in 'truly exceptional circumstances' where the person is destitute; has no other source of support and provision of support is necessary to avoid a breach of human rights. Section 4(2) and (3) of the Act enables the Secretary of State to provide facilities for the accommodation of failed asylum seekers and their dependants. She has made regulations specifying the criteria for determining whether to provide or continue providing accommodation to failed asylum seekers and their dependants. The criteria specified under the regulations are that the person appears to the Secretary of State to be destitute and one or more of the following additional conditions are satisfied[5]:

(a) they are taking all reasonable steps to leave the UK or place themselves in a position in which they are able to leave the UK, which may include complying with attempts to obtain a travel document to facilitate their departure;[6]

(b) they are unable to leave the UK by reason of a physical impediment to travel or for some other medical reason.[7] This criterion requires that the person is unable to leave the UK, (although it need not be literally impossible to leave); it is not sufficient that the person may have a medical condition making it undesirable in the interests of his or her treatment or prognosis to leave the UK;[8]

(c) they are unable to leave the UK because in the opinion of the Secretary of State there is no viable route of return available;[9]

(d) they have obtained permission for judicial review of a decision in relation to their asylum claim;[10]

(e) provision of accommodation is necessary to avoid a breach of their Convention rights.[11]

1   Since they cease to be asylum seekers within the statutory definition.

2   AI(TC)A 2004, s 9, inserting a new para 7A into Sch 3 to the NIAA 2002, in force 1 December 2004 by SI 2004/2999, art 2, Schedule.

3   'Section 4 Bail Accommodation', version 10, 1 July 2014 (on the UKVI website). As to the policy, see *R (on the application of Razai) v Secretary of State for the Home Department (Bail for Immigration Detainees intervening)* [2010] EWHC 3151 (Admin).

4   'Section 4 Support', version 29, 11 July 2014 (on the UKVI website).

5   The regulation making power is IAA 1999, s 4(5) and the regulations made are Immigration and Asylum (Provision of Accommodation to Failed Asylum Seekers) Regulations 2005, SI 2005/930, reg 3, in force 31 March 2005. The criteria for eligibility are set out on in the Section 4 Support Instruction and the Section 4 Support Review. See also the Section 4 guidance and Section 4 Transition Project (all on the UK Border Agency website).

6   In *R (on the application of Ahmed (Kareem)) v Asylum Support Adjudicator* [2008] EWHC 2282 (Admin), [2008] All ER (D) 12 (Oct), Silber J held that on the facts (no advantage taken of the voluntary assisted returns programme) both defendants were entitled to hold that it could not be said the claimant was taking all reasonable steps to leave the UK. The wording of the provision only applied to matters which arose in the UK and concerned leaving the UK. Even if it did not, there was no evidence to suggest that the route of return was not viable or was dangerous. A claim that a person was at risk on return contrary to Art 3 ECHR had already been considered in the unsuccessful immigration appeal and the asylum support adjudicator was entitled so to hold. Were Art 3 ECHR to be engaged, there was insufficient evidence to make good the proposition; see also *R (on the application of Guveya) v National Asyulm Support Service)* [2004] EWHC 2371 (Admin), [2004] All ER (D) 594 (Jul).

7   Immigration and Asylum (Provision of Accommodation to Failed Asylum-Seekers) Regulations 2005, SI 2005/930.

8   See *R (on the application of the Secretary of State for the Home Department) v Asylum Support Adjudicator, Osman (Mohammedi), Yillah (Zainab), Ahmad (Alhaj Adam) and Musemwa (Maggie)* [2006] EWHC 1248 (Admin), (2006) Times, 11 July.

9   In *R (on the application of Abdullah) v Secretary of State for the Home Department* (CO/3709/04), Charles J granted permission to apply for judicial review of decisions to refuse hard cases support to failed Iraqi asylum seekers other than on the basis that they return voluntarily to Iraq, as there was arguably no safe route of return. In *R (on the application of Rasul) v Asylum Support Adjudicator* [2006] EWHC 435 (Admin), [2006] ACD 62, SI 2005/930, reg 3(2)(c) was held to be satisfied where the Secretary of State has expressed an opinion that there was a viable route of return to a country for an asylum seeker. Such an opinion was in the nature of a policy decision and on appeal to the Asylum Support Adjudicators, there is no jurisdiction in that forum to enquire into the correctness of that opinion. Wilkie J observed that reg 3(2)(a) could be engaged on the basis that the Claimant was taking all reasonable steps to leave the UK or place himself in a position in which he is able to leave the UK, which may include complying with attempts to obtain a travel document to facilitate his departure. In *ASA 06/03/12859* the Chief Asylum Support Adjudicator considered *R (Rasul)* and declined to follow Wilkie J's observations in respect of reg 3(2)(a). She held that she could consider the reasonableness of steps taken but not whether it was reasonable to take a proposed step. Such proposed steps precluded from consideration included steps that would involve taking an alleged unsafe route of return. She did not consider that an asylum support adjudicator had jurisdiction to consider extra-territorial issues such as the risk incurred by taking a particular route. If the applicant had approached the International Organisation of Migration (IOM) to seek a voluntary return, the position might have been different.

10 SI 2005/930, reg 3(1), 3(2)(d), which also provides for the equivalents in Scotland and Northern Ireland. In *R v Immigration Appeal Tribunal and Lord Chancellor, ex p Mohammed Sarif Ali* [1999] Imm AR 48, Dyson J held that it was not unreasonable to use s 4 support for asylum seekers awaiting a test case on third country removals, whose asylum claims were not being decided substantively. In *R (on the application of NS) v First-tier Tribunal (Social Entitlement Chamber) and Secretary of State for the Home Department* [2009] EWHC 3819 (Admin), Stadlen J held that notwithstanding the requirement to obtain permission to apply for judicial review under reg 3(2)(d), it was an error for the Tribunal to find that permission to apply for judicial review was required to satisfy reg 3(2)(e) in circumstances where such an application for judicial review had been made and permission to proceed had yet to be granted.

11 SI 2005/930, reg 3(1), (2)(a)–(e). In *ASA/05/12/11497* the Chief Asylum Support Adjudicator considered an application for support where a fresh asylum application had been made. The

asylum support decision maker had to look at the matter on an individual basis. However, support should be granted unless the fresh claim for asylum simply rehearses previously considered material or contained no detail whatsoever. In *R (on the application of Mohammed Kareem Ahmed) v Asylum Support Adjudicator (2) Secretary of State* [2008] EWHC 2282 (Admin), [2008] ALL ER (D) 12 (Oct), Silber J held that a claim that a person was at risk on return contrary to Art 3 ECHR had already been considered in the unsuccessful immigration appeal and the asylum support adjudicator was entitled so to hold. Were Art 3 ECHR to be engaged, there was insufficient evidence to make good the proposition. See *R (on the application of NS) v (1) First-tier Tribunal (Social Entitlement Chamber) (2) Secretary of State for the Home Department* [2009] EWHC 3819 (Admin), [2009] All ER (D) 328 (Nov) in fn 11 above. In *R (on the application of Kiana and Musgrove) v Secretary of State for the Home Department* [2010] EWHC 1002 (Admin), [2010] NLJR 618, Supperstone QC held that it was lawful to refuse to support a failed asylum seeker support under section 4, to enable him to live with his family in the latter's accommodation, ie in accommodation not provided by the Secretary of State. He held that the offer of accommodation in premises other than that where his partner and child resided did not breach the applicant's rights under Art 8 ECHR. The question of whether a failed asylum seeker who makes fresh representations is eligible for IAA 1999, s 95 asylum support rather than s 4 support, on the basis that he or she is once again an 'asylum seeker' having regard to the application of Directive 2003/9/EC ('the Reception Directive') and *R (on the application of ZO (Somalia)) v Secretary of State for the Home Department* [2009] EWCA Civ 442 (now [2010] UKSC 36), has been the subject of differing decisions in the First-tier Tribunal. In AS/10/01/21325 the Principal Judge found that if the fresh representations have been recorded then the applicant is once again an asylum seeker. However, the reasoning in the decision is difficult to follow. By contrast in the latter decision of AS/10/03/22069 the Principal Judge reached a different result holding that s 4 support would suffice for compliance with the Reception Directive. In AS/10/02/21612 Judge Briden held that where a fresh claim had to be presented in person and this created a barrier for an individual applicant (s 4 support only being considered on presentation of the fresh claim), then support could nonetheless be provided under reg 3(2)(e).

14.174U The 'inability to leave the country' criterion was applied strictly in *Guveya*[1], where Moses J held that the fact that the Secretary of State had adopted a 'generous' policy of non-removal of failed asylum seekers to Zimbabwe did not mean that it was reasonable for the claimant to refuse to return voluntarily or that he was bound to be provided with accommodation. However, in *Nigatu*,[2] Collins J held that persons who had made representations which were not clearly unfounded in support of a fresh claim for asylum or under Article 3 of the ECHR were eligible, and in *Womba*,[3] an asylum support adjudicator held that only Immigration and Nationality Directorate (IND) caseworkers, and not NASS workers (the distinction may now be elided under the New Asylum Model (NAM) for case owners, although the training provided to them and designation of their formal competencies will still be material), were able to decide that representations were clearly unfounded. However, it has been held in the Administrative Court that *Womba* was incorrectly decided.[4] Where a failed asylum seeker makes representations purporting to be a fresh asylum or human rights claim and before the Secretary of State decides whether to accept the representations as such, a caseworker or local authority is entitled to form a view of the merits of the putative claim in order to decide whether the person must be supported in order to avoid a breach of his or her Convention rights. However, 'it is only in the clearest cases that it will be appropriate for the public body concerned to refuse relief on the basis of the manifest inadequacy of the purported fresh grounds'.[5] The Section 4 Support Instruction accepts that the submission of further representations seeking leave to remain where there is or will be a delay in serving a decision on those further representations (unless it is clear that the further representations are manifestly unfounded, or merely repeat the previous grounds or do not disclose any claim for asylum at all), or the submission of a late appeal out of time which is under consideration by the appellate authorities, are situations where the provision of hard cases support may be necessary to avoid a breach of Convention rights.[6] The Secretary of State's policy whereby she allowed herself 15 days (and in practice, longer) to decide applications for support under section 4 was held to be unlawful both by reference to Article 3 of the ECHR and to the Reception Directive.[7] The current policy provides as 'a general rule' that decisions should be made within five days, two in the case of people who are street homeless; families with children; disabled, elderly or pregnant; persons who have been subjected to torture, rape or other serious forms of psychological, physical or sexual violence or potential victims of trafficking.[8] An asylum seeker who is refused support under section 55 of the NIAA 2002 is not entitled to hard cases support.[9] Neither is an adult former asylum seeker who has failed to comply with removal directions, a person unlawfully in the UK in breach of the immigration laws or the adults in a family certified as having failed to take reasonable steps to leave voluntarily following final determination of their claim, save where support is necessary to avoid a breach of their Convention rights or their rights under the Community Treaties.[10] The regulations under section 4(5)[11] of the IAA 1999 allow conditions to be imposed on the continued provision of section 4 support, including a condition that the person in question performs or participates in specified community activities.[12] The AI(TC)A 2004 provided a new right of appeal to the asylum support adjudicators, now the First-tier Tribunal (Social Entitlement Chamber) in its capacity as the First-tier Tribunal (Asylum Support), in relation to the refusal or termination of support under section 4.[13] It is UK Border Agency policy, in cases of priority, to decide an application for support under s 4 within 48 hours, see *R (Matembera) v Secretary of State for the Home Department*.[14] Support provided under section 4 of the 1999 Act may be provided by a local authority in accordance with arrangements made by the Secretary of State under s 99(1) of the 1999 Act, following an amendment by section 43 of the IAN 2006.[15] In connection with this, an authority may incur reasonable expenditure in connection with preparing to enter into arrangements under section 4 of the 1999 Act, see section 99(4) of the 1999 Act as amended.[16] Accommodation under section 4 of the 1999 Act is excluded from the protective provisions of the Protection from Eviction Act 1977.[17]

[1]   *R (on the application of Guveya) v National Asylum Support Service* [2004] EWHC 2371 (Admin), [2004] All ER (D) 594 (Jul), a case with serious implications for asylum seeking families deprived of support under the NIAA 2002, Sch 3, para 7A (inserted by the AI(TC)A 2004, s 9 from 1 December 2004) if they fail to leave the country voluntarily or put themselves in a position where they are able to do so.

[2]   *R (on the application of Nigatu) v Secretary of State for the Home Department* [2004] EWHC 1806 (Admin) [2004] ACD 89, (2004) Times, 30 July.

[3]   ASA/05/04/9198.

[4]   *R (on the application of AW) v Croydon London Borough Council; R (on the application of A, D and Y) v Hackney London Borough Council* [2005] EWHC 2950 (Admin), (2006) BLGR 159.

[5]   Lloyd Jones J in R (on the application of AW) v Croydon London Borough Council.

[6]   Section 4 Support Instruction, p 24. From 14 October 2009, persons seeking section 4 accommodation will be refused unless they have attended an appointment to make further representations. If an applicant submits an application for section 4 solely on the basis that he or she has further representations awaiting consideration, the policy is to assess those further representations before the application for section 4 support is considered, ibid, pp 24–25. In particular cases this could lead to a person being refused section 4 support while awaiting their

appointment and being/verging on being destitute contrary to Art 3 ECHR. In such circumstances the application of the policy would be unlawful. See also *R (on the application of Erdogan (Sahsenem)) v Secretary of State for the Home Department* [2004] EWCA Civ 1087, para 21.

7 *MK v Secretary of State for the Home Department* [2012] EWHC 1896 (Admin).

8 'Section 4 Support', version 29, 11 July 2014, UKVI website.

9 At least, not while he or she remains an asylum seeker (as opposed to a failed asylum seeker who cannot leave, when hard cases support might be available under SI 2005/930, reg 3).

10 NIAA 2002, s 54, Sch 3, paras 1, 3, 6, 7, and 7A; SI 2005/930 reg 3(1), (2) above, unless they qualify under one of the other sub-paragraphs such as a medical condition precluding removal.

11 SI 2005/930, in force 31 March 2005. Subsections (5)–(9) were inserted into the IAA 1999, s 4 by the Asylum and Immigration (Treatment of Claimants etc) Act 2004, s 10(1), in force 1 December 2004 (SI 2004/2999). Section 10(1), (2), (6) and (7) were brought into force on 1 December 2004 by the Asylum and Immigration (Treatment of Claimants etc) Act 2004 (Commencement No 2) Order 2004, SI 2004/2999 and s 10(3), (4) and (5) were brought into force on 31 March 2005 by the Asylum and Immigration (Treatment of Claimants etc) Act 2004 (Commencement No 4) Order 2005, SI 2005/372. The Immigration and Asylum (Provision of Accommodation to Failed Asylum-Seekers) Regulations 2005, SI 2005/930 also came into force on 31 March 2005.

12 SI 2005/930, regs 4–6. The Joint Committee on Human Rights expressed concern that the performance of community service as a condition of subsistence support could violate Article 4 of the ECHR: 14th report Session 2003–2004: Asylum and Immigration (Treatment of Claimants) Bill, additional clauses, 5.7.04 (HL 130/HC 828). Community service conditions are not imposed at present. Other conditions which may be imposed include compliance with standards of behaviour, reporting and residence restrictions and with specified steps to facilitate removal: reg 6.

13 AI(TC)A 2004, s 10(3), inserting s 103(2A) into the NIAA 2002, in force 31 March 2005: SI 2005/372. The transfer to the First-tier Tribunal (Social Entitlement Chamber) was effected by the Transfer or Tribunal Function Order 2008, SI 2008/2833 and the First-tier Tribunal and Upper Tribunal (Chambers) Order 2008, SI 2008/2684.

14 In *R (on the application of Matembera) v Secretary of State for the Home Department* [2007] EWHC 2334 (Admin) interim relief was obtained by a destitute failed asylum seeker in circumstances where this policy was not followed. At an oral hearing permission to apply for judicial review was refused as s 4 accommodation was no longer required. Hodge J held there was no duty to provide support pending a decision whether to provide s 4 support, however long delay in assessing a claim might lead to a breach of rights under the ECHR. He further held that such a breach had been prevented by the intervention of the Court and that it was incumbent on the Secretary of State to put in place a system that avoided delay.

15 In force 16 June 2006, Immigration, Asylum and Nationality Act 2006 (Commencement No 1) Order 2006, SI 2006/1497.

16 In force 16 June 2006, Immigration, Asylum and Nationality Act 2006 (Commencement No 1) Order 2006, SI 2006/1497.

17 See s 3A(7A) of the Protection from Eviction Act 1977, as amended by s 43(4) of the IAN 2006 – in force 16 June 2006, Immigration, Asylum and Nationality Act 2006 (Commencement No 1) Order 2006, SI 2006/1497.

14.174V The support which may be provided is primarily accommodation, but the Secretary of State has accepted that it is 'full board'.[1] It was envisaged that meals rather than vouchers and cash would be provided.[2] For a time, £35 per week in voucher support was provided and no cash. Recently, a payment card has been introduced in place of vouchers, whereby £35 a week is allocated to the card but only £5 per week may be carried over to the following week, making it difficult to save up to bulk buy food at cheaper prices. Currently, most of the accommodation provided under these powers is outside London. All section 4 supported persons in London were to be transferred to the regions by the end of 2008 unless there was a so-called 'genuine need' to remain in London. If Part II of the 2002 Act is brought into force, section 4 accommodation may be provided in an accommodation centre.[3] Even though section 4, as amended by section 49 of the NIAA 2002, gives the Secretary of State a discretion to accommodate failed asylum seekers, in practice, for those who meet the criteria for its provision, it has become a right, and the former Immigration and Nationality Department's policy of not informing failed asylum seekers of its existence was held to be unlawful.[4] However, if support is withdrawn on the ground that in the Secretary of State's opinion there is a viable route of return to the asylum seeker's country[5], the asylum support adjudicator (now First-tier Tribunal (Asylum Support)) may consider only whether the Secretary of State held that opinion. The adjudicator (now First-tier Tribunal (Asylum Support)) may not determine whether there is in fact a viable route of return because that is a matter of policy and challengeable, if at all, by judicial review.[6]

1. NASS letter 3 April 2000 to 'Assistant' voluntary sector organisations involved in administering NASS support scheme, Annex A. In *R (on the application of MK) v Secretary of State for the Home Department* [2011] EWCA Civ 671, [2011] All ER (D) 158 (Apr) it was held that the power under s 4 to provide or arrange for the provision of facilities for the accommodation of a person did not permit the Secretary of State to provide stand-alone facilities, such as food vouchers, that were not linked to her provision or arrangement of accommodation.
2. NASS letter 3 April 2000 (see n 1 above), para 3.
3. NIAA 2002, s 23(5).
4. *R (on the application of Salih) v Secretary of State for the Home Department* [2003] EWHC 2273 (Admin), [2003] All ER (D) 129 (Oct), (2003) Times, 13 October.
5. So that the Immigration and Asylum (Provision of Accommodation to Failed Asylum-Seekers) Regulations 2005, SI 2005/930, r 3(2)(c) does not, or no longer applies.
6. *R (on the application of Rasul) v Asylum Support Adjudicator* [2006] EWHC 435 (Admin), [2006] All ER (D) 364 (Feb), [2006] ACD 62.

14.174W In respect of travel expenses, the Home Office has produced a policy called '*Travelling expenses policy: Contact management policy, process and implementation*', version 5, June 2006. This policy is made pursuant to section 69 of the NIAA 2002, a provision that permits the Secretary of State to make a payment in respect of travelling expenses incurred for the purpose of complying with a reporting restriction. The policy applies to both asylum seekers and failed asylum seekers. Expenses will be paid where a person has to attend a reporting centre and makes a journey of three miles or more to do so or where there are exceptional needs. In respect of travel to section 4 accommodation, see Policy Bulletin 28.[1] Under section 4(2) of the IAA 1999 the reference to 'facilities for the accommodation of a person' does not empower the Home Secretary to provide clothing to a failed asylum seeker or her child.[2] However, by section 43(7) of the IAN 2006, section 4 of the 1999 Act has been enlarged by the addition of subsections (10)–(11).[3] As a result, regulations may be made to permit a person provided with accommodation to be provided with services or facilities of a specified kind. By section 4(10)–(11) a voucher exchangeable for goods or services may be supplied, while money may not. Pursuant to this amendment, the Home Office has introduced the Immigration and Asylum (Provision of Services or Facilities) Regulations 2007.[4] These regulations allow an applicant to seek travel costs in respect of registering a birth or necessary medical treatment. By the regulations the Home Office are also able to provide for the cost of a birth certificate, one-off £250 vouchers for a pregnant or nursing mother and weekly vouchers to pregnant women and those with young children (£3 a week to a pregnant mother or mother with a child aged one or over, £5 a week to a mother with a child under one year old). Vouchers are also available to provide for clothing to children under sixteen years old (at £5 a week) and exceptional needs. There is also a power to provide facilities for official phone calls and correspondence.

[1] Policy Bulletin 28, Providing travelling expenses and reimbursing essential travel costs, version 3.0, 26 November 2008, paras 7.1 and 10.19.

[2] *R (on the application of W) v Secretary of State for the Home Department* [2006] EWHC 3147 (Admin), [2007] ACD 33.

[3] In force 16 June 2006, Immigration, Asylum and Nationality Act 2006 (Commencement No 1) Order 2006, SI 2006/1497.

[4] SI 2007/3627 in force 31 January 2008. See also policy document 'Section 4: additional services or facilities under the 2007 regulations', latest version 13 August 2013, UKVI website

SUPPORT FOR THOSE WITH SPECIAL IMMIGRATION STATUS

14.174X Under Part 10 of the Criminal Justice and Immigration Act 2008, not yet in force, the Secretary of State may designate a person who is (a) a 'foreign criminal' (as defined in the Act) who is liable to deportation but cannot be removed on account of obligations arising under the Human Rights Act 1998 and the ECHR, or (b) is a family member of someone who falls within (a). Persons with the right of abode, including British citizens, may not be designated. A designated person does not have leave to enter or remain in the United Kingdom, is subject to immigration control, is not to be treated as an asylum seeker or a former asylum seeker, and is not in the UK in breach of immigration laws. Such a designated person may not be granted temporary admission. Conditions may be imposed on a designated person, relating to residence, employment or occupation, and reporting to the police, Secretary of State or an immigration officer. Travel expenses in connection with compliance with reporting conditions, may be obtained under s 69 of the Nationality, Immigration and Asylum Act 2002. A designated person will not have access to welfare benefits as he will be excluded by s 115 of the Immigration and Asylum Act 1999. Conditions imposed may also prevent employment or other economic activity.

14.174Y Part 10 of the Criminal Justice and Immigration Act 2008 applies the asylum support regime under Pt VI of the Immigration and Asylum Act 1999, with modifications, to designated persons and their dependants. Support may be by way of providing accommodation appearing to the Secretary of State to be adequate for a person's needs, meeting what appear to be essential living needs, and by other ways which the Secretary of State thinks necessary to reflect the exceptional circumstances of a particular case. Support may not be provided wholly or mainly by way of cash unless the Secretary of State thinks it necessary to reflect the particular circumstances of a particular case (this restriction may be repealed, modified or disapplied by an order made by the Secretary of State). A notice to quit accommodation provided may be served where a person has ceased to be a designated person. Support under section 4 of the 1999 Act is not available to designated persons. The Secretary of State is relieved of the obligation under section 97 of the 1999 Act to have regard to the desirability of providing accommodation in a well-supplied area. Local authorities, registered social landlords, registered housing associations in Scotland and Northern Ireland and the Northern Ireland Housing Executive are relieved of the obligation to assist the Secretary of State in the provision of accommodation under s 100 of the 1999 Act in respect of designated persons. Part VI of the 1999 Act is further modified in that obligations arising under sections 101 (reception zones), 108 (failure of the sponsor to maintain), 111 (grants to voluntary organisations), and 113 (recovery of expenditure from sponsor) do not to apply in respect of designated persons. References in Part VI of the 1999 Act which require or permit the Secretary of State to have regard to the temporary nature of asylum support are to be read as requiring the Secretary of State to have regard to the nature and circumstances of support provided to the designated person.

14.174Z However, by section 134(6) of the CJIA 2008 as enacted, a designated person is not to be treated as a person from abroad who is not eligible for housing assistance as homeless under s 185(4) of the Housing Act 1996 or as a person subject to immigration control for the purposes of s 119(1)(b) of the Immigration and Asylum Act 1999 (homelessness: Scotland and Northern Ireland). Thus, for homelessness purposes a designated person is not to be disregarded in determining whether another person (a) is homeless or threatened with homelessness, or (b) has a priority need for accommodation. Section 134(6) has been repealed as it is no longer needed.[1] In addition, as with support provided under Pt VI of the 1999 Act to asylum seekers, there is a right of appeal to the First-tier Tribunal (Social Entitlement Chamber). After a designation lapses support may not be provided for a time thereafter unless (a) the person is granted leave to enter or remain in the United Kingdom or is notified by the Secretary of State or an immigration officer of a right of residence in the United Kingdom under the Community Treaties;[2] or (b) the person is made the subject of a deportation order under s 5 of the Immigration Act 1971.[3]

[1] Section 134(6) was repealed by the Housing and Regeneration Act 2008, ss 314, 321(1), Sch 15, Pt 3, paras 23, 24, Sch 16 and SI 2009/415, Art 4(b)(ii), from 2 March 2009. By section 135(7), an order made under s 10 of the Human Rights Act 1998 amending one of the homelessness provisions, s 185(4) of the Housing Act 1996 or s 119(1)(b) of the Immigration and Asylum Act 1999 (homelessness: Scotland and Northern Ireland), may also have repealed or amended s 134(6) of the Act. However, events have moved on. The Housing and Regeneration Act 2008, s 314, Sch 15 made amendments to the Housing Act 1996, the Housing (Scotland) Act 1987, the Housing (Northern Ireland) Order 1988 and the Immigration and Asylum Act 1999. The amendments have the intention of addressing the declaration of incompatibility made in *R (on the application of Morris) v Westminster City Council* [2005] EWCA Civ 1184, [2006] 1 WLR 505 so that the eligibility provisions of the housing legislation in question are not discriminatory contrary to Art 14 ECHR. The amendments came into force by the Housing and Regeneration Act 2008 (Commencement No 1 and Savings Provisions) Order 2009, SI 2009/415, Art 2 and repeal the provisions of the Criminal Justice and Immigration Act 2008 exempting designated person from this discrimination, on the basis that such discrimination no longer exists. Whether the amendments do actually remove all traces of discrimination is another matter.

[2] Support may be provided in respect of a period which begins when the designation lapses, and ends on a date determined in accordance with an order of the Secretary of State.

[3] Support may be provided in respect of (a) any period during which an appeal against the deportation order may be brought (ignoring any possibility of an appeal out of time with permission), (b) any period during which an appeal against the deportation order is pending, and (c) after an appeal ceases to be pending, such period as the Secretary of State may specify by order.

COMMUNITY CARE PROVISION FOR THOSE SUBJECT TO IMMIGRATION CONTROL

Asylum seekers

14.175 In *R v Westminster City Council, ex p A, M and X*[1] the Court of Appeal held that all destitute adult asylum seekers, able bodied as well as disabled, who were deprived of other support were entitled to assistance in the form of accommodation under section 21 of the National Assistance Act 1948 (NAA 1948).[2] This led in part to the asylum support legislation in the Immigration and Asylum Act 1999 and the creation of the National Asylum Support Service, which was designed to relieve local authorities of the responsibility for providing support to such asylum seekers. One of the stated purposes behind the IAA 1999 was also to reduce the perceived incentive provided by the availability of welfare benefits and community care provision, which was thought to attract economic migrants, as opposed to asylum seekers, to make applications for asylum in the UK.[3] Section 116 of the IAA 1999 was designed to amend section 21 of the NAA 1948 in order to prevent local authorities giving assistance to destitute adult asylum seekers or to anyone who was subject to immigration control if the need for care and attention arose solely from destitution or because of the physical or anticipated physical effects of being destitute.[4] Subject to section 21(1A), the criteria for eligibility for residential care under s 21(1)(a) of the NAA 1948 are that: (i) the person must have a need for 'care and attention' which is; (ii) as a result of his or her age, illness, disability, or other circumstances; and (iii) the support is not 'otherwise available to' him or her than by the provision of residential care.[5]

[1] *R v Westminster City Council*, ex p (1) A; (2) M; (3) *R v Lambeth London Borough Council, ex p P*; (4) X (1997) 1 CCLR 85, (1997), Times, 19 February.

[2] The position of support for lone children and adults with dependent children is considered below.

[3] 'Basis of a Safety Net Scheme' in White Paper 'Fairer, Faster and Firmer – A Modern Approach to Immigration and Asylum', July 1998, chapter 8, p 39.

[4] IAA 1999, s 116, inserting new sub-sections (1A) and (1B) into the NAA 1948, s 21.

[5] Section 21(1)(aa) deals with the position of expectant and nursing mothers, and the same criteria as to the need for care and attention which is not otherwise available to them applies to this category of persons.

14.176 In such a case, the House of Lords held in *Westminster v National Asylum Support Service* that the Secretary of State is relieved of any duty that would otherwise fall upon her or him to support that person under the asylum support provisions.[1] Their Lordships characterised the asylum support powers to provide support under the IAA 1999 as residual powers, which could be exercised if no other support was available for an asylum seeker. A failed asylum seeker in need of care and attention arising not solely from destitution, or because of the physical or anticipated physical effects of being destitute, who has an outstanding fresh asylum or human rights application that has yet to be accepted as a fresh claim, is similarly entitled to assistance in the form of accommodation from a local authority under the NAA 1948, rather than support from the Home Office under the IAA 1999, s 4. A local authority has a duty to provide residential accommodation for a destitute asylum seeker who suffers from a disability even if the disability would not generally require the provision of residential accommodation,[2] since all destitute asylum seekers are entitled to assistance under the NAA 1948, s 21 following the Court of

Appeal's decision in *R v Westminster City Council, ex p A, M and X*[3] unless specifically excluded by the insertion of subsection (1A) into that section by section 116 of the IAA 1999. Similarly, a failed asylum seeker or other person who is eligible for support under section 21 of the NAA 1948 would not be eligible for support under section 4 of the IAA 1999. That is because the eligibility for section 21 support would exclude the person from the statutory definition of 'destitute' which has to be satisfied in order to qualify for support under section 4.[4]

1   *R (on the application of Westminster City Council) v National Asylum Support Service* [2002] UKHL 38, [2002] 1 WLR 2956, [2002] 4 All ER 654, [2003] LGR 23, [20002] HLR 58, (2002) Times, 18 October.

2   *R (on the application of AW) v Croydon London Borough Council* [2007] EWCA Civ 266, [2007] 1 WLR 3168, [2007] LGR 417, (2007) Times, 11 May.

3   *R (on the application of Mani) v Lambeth London Borough Council and the Secretary of State for the Home Department* [2003] EWCA Civ 836, [2004] LGR 35, (2003) Times, 23 July.

4   *R (on the application of AW) v Croydon London Borough Council* [2007] EWCA Civ 266, [2007] 1 WLR 3168, [2007] LGR 417, (2007) Times, 11 May. For the position of nursing and expectant mothers under section 21(1)(aa), where the obligation falls on the Secretary of State, see *R (on the application of AG) v Leeds City Council* [2007] EWHC 3275 (Admin), [2007] All ER (D) 163 (Dec)

14.177 Authoritative guidance regarding the meaning of 'care and attention' was given by the House of Lords in *R (on the application of M) v Slough Borough Council*.[1] Lady Hale, giving the leading speech, stated that the natural and ordinary meaning of the words 'care and attention' is 'looking after'. Looking after means doing something for the person being cared for which he or she cannot or should not be expected to do autonomously. She gave a series of (non-exhaustive) examples and stated that the approach to defining what is a need for 'care and attention' must draw a reasonable line between the able-bodied and the infirm. The concept needed to be treated with some 'sensible flexibility' so as to allow a local authority to intervene before 'a present need . . . becomes a great deal worse'.[2] Lord Neuberger, agreeing with Lady Hale, added[3] that 'care and attention' does not involve the 'mere provision of physical things', emphasising that the mere need for accommodation or funds did not give rise to a need for 'care and attention' but recognising that without a home, money or access to food, a person may 'soon become' in need of care and attention. The assessment of 'care and attention' is as to current needs, not future needs. Thus in a series of cases, it has been held that an asylum seeker whose need for 'care and attention' is to any material extent made more acute by some circumstance other than mere lack of accommodation and funds, he or she can be entitled to assistance under the NAA 1948, if 'care and attention' is 'not otherwise available' to him or her.[4]

1   [2008] UKHL 52, [2008] 1 WLR 1808. This was affirmed by the Supreme Court in *R (on the application of S) v Westminster City Council* [2013] UKSC 27, [2013] 1 WLR 1445.

2   See [31–35] of Lady Hale's speech.

3   See [56] of Lord Neuberger's speech.

4   *R v Wandsworth London Borough Council, ex p O; R v Leicester City Council, ex p Bhikha* [2000] 1 WLR 2539, [2000] 4 All ER 590, CA; see also *R (on the application of PB) v Haringey London Borough Council* [2006] EWHC 2255 (Admin), [2000] HLR 175; *R (on the application of M) v Slough Borough Council* [2008] UKHL 52, [2008] 1 WLR 1808, [2008] 4 All ER 831, [2008] HLR 44, (2008) Times, 5 September; *R (on the application of Pajaziti (Rasim) and Pajaziti (Hylkije)) v Lewisham London Borough Council* [2007] EWCA Civ 1351; *R (on the application of Sharef v Coventry City Council* [2009] EWHC 2191 (Admin), and *R (on the application of Zarzour) v Hillingdon London Borough Council* [2009] EWCA

Civ 1529, [2010] NLJR 1075 for applications of these provisions in the context of subsequent case law. In Z at first instance, [2009] EWHC 1398 (Admin), Brennan J noted that it was present not future need that needed to be considered unless any improvement is likely to be practically immediate, and that care from friends and relatives did not mean that care and attention was 'otherwise available'. See also *Nassery v Brent London Borough Council* [2011] EWCA Civ 539, [2011] LGR 711, (2011) Times, 5 July as regards mental health and care and attention but see the Supreme Court's decision in *R (on the application of SL) v Westminster City Council* [2013] UKSC 27, [2013] 1 WLR 1445, referred to below at **14.178**.

14.178 Before the Supreme Court's decision in *SL v Westminster City Council*,[1] the approach was to find that a person is entitled to NAA 1948, s 21 where his or her need for 'care and attention' is to any material degree made more acute by some circumstance other than the lack of accommodation or funds. *SL v Westminster City Council* considered the ambit of 'not otherwise available'. Before the Court of Appeal, it was held that 'care and attention' was not otherwise available unless it would be reasonably practicable and efficacious to supply it without the provision of accommodation.[2] The Supreme Court in *SL v Westminster City Council* rejected the formulation adopted by the Court of Appeal in the same case, finding that what is involved in providing 'care and attention' must take some colour from its association with the duty to provide residential accommodation. While it is not confined to care and attention which can only be delivered in specialist residential accommodation, the individual's condition must be in some sense 'accommodation-related'. Giving the speech for the justices, Lord Carnwath held that 'not otherwise available' means that it has at least to be 'care and attention of a sort which is normally provided in the home (whether ordinary or specialised) or will be effectively useless if the claimant has no home.'[3]

[1] [2013] UKSC 27, [2013] 1 WLR 1445.
[2] Per Laws LJ at [37] and [44] of the judgment ([2011] EWCA Civ 954, [2012] 1 All ER 935).
[3] Per Lord Carnwath at [49], 1463F–G.

14.179 Where an asylum seeker has lost an appeal for leave to remain under Article 3 of the ECHR, has thereafter made an application to the European Court of Human Rights, and that Court has asked for the applicant not to be removed, the situation for asylum support purposes, is analogous to that when a fresh application for asylum is made and support is sought pending a decision on whether to consider the fresh application as a fresh claim, see *R (N) v Lambeth*.[1] Accordingly, in that case it was held that it was not correct for a local authority to apply its eligibility criteria based on the *Fair Access to Care Services Guidance (FACS)*.[2] The correct approach once again is to consider that an applicant with a need for care and attention which arises as the result of his or her age, illness, disability or other circumstances, which is not being met, is still entitled to assistance under the NAA 1948, if the need for care and attention is to any material extent made more acute by some circumstance other than mere lack of accommodation and funds. The potential availability of accommodation under section 4 of the IAA 1999 should not be taken into account when an assessment is made as to whether there is a duty under section 21 of the NAA 1948. Furthermore, pursuant to Schedule 3 to the NIAA 2002, a prior question as to eligibility for assistance under the NAA 1948 was to consider whether assistance was required to avoid a breach of rights under the ECHR. On a different point arising in a different case, where a destitute asylum-seeking parent is entitled to support under section 21 of the

NAA 1948 as a result of her need for care and attention as a person who is HIV positive, a local authority will have no power to provide care and assistance to her children, as its powers under section 21 are restricted to those who are aged 18 and over. In such a situation, as she and her dependants have additional needs which are not being met by section 21 and cannot be met by section 17 of the Children Act 1989 because of the provisions of section 122 of the IAA 1999, the Secretary of State should make arrangements with the local authority to make a financial contribution to cover the costs of supporting her children.[3]

1   *R (on the application of N) v Lambeth London Borough Council* [2006] EWHC 3427 (Admin), [2007] ACD 49. By the time of the appeal, see [2007] EWCA Civ 862, the local authority had agreed to undertake a re-assessment and so the appeal was considered to be of academic interest only. On that basis, the Court of Appeal did not consider it appropriate to consider the merits.
2   The *FACS Guidance* was replaced by the *Prioritising Needs in the context of Putting People First: A whole system approach to eligibility for social care* (April 2010).
3   *R (on the application of O) v Haringey London Borough Council* [2004] EWCA Civ 535, [2004] LGR 672, [2004] 2 FCR 219, [2004] 2 FLR 476, (2004) Times, 27 May.

Other persons subject to immigration control

14.180 Persons who are subject to immigration control and who are not asylum seekers may also be entitled to support under the NAA 1948 if their need arose for those same reasons and not merely because of an inability to access benefits or to obtain permission to work, or otherwise support themselves. For instance, where an overstayer was chronically ill as a result of being HIV positive, his needs arose from a combination of illness and destitution and he was held to be a person who was entitled to care and attention from his local authority under the Act.[1] However, the House of Lords has made it clear that the care and attention required must be care and attention from the local authority and must relate to matters other than a mere need for accommodation. Care and attention embraces a need for help with personal care, household tasks or supervision, where a person cannot or cannot reasonably be expected to manage these tasks himself.[2] A victim of domestic violence may also be entitled to care and attention under the Act.[3] Those who are unfit to return to their country of origin,[4] or who are prevented from returning home by factors outside their own control,[5] may also have a need for care and attention. In addition, failed asylum seekers may also have a need for care and attention.[6] However, the mere existence of mental illness does not give rise to a need for care and attention. The care and attention must in those circumstances be 'accommodation-related'.[7] However, any entitlement is subject to the provisions of Sch 3 to the NIAA 2002 and the Withholding and Withdrawal of Support (Travel Assistance and Temporary Accommodation) Regulations 2002.[8] Schedule 3 prevents a local authority from providing support to various categories of people defined by their nationality, their immigration status and whether they have failed to comply with removal directions or failed to take steps to leave the country,[9] save where the withdrawal or withholding of support would be a breach of either ECHR or EU rights.[10] In such cases the person gets through the gateway to mainstream support under para 1, including section 21 of the NAA 1948, because it is necessary to avoid a breach of those rights.[11] If a person has made a human rights application to stay in the UK or is otherwise not free to go, it may be necessary for a local authority to take a view as to its merits of that application in order to determine whether provision of support is necessary, whilst the Home Office considers whether the application for leave to remain should be allowed to avoid a breach of human rights that would be occasioned by return. However, it would only be if the local authority could properly characterise the human rights application as manifestly unfounded in the sense of being hopeless or abusive that it could withhold support on the basis that it was not necessary to avoid a breach of ECHR rights.[12] Whilst Sch 3 makes a person ineligible for the provision of 'support or assistance' it does not affect a person's eligibility for the provision of a personal adviser and a pathway plan under s 23C of the Children Act 1989 because these things are not 'support or assistance'.[13] It has been held to be lawful for a local authority to carry out a Sch 3 assessment to show that it had no power to provide assistance and then to refuse to conduct a community care assessment.[14] However, given that Sch 3 itself requires the exercise of a power or the performance of a duty to the extent necessary to avoid a breach of ECHR or EU rights, this approach may not be correct in every case.

[1] *R (on the application of M) v Slough Borough Council* [2004] EWHC 1109 (Admin), [2004] LGR 657, [2004] All ER (D) 283, Collins J. The Court of Appeal approved Collins J's judgment in *R (on the application of M) v Slough Borough Council* [2006] EWCA Civ 655, [2007] LGR 225, (2006) Times 13 June. However, see the judgment of the House of Lords, cited in fn 2 below, that care and attention required must be care and attention from the local authority and must relate to matters other than a mere need for accommodation.

[2] *R (on the application of M) v Slough London Borough Council* [2008] UKHL 52, [2008)]1 WLR 1808, [2008] 4 All ER 831, [2008] HLR 44, Times, 5 September 2008. See also *Nassery v Brent London Borough Council* [2011] EWCA Civ 539, [2011] LGR 711, (2011) Times, 5 July as regards mental health and care and attention; *R (on the application of SL) v City of Westminster and two others* [2011] EWCA Civ 954 on the relationship between care and attention and the provision of accommodation.

[3] *R (on the application of Khan) v Oxfordshire County Council* [2004] EWCA Civ 309, [2004] HLR 706, [2004] LGR 257. On the facts of the case she was not found to be entitled to care and attention under s 21.

[4] *R v Brent London Borough Council, ex p D* [1998] 1 CCLR 234.

[5] *R v Lambeth London Borough Council, ex p Sarhangi* [1999] 2 CCL Rep 145.

[6] *R (SL) v Westminster City Council* [2013] UKSC 27 per Lord Carnwath at [44]–[49], in particular [48]: 'it has at least to be care and attention of a sort which is normally provided in the home (whether ordinary or specialised) or will be effectively useless if the claimant has no home.'

[7] See, for example, *R (on the application of N) v Coventry City Council* [2008] EWHC 2786 (Admin).

[8] SI 2002/3078.

[9] NIAA 2002, Sch 3, paras 4–7A (para 7A inserted by the AI(TC)A 2004, s 9, in force from 1 December 2004 by the Asylum and Immigration (Treatment of Claimants etc) Act 2004 (Commencement No 2) Order 2004, SI 2004/2999). Section 44 of the IAN 2006 provides that the Secretary of State may make an order that para 7A of Sch 3 to the 2004 Act shall cease to have effect. Section 44 of the 2006 Act is not yet in force. At the time of writing, the Home Office have indicated that para 7A will remain in force, although it is not in practice applied. The provisions disqualify affected persons from support or assistance under the National Assistance Act, ss 21 and 29 (accommodation and welfare), the Health Services and Public Health Act 1968, s 45 (welfare of elderly), s 254 of, and Sch 20 to, the National Health Service Act 2006, or s 192 of, and Sch 15 to, the National Health Service (Wales) Act 2006 (social services), Children Act 1989, ss 17, 23C, 24A and 24B (welfare powers which can be exercised in relation to adults), and their Scottish and Northern Irish equivalents: Sch 3, para 1(1). The Law Commission Consultation Paper on Adult Social Care (No 192) (24 February 2010) contemplates that obligations arising under the Chronically Sick and Disabled Persons Act 1970, s 2 and the Mental Health Act 1983, s 117 could be added to the list of community care functions subject to an immigration based exclusionary regime, see Part 9, paras 9.76–9.81.

10 NIAA 2002, Sch 3, para 3.
11 NIAA 2002, Sch 3, para 3.
12 *R (on the application of B) v Southwark London Borough Council* [2006] EWHC 2254 (Admin), [2007] 3 FCR 457, [2007] ACD 35, applying *R (on the application of Kimani) v Lambeth London Borough Council* [2003] EWCA Civ 1150, [2004] 1 WLR 272, [2003] 3 FCR 222; *R (on the application of PB) v Haringey London Borough Council* [2006] EWHC 2255 (Admin), [2000] HLR 175; *R (on the application of AW) v Croydon London Borough Council*; *R (on the application of A, D and Y) v Hackney London Borough Council* [2005] EWHC 2950 (Admin), [2005] All ER (D) 251 (Dec), [2006] LGR 159 and *Clue v Birmingham City Council (Shelter intervening)* [2010] EWCA Civ 460, [2010] Fam Law 802, (2010) Times, 7 May.
13 *R (on the application of B) v London Borough of Southwark* (see fn 12 above).
14 *R (on the application of Sharef) v Coventry City Council* [2009] EWHC 2191 (Admin).

Exclusion from support

14.181 The categories of persons prima facie ineligible for support are: non-EEA nationals with refugee status abroad in another EEA state, and their dependants;[1] citizens of other EEA Member States and their dependants;[2] former asylum seekers who fail to co-operate with removal directions, and their dependants;[3] persons who are not asylum seekers and are in the UK in breach of the immigration laws;[4] and failed asylum seekers with families where the Secretary of State has certified that in her opinion they have failed to take reasonable steps to leave voluntarily, or to put themselves in a position to do so, after their appeals are finally determined.[5] No appeal lies against refusal or withdrawal of support on the basis that a provision of Schedule 3 applies, except in the last case.[6] A failed asylum seeker who claimed asylum at port and continues to be on temporary admission is not unlawfully in the UK and so is not caught by the exclusion of those in the UK in breach of immigration laws.[7] A local authority can make travel arrangements to return a person and consequential accommodation arrangements pending travel, where that person is accompanied by a dependent child, and (i) that person is an EEA national or his or her dependant or (ii) that person has refugee status in another EEA state or is his or her dependant.[8] Temporary accommodation may also be provided to a person in the UK in breach of UK immigration law, who is accompanied by a dependent child, where that person has not failed to comply with individual removal directions.[9] Where a woman with a dependent child, had an outstanding challenge to removal from the UK, and the local authority from whom she sought support had no power to make travel arrangements for her (as she was not an EEA national or a refugee in an EEA state), the local authority had the power to provide accommodation under Schedule 3 until such time as she failed to comply with any individual removal directions (which had not then been set).[10] Where a parent and his or her children are unlawfully present in the UK but have an outstanding application for leave to remain which either explicitly or implicitly raises Article 8 of the ECHR, the withholding or withdrawing of support to the family (if they are destitute) would be a breach of ECHR, Art 8.[11] Pending determination of a claim for judicial review arising from a failure by a local authority to exercise its powers under section 21 of the NAA 1948, the court can order the local authority to provide the claimant with care and assistance.[12]

1 NIAA 2002, Sch 3, para 4.
2 NIAA 2002, Sch 3, para 5.

3   NIAA 2002, Sch 3, para 6.
4   NIAA 2002, Sch 3, para 7. This category includes former asylum seekers (whether or not they have failed to comply with removal directions) present in the UK in breach of the immigration laws: *R (on the application of AW) v Croydon London Borough Council*; *R (on the application of A, D and Y) v Hackney London Borough Council* [2005] EWHC 2950 (Admin), [2005] All ER (D) 251 (Dec), [2006] LGR 159 and *R (on the application of M) v Slough Borough Council* [2008] UKHL 52, [2008] 1 WLR 1808, [2008] 4 All ER 831, [2008] HLR 44, (2008) Times, 5 September.
5   NIAA 2002, Sch 3, para 7A. People in this category are liable to lose support 14 days after receipt of a certificate from the Secretary of State that in his or her opinion they have failed without reasonable excuse to take reasonable steps to leave the UK voluntarily or to place themselves in a position in which they can do so: Sch 3, para 7A(1). It applies to their dependants: Sch 3, para 7A(2). An appeal may be brought against the decision under IAA 1999, s 103, and the First-tier Tribunal (Asylum Support) may annul the certificate or require the Secretary of State to reconsider: AI(TC)A 2004, s 9(3), (4).
6   See AI(TC)A 2004, s 9(3), in force 1 December 2004: SI 2004/2999.
7   *R (on the application of AW) v Croydon London Borough Council*; *R (on the application of A, D and Y) v Hackney London Borough Council* [2005] EWHC 2950 (Admin), [2005] All ER (D) 251 (Dec), [2006] LGR 159.
8   NIAA 2002, Sch 3, paras 8–9, Withholding and Withdrawal of Support (Travel Assistance and Temporary Accommodation) Regulations 2002, SI 2002/3078.
9   NIAA 2002, Sch 3, para 10, Withholding and Withdrawal of Support (Travel Assistance and Temporary Accommodation) Regulations 2002, SI 2002/3078.
10 *R (on the application of M) v Islington London Borough Council* [2004] EWCA Civ 235, [2005] 1 WLR 884, [2004] 4 All ER 709, [2004] 2 FLR 867, [2004] LGR 815, (2004) Times, 22 April, contradicting guidance previously given to local authorities by the Secretary of State in December 2002 which stated that support should be given for not more than 10 days.
11 See *Clue v Birmingham City Council (Shelter intervening)* [2010] EWCA Civ 460, [2010] Fam Law 802, (2010) Times, 7 May. The *Clue* judgment arguably calls into doubt the correctness of the decision in *R (on the application of Grant) v Lambeth London Borough Council* [2004] EWCA Civ 1711, [2005] 1 WLR 1781, [2005] LGR 81.
12 *R (on the application of AA) v Lambeth London Borough Council* [2001] EWHC 741 (Admin), (2002) 5 CCLR 36.

14.182 If a person has been given refugee status in another EEA state or is a national of an EEA state or a dependant of such a person, local authorities can make travel arrangements for him or her and his or her dependants to return to the relevant EEA state, and may accommodate them pending their departure.[1] There is no question here of having to wait for removal directions to be issued, and it is envisaged that accommodation will only have to be provided for a short period of time. In *R (on the application of K) v Lambeth London Borough Council*,[2] Lambeth had terminated interim support to a Kenyan woman with one child who was married to an Irish national from whom she had separated, provided on the basis that she was the dependant of an EEA national. She asserted that it was a breach of her rights under Articles 3 and 8 of the ECHR to refuse to support her whilst she exercised her right of appeal against the decision of the Secretary of State that her marriage was one of convenience giving rise to no EC rights. The court accepted that she was a spouse but distinguished her case from that of an asylum seeker with an outstanding appeal on the basis that there was nothing to stop her from returning to Kenya pending her appeal and that the state owed no duty under the Convention to a foreign national who had been permitted to enter the state's territory but could return home.

1   NIAA 2002, Sch 3, paras 8–9, Withholding and Withdrawal of Support (Travel Assistance and Temporary Accommodation) Regulations 2002, SI 2002/3078, reg 3.

² *R (on the application of Kimani) v Lambeth London Borough Council* [2003] EWCA Civ 1150, [2004] 1 WLR 272, [2003] 3 FCR 222.

14.183 Section 117 of the IAA 1999 modifies and thereby partially removes the duties placed on local authorities which arise from section 45 of the Health Services and Public Health Act 1968 (the duty to promote the welfare of the elderly) in respect of persons subject to immigration control when the need arises solely from destitution or the physical effects of such destitution. Section 254 and Schedule 20 to the National Health Service Act 2006 does the same for the duty to make arrangements to prevent illness and to provide care and aftercare, when the need arises solely from destitution or the physical effects of such destitution. The extent of the residual duties was not discussed in *R v Wandsworth London Borough Council, ex p O*,¹ but it would be reasonable to assume that the same principles will apply as in that case, ie that where the effects of destitution were aggravated by illness or other vulnerability, the duty remains. Paragraph 341 of the Explanatory Notes to the IAA 1999 would also suggest that this is the correct interpretation. A local authority has powers under section 2 of the Local Government Act 2000 to provide accommodation or assist someone to secure accommodation but this power too is in practice restricted to those who are not in need of care and assistance solely by reason of destitution caused by their not being entitled to welfare benefits and support.²

¹ *R v Wandsworth London Borough Council, ex p O; R v Leicester City Council, ex p Bhikha* [2000] 1 WLR 2539, [2000] 4 All ER 590.
² *R (on the application of Khan) v Oxfordshire County Council* [2004] EWCA Civ 309, [2004] HLR 706, [2004] LGR 257, (2004) Times, 24 March.

Provision of support

14.184 Where a person is entitled to assistance under the NAA 1948, existing case law relating to it will still be applicable. Therefore, local authorities will have no power to give assistance in cash.¹ Neither do they have the power to provide an individual with food vouchers, if they are not also providing accommodation. However, in that situation, the person could be in need of care and attention because he or she had no food (although there would have to be another reason, or no duty would arise) and the local authority should therefore consider whether it should secure residential accommodation for the person, even if he or she is not yet threatened with eviction.² The local authority does not have to provide residential accommodation within an institutional setting and can provide ancillary services, appropriate to the individual's needs, including board, as part of an overall package.³ Neither is it restricted to providing bed and breakfast accommodation.⁴ Health and social services authorities have a duty to provide residential accommodation free of charge to anyone who has been discharged from detention under section 3 of the Mental Health Act 1983.⁵ Schedule 3 to the NIAA 2002 does not apply to or limit this power.⁶ Where it appears to a local authority that any person for whom they may provide or arrange for the provision of community care services may be in need of such services, the local authority is under a duty to undertake a needs assessment.[7]

1 *R v Secretary of State for Health, ex p Hammersmith and Fulham London Borough Council* [1998] 31 HLR 475, [1999] LGR 354.
2 *R v Newham London Borough Council, ex p Gorenkin (Mikhail)* [1997–98] 1 CCL Rep 309.
3 *R v Newham London Borough Council, ex p Medical Foundation for the Care of Victims of Torture* [1997–98] 1 CCL Rep 227. For guidance on when the duty is discharged see *R v Royal Borough of Kensington and Chelsea, ex p Kujtim* (1999) 32 HLR 579, CA; see also *R (on the application of Zarzour) v Hillingdon London Borough Council* [2009] EWCA Civ 1529, [2010] NLJR 1075.
4 *R v Newham London Borough Council, ex p C* (1998) 31 HLR 567.
5 Mental Health Act 1983, s 117; *R v Richmond upon Thames London Borough Council, ex p Watson* [2001] QB 370, CA.
6 The provision is not listed in NIAA 2002, Sch 3, para 1(1). However, the Law Commission Consultation Paper on Adult Social Care (No 192) (24 February 2010) contemplates that obligations arising under the Chronically Sick and Disabled Persons Act 1970, s 2 and the Mental Health Act 1983, s 117, could be added to the list of community care functions subject to an immigration based exclusionary regime, see Part 9, paras 9.76–9.81. As regards the allocation of responsibility as between social services authorities under the Mental Health Act 1983, s 117 see *R (on the application of Hertfordshire County Council) v Hammersmith and Fulham London Borough Council* [2011] EWCA Civ 77, [2011] LGR 536, 119 BMLR 27 and *R (on the application of Sunderland City Council) v South Tyneside Council* [2011] EWHC 2355 (Admin).
7 National Health Service and Community Care Act 1990, s 47(1). However, it has been held to be lawful for a local authority to carry out a Schedule 3 assessment to show that it had no power to provide assistance, and then to refuse to conduct a community care assessment, see *R (on the application of Sharef) v Coventry City Council* [2009] EWHC 2191 (Admin). See also Council Directive 2003/9/EC OJ L 031, 06 February 2003, pp 0018–0025, Art 17, the Asylum Seekers (Reception Conditions) Regulations 2005, SI 2005/7, reg 4, *Policy Bulletin 83*, Duty to offer support, family unity, vulnerable persons, withdrawing support, and the requirement to have regard to the needs of vulnerable persons.

Support under the Children Act 1989

14.185 Before the Children Act 1989 came into force, the National Assistance Act 1948 contained a power to assist both adults and children in need of care and attention but the Children Act 1989 amended the 1948 Act to restrict its powers to those aged 18 or over.[1] Under the 1989 Act a local authority must take reasonable steps to identify the extent to which there are children in need in its area. Thereafter, it may assess the needs of a child who appears to be in need in its area.[2] The *Working together to Safeguard Children Guidance* provides statutory guidance on the approach to the assessment of needs, identifying required services and setting out who is to provide them.[3] A child will be in need where he or she is unlikely to achieve or maintain, or have the opportunity of achieving or maintaining, a reasonable standard of health or development without the provision for him or her of services by a local authority under Part 3 of the Children Act 1989; his or her health or development is likely to be significantly impaired, or further impaired, without the provision for him or her of such services; or he or she is disabled.[4] Where a child is aged 16 or 17 and eligible for homelessness assistance, he or she may seek assistance under the Children Act 1989 from a local social services authority. In principle such a child may also apply under Part 7 of the Housing Act 1996 for homelessness assistance, although this will not be relevant in the context of children who are subject to immigration control. The primary duty to accommodate a lone homeless child is under the Children Act 1989, section 20. Were he or she to be accommodated by the latter it would be under the Children Act 1989, section 20 see **14.188–14.189**. A child accommodated under section 20 for 13 weeks ending after he or she turns 16-years-old will be able to seek further accommodation and support under the children leaving care provisions of the Children Act 1989 after he or she turns 18, see **14.193–14.195**. Where the criteria for accommodation under the Children Act 1989, section 20 are met, the local social services authority, having been approached, cannot avoid its obligations by turning to the local housing authority exercising its functions under the Housing Act 1996.[5] Where the criteria for accommodation under the Children Act 1989, section 20 are met, a local social services authority may not decide that a child requires 'help with accommodation' under section 17 rather than performing what is in reality a duty under section 20.[6]

1   Children Act 1989, Sch 13, para 11.
2   Children Act 1989, Sch 2, paras 1 and 3.
3   www.gov.uk/government/uploads/system/uploads/attachment_data/file/281368/Working_tog ether_to_safeguard_children.pdf. The *Working Together* guidance came into force in April 2013. (The previous guidance, the *Framework for the Assessment of Children in Need and their Families* is no longer in force in England.) It is however notable that the *Working Together* guidance refers to the old guidance in its Annex and thus may still be relevant to the approach the local authority must take in assessing needs. There is separate guidance in respect of Wales.
4   Children Act 1989, s 17(10).
5   *R (on the application of S) v Sutton London Borough Council* [2007] EWCA Civ 790; *R (on the application of M) v Hammersmith and Fulham LBC* [2008] UKHL 14, [2008] 1 WLR 535, [2008] 4 All ER 271, [2008] 1 FLR 1384, (2008) Times, 3 March; and *R (on the application of G) v Southwark London Borough Council* [2009] UKHL 26, [2009] 1 WLR 34, [2008] 2 FLR 1762.
6   *R (on the application of G) v Southwark London Borough* [2008] EWCA Civ 877, [2009] 1 WLR 34, [2008] 2 FLR 1762; *R (on the application of H) v Wandsworth London Borough Council* [2007] EWHC 1082 (Admin), [2007] 2 FLR 822; and LAC (2003) 13 'Guidance on accommodating children in need and their families'.

Accommodation and support under section 17 of the Children Act 1989

14.186 The Children Act 1989 includes a general target duty for all local authorities to safeguard and promote the welfare of children within their area who are in need, to meet these needs by providing a range of appropriate services, and to promote the upbringing of such children by their families wherever that is consistent with promoting their welfare.[1] This duty may include the provision of accommodation and financial support to both the children and their families. Local authorities may owe a duty under section 17 to non-asylum seeking families who are subject to immigration control. Section 17 does not place an absolute duty on a local authority to provide accommodation in accordance with a family's assessed need; neither does it impose a specific duty to meet the needs of each individual child. It only places a general duty on a local authority to maintain a level and range of services sufficient to enable it to discharge its functions under the Act. Its more specific duties are contained in other sections of the Act.[2] However where a local authority children's services authority has decided to provide a child 'in need' with support, including accommodation and subsistence support, with his or her parents, it would be unlawful for the local authority to do so in a manner which leaves the family in a position of destitution.[3] In cases covered by Sch 3 to the NIAA 2002, the authority may provide accommodation and support only to the children, except in cases where this would lead to a breach of rights protected by the ECHR or the EC Treaties (ie EU law).[4] Local authorities must have regard to the best interests of the child and ask whether it would be in the child's best interests to be brought up with his or her family. Separation of the child from his or her family can only be justified if in the child's best interests and is proportionate.[5] Local authorities are not permitted to exercise their powers to provide accommodation and essential living needs to asylum seekers and their minor dependants whilst the Secretary of State is either providing them with support under section 95 of the Immigration and Asylum Act 1999 or there are reasonable grounds for believing that the asylum seeker would be entitled to asylum support and that if an application for asylum support were made, the Secretary of State would be under a duty to provide asylum support on the basis that there is a dependent child in the household.[6] Responsibility for supporting the children of asylum seekers lies with the Secretary of State. So where an able-bodied asylum seeker had two disabled minor dependants, no duty arose under section 17 of the Children Act 1989 and the Secretary of State was held to be responsible for providing adequate accommodation to meet the children's needs. It was held that in such circumstances, the Secretary of State should use his or her powers to request local authorities and social landlords to assist him or her to find adequate accommodation for the family.[7] However where what is required by the disabled minor dependents of an asylum seeker is support arising from their disabilities, those support needs which are additional to the essential living needs provided for under section 95, Immigration and Asylum Act 1999, shall be the responsibility of the local authority.[8]

---

[1]   Children Act 1989, s 17.

[2]   *R (on the application of G) v Barnet London Borough Council* [2003] UKHL 57, [2004] 2 AC 208, [2003] 3 WLR 1194, [2004] 1 All ER 97; *Blackburn-Smith v Lambeth London Borough Council* [2007] EWHC 767 (Admin), [2007] All ER (D) 64 (Apr).

[3]   *R (on the application of PO) v Newham London Borough Council* [2014] EWHC 2561 (Admin) at [47].

[4]   See the Children Act 1989, ss 17, 23C, 24A and 24B, and the Nationality, Immigration and Asylum Act 2002, s 54 and Sch 3; see also *R (on the application of Grant) v Lambeth London Borough Council* [2004] EWCA Civ 1711, [2005] 1 WLR 1781, [2005] LGR 81; *R (on the application of Conde) v Lambeth London Borough Council* [2005] HLR 452. See also *Clue v Birmingham City Council (Shelter intervening)* [2010] EWCA Civ 460, [2010] Fam Law 802, (2010) Times, 7 May on the need for local authorities: (a) to have regard to a material policy of the Secretary of State in deciding whether or not to withdraw support and offer to pay for travel to the country of origin in order to meet any human rights obligations arising under Sch 3 to the Nationality, Immigration and Asylum Act 2002, and (b) where any argument for leave to remain has been raised expressly or implicitly on Art 8 ECHR grounds that are not abusive or hopeless, not to refuse support where a person would have to forfeit his claim and leave the UK in consequence.

[5]   See the Children Act 1989, s 17(1)(b), promoting the child's upbringing with his or her family and *PO v Newham, supra* at [47]. See also the approach to the assessment of best interests in *ZH (Tanzania) v Secretary of State for the Home Department* [2011] UKSC 4; *HH v Deputy Prosecutor of the Italian Republic, Genoa* [2012] UKSC 25.

[6]   IAA 1999, s 122 (to be substituted by the NIAA 2002, s 47 from a date to be appointed). However, see *R (on the application of Refugee Action) v Secretary of State for the Home Department* [2014] EWHC 1033 (Admin) at [77].

[7]   *R (on the application of A) v National Asylum Support Service and Waltham Forest* [2003] EWCA Civ 1473, [2004] 1 WLR 752, [2004] 1 All ER 15, [2004] 1 FLR 704, (2004) HLR 24, (2003) Times, 31 October.

[8]   *R (on the application of Ouji) v Secretary of State for the Home Department* [2002] EWHC 1839 (Admin).

14.187 As regards the relationship between support under the Children Act 1989, section 17 and the Immigration and Asylum Act 1999, section 4 a local authority is not able to withdraw or withhold support automatically under section 17 where a child had been assessed as being in need on the basis that section 4 of the 1999 Act support was available; save where the Secretary of State was bound or had agreed to be bound to provide support and such support would meet the child's assessed needs.[1]

[1]   See *R (on the application of VC and K) v Newcastle City Council* [2011] EWHC 2673 (Admin), [2011] 43 LS Gaz R 22.

Accommodation under section 20 of the Children Act 1989

14.188 Responsibility to provide accommodation for an Unaccompanied Asylum Seeking Child (UASC) falls to a local authority under section 20(1) of the Children Act 1989 where the child is within its area and appears to the local authority to require accommodation as a result of there being no person with parental responsibility, the child having been lost or abandoned, or where the person who has been caring for the child is prevented (whether or not permanently, and for whatever reason) from providing him or her with suitable accommodation or care.[1] It is inevitable that a UASC will meet the criteria under section 20(1) as it is unlikely that there will be someone with parental responsibility able to provide him with accommodation and support. Where a child is accommodated under section 20, such a child will be 'looked after' by the local authority.[2] Accommodation provided under section 20(1) of the Children Act 1989 is not subject to the eligibility test in section 54 and Schedule 3 to the NIAA 2002. The Secretary of State does not provide asylum support to unaccompanied asylum seeking children for so long as they are minors. See further **14.193** below for continued support post-18 for UASCs.

[1]   See eg *R (on the application of Liverpool City Council) v Hillingdon London Borough Council* [2009] EWCA Civ 43, [2009] PTSR 1067, [2009] 1 FLR 1536, (2009) Times, 13 February, a case concerning a dispute between two local authorities as to which one was subject to a duty to accommodate a child under section 20 of the Children Act 1989.
[2]   See Children Act 1989, s22(1) defines circumstances where a child is 'looked after'.

14.189 Where a child is looked after by the local authority under section 22(1) of the Children Act 1989, it unlocks a suite of further duties owed to the child under sections 22 and 22A–22G of the Children Act 1989. A local authority who looks after a child under a care order pursuant to section 31 of the Children Act 1989 will assume legal parental responsibility for the child. For children looked after under section 20, Children Act 1989, the local authority will nevertheless assume corporate parental responsibility for the child, particularly if the child is a UASC as there will be no other person owing parental responsibility. As the corporate parent, the local authority owes a mandatory duty under section 22(3), Children Act 1989 to safeguard and promote the child's welfare. Like section 55 of the Borders Citizenship and Immigration Act 2009, section 22(3) requires the local authority to act in the child's best interests.[1] Under section 22(3A), the local authority is obliged to promote a child's educational achievement. For UASCs, this in particular means ensuring that they are in education which is both age appropriate and appropriate to their abilities.[2] Pursuant to section 22A and 22C, Children Act

1989, the local authority is obliged to arrange suitable accommodation for the looked after child, such accommodation must be arranged in accordance with his or her cultural, religious and personal needs.[3] In addition to accommodation, the local authority is also obliged to maintain the child in other ways under section 22B, the scope of which is undefined under the primary legislation.[4]

1 See *ZH (Tanzania) v Secretary of State for the Home Department* [2011] UKSC 4; *HH v Deputy Prosecutor of the Italian Republic, Genoa* [2012] UKSC 25.

2 See *R (on the application of KS) v Croydon London Borough Council* [2010] EWHC 3391 (Admin) where the Court declared the local authority in breach of section 19, Education Act 1996 and section 22(3A), Children Act 1989 for its failure to arrange education for three UASCs who are of compulsory schooling age. See also *Aiming High: Guidance on Supporting the Education of Refugee and Asylum Seeking Children*. webarchive.nationalarchives.gov.uk /20130401151715/http://www.education.gov.uk/publications/eorderingdownload/dfes -0287-2004.pdf. For Wales, see the All Wales Practice Guidance on Safeguarding and Promoting the Welfare of Unaccompanied Asylum Seeking Children and Young People. www. awcpp.org.uk/wp-content/uploads/2014/03/Safeguarding-and-Promoting-the-Welfare-of-Una ccompanied-Asylum-Seeking-Children-and-Young-People-All-Wales-Practice-Guidance.pdf

3 See also Care for Unaccompanied and Trafficked Children issued by the Department for Education. See also the Care Planning Placement and Case Review (England) Regulations 2010, SI 2010/959, Pt 3 and Sch 2.

4 See Care Planning Placement and Case Review (England) Regulations 2010, SI 2010, SI 2010/959, Pt 2 and Sch 1 on care planning. See also the statutory guidance, Volume 2: Care Planning Placement and Case Review (England) Regulations 2010.

14.190 Where a local authority considers that a person may be an adult, it may conduct an age assessment to establish the person's age. The Care for Unaccompanied and Trafficked Children statutory guidance emphasises that age assessments must not be carried out as a matter of course. They should only be carried out where there is 'significant doubt' as to whether the person is a child.[1] Where the person is a potential victim of trafficking and his or her age is uncertain, the EU Anti-Trafficking Directive (2011/36/EC) requires that UK public authorities presume the person is a child pending verification.[2] Thus if a person is trafficked, any assessment of age must be undertaken applying the presumption in favour of the person being a child as claimed. The correct approach to age assessment had proved highly contentious in terms of the procedural safeguards required to ensure fairness.[3] The 'right' to accommodation under the Children Act 1989, s 20(1) has been held not to be a civil right for ECHR, Article 6(1) purposes and that even if it were, the availability of judicial review was sufficient to ensure compliance.[4] However, in the same case on further appeal, the Supreme Court held that the duty under section 20(1) was owed to those who were as a matter of fact children and not just to those who appeared to the local authority to be children. Thus, whether or not a person is a child is a matter of objective precedent fact to be determined by the court and not the local authority.[5] Age is a fact which admits only one right answer and not determined by the evaluative judgment of a local authority or by the immigration authorities.[6] There is no burden on the person to prove his age.[7]

1 Statutory guidance can be found at www.gov.uk/government/consultations/care-for-unaccom panied-and-trafficked-children, paragraph 22.

2 Article 13(2) of the EU Anti-Trafficking Directive. See also Council of Europe Convention on Action against the Trafficking in Human Beings, art 10(3) and the Explanatory Note to the Convention, paragraph 136 which states: '136. *The point of paragraph 3 is that, while children need special protection measures, it is sometimes difficult to determine whether*

someone is over or under 18. Paragraph 3 consequently requires Parties to presume that a victim is a child if there are reasons for believing that to be so and if there is uncertainty about their age. Until their age is verified, they must be given special protection measures, in accordance with their rights as defined, in particular, in the United Nations Convention on the Rights of the Child.'

³   *R (on the application of B) v Merton London Borough Council* [2003] EWHC 1689 (Admin), [2003] 4 All ER 280, [2003] 2 FLR 888, (2003) Times, 18 July; *R (on the application of I) v Secretary of State for the Home Department* [2005] EWHC 1025 (Admin), (2005) Times, 10 June; *R (on the application of C) v Merton London Borough Council* [2005] EWHC 1753 (Admin), [2005] 3 FCR 42 and *R (on the application of NA) v Croydon London Borough Council* [2009] EWHC 2357 (Admin). In respect of the use of experts, see *R (on the application of A) v Croydon London Borough Council* [2008] EWHC 2921 (Admin), [2009] LGR 113, [2009] 3 FCR 499 and *R (on the application of WK); R (on the application of A) v Secretary of State for the Home Department* [2009] EWHC 939 (Admin), [2010] 1 FLR 193 at [33]–[34] and [45]–[47], [2009] Fam Law 659. See also *R (on the application of FZ acting by his litigation friend Parivash Ghanipour) v Croydon London Borough Council* [2011] EWCA Civ 59, [2011] LGR 445, [2011] PTSR 748 and *R (on the application of CJ (by his Litigation Friend SW)) v Cardiff City Council* [2011] EWCA Civ 1590, [2012] NLJR 68.

⁴   *R (on the application of A) v London Borough of Croydon; R (on the application of M) v London Borough of Lambeth* [2008] EWCA Civ 1445, [2009] PTSR 1011, [2009] 1 FLR 1325, [2009] 1 FCR 317.

⁵   *R (on the application of A) v Croydon London Borough Council; R (on the application of M) v Lambeth London Borough Council* [2009] UKSC 8, [2009] 1 WLR 2557, , [2010] 1 All ER 469.

⁶   *R (on the application of A) v London Borough of Croydon* [2009] UKSC 8, [2009] 1 WLR 2557 per Lady Hale at [26]–[27], [33] and Lord Hope at [51]–[54].

⁷   *R (CJ) v Cardiff City Council* [2011] EWCA Civ 1590 [2012] NLJR 68.

14.191 The importance of the correct fact of age cannot be underestimated. If a young person is a child and otherwise meets the qualifying criteria, he must be provided with accommodation and maintenance under sections 20(1) and 23(1) of the 1989 Act. This brings with it a wider range of services than other forms of housing and benefit provision. These include the services for young people who leave social services accommodation after they reach 18.¹ A person who is accepted as a child will also be provided with accommodation by children's services not by the Secretary of State for the Home Department under the asylum support scheme, which is for adults and families. Furthermore, as the Supreme Court in *A v Croydon* acknowledged, the Secretary of State also adopts different policies in relation to asylum seekers who are under 18.² If a claim is rejected when the child is under the age of seventeen and a half, the Home Secretary will not remove him or her for three years, or until the person reaches seventeen and a half, whichever is the earlier, unless there are adequate arrangements to look after him or her in the country of origin. Also, such children will not be detained under the Home Secretary's immigration powers, save in exceptional circumstances and then normally only overnight.³

¹   *R (on the application of M) v Hammersmith and Fulham London Borough Council* [2008] UKHL 14, [2008] 1 WLR 535, paras 20–24.

²   *R (on the application of A) v Croydon London Borough Council* [2009] UKSC 8 paras 5–8.

³   See Part 2 of the statutory guidance issued under the Borders Citizenship and Immigration Act 2009, s 55 *Every Child Matters: Change Matters. Statutory Guidance to the UK Border Agency on arrangements to safeguard and promote the welfare of children.* See further Enforcement Instructions and Guidance, chapter 55 para 55.9.3.

14.192 Since age assessments have such a significant impact on the way a person is supported and his or her application for leave to remain processed, there is a set of developed guidance on how assessments of age ought to be conducted. The guidance is colloquially called Merton guidelines, named after the first guideline case of *R (on the application of B) v Merton London Borough Council* [2003] EWHC 1689 (Admin) and developed further in subsequent case law. The purpose of an age assessment is to establish chronological age. The *Merton* guidelines seek to provide guidance on how a local authority may achieve this. The guidelines demand a holistic approach to the assessment of age, conducted by two qualified and experienced social workers. Neither physical appearance nor demeanour can or should be determinative of age. The Court of Appeal's judgment in *R (on the application of FZ acting by his litigation friend Parivash Ghanipour) v Croydon London Borough Council* [2011] EWCA Civ 59 affirmed the *Merton* guidelines and went further to demand a scrupulous standard of fairness which requires the assessing social workers to properly put adverse inferences relied upon to dispute a young person's age to him or her so that he or she can have an opportunity to clarify and/or rebut these inferences before a final conclusion is arrived at by the local authority assessors. There are two core aspects of the *Merton* guidelines, substantive guidance on the assessment, and procedural guidance on how to conduct the assessment. They can be summarised as follows:

As to the substance of an assessment:

(a)   The purpose of an age assessment is to establish the chronological age of a young person.

(b)   An assessing social worker is not entitled to simply look at a child and determine that he or she looks 18-years-old and, therefore, does not require an assessment of age, particularly where the child is claiming to be a child.[1]

(c)   Physical appearance is a notoriously unreliable indicator of age other than in the most obvious of cases.[2]

(d)   Demeanour has also been held to be notoriously unreliable.[3]

(e)   Caution must be taken in respect of any reliance on a young person's demeanour. As Collins J stated at [56] in *A and WK*:[4] 'What is meant by the observation that he appeared to be comfortable in his body? It is difficult to follow what this does mean and how a discomfort with a changing body can manifest itself.' It can only be relevant in the totality of the evidence before the assessors.

(f)   The decision on age must be dealt with on the particular facts of a particular unaccompanied asylum-seeking child.[5]

(g)   There is no burden of proof imposed on the child to prove his or her age in the course of the assessment.[6]

(h)   Benefit of any doubt is always given to the unaccompanied asylum-seeking child since it is recognised that age assessment is not a scientific process.[7]

As to the procedure:

(a)   There should be two qualified, properly trained and experienced social workers.[8] The assessors should be fully qualified and subject to the code of practice issued by the Health and Care Professional Council.[9]

(b)   The child should have an appropriate adult, be informed of the right to have one, and should have explained to him or her the purpose of an appropriate adult.[10]

(c)   The child should be told the purpose of the assessment.[11]

(d)   The young person should be told the assessment will be used not only by the local authority but also by the Home Office to whom the assessment will be disclosed.

(e)   The decision must be based on firm grounds and reasons for them must be fully set out and explained to the applicant (child).[12]

(f)   The approach of the assessors must be professional and sensitive to the young person. 'It was important to try to establish a rapport with the applicant and any questioning, while recognising the possibility of coaching, should be by means of open-ended and not leading questions. It was equally important for the assessors to be aware of the customs and practices and any particular difficulties faced by the applicant in his home society'.[13]

(g)   It is axiomatic that the child should be given a fair and proper opportunity, at a stage when a possible adverse decision is no more than provisional, to deal with important points adverse to his age case which may weigh against him.[14]

(h)   Providing the child a summary sheet of the outcome of the assessment *without* providing the child an opportunity to know the details of the adverse points, or an opportunity to respond to the adverse points *before* the outcome is finalised and communicated to the child cannot be said to be fair. It evidences the lack of any intention to ensure the assessment is a fair one.[15]

(i)   Assessments devoid of details and/or reasons for the conclusion are not compliant with the *Merton* guidelines.[16]

[1] *R (on the application of A) v Croydon London Borough Council; R (on the application of WK) v Secretary of State for the Home Department* [2009] EWHC 939 (Admin) per Collins J at [7] and [13]. See *Merton* per Stanley Burnton J at [37].

[2] *R (on the application of NA) v Croydon London Borough Council* [2009] EWHC 2357 (Admin) per Blake J at [27]; *AM v Solihull* [2012] UKUT 00118 (IAC).

[3] *NA v Croydon* at [28]; *AM v Solihull* at [19–21].

[4] [2009] EWHC 939 (Admin).

[5] *Merton* per Stanley Burnton at [37–38]. See also *FZ* per Sir Anthony May at [3].

[6] *FZ* at [3]. See also *R (on the application of CJ (by his Litigation Friend SW)) v Cardiff City Council* [2011] EWCA Civ 1590.

[7] [40] per Collins J in *A and WK*.

[8] per Collins J in *A and WK* [38].

[9] See the Court of Appeal in *R (on the application of A) v Croydon London Borough Council* [2008] EWCA Civ 1445 per Ward LJ at [68].

[10] *FZ* at [23–25].

[11] *FZ* at [3].

[12] per Collins J at [12] in *A and WK*.

[13] per Collins J at [13] in *A and WK*.

[14] *FZ* at [21]; *J v Secretary of State for the Home Department* [2011] EWHC 3071 (Admin) at [14]; *AAM (a child acting by his litigation friend, FJ) v Secretary of State for the Home Department* [2012] EWHC 2567 (QB) at [94(c)]; *Durani v Secretary of State for the Home Department* [2013] EWHC 284 (Admin) at [84–87]; *HTX v Secretary of State for the Home Department* [2013] EWHC 1962 (QB) at [22(c)].

[15] *FZ* at [22].

[16] *FZ* at [21–22]; *J v SSHD* at [16–17].

Accommodation and support for children leaving care

14.193 The Children Act 1989, Schedule 2, paragraphs 19A–19B, ss 23A–23E, 24, 24A–24D, makes provision for children who have been 'looked after' when they leave care. Further provision is made in the Care Leavers (England) Regulations 2010[1] and its Welsh equivalent.[2] Statutory guidance may be found in Volume 3: Transition to Adulthood for Care Leavers.[3] The main provisions governing the provision of accommodation, sections 23B, 23C, 23CA, 24A, and 24B of the Children Act 1989, are subject to the immigration-based eligibility criteria found in section 54 of, and Schedule 3 to, the NIAA 2002. In order to be 'looked after' a child must have been accommodated in the care of a local social services authority for a minimum period of 13 weeks, beginning after the child turned 14-years-old with at least one day of accommodation after the child's 16th birthday.[4] Accommodation provided under section 17 of the Children Act 1989 is expressly excluded from counting for the purposes of whether a child is 'looked after'.[5] See further **14.186–14.187** above. A child who has been accommodated for 13 weeks, who continues to be looked after, and who is aged 16 or 17 is an 'eligible child.'[6] For each eligible child the local authority must carry out an assessment of his or her needs with a view to determining what advice, assistance and support it would be appropriate for it to provide to him or her, while it is still looking after him or her and after it ceases to look after the child. Thereafter it must prepare a pathway plan for the child, keep that plan under regular review and appoint a personal advisor for the child.[7] A child who was, but is no longer a 'looked after' child, who is aged 16 or 17 is a 'relevant child'. The responsible local social services authority must take reasonable steps to keep in touch with the relevant child whether or not he or she is within its area. There are also continuing obligations in respect of pathway plans, and personal advisors and an obligation to keep in touch with the relevant child, even where it has lost touch.[8] The local authority is required to safeguard and promote the relevant child's welfare, and unless it is satisfied that his or her welfare does not require it, support him or her by maintaining him or her, maintaining or providing him or her with suitable accommodation, and providing support of such other description as may be prescribed. Support may be in cash.[9] Whether an eligible or relevant child, the local authority must appoint a personal adviser for the child.[10] The personal adviser's functions include (i) providing the child with advice (including practical advice) and support; (ii) participating in their assessment and preparation of their pathway plans; (iii) participating in reviews of their pathway plans; (iv) liaising with the local authority in the implementation of the pathway plan; (v) coordinating the provision of services to them, and to taking reasonable steps to ensure that they make use of such services; keeping informed about the child's progress and wellbeing; (vi) keeping a written record of contact with the child.[11] The adviser in effects acts as a 'go-between' between the local authority, and the child and as an advocate for the provision of appropriate support for the child. He or she should not also be the one making budgetary decisions about the provision of support to the child so as to avoid a conflict of interest that would prevent him or her from advocating on behalf of the child.[12]

[1]   SI 2010/2571.
[2]   Children (Leaving Care) (Wales) Regulations 2001, SI 2001/2189.

3 Published by the Department of Education at www.gov.uk/government/uploads/system/uploa ds/attachment_data/file/361534/CA1989_The_Children_Act_1989_guidance_and_regulation s_V3_0610.pdf.
4 Paragraph 19B, Schedule 2 to the Children Act 1989, Care Leavers (England) Regulations 2010, SI 2010/2571, reg 3.
5 Children Act 1989, s 22(1).
6 Children Act 1989, Sch 2, para 19B.
7 Children Act 1989, Sch 2, paras 19B, 19C; Care Leavers (England) Regulations 2010, SI 2010/2571, regs 6–8.
8 Children Act 1989, ss 23A(2), 23B(1)–(7), (11); Care Leavers (England) Regulations 2010, SI 2010/2571, reg 3.
9 Support may be in cash. See Children Act 1989, s 23B(8)–(9); see also Care Leavers (England) Regulations 2010, SI 2010/2571, reg 9.
10 See paragraph 19C, Schedule 2 to the Children Act 1989 for eligible children; and s 23B(2), Children Act 1989 for relevant children.
11 See regulation 44 of the Care Planning Placement and Case Review (England) Regulations 2010; reg 8 of the Care Leavers (England) Regulations 2010; reg 12 of the Children (Leaving Care) (Wales) Regulations 2001.
12 See Munby J at paras 28–31 of *R (on the application of J) v Caerphilly County Borough Council* [2005] EWHC 586 (Admin).

14.194 The Care Planning Placement and Case Review (England) Regulations 2010[1] govern the detail required for pathway needs assessments and pathway plans for eligible children. Similar principles apply in respect of relevant children pursuant to the Care Leavers (England) Regulations 2010.[2] In much the same way that the Child in Need section 17 assessment requires a holistic consideration of all aspects of a child's development, the pathway plan expects the local authority to consider the same, identifying the needs of the child in respect of his or her mental and physical health, emotional well-being, accommodation, identity, financial, education and other needs. The pathway plan should operate a 'realistic operational plan' which sets out what the needs are, what provision is to be arranged for the child, how it will be provided, by whom and by when.[3] The child must have an opportunity to participate in making the pathway plan, as must the child's personal adviser. The local authority must consult with other relevant professionals, for example, tutors, foster carers, support workers and health professionals involved with the child.[4] Given the specific duty under section 22(3A) of the Children Act 1989 on the local authority to promote the educational achievement of 'looked after' children, it is important that the pathway should consider provision for the child's education and vocational training. Provision of continuing, appropriate education and vocational training is fundamental to the parliamentary purpose behind section 22(3A) and the subsequent extension of leaving care duties owed to those care leavers in education under the Children Act 1989, sections 23C(6)–(7) and 23CA. Thus in any given pathway plan, the importance of ensuring that the educational and vocational training future of a looked after child, whether an eligible or relevant child, is properly secured.

1 SI 2010/959.
2 For Wales, see the Children (Leaving Care) (Wales) Regulations 2001, SI 2001/2189.
3 See *R (on the application of J) v Caerphilly County Borough Council* [2005] EWHC 586 (Admin) per Munby J. See also Kenneth Parker J in *R (on the application of A) v Lambeth London Borough Council* [2010] EWHC 2439 (Admin).
4 See regulation 43 to the Care Planning Placement and Case Review (England) Regulations 2010. See also *R (J) v Caerphilly CBC* [2005] EWHC 586 (Admin).

14.195 A 'former relevant child' is (a) a person who has been a relevant child and who would be one if under 18-years-old; and (b) a person who has been looked after by a responsible local authority when he turned 18-years-old and immediately before ceasing to be looked after was an eligible child. A former relevant child must be at least 18 and, subject to an important proviso, ceases to be one when he or she turns 21-years-old.[1] The responsible local authority who owes the leaving care duties is the local authority which last looked after the child before he turned 18.[2] Thus even if that authority places the child in an out of area placement for whatever reason: that authority retains legal responsibility for the care leaver post-18 even if some other local authority may owe concurrent duties under the Housing Act 1996 or under adult community care provisions such as those under the NAA 1948. The duties under sections 23C–23E of the Children Act 1989 owed to former relevant children derives from the young adult having previously been looked after and assumes that duties owed to the child as an eligible or relevant child had been complied with. Thus the legislation assumes that the young adult already has an appointed personal advisor, the appointment of which must continue post-18.[3] The legislation also assumes the existence of a pathway plan, which must be kept under review.[4] Underpinning both of these continuing duties is the duty on the local authority to keep in contact with the former relevant child post-18,[5] and the overarching role of the local authority as the good corporate parent.[6] The duty continues post-18 to provide such assistance as the former relevant child's welfare requires.[7] Where a former relevant child's pathway plan sets out a programme of education or training that extends beyond his or her 21st birthday, a duty to provide assistance to the extent that his or her educational needs require it, continues to subsist so long as the former relevant child continues to pursue that programme. In those circumstances, the duties to keep in touch, continue the appointment of a personal advisor and keep the pathway plan under review also continue to subsist. Any interruption in the former relevant child's programme of education or training must be disregarded if the local authority is satisfied that he or she will resume it, as soon as is reasonably practicable.[8] Provision is also made for further assistance to pursue education or training up to the age of 25 for those who had left care at the age of 21 but who wish to return to education. For these care leavers, the local authority owes a duty to carry out a further needs assessment and pathway plan to consider the assistance to be provided to the former relevant child to return to education.[9] Assistance to a former relevant child under section 23(C)(4) includes accommodation and financial support. The local authority, in considering whether to assist a former relevant child with accommodation must disregard the availability of asylum support or assistance under section 4 or section 9 of the IAA 1999.[10] For those in education, the scope of section 23C(4)(b) extends to funding 100 per cent of the former relevant child's accommodation,[11] and costs associated with education.[12]

---

[1] Children Act 1989, s 23C(1), (6).
[2] Children Act 1989, s 23C(1).
[3] Children Act 1989, s 23C(3)(a).
[4] Children Act 1989, s 23C(3)(b).
[5] Children Act 1989, s 23C(2).
[6] See para 1.14 of *The Children Act 1989 Guidance and Regulations Vol 2: Care Planning, Placement and Case Review* ('Care Planning Guidance'): 'the role of the corporate parent is to act as the best possible parent for each child they look after and to advocate on his/her behalf to secure the best possible outcomes'. See also *The Children Act 1989 Guidance and*

Regulations Vol 3: Transition to Adulthood statutory guidance ('Transition to Adulthood guidance') para 1.8 stating that the legislation and associated regulations and guidance are 'designed to ensure care leavers are given the same level of care and support that their peers would expect from a reasonable parent and that they are provided with the opportunities and chances needed to help them move successfully in to adulthood.' In particular see 1.10 of the same guidance stating that local authorities in arranging transitional care and other support for care leavers should ask itself the questions: (i) is this good enough for my own child?; (ii) does it provide a second chance if things don't go as expected?; (iii) is this tailored to their individual needs? Particularly if they are more vulnerable than other young people.

7   Children Act 1989, s 23C(4).
8   Children Act 1989, s 23C(2)–(4) and (6)–(8).
9   Children Act 1989, s 23CA.
10 *R (on the application of SO) v Barking and Dagenham London Borough Council* [2010] EWCA Civ 1101.
11 *R (on the application of Sabiri) v Croydon London Borough Council* [2010] EWHC 1236 (Admin).
12 *R (on the application of Kebede) v Newcastle City Council* [2013] EWCA Civ 960. However see *R (on the application of Nfuni) v Solihull Metropolitan Borough Council* [2013] EWHC 3155 (Admin) which suggests that a former relevant child's uncertain immigration status may affect the scope of the local authority's duty to accommodate and support a former relevant child's wish to continue to pursue education. *Nfuni* will need to now be read in the light of the new statutory guidance *Care of Unaccompanied and Trafficked Children* which at para 53 now stresses that a child's immigration status has 'no bearing on a local authority's duties to provide care leaving support. Unaccompanied children must be provided with the same support as for any care leaver.'

14.196 Some children do not accrue sufficient time as a 'looked after' child to be owed the full suite of leaving care duties. They may nevertheless qualify for advice and assistance. In respect of a person qualifying for advice and assistance by virtue of being between 16- and 21-years-old: (a) where a special guardianship order is or was in force; or (b) where he or she was looked after, accommodated or fostered, provision may be made where he or she needs assistance with employment, education and training. Depending on which provisions are satisfied, a power or a duty may arise to advise and befriend the person. Thereafter assistance may be given in kind, or in exceptional circumstances by providing accommodation (where accommodation may not be provided under section 24B of the Children Act 1989) or in cash.[1] There is also a power to provide assistance to a person falling within a particular class of persons who qualify for advice or assistance: (a) by contributing to expenses incurred by him or her in living near the place where he or she is, or will be, employed or seeking employment; and (b) by contributing to expenses incurred by the person in question in living near the place where he or she is, or will be, receiving education or training, or making a grant to enable him or her to meet expenses connected with his or her education or training. In respect of (a) this power may be exercised where he or she is under the age of 21, and in respect of (b) this power may be exercised where he or she is under the age of 25.[2] In respect of a former relevant child, it is the duty of the responsible local authority to provide assistance in accordance with (a) to the extent that his or her welfare requires it; and (b) to the extent that his or her welfare and his or her educational or training needs require it.[3] There is also a duty to give a former relevant child other assistance to the extent that his or her welfare requires it, in kind or in exceptional circumstances in cash.[4] In respect of the latter duty, it has been held that this does extend to the provision of accommodation.[5] Provision is also made for further assistance to pursue education or training up to the age of 25.[6]

1   Children Act 1989, ss 24(1)–(2), 24A(1)–(5).
2   Children Act 1989, s 24B(1)–(3); see **14.194–14.195** above; see also *R (on the application of Birara) v Hounslow London Borough Council* [2010] EWHC 2113 (Admin), [2010] 3 FCR 21.
3   Children Act 1989, s 23C(4)(a)–(b).
4   Children Act 1989, s 23C(4)(c) and s 23C(5).
5   *R (on the application of SO) v Barking and Dagenham London Borough Council* [2010] EWCA Civ 1101, [2011] 2 All ER 337, [2011] LGR 1.
6   Children Act 1989, s 23CA.

14.197 Where a local authority has 'looked after' unaccompanied minor asylum seekers between the ages of 14 and 18 so that they qualify for advice and assistance, and/or they qualify as former relevant children, prior to 7 November 2002 under section 17 or 20 of the Children Act 1989 and on or after that date under section 20 alone, it may owe those young persons an ongoing duty up to the age of 21: to provide them with any necessary support for accommodation and other support (including travel expenses, money for books and equipment or perhaps even course fees) to ensure that they can continue to fulfil their education or training needs, enter and remain in employment and the employment market, or meet other needs; and up to the age of 25: in respect of educational or training needs set out in a pathway plan.[1] Even if the local authority asserts that the child was only assisted under section 17 on or after 7 November 2002 when section 17 had ceased to be classified as a power to 'look after' the child,[2] there is a rebuttable presumption that the local authority should have been looking after an unaccompanied child under section 20 of the Children Act 1989, and thus owes the continuing duty.[3] Further, it has been held that in having provided accommodation to a child in need, as a lone child, a local authority was doing so pursuant to a duty under section 20 of the Children Act 1989 and it could not assert that the accommodation was provided pursuant to the exercise of a power under section 17 of the same.[4] For a former looked after child, as a former relevant child, the local authority is also under a duty to provide him or her with a pathway plan and a personal adviser.[5] If a young person who is over 18 has been granted refugee status, humanitarian protection or exceptional or discretionary leave, this support will be additional to any support he or she is entitled to from his or her local housing authority or from the Department for Work and Pensions. Those 16- or 17-year-olds who were previously looked after by a local authority are not entitled to claim income-based jobseeker's allowance, income support or housing benefit, and should continue to be supported by their local authority.[6] If the person who qualifies for advice and assistance and/or qualifies as a former relevant child is still an asylum seeker when he or she becomes 18, the Secretary of State will not ordinarily seek to disperse that person and will reimburse the local authority up to £140 for the cost of his or her accommodation (with the local authority obliged to meet any excess) so that he or she can remain in that local authority's area. In such circumstances the calculation of any asylum support to be paid will take into account the material support provided by the local authority.[7] A challenge by a local authority, to a decision by the Secretary of State to change the basis upon which it calculated its discretionary grant to local authorities, paid to support former unaccompanied asylum seeking children who had become former looked after children to whom the local authority was responsible for providing after care services, failed.[8] Where a formerly looked after child, as a former relevant child, aged 18 or over, who is being supported in that capacity by a local authority, has an undetermined application for leave to remain under the ECHR, Art 8, then a local authority will be under an obligation to support her or him to the extent necessary to avoid a breach of the individual's rights protected under the ECHR while in the UK. In considering the merits of the application for leave under Art 8, a local authority was confined to considering whether the application was 'manifestly unfounded' in the sense of being hopeless or abusive and its powers to scrutinise did not extend to assessing the merits of the application.[9]

[1]   Children Act 1989, ss 23, 23C, 23CA 24, 24A, 24B (as amended and inserted by the Children (Leaving Care) Act 2000, the Adoption and Children Act 2002 and the Children and Young Persons Act 2008).
[2]   Ie, as a result of the Children Act 1989, s 22 being amended by the Adoption and Children Act 2002, s 116(2) on 7 November 2002.
[3]   Local Authority Circular LAC(2003) 13 *Guidance on Accommodating Children in Need and Their Families* (2 June 2003); see also *R (on the application of Berhe) v Hillingdon London Borough Council* [2003] EWHC 2075 (Admin), [2004] 1 FLR 439, [2003] Fam Law 872 followed in *R (on the application of W) v Essex County Council* [2003] EWHC 3175 (Admin), [2003] All ER (D) 402 (Dec).
[4]   *R (on the application of H) v Wandsworth London Borough Council; R (on the application of Barhanu) v Hackney London Borough Council; R (on the application of B) v Islington London Borough Council and Secretary of State for Education and Skills* [2007] EWHC 1082 (Admin), [2007] 2 FCR 378, [2007] 2 FLR 822.
[5]   Children Act 1989, s 23C.
[6]   Children (Leaving Care) Act 2000, s 6; see also Children (Leaving Care) Social Security Benefits Regulations 2001, SI 2001/3074.
[7]   See the 'Children Leaving Care Act 2000 regulations and guidance' (DH), ch 2, paras 7–11; see also *Policy Bulletin 29, Transition at the Age of 18*, paras 3 and 6. However, see also *R (on the application of SO) v Barking and Dagenham London Borough Council* [2010] EWCA Civ 1101.
[8]   *R (on the application of Hillingdon London Borough Council) v Secretary of State for Education and Skills* [2007] EWHC 514 (Admin), [2007] All ER (D) 260 (Mar).
[9]   *R (on the application of B) v Southwark London Borough Council* [2006] EWHC 2254 (Admin), [2007] 3 FCR 457, [2007] 1 FLR 916; *Clue v Birmingham City Council (Shelter intervening)* [2010] EWCA Civ 460, [2010] 4 All ER 423, [2011] 1 WLR 99.

ACCESS TO HOUSING UNDER THE HOUSING ACTS

Allocation of social housing

14.198 A person who is subject to immigration control, as an alien, has the right to own property in the UK and to enter into a private tenancy agreement.[1] As a private sector tenant, he or she has the same rights to security of tenure, access to civil remedies in cases of disrepair or excessive rent rises as any other private tenant and may rely on the Protection from Eviction Act 1977.[2] He or she is also protected from discrimination on the basis of race, when seeking accommodation.[3] However, there is limited entitlement to housing benefit. Persons subject to immigration control will not generally be eligible for public sector housing under Part II of the Housing Act 1985.[4] Section 160A of the Housing Act 1996 in respect of Wales, and section 160ZA in respect of England, prevents local housing authorities from *allocating* public sector housing to persons from abroad, including those subject to immigration control under the 1996 Act,[5] those excluded from housing benefit by section 115 of the IAA 1999[6] and other classes as prescribed. Regulations under section 160A and section 160ZA prescribe categories of persons who are subject to immigration control or are other persons from abroad who may be allocated housing under Part VI of that Act. The regulations in force since 1 June 2006 are the Allocation of Housing and Homelessness (Eligibility) (England) Regulations 2006.[7] There are four classes of persons subject to immigration control who are eligible for housing: recognised refugees, persons with exceptional leave to remain such as discretionary leave, persons with indefinite leave to remain who are habitually resident in the common travel area, and those with humanitarian protection within the Immigration Rules.[8] A fifth category of persons originally identified as eligible for accommodation (nationals of a state which has ratified the European Convention on Social and Medical Assistance or the Council of Europe Social Charter and who are lawfully present and habitually resident) are no longer eligible under the regulations.[9] In addition, a sixth category, persons over 18, who left Montserrat after 1 November 1995 because of the effect on that territory of a volcanic eruption, are no longer eligible for assistance if they apply on or after 9 October 2006.[10] Thus the persons subject to immigration control who are eligible for assistance are:

- Class A – a person who is recorded by the Secretary of State as a refugee within the definition in Article 1 of the Refugee Convention and who has leave to enter or remain in the UK (since they are not excluded from having recourse to public funds);
- Class B – a person: (i) who has exceptional leave to enter or remain in the UK granted outside the provisions of the Immigration Rules (such as discretionary leave); and (ii) who is not subject to a condition requiring him to maintain and accommodate himself, and any person who is dependent on him, without recourse to public funds;
- Class C – persons who have indefinite leave to remain and are habitually resident in the common travel area (except for sponsored immigrants who have been here for less than five years and whose sponsor is still alive);
- Class D – persons granted humanitarian protection within the Immigration Rules.

Where a person is eligible for an allocation of housing but seeks to have taken into account as part of her household adult children who are themselves subject to immigration control, it was held in *R (on the application of Ariemuguvbe) v Islington LBC* that a local authority could lawfully conclude that it was not appropriate to consider those adult children as they were independent and were, in addition, subject to immigration control. In that case it was noted that providing accommodation to them would amount to having recourse to public funds in breach of conditions of entry to the UK.[11]

[1] Aliens Restriction Act 1914, s 17.
[2] *Akinbolu v Hackney London Borough Council* (1996) 29 HLR 259.
[3] Race Relations Act 1976, ss 20–21 and now Equality Act 2010.
[4] IAA 1999, s 118, concerning the grant of a tenancy or a licence to occupy housing accommodation by a local housing authority. See also the Persons subject to Immigration Control (Housing Authority Accommodation and Homelessness) Order 2000, SI 2000/706, Persons Subject to Immigration Control (Housing Authority Accommodation) (Wales) Order 2000, SI 2000/1036, and the Persons Subject to Immigration Control (Housing Authority Accommodation and Homelessness) (Amendment) Order 2006, SI 2006/2521. See

also the Persons Subject to Immigration Control (Housing Authority Accommodation and Homelessness) (Amendment) Order 2008, SI 2008/1768.

5   Housing Act 1996, s 160A(1), (3) (inserted by the Homelessness Act 2002, s 4 from 5 December 2002 and amended by the Localism Act 2011 from 29 April 2013). Housing Act 1996, s 160ZA inserted by the Localism Act 2011 from 29 April 2013.

6   Housing Act 1996, s 160A(4), as inserted.

7   SI 2006/1294 amended by the Allocation of Housing and Homelessness (Eligibility) (Amendment) Regulations 2014, SI 2014/435. In Wales the Allocation of Housing (Wales) Regulations 2003, SI 2003/239 (W 36) apply. In *Ehiabor v Royal Borough of Kensington and Chelsea* [2008] EWCA Civ 1074, [2008] All ER (D) 104 (May), it was held that a child born in the UK, who was not a British citizen, required leave to remain, and was thus subject to immigration control.

8   The Allocation of Housing and Homelessness (Eligibility) (England) Regulations 2006, SI 2006/1294, reg 3 as amended by the Allocation of Housing and Homelessness (Eligibility) (England) (Amendment) Regulations 2014/435 effective from 31 March 2014.

9   For non-EEA states which have ratified these agreements. For 'lawfully present', see *Szoma v Secretary of State for Work and Pensions* [2005] UKHL 64, [2006] 1 AC 564, [2006] 1 All ER 1. Prior to 3 April 2000, nationals of states which had signed the Convention and Charter and who were habitually resident here were also entitled to join the housing register. The category was removed by the Allocation of Housing and Homelessness (Amendment) (England) Regulations 2006, SI 2006/1093 save for applicants who before 20 April 2006 had made applications for an allocation of housing accommodation under Part 6 of the Housing Act 1996 and had not been notified by the local housing authority that they were ineligible for an allocation.

10   Allocation of Housing and Homelessness (Miscellaneous Provisions) (England) Regulations 2006, SI 2006/2527, the Allocation of Housing (Wales) (Amendment) Regulations 2006, SI 2006/2645.

11   *R (on the application of Ariemuguvbe) v Islington London Borough Council* [2009] EWCA Civ 1308, [2010] HLR 14.

14.199 Nationals of EEA states and their family members of any nationality, who are not subject to immigration control as they have an EU right of residence pursuant to the Immigration (European Economic Area) Regulations 2006,[1] Council Directive 2004/38/EC[2] or another enforceable European Union right, are classified as other persons from abroad and are ineligible for an allocation of housing unless their EU right of residence constitutes a qualifying right to reside. Persons not subject to immigration control, as other persons from abroad, (including nationals of EEA States and their family members) are ineligible for allocation of housing unless they are habitually resident in the common travel area and have a right to reside (ie as British citizens, Commonwealth citizens with the right of abode in the UK, Irish nationals, persons exempt from immigration control, and EEA nationals and family members with a right to reside, etc). However, if their only right to reside is an EEA right to reside as a jobseeker, a family member of a jobseeker or a person with an initial three month right to reside, they will be ineligible.[3] On a separate point, the following persons with a right to reside do not have to further establish that they are habitually resident in order to be eligible for accommodation: (a) an EEA national who is a worker; or (b) an EEA national who is self-employed; (c) an Accession state worker who is treated as a qualified person under the EEA Regulations (national of a state in eastern Europe that joined the European Union on 1 May 2004 or 1 January 2007, lawfully working in UK); (d) a family member of a person listed at (a)–(c); (e) a person with an EEA right to reside permanently (acquired other than by having completed five years of EEA rights to reside under the Immigration (European Economic Area) Regulations 2006);[4] (f) a person not subject to immigration control who left Montserrat after 1 November 1995 because of the effect of the volcanic eruption; (g) a person in the UK owing to deportation or removal from another country; (h) during the relevant period beginning at 4pm on 25 July 2006 and ending on 31 January 2007, a person who left Lebanon on or after 12 July 2006 because of the armed conflict there; and (i) a person (in practice any British national and his or her family members who have the right of abode in the UK) who arrived in Great Britain on or after 28 February 2009 but before 18 March 2011, immediately before arriving in Great Britain had been resident in Zimbabwe, and before leaving Zimbabwe, had accepted an offer, made by Her Majesty's Government, to assist that person to settle in the United Kingdom.⁵ Those entitled to housing accommodation may apply to a local housing authority for an allocation of housing, and their entitlement will be considered in line with the usual procedures contained in Part VI the Housing Act 1996. Those refused housing allocation on grounds of ineligibility have a right to written reasons for the refusal and to a review of the decision.⁶

1 SI 2006/1003.
2 In *Sheich (Habiba) v Bristol County Council* 5 BS 03394, HHJ Purcell held that an EEA national who was not employed and who was not a work seeker or otherwise a qualified person within the meaning of reg 5 of the Immigration (European Economic Area) Regulations 2000, SI 2000/2326 was eligible for housing assistance under Part VII of the Housing Act 1996, because she was in receipt of income support and fell within Class I of reg 3 of the Homelessness (England) Regulations 2000, SI 2000/701. That was the position confirmed by the Court of Appeal in *Barnet London Borough Council v Ismail* [2006] EWCA Civ 383, [2006] 1 WLR 2771, [2007] 1 All ER 922, [2006] HLR 23, Times 25 April 2006. Thereafter, the government amended the Allocation of Housing (England) Regulations 2002, SI 2002/3264, to revoke reg 4(d) and the Homelessness (England) Regulations 2000, to revoke reg 3(1)(i) which, respectively, had made those subject to immigration control but receiving income support or jobseeker's allowance eligible for an allocation of housing and housing assistance. See SI 2006/1093, reg 2(1). In respect of enforceable EU rights outside of the Immigration (European Economic Area) Regulations 2006,¹ Council Directive 2004/38/EC: in the homelessness case of *London Borough of Harrow v Ibrahim* (C-310/08), the Court of Justice found that a non-EEA national spouse of an EEA former worker, whose children were in education and for whom she was the primary carer, and who fell outside the scope of the rights of retained residence in Directive 2004/38/EC, could derive a right of residence on the sole basis of Article 12 of Regulation (EEC) 1612/68 without such a right being conditional on her having sufficient resources and comprehensive sickness insurance cover in host Member State. In a second homelessness case, *Teixeira v London Borough of Lambeth* (C-480/08), the Court of Justice held that an EEA former worker, whose child was in education and for whom she was the primary carer, and who fell outside the scope of the rights of retained residence in Directive 2004/38/EC, could derive a right of residence on the sole basis of Article 12 of Regulation (EEC) 1612/68 without such a right being conditional on her having sufficient resources and comprehensive sickness insurance cover in the host Member State. The court further held that the right of residence in the host Member State of the parent who is the primary carer for a child of a migrant worker, where that child is in education in that state, is not conditional on one of the child's parents having worked as a migrant worker in that Member State on the date on which the child started in education, and that the right of residence in the host Member State of the parent who is the primary carer for a child of a migrant worker, where that child is in education in that state, ends when the child reaches the age of majority, unless the child continues to need the presence and care of that parent in order to be able to pursue and complete his or her education. Both cases turned on the continuing efficacy and extent of Article 12 of Regulation (EEC) 1612/68 and the applicability and logic of the reasoning in *Baumbast v Secretary of State* (C-413/99) [2002] ECR I-7091 ECJ following the introduction of Directive 2004/38/EC, as well as the question of whether or not there was any requirement for primary carers to be self-sufficient. In *Barry (Mohammed) v Southwark London Borough Council* [2008] EWCA Civ 1440, [2009] 2 CMLR 269, [2009] ICR 437 it was held that two weeks' work at a tennis tournament was sufficient for a person to qualify as a worker and for the applicable machinery under reg 6(2) of the Immigration (European Economic Area) Regulations 2006 to enable him to retain worker status.

3 SI 2006/1294, reg 4(1). The three months' right of residence referred to is that conferred by SI 2006/1003, reg 13.
4 SI 2006/1294, reg 4(2) as amended as at 31 March 2014.
5 SI 2006/1294, reg 4(2), (i) was added by the Allocation of Housing and Homelessness (Eligibility) (England) (Amendment) Regulations 2009, SI 2009/358, from 18 March 2009.
6 Housing Act 1996, s 160ZA(9), (10) for England. Housing Act 1996, s 160A(9), (10) as inserted and s 167(4A)(d) for Wales.

Homelessness assistance

14.200 In respect of applications for homelessness assistance under Part VII of the Housing Act 1996, the eligible persons subject to immigration control are those listed at Classes A–D plus a Class E consisting of a person who is an asylum seeker whose claim for asylum is recorded by the Secretary of State as having been made before 3 April 2000 in one of three circumstances: (i) on arrival (other than on his re-entry) in the UK from a country outside the UK, the Channel Islands, the Isle of Man or the Republic of Ireland; (ii) within three months from the day on which the Secretary of State made a relevant declaration, and the applicant was in Great Britain on the day on which the declaration was made; or (iii) on or before 4 February 1996 by an applicant who was on 4 February 1996 entitled to benefit under regulation 7A of the Housing Benefit (General) Regulations 1987 (persons from abroad).[1] In respect of other persons from abroad, not subject to immigration control, who are eligible for assistance as homeless under Part VII of the Housing Act 1996, the list is the same as for those eligible for an allocation of housing under Part VI of the 1996 Act. By section 185(4) in Part VII of the 1996 Act a person from abroad who is not eligible for housing assistance shall be disregarded in determining whether a person falling within section 185(5) is homeless or threatened with homelessness, or has a priority need for accommodation. By section 185(5) this applies to a person who falls within Classes A–E of the regulations made in respect of persons subject to immigration control but who is not a national of an EEA state or Switzerland. In essence a person of any immigration status, irregular or otherwise, may be taken into account where the applicant is a British citizen, a Commonwealth citizen with the right of abode in the UK, an EEA or Swiss national or a family member of any nationality with an EU right of residence, an EEA national or Swiss national who falls within Classes A–E of persons subject to immigration control, or a person exempt from immigration control. However, a person with a non-qualifying immigration (ie irregular, subject to restrictions on recourse to public funds) of not specified by Classes A–E) status who is a person subject to immigration control, will fall to be excluded from being taken into account where the applicant falls within Classes A–E of the regulations made in respect of persons subject to immigration control. This has the effect of excluding members, including family, of an applicant's household, from being taken into consideration when decisions are being made to determine whether the applicant is homeless or in priority need. Even where persons subject to immigration control who do not qualify in their own right by virtue of their immigration status, are taken into account so that an eligible applicant (eg a British citizen, a Commonwealth citizen with the right of abode in the UK, etc) is considered homeless and/or in priority need, such persons are defined as 'restricted persons' (as having no leave to enter or remain or leave subject to maintaining and accommodating themselves and any dependants without recourse to public funds) and applications that rely upon them to secure a full homelessness duty under sections 193(2) or 195(2) of the Housing Act 1996 are defined as restricted cases whereby the duty arising may be performed in a sub-optimal way through the making of a private accommodation offer. Section 185 was amended so that section 185(4) and (5) take the form set out above.[2] In respect of section 185 prior to amendment, the Court of Appeal had declared section 185(4) to be incompatible with the ECHR, Article 8 (right to respect for family life) and Article 14, as it created a difference in treatment that is unjustified discrimination on grounds of national origin or a combination of nationality, immigration control, settled residence and social welfare.[3] The Housing and Regeneration Act 2008, Sch 15, amends the Housing Act 1996, the Housing (Scotland) Act 1987, the Housing (Northern Ireland) Order 1988 and the Immigration and Asylum Act 1999 in an attempt to remove the incompatibility. It creates a statutory regime that makes it easier for a local housing authority to perform a duty to persons forming a household, to whom a duty is owed because their number includes a person who lacks leave to remain or has such leave subject to a no recourse to public funds condition. However, there remain elements of discrimination in the new scheme. The 'Homelessness Code of Guidance for Local Authorities' was published by the Department for Communities and Local Government in July 2006. It came into force on 4 September 2006. This has been supplemented by the 'Homelessness change in the Localism Act 2011: supplementary guidance' published in November 2012.[4] Eligibility for assistance is considered at Chapter 9: Eligibility for Assistance, paras 9.1–9.25 and Annex 8 to Annex 13. For homelessness applicants, interim accommodation pending review under section 188(3) of the 1996 Act and pending appeal under section 204(4) of the 1996 Act is subject to section 54 and Schedule 3 to the NIAA 2002. Accommodation may only be provided to those falling within its provisions, if it is, and to the extent, necessary to avoid a breach of the ECHR or the EC Treaties (ie EU law).[5]

1   SI 2006/1294, reg 5. For the purpose of Class E (iii), a person does not cease to be an asylum seeker while he is eligible for housing benefit by virtue of: (a) regulation 10(6) of the Housing Benefit Regulations 2006, SI 2006/213; or (b) reg 10(6) of the Housing Benefit (Persons who have attained the qualifying age for state pension credit) Regulations 2006, SI 2006/214, as modified in both cases by para 6 of Sch 3 to the Housing Benefit and Council Tax Benefit (Consequential Provisions) Regulations 2006, SI 2006/217.
2   Housing and Regeneration Act 2008, s 314 and Sch 15, in force 2 March 2009 by the Housing and Regeneration Act 2008 (Commencement No 1 and Savings Provisions) Order 2009, SI 2009/415.
3   *R (on the application of Morris) v Westminster City Council; R (on the application of Badhu) v Lambeth London Borough Council* [2005] EWCA Civ 1184, [2006] 1 WLR 505, [2006] LGR 81, Sedley and Auld LLJ, Jonathan Parker LJ dissenting.
4   www.gov.uk/government/publications/homelessness-changes-in-the-localism-act-2011-supplementary-guidance
5   *R (on the application of Maryam Mohamed) v Harrow London Borough Council* [2006] HLR 18 and *Putans v Tower Hamlets London Borough Council* [2006] EWHC 1634 (Ch), [2007] HLR 126.

Local authority disposal of residential accommodation

14.201 A local authority's primary power to dispose of residential accommodation is provided for in Part II of the Housing Act 1985.[1] Section 118 of the

IAA 1999, which re-enacts section 9(1) of the Asylum and Immigration Act 1996 (AIA 1996) and makes additional provision, requires local housing authorities to ensure that, so far as is practicable, tenancies and licences to occupy housing accommodation are not *granted* under Part II of the Housing Act 1985 to persons subject to immigration control unless: (a) they are of a class specified in regulations, or (b) the licence or tenancy is granted under support arrangements for asylum seekers, failed asylum seekers or other qualifying persons subject to immigration control under IAA 1999, sections 4, 95 and 98.[2] For the purposes of section 118 of the IAA 1999, 'person subject to immigration control' means a person who requires leave to enter or remain under the Immigration Act 1971, whether or not such leave has been given.[3] In contrast to the eligibility schemes for Part VI and Part VII of the Housing Act 1996, there is no additional regulation of persons *not* subject to immigration control by way of a habitual residence test or a right to reside test. The classes of persons subject to immigration control who are specified for England and Wales are:

- Class A: a person recorded by the Secretary of State as a refugee within the definition in Article 1 of the Refugee Convention;
- Class B: a person:
  - (i) who has leave to enter or remain in the United Kingdom granted outside the provisions of the Immigration Rules; and
  - (ii) whose leave is not subject to a condition requiring him to maintain and accommodate himself, and any person who is dependent on him, without recourse to public funds;
- Class BA: a person who has humanitarian protection granted under the Immigration Rules;
- Class C: a person who has current leave to enter or remain in the United Kingdom which is not subject to any limitation or condition and who is habitually resident in the Common Travel Area other than a person:
  - (i) who has been given leave to enter or remain in the United Kingdom upon an undertaking given by another person (his 'sponsor') in writing in pursuance of the Immigration Rules to be responsible for his maintenance and accommodation;
  - (ii) who has been resident in the United Kingdom for less than five years beginning on the date of entry or the date on which the undertaking was given in respect of him, whichever date is the later; and
  - (iii) whose sponsor or, where there is more than one sponsor, at least one of whose sponsors, is still alive;
- Class D: a person who left the territory of Montserrat after 1 November 1995 because of the effect on that territory of a volcanic eruption;
- Class F: a person who is attending a full-time course at a specified education institution in a case where the housing accommodation which is or may be provided to him:
  - (i) is let by a housing authority to that specified education institution for the purposes of enabling that institution to provide accommodation for students attending a full-time course at that institution; and
  - (ii) would otherwise be difficult for that housing authority to let on terms which, in the opinion of the housing authority, are satisfactory;

- Class G: a person who is owed a duty under section 21 of the National Assistance Act 1948 (duty of local authorities to provide accommodation);
- Class H: a person who is either a child in need or a member of the family of a child in need;
- Class I: a person:
  - (i) who is owed a duty under sections 63(1) (interim duty to accommodate in case of apparent priority need), 65(2) or (3) (duties to persons found to be homeless) or 68(1) or (2) (duties to persons whose applications are referred) of the Housing Act 1985; (NB these provisions are no longer in force);
  - (ii) who is owed a duty under sections 188(1) (interim duty to accommodate in case of apparent priority need), 190(2) (duties to persons becoming homeless intentionally), 193(2) (duty to persons with priority need who are not homeless intentionally), 195(2) (duties in case of threatened homelessness) or 200(1), (3) or (4) (duties to applicant whose case is considered for referral or referred) of the Housing Act 1996; or
  - (iii) in respect of whom a local housing authority are exercising their power under section 194(1) (power exercisable after minimum period of duty under section 193) of the Housing Act 1996, (in force) (NB this provision is no longer in force);
- Class J: an asylum seeker to whom, or a dependant of an asylum seeker to whom, a local authority is required to provide support in accordance with regulations made under Schedule 9 to the 1999 Act (asylum support: interim provisions) (NB the interim provisions regime is no longer in force);
- Class K: a person who is attending a designated course, which is a full-time course, at an educational establishment in a case where the housing accommodation which is or may be provided to him by a local housing authority:
  - (i) is not and will not be let to him as a secure tenancy by virtue of paragraph 10 of Schedule 1 to the 1985 Act (student lettings which are not secure tenancies);
  - (ii) and would otherwise be difficult for that local housing authority to let on terms which, in the opinion of the local housing authority, are satisfactory;
- Class L: a person who has a secure tenancy within the meaning of section 79 of the 1985 Act (secure tenancies).

Eligibility for an *allocation* of housing is governed by section 160A of the Housing Act 1996.

1   Housing Act 1985, ss 32(1)–(3) and 44(1).
2   Persons Subject to Immigration Control (Housing Authority Accommodation and Homelessness) Order 2000, SI 2000/706, Art 3; Persons Subject to Immigration Control (Housing Authority Accommodation) (Wales) Order 2000, SI 2000/1036; Persons Subject to Immigration Control (Housing Authority Accommodation and Homelessness) (Amendment) Order 2006, SI 2006/2521; and the Persons Subject to Immigration Control (Housing Authority Accommodation and Homelessness) (Amendment) Order 2008, SI 2008/1768.
3   IAA 1999, s 118(6).

Asylum seekers, refugees and persons granted humanitarian protection and forms of discretionary leave

14.202 From 3 April 2000, asylum seekers are ineligible for housing authority accommodation if they are homeless, even if they are in priority need and not intentionally homeless.[1] They must instead apply to the Secretary of State for a decision on whether they are destitute. If they have accommodation but it is in a very poor state of repair, it is unlikely to be deemed adequate so as to preclude a finding of destitution.[2] If they are facing eviction from previous accommodation, the Secretary of State will only deem them destitute if the actual eviction is due to take place in 14 days or less.[3] In order to provide accommodation for asylum seekers, the Secretary of State enters into contractual arrangements with local authorities, registered social landlords and private landlords and companies. It does not enter into a contract with the asylum seekers themselves. The accommodation provider does not provide them with a tenancy agreement, but enters into an occupation agreement. Asylum seekers provided with accommodation by the Secretary of State are, therefore, not secure tenants, unless their landlord expressly notifies them that they have been given a secure tenancy.[4] This is the case even if they are occupying local authority accommodation. Neither can they be assured tenants.[5] In addition, they will not benefit from the Protection from Eviction Act 1977.[6] Once an asylum application has been finally determined,[7] the asylum seeker is expected to leave the accommodation provided by the Secretary of State within up to a further seven days.[8] However, if the Secretary of State does evict a person from accommodation she has previously provided to him or her, she would be expected to act reasonably in doing so.[9] If accommodation is provided under section 4 of the IAA 1999 (to a failed asylum seeker or other person on temporary admission or released from detention) then, as with accommodation provided by the Secretary of State under Part VI of the IAA 1999, the supported person will not benefit from the Protection from Eviction Act 1977,[10] will not have a secure tenancy unless expressly notified by the landlord that he or she does have a secure tenancy,[11] and will not have an assured tenancy.[12]

1   IAA 1999, Sch 16, amending Housing Act 1996, s 183(2); Allocation of Housing and Homelessness (Eligibility) (England) Regulations 2006, SI 2006/1294; Allocation of Housing and Homelessness (Eligibility) (England) (Amendment) Regulations 2006, SI 2006/2007; Allocation of Housing and Homelessness (Miscellaneous Provisions) (England) Regulations 2006, SI 2006/2527; Homelessness (Wales) Regulations 2006, SI 2006/2646; Allocation of Housing, Homelessness (Eligibility) (England) (Amendment) (No 2) Regulations 2006, SI 2006/3340; Allocation of Housing and Homelessness (Eligibility) (England) (Amendment) Regulations 2009, SI 2009/358; and Allocation of Housing and Homelessness (Eligibility) (Wales) Regulations 2009, SI 2009/393.
2   *Lismane v Hammersmith and Fulham London Borough Council* (1998) 31 HLR 427.
3   Asylum Support Regulations 2000, SI 2000/704, reg 7(a).
4   Housing Act 1985, Sch 1, para 4A.
5   Housing Act 1988, Sch 1, para 12A; Housing (Scotland) Act 1988, Sch 4, para 11B.
6   IAA 1999, Sch 14, para 73 excludes asylum seekers from security of tenure by inserting section 3A(7A) in to the Protection from Eviction Act 1977.
7   The claim is determined 28 days after a claim for asylum is accepted, or 21 days after a negative decision by the Secretary of State or (if there is an appeal) after the disposal of the appeal: IAA 1999, s 93(4), Asylum Support Regulations 2000, SI 2000/704, reg 2(2), as amended by SI 2002/472, reg 3, For final determination of a claim.
8   Asylum Support Regulations 2000, SI 2000/704, reg 22. The total period after the final decision on the claim could be 35 or 28 days (see fn 8 above), but a further two days is added for receipt of the relevant notices. See Ceasing Asylum Support, Asylum Process Guidance.

9   See *R v Newham London Borough Council, ex p Ojuri (No 5)* (1999) 31 HLR 631 and *R v Secretary of State for the Environment, ex p Shelter and the Refugee Council* (23 August 1996, unreported), QBD.

10   Immigration Asylum and Nationality Act 2006, s 43(4)(a), amending the Protection from Eviction Act 1977, s 3A(7A), with effect from 16 June 2006, see Immigration, Asylum and Nationality Act 2006 (Commencement No 1) Order 2006, SI 2006/1497.

11   Immigration Asylum and Nationality Act 2006, s 43(4)(d), amending Housing Act 1985, Sch 1, para 4A(1) with effect from 16 June 2006, SI 2006/1497.

12   Immigration Asylum and Nationality Act 2006, s 43(4)(f), amending Housing Act 1988, Sch 1, para 12A(1) with effect from 16 June 2006, SI 2006/1497.

14.203 If an asylum seeker has been granted refugee status, humanitarian protection, or exceptional or discretionary leave to remain and is homeless, eligible for assistance, in priority need and not intentionally homeless, he or she is entitled to local authority accommodation on the same basis as other homeless persons.[1] The local authority will also be under a duty to provide accommodation on a temporary basis whilst his or her entitlement to such accommodation is being assessed,[2] or pending a possible referral to another authority.[3] The House of Lords held that a successful asylum seeker was not obliged to seek assistance from the local authority to whose area he or she had formerly been dispersed, as dispersal accommodation provided by the Secretary of State on a no-choice basis could not give rise to residence of choice in that area for the purpose of establishing a local connection. Therefore, another local authority to whom the applicant may choose to apply for assistance under Part VII of the Housing Act 1996 could not seek to hold the 'dispersal' authority responsible for providing him or her with accommodation.[4] In response, the Government rushed through section 11 of the AI(TC)A 2004, which came into force on 4 January 2005, and effectively reverses that decision. It provides that a person has a local connection with the district of a local housing authority if he or she was (at any time) provided with accommodation in that district under section 95 of the IAA 1999 unless he or she was subsequently provided with accommodation in the district of another local housing authority.[5] Accommodation in an accommodation centre does not give rise to a local connection for housing purposes.[6] A homeless person, who was previously provided with accommodation in Scotland (otherwise than in an accommodation centre) under section 95 of the IAA 1999 at any time and has not been able to establish a local connection with a district of a local housing authority in either England and Wales or Scotland may only be provided with temporary accommodation and advice and assistance from his or her local housing authority for the period needed to give him or her a reasonable opportunity of securing accommodation.[7] Refugees and others who have been granted leave to remain may be able to show an alternative local connection through their employment, family associations or as a result of special circumstances.[8] Family associations may give rise to a local connection if they involve parents, siblings or people who previously were part of the same household.[9] A young person who was formerly an unaccompanied minor asylum seeker and who was looked after by a local authority for more than 13 weeks after the age of 14 and before the age of 18, who subsequently becomes homeless when he or she is no longer looked after, will be deemed to be in priority need for rehousing (as long as he or she is otherwise eligible for public housing for example as a refugee or as someone who has been granted humanitarian protection or exceptional or discretionary leave).[10]

1   Housing Act 1996, s 193 (as amended by the Homelessness Act 2002, from 31 July 2002).
2   Housing Act 1996, s 188 as amended.
3   Housing Act 1996, s 200, as amended.
4   *Al-Ameri v Kensington and Chelsea Royal London Borough Council; Osmani v Harrow London Borough Council* [2003] EWCA Civ 235, [2003] 2 All ER 1, [2003] 1 WLR 1289 affd [2004] UKHL 4, [2004] 2 AC 159, [2004] 1 All ER 1104.
5   Housing Act 1996, s 199(6), inserted by the AI(TC)A 2004 s 11(1), in force 4 January 2005: SI 2000/2999.
6   Housing Act 1996, s 199(7)(b), as inserted.
7   AI(TC)A 2004, s 11(2)–(3).
8   Housing Act 1996, s 199(1) (as amended).
9   *R v Hammersmith and Fulham London Borough Council, ex p Avdic* (1996) 30 HLR 1; *Munting v Hammersmith and Fulham London Borough Council* [1998] CLY 3017.
10   Homelessness (Priority Need for Accommodation) (England) Order 2002, SI 2002/2051, art 4.

Provision of accommodation

14.204 Accommodation provided by the Secretary of State should be adequate for the needs of the asylum seeker.[1] Ministerial statements suggest that the adequacy of the accommodation should be judged on the same basis as the suitability of accommodation provided to homeless persons under housing legislation.[2] It is likely that the need to access specialist hospital services, to ensure the safety, welfare and protection of children and to protect public health will be taken into account.[3] Other factors which may be taken into account are the location of members of the same ethnic or religious group, health needs, disability and dietary needs.[4] As asylum seekers do not hold the accommodation which they occupy under a tenancy, they are not protected by any implied repairing obligation if the property is in disrepair.[5] Occupation agreements drawn up by accommodation providers are unlikely to include express repairing obligations. However, if the accommodation is in such a state of disrepair that it could be said to be prejudicial to the health of asylum seekers or their dependants, they can seek an order in the magistrates' court (or in Scotland the sheriff) against a local authority, a registered social landlord or a private landlord.[6] If the accommodation is provided by a registered social landlord or a private landlord, they could also request inspection by an environmental health officer and, if appropriate, ask the local authority to serve an abatement notice.[7] If there is a significant risk of violence occurring to the asylum seeker or one of his or her dependants, as a result of racial harassment directed towards them, the Secretary of State should provide alternative accommodation.[8]

1   IAA 1999, s 96(1)(a).
2   Barbara Roche (Parliamentary Under-Secretary of State), Written Answer, 348 HC Official Report (6th series), col 593, 20 April 2000.
3   Lord Williams of Mostyn, 605 HL Official Report (5th series), col 1163, 20 October 1999. See now the duty to have regard to family unity and the needs of vulnerable persons, in Council Directive 2003/9/EC, the Asylum Seekers (Reception Conditions) Regulations 2005, SI 2005/7 and Policy Bulletin 83, Duty to offer support, family unity, vulnerable persons, withdrawing support, version 4.0, 14 October 2009.
4   NASS 1 Application Form, Asylum Support Guidance Notes, note 11.
5   Under Landlord and Tenant Act 1985, s 11.
6   Environmental Protection Act 1990, s 82.
7   Environmental Protection Act 1990, s 80.

8 *Policy Bulletin 81*, Racist Incidents, version 1.0, 21 June 2004.

14.205 Those persons who claimed asylum on arrival in the UK before 3 April 2000 and whose applications are not yet recorded as having been decided (other than on appeal) or abandoned, are still eligible for temporary accommodation as homeless persons under Part VII of the Housing Act 1996 if they are homeless, in priority need and not intentionally homeless.[1] They may also apply for housing benefit.[2] If they are homeless but not in priority need,[3] the local authority is not obliged to secure accommodation for them, but has a duty to provide advice and assistance in relation to finding alternative housing.[4] This may involve access to a rent deposit scheme, a hostel placement, a lodger scheme or fast tracking of housing benefit. An asylum seeker whose application is recorded as having been made within three months of a declaration of fundamental upheaval and whose claim is not yet recorded as having been decided (other than on appeal) or abandoned, will also be entitled to accommodation under homelessness legislation[5] and to housing benefit.[6] Such an asylum seeker will be deemed to be in priority need if, among other things, he or she is vulnerable on grounds of age, illness, pregnancy or disability or has dependent children or a pregnant partner.[7] If a single asylum seeker, who was eligible for housing but for the fact that he or she was not in priority need, is joined by a dependant with such needs on or after 3 April 2000, he or she will become eligible, if they enter as his or her dependants and if his or her application has not yet been recorded as decided.[8]

1 The Allocation of Housing and Homelessness (Eligibility) (England) Regulations 2006, SI 2006/1294, reg 5(1)(e). SI 2006/1294 revoked the Homelessness (England) Regulations 2000, SI 2000/701, reg 3(f);
2 Social Security (Immigration and Asylum) Consequential Amendments Regulations 2000, SI 2000/636, reg 12(6), (7)(a) and Housing Benefit and Council Tax Benefit (Consequential Provisions) Regulations 2006, SI 2006/217, Sch 3.
3 The most usual example of this is a single person in good health, with no dependants.
4 Housing Act 1996, s 192, as amended by the Homelessness Act 2002.
5 SI 2006/1294, reg 5(1)(e).
6 Social Security (Immigration and Asylum) Consequential Amendments Regulations 2000, SI 2000/636, reg 12(6), (7)(b) and Housing Benefit and Council Tax Benefit (Consequential Provisions) Regulations 2006, SI 2006/217, Sch 3.
7 HA 1996, s 189 as amended.
8 SI 2006/1294, reg 5(1)(e).

14.206 Amendments to Part VII of the Housing Act 1996 (homelessness), made by Order, have also been introduced to enable local authorities to disperse the small number of eligible homeless asylum seekers, ie those in Class E, to areas outside London and the south-east and for the receiving local authorities to place them in housing authority accommodation.[1] These regulations came into force on 6 December 1999 and continue in force until section 186 of the Housing Act 1996 is repealed. The latter was in fact repealed by sections 117(5), 169(3) and Sch 16 to the Immigration and Asylum Act 1999 but that provision is itself not yet in force. As a result section 186 of the Housing Act 1996 and the Homelessness (Asylum-Seekers) (Interim Period) (England) Order 1999 limp on although they must be little, if at all, used.

1 The Homelessness (Asylum-Seekers) (Interim Period) (England) Order 1999, SI 1999/3126 and the Housing Act 1996, s 186.

14.207 Persons who are subject to immigration control, but who qualify for public sector housing under housing legislation, will be allocated long-term accommodation by a local authority or a registered social landlord.[1] Their applications will be considered in accordance with the provisions of Part VI of the Housing Act 1996 or the equivalent parts of the appropriate housing legislation in Wales. Housing is allocated according to housing need and local authorities are required to draw up procedures by which they prioritise the allocation of their available housing stock.[2]

[1] A body which is registered (a) in England with the Regulator of Social Housing under the Housing and Regeneration Act 2008, Part 2 and (b) in Wales with the Welsh Ministers under Housing Act 1996, Pt I.
[2] Housing Act 1996, s 167 (as amended by the Homelessness Act 2002); DoE/ DoH Code of Guidance on the Housing Act 1996, Parts VI and VII. For eligibility and ineligibility for housing under section 160A of the 1960 Act as amended.

ACCESS TO EDUCATIONAL PROVISION

Pre-school, primary and secondary education

14.208 Although children may not be admitted to the UK for the purpose of state education,[1] access to state education for children between the ages of four and 16 is not subject to any restriction in the immigration legislation. Even if an adult's leave to remain is subject to the condition that they do not rely on public funds or they are illegal entrants or overstayers, they are entitled to send their children to school. Similarly, unaccompanied asylum seeking children and children who have been granted asylum, humanitarian protection or discretionary or exceptional leave to remain are also entitled to free education in maintained schools. Local authorities have a duty to provide school places to any child residing, temporarily or permanently, in their area, where that child forms part of the population of that area.[2] If the child is from an asylum-seeking family, the Secretary of State should inform the relevant education authority that a child is being dispersed to its area.[3] From September 2000 to March 2003, schools in dispersal areas were eligible for a one -off grant of £500 for each pupil they admitted from an asylum-seeking family which was supported by the Secretary of State.[4] Since then education authorities have been expected to absorb the costs of educating these children within the Standard Spending Assessment System.[5] Local education authorities also receive funding to provide free early education places to the most needy three-year-olds in their area. It is up to the authorities to set their own criteria of social need, which may include providing places to children from asylum-seeking families. As a matter of policy, in the case of children of asylum seekers and unaccompanied minors, asylum support caseworkers should defer dispersal if a child is in his or her final year at school or college and is about to take his or her final examinations at GCSE, AS or A level or their equivalent.[6]

[1] HC 395 of 1993–94 as amended, Appendix A – Attributes, para 124(a); see Chapter 8 above.
[2] Education Act 1996, s 13.
[3] See former *NASS Policy Bulletin 63, Education.*
[4] See *Ofsted report on The Education of Asylum-Seeking Pupils*, HMI 453 (October 2003).
[5] See former *NASS Policy Bulletin 63, Education.*
[6] *Policy Bulletin 31, Dispersal Guidelines*, para 6.5, version 5.0, September 2009.

14.209 If Part 2 of the NIAA 2002 is brought into force and asylum seekers are housed in accommodation centres, local authorities will be deprived of the power to admit children accommodated there to maintained schools or nurseries[1] unless the child in question is admitted to a community or foundation special school which had been named in a statement of special educational needs under section 324 of the Education Act 1996[2] or there is no educational provision at the centre provided under section 29(1)(f) of the NIAA 2002.[3] Local authorities and governors of maintained schools are also required to admit children to the school of their parents' choice, subject to resource considerations,[4] unless the child in question is resident in an accommodation centre.[5] This also applies to children with special educational needs[6] unless they are resident in an accommodation centre.[7] Children with special educational needs also have the right to be educated in mainstream schools if this is appropriate to their needs[8] unless they are resident in an accommodation centre.[9] Educational provision within accommodation centres will not be 'schools' as defined by section 4 of the Education Act 1996 but will be subject to school inspections[10] and reviews and assessments of educational needs.[11] Children of asylum seekers will also be entitled to free school meals.[12] Local education authorities also have a discretion to provide asylum seeking children with school uniform grants and bus passes.[13] Some schools have developed good models to assist the integration of children from asylum-seeking families into maintained schools.[14]

[1]   NIAA 2002, s 36(2).
[2]   NIAA 2002, s 36(3) as amended by the Children and Families Act 2014 at a date to be appointed (as at November 2014).
[3]   NIAA 2002, s 36(10).
[4]   School Standards and Framework Act 1998, ss 86, 94.
[5]   NIAA 2002, s 36(5) as amended by the Children and Families Act 2014 at a date to be appointed (as at November 2014).
[6]   Education Act 1996, Sch 27, paras 3, 8.
[7]   NIAA 2002, s 36(5)(e) as amended by the Children and Families Act 2014 at a date to be appointed (as at November 2014).
[8]   Education Act 1996, s 316(2)–(3).
[9]   NIAA 2002, s 36(5)(d). Children with special educational needs who are resident in an accommodation centre will be provided with education there unless this is incompatible with receiving the special educational provision which his or her learning difficulty calls for, the provision of efficient education for other children who are resident in the accommodation centre or the efficient use of resources: NIAA 2002, s 36(7), (8). If so, the education provider at the accommodation centre will advise the local education authority in writing that that there are special circumstances which call for it to provide for the particular child's special educational needs and it will be able to disapply the provisions of NIAA 2002, s 36 which prevented it from making such provision: NIAA 2002, s 37(1), (2). The Secretary of State can provide guidance to local authorities in relation to such eventualities but has not done so yet: NIAA 2002, s 37(3), (6).
[10] Education Act 2005, Part 1.
[11] Education Act 1996, s 329A, Children and Families Act 2014, s 36 for England (post-1 September 2014) and Learning and Skills Act 2000, s 140 for Wales.
[12] Education Act 1996, s 512ZB(4)(a)(iii).
[13] See former NASS Policy Bulletin 63, Education, para 8.
[14] See Ofsted report on 'The Education of Asylum-Seeking Children', HMI 453 (October 2003).

Further education

14.210 The Education Funding Agency (which supports the delivery of training and education to 16–19 year olds in England)[1] and the Skills Funding

Agency (which regulates adult further education and skills training in England) have replaced the Learning and Skills Council in England and are responsible for determining whether to fund further education for asylum seekers. In Wales further education funding is the responsibility of the Welsh Assembly Government's Department for Children, Education, Lifelong Learning and Skills; in Northern Ireland further education funding is the responsibility of the Department for Employment and Learning and in Scotland further education funding is the responsibility of the Scottish Funding Council. Colleges have discretion as to whether they accept asylum seekers onto their courses and most colleges do. Once a college has accepted an asylum seeker onto a course it can apply to the relevant funding body for funding for him or her.[2] Young persons who were looked after by a local authority for more than 13 weeks after they reached the age of 14 and before they became 18 may be entitled to assistance with the additional costs of travel, accommodation and books associated with attending further or higher education or training.[3] This may include assistance to pay for accommodation during vacations. Support by way of funding may also be available under the Children Act 1989 to young persons who have been 'looked after' and children leaving care. The detail of the current funding policy for England is given below.

[1] Previously known as the Young People's Learning Agency which was abolished in April 2012.
[2] See former *NASS Policy Bulletin 63, Education*, para 8.
[3] Children Act 1989, ss 23C(4)(b) and 24, 24A, 24B; Care Leavers (England) Regulations 2010, SI 2010/2571; see also *R (on the application of Sabiri) v Croydon London Borough Council* [2010] EWHC 1236 (Admin); *R (on the application of Kebede) v Newcastle City Council* [2013] EWCA Civ 960; *R (on the application of Berhe) v Hillingdon London Borough Council* [2003] EWHC 2075 (Admin), [2004] 1 FLR 439, [2003] Fam Law 872 and *R (on the application of W) v Essex County Council* [2003] EWHC 3175 (Admin), [2003] All ER (D) 402 (Dec); 'Guidance on Accommodating Children in Need and Their Families', LAC(2003)13.

14.211 In respect of further education funding, the broad policy framework for England is given in the Skills Funding Agency *Funding Rules 2014–2015*.[1]

Further information on Wales, Scotland and Northern Ireland can be found on the UKCISA website.

[1] www.gov.uk/government/uploads/system/uploads/attachment_data/file/308105/funding_rules _2014_to_2015_version_2.pdf

Higher education

14.212 Publicly funded educational institutions are permitted to charge higher fees for students of further[1] and higher[2] education, who do not qualify as 'home students'.[3] For higher education courses, individual higher education institutions are responsible for classifying students for fees purposes.[4] A student is likely to qualify as a 'home student' for the purposes of higher education courses if he or she falls within one of twelve categories:

(1) British citizens, those with the right of abode in the UK or with indefinite leave to remain here, who are ordinarily resident in the UK, who have been ordinarily resident[5] in the UK and Islands throughout

the three-year period preceding the first day of the first academic year of the course,[6] and that ordinary residence must not have been wholly or mainly for the purpose of receiving full-time education[7];

(2) persons who have acquired the EU/EEA permanent right of residence under Directive 2004/38/EC, and are settled in the UK thereby, who are ordinarily resident in the UK, who have been ordinarily resident in the UK and Islands throughout the three-year period preceding the first day of the first academic year of the course; and where the three year prior residence in the UK and Islands was wholly or mainly for the purpose of receiving full-time education, were ordinarily resident in the EEA, Switzerland or the Overseas territories[8], immediately before that period of residence;

(3) persons who are refugees; the spouses or civil partners of refugees on the date the refugees applied for asylum; and children of the refugees, spouses or civil partners who were so related on the date the refugees applied for asylum and who were under 18 on that date; who are ordinarily resident in the UK and Islands, have not ceased to be so resident since they were recognised as refugees or granted leave, and are ordinarily resident in UK on the first day of the first academic year of the course. The UKCISA Guidance 'Tuition fees: will I pay the "home" or "overseas" rate?' states that if a person is granted refugee status part way through a course, he or she will be liable to pay 'home fees' at the start of the next academic year. However, as the grant of refugee status merely recognises the fact that the person is a refugee and does not create this status, it is arguable that a refugee is entitled to a repayment of any additional fees paid as an 'overseas' student' before his or her status was formally recognised;

(4) persons granted humanitarian protection, discretionary leave or exceptional leave to remain when asylum is refused; their spouses or civil partners on the date the person applied for asylum; and children of the persons, spouses or civil partners who were so related on the date the person applied for asylum and who were under eighteen on that date;

(5) persons who are: (a) EEA or Swiss migrant workers; (b) EEA or Swiss self-employed persons; (c) family members of such persons mentioned (a)–(b); (d) EEA frontier workers or EEA frontier self-employed persons; (e) Swiss frontier employed persons or Swiss frontier self-employed persons; and (f) family members of persons mentioned in at (d)–(e); who are ordinarily resident in the UK on the first day of the first academic year of the course and ordinarily resident in the EEA, Switzerland and the overseas territories throughout the three-year period preceding the first day of the first academic year of the course. However, there is no requirement to be ordinarily resident in the UK on the first day of the first academic year of the course where persons are EEA frontier workers or EEA frontier self-employed persons, Swiss frontier employed persons or Swiss frontier self-employed persons or family members of such persons;[9]

(6) persons who are ordinarily resident in the UK on the first day of the first academic year of the course; have been ordinarily resident in EEA, Switzerland or the Overseas territories throughout the three-year

period preceding the first day of the first academic year of the course; and are entitled to support by virtue of Article 12 of Council Regulation (EEC) No 1612/68 as extended by the EEA Agreement;

(7) persons who are settled in the UK; left the UK and exercised a right of residence after having been settled in the UK; are ordinarily resident in the UK on the day on which the first term of the first academic year actually begins; have been ordinarily resident in the EEA, Switzerland or the overseas territories throughout the three-year period preceding the first day of the first academic year of the course; and where the prior ordinary residence was wholly or mainly for the purposes of receiving full-time education, were ordinarily resident in the EEA and Switzerland immediately beforehand.[10]

(8) persons who are either (a) EC nationals on the first day of an academic year of the course or (b) family members of a such a person, who are undertaking the course in the UK. All such persons must have been ordinarily resident in the EEA, Switzerland or the overseas territories throughout the three-year period preceding the first day of the first academic year of the course. The prior period of ordinary residence in the relevant territory must not during any part of the period referred to have been wholly or mainly for the purpose of receiving full-time education;

(9) persons who are EC nationals other than UK nationals on the first day of the first academic year of the course, who are ordinarily resident in the UK on the first day of the first academic year of the course, who have been ordinarily resident in the UK and Islands throughout the three-year period immediately preceding the first day of the first academic year of the course, and where prior periods of ordinary residence were wholly or mainly for the purpose of receiving full-time education, were ordinarily resident in the territory comprising the EEA, Switzerland or the overseas territories, immediately prior to that period of ordinary residence in the UK. Where a state acceded to the EC after the first day of the first academic year of the course and a person is a national of that state, the requirement to be an EC national other than a UK national on the first day of the first academic year of the course is treated as being satisfied;[11]

(10) the children of Swiss nationals who are entitled to support in the UK by virtue of the Swiss Agreement, who are ordinarily resident in the UK on the first day of the first academic year of the course, and who have been ordinarily resident in the EEA and Switzerland throughout the three-year period preceding the first day of the first academic year of the course. In a case where such prior ordinary residence referred to was wholly or mainly for the purpose of receiving full-time education, were ordinarily resident in the territory comprising the EEA, Switzerland and the overseas territories, immediately before that period of ordinary residence;

(11) the children of Turkish workers, who are ordinarily resident in the UK on the first day of the first academic year of the course, and who have been ordinarily resident in the EEA, Switzerland, Turkey and the overseas territories, throughout the three-year period preceding the first day of the first academic year of the course;

(12)   students studying under a formal exchange programme where fees have to be paid. (It is usual under such programmes for the fees to be waived.)

1   Eg GCSE, 'A' level and their equivalent, NVQ and access courses.
2   Eg Undergraduate, post-graduate, HND and HNC courses.
3   Education (Fees and Awards) Act 1983, s 1; Education (Fees and Awards) (England) Regulations 2007, SI 2007/779; and Education (Fees and Awards) (Wales) Regulations 2007, SI 2007/2310, Education (Student Fees, Awards and Support) (Amendment) (No 2) Regulations 2007, SI 2007/2263. See also the Education (Fees and Awards) (Wales) Regulations 2008, SI 2008/1259 (W126). For the position in respect of student support from 1 April 2008 see the Education (Student Support) Regulations 2009, SI 2009/1555.
4   In line with the Education (Fees and Awards) (England) Regulations 2007, SI 2007/779 (as amended by SI 2007/2263).
5   Ordinary residence was defined by the House of Lords in *Shah v Barnet London Borough Council* [1983] 2 AC 309 as 'abode in a particular place or country which [the person] has adopted voluntarily and for a settled purpose as part of the regular order of his life for the time being, whether of short or long duration'. Reasons for the residence can include business or profession, employment, health, family or merely love of the place. If a person is not lawfully present in the UK he or she cannot be ordinarily resident. For the purposes of the Fees Regulations a person who is ordinarily resident in the UK as a result of having moved from the Islands (Channel Islands, Isle of Man) for the purpose of undertaking a course is to be considered to be ordinarily resident in the Islands; see SI 2007/779, reg 2(8) as inserted by SI 2007/2263.
6   This will be calculated as the date closest to 1 January, 1 April or 1 September.
7   A person is treated as ordinarily resident in England; England and Wales; Great Britain; the UK; the UK and Islands; the EEA and Switzerland; the EEA, Switzerland and the overseas territories; or the EEA, Switzerland and Turkey if he would have been so resident but for the fact that he, his spouse or civil partner, his parent or in the case of dependent direct relative in the ascending line, his child or child's spouse or civil partner, is or was temporarily employed outside the area in question. Temporary employment includes Crown Service in the armed forces, serving outside the UK, service in the armed forces of an EEA State or Switzerland for any period which they serve outside the territory EEA and Switzerland, service in the armed forces of Turkey, during any period which they serve outside the EEA, Switzerland and Turkey; see SI 2007/779, reg 2(4)–(5).
8   Overseas territories means Anguilla; Aruba; Bermuda; British Antarctic Territory; British Indian Ocean Territory; British Virgin Islands; Cayman Islands; Falkland Islands; Faroe Islands; French Polynesia; French Southern and Antarctic Territories; Mayotte; Greenland; Montserrat; Netherlands Antilles (Bonaire, Curaçao, Saba, Sint Eustatius and Sint Maarten); Pitcairn, Henderson, Ducie & Oeno Islands; South Georgia and the South Sandwich Islands; St Helena and Dependencies (Ascension Island and Tristan de Cunha); St Pierre et Miquelon; the Territory of New Caledonia and Dependencies; Turks and Caicos Islands and Wallis and Futuna; see SI 2007/779, reg 2(1).
9   For categories (5)–(8) persons are treated as ordinarily resident in England, England and Wales, Great Britain, the UK, the UK and Islands, the EEA and Switzerland, the EEA, Switzerland and the overseas territories, or in the EEA, Switzerland and Turkey if they would have been so resident but for the fact that they, their spouses or civil partners, their parents or in the case of a dependent direct relatives in the ascending line, their children or their children's spouses or civil partners were temporarily receiving full-time education outside the area in question; see SI 2007/779, reg 2(6). For all categories, an area which was previously not part of the European Community or the EEA but at any time has become part of one or the other or both of these areas, is to be considered to have always been a part of the European Economic Area; see SI 2007/779, reg 2(7).
10 Persons have exercised a right of residence if they are UK nationals, family members of UK nationals for the purposes of Article 7 of Directive 2004/38 (or equivalent EEA Agreement and Swiss Agreement provisions) or persons who have rights of permanent residence who in each case have exercised rights under Article 7 of Directive 2004/38 (or equivalent EEA Agreement and Swiss Agreement provisions) in a state other than the UK or, in the case of persons who are settled in the UK and have rights of permanent residence, if they go to the state within the EEA and Switzerland of which they are nationals or of which the persons in relation to whom they are family members are nationals: SI 2007/779, Sch 1, para 8(2).

[11] Ie most recently for nationals of Bulgaria, Cyprus, the Czech Republic, Estonia, Hungary, Latvia, Lithuania, Malta, Poland, Romania, Slovakia and Slovenia.

14.213 Local authorities may lawfully impose eligibility criteria for awards. Financial assistance, called Student Support, is available in the form of student loans for tuition fees; maintenance grants or special support grants; student loans for maintenance; bursaries; extra help for those with a disability, children or adult dependants; and a college fee loan for graduate entrants to specified undergraduate courses at Oxford or Cambridge. Support is available for first-degree courses (either full time or sandwich), a Higher National Diploma, a Diploma in Higher Education or a Postgraduate Certificate in Education and some part-time courses. Mandatory award criteria are set out in the Education (Mandatory Award) Regulations 2003.[1] The criteria for eligibility for other student support is contained in the Education (Student Support) Regulations 2011.[2] In general, the following categories of persons are eligible for student support in England:[3]

(1) persons settled in the UK other than by having acquired the right of permanent residence: on the first day of the first academic year of the course must be ordinarily resident in England, ordinarily resident in the UK and Islands for the three-year period before the first day of the first academic year of the course, where the main purpose of residence in the UK and Islands must not have been full-time education during the three-year period;

(2) persons who are settled in the UK by virtue of having acquired the right of permanent residence (ie EU citizens and family members): on the first day of the first academic year of the course must be ordinarily resident in England, ordinarily resident in the UK and Islands for the three-year period before the first day of the first academic year of the course, and where the latter period of ordinary residence referred was wholly or mainly for the purpose of receiving full-time education, must have been ordinarily resident in the territory comprising the European Economic Area and Switzerland immediately before that three-year period;

(3) refugees and family members: must be: (a) a refugee; (b) spouse or civil partner on the date the refugee applied for asylum; or (c) child of a refugee, spouse or civil partner who was under 18 on the date the refugee applied for asylum; on the first day of the first academic year of the course must be ordinarily resident in England; and must have remained ordinarily resident in the UK and Islands;

(4) persons granted other leave when asylum claim refused: (a) persons granted humanitarian protection or discretionary leave or exceptional leave to remain when asylum is refused, (b) their spouses or civil partners on the date the person applied for asylum, and (c) children of the persons, spouses or civil partners who were so related on the date the person applied for asylum and who were under eighteen on that date; on the first day of the first academic year of the course must be ordinarily resident in England; and must have been ordinarily resident in the UK and Islands for three years before the first day of the first academic year of the course;

(5) EEA and Swiss workers or self-employed persons and their family members (not UK nationals): on the first day of the first academic year of the course must be ordinarily resident in England (this is not required

from EEA or Swiss frontier workers or self-employed persons or family members of the same), and must have been ordinarily resident in the EEA or Switzerland for three years prior to the first day of the first academic year of the course;

(6) persons ordinarily resident in England on the first day of the first academic year of the course; ordinarily resident in the territory comprising the European Economic Area and Switzerland throughout the three-year period preceding the first day of the first academic year of the course; and entitled to support by virtue of Article 12 of Council Regulation (EEC) No 1612/68 as extended by the EEA Agreement;

(7) persons settled in the UK: on the first day of the first academic year of the course must be ordinarily resident in England, the person or family member must have left the UK and exercised an EEA right of residence in the EEA or Switzerland after having been settled in the UK, must have been ordinarily resident in the EEA or Switzerland for the three-year period before the first day of the first academic year of the course, and if the prior period of residence was for the purpose of full-time education, must have been ordinarily resident in the EEA or Switzerland prior to the three-year period of ordinary residence;

(8) persons who are either EC nationals on the first day of the first academic year of the course or a family member of such a person, who are attending a designated course in England, or undertaking a compressed degree course, designated part-time course or a designated postgraduate course in England; who have been ordinarily resident in the territory comprising the EEA and Switzerland throughout the three-year period preceding the first day of the first academic year of the course; and whose ordinary residence in the territory comprising the EEA and Switzerland has not during any part of that three-year period been wholly or mainly for the purpose of receiving full-time education, although the latter stipulation does not apply to persons who are treated as being ordinarily resident in the territory comprising the EEA and Switzerland but who were outside that area for reasons of temporary employment. Where a state accedes to the EU after the first day of the first academic year of the course and a person is a national of that state or the family member of a national of that state, the requirement to be an EC national on the first day of the first academic year of the course is treated as being satisfied;

(9) EC nationals living in UK and Islands (not UK Nationals): on the first day of the first academic year of the course must be ordinarily resident in England, ordinarily resident in the UK and Islands for the three-year period before the first day of the first academic year of the course, and if the prior period of residence was for the purpose of full-time education, must have been ordinarily resident in the EEA or Switzerland prior to the three year-period of ordinary residence in the UK and Islands. Where a state accedes to the EU after the first day of the first academic year of the course and a person is a national of that state, the requirement to be an EC national other than a United Kingdom national on the first day of the first academic year of the course is treated as being satisfied;

(10) children of Swiss nationals living in the EEA or Switzerland: on the first day of the first academic year of the course must be ordinarily resident in England, must have been ordinarily resident in the EEA or Switzerland for three years before the first day of the first academic year of the course, and if the prior period of residence was for the purpose of full-time education, must have been ordinarily resident in the EEA or Switzerland prior to the three-year period of ordinary residence;

(11) children of Turkish workers living in the EEA, Switzerland or Turkey: must be the children of Turkish citizens ordinarily resident in the UK who are or have been lawfully employed in the UK, on the first day of the first academic year of the course must be ordinarily resident in England, and must have been ordinarily resident in the EEA, Switzerland or Turkey for three years before the first day of the first academic year of the course.

Further information on eligibility for student support may be found at www.direct.gov.uk/en/EducationAndLearning/UniversityAndHigherEducatio n/StudentFinance/index.htm.

[1] SI 2003/1994, as amended.
[2] SI 2011/1986.
[3] The current criteria for England, Wales, Scotland and Northern Ireland can be found on the UKCISA website.

ACCESS TO THE NATIONAL HEALTH SERVICE

14.214 The founding principle of the National Health Service was the provision of treatment which was free at the point of delivery, comprehensive and provided on the basis of need.[1] However, inroads were made into the principle of free treatment in the late 1980s, when the Secretary of State was empowered to make regulations imposing charges for non-emergency treatment on people who are not ordinarily resident in the UK.[2] The term 'overseas visitors' has been and is used in the relevant regulations to describe those who are not ordinarily resident.[3] The regulations permitted charges to be made.[4] These charges can be calculated at an appropriate commercial basis and the power to set these rates has been devolved to the Strategic Health Authorities, Primary Care Trusts, Foundation Trusts, and NHS Trusts in England.[5] Sections 38 and 39 of the Immigration Act 2014 (in force from 20 October 2014) now allows for the Home Office to impose a charge for health services on anyone who applies for 'immigration permission'. This means that anyone with limited leave to enter or remain in the UK, or leave to enter under entry clearance provisions, will now be subject to a financial charge if they wish to access the NHS. In the event that a person does not pay this charge, his or her application for leave to enter or remain may be refused by the Home Office. The amount of this charge is not yet specified. However, in considering what amount to charge an individual, the Home Office must have 'regard to the range of health services that are likely to be available free of charge.' Under the Immigration Act 2014, the Home Office also has the discretion to provide for an exemption, reduction or waiver of these financial charges.[6]

[1] The current duty for England is expressed at s 1 of the National Health Service Act 2006 and for Wales in the National Health Service (Wales) Act 2006.

2   See former National Health Service Act 1977, s 121 (as amended by ss 7(12) and (14) of the Health and Medicines Act 1988) and s 175 of the National Health Service Act 2006). For ordinary residence, see CHAPTER 4 above.

3   National Health Service (Charges to Overseas Visitors) Regulations 2011, SI 2011/1556, reg 2. A challenge to the definition of the term 'overseas visitor' and its application to a failed asylum seeker in order to justify the refusal of non-emergency treatment, was brought on the basis that he was not unlawfully in the UK as he had claimed asylum at port. The NHS Hospital Trust in question agreed to treat the person. However, in a collateral challenge to the related Department of Health Guidance 'Implementing the overseas visitors hospital charging regulations: Guidance for NHS trust hospitals in England', in *R (on the application of YA) v Secretary of State for Health* [2009] EWCA Civ 225, [2010] 1 WLR 279, [2010] 1 All ER 87, the Court of Appeal held that refused asylum seekers are not 'ordinarily resident' in the UK and therefore may not escape liability to charges, nor are they "awfully resident' in the UK so that they are otherwise exempt from charges albeit that they are overseas visitors. The court also held that the Guidance was unlawful, albeit that there was a discretion to withhold treatment, as the Guidance lacked sufficient clarity. As a result of the case the Department of Health issued new guidance which was most recently updated in August 2013. It can be found here: www.gov.uk/government/uploads/system/uploads/attachment_data/file/254530/ovs_visitors_guidance_oct13a.pdf.

4   National Health Service (Charges to Overseas Visitors) Regulations 2011, SI 2011/1556. Further regulations also modify the provision made in respect of the NHS in Wales and Scotland.

5   National Health Service (Charges to Overseas Visitors) Regulations 2011, SI 2011/1556, reg 4.

6   At the writing of this chapter, no orders or directions have been issued by the Secretary of State for the Home Department and it is unclear how charges will be imposed on those applying for 'immigration permission'.

Visits for the purpose of private medical treatment

14.215 Persons entering the UK as visitors for medical treatment are required to pay privately as a condition of entry and further leave to remain.[1] In such cases, the NHS can withhold treatment pending payment in advance for any treatment or an acceptable guarantee of the future payment for any such treatment.[2] In exceptional humanitarian circumstances where a person can satisfy the Secretary of State that the treatment which he or she needs is not available in his or her country of origin, that the necessary arrangements have been made to accommodate him and her and any authorised companion or child,[3] and that the necessary arrangements have been made for them to return home at the end of the treatment, no charge for that treatment will be made or recovered.[4]

1   HC 395, paras 51–56; see CHAPTER 8 above.
2   *R v Hammersmith Hospitals NHS Trust, ex p Reffell* (2000) 55 BMLR 130.
3   'Authorised' in this context means granted leave to enter the UK with the person obtaining a course of treatment in respect of which no charges are payable: National Health Service (Charges to Overseas Visitors) Regulations 1989, SI 1989/306, as amended by SI 2004/614, reg 1(2).
4   National Health Service (Charges to Overseas Visitors) Regulations 1989, SI 1989/306, as amended, reg 6A.

NHS hospital treatment

14.216 For an up-to-date list of persons entitled to free non-emergency NHS hospital treatment, see National Health Service (Charges to Overseas Visitors) Regulations 2011, SI 2011/1556.

14.217 Asylum seekers and refugees in particular suffer a high rate of medical problems, exacerbated by poverty, poor housing, and loss of status and family support.[1] The Department of Health has produced a resource pack to provide advice to local health and social care agencies in asylum support dispersal areas.[2] Asylum seekers should also be provided with their own Patient Held Health Records which they can take with them as they are dispersed around the country.[3]

[1]   See Refugee Health Consortium, *Promoting the Health of Refugees* (November 1998) published by ILPA. The incidence of mental illness is particularly high. See eg Brent and Harrow HA, 'Brent and Harrow Refugee Survey' (1995); Carey Wood and others, 'The settlement of refugees in Britain', HO Research Study No 1441 (HMSO, 1995); Health of Londoners Project 'Refugee Health in London – Key issues for public health', HOLP, c/o East London and City HA (1999); Home Office Online Report 13/03, *Asylum Seekers in Dispersal – Healthcare Issues* by Mark R D Johnson, The HARP Programme whose steering group is based at the University of East London can also provide a good source of information on current research and information at: www.harpweb.org.uk.

[2]   Caring for Dispersed Asylum Seekers: A Resource Pack, Department of Health, 19 June 2003.

[3]   This was developed by the Department of Health's Asylum Seeker Co-ordination Team and is downloadable from the Department of Health's website at www.dh.gov.uk They also produce a regular Asylum Seeker Newsletter.

14.218 For an up-to-date list of other individuals who have a more limited entitlement to free NHS hospital treatment for conditions which arose during a visit, see National Health Service (Charges to Overseas Visitors) Regulations 2011, SI 2011/1556. EEA or Swiss nationals in possession of a form S2 are eligible for treatment for the particular condition specified on the form and for which they have been referred to the UK.

14.219 Treatment in accident and emergency and casualty departments of NHS hospitals remains free of charge to anyone requiring such treatment regardless of their immigration status or nationality until the point at which he or she is admitted to the hospital as an in-patient or is referred to an out-patient clinic.[1] Also free is emergency treatment in an NHS walk-in centre.[2] The diagnosis and treatment of certain specified diseases such as TB, malaria, whooping cough, salmonella, etc, which are notifiable and to which specific public health enactments apply, is also free.[3] Treatment of sexually transmitted diseases, except for human immunodeficiency virus (HIV) and AIDS, at a special clinic for the treatment of sexually-transmitted diseases or on referral from such a clinic is also free of charge to all. Free services in connections with HIV or AIDS are limited to a diagnostic test and any counselling associated with such a test and its result.[4] Family planning services are also free to all.[5] Anyone who is detained in a hospital or received into guardianship under the Mental Health Act 1983 or any similar enactment or subjected to treatment under section 3(1) of the Powers of the Criminal Courts Act 1973 is also entitled to free treatment.[6] Treatment other than hospital treatment remains free (see below).[7]

[1]   National Health Service (Charges to Overseas Visitors) Regulations 2011, SI 2011/1556, reg 6.

[2]   SI 2011/1556 reg 6.

[3]   SI 2011/1556, reg 6.

[4]   SI 2011/1556, reg 6. The exclusion from free treatment of overseas visitors suffering from HIV/AIDS has been widely condemned among public health professionals, not only on humanitarian grounds but also on public health grounds, and many doctors have indicated that they will not comply.

⁵ SI 2011/1556, reg 6.
⁶ SI 2011/1556, reg 6.
⁷ SI 2011/1556, reg 6.

Primary care

14.220 At present, primary health care in the NHS is provided by general practitioners under GMS (general medical services) or PMS (personal medical services) contracts with the NHS or by NHS Walk-In Centres, NHS Direct or APMS (alternative provider medical services) usually provided by voluntary organisations. It is used to be managed by local Primary Care Trusts (PCT). This changed in April 2013 when PCTs ceased to exist and the Health and Social Care Act 2012 brought into being Clinical Commissioning Groups (CCG). The old PCT functions are now taken over by CCGs and local area teams (LATs). They share the responsibilities of commissioning services for their local communities. All GP practices are now belong to a CCG, which commission most services on behalf of patients, including emergency care, community care, planned hospital care, and mental health and learning disability services in their local areas. Anyone needing primary care can either approach his or her local CCG who will direct him or her to a local practice or he or she can apply to register with a local practice directly. Local practices have a discretion to register anyone as a permanent patient, regardless of his or her immigration status or nationality.[1] They may register a person as a temporary patient if he or she has lived in the practice's area for more than 24 hours but less than three months. Local practices may refuse to register a particular patient, but from 1 April 2004, they must have reasonable grounds for doing so which do not relate to the applicant's race, gender, social class, age, religion, sexual orientation, appearance, disability or medical condition.[2] General practitioners are obliged to treat anyone whose need for treatment is immediately necessary, in the opinion of the clinician, or where there is a need for emergency treatment. This treatment must be provided for 14 days or until he or she can register elsewhere, even if the patient is not accepted onto the practice's permanent list and there is no agreement to treat the person as a temporary patient.

[1] HSC 1999/018 Overseas visitors' eligibility to receive free primary care a clarification of existing policy together with a description of the changes brought in by the new EC health care form E128.
[2] National Health Service (General Medical Services) (Contracts) Regulations 2004, SI 2004/291, reg 17.

14.221 Refugees and those who have been granted Humanitarian Protection are entitled to free primary care, as defined in the previous paragraph, and if under 18 or in receipt of benefits, will not have to pay any prescription charges. It is no longer clear, following sections the Immigration Act 2014, sections 38–39 (into force on 20 October 2014) whether those with limited leave to remain will also benefit from free primary care. No orders have been made pursuant to these sections to set out how charges will be implemented and what exemptions apply. Asylum seekers who are supported by the Secretary of State are issued with an HC2 Certificate by the Secretary of State on behalf of the Department of Health. This will entitle them to free prescriptions, dental treatment, eye tests, wigs and fabric supports, travel costs to and from hospital and vouchers towards the cost of glasses.[1] Persons who are deemed to be ordinarily resident in the UK are similarly eligible.[2] At present, it is accepted that anyone who has been living in the UK for more than a year is ordinarily resident. This will include workers and students. Temporary visitors from EEA states and Switzerland, who are nationals of those states or who have been accepted as refugees or stateless persons there, are entitled to all necessary care for conditions which develop while they are here, including problems arising from a chronic condition.[3] They may be in possession of a European Health Insurance Card but there is no legal requirement to produce such evidence of entitlement. International transport workers and EEA and Swiss job-seekers may also have a European Health Insurance Card. EEA and Swiss residents may also be entitled to treatment for specific conditions noted on an S2. A person or his or her dependants who has had, at any time, not less than ten years continuous residence in the UK or not less than ten years continuous service as a Crown servant and who is in receipt of a UK pension is also entitled to free treatment for any conditions which develop while he or she is here. A person who is resident in an EEA state and has had ten years prior continuous residence in the UK is also entitled to free NHS treatment for any condition which develops whilst he or she is in the UK. A Turkish national who is lawfully in the UK and who is without sufficient resources to obtain private treatment is entitled to free treatment as a national of a state which has ratified the European Convention on Social and Medical Assistance.[4] Once accepted as a patient, the person concerned will be entitled to free NHS Primary Care services and to Secondary Care services referred to above which are not limited by immigration status or nationality. Asylum seekers and refugees will be entitled to both free Primary and Secondary NHS care, as will other individuals who fall within the exceptions referred to above. Persons who are not entitled to free Secondary Care will not be able to access it even if a referral is made by their GP or other Primary Care provider. This means that patients registered with a GP who need treatment for cancer, AIDS and other very serious conditions will only receive more specialist treatment if they pay for it out of their own resources. They will remain entitled to treatment in accident and emergency and casualty departments, and it is likely that there will be a significant increase in admissions to these departments of those suffering from very serious chronic or terminal illness which have gone untreated.

1   *Policy Bulletin 43, HC2 Certificates*, version 1.0, 30 November 2000.
2   *Shah v Barnet London Borough Council* [1983] 2 AC 309.
3   These categories are similar to those exempt from NHS charges for hospital treatment.
4   National Health Service (Charges to Overseas Visitors) Regulations 2011, SI 2011/1556, reg 23.

14.222 General dental practitioners cannot accept a patient on to their list on a temporary basis, in the same way that GPs may.[1] Ophthalmic opticians have a discretion to provide free treatment, subject to certain eligibility criteria.[2] Persons accepted as eligible for NHS treatment will be entitled to a free eye test and, if eligible under further regulations,[3] will be issued with an optical voucher if required. Asylum seekers and those who have been granted humanitarian protection or discretionary or exceptional leave to remain who are on a low income may also qualify for free optical and dental treatment and free prescriptions, even when they are not in receipt of asylum support or income support, by completing a form HCI, which can be obtained from the

NHS, the Benefits Agency or the Health Benefits Division. Pharmacists cannot dispense medication free to those who are required to pay prescription charges, and the NHS Counter Fraud and Security Management Services conduct random checks to see whether individuals have been falsely claiming to be exempt from charges.

¹ Health Service Circular HSCV 1999/018, DH 1 February 1999, para 31 (obsolete but not yet replaced).
² NHS (General Ophthalmic Services) Regulations 1986, SI 1986/975.
³ NHS (Optical Charges and Payment) Regulations 1997, SI 1997/818.

ACCESS TO EMPLOYMENT

14.223 A grant of temporary admission or bail can be made subject to a restriction prohibiting the person from taking employment or engaging in an occupation.¹ The concession which permitted asylum seekers on temporary admission to obtain permission to work if their application for asylum had not been determined within six months was withdrawn on 23 July 2002. Those who were already benefiting from the concession were permitted to continue to work until their application was finally determined. A person may apply for a grant of asylum during periods of extant leave to enter or remain where such leave includes permission to work. By applying for a grant of asylum such a person is making an application for an extension of leave to remain. While his or her application for such a variation of leave is under consideration and until his or her immigration appeal rights are exhausted, he or she will be permitted to continue to work by virtue of a statutory extension of his or her leave.² Where leave to enter or remain is curtailed by variation or revocation and where such leave had permitted a person to work, a statutory extension of leave will permit him or her to work until his or her immigration appeal rights are exhausted.³ However, Council Directive 2003/9/EC on the minimum standards for the reception of asylum seekers requires Member States to grant access to the labour market to asylum seekers who have waited for more than 12 months for their claim to be determined,⁴ and the Immigration Rules have been amended to enable such persons to apply for permission to take employment (although not to become self-employed or engage in a business or professional activity.⁵ Home Office guidance has been issued for dealing with applications for permission to work.⁶ A failed asylum seeker who makes a fresh application for leave to remain as part of a fresh claim for asylum, where such an application is awaiting the determination of the Secretary of State as to whether to grant leave and if not whether to recognise it as a fresh claim, falls within the material scope of Article 11(2) of Directive 2003/9/EC so that he or she may seek permission to work where a first decision on the fresh application has not been made within 12 months of its presentation and this delay cannot be attributed to the applicant.⁷ Asylum seekers who do not have permission to work may undertake voluntary activities.⁸ Supported asylum seekers wishing to take up vocational training will need the conditions attached to their temporary admission amended to allow unpaid employment, and any training allowance may impact on their eligibility for asylum support support.⁹ Failed asylum seekers may be required to perform unpaid work as a condition of continued entitlement to support under section 4 of the IAA 1999, although they are currently not so required.¹⁰ By section 59 of the IAN

2006, a person detained in a removal centre does not qualify for the national minimum wage in respect of work done in pursuance of removal centre rules.[11] In *R (on the application of Tekle) v Secretary of State for the Home Department*[12] it was held that the blanket policy denying permission to work to those who had made fresh asylum applications was unlawfully overbroad and unjustifiably detrimental to claimants who had to wait for as long as four years. The employment of an adult subject to immigration control, where that adult who is not permitted to work may give rise to liability to a civil penalty,[13] subject to a right to an administrative review and/or an appeal to a county court (or in Scotland to a sheriff) or to the commission of a criminal offence for knowingly employing an adult subject to immigration control without leave or subject to a condition preventing him or her from accepting his or her employment.[14]

[1] Immigration Act 1971, Sch 2, para 21(2), Sch 3, para 2(5).
[2] Immigration Act 1971, s 3C.
[3] Immigration Act 1971, s 3D.
[4] OJ L 31, 6 February 2003, p 18. See Directive 2003/9/EC, Art 11: where a first decision on an asylum application has not been made within one year of its presentation and this delay cannot be attributed to the applicant, a Member State (of the EU) shall decide the conditions for granting access to the labour market. Such access may not be withdrawn during an appeal that has suspensive effect until a negative decision on the appeal is notified. However, a Member State for reasons of labour market policies, may give priority to EU citizens, EEA nationals and legally resident third-country nationals.
[5] HC 395, paras 360–360E provide for the grant of permission to work upon application. An asylum applicant may apply to the Secretary of State for permission to take up employment. Where a decision on the asylum application has not been taken within a year of it being recorded, any permission to work granted must be in a shortage occupation category and must not include permission to become self-employed or to engage in a business or professional activity. The Secretary of State only considers such an application if, in his or her opinion, any delay in reaching a decision at first instance cannot be attributed to the applicant. Permission to take up employment is until such time as the asylum application is finally determined. Equivalent provision is made as regards further submissions and fresh claims for asylum.
[6] See Asylum Policy Instruction: Permission to Work (Version 6.0, 1 April 2014) at www.gov.uk/government/uploads/system/uploads/attachment_data/file/299415/Permission_to_Work_Asy_v6_0.pdf
[7] *R (on the application of ZO (Somalia)) v Secretary of State for the Home Department* [2010] UKSC 36. *In R (on the application of Sathakaran) v Secretary of State for the Home Department* [2009] EWHC 2916 (Admin), [2009] All ER (D) 212 (Oct) a mandatory order was made compelling the Secretary of State to grant permission to work, notwithstanding that the appeal was then pending before the Supreme Court in *R (ZO)* (above).
[8] *Policy Bulletin 72, Employment and Voluntary Activity*, version 3.0, 21 November 2008.
[9] *Policy Bulletin 72, Employment and Voluntary Activity*, version 3.0, 21 November 2008.
[10] Immigration and Asylum (Provision of Accommodation to Failed Asylum-Seekers) Regulations 2005, SI 2005/930, reg 4.
[11] In force 13 August 2006, see the Immigration, Asylum and Nationality Act 2006 (Commencement Order No 2) 2006, SI 2006/2226.
[12] [2008] EWHC 3064 (Admin), [2008] All ER (D) 120 (Dec).
[13] Immigration, Asylum and Nationality Act 2006, ss 15–20; see also the Immigration (Restrictions on Employment) Order 2007, SI 2007/2390, the Civil Penalties for Employers Code of Practice (February 2008) and the Avoiding Unlawful Discrimination Code of Practice (February 2008).
[14] Immigration, Asylum and Nationality Act 2006, ss 21 and 22.

Chapter 15

PENAL AND CARRIER SANCTIONS

INTRODUCTION

15.1 The following abbreviations are used in this chapter:

IA 2014	Immigration Act 2014
IA 1971	Immigration Act 1971
PACE 1984	Police and Criminal Evidence Act 1984
IAA 1999	Immigration and Asylum Act 1999
NIAA 2002	Nationality, Immigration and Asylum Act 2002
AI(TC)A 2004	Asylum and Immigration (Treatment of Claimants, etc) Act 2004
IAN Act 2006	Immigration and Nationality Act 2006
UKBA 2007	UK Borders Act 2007
BCIA 2009	Borders, Citizenship and Immigration Act 2009

Enforcement of immigration control has become a major policy issue preoccupying UK ministers and their EU counterparts. Immigration officers now have an array of powers which have transformed them into an immigration police force independent of the police.[1] Since the abolition of the UK Border Agency, the border enforcement wing of the Home Office is now named the Border Force, created on 1 March 2012 and describing itself as securing the UK border 'by carrying out immigration and customs controls for people and goods entering the UK'.[2] It is one of the agencies carrying out the enforcement functions described in this chapter, together with immigration officers, customs officials, other officials of the Secretary of State and the police, all operating within as well as at the UK's borders.

The Immigration Act 2014, which further extends the powers of immigration officers, is the latest stage in a process that began with the Nationality, Immigration and Asylum Act 2002 and continued to be a focus of legislative activity in later Acts, including, in particular, the UK Borders Act 2007 (UKBA 2007) and more recently the Borders, Citizenship and Immigration Act 2009 (BCIA 2009), Part 1 of which is entitled 'Border Functions'. The Prime Minister announced in July 2007 the intention to create a 'unified border force'[3] with the BCIA 2009 being a key manifestation of that aim.

In addition to these changes a welter of offences remain in place, including offences designed to criminalise immigrants and asylum seekers in their attempts to enter the country and in their resistance to leaving it. There are a number of overlapping enforcement mechanisms. For example, in a case where leave to enter has been obtained by deception, an immigrant might be summarily removed as an illegal entrant by the immigration service,[4] deported on conducive to the public good grounds by the Secretary of State[5] or prosecuted in the courts by the police,[6] with a possibility of a recommendation for deportation as part of the sentence.[7] We deal with deportation in CHAPTER 16 and removal in CHAPTER 17. In this chapter we deal with arrests by police and immigration officers, the criminal sanctions aimed at immigrants and asylum seekers and those who assist them, and the burgeoning sanctions against employers, carriers, and those who come into contact with immigrants. As far as the latter is concerned, a new tranche of sanctions is contained in the Immigration Act 2014, whose provisions add landlords to the list of people required to carry out checks on immigrants. On pain of a fine of up to £3000, they will be required to check the immigration status of potential tenants, since those without leave to remain or enter are barred under the 2014 Act from entering into residential tenancy agreements unless certain exceptions apply. The provisions are not yet in force at the time of writing, and it is doubtful whether landlords will be capable of verifying the true immigration status of individuals, a complex matter even for the experienced immigration practitioner. There is perhaps a risk that they may refuse to rent at all to anyone looking or sounding foreign.[8]

From the immigrant's point of view, the existence of a parallel set of criminal and administrative sanctions means that there is no knowing which way they are going to be dealt with. Unlike other sections of the population, those subject to immigration control are always in double jeopardy. The fact that they have been arrested by the police and charged with a criminal offence is no guarantee that they will not be summarily removed as an illegal entrant under the administrative powers.[9] The principle of double jeopardy is enshrined in section 28(4) of the IA 1971, which provides that:

> 'Any powers exercisable under this Act in the case of any person may be exercised notwithstanding that proceedings for an offence under this Part of this Act have been taken against them.'

The criminal law has been used increasingly frequently against those using deception or false documents on arrival, as well as those obtaining leave to remain by deception. Draconian offences to criminalise those arriving without documentation, contained in the Asylum and Immigration (Treatment of Claimants etc) Act 2004, are being enthusiastically deployed.[10] But the use of the criminal law against overstayers remains rare where immediate removal is a viable option;[11] and the IDI on overstayers, who come to notice while embarking, indicate that they 'should not be detained for prosecution'.[12] Although there has been a great increase in criminal sanctions in recent years, these are directed mainly at preventing the entry of immigrants and asylum seekers to the UK,[13] and at deterring employers from employing them.

In addition to the alternative procedures – criminal or administrative – for dealing with an offender against the immigration laws, immigrants also face the possibility of being held in detention under widely different powers. First there are the normal criminal law powers of detention in custody on suspicion of having committed an offence. These carry all the normal safeguards of the criminal law – the requirement to charge and bring before a court. But then there are the additional powers of detention contained in Schedules 2 and 3 to the IA 1971 pending a decision on whether the person is to be refused entry, or be removed as an illegal entrant or overstayer, or be made subject to a deportation order. Here there are few of the safeguards normally given to those suspected of a criminal offence, although detention must comply with common law and ECHR Article 5 standards. We deal with detention in Chapter 18 below.

[1]   The transformation of immigration officers into an immigration police force was given recognition in the Police and Justice Act 2006, s 41 of which makes provision for regulations being made to enable the Independent Police Complaints Commission (IPCC) to deal with complaints against immigration officers, other officials of the Secretary of State, designated customs officials, the Director of Border Revenue and persons exercising functions of the Director (see **15.2** below). The most recent Regulations are the UK Border Agency (Complaints and Misconduct) Regulations 2010, SI 2010/782 which revoke and remake, with certain amendments, the UK Border Agency (Complaints and Misconduct) Regulations 2009, SI 2009/2133. The 2010 Regulations provide for the IPCC to have oversight of serious complaints and conduct matters (including incidents where a death or serious injury has taken place) that arise as a result of immigration officers, officials and contractors exercising certain functions in relation to immigration, asylum and customs. They broadly mirror the arrangements for IPCC oversight of the police set out in Part 2 and Schedule 3 to the Police Reform Act 2002 and relevant secondary legislation.

[2]   www.gov.uk/government/organisations/border-force/about

[3]   In the first of the parliamentary statements, made in the light of the attempted bombings in London and Glasgow on 29 and 30 June 2007, the Prime Minister referred to the borders as 'the second line of defence' against terrorism, as well as against crime and illegal immigration. He announced that 'to strengthen the powers and surveillance capability of our border guards and security officers we will now integrate the vital work of the Borders and Immigration Agency, Customs and UK visas overseas and at the main points of entry to the UK, and we will establish a unified border force', HC Deb, 27 July 2007, vol 463, cc 842-3. See also 'Security in a Global Hub: Establishing the UK's New Border Arrangements', Cabinet Office (14 November 2007).

[4]   Immigration Act 1971 (IA 1971), Sch 2, para 9; see **17.9** and **17.10** below.

[5]   IA 1971, s 3(5)(a); *Immigration Appeal Tribunal v Patel (Anilkumar)* [1988] Imm AR 434, HL.

[6]   IA 1971, ss 24A (as amended by the Immigration and Asylum Act 1999, s 2(8), 26(1)(c)).

[7]   IA 1971, s 3(6).

[8]   As suggested by Frances Webber, a former editor of this work, writing for the Institute for Race Relations, see commentary on the Immigration Act 2014 at www.irr.org.uk/news/immigration-bill-passes-through-commons/

[9]   See *Anwar (Mohammed) Re* (DC No 448/77) (19 January 1978, unreported), where the Divisional Court held that the abandonment of criminal proceedings for illegal entry in favour of administrative removal of a suspected impostor was not an unreasonable exercise of the Secretary of State's discretion.

[10] Asylum and Immigration (Treatment of Claimants, etc) Act 2004 ('the AI(TC)A 2004'), s 2. The AI(TC)A 2004 also criminalises failure to cooperate with arrangements for removal, s 35.

11 The use of criminal sanctions against overstayers virtually ceased when rights of appeal against deportation were restricted in 1988 by the Immigration Act 1988, s 5.
12 IDI Ch 20 (Evasion of control), para 3.1. However, the IDI are silent on criteria for prosecution of those overstayers and illegal entrants discovered prior to embarkation. The detailed instructions from the Immigration Service Enforcement Directorate (ISED) covering evasion of control, illegal entry, deportation work, offences against the immigration laws and procedures for investigation, remain confidential.
13 The geographical reach of offences relating to entry has been extended to continental ports by the Channel Tunnel (International Arrangements) Order 1993, SI 1993/1813 the Channel Tunnel (Miscellaneous Provisions) Order 1994, 1994/1405and the Nationality, Immigration and Asylum Act 2002 (Juxtaposed Controls) Order 2003, SI 2003/2818; see eg. **15.37** fn 8, **15.48** fn 2 below.

POLICING THE BORDER

The Borders, Citizenship and Immigration Act 2009: an overview

15.2 Part 1 of the BCIA 2009 creates the legislative framework that allows customs functions performed at the border by Her Majesty's Revenue and Customs[1] (HMRC) to be performed concurrently by immigration officers and officials of the Secretary of State so as to create a unified border force within the Home Office.[2]

This part of the Act also provides for the Secretary of State to appoint, with the consent of the Treasury, a 'Director of Border Revenue'[3] who is responsible for 'customs revenue functions',[4] which is the term used in the Act to describe functions relating to taxes, duties and levies, traditionally areas of government, the administration of which has been independent of ministerial control, customs revenue functions being distinguished from customs policing functions.[5]

Part 1 provides for general customs functions (ie those not concerned with revenue and tax) to be exercisable by the Secretary of State, and for tax and revenue functions to be carried out under the direction of the Director of Border Revenue. Part 1 of the Act is therefore concerned with reorganising existing functions,[6] rather that creating new powers. In dealing with border functions, including customs functions, the Act makes important and detailed provisions on the use, sharing and disclosure of information subject to constraints and penalties for wrongful disclosure; and on powers of investigation, detention, inspection and oversight.

In the Explanatory Note to the BCIA 2009 the government described the new division of responsibilities. Its intention was that:

'officials of the UKBA[7] will exercise these functions on behalf of the Secretary of State and the Director of Border Revenue ("the Director") respectively. Non-revenue customs functions, for example, the prevention of drugs smuggling, will be a matter for the Secretary of State and general customs officials. Customs revenue functions, for example the collection of duties and taxes from passengers and on postal packets, and the prevention of smuggling of goods where such duties and taxes have not been paid, will be a matter for the Director and customs revenue officials.'

The government's intention was that 'UKBA's customs role will be focused on border-related matters, such as the importation and exportation of goods, while HMRC will continue to exercise revenue and customs functions inland'.

Sections 1 to 13 of Part 1 enable the Secretary of State and the Director of Border Revenue to exercise concurrently with the Commissioners for HMRC ('the Commissioners') functions which were previously exercised by the Commissioners and which relate to general customs matters and customs revenue matters. These sections also enable the Secretary of State to designate officials for the purpose of carrying out functions relating to general customs matters (referred to in the Act as 'general customs officials')[8] and the Director to designate officials of the Secretary of State for the purpose of carrying out functions relating to customs revenue matters (referred to in the Act as 'customs revenue officials').[9] General customs officials and customs revenue officials are collectively referred to in the Act as 'designated customs officials'.[10]

The BCIA 2009 confers on the Secretary of State, the Director of Border Revenue, general customs officials and customs revenue officials a wide range of powers. Those powers are set out in other legislation and were previously the sole province of HMRC. For example, the Secretary of State receives customs powers that previously belonged to the HMRC and one individual is able to be both an immigration officer and a customs official.

As a result, immigrants, asylum seekers and British nationals alike passing through UK ports are likely to be affected by the increased range of powers that a single official at the border enjoys under Part 1 of the BCIA 2009, and by the new information sharing powers.[11] Part 1 came into force on 21 July 2009, the day the BCIA 2009 was passed.[12]

Parts 3 and 4 of the BCIA 2009 also contain provisions relevant to the contents of this chapter. In Part 3, section 51 concerns fingerprinting of foreign nationals liable to automatic deportation and section 52 concerns detention at ports in Scotland. In Part 4, section 54 concerns trafficking of people for exploitation.

---

[1]   The Commissioners and the officers of the Revenue and Customs may together be referred to as Her Majesty's Revenue and Customs (Commissioners for Revenue and Customs Act 2005, s 4(1)).

[2]   Section 3 of the BCIA 2009 gives the Secretary of State a power to designate immigration officers and any other officials in his or her department as 'general customs officials'. Those designated persons are able to carry out 'general customs functions' (i.e. those not concerned with revenue and tax, set out at BCIA 2009, s 1(2), (3)) in the same manner as are exercised by officers of HMRC.

[3]   BCIA 2009, s 6.

[4]   BCIA 2009, s 7(2)–(4).

[5]   See *BT Trasporti SRL (in liq) v Revenue and Customs Comrs* [2010] UKFTT 287 (TC) at [9]–[12], for an example as to the overlapping functions of HMRC and the then UKBA in customs revenue matters.

[6]   BCIA 2009, s 38 describes a 'function' as 'any power or duty, including a power or duty that is ancillary to another power or duty'.

[7]   Now of course abolished such that the provisions can be read as a general reference to the Home Office or to the Home Office Border Force.

[8]   BCIA 2009, s 3.

[9]   BCIA 2009, s 11.

[10]   BCIA 2009, s 14(6).

[11]   BCIA 2009, ss 14–21.

[12]   BCIA 2009, s 58

THE PERSONNEL OF IMMIGRATION CONTROL

Functions of police, home office officials[1] and Secretary of State

[1] This is a general reference to immigration officers and designated customs officials.

15.3 The police have a number of different functions relating to immigration which can be summarised as:

(i) investigating criminal offences;
(ii) performing duties given to them under the IA 1971 in connection with the administration of immigration control;
(iii) conducting civil inquiries for the Home Office;
(iv) intelligence gathering.

We have already referred to their general powers under immigration law in **1.68** above. Here we deal with their arrest powers under the IA 1971. The Immigration and Asylum Act 1999, the Nationality, Immigration and Asylum Act 2002 and the Asylum and Immigration (Treatment of Claimants etc) Act 2004 have extended the powers of arrest of immigration officers considerably, and have given them powers of search, entry and seizure in respect of immigration offences equivalent to those of the police.[2] They have the power to use reasonable force if necessary in carrying out any of their functions.[3] The aim of the increase in their powers is to reduce dependency on the police, who previously carried out arrests and removals under the 1971 Act, by enabling immigration officers to perform these functions alone.[4] They are now a true immigration police force. The AI(TC)A 2004 bestowed yet more powers on immigration officers to arrest for offences formerly the sole province of the police and these powers were further extended under the UK Borders Act 2007.[5]

Further, sections 22–24 of the BCIA 2009 give immigration officers and designated customs officials powers similar to those exercised by HMRC in respect of the investigation of offences and detention of persons, subject to similar safeguards. The conferment of these powers is achieved by applying various provisions of the Police and Criminal Evidence Act 1984 (PACE 1984) to immigration officers and designated customs officials, including those with respect to the searching of premises; seizure of property; powers of arrest; searching of persons; places of detention; designation of custody officers; and imposition of custody time limits.

The provisions of PACE 1984 do not apply in Scotland. There, the powers of HMRC to investigate offences and detain suspects are contained in the Criminal Law (Consolidation) (Scotland) Act 1995. BCIA 2009, s 24, adds a new section 26C to that Act so as to make it applicable to criminal investigations conducted by designated customs officials.

Section 22 of the BCIA 2009 applies various provisions of PACE 1984 and of the Police and Criminal Evidence (Northern Ireland) Order 1989[6] (PACE (NI)) to criminal investigations conducted by designated customs officials in relation to a general customs matter or a customs revenue matter,[7] and to persons detained[8] by such designated customs officials.[9] Note that the wording of section 22(1) appears to indicate that section 22 does not apply to pure immigration officers (ie those who are not designated customs officials) or designated customs officials who are exercising their immigration officer functions only (and not their functions in relation to general customs or customs revenue matters). In effect, section 22 brings the powers available to designated customs officials into line with the powers available to HMRC. The government described the objective as being to ensure the 'seamless application of PACE to those officers transferring from HMRC to the UK Border Agency, until a further bespoke PACE application order is made in relation to the border force customs and immigration functions'.[10]

The reference to 'a further bespoke PACE application order' is a reference to the power given to the Secretary of State under section 23 of the BCIA 2009. This power enables the Secretary of State, by order, to apply various provisions of PACE and PACE (NI) to designated customs officials, and also to immigration officers, when they are either investigating offences or exercising powers of detention.[11] The Police and Criminal Evidence Act 1984 (Application to immigration officers and designated customs officials in England and Wales) Order 2013[12] has been made under this section. Part 2 of the Order applies to investigations conducted by immigration officers; Part 3 applies to investigations conducted, and persons detained, by designated customs officials. Hence the PACE provisions now appear to apply to both immigration officers and designated customs officials, simplifying the position created by section 22 of the BCIA 2009.

Where any provision of PACE 1984, confers a power on an immigration officer or designated customs official, and does not provide that the power may only be exercised with the consent of some other person, the official may use reasonable force, if necessary, in the exercise of the power.[13]

Detention custody officers, who are usually private sector employees, also have considerable powers, particularly search powers, although they have no independent powers of arrest.[14] And finally, the Secretary of State and immigration officers have extensive powers of coercive information gathering.[15]

Broadly, there are three types of arrest power under the IA 1971, as amended by the IAA 1999 and the Nationality, Immigration and Asylum Act 2002: (a) without a warrant on reasonable suspicion of certain immigration-related offences; (b) with a warrant on reasonable suspicion of immigration offences; and (c) administrative arrests for the purpose of detention and removal of persons refused leave to enter, absconders from temporary admission, illegal entrants, overstayers and persons in breach of conditions, persons awaiting deportation on conducive grounds or following a recommendation of deportation by a criminal court of persons reasonably suspected of being in those categories.

[2]   Immigration and Asylum Act 1999 (IAA 1999), ss 128–139.
[3]   IAA 1999, s 146(1). Paragraph 5 of Schedule 1 of the Immigration Act 2014 amends the wording of s 146 so that the power to use reasonable force is not limited to the exercise of powers under the 1971 and 1999 Act but applies to all 'the Immigration Acts'. SI 2014/1820: In force 28 July 2014.
[4]   Explanatory Note to IAA 1999, Pt VII; Mike O'Brien speech to Special Standing Committee, 13 May 1999.
[5]   Asylum and Immigration (Treatment of Claimants etc) Act 2004, s 14; UK Borders Act 2007, ss 1 and 18.
[6]   SI 1989/1341 (NI 12).
[7]   BCIA 2009, s 22(1)(a).

8   BCIA 2009, s 22(1)(b).

9   Section 22 of the BCIA 2009 does this by applying the Police and Criminal Evidence (Application to Revenue and Customs) Order (Northern Ireland) 2007, SR 2007/464 to those investigations. See also the Police and Criminal Evidence Act 1984 (Application to immigration officers and designated customs officials in England and Wales) Order 2013, SI 2013/1542 ('the 2013 PACE Order'), art 32 which disapplies the Police and Criminal Evidence Act 1984 (Application to Revenue and Customs) Order 2007, SI 2007/3175 to section 22, ensuring that it is no longer a PACE Order for the purposes of that section, albeit that it remains in force. The 2013 PACE Order came into force on 25 June 2013.

10   HL Comm Deb, 25 February 2009, vol 708 c 262, per Lord West of Spithead, Parliamentary Under-Secretary of State, Home Office.

11   BCIA 2009, s 23(1) and (2).

12   SI 2013/1542, in force 25 June 2013.

13   PACE (Application to immigration officers and designated customs officials in England and Wales) Order 2013, SI 2013/1542, arts 6 and 15.

14   IAA 1999, Sch 11, paras 2–3, Sch 12, paras 2–3; Detention Centre Rules 2001, SI 2001/238, made under IAA 1999, s 153.

15   See 15.25 below.

ARREST AND DETENTION

Arrest without warrant

15.4 A police or immigration officer has a power of arrest without warrant in respect of offences under sections 24 and 24A of the IA 1971, such as illegal entry, overstaying and obtaining leave by deception;[1] for various offences under sections 25, 25A and 25B of facilitating illegal entry into an EU Member State, or the arrival in the UK of asylum seekers and EU national deportees;[2] and for offences relating to false, altered or forged registration cards and possession of immigration stamps under section 26A and 26B.[3] Arrest by police officers without a warrant, for offences for which there is no specific statutory power of arrest without a warrant, can only be carried out if the conditions set out at section 24(5) of PACE 1984 are met.[4] Immigration officers also have a power of arrest without warrant for the offence of obstruction, but only where it would be impracticable to proceed by way of summons.[5] Under the Asylum and Immigration (Treatment of Claimants etc) Act 2004 immigration officers have arrest powers in relation to the most serious offences of trafficking under the Sexual Offences Act 2003 and the equivalent Scottish law, and trafficking for exploitation under the Act of 2004.[6] There is no power of arrest for offences (other than obstruction) connected with the administration of the 1971 Act, or by captains of ships or aircraft or operators of trains.[7]

A designated customs official may arrest without warrant anyone who is about to or is in the act of committing an offence, or whom the official has reasonable grounds to suspect is or is about to commit an offence, or whom the official reasonably suspects to be guilty of an offence.[8]

1   IA 1971, s 28A(1), inserted by IAA 1999, s 128. The power of arrest only applies to s 24(1)(d) offences (failing to report for a medical examination), if the officer applies for a warrant: IA 1971, ss 28A(2) and 28AA; see fn 1 at 15.9 below.

2   IA 1971, s 28A(3) as amended by Nationality, Immigration and Asylum Act 2002, s 144. The police power of arrest comes from Police and Criminal Evidence Act 1984, s 24. The power of summary arrest conferred by ss 24(1)–(3) of PACE 1984 is circumscribed by s 24(5).

[3]   These offences were added by Nationality, Immigration and Asylum Act 2002, s 146; powers of arrest are under IA 1971, s 28A(9), inserted by section 150 of the Nationality Immigration and Asylum Act 2002 (NIAA 2002).

[4]   PACE 1984, ss 24(4)–(5):

   '(4)   But the power of summary arrest conferred by subsection (1), (2) or (3) is exercisable only if the constable has reasonable grounds for believing that for any of the reasons mentioned in subsection (5) it is necessary to arrest the person in question.

   (5)   The reasons are: (a) to enable the name of the person in question to be ascertained (in the case where the constable does not know, and cannot readily ascertain, the person's name, or has reasonable grounds for doubting whether a name given by the person as his name is his real name); (b) correspondingly as regards the person's address; (c) to prevent the person in question: (i) causing physical injury to himself or any other person; (ii) suffering physical injury; (iii) causing loss of or damage to property; (iv) committing an offence against public decency (subject to subsection (6)); or (v) causing an unlawful obstruction of the highway; (d) to protect a child or other vulnerable person from the person in question; (e) to allow the prompt and effective investigation of the offence or of the conduct of the person in question; (f) to prevent any prosecution for the offence from being hindered by the disappearance of the person in question.'

[5]   IA 1971, s 26(1)(g); s 28A(5) of the IA 1971, inserted by s 128 of the IAA 1999. The provisions mirror the police' general power of arrest (PACE 1984, s 25) requiring either reasonable doubts as to the identity or address of the person or the risk of physical injury or loss or damage to property, to justify arrest without warrant.

[6]   Under the Asylum and Immigration (Treatment of Claimants etc) Act 2004, s 14(2)(n)–(p) (from 1 December 2004: SI 2004/2999).

[7]   IA 1971, ss 26 and 27.

[8]   PACE 1984, ss 24(2), (4) and (5) apply to immigration officers and designated customs officials by virtue of the 2013 PACE Order (see above at 15.3 fn 9) and the Police and Criminal Evidence (Application to Revenue and Customs) Order (Northern Ireland) 2007 SR 2007/464. This power does not limit any other power of arrest conferred on an immigration officer or designated customs official by any other enactment: see 2013 PACE Order, arts 7 and 16.

15.5 Under the Asylum and Immigration (Treatment of Claimants etc) Act 2004 police and immigration officers have powers of arrest without warrant of anyone reasonably suspected of not having an immigration document,[1] or of failing to comply with a requirement of the Secretary of State to enable removal.[2] In addition, immigration officers also have extensive powers of arrest without warrant for a large number of offences involving dishonesty, including conspiracy to defraud, bigamy, making false statements, offences under the Perjury Act, theft, obtaining by deception, false accounting, handling, forgery and the use and possession of false instruments, and equivalents in Scotland and Northern Ireland.[3] The power is available where an immigration officer is exercising a function under the Immigration Acts, such as conducting an interview or looking at seized documents, and forms a reasonable suspicion that the person has committed or attempted to commit one of the listed offences.[4] Under the UKBA 2007, immigration officers are also given a power to arrest without warrant persons suspected of making false or dishonest claims for asylum support contrary to sections 105 or 106 of the IAA 1999.[5] An immigration officer may also arrest a person without warrant if the officer reasonably suspects that the person has committed or is about to commit the new offence of assaulting an immigration officer.[6]

[1]   Asylum and Immigration (Treatment of Claimants etc) Act 2004, s 2(10) (in force 22 September 2004: s 48(1)).

[2]   AI(TC)A 2004, s 35(5) (in force 22 September 2004: s 48(1)).

3   AI(TC)A 2004, s 14(2) (in force 1 December 2004: SI 2004/2999).
4   AI(TC)A 2004, s 14(1) (in force 1 December 2004: SI 2004/2999).
5   UKBA 2007, s 18, inserting new section 109A of the IAA 1999.
6   UKBA 2007, s 23(1)–(3).

Arrest with a warrant

15.6 An immigration officer may arrest on a warrant from a JP (or a sheriff in Scotland) for failure to report to a medical officer,[1] or for the offence of employing someone not entitled to work in the UK.[2]

The BCIA 2009[3] confers on the Secretary of State, the Director of Border Revenue, general customs officials and customs revenue officials a wide range of powers. Those powers are set out in other legislation and were previously the sole province of HMRC. For example, section 138 of the Customs and Excise Management Act 1979 now confers on designated customs officials a power of arrest in respect of any person who has committed or is reasonably suspected of having committed any offence under the Customs and Excise Acts.[4]

1   Under IA 1971, s 24(1)(d); the power of arrest is created by IA 1971, s 28AA, inserted by Nationality, Immigration and Asylum Act 2002, s 152.
2   Under IAN 2006, s 21: see 15.98 ff below.
3   BCIA 2009, ss 1–13.
4   See PACE Act (Application to Revenue and Customs) Order 2007, SI 2007/3175, art 17, read with BCIA 2009, s 14(6).

Detention of suspects

15.7 Under sections 1 and 2 of the UK Borders Act 2007 (UKBA), the Secretary of State may designate suitably trained immigration officers, who are fit and proper for the purpose, to detain for up to three hours individuals who are liable to arrest by a constable under the Police and Criminal Evidence Act 1984[1] or its equivalent in Northern Ireland[2] or are subject to a warrant for arrest. The officer may then search the individual for weapons and evidence. He must also arrange for a constable to attend as soon as is reasonably practicable.[3] Anyone who absconds, assaults or obstructs an immigration officer carrying out these duties commits a summary offence, which can be punished by a fine or imprisonment.[4]

Section 52 of the BCIA 2009 amends sections 2, 3 and 60(1) of the UKBA 2007 and extends the permissive detention power in section 2 of the UKBA 2007 to designated immigration officers in Scotland. The provision enables an immigration officer designated under section 1 of the UKBA 2007 to detain, at a port in Scotland, an individual whom the immigration officer thinks is subject to a warrant for arrest. Detention may be for up to three hours pending the arrival of a constable. Section 52(3) amends section 60(1) of the UKBA 2007 so that the territorial scope of the powers of detention and enforcement by designated immigration officers under UKBA 2007, ss 1–4 extends to Scotland.

With respect to the related offences in section 3 of the UKBA 2007 – where, for example, a person absconds from detention under section 1 of that Act –

section 52(2) of the BCIA 2009 makes provision for the sentences for those offences in Scotland.

By virtue of section 58(3)(b) of the BCIA 2009, section 52 comes into force on such day as the Secretary of State may by order appoint.

A person arrested by a designated customs official must be taken to an 'office of the UKBA' and, if detained for more than six hours, must be taken to a 'designated office of the UKBA'.[5] A person is in UKBA detention if taken to a UKBA office after being arrested or, having attended a UKBA office voluntarily, is arrested there.[6] A person arrested by a designated customs official for an offence may not be kept in detention except in accordance with the provisions of Part IV of PACE 1984, including: that he or she is to be released if the grounds for detention cease to apply;[7] the Secretary of State is required to designate UKBA offices for the purpose of detaining arrested persons and to designate offices that appear to him or her to provide enough accommodation for that purpose;[8] a designated customs official must be appointed by the Secretary of State as custody officer at each designated office[9] and he or she is responsible for determining whether to charge, release, or authorise detention of the arrested person.[10] The custody officer is responsible for ensuring that the detained person is treated in accordance with PACE 1984 and any relevant Code of Practice and that a custody record is kept.[11] Periodic reviews of the person's detention are to be carried out by the custody officer in respect of a person charged and by a designated customs official of at least immigration officer or executive officer grade in respect of a person who has not been charged.[12]

Immigration officers and designated customs officials do not have power to charge a person with any offence or to release the person on bail.[13]

[1] PACE 1984, s 24(1), (2) or (3).
[2] Article 26(1), (2) or (3) of the Police and Criminal Evidence (Northern Ireland) Order 1989, SI 1989/1341 (NI 12).
[3] UKBA 2007, s 2(2). Detention under this section shall be treated as detention under the IA 1971 for the purposes of Part 8 (detained persons) of the IAA 1999, which means that no complaint can be made to the IPCC: Police and Justice Act 2006, s 41.
[4] UKBA 2007, s 3.
[5] PACE 1984, s 30. An office of the UKBA is defined as 'premises wholly or partly occupied by designated customs officials,' such that the effect of the provision remains the same in spite of abolition of the UKBA: BCIA 2009, s 22(4)(b). Throughout these paragraphs the terms 'UKBA office' and 'UKBA detention' are used since that continues to be the statutory wording.
[6] BCIA 2009, s 22(4)(a). This definition of UKBA detention does not cover persons detained under para 16 of Schedule 2 to the IA 1971 or para 2 of Schedule 3 to the Immigration Act 1971 or section 2 or 36 of the UKBA 2007. For fuller information about detention, see CHAPTER 18. In Northern Ireland only, a person may be transferred between UKBA detention and Revenue and Customs detention and between UKBA detention and police detention: BCIA 2009 s 22(6) and (6A): see the 2013 PACE Order, art1, in force 25 June 2013.
[7] PACE 1984, s 34.
[8] PACE 1984, s 35, modified by the 2013 PACE Order, art 22.
[9] PACE 1984, s 36, modified by the 2013 PACE Order, art 23.
[10] PACE 1984, s 37.
[11] PACE 1984, s 39.
[12] PACE 1984, s 40.
[13] Articles 4 and 13 of the 2013 PACE Order. Designated customs officials do not have the power to detain a person for an offence after he or she has been charged with that offence: see Police and Criminal Evidence Act 1984 (Application to Revenue and Customs) Order 2007, SI 2007/3175, art 4, read with BCIA 2009, s 14(6).

Custody time limits

15.8 The following section concerns detention arising from suspicion of the commission of criminal offences (detention for immigration purposes is dealt with in CHAPTER 18). A person may not be kept in UKBA detention for more than 24 hours without being charged,[1] unless a designated customs official, of at least the rank of inspector or senior executive officer, has reasonable grounds for believing that further detention is necessary to preserve evidence or obtain evidence by questioning in relation to the offence for which the person was arrested; that the offence is indictable and that it is being investigated diligently and expeditiously.[2] In that case, detention for up to 36 hours may be authorised. Thereafter, a designated customs official may apply to a magistrates' court for a warrant of further detention which may authorise up to 36 hours' further detention;[3] an application may be made to extend the warrant up to a maximum of 96 hours' detention from the earlier of the time of the person's arrival at the UKBA office and the time of the person's arrest.[4]

Each UKBA office is required to keep written records showing on an annual basis the numbers of people detained for more than 24 hours and subsequently released without charge, and of warrants for further detention.[5]

Nothing in Part IV of PACE 1984 affects the right of any detained person to apply for habeas corpus.

[1]   PACE 1984, s 41, modified by the 2013 PACE Order, SI 2013/1542, art 24. Once more 'UKBA detention' refers to detention at 'premises wholly or partly occupied by designated customs officials,' such that the provision continues to make sense following abolition of the UKBA: BCIA 2009, s 22(4)(b). See 15.7 above, fn 5 and 6 for the definition of 'UKBA detention.'
[2]   PACE 1984, s 42, modified by the 2013 PACE Order, art 25.
[3]   PACE 1984, s 43, modified by 2013 PACE Order, art 26.
[4]   PACE 1984, s 44.
[5]   PACE 1984, s 50, modified by the 2013 PACE Order, art 28.

Questioning and treatment of persons by designated customs officials

15.9 The custody officer is to ascertain and make a record of everything that a person has with him or her when brought under arrest to, or arrested at, a UKBA office and the person may be searched by a designated customs official.[1] A designated customs official or immigration officer of executive officer grade may authorise the carrying out of an intimate search if there are reasonable grounds for believing that the detained person has concealed on him or her anything which could cause injury to him or herself or to others.[2] Intimate samples may be taken from a person if a designated customs official of at least the grade of immigration officer or executive officer authorises the taking of samples and the person consents.[3]

A person detained is entitled to have one friend or relative or other person known to him or her and likely to take an interest in the person's welfare informed of his or her arrest and detention.[4]

A person arrested and held in custody at a UKBA office is entitled to consult a solicitor privately at any time.[5]

The PACE Codes of Practice are applicable to investigations by designated customs officers because a person other than a police officer charged with the duty of investigating an offence is obliged to have regard to any relevant provision of a code.[6]

[1] PACE 1984, s 54, modified by the 2013 PACE Order, art 29.
[2] PACE 1984, s 55, modified by the 2013 PACE Order, art 30.
[3] PACE 1984, s 62.
[4] PACE 1984, s 56.
[5] PACE 1984, s 58.
[6] PACE 1984, s 67(9).

Entry and search before arrest

15.10 Police and immigration officers have power to enter and search without a warrant any premises where they believe on reasonable grounds that a suspect is, in order to make an arrest for an offence of assisting a breach of immigration law or the arrival of asylum claimants under sections 25, 25A and 25B of the IA 1971.[1] Immigration officers' powers of entry and search without a warrant were vastly increased by the AI(TC)A 2004, to embrace offences such as fraud, bigamy, theft, handling stolen goods and perjury.[2] Where persons are suspected of making false or dishonest claims for asylum support contrary to sections 105 or 106 of the IAA 1999, immigration officers have the powers of entry, search and seizure they already had under the IA 1971.[3] Police and immigration officers also have power to enter and search business premises without a warrant, and arrest any suspected illegal entrants, over-stayers or persons who are in breach of conditions or who have used deception to remain.[4] With a warrant issued by a justice of the peace or sheriff, they may enter named premises, if need be by reasonable force, to search for and arrest a person suspected of an ever expanding list of offences,[5] such as illegal entry, overstaying, breach of conditions, failing to report for medical examination or to comply with conditions of temporary admission, unlawful disembarkation, entry or remaining by deception, and offences connected with registration cards and immigration stamps.[6] The offences of unlawful employment,[7] of not having an immigration document on arrival and of failure to cooperate with removal have now been added to the list of 'relevant offences' for the purpose of entry and search with a warrant.[8]

[1] Police power comes from the Police and Criminal Evidence Act 1984, s 17; immigration officers' from IA 1971, s 28C, inserted by IAA 1999, s 130, as amended by Nationality, Immigration and Asylum Act 2002, s 144.
[2] AI(TC)A 2004, s 14(3), in force 1 December 2004: SI 2004/2999. Police have these powers under PACE 1984: see fn 1 above.
[3] UKBA 2007, s 18, inserting new sections 109A and 109B of the IAA 1999.
[4] IA 1971, s 28CA, inserted by NIAA 2002, s 153. The power may be used for the purpose of making an arrest for the offences under s 24 or s 24A or under Sch 2, para 17 (the administrative provisions of the Act). The operation must be authorised by the Secretary of State (if performed by an immigration officer) or by a Chief Superintendent (for police), and the police or immigration officer must produce identity if the premises are occupied: IA 1971, s 28CA(2), (4). The authority expires after seven days: IA 1971, s 28CA(3).
[5] Starting with the Asylum and Immigration Act 1996, s 7, which applied to offences under s 24(1)(a), (aa) and (b) (illegal entry, entry by deception and overstaying). This was repealed (Sch 14, para 14) and replaced (s 129) by the IAA 1999, which extended the power to s 24(1)(d), (e), and (f), s 24A and s 25(2). The NIAA 2002, s 150(2) extended it to ss 26A and

26B (new offences in relation to immigration or asylum documents). Now it has been further extended by the AI(TC)A 2004, as set out below.

[6]   IA 1971, s 28B, inserted by IAA 1999, s 129 as amended by NIAA 2002, ss 144 and 150.

[7]   IAN 2006, s 21: see **15.94** ff below.

[8]   AI(TC)A 2004, ss 2(11), 35(6), in force 22 September 2004: AI(TC)A 2004, s 48(1).

Administrative arrest

15.11 Police and immigration officers also have extensive powers of arrest under Schedules 2 and 3 to the IA 1971 in support of the administration of the Act. The administrative powers under these provisions are not concerned with the task of catching and prosecuting offenders, but to facilitate examination of new arrivals and the removal of persons without leave to enter (including illegal entrants and overstayers) and deportees. The following may be arrested: persons who are required to submit to examination by an immigration officer on arrival in the UK, those who have been refused leave to enter the country or whose leave to enter is suspended, members of the crew of a ship or aircraft who are suspected of deserting ship or overstaying their leave, illegal entrants, overstayers, those awaiting deportation, and their family members.[1] Persons suspected of belonging to any of these categories may all be detained under the authority of an immigration officer or the Secretary of State for the purpose of examination, a decision on removal or being given removal directions.[2] The Immigration Act 2014 contains new enforcement powers in relation to the detention of persons so detained. Paragraph 1 of Schedule 1 inserts into paragraph 18(3) of Schedule 2 to the 1971 Act a power for an immigration officer to escort a person for this purpose.[3] There is also a new power for immigration officers to search a person so detained for anything which the person might use to cause physical injury to themselves or others or which they might use to escape from legal custody. It sets out the grounds which must exist before the power can be exercised, the extent of the search and sets out what may be seized and retained as a result of the search and for how long such items may be retained.[4] All these people may be arrested without warrant by an immigration officer or a police officer.[5] If they cannot be found, a justice of the peace or sheriff may issue a warrant to the police to enter premises where any of them is reasonably believed to be for the purpose of searching for and arresting that person. Reasonable force may be used in the execution of the warrant.[6] There is also a power to arrest those who have broken or are about to break bail conditions imposed by the appellate authorities,[7] or restrictions imposed by a court on those recommended for deportation.[8] A new category of administrative arrest was added by section 53 of IAN 2006 in deportation cases. The power of arrest with or without a warrant under paragraph 17 of Schedule 2 can be exercised in deportation cases when the notice of intention to deport is ready but has not yet been given to the prospective deportee. The purpose of this provision is to enable immigration officers and the police to seek a warrant in such circumstances under paragraph 17(2) to enter named premises in order to give the notice of intention to deport to the prospective deportee and at the same time to arrest him or her.

[1]   IA 1971, Sch 2, para 10A, inserted by Nationality, Immigration and Asylum Act 2002, s 73, assimilated the position of family members of groups covered by paras 8–10 of the Schedule (those refused leave to enter and illegal entrants), to family members of overstayers (IAA 1999, s 10(7)) who have always been liable to removal from the UK with the principal. The provision

enables the removal of British-born (but not British citizen) children of those remaining in the UK on temporary admission for lengthy periods before refusal of an asylum or human rights claim.

2   IA 1971, Sch 2, para 16(1), (1A) and (2), applied to the Secretary of State by NIAA 2002, s 62, applied to overstayers by IAA 1999, s 10(7) (save those falling within the transitional 'regularisation' provisions of s 9), and Sch 3, para 2 for deportees. Note Sch 2, para 16(2) which empowers detention on suspicion; previously, being in one of the categories, eg an illegal entrant, was a condition precedent for detention, and damages could be (and were) awarded for the detention of a person reasonably but incorrectly suspected of being an illegal entrant and detained under Sch 2.

3   Paragraph 18(3) of Sch 2 of IA 1971 already allows any person acting under the authority of an immigration officer to escort a person so detained.

4   Immigration Act 2014, Sch 1, para 2(1). SI 2014/1820 art 1(y): in force 28 July 2014.

5   IA 1971, Sch 2, para 17(1). A police or immigration officer may enter and search any business premises to arrest under para 17 without a warrant: IA 1971, s 28CA(1), inserted by NIAA 2002, s 153. See above.

6   IA 1971, Sch 2, para 17(2), as amended by IAA 1999, s 140(2), NIAA 2002, s 62.

7   IA 1971, Sch 2, paras 24(1), 33(1).

8   IA 1971, Sch 3, para 7.

Powers of arrest in control zones

15.12 Powers of arrest for arrestable offences, offences under the Immigration Acts and for administrative detention are exercisable by police in control zones in France and Belgium.[1] The control zones include Coquelles, Frethun, Paris Gare du Nord, Brussels Gare du Midi, Lille, Calais (ferryport and hoverport), Boulogne and Dunkirk.[2]

1   Channel Tunnel (International Arrangements) Order 1993, SI 1993/1813, art 6, Sch 3, para 2; Channel Tunnel (Miscellaneous Provisions) Order 1994, SI 1994/1405, arts 4–6, Sch 3; Nationality, Immigration and Asylum Act 2002 (Juxtaposed Controls) Order 2003, SI 2003/2818, arts 11–13.

2   The control zones are not set out in the 1993 and 1994 Orders, but the control zones in the ports of Calais, Boulogne and Dunkirk are set out in SI 2003/2818, Sch 1.

SEARCH AND SEIZURE OF EVIDENCE

Search for evidence of crime

15.13 Police and immigration officers may enter premises to search for and seize evidence on a warrant from a justice of the peace or sheriff[1] on reasonable grounds for belief that a 'relevant offence'[2] has been committed, that material evidence of substantial value to the investigation of the offence is on the premises (and does not consist of or include items subject to legal privilege, excluded material or special procedure material) and it is not practicable to enter without a warrant.[3] On arrest, premises, where the suspect was arrested or had been immediately before arrest, may be searched for evidence relating to the offence[4] without any warrant or other authority. In the more serious offences under sections 25, 25A or 25B of the IA 1971 premises suspected of being occupied or controlled by a suspect can be entered and searched, after arrest, by immigration officers, if they obtain the authorisation of a chief immigration officer.[5] An arrested suspect may be searched, outside or in the police station, for weapons, escape tools, evidence and documents.[6] Immigration officers have these ancillary powers of entry and search[7] in respect of the criminal offences of fraud, perjury, bigamy etc which they uncover in the course of their immigration duties.[8] With respect to the investigation of offences and detention of persons, the effects of the PACE Order made under section 23 of the BCIA 2009 (see at **15.3** above), include powers to search premises and seize articles. A designated customs official can apply to a justice of the peace for a search warrant[9] and to a circuit judge for an order giving him or her access to 'excluded material or special procedure material'[10] (ie certain types of confidential material). He or she may enter and search premises for the purpose of executing an arrest warrant or arresting a person for an indictable offence;[11] may enter and search any premises occupied or controlled by a person arrested for an indictable offence;[12] if lawfully on any premises, may seize anything which is on the premises if (inter alia) he or she has reasonable grounds to believe that it is evidence relating to an offence that he or she is investigating,[13] including information stored in electronic form.[14] When searching premises relying on a warrant, an immigration officer or designated customs official may search any person found on the premises where he or she has reasonable cause to believe that the person is in possession of material which is likely to be of substantial value to the investigation.[15] The powers of immigration officers and designated customs officials' to seize items are not limited to items that are evidence of offences in relation to which they have functions.[16] The designated customs official is obliged, if requested to do so, to provide a record of what is seized and a photograph or photocopy of seized material.[17] He or she may retain seized material for as long as necessary in all the circumstances.[18]

[1] For police officers this power derives from section 8(1) and (6) of PACE 1984. For immigration officers this power derives from IA 1971, s 28D.

[2] 'Relevant offences' are illegal entry, deception, overstaying and breach of conditions or restrictions, failure to report to a medical officer, unlawful disembarkation, assisting breaches of immigration law, helping asylum seekers to arrive, offences relating to registration cards and immigration stamps and employment offences by virtue of IA 1971, ss 24(1)(a)–(f), 24A, 25, 25A, 25B, 26A and 26B. See section 28D(4) of the IA 1971, as amended by NIAA 2002, ss 144(1), (6) and 150(3). They also include entry without a passport and failure to co-operate with removal: AI(TC)A 2004, ss 2(11), 35(6) (in force 22 September 2004: s 48(1)).

[3] IA 1971, s 28D(1) and (2) for immigration officers, PACE 1984, s 8(1) and (3) for police officers.

[4] Police have power under PACE 1984, s 18; immigration officers under IA 1971, s 28E, inserted by IAA 1999, s 132(1). For immigration officers, the power covers all offences under Pt III of IA 1971.

[5] IA 1971, s 28F, inserted by IAA 1999, s 133. Police have this power in respect of arrestable offences (including s 25 offences) by virtue of Police and Criminal Evidence Act 1984, s 18.

[6] Police powers of search of persons derive from PACE 1984, ss 32, 54, 55; immigration officers are given equivalent powers under IA 1971, ss 28G and 28H, inserted by IAA 1999, ss 134(1) and 135(1). A gap of over two hours between arrest and search however meant that the power of search on arrest was no longer available: *R (on the application of Hewitson) v Chief Constable of Dorset Police* [2003] EWHC 3296 (Admin), (2004) Times, 6 January (a case on PACE 1984, s 32 but applicable to immigration officers' powers of search). Immigration officers have no powers to conduct intimate body searches. However, designated customs officials have the same limited powers as HMRC officials to conduct intimate body searches only in respect of items that might cause injury: the Police and Criminal Evidence Act 1984 (Application to Revenue and Customs Order) 2007, SI 2007/3175, art 13, see also the 2013 PACE Order, SI 2013/1542, art 30.

[7] Ie, under IA 1971, ss 28C (entry and search before arrest), 28E and 28F (entry and search following arrest), 28G (search of arrested person) and 28I (seizure of materials).

[8] AI(TC)A 2004, s 14(3) (in force 1 December 2004: SI 2004/2999).

[9] PACE 1984, s 8, subject to safeguards in section 15 and if issued, to be executed in accordance with section 16. See also Article 19 of the 2013 PACE Order.

¹⁰ PACE 1984, s 9. The definition of excluded material and special procedure material is modified by Article 6 of the PACE Orders.
¹¹ PACE 1984, s 17.
¹² PACE 1984, s 18, modified by arts 10 and 20 of the 2013 PACE Order.
¹³ PACE 1984, s 19.
¹⁴ PACE 1984, s 20.
¹⁵ See the PACE Order 2013, arts 8 and 17.
¹⁶ PACE Order 2013, arts 9 and 18.
¹⁷ PACE 1984, s 21.
¹⁸ PACE 1984, s 22.

Search for evidence to assist nationality and immigration control

15.14 Similar powers as those described above exist on arrest or detention under the administrative provisions of Schedule 2 to the IA 1971. Thus there is power to search the premises of the arrested person,[1] or (with the authority of a chief immigration officer) premises controlled or occupied by the arrested person, to look for such things as documents which might establish the person's identity, nationality, citizenship, his or her country of embarkation and of destination.[2] Schedule 1 of the Immigration Act 2014 makes this power available in respect of persons who are arrested other than under that schedule and detained under paragraph 16 of Schedule 2 to the IA 1971, whether or not the arrest was carried out by a constable.[3] Additionally, but only for the purpose of examining new arrivals, immigration officers have the power to search a newly arrived ship or aircraft or anything on board it, or any vehicle taken off it, to find passengers.[4] They may search passengers and their luggage, their vehicle, and the ship, vehicle or aircraft on or in which they arrived, to check whether they have documents such as passports, other identity documents or any other documents immigration officers wish to see (which might, for example, be relevant to their intentions on entry).[5] Immigration officers also have extensive powers of examination and search under the Terrorism Act 2000.[6] Under the UK Borders Act 2007, immigration officers and the police (including civilian police) can apply for a warrant to enter and search premises for nationality documents where there are doubts about the British nationality of someone being held at a police station.[7] Nationality documents in relation to the arrested individual may be seized.[8]

[1] IA 1971, Sch 2, paras 25B and 25C, inserted by IAA 1999, ss 134(2) and 135(2). Immigration officers have no power to conduct an intimate body search.
[2] IA 1971, Sch 2, para 25A, inserted by IAA 1999, s 132(2).
[3] Immigration Act 2014, Sch 1, para 3. SI 2014/1820: In force 28 July 2014. Para 3 of Schedule 1 also inserts new sub-paragraphs (6A) and (6B) into paragraph 25A so that a warrant may be obtained to enter and search premises belonging to a third party (other than the arrested person) where there are reasonable grounds to believe that relevant documents may be found there. Paragraph 3(4) removes the power to retain relevant documents for so long as necessary in connection with the purpose for which the person was arrested and paragraph 3(5) inserts a new sub-paragraph (8A) so that the power to retain relevant documents is aligned with the retention powers in section 17 of the 2004 Act and section 46(3) of the 2007 Act.
[4] IA 1971, Sch 2, para 1(5). This power applies in control zones: see SI 1993/1813, Sch 4, para 1(11)(a).
[5] IA 1971, Sch 2, para 4(3).
[6] Terrorism Act 2000, s 53, Sch 7; see **5.31** above.
[7] UKBA 2007, ss 45 and 47.
[8] UKBA 2007, s 46.

15.15 There are in addition powers to detain vehicles, small ships and aircraft, used or intended to be used in connection with offences of assisting a breach of immigration laws or the arrival of asylum seekers and trafficking for exploitation, and vehicles in which clandestine entrants have arrived, either pending a criminal prosecution,[1] or pending the payment of a civil penalty.[2] In criminal cases the vehicle may be forfeited on conviction, and in civil cases it may be sold if the penalty remains unpaid.[3]

The NIAA 2002 gave police and immigration officers extensive additional powers to search business premises with and without a warrant and seize employee records, where they suspect overstayers and illegal entrants are or have been unlawfully employed. In broad terms, the preconditions of a search without a warrant are (a) the presence or suspected presence on the premises of illegal entrants, overstayers or people committing related offences,[4] (b) a reasonable belief that they are working there illegally, and (c) a reasonable belief that employee records, or other evidence, which will be of substantial value in investigating the employment offence, will be found there. Records may also be seized for the investigation of asylum support fraud.[5] An additional power to enter and search business premises for personnel records may be exercised, with a warrant, on a reasonable belief that an employer has provided inaccurate or incomplete information in response to a demand by the Secretary of State,[6] that gaps in the information provided will be filled by seizing records kept on the premises, and that it is not practicable to proceed without a warrant.[7]

[1] IA 1971, s 25D, inserted by IAA 1999, s 38, renumbered and substituted by Nationality, Immigration and Asylum Act 2002, s 144, applied to offences of trafficking for exploitation by AI(TC)A 2004, s 5(4) and (5) as from 1 December 2004: SI 2004/2999.
[2] See **15.97** below.
[3] IA 1971, s 25C, substituted for the original provision in s 25 by NIAA 2002, s 143; IAA 1999, s 37(5A), inserted by the NIAA 2002, Sch 8, para 11, as from a date to be appointed.
[4] Ie persons suspected of offences under IA 1971, ss 24(1) and 24A, or suspected of being liable to removal, under Sch 2, para 17.
[5] IA 1971, s 28FA, inserted by Nationality, Immigration and Asylum Act 2002, s 154.
[6] For powers of coercive information gathering see **15.25** below.
[7] IA 1971, s 28FB, as inserted. 'Business premises' are defined in NIAA 2002, s 155.

Customs powers in the Borders, Citizenship and Immigration Act 2009

15.16 The BCIA 2009 confers on designated customs officials wide-ranging powers previously exercised only by HMRC officials (see **1.1** above). These include various powers to conduct searches in respect of customs matters such as those given to HMRC officers in provisions of the Customs and Excise Management Act 1979 (CEMA 1979):[1] power to board a ship, aircraft or vehicle, to 'remain therein and rummage any part thereof';[2] power of access to ships, aircraft and vehicles in specified places and to break open any locked containers for which the keys are withheld;[3] powers to detain ships, aircraft or vehicles;[4] power to board and inspect an aircraft and to inspect goods loaded therein, documents relating to the aircraft and documents relating to goods and passengers carried therein;[5] and powers to board and search coasting ships and require production of documents.[6] Designated customs officials also have powers to require any person entering or leaving the UK to answer questions with respect to his or her baggage and anything carried by the person and to produce the baggage for examination;[7] powers to enter and search premises;[8] powers to seize or detain anything liable to forfeiture under the Customs and Excise Acts, including any ship, aircraft, vehicle, animal, or container used 'for the carriage, handling, deposit and concealment' of such things;[9] and power to search a person on board a ship or aircraft or entering or about to leave the UK, including to conduct a strip search and an intimate search where there are reasonable grounds to suspect that he or she is carrying any article in respect of which there is unpaid duty or the import or export of which is subject to prohibition or restriction.[10]

[1] General customs officials and customs revenue officials are both 'designated customs officials', see BCIA 2009, ss 14(6) and 38. A designated customs official means a general customs official or a customs revenue official.
[2] CEMA 1979, s 27.
[3] CEMA 1979, s 28.
[4] CEMA 1979, ss 29 and 34.
[5] CEMA 1979, s 33.
[6] CEMA 1979, s 72.
[7] CEMA 1979, s 78.
[8] CEMA 1979, ss 118C, 161, and 161A.
[9] CEMA 1979, ss 139 and 141.
[10] CEMA 1979, s 164; see fn 5 at **15.13** above.

Recovery of cash in summary proceedings

15.17 Chapter 3 (sections 289–303) of Part 5 of the Proceeds of Crime Act 2002 allows the police and customs officers to recover cash in summary proceedings, where it is reasonably suspected of having been obtained through unlawful conduct or of being intended for use in such conduct. Section 24 of the UK Borders Act 2007 extends these powers with suitable adaptions to immigration officers in relation to immigration offences as regards search powers under section 289 and in relation to the wider group of offences where they were given a power of arrest without warrant in the exercise of their immigration powers under section 14 of the Asylum and Immigration (Treatment of Claimants, etc) Act 2004 as regards seizure, detention and forfeiture.[1] Section 289 of the Proceeds of Crime Act 2002 (POCA 2002), as amended, confers upon a constable, immigration or customs officer various powers to search premises and people. Where the officer is lawfully on any premises (for instance exercising a power of entry to private premises under the IA 1971), and has reasonable grounds for suspecting that there is cash on the premises, which has been unlawfully obtained (and is therefore recoverable property) or that is intended for use in unlawful conduct. In the case of a person, the officer must have reasonable grounds for suspecting that the person is carrying cash which is recoverable property or that is intended by any person for use in unlawful conduct and that it is more than £1,000.[2] Section 290 requires prior approval for such searches to be given by a justice of the peace or, where this is not practicable in any case, a senior officer, unless it is not practicable to obtain such approval. There are Rules of Court as to the exercise of these powers[3] and a statutory Code of Practice which sets out how the powers of search are to be exercised, which will need to be adapted to the new situation.[4] Section 295[5] allows for an initial period of detention of seized property of 48 hours (not including weekends or public or bank holidays), which can be extended by order to three months, or by further order to not more than two years from the making of the first order. Orders for an extension to the 48-hour period may be made only where certain conditions are satisfied, for example, where there are reasonable grounds for suspecting that the property is recoverable property, and its continued detention is justified while its derivation is further investigated. Sections 298 to 300 concern forfeiture. The court may order forfeiture of detained cash if it is satisfied that it is recoverable property or intended for use in unlawful conduct (POCA 2002, s 298). There is a right of appeal to the Crown Court against orders or decisions not to order forfeiture under section 298.[6] Section 300 outlines how forfeited cash is to be applied. In relation to immigration powers, section 23(1) of the UK Borders Act 2007 allows any property that has been used for the purpose of committing, or facilitating the commission of, any immigration- or asylum-related offence to be forfeited to the Secretary of State rather than to the police. Section 301 allows for the release of the cash to persons who apply to the court if they can satisfy the court that they were deprived of the cash by unlawful conduct, that it was not recoverable property and that it belongs to him or her. Section 302 deals with various situations where compensation should be paid to the owner of detained cash. In immigration cases this is to be paid by the Secretary of State.[7]

1   The Home Affairs Committee had recommended in its 2004 report on Asylum Applications that these powers should be used to seize profits made by people traffickers and those who employ illegal labour. See 143 Home Affairs Committee, 2nd Report of 2003–04, Asylum Applications, HC 218-I, para 247.
2   Proceeds of Crime Act 2002 (Recovery of Cash in Summary Proceedings: Minimum Amount) Order 2006, SI 2006/1699 (reducing the amount from GBP 5,000).
3   The Magistrates' Courts (Detention and Forfeiture of Cash) Rules 2002, SI 2002/2998 prescribe the procedure to be followed for applications to a justice of the peace under section 290(1) for prior approval of a search for cash under section 289, for applications to a magistrates' court for the detention, further detention, forfeiture or release of cash seized under Chapter 3, and for applications to a magistrates' court for compensation. The rules were amended by the Magistrates' Courts (Detention and Forfeiture of Cash) (Amendment) Rules 2003, SI 2003/638, which inserted a new rule to make clear that any magistrates' court, wherever situated, has jurisdiction to hear applications under the rules.
4   POCA 2002, s 292 and the Proceeds of Crime Act 2002 (Cash Searches: Code of Practice) Order 2002, SI 2002/3115.
5   As amended by the Serious Organised Crime and Police Act 2005 (SOCPA 2005), s 100.
6   POCA 2002, s 299 as substituted by the SOCPA 2005, s 101.
7   UKBA 2007, s 24(2)(h).

Forfeiture of detained property

15.18 Section 143 of the Powers of Criminal Courts (Sentencing) Act 2000[1] gives a court, sentencing an offender, power to make a forfeiture order of any property used for the purposes of crime. Normally, the property will then go to the police. Section 25 of the UKBA 2007 provides that the court may order that the property be taken into the possession of the Secretary of State (and not of the police), but may only do so if the court thinks that the offence related to immigration or asylum, or was committed for a purpose connected with immigration or asylum.

1   Or Article 11 of the Criminal Justice (Northern Ireland) Order 1994, SI 1994/2795 (NI 15) in Northern Ireland.

Disposal of property

15.19 The power to dispose of property under s 26 of the UKBA 2007 by returning it to its rightful owner, selling it or keeping it applies to any property that has come into the possession of an immigration officer or the Secretary of State in relation to their immigration functions. This will include vehicles, ships or aircraft which have been used in clandestine entry to the UK or human trafficking. A magistrates' or Sheriff Court may make disposal orders on application being made by the Secretary of State.[1] Such an order shall not affect the right of any person to take legal proceedings for the recovery of the property, provided that the proceedings are started within six months of the date of the order.[2] Where the property in question has been forfeited under s 25, or under s 25C of the IA 1971, the applicant (if not the Secretary of State) has six months from the date of the order to apply to the court and must satisfy it (i) that the applicant did not consent to the offender's possession of the property, or (ii) that the applicant did not know and had no reason to suspect that the property was likely to be used, or was intended to be used, in connection with an offence.[3] The Immigration (Disposal of Property) Regulations 2008, SI 2008/786, came into force on 17 April 2008. The Regulations allow the Secretary of State to dispose, sell or retain property confiscated pursuant to powers under ss 25 and 26 of the UKBA 2007.

[1]   UKBA 2007, s 26(2).
[2]   UKBA 2007, s 26(3).
[3]   UKBA 2007, s 26(5).

Detainee custody officers

15.20 Detention custody officers look after people in immigration detention. They have power to search any detained person for whose delivery or custody they are responsible[1] and anyone else seeking to enter the place where the detained person is held.[2] They are authorised to use reasonable force if necessary.[3] They may enter business[4] and other[5] premises to search persons detained there by police or immigration officers. They have powers under the Detention Centre Rules to measure and photograph detainees[6] and to test them for drugs or alcohol.[7]

[1]   IAA 1999, Sch 11, Sch 13, para 2.
[2]   IAA 1999, Sch 11, Sch 13, para 2(2); the latter power does not authorise removal of clothing except for an outer coat, jacket or gloves.
[3]   IAA 1999, Sch 13, para 2(4).
[4]   IA 1971, s 28CA(5), (6) inserted by Nationality, Immigration and Asylum Act 2002, s 153.
[5]   IA 1971, Sch 2, para 17(3)–(5), inserted by NIAA 2002, s 64.
[6]   IAA 1999, Sch 12, para 1; Detention Centre Rules 2001, SI 2001/238, r 5.
[7]   IAA 1999, Sch 12, para 2; SI 2001/238, r 44.

Search powers under asylum support provisions

15.21 To enforce the draconian provisions on compulsory dispersal of asylum seekers and their dependants, the IAA 1999 contains powers of search of premises in which accommodation has been provided by 'a person authorised by the Secretary of State' (who could be a private hotel-owner) on a warrant, where there is reason to believe that the supported person or his or her dependants for whom the accommodation is provided are not living there, or the accommodation is being used for any other purpose, or any unauthorised person is living there.[1] This would presumably include putting up another family member or friend, running a small business (for example, as a mechanic or seamstress) from the room, as well as unauthorised sub-letting. Reasonable force may be used in entering premises under the warrant.[2] Where persons are suspected of making false or dishonest claims for asylum support contrary to sections 105 or 106 of the IAA 1999, immigration officers have the powers of entry, search and seizure they already have under the IA 1971.[3]

1   IAA 1999, s 125. See further **14.164–14.165** above.
2   IAA 1999, s 125(3)(b).
3   IA 1971, ss 28B and 28D and 28(4), 28E, 28G and 28H. In addition the powers contained in ss 28I, 28J, 28K, and 28L(1) apply: IAA 1999, s 109B(2).

SEARCH POWERS OF IMMIGRATION SERVICE COMMISSIONER

15.22 The Immigration Service Commissioner through his or her investigating officer has powers of entry of premises on a warrant where there are reasonable grounds for believing that immigration advice or services are provided by a registered person who is the subject of an investigation or complaint.[1] The Commissioner may require documents to be produced and remove computer data. A registered person who does not allow access, or otherwise obstructs or fails to cooperate, may have his or her registration cancelled.[2] The Commissioner also has powers of entry on a warrant to search for and seize material on the premises which is likely to be of substantial value to the investigation of an offence of unauthorised provision of immigration advice or services.[3] Schedule 7 of the Immigration Act 2014, not in force at the time of writing, will modify the framework for the Commissioner's power of entry in relation to non-criminal matters. The power may only be given effect if the Commissioner obtains a warrant from a magistrate or, in Scotland, a sheriff. The magistrate or sheriff may grant the warrant in relation to the exercise of any of the Commissioner's functions, not just the investigation of complaints. Thus the power of entry can be used for inspection purposes. The warrant may be granted in relation to private residences where they are being used or have been used to provide immigration advice or services. The sanction available to the Commissioner in relation to a person who fails without reasonable excuse to allow access to the premises is the cancellation of the person's registration. In other respects, the Commissioner's power of entry remains substantially the same.[4]

1   IAA 1999, Sch 5, para 7.
2   IAA 1999, Sch 5, para 7.
3   IAA 1999, s 92A, inserted by Asylum and Immigration (Treatment of Claimants etc) Act 2004, s 38, in force 1 October 2004: SI 2004/2523.
4   Immigration Act 2014, Sch 7, para 8(2), inserting a new para 10A into Sch 6 of the IAA 1999.

BIOMETRIC INFORMATION AND DOCUMENTS

15.23 Police (but not immigration officers) have power to take fingerprints from those charged with criminal offences.[1] Police, immigration officers and anyone else so authorised may take fingerprints, photographs or other identification measures in respect of anyone liable to be detained under the administrative provisions of Schedules 2 or 3 to the IA 1971.[2] The extension of this power to those liable to be detained, in addition to those already detained, arises from the Immigration Act 2014 and came into force on 28 July 2014.[3] Hence this new power allows for the identification of persons liable to detention by means of biometric checks, such as fingerprinting and photographing. This power to check biometrics is limited to the purpose of verifying identity as part of an immigration investigation and any biometrics are to be destroyed as soon as that purpose has been fulfilled.[4] Immigration officers were first given powers to fingerprint asylum seekers and their dependants (defined as spouses and children under 18) by the Asylum and Immigration Appeals Act 1993, with powers of arrest without warrant for those who fail to comply with a notice requiring their attendance for the purpose.[5] These powers were extended to other classes of person by the IAA 1999:

(i)   those who fail to produce a passport or other satisfactory evidence of identity when they are asked to do so by an immigration officer;

(ii)   those refused leave to enter, who have been granted temporary admission, who the immigration officer reasonably suspects will breach conditions of residence or reporting;

(iii)   those served with a notice to remove them as illegal entrants, overstayers, or after a deportation order;[6]

(iv)   those arrested under paragraph 17 of Schedule 2 (persons liable to be detained under paragraph 16);

(v)   asylum claimants;

(vi)   dependants of any of the above.[7]

The Secretary of State may serve written notice on any of the above persons requiring them to attend for fingerprinting at a specified place, on seven days' notice. Refusal to comply can be met with a number of responses. First, non-attenders can be arrested. Second, reasonable force can be used to take the prints.[8] Third, according to Home Office guidance, refusal to cooperate may result in no registration card being issued to the recalcitrant asylum seeker, or in refusal of the asylum claim on non-compliance grounds, or in adverse credibility findings.[9] Once taken, fingerprints can be kept indefinitely,[10] except in the case of British citizens and those with a right of abode, and their dependants, where there is a statutory requirement to destroy them as soon as reasonably practicable.[11]

In Part 3 of the BCIA 2009, section 51 extends the powers of authorised persons to take fingerprints under section 141 of the Immigration and Asylum Act 1999 to include 'foreign criminals' who are liable to automatic deportation under the UKBA 2007 provisions.[12] Section 51(2) of the BCIA 2009 excludes dependants of a foreign criminal from the section 141 fingerprinting provisions. Like various other provisions in the BCIA 2009 and earlier Immigration Acts, section 51 of the BCIA 2009 exemplifies the tendency in immigration legislation to meld immigration control and criminal justice functions. Section 51 came into force on 10 November 2009.[13]

[1] PACE 1984, ss 27, 61. They may be taken without consent at a police station in order to confirm or disprove involvement in an offence, on charge or after conviction of a recordable offence.

2   IA 1971, Sch 2, para 18(2); *Irawo-Osan v Secretary of State for the Home Department* [1992] Imm AR 337.

3   See section 9 of the Immigration Act 2014, SI 2014/1820 art 3(h).

4   See Explanatory Notes to Immigration Act 2014 para 67.

5   Asylum and Immigration Appeals Act 1993, s 3 (repealed by IAA 1999, s 169).

6   IAA 1999 s 141, amended by Asylum and Immigration (Treatment of Claimants etc) Act 2004, s 15 as from 1 October 2004: SI 2004/2523.

7   IAA 1999, s 141. Fingerprints may not be taken from a child under 16 except in the presence of a parent or carer: s 141(3). Children under five are not fingerprinted: API 'Fingerprinting' para 1.2.

8   IAA 1999, ss 142, 146, amended in relation to the use of force by Nationality, Immigration and Asylum Act 2002 s 153(2).

9   API 'Fingerprinting', para 3.

10 Detailed provisions for the destruction of fingerprints within specified periods, in the IAA 1999, s 143(3)–(8) and (14), were repealed by the Anti-terrorism, Crime and Security Act 2001, ss 36(1)(a), (2), 125 and Sch 8, Pt 3. The Immigration (PACE Codes of Practice No 2 and Amendment) Directions 2000 provide for the destruction of fingerprints, if taken with consent, in ten years, and if taken under IA 1971, Sch 2, para 18, as soon as reasonably practicable after they have been used for identity purposes. The API 'Fingerprinting' state that fingerprints will normally be destroyed after ten years: para 2.3.

11 IAA 1999, s 143(2), (9).

12 See UKBA 2007, ss 32–39.

13 See BCIA 2009, s 58(3)(b) and SI 2009/2731, art 3(a).

15.24 The purposes of the broad fingerprinting powers in relation to asylum seekers include detection of those who have made a claim before, in another identity, or in another EU Member State, to enable them to be refused or returned to the other Member State under the provisions of the Dublin Convention and Regulation (Dublin II).[1] Under the EU Eurodac regulations,[2] the fingerprints of all asylum seekers over 14 and other third country nationals who are apprehended crossing borders irregularly or are found 'illegally present' in any Member State,[3] are sent to a central unit for matching,[4] so as to enable concerted expulsion measures.[5]

1   For the Dublin Conventions see **12.148** ff above.

2   Council Regulation (EC) 2725/2000 concerning the establishment of 'Eurodac' for the comparison of fingerprints for the effective application of the Dublin Convention; Council Regulation (EC) 407/2002 laying down certain rules implementing regulation (EC) 2725/2000 (OJ L 062).

3   Regulation (EC) 2725/2000, arts 8, 11.

4   Regulation (EC) 2725/2000, art 4.

5   Council Directive 2001/40/EC on mutual recognition of decisions on expulsion of third country nationals (OJ L 149/341).

15.25 The Secretary of State was empowered under the IAA 1999 to make regulations enabling data on other external physical characteristics to be collected. Under the Nationality, Immigration and Asylum Act 2002 the power to collect, store and exchange biometric data was taken further.[1] Biometric data can now be required from applicants other than asylum claimants, including visitors. Regulations can be made requiring any applicant for entry clearance, leave to enter or leave to remain to provide 'information about external physical characteristics', including features of the iris or other parts of the eye.[2] So far, regulations have been limited to fingerprints.[3] The Immigration Act 2014 has enabled the Secretary of State to require biometric information from foreign nationals applying for Direct Airside Transit Visas (DATVs); and from non-EEA family members of EEA nationals, and other non-EEA nationals when applying for a document as evidence of their right to enter or remain in the UK, such as an EU residence card.[4] There is also a new power to make provision for biometric information to be provided in citizenship applications.[5] The first non-asylum applicants to be required to give fingerprints were Sri Lankans in July 2003, followed by applicants seeking entry clearance in Djibouti, Eritrea, Ethiopia, Kenya, Rwanda, Tanzania and Uganda.[6] The regulations enable the Secretary of State to pass on biometric data to policing and other agencies. The NIAA 2002 also enabled the Secretary of State to set up a voluntary scheme for the collection and storage of biometric data, to expedite the entry of frequent travellers.[7] Under the Immigration (Provision of Physical Data) Regulations 2006, which came into force on 4 July 2006, the requirement for people to provide information about their physical characteristics has been extended from fingerprints to fingerprints and photos of the person's head. The regulations are not limited to applicants seeking entry clearance in named posts overseas. They now apply to anyone. Unlike the previous regulations, they do not contain any power enabling the Secretary of State to pass on the biometric data to policing and other agencies but this can now be done under general powers to pass on information or to share it with other law enforcement agencies, as for example under powers given by IAN Act 2006, s 36 (duty to share information). Section 36 of the IAN Act 2006 has now been amended by section 21 of the BCIA 2009 (see further fn 1 at **15.32** below).

1   Nationality, Immigration and Asylum Act 2002, s 126.
2   NIAA 2002, s 126(9).
3   Immigration (Provision of Physical Data) Regulations 2003, SI 2003/1875 have been revoked and replaced by the Immigration (Provision of Physical Data) Regulations 2006, SI 2006/1743, as amended by the Immigration (Provision of Physical Data) (Amendment) Regulations 2011, SI 2011/177 which enabled biometric information to be taken from persons accredited for the 2012 London Olympic and Paralympic Games.
4   Immigration Act 2014, s 8, in force 28 July 2014: SI 2014/1820, art 3(g). The new provision also provides for biometric information submitted as part of an application to be recorded on any document issued as a consequence of that application.
5   Immigration Act 2014, s 10, in force 28 July 2014: SI 2014/1820, art 3(i). As per reg 9 of the Immigration (Provision of Physical Data) Regulations 2006, SI 2006/1743, any record of biometric information must be destroyed as soon as is reasonably practicable once the person becomes a British citizen.
6   SI 2003/1875, Schedule, as amended by SI 2004/474 and 1834. The Schedule to SI 2003/1875 was further amended in 2005 to include Congo, Holland and Vietnam, but this and all other amendments have been revoked and replaced by the Immigration (Provision of Physical Data) Regulations 2006, SI 2006/1743, as amended by the Immigration (Provision of Physical Data) (Amendment) Regulations 2011, SI 2011/177.
7   NIAA 2002, s 127, in force 10 December 2004: SI 2004/2998.

15.26 The Home Office planned to include biometric data in all new passports by the year 2005.[1] The requirement to provide physical data in advance of travelling to the UK, data which is then digitised, would enable the Home Office to achieve its ambition of 'e-borders', involving the automatic transmission of passenger information in real time at the point of departure (advanced passenger processing), with data-matching followed by the grant or refusal of authority to board the ship or aircraft.[2] Meanwhile, fingerprint information is stored in a microchip on asylum Application Registration Cards (ARC), together with a photographic image and information such as NASS status, languages spoken by the holder and family members, and employment status.[3] In November 2003, the Home Secretary announced the government's decision to introduce compulsory identity cards, incorporating biometric data such as fingerprints or an iris scan, for all legal residents of the UK, to start in 2007/8. Biometric residence cards would then be mandatory for all foreign nationals staying in the UK for over three months.[4]

1   Asylum and Immigration (Treatment of Claimants) Bill Standing Committee (Commons), 11th sitting, col 401, 27.1.03.
2   Ibid. This plan features in the five-year strategy document 'Controlling our borders: Making migration work for Britain: Five year strategy for asylum and immigration', Cm 6472, Feb 2005.
3   Hansard HC, 6 February 2002, col 974W, Angela Eagle. See 'Controlling our borders' at fn 2 above.
4   Hansard HC, 11 November 2003, col 171, David Blunkett.

Biometric immigration documents (BID)

15.27 The Identity Cards Act 2006 laid the statutory framework for the universal identity card, but that Act was revoked on the coming into force of the Identity Documents Act 2010. However, the separate scheme for biometric identity cards (BIDs), also referred to as biometric registration documents (BRD), for certain categories of foreign nationals under the UKBA 2007 has survived.[1] Regulations, pursuant to powers under that Act, now require those seeking leave to enter or remain for more than a cumulative period of six months' leave, asylum seekers and those non-EEA nationals applying to replace a stamp, sticker or other attachment in a passport to have a biometric identity card. Where a person fails to comply with a requirement made under these regulations a range of non-criminal sanctions are available, including a refusal to issue the biometric immigration document, disregarding or refusing the person's application for leave to remain, curtailment of existing leave and the imposition of a civil penalty notice.[2] A Code of Practice has also been brought into operation to deal with the use of immigration and civil penalties for those who refuse or fail to meet these new requirements.[3] For fuller information see **Chapter 3, 3.7–3.16.**

1   See UKBA 2007, s 15(1)(a), (b) and (c). The definition of biometric information for these purposes has been amended by s 11 of the Immigration Act 2014, inserting new sub-paragraphs (1A) to (1C) in s 15(1) such that it is now defined as 'information about a person's external physical characteristics (including in particular fingerprints and features of the iris, and any other information about a person's physical characteristics specified in an order made by the Secretary of State'. It cannot include information about a person's DNA. SI 2014/1820 art 3(j) in force 2 March 2014. Immigration includes asylum: UKBA 2007, s 15(1)(f).
2   The Immigration (Biometric Registration) (Objection to Civil Penalty) Order 2008, SI 2008/2830 deals with the procedure for objecting to the imposition of a civil penalty and this is backed up with the Immigration (Biometric Registration) (Civil Penalty Code of Practice) Order 2008, SI 2008/3049, introducing the Code of Practice on the imposition of a civil penalty.
3   The Immigration (Biometric Registration) (Civil Penalty Code of Practice) Order 2008, SI 2008/3049, made under s 9(1) of the UKBA 2007.

Electronic monitoring

15.28 Under provisions contained in the Asylum and Immigration (Treatment of Claimants etc) Act 2004, adults who are liable to detention but released on temporary admission by an immigration officer or the Secretary of State, or on bail, may be required to submit to electronic monitoring, in accordance with regulations under the Act, to ensure compliance with residence conditions or as an alternative to physical reporting.[1] Electronic monitoring may be by way of voice recognition,[2] tagging[3] or use of tracking technology,[4] all of which the Home Office has piloted.[5] Electronic monitoring could only be used with the consent of the subject, as an alternative to detention.

[1] Asylum and Immigration (Treatment of Claimants etc) Act 2004, s 36 (in force 1 October 2004: SI 2004/2523). No regulations had been made under the section at the time of writing.

[2] Voice recognition technology uses biometric voice recognition software to facilitate reporting over a telephone from a fixed land line from a fixed address at a notified time. This could obviate the need for people to report physically to a centre on a weekly basis. They would be given a particular number to ring in, and have their voice and location checked: Asylum and Immigration (Treatment of Claimants) Bill Standing Committee (Commons) 10th sitting, 22.1.04, col 363–4, Beverley Hughes.

[3] Tagging involves wearing a bracelet which emits a signal to a receiver at the subject's home address. The subject may be required to be at home for a particular hour in the week, or more frequently for people who present other kinds of risk, to confirm that they are complying with a residence restriction. That would often serve in lieu of physical reporting: ibid.

[4] Tracking involves using global positioning satellite technology to pinpoint the whereabouts of a subject on a continuous basis. It is in its infancy: ibid.

[5] Since electronic monitoring must, under the terms of the Act, comply with regulations which have not yet been promulgated, the legal basis for the pilot which started in October 2004 is unclear. The same goes for current attempts by Home Office presenting officers to seek to tag persons released on Immigration Act bail (see CHAPTER 18 below).

GETTING AND EXCHANGING INFORMATION

Other information-gathering powers

15.29 The IAA 1999 created a wide information exchange network between the Secretary of State on the one hand and, on the other, a range of agencies including the police, the National Criminal Intelligence Service (NCIS), the National Crime Squad (NCS) and Customs and Excise.[1] Information held by a chief officer of one of these agencies, a contractor or sub-contractor of the Home Office or 'any other specified person', may be supplied to the Secretary of State for immigration purposes, including the administration of control, the prevention, detection, investigation and prosecution of offences under the Immigration Acts, civil penalties (carrier sanctions), asylum support and other specified purposes.[2] Similarly, the Secretary of State is empowered to supply information held by him or her in connection with the exercise of immigration functions to chief officers of the same agencies.[3] The Secretary of State may also provide information (including fingerprints) to the authorities of a country to which he or she seeks to remove an undocumented person.[4] The 2002 Act added powers for the Commissioners of the Inland Revenue to supply address details to enable the Secretary of State to locate someone reasonably suspected not to have leave to enter or permission to work.[5] Information may also be provided to determine whether a person is of good character (in connection with a naturalisation application)[6] or for the purposes of the maintenance and accommodation requirements of the Immigration Rules.[7] Further, s 17 of the AI(TC)A 2004 enables the Secretary of State or an immigration officer to retain any document coming into their possession in the course of the exercise of an immigration function, while they suspect that a person to whom the document relates may be liable to removal from the UK and that retention of the document may facilitate the removal.[8] The Immigration, Asylum and Nationality Act 2006 (Commencement No 7) (Amendment) Order 2007, SI 2007/3580 brought into force certain provisions in the Immigration, Asylum and Nationality Act 2006, on a delayed date, on 31 March 2008.[9] Those provisions address information and its disclosure to law enforcement agencies, the power of Her Majesty's Revenue and Customs (HMRC) to obtain information, the provision of information to immigration officers, police powers regarding passenger and crew information, the duty to share information and the code of practice regarding that, and the disclosure of information for security purposes; and offences regarding the same.

[1]   Since the amalgamation of Customs and Excise with the Inland Revenue, provision was made to include the Revenue in this extensive information exchange, with confidentiality safeguards and a criminal offence of wrongful disclosure: UKBA 2007, ss 40–42. The main aim of the inclusion of the Inland Revenue in this wider gateway, according to the Home Affairs Committee, was to make tackling tax and National Insurance evasion a central feature of the drive against the employment of illegal labour, in which the tax authorities must make much greater efforts to tackle these in the informal economy. See 241 HC 775 2005–06, paras 453, 455. See also Home Office, UK Borders Bill: Regulatory Impact Assessment, January 2007, pp 5–6. The government repeatedly made it clear that they wanted as full access as possible to HMRC data to track down illegal immigrants.

[2]   IAA 1999, s 20. The Immigration (Supply of Information to the Secretary of State for Immigration Purposes) Order 2008, SI 2008/2077 provides that information held by certain persons may be supplied to the Secretary of State for use for 'immigration purposes'. These persons are the Secretary of State for Transport, the Secretary of State for Work and Pensions (for the purposes of functions relating to social security), and the Chief Constable of the British Transport Police Force (for the purposes of the prevention, detection, investigation or prosecution of criminal offences and safeguarding national security).

[3]   IAA 1999, s 21.

[4]   IAA 1999, s 13. The transfer of information is deemed 'necessary for reasons of substantial public interest' for the purposes of the Data Protection Act 1998: IAA 1999, s 13(4).

[5]   Nationality, Immigration and Asylum Act 2002, s 130. This gateway has been widened by the changes in the UKBA 2007, noted at fn 1, above.

[6]   Nationality, Immigration and Asylum Act 2002, s 131. The scope of police powers in relation to nationality inquiries has been widened to include information whether an applicant for registration listed in s 58(2) of the IAN 2006 is of good character; and in relation to decisions whether to deprive someone of their nationality under s 40 of the British Nationality Act 1981: UKBA 2007, s 43, amending s 131, above.

[7]   Nationality, Immigration and Asylum Act 2002, s 130.

[8]   AI(TC)A 2004, s 17. This power is so broad as to invite abuse.

[9]   The original commencement date was 31 December 2007: the Immigration, Asylum and Nationality Act 2006 (Commencement No 7) Order 2007, SI 2007/3138.

15.30 Part 1 of the BCIA 2009 creates the legislative framework for immigration officers and officials of the Secretary of State to exercise revenue and customs functions previously performed by HMRC so as to create a unified border force within the Home Office. The government said that Part 1 of the Act would establish 'a comprehensive framework covering the use and disclosure of customs information', including personal customs information' because 'information is obviously an essential tool in support of law enforcement and national security and is key to our ability to secure the border effectively'.[2] The legislative proposals gave rise to concern that they were part of 'a dangerous tendency to collect too much information and to give the various organs of the state too much power to share it with one another without the permission of the person about whom the information was collected'.[3]

Section 20 of the BCIA 2009 inserts new ss 41A and 41B into the UKBA 2007. That Act already provided for HMRC and the Revenue and Customs Prosecution Office (RCPO) to supply information to the Secretary of State in relation to various immigration and nationality functions,[4] subject to specified restrictions on further disclosure of that information.[5] The new provisions inserted by BCIA 2009, s 20 allow HMRC and RCPO or a person authorised to act on their behalf[6] to supply information[7] to a designated customs official, the Secretary of State, the Director of Border Revenue and a person acting on behalf of any of them[8] for the purpose of the exercise of their customs functions.[9] The provision applies equally to documents or articles coming into the possession of the HMRC or RCPO[10] and allows for the retention or disposal of such documents or articles.[11]

Further disclosure of the information, document or article by the recipient may not occur unless the disclosure[12] is for a purpose of a customs function and does not contravene any restriction imposed by the Commissioners for HMRC; or is made for the purpose of civil proceedings (whether in or outside the UK) and relating to a customs function, or is made for the purpose of a criminal investigation or criminal proceedings (whether in or outside the UK); or is made in pursuance of a court order; or is made with the consent (general or specific) of the HMRC or the RCPO; or is made with the consent of each person to whom the information relates. A person who makes a wrongful disclosure of information received from HMRC or RCPO may be liable to prosecution[13] (see also below at **15.93**).

[1] Defined in the BCIA 2009, ss 14(6) and 38 as 'information acquired or capable of being acquired as a result of the exercise of a general customs functions or a customs revenue function'.
[2] HL Deb, 25 March 2009, vol 709, c 691, per Lord West of Spithead, Parliamentary Under-Secretary of State, Home Office.
[3] PCB Deb, 9 June 2009, 1st sitting c 31, per Damian Green MP (Conservative), Shadow Minister for immigration.
[4] UKBA 2007, s 40.
[5] UKBA 2007, s 41.
[6] UKBA 2007, s 41A(5).
[7] UKBA 2007, s 41A(1).
[8] UKBA 2007, s 41A(2).
[9] UKBA 2007, s 41A(1).
[10] UKBA 2007, s 41A(3).
[11] UKBA 2007, s 41A(4).
[12] UKBA 2007, s 41B(2).
[13] Under UKBA 2007, s 42(1), as amended by BCIA 2009, s 20(2).

Coercive information gathering

15.31 The IAA 1999 contained a number of coercive provisions allowing the Secretary of State to require information from various sources. Property owners and managers could be required to provide information about premises and their occupants, for asylum support purposes.[1] The post office and other carriers could be required to provide redirection information for use in the prevention, detection, investigation and prosecution of criminal offences relating to asylum support, to check the accuracy of the information given about support or for other purposes relating to asylum support.[2] Marriage registrars were fixed with a duty to report suspicious marriages.[3] As of 14 July

2014, the duty on registration officials extends to information received in advance of a person giving notice of marriage or civil partnership.[4]

The Nationality, Immigration and Asylum Act 2002 took these coercive information-gathering powers yet further. Local authorities can be compelled by the Secretary of State to supply information to help find someone who is or has been living in their area, if the person is reasonably suspected of an offence of illegal entry, overstaying, breach of conditions or restrictions on stay, unlawful disembarkation, obtaining leave to enter or remain by deception, making false representations or using or possessing a false document.[5] Employers can be similarly compelled to provide information on an employee or former employee reasonably suspected of these offences, or offences in relation to asylum support, if the information is needed to establish their whereabouts, earnings or employment history.[6] A bank or building society can be compelled to provide relevant financial information which the Secretary of State reasonably believes it possesses about an account holder reasonably suspected of an asylum support offence.[7] In the case of employers and financial institutions, the Act requires written notice to be served specifying the information required and the manner and period in which it is to be provided. Failure to comply without reasonable excuse is an offence.[8]

[1] IAA 1999, s 126. To date, no regulations have been made under the section.
[2] IAA 1999, s 127. To date, no regulations have been made under this section.
[3] IAA 1999, s 24; Reporting of Suspicious Marriages and Registration of Marriages (Miscellaneous Amendments) Regulations 2000, SI 2000/3164; and Reporting of Suspicious Marriages (Northern Ireland) Regulations 2000, SI 2000/3233. The information required includes the names, dates of birth or ages of the parties, their marital status, address(es) and nationalities, the date, place and time of the marriage, the evidence produced of name, age, marital status and nationality, the reasons for the report and the full name of the reporting officer making the report. In the first year of its operation there were 700 reports. (Hansard HL, 24.6.02, col 1177, Lord Filkin). Note the AI(TC)A 2004, ss 19–25 which prevent marriage registrars from marrying non-EEA nationals who do not have entry clearance for the purpose of marriage, unless they have written permission from the Secretary of State to marry in the UK or fall within a specified class: see **11.47** below.
[4] Immigration Act 2014, s 56(2), amending s 24 of the 1999 Act (for marriages) and s 56(3), amending s 24A of the 1999 Act (for civil partnerships). See further **1.83**.
[5] Ie offences under IA 1971, ss 24, 24A and 26(1)(c) and (d): Nationality, Immigration and Asylum Act 2002, s 129.
[6] NIAA 2002, s 134.
[7] NIAA 2002, s 135.
[8] NIAA 2002, s 136.

Passenger information

15.32 The powers under the IA 1971 for immigration officers to demand passenger and crew lists from captains of ships and aircraft[1] arriving in the UK were modified by regulations made under the 1999 Act[2] to enable immigration officers to require much more detailed information, including passengers' gender, date of birth, travel document number, visa expiry date, ticket number and date and place of issue, the identity of the person booking the ticket, the method of payment, the passenger's travel itinerary and the names of all other passengers on the reservation.[3] Immigration officers may demand the information in relation to ships and aircraft expected to arrive and those which have left or are expected to leave the UK.[4] A senior officer may also require information about the expected arrival of any craft expected to carry non-EEA nationals.[5] There is provision in the Asylum and Immigration (Treatment of Claimants etc) Act 2004 to allow immigration officers to demand copies of particular passengers' travel documents as well, a power which would be targeted as individuals, rather than applied in a blanket manner, because of the huge delays which copying all passengers' documents would entail.[6] When the 'Authority–to–carry scheme' in section 124 of the Nationality, Immigration and Asylum Act 2002 is brought into force, the passenger information may be required in advance of boarding, to enable a check to be made against Home Office databases so that, if a passenger is identified as a security or immigration risk, authority to carry him or her may be refused.[7] A request to a carrier continues in force until withdrawn, and can last up to six months, or longer if renewed. The data required is not restricted to foreign nationals but can cover all passengers, including British and European citizens. However, up to now the power has been used for specific flights or flights from specific destinations. Additional powers exist under the Terrorism Act 2000 to require passenger information.[8] The effect of the Immigration and Police (Passenger, Crew and Service Information) Order 2008 is to enable immigration and police officers to (a) request specific passenger, crew and service information from air, sea and rail carriers in respect of movements into or out of the UK and (b) to specify the form and manner in which some of this data should be supplied.[9]

[1] IA 1971, Sch 2, para 27. The power to demand passenger and crew lists under para 27 of Sch 2 has been extended by s 31 of the IAN 2006. This information can now be obtained in advance of the arrival of the ship or aircraft in the UK and not just on arrival. Secondly, the duty to provide the lists applies to owners and agents of the ship or aircraft as well as the captain: Sch 2, para 27, as amended by the IAN 2006, s 31. Sections 32 and 33 of the same Act give the police new and additional powers to obtain from the owners, agents or captains of ships and aircraft details of passengers, crew, flight or voyage and freight. Provision is also made for information sharing between each of the different policing agencies, including immigration officers, in ss 36 to 41 of the IAN 2006. Section 36 of the IAN 2006 has now been amended by BCIA 2009, s 21 by adding designated customs officials; immigration officers; the Secretary of State in so far as he or she has general customs functions, immigration, asylum, or nationality functions and the Director of Border Revenue and any person exercising functions of the Director, to the list of persons required to share information relating to the passengers, crew and freight of ships and aircraft.
[2] IA 1971, Sch 2, para 27B, inserted by the IAA 1999, s 18.
[3] Immigration (Passenger Information) Regulations 2000, SI 2000/912.
[4] IA 1971, Sch 2, para 27B(1)(a) and (b). The power is exercisable in respect of a particular passenger or craft, or all passengers and/or all craft of the carrier.
[5] IA 1971, Sch 2, para 27C, inserted by the IAA 1999, s 19.
[6] Asylum and Immigration (Treatment of Claimants) Act 2004, s 16, amending the IA 1971, Sch 2, para 27B as from a date to be appointed.
[7] See **15.105** below.
[8] Terrorism Act 2000, Sch 7, para 17.
[9] For more details see the Explanatory Statement to the Immigration and Police (Passenger, Crew and Service Information) Order 2008, SI 2008/5.

CODES OF PRACTICE

15.33 The Codes of Practice issued under the Police and Criminal Evidence Act 1984 have always applied to persons who are not police officers who are investigating offences,[1] and have been held to apply to immigration officers exercising administrative powers in relation to illegal entrants and overstayers, at least if a criminal offence was potentially involved.[2] Now, in the exercise of powers of arrest, questioning, search, fingerprinting, entry and seizure –

whether investigating criminal offences or in the course of their IA 1971, Sch 2 functions – immigration officers are statutorily obliged to have regard to certain specified (but not all) provisions of the Codes of Practice.[3] Thus, when arresting a suspect without a warrant, whether for an immigration offence or for a related offence, immigration officers must have regard to all the provisions of Codes C, D and E.[4] When conducting interviews, they should not refuse access to solicitors, and questioning should be under caution and contemporaneously recorded.[5] But when arresting without warrant under the administrative provisions of the Schedule, none of the provisions of Code C relating to the conduct of interviews apply, according to the Codes of Practice Direction.[6] Where there is a Code breach, this does not necessarily mean that the immigration officer or Secretary of State cannot subsequently rely on what is said at an interview.[7] If it is not voluntary, has been obtained by force, inducement or oppression, or a statement has been made at a time of stress, it may be ruled out.[8] But if there is simply a failure to inform the applicant that his or her solicitor is available, all the court or Secretary of State need do is to be very careful to test the reliability of the answers.[9] By virtue of sections 22 and 23 of the BCIA 2009, provisions of PACE and PACE (NI) apply to persons detained, and investigations conducted, by immigration officers and designated customs officials (see **15.3** above).

[1]   Police and Criminal Evidence Act 1984, s 67(9).
[2]   *R v Secretary of State for the Home Department, ex p Ibrahim* [1993] Imm AR 124, QBD.
[3]   IAA 1999, s 145, Immigration (PACE Codes of Practice) Direction 2000, Immigration (PACE Codes of Practice No 2 and Amendment) Direction 2000 (on taking, retention and destruction of fingerprints).
[4]   The Detention, Treatment and Questioning of Persons by Police Officers; The Identification of Persons by Police Officers; Tape Recording of Interviews with Suspects.
[5]   See PACE Code C as applied by the Immigration (PACE Codes of Practice) Direction 2000, paras 6, 10, 11, and 12. Illegal entry interviews where no caution was administered were held inadmissible in the Scottish cases of *Oghonoghor v Secretary of State for the Home Department* 1995 SLT 733, OHCS and *Kim (Sofia) v Secretary of State for the Home Department* 2000 SLT 249, OHCS.
[6]   Immigration (PACE Codes of Practice) Direction 2000, Sch 1. In practice, immigration officers are likely to adhere to the relevant Code, as (broadly speaking) they have done in the past.
[7]   But see Oghonoghor v Secretary of State for the Home Department, Kim v Secretary of State for the Home Department, fn 5 above.
[8]   Evidence of a police interview was excluded by an adjudicator in a deportation appeal (breach of conditions) in *Oyefuwa* (18035).
[9]   *Ibrahim*, above at 129. In addition it should be recalled that Police and Criminal Evidence Act 1984, ss 76 and 78 (exclusion of evidence obtained unfairly or by oppression) do not apply to civil proceedings.

15.34 Powers of entry and search of premises, seizure of documents and search of the person, and similarly intrusive measures including the taking, transmission and storage of fingerprints and other biometric data, all constitute interference with privacy under Article 8 of the ECHR. To conform with the Convention, the exercise of the powers must be not only in accordance with the law but also must have a legitimate aim and be proportionate to the aim pursued.[1] If they are not (an extreme example might be a midnight, intrusive search causing damage looking for someone who has failed to report to a medical officer) damages would be recoverable.[2] Breaches of Article 8 would also be relevant to admissibility of evidence in criminal proceedings.[3]

[1]   *Chappell v United Kingdom* (1989) 12 EHRR 1; *Niemietz v Germany* (1992) 16 EHRR 97; *R (on the application of S) v Chief Constable of South Yorkshire; R (on the application of*

Marper) v *Chief Constable of South Yorkshire* [2002] EWCA Civ 1275, [2002] 1 WLR 3223,
[2003] 1 All ER 148 (retention of fingerprints and DNA). See **7.117** above.
[2]   Human Rights Act 1998, s 8.
[3]   In *A-G's Reference (No 3 of 1999)* [2001] 1 Cr App Rep 475, the House of Lords held that
use of a DNA sample which should have been destroyed was fair bearing in mind the powers
of discretionary exclusion of evidence under Police and Criminal Evidence Act 1984, s 78,
lawful and necessary for the investigation and prosecution of serious crime.

15.35 Complaints about immigration officers' exercise of their powers of
arrest, search and seizure under Part III of the IA 1971 can be made to the
Independent Police Complaints Commission (IPCC)[1] under the Police and
Justice Act 2006, s 41, which makes provision for regulations being made to
enable the IPCC to deal with complaints against immigration officers and
other officials of the Secretary of State about specified enforcement functions[2]
in immigration or asylum investigations, other than functions in relation to
removal centres and detained persons under Part VIII of the IAA 1999. The
most recent Regulations[3] provide for the IPCC to have oversight of serious
complaints and conduct matters (including incidents where a death or serious
injury has taken place) that arise as a result of UKBA officers, officials and
contractors exercising certain functions in relation to immigration, asylum and
customs. They broadly mirror the arrangements for IPCC oversight of the
police set out in Part 2 and Schedule 3 to the Police Reform Act 2002 and
relevant secondary legislation.

[1]   The IPCC was established under Part 2 of the Police Reform Act 2002. See now the
Independent Police Complaints Commission (Immigration and Asylum Enforcement
Functions) Regulations 2008, SI 2008/212, which came into force on 25 February 2008.
[2]   The 'enforcement functions' include powers of entry, powers to search persons or property,
powers to seize or detain property, powers of arrest and detention, powers of examination,
and powers in connection with the removal of persons from the UK.
[3]   The UK Border Agency (Complaints and Misconduct) Regulations 2010, SI 2010/782 which
revoke and remake, with certain amendments, the UK Border Agency (Complaints and
Misconduct) Regulations 2009, SI 2009/2133.

CRIMINAL OFFENCES

Illegal entry and deception

15.36 The criminal offence of illegal entry is defined in section 24(1)(a) of the
IA 1971. The offence cannot be committed by a British citizen.[1] It occurs if
contrary to the Act a person knowingly enters the UK without the leave of an
immigration officer or in breach of a deportation order. It requires actual entry,
and can only be committed on the day of entry.[2] It is a purely summary offence
punishable with a fine on level 5 or imprisonment up to six months.[3] The
extended time limit for prosecution applies.[4] Suspected offenders can be
arrested without warrant.[5] Normally the burden of proving an illegal entry is
on the prosecution, but an exception is made in cases brought within six
months of the date of entry, where the defendant must prove that he or she had
leave to enter.[6] Proof in such cases will be on the balance of probabilities, in
accordance with the normal rule of criminal law where the burden of proof is
reversed.[7] Whether the reverse burden would be held incompatible with the

presumption of innocence in Article 6(2) of the ECHR, and read as an evidential rather than persuasive burden, has yet to be tested in this context.[8]

1 IA 1971, s 24(1), as amended by British Nationality Act 1981, Sch 4, para 2(a).
2 *Grant v Borg* [1982] 2 All ER 257, [1982] 1 WLR 638, HL.
3 IA 1971, s 24(1), as amended by Criminal Justice Act 1982, ss 38 and 46, and by Asylum and Immigration Act 1996, s 6(a). A level 5 fine is presently £5,000 in England and Wales: Criminal Justice Act 1982, s 37 as amended by Criminal Justice Act 1991, s 17.
4 IA 1971, ss 24(3), 28(1). See below **15.67**.
5 IA 1971, s 28A, added by IAA 1999, s 128.
6 IA 1971, s 24(4)(b).
7 *R v Carr-Briant* [1943] KB 607, [1943] 2 All ER 156.
8 See *R v DPP, ex p Kebilene* [2000] 2 AC 326; *R v Lambert* [2001] UKHL 37, [2002] AC, [2001] 3 All ER 577. In cases involving regulatory offences, and in some cases involving true criminal offences, a reverse persuasive burden has been held proportionate: *R v Matthews* [2003] EWCA Crim 813, [2004] QB 690; *S v London Borough of Havering* [2002] EWCA Crim 2558, [2003] 1 Cr App Rep 602. See now on reverse burden of proof *R v Johnstone* [2003] UKHL 28, [2003] 3 All ER 884; *A-G's Reference (No 4 of 2002)*; *Sheldrake v DPP* [2004] UKHL 43, [2005] 1 AC 264.

15.37 The offence of using deception to enter or remain was added in 1996 and expanded in scope in 1999. It is set out in section 24A of the IA 1971. Again, it cannot be committed by a British citizen.[1] It occurs if, by means which include deception by him or her, a person:

(a)   obtains or seeks to obtain leave to enter or remain in the UK;[2] or
(b)   secures or seeks to secure the avoidance, postponement or revocation of enforcement action against him or her.[3]

The wording of the offence makes clear that the deception must be by the immigrant and not some third party. It must be material, ie instrumental in obtaining leave to enter, remain, etc,[4] although it does not have to be the sole effective means of obtaining entry, stay, etc. Deception can be carried out by conduct or conduct accompanied by silence as to a material fact, such as the silent presentation of a false passport.[5] 'Enforcement action' is defined to include removal directions, the making of a deportation order or removal in consequence of either. The offence is considerably broader in certain respects than the offence of illegal entry. It can be committed by seeking to enter, as well as by actually doing so. It extends to embrace action taken to remain in the UK, and to prevent or defer removal, as well as action taken to enter.[6] It has been used against failed asylum seekers who have sought asylum again under a different identity.[7] It can be committed in a control zone.[8] The offence is triable either way, with a fine up to the statutory maximum and/or up to six months' imprisonment on summary conviction, or a fine and/or up to two years' imprisonment on indictment.[9]

As regards sentence it was held in *R v Pit Heng Ding*[10] that there is no general difference in culpability between seeking to enter, seeking to remain in, the United Kingdom by deception (offences under section 24A(1)(a)) or using deception to prevent the authorities from discovering that the person is unlawfully in the country (an offence under section 24A(1)(b)). It was also said that the offences under the Identity Cards Act 2006, section 25(1) (re-enacted, with amendments, by the Identity Documents Act 2010, section 4) are not generically more serious than the offences under section 24A(1), notwithstanding that the maximum sentence for the offence under the 2006 Act was 10 years' imprisonment, as compared with two years for that under the 1971 Act.

But there was an understandable reason for that. The sentencing range under section 25 of the Identity Cards Act 2006 has to cater for the worst possible case, which may include the manufacture and distribution of false documents on a commercial basis, no doubt for potentially significant gain. That may cause far greater damage to the integrity of the border control system than could be caused by a single individual attempting to deceive the immigration authorities and thereby committing an offence whether under that Act or under section 24A(1) of the 1971 Act. The Court also accepted the distinction made in *R v Ovieriakhi*[11] between that type of case and one where an offender used the passport not for the direct purpose of avoiding or defeating border control but to obtain work or open a bank account. A sentence of between 12 and 18 months could be expected by an individual in the first case and a sentence less than 12 months in the second.

[1] IA 1971, s 24A(1), inserted by IAA 1999, s 28.
[2] This subsection was previously enacted as IA 1971, s 24(1)(aa), added by Asylum and Immigration Act 1996, s 4. It applies in a control zone as in the UK: Channel Tunnel (International Arrangements) Order 1993, art 5; Channel Tunnel (Miscellaneous Provisions) Order 1994, art 5; Nationality, Immigration and Asylum Act 2002 (Juxtaposed Controls) Order 2003, art 12.
[3] This sub-section was added by the IAA 1999.
[4] See discussion in the House of Lords during passage of the Asylum and Immigration Act 1996, which created the offence: 571 HL Official Report (5th series) col 1633, 1996.
[5] *Choudhry v Metropolitan Police Comr* (24 November 1984, unreported), QBD; R v Secretary of State for the Home Department, ex p Patel [1986] Imm AR 515, CA (cases relating to false representations under IA 1971, s 26(1)(c)). See **17.24** below.
[6] IA 1971, s 24A(2).
[7] *R v Nagmadeen* [2003] EWCA Crim 2004, [2003] All ER (D) 342 (Jun).
[8] Nationality, Immigration and Asylum Act 2002 (Juxtaposed Controls) Order 2003, SI 2003/2818, art 12.
[9] IA 1971, s 24A(3). When the offence was created in 1996 it was summary only. In *R v Ali (Nasir)* [2001] EWCA Crim 2874, [2002] 2 Cr App Rep (S) 32 a sentence of 18 months was reduced to 12 months on appeal for a Pakistani national pleading guilty to seeking leave to enter by deception by posing as an Afghani asylum seeker. Twelve-month sentences were upheld in *R v Nagmadeen* (fn 7 above) for Iraqi Kurds claiming asylum a second time under false names after their original claims were rejected and their appeals dismissed. An 18-month sentence for using false documents to re-enter the UK was reduced to nine months in *R v Rehman (Asif)* [2003] EWCA Crim 2473, [2003] All ER (D) 197 (Sep) where the motivation was to visit his sick mother at home and to avoid the inevitability of an asylum appeal being dismissed by his leaving the country. In *R v Kishientine* [2004] EWCA Crim 3352, [2005] 2 Cr App Rep (S) 156, a nine-month sentence was upheld for an entry by deception ten weeks before an asylum claim was made, and the court held that where a defence under s 31 did not apply (see **15.44** below), the sentencing judge was not obliged to assess the strength of any asylum claim made by the defendant. However, a four-month detention and training order imposed by a youth court on a 17-year-old asylum claimant was quashed as wrong in principle, and a conditional discharge substituted, in *R (on the application of K) v Crown Court at Croydon* [2005] EWHC 478 (Admin), [2005] 2 Cr App Rep (S) 578. The court emphasised the importance of the agent's role.
[10] [2010] EWCA Crim 1979, [2011] 1 Cr App Rep (S) 546, at paras 9, 11 and 14.
[11] [2009] EWCA Crim 452, [2009] 2 Cr App Rep (S) 607 (sentence reduced to 6 months).

15.38 It is important to distinguish the offences of illegal entry and entry by deception from the status of an illegal entrant. The status of illegal entrant requires no intention, or even knowledge, of a breach of immigration law, and includes those who enter without realising that they require and have no leave to enter or are subject to a deportation order.[1] The criminal offence, on the other hand, is only committed if done knowingly. Illegal entrants also include those who have obtained leave by another person's deception,[2] but entry by means of another person's deception cannot ground a criminal prosecution. Thus, persons who do not realise that they have no leave, and those who were brought in (usually as children) by the deception of another person (usually a relative), or those wrongly believed to be British citizens and so not granted leave to enter, cannot be prosecuted, even though they can be removed summarily as illegal entrants.[3]

1   See *R v Governor of Ashford Remand Centre, ex p Bouzagou* [1983] Imm AR 69, CA; *R v Secretary of State for the Home Department, ex p Yeboah* [1986] Imm AR 52 at 59, QBD. See **17.16** ff below.
2   IA 1971, s 33 as amended by Asylum and Immigration Act 1996, Sch 2, para 4). For the position under EC law, see **17.34** below.
3   *R v Governor of Ashford Remand Centre, ex p Bouzagou* above; *R v Secretary of State for the Home Department, ex p Khaled (Abdul)* [1987] Imm AR 67, QBD; *Mokuolo v Secretary of State for the Home Department* [1989] Imm AR 51, CA.

Non-production of passport

15.39 In the 1993 case of *Naillie*,[1] the House of Lords ridiculed the suggestion that the duty of passengers to produce a passport to an immigration officer on arrival[2] gave rise to criminal liability for non-production. Then in 2004, Parliament provided that it may do. A person commits a criminal offence punishable by up to two years' imprisonment if at a leave or asylum interview, he or she does not have a passport or other travel document which is in force and satisfactorily establishes his or her identity and nationality or citizenship.[3] If the passenger is travelling with a dependent child, it is also an offence not to have such documentation in respect of the child.[4] On the plain wording of the Act, the offence may be committed by a child who is travelling alone.[5] However, no offence is committed, if the interview takes place after the passenger has entered the UK, and he or she is able to provide the correct documentation within three days of the interview.[6] It is a defence for the accused person to prove that (a) he or she, or the child for whom he or she is responsible, is an EEA national, (b) he or she or the child is a family member of an EEA national exercising a Treaty right, (c) he or she has a reasonable excuse for not being in possession of a 'document of the kind' needed at the interview to prove identity, or (d) to produce a false document and to prove that it was used for all purposes in connection with their journey to the UK, or (e) to prove that at no stage of the journey to the UK did he or she have a passport or similar immigration document.[7] Deliberate destruction or disposal of the document is deemed not to be a reasonable excuse for non-possession at the interview, unless the destruction or disposal was beyond the passenger's control or was done for a reasonable cause (which does not include delaying the handling or resolution of a claim or application, increasing its chances of success or complying with the instructions or advice of a facilitator or someone offering advice, unless it is unreasonable to expect non-compliance with those instructions or advice).[8]

1   *R v Naillie; R v Kanesarajah* [1993] AC 674, [1993] 2 All ER 782, [1993] 2 WLR 927, [1993] Imm AR 462, [1993] 27 LS Gaz R 34, [1993] NLJR 848, 137 Sol Jo LB 145.
2   Under IA 1971, Sch 2, para 4.
3   Under Asylum and Immigration (Treatment of Claimants etc) Act 2004, s 2.
4   Asylum and Immigration (Treatment of Claimants etc) Act 2004, s 2(1) and (2). Failure to produce a document to an immigration officer on request gives rise to a presumption that the person does not have one: s 2(8). The penalty is six months or a fine up to the statutory

maximum if tried summarily; two years or a fine on indictment: AI(TC)A 2004, s 2(9). Eighty-six people were convicted in the first three months of the section's operation (Asylum Process Stakeholders Group, January 2005). In *R v Wang (Bei Bei)* [2005] EWCA Crim 293, [2005] 2 Cr App Rep (S) 492 a guideline case, the Court of Appeal reduced a sentence of ten months imposed on an 18-year-old girl on a guilty plea, to two months and quashed a recommendation for deportation. In *R v Safari and Zanganeh* [2005] EWCA Crim 830, [2006] 1 Cr App Rep (S) 1, the court, applying *Wang*, reduced a sentence of nine months imposed on a husband and wife to three months. But in *R v Ai (Lu Zhu)* [2005] EWCA Crim 936, [2006] 1 Cr App Rep (S) 18 the court, reducing a nine-month sentence to five months, held that a deterrent message had to be sent to agents that their clients faced a real risk of a custodial sentence in the UK. Ironically, the role and authority of the agent were held to be strong mitigating factors justifying the quashing of a custodial sentence against a 17-year-old in *R (on the application of K) v Crown Court at Croydon* [2005] EWHC 478 (Admin), [2005] 2 Cr App Rep (S) 578 a deception case: see **15.37** fn 9 above.

5   It is not the Home Office's intention that vulnerable people and in particular younger children should be convicted: Beverley Hughes (then Minister for Immigration, Citizenship and Counter-Terrorism), Asylum and Immigration (Treatment of Claimants) Bill Standing Committee (Commons) 8.1.04, col 15.
6   Asylum and Immigration (Treatment of Claimants etc) Act 2004, s 2(3).
7   Asylum and Immigration (Treatment of Claimants etc) Act 2004, s 2(4), (5) and (6). For EEA nationals and family members see **Chapter 6**.
8   Asylum and Immigration (Treatment of Claimants etc) Act 2004, s 2(7).

15.40 In *R v Navabi; R v Embaye*[1] the Court of Appeal refused to link offences under section 2 of the Asylum and Immigration (Treatment of Claimants etc) Act 2004 with a refugee's rights under Article 31 of the Refugees Convention and rejected the reverse burden of proof submission of the appellant. Kennedy LJ said (para 29):

'we see no reason to conclude that the burden of proof should be interpreted as being anything less than a legal burden. An evidential burden would do little to promote the objects of the legislation in circumstances where the prosecution would have very limited means of testing any defence raised.'

However, a later decision of the Administrative Court clearly undermines the judgment in *Embaye* and blunts the ambit of the offence, created by section 2 of the Asylum and Immigration (Treatment of Claimants etc) Act 2004. In *Thet v DPP*[2], the court held that a failure to produce a passport or other valid identity document at an immigration interview is not an offence under section 2, if throughout the journey to the UK either a false passport or no passport had been used. The Court held that the correct interpretation of section 2(4)(e) is that an immigration document refers only to a genuine 'in force' passport. If the passenger can prove that he or she travelled to the UK without at any stage having such a document then he or she has an absolute defence. This could mean that past convictees may now be able to have a remedy, if they apply for leave to appeal the conviction out of time to the Crown Court or, if convicted in the Crown Court, to the Court of Appeal.

1   *R v Navabi; R v Embaye* [2005] EWCA Crim 2865, (2005) Times, 5 December.
2   *Thet v DPP* [2006] EWHC 2701 (Admin), [2007] 2 All ER 425.

15.41 The criminalisation of arrival without travel documents is designed to address the large-scale destruction and disposal of documents before arrival, which creates problems in terms of tracing passengers back to particular carriers or ports of embarkation, and therefore delays their removal. It is based on the assumption that all passengers presenting themselves at immigration control must have had travel documents when they embarked, because carrier sanctions penalise carriers who bring undocumented passengers,[1] although the same assumption cannot be made in respect of clandestine entrants, who have left a container lorry during a ferry crossing or have been apprehended after the lorry has reached the UK. It is doubtful whether criminalising vulnerable people who have been forced to use unlawful methods to reach safety and who simply obey the instructions of agents bringing them in, is either lawful (having regard to the UK's Refugee Convention obligations)[2] or an efficient or humane way of dealing with the problem.

[1] For carrier sanctions see **15.106** ff below.
[2] Both the Home Affairs Committee and the Joint Committee on Human Rights expressed concern at the risk that the UK would, as a result of the creation of the offence, fail to discharge its obligations under Article 31 of the Refugee Convention (as to which see **12.11** above and **15.44** ff below) Home Affairs Committee, First Report of Session 2003–04, Asylum and Immigration (Treatment of Claimants) Bill, HC 109, paras 12–14; Joint Committee on Human Rights Fifth Report 2003–04, paras 11–14. It has been held at first instance that asylum seekers have no legitimate expectation that they will not be prosecuted on facts giving rise to the offence under s 2: *R v Chohan*, Isleworth CC, 3 February 2005 (HHJ McGregor-Johnson). But there should be no prosecution, or at least no conviction, where the actions are related to a bona fide quest for asylum: see *R v Uxbridge Magistrates' Court ex p Adimi* [1999] INLR 490 (at **15.44** below).

15.42 The use of criminal sanctions against those entering the UK illegally, or unable to produce travel documents at interview after arrival, has given rise to issues relating to the UK's obligations under both EU/EC law and under international law relating to refugees.

EU nationals

15.43 The Court of Justice of the European Union, formerly known as the European Court of Justice (and hereinafter referred to as the ECJ) has ruled that illegal entry or a failure to report their presence to the authorities does not affect an EU national's right of residence under EU law. However, these rights do not prevent any Member State from prosecuting such persons, provided that the penalty imposed is not so disproportionate to the gravity of the infringement that it becomes an obstacle to the free movement of persons.[1] EU nationals exercising Community rights do not require leave to enter,[2] and will rarely be illegal entrants, although an EU national entering the UK after an exclusion order was made against him, which had not been set aside, was held to have been properly characterised as an illegal entrant in the *Shingara* case,[3] and an EU national entering the UK in breach of a deportation order is an illegal entrant.

[1] *Case 118/75 Re Watson and Belmann* [1976] ECR 1185, ECJ (failure to report); *Royer 48/75* [1976] ECR 497, ECJ (clandestine entry); *R v Pieck*: C-157/79 [1981] QB 571, ECJ.
[2] By virtue of Immigration Act 1988, s 7.
[3] *Shingara v Secretary of State for the Home Department* [1999] Imm AR 257, CA.

Defences based on Article 31 of the Refugee Convention

15.44 The criminal sanctions laid down in the IA 1971 made no allowance for refugees who entered the UK illegally. But the combined effect of visa requirements and carrier sanctions has forced refugee claimants to adopt illegal methods in order to find safety. The growing use of false documents, either on entry to the UK or in transit via the UK to Canada and the US, led to numerous criminal prosecutions under the Forgery and Counterfeiting Act 1981 and under sections 24A and 26(1)(d) of the 1971 Act (falsification of documents). Since the coming into force of the Identity Documents Act 2010 prosecutions are normally under sections 4 or 6 of that Act.[1] Custodial sentences of up to nine months for offences relating to false documents were originally imposed (and upheld by the Court of Appeal), but are now likely to be much longer.[2] In *Ex p Adimi*[3] the Divisional Court denounced this practice as contrary to Article 31(1) of the Refugee Convention. This provides that contracting states should not impose penalties on refugees who enter their territory illegally, provided they present themselves without delay to the authorities. The court recognised that 'the combined effect of visa regimes and carriers' liability has made it well-nigh impossible for refugees to travel to countries of refuge without false documents'.[4] The broad purpose sought to be achieved by Article 31(1), it held, was 'to provide immunity for genuine refugees whose quest for asylum reasonably involved them in breaching the law', so that 'where the illegal entry or use of false documents or delay can be attributed to a bona fide desire to seek asylum whether here or elsewhere, that conduct should be covered by Article 31'.[5]

The protection of Article 31(1) applies not only to those ultimately recognised as refugees, but to those claiming asylum in good faith, and to those using false documents as well as clandestine entrants.[6] Since some element of choice is open to refugees as to where they may properly claim asylum, the phrase 'coming directly' should be interpreted in such a way that any merely short-term stopover en route to the intended sanctuary cannot forfeit the protection of the Article. The main touchstones by which exclusion from protection should be judged are the length of stay in the intermediate country, the reasons for delaying there (even a substantial delay in an unsafe third country would be reasonable were the time spent trying to acquire the means of travelling on), and whether or not the refugee sought or found there protection de jure or de facto from the persecution they were fleeing.[7] The requirement in the Article to 'present themselves without delay' was not necessarily breached by a failure to claim asylum on arrival.[8] Simon Brown LJ expressed the hope that prosecutions would be conducted only 'where the offence itself appears manifestly unrelated to a genuine quest for asylum'.[9] The court was divided on the issue of responsibility for ensuring compliance with Article 31; Newman J held that the Secretary of State for the Home Department should determine entitlement to the protection of Article 31(1) since it was analogous to a pardon, which was an executive act;[10] Simon Brown LJ did not feel able to impose such an obligation on the executive and believed that the magistrates' abuse of process jurisdiction could be invoked.[11]

---

[1] Sections 4 and 6 of the Identity Documents Act 2010 create new criminal offences relating to the possession of false identity documents. Section 6(1) makes it an offence for a person to have in their possession or control, without reasonable excuse, a false identity document or a genuine document that has been improperly obtained or relates to someone else, or equipment used for making false identity documents. Unless there is a reasonable excuse, these offences apply irrespective of any intent to use the documents or equipment. Section 6(2) prescribes a maximum penalty of two years' imprisonment, a fine or both, on indictment, and six months or a fine of £5000 on summary conviction. Under section 4(1) it is an offence for a person with 'an improper intention' to have in their possession or control a false or improperly obtained identity document which is known or believed to be false or improperly obtained. Improper intention here means an intention to use the document for establishing personal information

about that person, or allowing or inducing another to establish, ascertain or verify personal information about that person or anyone else. This offence carries a maximum sentence of ten years on indictment, or a fine, or both.

2   A sentence of eight months was held appropriate in *R v Singh (Daljit)* [1999] 1 Cr App Rep (S) 490, a 'guideline case' involving a guilty plea to using a false instrument in respect of an attempt to travel to Canada using a false passport. This level of sentencing has since been increased: see *R v Pit Heng Ding* [2010] EWCA Crim 1979, [2011] 1 Cr App Rep (S) 546, at paras 9,11 and 14, discussed at **15.37**, above. Evidence to the Home Affairs Committee in 2003 put the number of convictions at between 5,000 (JUSTICE) and under 1,000 (the government): First Report of Session 2003–04, Asylum and Immigration (Treatment of Claimants) Bill, HC 109, paras 12–14.

3   *R v Uxbridge Magistrates' Court, ex p Adimi*; *R v Crown Prosecution Service, ex p Sorani*; *R v Secretary of State for the Home Department, ex p Kaziu* [1999] INLR 490.

4   [1999] INLR 490 at 492G, per Simon Brown LJ. He held that Article 31 was justiciable in the UK courts through the doctrine of legitimate expectation, a conclusion he later described as 'suspect': see *European Roma Rights Centre v Immigration Officer at Prague Airport (United Nations High Comr for Refugees intervening)* [2003] EWCA Civ 666, [2003] INLR 374, para 51. Laws LJ described it as a 'constitutional solecism'. See further **12.11** above.

5   [1999] INLR 490 at 496D–E.

6   [1999] INLR 490 at 496F.

7   [1999] INLR 490 at 497A–C.

8   [1999] INLR 490 at 498E.

9   [1999] INLR 490 at 504C.

10   [1999] INLR 490 at 513F.

11   [1999] INLR 490 at 503C.

15.45 After the judgment in *Adimi* a statutory defence was enacted to charges of deception under section 24A of the IA 1971 or falsification of documents under section 26(1)(d) of the Act, charges under the Forgery and Counterfeiting Act 1981 (forgery, use and possession of false instruments), and under sections 4 and 6 of the Identity Documents Act 2010, by the IAA 1999, s 31.[1] The statutory defence is significantly narrower in its scope than the protection afforded by Article 31(1) of the Refugee Convention according to *Adimi*. It applies to those who have claimed refugee status, but whose cases have not yet been dealt with, if the prosecution cannot disprove beyond a reasonable doubt that they are refugees.[2] The legislation contains two aspects that more narrowly define the position than that advanced in *Adimi*; namely, in subsection (1) the requirement that anyone claiming protection must have applied for asylum as soon as is reasonably practicable after arrival in the UK[3], and in subsection (2) that a refugee who has stopped in another country outside the UK must show that he or she could not reasonably have been expected to be given Convention protection in that other country[4].

Section 31 provides that those wrongly convicted before the commencement of the section may apply to the Criminal Cases Review Commission for their cases to be referred to the Court of Appeal.[5] In *Hussain*[6] it was held that s 31 represented Parliament's interpretation of the UK's obligations under Article 31. A two-judge Divisional Court went further in *Pepushi*,[7] holding that s 31 was to be followed even if it put the UK in breach of the Refugee Convention. In *R v Makuwa*[8] the Court of Appeal held that in a prosecution to which s 31 of the IAA 1999 applied, the defendant's refugee status was a matter to be determined by proof; but the burden on the defendant was a merely evidential burden and provided he or she adduced sufficient evidence to raise the issue, the burden is then upon the prosecution to prove to the usual standard that the defendant is not a refugee. With regard to the other elements of the defence, the burden remains on the defendant.[9]

[1] Section 31(3) of the 1999 Act has been amended to insert a new para (aa), which extends the defence to the false documents offences in the 2010 Act.

[2] IAA 1999, s 31(1), (6); *R v Makuwa* [2006] EWCA Crim 175, [2006] 1 WLR 2755. A refused asylum seeker can seek to avail him or herself of the defence, and arguably the ruling in *Makuwa* also applies to the post decision situation.

[3] IAA 1999, s 31(1)(a) and (c).

[4] IAA 1999, s 31(2). See *R v Abdalla (Mohammed); R v V (M); R v Mohamed (Rahma Abukar); R v Nofallah* [2010] EWCA Crim 2400, [2011] 1 CR App Rep 35, CA, at [7]. The court noted (at [8]) that the decision in *Adimi* was subsequently affirmed by the House of Lords in *R v Asfaw* [2008] UKHL 31, [2008] 1 AC 1061, [2008] 3 All ER 775 in which the majority concluded that 'the Convention (and the amendment to the 1999 Act) was to be given a purposive construction consistent with its humanitarian aims. It was thus sufficient to include protection of refugees from the imposition of criminal penalties for infractions of the law reasonably or necessarily committed in the course of their flight from persecution, even if they had made a short term stopover in an intermediate country on route to the country of intended refuge.' The court further noted (at [9]) that although the full scope of s 31 was not determined by *Asfaw*:

> 'Lord Bingham did make clear that in order to satisfy the requirement of s 31(1)(c) the claim for asylum must be made as soon as was reasonably possible (which did not necessarily mean at the earliest possible moment: see para 16). Second, the fact that a refugee had stopped in a third country in transit was not necessarily fatal . . . Refugees had some choice as to where they might properly claim asylum and . . . the main touchstones by which exclusion from protection should be judged were the length of the stay in the intermediate country, the reasons for delaying there and whether or not the refugee sought or found protection de jure or de facto from the persecution from which he or she was seeking to escape: see also *R v MMH* [2008] EWCA Crim 3117 at paras 14–15.'

The principle that a stopover in a third country in transit was not necessarily fatal to a defence under section 31 was more recently confirmed by the Court of Appeal in *R v Mateta* [2013] EWCA Crim 1372, [2014] 1 All ER 152, where *Mohammed Abdullah* was followed.

[5] IAA 1999, s 31(8). In fact most convictions were in the magistrates' court, and could be reopened under Magistrates' Courts Act 1980, s 142(2), to enable the Crown to offer no evidence. Asylum seekers who were wrongly convicted and imprisoned have received compensation of up to £40,000: see *Abdi v Secretary of State for the Home Department* (2002) Legal Action, November. Home Office evidence to the Home Affairs Committee was that fewer than 20 people had successfully claimed compensation for wrongful conviction: Home Affairs Committee First Report of Session 2003–04, Asylum and Immigration (Treatment of Claimants) Bill, HC 109.

[6] *R (on the application of Hussain) v Secretary of State for the Home Department* [2001] EWHC 555 (Admin).

[7] *R (on the application of Pepushi) v Crown Prosecution Service* [2004] EWHC 798 (Admin),), (2004) Times, 21 May.

[8] *R v Makuwa* [2006] EWCA Crim 175, [2006] 1 WLR 2755.

[9] The Court followed the reasoning used in *R v Navabi; R v Embaye* [2005] EWCA Crim 2865, (2005) Times, 5 December where a reverse burden argument concerning the defences under s 2 of the Asylum and Immigration (Treatment of Claimants etc) Act 2004 was rejected.

15.46 In *R v Asfaw*[1] the House of Lords held that since section 31 of the 1999 Act was intended to give effect to Article 31 of the Refugee Convention, the defence provided by it should not be read as limited to offences attributable to a refugee's illegal entry into or presence in this country, but rather as providing immunity (if the conditions contained therein are fulfilled) from the imposition of criminal penalties for offences attributable to the attempt of a refugee to leave this country in the continuing course of a flight from persecution, even after a short stopover in transit.

They also dealt with the position where a defendant who has attempted to leave this country for another place of refuge using false documents is charged both with an offence to which the section 31 defence applies and with an offence of dishonesty to which it does not. The House held that to charge a defendant in this way was not an abuse of process, since the defence under s 31 applies only to a limited number of offences and since the prosecution are entitled to question whether the defendant is a refugee. If the defendant is not a refugee, then the defence will not avail him or her in respect of either count.[2] However, if the two counts relate to identical conduct and the second count is included in the indictment in order to prevent the defendant from relying on the defence, there will be strong grounds for contending that prosecuting that count is an abuse of process, since it would be unfair and contrary to the intention of the Act to convict the defendant on that count if he or she has successfully raised the defence in respect of the first count. The appropriate course of action in such circumstances is for the court to stay the prosecution of the second count pending the determination of the first count by the jury, and to maintain the stay if the defendant is acquitted.

It should be noted that the House was not concerned with section 31(2), which is drafted in narrower terms than Article 31, in that refugees who have stopped over in another country are protected only if they are able to show that they could not reasonably have been expected to be given protection under the Convention in that country, whereas under Article 31 a short-term stopover *en route* would not deprive the refugee of protection from prosecution. So although *Pepushi*[3] is still good law, it is likely that in the light of the thorough review of the history of art 31 in the speeches in *Asfaw*, the courts will adopt a generous approach to what refugees could 'reasonably have expected' by way of protection in third countries. In *R v Hasan*[4] the court held that it was reasonably arguable that H had a reasonable prospect of demonstrating that he came directly from a country where his life or freedom was threatened within the meaning of the Convention Relating to the Status of Refugees 1951 (United Nations), Article 31 and did not stop in another country. H would have had a reasonable prospect of relying on section 31 and defending the charge. H was not given advice specifically on the meaning of coming directly from a country where his life or freedom was threatened or on the ambit of section 31(2). The instant case was a case where the safety of conviction could be considered, notwithstanding the fact that H pleaded guilty. The conviction was quashed. As H had already served his sentence, it was not in the interests of justice to order a retrial.

The previous Asylum Policy Instructions (API) on section 31 and Article 31, updated to October 2006 and rebranded in October 2009, have been withdrawn and are under review. Many parts of the previous guidance were out of date and misleading and included incomplete references to the case law. Interim guidance dated September 2012 has been issued[5]. The interim API state that the role of the UKBA Criminal and Investigation teams is restricted to providing information and evidence to the CPS, which is relevant to the assessment of whether or not a defence under section 31 may apply.[6] The API also makes clear that *Asfaw*[7] establishes the availability of the statutory defence for offences attributable to a refugee's attempt to leave the UK in the continuing course of a flight from persecution and that the term 'coming directly' is to be interpreted liberally.[8]

[1]   *R v Asfaw* [2008] UKHL 31, [2008] 1 AC 1061, [2008] 3 All ER 775.
[2]   For an example of a case where the Court held that the defendant was not a refugee see *R v Evans (Fabien)* [2013] 1 Cr App Rep 34, where the court of Appeal held that while there was

evidence in the case that wealthy people in Jamaica were targeted by gangs, there was no evidence that returnees to Jamaica as a group, or persons deported to Jamaica as a sub-group, were specifically so targeted. The lesson of this case is that it is essential to have the necessary evidence ready at the criminal trial.

3   *R (on the application of Pepushi) v Crown Prosecution Service* [2004] EWHC 798 (Admin), (2004) Times, 21 May.
4   [2008] EWCA Crim 3117, [2008] All ER (D) 116 (Nov).
5   See paras [22]–[24], [30]–[33], [37]–[39], [44]–[46], [56]–[57].
6   API 'Section 31 of immigration and Asylum Act 1999 and Article 31 of the 1951 Refugee Convention'.
7   [2008] UKHL 31, [2008] 1 AC 1061, [2008] 3 All ER 775.
8   API para 7.

15.47 There has been considerable concern that, despite Article 31 and section 31, asylum seekers coming to the UK on false passports have been prosecuted, charged, and convicted without any reference being made by their legal advisers or the court to the existence of the section 31 defence. This problem was addressed by the Court of Appeal in *R v Abdalla (Mohammed)*[1]. In allowing three out of the four appeals the court said that it is critical that those advising a defendant charged with an offence to which the defence provided for by section 31 applies make clear the parameters of the defence so that the defendant can make an informed choice of whether to seek to advance it (at [10]). It was said that if the circumstances and instructions generate the possibility of mounting a defence under section 31, there is simply no excuse for a failure to do so and, at the same time, properly to note both the instructions received and the advice given. If these steps are taken, cases such as the four with which the court has just dealt, will not recur and considerable public expense will be spared (at [56]). The issue was more recently considered by the Court of Appeal in *R v Mateta*[2]. The Court held that there was an obligation on those representing defendants charged with possession of an identity document with improper intention to advise them of the existence of the defence. As to the circumstances in which a conviction may be set aside, where the defendant has been improperly advised and has pleaded guilty, the Court made it clear that it can entertain an application for leave to appeal against conviction either on the grounds that a tendered guilty plea was a nullity or more likely on a ground firmly based in the safety of the conviction. An appeal will only be successful, if the court believes the defence would quite probably have succeeded and concludes, therefore, that a clear injustice has been done.[3]

1   [2010] EWCA Crim 2400, [2011] 1 Cr App Rep 432, CA.
2   [2013] EWCA Crim 1372, [2014] 1 All ER 152, see above at **15.45**.
3   See *R v Boal* [1992] QB 591, 95 Cr App Rep 272, CA, per Simon Brown LJ at 278.

Facilitating unlawful immigration and assisting asylum seekers

15.48 Sections 25, 25A and 25B of the IA 1971[1] widen and extend the old facilitation provisions, and cover any act facilitating a breach of immigration law by a non-EU citizen (including a breach of another Member State's immigration law, and acts covered by the old offence of harbouring), helping asylum seekers to arrive in the UK, or helping EU citizens to enter the UK in breach of a deportation order or an exclusion order. The jurisdiction is wide and includes offences committed in the UK, by British nationals abroad, and covers actions performed in a control zone.[2] These are the most serious offences in the Act. On summary trial they carry a fine up to the statutory maximum[3] and imprisonment of up to six months, but it is rare for magistrates to accept jurisdiction, and on indictment a prison sentence of up to 14 years can be given.[4]

1   Sections 25–25C were substituted for section 25 of the 1971 Act (as amended) by the Nationality, Immigration and Asylum Act 2002, s 143, as from 10 February 2003 (Nationality, Immigration and Asylum Act 2002 (Commencement No 2) Order 2003, SI 2003/1) and subsequently amended by the insertion of subsections (7) and (8) by the Asylum and Immigration (Treatment of Claimants, etc) Act 2004, s 1(1), as from 1 October 2004 (Asylum and Immigration (Treatment of Claimants, etc) Act 2004 (Commencement No 1) Order 2004, SI 2004/2523).

2   See the Channel Tunnel (International Arrangements) Order 1993, art 5, Channel Tunnel (Miscellaneous Provisions) Order 1994, Nationality, Immigration and Asylum Act 2002 (Juxtaposed Controls) Order 2003, art 12.

3   The statutory maximum is presently £5,000: Magistrates' Courts Act 1980, s 32(9); Criminal Justice Act 1991, s 17.

4   IA 1971, s 25(6), s 25A(4), s 25B(4) as substituted. The original offence of facilitating illegal entry attracted a seven-year sentence. The IAA 1999 increased the maximum sentence to ten years. Sentencing decisions, such as *R v Le (Van Binh); R v Stark/* [1999] 1 Cr App Rep (S) 422, [1999] Crim LR 96, in which Lord Bingham CJ explained some of the relevant aggravating and mitigating features in this class of case, need to be read, bearing in mind the maximum sentence applicable at the time of the offence in the particular case.

15.49 Section 25 of the IA 1971 makes it an offence to do an act which facilitates the commission of a breach of immigration law by someone who is not an EU citizen, knowing or having reasonable cause to believe both that the act facilitates a breach of immigration law and that the individual assisted is not an EU citizen. 'Immigration law' includes the laws of any Member State regarding entitlement to enter, transit or be in a state[1], and the immigration laws of Member States are to be conclusively proved by a certificate from the government concerned.[2] Section 25 was amended into its present form by section 143 of the Nationality Immigration and Asylum Act 2002 and came into force on 10 February 2003. It applies only to breaches of immigration law by non-citizens of the EU (Third country Nationals or TCNs). It was enacted to conform with the UK's obligations under Council Directive 2002/90/EC.[3] The UK took part in the adoption and application of the Directive and it is binding on the UK, has become part of UK domestic law and if there is any incompatibility between the Directive and domestic law, the Directive prevails. Article 1 of the Directive provides:

'1.   Each Member State shall adopt appropriate sanctions on:

(a)   any person who intentionally assists a person who is not a national of a Member State to enter, or transit across, the territory of a Member State in breach of the laws of the State concerned on the entry or transit of aliens;

(b)   any person who, for financial gain, intentionally assists a person who is not a national of a Member State to reside within the territory of a Member State in breach of the laws of the State concerned on the residence of aliens.'

Article 2 provides that Member States should enact the laws and regulations necessary to comply with the Directive before 5 December 2004.

There are undoubted discrepancies between the Directive and section 25, as it has been interpreted by *R v Javaherifard and Miller*[4]. First section 25 makes it an offence to facilitate a non-EU national to be in the UK – in the sense of being 'present' – in breach of immigration laws. This is considerably wider and more punitive than the Directive which requires Member States to adopt sanctions against persons who assist a non-EU national to *reside within* the territory of a Member State in breach of the immigration laws of that State *on the residence* of aliens. Secondly, the *mens rea* is different. The *mens rea* required by the Directive is in each case *an intention to assist* and in the case of assisting to reside within a Member State there is an additional requirement that the assistance should be *for financial gain*. By contrast, section 25 imposes sanctions on entering, transiting across and being in the State and instead of intention to assist and financial gain it substitutes *knowledge or reasonable cause to believe*. Although the purpose of the Directive is to provide a common definition throughout the EU of the facilitation of illegal immigration and consequently to render more effective the implementation of penalties against it, it is not clear whether the more severe sanctions imposed by the UK law is incompatible with the Convention or whether the Directive is merely setting minimum standards.[5] Further, the difference in *mens rea* and the watering down of 'residence' into 'presence' allow one of the unintended by-products of illegal employment, namely, enabling the continuation of the worker's unlawful presence in the UK, to come within the ambit of section 25, when, arguably, it would not come within the ambit of the Directive.[6] Decisions are awaited.

[1] IA 1971, s 25(2) as substituted by the Nationality, Immigration and Asylum Act 2002, s 143.

[2] IA 1971, s 25(3) as substituted. 'Member State' includes a state on a list of 'Schengen Acquis' states: s 25(7); see Immigration (Assisting Unlawful Immigration) (Section 25 List of Schengen Acquis States) Order 2004, SI 2004/2877, which lists Norway and Iceland.

[3] Council Directive 2002/90/EC of 28 November 2002 defining the facilitation of unauthorised entry, transit and residence.

[4] [2005] EWCA Crim 3231, (2006) Times, 20 January.

[5] In its Preamble the Directive stated that measures should be taken to combat the aiding of illegal immigration both in connection with unauthorised crossing of the border in the strict sense and for the purpose of sustaining networks which exploit human beings (para 1). To that end it was *essential to approximate* existing legal provisions, in particular, . . . *the precise definition of the infringement in question and the cases of exemption* (our emphasis) (para 2). See also the Framework Decision 2002/946/JHA (which deals inter alia with minimum rules for penalties for illegal immigration).

[6] But see *Javaherifard and Miller* [2005] EWCA Crim 3231, (2006) Times, 20 January at para 50 ('If someone provides food, money or accommodation to an illegal entrant, knowing or having reasonable cause for believing that such acts facilitate him being in the country as an illegal entrant, he would be guilty of an offence and we see no reason why that should not be so. If food, money or accommodation is . . . not supplied with the knowledge that it will assist his presence as an illegal entrant but instead is supplied knowing that it will assist him simply as a human being, eg to avoid degradation or destitution, there would be no offence' – not perhaps a very convincing statement, given that 'knowledge' is used with two distinct meanings). Since an offence under s 25 can only be committed with guilty knowledge, providing legal advice to an illegal immigrant with a view to regularising his or her position or making an asylum claim (unless the claim is known to be false) does not amount to an offence.

15.50 The offence is defined broadly enough to encompass both the old offences of assisting illegal entry (whether by smuggling someone in a vehicle or by providing false documents for presentation at a port), assisting someone to remain by deception (for example by entering into a sham marriage or by procuring false documents),[1] and other forms of assistance which facilitate a breach of the immigration laws. In *R v Naillie*,[2] decided under the old law, it was held that in a prosecution for facilitation it was necessary to determine whether the persons whose entry was assisted were illegal entrants; a distinction was to be drawn between arrival and entry, and mere disembarkation without a passport was not enough to make the asylum seekers illegal entrants; that they did not seek to enter the UK in breach of the laws until they presented a false passport to an immigration officer or tried to pass out of the immigration control area without submitting to examination at all; that by requesting asylum without any attempt to deceive, they did not seek to enter in breach, and were not illegal entrants. In *Javaherifard and Miller*,[3] the court held that entry to the UK occurred at the point where someone crossed the border from the Republic into Northern Ireland and not at the point where they first present a passport. The court also held that it is not essential that the breach of immigration law itself should constitute an offence. *Naillie* has been distinguished in subsequent cases. It is said that it dealt with the routine position at an international port where there is a designated immigration control area and that the position is different where the would-be entrant intends to, and receives help to, evade immigration controls altogether before arriving in the UK.[4] Thus the offence is committed if the intending immigrants are discovered before entry in circumstances indicating their intention to enter illegally.[5] Under the amended section, the Crown no longer has to prove that those assisted are illegal entrants, but does have to prove that the acts facilitated a breach of the immigration laws, to the defendant's knowledge or reasonable belief.

The defence of necessity has been used at first instance when those smuggled in were refugees and smuggling was the only way to secure their safety from a threat of death or serious injury,[6] and an argument based on abuse of process succeeded in a case under the old provisions where a charge of helping asylum seekers was brought but dropped in favour of a facilitating illegal entry charge when the Crown realised it could not prove gain.[7] However, the defence afforded to refugees by Article 31 or section 31 (see **15.44–15.47** above) is not available to those smuggling refugees or otherwise helping them to arrive in breach of the immigration laws.[8]

Under the UKBA 2007, the territorial ambit of this section has been widened. It now applies to things done whether inside or outside the UK and does not depend on the nationality of the alleged offender.[9] In *R v Le (Van Binh)*[10] the Court of Appeal held, in relation to the original section 25(1)(a) (facilitating entry of illegal entrant), that the appropriate penalty for all but the most minor offences would be one of immediate custody; the offence frequently calls for deterrent sentences, the problem of illegal entry being on the increase; in determining the seriousness of a particular case, it is necessary to have regard, in particular, to whether the offence was an isolated act or had been repeated or there were previous convictions for like offences, to the motivation (commercial or humanitarian), to the identity and number of the entrants (strangers/family), to the degree of organisation and to the role played by each defendant.

In *R v Oliveira and Cina*[11] the Court of Appeal said that when sentencing under section 25 arising from a sham marriage, a court should begin with the common aggravating features, as set out in *Van Binh*, to which should be added recruitment of others to assist in the crime, and any exploitation or pressure, in the case of a racket providing services to others for money. It will also be necessary to look at the role of each offender within the organisation.

Right at the bottom of the range may be a single bogus ceremony, where one party has been blackmailed into taking part. The distinction between a sham marriage case and a case of forged or falsified documents for the purpose of evading immigration control will frequently be a distinction without a difference. Both are to provide a bogus authentication of presence. The marriage certificate is not itself a forgery, but is just as false as if it were. In reading previous cases it is important that the sentence bears in mind what the operative maximum sentence was at the time. On the one hand the lifting of the maximum is designed to deal with more extensive and serious forms of offence. These cases apart, the parliamentary signal is of significance to sentencing. Nevertheless a large number of the cases will be cases of a single transaction, where the offender is a party to the ceremony and a sentence will fall into a bracket of around 18 months to three years.

1   Ie, offences previously covered by IA 1971, s 25(1)(c).
2   *R v Naillie* [1993] AC 674, HL.
3   [2005] EWCA Crim 3231; [2006] INLR 302, [2006] Imm AR 185.
4   *R v Adams* [1996] Crim LR 593; *R v Eyck, R v Hadakoglu* [2000] 1 WLR 1389, [2000] INLR 277, CA; *R v Javaherifard and Miller* [2005] EWCA Crim 3231, [2006] INLR 302, [2006] Imm AR 185, 15.49 above.
5   In *R v Singh; R v Meeuwsen* [1973] 1 All ER 122, [1972] 1 WLR 1600, CA, the Court of Appeal held that acts both before and after the illegal entry could be relied on as facilitating that entry. That case concerned two men who assisted some illegal entrants to get away from the trailer, in which they were concealed, after it had left the port area. See also *R v Adams*; *R v Eyck, R v Hadakoglu* fn 4 above.
6   See *R v Martin* [1989] 1 All ER 652, 88 Cr App Rep 343, CA at 345–346, per Simon Brown J; *R v Pommell (Fitzroy Derek)* [1995] 2 Cr App Rep 601, CA; *R v Abdul-Hussain* [1999] Crim LR 570; R v Cairns [1999] 2 Cr App Rep 137, CA.
7   *R v KS*, Middlesex Guildhall, 3 October 1999, *HHJ Blacksall*. See (2000) Legal Action February, p 21.
8   *R v Alps (Rudolph)* (2 February 2001, unreported), CA.
9   UKBA 2007, s 30.
10   *R v Le (Van Binh)* [1999] 1 Cr App Rep (S) 422.
11   [2013] 2 Cr App Rep (S) 4.

15.51 The new section 25A of the IA 1971, inserted by the NIAA 2002,[1] is a reworking of the offence created in 1996 of facilitating the entry of asylum claimants. No element of smuggling is required to make out the offence; the asylum seekers do not need to be illegal entrants. The offence is aimed at those who, for gain, bring asylum seekers to the UK to enable them to claim asylum; it was intended to plug the gap disclosed by *R v Naillie*.[2] Since the right to seek and enjoy asylum is declared a fundamental human right by Article 14 of the UDHR, the criminalisation of those who assist asylum seekers to reach this country's shores for genuine humanitarian reasons was a controversial move on its introduction in 1996, and the government was at pains to stress that it was aimed at 'illegal racketeering activity' of 'those who make profit by facilitating the entry of asylum seekers'.[3] The definition of the offence is knowingly and for gain facilitating the arrival at or entry into the UK[4] of an individual known or reasonably believed to be an asylum seeker. An 'asylum seeker' is defined as a person who intends to claim that to remove him or her, or require him or her to leave the UK, would be contrary to the UK's obligations under the Refugee Convention or the Human Rights Convention.[5] The requirement of gain is now clearly part of the definition of the offence. The wording of the old section 25(1)(b), stating that the section did not apply to acts done 'otherwise than for gain', created confusion over the correct burden and standard of proof.[6] Section 25A exempts paid charity workers by asserting that the section does not apply to anything done by a person acting on behalf of an organisation which aims to assist asylum seekers and does not charge for its services.[7] A conspiracy to 'assist persons claiming asylum in the UK' is not an offence known to law.[8]

[1] Nationality, Immigration and Asylum Act 2002, s 143, in force 10 February 2003.
[2] [1993] AC 674, HL. The case distinguished between 'arrival' and 'entry'. The old s 25(1)(b) ('facilitating the entry of asylum claimants') still used the word 'entry' in the definition of the offence, enabling defence lawyers to argue, following *R v Naillie* that all their clients did was to facilitate arrival, not entry. The new section does not fall into this trap, using the word 'arrival' instead of the term of Art 'entry'. This change enabled the draftsman to do away with the sub-section exempting immigration lawyers from criminal responsibility for advising and assisting their clients (thereby facilitating the grant of leave to enter to them).
[3] See HL Official Report (5th series), cols 570–574, 20 June 1996.
[4] The words 'entry into' were added by UKBA 2007, s 29.
[5] IA 1971, s 25A(2) as inserted.
[6] See *R v Hunt* [1987] AC 352; *R v Duibi* (Harrow Crown Court, 30 March 1999, (2000) Legal Action February, p 21).
[7] IA 1971, s 25A(3) as inserted.
[8] *R v Hadi (Dawood)* [2001] EWCA Crim 2534, [2001] All ER (D) 450 (Oct).

15.52 The courts have been unwilling to apply the principle behind Article 31(1) of the Refugee Convention to allow those who smuggle in refugees for purely humanitarian reasons to escape penalty.[1] But in sentencing for the offence of facilitating illegal entry, the courts must have regard to whether, in particular, the motivation was commercial or humanitarian, as well as to whether the offence was an isolated act or repeated, the degree of organisation and the defendant's role. However, the Court of Appeal has deemed an immediate custodial sentence appropriate for all but the most minor offences.[2] Reported sentences range from six months for smuggling a husband[3] to six years for carrying large numbers in a specially adapted truck,[4] and eight years for conspiracy where 58 Chinese nationals suffocated to death in the lorry after the driver closed the air vents.[5] In addition to the penalties of fines and imprisonment, the Crown Court has very wide powers to order the forfeiture of any vehicle used or intended to be used for an offence under one of the sections, or a ship or aircraft carrying more than twenty entrants.[6] The vehicle or craft may be detained under the authority of a police or senior immigration officer pending prosecution, conviction and forfeiture,[7] and there are new powers on disposal of such property under section 26 of the UKBA 2007.

[1] See **15.50** fn 8 above.
[2] *R v Le (Van Binh)*; *R v Stark* [1999] 1 Cr App Rep (S) 422. A suspended sentence of 18 months was imposed in *R v Bellikli* [1998] 1 Cr App Rep (S) 135 (driving through immigration control with an illegal entrant concealed in van), because of exceptionally difficult domestic circumstances.
[3] *R v Ozdemir* [1996] 2 Cr App Rep (S) 64. In *R v Toor* [2003] EWCA Crim 185, [2003] 2 Cr App Rep (S) 349 a sentence of 30 months was upheld for bringing in a brother on another brother's passport with a substituted photograph.
[4] *R v Salem (Lofti ben)* [2003] EWCA Crim 2172, [2003] All ER (D) 123 (Aug): a truck driver had 24 illegal entrants hidden in the truck, and holes had been drilled to enable them to breathe and to communicate with him.
[5] *R v Wacker (Perry)* [2002] EWCA Crim 1944, [2002] Crim LR 839, [2003] QB 1207, [2003] 4 All ER 295.
[6] IA 1971, s 25C as substituted by Nationality, Immigration and Asylum Act 2002, s 143.
[7] IA 1971, s 25D, inserted by IAA 1999, s 38(2), and renumbered by Nationality, Immigration and Asylum Act 2002, s 144.

15.53 The new section 25B of the IA 1971[1] makes it an offence to assist the entry to the UK of an EU national in breach of a deportation or exclusion order. The section plugs the gap created by the new section 25, which excludes EU nationals from its remit. The offence is committed by doing an act which facilitates a breach of a deportation order in force against an EU citizen, knowing or having reasonable cause to believe that the act facilitates a breach of the order,[2] or, in a situation where the Secretary of State has personally excluded an EU citizen from the UK on public good grounds, doing an act which assists the person to arrive in, enter or remain in the UK, knowing or having reasonable cause to believe that the act has that effect and that the Secretary of State has made an exclusion order.[3]

[1]   IA 1971, s 25B, inserted by Nationality, Immigration and Asylum Act 2002, s 143.
[2]   IA 1971, s 25B(1).
[3]   IA 1971, s 25B(2).

15.54 Since a large part of the arrangements for assisting breaches of immigration laws, the illegal entry of EU nationals and for bringing asylum claimants will be made outside the UK, it is provided that acts committed abroad are triable in the UK, if committed by British citizens, British Overseas Territories citizens, British Overseas citizens, British Nationals (Overseas), British Protected Persons and British Subjects, and by companies incorporated in the UK.[1] As noted above, offences are triable in the UK if committed in control zones by persons of any nationality.[2]

[1]   IA 1971, ss 25(6), 25A(4), 25B(4) as substituted and inserted by Nationality, Immigration and Asylum Act 2002, s 143.
[2]   See **15.48** above, text and fn 2.

Trafficking offences

15.55 The Nationality, Immigration and Asylum Act 2002 created a new offence of trafficking in prostitution, making it an offence punishable by up to 14 years' imprisonment to arrange or facilitate a passenger's arrival in, travel within, or departure from the UK, (a) intending to exercise control over prostitution by the passenger in the UK or elsewhere, or (b) believing that another person would do so.[1] The Sexual Offences Act 2003 repealed these provisions and replaced them with an offence of trafficking for sexual exploitation, an offence much broader in its reach.[2] The offence was committed by intentionally arranging or facilitating the arrival in, travel within, or departure from the UK of a passenger, (a) intending to do anything to the passenger in any part of the world which involves the commission of a relevant offence, or (b) believing that another person is likely to do so.[3] In April 2014 a further amendment was made by the coming into force of section 109 of the Protection of Freedoms Act 2012.[4] This new offence is directed at trafficking individuals within *and outside* the UK with a view to sexual exploitation. This offence is committed by intentionally facilitating or arranging the arrival in, or entry into, the UK or another country of a person, or their travel within the UK or another country, or their departure from the UK or another country, with a view to that person's sexual exploitation. A huge range of sexual offences is incorporated within the definition of 'relevant offence'.[5] As with the offences of facilitating arrival at or entry into the UK, the courts have jurisdiction in trafficking cases over acts done in the UK or those done in the UK or abroad, if committed by British nationals of all categories, British Protected Persons or UK-incorporated companies.[6] The placing of the new trafficking for sexual exploitation offence in an immigration statute and then removing it to a sexual offences one raises the question of why it was in the immigration statute in the first place. Although facilitating is an essential element of the offence, it is quite different from the raft of offences dealing with facilitating unlawful immigration, in that there is a clearly identified victim in trafficking. Exercise of control over the victim by the initial trafficker or by others is a key characteristic of the offence. While the victim is nearly always going to have an unlawful immigration status (reason enough for placing it in an immigration statute), it is surprising that domestic immigration law and practice is entirely silent on the measures which need and ought to be taken to protect the victim. Indeed initial experience of the operation of the new laws is that they give authority and justification for rounding up women engaged in prostitution, who are very likely to have been the victims of trafficking, and speedily deporting them, while doing very little against their exploiters. It seems the government has turned its back on the vibrant discussion at UN and EC level on the central question of the protection of victims, which is to give them renewable short term and, in some cases, permanent stay in the country to which they have been taken.[7] Passing the criminal laws is easy; tackling the exploitation and protecting the victims cannot properly be ignored.[8]

[1] Nationality, Immigration and Asylum Act 2002, s 145 (subsequently repealed.

[2] Sexual Offences Act 2003, ss 139, 140, 141(1), Sch 6, 7, in force 1 May 2004: SI 2004/874.

[3] Sexual Offences Act 2003, ss 57–59.

[4] In force 6 April 2013: SI 2013/470. This inserts a new s 59A into the Sexual Offences Act 2003.

[5] SOA 2003, s 60, as amended by the UK Borders Act 2007, s 31(4) and the Protection of Freedoms Act 2012, s 109 (1) and (3)–(5) and s 115(2). The definition includes offences under Part I of the Act and under s 1(1)(a) of the Protection of Children Act 1978, equivalent offences in Northern Ireland, or anything done elsewhere which would be an offence in England, Wales or Northern Ireland.

[6] Nationality, Immigration and Asylum Act 2002, s 146(1), (2) (before repeal); SOA 2003, s 60(2) and (3). These provisions echo the jurisdictional reach of the courts for facilitators (see 15.48 above).

[7] Proposal for a Council Directive on the short-term residence permit issued to victims of action to facilitate illegal immigration or trafficking in human beings who cooperate with the competent authorities COM (2002) 71 final. This Proposal corresponds to recommendations issued by different international organisations on the fight against trafficking in human beings, eg. the Protocol to Prevent, Suppress and Punish Trafficking in Persons, especially Women and Children, supplementing the United Nations Convention Against Transnational Organized Crime, GA res 55/25, Annex II UN GAOR Supp (n° 49) at 60, UN Doc A/45/49 (Vol I) (2001). See further 'Integration of the human rights of women and the gender perspective violence against women', report of the Special Rapporteur on violence against women, its causes and consequences, Radhika Coomaraswamy, on trafficking in women, women's migration and violence against women, submitted in accordance with Commission on Human Rights Resolution 1997/44, Economic and Social Council, E/CN4/2000/68. See also Council of Europe, Parliamentary Assembly Recommendation 1545 (2002), 21.01.2002.

[8] In the CPS *Code for Crown Prosecutors* prosecutors are told that where a defendant or potential defendant is a victim of trafficking they should take cognisance of the CPS Guidance before initiating a prosecution.

15.56 The Asylum and Immigration (Treatment of Claimants etc) Act 2004 creates the offence of trafficking people for exploitation. The offence is designed to deal with the activities of 'snakeheads' and gangmasters who make vast profits bringing people in and making them work as debt slaves, or paying illegally low wages. The activities of these gangs came to public attention when 23 Chinese workers drowned collecting cockles on a Lancashire beach in February 2004. The offence is committed by arranging or facilitating the arrival, travel within the UK or departure of a passenger, intending to exploit the passenger in the UK or elsewhere or believing that another person is likely to do so.[1] As with the case of trafficking for sexual exploitation, the Protection of Freedoms Act 2012 has amended the AI(TC) A 2004 to cover trafficking within and outside the UK with a view to exploitation. The offence is largely directed at exploitation through labour.[2] The scope of the offence now includes facilitating or arranging the travel or departure of another person from another country with a view to their exploitation. Moreover, the offence can be committed by UK nationals, regardless of where the arranging or facilitating takes place, or which country is the country of arrival, entry, travel or departure. As with the new sexual exploitation offence, a non-UK national commits the offence if any part of the arranging or facilitating takes place in the UK or the UK is the country of arrival, entry, travel or departure.[3] Thus the 2013 amendments broaden the territorial reach of the offence and explicitly target foreign perpetrators if operating within or via the UK. As originally enacted, 'exploitation' was defined as:

(i)   behaviour contravening Article 4 ECHR (slavery and forced labour);

(ii)   encouraging, requiring or expecting the passenger to do anything which would amount to an offence under the Human Organ Transplant Act 1989;[4]

(iii)   subjecting the passenger to force, threats or deception to induce him or her to provide services or benefits of any kind or to enable someone else to acquire benefits; or

(iv)   requesting or inducing someone to undertake an activity because they are mentally or physically ill or disabled, young or have a family relationship, when another person without those characteristics is likely to refuse or resist.[5]

The latter definition has since been expanded through amendments by the BCIA 2009, section 54 of which modifies and expands the original definition of exploitation. Specifically, the original requirement in section 4(4)(d) of the AI(TC)A 2004 for an individual to have *been requested or induced to undertake an activity* has been replaced by a new provision that omits altogether the requirement for a request or inducement to undertake an activity.

The amendment seeks to plug a lacuna in the offence of trafficking of people for exploitation arising from the original definition of exploitation. That definition had proved inadequate, as it failed to encompass victims of trafficking who were entirely passive, for example, very young children and babies who could not, as such, be requested or induced to do anything.[6] Section 54 of the BCIA 2009 is intended to deal with this situation. It aims to ensure that victims of trafficking who play an entirely passive role in situations where they are used, or attempts are made to use them, for the purpose of obtaining services or benefits of any kind, are nonetheless protected.

By virtue of section 57(4)(b) of the BCIA 2009, section 54 extends to England and Wales and Northern Ireland only. It is inapplicable to Scotland where the existing definition of 'exploitation' will continue to apply, unless and until amended. Section 54 came into force on 10 November 2009.[7]

The offences carry maximum sentences of 14 years.[8] The provisions about detention and forfeiture of vehicles apply.[9]

In *R v SK*[10] the appellant was charged with an offence under section 4(1) of the Asylum and Immigration (Treatment of Claimants etc) Act 2004 of facilitating the entry into the UK of an individual with the intention of exploiting that individual. The complainant was brought to the UK ostensibly as the defendant's housekeeper but she was made to work almost 24 hours a day, was poorly fed, was never allowed out on her own and seldom with others, had little contact with her family back home, and such contact as she had with them was listened to and sometimes recorded by the appellant. The appellant was convicted and appealed to the Court of Appeal. Her conviction was quashed, it being held that the trial judge had failed properly to direct the jury on the effect of Article 4, ECHR. The court first analysed the case law of the Strasbourg Court in *Siliadin v France*[11] and *Rantsev v Cyprus and Russia*[12] and found assistance in what has been described as the hierarchy of the denial of personal autonomy to which Article 4 and thus section 4 of the 2004 Act relate.[13] In descending order of gravity 'slavery' stands at the top of the hierarchy, 'servitude' in the middle, and 'forced or compulsory labour' at the bottom. Forced labour connotes direct compulsion whereas compulsory labour impliedly includes *indirect* forms of compulsion as well. In most cases the distinction between the two is unnecessary. In his summing up to the jury the trial judge had not gone down this road and this meant that the conviction had to be quashed. The case is one further reminder to those prosecuting or defending in cases which involve immigration crimes that they have to move out of the narrow box of reliance only on domestic law.[14]

In *CN v United Kingdom*[15] the ECtHR further explored the limits of the section 4 offence, there in the context of considering whether the UK was in breach of its positive obligation under Article 4, ECHR to have in place criminal laws penalising forced labour and servitude. The applicant was kept in conditions amounting to domestic servitude. The Court found that while the criminal investigation into the applicant's treatment occasionally referred to slavery, forced labour and domestic servitude, the focus was on the offence of trafficking for exploitation set out in section 4 AI(TC)A 2004. Domestic servitude involved a complex set of dynamics, involving both overt and more subtle forms of coercion, to force compliance. Due to the absence of a specific offence of domestic servitude in UK law, the domestic authorities were unable to give due weight to those factors. Consequently, the investigation into the applicant's complaints of domestic servitude was ineffective and there was a violation of Article 4, ECHR.

1   AI(TC)A 2004, s 4 (in force 1 December 2004: SI 2004/2999).
2   Protection of Freedoms Act 2012, s110 in force 6 April 2013: SI 2013/470. This inserts new subparagraphs (1A)–(1C), (3A), (4A) and (4B) into s 4, AI(TC)A 2004.
3   Sections (4A) and (4B) AI(TC)A 2004.
4   Ie sale of organs.
5   AI(CT)A 2004, s 4(1)–(3).
6   See 'Woman smuggled Baby into the UK to qualify for housing priority', *Guardian*, 12 April 2008, concerning the case of Peace Sandberg.
7   See BCIA 2009, s 58(4)(b) and SI 2009/2731, art 3(a).
8   AI(CT)A 2004, s 4(4).

[9] AI(CT)A 2004, s 5(4).

[10] [2011] EWCA Crim 1691, [2011] 2 Cr App Rep 502, 175 CL&J 485. The court noted that a new offence of holding a person in slavery or servitude or requiring another person to perform forced or compulsory labour has been created by section 71 of the Coroners and Justice Act 2009.

[11] (Application 73316/01) (2005) 43 EHRR 287, 20 BHRC 654, ECtHR (a minor, who had been trafficked to France and made to perform unpaid domestic work for a family for 15 hours a day, seven days a week, was held to have been in servitude, contrary to Article 4).

[12] (Application 25965/04), (2010) 55 EHRR 1, 28 BHRC 313, ECtHR which concluded that in the light of present day conditions it was unnecessary to decide whether a victim of trafficking was thereby in slavery, servitude or forced labour and held that 'trafficking itself, within the meaning of Article 3(a) of the Palermo Protocol and Article 4(a) of the Anti-Traffick-ing Convention falls within the scope of article 4 of the Convention'. See **7.61** of the main text.

[13] This is based on Clayton and Tomlinson's 'The Law of Human Rights' (2nd edn), vol I, paras 9.17–9. 20 (on the concepts of 'slavery' and 'servitude') and para 9.25 (on the concept of 'forced or compulsory labour'.

[14] See *R v Abdalla (Mohammed)* [2010] EWCA Crim 2400 at **16.59**; *R v LM* [2010] EWCA Crim 2327, [2011] 1 Cr App Rep 135, [2011] Crim LR 425, at **16.87**.

[15] (Application 4239/08), (2013) 56 EHRR 24, 34 BHRC 1.

Don't penalise victims

Non punishment under Article 26 of the Anti-Trafficking Convention 2005

15.57 Under the Council of Europe Convention on Action against Trafficking in Human Beings 2005 (CETS No 197) ('the Anti-Trafficking Convention') the UK is bound to adopt legislative and other measures to identify and protect victims of trafficking. The process is described in CHAPTER **13** and much of the legislative and other steps taken by the UK authorities is summarised by the Court of Appeal its recent (criminal) decision in *R v LM*,[1] including the definition of trafficking in Article 4 of the Convention, the duty to identify victims of trafficking in Article 10 and the agencies set up to carry out the identification obligations. Here we concentrate on Article 26 which is headed 'Non punishment Provision' and provides as follows:

> 'Each party shall, in accordance with the basic principles of its legal system, *provide for the possibility of not imposing penalties* on victims for their involvement in unlawful activities to the extent that they have been compelled to do so.' (our emphasis)

According to the court in *LM*, the implementation of Article 26 in England and Wales is achieved through three mechanisms:

(1) English law recognises the common law defences of duress and necessity ('duress of circumstances').

(2) Specific rules have been made for the guidance of prosecutors in considering whether charges should be brought against those who are or may have been victims of trafficking.

(3) In the event that the duty laid on the prosecutor to exercise judgment is not properly discharged, the ultimate sanction is the power of the court to stay the prosecution for what is conveniently, if not very accurately, termed 'abuse of process'.

The court then deals with each of these in turn.

Duress and necessity. The court sets out the ambit and limitations of the common law defences of duress and necessity, otherwise known as duress of circumstances. If either applies then the case may be disposed of under the ordinary rules relating to these defences, although the same facts may also lead to discontinuance of the prosecution within the terms of the Convention.

CPS Guidance to prosecutors. The court points out that the special guidance to prosecutors issued by the CPS at the time of these offences, in order to comply with the Convention, imposes on them a duty which includes but is wider than consideration of these common law defences, so that even where there is no clear evidence of a credible common law defence, but the offence may have been committed as a result of *compulsion arising from the trafficking*, prosecutors should consider whether the public interest lies in proceeding to prosecute or not. This approach is consistent, said the court, with the requirements of Article 26, which, it is clear, uses the word 'compelled' in a general sense appropriate to international instrument, and is not limited to circumstances in which the English common law defences would be established. Although the latest CPS Guidelines are given in the context of consideration of immigration offences, the obligation under Article 26 is not confined to immigration offences, but extends to any offence where it may have been committed by a trafficked victim who has been compelled to commit it.

The ambit of the Article 26 obligation. The court points out (at [13]) that Article 26 does:

'not say that no trafficked victim should be prosecuted, whatever offence has been committed. It does not say that no trafficked victim should be prosecuted when the offence is in some way connected with or arises out of trafficking. It does not provide a defence which may be advanced before a jury. What it says is no more, but no less, than that careful consideration must be given to whether public policy calls for a prosecution and punishment when the defendant is a trafficked victim and the crime has been committed when he or she was in some manner compelled (in the broad sense) to commit it. Article 26 does not require blanket immunity from prosecution for trafficked victims. It follows that the application of Article 26 is fact sensitive in every case.'

At [14] the court ventures some general propositions without giving an exhaustive analysis of all possible factual situations.

Stay for abuse of process. The court accepts that the power to stay for 'abuse' exists as a safety net to ensure that the Article 26 obligation is not wrongly neglected in an individual case to the disadvantage of the defendant (at [18]). 'Thus the convention obligation is that a prosecuting authority must apply its mind conscientiously to the question of public policy and reach an informed decision. If it follows the advice in the earlier version of the guidance . . . . . then it will do so. If however this exercise of judgment has not properly been carried out and would or might well have resulted in a decision not to prosecute, then there will be a breach of the convention and hence grounds for a stay. Likewise, if a decision has been reached at which no reasonable prosecutor could arrive, there will be grounds for a stay. Thus in effect the role of the court is one of review. The test is akin to that upon judicial review,' but is not one of proportionality (at [19]).

From the above, it can be seen that this case is both important and complicated. For criminal practitioners it is not the straightforward situation of a common law defence, as the court has explained. It introduces a public law obligation based on an international treaty. It is an obligation which requires the exercise of discretion arising from different fact sensitive situations by the CPS and a full consideration of the factual situation and the lawfulness and rationality of a decision to proceed with a prosecution. It is therefore more complicated than the situation under Article 31 of the Refugee Convention. Considerable concern was expressed by the Court of Appeal over the failings of some practitioners properly to advise their clients or the courts with regard to criminal charges brought against victims of trafficking. The court said it is apparent that at present the provisions of the Convention, and particularly of Article 26, are not sufficiently known generally amongst the profession, even though the court had drawn attention to the importance of the terms of the Convention in the 2008 case of *R v O*.[2]

In *L v R, The Children's Comr for England and Equality and Human Rights Commission intervening*[3] the Court of Appeal considered, *inter alia*, the impact of EU Directive 2011/36/EU on Preventing and Combating Trafficking in Human Beings and Protecting its Victims, Article 8 of which is in similar terms to Article 26 of the Anti-Trafficking Convention' and provides an obligation on Member States to ensure that national authorities are entitled not to prosecute or impose penalties on victims of trafficking. The appellants, three of whom were child victims of trafficking, had argued that since the Directive was directly effective, the courts' obligation to safeguard the rights of trafficking victims was independent of its jurisdiction to review the a prosecutor's decision to bring or continue a prosecution. The Court held that issues relating to the age of the defendant, whether the defendant was a victim of trafficking and whether the alleged offences were an aspect of the defendant, were, in line with *LM*, to be resolved by the exercise of the jurisdiction to stay a prosecution, albeit that the Directive had become directly effective. When an abuse of process argument was advanced on behalf of an alleged victim of trafficking, the court would reach its own view on the basis of the material advanced in support of and against the continuation of the prosecution and would stay the prosecution if it disagreed with the decision to prosecute[4]. Where it is found that a defendant has been a victim of trafficking that will diminish culpability[5]. In the case where a defendant was alleged to be a child victim of trafficking, first the defendant's age had be ascertained, and second the evidence suggestive of trafficking had to be assessed. In the event that the defendant was found to be a victim of trafficking a distinct question for consideration was the extent to which the alleged offending behaviour was consequent on and integral to his exploitation. These were fact specific issues.[6]

The prosecution was under an obligation to disclose all material bearing on the issues of age, trafficking, exploitation and culpability. Where any issue arose it had to be dealt with head on at the first appearance, or alternatively raised at the plea and case management hearing, with the court adjourning as appropriate for further information from the UKBA (now the Home Office)and other authorities.[7]

1   [2010] EWCA Crim 2327.
2   [2008] EWCA Crim 283.
3   [2013] EWCA Crim 991.
4   Paras [13]–[18].
5   See para [13] per Lord Judge CJ: 'when there is evidence that victims of trafficking have been involved in criminal activities, the investigation and the decision whether there should be a prosecution, and, if so, any subsequent proceedings require to be approached with the greatest

sensitivity. The reasoning is not always spelled out, and perhaps we should do so now. The criminality, or putting it another way, the culpability, of any victim of trafficking may be significantly diminished, and in some cases effectively extinguished, not merely because of age (always a relevant factor in the case of a child defendant) but because no realistic alternative was available to the exploited victim but to comply with the dominant force of another individual, or group of individuals.'

6   Para [10].
7   Paras [29]–[31].

Breach of conditions and overstaying

15.58 A person who is not a British citizen commits a criminal offence if, having only a limited leave to enter or remain in the UK, he or she knowingly either:

(i)   remains beyond the time limited by the leave; or
(ii)   fails to observe a condition of the leave.[1]

Both these offences are summary only. The maximum penalty is six months' imprisonment and a fine at level 5,[2] and police and immigration officers may arrest suspected offenders without warrant.[3]

1   IA 1971, s 24(1)(b), as amended by British Nationality Act 1981, Sch 4, para 2.
2   Set at £5,000: Criminal Justice Act 1982, s 37(2), as amended by Criminal Justice Act 1991, s 17.
3   IA 1971, s 28A, inserted by IAA 1999, s 128.

15.59 Overstaying used to be the most common immigration offence but since overstayers' rights of appeal against deportation were restricted in 1988,[1] it has rarely been used. The wording of the offence gives rise to difficulty: 'having' a limited leave does not readily fit an offence of remaining beyond the leave. It is entirely appropriate for the second limb of the offence, where there must be an extant leave in order for there to be a breach of conditions.[2] To make sense of the wording, 'having' has to be interpreted as meaning 'having had', although such an interpretation of identical words in section 14 of the IA 1971 was rejected by the House of Lords in the case of *Suthendran*.[3] The offence of overstaying is defined as a continuing offence which is committed at any time when the immigrant knows that the time limited by his or her leave has expired and nevertheless remains in the UK.[4] There is no need for any provision to extend the time limits for prosecution. But a person cannot be prosecuted more than once in respect of the same limited leave.[5]

1   By Immigration Act 1988, s 5. The IAA 1999, s 10 made overstayers and those in breach of conditions of leave liable to administrative removal rather than deportation and removed rights of appeal (except on asylum or human rights grounds).
2   *Singh (Gurdev) v R* [1974] 1 All ER 26, [1973] 1 WLR 1444, DC.
3   Suthendran v Immigration Appeal Tribunal [1977] AC 359, [1976] 3 All ER 611, HL.
4   IA 1971, s 24(1A), inserted by Immigration Act 1988, s 6, except in relation to persons whose leave had expired before 10 July 1988, for whom the offence could only be committed on the day following the expiry of their leave: *Grant v Borg* [1982] 2 All ER 257, [1982] 1 WLR 638, HL.
5   IA 1971, s 24(1A), as amended.

15.60 Persons who applied before the expiry of their leave for further leave and who remain awaiting a decision on their application are not overstayers because their leave is extended by statute until the end of the period allowed for the bringing of an in country appeal, and while any appeal is pending.[1] These considerations give rise to evidential difficulties in that the expiry date on the leave stamp in a passport is not conclusive evidence that the accused has overstayed.[2]

[1] IA 1971, s 3C, substituted by the Nationality, Immigration and Asylum Act (NIAA) 2002, s 118, and as amended by IAN 2006, s 11, which came into force on 31 August 2006. The normal period allowed for the bringing of an appeal under NIAA 2002, s 82(1) is ten days: Asylum and Immigration Tribunal (Procedure) Rules 2005, SI 2005/230, r 7.

[2] See *Zoltak v Sussex Constabulary* [1983] CLY 1923 where a conviction for overstaying was quashed where the defendant had applied for an extension, and the application was date-stamped as received two days after his leave expired. The court held that since the application was made when it was posted (following *Lubetkin v Secretary of State for the Home Department* [1979–80] Imm AR 162) the prosecutor had not established that on the date of the alleged offence the defendant did not have deemed leave under the provisions of the Immigration (Variation of Leave Order) 1976, the precursor of s 3C.

15.61 A conviction for overstaying requires proof of knowledge. A belief that one's leave expires on a different date is a mistake of fact; so also is the belief that another person – a friend or agent – has made an application for an extension when this is not the case. There may be cases of illiterate persons or persons whose comprehension of English is so poor that they do not appreciate that their leave has expired, or persons whose employer has retained their passport and has never shown the employee the endorsement. Sheer forgetfulness, and oversight owing to the stress caused by bereavement, may be capable of providing good defences.[1]

[1] *Immigration Appeal Tribunal v Chelliah* [1985] Imm AR 192, CA; R v Bello (1978) 67 Cr App Rep 288, [1978] Crim LR 551, CA (dismissed on the facts).

15.62 Since the right of entry and residence of EEA nationals flows directly from the provisions of EU law and is not subject to the requirements of the IA 1971 to obtain leave to enter or remain,[1] it is difficult to see how an EEA national covered by the free movement provisions of the EC Treaty (now incorporated and renumbered into the Treaty of Lisbon) can commit the offence of overstaying under section 24(1)(b) of the 1971 Act by remaining after his or her residence permit expires. The 'no visa' rule, however, does not apply to members of the EEA worker's family who are not EEA nationals. They are required to obtain a family permit confirming their rights of entry under EU law (see CHAPTER 6 above). But their rights flow from EU law and provided they continue to qualify as members of the family, they should not be liable to criminal or administrative action for remaining beyond the time limited by their permit.

[1] *R v Pieck*: 157/79 [1981] QB 571, [1981] 3 All ER 46, ECJ; Immigration Act 1988, s 7.

15.63 Under section 8(1) of the IA 1971,[1] as we have seen, crews of ships, international trains and aircraft are allowed entry without leave until their ship, train or aircraft leaves the country again. Under section 24(1)(c) of the 1971 Act it is an offence if seamen or air or train crews stay longer than the temporary period of admission normally allowed under section 8(1) when their ship, train or aircraft docks, arrives or lands here. The extended time limit applies to such offences,[2] and they may be arrested without warrant by the police or immigration officers if with reasonable cause they are suspected of having committed such an offence.[3] This offence was intended in particular to catch seamen who deserted ship when it arrived in the UK, but it is a less effective way, from the authorities' point of view, than the extensive administrative powers of removal under Schedule 2 to the 1971 Act.

[1] Modified in relation to international trains by the Channel Tunnel (International Arrangements) Order 1993, SI 1993/1813, art 7, Sch 4, para 1(7); Channel Tunnel (Miscellaneous Provisions) Order 1994, SI 1994/1405, art 7.
[2] IA 1971, ss 24(3), 28.
[3] IA 1971, s 28A, inserted by IAA 1999, s 128.

15.64 Conditions can only be attached to a limited leave to remain, and the only conditions that can be attached to leave are a restriction on employment or occupation in the UK, a restriction on studies in the UK, a condition requiring an immigrant to maintain and accommodate him or herself and any dependants without recourse to public funds, or to register with the police, or to report to an immigration officer or the Secretary of State, or a condition about residence, or all six.[1] Thus there is no power to attach conditions to an indefinite leave, and where a limited leave is extended to become an indefinite leave any conditions automatically cease.[2] Where a limited leave is subject to conditions, an automatic extension of leave under the statutory provisions also extends the conditions.[3] However, a person can only be guilty of the offence of a breach of conditions during a period in which the conditions apply; where the leave itself has run out and is not extended by statute (whether by an application or by an appeal) there is nothing for the conditions to attach to and the conditions will lapse.[4] Thereafter a person may be guilty of overstaying the leave but not of contravening restrictions attached to it.[5] Thus a person who takes employment after the expiry of leave is not committing any additional offence by doing so (although his or her employer is: see **15.94** ff below). The same principles apply to persons who are required to register with the police; this requirement attaches to a leave and expires with the leave.[6] The offence is a continuing one in that the Crown is not confined to the first occasion of the breach of condition.[7] The extended time limit for prosecutions does not apply to an offence of breach of conditions, and a prosecution must, therefore, be brought within six months of the commission of the offence. Knowledge of the conditions is a prerequisite of the offence.

[1] IA 1971, s 3(1)(c), as amended by Asylum and Immigration Act 1996, Sch 2, para 1(1), the UK Borders Act 2007, s 16 and the Borders, Citizenship and Immigration Act 2009, s 50(1).
[2] IA 1971, s 3(3)(a).
[3] IA 1971, s 3C, as substituted by Nationality, Immigration and Asylum Act 2002 s 118; *Ali (Shaukat) v Chief Adjudication Officer* (1985) Times, 24 December, CA; *Rajendran (Kangeyan) v Secretary of State for the Home Department* [1989] Imm AR 512.
[4] *Suthendran v Immigration Appeal Tribunal* [1977] AC 359, [1976] 3 All ER 611, HL.
[5] *Singh (Gurdev) v R* [1974] 1 All ER 26, [1973] 1 WLR 1444, DC.
[6] *R v Naik* (1978) Times, 26 July, CA.
[7] *Manickavasagar v Metropolitan Police Comr* [1987] Crim LR 50, DC. See further *Singh (Gurdev)* above.

15.65 Where a person is given temporary admission – either pending a further examination on entry, or pending removal as an illegal entrant, overstayer or deportee – it is an offence to fail to observe any requirements as to residence, employment or occupation, or reporting to the police, an immigration officer or the Secretary of State, without reasonable excuse.[1] A person who has been placed on board a train, ship or aircraft pursuant to removal directions commits an offence if he or she disembarks, as does a person who embarks in contravention of an Order in Council made under the provision of the IA 1971 to permit retaliatory measures or hostage orders.[2] The extended time limits do not apply to any of the offences considered in this section.

[1] IA 1971, s 24(1)(e), as amended by Nationality, Immigration and Asylum Act 2002, s 62(9). The amendment reflects the fact that the Secretary of State has most of the powers of immigration officers in respect of entry. Failure to cooperate with electronic monitoring, once the requisite regulations are in force, will be treated for these purposes as failure to comply with a residence or reporting condition: Asylum and Immigration (Treatment of Claimants) Act 2004, s 36(2)(b), (3)(b). Immigration officers may arrest for this and offences under sections 24(1)(a), 24(1)(b), 24(1)(c), 24(1)(d) and 24(1)(f), 24A, 26A or 26B provided they have a warrant: s 28B; for arrest without a warrant, see **15.4** above.

[2] IA 1971, s 24(1)(f) and (g), modified in its application to the Channel Tunnel by the Channel Tunnel (International Arrangements) Order 1993, art 7(1), Sch 4, para 1(7).

Breach of immigration officers' directions

15.66 A variety of miscellaneous offences exist to back up the immigration officer's powers on examination and removal, although they have rarely been used in the past. Thus it is an offence to fail to comply with a direction to report to a medical officer of health, as directed, or to fail to attend or to submit to an examination required by such an officer.[1] There is a defence of reasonable excuse, which might apply, for example, to a refusal to undergo an examination which was not conducted by properly qualified medical staff. There used to be no power of arrest for this offence, but a power of arrest on warrant was created in 2002.[2] Immigration officers may search premises to effect an arrest with a warrant.[3]

[1] IA 1971, s 24(1)(d).
[2] IA 1971, s 28AA, inserted by Nationality, Immigration and Asylum Act 2002, s 152.
[3] IA 1971, s 28B, inserted by IAA 1999, s 129.

Failure to cooperate with arrangements for removal

15.67 The AI(TC)A 2004 creates the offence of failure without reasonable excuse to comply with a requirement of the Secretary of State imposed to facilitate the obtaining of a travel document and the person's deportation or removal.[1] The offence may be committed by failing to comply with a requirement to:

- provide information or documents to the Secretary of State or anyone else;
- obtain information or documents;
- provide fingerprints and submit to the taking of a photograph;
- submit to a process for the recording of information about external physical characteristics such as the iris;
- make or consent or cooperate with making an application to the representative of another government;
- cooperate with a process designed to enable determination of an application;
- complete a form accurately and completely;
- attend an interview and answer questions accurately and completely;

- make an appointment.[2]

Failure to comply can result in imprisonment for up to two years on indictment, or to six months or the statutory maximum fine on summary conviction.[3] The offence carries a power of arrest without warrant.[4] As the Joint Committee on Human Rights noted, the section would enable the administration to abuse its power by demanding information and cooperation which could then be used to facilitate the person's deportation later.[5] It could create grave dangers for those wrongly refused asylum and for any relatives in the home country.[6] Furthermore, if during the course of the interview there arises a suspicion that the detainee may have committed a criminal offence, the interview should immediately stop, the caution should be administered, and the suspect should be told of his or her right to a lawyer, and, in appropriate circumstances to consular access.

1 Asylum and Immigration (Treatment of Claimants etc) Act 2004, s 35(3). Home Office guidance indicates that once the defendant raises an excuse it is for the Crown to disprove it or show it was not reasonable. Examples of reasonable excuse given in the guidance are limited to medical emergencies or transport problems; but see fn 6 below. see Enforcement instructions and guidance, Chapter 18: 'Amended Instructions for documenting removals and the implementation of section 35 of the Asylum and Immigration (Treatment of Claimants) Act 2004 in non-compliant cases' at para 8,5 The guidance cites *R v Tabnak* [2007] EWCA Crim 380 as establishing that a fear of persecution could not amount to a reasonable excuse for these purposes.
2 AI(TC)A 2004, s 35(1), (2)(a)–(h).
3 AI(TC)A 2004, s 35(4).
4 AI(TC)A 2004, s 35(5).
5 Joint Committee on Human Rights 5th report session 2003–4, 10.2.04, para 79.
6 The court accepted in *R (on the application of Amirthanathan) v Secretary of State for the Home Department* (upheld in the Court of Appeal with no reference to this part of the judgment, as *Nadarajah v Secretary of State for the Home Department;R (on the application of Amirthanathan) v Secretary of State for the Home Department* [2003] EWCA Civ 1768, (2003) Sol Jo LB 24, that 'once an appeal is lodged it is inappropriate to require a person to give an interview to the authorities of the destination country to facilitate the obtaining of a travel document, since the interview might lead to information being provided which might put the claimant or his family at risk'.

Offences in connection with the administration of the Immigration Acts

15.68 There are a number of summary offences which serve to emphasise the extensive powers of immigration officers when conducting an examination on entry. Persons who refuse or fail to submit to such an examination,[1] who refuse or fail to produce information in their possession, or documents under their control which they are required to produce, or fail to complete a landing card or embarkation card, commit offences if they have no reasonable excuse.[2] It is also an offence to fail without lawful excuse to comply with any regulations regarding registering with the police or keeping hotel records.[3]

1 IA 1971, s 26(1)(a). The maximum penalties are now six months' imprisonment or a level 5 fine. The offences are summary only.
2 IA 1971, s 26(1)(b). It is arguable that a reasonable excuse not to provide information would exist, if the examination interview involves asking certain questions, without administering the caution and informing the person of his or her right to a lawyer and possible consular access. These are questions about criminal offences, such as not having valid travel documents contrary to AI(TC)A 2004, s 2, of which the passenger has become a suspect. See **15.39** ff above.

[3]   IA 1971, s 26(1)(f).

15.69 Two of these offences bear closer examination. The first is that of making a false statement under section 26(1)(c) of the IA 1971. It is an offence to make a return, statement, or representation which is known to be false or not believed to be true to an immigration officer or other person acting in the execution of a 'relevant enactment', either on a 1971 Act, Schedule 2 examination or otherwise.[1] 'Otherwise' means otherwise acting in execution of the relevant Act. So the phrase qualifies both the person to whom the statement is made and the circumstances in which it is made. A great many people act in the course of their employment in functions which promote the purposes of the Acts, but they are not acting in the execution of the 'relevant enactments'.[2] The offence is committed where the false statement is addressed to a person pursuing a right or duty under one of the relevant Acts to receive information, and includes immigration officers, entry clearance officers,[3] and perhaps also medical inspectors, police officers acting under the 1971 Act, Home Office officials who process applications to vary and the appellate authorities. The offence (along with all the other section 26 offences) may be committed in a control zone.[4] Prior to 1999, the offence could only be committed in relation to a person exercising functions under the 1971 Act. The amendments in 1999 and 2002 broadened the scope of the offence, which can now be committed by telling lies to a wider range of people – a detainee custody officer in a contracted-out detention centre[5] or to a NASS sub-contractor,[6] for instance, and can be committed by a much wider range of people in respect of a vastly wider range of functions. Lies told by a third party to an immigration officer who is searching a property for a person or for documents could be covered, since such a search is now a statutory function.

[1]   The phrase 'relevant enactments' was inserted and defined by IAA 1999, s 30, and amended by Nationality, Immigration and Asylum Act 2002, s 151. The 'relevant enactments' are defined as the IA 1971, the Immigration Act 1988, the Asylum and Immigration Appeals Act 1993, the IAA 1999 (apart from Part VI) or the Nationality, Immigration and Asylum Act 2002 (apart from Part 5).
[2]   *R v Clarke* [1985] AC 1037, [1985] 2 All ER 777, HL in which lies told to police investigating an offence under the IA 1971 were held not to constitute the offence since the officers were not acting 'in the execution of the Act'.
[3]   *R v Secretary of State for the Home Department, ex p Kwadwo Saffu-Mensah* [1991] Imm AR 43, QBD, affirmed on different grounds in the Court of Appeal [1992] Imm AR 185. Though made abroad, such representations may be prosecutable in the UK as an act done to obtain a benefit here, or having a real and substantial link with the UK: *R v Baxter* [1972] 1 QB 1, [1971] 2 All ER 359, CA; *DPP v Stonehouse* [1977] 2 All ER 909 at 913; *Somchai Liangsiriprasert v Government of the United States of America* [1991] 1 AC 225, PC – although the explicit territorial extensions elsewhere in the Act make such an implied extension unlikely, particularly in the penal context.
[4]   Nationality, Immigration and Asylum Act 2002 (Juxtaposed Controls) Order 2003, SI 2003/2818, art 12.
[5]   In respect of the functions performed under IAA 1999, Pt VIII in contracted-out detention centres.
[6]   In respect of the provision of accommodation; however these would more likely be charged as asylum support offences, for which see **14.81** below.

15.70 According to *Khawaja v Secretary of State for the Home Department* the Crown needs to prove that the false representation concerned was 'effective' in obtaining leave to enter, but subsequent cases have suggested that the deception need only be 'material' in the sense that it was likely to influence the decision to allow entry.¹ Nowadays, making false representations to immigration officers giving leave to enter, or to Home Office officials giving leave to remain or deciding on removal or deportation, is more likely to be charged as deception (if performed by the immigrant) or assisting a breach of immigration law or obstruction (if performed by third parties). These offences are committed if the means of entry, remaining, etc included deception.² Charging deception also gets round the technical problems described in **15.68** above and discussed in *R v Clarke*³ as to when a person was acting in the execution of the relevant Act.

¹ See **18.21** below. In *R v Secretary of State for the Home Department, ex p Castro* [1996] Imm AR 540, the court held that the deception of the mother was both effective and material in obtaining the leave for her children. The case was not a criminal case but a judicial review of a decision that the person was an illegal entrant, following *Khawaja v Secretary of State for the Home Department* [1984] AC 74, [1983] 1 All ER 765, [1983] 2 WLR 321, [1982] Imm AR 139, HL, which held that the offence was at the heart of illegal entry by deception. Perhaps more importantly the court decided that a deceit by the mother could be imputed to her children under s 26(1)(c), following *R v Secretary of State for the Home Department, ex p Khan* [1977] 1 WLR 1466, CA and an *obiter* in *R v Secretary of State for the Home Department, ex p Salim* [1990] Imm AR 316 at 323–4, and distinguishing *R v Immigration Officer, ex p Chan* [1992] 1 WLR 541, CA and *R v Secretary of State for the Home Department, ex p Kuet* [1995] Imm AR 274, CA.
² See **15.36** above.
³ *R v Clarke* [1985] AC 1037, [1985] 2 All ER 777, HL.

15.71 There is also an offence of obstructing an immigration officer or other person acting in execution of the IA 1971.¹ By analogy with the offence of obstructing a police officer, the offence would require some physical or other unlawful activity which prevents or impedes a person from carrying out some particular duty entrusted to them by the Act.² Where the obstruction consists of a refusal to do something requested by an immigration official, the offence will only be committed if there is a duty under the Act to do what is requested, such as permitting inspection of luggage by an immigration officer.³ The offence can be committed in a control zone.⁴ There is a restricted power of arrest without warrant for obstruction, on failure of the suspect to provide a reliable name or address.⁵ An additional offence of assaulting an immigration officer has been created by the UKBA 2007. A person who assaults an immigration officer commits a summary offence which can be punished by imprisonment or a fine or both.⁶ An immigration officer may arrest an offender without warrant if the officer reasonably suspects that the person has committed or is about to commit this offence and may enter premises and carry out searches in accordance with various IA 1971 powers, as we have seen.⁷

¹ IA 1971, s 26(1)(g).
² See R v Clarke [1985] AC 1037, [1985] 2 All ER 777, HL.
³ IA 1971, Sch 2, para 4.
⁴ Nationality, Immigration and Asylum Act 2002 (Juxtaposed Controls) Order 2003, SI 2003/2818, art 12.
⁵ IA 1971, s 28A(5), inserted by IAA 1999, s 128.
⁶ UKBA 2007, s 22(1). The levels of fine and imprisonment England and Wales, Northern Ireland and Scotland are set out at UKBA 2007, s 22(2)–(5).
⁷ UKBA 2007, s 23(1)–(3).

15.72 The final offences in connection with the administration of the Immigration Acts are in respect of documents and stamps. It is an offence to alter a certificate of entitlement, entry clearance, work permit or other document issued or made under or for the purposes of the IA 1971 or used for its purposes.[1] This might include police registration books. These are all documents emanating from the UK authorities. Furthermore it is an offence to use for the purposes of the 1971 Act, or to possess with intent to use, any passport, certificate of entitlement, entry clearance, work permit or other document which a person knows to be false or has reasonable cause to believe to be false.[2] The category of documents here is wider, and might include any document presented to an immigration officer or Home Office official for the purpose of obtaining leave to enter or remain. The reference to a document being false must be a reference to a false particular of a material kind to give the general character of falsity to the document.[3] The document concerned must actually be false for the offence to be committed;[4] the reasonable cause for belief in its falsity is necessary but not sufficient for the offence to be made out. It is likely that the defendant must actually believe the document to be false.[5] The penalties for this, as for the other 1971 Act, section 26 offences, are a fine on level 5 and up to six months' imprisonment.[6] If the possession or use of the false document is related to a bona fide quest for asylum, the section 31/Article 31(1) defence is available.[7]

[1] IA 1971, s 26(1)(d).
[2] IA 1971, s 26(1)(d).
[3] See Webster J in *R v Secretary of State for the Home Department, ex p Patel* [1986] Imm AR 208, QBD; affd [1986] Imm AR 515, CA.
[4] By analogy with the assisting offences of ss 25, 25A and 25B of the IA 1971, which have the same wording – those assisted must actually be illegal entrants or asylum claimants: see *R v Naillie* [1993] AC 674.
[5] By analogy with 'reasonable grounds for suspicion', which requires actual suspicion: *O'Hara v Chief Constable of Royal Ulster Constabulary* [1997] AC 286, HL. See discussion in *R v Secretary of State for the Home Department, ex p Rouse* (1985) Times, 25 November, QBD.
[6] IA 1971, s 26. The fine is currently £5,000: Criminal Justice Act 1982, s 37, as amended by Criminal Justice Act 1991, s 17.
[7] IAA 1999, s 31; Refugee Convention, art 31(1): see **15.44–15.46** above.

15.73 All the offences discussed in this section can be committed by British as well as non-British citizens. There is no power of arrest without warrant, and the offences must be prosecuted within six months, save the offences of false statements and false documents, in respect of which the extended time limit applies.

15.74 The NIAA 2002 created new offences relating to registration cards and immigration stamps. It is an offence to make a false registration card, or to alter a registration card with intent to deceive, or to use or attempt to use a false or altered card with intent to deceive, or to make something designed to be used in making or altering a card, or to possess a false or altered card or a forgery tool without reasonable excuse.[1] The offences, unlike those in s 26(1)(d), are triable either way, and making, altering or using carry a sentence of up to ten years' imprisonment on indictment, while offences of possession carry up to two years on indictment.[2] The registration card is defined as a document which carries information about a person (whether or not electronic) and is used by the Secretary of State in connection with an asylum claim (whether or not by that person).[3] The Immigration (Registration Card) Order 2008, SI 2008/1693 extends the definition of 'registration card' to include documents issued by the Secretary of State to a person wholly or partly in connection with a claim for support under s 4 of the Immigration and Asylum Act 1999 (whether or not made by that person). Support under s 4(1) is available to a number of classes of people subject to immigration control, including those with temporary admission, those released from detention and persons on bail under immigration provisions. The majority of people supported are destitute former asylum seekers whose claim for asylum was rejected and who are temporarily unable to leave the United Kingdom for reasons beyond their control. The offences of possession of an immigration stamp or a replica stamp without reasonable excuse[4] carry sentences up to two years on indictment.[5] Both offences carry powers of arrest without warrant[6] and the other ancillary powers of search of premises.[7]

1   IA 1971, s 26A, inserted by the Nationality, Immigration and Asylum Act 2002, s 148.
2   IA 1971, s 26A(5), (6). On summary trial they carry six months' imprisonment and/or a fine up to the statutory maximum.
3   The asylum registration card carries a wealth of information, including biometric information: see 15.23 above. Applicants and their dependants each have a card, which serves as evidence of their status in the UK. The anomaly between the penalties for offences under s 26 (including deception) and s 26A is likely to result in prosecution under s 26A rather than s 26.
4   IA 1971, s 26B, inserted by the Nationality, Immigration and Asylum Act 2002, s 148.
5   IA 1971, s 26B(4). On summary trial the penalties are as for the s 26A offences: see fn 2 above.
6   IA 1971, s 28A(9) inserted by the NIAA 2002, s 150.
7   IA 1971, s 28B(5) and s 28D(4), as amended by the NIAA 2002, s 150.

Extended time limit

15.75 Normally the time limit for bringing a prosecution for a summary offence is six months.[1] This normal time limit applies to most immigration offences, but, as already indicated, there are a number of offences to which the extended time limit, set out in section 28 of the IA 1971, applies. In particular, it applies to the offences of illegal entry, overstaying[2] and making a false statement or altering a document.[3] In England and Wales the extended time limit enables a magistrates' court to try an information if it is laid within three years after the commission of the offence and not more than two months after the date certified by a chief officer of police to be the date on which evidence sufficient to justify proceedings came to the notice of an officer of that police force.[4] In Scotland the certifying officer is the Lord Advocate[5] and in Northern Ireland, a police officer not below the rank of assistant chief constable.[6] The 'trial' of the information begins with the hearing of the information, not with the plea of not guilty, which only marks the need for a trial.[7] 'Evidence' means more than information given over the telephone, which would be inadmissible in proceedings.[8]

1   Magistrates' Courts Act 1980, s 127.
2   IA 1971, s 24(3).
3   IA 1971, s 26(2).
4   IA 1971, s 28(1)(a).
5   IA 1971, s 28(1)(b).
6   IA 1971, s 28(1)(c).
7   *Quazi v DPP* (1988) 152 JP 385.
8   *Enaas v Dovey* (1986) Times, 25 November

15.76 The operation of the extended time limit was illustrated in *Ex p Offei*,[1] where a certificate to enable an extended time limit to apply had been signed by the chief constable, but officers from the same force had interviewed the applicant in connection with his overstaying at least 18 months earlier than the two-month period to which the certificate related. As a result of the earlier interview, all the evidence needed to prosecute him for an offence against section 24(1)(b) of the IA 1971 was to hand. The Divisional Court quashed his conviction, holding that by reason of the earlier interview there was evidence sufficient to justify proceedings and the certificate was therefore a nullity. The court held that there would not have been sufficient evidence if the overstayer's whereabouts were unknown. It also held that the challenge to the validity of the certificate was for the High Court rather than the magistrates,[2] although a different view was taken in *Enaas v Dovey*,[3] which held that magistrates could go behind the certificate to see whether the decision of the chief of police was reasonable. Resolution of these conflicting views has not yet happened. The sufficiency of evidence is a matter for the chief of police's judgment, which can only be successfully challenged if it is unreasonable in a *Wednesbury*[4] sense. The extended time limit for prosecution is no longer of importance in relation to the offence of overstaying, since it can be prosecuted at any time until the person leaves the country (see **15.58** above), but it is still important in offences which are not continuing, such as illegal entry and using a false document.

[1]   *R v Clerk to Birmingham Justices, ex p Offei* (28 November 1985, unreported), QBD.
[2]   By analogy with the absence of the Director of Public Prosecutions' consent in *R v Angel* [1968] 2 All ER 607n, [1968] 1 WLR 669, CA.
[3]   (1986) Times, 25 November.
[4]   *Associated Provincial Picture Houses Ltd v Wednesbury Corpn* [1948] 1 KB 223, [1947] 2 All ER 680, CA.

Offences in relation to passports and acquisition of nationality

15.77 It is an offence punishable on summary conviction by a fine up to level 5[1] or up to three months' imprisonment, or both, for any person, for the purpose of procuring anything to be done or not to be done under the British Nationality Act 1981, knowingly or recklessly to make any statement which is false in a material particular.[2] The offence would be committed by a person lying about the length of his or her residence in the UK to obtain naturalisation, for example. The extended time limit for prosecution applies.[3]

[1]   Set at £5,000: Criminal Justice Act 1982, s 37(2), as amended by Criminal Justice Act 1991, s 17.
[2]   British Nationality Act 1981, s 46(1), as amended, penalty to be increased to 51 weeks by Criminal Justice Act 2003, s 280, Sch 26, para 29, as from a date to be appointed.
[3]   British Nationality Act 1981, s 46(3).

15.78 Making a statement which is to the person's knowledge untrue for the purpose of procuring a passport for him or herself or for any other person[1] is a more serious offence, triable either way and punishable on summary conviction by a fine up to the statutory maximum fine and/or up to six months' imprisonment, and on indictment by up to two years' imprisonment. Where a passport is actually obtained by a fraudulent application and used, it is more appropriate to charge an offence of obtaining property by deception;[2] the offence under this section is more appropriate where no passport is actually obtained.[3] A custodial sentence has been held appropriate for a first offence.[4]

[1] Criminal Justice Act 1925, s 36. This has become an arrestable offence by s 3 Criminal Justice Act 2003 (in force 29 January 2004: SI 2004/81), by adding it to Sch 1A to the Police and Criminal Evidence Act 1984 (see **15.4** fn 2 above).

[2] *R v Ashbee* [1989] 1 WLR 109, 88 Cr App R 357, CA.

[3] *R v Bunche* (1993) 157 JP 780, CA.

[4] *R v Walker* [1999] 1 Cr App Rep (S) 42, where an overstayer applied for a passport using a false name, date and place of birth. The sentence of 18 months was however reduced to nine months.

15.79 A passport is an 'instrument' for the purposes of 'relevant offences' under the Forgery and Counterfeiting Act 1981.[1] Relevant offences are forgery (making a false instrument),[2] using a false instrument,[3] possession of a false instrument with intent,[4] and possession of a false instrument without lawful authority or excuse.[5] All the offences are triable either way, punishable on summary conviction by a fine up to the statutory maximum or six months' imprisonment, and on indictment by a maximum of 10 years' imprisonment, save for possession without lawful authority when the maximum sentence on indictment is two years.[6] Persons presenting false passports at immigration control are frequently charged with the possession offences. The statutory defence under the IAA 1999, s 31, and Refugee Convention, Article 31 argument, apply to these offences.[7] The Asylum and Immigration (Treatment of Claimants etc) Act 2004 adds other 'immigration documents' to the definition of 'instrument' under the 1981 Act, including cards and adhesive labels carrying information about the person (which might be electronic), and about the leave granted, or given to confirm a right of residence under the Community Treaties.[8] For offences of possession of a false identity document or the means of creating one, see ss 4-6 of the Identity Documents Act 2010.[9]

[1] Forgery and Counterfeiting Act 1981, ss 8(1)(a), 5(5)(f).

[2] FCA 1981, s 1.

[3] FCA 1981, s 3.

[4] FCA 1981, s 5(1).

[5] FCA 1981, s 5(2).

[6] FCA 1981, s 6; the statutory maximum is £5,000: Magistrates' Courts Act 1980, s 32(9). See *R v Kolawole* (2004) Times, 16 November: 12–18 months is an appropriate sentence for use of a false passport for a person of good character on a guilty plea. See also cases cited at **15.36** fn 9 above.

[7] IAA 1999, s 31(3) and (4); see **15.44–15.46** above.

[8] Asylum and Immigration (Treatment of Claimants etc) Act 2004, s 3, inserting FCA 1981, s 5(5)(fa), 5(9)–(11) as from a date to be appointed.

[9] In *R v Buriticia-Castrillon; R v Omtade* [2008] EWCA Crim 1972, the Court of Appeal Criminal Division held that a sentence of 15 months' imprisonment for possession of a false identity document contrary to the Identity Cards Act 2006, s 25(1), the relevant offence prior to repeal by the Identity Documents Act 2010, was inappropriate and would be replaced by a sentence of 10 months' imprisonment where an appellant had used a false passport as a means of identification to obtain something to which they were entitled, namely to cash a cheque. See also *R v Hasan* [2008] EWCA Crim 3117, [2008] All ER (D) 116 (Nov), discussed at **15.46**, above.

Offences by persons connected with ships, aircraft, ports or trains

15.80 Captains of ships or aircraft, and managers of Eurostar through trains and shuttle trains, commit an offence if they allow people to disembark or leave the transport when required to prevent it, or fail to provide passenger lists, particulars of crew members, and information on non-EEA arrivals as required, or fail without reasonable excuse to comply with directions for a person's removal.[1] In the last-mentioned case, the owner or agent is also liable. Whether a demonstration by anti-deportation protesters or a refusal by other passengers to travel on a flight with a deportee constitute 'reasonable excuse' for failure to comply with directions for a passenger's removal has yet to be tested in the courts. Additionally, an owner or agent who arranges for a ship or aircraft to call at an unauthorised port, or who without reasonable excuse fails to provide landing or embarkation cards, commits an offence. The offences may be committed in a control zone.[2] They are all summary only and punishable by a fine up to level 5 and/or six months' imprisonment.[3] The Immigration Act 2014 amends the section 27 offence to provide that a failure by a carrier or port operator to comply with a direction issued under new paragraph 5B of Schedule 2 of the IA 1971 without reasonable excuse will be an offence under that section.[4]

[1] IA 1971, s 27, modified in relation to Channel Tunnel trains by the Channel Tunnel (International Arrangements) Order 1993, SI 1993/1813, Sch 4, para 1(9). The requirement to provide passenger lists and particulars of crew is contained in IA 1971, Sch 2, para 27(2); wider passenger information in Sch 2, paras 27B, and 27C, inserted by IAA 1999, ss 18 and 19 (Para 27B(4A) imposes a further duty on carriers to provide copies of travel documents requested by an immigration officer, breach of which will similarly be a criminal offence, inserted by the Asylum and Immigration (Treatment of Claimants etc) Act 2004, s 16.
[2] Nationality, Immigration and Asylum Act 2002 (Juxtaposed Controls) Order 2003, SI 2003/2818, art 12. This does not apply to captains of aircraft.
[3] IA 1971, s 27.
[4] Immigration Act 2014, Sch 8, para 7, in force 28 July 2014: SI 2014/1820. The new para 5B enables the Secretary of State to direct carriers and port operators to make specified arrangements for the exercise of functions by 'designated persons' who may exercise specified functions in relation to persons of a specified description. Hence a carrier may be required to make arrangements for designated persons to exercise the power of examination in respect of embarking passengers travelling on a specified route, or from a specified port. See Explanatory Notes to Immigration Act 2014, paras 425-431, Sch 8 allows for powers of examination exercisable by an immigration officer to be exercised by a designated person.

15.81 The Immigration and Nationality Act 2006 (IAN 2006), s 34 makes it a summary offence punishable by a fine or imprisonment, if any person fails, without reasonable excuse, to supply information on passengers or crews of ships or aircraft required to be given under section 32(2) or (3) of IAN 2006 or to give freight information required under section 33(2). Section 32(2) provides that the owner or agent of a ship or aircraft shall comply with any requirement by a constable of the rank of superintendent or above to provide passenger or service information; Section 32(3) requires a passenger or crew member to provide any information to the owner or agent for the purpose of providing information under subsection 2. Section 33 provides that the owner or agent of a ship or aircraft, or the owner or hirer of a vehicle, or persons responsible for the import of freight into or from the UK, shall provide freight information to a constable of the rank of superintendent or above if required to do so.

Failure to supply information by employers and financial institutions

15.82 An employer or financial institution which fails without reasonable excuse to comply with a requirement to supply information to the Secretary of State about a person commits an offence and may be sentenced to a maximum of three months' imprisonment or a fine on level 5 of the standard scale on summary conviction.[1] Where the offence is committed by a company, its director, manager, secretary or member may be criminally responsible.[2]

1 Nationality, Immigration and Asylum Act 2002, s 137, to be amended by increase of penalty to 51 weeks (from a date to be appointed) by Criminal Justice Act 2003, Sch 26, para 58.
2 NIAA 2002, s 138.

Offences in relation to detention

15.83 Assaulting a detainee custody officer (DCO), acting in accordance with escort arrangements or performing custodial functions, is an offence carrying a maximum sentence of six months' imprisonment and a fine at level 5.[1] Resistance to or wilful obstruction of a DCO in these circumstances carries a fine of up to level 3.[2] In addition, those detained at a removal centre and their visitors may be subject to a range of offences under Schedule 12 to the IAA 1999.[3] A detainee who fails to submit to a medical examination without reasonable excuse is guilty of an offence if there is an authorisation in force for the removal centre[4] and there are reasonable grounds to believe that the person is suffering from a specified disease.[5] Assisting detainees to escape, or bringing, sending or leaving anything at the centre with intent to facilitate an escape, carries a maximum sentence of two years on indictment.[6] Bringing or leaving alcohol to a centre is an offence, as is allowing alcohol to be sold or used (applied to DCOs and other staff.[7]) Bringing anything else into a centre, or taking something out, contrary to the rules, is a summary offence.[8]

1 IAA 1999, Sch 11, para 4.
2 IAA 1999, Sch 11, para 5.
3 IAA 1999, Sch 12 as amended by Nationality, Immigration and Asylum Act 2002, s 66.
4 Ie, under para 3(1) of the Schedule.
5 The Detention Centre (Specified Diseases) Order 2001, SI 2001/240 specifies 33 diseases including cholera, plague, measles and food poisoning. The penalties are up to six months' imprisonment or a fine on level 5: IAA 1999, Sch 12, para 3(5).
6 Or on summary conviction, six months or the maximum fine: IAA 1999, Sch 12, para 4.
7 The offences are summary only, carrying six months' imprisonment or a fine on level 3. IAA 1999, Sch 12, para 5.
8 The penalty is a fine up to level 3: IAA 1999, Sch 12, para 6.

Offences in relation to asylum support

15.84 The IAA 1999 removed virtually everyone subject to immigration control from mainstream social security benefits and created a new Home Office department, NASS, which provides limited subsistence support to destitute asylum seekers.[1] This support regime is enforced by a number of offences modelled on offences relating to social security:[2] false representations; dishonest representations and obstruction; and failure by a sponsor to maintain. They can be committed by corporate bodies, whose officers and even members may be liable if they have consented to or connived at the offence, or it is attributable to neglect on their part.[3] In Scotland, partnerships and partners may be liable in corresponding circumstances.[4] All the offences can be committed in relation to the support to be provided in accommodation centres set up under the Nationality, Immigration and Asylum Act 2002[5] as they apply to NASS and interim support provided under the IAA 1999. The powers of entry and search on a warrant issued by a magistrate to check for the presence of unauthorised persons or the absence of authorised ones[6] are of relevance in relation to these offences. The UKBA 2007 gives immigration officers a much bigger role in policing these offences. Immigration officers can arrest without warrant persons suspected of making false or dishonest claims for asylum support contrary to sections 105 or 106 of the IAA 1999.[7] Separately, Schedule 3 to the NIAA 2002, which provides for EEA nationals, their family members and persons with refugee status abroad to be given temporary support while their departure from the UK is arranged,[8] makes it a criminal offence to come back and seek assistance or accommodation or further repatriation assistance.[9] Other categories of person for whom limited welfare provision may be made commit an offence by failing to mention a previous request for assistance.[10] Both offences carry a maximum penalty of six months' imprisonment on summary conviction.[11]

[1] See CHAPTER 14 above.
[2] The new offences are in IAA 1999, ss 105–108, and are based on Social Security Administration Act 1992, ss 105 and 111–113.
[3] IAA 1999, s 109(1).
[4] IAA 1999, s 109(4).
[5] Nationality, Immigration and Asylum Act 2002, s 35.
[6] IAA 1999, s 125: see 15.21 above.
[7] IAA 1999, s 18, inserting new section 109A of the IAA 1999. The new section 109B(1) gives the immigration officers the powers of entry, search and seizure they already have under the IA 1971, ss 28B and 28D and 28(4), 28E, 28G and 28H. In addition the powers contained in ss 28I, 28J, 28K, and 28L(1) apply: IAA 1999, s 109B(2).
[8] NIAA 2002, Sch 3, paras 1, 4, 5 and 8.
[9] NIAA 2002, Sch 3, para 13(1).
[10] NIAA 2002, Sch 3, para 13(2).
[11] NIAA 2002, Sch 3, para 13(3).

15.85 The offence of false representations is committed by a person who, with a view to obtaining support for him or herself, or for any other person, makes a statement or representation he or she knows to be false in a material particular,[1] gives a document or information he or she knows to be false to someone performing asylum support functions,[2] fails to notify a relevant change of circumstances[3] or without reasonable excuse, knowingly causes another person to fail to notify such a change.[4] It is a summary offence, punishable by up to a level 5 fine or three months' imprisonment, or both.[5] There is no power of arrest without warrant. The Secretary of State may require employers and financial institutions to provide information in connection with an offence under this section,[6] and may seize and retain employee records.[7]

[1] IAA 1999, s 105(1)(a).
[2] IAA 1999, s 105(1)(b). Persons performing functions under Pt VI of the Act include officers of NASS and of local authorities who process applications for support. They could also include officers of registered social landlords and housing associations by virtue of s 100, employees of sub-contractors providing accommodation and support, including private landlords, and judges of the First-tier Tribunal (Asylum Support) by virtue of ss 102–103.

3   IAA 1999, s 105(1)(c). The relevant changes are set out in the Asylum Support Regulations 2000, SI 2000/704, reg 15(2), and include being joined by a dependant, receiving or getting access to any previously undeclared money or other asset, becoming employed or unemployed, changing one's name, marrying, forming a civil partnership, cohabiting with a spouse or civil partner, divorcing, separating, becoming pregnant, having a child, leaving school, sharing, moving or leaving accommodation, going into hospital or prison, leaving the UK and dying.
4   IAA 1999, s 105(1)(d).
5   IAA 1999, s 105(2), to be amended by increase in penalty to 51 weeks as from a date to be appointed by Criminal Justice Act 2003, s 280(3), Sch 26, para 53.
6   Under Nationality, Immigration and Asylum Act 2002, ss 134, 135: see **15.31** above.
7   IA 1971 ss 28FA, 28FB(5), inserted by NIAA 2002, s 154.

15.86 The offence of dishonest representations is committed by performing the same acts, but with a view to obtaining any benefit or advantage under Part VI of the IAA 1999 for him or herself or any other person. The acts must have been performed dishonestly.[1] The offence is a broad one and can be committed by landlords or providers of other services attempting to defraud NASS. The section is directed at cases of serious and calculated fraud, such as where a person makes a plan to extract as much from the Home Office as possible by deception.[2] This is evident from the penalties: it is triable either way, and punishable on summary conviction by a fine up to the statutory maximum or up to six months' imprisonment, or both, and on indictment by a fine and/or up to seven years' imprisonment[3]. The Secretary of State may require employers and financial institutions to provide information in connection with an offence under this section,[4] and may seize and retain employee records.[5]

1   IAA 1999, s 106(1).
2   Explanatory notes to IAA 1999, s 106.
3   IAA 1999, s 106(2).
4   Under Nationality, Immigration and Asylum Act 2002, ss 134, 135: see **15.31** above.
5   IA 1971, ss 28FA, 28FB(5), inserted by NIAA 2002, s 154.

15.87 The offence of delay or obstruction is committed by intentionally delaying or obstructing someone exercising asylum support functions, or refusing or neglecting to answer a question, give information or produce a document when required to do so.[1] It is summary only and punishable by a fine up to level 3.[2] There is no power of arrest without warrant.

1   IAA 1999, s 107(1). For persons exercising functions under Pt VI of the Act, see Chapter 14 and **14.177**ff above.
2   IAA 1999, s 107(2).

15.88 The offence of failure to maintain is committed by a sponsor (a person who has given a written undertaking under the Immigration Rules to be responsible for the maintenance and accommodation of another person) who, during the period covered by the undertaking, persistently refuses or neglects, without reasonable excuse, to maintain the person in accordance with the undertaking, with the result that support has to be provided under Part VI of the IAA 1999.[1] A sponsor is not to be taken to have refused or neglected to maintain another person by reason only of anything done or omitted in furtherance of a trade dispute.[2] The proviso that the refusal or neglect must be without reasonable excuse was added at Report stage, after the minister had made clear that 'it is not our intention to catch people who might become ill or unable to support the person for a genuine reason'.[3] Sponsored immigrants are not entitled to social security benefits for at least five years unless their sponsor dies,[4] and so the offence, which requires receipt of support in consequence of the failure to maintain, can, it appears, only be committed if the sponsored immigrant concerned applies for asylum as a refugee or under Article 3 of the ECHR[5] and receives asylum support because of the sponsor's failure. The offence is summary only and punishable by a fine up to level 4 or a maximum of three months' imprisonment, or both.[6] There is no power of arrest without warrant.

[1] IAA 1999, s 108(1).
[2] IAA 1999, s 108(3).
[3] HC Official Report, Special SC (Immigration and Asylum Bill), 21st sitting, 11 May 1999, col 1422; 606 HL Official Report (5th series) cols 839–842, 2 November 1999.
[4] By IAA 1999, s 115 and the Social Security (Immigration and Asylum) Consequential Amendments Regulations 2000, SI 2000/636, Schedule, paras 2 and 3.
[5] See interpretation section, IAA 1999, s 94(1).
[6] IAA 1999, s 108(2). Level 4 is currently £2,500: Criminal Justice Act 1982, s 37(2), as amended by Criminal Justice Act 1991, s 17. The penalty is to be increased to 51 weeks as from a date to be appointed by Criminal Justice Act 2003, s 280(3), Sch 26 para 53.

Offences in relation to provision of immigration advice or services

15.89 The Immigration Acts police not just immigrants and asylum seekers, but also those who advise and represent them. In response to widespread disquiet at the abuse and exploitation of immigrants and asylum seekers by lawyers and by unqualified consultants, Part V of the IAA 1999 created a structure of authorisation or registration within which advice and services are to be provided.[1] Essentially, no one may provide immigration advice or services unless he or she is registered with the Immigration Services Commissioner,[2], or authorised by a designated professional body[3], or a designated qualifying regulator[4] (or employed or supervised by such a person),[5] or, like a student union, is exempt.[6] The Commissioner has a duty to investigate complaints regarding the competence or fitness of persons providing advice, or alleging breaches of Commissioners' rules and Code of Practice,[7] and may decline or cancel registration.[8] As of July 2014 there is a new power to carry out inspections of the activities and businesses of registered persons.[9] The First-tier Tribunal hears appeals and disciplinary charges arising from the Commissioner's decisions, or the disciplinary body with jurisdiction over the service provider (if he or she is a solicitor, legal executive or barrister). The disciplinary body may make restraining orders restricting, suspending or prohibiting the advice or services of the individual or firm concerned.[10] In the course of an investigation, the Commissioner has power to enter and search premises where it is believed on reasonable grounds that advice is being provided, and may require the production of documents or information held on a computer, which may be copied or removed.[11]

[1] IAA 1999, s 84.
[2] IAA 1999, s 84(2)(a) and (b). The Commissioner is created by s 83. Fees for initial registration are £1,750 for an organisation with up to four advisers, £1,960 for between five and nine, and £2,370 for ten or more. The fees for continued registration are £1,290; £1,600 and £2,115 respectively: Immigration Services Commissioner (Application Fee) Order 2011, SI 2011/1366. Applicants must demonstrate competence and fitness to provide immigration advice.

3   The full list is set out in the IAA 1999, s 86(1) as the Law Society of Scotland, the Law Society of Northern Ireland, the Faculty of Advocates and the General Council of the Bar of Northern Ireland. There is provision to amend the list after consultation: s 86(2)–(7). A body can be removed from the list if it consistently fails to supervise its members properly.

4   Ie the Law Society, the Institute of Legal Executives and the General Council of the Bar, IAA 1999, s 86A, inserted by the Legal Services Act 2007, s 186, Sch 18, Pt 1, paras 9,14. In response to the ISC's concerns, the Law Society has set up an accreditation scheme for immigration solicitors. The Bar Council's (voluntary) scheme appears to have fallen into desuetude.

5   IAA 1999, s 84(2)(c) and (f). Paras (d) and (e) deal with those registered or authorised in another EEA state.

6   Educational institutions, student unions and health sector bodies are exempt: IAA 1999 (Part V Exemption: Educational Institutions and Health Service Bodies) Order 2001, SI 2001/1403. Employers providing immigration advice or services free to (prospective) employees who have been granted work permits, for them and their families, are exempt: IAA 1999 (Part V Exemption: Relevant Employers) Order 2003, SI 2003/3214. So too are licensed sponsors of Tier 2 and Tier 4 migrants under the Points Based System: IAA 1999 (Part V Exemption: Licensed Sponsors Tiers 2 and 4) Order 2009, SI 2009/506. These exempted categories are subject to the proviso that immigration advice or services provided about matters not related to migrants' applications, or to any immediate family members' dependant applications, may still give rise to criminal prosecution under s 84.

7   IAA 1999, Sch 5, para 5.

8   IAA 1999, Sch 5, para 6(3), Sch 6, paras 2 and 3.

9   IAA 1999 Sch 5, para 4A as inserted by the Immigration Act 2014, Sch 7, para 6. In force 28 July 2014: SI 2014/1820.

10   IAA 1999, ss 89(8), 90(1), Sch 5, para 9(3).

11   IAA 1999, Sch 5, para 7, as amended by Nationality, Immigration and Asylum Act 2002, s 140, which extends the power of entry to investigations on the Commissioner's own initiative.

15.90 The Immigration Act 2014 makes amendments to Part V of the IAA 1999 concerning the regulation of immigration advisors and service providers. Under provisions not yet in force at the time of writing,[1] the Commissioner's general power to exempt advisors from the requirement to be registered and pay a fee, is removed.[2] The Secretary of State is granted a new power to require or authorise the Commissioner to waive all or part of a registration fee in particular cases. The power is expected to be used to require the Commissioner to waive registration fees for advisors who do not charge for their services.[3] The Commissioner's existing power to cancel registration becomes a duty in certain circumstances including where the Commissioner considers that the person is no longer competent or is otherwise unfit to provide immigration advice and services.[4] Where such cancellation is on the grounds that an adviser is no longer competent or is otherwise unfit, such a decision is appealable to the First-tier Tribunal under section 87(3) of the 1999 Act.[5] The Tribunal may, on an application made to it by the Commissioner, suspend a person's registration where the person is charged with a dishonesty or deception offence, an indictable offence; or certain immigration offences. Such suspension will have effect until the person is acquitted, or the charge withdrawn, or the proceedings are discontinued or an order is made for the charge to lie on the file. Where the person is convicted, the suspension will continue to have effect until the Commissioner has cancelled the person's registration (in circumstances where cancellation is mandatory) or decided whether or not registration should cancelled (where cancellation is discretionary). Persons suspended will, for the period of their suspension, not be treated as registered persons for the purposes of section 84 of the 1999 Act.[6]

1 Save for Sch 7, para 6 in force 28 July 2014 concerning the power to inspect the business and activities of registered persons, see **15.22** above and fn 9 of **15.95**.
2 Immigration Act 2014, Sch 7, paras 2(1) and 2(2)
3 Schedule 7, para 3, see also Explanatory Notes to the 2014 Act at para 367.
4 Schedule 7 para 4(4), inserting a new para 4A into Sch 6 of the IAA 1999. The other circumstances are where the person asks for their registration to be cancelled; or dies; or where the organisation concerned is dissolved or wound up; where the person is convicted of certain immigration offences; where The Tribunal directs the Commissioner to cancel a person's registration.
5 Schedule 7 para 4(1).
6 Schedule 7 para 5(3), inserting a new para 4B into Sch 6 of the IAA 1999.

15.91 It is an offence for an unqualified person (one who is not registered, authorised or exempt), or for someone subject to a restraining order, to provide immigration advice or services.[1] The offence is triable either way, and is punishable on summary conviction with a fine up to the statutory maximum or up to six months' imprisonment, or both, and on indictment by a fine or up to two years' imprisonment, or both.[2] Where it is committed by a corporate body, the company's officers (director, manager, secretary, etc) or members may be liable if they are proved to have connived in the offence or it is attributable to neglect on their part.[3] In Scotland, partners are liable in corresponding circumstances where the offence is committed by a partnership.[4] Since 2001 when the Office of the Immigration Services Commissioner came into being, 182 people have been prosecuted with a further 110 being cautioned.[5]

1 IAA 1999, s 91(1). In *R v K* [2008] EWCA Crim 1900, [2009] 1 All ER 510, the appellant, who had been called to the Bar but had not completed pupillage, was charged with two offences under s 91 for providing immigration services. Despite being described as 'scrupulous to keep within the law' and having appropriate professional indemnity insurance, his appeal was dismissed. K was not subject to the regulatory provisions of the Bar Code of Conduct and accordingly not 'authorised by a designated professional body' within the meaning of s 84(2)(b) of the 1999 Act; it was the amenability to regulation of the person offering services under that provision which was important under that provision. In the view of the court, it was difficult to see how the Bar Council would wish to authorise a person to perform services for which being a practising barrister provided legal eligibility while at the same time abdicating any regulatory control over the performance of such services (see paras [20]–[23]).
2 IAA 1999, s 91(1).
3 IAA 1999, s 91(3)–(5).
4 IAA 1999, s 91(6)–(7).
5 OISC Annual Report 2013/14.

15.92 The Asylum and Immigration (Treatment of Claimants etc) Act 2004 creates an offence, punishable by a fine on level 4, of offering or advertising immigration advice and services which would be unlawful.[1] An extended time limit of two years applies.[2] The AI(TC)A 2004 also creates powers of entry, search and seizure of evidential material on a warrant, on reasonable grounds to believe that an offence of unlawful provision of advice or services has been committed.[3] It is an offence to obstruct the Immigration Services Commissioner in the exercise of these powers of entry, search and seizure, punishable by up to six months' imprisonment and/or a fine on level 5.[4]

1 IAA 1999, s 92B, inserted by Asylum and Immigration (Treatment of Claimants etc) Act 2004, s 39 in force 1 October 2004: SI 2004/2523, art 2, Schedule.

² For extended time limits see **15.75** above.
³ IAA 1999, s 92A, as inserted.
⁴ IAA 1999, s 92A(5), (6), as inserted.

Offences of disclosure

15.93 There are a number of offences relating to disclosure of confidential information. First, someone, who is or has been the Immigration Services Commissioner, or an agent or staff member of a Commissioner, commits an offence if, without lawful authority, he or she knowingly or recklessly discloses information relating to an identified or identifiable individual or business which was obtained by the Commissioner for the purposes of the IAA 1999 and is not in the public domain.[1] The offence is triable either way and punishable by a fine. Second, it is an offence for a private sector employee at a detention centre or on escort duties to make unauthorised disclosure of information relating to a particular detainee acquired in the course of his or her employment.[2] The maximum penalty for this offence, also triable either way, is a fine up to the statutory maximum or six months' imprisonment or both on summary conviction, and on indictment, two years' imprisonment.

Section 18 of the BCIA 2009 makes unauthorised disclosure of personal customs information a criminal offence carrying a maximum penalty of two years' imprisonment and a fine. The offence is triable either way, that is either: summarily, where the maximum penalty will be 12 months' imprisonment (in England and Wales) or six months' imprisonment (in Northern Ireland), or a fine not exceeding the statutory maximum (currently £5,000), or both; or on indictment, when the maximum penalty will be two years' imprisonment, or a fine, or both.

Provision is also made for penalties in Scotland and Northern Ireland. In relation to an offence under section 18 committed before the commencement of section 282 of the Criminal Justice Act 2003, the reference to 12 months has effect as if it were a reference to six months.

Section 42 of the UKBA 2007, as amended by BCIA 2009, s 20(2), creates an offence of wrongful disclosure of certain information supplied by HMRC, the Revenue and Customs Prosecution Office or those authorised to act on behalf of either of them. The offence is committed where a person in disclosing the information which relates to an identifiable natural or legal person contravenes the statutory duty of confidentiality.[3] The offence is triable either way, that is either: summarily, where the maximum penalty will be 12 months' imprisonment, or a fine not exceeding the statutory maximum, or to both; or on indictment, when the maximum penalty will be two years' imprisonment, or a fine, or to both.

¹ IAA 1999, s 93(4).
² IAA 1999, s 158.
³ Defined by UKBA 2007, s 41.

EMPLOYER SANCTIONS

Introduction

15.94 The Asylum and Immigration Act 1996 created an offence for employers who employed persons aged 16 or over, who were subject to immigration control and were not entitled to work in the UK or not free to take the particular employment.[1] Only in cases of a legally binding obligation to work in exchange for remuneration would section 8 apply.[2] The offence is one to which the search, entry, arrest and seizure provisions of the IA 1971 apply.[3] In its report on gangmasters issued in September 2003, the Select Committee on the Environment, Fisheries and Food expressed itself 'appalled by the lack of priority given' to their illegal activities. Describing government enforcement in the area as 'perfunctory and un-coordinated', the Select Committee complained that 'no significant resources' were allocated, no targets set and no minister took overall responsibility.[4] We dealt with this quite fully in the 6th edition of this work (see **15.82** ff). Sections 15 to 26 of IAN 2006 entered into force on 29 February 2008[5] creating a new statutory regime covering employer sanctions. Thus, the above commentary only applies to offences committed before the entry into force of sections 15 to 26.

[1] Asylum and Immigration Act 1996, s 8.
[2] Letter from Immigration and Nationality Directorate to Commission for Racial Equality, 7 July 1997.
[3] Asylum and Immigration Act 1996, s 8(10) as inserted by Nationality, Immigration and Asylum Act 2002, s 147 from 1 April 2003. Note that the 2002 Act also provided for the extended time limit under IA 1971, s 28(1) to apply to prosecutions under the section (see **14.65** above), but as the provision was repealed from 1 October 2004 (SI 2004/2523) by s 6 Asylum and Immigration (Treatment of Claimants, etc) Act 2004.
[4] Select Committee on the Environment, Fisheries and Rural Affairs: Gangmasters, report and minutes of evidence issued 18 September 2003. The report describes 'Operation Gangmaster' which was set up in 1998 to coordinate enforcement activity between the Department of Work and Pensions, the Inland Revenue, Customs & Excise, the IND and others including DEFRA as required. It notes that between 35% and 50% of a casual workforce of around 70,000 in agriculture are supplied by gangmasters, of whom around 20% are committing a wide range of offences. See now the Gangmasters (Licensing) Act 2004.
[5] Immigration Asylum and Nationality Act 2006 (Commencement No 8 and Transitional and Saving Provisions) Order 2008, SI 2008/310.

15.95 Employer sanctions have been put on an entirely new statutory footing under sections 15–26 of IAN 2006, the result being that sections 8 and 8A of the Asylum and Immigration Act 1996 have been repealed.[1] The sanctions have two main prongs: (1) the imposition of a civil penalty by the Home Office, the details of which are now contained in an order which came into force on 29 February 2008;[2] and (2) a criminal offence of knowingly employing someone whose immigration status does not permit them to work. Unlike section 8 of IAA 1999 the offence is not one of strict liability: knowledge that the employee has no permission to work is required.[3] In the normal case employees should have leave to enter or remain without any conditions attached to their leave restricting or prohibiting employment with that employer. But what about persons who are given temporary admission and are allowed to work? Section 24 of IAN 2006 provides that where such persons have been granted temporary admission,[4] they are to be treated as if they had been granted leave to enter and as if any restriction on employment imposed by the temporary admission was a condition of leave. The practical effect of this is that an employer is not liable to a civil penalty and commits no criminal offence if he or she employs someone who does not have leave to enter or remain, but has been given temporary admission or release from detention without any condition restricting or prohibiting employment. The clear policy is to primarily employ the civil sanctions and only resort to the criminal provisions for deliberately recalcitrant employers. The system of civil penalties is designed to encourage employers to comply with their legal obligations, without criminalising those who slip up.[5] It is said that:

> 'the illegal working provisions form part of a balanced package of measures to prevent illegal migrant working in the UK, incorporating additional support for law abiding employers through verification services, the points based scheme and identity cards for foreign nationals. The . . . system needs to reflect a proportionate approach to non-compliance, whilst providing a sufficient deterrent effect so that employers will not want to risk their profits and reputation by using slipshod employment practices and employing illegal migrant workers.'[6]

---

[1] IAN 2006, s 26 and Sch 3, which come into force on 29 February 2008: Immigration Asylum and Nationality Act 2006 (Commencement No 8 and Transitional and Saving Provisions) Order 2008, SI 2008/310.

[2] Immigration (Restrictions on Employment) Order 2007, SI 2007/3290, as amended by the Immigration (Restrictions on Employment) (Codes of Practice and Amendment) Order 2014, SI 2014/1183: in force 16 May 2014. The maximum penalties are set out in the Immigration (Employment of Adults Subject to Immigration Control) (Maximum Penalty) Order 2008, SI 2008/132 as amended by the Immigration (Employment of Adults Subject to Immigration Control) (Maximum Penalty) (Amendment) Order 2014, SI 2014/1262. These Orders fix the maximum civil penalty at £20 000 for contraventions of s15 IAN 2006 committed on or after 16 May 2014. The maximum penalty is £10 000 for contraventions committed before that date.

[3] See below at **15.100**.

[4] Or release from detention under paragraph 21(1) of Schedule 2 to the IA 1971.

[5] Explanatory Memorandum to Immigration (Restrictions on Employment) Order 2007, para 7.1.

[6] Explanatory Memorandum, para 7.5.

Civil penalty

15.96 Section 15 of IAN 2006 provides that an employer is liable to a civil penalty[1] if he or she employs someone aged 16 or over, who is subject to immigration control and:

(a)   has not been granted leave to enter or remain in the UK; or

(b)   has a leave which–

    (i)   is invalid;

    (ii)   has ceased to have effect (by reason of curtailment, revocation, cancellation, passage of time or otherwise); or

    (iii) is subject to a condition preventing him or her from accepting the employment.[2]

Much of the new civil penalty regime depends upon the provisions of the Immigration (Restrictions on Employment) Order 2007[3] and the Immigration (Employment of Adults Subject to Immigration Control) (Maximum Penalty) Order 2008[4] which imposes a maximum penalty of £20,000.[5] Under the Restrictions Order an employer has an excuse not to pay the civil penalty if he or she complies with the prescribed requirements set out in the Order.[6] But the excuse will not help the employer if it can be shown that he or she knew that the employment of the employee was unlawful.[7] Section 15 describes the matters to be covered in the penalty notice[8] and sets out the parameters of the regulation making power of the Secretary of State. Section 15(5) makes it clear that he or she can issue a penalty notice without having to investigate whether the employer is likely to have an excuse for the illegal employment. This puts the burden of proving an excuse on the employer. But showing that the business has complied with any of the prescribed requirements may not be enough, if the Secretary of State can show that the employer knew, at any time during the period of employment, that the employee was being unlawfully employed.

[1]   IAN 2006, s 15(2). The subsection refers to a prescribed maximum which is currently £20 000; see **15.94**, fn 2.
[2]   As amended by the Immigration (Restrictions on Employment) (Codes of Practice and Amendment) Order 2014, SI 2014/1183.
[3]   As amended by the Immigration (Employment of Adults Subject to Immigration Control) (Maximum Penalty) (Amendment) Order 2014, SI 2014/1262.
[4]   IAN 2006, s 15(1)(a) and (b).
[5]   See **15.95**, fn 2. For contraventions of s15 committed solely prior to the coming into force of the 2014 Order on 16 May 2014, but after commencement of the 2007 Restrictions Order on 29 February 2008, the maximum penalty is £10 000.
[6]   See Immigration (Restrictions on Employment) Order 2007, SI 2007/3290, arts 2, 3 4,4A and 6.
[7]   IAN 2006, s 15(4).
[8]   The penalty notice must state such things as: (a) why the Secretary of State thinks the employer is liable; (b) must state the amount of the penalty; (c) must specify a date, at least 28 days after the date specified in the notice, by which the penalty must be paid; (d) specify how it must be paid; (e) explain how the employer may object to the penalty; and (f) explain how the Secretary of State may enforce the penalty: IAN 2006, s 15(6).

15.97 Under the Immigration (Restrictions on Employment) Order 2007,[1] Articles 3, 4 and 4A together with the Schedule, describe how an employer will be excused from paying a penalty under section 15 of the IAN 2006 for either the duration or the remainder of the employment. First, when the employee or prospective employee presents a document or combination of documents that demonstrates an entitlement to work in the UK for an indefinite period, as contained in List A,[2] no further checks are required during that employment[3] Secondly, where an employee or prospective employee can demonstrate entitlement to work for a limited period and is able to produce a document or combination of documents from part 1 of list B[4] the employer is excused from paying a penalty for the duration of the leave, and, if satisfied that the employee has an outstanding application to vary his or her leave or a pending appeal, for a further 28 days or until the Secretary of State terminates the right to undertake employment.[5] Thirdly, where the employer obtains a Positive Verification Notice issued by the Home Office Employer Checking Service indicating the employee's permission to stay and do the work in question, or the employee presents a document or combination of documents from part 2 of List B[6], the employee is excused from any penalty for six months beginning with the date of the Notice.[7] Once the employer is given the documents he or she must then meet the stringent requirements set out in Article 6. They are:

(a)   to take all reasonable steps to check the validity of the document and retain a record of the date on which any check was made;

(b) to retain securely the copy or copies for a period of not less than two years after the employment has come to an end;

(c) to satisfy himself or herself that any photograph contained in the document is of the prospective employee or employee;

(d) to satisfy himself or herself that any date of birth in a document is consistent with the appearance of the prospective employee or employee;

(e) to take all other reasonable steps to check that the prospective employee or employee is the rightful owner of the document;

(f) if the document is not a passport . . . the employer retains a copy of whole of the document in a format which cannot be subsequently altered;

. . .

[(g) if the document is a passport . . . , the employer retains a copy of the following pages of that document in a format which cannot be subsequently altered—

 (i) . . . ;

 (ii) any page containing the holder's personal details including nationality;

 (iii) any page containing the holder's photograph;(iv) any page containing the holder's signature;

 (v) any page containing the date of expiry; and(vi) any page containing information indicating the holder has an entitlement to enter or remain in the UK and undertake the work in question; and

If the employee is a student with permission to work for limited weekly hours during term time, the employer must retain details of the term and vacation dates of the employee's course.[8]

Article 5 together with the Schedule provides that an employer is only excused from paying a penalty if documents have been provided prior to the commencement of employment. Article 7 prevents employers from retaining documents for any period longer than is necessary for the purposes of satisfying Article 6.

[1] SI 2007/3290.

[2] List A

 (1) A passport showing that the holder, or a person named in the passport as the child of the holder, is a British citizen or a citizen of the United Kingdom and Colonies having the right of abode in the United Kingdom.

 (2) A passport or national identity card showing that the holder, or a person named in the passport as the child of the holder, is a national of a European Economic Area country or Switzerland.

 (3) A registration certificate or document certifying permanent residence issued by the Home Office to a national of a European Economic Area country or Switzerland.

 (4) A permanent residence card issued by the Home Office to the family member of a national of a European Economic Area country or Switzerland.

 (5) A current biometric immigration document issued by the Home Office to the holder which indicates that the person named in it is allowed to stay indefinitely in the United Kingdom, or has no time limit on their stay in the United Kingdom.

 (6) A current passport endorsed to show that the holder is exempt from immigration control, is allowed to stay indefinitely in the United Kingdom, has the right of abode in the United Kingdom, or has no time limit on their stay in the United Kingdom.

 (7) A current immigration status document issued by the Home Office to the holder with an endorsement indicating that the person named in it is allowed to stay indefinitely in the United Kingdom or has no time limit on their stay in the United Kingdom, when produced in combination with an official document giving the person's permanent National Insurance Number and their name issued by a Government agency or a previous employer.

 (8) A full birth certificate issued in the United Kingdom which includes the name(s) of at least one of the holder's parents, when produced in combination with an official

document giving the person's permanent National Insurance Number and their name issued by a Government agency or a previous employer.

(9) A full adoption certificate issued in the United Kingdom which includes the name(s) of at least one of the holder's adoptive parents when produced in combination with an official document giving the person's permanent National Insurance Number and their name issued by a Government agency or a previous employer.

(10) A birth certificate issued in the Channel Islands, the Isle of Man or Ireland, when produced in combination with an official document giving the person's permanent National Insurance Number and their name issued by a Government agency or a previous employer.

(11) An adoption certificate issued in the Channel Islands, the Isle of Man or Ireland, when produced in combination with an official document giving the person's permanent National Insurance Number and their name issued by a Government agency or a previous employer.

(12) A certificate of registration or naturalisation as a British citizen, when produced in combination with an official document giving the person's permanent National Insurance Number and their name issued by a Government agency or a previous employer.

3 Article 3.
4 List B—Part 1

(1) A current passport endorsed to show that the holder is allowed to stay in the United Kingdom and is allowed to do the type of work in question.

(2) A current biometric immigration document issued by the Home Office to the holder which indicates that the person named in it is allowed to stay in the United Kingdom and is allowed to do the work in question.

(3) A current residence card (including an accession residence card or a derivative residence card) issued by the Home Office to a non-European Economic Area national who is a family member of a national of a European Economic Area country or Switzerland or who has a derivative right of residence.

(4) A current immigration status document containing a photograph issued by the Home Office to the holder with an endorsement indicating that the person named in it is allowed to stay in the United Kingdom and is allowed to do the work in question, when produced in combination with an official document giving the person's permanent National Insurance Number and their name issued by a Government agency or previous employer.

5 See Article 4, as amended by SI 2014/1183, arts 2 and 3, in force 16 May 2014.
6 List B—Part 2

(1) A certificate of application issued by the Home Office under regulation 17(3) or 18A(2) of the Immigration (European Economic Area) Regulations 2006, to a family member of a national of a European Economic Area country or Switzerland stating that the holder is permitted to take employment which is less than 6 months old.

(2) An application registration card issued by the Home Office stating that the holder is permitted to take the employment in question.

7 Article 4A, as inserted by SI 2014/1183, arts 2 and 3, in force 16 May 2014.
8 Article 6(2), as inserted by SI 2014/1183, arts 2 and 5, in force 16 May 2014.

15.98 Employers can object to a penalty notice on three grounds:

(a) that they are not liable to the imposition of the penalty;
(b) they have complied with the required prescribed requirements and have an excuse for the employment; or
(c) the penalty is too high.

To make an objection the employer must give a written notice of objection, served within the time period prescribed and giving reasons for the objection.[1] Article 8 of the Immigration (Restrictions on Employment) Order 2007 prescribes the manner in which an objection against a penalty must be made. As a minimum it should contain the penalty reference number; the name and contact address of the employer; the name and contact address of the employee in respect of whom the penalty was issued; full grounds of objection; full details of the employer's ability to pay if the employer is simply requesting permission to pay by instalments; and in cases where the employer has appealed to a county or Sheriff Court confirmation and details of the appeal. The objection must be signed, dated and served upon the Secretary of State at the address set out in the penalty notice within 28 days of the date specified in the penalty notice.[2] In deciding what to do he or she must have regard to the Code of Practice, issued under section 19 of IAN 2006, which will set out the criteria to be applied in determining the amount of the civil penalty.[3] The Secretary of State must then determine the objection within 28 days from the date on which the notice of objection was served on her or such longer period as may be agreed between herself and the employer.[4] She may cancel the penalty, reduce it, increase it, or determine to take no action.[5] If the penalty is increased a new notice must be issued.[6] If the penalty is reduced, the Secretary of State must inform the objector of the reduced amount.[7]

1 IAN 2006, s 16(3).
2 SI 2007/3290, art 9.
3 IAN 2006, s 17(3).
4 SI 2007/3290, art 10 and IAN 2006, s 16(5)(b).
5 IAN 2006, s 16(4).
6 IAN 2006, s 16(5)(c).
7 IAN 2006, s 16(5)(d).

15.99 In addition to objection, there is an appeal to the county court in England and Wales and Northern Ireland or to the Sheriff Court in Scotland.[1] Employers can appeal on the grounds that they are not liable to the penalty, the amount is too high or they are excused payment because of compliance with the specified requirements.[2] The court can allow the appeal and cancel the penalty, allow the appeal and reduce the penalty, or dismiss the appeal.[3] An appeal is a rehearing of the decision to impose a penalty and the court must have regard to the Code of Practice under section 19 of IAN 2006 and any other matters the court thinks relevant, including matters of which the Secretary of State was unaware.[4] The appeal must be brought within a 28-day time period beginning with the 'relevant date'[5] defined according to the Secretary of State's response to the employer's notice of objection.[6]

Prior to 28 July 2014 an appeal could be brought by an employer irrespective of whether he or she has made an objection under section 16 of IAN 2006. However as the result of section 44 of the Immigration Act 2014, employers are now required to give a notice of objection before exercising their right of appeal.[7] Also prior to this date any civil penalty imposed by the Secretary of State could be recovered as debt, under section 18 of IAN 2006. As the result of new subsections 1 to 1D of section 18[8], the Secretary of State may enforce a penalty as if it were a debt due under a court order. The amendment allows an outstanding penalty to be registered with the civil court, after which enforcement action may be commenced immediately. Thus the need for the Secretary of State to first make an application to the court for a substantive order for payment will be eliminated.

1 IAN 2006, s 17(6).
2 IAN 2006, s 17(1).
3 IAN 2006, s 17(2).
4 IAN 2006, s 17(3).
5 IAN 2006 s 17(4B), as inserted by s 44 Immigration Act 2014. SI 2014/1820, art 3(p) in force 28 July 2014.

[6] See subsections (4C)–(4E), as inserted by s 44 Immigration Act 2014. SI 2014/1820, art 3(p) in force 28 July 2014.

[7] IAN 2006, s 17(4A) as inserted by s 44 Immigration Act 2014. SI 2014/1820, art 3(p) in force 28 July 2014.

[8] As inserted by s 45 Immigration Act 2014. SI 2014/1820, art 3(q). For transitory and saving provisions see art 6.

Criminal offence

15.100 The second sanction is the creation of a criminal offence of employing a person knowing that they are an adult subject to immigration control:

(a)   who has not been granted leave to enter or remain (unless granted permission to work by the Secretary of State); or

(b)   whose leave to remain is–

    (i)   invalid;

    (ii)   has ceased to have effect (whether by reason of curtailment, revocation, cancellation, passage of time or otherwise); or

    (iii)   is subject to a condition preventing him or her from accepting the employment.[1]

On summary conviction, the maximum penalty is six months' imprisonment in England and Wales (12 months once section 154(1) of the Criminal Justice Act 2003 is commenced), six months in Scotland or Northern Ireland, or a fine up to the statutory maximum or both.[2] This offence replaces the offence under section 8 of the AIA 1996, following the entry into force of section 21 of IAN 2006.

[1] IAN 2006, s 21(1), which came into force on 29 February 2008: Immigration Asylum and Nationality Act 2006 (Commencement No 8 and Transitional and Saving Provisions) Order 2008, SI 2008/310.

[2] IAN 2006, s 21(2) and (4).

15.101 The criminal offence applies not only to individual employers but also to companies and partnerships. Section 22 of IAN 2006 defines the liability of bodies corporate, their officers and employees, and of members of partnerships in relation to the criminal offence in section 21 of the Act. Section 22(1) deals with the question of knowledge and enacts that if a person who has responsibility within a body (whether corporate or not) for an aspect of the employment knows relevant facts about an employee, that person's knowledge is imputed to the body. Section 22(2) provides that where an offence under section 21(1) is committed by a body corporate with the consent or connivance of an officer of the body, the officer as well as the body should be treated as having committed the offence. Officers include a director, manager or secretary, a person purporting to act as such and, in the case of bodies managed by its member, a member.[1] Where the offence is committed by a partnership and a partner or a person purporting to act as a partner has consented or connived at the offence, that person, as well as the partnership, is to be treated as having committed the offence.[2] Where an offence under section 21 is being investigated, immigration officers have the powers of arrest, entry and search given by sections 28B and 28D, 28E, 28G and 28H of the IA 1971.[3]

[1] IAN 2006, s 21(3), which came into force on 29 February 2008: Immigration Asylum and Nationality Act 2006 (Commencement No 8 and Transitional and Saving Provisions) Order 2008, SI 2008/310. This applies to the following fns 2 and 3 below.
[2] IAN 2006, s 22(4).
[3] IAN 2006, s 21(3).

Codes of Practice

15.102 Section 19 of the IAN 2006 provides for a Code of Practice to specify the factors to be considered by the Secretary of State in determining the amount of the penalty to be imposed on the employer. This includes whether any previous penalty notices have been issued on the employers in the preceding three years, whether follow up checks have been undertaken by the employer, if required, and whether the employer reported his or her suspicions of immigration abuse, or co-operated with the Home Office. Article 11 of the Immigration (Restrictions on Employment) Order 2007[1] brought into force this Code of Practice; an updated Code was brought into force by Article 10 of the Immigration (Restrictions on Employment) (Codes of Practice and Amendment) Order 2014.[2] The creation of the offence under section 8 of the Asylum and Immigration Act 1996 was deeply controversial, with many believing it would exacerbate and entrench racial discrimination in employment while not preventing illegal working, but driving it further underground to yet more exploitative conditions. Section 8A of the Asylum and Immigration Act 1996, added by the IAA 1999, obliged the Secretary of State to issue a Code of Practice for employers to avoid racial discrimination in complying with the requirements of the statutory defence under section 8(2). Section 23 of IAN 2006 provides for a Code of Practice specifying what an employer should or should not do in order to ensure that while avoiding the liability of a penalty or committing an offence of knowingly employing an illegal worker, the employer also avoids contravening race relations laws.[3] Article 12 of the Immigration (Restrictions on Employment) Order 2007[4] brought into force this Code of Practice. The updated code is brought into force by Article 11 of the Immigration (Restrictions on Employment) (Codes of Practice and Amendment) Order 2014.[5]

[1] SI 2007/3290.
[2] SI 2014/1183, in force 16 May 2014: 'Code of practice on preventing illegal working: Civil penalty scheme for employers'.
[3] The Race Relations Act 1976 or the Race Relations (Northern Ireland) Order 1997, as amended.
[4] SI 2007/3290.
[5] SI 2014/1183. In force 16 May 2014: 'Code of practice for employers: Avoiding unlawful discrimination while preventing illegal working'.

Unlawful employment of EU accession workers

15.103 The accession of 10 new members to the EU in May 2004 and of Bulgaria and Romania on 1 January 2007 created two further offences for employers. Eight of these new States in May 2004 did not have immediate rights of free movement for workers. Their nationals were subject to UK national law for a five-year period until 30 April 2009. Meanwhile, the UK government created a registration scheme, giving workers from these new Eastern European accession Member States very wide rights to work, provided they were registered and their employer was authorised.[1] It was thereby an offence for an employer to employ an accession worker requiring registration during a period when the employer was not an authorised employer in relation to the worker.[2] In the case of Bulgarian and Romanian nationals, employers would commit a criminal offence under the Accession (Immigration and Worker Authorisation) Regulations 2006[3] if the employee did not hold an accession worker authorisation document; or the worker authorisation document was subject to conditions that preclude him or her from taking up the employment. On 23 November 2011, Immigration Minister Damian Green announced that the restrictions in place regarding Bulgarian and Romanian nationals would remain in place until the end of December 2013.[4] Since the lifting of the restrictions the criminal penalty in the 2006 Regulations no longer applies.

[1] The scheme is described in detail at **6.13**.
[2] The Accession (Immigration and Worker Registration) Regulations 2004, SI 2004/1219, reg 9, now revoked as of 1 May 2011 by SI 2011/544, reg 2.
[3] SI 2006/3317, reg 12.
[4] Via the Accession (Immigration and Worker Authorisation) (Amendment) Regulations 2011, SI 2011/2816.

15.104 Following the accession of Croatia to the EU on 1 July 2013 a similar scheme requiring worker authorisation documentation now applies to Croatian workers.[1] Under the Accession of Croatia (Immigration and Worker Authorisation) Regulations 2013, it is an offence for an employer knowingly to employ a Croatian national subject to worker authorisation where the employee does not hold a valid accession worker document or is prohibited from undertaking the employment because of a condition in his accession worker authorisation document.[2] Where an offence is being investigated immigration officers have the powers of entry, search and arrest given by sections 28B, 28D, 28E, 28G and 28H of the 1971 Act.[3]

Regulation 11 provides for a civil penalty where an employer employs a Croatian worker subject to the authorisation scheme if the employee is not the holder of a valid accession worker authorisation document or is in breach of a condition of such a document. The Secretary of State may give a penalty notice imposing a penalty of up to £5000 under this regulation, specifying why the employer is liable to the penalty; the amount of the penalty; how it is to be paid; specifying a date at least 28 days after the date specified in the notice, before which the penalty must be paid; explaining how the employer may object to the penalty and how it may be enforced.[4]

An employer is excused from paying the penalty if he can produce an accession worker authorisation document authorising the employment in question; an EEA registration certificate stating that the holder has unconditional access to the UK labour market, or a document confirming that the employee is not an accession State national subject to worker authorisation.[5] Alternatively the employer is excused if he complies with the stringent requirements set out in regulation 11(6).[6] Regulations 12 and 13 set out the scheme for objecting and appealing against a penalty notice. The Code of Practice issued by the Secretary of State under section 23 of the IAN 2006 is applicable to offences under the Regulations.[7]

1   For further details of accession workers see CHAPTER 6.
2   Accession of Croatia (Immigration and Worker Authorisation) Regulations 2013, SI 2013/1460, reg 15. On summary conviction, the maximum penalty is six months' imprisonment in England and Wales (51 weeks once s 281(5) of the Criminal Justice Act 2003 comes into force), six months' imprisonment in Scotland or Northern Ireland, a fine up to the statutory maximum, or both.
3   Ibid, reg 15(3).
4   Ibid, reg 11(4).
5   This may be either a passport, national identity card or other travel document: 2013 Regulations, Reg 11(5)(iii).
6   These requirements involve employers taking all reasonable steps to check the validity of the document, satisfying themselves that the date of birth is consistent with the appearance of the employee or prospective employee, taking all reasonable steps to check that the employee or prospective employee is the rightful holder of the document, and securely retaining a dated copy of the whole of the document in a format which cannot be subsequently altered for a period of not less than two years after it has come to an end.
7   By virtue of 2013 Regulations, reg 11(9).

15.105 As we have seen at **15.31** and **15.82** above, employers can be obliged to provide information to the Secretary of State about someone suspected of an immigration offence or irregularity, on pain of imprisonment. However, the information thus obtained cannot be used in a prosecution against the employer under section 21 of the IAN 2006.[1] Employers' premises may also be searched and employee records seized,[2] and there is no such constraint on the use of material seized.

1   Nationality, Immigration and Asylum Act 2002, s 139.
2   IA 1971, ss 28FA, 28FB, inserted by the Nationality, Immigration and Asylum Act 2002, s 154.

CARRIERS' LIABILITY

15.106 Ever since the first carriers' liability legislation in the UK, passed in 1987 in a panic response to the arrival of a flight containing 58 Sri Lankan Tamils with no visas, carrier sanctions have been one of the favourite and well-used weapons in the armoury against illegal entrants and asylum seekers (too often seen as synonymous).[1] Despite concerns that they undermine the fundamental right to seek and enjoy asylum set out in Article 14 of the UDHR and the right to leave one's own country enshrined in Article 12 of the International Covenant on Civil and Political Rights,[2] and despite overwhelming evidence that carrier sanctions do not deter immigration or the quest for asylum, but merely drive up the price and the human cost,[3] the UK government, in common with its European partners, continues the restrictive policies, which both make legal entry well-nigh impossible and penalise all those involved, however inadvertently, in illegal entry.[4] The most recent turn of the screw is the penalties for carriers of clandestine entrants, introduced in 1999, to join the original penalties for carriers of inadequately documented passengers – themselves extended to cover almost all forms of transport. A formidable range of powers is deployed to enforce carrier sanctions. The provisions are all contained in Part II of the IAA 1999, as amended by the Nationality, Immigration and Asylum Act 2002.[5] It has now been decided at High Court level that the penalty regime extends to the control zones in France as well as the UK. In *Bogdanic v Secretary of State for the Home Department*,[6] the court was required to determine a preliminary issue arising from an appeal to the county court by a lorry driver/carrier (B) against civil penalties imposed on him under the Immigration and Asylum Act 1999 Pt II. The issue is whether liability to pay a penalty extended to immigration control zones in France as well as those in the United Kingdom. The court held that they did so extend, when one considered all the indicators of the legislators' intention in the original and amending legislation. Sales J followed the interpretive approach in *Inco Europe Ltd*,[7] which allowed limited scope for rectification of drafting defects.

[1] See for example the Resolution on manifestly unfounded applications for asylum drafted by the Ad Hoc Group on Immigration and adopted at the Council of Ministers' meeting of 30 November 1992, which described as 'unlawful' the actions of asylum seekers who travelled to another continent rather than availing themselves of local protection.

[2] Among the vast critical literature see James Hathaway 'Harmonizing for Whom? The Devaluation of Refugee Protection in the Era of European Economic Integration' (1993) 26 Cornell International Law Journal 719; UNHCR Position on Conventions Recently Concluded in Europe (Dublin and Schengen Conventions), Aug 16 1991; International Law Association International Committee on the Status of Refugees, *Restrictive Measures in Europe* 21 (1992).

[3] Every year hundreds of would-be asylum claimants from sub-Saharan Africa, Iraq, Afghanistan and other refugee-producing areas of the world die attempting to cross the sea to Europe in small boats, or hiding in the holds of ships or in the undercarriages of aircraft or in lorries. The discovery of 35 migrants from Afghanistan inside a shipping container in Tilbury docks on 16 August 2014, one of whom died, is a timely reminder of this ongoing problem.

[4] See John Morrison The trafficking and smuggling of refugees UNHCR (July 2000).

[5] Nationality, Immigration and Asylum Act 2002, s 125, Sch 8.

[6] [2014] EWHC 2872 (QB).

[7] *Inco Europe Ltd v First Choice Distribution* [2000] 1 WLR 586. See also *R v Secretary of State for the Environment, Transport and the Regions, ex p Spath Holme Ltd* [2001] 2 AC 349 at paras 42, and 45-46.

Liability for clandestine entrants

15.107 The IAA 1999 imposed a fixed penalty of £2,000 for each clandestine entrant brought in by carriers, with no flexibility to reflect mitigating factors, no rights of appeal and a reverse burden of proof on the carrier to establish one of the statutory defences. It also gave the Secretary of State draconian powers of seizure and detention of vehicles. This combination of features was held by a majority of the Court of Appeal in *Roth*[1] to render the provisions incompatible with Article 6 and Article 1 of Protocol 1 of the ECHR. The provisions have been significantly modified as a result. Fixed penalties have been replaced by discretionary variable penalties, to be assessed with reference to a Code of Practice.[2] A right of appeal exists against liability for a penalty and its amount.[3] Safeguards attend the seizure and detention of vehicles.[4]

[1] *International Transport Roth GmbH v Secretary of State for the Home Department* [2002] EWCA Civ 158, [2002] 3 WLR 344.

[2] Level of penalties: Code of Practice under IAA 1999, ss 32(2), 32A, inserted by Nationality, Immigration and Asylum Act 2002, Sch 8, para 3.

[3] IAA 1999, s 35A, inserted by NIAA 2002, Sch 8, para 8.

[4] IAA 1999, s 36A, inserted by NIAA 2002, Sch 8, para 10.

15.108 Section 32 of the IAA 1999 (as amended) allows the Secretary of State to impose a penalty on persons responsible for a clandestine entrant. A clandestine entrant is defined as someone who either claims or intends to claim asylum or evades or tries to evade immigration control, having arrived in the UK concealed in a vehicle, ship, aircraft or rail freight wagon; passed or tried to pass through immigration control concealed in a vehicle; or arrived in the UK on a ship or aircraft, after embarking outside the UK concealed in a vehicle.[1] Aircraft includes hovercraft and a vehicle includes a trailer, semi-trailer, caravan or anything else designed for towing.[2] The owner and captain of the ship or aircraft, the train operator and the owner, hirer and driver of the vehicle (or operator, if the vehicle was a trailer) in or on which the clandestine entrant was concealed, are all 'responsible persons'.[3] All 'responsible persons' are potentially liable for a penalty up to a prescribed maximum[4] in respect of each clandestine entrant or concealed person carried.[5] 'Immigration control' for the purposes of the section includes any UK immigration control operated in a prescribed control zone outside the UK, and carriers are liable for the arrival of clandestine entrants in such a control zone.[6]

1   IAA 1999, s 32(1) as amended by Nationality, Immigration and Asylum Act 2002, Sch 8, para 2.
2   IAA 1999, s 43.
3   IAA 1999, s 32(5), (5A) and (6), as amended by Nationality, Immigration and Asylum Act 2002, Sch 8, para 2(5)–(7). But the provisions are not yet in force in relation to ships and aircraft.
4   The maximum currently prescribed by the Carriers' Liability Regulations 2002, SI 2002/2817, reg 3(1) is £2,000, with a maximum aggregate penalty of £4,000. The Secretary of State must have regard to the provisions of a Code of Practice on the level of penalty in determining the amount of any penalty: IAA 1999, s 32A, inserted by NIAA 2002, Sch 8, para 3.
5   IAA 1999, s 32(2) and (4), as amended by NIAA 2002, Sch 8, para 2.
6   IAA 1999, s 32(10). The part of France situated at Coquelles, which is a control zone for international purposes, is prescribed by SI 2000/685, reg 5. The Nationality, Immigration and Asylum Act 2002 (Juxtaposed Controls) Order 2003, SI 2003/2818, art 2, Sch 1 added Calais, Boulogne and Dunkirk.

15.109 The statutory definition of 'clandestine entrants' for whom responsible persons may incur penalties is far broader than its everyday usage. It includes not just those who try to enter without seeing (or being seen by) an immigration officer, but also those who present themselves at immigration control and claim asylum after stowing away on a ship or aircraft, or hidden in a lorry or rail freight wagon for the journey. In such a case the owner and captain of the ship or aircraft, or manager of the train in which they stowed away, or the owner, hirer and driver or operator of the lorry or trailer would all be potentially liable to pay a penalty. It also includes asylum seekers who present themselves at immigration control in, say, Dover having hidden in a vehicle in Ostend to embark on a cross-Channel ferry and got out of the vehicle during the crossing to leave the boat as a foot passenger. In such a situation, the owner, hirer or the driver of the vehicle in which they hid at Ostend would in theory be liable, although not the owner or captain of the ferry.[1] The provisions apply to private as well as public vehicles, so all car drivers must check that their vehicles are not concealing extra passengers, that windows are fully closed and doors and car boots fully locked before driving on to the cross-Channel ferry on their return from a continental holiday, to avoid liability. The provisions are not yet in force in relation to ships and aircraft, only in relation to vehicles (including buses, coaches, lorries and cars) and freight trains. They were held in *Roth*[2] not to amount to a restriction on free movement under EC law.

1   See IAA 1999, s 32(6). This would not apply if the ferry came from a designated port in a
     control zone (Calais, Boulogne or Dunkirk) because controls are carried out there: National-
     ity, Immigration and Asylum Act 2002 (Juxtaposed Controls) Order 2003, SI 2003/2818.
2   *International Transport Roth GmbH v Secretary of State for the Home Department* [2002]
     EWCA Civ 158 [2002] 3 WLR 344.

15.110 When a carrier becomes potentially liable for a penalty under section 32 of the IAA 1999 as amended, there are three statutory defences, the
burden of proof in each being on the carrier:

(i)   duress;[1] or
(ii)   that the carrier did not know and had no reasonable grounds for
       suspecting that a clandestine entrant might be concealed in the trans-
       porter; that an effective system for preventing the carriage of clandes-
       tine entrants was in operation in relation to the transporter; and that
       system was properly operated on the occasion in question;[2] or
(iii) (for rail freight), that the carrier knew or suspected that a clandestine
       entrant was or might be concealed in a rail freight wagon but could not
       stop the train or the shuttle of which the wagon formed a part without
       endangering safety, and an efficient system was in operation for
       preventing the carriage of clandestine entrants and was operated
       properly on the occasion in question.[3]

If a defence of duress is successfully relied on, every other responsible person
is entitled to the benefit of the defence.[4] Codes of Practice have been issued
which detail the precautions which should be taken by owners, hirers,
operators and drivers of road haulage and other commercial vehicles, buses
and coaches and private vehicles;[5] and those operating rail freight transport.
Regard will be had to its provisions in determining whether the system in
operation is effective for the purposes of the IAA 1999, section 34(3) defence.[6]

1   IAA 1999, s 34(2).
2   IAA 1999, s 34(3).
3   IAA 1999, s 34(3A), inserted by Nationality, Immigration and Asylum Act 2002, Sch 8,
     para 6.
4   IAA 1999, s 34(6) as amended by NIAA 2002, Sch 8, para 6.
5   The Prevention of Clandestine Entrants: Civil Penalty: Code of Practice for Vehicles was
     brought into force by the Carriers' Liability (Clandestine Entrants) (Code of Practice) Order
     2000, SI 2000/684, on 3 April 2000. On 1 March 2004, this was superseded by the Carriers'
     Liability (Clandestine Entrants) (Revised Code of Practice for Vehicles) Order 2004, SI
     2004/250. The revised Code inserts references to the additional control zones outside the UK
     prescribed by the Carriers' Liability (Amendment) Regulations 2004 for the purposes of
     section 32(10) of the 1999 Act. The latest version of this Code appears at: www.gov.uk/gov
     ernment/uploads/system/uploads/attachment_data/file/257187/levelofpencodeofpractice.pdf.
     There has also been a Code of Practice for Rail Freight, which was brought into force by the
     Carriers' Liability (Clandestine Entrants) (Code of Practice for Rail Freight) Order 2001, SI
     2001/312, on 1 March 2000; and one for freight shuttle wagons brought into force by the
     Carriers' Liability (Clandestine Entrants) (Code of Practice for Freight Shuttle Wagons) Order
     2001, SI 2001/3233.
6   IAA 1999, s 34(4).

15.111 Once the responsible persons are served with a penalty notice,
payment must be made within 60 days[1] unless a notice of objection is served
within 28 days,[2] in which case the Secretary of State decides whether to cancel,
reduce, uphold or increase the penalty.[3] There is a right of appeal to a county

court (or sheriff's court in Scotland)[4] against the imposition of a penalty or its amount, and the court may cancel or reduce the penalty or dismiss the appeal, which is by way of rehearing, having regard to the relevant Codes of Practice.[5] An appeal may be brought whether or not a notice of objection has been given or the penalty reduced or increased by the Secretary of State.[6] Now that the appeal system is in place, the Divisional Court's advice in *Balbo Auto Transporti*[7] to raise defences during enforcement proceedings is no longer appropriate, and is precluded by statute.[8] If a penalty notice has been given, a senior officer may detain a vehicle, small ship, small aircraft or rail freight wagon until all penalties and expenses are paid, but only if the driver is the owner or hirer or their employee or the penalty notice has been given to the owner or hirer,[9] and only if the officer believes there is a significant risk that the penalty will not be paid otherwise and no alternative security has been given.[10] Senior officers have the power to detain a relevant vehicle, small ship, small aircraft or rail freight wagon ('the transporter') pending (a) a decision whether to issue a penalty notice, or (b) its issue, or (c) a decision after issue of the penalty notice, whether to detain the transporter until all penalties and expenses have been paid, but such a 'provisional' detention' may not be exercised in any case for longer than is necessary in the circumstances, and may not exceed 24 hours following the first search of the transporter by an immigration officer after it arrived in the UK.[11] Application may be made to the county court for release of the transporter by anyone whose interests may be affected by detention.[12] On such an application, there is no longer any requirement to show a 'compelling need' to have the transporter released, as before, but the court is obliged to consider the extent of the hardship caused by its detention and the extent of the responsibility of the applicant, and any other relevant matter including the security provided and the risk of non-payment and doubts about liability.[13] The powers to detain transporters on non-payment of penalties are wider and the criteria for their release by a court more stringent.[14] Subject to any appeal or court order for release, the Secretary of State is empowered to sell the transporter after 12 weeks if the penalty is not paid.[15]

[1] Period defined by the Carriers' Liability Regulations 2002, SI 2002/2817, reg 4.
[2] Period defined by SI 2002/2817, reg 6.
[3] IAA 1999, s 35 as amended by Nationality, Immigration and Asylum Act 2002, Sch 8, para 7. He must do so within 70 days of the issue of the penalty notice: SI 2002/2817, reg 7.
[4] IAA 1999, s 43 as amended by NIAA 2002, Sch 8, para 15; the court may transfer the proceedings to the High Court or Court of Session.
[5] IAA 1999, s 35A, added by NIAA 2002, Sch 8, para 8.
[6] IAA 1999, s 35A(6).
[7] *R (on the application of Balbo B & C Auto Transporti Internationali) v Secretary of State for the Home Department* [2001] EWHC 195 (Admin), [2001] 4 All ER 423, [2001] 1 WLR 1556.
[8] IAA 1999, s 35(11), inserted by NIAA 2002, Sch 8, para 7(5).
[9] IAA 1999, s 36(1), (2A) as amended by NIAA 2002, Sch 8, para 9.
[10] IAA 1999, s 36(2), as inserted.
[11] IAA 1999, s 36(2B), (2C) as inserted.
[12] IAA 1999, s 37(2), (3), (3A), (3B) as amended and inserted. For 'court' see fn 4 above. In England, Wales and Northern Ireland; in Scotland, the sheriff or the Court of Session: IAA 1999, s 43.
[13] IAA 1999, s 37(3B) as inserted.
[14] IAA 1999, s 36A, inserted by NIAA 2002, Sch 8, para 10. The power is not to be exercised while an appeal against a penalty is pending or could be brought: s 36A(5). A court may release a transporter detained for non-payment of a penalty only if it considers that detention

is unlawful or if the penalty notice was not issued to the owner or employee and the court considers release the right course: s 37(3A), (7) as amended and inserted.

[15] IAA 1999, s 37(5A), inserted by NIAA 2002, Sch 8, para 11. The power of sale lapses if not exercised within a prescribed period, which is currently 60 days: s 37(5B) as inserted, SI 2002/2817, reg 11.

Liability for inadequately documented passengers

15.112 An EC Directive[1] requires Member States to enforce carriers' responsibility to check passengers' travel documents and to impose penalties on carriers which do not comply. The UK has had carriers' liability legislation to this effect in force since 1987,[2] but the provisions have been overhauled by the Nationality, Immigration and Asylum Act 2002. Section 40 of the IAA 1999, as substituted by the NIAA 2002,[3] imposes a fixed penalty of £2,000 on owners of ships or aircraft[4] on which passengers arrive who require leave to enter the UK[5] and fail, if required, to produce to an immigration officer an immigration document and a visa of the required kind[6] An 'immigration document' is a passport or a document relating to a non-British citizen serving the same purpose as a passport.[7] It must be in force and must satisfactorily establish the identity and nationality or citizenship of the holder, thus penalising carriers for passengers' possession of false documents, although carriers are entitled to regard a document as authentic and belonging to the holder unless the contrary is reasonably apparent.[8] No penalty is payable if the owner shows that the now undocumented passenger produced a document on embarkation.[9] Guidance has been issued to carriers on passport and visa requirements.[10]

[1] Directive 2001/51/EC of 28 June 2001.

[2] Immigration (Carriers' Liability) Act 1987, rushed through Parliament in response to the arrival of a group of 58 Tamil asylum seekers on one flight from Sri Lanka.

[3] Nationality, Immigration and Asylum Act 2002, Sch 8, para 13.

[4] Not vehicles or trains, although the section can be amended by order to include trains: IAA 1999, s 40(7), (8) as substituted.

[5] Ie excluding British nationals, those with the right of abode, EEA and Swiss nationals (who do not require leave to enter under IA 1988, s 7), and diplomats, who are exempt from immigration control: IAA 1999, s 40(1) as substituted.

[6] IAA 1999, s 40(1), (2) as substituted. A visa might include a transit visa if one is required by passengers of that nationality: IAA 1999, s 40(6). The power to require transit passengers to hold a transit visa is contained in s 41 (in force 8 December 2002). Persons requiring transit visas are set out in the Immigration (Passenger Transit Visas) Order 2003, SI 2003/1185, as successively amended on 11 occasions and most recently by the Immigration (Passenger Transit Visa) (Amendment) Order 2014 SI 2014/1514. The list of countries is contained in the Schedule to SI 2003/2628 read with the successive amendments. At the time of writing the list is Afghanistan, Albania, Algeria, Angola, Bangladesh, Belarus, Burma, Burundi, Cameroon, Congo, Democratic Republic of Congo, Ecuador, Eritrea, Ethiopia, Egypt, Former Yugoslav Republic of Macedonia, Gambia, Ghana, Guinea, Guinea-Bissau, India, Iran, Iraq, Ivory Coast, Jamaica, Kenya, Lebanon, Lesotho, Liberia, Libya, Malawi, Moldova, Mongolia, Nepal, Nigeria, Pakistan, Palestinian Territories, China, Rwanda, Senegal, Serbia and Montenegro, Sierra Leone, Somalia, Sri Lanka, South Africa, Sudan, Swaziland, Syria, Tanzania, Turkey, Uganda, Venezuela (unless the passport contains biometric information in an electronic chip) Vietnam (unless the holder has a diplomatic or official passport) and Zimbabwe. There is a limited exemption for passengers travelling via the UK to or from Canada, Australia, New Zealand and the US (SI 2005/492). The arrival without a visa of nationals of countries to whom the Transit Without a Visa (TWOV) concession does not apply, and of passengers accepted for transit under TWOV who are subsequently denied onward carriage by an airline while in the UK, will render the inward carrier liable. See the

guidance: *Charging Procedures: A guide for carriers*, to be found at www.gov.uk/government
/uploads/system/uploads/attachment_data/file/275926/Charging_Guide_Jan_2014_Version
_6.pdf

7   IAA 1999, s 40(9) as substituted.
8   IAA 1999, s 40(5) as substituted. One of the complaints in the *Hoverspeed* case (*R v Secretary
     of State for the Home Department, ex p Hoverspeed* [1999] INLR 591) was that under French
     law it is a criminal offence for unauthorised persons, including carriers, to conduct identity
     checks, as opposed to documentary checks, but this did not allow the company to claim the
     benefit of the defence under this subsection.
9   IAA 1999, s 40(4) as substituted.
10   See *Charging Procedures: A Guide for Carriers*, as above (fn 6).

15.113 If the Secretary of State decides to impose a penalty under section 40,
she must notify the carrier of the reasons for doing so, specify the amount, set
the date and manner of payment, and inform the carrier of the provisions for
objecting to the imposition of a penalty. The notice must also explain the steps
the Secretary of State may take to recover the charge.[1] If an objection is made
in accordance with the procedure,[2] the Secretary of State may cancel the
charge.[3] The time limits for making an objection and for the Secretary of State
to make a decision in response are the same as for carriers of clandestine
entrants.[4] There are also similar appeal rights to those operating in the case of
clandestine entrants,[5] but the power to detain or sell transporters has been
abolished, since liability no longer applies to vehicles.[6]

1   IAA 1999, s 40A, inserted by Nationality, Immigration and Asylum Act 2002, Sch 8, para 13,
     in force 8 December 2002: SI 2002/2811.
2   IAA 1999, s 40A(3), (4), Carriers' Liability Regulations 2002, SI 2002/2817, reg 6.
3   IAA 1999, s 40A(5) as inserted.
4   IAA 1999, s 40A as inserted; Carriers' Liability Regulations 2002, SI 2002/2817. See **15.111**
     above.
5   IAA 1999, s 40B as inserted. See **15.111** above.
6   IAA 1999, s 42 was repealed by NIAA 2002, Sch 8, para 14.

15.114 The current Home Office guidance for carriers facing penalties under
section 40[1] sets out some of the situations in which immigration inspectors
would normally be prepared to waive a charge:[2]

- the passenger is a child travelling as part of an organised school group,
  in the care of a responsible adult;
- the passenger has arrived on a flight or ship which, following departure,
  has been diverted to the UK due to medical emergency, urgent
  mechanical problems, severe weather conditions or other severe and
  unforeseen emergencies requiring diversion to a UK port;[3]
- the passenger is a stowaway and the carrier has taken all reasonable
  security and searching measures to ensure that no unauthorised persons
  board;[4]
- the carrier has no realistic alternative to bringing the passenger to or via
  the UK, eg where the law or government of another country requires it
  (unless the carrier had previously passenger through the UK without the
  documents required for that purpose, eg if the passenger had passed
  through the UK in direct transit without a necessary visa for his final
  destination or for any intermediate destination);
- the carrier acted on the advice of a UK government representative and
  it was reasonable to rely on that advice;[5]

- the case is the first to arise from a particular route from that port to the UK;[6]
- at the time of check-in the passenger was in imminent and self-evident danger of his or her life, and had no reasonable means of obtaining the necessary documents, and the UK was the only or clearly the most appropriate destination, and the carrier had no opportunity to verify his or her acceptability with the UK authorities;[7]
- there are exceptional compelling compassionate reasons or other compelling circumstances justifying waiver.[8]
- in the case of an used visa, the Border Force officer's endorsement is not placed on the same page, or on an adjacent page. A charge may be waived if the date of the endorsement is unclear.

In addition, it appears to be the government's policy to waive or refund the charge in respect of passengers ultimately granted full refugee status (a concession not extended to those admitted for any other reason).[9] Charges will also be waived for visa nationals arriving by air who qualified for a visa waiver under the Transit without Visa concession, where the passenger had the necessary documentation for his or her ultimate destination and the carrier genuinely believed that their sole purpose was to pass through the UK in onward passage. The waiver will not apply, if the passenger is subsequently denied onward carriage by the airline, while in the UK, owing to detection of inadequate documentation.[10] Carriers may also escape liability by achieving and retaining Approved Gate Check (AGC) Status, for which they have to fulfil stringent criteria for checking passengers' documentation prior to embarkation.[11] As of October 2012, there were 441 routes to the UK with Advanced Gate Check status.[12]

[1]   The current version of this guidance: *Charging Procedures, a Guide for Carriers* is available at www.gov.uk/government/uploads/system/uploads/attachment_data/file/275926/Charging_Gu ide_Jan_2014_Version_6.pdf
[2]   See Appendix A for the list of circumstances.
[3]   The waiver will not apply where it was known prior to departure that the destination would be the UK or where a decision is subsequently taken to divert to the UK for commercial reasons only. (*Charging Procedures* Appendix A, fn 1 above).
[4]   In deciding whether a charge will be imposed in this scenario, account will be taken of the carrier's previous record in carrying unauthorised persons and co-operation with the UK Border Force in seeking to prevent the carriage of such persons, in particular whether the carrier has made proper use of effective equipment used to search vehicles and containers. The guidance states that current Home Office policy is not to impose section 40 charges where the persons concerned can be shown to have boarded vessels concealed in vehicles (*Charging Procedures* Appendix A, fn 1 above).
[5]   A number of ports and airports overseas now have UK liaison immigration officers (LIOs) or airline liaison officers (ALOs) permanently based there, advising carriers on passengers' eligibility to travel and authenticity of their documentation. They are responsible for preventing many hundreds of passengers, including refugees, from embarking on journeys to the UK. See *European Roma Rights Centre v Immigration Officer at Prague Airport (United Nations High Comr for Refugees intervening)* [2003] EWCA Civ 666, [2003] INLR 374; revsd [2004] UKHL 55, [2005] 2 WLR 1. See also Morrison *The Trafficking and Smuggling of Refugees* (July 2000), UNHCR p 40; UNHCR *Interception of Asylum seekers and Refugees: The international framework and recommendations for a comprehensive approach* Standing Committee, 9 June 2000 [EC/50/SC/CRP.17].
[6]   Again, a charge may not be waived if the carrier has failed to act on advice previously given by UK Border Force to avoid inadequately documented passengers being carried in similar circumstances, A waiver in this scenario is unlikely to be granted more than once (*Charging Procedures* Appendix A, fn 1 above).
[7]   The advised course of action under the guidance is to contact the nearest UNHCR office or UK representative. (*Charging Procedures* Appendix A, fn 1 above).

8   Carriers are advised to ascertain whether a waiver is likely to be given pre-embarkation if possible (*Charging Procedures* Appendix A, fn 1 above).
9   In the wording of the policy: 'a credit may arise (on your account) . . . if a charge that has been paid is later waived, perhaps because the person concerned has been granted refugee status (*Charging Procedures* at para 8.3, fn 1 above),'
10 See *Charging Procedures* (fn 1 above), para 2.6 for detailed requirements of this concession. See **15.112** fn 6 above for a list of countries whose nationals require transit visas.
11 The criteria for Advanced Gate Check status are an audited high standard of document checking and security procedures at the port of embarkation, a good level of cooperation from the carrier and a satisfactory record in relation to carriers' liability responsibilities: *Charging Procedures* (fn 1 above), section 9.
12 Home Office consultation document on carriers' liability penalty charges, October 2012, at w ww.gov.uk/government/uploads/system/uploads/attachment_data/file/147875/consultation-im pact-assessment.pdf

15.115 In the *Hoverspeed* case[1] the company, which had incurred (disputed) liabilities of almost £500,000 for carrying inadequately documented passengers, mostly passengers without a valid or current visa, sought declarations that the carriers' liability legislation offended against EC law in two distinct ways: (i) it constituted an unlawful restriction on the company's right to provide services, contrary to Article 49 EC (ex Article 59); (ii) it constituted an unlawful interference with the free movement rights of EEA nationals and their families who were subjected to documentary checks, an interference which the company was entitled to rely on. The Divisional Court rejected both arguments. Simon Brown LJ made the point that the Schengen Convention,[2] incorporated into EU law via the Amsterdam Treaty, obliged Member States (except the UK, Ireland and Denmark, which have opted out) to impose carrier sanctions, making it realistic to assume that it was compatible with EC law,[3] and held that the legislation did not impose measures so disproportionate as to thwart the central purpose of the EC Treaty, the free movement of persons, and so did not constitute a restriction for the purposes of Article 49 EC (ex Article 59).[4] If it did amount to a restriction, it was justified on public policy grounds, in the interests of immigration control, as an essential adjunct to the effective operation of the visa system.[5] Nor did it impede free movement of EEA nationals, who suffered only a brief though careful documentary check which had no perceptible effect on their freedom to travel.[6] In the course of his judgment he accepted implicitly that carrier sanctions deprived asylum seekers of any choice as to the country of asylum,[7] a choice which he held in the later *Adimi* case[8] to be open to asylum seekers on a limited basis as part of the international obligations towards refugees.

1   *R v Secretary of State for the Home Department, ex p Hoverspeed* [1999] INLR 591.
2   Article 26(2) of the Schengen Convention.
3   *Hoverspeed* above, at 603A.
4   *Hoverspeed* above, at 607H.
5   *Hoverspeed* above, at 608D. In *International Transport Roth GmbH v Secretary of State for the Home Department* [2002] EWCA Civ 158 [2002] 3 WLR 344) the CA held that the scheme penalising carriers of clandestine entrants did not breach EC law either.
6   *Hoverspeed* above, at 612H.
7   *Hoverspeed* above, at 599H.
8   *R v Uxbridge Magistrates' Court, ex p Adimi* [1999] INLR 490 at 496H–497F.

15.116 It is clear from the terms of the IAA 1999, as amended, and the guidance, that imposing a penalty on carriers is a matter of both jurisdiction and discretion. Under section 1 of the original Immigration (Carriers'

Liability) Act 1987, liability was imposed where undocumented passengers arrived in the UK or did not possess the necessary visas, but the carriers had a defence if the passenger had shown them travel documents at the port of departure, whose falsity was not reasonably apparent. In the *Hoverspeed* case Simon Brown LJ appears to have treated this as a jurisdictional threshold, which it was for the court, not the Home Office, to decide.[1] If correct, this suggests that the power to impose a penalty depends upon the establishment of jurisdictional or precedent facts. But once the jurisdictional basis is established, then there is room for a further challenge to the exercise of the Secretary of State's discretion, for example, in setting the standards of scrutiny he or she would expect from carriers, before deciding to enforce the penalty. As Simon Brown LJ said, 'it is ultimately for the court to decide, in any given case, whether the Secretary of State is, by his officials, setting impermissibly high standards for the detection of forged or otherwise inadequate travel documents'.[2] This puts the carrier regime on the same basis as immigration detention, which can give rise to a jurisdictional challenge as well as a challenge on traditional public law principles to a particular policy of detention. The distinction is important, but is unlikely to be tested in the higher courts, given the newly established rights of appeal.

[1] *R v Secretary of State for the Home Department, ex p Hoverspeed* [1999] INLR 591, QBD, at 602A. On precedent fact cases, see *R v Governor of Brixton Prison, ex p Ahsan (or Ahsen or Ahson)* [1969] 2 QB 222, QBD (proof that arrest took place within 24 hours of A's entry into the UK); *Khawaja v Secretary of State for the Home Department* [1984] AC 74, at 97E (Lord Fraser), 110E and 111E (Lord Scarman), 122–124 (Lord Bridge) (proof of illegal entry); *Tan Te Lam v Superintendent of Tai A Chau Detention Centre* [1997] AC 97, 111B–E and 113E–D, PC (proof that detention is 'pending removal').

[2] *Hoverspeed* above, at 602C. Contrast *R v Governor of Durham Prison ex p Singh* [1984] 1 WLR 704, QBD and *Tan Te Lam v Superintendent of Tai A Chau Detention Centre* [1997] AC 97, at 113E–D, PC (probably both jurisdictional challenges according to Mance LJ in *R (on the application of Khadir) v Secretary of State for the Home Department* [2003] EWCA Civ 475, [2003] INLR 426, at para 72) with *Nadarajah v Secretary of State for the Home Department* [2004] INLR 139, CA (challenge to policy not to treat removal as imminent, when judicial proceedings have been initiated). See further CHAPTER 17 below.

15.117 The carrier sanction regime imposes on carriers the duty of trying to apply the correct visa requirements on its passengers, and, inevitably, they will get it wrong. Does this make them liable for refusing to carry someone, because they wrongly believe that they do not have the correct travel documents? In *Naraine v Hoverspeed*[1] a British citizen of Asian/Caribbean origin holding a British visitor's passport (BVP), who was refused access to a hovercraft to France on a day trip, lost his claim against Hoverspeed on the ground that the company's action was dictated by French insistence on visas for BVP holders and the need to follow its carrier sanction regime, which was not in breach of EC law, and there was no racial discrimination since all BVP holders were treated in the same way. But in *Farah v British Airways and Home Office*,[2] an appeal against the striking out of a negligence claim, Somali nationals, who had been refused access to a British Airways flight in Cairo on the advice of an airline liaison officer and were subsequently deported to Ethiopia, were held entitled to pursue a claim against the Home Office for the wrong advice, since loss, including non-economic loss, was eminently foreseeable and it was arguable that the airline liaison officer owes a duty of care to passengers to give correct and accurate advice to airlines as to the validity of documents issued at a British diplomatic post overseas.

1   (1999) Independent, 18 November; [1999] CLY 2273.
2   *Farah v British Airways plc and Home Office* (2000) Times, 26 January, CA.

LANDLORD SANCTIONS

15.118 Sweeping proposals contained in the Immigration Act 2014 came into force on 1 December 2014 and two new statutory instruments have been made to explain and enforce the new provisions. They are the Immigration (Residential Accommodation) (Prescribed Requirements and Codes of Practice) Order 2014[1] and the Immigration (Residential Accommodation) (Prescribed Requirements and Codes of Practice) Order 2014,[2] both of which come into force on 1 December 2014. Given our publication deadlines it is too late to comment on the new Orders. Under the new law[3] all non-British, non-EEA and non-Swiss citizens who require leave to enter or remain in the UK but do not have it, or whose leave to enter or remain is subject to a condition preventing them from occupying premises, are disqualified from entering into a residential tenancy agreement.[4] All arrangements where a person is permitted to occupy a property as their only or main residence in return for the payment of rent are residential tenancy agreements, unless the arrangement falls into one of the exclusions set out in Schedule 3.[5] Accommodation for which no rent is paid, such as convents or monasteries, does not fall within this definition, and so is not subject to the restriction on letting, nor is accommodation which is not used by a person as their only or main home. So, for example, holiday accommodation will not ordinarily be captured, as for most people it will not provide their only or main home, but if somebody chooses to live in a hotel, the arrangements for that person will be captured. The list of excluded properties in Schedule 3 includes social housing, care homes and refuges. Student accommodation organised by universities and colleges is also exempt. Subsection (7) creates a power to amend Schedule 3, in case further categories of agreement need to be excluded from these provisions, or some should be brought within the scope of the restriction. The order is subject to the affirmative resolution procedure.

1   SI 2014/2873.
2   SI 2014/2874.
3   Chapter 1: Residential Tenancies, ss 20-33 Immigration Act 2014. It appears that there has been Ministerial agreement that the scheme will initially apply on a pilot basis. Details of the pilot have not yet been made public (See JCWI: *Immigration Act 2014 Summary of Provisions*, available at www.jcwi.org.uk/sites/default/files/Immigration%20Act%202014%20Summary %20Provisions_0.pdf
4   Immigration Act 2014, s 21.
5   Immigration Act 2014, s 20(2)–(4).

15.119 Under the scheme landlords have a duty to check their tenants' immigration status. The Secretary of State is empowered under section 23 to impose a penalty of up to £3,000[1] for each disqualified adult a landlord allows to occupy property. The penalty also applies to agents contracted by a landlord to carry out checks on an occupant's right to rent.[2] An agent may be liable where they act in the course of a business, so for instance letting agents who make status checks on tenants, the landlord cannot simply pass the checking burden on by asking a friend to carry out the checks for them. The agreement with the agent must be made in writing.

Section 24 of the 2014 Act sets out the statutory excuses available to landlords. An excuse can be established if the landlord carries out checks according to the prescribed requirements and the carrying out of those requirements do not show that the prospective occupant was disqualified. Subsections (3) and (4) set out the duration before a tenancy commences within which the checks must be carried out. In the case of those with permanent status in the UK, the checks may be carried out at any time before the tenancy is entered into. For those subject to immigration control and/or who have a limited right to rent the checks must be carried out within a set period prior to the commencement of the tenancy. This period will be specified by order. This is to prevent a perverse scenario whereby checks reveal a person's leave will expire prior to the commencement of the tenancy but a landlord is nevertheless able to rent to them because they had valid leave at the time the check was carried out. The section further provides that if an occupant's leave expires during a tenancy the landlord can establish an excuse by carrying out repeat checks at the specified intervals, (or arranging for an agent to do so), and by then telling the Secretary of State that a disqualified person is in their property if the repeat check identifies that the person's limited right to rent is no longer valid. They must make this report as soon as reasonably practicable after making the repeat check.[3]

¹   Immigration Act 2014, s 23(1)–(2),
²   Immigration Act 2014, s 25.
³   Immigration Act 2014, s 24(6).

15.120 As with the sanctions scheme for employers, landlords may object to or appeal against a penalty notice. A landlord may object to liability for imposition of a penalty or to the amount, or on the basis that he is not the liable party, or has complied with the requirements set out in section 24 for landlords, or section 26 for agents, or that the penalty given is too high in the circumstances.[1] The objection must be made in writing to the Secretary of State within a prescribed period to be specified by order and must give reasons.[2] The Secretary of State must consider the objection, with regard to a Code of Practice issued under section[3]; and may decide to cancel the penalty, change the amount which must be paid as a result of the objection either by reducing or increasing it, or take no action and leave the penalty notice as it stands. The Secretary of State must notify the agent or landlord of the decision within a set period that will be set out by order.[4]

Section 30 sets out the appeals regime. There is a right of appeal where the landlord or agent wishes to challenge the Secretary of State's decision on their objection to a penalty, and ensures a right of appeal should the Secretary of State fail to respond to an objection within the required timeframe. An appeal may be brought on the basis that there is no liability for a penalty, that the penalty is too high, or that payment is excused on the basis of compliance with the specified requirements.[5] On appeal the court[6] may allow the appeal and cancel or reduce the penalty, or dismiss the appeal.[7]

Subsection 3 provides that the appeal is a re-hearing of the Secretary of State's decision to impose a penalty and is to be determined having regard to the Code of Practice that has effect at the time of the appeal and any other matters which the court thinks relevant (including mattes of which the Secretary of State was unaware. As with the new regime for employers imposed under the 2014 Act[8], the right of appeal only arises if the landlord or agent has already made an objection under section 29 before an appeal may be brought.[9] Any appeal must be brought within 28 days of the 'relevant date', defined according to the outcome of the objection under section 29.[10] Section 31 provides that a penalty due to the Secretary of State may be recovered as though it were due under an order of a court. In other words, the Secretary of State may take action to recover money owed under a penalty notice without first issuing a substantive claim with a court. Instead the debt may be registered with the court, and enforcement action pursued without further order.

1   Immigration Act 2014, s 29(1) and (2).
2   Immigration Act 2014, s 29(3).
3   The Code of Practice must set out the criteria to be applied in deciding whether to impose a penalty and the amount of the penalty, guidance on when a person will be considered to be using premises as their 'only or main residence', and details of the steps landlords will reasonably be expected to take to determine the identity of those occupying the premises under the terms of a residential tenancy agreement: section 32 of the Immigration Act 2014.The whole scheme is quite likely to result in racially discriminatory refusals of tenancies. Section 33 of the Act seeks to deal with this. Under section 33 the Code of Practice must specify how a landlord can avoid contravening the Equality Act 2010 and the Race Relations Order 1997. The Secretary of State also has a duty under this section to consult the Commission for Equality and Human Rights and the Equality Commission for Northern Ireland. Before publication a draft Code must be laid before Parliament and representations about the draft Code considered. See now the Immigration (Residential Accommodation) (Prescribed Requirements and Codes of Practice) Order 2014, SI 2014/2873, which came into force on 1 December 2014.
4   Immigration Act 2014, s 29(4)–(6).
5   Immigration Act 2014, s 30(1).
6   The Court is the county court in England or Wales, if the residential tenancy relates to premises in England or Wales, to the county court in Northern Ireland if the premises are in Northern Ireland and the Sheriff Court if the premises are in in Scotland: IA 2014, s 30(10).
7   Immigration Act 2014, s 30(2).
8   See **15.99** above.
9   Immigration Act 2014, s 30(5).
10 Immigration Act 2014, s 30(6)–(9).

Chapter 16

DEPORTATION AND REPATRIATION

DEPORTATION

Introduction

16.1 The following abbreviations are used in this chapter:

CJA	Criminal Justice Act
EIG	Enforcement Instructions and Guidance:see: www.ukba.homeoffice.gov.uk/policyandlaw/guidance
ERS	Early Removal Scheme
ERED	ERS eligibility date
FNP	Foreign national prisoner
HDC	Home Detention Curfew Home Detention Curfew
PS1	Prison Service Instruction
PSO	Prison Service Orders

Deportation is the process whereby a non-British citizen can be compulsorily removed from the UK and prevented from returning unless the deportation order is revoked.[1] A deportation order operates to cancel leave to remain.[2] Furthermore, a successful appeal or revocation decision does not operate to reinstate that leave to remain, allowing the Secretary of State in those circumstances to grant short term successive periods of leave to remain under Paragraph 399B of the Immigration Rules, even where the appellant previously had indefinite leave to remain, to allow review until the obstacle to deportation is removed.[3] But deportation has an effect long after the removal. A deportation order continues in force until revoked. Deportation is thus to be distinguished from other forms of compulsory removal which only bring a particular application or entry to an end, although they may create difficulties for an immigrant seeking to enter in the future. These various powers are not mutually exclusive: being an illegal entrant or a psychiatric patient does not prevent the exercise of the power to deport, provided the conditions for deportation exist.[4]

---

[1]   Immigration Act 1971, s 5(1) and (2).

[2]   Immigration Act 1971, s 5(1).

[3]   *R (on the application of George (Fitzroy)) v Secretary of State for the Home Department* [2014] UKSC 28.

[4]   See *Patel (Yanus) v Immigration Appeal Tribunal* [1989] Imm AR 416, CA. As to the alternative use of deportation or Mental Health Act 1983 powers see *R v Immigration Appeal Tribunal and the Secretary of State for the Home Department, ex p Alghali* [1986] Imm AR 376; *X v Secretary of State for the Home Department* [2001] 1 WLR 740, [2001] INLR 205, CA; *MJ (Angola) v Secretary of State for the Home Department* [2010] EWCA Civ 557, [2010] All ER (D) 209 (May). See further CHAPTER 16.

16.2 In 2006, populist agitation in the media led to a public outcry over foreign prisoners being released from prison at the end of their sentences without being considered for deportation. This led initially to amendment of the Immigration Rules and thousands of people being considered for deportation in circumstances where prior to that date such consideration would have been unlikely. It also led to foreign nationals (or in some instances those with 'foreign sounding' names) being refused release from prison on their release date or being recategorised from open prison conditions to closed conditions. By the end of 2007, radical statutory changes had been enacted by Parliament requiring the Secretary of State to make an 'automatic deportation order' in prescribed circumstances and introducing a presumption of detention.[1] The incremental tightening of deportation processes continued with the introduction into the Immigration Rules on 9 July 2012 of new provisions introducing for the first time a set of criteria by reference to which the impact of Article 8 in criminal deportation cases was to be assessed.[2] It has culminated to date in the Immigration Act 2014 incorporation into primary legislation a series of 'considerations' designed to dictate the approach to Article 8 assessment by decisionmakers[3] and further by the introduction of a new certification process rendering non-suspensive the appeal rights of deportees absent demonstration of serious and irreparable harm.[4]

[1]   UK Borders Act 2007, ss 32–39.
[2]   Statement of Changes to the Immigration Rules HC194, paras 390–399A.
[3]   Immigration Act 2014, ss 17A–17C.
[4]   Immigration Act 2014, s 19.

History of the power to deport

16.3 Deportation was a power originally confined to aliens,[1] or foreign nationals. Since the late eighteenth century it has always been regulated by statute or an Order made under statute, the last being the Aliens Order 1953.[2] For example, there was power under the Aliens Order 1953 to deport aliens on the ground that to do so was conducive to the public good.[3] In 1962 the first provisions enabling the deportation of Commonwealth citizens were introduced. But at first deportation was only available on the recommendation of a criminal court following a conviction, including convictions for immigration offences under the Commonwealth Immigrants Act 1962.[4] In 1969 the Secretary of State for the Home Department was given the power to initiate deportation proceedings against Commonwealth citizens who were in breach of their conditions of admission.[5] With the coming into force of the Immigration Act 1971 in 1973, the position of Commonwealth immigrants and aliens was made broadly the same. Anyone (except exempt persons including certain Commonwealth citizens, see below) could be deported for overstaying or breaching conditions of leave; on grounds that it was conducive to the public good; for belonging to the family of someone being deported on these grounds; or on a recommendation in a criminal case.[6]

[1]   Ie not Commonwealth citizens. Defined in British Nationality Act 1981, s 50(1).
[2]   SI 1953/1671, made under the Aliens Restriction Act 1914 and the Aliens Restriction (Amendment) Act 1919, which were temporary laws renewed each year under the Expiring Laws Continuance Acts. For arguments about the Prerogative, see CHAPTER 1, above.
[3]   Aliens Order 1953, art 20(2)(b), now repealed.
[4]   Commonwealth Immigrants Act 1962 and 1968, s 6, now repealed.

⁵ Immigration Appeals Act 1969, s 16, now repealed.
⁶ Immigration Act 1971, unamended, s 3(5), (6).

16.4 The law distinguished between illegal entrants, who (like those refused leave to enter) could be removed without further ado,¹ and those who had entered lawfully but had breached conditions or overstayed. The latter were made subject to deportation (connoting not just removal but prohibition on re-entry), but had the protection of an in-country appeal right before this was done. In one of its more dramatic reforms, the Immigration and Asylum Act 1999 removed this distinction. From 2 October 2000, overstayers, those breaching conditions of their leave and persons obtaining leave by deception, together with their families, became subject to administrative removal procedures identical to those applying to illegal entrants.² Only those protected by transitional provisions and those participating in a regularisation programme were excepted.³

¹ Immigration Act 1971, Sch 2, para 9.
² Immigration and Asylum Act 1999, s 10. See CHAPTER 17 below.
³ Immigration and Asylum Act 1999, s 9, Sch 15, para 12.

DEPORTATION – LIABILITY AND EXEMPTION

Non-British citizens

16.5 A British citizen cannot be deported.¹ If someone becomes a citizen (or acquires the right of abode and is therefore deemed to be a citizen for the purposes of the Immigration Acts) any deportation order ceases to have effect.² The term 'British citizen' includes a Commonwealth citizen who had the right of abode in the UK before 1983.³ Thus a Commonwealth woman married to a British citizen before 1983 is not liable to be deported.⁴ Section 65 of the new Immigration Act 2014, inserts new paragraphs 4E to J, to allow certain citizens of the UK and colonies to register by entitlement, where there was no acquisition of citizenship by birth, as a consequence of the father not being married to the mother. Where the deportee was historically denied citizenship as a result of discriminatory legislation, deportation may amount to a breach of Articles 8 and 14 ECHR.⁵ There is no legal bar in UK domestic law to deporting a British Overseas Territories citizen or a British Overseas citizen,⁶ and in the case of British Overseas citizen visitors there can be no legitimate expectation that they will not be deported.⁷ In practice, however, it is extremely difficult as there appears to be little obligation on the country of former residence to receive them back.⁸ Equally, there is no bar on the deportation of EEA nationals or Turkish nationals and their dependants who have rights to reside as employed or self-employed persons under the Turkey-EC Association Agreement, but special rules apply.⁹ There is no statutory bar on the deportation of Convention refugees, although the Immigration Rules preclude the making of a deportation order against anyone whose removal would breach the UK's obligations under the Refugee Convention or the ECHR.¹⁰ There are provisions for revoking both citizenship and the right of abode. See CHAPTERS 2 and 4, above. If this action was taken successfully such people would become liable for deportation. Where British Citizenship is in dispute, the onus is on the person facing deportation, who asserts their entitlement, to prove it.[11]

1 Immigration Act 1971, ss 3(5), 6(2).
2 Immigration Act 1971, s 5(2). This contrasts with the position under the old law of an alien who became a British subject after the making of a deportation order: see *C v E* (1946) 62 TLR 326.
3 Immigration Act 1971, s 2, as amended by British Nationality Act 1981.
4 Immigration Act 1971, ss 2(2) and 5(2). But if the marriage took place after a deportation order had been signed, then she would not be deemed to be a British citizen.
5 *R (on the application of Johnson) v Secretary of State for the Home Department* [2014] EWHC 2386 (Admin) (17 July 2014), Dingemans, J set out the five questions to be asked in approaching Article 14 cases and held that where a deportee would have been denied citizenship during his minority, as a result of discriminatory legislation that did not entitle the illegitimate children of British fathers to automatically acquire citizenship, if on the balance of probabilities such an application would have been successful, but for the discrimination, deportation would amount to a breach of Article 8. Although deporting foreign criminals was deemed to be conducive to the public good, treating the deportee as a foreign criminal amounted to a breach of his rights under Article 14, when read in conjunction with Article 8.
6 See *R v Immigration Appeal Tribunal, ex p Sunsara* [1995] Imm AR 15.
7 *Patel v Secretary of State for the Home Department* [1993] Imm AR 392, CA.
8 See *R v Chief Immigration Officer, Gatwick Airport, ex p Singh (Harjendar)* [1987] Imm AR 346, QBD. The absence of evidence that the country specified in the removal direction would accept a person did not remove the Secretary of State's power to deport: *Sunsara* above.
9 See further CHAPTER 6 above.
10 See *Raziastaraie v Secretary of State for the Home Department* [1995] Imm AR 459, CA. (any primary/secondary legislative source now it has been deleted from the Immigration Rules?)
11 Nationality, Immigration and Asylum Act 2002, s 117D(5) newly inserted by s 19 of the Immigration Act 2014.

Exemption from deportation

Diplomatic exemption

16.6 Under section 8(3) of the Immigration Act 1971 and the Immigration (Exemption from Control) Order 1972[1] made under section 8(2), as we have seen in CHAPTER 5 above, exemption from immigration control is given to diplomats and international functionaries. In some cases full immunity is given, including immunity from deportation, but in other cases the exempted category of person can still be deported on grounds conducive to the public good. Where someone is subject to an exemption, normally the exemption will extend to members of their family who form part of their household.[2] Whether someone falls within this category sometimes can be difficult to determine.[3] Diplomats who are the subject of a *demarche* under Article 9(1) of the Vienna Convention on Diplomatic Relations are probably not deportable, even though they cease to have diplomatic exemption, because they normally leave before the 'expiry of a reasonable period in which to do so', and because Article 39(2) and (4), which are part of UK law,[4] provide that their privileges and immunities continue until that time or until they leave the country.

1 SI 1972/1613.
2 See CHAPTER 5 above.
3 *Gupta v Secretary of State for the Home Department* [1979–80] Imm AR 52 at 57; *R v Secretary of State for the Home Department, ex p Bagga* [1990] Imm AR 413, CA.
4 Diplomatic Privileges Act 1964.

Five-year rule for Irish and Commonwealth citizens

16.7 Certain Commonwealth[1] and Irish citizens, who were ordinarily resident in the UK when the Immigration Act 1971 came into force, are exempted from liability for deportation.[2] Under earlier laws, Commonwealth or Irish citizens could not be deported if they had completed five years ordinary residence, excluding any long periods spent in prison.[3] At the same time, no Commonwealth or Irish citizen could be deported on conducive to the public good grounds. These exemptions were continued in the circumstances set out in section 7 of the 1971 Act for Commonwealth and Irish citizens who became ordinarily resident in the UK on or before 1 January 1973, when the 1971 Act came into force, and were Commonwealth or Irish citizens at that time.[4] The burden of proving entitlement to the exemption is on the proposed deportee, and not the authorities.[5] Essentially this means showing that they have been 'ordinarily resident' for the requisite period.

1. For Commonwealth citizens see British Nationality Act 1981, s 37, Sch 3. For nationals of Pakistan and South Africa see **16.12** below.
2. Immigration Act 1971, s 7(1)(b). The subsection was modified by Immigration and Asylum Act 1999, Sch 14, para 46, applying the exemption to those who would formerly have been deported but are now subject to administrative removal by virtue of s 10.
3. Commonwealth Immigrants Act 1962, s 7(2), now repealed, and see *R v Edgehill* [1963] 1 QB 593, [1963] 1 All ER 181, CCA.
4. Immigration Act 1971, s 7(1), as amended by Immigration and Asylum Act 1999, Sch 14, para 46.
5. Immigration Act 1971, s 7(5).

16.8 Commonwealth and Irish citizens cannot be deported on any ground, or recommended for deportation by a criminal court) if they were ordinarily resident at 1 January 1973 and have been so for the five years prior to the decision or conviction.[1] The five years must have been completed at the time of the decision or conviction, not the date of the actual making of the order.[2] The date on which a decision to deport is made is a matter of fact, not law, and is not necessarily the date when notice of it is given to or reaches the potential deportee.[3]

1. Immigration Act 1971, s 7(1)(b), substituted by the Nationality, Immigration and Asylum Act 2002, s 75, and (c). Section 7(1)(a) (which exempted Commonwealth and Irish citizens from deportation on public good grounds if they were ordinarily resident on 1 January 1973 and at all times until the date of the decision) was repealed as redundant (NIAA 2002, s 75). See *R v Secretary of State for the Home Department, ex p Olashehinde* [1992] Imm AR 443, QBD.
2. *Mehmet v Secretary of State for the Home Department* [1977] Imm AR 68, CA.
3. *Rehman v Secretary of State for the Home Department* [1978] Imm AR 80. Contrast *Rafiq v Secretary of State for the Home Department* [1998] Imm AR 193, CA: a grant of leave is not effective until communicated. See also on the communication of decisions *R (on the application of Anufrijeva) v Secretary of State for the Home Department* [2003] UKHL 36, [2003] Imm AR 570, [2003] INLR 521. The practice of serving deportation decisions on the file when the person's whereabouts were unknown, prevalent until 1986 when it was abandoned as unfair, meant that many long-term overstayers were not aware of deportation decisions, and even deportation orders, against them for many years. The 2003 Notices Regulations (SI 2003/658) revive the power. See CHAPTER 20 below.

16.9 Normally a person is not to be treated as ordinarily resident at a time when he or she is in this country 'in breach of the immigration laws'.[1] But for the purposes of this exemption from deportation, the position is different. Section 7(2) of the Immigration Act 1971 provides that a person who has at any time become ordinarily resident is not to be treated for the purposes of the exemption as having ceased to be so by reason only of having remained in breach of the immigration laws. Deserting seamen[2] and illegal entrants[3] will not gain exemption, only those who entered lawfully and subsequently overstayed. For example, in the case of *R v Immigration Appeal Tribunal, ex p Perdikos*[4] the applicant returned to this country while he was still subject to a deportation order. Woolf J held that he never acquired ordinary residence, and so could not benefit from the deportation exemption.

1   Immigration Act 1971, s 33(1); see CHAPTER 4 above.
2   *Re Abdul Manan* [1971] 2 All ER 1016, [1971] 1 WLR 859, CA: a deserting seaman had never become ordinarily resident since he was guilty of an offence when he deserted ship, and continued to be so during the whole period of his stay in this country.
3   *R v Bangoo* [1977] Imm AR 33n, CA; *R v Immigration Appeal Tribunal, ex p Perdikos* (1981) 131 NLJ 477.
4   (1981) 131 NLJ 477, following Manan above. See further *R v Secretary of State for the Home Department, ex p Margueritte* [1983] QB 180, [1982] 3 All ER 909, CA; *Immigration Appeal Tribunal v Chelliah* [1985] Imm AR 192, CA; *R v Secretary of State for the Home Department, ex p Oni* (CO 2863/1998) (25 October 1999, unreported).

Special circumstances of Irish nationals

16.10 Following a ministerial statement on 19 February 2007 concerning the deportation of Irish Nationals[1] the only criteria under which an Irish national may be considered for deportation are:

(i)   a court has recommended deportation in sentencing; or
(ii)   the Secretary of State concludes that due to the exceptional circumstances of the case the public interest requires deportation.

Exceptional circumstances will be rare. The guidance given suggests that deportation might be considered where an offence involves national security matters or crimes that pose a serious risk to the safety of the public or section of the public.[2] This might be where a person has been convicted of a terrorism offence, murder or a serious sexual or violent offence and is serving a sentence of ten years or more. Deportation action must be agreed at director level.

1   Hansard, 19 February 2007, Column 3WS.
2   Home Office Policy: 'European Economic Area (EEA) Foreign National Offender Cases v3.0'.

Section 1(5) cases

16.11 Until August 1988, a Commonwealth woman married to a Commonwealth man settled here before 1 January 1973 was not liable to be deported, even if the marriage was a sham one.[1] Children under 16 at the time of the decision to deport also benefitted.[2] This exemption disappeared with the repeal of section 1(5) of the Immigration Act 1971 by the Immigration Act 1988,[3] and it is doubtful if any privilege or right under section 1(5) was preserved by section 16 of the 1988 Act after the repeal.[4]

1   This was because of the saving provision of s 1(5) of the Immigration Act 1971 combined with provisions allowing such women to register as British on marriage. See *Secretary of State for the Home Department v Huseyin* [1988] Imm AR 129, CA; this did not apply to alien wives of Commonwealth citizens: see *O'Shea v Secretary of State for the Home Department* [1988] Imm AR 484, CA. It did not apply if the marriage took place after the deportation order had been signed: *R v Secretary of State for the Home Department, ex p Hayden* [1988] Imm AR

555, QBD. Nor did it apply to husbands of women settled here: *Singh (Bahadur) v Immigration Appeal Tribunal* [1988] Imm AR 582.

2   *Menn v Secretary of State for the Home Department* [1992] Imm AR 245, CA.
3   Immigration Act 1988, s 1.
4   *Menn* above; *R v Secretary of State for the Home Department, ex p Delpratt* [1991] Imm AR 5n, QBD; see also *R v Secretary of State for the Home Department, ex p Ovakkouche* [1991] Imm AR 5, QBD.

Application to citizens of Pakistan and South Africa

16.12 Pakistan withdrew from the Commonwealth on 30 January 1972. Section 1 of the Pakistan Act 1973, passed on 25 July 1973 and in force on 1 September 1973, enacted that citizens of Pakistan ceased to be Commonwealth citizens at commencement. But transitional provisions enabled citizens of Pakistan to retain some of their rights as Commonwealth citizens for long enough to register as citizens of the UK and colonies (CUKC).[1] In 1989 Pakistan rejoined the Commonwealth.[2] Thus from 1 October 1989 its citizens have been able to claim exemption again if they fulfilled the residence conditions set out above.[3] On 22 November 2007, Pakistan was suspended from the Commonwealth and remains suspended at the time of writing. In 1994 South Africa rejoined the Commonwealth, and its citizens became able to claim exemption if they fulfilled the residence conditions set out above.[4]

1   By deeming them Commonwealth citizens until 31 August 1974, giving one year to apply for registration as a CUKC. If such an application was made, deemed Commonwealth citizenship continued pending its determination. Those not applying in time lost eligibility for the exemption.
2   British Nationality (Pakistan) Order 1989, SI 1989/1331.
3   In *Siddique* (16050) (7 January 1998, unreported), IAT, a Pakistan national relied on the transitional provisions to found exemption from deportation on the ground of ordinary residence on 1 January 1973 and for five years preceding the decision.
4   See British Nationality (South Africa) Order 1994, SI 1994/1634, which came into force on 26 July 1994.

Grounds of deportation

16.13 A person who is not a British citizen and not exempt is liable to deportation from the UK in the following circumstances:

(i)   following conviction for a criminal offence attracting at least one single sentence of imprisonment of 12 months or more;[1]
(ii)   the Secretary of State deems his or her deportation to be conducive to the public good;[2]
(iii) another member of the family to which he or she belongs is to be deported;[3]
(iv)   a court recommends deportation in the case of a person over the age of 17 after conviction of an offence punishable by imprisonment.[4]

Prior to 2 October 2000, a person would have been liable to deportation in certain circumstances in which he or she is now liable to administrative removal.

1   UK Borders Act 2007, s 32.
2   Immigration Act 1971, s 3(5)(a), as amended by Immigration and Asylum Act 1999, Sch 14, para 44(2).

[3] Immigration Act 1971, s 3(5)(b), as amended.
[4] Immigration Act 1971, s 3(6).

AUTOMATIC DEPORTATION OF FOREIGN CRIMINALS

16.14 The UK Borders Act 2007 (Commencement No 3 and Transitional Provisions) Order 2008, SI 2008/1818 brought into force as from 1 August 2008 the automatic deportation provisions contained in section 32–38 of the UK Borders Act 2007. The provisions apply to any person convicted after the passing of the Act, however, and not just those convicted after the provisions bringing the UK Borders Act 2007 into force.[1] Section 32[2] introduces a statutory presumption that a deportation to which section 32 applies is conducive to the public good for the purpose of section 3(5)(a) of the 1971 Act. The section established two categories or 'conditions' of foreign national convict who may be subject to the automatic procedure:

- Condition 1: those who have been sentenced to a period of at least 12 months' imprisonment;[3]
- Condition 2: those sentenced to a period of imprisonment following conviction for serious criminal offences as specified by order of the Secretary of State (Nationality, Immigration and Asylum Act 2002, section 72(2)(a).[4]

[1] See *AT (Pakistan) & Anor v Secretary of State for the Home Department* [2010] EWCA Civ 567, [2010] NLJR 806 in which Hooper LJ held that Parliament intended that section 32 would apply to any person convicted after the passing of the Act and before it came into force, unless the Secretary of State by statutory instrument ordered otherwise, which he did not do. See also: *R (on the application of Hussein) v Secretary of State for the Home Department* [2009] EWHC 2492 (Admin), [2009] All ER (D) 207 (Oct).
[2] UK Borders Act 2007, s 32(4).
[3] UK Borders Act 2007, s 32(2).
[4] UK Borders Act 2007, s 32(3). Not in force at the time of writing.

16.15 Automatic deportation is constrained only by the operation of certain statutory exceptions and may be resisted where a foreign national can demonstrate removal would breach the Refugee and Human Rights Conventions, or European Community law, or where the Secretary of State thinks the foreign criminal was under the age of 18 on the date of conviction.[1] There are transitional provisions for those in custody at the time of commencement or whose sentences are suspended. This is provided such a person has not been served with a notice of a decision to make a deportation order under s 5 of the Immigration Act 1971 before commencement.

[1] UK Borders Act 2007, s 33. See further **16.19** below.

16.16 By operation of section 38(1)(a) of the 2007 Act a sentence of imprisonment for 12 months does not include the following:

(i) a suspended sentence unless a court subsequently orders that it take effect – section 38(1)(a);

(ii) consecutive sentences that individually are less than 12 months in duration but amount in aggregate to 12 months or more – section 38(1)(b).

Further whilst 'imprisonment' under sections 38(1)(c) and 38(2)(b) includes a reference to 'detention', in an institution other than a prison (including, in particular, a hospital or an institution for young offenders), this does not include detention under immigration powers for the purpose of effecting removal or pursuing deportation action. It is also arguably the case that also it does not include military detention in a Military Corrective Training Centre (MCTC) either for civilians, servicemen and women convicted by a Court Martial of an offence under the Armed Forces Act 2006. That position is supported by the following:

(i)   The MCTC describes itself as 'an establishment that provides corrective training for those servicemen and women sentenced to periods of detention: it is not a prison'.

(ii)   Inspection by HMIP is carried out by invitation only as it does not fall under the statutory remit of the prison inspectorate.

(iii)   The Courts Martial have powers to sentence those convicted of a military offence to imprisonment, but also possess a number of discrete punishments under s 164 of the Armed Forces Act 2006 that are not available to civilian courts, such as serving a term of corrective training or detention as an alternative to imprisonment. Thus detention in MCTC is not a characterisable as imprisonment, but rather is a lesser or separate sentence than imprisonment.[1]

(iv)   It is not a detention facility in which those sentenced to imprisonment, who for reasons of minority or mental state can serve out their term in a prison establishment. MCTC cannot, under its own remit, accept those sentenced to serve a term of imprisonment, only those sentenced to detention or on remand awaiting Court Martial.

(v)   Military offences that are deemed sufficiently serious to attract 12 months corrective detention may not amount to criminal offences in a civilian environment since military operational factors apply to aggravate severity of misconduct. Courts Martial apply different guide-lines[2] when sentencing military offenders to those applied in civilian courts, thus had an offender facing a sentence of 12 months in corrective military detention instead been convicted in a civilian court, he may have been sentenced to a lesser period or received a non custodial sentence (paras 3.4.9, 5.8.7).

(vi)   Arguably, foreign national servicemen and women should not be liable to deportation under the automatic deportation scheme as a result of 12 months detention in MCTC.

To date the Home Office have withdrawn deportation decisions on MCTC detained cases, with the effect that there is currently no caselaw on this point.

[1]   Guidance on Sentencing in the Court Martial version 4 (www.justice.gov.uk/downloads/cour ts/judge-advocate-general/guidance-sentencing-court-martial.pdf).and *R v Holmes* [2004] EWCA Crim 3180 at 12; *R v Birch* [2011] EWCA Crim 46 at 11.

[2]   Guidance on Sentencing in the Court Martial version 4 (www.justice.gov.uk/downloads/cour ts/judge-advocate-general/guidance-sentencing-court-martial.pdf).

16.17 HC 951 amended the Immigration Rules in order to bring them in line with the new statutory powers. Paragraphs A362 to 368 of the Immigration Rules now provide the framework describing when liability to deportation may arise. Paragraph 378 was amended and provides that the prohibition on making a deportation order while an appeal is pending does not apply to automatic deportation cases. The Immigration (Notices) (Amendment) Regulations 2008[1] and the Immigration (Notices) (Amendment) (No 2) Regulations 2008[2] add a decision that a person is a foreign criminal to the list of immigration decisions which require a notice of appeal rights to be served on the individual concerned, however those rights will be restricted by the new amendments to section 82 Nationality, Immigration and Asylum Act 2002, now that section 117A–117D of the Act, inserted by section 19 of the Immigration Act 2014, is in force.

[1] SI 2008/684.
[2] SI 2008/1819.

16.18 Section 34 of the 2007 Act governs the timing of the making of the deportation order. Apart from precluding the making of an order under section 32 while any criminal sentence is under appeal or could be brought,[1] the section gives the Secretary of State complete discretion as to timing. There is no restriction on the making of an order under section 32 whilst any appeal against that process is before the IAC.[2]

[1] UK Borders Act 2007, s 34(2).
[2] UK Borders Act 2007, s 35 modifies s 79 of Nationality, Immigration and Asylum Act 2002, which is the section which normally prevents a deportation order being made while an appeal is brought, so that the section does not apply in cases of automatic deportation orders made under s 32 of the 2007 Act.

16.19 There are listed exceptions to the statutory requirement to treat the deportation of a foreign criminal as conducive to the public good and to impose a mandatory duty to deport. These are where the person benefits from one or the other exemptions from deportation under sections 7 and 8 of the Immigration Act 1971,[1] and one of the following exceptions apply:

(i)   where deportation would breach either foreign criminals' human rights or their rights under the Refugee Convention;[2]

(ii)   where the SSHD 'thinks' that the foreign criminal was under 18 on the date of conviction;[3]

(iii)   where removal of foreign criminals would breach their rights under the Community treaties;[4]

(iv)   where foreign criminals are subject to extradition proceedings;[5] or

(v)   where they are subject to certain provisions of mental health legislation specified in this exception;[6]

(vi)   where the Secretary of State thinks that the application of section 32(4) and (5) would contravene the UK's obligations under the Council of Europe Convention on Action against Trafficking in Human Beings (done at Warsaw on 16 May 2005).[7]

It should be noted that these exceptions simply remove the requirement to make a deportation order; they do not prevent the making of one.[8] Moreover, even if exceptions (i) or (iv) apply, deportation must still be treated as conducive to the public good.[9] Consequently where an exception does apply, there is at least a theoretical possibility that deportation may still be pursued under section 3(5)(a) of the Immigration Act 1971 or, in the case of EEA nationals and their family members who are exercising Treaty rights, under the

Immigration (European Economic Area) Regulations 2006. Of these exceptions, the most frequently relied on is the human rights exception, with particular reliance placed on Article 8 ECHR.

1   UK Borders Act 2007, s 33(1).
2   UK Borders Act 2007, s 33(2).
3   UK Borders Act 2007, s 33(3).
4   UK Borders Act 2007, s 33(4).
5   UK Borders Act 2007, s 33(5).
6   UK Borders Act 2007, s 33(6).
7   Sub-s (6A) was inserted by the Criminal Justice and Immigration Act 2008, s 146. Date in force: 1 April 2009: see SI 2009/860, art 2(1)(d).
8   UK Borders Act 2007, s 33(7).
9   UK Borders Act 2007, s 33(7).

16.20 Where automatic deportation does not apply because one of the exceptions operates – for example, that the appellant was under 18 at date of conviction – but the Home Office wish to proceed with deportation under section 3(5)(a) of the 1971 Act, relevant case law decided in respect of pre-automatic deportations remains applicable. In such cases, in line with Court of Appeal guidance in *N (Kenya)*,[1] the Immigration Judge must attach weight to the Secretary of States view of the public good and public interest, because the case is a straightforward conducive deportation under section 3(5)(a) without any statutory presumption.[2] Where the exception is a breach of rights under the Refugee Convention, the Secretary of State's focus is almost certain to be on the exception to the principle of non-refoulment in Article 33(2) of the Refugee Convention[3] and the presumptions that the person has been convicted of a particularly serious crime and is a danger to the community contained in the NIAA 2002, section 72(2).[4]

1   *R (on the application of N) v Secretary for State for the Home Department* [2004] EWCA Civ 1094, [2004] 37 LS Gaz R 36, (2004) Times, 13 September. See also in *OP (Jamaica) v Secretary of State for the Home Department* [2008] EWCA Civ 440, [2008] All ER (D) 06 (May).
2   *BK (Deportation – s.33 'exception' UKBA 2007 – public interest) Ghana* [2010] UKUT 328 (IAC) (chaired by Sedley LJ).
3   The non-refoulment duty does not apply to 'a refugee whom there are reasonable grounds for regarding as a danger to the security of the country in which he is, or who, having been convicted by a final judgment of a particularly serious crime, constitutes a danger to the community . . . '.
4   See *AQ (Somalia) v Secretary of State for the Home Department* [2011] EWCA Civ 695, and *TB (Jamaica) v Secretary of State for the Home Department* [2008] EWCA Civ 977, (2008) Times, 9 September. See **12.99–12.100**, above.

16.21 In most contested cases of automatic deportation the most common defence is Article 8, ECHR. Comments on new case law are at **16.44**. However, the newly amended Paragraph A362 of the Immigration Rules states that 'where Article 8 is raised in the context of deportation under Part 13 of these Rules, the claim under Article 8 will only succeed where the requirements of these rules as at 28 July 2014 are met, regardless of when the notice of intention to deport or the deportation order, as appropriate, was served'. Thus for the majority of appeals on Article 8 grounds to be successful, they must engage the more limited interpretation of Article 8 contained within section 117C of the Nationality Immigration and Asylum Act 2002[1] and in the

Immigration Rules at Paragraphs A398 to 399A.[2]

[1]   As amended by Immigration Act 2014, s 19.
[2]   HC 395. As amended by Statement of Changes to the Immigration Rules, HC 194.

The effect of the automatic deportation regime

16.22 The automatic deportation process placed the law and underlying policy with regard to deportation in some disarray Provisions relating to a recommendation for deportation by a court were neither amended nor repealed, but plainly the scope for making a recommendation was severely curtailed in view of the breadth of the provisions for automatic deportation and to the established criteria for making a recommendation for deportation.[1] In *R v Hakimzadeh*,[2] the Court of Appeal approved an adjustment in the structure of a sentence in order to avoid the automatic deportation provisions, where the appellant was to be sentenced for a series of thefts over a long period of time from the British Library and the Bodleian Library and faced automatic deportation under section 32 if he was sentenced to a single term of imprisonment of 12 months for at least one offence. The Court adjusted his single sentence of 12 months to two separate sentences; one of nine months and the other of three months to run consecutively, thus avoiding automatic deportation, which clearly none of the judges thought was an appropriate outcome.

[1]   See *Archbold: Criminal Pleading, Evidence and Practice* (2010) Sweet & Maxwell, 5.919.
[2]   [2009] EWCA Crim 959, [2010] 1 Cr App Rep (S) 49, [2009] Crim LR 676.

16.23 Further, the prevailing approach to deportation is at odds with the evaluative approach applied by the criminal courts when sentencing. For instance, when a convicted criminal is sentenced the main focus is on the following – the nature of the crime, the impact on the victims, the extent and nature of the defendant's criminality, his or her background and the risk he or she poses to the public. The deterrent element of the sentence, if applied, focuses on the nature of the crime rather than the individual in the dock. Sentencing is a sophisticated, complex and well worked exercise. In deportation the considerations are different. Except for the purposes of a criminal appeal, it is not a sentence and is not, therefore to be seen as punishment, although for many it is just that, especially in cases where a marriage and family ties are broken.[1] The main policy imperatives behind it are deterrence, expressing society's revulsion towards the criminal conduct and protection of the public. There is often an overlap between protection and deterrence. The theory is that if it is an effective deterrent there will be less crime and therefore the public will be safer. If there is a high risk of the deportee reoffending then it does not much matter which of these two policy imperatives apply. The problem lies in those cases where the offender is rehabilitated or presents a very low risk to the public. In *R (on the application of N) v Secretary for State for the Home Department*[2] and in *OP (Jamaica) v Secretary of State for the Home Department*[3] the Court of Appeal has identified the Secretary of State's policy as one of deterrence and held that it will be an error of law if the lower Tribunal does not give appropriate weight to that policy (see **16.44** below). Appropriate weight will not have been given, if the Tribunal places too much emphasis on the rehabilitation of the offender. Despite a strong dissenting judgment by Sedley LJ objecting to the appropriation of the adjudicator's discretion in *N (Kenya)*, this has been the applicable law since 2004.

[1] See *AT (Pakistan) v Secretary of State for the Home Department* [2010] EWCA Civ 567 in which the Court of Appeal rejected argument that the automatic deportation process was characterisable as a 'penalty' for the purposes of Article 7 of the ECHR, holding that it was 'a measure of this kind taken in pursuance, not of the criminal law but of the law on aliens is not in itself penal in character', and finding that it was directed at avoiding re-offending by foreign criminals in the UK which permitted its characterisation as preventive rather than punitive for the purposes of Article 7.

[2] [2004] EWCA Civ 1094, [2004] 37 LS Gaz R 36, (2004) Times, 13 September.

[3] [2008] EWCA Civ 440, [2008] All ER (D) 06 (May).

16.24 Under the regime operating prior to automatic deportation, a decision to deport on conducive grounds was a matter of discretion for the Secretary of State, guided by consideration of all relevant factors, including those set out in the now deleted paragraph 364 of the Immigration Rules and by the need to have regard to paragraph 380 which provided that a deportation order will not be made against any person if his or her removal in pursuance of the order would be contrary to the UK's obligations under the Refugee Convention or the ECHR. By contrast, in a case of automatic deportation, deportation is deemed to be conducive to the public good by section 32(4) of the UK Borders Act 2007. So the Secretary of State has no discretion, and thus the principle of *N (Kenya)*[1] that weight must be afforded to the Secretary of State's policy does not apply as it would in a case of discretionary deportation.[2] So, when the tribunal is considering the human rights exception and comes to proportionality, the starting point will be that the Secretary of State has been obliged to make a deportation order by virtue of section 32(2) of the UK Borders Act 2007 and by section 32(4) the deportation is deemed to be conducive to the public good.[3] This determination was approved by the Court of Appeal in *RU (Bangladesh)*[4], where Aikens LJ thought that because, by statute, the deportation of *'foreign criminals'* is deemed to be conducive to the public good, the constituents of that 'public good' must continue to include those particular facets of 'the public interest' summarised by Wilson LJ in *OH(Serbia)*.[5] The 'facets' Wilson LJ identified were:

(a)   the risk of re-offending by the person concerned;

(b)   the need to deter foreign nationals from committing serious crimes by leading them to understand that, whatever the other circumstances, one consequence of them may well be deportation; and

(c)   the role of deportation as an expression of society's revulsion at serious crimes and in building public confidence in the treatment of foreign citizens who have committed serious crimes.

However, that still leaves open two questions: first, what weight is generally to be attached to those public interest factors in the proportionality exercise; is it the same or more than was accorded under the pre-UK Borders Act regime? Second, should any separate or additional weight be given to the SSHD's own judgement on the weight of those factors in a particular case, as expressed in the Decision Letter.

1   *N (Kenya) v Secretary of State for the Home Department* [2004] EWCA Civ 1094, (2004) INLR 612.
2   *Omotunde (best interests – Zambrano applied – Razgar) Nigeria* [2011] UKUT 247 (IAC) (25 May 2011). See also *MK (deportation – foreign criminal – public interest) Gambia* [2010] UKUT 281 (IAC); *RG (Automatic deportation) SS 33(2)(a) exception Nepal* [2010] UKUT 273 (IAC).
3   *MK (deportation-foreign criminal-public interest) Gambia* [2010] UKUT 281 (IAC); [2011] Imm AR 60 at [30].
4   *RU (Bangladesh) v Secretary of State for the Home Department* [2011] EWCA Civ 651, [2011] All ER (D) 38 (Jun) (8 June 2011); *OH (Serbia) v Secretary of State for the Home Department* [2008] EWCA Civ 694, [2009] INLR 109.
5   *OH (Serbia) v Secretary of State for the Home Department* [2008] EWCA Civ 694, (2009) INLR 109. Wilson LJ also emphasised that the primary responsibility for the public interest was that of the SSHD, who would be likely to have a broader and better informed view of that interest than would a tribunal. *OH (Serbia)* was followed in *DS (India) v Secretary of State for the Home Department* [2009] EWCA Civ 544 at [37], [2009] All ER (D) 110 (Jun) where the court held that the public interest in deportation of those who commit serious crimes extends to deterring and preventing serious crime generally and to upholding abhorrence of such offending.

16.25 In an earlier case, *AP (Trinidad & Tobago)*[1] Carnwath LJ suggested in obiter comment that, as what was conducive to the public good had been given parliamentary endorsement, it was arguable that greater weight should be given to such factors when drawing the balance of proportionality under Article 8. However, these judicial statements are at present no more than thoughts and suggestions. It should be recalled that after Judge LJ (as he then was) had referred in *N (Kenya)*[2] to the facet of public interest which included the need for deterrence and the inclusion of public revulsion, he had also made it clear that:

> 'The adjudicator must form his own independent judgement. Provided he is satisfied that he would exercise the discretion differently to the SSHD he must say so. Nevertheless in every case he should at least address the SSHD's prime responsibility for the public interest and the public good and the impact that these matters will probably have had on the exercise of his discretion.'

That approach retained relevance even after the introduction of automatic deportation, the Courts concluding that whilst the public interest in deportation had been established by legislation, its content and extent in a particular case still had to be separately evaluated, initially by the Home Secretary and thereafter if necessary by the tribunal, where proportionality comes into question.[3]

1   *AP (Trinidad & Tobago) v Secretary of State for the Home Department* [2011] EWCA Civ 551, [2011] All ER (D) 108 (May) (12 May 2011).
2   *N (Kenya)* at [83].
3   In *Gurung v Secretary of State for the Home Department* [2012] EWCA Civ 62 for example the Court of appeal held that whilst the advent of automatic deportation no longer required the Home Secretary to form her own view of where the public interest lay when deciding on the need to deport a foreign criminal falling within the statute, the public interest was not only to be treated as by definition served by deporting foreign criminals; it was also among the factors capable of affecting the proportionality of deporting them if that arose, it being found that while the public interest in deportation has already been established by legislation, its content and extent in the particular case had to be separately evaluated.

16.26 More recently in *SS (Nigeria) v Secretary of State for the Home Department* the Court of Appeal reiterated that every intrusion by the State upon the freedom of the individual stood in need of justification, and any interference which is greater than that required for the State's proper purpose could not be justified, observing that the principle of minimal interference justified these ideas as linked imperatives for the avoidance of arbitrary rule; and thereby locked them into the concept of was 'necessary in a democratic society'. The Court proceeded to find, however, that the breadth of the margin the State enjoyed was conditioned by context, and in particular driven by two factors:

(1)   the nature of the public decision, and
(2)   its source, concluding that where the decision applies State policy which is general or strategic in nature, and where the policy source is primary legislation, the margin would be correspondingly broad.[1]

---

[1]   *SS (Nigeria) v Secretary of State for the Home Department* [2013] EWCA Civ 550. The Court found that the principle of minimal interference meant that the fundamental right in question in the case could never, lawfully, be treated as a token or a ritual - the margin of discretionary judgment enjoyed by the primary decision-maker, though variable, meaning that the court's role was kept in balance with that of the elected arms of government; and that this served to quieten constitutional anxieties that the Human Rights Act 1998 drew judges onto ground they should not occupy.

16.27 As is well known, the deportation regime changed again on 9 July 2012 when a wholly revised version of Part 13 of the Immigration Rules was introduced by the Secretary of State through the Statement of Changes HC194. Under the revised scheme the assessment exercise falling to be performed shifted again as the Secretary of State endeavoured to dictate how the balance should be struck between individual rights under Article 8 and the public interests in protecting the public from foreign criminals, the wanted aim being that henceforth '*a decision taken in accordance with the Rules will, other than in exceptional cases, [be] compatible with Article 8*'.[1] Under those rules a foreign national offender sentenced to up to four years imprisonment was required to demonstrate their inclusion within one of the exceptions to deportation as outlined in paragraphs 399 and 399A of the Immigration Rules. Those who could not and those sentenced to four years or more imprisonment can demonstrate that the public interest in deportation would be outweighed only in very exceptional circumstances.

---

[1]   Home Office Statement, 13 June 2012.

16.28 The exigencies of that scheme were explained, and to a material extent, tempered by decisions of the Courts, in particular *MF(Nigeria) v Secretary of State for the Home Department*[1] in which the Court of Appeal held inter alia that whilst the Immigration Rules contained in Part 13 constituted a complete code for the purposes of an Article 8 assessment such that very compelling reasons would be required to outweigh the public interest in deportation where an individual fell outwith the criteria laid down in paragraphs 398–399A, Those compelling reasons were encapsulated in the 'exceptional circumstances' threshold specified in the rules the determination of which would be the product of an application of the proportionality test required by the Strasbourg jurisprudence. The critical aspects of the judgment bear repetition:

'40.   Does it follow that the new rules have effected no change other than to spell out the circumstances in which a foreign criminal's claim that deportation would breach his article 8 rights will *succeed*? At this point, it is necessary to focus on the statement that it will only be "in exceptional circumstances that the public interest in deportation will be outweighed by other factors". [Counsel for the Secretary of State] submits that the reference to exceptional circumstances serves the purpose of emphasising that, in the balancing exercise, great weight should be given to the public interest in deporting foreign criminals who do not satisfy paras 398 and 399 or 399A. It is only exceptionally that such foreign criminals will succeed in showing that their rights under article 8(1) trump the public interest in their deportation.

41.   We accept this submission . . .

42.   . . . in approaching the question of whether removal is a proportionate interference with an individual's article 8 rights, the scales are heavily weighted in favour of deportation and something very compelling (which will be "exceptional") is required to outweigh the public interest in removal. In our view, it is no coincidence that the phrase "exceptional circumstances" is used in the new rules in the context of weighing the competing factors for and against deportation of foreign criminals.

43.   The word "exceptional" is often used to denote a departure from a general rule. The general rule in the present context is that, in the case of a foreign prisoner to whom paras 399 and 399A do not apply, very compelling reasons will be required to outweigh the public interest in deportation. These compelling reasons are the "exceptional circumstances".

44.   We would, therefore, hold that the new rules are a complete code and that the exceptional circumstances to be considered in the balancing exercise involve the application of a proportionality test as required by the Strasbourg jurisprudence. We accordingly respectfully do not agree with the UT that the decision-maker is not "mandated or directed" to take all the relevant article 8 criteria into account (para 38).'

Importantly the Court in *MF(Nigeria)* recognised that where paragraphs 399 and 399A did apply, determination of the issues arising within them would likely involve questions of evaluation as well as hard-edged fact, such as whether it would be 'reasonable' to expect a child to leave the UK or whether there are 'insurmountable obstacles'. In so finding the Court held that, provided appropriate and substantial weight was given to the public interest as described by the rules, a Tribunal could properly undertake a reasoned evaluation of all of the issues in the case so as to record favourable findings on exceptional grounds, as in fact the Upper Tribunal had done effectively and lawfully in that instance.

¹   [2013] EWCA Civ 1192, [2014] 1 WLR 544.

16.29 The Secretary of State has now responded by further modifying her rules, substituting the 'exceptional circumstance' threshold for one of 'very compelling circumstances over and above those described in paragraphs 399 and 399A',¹ and further still by importing a range of considerations material to the disposal of Article 8 applications and deportation cases in particular into primary legislation in the form of section 117A-17D of the Immigration Act 2014.² It remains to be seen to what extent those new reforms will impact on the nature and extent of the evaluative exercise falling to be performed outwith rule and statute. The particulars of the new scheme and its operation in practice are considered in greater detail at **16.44** where some intitial views are advanced as to the impact of the same.

1   Statement of Changes HC 532 amending paragraph 398; IDI's Chapter 13, Version 5, Section
     6.
2   Amending Nationality, Immigration and Asylum Act 2002, s 117.

16.30 Even under the Secretary of State's new codified system the criminal conduct which informs the public interest in deportation remains susceptible to and indeed requires a case specific evaluation in the context of a proportionality review. The Immigration Directorate Instructions recognising the following factors as 'adding' to the case for deportation:

- Even within a scheme which purports to codify the public interest side of the equation, however, there remains an obligation in the context of an evaluation of the proportionality of enforcement action, to assess the character of the offending behaviour and to assess too the prospective risk the deportee would represent. The Home Office recognises the same in its IDI's[1] the more serious the offence;
- the more criminal convictions a foreign criminal has;
- where there is a high risk of reoffending;
- where the offender has not accepted responsibility for his offending or expressed remorse;
- the commission of other offences overseas;
- presentation with a particularly poor immigration record.

Whilst the examples furnished in the IDI's are stated to 'add' to the case for enforcement, they necessarily operate conversely so as to reduce the public interest in deportation where it can be shown that none aggravating features are present.[2] If the presence of those factors elevates the public interest in deportation, then the absence of the same must operate conversely, a reality which bears emphasis when advancing a case in opposition to enforcement action founded on family and private life interests.[3]

1   IDI Chapter 13 – Criminality Guidance in Article 8 ECHR Cases V5.0 (28 July 2014) Section
     2.3.
2   See further Chapter 15.20F-H regarding the relevance of propensity to re-offend.
3   As to which consider IDI Chapter 13, Section 2.5.3 which identifies *'the greater the public
     interest in deportation, the stronger the countervailing factors need to be to succeed'* from
     which one can clearly articulate the contrary position.

16.31 Further to the above it should be noted that on past authority it was acknowledged that it was not every conviction that could legitimately result in a deportation, the Court's emphasising that it was not the label attached to an offence but its factual circumstances that best indicated the nature of the conduct and its repercussions on the public domain.[1] Further although recidivism and a propensity to commit further offences has long been recognised not to be essential preconditions to the exercise of the power to deport, they were recognised to be generally material considerations when considering the merits of a decision.[2] It is relevant to note too that certain offences have been held to cause such deep public revulsion that as a matter of public policy, deportation of their perpetrators is required including: convictions for importing or supplying dangerous drugs,[3] for rape,[4] incest,[5] violent robbery[6] and arson,[7] even in such cases human rights, compassionate or other relevant circumstances have been held to outweigh the public good.[8]

1   *R v Immigration Appeal Tribunal, ex p Florent* [1985] Imm AR 141, CA.
2   *Andrews (Joseph)* [2002] UKIAT 07598: 'propensity to re-offend is a significant factor in determining whether deportation is correct'. Where the deportee is an EU national, propensity to re-offend is generally (although not invariably) necessary to the exercise of the deportation power: *R v Bouchereau* [1978] QB 732 para 29 and see CHAPTER 6, above. The Court of Appeal has held in *N (Kenya)* [2004] UKIAT 00009 that for serious offending deportation may be necessary as an example to other actual or potential criminals 'even where there was a low or no risk of further offending' (Judge LJ at para 87). The Tribunal has made plain in *Kendeh* (IA/02279/2006) 1 March 2007. however, that 'the decision in N could not be read to mean that engagement in serious criminal activities of non-nationals must inevitably and in every case result in dismissal of challenges to the Secretary of State's order of deportation'; *Said v Immigration Appeal Tribunal* [1989] Imm AR 372, CA; *Martinez-Tobon v Immigration Appeal Tribunal* [1988] Imm AR 319, CA; *R (on the application of Samaroo) v Secretary of State for the Home Department* [2001] EWCA Civ 1139, [2002] INLR 55.
3   *R v Secretary of State for the Home Department, ex p Marchon* [1993] Imm AR 384, CA; *R (on the application of Samaroo) v Secretary of State for the Home Department* (CO 4973/1999) (20 December 2000, unreported), affd [2001] EWCA Civ 1139, [2001] UKHRR 1150, [2002] INLR 55. But see below.
4   *Galoo* (00TH0009): 'rape strikes at the roots of society, including the sanctity of the family'. See also *N (Kenya)* [2004] UKIAT 00009 (upheld by the Court of Appeal at [2004] EWCA Civ 1094, [2004] INLR 612); *Ayodele v Secretary of State for the Home Department* [2003] EWCA Civ 5 (permission hearing).
5   *Goremsandu v Secretary of State for the Home Department* [1996] Imm AR 250, CA.
6   *Florent* above; *R (on the application of Schmelz) v Immigration Appeal Tribunal* [2004] EWCA Civ 29, [2004] All ER (D) 87 (Jan) (EU national).
7   *Escudero* (20525) (8 March 1999, unreported).
8   See the European Community case, *R v Bouchereau* [1978] QB 732, particularly AG Warner at 742b–c; but see also *Calfa (Criminal Proceedings against)*: C-348/96 [1999] ECR I-11.

16.32 It may be material also in the context of a public interest assessment to be able to identify examples of inconsistency or unfairness in the way the system has been applied as between one person and another,[1] given that disparate treatment between like cases has in the past founded successful appeals.[2] Such comparisons of individual cases are likely to be rare because one case is rarely identical with another. Considerations of fairness may impinge too on the decision making process where there are indicators of mismanagement by the Secretary of State which has had the effect of causing some disadvantage or detriment. The Court of Appeal has held for example that the Secretary of State ought to take into account when assessing whether enforcement action is appropriate that there has been a past history of mishaps, such as a failure to grant leave to remain under the Minors policy when dealing with the case. Where the result has been that the applicant has lost the opportunity to live lawfully in the UK and to work lawfully whilst here, this should be regarded as a relevant consideration.[3]

1   *Alsawaf v Secretary of State for the Home Department* [1988] Imm AR 410, CA.
2   See *R v Secretary of State for the Home Department, ex p Sheikh (Shafat Ahmed)*, (DC/260/81) (4 February 1982), QBD, in which the inconsistent treatment of two brothers, both innocent beneficiaries of corruptly obtained leave, founded a successful challenge.
3   *SL (Vietnam) v Secretary of State for the Home Department* [2010] EWCA Civ 225.

16.33 The public interest in deportation may be affected by other factors peculiar to an applicant including considerations relating to their health, particularly where these impact on the offending act, or on the question of propensity. In *MM (Zimbabwe) v Secretary of State for the Home Department* for instance it was recognised by the Court of Appeal that where evidence suggested (despite not guaranteeing) that an appellant would not have offended but for his mental health problems and would not re-offend in the future this can have a bearing on the public interest in deportation, and the consequent proportionality of such action.[1] The Court emphasised though that when considering the risk to the public of his continued presence in this country it was recognised to be of great importance to assess the extent to which continued medication and support would remove the risk of further offending – if the correct conclusion was that although the risk could never be said to have been entirely removed, it would, for practical purposes, be minimal, that was a powerful factor in considering the proportionality of the deportation order.

[1]   [2012] EWCA Civ 279.

16.34 Of course the picture is quite different under EC law, where the focus is on the risk to society posed by individual being deported and general deterrence has no part to play.[1] And what about the criminal court's power to recommend deportation? As we discuss the *Nazari*, *Carmona* and *Caird* guidelines still apply. But what is the point of it all, if the end result is a foregone conclusion and the input of the trial judge is of no consequence since the new focus is entirely on the Secretary of State's pre-determined view of the offence? Is the individual criminality and dangerousness of the offender of no consequence? Are mitigating or aggravating circumstances unimportant? Is the assessment of the risk posed by the offender by the time of his or her release of little or no relevance? The problem does not lie in dealing with those who have no ties to the UK or pose a serious risk to the public. It is the others. The automatic deportation powers in UK domestic law are so out of kilter with human rights and community law for those who do have ties to this country. It is clear that beyond the new direction of the law on deportation there is another consideration. If the reason for deportation at the end of the sentence is the protection of the public, this can only mean the British public. The international drug dealer, the terrorist and the psychopath will each be released to another country where he is she will, unless facing charges be free to engage in crime. This will be particularly true of sex offenders being removed to countries where there are none of the safeguards of a sex offenders' register. Deportation then risks becoming the means of exporting and circulating crime – 'not in my back yard – you can have them'. Some serious rethinking needs to be done.

[1]   It is also quite possible that no-one in the country of return will have any information of the offences for which the person is being deported. See the very interesting document reproduced in *HH (Iraq)* [2007] UKAIT 00036, 1 February 2008, which sets out the restricted circumstances in which criminal convictions can be disclosed to foreign governments, consistently with the Data Protection Act 1998 and the Human Rights Act 1998.

DEPORTATION CONDUCIVE TO PUBLIC GOOD

16.35 The power to deport on public good grounds has existed in the case of foreign nationals for most of the last century, and before that under various earlier statutes. The same power existed for Commonwealth citizens after the Commonwealth Immigrants' Act 1962 and both powers were amalgamated in the Immigration Act 1971. There was no right of appeal until 1969 and the decided cases in the High Court under the earlier Aliens laws all favoured the executive, although the judges proclaimed their ability to protect the liberty of the subject.[1] The power is now contained in section 3(5)(a) of the Immigration Act 1971, as amended. A special regime applies to political cases, as we shall see.[2] The UK Borders Act 2007 now provides a statutory basis for stating that the deportation of a foreign criminal satisfying the relevant criteria is conducive to the public good.[3] The most frequent use of the power has been against convicted criminals who have not been recommended for deportation by the court which sentenced them.[4] Although the use of the conducive power to deport in criminal cases has been largely overtaken by automatic deportation we have retained and updated the following paragraphs, because the rules on conducive deportations still play a residual part in the deportation process in relation to criminal offending.

[1]   *R v Governor of Brixton Prison, ex p Sarno* [1916] 2 KB 742 at 749 and 752 ('if it was clear that an act was done by the executive with the intention of misusing those powers, this court would have jurisdiction to deal with the matter'); *R v Chiswick Police Station Superintendent, ex p Sacksteder* [1918] 1 KB 578 at 586–587, CA ('if that order is . . . practically a sham . . . it seems to me the court can go behind it'); cf *R v Governor of Brixton Prison, ex p Bloom* (1920) 85 JP 87 at 88. See further *R v Secretary of State for Home Affairs, ex p Duke of Chateau Thierry* [1917] 1 KB 922; *R v Home Secretary, ex p Bressler* (1924) 88 JP 89; see *C v E* (1946) 62 TLR 326; *R v Governor of Brixton Prison, ex p Soblen* [1963] 2 QB 243, [1962] 3 All ER 641. See A W Brian Simpson *In the Highest Degree Odious* (1994) for an illuminating review of the treatment of aliens under wartime and emergency regulations.

[2]   See CHAPTER 22 below.

[3]   UK Borders Act 2007, s 32(4).

[4]   The failure or even the reasoned refusal of a criminal court to make a recommendation does not prevent the minister initiating deportation proceedings under s 3(5)(a): see *Martin* [1993] Imm AR 161, IAT; *R v Secretary of State for the Home Department, ex p Figueiredo* [1993] Imm AR 606, QBD; *M v Secretary of State for the Home Department* [2003] EWCA Civ 146, [2003] INLR 306; *Jaroudy* [2002] UKIAT 06653.

CRIMINAL CONVICTIONS

16.36 The existence of the power to deport on public good grounds based on criminal convictions is not in doubt.[1] The automatic deportation custody thresholds operate only in respect of a twelve month custodial sentence for a single offence, and, as has been seen, does not operate in respect of suspended sentences and offences committed whilst a juvenile.[2] Those categories of offender, however, are not immune from deportation, as section 3(5)(a) of the Immigration Act 1971 continues to operate out with the automatic deportation regime. Its use is generally confined to cases where, for example, the offender is under 18, on the basis of an aggregate of time spent in custody for convictions over a specified period, on the basis of a 'series' of comparatively minor convictions,[3] or in respect of particular categories of offending.[4] Where too the Home Office seeks to exercise the facility to pursue deportation solely on the basis of one or more overseas conviction, those cases too fall to be assessed outside the automatic statutory deportation regime as they do not meet the definition of a foreign criminal set out at section 117D(1) of the Nationality, Immigration and Asylum Act 2002 (as amended by Immigration Act 2014), and further do not fall within the criminality thresholds set down in the rules at paragraph 398. The Home Office in the IDI's nonetheless directs caseworkers that the Rules, be used as a guide, because 'they reflect Parliament's view of the balance to be struck between an individual's right to private and family life and the public interest'.[5] Those falling into this category who succeed in resisting deportation are granted leave outside the rules for period not exceeding 30 months.[6]

[1] *R v Immigration Appeal Tribunal, ex p Florent* [1985] Imm AR 141, CA.
[2] Section 38(1)(a)–(c) UK Borders Act 2007.
[3] EIG, Chapter 12.
[4] The Secretary of State has previously designated the supply of class A, B or C drugs as warranting deportation regardless of sentence length: EIG, 'Important changes to our deportation policy', operative from 1 August 2008.
[5] IDIs: Chapter 13 – Criminality Guidance in Article 8 ECHR Cases V5.0 (28 July 2014) Section 2.7.1.
[6] IDIs: Chapter 13 – Criminality Guidance in Article 8 ECHR Cases V5.0 (28 July 2014) Section 2.7.2.

POLITICAL DEPORTATIONS

16.37 Deportation may be deemed conducive to the public good as being in the interests of national security or of the relations between the UK and another country, or for other reasons of a political nature. In *Rehman*[1] the House of Lords, endorsing the Court of Appeal's judgment, held that 'national security', 'international relations' and 'other political reasons' may overlap, and gave an extremely broad meaning to the phrase 'national security'. Rejecting the approach of the SIAC, which had held that endangering national security required engagement in, promotion or encouragement of violent activity targeted at the UK, its system of government or its people,[2] their Lordships agreed with the Court of Appeal that the promotion of terrorism against any state is capable of being a threat to the UK's national security, since increasingly the security of one country is dependent upon the security of others, so that any activity likely to create a risk of adverse repercussions, including conduct which could have an adverse effect on the UK's relationship with a friendly state, could threaten the UK's national security. Thus planning and organisation in the UK of terrorist acts abroad could found deportation,[3] although the Secretary of State would have to show that there was a real possibility of adverse repercussions in terrorist cases.[4] The House also endorsed the Court of Appeal's distinction between proof and evaluation; the Secretary of State's reasons are not counts on an indictment, and the task is evaluative and predictive, using a global approach to assess whether the subject is a danger to national security.[5] Nevertheless, the assertions on which the Secretary of State bases her evaluation of danger must be reliable, and suspicious circumstances do not necessarily make for a reasonable suspicion so as to justify deportation.[6] Public good grounds for deportation may also include assisting the proliferation of another country's nuclear capability contrary to international treaty.[7] We deal with this in more detail in Chapter 22, which deals with appeals to SIAC.

[1] *Secretary of State for the Home Department v Rehman* [2001] UKHL 47, [2001] 3 WLR 877, [2002] INLR 92, [2002] Imm AR 98, affirming *Secretary of State for the Home Department v Rehman (Shafiq ur)* [2000] INLR 531.
[2] *Rehman (Shafiq ur) v Secretary of State for the Home Department* [1999] INLR 517 (SIAC).
[3] See *Rehman* above, per Lord Slynn at para 18, Lord Steyn (para 28), Lord Hoffmann (para 49). See also *Singh (Raghbir) v Secretary of State for the Home Department* [1996] Imm AR 507 at 510, CA.
[4] *Rehman* above, para 16.

5   *Rehman* above, para 29 (Lord Steyn), 49 (Lord Hoffmann).
6   *M v Secretary of State for the Home Department* [2004] EWCA Civ 324, [2004] 2 All ER 863 (permission), where SIAC's decision to quash a deportation order and a certificate under Anti-terrorism, Crime and Security Act 2001, s 21 was upheld: see **16.43** below.
7   *R v Secretary of State for the Home Department, ex p Saleem* (23 July 1996, unreported), QBD.

OTHER CONDUCIVE DEPORTATIONS

16.38 The circumstances other than criminal behaviour (apart from political cases) where the public good power can be exercised are not defined. Whatever they are, it is for the Secretary of State to prove the detrimental conduct complained of and to demonstrate that it impinges on the public domain. It has been held that a sham marriage qualifies because it undermines a fundamental institution of society,[1] though the appellate body must be careful that all the elements of a sham marriage are proved.[2] This ground, although still available, is unlikely to be used again, since obtaining leave by deception is now a ground for administrative removal, without an in country appeal, under section 10 of the Immigration and Asylum Act 1999. Criminal associations which have not led to a conviction might be a further basis, and evidence of spent convictions and of a charge that had been withdrawn from a jury have been held to be admissible but not as a basis without more for justifying deportation.[3] Further, whilst the Secretary of State may rely on inferences drawn from such past conduct and events,[4] there will likely be difficulty in proving the acts complained of. The standard is the civil burden of proof, but flexibly applied, so that the graver the allegation the more certain the proof required.[5] The commission of offences abroad might be a ground for a public good deportation,[6] so long as it is not disguised extradition[7] and does not breach the person's human rights.

1   *R v Immigration Appeal Tribunal, ex p Cheema* [1982] Imm AR 124. See below.
2   *R v Immigration Appeal Tribunal, ex p Khan (Mahmud)* [1983] QB 790.
3   In *R (on the application of V) v Asylum and Immigration Tribunal & Anor* [2009] EWHC 1902 (Admin) Hinkinbottom J held that given strict rules of evidence are waived by rule 51(1) of the Asylum and Immigration (Procedure) Rules 2005, it was open to the AIT (now IAC) to admit evidence of spent convictions and of a charge that had been withdrawn from a jury, though it was held that it was likely much weight might be given to those sources.
4   *Martinez-Tobon v Immigration Appeal Tribunal* [1988] Imm AR 319, CA.
5   *Khawaja v Secretary of State for the Home Department* [1984] AC 74.
6   *El-Awam* (12807) (14 December 1995, unreported).
7   A decision to deport on conducive grounds for a conspiracy triable abroad is lawful provided the purpose is not to surrender the deportee without the benefit of extradition safeguards, but if during the process an extradition request is received, there are powerful reasons of comity for giving it priority: *Caddoux, Re* [2004] EWHC 642 (Admin), [2004] All ER (D) 498 (Mar), para 6. Using deportation to bypass the safeguards of extradition could also amount to an abuse of process: *R v Mullen* [2000] QB 520, CA; *R v Horseferry Road Magistrates' Court, ex p Bennett* [1994] 1 AC 42, HL; *R v Bow Street Magistrates, ex p Mackeson* (1982) 75 Cr App Rep 24, CA.

Deception of the Home Office

16.39 Where the Home Office has been misled into granting an indefinite leave to remain, it can base a decision to deport under section 3(5)(a) of the Immigration Act 1971 on that ground.[1] This may involve false allegations as to marital status, or as to the continued existence of cohabitation at a time when the parties are living separately, or a fabricated claim to refugee status. Whether there has been a deception is a matter of fact to be proved to the satisfaction of the Tribunal on a civil balance of proof, flexibly applied to take into account the gravity of the allegation.[2] Fraud must be 'clear and manifest' to justify deportation of someone granted indefinite leave to remain as a refugee.[3] In *Patel*[4] Lord Bridge reconsidered and withdrew his dictum in *Khawaja*[5] that the power could not be used to deport someone who told lies on entry if his or her conduct thereafter was perfectly satisfactory, and lies on entry may form the basis of a later deportation on conducive grounds,[6] although administrative removal as an illegal entrant is easier[7] and therefore far more likely.

[1] *Re Owusu-Sekyere* [1987] Imm AR 425, CA. However, administrative removal under s 10 of the Immigration and Asylum Act 1999 (as amended by Nationality, Immigration and Asylum Act 2002, s 74) is also available for anyone who uses deception in seeking (whether successfully or not) leave to remain, and Home Office deport policy directs caseworkers to the administrative removal process in respect of any deception used to obtain settlement which took place after 1 October 1996: EIG Chapter 12.2.

[2] *Tahir v Immigration Appeal Tribunal* [1989] Imm AR 98, CA.

[3] *R (on the application of Saribal) v Secretary of State for the Home Department* [2002] EWHC 1542 (Admin), [2002] All ER (D) 379 (Jul).

[4] *R v Immigration Appeal Tribunal, ex p Patel (Anilkumar Ravindrabhai)* [1988] AC 910, [1988] Imm AR 434; see also *R v Immigration Appeal Tribunal, ex p Karim* [1986] Imm AR 428 (use of a false identity).

[5] *Khawaja v Secretary of State for the Home Department* [1984] AC 74, [1983] 1 All ER 765, HL.

[6] *R v Secretary of State for the Home Department, ex p Chaumun* [1999] INLR 479.

[7] Immigration Act 1971, Sch 2, para 9; see CHAPTER 17 below.

DEPORTATION OF FAMILY MEMBERS

16.40 The power to deport on public good grounds has applied to members of a family for the best part of a century.[1] Under section 3(5)(b) of the Immigration Act 1971,[2] the Secretary of State possesses the power to deport the dependent spouse, civil partner[3] and dependent children of an immigrant where the spouse, civil partner or parent respectively (hereafter called the principal deportee) has been deported or is ordered to be deported. In the past this power was only likely to be used where the family were all settled in the UK; where the family had a limited leave in consequence of the principal's status, then an extension of that leave would normally be refused on a decision to deport the principal deportee. But current Home Office policy is to use the family deportation provisions 'to avoid a possible Article 8 challenge'.[4] Under a family deportation, not only a spouse but also any children under 18 may be deported, even where they are the children of the dependent spouse and not the principal's own.[5] Adopted[6] and illegitimate children may also be deported, but not natural children who have been adopted by someone else.[7] For the purposes of this section, 'wife' includes each of two or more wives.[8] A dependent spouse who is separated from the principal remains a member of the family of the principal deportee until divorce and would still be liable to family deportation. However, the Immigration Rules make plain that the Secretary of State will not deport a dependent spouse who has qualified for settlement in his or her own right or has been living apart from the principal deportee.[9]

tion, even if this is the only part of the sentence against which an appeal is made.[2] But in those cases in which no appeal lies to the Court of Appeal from a sentence of a lower court, no appeal can be made to that court against a recommendation.[3] Until the 2002 Act, there was no appeal to the immigration appellate authorities[4] if the Secretary of State decides to follow the recommendation, except on asylum, human rights or race discrimination grounds,[5] but that decision attracts a right of appeal to the First-tier Tribunal on human rights grounds under section 82 of the Nationality, Immigration and Asylum Act 2002, which will shortly be amended by section 15 of the Immigration Act 2014, to limit the appeals which may be pursued, also the grounds on which the appeal may be brought, under the newly amended section 84 of the Nationality, Immigration and Asylum Act 2002. Appeals against liability to deportation. Human rights claims by those liable to deportation on conducive grounds[6] or on recommendation by a criminal court[7] may be certified by SSHD, such that the appeal may only be pursued out of country, on the ground that removal of the appellant would not be unlawful under section 6 of the Human Rights Act 1998[8], or on the ground that the appellant would not face a serious risk of real irreversible harm if removed to the country proposed.[9]

1. Immigration Act 1971, s 6(5)(a), as amended by Race Relations Amendment Act 2000.
2. See *R v Edgehill* [1963] 1 QB 593, [1963] 1 All ER 181, CCA on a similar provision in the repealed Commonwealth Immigrants Act 1962.
3. *R v Lynch* [1965] 3 All ER 925, [1966] 1 WLR 92, CCA.
4. Under Immigration and Asylum Act 1999, s 63.
5. The right of appeal on asylum grounds attached to the Secretary of State's refusal to revoke a deportation order made on the criminal court's recommendation, under Immigration and Asylum Act 1999, s 69(4). The human rights and race discrimination appeal was conferred by Immigration and Asylum Act 1999, s 65, a wide, free-standing right of appeal against any decision relating to entitlement to enter or remain in the UK.
6. Immigration Act 1971, s 3(5)(a).
7. Immigration Act 1971, s 3(6).
8. Nationality, Immigration and Asylum Act 2002, s 94B(2), as amended by the new s 17(3) of the Immigration Act 2014.
9. Nationality, Immigration and Asylum Act 2002, s 94B(3), as amended by the new s 17(3) Immigration Act 2014.

16.46 No court may recommend a person for deportation unless he or she has been given seven days' notice in writing.[1] If the notice has not been served in time, the hearing may be adjourned, even after conviction, to enable the notice to be served.[2] The court needs a 'full inquiry into all the circumstances' and counsel should be invited to address the court specifically on the issue of a recommendation.[3] Where a court decides to make a recommendation, full reasons for the decision should be given, in fairness to the offender and in order to assist the Secretary of State with the ultimate decision as to whether to proceed with deportation.[4] A failure by the sentencing court to provide any, or any adequate, reasoning does not automatically lead to a recommendation being quashed, however, since the Court of Appeal has the power to give its own reasons where it considers deportation appropriate.[5] Similarly, a failure by the prosecution to give the requisite seven days' notice under s 6(2) does not necessarily invalidate the recommendation.[6]

1. Immigration Act 1971, s 6(2). The proper course is to attach the acknowledgment of service of the notice to the case file, to avoid later disputes: *R v Edgehill* [1963] 1 QB 593, [1963] 1 All ER 181, but this is not essential, and service may be inferred from strong circumstantial evidence: *R v Rodney* [1996] 2 Cr App Rep (S) 230; *R v Adomako* [1998] EWCA Crim 3019.
2. Immigration Act 1971, s 6(2).

³ *R v Nazari* (1980) 71 Cr App Rep 87; *R v Escauriaza* (1987) 9 Cr App Rep (S) 542; *R v Omojudi* (1992)13 Cr App Rep (S) 346; *R v Frank* (1991) 13 Cr App Rep (S) 500.

⁴ *R v Nazari* above; *R v Rodney* [1998] INLR 118, [1996] 2 Cr App Rep (S) 230; *R v Bozat* [1997] 1 Cr App Rep (S) 270; *R v Dosso* [1998] EWCA Crim 3180; *R v Ntua* [1999] EWCA Crim 1520.

⁵ *R v Abdi (Liban)* [2008] 1 Cr App Rep (S) 87, CA.

⁶ *R v Rodney* above; *R v Bozat* above; *R v Green (Steven)* [1997] EWCA Crim 2661; *R v Dudeye (Said)* [1998] 2 Cr App Rep (S) 430.

Guidelines for criminal courts

16.47 The power to make a recommendation must be exercised judicially and is concerned with criminal behaviour rather than the enforcement of an immigration policy.[1] The court is not under an obligation to recommend deportation in serious cases concerning evasion of immigration controls (such as forging passports or organising illegal entry)[2] and the question whether to recommend deportation should be decided quite independently of the immigration status of the offender.[3] The basic statement of principle to guide the criminal courts was set out in the decision in *R v Caird*.[4] In quashing a recommendation for deportation against one of the defendants, the court stated that it wished to emphasise:

> 'that the courts when considering a recommendation for deportation are normally concerned simply with crime committed and the individual's past record and the question as to what is their effect on the question of potential detriment to this country of the appellant remaining here. It does not embark, and indeed is in no position to embark, upon the issue as to what is likely to be his life if he goes back to his country of origin. That is a matter for the Home Secretary.'

Caird was cited with approval and amplified in the leading case of *R v Nazari*,[5] where the widely differing cases of four appellants were dealt with together and the Court of Appeal set out a series of guidelines for courts. These cases have now been supplemented by *R v Carmona*.[6] The criminal courts are concerned with potential detriment to the UK, and assessing potential detriment is a question of fact in each case, involving consideration of matters other than the gravity of the offence. Detriment refers to the potential harm caused by the defendant's criminal behaviour, and not such matters as receipt of welfare benefits[7] or immigration status.[8] A comparatively minor offence will not make continued presence a detriment;[9] the important issue is the defendant's likely future conduct.[10] The likelihood of re-offending is usually relevant; indeed the EC criteria have to all intents and purposes been assimilated into domestic criminal law.[11] In *R v Abdi (Liban)*,[12] it was held that there was no inconsistency between the judge's conclusion that the criteria for significant risk under s 229 of the Criminal Justice Act 2003 had not been satisfied and his decision to make a recommendation for deportation on the basis that there was a degree of risk of re-offending (although not sufficient to amount to dangerousness under s 229) and that serious harm would undoubtedly result from any re-offending.

¹ See *Arthur Rogerson 'Deportation'* [1963] PL 305 at 309; Graham Zellick 'The Power of The Courts To Recommend Deportation' [1973] Crim LR 612; the Wilson Committee on Immigration Appeals (1967) Cmnd 2739, para 94.

² *R v Akan* (1972) 56 Cr App Rep 716, CA; *R v Anno-Firempong* [1997] EWCA Crim 1054 (possession of a false passport boarding an aircraft for Canada); *R v Dosso* [1998] EWCA Crim 3180 (assisting illegal entry).

3   The relevant considerations were the offender's history, particularly criminal history, and the gravity of the offence: *R v Khandari*, 24 April 1979, Bridge LJ. A similar view was expressed in *Miller v Lenton* (1981) 3 Cr App Rep (S) 171; *R v Nunu* (1991) 12 Cr App Rep (S) 752, CA. See also *R v Stefanski, R v Kwiek* [2002] EWCA Crim 1810. However, in *R v Benabbas (Ahmed)* [2006] 1 Cr App Rep (S) 550, [2005] EWCA Crim 2113, it was said that there was a distinction to be drawn between the person who had entered the UK by fraudulent means and the person who was in this country unlawfully and who was convicted of an offence unconnected with his status and the circumstances in which he had entered the country. The public interest in preventing the fraudulent use of passports to gain entry or support residence was of considerable importance and deserved protection; where the essential gravamen of the offence for which the offender was being sentenced was itself an abuse of the immigration laws, the issue of detriment, when applying *R v Nazari* [1980] 1 WLR 1366) was intimately bound up with the protection of public order afforded by confidence in a system of passports; therefore, the approach identified in *R v Khandari* was inappropriate to the offence of entering without a passport, although it might be appropriate where the defendant had immediately claimed asylum upon entry (because the asylum claim would be assessed by the Secretary of State, who was best left to consider it without any possible complication arising from a recommendation for deportation).

4   (1970) 54 Cr App Rep 499, CA.

5   [1980] 3 All ER 880 at 885–886, 71 Cr App Rep 87.

6   [2006] EWCA Crim 508, [2006] 2 Cr App Rep (S) 662.

7   *R v Serry* (1980) 2 Cr App Rep (S) 336, [1980] LS Gaz R 1181, CA.

8   But see fn 3 above.

9   *R v Kraus* (1982) 4 Cr App Rep (S) 113, CA; *R v Compassi* (1987) 9 Cr App Rep (S) 270, CA; *R v Okelola* (1992) 13 Cr App Rep (S) 560, CA. In *R v Williams (Vivian)* [1996] EWCA Crim 354, the Court of Appeal treated sexual abuse on and impregnation of a 12-year-old stepdaughter as a relatively minor offence not meriting deportation, although such offences are deemed to merit at least ten years' absence from the UK by the Home Office: see IDI Dec 00, Ch 13, Annex A, 'Period normally appropriate for revocation', and such a decision is, one hopes, inconceivable today. However, a conspiracy to defraud (cashing giros) was deemed sufficiently serious in *R v Lembo, R v Mobonda, R v Mukwete* [2003] EWCA Crim 3246. In *R v Tangestani-Najad* [1998] EWCA Crim 1970, assault occasioning actual bodily harm on a tenant by a landlord with previous convictions was deemed not serious enough to merit deportation.

10   *R v David* (1980) 2 Cr App Rep (S) 362, CA; *R v Tshuma* (1981) 3 Cr App Rep (S) 97; *R v Altawel* (1981) 3 Cr App Rep (S) 281 and other cases cited in Thomas Current Sentencing Practice Part K.

11   *R v Escauriaza* (1987) 87 Cr App Rep 344, CA; *R v Spura* (1988) 10 Cr App Rep (S) 376, CA. Note the different approach under the Immigration Act 1971, s 3(5)(a), for which see *R (on the application of Samaroo) v Secretary of State for the Home Department* (CO 4973/1999) (20 December 2000, unreported) (affd [2001] EWCA Civ 1139, [2001] UKHRR 1150, [2002] INLR 55).

12   [2008] 1 Cr App Rep (S) 87, CA.

16.48 The second guideline gleaned from *Nazari, Carmona* and *Caird* is that the (criminal) courts are not concerned with the political system in the offender's home country, or with what is likely to be the offender's life there.[1] The guidance was adopted because of the difficulties and undesirability of their making such an assessment, particularly if there may be a long period of imprisonment between the conviction and the execution of the deportation order, during which time there may be a change of circumstances.[2] In the previous edition of this work[3] we suggested that this policy would need to be modified in the light of the court's primary obligation under the Human Rights Act 1998.[4] The Court of Appeal has taken a different view, generally refusing to embark on investigation into conditions awaiting proposed deportees in the home country and leaving these matters to the Secretary of State.[5] Given the introduction of a right of appeal against the subsequent decision of the Secretary of State,[6] this arrangement is compatible with the UK's obligations under Article 13 of the ECHR.[7]

1   *R v Caird* (1970) 54 Cr App Rep 499, CA; *R v Nazari* [1980] 3 All ER 880, 71 Cr App Rep 87. The policy was subject to exceptions, where there was cogent evidence of the consequences of deportation, and where the anticipated deportation was reasonably proximate to the decision: see eg *R v Dudeye (Said)* [1998] 2 Cr App Rep (S) 430 (recommendation against young Somali refugee for robbery quashed in light of circumstances in Somalia).
2   *R v Uddin* [1971] Crim LR 663, CA; *R v Caird* above.
3   Fifth edition, 15.27.
4   As a public authority under Human Rights Act 1998, s 6: see **7.18** above.
5   See *R v Chen (Ling)* [2001] EWCA Crim 885; *R v Lembo, R v Mobonda, R v Mukwete* [2003] EWCA Crim 3246.
6   Nationality, Immigration and Asylum Act 2002, s 82(2)(j) (from 1 April 2003); previously (from 2 October 2000) a decision to act on a recommendation was appealable on human rights grounds under Immigration and Asylum Act 1999, s 65, and on asylum grounds by seeking revocation of a deportation order and appealing refusal under s 69(4). These provisions have now been amended by s117 of the Immigration Act 2014, so as to limit the grounds on which appeals may be brought and to enable certification by SSHD of in country appeals on the new s 94B of the Nationality, Immigration and Asylum Act 2002 grounds.
7   Before 2 October 2000 the Secretary of State's decision to act on a recommendation could be judicially reviewed as *Wednesbury* unreasonable if it violated fundamental rights: see *R v Secretary of State for the Home Department, ex p M* [1999] Imm AR 548 (decision to deport AIDS sufferer following court recommendation). For the effect of art 13 of ECHR see **7.125** above.

16.49 The third *Nazari* guideline[1] is that the criminal courts will have regard to the effect of any recommendation on innocent third parties. The courts have no desire to break up families and force spouses to choose between the interests of their children or the future of their marriage.[2] In *Nazari* the guideline reflects the need for compliance with Article 8 ECHR; the courts will consider whether deportation would result in interference with family or private life (ie whether the proposed deportee has family or other ties in the UK which would be interfered with by deportation, eg if family members could not reasonably be expected to accompany the deportee abroad) and if such interference would result, whether it is proportionate to the legitimate aim of preventing crime or disorder – which requires balancing matters such as the prevalence and gravity of the crime and its impact on society against the family or private life considerations. The reported cases show that the Court of Appeal has generally applied this guideline with care and in a more generous spirit than have the appellate authorities in 'conducive to the public good' deportations.[3] However, in *Carmona* the court veered away from the *Nazari* position on the importance of the ECHR in deciding to make a recommendation. There it was held that notwithstanding the Human Rights Act 1998, there is no need for a sentencing court to consider the rights of an offender under Articles 2 (right to life), 3 (prohibition of torture) and 8 (right to respect for private and family life) of the ECHR, when considering whether to make a recommendation. These, the court held, are for the Secretary of State to consider when deciding whether to act on the recommendation, as is the effect of deportation on the family of the offender. Accordingly, in the case of non-EU citizens the only question to be addressed is whether the offender's continued presence in this country is contrary to the public interest. That approach was subsequently confirmed by *DA (Colombia) v Secretary of State for the Home Department*[4] where the Court of Appeal again held that a sentencing judge should consider only matters relating to past, present and possible future offences when deciding whether or not to make a recommendation to deport, and reiterated that it was for the Secretary of State alone to take account of ECHR matters and any other considerations that are personal to the offender and his family when he or she comes to consider whether or not to make a deportation order under section 5(1) of the Immigration Act 1971. The latter approach is more in line with the decision in *Samaroo, where the* Court held that in certain circumstances the sheer gravity of an offence, absent the propensity to repeat it, can override family or private life interests under Article 8(2) of the ECHR.[5]

The third *Nazari* guideline has been greatly diminished to vanishing point, first by *Carmona* and now by *Kluxen*[1] where it was said that a criminal court should not take into account the rights of the offender under the ECHR, the effect the recommendation may have on innocent persons not before the court, or the political situation in the country to which he may be deported, as all of these are matters for the Secretary of State.[6]

[1] [1980] 3 All ER 880 at 886, 71 Cr App Rep 87.
[2] *R v Craviato* (1990) 12 Cr App Rep (S) 71; *R v Odendaal* (1991) 13 Cr App Rep (S) 341; *R v Shittu* (1992) 14 Cr App Rep (S) 283.
[3] See eg *R v Ifekwe* [1997] EWCA Crim 1691; *R v Mounganga* [1999] EWCA Crim 1706; *R v Zand-Lashami* [1999] EWCA Crim 1723; *R v Stefanski, Kwiek* [2002] EWCA Crim 1810.
[4] [2009] EWCA Civ 682.
[5] *R (on the application of Samaroo) v Secretary of State for the Home Department* [2001] EWCA Civ 1139, [2002] INLR 55, a judgment by the civil division of the court, reviewing the Secretary of State's decision rather than hearing an appeal against a Crown Court judge's recommendation.
[6] *R v Kluxen; R v Rostas* [2010] EWCA Crim 1081, [2011] 1 Cr App Rep (S) 249, [2010] Crim LR 657.

16.50 What then is the picture which emerges from the case law? First, an isolated offence, even of a serious nature, committed by a person of previous good character whose behaviour while in the UK has been otherwise satisfactory may well not indicate that there is a potential detriment if he or she remains.[1] Secondly, the case law does not necessarily mean that it is wrong to make a recommendation against an offender with no previous convictions, particularly for a serious offence of a deliberate character, as was made clear in *Nazari* and other subsequent cases.[2] Thirdly, the courts are not concerned with the political systems which operate in other countries. Such matters are for the Secretary of State.[3] The fact that the offender has been granted refugee status does not prevent the court from making a recommendation for deportation,[4] but it is likely to prevent actual deportation (see below). Fourthly, as regards the terms of paragraph 2(1) of Schedule 3 to the Immigration Act 1971 do not create a presumption that an offender who has been recommended for deportation, but who is not serving a sentence, is to be detained pending the making of a deportation order.[5]

[1] See *R v David* (1980) 2 Cr App Rep (S) 362, CA (theft of passport by man with previous convictions in distant past, recommendation quashed); *R v Tshuma* (1981) 3 Cr App Rep (S) 97, CA (arson by young woman under emotional stress, recommendation quashed); and *R v Altawel* (1981) 3 Cr App Rep (S) 281, CA (obtaining student grant by deception, recommendation quashed).
[2] *R v Kouyoumdjian* (1990) 12 Cr App Rep (S) 35, CA (fraudulent trading involving debts of about 400,000 GBP); *R v Ahemed (Lukman Yakub)* [2005] EWCA Crim 1954, [2006] 1 Cr App Rep (S) 419 (entering marriage as part of a 'well thought out scheme of deception' designed to obtain an immigration advantage).
[3] *Nazari*, above; *R v Antypas* (1972) 57 Cr App Rep 207, CA; and *Carmona*, above.

[4] See *R v Villa and Villa* (1992) 14 Cr App Rep (S) 34, CA); *R v Antypas* (1972) 57 Cr App R 207, CA; and *Carmona*, above.

[5] *R (on the application of Sedrati) v Secretary of State for the Home Department* (17 May 2001, unreported), QBD (Moses J) ([2001] EWHC 418 (Admin)); from which it follows that it is unlawful not to release a person satisfying the criteria for release from custody pending the making of a deportation order unless there has been some conscious decision authorising continued detention until that time: *R (on the application of Vovk) v Secretary of State for the Home Department* [2007] ACD 48, QBD (Calvert Smith J).

16.51 The scope for making a recommendation has been severely curtailed in the light of the breadth of the provisions for automatic deportation and the established criteria for making a recommendation for deportation, and criminal courts appear to be using it less and less where the sentence passes the threshold of twelve months for automatic deportation; but there is new authority on its use where the sentence falls below twelve months. In *R v Kluxen*[1] the Court of Appeal said that if the court is, exceptionally, considering recommending deportation in such a case, it should apply the tests in *R v Nazari*[2] and *Bouchereau*,[3] which the court considered for practical purposes to be the same, whether or not the offender is a citizen of the EU. However, in the court's view, the issue of a recommendation is only ever likely to arise in the case of an offender with a long record of relatively minor offending who receives a custodial sentence of less than twelve months or in cases involving the use of false identity documents.[4] *R v Brown*[5] was such a case. The Court of Appeal applied *Kluxen* in upholding a recommendation for deportation where the offender, of previous good character, was sentenced to a total of ten months' imprisonment on conviction of four offences arising out of her claims for income support and housing and council tax benefit. Her false claims were made possible by her use of her passport, in which there was a forged stamp purporting to show she had indefinite leave to remain, when in fact she had limited leave with the usual condition of no recourse to public funds.

[1] See *R v Kluxen; R v Rostas* [2010] EWCA Crim 1081, [2011] 1 Cr App Rep (S) 249, [2010] Crim LR 657.

[2] *R v Nazari* [1980] 3 All ER 880, [1980] 1 WLR 1366, CA.

[3] Case 30/77 *R v Bouchereau* [1978] QB 732, [1981] 2 All ER 924n, ECJ.

[4] See *R v Maya (Didi Roc)* [2009] EWCA Crim 2427, [2010] 2 Cr App Rep (S) 85, 173 CL&J 748.

[5] *R v Brown (Romeka)* [2010] EWCA Crim 1807, [2011] 1 Cr App Rep (S) 482. Brown is in line with the earlier *R v Okhotnikov (Ivan)* [2008] EWCA Crim 1190, [2009] 1 Cr App Rep (S) 188, where it was said that that involvement in the production and dissemination of false driving documents and passports to foreign nationals could be viewed as undermining the good order of society.

16.52 *Nazari* did not deal with the position of EC nationals and others deriving rights from EC law.[1] This has now been remedied in the recent decision of the Court of Appeal in *R v Carmona*[2]. The European Court of Justice held in *R v Bouchereau* Case 30/77, [1978] QB 732, 66 Cr App R 202, that a recommendation for deportation was a 'measure' for the purposes of Directive 64/221, and that accordingly a recommendation could be made only in accordance with Article 48 of the Treaty of Rome (now Article 39) and the Directive. In *Carmona* the court acknowledged the possibility that whereas a recommendation for deportation may have been a 'measure' for the purposes of Directive 64/221, it might well not be a 'decision' for the purposes of the Citizens' Directive of 2004 and the Regulations to give it effect in domestic law[3] (any 'decision' being made by the Secretary of State), but it was of the opinion that the provisions of the Directive would have a significant effect on the exercise by courts of the power to recommend deportation, 'since it would not be right to make a recommendation . . . where the Directive precludes actual deportation' (para 3). It is likely, therefore, that courts dealing with persons covered by the Directive and Regulations will apply the public policy principles set out in Article 27 of the Directive, as elaborated by regulation 21(5) of the 2006 regulations.[4]

[1]   Such as Turkish nationals enjoying rights under the Ankara Agreement: *Nazli v Stadt Nürnberg* Case C-340/97, [2000] ECR I-957.
[2]   [2006] EWCA Crim 508, [2006] 2 Cr App Rep (S) 662.
[3]   Council Directive 2004/38/EC (Citizens' Directive), art 27(2); Immigration (European Economic Area) Regulations 2006, SI 2006/1003, reg 21(5).
[4]   See Archbold 2008, para 5-519.

16.53 As to the relevance of Articles 27 and 28 of the Citizens' Directive (2004/38/EC) and the 2006 EEA Regulations, the court held in *Kluxen*, above, as in *R v Carmona*[1], that a recommendation is not a 'decision' for the purposes of the Directive, but it dissented from the view expressed in *R v Carmona* that those provisions would have a significant effect on the exercise of the power to recommend deportation 'since it would not be right to make a recommendation . . . where the Directive precludes actual deportation' (see main text).

[1]   [2006] EWCA Crim 508, [2006] 1 WLR 2264, [2006] 2 Cr App Rep (S) 662.

16.54 In considering whether to deport an offender in respect of whom a recommendation has been made by the courts,[1] the factors to be taken into account by the Secretary of State in exercising his or her discretion are the same as in conducive to the public good cases.[2] Although a recommendation by a sentencing judge carries weight and may afford a presumption in favour of deportation, and although the reasoning of the sentencing judge is a material factor for the Secretary of State, the recommendation simply initiates the Secretary of State's task; it is essentially dealing with an assessment made, when the offender is sentenced, of the potential detriment to the UK of the offender's criminal behaviour and, in particular, his or her likely future conduct.[3] By the time the Secretary of State makes a decision, the offender will be near the end of his or her sentence, and may be rehabilitated and at little or no risk of re-offending. Clearly the sentencing judge's reasons and decision should not be substituted for what the Secretary of State has to decide.[4] But the fact that the sentencing judge made no reference to a recommendation when sentencing should not lead to the inference that he or she decided deportation was inappropriate;[5] and even a reasoned refusal of a recommendation, or a decision by the Criminal Division of the Court of Appeal to quash a recommendation made by the sentencing judge, does not create a presumption that the Secretary of State must follow, because of the wider range of factors considered by him or her. In this situation, however, the Secretary of State must apply the principle of proportionality. The court's judgment is a relevant matter, and reasons must be given for taking a different view,[6] though the Secretary of State need only have regard to and comment upon those remarks of the criminal court which were within its expertise.[7] Convictions which are reported to the Home Office by police include those where a recommendation for deportation is made, convictions for an offence under the Immigration Act 1971,[8] convictions for violence against the person or drugs resulting in a custodial sentence (including a suspended sentence) or hospital order; convictions for any offence resulting in a custodial sentence of 12 months or more.[9] A decision to deport should not usually be based on spent convictions.[10]

1　See **16.44–16.46** above.
2　HC 395, para 364.
3　*R v Caird* (1970) 54 Cr App Rep 499, CA.
4　*R v Secretary of State for the Home Department, ex p Dinc* [1999] Imm AR 380, [1999] INLR 256, CA.
5　*Jaroudy* [2002] UKIAT 06653.
6　*M v Secretary of State for the Home Department* [2003] EWCA Civ 146, [2003] INLR 306.
7　*DA (Colombia) v Secretary of State for the Home Department*, above.
8　For such offences, see CHAPTER 15 above.
9　IDI, Ch 13, s 4, para 2. Police also have discretion to report any other conviction in exceptional circumstances.
10　IDI, Ch 13, s 4, para 5.1. The IDI sets out the relevant provisions of the Rehabilitation of Offenders Act 1974. The exception to non-reliance on spent convictions is where justice cannot otherwise be done, eg where the person has delayed enforcement action by going to ground.

THE DECISION TO DEPORT – CONSIDERATION OF MERITS

16.55 The statutes and rules governing deportation have changed significantly over the period 2007–2014, as respective Governments responded to public concerns over immigration generally. Drivers of change have included the Home Office's incompetent management of the enforcement processes in particular, repeated adjustment of the regime operating in respect of FNP's; the much vaunted ambition since 2012 of elevating the public interest in deportation and the associated codification within the rules and then legislation of considerations which will determine the outcome of any ECHR Article 8 based objection to deportation. The following part of the Chapter outlines the critical aspects of the various rules-based regimes which have operated over the specific time. It also evaluates the impact of the recent changes introduced by the Immigration Act 2014. In determining which rules operate in an individual case it is necessary to check out the transitional provisions appended to the various Statements of Changes. These are considered within the respective sections below. The relevant rules will generally be those which were operative at the date a decision to deport was notified, and not the date of service of notice of liability to deportation, that position applying too in respect of an assessment of whether a particular policy is in force.[1] Unfortunately the transitional provisions of a rule change are not reproduced in the Consolidated Version of the Rules updated and available on the Home Office website. The Consolidated Rules do not give any footnotes or other information about when, where or how a rule has been changed, substituted or by what Statement of Change these things have been effected. Dates and indications when and in what way rules have been changed can, however, be found in Part 2 of this work.

1　*CW (Jamaica) v Secretary of State for the Home Department* [2013] EWCA Civ 915; *SS (India) v Secretary of State for the Home Department* [2010] EWCA Civ 388, [2010] All ER (D) 71 (Apr). See also: EIG, Ch 12, 'Concessions'.

The system under paragraph 364, HC 395

16.56 The general rule for deportations until 9th July 2012 was contained in paragraph 364 of HC 395. That rule applied to decisions to deport on conducive grounds or for family reasons or where a criminal court made a recommendation to deport but gives a sentence below the automatic deportation threshold.

16.57 The rule introduced, for the first time, a presumption that the public interest required doing away with the system which had existed, which saw in the old rules, the public interest balanced against all the compassionate circumstances of the case and all the other relevant factors that had to be taken into account, some adding weight to the public interest and some weakening it. For the first time it was made explicit that the public interest would rarely be outweighed, unless deportation would be contrary to either the obligations under the Human Rights Convention or the Refugee Convention and Protocol. If it is not, it was to be only in exceptional circumstances that the decision to deport will be rejected.

16.58 Paragraph 364 applied to all conducive deportations, not just those based upon criminal offending. However, the amendments were introduced with foreign national prisoners and very little else in mind.[1] In that respect they and the case law based on them had been very much overtaken by the introduction of the automatic deportation provisions. The main focus of the new rule was on persons who have been convicted of crime and are coming to the end of a sentence of imprisonment or other form of custody. Fixing where the public interest lies depended first, upon certain broad generalities of policy, which can be narrow or wide, such as the prevention and punishment of crime and the interests of public safety, but, secondly, on very fact-specific factors relating to the particular case, like the nature of the criminal offending and the risk posed by the particular offender. In practice, the Secretary of State issued guidance to the effect that deportation would be considered where a non-EEA national is convicted of a criminal offence and sentenced to twelve months or more or has two or three sentences over a period of five years or more. In *OP (Jamaica) v Secretary of State for the Home Department*[2] the Court of Appeal held, following *R (on the application of N) v Secretary for State for the Home Department*[3] that proper weight must be given to the Secretary of State's policy on deportation, and in particular to the fact that she has taken the view, in the public interest, that serious crimes of violence are sufficiently serious to warrant deportation. In such circumstances, her assessment had to be taken as a given, unless it is palpably wrong. At the same time we are reminded by the decision in *DW (Jamaica) v Secretary of State for the Home Department*,[4] that where the AIT (now IAC) dismissed the claimant's appeal against deportation, stating that someone who committed a serious offence in the United Kingdom could not be permitted to remain here, this was a misdirection of law and the decision could not stand unless it was inevitable that it would have come to the same conclusion if properly directed.

[1] See the Home Secretary's Written Ministerial Statement of 23 May 2006 (Official Report, Column 80 WS).
[2] [2008] EWCA Civ 440, [2008] All ER (D) 06 (May).
[3] [2004] EWCA Civ 1094, [2004] INLR 612.
[4] [2008] EWCA Civ 1587, [2008] All ER (D) 261 (Oct).

16.59 This rule indicated that the task in a deportation case was one of discretion rather than the application of a precise code having mandatory effect. In exercising discretion, the task of the decision maker was essentially one of reaching a fair balance between the public interest and the personal interests of the proposed deportee. The aim was an exercise of power which was proportionate and fair. This jurisdiction existed from 1969 and no question of deference to the Secretary of State arose prior to the coming into force of the Human Rights Act 1998 in October 2000.[1] The paragraph characterised the essential issue in most cases but it was not intended to be exhaustive or comprehensive. It was not designed to restrict what were relevant factors or to limit the consideration of factors simply to compassionate ones.[2] In *Idrish*[3] the Tribunal held that the strength of the public interest in deporting could and should be assessed in the light of all circumstances.

[1]   Compare *Singh (Bakhtaur) v Immigration Appeal Tribunal* [1986] 2 All ER 721, [1986] 1 WLR 910, [1986] Imm AR 352, HL, with *R (on the application of N) v Secretary of State for the Home Department* [2004] EWCA Civ 1094, [2004] INLR 612.
[2]   *Singh (Bakhtaur) v Immigration Appeal Tribunal*, above.
[3]   *Idrish* [1985] Imm AR 155, IAT.

16.60 Everything that was properly persuasive for or against deportation, including the background situation in the country to which deportees are to be deported[1] should be considered. The impact of the proposed deportation on third parties, whether family,[2] work colleagues, employees,[3] police[4] or members of a local community, is always a relevant circumstance and it does not have to be squeezed into the category of compassionate circumstances.[5] Only what was irrelevant to a decision to deport could be excluded (such as the threat of industrial action or other forms of unrest either in support of or against deportation, matters to which it would be improper for the minister to have regard).[6] Paragraph 364 had been introduced into the rules in September 2000 by Cm 4851 at a time when overstaying and breach of conditions had been separated from deportation on conducive grounds and was dealt with by removal. The paragraph contained no express presumption in favour of deportation which weighted the balance against foreign criminals, and it set out a list of different factors for and against deportation to be taken into account. That period came to an end in the years between 2006 and 2007. First, paragraph 364 was substituted by a new paragraph.[7] First, where there was deportation on conducive grounds, there was now an express presumption in favour of deportation. Second, although all relevant factors still had to be taken into account the scales were to be heavily weighted and only in exceptional circumstances would the public interest in deportation be outweighed. This plus the introduction of automatic deportation in 2007 ushered in a new era for deporting foreign criminals, but still left the door open to Article 8 arguments under the ECHR. These changes were nothing compared with the programme for deportation introduced in July 2012.

[1]   *Kamara (Elizabeth) (20155)*; *Kamara (Mohammed) (21814)*; *Kapusnik (00TH01897)*.
[2]   *Tantono* [2002] UKIAT 00356, where the effect of deportation on the children of a long-term resident convicted of manslaughter and false imprisonment in exceptional circumstances prevented his deportation. See also: *SS (India) v Secretary of State for the Home Department* [2010] EWCA Civ 388, [2010] All ER (D) 71 (Apr); *AF (Jamaica) v Secretary of State for the Home Department* [2009] EWCA Civ 240; *KB (Trinidad and Tobago) v Secretary of State for the Home Department* [2010] EWCA Civ 11 (see **16.36** above).

3   *Leong* (5055), IAT where deportation would have resulted in a loss of employment for persons settled here.
4   But the desire of police officers to retain the services of a valuable informer was held not decisive against deportation in *CM v Secretary of State for the Home Department* [1997] Imm AR 336.
5   *Singh (Bakhtaur) v Immigration Appeal Tribunal* [1986] 2 All ER 721, [1986] 1 WLR 910, [1986] Imm AR 352, HL.
6   *Singh (Bakhtaur)* fn 5 above; *CM* fn 4 above.
7   HC 1337 which came into effect on 20 July 2006.

The Rules post 9th July 2012 – Statement of Changes HC 194

16.61 In June 2012 the Home Office announced its intention to codify the interpretation of Article 8 ECHR.[1] They made it quite clear that Article 8 was the lingering problem of deporting foreign criminals and that they were going to do something about it. The first step was taken in the Statement of Changes HC 194 which came into effect on 9 July 2012. Rules 364, 364A, 367 and 380 were deleted,[2] A presumption that the public interest required deportation was inserted in the rules together with a rule-based application of the government's interpretation of the main factors relevant to an Article 8 claim (paragraphs 396 to 399C).[3] The new rules applied to all those facing deportation on or after 9 July 2012 regardless of when the notice of intention to deport or the deportation order was served, the relevant date for determining the applicable rule being the date of decision to deport.

1   'Statement of Intent: Family Migration', June 2012, see para 38 onwards
2   Inserted by HC 194, para 112.
3   Inserted by HC 194, para 114.

16.62 The Immigration Rules expressly provide that a deportation order will not be made against a person with a well-founded fear of persecution,[1] or a person whose removal would be in breach of the UK's obligations under the ECHR.[2] Deportation will not take place where the consequences of return would be disproportionately severe.[3] Although risk may be mitigated in the presence of assurances from a receiving State as to treatment on return,[4] or evidence in a medical case that appropriate and adequate steps would be taken to manage risk by the sending or receiving States.[5] The Secretary of State may revoke indefinite leave to remain where the person would be liable to deportation but cannot be deported for legal reasons (ie, because deportation would be in breach of the Human Rights Convention).[6]

1   HC 395, para 397 (formerly para 380). This does not prevent the deportation of a refugee, simply because he or she has in the past been granted refugee status, if by his or her criminal activities the protection of the Refugee Convention has been lost: *Raziastaraie v Secretary of State for the Home Department* [1995] Imm AR 459, CA, or if leave to remain was never granted and the circumstances in which he or she was recognised as a refugee have ceased to exist: *N (Kenya)* [2004] UKIAT 00009. But no removal could take place if a real risk engaging the ECHR exists.
2   HC 395 para 397, inserted by HC 194, para 380 having been deleted.
3   *Kim* (11041) (Korean national convicted of several homicides, appeal allowed on basis of double jeopardy and possibility of execution); *Oyedeji* (19618) (drugs, serious possibility of arrest and charge on return, which would be double jeopardy, and life-threatening detention conditions); *Tantono* [2002] UKIAT 00356 (human rights situation in Indonesia). See further: *AF (Jamaica) v Secretary of State for the Home Department* [2009] EWCA Civ 240; *KB (Trinidad and Tobago) v Secretary of State for the Home Department* [2010] EWCA Civ 11 (at **16.60** above). See also cases on arts 3 and 8 of the ECHR in Chapter 7, above.

[4]   In *Othman (Abu Qatada) v United Kingdom* (Application 8139/09) [2012] ECHR 56 it was
      held by the ECtHR that without assurances from the Jordanian Government, there would be
      a real risk of ill-treatment of a high profile Islamist and that, even where government
      assurances from the receiving country are obtained, caution should attached to any diplomatic
      assurances, The applicant's deportation to Jordan was held in that case not be in violation of
      Article 3 of the Convention given the diplomatic assurances provided in the case. Deportation
      to Jordan was, however, held to be in violation of Article 6 of the Convention given the
      concrete and compelling evidence that the Applicant's co-defendants were tortured into
      providing the case against him. Following later assurances by the Jordanian government that
      no evidence would be called if it had or might have been obtained by torture, Mr Othman
      returned to Jordan and was in due course acquitted of all charges against him.
[5]   *Balogun v The United Kingdom* (Application 60286/09) [2012] ECHR 614 held that where
      appropriate and adequate steps were taken by the relevant authorities to mitigate a risk of
      suicide this will weigh against a conclusion that the high threshold of Article 3 has been
      reached. In that case it was noted that the UK Government were now fully aware of the suicide
      risk posed by the applicant to himself and could be relied upon to take the necessary steps to
      minimise such risks.
[6]   Nationality, Immigration and Asylum Act 2002, s 76(1).

16.63 In relation to Article 8 the rules laid down at HC 395, paragraphs 398
to 399C were intended to be a complete code of how the proportionality
balance under that provision of the ECHR should be struck. The rules maintained the presumption that the public interest required a persons removal
where they were liable to deportation was retained.[1] The Rules proceeded to
present a framework informed by the length of sentence of imprisonment[2],
whereby those who were sentenced to less than four years imprisonment could
avoid deportation if their case fell within the circumstances outlined in
rule 399 (family life) or rule 399A (private life). As to the former paragraph 399 provided that deportation could be avoided on family life case in
the following limited circumstances:

(a)   where the deportee had a genuine and subsisting parental relationship
       with a minor child present in the UK who was either British or had
       resided in the jurisdiction for the seven years prior to the application
       and could not reasonably be expected to leave the UK, and where there
       were no other family members able to care for the that child in the UK;[3]
(b)   Where the deportee had lived continuously in the UK with valid leave
       for 15 years and was in a genuine and subsisting relationship with a
       partner in the UK who was either British, settled or present as a Refugee
       or with Humanitarian protection, with whom family life could not
       continue outside the UK due to the existence of insurmountable
       obstacles.[4]

With regard to private life cases paragraph 399A afforded a platform from
which to resist deportation where either the person has lived continuously in
the UK for at least 20 years immediately preceding the date of the immigration
decision[5], or they were aged under 25 years and had lived more than half their
lives in the UK[6]. In each case the rules required the deportee additionally to
demonstrate that they had no ties (including social, cultural or family) with the
country to which he would have to go if required to leave,[7] and specified that
periods spent in prison would be discounted from the assessment of period of
residence.

[1]   *R (on the application of George (Fitzroy)) v Secretary of State for the Home Department*
      [2014] UKSC 28

2   HC 395, para 398 and Explanatory Memorandum to Statement of Changes HC 194 and see *McLarty (Deportation – balance)* [2014] UKUT 00315 (IAC).
3   Paragraph 399(a), Immigration Rules HC 194. See **16.79** below for the subsequent amendment of this Rule.
4   Paragraph 399(b), Immigration Rules HC 194. In *Ogundimu (Article 8 – new rules) Nigeria* [2013] UKUT 60 (IAC) the Tribunal offered an interpretation of 'insurmountable obstacles', observing that it was not intended to mean an obstacle that literally could not be surmounted, concluding that where Article 8 rights would be breached that may well satisfy the test, as may the loss of benefit obtained by a child by reason of their British or EU citizenship. See further *Sanade, Harrison & Walker v Secretary of State for the Home Department* [2012] UKUT 00048(IAC). See **16.80** for subsequent amendment to this rule.
5   Immigration Rules HC194, para 399A(a).
6   Immigration Rules HC194, para 399A(b).
7   In *Ogundimu (Article 8 – new rules) Nigeria* [2013] UKUT 60 (IAC) the Tribunal found that the term 'no ties (social, cultural or family)' should be afforded its ordinary meaning, proceeding to conclude it involved a concept of something more than merely remote and abstract links to the country of proposed deportation or removal, rather it required there be a continued connection to life in that country in the form of something that tied then in a meaningful way to it.

16.64 Where paragraphs 399 and 399A, HC 194 did apply this did not operate so as to remove the necessity for considered case specific evaluation. As the Court in *MF (Nigeria)*[1] observed resolution of the issues arising under the rules may involve questions of evaluation as well as hard-edged fact, such as whether it would be 'reasonable' to expect a child to leave the UK or whether there are 'insurmountable obstacles'. In relation to the policy objectives that an individual's personal circumstances have to be weighed against, these have been referred to in many cases.

1   [2013] EWCA Civ 1192, [2014] 1 WLR 544.

16.65 When assessing qualification under the applicable rules there is no 'near miss' principle operative. Where an appellant misses satisfying the requirements of the rules even by a small margin, and contends that his removal from the UK will breach his rights under Article 8, the requirement of immigration control are not weakened by the degree of non-compliance with the Immigration Rules.[1] The decision of the Supreme Court in *Patel v Secretary of State for the Home Department; Alam v Secretary of State for the Home Department* is notable in the above regard, Lord Carnwath holding that the 'the balance [between the Article 8(1) interest and legitimate aim pursued] drawn by the rules may be relevant to the consideration of proportionality,' and that, *'the practical or compassionate considerations which underlie the policy [i.e. the rule] are also likely to be relevant to the cases of those who fall just outside it, and to that extent may add weight to their argument [under Article 8]'*[2]. The concept of a 'near-miss' falls to be distinguished from the de minimis principle which may have application on the basis that if a departure from a rule were truly de minimis, the rule may be considered to have been complied with.[3]

1   *Miah v Secretary of State for the Home Department* [2012] EWCA Civ 261 (7 March 2012).
2   [2013] UKSC 72, [2014] AC 651, [2014] 1 All ER 1157 at 55.
3   *Miah and others* ante.[2012] EWCA Civ 261.

16.66 Under the Rules those falling outwith the categories particularised in paragraphs 399 and 399A HC194, or those who had been subject to a custodial sentence in excess of four years were stated to enjoy no entitlement to remain under the rules save upon the demonstration of exceptional circumstances.[1] Assessment of whether such exceptional circumstances existed fell to be performed by reference to established domestic and Strasbourg jurisprudence.[2] It could only be answered in the context of whether there were factors not covered by the Rules which gave rise to the need to consider Article 8 further ie whether there are there any 'compelling circumstances' that would justify a detailed examination taken outside of the Rules[3]. Those matters would not include the considerations identified in *Üner v Netherlands*[4] as material to a determination of the proportionality of enforcement action in cases of criminal conduct, the Court of Appeal in *LC (China) v Secretary of State for the Home Department* finding that they had been subsumed into the Immigration Rules with the effect that there was no obligation to perform a discrete assessment by reference to the same in the context of an exceptionality review.[5]

[1] MF (Nigeria) v Secretary of State for the Home Department [2013] EWCA Civ 1192 and Kabia (MF: Para 298-Exceptional Circumstances) [2013] UKUT 00569 IAC and R (on the application of MM (Lebanon) v Secretary of State for the Home Department 2014 EWCA Civ 985.

[2] Miah v Secretary of State for the Home Department [2012] EWCA Civ 261, [2013] QB 35, [2012] 3 WLR 492; Nagre [2013] EWHC 720 (Admin); Gulshan [2013] UKUT 640, Shahzad (Article 8: legitimate aim) [2014] UKUT 00085 (IAC).

[3] Nagre at 31.

[4] (2006) 45 EHRR 421. The factors set down by the Court were outlined at paragraphs 57 and 58 and included the following:

(i)   the nature and seriousness of the offence committed by the applicant;
(ii)   the length of the applicant's stay in the country from which he isto be expelled;
(iii)   the time elapsed since the offence was committed and the applicant's conduct during that period;
(iv)   the nationalities of the various persons concerned;
(v)   the applicant's family situation such as the length of the marriage and other factors expressing the effectiveness of a couple's family life;
(vi)   whether the spouse knew about the offence at the time when he or she entered into a family relationship;
(vii)   whether there are children of the marriage, and if so, their age;
(viii)   the seriousness of the difficulties which the spouse is likely to encounter in the country to which the applicant is to be expelled;
(ix)   the best interests and well-being of the children, in particular the seriousness of the difficulties which any children of the applicant are likely to encounter in the country to which the applicant is to be expelled;
(x)   the solidity of social, cultural and family ties with the host country and with the country of destination.

[5] LC (China) v Secretary of State for the Home Department [2014] EWCA Civ 1310, [2014] All ER (D) 134 (Oct).

16.67 In evaluating exceptional circumstances and whether they apply, the Court of Appeal accepted in *MF (Nigeria)* that in the balancing exercise, great weight should be attached to the public interest for those who do not satisfy paragraphs 398, 399 or 399A. In 'precarious' family life cases, where family life was established when immigration status was uncertain, that it was likely to be only in the most exceptional of circumstances that the removal of the deportee would be likely to violate Article 8. Exceptionality was considered to be a likely factual characteristic of a claim that properly succeeds rather than a legal test to be met. In this context, 'exceptional' has been held to mean circumstances in which deportation would result in unjustifiably harsh consequences for the individual or their family such that a deportation would not be proportionate[1]. The Court held that whether there are 'very compelling reasons' or exceptional circumstances to engage Article 8 will be the product of a proportionality test in accordance with Strasbourg jurisprudence. What amounts to exceptional circumstances or very compelling circumstances is very much fact dependent but must necessarily be seen in the context of the articulated will of Parliament in favour of deportation. Thus 'exceptional' or 'compelling' must describe the end result of the proportionality weighing exercise[2].

1   *MF (Nigeria) ante; Nagre ante; Kabia (MF: Para 298-Exceptional Circumstances)* [2013] UKUT 00569 IAC.
2   *McLarty (Deportation – proportionality balance)* [2014] UKUT 00315 (IAC).

Settled migrant children

16.68 Deficiencies in the construction of paragraphs 399 and 399A, as amended by HC 194, were identified by the Tribunal so as to admit of exceptionality in a number of cases. Most notably in in *Ogundimu*[1] the tribunal observes that the new rules made no attempt to reflect one of the most important Strasbourg decisions on deportation, that of *Maslov*[2] and that the ratio of that decision continued to apply, so that very serious reasons were required to justify expulsion of a settled migrant who had lawfully spent all or the majority of their childhood in the UK.[3] Even in such cases, however, deportation may be justified where offences perpetrated are very serious and where too they were committed during majority.

1   *Ogundimu (Article 8 – new rules) Nigeria* [2013] UKUT 60 (IAC).
2   *Maslov v Austria* [2008] ECHR 546. Note that Maslov does not apply where the appellant has no right to be in the UK, as to which see: *Darko v Secretary of State for the Home Department* [2012] EWCA Civ 39; *Richards v Secretary of State for the Home Department* [2013] EWCA Civ 244.
3   *Balogun v United Kingdom* (Application 60286/09) [2012] ECHR 614. The ECtHR held that the possession of Class A drugs with intent to supply for which a sentence of three years was given was undoubtedly very serious particularly in light of the fact that the majority of the applicant's offences were committed when he was already an adult, the Court proceeding to find that the applicant could not excuse his past criminal conduct by reference to his upbringing and that his removal would not be disproportionate.

Best interests considerations

16.69 The rules were also found to be deficient by reason of their failure to differentiate, when assessing the seriousness of offending for the purposes of deportation, between offences committed during a person's minority and those perpetrated following the attainment of majority, the Grand Chamber in *Maslov*[1] again having confirmed that 'when assessing the nature and seriousness of the offences committed by an applicant, it has to be taken into account whether he or she committed them as a juvenile or as an adult'.[2]

1   *Maslov v Austria* [2008] ECHR 546.
2   *Green (Article 8 – new rules)* [2013] UKUT 254 (IAC).

16.70 Issue was also raised by authority with regard to the question of how far the new rules adequately address the best interests of children, the provision in paragraph 399(a) that a deportee who enjoyed a genuine and subsisting relationship with a qualifying child may nonetheless be expelled if there were another family member able to care for that child being clearly inconsistent with primary legislation, a fully ratified international treaty and a Supreme Court decision: respectively section 55 of the Borders, Citizenship and Immigration Act 2009, the UN Convention on the Rights of the Child and *ZH Tanzania* [2011] UKSC 4.[1]

[1]   *Ogundimu (Article 8 – new rules) Nigeria* [2013] UKUT 60 (IAC).

16.71 The presence of children, even where they are settled or British, has been held not to preclude deportation action automatically, In *ZH (Tanzania) v Secretary of State for the Home Department*[1] the Supreme Court itself recognised that the interests of the children, and in particular with regard to nationality, whilst very important, were not trump cards over all other policy considerations which included ' . . . the need to maintain firm and fair immigration control'. The Court of Appeal in *SS (Nigeria) v Secretary of State for the Home Department*[2] subsequently holding that the practical bite of the primacy of the best interests of the child would vary with the case in hand. It characterised 'a primary consideration' as meaning a consideration of substantial importance, noting that in a child case the right in question (the child's best interests) is always a consideration of substantial importance, but proceeded to observe that those interests could be displaced that the more pressing the public interest in removal or deportation, the stronger must be the claim under Article 8 if it is to prevail, observing that the nature of the public interest in criminal deportation cases was vividly informed by the fact that by Parliament's express declaration that the public interest is injured if the criminal's deportation is not effected and such a result could only be justified by a very strong claim indeed. More recently still the Court of Appeal in *LC (China) v Secretary of State for the Home Department*[3] has held that the fact that the children of a deportee have British Citizenship may not be an automatic barrier to enforcement action.

[1]   [2011] UKSC 4, [2011] 2 AC 166, [2011] 2 All ER 783.
[2]   [2013] EWCA Civ 550, [2013] All ER (D) 281 (May).
[3]   [2014] EWCA Civ 1310.

16.72 Obviously any failure to recognise and reflect within a decision on deportation that the best interest of a child were a primary consideration would flaw the same without more, even in cases where the offending behaviour informing enforcement action was serious. The Court of Appeal holding that the interests of family life may surmount the public interest in deportation, and ordering an appeal back to the IAC in *AF (Jamaica) v Secretary of State for the Home Department*[1], a case in which the appellant had been sentenced to a lengthy custodial sentence for Class A drug supply, having found the third-party interests of a partner and child had been accorded insufficient weight by the Tribunal. The importance of treating the best interests of affected children as a primary consideration and the significance of their British and EU citizenship was emphasised in *Omotunde (best interests – Zambrano applied – Razgar) Nigeria*.[2]

[1]   [2009] EWCA Civ 240, [2009] All ER (D) 261 (Mar). See further *KB (Trinidad and Tobago) v Secretary of State for the Home Department* [2010] EWCA Civ 11, [2010] 1 WLR 1630.
[2]   [2011] UKUT 00247 (IAC).

16.73 The fact that deportation may breach Article 8 where a parent has contact with a child present in the UK, means that it is obviously desirable to resolve the issue of an entitlement to such parent/child contact, where the matter is contentious, so as to to enable a just disposal of the proportionality issues. Consequently where such proceedings are in train before the family courts and deportation would serve to deny or undermine that parent's ability to pursue the same the ECtHR has long held that pursuit of the enforcement exercise may amount to a violation.[1] That position has been adhered to consistently by domestic Courts most significantly by the Court of Appeal in *Mohan v Secretary of State for the Home Department*,[2] where the Vice President, Maurice Kay LJ, set out and endorsed guidance previously laid down by the Upper Tribunal in a case called *RS (immigration and family court proceedings) India*[3] which reads as follows:

> 'In our judgment, when a judge sitting in a immigration appeal has to consider whether a person with a criminal record or adverse immigration history should be removed or deported when there are family proceedings contemplated, the judge should consider the following questions:
> (i)   Is the outcome of the contemplated family proceedings likely to be material to the immigration decision?
> (ii)   Are there compelling public interest reasons to exclude the claimant from the United Kingdom, irrespective of the outcome of the family proceedings or the best interests of the child?
> (iii) In the case of contact proceedings initiated by an appellant in an immigration appeal, is there any reason to believe that the family proceedings have been instituted to delay or frustrate removal and not to promote the child's welfare?
> (iv) In assessing the above questions, the judge will normally want to consider: the degree of the claimant's previous interest in and contact with the child, the timing of the contact proceedings and the commitment with which they have been progressed, when a decision is likely to be reached, what materials (if any) are already available or can be made available to identify pointers to where the child's welfare lies.'

---

[1] *Moser v Austria* [2007] 1 FLR 702 at 67 to 69, and *Ciliz v Netherlands* [2002] FLR 469 at 70 to 73.
[2] [2012] EWCA Civ 1363. See further: *R (on the application of Singh) v Secretary of State for the Home Department* [2014] EWHC 461 (Admin).
[3] [2012] UKUT 00218 IAC.

16.74 The mere possibility of family proceedings being issued would not have the effect of obliging a stay in extant deportation proceedings, the Upper Tribunal so finding when it determined a Judicial Review against a first instance decision of the First Tier in *Mohammed (Family Court proceedings-outcome)*[1]. The Upper Tribunal confirmed that following the coming into force on 22 April 2014 of the Children and Families Act 2014, there was nothing in the guidance given in, *RS* or *Mohan* or in the previous case law that supported the notion that the mere possibility of an application being made or pursued for contact or residence was a relevant criterion for an immigration judge or panel to take into account when deciding whether to adjourn an appeal or to direct a grant of discretionary leave in order to enable Family Court proceedings to be pursued. The guidance being concerned with whether there was a realistic prospect of the Family Court making a decision that would have a material impact on the relationship between a child and the parent facing deportation. The Upper Tribunal considered the new statutory provisions relating to Article 8, set out in section 117A–D of the Immigration Act 2014, meant that the appeal could not have succeeded under the old or new regimes.

¹ [2014] UKUT 00419 (IAC). See further: *KG (Jamaica) v Secretary of State for the Home Department* [2014] EWCA Civ 453.

16.75 Indeed it is notable that in *SS (Nigeria)*¹ the Court of Appeal found that the circumstances in which the Tribunal might be required to cause further inquiries to be made, or evidence to be obtained, in cases affecting children were likely to be extremely rare. The Court concluded that in the vast majority of such cases the Tribunal would expect the relevant interests of the child to be drawn to the attention of the decision-maker by the applicant, so that the decision-maker could then make such additional inquiries as might appear appropriate.

¹ *SS (Nigeria) v Secretary of State for the Home Department* [2013] EWCA Civ 550.

Medical cases

16.76 An exceptional case may be made out where there are medical issues affecting the deportee. Those issues could be an additional factor to be weighed in the balance, with other considerations relevant to Article 8 ECHR. Medical issues may be a decisive factor in a case where the deportees have established a strong family and private life in the United Kingdom based on their family ties, their illness, their dependency on particular clinicians and their medication, taken together with the obligation under the Mental Health Act 1983 to provide them with community care after discharge.¹ A finding in favour of the deportee in the above regard would need not to involve a comparison between medical facilities here and those in the country of origin, and so would not need to offend the principle expressed in *N v United Kingdom*² that the United Kingdom is under no Convention obligation, except in the most exceptional circumstances, to provide medical treatment here when it is not available in the country to which the appellant is to be deported.

¹ *MM (Zimbabwe) v Secretary of State for the Home Department* [2012] EWCA Civ 279 (13 March 2012).
² (Application no 26565/05), (2008) 47 EHRR 885, (2008) Times, 6 June, ECtHR.

The Rules post 28th July 2014 – Statement of Changes HC 532

16.77 The Immigration Rules relating to deportation were further amended with effect from 28 July 2014 by Statement of Changes HC 532. Paragraphs 378 and 386 were amended so as to fit in with the non-suspensive deportation appeal regime introduced by the Immigration Act 2014 and paragraphs 398-399D were updated to bring the rules into line with the new provisions of the Immigration Act 2014¹. The new rules apply to decisions made on or after 28 July 2014, regardless of whether the application was made before that date². Whilst the modified rules do not purport to make any substantial changes to the policies contained in the 9 July 2012 provisions, in practice they have that effect, in that they have encouraged the Secretary of State to assert that the statutory framework or code is complete, and has now replaced previous caselaw in relating to the interpretation of public interest factors.[3] We shall see.

1   See Immigration Act 2014 (Commencement No 1, Transitory and Saving Provisions) Order 2014, SI 2014/1820. See also Immigration Act 2014 (Commencement No 3, Transitory and Saving Provisions) Order 2014, SI 2014/2771.
2   Paragraph A279 of the Rules is amended by HC 532 to read as follows: '*Paragraphs 398-399D apply to all immigration decisions made further to applications under Part 8 and paragraphs 276A–276D where a decision is made on or after 28 July 2014, irrespective of the date the application was made*'.
3   Chapter 13 IDIs 'Deportation'.

16.78 The impact of decision of the Court of Appeal in *MF(Nigeria)* is reflected in the removal from paragraph 398 of the controversial 'exceptional circumstances' test,[1] to be replaced by the following: 'the public interest in deportation will only be outweighed by other factors where there are very compelling circumstances over and above those described in paragraphs 399 and 399A'. The language is obviously taken directly from the Court of Appeals description in *MF(Nigeria)*[2] of what 'exceptionality' translated to in practice in the context of a rules based review, and as such does not materially alter the evaluative approach.

1   See Explanatory Statement to HC 532 10 July 2014.
2   *MF(Nigeria)* at 43.

16.79 Paragraph 399 also saw quite substantial changes under HC532. Firstly, for those seeking to resist deportation on the basis of relationship with a child, the paragraph 399(a)(ii)(a) test of reasonableness when assessing relocation of a child has been replaced by one of undue harshness. The test of there being 'no other family member who is able to care for the child in the UK' at paragraph 399(a)(ii)(b) is replaced with a similar 'unduly harsh' test with regard to the impact of separation. As to what the unduly harsh threshold will require, that remains to be clarified by caselaw. The Secretary of State's instructions appear to go further than the wording of the rules by adding the adjectives 'severe' and 'cruel'. She suggests that satisfaction of the test would require evidence that the consequences of resettlement would be 'excessively harsh, severe or cruel'[1]. This is in effect an attempt to assimilate the Article 8 requirements with some of those in Article 3 ECHR.

1   Chapter 13 IDIs 'Deportation' at paragraph 2.5.2.

16.80 The previous test for links to the UK through a spouse set down in paragraph 399(b) is also replaced with the following:

(i)   the relationship was formed at a time when the person (deportee) was in the UK lawfully and their immigration status was not precarious; and

(ii)   it would be unduly harsh for that partner to live in the country to which the person is to be deported, because of compelling circumstances over and above those described in paragraph EX.2. of Appendix FM; and

(iii)   it would be unduly harsh for that partner to remain in the UK without the person who is to be deported.

As can be seen the controversial 'insurmountable obstacles' threshold was withdrawn to be replaced by what is likely to be an equally onerous 'unduly harsh' test. The fixed benchmark of 15 years' residence is replaced too with a more discretionary approach. The requirement that the relationship commenced when the deportee's status was not precarious is an absolute bar to success in many cases, though, and cannot possibly be considered consistent with a proper human rights assessment. A limited dispensation for those with refugee leave or humanitarian protection is removed at paragraph 399(b). For deportation to be averted on the basis of the person's own private life which required 20 years for those over 25 and 'half of life' for those under 25, the replacement provisions are:

(a)   the person has been lawfully resident in the UK for most of his life; and

(b)   he is socially and culturally integrated in the UK; and

(c)   there would be very significant obstacles to his integration into the country to which it is proposed he is deported.

Paragraph 399B is also modified so as to include modified provisions for the revocation of a deportation order. We deal with this at **16.113** below.

THE IMMIGRATION ACT 2014

16.81 As indicated above the rule changes introduced in July 2014[1] were intended to give effect to the statutory code for the proportionality assessment under Article 8 ECHR being put in place by the Immigration Act 2014. The 2014 Act inserts a new Part 5A into the Nationality, Immigration and Asylum Act 2002, the purpose of which is to set in stone the considerations a court or tribunal must have regard to in assessing the public interest considerations under Article 8 ECHR. Section 19 of the new Act introduces sections 117A–D into the 2002 Act so as to set out a series of mandatory requirements on courts and tribunals in judging decisions made under the Immigration Acts in order to determine whether these decisions are in breach of a person's Article 8 rights and unlawful under section 6 of the Human rights Act 1998.

[1]   HC 395, paras 398–399A.

16.82 In the context of deportation the critical aspects of Part 5A of the 2002 Act are contained in sections 117A and 117C. The former states that judges 'must have regard to the various considerations'. A statutory provision mandating 'consideration' of particular issues is not without precedent in the immigration context. Section 8 of the Asylum and Immigration (Treatment of Claimants etc) Act 2004 introduced a similar obligation in the context of credibility assessments in asylum cases, stating that judges 'shall take account, as damaging the claimant's credibility, of any behaviour to which this section applies'. The new Part 5A duty is more weakly expressed than section 8 of the 2004 Act. In particular no similar steer is given in the new Part 5A regarding the outcome of the judge's consideration of Tthe factors stated to be relevant. Importantly too the Court of Appeal proceeded in *JT (Cameroon) v Secretary of State for the Home Department* [2008] EWCA Civ 878 to interpret section 8 as no more than a 'reminder' that conduct coming within the categories detailed in the provisions was capable of impacting upon credibility. in so finding Lord Justice Pill, giving the leading judgment, held that the provision did not offend against constitutional principles:

'Section 8 can thus be construed as not offending against constitutional principles. It is no more than a reminder to fact-finding tribunals that conduct coming within the categories stated in section 8 shall be taken into account in assessing credibility. If there was a tendency for tribunals simply to ignore these matters when assessing credibility, they were in error. It is necessary to take account of them. However, at one end of the spectrum, there may, unusually, be cases in which conduct of the kind identified in section 8 is held to carry no weight at all in the overall assessment of credibility on the particular facts. I do not consider the section prevents that finding in an appropriate case. Subject to that, I respectfully agree with Baroness Scotland's assessment, when introducing the Bill, of the effect of section 8. Where section 8 matters are held to be entitled to some weight, the weight to be given to them is entirely a matter for the fact-finder'.

A similar approach may be adopted by the tribunals and courts. It is likely that a pragmatic view will be taken by the Courts, given that the matters framed in section 117C, to which 'consideration' must be given, are ones to which immigration judges are already having regard under both the rules[1] and established jurisprudence. No decision maker, immigration adviser or tribunal will have any difficulty in having regard to a consideration that the section identifying in its precursors for instance that 'the deportation of foreign criminals is in the public interest;' before proceeding to state uncontroversially or that 'the more serious the offence committed the greater is the public interest in deportation of the criminal'.[2] The section then distinguishes between two categories of foreign national offender by reference to familiar custodial sentence thresholds of four years and over[3] and up to four years,[4] before describing, in respect of each, the considerations operating as exceptions to the enforcement activity otherwise mandated by the sentences imposed.[5]

[1]   Nationality, Immigration and Asylum Act 2002, s 117C(1).
[2]   Nationality, Immigration and Asylum Act 2002, s 117C(2).
[3]   Nationality, Immigration and Asylum Act 2002, s 117C(6).
[4]   Nationality, Immigration and Asylum Act 2002, s117C(3).
[5]   Nationality, Immigration and Asylum Act 2002, s 117C(4) and (5).

16.83 In respect of those sentenced to imprisonment of four years or more the public interest requires deportation, subject to the operation of two exceptions:

Exception 1 applies where deportee:

(a)   has been lawfully resident in the United Kingdom for most of his or her life,
(b)   is socially and culturally integrated in the United Kingdom, and
(c)   there would be very significant obstacles to their integration into the country to which deportation is proposed.[1]

Exception 2 applies where a deportee has:

(a)   a genuine and subsisting relationship with a qualifying partner, or
(b)   a genuine and subsisting parental relationship with a qualifying child, and the effect of C's deportation on the partner or child would be unduly harsh.[2]

In the case of a foreign criminal who has been sentenced to a period of imprisonment of at least four years, the public interest requires deportation unless there are very compelling circumstances, over and above those described in Exceptions 1 and 2.[3] Section 117C(7) concludes by directing that the considerations in the preceding sub-sections 'are to be taken into account where a court or tribunal is considering a decision to deport a foreign criminal only to the extent that the reason for the decision was the offence or offences for which the criminal has been convicted'. This makes plain that if extraneous factors dictated the institution of deportation action, for instance considerations of national security or public health, then section 117C would not be operative.[4]

[1]   Nationality, Immigration and Asylum Act 2002, s 117C(4).
[2]   Nationality, Immigration and Asylum Act 2002, s 117C(5).
[3]   Nationality, Immigration and Asylum Act 2002, s 117(6).
[4]   Nationality, Immigration and Asylum Act 2002, s 117(7).

Article 8 and Proportionality under the new regime

16.84 In the IDIs on Criminality Guidance, the Secretary of State explicitly instructs her caseworkers that there is now no obligation to assess Article 8 proportionality issues against authority preceding the implementation of the new Immigration Rules and the changes wrought by the Immigration Act 2014 in respect of decisions made after 28th July 2014:

> 'Decision-makers must not make decisions on the basis of case law established before commencement of section 19 of the Immigration Act 2014 (28 July 2014) or refer to such case law in decision letters. Decisions must be taken solely on the basis of the Immigration Rules, which Part 5A of the 2002 Act underpins. The courts will develop new case law in relation to the public interest statements'.[1]

That bold assertion may be seen as having been endorsed by the Court of Appeal decision in *LC (China) v Secretary of State for the Home Department*,[2] in which it was suggested, in respect of the preceding rules, that previous case law of the ECtHR has been subsumed into the Immigration Rules with the effect that a decision maker does not therefore need to give it further thought. Consequently there was no error of law by the UT in failing to consider in explicit terms the factors identified in *Üner*.[3] It should be noted that *LC (China)*, *SS (Nigeria)*[4] and *MF (Nigeria)*[5] are very specific to deportation. They all emphasise the great weight to be attached to the public interest in the deportation of foreign criminals and the importance of the policy in that regard to which effect has been given by Parliament in the UK Borders Act 2007 concerning automatic deportation. In *LC (China)*, Moore-Bick LJ distinguished deportation of foreign criminals with those cases concerned with the removal of persons who were in the UK country illegally (para 25).

[1]   IDIs: Chapter 13 – Criminality Guidance in Article 8 ECHR Cases V5.0 (28 July 2014), Section 2.8.1.
[2]   [2014] EWCA Civ 1310, at 26,
[3]   *Üner v The Netherlands* (2006) 45 EHRR 421.
[4]   *SS (Nigeria) v Secretary of State for the Home Department* [2013] EWCA Civ 550, [2014] 1 WLR 998.
[5]   *MF (Nigeria) v Secretary of State for the Home Department* [2013] EWCA Civ 1192, [2014] 1 WLR 544.

PROCEDURE AND APPEALS

Making and notifying a decision

16.85 Rights of appeal in the context of deportation have been radically altered by the Immigration Act 2014. Decisions to make deportation orders; to refuse to revoke a deportation order and decisions that the automatic deportation provisions apply are no longer appealable under Nationality, Immigration and Asylum Act 2002 if they were made on or after 10th November 2014.[1] Nor are they appealable by someone who became a foreign criminal on or after 20th October 2014 or by someone being deported as belonging to the family of such a person.[2] Individuals falling into those categories will have rights of appeal against refusal of a protection or human rights claim or revocation of protection status. However, there will be many individuals with rights of appeal against deportation decisions taken before the 2014 Act provisions came into effect. What follows will begin by describing the rights of appeal available to them. In two of the three cases where a person is liable to deportation, the initiative is taken by the Secretary of State for the Home Department. Save where a decision is required by statute to be taken by the Secretary of State personally,[3] administrative arrangements can be made for departmental officers to exercise these powers. The Secretary of State is entitled to act through departmental civil servants, pursuant to the *Carltona* principles,[4] including immigration officers.[5] Decisions to deport on the grounds of public good other than political cases, and decisions to deport family members, are taken by the UKIV officials. A deportation order may not be made on the recommendation of a court while an appeal against the recommendation, or against conviction, is pending or can be brought (or in Scotland, for 28 days after the recommendation),[6] but subject to this the Secretary of State may choose when to act on the recommendation.[7] Since Parliament gave all proposed deportees a right of appeal against the Secretary of State's decision,[8] the distinction between the practice in relation to those recommended for deportation and those not recommended is unimportant. In all criminal cases, the Secretary of State waits until near the end of the sentence,[9] and then reviews the case in the light of any changed circumstances since conviction and sentence. For this purpose representations are normally sought from the proposed deportee before the decision is reached.[10]

[1] Immigration Act 2014, s 15 and The Immigration Act 2014 (Transitional and Saving Provisions) Order 2014, SI 2014/2928.

[2] Immigration Act 2014, s 15 and The Immigration Act 2014 (Commencement No 3, Transitional and Saving Provisions) Order 2014, SI 2014/2771.

[3] Under eg Nationality, Immigration and Asylum Act 2002, s 97. The decision need not be signed personally: *Re Khan (Amanullah)* [1986] Imm AR 485.

[4] *Carltona Ltd v Works Comrs* [1943] 2 All ER 560, CA.

[5] *R v Secretary of State for the Home Department, ex p Oladehinde* [1991] 1 AC 254, [1990] 3 All ER 393, [1990] 3 WLR 797, HL.

[6] Immigration Act 1971, s 6(6). This provision will be maintained for automatic deportation under the UK Borders Act 2007.

[7] *R (on the application of Samaroo) v Secretary of State for the Home Department* [2001] EWCA Civ 1139, [2001] UKHRR 1150, [2001] UKHRR 1150, [2002] INLR 55.

[8] Nationality, Immigration and Asylum Act 2002, s 82(2)(j).

[9] This is because in most cases, the risk of re-offending, which is generally assessed by prison staff with reference to evidence of the proposed deportee's performance in rehabilitation programmes etc, is relevant to the balancing exercise. A Tribunal disagreeing with an assessment by a trained probation officer, whose job it is to assess risk would have to do so on a reasoned basis, see *AM v Secretary of State for the Home Department* [2012] EWCA Civ

1634. For the effect of lapse of time, see Case 131/79 *R v Secretary of State for the Home Department, ex p Santillo* [1980] ECR 1585, [1980] 2 CMLR 308.

[10]   *Ayo v Immigration Appeal Tribunal* [1990] Imm AR 461, CA. Inviting further representations from a deportee does not mean that the original decision is flawed: *R v Secretary of State for the Home Department, ex p Amoa* [1992] Imm AR 218, QBD.

16.86 A decision to deport must be notified in accordance with the Immigration (Notices) Regulations 2003.[1] A decision to deport following a recommendation by a criminal court is appealable and consequently requires the Secretary of State to give written notice.[2] The notice must include or be accompanied by a statement of the reasons for the decision, indicate the country or territory to which it is proposed to remove the person, and indicate the right of appeal and how it may be exercised.[3] Amplification of the reasons for a decision to deport is permissible consequent to notification,[4] although a decision-maker may not switch to a different statutory category.[5] The appellate authority may not allow an appeal solely on the basis of a defect in the notice, if the decision itself was in accordance with the law and the rules.[6] The Regulations allow service of the notice either at an address provided for correspondence by the person or his or her representative, or (where there is no such correspondence address) at the last known or usual home or business address of either the proposed deportee *or* the representative.[7] Service may be achieved by fax transmission in addition to the traditional methods of hand and post (recorded delivery).[8] Under the old rules, if the Secretary of State or his officers had no knowledge of the whereabouts or place of abode of a prospective deportee, service could be dispensed with altogether, and there was no necessity for re-service of the notice if the deportee was subsequently located.[9] Although deemed intra vires by the courts,[10] the power was abandoned in 1986 as unfair and ineffective.[11] It was revived in the 2003 Regulations; where the person's whereabouts are unknown and the decision-maker has no address or only a defective, false or out-of-date address for him or her, and no representative appears to be acting, notice is deemed given when it is put on the file with a note of the circumstances.[12] When the subject of the notice is located, he or she is to be given a copy notice, but this will not generate the right to an in-time appeal.[13] See CHAPTER 20 below.

[1]   SI 2003/658, reg 4. The Regulations apply to deportation appeals generated under s 15 of the Immigration Act 1971 which have arisen as a result of the regularisation procedures under s 9 of the Immigration and Asylum Act 1999: see reg 3.

[2]   A decision to deport following a recommendation by a judge (s 3(6), Immigration Act 1971) has been appealable since 1 April 2003 (by Nationality, Immigration and Asylum Act 2002, s 82(2)(j)). Prior to that date notice of the decision was not required under the corresponding notices Regulations (SI 2000/2246) unless an asylum claim or human rights allegation was made.

[3]   SI 2003/658, reg 5.

[4]   *R v Immigration Appeal Tribunal, ex p Hubbard* [1985] Imm AR 110; *R v Immigration Appeal Tribunal, ex p Dukobo* [1990] Imm AR 390.

[5]   *Wah (Yau Yak) v Home Office* [1982] Imm AR 16, CA; *R v Immigration Appeal Tribunal, ex p Mehmet (Ekrem)* [1977] Imm AR 56, QBD; *Parsaiyan v Visa Officer, Karachi* [1986] Imm AR 155. For further discussion see CHAPTER 20 below.

[6]   *R v Immigration Appeal Tribunal, ex p Jeyeanthan* [1999] 3 All ER 231, [2000] 1 WLR 354, CA.

[7]   SI 2003/658, reg 7(1)(c)(ii). The election is that of the Secretary of State, so a notice may be sent to the deportee's last known address even if it is known that he or she no longer lives there: *Singh (Pargan) v Secretary of State for the Home Department* [1993] Imm AR 112, (although in such a case, there is the option of 'service on the file' in accordance with reg 7(2): see below). Service at the last known address has been held valid under previous regulations

despite the person's request that notices be served on the representative: *Tongo v Secretary of State for the Home Department* [1995] Imm AR 109, CA, but this decision would be unlikely under the current regulations and in the light of the importance given to actual notice of adverse decisions in cases such as *R v Secretary of State for the Home Department ex p Saleem (Asifa)* [2000] Imm AR 529, [2000] INLR 413, CA and *R (on the application of Anufrijeva) v Secretary of State for the Home Department* [2003] UKHL 36, [2003] Imm AR 570, [2003] INLR 521.

8 SI 2003/658, reg 7(1). A notice sent by post is deemed to have been received two business days after posting: reg 7(4)–(6).

9 SI 1984/2040, reg 3(4); *Singh (Pargan)* above at 117; *R v Secretary of State for the Home Department, ex p Brew* [1988] Imm AR 93, QBD.

10 *Singh (Pargan)* above; *Rhemtulla v Immigration Appeal Tribunal* [1979–80] Imm AR 168, CA.

11 Under a policy DP5/86; see *R v Secretary of State for the Home Department, ex p Chew and Popatia* [2001] Imm AR 46, [2000] INLR 587, **18.52** below.

12 SI 2003/658, reg 7(2).

13 The time for appealing would run from the date the notice was placed on the file: SI 2003/658, reg 7(3). Immigration service caseworkers are advised not to re-serve decisions to deport on missing overstayers who are found, presumably since such re-service would be likely to generate an in-time appeal (Operational Enforcement Manual Ch 16, 'Service of notice of intention to deport'). Query whether this advice is good in the light of the landmark decision of the House of Lords in *R (on the application of Anufrijeva) v Secretary of State for the Home Department* [2003] UKHL 36, [2003] Imm AR 570, [2003] INLR 521.

Right of appeal pre- Immigration Act 2014

16.87 When a decision to deport is taken, whether on conducive grounds (other than political cases) or on family grounds, or following a recommendation by a criminal court, there is currently a right of appeal to the AIT under section 82(2)(j) of the Nationality, Immigration and Asylum Act 2002.[1] Automatic deportation is a separate immigration decision and there will be a right of appeal under section 82(3A) of the 2002 Act. Notice of appeal should be served within ten working days of the decision being notified[2] (or within five working days if the person is in detention),[3] though there is provision for an extension of time where 'special circumstances' can be demonstrated.[4] For the time being the right of appeal comes after the decision to deport, but before the making of a deportation order except for in the case of an automatic deportation order (see below). The sequence is thus decision, appeal, deportation order. The clear distinction between a 'decision to deport' and a 'deportation order' should be noted. Both the decision to deport and a refusal to revoke a deportation order are 'immigration decisions' for the purposes of the appeal provisions of the 2002 Act.[5] An appeal against a decision to deport is in-country,[6] subject to certification under section 94 and 94B of the 2002 Act, an appeal against refusal to revoke a deportation order cannot be exercised while the appellant is in the UK, unless he or she is an EEA national or a member of the family of an EEA national relying on Community rights, or has made an asylum or human rights claim in the UK.[7] In such a case, however, the in-country appeal is not limited to those grounds.[8] The Tribunal will typically direct service upon the appellant, by the Secretary of State, of a number of documents that form the case in favour of deportation, such as the sentencing remarks of the criminal judge and all criminal antecedents. Failure to serve or disclose key documents that form the case against the appellant may engage Article 6 and common law rules of fairness. However, the balancing exercise in disclosure and the public interest where the case involves national security matters may be weighted differently.[9] Those liable to deportation who seek to assert an asylum claim in the detained fast track may experience difficulties obtaining evidence to assert their case that may undermine the effectiveness of the remedy available.[10]

1 The right to appeal against a decision taken after a recommendation by a criminal court is new. Any remaining overstayers who applied, prior to 9 October 2000, to regularise their position under the Immigration and Asylum Act 1999, s 9 and are still awaiting a decision, may also appeal under this section, if their application is rejected. Section 82(2) embraces all decisions to deport under Immigration Act 1971, s 5. In political cases the appeal is to the SIAC: Nationality, Immigration and Asylum Act 2002, s 97, Special Immigration Appeals Commission Act 1997, s 2 (as amended).

2 Asylum and Immigration Tribunal (Procedure) Rules 2005, SI 2005/230, r 7(1)(b) read with r 57(1)(b) (calculation of time).

3 Asylum and Immigration Tribunal (Procedure) Rules 2005, r 7(1)(a).

4 SI 2005/230, r 10. See also Chapter 20 below.

5 Nationality, Immigration and Asylum Act 2002, s 82(1), (2)(j) and (k).

6 NIAA 2002, s 92(1), (2).

7 NIAA 2002, s 92(4); however an in-country appeal under s 92(4) may not be brought if the Secretary of State certifies that the asylum or human rights claim concerned is clearly unfounded: s 94(2); see Chapter 19, below.

8 This is clear from the wording of ss 82, 84 (grounds of appeal), 85(1) (matters to be considered) and 92(4) (in-country appeals). Appeal rights under the 2002 Act are thus wider than under the provisions of either the 1999 or the 1971 Acts. But in a family deportation, the appeal of the family member (a UK-born child of the person subject to a deportation order) is predicated on the deportation of the principal and cannot be used as a lever to re-open the issue of the principal's deportation: *N v Secretary of State for the Home Department* [2001] EWCA Civ 688, [2001] All ER (D) 220.

9 Court of Appeal *R (on the application of BB) v Special Immigration Appeals Commission and another* [2012] EWCA Civ 1499 (19 November 2012).

10 European Court of Human Rights *IM v France* (Application 9152/09).

Certification of Deportation applications under the new regime

16.88 Section 17(2) and (3) of the Immigration Act 2014 substitute a new section 92 for the exiting one and inserts a new section 94B after the existing 94A of the Nationality, Immigration and Asylum Act 2002. In combination they introduce significant new limitations on the facility of those subject to deportation action to exercise a right of appeal in-country prior to the commencement of enforcement action.

Section 17(2), now that it has effect, by modifying the existing section 92 of the NIAA 2002 to remove the suspensive appeal protection in deportation cases whenever the Secretary of State makes a certification decision under the newly inserted section section 94B. It gives the Secretary of State the power to certify as clearly unfounded human rights claims made by persons liable to deportation under section 3(5)(a) or 3(6) of the Immigration Act 1971,[1] allowing a right to an in country appeal only in exceptional circumstances.

1 Nationality, Immigration and Asylum Act 2002, s 94B(1)(a), (b).

16.89 Section 17(3) took effect on the 28 July 2014 before the implementation of section 17(2). The commencement order introducing section 17(3) contained 'transitional and saving provisions' at Article 4,[1] which provides that until section 17(2) of the Act comes into force for all purposes, section 92 has effect in any case in which a foreign criminal[2] has made a human rights claim which the Secretary of State has certified under section 94B as if:

- a decision to make a deportation order under section 82(2)(j) of the 2002 Act no longer carries an in country right of appeal;
- making a human rights or asserting an EU treaty right no longer confers an in country right of appeal under section 92(4)(a) and (b).

It is apparent then that the new certification regime will then enter force in two stages. Under stage 2, the Immigration Act 2014 (Commencement No 3, Transitional and Saving Provisions) Order 2014, SI 2014/ 2771 brought section 17(2) into force on 20 October 2014. It revoked article 4 of the Immigration Act 2014 (Commencement No 1, Transitional and Saving Provisions) Order 2014 (article 14) but has made new transitional provisions for any case in which a foreign criminal has made a human rights claim which the Secretary of State certified under section 94B prior to 20th October 2014, whereby section 92 of the 2002 Act, which deals with appeals from within the United Kingdom, continues to have effect as if:

- A decision to make a deportation order under section 82(2)(j) of the 2002 Act no longer carries an in country right of appeal;
- A decision refusing an asylum or human rights claim under section 92(4)(a) no longer carries an in-country right of appeal;
- A claim by an EEA national or family member of such national that a refusal of entry to or residence in the UK is a breach of their rights under EU law under section 92(4)(b) no longer carries an in-country right of appeal;

Whilst the First Stage alone was operative it was not be possible for the Secretary of State to make a certificate under section 94B that would have the effect of stifling an appeal which was already pending as at 28 July 2014: because the appeal has arisen with the enjoyment of the full protection conferred by section 92 as in force before the possibility of 'reading out' its 'in-country' protections arose.[3] Under Stage 2, so far as they concern deportation appeals, articles 9 and 10 of SI 2014/2771 make transitional and saving provision in relation to section 17(2) of the 2014 Act, which inserts a new section 92 into the 2002 Act. Article 9 makes saving provision in relation to the 'saved provisions' so that they continue to have effect, and the relevant provisions do not have effect, other than so far as they relate to the persons in article 10. The 'saved provisions' include Part 5 of the 2002 Act, which includes section 92. The persons referred to in article 10 are a person ('P1') who becomes a foreign criminal under section 117D(2) of the 2002 Act on or after 20th October 2014 or their family members. The effect of the saving provision is that only the persons in articles 10 (the newly convicted and sentenced foreign criminal and his or her family members) will be subject to the new appeals provisions in section 82(2), as inserted by section 15(2) of the Immigration Act 2014, which provide a right of appeal to the First-tier Tribunal where a person's protection claim or human rights claim has been refused, or their protection status has been revoked.

[1]   The Immigration Act 2014 (Commencement No 1, Transitory and Saving Provisions) Order 2014, SI 2014/1820, art 4.
[2]   As defined in NIAA 2002, s 117D(2), inserted by s 19 Immigration Act 2014, s 19.

[3] Support of that proposition may be derived from *R (on the application of AM (Somalia)) v Secretary of State for the Home Department* [2009] EWCA Civ 114.

16.90 For those cases in respect of which the appealable decision is generated post 28 July 2014 the language of section 94B anticipates that certification may be permissible at any stage in the course of the application or appeal process.[1] The legality of imposition of such a certificate post decision, and upon an appeal having been lodged would have to be appraised in the context of the Court of Appeal's decision in *AM(Somalia)*.[2] Such a step would likely falter on rationality grounds in all events, the inconsistency of the Secretary of State's positions, absent some manifest change in circumstances, obliging substantial justification. It is likely with such considerations in mind that the Secretary of State signals in her casework instructions that post-decision certification will only be contemplated following on from an initial negative appeal determination, in circumstances where a linked element of the appeal relating to asylum or Article 3 protection which would ordinarily be amenable to certification under section 94B (see below) has not been pursued to the Upper Tribunal.[3] The guidance deals with when to certify under section 94B as follows:

'3.10 Case owners need to bear in mind that it is possible to certify under section 94B at any stage in the process as long as the person has not exhausted their appeal rights. In practice, this means that if a claim is not certified at the initial decision stage, and either party challenges the decision of the First-tier Tribunal (or that of the Upper Tribunal), the case owner must consider whether it is appropriate to certify the claim before it is heard by the Upper Tribunal (or Court of Appeal).

3.11 For example, if a person has an in-country appeal against the refusal of a non-protection claim solely because they were entitled to an in-country appeal against the refusal of a protection claim, and the appeal progresses to the Upper Tribunal (regardless of whether it was allowed or dismissed at the First-tier Tribunal), it may be the case that the protection claim is no longer relied upon, and the only part of the claim that remains is an Article 8 claim. If so, and there is not a real risk of serious irreversible harm, and the person is otherwise removable (eg a travel document is now available), it is likely that certification will be appropriate.'

[1] Nationality, Immigration and Asylum Act 2002, s 94B(1)(a)–(b).
[2] *R (on the application of AM (Somalia)) v Secretary of State for the Home Department* [2009] EWCA Civ 114.
[3] Section 94B certification guidance for Non-European Economic Area deportation cases Version 2.0 20 October to be found at: (www.gov.uk/government/uploads/system/uploads/at tachment_data/file/336866/Section_94B.pdf)-paragraphs 3.10–3.11.

16.91 Certification under section 94B is discretionary and not mandatory, as evidenced by the use of the term 'may' in section 94B(2) and (3) as opposed to 'shall'.[1] The application of a certificate is subject only to the Secretary of State's being satisfied that enforcement action would be consistent with the Human Rights Act 1998[2] and would not result in the deportee 'facing a real risk of serious irreversible harm'.[3] Satisfaction of the former requirement is implicit in any decision the Secretary of State in which she authorises the commencement of deportation action. The Section 94B certification guidance also deals with dual certification. The instruction to caseholders is that 'If a protection claim is certified under sections 94 or 96, but it is not possible to certify a linked Article 8 claim (or other non-protection human rights claim) under either of those powers, then consideration must be given to certifying the Article 8 claim under section 94B as long as there is not a real risk of serious irreversible harm.'[4]

1   NIAA 2002, s 94B(2). Compare with s 94(3), NIA 2002.
2   NIAA 2002, s 94B(2).
3   NIAA 2002, s 94B(3).See s 94B certification guidance, Real risk of serious irreversible harm at paras 3.3 -3.8.
4   Section 94B certification guidance, para 3.9.

16.92 The threshold test applicable to certification of cases as clearly unfounded under section 94, and the evaluative processes relevant to the determination of whether certification is permissible are discussed elsewhere in this text.[1] Turning then to the 'real risk of serious irreversible harm' test. It has its origins in the European Court of Human Rights Grand Chamber decision in *De Souza Ribeiro v France.*[2] The section 92B test mirrors the approach taken by the Court to the determination of interim measures under Rule 39 of the Rules of Procedure.[3]

1   See **Chapter 20**.
2   *De Souza Ribeiro v France* (Application no 22689/07).
3   Rules of the Court, 4 November 1998. The section 94B Guidance, version 2 states that the irreversible risk part of the test is derived from that applied by the European Court when determining Rule 39 applications para 3.3, but only covers the period between deportation and the conclusion of any appeal and will not be met solely because the person will be separated from family members in the UK during that period: para 3.4, version 2.

16.93 In *De Souza and Ribeiro* the European Court of Justice drew a clear distinction between a complaint concerning the risk of exposure to a breach of Articles 2 and 3 and one presented in respect of Article 8 ECHR. As to the former the Court found that in view of the importance the Court attached to those provisions and *'given the irreversible nature of the harm that might occur if the risk of torture or ill-treatment alleged materialised, the effectiveness of the remedy for the purposes of Article 13 requires imperatively that the complaint be subject to close scrutiny'* and further that *'effectiveness also requires that the person concerned should have access to a remedy with automatic suspensive effect'.*[1] That position mirrors the Court's assiduous approach to the application interim measures in cases where an applicant is threatened with a danger of torture and death.[2] Appropriately then, the Home Office has accepted that Article 3 and refugee cases should not be certified under the new power contained in section 94B if such certification had been considered and ruled out by reference to existing provisions contained in section 94(3) and (5) and section 96.[3]

1   *De Souza Ribeiro v France* at para 82.
2   *Soering v United Kingdom* (1989) 11 EHRR 439, ECtHR; *D v United Kingdom* (1997) 24 EHRR 423; *Chahal v United Kingdom* (1996) 23 EHRR 413.
3   Guidance at paragraph 3.5.

16.94 The Court in *De Souza Ribeiro* observed that position assumed in respect of Article 2 and 3 may not automatically apply in respect of Article 8. They said:

'83. By contrast, where expulsions are challenged on the basis of alleged interference with private and family life, it is not imperative, in order for a remedy to be effective, that it should have automatic suspensive effect. Nevertheless, in immigration matters, where there is an arguable claim that expulsion threatens to interfere with the alien's right to respect for his private and family life, Article 13 in conjunction with Article 8 of the Convention requires that States must make available to the individual concerned the effective possibility of challenging the deportation or refusal-of-residence order and of having the relevant issues examined with sufficient procedural safeguards and thoroughness by an appropriate domestic forum offering adequate guarantees of independence and impartiality.'[1]

Despite the Court's generally cautious approach, described above, the Court has intervened with Rule 39 interim measures in a family life case. In *Nunez v Norway*,[2] the Court stated that children should not always suffer the negative consequences of the fraudulent conduct of a mother and that the authorities should always examine the effect an expulsion has on the possibilities of children being able to enjoy private and/or family life as protected by Article 8 ECHR. The Court considered that 'exceptional circumstances' may make it necessary to accord primacy to the interests of dependent children – even if that would imply that a parent must be allowed residence as well (and the mother had a very poor immigration history having been convicted of serious offences of dishonesty regarding her past obtaining of visas).

[1] *De Souza Ribeiro v France* at para 83.
[2] *Nunez v Norway* (Application no 55597/09; 28 June 2011.

16.95 In fact it is likely that the impact of such certification on the Article 8 interests of third parties, particularly minor children, invoking the ratio of the House of Lords in *Beoku-Betts v Secretary of State for the Home Department*,[1] will prove a central platform from which to challenge certification, given that on a section 94B(3) certification the Secretary of State will be concerned only with ruling on whether the deportee would face a 'real risk of serious irreversible harm'. The term 'real risk' is a relatively low threshold and has the same meaning as when used to ascertain whether removal would breach ECHR Article 3. However, the terms 'serious' and 'irreversible' must be given their ordinary meanings. 'Serious' indicates that the harm must meet a minimum level of severity, and 'irreversible' means that the harm would have a permanent or very long-lasting effect. If the human rights claim is based on Article 8, case owners must consider not only the impact on the foreign criminal's rights, but also those of any partner or child.[2]

[1] *Beoku-Betts v Secretary of State for the Home Department* [2008] UKHL 39, [2009] AC 115, [2008] 4 All ER 1146, [2008] 3 WLR 166.
[2] The section 94B Guidance, version 2, para 3.4.

16.96 The Section 94B Guidance sets out different scenarios: (i) where there is a risk and (ii) where there is no risk. This exercise is in itself a risky business since all these cases will be very much fact-specific. The different scenarios are at paragraphs 3.6 (a real risk of serious irreversible harm is unlikely) and 3.7 (cases where the test is met). There then follows a paragraph which seems to speak out of both corners of the Secretary of State's mouth. On the one hand (now mixing my metaphors!) the onus is on the Secretary of State to demonstrate that there is not a real risk of serious irreversible harm. On the other hand if a person claims that a non-suspensive appeal would risk serious irreversible harm, the onus is on that person to substantiate the claim with documentary evidence, preferably from official sources.[1]

[1] Section 94B Guidance, version 2 at para 3.8.

16.97 Reference to the Secretary of States Guidance version 1 affords valuable indications in addition to those already referred to in Version 2 as to how case holders are expected to assess whether to certify. In particular it provided that section 94B should only be used where certification is not otherwise feasible under sections 94 or 96 of the NIAA 2002;[1] It also indicated that those engaged in family proceedings would not be automatically excepted from certification,[2] a matter which looks as if it has been quietly dropped, because: (a) it is likely to prove controversial if put into practice; (b) it must have become clear that even a short break in residence could potentially prejudice the pursuit of litigation before the family courts; and (c) the practice would arguably be contrary to rulings of the European and domestic courts in cases such as *Ciliz v Netherlands*[3] and MS (Ivory Coast) v Secretary of State.[4]

[1] Guidance, version 1, at para 3.7.
[2] See Guidance, version 1 at paras 4.2, 4.3, and 4.6.
[3] *Ciliz v Netherlands* [2000] ECHR 365.
[4] *MS (Ivory Coast) v Secretary of State for the Home Department* [2007] EWCA Civ 133.

16.98 Where a certificate is applied, that decision will be susceptible to judicial review in the ordinary way, and that process may itself be pursued as in-country. The availability of that remedy and its suspensive effect may well have the effect of rendering the certification process a costly and time consuming one for the Secretary of State, and one which in consequence will fail to deliver on the purposes of the amendments to section 94. The hurdle for deportees of course will primarily be a financial one given the limited facility to secure funding for judicial review in Article 8 cases, with the effect that many certification decisions may well go unchallenged. See further on legal aid, Chapter 1, above.

16.99 As a result of the root and branch changes to the right of appeal, we no longer deal with the process of appeal against a deportation order under the old order. Those seeking information should consult earlier editions of this work; See eg 15.58ff (ordinary appeals) and 15.59 (deportation appeals in national security cases before SIAC) in the 8th edition.

Deportation of EEA nationals

16.100 The deportation of EEA nationals is subject to special rules which provide both procedural safeguards and more rigorous justification for deportation and other exclusions from a Member State. The rules do not just cover deportation cases but all exclusions and removals. They are dealt with in detail in Chapter 6, above. The provisions, sometimes referred to as the public policy proviso are contained in Articles 27 to 33 of Directive 2004/38/EC (the Citizens' Directive), Chapter VI. Articles 27 and 28 together with the procedural safeguards in Articles 30 (notification of decision) and 31 (Procedural safeguards) are the key provisons so far as deportation of EEA nationals and their family members are concerned.

The provisions of the Citizens' Directive have also been transposed into domestic law by the Immigration (European Economic Area) Regulations 2006.[1] They provide that those EEA nationals and their family members (who may not be EEA nationals themselves), who would otherwise be entitled to reside in the UK under the 2006 Regulations may only be removed on grounds of public policy, public security or public health in accordance with regulation 19(3)(b) of the 2006 Regulations. Any decision to remove must be taken in accordance with the principles laid down in Articles 27 and 28 of the Citizens Directive or regulation 21 of The Immigration (European Economic Area) Regulations 2006 Summarising what is explained in more detail in CHAPTER 6, above, there are two critical questions: (i) does the appellant's conduct manifest a real and sufficiently serious threat to a fundamental interest of society, and (ii) if so is it proportionate in all the circumstances to deport him or her?[2] Two further issues need to be mentioned in this chapter.

[1] Immigration (European Economic Area) Regulations 2006, SI 2006/1003.
[2] See *Machado v Secretary of State for the Home Department* [2005] EWCA Civ 597, [2005] All ER (D) 289 (May).

16.101 First, the public policy proviso is contained within the Citizens Directive[1] which is concerned with the right of residence of those EU nationals who have exercised their free movement rights by moving from one Member State to another. But other EU citizens have a right of residence outwith the Citizens Directive; The right may arise directly from Articles 20 and 21 of TFEU which deal with rights pertaining to EU citizenship: see the *Zambrano*[2] and *Dereci*[3] decisions. In the Case of *Nazli*[4] the CJEU has already extended the Public policy proviso to Turkish nationals and by parity of reasoning the pulic order and security provisions must also extend to those EU citizens and their family members,who benefit from the *Zambrano/Dereci* rights of residence. Secondly, there is the issue of what is sometimes referred to as other family members. In the Case of *Rose*[5] the Upper tribunal held that they cannot rely on Articles 27 or 28 of the Citizens Directive. In the Supplement to the 8th edition we argued that that case was wrongly decided and gave full reasons for that view. We still hold to our position and would refer the reader to the Supplement at 15.

[1] Council Directive 2004/38 EC.
[2] *ZambraNo*
[3] *Dereci.*
[4] *Nazli.*
[5] *Rose (Automatic deportation – Exception 3) Jamaica* [2011] UKUT 00276 (IAC).

16.102 In *Land Baden-Wurttemberg v Tsakouridis*[1] the CJEU examined the factors making expulsion of an EU national or a family member with long term residence in the host member state residence appropriate following criminal conviction for serious crime. The Court held *inter alia* that in considering whether expulsion of a criminal is proportionate:

- a balance must be struck more particularly between the exceptional nature of the threat to public security as a result of the personal conduct of the person concerned, assessed if necessary at the time when the expulsion decision is to be made, by reference in particular to the possible penalties and the sentences imposed, the degree of involvement in the criminal activity, and, if appropriate, the risk of reoffending, on the one hand, and, on the other hand, the risk of compromising the social rehabilitation of the Union citizen in the State in which he or she has become genuinely integrated;

- the concept of 'imperative grounds of public security' presupposes not only the existence of a threat to public security, but also that such a threat is of a particularly high degree of seriousness, as is reflected by the use of the words 'imperative reasons';
- an expulsion measure must be based on an individual examination of the specific case and can be justified on imperative grounds of public security only if, having regard to the exceptional seriousness of the threat, such a measure is necessary for the protection of the interests it aims to secure, provided that that objective cannot be attained by less strict means, having regard to the length of residence of the Union citizen in the host Member State and in particular to the serious negative consequences such a measure may have for Union citizens who have become genuinely integrated into the host Member State;
- a sentence of five years' imprisonment cannot lead to an expulsion decision, as provided for in national law, without the relevant factors being taken into account, which is for the national court to verify.

Tsakouridis was followed by the Court of Appeal in *FV (Italy) v Secretary of State for the Home Department* [2] The Court elaborated on the findings of the CJEU. They held that:

- although a period of imprisonment does not count towards the five years residence necessary under regulation 21(3) of the EEA Regulations 2006 to establish a permanent right of residence or towards the ten years residence required under regulations 21(4), the continuity of residence for the purpose of regulation 21(4)(a) (ten years residence) is not broken by a period of imprisonment.
- A period in prison during the ten years immediately prior to the decision to deport does not automatically mean that the EEA national must lose his or her 'enhanced protection'.
- Time spent in prison before an expulsion decision is made does not of itself defeat integration, for the decision turns on an overall qualitative assessment having regard to all relevant factors, including the length of residence, family connections, any interruptions in integration, and severance of links with the state of origin.

[1]   [2011] 2 CMLR 11.
[2]   [2012] EWCA Civ 1199 (14 September 2012).

16.103 In *R (on the application of Essa) v Upper Tribunal (Immigration & Asylum Chamber)* [1] the Court of Appeal deals with rehabilitation and the way it was dealt with in the judgment in *Tsakouridis*. In applying regulation 21 of the EEA Regulations, the decision maker must consider whether a decision to deport may prejudice the prospects of rehabilitation from offending in the host country, and weigh that risk in the balance when assessing proportionality under regulation 21(5)(a) – in most cases, this will necessarily entail a comparison with the prospects of rehabilitation in the receiving country.

The Court indicated that there is a European dimension to the proportionality exercise which widens consideration beyond the interests of the expelling Member State and those of the foreign criminal. This in turn echoes the observation of Carnwath LJ in *Batista (Valentine) v Secretary of State for the Home Department*[2] where he said that even in respect of those deemed sufficiently dangerous to justify deportation under the EEA rules, common sense would suggest a degree of shared interest between the EEA countries in helping progress towards a better form of life and there seemed no reason why this may not be taken into account in the overall balance of proportionality.

[1]   [2012] EWCA Civ 1718, [2013] All ER (D) 12 (Jan).
[2]   [2010] EWCA Civ 896, [2010] All ER (D) 323 (Jul).

Burden of proof on residence

16.104 *R (on the application of A, B and C) v Secretary of State for the Home Department*[1] deals with the burden of proof in establishing that an EEA national was neither resident nor permanently resident. The court held that the burden was on the Secretary of State where she wished to prove an entitlement to deport someone on public policy or public security grounds, at least where the proposed deportees had established a prima facie evidential case for being resident within the EEA Regulations so that the burden of proof would have shifted to the defendant to show the contrary. If no additional evidence was provided to shift the burden back again, proposed deportees person would be legally resident here once the state had treated them as being so resident for example by granting them child tax credits and having them rehoused by a local housing authority as a social tenant.

[1]   [2013] EWHC 1272 (Admin) (22 May 2013) (Anthony Thornton QC sitting as a Deputy High Court judge).

Certification under the new regime in EEA cases

16.105 A comparable certification regime was also introduced on the 28 July 2014 for EEA deportation cases by the Immigration (European Economic Area) (Amendment) (No 2) Regulations 2014.[1] The new Regulations amend the Immigration (European Economic Area) Regulations 2006 so that an appeal against a deportation decision under regulation 19(3)(b) can still be lodged in the UK but no longer suspends removal proceedings, except where:

- The Secretary of State has not certified that the person would not face a real risk of serious irreversible harm if removed to the country of return before the appeal is finally determined.
- The person has made an application to the courts for an interim order to suspend removal proceedings (eg judicial review) and that application has not yet been determined, or a court has made an interim order to suspend removal.

Where an interim order to suspend removal proceedings is initiated, the Secretary of States guidance[2] indicates that removal will not be suspended unless the order is made where:

- the notice of a decision to make a deportation order is based on a previous judicial decision;
- or the person has had previous access to judicial review;
- or the removal decision is based on imperative grounds of public security.

The Secretary of States guidance Version 1 sets the same test phase and criteria as apply in non EEA cases to this category of deportation.

1   SI 2014/1976.
2   Section 94B Guidance, version 1.

16.106 One notable difference between EEA and Non-EEA cases subject to such certification is that persons removed from the United Kingdom under the Regulation can apply to re-enter in order to make submissions in person at their appeal hearing by operation of Article 31(4) of Directive 2004/38/EC which states:

'Member States may exclude the individual concerned from their territory pending the redress procedure, but they may not prevent the individual from submitting his/her defence in person, except when his/her appearance may cause serious troubles to public policy or public security or when the appeal or judicial review concerns a denial of entry to the territory.'

The guidance purports to limit this provision to cases where the appeal was lodged in time, an appeal hearing date has been set and the person wants to make 'submissions' in person. It is not clear whether a person with a legal representative would necessarily qualify for entry under this approach.[1] Further, the guidance states that permission for entry must be sought in advance: simply turning up at the border will lead to refusal of admission.[2]

1   Section 94B Guidance.
2   Section 94B Guidance.

SUCCESSFUL APPEALS

(i) Pre-October 2014

16.107 If the appeal is allowed, the decision is reversed but the Tribunal has no power to direct the grant of leave to remain in non-human rights cases.[1] It may direct that appropriate leave be granted, where there has been a finding that deportation would be in breach of human rights.[2] If the proposed deportee's leave has expired, and the Home Office has not renewed it pending appeal, leave to remain will normally be granted in order to regularise the position. But this does not follow as a matter of course. Immigrants who succeed in an appeal should not, therefore, leave the country for a celebratory holiday until leave has been obtained.[3] If they do, they have no right to be treated as a returning resident and would have no other claim to re-enter. The Tribunal has no power to grant a stay of deportation, for example because of the political situation then pertaining in a country,[4] but a determination that deportation is not currently the right course on the merits could be properly made without prejudice to a future exercise of the power if the person's behaviour merits deportation. In one case an adjudicator allowed the appeal on the grounds that the applicant was a genuine student who should be given a further opportunity to progress with his studies.[5] But where an appeal was unsuccessful, a period of grace, to allow the appellant to finish his course and make a voluntary departure, did not constitute fresh leave, and the Secretary of State was entitled to sign a deportation order when he did not leave.[6]

[1] *R v Immigration Appeal Tribunal, ex p Singh (Mahendra)* [1984] Imm AR 1, QBD. See CHAPTER 20 below. The Tribunal may recommend this course, however.
[2] *Sharif (Omeed)* [2002] UKIAT 00953.
[3] *R v Secretary of State for the Home Department, ex p Botta* [1987] Imm AR 80, QBD.
[4] *Yuksel* [1976] Imm AR 91, IAT.
[5] *Youssef* (TH114300 Adjudicator); see also *Dexter* (4980) unreported.
[6] *R v Secretary of State for the Home Department, ex p Smith* [1996] Imm AR 331. For a similar categorisation of 'packing up time', see *R (on the application of Hindawi) v Secretary of State for the Home Department; R (on the application of Headley) v Secretary of State for the Home Department* [1977] Imm AR 89, CA; but cf Lord Russell in *Suthendran v Immigration Appeal Tribunal* [1977] AC 359 at 372 and *Halil v Davidson* [1979–80] Imm AR 164, HL. *Ex p Smith* was decided before administrative removal replaced deportation for overstaying; Home Office practice now would be to sign the order but defer its implementation for the relevant period.

(ii) Under the new appeal regime

16.108 The version 2 Guidance makes it clear that where a foreign criminal's out-of-country appeal against the refusal of a non-protection human rights claim succeeds, the foreign criminal is entitled to return to the UK and the deportation order must be revoked.[1] At paragraph 4.2 it is said that 'Consideration must be given to whether the Home Office should pay for the foreign criminal's journey back to the UK if this is requested by the foreign criminal.' The rest of the paragraph then deals with the factors which should be taken into consideration in I considering whether to pay for the foreign criminal's journey back to the UK.[2] These are:

- the quality of the Home Office's decision to refuse the human rights claim;
- whether the appeal was allowed on the basis of evidence or information that the foreign criminal failed to submit to the Home Office in advance of his deportation despite a section 120 warning, and if so, whether there is any reasonable explanation for this;
- whether there is evidence that if the Home Office does not pay for the return journey the foreign criminal be unable to return to the UK even though the human rights decision requires him to be able to return.

[1] Section 94B certification guidance for Non-European Economic Area deportation cases Version 2.0 20 October 2014, para 4.1, to be found at: www.gov.uk/government/uploads/sy stem/uploads/attachment_data/file/336866/Section_94B.pdf.
[2] Ibid, para 4.2 and 4.3.

Detaining deportees

16.109 The power to detain deportees arises at three stages; first when a court recommends deportation;[1] secondly when the decision to deport is made,[2] and thirdly when the deportation order is signed.[3] At all three stages there is also the option of bail or release on temporary admission, subject to requirements as to residence and so forth.[4] A separate system operates with regard to those subject to automatic deportation.[5] The position is dealt with more fully in the chapter on detention (CHAPTER 18 below).

1   Immigration Act 1971, Sch 3, para 2(1). For the legality of detention pending the implementation of a recommendation to deport, see *Re Nwafor* [1994] Imm AR 91, QBD.
2   Immigration Act 1971, Sch 3, para 2(2); HC 395, para 382.
3   Immigration Act 1971, Sch 3, para 2(3).
4   Immigration Act 1971, Sch 3, para 2 as amended by Immigration and Asylum Act 1999, s 54, from 10 February 2003 (Immigration and Asylum Act 1999 (Commencement Order No 12) 2003, SI 2003/2).
5   UK Borders Act 2007, s 36.

Voluntary or supervised departure

16.110 Persons liable to deportation who are not detained may leave the UK voluntarily, paying for their own passage and leaving under their own auspices, at any time before a deportation order is signed.[1] This may require liaison with the port if travel documents are held. The advantage of this option is that it does not preclude a future return under the Immigration Rules, since the power to sign a deportation order can only be exercised when the person is in the UK.[2] If it is known that a person has embarked, enforcement action will cease.[3] For this reason it may be unfair to reject representations to remain on compassionate grounds and sign a deportation order before giving the opportunity for a voluntary departure.[4] However, the benefits of voluntary departure can easily be lost, if the reasons for the decision to deport are used to exclude the person from the UK on an attempt to re-enter.[5] Voluntary departure is not the same thing as supervised departure. Reference to supervised departure has been deleted from the current Immigration Rules, but it remains in the IDI, which suggest that it would be appropriate where a person agrees to leave immediately and signs a waiver regarding appeal rights.[6] Supervised departure may be at the individual's or the Secretary of State's expense.[7] Like other voluntary departures, supervised departure does not debar the subject from re-entering.[8]

1   Voluntary departure is not to be confused with being deported in travel arranged and paid for by the deportee, so as to make it less stressful and saving public funds: *Babalola* (0000926), IAT (unreported).
2   Immigration Act 1971, s 5(1).
3   IDI (Dec 07), Ch 13, s 1, para 10.1.
4   The argument was unsuccessful on its facts in *R v Secretary of State for the Home Department, ex p Brew* [1988] Imm AR 93.
5   See HC 395, para 320(18), (19).
6   IDI (Dec 07), Ch 13, s 1, para 10.2.
7   Section 5(6) of the Immigration Act 1971, as amended by para 2 to the Schedule to the Immigration Act 1988, refers to persons liable to deportation who leave the UK to live permanently abroad and enables the Secretary of State to meet their expenses. Undoubtedly such funding will be a relevant consideration if the person seeks to return.
8   IDI, Ch 13, s 1, para 9.3.

SIGNING THE DEPORTATION ORDER

16.111 In criminal cases, where a recommendation has been made by the courts, the Secretary of State may not make a deportation order until the convicted person has exhausted all rights of appeal or until the time for bringing an appeal has expired (in Scotland, until the expiry of 28 days from the date of the recommendation).[1] In all cases, where no appeal is lodged or if the appeal is dismissed, the order for deportation is submitted to the minister for signature.[2] Earlier Immigration Rules stated that the submission would include a summary of the facts of the case, written confirmation of the dismissal of any appeal, and a note of any other relevant information, whether or not it was available to the courts or the appellate authorities.[3] It is believed that the practice remains the same. In *Sanusi*[4] the Court of Appeal held that the Secretary of State could not make a deportation order between the making of an asylum application and the notification of a decision on it, because of the statutory prohibition on removal (then section 6 of the Asylum and Immigration Appeals Act 1993). The case was reversed by statute.[5] Hitherto, it has been assumed that the signing of the deportation order by the Secretary of State is what made it effective. Thus it could be said if the order is signed while the proposed deportee is in the UK but he or she leaves without becoming aware of it, it is still effective; and in one case it was held that a failure to serve the order and the return of the person's passport with an uncancelled indefinite leave stamp did not give rise to a legitimate expectation that the order would not be enforced.[6] It is now established, not just arguable, that a deportation order is not 'in force' unless it is notified and detention prior to notification would be unlawful: *R (on the application of S) v Secretary of State for the Home Department* [2011] EWHC 2120 (Admin), 175 CL&J 551 (5 August 2011).

[1] Immigration Act 1971, s 6(6). Now that there is a right of appeal to the Tribunal against the decision of the Secretary of State to follow a court recommendation under NIAA 2002, s 82(2), (2)(j), no order may be submitted to the minister until appeal rights are exhausted.

[2] Normally the order is signed by the Home Office immigration minister, but contentious cases may be referred to the Secretary of State for the Home Department for signature: IDI Ch 13, s 1.

[3] HC 251, para 157.

[4] *R v Secretary of State for the Home Department, ex p Sanusi* [1999] INLR 198, [1999] Imm AR 334.

[5] Immigration and Asylum Act 1999, s 15, Sch 4, para 20; see now Nationality, Immigration and Asylum Act 2002, s 77(4)(b).

[6] *Dey (Sri Kumar) v Secretary of State for the Home Department* [1996] Imm AR 521, CA.

Removal of deportees

16.112 Following the making of a deportation order, removal directions may be set.[1] Removal must be to the country of nationality, or to any other country to which there is reason to believe the deportee will be admitted.[2] Where the person is serving a prison sentence, arrangements for removal will be made to coincide with his or her release wherever possible.[3] The costs of removal are always defrayed by the Secretary of State rather than the carrier.[4] For removal see CHAPTER 17 below. Under EC Directive 2001/40 on the mutual recognition of expulsion decisions a decision on expulsion issued in one Member State is enforceable in another; so a deportee from the UK could find him or herself deported from any other EU country he or she attempted to enter while the deportation order is still in force.[5] A person who is already the subject of a deportation order but who subsequently leaves the UK of his or her own volition is regarded as having 'deported' him or herself irrespective of whether the persons were aware of the signing of a deportation order against them.[6] This guidance must be of dubious legality, especially in light of the House of Lords ruling in *R (on the application of Anufrijeva).*[7]

[1] The subject of a deportation order who disappears may be removed in pursuance of the order if he or she comes to light within three months, provided the circumstances are unchanged and no undertaking was given to review the case; otherwise the case is to be referred for further consideration: Operational Enforcement Manual 'Deportation', para 18.6.
[2] Immigration Act 1971, Sch 3, para 1.
[3] This was stated in the former IDI, Ch 13, s 1, para 6, but the current IDI (Aug/2006) makes no reference to this. The practice of the Parole Board in refusing early release to prisoners subject to deportation action was held to violate art 14 with art 5 in *R (on the application of Hindawi) v Secretary of State for the Home Department; R (on the application of Headley) v Secretary of State for the Home Department* [2004] EWHC 78 (Admin), (2004) Times, 5 February. Sections 259–260 of the Criminal Justice Act 2003 (not yet in force) provides for early release for prisoners liable for deportation or administrative removal. (They can be returned to prison if they return to the UK before the expiry of their sentence: s 261.)
[4] Operational Enforcement Manual, 'Deportation', para 19.1 (unless a deportation order is made in respect of someone refused at the port, eg a drugs courier, in which case removal is the responsibility of the refusing port: ibid).
[5] OJ 2001 L 150/47, which was supposed to have been implemented by 2 December 2002.
[6] IDI, Ch 13, s 1, para 10.
[7] See further **16.111**, above.

REVOCATION OF DEPORTATION ORDERS

16.113 The effect of a deportation order is to invalidate any leave to enter or remain in the UK given before the order is made or while it is in force.[1] A deportation order comes into force on the day it is signed rather than when it is served.[2] There are statutory provisions for when it ceases to apply. The order ceases to have effect automatically:

(1)   if the deportee becomes a British citizen;[3]
(2)   if the relationship between the deportee and his spouse or civil partner deported under a family order 'comes to an end those family members may seek re-admission under the rules';[4]
(3)   similarly in the case of children deported under a family order, as soon as they reach the age of 18.[5]

An order may also become invalid if the deportee has become a family member of an EEA national exercising Treaty rights in the UK.[6] In all other circumstances a deportation order continues in force until it is revoked by a further order of the Secretary of State.[7]

[1] Immigration Act 1971, s 5(1).
[2] *Peerbocus* [1987] Imm AR 331; *Dey (Sri Kumar) v Secretary of State for the Home Department* [1996] Imm AR 521, CA.
[3] Immigration Act 1971, s 5(2). But an order is not revoked merely because a Commonwealth citizen marries a British citizen after the order is signed: *R v Secretary of State for the Home Department, ex p Hayden* [1988] Imm AR 555, QBD.
[4] Immigration Act 1971, s 5(3), (4); HC395, para 389(ii).
[5] Immigration Act 1971, s 5(3), (4); HC395, para 389(i).
[6] See CHAPTER 6 above.
[7] Immigration Act 1971, s 5(2). A deportation order cannot be impliedly revoked and the grant of entry clearance while the order is in existence does not have this effect: *Watson* [1986] Imm AR 75.

16.114 An application for revocation of a deportation order can be made to either an entry clearance officer or the Home Office.[1] Where there has been an automatic deportation there is power to revoke it under section 5(2) of the Immigration Act 1971, but section 32(6) of the 2007 Act substantially constricts the exercise of that power[2] An application for revocation may be made at any time even prior to its enforcement, and will be considered in light of all the circumstances advanced, including any compassionate factors[3] The rules make plain, however, that it will be the 'proper course' to maintain an order for persons convicted of an offence carrying a custodial sentence of up to four years where an application is received within ten years of its having been made, and for those sentenced to periods in excess of that that position will prevail 'at any time'.[4] In other cases, revocation of the order will not normally be authorised unless the situation has been materially altered, either by a change of circumstances since the order was made, or by fresh information coming to light.[5] The rules also specify that where paragraph 398 applies, in the absence of a deportee fitting within the parameters of either paragraph 399 or 399A 'it will only be in exceptional circumstances that the public interest in maintaining deportation will be outweighed by other factors'.[6] Further, even where a deportation order is revoked, however, that still does not entitle the person to re-enter the UK, but merely to qualify for admission under the Immigration Rules.[7]

[1]   Modernised Guidance 'Revocation of deportation order: requests made from outside the UK' Version 3.0 (valid from 23 January 2014) at page 4.
[2]   See *SB (Jamaica) v Secretary of State for the Home Department* [2010] EWCA Civ 1569.
[3]   HC 395, para 390.
[4]   HC 395, para 391(a) and (b). The changes were made with effect from 13 December 2012 pursuant to introduction of section 56A of the UK Borders Act 2007 (as inserted by section 140 of the Legal Aid, Sentencing and Punishment of Offenders Act 2012) which gained effect on 1 October 2012, and which enabled the Secretary of State through her rules to render section 4(1), (2) and (3) of the Rehabilitation of Offenders Act 1974 inapplicable to particular 'immigration decision', which she duly did in respect of refusals of application for revocation: See further: Modernised Instructions 'Rehabilitation of Offenders Act' (Version 2.0, valid from 9 December 2013). Whilst the limitation operates only in respect of convictions which became spent after implementation of the new scheme, the IDI's direct that a decision to refuse to revoke an order based on a conviction which is spent and which relies on the provisions of the Rehabilitation of Offenders Act 1974 'can be proposed by an EO caseworker, but must be authorised and agreed at senior caseworker level, which must be at HEO or SEO'. Modernised Guidance 'Revocation of deportation order: requests made from outside the UK' – v3.0 (valid from 23 January 2014) page 19.
[5]   HC 395, para 391A.
[6]   HC 395, para 390A.
[7]   HC 395, para 392.

16.115 If an application for revocation is refused there was until 20 October 2014 an automatic right of appeal against the refusal, which was exercisable in-country and the deportee remained in the jurisdiction at the date of decision.[1] Where the Secretary of State certifies that the appellant's continued exclusion is in the interests of national security or the relationship between the UK and another country, or that the decision to refuse revocation was taken wholly or partly on information which he or she believes should not be made public for similar or other public interest reasons, the appeal lay with SIAC.[2] Such an appeal would usually be out of country.[3] However, where a fresh asylum or human rights claim had been made as part of the application for revocation then this qualified the claimant for an in-country right of appeal under section 92(4)(a) irrespective of whether the fresh claim qualifies under Immigration Rule 353, unless the claim was certified clearly unfounded under section 94, or 94B on or after 28 July 2014[4] or excluded under section 96.[5] A similar situation prevails in circumstances where it is asserted that the decision breached his or her Community law rights, in which case the appeal was in-country.[6] With commencement of section 15 of the Immigration Act 2014 in respect of deportation cases,[7] however, all those made subject to a deportation order on or after 20 October 2014 will derive a right of appeal under the modified section 82(1) of the 2002 Act. The changed statutory framework does not restrict the facility to raise an appeal against revocation any further than the position that previously prevailed such an appeal remaining non-suspensive under amended provisions introduced in section 92 on the basis of the introduction of a protection or human rights claim,[8] subject of course to the extended certification regime.

[1]   Nationality, Immigration and Asylum Act 2002, s 82(2)(k).
[2]   Nationality, Immigration and Asylum Act 2002, s 97; Special Immigration Appeals Commission Act 1997, s 2 (as amended by s 114 and NIAA 2002, Sch 7).
[3]   Nationality, Immigration and Asylum Act 2002, s 92(1).
[4]   See **16.88** above with regard to the new certification scheme introduced pursuant to amendment of s 94 by the Immigration Act 2014.
[5]   *R (on the application of BA (Nigeria)) v Secretary of State for the Home Department* [2009] EWCA Civ 119, [2009] QB 686, [2009] 2 WLR 1370 as qualified by *R (on the application of ZA (Nigeria)) v Secretary of State for the Home Department* [2010] EWCA Civ 926.
[6]   Nationality, Immigration and Asylum Act 2002, s 92(4). There is no provision for certifying clearly unfounded a revocation appeal resting on Community law.
[7]   The Immigration Act 2014 (Commencement No 3, Transitional and Saving Provisions) Order 2014, Articles 2, 9 and 10.
[8]   Human rights claim is defined for general purposes within art 10(5) of the Commencement Order No 3. The Defendant in her IDI's indicates such a claim will be treated as having been made where, on service of a notice to deport, in respect of which she is required to invite a written response within 20 day (treated as a section 120 warning) from the potential deportee, human rights issues are raised in that reply: see: IDI Chapter 13' Deporting Non-EEA Foreign Criminals (Version 1.0, October 2014) para 4.1.

Returned deportees

16.116 Where someone returns to the UK in breach of a deportation order, he or she may lawfully be deported under the original order.[1] But every case should be considered in the light of all the relevant circumstances.[2] A person who enters in breach of a deportation order is an illegal entrant[3] and a person who does so knowingly is, in addition, guilty of a criminal offence.[4]

[1]   Immigration Act 1971, s 5(5).
[2]   HC 395, para 388; *Alsawaf v Secretary of State for the Home Department* [1988] Imm AR 410, where the country of proposed destination refused to accept the deportee.
[3]   Immigration Act 1971, s 33(1). A decision to remove an illegal entrant attracts an appeal under s 82(2)(h) of the Nationality, Immigration and Asylum Act 2002, but it does not suspend removal unless an asylum or human rights claim has been made which is not certified as clearly unfounded, or the subject asserts a right under the Community Treaties: ss 92(1), (4), 94.
[4]   Immigration Act 1971, s 24(1)(a); *R v Secretary of State for the Home Department, ex p Yeboah* [1986] Imm AR 52, QBD.

16.117 Where there has been an automatic deportation there is power to revoke it under section 5(2) of the Immigration Act 1971, but section 32(6) of the 2007 Act substantially constricts the exercise of that power and sections 94(2) and 96(1) of the 2002 Act enable the Secretary of State to issue certificates in such cases and to prevent a series of unmeritorious appeals proceeding through the tribunal system.[1]

[1] See *SB (Jamaica) v Secretary of State for the Home Department* [2010] EWCA Civ 1569.

REPATRIATION AND ASSISTED VOLUNTARY RETURN

Voluntary repatriation

16.118 Section 5(6) of the 1971 Act empowers the Secretary of State to meet the expenses (including travelling expenses for members of the family or household) of someone liable for deportation, who leaves the UK voluntarily to live permanently abroad.[1] Similar, but broader provision is made for others who wish to live abroad. In November 2002, section 58 of the 2002 Act repealed the voluntary repatriation scheme under the Immigration Act 1971,[2] and replaced it with a new scheme to assist 'voluntary leavers'.[3] The section provides arrangements to help those (not British citizens or EEA nationals) who are leaving the UK for a place where they hope to take up permanent residence, where the Secretary of State thinks it is in their interests to leave and they wish to do so. The help they may be given includes resettlement expenses and expenses of 'explore and prepare' trips to help people decide whether they wish to leave and if so, to make preparations for leaving.[4] The scheme is not meant to provide a facility for repatriating visitors or those subject to a deportation order.[5] A person settled in this country who makes use of public funds for resettlement will not be able to claim re-entry as a returning resident, but are not required to sign an undertaking not to return, and may be admitted if they otherwise qualify under the rules.[6] The 2002 Act also enables financial support to be given to international organisations working in the field of international migration, including resettlement of refugees overseas.[7]

[1] Immigration Act 1971 s 5(6); see **16.110** fn 7 above.
[2] The old 'voluntary repatriation' scheme was under s 29 Immigration Act 1971. It was administered by the International Social Services of the UK, and was intended to help those persons who have failed to settle satisfactorily in the UK and who wished to leave but lacked the means to do so. Only travel costs, and no resettlement expenses, could be provided. 2,545 individuals were assisted between 1972 and 1995: *Hansard* (HC) 5 February 1996, col 48.
[3] 'Voluntary leavers' are defined in Nationality, Immigration and Asylum Act 2002, s 58(1).
[4] Nationality, Immigration and Asylum Act 2002, s 58(2), (3). See also the explanatory notes to the Act.
[5] IDI May 04, Ch 19, s 6, 'Voluntary repatriation' para 1.
[6] HC 395, para 18(iii); IDI above para 3.
[7] Nationality, Immigration and Asylum Act 2002, s 59. The organisations to be funded under this section are the International Organisation for Migration, which is heavily involved in 'voluntary return' programmes for failed asylum seekers (including unaccompanied minors), and UNHCR.

16.119 Chapter 46 of the Secretary of State's Enforcement Instruction and Guidance (EIG) describes the existing Assisted Voluntary Return (AVR) programmes which are developed and managed by the Assisted Voluntary Return Team based in UKBA/Immigration Group/Directorate of Central Operations and Performance/Removals Logistics. AVRs differ from voluntary departures as the mechanics of the return are handled by the International Organization for Migration (IOM) allowing for return of individuals from nationalities that could not otherwise be removed.

16.120 There are three major AVR programmes as follows.

(1)   The Voluntary Assisted Return and Reintegration Programme (VARRP) which is managed by Refugee Action and is intended for individuals who have asylum applications pending, or have been refused asylum and are appealing against the decision, or have been refused asylum and exhausted the appeals process; who have not withdrawn their asylum application, have been refused asylum and granted discretionary leave outside the immigration rules and whose criminal offences solely amount to immigration offences. The programme, however, is not available for the immigration detainees who have had directions set for their removal, for convicted prisoners subject to deportation orders or for anyone that has in the past been convicted of a serious immigration offence. Also excluded are unaccompanied children, and the dependants of those who did not claim asylum, or those who might be eligible under the pilot scheme set out at (3) below.

(2)   The second existing programme, Assisted Voluntary Return for Irregular Migrants (AVRIM), also managed by Refugee Action, is intended to assist with repatriation of victims of trafficking, illegal entrants who have been smuggled from abroad, individuals that entered the UK illegally, individuals that have been granted conditional leave to remain but breached one or more conditions of that leave, and individuals detained by the UKBA solely in relation to immigration offences where they have been assessed as violent or posing a threat to detention staff. The programme is not open to convicted prisoners subject to deportation orders, those who have been convicted of a serious immigration offence, those who have been granted humanitarian protection, ILR or refugee status, those who have sought asylum and have not withdrawn the application, those who entered the UK with valid leave and for non asylum reasons, and the immigration detainees that had removal directions set against them presently or in the past.

(3)   The third programme is the Pilot Assisted Voluntary Return for Families and Children programme, managed by Refugee Action, will be available to family groups comprising of 1 adult parent or legal guardian and at least one child (under 18) and from unaccompanied children (under 18) who have made an asylum claim or have been accepted as a victim of trafficking or have otherwise entered the UK illegally. The scheme is not open to those who are involved in pending criminal proceedings, or where any member of the family has a Deportation Order against them, to convicted prisoners, those who have leave to remain or have been convicted of a serious immigration offence.

Prison repatriation

16.121 The Council of Europe Convention on the Transfer of Sentenced Persons 1983 provided for repatriation to enable prisoners sentenced abroad to serve their sentences in their home country, with the consent of the prisoner and the agreement of the two countries concerned. Under the Convention the prisoner must have at least six months of his or her sentence left to serve and be a national of the state to which he or she is to be transferred. There should be no outstanding appeal to a higher court against sentence or conviction. The Repatriation of Prisoners Act 1984 was enacted to give effect to the Convention in UK law. British prisoners convicted overseas may be repatriated to complete their sentence in a British jail or other institution, and overseas prisoners in UK jails may be sent back to their own countries to complete their sentences. Under the 1984 Act any repatriation must take place under an international arrangement, such as the Council of Europe Convention or some bilateral arrangement between the UK and another government,[1] and consent must be given by the prisoner and the two countries concerned.[2] Transfer in and out is effected at the British end by a warrant issued by the Secretary of State for Justice authorising transfer of a prisoner under the Act to another country that has a Prison Transfer Agreement (PTA) with the UK. In outward transfers this authorises the taking of a prisoner to any place in any part of the UK, his or her delivery at a place of departure to the custody of an agent of the transfer country and the removal of the prisoner from the UK.[3] In inward transfers the 1984 Act authorises the return of prisoners to the UK and their subsequent detention in a prison, hospital or other institution as authorised by the Secretary of State's warrant.[4] Once a prisoner has been transferred back to the UK the Secretary of State has the power to give that person a pardon and is not prevented from doing so by the 1983 Convention.[5] A prisoner who is in the UK or on board a British ship, aircraft or hovercraft is deemed to be in the legal custody of the Secretary of State.[6] A prisoner who escapes can be arrested by the police without warrant.[7] The provisions of the 1984 Act do not apply to anyone who is detained in pursuance of a sentence of the International Criminal Court.[8]

[1]   Repatriation of Prisoners Act 1984, ss 1(1) and 8(1).
[2]   Repatriation of Prisoners Act 1984, s 1(1)(b) and (c). The Habeas Corpus Act of 1679, s 11 forbids the sending of any person as a prisoner out of the realm (ie, without his or her consent) and imposes the penalty of life imprisonment upon anyone taking part in such illegal repatriation or deportation. But s 12 exempts from this prohibition any persons, who 'by contract in writing agree with . . . any merchant or owner of any plantation, or other persons whatsoever, to be transported to any parts beyond the seas'.
[3]   Repatriation of Prisoners Act 1984, s 2.
[4]   Repatriation of Prisoners Act 1984, s 3.
[5]   *R (on the application of Shields) v Secretary of State for Justice* [2008] EWHC 3102 (Admin), (2009) Times, 14 January.
[6]   Repatriation of Prisoners Act 1984, s 5(2).
[7]   Repatriation of Prisoners Act 1984, s 5(5).
[8]   International Criminal Court Act 2001, s 42(5)(a).

16.122 Section 44 of the Police and Justice Act 2006 amends section 1 of the Repatriation of Prisoners Act 1984, except as regards Scotland, to enable transfers of serving foreign prisoners to take place without their consent except in those cases where the Prisoner Transfer Agreement (PTA) makes consent obligatory. When a decision is taken to repatriate a prisoner to serve his or her sentence in his or her home country, the Home Office will be informed of this decision and asked to serve a deportation order prohibiting that person's return to the UK.[1] Because of the overcrowding crisis in British prisons, the Home Secretary has set up a scheme to encourage foreign prisoners to volunteer for a transfer to their home country under a Prisoner Transfer Agreement (PTA) to serve the rest of their sentence there. Under the scheme they will be provided with 'reintegration assistance' in their home country.[2] Under Home Office policy 'Repatriation of FNO' to be eligible for transfer the prisoner must:

(a)   Be from a country which has signed a repatriation agreement with the UK, as listed in the Council of Europe Website and NOMS list of countries who have a PTA. For more information, see related link: Prison Service instruction – 52/2011.

(b)   Be a national of the country to which repatriation is requested. In exceptional circumstances, consideration will be given to requests from non-national residents of the proposed country of repatriation, for example, family members of nationals from the country of repatriation.

(c)   Have a sentence that is final and enforceable, and all appeal rights exhausted.

(d)   Have at least six or 12 months of their sentence left to serve, depending on the terms of the relevant PTA arrangement, or if they are serving a life sentence.

(e)   Not have outstanding criminal proceedings against them in the UK.

(f)   Before any repatriation, a deportation order needs to have been signed and served.

[1]   IDI, Ch 13, s 1, para 4.
[2]   Letter Home Office to Prison Reform Trust (9 October 2006). A news report in March 2008, stated that each prisoner would receive £3,000 integration payment. According to the Home Office, more than 4,200 foreign prisoners were deported in 2007 – 80% more than the previous year. It said the Facilitated Returns Scheme helped achieve that figure.

RECATEGORISATION

16.123 The Prison Rules 1999[1] specify that prisoner classification shall be determined according to age, temperament and record.[2] A blanket ban on the transfer of FNPs to open prisons was removed under a Prison Service Instruction (PSI) issued in 2002, which stated that: 'FNP's must now be risk assessed as to their suitability for categorisation and allocation to open conditions on an individual basis in the same way as all other prisoners'.[3] The instruction made plain that, whilst deportation status remained a major factor in the risk assessment process, it could be taken into account only in so far as it is might be indicative of the likelihood of abscond and not as a determinative factor precluding allocation to open conditions.

[1]   The Rules which are enacted under section 47(1) of the Prisons Act 1952 affords the Secretary of State the power to make rules: '. . . . for the regulation and management of prisons . . . . and for the classification, treatment employment discipline and control of persons required to be detained therein.'
[2]   Paragraph 7 of the Prison Rules 1999 states: 'Prisoners shall be classified in accordance with any directions of the Secretary of State having regard to their age, temperament and record and with a view to maintaining good order and facilitating training, and in the case of convicted prisoners of furthering the purpose of their training and treatment as provided . . . .'.
[3]   PSI 35/2002.

16.124 Subsequent PSOs and PSIs outline the most up-to-date criteria governing the categorisation of FNPs.[1] The guidance, whilst advocating individualised assessment, is often interpreted by the Prison Service as promoting deportation status as the sole determining factor, since the applicable PSO requires the prison to assume that deportation will occur absent a clear indication to the contrary. The result is that reallocation of FNPs to open conditions is frequently refused as being a general risk, despite favourable reallocation assessments based on the prisoners' conduct. It is also noteworthy, and incongruous, that the directions to the parole board on the transfer of lifers to open conditions[2] contain no equivalent provisions, such that lifers liable to deportation may face fewer barriers than other FNPs as they progress towards release. The case law in fact discourages adherence to the narrow approach encouraged by the PSOs, with its emphasis on absconding. Ouseley J in *R (on the application of Cooper (Michael Ivan)) v Secretary of State for the Home Department* emphasised that the requirements for categorisation involved a consideration of the likelihood that a prisoner will seek to escape, and of the level of risk which they would pose to the public were they to do so.[3]

[1]   PSO 4630 under section *'Security Classification Policy and Allocation to Open Conditions'* states as follows: 'The overriding purpose of security classification is to ensure that prisoners are retained in custody with a level of security which is consistent with the need to prevent escape and to protect the public. Any increased likelihood of deportation for Foreign Nationals given a custodial sentence may increase the risk of escape or absconding. This risk should be taken into account when considering foreign national prisoners for Category D and allocation to open conditions'. It continues under the section entitled *'Mandatory'* to state: 'Before a foreign national prisoner is classified, the individual risk must be assessed on the assumption that deportation will take place, unless a decision not to deport has already been taken by the IND; a decision which must be recorded in the prisoner's record'. It continues: 'Each case must be individually considered on its merits but the need to protect the public and ensure the intention to deport is not frustrated is paramount. Category D will only be appropriate where it is clear that the risk is very low. PSI 40/2011 remains effective until 1 September 2015 and replaces PSI 35/2002 *Allocation of Deportees to Open Conditions*, as of 1 September 2011. It provides, at paragraph 25, that *'Prisoners liable to enforcement proceedings under the Immigration Act are considered for categorisation to Category D in the same way as other prisoners, and must have their security category reviewed. If a deportee is being considered for open conditions however, the Request for Information form sent to Criminal Casework Directorate in UKBA must have been returned before a prisoner is moved from the closed estate.* It is not UKBA's decision whether or not a deportee should proceed to open conditions. That decision lies with the prison. UKBA are consulted in case they have any additional information which might impact on the risk assessment process – for instance that the prisoner may try to evade an eventual deportation by absconding (and not merely that the subject is likely to be deported). The final decision will be for the Governor of the closed prison carrying out the recategorisation and allocation review.'

[2]   Issued by the Secretary of State in August 2004 pursuant to section 32(6) of the Criminal Justice Act 1991.

[3]   [2005] EWHC 1715 (Admin), [2005] All ER (D) 470 (Jul). See also *R (on the application of Brownhill) v Secretary of State for the Home Department* [2006] EWHC 1213 (Admin).

16.125   In instances where PSO 4630 is interpreted so as to exclude an FNP on the basis of a supposed heightened risk of absconding, the decision of the Prison Service may be amenable to challenge by way of judicial review, on the grounds that the policies relating to FNPs are incompatible with Rule 7 of the Prison Rules[1] and that it is irrational to rely upon deportation status as the sole determining factor in the categorisation process. In *R (on the application of Manhire) v Secretary of State for Justice*[2] it was held that the refusal of the Governor to transfer the claimant FNP to an open prison was unlawful due to the improbability of him being removed to Zimbabwe at the end of his sentence, his settled family circumstances, and the hugely disproportionate effect that absconding would have on his appeal against deportation. This demonstrates a willingness by the courts to adopt a more common-sense approach and to intervene in appropriate cases.

1   As at the end of July 2010 there is a judgment pending in which the court will rule upon whether the categorisation policies relating to FNPs are *ultra vires* Rule 7: *R (on the application of Omoregbee) v Secretary of State for Justice* [2010] EWHC 2658 (Admin).

2   [2009] EWHC 1788 (Admin).

HOME DETENTION CURFEW

16.126 The Home Detention Curfew (HDC) scheme was first introduced under the Crime and Disorder Act 1998, and since 3 December 2012, post amendment of existing legislation by Legal Aid, Sentencing and Punishment of Offenders Act 2012, there is a single HDC scheme regulated by section 246 of the Criminal Justice Act 2003. Under the scheme the Secretary of State has a discretion to release prisoners early on 'tag'; as long as they are not excluded from the scheme under the statute. Such prisoners are eligible to be released on licence after serving a requisite period, which is determined by reference to their sentence length. Prisoners currently liable to removal from the UK fall into the excluded categories, and are defined under section 259 of the 2003 Act as follows:

- those liable to deportation under section 3(5) of the Immigration Act 1971 who have been notified of a decision to make a deportation order against them;[1]
- those liable to deportation under section 3(6) of the Immigration Act 1971;
- those notified of a decision to refuse leave to enter the UK;
- illegal entrants within the meaning of section 33(1) of that Immigration Act 1971,
- those liable to removal under section 10 of the Immigration and Asylum Act 1999.

The discretion to authorise the release of a prisoner on HDC is exercised by the Governor of the prison where the prisoner is detained, on behalf of the Secretary of State. PSO 6700 sets down the policy and procedure on implementation of the HDC, and has since been updated by PSIs 31/2003 and 31/2006. The Administrative Court addressed the impact and relevance of a prisoner's immigration status in *R (on the application of Serrano) v Secretary of State for Justice*[2]:

(a)   First, a prisoner's immigration status is relevant to whether he or she should be granted HDC and a prisoner who is going to be deported falls outside the scope of HDC, the purpose of which is to manage resettlement in the community;

(b)   Second, and in the absence of any challenge to the statutory provisions themselves, once a decision has been made by the SSHD that a prisoner will be deported pursuant to the automatic deportation provisions of section 32 of the UK Borders Act 2007, the prisoner becomes statutorily ineligible for HDC, and there is then no obligation on the SSJ to consider the grant of HDC unless and until the SSHD's decision is in fact successfully challenged;

(c) Third, in a case where no decision has yet been made by the SSHD whether a prisoner who is subject to the automatic deportation provisions is entitled to rely on one of the exceptions in section 33, the Prison Service should seek information from UKBA as to the prisoner's immigration status and UKBA's proposals;

(d) Fourth, the SSJ, acting through the Prison Service, has a duty to consider HDC when no decision on deportation has yet been made, albeit that in a case where an IS 91 has been issued, it will in general be a lawful exercise of the SSJ's discretion to refuse release on HDC, having regard to the purpose for which such release exists;

(e) Fifth, exercise of the SSJ's discretion in accordance with these principles does not constitute unlawful discrimination contrary to Article 14 of the Convention in combination with Article 5.

1 FNPs with leave to remain, including indefinite leave, are susceptible to deportation under either s 3(5)(a) of the Immigration Act 1971. If their leave has not been curtailed or revoked, however, and the Secretary of State has not issued notice of intention to deport as of their eligibility date for HDC they cannot be excluded, as is sometime done, solely on the basis that deportation proceedings may be initiated against them.
2 [2012] EWHC 3216 (Admin), [2012] All ER (D) 217 (Nov).

EARLY REMOVAL AND INDUCEMENT TO DEPART

Early removal scheme

16.127 To alleviate the disparity which arose as a result of the exclusion from the HDC of those who were liable to removal, section 260 of the Criminal Justice Act 2003 (CJA 2003) introduced a mandatory early release scheme for determinate sentenced foreign national offenders which impacted on persons liable to removal from the UK.[1] The Early Removal Scheme (ERS) came into effect in April 2005 and enables eligible FNPs to secure their discharge from prison, for the sole purpose of effecting removal,[2] before the end of their sentence. Initially prisoners were entitled to be released at a stage in the sentence equivalent to that at which they would otherwise have been released on HDC. However, the Early Removal of Short-Term and Long-Term Prisoners (Amendment of Requisite Period) Order 2008, SI 2008/977, expanded the early release scheme so as to enable FNPs to be removed from prison, up to 270 days before the halfway point in the sentence. This disparity was unsuccessfully challenged by a UK national prisoner who argued that the acceleration of the date at which FNPs could be released discriminated against him since he could only be released up to 135 days before that point on HDC.[3] PSI 4/2013, which updates PSI 38/2012, provides details of the relevant legislation governing the ERS. When the scheme was first introduced, a number of categories of prisoner were statutorily excluded from the early removal scheme, but those exclusions were removed on 3 November 2008, following commencement of provisions in the Criminal Justice and Immigration Act 2008, meaning all classes of foreign national prisoner are now eligible for the scheme, save for the following:

(a) those with an indeterminate sentence, who will be dealt with by way of the tariff expired removal scheme, in accordance with PSI 18/2012;

(b) those who are on remand;

(c)   those who are detained under immigration powers;

(d)   those who are subject to further criminal proceedings, confiscation order or further custodial requirements.

Where a FNP is removed under the ERS but re-enters the UK before the sentence expiry date he is liable to be detained to serve out his sentence.[4]

---

[1]   See s 49A of the Criminal Justice Act 1991 (as amended by Sch 20 of the CJA 2003) and ss 259–261 of the CJA 2003. Baroness Scotland of Asthal (made the following statement on the ERS on behalf of the Government in the course of debates on the CJA 2003:

'My Lords, this group of amendments deal with foreign national prisoners who make up a rising proportion of the prison population. About 800 foreign national prisoners are deported or otherwise removed each year. Those liable to deportation at the end of the custodial portion of their prison sentences are currently ineligible for the early release arrangements available to other prisoners. The purpose of these amendments is therefore to introduce an early removal scheme for this group of prisoners. Eligible prisoners will be deported up to a maximum of 135 days early, depending on sentence length. The scheme will save a small number of prison places. But, as importantly, it will provide fairer release and removal arrangements for prisoners who are ineligible for the early release provisions available to other prisoners'.
[Lords Hansard text for 5 November 2003, Column 900, page 132, line 22].

[2]   CJA 1991, s 46A(3); CJA 2003, s 259(3).

[3]   *R (on the application of Brooke) v Secretary of State for Justice* [2009] EWHC 1396 (Admin), [2009] All ER (D) 272 (Oct).

[4]   CJA 1991, s 46B(1)–(7); CJA 2003, s 261.

16.128 The ERS properly implemented enables FNPs to obtain their release, and hence removal, up to 270 days prior to their conditional or unconditional release dates. All FNPs were made presumptively eligible for the scheme unless they fell into a statutorily excepted offender category (above), there were exceptional or compelling reasons to exclude them, or they were irremovable due to practical impediments. Implementation of the ERS was governed by the Prison Service through Chapter 9 of its PSO 6000, which has since been replaced by PSI 4/2013. The scheme has now been integrated with the Immigration Repatriation and Removal Services PSI 52/2011. There are four recognised stages to the determination of eligibility under the ERS (although Scotland has introduced ERS since 4 November 2011, it follows a slightly different process and Northern Ireland have yet to adopt the scheme):

- *Stage 1* – the Prison Parole Clerk ascertains whether the deportee can be considered for the ERS. This is arguably the most involved aspect of the process, with the Clerk having to ascertain whether the Claimant is: facing further charges; is subject to consecutive sentences, or; there are other exceptional or compelling reasons to exclude.

- *Stage 2* – charges the Home Office with determining whether removal is lawful and practical. A standardised referral form is sent to the criminal casework department. CC are required to confirm that an applicant is subject to immigration control and is amenable to enforcement action, that there are no pending judicial proceedings challenging removal, and that the applicant is adequately documented so that enforcement action is feasible.

- *Stage 3* – the process concludes with a reference back to the Prison Governor to reassess whether, in the intervening period, between stages there have emerged any exceptional compelling reasons which render the prisoner ineligible. If not then the Prison Governor will issue a decision and removal may proceed at the commencement on or after the ERED.

- *Stage 4* – the prisoner is removed from prison and transferred to immigration detention and thereafter removed to his country of origin.

A fairly rigorous timetable for determination of eligibility was set down in PSO6000[1] with the main amendment from PSI 52/2011 being the reduction in the deadline for the governor to notify the Home Office of a potential ERS case going from 30 days to five. The Prison Service has generally adhered to the timetable set down. The Home Office at stage 2, however, have frequently failed to process referrals with the result that prisoners presumptively eligible for the ERS often lose, wholly or in part, the benefit of the scheme. The Courts have held, however, that there is no obligation on the Immigration Service to adhere to the said timetable, or indeed to conclude the assessment of eligibility prior to the ERED, it being determined that those presumptively eligible for the ERS possessed no more than a legitimate expectation, derivable from Statute and the PSO, that their case would be considered prior to the expiration of the eligibility period.[2] Where the conduct of the Immigration or Prison Service appears likely to deprive those presumptively eligible to the benefit of the Scheme, a remedy exists, however, by way of judicial review, the FNP seeking a mandatory order requiring the Secretary of State to act. Whether such an order is granted is then decided pursuant to a determination by the High Court of whether the consequent frustration of the individual's expectation was so unfair as to be a misuse of the authority's power.[3]

[1] In the case of an FNP detained for 12 months the process is estimated to take 13 weeks with a start date enabling resolution of eligibility prior to the ERED. Where a sentence is for shorter periods PSO6000 indicates the time frame may be circumvented.

[2] As per Newman J in *R (on the application of Christian) v Secretary of State for the Home Department* [2006] EWHC 2152 (Admin), [2006] All ER (D) 35 (Jul) where he found in terms:

   (a)   the SSHD was not under a statutory obligation to determine eligibility prior to the ERED date and that the breadth of the discretion afforded under section 46A(1) of CJA 1991 and section 259(1) of CJA 2003 ensured that he had acted in accordance with his statutory obligations provided he determined eligibility and effected the removal of those deemed eligible within the ERS period (ie the period from the ERED to 14 days prior to the prisoner's conditional or unconditional release dates);

   (b)   that PSO 6000 was incapable of establishing the legitimate expectation argued for. It was merely instruction and direction to the Prison Service to achieve desired standards of administration. The IND's own instructions promised no more than that removal would be effected as expeditiously as possible and this was not a clear and unambiguous promise;

   (c)   accordingly those presumptively eligible for the ERS had a legitimate expectation, derivable from statute and Instruction, only that there case would be considered within the eligibility period, could expect no more than that their cases would be processed within the ERS period (as above);

   (d)   that the SSHD's delay was not evidence of maladministration as on the court's construction of the statute the SSHD was afforded the whole of the ERS period within which to determine eligibility.

[3] *R (on the application of Christian) v Secretary of State for the Home Department.* fn 2 above.

16.129 Challenge to the interpretation of the operation of the ERS as set out in *Christian* may theoretically be possible under Article 5 and 14 of the ECHR, however. Whilst in *R (on the application of Hindawi) v Secretary of State for the Home Department*,[1] Lord Bingham held that 'a prisoner sentenced to a determinate term cannot seek to be released at any earlier time than that for which domestic law provides, and that 'during the currency of a lawful sentence, article 5(4) has no part to play', it was none the less held that Article 14 could be invoked to prevent discrimination occurring in the parole arrangements existing at that time.[2] This argument derives some support from *Csoszanszki v Sweden*[3] in which it was accepted that an early release scheme can give rise to a reasonable expectation that the de facto period of imprisonment will be shorter than the period imposed by the court and that accordingly the individual's detention may become unlawful if it is seen to become arbitrary. An Article 14 ECHR argument may then be raised in reliance upon the prima facie breach of Article 5: the interpretation of the court in *Christian* operating so as to reinforce (as opposed to relieve) pre-existing inequalities in the treatment of FNPs, the ERS not achieving parity with the HDC in practice in terms of prisoners' eligibility to early release.

1   [2006] UKHL 54, [2007] 2 All ER 1.
2   See **16.87** below.
3   (Application No 22318/02) (27 June 2006, unreported).

The Criminal Justice and Immigration Act 2008

16.130 The Criminal Justice and Immigration Act 2008 made amendments to the various powers to enable foreign prisoners to be released early and returned to their country of nationality. Section 15 amended section 35(1) of the Criminal Justice Act 1991 in its application to prisoners liable to removal from the UK. Section 33 amended the early removal of prisoners from the UK under the Criminal Justice Act 1991 and section 34 made amendments to deal with removal under Part 12 of the Criminal Justice Act 2003.

Other inducements to depart

16.131 A person liable to be sentenced by a criminal court or punished for contempt of court may be encouraged to avoid punishment by agreeing to a voluntary departure and not to return to the UK. This inducement was used in the nineteenth century for convicted prisoners, who were offered free pardons if they left the UK.[1] There were a number of contempt cases where the application to commit was adjourned *sine die* on the agreement to depart.[2] The more frequent technique of persuasion has been the use of a bind-over at common law to come up for judgment when called on to do so upon terms that the person leaves the UK within a specified time and does not return within a specified number of years.[3] There is no power to make such a condition under the Justices of the Peace Act 1361[4] or a probation order,[5] and it can only be made in lieu of and not in addition to a sentence of the court.[6] The Court of Appeal has held that consent remains free even though given in the face of the alternative of imprisonment.[7] The making of such a bind-over was considered to be a purely internal situation and therefore not contrary to community law in the case of *R v Saunders*.[8] But it is unlikely to survive litigation under the Human Rights Act 1998.[9]

1   O Higgins 'Voluntary Deportation' [1963] Crim LR 680.
2   *Yager v Musa* [1962] Crim LR 240; *Smith v Smith* (1963) Times, 23 August.

3 See D Williams 'Suspended Sentence at Common Law' [1963] PL 441; Supreme Court Act 1981, s 79.

4 *R v Ayu* [1958] 3 All ER 636, [1958] 1 WLR 1264.

5 *R v McCartan* [1958] 3 All ER 140, [1958] 1 WLR 933.

6 *R v Ayu* above; *R v Governor of Brixton Prison, ex p Havilde* [1969] 1 All ER 109, [1969] 1 WLR 42.

7 *R v Williams* [1982] 3 All ER 1092, [1982] 1 WLR 1398.

8 Case C-175/78 [1980] QB 72.

9 On bind-overs see *Steel v United Kingdom* (1998) 28 EHRR 603. On the prohibition of exile in international law see Nuala Mole 'Constructive deportation' (1995) EHRLR 64.

Chapter 17

REMOVAL AND OTHER EXPULSION

INTRODUCTION

17.1 The following abbreviations are used in this Chapter:

IA 2014	Immigration Act 2014
IAA 1999	Immigration and Asylum Act 1999
NIAA 2002	Nationality, Immigration and Asylum Act 2002
IAN Act 2006	Immigration and Nationality Act 2006

In this chapter we examine the grounds for administrative removal from the UK and the means by which it is achieved. In contrast to removal by deportation, which we dealt with in the last chapter, there is no formal ban on return in cases of summary administrative removal, as set out in s 5(1) of the Immigration Act 1971. A series of rule changes have, however, introduced a variety of bans of between one year and ten years on return to the UK that apply in different circumstances where a person is removed from the UK or, in some circumstances, makes a voluntary departure. Details of these amendments to paragraph 320 of HC 395 are contained at **3.136ff**, above.

At the time of writing, substantial changes to the power of administrative removal had been passed into law by section 1 of the Immigration Act 2014 (IA 2014). If brought into full effect, this has the effect of entirely replacing section 10 of the Immigration and Asylum Act 1999 (IAA 1999) as amended, which was the principal means by which administrative removals were carried out.[1] IA 1999 also repeals section 47 of the IAN 2006, a source of considerable litigation on the issue of administrative removal in recent years. This text addresses the old powers and the new ones. [2] These amendments are yet to be brought fully into force and it was unknown what, if any, transitional arrangement might be put in place when the new powers do come into effect. This text therefore addresses the old powers and the new ones.

[1] At the time of writing, The Immigration Act 2014 (Commencement No 3, Transitional and Saving Provisions) Order 2014, SI 2014/2711 had brought into effect IA 2014, s 1, along with some other provisions of the IA 2014, but only in respect of two groups of migrants: foreign criminals and students who make Tier 4 applications on or after 20 October 2014. Saving provisions apply.

[2] IA 2014, Sch 9, para 5.

17.2 Under section 10 of the IAA 1999, immigrants who are liable to removal are those refused leave to enter; illegal entrants; overstayers, and those in breach of their conditions of stay; those using deception to remain; former refugees; family members of those liable to removal, and crew members remaining unlawfully. The Nationality, Immigration and Asylum Act 2002 (NIAA 2002) made it possible for the first time to remove persons who attempted but failed to obtain leave to remain using deception;[1] former refugees[2] and the UK-born children of all those liable to removal including illegal entrants and persons refused leave to enter.[3] The powers of removal were by and large unchanged save for these extensions; removal of those refused leave to enter, illegal entrants, their family members and sea and air crews is dealt with in Schedule 2 to the Immigration Act 1971,[4] and of the other groups in section 10 of the IAA 1999 and the Immigration (Removal Directions) Regulations 2000.[5] Removal of asylum claimants to 'safe third countries' under sections 11 and 12 of the 1999 Act is dealt with in CHAPTER 12 above. In addition, there are provisions for the summary removal of sea, air and train crews who are in the UK illegally, and for detained psychiatric patients and members of visiting forces.

1   IAA 1999, s 10(1)(b), substituted by the NIAA 2002, s 74, from 10 February 2003: SI 2003/1, art 2.
2   IAA 1999, s 10(1)(ba), inserted by the NIAA 2002, s 76(7), from 10 February 2003: SI 2003/1.
3   Immigration Act 1971, Sch 2, para 10A, inserted by the NIAA 2002, s 73(1), from 10 February 2003: SI 2003/1.
4   Immigration Act 1971, Sch 2, paras 8–15 as amended.
5   SI 2000/2243.

17.3 Under the new amended section 10 of the IAA 1999 to be introduced by section 1 of the IA 2014, the power to remove is very differently conceived. The new section 10 introduces a general power to remove any person who 'requires leave to enter or remain in the United Kingdom but does not have it': section 10(1). In sharp contrast to the prior version of section 10, no consideration is necessary as to how the person came to be in the situation of requiring leave but not having it. The general removal power also applies to a member of family of the person facing removal: section 10(2). The definition of family member is examined further below.

REMOVAL UNDER THE IMMIGRATION ACT 2014

17.4 The intention of the new section 10 of the IAA 1999 brought into effect by section 1 of the IA 2014 is to drastically simplify the process of administrative removal. During the passage of the Immigration Act 2014, Lord Taylor of Holbeach stated that: 'our current system for removal is too complex. It requires a number of decisions and notices to be made and served. Separate refusal and removal decisions can cause confusion to migrants as to when they need to leave the UK and lead to legal challenges being made later in the process' and that the intention was to 'move to a system where only one decision is made and served, giving, refusing or varying leave. Following that decision, those who require leave but do not have it will be removable.'[1] When combined with the limited rights of appeal under the regime of the IA 2014, which omit any right of appeal against a decision to make removal directions or otherwise against a decision under the amended section 10 of the IAA 1999, the amendment certainly achieves administrative simplicity and a reduction in the scope for legal challenges.

1   Hansard HL, 3 Mar 2014 : Columns 1118-9 per the Lord Taylor of Holbeach.

17.5 In the case of a person who has no leave at all, such as an overstayer or an illegal entrant, the amended section 10 of the IAA 1999 imparts to the Secretary of State for the Home Department a general power to remove. No notice is required for section 10(1) to take effect. It is not necessary to serve such a person with a notice of decision to make removal directions, and any similar notice that a person is removable under section 10 that is issued in future will in any event not carry a right of appeal because appeal rights are tied to the making and refusal of a protection or human rights claim. Arrangements will need to be made by the Secretary of State for the Home

Department with a relevant carrier and removal directions will be set under paragraph 8 of Schedule 2 of the IA 1971 (or Schedule 3 of the IA 1971 if a deportation order is in force).[1]

[1] IAA 1999, s 10(7)-(9).

17.6 In the case of a person who has leave but where an application for further leave is refused or where a curtailment decision is made, that person will receive written notice of the decision to give, refuse or vary leave as required by section 4 of the IA 1971. The amended version of section 10 of the IAA 1999 does not on the face of it permit removal of a person who does possess leave but who obtained that leave by deception or who has breached a condition of leave, unlike the prior version. The prior version included provision for leave to be invalidated by service of a section 10 decision but the new version contains no equivalent.[1]

[1] See prior version of IAA 1999, s 10(8).

17.7 The amended section 10 of the IAA 1999 also includes a power to remove defined family members of a person who requires leave but does not possess it.[1] In contrast to the person who requires leave but does not have it, notice is required for the removal of a family member.[2] The effect of service of such a notice is that it invalidates any leave to enter or remain in the United Kingdom previously given to the family member.[3] Member of family is defined to include partner, parent, adult dependent relative or child or child living in the same household where the person facing removal has care of the child and a child is specifically defined as a child under the age of 18.[4] The definition is intended to be wide and to extend to a situation 'where children are being looked after by someone other than a parent, such as an older sibling, a grandparent or another adult family member'.[5] To be removable under this power, the member of the family must either have leave to enter or remain on the basis of family life with the person facing removal or, in the opinion of the Secretary of State or immigration officer, if making an application for leave would not be granted leave in his or her own right but would be granted leave on the basis of family life with the person facing removal if the person facing removal themselves had leave.[6] Where a family relationship or relationship of dependency has broken down, the family member will instead be considered for removal in their own right.[7] The removal power does not apply if the family member is a British citizen or has an enforceable EU right to reside.[8]

[1] IAA 1999, s 10(2).
[2] IAA 1999, s 10(2) and regulations made under s 10(10).
[3] IAA 1999, s 10(6).
[4] IAA 1999, s 10(3) and (11).
[5] Hansard HL, 1 Apr 2014: Column 860 per the Lord Taylor of Holbeach
[6] IAA 1999, s 10(4).
[7] Hansard HL, 1 Apr 2014 : Column 860 per the Lord Taylor of Holbeach.
[8] IAA 1999, s 10(5).

17.8 Family members who are children benefit from some additional protections conferred by further amendments introduced by sections 2 and 3 of the Immigration Act 2014.[1] Section 2 of the IA 2014 introduces a new section 78A of the NIAA 2002 which provides two protections for children once any appeal rights have been exhausted. Firstly, the child may not be removed unless

28 days has passed since both the parent or carer and the child exhausted their appeal rights.[2] Secondly, the child's parent or carer may not be removed if this would leave the child without a parent or carer living with him or her in the UK.[3] The definition of 'relevant parent or carer' is that the person must be (i) a parent of the child or have care of the child, and (ii) be living in a household in the United Kingdom with the child.[4] The removal of a parent or carer who does not reside with the relevant child or an unaccompanied child therefore does not trigger the protection of section 78A of the NIAA 2002. It is unclear whether these protections come into effect if no appeal was pursued but it is certainly arguable that the framing of section 78A(3) brings the protections into effect whether or not an appeal was pursued providing there is no current appeal and none can be brought (ignoring the possibility of an out of time appeal). Section 3 of the IA 2014 came into force on 28 July 2014 and inserts a new section 54A into the Borders, Citizenship and Immigration Act 2009 (BCIA 2009) to provide statutory footing for the Independent Family Returns Panel ('the panel'). The Secretary of State is obliged to consult (but not abide by decisions of) the panel 'on how best to safeguard and promote the welfare of the children of the family' in each family returns case and in each case where the Secretary of State proposes to detain a family in pre-departure accommodation, on the suitability of so doing, having particular regard to the need to safeguard and promote the welfare of the children of the family.[5] A 'family returns case' is defined as a case where removal of a child is going to take place along with removal of a person who is a parent of the child or has care of the child and is living in a household in the United Kingdom with the child.[6]

1   At the time of writing these sections, like IA 2014, s 1, had not been commenced.
2   NIAA 2002, s 78A(2)(a).
3   NIAA 2002, s 78A(2)(b).
4   NIAA 2002, s 78A(1)(b).
5   BCIA 2009, s 54A(2). Pre departure accommodation is defined by reference to Part 8 NIAA 2002 as amended by s 6 of the IA 2014.
6   BCIA 2009, s 54A(3).

REMOVAL OF ILLEGAL ENTRANTS AND OVERSTAYERS

17.9 Historically the treatment of illegal entrants liable to summary removal[1] was in stark contrast to the position of those who had entered lawfully but breached conditions or remained beyond the time limited by their leave. Prior to 2 October 2000 (the coming into force of the relevant provisions of the IAA 1999), overstayers and those in breach of conditions were liable to deportation,[2] but had an in-country right of appeal, which allowed the appellate authority to look at the merits of their case, if they had been here for more than seven years or if the decision to deport followed a curtailment decision.[3] Illegal entrants had no in-country right of appeal and could only challenge the decision to treat them as illegal entrants by way of judicial review.[4] Yet both might have long-established roots in the community. The pre Immigration Act 2014 version of section 10 of the IAA 1999 levelled down the treatment of the two groups by making overstayers subject to the same summary removal process as illegal entrants, a process brought to a conclusion by the amended version of section 10. The safeguard of an in-country right of appeal, which has the effect of suspending removal during the appeal process, was still available to those presenting a claim on asylum and human rights grounds, but in a decreasing proportion of cases.[5] The appeals provisions of the IA 2014 bring the process of removal of procedural protections to a conclusion by entirely removing the right of appeal other than where a protection or human rights claim is made and is rejected.[6]

[1]   Immigration Act 1971, Sch 2, para 9 as amended by Asylum and Immigration Act 1996, Sch 2, para 6; see Lord Bridge in *Khawaja v Secretary of State for the Home Department* [1983] UKHL 8 (10 Feb 1983) ;[1984] AC 74 at paras 106-111.

[2]   Immigration Act 1971, s 3(5)(a) as originally enacted, s 5: see CHAPTER 16 above.

[3]   Immigration Act 1971, s 15, as amended by Immigration Act 1988, s 5; see also Immigration (Restricted Right of Appeal Against Deportation) (Exemption) Order 1993, SI 1993/1656.

[4]   The only suspensive appeal against removal was on asylum grounds. The right of appeal against removal directions under s 16 of the Immigration Act 1971, and subsequently s 66 of the IAA 1999, was exercisable only after removal, and jurisdiction was limited to whether the power in law exists. See now NIAA 2002, s 82(2)(g)–(i).

[5]   See NIAA 2002, s 82(2)(g)–(ia) (previously there were separate appeals under the IAA 1999, s 69(5) for asylum applicants, and s 65 for human rights claimants). The suspensive effect of such appeals is provided by s 92(4)(a) of the NIAA 2002, but can be avoided by a certificate that the claim is clearly unfounded under s 94: see CHAPTERS 7, above and 19.

[6]   IA 2014, s 15.

Definition of illegal entry

17.10 An illegal entrant is defined in section 33(1) of the Immigration Act 1971 as:[1]

'a person:

(a)   unlawfully entering or seeking to enter in breach of a deportation order or of the immigration laws; or

(b)   entering or seeking to enter to enter by means which include deception by another person,

and includes also a person who has entered as mentioned in paragraph (a) or (b) above.'

The definition of 'illegal entrants' thus covers three stages:

- those who enter;
- those who seek to enter;
- those who have entered.

[1]   As amended by Asylum and Immigration Act 1996, Sch 2, para 4. See also IAA 1999, s 167(2), which provides that 'illegal entrant' has the same meaning as in the Immigration Act 1971.

17.11 By section 11(1) of the Immigration Act 1971 'entry' is distinguished from 'arrival'.[1] Usually passengers 'arriving' at a port or airport are deemed not to 'enter' the UK until they have (1) disembarked from their ship, aircraft or Channel Tunnel train;[2] and (2) left the areas reserved for immigration control.[3] If detained or temporarily admitted or released while liable to detention,[4] they are deemed not to have 'entered'. By contrast, those who arrive at a remote beach or private landing strip or away from a designated port or airport are treated as 'entering' as soon as they leave their ship or aircraft.[5] These statutory distinctions between 'arriving' and 'entering' may help distinguish between someone seeking to enter and someone who has entered.

[1]   See also 3.56 above.

2   In relation to Channel Tunnel trains, which are designated control areas while passing through control zones in France and Belgium, passengers 'enter' the UK by remaining on the train after it ceases to be a control area: Immigration Act 1971, s 11 modified in relation to Channel Tunnel by SI 1993/1813, art 7(1), Sch 4, para 1(5), and in relation to frontier controls between the UK, France and Belgium by SI 1994/1405, art 7.

3   The area is defined by s 11(1) of the Immigration Act 1971 as such area at the port 'as may be approved for this purpose by an immigration officer'. Thus, stowaways who claimed asylum before the ferry bringing them to the UK docked were not illegal entrants: *Ex p Karakoc, ex p Karatas* (CO 694, 695/2000) (16 May 2000, unreported), and stowaways in a lorry on the Eurostar shuttle who took steps to alert the immigration service of their presence and to make an asylum claim immediately on entering the UK, and before leaving the designated control area, were not illegal entrants: *Ex p Uzun, ex p Karadag* (CO 2089, 2090/2000) (10 July 2000, unreported), (permission granted, Home Office conceded that such persons could not be treated as having entered or having sought to enter illegally).

4   Immigration Act 1971, s 11(1) as amended, inserting references to IAA 1999, Part III, NIAA 2002, ss 62, 68, all of which provide for temporary admission or release on bail, which displaces the presumption of entry by leaving immigration control.

5   Thus, asylum seekers hidden in a lorry who sought asylum on arrival at the freight port of Immingham were illegal entrants because the port is not a designated port for immigration purposes: *R v Secretary of State for the Home Department, ex p Uluyol and Cakmak* [2001] INLR 194. In *R v Javaherifard* [2005] EWCA Crim 3231, (2006) Times, 20 January, [2005] All ER (D) 213 (Dec), the Court of Appeal explained that section 11 has no application to entry by land; that those who disembark from a boat otherwise than at a port enter on disembarkation, as do those who disembark at a port which has no designated immigration area; and that section 11 does not apply to those who have already entered the UK overland or on an earlier disembarkation.

17.12 The provisions of the IAA 1999 and Orders made under it to grant or refuse leave to enter 'before arrival in the United Kingdom', and for entry clearance 'to have effect as leave to enter the United Kingdom',[1] mean that a person who has obtained leave to enter by deception, becomes an illegal entrant before leaving his or her own country. He or she would then be liable to removal on arrival in the UK.[2]

1   Immigration Act 1971, s 3A, inserted by IAA 1999, s 1 makes 'further provision as to leave to enter'. See Immigration (Leave to Enter and Remain) Order 2000, SI 2000/1161, art 2; and 3.58 above.

2   Immigration Act 1971, Sch 2, para 9(1), (2).

17.13 It is not entirely clear why those seeking to enter should be treated as illegal entrants (unless it is facilitate the prosecution of those assisting them under section 25 or 25B of the Immigration Act 1971).[1] For if they are caught before they succeed in entering, they can be examined by immigration officers and, if necessary, refused entry and removed without being classified as illegal entrants.[2] Home Office policy is to do exactly that in most cases.[3] However, there are two differences which may follow from classifying someone seeking to enter as an illegal entrant:

(i)   the safeguards given to those seeking to enter lawfully do not apply; an illegal entrant is not entitled to a notice of refusal of entry within 24 hours of examination or further examination and a deemed leave to enter if this provision is not fulfilled;[4]

(ii)   under the regime before commencement of the appeals provisions of the Immigration Act 2014, an illegal entrant had no right of appeal on the merits under section 82 of the NIAA 2002 against a refusal of leave to enter,[5] although illegal entrants and their dependants may appeal against a decision to remove them, and unlike their predecessors, the appeal provisions of the 2002 Act do not limit the appellant to a contention that the decision was not in accordance with the law.[6] The appeal rights are not ordinarily exercisable in-country however.[7]

A person who arrives at immigration control without a valid passport (whether an asylum seeker or not) is not seeking to enter in breach of the immigration laws unless he or she intends to deceive the immigration officer, and so cannot be treated as an illegal entrant,[8] despite the enactment of the criminal offence of having no immigration document.[9]

[1] Those who assist the arrival of asylum seekers may be prosecuted even though their entry or proposed entry is not unlawful, but only if they do so for gain: Immigration Act 1971, s 25A, inserted by NIAA 2002, s 143, replacing s 25(1)(b) of the IA 1971, which was itself added by Asylum and Immigration Act 1996, s 5.

[2] Immigration Act 1971, Sch 2, para 8.

[3] 'People who seek leave to enter at arrivals in breach of a deportation order or by verbal deception or misrepresentation should normally be refused leave to enter at on-entry control and dealt with as a passenger refusal. The same applies to clandestines, including stowaways, who bring themselves voluntarily to the notice of the immigration officer at or before control. But a person detected after control should be dealt with as an illegal entrant (except at Cheriton): IDI, Ch 20, para 2.4.

[4] Immigration Act 1971, Sch 2, para 6(1), as amended by Immigration Act 1988. In *Hussain (Maqbool), Re* (4 May 1976, unreported), DC the Divisional Court said that the time limit in this para does not apply to an illegal entrant; but this was a case of someone who had entered illegally rather than someone seeking to enter.

[5] An illegal entrant who seeks leave to enter is unlikely to fulfil the eligibility criteria outlined in NIAA 2002, s 88(1)–(2). But there is a right of appeal against removal: see text and fnn 6, 7 below.

[6] Under NIAA 2002, s 82(2)(g)–(i); there is no restriction in Part V of the 2002 Act prohibiting illegal entrants from invoking any of the grounds of appeal set out in s 84 of the Act.

[7] NIAA 2002, s 92(1), (2). But the appeal rights of illegal entrants who raise EC Treaty, asylum or human rights grounds in support (s 84(1)(d), 84(1)(g)) are suspensive unless (in the case of asylum or human rights grounds) certified unfounded under s 94(2) as amended by s 27 Asylum and Immigration (Treatment of Claimants, etc) Act 2004: s 92(4); see CHAPTER 19 below. Suspensive asylum and human rights appeals were formerly provided by IAA 1999, ss 65, 69(5).

[8] *R v Naillie* [1993] AC 674, [1993] 2 All ER 782, [1993] Imm AR 462, HL.

[9] Asylum and Immigration (Treatment of Claimants) Act 2004, s 2; see **17.30** below.

17.14 As we have seen, an illegal entrant is a person (a) unlawfully entering or seeking to enter the UK in breach of a deportation order or of the immigration laws, or (b) entering or seeking to enter by means which include deception by another person. The 'immigration laws' means the Immigration Act 1971 and any law for purposes similar to this Act.[1] In order to sustain an allegation of illegal entry, it is therefore necessary to show that the person has entered in breach of some statutory provision. To enter clandestinely without leave is, of course, such a case, if entry is in breach of the requirement of section 3(1) of the IA 1971 that a person 'shall not enter unless given leave to do so in accordance with the Act'. Entry in breach of the immigration laws is a wider concept than entry in breach of section 3(1), and will include not only the offence of illegal entry under IA 1971, section 24(1)(a) but also (most commonly) entry by deception in breach of sections 24A and 26(1)(c) of the Act.[2] The use of the word 'unlawfully' in the definition does not appear to add anything, since it is difficult to envisage any entry in breach of the immigration laws which would be regarded as lawful. In *Ex p Bouzagou*,[3] which concerned a man who had entered the UK from the Republic of Ireland without knowing that he was entering in breach of the immigration law, the court held that the word 'unlawfully' did not import a requirement of mens rea (ie an awareness of illegality) into the definition. Thus it would appear that the only possible entry in breach of the immigration laws which is not unlawful is an involuntary act or one compelled by necessity,[4] as where an aircraft develops a fault and is forced to land or a boat is forced ashore by bad weather.

[1] Immigration Act 1971, s 33(1). See also s 61(2) of the UK Borders Act 2007 as amended defining 'the Immigration Acts'.

[2] For the criminal offences of illegal entry, deception etc, see CHAPTER 15 above.

[3] *R v Governor of Ashford Remand Centre, ex p Bouzagou* [1983] Imm AR 69, CA. See also *Ali (Ifzal) v Secretary of State for the Home Department* [1994] Imm AR 69. Normally 'unlawfully' means 'without lawful justification or excuse', and does not connote a mental element: see Archbold Criminal Pleading, Evidence and Practice (Sweet & Maxwell, 2005) para 17.44.

[4] See *R v Conway* [1989] QB 290, 88 Crim App Rep 159, CA; R v Martin (1989) 88 Cr App Rep 343, CA; *R v Abdul-Hussain* [1999] Crim LR 570, CA (hijacking an aircraft and bringing it to the UK); *R v Safi (Ali Ahmed)* [2004] 1 Cr App Rep 14, CA (Afghanistan hijacking case).

17.15 There are four kinds of possible illegal entry under the Immigration Act 1971:

- entry without leave;
- entry in breach of a deportation order;
- entry through the common travel area; and
- entry by deception, use of false documents and corruption.

Effectively, the first three are 'no leave' cases and in the fourth leave is granted but deception is involved. The entry without leave and subsequent overstay of crew members is dealt with at **17.54** below.[1]

[1] For the history of the powers of removal of illegal entrants see the fourth edition at 16.1–16.6.

NO LEAVE CASES

17.16 Entry to the UK without leave normally constitutes a breach of section 3(1)(a) of the Immigration Act 1971, which requires that, unless otherwise provided, a person who is not a British citizen shall not enter the UK unless given leave to enter in accordance with the Act. Such persons will be illegal entrants within the statutory definition (having entered the UK in breach of the immigration laws). However, the spectrum of persons who are illegal entrants on this basis varies greatly. At one end are clandestine entrants, who evade immigration control and knowingly enter without leave; at the other end are the entirely blameless victims of someone else's fraud or mistake. Clandestine entrants who enter without leave will include those who go through immigration control hidden in the back of container lorries,[1] slip through the airport terminal,[2] or land on a remote beach at night.[3] There are also those the circumstances of whose entry are unknown, but who cannot show that leave was granted,[4] or can only point to a leave which is forged.[5]

[1] See **17.11** fnn 3 and 5, above.

[2] See *Re Hassan* [1976] 2 All ER 123, DC.

[3] See *R v Governor of Brixton Prison, ex p Ahsan* [1969] 2 QB 222, [1969] 2 All ER 347, DC.

[4] Leave no longer has to be in writing in every case: Immigration (Leave to Enter and Remain) Order 2000, SI 2000/1161, art 8. But the burden of proof as to the date and manner of entry is on the entrant: see SI 2000/1161, art 11. See CHAPTER 3 above.

5   *R v Secretary of State for the Home Department, ex p Musawwir* [1989] Imm AR 297, QB.

17.17 Particular problems arise over mistakes or ignorance of the law. There are considerable numbers of people who do not need leave to enter, in view of their citizenship, the common travel area, EEA, diplomatic exemptions and so forth.[1] Because of the complexity of the law and the Immigration Rules, it is easy for both travellers and immigration officers to make mistakes. For example, people come from Ireland not knowing that their particular group needs leave to enter; others are wrongly allowed through immigration control by immigration officers who mistakenly think that they do not need leave. The law is harsh. They are all illegal entrants.[2] It was formerly thought that people who submitted to immigration control and were mistakenly passed through by the immigration service had been examined and were the beneficiaries of a deemed leave under the Immigration Act 1971, Schedule 2, paragraph 6.[3] But the case law makes it clear that such a deemed leave only arises where an immigration officer carries out an examination intending to give a limited leave or to refuse leave, but fails to record the decision within the appropriate time limits.[4] Thus persons who are wrongly assumed to be British citizens may later find themselves being treated as illegal entrants through no fault of their own.[5] Yet others become illegal entrants even though they have been examined and an open date stamp has been placed in their passport, indicating exemption from control.[6] Again the law is harsh, since here it is the immigration officer's mistake in allowing them entry without leave which founds the illegality.[7] These cases are to be contrasted with the case where the immigration officer's mistaken grant of leave is valid.[8]

1   The list of exemptions from leave is at **3.55** above. See *R v Secretary of State for the Home Department, ex p Wuan* [1989] Imm AR 501.
2   *R v Governor of Ashford Remand Centre, ex p Bouzagou* [1983] Imm AR 69, CA; *R v Secretary of State for the Home Department, ex p Mohan* [1989] Imm AR 436.
3   *R v Secretary of State for the Home Department, ex p Malik* (2 October 1987, unreported), QBD. See Chapter **3**, above.
4   *Secretary of State for the Home Department v Thirukumar* [1989] Imm AR 402, CA; *Rehal v Secretary of State for the Home Department* [1989] Imm AR 576, CA; *R v Secretary of State for the Home Department, ex p Kumar* [1990] Imm AR 265.
5   *R v Secretary of State for the Home Department, ex p Khaled (Abdul)* [1987] Imm AR 67; *Mokuolo v Secretary of State for the Home Department, Ogunbiyi v Secretary of State for the Home Department* [1989] Imm AR 51, CA.
6   *R v Secretary of State for the Home Department, ex p Bagga* [1990] Imm AR 413, CA. See **3.53** above.
7   In view of the more relaxed requirements for notice of leave under the IAA 1999, there is doubt whether these decisions remain relevant: see **3.89** above.
8   *R v Secretary of State for the Home Department, ex p Ram* [1979] 1 All ER 687, [1979] 1 WLR 148, DC. See **3.92** above.

17.18 The case of *Noor Nawal Khan*[1] illustrates the absurdities of this doctrine. At the time of his birth in Pakistan in 1971, Mr Khan was a citizen of the UK and colonies by descent. He became a British Dependent Territories citizen on the coming into force of the British Nationality Act 1981. On arrival in the UK in 1992, he presented his passport describing him (correctly) as a British Dependent Territories citizen, although he believed himself entitled to enter and depart from the UK freely by reason of his father's registration as a CUKC in 1965 at the British Sovereign Base in Cyprus. Initially granted temporary admission whilst his claim was investigated, he later received a letter from a chief immigration officer informing him that his 'British nationality had been resolved', that he was 'deemed to be a British citizen' and that he could apply for a British passport describing him as such. His subsequent application for registration as a British citizen, however, was rejected and the letter from the chief immigration officer was held to be incorrect, although he was told he could re-apply for registration later. When he applied for leave to remain as a working holidaymaker, the Home Office responded by informing him that he was an illegal entrant with no claim to remain and that he should 'now make arrangements to return to Pakistan'. Fortunately, on judicial review McCullough J held that the decision declaring Mr Khan to be an illegal entrant and telling him that he should 'now' leave the country was 'altogether excessive and out of proportion to the occasion'. Once it had been decided that he was not going to be allowed to remain to enable him to apply again for British citizenship, 'fairness demanded that he should have been invited to make representations to argue the contrary'.

[1]   *R v Secretary of State for the Home Department, ex p Khan (Noor Nawal)* (9 May 1997, unreported) (McCullough J).

Breach of deportation order

17.19 A deportation order is defined by section 5(1) of the Immigration Act 1971 as an order requiring a person to leave and prohibiting him or her from entering the UK (see CHAPTER 16) The section provides that a deportation order against a person invalidates any leave to enter or remain in the UK given before the order was made or while it is in force. What this means is that if someone subject to a deportation order still in force manages to obtain leave to enter, this will be invalidated by section 5(1). Questions of deception do not arise. The statutory invalidation of leave operates whether the deportee obtained it by deception or through the immigration officer's mistake.[1] The immigration authorities can make arrangements for the removal of deportees under the existing deportation order.[2] The only gain from removing them as illegal entrants is that sometimes the airline or shipping company can be made to pay their return fare, whereas in a deportation it is the British government which pays.[3]

[1]   *R v Secretary of State for the Home Department, ex p Yeboah* [1986] Imm AR 52.
[2]   Immigration Act 1971, Sch 3, para 1; on procedure see Immigration Rules, HC 395, para 388.
[3]   See **17.66** and **17.68** below for arrangements for removal of illegal entrants and deportees respectively.

17.20 Most returning deportees will be illegal entrants because they have no leave.[1] They would still be illegal entrants if the words 'in breach of a deportation order' were omitted from the definition of illegal entrants in section 33(1) of the Immigration Act 1971. But these words are essential for those who do not need leave to enter the UK, such as Irish citizens and deportees of other nationalities who return through Ireland, or EEA nationals exercising free movement rights.[2] The operation of the deportation order is unaffected by the leave-free travel provisions of the EEA or common travel area.[3] Deportees of other nationalities who return to the UK on a local journey from Ireland do not need leave to enter, but are illegal entrants because their return is in breach of the deportation order. Where someone has been deported from the Channel Islands or the Isle of Man the order has the same effect as if it was a UK deportation order,[4] and the person who tries to enter the UK in breach of it would be an illegal entrant.

1   Immigration Act 1971, s 5(1).
2   *See eg Shingara v Secretary of State for the Home Department* [1999] Imm AR 257, CA.
3   Immigration Act 1971, ss 1(3) and 9(4).
4   Immigration Act 1971, Sch 4, para 3(1).

Entry through the common travel area

17.21 Those who arrive in this country after a local journey[1] from Ireland, the Channel Islands or Isle of Man – all parts of the common travel area – do not normally require leave to enter[2] and so unless they have arrived in breach of a deportation order they will not usually be illegal entrants.[3] But there are a number of exceptions. Those arriving from the Channel Islands or the Isle of Man will be illegal entrants if:

- their presence there was unlawful;[4] or
- they have previously been refused entry to the UK and have not been given a later leave to enter or remain.[5]

1   For the definition of a local journey, see Immigration Act 1971, s 11(4).
2   IA 1971, s 1(3). Generally on the common travel area see CHAPTER 6 above.
3   By IA 1971, s 9(4) leave-free travel within the common travel area under s 1(3) does not affect the operation of a deportation order.
4   IA 1971, Sch 4, para 4.
5   IA 1971, s 9(4)(b).

17.22 For arrivals from Ireland the position is more complicated. A distinction has to be made between citizens of the Republic and other nationals who come via Ireland. Citizens of the Republic will only be illegal entrants if: (1) they are returning deportees; or (2) they return after being refused entry for national security reasons.[1] Other nationals who come via Ireland will be illegal entrants if they need leave to enter the UK under the Immigration (Control of Entry through Republic of Ireland) Order 1972[2] and enter without it.[3] Even if they are unaware that they ought to have obtained leave,[4] they can nevertheless be treated as illegal entrants in the following circumstances:[5]

(i)   they have previously been refused entry to the UK and have not been given later leave to enter or remain;[6]
(ii)   although arriving on an aircraft which began its flight in the Republic they entered the Republic in transit from another country and did not obtain leave to land;[7]
(iii) they are visa nationals who have no valid visa to enter the UK;[8]
(iv)   they entered the Republic unlawfully from a place outside the common travel area;[9]
(v)   they entered the Republic from the UK or Northern Ireland when they were illegal entrants or overstayers there;[10]
(vi)   directions have been given to exclude them from the UK on the ground that their exclusion is conducive to the public good.[11]

1   Immigration Act 1971, s 9(4)(a). Here, the EC law public policy derogation will apply: see CHAPTER 6 above.

2   SI 1972/1610 (as amended by SI 1979/730, SI 1982/1028, SI 1985/1854, SI 1987/2092, SI 2000/1776); see CHAPTER 5 above.

3   They 'enter' the UK as soon as they leave their ship or plane (unless they have been examined by an immigration officer on board, and immigration officers do not usually travel on board): see Immigration Act 1971, s 11(1) and (2). So unless they obtain leave before leaving Ireland, they will already have become illegal entrants by the time they find an immigration officer on arrival.

4   *R v Governor of Ashford Remand Centre, ex p Bouzagou* [1983] Imm AR 69, CA; *R v Secretary of State for the Home Department, ex p Mohan* [1989] Imm AR 436.

5   See further 5.30 above.

6   IA 1971, s 9(4)(b).

7   SI 1972/1610 as amended, art 3(1)(a).

8   SI 1972/1610 as amended, art 3(1)(b)(i).

9   SI 1972/1610 as amended, art 3(1)(b)(ii).

10 SI 1972/1610 as amended, art 3(1)(b)(iii). In *R v Secretary of State for the Home Department, ex p Wuan* [1989] Imm AR 501 a British Dependent Territories citizen from Hong Kong entered the UK when exempt from control as a member of the armed forces; he left for the Republic of Ireland after he ceased to be exempt; it was held that he was not excluded from the common travel area as an overstayer and had accordingly been given a deemed leave on his re-entry to the UK.

11 SI 1972/1610 as amended, art 3(1)(b)(iv).

DECEPTION, FALSE DOCUMENTS AND CORRUPTION

17.23 The amended definition of 'illegal entrant' in section 33 of the Immigration Act 1971 (**17.10** above) is incomplete and still does not provide a satisfactory basis for illegal entry by deception, except where the deception is by a third party. Instead we have to look to the criminal provisions of the Act in much the same way as did the House of Lords in *Khawaja*.[1] Entry by deception occurs where the entrant: (i) makes or causes to be made a false representation contrary to section 26(1)(c) of the Immigration Act 1971 and such deception is the effective means of entry;[2] (ii) enters the UK by means including deception, contrary to section 24A of the 1971 Act;[3] or (iii) enters or seeks to enter by means which include deception by another person.[4] The decision in *Khawaja*[5] established that leave to enter is obtained in breach of the Act if the effective means of obtaining it is the commission of the offence of making a false representation under section 26(1)(c) of the 1971 Act.[6] The court held that the entrant had no duty of candour,[7] and is not deemed to be aware of all the Immigration Rules and conditions for entry. They doubted whether a person who was personally innocent of any fraud could be removed as an illegal entrant by reference to section 26(1)(c).[8] This part of the judgment has been superseded by the extension of the definition of illegal entry to include entry by means of deception by a third party.[9] The creation of a new criminal offence of obtaining or seeking to obtain leave to enter by deception[10] provides a clear statutory foundation for illegal entry by deception.

1   *Khawaja v Secretary of State for the Home Department* [1984] AC 74, [1984] 1 All ER 765, HL.

2   For ingredients of offence see CHAPTER 15, above.

3   For ingredients of offence see CHAPTER 15, above.

4   See definition of illegal entrant, Immigration Act 1971, s 33(1)(b).

5   *Khawaja v Secretary of State for the Home Department* [1984] AC 74, [1984] 1 All ER 765, HL.

6   *Khawaja* above at 118–119, per Lord Bridge.

7   Imposed on immigrants in the 1979 case of *Zamir v Secretary of State for the Home Department* [1980] AC 930, [1980] 2 All ER 768, HL.

8 *Khawaja* above at 199, per Lord Bridge.
9 Immigration Act 1971, s 33(1) as amended by Asylum and Immigration Act 1996, Sch 2, para 4. This statutory creation put an end to 20 years' debate in the courts: see *Khan v Secretary of State for the Home Department* [1977] 3 All ER 538, [1977] 1 WLR 1466, CA; *Khawaja v Secretary of State for the Home Department* [1984] AC 74, [1984] 1 All ER 765, HL; *R v Immigration Officer, ex p Chan* [1992] Imm AR 233, CA; *Hamid v Secretary of State for the Home Department* [1993] Imm AR 216, CA; *R v Secretary of State for the Home Department, ex p Kuet* [1995] Imm AR 274, CA.
10 IA 1971, s 24A, inserted by Asylum and Immigration Act 1996, s 4 and amended by IAA 1999, s 28.

17.24 Deception in illegal entry cases involves representations made to the immigration officer at the port of entry and to an entry clearance officer at an overseas post.[1] Knowledge of falsehood is a key element. The deception may take a variety of forms. It may involve landing cards filled out on the plane, answers given to questions by an immigration officer, an entry clearance officer or medical inspector, as well as a whole host of representations which the courts have implied from the mere presentation of a passport, and representations by conduct.[2]

1 *R v Secretary of State for the Home Department, ex p Kwadwo Saffu-Mensah* [1991] Imm AR 43, QBD.
2 See *Akinde v Secretary of State for the Home Department* [1993] Imm AR 512, CA; *Al-Zahrany (Rasmish) v Secretary of State for the Home Department* [1995] Imm AR 510, CA; *R v Secretary of State for the Home Department, ex p Awan* [1996] Imm AR 354, QBD; *R v Secretary of State for the Home Department, ex p Kuteesa (Bruce Kikule)* [1997] Imm AR 194, QBD.

17.25 The fact that leave no longer lapses when the holder leaves the common travel area[1] means that, if leave was obtained by deception, the holder enters illegally each time he or she enters the UK using it. What of the situation where leave obtained by deception lapses and fresh leave is sought on entry? For example, a returning resident seeking entry after more than two years away presents a passport endorsed with a previous indefinite leave to enter; strictly, the representation of indefinite leave, and thus eligibility as a returning resident, is accurate, as leave is not vitiated or rendered non-existent by deception; but if the presenter of the passport knows that the previous leave was improperly obtained, the judges will infer an implied representation that the leave was a lawful one.[2] Offering a passport containing a student leave implies a representation that the holder had validly been granted leave as a student.[3]

1 Immigration (Leave to Enter and Remain) Order 2000, SI 2000/1161, art 13: see **3.3** above.
2 *R v Secretary of State for the Home Department, ex p Patel* [1986] Imm AR 515, CA; *R v Secretary of State for the Home Department, ex p Salim* [1990] Imm AR 316, QBD.
3 *Durojaiye v Secretary of State for the Home Department* [1991] Imm AR 307, CA.

17.26 Where the passport contains an entry clearance, a representation is implied: (i) that entry clearance was validly obtained; and (ii) that the person seeks entry for that purpose and no other.[1] The representation may be a silent one; although the duty of candour has gone, judicial enthusiasm for implying representations from the silent presentation of a passport has almost plugged the gap.[2] Each case will depend on its own facts, however, and an entrant who has reason to believe that a previous irregularity has been cured or pardoned will not be guilty of misrepresentation as to the nature of a previous leave.[3]

Where there has been no contact at all between the immigrant and the immigration officer or entry clearance officer, there is no representation of any kind.[4] In *Doldur*[5] (where between the grant of a settlement visa as a dependent son and entry the applicant had married) the Court of Appeal held (by a majority) that it was not an irresistible inference that he failed to reveal his marriage because he knew that to do so would affect his chances of entry. Rather, it was a reasonable inference that the applicant believed his marriage did not alter the fact that he entered as his father's dependant and would remain so until he found a job and could provide for his wife himself. The applicant had been asked no questions on arrival by the immigration officer and (in the words of Evans LJ) seeking to rely on his failure to volunteer information as a positive misrepresentation came very close to contending that he owed a duty of candour.[6] In *James* two adult twins who were mentally impaired were brought to the UK as visitors by their aunt, who subsequently died. The twins' admission that they had always wanted to live in the UK did not make them illegal entrants, because there was no evidence that this was the aunt's intention and they themselves had had no dealings with the immigration officer.[7]

1 *R v Secretary of State for the Home Department, ex p Kwadwo Saffu-Mensah* [1991] Imm AR 43, QBD (husband intending to join wife permanently if she would have him obtains entry clearance as visitor). See also *Al-Zahrany (Rasmish) v Secretary of State for the Home Department* [1995] Imm AR 510, CA; *R v Secretary of State for the Home Department, ex p Awan* [1996] Imm AR 354, QBD. Note that Immigration Act 1971, Sch 2, para 2A(2A), inserted by Asylum and Immigration (Treatment of Claimants) Act 2004, s 18 (in force 1 October 2004: SI 2004/2523), provides for examination of passengers with entry clearance for the express purpose of cancelling their leave if their purpose on entry is not that for which the entry clearance was issued.

2 See cases referred to at **17.23** above. Silent presentation of a passport showing an earlier leave to enter obtained by false representations amounts to a fresh false representation: *R v Secretary of State for the Home Department, ex p Patel* [1986] Imm AR 515, CA. Re-entry on the basis of leave to enter obtained by a false representation is a fresh false representation which carries forward from one trip to the next *ad infinitum*: see *Khatun (Layla)* [1993] Imm AR 616, IAT (false representation made in 1969 still effective in 1992).

3 *R v Secretary of State for the Home Department, ex p Addo* (1985) Times, 18 April, QBD, followed in *R v Secretary of State for the Home Department, ex p Okunbowa* (19 November 1985, unreported), QBD.

4 *R v Secretary of State for the Home Department, ex p Dordas* [1992] Imm AR 99, QBD (ill-treated domestic servant, who decided before she left Kuwait to run away in the UK if the opportunity arose, was not an illegal entrant where her entry clearance was obtained by her employer and at the port her passport was also presented by him).

5 *Doldur v Secretary of State for the Home Department* [1998] Imm AR 352. For a case on the other side of the line see *Jahangir v Secretary of State for the Home Department* (11 December 1996, unreported), CA.

6 See also *R v Secretary of State for the Home Department, ex p Wilson* [2001] EWHC 115 (Admin), in which visit leave was held not to have been obtained by deception, although an intention to remain with a settled spouse existed, because there were no questions on the length of the visit and the applicant was unaware of the visa requirement for family reunion.

7 *R v Secretary of State for the Home Department, ex p James* (CO 1955, 1956/92) (27 May 1994, unreported), QBD (Sedley J).

17.27 In *Choudhry v Metropolitan Police Comr*[1] the Divisional Court found that an application to the Home Office to remain on the ground of marriage carried with it an implied representation that it was a 'genuine' marriage and not a marriage of convenience entered into solely to persuade the Home Office to grant leave. The judgment was given on the basis that the implied representation was of general application and not confined to the particular defendant, with his particular knowledge of the Immigration Rules relating to husbands. Unfortunately, the court did not refer to older cases dealing with marriages of convenience.[2] A marriage solely for immigration and nationality purposes is nevertheless a valid one; it is for the Home Office to consider whether it also complies with the Rules.[3] The decision in *Choudhry* turns a perfectly accurate statement of the law into a deception. The fact of marriage is by no means conclusive of immigration and nationality status; such matters as the parties' intention to cohabit and their financial security are further criteria which may need to be satisfied.[4] To import into a statement that the parties are married further representations that the marriage has qualities required to give the spouse admission under the Rules is to turn application and investigation upside down. It is strongly arguable that the decision in *Choudhry* was wrong. Too great a readiness to find false representations risks bringing back the duty of candour via the back door. It is to be hoped that the issue may fall for reconsideration.

[1]   (24 November 1984, unreported), DC.
[2]   *Silver (otherwise Kraft) v Silver* [1955] 2 All ER 614, [1955] 1 WLR 728; *Vervaeke v Smith* [1983] 1 AC 145, [1982] 2 All ER 144, HL; *Puttick v A-G* [1980] Fam 1, [1979] 3 All ER 463.
[3]   Until the British Nationality Act 1981 came into force on 1 January 1983, Commonwealth citizens marrying patrial men automatically became patrial, no matter what the purpose of the marriage, provided merely that it was a valid one. If, however, fraud had been used, the courts might refuse to grant any relief: see *Puttick v A-G* above
[4]   The further criterion that the 'primary purpose' of the marriage should not be settlement was withdrawn from 5 June 1997 (one of the first acts of the new Labour government in honouring a manifesto commitment): see HC 26, amending Pt 8 of HC 395.

Effective deception

17.28 In *Khawaja* the House of Lords held that deception or fraud must be the effective, or one of the effective means, of obtaining leave to enter, so as to make the contravention of the Immigration Act 1971 and the obtaining of leave two inseparable elements in the single process of entry.[1] This was further explained in *Bugdaycay*,[2] where the House of Lords held that the question of whether a fraud was effective in obtaining entry could only be considered in the light of the application actually made and it was irrelevant that the person might have been admitted in some other capacity. In *Khawaja, Lord Bridge* thought that useful guidance as to what constituted effective means was given in the earlier case of *Jayakody*.[3] There the Court of Appeal held that the fraud must be decisive of the application, *ie* in all probability the leave would have been refused but for the deception. Thus a failure to reveal one of the purposes of an otherwise genuine visit, or to tell the immigration officer that a spouse was resident in the UK, might not be decisive of the grant or refusal of leave to enter. But the binding effect of *Jayakody* has been watered down by subsequent cases, which have moved the focus away from 'effective means' to mere 'materiality'. First, in *Durojaiye v Secretary of State for the Home Department*[4] Staughton LJ said that false answers to questions about a student's hours of attendance at college plainly were 'material in the sense it was likely to influence the decision'. This was followed by Laws J in *Ex p Ming*,[5] holding that a representation was material if, on revelation of the truth, 'at the very least further inquiries would have been made'. And in *Kaur (Sukhjinder) v Secretary of State for the Home Department*[6] (an appeal against refusal of leave to enter on the ground that material facts were not disclosed for the purpose of obtaining a visa) Ward LJ stated that the time had come 'to put the *Jayakody* test to rest' as being 'quite inconsistent' with *Bugdaycay*[7] and *Durojaiye*.[8] He agreed expressly with Staughton LJ's analysis in *Durojaiye* as being the 'appropriate test'. However, *Khawaja* is still binding authority, and, by bedding *Jayakody*, the Court in *Kaur* cannot have intended to substitute 'mere materiality' for 'effective means' as the proper test for establishing the causal connection between the deception practised and the leave to enter granted by the immigration officer. That would be too much of a watering down. What is clear, however, is that the wording of the section 24A offence, inserted into the IA 1971 in 1999,[9] endorses the view put forward in *Khawaja* that the deception employed need only have been one of the factors leading to the grant of leave to enter, an effective but not necessarily decisive one.

[1] *Khawaja v Secretary of State for the Home Department* [1984] AC 74 at 118E, per Lord Bridge.

[2] *Bugdaycay v Secretary of State for the Home Department* [1987] AC 514, where a visitor failed to disclose his intention of applying for asylum. He was held to be an illegal entrant despite the fact that he would not have been removable had he claimed asylum.

[3] *R v Secretary of State for the Home Department, ex p Jayakody* [1982] 1 All ER 461, [1982] 1 WLR 405, CA.

[4] [1991] Imm AR 307, CA.

[5] *R v Secretary of State for the Home Department, ex p Ming* [1994] Imm AR 216, Laws J See also *R v Secretary of State for the Home Department, ex p Castro* [1996] Imm AR 540 where Dyson J was satisfied that deception was the effective means of obtaining leave to enter, but thought it 'may' have been sufficient for the Secretary of State to show that deception was material in the sense of being likely to influence the decision.

[6] [1998] Imm AR 1, CA.

[7] [1987] 1 AC 514, see fn 2 above.

[8] [1991] Imm AR 307, CA.

[9] IAA 1999, s 28.

17.29 There is substantial case law on the existence and effect of deception.[1] In the past particular problems were created where the Immigration Rules allowed a switch in categories from visitor to student or dependent relative status.[2] It was not permissible to come in with leave in one category with a fixed intention of applying to vary to another.[3] Although it was acknowledged by authority that there was a difference between a wish and an intention,[4] the courts are prepared to draw the inference of deception where all the circumstances warrant it.[5]

[1] See, for example, *Olusanya (Olugbenga), Re* [1988] Imm AR 117, QBD (intending student gained entry as visitor); *R v Secretary of State for the Home Department, ex p Mahoney* [1992] Imm AR 275, QBD (visitor, always intended to study); *Tadimi v Secretary of State for the Home Department* [1993] Imm AR 90, CA (doing work inconsistent with student status); *R v Secretary of State for the Home Department, ex p Ahmed* [1993] Imm AR 242, QBD and *R v Secretary of State for the Home Department, ex p Miah* [1994] Imm AR 279, QBD (son pretending to be single when in fact married); *R v Secretary of State for the Home Department, ex p Zeenat Bibi* [1994] Imm AR 326, QBD (spouse posing as unmarried visitor). For instances where a deception was immaterial, see *R v Secretary of State for the Home Department, ex p Miah* [1989] Imm AR 559, CA; *R v Secretary of State for the Home Department, ex p Khan (Hiram)* [1990] Imm AR 327, CA.

[2] Immigration Rules HC 395, para 60, 298. The introduction of mandatory entry clearance for all categories of entry over six months will eventually mean the end of post-entry switching from visitor to settlement categories, and therefore the end of this line of cases.

[3] *Adesina v Secretary of State for the Home Department* [1988] Imm AR 442, CA; *Ex p Mahoney* above. Cf *R v Immigration Appeal Tribunal, ex p Coomasaru* [1983] 1 All ER 208,

[1982] Imm AR 77 (returning residents entering as visitors, fixed intention to settle qualifies them as returning residents rather than as illegal entrants). This scenario is much less likely in any event since the Immigration (Leave to Enter and Remain) Order 2000, SI 2000/1161, art 13.
4   See *Masood v Immigration Appeal Tribunal* [1992] Imm AR 69, per Glidewell LJ.
5   *R v Secretary of State for the Home Department, ex p Brakwah* [1989] Imm AR 366, QBD; *R v Secretary of State for the Home Department, ex p Nwanurue* [1992] Imm AR 39, QBD.

Invalid documents and third party deception

17.30 Although section 24A of the Immigration Act 1971 gives a firmer jurisprudential basis for illegal entry by deception, it only deals with deception by the person seeking to enter or remain, not deception by third parties. However, the amendment of the statutory definition of illegal entrant in section 33(1) in 1996[1] put to rest the question of third party deception, left open by the House of Lords in *Khawaja*,[2] and made it clear beyond doubt that the innocent proffering of false documents now makes the person proffering them an illegal entrant. The use of a false document, the falsity of which is unknown to the entrant, will now be dealt with as 'means which include deception by another'. But the person must have entered or be seeking to enter by means of the false documents; so where someone travels on forged documents but claims asylum at the immigration desk without seeking entry on the basis of the documents, the person is not an illegal entrant.[3] The need for a causal nexus between the offence and the entry makes it unlikely that the mere failure to produce a valid immigration document at a leave or asylum interview – although an offence under section 2 of the Asylum and Immigration (Treatment of Claimants etc) Act 2004 – could make the person an illegal entrant by entry in breach of the immigration laws.[4]

1   Asylum and Immigration Act 1996, Sch 2, para 4.
2   *Khawaja v Secretary of State for the Home Department* [1984] AC 74.
3   *R v Naillie* [1993] AC 674, [1993] 2 All ER 782, HL. However, intending immigrants discovered before entry in circumstances indicating an intention to enter illegally have been treated as illegal entrants for the purpose of convicting a facilitator in *R v Eyck, R v Hadakoglu* [2000] INLR 277.
4   For discussion of this offence see CHAPTER 15, above.

Breaking conditions of temporary admission

17.31 Where a person's examination is left unfinished for further inquiries to be made, he or she may be given temporary admission under paragraph 21 of Schedule 2 to the Immigration Act 1971. Under section 11 of the Act persons on temporary admission are not deemed to have 'entered' the UK unless they have 'otherwise entered'. Absconders and those in breach of conditions of temporary admission may be detained, refused leave and summarily removed,[1] but, according to the Court of Appeal in *Akhtar v Governor of Pentonville Prison*,[2] they may also be treated as illegal entrants either on the basis that they were seeking entry by deception or that by breaking conditions of temporary admission they have 'otherwise entered' the UK without obtaining leave to enter.[3] But not every breach of temporary admission will make a person an illegal entrant, or at least liable to removal, unless, according to Evans LJ, the breach is sufficiently serious and deliberate to amount to an entry or an attempt to enter without leave.[4] This decision seems an unnecessary complication, which stretches the already fictional concept of 'entry' created by section 11. There are already adequate ways of dealing with those in breach of the conditions of their temporary admission (see **CHAPTER 18**, below), without the introduction of this kind of legal sophistry. In any event the test suggested by Evans LJ may well be unworkable, because the subjective intention of the absconder, almost certainly unaware of the conceptual subtleties imposed on us by section 11, will be an intention to remain, not to enter.

[1] Immigration Act 1971, Sch 2, paras 6, 8 and 21(1) and (4). For further discussion of temporary admission, see **3.95–3.96**, above.

[2] *Akhtar v Governor of Pentonville Prison* [1993] Imm AR 424, CA; see also *R v Secretary of State for the Home Department, ex p Khan (Taj Mohammed)* [1985] Imm AR 104, CA. See **17.36** below.

[3] See *Akhtar* above at 431, per Sir Thomas Bingham MR.

[4] *Akhtar* above at 431, per Evans LJ. We suggest that only absconding, and not breach of employment restrictions or of the draconian residence conditions which are envisaged in Immigration Act 1971, Sch 2, para 21(2B), would constitute illegal entry, since the latter does not indicate an intention to 'enter'. Escape from a removal centre would probably constitute illegal entry.

Leave to enter obtained by corruption or forgery

17.32 A forged leave to enter is clearly no leave at all.[1] A leave to enter obtained in knowing reliance on an entry clearance or a work permit itself obtained by corruption would be a leave obtained by fraud (because the proffering of such a permit or endorsement carries a representation that it was duly obtained).[2] But if the entrant was unaware of the corruption and was not party to any false or corrupt procurement of leave to enter he or she would be able to rely on such leave if it was issued by someone who had the authority to do so, particularly since an immigrant is not to be penalised for the errors or dishonesty of public officials.[3] If an innocent immigrant presents an entry clearance or work permit obtained by corruption to which he or she has not been a party, it is hard to see why such document, issued by a person with authority to do so, and who is the ostensible agent or alter ego of the Secretary of State, cannot be relied on, since neither it nor any leave obtained in reliance on it has been obtained by deception on anyone's part – or it could be said that the endorsement of the passport by the corrupt official constitutes third-party deception just as forgery of a visa does. On either interpretation of the situation the burden of proof is on the Secretary of State and it is a heavy burden.[4] It may also be one of these rare cases where the Secretary of State will need to call evidence at an appeal hearing.

[1] *R v Secretary of State for the Home Department, ex p Musawwir* [1989] Imm AR 297.

[2] See **17.26** above.

[3] *R v Secretary of State for the Home Department, ex p Kuet* [1995] 2 All ER 891 (*sub nom Ku*), [1995] Imm AR 274, CA, observations of Sir Thomas Bingham MR.

[4] *Khawaja v Secretary of State for the Home Department* [1984] AC 74, [1984] 1 All ER 765, HL; In *Re B (children) (sexual abuse: standard of proof)* [2008] UKHL 35, [2009] AC 11. See further **17.51** below.

Persons claiming to be British citizens

17.33 Persons who are British citizens cannot be removed as illegal entrants, even if they entered under some other nationality.[1] The difficulty, however, may lie in proving the entitlement. Unusually for illegal entry cases, the burden of proof rests on the immigrant concerned.[2] Section 3(9) of the Immigration Act 1971 requires proof of the right of abode by means either of a UK passport describing the holder as a British citizen (or a CUKC with the right of abode), or a certificate of entitlement certifying such right of abode. This will satisfy the initial burden and it will then be for the Home Office to demonstrate that the documents were improperly obtained or that the holder was not entitled to them.[3] In *Obi*[4] the burden of proof was everything (since it was accepted that if it lay on the Secretary of State it was not one he could discharge). The applicant had produced a UK passport describing him as a British citizen. The Secretary of State accepted that the passport described Mr Obi as a British citizen, but contended that until the applicant proved that he was Mr Obi, the passport was not one describing 'him' as a British citizen. The physical possession of a UK passport alone would not satisfy the section 3(9) test (for example, if it was believed to be stolen or forged the burden could not be discharged until the bearer could show him- or herself to be the person described in the passport). But here it was undisputed both that the person described in the passport as a British citizen had applied for it in Liverpool and that that person was the applicant (the photograph being indisputably his). Sedley J held that no further burden lay on the applicant. Where such an allegation is made in the course of illegal entry proceedings, the case is one within *Khawaja* principles. It should be noted that production of a birth certificate in the name of the applicant[5] or an identity document is not proof of British citizenship so as to shift the burden of proof on to the Secretary of State.[6] For disputed citizenship and deprivation of citizenship obtained by fraud see CHAPTER 2, above.

[1]   Immigration Act 1971, s 1(1).
[2]   Immigration Act 1971, s 3(8); see *Re Bamgbose* [1990] Imm AR 135, CA where a birth certificate did not discharge the burden as there was a dispute as to whether it truly related to the applicant. In *Mokuolo v Secretary of State for the Home Department* [1989] Imm AR 51, CA a statement as to birth in the UK in a Nigerian passport was similarly not sufficient.
[3]   A passport or certificate of entitlement are the means specified in the Immigration Act 1971 for proving citizenship: see s 3(9); Sch 2, para 3.
[4]   *R v Secretary of State for the Home Department, ex p Obi* [1997] Imm AR 420 QBD.
[5]   *Re Bamgbose* [1990] Imm AR 135, CA.
[6]   *Minta v Secretary of State for the Home Department* [1992] Imm AR 380, CA (British visitors passport (BVP), now discontinued).

Nationals of EEA and Association Agreement States

17.34 Similar considerations as operate in relation to British citizens apply to EEA nationals. Under the Citizens' Directive,[1] to EU citizens, and under the Immigration (European Economic Area) Regulations 2006,[2] EEA nationals must be admitted as of right to the UK if, on arrival, they produce a valid national identity card or passport issued by another EEA state,[3] unless there are public policy reasons for their exclusion.[4] Community rights, as we have seen, flow from EC law and do not need any grant of leave under the Immigration Act 1971.[5] Entry in breach of the immigration laws will be a rare and exceptional thing, but can occur if someone enters clandestinely without any intention of exercising free movement rights, uses a false identity card or passport, or enters in breach of a deportation order. The Court of Appeal held in *Shingara*[6] that it occurred when an EEA national entered after being excluded pursuant to a validly imposed exclusion order which complied with Council Directive (EEC) 64/221. Where an EEA national has entered illegally, removal can only take place in accordance with the public policy provisions of the Citizens' Directive,[7] and must not be discriminatory or disproportionate to the limited rights of Member States to impose penalties for infringements of their national procedures.[8]

[1]   Directive 2004/38/EC, art 6. Initial entry is for a period of up to three months without any conditions or formalities.
[2]   SI 2006/1003, reg 13.
[3]   SI 2006/1003, reg 11.
[4]   SI 2006/1003, reg 21.
[5]   *R v Pieck* [1981] QB 571; Immigration Act 1988, s 7(1); see CHAPTER 6 above.
[6]   *Shingara v Secretary of State for the Home Department* [1999] Imm AR 257, CA.
[7]   Directive 2004/38/EC, Chapter VI, as transposed into domestic law by the Immigration (European Economic Area) Regulations 2006, SI 2006/1003, Part 4.
[8]   *EC Commission v Belgium* [1990] 2 CMLR 492, ECJ; *Re Royer* [1976] 2 CMLR 619, ECJ; *Re Watson and Belmann* [1976] 2 CMLR 552, ECJ.

Refugees

17.35 Illegal entrants who are refugees cannot be removed to a country where they have a well-founded fear of persecution,[1] unless they are excluded from the protection of the Refugee Convention consequent to the commission of a particularly serious crime and constitute a danger to the community of the UK,[2] and even then they cannot be removed if substantial grounds exist for believing that they face a real risk of treatment contrary to Article 3 ECHR: see CHAPTER 7, above.

[1]   See CHAPTER 12 above; Refugee Convention, art 33.
[2]   NIAA 2002, s 72; CHAPTER 12, above. Former refugees may be removed: see **17.52** below.

The decision to remove as an illegal entrant

17.36 Although the immigration officer is the official responsible under statute for the decision that a person is to be treated as an illegal entrant and removed,[1] in practice the distinction between immigration officers and other Home Office immigration case workers is often blurred and an initial decision by immigration officers will be referred to a non-immigration officer team, especially where there needs to be a decision whether or not to grant leave to remain, a decision which is for the Secretary of State for the Home Department to take under section 4(1) of the Immigration Act 1971. The fact that a person has entered illegally does not oblige the Secretary of State to proceed to summary removal, as there is always a discretion to allow the person to stay.[2]

[1]   Immigration Act 1971, Sch 2, para 9. Modifications to Sch 2 made by the Immigration (Entry Otherwise than by Sea or Air) Order 2002, SI 2002/1832 give the same power to the Secretary of State when the illegal entrant arrives from Ireland.
[2]   See *Afunyah v Secretary of State for the Home Department* [1998] Imm AR 201. Contrast *R v Secretary of State for the Home Department, ex p Urmaza* [1996] COD 479 (seaman

deserter was illegal entrant and it was not open to Secretary of State not to treat him as one). See further, on the need for an immigration official to exercise discretion whether or not to treat a person who is an illegal entrant as such, *R v Secretary of State for the Home Department, ex p Uluyol and Cakmak* [2001] INLR 194. The Home Office policy on when to treat port cases as illegal entrants is set out in IDI, Ch 20, para 2.4.

17.37 Once it is established that the person is an illegal entrant and that the immigration officer or Secretary of State is going to treat the person as such, the practice prior to the commencement of the Immigration Act 2014 version of section 10, IAA 1999 was to serve an IS 151A notice. There is no statutory requirement to do so, since it is not a decision to give or refuse leave, nor a notice of an immigration decision,[1] since it is not a decision to remove.[2] The service of such notice is significant in its own right, however, in that it dates the 'commencement of enforcement action' for the purposes of rules, policies and concessions based on long residence, marriage or other ties which the person may seek to rely on to argue that he or she should not be removed.[3]

[1] Ie, one of the decisions listed in the NIAA 2002, s 82(2).
[2] In practice the IS 151A notice is now generally served together with the IS 151A part 2: See Enforcement Instructions and Guidance, ch 50. The notice of decision to remove gives rise to appeal rights and so attracts the provisions of the Notices Regulations: see Immigration (Notices) Regulations 2003, SI 2003/658, reg 4. See also the revoked marriage policy (DP/3/96) and revoked policies on children (DP/4/95 and DP 5/96) described in previous editions.
[3] See **11.61** above for the policies relating to marriage; see CHAPTER **11** for those relating to children, and **17.58** below for the long-residence rule.

Identifying victims of trafficking

17.38 The Enforcement Instructions and Guidance (EIG)[1] contain detailed guidance on identifying victims of trafficking, many of whom will have been illegal entrants. Trafficking is defined in the Palermo Protocol which is one of two Protocols under the UN Convention against Transnational Organised Crime (UNTOC). The Palermo Protocol aims to prevent, suppress and punish trafficking in persons, especially women and children, and was signed by the UK on 14 December 2000 and ratified on 9 February 2006. One of its main aims is to protect and assist the victims of such trafficking, with full respect for their human rights.[2] It was the first international instrument to define and address the trafficking problem. It has since been supplemented by the Council of Europe Convention on Action against Trafficking in Human Beings, adopted on 3 May 2005. The Guidance deals with means by which UKBA (now known as UK Immigration and Visas) officers are to identify victims of trafficking, sets out the procedures to be followed and the circumstances where, instead of removal, renewable residence permits are to be issued to victims if the competent authority believes their stay to be necessary owing to their personal situation or for the purpose of their co-operation with the competent authorities in investigation or criminal proceedings.[3] These matters are more fully detailed in CHAPTER **13**, above.

[1] EIG, ch 9.
[2] EIG, ch 9, para 9.1.
[3] European Convention on Action Against Trafficking in Human Beings, art 14.2.

Later leave to enter or remain

17.39 Prior to the amendment of section 10 of the IAA 1999 by the Immigration Act 2014, the power of removal only arose under paragraph 9 of Schedule 2 to the Immigration Act 1971 where the illegal entrant has not been given 'leave to enter or remain':[1]

'(1)   Where an illegal entrant is not given leave to enter or remain in the United Kingdom, an immigration officer may give any such directions in respect of him as in a case within paragraph 8 above as are authorised by paragraph 8(1);

(2)   any leave to enter the United Kingdom which is obtained by deception shall be disregarded for the purposes of this paragraph.'

This reflects the discretion of the immigration officer or Secretary of State to decide whether or not to allow an illegal entrant to remain in the UK. Paragraph 9(2) was added to resolve the difficulty caused by the decision in *Khawaja*[2] to the effect that leave obtained by deception remained valid.[3] However, leave granted on a completely different basis (eg as a refugee) in ignorance of initial illegal entry (as, say, a visitor) cannot be disregarded, and would prevent removal, since the initial deception played no role in the grant of the new leave. The paragraph does not, however, cover the position of those who entered lawfully, but who subsequently obtained leave to remain by deception. Persons in this category who have left the UK and re-entered are clearly illegal entrants on re-entry with their original leave. Those who have obtained leave to remain by deception and have not left the country since are not illegal entrants, but may be summarily removed under section 10 of the IAA 1999.[4]

[1]   Immigration Act 1971, Sch 2, para 9(1), as amended by Asylum and Immigration Act 1996, Sch 2, para 6.
[2]   *Khawaja v Secretary of State for the Home Department* [1984] AC 74, HL.
[3]   The section gives statutory effect to the Court of Appeal decision in *R v Secretary of State for the Home Department, ex p Lapinid* [1984] 3 All ER 257, [1984] 1 WLR 1269, that Sch 2 para 9 to the Immigration Act 1971 must exclude leave obtained by deception, or any extension of it. Following *Azam v Secretary of State for the Home Department* [1974] AC 18, HL, an extension of leave granted by the Home Office prevented removal under para 9 even if based on the initial deception – a construction now excluded by para 9(2).
[4]   See **17.51** below. Prior to the 1999 Act such persons had to be deported on 'conducive to the public good' grounds (Immigration Act 1971, s 3(5)(b), as originally enacted).

17.40 Section 73 of the NIAA 2002 provides for the removal of the family members of illegal entrants.[1] Previously, the UK-born children of illegal entrants could not be removed, although young children would normally be taken by their departing parent at public expense. But it was up to the family whether they were taken or left in the care of friends or family in the UK, and they were not removable.[2] Section 73 was to be repealed by the Immigration Act 2014 at a date to be fixed, presumably at the same time that the new section 10 of IAA 1999 was to be commenced.[3]

[1]   Inserting a new para 10A into Sch 2 to the Immigration Act 1971.
[2]   Children born in the UK do not need leave to remain, so long as they do not leave the country, but they need leave to return: HC 395, para 304; see **11.81** above.
[3]   IA 2014, Sch 9, para 7 repealing s 73(2)–(4) of the NIAA 2002.

OVERSTAYERS, BREACHERS OF CONDITIONS OF STAY AND OTHERS

17.41 As discussed earlier in this Chapter, section 1 of the Immigration Act 2014 entirely replaces section 10 of the Immigration and Asylum Act 1999, along with all of the later amendments to section 10. The new version of section 10 makes no distinction between overstayers, breachers of conditions of stay and others, so this part of the chapter is relevant principally to removals under the regime before commencement of section 1 of the IA 2014.

From 2 October 2000 the following categories of individual who were formerly subject to deportation action became subject to administrative removal procedures identical to those which apply to illegal entrants and those refused leave to enter:

- persons overstaying their limited leave;
- persons breaching a condition of their limited leave;
- those whose continued stay was obtained by deception; and
- family members of any of the above.[1]

Of these, only overstayers and those in breach who applied before 2 October 2000 for leave to remain in accordance with a specially constituted regularisation scheme were excluded from these procedures.[2] Those who qualified under the scheme, together with their dependants, remain subject to pre-existing arrangements.[3] The 2002 Act added two further categories of persons who may be administratively removed:

- those unsuccessfully using deception in seeking leave to remain;[4]
- persons ceasing to be refugees, whose indefinite leave to remain has been revoked.[5]

Under the removal provisions for the categories listed above, the person to be removed will be given written notice of the decision,[6] following which the immigration officer may authorise detention or make an order restricting residence, employment or occupation, or imposing reporting conditions pending removal.[7] Section 48 of the Immigration, Asylum and Nationality Act 2006 (IAN 2006) amends section 10(8) of the IAA 1999, so that notification of a decision to remove in accordance with that section invalidates any leave to enter or remain in the UK which was previously given to the person. Prior to this amendment, leave was invalidated only at the point at which removal directions were given under section 10. Invalidation of the person's leave has the effect of stopping access to any benefits, financial or otherwise, which may have been conditional on the leave.

---

[1] IAA 1999, s 10(1); HC 395, para 395B as amended by Cm 4851. The first two categories were formerly liable to deportation under old s 3(5)(a) of the Immigration Act 1971, the third under s 3(5)(aa) and the last under s 3(5)(c).

[2] IAA 1999, s 10(2). The regularisation scheme is set out in s 9 of the IAA 1999. It closed on 2 October 2000. The Home Office said it had completed the exercise of processing all applications in August 2003. By November 2002 (the latest figure for which statistics are available), 2,954 applications under the scheme had been granted and 425 refused (WA 28.11.02, col 424W).

[3] Ie, they are subject to deportation action under former Immigration Act 1971, s 3(5)(a): IAA 1999, s 10(2), NIAA 2002 (Commencement No 4) Order 2003, SI 2003/754, Sch 2, para 6(2).

[4] IAA 1999 s 10(1)(b) as amended by NIAA 2002, s 74, from 10 February 2003 (SI 2003/1).

[5] IAA 1999 s 10(1)(ba), inserted by NIAA 2002, s 76(7), from 10 February 2003: SI 2003/1.

[6] HC 395, para 395E inserted by Cm 4851.

7   HC 395, para 395F as inserted. See also Home Office Operational Guidance Notes Ch 11, Administrative removal procedures.

17.42 In addition to those who were subject to administrative removal under the pre Immigration Act 2014 version of section 10 of the IAA 1999, there was an additional category who could be removed under section 47 of the Immigration, Asylum and Nationality Act 2006 (IANA 2006) as amended by the Crime and Courts Act 2013 (CCA 2013).[1] These were those who had their leave extended under sections 3C and 3D of the Immigration Act 1971 (as amended but prior to the commencement of paragraph 21 of Schedule 9 of the Immigration Act 2014). Section 3C extends leave where an application for further leave is made during the currency of the original leave but not decided before that leave expires. The section extends leave during any period when: (i) the application for variation is neither decided nor withdrawn; (ii) an in-country and in-time appeal under section 82 of the 2002 Act may be brought; (iii) a section 82 appeal is pending. Section 3D applies where a person's leave to enter or remain in the UK has either been varied (so he or she has no further right to remain) or is revoked. The section extends the person's leave during the period when an appeal under section 82(1) of the 2002 Act against the variation or revocation 'could be brought' or when such an appeal 'is pending'.[2] The original version of section 47 of the IANA 2006, which came into force on 1 April 2008, led to considerable litigation in the immigration tribunal and higher courts. Ultimately section 47 was interpreted as being incapable of being used to inform an immigrant of a removal decision in a notice which also contained a decision refusing to vary his leave to remain, rendering a very significant number of decisions by the Secretary of State unlawful, and it was held that there was no obligation to make a removal decision at the same time as a refusal to vary leave decision.[3] On a pragmatic basis, this led the tribunal to 'split' decisions under appeal, allowing appeals against section 47 decisions as being not in accordance with the law but going on substantively to determine any other grounds of appeal.[4] The procedural issue was dealt with by an amendment to section 47 by the Crime and Courts Act 2013 before section 47 of the IANA 2006 along with section 10 of the IAA 1999 were repealed and entirely replaced by a new unified removal power by section 1 of the Immigration Act 2014 as described earlier.

1   CCA 2013, s 51, commenced 8 May 2013.
2   See respectively Immigration Act 1971, s 3D(2)(a) and (b). Section 104 of the 2002 Act defines what is included by the term 'pending appeal'. It starts when the appeal is instituted and finishes when it is finally determined, withdrawn or abandoned.
3   *Ahmadi (Javad) v Secretary of State for the Home Department* [2013] EWCA Civ 512, [2013] 4 All ER 442; *Patel v Secretary of State for the Home Department* [2013] UKSC 72, [2014] AC 651. See further below.
4   *Adamally (Section 47 Removal Decisions: Tribunal Procedures)* [2012] UKUT 414 (IAC), approved by the Court of Appeal in *Rahman (Md Mahamudur) v Secretary of State for the Home Department* [2014] EWCA Civ 11.

Exemption from administrative removal

17.43 Since administrative removal powers only apply to those who have had leave to enter the UK, British citizens and those with the right of abode, EEA nationals and their dependants, and persons exempt from control under section 8 of the Immigration Act 1971 would normally be exempt from administrative removal, since none of them needs leave to enter. However, the EEA Regulations 2006 make provision for removal of EEA citizens who are to be expelled or excluded under the public policy provisions of the Regulations[1] or because they have entered or sought to stay by reason of fraud or a marriage of convenience[2] by using the mechanisms of removal under domestic law.[3] Additionally, Commonwealth and Irish citizens who are exempt from deportation because they were ordinarily resident in the UK on 1 January 1973 and have been ordinarily resident for the five years immediately preceding the decision,[4] are also exempt from removal under section 10 of the IAA 1999.[5]

[1] Immigration (European Economic Area) Regulations 2006, SI 2006/1003, regs 19–21.
[2] Directive 2004/38/EC, art 35 and SI 2006/1003, reg 2(1) – definitions of 'civil partner' and 'spouse': see further *TC (Kenya) v Secretary of State for the Home department* [2008] EWCA Civ 543.
[3] SI 2006/1003, regs 22–24.
[4] For exemption from deportation see **16.5** ff; for ordinary residence in this context see **16.9** above.
[5] IAA 1999, s 10(10), applying Immigration Act 1971, s 7(1)(b) as substituted by NIAA 2002, s 75, from 10 February 2003: SI 2003/1.

Overstaying and breach of conditions

17.44 Leave to enter the UK may be given for a limited period, and may be subject to a condition restricting employment or occupation, studies, precluding recourse to public funds in maintenance or accommodation, requiring registration with the police, reporting to an immigration officer or the Secretary of State; or being subject to a condition about residence.[1] Before the enactment of section 1 of the Immigration Act 2014 and the introduction of the new unified removal power, failing to observe any of these conditions or remaining beyond the time limited by the leave made a person liable to removal under section 10 of the IAA 1999. Thereafter, there needed to be a decision to remove, which involved the exercise of a discretion; see **17.55** below. The burden of proving overstaying or breach of conditions is on the Home Office. The Secretary of State must establish the facts which give rise to the power to remove, although reasonable suspicion is enough to justify detention. There are, however, one or two areas of difficulty. What are the ingredients of overstaying and breach of conditions which need to be proved in order to justify removal under section 10 of the 1999 Act?

[1] Immigration Act 1971, s 3(1)(c), as amended by the UK Borders Act 2007, s 16 and Borders, Citizenship and Immigration Act 2009, s 50.

17.45 The words in the pre-Immigration Act 2014 section 10(1)(a) of the IAA 1999 referring to persons 'having only a limited leave to remain' suggest the existence of a current leave either at the time of the breach or of the decision to remove, but this would make the provision inoperative as far as overstaying is concerned. The words are confusing, and in the context of overstaying the established view is that they need to be read as 'having had' leave.[1] To establish overstaying, the date of the expiry of leave will clearly need to be proved. Normally this can be done by looking at the passport, but where the passport is not available, or where leave was granted by other means, such as orally or by Email, no assumption may be made as to the date and duration of any leave granted. While the Home Office must prove overstaying as a precedent fact to the exercise of the power to remove, the provisions of the Immigration (Leave to Enter and Remain) Order 2000[2] impose a burden on the recipient of an oral leave, or a leave granted through a responsible third party, to establish the manner and date of his or her entry into the UK. The date of expiry of leave is not conclusive on the issue of overstaying, since if a valid in-time application for a variation was made prior to the expiry of limited leave, that leave is extended by statute while the decision on the variation application is pending and, if the decision is negative, while an in-time appeal could be brought and while any appeal is pending.[3]

1 See *Suthendran v Immigration Appeal Tribunal* [1977] AC 359, [1977] Imm AR 44, HL where this argument failed in relation to the similar construction of appeal rights under s 14 of the Immigration Act 1971. See further *Sabbagh* [1986] Imm AR 244.
2 SI 2000/1161, art 11.
3 Immigration Act 1971, s 3C, as substituted by the NIAA 2002, s 118 from 1 April 2003 (Nationality, Immigration and Asylum Act 2002 (Commencement No 4) Order 2003, SI 2003/754), replacing s 3 and Sch 4, para 17(1) IAA 1999. Transitional provisions in SI 2003/754, art 3, Sch 2, para 2 provide that the terms of the amended s 3C shall apply to all decisions made on or after 1 April 2003 whenever the application to vary was submitted. Statutory leave lapses if the applicant or appellant leaves the UK: Immigration Act 1971, s 3C(3) as amended. Note that the Immigration Act 2014 limits the extension of leave under s 3C, IA 1971 to applications for administrative review: see para 21 to Sch 9, yet to be commenced at the time of writing.

17.46 An issue which arose in the earlier case law on deportation was whether past overstaying or breach of conditions justifies removal. Past breaches of conditions were held to found liability for deportation in *Sabir*,[1] but different considerations may arise now that the response is summary removal in respect of which there is generally no suspensive merits appeal.[2] The use of the present tense in the reference to not observing a condition of leave or remaining beyond the time limited suggests that only current overstaying and breach of conditions founds liability to removal, not an historical breach, so that someone who has been granted further leave to remain after overstaying cannot be removed. In our view this is the only sensible construction; it is inconceivable that the grant of a fresh leave after overstaying could leave a residual liability to summary removal under the pre Immigration Act 2014 section 10 of the IAA 1999 because of a past overstay or breach of conditions. It would be different if there were further overstaying or breaches. If a fresh leave was granted in ignorance of past overstay or breach, liability for summary removal would in any event result, if it were shown that the failure to refer to the past breaches constituted deception. If no deception was employed to obtain the fresh leave, and the past breaches were sufficiently severe to warrant enforcement action, we suggest the right course would be to make a decision to deport under section 3(5)(a) of the Immigration Act 1971 (deportation conducive to the public good). This would at least give rise to an appeal on the merits.

1 *Sabir* [1993] Imm AR 477. The Tribunal failed in that case to address the question as to whether liability to removal for breach of conditions continues once fresh leave is granted, which is not subject to the relevant condition.
2 For appeal against removal see CHAPTER 19, below.

17.47 If there is no extant leave, no conditions attach to it, so there can be no liability to removal for breach of conditions where the alleged breach occurs after leave expires. But leave extended under section 3C of the Immigration Act 1971 will be subject to the same conditions as the original leave. Thus, if a person who had leave with a condition prohibiting employment, works while an appeal against refusal of an extension is pending, he or she becomes liable to removal for breach of conditions under the pre Immigration Act 2014 section 10 of the IAA 1999.[1] But section 3C of the Immigration Act 1971 has been amended so that a leave is only extended during an appeal period if the person has a right to an in-country appeal.[2]

[1] Statutory leave pending appeal under IAA 1999, Sch 4, para 17(1) (repealed by NIAA 2002, Sch 9 with effect from 1 April 2003) made this explicit, but the NIAA 2002 provisions are no less clear in intention and effect.

[2] IAN 2006, s 11, which came into force on 31 August 2006. Note that the Immigration Act 2014 limits the extension of leave under s 3C, IA 1971 to applications for administrative review: see para 21 to Sch 9, yet to be commenced at the time of writing.

17.48 What happens if someone overstays or breaches conditions and then becomes exempt from immigration control under section 8(1) of the Immigration Act 1971? Cases under the old law established that exemption simply removed the person from control for the period of the exemption, so that liability to removal arising before the exemption continued to exist after the exemption ended.[1] But if leave was still current on termination of the exemption there was no continuing liability to enforcement action.[2] The position is not clear now that statutory leave of 90 days operates automatically at the end of the exemption if the person requires leave and does not have it.[3] One view is that removal could be enforced in this situation, since removal directions under section 10 of the IAA 1999 invalidate any leave granted before they were made, or while they are in force.[4] Another view is that the pre-1999 Act position still holds. Alternatively, since the 90-day leave is statutory, it is unaffected by what happened pre-exemption.

[1] See *Sabbagh* [1986] Imm AR 244; *Noorhu* [1984] Imm AR 190, IAT.
[2] *Ashiwaju* [1994] Imm AR 233, IAT.
[3] Immigration Act 1971, s 8A(2), inserted by IAA 1999, s 7.
[4] IAA 1999, s 10(8).

17.49 In cases of breach of conditions, the Home Office must show that the conditions are ones which may be lawfully imposed – there are only six conditions which may be lawfully imposed on a grant of leave: restrictions on employment or occupation; restriction on studies; no recourse to public funds; registration with police; reporting to an immigration officer or the Secretary of State; or being subject to a condition about residence[1] – and that they have been properly notified.[2] This is particularly important with visit leave, which may be granted orally, and normally will be subject to conditions restricting working and precluding recourse to public funds. However, a person does not need to be knowingly an overstayer or in breach of conditions to be liable to removal (knowledge founds liability to criminal prosecution),[3] although in considering whether removal is justified by reference to the factors set out in the Immigration Rules, lack of knowledge will be highly relevant.[4]

[1] Immigration Act 1971, s 3(1)(c), as amended by the UK Borders Act 2007, s 16 and Borders, Citizenship and Immigration Act 2009, s 50. Before this latter amendment, failure by a student to maintain 15 hours a week attendance on a course would not place him or her in breach of a condition attached to the leave to enter, so as to render that person liable to removal under section 10 of the IAA 1999, although it could give rise to curtailment of student leave under

Immigration Act 1971, s 3(3)(a), or refusal of an extension (HC 395 para 323): *R (on the application of Zhou) v Secretary of State for the Home Department* [2003] EWCA Civ 51, [2003] 12 LS Gaz R 30.

2   IA 1971, s 4(1). Conditions are an integral part of leave and must be notified in writing along with the leave, unless the leave is visit leave granted orally by Immigration (Leave to Enter and Remain) Order 2000, SI 2000/1161, art 8(3).

3   IA 1971, s 24(1)(b).

4   HC 395, para 395C, inserted by Cmd 4851; see *Hanif* [1985] Imm AR 57, IAT.

17.50 Another issue is whether every overstay or breach of conditions, however trivial, gives rise to liability to removal under the pre Immigration Act 2014, section 10 of the IAA 1999. The likely answer is that all breaches give rise to liability, but trivial breaches are likely to be condoned.[1] In *R (on the application of Lim) v Secretary of State for the Home Department*[2] the Divisional Court noted that nothing obliges the Home Secretary to remove every non-British citizen who commits an infraction, however inconsequential, of his or her conditions of leave to remain, especially where the occurrence of the infraction is itself in issue. A decision to remove always involves the exercise of a discretion, and could be challenged where, for example, Home Office policy is to overlook a minor breach or a short overstay, since it would be inconsistent with good administration and unfair to remove someone on that basis. For example, anyone whose leave is subject to a condition of no recourse to public funds may be liable to summary removal if he or she claims any welfare or social security benefits or homeless persons housing.[3] However, Home Office policy in relation to settlement is not to refuse in the case of strictly temporary recourse to public funds;[4] it would thus be unreasonable to remove someone on this basis. Similar considerations apply to an overstay of a few weeks. In cases of alleged working in breach of employment conditions, the IDI state there must be firm and recent evidence (within six months) of working in breach.[5]

1   See *R v Secretary of State for the Home Department, ex p Amoa* [1992] Imm AR 218, QBD; *R v Newham London Borough Council, ex p Ajayi* (1994) 28 HLR 25 (deportation). Home Office instructions state that working in breach must be recent (within the past six months), and of sufficient gravity to warrant removal: Operational Enforcement Manual, Section B, Ch 10, para 10.6.4. Action may be appropriate where it appears that a student's main purpose in being in the UK is work rather than study: para 10.6.5, and persons who have overstayed for only a short period may be removed if there is reason to believe that they have no intention of leaving the UK: ibid 10.6.3.

2   *R (on the application of Lim) v Secretary of State for the Home Department* [2006] EWHC 3004 (Admin), [2006] All ER (D) 410 (Nov).

3   For the definition of public funds see HC 395, para 6 and 6A.

4   See eg IDI (Mar 06), Ch 8, Annex F, para 8.

5   IDI, Ch 13, s 2, para 2.1.2.

Use of deception in seeking leave to remain

17.51 A person who obtained leave to remain by deception was for the first time rendered liable to removal (as opposed to deportation) by the pre-Immigration Act 2014, section 10 of the IAA 1999.[1] Section 74 of the Nationality, Immigration and Asylum Act 2002 substantially extended liability to removal in this category, which was then triggered by any use of deception by a person seeking leave to remain, 'whether successful or not'.[2] The amendment appears to render irrelevant the proposition that any deception must have been 'effective' in order to permit initiation of enforcement action.[3] The wording of the section indicates that the deception must be that of the applicant him- or herself rather than that of a third party, although it can clearly include the use of false documents as well as the making of false representations. Leave granted on the basis of such deception would be invalidated by the issue of removal directions,[4] but deception must be proved to a high degree of probability.[5] Removal for practising deception only applies to persons who have practised deception from 1 October 1996.[6] If it appears that leave to remain was obtained by deception prior to that date this does not stop the case being referred for possible deportation action on non-conducive grounds under s 3(5)(a) of the Immigration Act 1971.[7] Leave obtained by deception was under the regime prior to commencement of the Immigration Act 2014 invalidated when notice of removal was given, not when removal directions were given.[8]

[1] IAA 1999, s 10(1)(b).
[2] IAA 1999, s 10(1)(b) as amended by the NIAA 2002, s 74. Section 76 of the NIAA 2002 enables the Secretary of State to revoke ILR granted by deception even where the person cannot be removed for legal or practical reasons (eg art 3 ECHR, or no direct flights to the country or territory concerned). See **4.10** above.
[3] See the discussion at **17.17–17.23** above on what constitutes deception, and what is a material deception in leave to enter cases.
[4] IAA 1999, s 10(8).
[5] *Khawaja v Secretary of State for the Home Department* [1983] UKHL 8(10 Feb 1983) [1984] AC 74 paras 76-77 (Lord Scarman) and 111 (per Lord Bridge.
[6] IDI, Ch 13, s 2, para 2.2.
[7] See fn 6 above.
[8] IAA 1999, s 10(8), amended by the IAN 2006, s 48, which came into force on 16 June 2006.

Persons ceasing to be refugees

17.52 The NIAA 2002 provides that refugees may have their indefinite leave to remain revoked if they voluntarily avail themselves of the protection of their country of nationality, voluntarily re-acquire a lost nationality, acquire the nationality or avail themselves of the protection of a country other than the UK, or voluntarily establish themselves in the country in respect of which they were granted refugee status.[1] Once indefinite leave is revoked, they are liable to removal.[2] There is a right of appeal against revocation of indefinite leave, and a separate right of appeal against removal after revocation.[3]

[1] NIAA 2002, s 76(3)(a)–(d), reflecting the provisions of the Refugee Convention, art 1C(1)–(4). The Act does not provide for revocation of the indefinite leave of refugees where the circumstances in their country of origin have changed fundamentally (Art 1C(5) of the Convention), reflecting the Secretary of State's policy only to withdraw ILR on the basis of a voluntary act by a refugee incompatible with continuing refugee status: Lord Bassam of Brighton, *Hansard* (HL) 17July 2002, col 1331. See further: *Secretary of State for the Home Department v MW (National passport: re-availment of protection) Pakistan* [2004] UKIAT 0013, a significant case in that the Tribunal applied the principle of re-availment of national protection to humanitarian protection. See further **12.86** ff above.
[2] IAA 1999, s 10(1)(ba), inserted by NIAA 2002, s 76(7).
[3] NIAA 2002, s 82(2)(f) (right of appeal against revocation), as amended by IAN Act 2006, s 2.

Family members

17.53 Where directions have been given for the removal of a person under the pre-Immigration Act 2014 section 10 of the IAA 1999, his or her family members are also liable to removal under section 10 provided those family members were notified no more than eight weeks after the departure of the first person.[1] The detailed criteria for removal of family members mirror those for deportation of family members, at **16.40** and **16.41**, to which reference should be made. Section 5(4) of the Immigration Act 1971 now provides that the civil partner of a man or woman, who is or has been ordered to be deported, can be a member of that person's family for the purposes of deportation.[2] Family members are the non-settled spouse or civil partner, or children under the age of 18 belonging to the family of a person in respect of whom removal directions have been given under section 10.[3]

[1]   IAA 1999, s 10(1)(c), (3), as amended by the NIAA 2002, s 73.
[2]   Immigration Act 1971, s 5(4), as amended by Civil Partnership Act 2004, s 261(1) and Sch 27, para 37(a), which came into force on 5 December 2005.
[3]   IDI, Ch 13, s 2, para 2.4.

SEA, AIR AND TRAIN CREWS

17.54 Seamen and air and train crews are a special category, as we have seen.[1] Section 8(1) of the Immigration Act 1971 provides that they may enter the UK without leave, and remain until the departure of the ship, aircraft or train in which they are required by their engagement to leave. This concession is subject to exceptions, and means that crew members can be treated as illegal entrants if they require leave to enter and enter without it. They also become illegal entrants if they desert their ship, plane or train and remain in this country. This is because of the provisions of section 11(5) of the Act which provide that someone who enters the UK lawfully under section 8(1) and seeks to remain beyond the section 8(1) time limit is to be treated as 'seeking to enter the UK'.[2] However, these distinctions are somewhat academic, because Schedule 2 to the Act gives immigration officers powers to order the removal of crew members who overstay, or who the immigration officer reasonably suspects of intending to do so.[3] In view of these draconian powers there is perhaps no need to declare seamen or air or train crews illegal entrants and to treat them as such.

[1]   See 6.31 above.
[2]   See *R v Secretary of State for the Home Department, ex p Urmaza* [1996] COD 479 where Sedley J held that a seaman deserter was an illegal entrant on this analysis. DP/2/93 applied to 'all illegal entry cases' and on the plain and ordinary meaning of such words it was not open to the Secretary of State to contend that it did not apply to the applicant as a seaman deserter. Contrast this approach with *Afunyah v Secretary of State for the Home Department* [1998] Imm AR 201, CA.
[3]   Immigration Act 1971, Sch 2, paras 12 and 13, modified in relation to Channel Tunnel trains by SI 1993/1813, Sch 4, para 1(11)(n).

USE OF DISCRETION IN SECTION 10 REMOVAL CASES

17.55 The fact that a person is liable to be removed, does not always mean, as we have seen, that he or she should be removed. The Immigration Rules set out a mechanism for the Secretary of State to take into account certain factors in exercising discretion. Prior to its abolition from 13 February 2012, paragraph 395C imposed a positive duty on the Secretary of State to take into account factors which were identical to the factors previously set out for deportation cases in HC 395, para 364, before its amendment by HC 1337 on 20 July 2006.[1] Paragraph 395C required consideration of all relevant circumstances, including: age; length of residence and strength of connections with the UK; personal history, including character, conduct and employment record; domestic circumstances; criminal record; compassionate circumstances; and representations made on the person's behalf. They are discussed in detail at **16.60** ff above. Paragraph 395C was replaced with paragraph 353B, which merely requires the Secretary of State to consider any further submissions that are made by a person which do not amount to a fresh human rights or asylum claim under paragraph 353. In considering such submissions the Secretary of State will also have regard to the migrant's:

(i)   character, conduct and associations including any criminal record and the nature of any offence of which the migrant concerned has been convicted;

(ii)   compliance with any conditions attached to any previous grant of leave to enter or remain and compliance with any conditions of temporary admission or immigration bail where applicable;

(iii)   length of time spent in the United Kingdom spent for reasons beyond the migrant's control after the human rights or asylum claim has been submitted or refused; in deciding whether there are exceptional circumstances which mean that removal from the United Kingdom is no longer appropriate.

[1]   See HC 395, para 395A–395D, as amended by Cmd 4851.

17.56 A problem arises for many migrants who have previously had and perhaps still have leave to remain but who do not qualify for new or further leave under any of the conventional Immigration Rule categories yet do have a case that might succeed under paragraph 353B or, before it, paragraph 395C. The cases of the applicants in *Mirza*[1] illustrate the point. In one of the cases the applicant, on a work permit, had breached the rules by changing her employer and so was disqualified from obtaining indefinite leave to remain, but claimed that she should not be removed because her breach was innocent and insubstantial: she was permitted to work for one firm of accountants but began to work for another. In another case a student who had been legitimately judged not to be making satisfactory progress as a student and so had been refused further leave to remain, accepted that he was struggling but asked for one more try. Another applicant had ticked the 'No' box for criminal convictions on his application for further leave when he had incurred two fines with penalty points for road traffic offences. He said that he did not appreciate that this constituted a criminal record. Another who entered lawfully as a highly skilled migrant, was refused leave to remain as a general migrant because she did not disclose a criminal conviction incurred by her husband.

The problem for these applicants prior to commencement of the removals and appeals provisions of the Immigration Act 2014 was that they had to become overstayers and in breach of the criminal law, before they had the opportunity of being presented with an appealable decision in which they would get the chance to argue why, despite the refusal of leave to remain, they should not be removed. This comes about, as the court put it in *Mirza*, because: 'each of these appellants is being denied a removal decision, following a legitimate refusal of leave to remain, as part of a generalised practice, either manifested in or deriving from the internal organisation of the Border Agency, of separating the two decisions by a frequently substantial period of time.' (at [40]).[2]

Following considerable litigation on this point the Supreme Court settled the question of the Secretary of State's obligations in the case of *Patel v Secretary of State for the Home Department* [2013] UKSC 72[2014] AC 651. The Supreme Court held that the Secretary of State was not obliged to issue a removal decision at the same time as, or immediately after, refusing an individual's application for a variation of his leave to remain in the United Kingdom. Thus, any failure to issue a removal decision did not render the refusal unlawful.

1   *R (on the application of Mirza) v Secretary of State for the Home Department* [2011] EWCA Civ 159.
2   The effect of this case law is mitigated in some cases by the Home Office policy entitled *Requests for Removal Decisions*, located within the Modernised Guidance. This provides that where a pre-action protocol letter is sent prior to commencement of an application for judicial review and certain conditions are met (including that there are children affected by the decision in question) then a removal decision will be made and a right of appeal thereby normally generated.

17.57 For those who are not lawfully in the UK, when they apply for leave to remain, it was held prior to the commencement of the unified removal power introduced by the Immigration Act 2014 that it would be contrary to the policy and objects of the 2002 Act to impose an obligation on the Secretary of State, when refusing an overstayer's application for leave to remain, to make at the same time an appealable refusal decision, so as to confer a right of appeal.[1] Where a person had already previously been the subject of a removal decision and later applied for leave on human rights or discretionary grounds, this permitted the Secretary of State to refuse the human rights claim but take no removal action and thereby not trigger any right of appeal, leaving the person either to wait for removal action and a right of appeal or challenge the refusal by way of an application for judicial review.

1   *R (on the application of Daley-Murdock) v Secretary of State* [2011] EWCA Civ 161, [2011] NLJR 327, [2011] NLJR 365 (23 February 2011). See also *TE (Eritrea)* [2009] EWCA Civ 174.

THE LONG RESIDENCE RULE

17.58 The 'long residence' rule started life as a Home Office concession but it was incorporated into the Immigration Rules on 1 April 2003.[1] It originated in the UK's ratification in 1969 of the European Convention on Establishment. Article 3(3) of the Convention provided that nationals of any contracting state who had been lawfully resident for over ten years in the territory of another party could only be expelled for reasons of national security or for particularly serious reasons relating to public order, public health or morality. The Home Office, when implementing this Article, extended it in three respects:

- to include all foreign nationals;

- to grant indefinite leave rather than simply refrain from removal; and
- to allow those who have been in the UK illegally to benefit, but not until they have completed 14 years' continuous residence.

However, substantial changes were introduced on 9 July 2012 and further modifications were made on 28 July 2014.[2] The provision for settlement to be granted after ten years of continuous lawful residence was retained but what had become known as 'the 14 year rule' for those who had attained 14 years of residence whether lawful, unlawful or mixed, was replaced with a set of rules on different periods of residence. These rules do not immediately lead to settlement but instead place a migrant on the 10 year route to settlement; 30 months of leave is granted at a time and after 120 months the migrant can potentially qualify for Indefinite Leave to Remain, assuming other relevant criteria are also satisfied.[3] These rules are now set out in a new subsection of the Immigration Rules that is entitled 'Private life', presumably in order to suggest an implementation of human rights considerations within the Immigration Rules in line with Government policy.[4] The relevant periods of continuous residence (lawful, unlawful or mixed and excluding periods in prison) are 20 years for all migrants, a period of seven years for children but with the added proviso that it must also be unreasonable for the child to leave the UK, a period of half of life for migrants aged between 18 and 25 and for migrants over the age of 18 further provision is made for those with less than 20 years of continuous residence if there would be very significant obstacles to the person's integration into the country to which he or she would have to go if required to leave the UK.[5]

The long residence rules perpetuate the distinction between lawful residence, which confers eligibility for settlement after ten years,[6] and residence partly or wholly unlawful, conferring eligibility only after these varying tariffs and additional conditions.[7] In either case, the residence must be continuous. Continuity of lawful residence may be broken by gaps of more than 28 days caused by late applications to renew leave, even if the lateness is known and is condoned by the grant of further leave.[8] Continuity of residence will not be broken by short absences of six months or less at any one time during periods of leave, but will be broken by removal, deportation or departure after refusal of leave to enter; departure from the UK with a clear intention not to return or in circumstances where there was no reasonable prospect of lawful return; by a custodial sentence or hospital order; or by a cumulative total of 18 months outside the UK.[9] In *TT (Long residence – 'continuous residence' – interpretation) British Overseas Citizen*[10] it was held that a period of continuous residence, as defined in HC 395, para 276A(a), is not broken in circumstances where a person with leave to remain in the United Kingdom obtains further leave from an Entry Clearance Officer while temporarily outside the United Kingdom prior to the expiry of the leave to remain.[11]

1   HC 395, paras 276A–E, inserted by HC 538. In *OS (10 years' lawful residence) Hong Kong* [2006] UKAIT 00031 (20 March 2006), the Tribunal noted that the 'long residence' concession had not been withdrawn when the rules relating to long residence were introduced. The Tribunal ruled that paragraphs 276A–D of the Immigration Rules (HC 395) stand alongside the published concession in long residence cases. The rules mean what they say and a person who does not meet the requirements of the rules may still get the benefit of the Secretary of State's exercise of discretion in his favour under the concession. Under the concession, there is no absolute requirement that every day of residence during the ten years be a day of lawful residence.

2   HC 194 and HC 532 respectively.
3   HC 395, paras 276BE-276DG inserted by HC 194.
4   HC 395, paras 276ADE-276DH
5   HC 395, para 276ADE inserted by HC 194 sets out the basic tariffs. The additional criterion of it being unreasonable for a child with seven years of residence to leave the UK was inserted by HC 760 on 13 December 2012. The test applicable for migrants over the age of 18 with less than 20 years of residence was originally 'no ties (including social, cultural or family) with the country to which he would have to go if required to leave the UK' but was amended to the text shown in the main body of the paragraph above by HC 532 on 28 July 2014. For interpretation of the earlier 'no ties' provision see *Ogundimu (Article 8 – new rules) Nigeria* [2013] UKUT 60 (IAC).
6   Lawful residence means continuous residence pursuant to leave to enter or remain, temporary admission where leave is subsequently granted, or an exemption from control: HC 395, para 276A(b). The IDI, Ch 18 para 7 assert that a person who is still exempt from control cannot apply for ILR, but the rule does not require an applicant to have current leave to remain in order to qualify, and on the face of it would not preclude an application from someone whose exemption from control was extant but about to end.
7   The distinction was first made in 1987; see 5th edition 16.43. The 14 years' residence under the rule excludes any period spent in the UK following service of notice of liability to removal, of removal directions under Sch 2 to the IA 1971 or s 10 of the IAA 1999, or of a notice of intention to deport: HC 395 para 276B(i)(b) as amended by Cmd 6339 on 24 Sep 2004. This reflects the case law under the previous policy: see *R v Secretary of State for the Home Department, ex p Ofori* [1994] Imm AR 34, CA; *R v Secretary of State for the Home Department, ex p Musah* [1995] Imm AR 236, *Hussain and Begum v Immigration Appeal Tribunal and Secretary of State for the Home Department* [1991] Imm AR 413, although this was held only to apply when the person became aware of the notice: *R v Secretary of State for the Home Department, ex p Chew and Popatia* [2000] EWHC 556 (QB), [2001] Imm AR 46, [2000] INLR 587.
8   'Lawful residence' in the context of these rules has a clear legal meaning. A failure to make an application for an extension of leave before the expiry of the current leave means that the provisions for a statutory extension of leave under section 3C of the Immigration Act 1971 is not triggered; so there is a gap where there is no leave and the person becomes an overstayer and the residence becomes unlawful. Obviously a person can become an overstayer for a whole variety of reasons stretching over quite a wide spectrum from those who deliberately flout the law to those who are prevented from applying in time through illness, forgetfulness or because their funds from home have been delayed through no fault of their own.
9   HC 395, para 276A(a). On the 18-month absence, see *LL (China) v Secretary of State for the Home department* [2009] EWCA Civ 617; *R (on the application of Demchigdorj) v Secretary of State for the Home Department* [2010] All ER (D) 49 (Aug), [2010] EWHC 2085 (Admin). For cases on continuity of residence under the old policy see the 6th edition of this work, 16.43 text and fn 4.
10 [2008] UKAIT 00038.
11 [2008] UKAIT 00038. This approach is now incorporated into the Home Office Long Residence Modernised Guidance.

17.59 The incorporation of the original concession into the rules has not been without considerable difficulties. The main litigation has arisen in relation to continuity of lawful residence pursuant to leave to enter or remain and the exercise of discretion, where there has been one or more gaps in the continuity of lawful residence.[1] Most of the cases concern students, who for one reason or another have made late applications for extensions of their leave but their leave has been extended without any questions being raised by the Home Office. Under the original concession[2] short gaps of this kind could be overlooked. Under the Immigration Rules no allowance for short gaps is made for applications before 9 July 2012.[3] We have seen, the concession and the rules existed side by side until 1 March 2006, when the concession was withdrawn. There was then a three-year period where there was no discretion to overlook gaps in lawful continuity. Then, in April 2009, new IDIs were published which restored a discretion to overlook short gaps, a discretion that has been retained since then. A person who applied during the three-year gap was therefore subject to a strict approach under the rules. For those that have applied with gaps in lawful residence during the currency of a discretion, if there has been a failure to consider the terms of the 'concession' properly, or at all, they are able to rely on the ground of appeal that the decision is not in accordance with the law.[4]

1   *OS (10 years' lawful residence) Hong Kong* [2006] UKAIT 00031; *SA (long residence concession) Bangladesh* [2009] UKAIT 00051; *LL (China)* [2009] EWCA Civ 617; *MD (Jamaica) v Secretary of State for the Home Department* [2010] EWCA Civ 213 and, more generally, *Mahad (previously referred to as AM) (Ethiopia) v Entry Clearance Officer* [2009] UKSC 16.
2   The terms of the old concession are set out in the AIT determination in *OS (10 years' lawful residence) Hong Kong* [2006] UKAIT 00031.
3   HC 395, para 276A and 276B.
4   Under NIAA 2002, s 84(1)(e)).

17.60 The question of lawfulness must be decided on the basis of the law and policy in operation at the time of the Secretary of State's decision and the statutory provision in NIAA 2002, section 85(4) allowing post-decision evidence to be adduced does not apply.[1] It is not, therefore open to an appellant on a 'not in accordance with the law' challenge to rely on the new concessions introduced if the decision on his or her application was made before that date. However, when it comes to a human rights assessment under Article 8 ECHR the immigration judge must have regard to the current position, not (as when looking to see whether the decision was 'in accordance with the law') the position at the date of decision. If at the date of the hearing there is in existence a policy which gives a discretion to overlook a short gap in the continuity of the appellant's lawful residence, that policy must clearly be taken into consideration by the immigration judge.[2]

1   *AG (Policies; executive discretion; Tribunal's powers) Kosovo* [2008] UKAIT 00082; *SA (long residence concession) Bangladesh and MD (Jamaica)* (fn 3 above).
2   *SA (long residence concession) Bangladesh* [2009] UKAIT 00051.

17.61 As intimated earlier, an applicant on the basis of 10 years of continuous lawful residence is eligible for indefinite leave immediately.[1] An applicant on the basis of the differing tariffs and conditions at paragraph 276ADE of the rules is only eligible for a grant of 30 months of leave. This period can be extended and the applicant eventually becomes eligible for indefinite leave after 120 months of such leave.[2] The grant of indefinite leave under the rules on the grounds of long residence or private life depends on the applicant fulfilling all the preconditions of leave and having a knowledge of English and of life in the UK.[3] If the main preconditions are not fulfilled, leave is to be refused, but if the only failure is the knowledge of English or life in the UK, an extension of stay of up to two years may be granted to an applicant under the 10 years continuous lawful residence route.[4] If an applicant under the other routes at paragraph 279ADE is ineligible for ILR by reason of a failure of the knowledge of English or life in the UK test that person would be eligible for a further extension of leave of 30 months, there being no maximum number of extensions that can be sought or granted. Even if all the preconditions are fulfilled the grant of leave on the basis of long residence or private life is discretionary ILR will only be granted to an applicant under the 10 years continuous lawful residence route if there are no reasons, having regard to the public interest, making it undesirable to do so, taking into account age, strength of connections in the UK, personal history including character, conduct, associations and employment record, domestic and compassionate circumstances, and representations from third parties.[5] Under the private life routes at paragraph 276ADE different criteria apply and an application for ILR can be refused if the suitability criteria at Appendix FM are not satisfied and there are no reasons why it would be undesirable to grant the applicant indefinite leave to remain based on the applicant's conduct, character or associations or because the applicant represents a threat to national security.[6]

[1]   HC 395, para 276B.
[2]   HC 395, para 276BE to 276DH.
[3]   HC 395, para 276B and 276DE.
[4]   HC 395, paras 276A1 and 276A2.
[5]   HC 395, para 276B(ii).
[6]   HC 395, para 276DE.

17.62 In *Aissaoui v Secretary of State for the Home Department*[1] the Court of Appeal held that it was wrong to approach the public interest reasons in HC 395, para 276B(ii) in a too literal way, because this would risk automatically excluding in the public interest from the long residence rule many who, absent other factors, are intended to have the benefit of that rule. The Court warned that *MO (Long residence rule – public interest proviso) Ghana*[2] should be treated with caution. The Court ruled that the immigration judge had erred in determining that an overstayer had deliberately tried to avoid detection, by engaging in employment under the name and national insurance number of another person. In *ZH (Bangladesh) v Secretary of State for the Home Department*[3] the Court of Appeal held that the public interest in an unlawful stay which had lasted 14 years or more was treated by the Immigration Rules, para 276B as met by a grant of indefinite leave to remain provided that there were no countervailing factors which tilted the public interest balance the other way. The use of a false identity might be a relevant factor in gauging where the public interest lay, but nothing in the rule accorded it any given weight, much less made it decisive. The Court said that MO should not in future be cited on para 276B(i)(b) appeals even as persuasive authority. Even the Secretary of State's own guidance recognised that applicants under the 14-year rule, if they were to be successful, must be expected to have worked unlawfully for much of their time in the UK.

In *AA (Spent convictions) Pakistan*[4] the Tribunal held that convictions that are 'spent' for the purposes of the Rehabilitation of Offenders Act 1974 should not normally be the subject of reference in appeals before the Tribunal. The exception is in s 7(3) of the 1974 Act, which allows spent convictions to be proved if the interests of justice require it: it is for the respondent to prove that they do. To rely on a spent conviction without considering whether justice could be done without it, is an error of law.

[1]   [2008] EWCA Civ 37, [2008] All ER (D) 92 (Feb).
[2]   [2007] UKAIT 00014.
[3]   [2009] EWCA Civ 8, [2009] All ER (D) 118 (Jan).
[4]   [2008] UKAIT 00027 (25 March 2008).

REMOVAL DIRECTIONS

17.63 Removal can only take place if directions are properly given in accordance with paragraphs 8–10 of Schedule 2 to the IA 1971. The statutory provisions for making removal directions have a coherent structure: the various powers to give directions comprise a progression in which each envisages directions less specific than the last. The first stage is directions for removal in the very vessel (ship or aircraft) in which the person arrived (para 8(1)(a)). The second is directions for removal in any specified vessel owned or operated by the same carrier as brought the person to the UK (para 8(1)(b)). The third is directions to that carrier to remove the person in any specified or indicated vessel (even if the carrier is not the vessel's owner or agent) to a specified country or territory (para 10(1)). The last is directions for removal 'in accordance with arrangements to be made by the Secretary of State' to any country or territory to which the person could have been removed under the previous two powers paragraph 10(2).[1] Directions may be given, a deportation order may be signed, and any other preparatory steps to facilitate removal may be undertaken, at any time while a claim for asylum or a suspensive appeal is pending.[2] With the exception of certain deportation appeals certified under section 94B of the NIAA 2002 as amended by the Immigration Act 2014, actual removal cannot, however, be effected until a decision on the asylum claim is notified and any in-country rights of appeal are exhausted.[3] Removal directions are not mere notifications to the carrier of its obligations, but are part of the machinery for removal. An immigrant affected by a direction is therefore entitled, in appropriate circumstances, to challenge its validity.[4] In *DJ v Secretary of State for the Home Department*, under the regime in place before section 1 of the Immigration Act 2014 came into effect, the Tribunal considered the effect of removal directions which were defective in that there was no indication on their face whether the Secretary of State was removing the person as an illegal entrant, an overstayer or other 'immigration offender', as required by the Notice Regulations,[5] and held that where reasons had been provided in a separate letter there was substantial compliance.[6]

[1]   *Jazayeri v Secretary of State for the Home Department* [2001] INLR 489, para 15.
[2]   Nationality Immigration and Asylum Act 2002, ss 77(4) and 78(3), subject to ss 79 and 92. It used to be thought that a direction was only valid if it indicated clearly that the immigrant was then, and not at some future unspecified date, required to be removed: see *R v Immigration Officer, ex p Shah* [1982] 2 All ER 264, [1982] 1 WLR 544, DC (a direction to the airline to remove the applicant to India 'as soon as his application to enter the UK is finally resolved' was held invalid); *R (on the application of Khadir) v Secretary of State for the Home Department* [2003] EWCA Civ 475, [2003] INLR 426, para 46 (dictum by Chadwick LJ that, at a time when there were no flights to the Kurdish Autonomous Zone and no possibility of return to Baghdad, it was difficult to see how directions for the removal of an Iraqi Kurd 'by scheduled airline to Iraq at a time and date to be notified' could have been thought appropriate or to be an effective exercise of the power conferred by Sch 2 to the Immigration Act 1971); contrast *Jayazeri v Secretary of State for the Home Department* [2001] INLR 489 IAT (immigration officers directions for removal 'at a time and date to be notified' upheld); *Hussain* [2002] UKIAT 03419; *Messar* [2002] UKIAT 00846. In *Hashemi* [2002] UKIAT 02975 the Tribunal thought such a notice could well be invalid, but that the defect could be remedied by amendment prior to determination of an appeal.
[3]   NIAA 2002, ss 77(1) and 78(1).
[4]   *R v Immigration Officer, ex p Shah* [1982] 2 All ER 264, [1982] 1 WLR 544; *Singh (Parshotam) v Secretary of State for the Home Department* [1989] Imm AR 469, CA.
[5]   See **CHAPTER 19**, below.

6   *DJ v Secretary of State for the Home Department (Defective Notice of Decision) Iraq* [2004] UKIAT 00194.

Removal after refusal of leave to enter

17.64 Where passengers arriving in the UK are refused leave to enter, an immigration officer may arrange for their removal by the owners or agents of the aircraft or ship which brought them in.[1] If such arrangements are made within two months the carriers must bear the costs of removal, and they are also liable if removal is not effected within this timescale but the immigration officer has given them written notice of the intention to remove.[2] In calculating the period of two months, any period during which an appeal is pending under the Immigration Acts is to be disregarded.[3] As indicated above, enforcement action cannot normally be effected whilst a suspensive right of appeal under section 82(1) of the NIAA 2002 is pending. However, as we saw in the last paragraph, there is no statutory prohibition on the giving of removal directions (or the initiation of other preparatory steps to facilitate removal) whilst a claim for asylum or appeal proceedings are outstanding.[4] Where directions are issued in respect of a principal applicant, directions may also be given in respect of family members.[5] The failure to remove a person refused leave to enter within two months, or to make arrangements or give notice to the carriers of proposed removal, does not prevent later removal.[6] But after two months the Secretary of State for the Home Department takes responsibility for the removal and must pay for it.[7] The government will pay the cost of removal when removal under the normal procedure is 'not practicable' or would be 'ineffective' and special arrangements have to be made.[8] A captain of a ship or airline who is told to remove someone and fails, without reasonable excuse, to comply, commits a criminal offence and is liable to a fine or imprisonment.[9] In this context it is also material to note that the IAA 1999 for the first time provided that directions for removal may include provision that the person being removed have an escort, which the carrier may be required to pay for.[10]

1   Immigration Act 1971, Sch 2, para 8(1). There is no specific provision for the removal of persons whose advance leave to enter is cancelled under Sch 2, para 2A(8), who are left in limbo, unable to enter the UK without leave but apparently irremovable until a further decision to refuse leave to enter.

2   IA 1971, Sch 2, para 8(2), as amended by Immigration Act 1988, Sch, para 9. The modification of para 8 by the Immigration (Entry otherwise than by Sea or Air) Order 2002, SI 2002/1832, provides for the Secretary of State to defray the costs of returning persons entering or seeking to enter via the land border through the Republic of Ireland.

3   IA 1971, Sch 2, para 8(2), as amended by NIAA 2002, Sch 7, para 4.

4   NIAA 2002, ss 77 and 78. Sch 9 to the Act repealed the IAA 1999, Sch 4, Pt II, para 10 which precluded the making of removal directions and provided that directions previously issued ceased to have effect while an appeal was pending, from 1 April 2003.

5   IA 1971, Sch 2, para 10A, inserted by NIAA 2002, s 73 from 10 February 2003 (SI 2003/1). Read literally, the amendment would allow immigration officers to remove UK-based family members of a visitor refused leave to enter, which would clearly be absurd. The Explanatory Notes to the 2002 Act state that its purpose is to remove UK-born children of those who have been on temporary admission for some time, and of illegal entrants.

6   IA 1971, Sch 2, para 10(1)(b). See *Rahman (Mohammed) v Secretary of State for the Home Department* [1995] Imm AR 488, CA; *R v Secretary of State for the Home Department, ex p Al-Zahrany* [1995] Imm AR 283.

7   IA 1971, Sch 2, para 10(3).

[8] IA 1971, Sch 2, para 10(1)(a). In *Jayazeri v Secretary of State for the Home Department* [2001] INLR 489 (starred), a starred Tribunal held that an immigration officer could issue directions under this paragraph without express delegation from the Secretary of State.

[9] IA 1971, s 27(a). This measure forms part of the range of measures, including carriers' liability, penalties for inadvertent carriage of stowaways and employer sanctions, which implicate private companies and individuals in the enforcement of immigration control.

[10] IAA 1999, s 14. Regulations may require the carrier to arrange for the escort's return to the UK and for his or her remuneration. No regulations have yet been made under the section.

17.65 Apart from the time limit which determines who is to pay for removal, there is no express requirement on the part of the authorities to act quickly. In *Rafiq*[1] the Divisional Court had held that it was entirely reasonable to delay for six weeks the giving of directions for removal, until the Home Office had discovered whether or not the applicant would be admitted to Pakistan. The alternative course would have been to direct his removal without establishing whether the directions would be effective. But where a person is in custody pending removal, there is a requirement to act reasonably promptly; otherwise detention may become unlawful.[2] The NIAA 2002[3] allows persons in respect of whom removal directions have been or might be set, but who cannot be removed for practical or legal reasons, to be treated as 'liable to detention' for the purpose of granting temporary admission, even though they cannot actually be detained.[4]

[1] *R v Secretary of State for the Home Department, ex p Rafiq (Mohammed)* [1970] 3 All ER 821.

[2] *R v Governor of Durham Prison, ex p Singh* [1984] 1 All ER 983, [1984] 1 WLR 704, [1983] Imm AR 198, QBD.

[3] NIAA 2002, s 67.

[4] *R (on the application of Khadir) v Secretary of State for the Home Department* [2003] EWCA Civ 475, [2003] INLR 426, upheld on appeal by the House of Lords. For more details see **3.43**, above.

Removal of illegal entrants

17.66 Precisely the same removal procedure operates in the case of illegal entrants (assuming of course that the illegal entrant can in fact be removed),[1] save that the two-month time limit for immigration officers' directions does not apply.[2] Illegal entrants who are discovered as stowaways coming off a particular ferry may clearly be the subject of directions to the captain, but in the case of illegal entrants who are not detected at the port, it will rarely be 'practicable' or 'effective' to identify or issue directions to the company which brought them in; in which case responsibility falls on the Secretary of State, who bears the costs.[3] Where directions are issued for the removal of an illegal entrant, directions may also be given for the removal of family members.[4]

[1] See *R v Secretary of State for the Home Department, ex p Yu and Lin* (CO 393/1999, CO 4621/1999) where permission was granted for judicial review of the failure to remove or to regularise Chinese illegal entrants for over four years while travel documents were awaited from the Chinese authorities. The matter never reached full hearing because the travel documents were finally issued and removal was effected.

[2] Immigration Act 1971, Sch 2, para 9, referring to para 8(1). See *Rahman v Secretary of State for the Home Department* [1995] Imm AR 488, CA. The modification of para 9(1) by the Immigration (Entry otherwise than by Sea or Air) Order 2002, SI 2002/1832, provides for the Secretary of State to defray the costs of returning persons entering or seeking to enter illegally via the land border through the Republic of Ireland.

[3] IA 1971, Sch 2, para 10(1)(a), 10(3).

4   Immigration Act 1971, Sch 2, para 10A, inserted by NIAA 2002, s 73(1). This allows UK-born children of illegal entrants to be removed, although the breadth of the power would need to be limited by reasonable criteria such as age, length of residence in the UK etc.

Removal under section 10 of the Immigration and Asylum Act 1999

17.67 For persons subject to administrative removal, including those whose indefinite leave to remain has been revoked under section 76(3) of the NIAA 2002,[1] but excluding those overstayers subject to the deportation procedure under transitional provisions[2] and those who would be exempt from deportation,[3] directions are set by the Secretary of State as if after refusal of leave or illegal entry.[4] Under the scheme in place before commencement of section 1 of the Immigration Act 2014, issue of removal directions immediately invalidated any extant leave.[5] The costs of removal, so far as reasonably incurred, will be borne by the Secretary of State.[6] Family members may be removed if directions have been issued in respect of the person to whose family they belong, provided the Secretary of State has given written notice of the intention to remove.[7] If removal as a dependant is proposed then directions must be given within eight weeks of the departure of the principal to whose family they belong.[8]

1   Ie, those ceasing to be refugees: IAA 1999, s 10(1)(ba), inserted by NIAA 2002, s 76(7).
2   Ie, overstayers or those in breach of conditions served with a notice of intention to deport before 2 October 2000, or who applied for regularisation under s 9 of the IAA 1999 and have been served with a notice of intention to deport since: Nationality, Immigration and Asylum Act 2002 (Commencement No 4) Order 2003, SI 2003/754, art 3 and Sch 2, para 6(2): see **17.41** above.
3   IAA 1999, s 10(10), inserted by NIAA 2002, s 75.
4   IAA 1999, s 10(7); see the Immigration (Removal Directions) Regulations 2000, SI 2000/2243.
5   IAA 1999, s 10(8). Leave may be extant although obtained by deception, or in cases of breach of conditions.
6   IAA 1999, s 10(9).
7   IAA 1999, s 10(1)(c) and 10(3) (s 10(3) substituted by NIAA 2002, s 73(2) from 10 February 2003 (SI 2003/1). Directions for the removal of family members cannot take effect if they cease to be family members (eg by divorce, leaving home or turning 18): s 10(5A) as inserted.
8   IAA 1999, s 10(4), as substituted.

Removal of deportees

17.68 For persons subject to deportation action, the arrangements for removal are set out in Schedule 3 to the Immigration Act 1971.[1] The cost again falls on the Secretary of State for the Home Department, except where the deportees are made to pay for their own removal.[2] A deportation order may not be made whilst an appeal against deportation under section 82(1) of the NIAA 2002 may be brought or is pending,[3] but may be made in respect of a person who has a claim for asylum pending.[4] Thus a person who does not claim asylum until a deportation appeal has been dismissed may have an order made against him or her, though plainly it cannot be effected while the claim is being determined.[5]

1   IA 1971, Sch 3, para 1.
2   IA 1971, Sch 3, para 1(4).

3 NIAA 2002, s 79, in force 1 April 2003 (SI 2003/754 art 2, Sch 1), applied to appeals under the old appeals provisions by art 3 and Sch 2, para 1(4).

4 NIAA 2002, s 77(4), applying to claims pending both before and after 31 March 2003 (SI 2003/754 arts 2, 3, Sch 1, Sch 2, para 1(2)).

5 NIAA 2002, s 77(1).

Removal of sea, air and train crews

17.69 Here the removal arrangements are very similar to those of persons refused entry. Initially, responsibility for removal and its costs are borne by the owners or agents of the ship or aircraft or train manager of whose crew the person to be removed is a member, but if this is not practicable or would be ineffective the alternative removal arrangements are paid for by the government.[1] In the case of *Ex p Urmaza*,[2] Sedley J had to consider when enforcement action began against a deserting seaman who had married and resided in this country. He concluded that it was when removal directions were given and not when the exemption from obtaining leave to enter was revoked, and thus the enforcement policy applied in the same way as other cases.

1 Immigration Act 1971, Sch 2, paras 12–14.
2 *R v Secretary of State for the Home Department, ex p Urmaza* [1996] COD 479, (1996) Times, 23 July.

COUNTRIES TO WHICH REMOVAL IS POSSIBLE

17.70 The range of countries to which removal may be effected varies according to the immigration status of the person being removed. Overstayers etc and deportees may only be removed to a country:

- of which they are nationals or citizens; or
- to which there is reason to believe they will be admitted.[1]

Illegal entrants and those refused entry can be removed to a wider range of countries:

- of which they are nationals or citizens;
- in which they obtained a passport or identity documents;[2]
- from which they embarked for the UK; or
- to which there is reason to believe they will be admitted.[3]

The power to return those refused leave to enter to the country of embarkation or any country to which there is reason to believe that they will be admitted provides the statutory basis for the removal of asylum claimants to 'safe' third countries without determining their claim under section 33 of and Schedule 3 to the Asylum and Immigration (Treatment of Claimants, etc) Act 2004. Members of a ship or aircrew may additionally be removed to the country where they were engaged.[4]

1 Immigration (Removal Directions) Regulations 2000, SI 2000/2243, reg 4(2); Immigration Act 1971, Sch 3, para 1.
2 The Tribunal in *Matanoviq* [2002] UKIAT 01874 was of the view that 'other document of identity' in Sch 2, para 8(1)(c)(ii) of the IA 1971 has to be read *ejusdem generis* as 'passport' – the provision appears to require some document of identity issued at some stage by the state authorities of the country in question, which will at least raise an inference that the holder has a right to be there.

³   Immigration Act 1971, Sch 2, paras 8(1)(c)(i)–(iv) and 10(1). 'Admitted' does not mean admitted for an indefinite period: *Alsawaf v Secretary of State for the Home Department* [1988] Imm AR 410, CA.
⁴   IA 1971, Sch 2, para 12(2)(c)(iv).

17.71 The country of nationality or citizenship may under the rules of international law be bound to receive its own nationals.¹ There is, therefore, usually no problem about admission.² But where persons are being removed to other countries, there may be difficulties. There is nothing in the legislation which suggests that the immigration authorities must check on whether a person will be admitted before directing their removal to that country. But it is not enough for the Secretary of State to conclude that a person ought to be admitted to a country which is not obliged to accept him or her if there is no evidence that admission is likely to be granted.³

¹   See CHAPTER 7 above.
²   This is subject to proof of nationality: see discussion at **17.73** below on measures related to the provision of travel documents for removal.
³   *R v Secretary of State for the Home Department, ex p Yasine (or Yassine)* [1990] Imm AR 354.

17.72 Since 2006, it has been permissible to specify multiple countries in removal directions.¹ In *MS (Palestinian Territories)*² the Supreme Court held that the proposing of a destination country in removal directions is not an integral part of an immigration decision and does not form part of the subject of a statutory appeal. The Court concluded that there is no right of appeal against an immigration decision under section 82(2)(h) on the ground that the country or territory stated in the notice of the decision is not one that would satisfy the requirements of para 8(1)(c) of Schedule 2 to the 1971 Act.

¹   Immigration (Notices) (Amendment) Regulations 2006, SI 2006/2168.
²   *MS (Palestinian Territories) v Secretary of State for the Home Department* [2010] UKSC 25.

CARRYING OUT REMOVAL

17.73 Those liable to be removed from the UK, particularly illegal entrants, will often possess no valid travel documents (or none at all) and no proof of identity or nationality. The authorities of the state to which removal is proposed may, not unreasonably, require production of identification data to enable them to confirm the person's nationality before issuing a travel document. Although under the Immigration Act 1971 wide powers existed to deal with this situation,¹ the process usually required the co-operation of the proposed returnee, which was not always forthcoming. Rejected asylum seekers in particular resisted giving information which they feared might endanger families at home. In the first instance judgment in *Amirthanathan*, the Administrative Court recognised this fear as well-founded in cases where an appeal had been lodged:

> 'It is inappropriate to require a person to give an interview to the authorities of the destination country to facilitate obtaining a travel document, since the interview might lead to information being provided which might put the claimant or his family at risk'.²

The IAA 1999 empowered the Secretary of State to release to the authorities of the proposed country of removal identification data on the returnee, such as fingerprints.[3] Provisions of the Data Protection Act 1988 forbidding transfer of personal data to states outside the EEA were avoided by deeming the transfer of such personal data 'necessary for reasons of substantial public interest'.[4] Finally, the Asylum and Immigration (Treatment of Claimants etc)Act 2004 forces returnees to cooperate in their own removal by making it a criminal offence punishable by two years' imprisonment to fail without reasonable excuse to cooperate in endeavours to obtain travel documents.[5] The Act also enables the Secretary of State or an immigration officer to retain any document which comes into their possession in the exercise of an immigration function, while there is a suspicion that the person to whom it relates may be liable to removal and that retention of the document might facilitate the removal.[6]

[1] Immigration Act 1971, Sch 2, para 18(2) and (2A), allowing immigration officers, police, prison officers and anyone else authorised by the Secretary of State to photograph, measure, fingerprint and otherwise identify detainees, and para 18(3), allowing them to take detainees anywhere necessary to establish their citizenship, and to make arrangements for their admission to another country.

[2] *R (on the application of Amirthanathan) v Secretary of State for the Home Department* [2003] EWHC 2595 (Admin), [2003] All ER (D) 29 (May) at para 39. This aspect of the judgment was not dealt with by the Court of Appeal at [2003] EWCA Civ 1768, [2003] All ER (D) 129 (Dec). However, in *R v Secretary of State for the Home Department, ex p Z* [1998] Imm AR 516, Moses J had held that the power to make removal directions implied a power to obtain the information required to implement the directions, and failure to co-operate would empower the Secretary of State to detain under Immigration Act 1971, Sch 2, para 18(2).

[3] IAA 1999, s 13.

[4] IAA 1999, s 13(4), which renders inapplicable the eighth principle of Sch 1 to the Data Protection Act 1998, prohibiting transfer of personal data to countries outside the EEA unless an adequate level of protection in relation to its processing is guaranteed. The only express limitation is that the Secretary of State must not disclose whether or not an asylum claim has been made (s 13(3)). This miserable sole safeguard is wholly inadequate to protect those whose national authorities are made aware by the transfer of identification data that they are in the UK without travel documents and that they are shortly to be returned home.

[5] Asylum and Immigration (Treatment of Claimants, etc) Act 2004, s 35, in force 22 July 2004 (s 48(1)).

[6] Asylum and Immigration (Treatment of Claimants, etc) Act 2004, s 17, in force 1 December 2004 (SI 2004/2999).

17.74 To ensure that directions for removal are effective against the captain of a ship or airline or against the owners or agents, it is made a criminal offence for them to disobey directions without reasonable excuse.[1] Where directions for removal have been given, the person to be removed may be placed, under the authority of an immigration officer or the Secretary of State, on board any ship or aircraft in which that person is to be removed in accordance with those directions.[2] Detainee custody officers are empowered to use force in the exercise of their functions,[3] and force has certainly been used, on occasion with fatal effects.[4] Once the person is on board, it becomes the responsibility of the captain of the ship or aircraft to prevent them escaping. For this purpose they may be detained until removal is fulfilled.[5] A captain who knowingly lets such persons disembark commits a criminal offence and is liable to a fine or imprisonment.[6] Where a person who is being removed threatens suicide, or gives any indication that he or she may attempt suicide, immigration officers are under instruction to seek the port medical inspector's opinion of the person's state of mind and not to pursue removal without reference to the passenger casework section of the Immigration Service.[7] The IAA 1999 has provision for escorts to accompany the removed person, to be specified in the removal directions.[8] The section empowers the Secretary of State to make regulations regarding the costs of such escorts.[9] A person's removal under the provisions of section 5, Schedule 2 or Schedule 3 to the IA 1971 is not precluded by a travel restriction order under the Criminal Justice and Police Act 2001.[10]

1. Immigration Act 1971, s 27(a)(ii) and (b)(iii).
2. IA 1971, Sch 2, paras 11 and 15; Sch 3, para 1(3) (modifed in relation to the Channel Tunnel by SI 1993/1813, art 7(1), Sch 4, para 1(11); in relation to controls between the UK, France and Belgium by SI 1994/1405, art 7, and in relation to certain persons entering or seeking to enter through the Republic of Ireland by SI 2002/1832).
3. IAA 1999, Sch 11, Sch 13, para 2(4).
4. In the case of Joy Gardner, who died after being gagged with 13 feet of tape in addition to being manacled and handcuffed in August 1993, and in the case of Jimmy Mubenga who died after being restrained in the process of removal in 2010. Other deportees have been seriously injured by the use of inappropriate restraint, and protests by passengers at excessive physical restraint of deportees on aircraft became increasingly common. The government now regularly uses special charter flights. See eg Amnesty International *Cruel, inhuman or degrading treatment during forcible deportation* (July 1994); Medical Foundation *Harm on removal: Excessive force against failed asylum seekers* (October 2004).
5. IA 1971, Sch 2, para 16(4) – this is a very clumsily worded paragraph and our interpretation involves placing the words 'or before the directions for his removal have been fulfilled . . . ' after 'an immigration officer'.
6. IA 1971, s 27(a)(i). This is an absolute offence with no room for 'reasonable excuse'. Where the condition of a deportee or other compelling factors such as an on-board protest dictate removal of the deportee from the aircraft, the captain would have to obtain the permission of the immigration officer or the Secretary of State to avoid criminal liability.
7. IDI (Sep 04), Ch 9, s 6, para 5.
8. IAA 1999, s 14.
9. No regulations have been made under this section.
10. Ie, under Criminal Justice and Police Act 2001, s 33 (travel restriction order against certain persons convicted of drug trafficking offences). Section 37 provides that an order under the Act does not prevent removal under prescribed powers, and the removal powers are set out in the Travel Restriction Order (Prescribed Removal Powers) Order 2002, SI 2002/313, Schedule.

EUROPEAN CO-OPERATION

17.75 Removal of illegal entrants and overstayers is a major preoccupation of immigration authorities not just of the UK government but throughout the European Union. Several measures have been adopted to facilitate cooperation on expulsion, including Council Directive 2001/40 on the mutual recognition of decisions on expulsion of third country nationals,[1] which the UK has opted into and which was required to be implemented in national law by 2 December 2002. The Directive enables expulsion decisions made against third country nationals in one Member State to be enforced in another. The expulsion decisions concerned must be based on conviction of an offence punishable by 12 months' or more imprisonment, serious grounds for believing that the person has committed or intends to commit a serious criminal offence, or failure to comply with national rules on the entry or residence of aliens.[2] The UK has also opted into implementation measures such as the Decision on joint expulsion flights.[3]

1. Directive 2001/40, OJ 2001 L 150/47.
2. Directive 2001/40, art 3. The provisions do not apply to family members of EU nationals: art 1.
3. OJ 2004 L 261/28.

COMPULSORY REMOVAL OF MENTALLY DISORDERED PATIENTS

17.76 Section 86 of the Mental Health Act 1983,[1] empowers the Secretary of State for the Home Department to authorise the removal to any country abroad of certain detained patients who have been given leave to enter or remain, but do not have a right of abode in the UK and who are receiving in-patient treatment for mental disorder.[2] The power originated with the Lunacy Act 1890, under which aliens detained as persons of unsound mind could be returned to their own country at the request of their family or friends, a right of initiative removed by the Mental Health Act 1959. The Secretary of State's powers of removal of mental patients were increased by the Immigration Act 1971[3] and the British Nationality Act 1981[4] to embrace all patients without the right of abode. The main purpose of the power, according to the government, is to 'enable patients who are either irrationally opposed to their removal, or are unable to express a view, to be compulsorily removed to another country when this is judged to be in their best interests. It is also used to enable patients to be kept under escort on their journey home if this is necessary'.[5] Before exercising these powers the Secretary of State must have obtained the approval of an appropriate Tribunal[6] and must be satisfied that proper arrangements have been made for the removal of patients and for their care or treatment, and that removal is in their interests.[7] Where a mentally disordered patient is liable to removal under some other provision of the IA 1971, for example because he or she is on temporary admission, the Secretary of State is not obliged to use this procedure for removal of psychiatric patients, so the safeguard of the Mental Health Review Tribunal does not apply.[8] As removal under section 30 is not an 'immigration decision' within the meaning of section 82 of the NIAA 2002, there is no right of appeal, and a challenge would have to be by way of judicial review.[9] Removal under this section is not prevented by a travel restriction order.[10] On arrival at their destination, any orders or directions made in respect of them will cease to have effect, except that in the case of patients who were subject to a Hospital Order and a Restriction Order when they were removed, both Orders will remain in force.[11] There is nothing to prevent patients who have been removed from applying for re-admission to the UK at any time.[12] The removal powers are, however, draconian and need very rigorous adherence to the safeguards to avoid non-compliance with due process and private life requirements of the ECHR.

---

[1] The 1983 Act applies only to England and Wales but is extended to Northern Ireland by the Mental Health (Northern Ireland) Order 1986, and amended by the Mental Health (Northern Ireland Consequential Amendments) Order 1986.

[2] Mental disorder was substituted for psychiatric illness by the Mental Health Act 2007, s 1(4), Sch 1, para 15.

[3] Immigration Act 1971, s 30(1).

[4] British Nationality Act 1981, s 39(7).

[5] White Paper *The Review of the Mental Health Act 1959* (Cmd 7320) para 8.26. Powers of escort are now expressly contained in IAA 1999, s 14, and are not confined to psychiatric patients.

[6] Mental Health Act 1983, s 86(3) as amended by SI 2008/2883, art 9, Sch 3, para 62. An appropriate Tribunal is the First Tier Tribunal (Mental Health) in England and the Mental Health Review Tribunal for Wales, as set up by s 65(1) of the Mental Health Act 1983. In Northern Ireland it is the Mental Health Review Tribunal for Northern Ireland and the Secretary of State is to be construed as the Department of Justice in Northern Ireland: s 86(3) and (4).

[7] Mental Health Act 1983, s 86(2).

[8] *X v Secretary of State for the Home Department* [2001] 1 WLR 740, [2001] INLR 205, CA.

⁹ See (under the old appeal provisions) *R v Immigration Appeal Tribunal and the Secretary of State for the Home Department, ex p Alghali* [1986] Imm AR 376, QBD.

¹⁰ Ie, under Criminal Justice and Police Act 2001, s 33 (travel restriction order against certain persons convicted of drug trafficking offences). Section 37 provides that an order under the Act does not prevent removal under prescribed powers, and removal under Mental Health Act 1983, s 86 is among the prescribed removal powers set out in the Travel Restriction Order (Prescribed Removal Powers) Order 2002, SI 2002/313, Schedule.

¹¹ Mental Health Act 1983, s 91. For the power to remove restricted patients, see *MJ (Angola) v Secretary of State for the Home Department* [2010] EWCA Civ 557.

¹² But a compulsory order under s 37 of the Mental Health Act 1983 takes effect on a patient's return: s 91(2).

REMOVAL OF DESERTERS FROM FRIENDLY FORCES

17.77 The position of deserters or absentees without leave in the UK from friendly foreign forces is governed by the Visiting Forces Act 1952, under which deserters can be arrested, detained and removed from the UK.[1] Arrest must be by warrant granted either to the police or army personnel. The person is then brought before a court which decides whether they should be handed over for trial as a deserter to the country concerned. Court proceedings can be dispensed with if the deserter surrenders voluntarily at a police station. As in extradition proceedings the magistrates' courts' powers are subject to *habeas corpus* proceedings or judicial review. This is how the provisions work.

1. The Visiting Forces Act 1952 Part II, as amended. For more details, see the amended statute at the government website at: www.statutelaw.gov.uk. The 1952 Act applies mostly to forces of Commonwealth countries, but also to any other countries authorised by Order in Council. In particular it applies to the forces of Antigua and Barbuda, Australia, Bahamas, Bangladesh, Barbados, Belize, Bermuda, Botswana, Brunei, Cameroon, Canada, Republic of Cyprus, Dominica, Fiji, The Gambia, Ghana, Grenada, Guyana, India, Jamaica, Kenya, Kiribati, Lesotho, Malawi, Malaysia, Maldives, Malta, Mauritius, Mozambique, Namibia, Nauru, the New Hebrides, New Zealand, Nigeria, Pakistan, Papua New Guinea, Saint Christopher and Nevis, Saint Lucia, Saint Vincent and the Grenadines, Seychelles, Sierra Leone, Singapore, Solomon Islands, South Africa, Sri Lanka, Swaziland, Tanzania, Tonga, Trinidad and Tobago, Tuvalu, Uganda, Vanuatu, Western Samoa, Zambia, Zanzibar and Zimbabwe: see Visiting Forces Act s 1(1) as amended; Visiting Forces Act (Application to Bermuda) Order 2001, SI 2001/3922. It also applies under designation orders made under s 1(2) of the 1952 Act to Albania, Armenia, Austria, Azerbaijan, Belarus, Belgium, Bulgaria, Czech Republic, Denmark, Estonia, Finland, France, Georgia, Germany, Greece, Hungary, Italy, Latvia, Lithuania, Luxembourg, Kazakhstan, Kyrgystan, Former Yugoslav Republic of Macedonia, Moldova, Netherlands, Norway, Poland, Portugal, Romania, Russia, Slovakia, Slovenia, Spain, Sweden, Switzerland, Turkey, Turkmenistan, Ukraine, United States of America and Uzbekistan (see SI 1999/1736, Sch 1, See 3 *Halsbury's Laws* (4th edn) p 936. The Act also applies, with adaptations, to any headquarters or organisation set up in pursuance of arrangements for defence (International Headquarters And Defence Organisations Act 1964, s 5); SI 1999/1736, art 3(2).

17.78 Section 13(1) of the Visiting Forces Act 1952 (as substituted)[1] applies the Army Act 1955, sections 186–188[2] and 190 (which allows for the apprehension, detention and delivery into military custody of deserters and absentees without leave from the regular forces)[3] to deserters and absentees from forces of any country to which the section applies. But first there must be a request (either specific or general) of the appropriate authority of the country to which the person belongs and a certificate that he or she is a deserter or absentee. Section 13(3) states that references in the sections of the 1955 Act to the delivery of a person into military custody shall be construed as references

...ne handing over of that person to such authority of the country to which he or she belongs, at such place in the UK as may be designated by the appropriate authority of that country.

[1] Section 13(1)–(3) substituted by the Revision of Army and Air Force Acts (Transitional Provisions) Act 1955, s 3, Sch 2, para 17(1).

[2] Section 186 of the Army Act 1955 gives power to arrest suspected deserters/absentees to a constable, or if none is available, any officer, warrant officer, NCO or soldier of the regular forces. A warrant for the arrest of a suspect as aforesaid can be issued by anyone having authority to issue warrants for arrest of persons charged with crime. A person in custody by virtue of s 186 shall be brought before a court of summary jurisdiction as soon as practicable. If the person admits being a deserter and the court is satisfied with the truth of the admission, or if he denies it but the court is satisfied that (a) he is under military law and (b) that there is sufficient evidence for him to be tried for desertion, the court shall deliver him into military custody, but otherwise discharge him (s 187). If a person surrenders himself to the police as a deserter and it appears to the police that he is telling the truth, the police may deliver him into military custody without taking him to court (s 188). Governors of police stations and persons in charge of prisons are under a duty to receive deserters and detain them until they can be delivered into military custody (s 190).

[3] Visiting Forces Act 1952, s 13(2) as substituted. Under s 14 (as amended by SI 1964/488) the magistrates' court will require two certificates: (1) stating that the country concerned has made a request for the exercise of the 1952 Act (this is signed by the Secretary of the Defence Council); and (2) stating that the person is a deserter or an absentee without leave (this is signed by the officer commanding a unit or detachment of any of the forces of the country concerned).

17.79 Section 13 of the Visiting Forces Act 1952 does not apply just to deserters from visiting forces (ie those stationed in the UK) but also to all the forces of a country to which the section applies. In *R v Thames Justices, ex p Brindle*[1] an American citizen resident in England returned to the US, joined the army and was posted to Germany, deserted and came to England where he was arrested for other offences and ordered by the magistrate to be handed into the custody of the US military authorities on completion of his sentence. The Court of Appeal held that although Part I of the 1952 Act (ss 1–12) applied just to visiting forces as defined in section 12(1), section 13 applied to deserters from the 'forces of any designated country' without a limitation to visiting forces.

[1] [1975] 3 All ER 941, [1975] 1 WLR 1400, CA.

17.80 The procedure and standard of proof to be applied by a magistrates' court in such cases was spelt out by the Divisional Court in *R v Tottenham Magistrates' Court, ex p Williams*.[1] Mr W, a Nigerian lawfully settled in the UK, was arrested as a deserter from the Nigerian airforce, but claimed that his engagement had terminated before he came to the UK. The magistrate had ordered his surrender on the basis that he was the person named in a certificate signed by an officer commanding a unit of the Nigerian forces who stated that Mr W was a deserter. She did not take into account the evidence and statement of Mr W. The Divisional Court quashed the decision. Donaldson LJ pointed out that there was a very heavy onus and that no one was to be imprisoned or delivered into the custody of any authority, whether British or Nigerian, save in strict compliance with the law. As Mr W did not admit he was legally absent, two things had to be proved under the Visiting Forces Act 1952 procedure:

- that Mr W was subject to Nigerian military law. The magistrates had to be satisfied beyond reasonable doubt – the criminal standard of proof; and
- if so, that there was sufficient evidence to justify his being tried in Nigeria for desertion.

This is the less onerous test applied to committal proceedings. In deciding both questions magistrates had to consider all the evidence tendered and not just that of the prosecution. In *Re Virdee*[2] the Divisional Court held that proceedings under the Visiting Forces Act 1952 were quasi-criminal, like the exercise of extradition powers, and so not affected by Article 48 EC (now art 39), since the purpose both of extradition and of handover under section 13 was a trial by a foreign court with a view to punishment, rather than exclusion from the UK.

[1]   [1982] 2 All ER 705, DC.
[2]   [1980] 1 CMLR 709, DC.

EXTRADITION

17.81 Extradition is another form of compulsory removal and is a topic beyond the scope of this work.[1] There may be an overlapping of extradition and immigration law where a fugitive offender is refused leave to enter the country and enters unlawfully, or resists extradition on the ground of being a refugee. The Extradition Act 2003[2] provides for 'fast-track' extradition procedures to EU Member States without consideration of evidence, and simplifies procedures under the previous legislation. For the first time, the 2003 Act deals with asylum claims by persons in respect of whom extradition warrants are issued. It provides that a person must not be extradited in pursuance of the warrant before the asylum claim is finally determined.[3] These provisions are in addition to the ban on extradition where a prosecution is brought for a Refugee Convention reason or where the offender is likely to be prejudiced at trial for a Convention reason, which have been carried forward into the 2003 Act.[3] Finally, once an extradition judge has decided that the offence is an extradition offence and that there is no statutory bar to extradition, he or she must decide if extradition is compatible with the person's rights under the Human Rights Convention, and if not, must discharge the offender.[4] Administrative removal should not be used in order to circumvent extradition safeguards, but provided immigration powers are used lawfully and bona fide, removal may be ordered to any destination permitted under the statute, including the country requesting extradition.[5] In extradition proceedings in relation to whether an individual convicted in his absence would receive a retrial that accorded with the European Convention on Human Rights 1950, Protocol 1 Article 6 if extradited, it was unnecessary to examine what a requesting state did in practice provided that the Convention was unequivocally incorporated into its body of laws and that the terms of the Convention would prevail if any conflict arose between it and those laws.[6] Occasionally a deportation case will also be subject to extradition or repatriation proceedings. These proceedings will make no difference to the consideration of whether deportation should go ahead. Deportation consideration and extradition/repatriation proceedings should continue simultaneously.[7]

1 See Sambel and Jones *Extradition Law Handbook* (2004); Stanbrook and Stanbrook *Extradition Law and Practice* (2000).

2 In force 1 January 2004, except for cases where a request was received on or before 31 December 2003 (which will be dealt with under the Extradition Act 1989).

3 Extradition Act 2003, ss 39 (Category 1 territories), 121 (Category 2 territories). The Category 1 territories are defined as the EU Member States by the Extradition Act 2003 (Designation of Part 1 territories) Order 2003, SI 2003/3333, amended by SI 2004/1898), No state which retains the death penalty can be included in Category 1: Extradition Act 2003, s 1(3). The Category 2 territories are set out in the Extradition Act 2003 (Designation of Part 2 territories) Order 2003, SI 2003/3334, amended by SI 2004/1898). The ban on extradition before an asylum claim is 'finally determined' (defined for this purpose to include appeals) is lifted where extradition is to an EU Member State which has accepted responsibility under standing arrangements for determining the asylum claim, or where the person's life and liberty will not be threatened in that state, which will not *refoule* the person in breach of the Refugee Convention, and the person is not a national or citizen.

4 Extradition Act 2003, ss 21 (Category 1 territories); 87 (Category 2 territories).

5 *Re Caddoux* [2004] EWHC 642 (Admin), [2004] All ER (D) 498 (Mar); *R v Mullen* [2000] QB 520, CA; *R v Horseferry Road Magistrates' Court, ex p Bennett* [1994] 1 AC 42, HL; *R v Bow Street Magistrates, ex p Mackeson* (1981) 75 Cr App Rep 24, CA. For permitted destination countries, see **17.70** above.

6 *Chen (An) v Government of Romania* [2006] EWHC 1752 (Admin), [2006] All ER (D) 265 (Jun).

7 IDI, Ch 13, s 1, para 4.

Chapter 18

DETENTION AND BAIL

EIG	Enforcement Instructions and Guidance
ECHR	European Convention of Human Rights and Freedoms
FTT	First Tier Tribunal (IAC)
ECO	Entry Clearance Officer
NOMS	National Offender Management Service
OEM	Operation Enforcement Manual
PSO	Prison Service Order
PSI	Prison Service Instruction
SIAC	Special Immigration Appeal Commission
SLA	Service Level Agreement
UT	Upper Tribunal (IAC)

INTRODUCTION

18.1 The introduction by the Immigration Act 1971 (IA 1971) of administrative detention of those liable to deportation or removal was a dramatic constitutional innovation[1] which has been much relied upon by the state. The use of detention for immigrants and asylum seekers has increased continuously and detention remains a central focus of government policy as the key to fast tracking of asylum cases and enforcement. A policy intention behind the Nationality, Immigration and Asylum Act 2002 (NIAA 2002), with its reception, accommodation and removal centres,[2] was to normalise the use of detention as an inevitable part of the examination process, to be used in part as a matter of administrative convenience for processing claims quickly. In the 2002 White Paper *Secure Borders, Safe Haven*, what was then the Oakington fast track facility was described as 'a central plank of asylum policy'.[3] Up to 250 applicants were held in the centre at any one time and their claims were to be processed within one week. The Government estimated at the time that up to 13,000 applicants could be processed in any one year.[4] In March 2003 the Home Office extended this procedure to Harmondsworth Removal Centre and introduced a scheme which has as its cornerstone detention throughout the entire process of the asylum claim, including any appellate remedies, which is intended to be completed within five weeks.[5] In May 2005, the Detained Fast Track (DFT) system was expanded to include the processing of adult female claimants at Yarl's Wood. Claimants in the DFT process with an in-country right of appeal may be detained only at sites specified in the relevant statutory instrument (currently the Tribunal Procedure (First-tier Tribunal) (Immigration and Asylum Chamber) Rules 2014/2604 which replaced the old Fast Track Procedure Rules on 20 October 2014.[6] The current designated sites are Harmondsworth, Yarl's Wood, Colnbrook and Campsfield. Since the autumn of 2006, Yarl's Wood has also dealt with female detained non-suspensive appeal cases (NSA) as well as female DFT cases. Oakington has now closed although it remains a designated site (SI 2005/560) Yarl's Wood and Dungavel have been used to detain families with children. This practice of detaining families was challenged unsuccessfully in the case of *R (on the application of Suppiah) v Secretary of State for the Home Department*.[7] The detention of children in inappropriate accommodation can potentially engage Article 3 of the ECHR (*Popov v France* (39472/07; 39474/07) as well as Article 5 ECHR (see eg *Kanagaratnam v Belgium* (15297/09))). A failure to take account of the best interests of the child can render the decision to detain unlawful (*R (on the application of Abdollahi) v Secretary of State for the Home Department*).[8]

With the coming into force of section 6 of the Immigration Act 2014 (IA 2014) the 'pre-departure accommodation' in which families are held is now on a statutory footing distinct from short-term holding facilities. The current 'pre-departure accommodation' is Cedars which opened in August 2011 and to which people may be sent following reference by the Family Returns Panel. It is run by G4S and a range of services are provided, controversially, by Barnardos.

There are currently ten removal/detention centres, eight run by private contracted firms[9] and two by HMP service.[10] There are up to 30 smaller temporary holding facilities, typically at airports, and people continue to be detained in police cells and in prisons. These are apparently subject neither to the Detention Centre Rules nor the Prison Service Instructions, a regrettable lacuna. The fall out from the political crisis relating to Foreign National Prisoners (FNPs) resulted in detention becoming virtually routine for former FNPs at the end of their criminal sentences. This was sanctioned by the operation of an undisclosed and unlawful policy,[11] but the practice has since been effectively codified through the UK Borders Act 2007 (UKBA 2007) with the introduction of automatic deportation for a significant number of offenders,[12] the extension of the power to detain pending consideration of whether or not to deport[13] and policy which operates a strong presumption in favour of detention for former FNPs.[14] This policy has been upheld as lawful by the Supreme Court (*R (on the application of Lumba) v Secretary of State for the Home Department*).[15]

[1] *Secretary of State for the Home Department v Pankina* [2010] EWCA Civ 719.
[2] A process under which asylum seekers may be detained where it appears that their claim is straightforward and capable of being decided quickly was introduced at Oakington in March 2000. Detention for this purpose was at that time commonly referred to as being under 'Oakington criteria'. This was supposed to be seven days, but is now sometimes measured in weeks, to enable their claim for asylum to be determined within that period; see below at 17.32. The legality of the policy was upheld by the House of Lords in *R (on the application of Saadi) v Secretary of State for the Home Department* [2002] 1 WLR 3131 and by the European Court of Human Rights in *Saadi v United Kingdom* (2008) 47 EHRR 427. The current policy which includes continuing detention during the appeals process was held to be unlawful in respect of the delays in facilitating access to legal representation, carrying an 'unacceptably high risk of unfairness' in *Detention Action v Secretary of State for the Home Department (Equality Human Rights Commission intervening)* [2014] EWHC 2245 (Admin).
[3] White Paper Secure Borders, Safe Haven (2002 Cm 5387) at para 4.69.
[4] Cm 5387, para 4.72.
[5] In *R (on the application of Refugee Legal Centre) v Secretary of State for the Home Department* [2004] EWCA Civ 1481, [2004] All ER (D) 201 (Nov) the Court of Appeal concluded that the procedure provided a fair opportunity for asylum seekers to put their case provided that a policy was formulated to enable the strict timetable for processing the claim to be adapted in individual cases. The process was put on a statutory footing as far as appeals were concerned with the introduction of the Asylum and Immigration Tribunal (Fast Track Procedure) Rules 2005, SI 2005/560, which provided at rule 30 for transfer out of the fast track procedure which should bring detention to an end. This is now included in para 4 of Sch 1 to the Tribunal Procedure (First-tier Tribunal) (Immigration and Asylum Chamber) Rules 2014, SI 2014/2604 which replaced the the the old Fast Track Procedure Rules on 20 October 2014. See also the decision in *Detention Action v Secretary of State for the Home Department (Equality Human Rights Commission intervening)* [2014] EWHC 2245 (Admin) above.
[6] SI 2005/560.

7 [2011] EWHC 2 (Admin)
8 [2013] EWCA Civ 366
9 Brook House, near Gatwick Airport. Opened March 2009. Contractors G4S Group. Relatively short-term accommodation for 448 male detainees. Campsfield House, Kidlington, Oxon. Opened 1993. Contractors Mitie. Long-term accommodation for 216 male detainees. Colnbrook, near Heathrow Airport. Opened August 2004. Contractors – Serco. IRC and short-term holding facility for 420 males and females. Accommodation for 318 male detainees. Dungavel, Strathaven, South Lanarkshire. Previously a hunting lodge and an open prison. Opened as IRC September 2001. Contractors – GEO. Accommodation for 249 people. Harmondsworth, near Heathrow Airport. Opened 2001. Contractors GEO Group. Long-term accommodation for 661 male detainees. Oakington has now closed. Tinsley House, near Gatwick Airport. Opened 1996. Contractor – G4S. Accommodation for 119 males and up to eight families. Yarl's Wood, Bedford. Opened November 2001. Contractor – Serco. Accommodation for 314 single females and 54 family spaces. Cedars opened in August 2011. Run by G4S and Barnados and can accommodate up to nine families. HMP Verne has been designated an Immigration Removal Centre following an announcement in 2013, but the plans were put in hold in March 2014. It remains a prison although it is currently housing immigration detainees. Further information can be obtained from Gatwick Detainees Welfare Group (GDWG): www.gdwg.org.uk/ and HM Inspectorate of Prisons at www.gov.uk/government/o rganisations/hm-inspectorate-of-prisons.
10 Dover, Western Heights, Port of Dover. Previously a young offenders' institution; re-designated IRC April 2002. Run by HM Prison Service. Accommodation for 280 male detainees. Haslar, Gosport, Hants. Formerly a naval barracks and young offenders' institution, re-opened as IRC June 1989. Run by HM Prison Service. Accommodation for 170 male detainees. Lindholme, Hatfield Woodhouse, near Doncaster. Formerly part of RAF Lindholme ceased operating as an IRC in January 2012. *R (on the application of WL (Congo)) v Secretary of State for the Home Department; R (on the application of KM (Jamaica)) v Secretary of State for the Home Department* [2010] EWCA Civ 111.
11 *R (on the application of Lumba) v Secretary of State for the Home Department* [2011] UKSC 12.
12 UKBA 2007, s 32.
13 UKBA 2007, s 36(1). In answer to a parliamentary question on 4 February 2010 the then under Secretary of State, Home Office (Lord West of Spithead) stated that there were 1,250 time served FNPs (1,168 men and 82 women) in the UKBA's detention estate. This excludes an unknown number of former FNPs remaining in prison facilities. For the week commencing 2 December 2013 there were 957 immigration detainees held in prisons (Immigration Minister Mark Harper in response to a question from Sarah Teather MP on 10 December 2013). During the whole of 2013 some 30,000 people were detained under immigration administrative powers.
14 UKBA 2007, s 36(1) and (2); Enforcement Instructions and Guidance, ch 55.
15 [2011] UKSC 12

18.2 The actual use of the power to detain is, however, restricted by the availability of accommodation space[1] and the need for a rational policy for determining who is to be detained and in what circumstances given that not everybody liable to detention can be detained. Detention, therefore, remains in principle and in practice for the majority of cases other than the DFT and FNPs a measure of last resort to be utilised at the end of the determination process immediately prior to removal. The broad powers of administrative detention are also limited in a number of important ways by implied statutory restrictions, Home Office policy and human rights law, and are subject to increasing judicial scrutiny, particularly in the Administrative Court on judicial review. These limitations and safeguards were, however, suspended for certain foreign nationals suspected of involvement in international terrorism linked to Al Qaeda with the enactment of Part 4 of the Anti-terrorism Crime and Security Act 2001 (ATCSA 2001), which sanctioned indeterminate detention without trial, requiring derogation from Article 5 of the ECHR and ousting the jurisdiction of the High Court on *habeas corpus* or judicial review.[2] In *A v*

Secretary of State for the Home Department; X v Secretary of State for the Home Department,[3] the House of Lords ruled that the derogation from Article 5 of the ECHR was discriminatory and disproportionate, quashed the Derogation Order,[4] and made a declaration that the provisions of the 2001 Act which allowed indefinite detention were incompatible with Articles 5 and 14 of the ECHR. The Prevention of Terrorism Act 2005 (PTA 2005), itself now repealed, was introduced in March 2005 replacing indefinite detention with control orders which allowed for the imposition of severe restrictions on the movement and association of the controlled person. They entailed a combination of confinement at home during specified hours, curfews, electronic tagging, geographical restrictions, requirements for permission to meet others both inside and outside of the home as well as prohibition on communication by telephone, access to the Internet, banking and travel.[5] Control orders could be imposed on both British and Foreign nationals. Control orders which imposed the most extreme combination of obligations including 18 hours' confinement within the premises, with restrictions on visitors inside and meetings outside the premises and confinement within a small, strictly defined geographical area were held to amount to a 'deprivation of liberty' in breach of Article 5 of the ECHR and therefore were struck down as ultra-vires.[6] The House of Lords did, however, uphold other less intrusive orders with periods of confinement of 12 hours[7] and 14 hours with less severe restrictions on association inside and outside of the premises.[8] A 16-hour curfew was held to constitute a deprivation of liberty because of the additional acute social isolation owing to the particular location and the consequent lack of association with family and community that the person previously enjoyed.[9] The rulings on these cases are an important exposition of what constitutes a deprivation of liberty within the meaning of Article 5, accepting and following the guidance of the EctHR in *Guzzardi v Italy*[10] which rejected the requirement of complete physical confinement or restraint and held that deprivation of liberty may take numerous other forms; whether there is a deprivation of liberty will depend on 'a whole range of criteria such as the type, duration, effects and manner of implementation of the measures in question'.[11] The Terrorism Prevention and Investigation Measures Act 2011 (TPIMA 2011) abolished the control order regime in its entirety and has replaced it with a regime of 'TPIMs' which contain less stringent restrictions than those that were available under the control order regime. The obligations imposed by TPIMs include a condition of residence, restrictions on travel (both overseas and to excluded areas), restrictions on the use of bank accounts or property, restrictions on the use of communications devices or other communication, restrictions on work and study, electronic tagging.[12] Although significantly less intrusive than the control order regime the measures remain a grave interference with personal liberty.

[1] In the first half of 2010, 12,995 people were detained under Immigration Act powers. In the second quarter of 2010, 115 children were detained under Immigration Act powers: 'Control of Immigration: Quarterly Statistical Summary, United Kingdom: April – June 2010' (26 August 2010) Home Office. The number of people detained under Immigration Act powers has been steadily climbing and reached 30,113 in the year to March 2014, a rise of 5% on the previous year. Home Office Statistics, January to March 2014.

[2] The Special Immigration Appeal Commission (SIAC) had exclusive jurisdiction in respect of challenges to the derogation: ATCSA 2001, s 30. Part IV of the ATCSA 2001 (ss 21–32) was repealed by the PTA 2005, s 16 on 14 April 2005.

[3] *A v Secretary of State for the Home Department; X v Secretary of State for the Home Department* [2004] UKHL 56, [2005] 2 WLR 87 [2005] 2 AC 68.

4   Human Rights Act 1998 (Designated Derogation) Order 2001, SI 2001/3644, quashed by the
     House of Lords in *A*, above.
5   PTA 2005, s 1.
6   *Secretary of State for the Home Department v JJ* [2007] UKHL 45, [2008] 1 All ER 613,
     [2008] 1 AC 385.
7   *ES v Secretary of State for the Home Department* [2007] UKHL 47, [2008] 1 All ER 699,
     [2008] 1 AC 499.
8   *Secretary of State for the Home Department v AF* [2007] UKHL 46, [2008] 1 All ER 657 and
     *Secretary of State for the Home Department v AH (proceedings under the Prevention of
     Terrorism Act 2005)* [2008] EWHC 1018 (Admin), where a 14-hour curfew was treated as a
     border line case because of the additional social isolation.
9   *Secretary of State for the Home Department v AP* [2010] UKSC 24.
10   *Guzzardi v Italy* (1980) 3 EHRR 33.
11   *Guzzardi*, paras 92–95.
12   TPIMA 2011, Sch 1.

18.3 We will examine in this chapter the limits to the power to detain under the Immigration Acts and the special provisions in national security cases; the power to grant bail by immigration officers, the First-tier Tribunal, the Special Immigration Appeals Commission (SIAC) and by the Administrative Court while proceedings are pending before it, as well as the availability of *habeas corpus* and judicial review to challenge the lawfulness of the detention itself. An overview will also be given of the available remedies in cases of unlawful detention.

18.4 The original powers of detention are to be found in Schedule 2, paragraph 16 and Schedule 3 to the Immigration Act 1971 (IA 1971), as later amended by the 1999, 2002, 2006, 2007 and 2014 Acts. Historically the exercise of those powers to detain immigrants was made ancillary to other immigration measures; essentially they were holding powers pending administrative acts of examination, removal or deportation. Section 62 of the NIAA 2002 not only gave the Secretary of State the power to detain, where previously this had been the preserve of immigration officers,[1] but also extended those powers, first, by linking them to the taking of putative decisions rather than just administrative action, so that a person can be detained, for example, *pending* a decision whether or not to give directions for his or her removal as an overstayer or illegal entrant.[2] Secondly, detention was made possible where the Secretary of State has a reasonable, albeit mistaken, belief that he or she has the power to detain or release someone in any of the situations covered by the statutory powers.[3] In principle, therefore, the Secretary of State acquired more open-ended powers of detention, although as we shall see, in practice, stated policy still significantly restricts and refines the exercise of this broad discretion. The United Kingdom Border Act 2007 (UKBA 2007) continued this trend by creating new powers to detain under section 36(1) of the Act while (a) the Secretary of State considers whether the automatic deportation provisions under section 32(5) apply, and (b) if she thinks they do, pending the making of a deportation order. In *Rashid Hussein v Secretary of State for the Home Department* the court proceeded, without argument, on the basis that section 36(1)(a) and (b) were alternatives.[4] It did emphasise, however, that it was incumbent on the Secretary of State to identify under which specific provision – section 36(1)(a) or (b) – the person is detained because there is a right to know the power under which the person is being held; the preconditions are different and in any challenge the detainee needs to know at what target he or she needs to aim.

1   Previously the Secretary of State only had powers under IA 1971, Sch 3 to detain or release a person against whom deportation action was being taken, and to grant temporary admission to (but not detain) a person claiming asylum (including a claim that removal would be in breach of the person's human rights) on arrival at a port (Immigration (Leave to Enter) Order 2001, SI 2001/2590, Art 3).
2   NIAA 2002, s 62(1)(a); IA 1971, Sch 2, para 16(2), as amended by Immigration and Asylum Act 1999, s 140(1) and Sch 14, para 60 and by NIAA 2002, s 73(5).
3   *R (on the application of Hussein (Rashid)) v Secretary of State for the Home Department* [2009] EWHC 2492 (Admin) at para 41, [2009] All ER (D) 207 (Oct).
4   NIAA 2002, s 62(7); IA 1971, Sch 2, para 16(2) as amended.

18.5 Detention in connection with immigration is a lawful purpose under Article 5(1)(f) of the ECHR, if used to prevent someone effecting an unauthorised entry into the country or with a view to removal, but the power to detain is still (both under the ECHR and at common law) circumscribed and strictly limited to the stated statutory purpose which is a condition precedent for the exercise of the discretion.[1] Using deportation as a means of securing ulterior objects may render the detention ultra vires. In *R v Governor of Brixton Prison, ex p Soblen*,[2] the Court of Appeal held that it was incumbent upon the court to distinguish between a deportation 'done for an authorised purpose' which is lawful and deportation 'done professedly for an authorised purpose, but in fact for a different purpose with an ulterior object', in which case it would be unlawful. It was therefore:

'. . . open to these courts to inquire whether the purpose of the Home Secretary was lawful or an unlawful purpose, Was there a misuse of the power or not? The courts can always go behind the face of the deportation order in order to see whether the powers entrusted by Parliament have been exercised lawfully or not'.

This reflects the position under Article 5(1)(f) of the ECHR where detention pending a deportation which was a disguised extradition was held to be unlawful and in breach of Article 5(1) of the ECHR.[3] In *HXA v Home Office*,[4] applying this approach, a decision to detain a national security suspect pending deportation to Iraq under Schedule 3 to the IA 1971 was held to be unlawful because the deportation had an ulterior and conditional purpose, namely to secure arrest and detention in Iraq which were beyond the powers contained in the IA 1971. Detention for the welfare of a suicidal detainee is outwith the limited purpose of detention under the Immigration Acts.[5] Detention pending removal when there is no practical prospect of effecting removal at all will also render the use of the power unlawful and ultra vires.[6] The exercise of the statutory power to detain is also impliedly limited to the period of time reasonably necessary for the purpose of effecting removal; what is a reasonable period depends on the facts of the case.[7] A failure to pursue deportation with adequate diligence will render detention unlawful both by reference to Article 5 of the ECHR and under common law.[8] Under the IA 1971 there was strict liability – either the person was detained for the stated purpose or they were not. However, section 140 of the Immigration and Asylum Act 1999 amended the IA 1971, requiring only that the detainor had 'reasonable grounds for suspecting' that the person is someone in respect of whom removal directions may be given because, for example, the person is an illegal entrant, or has been refused leave to enter.[9] This does not affect the Administrative Court's jurisdiction on judicial review in a challenge to the lawfulness of the removal directions: whether the detainee is actually removable or an illegal entrant is still a precedent fact question for the Court. Moreover, it would follow that if the objective facts of, for example, illegal entry could not be established, there would be no lawful power to continue to detain after a reasonable period for investigation of the facts, however reasonable the suspicion. Having reasonable grounds for suspecting the relevant precedent fact is, however, as we shall see, a potential defence to a claim for false imprisonment; the detention is authorised if the relevant suspicion is established and objective and rational grounds for the suspicion exist

[1] *Khawaja v Secretary of State for the Home Department* [1984] AC 74 (illegal entry); *R (on the application of Khadir) v Secretary of State for the Home Department* [2005] UKHL 39, [2006] 1 AC, 207, [2005] 4 ALL ER 114 (removal); *Tan Te Lam v Superintendent of Tai A Chau Detention Centre* [1997] AC 97, [1996] 4 All ER 256, PC, approving *R v Governor of Durham Prison, ex p Singh* [1983] Imm AR 198; followed in *Mahmod (Wasfi Suleman), Re* [1995] Imm AR 311, QBD, where Laws J said: 'While of course Parliament is entitled to confer power of administrative detention without trial, the courts will see to it that . . . the statute that confers it will be strictly and narrowly construed and its operation and effect will be supervised by the court according to high standards'.

[2] [1963] 2 QB 243.

[3] *Bozano v France* (Application 9990/82), (1986) 9 EHRR 297, ECtHR.

[4] [2010] EWHC 1177 (QBD).

[5] *R (on the application of AA) v Secretary of State for the Home Department* [2010] EWHC 2265 (Admin). This view was tentatively endorsed in *R (on the application of OM acting by her litigation friend, the Official Solicitor) v Secretary of State for the Home Department* [2011] EWCA Civ 909 at para 32 and *R (on the application of Das) v Secretary of State for the Home Department* [2014] EWCA Civ 45 at 68.

[6] See *R (on the application of I) v Secretary of State for the Home Department* [2002] EWCA Civ 888 [2003] INLR 196 and *A (Somalia)* [2007] EWCA Civ 2004 for the relevance of individual circumstances relating to the significance of the risk of absconding or reoffending and co-operation with the removal process.

[7] See *Tan Te Lam*, above.

[8] *R (on the application of JS (Sudan)) v Secretary of State for the Home Department* [2013] EWCA Civ 1378; *Massoud v Malta* (Application No 24340/08).

[9] IA 1971, Sch 2, para 16(2), amended by Immigration and Asylum Act 1999, s 140(2); for the Secretary of State's equivalent power to detain on suspicion see NIAA 2002, s 62(7).

18.6 Nevertheless, what constitutes reasonable grounds in this context has yet to be defined and its compatibility with Article 5 of the ECHR determined. In Article 5(1)(f) cases, detention is only authorised for the purposes of preventing unauthorised entry and where action is being taken with a view to deportation, and not in circumstances where there is a reasonable suspicion to that effect. Reasonable suspicion for this purpose is not necessarily the same as that required to constitute a suspicion of commission of a criminal offence justifying a simple arrest and limited detention for further investigation. The context, circumstances and the consequences to the individual, particularly in respect of the length of detention, are relevant to the test to be applied.[1] Moreover the question of whether or not the grounds are reasonable itself requires an assessment of objective circumstances which is to be determined by the court[2] and can be challenged on ordinary administrative law principles.[3] An error of law on the part of the detainor, even if entirely understandable, would not constitute reasonable grounds for the relevant suspicion.[4] An example in the immigration context is derived from the unreported case of *N v Home Office*[5] where an immigration officer entirely misconstrued an application under the regularisation scheme for overstayers under s 9 of the Immigration and Asylum Act 1999 as simply a long residence application, thereby failing to determine the application under the scheme. The officer then practice.[1] The government's decision not to implement sections 44–52 of the IAA 1999, which provided for automatic bail hearings, and to repeal them in section 68 of the NIAA 2002,[2] is to be regretted as a lost opportunity to provide greater access to scrutiny of decisions to detain, particularly for those held in long-term detention, many of whom are inadequately represented and in the light of the fact that the system of internal reviews required by rule 9 of the Detention Centre Rules 2001, SI 2001/238, and stated policy has been shown, where it operates at all, to be inadequate.[3] The government has, by contrast, with the Immigration Act 2014 sought to *reduce* the circumstances in which bail can be sought.[4] We shall deal with bail, temporary admission and release on conditions, and note that, there is still no statutory time limit on the period of examination pending a decision on whether or not to grant leave to enter nor on the period of detention itself.[5] The European Union in Directive 2008/115/EC[6] has set maxiumum time limits for detention during the procedures for return which are limited to six months[7] and thereafter for a maximum of 12 months if all reasonable efforts have been taken, but the removal operation is frustrated due to lack of co-operation by the third-country national or there are delays in obtaining the necessary documentation from third countries.[8] The UK has not implemented this Directive and the last government indicated that it had no plans to do so, although it was suggested that 'current practices on the return of illegal third-country nationals are broadly in line with the terms of the Directive'.[9] The IAA 1999[10] and detention rules made under it[11] for the first time regulated immigration detention centres and the powers and duties of custodians, and provide a statutory basis (albeit not in primary legislation) for the giving of written reasons for detention.[12] UKVI also issues detailed Operating Standards.[13] These set out expectations in a wide range of areas as to how detention centres will be managed. The Foreword to the consolidated Operating Standards states that they are designed to:

> 'build on the Detention Centre Rules and to underpin the arrangements we have for the management of removal centres. They are important because they provide a means of raising standards and they are also a means of achieving a level of consistency across the removal estate. They are also a public document and this makes transparent the way we expect detainees to be treated and how our centres operate more generally.'

Detention Services Orders (DSOs) are also issued by UKBA to set out policy and advice on specific areas.[14] For the increasing number of migrants detained in prisons protection is provided by Prison Service Orders[15] and Prison Service Instructions.[16] There are no obvious equivalent protections for those detained in Short Term Holding Facilities.

---

[1] *Secretary of State for the Home Department v Thirukumar* [1989] Imm AR 402.

[2] NIAA 2002, s 68(6), in force 10 February 2003: NIAA Act 2002 (Commencement No 2) Order 2003, SI 2003/1.

[3] *R (on the application of Kambadzi) v Secretary of State for the Home* [2011] UKSC 23.

[4] Section 7 of the IA 2014 which amends Schedule 2 to the IA 1971 so as to prevent a second application for bail being made within 28 days of a refusal at a hearing without a '*material change in circumstances*' (Sch 2, para 25), and to prevent bail being granted where removal directions have been given (Sch 2, para 22).

[5] A statutory time limit on Immigration Act detention was considered and rejected during the passage of the IAA 1999: see 603 HL Official Report (5th series) col 220, 29 June 1999; 605 HL Official Report (5th series) col 1248, 20 October 1999. An implied time limit for detention during consideration of whether or not to deport a person under s 36 of the UK Borders Act

2007 was rejected by the Court of Appeal in *R (on the application of JS (Sudan)) v Secretary of State for the Home Department* [2013] EWCA Civ 1378 at para 31.
[6] Directive 2008/115/EC of the European Parliament and of the Council of 16 December 2008 on common standards and procedures in Member States for returning illegally staying third-country nationals.
[7] Directive 2008/115/EC, Art 15.5.
[8] Article 15.6.
[9] Statement to Parliament by the then Minister Phil Woolas, November 2009. HC Col 690W.
[10] See Pt VIII of the IAA 1999 (ss 147–159).
[11] The Detention Centre Rules 2001, SI 2001/238. Note that detention centres' name was changed to removal centres by the NIAA 2002, s 66(4).
[12] SI 2001/238, r 9(1).
[13] www.gov.uk/government/uploads/system/uploads/attachment_data/file/257352/operatingstandards_manual.pdf.
[14] www.gov.uk/government/collections/detention-service-orders
[15] www.justice.gov.uk/offenders/psos.
[16] www.justice.gov.uk/offenders/psis.

IMMIGRATION OFFICERS' POWERS TO DETAIN

18.9 The code for regulating the examination and admission of non-nationals to UK territory is contained within the Immigration Acts 1971 to 2014. Incidental to the power to examine or remove a non-national is the ancillary power to detain pending the conclusion of such examination or removal. Under para 16 of Sch 2 to the IA 1971, immigration officers are authorised to detain in the following situations:

(1) persons arriving in the UK may be detained pending examination by an immigration officer to establish whether they need or should be granted leave to enter.[1]

(2) There is now a power to detain those who are seeking to leave the UK for a period not exceeding 12 hours if they have been required by a notice in writing to submit to further examination under paragraph 3(1A) of Schedule 2 to the IA 1971 in order to establish whether they are British citizens or to check their identity, whether they entered lawfully, complied with conditions of leave and whether or not their return to the UK is prohibited or restricted.[2]

(3) Those who, on arrival in the UK with leave to enter granted prior to arrival, have been examined under para 2A of Sch 2 to the IA 1971[3] and had their leave suspended, may be detained pending completion of the examination and a decision on whether to cancel leave.[4]

(4) those refused leave to enter and those reasonably suspected of having been refused leave to enter[5] may be detained pending the giving of directions for their removal from the UK;[6]

(5) Illegal entrants and those reasonably suspected of being illegal entrants may be detained, pending a decision on whether to issue removal directions and pending removal in pursuance of directions.[7]

(6) Those who, having limited leave to enter or remain, do not observe a condition attached to their leave or remain beyond their leave or who have sought or obtained leave to remain by deception, or whose indefinite leave to remain has been revoked, or are reasonably suspected of being such persons, may be detained pending a decision to remove them or pending removal.[8]

(7)   Members of the family of someone who has been given removal directions as described in the previous four paragraphs.[9]

(8)   Members of the crew of a ship, aircraft or train who remain beyond the leave granted to enable them to join their ship, aircraft or train, or abscond having lawfully entered without leave, or are reasonably suspected of doing so, may also be detained.[10]

(9)   A person claiming a right of admission as the family member of an EEA national or as a family member who has retained a right of residence or as a person with a permanent right of residence under the EEA Regulations whilst the person's claim is being examined.[11]

(10) A person claiming a right of admission as an EEA national where there is reason to believe that he or she may be excluded from the UK on grounds of public policy, public security or public health pending examination of the claim, or subject to a deportation or exclusion order.[12]

(11) A person refused admission to the UK because he or she does not qualify under the EEA Regulations, pending his or her removal from the UK.[13]

(12) A person whose EEA residence card or family permit has been revoked on arrival by an immigration on the grounds that he or she is not a family member of a qualified person or of an EEA national with a right of residence or does not possess a right of residence him or herself or if the revocation is justified on public policy, public security or public health grounds, or because of an alleged abuse of rights pending removal from the UK.[14]

(13) A person refused admission as a family member of an EEA national, a family member who has retained a right of residence or other person with a right of residence under the EEA Regulations on grounds of public policy, public security or public health, because of the existence of a deportation order or exclusion order, or because of the alleged possibility of an abuse of the right to reside, pending removal from the UK.[15]

(14) A person who does not have or ceases to have a right to reside under the EEA Regulations pending his or her removal.[16]

(15) A person who enters or seeks to enter in breach of a deportation order;[17]

(16) Immigration officers designated by the Secretary of State can detain an individual for up to three hours if they think the individual may be liable to arrest by a police officer under the Police and Criminal Evidence Act 1984, section 24(1)–(3)[18] (ie as someone who is about to commit, is committing or has committed an offence or is reasonably suspected of doing or having done so).

The Immigration, Asylum and Nationality Act 2006 (IAN 2006), section 47[19] enables the Secretary of State to make a decision that a person with statutory leave[20] is to be removed from the UK by way of directions to be given by an immigration officer. The administrative provisions of the IA 1971, Schedule 2, including the power to detain under paragraph 16 apply in relation to directions given by an immigration officer under section 47.[21] However, this does not mean that an immigration officer can detain a person as soon as a section 47 decision is made against him or her, a decision which may be made at the same time as, eg a decision refusing to extend the person's leave to remain. That is because an immigration officer will only be able to detain if there are 'reasonable grounds for suspecting that a person is someone in respect of whom' removal directions may be given.[22] The immigration officer will only be able to give removal directions 'if and when' the statutory leave ends;[23] whilst an appeal might be brought or an appeal is pending, the immigration officer has no power to give removal directions and so will be unable to have reasonable grounds for suspecting that removal directions may be given.[24] Persons may be detained under Schedule 2, paragraph 16 anywhere the Secretary of State directs.[25] An Immigration Officer may search a person detained under paragraph 16 of Schedule 2 to the IA 1971 for any object which might be used to cause injury to others or to escape lawful custody.[26]

[1]   IA 1971, Sch 2, para 16(1).
[2]   IA 1971, Sch 2, para 16(1B) inserted by s 42(2) of the Immigration, Asylum and Nationality Act 2006; SI 2006/2226, Art 3, Sch 1.
[3]   IA 1971, Sch 2, para 2A (inserted by the IAA 1999, Sch 14, para 57) allows examination on entry of those granted leave prior to entry, to establish (i) if there has been a change circumstances since that leave was given; (ii) whether that leave was obtained as a result of false information or a failure to disclose material facts; (iii) if there are medical grounds on which that leave should be cancelled; (iv) if it would be conducive to the public good for that leave to be cancelled. Paragraph 2A(2A), inserted by the Asylum and Immigration (Treatment of Claimants, etc) Act 2004, s 18, adds a further ground for holders of entry clearance; and (v) whether the person's purpose in arriving in the UK is different from that specified in the entry clearance.
[4]   IA 1971, Sch 2, para 16(1A), inserted by the IAA 1999, Sch 14, para 60.
[5]   Ie, suspected of having absconded from temporary admission having been refused leave to enter.
[6]   IA 1971, Sch 2, paras 8, 16(2), as amended by the IAA 1999, s 140(1); and the NIAA 2002, s 73(5).
[7]   IA 1971, paras 9, and 16(2), as amended. Note that the amended wording of para 16(2) allows detention of suspected illegal entrants as well as those who actually are illegal entrants, although actual illegal entry will still be a precedent fact founding the power to remove: see 17.6 above.
[8]   IAA 1999, s 10(1)(a), (b), (ba) and (7). The latter applies the provisions of the IA 1971, Sch 2, para 16.
[9]   IA 1971, Sch 2, para 10A, 16(2) inserted and amended by the NIAA 2002, s 73(1) and 73(5) respectively; IAA 1999, s 10(1)(c) and (7).
[10] IA 1971, Sch 2, paras 12–14, 16(2), modified in relation to Channel Tunnel train crews by the Channel Tunnel (International Arrangements) Order 1993, SI 1993/1813, Sch 4, para 1(11)(n) and (p).
[11] Immigration (European Economic Area) Regulations 2006, SI 2006/1003, reg 22(1)(a).
[12] SI 2006/1003, reg 22(1)(b).
[13] SI 2006/1003, reg 23(1)(a).
[14] SI 2006/1003, reg 23(1)(a).
[15] SI 2006/1003, reg 23(1)(b).
[16] SI 2006/1003, reg 24(2).
[17] SI 2006/1003, reg 24(4).
[18] UKBA 2007, s 2(1) for designated immigration officers brought into effect on 31 January 2008 by SI 2008/99.
[19] As amended by s 51(3) of the Crime and Courts Act 2013.
[20] Ie leave under the IA 1971, s 3C(2)(b), as amended, or s 3D(2)(a), as inserted by the IAN 2006, s 11 – which is leave extended following a refusal to vary leave, a variation or a revocation of leave whilst an appeal may be brought and whilst any appeal is pending. These provisions will be affected by the appeals provisions of the Immigration Act 2014 (IA 2014) if and when they come into force, although it is likely that equivalent provisions will remain.
[21] IAN 2006, s 47(3).
[22] IA 1971, Sch 2, para 16(2).
[23] IAN 2006, s 47(1).

24 The Minister (Tony McNulty) gave an assurance in Parliament that s 47 (as originally drafted) did not create any new power to impose restrictions on a person, eg to detain him or her, whilst the person has statutory leave: *Hansard*, 29.3.06, col 906.
25 IA 1971, Sch 2, para 18(1): see 17.21 below.
26 Para 18A of Schedule 2 to the Immigration Act 1971 as inserted by para 2 of Sch 1 to the IA 2014.

18.10 In the case of a port or illegal entrant asylum claimant, the examination referred to in Schedule 2 to the IA 1971, pending a decision on leave to enter, may embrace the whole asylum determination procedure, impliedly limited only by a period reasonably necessary to conduct the examination and come to the relevant decision.[1] The exercise of this power need not have regard to the individual's propensity to abscond, as ruled by the House of Lords which upheld the immigration officer's power to detain for up to 10 days in order to facilitate speedy decision making by ensuring the claimant's availability for interview at any time.[2] The European Court of Human Rights agreed with the House of Lords that detention of an asylum seeker, who presented no risk of absconding and was only detained for reasons of administrative convenience, did not breach Article 5(1)(f). The Court so held even though there was no suggestion that the applicant would seek to enter or remain unlawfully and no suggestion that he was anything other than a bona fide asylum seeker; notwithstanding that, his detention was said to be for the purpose of preventing an unauthorised entry. The Court adopted a literal interpretation and concluded that until granted leave to enter, the applicant was not authorised to enter even though he might be granted temporary admission. The Grand Chamber has upheld these conclusions.[3] Whilst section 77 of the NIAA 2002 reproduces the protection against removal pending the determination of an asylum claim formerly contained in section 15 of the IAA 1999,[4] section 77 also provides that directions for removal may be given, preparatory steps to facilitate removal may be taken, and a deportation order may be served during that period.[5] The amended provisions of paragraph 16(2) of Schedule 2 of the IA 1971 ensure that the prohibition on removal does not preclude the power to detain and prevents a claim for unlawful detention on the basis that there is no power of removal and therefore no lawful purpose for the detention.[6]

1 *R (on the application of Saadi) v Secretary of State for the Home Department* [2002] UKHL 41, [2002] 1 WLR 3131, [2002] INLR 523.
2 *R (on the application of Saadi) v Secretary of State for the Home Department* above.
3 *Saadi v United Kingdom* (Application No 13229/03) [2006] All ER (D) 125 (Jul), EctHR. Judgment by the Grand Chamber given on 29.1.2008. *Saadi v United Kingdom* (Application 13229/03)(2008) 47 EHRR 427, (2008) Times, 4 February
4 Ministers confirmed however, during the passage of the 1999 Act, that no directions or deportation order would be served until a negative determination: Lord Williams of Mostyn, 605 HL Official Report (5th series) col 785; 606 HL Official Report (5th series) cols 766–767.
5 NIAA 2002, s 77(4).
6 *R v Secretary of State for the Home Department, ex p Khan* [1995] Imm AR 348, CA.

TEMPORARY ADMISSION

18.11 For those liable to be detained pending examination under Schedule 2, paragraph 16(1) and (1A) (but note not paragraph (1B))[1] and removal under any of the Schedule 2 powers in the IA 1971, the main alternative to incarceration is the grant of temporary admission to the UK.[2] The power can be exercised by both immigration officers and the Secretary of State[3] by giving written notice.[4] There is no power to grant temporary admission instead of granting leave to enter (eg in circumstances where the Secretary of State accepts that a person cannot be removed because removal would breach his or her human rights but considers it 'inappropriate' to grant discretionary leave); temporary admission may only be granted whilst an application for leave to enter is being considered or pending removal from the UK.[5] Those temporarily admitted are deemed not to have entered the UK.[6] The House of Lords has held that whilst the purpose of section 11 of the IA 1971 was to exclude a person temporarily admitted from the rights available to those granted leave to enter, in particular the right to seek an extension of leave to remain, a person granted temporary admission was nonetheless 'lawfully present' in the United Kingdom for the purposes of social security entitlement.[7] The status may be subject to significant restrictions as to residence, employment or occupation, and may require reporting to the police or an immigration officer. Section 36(2) of the Asylum and Immigration (Treatment of Claimants etc) Act 2004 (AI(TC)A 2004) provided the power to make a residence restriction subject to electronic monitoring[8] or impose electronic monitoring as an alternative to a reporting restriction.[9] The restrictions may be varied by either an immigration officer or the Secretary of State, who may each vary conditions imposed by the other.[10] The grant of temporary admission is without prejudice to the exercise of the power to detain. A failure to observe any restriction imposed under these provisions can be grounds for detaining or re-detaining and, in the absence of any reasonable excuse may also constitute a criminal offence under section 24(1)(e) of the IA 1971. On the other hand the power to re-detain does not require breach of conditions of temporary admission, although it might be condemned as arbitrary if there was no actual or anticipated breach.[11] The residence restrictions may include prohibitions on residence in a specified area, or a condition requiring residence in specified accommodation provided under section 4 of the IAA 1999,[12] and prohibiting absence from it, in accordance with regulations.[13] An additional residence restriction may be imposed on asylum seekers and their dependants, requiring them to reside at a specified location for a period not exceeding 14 days in order to attend an induction programme being held nearby.[14] A person released from immigration detention may apply for permission to work if he or she is an asylum clamant and a first instance decision has not been made within a year of making the asylum claim or fresh claim for asylum.[15] Otherwise released detainees who are liable to deportation or removal as illegal entrants or under the IAA 1999, s 10 will not be given permission to work.[16] Reporting to the police or the immigration service should not normally be required more than once a month, and if a non-Criminal Casework Directorate (CCD) case remains unresolved for three years, should be lifted.[17] The Secretary of State may make a payment to cover travel expenses incurred in complying with a reporting restriction.[18] Section 71 of the NIAA 2002 permits similar restrictions to be imposed on those who have extant leave to enter or remain at the time of making a claim for asylum as can be imposed on other asylum seekers who are given temporary admission under paragraph 21 of Schedule 2 to the IA 1971, and similar powers of detention for breach of restrictions.[19]

---

[1]   IA 1971, Sch 2, para 21, amended by IAN 2006, s 42(4); SI 2006/2226, art 3, Sch 1. See further CHAPTER 3 (temporary admission).

2   It appears that those detained for up to 12 hours seeking to leave the UK cannot be granted temporary admission.
3   IA 1971, Sch 2, para 21 (immigration officers); NIAA 2002, s 62(3)(b) (Secretary of State).
4   IA 1971, Sch 2, para 21(1), (2), as amended by Immigration Act 1988, Schedule, para 10.
5   *R (on the application of GG) v Secretary of State for the Home Department* [2006] EWHC 1111 (Admin), (2006) Times, 14 June, [2006] All ER (D) 143 (May); *affd sub nom S v Secretary of State for the Home Department (sub nom R (on the application of GG) v Secretary of State for the Home Department)* [2006] EWCA Civ 1157, [2006] All ER (D) 30 (Aug), upheld in *S v Secretary of State for the Home Department (sub nom R (on the application of GG) v Secretary of State for the Home Department)* [2006] EWCA Civ 1157, [2006] All ER (D) 30 (Aug).
6   IA 1971, s 11(1), referred to as a fictional status by Chadwick LJ in *R (on the application of Khadir) v Secretary of State for the Home Department* [2003] EWCA Civ 475, [2003] INLR 426 at para 57.
7   *Szoma v Secretary of State for the Department of Work and Pensions* [2005] UKHL 64, [2006] 1 AC 564.
8   AI(TC)A 2004, s 36(2).
9   AI(TC)A 2004, s 36(3).
10 IA 1971, Sch 2 para 21(2); NIAA 2002, s 62(4)(a), (b).
11 Persons liable to be detained under IA 1971, Sch 2, para 16, who may be arrested under para 17, include those on temporary admission: *R (on the application of Khadir) v Secretary of State* above.
12 Section 4 of the IAA 1999 empowers the Secretary of State to provide accommodation for persons temporarily admitted or released from detention, the immigration equivalent of bail hostels. Amendments made by NIAA 2002, s 49 extends the provision of such temporary accommodation to failed asylum seekers. See the Immigration and Asylum (Provision of Accommodation to Failed Asylum Seekers) Regulations 2005, SI 2005/930.
13 IA 1971, Sch 2, para 21(2A)–(2E), inserted by IAA 1999, Sch 14, para 62. No regulations have been made under these paragraphs, although the provision of accommodation under s 4 of IAA 1999 is regulated by SI 2005/930, see above.
14 NIAA 2002, s 70(1). A programme of induction means education about the nature of the asylum process: NIAA 2002, s 70(3).
15 HC 395, para 360, introduced on 1 April 2005 in line with a European Directive on asylum seekers' right to work. See also *R (on the application of ZO (Somalia)) v Secretary of State for the Home Department* [2010] UKSC 36.
16 Enforcement Instructions and Guidance (EIG), paras 23.9.3 and 23.9.5.
17 EIG, para 55.20.2.
18 NIAA 2002, s 69(1).
19 Ie, under IA 1971, Sch 2, para 16: NIAA 2002, s 71(3)(b).

18.12 Those on temporary admission are excluded from income support and related benefits, but if they are asylum claimants, may be eligible for NASS support whilst their application or appeal is outstanding. Thereafter they only have access to hard cases support, with the qualification, introduced in 2003, that those who can leave the jurisdiction, but choose not to, are excluded even from this minimal support. See CHAPTER 14. This state of affairs was the subject of litigation in the case of *Khadir*,[1] where the Administrative Court held that under the IA 1971 Act, temporary admission was not available when the power to detain no longer exists, and consideration had to be given to the grant of leave to remain. The case concerned Iraqi Kurds who could not safely be returned to Iraq because of the practical impossibility of return directly to the Kurdish Autonomous Region, and it could not, therefore be said that removal was 'pending' for the purpose of paragraph 16 of Schedule 2 to the IA 1971. If removal was not pending then the person was not liable to be detained and consequently there was no power to grant temporary admission, with its associated reporting, residence and employment restrictions. The House of Lords[2] however decided that both Crane J and the Court of Appeal were wrong to have held that removal was not 'pending' for the purpose of the IA

1971, Schedule 2, paragraph 16, if it was not possible to effect removal within a reasonable or tolerable time. A person's removal would be 'pending' for as long as an immigration officer or the Secretary of State intended to remove the person and there was some prospect of achieving the person's removal. The person would remain liable to be detained until one or both of the intention to remove and the prospect of removal ceased. The line of cases following *Ex p Singh*[3] and holding that the power to detain was implicitly limited to the period reasonably necessary for the purpose of effecting removal were concerned with the exercise but not the existence of the power to detain.[4] Accordingly, it was unnecessary to have enacted the NIAA 2002, section 67.[5]

[1] *R (on the application of Khadir) v Secretary of State for the Home Department* (CO/5118/2001) (29 July 2002, unreported), Crane J. This part of the judgment was upheld at [2003] EWCA Civ 475, [2003] INLR 426, per Chadwick LJ at paras 52–53 but overturned by the House of Lords [2005] UKHL 39, [2006] 1 AC 207, [2005] 4 All ER 114.

[2] *R (on the application of Khadir) v Secretary of State for the Home Department* [2005] UKHL 39, [2006] 1 AC 207, [2005] 4 All ER 114, [2005] 3 WLR 1.

[3] *R v Governor of Durham Prison, ex p Singh* [1984] 1 All ER 983, [1984] 1 WLR 704, [1983] Imm AR 198, QBD. See further 17.42 of the main text.

[4] See fn 1 above.

[5] See fn 1 above.

18.13 Section 67 of the NIAA 2002 was specifically drafted to deal with the apparent problems raised in *Khadir*[1] and came into force with retrospective effect.[2] It provides a revised definition of 'person liable to detention'. Persons are included within the definition if the only reason why they cannot be detained is that: (a) they cannot presently be removed from the United Kingdom, because of a legal impediment connected with the United Kingdom's obligations under an international agreement;[3] (b) there are practical difficulties impeding or delaying the making of arrangements for their removal from the United Kingdom; or (c) practical difficulties, or demands on administrative resources, are impeding or delaying the taking of decisions in respect of them.[4] Section 67 does not authorise detention in those circumstances, but does authorise temporary admission to be granted. This expressly allows conditions and restrictions to be imposed on those in the situation of the applicants in *Khadir* but the broad and extended definition of 'pending' made this provision unnecessary in the removal context.

[1] *R (on the application of Khadir) v Secretary of State for the Home Department* [2003] EWCA Civ 475, [2003] INLR 426.

[2] NIAA 2002, s 67(3).

[3] NIAA 2002, s 67(2). The description of legal obligations under the Human Rights Act as a 'legal impediment' to the exercise of the power of removal is an extraordinary example of the mind-set of the government towards asylum seekers' rights.

[4] It is to be noted that s 67(2) is not exhaustive and there may be situations where it does not apply, for example, the policy of non-removal adopted for a time by the Home Office in respect of Zimbabwean nationals, which does not appear to fall within the ambit of s 67(2), because the Secretary of State expressly disavowed human rights considerations as the rationale for it. Instead it was said to be 'based on political rather than legal grounds. It is not in place because it is considered unsafe for failed asylum seekers to return to Zimbabwe': see *Dowu v Secretary of State for the Home Department* [2003] EWCA Civ 753.

SPECIAL IMMIGRATION STATUS

18.14 The Criminal Justice and Immigration Act 2008 will, if and when the relevant provisions come into force, enable the Secretary of State to give a new 'special immigration status' to designated individuals.[1] The Secretary of State will be able to designate individuals falling within the statutory definition of 'foreign criminal' but whose deportation would be in breach of an ECHR right and he or she may also designate 'family members' of such a person.[2] A foreign criminal is a person who has been convicted and sentenced to at least two years' imprisonment for an offence in the UK or has been convicted and sentenced to at least two years' imprisonment outside the UK and could have been sentenced to at least two years for a similar offence in the UK[3] or convicted of a specified offence[4] or has been excluded from the Refugee Convention under Article 1F.[5] A person with special immigration status will not have leave to enter or remain[6] or temporary admission[7] but a status that is regulated entirely by this Act. Conditions as to residence, employment or occupation, reporting and monitoring may be imposed, breach of any of which is a criminal offence.[8] Support is to be provided by a modified asylum support regime.[9] The purpose behind these provisions may have largely been fulfilled by the policy of granting six months' discretionary leave where persons fall under Article 1F of the Refugee Convention.[10]

[1]   Criminal Justice and Immigration Act 2008 (CJIA 2008), ss 130(1) and 132.
[2]   CJIA 2008, s 130(2), (3).
[3]   CJIA 2008, s 131(1), (2).
[4]   CJIA 2008, s 131(3).
[5]   CJIA 2008, s 131(4).
[6]   CJIA 2008, s 132(1).
[7]   CJIA 2008, s 132(4)(b).
[8]   CJIA 2008, s 133.
[9]   CJIA 2008, ss 134 and 135.
[10] www.gov.uk/government/uploads/system/uploads/attachment_data/file/257436/restricted-lea ve-article-1f-pdf.pdf. This policy was introduced on 2 September 2011.

SECRETARY OF STATE'S POWERS TO DETAIN

18.15 The NIAA 2002 gave the Secretary of State the following powers to detain:

(1)   The power to detain pending a decision whether to direct removal pursuant to the Secretary of State's powers under Schedule 2 to the IA 1971, and pending removal.[1]

(2)   The power to detain persons seeking leave to enter the UK[2] who have made an asylum or human rights claim or who have sought departure from the immigration rules, pending the Secretary of State's examination, decision whether to grant or refuse leave to enter, decision whether to remove following refusal, and removal.[3]

(3)   The power to detain where the Secretary of State has reasonable grounds to suspect that he or she may make one of the specified decisions above.[4]

(4)   The power to detain persons who make a claim for asylum when they have leave to enter or remain and who fail to comply with restrictions imposed on them.[5]

In addition to these powers, the Secretary of State has always had wide powers to detain persons liable to deportation, contained in Schedule 3 to the IA 1971. Detention may occur in the following situations:

(1) *Court recommendation.* Where a recommendation for deportation made by a court is in force and the person is not detained pursuant to the sentence or order of any court, he or she must be detained pending the making of a deportation order,[6] unless *either* the court by which the recommendation is made, or an appeal court[7] otherwise directs, *or* the Secretary of State directs that the person be released pending further consideration of the case, *or* he or she is released on bail.[8]

(2) *Decision to deport.* Where notice has been given to a person of a decision to make a deportation order under section 3(5) of the IA 1971,[9] and that person is not detained pursuant to the sentence or order of a court, he or she may be detained under the authority of the Secretary of State pending the making of the deportation order.[10] IAN 2006, section 53 came into force on 31 August 2006 with the effect that a person will be liable to detention not only (as the law previously stood) when he or she has been given notice of a decision to make a deportation order but also when there is such a notice ready to be given to the person. A police or immigration officer has the power to arrest the person once notice of a decision to make a deportation order is ready to be given.[11]

(3) *Deportation order made.* Persons against whom a deportation order is in force may be detained under the authority of the Secretary of State pending their removal or departure from the UK. If they are already detained under either of the previous provisions they shall continue to be detained unless the Secretary of State directs otherwise or they are released on bail.[12] Which provision a person was detained under may have some significance as it can affect whether or not a breach of a relevant public law policy will give rise to a false imprisonment.[13]

In cases (2) and (3) above, the powers of arrest, entry, search and seizure possessed by immigration officers under Schedule 2 to the IA 1971 in relation to persons detained pending removal also apply to detained deportees.[14] Detained deportees may also benefit from the bail provisions in paras 22 to 23 of Schedule 2 to the IA 1971.[15] A person admitted to or residing in the UK under the EEA Regulations may be detained under the powers contained in the IA 1971, Schedule 3 if a decision is taken to remove the person on the grounds that he or she does not have or no longer has a right of admission or residence under the Regulations or the person's removal is justified on public policy, public security or public health grounds.[16] Such a person may also be detained where the Secretary of State has reasonable grounds for suspecting that he is a person who may be removed under the power in regulation 19(3).[17]

---

[1] Ie, directions to remove persons refused leave to enter, illegal entrants and members of their families, and overstaying crew members in the situations described at the IA 1971, Sch 2, paras 10, 10A and 14: NIAA 2002, s 62(1)(a), (b).

[2] Ie, port claimants or illegal entrants.

[3] NIAA 2002, s 62(2), (3)(a). The powers on which the power to detain is contingent are set out in the Immigration (Leave to Enter) Order 2001, SI 2001/2590, art 2, made under the IA 1971, s 3A (inserted by the IAA 1999, s 1).

[4] NIAA 2002, s 62(7).

[5] NIAA 2002, s 71(1)–(3).

6. IA 1971, Sch 3, para 2(1), as amended by AI(TC)A 2004, s 34(1). Before amendment by the AI(TC)A 2004, the paragraph allowed (or arguably required) the release of a person recommended for deportation who was on bail from the criminal court. See explanatory Notes to the AI(TC) Bill (HL), para 109.

7. The appeal court may direct release while upholding the recommendation: IA 1971, Sch 3, para 2(1A), inserted by the Criminal Justice Act 1982, s 64, Sch 10.

8. IA 1971, Sch 3, para 2(1), as amended by the IAA 1999, s 54(3) which finally came into force on 10 February 2003: SI 2003/2. The paragraph has no application where the person is serving a sentence or on remand to a criminal court: see *Re Nwafor* [1994] Imm AR 91, QBD.

9. Deportation deemed conducive to the public good, and of family members of deportees: IA 1971, s 3(5), as substituted by the IAA 1999, s 169 and Sch 14, para 44(2).

10. IA 1971, Sch 3, para 2(2), as amended the AI(TC)A 2004, s 34(2).

11. SI 2006/2226.

12. IA 1971, Sch 3, para 2(3), as amended by the IAA 1999, s 54(3) (in force 10 February 2003: SI 2003/2).

13. *R (on the application of Francis) v Secretary of State for the Home Department* [2014] EWCA Civ 718.

14. These powers do not apply to those detained by the Secretary of State following a recommendation for deportation: IA 1971 Sch 3, para 2(4) as amended by the IAA 1999.

15. IA 1971, Sch 3, para 2(4A), inserted by the IAA 1999.

16. Immigration (European Economic Area) Regulations 2006, SI 2006/1003, reg 24(3).

17. Immigration (European Economic Area) Regulations 2006, SI 2006/1003, reg 24(1); reg 19(3).

18.16 The Secretary of State's powers to detain 'foreign national prisoners' were greatly increased by the UKBA 2007[1] which allows for the Secretary of State to detain a person who has served a period of imprisonment whilst the Secretary of State considers whether the provision for 'automatic deportation'[2] applies and if the Secretary of State thinks that it does, pending the making of the deportation order.[3] The powers to detain under section 36 of the UKBA 2007 are available in respect of 'a person who has served a period of imprisonment' which means a person who has served the whole of the custodial period of his or her sentence, not just some part of it.[4] The provision for 'automatic deportation' applies to people who are not British citizens who have been convicted in the UK and sentenced to at least 12 months' imprisonment (for a single offence) or, although this is not yet in force, to a period of imprisonment for an offence specified by an order made under section 72(4)(a) of the NIAA 2002.[5] Where a deportation order is made under that provision the Secretary of State 'shall' exercise the power to detain pending removal from the UK[6] 'unless in the circumstances the Secretary of State thinks it inappropriate'.[7] The statutory provisions appear to operate no express presumption when detention is authorised under section 36(1) and will be construed as a presumption in favour of release. While the power in section 36(2) of the Act to detain following the making of an automatic deportation order under the UKBA 2007 appears at first blush to be in mandatory terms, which would suggest that it also amounts to a statutory warrant, the authors consider that the wording in section 36(2) is so widely drawn as to amount to a discretion.[8] In *R (on the application of Hussein (Rashid)) v Secretary of State for the Home Department* it was confirmed that these provisions applied retrospectively to convictions made between the passage of the Act on the 1 November 2007 and its commencement on 1 August 2008.[9] The Court also held detention under section 36(1)(a) to be compatible with Article 5(1) of the ECHR even though it allows for detention before a decision is made as to whether or not deportation action should be pursued. This was still said to be detention with a 'view to deportation'. An attempt to try to confine the acceptable lengths of time for detention under section 36(1)(a) to fast track time frames was rejected but the court emphasised the need for expeditious consideration of any claims. The Court of Appeal in *R (on the application of JS (Sudan)) v Secretary of State for the Home Department*[10] again rejected any attempt to set a 'yardstick' for consideration of claims. The Court however approved Nicol J's decision that application of the *Hardial Singh* principles under section 36(1)(a) is coloured by the fact that detention can only be lawful under that section specifically for the purpose of deciding whether the exceptions to automatic deportation apply.[11] It is clear from *JS (Sudan)* that, depending on the facts, it may be necessary for the Secretary of State to begin the task of examining whether a person should be deported prior to a person entering immigration detention.[12] Policy refers to the need for early consultation with relevant bodies particularly if the case concerns deportation of individuals with children.[13] Increasingly in practice however people are being detained for substantial periods under section 36(1) and invariably for months rather than weeks. In such cases the question of whether or not the Secretary of State has diligently applied herself to the consideration of the automatic detention criteria will be important. In *JS (Sudan)* the claimant's challenge succeeded because of substantial unexplained delays, which it might be considered would not have occurred had he been on bail.[14] Cases where children are concerned appear to be proving particularly problematic because no proper assessment can be made about the interests of the children if they cannot be reunited with a parent, especially a mother, prior to removal because the parent is detained and may have been detained for lengthy periods of time.

1   UKBA 2007, s 36.
2   Ie that the person is a 'foreign criminal' against whom the Secretary of State must make a deportation order under the UKBA 2007, s 32(5).
3   Presently, the detention powers under s 36 apply only in relation to those liable to automatic deportation because they have been sentenced to imprisonment for 12 months or more. They do not apply in relation to those liable because they have been imprisoned for an offence specified by order of the Secretary of State. See the UK Borders Act 2007 (Commencement No 3 and Transitional Provisions) Order 2008, SI 2008/1818.
4   *R (on the application of Aitouaret) v Secretary of State for the Home Department* [2010] EWHC 3136 (Admin), [2010] NLJR 1570.
5   UKBA 2007, s 32. The order referred to is currently the Nationality, Immigration and Asylum Act 2002 (Specification of Particularly Serious Crimes) Order 2004, SI 2004/1910.
6   Section 36(2) of the UKBA 2007, referring to the power under the IA 1971, Sch 3, para 2(3).
7   UKBA 2007, s 36(2). Policy in EIG, para 55.1.2. states that the presumption in favour of liberty continues to be applied but will often be displaced in the light of any risk of reoffending and absconding. Substantial weight is to be given to any harm to the public caused by the risk of reoffending (para 55.1.3) and the more serious the past offending behaviour the more weight will be attached to it as a factor in favour of detention (paras 55.3.A and 55.3.2–55.3.2.12). For serious offences such as crimes which are violent, sexual, drug related and similar offences, particularly compelling factors will be required (para 55.1.3). Those assessed as low to medium risk of reoffending and harm to the public should, however, generally be considered for management by rigorous contact management under the instructions in para 55.20.5, which refers to release subject to extensive conditions including electronic tagging (para 55.3.2.11).
8   UKBA 2007, s 36(2). ' . . . . the Secretary of State shall exercise the power of detention under paragraph 2(3) of Schedule 3 to the Immigration Act 1971 . . . . unless in the circumstances the Secretary of State thinks it inappropriate.'.
9   [2009] EWHC 2492 (Admin) at [28]. The approach of Nicol J was approved by the Court of Appeal in *AT (Pakistan) v Secretary of State for the Home Department* [2010] EWCA Civ 567.
10 [2013] EWCA Civ 1378

[11] Nicol J stated: 'i) The Secretary of State must intend to deport the person unless one of the exceptions in s 33 applies and can only use this power to detain for the purpose of examining whether they do. The Secretary of State must have this conditional intention because otherwise it would not be possible for him to say that detention was pursuant to action with a view to deportation . . . ii) The detainee may only be detained for a period that is reasonable in all the circumstances . . . iii) If, before the expiry of the reasonable period it becomes apparent that the Secretary of State will not be able to effect deportation within that reasonable period he should not seek to exercise the power of detention. No change is necessary to the formulation here, but this principle will be infringed if detention continues even though it is apparent that either resolution of the question of whether any of the exceptions in s 33 is applicable, or any subsequent deportation, or both together, will take more than a reasonable time. iv) The Secretary of State should act with reasonable diligence and expedition to determine whether any of the exceptions in s 33 is applicable.'*R (on the application of Hussein (Rashid)) v Secretary of State for the Home Department* [2009] EWHC 2492 (Admin) at para 44, approved by the Court of Appeal in *R (on the application of JS (Sudan)) v Secretary of State for the Home Department* [2013] EWCA Civ 1378 at para 15.

[12] At para 50.

[13] Criminal Casework Directorate: Children and Family Cases Process Instructions. See also *R (on the application of Abdollahi) v Secretary of State for the Home Department* [2013] EWCA Civ 366.

[14] There were a total of 12 months of administrative inactivity out of a period of 15 months' detention. See also *R (on the application of Ismail) v Secretary of State for the Home Department* [2013] EWHC 3921 (Admin).

Restriction orders

18.17 In each of these cases, including the case of recommendations by the courts, an alternative to detention is provided. On the Secretary of State's direction, the person may instead be subjected to a restriction order which places him or her under such restrictions as to residence, employment or occupation and a requirement to report to the police or immigration officer, as the Secretary of State may from time to time notify in writing.[1] The restrictions mirror those which an immigration officer may impose on temporary admission, for which see 17.11 above.

[1] IA 1971, Sch 3, para 2(5) and (6), as substituted by the CJA 1982, s 64, Sch 10 and amended by the IA 1988, Sch, para 10; Asylum and Immigration Act 1996, Sch 2, para 13. Applied by the UK Borders Act 2007, s 36(5) to detention under s 36(1) of that Act.

Accommodation centres

18.18 Section 16 of the NIAA 2002 gave the Home Secretary power to set up accommodation centres to house destitute asylum seekers and their dependants. The provision has never been come into force and there are no signs that it will be.

Prisoners recommended for deportation

18.19 The qualified requirement to detain those recommended for deportation pending the decision of the Secretary of State was the subject of considerable criticism, as long ago as 1978, on the grounds that it resulted in unnecessary detention in custody of such persons, either at the end of a prison sentence or immediately, where a non-custodial sentence had been given. In

July 1978, partly in response to these criticisms, the Home Office issued a circular to the courts[1] reminding them that because of appeal rights, a person recommended for deportation may spend at least five weeks in detention; that the Secretary of State would not necessarily be in a position to decide whether to exercise his or her discretion to release the person if the court had not already done so; and that courts might wish to bear in mind, when considering whether or not to release, the principal grounds for withholding bail in criminal proceedings under the Bail Act 1976. The circular also reminded the courts of the importance of submitting a certificate of recommendation without delay to the Home Office. The clear intention of the circular was to make release the rule rather than the exception. It became clear, however, that this guidance was not being followed by the Secretary of State, and instead, up until 2001 the Home Office proceeded on the basis that Schedule 3 created a presumption in favour of detention, at the end of a prison sentence, to enable a decision to be reached whether or not to deport. This presumption would only be displaced by exceptional circumstances. In *Sedrati*[2] the government conceded that this approach was wrong in law, and the Court made a declaration that there was no presumption under paragraph 2 of Schedule 3 to the IA 1971 in favour of detention after the end of the deportee's prison sentence. By the terms of the declaration however, following this approach, it has been held that if the Secretary of State does not make a decision to deport a person who has been recommended for deportation by the Court, his or her continued detention after completion of the prison sentence would be unlawful.[3] The fact that the criminal court could have, but did not, recommend deportation may be an important factor in favour of relase.[4] However, in *WL (Congo)*,[5] the Court of Appeal concluded that the Secretary of State had been wrong to make the concession that there was no presumption in favour of the detention of a person against whom there was a recommendation to make a deportation order and overruled *Sedrati)*. The Supreme Court in *Lumba* found it '*puzzling*' that the Court of Appeal had reached this conclusion since the declaration made following the *Sedrati* case had concerned only 2(2) and 2(3) which clearly created no presumption.[6] Following the decision of the Court of Appeal in *R (Francis) v Secretary of State for the Home Department*,[7] it is now unequivocally the case that where a person has been recommended for deportation the statute requires detention. The effect of this is that the 'statutory warrant' to detain is unaffected by public law errors bearing on the decision to detain such as those that gave rise to a false imprisonment in *Lumba*. The same applies to detention under paragraph 2(3) of Schedule 3 once the recommended deportation order has been made.[8] The Court emphatically held that whatever the position for public law breaches the *Hardial Singh* principles continue to apply to such cases, and any breach thereof will give rise to a false imprisonment and damages. Cases like *Sedrati* had revealed the absence of any effective procedural safeguards for those detained at the completion of criminal sentences. Section 54 of the IAA 1999 assimilated the position of persons detained for deportation (whether after a recommendation, a notice of intention to deport or a deportation order) to that of persons detained by immigration officers, and they can apply to an immigration officer for release or to the Tribunal for bail.[9]

[1] Home Office Circular No 113/1978 'Immigration Act 1971: Detention Pending Deportation'.

2   *R (on the application of Sedrati) v Secretary of State for the Home Department* [2001] EWHC Admin 418. However, see the effect of *R (on the application of Francis) v Secretary of State for the Home Department* [2014] EWCA Civ 718.

3   *R (on the application of Vovk) v Secretary of State for the Home Department* [2006] EWHC 3386 (Admin), [2006] All ER (D) 171 (Dec). The Court of Appeal appeared to doubt this reasoning in *R (on the application of Francis) v Secretary of State for the Home Department* [2014] EWCA Civ 718 at para 28. See also *R (on the application of Singh) v Secretary of State for the Home Department* [2011] EWHC 1402 (Admin). The relevance of this case has in any event largely been overtaken by the operation of the automatic deportation provisions in the UKB A 2007.

4   *R (on the application of Faulkner) v Secretary of State for the Home Department* [2005] EWHC 2567 (Admin), [2005] All ER (D) 03 (Nov).

5   *R (on the application of WL (Congo)) v Secretary of State for the Home Department; R (on the application of KM (Jamaica)) v Secretary of State for the Home Department* [2010] EWCA Civ 111.

6   *R (on the application of Lumba) v Secretary of State for the Home Department* [2011] UKSC 12.

7   [2014] EWCA Civ 718.

8   The Court referred with apparent approval to the passage in *Choy v Secretary of State for the Home Department* [2011] EWHC 365 (Admin) in which Bean J had noted that the situation might be different if the Secretary of State had irrationally refused release. This view accords with what was said by Lord Diplock in *Holgate-Mohammed v Duke* [194] AC 437.

9   IA 1971, Sch 3, para 2(4A), inserted by I AA 1999, s 54(4), in force 20 February 2003. For bail under the IA 1971, Sch 2, para 22, see **18.67** below.

Foreign national prisoners – treatment in detention

18.20 The Secretary of State also adopted policies and practices with regard to prisoners subject to possible deportation. Firstly, they were not permitted to be held in Category D open prison conditions whilst serving their prison sentences. Secondly, detainees subject to deportation after the completion of a criminal sentence of 12 months or more were not eligible for transfer to immigration facilities at the end of their sentence, but had to remain within the prison system on conditions which are substantially inferior to those of a sentenced prisoner or an immigration detainee.[1] After the *Sedrati* litigation a consent order between the parties made clear that this policy would be revised so that transfer would depend on the individual circumstances of the prisoner.[2] Thirdly, there were the provisions of the Criminal Justice Act 1991, ss 35(1) and 46(1), (introduced following the 1988 Carlisle Committee report) which left entirely to the Secretary of State the decision whether long term prisoners who are liable to removal should be released on licence.[3] Prisoners not liable to be removed have a right to have their cases referred to the Parole Board. In *Hindawi*[4] the House of Lords overruled the Court of Appeal and upheld a decision of the Administrative Court that this situation constituted unlawful discrimination on the grounds of nationality contrary to Article 14 read together with Article 5 of the ECHR. Lord Bingham of Cornhill described the differences in treatment of foreign nationals as an 'indefensible anomaly' and 'no longer capable of rational justification'.[5] The somewhat surprising conclusion of the Court of Appeal that the case fell outside of the ambit of Article 5 of the ECHR altogether on the basis that detention pursuant to the criminal sentence was lawful and that procedures for release did not engage questions of liberty was flatly rejected.[6] Together with the case of *A v Secretary of State for the Home Department*[7] the House of Lords made it clear that the immigration status of the person is not determinative in matters affecting liberty but not connected with immigration control. On 1 May 2009, the UKBA and the National Offender Management Service (NOMS) in the Ministry of Justice agreed and implemented a service level agreement (SLA) to transfer certain FNPs[8] into designated hub prisons where FNPs would make up the whole or the majority of the prison population. The purpose of this SLA was largely to ensure effective implementation of the deportation process for FNPs. Individual transfers under the SLA may be successfully challenged on the basis that consideration was not being given to the particular circumstances of the prisoner. The High Court also granted a declaration in judicial review proceedings brought by the Equality and Human Rights Commission that the SLA was formulated and implemented in breach of the duties under section 71 of the Race Relations Act 1976 and section 49A of the Disability Discrimination Act 2005.[9] Particular concerns have been that transfers took place without regard to maintaining family ties and access to legal representation, many of the hub prisons being in remote locations. Despite the concerns raised by the HM Inspector of Prisons about the treatment of FNPs in the prison estate no special measures had been taken to address, for example, the incidence of race and religious discrimination experienced by FNPs and the lack of access to adequate translation or interpretation facilities. The present SLA has not been disclosed but provides by its terms that 600 beds are made available by NOMS for immigration detention purposes. The Secretary of State's policy provides that those who are detained in prison following the completion of their sentence will remain there until this figure is reached, before being transferred to the IRC estate on a first-come-first-served basis subject to the risk-based criteria in the policy.[10] This is not to be confused with the separate cap on the number of time-served prisoners on the IRC estate 'in the interests of maintaining security and control'. The cap may also be used for the troublingly nebulous purpose of meeting 'changing operational priorities'.[11]

---

[1] Operation Enforcement Manual (OEM), para 38.8 (previous version)

[2] *R (on the application of Sedrati) v Secretary of State for the Home Department* [2001] EWHC 418 (Admin). The information comes from counsel and is not referred to in the very short judgment of the court. However, the policy, which is now in Chapter 55 of the Enforcement Instructions and Guidance, has been steadily creeping towards a system whereby people who are being detained pending deportation following prison sentences will remain in prison see 18.23 below.

[3] Since the coming into force of the Coroners and Justice Act 2009 the Secretary of State's discretion is significantly curtailed where a Parole Board recommends release.

[4] *R (on the application of Hindawi) v Secretary of State for the Home Department* [2004] EWHC 78 (Admin), (2004) Times, 5 February; revsd [2004] EWCA Civ 1309, [2005] 1 WLR 1102, sub nom *Hindawi v Secretary of State for the Home Department* (2004) Times, 26 October; revsd [2006] UKHL 54, [2007] 2 All ER 1.

[5] *Hindawi* (above), para 38.

[6] *Hindawi* (above) per Lord Bingham of Cornhill at paras 18–20.

[7] *A v Secretary of State for the Home Department* [2004] UKHL 56, [2005] 2 WLR 87.

[8] FNPs who meet deportation criteria of being: (i) sentenced to 12 months; or (ii) fit the aggregate sentence rule (12 months); (iii) court recommended for deportation; and (iv) have less than three years but more than one month of sentence left to serve and FNPs who do not meet the deportation criteria: sentenced to less than 12 months but have more than one month of sentence left to serve. At the time it applied only to category C prisons.

[9] *R (on the application of Equality and Human Rights Commission) v Secretary of State for Justice* [2010] EWHC 147 (Admin).

[10] Chapter 55 of the Enforcement Instructions and Guidance 55.10.1. The blanket detention policy (not to be confused with the separate cap on the number of FNPs in the IRC estate

Chapter 55 EIG) is likely to be challenged in the forthcoming cases of *Lemtelsky* and *Idira*. The number of 600 was increased to 1000 for a period in 2012.
11   Chapter 55.10.1.

National security

18.21 There is no power to detain simply on national security grounds. Persons whose deportation is deemed to be conducive to the public good on grounds of national security[1] can be detained under the provisions of Schedule 3 to the IA 1971, which apply to all deportations, pending a decision to make a deportation order[2] and, where a deportation order is in force, pending removal or departure from the UK.[3] National security concerns are of course relevant to the lawfulness of continued detention and would justify continued detention while deportation is pending.[4] This includes cases based upon allegations of involvement in terrorism.[5] Special provision was made in Part IV of the ATCSA 2001 for the indefinite detention of those foreign nationals, who could not be safely removed or deported from the UK, if the Secretary of State certified that he or she: (a) reasonably believed that the person's presence in the UK was a risk to national security, and (b) reasonably suspected that the person was an international terrorist.[6] However, in *A (FC)*,[7] the House of Lords ruled that the derogation from Article 5 of ECHR was discriminatory and disproportionate, quashed the Derogation Order,[8] and made a declaration that s 23 of the ATCSA 2001, which allowed indefinite detention was incompatible with Articles 5 and 14 of ECHR. The government refused to release the detainees,[9] until new laws were enacted introducing control orders, allowing the men to be placed under conditions of 'house arrest' and other restrictions on liberty,[10] the legality of which was been considered by the House of Lords in a series of cases *JJ and 0rs*,[11] *Secretary of State for the Home Department v MB*,[12] *Secretary of State for the Home Department v AF*[13] and the Supreme Court in *Secretary of State for the Home Department v AP*.[14]

1   IA 1971, s 3(5)(a).
2   IA 1971, Sch 3, para 2(2): see 17.14 above.
3   IA 1971, Sch 3, para 2(3).
4   Such considerations could also be relevant to the period of time which the Court would consider reasonable for the Secretary of State to arrange removal, by parity of reasoning with Simon Brown LJ's observations in *R (on the application of I) v Secretary of State for the Home Department* [2003] INLR 196, [2002] EWCA Civ 888 (para 29) to the effect that a substantially longer period of time would be afforded if there was clear evidence that the person would abscond or re-offend.
5   Terrorism under the anti-terrorist legislation is defined in s 1 of the Terrorism Act 2000. It has an exceptionally wide meaning, covering the use or threat of action to advance a political, religious, racial or ideological cause and either involves the use of firearms and explosives or is designed to influence government or to intimidate the public or a section of the public. Action means serious violence against he person or endangering someone's life, serious damage to property, serious risk to health and safety of the public or a section of the public or designed to seriously interfere with or seriously disrupt an electronic system.
6   ATCSA 2001, s 21.
7   *A v Secretary of State for the Home Department; X v Secretary of State for the Home Department* [2004] UKHL 56, [2005] 2 WLR 87, [2005] 2 AC 68.
8   Human Rights Act 1998 (Designated Derogation) Order 2001, quashed by the House of Lords *A and X*, above.
9   Applications were therefore lodged in Strasbourg and the breach of Article 5(1) was upheld by the Court in *A v United Kingdom* (Application No 3455/05) *(2009) 49 EHRR 625, (2009) Times, 20 February*. The ECtHR also held that there was a breach of Article 5(4) ECHR in

cases where insufficient disclosure of the cases against the detainee had been made to provide an effective opportunity to challenge the case against him. See CHAPTER 21.

10 Hansard HC (2005) 25 January, Statement by Home Secretary; see now repealed PTA 2005, s 1.

11 *Secretary of State for the Home Department v JJ* [2007] UKHL 45, [2008] 1 All ER 613, [2008] 1 AC 385 see 17.2.

12 [2007] UKHL 46, [2008] 1 AC 440.

13 [2009] UKHL 28, [2009] 3 WLR 74.

14 [2010] UKSC 24. The TP IMA 2011 abolished the control order regime and replaced it with a regime of 'TPIMs' which contain less stringent restrictions.

Power of arrest

18.22 In cases where persons are liable to detention either under the authority of the Secretary of State or of an immigration officer, they may be arrested without warrant by a police or immigration officer.[1] The power of arrest without warrant applies to persons released on bail by immigration officers or by the Tribunal, for reasonable cause; see **18.68** and **18.69** below. In addition, warrants may be issued to the police for the purpose of searching for and arresting such persons.[2]

1 IA 1971, Sch 2, para 17(1) and Sch 3, para 2(4). This does not, however, apply to those recommended for deportation by a court, presumably because if they are not detained, it is by direction of the Secretary of State or because they have been released on bail; see 17.19 above. The powers of arrest are additional to the power to arrest those in breach of release or bail conditions under Sch 2, para 24 and Sch 3, para 7: see 17.64 ff below.

2 IA 1971, Sch 2, para 17(2), para 24(1)(b) and Sch 3, para 2(4).

WHY, WHERE AND HOW DETAINED

Place of detention

18.23 The Immigration (Places of Detention) Direction 2014 sets out the places in which a person may be detained under immigration powers. They are, exhaustively, places used by immigration officers for their functions (including ports of entry and control zones), short-term holding facilities (including police stations, Tribunals and courts or places of detention nearby), pre-departure accommodation (see below **18.32**), any hospital, prison and young offenders' facilities, mobile detention centres and the Immigration Removal Centre estate. Those detained pending deportation rather than removal may be detained in any of these places other than those places used by immigration officers for their functions. People may not be detained in certain places (including short-term holding facilities such as police cells) for more than five consecutive days, or seven where it is proposed to issue removal directions.[1]

The use of mainstream prison for the detention of immigrants and asylum seekers has been controversial and the Home Office in the past expressed a commitment which has never been fulfilled to stop its use. At para 4.78 of the 2002 White Paper (*Secure Borders, Safe Haven* (Cm 5387, February 2002)) the government repeated that their strategy was to '*eliminate . . . reliance on this accommodation, subject to limited exceptions*'. The use of local prisons was withdrawn, including use of dedicated accommodation at HMP Rochester, and the Home Office adopted a policy of redesignation of immigration facilities within mainstream prisons at HMP Haslar, HMP Lindholme and HMYOI Dover as removal centres subject to the Detention Centre Rules. UNHCR has stated that in its view asylum seekers and refugees should never be placed with common criminals: UNHCR *Guidelines on the Applicable Criteria and Standards relating to the Detention of Asylum Seekers and Alternatives to Detention* (September 2012) Guideline 8. The practice does however continue. However, the policy now appears to have changed with a particular emphasis on the detention of those who have committed criminal offences in prison after their sentences have expired and prior to deportation (see **18.20** above).

Holding an immigration detainee with a convicted prisoner is prohibited unless the detainee gives their express consent.[2] A breach of comparable provisions was held to be a breach of Art 5 of the ECHR in *Chahboub*.[3] In cases challenging the fact of, or the conditions of, detention in a prison proceedings should be against, or include, the Ministry of Justice.[4]

The vast majority of those detained are held in immigration service detention, which consists of dedicated immigration facilities run by private security firms and subject to the Detention Centre Rules. Chapter 55 of the Enforcement Instructions Guidance previously held that immigration detainees would only be held in prison establishments when they present specific risk factors that indicate that they pose a serious risk to the stability of immigration removal centres. Now the policy is that all proposed deportees completing prison sentences will remain in the prison estate until the number of allocated beds under the Service Level Agreement between UKVI and the National Offender Management Service (NOMS), presently 600, is reached (see **18.20** above). Thereafter they will be moved to detention centres on a first-come-first-served basis subject to certain risk factors.[5] The risk factors divide people into those whose detention on the IRC estate will only be appropriate in '*very exceptional circumstances*' (such as eg those perceived to be a threat to national security), those who will '*normally*' remain in prison (such as those who have committed certain sexual offences or previously escaped from custody) and those whose transfer '*may*' be inappropriate (such as those whose behaviour in prison or detention has suggested they pose a risk, or those who are refusing food and fluids).[6]

Any individual may request a transfer and written reasons will be given if this is rejected. Separately from the policy of using the places made available under the SLA before transfer to the prison estate is considered, the Guidance provides that in the interests of maintaining security and control in the UKBA detention estate as a whole, a cap is placed on the total number of time-served FNPs who may be held in the estate at any one time. Where this cap is reached, time-served FNPs will continue to be held in prisons even if there may be free space in IRCs. The level of the cap may change to meet '*changing operational priorities*'. Prompt consideration must be given to any request by time-served FNPs to transfer to the UKBA detention estate and reasons for deciding not to transfer an individual must be recorded, as must the reasons for any delay in transfer.[7]

---

1   The Immigration (Places of Detention) Direction 2014 (No 2). Chapter 55 of the Enforcement Instructions and Guidance provides at para 55.13.2 that detainees should preferably spend only one night in police cells, with a 'normal maximum' of two nights.

² Prison Rules 1999 (1999/728), r 7 and PSO/4600 applied to immigration detainees by PSI/52/2011.

³ *R (on the application of Chahboub) v Secretary of State for the Home Department* [2009] EWHC 1989 (Admin).

⁴ See discussion in *Chahboub* above and *R (on the application of Hussein) v Secretary of State for the Home Department* [2009] EWHC 2506 (Admin), [2009] All ER (D) 133 (Oct) However see also *R(on the application of Mcfarlane) v Secretary of State for the Home Department* [2010] EWHC 3081 (Admin) which held that .the decision as to where a person was to be detained was '*essentially an operational*' one for the Secretary of State.

⁵ PSI 52/2011, which is still in force, states at 2.68 that '*Immigration detainees should only remain or be moved into prison establishments when they present specific risk factors that indicate they pose a serious risk of harm to the public or to the good order of an Immigration Removal Centre, including the safety of staff and other detainees, which cannot be managed within the regime applied in Immigration Removal Centres.*' The conflict between that policy and the policy in Chapter 55 EIG and the Service Level Agreement is apparently stark.

⁶ EIG, para 55.10.1.

⁷ EIG, para 55.10.1. It was recognised in *Rashford v Secretary of State for the Home Department* [2010] EWHC 2200 (QB), [2010] All ER (D) 13 (Sep) that removal from a detention centre to a prison is an important and potentially detrimental step so far as a detainee is concerned, and that it was strongly arguable consistent with general principles of public law that a person affected by such a decision should be given reasons and an opportunity to make representations about such a step. A failure to do this would be susceptible to judicial review. However see also *R (Mcfarlane) v Secretary of State for the Home Department* [2010] EWHC 3081 (Admin).

18.24 Rule 11 of the Detention Centre Rules sets out the conditions of detention for families and minors[1] and provides that family members are entitled to enjoy family life save to the extent necessary in the interests of security and safety.[2] The accommodation must be suitable to meet the needs of minors and families and everything reasonably necessary for the protection, safety and well being and the maintenance and care of infants and children shall be provided. In December 2010 the Government announced its plans to end the detention of children.[3] Unsurprisingly, this has not been achieved, although there have been improvements. The IA 2014 places 'pre-departure accommodation', which is where families are now primarily held, on a statutory footing that is distinct from short-term holding centres. A child or family may not be detained in eparture accommodation for longer than 72 hours, or 7 days with Ministerial authorisation.[4] The Act also places on a statutory footing the existence and role of the Family Returns Panel (itself introduced in March 2011), which must be consulted in every case where the Secretary of State proposes to detain a family in pre-departure accommodation 'on the suitability of so doing', or proposes to remove a child with an adult from the same household, parent or carer.[5] The detention of families may generally only be in pre-departure accommodation and may only be as a last resort.[6] The current 'pre-departure accommodation' is Cedars which opened in August 2011. It is run by G4S but a range of services are provided by Barnardo's which has received criticism as a result for colluding in the detention of children. It has been argued that without Barnardos' assistance the experience of detained families in the stressful period prior to removal would be significantly worse.[7] The IA 2014 introduces new restrictions on the detention of unaccompanied minors, who may only be detained under s 16(2) of the IA 1971 in a short-term holding facility and for a maximum of 24 hours. Detention in these circumstances is only permissible where removal directions are in force or likely to be made.[8] Minors may otherwise only be detained in a place of safety as defined in the Children and Young Persons Act 1933 which includes any home provided by a local authority, any remand home or police station or any hospital, surgery or other suitable place the occupier of which is willing temporarily to receive the child.[9] They may not 'under any circumstances' be detained in an Immigration removal Centre. In *R (S)*[10] the Court upheld the legality of the Secretary of States' policy with regard to the detention of families with children under the fast track regime and generally, including finding the policy consistent with the UN Convention on the Rights of the Child (UNCRC), Arts 3 and 37(b). However, on the facts the detention of a mother and her two young children after the conclusion of the fast track procedure was unlawful because it was not warranted by the Secretary of State's policy as it then stood – there were not sufficiently strong grounds to justify detention and because the period of detention (two months) was unreasonable given the age of the children. Moreover, the prolonged detention of just over five months had serious repercussions; the mother became a suicide risk and the damage to the health and welfare of the youngest child who developed anaemia and rickets whilst detained led the court to conclude that there had been a breach of the right to respect for physical integrity protected by Article 8 of the ECHR. This case is a salutary example of the risks involved in detention of children. The evidence about the standard of medical care was of particular concern although the judge came to no final conclusion as to its legality holding the Secretary of State responsible for the foreseeable and avoidable harm that the child suffered. Significant and extensive research demonstrating the harm caused to children in immigration detention is available.[11] Concern about the impact on children has been widespread but the organisations, Bail for Immigration Detainees and Medical Justice, have been particularly effective in identifying and documenting the nature and extent of the damage to children's mental and physical health.

1 Detention Centre Rules 2001, SI 2001/238.

2 SI 2001/238, r 11.

3 On 16 December 2010 it was announced that the family unit at Yarl's Wood would close with immediate effect.

4 Immigration Act 2014, s 6 amending s 147 of the IAA Act 1999. Stays longer than 72 hours will only be permitted in *'exceptional circumstances'*. Mothers with infant children may be detained in mother and baby units in prison subject to advice from the Family Returns Panel Ch 55 EIG 55.9.4.

5 Section 55A of the Borders, Citizenship and Immigration Act 2009 as inserted by s 3 of the IA 2014. There is a power to make regulations regarding the Panel but none have been laid as yet.

6 Ch 55 EIG 55.9.4 and Ch 45b EIG at 5.0. The policy states that there may be rare occasions where it will be necessary for a family to be detained at Tinsley House, or for one member of a family who presents a risk to be detained in an IRC. Otherwise, the only permissible place for a family to be held is a non-residential short-term holding facility or pre-departure accommodation (Cedars). The government has said that detention in short-term holding centres or Tinsley House is expected to happen to a *'few dozen families each year, usually for less than 24 hours' Ending Child Immigration Detention*, Melanie Gower, Home Affairs Section, 4 September 2014.

7 There are substantial facilities available in the Cedars accommodation which are not available elsewhere. 'Each apartment has a kitchen and lounge area, family bathroom and up to three bedrooms (to accommodate up to six people). Families can eat in communal areas or take food from the cafeteria to cook in their own apartments. Facilities within the accommodation centre include children's play areas and exercise facilities, access to the internet, 24 hour healthcare including daily access to a GP and a prayer room.' *Ending Child Immigration Detention*, Melanie Gower, Home Affairs Section, 4 September 2014. It is unquestionably detention however. See *Does Baranardo's Legitmise Child Detention* by Frances Webber, Institute of Race Relations, 17 March 2011 and *Cedars: Two Years On*, Baranardo's, April 2014.

8 Para 18B of Sch 2 to the IA 1971 as inserted by s 5 of the IA 2014.

[9] Chapter 55 of the Enforcement Instructions and Guidance 55.9.3; Children and Young Persons Act 1933, s 107.

[10] *R (on the application of S) v Secretary of State for the Home Department* [2007] EWHC 1654 (Admin), [2007] All ER (D) 290 (Jul).

[11] Royal College of Paediatrics and Child Health, Royal College of General Practitioners, Royal College of Psychiatrists and Faculty of Public Health: Inter Collegiate Briefing Paper: '*Significant Harm – the effects of administrative detention on the health of children, young people and their families*' delivered in December 2009; and the study by Lorek et al, 'The mental and physical health difficulties of children held within a British immigration detention center: A pilot study', *Child Abuse and Neglect* 33 (2009), 573–585; '*Significant Harm: the effects of immigration detention on the health of children and families in the UK*' – Joint Statement and Briefing Paper by Royal College of Paediatrics and Child Health, Royal College General Practitioners, Royal College of Psychiatrists and Faculty of Public Health (December 2009); *Fast-Tracked Unfairness Detention and Denial of Women Asylum Seekers in the UK*, Human Rights Watch (February 2010); '*State Sponsored Cruelty*' Children in immigration detention Medical Justice (September 2010).

18.25 Detainees can be, and are, transferred from England to Scotland to be held at Dungavel Detention Centre. This has repercussions for legal representation and access to the courts because of Scotland's separate legal jurisdiction.[1] It can lead to complexity and confusion, with lawyers acting in both jurisdictions on different aspects of an individual's case. It can also cause delay in seeking bail. This was a feature of the *Konan* case which was observed to have 'created real difficulties for the claimants in pursuing their legal remedies'.[2] This would amount to a legitimate reason for objecting to a proposed transfer to or from Dungavel. Consideration should also be given to the impact on any family ties if detainees are moved many miles from their family's home. Frequent transfers, which are a feature of prolonged detention, also present difficulties for access to legal representatives and there is inefficiency in coordinating the location of bail applications with the removal centre.

[1] See *Gardi v Secretary of State for the Home Department* [2002] EWCA Civ 1560, [2002] INLR 557, for the complications that can arise in the case (Court of Appeal's judgment nullified because of lack of jurisdiction, first instance appeal having been heard in Scotland).

[2] *R (on the application of Konan) v Secretary of State for the Home Department* [2004] EWHC 22 (Admin), [2004] All ER (D) 151 (Jan) at para 13. Similar issues arose in *Fardous v Secretary of State for the Home Department* [2014] EWHC 3061 (QB) where the defendant initially contended that the claimant was estopped from bringing a civil action for false imprisonment because of an application for judicial and liberation brought earlier in Scotland, which the claimant had been unable to pursue because he was transferrd to England before the matter reached court. The point was not pursued at the hearing.

Conditions of detention

18.26 The Detention Centre Rules 2001 make provision for minimum conditions of detention by requiring that the detention facilities: (i) have been certified as having lighting, heating, ventilation and fittings adequate for health;[1] (ii) the detainee is provided with clothing adequate for warmth and health;[2] and the detainee is provided with toilet articles necessary for health and cleanliness.[3] Rule 34 is an important safeguard which requires that every detained person shall, unless he does not consent, be given a physical and mental examination within 24 hours of his admission to a detention centre.[4] The case of *R (on the application of D) v Secretary of State for the Home Department; R (on the application of K) v Secretary of State for the Home Department*[5] revealed that this rule had never been complied with at Oakington because of a failure to make financial provision to put it into effect and later a decision that it was not considered necessary. The Court condemned this failure and declared both the Secretary of State and Group 4 had acted unlawfully with the consequence that both D and K had been unlawfully detained. Had the medical examination been carried out it would have provided independent evidence that the claimants were victims of torture and therefore, according to the Secretary of State's policy on detention, ought not to have been detained. *In EO (Turkey) v Secretary of State for the Home Department*[6] it was held that the failure to carry out a Rule 34 examination within 24 hours was a public law failing bearing on the decision to detain applying the decision of the Supreme Court in *R R (on the application of Kambadzi) v Secretary of State for the Home Department*[7]. The definition of torture, for the purposes of the Rules, was held not to be limited to acts by state parties but to include: 'any act by which severe pain or suffering, whether physical or mental, is intentionally inflicted on a person for such purposes as obtaining from him or a third person information or a confession, punishing him for an act he or a third person has committed, or intimidating or coercing him or a third person, or for any reason based upon discrimination of any kind'. Rule 40 provides for segregation of detainees and solitary confinement which requires authorisation by a removal centre manager for the first 24 hours (r 40(1) and thereafter by the Secretary of State).[8] Written reasons must be given to the detainee within two hours of removal to the segregation unit, and notice of what has happened must be provided to the visiting community, a medical practitioner and the manager of religious affairs without delay.[9] Detainees must be visited at least once a day during their segregation by the Removal Centre Manager, a medical practitioner and an Officer of the Secretary of State.[10] There are no published criteria for segregation, and there is no available procedure, unlike in criminal prisons, to challenge a decision to segregate a detainee. This gives rise to potential challenge under Article 8 and/or Article 5(4) of the ECHR.[11] The European Committee for the Prevention of Torture places particular emphasis on three fundamental rights, namely the right of detained persons to inform a close relative or another third party of their choice of their situation, to have access to a lawyer, and to have access to a doctor.[12] The UN Working Group on Arbitrary Detention, visiting in 1998, found that the main problem for detainees was in access to lawyers, and obtaining information about their case.[13] The Chief Inspector of Prisons (HMCIP) has a duty to inspect, in addition to immigration removal centres, Short Term Holding Facilities (STHFs) and escort arrangements. Section 46 of IAN 2006 amended section 5A(5A) of the Prison Act 1952 to put these powers on a statutory footing. It means that inspection of STHFs, pre-departure accommodation and escort arrangements are in line with the position on immigration removal centres, which were made subject to statutory inspection by section 152(5) of the IAA 1999. IAN 2006, section 59 disqualifies detainees in removal centres from entitlement to the national minimum wage.

[1] Detention Centre Rules 2001, SI 2001/238, r 15(3). The centres are subject to inspection by HM Prisons Inspectorate, and the inspection reports are all available online from the Ministry of Justice website.
[2] SI 2001/238, r 12(2).
[3] SI 2001/238 r 16(2), (3).
[4] SI 2001/238 r 34(1)
[5] [2006] EWHC 980 (Admin), 150 Sol Jo LB 743.
[6] [2013] EWHC 1236 (Admin).

7   [2011] UKSC 23.

8   SI 2001/238, r 40(3), where the detention centre is directly managed. Where it is contracted out, solitary confinement always requires authorisation (although the centre manager may assume the Secretary of State's responsibility in cases of urgency, provided the Secretary of State is notified as soon as possible: r 40(1), (2).

9   SI 2001/238, r 40(5), (6).

10   SI 2001/238, r 40(9).

11   But see *R (on the application of Munjaz) v Mersey Care NHS Trust* [2003] EWCA Civ 1036, [2004] QB 395 and in the House of Lords [2005] UKHL 58. See also the decision of the European Court of Human Rights in that case *Munjaz v United Kingdom* (2913/06).

12   Report on visit to UK and Isle of Man by the Committee for the Prevention of Torture and Inhuman or Degrading Treatment or Punishment, March 2005 (CPT Inf/2005 1). The most recent report (CPT/Inf (2014) 11) recommends that it is ensured that those in segregation are permitted their one house exercise per day.

13   UN Working Group on Arbitrary Detention *Report on a visit to the UK on the issue of immigrants and asylum seekers*, E/CN.4/1999/63/Add.3 (1998). The CPT report of 27 March 2014 (CPT/Inf (2014) 11) expressed concern at the use of other detainees as interpreters.

18.27 It is also important to note that the place and conditions of detention are relevant to the lawfulness of the deprivation of liberty under Article 5(1) of the ECHR and whether the detention is arbitrary because there must be 'some relationship between the ground of permitted deprivation of liberty relied upon and the place and conditions of detention'.[1] Thus the detention of a mentally ill man accused of a criminal offence on remand in an ordinary criminal prison was held to be unlawful because it should have been effected in a hospital, clinic or other appropriate institution consistent with the provisions of Article 5(1)(e).[2] Likewise a juvenile in need of educational supervision should not be detained in a prison where no education is available.[3] By analogy a mentally ill immigrant detained in a detention centre or mainstream prison as opposed to a hospital may be unlawfully detained in breach of Article 5.[4] Failures to transfer a detainee to a mental hospital under section 48 of the Mental Health Act 1983 can be challenged by way of judicial review.[5] Detention of a mentally ill person cannot be justified on grounds of their own well being and to prevent suicide.[6]

1   *Saadi v United Kingdom* (2008) 47 EHRR 427 at para 69. See further CHAPTER 16 above. See also *R (on the application of Krasniqi) v Secretary of State for the Home Department* [2011] EWCA Civ 1549.

2   *Aerts v Belgium* (2000) 29 EHRR 50, at para 46. See also the decision of the *Grand Chamber in Ashingdane v United Kingdom* (1985) 7 EHRR 528 at para 44.

3   See *Bouamar v Belgium* (1988) 11 EHRR 1.

4   Chapter 55 of the Enforcement Instructions and Guidance provides at para 55.10 that unless there are very exceptional circumstances, those suffering serious mental illness which cannot be satisfactorily managed in detention should not be detained although in exceptional cases it may be necessary for detention at a removal centre or prison to continue while individuals are being, or waiting to be, assessed, or are awaiting transfer under the Mental Health Act.

5   In *R (on the application of D) v Secretary of State for the Home Department and National Assembly for Wales* [2004] EWHC 2857 (Admin), [2005] MHLR 17, Stanley Burnton J held at [33] that there was a duty in the equivalent power under section 47 of the 1983 Act 'to expeditiously take reasonable steps to obtain appropriate medical advice, and if that advice confirms the need for transfer to hospital to take reasonable steps within a reasonable time to effect transfer'. That principle was extended by Singh J to immigration detainees in *R (on the application of HA (Nigeria)) v Secretary of State for the Home Department* [2012] EWHC 979 (Admin) at para 170.

6   *R (on the application of AA) v Secretary of State for the Home Department* [2010] EWHC 2265. This view was tentatively endorsed in *R (on the application of OM acting by her litigation friend, the Official Solicitor) v Secretary of State for the Home Department* [2011]

EWCA Civ 909 at para 32 and *R (on the application of Das) v Secretary of State for the Home Department* [2014] EWCA Civ 45 at 68.

Reasons for detention

18.28 There is no requirement in primary legislation for reasons to be given for detention, despite the obligation in Article 5(2) of the ECHR.[1] The 1998 White Paper contained a commitment for written reasons to be given on initial detention and at monthly intervals thereafter, or shorter periods in cases involving families.[2] Since October 1999 immigration officers have served written reasons in the IS 91 in the form of a checklist.[3] They are instructed to ensure that the contents of the checklist are interpreted into the detainee's language.[4] Rule 9 of the Detention Centre Rules 2001[5] represents the first statutory requirement for written reasons for detention, and incorporates the commitment that reasons be given monthly and not just on first detention. The EIG requires regular reviews of detention, in order to determine whether continued detention remains lawful and consistent with detention policy.[6] One of the consistent failings of the immigration service, even where they have carried out the review, has been a failure to serve the reasons for continued detention on the detainee, even where there have been significant changes in circumstances between the reviews. In *Ex p B*[7] the failure of the Secretary of State to consider 'carefully and urgently' new circumstances that had emerged, relating to the merits of the claim for asylum and the availability of sureties, led the court to rule that the continued detention of the claimant was unlawful. The need for such a review was described by Kay J as 'imperative'. Human rights implications should be considered as part of the regular review.[8] In *Faulkner* it was held that there was an obligation to inform a person of the essential factual and legal grounds for his or her detention and that failure to give reasons for detention made the detention unlawful.[9] In *R (on the application of SK)*[10] the failure to provide written reasons for the detention following monthly reviews was severely criticised as not only non-compliant with rule 9(1) of the 2001 Rules but a breach of a fundamental and constitutional principle which requires notice to the person for a decision to have legal effect.[11] The Supreme Court in *Kambadzi*[12] held that the failure to carry out these reviews as required by Chapter 38 of the Operational Enforcement Manual (the precursor to Chapter 55 of the Enforcement Instructions and Guidance) was sufficiently closely connected to the lawful authority to detain that it gave rise to a false imprisonment. In *Saadi v United Kingdom* the European Court of Human Rights held that there was a breach of the obligation under Article 5(2) of the Convention to inform a person 'promptly' of the reasons for his arrest in circumstances where an asylum seeker was not told for 76 hours why he was being detained at Oakington Detention Centre. However, the Court did not treat this as having an impact on the legality of the detention under Article 5(1)(f) of the ECHR.[13] In the context of discussing whether, and if so in what circumstances public law error would make detention unlawful, Lord Hope highlighted that in *Saadi*[14] it was not argued 'that the muddle about reasons rendered the decision to detain unlawful'.[15] Nevertheless, *Saadi* is authority for holding detention in the fast track to be lawful even if the reasons given are not the real reasons for detention.[16]

1   See **7.71** above.
2   *Fairer, Faster and Firmer – a Modern Approach to Immigration and Asylum* (Cm 4018, July 1998).
3   The use of a checklist has been criticised as contrary to UNHCR's requirements of individualised written reasons, and there are indications that the checklist often masks the real reasons for detention: see Leanne Weber *Deciding to detain* (University of Cambridge Institute of Criminology, 2000).
4   EIG, para 55.6.3. Detainees are also to be told the power under which they are detained and 'there must be a properly evidenced and fully justified explanation of the reasoning behind the decision to detain placed on file in all detention cases.'
5   SI 2001/238.
6   EIG, para 55.8 requiring reviews of detention following specified periods of detention and by officials of specified seniority.
7   *R v Special Adjudicator and Secretary of State for the Home Department, ex p B* [1998] INLR 315, QBD. See also *R v Secretary of State for the Home Department, ex p Brezinski and Glowacka* 19 July 1996 [1997] CLY 2880.
8   EIG, para 55.8.
9   *R (on the application of Faulkner) v Secretary of State for the Home Department* [2005] EWHC 2567 (Admin), [2005] All ER (D) 03 (Nov). See also *R (Rashid Hussein) v Secretary of State for the Home Department* [2009] EWHC 2492 (Admin) para 41 and at 17.4 above.
10   *R (on the application of SK) v Secretary of State for the Home Department* [2008] EWHC 98 (Admin) (later referred to as *Kambadzi in the Supreme Court*).
11   *R (on the application of SK) v Secretary of State for the Home Department* [2008] EWHC 98 (Admin).
12   *R (on the application of Kambadzi) v Secretary of State for the Home* [2011] UKSC 23; [2011] 1 WLR 1299].
13   *Saadi v United Kingdom* (Application 13229/03) (2006) Times, 3 August, [2006] All ER (D) 125 (Jul), ECtHR and Grand Chamber (2008) 47 EHRR 17
14   *R (on the application of Saadi) v Secretary of State for the Home Department* [2002] UKHL 41, [2002] 4 All ER 785, [2002] 1 WLR 3131.
15   *R (on the application of Kambadzi) v Secretary of State for the Home Department* [2011] UKSC 23, para 45, [2011] 4 All ER 975, [2011] 1 WLR 1299.
16   *R (on the application of Suckrajh) v Asylum and Immigration Tribunal* [2011] EWCA Civ 938, [2011] All ER (D) 292 (Jul).

POLICY AND CRITERIA FOR DETENTION

18.29 The criteria for detention are based on a series of policy statements set out in Immigration Service Instructions to staff on detention dated 3 December 1991 and 20 September 1994,[1] factors set out in two White Papers of 1998 and 2002,[2] and now incorporated in a single detailed document, the Enforcement Instructions and Guidance, Chapter 55.[3] The 1991 and 1994 criteria were confidential and only came to the attention of practitioners through accidental disclosure. The policy in Chapter 55 is among the most frequently amended policies in immigration law. The most significant recent developments have been in respect of the treatment of former FNPs. The general policy, save for FNPs, is set out in Chapter 55.1 of the EIG and can be summarised as follows:

(i)   detention, save for the DFT, is only to be used as a last resort;
(ii)   detention will usually only be appropriate to effect removal, establish identity or the true basis of the claim, or prevent absconding;

(iii)   detention in the DFT presently at Campsfield House, Colnbrook House, Harmondsworth and Yarls Wood Immigration Removal Centres[4] will only be used where it appears that the claim can be decided quickly; and

(iv)   people should not be detained for lengthy periods if it would be practical to effect detention later in the process once appeal rights have been exhausted.[5]

Chapter 55 of the EIG reiterates that:

'1.   there is a presumption in favour of temporary admission or temporary release. There must be strong grounds for believing that a person will not comply with conditions of temporary admission or release for detention to be justified.

2.   All reasonable alternatives to detention must be considered before detention is authorised.

3.   Each case must be considered on its individual merits, including consideration of the duty to have regard to the need to safeguard and promote the welfare of any children involved.'

It goes on to say, 'Once detention has been authorised, it must be kept under close review to ensure that it continues to be justified' (at para 55.3.1.). The factors identified in the policy statements as relevant to the exercise of the power to detain are as follows:

(i)   the likelihood of the person being removed and after what timescale;

(ii)   previous absconding from detention;

(iii)   previous failure to comply with conditions of temporary release or bail;

(iv)   evidence of a determined attempt to breach the immigration laws (eg entry in breach of a deportation order, attempted or actual clandestine entry);

(v)   history of compliance with the requirements of immigration control – eg by applying for a visa, further leave, etc;

(vi)   ties with the UK evidenced by close relatives (including dependants) in the country, a settled address, employment;

(vii)   the individual's expectations about the outcome of the case and any factors which would provide an incentive to keep in touch, such as an outstanding application for judicial review, representations or an appeal;

(viii)   the risk of offending or harm to the public (requiring consideration of the likelihood of harm *and* the seriousness of the harm if the person does offend);

(ix)   whether the person is under 18;

(x)   a history of torture;

(xi)   the physical or mental health of the subject; and

(xii)   the impact of detention on any relevant children.[6]

---

[1]   Cited in *R v Secretary of State for the Home Department, ex p Brezinski and Glowacka* (19 July 1996, [1997] CLY 2880), Kay J.

[2]   Fairer, Faster and Firmer – a Modern Approach to Immigration and Asylum (Cm 4018, July 1998); Secure Borders, Safe Havens: Integration with Diversity in Modern Britain (Cm 5387, February 2002).

[3]   EIG, Chapter 55 which replaced Chapter 38 Operational Enforcement Manual, relevant paragraphs of which are referred to below.

[4]   The removal centres specified for fast track asylum applicants (see 12.111) under SI 2005/560, Sch 2. The now-closed Oakington IRC is still included in the Schedule.

5 For the way in which decisions to detain are actually taken see Leanne Weber's valuable study Deciding to detain (17.28 fn 3 above).

6 These factors were all set out in the 1991 policy, ISC 26/1991 and now in the EIG, Chapter 55.

18.30 The Immigration Service has designed a form, the IS91R, which identified six justifications for detention and which is intended to inform the detainee of the reasons for their detention. It is an important part of the published policy.[1] The specified reasons are as follows:

(1)   You are likely to abscond if given temporary admission or release.
(2)   There is insufficient reliable information to decide on whether to grant you temporary admission or release.
(3)   Your removal from the United Kingdom is imminent.
(4)   You need to be detained whilst alternative arrangements are made for your care.
(5)   Your release is not considered conducive to the public good.
(6)   I am satisfied that your application may be decided quickly using the fast track asylum procedure.

The most significant issues in the application of the policy, save for former FNPs, are normally: (i) the assessment of the timescale for removal and whether removal can said to be *imminent* – the criteria adopted by the Home Office as the touchstone for detention at the end of the process; and (ii) the effect of outstanding legal obstacles to removal, including outstanding applications, representations, and, in particular, legal proceedings by way of appeals and judicial review, each of which is accepted as providing an incentive to comply with conditions of release[2] and meaning that removal is not imminent. The EIG say that removal is 'imminent' if 'a travel document exists, removal directions are set, there are no outstanding legal barriers and removal is likely to take place in the next four weeks'.[3] Even prior to the adoption of this definition of 'imminent', detention could not be justified on the ground that removal was imminent when removal directions were not even given until four weeks after the person was detained.[4] In *Nadarajah and Amirthanathan*[5] N was detained, although the immigration officer knew that judicial review proceedings were about to be issued. In A's case, he was detained after his human rights claim was rejected, even though the immigration officer knew he had a right of appeal, which he intended to exercise. The detention policy was described by a senior executive officer in the Home Office, who explained that 'an application for judicial review suspends removal of the claimant and it would be most unlikely that detention would be maintained throughout protracted judicial review proceedings'. The Court held that two important aspects of the Secretary of State's policy were that (i) 'removal will not be treated as imminent once proceedings which challenge the right to remove have been initiated'; and (ii) when deciding whether removal is imminent no regard would be paid to a statement that proceedings challenging removal would be initiated.[6] The court upheld the finding in the Administrative court that it was not realistic to say that removal was imminent in either case and dismissed the Secretary of State's appeals.

1 Referred to in para 55.6.3 of the EIG; *R (on the application of Amirthanathan) v Secretary of State for the Home Department* [2003] EWCA Civ 1768, [2004] INLR 139, at para 55. The form includes a risk assessment at IS91RA which should be carried out in advance of detention.

2   EIG, para 55.1.3.
3   EIG, para 55.3.2.4. By contrast, the OEM which the EIG replaced did not define 'imminent'
      so that in *R (on the application of Ahmed) v Secretary of State for the Home Department*
      [2008] EWHC 1533 (Admin), [2008] All ER (D) 29 (Jul), a case concerned with the OEM,
      the Court could hold that removal could be imminent even in the absence of removal
      directions. See *FM v Secretary of State for the Home Department* [2011] EWCA Civ 807,
      [2011] All ER (D) 125 (Jul) for the meaning and significance of 'imminent' removal.
4   *R (on the application of K) v Secretary of State for the Home Department* [2008] EWHC 1321
      (Admin).
5   *R (on the application of Amirthanathan) v Secretary of State for the Home Department* [2003]
      EWCA Civ 1768, [2004] INLR 139.
6   [2003] EWCA Civ 1768 at para 58. The court summarised the policy as follows (para 28):
      'Where proceedings have been initiated which challenge the right to remove an immigrant, it
      is not the policy of the Secretary of State to detain an immigrant on the ground that his
      removal is imminent. Normally, in such circumstances he will be granted temporary admission
      pending the result of those proceedings'.

18.31 The policy on judicial review is set out in the Enforcement Instructions and Guidance at Chapter 60. Ongoing proceedings, either judicial review or appeals, are treated as an incentive to comply with conditions of release. Normally a person will not be detained or if detained, will be released once proceedings are lodged[1] (as long as they are not subject to an expedited process[2]) because removal is no longer imminent.[3] The question which arose in *Amirthanathan* was the effect of solicitors indicating a genuine intention to initiate proceedings. The published policy was silent as to this matter, but solicitors acting on behalf of the claimants proceeded on the basis that such an indication meant detention would not normally take place. The Secretary of State, however, revealed that, although not publicly disclosed, the actual policy of the immigration service when considering the imminence of removal was to 'disregard information from those acting for asylum seekers that proceedings were about to be initiated, however credible that information might be'. The Court held that it was unlawful to rely upon this undisclosed policy[4] which was at odds with the published statements, because it was not accessible, and a detention based on factors at odds with the Home Office's published policy was in breach of Article 5(1)(f) of the ECHR. At the heart of this important decision is the bugbear that properly prepared notices by solicitors that they intend to challenge decisions to remove are often ignored and clients are placed in detention for a matter of days until the proceedings are lodged and then have to be released because removal is not imminent. In *Amirthanathan* the Court of Appeal considered that if such a practice was part of an accessible and published policy it would be neither arbitrary nor irrational,[5] but did not go into the matter fully.[6] The distress, disruption and cost of such a practice hardly seems sensible and it does not, on its face, appear consistent with the general policy of using detention as a last resort to deal with cases of imminent removal or high risk of absconding. The present policy provides that removal directions will remain in place where a threat of judicial review is obtained pending receipt of a Crown Office reference or Upper Tribunal reference, save in certain Port cases.[7] The policy of giving notice of removal for only five working days if the person is not detained (three days if they are) was referred to in *Amirthanathan*, with the Home Office explaining that the policy does not carry with it the implication that detention will not take place during the five-day period, only that removal will not be effected, in order to permit access to the court.[8] The Court of Appeal's endorsement of this approach is a general one only and does not prevent challenge to its application in any individual case, particularly where there may be other factors such as health or family ties to consider in detaining the individual. In *Amirthanathan* the Secretary of State made clear that it is not his policy 'to detain whenever removal is imminent, but only where there is some additional reason for detaining',[9] for example, if detention is necessary for an orderly removal.[10] This was explained by the court on the basis that imminence of removal is a *reason* for detention but the risk of a failure to comply is the *justification*.[11] The Secretary of State also indicated that the categories set out in IS91 are not exhaustive and there may be other reasons not specifically set out justifying the decision to detain.[12] However, the policy is not inflexible and the Secretary of State can defer a decision about releasing a person until the grounds have been served and can be considered and a decision taken on whether or not to seek to expedite the appeal or judicial review.[13] The time to determine this question and to seek expedition is, however, limited especially in cases were families with children are detained.[14] The fact that expedition is sought will not avail the Secretary of State if there has been an error as to the underlying merits of the case and the time that it would take for removal to lawfully take place.[15]

1   *R (on the application of Konan) v Secretary of State for the Home Department* [2004] EWHC 22 (Admin), [2004] All ER (D) 151 (Jan) where appeal rights had been exhausted but removal was challenged on the basis of a fresh claim for asylum and on human rights grounds. The Administrative Court held that the detention was unlawful from the date that judicial review proceedings were lodged, because it was inconsistent with the then stated policy to continue to detain in those circumstances.

2   EIG, Ch 60, Section 11 sets out cases that may be suitable for an expedited process, namely where: the claimant is in detention, the claimant's family is in the family returns process, the claim appears to be without merit, the claim is an abuse of process, the issue of public safety arises, the decision-making process has previously been subject to accelerated timescales (eg such as NSA cases, DFT), there is a risk of self-harm, the claimant is/was to be removed as part of an enforcement operation (eg such as a special charter flight), for Third Country Unit and Criminal Casework Directorate cases expedition will be agreed directly with Treasury Solicitors.

3   EIG, Ch 60, Section 11.1 provides that 'Cases must only be expedited where we are confident that we can complete removal quickly if the permission application is refused. Normally detention is maintained while a JR permission application is expedited as it is considered removal is still imminent'.

4   There are a number of cases where the Secretary of State fails to act consistently with stated policy, and when challenged pulls out of the hat the white rabbit of a different and undisclosed understanding of policy, which is at odds with the plain terms of the published criteria. See *NF (Ghana) v Secretary of State for the Home Department* [2009] INLR 93 (7-year concession); *R (on the application of Amirthanathan) v Secretary of State for the Home Department* [2003] EWCA Civ 1768, [2004] INLR 139; *R (on the application of Gashi) v Secretary of State for the Home Department* [2003] EWHC 1198 (Admin); *R v Secretary of State of the Home Department, ex p Nicholas* [2000] Imm AR 334, QBD. What the policy means is an objective 'hard edged question for the court': *R (on the application of Anam) v Secretary of State for the Home Department* [2009] EWHC 2496 (Admin) where the authorities were reviewed, at paras 49–50. See also the secret unlawful policy, which directly contradicted the published policy, disclosed in the Lumba litigation:*R (on the application of Lumba) v Secretary of State for the Home Department* [2011] UKSC 12.

5   In *R (on the application of Mpasi) v Secretary of State for the Home Department* [2007] EWHC 2562 (Admin), [2007] All ER (D) 103 (Nov) it was held that the judgment in *Nadarajah* which made public the undisclosed policy meant that it could no longer be said that the policy was not sufficiently accessible even though at the time of the decision in the case it had not been included in the published policy – see paragraph 49.

6   *Amirthanathan* above, para 63.

7   EIG, CH 60, Sections 5-6.

8   *Amirthanathan* para 59; see also *R (on the application of Pharis (Ben)) v Secretary of State for the Home Department* [2004] EWCA Civ 654 para 15, [2004] 3 All ER 310, where the Court

of Appeal referred to the consequential arrangements between the Treasury Solicitor and the IND and the High Court known as the Concordat, whereby it was agreed that removal directions would not be implemented following the lodging of an application for judicial review pending the decision of the court on the papers, as to whether to grant permission and if renewed, until the judicial review process was exhausted. The Court of Appeal had been following a similar, unformalised practice. The court stated at para 17 that the practice need not continue in respect of judicial reviews taken to the Court of Appeal, citing abuse of the system as the justification and indicated that an express application for a stay should be made in accordance with CPR 52.7 which states that, unless the appeal court or the lower court orders otherwise, an appeal should not operate as a stay of any order or decision of the lower court. Appeals from the Upper Tribunal (IAC) are, however, excepted and do act as a stay: see CPR 52.7(b). The High Court when refusing applications for judicial review on the papers will indicate that any renewal of the application need not act as a stay on removal if it is considered an unmeritorious case and only the grant of an injunction would prevent removal in those circumstances.

9   Secretary of State's submission at para 42 and the Court of Appeal's summary at para 56.
10 [2004] EWCA Civ 654, at para 57.
11 [2004] EWCA Civ 654, para 56.
12 [2004] EWCA Civ 654, para 42.
13 *Nadarajah v Secretary of State for the Home Department* [2003] EWCA Civ 1768, 148 Sol Jo LB 24 See also para 58 of *R (on the application of Mpasi) v Secretary of State for the Home Department* [2007] EWHC 2562 (Admin), [2007] All ER (D) 103 (Nov). The facts of *Mpasi* were very unusual and the grounds were substitute grounds. The original claim had been largely determined by the time the Secretary of State was notified that the application had been lodged. In this unusual context there was the possibility of expediting the judicial review application so that the case fell outside of the normal range of cases and it could reasonably be said that removal was still imminent and would be within 28 days rather than the three to four months that it usually takes for a permission application to be decided.
14 *R (on the application of I) v Secretary of State for the Home Department* [2010] EWCA Civ 727; *R (on the application of Nukajam) v Secretary of State for the Home Department* [2010] EWHC 20 (Admin).
15 *R (on the application of Nukajam)* above and *HA v Secretary of State for the Home Department* [2010] EWHC 1940 (QB).

Special categories of detainee

18.32 In its 1998 White Paper,[1] the government set out certain special categories of asylum seeker whose detention would not normally be appropriate. This was set out in the Operational Enforcement Manual (OEM) Chapter 38, which has now been replaced by Chapter 55 of the EIG. It identifies[2] a number of 'special cases' which, in the current version, are:

(1)   *Pregnant women* should normally be detained only in very exceptional circumstances. Exceptions to that are cases where there is a clear prospect of early removal and medical advice does not suggest that confinement before removal, or women who are less than 24 weeks' pregnant who may be detained at Yarl's Wood as part of the fast-track process.[3]

(2)   *Cohabiting spouses of British nationals* save for FNP cases not dealt with by the Criminal Cases Directorate may only be detained with the authority of an inspector or senior caseworker and where 'strong representations' continue to be received, the decision to detain must be reviewed by an Assistant Director.[4]

(3)   *Spouses of EEA nationals* save for FNP cases should not be detained unless there is strong evidence that the EEA national spouse is no longer exercising treaty rights in the UK or it can be proved that the marriage was one of convenience and the parties had not intention to live together from the outset of the marriage;[5]

(4)   *Unaccompanied children* should only ever be detained in very exceptional circumstances where it is necessary for the child's care and safety and then only overnight and for the shortest possible time whilst alternative arrangements are made. In the absence of responsible family or friends, unaccompanied minors and those under 18 will be placed in the care of the local authority. In criminal deportation cases, a person under 18 may be detained in exceptional circumstances where it can be shown that they pose a serious risk to the public and a decision to deport or remove has been taken. Children may be detained for the purpose of removing them but only on the day of planned removal and detention must be authorised by an Assistant Director.[6] Children may only be detained in a place of safety or a short-term holding facility.

(5)   *Age dispute cases*: where age is disputed, Home Office policy[7] is to accept that a person is a child unless:
   (a)   There is credible and clear documentary evidence that they are 18 or over. OR
   (b)   A Merton compliant age assessment by a local authority is available stating that they are 18 years of age or over. OR
   (c)   Their physical appearance/demeanour very strongly suggests that that they are significantly over 18 years of age and no other credible evidence exists to the contrary[8] OR
   (d)   *All* of the following apply:
      (i)   The individual, prior to detention, gave a date of birth that would make them an adult and/or stated they were an adult; and
      (ii)   only claimed to be a child after a decision had been taken on their asylum claim; and
      (iii) only claimed to be a child after they had been detained; and
      (iv)   has not provided credible and clear documentary evidence proving their claimed age; and
      (v)   does not have a Merton compliant age assessment stating they are a child; and
      (vi)   does not have an unchallenged court finding indicating that they are a child; and
      (vii) their physical appearance/demeanour very strongly suggests that they are 18 years of age or over.

Unless there is either a Merton-compliant[9] age assessment available or documentary evidence, a second officer must make an assessment. If new evidence is acquired the decision to treat the person as an adult must be reviewed. Where a person has been treated as an adult by a criminal court and there is no credible evidence that they are a child they be referred for a Merton-compliant age assessment. A person claiming to be a child should be afforded the benefit of any doubt. The question of whether a person is a child or not is one of precedent fact for the purposes of the Children Act 1989 to be decided by the Court on an application for judicial review (*R(A) v London Borough of Croydon*[10]). The Supreme Court has also held however that the mere fact that a person detained on the basis of a Merton-compliant age assessment turns out, in fact, to be a child will not render detention unlawful (*R(AA)Afghanistan v Secretary of State for the Home Department*[11]). In order for the Secretary of State to lawfully detain a person claiming to be a child in reliance on a local authority age assessment it is necessary for the Officer to see the assessment and to evaluate whether it in fact complies with the *Merton* criteria.[12] The Secretary of State must always make a reference to a local authority where an unaccompanied child is encountered, and where that child is detained and a reference is not made sufficiently quickly, in particular to facilitate questioning, that may render detention unlawful.[13]

(6) *Families*: the introduction of 'pre-departure accommodation', placed on a statutory footing by the Immigration Act 2014[14], represents a policy shift away from the detention of families and ends, on a cosmetic level, their detention in Immigration Removal Centres[15]. Closer scrutiny shows that 'pre-departure accommodation' [see **18.24** above] is in fact detention, albeit with certain facilities and support from Barnardo's. This form of detention is to be used as a '*last resort*' and for the shortest possible time.[16] The policy provides that in certain '*rare*' circumstances it may be necessary to detain a family in Tinsley House or separate a member of the family considered to be a risk for detention in the IRC estate. Stays at pre-departure accommodation are normally limited to 72 hours but may, in exceptional circumstances and with Ministerial authority, be extended up to seven days. The policy aims to take account of the best interests of the child (which following the decision of the Supreme Court in *ZH (Tanzania) v Secretary of State for the Home Department*[17] must be a 'primary consideration') and is directed towards minimising the use of detention in family cases. A failure of the Secretary of State to have regard to the statutory duty under section 55 of the Borders, Citizenship and Immigration Act 2009 to safeguard and promote the best interests of the child, and the policies made thereunder, can lead result in detention being unlawful.[18] Similarly, a failure to have regard to the section 55 duty and the policies regarding the separation of families was held by the Court of Appeal to render detention unlawful in *R (on the application of Abdollahi) v Secretary of State for the Home Department*.[19]

---

1 *Fairer Faster and Firmer – A Modern Approach to Immigration and Asylum* (Cm 4018, July 1998).

2 For detention of families see *A Few Families Too Many: Detention of Asylum-Seeking Families in the UK* Emma Cole, Bail for Immigration Detainees, London, March 2003.

3 EIG, para 55.9.1. For the experiences of women in detention see for example Sarah Culter and Sophia Ceneda They took me away: women's experiences of immigration detention in the UK (BID and Refugee Women's Project, 2004).

4 EIG, para 55.9.2.

5 EIG, para 55.9.2.

6 EIG, para 55.9.3.

7 It is important to consider Ch 55.9.3.1 EIG in conjunction with the Assessing Age policy and Detention Services Order 14/2012.

8 A statement accompanying the announcement of the change in policy on 30 November 2005, referring to cases where (as it then was) 'appearance very strongly indicates that they are

significantly over 18', stated that '[this category] is intended for the fairly exceptional case – for claimants appearing to be in their 30s or older'.

⁹ For age assessment see **11. 6, 11.121** and **12.120** above. The leading cases on age assessment are *R (on the application of B) v Merton London Borough Council* [2003] EWHC 1689 (Admin), [2003] 4 All ER 280 (12.117 above) and *R (on the application of FZ acting by his litigation friend Parivash Ghanipour) v Croydon London Borough Council* [2011] EWCA Civ 59, which elaborates and clarifies the criteria set out in Merton. In *R (on the application of A) v Croydon London Borough Council* [2009] UKSC 8 the Supreme Court left open the appeal from the Court of Appeal's judgment ([2008] EWCA Civ 1445) that a local authority decision to provide accommodation under the Children Act 1989 was the determination of a civil right for the purposes of Article 6 of the ECHR. In *R (on the application of HBH) v Secretary of State for the Home Department* [2009] EWHC 928 (Admin) there was a successful challenge to the old age dispute policy where its application led the Home Office to refer a disputed child as if he were an adult to the police for prosecution under the AI (TC)A 2004, s 2.

¹⁰ [2009] UKSC 8

¹¹ [2013] UKSC 49

¹² *R (on the application of J) v Secretary of State for the Home Department* [2011] 3073 (Admin) at para 31; *AAM (a child acting by his litigation friend, FJ) v Secretary of State for the Home Department* [2012] EWHC 2567 (QB) at para 110 (Note: the Supreme Court in *R (on the application of AA) v Secretary of State for the Home Department* [2013] UKSC 49 overturned part of Lang J's judgment but endorsed this element); *Durani v Secretary of State for the Home Department* [2013] EWHC 284 (Admin) at para 88-90. It was held, by contrast, in *VS v Home Office* [2014] EWHC 2483 (QB) that 'something less' than a full Merton-compliant assessment could be seen by the officers (although something more than a mere results pro forma). This is a problematic judgment and is currently subject to appeal.

¹³ See *VS v Secretary of State for the Home Department* [2014] EWHC 2483 (QB) applying *R (on the application of AN (a child) and FA (a child)) v Secretary of State for the Home Department* [2012] EWCA Civ 1636; 'Every Child Matters. Change for Children: Statutory Guidance to the UK Border Agency on making arrangements to safeguard and promote the welfare of children', the guidance made under s 55(3) of the Borders, Citizenship and Immigration Act 2009 (BCIA 2009) at s 2.19. Article 37 of the UN Convention on the Rights of the Child provides that the detention of a minor should only be as 'a last resort'.

¹⁴ Section 6, IA 2014 amending s 147 of the IAA1999.

¹⁵ EIG Ch 55.9.4; Ch 45b 5.0. The previous policy considered in *R (on the application of Suppiah) v Secretary of State for the Home Department* [2011] EWHC 2 (Admin) which shares many features with the present policy was interpreted by Wyn Williams J as meaning that detention of families should only be authorised in 'exceptional circumstances'. (at para 25). He acknowledged the significant evidence adduced by the claimants that 'detention is inherently and seriously harmful to the health and development of children' (at para 107) and considered that 'no one can seriously dispute that detention is capable of causing significant and, in some instances, long lasting harm to children' (at para 111).

¹⁶ In *R (Suppiah) v Secretary of State for the Home Department* [2011] EWHC 2 (Admin) Wyn Williams J held that the failure to have regard to the s 55 of the BCIA 2009 duty before detention rendered detention unlawful (at paras 167, 200 and 205). The policy itself, as it then stood, was held to be lawful.

¹⁷ [2011] UKSC 4

¹⁸ In the unusual circumstances of that case only nominal damages were awarded. The relevant policies on the separation of families are Children and Family Cases Process Instruction and Criminal Casework: Detention of Families.

¹⁹ [2013] EWCA Civ 366. Previous case law had held that detention of a family should take place as close to removal as possible. This was the approach of Collins J in *R (on the application of Konan) v Secretary of State for the Home Department* [2004] EWHC 22 (Admin), [2004] All ER (D) 151 (Jan), having heard full argument on the effect of changes to the old policy indicated by correspondence and the 2002 White Paper. In *R (on the application of I) v Secretary of State for the Home Department* [2010] EWCA Civ 727 the Court of Appeal held that a delay of more than three days in releasing an asylum seeker and his children after the commencement of judicial review proceedings, that had not been expedited, challenging the refusal of the asylum and human rights claims was unreasonable and the consequent 11 days further detention was unlawful. Concerns relating to the practice of detaining children have been consistently expressed, for example by the Official Solicitor to the Standing Committee on the IAA 1999; HM Chief Inspector of Prisons in various reports, the Children' Commis-

sioner for England in various reports; the Joint Chief Inspectors Report on Arrangements to Safeguard Children (July 2005), Every Child Matters: Change for Children 2006 and the JCHR: the Treatment of Asylum Seekers Tenth Report of session 2006–07 (30 March 2007), as well as by NGOs such as the Refugee Children's Consortium, the Medical Foundation for Victims of Torture, Bail for Immigration Detainees Amnesty International: Seeking Asylum is Not a Crime (June 2005); Childrens Society submissions to the JCHR, Save the Children: No place for a Child (February 2005) and IPLA: Child First, Migrant Second: Ensuring that Every Child Matters (February 2006), Seeking Asylum Alone (November 2006) and When is a Child not a Child (May 2007); Sarah Cutler, Detention of asylum seeking children, Childright (June 2002); Alison Harvey, Briefing on Detention of Asylum Seeking Children and Young People, Medical Foundation (September 2000). See also reports referred to at **18.24**, fn 11 above.

18.33 The EIG sets out groups considered unsuitable for detention, who should be detained only in very exceptional circumstances; they are:[1]

(i) unaccompanied children and young persons under the age of 18;

(ii) the elderly, especially where significant or constant supervision is required which cannot be satisfactorily managed within detention;

(iii) pregnant women, unless there is the clear prospect of early removal and medical advice suggests no question of confinement prior to this;

(iv) those suffering from serious medical conditions which cannot be satisfactorily managed within detention;

(v) those suffering serious mental illness which cannot be satisfactorily managed within detention. In exceptional cases it may be necessary for detention at a removal centre or prison to continue while individuals are being or awaiting to be assessed, or are awaiting transfer under the Mental Health Act;

(vi) those where there is independent evidence that they have been tortured;[2]

(vii) people with serious disabilities which cannot be satisfactorily managed within detention; and

(viii) persons identified by the Competent Authorities as victims of trafficking.[3]

In *R (on the application of Lumba) v Secretary of State for the Home Department*[4] Lord Dyson stated that 'immigration detention powers *need* to be transparently identified through formulated policy statements' He held that Chapter 55 of the EIG, read in conjunction with the Detention Centre Rules and other relevant policy guidance, is the means by which immigration detention powers are saved from arbitrariness. Breach of this policy will generally render detention unlawful as it bears directly on the decision to detain.[5]

[1] EIG, para 55.10.
[2] See eg *R (on the application of D) v Secretary of State for the Home Department; R (on the application of K) v Secretary of State for the Home Department* [2006] EWHC 980 (Admin), 150 Sol Jo LB 743; *R (on the application of PB) v Secretary of State for the Home Department* [2008] EWHC 364 (Admin); *R (on the application of MT) v Secretary of State for the Home Department* [2008] EWHC 1788 (Admin); and *E v Home Office* (10 June 2010) (Claim No 9 CLO/651). The leading case on these issues is now *R(on the application of EO) v Secretary of State of the Home Department* [2013] EWCA Civ 1099.
[3] See CHAPTER 13 above for the UK's procedures for identifying victims of trafficking.
[4] [2011] UKSC 12.
[5] Ibid. See also *R (on the application of Francis) v Secretary of State for the Home Department* [2014] EWCA Civ 718 as to whether damages will follow for the tort of false imprisonment.

Detainees with mental health problems

18.34 Perhaps the greatest volume of litigation arising from these categories has concerned those suffering from mental health problems.[1] An earlier incarnation of the policy required that those suffering from serious medical conditions '*or the mentally ill*' would not be detained.[2] On 26 August 2010 this was changed to the version set out above which only prohibited the detention of those with conditions that could not be satisfactorily managed in detention. In respect of general medical conditions, it was accepted by the Court of Appeal in *R (on the application of MD (Angola)) v Secretary of State for the Home Department*[3] that this was not a policy change but rather a more explicit statement of already existing policy. Singh J in *R (on the application of HA (Nigeria)) v Secretary of State for the Home Department*[4] held in respect of those suffering from mental health problems that this change had been unlawful as a result of the Secretary of State's failure to have regard to her duties under the Race Relations Act 1976 and the Disability Discrimination Act 2005.[5] However, in a case heard two days after that decision the Court of Appeal in *LE (Jamaica) v Secretary of State for the Home Department*[6] considered that there had not, in effect, been any material change in the policy at all.[7] The Court also held, obiter, that unlike in the context of a *Hardial Singh* analysis, the question for the Court on an application for judicial review of the decision to detain where a breach of policy was alleged was whether or not the Secretary of State had acted rationally by reference to the *Wednesbury* test.[8] That position endorsed the view of the Court of Appeal in *R (on the application of OM acting by her litigation friend, the Official Solicitor) v Secretary of State for the Home Department*[9] where it was also held that where a person is unlawfully detained by reference to a relevant policy, only nominal damages will be awarded if that person '*could and would*' have been detained in any event.

In *R (Anam) v Secretary of State for the Home Department*[10] it was held that the policy is only engaged 'where there is available objective medical evidence establishing that a detainee is, at the material time, suffering from mental health issues of sufficient seriousness as to warrant consideration of whether his circumstances are sufficiently exceptional to warrant his detention'. That view was endorsed by the Court of Appeal in what is now the leading case on the detention of those suffering from mental health problems *R (Das) v Secretary of State for the Home Department*.[11] In that case the Court of Appeal rejected the restrictive interpretation of the policy by Sales J at first instance, who had held that in order to trigger the policy the level of ill-health had to be around the level that would merit compulsory detention under the Mental Health Act 1983. The Court considered that for the policy to bite: (i) there must be a diagnosis of mental illness, (ii) the person concerned must be 'suffering' as a result of that illness, and (iii) it must be one which cannot be satisfactorily managed in detention. The mere fact of diagnosis is insufficient. 'The effects of the illness on the particular individual, the effect of detention on him or her, and on the way that person's illness would be managed if detained must also be considered.'[12]

Where the policy does bite there is a high hurdle to be overcome to justify detention. For the purposes of the policy not to detain those in respect of whom there is independent evidence of torture, an expert report applying the Istanbul protocol will not be excluded from consideration simply because the author has begun with the claimant's account. It is the *'evidence'* that is required to trigger the policy rather than proof.[13] Similarly, a person's credibility is not relevant to the question of whether or not there is independent evidence of torture, but may be relevant to the question of whether there are exceptional circumstances to justify detention in any event.[14] In respect of disabled persons, the Secretary of State has a statutory obligation to consider whether the detention estate has appropriate facilities and processes for disabled detainees generally and, before detaining a disabled individual, to carry out an assessment in relation to his or her needs.[15] Neither that obligation, nor the requirements of the EIG are satisfied by considering whether the individual is medically fit to be detained but not the wider issue of the effect of the detainee's disability on his or her experience of detention including matters such as increased distress, pressure, loss of privacy and dignity and embarrassment.[16] These are all matters relevant both to the question whether detention was lawful in the first place and for *Hardial Singh* purposes, the length of a reasonable period during which the person may be detained. In *IM (Nigeria) v Secretary of State for the Home Department*[17] the court considered the extreme situation of a person whose fitness for detention was being affected by the fact that he was refusing food and fluids and apparently near death. It was held that he could be lawfully detained in a hospital if not fit for detention in an IRC.[18]

1   There have been many cases over the years where there was medical evidence that a detainee was suffering from mental illness and as a consequence the detention was held to be unlawful owing to the Secretary of State's failure properly to apply the policy (as it then was) of not detaining mentally ill people save in very exceptional circumstances – *R (on the application of MMH) v Secretary of State for the Home Department* [2007] EWHC 2134 (Admin),(but see *R (on the application of Das) v Secretary of State for the Home Department* [2014] EWCA Civ 45 at para 51); *R (on the application of Hussain) v Secretary of State for the Home Department* [2007] EWHC 2134 (Admin), 151 Sol Jo LB 1228; and *R (on the application of MC (Algeria)) v Secretary of State for the Home Department* [2010] EWHC 2265 (Admin). See, however, *R (on the application of Anam) v Secretary of State for the Home Department* [2009] EWHC 2496 (Admin) and *MC v Secretary of State for the Home Department* [2010] EWCA Civ 347. It is to be noted that in *MC* the Court of Appeal construed mental illness broadly to mean the mentally disordered and to include those like MC who were diagnosed with a personality disorder.
2   Failure to apply the earlier version of the policy in paragraph 55.10 of the EIG that those suffering from mental illness would normally be considered suitable for detention only in very exceptional circumstances rendered the detention unlawful: *R (on the application of T) v Secretary of State for the Home Department* [2011] EWHC 370 (Admin). The court has accepted that the mental illness required a level of seriousness to engage the policy but it was for the decision maker to address this and it was not sufficient to simply state that there was 'no risk of suicide' since this is not the criteria in the policy. The detention was consequently unlawful: *R (on the application of SRH) v Secretary of State for the Home Department* [2007] EWHC 2134 (Admin), paras 48–49, *151 Sol Jo LB 1228.*
3   [2011] EWCA Civ 1238.
4   [2012] EWHC 979 (Admin).
5   The Secretary of State undertook to conduct an Equality Impact Assessment within seven days of judgment being handed down. The Secretary of State appealed the decision of Singh J but withdrew that appeal following the decision of the Court of Appeal in *R (on the application of LE (Jamaica)) v Secretary of State for the Home Department* [2012] EWCA Civ 597.
6   [2012] EWCA Civ 597.
7   *LE (Jamaica) v secretary of State for the Home Department* [2012] EWCA Civ 597 at para 41.
8   *LE (Jamaica) v Secretary of State for the Home Department* [2012] EWCA Civ 597 at para 29. That approach has since been treated as correct. See eg *R (on the application of O) v Secretary of State for the Home Department* [2014] EWCA Civ 990 at para 39.
9   [2011] EWCA Civ 909.
10 [2009] EWHC 2496 (Admin).

11 [2014] EWCA Civ 45.

12 The Court of Appeal in *R (O) v Secretary of State for the Home Department* held that an illness could be satisfactorily managed where, objectively considered, 'the treatment would generally be regarded as acceptable medical practice for dealing with this condition appropriately, which may mean keeping the condition stable . . . it would not necessarily mean treatment that provided the hope of recovery.' (para 48).

13 *R (on the application of AM) v Secretary of State for the Home Department* [2012] EWCA Civ 521 at para 29.

14 *R (on the application of EO) v Secretary of State for the Home Department* [2013] EWHC 1236 (Admin).

15 *R (on the application of BE) v Secretary of State for the Home Department* [2011] EWHC 690 (Admin). Section 49A of the Disability Discrimination Act 1995 was repealed shortly after this case was handed down with the coming into force of the Equality Act 2010. As to the application of the Equality Act 2010 duty see *R (on the application of S) v Secretary of State for the Home Department* [2014] EWHC 50 (Admin).

16 *R (on the application of BE) v Secretary of State for the Home Department* [2011] EWHC 690 (Admin), [2011] All ER (D) 298 (Mar), para 160.

17 [2013] EWCA Civ 1561.

18 The Court was considering in particular the interaction of the policy with DSO 03/13 brought in to deal with the increasing problem of hunger striking. The circumstances of this case were extreme: the Court considered that the *Hardial Singh* principles had not been breached because the appellant's condition was not yet '*irreversible*'. The problem of hunger striking is an indictment of the lengthy periods of detention experienced by many.

Detention of foreign national prisoners

18.35 Between April 2006 and 9 September 2008 the Secretary of State's published policy on detention of Foreign National Prisoners (FNPs) was that there was a presumption in favour of release. In fact, throughout that time the Secretary of State applied a near blanket ban on release of FNPs, irrespective of whether removal could be achieved. The secret policy, which was not published until 9 September 2008, contained a presumption in favour of detaining foreign national prisoners convicted of serious offences after completion of their sentences and pending deportation for as long as there was a realistic prospect of removal within a reasonable period of time.[1] Application of such a presumption was held to be unlawful in proceedings in the High Court.[2] However, on appeal the Court of Appeal held that the provisions in paragraph 2(1) of Schedule 3 to the IA 1971 should be construed creating a presumption in favour of detention pending deportation for those recommended for deportation. Thus it was not unlawful for the Secretary of State to adopt a policy for the purposes of paragraph 2(2) and (3) of Schedule 3 containing such a presumption provided that it did not operate as a blanket policy precluding consideration of the individual case. The Supreme Court in the ground-breaking case of *R (on the application of Lumba) v Secretary of State for the Home Department*[3] concluded that the policy was unlawful and that as it bore on the decision to detain it rendered the detention of the claimants unlawful. However, it was held that where they would have been detained even had the correct policy been applied they would only be entitled to nominal damages. Practitioners are increasingly seeing very long periods of detention for FNPs. Since the crisis of April 2006 which led to automatic deportation more and more foreign nationals (and occasionally British citizens unable to prove their nationality) are reflexively detained for very long periods. The evident danger, as experience is showing, is that in practice no proper regard will be had to the rehabilitative impact of the prison sentence or the propensity to reoffend as well as to individual factors such as mental health problems and the impact of continued detention on family life. Detention is also likely to be prolonged and of excessive duration given that many FNPs have complex cases and will have in-country rights of appeal. The Court of Appeal in *R (on the application of Francis) v Secretary of State for the Home Department*[4] revived the distinction between detention under paragraph 2(1) of the Schedule (and thereafter under paragraph 2(3)) and paragraph 2(2) (and thereafter under paragraph 2(3)). The Court held that in the former circumstances damages for false imprisonment will follow for a breach of the *Hardial Singh* principles but not for a breach of a public law rule, as the underlying lawfulness of detention was not undermined by such a breach. The current version of the policy in Chapter 55 of the EIG does in fact continue to operate a presumption in favour of release in respect of foreign national prisoners but where the 'deportation criteria' are met, substantial weight should be given to the risk of reoffending and of absconding as rebutting the presumption. The deportation criteria are for a non-EEA national, convicted in the UK and sentenced to 12 months' imprisonment or two or more sentences amounting to 12 months or more in total over the past five years or a custodial sentence of any length for a serious drugs offence.[5] In the case of EEA nationals, the criteria for deportation are a sentence of at least 24 months' imprisonment. Greater weight is to be given to the risk of further offending and harm to the public according to the seriousness of the offence to the extent that in relation to violent, sexual and drug related offences, release is likely only if there are 'particularly compelling' factors in favour of release.[6] Where removal is 'imminent' detention 'will usually be appropriate and removal is said to be imminent if a travel document exists, removal directions are set, there are no outstanding legal barriers to removal and removal is likely to take place in the next four weeks.[7] Where removal is not imminent, risk of absconding is to be considered. Among the factors said to indicate such a risk is conduct of the individual frustrating removal, including by not co-operating with attempts to document him or her.[8]

[1] *R (on the application of Lumba) v Secretary of State for the Home Department* [2011] UKSC 12.

[2] *R (on the application of Abdi) v Secretary of State for the Home Department* [2008] EWHC 3166 (Admin). Davis J considered that the presumption in favour of detention was unlawful because it was not authorised by the statutory power, the Immigration Act 1971, Sch 3, para 2 as construed in *R (on the application of Sedrati) v Secretary of State for the Home Department* [2001] EWHC 410 (Admin). The Secretary of State for the Home Department cross appealed on this finding in *R (on the application of WL (Congo)) v Secretary of State for the Home Department* [2010] EWCA Civ 111 and the court held that the declaration in *Sedrati* was wrong in law. The Supreme Court found that conclusion 'somewhat puzzling' since paragraph 2(2) and 2(3) of Schedule 3 do not create any presumption. For further consideration of the distinction between paragraph 2(2) and paragraph 2(1) of the Schedule see *R (on the application of Francis) v Secretary of State for the Home Department* [2014] EWCA Civ 718.The current version of the policy does not include a presumption in favour of detention.

[3] [2011] UKSC 12

[4] [2014] EWCA Civ 718

[5] EIG, para 55.1.2.

[6] EIG, para 55.3.2.

[7] EIG, para 55.3.2.4.

[8] EIG, para 55.3.2.5.

18.36 The Detention Centre Rules[1] provide for medical examination of all immigration detainees within 24 hours of admission to the removal centre, and oblige the medical practitioner to report to the centre manager, who must send a copy of the report to the Secretary of State, any case where the detainee may have been the victim of torture, or is potentially suicidal, or whose health is likely to be injuriously affected by detention or detention conditions, or who becomes seriously ill, is injured or is removed to hospital on account of mental disorder.[2] These are essential requirements which must be observed if the policy in Chapter 55 of the Enforcement Instructions and Guidance is to be properly applied, since it provides the only effective opportunity at an early stage of detention to obtain relevant information about the person's history and the state of his or her physical and mental health given the lack of any effective prior screening by the Immigration Service. Compliance with these rules is essential therefore to prevent detention of those categories of persons deemed unsuitable for detention. The case of *R (on the application of D) v Secretary of State for the Home Department; R (on the application of K) v Secretary of State for the Home Department*[3] revealed the wholesale and deliberate failure to operate these Rules at Oakington. The Chief Inspector of Prisons has also issued a number of critical reports about the lack of compliance in other removal centres and the persistent failure of the Home Office to act upon Rule 35 notices when they were provided by detention centre staff.[4] These failures led to a number of challenges to the legality of detention of victims of torture[5] and in a civil claim to the award of exemplary damages in the sum of £25,000.[6] Once material, usually medical evidence, is produced to demonstrate that the person falls within one of the vulnerable categories it is incumbent upon the Secretary of State to review the decision to detain and to apply the policy.[7] In *R (on the application of SRH) v Secretary of State for the Home Department*[8] a failure to consider the policy and grapple with a medical report diagnosing mental illness flawed the decision to detain.

[1]   Detention Centre Rules 2001, SI 2001/238.
[2]   SI 2001/238, rr 34–36. A number of reputable organisations including the Medical Foundation for the Care of Victims of Torture and Bail for Immigration Detainees have consistently reported that torture victims were being detained too frequently. See eg Alison Harvey, 'The detention of asylum seekers', a conference paper given at the University of Cambridge Institute of Criminology, 20 March 2001. See also Leanne Weber *Deciding to detain* (17.28 fn 3 above).
[3]   [2006] EWHC 980 (Admin), 150 Sol Jo LB 743, [2006] All ER (D) 300 (May).
[4]   Reports by the Chief Inspector of Prison following visits to Yarl's Wood in May 2005, Harmondsworth, September 2006 and Campsfield in January 2007. In *E v Home Office (10 June 2010)* (Claim No 9CLO/651), Collins HHJ concluded that 'the failure to have an adequate system for dealing with Rule 35 cases after the warnings of the Inspector of Prisons was outrageous and as grave a failure on the part of the Home Office and its contractors as can be imagined . . . '. The procedure for handling reports is now contained within Detention Services Order 17/2012. See also the policy Detention Rule 35 Process.
[5]   *R (on the application of PB) v Secretary of State for the Home Department* [2008] EWHC 364 (Admin); *R (on the application of MT) v Secretary of State for the Home Department* [2008] EWHC 1788 (Admin); *E v Home Office (10 June 2010)* (Claim No 9CLO/651); *R (on the application of EO) v Secretary of State for the Home Department* [2013] EWHC 1236 (Admin). In *R (on the application of RT) v Secretary of State for the Home Department* [2011] EWHC 1792 (Admin), [2011] All ER (D) 116 (Jul) detention was found to be unlawful owing to failure to comply with rule 34 of the Detention Centre Rules. Although the claimant had declined to be medically examined, she had referred in her screening interview to having been tortured so that the defendant's failure to advise her that it was in her interests to be examined was a 'conspicuous failure' to apply the rule.
[6]   *E v Home Office* (fn 4 above).

7   See Detention Rule 35 Process in respect of asylum seekers and Detention Services Order 17/2012.
8   [2007] EWHC 2134 (Admin), 151 Sol Jo LB 1228. See **18.33** above.

Fast track detention

18.37 The use of detention to facilitate accelerated determination of asylum claims and the removal of unsuccessful applicants has become a significant practice. In March 2000, the much wider use of detention was sanctioned by the government in a parliamentary answer[1] amending the White Paper[2] criteria in respect of detention originally at Oakington, a reception centre for holding asylum seekers whose claims were expected to be processed quickly.[3] Later in *Saadi*, as we have seen above, the House of Lords and subsequently the European Court of Human Rights upheld the legality of this kind of detention.[4] More recently, the High Court held in *R (Detention Action) v Secretary of State for the Home Department* that while lawful in its terms, carried an unacceptable risk of unfairness for vulnerable applicants due to the fact that lawyers did not have sufficient time to 'do what needs doing'. The Court refused to issue any further relief than a declaration that as at 9 July 2014 the DFT system: 'created an unacceptable risk of unfair determinations for those vulnerable or potentially vulnerable applicants . . . who did not have access to lawyers sufficiently soon after induction to enable instructions to be taken and advice to be given before the substantive interview'.[5] Asylum applicants, whatever their country of origin, may be detained whilst their asylum claims are determined if their claims appear to be ones where 'it appears that a quick decision is possible'.[6] The current designated sites for fast tracking are Harmondsworth, Yarl's Wood and Colnbrook.[7] The following are unlikely to be considered suitable for the DFT:

(i)   women who are 24 or more weeks pregnant;

(ii)   family cases (families with at least one minor chid, where that child is solely or principally dependent on the main applicant);

(iii)   those who are unaccompanied asylum seeking children, whose claimed date of birth is accepted by the UKVI;

(iv)   those with a physical or mental condition which cannot be adequately treated within a detained environment, or for practical reasons managed within a detained environment (such as contagious or infectious disease);

(v)   those with a disability which cannot be easily managed within a detained environment;

(vi)   those who clearly lack the mental capacity or coherence to sufficiently understand the asylum process and/or cogently present their claim;

(vii)   those for whom there has been a reasonable grounds decision taken (and maintained) by a competent authority stating that the applicant is a potential victim of trafficking or where there has been a conclusive decision taken by a competent authority stating that the applicant is a victim of trafficking; and

(viii) those in respect of whom there is independent evidence of torture.

Originally it was intended that the fast track would apply to claims that were both obviously well-founded as well as the obviously unfounded. Fast-tracking was advanced as beneficial to asylum seekers with meritorious claims because they would get a speedy decision. This has been relied on as justification for the measure by the courts domestically and in Strasbourg in the *Saadi* litigation.[8] However, in reality it is almost exclusively applied to claims thought likely to be refused and it is a procedure in which all but a tiny fraction of claims are rejected and a majority certified as unfounded. Assessment of suitability for the fast track has to continue throughout the claim and if at any stage evidence comes to light indicating that the individual is no longer suitable for the detained fast track or the detained non-suspensive appeals procedure then he or she must be removed from the procedure.[9]

1   346 HC Official Report (6th series) written answers col 263N, 16 March 2000, Barbara Roche.
2   Cm 4018, above.
3   Detention there was to be for a period of seven days, while applicants were interviewed and an initial decision made. If a decision has not been taken, the applicant would be granted temporary admission or transferred to longer-term detention; if refused, a decision about further detention would be made in accordance with normal criteria: ibid; see *R (on the application of Saadi) v Secretary of State for the Home Department* [2002] UKHL 41, [2002] INLR 523. As noted in the *Detention Action* case, the times are now on average up to four times what was contemplated in *Saadi*.
4   *R (on the application of Saadi) v Secretary of State for the Home Department* [2002] UKHL 41, [2002] INLR 523.
5   *R (on the application of Detention Action) v Secretary of State for the Home Department* [2014] EWHC 2245 (Admin) at para 196. The decision to refuse further relief ([2014] EWHC 2525 (Admin)) was then upheld by the Court of Appeal in *R (Detention Action) v Secretary of State for the Home Department* [2014] EWCA Civ 1270.
6   Detained Fast Track Processes. See also EIG, Chapter 55.4.
7   Tribunal Procedure (First-tier Tribunal) (Immigration and Asylum Chamber) Rules Rules 2014, SI 2014/2604, Schedule, para 2. EIG, para 55.4 and Detained Fast Track Processes continue to refer to Campsfield as a designated centre but it has not been included in the new Procedure Rules.
8   *Saadi v United Kingdom* (2008) 47 EHRR 427, para 77, (2008) Times, 4 February.
9   *R (on the application of the Refugee Legal Centre) v Secretary of State for the Home Department* [2004] EWCA Civ 1481. Tribunal Procedure (First-tier Tribunal) (Immigration and Asylum Chamber) Rules 2014/2604, Schedule, para 14. Detained Fast Track Processes.

18.38 The Harmondsworth scheme[1], first piloted in March 2003, extended the Oakington fast track procedure to single male asylum applicants who were considered to have straight forward claims and were from countries believed by the Secretary of State to raise in general no serious risk of persecution. The appeal process is also greatly curtailed, with the whole process, including any onward appeal or reconsideration, intended to take no more than 28 days.[2] Significantly, however the applicant remains detained throughout the entire period. In *R (on the application of Refugee Legal Centre) the Court of Appeal* held that the scheme was just flexible enough to be lawful.[3] Following that case, the Home Office published a policy document on the subject of 'flexibility' in the fast track processes indicating how the fast track timetable might be applied given that it claims to be built on 'an overriding principle of fairness'.[4] In May 2005 the fast track was extended to include women who could be detained at Yarls Wood.

1   Originally, fast track claimants were detained only at Harmondsworth, although there is now provision for their detention at Colnbrook and Yarl's Wood too: see Tribunal Procedure (Frist-tier Tribunal) (Immigration and Asylum Chamber) Rules 2004, SI 2004/2604, para 2 , Unlike those detained under the old Oakington scheme, Harmondsworth fast track claimants all have an in-country right of appeal, under the rules: see **20.46** below.

2   For the fast track appeal process see CHAPTER 20, and particularly **20.46**. *Detention Action v Secretary of State for the Home Department (Equality Human Rights Commission intervening)* [2014] EWHC 2245 (Admin) at para 81.

3   *R (on the application of Refugee Legal Centre) v Secretary of State for the Home Department* [2004] EWCA Civ 1481, [2004] All ER (D) 201 (Nov), upholding Collins J at [2004] EWHC 684 (Admin), [2004] Imm AR 142.

4   Detained Fast Track Processes: Operational Instruction; Flexibility in the fast track process, 26 April 2005. The present policy is Detained Fast Track Processes – Timetable Flexibility.

18.39 The difficulty in practice is that, prior to detention, there is no effective screening (apart from determining the person's nationality), to find out if fast tracking is suitable or if any of the general policy considerations militating against detention apply. The DFT List makes it clear that screening staff are not expected to engage in any analysis of asylum claims or to question claimants and when screened applicants are expressly told that they will not be asked any questions about the substance of their asylum claims. Furthermore, there is normally no effective screening to see whether the person is a torture victim, has mental health problems or other special medical needs such that they are otherwise unsuitable for the DFT. The lack of any adequate investigation on arrival creates the real possibility, in our view, of arbitrary detention based on nationality and in breach of stated policy. The Detention Centre Rules provide for new arrivals to a detention centre to be medically examined within 24 hours of arrival and for the medical practitioner conducting the examination to report any concern that the detainee may have been the victim of torture to the Secretary of State.[1] The objective is in part to ensure that victims of torture are identified and so not subject to the fast-track procedure and to being detained in breach of the policy. However, deliberately and in breach of the statutory obligation under the Detention Centre Rules, medical examinations at Oakington detention centre were routinely delayed beyond 24 hours. Continued detention beyond the point at which a person should have been identified, by a timely medical examination, as a victim of torture and so released in accordance with the detention and fast-track policies was held to be unlawful.[2] The case of *Renford Johnson*[3] is also indicative. Mr Johnson, a Jamaican national in his sixties, was detained at Oakington in circumstances where his claim could not be determined within the seven-day period but nevertheless, and despite the requirement for reviews, remained detained at Oakington pending a decision on his claim for over five weeks. Jack J held that the detention became unlawful after six days, when it was clear that the claim could not be determined speedily, and roundly rejected the surprising submission on behalf of the Secretary of State that seven days 'was merely a target' on the basis that it was 'wholly contrary' to the Department's submissions in *Saadi* and the basis on which the lawfulness of such detention was upheld by the House of Lords in that case.[4] He also held unlawful the period of Oakington detention after the decision on the claim, as it was contrary to the general policy, there being no basis for concluding that Mr Johnson would not co-operate or that he might abscond.[5] It would now appear following the decision in *Detention Action v Secretary of State for the Home Department (Equality Human Rights Commission intervening)*[6] that detention during any appeal proces following a decision is still detention under the DFT criteria rather than under the general Ch 55 EIG policy. Following *Renford Johnson* the Home Office revised the fast track detention policy, stating that the timetable for processing claims was only a guide and that if the timetable could not be adhered to, detention would continue beyond the 10 to 14-day timescale which was the subject of the litigation in *Saadi*, if 'the indications are that we can make and serve a decision within a reasonable timescale'. The revised policy also states that detention may be prolonged, if merited according to the general detention criteria, and could continue after service of a decision.[7] Application of the fast track procedures proved particularly controversial in disputed minors cases, where expert reports necessary to displace assumptions of adulthood[8] cannot normally be performed within the usual seven-day period, leading to delays and/or the reconsideration of cases where interviews have taken place, during which period claimants remain in detention. Detention and fast-tracking is patently unsuitable in such cases.[9] The change in the age dispute policy[10] has substantially reduced the number of disputed children in the fast track system.

1   SI 2001/238, rr 34 and 35.
2   *R (on the application of D) v Secretary of State for the Home Department; R (on the application of K) v Secretary of State for the Home Department* [2006] EWHC 980 (Admin), 150 Sol Jo LB 743, [2006] All ER (D) 300 (May). However, where an asylum seeker claimed to have been tortured, there was no obligation on the Secretary of State to carry out an earlier medical examination than required by the Detention Centre Rules in order to determine whether, by reason of being a torture victim, the person was unsuitable for the fast-track – *HK (Turkey) v Secretary of State for the Home Department* [2007] EWCA Civ 1357, [2007] All ER (D) 310 (Dec). Where an allegation of past torture is made this cannot simply be ignored by the decision maker *E v Home Office* (Claim No (CL01651) (10 June 2010 unreported).
3   *R (on the application of Johnson (Renford)) v Secretary of State for the Home Department* [2004] EWHC 1550 (Admin).
4   *R (Johnson)* above at para 32.
5   *R (Johnson)* above at para 34.
6   [2014] EWHC 2245 (Admin).
7   Desmond Browne (Minister for Citizenship and Immigration) Hansard HC, 16 Sept 2004, Column 157–158 WS.
8   See 17.32 above.
9   For a challenge to the practice of detention while age disputes are resolved, see *R (on the application of I) v Secretary of State for the Home Department* [2005] EWHC 1025 (Admin).
10 See **18.33** above.

UNHCR Guidelines for detention of asylum seekers

18.40 The UNHCR has issued guidelines relating to the detention of asylum seekers.[1] These guidelines include the general principle that it is inherently undesirable to detain asylum seekers and there should be a presumption against detention which should be used as a last resort.[2] UNHCR considers that there are only three purposes for which detention may be justified, namely public order, public health, and national security. The broad categories identified by UNHCR[3] are:

(i)   to prevent absconding and/or in cases of likelihood of non-cooperation;
(ii)   in connection with accelerated procedures for manifestly unfounded or clearly abusive claims;
(iii)   for initial identity and/or security verification;
(iv)   in order to record, within the context of a preliminary interview, the elements on which the application for international protection is based, which could not be obtained in the absence of detention; and
(v)   to protect public health or national security.

Detention as a penalty for illegal entry or to deter illegal entrants, or on the grounds that they will be expelled (before a decision on their claims) are expressly said by UNHCR not to justify detention.[4] Alternatives to detention must be considered. Unaccompanied minors should not be detained[5]. The latest version of the Guidance stresses the need for account to be taken of the individual circumstances of asylum seekers in the decision to detain, and sets out certain categories (such as unaccompanied minors) for specific consideration. Those categories are victims of trauma or torture, children, women, potential victims of trafficking, asylum seekers with disabilities, older asylum seekers, and lesbian, gay, transgender and intersex asylum seekers.[6] The Guidelines require that detainees be provided with reasons for detention in a language the detainee can understand; medical screening to identify trauma or torture victims; the segregation of asylum seekers from criminal prisoners; the segregation of men and women, and children from adults, unless they are part of a family group; rights to communicate with the outside world, with family, friends and consular officials; the right to challenge detention, with appropriate legal advice and assistance; the right to prompt medical attention; and educational, social, religious and cultural rights. The Guidelines also refer to the UN Body of Principles for the Protection of all Persons under any form of Detention or Imprisonment 1988,[7] which set out indispensable procedural safeguards for detainees. The UN Working Group on Arbitrary Detention has also observed that it is 'inherently unjust' to detain people who have been in the UK for 10 or 12 years and have put down roots.[8]

1   UNHCR *Guidelines on the applicable Criteria and Standards relating to the Detention of Asylum Seekers and Alternatives to Detention* (21 September 2012). This document updates and replaces the 1999 Guidelines.
2   UNHCR *Guidelines* above, Introduction and Guideline 4.
3   Set out in UNHCR *Guidelines* above, Guideline 4.
4   UNHCR *Guidelines* above, Guideline 4.
5   UNHCR *Guidelines* above, Guideline 9.2. The UN Working Group on Arbitrary Detention, in its report on detention of immigrants and asylum seekers, stated that unaccompanied minors should never be detained: Commission on Human Rights, 55th Session, 18 December 1998, E/CN.4/1999/63 Add 3, para 37. See also UNCRC: General Comment No 6 (2005) Treatment of Unaccompanied and Separated Children Outside their Country of Origin (1 September 2005).
6   UNHCR *Guidelines* above, Guideline 9. See also Detention Centre Rules 2001, SI 2001/238, rr 35 and 36, **18.35** above, and the Enforcement Instructions and Guidance Chapter 55 17.33 above.
7   UNGA 43/173, 1988; A/RES/43/173.
8   UN Commission on Human Rights, 55th Session, 18 December 1998, E/CN.4/1999/Add.3, paras 22–23.

Children

18.41 Specific guidance has also been issued by UNHCR in respect of refugee children. UNHCR's clear view is that children should not in principle be detained at all. It has adopted the wording of Article 37 of the CRC which holds that 'because detention can be very harmful to refugee children it must be used only as a measure of last resort and for the shortest appropriate period of time'. Article 37 of the CRC also expressly requires humane conditions, protection from physical abuse, the need to keep a family together, and access to education and play. These requirements are reflected in the UNHCR Guidelines referred to above. Reference is also made to the UN General

Assembly's detailed standards which apply whenever juveniles are deprived of their liberty.[1] Article 2 of these standards reiterates that deprivation of the liberty of a juvenile should be a measure of last resort and for the minimum necessary period, and should be limited to exceptional cases. See **18.32** above.

[1] UN Rules for the Protection of Juveniles Deprived of Liberty (1990) (UN General Assembly Resolution 45/113, 14 December 1990). See also UNHCR Guidelines on Separated Children (1997) and see UNHCR and Save the Children: Separated Children in Europe Statement of Good Practice, 3rd edn (2004). See also The UNHCR *Guidelines on the applicable Criteria and Standards relating to the Detention of Asylum Seekers and Alternatives to Detention* (21 September 2012) gives detailed guidance on the position of children at Guideline 9.2.

18.42 The legal relevance of the UN Convention on the Rights of the Child and the requirement to treat the best interests of the child as a primary consideration, has had a vexed history particularly given the UK's reservation, now withdrawn, from the UNCRC in immigration related matters.[1] The EU Reception Directive[2] at paragraph 18(1) put the issue beyond argument as far as reception arrangements for asylum seekers were concerned since it expressly provides that 'the best interests of the child shall be a primary consideration for member states' when implementing the provisions of the Directive which involve minors. The debate is now dead following the introduction of the duty in section 55 of the BCIA 2009 which requires the functions of the UKBA to be 'discharged having regard to the need to safeguard and promote the welfare of children who are in the United Kingdom'[3] and obliges decision makers to have regard to guidance issued under these provisions.[4] This guidance, Every Child Matters, issued in November 2009[5] is a highly significant development and expressly states that the UKVI must act in accordance with Article 3 of the UNCRC.[6] Decisions to detain or maintain detention of adults with children and to detain children themselves must therefore treat the interests of the children as a primary consideration and have regard to the need to safeguard and promote the welfare of children.[6] There has moreover been a succession of policies which expressly deal with detention that affects children and in particular the decision to split families.[7] The breach of the obligation to take account of the best interests of the child, or to contact the Office of the Children's Champion in certain circumstances as required by policy, is a public law error that bears on the decision to detain such that it will render detention unlawful.[8] *R (on the application of Abdollahi) v Secretary of State for the Home Department*[9]). Where EU law is engaged and the Charter of Fundamental Rights therefore applies Articles 24(1) and 24(2) require that:

'Children shall have the right to such protection and care as is necessary for their well-being . . . In all actions relating to children, whether taken by public authorities or private institutions, the child's best interests must be a primary consideration.'[10]

[1] The Secretary of State succeeded initially in persuading the courts that the UNCRC had no relevance to the exercise of discretion, as an unincorporated Treaty in cases such as *R v Secretary of State for the Home Department, ex p Gangadeen* [1998] INLR 206. However, the position changed with the incorporation of the European Convention on Human Rights into domestic law and the requirement to interpret its provisions consistently with other human rights instruments eg: *Golder v United Kingdom* (1975) 1 EHRR 524; *Al–Adsani v United Kingdom* (2002) 34 EHRR 11; *T and V v United Kingdom* (1999) 30 EHRR 121 at para 76; *Pini and Bertani v Romania* (Application 78028/01)) (2004) 40 EHRR 312, [2005] 2 FLR 596. For a review of some of the other relevant authorities, see *R (on the application of the Howard League for Penal Reform) v Secretary of State for the Home Department* [2002]

EWHC 2497 (Admin), [2003] 1 FLR 484, per Munby J at paras 51–52. In *Singh v Entry Clearance Officer, New Delhi* [2004] EWCA Civ 1075, [2004] INLR 515 the Secretary of State himself had submitted, and the court accepted, that Article 8 of the ECHR had to be interpreted consistently with other principles of international law of which it forms part including the UN Convention on the Rights of the Child (CRC). Furthermore there is no justifiable distinction in respect of children who are foreign nationals and who find themselves in detention under the Immigration Acts and the position of British children detained in Young Offenders' Institutions or accommodated with a parent serving a criminal sentence who had rights: (i) to be treated as other children; (ii) subject to the protection of the Children Act 1989; and (iii) for their best interests to be the primary consideration consistent with international norms: *R (on the application of the Howard League for Penal Reform) v Secretary of State for the Home Department* [2002] EWHC 2497 (Admin), [2003] 1 FLR 484 and *R (on the application of P) v Secretary of State for the Home Department* [2001] EWCA Civ 1151, [2001] 1 WLR 2002.

2 Council Directive (2003/9/EC) of 27 January 2003 laying down minimum standards for the reception of asylum seekers (The Reception Conditions Directive 2003/9/EC). On detention of children, see materials cited at 17.32 fn XX above. The United Kingdom has not signed up to the recast directive (2013/33/EU).

3 Section 55 of the BCIA 2009 which replaced sn 21 of the UKBA 2007 and the obligation to take account of the old Code of Practice For Keeping Children Safe from Harm issued under that section.

4 BCIA 2009, s 55(3) and (5).

5 *Every Child Matters: Change for Children: Statutory Guidance to the UK Border Agency on making arrangements to safeguard and promote the welfare of children* (November 2009).

6 Guidance as to the meaning of the obligation was provided by the Supreme Court in the seminal decision of *ZH(Tanzania) v Secretary of State for the Home Department* [2011] UKSC 4 and *HH v Deputy Prosecutor of the Italian Republic, Genoa* [2012] UKSC 25.

7 The Criminal Casework Directorate: Children and Family Cases Process Instruction policy, which appears to have been withdrawn, included an obligation to consult the Office of the Children's Champion before a decision was made to split a family with detention or with deportation, which are to be considered separately (*R (on the application of Abdollahi) v Secretary of State for the Home Department* [2012] EWHC 878 (Admin) confirmed by the Court of Appeal in *R (on the application of Abdollahi) v Secretary of State for the Home Department* [2013] EWCA Civ 366). The present policy Detention of Families also requires consultation with the Office of the Children's Champion. The policy focuses almost exclusively on the relationship between parents and children but the s 55 duty itself is certainly wider than that. See also the Guidance in Ch 55 EIG.

8 (*R (on the application of Abdollahi) v Secretary of State for the Home Department* [2013] EWCA Civ 366).

9 [2013] EWCA Civ 366

10 *Every Child Matters: Change for Children*, as above, para 2.7.

LIMITS TO THE POWER TO DETAIN

General principles

18.43 The right to liberty is a fundamental right and in the domestic common law there is a presumption of liberty which flows from the Magna Carta.[1] It is a pre-eminent right and a foundation stone of freedom in a democracy. According to Lord Bingham of Cornhill:[2] 'Freedom from executive detention is arguably the most fundamental and probably the oldest, the most hard won and the most universally recognised of human rights . . . .'. It means no person within the jurisdiction can be deprived of his or her liberty without cause, irrespective of their immigration status or nationality.[3] The 'principle that must lie at the heart of any discussion as to whether a person's detention can be justified' is that 'the liberty of the subject can be interfered with only upon grounds that the court will uphold as lawful'.[4] This right was reflected in the Immigration Service Instructions to staff on detention issued in 1991 and

1994 and repeated in the Operational Enforcement Manual and its successor, the EIG, which the courts have confirmed embodies a presumption in favour of release.[5] The Secretary of State's detention policy, currently in the EIG, is necessary to avoid the arbitrariness characteristic of a broad discretion that is not narrowly defined and in order to give effect to the *Hardial Singh* principles.[6] The rule of law requires that how immigration detention powers are to be exercised should be transparently identified by means of policy statements.[7] They must be published because an individual has a right to know the policy according to which he or she may be detained in order to be able to make informed and meaningful representations and to challenge any adverse decision.[8] Although, as we have seen there are notable exceptions to this as far as those subject to the DFT process is concerned. The Secretary of State did operate a secret policy for a time in respect of FNPs that effectively reversed the presumption[9], although the present incarnation of the EIG provides a presumption in favour of release even for FNPs (albeit with major caveats).

[1] The right to personal liberty is described by Blackstone as an 'absolute right inherent in every Englishman' see Clayton & Tomlinson *The Law of Human Rights* (OUP, 2000) p 449; *S-C (mental patient: habeas corpus), Re* [1996] QB 599, 603. The right is no longer confined to Englishmen; it now extends to women and foreign nationals: see fn 3, below. In *R (on the application of Lumba) v Secretary of State for the Home Department* [2011] UKSC 12 Lord Collins at para 219 endorsed Lord Bingham's suggestion in his 2010 book The Rule of Law that the provisions of Magna Carta '*are words which should be inscribed on the stationery of the . . . Home Office.*'

[2] Lord Bingham 'Personal Freedom and the Dilemma of Democracies' (2003) 52 ICLQ 841–858.

[3] *Khawaja v Secretary of State for the Home Department* [1984] AC 74, per Lord Scarman at 110–112; *R (on the application of Abbasi) v Secretary of State for Foreign and Commonwealth Affairs* [2002] EWCA Civ 1598, (2002) Times, 8 November, [2003] 3 LRC 297, [2003] UKHRR 76, paras 59–60; *A v Secretary of State for the Home Department; X v Secretary of State for the Home Department* [2004] UKHL 56, [2005] 2 WLR 87.

[4] Lord Hope in *R (on the application of Kambadzi) v Secretary of State for the Home Department* [2011] UKSC 23, para 49, [2011] 4 All ER 975, [2011] 1 WLR 1299, citing *R v Governor of Brockhill Prison, ex p Evans (No. 2)* [2001] 2 AC 19, 35, [2000] 4 All ER 15, HL.

[5] *Minteh (Lamin) v Secretary of State for the Home Department* (8 March 1996, unreported), CA, ILD 1996 Vol 3. The stated policy was to 'grant temporary admission/release whenever possible and to authorise detention only where there is no alternative. The aim is to free detention space for all those who have shown a real disregard for the immigration laws and whom we expect to remove within a realistic timetable'. The presumption of release was confirmed in the 1998 White Paper: *Fairer, Faster, Firmer – A Modern Approach to Immigration and Asylum* (Cmd 4018, July 1998).

[6] Lord Hope in *Kambadzi*, paras 42 and 51.

[7] *R (on the application of Lumba) v Secretary of State for the Home Department* [2011] UKSC 12, [2011] 4 All ER 1, [2011] 2 WLR 671, Lord Dyson, para 34.

[8] *R (Lumba)*, Lord Dyson, paras 34–38.

[9] See *R (on the application of Lumba) v Secretary of State for the Home Department* [2011] UKSC 12.

18.44 The court's duty is jealously to guard the liberty of the person and to require clear words in a statute to take away liberty and to interfere with fundamental rights.[1] Broad statutory discretions to detain should be construed narrowly and strictly ensuring that they are only exercised for the proper statutory purpose.[2] There is currently no statutory time limit placed on administrative detention but the power is impliedly limited to a duration and circumstances consistent with that statutory purpose and which are reasonable.[3] The lawfulness of a detention therefore depends on a number of considerations:

(i) whether it is or continues to be for the statutory purpose for which the power is given;

(ii) whether the detention has gone on or will go on for longer than is reasonably necessary for the purpose for which it is authorised; and

(iii) whether the exercise or continued exercise of the power is in accordance with administrative law principles of rationality, fairness and reasonableness, and in particular, whether the exercise of discretion is consistent with stated policy;[4] and

(iv) as an overriding consideration embracing some of the above factors, whether the detention is for a lawful purpose, is prescribed by law and is proportionate to its legitimate aim under Article 5(1)(f) of the ECHR.

The third principle may be described following the Supreme Court decision in *R (on the application of Lumba) v Secretary of State for the Home Department*[5] as meaning that detention will be rendered unlawful by a breach of a public law rule that bears on and is relevant to the decision to detain. That decision was followed by the decision in *R (Kambadzi) v Secretary of State for the Home Department*[6] in which it was held that the detention of the appellant was unlawful as a result of the failure to adequately review his detention as required by the Operations Enforcement Manual (now replaced by the EIG) and the Detention Centre Rules 2001. The Court considered that the requirement to regularly review detention was sufficiently closely connected to the authority to detain to provide a further qualification to the discretion to detain under the statute.[7] Because the claimants in *Lumba* and *Kambadzi* had been unlawfully detained the Secretary of State was liable for the tort of false imprisonment and they were entitled to a declaration to that effect as well as nominal damages. However, the Supreme Court held by a majority in *Lumba* that causation did not affect whether or not detention was unlawful per se (in contrast with the Court of Appeal's decision). However, the majority held that where detention is rendered unlawful by a public law error, but that person would have been detained in any event, only nominal damages would follow. The Court of Appeal in *R (on the application of OM acting by her litigation friend, the Official Solicitor) v Secretary of State for the Home Department*[8] held that the question for the Court is whether it can be shown that the person 'could and would' have been detained in any event. It has since been held by the Court of Appeal in *R (on the application of Francis) v Secretary of State for the Home Department*[9] that detention pursuant to paragraph 2(1) of Schedule 3 to the IA 1971, where a person has been detained pursuant to a court recommendation for deportation, and following the making of that order under paragraph 2(3), is to be distinguished from detention under paragraph 2(2), following the notice of intention to make a deportation order, and thereafter under paragraph 2(3). In the former case, because of the language of the statute which requires that the Secretary of State 'shall' detain a person whom a court has recommended for deportation, breach of a public law rule will not give rise to a false imprisonment even if a court quashes the decision to detain and requires it to be retaken. The Court was nevertheless clear in *Francis* that irrespective of this 'statutory warrant' to detain a breach of the *Hardial Singh* principles would nevertheless give rise to a false imprisonment and therefore a declaration and damages. It remains to be seen how the detention provisions within the UKBA 2007 are to be interpreted in light of the decision in *Francis* and that interpretation will be of great significance. Certainly the power to detain while the Secretary of State considers whether deportation is appropriate set out in section 36(1) of the Act is discretionary and directly analogous to the power in paragraph 2(2) of Schedule 3 to the IA 1971. While the power in section 36(2) of the Act to detain following the making of an automatic deportation order under theU-KBA 2007 appears at first blush to be in mandatory terms, which would suggest that it also amounts to a statutory warrant, the authors consider that the wording in section 36(2) is so widely drawn as to amount to a discretion.[10]

---

[1] *Tan Te Lam v Superintendent of Tai A Chau Detention Centre* [1997] AC 97; *R v Secretary of State for the Home Department, ex p Simms* [1999] 3 WLR 328, 341F.

[2] In *Mahmod (Wasfi Suleman), Re* [1995] Imm AR 311 Laws J stated the position as follows 'While of course Parliament is entitled to confer power of administrative detention without trial, the courts will see to it that . . . the statute that confers it will be strictly and narrowly construed and its operation and effect will be supervised by the court according to high standards'. See also *R (on the application of Lumba) v Secretary of State for the Home Department* [2011] UKSC 12 per Lord Dyson at para 53. The mischief of administrative detention was neatly summarised by Lady Hale in *Kambadzi v Secretary of State for the Home Department* [2011] UKSC 23 at paragraph 63 as this: 'No court had ordered or authorised or approved this detention. The trial judge . . . had not even recommended it. A Government official decided to lock him up, on the face of it until a Government official decided to take the next step'.

[3] *R v Governor of Durham Prison, ex p Singh* [1984] 1 WLR 704 approved by the PC in *Tan Te Lam* and applied in *Mahmod (Wasfi Suleman), Re* [1995] Imm AR 311 and reviewed and approved by the House of Lords in *R (on the application of Khadir) v Secretary of State for the Home Department* [2005] UKHL 39, [2006] 1 AC 207 and the Supreme Court in *R (on the application of Lumba) v Secretary of State for the Home Department* [2011] UKSC 12 as relevant to the exercise of the discretion to detain rather than the existence of the power to detain itself.

[4] *R (on the application of Lumba) v Secretary of State for the Home Department* [2011] UKSC 12; *R (Kambadzi) v Secretary of State for the Home Department* [2011] UKSC 23. *R (on the application of Amirthanathan) v Secretary of State for the Home Department* [2003] EWCA Civ 1768, [2004] INLR 139; *R v Special Adjudicator and Secretary of State for the Home Department, ex p B* [1998] INLR 315, *R (on the application of Konan) v Secretary of State for the Home Department* [2004] EWHC 22 (Admin), [2004] All ER (D) 151 (Jan).

[5] [2011] UKSC 12.

[6] [2011] UKSC 23.

[7] It is not every breach of a public law rule that will be sufficiently closely connected to the authority to detain to render detention unlawful, as Lord Dyson made clear in *R (Lumba) v Secretary of State for the Home Department* [2011] UKSC 12 at para 68. The examples given by Lord Dyson of public law breaches that would not be sufficiently closely connected to the authority to detain to render detention unlawful were detention approved by an official of the wrong rank or detention in conditions different to those prescribed by policy.

[8] [2011] EWCA Civ 909.

[9] [2014] EWCA Civ 718.

[10] UKBA 2007, s 36(2): ' . . . the Secretary of State shall exercise the power of detention under paragraph 2(3) of Schedule 3 to the Immigration Act 1971 . . . unless in the circumstances the Secretary of State thinks it inappropriate.'

18.45 In *WL (Congo)*[1] the Court of Appeal went further in departing from the approach of Lord Phillips MR in *Nadarajah*[2] which treated the obligation to comply with published policy as 'law' for the purposes of Article 5(1) and the need for deprivation of liberty to be in accordance with a procedure prescribed by law.[3] In *WL (Congo)* the Court of Appeal drew a distinction between compliance with stated policy required by a legitimate expectation and a specific legal requirement. However, Article 5(1) 'lays down the obligation to conform to the substantive and procedural rules of national law'[4] and in this context, it is unclear why a breach of a legitimate expectation arising from a failure to apply published policy is not a breach of national law and, therefore, Article 5(1).

The Supreme Court, sitting as a panel of nine judges, allowed the detainees' appeals in *WL (Congo)*.[5] It agreed with the Court of Appeal that the policy pursuant to which they were held was unlawful so that a public law error had been made by the Secretary of State. It was a blanket policy to detain foreign national prisoners and so fettered the exercise of discretion by admitting no possibility of exceptions; it was inconsistent with the published policy that contained a presumption in favour of release and (contrary to what the Court of Appeal had held) it should have been published. However, it rejected the Court of Appeal's conclusion that the decisions to detain were not unlawful because the appellants' detention would have been inevitable even if the lawful, published policy rather than the unlawful policy had been applied. Neither administrative law nor the tort of false imprisonment allows such a 'defence of causation' whereby an unlawful authority to detain may be rendered lawful by reference to how the executive could and would have acted had it not made the legal error[6]: 'where the power has not been lawfully exercised, it is nothing to the point that it could have been lawfully exercised'.[7] A trespass to the person, such as false imprisonment, is actionable per se, ie whether or not damage is suffered and even if the person does not know that he or she is detained.[8] In public law terms, there is no difference between a detention which is unlawful because there was no statutory power to detain and one which, although authorized by statute was made in breach of a rule of public law; both are ultra vires.[9] To render the detention unlawful, 'the breach of public law must bear on and be relevant to the decision to detain' so that, for example, a decision made by an official of a different grade to that specified in the policy or to detain a person in different conditions to those specified would not.[10] On the other hand, failure to carry out the reviews of detention required by the policy was such an error, albeit a breach of a procedural rather than a substantive requirement.[11] Whilst the breach of public law duty must be one capable of affecting the result it does not have to be shown that the result would have been different had there been no breach.[12]

---

[1] *R (on the application of WL (Congo)) v Secretary of State for the Home Department* [2010] EWCA Civ 111, paras 77–79. This is the same case as Lumba. It is only the reference which is different

[2] *Nadarajah v Secretary of State for the Home Department* [2003] EWCA Civ 1768, 148 Sol Jo LB 24.

[3] *Nadarajah v Secretary of State for the Home Department*, fn 2 above, paras 54, 64–67.

[4] See for example, *Eminbeyli v Russia* [2009] ECHR 359, para 43.

[5] *R (on the application of Lumba) v Secretary of State for the Home Department* [2011] UKSC 12, [2011] 2 WLR 671, Lords Hope, Walker, Kerr, Dyson and Baroness Hale: Lords Phillips, Brown and Rodger dissenting.

[6] *R (Lumba)*, Lord Dyson, para 71.

[7] *R (Lumba)*, Lord Dyson, para 62.

[8] *R (Lumba)*, Lord Dyson, para 64, citing *Murray v Ministry of Defence* [1988] 2 All ER 521, [1988] 1 WLR 692, HL.

[9] *R (Lumba)*, Lord Dyson, para 66 citing *Boddington v British Transport Police* [1999] 2 AC 143, [1998] 2 All ER 203, HL.

[10] *R (Lumba)*, Lord Dyson, para 68.

[11] *R (on the application of Kambadzi) v Secretary of State for the Home Department* [2011] UKSC 23, [2011] 4 All ER 975, [2011] 1 WLR 1299.

[12] *R (Lumba)*, Baroness Hale, para 207.

The purpose and length of detention

18.46 The purpose for which detention is authorised is spelt out in the Immigration Acts. As we have seen above, administrative detention under the IA 1971 is authorised pending examination or further examination, a decision on the grant, refusal or cancellation of leave, pending consideration of and making of a deportation order, the giving of removal directions and pending the removal of the person from the UK. Detention is not authorised for any other purpose.[1] Thus, detention as a deterrent to would-be asylum claimants[2] or a practice of routine detention of particular nationalities, of heads of households or of undocumented passengers which was not for one of the above purposes would be unlawful in domestic law as well as under Article 5 of the ECHR.[3] Detention in order to facilitate 'spiriting away of the claimants from the jurisdiction before there was likely to be time for them to obtain and act upon legal advice or apply to the court' would be for an improper purpose and therefore unlawful.[4] In *Saadi*[5] the House of Lords held that detaining recently arrived asylum seekers in order to process their claims quickly and efficiently was lawful both under domestic and ECHR law, even although there was no risk of any of the applicants absconding. Thus the power to detain pending examination is not subject to any need to show that detention is necessary to prevent the applicants running away, nor is it limited to those who cannot appropriately be granted temporary admission.[6] Likewise detention with a view to deportation or removal does not require that it is necessary to detain the person in order to effect removal, the only restriction is that it be for the immigration purpose.[7]

[1] See IA 1971, Sch 2, paras 2, 2A and 16; Sch 3, para 2, NIAA 2002, s 62; UKBoA 2007, s 36: 18.9–18.15 above.

[2] See *Amuur v France* (1996) 22 EHRR 533, para 43.

[3] Absent reasonable suspicion of an arrestable offence police have no power to detain an asylum seeker not carrying identity documents to check immigration status, and a four-hour detention sounded in damages of £2,000 in *Okot v Metropolitan Police Comr*, 1 September 1995, Central London Trial Centre (reported in (1996) Legal Action, February, p 12).

[4] *R (on the application of Karas) v Secretary of State for the Home Department* [2006] EWHC 747 (Admin), [2006] All ER (D) 107 (Apr), Munby J at 84 and *R (on the application of Collaku) v Secretary of State for the Home Department* [2005] EWHC 2855 (Admin) at 14-15.

[5] *R (on the application of Saadi) v Secretary of State for the Home Department* [2002] UKHL 41, [2002] 1 WLR 3131; [2002] INLR 523, followed in *ID v Home Office* [2005] EWCA Civ 38, [2005] All ER (D) 253 (Jan), [2006] 1 WLR 1003. (a civil claim for damages).

[6] *Saadi*, above at paras 22–24; *ID v Home Office* [2005] EWCA Civ 38, at para 25.

[7] *Chahal v United Kingdom* (1996) 23 EHRR 413; *Conka v Belgium* (Application No 51564/99), (2002) 11 BHRC 555; *R (on the application of Sezek) v Secretary of State for the Home Department* [2002] 1 WLR 348 at 13.

18.47 The limits of the power to detain in domestic law were spelt out in the seminal case of *Ex p Hardial Singh*[1] the principles of which have been reaffirmed by the Supreme Court in *R (on the application of Lumba) v Secretary of State for the Home Department*[2]. The case concerned the power given to the Secretary of State authorising the detention of a person against whom a deportation order had been made. The principles set out in the case apply to all administrative detentions.[3] It was held that this particular power authorised the detention of the applicant only pending his removal[4] and could not be used for any other purpose. Secondly, the period during which the power to detain could lawfully be exercised was thereby implicitly limited to the period reasonably necessary to achieve that purpose. Thirdly, it was implicit that the Secretary of State should exercise all reasonable expedition to ensure that all necessary steps were taken for the removal of the applicant within a reasonable time. A failure by the immigration authority responsible for detention to take the action it should take, or to take it sufficiently promptly, renders the detention unlawful.[5] Singh had been detained for five and a half months whilst the Home Office were seeking the necessary travel documents to return him to India. *Hardial Singh* was followed by the High Court in the case of *Mahmod*,[6] where a 10-month detention to obtain travel documents to effect removal was held to be excessive, and was approved by the Privy Council when reviewing the lengthy detention of Vietnamese asylum seekers in Hong Kong.[7] Prolongation of detention pending exhaustion of the judicial process is not necessarily unlawful, though the relevance of those proceedings will vary from case to case[8] Dyson LJ provided a useful though not exhaustive list of the circumstances relevant to the question of reasonableness of the period of detention:

"the length of the period of detention; the nature of the obstacles which stand in the path of the Secretary of State preventing a deportation; the diligence, speed and effectiveness of the steps taken . . . to surmount such obstacles; the conditions in which the detained person is being kept; the effect of detention on him and is family; the risk that if he is released from detention he will abscond; and the danger that, if released, he will commit criminal offences'. [para 48]'

Where there had been lengthy detention, the Court warned that there must be cogent evidence of a risk of re-offending and not merely a risk of absconding to justify further indeterminate detention,[8] but also warned against detention simply to prevent the commission of crime, which would be incompatible with Article 5(1)(f) of the ECHR. An undertaking to 'take no steps to remove' an applicant once judicial review proceedings had been issued has been held not to preclude detention.[9]

1   *R v Governor of Durham Prison, ex p Singh (Hardial)* [1984] 1 All ER 983, [1984] 1 WLR 704, [1983] Imm AR 198, QBD approved by the Privy Council in *Tan Te Lam v Superintendent of Tai A Chau Detention Centre* [1997] AC 97, [1996] 4 All ER 256, PC, and applied by the House of Lords in *R (on the application of Saadi) v Secretary of State for the Home Department* [2002] UKHL 41, [2002] 1 WLR 3131, [2002] INLR 523 to detention pending examination of a claim as well as removal. The case was approved by the Supreme Court in *R (on the application of Lumba) v Secretary of State for the Home Department* [2011] UKSC 12.

2   [2011] UKSC 12

3   *R (on the application of Saadi) v Secretary of State for the Home Department* [2002] UK HL 41, [2002] 1 WLR 3131, [2002] INLR 523. See also *R (on the application of Francis) v Secretary of State for the Home Department* [2014] EWCA Civ 718.

4   Removal would be pending for 'so long as the Secretary of State remains intent on removing the person and there is some prospect of achieving this' – Lord Brown in *R (on the application of Khadir) v Secretary of State for the Home Department* [2005] UKHL 39, [2006] 1 AC 207. How slight the prospect of removal may be for removal nevertheless to be 'pending' is shown by, for example *R (on the application of SK) v Secretary of State for the Home Department* [2008] EWHC 98 (Admin) (removals to Zimbabwe pending, notwithstanding the policy not to remove whilst protracted litigation ongoing); *R (Bashir) v Secretary of State for the Home Department* [2007] EWHC 3017 (Admin) (removal to Iraq pending even though forced removal presently impossible and had been for a long due to the danger to staff involved in removals); *R (on the applilcation of Milnyali) v Secretary for the Home Department* [2007] EWHC 2411 (Admin) (notwithstanding present impossibility of removal to Algeria because the Algerian authorities did not accept the claimant was Algerian, there was sufficient prospect that they would eventually change their mind. It is important not to conflate the existence of

the power to detain (which depends on whether removal is pending) and its lawful exercise, which is a separate question determined by reference to the four *Hardial Singh* principles.

5 In *R v Special Adjudicator and Secretary of State for the Home Department, ex p B* [1998] INLR 315 continued detention after an asylum seeker had established his identity was held unlawful on the basis, inter alia, that the Home Office had had long enough to check the information he provided. See also *R (on the application of JS (Sudan)) v Secretary of State for the Home Department* [2013] EWCA Civ 1378 and *R (on the application of Ismail) v Secretary of State for the Home Departmentnt* [2013] EWHC 3921 (Admin).

6 *Mahmod (Wasfi Suleman), Re* [1995] Imm AR 311.

7 *Tan Te Lam v Superintendent of Tai A Chau Detention Centre* [1997] AC 97, [1996] 4 All ER 256, PC.

8 The Supreme Court in *R (on the application of Lumba) v Secretary of State for the Home Department* [2011] UKSC 12 rejected an 'exclusionary' approach to periods of detention while challenges to removal are ongoing, and considered that the weight to be accorded to those periods will depend on the facts of the case, including whether or not the claim was hopeless (at para 121).

8 *I v Secretary of State for the Home Department* above, per Simon Brown LJ at para 37. The relevance of a risk of absconding should not be overstated. It cannot be treated a trump card irrespective of other factors in the case, not least the length of the period of detention (per Dyson LJ para 35); such a result would be 'a wholly unacceptable outcome where human liberty is at stake'. The same view was endorsed again in *R (on the application of Lumba) v Secretary of State for the Home Department* [2011] UKSC 12. Mitting J in *R (on the application of Wang) v Secretary of State for the Home Department* [2009] EWHC 1578 (Admin) treated a 30-month detention as 'right at the outer limits of the period of detention which can be justified on *Hardial Singh* principles except in the case of someone who has in the past committed very serious offences and who may go on to commit further such offences or who poses a risk to national security' (at 27). In *Fardous v Secretary of State for the Home Department* [2014] EWHC 3061 (QB) it was held that 'a period of detention of 12 months or more will always require anxious scrutiny. Such periods of detention may well be lawful, and may continue to be so for substantially longer periods, but great care is required in concluding that this is so in any particular case.' (para 41).

9 *R v Secretary of State for the Home Department, ex p Singh (Jaswinder)* [1997] Imm AR 166, OHCS.

18.48 The question of what is a reasonable period for carrying out the statutory purpose of effecting a person's removal from the UK is a question of fact and depends on all of the circumstances of the particular case.[1] The European Union has fixed an overall 18-month limit to the period during which a person may be detained for immigration purposes: 6 months pending the removal process and 12 months to effect the removal if delay is caused by documentation problems arising from the actions of the detainee or the third country[2] but no such time limits currently restrict detention in the UK and it is regrettably possible for individuals, particularly former FNPs, to be held for periods substantially in excess of 18 months. It is not necessary for the defendant to be able specify how long it will take before a detainee can be removed or even to be certain that removal will take place for there to be a sufficient prospect of removal within a reasonable time so as to justify detention.[3] Whether time during which a detainee is challenging removal from the UK should be left out of account when deciding whether a reasonable period of time has elapsed has proved controversial. The Secretary of State has advocated an 'exclusionary rule' whereby such time should generally be left out of account and the Court of Appeal may have accepted that in *WL (Congo)* where it said: 'as a matter of principle, a FNP cannot complain of the prolongation of his detention if it is caused by his own conduct'.[4] However, the rule has been rejected by the Court of Appeal[5] and by the Supreme Court. The latter rejected the exclusionary rule on the basis that there was no warrant for so mechanistic an approach to the determination of what is reasonable in all the circumstances[6] and for the restricted judicial oversight of the legality of detention that would result.[7] It would wrongly exclude consideration of delays occurring within the appeal process which were not the fault of the detainee but of the respondent or the court or tribunal[8] and would discount potentially long periods of detention and the effects that they might have whilst prima facie meritorious challenges are pursued.[9] There was no obstacle in principle or practice to the Court making an assessment of the prima facie merits of a challenge to removal in order to assess the weight to be given to time detained in its pursuit.[10] The rule is inconsistent with *Chahal* where the European Court of Human Rights took account of the period during which the applicant was challenging his deportation to determine whether detention exceeded a reasonable period.[11] The merits of a challenge to the decision to remove may also be relevant to the issue of whether there is a realistic prospect of removal within a reasonable period. That a decision to remove made without regard to the welfare of the detainee's children was obviously flawed and would have to be revisited had an impact on whether the detainee could be removed within a reasonable period.[12] The illegality of the directions given for the claimant's removal and to enforce which, he was detained was relevant to the legality of his detention.[13]

1 *R (on the application of A) v Secretary of State for the Home Department* [2007] EWCA Civ 804, para 45, (2007) Times, 5 September.
2 Directive 2008/115/EC of the European Parliament and of the Council of 16 December 2008 on common standards and procedures in Member States for returning illegally staying third-country nationals.
3 *R (on the application of MH) v Secretary of State for the Home Department* [2010] EWCA Civ 1112, [2010] All ER (D) 288 (Oct).
4 *R (on the application of WL (Congo)) v Secretary of State for the Home Department* [2010] EWCA Civ 111.
5 *Secretary of State for the Home Department v Abdi* [2011] EWCA Civ 242, (2011) Times, 11 March.
6 *R (on the application of Lumba) v Secretary of State for the Home Department* [2011] UKSC 12, [2011] 4 All ER 1, [2011] 2 WLR 671, Lord Dyson, para 116.
7 *R (Lumba)*, Lord Dyson, para 118.
8 *R (Lumba)*, Lord Dyson, para 117.
9 *R (Lumba)*, Lord Dyson, para 118.
10 *R (Lumba)*, Lord Dyson, para 120.
11 *R (Lumba)*, Lord Dyson, para 119.
12 *R (on the application of SM) v Secretary of State for the Home Department* [2011] EWHC 338 (Admin), [2011] All ER (D) 53 (Mar). See also *R (on the application of Abdollahi) v Secretary of State for the Home Department* [2013] EWCA Civ 366 and the decision at first instance *R (on the application of Abdollahi) v Secretary of State for the Home Department* [2012] EWHC 878 (Admin) for detention rendered unlawful on the basis of a breach of policy due to a failure to consider the best interests of children.
13 *R (on the application of Qader) v Secretary of State for the Home Department* [2011] EWHC 1956 (Admin), [2011] All ER (D) 13 (Jul).

18.49 A Lack of cooperation with removal and the risks of absconding and committing further offences are also relevant to the reasonableness of the length of detention, but again, all will turn on the particular facts of the case. These issues were considered in *R (on the application of A (Somalia)) v Secretary of State for the Home Department*.[1] The appellant in that case had been held in administrative detention for a month short of three years following a criminal sentence. He was appeal rights exhausted. The judge at first instance held that he was detained unlawfully for 20 months of that period because, although he could have returned voluntarily to Somalia, he refused to do so and it was not possible to enforce his removal. The Court of Appeal held unanimously that his refusal to return to Somalia voluntarily was relevant to the assessment of whether he would abscond if released.[2] The risk of absconding was held to be relevant because absconding would hinder or prevent his removal from the UK and his removal was the very purpose for which the statute authorised detention. The majority went much further and also found that his ability to return voluntarily was important because it meant that 'the loss of liberty involved in the individual's continued detention is a product of his own making'.[3] That the claimant refused to return voluntarily because of the 'volatile and chaotic' situation in Somalia was said not to be relevant to assessing the lawfulness of continued detention. Keene LJ accepted that whilst the refusal to return voluntarily was of some relevance it was not of 'fundamental importance' as asserted by the Secretary of State and he questioned whether refusal to accept voluntary departure could justify detention in a case where there was no real risk of absconding.[4] The Supreme Court considered the significance of refusal by a detainee to return voluntarily to his or her country in *R (on the application of Lumba)* and the approach of Keene LJ was in large part vindicated. It would be relevant to the assessment of what is a reasonable period if a risk of absconding could be inferred from the refusal, but it would be wrong to draw such an inference in every case. Refusal to return cannot be held against a person if return is in any event not possible for extraneous reasons. Nor is it relevant if the person is pursuing a claim to remain in the UK or a challenge to removal, particularly an asylum or human rights claim. If the person is not pursuing any legal remedy, refusal to accept voluntary return would be of limited relevance only and certainly not a 'trump card' justifying detention until deportation can be effected.[5] The Secretary of State does not have power to detain indefinitely any person who refuses to depart voluntarily even where that refusal is the sole reason the person cannot be removed.[6] This was the conclusion in *R (on the application of Rostami) v Secretary of State for the Home Department*.[7] That conclusion accords with the view of the European Court of Human Rights as expressed in the case of *Mikolenko v Estonia*.[8] In that case, detention of a Russian national for three years and eleven months was held to be in breach of Article 5(1)(f) and not with a view to deportation because expulsion having become virtually impossible because for all practical purposes it required [the detainee's] co-operation which he was not willing to give'. In *R (A (Somalia)* the court also held unanimously that the risk that the appellant would reoffend if released was relevant because the statutory purpose for which he was detained was to effect his removal, such removal having been ordered for the very reason that his propensity to commit serious offences meant that his presence was not conducive to the public good. The risks of reoffending and absconding were described by the Supreme Court in *R (on the application of Lumba)* as being of *'paramount'* importance. In the evaluative process of assessing the reasonableness of detention, it has been held that concept of *'burden of proof'* may not be helpful, a decision that sits ill with the principle that it is for the jailer to justify the curtailment of liberty.[9]

[1] *R (on the application of A) v Secretary of State for the Home Department* [2007] EWCA Civ 804, para 45, (2007) Times, 5 September.

[2] It had been found by the judge at first instance that the appellant would abscond if he considered that necessary to remain in the UK.

[3] Toulson LJ, para 54, Longmore LJ agreeing. Toulson LJ said that 'where there is a risk of absconding and a refusal to accept voluntary repatriation, those are bound to be very

important facts, and likely often to be decisive factors'. Contrast Dyson LJ in *R (on the application of I) v Secretary of State for the Home Department* [2002] EWCA Civ 888, para 51, [2002] All ER (D) 243 (Jun) 'the mere fact (without more) that a detained person refuses the offer of voluntary repatriation cannot make reasonable a period of detention which would otherwise be unreasonable'.

4   *R (on the application of A) v Secretary of State for the Home Department*, para 79, although accepting that the individual's ability to avoid detention by his voluntary act of returning was of relevance, it was not of 'fundamental importance'.

5   *R (on the application of Lumba) v Secretary of State for the Home Department* [2011] UKSC 12, paras 122–128. So, for example, in *Sino v Secretary of State for the Home Department* [2011] EWHC 2249 (Admin), [2011] All ER (D) 128 (Aug) a reasonable period had been exceeded in respect of a claimant whose refusal to disclose reliable information impeded his removal to Algeria.

6   *R (on the application of Bashir) v Secretary of State for the Home Department* [2007] EWHC 3017 (Admin), [2007] All ER (D) 493 (Nov), para 20. Lord Justice Dyson said in *R (on the application of Mamki) v Secretary of State for the Home Department* [2008] EWCA Civ 307, [2008] All ER (D) 95 (Apr): 'however grave the risk of absconding and reoffending, there must come a time when it can no longer be said that the detention is reasonable'. He repeated that view in the Supreme Court giving the lead judgment in *R (on the application of Lumba) v Secretary of State for the Home Department* [2011] UKSC 12 at para 144.

7   [2009] EWHC 2094 (Admin). See also *Sino v Secretary of State for the Home Department* [2011] EWHC 2249 (Admin).

8   [2009] ECHR 1471 (Applciation No 106645/05) (8 October 2009) at para 65. See also *Massoud v Malta* [2010] ECHR 1197 at para 67.

9   *R (on the application of JS (Sudan)) v Secretary of State for the Home Department* [2013] EWCA Civ 1378 at paras 44-46.

18.50 *R (on the application of A) v Secretary of State for the Home Department*[1] was applied in a number of cases in which claimants were detained pending removal to Iraq pursuant to decisions to deport made in consequence of their criminal offences. Whilst voluntary return by scheduled flight to Baghdad was possible, enforced removal was not because, following Foreign Office advice, conditions in Iraq were too dangerous for the escorts needed to accompany deportees.[2] The claimants refused to return voluntarily. In *MMH* Beatson J held that the detention of one claimant for 13 months, the other for 9 months was not unlawful having regard to their refusal to depart voluntarily 'so that their detention was a product of their own making' and the significant risk that they would abscond.[3] In another, factually similar case, 11 months' detention was held not to be unlawful.[4] In a case that was also factually similar save that the claimant had been detained for 23 months, Mitting J held that the claimant's detention had become unlawful.[5] He did so because 23 months 'on any view must be at or near the top of the period during which detention can lawfully occur'; the claimant had not committed 'truly grave offences' such as those in *R (A) v Secretary of State for the Home Department* 'repetition of which would put the public at very grave risk'; whilst the risk of absconding was significant it was not as high as in *R (A) v Secretary of State for the Home Department* and whereas in *R (A) v Secretary of State for the Home Department* the period of detention had come to an end by the time the case was considered by the Court, detention in this case was continuing with no indication of when it might end. With 'some hesitation' the Court of Appeal held because of the substantial risk of absconding and the 'very high risk' of reoffending that detention had not become unlawful after 15 1/2 months, even though there was 'no immediate prospect that deportation will take place' (because it was too dangerous to escort the appellant to Baghdad).[6] Where detention was during a period that removal was prevented by a Rule 39 indication arising out of the situation in Somalia, the Court of

Appeal in *R (Muqtaar) v Secretary of State for the Home Department*[7] rejected an argument that detention was unlawful by virtue of the fact that the Secretary of State could not identify a time by which removal would occur.[8] Richards LJ echoed his reasoning in *R (on the application of MH) v Secretary of State for the Home Department*[9] that '[there] can . . . be a realistic prospect of removal without it being possible to specify or predict the date by which, or period within which, removal can reasonably be expected to occur and without any certainty that removal will occur at all.' He rejected the argument that this approach could not survive *R (on the application of Lumba) v Secretary of State for the Home Department*[10] and *Mikolenko v Estonia*.[11] Mitting J described 30 months' detention in *R (on the application of Wang) v Secretary of State for the Home Department*[12] as a period 'right at the outer limit' of the period during which a person could lawfully be detained. The Court of Appeal in *R (on the application of MH) v Secretary of State for the Home Department*[13] described a period of 38 months as 'a very long period indeed . . . [requiring] the most anxious scrutiny'.[14] The Court in *R(MH) v Secretary of State for the Home Department* was also clear that the longer detention endures, the 'greater the degree of certainty and proximity of removal' is required to justify it. Some useful context is provided by Presidential Guidance Note No 1 of 2012 which gives the following guidance to FTT Judges considering bail applications:

> 'The senior courts have been reluctant to specify a period of time after which the length of detention will be deemed excessive and as a result that bail should be granted. Each case turns on its own facts and must be decided in light of its particular circumstances. However, it is generally accepted that detention for three months would be considered a substantial period of time and six months a long period. Imperative considerations of public safety may be necessary to justify detention in excess of six months.'

Where removal is delayed by the individual's failure to co-operate with attempts to document him or her, the period of time during which detention is lawful is increased.[15] However, where the Secretary of State could not give an indication of how much longer it would take to document an individual and admitted that an 'impasse' had been reached in attempting to do so, detention had become unlawful after 18 months.[16] The Court has looked in recent years at general evidence about securing removal of undocumented individuals to particular countries including Morocco[17], Algeria[18], Somalia[19], Russia[20], Iran[21], together with evidence specific to the individual claimants, sometimes drawing inferences from the defendant's failure to produce evidence[22] supporting an expectation that removal may be anticipated within a reasonable period.

1   *R (on the application of A) v Secretary of State for the Home Department* [2007] EWCA Civ 804, (2007) Times, 5 September.
2   See *Secretary of State's evidence, recited in R (on the application of MMH) (and SRH) v Secretary of State for the Home Department* [2007] EWHC 2134 (Admin), 151 Sol Jo LB 1228 at para 18.
3   18.49, fn 4 above. Beatson J accepted that the risk of absconding was less than in *R (A) v Secretary of State for the Home Department* and that there was not the risk of grave criminal offences being committed were they to be released so that detention for as long as that in in that case would not necessarily be justified.
4   *R (on the application of M) v Secretary of State for the Home Department* [2007] EWCA Civ 3115.
5   *R (on the application of Bashir) v Secretary of State for the Home Department* [2007] EWHC 3017 (Admin).

6   *R (on the application of Mamki) v Secretary of State for the Home Department* [2008] EWCA Civ 307, [2008] All ER (D) 95 (Apr).

7   [2012] EWCA Civ 127.

8   It was held in *Secretary of State for the Home Department v Abdi* [2011] EWCA Civ 242 that the fact of a Rule 39 indication did not render further detention unlawful on the apparently narrower basis that 'the Court may revoke that order on the basis of representations made by the Home Secretary or a decision of that court or of our courts.'

9   [2010] EWCA Civ 1112.

10 [2011] UKSC 12.

11 [2009] ECHR 1471.

12 [2009] EWHC 1578 (Admin).

13 [2010] EWCA Civ 1112.

14 *R (MH) v Secretary of State for the Home Department* [2010] EWCA Civ 1112. The appellant in MH had committed a number of serious offences including robbery. By contrast, in the case of *Fardous v Secretary of State for the Home Department* [2014] EWHC 3061 (QB) in which there was no risk of offences it was held that 'a period of detention of 12 months or more will always require anxious scrutiny. Such periods of detention may well be lawful, and may continue to be so for substantially longer periods, but great care is required in concluding that this is so in any particular case.'

15 *R (on the application of Qaderi) v Secretary of State for the Home Department* [2008] EWHC 1033 (Admin), [2008] All ER (D) 148 (May); *R (on the application of Jamshidi) v Secretary of State for the Home Department* [2008] EWHC 1990 (Admin), [2008] All ER (D) 304 (Jun) but see *R (on the application of Rostami) v Secretary of State for the Home Department* [2009] EWHC 2094 (Admin), *Sino v Secretary of State for the Home Department* [2011] EWHC 2249 (Admin), [2011] All ER (D) 128 (Aug) and *Mikolenko v Estonia (Application No 10664/05)* (8 October 2009).

16 *R (on the application of Oppong) v Secretary of State for the Home Department* [2008] EWHC 2596 (Admin), [2008] All ER (D) 87 (Oct). See, however, the decisions of Richards LJ in *R (MH) v Secretary of State for the Home Department* [2010] EWCA Civ 1112 and in *R (on the application of Muqtaar) v Secretary of State for the Home Department* [2012] EWCA Civ 1270 above.

17 *R (on the application of Raki) v Secretary of State for the Home Department* [2011] EWHC 2421 (Admin), [2011] All ER (D) 60 (Oct); *R (on the application of Mjemer) v Secretary of State for the Home Department* [2011] EWHC 1514 (Admin), [2011] All ER (D) 134 (May), *R (on the application of Noureddine) v Secretary of State for the Home Department* [2012] EWHC 1707 (Admin), *R(on the application of Mohammed) v Secretary of State for the Home Department* [2014] EWHC 972 (Admin), *R (on the application of Lemtelsi) v Secretary of State of the Home Department* [2014] EWHC 2750 (Admin), *Fardous v Secretary of State for the Home Department* [2014] EWHC 3061 (QB).

18 *Sino v Secretary of State for the Home Department* [2011] EWHC 2249 (Admin), [2011] All ER (D) 128 (Aug), *R (on the application of Badah) v Secretary of State for the Home Department* [2014] EWHC 364 (Admin), *Idira v Secretary of State for the Home Department* [2014] EWHC 1724 (Admin). See also *Massoud v Malta* [2010] ECHR 1197.

19 *R (on the application of MH) v Secretary of State for the Home Department* [2010] EWCA Civ 1112, [2010] All ER (D) 288 (Oct), *R(Muqtaar) v Secretary of State for the Home Department* [2012] EWCA Civ 1270, *R (on the application of Ismail) v Secretary of State for the Home Department* [2013] EWHC 3921 (Admin), *R(Abdi) v Secretary of State for the Home Department* [2014] EWHC 2641 (Admin) (a further claim involving the appellant in *R(A) v Secretary of State for the Home Department* [2007] EWCA Civ 804, see also *Abdi v United Kingdom* (2013) 57 EHRR 16).

20 *R (on the application of Yegorov) v Secretary of State for the Home Department* [2011] EWHC 3358 (Admin). See also *Mikolenko v Estonia* (Application No 10664/05).

21 *R (on the application of MA) v Secretary of State for the Home Department* [2010] EWHC 2350 (Admin), [2010] All ER (D) 133 (Sep); *R (on the application of BE) v Secretary of State for the Home Department* [2011] EWHC 690 (Admin), [2011] All ER (D) 298 (Mar), *R (on the application of FH (Iran)) v Secretary of State for the Home Department* [2013] EWHC 1092 (Admin), *R(on the application of JM) v Secretary of State for the Home Department* [2014] EWHC 4430 (Admin).

22 See *R (on the application of I) v Secretary of State for the Home Department* [2010] EWCA Civ 727, [2010] All ER (D) 244 (Jun) where Munby LJ warned that the Secretary of State could expect adverse inferences to be drawn from deficiencies in her response to a claim, applied in *R (Mounir Raki)*. See also the discussion at para 21 of the decision at first instance

in *R (on the application of Das) v Secretary of State for the Home Department* [2013] EWHC 682 (Admin) and *R (on the application of JS (Sudan)) v Secretary of State for the Home Department* [2013] EWCA Civ 1378 at para 60.

18.51 The Court of Appeal held in *R(Krasniqi) v Secretary of State for the Home Department* that:

'to found a claim in damages for wrongful detention, it is not enough that, in retrospect, some part of the statutory process is shown to have taken longer than it should have done. There is a dividing-line between mere administrative failing and unreasonableness amounting to illegality'.[1]

That position has been subsequently endorsed, and repeatedly relied upon by the Secretary of State in support of the proposition that the fourth *Hardial Singh* principle, the requirement of diligence in attempts to remove, is unlikely to give rise to a false imprisonment. This has been a matter of some concern as practitioners will have noted, particularly following the introduction of the automatic deportation regime which allows for detention while deportation is under consideration, lengthy detention and slow decision-making. It is now clear that where the Secretary of State does not act with adequate diligence in seeking to remove someone (or in deciding whether an exception to the automatic deportation criteria applies, as relevant) that will give rise to a false imprisonment. The Court of Appeal in *R (Saleh) v Secretary of State for the Home Department* held that where 12 months of the appellant's detention was largely unaccounted for in administrative terms, nine months of that time was unlawful having crossed the line referred to in *Krasniqi*. The Court was unimpressed by the decision at first instance in relation to this lengthy period that 'more expedition would have been ideal, but the delay was not unlawful'.[2] That finding was considered by the Court of Appeal to be 'a totally inadequate analysis of whether or not the deprivation of this individual's liberty was reasonable in all the circumstances.' That decision was followed by Lang J in the case of *R (on the application of Ismail) v Secretary of State for the Home Department* [2013] EWHC 3921 (Admin) where a 'dilatory and in some respects incompetent' investigation into whether the claimant should be deported led to a finding that he had been detained unlawfully.[3] These domestic decisions mirror to some extent the Strasbourg jurisprudence as it has been clear from at least the decision in *Mikolenko v Estonia* (Application No 10664/05) that a failure to seek a detainee's removal with adequate diligence and expedition will give rise to a breach of Article 5(1)(f).[4] The Court in *Massoud v Malta* [2010] ECHR 1197 looked in detail at the means by which the Maltese authorities had sought the applicant's removal to Algeria and found them inadequate, giving rise to a breach of Article 5.[5]

[1] *R (on the application of Krasniqi) v Secretary of State for the Home Department* [2011] EWCA Civ 1549 at para 12.

[2] *Saleh v Secretary of State for the Home Department* [2013] EWHC 61 (Admin) per DHCJ Mott at para 45.

[3] At para 115. The Secretary of State's officers sought to blame the claimant for the delay, and the Court found that it had been presented with an 'untruthful explanation for the delay in progressing the investigation into deportation to Somalia' (para 87). The Immigration Judge who had refused to grant the claimant bail had, moreover, also been presented with inaccurate information (para 90).

[4] At para 59, 63 and 68. See also *Chahal v United Kingdom* (1996) 23 EHRR 413 at 113 referring to earlier jurisprudence.

[5] *Massoud v Malta* [2010] ECHR 1197 at para 66: 'Although the identity and nationality of the applicant had been determined, the Government submitted that repatriation had been difficult

as the applicant was undocumented, the Algerian authorities had refused to issue the relevant documents and the applicant had been unwilling to cooperate. The Court notes that the Government have not submitted any details as to the procedures initiated save that the police had attempted to obtain such documents through the intervention of the Ministry of Foreign Affairs. They have not submitted information about the frequency of such requests or whether any other avenues were explored. The Court considers that while it is true that the Maltese authorities could not compel the issuing of such a document, there is no indication in the Government's observations that they pursued the matter vigorously or endeavoured entering into negotiations with the Algerian authorities with a view to expediting its delivery . . . '

18.52 Continued detention may be inherently unreasonable having regard to the circumstances of the case or it may be so because of the absence of any material distinction between the case in hand and those 'normal' cases in which conditional release is granted.[1] In *Sokha*[2] Lord Prosser highlighted the difference between the Scottish courts' approach to detention and that in England. In Scotland the risk of absconding, which is an inevitable concomitant of liberty, was, he said, not normally regarded by the Secretary of State as justifying continued detention, so that for such detention to be reasonable there had to be some feature in the particular case which indicated that there was a greater risk of absconding than usual. The decision was followed in *Rafaqat Ali*[3] where the Outer House of the Court of Session found detention lawful on the basis that the particular applicant had not employed a 'normal' degree of deception, but a 'degree and duration going far beyond the normal case of illegal immigration'.

[1] For an unreasonable exercise of the discretion to detain in the English courts in another context, see *Holgate-Mohammed v Duke* [1984] AC 437 at 444, 446 where Lord Diplock's comments on the unreasonable exercise by a police officer of a lawful power of arrest could also apply to immigration officers. See also *R v Special Adjudicator and Secretary of State for the Home Department, ex p B* [1998] INLR 315.
[2] *Sokha v Secretary of State for the Home Department* [1992] Imm AR 14, CS.
[3] *Ali (Rafaqat) v Secretary of State for the Home Department* [1999] SCLR 555, OHCS. However see *HK v Secretary of State for the Home Department* [2009] CSOH 35 which suggests that the approach of the Court of Appeal in *R (on the application of A) v Secretary of State for the Home Department* [2007] EWCA Civ 804 may now be not applicable in Scotland, at least in so far as the Cort making a decision on the facts for itself. See also *TP (Jamaica) v Secretary of State for the Home Department* [2009] CSOH 25.

18.53 In cases where the detention is not for one of the statutory purposes, either because there is no prospect of effecting removal or it is for an extraneous reason unauthorised by the provisions, the challenge goes to the power to detain and is a precedent fact question for the court.[1] The question of whether there is or will be unreasonable delay in effecting the removal, rendering the detention unlawful, goes to the exercise of the power to detain. It is for the court to determine whether in the circumstances the delay is or will be unreasonable. The court is not limited to making an assessment on *Wednesbury* grounds of the Secretary of State's view that the detention was for a reasonable period.[2] The Court of Appeal has held that in making that assessment the concept of 'burden of proof' is 'neither apt nor useful'.[3]

[1] *R (on the application of Khadir) v Secretary of State for the Home Department* [2003] EWCA Civ 475, [2003] INLR 426; *Tan Te Lam v Superintendent of Tai A Chau Detention Centre* [1997] AC 97, [1996] 4 All ER 256, PC; and *Khawaja v Secretary of State for the Home Department* [1984] AC 74. The same is not true, however, for the question of whether or not a person is a child for the purposes of the Secretary of State's obligations under s 55 of the BCIA 2009; (*R (on the application of AA) v Secretary of State for the Home Department* [2013] UKSC 49).

2   *R (on the application of A) v Secretary of State for the Home Department* [2007] EWCA Civ
804; *Youssef v Home Office* [2004] EWHC 1884 (QB), [2004] NLJR 1452 applied in *R (on
the application of Karas) v Secretary of State for the Home Department* [2006] EWHC 747
(Admin), [2006] All ER (D) 107 (Apr); *R (on the application of S) v Secretary of State for the
Home Department* [2007] EWHC 1654 (Admin), [2007] All ER (D) 290 (Jul); *HXA v Home
Office* [2010] EWHC 1177 (QB), *R(MH) v Secretary of State for the Home Department*
[2010] EWCA Civ 1112 applied in R*Fardous v Secretary of State for the Home Department*
[2014] EWHC 3061 (QB) at para 17. In *R (on the application of Lumba) v Secretary of State
for the Home Department* [2011] UKSC 12 at para 30 Lord Dyson accepted that 'the Hardial
Singh principles reflect the basic public law duties to act consistently with the statutory purpos
. . . and reasonably in the Wednesbury sense . . . .'

3   *R (on the application of JS (Sudan)) v Secretary of State for the Home Department* [2013]
EWCA Civ 1378 at para 45.

Policy cases

18.54 It is well established and accepted that a failure by the Secretary of State
to follow his own policy constitutes an error of law,[1] although there has been
debate about precisely what kind of error such a failure would be: ie whether
a breach of a legitimate expectation, unfairness or abuse of power.[2] It is now
clear following the decision in *R (on the application of Lumba) v Secretary
of State for the Home Department* [2011] UKSC 12 that as far as the
lawfulness of detention is concerned, the question is whether there has been a
material public law error bearing on the decision to detain. There is no further
need for the action to be an abuse of power.[3] A failure to act consistently with
published policy entitles the court to quash the decision, grant a declaration
and order the decision to be retaken.[4] In the case of a person who is detained
other than following a court order for deportation[5] there will also be false
imprisonment and an entitlement to at least nominal damages.[6] If the
defendant can show that the detained person could and would have been
detained had the policy been properly applied, there will be no award of
substantial damages and only nominal damages will follow.[7] An pre-*Lumba*
example was *Ex p B*[8] where Kay J held it was unlawful to detain an asylum
seeker for two months after his identity had been established and sureties had
been offered because there had been a failure to apply the relevant policy
criteria and in particular a failure, following a change of circumstances in the
claimant's case, to reconsider detention in accordance with the criteria.[9] It
follows from these cases that decisions to detain people in the categories
referred to in **18.32** above such as torture victims, certain people who are
mentally ill, or unaccompanied minors, for example, would normally be
unlawful, because the policy of the Home Office is normally not to detain these
categories of person. It would be incumbent on the Home Office officials to set
out fully the reasons for departing from stated policy in any given case.[10]
Furthermore, if the decision maker is to show that the policy has been properly
applied, he or she must give detailed reasons explaining why the decision to
detain has been taken and on what basis considerations within the policy
pointing for and against detention have been taken into account.[11] These
reasons are then open to scrutiny by the courts. A decision to detain could also
be unlawful if the Secretary of State's reasons disclosed reliance upon a
mistaken understanding of the detainee's immigration history in making the
decision to detain and therefore failed to have regard to matters that according

to the policy weighed against detention.[12]

1   *R v Secretary of State for the Home Department, ex p Khan (Asif Mahmood)* [1984] 1 WLR 1337; *R (on the application of Abbasi) v Secretary of State for Foreign and Commonwealth Affairs* [2003] UKHRR 76, [2002] EWCA Civ 1598; *NF (Ghana) v Secretary of State for the Home Department* [2009] INLR 93; *AF (Jamaica) v Secretary of State for the Home Department* [2009] EWCA Civ 240; *(SS (India) v Secretary of State for the Home Department* [2010] EWCA Civ 388; *R (on the application of Lumba) v Secretary of State for the Home Department* [2011] UKSC 12.

2   *R (on the application of WL (Congo)) v Secretary of State for the Home Department; R (on the application of KM (Jamaica)) v Secretary of State for the Home Department*) [2010] EWCA Civ 111 and *ID v Home Office* [2005] EWCA Civ 38. See the discussion in *R (on the application of Lumba) v Secretary of State for the Home Department* [2011] UKSC 12.

3   *R (on the application of Amirthanathan) v Secretary of State for the Home Department* [2003] EWHC 1107 (Admin) at para 36 records the Secretary of State's concession to that effect; see *R (on the application of Naderajah and Amirthanathan) v Secretary of State for the Home Department* [2003] EWCA Civ 1768, [2004] INLR 139, CA; *R (on the application of Konan) v Secretary of State for the Home Department* [2004] EWHC 22 (Admin), [2004] All ER (D) 151 (Jan). *R (on the application of Lumba) v Secretary of State for the Home Department* [2011] UKSC 12; *R (on the application of Francis) v Secretary of State for the Home Department* [2014] EWCA Civ 718.

4   See the discussion in *R (on the application of Lumba) v Secretary of State for the Home Department* [2011] UKSC 12 at para 69.

5   See **18.35** and **18.43** above.

6   *R (on the application of Lumba) v Secretary of State for the Home Department* [2011] UKSC 12; *R (Francis) v Secretary of State for the Home Department* [2014] EWCA Civ 718.

7   *R (on the application of OM acting by her litigation friend, the Official Solicitor) v Secretary of State for the Home Department* [2011] EWCA Civ 909.

8   *R v Special Adjudicator and Secretary of State for the Home Department, ex p B* [1998] INLR 315.

9   See also *R v Secretary of State for the Home Department, ex p Brezinski and Glowacka* (CO 4251/1995 and CO 4237/1995) [1997] CLY 2880 cited in *Ex p B* [1998] INLR 315 at 317–318; *R (on the application of Konan) v Secretary of State for the Home Department* [2004] EWHC 22 Admin; *R (on the application of Johnson) v Secretary of State for the Home Department* [2004] EWHC 1550 (Admin).

10   *R v Secretary of State for the Home Department, ex p Amankwah* [1994] Imm AR 240, QBD (decision quashed for unfairness).

11   *R (on the application of SRH) v Secretary of State for the Home Department* [2007] EWHC 2134 (Admin), paras 48–49, 151 Sol Jo LB 1228. Approved in *R (on the application of LE (Jamaica)) v Secretary of State for the Home Department* [2012] EWCA Civ 597 at para 33.

12   Such as the incentive not to abscond given to a family of failed asylum seekers by the making of an order for reconsideration of one family member's appeal; the fact that the family would be split because the family member whose appeal was still pending could not be detained and that the mentally disabled but at liberty son would be left without family support: *R (on the application of E) v Secretary of State for the Home Department* [2006] EWHC 3208 (Admin).

18.55 Since the judgment of the Court of Appeal in *ID v Home Office*[1] it had been settled law that public law errors including a failure to apply published policy could in principle found a claim for damages for the tort of false imprisonment in immigration detention cases provided that the error was causative of the decision to detain. That was followed by Davies J in *D and K*[2] and consistently applied at the High Court level. The approach was in fact endorsed in *WL (Congo)*[3] although the Court of Appeal took a different view of whether the obligation to consider policy constituted law for the purposes of Article 5(1) ECHR to that taken in *Nadarajah*.[4] In *SK*[5] the Court of Appeal likewise affirmed this approach. In *D and K*[6] the claimants proceeded on the basis that the burden was upon them to demonstrate that, on a balance of probabilities, proper application of the policy would have led to their release. In *Abdi*,[7] after argument, Davies J took the view that the burden was upon the

Secretary of State and in *WL (Congo)*[8] the court appeared to endorse this approach treating the breach of policy as the operative cause of the detention unless detention was otherwise inevitable, eg because of the risk of absconding or offending. The position is now clear following the decisions of the Supreme Court in *R (Lumba) v Secretary of State for the Home Department*[9] and *R (on the application of Kambadzi) v Secretary of State for the Home Department*[10] that breach of a policy bearing on the decision to detain will render detention unlawful, provided that the policy is 'sufficiently closely related to the authority to detain to provide a further qualification of the discretion' to detain[11] There is no need to demonstrate that the error was causative of the decision to detain; causation is relevant to damages rather than liability. In deciding whether there has been a material breach of a relevant policy the question is not for the Court, as it would be where the *Hardial Singh* principles are in issue, but rather whether the policy has been rationally applied.[12]

[1] [2006] 1 WLR 1003, [2005] EWCA Civ 38.

[2] [2006] EWHC 980.

[3] [2010] 1 WLR 2168.

[4] *R (on the application of Nadarajah and Amirthanathan) v Secretary of State for the Home Department* [2003] EWCA Civ 1768, [2004] INLR 139.

[5] [2003] EWCA Civ 1786, [2004] INLR 139.

[6] *R (on the application of D) v Secretary of State for the Home Department; R (on the application of K) v Secretary of State for the Home Department* [2006] EWHC 980 (Admin), 150 Sol Jo LB 743. This view survived the decision of the Supreme Court in *R (on the application of Lumba) v Secretary of State for the Home Department* [2011] UKSC 12 with the decision of Haddon-Cave J in *R (on the application of Belkasim) v Secretary of State for the Home Department* [2012] EWHC 3109 (Admin) where it was held that a breach of Rules 34 and 35 was not sufficient without more to give rise to a false imprisonment. Burnett J declined to follow *R (on the application of EO) v Secretary of State for the Home Department* [2013] EWHC 1236 (Admin) and in *R (on the application of DK) v Secretary Of State For Home Department* [2014] EWHC 3257 (Admin) Haddon-Cave J himself accepted that his approach in *Belkasim* was 'obviously wrong' at para 188.

[7] *R (on the application of Abdi and others) v Secretary of State for the Home Department* [2008] EWHC 3166 Admin.

[8] *R (on the application of WL (Congo))* [2010] EWCA Civ 111.

[9] [2011] UKSC 12

[10] [2011] UKSC 23

[11] *R (on the application of Kambadzi) v Secretary of State for the Home* [2011] UKSC 23 at para 51.

[12] *R (on the application of LE (Jamaica)) v Secretary of State for the Home Department* [2012] EWCA Civ 597 at para 29 approved in *R (on the application of O) v Secretary of State for the Home Department* [2014] EWCA Civ 990 at para. 38.

18.56 If there is an issue as to what precisely the policy is, this will be determined objectively by the court in accordance with the language employed by the minister and the proper context of the policy.[1] This is in line with the requirements of Convention law that a policy must also be sufficiently clear and certain to ensure fairness and be sufficiently accessible and precise to meet the standards of Convention legality.[2] In three cases relating to the policy of not sending asylum seekers to safe third countries if they had family ties in the UK the court found in favour of the claimant's claim as to the disputed terms of the policy: *Gashi*[3] (the correct approach to the term 'claim for asylum'); *Amirthanathan*[4] (the term 'asylum seeker'); and *R v Secretary of State for the Home Department, ex p Nicholas*[5] (whether the policy was limited to spouses only where the marriage took place before flight to the UK).

1   In *re Mcfarland* [2004] UKHL 17, 2004] 1 WLR 1289; *R (on the application of Raissi) v Secretary of State for the Home Department* [2008] EWCA Civ 72 and *R (on the application of Anam) v Secretary of State for the Home Department* [2009] EWHC 2496 (Admin); *R (on the application of Gashi) v Secretary of State for the Home Department* [2003] EWHC 1198 (Admin), [2003] All ER (D) 338 (May), paras 11–12; *R (on the application of Amirthanathan) v Secretary of State for the Home Department* [2003] EWCA Civ 1768, [2004] INLR 139 at para 25, *R v Director of Passenger Rail; Franchising, ex p Save Our Railways* [1996] CLC 589, *R (on the application of MD (Angola)) v Secretary of State for the Home Department* [2011] EWCA Civ 1238 at para 12, *R (on the application of LE (Jamaica)) v Secretary of State for the Home Department* [2012] EWCA Civ 597 at para 29. See also *IM (Nigeria) v Secretary of State for the Home Department* [2013] EWCA Civ 1561 at para 41.
2   *R (on the application of Gillan) v Metropolitan Police Comr* [2006] UKHL 12, [2006] 2 AC 307 and *R (on the application of Amirthanathan) v Secretary of State for the Home Department* [2003] EWCA Civ 1768, [2004] INLR 139, paras 64–67, *R (on the application of Lumba) v Secretary of State for the Home Department* [2011] UKSC 12 at para 28.
3   *R (on the application of Gashi) v Secretary of State for the Home Department* [2003] EWHC 1198 (Admin), [2003] All ER (D) 338 (May), paras 11–12.
4   *R (on the application of Amirthanathan) v Secretary of State for the Home Department* [2003] EWCA Civ 1768, [2004] INLR 139 at para 25.
5   [2000] Imm AR 334.

EUROPEAN CONVENTION ON HUMAN RIGHTS

18.57 Detention must also be compatible with Article 5 of the ECHR to be lawful. We deal with this Article in detail in **Chapter 7**. Here we simply remind readers that the central purpose of the Article is to prevent arbitrary interference with the personal liberty of the individual, which is both a substantive and procedural right.[1] Article 5 consists of specific provisions, contained in Article 5(1)(a)–(f), restricting the circumstances in which persons can be lawfully denied their liberty. This list is exhaustive of the grounds for lawful detention.[2] Article 5(4) entitles anyone detained to have access to a speedy review by a court of the legality of the detention,[3] and Article 5(5) uniquely gives detainees an enforceable right to compensation for any breach of Article 5(1). In any action to test the legality of detention, it is for the decision maker to establish that detention is authorised by a competent authority,[4] and that authority has the burden of establishing the lawful basis and justification for the detention,[5] by showing that:

(i)   it is to prevent unauthorised entry[6] or with a view to deportation or expulsion,[7] or for another purpose expressly permitted by Article 5 of the ECHR (such as prevention of the commission of crime,[8] lawful detention for non-compliance with an order of a court,[9] lawful detention of a minor for educational supervision[10] or lawful detention of persons of unsound mind);[11]

(ii) it is in accordance with domestic law[12] and with the requirements of precision and predictability; and[13]

(iii) it is proportionate to its aim.[14]

Article 5 of the ECHR also requires that there should be some connection between the ground of deprivation of liberty and the place and conditions of detention.[15]

1   *Chahal v United Kingdom* (1996) 23 EHRR 413.
2   See *Ireland v United Kingdom* (1978) 2 EHRR 25, para 194.

3   *Chahal v UK* (1996) 23 EHRR 413.
4   *Grauslys v Lithuania* (36743/97), 10 October 2000, ECtHR.
5   *Zamir v United Kingdom* (1983) 40 DR 42, para 102.
6   *Amuur v France* (1996) 22 EHRR 533 at para 43; *Saadi v United Kingdom* [2008] ECHR 80.
7   *Chahal v UK* (1996) 23 EHRR 413; *Bozano v France* (1986) 9 EHRR 297; *Conka v Belguim* (2002) 11 BHRC 555 at para 38; *Mayeka and Mitunga v Belgium* (2008) 46 EHRR 23.
8   ECHR, Art 5(1)(c).
9   ECHR, Art 5(1)(b).
10 ECHR, Art 5(1)(d).
11 ECHR, Art 5(1)(e).
12 *Raninen v Finland* (1998) 26 EHRR 563, para 46; *R v Governor of Brockhill Prison, ex p Evans (No 2)* [2001] 2 AC 19, [2000] 3 WLR 843.
13 The three requirements of Convention legality have been formulated by the ECtHR as follows: (i) the interference in question must have some basis in domestic law; and (ii) the law must be accessible; and (iii) the law must be formulated so that it is sufficiently foreseeable: *Sunday Times v United Kingdom (No 1)* (1979) 2 EHRR 245; *Silver v United Kingdom* (1983) 5 EHRR 347; *Malone v United Kingdom* (1984) 7 EHRR 14. See further Lord Hope in *R v Governor of Brockhill Prison, ex p Evans (No 2)* [2001] 2 AC 19 at 38C–E, [2000] 3 WLR 843; *R (on the application of Gillan) v Metropolitan Police Comr* [2006] UKHL 12, [2006] 2 AC 307; *Nadarajah v Secretary of State for the Home Department* [2003] EWCA Civ 1768; *R (on the application of Lumba) v Secretary of State for the Home Department* [2011] UKSC 12.
14 Per *Lord Hope* in *R v Governor of Brockhill Prison, ex p Evans (No 2)*, above. Place and conditions of detention are also relevant to proportionality: see *Aerts v Belgium* (1998) 29 EHRR 50.
15 See *Aerts v Belgium* (2000) EHRR 29 at para 46 and *Ashingdane v United Kingdom* (1985) 7 EHRR 528 at para 44.

18.58 Detention for purposes which are plainly not within Article 5(1)(f), such as detaining heads of household so as to deter other family members from absconding, is not lawful, unless based on reasonable apprehension that the person is otherwise likely to abscond.[1] Similar considerations apply to detention of particular nationalities. The so-called 'special exercises', involving detention of nationals of particular countries,[2] and nationality criteria for detention operated at Oakington,[3] gave rise to concern that detention is not justified by the facts of the particular case but by reference to a policy decision on the approach to claimants of a particular nationality, often appearing to be motivated by the numbers arriving rather than the context of the claim. The *Saadi* litigation[4] involved Iraqi Kurds who had been arriving in the UK in increasing numbers, whose claims were said to be suitable for fast tracking despite presenting complex issues of law.[5]

1   *R v Secretary of State for the Home Department, ex p Ferko* (CO 4205/1997) (11 December 1997, unreported), Kay J.
2   See exchange of correspondence between Bail for Immigration Detainees and the Immigration Service Enforcement Directorate, 26 and 30 October 2000.
3   Under the old Operational Enforcement Manual para 38.3.1. now replaced by the EIG Chapter 55. See 17.36 above.
4   *R (on the application of Saadi) v Secretary of State for the Home Department* [2002] UKHL 41, [2002] 1 WLR 3131, [2002] INLR 523; *Saadi v United Kingdom* [2008] ECHR 80.
5   See *Gardi v Secretary of State for the Home Department* [2002] 1 WLR 2755, [2002] INLR 499 (decision annulled at [2002] INLR 557, for want of jurisdiction, the adjudicator having sat in Glasgow, and has no value other than as an interesting opinion of a Lord Justice, sitting without jurisdiction). This decision records the undertaking of the Home secretary that no-one from the Kurdish autonomous region would be returned there via other parts of Iraq until it was safe to do so; and this froze the position, so that in practice none had been removed: *R (on the application of Khadir) v Secretary of State for the Home Department* [2003] EWCA Civ 475, [2003] INLR 426.

CHALLENGING DETENTION IN THE HIGH COURT

Habeas corpus and judicial review

18.59 A challenge to detention in the High Court may be made either by *habeas corpus* or judicial review. Although many of the technical and procedural complexities of the parallel jurisdictions that have concerned the courts in the past no longer apply,[1] the distinction between the two remedies is that *habeas corpus* goes to the power to detain and judicial review to the broader exercise of the discretion to detain (although the latter clearly also includes the former). *Hardial Singh*[2] was a *habeas corpus* application where the lawful power to detain was impliedly limited to a period reasonably necessary to enable enforcement of a decision to remove to be carried out. In *Ex p Muboyayi*[3] the Court of Appeal made it clear that *habeas corpus* is not available if the real challenge is to an underlying administrative decision, such as a refusal of entry, which involves making a judgment after consideration of a number of circumstances and factors. The appropriate remedy in such a case is judicial review. It is also not appropriate to use *habeas corpus* to challenge an immigration judge's conclusion that he or she had no jurisdiction to grant bail pending an appeal.[4] A *habeas corpus* application, while appropriate where the challenge is to the jurisdiction to detain, may also be used to challenge the compatibility of detention with ECHR, Article 5(1) if the challenge relates to whether detention is being used for the limited purposes in Article 5(1)(f) other challenges including the requirements of proportionality.

[1] In *Barker v Barking, Havering and Brentwood Community Healthcare NHS Trust (Warley Hospital)* [1999] 1 FLR 106, Lord Woolf (then MR) expressed his wish to combine the two remedies and to make an order for *habeas corpus* on an application for judicial review, to avoid two sets of proceedings, and added that until that time every effort should be made to harmonise the proceedings. Extra-judicial comments to the same effect were made by Simon Brown LJ in a 1999 lecture to the Administrative Bar Association.

[2] *R v Governor of Durham Prison, ex p Singh (Hardial)* [1984] 1 WLR 704.

[3] *R v Secretary of State for the Home Department, ex p Muboyayi* [1991] 3 WLR 442 at 448F. See also *R v Secretary of State for the Home Department, ex p Cheblak* [1991] 2 All ER 319, CA. See, however, the obiter comments of the Supreme Court in *R (on the application of AA) v Secretary of State for the Home Department* [2013] UKSC 49.

[4] *Re Maybasan* [1991] Imm AR 89, QBD. Habeas corpus was granted where the immigration service had instructed the police to detain an asylum seeker who was on bail to the immigration judge under the IA 1971, Sch 2, para 22, to effect her removal, in purported exercise of the power to detain for this purpose under para 16(2) of the Schedule. The court held that once bail had been granted by an immigration judge, it was for him or her to determine whether re-detention was appropriate by reference to the strict conditions of para 24 of the Schedule.

18.60 The main substantive advantage of *habeas corpus* is that, once illegality is established, the writ must be issued and there is no discretion to withhold relief as in the judicial review jurisdiction. In the past there were also some clear procedural advantages in seeking *habeas corpus*, though these are now largely historical.[1] Although there are no time limits for a *habeas* application, delay may be fatal to the application. In *Sheikh*[2] the Court of Appeal held that a *habeas corpus* application seeking to challenge a determination of illegal entry which founded a past detention, made some time after the failure of a renewed application for judicial review, itself years out of time, undermined the principle of finality in litigation and was an abuse of process. Where there is a challenge to the legality of a detention governed by paragraph 16 of

Schedule 2 to the IA 1971, it is no answer to an application for *habeas corpus* to rely on the provision of paragraph 18(4) of that Schedule, which provides that 'a person shall be deemed to be in legal custody at any time when he is detained under paragraph 16'. Criticism of views to the contrary expressed in a number of cases[3] was accepted 'unreservedly' in *Ex p Muboyayi*.[4] The object of paragraph 18 is to provide that once an order of detention is made the person named in that order may be kept in custody anywhere the Secretary of State directs.[5] The bail jurisdiction of the Special Immigration Appeals Commission (SIAC) does not oust the *habeas corpus* jurisdiction of the High Court[6] except in the now defunct anti-terrorist detention cases.[7] SIAC decisions on bail are also amenable to challenge by way of judicial review.[8] Judicial review is far more widely used and the more flexible and effective remedy available to challenge unlawful decisions to detain. Unlike *habeas corpus*, it covers cases where the detention is authorised by the statutory provisions but where the exercise of the discretion to detain is challenged on public law grounds. The most common grounds for judicial review in detention cases in recent years has been a failure by the Home Office to apply its stated policy for detention[9] and breach of the *Hardial Singh* principles. It is also possible to seek damages in judicial review if an action for the common law tort of false imprisonment can be established[10] or if there is a breach of Article 5 of the ECHR.[11] In *R (on the application of AA) v Secretary of State for the Home Department*[12] Lord Toulson giving the majority judgment suggested, without deciding the point, that in the context of a challenge to detention on the basis of disputed age where a local authority was not involved the scope of habeas corpus might extend to allowing the Court to determine a child's age for itself.[13]

[1] See Woolf MR in *Barker v Barking, Havering and Brentwood Community Healthcare NHS Trust (Warley Hospital)* [1999] 1 FLR 106.

[2] *R v Secretary of State for the Home Department, ex p Sheikh* [2001] INLR 98, CA. See also *R v Governor of Pentonville Prison, ex p Tarling* [1979] 1 WLR 1417; *R v Secretary of State for the Home Department, ex p Ali (Momin)* [1984] 1 WLR 663.

[3] *R v Secretary of State for the Home Department, ex p Cheblak* [1991] 2 All ER 319, CA; *Re Olusanya* [1988] Imm AR 117, DC.

[4] *R v Secretary of State for the Home Department, ex p Muboyayi* [1991] 3 WLR 442.

[5] *R v Secretary of State for the Home Department, ex p Greene* [1942] 1 KB 87 at 117, per Goddard LJ.

[6] In the matter of *Youseff* (CO 706/1999) (2 March 1999), QBD [2000] 6 (1) ILD.

[7] The ATCSA 2001 gave exclusive jurisdiction to the Special Immigration Appeals Commission (SIAC) in respect of all matters relating to detention of suspected international terrorists under s 23 of the Act, including the derogation from Art 5 of the ECHR, and for these purposes gives SIAC all the powers of the High Court: s 30(3)(c), with a right of appeal to the Court of Appeal in respect of a refusal or grant of bail by SIAC: ATCSA 2001, s 24(4), (5), inserted by Asylum and Immigration (Treatment of Claimants, etc) Act 2004, s 32. Part IV of the ATCSA 2001 (ss 21–32) was repealed by the PTA 2005, s 16 on 14 April 2005.

[8] *R (on the application of Cart) v Upper Tribunal; U v Special Immigration Appeals Commission; XC v Special Immigration Appeals Commission* [2009] EWHC 3052 (Admin), [2010] 1 All ER 908, [2010] 2 WLR 1012, [2010] STC 493. Affirmed in *R (Cart) v the Upper Tribunal* [2011] UKSC 28.

[9] See above under 'Policy cases'.

[10] *R (on the application of Lumba) v Secretary of State for the Home Department* [2011] UKSC 12.

[11] Human Rights Act 1998, s 8(1)–(4).

[12] [2013] UKSC 49

[13] 'The court's habeas corpus jurisdiction is a creation of the common law, although it has also been the subject of numerous statutes. The courts have power to develop it where necessary in order to achieve effective justice in matters of personal liberty . . . . Although it is unnecessary

to decide the point, I am sympathetic to the view that the court's habeas corpus jurisdiction in this type of situation should not be confined to determining whether the Secretary of State had acted lawfully in the detention of the claimant, but should extend to enable the court to make a fresh determination of the claimant's age, which would necessarily impact on the lawfulness of his continued detention . . . In practical terms it would mean that the court is able to reach a final determination of the claimant's age not only when his rights under the Children Act depend on it but more fundamentally when his liberty depends on it.' Lord Carnwath strongly dissented.

18.61 In both *habeas corpus* and judicial review, the Secretary of State has the burden of demonstrating that the power to detain exists and that the detention is for a purpose authorised by the statute.[1] Since the issues involve liberty, the burden on the Secretary of State is a heavy one.[2] In judicial review, as in *habeas corpus* cases, the court will determine as a precedent fact whether the power to detain exists, for example, whether or not the person is an illegal entrant[3] and it is for the court to decide for itself whether the power to detain has been lawfully exercised. This includes the *Hardial Singh* questions of whether the detention is for a period which is reasonably necessary to effect the statutory purpose.[4] The Court will subject lengthy periods of detention to 'the most anxious scrutiny'.[5] In *Youssef v Home Office*[6] the judge rejected the contrary submission of the Home Office that in assessing the legality of the detention, the standard is a *Wednesbury* standard.[7] This was approved by the Court of Appeal in *R (A) Somalia*.[8] Although *Youssef* was a civil action for damages for false imprisonment, the court applied the same principles as in public law proceedings. The issue was whether there had been a failure to exercise all reasonable expedition to ensure removal took place within a reasonable period of time. Although this involved determining difficult questions of fact, including whether there was any realistic chance of the government obtaining workable guarantees from the Egyptian government that the plaintiff would not be subjected to torture or ill treatment if returned, the judge held that the court was entitled to come to its own judgment on these matters.[9] In so doing 'the court would have regard to all of the circumstances and in so doing make allowance for the way that the government functions and be slow to second-guess the Executive's assessment of diplomatic negotiations'.[10] On appeal to the Court of Appeal, the Court should make its own assessment of the legality of detention at the time of the hearing before it, doing so in the light of the up to date material unless there were circumstances making it inappropriate for the Court to do so.[11]

[1]   *Hicks v Faulkner* (1881) 8 QBD 167 affirmed (1882) 46 LT 127, CA; *Tan Te Lam v Superintendent of Tai A Chau Detention Centre* [1997] AC 97, [1996] 4 All ER 256, PC. See, however, the decision of the Court of Appeal in *R (on the application of JS (Sudan)) v Secretary of State for the Home Department* [2013] EWCA Civ 1378 to the effect that when the Court is analysing reasonableness for the purposes of the *Hardial Singh* assessment, consideration of burden of proof is 'neither apt nor useful' (at para 45).

[2]   *Khawaja v Secretary of State for the Home Department* [1984] AC 74 and *Tan Te Lam v Superintendent of Tai A Chau Detention Centre* (above).

[3]   *Khawaja* above.

[4]   See **18.52** above.

[5]   *R (on the application of MH) v Secretary of State for the Home Department* [2010] EWCA Civ 1112, [2010] All ER (D) 288 (Oct).

[6]   *Youssef v Home Office* [2004] EWHC 1884 (QB), [2004] NLJR 1452, QBD at paras 62–63 followed in *R (on the application of S) v Secretary of State for the Home Department* [2007] EWHC 1654 (Admin), [2007] All ER (D) 290 (Jul).

[7]   Ie, that the decision to treat the person as liable to detention is one which could reasonably be reached: *Associated Provincial Picture Houses Ltd v Wednesbury Corpn* [1948] 1 KB 223.

⁸ *R (on the application of A) v Secretary of State for the Home Department* [2007] EWCA Civ 804 per Toulson LJ at para 62J and Keane LJ at paras 71–75. See also the decision in *R(MH) v Secretary of State for the Home Department* [2010] EWCA Civ 1112.

⁹ *Youssef v Home Office*, fn 5 above, at para 62.

¹⁰ *Youssef v Home Office*, fn 5 above, at para 63. In the event it was held that the claimant had been unlawfully detained for a two week period prior to his release, when it should have been apparent to the Home Secretary that there was no realistic prospect of removing the claimant in compliance with Art 3 of the ECHR. The case provides a unique and extraordinary insight into the political, bureaucratic and diplomatic machinations involved in such cases, and illustrates the significant advantages of civil claims in terms of disclosure of documents in comparison with disclosure in habeas or judicial review proceedings (as to which see below).

¹¹ *R (on the application of Lumba) v Secretary of State for the Home Department* [2011] UKSC 12, para 145.

Damages, judicial review and county court actions

18.62 Although CPR Part 54 provides for the Administrative Court to award damages in addition to other relief on an application for judicial review,¹ it has no jurisdiction to entertain a claim for damages alone.² Further, there are no facilities whereby a jury may be empanelled in the Administrative Court to try an action for damages for false imprisonment,³ and contested actions involving a human rights element often require cross-examination which is often more conveniently provided for outside the Administrative Court list.⁴ In *R (on the application of Wilkinson) v Responsible Medical Officer, Broadmoor Hospital Authority*⁵ Hale LJ said that it should not matter whether proceedings in respect of forcible treatment of detained patients were brought by way of an ordinary action in tort, an action under s 7(1) of the Human Rights Act 1998, or judicial review.⁶ In *ID v Home Office*⁷ the Court of Appeal expressed the hope that claims of procedural exclusivity might fall away under the CPR regime,⁸ and held that if proceedings are viable, they can be properly brought as a private law action in the county court or begun as a judicial review challenge in the Administrative Court.⁹ Where a claim for damages for false imprisonment is made ancillary to a public law challenge in the Administrative Court, the damages claim survives even if the underlying immigration decision is quashed or settled and thereby falls away and/or the person is released from detention. In *BA v Secretary of State for the Home Department (Bail for Immigration Detainees intervening)*¹⁰ the Court of Appeal considered an argument that bringing a civil claim for false imprisonment following dismissal of a judicial review claim which had obliquely raised the lawfulness of detention was an abuse of process. The Court held that in the circumstances of the case it was not. It also held, however, that generally in circumstances where a detention claim could be made as part of a judicial review claim it should be so made. There may therefore be circumstances in which failing to make such a claim gives rise to an abuse should a civil claim then be brought.¹¹ It often happens that the person has been released from detention before the conclusion of proceedings challenging the detention, but this does not prevent the Administrative Court determining the issue, granting a declaration as to the legality of the past detention and, where appropriate, awarding damages.¹² Recent decisions of the Administrative Court have expressed concern about claims for damages that could be bought in the County Court or the Queen's Bench Division continuing in the Administrative Court when no further public law remedy is sought beyond a declaration.[13]

1 Senior Courts Act 1981, s 31(4); CPR 54.3(2).
2 CPR 54.3(2).
3 See the County Courts Act 1984, s 66(3)(b) and the Senior Courts Act 1981, s 69(1)(b).
4 *R (on the application of Wilkinson) v Responsible Medical Officer Broadmoor Hospital* [2001] EWCA Civ 1545, [2002] 1 WLR 419 at para 62.
5 *R (on the application of Wilkinson) v Responsible Medical Officer, Broadmoor Hospital Authority* [2001] EWCA Civ 1545, [2002] 1 WLR 419 at para 62. See also Simon Brown LJ at para 24, and *R (on the application of P) v Secretary of State for the Home Department* [2001] EWCA Civ 1151 at [120], [2001] 1 WLR 2002, 2037.
6 *ID v Home Office* [2005] EWCA Civ 38, [2005] All ER (D) 253 (Jan), [2006] 1 WLR 1003 at para 104.
7 The court referred to Lord Woolf MR in *Clark v University of Lincolnshire and Humberside* [2000] 1 WLR 1988 at paras 25–27 and 32–39, who said that the relevant question was not whether 'the right procedure' had been adopted, but whether the protection provided by (then) RSC Order 53 had been flouted in circumstances which were inconsistent with the proceedings being able to be conducted justly in accordance with the general principles contained in CPR Part 1. 'These principles are central to determining what is now due process,' (para 39).
8 See *Swaran v Secretary of State for the Home Department* [2014] EWHC 1062 (Admin).
9 'To restrict access to justice by insisting on proceeding by way of CPR Part 54 in a damages claim would in such circumstances amount to the antithesis of the overriding objective in CPR Part 1' (para 106, per Brooke LJ).
10 [2012] EWCA Civ 944
11 The Court also held that where permission had been refused and a claim determined it would not generally be permissible to bring a challenge in civil proceedings on the same issues, although there would not technically be an issue estoppel and the matter would be fact sensitive (at para 27).
12 In *R (on the application of Konan) v Secretary of State for the Home Department* [2004] EWHC 22 (Admin), [2004] All ER (D) 151 (Jan) the claimant had been on adjudicator bail for several months and had been given a limited leave to remain by the time of the hearing of the challenge to the lawfulness of the detention.
13 *R (Swaran) v Secretary of State for the Home Department* [2014] EWHC 1062 (Admin); *R (on the application of DK) v Secretary Of State For Home Department* [2014] EWHC 3257 (Admin). In practice the Secretary of State is often reluctant to agree to transfer proceedings.

SOME DAMAGE AWARDS

18.63 Damages, including aggravated and exemplary damages[1] can only be awarded if the claimant is able to establish a private law cause of action which in the ordinary case will be a claim for false imprisonment and/or possibly misfeasance in public office[2] or a claim under the Human Rights Act 1998.[3] Below are some cases where damages have been awarded:

- In *R v Secretary of State for the Home Department, ex p Honegan*[4], a settlement of £17,000 was agreed for four days' detention over Christmas, following a judgment that the refusal of leave to enter on which the detention depended was irrational. £17,000 was awarded for detention of a British citizen and her infant child for approximately five days following a successful judicial review of her detention in *R v Secretary of State for the Home Department, ex p Ejaz*.[5]
- In *ex p AKB*[6] the damages claim was transferred to the Queens Bench Division for assessment by a Master, who awarded £10,000 for 63 days of unlawful detention (which followed a substantial period of lawful detention) and £8,000 for damages for exacerbation of a psychiatric condition.

- In *Konan*[7] above), £60,000 was awarded to the claimant mother and child for six months' detention, including a sum for deterioration in the mother's mental health and the stress of caring for a sick infant in difficult circumstances.

- In *R (on the application of Q) v Secretary of State for the Home Department*[8], a claim for unlawful detention and removal of a Kosovan family was resolved by consent on 28 January 2004, with £7,500 each for the father and children's claims for a day's detention prior to removal and a further six days' detention on return. The mother obtained damages of £18,500, reflecting the exacerbation of her psychiatric condition.

- In *R (on the application of Johnson) v Secretary of State for the Home Department*[9], where £15,000 was agreed in settlement of Mr Johnson's claim for 32 days of unlawful detention after it became apparent that his claim was not suitable for fast tracking at Oakington.

- In *Youssef v Home Office*[10] the claim was settled in the sum of £9,000 for the two weeks of unlawful detention following the lengthy period of lawful detention.

- In *R (on the application of Beecroft) v Secretary of State for the Home Department*[11], basic damages of £32,000 were awarded for 6 months of unlawful detention with £6,000 of aggravated damages because of failure to apply the Detention Centre Rules intended to avoid detention of torture victims and the defendant's failure to respond with due diligence to claims that the individual was unlawfully detained.

- Following a liability finding in *R (on the application of S) v Secretary of State for the Home Department*[12], in an unreported decision Master Leslie in *S, C and D v Home Office*[13] determined quantum for the unlawful detention for three and a half months (108 days) of a young mother and for one of her two young children. The Master determined that the mother should be awarded £25,000 basic damages, £5,000 aggravated damages and £5,000 exemplary damages and the child should be awarded £20,000 basic damages, £5,000 aggravated damages and £7,500 exemplary damages.

- *Muuse v Secretary of State for the Home Department*[14] was an appeal from a decision of the High Court[15] where, having found liability for a period of unlawful detention of 128 days which followed a period of lawful custody between 8 February and 18 July 2006, the judge awarded £25,000 basic damages, £7,500 aggravated damages and £27,500 exemplary damages. On the question of exemplary damages the Court of Appeal held, upholding the award of exemplary damages, that the requirement of oppressive, arbitrary or unconstitutional conduct did not need to be qualified by further looking for malice, fraud, insolence, cruelty or similar specific conduct. M's unlawful imprisonment was not merely unconstitutional but was an outrageous and arbitrary exercise of executive power which called for an award of exemplary damages by way of punishment, to deter and to vindicate the strength of the law. There had been no parliamentary or other enquiry into M's case and no minister or senior official had been held accountable. The only way the misconduct had been exposed was by the court action.

- In an unreported judgment from the Central London Court of *E v Home Office*[16], following a contested trial on liability and a finding that the claimant, a torture victim, had been unlawfully detained for a month, the court awarded global damages of £57,500 made up of £12,500 basic damages for false imprisonment, £10,000 aggravated damages, and £10,000 damages for exacerbation of a psychiatric injury. In additionally awarding £25,000 exemplary damages, the judge, HHJ Collins, felt constrained by authority from awarding more than this noting that 'the failure to have an adequate system for dealing with Rule 35 cases, notwithstanding a warning by the Inspector of Prisons, was as grave a failure on the part of the Home Office and its contractors as can be imagined in the context of this sort of case. A true punishment of the Home Office to reflect the gravity of the situation would run into sums far in excess of those which the court is legally authorised to award' [para 20 of the quantum judgment]. The judge also awarded indemnity costs for the entirety of the proceedings noting that although the claimant had made a part 36 offer shortly before trial noting that 'the Defendant . . . fixed on the intention not to call any of the witnesses who might have illuminated some of the questions on which I felt obliged to decide in favour of the claimant and has made no offer of their own. It seems to me an extraordinary way to conduct litigation, to approach it on the basis that you know you are not going to be able to call the relevant witnesses and you still do not make an offer to settle. It seems to me this is no way to conduct litigation ten years after the advent of the Civil Procedure [Rules] and this conduct seems totally out of the norm and is totally unreasonable.'
- In *R (on the application of MK) v Secretary of State*[17] the Court of Appeal awarded £12,500 basic and £5,000 aggravated damages following 24 days' detention. In *R (on the application of J) v Secretary of State for the Home Department*[18] Coulson J awarded £7,500 for four days' detention, and aggravated damages of £2,500. He held that the fact of the claimant's age was not an aggravating factor as it gave rise to the unlawfulness itself, although his treatment was.
- In *R (on the application of Lamari) v Secretary of State for the Home Department*[19], where the claimant was detained in breach of an undertaking given to the court (resulting in a contempt), basic damages of £10,000 were awarded for seven days' detention, with aggravated damages of £5,000 and a further £10,000 exemplary damages in view of the '*outrageous*' conduct.
- In R *R (on the application of Supawan) v Secretary of State for the Home Department*[20] a period of 15 days' detention gave rise to basic damages in the sum of £9,000.
- One case that is a bit different is *R (on the application of Nab) v Secretary of State for the Home Department*[21] where the claimant was awarded £75 per day for the 82 days of unlawful detention that followed a substantial period of lawful detention. The judge rejected the suggestions that there was contributory negligence or failure to mitigate his loss by the claimant who would have been removed rather than detained but for his refusal to sign a form. However, he held that

that was relevant to quantum; the claimant was entitled to less even than the award in *R v Governor of Brockhill Prison, ex p Evans (No 2)*[22] because 'the unusual situation here was that the claimant chose detention in the United Kingdom over freedom in Iran'.

1 Aggravated and exemplary damages need to be specifically pleaded: CPR 16.4(1)(c).

2 See, eg *R (on the application of Bernard) v Enfield London Borough Council* [2002] EWHC 2282 (Admin), [2003] UKHRR 148; *Anufrijeva v Southwark London Borough Council* [2003] EWCA Civ 1406, [2004] 1 All ER 833.

3 The principles of misfeasance are beyond the scope of this book; see *Bourgoin SA v Ministry of Agriculture* [1986] QB 716; *Three Rivers District Council v Bank of England (No 3)* [2003] 2 AC 1, [2000] 2 WLR 1220. Detention and forcible removal from the jurisdiction without any or any adequate notice to the claimant and in particular his or her legal representative, with refusal to stay removal for legal proceedings to be initiated or even after their initiation, could found a misfeasance claim; see *R (on the application of Changuizi) v Secretary of State for the Home Department* [2002] EWHC 2569 (Admin), [2003] Imm AR 355; *R (on the application of Q) v Secretary of State for the Home Department* (CO/5162/2003). See *Conka v Belgium* (2002) 34 EHRR 54 1298. In *Muuse v Secretary of State for the Home Department* [2010] EWCA Civ 453 the judge's finding on misfeasance was not upheld because although he had considered the officials' state of mind as regards the consequences to M, the judge had not made an express finding as to the state of their mind in respect of legality and had not expressly found that the officials acting on behalf of the Secretary of State were recklessly indifferent to the legality of their actions.

4 (13 March 1995, unreported), QBD.

5 [1994] Imm AR 300, CA.

6 [1998] INLR 315.

7 [2004] EWHC 22 (Admin), [2004] All ER (D) 151 (Jan)

8 (CO/5162/2003).

9 [2004] EWHC 1550 (Admin).

10 [2004] EWHC 1884 (QB).

11 [2008] EWHC 3189 (Admin), [2008] All ER (D) 46 (Dec).

12 [2007] EWHC 1654 (Admin), [2007] All ER (D) 290 (Jul).

13 (HQ09X01155) (9 October 2009).

14 [2010] EWCA Civ 453.

15 [2009] EWHC 1886, QB.

16 (Claim No 9CL01651) (10 June 2010, unreported).

17 [2010] EWCA Civ 980.

18 [2011] EWHC 3073 (Admin).

19 [2013] EWHC 3130 (QB).

20 [2014] EWHC 3224 (Admin).

21 [2011] EWHC 1191 (Admin), [2011] All ER (D) 123 (May).

22 [1999] QB 1043, [1998] 4 All ER 993.

No damage cases

18.64 The Supreme Court in *R (on the application of Lumba) v Secretary of State for the Home Department*[1] rejected the proposition that detention was not unlawful due to public law error if the person would have been detained even if the public law error had not been made, though it did hold that in such circumstances the claimant would be entitled only to nominal damages because he or she would not in fact have suffered loss.[2] For the detainee to be entitled to substantial and not just nominal damages would depend upon normal compensatory principles, although the burden of proof may be on the Secretary of State; he or she would be entitled to substantial damages unless it could be shown on a balance of probabilities that detention would have occurred even if the decision had been made lawfully.[3]

1 [2011] UKSC 12.

2   *R (on the application of Lumba) v Secretary of State for the Home Department* [2011] UKSC 12, [2011] 4 All ER 1, [2011] 2 WLR 671.
3   *R (on the application of OM acting by her litigation friend, the Official Solicitor) v Secretary of State for the Home Department* [2011] EWCA Civ 909, [2011] All ER (D) 02 (Aug).

18.65 In *ID v Home Office*[1] a Czech Roma family consisting of parents and two young daughters were detained in Oakington, Yarlswood and Campsfield detention centres and were all suffering from post-traumatic stress disorder and depression as a result of their experiences. The detentions resulted from decisions of immigration officers, purportedly exercising their powers under Schedule 2 to the IA 1971. The claimants started actions for declarations and damages in the county court, which were struck out at the instigation of the Home Office. They appealed to the Court of Appeal. The Home Office argued on two main fronts. First, they said that the immigration officers were immune from suit. Secondly, they argued that the complainants' remedy was limited to a declaration that the act was unlawful and/or a quashing order, by way of judicial review and not an action in the county court. They lost on each of these arguments. First, the court rejected the argument that foreign nationals who have not been granted leave to enter this country fall into a very special category.[2] The court held that by 1924 it was clear that aliens lawfully within this country in time of peace were accorded the same civil rights as British citizens,[3] and that in *Khawaja* Lord Scarman put it beyond doubt that the rule of law extended to aliens subject to administrative detention.[4] Secondly, the court held that immigration officers were not immune from being sued.[5] Thirdly, they held that, following: (i) the Human Rights Act and the need to read domestic law in the light of Article 5 of ECHR and (ii) the House of Lords decision in *Evans*,[6] Home Office officials could be sued for false imprisonment on a strict liability basis, and that a complainant was not confined to seeking a declaration or quashing order[7] through judicial review or *habeas corpus* proceedings in the Administrative Court. This early landmark decision cleared away obstacles previously blocking the path of the would-be claimant who has been wrongfully imprisoned without trial. In his judgment Brooke LJ set out the background to this growing area of litigation:

'The evidence of the interveners showed, however, that when the Home Office determined to embark on the policy of using powers of administrative detention on a far larger scale than hitherto, the practical implementation of that policy threw up very understandable concerns in individual cases. The transition from a world where decisions affecting personal liberty are made by officials of the executive who operate according to unpublished criteria, and where there is no way of compensating those who lose their liberty through administrative muddles and misfiling, to a world where the relevant criteria have to be published and where those officials are obliged to ensure that their decisions are proportionate and to justify them accordingly, is bound to be an uneasy one in the early years, and mistakes are bound to be made. But so long as detention, which may cause significant suffering, can be directed by executive decision and an order of a court (or court-like body) is not required, the language and the philosophy of human rights law, and the common law's emphatic reassertion in recent years of the importance of constitutional rights, drive inexorably, in my judgment, to the conclusion I have reached.'[8]

This decision was a forerunner for the more recent decisions such as that of the Supreme Court in *R (on the application of Lumba) v Secretary of State for the Home Department*[9] [2011] UKSC 12 and *R (on the application of Kambadzi) v Secretary of State for the Home*[10], in which Lady Hale said:

'No court had ordered or authorised or approved this detention. The trial judge who sentenced Mr Kambadzi for his crimes had not even recommended it. A Government official decided to lock him up, on the face of it until a Government official decided to take the next step. But no-one suggests that paragraph 2 of Schedule 3 gives the Government an unlimited power to authorise a person's indefinite detention without trial. Everyone knows that there are limits. Everyone also knows that if those limits are exceeded, the detention becomes unlawful. Everyone also knows that a person who is unlawfully detained is entitled, not only to be released, but to claim compensation for having been unlawfully detained. The person responsible for the unlawful detention is liable even if he acted in good faith and without any negligence . . . '

1 *ID v Home Office* [2005] EWCA Civ 38, [2006] 1 All ER 183, [2006] 1 WLR 1003.
2 Counsel argued that the power of a state to control immigration is well recognised in international law and under the ECHR (see Lord Slynn in *R (on the application of Saadi) v Secretary of State for the Home Department* [2002] UKHL 41, [2002] 1 WLR 3131 at para 31), and that this right extends beyond the simple control of entry to encompass the treatment of aliens and the control of their activities whilst they are present or resident in the state, citing *Nishimura Ekiu v United States of America* 142 US 651, 659 (1892); *Musgrove v Chun Teeong Toy* [1891] AC 272, 283; and *A-G for Canada v Cain* [1906] AC 542, 546; and Lord Denning MR in *R v Governor of Brixton Prison, ex p Soblen* [1963] 2 QB 243 at 300, citing Sir William Blackstone's Commentaries (Vol 1, 1765) at pp 259–260 to the effect that strangers who came spontaneously were liable to be sent home whenever the king saw occasion.
3 *Johnstone v Pedlar* [1921] 2 AC 262.
4 *Khawaja v Secretary of State for the Home Department* [1984] AC 74 per Lord Scarman at 111–112, who said that this principle had been in the law at least since Lord Mansfield freed 'the black' in *Sommersett's Case* (1772) 20 State Tr 1.
5 The court cited well known authority, including *Eleko (Eshugbayi) v Officer Administering the Government of Nigeria* [1931] AC 662 per Lord Atkin at 670; '[I]n English law every imprisonment is prima facie unlawful and . . . it is for a person directing imprisonment to justify his act. The only exception is in respect of imprisonment ordered by a judge, who from the nature of his office cannot be sued, and the validity of whose judicial decisions cannot in such proceedings as the present be questioned' (*Liversidge v Anderson* [1942] AC 206, per Lord Atkin at 245). 'The law attaches supreme importance to the liberty of the individual and if he suffers a wrongful interference with that liberty it should remain actionable even without proof of special damage': *Murray v Ministry of Defence* [1988] 1 WLR 692, per Lord Griffiths at 703–3).
6 *R v Governor of Brockhill Prison, ex p Evans (No 2)* [2001] 2 AC 19, where Lord Steyn relied on the first of Lord Atkin's dicta (above) as the traditional common law view, supporting an entitlement to compensation on the ground of false imprisonment where the executive can no longer support the lawfulness of the detention (at 28).
7 In so ruling the court distinguished (almost to the point of overruling, which they cannot do because of the doctrine of binding precedent) *W v Home Office* [1997] Imm AR 302, 309 and 311 and *Ullah (Mohammed) v Secretary of State for the Home Department and Immigration Officer* [1995] Imm AR 166.
8 *ID v Home Office* [2005] EWCA Civ 38, [2006] 1 All ER 183, [2006] 1 WLR 1003 at paragraph 130. A starting point for the assessment of damages should be the guidance given in relation to false imprisonment claims, developed in the context of civil actions against the police, for which see *Thompson v Metropolitan Police Comr* [1998] QB 498, [1997] 3 WLR 403; *Lunt v Liverpool City Justices* (5 March 1991, unreported), CA. This was the approach adopted by Mitting J in *E v Secretary of State for the Home Department* [2006] EWHC 2500 (Admin) who applied Thompson where an award of £3,000 had been made for the first 24 hours that the claimant was kept in police custody. Mitting J adjusted that figure to £3,750 to account for inflation and stated that an award of £6,000 would be made for detention that was short of three full days. For recent damages awards, see **18.64** above in the preceding paragraph.
9 [2011] UKSC 12.
10 [2011] UKSC 23 at para 63.

PAYING FOR DETENTION

18.66 The expense of detention will normally be the responsibility of the immigration authorities. However, carriers may be required to pay the detention costs (up to a maximum of 14 days) of those who are removed after being refused leave to enter,[1] except those passengers holding a certificate of entitlement, entry clearance or work permit,[2] or any person who successfully appeals.[3] Carriers may also be required to pay the detention costs of illegal entrants[4] or absconding or overstaying crew members who are facing removal.[5] No liability arises in the case of those held to be illegal entrants by deception whose leave was not cancelled within 24 hours of its grant.[6] A person facing deportation may find his or her money used to defray the costs of detention.[7] In a Parliamentary answer given by Mark Harper MP on 9 September 2013 the annual cost of detaining a person on the IRC estate in the year 2013-2014 was said to be £37,230, or £102 per day.[8]

[1] IA 1971, Sch 2, para 19(1). The 14-day limitation was inserted by the Asylum and Immigration Act 1996, Sch 2, para 8.
[2] IA 1971, Sch 2, para 19(2).
[3] IA 1971, Sch 2, para 19(3).
[4] IA 1971, Sch 2, para 20(1)(a).
[5] IA 1971, Sch 2, para 20(1)(b).
[6] IA 1971, Sch 2, para 20(1A) (inserted by Asylum and Immigration Act 1996, Sch 2, para 9), referring to para 6(2) (cancellation of leave within 24 hours of grant by immigration officer).
[7] IA 1971, Sch 3, para 1(4).
[8] HC Deb, 31 October 2013, Column 538W). This figure has remained roughly constant since 2011 (29 Jun 2011: Column WA443).

PROVISIONS FOR RELEASE OR BAIL

18.67 In all cases where the Secretary of State or immigration officers have a power to detain, they also have a power to release. The power to grant temporary admission or a restriction order as an alternative to detention has been described in 17.11 and 17.17 above. In addition, everyone detained under the IA 1971 may seek bail from the immigration authorities or the First-tier Tribunal under paragraphs 22 and 34 of Schedule 2 to the IA 1971.[1] Those awaiting appeal may apply for bail to the First-tier Tribunal under paragraph 29 of Schedule 2, and there are in addition possibilities of obtaining bail in judicial review or *habeas corpus* proceedings. The grant of bail is distinct from the issue of the lawfulness of the detention[2] (although the issues of eligibility for bail and lawfulness of detention are sometimes difficult to separate).[3] Bail is, therefore, not an alternative remedy that must be exhausted before proceedings for judicial review challenging the legality of detention can be sought, and refusal of bail is irrelevant to the question of the legality of the decision to detain, so that such a challenge cannot be properly characterised as a collateral challenge to the refusal of bail. Moreover, in practice immigration judges are not always provided with accurate reasons and information by the Home Office in bail summaries and they may well have refused bail on an erroneous basis.[4] We describe below the provisions for release on bail under the IA 1971 and in *habeas corpus* and judicial review proceedings.

[1] As amended by Asylum and Immigration Act 1996, Sch 2, para 11, Immigration and Asylum Act 1999, Sch 14, para 63, AI(TC)A 2004, s 26(7), Sch 2, Pt 1. The bail provisions apply to those detained by the Secretary of State under NIAA 2002, s 62: s 62(3).

2   See *In the matter of Youssef* (CO 706/1999) (2 March 1999), QBD [2000] 6 (1) ILD.
3   In *R (on the application of Konan) v Secretary of State for the Home Department* [2004] EWHC 22 (Admin), [2004] All ER (D) 151 (Jan) the court rejected the Secretary of State's submissions that bail was an alternative remedy to judicial review challenging the legality of the detention. The distinction between the two remedies was clear and the court confirmed that when an immigration judge is considering bail he or she is not determining the lawfulness of the detention. See para 30.
4   *R (on the application of Konan)* above, at para 26 and *R (on the application of Johnson (Renford)) v Secretary of State for the Home Department* [2004] EWHC 1550 (Admin), para 36.

New arrivals and those detained for removal: bail under the Immigration Act 1971

18.68 The right to apply for bail has been achieved through the accretion of amendments to Schedule 2 to the IA 1971 by the Asylum and Immigration Act 1996, the Immigration and Asylum Act 1999 and the NIAA 2002. It applies to new arrivals detained for more than seven days pending examination,[1] and anyone detained pending a decision on cancellation of leave to enter,[2] or after refusal of leave to enter pending removal directions,[3] or as a suspected illegal entrant or overstayer detained pending the giving of directions,[4] or persons detained following a decision to deport or a recommendation for deportation or a deportation order.[5] Bail may be granted by a chief immigration officer[6] or by the Secretary of State[7] or by the First-tier Tribunal,[8] on the person's own recognisance (or bail bond in Scotland), with a condition to appear before an immigration officer at a time and place notified in writing,[9] and other conditions may be imposed to secure the appearance of the person bailed at the requisite time and place.[10] Immigration officers and police may arrest those in breach of bail or those they reasonably believe will breach, are breaching or have breached conditions,[11] or on notice in writing of a surety that the released person is likely to breach a condition and that the surety wishes to withdraw.[12] A person arrested under these circumstances must be brought before an immigration judge or a justice of the peace as soon as reasonably practicable and in any event within 24 hours to decide whether detention or release should be ordered.[13] There is provision for the forfeiture of the recognisance or bail bond in case of breach of bail.[14] Bail may also be granted to persons against whom removal directions have been set,[15] however following the Immigration Act 2014 bail may not be granted without the consent of the Secretary of State where directions are in place for a removal date within 14 days of the proposed release date.[16] A person may be released on bail pending examination or pending removal subject to a requirement to appear before an immigration officer at a particular time and place.[17] An immigration officer may vary that requirement by notice in writing[18] so as to require an earlier appearance before an immigration officer than that directed by the Tribunal. However, the power to do so is subject to implied limitation; an immigration officer could not merely rely on reasserting the underlying power to detain because that would undermine the basis upon which the Tribunal had granted bail. There would need to be a material change of circumstances since the Tribunal granted bail for this power to be exercised lawfully and compatibly with Article 5(4) of the ECHR.[19] Following the introduction of the Immigration Act 2014 the

Tribunal is required to dismiss without a hearing any application for bail made within 28 days of the date on which an application was refused by the Tribunal, unless the applicant can demonstrate a material change in circumstances.[20]

1   IA 1971, Sch 2, para 22(1)(a), (1B), as amended by Asylum and Immigration Act 1996, Sch 2, para 11(1)–(3). The bail provisions apply to those detained by the Secretary of State under Nationality, Immigration and Asylum Act 2002, s 62 by virtue of s 62(3).

2   IA 1971, Sch 2, para 22(1)(aa), inserted by Immigration and Asylum Act 1999, Sch 14, para 63. There is no seven-day waiting requirement in relation to this category, or indeed to anyone except new arrivals seeking leave to enter.

3   IA 1971, Sch 2, para 22(1)(b), applied to persons detained by the Secretary of State under NIAA 2002, s 62 by NIAA 2002, s 62(3).

4   IA 1971, Sch 2, para 22(1)(b) applied as above by the NIAA 2002.

5   Immigration and Asylum Act 1999, s 54, extending paras 22–25 of Sch 2 to the IA 1971 to those detained under the relevant provisions of Sch 3, para 2. The sentencing court or the appeal court may also release on bail: *R v Governor of Holloway Prison, ex p Giambi* [1982] 1 All ER 434. The appeal court may grant bail pending an appeal against a recommendation, under Criminal Appeal Act 1968, s 19: *R v Ofori; R v Tackie* (1993) 99 Cr App Rep 219, and may direct release while upholding the recommendation: IA 1971, Sch 3, para 2(1A), inserted by Criminal Justice Act 1982, s 64, Sch 10, paras 1 and 2.

6   The EIG at Chapter 57 sets out detailed guidance on the use of bail as an alternative to detention. The factors to consider include the likelihood of absconding, the likely delay pending any conclusive decision or disposal of an appeal, diligence, speed and effectiveness of the steps taken by the Immigration Service to effect removal; any special reasons for detention (such as those in EIG, para 57.3), the reliability and standing of sureties and (in deportation cases) the views of the relevant senior caseworker in the relevant casework section (57.5). It expects sureties to have enough money or disposable assets to be able to pay the sum if bail is forfeited; be aged over 18 and settled in the UK; be a householder or at least well established in the place where he or she lives; without a criminal record; not to have come to adverse notice in other immigration matters particularly bail cases or applications for temporary admission and have a personal connection with the applicant or to be acting on behalf of a reputable organisation with an interest in the detainee's welfare. The Guidance recognises that the amount of bail has to be viewed in relation to the means of the applicant and his or her sureties but identifies a figure of between £2,000 to £5,000 as 'normally appropriate'. An inflexible approach to these factors and the 'normal' requirement for sureties in the stated sums may be unlawful if applied without proper regard to its necessity in individual cases: see 17.39 below. In refusing bail the exceptions in IA 1971, Sch 2, para 30 can be used.

7   NIAA 2002, s 68.

8   IA 1971, Sch 2, para 22(1A), as amended by Asylum and Immigration (Treatment of Claimants, etc) Act 2004, s 26(7), Sch 2, Pt 1.

9   IA 1971, Sch 2, para 22(1A).

10   IA 1971, Sch 2, para 22(2).

11   IA 1971, Sch 2, para 24(1)(a), without a warrant, and para 17(2), with a warrant for entry into premises.

12   IA 1971, Sch 2, para 24(1)(b).

13   IA 1971, Sch 2, para 24(2).

14   IA 1971, Sch 2, para 23.

15   IA 1971, Sch 2, para 34, applying the provisions of para 22 as to release on bail, and paras 23–25 relating to arrest, forfeiture of recognisance and bail procedures, to persons detained for removal. The paragraph is applied to those detained by the Secretary of State under the NIAA 2002, s 62 by NI 2002, s 62(3).

16   IA 1971, Sch 2, para 22(4).

17   IA 1971, Sch 2, para 22(1A).

18   IA 1971, Sch 2, para 22(1A).

19   *Re Mahmood* [2006] EWHC 228 (Admin), [2006] All ER (D) 303 (Feb). There is no power outside of the provision of para 24 of Sch 2 to the 1971 Act to detain a person on bail. The same approach was adopted in a further cases which following interim release was settled.

20   IA 1971, Sch 2, para 25(2) as inserted by the IA 2014, s7(3). To be achieved via procedure rules.

Bail pending appeal

18.69 Persons detained under Schedules 2 and 3 to the IA 1971 are eligible for bail if they have an in-country appeal pending before the First-tier Tribunal.[1] Bail on appeal may be granted by a chief immigration officer or police inspector[2] as well as by the First-tier Tribunal.[3] The grant of bail is discretionary, and may be withheld on grounds of previous non-compliance, prevention of crime, public health and protection for appellants vulnerable through mental disorder or youth.[4] It may be subject to the giving of sureties or recognisance and to conditions.[5] The Schedule provides that where removal directions are in force for removal within 14 days of the date of proposed release, the consent of the Secretary of State to bail must be obtained.[6] In *Ex p Alghali*[7] the court held that, since directions for removal are of no effect while an appeal is pending, the consent of the Secretary of State is not needed. However, the NIAA 2002 provides that, although a person may not be removed from the UK under the Immigration Acts pending an appeal under section 82, removal directions may be given.[8] The effect of this provision, read literally, would be to make all bail pending appeal subject to the Secretary of State's consent. Such an interpretation would be an unsustainable restriction on the powers of the appellate authorities to grant bail, and would offend against Art 5(4) of the ECHR.[9] Immigration officers and police officers may arrest persons released on bail pending appeal on reasonable grounds for believing that the person is likely to break the conditions of bail, or is breaking or has broken such conditions,[10] or on written notice by a surety that he or she no longer wishes to stand surety because of a belief that the person on bail will not appear.[11] There are powers for the Tribunal to forfeit any recognisance in whole or in part,[12] in which case a magistrates' court is specified to recover the sum.[13] Following the introduction of the Immigration Act 2014 the Tribunal is required to dismiss without a hearing any application for bail made within 28 days of the date on which an application was refused by the Tribunal, unless the applicant can demonstrate a material change in circumstances[14]

1   IA 1971, Sch 2, para 29(1), as amended by NIAA 2002, Sch 7 from 1 April 2003 (SI 2003/754) to provide for bail pending all appeals under Part 5 of the 2002 Act (see **19.15**).
2   IA 1971, Sch 2, para 29(2) as amended by AI(TC)A 2004, s 26(7), Sch 2, Pt 1.
3   IA 1971, Sch 2, para 29(3) as amended.
4   IA 1971, Sch 2, para 30(2) as amended.
5   IA 1971, Sch 2, para 29(3), (5), 30(2) as amended.
6   IA 1971, Sch 2, para 30(1) as amended by the IA 2014, s 7(5).
7   *R v Immigration Appeal Tribunal, ex p Alghali* [1984] Imm AR 106, QBD.
8   NIAA 2002, s 78(1)(a), (3)(a).
9   In such a situation, however, the appellant could rely on paras 22 and 34 of Sch 2 (grant of bail pending removal), which is not subject to the Secretary of State's consent. The potential problem appears to have been to some extent remedied by the IA 2014 which means that the Secretary of State's consent is only required where removal is scheduled within 14 days of the proposed release date.
10 IA 1971, Sch 2, para 33(1)(a). Even this could offend against the requirements of Art 5(4) of the EHCR; see above.
11 IA 1971, Sch 2, para 33(1)(b).
12 IA 1971, Sch 2, para 31(1).
13 IA 1971, Sch 2, para 31(2)–(5).
14 IA 1971, Sch 2, para 33A as inserted by the IA 2014, s 7(6). To be achieved via procedure rules.

18.70 The Upper Tribunal does not have power to grant bail; the power is conferred on the First-tier Tribunal.[1] Nor is there a right of appeal to the Upper Tribunal from a bail-related decision of the First-tier Tribunal, such decisions being 'excluded decisions' and thus not appealable.[2]

[1] IA 1971, Sch 2, paras 22 and 29 and Sch 3, para 2(4A).
[2] Tribunals, Courts and Enforcement Act 2007, s 11(1) and the Appeals (Excluded Decisions) Order 2009, SI 2009/275, art 2(b).

Bail before the Special Immigration Appeals Commission

18.71 The provisions of the IA 1971 in relation to bail are modified in respect of the following persons:

(i)   those detained under provisions of the IA 1971 or the NIAA 2002 whose detention has been certified by the Secretary of State as necessary in the interests of national security;[1]
(ii)   those detained under either Act following a decision to refuse leave to enter on the ground that exclusion is in the interests of national security;[2]
(iii)   those detained following a decision to deport on national security grounds.[3]

The modifications are set out in Schedule 3 to the Special Immigration Appeals Commission Act 1997. In all national security cases it is the Special Immigration Appeals Commission which has the power to grant bail, not immigration or police officers or the Tribunal.[4] This applies both to new arrivals and to appellants.[5] Provisions as to arrest for breach of bail and forfeiture of recognisances are modified accordingly.[6]

[1] Special Immigration and Appeals Commission Act 1997, s 3(1) (as amended by SI 2003/1016 Art 3, Sch, para 10(2)(a). Until March 2005 the list included those detained under s 23 of the ATCSA 2001 who were certified as suspected international terrorists under s 21 of the Act: ATCSA 2001, s 24(2).
[2] SIACA 1997, s 3(2)(b).
[3] SIACA 1997, s 3(2)(c).
[4] SIACA 1997, Sch 3, para 1, as amended by AI(TCA) 2004, s 26(7), Sch 2, Pt 1.
[5] SIACA 1997, Sch 3, para 4 as amended, substituting references to the Tribunal with references to the Commission.
[6] SIACA 1997, Sch 3, paras 2–8 as amended.

Bail procedure before the First-tier Tribunal

18.72 The procedure governing bail applications before the immigration appellate authority is governed by Part 5 of the Tribunal Procedure (First-tier Tribunal)(Immigration and Asylum Chamber) Rules 2014[1] A bail application must be made by filing an application notice in the prescribed form with the First-tier Tribunal.[2] The notice must contain the full name, date of birth and date of arrival in the UK of the applicant; the address where he or she is detained; whether an appeal is pending; a bail address (or reason why no such address is given); the amount of any recognisance offered; the names, addresses, occupations and dates of birth of any persons who have agreed to stand as sureties and the amounts offered by them; the grounds of the application and if a previous application has been refused, full details of any material change in circumstances. If an interpreter is required for the hearing this must also be stated.[3] The application must be signed by the applicant or a representative or (if the detainee is a minor or for some other reason is incapable of acting) by a person acting on his or her behalf.[4] Where an application for bail is filed within 28 days of a refusal of bail, the Tribunal must determine whether the detained person has shown that there has a material change in circumstances. If not, the application must be dismissed without a hearing[5]. If the Secretary of State's reasons for opposing bail include that removal directions have been set, a copy of those directions must be provided.[6] Otherwise, the appellate authority must as soon as reasonably practicable serve a copy on the Secretary of State and fix a hearing.[7] The Secretary of State must file a written statement of reasons for contesting the application (if it is contested) not later than 2.00 pm on the working day before the hearing, or where notice was received less than 24 hours before that time, as soon as reasonably practicable.[8] The First-tier Tribunal must serve written notice of its decision on the parties and where bail is granted the person having custody of the applicant.[9] If bail is granted the notice must include the conditions of bail, and the amount in which the applicant and any sureties are to be bound.[10] Where bail is refused or forfeiture of a recognizance is ordered, the notice must include reasons.[11] The Rules provide explicitly for the Tribunal to set conditions and a recognizance, with that recognizance to be taken by a specified person at a future date.[12] Applicants must be released once the person in whose custody they are has received a copy of a decision to grant bail and is satisfied that any recognisances have been entered into.[13] There are some variations in form to rules 37 to 41 for applications for bail made in Scotland, for example where cautioners replace sureties and deposits are given by both applicants and cautioners, and rule 42 is replaced.[14]

[1] SI 2014/2604 which on 20 October 2014 replaced SI 2005/230.
[2] SI 2014/2604, r 38(1). The relevant form, B1, is available from the Tribunal website.
[3] SI 2014/2604, r 38(2)–(3).
[4] SI 2014/2604, r 39(3) as required by the IA 2014, s 7(3) and (6).
[5] 2014/2604, r 40(2).
[6] SI 2014/2604, r 38(5). If bail is granted subject to a recognisance or surety, the recognisance or surety must also be in writing and must state the amount agreed and that the applicant or surety understands the bail decision and agrees to pay that amount of money if the applicant fails to comply with the conditions set out in the bail decision: SI 2014/2604, r 42(1). The recognisance must be signed by the applicant or surety and filed with the Tribunal: r 42(2).
[7] SI 2014/2604, rr 38(6), 39(1).
[8] SI 2014/2604, r 40.
[9] SI 2014/2604, r 41(1)(b).
[10] SI 2014/2604, r 41(2).
[11] SI 2014/2604, r 41(3).
[12] SI 2014/2604, rr 41(4), 43.
[13] SI 2014/2604, r 43.
[14] SI 2014/2604, r 44.

Bail guidance for judges

18.73 Guidance to the judiciary on the bail process has been provided in the form of Presidential Guidance Note No 1 of 2012 *Bail Guidance For Judges Presiding Over Immigration And Asylum Hearings* after an absence of guidance for some years. The Guidance Note provides that 'a First-tier

Tribunal Judge will grant bail where there is no sufficiently good reason to detain a person and lesser measures can provide adequate alternative means of control.[1] The fact that detention in a given case might be successfully challenged is considered to be a matter weighing in favour of bail.[2] Similarly if a policy has not been followed that might undermine detention. [3] The guidance provides that the Respondent should produce evidence of any risks referred to, rather than merely relying on generic policy statements to which a Judge is 'unlikely to give significant weight'. [4]Failure to serve a bail summary may lead to the application being treated as unopposed, though the circumstances will be carefully considered.[5]Where a person is already subject to license conditions they should not be given conditions of bail inconsistent with them and the need for such conditions may in any event be less pressing.[6] In considering the length of detention the guidance provides that 'three months would be considered a substantial period of time and six months a long period. Imperative considerations of public safety may be necessary to justify detention in excess of six months.'[7] In family cases detention should be compatible with both Article 8 of the ECHR and section 55 of the CSIA 2009.[8] Parties have an obligation to bring to the Judge's attention any relevant evidence in their possession[9]. Bail should not be refused unless there is good reason, and it is for the respondent to show that good reason exists.[10] Where bail is to be granted, detailed guidance is provided as to appropriate conditions.[11] Bail in principle may be granted with further information or evidence to be produced.[12] In *Lamin Minteh* the Court of Appeal held unlawful the declared practice of an adjudicator not to grant bail if there were no sureties regardless of whether there was evidence that the applicant was likely to abscond.[13] In *AKB* it was held that an adjudicator had to justify his decision to refuse bail; it was not good enough to say merely that there was a chance the applicant might abscond.[14] A failure to apply these guidelines, or action which is inconsistent with them, may be a ground for judicial review of a refusal of bail.

[1]   Para 4.
[2]   Para 5. The guidance is clear however that a bail application is not a challenge to the lawfulness of detention. See also *R (on the application of Konan) v Secretary of State for the Home Department* [2004] EWHC 22 (Admin), [2004] All ER (D) 151 (Jan).
[3]   Para 7.
[4]   Para 8, paras 12-13, para 28.
[5]   Para 10.
[6]   Para 15.
[7]   Para 19. See also para 21: 'Detention of over a year has been held to be proportionate where there is a high risk of the applicant causing serious harm to the public. On the other hand, a period of weeks might be disproportionate where one of the effects of detention is to keep a parent apart from young children.' Referring to *R (on the application of MXL) v Secretary of State for the Home Department* [2010] EWHC 2397 (Admin).
[8]   Para 21.
[9]   Para 29.
[10] Para 27.
[11] Paras 32-44.
[12] Paras 45-54.
[13] *Minteh (Lamin) v Secretary of State for the Home Department* (396/5400/D) (8 March 1996, unreported), CA.
[14] *R v Secretary of State for the Home Department, ex p AKB* [1996] 3 (2) ILD, QBD.

Procedures before the Special Immigration Appeals Commission

18.74 Procedures for bail hearings before the Special Immigration Appeals Commission are more formal than other bail hearings, and are contained in the Commission's Procedure Rules.[1] A bail application must be in writing and must contain particulars of the full name of the applicant, his or her date of birth, date of arrival in the UK, the address where he or she is detained, whether there are any proceedings pending before the Commission to which the applicant is a party, a bail address, the amount of any recognisance offered, the names, addresses and occupations of any potential sureties and the amounts they might offer, the grounds of the application and any change in circumstances since a previous unsuccessful application.[2] Where an application for bail is filed the Commission must as soon as reasonably practicable serve a copy on the Secretary of State and fix a hearing.[3] The Secretary of State must file a written statement of his reasons for contesting he application not later than 2.00 pm before the day of the hearing or, where he has received notice less than 24 hours before that time, as soon as reasonably practicable.[4] The Secretary of State can object to the written statement being disclosed to the applicant or his representatives and a closed hearing may be held[5] for the Commission to decide whether the objection to disclosure should be upheld.[6] SIAC must order the disclosure of sufficient material to provide the appellant with an effective opportunity to challenge the case for withholding bail in order to comply with the requirements of Article 5(4) of the ECHR.[7] That means that SIAC is not permitted to rely on earlier findings based on closed material in order to set bail conditions.[8] The applicant's interests are represented by a Special Advocate during the closed session.[9] To date, all those with appeals before the Special Immigration Appeals Commission have been detained except for the appellant Rehman,[10] who was on temporary admission for the entire period of the proceedings In only one case of those detained under the Anti-terrorism, Crime and Security Act 2001 was bail granted[11] but the Commission has since granted bail in a significant number of cases of detainees facing deportation on national security grounds. Practice in this regard has significantly changed in recent years with several SIAC appellants now on bail albeit on very strict conditions similar to, and in some cases stricter than, Control Orders and up to 24-hour house arrest.[12] In *XC, UF and U v Secretary of State for the Home Department*[13] whilst confirming SIAC's long standing approach of weighing the risks on release of absconding and to national security against the means to limit or contain those risks,[14] SIAC signalled what is described as a new 'precautionary approach' to the grant of bail after the judgment of the Divisional Court in *U and XC* concluded that SIAC could not withhold decisive closed material when considering bail applications compatibly with Article 5(4) of the ECHR.[15] The likely rationale for this lies in the dogmatic refusal by the security services to disclose the use and product of telephone taps and other covert surveillance.

---

[1] Special Immigration Appeals Commission (Procedure) Rules 2003, SI 2003/1034, Part 6, rr 28–31.

[2] SI 2003/1034, r 29(1), (2)(a)–(h). The application must also state whether the applicant requires an interpreter at the hearing and if so, for what language and dialect, and must be signed by the applicant or his or her representative or (for those incapable of acting by childhood or other reason) someone acting on his or her behalf. These rules are virtually identical to the bail provisions before the Tribunal, at 17.61 above. Where an applicant is over 18 he must also confirm if he is prepared to be subjected to electronic monitoring (r 29(fa)).

[3] SI 2003/1034, r 30(1).

4   SI 2003/1034, r 30(2).
5   SI 2003/1034, r 37.
6   SI 2003/1034, r 38.
7   *U v Special Immigration Appeals Commission; XC v Special Immigration Appeals Commission* [2009] EWHC 3052.
8   *R (on the application of BB) v Special Immigration Appeals Commission* [2011] EWHC 336 (Admin).
9   SI 2003/1034, r 38(2).
10   *Secretary of State for the Home Department v Rehman* [2002] Imm AR 98, HL.
11   In *G v Secretary of State for the Home Department* [2004] EWCA Civ 265, [2004] 1 WLR 1349, the Commission granted bail despite upholding the Secretary of State's certificate under the ATCSA 2001, s 21 (suspected international terrorist), on health grounds. The Court of Appeal held it had no statutory jurisdiction to hear the Secretary of State's appeal (this lacuna led to the enactment of AI(TC)A 2004, s 32, providing an appeal to the Court of Appeal against the grant or refusal of bail by SIAC) but reconstituted itself into a Divisional Court to hear a judicial review of the grant of bail. G was released on house arrest, under draconian conditions described by the House of Lords in *A v Secretary of State for the Home Department; X v Secretary of State for the Home Department* [2004] UKHL 56, [2005] 2 WLR 87 at para 35. The ATCSA detention and bail provisions lapsed in April 2005.
12   Bail has been granted in the cases, for example, of *U* (although since revoked) *Y, ZZ, BB, YY, PP, VV, O* (although since revoked), *AF, T, H,A, G, AA, W*, and *Abu Rideh*.
13   SC/77/2009, SC/80/2009 and SC/32/2005 (*21 December 2009*)
14   *A v Secretary of State for the Home Department* (SC/3-39/2005) (*20 October 2005*), where SIAC identified the question as being 'Are we satisfied that there is a real risk that, if released on bail, subject to whatever conditions may be imposed, an applicant would abscond, in the sense of not turning up to the hearing as required, and are we satisfied that there would be a real risk to national security if he were meanwhile on such bail, whether having absconded or even if he had not absconded?' See also *U, Y, Z, BB and VV* (*March 2009*): *EV v Secretary of State for the Home Department* SC/67/2008 (*7 April 2009*).
15   SIAC set out its new approach as follows: 'In the case of a new appellant, it is unlikely that the national security case will be fully deployed at the start, at least in the open material. We do not start with a presumption that he *must* be detained but, save in exceptional cases, we are unlikely to be able to determine, at least on the open material, whether or not the two risks could be managed if an appellant were to be admitted to bail. A precautionary approach will be adopted. Removal of the vital tool of reliance on closed material will make it unlikely that SIAC will grant bail'. In *R (on the application of U) v Special Immigration Appeals Commission* [2010] EWHC 813 (Admin) and *R (on the application of BB) v Special Immigration Appeals Commission* [2011] EWHC 336 (Admin) the cautionary approach was touched upon, but in neither case was it considered necessary to determine whether it was lawful.

18.75 The IAA 1999 enabled the Secretary of State by regulation to make new provisions in relation to bail applications for those detained under the IA 1971 (or section 62 of the NIAA 2002).[1] The regulations may confer a right to bail in prescribed circumstances,[2] may create or transfer jurisdiction for bail hearings,[3] provide where bail applications may be held,[4] the procedure to be followed[5] and the circumstances and conditions where an applicant may be released on bail.[6] They may amend or repeal any enactment relating to bail.[7] Any such regulations must provide that the authority which hears the bail application is the same one as hears the appeal.[8] The Lord Chancellor must approve the regulations.[9] None have been made to date since the coming into force of this provision in February 2003.

1   IAA 1999, s 53(1) in force since 10 February 2003 (SI 2003/2), as amended by NIAA 2002, s 62(13).
2   IAA 1999, s 53(2).
3   IAA 1999, s 53(3)(a) as amended.
4   IAA 1999, s 53(3)(b).
5   IAA 1999, s 53(3)(c).
6   IAA 1999, s 53(3)(d).
7   IAA 1999, s 53(3)(e).

8   Ie, a bail hearing must be heard by the Special Immigration Appeals Commission if the appeal
    is to that body: IAA 1999, s 53(4), amended by NIAA 2002, Sch 7, para 28.
9   IAA 1999, s 53(6). In Scotland the consent of the Scottish Ministers must be obtained: s 53(7).

Bail pending judicial review or habeas corpus

18.76 The statutory scheme for release on bail is now, as has been seen above, comprehensive. The remaining notable *lacuna*, is the inability to apply for bail for new arrivals until seven days have elapsed.[1] In this context the only available remedy is by way of judicial review of the refusal to release.[2] The Higher Courts will entertain bail applications pursuant to their inherent jurisdiction pending the hearing of an application for judicial review, notwithstanding the availability of bail from the appellate authority.[3] In *Ex p Turkoglu*[4] the Court of Appeal reviewed the position regarding bail in judicial review cases and held that the High Court has jurisdiction to grant bail on an application for permission to apply for judicial review or a substantive application as part of the power to grant ancillary orders. Where the High Court judge refuses bail in such a case, an appeal lies to the Court of Appeal.[5] But bail in this context is ancillary to some other substantive proceeding, and if the High Court refuses permission for judicial review it is *functus officio* and therefore has no jurisdiction to grant bail. The Court of Appeal has its own inherent jurisdiction on a renewed application for permission. Where there is a statutory right to apply for bail, it should generally be sought from the appellate authority, but in *Ex p Kelso*,[6] Collins J held that, where such an application could result in a further application for judicial review if returned to an adjudicator who refused bail or imposed unsatisfactory conditions, and where the matter can be dealt with expeditiously, it was appropriate for the High Court to entertain the application.[7]

1   IA 1971, Sch 2, para 22(1B).
2   *Vilvarajah (Nadarajah) v Secretary of State for the Home Department* [1990] Imm AR 457.
3   Senior Courts Act 1981 s 15(3) and 19, and see *R (on the application of Sezek) v Secretary of State* [2001] INLR 675 and *R (on the application of Doku) v Secretary of State for the Home Department* (C/2000/3360) (30 November 2000, unreported), CA.
4   *R v Secretary of State for the Home Department, ex p Turkoglu* [1988] QB 398, [1987] 2 All ER 823.
5   *Turkoglu* above.
6   *R v Secretary of State for the Home Department, ex p Kelso* [1998] INLR 603, QBD.
7   See also *R v Secretary of State for the Home Department, ex p Taher* (CO 3106/99) (24 September 1999, unreported), HC.

18.77 In *Kelso*[1] Collins J also retrieved the High Court's original jurisdiction to grant bail on the merits (as opposed to a jurisdiction to determine the reasonableness of detention on *Wednesbury* grounds), by adverting to the distinction drawn in *Vilvarajah*[2] between detention in respect of which statutory bail was not available and detention in respect of which it was. Only in the former case, where it was in effect the discretion to grant temporary admission that was in issue, was the jurisdiction limited to a *Wednesbury* review. In the latter case, the court's inherent jurisdiction allowed it to decide for itself on the material before it whether bail should be granted as an adjunct to the proceedings, and virtually all immigration detention now falls within that category.[3] *Kelso* was approved by the Court of Appeal in *Doku*,[4] a case involving detention pursuant to a recommendation for deportation. However, in *Sezek*[5] the Court of Appeal emphasised that significant weight had to be given to the fact that the Secretary of State had decided that the person should be detained and to the reasons why he had opposed release of that person. Reference was also made to the need for consideration to be given to the detention policy. The incorporation of Article 5 of the ECHR, as the court observed in *Sezek* at para 15, means that the distinction between the judicial review and the bail jurisdiction is less significant since the standards of the court scrutiny and the requirements that the Secretary of State demonstrate that the decision is justified and proportionate are the same. Judicial review is available to challenge a refusal of bail by an adjudicator.[6] In *ex p B*[7] the challenge was initially to both the refusal of bail and the Secretary of State's underlying decision to detain. Bail is not an alternative remedy where the decision of the Secretary of State to detain is unlawful, and the grant or refusal of bail is irrelevant to a judicial review of the legality of detention.[8] Even if the detainee is released on bail any previous period of detention, which is unlawful, can be the subject of judicial review proceedings seeking a declaration and damages under the common law and/or Article 5(5) of ECHR. In *ex p B* the claimant had been released by the Secretary of State following the grant of permission in the judicial review and in *Konan*[9] the claimant had been released on bail by an Adjudicator prior to the grant of permission in a judicial review challenging substantive decision in the case as well as a challenge to the lawfulness of the detention.

[1]   *R v Secretary of State for the Home Department, ex p Kelso* [1998] INLR 603, QBD.
[2]   *Vilvarajah (Nadarajah) v Secretary of State for the Home Department* [1990] Imm AR 457, CA.
[3]   *Kelso* above, at 606.
[4]   *R (on the application of Doku) v Secretary of State for the Home Department* (C/2000/3360) (30 November 2000, unreported), CA.
[5]   *R (on the application of Sezek) v Secretary of State* [2001] INLR 675.
[6]   *R v Secretary of State for the Home Department, ex p Brezinski and Glowacka* (CO 4251/1995 and CO 4237/1995) [1997] CLY 2880.
[7]   *R v Special Adjudicator and Secretary of State for the Home Department, ex p B* [1998] INLR 315.
[8]   See also *R (on the application of Konan) v Secretary of State for the Home Department* [2004] EWHC 22 (Admin), [2004] All ER (D) 151 (Jan).
[9]   *R (on the application of Konan) v Secretary of State for the Home Department* [2004] EWHC 22 (Admin), [2004] All ER (D) 151 (Jan).

Chapter 19

RIGHTS OF APPEAL AND ADMINISTRATIVE REVIEW

BACKGROUND AND STRUCTURE OF THE APPEALS SYSTEM

Background

19.1 'The right of access to justice . . . . is a fundamental and constitutional principle of a legal system'[1] and 'a right of access to a tribunal or other adjudicative mechanism established by the state is just as important and fundamental as a right of access to the ordinary courts'.[2] Appeals may be brought against some decisions relating to immigration status: to whom, in what circumstances and with what effect have been altered by each successive

Immigration Act in the ways summarised below. Following the historical introduction, the rest of this chapter describes the circumstances in which there is a right of appeal and some of the restrictions and limitations on appeal rights. It also describes the ways in which appeal rights will be affected by the bringing into force of the appeals provisions in the Immigration Act 2014 (IA 2014).[3] CHAPTER 20 will describe how the rights of appeal are exercised and how appeals are determined by the First-tier Tribunal (FT) and CHAPTER 21 will describe further appeals – to the Upper Tribunal (UT) and the Court of Appeal and judicial review. Immigration appeals have been heard by adjudicators, special adjudicators, the Immigration Appeal Tribunal (IAT) (together, the Immigration Appellate Authority), the Asylum and Immigration Tribunal (AIT) and now by the First-tier Tribunal Immigration and Asylum Chamber and the Upper Tribunal Immigration and Asylum Chamber, which we refer to as FT and UT. The UT and FT took over the earlier jurisdiction in February 2010 (see **19.10** below). Specific reference to one or other of these bodies will be made where necessary in these chapters, but otherwise reference will be to the generic 'tribunal' including any or all of them.

[1]   *R (on the application of Anufrijeva) v Secretary of State for the Home Department* [2003] UKHL 36, [2004] 1 AC 604, per Lord Steyn at para 26.
[2]   *R v Secretary of State for the Home Department, ex p Saleem (Asifa)* [2000] EWCA Civ 186, [2000] 4 All ER 814, per Hale LJ.
[3]   The editors hereby acknowledge the assistance provided in doing this by the submissions and training materials on the legislation produced by the Immigration Law Practitioners' Association, and in particular, by Alison Harvey, Steve Symonds, and Alison Pickup.

19.2 The 1969 Immigration Appeals Act, passed in response to the Wilson Committee report,[1] had provided Commonwealth citizens (but not aliens) with appeals against exclusion, removal and other decisions affecting immigrants. The appellate system thus set up was not intended in any way to undermine an effective immigration control. It was calculated to ease the fears of racial discrimination that immigration restrictions, imposed on Commonwealth immigrants for the first time only seven years previously in 1962, had provoked by seeing that the controls were imposed fairly; to provide 'a sense of protection against oppression and injustice, and . . . reassurance against fears of arbitrary action on the part of the Immigration Service',[2] and to ensure a more consistent and rational decision-making process. It was intended to be informal and largely inquisitorial; legal representation was not envisaged as necessary; it was for Commonwealth citizens only; and it did not provide appeals against deportation or other restrictive action 'on grounds which are primarily of a political nature'.[3] The Immigration Act 1971 (IA 1971) adopted the scheme of IAA 1969 and extended it to aliens, who had hitherto had no appeal rights. There were, however, important gaps in the scheme. Those who were refused leave to enter and had no entry clearance could exercise their rights of appeal only from abroad – a devastating disadvantage in asylum cases. There was no appeal against a proposed deportation where the decision had been made following a recommendation of a criminal court, nor against a decision to remove those deemed illegal entrants. Persons excluded, refused leave to enter or remain or subjected to deportation action on national security or political grounds had no right of appeal, only a right to an extra-statutory advisory procedure involving no disclosure of the grounds of proposed exclusion.[4]

[1]   Committee on Immigration Appeals, set up in 1966, chaired by Sir Roy Wilson QC (Cmnd 3387, 1967).
[2]   Cmnd 3387, para 85.
[3]   Cmnd 3387, para 191.
[4]   See the fourth edition of this book 15.52–15.57.

19.3 IA 1971 provided suspensive appeal rights to everyone who was subject to deportation as an overstayer or for breaching conditions of stay, in acknowledgment of the fact that, unlike illegal entrants, they had been admitted to the UK lawfully and so had a right to be heard before removal. The undermining of that distinction began in 1988, with the introduction of restricted rights of appeal for those whose last entry to the UK was within seven years of the decision to deport.[1] Adjudicators were henceforth precluded from reviewing the merits of the deportation decision in such cases.[2]

[1]   Immigration Act 1988, s 5; exceptions to the seven-year rule were laid by statutory instrument, but resulted in arbitrary distinctions between those who had a right of appeal and those who did not.
[2]   For a salutary case of the exercise of such discretion, see *Idrish* [1985] Imm AR 155. The removal of a right of appeal immediately led to harsher decisions being taken: see observations of Lord Griffiths in *R v Secretary of State for the Home Department, ex p Oladehinde* [1991] 1 AC 254, [1990] 3 All ER 393, [1990] 3 WLR 797.

19.4 By 1993 the big issue in immigration law was asylum. The lack of suspensive appeal rights for refused asylum seekers who claimed on arrival had led to litigation at the European Court of Human Rights.[1] The Asylum and Immigration Appeals Act 1993 introduced rights of appeal before removal for nearly all asylum seekers, including those who were to be removed to an EU Member State through which they had travelled to get to the UK, but removed the appeal rights of rejected visitors, short-term students and all applicants who did not possess either the requisite documents or the necessary age or nationality qualifications.

[1]   *Vilvarajah v United Kingdom* (1991) 14 EHRR 248. The judgment, which appeared after the 1993 Bill was published, in fact upheld the government's submission that judicial review of an adverse asylum decision was an effective remedy for the purposes of Article 13 to prevent a breach of Article 3 (exposure to torture or inhuman or degrading treatment by return to Sri Lanka), reversing the Commission on this point.

19.5 The accelerating integration of the UK into Europe marked in 1993 by the Treaty of European Union, and by proliferating inter-governmental measures on immigration and more particularly on asylum, had its impact on immigration appeals. The Immigration (EEA) Order 1994, SI 1994/1895 partially resolved the problem of EEA nationals and their families who, by virtue of the fact of not requiring leave to enter under IA 1971, had found themselves deprived of appeal rights against exclusion, removal and deportation. The embarrassing number of successful appeals against the removal of asylum seekers to the 'safe' countries of the EU,[1] on the grounds that *refoulement* from these countries to the country of persecution could not be ruled out, led to the abolition of the in-country appeal for this group of asylum seekers in the Asylum and Immigration Act 1996.[2] That Act, the first product of a co-ordinated European approach to asylum,[3] also curtailed the appeal rights of others, whose appeals were 'certified' for a variety of reasons, including the country they fled from, the timing of their claim and its nature.[4] The latter group of claimants had a first instance appeal but none to the Immigration Appeal Tribunal. Neither the 1993 nor the 1996 Act brought appeal rights to persons who could not claim to be refugees but whose removal arguably breached fundamental human rights, an omission which led to the proliferation of challenges to removal by judicial review, with particular reference to Article 3 and Article 8 of the ECHR.[5]

[1] Under ad hoc arrangements preceding the Dublin Convention, which came into force in 1997: see **12.139** ff.

[2] Sections 2, 3.

[3] See eg the Resolution on manifestly unfounded applications for asylum, anticipating the coming into force of the Dublin Convention, produced by the EU Member States' Ad hoc Group on Immigration and agreed at the immigration ministers' meeting of 30 November 1992, whose principles were reflected in Asylum and Immigration Act 1996, s 1 (now Asylum and Immigration (Treatment of Claimants, etc) Act 2004, s 33 and Sch 3).

[4] Asylum and Immigration Act 1996, s 1, amending Asylum and Immigration Appeals Act 1993, Sch 2, para 5.

[5] See eg *R v Secretary of State for the Home Department, ex p Kebbeh* [1999] EWHC 388 (Admin), Hidden J) on removal of disabled applicant to destitution and despair in Gambia (Article 3); *R v Secretary of State for the Home Department, ex p Ahmed and Patel* [1998] INLR 570; *R v Secretary of State for the Home Department, ex p Gangadeen* [1998] Imm AR 106; *R v Secretary of State for the Home Department, ex p Ali (Arman)* [2000] INLR 89 (Article 8).

19.6 In response to the European Court of Human Rights' condemnation in *Chahal*[1] of the lack of judicial scrutiny of national security-based deportation and detention, and similar criticisms by the European Court of Justice in *Shingara and Radiom*,[2] an appeal against exclusion, refusal of leave to enter or remain, or deportation on political or security grounds was introduced by the Special Immigration Appeals Commission Act 1997.[3] The intention was specifically to protect the UK against further findings of violations of Article 3 of the ECHR in such cases – although the machinery for a direct human rights appeal (as opposed to an asylum appeal) was not provided until the Human Rights Act 1998 and the human rights appeal of the Immigration and Asylum Act 1999 came simultaneously into force on 2 October 2000.

[1] *Chahal v United Kingdom* (1996) 23 EHRR 413.

[2] C-65/95, C-111/95, [1997] 3 CMLR 703.

[3] See Chapter **22**.

19.7 The Immigration and Asylum Act 1999 (IAA 1999) completed the process, begun in 1988, of removing the distinction between illegal entrants on the one hand, and overstayers and those in breach of conditions on the other, by taking the latter out of the deportation process altogether and in the process removing their rights of appeal.[1] But IAA 1999 introduced a free-standing appeal, suspensive of removal, which could be resorted to by anyone who asserted that the effect of any decision affecting his or her entitlement to enter or remain in the UK would be to breach the appellant's human rights or was racially discriminatory.[2] The appeal bridged the gap in international protection by ensuring that (subject to procedural requirements) human rights or discrimination arguments could be aired in all cases prior to removal. The only exception to the suspensive appeal was where an asylum claimant was to be removed to an EU Member State or another designated third country,[3] and the Secretary of State certified as manifestly unfounded a claim that such removal would breach the person's human rights.[4] To prevent what were seen as abusive and repetitious applications and multiple appeals, IAA 1999 introduced the one-stop appeal system.[5] Its rationale was simple – that all issues relating to a person's right to stay in the UK, and that of his or her family, should wherever possible be dealt with in one appeal, but the procedures designed to effect it were needlessly obscure and complex.

---

1   IAA 1999, s 10.
2   IAA 1999, s 65 as amended by the Race Relations (Amendment) Act 2000.
3   Under IAA 1999, ss 11 or 12; for designated countries see Asylum (Designated Safe Third countries) Order 2000, SI 2000/2245.
4   IAA 1999, ss 11(3), 12(5) and (6), 72(2)(a) as amended by the Race Relations (Amendment) Act 2000.
5   IAA 1999, ss 73–76; the Immigration and Asylum Appeals (One-stop Procedure) Regulations 2000, SI 2000/2244.

19.8 The appeal provisions in Part 5 of the Nationality, Immigration and Asylum Act 2002 (NIAA 2002) attempted to simplify appeal rights, by replacing disparate rights of appeal against various immigration decisions with a generic right of appeal against an 'immigration decision',[1] and by defining and bringing together the grounds of appeal which may be deployed.[2] Certain little-used appeal rights, such as the right of appeal against destination and the right of appeal against the decision that a person requires leave to enter, were abolished (although the lawfulness of a destination, and a requirement for leave, may be the subject of argument in the new appeals).[3] The one-stop procedure was simplified.[4] More controversially, NIAA 2002 removed suspensive rights of appeal from anyone (and not only those being removed to third countries), whose asylum or human rights claim was certified clearly unfounded,[5] and created a quasi-presumption in favour of certification in respect of listed countries,[6] which meant that for the first time since 1993, a person could be returned to the country where he or she asserted a fear of persecution before being able to appeal against the removal. Another controversial curtailment of rights of access to the courts was the replacement of judicial review[7] of an Immigration Appeal Tribunal's refusal of permission to appeal by statutory review, a purely paper review, and one subject to much stricter time limits than judicial review.[8] The jurisdiction of the Tribunal, historically embracing both fact and law, was reduced to points of law only.[9] NIAA 2002 also contained provision for costs awards to be made, and for public funding to be withheld in unmeritorious cases in the Tribunal.[10]

---

1   NIAA 2002, s 82(1), (2).
2   NIAA 2002, s 84(1).
3   On the ground that the decision is 'not in accordance with the law' under section 84(1)(e).
4   NIAA 2002, ss 96, 120.
5   NIAA 2002, s 94.
6   When the appeals provisions came into force (1 April 2003) and for the transitional provisions (from November 2002), the listed countries were the ten EU accession states; these states were removed from the list on 1 May 2004 when they joined the EU. Other states were added by statutory instrument.
7   Although it was accepted in *R (on the application of G) v Immigration Appeal Tribunal; R (on the application of M) v Immigration Appeal Tribunal* [2004] EWHC 588 (Admin), [2004] 3 All ER 286, [2004] 1 WLR 2953; affd, [2004] EWCA Civ 1731, [2005] 2 All ER 165, [2005] 1 WLR 1445 (upholding the Administrative Court's judgment at [2004] EWHC 588 (Admin)) that the NIAA 2002 did not oust judicial review, either expressly or by implication, the Court of Appeal held that statutory review provided an adequate and proportionate protection of the rights of asylum seekers, so that the court could decline to hear an application for judicial

review of issues which had been or could have been the subject of a statutory review. The court observed that the fact that immigrants and asylum claimants have no vested right to remain in the UK provides objective justification for any discrimination involved in the restriction of review rights.

8   NIAA 2002 (before amendment), s 101(2).
9   NIAA 2002, s 101(1).
10 NIAA 2002, s 101(3)(d) in relation to statutory review, and s 106(3) at Tribunal level (providing a rule-making power).

19.9 The Asylum and Immigration (Treatment of Claimants, etc) Act 2004 replaced adjudicators and the Immigration Appeal Tribunal with a single-tier appellate authority. By amendment to NIAA 2002,[1] the Act created the Asylum and Immigration Tribunal (AIT) to hear all immigration and asylum appeals (save those involving national security, which continued to be heard by the Special Immigration Appeals Commission). The passage of the 2004 Act was marked by an unprecedented attempt by the Secretary of State and the Lord Chancellor's Department to oust the jurisdiction of the higher courts in immigration and asylum matters. The AIT's decision was not to be the subject of any appeal or review (save for allegations of bad faith), except on a reference from the AIT itself.[2] The ouster clause was condemned by the Select Committee on Constitutional Affairs[3] and did not survive the wrath of the House of Lords. The replacement review provisions[4] allowed for a tribunal's decision to be reconsidered by the tribunal and to be remade if the original decision contained a material error of law. The Immigration, Asylum and Nationality Act 2006 (IAN 2006) made a number of further changes affecting appeals, which we deal with as they arise in the paragraphs which follow. This is also the case with the UK Borders Act 2007, and the Crime and Courts Act 2013, as and where these provisions affect appeals against deportation decisions.

1   NIAA 2002, s 81, substituted by Asylum and Immigration (Treatment of Claimants, etc) Act 2004, s 26(1), in force 4 April 2005.
2   Asylum and Immigration (Treatment of Claimants, etc) Bill, cl 11.
3   Select Committee on Constitutional Affairs, Second Report (2003–04 session), March 2004. The report quotes evidence from (inter alia) Hugh Tomlinson QC, Nicholas Blake QC (on behalf of the Bar Council), Ouseley J and Collins J on the constitutional impropriety of the ouster clause.
4   Nationality, Immigration and Asylum Act 2002, s 103A.

19.10 The Asylum and Immigration Tribunal was abolished on 15 February 2010 and its functions were transferred to the FT[1] created by the Tribunals, Courts and Enforcement Act 2007. The Act followed the Leggatt review of tribunals[2] and a government White Paper[3] and provided the statutory framework for the restructuring of more than 60 disparate tribunal jurisdictions, concerned with subjects as diverse as, eg social security, tax, land registration, criminal injuries compensation and war pensions as well as immigration and asylum into a single, two-tier jurisdiction.[4] There is a right of appeal from the FT to the UT[5] with the permission of the FT or UT[6] on a point of law.[7] There is a further right of appeal from the UT to the Court of Appeal, with the permission of the UT or the Court of Appeal.[8] Such permission may be granted only if the UT or the Court considers that the appeal would raise some important point of principle or practice or there is some other compelling reason for the appeal to be heard.[9] The Act also provides for the UT to exercise a 'judicial review jurisdiction'[10] in respect of any class of cases identified for the purpose. See further, CHAPTER 21 as to the classes that have been defined by directions.

1   Transfer of Functions of the Asylum and Immigration Tribunal Order, 2010, SI 2010/21, Art 2, made under the Tribunals, Courts and Enforcement Act 2007, ss 30(1) and (4) and 31(1), (2) and (7).
2   Report of the Review of Tribunals by Sir Andrew Leggatt: 'Tribunals for Users, One System, One Service' (HMSO, 2001).
3   Secretary of State for Constitutional Affairs: 'Transforming Public Services: Complaints, Redress and Tribunals' (2004) Cm 6243.
4   Sir Robert Carnwath, Senior President of Tribunals Tribunal Justice – a New Start [2009] PL 48. See also Edward Jacobs, *Tribunal Practice and Procedure: Tribunals under the Tribunals, Courts and Enforcement Act 2007* (2009), Legal Action Group, and 'Tribunal Reform: A New Coherent System', The Hon Mr Justice Hickinbottom [2010] JR 103.
5   Tribunals, Courts and Enforcement Act 2007, s 11(2).
6   Tribunals, Courts and Enforcement Act 2007, s 11(3) and (4). A decision of the UT to refuse permission to appeal to itself is, despite arguments to the contrary advanced by the Secretary of State, a decision capable of being challenged by way of Judicial Review, albeit that the grounds on which such an application may be brought are limited to the 'second appeals test' applied in appeals from the UT to the Court of Appeal, it is a paper application only, and is subject to a strict 16–day time limit: See *R (on the application of Cart) v Upper Tribunal* (Rev 1) [2011] UKSC 28, and CPR 54.7A.
7   Tribunals, Courts and Enforcement Act 2007, s 11(1).
8   Tribunals, Courts and Enforcement Act 2007, s 13.
9   Tribunals, Courts and Enforcement Act 2007, s 13(6).
10 Tribunals, Courts and Enforcement Act 2007, s 15.

19.11 The IA 2014 amends Part 5 of the NIAA 2002 so as to sweep away the rights of appeal described above. It has not come fully into force, but if it does the only decisions against which appeals may be brought will be EEA decisions and decisions by the Secretary of State to refuse a protection claim (ie a claim for asylum or humanitarian protection) to refuse a human rights claim or to revoke protection status.[1] Gone will be the long established rights of appeal against refusal of entry clearance, leave to enter or remain, and decisions to remove and to deport. The government justified this by castigating the existing system of appeals as being too complex and slow, and providing opportunities for the exercise of multiple appeal rights to obstruct expulsions from the UK.[2] However, more than 40 per cent of all immigration appeals to the FT are allowed[3] so the principal effect of the abolition of appeal rights will be to take away an important, accessible, and effective remedy against injustice.

1   IA 2014, s 15(2), substituting a new NIAA 2002, s 82.
2   See for example, *Immigration Bill Factsheet Appeals*: (clauses 11–13) Home Office, October 2013; *Impact Assessment of Reforming Immigration Appeal Rights*, 15 July 2013, Home Office; Home Secretary, Theresa May, HC Hansard Debates, 22 October 2013, Col 161.
3   *Tribunal Statistics Quarterly: April to June 2014*, Ministry of Justice, 11 September 2014: showed 42 per cent allowed in the financial year 2013/14; in 2012/13, 44 per cent of appeals were allowed; in 2011/12, 45 per cent of appeals were allowed; and in 2010/2011, 48 per cent were allowed: *Tribunal Statistics Quarterly (including Employment Tribunals and EAT): April to June 2013*, 12 September 2013, Ministry of Justice, Table 2.5.

19.12 At the time of writing the appeals provisions in the IA 2014[1] have been brought into force by two orders,[2] the second having been made shortly after the first when the government realised that the first order brought too few of those liable to deportation within the 2014 Act provisions. Thus the 2014 Act provisions apply only in respect of the following:

(1)   a person who becomes a foreign criminal within the meaning of NIAA 2002, s 117D (ie a non-British citizen, convicted in the UK and sentenced to a period of imprisonment of at least 12 months or who has been convicted of an offence that caused serious harm or who is a persistent offender) on or after 20 October 2014;[3]

(2)   a person liable to deportation from the UK because he or she belongs to the family of a person in (1);[4]

(3)   a person who is a 'foreign criminal' against whom a deportation decision (ie a decision to make a deportation order or to refuse to revoke a deportation order or a decision under the automatic deportation provisions of the UK Borders Act 2007, s 32(5)) was made on or after 10 November 2014;[5]

(4)   a person against whom a deportation decision is made on or after 10 November 2014 and who is liable to deportation as belonging to the family of a person in (3);[6]

(5)   a person who makes an application as a Tier 4 Migrant on or after 20 October 2014;[7]

(6)   a person who makes an application as a partner of a Tier 4 Migrant on or after 20 October 2014;[8]

(7)   a person who makes an application as the child of a Tier 4 Migrant on or after 20 October 2014.[9]

If a person in (5)–(7) subsequently makes an application for leave to enter or remain other than as a Tier 4 Migrant or Tier 4 Migrant's family member then the IA 2014 appeals provisions will not apply.[10] The appeal rights conferred by Part 5 of the NIAA 2002, unamended by the IA 2014, will continue to be available to everyone else who is the recipient of an immigration decision unless there is a further commencement order.

[1]   Viz., ss 15, 17(2) and Sch 9, Pt 4, paras 3–7.
[2]   The IA 2014 (Commencement No 3, Transitional and Saving Provisions) Order 2014, SI 2014/2771 and The IA 2014 (Transitional and Saving Provisions) Order 2014, SI 2014/2928.
[3]   SI 2014/2771, art 9.
[4]   SI 2014/2771, art 9.
[5]   SI 2014/2928, art 2(1)(b)(i).
[6]   SI 2014/2928, art 2(1)(b)(ii).
[7]   SI 2014/2771, art 9.
[8]   SI 2014/2771, art 9.
[9]   SI 2014/2771, art 9.
[10] SI 2014/2771, art 11(2).

RIGHTS OF APPEAL

19.13 Although the FT was created by the Tribunals, Courts and Enforcement Act 2007, the circumstances in which an appeal may be brought to the FT are set out in Part 5 of NIAA 2002, regulations 25–30 of the Immigration (European Economic Area) Regulations 2006[1] and in national security cases, the Special Immigration Appeals Commission Act 1997, ss 2 and 2B. For a long time after the replacement of the Asylum and Immigration Tribunal by the FT and UT in February 2010, the Asylum and Immigration Tribunal (Procedure) Rules 2005 continued to govern the procedure of the FT.[2]

However, from 20 October 2014, the FT has its own bespoke rules: the Tribunal Procedure (First-tier Tribunal) (Immigration and Asylum Chamber) Rules 2014, the Schedule to which contains procedure rules relating to the Fast Track procedure.[3] Rules regarding the service of notices are contained in the Immigration (Notices) Regulations 2003.[4] Appeals to the SIAC have their own special procedure rules.[5]

[1] SI 2006/1003.
[2] SI 2005/230.
[3] SI 2014/2604.
[4] SI 2003/658.
[5] Special Immigration Appeals Commission (Procedure) Rules 2003, SI 2003/1034.

19.14 Subject to the exceptions and qualifications discussed below, appeals can be brought:

(1)   against an 'immigration decision' as defined in section 82 of NIAA 2002. This right of appeal is to be abolished by the IA 2014, but at the time of writing, commencement of the provisions in that Act amending section 82 is limited, as described in paragraph **19.12** above;

(2)   against the refusal of an asylum claim if leave to enter or remain for a period exceeding one year has been granted, or if periods of leave to enter or remain exceeding one year in aggregate have been granted.[1] This right of appeal is also to be abolished by the IA 2014, but at the time of writing, the relevant provisions in that Act have been commenced only to the limited extent described in paragraph **19.12** above;

(3)   against a decision curtailing or refusing to extend limited leave to enter or remain given on asylum grounds, following a decision that the person is not a refugee but with the result that the person has leave in some other capacity.[2] This right of appeal is also to be abolished by the IA 2014, but at the time of writing, the relevant provisions in that Act have been commenced only to the limited extent described in paragraph **19.12** above;

(4)   against an 'EEA decision'.[3] Provision for appeals against EEA decisions is made by NIAA 2002, s 109 and the regulations made under section 109. Section 109 is unaffected by the IA 2014; and

(5)   against a decision by the Secretary of State to make an order depriving a person of his or her citizenship.[4]

[1] NIAA 2002, s 83.
[2] NIAA 2002, s 83A, inserted by IAN 2006, s 1.
[3] As defined in the Immigration (European Economic Area) Regulations 2006, SI 2006/1003, reg 2(1) which provide for a right of appeal against EEA decisions: NIAA 2002, s 109(1).
[4] British Nationality Act 1981, s 40A, inserted by NIAA 2002, s 4.

IMMIGRATION DECISIONS

19.15 The IA 2014 will abolish the right of appeal against an 'immigration decision' conferred by NIAA 2002, s 82, however as noted above, at the time of writing it has commenced only in respect of limited categories of persons: see paragraph **19.12**. The following are the 'immigration decisions' against which an appeal may still be brought other than by people falling within those categories:

(1)   refusal of leave to enter the UK,[1] including cancellation by an immigration officer of leave which the person had before arrival in, or return to, the UK;[2]

(2)   refusal of entry clearance;[3]

(3)   refusal of a certificate of entitlement to the right of abode under section 10 of the NIAA 2002;[4]

(4)   refusal to vary a person's leave to enter or remain in the UK if the result of the refusal is that the person has no leave to enter or remain;[5]

(5)   variation of a person's leave to enter or remain in the UK if when the variation takes effect the person has no leave to enter or remain;[6] This type of immigration decision includes cancellation of a person's non-lapsing leave whilst he or she is outside the UK; [7]

(6)   revocation under s 76 of the NIAA 2002 of indefinite leave to enter or remain;[8]

(7)   a decision that a person is to be removed from the UK by way of directions under s 10(1)(a), (b), (ba) or (c) of the IAA 1999 (ie as an overstayer; a person who has breached a condition of his or her leave to enter or remain; a person who has obtained leave to remain by deception; a person whose indefinite leave as a refugee has been revoked because the person has availed him or herself of the protection of the country from which asylum was sought or of another country or as the family member of someone being removed on these grounds).[9] In respect of a person with current leave the Secretary of State could curtail the person's leave (which would be an immigration decision of the kind mentioned in (5) above) as well as, or instead of, making a section 10 decision to give removal directions. However, if the Secretary of State chooses to make a section 10 decision only, that decision cannot be construed as also being a decision to vary the leave by curtailing it.[10]

(8)   a decision that an illegal entrant is to be removed from the UK;[11]

(9)   a decision that a person is to be removed from the UK by way of directions under para 10A of Sch 2 to the IA 1971 (ie as the family member of a person being removed as an illegal entrant or after refusal of leave to enter;

(10)   a decision to make a deportation order under s 5(1) of the IA 1971);[12]

(11)   a decision to make a deportation order under s 5(1) of the IA 1971, (other than a decision to make an 'automatic deportation' order against a 'foreign criminal' as defined in the UK Borders Act)[13] either following a recommendation to deport by a court under s 3(6) or on the ground that the person's deportation, or that of a family member, is deemed conducive to the public good under s 3(5);[14]

(12)   a decision by the Secretary of State that the UK Borders Act 2007, s 32(5) applies, ie that the person is a 'foreign criminal' (as defined) against whom the Secretary of State must make a deportation order;[15]

(13)   a refusal to revoke a deportation order;[16] including refusal to revoke an 'automatic deportation order', (ie, one made in accordance with the UK Borders Act 2007, s 32);[17]

(14)   a decision to give directions for the removal of an overstaying member of the crew of an aircraft or ship under para 12 of Sch 2 to the IA 1971;[18]

(15) a decision that a person is to be removed by way of directions given under s 47 of the IAN 2006;[19]

(16) a decision of the Secretary of State to make an order under the IA 1971, s 2A depriving a person of his or her right of abode on the ground that it would be conducive to the public good for the person to be excluded or removed from the UK.[20]

[1] NIAA 2002, s 82(2)(a).

[2] Immigration Act 1971, Sch 2, para 2A(9), including leave to enter or remain which had been given by an immigration officer or the Secretary of State for a period of more than six months so that it did not lapse on the person's departure from the UK and thus remained in force on his or her return: Immigration (Leave to Enter and Remain) Order 2000, SI 2000/1161.

[3] NIAA 2002, s 82(2)(b).

[4] NIAA 2002, s 82(2)(c).

[5] NIAA 2002, s 82(2)(d). If on being refused an extension of leave the person has leave that continues, even if only for some days, the refusal is not an 'immigration decision': *SA (Pakistan)* [2007] UKAIT 00083.

[6] NIAA 2002, s 82(2)(e). The variation 'takes effect' when it is notified to the person, not on the day when the leave is brought to an end by the variation if that happens at a later date than the notification. Consequently, a curtailment of leave which foreshortens but does not extinguish leave is not an 'immigration decision' because when it takes effect, the person still has leave: *R (on the application of Araromi) v Secretary of State for the Home Department* [2007] EWHC 2765 (Admin).

[7] *R (on the application of MK (Tunisia)) v Secretary of State for the Home Department* [2011] EWCA Civ 333.

[8] Ie revocation of indefinite leave to enter or remain because the person (i) is liable to deportation but cannot be deported for legal reasons (eg because deportation would breach Article 3 of the ECHR), (ii) obtained the leave by deception and would be liable to removal as a result but cannot be removed for legal or practical reasons, (iii) obtained the leave as a refugee but ceases to be a refugee as a result of a voluntary acquisition of nationality, establishment or availment of protection of his or her own or another country, or (iv) is a dependant of a person to whom (iii) applies. NIAA 2002, s 82(2)(f).

[9] NIAA 2002, s 82(2)(g).

[10] The tribunal had held in *CD (India)* [2008] UKAIT 00055 that it could be so construed but that proposition has been rejected by the Administrative Court in *R (on the application of Saleh) v Secretary of State for the Home Department* [2008] EWHC 3196 (Admin) and *R (on the application of Yu) v Secretary of State for the Home Department* [2008] EWHC 3072 (Admin) and by the Court of Appeal in *R (on the application of RK (Nepal)) v Secretary of State for the Home Department* [2009] EWCA Civ 359.

[11] NIAA 2002, s 82(2)(h).

[12] NIAA 2002, s 82(2)(i).

[13] UK Borders Act 2007, s 35(3), inserting the NIAA 2002, s 82(3A) in respect of a decision to make a deportation order in accordance with the UK Borders Act 2007, s 32(5).

[14] NIAA 2002, s 82(2)(j). A decision to make a deportation order following a recommendation by a court was not previously appealable. The Immigration Rules relating to deportation were radically amended on 20 July 2006 and again from 9 July 2012 by HC194. However, paras 378 and 381 of HC 395, as substituted from 2 October 2000 by HC 4851, have still not been brought up to date to reflect the creation of a right of appeal against a decision to make a deportation order following the recommendation of a court. The Rules (HC 395, para 378) wrongly state that there is no right of appeal against such a decision.

[15] UK Borders Act 2007, s 35(3), inserting the NIAA 2002, s 82(3A). In *Greenwood (Automatic Deportation: Order of Events)* [2014] UKUT 00342 (IAC), the UT held that: 'In an appeal against automatic deportation there is no appeal against a decision to deport or against the order to deport, but only against the decision that s 32(5) applies.'

[16] NIAA 2002, s 82(2)(k).

[17] *R (on the application of Mehmet) v Secretary of State for the Home Department* [2011] EWHC 741 (Admin), [2011] All ER (D) 28 (Apr). See also *R (on the application of AL (Angola)) v Secretary of State for the Home Department* [2010] EWCA Civ 1611 .

[18] NIAA 2002, s 82(2)(ia) as inserted by the Asylum and Immigration (Treatment of Claimants, etc) Act 2004, s 31, thereby restoring the old right of appeal which disappeared when NIAA 2002 was originally enacted.

[19] NIAA 2002, s 82(2)(ha). The Immigration, Asylum and Nationality Act 2006, s 47 which enables the Secretary of State to make the immigration decision that a person who has statutorily extended leave (ie by operation of the IA 1971, s 3C – leave pending a decision or an appeal) is to be removed from the UK after the leave ends and inserts s 82(2)(ha) into the NIAA 2002.

[20] NIAA 2002, s 82(ib). The power to make such orders and the corresponding right of appeal were created by the IAN 2006, s 57.

19.16 Decisions which are not appealable 'immigration decisions' for the purposes of section 82(1) of the NIAA 2002 (unamended by IA 2014) and which do not, therefore, give rise to a right of appeal under section 82 include:

- refusal of asylum;[1]
- refusal of a human rights claim;
- refusal to treat representations as a fresh human rights claim or claim for asylum;[2]
- refusal to grant a work permit;[3]
- the imposition of conditions of leave or refusal to revoke conditions;[4]
- the grant of a lesser period of leave than that sought;[5]
- refusal to grant leave to a person who had no leave at the date of the application;
- a decision of the competent authority that a person is not a victim of trafficking.[6]

The cancellation of leave when the holder is outside the common travel area, which did not previously attract a right of appeal, now does so because of the changed wording of the appeals provisions of section 82.[7]

[1] The refusal of asylum is not an 'immigration decision' for the purposes of s 82 of the NIAA 2002, unamended by the IA 2014, although it may be appealable under the limited circumstances dealt with by s 83 or s 83A considered in the next two paragraphs. Moreover, refusal of a claim for asylum or humanitarian protection will be appealable decisions under section 82 as substituted by the IA 2014, s 15(2).

[2] *R (on the application of ZA (Nigeria)) v Secretary of State for the Home Department* [2010] EWHC 718 (Admin).

[3] Work permit decisions were until 2001 the province of the Department of Work and Pensions or its previous incarnations, and although they were brought under the umbrella of the Home Office in 2001 there was still no appeal right. Work Permits have in any event been replaced by Tier 2 of the Points Based Scheme, and no applications for Work Permits have been possible since 27 November 2008.

[4] Conditions imposed under s 3(1)(c) of the IA 1971 were appealable under that Act, but were excluded under the IAA 1999, and their continued exclusion is achieved by the definition of 'immigration decision' in the NIAA 2002, s 82. Nor will there be any opportunity to challenge conditions of leave in the amended NIAA 2002, s 82 after amendment by IA 2014, s 15 (to be commenced).

[5] Curtailment of leave is however appealable as an immigration decision if it results in the person having no leave: s 82(2)(e).

[6] *R (on the application of AA (Iraq)) v Secretary of State for the Home Department* [2012] EWCA Civ 23.

[7] Under the Immigration (Leave to Enter and Remain) Order 2000, SI 2000/1161, art 13(2): NIAA 2002, s 82(2)(d). The wording of the appeals provisions of the 1999 Act (IAA 1999, s 61), couched in terms of being 'required to leave the UK within 28 days', manifestly precluded appeals against variation or refusal to vary leave while the holder was abroad. This wording was not repeated in the 2002 Act.

REFUSAL OF ASYLUM AND PROTECTION CLAIMS

19.17 When the IA 2014, s 15(2) is commenced, a decision by the Secretary of State to refuse a protection claim (ie a claim that removal from the UK would breach the UK's obligations under the Refugee Convention, or to a person eligible for humanitarian protection) will be one of the three kinds of decision appealable under NIAA 2002, s 82. At the time of writing, however, the IA 2014, s 15(2) has been commenced only to the limited extent described above in paragraph **19.12**. The new section 82 defines 'protection claim' for the purposes of Part 5 of the Act as a claim made by a person that his or her removal from the UK would breach the UK's obligations under the Refugee Convention, or the UK's obligations in relation to persons eligible for a grant of humanitarian protection.[1] The statutory definition makes no provision for the 'fresh claims' Immigration Rule to play a part in identifying a claim, by contrast to the prospectively amended definition of asylum and human rights claims in NIAA 2002, s 113. In the absence of such provision, refusal of a protection claim would be an appealable decision even if the person had previously made an unsuccessful claim and even if the new claim was not treated as a 'fresh claim'.[2]

1   NIAA 2002, s 82(2)(a), as substituted by IA 2014, s 15(2).
2   By analogy with *R (on the application of BA (Nigeria)) v Secretary of State for the Home Department* [2009] UKSC 7.

19.18 Save to the extent that the IA 2014, s 15(3) has been commenced, refusal of a claim for asylum is an appealable decision only if the person refused asylum has been granted leave to enter or remain for a period exceeding one year, or for periods exceeding one year in aggregate.[1] The grant of leave must follow the refusal of asylum; leave granted for more than a year but prior to the refusal of asylum will not suffice.[2] In this context, refusal of a claim for asylum includes a claim for humanitarian protection, or subsidiary protection, as well as a claim under the refugee Convention.[3] The grant of leave is the trigger, not the subject matter, of the right of appeal, and there does not have to be a nexus between the refusal of asylum and the grant of leave.[4] The two do not have to occur at the same time and a person may appeal under section 83 against the refusal of an asylum claim even if he or she has already challenged the refusal of that claim in the context of an appeal against an earlier 'immigration decision'.[5] A grant of indefinite leave to enter or remain is leave 'for a period exceeding one year' and so attracts the right of appeal under section 83.[6] The refusal of an asylum claim does not otherwise attract a right of appeal. A person refused asylum without being granted leave to enter or remain for more than a year may only appeal if, as well as being refused asylum, he or she is the subject of an 'immigration decision' within the meaning of section 82(2) of NIAA 2002. So, for example, if an overstayer or an illegal entrant made a claim for asylum and that claim was refused, the refusal of asylum would not be an appealable immigration decision. The person would only be able to appeal if an immigration decision was made to give directions for his or her removal from the UK. An appeal could then be brought against the immigration decision on the ground that removal would be contrary to the Refugee Convention.

1   NIAA 2002, s 83.

[2]   *R (Omondi) v Secretary of State for the Home Department* [2009] EWHC 827 (Admin); *Win (s 83 – order of events)* [2012] UKUT 00365 (IAC).
[3]   *FA (Iraq) v Secretary of State for the Home Department* [2010] EWCA Civ 696.
[4]   *R (on the application of Omondi) v Secretary of State for the Home Department* [2011] EWHC 627 (Admin) and, on appeal *AS (Somalia) v Secretary of State for the Home Department* [2011] EWCA Civ 1319.
[5]   *Abiyat (rights of appeal) Iran* [2011] UKUT 314 (IAC).
[6]   *S v First Tier Tribunal* [2011] EWHC 627 (Admin) and, on appeal *AS (Somalia) v Secretary of State for the Home Department* [2011] EWCA Civ 1319, [2011] 46 LS Gaz R 20.

19.19 Circumstances in which a refusal of asylum will not attract a right of appeal (prior to commencement of IA 2014, s 15(2)) include: where a person with extant leave to enter or remain makes an asylum claim and, when asylum is refused, the person still has leave but the leave was for one year or less;[1] where a person with extant leave to enter or remain is refused asylum but granted leave in some other capacity but the total period of leave is one year or less;[2] where an overstayer or illegal entrant makes a claim for asylum and, although asylum is refused, no decision to remove the person is made.[3] In such circumstances the asylum seeker's only remedy against the refusal of asylum would be judicial review.

[1]   This situation might have attracted an appeal under IAA 1999, s 69(3), but not under NIAA 2002, s 82(2)(d) because the applicant still has leave to enter or remain, or under s 83, because the leave was for a year or less.
[2]   This situation attracted an appeal under IAA 1999, s 69(3) but not under NIAA 2002, s 82(2)(e) because the applicant has leave when the variation takes effect, nor under s 83, because the leave is for a year or less.
[3]   There is no right of appeal in the absence of an 'immigration decision' under s 82(2)(g)–(i).

19.20 Section 83A of the NIAA 2002 provides a right of appeal for a person previously recognised as a refugee where the Secretary of State decides that the person is no longer a refugee, but, following that decision the person has leave to remain in the UK in some other capacity. This right of appeal was created following the change in policy whereby those recognised as refugees are given limited instead of indefinite leave to enter or remain.[1] As a result of this change of policy the question of whether a person continues to be entitled to refugee status will routinely arise – either when the person applies for further leave to remain or upon active review by the Secretary of State. The purpose of the right of appeal is to provide the opportunity for those who the Secretary of State decides are no longer refugees (following an 'active review'[2] or in response to an application for further leave to remain as a refugee) but who have leave in some other capacity to litigate the issue of their entitlement to refugee status.[3] It is not altogether clear how the right of appeal will arise. The appeal is against the decision to curtail or to refuse to extend leave to enter or remain to a person against whom there is a decision that he or she is not a refugee. However, the right of appeal is only available to a person who, following the decision that he or she is not a refugee, has limited leave to enter or remain other than as a refugee. It may be that the words 'as a refugee' have to be read into section 83A(2) so that it reads: 'The person may appeal to the Tribunal against the decision to curtail or to refuse to extend his limited leave *as a refugee*'.

[1]   Since 30 August 2005, those recognised as refugees have been granted leave to enter or remain for five years.
[2]   See asylum CHAPTER 12.

3   See Immigration, Asylum and Nationality Act 2006, Explanatory Notes, para 14.

EEA decisions

19.21 Since EEA nationals and their family members[1] do not require leave to enter, and must be admitted[2] (unless there are good reasons based on public policy, public security or public health for their exclusion),[3] the appeals regime which applies to them is a modified one.[4] An EEA national or a family member of an EEA national (or a person claiming to be an EEA national or a family member) may appeal to the FT or, in appropriate cases, to the SIAC against an 'EEA decision'.[5] An EEA decision is a decision made under the Immigration (European Economic Area) Regulations 2006 ('the Regulations') concerning a person's entitlement to be admitted to the UK, his or her entitlement to be issued with, have renewed or not have revoked a registration certificate, residence card, document certifying permanent residence or permanent residence card residence permit or residence document or the person's removal from the UK.[6] However, a person claiming to be an EEA national may not appeal under the Regulations unless he or she produces a valid national identity card or passport issued by an EEA State,[7] and someone claiming to be a family member of an EEA national may not appeal under the Regulations unless he or she can produce an EEA family permit or other proof of the relationship.[8]

1   As defined in regulation 7 of the Immigration (European Economic Area) Regulations 2006, SI 2006/1003, reg 7(1).
2   SI 2006/1003, reg 11.
3   SI 2006/1003, reg 19.
4   NIAA 2002, s 109(1).
5   SI 2006/1003, reg 26.
6   SI 2006/1003, reg 2.
7   SI 2006/1003, reg 26(2).
8   SI 2006/1003, reg 26(3). It was an error of law for the tribunal to reject a Church of England marriage certificate as being 'other proof that he is related as claimed to an EEA national': *R (on the application of Adetola) v First-tier Tribunal (Immigration and Asylum Chamber)* [2010] EWHC 3197 (Admin), [2011] 2 FLR 611, [2011] Fam Law 235.

DEPRIVATION OF CITIZENSHIP

19.22 Under provisions within the British Nationality Act 1981 (BNI 1981) the Secretary of State may by order deprive a person of his or her citizenship if the Secretary of State is satisfied that deprivation is conducive to the public good[1] or for obtaining citizenship by registration or naturalisation by fraud, false representation, or concealment of a material fact.[2] The Secretary of State must give the person notice of the decision to make the order[3] and the person given that notice may appeal against the decision before the order is made.[4] Under the old provisions for deprivation of citizenship in the 1981 Act,[5] there was no right of appeal against a decision to deprive a person of his or her British citizenship, although there was a right to appear before a specially appointed committee of inquiry. The 1981 Act provisions were never in fact invoked, and have been abolished and replaced by an appeal to the FT[6] or, if the decision was taken wholly or partly in reliance on information which the Secretary of State believes should not be made public for national security, political or other public interest reasons, to the SIAC.[7]

1   British Nationality Act 1981, s 40(2), as substituted by IAN 2006, s 56. Contrast this
    provision where the criterion for deprivation of citizenship is equated with that for the
    deportation of a non-citizen with the provision it replaces which required the Secretary of State
    to be satisfied that the person has done something which is seriously prejudicial to the vital
    interests of the UK.
2   BNA 1981, s 40(3) and (6) as substituted by NIAA 2002, s 4.
3   BNA 1981, s 40(5) as substituted.
4   BNA 1981, s 40A, inserted by NIAA 2002, s 4.
5   BNA 1981, s 40(6)–(9) (before amendment).
6   Under BNA 1981, s 40A(1) as inserted and amended by Asylum and Immigration (Treatment
    of Claimants, etc) Act 2004, Sch 2, para 4.
7   BNA 1981, s 40A(2) as inserted; Special Immigration Appeals Commission Act 1997, s 2B
    (inserted by NIAA 2002, s 4(2)).

HUMAN RIGHTS AND RACE DISCRIMINATION

19.23 When IA 2014, s 15(2) is commenced there will be a right of appeal
against refusal of a human rights claim. However, at the time of writing, the
provision has been commenced only to the limited extent described in
paragraph **19.12** above. Otherwise, only decisions of the kind set out above at
paragraph **19.14** above attract a right of appeal. Human rights and race
discrimination grounds can be relied on in appeals against immigration
decisions,[1] including EEA decisions,[2] and race discrimination claims can
sometimes be litigated in the county court.[3]

1   Under NIAA 2002, s 84(1)(b), (c) and (g). Section 84(1)(b) now provides, subsequent to
    amendment by the Crime and Courts Act 2013, s 51(1), a ground that 'the decision is unlawful
    by virtue of . . . [Article 20A of the Race Relations (Northern Ireland) Order 1997] [or by
    virtue of section 29 of the Equality Act 2010 (discrimination in the exercise of public
    functions, etc) so far as relating to race as defined by section 9(1) of that Act].
2   Immigration (European Economic Area) Regulations 2006, SI 2006/1003, reg 26(7) and Sch
    1.
3   See section 57A of the Race Relations Act 1976, which precludes the bringing of a claim where
    the issue of discrimination was or could have been raised in the immigration proceedings or it
    was raised and decided against the applicant. Equality Act 2006, s 67 has similar effect in
    respect of claims relating to discrimination on grounds of religion or belief under s 66 of that
    Act.

VENUE

19.24 Appeals against 'immigration decisions', 'EEA decisions', refusals of
asylum, curtailment of or refusal to extend leave as a refugee, refusal of a
protection claim, refusal of a human rights claim, revocation of protection
status, and deprivation of citizenship are normally made to the FT.[1] However,
a small number of people are excluded from the normal system of appeals
because of the political or national security grounds of the decision, and must
instead appeal to the SIAC.[2] The excluded decisions are:

(1)   a personal decision of the Secretary of State taken wholly or partly on
      the ground that the person's removal or exclusion from the UK is in the
      interests of national security or in the interests of the relationship
      between the UK and another country;[3]

(2) a decision taken in accordance with a personal direction from the Secretary of State, identifying the person to whom the decision relates and wholly or partly on national security or diplomatic grounds;[4]

(3) a decision taken wholly or partly in reliance on information which the Secretary of State personally certifies should not be made public for national security, diplomatic or other public interest reasons;[5]

(4) a decision to deprive a person of his or her citizenship taken wholly or partly in reliance on information which the Secretary of State certifies should not be made public for national security, diplomatic or other public interest reasons.[6]

1 NIAA 2002, s 82(1) (against immigration decisions); s 83(2) (against refusal of asylum); s 83A (against curtailment of or refusal to extend leave as a refugee); Immigration (European Economic Area) Regulations SI 2006/1003, reg 26(6) (against EEA decisions); and British Nationality Act 1981, s 40A(1) (inserted by section 4 of NIAA 2002) (against deprivation of citizenship).

2 Special Immigration Appeals Commission Act 1997, s 2(1) (in respect of immigration decisions and refusals of asylum and curtailment of or refusal to extend leave as a refugee), s 2B (inserted by NIAA 2002, s 4(2) (in respect of deprivation of citizenship); Immigration (European Economic Area) Regulations 2006, SI 2006/1003, reg 28(1) (in respect of EEA decisions).

3 NIAA 2002, s 97(1)(a), (2) and (4) in the case of immigration decisions, refusals of asylum and curtailment of or refusal to extend leave as a refugee; in the case of EEA decisions, the Immigration (European Economic Area) Regulations 2006, SI 2006/1003, reg 28(1), (2)(a) and (3).

4 NIAA 2002, s 97(1)(b), (2) and (4) in the case of immigration decisions, refusals of asylum and curtailment of or refusal to extend leave as a refugee; in the case of EEA decisions, the Immigration (European Economic Area) Regulations 2006, SI 2006/1003, reg 28(1), (2)(b) and (3).

5 NIAA 2002, s 97(3) and (4) in the case of immigration decisions, refusals of asylum and curtailment of or refusal to extend leave as a refugee; in the case of EEA decisions, the Immigration (European Economic Area) Regulations 2006, SI 2006/1003, reg 28(1) and (4).

6 British Nationality Act 1981, s 40A(2) as inserted by NIAA 2002, s 4.

EXCLUSION OF THE RIGHT OF APPEAL

19.25 The right of appeal against an immigration decision is presently excluded in the following cases:

(1) against a refusal of leave to enter, refusal of entry clearance, refusal to vary a leave to enter or remain, or a variation of leave to enter or remain taken on the ground that the person—

(i) does not satisfy a requirement as to age, nationality or citizenship specified in the Immigration Rules.[1] This would mean, for example, that a person refused leave to enter for settlement to join a parent on the ground that he or she was not under the age of 18, the requirement as to age contained in the rules, would not be able to appeal against the refusal;[2]

(ii) does not have an immigration document, ie an entry clearance, a passport, a work permit or other immigration employment document;[3]

(iii) failed to supply a medical report or medical certificate in accordance with a requirement of the Immigration Rules;[4]

    (iv)   is seeking to be in the UK for a period greater than that permitted by the Immigration Rules,[5] for example, an ordinary visitor seeking to enter the UK for more than six months;[6]

    (v)   is seeking to enter or remain in the UK for a purpose other than one permitted by the Immigration Rules;[7] or

    (vi)   is a dependant of a person in (i)–(v).[8]

However, a person otherwise excluded from appealing for these reasons may bring an appeal on human rights grounds, Equality Act 2010, race discrimination grounds or asylum grounds.[9] The exclusion of the right of appeal in the above cases is characterised as 'ineligibility' in the NIAA 2002.[10] The tribunal has highlighted that the 'ineligibility' provision operates where the decision is 'taken' on a particular ground, not where it is stated to have been taken on a particular ground. Consequently, so it held, albeit hesitantly, if the stated reason was one giving rise to ineligibility but it was apparent that the decision was not taken on the stated ground, eg because it bore no relation to the application that had been made then the right of appeal would not be excluded;[11]

(2)   against refusal of entry clearance as a visitor, short-term or prospective student or the dependant of such a student, although an appeal may be brought on Equality Act 2010 (race discrimination or human rights grounds);[12]

(3)   against refusal of entry clearance which was or had to be applied for under the Points Based Scheme unless the application for entry clearance was made for the purpose of visiting a person of a prescribed class or description or entering as the dependant of a person in prescribed circumstances; the provision does not exclude an appeal brought on race discrimination or human rights grounds;[13]

(4)   against refusal of entry clearance taken on grounds which relate to a provision of Immigration Rules specified for the purpose of the relevant statutory provision by order of the Secretary of State, except that an appeal could still be brought on race discrimination or human rights grounds.[14] No Immigration Rules have been specified for this specific purpose;

(5)   against refusal of leave to enter unless the person holds an entry clearance on arrival in the UK and the purpose of entry specified in the entry clearance is the same as that specified by the person when applying for leave to enter.[15] A person who arrives in the UK with non-lapsing leave[16] but no entry clearance will not be prevented by the want of entry clearance from appealing against cancellation of the leave. The cancellation of leave will be treated as a refusal of leave to enter and the cancelled leave as entry clearance.[17] The Tribunal has given the provision excluding the right of appeal against refusal of leave to enter a very narrow construction, holding that it does not operate against a person who is treated as having obtained leave to enter prior to arrival in the UK because he or she holds an entry clearance.[18] The provision does not exclude an appeal on asylum, human rights or race discrimination grounds;[19]

(6)   against a refusal of leave to enter the UK or a refusal of entry clearance taken by the Secretary of State personally on the grounds of the public good[20] although the bringing of an appeal on human rights, race discrimination and (in the case of a refusal of leave to enter) asylum grounds is not prevented.[21]

However, to the extent that the IA 2014, s 15(2) has been commenced, the right of appeal that is presently excluded in the circumstances described above will be abolished entirely. The statutory provisions that currently operate to exclude the right of appeal will themselves be repealed.[22] A right of appeal is also excluded in the following circumstances, applicable whether or not the 2014 Act is in force:

(7)   against a second immigration decision or a second decision to refuse a protection or human rights claim or revocation of protection status where there has been an earlier right of appeal, if the Secretary of State issues a certificate under NIAA 2002, s 96 (as to which, see below); and

(8)   against an EEA decision, where the appellant cannot produce proof of EEA nationality or membership of an EEA national's family.[23]

---

1   NIAA 2002, s 88(1) and (2)(a).

2   See HC 395, para 297(ii).

3   NIAA 2002, s 88(1), (2)(b) and (3). Clearly, this means the 'required' immigration document; entry clearance for visa nationals, work permits for those coming to work etc. IA 1971, Sch 2, para 4, and the Immigration Rules, HC 395, para 11, require persons arriving in the UK to produce a valid national passport or other document satisfactorily establishing their identity and nationality. Thus, if a passport is required it must be valid and must satisfactorily establish the person's identity (*MC (Gambia)* [2008] UKAIT 00030) and a work permit must be current, not expired (*DS (India)* [2008] UKAIT 00035. Note that s 88 applies not only to refusal of leave to enter but also to refusal of variation. Thus, a visitor seeking to remain for a purpose for which entry clearance is required would not get a right of appeal against refusal, for want of the relevant entry clearance: *R v Secretary of State for the Home Department, ex p Ahmed* [1995] Imm AR 590; on appeal [1996] Imm AR 260, CA.

4   NIAA 2002, s 88(2)(ba), inserted by the Immigration and Asylum Act 2006, s 5, from 31 August 2006.

5   NIAA 2002, s 88(1) and (2)(c).

6   See HC 395, para 41(i).

7   NIAA 2002, s 88(1) and (2)(d). Previously someone seeking to enter or remain for a purpose outside the Rules could appeal on the merits, since where there was no rule, there could be no request to the Secretary of State to depart from the rules: see *Rahman (Jinnah)* [1989] Imm AR 325 (a refugee recognised elsewhere seeking to transfer his status to the UK), see Fifth edition at 18.75. There is however an appeal on human rights grounds.

8   NIAA 2002, s 88(1) and (2).

9   NIAA 2002, s 88(4).

10   See headnote to the NIAA 2002, s 88.

11   *AM (Ghana)* [2009] UKAIT 0002.

12   NIAA 2002, s 88A. Prior to amendment by the Crime and Courts Act 2013, s 52(1), section 88A permitted certain appeals to be brought against refusal of entry clearance in certain categories of family visitor.

13   NIAA 2002, s 88A, substituted by Immigration, Asylum and Nationality Act 2006, s 4 in place of the previous s 88A but only to the extent that the application for entry clearance was of a kind identified in Immigration Rules as required to be made under the points based scheme (SI 2008/310, arts 3 and 4).

14   NIAA 2002, s 88A as inserted by Asylum and Immigration (Treatment of Claimants, etc) Act 2004, s 29 but substituted by Immigration, Asylum and Nationality Act 2006, s 4(1) subject to the savings in SI 2008/310, Arts 3 and 4.

15   IAA 2002, s 89(1) as substituted by the Immigration, Asylum and Nationality Act 2006, s 6, from 31 August 2006. The 'purpose' which has to be the same is the purpose specified by the person when applying for entry clearance and when arriving in the UK; the right of appeal is not excluded even if the immigration officer believes that the specified purpose is not the real

purpose for which entry is sought: *R (on the application of Aiyegbeni) v Secretary of State for the Home Department* [2009] EWHC 1241 (Admin).

[16] Ie leave to enter or remain which a person has when he or she leaves the UK and which was conferred either by an entry clearance (other than a visit visa) or was given by an Immigration Officer or the Secretary of State for a period of more than six months – Immigration (Leave to Enter and Remain) Order 2000, SI 2000/1161, art 13(2).

[17] IA 1971, Sch 2, para 2A(9).

[18] *GO (Nigeria)* [2008] UKAIT 00025.

[19] NIAA 2002, s 89(2) as substituted by the Immigration, Asylum and Nationality Act 2006, s 6.

[20] IA 2014, Sch 9, para 37.

[21] NIAA 2002, s 98(1)–(3).

[22] NIAA 2002, s 98(4), (5).

[23] EEA nationals must produce a valid national ID card or passport issued by an EEA Member State, and family members must produce an EEA family permit or other proof of the relationship: Immigration (European Economic Area) Regulations 2006, SI 2006/1003, reg 26(2) and (3).

OTHER RESTRICTIONS ON SCOPE OR SUBJECT-MATTER OF APPEALS

Third country cases

19.26 The restrictions imposed by the 1999[1] and 2002 Acts[2] on an asylum or human rights claimant's right of appeal against a decision to remove him or her to a third country have been extended by the 2004 Act which replaces the earlier provisions. Under Schedule 3 to the Asylum and Immigration (Treatment of Claimants, etc) Act 2004, presumptions of safety apply to varying degrees depending on the destination country. If it is an EU Member State (except Croatia), Iceland, Norway, or Switzerland, or another specified state,[3] the statutory presumption is that that state is deemed safe (ie a place where the claimant's life or liberty is not under threat by reason of race, religion, nationality, membership of a particular social group or political opinion, and which will not send the claimant elsewhere in contravention of the ECHR or otherwise than in accordance with the Refugee Convention).[4] Other specified states are deemed safe in respect of the Refugee Convention, but there is no statutory presumption that they will not remove the claimant in contravention of the Human Rights Convention.[5] Yet other specified states are deemed safe vis-à-vis Refugee Convention obligations for the particular individual.[6] In each case, the statutory presumption of safety, however cast, precludes an appeal on grounds which are inconsistent with it. This restriction is discussed at paragraph **12.143** ff above.

[1] IAA 1999, ss 11 and 12.

[2] NIAA 2002, s 80 (repealing and replacing IAA 1999, s 11).

[3] Asylum and Immigration (Treatment of Claimants, etc) Act 2004, Sch 3, Part 2 (paras 2–6), entitled 'First list of safe countries (Refugee Convention and Human Rights)' deal with EU Member States (except Croatia and Iceland, Norway and Switzerland; Part 3 (paras 7–11), entitled 'Second list of safe countries (Refugee Convention and Human Rights)' with states to be specified (none are so specified at time of writing).

[4] AI(TC)A 2004, Sch 3, para 3(2)(a)–(c).

[5] AI(TC)A 2004, Sch 3, Part 4, paras 14–16, entitled 'Third list of safe countries: Refugee Convention only', para 13(2)(a), (b). No states have yet been specified under this Part.

[6] AI(TC)A 2004, Sch 3, Part 5, paras 17–19, entitled 'Countries certified as safe for individuals'. This Part does not contain a statutory presumption of safety, but precludes appeal on a ground which is inconsistent with the Secretary of State's opinion.

IN-COUNTRY APPEALS AGAINST 'IMMIGRATION DECISIONS'

19.27 A person may not appeal against an immigration decision from within the UK unless his or her appeal is one to which s 92 of the NIAA 2002 applies or, although section 92 does not apply, the tribunal nevertheless hears the appeal without objection from the parties.[1] The IA 2014 substitutes a new section 92 (however, at the time of writing the original section 92 is preserved in respect of appeals against immigration decisions).[2] The new section 92 will be discussed below. The following discussion refers to the original, preserved section 92. Section 92 applies to immigration decisions of specified kinds and to all immigration decisions if certain kinds of claims have been made by the person. Thus it applies in the following circumstances:

(1) where the person has made a human rights claim or asylum claim[3] to the Secretary of State whilst in the UK and the claim is not certified by the Secretary of State as 'clearly unfounded' then the person can appeal against any immigration decision from within the UK.[4] If the person has previously made an asylum or human rights claim it is not necessary for the Secretary of State to accept a subsequent claim as being a 'fresh claim'[5] for section 92 to apply; the making of the claim is sufficient by itself;[6]

(2) an appeal against any kind of immigration decision can be brought from within the UK if the person is an EEA national or the family member of an EEA national and makes a claim to the Secretary of State that the decision breaches his or her community law rights;[7]

(3) where the appeal is against refusal of entry clearance the appeal cannot be brought from within the UK unless (1) or (2) above applies.[8] However, in practice there are likely to be few instances in which a person refused entry clearance could nevertheless gain admittance to the UK to appeal against the refusal;

(4) an appeal against refusal of leave to enter can be brought from within the UK if the person has an entry clearance.[9] However, if the refusal is on the ground that the leave to enter is being sought for a purpose other than one specified in the entry clearance, the person cannot rely upon the entry clearance to have an in-country appeal;[10]

(5) a person arriving in the UK with non-lapsing leave can appeal in-country against the cancellation of the leave[11] unless the cancellation of leave is on the ground that the person's purpose in arriving in the UK is different from that specified in the non-lapsed leave;[12]

(6) an appeal against refusal of leave to enter (or cancellation of leave treated as refusal of leave to enter) can be brought in-country, even if the grounds of refusal would otherwise prevent the appeal being brought in-country if the person is a British national[13] who holds a work permit and is in the UK;[14]

(7) an appeal against refusal of a certificate of entitlement to the right of abode can be brought in-country;[15]

(8) an appeal against a refusal to vary leave to enter or remain can be brought in-country;[16]

(9) an appeal against a variation or curtailment of leave can be brought in-country.[17] If the appealable variation takes the form of cancellation of a person's non-lapsing leave whilst he or she is outside the country, the person is entitled to appeal from within the UK, and thus to re-enter

the UK during the period within which notice of appeal could be given. That is because during that period, the person's leave is extended by IA 1971, s 3D.[18] However, the person may not re-enter the UK for the purpose of bringing an appeal if the Secretary of State personally certifies that the decision was taken on the ground that it is no longer conducive to the public good for the person to have leave.[19] A decision to give removal directions under section 10 of the Immigration and Asylum Act 1999 against a person with extant leave to enter or remain cannot be construed as also being a variation of leave and thus appealable in-country.[20]

(10)   an appeal against revocation of indefinite leave to remain as a refugee under the NIAA 2002, s 76 can be brought in-country;[21]

(11)   an appeal against a decision to remove the person as an overstayer, for breach of conditions, for deception in obtaining or seeking to obtain leave to remain, as a person whose indefinite leave to remain as a refugee has been revoked or as a family member of such a person cannot be brought in-country,[22] unless (1) or (2) above applies;

(12)   an appeal against a decision to remove a person as an illegal entrant cannot be brought in-country,[23] unless (1) or (2) above applies;

(13)   an appeal against a decision to remove a person as the family member of a person against whom removal directions have been given as an illegal entrant or following refusal of leave to enter cannot be brought in-country,[24] unless (1) or (2) above applies;

(14)   an appeal against a decision that a person with statutorily extended leave, is to be removed from the UK may be brought in-country;[25]

(15)   a decision to remove a member of a sea or aircrew who failed to embark with his or her ship or aircraft[26] may not be appealed in-country unless (1) or (2) above applies;

(16)   a decision to make an order that a person's right of abode be removed[27] cannot be appealed whilst the person is in the UK unless (1) or (2) above applies;

(17)   an appeal against a decision to make a deportation order can be brought in-country;[28] but a decision that the appellant is someone against whom an automatic deportation order is to be made is appealable in-country only if (1) or (2) above applies;

(18)   an appeal cannot be brought in-country against a refusal to revoke a deportation order,[29] unless (1) or (2) above applies;

(19)   where the Secretary of State certified before 1 October 2004 that an asylum seeker was being removed to a safe third country under sections 11(2) or 12(2) of the IAA 1999[30] (ie to countries which are members of the European Community or otherwise designated as a safe countries), unless the person makes a human rights claim which is not certified clearly unfounded;[31]

(20)   where the Secretary of State certifies after 1 October 2004 that an asylum or human rights claimant is to be removed to a safe third country under Sch 3 to the 2004 Act, and certifies the human rights claim clearly unfounded, he or she may not bring an appeal in country.[32]

---

[1]   *Pengeyo v Secretary of State for the Home Department* [2010] EWCA Civ 1275. In *R (on the application of Nirula) v First-Tier Tribunal (Asylum and Immigration Chamber)* [2012] EWCA Civ 1436, the Court of Appeal rejected the proposition that the Secretary of State was

obliged to raise an objection, on jurisdictional grounds, to an appeal proceeding before the FT; this was a point that the FT was capable of raising for itself. Further, the Secretary of State can be treated as having raised a jurisdictional point in any event, merely by asserting within a notice of immigration decision that an appeal against such decision could only be brought after departure from the UK.

2   IA 2014 (Commencement No 3, Transitional and Saving Provisions) Order 2014, SI 2014/2771, arts 1(2)(d) and 9.

3   Within the meaning of NIAA 2002, s 113.

4   NIAA 2002, s 92(4)(a).

5   Within the meaning of para 353 of the Immigration Rules. See *ZT (Kosovo) v Secretary of State for the Home Department* [2009] UKHL 6, [2009] 1 WLR 348.

6   *R (on the application of BA (Nigeria)) v Secretary of State for the Home Department* [2009] UKSC 7. It should be noted that unless an immigration decision is made the person making an asylum or human rights claim has no right of appeal at all, whether from within or without the UK. The making of the asylum or human rights claim does not by itself attract a right of appeal, nor does a decision refusing to accept the claim as a 'fresh claim': *R (on the application of ZA (Nigeria)) v Secretary of State for the Home Department* [2010] EWHC 718 (Admin).

7   NIAA 2002, s 92(4)(b).

8   NIAA 2002, s 92. Refusal of entry clearance is an immigration decision under s 82(2)(b) and so not one of the decisions to which s 92(2) applies.

9   NIAA 2002, s 92(3).

10 NIAA 2002, s 92(3C).

11 By reliance on the NIAA 2002, s 92(3) because the leave is treated as entry clearance and the cancellation of the leave as refusal of leave to enter (IA 1971, Sch 2, para 2A(9)).

12 NIAA 2002, s 92(3A) and (3B).

13 Ie a British Overseas Territories citizen, a British Overseas citizen, a British National (Overseas), a British Protected person or a British subject: NIAA 2002, s 92(3D)(c), inserted by the Asylum and Immigration (Treatment of Claimants, etc) Act 2004, s 28.

14 NIAA 2002, s 92(3D), as inserted. Before the 2004 Act amendment, possession of a work permit was by itself sufficient to confer an in-country right of appeal against refusal of leave to enter.

15 NIAA 2002, s 92(1) applying because such a decision is an immigration decision under s 82(2)(c), one of those listed in s 92(2).

16 NIAA 2002, s 92(1) applying because such a decision, being an immigration decision under s 82(2)(d) of the Act, and therefore one to which s 92(2) applies.

17 Being an immigration decision of a kind specified in the NIAA 2002, s 82(2)(e) and to which section 92(2) therefore applies.

18 *R(MK (Tunisia)) v Secretary of State for the Home Department* [2011] EWCA Civ 333 .

19 NIAA 2002, s 97B, introduced by Crime and Courts Act 2013, s 53(3) in response to *R (MK (Tunisia)) v Secretary of State for the Home Department.*

20 *R (on the application of RK (Nepal)) v Secretary of State for the Home Department* [2009] EWCA Civ 359. See further **19.15** fn 10, above.

21 Because it is an immigration decision listed in the NIAA 2002, s 92(2).

22 By virtue of the IAA 1999, s 10: removal is an immigration decision under the NIAA 2002, s 82(2)(g) which is not in the list of decisions appealable within the UK in s 92(2).

23 Ie under the IA 1971, Sch 2, para 9. Such a decision is an immigration decision under the NIAA 2002, s 82(2)(h) and so not one of the decisions that can be appealed in-country by operation of the NIAA 2002, s 92(2).

24 Ie under the IA 1971, Sch 2, para 10A, inserted by the NIAA 2002, s 73(1), which is an immigration decision under the IAA 2002, s 82(2)(i) but not one of those listed in section 92(2).

25 IAN 2006, s 47 adding such a decision to the list of immigration decisions to which the NIAA 2002, s 92(2) applies.

26 NIAA 2002, s 82(2)(ia).

27 NIAA 2002, s 82(2)(ib).

28 NIAA 2002, s 82(2)(j).

29 Ie an immigration decision under the NIAA 2002, s 82(2)(k).

30 NIAA 2002, s 93, repealed by the Asylum and Immigration (Treatment of Claimants, etc) Act 2004, ss 33(3)(b), 47, Sch 4 from 1 October 2004. For the transitional provisions see SI 2004/2523, Art 3. By the Asylum (Designated Safe Third Countries) Order 2000 SI

2000/2245, Canada, Norway, Switzerland and the United States of America are designated safe third countries. IAA 1999, ss 11 and 12 were substituted by the NIAA 2002, s 80, also repealed by the AI(TC)A 2004, s 33(2).
31 NIAA 2002, s 93(2), repealed as above.
32 Asylum and Immigration (Treatment of Claimants, etc) Act 2004, Sch 3, paras 5, 10, 15, 19.

19.28 As can be seen from the foregoing paragraph, whether an appeal can be brought in-country depends in many cases on whether the person 'has made an asylum claim, or a human rights claim, while in the United Kingdom'.[1] If the person has made such a claim, the NIAA 2002, s 92 applies and the appeal can be brought in-country. In this context, an asylum or human rights claim is defined by the NIAA 2002, s 113 as a claim made to the Secretary of State at a place designated by her that to remove the person would breach the UK's obligations under the Refugee Convention or the person's rights under the European Convention on Human Rights.[2] Section 113, as currently in force, applies both to initial and subsequent asylum and human rights claims; it is not necessary for the subsequent claim to be accepted by the Secretary of State as a 'fresh claim'[3] in order for it to fall within the s 113 definition[4] and thus for section 92 to apply. However, there does have to be a new claim; the fact of having made a claim in the past is not sufficient.[5] If and when the new section 113[6] is brought into force, the subsequent claim will not fall within the definition of asylum or human rights claim unless the Immigration Rules relating to fresh claims are satisfied. Prior to 4 April 2005 (when appeals to the Asylum and Immigration Tribunal replaced appeals to adjudicators), an asylum or human rights claim within the statutory definition could be made by including an asylum or human rights ground in a notice of appeal. That was because the Procedure Rules then applicable provided for notice of appeal to be given to the Secretary of State.[7] The AIT Procedure Rules 2005 required notice of appeal to be given to the Tribunal[8] not to the Secretary of State, so that an asylum or human rights ground contained in a notice of appeal does not meet the current statutory definition of a claim (both in respect of the person to whom and the place where such a claim must be made) and therefore would not entitle the person to an in-country right of appeal.[9] Similarly under the Tribunal Procedure Rules[10] notice of appeal is given to the Tribunal. It was said by the Administrative Court in *Nirula* that the human rights or asylum claim has to have been made prior to the immigration decision, if it is to enable an appeal to be brought in country.[11] However, whilst the Court of Appeal upheld the decision in *Nirula*, it deliberately refrained from endorsing that part of the Court's reasoning.[12] To have done so would have been to uphold a conclusion that was not necessitated by the language of the statute, but that would have been completely at odds with the presumption that Parliament intends to legislate justly, fairly, and reasonably.[13] Consider, for example, a settled person unexpectedly served with an appealable decision to remove her, perhaps because she belongs to the family of an immigration offender.[14] It is barely conceivable that as a person enjoying indefinite leave to remain she would have had any reason to have made an asylum or human rights claim before such a decision was made. It is equally inconceivable that Parliament would have legislated, other than by unambiguous provision, to allow appeals brought on asylum and human rights grounds to be in-country, but not in the circumstances of the kind postulated. The prospectively amended section 113 does not specify the person to whom the asylum or human rights claim must be made, nor the place where the claim must be made.

1 NIAA 2002, s 92(4)(a).
2 NIAA 2002, s 113. Immigration, Asylum and Nationality Act 2006, s 12 will substitute new definitions of an asylum claim and a human rights claim in the NIAA 2002, s 113 but is not yet in force.
3 Immigration Rules, para 353.
4 *BA (Nigeria) v Secretary of State for the Home Department* [2009] UKSC 7, [2009] 3 WLR 1253.
5 *R (on the application of Etame) v Secretary of State for the Home Department* [2008] EWHC 1140 (Admin), [2008] 4 All ER 798 which was approved by the Court of Appeal on this point in *R (on the application of BA (Nigeria)) v Secretary of State for the Home Department* [2009] EWCA Civ 119.
6 As substituted by the Immigration and Asylum Act 2006, s 12, but not yet in force.
7 *SS (Turkey)* [2006] UKAIT 00074.
8 Asylum and Immigration Tribunal (Procedure) Rules 2005, SI 2005/230, r 6(2).
9 *SS (Turkey)*.
10 Tribunal Procedure (First-tier Tribunal) (Immigration and Asylum Chamber) Rules 2014 SI 2014/2604, with effect from 20 October 2014.
11 *R (on the application of Nirula) v First-Tier Tribunal* [2011] EWHC 3336. Nirula was followed on this point in *R (on the application of Alighanbari) v Secretary of State for the Home Department* [2013] EWHC 1818 (Admin), but both parties had agreed that *Nirula* was correctly decided on the issue.
12 *R (on the application of Nirula) v First-Tier Tribunal (Asylum and Immigration Chamber)(IAC)* [2012] EWCA Civ 1436.
13 *Hampstead Heath Winter Swimming Club v Corpn of London* [2005] EWHC 713 (Admin) and *R (on the application of S) v Secretary of State for the Home Department* [2007] EWCA Civ 546 where Carnwath LJ referred to 'the principles of fairness and consistency which underlay the whole statutory scheme'.
14 Under the Immigration and Asylum Act 1999, s 10(1)(c).

EEA DECISIONS

19.29 In general a person may not appeal from within the UK against an EEA decision refusing admission to the UK, making an exclusion order, refusing to revoke a deportation or exclusion order, refusing to issue an EEA family permit, to revoke, or to refuse to issue or renew any document under these Regulations where that decision is taken at a time when the relevant person is outside the United Kingdom, or to remove a person who entered or sought entry in breach of a deportation or exclusion order.[1] However, in respect of decisions to refuse to admit to the UK or to make an exclusion order, the appeal may be brought whilst the person is in the UK if: (a) the person held an EEA family permit, a registration certificate, a residence card, a derivative residence card, a document certifying permanent residence, a permanent residence card or qualifying EEA State residence card on arrival in the UK, or can otherwise prove that he or she is resident in the UK; (b) the person has been in the UK with temporary admission or in immigration detention for three months or more when given notice of the decision; or (c) has made an asylum or human rights claim (or both), unless the Secretary of State has certified that the claim or claims is or are 'clearly unfounded'.[2] An appeal against a decision to remove a person from the UK after entering in breach of a deportation or exclusion order may be brought from within the UK if the person has made an asylum or human rights claim (or both), unless the Secretary of State has certified that the claim or claims is or are clearly unfounded.[3] Even if an asylum or human rights claim is made in the UK, an appeal against an EEA decision refusing to revoke a deportation order may only be brought from outside the

UK.[4]

1   Immigration (European Economic Area) Regulations 2006, SI 2006/1003, reg 27(1).
2   SI 2006/1003, reg 27(2), as amended.
3   SI 2006/1003, reg 27(3).
4   *R (on the application of BXS) v Secretary of State for the Home Department* [2014] EWHC 737 (Admin), appeal to the Court of Appeal pending at the time of writing.

CERTIFICATION OF ASYLUM AND HUMAN RIGHTS CLAIMS

19.30 By certifying an asylum or human rights claim under NIAA 2002, s 94 as 'clearly unfounded', the Secretary of State can prevent an appeal from being brought from within the UK if, but for the asylum or human rights claim, it would have to have been brought after the person had left the UK.[1] Moreover, if a person makes an asylum or human rights claim which is certified as 'clearly unfounded' he or she is thereby prevented from appealing in-country against the following immigration decisions which would, without the asylum or human rights claim, have been appealable in-country: refusal of a certificate of entitlement to the right of abode; refusal to vary leave; variation of leave and a decision to remove a person with statutorily extended leave.[2] Certification of an asylum or human rights claim as clearly unfounded cannot prevent an appeal from being brought in-country against revocation of indefinite leave under NIAA 2002, s 76 or against a decision to make a deportation order.[3] Nor can it prevent an appeal from being brought in-country if a community law claim has been made by an EEA national or a family member of an EEA national.[4] However, if the Secretary of State certifies that it is proposed to remove the person to a country of which he or she is not a citizen and that there is no reason to believe that the person's rights under the ECHR will be breached in that country, then the making of an asylum, human rights or community law claim do not entitle the person to appeal in-country.[5] Certification under NIAA 2002, s 94 only prevents an appeal from being brought and 'brought' in this context refers to the single event of instituting an appeal; it does not refer to the subsequent process.[6] Thus, once notice of appeal has been given, an appeal cannot be stopped by the issue of a certificate under NIAA 2002, s 94.

1   NIAA 2002, s 94(2), the effect of the certificate being to prevent reliance on s 92(4)(a).
2   NIAA 2002, s 94(1A) inserted by the Asylum and Immigration (Treatment of Claimants, etc) Act 2004, s 27.
3   Because NIAA 2002, s 94(1A) does not disapply s 92(2) in respect of immigration decisions specified in s 82(2)(f) and (j). However, after commencement of IA 2014, ss 15 and 17(2) (date to be notified), appeals against refusals of a 'protection claim' as defined under the new s 82(1)(a) of NIAA 2002, or of a 'human rights claim' (NIAA 2002, s 82(1)(b)) may be certified under s 94(1) or (7), or NIAA 2002, s 94B even after an appeal has been brought from within the UK, such that the appeals must to be continued from outside the UK.
4   Because NIAA 2002, s 94 has no effect on the application of s 92(4)(b).
5   NIAA 2002, s 94(7).
6   *R (on the application of AM (Somalia)) v Secretary of State for the Home Department* [2009] EWCA Civ 114. However, see footnote 3 above as to the position after commencement of IA 2014, ss 15 and 17(2).

IN COUNTRY APPEALS: POST-IMMIGRATION ACT 2014

19.31 The IA 2014 substitutes a new section 92 in the NIAA 2002. At the time of writing, it has been brought into effect only in relation to those persons for whom the 2014 Act rights of appeal have been substituted for the pre-2014 Act rights of appeal. In other words, it applies to those who become foreign criminals on or after 20 October 2014 and persons liable to deportation as their family members;[1] 'foreign criminals' and those belonging to the families of foreign criminals against whom deportation decisions are made on or after 10 November 2014;[2] those who applied for leave to remain as a Tier 4 migrant on or after 20 October 2014, and those applying for leave to remain as a partner or child of such a person.[3] If the new section 92 applies, an appeal against refusal of a protection claim must be brought from within the UK[4] unless the Secretary of State certifies the person's claim as clearly unfounded, or certifies that the person is to be removed to a third country of which he or she is not a citizen, and where there is no reason to believe that the person's human rights would be breached[5] or the person claims that removal to the specified safe third country would breach the refugee convention.[6] In those circumstances, the appeal must be brought from outside the UK. An appeal against refusal of a human rights claim must be brought from within the UK[7] unless the human rights claim was made whilst the person was outside the UK[8] or the Secretary of State certifies the claim as being clearly unfounded, or that the person is to be removed to a country of which he or she is not a citizen, and there is no reason to believe that the person's human rights would be breached there.[9] In those circumstances, the appeal must be brought from outside the UK.[10] An appeal against revocation of protection status must be brought from within the UK if the decision to be appealed against was made whilst the person was in the UK; if the decision was made whilst the person was outside the UK, the appeal must be brought from outside the UK.[11]

[1]   IA 2014 (Commencement No 3, Transitional and Saving Provisions) Order 2014, SI 2014/2771, arts 1(d), 2(d) and 9.
[2]   IA 2014 (Transitional and Saving Provisions) Order 2014, SI 2014/2928, art 2.
[3]   SI 2014/2771, arts 1(d), 2(d) and 9.
[4]   NIAA 2002, s 92(2), as substituted by IA 2014, s 17(2).
[5]   NIAA 2002, s 92(2)(a), as substituted by IA 2014, s 17(2), providing for certification under NIAA 2002, s 94(1) or 94(7) (as amended by IA 2014, Sch 9, para 38).
[6]   NIAA 2002, s 92(2)(b) (as substituted by IA 2014, s 17(2)).
[7]   NIAA 2002, s 92(3), as substituted by IA 2014, s 17(2).
[8]   NIAA 2002, s 92(4), as substituted by IA 2014, s 17(2).
[9]   NIAA 2002, s 92(3)(a), as substituted by IA 2014, s 17(2), providing for certification under the NIAA 2002, s 94(1) or s 94(7) as amended by IA 2014, Sch 9, para 38.
[10]   NIAA 2002, s 92(3).
[11]   NIAA 2002, s 92(5) (as substituted by IA 2014, s 17(2)).

19.32 The IA 2014 has created a new power to certify human rights claims by introducing section 94B into the NIAA 2002. Its purpose is to ensure that appeal rights available to a person liable to deportation should generally be exercised from outside the UK. If such a certificate is issued to a person, any appeal that he or she may bring against refusal of the human rights claim must be brought or continued from outside the UK.[1] A certificate may be issued to a person who has made a human rights claim if he or she is liable to deportation because the Secretary of State deems deportation conducive to the public good or because deportation has been recommended by the court (but not where liability arises as a result of belonging to a deportee's family). The Secretary of State may certify the claim if she or he considers that removal pending the outcome of the appeal would not be unlawful under Human Rights Act 1998, s 6 (ie, that it would not be incompatible with a Convention right). A certificate may be issued before an appeal is commenced or whilst it is ongoing. The provision highlights that that ground upon which a claim may be certified includes, in particular, that the person would not, before the appeals process is exhausted, face a real risk of serious irreversible harm if removed. The reference to 'serious irreversible harm' is redolent of the European Court of Human Rights criterion for making a rule 39 interim measure.[2] The Home Office's guidance is that a claim made wholly or partly on article 2 or 3 grounds may not be certified under this provision.[3] It is also important to note that even if removal pending determination of an appeal would not create a real risk of serious irreversible harm, it may nevertheless be unlawful under the HRA 1998, s 6.

[1] NIAA 2002, s 92(3)(a) and s 92(6) (as substituted by IA 2014 s 17(2)).
[2] European Court of Human Rights Practice Direction on Interim Measures.
[3] Home Office: *Section 94B Certification guidance for Non-European Economic Area deportation cases*, para. 2.4 (version 2.0, 20 October 2014).

19.33 Although the effect of section 94B is to prevent appeals against refusal of a human rights claim under the new, 2014 Act appeals provisions from being brought or continued[1] the commencement provisions operate so that a certificate under section 94B can prevent an in-country appeal against an immigration decision to make a deportation order, to refuse to revoke a deportation order, or a decision that the automatic deportation provisions applied. From 28 July 2014 until 20 October 2014, if the Secretary of State issued a certificate under section 94B in respect of a 'foreign criminal'[2] who made a human rights claim, he or she would not be able to rely upon section 92 to appeal whilst in the UK against one of those immigration decisions.[3] The 2014 Act appeals provisions would apply to those who become foreign criminals on or after 20 October 2014, or against whom a deportation decision is made on or after 10 November 2014.[4]

[1] That is, it prevents appeals under the substituted NIAA 2002, s 82 against refusal of an asylum claim from being brought, or continued by operation of the substituted NIAA 2002, s 92.
[2] As defined in NIAA 2002, s 117D.
[3] The IA 2014 (Commencement No 1, Transitory and Saving Provisions) Order 2014, SI 2014/1820, articles 3 and 4; article 4 and the IA 2014 (Commencement No 3, Transitory and Saving Provisions) Order 2014, SI 2014/2771, arts 14, 15.
[4] SI 2014/2771, arts 9, 10 and SI 2014/2928.

19.34 An appeal against refusal of a protection or human rights claim brought whilst the appellant is in the UK may not be continued in the UK if the Secretary of State: (a) certifies the claim to which the appeal relates as clearly unfounded,[1] or (b) certifies that the appellant is to be removed to a country of which he or she is not a citizen and there is no reason to believe that the person's human rights would be breached there[2] or, (c) in the case of a person liable to deportation, the Secretary of State certifies that removal would not be unlawful under the HRA 1998, s 6.[3] In addition, where a section 94A certificate is issued (in accordance with the provisions referred to in the previous paragraph) an appeal against an immigration decision to make, or to refuse to revoke a deportation order, or that the automatic deportation provisions apply, may not be continued whilst the appellant is in the UK. This marks a significant contrast with the certification provisions in force prior to IA 2014 when the issue of a certificate could prevent an appeal from being commenced but had no effect upon an appeal that had already been instituted.[4] However, even though an appeal may not be continued in these circumstances, the appeal remains pending[5] because certification of an appeal that has been instituted is not one of the events exhaustively identified in the statutory definition of 'pending' that brings an appeal to an end. As discussed in the following paragraph, a person who has a pending appeal may not be removed from the UK whilst his or her appeal is pending. Thus, whilst a person in respect of whom a section 94B certificate is issued after commencing an appeal may not continue the appeal whilst still in the UK, he or she may not be removed either.[6] Moreover, whilst the person remains irremovable owing to the pending appeal, a deportation order made under the automatic deportation provisions[7] does not have the effect of invalidating the person's leave.[8] Evidently, Parliament's intention in enacting the new certification provisions was not to discard the long established principle that a person with a pending appeal should not be removed whilst the appeal is pending but to introduce an incentive to depart the UK to such a person, in the form of having to be outside the UK to continue the appeal.

1   NIAA 2002, s 94(2).
2   NIAA 2002, s 94(7).
3   NIAA 2002, s 94B, as inserted by IA 2014, s 17(3).
4   *R (on the application of AM (Somalia)) v Secretary of State for the Home Department* [2009] EWCA Civ 114.
5   Within the meaning of NIAA 2002, s 104.
6   NIAA 2002, s 78 which is not amended by IA 2014, indicating that Parliament's intention continues to be that a person with a pending appeal may not be removed from the UK.
7   Under the UK Borders Act 2007, s 32(5).
8   NIAA 2002, s 79(4).

SUSPENSORY EFFECT OF AN APPEAL

19.35   Once an appeal to the tribunal against an 'immigration decision' or a decision to refuse a protection claim, a human rights claim or to revoke protection status under section 82(1) of NIAA 2002[1] is pending, then the appellant cannot be removed from or required to leave the UK.[2] However, removal directions can be given, or a deportation order made, while the appeal is pending[3] although a deportation order (other than an 'automatic deportation order' against a 'foreign criminal'[4]) may not be made if an appeal has been or could be brought against the decision to make the deportation order.[5] Appeals against EEA decisions refusing admission to or removing or deporting from the UK are of suspensive effect[6] but appeals against refusal to issue or renew or to revoke a registration certificate or residence card are not.[7] If the Secretary of State certifies that the decision to make a deportation order was taken on national security grounds, a deportation order can be made even if there is a right of appeal against the decision to make the deportation order.[8] An appeal is 'pending' once it is 'instituted',[9] ie by giving notice of appeal in accordance with the Tribunal Procedure rules[10] even if the Tribunal makes a decision[11] that the notice of appeal was given out of time if the evidence shows that the notice of appeal was given in time.[12] An appeal remains 'pending' until it is finally determined, withdrawn or abandoned or until it lapses.[13] An appeal is not finally determined while an application for permission to appeal to the Upper Tribunal or to the Court of Appeal could be made or is awaiting determination or has been granted and the appeal is awaiting determination or an appeal has been remitted to the tribunal or Upper Tribunal and is awaiting determination.[14] The earlier definition of the period during which an appeal was pending said that an appeal is not pending where an application for reconsideration or for permission to appeal has been or could be made outside the time limits provided under the Procedure Rules[15] and it was construed so that if the Court of Appeal granted permission to appeal on an application brought out of time, the appeal was once again 'pending'.[16] The current statutory provision does not exclude the period during which an out of time application for permission to appeal is pending. There have been a significant number of occasions when administrative failure or incompetence on the part of the immigration authorities has resulted in the illegal removal of individuals whose pending appeals constituted a statutory bar to removal.[17]

[1]   ie, an appeal under section 82(1) either before or after its amendment by the IA 2014.

[2]   NIAA 2002, s 78(1)(a), (b). This provision also applies to appeals under 'the old appeals provisions' (eg appeals under the 1971 Act against deportation as an overstayer under the transitional provisions): see the Nationality, Immigration and Asylum Act 2002 (Commencement No 4) Order 2003, SI 2003/754, Sch 2, para 1(3).

[3]   NIAA 2002, s 78(3).

[4]   UK Borders Act 2007, s 35(2), amending NIAA 2002, s 79 so that it does not apply to deportation orders made in accordance with the UK Borders Act 2007, s 32(5).

[5]   NIAA 2002, s 79.

[6]   Immigration (European Economic Area) Regulations 2006, SI 2006/1003, reg 29.

[7]   *R (on the application of Abdullah) v Secretary of State for the Home Department* [2009] EWHC 1771 (Admin).

[8]   NIAA 2002, s 97A(2)(a).

[9]   NIAA 2002, s 104(1)(a).

[10]   Tribunal Procedure (First-tier Tribunal) (Immigration and Asylum Chamber) Rules 2014. *R (on the application of Erdogan) v Secretary of State for the Home Department* [2004] EWCA Civ 1087, [2004] All ER (D) 421, decided in relation to Asylum and Immigration Tribunal (Procedure) Rules 2005, SI 2005/230, r 6(1) which is materially similar.

[11]   SI 2005/230, r 10(6).

[12]   *EA (Ghana)* [2006] UKAIT 00036.

[13]   NIAA 2002, s 104(1)(b). An appeal 'lapses' by virtue of s 99 of NIAA 2002 when a certificate is issued under s 97 or 98 (national security or other public good grounds). The section also provides for appeals to lapse following certification under s 96 (earlier appeal raising similar grounds), but following its amendment by Asylum and Immigration (Treatment of Claimants, etc) Act 2004, as from 1 October 2004 (SI 2004/2523), s 96 cannot be applied to appeals in progress: s 96(7).

[14]   NIAA 2002, s 104(2) (substituted by the Transfer of Functions of the Asylum and Immigration Tribunal Order 2010, SI 2010/21 from 15 February 2010).

[15]   NIAA 2002, s 104(2)(a) and (d) as substituted; see *R (on the application of Erdogan) v Secretary of State for the Home Department* [2004] EWCA Civ 1087, [2004] All ER (D) 421 (Jul), decided under the unamended provisions of s 104, where the Court of Appeal reversed the Administrative Court's decision that an asylum claimant had an appeal 'pending' (and so did not lose asylum support) when what he had pending was an application for permission to appeal out of time. However, the court (and the Secretary of State) agreed that once permission has been given to appeal out of time, the appeal has been (re)-instituted and is again pending: para 13. For out of time appeals see further CHAPTER 20 below.

[16]   *YD (Turkey) v Secretary of State for the Home Department* [2006] EWCA Civ 52, [2006] 1 WLR 1646.

[17]   See for example *R (on the application of E) v Secretary of State for the Home Department* [2006] EWHC 3208 (Admin).

19.36 In cases where there is a dispute as to whether the right of appeal is in-country or out-of-country (eg a dispute as to whether the appellant had made an asylum or human rights claim before the relevant decision was made, or whether a current entry clearance when refused leave to enter, or sought leave to enter for a different purpose), can the appellant seek to have the issue determined by the Tribunal, or does he or she have to bring judicial review proceedings to determine whether the appeal is in-country? Under earlier procedure rules, where a notice of appeal is lodged from within the UK, removal could only be effected once the dispute is finally determined against the appellant by the appellate authority.[1] The 2005 Procedure Rules made provision for the Tribunal to determine the timeliness of an appeal as a preliminary issue,[2] but not for any wider issues of validity to be determined as such. To the contrary, they provide that where a person has given notice of appeal but there is no relevant decision (defined as a decision against which there is an exercisable right of appeal to the Tribunal), the Tribunal must not accept the notice of appeal, but must notify the person who gave the notice, and the respondent, and take no further action.[3] Similar provision is made by the current Tribunal Procedure Rules.[4]

1 See *Lokko* [1990] Imm AR 111, decided under the Immigration Appeals (Procedure) Rules 1984, SI 1984/2041.
2 Asylum and Immigration Tribunal (Procedure) Rules 2005, SI 2005/230, r 10.
3 SI 2005/230, r 9.
4 Tribunal Procedure (First-tier Tribunal) (Immigration and Asylum Chamber) Rules 2014, SI 2014/2604, r 22.

19.37 Where the appeal suspends removal, the ban on removal pending appeal does not however prevent detention under the administrative provisions of Schedules 2 and 3 to IA 1971. The powers to give directions for a person's removal or to make a deportation order against him or her whilst an appeal is pending enable those powers of detention to be exercised.[1] For the exercise of detention powers under these provisions see Chapter 18 above.

1 NIAA 2002, s 78(3).

19.38 An appeal under NIAA 2002, s 82(1) against the refusal to vary leave which is an immigration decision under section 82(2)(d) has similar effect. A person's leave is extended by Immigration Act 1971, s 3C whilst any appeal under section 82(1) against 'the decision on the application' could be brought or is pending,[1] as long as the application for leave to remain was made before the original leave expired and the decision on the application to vary leave was made after the original leave expired.[2] It is unclear what effect IA 2014, substituting a new section 82, will have on the operation of IA 1971, s 3C. On one view, the new section 82(1) does not provide a right of appeal against 'the decision on the application for variation'. It only provides rights of appeal against refusal of protection and human rights claims or revocation of protection status, and those are not the kinds of appeal to which IA 1971, s 3C refers. On another and better view, if a person who has leave to enter or remain makes a human rights or protection claim, the claim is, in substance, an application to vary the person's leave, and the refusal of such an application is, in substance, a decision on the application for variation. The appeal under section 82(1) against the decision to refuse the protection or human rights claim is, therefore, in substance, an appeal against the decision on the application for variation, and so section 3C applies. The second view better reflects what Parliament must have intended when, by the 2014 Act it amended section 3C to align it with the new section 82 by providing for administrative review, but leaving untouched those parts of section 3C relating to section 82(1) appeals.

[1] IA 1971, s 3C(2)(b) and (c) (inserted by IAA 1999, s 3; substituted by NIAA 2002, s 118).
[2] IA 1971, s 3C(1).

19.39 The effect of a decision to curtail[1] or revoke[2] leave, so that the person has no leave is similarly suspended by IA 1971, s 3D. It provides that the variation or revocation is not to take effect whilst an appeal could be brought or is pending against the variation or revocation. If a person's leave is cancelled whilst he or she is outside the UK, the leave is extended by section 3D during the period when an appeal against the decision could be brought.[3] The substitution of section 82 by section 15(2) of the 2014 Act is likely to mean that a person in respect of whom such a decision is made will not have statutorily extended leave by virtue of an appeal because they will no longer be appealable decisions. A deportation order (apart from an 'automatic deportation order' against a 'foreign criminal'[4]) may not be made against a person whilst an appeal against the decision to make a deportation order could be brought or is pending[5] unless the Secretary of State certifies the decision to deport as having been made on national security grounds.[6] Under section 47 of IAN 2006 the Secretary of State is able to make a decision that a person with statutorily extended leave (ie leave extended pending a decision on an application or an appeal) is to be removed by directions to be given by an immigration officer.[7]

[1] NIAA 2002, s 82(2)(e).
[2] NIAA 2002, s 82(2)(f).
[3] E1 / (OS Russia) v Secretary of State for the Home Department [2012] EWCA Civ 357.
[4] UK Borders Act 2007, s 35(2), inserting new subsections (3) and (4) into NIAA 2002, s 79.
[5] NIAA 2002, s 79.
[6] NIAA 2002, s 97A(2)(a).
[7] IAN 2006, s 46 was amended on 8 May 2013 by operation of the Crime and Courts Act 2013, s 51(3) to make it clear that a section 47 removal decision may be made at the same time as a refusal to vary leave; prior to its amendment, the provision was unworkable and decisions made under it were unlawful: *Ahmadi (Javad) v Secretary of State for the Home Department* [2013] EWCA Civ 512.

19.40 An appeal against an EEA decision to refuse to admit a person to the UK prevents his or her removal from the UK, any removal directions previously given cease to have effect, except insofar as they have already been carried out, and no directions may be given while an appeal against exclusion is pending.[1] Similarly, any directions for the removal of the appellant after revocation of the residence permit or under section 10 of IAA 1999 or Schedule 3 to IA 1971, are not to take effect while the appeal is pending.[2] This means that in deportation cases, and in cases analogous to overstayer removal, directions may be given during the period while the appeal is pending so long as they are not acted on. The detention powers contained in Schedules 2 and 3 to IA 1971 continue to apply despite the freezing of removal directions.[3] No deportation order is to be made against an EEA national under section 5 of the 1971 Act while the deportation appeal is pending.[4]

[1] Immigration (European Economic Area) Regulations 2006, SI 2006/1003, reg 29(2).

² SI 2006/1003, reg 29(3).
³ SI 2006/1003, reg 29(4).
⁴ SI 2006/1003, reg 29(6), see **19.49** below.

ISSUES ARISING ON PARTICULAR APPEALS

19.41 Although section 82 of NIAA 2002 created a single right of appeal against an immigration decision, particular issues arise in relation to appeals in specific situations. We dealt above with exclusion of appeal rights; in this section we look at difficulties which have arisen in respect of particular types of appeal.

Entry clearance appeals

19.42 Legislation prior to IAN 2006 introduced ever more exclusions from and qualifications to the general right of appeal against refusal of entry clearance. From 1 April 2008, IAN 2006, s 4 substituted a new section 88A (for NIAA 2002, sections 88A, 90 and 91) the effect of which was that, an appeal may only be brought if the application for entry clearance was made to visit a person of a class specified by statutory instrument,¹ or to join a person as a dependant in similarly specified circumstances. In addition, an appeal against refusal of entry clearance could be brought on human rights, or race discrimination grounds.² Section 52 of the Crime and Courts Act 2013 repealed section 88A(1)(a) of NIAA 2002 (allowing certain visitor appeals) with effect from 25 June 2013³ with the result that refusal of an application for entry clearances as a family visitor made after that date no longer attracted a right of appeal. This is part of a process whereby unappealable power is being shifted to ECOs, who are becoming the main body granting leave to enter but doing so in the country of departure, while immigration officers at ports of entry are becoming more and more a police force at the ports for terrorists, drug and people traffickers and other criminals. The worry is that as the borders of the UK are shifted to the country of departure, immigration decisions are becoming more and more part of a system without checks and balances.

¹ The last of which was the Immigration Appeals (Family Visitor) Regulations 2012, SI 2012/1532.
² NIAA 2002, s 88A.
³ By operation of the Crime and Courts Act 2013 (Commencement No 1 and Transitional and Saving Provision) Order 2013, SI 2013/1042.

Refusal of leave to enter

19.43 In relation to appeals against refusal of leave to enter, the main issue used to be whether the right of appeal was exercisable in-country or out of country. Now (since IAN 2006, s 6 came into force¹) the main issue is whether there is a right of appeal at all against refusal (or cancellation) of leave to enter. This will usually depend on the person holding an entry clearance (or leave granted before the person's arrival in the UK, deemed to be an entry clearance for this purpose²) and then seeking entry for the same purpose as that specified in the entry clearance.³ That gives rise to considerable scope for disputes over issues of jurisdictional fact – did the person seek entry for a different purpose to that specified in the entry clearance or did the person seek entry for the same purpose – resolution of which may determine whether the person has a right of appeal. The FT does not have an adequate procedure for resolving such disputes: it is required to decide without a hearing, whether there is an appealable immigration decision.[4] If a person is able to appeal against refusal of leave to enter because the person holds or is deemed to hold entry clearance, the appeal will be in-country.[5] The making of an asylum or human rights claim or a claim to enter as an EEA national or family member of an EEA national also enables an appeal against refusal of leave to enter to be brought[6] and to be brought in-country[7] unless the asylum or human rights claim is certified as clearly unfounded.[8] Whilst a person who does not otherwise qualify to appeal against refusal of leave to enter can bring an appeal on race discrimination grounds,[9] such an appeal may not be brought whilst the person is in the UK.[10]

[1]   On 31 August 2006, substituting a new NIAA 2002, s 89.
[2]   Immigration Act 1971, Sch 2, para 2A(9).
[3]   NIAA 2002, s 89(1).
[4]   Asylum and Immigration Tribunal (Procedure) Rules 2005, SI 2005/230, r 9. From 20 October 2014, under r 22 Tribunal Procedure (First-tier Tribunal) (Immigration and Asylum Chamber) Rules 2014, SI 2014/2604.
[5]   NIAA 2002, s 92(3). However, by section 92(3A)–(3C), the appeal may not be brought in-country if leave was refused or cancelled on the ground that it was being sought for a purpose different to that specified in the entry clearance or deemed entry clearance. It is not easy to envisage circumstances in which these provisions would operate; unless entry was sought for the same purpose there would be no right of appeal to be exercised either in or out of the UK.
[6]   NIAA 2002, s 89(2).
[7]   NIAA 2002, s 92(4).
[8]   NIAA 2002, s 94(2).
[9]   IAN 2006, s 6 (creating new NIAA 2002, s 89(2)).
[10] Because NIAA 2002, s 92 does not apply to such an appeal.

Variation or refusal to vary leave

19.44 An appeal against a variation or refusal to vary a person's leave to enter or remain may only be brought if, as a result of that immigration decision the person has no leave to enter or remain.[1] This contrasts with the predecessor 'variation appeal' under IAA 1999,[2] where an appeal could be brought if the person's leave would expire within 28 days of being notified of the decision.[3] The Home Office frequently prevents people from acquiring a right of appeal by notifying refusal to vary leave before the expiry of current leave.[4] In order to obtain a right of appeal, the recipient of such a decision would have to make a further application for the leave to be varied, including payment of the prescribed fee, before it expired, or otherwise commit the offence of becoming an overstayer, and waiting for an administrative removal decision under IAA 1999, s 10.

[1]   NIAA 2002, s 82(2)(d).
[2]   IAA 1999, s 61.
[3]   That in turn contrasted with its predecessor, the 'variation appeal' under IA 1971, s 14, which provided appeal rights against any variation or refusal to vary leave. It was these provisions which enabled appeals to be brought against unwelcome conditions or a lesser leave than that sought.
[4]   As in *SA (Pakistan)* [2007] UKAIT 00083, for example.

19.45 Under the 1971 Immigration Act the right of appeal against a refusal to vary leave was limited to situations where there was an existing leave at the time of the lodging of the appeal.[1] In *Subramaniam* in the Court of Appeal[2] and in *Suthendran* in the House of Lords[3] it was decided by a majority of the judges that on its true construction IA 1971, s 14(1), the precursor of IAA 1999, s 61, and in similar terms, gave a right of appeal to 'a person who has a limited leave under this Act' and not to 'a person who has had' such limited leave. Thus there was no right of appeal under section 61 of the IAA 1999 for a person whose limited leave to remain in the UK had expired at the time of applying for a variation[4] and the position is the same under the current statutory provisions relating to variation appeals.[5] The interpretation adopted by the majority in the House of Lords in *Suthendran* also meant that someone whose application was made in time, but whose limited leave expired before the Home Office reached a decision, would have no right of appeal. The majority of the House of Lords realised this, but said that the injustice could be cured by administrative means. The 'leave gap' was closed by the Variation of Leave Order 1976;[6] it is now dealt with by s 3C of the 1971 Act[7] which was discussed above.

1   *Akhtar v Secretary of State for the Home Department* [1991] Imm AR 232, CA; see also *Wa-Selo v Secretary of State for the Home Department* [1990] Imm AR 76, CA.
2   *R v Immigration Appeal Tribunal, ex p Subramaniam* [1977] QB 190, [1976] 3 All ER 604.
3   *Suthendran v Immigration Appeal Tribunal* [1977] AC 359, [1976] 3 All ER 611.
4   Since all applications (with some exceptions such as EEA, asylum and Article 3 of the ECHR or discrimination ones) must be on prescribed forms, which must be completed in full and sent with all requisite documents and fees to constitute a valid application, the effect of a letter seeking further leave, or (previously a common practice among students) the mere sending in of a passport to the Home Office for further endorsement, will be that no valid application has been made prior to expiry of leave, and so no right of appeal will accrue: see HC 395, para 32 as amended by HC 329 and HC 704.
5   *SA (Ghana)* [2007] UKAIT 0006.
6   SI 1976/1572, as amended by SI 1989/1005, known as 'VOLO', and deemed leave under the Order was known as VOLO leave.
7   Inserted by the IAA 1999, s 3, substituted by the NIAA 2002, s 118.

APPEALS AGAINST DECISIONS TO GIVE REMOVAL DIRECTIONS

19.46 There has been much litigation about whether the Secretary of State has any obligation to make a decision to remove a person at the same time as making a variation decision, or in respect of a person without leave to remain who has unsuccessfully applied for leave. It may seem odd that immigrants have asked the courts to require the Secretary of State to make removal decisions against them but the rationale has been that such decisions provide the individual with an opportunity to argue his or her case before the tribunal. Disputes as to whether a removal decision under IAN 2006, s 47 should be served at the same time as, or shortly after a decision under NIAA 2002, s 82(2)(d) refusing to vary leave (see *TE (Eritrea)* [2009] EWCA Civ 174, *R (on the application of Mirza) v Secretary of State for the Home Department* [2011] EWCA Civ 159 were brought to an end in *Patel v Secretary of State for the Home Department* [2013] UKSC 72 in which the Supreme Court held that there was no such obligation. Further, section 47 of the 2006 Act was amended on 8 May 2013 by operation of the Crime and Courts Act 2013, s 51(3) to make it clear that a section 47 removal decision may be made at the same time as a refusal to vary leave, or at any other time thereafter. Further, upon commencement of IA 2014, s 15, and Schedule 9, para 5 of that Act (to be notified), a decision under section 47 of the 2006 Act will not only cease to be an appealable decision, but section 47 will be repealed altogether, as an amended section 10 of the Immigration and Asylum Act 1999 (amendment to take place by operation of IA 2014, s 1: to be commenced) widens the scope of section 10 of the 1999 Act to include removal of persons who would previously have been removable under section 47 of the 2006 Act. There is no general obligation on the Secretary of State to make appealable decisions in respect of overstayers who have sought and been refused leave to remain.[1]

1   *R (on the application of Daley-Murdock) v Secretary of State* [2011] EWCA Civ 161, [2011] NLJR 327, [2011] NLJR 365.

APPEALS BY EEA NATIONALS: REFUSAL TO ISSUE OR TO RENEW, OR REVOCATION OF RESIDENCE DOCUMENTS

19.47 Refusal to issue or to renew a residence permit or document to an EEA national or family member in the UK, or revocation of such a document, is the EEA equivalent of variation or refusal to vary leave to enter or remain. There is a right of appeal to the Tribunal against a refusal or revocation, exercisable in the UK. If the decision is on grounds relating to national security, diplomatic or political reasons and is followed by a decision to remove, there is a right of appeal to the SIAC instead.[1] In *Boukssid v Secretary of State for the Home Department*, the Court of Appeal held that an EEA national or family member, seeking indefinite leave to remain but granted a five-year residence permit instead, has no right of appeal under the domestic law, because that depends on having limited leave under UK law, and there is no refusal of a residence permit so as to bring into play the appeal provisions of the Regulations. The only remedy in this situation is judicial review.[2] However, in *Baumbast* the Tribunal accepted an argument based on paragraph 255 of HC 395 that the only method of granting indefinite leave under paragraph 255 was to endorse the residence permit to show permission to remain in the UK indefinitely and therefore by necessary inference, to grant a permit. If that endorsement was refused, that amounted to a refusal of a residence permit, against which there was a right of appeal.[3]

1   Immigration (European Economic Area) Regulations 2006, SI 2006/1003, reg 28.
2   *Boukssid v Secretary of State for the Home Department* [1998] INLR 275, CA, decided under equivalent provisions of IA 1971 and the Immigration (European Economic Area) Order 1994, SI 1994/1895.
3   *Baumbast* (21263) (8 June 1999, unreported), IAT, also decided under IA 1971 and the Immigration (European Economic Area) Order 1994.

DEPORTATION APPEALS

19.48 Since overstayers and those in breach of conditions of leave are no longer deported but administratively removed from the UK,[1] subject to transitional provisions affecting those served with a deportation notice or who applied to regularise their stay before 2 October 2000,[2] the range of people who are deported, and so enjoy a right of appeal before removal, is limited.

However, numbers of persons subject to deportation proceedings on grounds of criminality have increased since the commencement of the UK Borders Act 2007. Those subject to deportation currently include persons recommended for deportation by a criminal court, those whose deportation the Secretary of State deems to be conducive to the public good, 'foreign criminals' subject to automatic deportation under the UK Borders Act 2007, s 32, and their family members.[3] An appeal against a decision to make a deportation order is to the Tribunal,[4] and no order (other than an 'automatic deportation order' against a 'foreign criminal')[5] is to be made while such an appeal may be brought[6] or while it is pending[7] unless the Secretary of State certifies that the decision to make the deportation order was on grounds of national security.[8] A decision to make a deportation order which states that it is made in accordance with section 32(5) of the UK Borders Act 2007 (ie an automatic deportation order) is not an appealable 'decision to make a deportation order', but the Secretary of State's decision that section 32(5) applies is an appealable immigration decision[9] and such an appeal may be referred to as 'an appeal against an automatic deportation order'.[10] Once a deportation order is made, any pending appeal against refusal of leave to enter, refusal of a certificate of entitlement, refusal to vary, variation of or revocation of leave to enter or remain under section 82 of NIAA 2002 is to be treated as finally determined.[11] The provisions of Schedule 3 to IA 1971 apply to proposed deportees, who may be detained or granted temporary release or bail pending appeal.[12] If the grounds for the decision to deport are national security, diplomatic or political, the appeal is not to the Tribunal[13] but to the SIAC.[14] There is a right of appeal against a refusal to revoke a deportation order[15] but it may not be exercised from within the UK unless an asylum or human rights claim has been made and has not been certified clearly unfounded,[16] or an EEA national or family member of an EEA national claims that the decision breaches rights under Community law.[17] A decision to make a deportation order against a Bulgarian or Romanian national or their family members or refusing to revoke a deportation against such a person prior to 1 January 2007 is treated after that date as a decision to remove under the Immigration (European Economic Area) Regulations and any pending appeal is treated as an appeal brought under those Regulations.[18] A refusal to revoke based on a personal decision by the Secretary of State that the applicant's exclusion from the UK would be conducive to the public good is not appealable to the Tribunal but may be appealed to the SIAC.[19]

1   IAA 1999, s 10. See also prospective amendment IAA 1999, s 10 by IA 2014, s 1 widening the scope of persons who may be administratively removed under section 10.
2   IAA 1999, s 9 and Sch 15, paras 11 and 12, Immigration (Regularisation Period for Overstayers) Regulations 2000, SI 2000/265. The transitional provisions of Sch 15 enable these people to have a deportation appeal on the merits if they had been in the UK for seven years by the date of decision, and an appeal limited to whether the precedent conditions for deportation have been made out, if not, under IA 1971, s 15, Immigration Act 1988, s 5 and Immigration (Restricted Right of Appeal against Deportation) (Exemption) Order 1993, which are to continue to have effect in relation to this class of person notwithstanding their repeal.
3   IA 1971, s 3(5) and (6), as amended by IAA 1999, Sch 15, para 44(2), and the UK Borders Act 2007, s 32. For the factors to be considered in deportation appeals, see CHAPTER **16** above.
4   NIAA 2002, s 81 (substituted by section 26 of the Asylum and Immigration (Treatment of Claimants, etc) Act 2004), s 82(1) as amended, s 82(2)(j).
5   UK Borders Act, s 35(2), amending NIAA 2002, s 79.
6   NIAA 2002, s 79(1)(a).
7   NIAA 2002, 79(1)(b).

8   NIAA 2002, s 97A(2)(a).
9   NIAA 2002, s 82(3A). See also *Greenwood (Automatic Deportation: Order of Events)* [2014] UKUT 00342 (IAC) to the same effect.
10 NIAA 2002, s 83(3A)(b).
11 NIAA 2002, s 104(5).
12 For detention pending deportation, and bail pending appeal, see CHAPTER **18** above.
13 NIAA 2002, s 97.
14 Special Immigration Appeals Commission Act 1997, s 2(1), as amended; Immigration (European Economic Area) Regulations 2006, 2006/1003, reg 28.
15 NIAA 2002, s 82(2)(k).
16 NIAA 2002, ss 92(4)(a), 94(2) as amended by Asylum and Immigration (Treatment of Claimants, etc) Act 2004, s 27 (from 1 October 2004).
17 NIAA 2002, s 92(4).
18 Accession (Immigration and Worker Authorisation) Regulations 2006, SI 2006/3317, reg 8.
19 See fn 11 above.

EEA PUBLIC POLICY DECISIONS TO REMOVE

19.49 Removal of an EEA national or family member on public policy, public security or public health grounds[1] is equivalent to a deportation on conducive grounds, and section 5 of, and Schedule 3 to IA 1971 apply.[2] Where national security, diplomatic or political reasons underlie the decision, the appeal is to the SIAC,[3] otherwise, it is to the Tribunal.[4] The appeal is in-country and suspends removal.[5] An appeal against a refusal to revoke a deportation order is, however, out-of-country under the regulations.[6]

1   Immigration (European Economic Area) Regulations 2006, SI 2006/1003, reg 19(3)(b).
2   SI 2006/1003, reg 24(3).
3   SI 2006/1003, reg 28.
4   SI 2006/1003, reg 26(6). Regulation 26(7) applies the relevant sections of NIAA 2002.
5   SI 2006/1003, reg 29(6). It is in-country by virtue of its omission from the list of out-of-country appeals at SI 2006/1003, reg 27.
6   SI 2006/1003, reg 27(1)(b) subject to the exceptions in regulation 27(2).

APPEALS AGAINST REMOVAL: OVERSTAYERS, ILLEGAL ENTRANTS, SHIP AND AIRCREWS

19.50 Illegal entrants,[1] overstayers (including overstaying crew members),[2] those in breach of conditions, persons who have remained in the UK by deception and their family members may be summarily removed by directions given by an immigration officer.[3] They have an unrestricted right of appeal against the decision to remove them[4] (by contrast to the right of appeal that existed under the IAA 1999, which was limited to challenging the existence of the power to remove on the grounds stated in the notice).[5] However, the right of appeal may only be exercised after removal[6] unless the person has made an asylum or human rights claim, which has not been certified clearly unfounded[7] or a claim that the decision breaches Community law, whilst in the UK.[8] An appeal against refusal of leave to enter is not an appeal against removal directions, even though the notice of decision may include such directions or refer to an intention to give them.[9] Similarly, an appeal against a decision that an illegal entrant is to be removed by way of removal directions is concerned with the decision in principle to remove but not whether the proposed destination is one to which there is power to remove the person.[10]

1   See CHAPTER 17 above.
2   See CHAPTER 5 above.
3   Under the IA 1971, Sch 2, paras 9, 10, 12(2), 13(2), and the IAA 1999, s 10; (see CHAPTER 17).
4   NIAA 2002, s 82(2)(g),(h), (i) and (ia) (s 82(2)(ia) inserted by the Asylum and Immigration (Treatment of Claimants, etc) Act 2004, s 31 from 1 October 2004.
5   IAA 1999, s 66; (see Fifth edition at 18.25–18.26).
6   NIAA 2002, s 92(1).
7   NIAA 2002, s 92(4)(a) and 94(2) as amended by the Asylum and Immigration (Treatment of Claimants, etc) Act 2004, s 27 from 1 October 2004 (SI 2004/2523).
8   NIAA 2002, s 92(4)(b).
9   *MA (Somalia) v Secretary of State for the Home Department* [2009] EWCA Civ 4, [2009] All ER (D) 65 (Jan).
10 *MS (Palestinian Territories) v Secretary of State for the Home Department* [2010] UKSC 25.

EEA DECISIONS TO REMOVE ON GROUNDS OF NON-QUALIFICATION

19.51 A person may be removed from the UK if, having been admitted or having acquired a right to reside under the Immigration (European Economic Area) Regulations 2006 the person does not have a right of residence or the right ceases.[1] Removal of this group is equivalent to removal of overstayers under section 10(1)(a) of IAA 1999, which is to apply.[2] There is no right of appeal on the ground that the person is an EEA national unless the appellant produces a valid national identity card or passport issued by an EEA state.[3] A person claiming to be a family member for the purposes of an appeal must produce a family permit or other proof of relationship.[4] An appeal against removal may rely on asylum, human rights or race discrimination grounds.[5] If removal involves the cancellation of a non-EU citizen's residence card or equivalent earlier document on the grounds of a marriage of convenience, removal must be proportionate and subject to the procedural safeguards provided for in Articles 30 and 31 of the Citizens' Directive.[6]

1   SI 2006/1003, reg 19(3)(a).
2   SI 2006/1003, reg 24(2).
3   SI 2006/1003, reg 26(2).
4   SI 2006/1003, reg 26(3).
5   SI 2006/1003, reg 26 (7) and Sch 1, applying Nationality, Immigration and Asylum Act, s 84(1)(b)–(e), (g) to appeals under the regulations.
6   Directive 2004/38/EC, Art 35.

APPEALS OBJECTING TO DESTINATION

19.52 The previous legislation provided a right of appeal to an adjudicator on the ground of an objection to the country or territory to which the appellant was to be removed.[1] That right of appeal has not been reproduced by NIAA 2002. The destination to which it is proposed that a recipient of an immigration decision is to be removed is not part of the decision and cannot be challenged in an appeal as being not in accordance with the law.[2] However, the destination may be challenged on the ground that removal there (which includes an assessment of the safety of the route of return), would breach the

UK's obligations under the Refugee Convention or the ECHR.[3]

[1] IAA 1999, s 67. The destination appeal, which was not founded on legal arguments about the Secretary of State's power to remove to the particular destination, but on the appellant's preference, was rarely used, largely because it was necessary to stipulate an alternative destination and show by evidence that the appellant was likely to be accepted there (see the Fifth edition at para 18.52).

[2] *MS (Palestinian Territories) v Secretary of State for the Home Department* [2010] UKSC 25.

[3] *HH (Somalia) v Secretary of State for the Home Department* [2010] EWCA Civ 426.

ONE-STOP APPEALS

19.53 The one-stop appeal is not a term of art but describes features of immigration appeals first introduced by IAA 1999[1] and now in a third incarnation,[2] which stands to be amended further still, by operation of IA 2014, Sch 9, para 5, which will substitute a new form of NIAA 2002, s 120 in place of the existing provision. It applies only to in-country appeals. The basic idea, as its name suggests, is that all the grounds relied on to remain in the UK should be considered in the course of a single appeal, so as to avoid delay and abuse. The positive aspect of the one-stop appeal, therefore, is that the FT is obliged to consider all matters which have been raised by the appellant, whether on the original application or in response to a 'one-stop' notice.[3] The negative aspect of the procedure is that service of such a notice, or an earlier right of appeal, will generally preclude an appeal against a second immigration decision which relies on a matter which should have been, but was not raised earlier.[4] Section 47 of IAN 2006[5] was intended to further the policy of 'one-stop appeals' enabling a decision to remove to be made at the same time as a variation decision thereby obviating the need for a sequence of appealable decisions in respect of the same person.

[1] Sections 73–76; (see Fifth edition, 18.20ff).

[2] NIAA 2002, ss 96 and 120 simplified the procedure. Amendments by the Asylum and Immigration (Treatment of Claimants, etc) Act 2004, s 30 (from 1 October 2004) simplify the s 96 provisions further.

[3] NIAA 2002, s 85(2), (3).

[4] NIAA 2002, s 96(1), (2) as substituted by Asylum and Immigration (Treatment of Claimants, etc) Act 2004, s 30.

[5] Which itself stands to be repealed by IA 2014, Sch 9, para 5.

19.54 Until section 120 of the NIAA 2002 is amended by the IA 2014, the Secretary of State or an immigration officer may serve a notice under section 120 on an applicant for leave to enter or remain, or the subject of an immigration decision (such as deportation or removal),[1] at any time, whether before or after the decision.[2] The notice requires the person to state reasons for wishing to enter or remain, for being permitted to do so, or why he or she should not be removed or required to leave (other than those forming the basis of the application, or already relied on to resist the decision).[3] The response to the one-stop notice or warning is the 'Statement of Additional Grounds'. There is no statutory time limit for the making of a Statement nor are there any statutory provisions as to the form in which such a Statement is to be made. There is no statutory requirement for the Secretary of State or immigration officer to respond to a statement of additional grounds,[4] but there is a statutory obligation on the Tribunal hearing an appeal to consider any further grounds relied on in such a statement.[5] The additional grounds could be further grounds for leave to enter or remain under the Immigration Rules, under a relevant Home Office policy, asylum or human rights or discrimination grounds. So for example, a person refused leave to enter as a visitor at the port, served with a section 120 notice, might claim asylum or adduce human rights grounds for seeking to enter, which would then give rise to an in-country appeal (unless certified as clearly unfounded);[6] an asylum claimant waiting for his or her claim to be processed might marry or enter a relationship which could form the basis of a human rights claim under Article 8 of the ECHR; or a person seeking leave to remain under the student rules, who has been living with someone settled in the UK for two years, may seek to rely on the unmarried partners' rule, and on Article 8 of the ECHR, in the Statement of Additional Grounds, asserting that the decision is not in accordance with the law[7] and Immigration Rules[8] and is incompatible with the appellant's Convention rights;[9] a person whose application for leave to remain to study on a particular course was refused might put forward an application for further leave to pursue a different course of study.[10] The Court of Appeal considered these provisions in linked appeals where one appellant had applied for leave to remain to establish herself in business under the applicable Immigration Rule; in her statement responding to a one-stop notice she made an application under the Immigration Rules relating to the International Graduate Scheme. The other appellant had sought leave to remain under the '10-year rule' but made an application for leave to remain as a student in her one-stop statement. The Court held that the Tribunal was required to consider both of the applications included in the one-stop statements.[11] We consider further in CHAPTER 20 the extent of the Tribunal's jurisdiction to consider matters not raised before the original decision-maker.

1   NIAA 2002, s 120(1)(a), (b). These provisions replace the complicated procedures under ss 74 and 75 of IAA 1999, which provided for different one-stop procedures and notices in respect of specified applicants and appellants.
2   NIAA 2002, s 120(2). The flexibility provided by the section contrasts with the previous provisions (fn 1 above), which required the notice to be served at a particular point in the procedure which differed according to the application and the status of the applicant. Service of a notice under the section is not obligatory, but the Asylum Policy Instructions (API) indicate that it would be appropriate where an application is unlikely to be successful and it would be helpful to establish whether the applicant intended to put forward any other matters on appeal or to resist enforcement, and particularly where it is believed that an asylum or human rights claim may be made; or where a decision to remove or deport is going to be made or a person who has not previously had a one-stop warning is being considered for removal (API: Appeals: the One-Stop Procedure Warnings and Certificates), para 2.1. Most refusal decisions now incorporate one-stop warnings as a final or penultimate paragraph.
3   NIAA 2002, s 120(2), (3).
4   Under the previous scheme, procedure rules required the Secretary of State to respond to statements of additional grounds by supplementary refusal notices; this requirement was rarely observed, leading to problems for adjudicators who were unsure whether they were required to deal with all the issues notwithstanding the Secretary of State's failure (following *Haddad* [2000] INLR 117), or whether to insist on their role as an appellate body rather than a first-instance decision maker. The current IDI (fn 4 above), says that a statement of additional grounds must be considered, even if it arrives after a decision has been taken or an appeal lodged but (in contrast to earlier instructions) it says nothing about the Secretary of State responding to the maker of the statement either by letter or by amending the notice of decision.
5   NIAA 2002, s 85(2), (3). The section does not confer broader jurisdiction than the Tribunal has under s 84(1), so the additional grounds relied on must relate to one or other of the appeal grounds under that section.
6   Ie under NIAA 2002, s 94(2). In this example, there would have been no appeal if the asylum or human rights grounds had not been raised, because of section 88: see **19.30** above.
7   NIAA 2002, s 84(1)(e).

8   NIAA 2002, s 84(1)(a).

9   NIAA 2002, s 84(1)(c) and/or (g).

10 Making such a statement would enlarge the Tribunal's jurisdiction (if it did not have it already) so as to enable it to consider whether the appellant's newly stated grounds met the requirements of the Immigration Rules and to allow the appeal if they did. The Tribunal would not be restricted to determining only whether the application as originally put forward could meet the requirements of the Immigration Rules at the date of hearing, as held in *EA (Nigeria)* [2007] UKAIT 00013 (although without considering NIAA 2002, s 85(2)).

11 *AS (Afghanistan) v Secretary of State for the Home Department* [2009] EWCA Civ 1076. In *Patel v Secretary of State for the Home Department* [2013] UKSC 72, the Supreme Court agreed with the majority in *AS (Afghanistan) v Secretary of State* [2011] 1 WLR 385, that section 85(2) of the 2002 Act imposes a duty on the tribunal to consider any potential ground of appeal raised in response to a section 120 notice, even if it does not directly relate to the issues considered by the Secretary of State in the original decision.

19.55 The IA 2014 will substitute a new section 120 in the NIAA 2002.[1] The section will apply to a person who has made a protection claim or human rights claim, made an application to enter or remain in the UK, or a decision to deport or remove the person has been made.[2] The person may be served with a notice requiring him or her to set out his or her reasons for wishing to enter or remain in the UK, the grounds on which the person should be permitted to enter or remain in the UK, and any grounds on which the person should not be removed from or required to leave the UK. There is further provision[3] giving rise to an obligation on the person to file a further statement as soon as is reasonably practicable upon having additional reasons for remaining in the UK.

1 Upon commencement of IA 2014, Sch 9, para 55.

2 NIAA 2002, s 120(1), as substituted.

3 NIAA 2002, s 120(5) as substituted.

CERTIFICATION UNDER SECTION 96

19.56 The certification procedure under section 96[1] precludes a second or subsequent appeal against an immigration decision or, after commencement of the 2014 Act appeals provisions, a second or subsequent appeal under section 82(1) in two situations:

(i)   where the Secretary of State or an immigration officer certifies that the person was notified of a right of appeal against another decision (regardless of whether an appeal was brought or has been determined), where the new claim or application relates to a matter which could have been raised in an appeal against the old decision, and there is no satisfactory reason for the failure to raise it;[2]

(ii) where the Secretary of State or an immigration officer certifies that the person received a section 120 notice in respect of an earlier application or decision, should have raised the matter on which he or she now seeks to rely in a statement made in response to the notice, and there is no satisfactory reason for the failure to raise it.[3]

Thus, the one-stop procedure rests simply on a failure to raise the matter now relied on at an earlier stage – either on appeal, if there was an opportunity to appeal at an earlier stage, or in a statement of additional grounds in response to a one-stop notice. In this context, 'matter' has been defined broadly so that it is not restricted to being an 'issue' of a kind that might constitute a ground of appeal but may also be 'evidence'.[4] The certification procedure only comes into play to block an appeal, in a situation where otherwise, there would have been one, ie where a further immigration decision under section 82 of NIAA 2002 is taken in respect of someone who has previously made an application or been the subject of an earlier immigration decision. It does not apply where there is no such further immigration decision. Thus, it might apply to prevent a human rights appeal against a decision to remove an overstayer who had previously appealed against refusal to vary leave but had not raised human rights grounds on that appeal,[5] or to block an asylum claim, put forward late, after refusal of leave to enter on other grounds, and not referred to in response to a one-stop notice.[6] A further asylum or human rights claim made after the rejection of an earlier claim would not usually result in the making of an 'immigration decision'[7] unless it met the requirements of a fresh claim contained in the Immigration Rules.[8] and certification under section 96 is only considered once the Secretary of State has accepted further representations as a fresh claim for this purpose.[9] The simplified provisions thus make a much better fit with these 'fresh claims' provisions. The principal issue for the Secretary of State or the immigration officer under section 96 is whether the reasons for the failure to put forward the new matter are satisfactory, which has to be determined having regard to all relevant circumstances which, in an asylum or human rights case, would include the possible consequences for the would-be appellant of being removed without a hearing.[10] Even if the decision maker finds there was no satisfactory explanation, he or she is not obliged to certify but has a discretion to exercise and an obligation in doing so to have regard to all relevant considerations including the gravity of the person's claim.[11] Reasons need to be given by the decision-maker to explain why the discretion was exercised in favour of certification.[12] Earlier APIs indicated that a significant change of circumstances in the country of origin since an asylum appeal would be a satisfactory reason for failure to raise those circumstances on the appeal, as would the establishment of an appropriate relationship since the appeal which attracts the guarantees of Article 8 of the ECHR.[13] A serious failure by a representative to put forward a vital issue which would have had a significant impact on the outcome of the appeal might also be a satisfactory reason for the applicant's failure. We had continued that last sentence in an earlier edition saying 'provided that there is evidence to support the allegation and the matter is serious enough to justify a formal complaint to the representative's regulatory body or the OISC', but it has been held that neither corroborative evidence nor representative's default of that seriousness are always necessary in order to establish a 'satisfactory reason'.[14]

1   NIAA 2002, s 96(1), (2), substituted by Asylum and Immigration (Treatment of Claimants, etc) Act 2004, s 30 from 1 October 2004. Section 96 will be further amended by operation of IA 2014, Sch 9, para 41; to be commenced.

2   NIAA 2002, s 96(1) as substituted. This limb applies to earlier appeals under IAA 1999 as well as NIAA 2002: NIAA 2002, Sch 6, para 4(a). It does not require a s 120 notice to have been served, provided the earlier immigration decision gave rise to a right of appeal where the new matter could have been raised. It does not matter whether the applicant chose not to appeal, or withdrew or abandoned the appeal. Earlier APIs gave examples of what might constitute a satisfactory reason for not having raised a matter previously – if the new matter could not be raised on the appeal (eg because the Tribunal refused to allow it to be, or because it arose after the appeal), that would be a satisfactory reason for its not having been raised. The current IDI which deals with the one-stop procedure (Ch 12, s 3) is silent on that issue.

3   NIAA 2002, s 96(2) as substituted. This limb does not require the applicant to have had an earlier right of appeal, but would apply where for example, a one-stop notice was issued in respect of an earlier immigration decision and had the applicant responded, relying on the human rights or asylum claim he or she now seeks to raise, that would have generated a right of appeal. It applies where a one-stop notice was served under earlier legislation: see NIAA 2002, Sch 6, para 4(b)–(c).

4   *R (on the application of Khan (Mohammad Iqbal)) v Secretary of State for the Home Department* [2014] EWCA Civ 88.

5   Ie someone who had already had a right of appeal under NIAA 2002, s 82(2)(d) or its predecessor, and who now seeks to appeal in-country under s 82(2)(g) by the application of s 92(4)(a). However, for s 96(1) to bite, the person must, we suggest, have been notified of the obligation to disclose additional grounds before the earlier appeal, whether by service of a one-stop notice or otherwise.

6   NIAA 2002, s 96(2) as substituted. In this scenario, the claimant could have had an earlier appeal, relying on s 92(4)(a), had he or she made the asylum claim in response to the one-stop warning.

7   A situation where the further asylum or human rights claim which does not meet the requirements of paragraph 353 of HC 395 should nevertheless attract a new immigration decision is where the person is subject to a deportation order and applies for the deportation order to be revoked on the basis of the putative fresh claim; the Secretary of State would have to make a decision on the application to revoke the deportation order even if she does not accept a fresh claim. Refusal to revoke the deportation order is an appealable immigration decision: NIAA 2002, s 82(2)(k). HC 395, para 353: see **12.185** above.

8   See API (fn 2 above), para 3.1.

9   API (fn 2 above), para 3.2.

10 *R (on the application of J) v Secretary of State for the Home Department* [2009] EWHC 705 (Admin).

11 As fn 10 above.

12 *R (on the application of Mahmood) v Secretary of State for the Home Department* [2014] EWHC 259 (Admin).

13 API (fn 2 above), para 3.2.

14 By Stadlen J in *R (J) v Secretary of State for the Home Department* [2009] EWHC 705 (Admin).

TRANSITIONAL PROVISIONS

19.57 The rapid changes in legislation and rules regarding appeals make it necessary to know which provisions apply in any given case. It is particularly important to check which procedure rules apply in a 'transitional' situation.[1] Sometimes the legislation or the rules themselves contain clear and comprehensive transitional provisions.[2] When they do not, or a gap in the provisions is identified, there are a number of principles to bear in mind. First, Parliament can be assumed not to intend to produce unfair results,[3] so that a construction of a statute which appears retrospectively to remove rights of appeal is unlikely to be upheld, and if no specific provision is made, appeals pending under previous legislation proceed. Secondly, however, a right of appeal does not crystallise until a decision is made, so the restriction of rights of appeal in a statute is not unfair to those who have not yet received adverse decisions.[4] The Tribunal has been scathing on occasion about transitional provisions contained in Commencement Orders: in *Pardeepan* it expressed dismay at the restriction of appeals on human rights grounds to events post-dating 1 October 2000,[5] and in *ZA (Ethiopia)*[6] it complained that the transitional provisions made in a commencement order under NIAA 2002 regulating appeals submitted before that Act came into force[7] had 'some claim to be the worst drafted . . . order ever passed by Parliament.[8] *ZA (Ethiopia)* related to an asylum appeal under IAA 1999 which was dismissed in November 2003 (after

NIAA 2002 came into force). A human rights appeal was allowed. Following the grant of permission to appeal to the Tribunal, the Secretary of State granted three years' humanitarian protection. The question for the Tribunal was whether this led to deemed abandonment of the appeal under IAA 1999, or whether, as the appellant argued, the gap in the transitional provisions enabled her to proceed with her appeal. The Tribunal held that the old appeal provisions applied.[9] In another case, the Administrative Court held that a certificate issued under statutory provisions that had been repealed and replaced with new provisions to similar effect some days before it was issued had no legal effect; in particular, it could not prevent the person from appealing.[10]

[1] See for example *R (on the application of Ebadi) v Immigration Appeal Tribunal* [2004] EWHC 1645 (Admin), [2004] All ER (D) 228 (Jun), where the Tribunal had applied the wrong procedure rules in demanding good reason for the submission of late evidence.
[2] Eg, Asylum and Immigration Act 1996, s 1, inserting into the Asylum and Immigration Appeals Act 1993 provisions restricting appeal rights in respect of designated countries, which stated that its provisions applied to all appeals after the Act came into force 'irrespective of the date of the asylum claim': see *R v Secretary of State for the Home Department and Special Adjudicator, ex p Chowdry (Nargis)* (QBCOF 97/1715/D) (2 February 1998, unreported), CA.
[3] See eg *R (on the application of Kariharan) v Secretary of State for the Home Department* [2002] EWCA Civ 1102, [2003] QB 933, construing 'decision relating to entitlement to enter and remain' (IAA 1999, s 65) to determine whether removal directions issued after the coming into force of that Act following a notice to an illegal entrant and an asylum appeal attracted a right of appeal under s 65.
[4] *R v Secretary of State for the Home Department, ex p Mundowa* [1992] 3 All ER 606 (overstayer who expected to have right of appeal on merits against deportation, but had not been served with notice of intention to deport before Immigration Act 1988, s 5, restricting right of appeal, came into force, held not to be prejudiced as he had no right of appeal until service of notice).
[5] *Pardeepan v Secretary of State for the Home Department*, [2002] Imm AR 249, [2000] INLR 447.
[6] [2004] UKIAT 00241, [2004] Imm AR 538.
[7] Nationality, Immigration and Asylum Act 2002 (Commencement No 4) Order 2003, SI 2003/754 (amended by SI 2003/1040 and SI 2003/1339) Sch 2, paras 3, 4.
[8] [2004] UKIAT 00241, [2004] Imm AR 538, para 17.
[9] [2004] UKIAT 00241, [2004] Imm AR 538, at paras 18–19.
[10] *R (on the application of Mahamed) v Secretary of State for the Home Department* [2008] EWHC 1312 Admin. For discussion of transitional provisions in the different context of exclusion from *non-refoulement* protection, see *SB (Haiti - cessation and exclusion)* [2005] UKIAT 00036.

ADMINISTRATIVE REVIEW

19.58 In place of some of the rights of appeal swept away by the IA 2014 the government has provided for 'administrative review' by means of a statement of changes in the Immigration Rules.[1] Administrative review will involve a Home Office caseworker or Immigration Officer reviewing an eligible decision taken by one of his or her colleagues to see whether it is 'wrong because of a case working error'.[2] An eligible decision is a refusal of an application made on or after 20 October 2014 for leave to remain as a Tier 4 Migrant, or a dependant of a Tier 4 Migrant.[3] The rules exhaustively list 'case working errors' that are instances of when the original decision-maker applied the wrong rule; applied the rules incorrectly; wrongly calculated the period of leave held or granted; failed to consider all the evidence submitted; considered some or all of the evidence incorrectly; reached an unreasonable decision on the credibility of the applicant; incorrectly based the decision on the supporting documents not being genuine or not meeting a requirement of the Immigration Rules; or incorrectly refused the application on the basis that it was made more than 28 days after the person's leave had expired, or the original decision-maker failed to apply the Secretary of State's relevant published policy and guidance.[4] The person carrying out the administrative review will only consider evidence submitted in support of the original application unless new evidence is submitted to establish that the original decision-maker: failed to consider all the evidence; reached an unreasonable decision on credibility; incorrectly based the decision on documents not being genuine; or incorrectly refused the application on the basis of the applicant having overstayed for more than 28 days.[5] Administrative review may result in the decision being upheld, or withdrawn, or in reasons for the decision being withdrawn, or new reasons being given.[6]

[1] HC 693, 16 October 2014, introducing new 'Appendix AR.
[2] Appendix AR, Introduction and para AR1.1.
[3] Appendix AR para. AR3.2.
[4] Appendix AR para AR3.4.
[5] Appendix AR para AR2.4.
[6] Appendix AR para AR2.2.

19.59 The Immigration Rules make detailed provision as to the procedure to be followed in connection with administrative review.[1] The application has to be made whilst the applicant is in the UK[2] within 14 days of receiving the eligible decision, or, if the person is detained under the Immigration Acts, within seven days.[3] The Secretary of State may extend the time limit if satisfied that it would be unjust not to do so, and the application was made as soon as is reasonably practicable.[4] The application may be made online, or by completing a specified application form to be sent by post or courier.[5] An application will be treated as invalid if not made in accordance with the procedural requirements of the Immigration Rules, including requirements about specified documents, payment of the requisite fee, and the completion of sections of the application form indicated as being mandatory.[6]

[1] Paragraphs 34L–34Y, as inserted by HC 693, 16 October 2014.
[2] Paragraph 34Q.
[3] Paragraph 34R.
[4] Paragraph 34R(2).
[5] Paragraphs 34U and 34V.
[6] Paragraph 34N.

Chapter 20

APPEALS TO THE FIRST-TIER TRIBUNAL

THE FIRST-TIER TRIBUNAL

20.1 The rights of appeal described in the previous chapter are exercisable before the First-tier Tribunal. The First-tier Tribunal (FT) was created by section 3 of the Tribunals, Courts and Enforcement Act 2007 (TCEA 2007) to exercise the functions conferred on it by the TCEA or by any other Act. In the immigration context, those functions are hearing immigration appeals[1] and applications for bail and bail-related matters,[2] deciding applications for permission to appeal to the Upper Tribunal (UT)[3] and reviewing its own decisions.[4] References to 'the Tribunal' in the appeals part of the Nationality, Immigration and Asylum Act 2002 (NIAA 2002) are references to the FT.[5] Together with the UT it is presided over by the Senior President of Tribunals.[6] The Senior President is required to have regard to the need for the FT and UT to be accessible; for proceedings before them to be fair and handled quickly and efficiently; for their members to be 'experts in the subject-matter of, or the law to be applied in cases in which they decide matters' and the need to develop innovative methods of resolving disputes.[7] The FT consists of 'judges and other members'[8] and is organised into chambers,[9] one of which is the Immigration and Asylum Chamber.[10] Each chamber is presided over by one or two Chamber Presidents[11] appointed by the Lord Chancellor.[12] FT judges are appointed by the Lord Chancellor and a person is eligible for appointment if he or she is qualified as a solicitor, barrister or, in Scotland, an advocate and has at least five years' experience of law-related activities.[13] The Lord Chancellor may also transfer judges from other tribunals into the FT or UT and has done so in respect of the members of the Asylum and Immigration

Tribunal.[14] In addition, judges of the UT,[15] Court of Appeal and High Court judges, circuit judges, county court judges (in Northern Ireland) and district judges are ex officio judges of the FT.[16] The Lord Chancellor may appoint 'other members' to the FT, those eligible for appointment being holders of qualifications prescribed in an order made by the Lord Chancellor.[17]

1 Under Nationality, Immigration and Asylum Act 2002, ss 82, 83 and 83A and under the Immigration (European Economic Area) Regulations 2006, SI 2006/1003, reg 26.
2 Under Immigration Act 1971, Schs 2 and 3.
3 TCEA 2007, s 11(4)(a).
4 TCEA 2007, s 9.
5 NIAA 2002, s 81, as substituted from 15 February 2010 by SI 2010/21.
6 TCEA 2007, s 2(3).
7 TCEA 2007, s 7.
8 The FT is presently organised into the Social Entitlement Chamber; the War Pensions and Armed Forces Compensation Chamber; the Health, Education and Social Care Chamber; the Tax Chamber and the General Regulatory Chamber as well as the Immigration and Asylum Chamber: First-tier Tribunal and Upper Tribunal (Chambers) Order 2008, SI 2008/2684, art 2.
9 TCEA 2007, s 7(2).
10 TCEA 2007, s 7(7).
11 TCEA 2007, s 3(4). The first Senior President was (then) Lord Justice Carnwath; he has been succeeded by Lord Justice Sullivan.
12 TCEA 2007, s 2(3).
13 TCEA 2007, ss 4(1)(a) and 50–52 and Sch 2, para 1.
14 TCEA 2007, s 31(2)(b) and Transfer of Functions of the Asylum and Immigration Tribunal Order 2010, SI 2010/21, art 3.
15 TCEA 2007, s 4(1)(c).
16 TCEA 2007, s 6.
17 TCEA 2007, s 4(3).

20.2 The Senior President of Tribunals is required to decide the number of members of the FT who are to decide any matter and in doing so, to have regard to the need for members to have particular expertise, skills or knowledge.[1] To that end, the Senior President's 'Practice Statements'[2] specify the composition of the FT for deciding particular matters. One FT judge is to decide upon: whether notice of appeal was given in time[3] or time should be extended;[4] the giving of directions;[5] appeals which are to be determined without a hearing;[6] applications for bail;[7] the issue of witness summonses;[8] whether an appeal is abandoned or finally determined.[9] Decisions on applications to extend time for appealing in 'imminent removal cases';[10] and to the FT for permission to appeal to the UT[11] and on review of a decision of the FT[12] are to be made by a FT judge approved by the Senior President for dealing with such matters. All other matters and appeals are to be decided by one FT judge or a panel of two or three members of whom at least one is a FT judge and no more than one is another member.[13] The Chamber President is to decide whether an appeal or another matter is to be decided by more than one member, although the power to make such decisions may be delegated to another FT judge.[14]

1 The First-tier Tribunal and Upper Tribunal (Composition of Tribunal) Order 2008, SI 2008/2835, art 2.
2 Practice Statements: Immigration and Asylum Chambers of the First-tier Tribunal and the Upper Tribunal, 10 February 2010.
3 Practice Statements: para 2.1(1).
4 Practice Statements: para 2.1(1).
5 Practice Statements: para 2.1(5).
6 Practice Statements: para 2.1(6).

7 Practice Statements: para 2.1(7).
8 Practice Statements: para 2.1(8).
9 Practice Statements: para 2.1(9).
10 Practice Statements: para 2.1(2).
11 Practice Statements: para 2.1(11).
12 Under TCEA 2007, s 9, Practice Statements: para 2.1(10).
13 Practice Statements: para 2.1(3)
14 Practice Statements: para 2.3.

THE IMMIGRATION ACT 2014

20.3 The Immigration Act 2014 (IA 2014), to the extent that it is brought into force[1], makes sweeping changes to the appeals provisions in Part 5 of the NIAA 2002. Not only does the Act abolish rights of appeal, it reduces the available grounds of appeal; it imposes limits upon what the tribunal may consider; and it curtails the powers of the tribunal, including, removing its power to make directions for the purpose of giving effect to its decision on an appeal. At the time of writing the amendments have been brought into effect only in relation to seven categories of person.[2] They are as follows.

(1)   Those who become foreign criminals on or after 20 October 2014.[3] In this context, a 'foreign criminal' is someone who is not British; has been convicted in the UK of an offence; and has been sentenced to a period of imprisonment of at least 12 months or has been convicted of an offence that has caused serious harm or is a persistent offender.[4]

(2)   Those liable to deportation under Immigration Act 1971 (IA 1971), s 3(5)(b) because they belong to the family of a person who became a foreign criminal on or after 20 October 2014.[5]

(3)   'Foreign criminals' (as defined in (1) above) against whom a 'deportation decision' (ie a decision to make a deportation order; a decision to refuse to revoke a deportation order or a decision under the automatic deportation provisions of the UK Borders Act 2007, s 32(5)) was made on or after 10th November 2014.[6]

(4)   Those against whom a deportation decision was made on or after 10th November 2014 in respect of a person liable to deportation because he or she belongs to the family of a person to whom (3) applies.[7]

(5)   Those persons who make an application on or after 20 October 2014 for leave to remain as a Tier 4 Migrant.[8]

(6)   Those persons who apply for leave to remain as the partner of a Tier 4 Migrant on or after 20 October 2014.[9]

(7)   Those persons who apply for leave to remain as the child of a Tier 4 Migrant on or after 20 October 2014.[10]

The amended appeals provisions do not apply to people in the fifth, sixth and seventh categories who subsequently make an application for leave to enter or leave to remain in a category other than as a Tier 4 Migrant or family member of a Tier 4 Migrant, and as long as the application is not a protection or human rights claim made in the UK but not at a port.[11] (In other words, the IA 2014 appeals provisions will apply to a person in these categories who makes an in-country protection or human rights claim.) Moreover, in relation to people in the fifth, sixth and seventh categories who subsequently make further applications for leave to enter or remain, the amended appeals provisions will not apply where 'an immigration decision under section 82(2)' of the NIAA 2002 is taken or an asylum decision appealable under sections 83 or 83A of the NIAA 2002 is taken.[12] In respect of people who do not fall into the seven categories identified above, the appeals provisions in Part 5 of the NIAA 2002 will continue to apply, unamended by the Immigration Act 2014.[13] Thus there will be two sets of appeals provisions continuing for the foreseeable future: 'pre-Immigration Act 2014 appeals provisions' and 'post-Immigration Act 2014 appeals provisions'. Therefore, what follows will first describe the appeals provisions as they currently are (save in respect of the seven categories of people identified above). It will then describe the appeals provisions as amended by the IA 2014. Finally, it will outline the process of bringing, hearing and deciding appeals, which should be broadly be the same whether or not the IA 2014 provisions apply.

[1]   IA 2014, s 75(3).
[2]   Immigration Act 2014, s 73(1).
[3]   The Immigration Act 2014 (Commencement No 3, Transitional and Saving Provisions) Order 2014, SI 2014/2771, arts 2(b), 9 and 10(a).
[4]   The definition in NIAA 2002, s 117D(2), applied by SI 2014/2771, art 10(a).
[5]   SI 2014/2771, arts 2(b), 9 and 10(b).
[6]   The Immigration Act 2014 (Transitional and Saving Provisions) Order 2014, SI 2014/2928, art 2.
[7]   SI 2014/2928, art 2
[8]   SI 2014/2771, arts 2(b), 9 and 11(1)(a).
[9]   SI 2014/2771, arts 2(b), 9 and 11(1)(b).
[10] SI 2014/2771, arts 2(b), 9 and 11(1)(c).
[11] SI 2014/2771, art 11(2).
[12] SI 2014/2771, art 11(3), (4).
[13] SI 2014/2771, arts 1(e) and 9.

PRE-IMMIGRATION ACT 2014 POWERS OF THE FIRST-TIER TRIBUNAL

20.4 On an appeal, the power of the FT to decide the appeal one way or the other is contained in section 86 of the NIAA 2002.[1] It also has a jurisdiction to determine as a preliminary issue whether a notice of appeal is out of time, and if so, whether the appeal should be allowed to proceed.[2] We deal with this preliminary issue jurisdiction at **20.70** below. The FT has a power to make directions if it allows an appeal in order to give effect to its decision.[3] It has the power to review its own decisions[4] and to give permission to appeal from its decisions to the UT.[5]

[1]   As amended by Asylum and Immigration (Treatment of Claimants, etc) Act 2004, Sch 2, para 18 from 4 April 2005. The section is in similar, although not identical terms, to its predecessors, the Immigration and Asylum Act 1999 (IAA 1999), Sch 4, para 21 and Immigration Act (IA 1971), s 19, the old jurisdiction provisions.
[2]   The Tribunal Procedure (First-tier Tribunal) (Immigration and Asylum Chamber) Rules 2014, SI 2014/2604, r 20.
[3]   NIAA 2002, s 87 (as amended by Asylum and Immigration (Treatment of Claimants, etc) Act 2004, Sch 2, paras 18, 19 from 4 April 2005), but to be repealed by IA 2014, Sch 9, para 37.
[4]   TCEA 2007, s 9.
[5]   TCEA 2007, s 11(4)(a).

20.5 Section 86(3) of NIAA 2002 provides that the FT must allow the appeal if it thinks that:

(1) a decision against which the appeal is brought or is treated as being brought was not in accordance with the law (including Immigration Rules);[1] or

(2) a discretion exercised in making a decision against which the appeal is brought or is treated as being brought should have been exercised differently.[2]

The tribunal has no power to quash the decision against which an appeal is brought, but the effect of a decision to allow an appeal is that the decision maker may no longer rely on the decision appealed against. If the decision was a response to an application for leave to enter or remain, then the application remains outstanding[3] and, if the decision is held to be not in accordance with the law, a lawful decision is yet to be made.[4] Otherwise, the FT must dismiss the appeal.[5] A decision to remove someone from the UK is not to be regarded as unlawful if it could have lawfully been made by reference to another provision.[6] A decision by the Secretary of State not to depart from the rules may not be reviewed on the merits, but may be reviewed to see whether it is in accordance with the law.[7]

[1] NIAA 2002, s 86(3)(a), amended by Asylum and Immigration (Treatment of Claimants, etc) Act 2004, Sch 2, para 18.
[2] NIAA 2002, s 86(3)(b) as amended. On the issue of discretion see *Pearson v Immigration Appeal Tribunal* [1978] Imm AR 212, CA.
[3] *Greenwood (Automatic deportation: order of events)* [2014] UKUT 00342 (IAC).
[4] *Naved (Student – fairness – notice of points)* [2012] UKUT 14 IAC.
[5] NIAA 2002, s 86(5) as amended.
[6] NIAA 2002, s 86(4), which prevents technical appeals brought solely on the basis that, for example, an illegal entrant has been served with directions to an overstayer. Earlier statutory provisions in IAA 1999, Sch 4, para 24, which compelled the appellate authorities to dismiss appeals brought by illegal entrants and those against whom a deportation order is extant, needed modification to bring them into line with the Human Rights Act 1998. See *VN (Iran)* [2010] UKUT 303 (IAC).
[7] NIAA 2002, s 86(6). See **20.9** ff below.

20.6 The powers of the FT need to be read in the context of the statutory grounds of appeal, set out in section 84 of NIAA 2002, and the matters which the FT is obliged to consider under section 85 of the Act. An appeal against an immigration decision under section 82(1) must be brought on one or more of the statutory grounds. These are:

(a) the decision is not in accordance with Immigration Rules;[1]

(b) the decision is unlawful by virtue of article 20A of the Race Relations (Northern Ireland) Order 1997 or section 29 of the Equality Act 2010 (discrimination in the exercise of public functions etc) so far as relating to race as defined by s 9(1) of that Act;[2]

(c) the decision is unlawful under section 6, Human Rights Act 1998 (public authority not to act contrary to Human Rights Convention) as being incompatible with the appellant's Convention rights;[3]

(d) the appellant is an EEA national or a member of the family of an EEA national and the decision breaches the appellant's rights under the Community Treaties in respect of entry to or residence in the UK;[4]

(e) the decision is otherwise not in accordance with the law;[5]

(f) the person taking the decision should have exercised differently a discretion conferred by Immigration Rules;[6]

(g)   removal in consequence of the decision would breach the UK's obligations under the Refugee Convention or would be unlawful under
section 6, HRA 1998 as being incompatible with the appellant's Convention rights.[7]

Even if an appellant is able to bring an appeal from within the UK only because
of having made an asylum or human rights claim,[8] the appeal is not restricted
to the asylum or human rights grounds of appeal, but all of the statutory
grounds are available.[9]

[1]   NIAA 2002, s 84(1)(a). NIAA 2002 is the first to define and delimit exhaustively the permitted
grounds of appeal, but s 84 merely makes explicit what were previously implicit limitations
drawn by the scope of appellate jurisdiction. A useful definition of a 'ground' is 'the
application of particular legal rules to a set of facts to produce a legal result in the case in
question': *R (on the application of Borak) v Secretary of State for the Home Department*
[2005] EWCA Civ 110, [2005] All ER (D) 163 (Jan) (in the context of NIAA 2002, s 96 before
amendment).

[2]   NIAA 2002, s 84(1)(b) as amended by SI 2011/1060, SI 2003/341 and Crime and Courts Act
2013, s 51(1); see for example *European Roma Rights Centre v Immigration Officer at Prague
Airport* [2004] UKHL 55, [2005] 2 WLR 1, where the House of Lords upheld a claim of race
discrimination in the operation of pre-entry screening at Prague Airport.

[3]   NIAA 2002, s 84(1)(c). This ground is most apt in appeals against refusal of entry clearance,
where this is said to breach the positive obligation to respect family life (ECHR, art 8).

[4]   NIAA 2002, s 84(1)(d).

[5]   NIAA 2002, s 84(1)(e).

[6]   NIAA 2002, s 84(1)(f).

[7]   NIAA 2002, s 84(1)(g). Note that this ground embraces both Refugee and Human Rights Convention grounds, unlike ground (c); that is because in situations other than removal there is no
question of the Refugee Convention's *non-refoulement* obligation being breached.

[8]   NIAA 2002, s 92(4)(a).

[9]   *SA (Bangladesh)* [2005] UKAIT 00178.

20.7 An appeal under section 83 or 83A of the Act must be brought on the
ground that removal of the appellant would breach the UK's obligations under
the Refugee Convention[1] or under the Qualification Directive. The rationale
for the appeals under sections 83 and 83A is to enable refugees to litigate the
issue of their entitlement to status[2] and the corresponding rights that recognition brings under the Refugee Convention.[3] Attempts to argue human rights
grounds in section 83 appeals have failed because of the wording of the
section and of section 84(3), and because appellants have leave to remain in
the UK, and will be able to argue human rights grounds if and when that leave
is not renewed, bringing removal into prospect.[4] However, the EU law
'principle of equivalence' (whereby domestic legal rules governing actions
intended to ensure the protection of rights conferred by Community law
should not be less favourable than rules governing similar domestic actions)
applies because of the similarity of refugee status and humanitarian protection.[5] Therefore, it requires sections 83 and 83A to be read so as to allow an
appeal to be brought on the ground that the refusal is contrary to the
UK's obligation under the Qualification Directive not to remove a person
entitled to subsidiary protection.[6] The Supreme Court decided to make a
reference to the CJEU in the case of *FA (Iraq) v Secretary of State for the Home
Department*[7] but the Secretary of State subsequently withdrew her appeal
before a reference was made.

[1]   NIAA 2002, s 84(3) (for s 83 appeals) and 84(4) (for s 83A appeals).

[2]   For the duty to determine claims, see *Robinson (Anthonypillai Francis) v Secretary of State for
the Home Department and Immigration Appeal Tribunal* [1997] Imm AR 568; *Saad v*

Secretary of State for the Home Department, Diriye v Secretary of State for the Home Department, Osorio v Secretary of State for the Home Department [2001] EWCA Civ 2008, [2002] Imm AR 471, [2002] INLR 34.

3   See in particular Convention Relating to the Status of Refugees, arts 17–30, **12.101** above.

4   See *P (Yugoslavia)* [2003] UKIAT 00017; *LA (Eritrea)* [2004] UKIAT 00113. In *SS (Somalia)* [2005] UKAIT 00167 the Tribunal held that there was no jurisdiction to allow a s 83 appeal on the ground that the decision was 'not in accordance with the law'. See also *AN (Albania)* [2007] UKAIT 00097.

5   'Humanitarian protection' is the means by which the UK fulfils its obligation under art 18 of the Council Directive (2004/83/EC) of 29 April 2004 on minimum standards for the qualification and status of third country nationals or stateless persons as refugees or as persons who otherwise need international protection and the content of the protection granted ('the Qualification Directive') to provide 'subsidiary protection status'.

6   *FA (Iraq) v Secretary of State for the Home Department* [2010] EWCA Civ 696.

7   [2011] UKSC 22.

Scope of appeal

20.8 In accordance with the principle of 'one-stop' appeals (see **19.53** above), an appeal under section 82(1) is to be treated by the FT as including an appeal against any decision in respect of which the appellant has a right of appeal under the section.[1] This simply means that it is not necessary for an appellant to lodge separate appeals in respect of different immigration decisions.[2] Circumstances in which an immigrant would receive more than one immigration decision simultaneously might include: refusal of further leave to remain and a decision to deport on conducive grounds or following a recommendation for deportation or a decision that the person whose application for variation of leave is refused[3] is to be given removal directions under section 47 of the Immigration, Asylum and Nationality Act 2006 (IANA 2006).[4] This also means that the tribunal may give a 'differential determination' allowing an appeal in respect of one of the decisions appealed against, but dismissing it in respect of another.[5] Section 85(2) obliges the FT to consider additional grounds raised by the statement of additional grounds served in response to a one-stop notice, whether those grounds were served before or after the appeal was lodged,[6] if they fall within the scope of section 84(1). Section 86(2) re-emphasises the duty of the FT to determine any matter raised as a ground of appeal or which section 85 obliges it to consider. The wording of section 86(3), requiring the FT to allow appeals against decisions against which 'the appeal is brought *or is treated as being brought*',[7] brings these additional grounds within the scope of the appeal.

1   NIAA 2002, s 85(1). This section does not oblige the FT to consider issues not raised by the appellant, subject to Refugee Convention obligations (*Robinson (Anthonypillai Francis) v Secretary of State for the Home Department and Immigration Appeal Tribunal* [1997] Imm AR 568).

2   Explanatory notes to NIAA 2002, para 224.

3   Appealable under NIAA 2002, s 82(2)(d) or (e).

4   Appealable under NIAA 2002, s 82(2)(ha).

5   *Adamally and Jaferji* [2012] UKUT 414 (IAC); *Rahman (Md Mahamudur) v Secretary of State for the Home Department* [2014] EWCA Civ 11.

6   NIAA 2002, s 85(2), (3). Note that there is no statutory requirement for the Secretary of State to respond to a statement of additional grounds, and if there is no response, the FT would effectively be a first-instance decision maker in relation to these grounds. Although the language of a statement of additional grounds does not have to be legalistic, and complaints in Home Office refusal letters that the appellant has failed to specify which articles of the Convention are relied on are unjustified, the FT need consider only assertions which can

be construed as grounds of appeal within s 84(1)(a)–(g). 'I fear torture' or 'I will be separated from my family' would obviously fall within their scope.

7   NIAA 2002, s 86(3)(a) and (b).

'In accordance with the law'

20.9 The FT must allow an appeal if the decision which is the subject of the appeal was not in accordance with the law, including Immigration Rules. Legal incompatibility of decisions with the Immigration Rules is dealt with below. What does this limb of the appeal jurisdiction cover? This question has given rise to much litigation. The law is clearly something distinct from and much wider than the Immigration Rules or the 'immigration laws', both of which are terms of Art used and defined in IA 1971.[1] Little difficulty is encountered where the FT is called upon to construe and interpret the immigration or nationality laws, or some other applicable statutory provision, or to refer to the common law for the meaning of such terms as domicile, ordinary residence and the like. Clearly, the FT is also required to ensure that the respondent's decision was not incompatible with EC law and the refugee and human rights Conventions.[2] Thus an 'EEA decision' to refuse a residence card, made in accordance with the EEA Regulations,[3] would be 'not in accordance with the law' if the appellant had a Community law right of residence, albeit one to which the Regulations do not give effect.[4] The scope of this duty has given rise to some difficulty. In *SS (Malaysia)*,[5] a starred Tribunal held that the phrase 'not in accordance with the law' in the appeal provisions of the Immigration and Asylum Act 1999 (IAA 1999) did not extend to incompatibility with the Convention rights of the appellant's UK-resident mother, and that the invocation of the general jurisdiction attempted to subvert the express limitation of the scope of the appeal to the appellant's human rights. The House of Lords has held that there was no such limitation on the scope of an appeal brought under the IAA 1999 and that the Tribunal was required to consider the impact of the decision on the human rights of any affected non-appellants.[6] It is also significant that the Tribunal's power under the 2002 Act to allow an appeal if the decision is 'not in accordance with the law' is not, as it was under IAA 1999, 'subject to any restrictions on the grounds of appeal'.[7] Another potential difficulty arises from the historical focus of the section: the FT is required to allow the appeal if the decision 'was' not in accordance with the law, whereas the focus of appeals on asylum and human rights grounds is the future. Can it be said that a historical decision was not in accordance with the law because of unforeseeable events which have happened since – whether a coup at home or a marriage in the UK? The provisions of ss 85 and 86(2) expressly require consideration of such events, and we suggest that s 86(3) must be read, in appeals depending on asylum or human rights grounds, as if it required an appeal to be allowed if the decision 'would not be in accordance with the law if implemented now'.[8]

1   IA 1971, s 33. The definition covers all the Immigration Acts, a phrase itself defined by the UK Borders Act 2007, s 61. If the intention of Parliament had been to confine the appellate jurisdiction to checking whether the decision or action was in accordance with the immigration laws, the use of that phrase would have been entirely apt.

2   In asylum appeals, the Tribunal is required to ensure that its decisions comply with the European Council Directive 2004/83/EC on minimum standards for the qualification and status of third country nationals and stateless persons as refugees or persons who otherwise

need international protection (30.9.04, OJ L304/12), ie are no less favourable than the provisions of the Directive, although they may be more favourable. It is also necessary to ensure that decisions make the best interests of a child a primary consideration, a requirement incorporated in the Qualification Directive, art 18.5; Council Directive 2003/9/EC on minimum standards for the reception of asylum seekers, OJ 2003 L31/18, art 18. A similar requirement in the Temporary Protection Directive is incorporated in the Immigration Rules, HC 395, para 356B, inserted by HC 164.

3 Immigration (European Economic Area) Regulations 2006, SI 2006/1003.

4 *MDB (Article 12, 1612/68) Italy* [2010] UKUT 161 (IAC).

5 *SS (Malaysia)* [2004] UKIAT 00091, [2004] Imm AR 153 (starred). IAA 1999, Sch 4, para 21, required an adjudicator to allow an appeal against a decision which was not in accordance with the law, 'subject to any restrictions on the grounds of appeal'. SS, an adult son who sought to join his mother in the UK, could not succeed on his s 59 appeal against refusal of entry clearance under the Immigration Rules, para 317 (distressed relatives) since the exceptional compassionate circumstances related to his mother and not himself, so he was forced to rely on s 65 (human rights appeal), which referred to a breach of 'his human rights'.

6 *Beoku-Betts v Secretary of State for the Home Department* [2008] UKHL 39.

7 Immigration and Asylum Act 1999, Sch 4, para 21(2).

8 The Tribunal appears to have accepted that this is the correct interpretation of the phrase in an appeal raising asylum grounds, in *OB (Somalia)* [2005] UKIAT 00056.

20.10 Another difficult issue, which has dogged the appellate authorities and the courts for decades, has been the question of how far the appellate authorities can and must have regard to the general principles of administrative law when considering the actions and decisions of the Secretary of State or an immigration officer, where these involve the exercise of a discretion. In the case of *Singh*[1] the House of Lords held that the appellate authorities were not precluded from examining any aspect of the Secretary of State's broad discretion in deportation cases. Lord Bridge reasoned that the appellate jurisdiction to determine whether a decision was in accordance with the law had to embrace the general requirements of administrative law and so an appeal would be allowed if the Secretary of State had failed to have regard to all relevant circumstances.[2] He equated the adjudicator's jurisdiction with the supervisory jurisdiction of the High Court in such circumstances. The judgment in *Singh* gave rise to almost two decades of litigation on the scope of appellate jurisdiction.[3] Much of it was concerned with appeals against decisions taken outside the Immigration Rules, where appellants argued that refusal, while in accordance with Immigration Rules, failed to have regard to relevant policies (such as the Somali family reunion policy which operated in the 1980s and 1990s, the various marriage and cohabitation policies and the long residence policy), and thus breached the general principles of administrative law referred to by Lord Bridge in *Singh*. In *Abdi*,[4] the Court of Appeal, while observing that 'it is not obvious that Parliament intended adjudicators to have the power to examine the validity of the Home Secretary's decision by reference to all the matters that would be relevant for a judicial review of that decision', went on to 'proceed on the footing that if it can be shown that the Home Secretary failed to act in accordance with established principles of administrative or common law, for example if he did not take account of or give effect to his own published policy, that was 'not in accordance with the law'.[5] The Court of Appeal's endorsement of this principle in *Abdi* was followed in *Hersi*.[6] The court in *Abdi* held that the exercise of discretion outside the rules was flawed if refusal was predicated on misapprehension of material facts, which was held to be a further head of illegality.[7] The Tribunal now accepts that the statutory grounds of appeal[8] enable it to entertain challenges to immigration decisions based on public law grounds such as breach of a legitimate expectation;[9] procedural unfairness in the making of the decision[10] and failure to apply a relevant policy.[11] The tribunal may determine whether a decision that an individual is not a victim of trafficking, made the decision to remove unlawful, as being not in accordance with the Secretary of State's policy relating to the identification and treatment of victims of trafficking.[12] If the Immigration Directorate Instructions provide for a relaxation or generous interpretation of the requirements of the rules, withholding the benefit of such a concession would be not in accordance with the law.[13] Where a decision is 'not in accordance with the law' owing to failure to apply a policy, the tribunal should allow the appeal, remitting the case to the decision maker to apply the policy unless the only reasonable outcome when the policy is applied would be a decision in the appellant's favour.[14] So, for example, the terms of the policy relating to entry clearance applications by overage dependents of former members of the UK armed forces were not sufficiently precise to admit of only one possible outcome, meaning that the tribunal was wrong to have directed grants of entry clearance.[15] On the other hand, the tribunal could properly hold that 'the result would be inevitable' if the entry clearance officer was to apply the policy allowing a departure from the requirement of the rules that a domestic worker should be travelling with the employer if they are to be granted entry.[16] Refusal to vary a student's leave to remain on the ground that his college's sponsorship licence had been revoked was held to be unlawful because it was in breach of the requirements of fairness in circumstances where he had no prior knowledge of the revocation, no proper opportunity to make representations to the Secretary of State, and no opportunity to find an alternative course before the decision was made.[17] Focus by the tribunal on the decision making process may be necessary where the statutory scheme prevents a decision being revisited on the basis of new evidence.[18] However, where the tribunal can conduct an unfettered reassessment of the substance of the decision, eg by determining for itself the appellant's age, it will not decide the appeal merely by reference to whether the respondent's decision making process was lawful.[19] The tribunal has accepted that it would have to allow an appeal on the ground that if applicable secondary legislation was shown to be ultra vires, a decision made in accordance with that secondary legislation would nevertheless be 'not in accordance with the law'.[20]

[1]   *Singh (Bakhtaur) v Immigration Appeal Tribunal* [1986] 2 All ER 721, [1986] Imm AR 352, HL.

[2]   *Associated Provincial Picture Houses Ltd v Wednesbury Corpn* [1948] 1 KB 223, [1948] 2 All ER 680 – the origin of the 'Wednesbury unreasonable' test in administrative law.

[3]   For a detailed exposition see 5th edition, 18.64–18.87.

[4]   *Abdi (Dhudi Saleban) v Secretary of State for the Home Department* [1996] Imm AR 148, CA.

[5]   *Abdi*, ibid at 157.

[6]   *Hersi, Uslusow, Nur, Warsame and Kahie v Secretary of State for the Home Department* [1996] Imm AR 569, CA.

[7]   *Abdi*, fn 4 above; see now, on material mistake of fact, *E v Secretary of State for the Home Department* [2004] EWCA Civ 49, [2004] 2 WLR 1351. In such cases, the normal approach was for the Tribunal to find the relevant facts and to state that the issue remained outstanding, for determination on those facts, by the decision maker. For the impact of human rights jurisdiction see 20.25 below.

[8]   NIAA 2002, s 84(1)(e).

[9]   *AA (Pakistan)* [2008] UKAIT 00003, rejecting the Secretary of State's submission to the contrary in this case.

10   *BO (Nigeria)* [2004] UKIAT 0026; *Naved (Student – fairness – notice of points)* [2012] UKUT 14 (IAC).

11   *AG (Kosovo)* [2007] UKAIT 0082 and *HH (Iraq)* [2008] UKAIT 0051.

12   *AS (Afghanistan) v Secretary of State for the Home Department* [2013] EWCA Civ 1469.

13   *ZH (Bangladesh) v Secretary of State for the Home Department* [2009] EWCA Civ 8 at [31]-[33].

14   *AG (Kosovo)* [2007] UKAIT 82.

15   *KG (Nepal)* [2011] UKUT 000117 (IAC) and *Pun (Nepal)* [2011] UKUT 00377 (IAC).

16   *Ozhogina and Tarasova (Russia)* [2011] UKUT 00197 (IAC).

17   *Thakur (Bangladesh)* [2011] UKUT 00151 (IAC) and *Patel (India)* [2011] UKUT 00211 (IAC). The tribunal has emphasised that the jurisdiction to allow an appeal because a decision is unfair relates to the procedural rather than substantive features of the decision: *Marghia (Procedural fairness)* [2014] UKUT 366 (IAC) and *Fiaz (Cancellation of leave to remain – fairness)* [2012] UKUT 00057 IAC.

18   ie where NIAA 2002, s 85A applies.

19   *KA (Afghanistan) v Secretary of State for the Home Department* [2012] EWCA Civ 1420.

20   *IH (Eritrea)* [2009] UKAIT 00012 with which the Court of Appeal agreed on this point in *EN (Serbia) v Secretary of State for the Home Department* [2009] EWCA Civ 630. The court indicated that in such a situation it might have been appropriate for the AIT to adjourn proceedings to enable the vires of the legislation to be challenged in the Administrative Court but that, owing to its composition including High Court judges, the new tribunal structure would not need to act with such restraint.

20.11 It used to be a general rule that, if an application called for the exercise of a discretion which had not in fact been exercised, the decision was not in accordance with the law, and an appeal would be allowed to the extent that the Secretary of State should reconsider the case.[1] This was based on the principle that the appellate authority was not an original decision taker and, therefore, could not determine an application which had been made to the Secretary of State but not determined prior to appeal.[2] The rule has undergone modification in the asylum and human rights context, given the different nature of the appellate jurisdiction in these fields, where it has been held to be more of an extension of the original decision-making function.[3] The Tribunal held in *Haddad*,[4] an appeal against a refusal of asylum on 'non-compliance' grounds,[5] that the adjudicator had no power to remit an unconsidered claim to the Secretary of State for reconsideration, and should deal with the asylum claim on the merits, if necessary as a primary decision maker. The Court of Appeal endorsed this conclusion in *Zaier*,[6] holding that the adjudicator had no power to remit claims to the Secretary of State for reconsideration.[7] It is thus not uncommon, and certainly not unlawful, for a Tribunal to decide an asylum or human rights claim raised for the first time in a statement of additional grounds served with the notice of appeal and not considered by the Secretary of State, or indeed, raised for the first time by way of a late amendment to the grounds of appeal, and as indicated above, the wording of sections 85 and 86 of NIAA 2002 now suggests that the Tribunal could not lawfully decline to do so. In previous editions we suggested that outside the asylum and human rights context, if the decision maker failed to apply the correct rule or failed to exercise a discretion, the Tribunal should find the decision 'not in accordance with the law' and so still outstanding before the Secretary of State. However, it is now clear that there is no practical or legal obstacle to the Tribunal acting as, in effect, the primary decision maker and so it may not be necessary to remit a matter to the Secretary of State.[8] In *Yau Yak Wah*[9] the Court of Appeal held that a decision was not in accordance with the law where the Secretary of State had failed to give separate consideration to the case of each appellant in a case involving different members of a family, and thus failed to exercise discretion.

1 Sometimes this was expressed as the matter remaining outstanding before the decision maker: see eg *Ibeakanma* (18632) (25 September 1998, unreported), IAT; *Adeyemi* (17115) (20 May 1998, unreported), IAT. See *H (Somalia)* [2004] UKIAT 00027.
2 *R v Immigration Appeal Tribunal, ex p Malik* (1981) Times, 16 November, Forbes J.
3 *Ravichandran (Senathirajah) v Secretary of State for the Home Department* [1996] Imm AR 97 (asylum); *R (on the application of Razgar) v Secretary of State for the Home Department* [2004] UKHL 27, [2004] 3 WLR 58 (human rights).
4 [2000] INLR 117, IAT.
5 For 'non-compliance' refusals of asylum under HC 395, para 340 see **12.129** above.
6 *R (on the application of Zaier) v Secretary of State for the Home Department* [2003] EWCA Civ 937, [2003] All ER (D) 153 (Jul).
7 However, *Zaier* was an appeal under the Asylum and Immigration Appeals Act 1993, s 8, in which the jurisdiction of the adjudicator was limited to consideration of whether the removal of the appellant would breach the UK's Refugee Convention obligations. In that context, the court held that there was no power to do anything other than to determine the appeal, and that the direction to the Secretary of State to reconsider the asylum claim on its merits was not a procedural direction relating to the just, timely and effective disposal of the appeal, but related to a substantive issue. Following *Mwanza* [2001] Imm AR 557, CA, the court held the direction *ultra vires* the procedure rules. The court did not consider whether the 'not in accordance with the law' jurisdiction (then contained in IAA 1999, Sch 4, para 21) would allow an adjudicator to allow an appeal against the non-compliance decision to the extent of holding that the claim remained outstanding before the Secretary of State.
8 *AS (Afghanistan) v Secretary of State for the Home Department* [2009] EWCA Civ 1076. See **20.23** below.
9 *Wah (Yau Yak) v Home Office* [1982] Imm AR 16, CA.

20.12 The Court of Appeal held in *Manshoora Begum*[1] that an immigration rule, requiring certain classes of dependent relatives seeking entry to the UK to show (*inter alia*) that they enjoyed a standard of living substantially below that of their own country, was irrational and *ultra vires* IA 1971, under which it was promulgated. The question whether the Tribunal itself has the power to hold rules *ultra vires* and invalid, rendering decisions made under them 'not in accordance with the law', has in the past been answered in the negative by the Tribunal itself.[2] A starred Tribunal in *Pardeepan*[3] suggested without deciding that the *vires* of a commencement order under IAA 1999 were a matter for the High Court, and in *Koprinov*[4] a Tribunal chaired by the President held it had no jurisdiction to decide whether a rule was *ultra vires*. However, the Tribunal changed its mind on this issue[5] in the light of the House of Lords decision in *Foster*[6] and the Court of Appeal has held that the Tribunal could disapply unlawful secondary legislation.[7] Since the Human Rights Act came into force the question of the compatibility of secondary legislation and rules with Convention rights arises and the Tribunal has disapplied rules whose application in the particular case would result in a disproportionate interference with family or private life rights.[8]

1 *R v Immigration Appeal Tribunal, ex p Begum (Manshoora)* [1986] Imm AR 385.
2 The Court of Appeal in *Begum* assumed that the Tribunal did not possess this power, although in the later case of *Chief Adjudication Officer v Foster* [1993] AC 754, [1993] 1 All ER 705 the House of Lords, considering an analogous power possessed by the Chief Adjudication Officer on an appeal from a Social Security Appeal Tribunal, ruled that the Social Security Commissioner could determine the *vires* of a regulation under his or her 'erroneous in point of law' jurisdiction.
3 *Pardeepan v Secretary of State for the Home Department* [2002] Imm AR 249, [2000] INLR 447. The Tribunal proceeded on the basis that the order was intra vires. See also *Singh (Pawandeep)* (18465) (16 March 1999, unreported), IAT, where the Tribunal held that it had no power to determine whether the rules on adoption ran counter to the statutory scheme of the Adoption Act. In refusing leave to appeal, however, Buxton LJ was prepared to accept,

without deciding, that the Tribunal would have jurisdiction to enter upon that inquiry in an appropriate case, although in this case the rule was not *ultra vires*: SLJ 99/6917/4, 2 December 1999.

4 (01TH 00091) (5 February 2001, unreported).
5 *IH (Eritrea)* [2009] UKAIT 00012.
6 *Foster v Chief Adjudication Officer* [1993] AC 794.
7 *EN (Serbia) v Secretary of State for the Home Department* [2009] EWCA Civ 630.
8 See eg *R v Secretary of State for the Home Department, ex p Ali (Arman)* [2000] Imm AR 134, [2000] INLR 89; *Begum (Husna) v Entry Clearance Officer, Dhaka* [2001] INLR 115; *Boadi v Entry Clearance Officer, Ghana* [2002] UKIAT 01323, [2003] INLR 54 for discussions on interpretation and application of rules so as to give effect to human rights. See **7.15** above. The Tribunal is not given power to strike down legislation which is incompatible with the Convention, or to give a declaration of incompatibility: see **7.17** above.

Scottish or English law

20.13 The Immigration Acts and Rules apply throughout the UK and there is a unified appellate authority. This should mean that the law is the same in both Scotland and England. There are divergences in higher court decisions, particularly in areas such as detention,[1] in the exclusion of unfairly obtained evidence in illegal entry decisions,[2] and over the issue of delay in judicial review,[3] but in asylum cases at least, the distinctions between Scottish and English decisions are more apparent than real. Two questions arise. The first is a choice of law and the second a choice of jurisdiction. First, if there is a conflict between the Scottish and English decisions, which law should the Tribunal apply? In *Akbar*[4] the Tribunal suggested that if the judicial approach differs in any material way, it will be for the appellate authority to decide with which legal system the case is most closely connected. Secondly, can appellants choose whether to litigate in Scotland or England? At Tribunal level, the matter does not arise, since there is no distinct appellate unit in either jurisdiction. In applications for review and in appeals from determinations by the Tribunal the choice of jurisdiction is determined by statute. The appeal goes to the Court of Session where the determination of the Tribunal is made in Scotland and in all other cases to the Court of Appeal;[5] the application for review of a Tribunal decision made in Scotland goes to the Outer House of the Court of Session, and otherwise, to the Administrative Court.[6] Decisions of the Tribunal in Northern Ireland go on appeal to the Northern Ireland Court of Appeal and on review to the High Court in Northern Ireland.[7] Where the appeal was decided determines the jurisdiction in which the application for review or appeal from the Tribunal is made and if an appeal is reconsidered, it is 'decided' in the place where the reconsideration took place.[8]

1 *Sokha v Secretary of State for the Home Department* [1992] Imm AR 14, CS.
2 *Oghonoghor v Secretary of State for the Home Department* 1995 SLT 733; *Kim (Sofia) v Secretary of State for the Home Department* 2000 SLT 249, OHCS, Lord Abernethy.
3 *Singh (Gurjit)* (14 March 2000, unreported), OH CS, Lord Nimmo Smith.
4 (8670), IAT.
5 NIAA 2002, s 103B(5), (6) (inserted by the Asylum and Immigration (Treatment of Claimants, etc) Act 2004, s 26). The Court of Appeal's decision in *Gardi v Secretary of State for the Home Department* [2002] EWCA Civ 750 [2003] Imm AR 39, [2002] INLR 499 was nullified (see *Gardi v Secretary of State for the Home Department (No 2)* [2002] EWCA Civ 1560, [2002] INLR 557) because it transpired that the decision on appeal emanated from an adjudicator sitting in Scotland, and so should have gone to the Court of Session under the previous provisions, IAA 1999, Sch 4, para 23(3).

6   NIAA 2002, s 103A(9), (10) as inserted. Although prior to the NIAA 2002 there was no statutory jurisdictional bar on the High Court hearing applications for review of decisions from adjudicators in Scotland, Jackson J declined jurisdiction in *R (on the application of Majead) v Secretary of State for the Home Department* [2002] EWHC 2299 (Admin), citing by analogy the provisions of the IAA 1999 (above). See the Court of Appeal's judgment at [2003] EWCA Civ 615 and *Tehrani v Secretary of State for the Home Department* [2006] UKHL 47, [2007] 1 AC 521, [2007] 1 All ER 559.
7   NIAA 2002, s 103A(9)(c).
8   *HT (Cameroon) v Secretary of State for the Home Department* [2008] EWCA Civ 1508, [2009] All ER (D) 24 (Jan).

20.14 In applications for judicial review of decisions of the Secretary of State, the question is not so easily determined: the English Administrative Court or the Scottish Court of Session may each have or claim jurisdiction. In *Sokha*[1] the Court of Session resolved the matter by the application of the doctrine of *forum non conveniens*, and rejected jurisdiction in a case with no Scottish connection. Although strong preference should be given to the forum chosen by the applicant, particularly where the alternative jurisdiction is another part of the UK, rather than a wholly foreign country, this preference may be overcome if the respondent can 'establish that there is another available forum which is clearly and distinctly more appropriate', although less advantageous.[2]

1   *Sokha v Secretary of State for the Home Department* [1992] Imm AR 14, Ct of Sess.
2   *Spiliada Maritime Corpn v Cansulex Ltd, The Spiliada* [1987] AC 460, per Lord Goff; *Trendtex Trading Corpn v Crédit Suisse* [1982] AC 679; Abidin Daver, The [1984] AC 398 at 411. The Court of Appeal held in *Majead* [2003] EWCA Civ 615 that judicial review should be brought in the country where the appeal was heard.

'Including Immigration Rules'

20.15 For the purposes of section 86(3)(a), 'the law' includes 'Immigration Rules' but is not synonymous with them. We have considered above situations where it is argued that the Immigration Rules themselves do not adequately reflect the relevant law.[1] But, in many if not most cases, the Tribunal's first port of call, if not its last, will be the Immigration Rules. If a decision is not in accordance with Immigration Rules, the appeal should be allowed, subject to the proviso already referred to (that a removal decision will not be invalid because the wrong provision is cited, if the person is removable under another provision).[2] The rules to be considered by the Tribunal are (absent transitional provisions or a properly established legitimate expectation to the contrary) those applicable at the time of the decision appealed against, not those applicable at the time the application was made or those applicable at the time of the hearing.[3] However, at least in respect of the Immigration Rules intended to codify Article 8, ECHR as applied to deportation decisions, the rules to be applied are those in force at the time that the tribunal considers the matter, even if they were not in force at the time of the decision.[4] Thus, where the wrong rule is applied, and the decision is based on grounds which are inapplicable to the applicant, the decision is not in accordance with rules;[5] nor is it in accordance with Immigration Rules where the evidence before the Tribunal establishes the appellant's eligibility for entry under the relevant rule.[6] Because of this provision the Immigration Rules have the force of law for the purposes of appeals, though not for other purposes.[7] The case law reflects some conflict between two principles: on the one hand, the appellate authority must ensure that the decision is in accordance with Immigration Rules generally, implying a broad jurisdiction;[8] on the other, it is only entitled to determine that which is before it for determination.[9] The position may be summarised as follows.

(1) The Tribunal is not restricted to the particular rule or part of a rule relied on in the notice of decision or explanatory statement, but, having found the facts, is entitled to apply the Immigration Rules applicable to the case having regard to those facts, subject to giving the parties a fair opportunity to deal with the issue.[10] This applies whether the new rule involves mandatory refusal or the exercise of discretion.[11] However, if the facts known to the decision maker could support a ground for refusal that is not cited in the notice of decision, the Tribunal is entitled to assume that that potential ground for refusal is not relied on and is not in issue in the appeal.[12]

(2) The Tribunal is not entitled, however, to go behind a finding of fact of the Secretary of State favourable to the appellant.[13]

(3) Similarly, the respondent may seek to rely on a new rule applicable to the facts, subject to providing the appellant with a fair opportunity to deal with the new rule, by amendment of the refusal decision or the issue of a new explanatory statement.[14]

(4) The respondent may not, however, seek to alter the statutory basis of its decision, eg by relying on a wholly different deportation power in the IA 1971 from that originally exercised.[15]

(5) The principle for appellants is that if they make clear the facts that they rely on when making their application, they are not required to set out all the different potentially applicable Immigration Rules.[16] They must be permitted to ventilate on appeal eligibility under rules other than those previously considered by the respondent,[17] provided the fact found forms part of the basis of the decision, since to hold otherwise would mean that the scope of the right of appeal would be confined to the basis on which the respondent chose to frame it.[18] The pre-2002 Act cases suggest that there is no jurisdiction to allow an appeal against a decision on the basis that if the application had been made on another ground it might have qualified under another section of the rules,[19] particularly if the grounds are mutually exclusive but this restriction no longer applies, given the one-stop principle and its draconian enforcement by the NIAA 2002, section 96 on the one hand, and on the other, the broad jurisdiction of the FT.[20]

(6) The Tribunal may on its own initiative have regard to any particular rule that bears on the case put forward by the appellant with regard to the decision or action appealed against,[21] but it is not required to conduct a roving inquiry into whether the facts could fit any conceivable rule in the absence of submissions to that effect[22] or reference to the rule in the grounds of appeal as originally formulated or subsequently amended.[23]

(7) The appellant may raise wholly new matters on appeal, in response to a one-stop warning, by providing a statement of additional grounds and the Tribunal is required to decide whether they entitle the appellant to succeed, even if the Secretary of State has not considered them.[24] Where no one-stop warning has been issued, we suggest that the appellant may raise any new matters by amendment to the grounds of

appeal (subject to the consent of the Tribunal, which ought to give consent, provided the respondent is given a fair opportunity to deal with the new issues) otherwise, once more the scope of the appeal would be determined by the respondent, in this case by its failure to serve a one-stop notice.[25] In our view, the function of the one-stop notice is only to allow certification[26] to prevent the bringing of a later appeal. It is not a precondition to the exercise of the Tribunal's broad, primary jurisdiction which is founded on the other statutory provisions including NIAA 2002, section 85(4) which allows the Tribunal to consider evidence about 'any matter' so long as it is relevant to the 'substance of the decision'.[27]

(8) Given the obligation on the Tribunal to consider circumstances in existence at the date of the hearing[28] (other than in entry clearance appeals and appeals against refusal of a certificate of entitlement), an appellant able to show that he or she meets the requirements of the rules at the time of the hearing should be entitled to succeed on the ground that the decision was not in accordance with the rules even if he or she did not qualify at the time of the decision.[29]

---

[1] See also *M & A v Secretary of State for the Home Department* [2003] EWCA Civ 263, [2003] Imm AR 4, where the Court of Appeal emphasised that the rules must be given a purposive construction, so that the requirement that there be 'adequate accommodation' for children seeking to join parents would not be met when there were serious welfare concerns about the children living with their parents.

[2] NIAA 2002, s 86(4).

[3] *PP (India)* [2005] UKAIT 00141; *MO (Nigeria)* [2007] UKAIT 00057; *EO (Turkey)* [2007] UKAIT 00062; *AA (Pakistan)* [2008] UKAIT0 0003; *MO (Nigeria) v Secretary of State for the Home Department* [2008] EWCA Civ 308, [2009] 1 WLR 126; *Odelola v Secretary of State for the Home Department* [2009] UKHL 25.

[4] *YM (Uganda) v Secretary of State for the Home Department* [2014] EWCA Civ 1292, although the point was conceded. This is unlikely to be the last word on the matter.

[5] *R v Immigration Appeal Tribunal, ex p Khan* [1975] Imm AR 26. This happens most frequently in cases involving family settlement, where for example the 'living alone in the most exceptional compassionate circumstances' test is wrongly applied to an appellant. This does not, of course, mean that the appellant would succeed on the merits under the correct rule, and there would be no point in allowing the appeal to the extent of holding that the issue remains outstanding before the Secretary of State or ECO for reconsideration under the correct rule, if it would make no difference to the result. That is why the Tribunal may – and perhaps should – instead consider the appeal under the correct rule, subject to giving the appellant a fair opportunity to deal with the issue; see below.

[6] For a case which illustrates both the 'law' and 'rules' jurisdiction neatly, see *Ibeakanma* (18632) (25 September 1998, unreported).

[7] *Pearson v Immigration Appeal Tribunal* [1978] Imm AR 212; *R v Secretary of State for the Home Department, ex p Hosenball* [1977] 3 All ER 452, [1977] 1 WLR 766, CA; *Singh (Bakhtaur) v Immigration Appeal Tribunal* [1986] 2 All ER 721, [1986] Imm AR 352, HL; *R (on the application of Munir) v Secretary of State for the Home Department (Joint Council for the Welfare of Immigrants intervening)* [2012] UKSC 32; *R (on the application of Alvi) v Secretary of State for the Home Department* [2012] UKSC 33.

[8] *R v Immigration Appeal Tribunal, ex p Khan* [1975] Imm AR 26; *R v Immigration Appeal Tribunal, ex p Hubbard* [1985] Imm AR 110, QBD.

[9] *R v Immigration Appeal Tribunal, ex p Akhtar* (1982) 126 Sol Jo 430, QBD. The Tribunal leant towards this approach in *Immigration Officer (Nigeria)* [2004] UKIAT 00179, holding that applicants for entry clearance 'are entitled to assume that their ability to satisfy particular requirements of the rules has not been put in issue unless the entry clearance officer unequivocally puts it in issue'. Although the Tribunal recognised that the immigration judge could give the appellant express notice that another requirement of the rules is being put in issue, it went on to observe that the injustice to the appellant caused by the delay inherent in such a procedure was likely to outweigh that caused by assuming that requirements not put in issue were in fact met.

10   *R v Immigration Appeal Tribunal, ex p Hubbard* [1985] Imm AR 110; *R v Immigration Appeal Tribunal, ex p Malik* (1981) Times, 16 November, QBD; *Agyen-Frempong v Immigration Appeal Tribunal* [1988] Imm AR 262, CA; see also *Entry Clearance Officer, Manila v Brey* [2002] UKIAT 06655; *CP (Dominica)* [2006] UKAIT 0040; *JF (Bangladesh)* [2008] UKAIT 0008.
11   *Tahir (Nadeem) v Immigration Appeal Tribunal* [1989] Imm AR 98, CA.
12   *RM (India)* [2006] UKAIT 00039.
13   *R v Immigration Appeal Tribunal, ex p Hubbard* [1985] Imm AR 110. There is a distinction between a positive finding of fact or credibility by the Secretary of State, which the Tribunal should not seek to subvert, and a mere failure to take the point by the Secretary of State, which leaves the Tribunal free to do so: *Carcabuk and Bla* (00TH01426) (18 May 2000, unreported), IAT. But see *Immigration Officer (Nigeria)* [2004] UKIAT 00179 (fn 8 above).
14   *R v Immigration Appeal Tribunal, ex p Hubbard* [1985] Imm AR 110; *Parsaiyan* [1986] Imm AR 155, IAT; *Uddin v Immigration Appeal Tribunal* [1991] Imm AR 134, CA.
15   *R v Immigration Appeal Tribunal, ex p Mehmet (Ekrem)* [1978] Imm AR 46; *Secretary of State for the Home Department v Ziar (Salah)* [1997] Imm AR 456, [1997] INLR 221 (grounds for certification of claim).
16   *Khatun (Kessori) (4272).*
17   *SZ (Bangladesh)* [2007] UKAIT 00037.
18   *Rahman (Aklakur)* (00/TH/00307) (10 March 2000, unreported), IAT.
19   *Uddin (Hawa Bibi) v Immigration Appeal Tribunal* [1991] Imm AR 134, CA (application on the basis of marriage which was found invalid; appeal raised issue of common law relationship).
20   In particular, the omission of the definite article in s 84(1)(a) and the breadth of the matters to be considered in s 86(2)(b) and s 85(2), (4). For the position under the old law see *Hussain (Shabir)* [1991] Imm AR 483 (IAT).
21   *Uddin (Hawa Bibi) v Immigration Appeal Tribunal* [1991] Imm AR 134, CA; *R v Immigration Appeal Tribunal, ex p Ali (Tohur)* [1987] Imm AR 189, QBD; whether the appellate authority ought to do so was reserved in Court of Appeal [1988] Imm AR 237. In *Seymour (Selwyn)* [2002] UKIAT 00594 the Tribunal accepted that the adjudicator could have dealt with the appeal on the alternative basis put forward by the appellant.
22   *Ali (Mohammed Fazor) v Secretary of State for the Home Department* [1988] Imm AR 274, CA; *R v Immigration Appeal Tribunal, ex p Uddin (Hawa)* [1990] Imm AR 309, QBD; on appeal [1991] Imm AR 134, CA; *Robinson (Anthonypillai Francis) v Secretary of State for the Home Department and Immigration Appeal Tribunal* [1997] Imm AR 568, CA. But see text and fn 19 above.
23   *SZ (Bangladesh)* [2007] UKAIT 00037.
24   *AS (Afghanistan) v Secretary of State for the Home Department* [2009] EWCA Civ 1076.
25   Cf *Rahman (Aklakur)*, fn 17 above.
26   Under NIAA 2002, s 96.
27   See further **20.23**.
28   NIAA 2002, s 85(4).
29   *LS (Gambia)* [2005] UKAIT 00085.

20.16 Where a requirement of a rule has been waived by the Secretary of State, whether in the individual case or in the class of case to which the appellant belongs, it cannot be applied to the appellant without good cause, and a decision which did so would not be in accordance with the law.

Discretion should be exercised differently

20.17 Where persons are subject to immigration control, the Secretary of State for the Home Department and immigration officers have a general discretion as to who should be admitted and in what circumstances. Section 4(1) of IA 1971 gives the responsibility to immigration officers of granting leave to enter and that of leave to remain to the Secretary of State. Under section 3(2) of IA 1971, the Secretary of State is empowered to make Immigration Rules as to the practice to be followed in the administration of the

Act for regulating the entry into and stay in the UK of persons required by the Act to have leave to enter. Thus, it is clear that under IA 1971 the Secretary of State has a general and wide discretion to determine who can be admitted to the UK and in what circumstances, both through the guidelines set out in the Immigration Rules and in particular cases or situations not covered by the rules.[1] The Immigration Directorate Instructions (IDI) and the Asylum Policy Instructions (API), and other published material such as ministerial statements and parliamentary answers, provide detailed guidelines as to the exercise of discretion both inside and outside the Immigration Rules. Although many published policies have been brought within the Immigration Rules following the coming into force of the HRA 1998, dealing with matters such as the admission of children for adoption, the admission and stay of domestic workers, the treatment of spouses who have suffered domestic violence during their 'probationary period' in the UK and the 'long residence' rule,[2] other policies, dealing with the bringing of enforcement action against family members of those with residence rights in the UK,[3] or the grant of indefinite leave and family reunion rights to those with discretionary leave to remain,[4] have not. There are also cases where the Secretary of State will allow someone to remain exceptionally, in the exercise of his or her general discretion, although the Immigration Rules expressly say that they should not qualify.

[1] In *R v Secretary of State for the Home Department, ex p Ahmed and Patel* [1998] INLR 570 there was an inconclusive discussion on whether the extra-rules discretion in relation to the admission of aliens was derived from the statute or the prerogative. See *R v Immigration Appeal Tribunal and Immigration Appeal Adjudicator (R G Care), ex p Secretary of State for the Home Department* [1990] Imm AR 166. The issue remains unresolved, but of little importance given the equal reviewability of both types of discretion following the GCHQ case, *Council of Civil Service Unions v Minister for the Civil Service* [1985] AC 374.
[2] See HC 395, paras 316A (admission of children for adoption, see **11.110** above); 159A (domestic workers, see **10.41** above); 289A (domestic violence, see **11.56** above); 276A (long residence, see **17.58** above).
[3] For these policies see **11.60**, **11.119** and **16.48** above.
[4] For family reunion for those with these forms of leave see **12.191** above.

Discretion consistent with the rules

20.18 In cases where the application of an immigration rule involves the exercise of a discretion or where no rules apply to or mandate a particular exercise of a statutory discretion (eg to revoke indefinite leave to remain under NIAA 2002, s 76 or to give directions for removal under IAA 1999, s 10 or deeming a person's deportation conducive to the public good under IA 1971, s 3(5)(a)[1]), s 86(3)(b) of NIAA 2002 empowers the appellate authorities to review[2] the exercise of the discretion on the merits.[2] In other words the Tribunal is not limited to determining whether the original decision was in accordance with the law, including Immigration Rules, but is required to consider whether the discretion should be exercised differently.[3] Whether there has been fresh evidence or not,[4] whether the evidence discloses a different factual situation to that before the original decision maker or not, the Tribunal may exercise discretion differently and allow the appeal, or may uphold the decision on different grounds.[5] This is a very wide power, particularly in the context of a deportation appeal, which is a balancing exercise in which all relevant factors are weighed.[6] However, the Court of Appeal in *N (Kenya)*, while acknowledging the breadth of the power, nonetheless set limits which appear to require deference to the policy reasons for the Secretary of State's decision.[7]

1 *Bah (EO (Turkey) – Liability to deport)* [2012] UKUT 00196 (IAC).
2 One example of a decision involving the exercise of such a discretion is a decision to give removal directions under IAA 1999, s 10, made in accordance with HC 395, para 395C – see *EO (Turkey)* [2007] UKAIT 00062 where that was conceded to be the case by the Secretary of State, and *R (on the application of Mirza) v Secretary of State for the Home Department* [2011] EWCA Civ 159 where, contrary to the Secretary of State's submission, it was held to be the case.
3 *R v Immigration Appeal Tribunal, ex p Desai* [1987] Imm AR 18.
4 *Begum (Zakia) v Visa Officer, Islamabad* [1988] Imm AR 465.
5 *Tahir (Nadeem) v Immigration Appeal Tribunal* [1989] Imm AR 98, CA. It would be unlawful for a tribunal to approach the issue of the exercise of discretion as if it was conducting a judicial review rather than exercising the original statutory discretion: *KA (Turkey) v Secretary of State for the Home Department* [2012] EWCA Civ 1183.
6 *R v Immigration Appeal Tribunal, ex p Bakhtaur Singh* [1986] Imm AR 352 at 361; *R v Immigration Appeal Tribunal, ex p Dhaliwal* [1994] Imm AR 387 at 391.
7 *R (on the application of N) v Secretary of State for the Home Department* [2004] EWCA Civ 1094, [2004] INLR 612, para 64, but see Sedley LJ's dissenting remarks, at [74], [77], with which we respectfully agree.

Discretion to depart from the rules

20.19 As we have seen, section 86(6) of NIAA 2002 imposes limits on the use of the Tribunal's power to decide that discretion should have been exercised differently. It provides that refusal to depart from or to authorise departure from the Immigration Rules is not an exercise of discretion for the purposes of section 86(3)(b). The Tribunal's jurisdiction to review the decision in such a case is limited to deciding whether it is not in accordance with the law, which has been considered above.[1]

1 This was held in *Singh v Secretary of State for the Home Department* [1991] Imm AR 195 to apply to an application for further exceptional leave to remain, following the grant of a period of exceptional leave to remain: the Secretary of State was entitled to refuse under the rules, limiting the adjudicator's jurisdiction on appeal. Now, there would be no appeal against such a refusal of an application to remain 'for a purpose outside the rules' (NIAA 2002, s 88(2)(d)), except on human rights or discrimination grounds, ie compatibility with the Race Relations Act 1976 or with the Human Rights Convention, under s 84(1)(b), (c) or (g).

20.20 A request to depart from the rules arises where there is a rule requiring mandatory refusal of the application. This applies even where the Secretary of State has a policy outside the rules, thereby indicating that the discretion will normally be exercised within the terms of the policy and not the rules. A discretion exercised under the rules instead of the policy will, in such a situation, be 'not in accordance with the law' but the appellate authority cannot substitute its own decision on the merits. In *Abdi*[1] the Court of Appeal rejected the argument that a policy constituted a revised legal framework whereby the Secretary of State has agreed to depart from the rules. In *Kausar*[2] the Tribunal agreed that the policy of the Secretary of State – in applying the maintenance and accommodation criteria in family reunion cases so as to exclude only those whose arrival would cause additional recourse to public funds – appeared a de facto amendment to the rules by way of concession, but insisted that, while the adjudicator should make formal findings on the evidence, it could not take the decision itself on the basis of the concession.

1 *Abdi (Dhudi Saleban) v Secretary of State for the Home Department* [1996] Imm AR 148, CA.

2   *Kausar v Entry Clearance Officer, Islamabad* [1998] INLR 141, IAT, followed in *Bi (Sakina)*
[2002] UKIAT 01092, IAT. See *AG (Kosovo)* [2007] UKAIT 0082 where the Tribunal suggests
that if a policy creates a presumption in favour of leave rather than simply describing how
discretion should be exercised and on the facts there is nothing to displace the presumption
then the appellant would be entitled to succeed substantively and not just to have the Secretary
of State being required to make a new decision.

Discretion in the making of EEA decisions

20.21   Some EEA decisions involve the exercise of a discretion by the Secretary
of State.[1] A person against whom such a decision is made would be entitled to
have his or her appeal allowed if the Tribunal thought the discretion should
have been exercised differently.[2]

1   Eg the issue of a family permit to an extended family member under the Immigration
(European Economic Area) Regulations 2006, SI 2006/1003, reg 16(5) or of a residence card
to an extended family member under reg 17(4) or to remove a person who has ceased to have
a right to reside under the regulations or whose removal may be justified on public policy
grounds under reg 19(3) or refusals to issue, renew or decisions to revoke residence
documentation under reg 20.
2   *FD (Algeria)* [2007] UKAIT 00049 under NIAA 2002, s 86(3)(b), applied by Sch 1 to SI
2006/1003.

Reviewing questions of fact

20.22   In the exercise of its appellate jurisdiction under NIAA 2002, s 86(3),
the Tribunal can review the facts on which the decision under appeal was
based. This power of review is no longer explicit, as it was under the 1971 and
1999 Acts,[1] but is to be implied by the provisions concerning evidence, and by
the case law. In all appeals except appeals under section 82(1) against refusal
of entry clearance or certificate of entitlement, the Tribunal 'may consider
evidence about any matter which it thinks relevant to the substance of the
decision, including evidence which concerns a matter arising after the date of
the decision'.[2] In entry clearance and certificate of entitlement appeals, the
Tribunal is limited to considering 'only the *circumstances appertaining* at the
time of the decision to refuse'[3] even where it is said that the decision breaches
the appellant's human rights.[4] Evidence of post-decision facts may be considered to the extent that those facts illuminate the 'circumstances appertaining at
the time of the decision'; evidence of post-decision devotion, for example,
showing that a couple intended to live together at the time of the decision.[5] A
post-decision job offer was not evidence of circumstances appertaining at the
time of the decision that could be relied on in an appeal against refusal of entry
clearance.[6] In so far as an appeal relates to a decision on an application for
leave to enter or remain under the points based system and relies on the
grounds that the decision was not in accordance with the rules, the law or
involved a discretion that should have been exercised differently, the Tribunal
may only consider evidence submitted by the appellant with the application or
evidence intended to authenticate a document or to address reliance by the
respondent on grounds for refusal unrelated to the acquisition of points.[7]
Otherwise, if Parliament intended to reverse a long line of case law and limit
the Tribunal to *evidence* which was before the decision maker at the time of the
decision to refuse, it would have said so. This means that as far as questions
of fact are concerned the Tribunal is not confined to the evidence which was

before the immigration authority when they reached their decision or took action, but can consider all the evidence, including any further evidence found since the decision was taken, and in non-entry clearance or certificate of entitlement cases, evidence of facts which have arisen since, too. The Tribunal's fact-finding powers give it a different function from that of the Administrative Court on judicial review or statutory review, or the Court of Appeal, where the court is generally confined to the material which the minister or other body had before them.[8] In immigration appeals the Tribunal goes into the facts again,[9] and can correct factual errors made by the immigration authority,[10] and hear of facts which were unknown to the decision maker.[11] Whilst in entry clearance appeals the Tribunal should accord some respect to the views of the entry clearance officer who has interviewed the appellant,[12] it does not need to have fresh evidence before reversing the entry clearance officer's assessment.[13] By reason of this jurisdiction, and the power to determine exercises of discretion, the appellate authority can correct irrationality (eg failures to take into account important and relevant facts) and procedural unfairness (eg a failure to interview) without having to classify them as errors of law. The facts found by the Tribunal, certainly after hearing oral evidence, bind the Secretary of State unless they are perverse.[14]

[1] IA 1971, s 19(2); IAA 1999, Sch 4, para 21(3).

[2] NIAA 2002, s 85(4), amended by Asylum and Immigration (Treatment of Claimants, etc) Act 2004, Sch 2, para 18.

[3] NIAA 2002, s 85(5) as amended. So, for example, it was an error of law to allow an appeal against refusal of entry clearance on art 8 grounds by reference to the fact of the birth of a child more than one year after the decision appealed against – *SA (Pakistan)* [2006] UKAIT 00018.

[4] *AS (Somalia) v Secretary of State for the Home Department* [2009] UKHL 32, [2009] 1 WLR 1385. Their Lordships observed that there might be cases, for example where very young children or vulnerable adults were involved, in which respect for family life cried out for attention. The delay resulting from the need to start the procedure afresh, and to find the money to do so, might result in a finding that the application of s 85(5) in such cases was disproportionate. Thus the possibility remained for a declaration of incompatibility in an individual case, if the circumstances were so clearly focused as to enable the precise nature of the incompatibility with the applicant's art 8 rights to be identified. See also *BK (India)* [2014] CSOH 109; 2014 GWD 24-462.

[5] *DR (Morocco)** [2005] UKIAT 00038.

[6] *SF (Afghanistan) v Entry Clearance Officer* [2011] EWCA Civ 758.

[7] UK Borders Act 2007, s 19 inserting a new s 85A into NIAA 2002, commenced by SI 2011/1293. The provision would not prevent reliance on evidence that had not been before the original decision maker that was intended to support a different ground, eg that the decision breached art 8: *Alam (Bangladesh)* [2011] UKUT 424 (IAC).

[8] See *Ashbridge Investments Ltd v Minister of Housing* [1965] 3 All ER 371 at 374, CA. See 7.19 above for the role of the courts in human rights cases.

[9] *R v Immigration Appeal Tribunal, ex p Hubbard* [1985] Imm AR 110, QBD.

[10] *R v Secretary of State for the Home Department, ex p Husbadak* [1982] Imm AR 8.

[11] *R v Immigration Appeal Tribunal, ex p Hassanin* [1987] 1 All ER 74, [1986] 1 WLR 1448, CA.

[12] See *R v Immigration Appeal Tribunal, ex p Kwok On Tong* [1981] Imm AR 214, DC; *R v Immigration Appeal Tribunal, ex p Singh (Mahendra)* [1984] Imm AR 1, QBD. But the degree of deference due should not be exaggerated: *R (on the application of Hamfi) v Immigration Appeal Tribunal and Secretary of State for the Home Department* [2004] EWHC 939 (Admin), Collins J.

[13] *Begum (Zakia) v Visa Officer, Islamabad* [1988] Imm AR 465; *Entry Clearance Officer, Karachi v Ahmad (Zafar)* [1989] Imm AR 254.

[14] *R v Secretary of State for the Home Department, ex p Danaie* [1998] INLR 124, [1998] Imm AR 84, CA.

THE TRIBUNAL AS PRIMARY DECISION MAKER

20.23 It is now clear that the effect of the 2002 Act appeals provisions is to extend the appellate jurisdiction so as to make the Tribunal an extension of the administrative decision making process in respect of a wider range of issues than just asylum and human rights appeals.[1] So, for example, it would be an error of law for the Tribunal to decline to determine whether an appellant had a Community law right to remain in the UK[2] or whether a decision was contrary to the best interests of an affected child[3] on the ground that the Secretary of State had not yet made a decision on the issue. The terms in which some of the provisions of the rules relating to the points-based system are framed mean that the tribunal cannot allow an appeal, unless specified facts are found to have existed at the time of the application,; eg the requirement that an individual should hold a particular sum for three months at the time of the application for leave to remain is not met by evidence of having had that sum for three months at the time of the hearing,[4] nor is the requirement to have a qualification at the time of application satisfied by having the qualification at the time of the hearing.[5] However, it is the nature and substantive content of the requirements of the points based system rather than any jurisdictional limitation that prevents the Tribunal from acting as primary decision maker in such cases.[6]

If a person makes a statement in response to a one-stop notice the Tribunal is required to determine whether its contents establish an entitlement to enter or remain in, or not to be removed from, the UK even if they have not been considered by the Secretary of State prior to the appeal.[7] The tribunal would be obliged to consider the contents of the statement even if it was not made until the appeal was being redetermined by the Upper Tribunal.[8] That is so whether the statement contains an asylum or human rights claim or a claim under some category of the Immigration Rules or a policy or concession other than that on which the original application was based. However, the Secretary of State is not obliged to serve a one-stop notice.[9] Nevertheless, the approach adopted by the majority in *AS (Afghanistan)* which was endorsed by the Supreme Court in *Patel*[10] means that the Tribunal can consider any matter, including a matter arising after the decision which is relevant to the substance of the decision[11] regardless of whether a one-stop notice has been served. The 'substance of the decision' is not the decision maker's reasoned response to the particular application or factual situation that was before it,[12] but is one of the immigration decisions enumerated in section 82[13] and a 'matter' includes anything capable of supporting a fresh application to the decision maker.[14] The only restriction on the matters that the Tribunal can consider is that they have to be relevant to the substance of the decision and they are relevant to the substance of the decision if they are capable of making good one of the grounds of appeal or otherwise making the Tribunal decide to allow the appeal.[15]

[1] See *Ravichandran v Secretary of State for the Home Department* [1996] Imm AR 97 at 112 in respect of asylum appeals and *R (on the application of Razgar) v Secretary of State for the Home Department* [2004] UKHL 27, [2004] 3 WLR 58, at [15] for human rights appeals.

[2] *VM (Zambia) v Secretary of State for the Home Department* [2009] EWCA Civ 521.

[3] *DS (Afghanistan) v Secretary of State for the Home Department* [2011] EWCA Civ 305.

[4] *Secretary of State for the Home Department v Pankina* [2010] EWCA Civ 719, [2011] QB 376, [2011] 1 All ER 1043.

[5] *AQ (Pakistan) v Secretary of State for the Home Department* [2011] EWCA Civ 833, [2011] All ER (D) 182 (Jul). See also *Ali (Mansoor) v Secretary of State for the Home Department* [2013] EWCA Civ 1198 and *Raju v Secretary of State of the Home Department* [2013] EWCA Civ 754, rejecting the proposition that an application continued until the time the Secretary of State made her decision on the application so that a qualification obtained by then could be relied upon.

[6] See Sullivan LJ's judgment in *AQ (Pakistan) v Secretary of State for the Home Department* [2011] EWCA Civ 833 explaining that the discussion in *AS (Afghanistan) v Secretary of State for the Home Department* [2009] EWCA Civ 1076, [2010] 2 All ER 21, [2011] 1 WLR 385 was not concerned with the points based system or other applications concerned with 'a fixed historic time line' – the phrase used in *MS (Pakistan)* [2010] UKUT 117 (IAC).

[7] So the majority of the Court of Appeal (Moore-Bick and Sullivan LJJ, Arden LJ dissenting) held in *AS (Afghanistan) v Secretary of State for the Home Department* [2009] EWCA Civ 1076, interpreting NIAA 2002, ss 85(2) and 120.

[8] *MU (Bangladesh)* [2010] UKUT 442 (IAC).

[9] *Lamichhane v Secretary of State for the Home Department* [2012] EWCA Civ 260.

[10] *Patel v Secretary of State for the Home Department* [2013] UKSC 72.

[11] NIAA 2002, s 85(4).

[12] As the Tribunal had held in *EA (Nigeria)* [2007] UKAIT 00013; *SZ (Bangladesh)* [2007] UKAIT 00037 and *NA (Tier 1 Post-Study Work-funds)* [2009] UKAIT 00025.

[13] *AS (Afghanistan) v Secretary of State for the Home Department* [2009] EWCA Civ 1076.

[14] *AS (Afghanistan)*, ibid.

[15] The majority of the court in *AS (Afghanistan)* considered that the broad, primary jurisdiction of the Tribunal depended for its existence on a one-stop notice having been served. We would say that is obiter. Whether a one-stop notice is served determines whether the Secretary of State can later use his or her powers to certify an appeal or claim under s 96 but not the jurisdiction of the Tribunal.

Determining liability for removal

20.24 Section 86(4) provides that for the purposes of subsection (3), a decision that a person should be removed from the UK under a provision is not to be regarded as unlawful if it could have been lawfully made by reference to removal under another provision. Thus, if the Tribunal determines that a person appealing against a decision to remove as an overstayer is an illegal entrant, or vice versa, the error in categorisation does not per se make the decision unlawful.[1] This does not mean that the appeal must be dismissed,[2] only that it should not be allowed on that basis. In the majority of appeals, it makes no difference at all whether the person is to be removed under one power or another, since the issue is whether removal would breach Refugee Convention or human rights obligations. This does not mean that illegal entry should be conceded in the absence of evidence; it still carries a stigma greater than overstaying an initial lawful stay, and could result in differential treatment on an application to return. In *Khawaja*[3] the House of Lords held that a person only became an illegal entrant by deception when the Home Office declared them to be such, and thus, in cases where the Secretary of State did not assert illegal entry, Tribunals should not attempt to usurp this function.[4] Section 86(4) does not give the Secretary of State the right to remove a person to a destination other than that permitted by the terms of Schedule 2, paragraph 8(1)(c) to IA 1971.[5] However, the question of whether directions can lawfully be given under that provision to the destination indicated in the notice of the immigration decision (eg because the destination is not the appellant's country of nationality or a territory from which he or she embarked for the UK or to which there is reason to believe he or she would be admitted) is not one that can be addressed by the Tribunal but can only be determined if and when removal directions are actually given.[6] Whether removal to the proposed destination would breach the UK's obligations under the Refugee Convention or ECHR is a separate matter that can be determined by the Tribunal, even if removal directions have not been given.[7]

[1] NIAA 2002, s 86(4).
[2] This was previously the position if an appellant was held to be an illegal entrant: see IAA 1999, Sch 4, para 24(1) and (3).
[3] *Khawaja v Secretary of State for the Home Department* [1984] AC 74, [1983] 1 All ER 765, HL.
[4] *Watson v Immigration Officer, Gatwick* [1986] Imm AR 75, IAT. See also *R v Secretary of State for the Home Department, ex p Jayakody* [1982] 1 All ER 461, [1982] 1 WLR 405, CA; *R v Immigration Appeal Tribunal, ex p Akhtar* (1982) 126 Sol Jo 430, QBD.
[5] See **17.64** ff above.
[6] *MS (Palestinian Territories) v Secretary of State for the Home Department* [2010] UKSC 25.
[7] *HH (Somalia) v Secretary of State for the Home Department* [2010] EWCA Civ 426. See **20.25** below.

The appellate jurisdiction in asylum and human rights appeals

20.25 While the jurisdiction of the Tribunal set out in section 86(3) of the NIAA 2002 applies equally to an appeal on asylum or human rights grounds under section 84(1)(g), in cases where no other appeal grounds are available, the ground of appeal is that the appellant's removal in consequence of the decision would breach the UK's obligations under the Refugee Convention or would be unlawful under section 6 of the HRA 1998 as incompatible with the Human Rights Convention.[1] This has positive and negative consequences for the Tribunal's jurisdiction on appeal. On the one hand, even where the Secretary of State has failed to consider a claim substantively but has refused an application for failure to attend an interview or complete a statement of evidence form, the Tribunal on appeal must decide whether the appellant's removal is in breach of the Refugee Convention (and, we suggest, the Human Rights Convention too).[2] An appeal on asylum grounds requires the Tribunal to decide whether, if returned at the time of the hearing before the Tribunal, the appellant would face a real risk of persecution or serious harm, even if for practical, political or other reasons the Home Office is not at that time removing persons to the country concerned.[3] Human rights and asylum issues can arise in relation to the method, route, timing or destination of removal consequent on an immigration decision.[4] It is now clear that the Tribunal is required to deal with such issues and cannot throw up its hands, leaving them to be litigated if and when removal directions are given rather than as part of the appeal against the immigration decision. Thus, if it can be shown either directly or by implication, what route or method of return is envisaged, the Tribunal is obliged to consider any asylum or human rights issues that are raised in relation to the process of return.[5] Moreover, European Community law[6] now requires states to determine whether an individual is entitled to refugee status or subsidiary protection status within a reasonable period, rather than at the end of a period in limbo after asylum has been refused, an appeal dismissed and removal directions are finally set. Community law also requires an asylum seeker to be provided with an effective remedy if the individual is found not to be entitled to status. In that context, given that risks consequent upon the process of return are integral to assessing entitlement to status under Community law, the Secretary of State may be required by the Tribunal to adduce evidence as to the route and method of return if not already apparent.[7] If the Tribunal rejects the appellant's claim to be a national of the country in which he or she claims to be at risk it need not go on to determine whether the person's removal there would in fact breach his or her human rights so long as the Secretary of State undertakes not to remove the person to that country.[8] The absence of removal directions does not prevent the Tribunal from determining whether, if the appellant was eventually removed, he would be refused entry to his country of habitual residence and whether such refusal would amount to persecution; the relevant ground for appeal ('removal in consequence of the immigration decision would breach the Refugee Convention'[9]) required a hypothetical question to be addressed and did not require the existence of removal directions.[10] There may be no prospect of imminent removal as a result of an immigration decision because the appeal is against a variation decision as opposed to a removal decision or in cases where, for practical or policy reasons there is no foreseeable prospect of removal. In such cases the Tribunal is not relieved of the obligation to determine any human rights grounds that may be raised;[11] the question for the Tribunal is whether removal in consequence of the decision would breach the appellant's human rights.[12] Even if the Secretary of State gave an undertaking not to remove the appellant whilst she was involved in contact proceedings relating to her children, she would be entitled to succeed in her appeal if she could make good the hypothesis that, at the time of the hearing, removing her and thereby preventing her from participating in the contact proceedings would breach her human rights.[13] Similarly, an undertaking by the Secretary of State not to remove a minor until and unless adequate reception arrangements had been made did not relieve the Tribunal of the obligation to determine the appeal in the light of what the evidence showed about the actually existing reception arrangements at the time of the hearing. Nor would an undertaking by the Secretary of State not to remove the appellant until properly monitored assurances from the destination country were in place relieve the tribunal of the obligation to determine whether removal in the circumstances pertaining at the time of the hearing (including the absence of suitable assurances) would breach Article 3 of the ECHR.[14] Otherwise the Tribunal would be denying the appellant the statutory right of appeal and instead delegating part of the decision to the Secretary of State.[15] An appeal under section 82 which suspends removal because the person has made an asylum or human rights claim in the UK which has not been certified clearly unfounded[16] (or a claim under Community law, for that matter),[17] is not limited to those grounds, however, but may include any or all of the statutory grounds under section 84(1).[18] Such an appeal might encompass the lawfulness of the proposed removal destination, or arguably the lawfulness of the asylum procedure applied to a minor.[19] However, this does not apply to an appeal against refusal of leave to enter or refusal to vary leave where a ground of refusal is ineligibility; in such a case, any appeal may be brought only on discrimination, human rights or asylum grounds.[20]

[1] NIAA 2002, s 86(3) read with s 84(1)(g), see also s 84(1)(c).

[2] *Haddad (Ali)* [2000] INLR 117, *Busuulwa (01TH 00239), IAT*; see fn 1. Paragraph 340 (non-compliance refusals) applies to asylum claims, while para 322(10) is an equivalent in non-asylum cases; and the principles of *Haddad* apply to removal which would breach either Convention. For a discussion of the wording of s 86(3) in relation to appeals on asylum and human rights grounds see **20.25** above.

3 *Saad v Secretary of State for the Home Department, Diriye v Secretary of State for the Home Department, Osorio v Secretary of State for the Home Department* [2001] EWCA Civ 2008, [2002] Imm AR 471, [2002] INLR 34; *R (Secretary of State for the Home Department) v Immigration Appeal Tribunal; R (on the application of Hwez) v Secretary of State for the Home Department* [2001] EWHC 1597 (Admin), [2002] Imm AR 116. The difference between the Refugee and Human Rights Convention is that recognition under the Refugee Convention confers a particular status in international law: *L (Ethiopia)* [2003] UKIAT 00016, paras 62–63.

4 *GH (Iraq) v Secretary of State for the Home Department* [2005] EWCA Civ 1182 and *AG (Somalia) v Secretary of State for the Home Department* [2006] EWCA Civ 1342, [2006] All ER (D) 189 (Oct).

5 *HH (Somalia) and Ors v Secretary of State for the Home Department* [2010] EWCA Civ 426.

6 In the shape of Council Directive 2004/83/EC ('the Qualification Directive') and Council Directive 2005/85/EC ('the Procedures Directive').

7 So the Court of Appeal held, obiter, in *HH (Somalia) and Ors.*

8 *MA (Somalia) v Secretary of State for the Home Department* [2009] EWCA Civ 4, [2009] All ER (D) 65 (Jan).

9 NIAA 2002, s 84(1)(g).

10 *AK v Secretary of State for the Home Department* [2006] EWCA Civ 1117, [2006] All ER (D) 470 (Jul).

11 *JM v Secretary of State for the Home Department* [2006] EWCA Civ 1402, overturning *JM (Liberia)* [2006] UKAIT 0009*.

12 NIAA 2002, s 84(1)(g).

13 *MS (Ivory Coast) v Secretary of State for the Home Department* [2007] EWCA Civ 133, (2007) Times, 27 March.

14 *J1 v Secretary of State for the Home Department* [2013] EWCA Civ 279.

15 *CL (Vietnam) v Secretary of State for the Home Department* [2008] EWCA Civ 1551, (2009) Times, 7 January. In *J1 v Secretary of State for the Home Department* Elias LJ said: 'the fundamental constitutional principle is that it is for the court to determine whether a refusal by the Secretary of State to grant asylum will involve a breach of the asylum seeker's rights under the Human Rights Convention. This is not simply a *Wednesbury* review of the Secretary of State's decision. In any article 3 case the court is answering the hypothetical question whether the appellant would face a real risk on the basis of the evidence before the court at the time of its determination' ([96]).

16 ie under NIAA 2002, s 94.

17 NIAA 2002, s 92(4).

18 *SA (Bangladesh)* [2005] UKAIT 00178.

19 NIAA 2002, s 84(1)(e); see *Shaqiri* [2002] UKIAT 04159; *Melikli* [2002] UKIAT 07428.

20 NIAA 2002, s 88; see **19.24** above. Arguably, once an appeal has been brought on asylum or human rights grounds, ss 85 and 86 oblige the Tribunal to consider all the issues as set out there.

Discrimination appeals

20.26 Section 84(1)(b) of NIAA 2002 provides that a person may appeal against an immigration decision on the ground that it is unlawful by virtue of section 29 of the Equality Act 2010. However, an allegation of racial discrimination in (for example) refusal of leave to enter, does not make an appeal suspensive of removal, as it does if a human rights or asylum claim is made. In many cases, this would not present a problem, since the two grounds – race discrimination and human rights – would be likely to co-exist (for example, where the allegation related to refusal of leave to enter to visit family members).[1] But where the allegation related to refusal of leave to enter as a business visitor, and there were no relevant human rights grounds, the discrimination appeal would (in the absence of entry clearance) have to be conducted from abroad.

[1] This might breach ECHR, Art 14 together with Art 8, and so be appealable under NIAA 2002, s 84(1)(c) and/or (g), as well as on race discrimination grounds: s 84(1)(b).

Giving directions where an appeal is allowed

20.27 Under section 87(1) of the NIAA 2002, where an appeal is allowed, the Tribunal may give a direction for the purpose of giving effect to the decision.[1] A direction is part of the Tribunal's decision on appeal, for the purposes of an application for review.[2] The person responsible for making the immigration decision must act in accordance with any relevant direction,[3] but directions have no effect while an in-time onward appeal to the UT or Court of Appeal may be brought, or has been brought and has not been finally determined.[4] The power to make directions under this section is a completely separate power from the power of the Tribunal to give procedural directions for the conduct of the appeal, which is contained in the Procedure Rules.[5] Directions under the section (i) can only be given where an appeal is allowed, (ii) to give effect to the decision.[6]

By contrast to previous statutory regimes, the tribunal's power to give directions is not restricted to circumstances where a direction would be necessary.[7] In an appeal against refusal of entry clearance, a direction should not be made unless the tribunal is satisfied that the requirements of the requisite rule will be met in the foreseeable future. But if the tribunal is satisfied of that, it may direct a grant of entry clearance, particularly if a child or other vulnerable person is involved.[8] Where an application for entry clearance is made for settlement and an appeal against a refusal is allowed, there is little difficulty in directing that entry clearance should be issued in the capacity sought. This is because all relevant issues will now have been determined in favour of an appellant. The entry clearance officer will be bound by this direction in the absence of an appeal. But where the appeal is against a refusal of entry in some limited capacity, as a family visitor, an au pair or a student, it is likely that the passage of time since the decision will have led to a change of circumstances. The Tribunal has suggested that entry clearance should not generally be directed in these cases.[9] If the immigrant still seeks entry, the matter should be remitted for reconsideration by the entry clearance officer in the light of the decision.[10] In such circumstances the entry clearance officer would be bound by the positive findings in favour of the appellant unless it can be proved to a high civil standard that the findings were obtained by fraud,[11] but other issues such as *present* intentions or ability to maintain[12] and any changes in the Immigration Rules since the original decision would need to be considered.[13] The direction given for the grant of entry clearance on a successful appeal is spent when such entry clearance is granted, and the failure of an appellant to use it does not oblige an entry clearance officer to grant another years later without a further decision.[14]

[1] NIAA 2002, s 87. The power to make directions was formerly contained in the IAA 1999, Sch 4, para 21(5) and para 22(5)–(7). The statutory power to make recommendations when allowing an appeal was rarely used and has been abolished.
[2] NIAA 2002, s 87(4), amended by the Asylum and Immigration (Treatment of Claimants, etc) Act 2004, Sch 2, para 19(b).
[3] NIAA 2002, s 87(2).

4   NIAA 2002, s 87(3).
5   See the Tribunal Procedure (First-tier Tribunal)(Immigration and Asylum Chamber) Rules
     2014, SI 2014/2604, r 4(2).
6   Thus, the Secretary of State cannot be directed to issue a fresh refusal letter as a condition of
     defending a decision on appeal. The asylum rules are procedural, not substantive: *Mwanza v
     Secretary of State for the Home Department* [2001] Imm AR 557, [2001] INLR 616, CA;
     followed in *R (on the application of Emlik) v Immigration Appeal Tribunal* [2002] EWHC
     1279 (Admin), [2002] All ER (D) 209 (Jun); *R (on the application of Zaier) v Immigration
     Appeal Tribunal* [2003] EWCA Civ 937, [2003] All ER (D) 153 (Jul), holding further that
     there was no power under IAA 1999 to remit an asylum claim to the Secretary of State for
     redetermination. Directions issued for a purpose other than that of giving effect to the decision
     on appeal are of no effect: *Secretary of State for the Home Department v Fardy* [1972] Imm
     AR 192; *R v Immigration Appeal Tribunal, ex p Singh* [1984] Imm AR 1, QBD.
7   *SP (South Africa)* [2011] UKUT 00188 (IAC).
8   ibid.
9   *MG (Jamaica)* [2004] UKIAT 00140, [2004] Imm AR 377, following *Immigration Officer,
     Heathrow v Obeid* [1986] Imm AR 341; *EA (Ghana)* [2005] UKIAT 00108 and *EB (Ghana)*
     [2005] UKIAT 00131.
10   An alternative approach might be to direct entry clearance conditional on the production of up
     to date documents; *Visa Officer, Aden v Thabel* [1977] Imm AR 75. However, in *S (Yemen)*
     [2003] UKIAT 00008, the Tribunal held directions to an ECO to investigate the spon-
     sor's property and domestic circumstances inappropriate, they were not direction for giving
     effect to a decision to allow a family visitor appeal, but for *not* giving effect to it unless satisfied
     on matters relevant to the genuineness of the visit.
11   *R v Immigration Appeal Tribunal, ex p Miah (Lulu)* [1987] Imm AR 143, QBD; *R v Secretary
     of State for the Home Department, ex p Yousuf* [1989] Imm AR 554; *R (on the application
     of Saribal) v Secretary of State for the Home Department* [2002] EWHC 1542 (Admin),
     [2002] INLR 596, [2002] All ER (D) 379 (Jul). See, however, *R (on the application of
     Rahman) v Entry Clearance Officer* [2006] EWHC 1755 (Admin); whilst following a
     successful appeal against refusal of entry clearance, the ECO could not embark on further
     enquiries intended to circumvent the decision on the appeal, the ECO was nevertheless obliged
     to determine on the facts before him or her, including those that might establish earlier
     deception on mistake of fact, whether entry clearance should be granted; *R (on the application
     of Haider) v Entry Clearance Officer* [2009] EWHC 3008 (Admin) – ECO ordered to grant
     entry clearance in order to give effect to the Tribunal's decision to allow an appeal against
     refusal of entry clearance on art 8 grounds.
12   However, in the absence of an appeal, the failure to give directions to give effect to a
     determination relating to the subsistence of a marriage did not entitle the Secretary of State to
     issue a fresh decision after the marriage had broken down, and the applicant was entitled to
     the benefit of the positive determination: *R (on the application of Boafo) v Secretary of State
     for the Home Department* [2002] EWCA Civ 44, [2002] 1 WLR 1919.
13   *R (on the application of Khan) v Entry Clearance Officer, New Delhi* [2010] EWHC 517
     (Admin) upholding the decision of an ECO who refused entry clearance after a successful
     appeal by the appellant, relying on the new para 320(7A) of the Immigration Rules which
     made refusal of entry clearance mandatory rather than discretionary where there had been
     reliance on false documents.
14   *R v Secretary of State for the Home Department, ex p Moon* [1997] INLR 165, QBD. See also
     Hashim (6421), where directions were quashed by consent because there had been a change of
     circumstances and a fresh application for entry between the original decision and the appeal.

20.28 If on appeal the Tribunal finds that an appellant is a British citizen,
directions may be given to the respondent for the issue of a certificate of
entitlement to the right of abode.[1] In deportation cases, the question whether
indefinite leave to remain or limited leave should be given following a
successful appeal is one for the Secretary of State.[2] Similarly, following a
successful appeal on human rights grounds, it is for the Secretary of State to
decide on the length of leave to be granted.[3] The question of what directions
it is lawful or appropriate to give on allowing an asylum appeal is unresolved,
with divisions of the Tribunal holding on the one hand that the appellate
authorities are entitled to give directions declaring that the appellant was a

refugee at the date of decision, as well as the date of hearing,[4] and on the other, that it is not necessary for giving effect to the decision to direct the grant of status or its backdating, since the only direction required is leave to enter.[5] In our view, the latter view cannot be correct given that the withholding of refugee status would be contrary to the Convention, and effect is given to a successful asylum appeal not merely by the grant of leave, but specifically by granting recognition, whether or not that recognition must be backdated.[6] Where an asylum appeal was allowed but the appellant had by then been returned to the country of persecution (in a pre-1993 case where an appeal was not suspensive), the question arose whether directions should order his return to the UK.[7] The Tribunal decided that in view of the time that had passed since his removal and the lack of current knowledge of his circumstances, the appropriate direction was that, should he apply to a British post abroad, consideration should be given to the application as if he were in the UK. Clearly in such a case the entry clearance officer would be bound by the factual findings as to the past treatment of the appellant.

The same reasoning should apply where an asylum seeker leaves the UK voluntarily before promulgation of the determination of his or her appeal.[8] We suggest that where a non-suspensive appeal takes place fairly speedily on removal, and is successful, there is no reason why directions should not be issued for the Secretary of State or his officers to use their best endeavours to facilitate the return of the appellant to the UK by the issue of an appropriate entry clearance.

[1]   *Rahman and Akhter* (00307) (10 March 2000, unreported), IAT.
[2]   *R v Secretary of State for the Home Department, ex p Botta* [1987] Imm AR 80; *Rathiesh* (14648) 14 March 1997, IAT.
[3]   *Sharif (Omeed)* [2002] UKIAT 00953. For the Secretary of State's policy on the period of discretionary leave granted, see **7.126** and **12.175** above.
[4]   *Haibe* [1997] INLR 119, IAT; *Belvue* (11834a), in accordance with the fact that refugees are recognised, not created, by the grant of refugee status: *Khaboka (Alimas) v Secretary of State for the Home Department* [1993] Imm AR 484, CA.
[5]   *Merzouk* [1999] INLR 468, IAT.
[6]   In *Altun (Guluzar)* (16628) (17 July 1998, unreported), the Tribunal held that 'there is nothing in the 1951 Convention which requires the determination of a notional point at which [an appellant] became a refugee', but accepted that the adjudicator could declare the appellant to be one.
[7]   *Kondo* (10413). There are as yet no reported determinations regarding the issue of directions to give effect to successful non-suspensive asylum or human rights appeals under NIAA 2002.
[8]   Pending in-country appeals are treated as abandoned on departure from the UK.

20.29 Directions may be given in extra-rules cases. Thus appropriate directions where the Secretary of State has failed to give effect to a policy will be that the respondent gives consideration to the case in accordance with the relevant policy and in the light of the evidence available to him or her and the facts found by the Tribunal. It would not be appropriate for the Tribunal to direct the grant of entry clearance: the appellant's right is for the case to be considered in accordance with the policy, not an eventual decision in his or her favour.[1]

[1]   *Kausar v Entry Clearance Officer, Islamabad* [1998] INLR 141. See also *Antonipillai* (16588) (12 May 1998, unreported), IAT; *H (Somalia)* [2004] UKIAT 00027.

20.30 Directions should not be given without the parties having an opportunity to make submissions,[1] and if necessary to call evidence.[2] Under the pre-NIAA 2002 appeals provisions, directions did not need to be given at the same time as the decision allowing the appeal.[3] This was sensible as most decisions are delivered by post when there is no opportunity for oral argument on what directions are necessary. Thus a successful appellant could return to the appellate authority within a reasonable time after the appeal had been allowed to seek directions. This might also have provided some sanction against an obdurate entry clearance officer or immigration officer. There is a question mark over whether under the present appeal provisions it would be possible for the FT to make directions after determining the appeal because, at least for the purpose of the right of appeal to the UT, the directions are to be treated as part of the decision on the appeal.[4] Directions to give effect to a decision under section 86 of NIAA 2002 (which are matters of substance) should not be confused with procedural directions under the Procedure Rules.[5] These are matters of procedure to which we turn below. Equally, they should not be confused with recommendations made to the Secretary of State when the Tribunal dismisses an appeal. These are purely gratuitous and have no basis in the Act or procedure rules.

1   *Immigration Officer, Heathrow v Adac-Bosompra* [1992] Imm AR 579. The old rule that directions could only be given at the request of a party, expressed in *Yousuf, ex p* [1990] Imm AR 191, has been superseded by the coming into force of the HRA 1998: *Hamad* [2002] UKIAT 07240.
2   The Court of Appeal in R *(on the application of Boafo) v Secretary of State for the Home Department* [2002] EWCA Civ 44, [2002] Imm AR 383, [2002] INLR 231 agreed with the Tribunal's observations in *Yousuf* [1990] Imm AR 191.
3   *Yousuf* [1990] Imm AR 191, approved in *Boafo* above.
4   NIAA 2002, s 87(4).
5   Tribunal Procedure (First-tier Tribunal)(Immigration and Asylum Chamber) Rules 2014, SI 2014/2604, r 4(3).

20.31 Directions are to be treated as part of the determination of the appeal for the purposes of section 11 of the TCEA 2007,[1] enabling the parties to appeal to the UT against a direction or a refusal to make one. However, directions are probably not appealable to the Court of Appeal,[2] although a Tribunal's determination that it has no power to give directions would be appealable for error of law.

1   NIAA 2002, s 87(4), amended by Asylum and Immigration (Treatment of Claimants, etc) Act 2004, Sch 2, para 19.
2   The wording of s 87(4) strongly indicates that directions are *not* part of the decision for the purposes of TCEA 2007, s 13 which gives the right of appeal to the Court of Appeal.

THE EFFECT OF AN APPEAL ALLOWED WITHOUT DIRECTIONS

20.32 The making of a direction is not necessary in order to give a determination binding effect upon the respondent, at least where entitlement to status such as indefinite leave to remain on marriage grounds is in issue.[1] Once an appeal against refusal of leave to enter has been allowed and there is no further appeal there is a clear duty on the Secretary of State to give effect to the immigration judge's decision;

'it would strike at the heart of the independent appeal system . . . if the Secretary of State felt free to deliberately circumvent an adverse decision by the Tribunal simply because he disagreed with the outcome on the merits'.[2]

The principle is that 'the decision of the Tribunal is binding on the parties and in particular on the Home Secretary'.[3] Thus the Secretary of State could not lawfully withhold refugee status by reference to a 'particularly serious offence' committed by the appellant before he won his appeal on Refugee Convention grounds and when the fact of the offence had been considered by the Tribunal;[4] nor could humanitarian protection be denied on the ground that the successful appellant was excluded by virtue of his conviction for threats to kill in circumstances where the Secretary of State could have, but did not rely on the conviction to argue for exclusion before the Tribunal.[5] An appellant who succeeds in an appeal on Refugee Convention grounds has been said to have refugee status in both domestic and international law from that moment onwards.[6] Where an appeal is allowed on human rights grounds against a decision to remove the appellant, the Secretary of State has a discretion as to the period of leave to enter or remain that should be granted and is not necessarily obliged to grant indefinite leave.[7] However, that discretion has to be exercised in the light of the particular findings made by the Tribunal and the potentially applicable rules and policies so that a grant of discretionary leave was unlawful where the Tribunal's findings made clear that the appellant was entitled to humanitarian protection.[8]

[1] R (on the application of Boafo) v Secretary of State for the Home Department [2002] EWCA Civ 44.

[2] R (on the application of GG) v Secretary of State for the Home Department [2006] EWHC 1111 (Admin), (2006) Times, 14 June, [2006] All ER (D) 143 (May); affd sub nom S v Secretary of State for the Home Department (sub nom R (on the application of GG) v Secretary of State for the Home Department) [2006] EWCA Civ 1157, [2006] All ER (D) 30 (Aug), upheld in S v Secretary of State for the Home Department (sub nom R (on the application of GG) v Secretary of State for the Home Department) [2006] EWCA Civ 1157, [2006] All ER (D) 30 (Aug). However, there is no causes of action estoppel where the Secretary of State makes a new, adverse decision that is the same as a previous decision overturned on appeal: Mubu (Immigration appeals – res judicata) [2012] UKUT 398 (IAC).

[3] TB (Jamaica) v Secretary of State for the Home Department [2008] EWCA Civ 977, (2008) Times, 9 September. The Tribunal's decision in MM (Pakistan) [2008] UKAIT 00040 that entry clearance could lawfully be refused to a successful appellant upon his further application, by reference to the same facts as had been before the Tribunal is incompatible with these authorities.

[4] Secretary of State for the Home Department v TB (Jamaica), ibid.

[5] R (on the application of Erdogen) v Secretary of State for the Home Department [2008] EWHC 2446 (Admin), [2008] All ER (D) 102 (Sep). Similarly, the Secretary of State may not rely on evidence of deception that could have been produced at an appeal, to justify curtailment of leave: Chomanga (Zimbabwe) [2011] UKUT 00312 (IAC). Nor may the Secretary of State rely on evidence that could have been produced at an appeal to revisit findings of fact made by the tribunal: AM (Pakistan) v Secretary of State for the Home Department [2011] EWCA Civ 872.

[6] R (on the application of Mwangi) v Secretary of State for the Home Department [2008] EWHC 3130 (Admin).

[7] R (on the application of Farinloye) v Secretary of State for the Home Department [2010] EWCA Civ 203, [2010] All ER (D) 106 (Mar).

[8] R (on the application of Jenner) v Secretary of State for the Home Department [2010] EWHC 132 (Admin).

Recommendations when an appeal is dismissed

20.33 There is no statutory power to make a recommendation when a case is dismissed, and a recommendation forms no part of the Tribunal's determination.[1] Although the Tribunal has a practically unfettered discretion to make extra-statutory comments as to any appropriate future course of action if it thinks fit, the ability to succeed on appeal on human rights grounds has reduced the necessity and utility of extra-statutory recommendations in most cases. Indeed, the Tribunal has repeatedly held that in the light of its human rights jurisdiction, such extra-statutory recommendations are not only unnecessary but positively undesirable.[2] However, the Administrative Court in *Shillova* referred to their continuing utility in situations where no asylum or human rights issues are engaged but it might be proper to draw to the Secretary of State's attention considerations of fairness, or the appellant's value to the community of the UK, or other considerations[3] Tribunals have made or endorsed extra-statutory recommendations in a variety of situations, either in general terms or limited to a specific objective.[4] Tribunals can hear evidence which is relevant only to a hoped-for recommendation, but if they decline to do so, or to adjourn the case so that such evidence can be called at a later date, or refuse to consider making a recommendation, or refuse to make one on the basis of the evidence which they have already heard, the High Court will not intervene.[5] This is so even where the refusal to make a recommendation is based on a material misapprehension of the facts, since the remedy lies against the Secretary of State if he or she adopts flawed findings of fact.[6] The Court of Appeal has given new life to the old practice of making recommendations by inviting the Tribunal to specify steps relating to the modalities of removal that must be taken by the respondent to avoid the appellant's human rights being breached upon being removed and to rely on the assumption that the specified steps will be taken in order to dismiss the appeal.[7]

[1]   *R v Immigration Appeal Tribunal, ex p Chavrimootoo* [1995] Imm AR 267, QBD; *R v Immigration Appeal Tribunal, ex p Anderson* (CO 1048/99) (14 March 2000, unreported), QBD; *Khatib-Shahidi v Immigration Appeal Tribunal* [2001] Imm AR 124, [2000] INLR 491, CA.

[2]   *Berisha (HR/8328/01)*; *Gokteke* [2002] UKIAT 06608; *AM (Angola)* [2004] UKIAT 00146, where the adjudicator, dismissing a human rights appeal, made a recommendation on the basis that it would be 'entirely lacking in humanity' to return the appellant's pregnant wife to 'that terrible place'.

[3]   See *R (on the application of Shillova) v Secretary of State for the Home Department* [2002] EWHC 1468 (Admin), [2002] INLR 611. Where a student had been very depressed as a result of criminal injuries but had improved in attendance and achievements since the decision, a recommendation might be appropriate: *S (India)* [2003] UKIAT 00043.

[4]   Thus in *Secretary of State for the Home Department v Okoth* [2002] UKIAT 06750, the Tribunal made a recommendation to enable the claimant to remain for his final nursing exams.

[5]   *R v Immigration Appeal Tribunal, ex p Chavrimootoo* [1995] Imm AR 267, QBD; *R v Immigration Appeal Tribunal, ex p Nalongo* [1994] Imm AR 536; *Wadia v Secretary of State for the Home Department* [1977] Imm AR 92; *Gillegao v Secretary of State for the Home Department* [1989] Imm AR 174; *R v Secretary of State for the Home Department, ex p Kumar* [1993] Imm AR 401, QBD; *R v Immigration Appeal Tribunal, ex p Anderson* (CO 1048/99) (14 March 2000, unreported); *Khatib-Shahidi v Immigration Appeal Tribunal* [2001] Imm AR 124, CA.

[6]   *Khatib-Shahidi v Immigration Appeal Tribunal* [2001] Imm AR 124, CA.

[7]   *AG (Somalia) v Secretary of State for the Home Department* [2006] EWCA Civ 1342, [2006] All ER (D) 189 (Oct).

20.34 The policy of the Secretary of State is to accept an extra-statutory recommendation in dismissed or withdrawn appeals 'only where the written determination discloses clear exceptional compassionate circumstances which have not been previously considered and which would merit the exercise of my discretion outside the Immigration Rules'.[1] A failure to follow a recommendation did not betray any promise made on behalf of the Department.[2] In considering any recommendation or further application, the Secretary of State is bound by factual findings of the Tribunal after oral evidence,[3] unless these factual findings are themselves unsustainable.[4]

[1]   42 HC Official Report (6th series) col 173, 23 July 1996. For the former policy on recommendations see 4th edition of this book at 18.117.

[2]   *R v Secretary of State for the Home Department, ex p Sakala* [1994] Imm AR 143, CA; *R v Secretary of State, ex p Alakesan* [1997] Imm AR 315, QBD; *R v Secretary of State for the Home Department, ex p Gardian* (1996) Times, 1 April, CA; *R v Secretary of State for the Home Department, ex p Banu* [1999] Imm AR 161.

[3]   The Secretary of State was not in the past bound by the Tribunal's assessment of country conditions: see eg *Elhasoglu v Secretary of State for the Home Department* [1997] Imm AR 380; *Kamara v Secretary of State for the Home Department* [1997] Imm AR 105, CA. With the advent of country guidance cases, it is arguable that the Secretary of State could not reject a recommendation on the basis of its assessment of country conditions which wholly disregarded a recent country guidance case, particularly if the case contained criticism of its CIPU assessment.

[4]   *R v Secretary of State for the Home Department, ex p Danaie* [1998] Imm AR 84, [1998] INLR 124, CA; *R (on the application of Saribal) v Secretary of State for the Home Department* [2002] EWHC 1542 (Admin), [2002] INLR 596, [2002] All ER (D) 379 (Jul).

POST-IMMIGRATION ACT 2014 POWERS OF THE FIRST-TIER TRIBUNAL

20.35 As described in the previous chapter, the Immigration Act 2014 amends the NIAA 2002, s 82 so that there will be rights of appeal against only three decisions: refusal of a protection claim; refusal of a human rights claim or revocation of protection status.[1] The Act also amends NIAA 2002, s 84 to restrict the grounds upon which an appeal may be brought. The extent to which these amendments are presently in force is described in **20.3** above. Under the amended appeal provisions, an appeal against refusal of a protection claim must be brought on one or more of the grounds that by removal of the appellant would breach the UK's obligations under the Refugee Convention or in respect of a person eligible for a grant of humanitarian protection, or would be unlawful under s 6 of the HRA 1998 (ie incompatible with an ECHR right).[2] An appeal against refusal of a human rights claim must be brought on the ground that the decision is unlawful under s 6 of the HRA 1998.[3] An appeal against revocation of protection status must be brought on one or both of the grounds that the decision breaches the UK's obligations under the Refugee Convention or in relation to persons eligible for a grant of humanitarian protection.[4] A person whose protection status has been revoked will not be able to bring an appeal on the ground that the decision is incompatible with his or her human rights, even though the consequence of the decision may be removal from the UK. Gone are the grounds of appeal that the decision was not in accordance with the rules or the law, the EU treaties or the race discrimination legislation, or that discretion should have been exercised differently.[5]

1 NIAA 2002, s 82, as substituted by IA 2014, s 15(2).
2 NIAA 2002, s 84(1) as substituted by IA 2014, s 15(4). The new human rights ground no longer qualifies the unlawfulness under the Human Rights Act 'as being incompatible with the appellant's Convention rights' as the ground in its current form does. However, thanks to *Beoku-Betts v Secretary of State for the Home Department* [2008] UKHL 39 those words had in any event ceased to restrict an appeal to consideration of whether the decision breached the appellant's human rights, excluding consideration of whether it breached the human rights of non-appellants.
3 NIAA 2002, s 84(2), as substituted by IA 2014, s 15(4).
4 NIAA 2002, s 84(3), as substituted by IA 2014, s 15(4).
5 NIIA 2002, s 84, as substituted by IA 2014, s 15(4).

20.36 The grounds of appeal 'that removal of the appellant from the United Kingdom would breach the United Kingdom's obligations in relation to persons eligible for humanitarian protection'[1] or that 'the decision to revoke the appellant's protection status breaches the United Kingdom's obligations in relation to persons eligible for a grant of humanitarian protection'[2] are new. The IA 2014 says that 'humanitarian protection' is 'to be construed in accordance with the immigration rules'.[3] It is not immediately obvious that the UK can have obligations in relation to a person whose status is to be construed in accordance with Immigration Rules when the rules are but 'statements of administrative policy: an indication of how at any particular time the Secretary of State will exercise her discretion with regard to the grant of leave to enter or remain': an indication of how at any particular time the Secretary of State will exercise her discretion with regard to the grant of leave to enter or remain'.[4] However, it is clear that the rules dealing with humanitarian protection were implemented to give effect to the UK's obligations under the Qualification Directive.[5] It should follow that the rules and 'the obligations in relation to persons eligible for humanitarian protection' to which the statute refers should be construed in accordance with the Qualification Directive. The Directive imposes numerous obligations on the UK in relation to persons eligible for international protection (some but not all of which are referred to in the rules) over and above the non-refoulement obligation eg to issue a residence permit valid for at least one year,[6] to issue a travel document,[7] to permit access to employment[8] and education,[9] and to allow freedom of movement.[10] That means that if humanitarian protection is revoked (eg on grounds that the person is excluded from humanitarian protection[11]) but the person is permitted to remain with 'restricted leave' for a period of six months subject to conditions such as residence, reporting and a prohibition on taking employment or engaging in studies,[12] then the person would be able to contend that the revocation of humanitarian protection breaches those obligations. Similar obligations in addition to non-refoulement are imposed on the UK by the Refugee Convention so that a person whose leave to enter or remain as a refugee is revoked, but who is given 'restricted leave' or some other status, would also be able to appeal against the revocation on the ground that it breaches the UK's obligations under the Refugee Convention.

1 NIAA 2002, s 84(1)(b), as substituted by IA 2014, s 15(4).
2 NIAA 2002, s 84(3)(b), substituted by IA 2014, s 15(4).
3 NIAA 2002, s 82(2)(d), as substituted by IA 2014, s 15(2).
4 *Odelola v Secretary of State for the Home Department* [2009] UKHL 25, per Lord Brown at [35].

[5] Explanatory Memorandum to the Statement of Changes in Immigration Rules laid on 18 September 2006 (Cm 6918), explaining that the rules dealing with humanitarian protection were introduced to implement Council Directive 2004/83/EC of 29 April 2004 on minimum standards for the qualification and status of third-country nationals or stateless persons as refugees or as persons who otherwise need international protection and the content of the protection provided ('the Qualification Directive').
[6] Qualification Directive, art 24(2); Immigration Rules, para 339Q.
[7] Qualification Directive, art 25, Immigration Rules, para 344A.
[8] Qualification Directive, art 26; Immigration Rules, para 344B.
[9] Qualification Directive, art 27. Not referred to in the Immigration Rules.
[10] Qualification Directive, art 32. Not referred to in the Immigration Rules.
[11] Immigration Rules, para 339G.
[12] Conditions of a kind typically imposed under the Secretary of State's 'Restricted Leave policy: asylum casework instruction', 28 May 2012.

20.37 NIAA 2002, section 85, which makes provision about what the tribunal has to consider, will be amended.[1] The tribunal will still have to treat the appeal as including an appeal against any decision in respect of which the appellant has a right of appeal under section 82.[2] It will also have to consider any matter raised by the appellant in a statement in response to a 'one-stop notice',[3] whether made before or after commencement of the appeal if the matter constitutes a ground of appeal.[4] The scope for this to have effect will be attenuated; an appellant could raise a human rights ground of appeal against refusal of a protection claim or a protection ground of appeal against refusal of a human rights claim. Surprisingly, the section does not make express provision for the tribunal to consider evidence; section 85 currently provides for the tribunal to 'consider evidence about any matter', but that is to be amended by the IA 2014 so that what the tribunal has to consider is 'any matter', not 'evidence about any matter'.[5] However, its capacity to consider evidence must be implicit, otherwise it would be incapable of considering matters as required by the statute. There is express provision for the tribunal to consider a matter arising after the date of the decision and to do that it will have to be able to consider evidence.[6] The tribunal will only be able to consider a new matter if the Secretary of State consents to the tribunal doing so.[7] However, that provision does not mean that the tribunal may only consider new evidence if the Secretary of State consents. The word 'matter' used elsewhere in the statute has been interpreted broadly so as to include 'evidence' as well as 'issue', but for the purpose of section 85 'new matter' is narrowly defined so as to require more than just evidence.[8] For something to be a new matter it has to constitute a ground of appeal that has not previously been considered by the Secretary of State in the context of making the decision being appealed against or in the context of a statement made in response to a 'one-stop notice'.[9] So, for example, a person appealing against refusal of a protection claim would be free to adduce new evidence to support the matter that they have already raised (ie that removal from the UK would breach the UK's obligations under the Refugee Convention), but would need the Secretary of State's consent to bring evidence to show that removal would also breach Article 8 of the ECHR if that issue had not previously been considered by the Secretary of State. Where a human rights claim is made from outside the UK, the tribunal will not be restricted to considering circumstances appertaining at the time of the decision as it currently is when hearing an appeal against refusal of entry clearance.[10] As with appeals against refusals of protection and human rights claims made in the country, the statutory grounds have to be determined by reference to circumstances at the time of the determination: the question is a prospective one, ie whether removal 'would' breach the UK's protection obligations or 'would be unlawful' under section 6 of the HRA 1998.

1   IA 2014, s 15(5).
2   NIIA 2002, s 85(1) which is unaffected by the 2014 Act.
3   ie notice of a 'requirement to state additional grounds for application' served under NIAA 2002, s 120.
4   NIIA 2002, s 85(2).
5   IA 2014, Sch 9, para 34.
6   NIAA 2002, s 85(4).
7   NIAA 2002, s 85(5), as substituted by IA 2014, s 15(5). During the passage through Parliament of what became the Act, the minister stated that it was intended the Home Office would publish guidance about when consent would or would not be given.
8   The word 'matter' in NIAA 2002, s 96 has been interpreted to mean 'evidence' as well as 'issue': *Khan (Mohammad Iqbal) v Secretary of State for the Home Department* [2013] EWHC 601(Admin) and *R (on the application of Khan (Mohammad Iqbal)) v Secretary of State for the Home Department* [2014] EWCA Civ 88. During the passage through Parliament of what became the Immigration Act 2014, the minister confirmed that s 85(5) was not referring to new evidence: Hansard HL, 1 April 2014, col 892, Lord Wallace of Tankerness.
9   NIAA 2002, s 85(6), as substituted by IA 2014, s 15(5).
10 NIAA 2002, s 85A, which contained exceptions to the general rule set out in s 85, including the exception in relation to entry clearance applications, is to be repealed by IA 2014, Sch 9, para 35.

20.38 NIAA 2002, section 86 is substantially amended by the IA 2014. The tribunal will continue to be obliged to determine any matter raised as a ground of appeal and any matter that it is required to consider by section 85. Thus it will have to decide whether or not removal or revocation of protection status will breach the UK's protection or ECHR obligations. What it will no longer be able to do is allow or dismiss an appeal or decide that discretion should have been exercised differently.[1] Nor will the tribunal be able to make directions that the immigration decision maker will have to comply with.[2] Nevertheless, if the tribunal determines that removal would breach the UK's protection or human rights obligations, the Secretary of State would be obliged to act in accordance with its decision for the reasons discussed above in **20.32**.

1   IA 2014, Sch 9, para 36, deleting sub-ss (3) to (6) of NIAA 2002, s 86.
2   IA 2014, Sch 9, para 37, repealing NIAA 2002, s 87.

20.39 There will be little remaining scope for the tribunal to act as the primary decision maker,because the appeal will be confined to consideration of the decision on a claim by reference only to the criteria that the decision maker will (or should) have applied (ie whether removal would breach the UK's protection obligations or human rights laws). It will only be if the Secretary of State permits the tribunal to consider a 'new matter' that the tribunal will be a primary decision maker.

The IA 2014 will also effect important changes to the certification provisions.

COSTS

20.40 The FT and the UT have power to make orders in respect of the costs of and incidental to proceedings.[1] However, the power is subject to Tribunal

Procedure Rules.[2] The 2005 Procedure Rules limited the tribunal's power to make costs orders to ordering the respondent to pay an amount no greater than the fee paid by the appellant for bringing the appeal.[3] That power is retained by the 2014 Procedure Rules.[4] The 2014 Procedure Rules also give the tribunal power to make wasted costs orders.[5] Such orders may be made against a legal or other representative or an employee of the representative.[6] A 'legal or other representative' is 'any person exercising a right of audience or right to conduct proceedings' on behalf of a party.[7] The jurisdiction to make such orders is one that should be approached with considerable caution, so as to avoid it being a deterrent to advocates from discharging their obligations to promote and protect fearlessly, by all proper and lawful means, the best interests of their clients.[8] 'Wasted costs' are any costs incurred by a party as a result of any improper, unreasonable or negligent act or omission on the part of any legal or other representative or the representative's employee.[9] Costs incurred by a party which the tribunal considers unreasonable to expect that party to pay in the light of any such act or omission occurring after the costs were incurred are also 'wasted costs'.[10] One situation in which costs might be awarded on this basis would be where the decision maker unreasonably withdraws the decision being appealed against. The provisions refer to 'any' legal or other representative, and so include the party's own representative[11] and his or her opponent's representative. They also refer to 'any costs incurred by a party' and so may be those of the winning or losing party. The tribunal may make an order in respect of the costs incurred in applying for wasted costs.[12] The tribunal may also make an order in respect of costs if a person has acted unreasonably in bringing, defending or conducting proceedings.[13]

[1] TCEA 2007, s 29(1) and (2).
[2] TCEA 2007, s 29(3).
[3] SI 2005/230, r 23A and in the fast track, SI 2005/560, r 6(h).
[4] Tribunal Procedure (First-tier Tribunal) (Immigration and Asylum Chamber) Rules, SI 2014/2604, r 9(1).
[5] SI 2014/2604, r 9(2).
[6] TCEA 2007, s 29(4)(b) and SI 2014/2604, r 9(2)(a).
[7] TCEA 2007, s 29(6). The definition includes barristers not just when they are exercising rights of audience, but also when they engage in conduct immediately relevant to the exercise of a right of audience, such as drafting documents: *Medcalf v Weatherill* [2002] UKHL 27 at [20].
[8] *Medcalf v Weatherill*, [56].
[9] TCEA 2007, s 29(5)(a).
[10] TCEA 2007, s 29(5)(b).
[11] In the context of wasted costs under Senior Courts Act 1981, s 51(6), it is open to a litigant to seek a wasted costs order against his or her own representatives: *Brown v Bennett (No 1)* [2002] 1 WLR 713 at [30].
[12] SI 2014/2604, r 9(2)(a).
[13] SI 2014/2604, r 9(2)(b).

20.41 The concepts of 'improper', 'unreasonable' and 'negligent' that appear in TCEA 2007, s 29(5) are well-known terms in the context of wasted costs.[1] 'Improper' conduct would include any significant breach of a substantial duty imposed by a relevant professional code of conduct, but extends beyond that to conduct which would be regarded as improper according to a consensus of professional (including judicial) opinion, even if it does not violate the letter of a professional code.[2] 'Unreasonable' describes conduct that is vexatious, designed to harass the other side rather than advance the resolution of the case. Conduct is not unreasonable merely because it led to an unsuccessful outcome; 'the acid test is whether the conduct permits of a reasonable explanation'.[3] 'Negligent' means failing to act with the competence reasonably to be expected of ordinary members of the profession and requires proof of nothing less than would have to be proved in a claim for negligence.[4] A legal representative does not act improperly, unreasonably or negligently by acting for a party who pursues a claim or defence which is plainly doomed to fail.[5] However, it would be different if the representative lent his or her assistance to proceedings which are an abuse of process eg proceedings used for reasons unconnected with success in the litigation or pursuing a case he or she knows to be dishonest.[6] In the context of judicial review, it was improper, unreasonable and negligent conduct to advance an application for judicial review where the basis of the case was 'fatally undermined' by the claimant's own expert evidence and where the representatives must have thought that the 'glaring inconsistency' between the claim advanced and the evidence could be camouflaged.[7] In that case, the full amount of the respondent's costs were ordered against the claimant's representative because the application for judicial review was 'flawed from start to finish'.[8]

[1] *R (on the application of Okondu and Abdussalam) v Secretary of State for the Home Department (wasted costs; SRA referrals; Hamidi) IJR* [2014] UKUT 377 (IAC).
[2] *Ridehalgh v Horsefield* [1994] EWCA Civ 40, Sir Thomas Bingham MR.
[3] ibid.
[4] ibid.
[5] ibid.
[6] ibid.
[7] *R (Okondu and Abdussalam)* paras 38, 39.
[8] *R (Okondu and Abdussalam)* para 40.

20.42 The tribunal may make an order for costs on its own initiative or on the application of a person.[1] An application may be made orally at a hearing or in writing, sent or delivered to the tribunal and the person against whom the order is sought.[2] A schedule of the costs claimed may accompany the application so as to allow summary assessment by the tribunal.[3] An application may be made at any time during the proceedings and must be made within 28 days of the tribunal sending notice of its decision disposing of the proceedings or notice that a withdrawal of the appeal (including deemed withdrawal upon withdrawal of the decision appealed against) has taken effect.[4] The tribunal may not make an order for costs against a person without first giving that person an opportunity to make representations.[5] A judge deciding whether to make an order against a legal representative would have to bear in mind that the representative may be prevented by legal professional privilege from revealing what advice they gave to and instructions they received from their client, and would thus be prevented from properly defending their conduct; in those circumstances, the judge must give the benefit of any doubt to them.[6]

The test for deciding whether to make an order should involve addressing three issues.

(1) Has the legal representative of whom complaint is made acted improperly, unreasonably or negligently?
(2) If so, did such conduct cause the applicant to incur unnecessary cost?
(3) If so, is it, in all the circumstances, just to order the legal representative to compensate the applicant for the whole or any part of the relevant costs?[7]

The amount of costs to be paid may be determined by summary assessment by the tribunal; agreement between the paying person and the person entitled to receive the costs; or detailed assessment.[8]

¹ Tribunal Procedure (First-tier Tribunal)(Immigration and Asylum Chamber) Rules 2014, SI 2014/2604, r 9(3).
² SI 2014/2604, r 9(4)(a).
³ SI 2014/2604, r 9(4)(b).
⁴ SI 2014/2604, r 9(5).
⁵ SI 2014/2604, r 9(6).
⁶ *Ridehalgh v Horsefield* [1994] EWCA Civ 40.
⁷ ibid.
⁸ SI 2014/2604, r 9(9).

PROCEDURE ON APPEALS

20.43 Proceedings before the FT and the Special Immigration Appeals Commission (SIAC) are civil proceedings, and save where special provision is made, must be regarded as governed by the ordinary principles and practice relating to civil proceedings.[1] These appellate bodies are public authorities under the HRA 1998, and are therefore subject to an overriding duty to ensure compliance with the rights guaranteed by the Human Rights Convention.[2] However, the European Court of Human Rights (ECtHR) has repeatedly held that 'the right of an alien to reside in a country is a matter of public law' and is thus not a 'civil right' for the purposes of ECHR, art 6 (fair trial in determination of civil rights and obligations),[3] and the Tribunal has simultaneously held that its procedures are art 6 compliant, and that art 6 does not apply to its procedures or to procedural provisions of the relevant Acts.[4] The Court of Appeal has come close to accepting that the Qualification Directive creates an individual right to asylum falling within the category of 'civil rights' to which art 6 applies but held that it could not take that step because of the weight of Strasbourg authority to the contrary.[5] The duty of fairness imposed on the Tribunal is thus more likely to be derived from the high common law standards of fairness applied by the higher courts to immigration appeals of all kinds, and particularly to those raising issues of international protection.[6]

¹ *Prendi* (01LS00060) (8 August 2001, unreported), IAT.
² See HRA 1998, s 6(3); *MNM* (00TH02423); *SK* [2002] UKIAT 05613 (starred); see **7.16** above.
³ *Agee v United Kingdom* (1976) 7 DR 164; *P v United Kingdom* (13162/87) (1987) 54 DR 211, *Bozano v France* (1984) 39 DR 119; *Maaouia v France* (Application 39652/98) (2000) 33 EHRR 1037, 9 BHRC 205; *Ilic v Croatia* (Application 42389/98) (19 September 2000, unreported); *Mamatkulov and Abdurasulovic v Turkey* (Applications 46827/99 and 46951/99) (6 February 2003)2003) Times, 13 March, 14 BHRC 149. Procedural safeguards have been held by the ECtHR to be vital ingredients of substantive Convention rights: see eg *Chahal v United Kingdom* (1996) 23 EHRR 413; *McCann v United Kingdom* (1995) 21 EHRR 97; *Kaya v Turkey* (1998) 28 EHRR 1; see also **7.47** above. The European Court has also emphasised the importance of effective remedies under ECHR, art 13 (deemed incorporated in practice and so not set out in the Schedules to the HRA 1998).
⁴ See *AM ('Upgrade' appeals) (Afghanistan)* [2004] UKIAT 186.
⁵ *R (on the application of MK) v Secretary of State for the Home Department* [2010] EWCA Civ 115.
⁶ See eg *R v Secretary of State for the Home Department, ex p Fayed* [1998] 1 WLR 763; *R v Secretary of State for the Home Department, ex p Saleem (Asifa)* [2000] Imm AR 529, [2000] INLR 413, CA; *Ravichandran v Secretary of State for the Home Department* [2000] Imm AR

10, CA; *R (on the application of the Refugee Legal Centre) v Secretary of State for the Home Department* [2004] EWCA Civ 1481, [2004] All ER (D) 201 (Nov); *R (on the application of Anufrijeva) v Secretary of State for the Home Department* [2003] UKHL 36, [2003] Imm AR 570, [2003] INLR 521.

20.44 Subject to that overriding duty, the practice and procedure on appeals is governed by the Immigration (Notices) Regulations 2003,[1] the Tribunal Procedure Rules[2] and Practice Directions given by the Senior President of Tribunals or by a Chamber President.[3] The Tribunal Procedure Rules are made by the Tribunal Procedure Committee[4] composed of the Senior President of Tribunals (or his or her nominee); three appointees of the Lord Chancellor with experience of Tribunal practice and one nominated by the Administrative Justice and Tribunals Council; three appointees of the Lord Chief Justice including a judge of each of the FT and UT and a non-judge member of the FT or UT; an appointee of the Lord President of the Court of Session and up to four individuals who may be appointed for their knowledge and experience of a particular issue or subject area.[5] The Committee must consult before making rules and the rules made by the committee must be signed by a majority of its members.[6] The Lord Chancellor may then allow or disallow the rules with those that are allowed being contained in a statutory instrument, subject to negative resolution of Parliament and coming into force on a day directed by the Lord Chancellor.[7] The Rules may provide, *inter alia*, for functions of the FT or UT to be delegated to staff of the Tribunal; for time limits in relation to initiating or taking any step in proceedings; for the Tribunals to exercise its powers of its own initiative; for dealing with matters without a hearing or for hearings in private; for proceedings without notice; for conferring additional rights of audience; for the production of evidence; for the disclosure or non-disclosure of information received during the course of proceedings; for the rules to refer to Practice Directions instead of making provision about a matter; for errors to be corrected and for decisions to be set aside on procedural grounds.[8] The TCEA 2007 allows for the procedure rules of a Tribunal whose functions are transferred into the FT to be modified and deemed, by order of the Lord Chancellor, Tribunal Procedure Rules.[9] Thus, the Asylum and Immigration Tribunal (Procedure) Rules 2005[10] and the Asylum and Immigration Tribunal (Fast Track Procedure) Rules 2005[11] as amended,[12] had effect from 15 February 2010 as if they were Tribunal Procedure Rules[13] applying to proceedings before the FT of the Immigration and Asylum Chamber.[14] These Rules were replaced by the Tribunal Procedure (First-tier Tribunal)(Immigration and Asylum Chamber) Rules 2014 with effect from 20 October 2014.[15] The overriding objective of these Rules is to enable the tribunal to deal with cases fairly and justly and the tribunal must seek to give effect to the overriding objective when it exercises any power under the Rules or interprets any rule or Practice Direction.[16] The Senior President of Tribunals gave Practice Directions and made Practice Statements for the Immigration and Asylum Chambers of the FT Tribunal and the Upper Tribunal on 10 February 2010, which came into force on 15 February 2010.[17] The Senior President of Tribunals also made a Practice Direction on child, vulnerable adult and sensitive witnesses.[18] The Chamber Presidents have issued guidance on various matters, eg on child, vulnerable adult and sensitive appellants[19] and fee awards in immigration appeals.[20]

[1]   SI 2003/658, made under NIAA 2002, s 105.

[2] Made under TCEA 2007, s 22.
[3] TCEA 2007, s 23.
[4] TCEA 2007, s 22(2).
[5] TCEA 2007, s 22(3) and Sch 5, Pt 2.
[6] TCEA 2007, s 22(3) and Sch 5, Pt 3.
[7] TCEA 2007, s 22(3) and Sch 5, Pt 3.
[8] TCEA 2007, s 22(1) and (3) and Sch 5, Pt 1.
[9] TCEA 2007, s 31(7).
[10] SI 2005/230.
[11] SI 2005/560.
[12] Transfer of Functions of the Asylum and Immigration Tribunal Order 2010, SI 2010/21, art 4.
[13] By SI 2010/21.
[14] SI 2005/230, r 3 (note the definition of 'Tribunal' in r 2) and SI 2005/560, r 3.
[15] SI 2014/2604, r 1(1), providing for commencement.
[16] 'Dealing with a case fairly and justly includes: dealing with the case in ways proportionate to the importance of the case, the complexity of the issues, the anticipated costs and the resources of the parties and the tribunal; avoiding unnecessary formality and seeking flexibility in the proceedings; ensuring so far as practicable that the parties are able to participate fully in the proceedings; using any special expertise of the tribunal effectively and avoiding delay so far as compatible with proper consideration of the issues': SI 2014/2604, r 2.
[17] The Practice Directions were subsequently amended on 1 November 2013 and new Practice Statements were issued on 25 September 2012. Available from: www.tribunals.gov.uk.
[18] Practice Direction: First Tier and Upper Tribunal: Child, Vulnerable Adult and Sensitive Witnesses, 30 October 2008.
[19] Joint Presidential Guidance Note No 2 of 2010.
[20] Joint Presidential Guidance: 'Fee Awards in Immigration Appeals'.

Procedures: Transitional provisions

20.45 Paragraph 19.37 of the previous edition of this book deals with the provisions that were made for the transfer of proceedings from the Asylum and Immigration Tribunal, abolished on 15 February 2010, to the First-tier and Upper Tribunal, and for onward appeals to the Court of Appeal.

Normal and fast track appeals

20.46 Appeals against immigration decisions, other than those dealing with national security, all come to the FT, as will appeals against refusals of protection or human rights claims and revocation of protection status, when the appeals provisions in the Immigration Act 2014 come into force. But there are different procedures and, more significantly, different timescales, depending on whether the appeal is in the normal track or the fast track. We discussed earlier, at **12.112**, the detention of single male asylum claimants from countries deemed 'safe' by the Home Office, and their subjection to fast track processing of their claim, in procedures which the Court of Appeal in the *Refugee Legal Centre* case held at the edge of illegality for unfairness, but just flexible enough to avoid it.[1] Those on the fast track have an in-country appeal, regulated by the fast track rules in the Schedule to the Tribunal Procedure (First-tier Tribunal)(Immigration and Asylum Chamber) Rules 2014.[2] The Fast Track Rules apply where the person giving notice of appeal was in detention under the Immigration Acts[3] in a specified removal centre when served with the notice of the decision which is the subject of the appeal, and has been continuously in detention since.[4] The Court of Appeal acknowledged that concerns raised by the UNHCR about the fast track are important, including insufficient clarity about the policy for applying fast track procedures; the allocation of complex cases to the procedure; and the failure to give or record adequate reasons for allocating a case to the fast track.[5]

1   *R (on the application of the Refugee Legal Centre) v Secretary of State for the Home Department* [2004] EWCA Civ 1481, [2004] All ER (D) 580 (Mar), upholding Collins J at [2004] EWHC 684 (Admin). The court required the Secretary of State to formulate a written policy stating when the normal timescales would be adapted to the individual claimant's needs. Fast track claimants did not have to be single; it was physical constraints, not policy, which precluded the admission of partners and children to the fast track accommodation: *R (on the application of Kpandang) v Secretary of State for the Home Department* [2004] EWHC 2130 (Admin), [2004] All ER (D) 555 (Jul).
2   SI 2014/2604, in force from 20 October 2014, replacing the Asylum and Immigration Tribunal (Fast Track Procedure) Rules 2005, SI 2005/560 which came into force 4 April 2005 (replacing the Immigration and Asylum (Fast Track Procedure) Rules 2003, SI 2003/801) and the Transfer of Functions of the Asylum and Immigration Tribunal Order 2010, SI 2010/21, art 4 by which they were deemed to be Tribunal Procedure Rules. This group is to be distinguished from the 'NSA' or non-suspensive appeal group, who are also asylum claimants coming from countries deemed safe, but including families with children. The latter group, generally coming from countries listed in NIAA 2002, s 94(4), are also detained and subject to speedy determination of their asylum claims, but refusal generally leads to immediate removal, and the right of appeal against the immigration decision may only be exercised from abroad. The normal procedure rules apply to non-suspensive appeals.
3   Defined in Asylum and Immigration (Treatment of Claimants, etc) Act 2004, s 44. The specified places of detention are Colnbrook House, Harmondsworth Immigration Removal Centre and Yarlswood Immigration Removal Centres: SI 2014/2604, Schedule, r 2(3).
4   SI 2014/2604, r 2(1).
5   *R (on the application of Suckrajh) v Secretary of State for the Home Department* [2011] EWCA Civ 938, [2011] All ER (D) 292 (Jul).

20.47 Rule 14 of the Fast Track Rules regulates transfer of cases out of the fast track into the normal appeal procedures, and applies both to first appeals and to applications to the FT for permission to appeal to the UT. It provides that the Tribunal must transfer cases out of the fast track if all parties consent or if the tribunal is satisfied that the case cannot justly be determined within the fast track timescales.[1] Refusal of an adjournment, needed to obtain expert evidence to answer the case against the asylum seeker on the basis that removal from the fast track would necessarily result, was held to be unlawful.[2] There is no longer specific provision to transfer a case from the fast track if the respondent has failed to comply with a direction or provision of the rules.[3] The Fast Track Rules cease to apply if the appellant is released from detention.[4] When the Tribunal orders transfer out of the fast track, it has power to adjourn a hearing and give directions.[5] Once the Fast Track Rules cease to apply, the principal procedure rules apply, with their time limits.[6]

1   SI 2014/2604, Schedule, r 14(1). The predecessor to that rule required not only that the case could not be justly determined, but also 'exceptional circumstances': see *SH (Afghanistan) v Secretary of State for the Home Department* [2011] EWCA Civ 1284. In the *Refugee Legal Centre* case (**20.46**, fn 1 above), the Home Office acknowledged that complex cases, those with medical issues or requiring expert evidence were not suitable for the fast track. The evidence before the court in that case was that of 1,438 claimants on the fast track, 151 were taken off the fast track before a decision and a further 270 pending appeal. But in *K (Côte d'Ivoire)* [2004] UKIAT 00061, the Tribunal rejected the argument that a case with complex facts, which necessitated a two-day hearing and an adjournment, should have been transferred out.
2   *SH (Afghanistan) v Secretary of State for the Home Department* [2011] EWCA Civ 1284, [2011] All ER (D) 55 (Nov).
3   As there was in SI 2005/560, r 31(1)(c).
4   SI 2014/2604, r 1(5).

[5]   SI 2014/2604, Schedule, r 14(2).
[6]   SI 2014/2604, r 1(5).

20.48 In the *Refugee Legal Centre* case, the Court of Appeal acknowledged that in some cases, transfer out of the fast track process at the appeal stage is too late; the appeal would be flawed by the fundamental unfairness of the determination process which has resulted in an interview which should not be relied on, still less be used as the basis of arguments about discrepancies and credibility.[1] Collins J observed at first instance that he could not believe that any competent representative would let his or her client be treated unfairly without intervening,[2] and it is clearly vital that representatives make vigorous representations in writing about any unfairness, including that arising by refusal to remove a case from the fast track at the initial determination stage. However, if representations are rejected, should the representative seek transfer at the appeal stage, or should he or she seek judicial review of the refusal of the Secretary of State to transfer out of the fast track at the earlier stage? In *Sunalla*,[3] Moses J agreed that an asylum determination procedure in the course of which the claimant had been interviewed for a total of 23 hours was likely to be unfair, and that such unfairness could not be cured on appeal, but refused permission for judicial review, because the claimant had not waited for an asylum decision. Thus, where the Secretary of State has refused to transfer an asylum claimant out of the fast track procedure, the proper course would seem to be to await initial decision to see whether the refusal has led to prejudice, and if so, to seek judicial review of the unfair procedure, with reference to the prejudice caused, while at the same time lodging a protective appeal.

[1]   *R (on the application of the Refugee Legal Centre) v Secretary of State for the Home Department* [2004] EWCA Civ 1481, [2004] All ER (D) 580 (Mar).
[2]   *R (Refugee Legal Centre) v Secretary of State for the Home Department* [2004] EWHC 684 (Admin).
[3]   *R v Secretary of State for the Home Department, ex p Sunalla* (CO/2362/98).

Non-suspensive appeals

20.49 Non-suspensive appeals are appeals from decisions taken when the claimant is in the UK but which have to be conducted from abroad. The term is usually applied to appeals on asylum or human rights grounds which have been certified clearly unfounded under section 94 of NIAA 2002.[1] Such appeals are not subject to special procedure rules, as fast track appeals are, but time for lodging the appeal runs from the date of departure rather than the date of service of the decision,[2] and non-standard directions may be given.[3] For example, after the High Court ruled that the Ahmadi family, who had sought sanctuary in a mosque, had been unlawfully removed to Germany, the Secretary of State persuaded the court not to order their return by pointing to the ability of the appellate authority to expedite a hearing of their appeal, with video link facilities to enable them and their medical witnesses to give evidence.[4]

[1]   As amended by Asylum and Immigration (Treatment of Claimants, etc) Act 2004, s 27, in force 1 October 2004.
[2]   Tribunal Procedure (First-tier Tribunal)(Immigration and Asylum Chamber) Rules 2014, SI 2014/2604, r 14(3).

3   SI 2014/2604, r 4(2). For directions see **20.87** below.
4   *R (on the application of Ahmadi) v Secretary of State for the Home Department* [2002]
    EWHC 1897 (Admin), [2002] All ER (D) 52 (Sep). It would not be in every case that the
    Secretary of State would offer to pay for an appellant's legal representative to be with the
    appellant to offer advice and assistance, however, as happened in that case.

Notices of action or decision

20.50 The first stage in the appeal procedure is for notice of the decision of the
immigration authority in question to be given to the immigrant. Provision for
this is made by the Notice Regulations[1] under which a written notice of any
appealable decision is to be given to the person in respect of whom the decision
is made.[2] The Notices Regulations have been amended so that they make
different provision according to whether or not the IA 2014 appeals provisions
apply,[3] those provisions having been commenced only in respect of persons in
the situations described in **20.3** above. Where the IA 2014 appeals provisions
do not apply, the Notices Regulations require notice to be given of an
immigration decision or EEA decision,[4] or of a grant of leave if, as a result, the
person has a right of appeal under section 83[5], or a decision that a person is
no longer a refugee that is appealable under section 83A[6] of NIAA 2002. The
notice must be given to the person in respect of whom the decision or action
is taken.[7] If the notice is given to the person's representative, it is deemed to
have been given to the person.[8] Where the IA 2014 appeals provisions apply,
the Notices Regulations only require notice to be given of EEA decisions and
decisions that are appealable under NIAA 2002, section 82(1) as amended ie
refusal of a protection or human rights claim or revocation of protection
status.[9]

1   Immigration (Notices) Regulations 2003, SI 2003/658 as amended, made under NIAA 2002,
    s 105.
2   SI 2003/658, reg 4(1).
3   By SI 2014/2768, reg 3 of which makes transitional provision.
4   SI 2003/658, reg 4(1).
5   SI 2003/658, reg 4(2).
6   SI 2003/658, reg 4(2A) (as inserted by SI 2006/2168).
7   SI 2003/658, reg 4(1).
8   SI 2003/658, reg 7(1); Immigration (Leave to Enter and Remain) Order 2000, SI 2000/1161,
    arts 8(2), 10(1).
9   SI 2003/658, as amended by SI 2014/2768, reg 3.

20.51 A decision may be given by hand or sent by recorded delivery, post or
by fax, electronically, by document exchange or by courier[1] to the applicant or
his or her representative or the applicant or representative may collect the
decision.[2] In the case of an unrepresented minor, the notice may be given to the
child's parent or guardian or to another adult who has responsibility for the
child.[3] If no address is known, the decision may be 'served on the file'.[4] A
refusal of leave to enter or variation of leave complying with section 4(1) of the
Immigration Act 1971 will be deemed to comply with the regulations if
accompanied by the prescribed information,[5] which must otherwise be contained in the notice.

1   SI 2003/658, reg 7(1)(c)(i), (ii).
2   SI 2003/658, reg 7(1)(f).
3   SI 2003/658, reg 7(7).

4   SI 2003/658, reg 7(2). For service, including 'service on the file', see CHAPTER 20 below.
5   *R (on the application of Hashimi) v Secretary of State for the Home Department* [2002]
     EWCA Civ 728, [2002] INLR 377. A letter to an MP serves as notice for the purposes of IA
     1971, s 4(1).

20.52 The Notices Regulations[1] specify what must be contained in the notice, or in a statement accompanying the notice. The specifications are different depending upon whether the decision is appealable under the IA 2014[2] or under appeals provisions unaffected by the IA 2014.[3] If the decision is an EEA decision or is appealable under NIAA 2002, section 82(1) (unamended by the IA 2014, section 82(1)), or under NIAA 2002, sections 83 or 83A, the notice must contain the following information:

(1)   the reasons for the decision;[4]
(2)   the country or territory to which the person is to be removed, where the notice refers to the giving of directions for removal from the UK. If it appears to the decision maker that a person may be removable to more than one country then the notice can specify more than one destination country;[5]
(3)   details of the person's right of appeal and the statutory provision on which the right of appeal is based;[6]
(4)   whether or not the appeal may be brought whilst in the UK;[7]
(5)   the grounds on which the appeal may be brought;[8]
(6)   the facilities available for advice and assistance in connection with the appeal;[9]
(7)   the time limit for bringing the appeal, the address to which the notice of appeal should be sent or taken by hand, or a fax number to which it may be sent;[10]
(8)   reference to any provision under Part 5 of NIAA 2002 that limits or restricts the right of appeal.[11]

The notice must also be accompanied by a notice of appeal. The notice of decision need not contain the information about appeal rights, or be accompanied by a notice of appeal, if the decision would not be appealable other than on race discrimination, asylum or human rights grounds.[12] However, if a person is served with notice of such a decision and then makes an asylum, human rights or race discrimination claim, the decision maker must, as soon as practicable, re-serve the notice of decision including the requisite appeal information and forms.[13]

The tribunal has held that if a notice of an immigration decision conceals from the recipient that they have a right of appeal against a variation decision, albeit one restricted to human rights, asylum or race discrimination grounds,[14] then the person's leave is statutorily extended until after he or she makes an asylum, human rights or race discrimination claim and the Secretary of State responds by re-serving the immigration decision.[15] This is because IA 1971, sections 3C and 3D extend a person's leave during the period in which an appeal could be brought against a variation of or refusal to vary the leave. The effect of the Notices Regulations is that the period during which an appeal could be brought extends until after the immigration decision is reserved following the making of such a claim, however long that may be after the original decision. Whilst at first glance a surprising conclusion, it is a response to the Notices

Regulations being drafted in such a way as to subvert their statutory purpose of informing people about their rights of appeal,[16] particularly in respect of matters as critical as asylum, human rights and race discrimination.

1 The Immigration (Notices) Regulations 2013, SI 2003/658.
2 ie NIAA 2002, s 82(1) as amended by the IA 2014, s 15.
3 The Immigration (Notices) (Amendment) Regulations 2014, SI 2014/2768, transitional provision in reg 3.
4 SI 2003/658, reg 5(1)(a). If the decision is the grant of leave and refusal of asylum, the notice must contain the reasons for the refusal of asylum: reg 5(2). A letter setting out the reasons for refusal is generally served with (or ahead of) the formal notice of decision, and such an arrangement meets the reasons requirement.
5 ie a refusal of leave to enter, a decision to remove or to deport (under NIAA 2002, s 82(2)(a), (g)–(j)): SI 2003/658, reg 5(1)(b), as amended by SI 2006/2168. For the validity of a decision notice containing no destination country, or one which appears not to comply with the requirements of IA 1971, Sch 2, para 8(1)(c) or Sch 3, para 1, see **17.67–17.68** above.
6 SI 2003/658, reg 5(3)(a).
7 SI 2003/658, reg 5(3)(b).
8 SI 2003/658, reg 5(3)(c).
9 SI 2003/658, reg 5(3)(d).
10 SI 2003/658, reg 5(4).
11 eg a statement under Asylum and Immigration (Treatment of Claimants, etc) Act 2004, Sch 3, paras 15(3), 19 (prohibited grounds of appeal): SI 2003/658, reg 5(5).
12 SI 2003/658, reg 5(6).
13 SI 2003/658, reg 5(6), (7). Time for appealing runs from re-service: reg 5(8).
14 As permitted by the Immigration (Notices) Regulations 2003, SI 2003/658, reg 5(6).
15 Under reg 5(7) of the Immigration (Notices) Regulations. See *CHH (Jamaica)* [2011] UKUT 121 (IAC).
16 NIAA 2002, s 105 and *Singh (Pargan) v Secretary of State for the Home Department* [1992] 4 All ER 673, [1992] 1 WLR 1052, HL.

20.53 In respect of decisions that are appealable under the IA 2014 ie refusal of a protection claim, a human rights claim or revocation of protection status, the notice of decision has to include or be accompanied by the following information:[1]

(1)   the reasons for the decision;
(2)   details of the person's right of appeal and the statutory provision on which it is based;
(3)   whether or not the appeal may be brought whilst in the UK;
(4)   the grounds on which the appeal may be brought;
(5)   the facilities available for advice and assistance in connection with the appeal;
(6)   information about the process for providing notice of appeal to the tribunal;
(7)   the time limit for providing that notice.

1 SI 2003/658, reg 5, as amended by SI 2014/2768.

20.54 Where a notice fails to comply with any of these requirements, do the defects invalidate the notice, or is the notice still good? Guidance on this question was given by the Court of Appeal in *Jeyeanthan*,[1] a case about a notice of appeal lacking the necessary declaration. The Master of the Rolls said that:

'the important question [is] what the legislator should be judged to have intended should be the consequence of non-compliance. This has to be assessed on a consideration of the language of the legislation against the factual circumstances of the non-compliance. In the majority of cases it provides limited, if any, assistance to inquire whether the requirement is mandatory or directory . . . Procedural requirements are designed to further the interests of justice and any consequence which would achieve a result contrary to those interests should be treated with considerable reservation.'

He suggested that three questions were likely to arise:

(a) Is the statutory requirement fulfilled if there has been substantial compliance with the requirement and, if so, has there been substantial compliance in the case in issue even though there has not been strict compliance? (The substantial compliance question.)

(b) Is the non-compliance capable of being waived, and if so, has it been, or can it and should it be waived in this particular case? (The discretionary question.)

(c) If it is not capable of being waived or is not waived then what is the consequence of the non-compliance? (The consequences question.)[2]

These considerations were expressed to apply to procedural requirements for both sides and at all stages of the appeal process. A notice which fails to tell an appellant of a right of appeal is likely to be held invalid, so that time would not begin to run for the purpose of appealing.[3] More recent guidance given by the House of Lords is that the emphasis ought to be on the consequences of the non-compliance, asking whether it was the legislative intention that an act done in breach of procedural requirements should be invalid.[4] So, for example, where a notice of decision to make a deportation order failed to specify the country to which the appellant was to be removed, the appellant, by giving notice of appeal effectively waived the requirement and all the parties knew to which country the appellant was to be deported and so were not prejudiced by the non-compliance. In those circumstances no prejudice was caused by the deficiency so that the notice was held to be valid.[5] A notice of immigration decision that referred to the wrong statutory provision[6] as a basis for certifying an asylum claim as clearly unfounded was not for that reason invalid: there was a power to certify the claim, albeit under a different provision and the recipient of the decision was left in no doubt as to its legal consequences.[7] On the other hand, where a claimant's indefinite leave to remain had been cancelled on national security grounds while he was outside the country, and the decision notice had informed him that he had an out-of-country right of appeal but wrongly failed to inform him that he had an in-country right of appeal, the notice of decision was unlawful and would be quashed.[8]

1   *R v Immigration Appeal Tribunal, ex p Jeyeanthan; Ravichandran v Secretary of State for the Home Department* [2000] 1 WLR 354, [2000] Imm AR 10, [2000] INLR 241.

2   *Jeyeanthan*, ibid [2000] INLR 241 at 247. The court held that the Secretary of State's failure to make a declaration of truth on the form meant there was not substantial compliance (disapproving *R v Immigration Appeal Tribunal, ex p Nicholapillai* [1998] Imm AR 232) but that the non-compliance had in one case been waived and in the other had had no adverse consequences. See also *Hussain (Halgurd)* [2002] UKIAT 03419.

3   See *Akhuemonkhan v Secretary of State for the Home Department* [1998] INLR 265, where an appeal was allowed against a notice from the appellate authority of 'abandonment of appeal' with no indication of appeal rights. See also *Odomusu* (17109) 22 May 1998, IAT, a decision involving failure to serve notices on the children of a proposed deportee including rights of voluntary departure and of appeal. In *Mohamed (Omar) v Secretary of State for the Home Department* [2002] UKIAT 04634 the Tribunal held that notice of a decision giving exceptional leave to remain was a valid grant of leave, in spite of its failure to comply with the requirement in the Notice Regulations to inform the recipient of the statutory provisions under

which he could appeal. However, that failure would prevent the Secretary of State from taking any point as to the timeliness of any appeal brought against that decision. See also *ZA (Ethiopia)* [2004] UKIAT 00241, [2004] Imm AR 538, where an appellant was granted humanitarian protection after refusal of asylum but not advised of her appeal rights; time was not held to run against the appellant until she received a proper notice informing her of her right to appeal.

4 *R v Soneji* [2006] 1 AC 340.
5 *JN (Cameroon) v Secretary of State for the Home Department* [2009] EWCA Civ 307. The Court of Appeal doubted whether, in any event, non-compliance with the Notices Regulations could render a decision invalid.
6 NIAA 2002, s 94(2) instead of s 94(1A).
7 *R (on the application of Huang) v Secretary of State for the Home Department* [2011] EWHC 2069 (Admin), [2011] All ER (D) 87 (Aug).
8 *EI/(OS Russia) v Secretary of State for the Home Department* [2012] EWCA Civ 357.

Giving notice of decision

20.55 Elementary fairness supports the principle that a decision takes effect only on communication.[1] As we shall see, the Notices Regulations[2] do not always give effect to this principle, sometimes prioritising firm immigration control over fairness. The regulations contain no requirement that notice be given 'as soon as practicable' after a decision is taken. Cases under previous regulations[3] indicated that the notice could be sent to the last-known or usual place of abode even when the Home Office knew that the appellant was not there,[4] or had been asked to send it to the appellant's legal representative.[5] In *ex p Yeboah and Draz*,[6] where a letter was sent by post but not received by its intended recipient, the Court of Appeal held that the Interpretation Act 1978, section 7 did not enable the appellant to disprove the presumption of receipt by evidence of actual non-receipt. This harsh decision was reversed by statute,[7] following another Court of Appeal decision, *Saleem*,[8] which made it clear that such irrebuttable presumptions which deprived appellants of appeal rights were no longer acceptable in the new climate.

The 2000 Procedure Rules required the notice of the decision to be 'received' in most cases before time limits for appealing started to run.[9] The 2003 Rules that replaced them, and their 2005 successors, required notice to be 'served'.[10] The current (2014) Tribunal Procedure Rules no longer talk about documents being 'served', but instead refer to documents being 'provided', 'sent', 'delivered,' left with the person, or 'received'.[11] Time for appealing starts to run once the person is 'sent'[12] the notice of decision if the appellant is in the country and may appeal from within the UK.[13]

There is a lacuna in the Procedure Rules as currently drafted in respect of such an appellant to whom the decision is not sent, but is given by hand or collected by the person.[14] Time does not start to run against that person because the decision has not been 'sent', at least on a literal reading of the Procedure Rules and having regard to the deliberate distinctions that they make between notices being 'sent', 'received', 'provided' and left with an individual. If the individual with an in-country right of appeal is in the fast track, time runs from when he or she is 'provided' with the notice of appealable decision,[15] something which may be accomplished by giving it to the person by hand or leaving it with the person, but not by sending it unless there is also evidence of the document being received. If the appellant is out of the country when the decision is made, time runs from when they 'receive' the notice,[16] which is deemed to be on the

28th day after posting unless the contrary is proved.[17] In the case of a decision made whilst the person is in the UK but which is appealable only from outside the UK, time runs from the person's departure from the UK.[18] If time starts running when a document is sent, the time within which notice of appeal must be given may end without the person actually receiving the notice of decision. No doubt such an eventuality would be relevant to the exercise of the discretion to extend time for appealing.[11] Time will not start to run against an appellant if the decision was not given to the person by one of the means provided for in the Notices Regulations eg by sending it by ordinary post rather than recorded delivery.[19] The use of a courier service by entry clearance officers did not constitute good service[20] until the Notices Regulations were amended to allow for the giving of notice by courier.[21]

[1] *R (on the application of Anufrijeva) v Secretary of State for the Home Department* [2003] UKHL 36, [2003] Imm AR 570, [2003] INLR 521, per Lord Steyn at [30]. The individual concerned must, he ruled, be in a position to challenge the decision in the courts ([26]). Lord Millett held that the presumption that notice of a decision must be given to the person adversely affected by it before it can have legal effect is a strong one (at [43]).

[2] Immigration (Notices) Regulations 2003, SI 2003/658, made under NIAA 2002, s 105.

[3] Immigration Appeals (Notices) Regulations 1984, SI 1984/2040.

[4] *Singh (Pargan v Secretary of State for the Home Department* [1993] Imm AR 112 at 118, HL.

[5] *Tongo v Secretary of State for the Home Department* [1995] Imm AR 109, CA.

[6] *R v Secretary of State for the Home Department, ex p Yeboah, R v Secretary of State for the Home Department, ex p Draz* [1987] Imm AR 414, CA.

[7] IAA 1999, Sch 4, para 2; see also Immigration and Asylum Appeals (Procedure) Rules 2000, SI 2000/2333, r 48(2), succeeded by the Immigration (Notices) Regulations 2003, SI 2003/658, reg 7(4); Immigration and Asylum Appeals (Procedure) Rules 2003 SI 2003/652, r 54(5).

[8] *R v Secretary of State for the Home Department, ex p Saleem (Asifa)* [2000] Imm AR 529, [2000] INLR 413.

[9] SI 2000/2333, r 6.

[10] Asylum and Immigration Tribunal (Procedure) Rules 2005, SI 2005/230, r 7(1) (replacing the Immigration and Asylum Appeals (Procedure) Rules 2003, SI 2003/652, r 7); Asylum and Immigration Tribunal (Fast Track Procedure) Rules 2005, SI 2005/560, r 8.

[11] Tribunal Procedure (First-tier Tribunal)(Immigration and Asylum Chamber) Rules 2014, SI 2014/2604, eg rr 12(1), 19(3)(b).

[12] SI 2003/658, reg 7(1) makes provision about the sending of notices.

[13] SI 2014/2604, r 19(2).

[14] SI 2014/2604, r 19(3)(b).

[15] SI 2003/658, r 7(4).

[16] SI 2014/2604, Sch, r 5(1).

[17] SI 2014/2604, r 19(2)(a).

[18] SI 2003/658, r 7(1)(a) and (g).

[19] SI 2014/2604, r 20(1) and 4(3).

[20] *OI (Nigeria)* [2006] UKIAT 00042.

[21] SI 2003/658, reg 7(1)(a).

20.56 Where an unrepresented person's whereabouts are unknown to the decision maker and there is no reliable address for the person, the Notices Regulations provide for notice of a decision to be deemed to have been given to the person by placing the notice on the file.[1] If the person is subsequently located, then he or she is to be given a copy of the notice.[2] However, according to the Notices Regulations, the time limit for bringing an appeal is to be calculated from the time when the notice was deemed to have been given by placing it on the file.[3] It is at the very least doubtful whether the Notices Regulations can lawfully make provision about when time for giving notice of appeal is to start running. The primary legislation under which they are made allows the Notices Regulations to require a person to be given written notice of a decision and for the notice to state various matters.[4] Provision as to time limits for initiating appeal proceedings is a matter for Tribunal Procedure Rules,[5] not Notices Regulations.

1   Immigration (Notices) Regulations 2013, SI 2003/658, reg 7(2). Paragraph 18.62, fn 2 in the 4th edition of this work refers to cases about similar rules in earlier Notices Regulations.
2   SI 2003/658, reg 7(3).
3   SI 2003/658, reg 7(3) as substituted by SI 2014/2768.
4   NIAA 2002, s 105.
5   TCEA 2007, s 22 and Sch 5, para 4.

One-stop notice

20.57 Section 120 of the NIAA 2002 enables the Secretary of State or an immigration officer to serve a notice on a person requiring the person to state any 'additional grounds' they have for entering or remaining in the UK or not being removed from the UK. The provision in force at the time of writing may be replaced by a new s 120 to be substituted by the Immigration Act 2014.[1] What follows will describe the provision currently in force and then the provision with which it is to be replaced. A notice under section 120 of the NIAA 2002 can be served by the Secretary of State or an immigration officer at any time during the course of an application or on refusal, or before, on or after a decision to remove or deport is made.[2] The notice requires the person to state his or her reasons for wishing to enter or remain in the UK, any grounds on which he or she should be permitted to enter or remain in the UK and any grounds on which he or she should not be removed from or required to leave the UK.[3] There is no time limit within which the applicant must return a statement of additional grounds, and no obligation for the Home Office to wait for a statement before making a decision, or to issue a supplementary decision relating to the matters raised in the statement. The effect of serving the s 120 notice is to give jurisdiction to the appellate authority to consider anything contained in the statement of additional grounds,[4] and to deprive the appellant of a second appeal on any grounds which should have been contained in the statement and/or considered on appeal, but were not.[5] To the extent that the new section 120 is in force, the Secretary of State or an immigration officer will be able to serve a notice on a person who has made a protection or human rights claim or an application to enter or remain in the UK, or against whom a decision to deport or remove may be taken. The notice will require the person to state their reasons for wishing to enter or remain in the UK; any grounds on which the person should be permitted to enter or remain; and any grounds on which the person should not be removed or required to leave. The 'grounds' which a person is required to state are the same as those on which an appeal may be brought, namely that removing the person or revoking the person's protection status would breach the UK's obligations under the Refugee Convention or to a person eligible for humanitarian protection, or if removing the person would be in breach of ECHR obligations. If the person's circumstances change so that they have additional reasons or grounds for entering, staying in or not being removed from the UK, the person must set them out in a further statement.

1   IA 2014, ss 73(6), 75(1), Sch 9, para 55.

2   NIAA 2002, s 120(1). The API 'Appeals: One-stop Procedure' state that in asylum cases, the
     one-stop warning would normally be given during induction (see **12.113**).
3   NIAA 2002, s 120(2). The statement in response need not repeat reasons or grounds set out
     in any application which has already been made: s 120(3).
4   By virtue of NIAA 2002, s 85(2). This applies whether the statement under s 120 was made
     before or after the appeal was commenced: s 85(3).
5   NIAA 2002, amended by Asylum and Immigration (Treatment of Claimants, etc) Act 2004,
     ss 30, 96(1), (2). This applies whether the appellant has been outside the UK since the
     requirement under s 120 arose: s 96(5). See *TN (Zimbabwe)* [2014] CSOH 85 and *ANR
     (Pakistan)* [2013] CSOH 107.

Grounds for decision

20.58 Under IA 1971 and IAA 1999, where a statement of the reasons for the
decision or action is included in a notice, it was 'conclusive of the person by
whom and of the ground on which any decision or action was taken'.[1] This
gave rise to considerable litigation. Although NIAA 2002 contains no such
provision rendering the grounds of a decision conclusive, the distinction drawn
by the old case law still holds good. That case law established that where the
grounds given reflected the Immigration Rules, the statutory finality did not
prevent the immigration officer or Secretary of State amending the notice by
varying or amplifying the reasons for the decision,[2] but if a decision was based
on a statutory ground, the notice was in reality 'conclusive'. The principle is
illustrated in the old case law on deportation. There used to be various
statutory grounds for deportation: overstaying; breach of conditions; conducive to the public good; being a family member of a proposed deportee. A
decision maker could not switch between these statutory categories,[3] and we
believe that an attempt to amend the grounds of a deportation decision from
conducive grounds to being the family member of a proposed deportee,[4] or
vice versa, without service of a fresh notice of decision, would still be held
impermissible.[5]

1   IA 1971, s 18(2) and IAA 1999, Sch 4, para 1(2).
2   Grounds for a decision must always be contained in the notice, but not always reasons. A
     ground for a decision to deport is that deportation is conducive to the public good; reasons,
     which might relate to criminal, political or other anti-social behaviour, would need to be
     stipulated. A ground for refusal of leave to enter as a visitor is that the person is not genuinely
     seeking leave to enter for the period sought; further reasons have been held unnecessary for the
     purposes of the notice requirements. In *R v Immigration Appeal Tribunal, ex p Hubbard*
     [1985] Imm AR 110 Woolf J doubted whether it was right or sensible to draw a distinction
     between grounds and reasons and held that the appellate authorities were not restricted on an
     appeal to the grounds or reasons specified in the notice of refusal. See **20.83** above. An
     adjudicator's refusal to allow the respondent entry clearance officer to amend a notice to
     include consideration of para 317 of the Immigration Rules was criticised by the Tribunal in
     Entry Clearance Officer, Manila v Brey [2002] UKIAT 06655. The Senior President of
     Tribunals Practice Directions, 10 February 2010, para 7.4 envisages that the respondent may
     amend the notice of decision, at 6.4.
3   *R v Immigration Appeal Tribunal, ex p Mehmet (Ekrem)* [1977] Imm AR 56, QBD; *Parsaiyan
     v Visa Officer, Karachi* [1986] Imm AR 155. See also *R v Secretary of State for the Home
     Department, ex p Cheblak* [1991] 2 All ER 319.
4   ie from deportation under s 3(5)(a) of IA 1971 to deportation under s 3(5)(b).
5   The distinction was particularly important where the appellate jurisdiction was confined to
     deciding whether there was power to implement the decision for the reason stated in the
     notice: in such a case the Secretary of State could not amend the notice so as to increase the
     jurisdiction of the appellate authority to take into account reasons not initially stated in the
     grounds of decision; *Egbale v Secretary of State for the Home Department* [1997] INLR 88,
     IAT. See also *Secretary of State for the Home Department v Ziar (Salah)* [1997] Imm AR 456,

[1997] INLR 221, IAT, a case on the statutory certification of an appeal. Since the effect of certification was to preclude a further appeal (from the adjudicator to the Immigration Appeal Tribunal), certification had to be based on the appropriate statutory ground and could not be amended in the course of the appeal.

Notice of appeal

20.59 An appeal is started by providing a notice of appeal to the Tribunal.[1] The notice of appeal must:

(i) set out the grounds of appeal;

(ii) be signed and dated by the appellant or the appellant's representative. If it is signed by the appellant's representative, the representative must certify in the notice that it was completed in accordance with the appellant's instructions;

(iii) state whether the appellant requires an interpreter, giving the language and dialect;

(iv) state whether the appellant intends to attend at any hearing; and

(v) state whether the appellant will be represented at any hearing.[2]

The notice must be accompanied by a copy of the notice of decision which is the subject of the appeal or, if that is not practicable, the reasons why it is not.[3] It must also be accompanied by any statement of reasons for the decision; any documents in support of the appellant's case which have not been supplied to the respondent; an application for the Lord Chancellor to issue a certificate of fee satisfaction; and any further information or documents required by an applicable Practice Direction.[4] The notice of appeal must be in English.[5] Cases under earlier Procedure Rules suggest that many of the requirements in the notice are not mandatory, and failure to include some of the information required would not invalidate an appeal.[6] The guidance provided by the Court of Appeal case of *Jeyeanthan*[7] has resonance here, although the language of the Procedure Rules is very strict. Even if non-compliance with procedural rules relating to the notice of appeal does not invalidate the notice, it would enable the tribunal to dispose of the appeal without a hearing if satisfied that it was appropriate in all the circumstances.[8]

1   Tribunal Procedure (First-tier Tribunal)(Immigration and Asylum Chamber) Rules 2014, SI 2014/2604, r 19(1).

2   SI 2014/2604, r 19(4).

3   SI 2014/2604, r 19(5)(a).

4   SI 2014/2604, r 19(5)(b)-(e).

5   SI 2014/2604, r 12(5)(a).

6   *Jarvis* [1994] Imm AR 102; *R v Immigration Appeal Tribunal, ex p Begum (Hamida)* [1988] Imm AR 199, QBD; *Re Sogunle* [1994] Imm AR 554. The intention is not to sanction appellants who, through no fault of their own, have failed to complete the form fully or correctly, but to encourage them to do so in order for their appeal to be handled promptly: DCA document following consultation on procedure rules, 8 February 2005; *HH (Serbia)* [2006] UKAIT 00063.

7   *R v Immigration Appeal Tribunal, ex p Jeyeanthan; Ravichandran v Secretary of State for the Home Department* [2000] 1 WLR 354, [2000] Imm AR 10, [2000] INLR 241. See 20.54 above.

8   SI 2014/2604, r 25(1)(e).

Fees for bringing an appeal

20.60 A person wishing to bring an appeal must pay a fee unless an exemption applies.[1] Exemptions apply in relation to the following:

(1) appeals against specific kinds of decision. In other words, decisions to take away certain kinds of status (deprivation of the right of abode or citizenship, or revocation of indefinite leave to remain) and removal decisions (decisions in relation to deportation; to remove an illegal entrant or an illegal entrant's family member or a crew member; to remove under IAA 1999, section 10 or Immigration, Asylum and Nationality Act 2006, section 47; or to remove a person in the UK with EU rights of residence).[2]

(2) appeals brought by persons to whom the 2005 Fast Track Procedure Rules apply.[3] Those rules have been revoked and replaced by the Fast Track Rules contained in the Schedule to the First-tier Tribunal Procedure Rules.[4] The provisions for exceptions to the requirement to pay a fee have not been amended to reflect the introduction of new Fast Track Procedure Rules. Presumably this is a result of oversight rather than an intention that those in the detained fast-track should be required to pay a fee to bring an appeal. The fact of that oversight may constitute 'exceptional circumstances' of the kind that enable the Lord Chancellor to reduce or remit the fee.[5]

(3) an appeal brought by a person in receipt of asylum support.[6]

(4) an appeal brought by a person in receipt of legal aid.[7]

(5) an appeal brought by a person for whose benefit services are provided under section 17 of the Children Act 1989.[8]

(6) circumstances where there is an international agreement whereby no fee is payable in respect of proceedings.[9]

In addition, the Lord Chancellor may defer payment of a fee where the appeal is brought on the grounds that the decision would breach the UK's obligations under the Refugee Convention or the Qualification Directive.[10] The fee is £80 for an appeal to be determined without a hearing, or £140 if it is to be determined with a hearing.[11] The notice of appeal must be accompanied by an application for the Lord Chancellor to issue a certificate of fee satisfaction.[12] The Lord Chancellor must issue such a certificate if:

(i) the requisite fee has been paid;

(ii) an undertaking has been given by or on behalf of an appellant to pay promptly by BACS or international money transfer;

(iii) no fee is payable;

(iv) payment is to be deferred; or

(v) the appellant has applied to the Lord Chancellor for the fee to be reduced or remitted.[13]

The FT may not accept a notice of appeal if the Lord Chancellor has refused to issue a certificate.[14] If a certificate is revoked, the appeal is automatically struck out.[15] An appeal that has been struck out may be reinstated on application by the appellant (made in writing within 14 days of the tribunal sending notification that the appeal has been struck out or within 28 days if the appellant is outside the UK[16]) if the Lord Chancellor has issued a new certificate.[17] If an appeal is allowed, the FT may order the respondent to pay an amount up to the value of any fee paid or payable by the appellant.[18]

1 First-tier Tribunal (Immigration and Asylum Chamber) Fees Order 2011, SI 2011/2841, made
under TCEA 2007, s 42.
2 SI 2011/2841, art 5(1)(a).
3 SI 2011/2841, art 5(1)(b).
4 Tribunal Procedure (First-tier Tribunal)(Immigration and Asylum Chamber) Rules 2014, SI
2014/2604, r 45 of which revokes the Asylum and Immigration Tribunal (Fast Track
Procedure) Rules 2005, SI 2005/560 in their entirety.
5 Under SI 2011/2841, art 7.
6 SI 2011/2841, art 5(3).
7 SI 2011/2841, art 5(2).
8 SI 2011/2841, art 5(4).
9 SI 2011/2841, art 5(5).
10 SI 2011/2841, art 6.
11 SI 2011/2841, art 3(3).
12 SI 2014/2604, r 19(5)(d).
13 SI 2011/2841, art 8(1).
14 SI 2014/2604, r 22(2)(b).
15 SI 2014/2604, r 7(1).
16 SI 2014/2604, r 7(3).
17 SI 2014/2604, r 7(2).
18 SI 2014/2604, r 9(1). The power to make a 'fee award' is the subject of the Joint Presidential
Guidance: 'Fee Awards in Immigration Appeals', which says the starting point is that a
successful appellant should be able to recover the whole fee, but that that might be displaced
by the conduct of the appellant or the fact that the decision on the appeal was the result of
evidence that could or should have been produced earlier.

Grounds of appeal

20.61 The notice of appeal is required to set out the grounds of appeal,[1] but
unlike the previous procedure rules, there is no requirement to provide reasons
in support of the grounds.[2]

1 Tribunal Procedure (First-tier Tribunal)(Immigration and Asylum Chamber) Rules 2014, SI
2014/2604, r 19(4)(a) or Schedule, r 3(2)(a) in the case of fast track appeals.
2 Asylum and Immigration Tribunal (Procedure) Rules 2005, SI 2005/230, r 8(1)(d).

Starting an appeal

20.62 An appeal is started by providing a notice of appeal to the tribunal.[1] A
person in the detained fast-track may instead give the notice of appeal to the
person who has custody of him or her,[2] but that option is no longer available
generally to those detained under the Immigration Acts.[3] Nor is it open to a
person outside the UK wishing to appeal against refusal of entry clearance to
give the notice of appeal to an entry clearance officer instead of directly to the
tribunal.[4] The notice of appeal has to be provided to the tribunal by post, fax
or email or by other method of delivery to an address, fax number or email
address identified for the purpose by the tribunal.[5]

1 Tribunal Procedure (First-tier Tribunal) (Immigration and Asylum Chamber) Rules 2014, SI
2014/2604, r 19(1).
2 SI 2014/2604, Sch, r 4(1).
3 As it had been under Asylum and Immigration Tribunal (Procedure) Rules 2005, SI 2005/230,
r 6(3).
4 SI 2005/230, r 6(6).

[5] SI 2014/2604, r 12(1). If the notice of appeal is sent to the wrong address and cannot be traced, the Tribunal is entitled to conclude that no valid appeal has been lodged: *Adeniyi v Secretary of State for the Home Department* [1995] Imm AR 123, CA; *Shaffi v Secretary of State for the Home Department* [1990] Imm AR 468.

Time limits for appealing

20.63 The time limit for appealing varies according to whether the appellant is in the UK or abroad when served with notice of the decision and, if the appellant is in the UK, whether he or she is entitled to stay in the UK whilst appealing and whether he or she is in the detained fast track procedure. If notice of the decision is not served in accordance with the Immigration (Notices) Regulations 2003, time does not begin to run against the appellant.[1] Where the appellant is in the UK and the appeal may be brought in-country, then the notice of appeal must be received by the tribunal no later than 14 days after the person is sent the notice of decision against which he or she is appealing.[2] The same time limit applies if the person is detained under the Immigration Acts[3] unless he or she is in the detained fast-track when provided with the decision, in which case the notice of appeal must be provided to the tribunal or the person with custody of the appellant no more than two working days later.[4] If the appellant is in the UK when provided with notice of the decision, but may not appeal whilst in the UK owing to a provision of the NIAA 2002, then the notice of appeal has to be received by the tribunal not later than 28 days after the person's departure from the UK.[5] If the person was outside the UK when he or she received the notice of decision[6], the notice of appeal has to be provided to the tribunal no more than 28 days later.[7] The notice of appeal must be provided to the tribunal by midnight on the last day of the period allowed by the rules for giving notice of appeal.[8] However, if the last day of this period is not a working day, then notice of appeal is given in time if given on the next working day.[9] A working day is any day except a Saturday or Sunday, Christmas Day, Good Friday or a bank holiday[10] and the period 27-31 December inclusive.[11]

[1] See for example, *FO (Nigeria)* [2007] UKAIT 00093.
[2] Tribunal Procedure (First-tier Tribunal)(Immigration and Asylum Chamber) Rules 2014, SI 2014/2604, r 19(2).
[3] By contrast to the Asylum and Immigration Tribunal (Procedure) Rules 2005, SI 2005/230, r 7(1)(a), which provided a shorter time for a detainee.
[4] ie detained in Colnbrook House, Harmondsworth or Yarl's Wood Immigration Removal Centre at the time of being provided with the notice of decision: SI 2014/2604, Schedule, rr 2 and 5(1).
[5] SI 2014/2604, r 19(3)(a).
[6] Deemed to be on the 28th day after posting if sent to a place outside the UK: Immigration (Notices) Regulations 2003, SI 2003/658, reg 7(4)(b).
[7] SI 2014/2604, r 19(3)(b).
[8] SI 2014/2604, r 11(1).
[9] SI 2014/2604, r 11(2).
[10] Within the meaning of the Banking and Financial Dealings Act 1971, s 1.
[11] SI 2014/2604, r 1(4).

20.64 The current procedure rules no longer make adequate provision for NIAA 2002, section 83 appeals, presumably because it was assumed when drafting them, wrongly as it turned out, that there would no longer be section 83 appeals from 20 October 2014 onwards.[1] The problem is that section 83 gives a right of appeal against a refusal of asylum to a person who has been granted leave to enter or remain for more than one year. The current procedure rules require notice of appeal to be provided no more than 14 days after the person is sent the notice of decision against which the appeal is brought.[2] That would be unproblematic if the refusal of asylum and the grant of leave for more than a year are simultaneous. However, if the grant of leave for more than one year does not happen until some time after the refusal of asylum, the right of appeal may not accrue until after the time for appealing has passed. The 2005 procedure rules accommodated for that possibility by modifying the general rule about time for appealing running from the date of service of the appealable decision, so that time would instead run from the date on which the appellant was granted leave that would result in the person having leave for more than one year.[3] No doubt the tribunal will treat the failure by the current rules to make similar provision as sufficient reason to justify extending time for appealing against refusal of asylum.

[1] Because IA 2014, s 15(3) repeals NIAA 2002, ss 83 and 83A. However, NIAA 2002, ss 83 and 83A are saved by arts 9 and 11(3)(b) of SI 2014/2771, the commencement order that brought IA 2014, s 15 into effect on 20 October 2014, the same day as SI 2014/2604 came into effect.

[2] SI 2014/2604, r 19(1).

[3] Asylum and Immigration Tribunal (Procedure) Rules 2005, SI 2005/230, r 7(3).

20.65 The existence of a time limit for appealing against the actions or decisions of the immigration authorities can mislead would-be appellants into thinking that if they merely adhere to the time limit they will be able to enjoy their full right of appeal. There are, however, situations where this may not be the case. For example, persons refused entry generally have a right of appeal without having to leave the UK if they had an entry clearance on arrival.[1] But the existence of a right of appeal does not in itself operate as a stay on removal. It is only once an appeal is 'pending', ie once notice of appeal has been given, that a person otherwise removable may not be removed from the UK.[2] Thus if such appellants delay giving notice of appeal they may in fact find themselves being removed from the UK. They still have a right of appeal, but can only exercise it from abroad, whereas if they had given notice of appeal before their departure they would have been allowed to remain until their appeal was heard.

[1] NIAA 2002, s 82(2)(a) and s 92(3) (as amended by s 28, Asylum and Immigration (Treatment of Claimants, etc) Act 2004); see **19.26** above.

[2] NIAA 2002, ss 78(1), 104(1).

Late notice of appeal

20.66 Where a notice of appeal is given outside the applicable time limit, the notice of appeal must include an application for an extension of time for appealing and must state the reasons for failing to give the notice in time.[1] The rules contain provision for disputes as to whether the notice was served in time or not. If the notice appears to the Tribunal to have been given late, but does not include an application for an extension of time, then, unless it decides on its own initiative to extend time, the Tribunal must notify the person giving notice of appeal that it proposes to treat the appeal as out of time.[2] If the intending appellant contends that the notice of appeal was in fact given in time or that time for providing the notice of appeal should be extended, the person may give written notice and supporting evidence in writing to that effect to the tribunal.[3] There are no time limits within which that notice must be given as there were under the previous Procedure Rules.[4] The tribunal has to decide whether notice of appeal was or was not given in time and whether to extend time as a preliminary issue, giving written notice of its decision and reasons to the parties.[5] The previous Procedure Rules dictated that these issues had to be decided without a hearing; under the current rules, the tribunal has a discretion to have a hearing to decide them.[6]

If the Tribunal decides to treat a notice of appeal as being out of time but evidence clearly shows that it was given in time, the Tribunal can ignore the previous decision and treat the appeal as pending.[7] If notice of appeal has or appears to have been given out of time and the respondent notifies the tribunal that directions have been given for the person's removal within five days of the notice of appeal being received, the tribunal must 'if reasonably practicable' make a decision as to timeliness or extending time before the date and time proposed for removal. The tribunal may notify the person orally, including by telephone, that there is a preliminary issue as to timeliness, and may receive evidence orally, including by telephone, to determine the issue.[8] The Fast Track Rules provide for the determination of whether a notice of appeal was given late and whether time for appealing should be extended as a preliminary issue at the hearing fixed for determination of the appeal.[9]

[1] Tribunal Procedure (First-tier Tribunal)(Immigration and Asylum Chamber) Rules 2014, SI 2014/2604, r 20(1).
[2] SI 2014/2604, r 20(2). This rule does not refer to the 'appellant', but the 'persons'; the 'person' does not become an 'appellant', with all the protections that word entails, until or unless the appeal has been accepted as timely or an extension of time has been given. This reasoning accords with that of the Tribunal in *B (Zimbabwe)* [2004] UKIAT 00076.
[3] SI 2014/2604, r 20(3).
[4] Asylum and Immigration Tribunal (Procedure) Rules 2005, SI 2005/230, r 10(4).
[5] SI 2014/2604, r 20(5).
[6] SI 2014/2604, r 20(4). Compare SI 2005/230, r 10(6).
[7] *EA (Ghana)* [2006] UKAIT 00036. Where an in-time application is treated, through no fault of the tribunal, as being out of time, the tribunal's decision would be based on mistake of fact and justice would demand its quashing: *R (on the application of Tataw) v Immigration Appeal Tribunal* [2003] EWCA Civ 925, [2003] INLR 585.
[8] SI 2014/2604, r 21.
[9] SI 2014/2604, Schedule, r 5(3).

20.67 In fast track cases, the tribunal may not extend the time for giving notice of appeal unless it considers that it is in the interests of justice to do so.[1] In non-fast track cases, time may be extended by exercising the tribunal's general case management power to extend time for complying with a rule.[2] The overriding objective of dealing with cases fairly and justly provides the criteria for the exercise of that power.[3] The criteria are similar in fast track cases to those that applied generally under the previous rules,[4] whilst the criteria for non-fast track cases are significantly broader under the current rule. The guidance given by the tribunal under the previous rules will thus have some resonance, particularly in fast track cases, but will not be determinative. That guidance[5] was that the starting point would be the explanation for the lateness of the notice of appeal. The explanation would need to be supported by such evidence as is available. Admitted delay by the appellant's representative might be a satisfactory explanation. An extension of time could be granted no matter how long the delay, provided it was satisfactorily explained. Time would only be extended in the absence of a satisfactory explanation if there were exceptional reasons for doing so. Other factors to be considered include the merits of the grounds of appeal, and the consequences for the appellant of the decision. Mistakes, breaches of rules of procedure or very long delays on the part of the respondent might make it unjust or disproportionate not to extend time for appealing. Older cases about extending time for appealing are cited in 20.54 of the 8th edition of this work.

¹   Tribunal Procedures (First-tier Tribunal)(Immigration and Asylum Chamber) Rules 2014, SI 2014/2604, Schedule, r 5(2).
²   SI 2014/2604, rr 4(3)(a), 20(1).
³   SI 2014/2604, r 2(3)(a).
⁴   Asylum and Immigration Tribunal (Procedure) Rules 2005, SI 2005/230, r 10(5).
⁵   *BO (Nigeria)* [2006] UKAIT 00035.

20.68 The Procedure Rules indicate that both decisions on timeliness of a notice of appeal, and whether to extend time, are preliminary decisions.¹ As such they are 'excluded decisions' against which there is no right of appeal from the FT to the UT.² A decision on the validity of a purported appeal is treated the same as an exercise of discretion not to extend time, although the two decisions could not be more different, as the Tribunal in *B (Zimbabwe)* explained.³ The only remedy for an unlawful decision that an appeal was lodged out of time is judicial review. However, the Tribunal has taken the view that if it is persuaded that such a decision was wrongly made because notice of appeal was in fact given in time, it would be 'entitled, indeed required, when made aware of its error to deal with the appeal in a proper way'.⁴

¹   Tribunal Procedures (First-tier Tribunal)(Immigration and Asylum Chamber) Rules 2014, SI 2014/2604, r 20(4).
²   TCEA 2007, s 11(1), (5)(f) and (6)(b) and Appeals (Excluded Decisions) Order 2009, SI 2009/275, art 3(m) as inserted by the Tribunals, Courts and Enforcement Act 2007 (Miscellaneous Provisions) Order 2010, SI 2010/41.
³   A decision on the preliminary issue of time was held to be a determination under the 1971 Act (making it appealable) in *Jaayeola* (14819) (2 April 1997). The definition of 'determination' under the 2000 Procedure Rules as a decision to allow or dismiss an appeal, excluded a decision on time, with the Tribunal holding in *B (Zimbabwe)* [2004] UKIAT 00076 that once it had been established that a notice of appeal was out of time and an extension of time was refused, there was no valid appeal for the purpose of any onward appeal. However, in *MM (Burundi)* [2004] UKIAT 00182 the Immigration Appeal Tribunal held that however 'determination' was defined, it had jurisdiction to hear an appeal on a point of law relating to an adjudicator's decision that an appeal was invalid, which included the issue of timeliness (although not the exercise of discretion). The omission of any definition of 'determination' in the relevant part of the NIAA 2002 and the 2003 Rules enabled the Tribunal to reinstate a decision on timeliness as a 'determination', holding that a decision on time determined the appeal by bringing it to an end.
⁴   *SB (Pakistan)* [2008] UKAIT 00053 (Tribunal had wrongly held that the appellant was not a 'family visitor' and therefore not entitled to appeal against refusal of entry clearance), following *EA (Ghana)* [2006] UKAIT 00036 where the Tribunal set aside its earlier erroneous decision that notice of appeal had been given late.

20.69 The rules do not specify a maximum period by which time for appealing may be extended; neither is a maximum imposed by statute.¹ However, once the time limit imposed by the Procedure Rules is past, any statutory leave which a person had as a result of an in-time application for an extension of leave ends, leaving the person vulnerable to removal.² Similarly, an appeal is no longer 'pending' for the purposes of asylum support etc³

However, if an extension of time for appealing is granted, the appeal reverts to 'pending' status, any statutory leave the person held resumes,[4] and the person cannot be removed.[5]

[1] In variation appeals, there used to be a maximum delay of 14 days, beyond which time for lodging an appeal could not be extended, because of the complexities to which s 14 of IA 1971 gave rise, for which see 5th edition at 18.105.

[2] IA 1971, s 3C(2)(b) as substituted by NIAA 2002, s 118 (s 3C inserted by IAA 1999, s 3), which extends leave during the period while (*inter alia*) an appeal under s 82 could be brought (ignoring any possibility of an appeal out of time with permission).

[3] NIAA 2002, s 104. See *R (on the application of Erdogan) v Secretary of State for the Home Department* [2004] EWCA Civ 1087, [2004] All ER (D) 421 (Jul), where the Court of Appeal reversed the Administrative Court's decision that an asylum claimant had an appeal 'pending' for the purposes of s 104 (and so did not lose asylum support) when what he had pending was an application for permission to appeal out of time. However, the court (and the Secretary of State) agreed that once permission has been given to appeal out of time, the appeal has been (re)-instituted and is again pending.

[4] IA 1971, s 3C(2)(c) as inserted and substituted.

[5] NIAA 2002, s 78.

Invalid notice of appeal

20.70 Rule 22 of the Procedure Rules specifies two situations in which the Tribunal must not accept a notice of appeal.[1] The first is where there is no appealable decision[2] ie a decision from which there is right of appeal to the tribunal.[3] The second is where the Lord Chancellor has refused to issue a certificate of fee satisfaction.[4] In either of those situations, the Tribunal must notify the would-be appellant and the respondent that it does not accept the notice of appeal and take no further action. The Senior President's Practice Statements highlight that the Procedure Rules make no provision for the issue of validity to be determined by means of a hearing or by reference to any representations of the parties.[5] It would be extraordinary if the Practice Statements were intended to suggest that the FT was to close its eyes to any representations accompanying the notice of appeal as to its validity. A decision taken under r 9, without a hearing, is a 'procedural or preliminary decision' ie an excluded decision and thus not appealable to the UT.[6] If a notice of hearing is given or if the appeal actually proceeds to a hearing it is not thereby deemed to be a valid appeal.[7] However, if there is a hearing and only then does the Tribunal decide that the notice of appeal was invalid because there was no appealable decision, the Tribunal's decision to that effect should not be characterised as an 'excluded decision'. The Practice Statements say that such a decision should take the form of a 'determination'[8] which by definition is not a procedural, ancillary or preliminary decision.[9] Adopting this practice is consistent with the Court of Appeal's decision in *JH (Zimbabwe)*[10] which held that it was wrong for the Tribunal to have purported to dispose of an appeal that had been heard by using the r 9 procedure rather than in the form of a reviewable or appealable determination.

[1] Tribunal Procedures (First-tier Tribunal)(Immigration and Asylum Chamber) Rules 2014, SI 2014/2604, r 22(2).

[2] SI 2014/2604, r 22(2)(a).

[3] SI 2014/2604, r 1(4).

[4] Tribunal Procedures (First-tier Tribunal)(Immigration and Asylum Chamber) Rules 2014, SI 2014/2604, r 22(2)(b).

5 Practice Statements: Immigration and Asylum Chambers of the FT Tribunal and the Upper Tribunal, 10 February 2010, para 3.2.
6 Practice Statements, para 3.3 and TCEA 2007, ss 9(1) and 11(1).
7 Practice Statements, para 3.4.
8 Practice Statements, para 3.4.
9 Asylum and Immigration Tribunal (Procedure) Rules 2005, SI 2005/230, r 2.
10 *JH (Zimbabwe) v Secretary of State for the Home Department* [2009] EWCA Civ 78, [2009] All ER (D) 193 (Feb); in that case the rule 9 decision was made only after the appeal had been determined substantively and then returned to the Tribunal from the Court of Appeal. In *AS (India) v Secretary of State for the Home Department* [2009] EWCA Civ 1495 the court rejected the contention that *JH (Zimbabwe)* was confined to its unusual facts and held it was authority for the proposition that there was no good reason of principle or policy why the Tribunal's decision on an appeal that it lacked jurisdiction should be excluded from review or further appeal. See also *Abiyat (Iran)* [2011] UKUT 314 (IAC).

Imminent removal cases

20.71 As we have seen, the determination of the timeliness of an appeal or whether to extend time is a preliminary issue decided without reference to the immigration authorities. Rule 21 of the procedure rules applies where removal directions have been issued against an appellant and it is proposed to remove him or her within five calendar days of the date on which the notice of appeal was given. On notification of this by the respondent, the Tribunal must, if reasonably practicable, make a preliminary decision as to timeliness under rule 20 before the proposed date and time of removal,[1] and may notify the appellant orally, including by telephone, that it believes the appeal is out of time;[2] shorten the time for the appellant to give evidence in support of a contention that the appeal notice was filed in time;[3] and direct that such evidence be given orally, including by telephone, and hold a hearing or telephone hearing to receive the evidence.[4] In fast track cases, the tribunal is also required to make a decision about timeliness as soon as reasonably practicable if notified that directions have been set for the appellant's removal within five days of the notice of appeal being received.[5] Whether the intending appellant is protected from removal if the decision on the timeliness or validity of the appeal is not made before the projected removal is due to take place is not spelt out by the rules. Clearly, while an appeal is 'pending' for the purposes of section 78 of the NIAA 2002, removal would be unlawful.[6] Where there is a dispute about timeliness, we suggest that until it is resolved, the appeal must be treated as pending; the intending appellant must be protected from removal pending the Tribunal's decision on the issue, to give effect to elementary considerations of fairness (particularly where fundamental rights are engaged).[7] Somewhat different considerations apply where the appeal is admittedly out of time and the Tribunal is being asked to exercise discretion to extend time, since in such a situation, the appeal is no longer 'pending',[8] although given the importance of the appeal, it would arguably be unfair to remove, particularly where there was a good reason for the failure to file the appeal in time.[9]

1 Tribunal Procedures (First-tier Tribunal) (Immigration and Asylum Chamber) Rules 2014, SI 2014/2604, r 21(1), (2). Applications in imminent removal cases will normally be dealt with by a FT judge approved by the Senior President to make such decisions: Senior President's Practice Directions, 10 February 2010.
2 SI 2014/2604, r 21(3)(a).
3 SI 2014/2604, r 21(3)(b).
4 SI 2014/2604, r 21(3)(c).

⁵ SI 2014/2604, Schedule, r 5(4).
⁶ ie the prohibition on removal of appellants pending appeal: see **19.35** above. Previously, the submission of a notice of appeal was enough to halt removal: *Secretary of State for the Home Department v Omishore* [1990] Imm AR 582; *Secretary of State for the Home Department v Ibrahim* [1994] Imm AR 1.
⁷ See the observations of Sedley LJ on the balance between administrative convenience and fairness in *R (on the application of the Refugee Legal Centre) v Secretary of State for the Home Department* [2004] EWCA Civ 1481, [2004] All ER (D) 580 (Mar) at [6], and see *R v Secretary of State for the Home Department, ex p Fayed* [1998] 1 WLR 763 at 777. Premature removal which wrongly prevented the appellant from putting human rights arguments could well breach procedural requirements inherent in the relevant rights, cf *Ciliz v Netherlands* [2000] 2 FLR 469; *Conka v Belgium (51564/99)* (2002) 34 EHRR 1298, 11 BHRC 555, ECtHR.
⁸ *R (on the application of Erdogan) v Secretary of State for the Home Department* [2004] EWCA Civ 1087, [2004] All ER (D) 421 (Jul).
⁹ Cf the situation of the appellant MM in the case of that name, *MM (Burundi)* [2004] UKIAT 00182 (starred), where the appellant's house had burned down at the crucial time, or even, less dramatically, that of the appellant in *Erdogan* (above), whose appeal was lodged out of time because of a postal strike. The court in *Erdogan* (para 20) remarked that the power of the Secretary of State to remove a person who was seeking an extension of time to appeal to the Tribunal would be subject to the supervisory role of the Administrative Court in judicial review to give protection where necessary.

Respondent's duty to file appeal papers

20.72 Once the notice of appeal has been filed with the FT, it must serve a copy on the respondent, together with any accompanying documents or information[1] and must do so immediately, if the appeal is in the fast track.[2] The respondent must then file the notice of the decision to which the notice of appeal relates, any other document giving reasons for that decision, any statement of evidence form or application completed by the appellant any record of interview with the appellant relating to the decision under appeal, any unpublished document referred to in the decision notice or reasons for refusal letter or relied on by the respondent, and notice of any other appealable decision made in relation to the appellant.[3] If in the light of the grounds of appeal and accompanying documents the respondent intends to change or add to the grounds or reasons for their decision, they have to provide the appellant and the tribunal a statement of whether they oppose the appellant's case and the grounds for doing so.[4] In appeals against a refusal of entry clearance or of an EEA family permit, the respondent is required to file the same documents as well as a statement of whether the respondent opposes the appellant's case and, if so, the grounds upon which it is opposed.[5] The respondent is required to file and serve their documents in response to the notice of appeal within 28 days of being sent the notice[6] or within two working days in a fast track case.[7] If the respondent fails to serve any of the unpublished documents referred to in the notice or reasons for refusal, the tribunal is entitled to conclude that neither the documents nor the passages referring to them continue to form part of the respondent's case.[8] The requirement on the respondent to file and serve its documents within 28 days of being provided with a notice of appeal displaces the Tribunal's former policy of allowing entry clearance officers 19 weeks in which to file documents with the Tribunal in appeals against refusal of settlement, a policy which was held to be rational and lawful.[9] This was in part because the Tribunal operates a system to expedite appeals in cases where there are compelling compassionate circumstances; requests for expedition under the scheme are made to the Duty Immigration Judge at the AIT's Operational Support Centre in Loughborough.[10] The tribunal was extremely scathing about the 'usual practice'[11] of entry clearance officers of not complying with the obligation to produce documents for the appeal and instead to treat judicial directions and procedure rules 'with utter disdain'.[12]

1   Tribunal Procedures (First-tier Tribunal)(Immigration and Asylum Chamber) Rules 2014, SI 2014/2604, r 19(6).
2   SI 2014/2604, Schedule, r 6.
3   SI 2014/2604, r 24 and in fast track cases, Schedule, r 7.
4   SI 2014/2604, r 24(2).
5   SI 2014/2604, r 23.
6   SI 2014/2604, rr 23(2) and 24(3).
7   SI 2014/2604, Schedule, r 7.
8   *MH (Pakistan)* [2010] UKUT 00168 (IAC); *Cvetkovs (Latvia)* [2011] UKUT 00212 (IAC).
9   *R (on the application of Uddin) v Asylum and Immigration Tribunal; R (on the application of Ali) v Asylum and Immigration Tribunal* [2006] EWHC 2127 (Admin), [2006] All ER (D) 36 (Aug).
10 See *R (Uddin)*, ibid.
11 *AO (Nigeria)* [2008] UKAIT 00073.
12 *AW (Pakistan)* [2008] UKAIT 00072.

20.73 After a notice of appeal has been filed and forwarded to the respondent, and the appeal documents have been sent in, a number of further steps may be taken before the appeal comes on for a hearing or is determined. The FT may hold a case management review hearing, and may issue directions relating to the conduct of the appeal, to determine the form of the appeal, whether there is to be a hearing, whether it is to be before a single immigration judge or a panel, the time it will take, the evidence, documentary and oral, that will be given and the issues to be addressed.[1] There is provision to allow the grounds of appeal to be varied during the course of the appeal.[2] The immigration authorities may reverse, withdraw or vary their decision – which will lead to the appeal being treated as abandoned[3] (other than in the case of an appeal against refusal of asylum under section 83 of NIAA 2002).[4] The FT may decide to determine an appeal without a hearing.[5] Some of these steps will now be examined more closely.

1   Tribunal Procedures (First-tier Tribunal)(Immigration and Asylum Chamber) Rules 2014, SI 2014/2604, rr 4, 5.
2   SI 2014/2604, r 19(7), Schedule, r 3(4) in fast track cases.
3   NIAA 2002, s 104(4).
4   The appeal against refusal of asylum is only available once leave exceeding a year in total has been granted; thus the grant of further leave will not affect a pending s 83 appeal.
5   SI 2014/2604, r 25, Schedule, r 9 in fast track cases.

Parties to an appeal

20.74 The parties to an appeal will be the appellant (ie the person who has given a notice of appeal to the FT against an appealable decision in accordance with the Procedure Rules),[1] and the respondent (ie the decision maker specified in the notice of decision against which a notice of appeal has been provided).[2] The United Nations High Commissioner for Refugees (UNHCR) may become a party in any appeal where the appellant has made an asylum claim if notice is given to the tribunal of the UNHCR's wish to participate in any proceedings.[3]

1   Tribunal Procedures (First-tier Tribunal)(Immigration and Asylum Chamber) Rules 2014, SI 2014/2604, r 1(4). Note that a person who submits a notice of appeal is not an appellant; that condition is only met if (i) the notice is against an appealable decision and (ii) the notice is served 'in accordance with these Rules'. For timeliness and compliance with other requirements relating to the notice of appeal see **20.66** and **20.70** above.

2   Tribunal Procedures (First-tier Tribunal)(Immigration and Asylum Chamber) Rules 2014, SI 2014/2604, r 1(4).

3   SI 2014/2604, r 8(3).

Certification of pending appeal

20.75 The Secretary of State or an immigration officer may, while an appeal to the Tribunal is pending, issue a certificate under section 97 or 98 (national security, diplomatic or public interest issues justifying exclusion or removal from the UK). In each case, the certificate has the effect of putting an end to the proceedings before the Tribunal.[1] The Procedure Rules require the Secretary of State to notify the Tribunal of any such certification, whereupon the Tribunal must notify the parties, and take no further action on the appeal.[2] There is no longer any power for the Secretary of State or an immigration officer to certify a pending appeal under s 96 (earlier right of appeal); although an appeal can be prevented by a certificate under the section, it cannot be brought to an end once lodged.[3] Similarly, although certification of an asylum or human rights claim as 'clearly unfounded' may prevent an appeal from being brought (which the Court of Appeal has held in this context to mean commenced) whilst the appellant is in the UK,[4] such a certification cannot prevent an appeal that has already been commenced from being continued in the UK.[5]

1   See the NIAA 2002, s 99, amended by the Asylum and Immigration (Treatment of Claimants, etc) Act 2004.

2   Tribunal Procedures (First-tier Tribunal) (Immigration and Asylum Chamber) Rules 2014, SI 2014/2604, r 18.

3   NIAA 2002, s 96(7), as amended.

4   NIAA 2002, s 94(2).

5   *R (on the application of AM (Somalia)) v Secretary of State for the Home Department* [2009] EWCA Civ 114, [2009] All ER (D) 248 (Feb).

Withdrawal of appeals

20.76 All appeals may be withdrawn or abandoned. What are the distinctions between withdrawal and abandonment, and what are the consequences? Withdrawal of an appeal implies a positive act (giving notice of withdrawal of the appeal, specifying reasons for the withdrawal),[1] while abandonment suggests a passive failure to prosecute the appeal, or an action incompatible with pursuing it whereby it is deemed abandoned by statute. The tribunal is required to treat an appeal as withdrawn, unless there are good reasons not to, if the respondent notifies the tribunal that it has withdrawn the decision appealed against, specifying its reasons for withdrawing the decision.[2] Withdrawal of the decision being appealed against would be amenable to judicial review if, for example, it could be shown that it was done with a view to gaining some procedural advantage as opposed to conducting a genuine reconsideration which might lead to a change of mind.[3] Such grounds for judicial review would no doubt constitute good reasons to treat the appeal as continuing. In the case of a deemed withdrawal,[4] the positive act is that of the respondent rather than the appellant. The distinction between withdrawal and abandonment vanishes with the concept of 'deemed abandonment' when the appellant is granted leave to enter or remain in the UK.[5] The 2014 Procedure Rules no longer deal with the situation arising on the death of an appellant. The 2005 Rules gave the tribunal a discretion to treat the appeal as withdrawn or to allow the appellant's representative to continue the appeal, but that has not been reproduced in the 2014 Rules.[6] If an appeal is withdrawn or treated as withdrawn, the Tribunal must serve on the parties notification that a withdrawal has taken effect and the appeal is no longer regarded by the tribunal as pending.[7] Whether the giving of such a notice is a 'procedural, ancillary or preliminary decision in relation to an appeal'[8] and as such an 'excluded decision' against which there is no right of appeal from the FT to the UT[9] remains to be determined. It is clear that whether an appeal has been withdrawn is a matter for the Tribunal and the courts, not for the Secretary of State.[10] Where an appeal is validly withdrawn prior to the hearing, and the withdrawal accepted by the Tribunal, the appeal does not go into a state of suspended animation, but ceases to exist,[11] and any determination of the appeal (on the merits) is a nullity.[12] The consequences of withdrawal of the immigration decision appealed against before the Upper Tribunal are different and are discussed below.

[1] Tribunal Procedures (First-tier Tribunal)(Immigration and Asylum Chamber) Rules 2014, SI 2014/2604, r 17(1).
[2] SI 2014/2604, r 17(2).
[3] *R (on the application of Glushkov) v Secretary of State for the Home Department* [2008] EWHC 2290 (Admin) and *R (on the application of Chichvarkin) v Secretary of State for the Home Department* [2010] EWHC 1858 (Admin) and [2011] EWCA Civ 91.
[4] SI 2014/2604, r17(2),
[5] NIAA 2002, s 104(4)(a).
[6] Asylum and Immigration Tribunal (Procedure) Rules 2005, SI 2005/230, r 17(2A).
[7] SI 2014/2604, r 17(3).
[8] Appeals (Excluded Decisions) Order 2009, SI 2009/275, art 3(m).
[9] TCEA 2007, s 11(1).
[10] *Entry Clearance Officer v Hughes* (01TH01147) (22 May 2001, unreported), IAT; see fn 15 below.
[11] *Adewole* (18538) (22 September 1998, unreported), IAT; *Singh (Nachtar) v Secretary of State for the Home Department* [1991] Imm AR 195; *Osman (Ayse)* [1993] Imm AR 417.
[12] *Kirungi* (13111) (20 March 1996, unreported), IAT. But see *Entry Clearance Officer v Hughes* (01TH01147) (22 May 2001, unreported), where the Tribunal dismissed (albeit on technical grounds) an ECO appeal against an adjudicator's decision allowing an appeal that had apparently been withdrawn, although the Tribunal had doubts about the circumstances of the withdrawal.

20.77 A particular difficulty in practice has been whether the person withdrawing an appeal has the necessary instructions and authority to do so.[1] The general rule that a retainer of a solicitor includes authority to compromise an action or withdraw unless contrary instructions are expressly given,[2] does not appear to apply in immigration appeals,[3] and a solicitor without instructions has been held to have no authority to withdraw an appeal.[4] Where there is authority, withdrawal will be effective.[5] The old case law indicates that an employer or someone who has no right of audience at the appeal may validly withdraw an appeal,[6] even if that person is not registered or exempt under

Part V of IAA 1999.[7] An appellant whose appeal has been withdrawn can apply to the Tribunal for the withdrawal to be treated as invalid and if such an application is made, the Tribunal will set the matter down for hearing on that issue.[8] If there was a formally effective withdrawal of the appeal, the appellant will have to satisfy the Tribunal on a balance of probabilities that the withdrawal was not the result of a deliberate and informed decision by the appellant, eg that the appellant did not understand the nature and consequences of the withdrawal.[9]

[1] See *R v Diggines, ex p Rahmani* [1985] QB 1109, [1986] Imm AR 195; *R v Immigration Appeal Tribunal, ex p Pollicino* [1989] Imm AR 531, QBD; *Nessa v Secretary of State for the Home Department* [1985] Imm AR 131, CA.

[2] 44 *Halsbury's Laws* (4th edn) para 121.

[3] See *R v Diggines, ex p Rahmani* [1985] QB 1109, [1986] Imm AR 195.

[4] *Singh v Secretary of State for the Home Department* [1991] Imm AR 195.

[5] *Attivor v Secretary of State for the Home Department* [1988] Imm AR 109. The API (Appeals: Withdrawal, para 2.3) state that if the representatives who submitted the appeal write to withdraw it, it would normally be appropriate to accept subsequent correspondence from them stating that the appeal is to be withdrawn, but that care should be taken when the appellant has instructed a number of representatives during the course of an application; where there is doubt about a withdrawal by a representative, the appellant should be asked to confirm the withdrawal personally in writing. The API states that the final decision to accept or reject a withdrawal by a representative rests with the Tribunal. The instructions are likely to be amended to reflect the loss of the immigration authorities' role in receiving appeal notices.

[6] *Tanakloe v Secretary of State for the Home Department* [1991] Imm AR 611.

[7] See Tribunal Procedures (First-tier Tribunal)(Immigration and Asylum Chamber) Rules 2014, SI 2014/2604, r 10(4).

[8] *AP (Pakistan)* [2007] UKAIT 00022.

[9] *AP (Pakistan)*, ibid.

Abandonment of appeal

20.78 The 2014 Procedure Rules, like the 2005 Rules (but unlike earlier rules), do not make specific provision for abandonment by an appellant in the sense of simple failure to prosecute their appeal.[1] They provide only for statutory abandonment of the appeal.[2] An appeal under section 82 of NIAA 2002 brought by a person whilst in the UK is deemed abandoned by statute in two specific situations: (i) the appellant leaving the UK;[3] (ii) the appellant being granted leave to enter or remain[4] (or, in an EEA appeal, a registration certificate, residence card, a document certifying permanent residence or a permanent residence card under the Immigration (European Economic Area) Regulations 2006 or a registration certificate under the Accession (Immigration and Worker Registration) Regulations 2004).[5] If any party to a pending appeal becomes aware that an appellant has left the UK or has been granted leave or that a deportation order has been made against the appellant or a document recognising an EEA right, they must notify the Tribunal, which must, in turn, serve notice on the parties informing them that the appeal is being treated as abandoned and thereafter take no further action in relation to the appeal.[6] The same procedure applies to an appeal which is treated as 'finally determined' when a deportation order is made against the appellant.[7] The Court of Appeal held in *Shirazi*[8] that statutory abandonment provisions in IAA 1999[9] did not apply to appeals to itself, so that someone leaving the UK (and returning) while an appeal to the Court of Appeal was pending was not deprived of that appeal by statute.[10] The position was probably the same under the 2002 Act provisions for appeals to the Court of Appeal because the distinction was maintained between appeals 'under section 82(1)', those being the appeals subject to the statutory abandonment provisions, and 'a further appeal' to the Court of Appeal under ss 103B and 103E to which the abandonment provisions made no direct reference. Moreover, a similar distinction can now be made between an appeal to the FT under NIAA 2002, s 82 and appeals to the Upper Tribunal that are brought under TCEA 2007, s 11. The abandonment provisions in NIAA 2002, s 104 apply only to the appeal under NIAA 2002, s 82 so that there is no basis in the primary legislation for treating an appeal to the Upper Tribunal as abandoned if the appellant leaves the UK or is granted leave to enter or remain. However, the UT's Procedure Rules do contemplate, wrongly we think, NIAA 2002, s 104 applying to appeals to the UT.[11] Deemed abandonment on departure from the UK does not apply to cases involving EEA nationals or their family members.[12] A pending appeal is deemed abandoned by operation of statute as soon as leave to enter or remain is granted, so that there is no longer an appeal before the Tribunal,[13] but only an actual grant of leave by way of notice in writing has this effect; an undertaking by the respondent to grant leave does not result in the appeal being abandoned.[14] Where an asylum seeker's appeal under NIAA 2002, s 82 is treated as abandoned as a result of a grant of leave to enter or remain, they acquire a new right of appeal under section 83(1), if the leave granted or the aggregate of that and any previous leave exceeds one year. However, a new notice of appeal must be filed in order to exercise that right of appeal; an abandoned s 82 appeal cannot be varied so as to become a s 83 appeal, because there is no appeal left to vary.[15] The Immigration Asylum and Nationality Act 2006 changed the statutory abandonment provisions[16] in three ways. First, it is only appeals brought whilst the appellant is in the UK that are treated as abandoned if the appellant leaves the country or is granted leave;[17] an appeal brought from outside the UK eg against refusal of entry clearance would not be statutorily abandoned. This means that a person who brought an appeal from outside the UK (eg against refusal of entry clearance) will not have the appeal treated as abandoned if they are granted leave to enter whilst the appeal is pending[18] or having entered the UK, leaves. Second, if an appellant is granted leave for a period exceeding 12 months they will be able to continue with the appeal on Refugee Convention grounds if the person gives notice to the Tribunal within 28 days of receiving the grant that he or she wishes to continue with the appeal.[19] If such notice is given, the statutory abandonment provision does not apply. Third, a grant of leave will not prevent an appeal from being continued on race discrimination grounds[20] so long as notice of the wish to continue with the appeal is given in accordance with Tribunal Procedure Rules.[21] However, the current procedure rules make no provision for the appellant to give notice of his or her wish to continue with the appeal on race discrimination grounds. Presumably, that is because the procedure rules were drafted on the assumption that the Immigration Act 2014 would have repealed the provision for appealing on race discrimination grounds by the time they came into force.

[1] For example, the Immigration and Asylum Appeals (Procedure) Rules 2000, SI 2000/2333, r 32 provided that the appellate authorities could treat failure to attend a hearing or to comply with directions as tantamount to abandonment of the appeal: see *Gremesty* [2001] INLR 132, IAT.

[2] Tribunal Procedures (First-tier Tribunal) (Immigration and Asylum Chamber) Rules 2014, SI 2014/2604, r 16.

[3] NIAA 2002, s 104(4)(b): *Dupovac v Secretary of State for the Home Department* [2000] Imm AR 265 (referring to equivalent provisions in s 33(4) of IA 1971, inserted by the Asylum and Immigration Act 1996). However, the appeal is not to be treated as abandoned by operation of that provision if the appellant 'leaves the United Kingdom' as a result of being illegally removed by the Secretary of State: *Muja* [2002] UKIAT 05107. The Court of Appeal cast further doubt on the applicability of the section to all cases of 'leaving' the UK in *Shirazi v Secretary of State for the Home Department* [2003] EWCA Civ 1562, [2004] 2 All ER 602, doubting whether a mere day trip to Calais would activate the abandonment provision, but did not decide the issue.

[4] NIAA 2002, s 104(4)(a). A third 'deemed abandonment' of an appeal, under s 58(10), IAA 1999, applied where a deportation order was made against an appellant; under NIAA 2002, however, appeals are to be treated as finally determined, rather than abandoned, in this situation: NIAA 2002, s 104(5): see fn 7 below.

[5] Immigration (European Economic Area) Regulations 2006, SI 2006/1003, Sch 2, para 4(2); SI 2004/1219.

[6] SI 2014/2604, r 16.

[7] Under NIAA 2002, s 104(5): see SI 2014/2604, r 16.

[8] *Shirazi v Secretary of State for the Home Department* [2003] EWCA Civ 1562, [2004] INLR 92.

[9] Under IAA 1999, s 58.

[10] The decision depended partly on the distinction in the Act itself (reproduced in NIAA 2002 provisions) between appeals under the relevant Part of the Act, and 'further appeals', and partly on the inherent jurisdiction of the Court of Appeal. The same logic would apply to deemed abandonment by grant of leave to enter or remain. Any other interpretation of the abandonment provisions would deprive the Court of Appeal of its inherent discretion to consider appeals involving important legal or policy issues even though the grant of leave has made the issue academic in the particular case.

[11] Tribunal Procedure (Upper Tribunal) Rules 2008, SI 2008/2698, r 17A.

[12] See *Baumbast* (21263) (8 June 1999, unreported), IAT and the Immigration (European Economic Area) Regulations 2000, SI 2000/2326 (as amended by SI 2003/549), reg 27(4).

[13] NIAA 2002, s 104(4)(a); *Kanyenkiko v Secretary of State for the Home Department* [2003] EWCA Civ 542, [2003] All ER (D) 348 (Feb) (on the equivalent provisions under IAA 1999, s 58(9)). For the effect of transitional provisions, where leave to remain was granted after the coming into force of the appeal provisions of NIAA 2002 but the appeal was brought under IAA 1999, see *ZA (Ethiopia)* [2004] UKIAT 00241, [2004] Imm AR 538.

[14] *Mohamed (Omar) v Secretary of State for the Home Department* [2002] UKIAT 04634.

[15] *Kanyenkiko v Secretary of State for the Home Department* (see fn 12 above).

[16] IAN 2006, s 9, amending NIAA 2002, s 104, commenced on 13 November 2006 by SI 2006/2838.

[17] By virtue of the old s 104(4) being substituted and a new s 104(4A) inserted.

[18] As happened in *SS (Nigeria)* [2007] UKAIT 00026.

[19] SI 2014/2604, r 16(3).

[20] Thereby avoiding the potential injustice under the unamended provision, considered in *Emunefe v Secretary of State for the Home Department* [2005] EWCA Civ 2002. An appellant could pursue a race discrimination claim in civil proceedings under the Race Relations Act 1976, s 57(1) once the Tribunal appeal was abandoned unless the Tribunal had made an adverse decision on the race discrimination. The Tribunal might have made the adverse decision wrongly but the abandonment of the appeal to the Tribunal would have prevented the appellant from overturning that part of the decision.

[21] NIAA 2002, s 104(4C).

20.79 The Procedure rules about certification, withdrawal and abandonment are drafted in very similar terms.[1] In each case, the Tribunal apparently acknowledges a state of affairs which means there is no longer an appeal before it, by notifying the parties. It was doubtless the draftsman's intention to assimilate the situations, so that notices of withdrawal and abandonment were no different from certification. But in fact there are profound differences. The Secretary of State's certification is final and decisive in a way that an appellant's withdrawal of an appeal, even deemed withdrawal and deemed abandonment, is not. We have referred earlier to the substantial case law on withdrawal and on deemed abandonment.[2] Whether an appeal can be brought against the giving of a notice that an appeal is being treated as abandoned or withdrawn depends on whether there is 'a decision' of the Tribunal and if there is, whether it is an excluded decision.[3] The giving of such a notice requires the making of a decision by the Tribunal that the relevant state of affairs exists. That 'a decision' as opposed to a mere acknowledgment of an existing state of affairs is involved is clear from the Senior President's Practice Statements which list among decisions for the Tribunal 'any determination that an appeal be dismissed as abandoned or finally determined'.[4] Moreover, the notice of abandonment or withdrawal is also dispositive of the appeal proceedings. For one or both of those reasons, such notices have been treated as appealable decisions under previous appeal provisions.[5] It is not obvious that a decision having the effect that a pending appeal comes to an end can properly be characterised as a 'procedural, ancillary or preliminary decision made in relation to an appeal'[6] and a 'determination', the form in which a decision on abandonment is taken,[7] is by definition not 'procedural, ancillary or preliminary'.[8]

1   Tribunal Procedures (First-tier Tribunal)(Immigration and Asylum Chamber) Rules 2014, SI 2014/2604, rr 16, 17, 18.
2   See **20.76** ff above.
3   TCEA 2007, ss 11(1) and 13(1).
4   Practice Statements: Immigration and Asylum Chambers of the First-tier Tribunal and the Upper Tribunal, para 2.1(9), 10 February 2010.
5   *Gremesty* [2001] INLR 132, IAT. See also, under previous rules, *Akhuemonkhan* [1998] INLR 265, IAT; *Secretary of State for the Home Department v Ibrahim* [1994] Imm AR 1; *Secretary of State for the Home Department v Munchula* [1996] Imm AR 344; *R v Immigration Appeal Tribunal, ex p Lila* [1978] Imm AR 50; *MM (Burundi)* [2004] UKIAT 00182, [2004] Imm AR 515, [2004] INLR 327 (starred).
6   As it would have to be in order to be treated as an 'excluded decision' – TCEA 2007, ss 11(1) and 13(1) and Appeals (Excluded Decisions) Order 2009, SI 2009/275, art 3(m).
7   Practice Statements: para 2.1(9).
8   Asylum and Immigration Tribunal (Procedure) Rules 2005, SI 2005/230, r 2.

Defining the issues pre-hearing

20.80 The respondent is, as we have seen, required to file with the Tribunal and serve on the appellant the notice of the decision or decisions appealed against, any other document served on the appellant giving reasons for the decision, and evidence which has come into being during the decision making process, such as statement of evidence forms, records of interview and any unpublished material referred to in the decision or reasons, or otherwise relied on by the respondent.[1] The respondent's duty to produce 'any unpublished material . . . otherwise relied on by the respondent' is wider than before, and is designed to ensure that appellants are not taken by surprise. However, there may well be other evidence or information which the appellant requires from the Home Office.[2] There is, surprisingly, no power of discovery of documents in the Procedure rules,[3] but there are other ways of achieving the same result. In the exercise of its powers to give directions, the Tribunal may require a party to provide documents, information, evidence or submissions to the tribunal or to a party;[4] to provide a bundle for a hearing;[5] or it may give directions as to the issues on which it requires evidence or submissions, the nature of such evidence or submissions, and the manner in which they are to be provided.[6] The list of possible directions is not exhaustive.[7] However, directions may only be given in relation to procedural matters; they may not require the Secretary of State to take a substantive step, such as issuing a fresh refusal letter,[8] interviewing an appellant[9] or reconsideration of an asylum claim (even where asylum had wrongly been refused on grounds of non-compliance with procedure).[10] But a direction could properly be made requiring the Secretary of State to provide reasons for refusing asylum on the merits where the only reasons given were that the appellant had failed to submit a statement or attend for interview.[11] While the main use of directions has been to control appellants' cases, they are apt to extract from the respondent in advance all evidence on which it seeks to rely, and also evidence in its possession which might assist the appellant. Practice Directions require both parties to provide to the Tribunal and the other party any amendments, proposed amendments or applications to vary grounds of appeal or notices of decision at the case management review hearing. At the end of the hearing, the Tribunal is to give written confirmation to the parties of any issues that have been agreed at the CMR hearing as being relevant to the determination of the appeal, and any concessions made by a party at the CMR hearing[12] (although it is unlikely that these concessions would be irrevocable, particularly if they are made before all the evidence is available).

[1] Tribunal Procedures (First-tier Tribunal) (Immigration and Asylum Chamber) Rules 2014, SI 2014/2604, rr 23, 24; see **20.72** above.

[2] It may, for example, be necessary to seek further particulars relating to an anonymous allegation. In an asylum case involving a person who had been suspected of support for terrorism by British police, it would be very important to find out whether any information about the appellant had passed between the British authorities and those of the appellant's country.

[3] *R v Adjudicator (RG Care), ex p Secretary of State for the Home Department* [1989] Imm AR 423, QBD.

[4] Tribunal Procedures (First-tier Tribunal)(Immigration and Asylum Chamber) Rules 2014, SI 2014/2604, r 4(3)(d).

[5] SI 2014/2604, r 4(3)(i).

[6] SI 2014/2604, r 14.

[7] This is apparent from the words 'in particular and without restricting the general powers in paragraphs (1) and (2)' in SI 2014/2604, r 4(3).

[8] *Mwanza v Secretary of State for the Home Department* [2001] INLR 616.

[9] *R (on the application of Zaier) v Immigration Appeal Tribunal* [2002] EWHC 2215 (Admin), [2002] All ER (D) 70 (Oct).

[10] *R (on the application of Emlik) v Immigration Appeal Tribunal* [2002] EWHC 1279 (Admin), [2002] All ER (D) 209 (Jan).

[11] *Secretary of State for the Home Department v Razi* (2001) 01TH1836; *Secretary of State for the Home Department v Tekle* [2002] UKIAT 00704.

[12] Senior President's Practice Directions, 10 February 2010, para 7.

20.81 An application for a direction requiring the provision of further information is particularly important in cases where the Secretary of State makes a positive assertion, eg that the unauthorised disclosure of an asylum claim to the authorities of the appellant's country will not affect his or her safety on return,[1] or that a particular practice operates at the airport of a particular country, or that a document is not genuine. It is possible to obtain information or documents by summoning a witness to answer questions or to produce documents,[2] subject only to the limitation that a party or witness may not be compelled to give evidence or produce a document that he or she could not be compelled to give or produce in civil proceedings.[3] Where the respondent is asserting some matter, such as fraud or forgery of documents, the burden of proof is on the respondent, and the more serious the allegation, the clearer and more direct the proof should be.[4] In such cases a failure to produce or call evidence in support of the allegations should result in the respondent's allegations remaining unproven or of very little weight.[5]

[1] *R v Immigration Appeal Tribunal, ex p Agbenyenu* [1999] Imm AR 460, QBD. However, in *FZ* [2003] UKIAT 00315, [2003] Imm AR 633, the Tribunal held that the Secretary of State was under no duty to embark on an investigation to identify evidence not in his hands, and that any duty of disclosure on the Secretary of State would generally be discharged by production of a relevant Country Information and Policy Unit (CIPU) report.

[2] Tribunal Procedures (First-tier Tribunal)(Immigration and Asylum Chamber) Rules 2014, SI 2014/2604, r 15.

[3] SI 2014/2604, r 15(3).

[4] *Ali v Secretary of State for the Home Department* [1984] 1 All ER 1009, [1984] Imm AR 23, CA. See **20.124** below.

[5] See *R v Immigration Appeal Tribunal, ex p Cheema* [1982] Imm AR 124 at 133, CA.

20.82 Quite apart from these means of obtaining information, an individual is entitled to a copy of any information about him or her[1] that is held by any 'data controller'[2] such as the Immigration Service or Home Office or other government department.[3] Such information (for example, a copy of the individual's Home Office file) is to be provided when the individual makes a request in writing to the data controller and pays such a fee as may be required.[4] To obtain a copy of his or her Home Office file, an individual should write to the DPU SAR, UK Border Agency, Lunar House, 40 Wellesley Road, Croydon CR9 2BY enclosing a cheque or postal order for £10, payable to 'The Home Office Accounting Officer'. In addition to the written 'Subject Access Request', 'sufficient personal information to enable us to uniquely identify you – for example a copy of your passport or driver's licence, original utility bills, and your Home Office reference number if you have one' must be included. If the application is made on behalf of someone else, the person's original, signed form of authority must be included.[5] The request for information must be complied with within 40 days.[6] The obligation to disclose information is subject to exemptions relating, *inter alia*, to the safeguarding of national security,[7] the prevention and detection of crime and the prosecution of criminals.[8]

[1] Data Protection Act 1998 (DPA 1998), ss 7(1)(c)(i) and 8(2).

[2] DPA 1998, s 1(1).

[3] DPA 1998, s 63.

[4] DPA 1998, s 7(2). The fee that may be required is up to a maximum of £10. See Data Protection (Subject Access) (Fees and Miscellaneous Provisions) Regulations 2000, SI 2000/191, reg 3.

[5] 'Requests for personal data', document on UKBA website.

[6] DPA 1998, s 7(8) and (10).

[7] DPA 1998, s 28.

[8] DPA 1998, s 29.

Reasons for the decision or action appealed

20.83 The giving of reasons is a substantial matter. The Notices Regulations[1] require that reasons should be given when the decision or action is notified to the appellant, as seen above. The giving of reasons for an administrative decision adversely affecting rights of residence, family life, and even more fundamental rights protected by the Refugee Convention, is increasingly seen as vital for compliance with standards of fairness at common law,[2] and for compatibility with the Human Rights Convention.[3] It is for this reason thought that unless the notice of refusal is amended, it is not possible for the immigration authority to rely upon an entirely different reason for refusal at the hearing. The extent to which the reasons may be amended to reflect the true reasons for the decision and the extent to which the Tribunal is tied to the reasons contained in the notice and decision letter, when it comes to the hearing of the appeal, have already been considered.[4] The position under IA 1971 was that the notice of decision and explanatory statement were preliminary definitions of the issues between the parties on appeal, but with the probable exception of statutory grounds (eg for deportation), not necessarily conclusive.[5] Certainly, the jurisdiction of the Tribunal is wide enough, at least in cases where the Refugee Convention is engaged, to oblige it to measure its view of the facts[6] against the applicable statutes, rules, policies, Convention and administrative law standards, whether or not these have been expressly referred to, with the Court of Appeal decision in *Robinson*[7] providing the parameters of this duty.[8] So, where an asylum claim has been refused for reasons of non-compliance with the asylum determination procedure (eg failure to attend an interview), the Tribunal has held that the appellate authority has an obligation to decide for itself whether the appellant's removal would be contrary to the Refugee Convention.[9] A fair hearing demands a proper opportunity to meet the case made. In this connection it is important to recall that the Tribunal has power to limit the issues on appeal.[10] This provides an opportunity to agree facts and legal issues which once agreed, should not be reopened unless patently wrong.[11]

[1]   Immigration (Notices) Regulations 2003, SI 2003/658, reg 5(1)(a).
[2]   See eg *Stefan v General Medical Council* [1999] 1 WLR 1293; *R v Secretary of State for the Home Department, ex p Zighem* [1996] Imm AR 194.
[3]   *Stefan v General Medical Council* [1999] 1 WLR 1293; *R v Higher Education Funding Council, ex p Institute of Dental Surgery* [1994] 1 WLR 242.
[4]   See **20.58** above.
[5]   Woolf J in *R v Immigration Appeal Tribunal, ex p Hubbard* [1985] Imm AR 110.
[6]   NIAA 2002, s 85(4).
[7]   *Robinson (Anthonypillai Francis) v Secretary of State for the Home Department and Immigration Appeal Tribunal* [1997] Imm AR 568, CA.
[8]   *Rahman and Akhter (00307)* (10 March 2000, unreported), IAT; *Kaur (Sukhinder) v Secretary of State for the Home Department* [1998] Imm AR 1, CA; *R (on the application of Naing) v Immigration Appeal Tribunal; R (on the application of Eyaz) v Immigration Appeal Tribunal* [2003] EWHC 771 (Admin), [2003] All ER (D) 337 (Mar).
[9]   *Haddad (Ali)* [2000] INLR 117, IAT.
[10] Tribunal Procedures (First-tier Tribunal)(Immigration and Asylum Chamber) Rules 2014, SI 2014/2604, r 14(1)(a).
[11] See *R v Immigration Appeal Tribunal, ex p Akhtar and Bowen* (1982) 126 Sol Jo 430, QBD.

20.84 Where a question of fact (eg the credibility of an appellant's evidence) is conceded by the immigration authority, either in its decision letter or at a hearing, through the Home Office presenting officer, the concession must be accepted by the Tribunal.[1] But a concession is a positive act; mere failure to put a fact in issue in a refusal letter or to cross-examine on a fact or even to cross-examine at all, does not amount to a concession.[2] A concession may be withdrawn before the Tribunal, but it is for the Tribunal to decide whether to permit withdrawal of the concession taking account of all the circumstances, including whether the appellant would be prejudiced by the withdrawal.[3] However, the Tribunal is not required to undertake an analysis applying public law principles to the decision to withdraw the concession or to be satisfied that something new has arisen to justify the withdrawal.[4] Whether a concession was actually made may subsequently become a disputed question of fact[5] underlining the desirability of the parties reducing to writing any concession that is made.[6]

[1] *R (on the application of Ganidagli) v Secretary of State for the Home Department* [2001] INLR 479; see also *Carcabuk and Bla v Secretary of State for the Home Department (00TH01426)* (although not starred because the Tribunal consisted of only two members, this decision is to be regarded as binding).

[2] *Carcabuk and Bla*, ibid. But see *MS (Sri Lanka) v Secretary of State for the Home Department* [2012] EWCA Civ 1548: where evidence was given addressing an issue raised in a refusal letter and the appellant was not cross examined in relation to that evidence, it would be unfair for the tribunal to decide against the appellant on that issue.

[3] *Davoodipanah v Secretary of State for the Home Department* [2004] EWCA Civ 106, [2004] INLR 341; *R (on the application of Ivanuskiene) v Special Adjudicator* [2001] EWCA Civ 1271, [2002] INLR 1, (2001) Times, 18 September (relating to a concession on the law, based on the law at the time of the appeal hearing); *Secretary of State for the Home Department v Abdalla* [2002] UKIAT 01900.

[4] *NR (Jamaica) v Secretary of State for the Home Department* [2009] EWCA Civ 856.

[5] See eg *R (on the application of Kantharajah) v Secretary of State for the Home Department* [2003] EWHC 1456 (Admin), [2003] All ER (D) 77 (Jun).

[6] *R (on the application of Ganidagli) v Secretary of State for the Home Department* [2001] INLR 479; *Kalidas (Agreed facts – best practice)* [2012] UKUT 00327 (IAC).

Amending the grounds of appeal

20.85 The Court of Appeal's observation in *Zenovics*[1]

'The formulation of grounds of appeal is done rapidly, often by people with no mastery of either English law or the English language. All this in an area where the law is riddled with obscurities and regularly amended by primary or secondary legislation and by rules'.

explains the need for appellants to be able to amend their grounds of appeal. Further, the real scope of an appellant's case often does not become clear until much of the preparatory work on an appeal has been done and certainly long after notice of appeal has been given. A wide discretion to allow grounds of appeal to be varied in asylum and human rights appeals is particularly necessary, bearing in mind the serious consequences of a wrong decision[2] and the principle that all possible grounds for seeking to remain should be dealt with in a single appeal. The Procedure Rules provide that the appellant may vary his or her grounds only with its permission.[3] Permission is of course not required to serve a statement in response to a one-stop notice under NIAA 2002, s 120 and the tribunal is obliged to consider any matter raised in the statement that constitutes a ground of appeal[4] (except to the extent that the new NIAA 2002, s 85 is brought into force so that the Secretary of State will have to consent to the tribunal considering such matters).[5] There is no limitation to the power to permit the grounds of appeal to be varied under the 2014 Procedure Rules, other than the overriding objective to secure that proceedings before the Tribunal are dealt with fairly and justly;[6] and there are likely to be few, if any, circumstances where it would be right for permission to be refused.[7] Were the application to vary the grounds to be refused, the appellant could not, we suggest, reasonably be prevented by certification from relying on the new grounds in a future appeal.[8] Practice Directions require appellants to notify the Tribunal and the respondent at the case management review hearing of any application to amend the grounds of appeal, and any amendments to the reasons in support of the grounds.[9]

1   *R (on the application of Zenovics) v Secretary of State for the Home Department* [2002] EWCA Civ 273, [2002] INLR 219.
2   *Dyli v Secretary of State for the Home Department (No 2) (01TH1010).*
3   Tribunal Procedures (First-tier Tribunal)(Immigration and Asylum Chamber) Rules 2014, SI 2014/2604, r 19(7).
4   NIAA 2002, s 85(2) (duty of Tribunal to consider additional grounds responding to one-stop notice).
5   NIAA 2002, s 85(5), as substituted by IA 2014, s 15(5), currently in force only to the extent provided by SI 2014/2771: see **20.3**.
6   SI 2014/2604, r 2(1).
7   Cases such as *FF (Iran)* [2004] UKIAT 00192, where a late application to vary grounds of appeal to the Immigration Appeal Tribunal from an adjudicator's determination, have no application to first instance appeals, where both law and factual issues are at large. But note the observation of the Tribunal that outline submissions do not amount to varied grounds of appeal or an application to vary.
8   ie under NIAA 2002, s 96(1), (as substituted by Asylum and Immigration (Treatment of Claimants, etc) Act 2004, s 30), which permits a second claim to be certified, thereby precluding appeal, if it relies on a matter which could have been raised on an earlier appeal. That condition cannot be satisfied if the Tribunal prevented an appellant from raising the matter on the earlier appeal by refusing to permit a variation of the grounds of appeal.
9   Senior President's Practice Directions, 10 February 2010, paras 7.3 and 7.4.

Notice of hearing

20.86 When the Tribunal fixes a hearing, it must give each party notice of the time and place of the hearing and notice of any adjourned or postponed hearing, as well as any changes to the time and place of the hearing.[1] There is no longer special provision for appeals relating to asylum claims requiring them to be listed by a particular time after notice of appeal is given.[2] Practice Directions provide for the Tribunal to direct that a case management review (CMR) hearing will be held in respect of in-country appeals in the FT.[3]

1   Tribunal Procedures (First-tier Tribunal)(Immigration and Asylum Chamber) Rules 2014, SI 2014/2604, r 26.
2   As there had been in the 2005 Procedure Rules, SI 2005/230, r 23(1), (2).
3   Senior President of Tribunals Practice Directions: Immigration and Asylum Chambers of the First-tier Tribunal and the Upper Tribunal, 10 February 2010, para 7.

CASE MANAGEMENT AND DIRECTIONS

20.87 Subject to the procedure rules, the tribunal may regulate its own procedure[1] and may vary any time limit imposed on a party by the procedure rules, a Practice Direction or a direction. The tribunal may give a direction in relation to the conduct or disposal of proceedings at any time and it may give directions that amend, suspend or set aside earlier directions.[2] A party can apply for a direction to be made either by means of a written application or orally at a hearing,[3] and a party may challenge a direction made by the tribunal by applying for another direction which would amend, suspend or set aside the first direction.[4] Case management by the tribunal includes decisions about whether the case should be heard by an immigration judge or a panel of judges; defining the issues, including any preliminary issues;[5] whether the appeal is to be determined without a hearing[6], or joined with another appeal in one hearing[7]; readiness for the full hearing of the appeal; and the preparation and presentation of evidence.

We have dealt with defining the issues at **20.80** above. Now, we turn our attention to other aspects of case management. Decisions as to the constitution of the Tribunal to hear an appeal (ie whether the appeal should be heard by one immigration judge or by a panel) are for the Chamber President or for an FT judge to whom the making of such decisions is delegated.[8] A single FT judge will conduct a case management review hearing, give directions to the parties and deal with other preliminary or incidental matters.[9] The Tribunal must send written notice of any direction to every party and any other person affected by the direction, unless it considers that there is good reason not to do so.[10] There may be directions as to the issues on which evidence and submissions are required by the tribunal; the nature of the evidence and submissions required; the number of witnesses to be heard; whether the parties are required or permitted to provide expert evidence; and the manner in which evidence or submissions are to be provided, which may be orally at a hearing or in writing.[11] The power to direct that witness statements stand as evidence in chief is not subject to the appellant's consent, although this does not mean that at the hearing the appellant should not have the opportunity of adding to the witness statement anything necessarily supplementary to it to bring it to life.[12] Directions may also require parties to file and serve, within specified time limits, statements of the evidence to be called, skeleton arguments, chronologies, paginated and indexed bundles of the documentary evidence to be relied on, time estimates, lists of witnesses, a chronology and details of any interpreter required. Directions may limit the number or length of documents a party may rely on (particularly useful in asylum appeals where 'standard bundles' of over 300 pages are frequently served), the length of oral submissions and the time allowed for examination and cross-examination of witnesses.[13] The Senior President of Tribunals Practice Directions contain detailed provision about the instruction of experts and the form and content of expert reports.[14] Directions may provide for a hearing to be conducted or evidence given or representations made by video link or by other electronic means.[15] The tribunal may make an order prohibiting publication or disclosure of any matter likely to lead members of the public to identify any person whom the tribunal considers should not be identified.[16]

1   Tribunal Procedures (First-tier Tribunal)(Immigration and Asylum Chamber) Rules 2014, SI 2014/2604, r 4(1).
2   SI 2014/2604, r 4(2).
3   SI 2014/2604, r 5(1), (2).
4   SI 2014/2604, r 5(5).
5   SI 2014/2604, r 14(1)(a).
6   SI 2014/2604, r. 25.
7   Practice Statements: Immigration and Asylum Chambers of the First-tier Tribunal and the Upper Tribunal, 10 February 2010, para 2.3.
8   SI 2014/2604, r 4(3)(b). This might happen where the appeals raise some common question of fact or law, relate to decisions in respect of members of the same family, or where it is desirable for some other reason that they be heard together.
9   Practice Statements, para 2.1.
10 SI 2014/2604, r 5(4).
11 SI 2014/2604, r 14.

[12] *R v Secretary of State for the Home Department, ex p Singh* [1998] INLR 608, CA (permission). Senior President's Practice Directions, 10 February 2010, para 7.7 says that 'in normal circumstances a witness statement should stand as evidence in chief', but acknowledges that 'there may be cases where it will be appropriate' for appellants or witnesses to add to or supplement their statements. It is a rare case where it is *not* necessary to give such opportunity, at least to appellants.

[13] The current procedure rules no longer make specific provision to this effect, but these are matters falling within the tribunal's general power to give directions.

[14] Practice Directions: Immigration and Asylum Chambers of the First-tier Tribunal and the Upper Tribunal, 10 February 2010, para 10.

[15] The current procedure rules do not make specific provision for this, but SI 2014/2604, r 4(3)(g) does refer to the tribunal's power to 'decide the form of any hearing' and r 14(1)(e) provides for the tribunal to make directions about 'the manner in which any evidence or submissions are to be provided'. Hearings by video link routinely occur in Field House in London with the parties appearing by means of a video link in another hearing centre. It has been used to enable appellants to give evidence from outside the UK: see eg *R (on the application of Ahmadi) v Secretary of State for the Home Department* [2002] EWHC 1897 (Admin), [2002] All ER (D) 52 (Sep) at [1926]. The refusal by a Tribunal to permit a witness to give evidence over the telephone from Cameroon was held to be at least arguably unlawful in *R (on the application of AM (Cameroon)) v Asylum and Immigration Tribunal* [2007] EWCA Civ 131.

[16] SI 2014/2604, r 13(1).

CASE MANAGEMENT REVIEW HEARINGS

20.88 Provision for case management review hearings and the making of directions is contained in the Senior President's Practice Directions.[1] The Tribunal may direct that there is to be a case management review hearing where the appellant is in the UK and has a right of appeal exercisable whilst in the UK.[2] Failure by a party or his or her representative to attend may result in the appeal being determined without a hearing or in the party's absence.[3] At the hearing, the appellant is required to provide the Tribunal and the respondent with particulars of any application to amend the grounds of appeal or the reasons in support of the grounds of appeal and of any witnesses whose written or oral evidence is to be relied on and a draft of any directions sought.[4] The respondent is required to file and serve at the hearing any amendment to the notice of decision or other document giving reasons for the decision and a draft of any direction sought.[5] Prior to the hearing, standard directions are normally given with the notice of hearing.[6] They require, not later than five days before the full hearing or ten days in the case of an out-of-country appeal, the appellant to file and serve witness statements of the evidence to be called; a paginated and indexed bundle of all documents relied on with a schedule identifying essential passages; a skeleton argument and a chronology. They also require the respondent to file and serve at least five days before the hearing, a paginated and indexed bundle of all the documents relied on with a schedule identifying relevant passages and a list of any authorities relied on. At the end of the case management hearing, the Tribunal should give to the parties any further written directions[7] and written confirmation of any issues that have been agreed as being relevant to determination of the appeal and any concessions made by a party.[8]

[1] Senior President of Tribunals Practice Directions: Immigration and Asylum Chambers of the First-tier Tribunal and the Upper Tribunal, 10 February 2010 ('Senior President's Practice Directions').

2 Senior President's Practice Directions, para 7.1. Under the Asylum and Immigration Tribunal Practice Directions, 30 April 2007, a case management review hearing were a matter of course for asylum appeals unless the Tribunal directed otherwise.

3 Senior President's Practice Directions, para 7.2, referring to the Asylum and Immigration Tribunal Procedure Rules, SI 2005/230, rr 15(2) and 19(1).

4 Senior President's Practice Directions, para 7.3.

5 Senior President's Practice Directions, para 7.4.

6 Senior President's Practice Directions, para 7.5.

7 Senior President's Practice Directions, para 7.6.

8 Senior President's Practice Directions, para 7.8.

20.89 What effect does non-compliance with a direction, a Practice Direction or a provision of the Procedure Rules have on the appeal? An irregularity resulting from a non-compliance does not by itself render void the proceedings or any step in the proceedings.[1] If there has been non-compliance by a party, the tribunal may take such action as it considers just, which may include waiving the requirement, requiring the failure to be remedied or referring the matter to the Upper Tribunal to exercise its 'supplementary powers'.[2] These supplementary powers that the Upper Tribunal may be asked to exercise are those that relate to a person's failure to comply with a requirement imposed by the tribunal to attend or make themselves available to give evidence; to swear an oath; to give evidence; or to produce a document or facilitate the inspection of a document or any other thing including premises. In relation to these matters, the Upper Tribunal's powers are the same as those of the High Court[3] and would extend, for example, to enforcement of its directions by means of contempt proceedings. Another course of action that the tribunal might take is to determine the appeal without a hearing, but it would have to be satisfied that that is the appropriate course in all the circumstances, including the extent of, and any reasons for, the failure.[4] Consideration of 'all the circumstances' would require the Tribunal to take account of whether there was evidence of previous failure by the party to comply with a direction or rule.[5] The power to determine an appeal without a hearing for non-compliance with directions should be exercised with extreme caution, and will rarely, if ever, be appropriate if the party in default is present.[6] It is no longer possible for the Tribunal to dismiss the appeal without consideration of the merits where the party failing to comply with the procedure rule or the direction is the appellant, a power contained in previous procedure rules which gave rise to considerable unfairness and litigation. The rules no longer require the tribunal to consider evidence filed later than directed, only if satisfied that there is good reason to do so;[7] instead it has the broad general power to take such action as it considers just.[8] Whilst that power might enable the tribunal to decline to consider the late evidence, 'as a general principle, the requirement to ensure that justice is done in appeals requiring the most anxious scrutiny will in most cases outweigh the understandable desire on the part of the appellate authority to ensure that its directions and the provisions of the procedure rules are not flouted with impunity'.[9] It would be pointless to exclude a witness statement not served in time because even if it is excluded, the appellant would still be entitled to call the witness to give oral evidence.[10]

1 Tribunal Procedures (First-tier Tribunal)(Immigration and Asylum Chamber) Rules 2014, SI 2014/2604, r 6(1).

2 SI 2014/2604, r 6(2), (3).

3 Tribunals, Courts and Enforcement Act 2007, s 25.

4 SI 2014/2604, r 25(1)(e).

5   *R (on the application of Karagoz) v Immigration Appeal Tribunal* [2003] EWHC 1228 (Admin). Since determination without a hearing generally prejudices the appellant and not the respondent, it is the appellant's default that will usually lead to the invocation of the rule.

6   *Meflah (Mohamed) v Secretary of State for the Home Department* [1997] Imm AR 555, IAT; *R v Immigration Appeal Tribunal, ex p S* [1998] Imm AR 252, [1998] INLR 168. Although these cases were decided before an express power existed to dispense with a hearing, the overriding objective – and so the framework within which the appellate authority must exercise its discretion – remains the same.

7   As provided by SI 2005/230, r 51(4), applied to fast track appeals by SI 2005/560, r 27. The immigration judge must not automatically exclude late evidence but must apply the 'good reason' test and consider whether the appeal should be adjourned to avoid prejudice to the other side: *MD (Pakistan)* [2004] UKIAT 00197. The 'good reason' applies to the admission of the evidence, and not to the reason for its lateness: *SA (Sri Lanka)* [2005] UKIAT 00028.

8   SI 2014/2604, r 6(2).

9   *AK (Iran)* [2004] UKIAT 00103. See also *KK (Afghanistan)* [2004] UKIAT 00258.

10   *MA (Somalia)* [2007] UKAIT 00079.

TRIBUNAL HEARINGS

Dispensing with a hearing

20.90 The Tribunal has separate powers to determine an appeal without a hearing,[1] and to determine the appeal following a hearing in the absence of a party.[2] Here we consider determination of an appeal without a hearing at all. Under the 2014 Procedure Rules, the tribunal must hold a hearing before making a decision that disposes of proceedings, except where:

(1)   the appeal lapses pursuant to section 99 of the NIAA 2002, ie where the appeal has been certified under section 97 (certification on national security grounds) or s 98 (certification on other grounds of public good) of the Act;[3]

(2)   the appeal is treated as abandoned pursuant to section 104(4) of the NIAA 2002, ie as a consequence of the appellant being granted leave to enter or remain or leaving the UK;[4]

(3)   on a deportation order being made with the result that an appeal against refusal of leave to enter, refusal of a certificate of entitlement to the right of abode, variation or refusal to vary a person's leave or revocation of a person's indefinite leave is treated as finally determined, by operation of the NIAA 2002, section 104(5);[5]

(4)   the appeal is withdrawn, or is treated as withdrawn by virtue of rule 17, on the respondent withdrawing the decision;[6]

(5)   all the parties to the appeal consent or do not object to the appeal being determined without a hearing;[7]

(6)   the appellant is outside the UK and unrepresented, or represented by someone who does not have an address for service in the UK;[8]

(7)   it is impracticable to give the appellant notice of a hearing;[9]

(8)   a party has failed to comply with a provision of the Procedure Rules or a direction of the Tribunal, and the Tribunal is satisfied that in all the circumstances, including the extent of the failure and any reasons for it, it is appropriate to determine the appeal without a hearing;[10]

(9) the Tribunal is satisfied that it can justly determine the matter without a hearing and it has given the parties notice of its intention to do so and an opportunity to make written representations as to whether there should be a hearing;[11]

(10) the appeal is struck out owing to revocation of a certificate of fee satisfaction;[12]

(11) in fast track cases, there must be a hearing of the appeal unless the appeal lapses, is treated as abandoned or withdrawn, or the parties consent to the appeal being decided without a hearing.[13]

The power to dispense with a hearing must be exercised by the Tribunal personally rather than a member of the administrative staff.[14]

[1] Tribunal Procedures (First-tier Tribunal) (Immigration and Asylum Chamber) Rules 2014, SI 2014/2604, r 25.

[2] SI 2014/2604, r 28. The Tribunal should be clear to distinguish between the two situations and should make it clear which procedure it is adopting: *Abali (15543)* (6 October 1997, unreported), IAT; *JZ (Ivory Coast)* [2004] UKIAT 00102.

[3] SI 2014/2604, rr 18, 25(1)(f).

[4] SI 2014/2604, rr 16, 25(1)(f). For abandonment of appeals, see **20.78** above.

[5] SI 2014/2604, r 16(1)(c).

[6] SI 2014/2604, r 17. For withdrawal of appeals see **20.76** above.

[7] SI 2014/2604, r 25(1)(a).

[8] SI 2014/2604, r 25(1)(c). Before proceeding without a hearing under the rule, the Tribunal must notify both parties and give them an opportunity to make further representations: *Entry Clearance Officer v TMG (Turkey, South Africa, Colombia)* [2004] UKIAT 00028; *PP (India)* [2004] UKIAT 00128. On unrepresented appellants, see *R v Diggines, ex p Rahmani* [1985] QB 1109, [1986] Imm AR 195, HL, where it was held that UKIAS had not ceased to act for the appellant, although it had lost her new address; before proceeding under this rule, the adjudicator should have required an unambiguous declaration from UKIAS either that its instructions had been withdrawn or that it had no instructions.

[9] SI 2014/2604, r 25(1)(d).

[10] SI 2014/2604, r 25(1)(e). The power to dispense with a hearing for non-compliance with directions should be used very sparingly, and probably not at all when parties have appeared for the hearing: *MD (Pakistan)* [2004] UKIAT 00197. Where the appellant was not personally at fault when the representative filed the reply to the notice of hearing late, the appeal should not have been determined without a hearing: *K (Afghanistan)* [2004] UKIAT 00043. While it may be legitimate for an immigration judge to decide to proceed without a hearing, or a further hearing, after a failure to comply with directions, and even to decide to pass the case to another immigration judge, the second immigration judge must not determine the case as if he or she was the original immigration judge: *JZ (Ivory Coast)* [2004] UKIAT 00102.

[11] SI 2014/2604, rr 25(1)(g) and (2). Where both parties want a hearing, it would rarely be appropriate to dispense with one: *MD (Pakistan)* [2004] UKIAT 00197, and never when credibility is in issue: *Federation of Canadian Sikh Societies v Canadian Council of Churches* [1985] 1 SCR 178 (cited in *R v Immigration Appeal Tribunal, ex p S* [1998] Imm AR 252 at 267 and *R v Secretary of State for the Home Department, ex p Yousaf* [2000] INLR 432).

[12] SI 2014/2604, r 7.

[13] SI 2014/2604, Schedule, r 9.

[14] *Singh (Piara) (7069)*, IAT.

The hearing

20.91 Every appeal must be considered at a hearing before an immigration judge or a panel of immigration judges unless a provision of the Procedure Rules or any other enactment permits or requires the Tribunal to dispose of an appeal without a hearing.[1] The rules allow the tribunal to decide the form of any hearing[2] and the manner in which evidence and submissions are to be provided,[3] which presumably would include by video link or other electronic means,[4] opening up for the first time the possibility of appellants giving evidence in their own out-of-country appeals.[5] The procedure rules no longer dictate a period within which an appeal has to be heard, unless the appeal is in the fast track, in which case a hearing date should be fixed no more than three days after the respondent is supposed to file their documents with the tribunal.[6] There is nothing in the procedure rules as to where hearings may take place. The Tribunal is not required to list an appeal at the hearing centre that is closest or most convenient for the appellant. An appellant has no legitimate expectation that the date of the hearing will not be brought forward, only that it will not be changed without reasonable notice.[7]

1   Tribunal Procedures (First-tier Tribunal)(Immigration and Asylum Chamber) Rules 2014, SI 2014/2604, r 25(1).
2   SI 2014/2604, r 4(3)(g).
3   SI 2014/2604, r 14(1)(e).
4   The current rules do not make express provision for hearings by video link. although the previous rules did: SI 2005/230, r 45(4)(h). A party has no right to give evidence by those means and whether the party may do so is a matter for the tribunal's discretion: *Nare (Zimbabwe)* [2011] UKUT 443 (IAC) gives detailed guidance.
5   See by way of example, *R (on the application of Ahmadi) v Secretary of State for the Home Department* [2002] EWHC 1897 (Admin), [2002] All ER (D) 52 (Sep).
6   SI 2014/2604, Schedule, r 8(1).
7   SI 2005/230, r 46; *R v Immigration Appeal Tribunal, ex p Shandar* [2000] Imm AR 181.

Proceeding in a party's absence

20.92 The tribunal may hear an appeal in a party's absence if satisfied that the party has been notified of the hearing or that reasonable steps have been taken to notify the party of the hearing, and that it is in the interests of justice to proceed.[1] The Tribunal has set out guidelines for immigration judges on how to proceed where the Home Office is not represented, attached to the starred case of *MNM*.[2]

1   Tribunal Procedures (First-tier Tribunal)(Immigration and Asylum Chamber) Rules 2014, SI 2014/2604, r 28.
2   *MNM* (00TH 02423) (starred) (1 November 2000), IAT ('the *Surendran* guidelines').

20.93 Most of the case law concerns allegations of non-receipt of notices of hearing, leading to hearings in the absence of appellants. Parties have to identify an address to which documents provided by the tribunal or any other person are to be sent.[1] The respondent is obliged to notify the Tribunal if they know that the appellant has changed address.[2] If the party is represented, the representative is required to provide written notice of their address.[3] Thereafter, any document may be provided to the representative instead of to the party,[4] and any document provided to the appellant must be copied to the representative.[5] A document provided to a person who has notified the tribunal that they are acting as the representative for a party is deemed to have been provided to that party.[6] But all deemed service must arguably be subject to a proviso, whether or not expressly stated, allowing proof of non-receipt.[7] Procedural requirements are designed to further the interests of justice.[8] The Tribunal is obliged to consider an allegation of non-receipt of the notice of hearing in an application for permission to appeal.[9] It would be a 'strong step' not to accept the assertion of any professional person that a notice sent otherwise than by recorded delivery had not been received.[10] Giving notice of hearing is not legally adequate if the name on the envelope is incorrect.[11] Earlier decisions on judicial review suggest that where a direction requires a certificate of readiness to be submitted, failing which the party is to appear on the date in the notice, and a certificate of 'unreadiness' is sent in, the Tribunal is entitled to proceed in the absence of the appellant and the representative,[12] but most reported cases indicate that a failure by a representative to comply with procedural requirements should not prejudice the appellant to the extent of preventing his or her attendance to give oral evidence, where this is necessary for the just disposal of the appeal.[13]

1   Tribunal Procedures (First-tier Tribunal)(Immigration and Asylum Chamber) Rules 2014, SI 2014/2604, r 12(1).
2   SI 2014/2604, r 12(3).
3   SI 2014/2604, r 10(3).
4   SI 2014/2604, r 10(5).
5   SI 2014/2604, r 10(6).
6   SI 2014/2604, r 12(4).
7   Following *R v Secretary of State for the Home Department, ex p Saleem* [2000] Imm AR 529, [2000] INLR 413, upholding Hooper J at [1999] INLR 621. See also *R (on the application of Hasa) v Immigration Appeal Tribunal* [2003] EWHC 396 (Admin), [2003] All ER (D) 232 (Feb).
8   *Ravichandran v Secretary of State for the Home Department* [2000] 1 WLR 354 at 359, per Lord Woolf MR.
9   *R v Immigration Appeal Tribunal, ex p Susikanth* [1998] INLR 185, CA, and grounds explaining non-attendance at a hearing as caused by solicitor error gave an explanation for non-attendance: *R (on the application of Habyl) v Immigration Appeal Tribunal* [2002] EWHC 2313 (Admin), [2002] All ER (D) 237 (Oct). The old case of *Al-Mehdawi v Secretary of State for the Home Department* [1990] 1 AC 876, in which the House of Lords held that a representative's failure to send the notice of hearing to the appellant did not ground an allegation of procedural impropriety in the subsequent hearing, where the appellant was absent and unrepresented, has been held inapplicable to cases in which human rights or asylum issues are engaged: *Haile v Immigration Appeal Tribunal* [2001] EWCA Civ 663, [2002] Imm AR 170, [2002] INLR 283; cf *E v Secretary of State for the Home Department* [2004] EWCA Civ 49, [2004] 2 WLR 1351; *FP (Iran) and MB (Libya) v Secretary of State for the Home Department* [2007] EWCA Civ 13.
10 *R (on the application of Karagoz) v Immigration Appeal Tribunal* [2003] EWHC 1228 (Admin); *R (on the application of Simeer) v Immigration Appellate Authority* [2003] EWHC 2683 (Admin), [2003] All ER (D) 419 (Oct), holding that it was irrational for the IAT to reject as without foundation the assertion made in grounds of appeal to the IAT that notice of hearing had not been received. But see *R (on the application of Maqsood) v Special Adjudicator and Secretary of State for the Home Department* [2002] Imm AR 268 where the claimant's solicitor's evidence of non-receipt of the notice of hearing was rejected.
11 *Choudhry* (15911) (7 January 1998, unreported), IAT. See also *Idrissi v Secretary of State for the Home Department* [2001] EWCA Civ 235, [2001] All ER (D) 390 (Feb) where a decision was quashed on the basis that the Tribunal proceeded on a mistaken view of the facts (ie a belief that the appellant had been properly served), when an administrative mistake led to a notice of hearing going to the wrong representative.
12 *R v Secretary of State for the Home Department, ex p Butt* [1999] Imm AR 341, QBD; *R v Special Adjudicator, ex p Arshad* (CO 1145/97) (15 April 1997, unreported), QBD.
13 *K (Afghanistan)* [2004] UKIAT 00043; see also cases cited at fnn 9–10 above.

20.94 In exercising the power to proceed in a party's absence, the Tribunal must act fairly.[1] It would be wise for an immigration judge to take the precaution of trying to find out why a party was absent, eg by making a telephone call to his or her representative before deciding to proceed in the party's absence.[2] However, the Tribunal is not obliged to accept any excuse for non-attendance at face value. In particular, the Tribunal is not obliged to accept a medical certificate which does not explain why a party is unable to attend.[3] The Tribunal must specify precisely why it is proceeding in the absence of a party, ie which particular provision of the rule it is relying on.[4] If it proceeds, it must allow or dismiss the appeal.[5]

[1] *Singh (Reshan) and Kaur v Secretary of State for the Home Department* [1993] Imm AR 382 (if hearing is described as pre-hearing review, it is unfair to proceed in the absence of appellant, as if it was the final hearing). But see *R (on the application of Maqsood) v Special Adjudicator and Secretary of State for the Home Department* [2002] Imm AR 268.

[2] *R (on the application of Karagoz) v Immigration Appeal Tribunal* [2003] EWHC 1228 (Admin) and *R (on the application of Simeer) v Immigration Appellate Authority* [2003] EWHC 2683 (Admin), [2003] All ER (D) 419 (Oct).

[3] *R v Immigration Appeal Tribunal, ex p Baira* [1994] Imm AR 487, QBD; *Deen-Koroma (Jeneba) v Immigration Appeal Tribunal* [1997] Imm AR 242, CA; *R v Secretary of State for the Home Department, ex p Lal Singh* [1998] Imm AR 320, QBD.

[4] *Jan (7063), IAT; Deb* [1990] Imm AR 14.

[5] *Ali (Shaharia)* [1999] INLR 108, IAT. Additionally, if the immigration judge accepts material from the party in whose absence they are proceeding, that is tantamount to reopening the hearing, obliging the immigration judge to reconsider whether it is appropriate to proceed in the party's absence: *Feghali* (16602) (25 November 1998, unreported), IAT.

Representation

20.95 Parties may be represented by any person not prohibited from acting by section 84 of IAA 1999.[1] A representative has all the powers of the party he or she is representing, such as the giving or receipt of notices, apart from signing a witness statement.[2] Documents that are to be given to a party must be given to their representative; a document given to an appellant must also be given to their representative, but a document given to the representative need not be given to the represented party as well.[3] Persons are entitled to assume that a represented party continues to be represented by the appointed representative until the party or the representative gives written notice to the contrary.[4]

[1] Tribunal Procedures (First-tier Tribunal)(Immigration and Asylum Chamber) Rules 2014, SI 2014/2604, r 10(1). This includes qualified lawyers or registered or exempted immigration service providers: see CHAPTER 1 above. The AIT Practice Directions, 30 April 2007, para 8B said that a sponsor who is not prohibited by s 84 from representing an appellant may appear as his or her representative. The Senior President's Practice Directions of 10 February 2010 are silent about sponsors. An unqualified person may represent a person before the tribunal so long as they are doing so other than in the course of a business; and as such the tribunal had been wrong to prevent an appellant's family friend from representing her: *RK (Bangladesh)* [2011] UKUT 00409 (IAC).

[2] SI 2014/2604, r 10(4). Whether a representative's purported withdrawal of an appeal can bind the appellant is discussed at **20.76** above. On the issue of whether representatives' failure to comply with procedural requirements such as time limits for appealing, responses to directions etc should deprive personally blameless appellants of appeal rights, the courts have tended towards greater leniency in recent years, at least where human rights or asylum issues are engaged: see **20.93** above.

[3] SI 2014/2604, r 10(5) and (6).

[4] SI 2014/2604, r 10(6).

Adjournments

20.96 The Tribunal has power to adjourn a hearing, to be exercised in accordance with the overriding objective.[1] It is no longer circumscribed as it was in the 2005 Procedure Rules by procedural requirements and by a prohibition on the tribunal adjourning unless satisfied that the appeal cannot otherwise be justly determined.[2] It cannot be said of the 2014 Rules, as it was of earlier rules, that they are 'hostile to adjournments in general'[3] and that that hostility should inform decisions on adjournment applications. Where adjournments are sought on the grounds of health, the higher courts have generally been content to leave it to the immigration judge's judgment,[4] so long as he or she has given an adequate opportunity to respond to objections to medical evidence.[5] In such a case, the Tribunal is obliged to make a conscientious judgment as to whether justice calls for an adjournment, taking into account the nature of the appellant's condition and the evidence about when, if ever, the appellant would be able to give evidence.[6] Where adjournments have been sought on grounds of the appellant's need to find representation, the higher courts have frowned upon what was a more liberal approach by the Tribunal,[7] which in asylum appeals such as *Ajeh*[8] had said that 'whether or not an appellant is articulate, the need for representation at the hearing . . . appears almost axiomatic given the obligation to give the most anxious scrutiny to cases of this kind'[9]. However, in, *ex p Ghaly*[10] Sedley J issued a reminder that 'the question of adjournment . . . frequently throws up fundamental issues of fairness. If the maxim 'both sides are to be fairly heard' is to have any effect, it means that each side has to have a fair opportunity of preparing to deal with what the other side is going to say'.[11] In *Okiji*[12] the Tribunal deprecated the refusal of an adjournment when counsel was taken ill and the adjudicator had, in refusing, referred to the 'normal practice of the Bar' in sending a replacement 'even at one moment's notice'. It observed that the traditions of the Bar were 'not always consistent with the interests of the appellant'.[13] The withdrawal of a representative at a hearing (other than when an appellant withdraws instructions) has been held a good reason to adjourn.[14] An adjournment to enable the appellate authority to provide an interpreter of the kind that the appellant had originally requested should not have been refused.[15]

[1] Tribunal Procedures (First-tier Tribunal)(Immigration and Asylum Chamber) Rules 2014, SI 2014/2604, r 4(3)(h).

[2] SI 2005/230, r 21.

[3] *Secretary of State for the Home Department v DD (Croatia)* [2004] UKIAT 00032 (starred).

[4] See eg *R v Secretary of State for the Home Department, ex p Odubanjo* [1996] Imm AR 504, QBD (adjudicator entitled to use common sense regarding a pregnant appellant who felt unwell at the hearing); *R v Immigration Appeal Tribunal, ex p Choudhury (Kawsar)* (1999/6451/C) (2 November 1999, unreported), CA (adjudicator entitled to refuse adjournment having regard to medical evidence and appellant's demeanour and ability to answer questions at the hearing).

[5] *Chisthi (14953)* (12 May 1997, unreported); *Awadh (12783)* (7 December 1995, unreported); *Gheorghiu (12850)* (28 December 1995, unreported). See also *WT (Ethiopia)* [2004] UKIAT 00176, where the Tribunal held that obtaining an appointment with the Medical Foundation did not (on the particular facts) justify granting an adjournment (but note the comments indicating that in such a case the Secretary of State might be more receptive to a fresh claim). For adjournments to obtain evidence see below.

[6] *Ramirez v Secretary of State for the Home Department* [2001] EWCA Civ 1365, [2002] Imm AR 240.

[7] In *R (on the application of Bogou) v Secretary of State for the Home Department and Immigration Appeal Tribunal* [2000] Imm AR 494, Maurice Kay J pointed to the tightening of the criteria for adjourning between the Asylum Appeals (Procedure) Rules 1993 and 1996, SI 1993/1661 and SI 1996/2070 and to the failure of Tribunal jurisprudence to reflect that change. In *R v Special Adjudicator, ex p Nitcheu* (00/5158/C) (7 March 2000), CA (renewed permission application) a refusal to adjourn for legal representation for an appellant who had lost his representation through compulsory dispersal was upheld. See also *R v Special Adjudicator, ex p Kotovas* [2000] Imm AR 26; *R v Immigration Appeal Tribunal, ex p Adrees*

(95/5564/D) (18 April 1996, unreported), CA; *R v Secretary of State for the Home Department, ex p Janneh* [1997] Imm AR 154; *R v Secretary of State for the Home Department, ex p Twaha* (CO/4073/98) (1 December 1999), QBD.

8   (13853) (30 August 1996, unreported), IAT, followed in (*inter alia*) *Cabrera* (17123) (21 May 1998, unreported); *Kyeyune* (18153) (25 November 1998, unreported). The liberal approach is not evident in entry clearance cases, see eg *Musa (Ibne)* [2002] UKIAT 07625.

9   The Tribunal's view of the importance of representation in asylum and human rights appeals reflected those of the Genn Report *Representation before Tribunals* (1989) Hazel and Yvette Genn, the Legal Aid Board (now Legal Services Commission), *Access to quality services in the immigration category* (May 1999), and of the Lord Chancellor's Advisory Committee on Legal Education and Conduct *Improving the quality of immigration advice and representation: A report*, ACLEC (July 1998).

10 *R v Secretary of State for the Home Department, ex p Ghaly* (27 June 1996, unreported), QBD.

11 See also the guidance in *R v Kingston-upon-Thames Justices, ex p Martin* [1994] Imm AR 172, DC, which was held to apply, together with that in *Macharia* [2000] Imm AR 190, 196 to adjournments in human rights cases, so that refusal to await a psychiatric report on a rape victim, due in days and likely to assist in a human rights appeal, was held *Wednesbury* unreasonable in *R (on the application of Fanna) v Secretary of State for the Home Department* [2002] EWHC 777 (Admin), [2002] All ER (D) 16 (Mar).

12 (13079) (7 March 1996), IAT.

13 See also *Bozkurt* (11783) (19 January 1995, unreported); *Muia* (17223) (29 May 1998, unreported), IAT.

14 *Kandeepan* (15124), IAT; particularly where the claimant had been ill-served by that representative: *R (on the application of Dirisu) v Immigration Appeal Tribunal* [2001] EWHC 970 (Admin), [2001] All ER (D) 449 (Nov). But see *AD (Algeria)* [2004] UKIAT 00155, where the Tribunal held that it would be wrong to adjourn an appeal merely because of the withdrawal or threatened withdrawal of a representative, where otherwise there was no merit in an adjournment request.

15 *AT* [2002] UKIAT 02883.

20.97 It may be necessary to adjourn to enable a party to obtain further evidence where the evidence was not available at the hearing.[1] It was an error of law for the Tribunal to refuse an adjournment to obtain further evidence on a material issue in circumstances where the reliability of the existing evidence on that issue had not been questioned prior to the hearing.[2] The tribunal could not both refuse an adjournment, sought to enable an appellant to produce medical evidence of having been tortured, on the ground that the refusal to adjourn did not prevent just disposal of the appeal, and at the same time reject the account of being tortured because of the absence of medical evidence.[3] Where an adjournment was sought to enable the appellant to call corroborative witnesses, it was wrong for the Tribunal to refuse on the ground that the appellant was capable of giving evidence on the same issue herself, given that the very purpose of calling the witnesses was to repair the appellant's damaged credibility.[4] Where the Tribunal permits a party to adduce evidence not previously sent to the other party, there must be an adjournment if necessary to avoid prejudice.[5] The tribunal should be cautious before adjourning to await a pending appellate decision, but adjournment may be necessary if the anticipated decision will have a critical impact on the outcome of the appeal.[6] In *Kimbesa*[7], a refusal to adjourn was quashed where, shortly before an asylum appeal hearing, the appellant's brothers, whose claims rested on the same facts, had arrived in the UK. Ognall J held that it was unfair to expect the brothers to have their accounts tested in an appeal hearing before they had been interviewed on their claim. In *Rajan*,[8] a starred Tribunal case, Collins J distinguished *Kimbesa*, and held that it was not authority for the proposition that wherever there was a concurrent application by a relative an adjournment was in the interests of justice, although the existence of concurrent applications by family members was a relevant consideration which may point to an adjournment in an appropriate case. A refusal to adjourn a hearing is clearly a procedural decision which is not per se susceptible to appeal or review, but a wrongful refusal would give a ground for appeal or review of the subsequent decision on the appeal.[9]

1 *R v Medical Appeal Tribunal (Midlands Region), ex p Corrarini* [1966] 1 WLR 883; *Kondo* (10413) (12 November 1993, unreported), IAT; *Sarica* (15363) (21 August 1997, unreported), IAT; or to obtain a translation: *Getener (14799)*, IAT. *R (on the application of Fanna) v Secretary of State for the Home Department* [2002] EWHC 777 (Admin), [2002] All ER (D) 16 (Mar): it was irrational for the adjudicator both to refuse to adjourn the appeal to enable production of a psychological report and to refuse to agree to receive the report after the hearing, bearing in mind the possible consequences in a human rights case of preventing reliance on potentially cogent evidence. See *R (on the application of RQ (Jordan)) v Secretary of State for the Home Department* [2014] EWHC 559 (Admin).
2 *Shkembi v Secretary of State for the Home Department* [2005] EWCA Civ 1592, [2005] All ER (D) 323 (Nov).
3 *Ntoya* [2002] UKIAT 00155.
4 *AS (Pakistan) v Secretary of State for the Home Department* [2007] EWCA Civ 703, [2007] All ER (D) 253 (Jun).
5 *Macharia v Immigration Appeal Tribunal* [2000] INLR 156, CA. The principle applies to any other situation in which the other party risks being taken by surprise, eg by a new ground of decision, or a new ground of appeal, or by the Tribunal taking a point not raised by the parties.
6 *AB (Sudan) v Secretary of State for the Home Department* [2013] EWCA Civ 921. See also *TR (Pakistan)* [2011] UKUT 33 (IAC).
7 *R v Secretary of State for the Home Department, ex p Kimbesa* (29 January 1997, unreported), Ognall J.
8 Rajan (Munigesu) (01TH00244)
9 On an application for permission to appeal against a decision on an appeal where a ground relates to refusal to adjourn to produce evidence, the relevant evidence should be produced for the review or appeal court, to demonstrate that it would have made a difference: see *R (on the application of Bosombanguwa) v Immigration Appeal Tribunal and Secretary of State for the Home Department* [2004] EWHC 1656 (Admin), [2004] All ER (D) 260 (Jul).

20.98 The Practice Direction requires an application for an adjournment to be made not later than 5pm one clear working day before the date of the hearing,[1] supported by full reasons and made in accordance with the Procedure Rules.[2] A later application must be made at the hearing, and requires the attendance of the party or representative.[3] Only in the most exceptional circumstances will a late application for an adjournment be considered without the attendance of a party or representative.[4] Parties must not assume that an application will be successful, and must check with the Tribunal, since if the application is not granted and they fail to attend, the Tribunal may proceed in their absence if there is no satisfactory explanation for their non-attendance.[5]

1 Senior President's Practice Directions: Immigration and Asylum Chambers of the First-tier Tribunal and the Upper Tribunal, 10 February 2010, para 9.1.
2 Senior President's Practice Directions, para 9.3.
3 Senior President's Practice Directions, para 9.4.
4 Senior President's Practice Directions, para 9.5.
5 Senior President's Practice Directions, paras 9.6, 9.8.

20.99 Hearings of fast track appeals may only be adjourned if the appeal could not justly be decided if the hearing were to be concluded on the date fixed, and there is a date no more than ten days later upon which the tribunal can conclude the hearing and justly determine the appeal.[1] If the tribunal is satisfied that the case cannot justly be decided within that timescale, it must order that the Fast Track Rules cease to apply.[2] Fairness would require an adjournment if necessary to enable an appellant to answer the case against him or her by obtaining expert evidence, even if the inevitable result would be removal of the case from the Fast Track.[3]

[1] Tribunal Procedures (First-tier Tribunal)(Immigration and Asylum Chamber) Rules 2014, SI 2014/2604, Schedule, r 12.
[2] SI 2014/2604, Schedule, r 14.
[3] *SH (Afghanistan) v Secretary of State for the Home Department* [2011] EWCA Civ 1284.

Procedure at the hearing

20.100 There is extensive jurisprudence from the Tribunal and the higher courts on the scope of the duty of fairness in immigration appeals. At the hearing, each party may address the Tribunal, give evidence and call witnesses, and put questions to any witness. Each party should also be given an opportunity to make representations on the evidence (if any) and on the subject matter of the appeal generally. Where evidence is taken, the representations are normally made after the evidence is completed. The issues addressed, the oral and documentary evidence received and the submissions entertained may be limited in accordance with directions previously given and with the time estimate put in by the parties.[1] However, the Tribunal should not prevent an advocate from developing their submissions.[2] The Tribunal has power to conduct the proceedings in the manner it considers appropriate in the circumstances for ascertaining the matters in dispute and determining the appeal.[3] In doing so it must act fairly,[4] and should give an appellant a chance to comment on any adverse material in the evidence.[5] Whilst it is preferable that complaints about judicial conduct should be raised at the hearing rather than waiting for a subsequent appeal, the difficulty of raising such a complaint with a judge who may go on and decide the appeal has been acknowledged.[6] However, fairness does not require that every point that may be decided against an appellant should first of all be put to him or her; whether this is necessary depends on the circumstances of the particular case.[7] The Tribunal is not obliged to accept an improbable account simply because it has not been tested.[8] The Tribunal should not refuse to allow cross-examination of any witness who has been called to give oral evidence.[9] In cross-examining an appellant, the respondent is not limited to the issues raised in the 'reasons for refusal letter'.[10] The Tribunal's provisional conclusions should not be indicated at the outset of the hearing.[11] If an immigration judge has particular knowledge or experience relevant to the facts in issue, that should be made known to the parties and they should be invited to state whether they have any objection to that immigration judge hearing the appeal.[12] An immigration judge's personal knowledge should not be taken into account in a manner that may suggest bias.[13] If the Tribunal has access to relevant evidence not produced by the parties, their attention should be drawn to it.[14] A Tribunal may take into account material that comes to light after the hearing, but must inform the parties of its intention to do so and afford them an opportunity to comment on it.[15] If, having heard the evidence, the Tribunal expresses a positive view as to the credibility of the appellant, the hearing should be reconvened and submissions invited if the Tribunal subsequently changes its mind.[16] Similarly, if at the end of the hearing, the Tribunal indicates that the appeal is to be allowed, it may change its mind when giving a written determination, but only after inviting the parties to make further representations[17] unless the announcement of the provisional view had no impact on the way in which the case was put.[18] The parties should be given an opportunity to deal with any case they have not referred to which appears to be determinative or call for argument,[19] although immigration judges are entitled to take account of well-known Tribunal decisions, meaning those given under the Tribunal's reporting system, even if neither party has cited them.[20] In an asylum appeal, the Tribunal may introduce the issue of internal flight even if the Secretary of State has not, but should be cautious about doing so and must give the parties an opportunity to deal with it.[21] All representatives, including respondents', are under a duty to assist the Tribunal by presenting it with all relevant case law, including that contrary to the argument put forward.[22] The respondent must put to a witness any matter said to undermine the witness' credibility,[23] and must not knowingly mislead the court by not disclosing material which detracts from its case.[24] The respondent has an obligation, at least in asylum and human rights cases, to place the Tribunal in a position to make an informed decision on the issues before it;[25] Thus, for example, the respondent must produce any evidence about which he or she knows or ought to know and which shows that an 'authoritative' Tribunal decision does not accurately describe material conditions in the appellant's country.[26] The respondent is also obliged to inform the Tribunal of any policy that is or may be relevant to the issues in the case and failure to comply with that obligation may result in the Tribunal, through blameless ignorance of a relevant policy, making a decision that is unlawful.[27] It may be that asylum and human rights is a field where, since the court has an overriding obligation to ensure the highest standards of fairness, litigation privilege would not allow a party to refuse production of an expert report.[28] There is a need to be especially vigilant in fast track appeals, where each stage in the appeal process follows very swiftly, and the Tribunal must take care not to allow itself to be misdirected by the Secretary of State on the objective evidence.[29]

[1]   See **20.87** above and *R v Secretary of State for the Home Department, ex p Singh* [1998] INLR 608, CA, upholding an adjudicator's refusal to allow a witness to add orally to her statement, which was the subject of a direction that it stand as evidence in chief.

[2]   *Katrinak v Secretary of State for the Home Department* [2001] EWCA Civ 832, [2001] INLR 499.

[3]   See the discussion of case management above.

[4]   So, for example, where an appellant put in a report from Amnesty International concerning the dangers facing failed asylum seekers from Algeria, which was unchallenged by the presenting officer, the adjudicator should not have rejected the evidence without allowing the appellant to adduce further evidence to confirm it: *Kriba v Secretary of State for the Home Department* 1998 SLT 1113, OHCS (Scot). And after an appellant had given evidence in the absence of the respondent's representative, whose inability to attend the hearing was the fault of the appellate authority, the hearing should not have proceeded, in fairness to the respondent, but should have been transferred: *Secretary of State for the Home Department v I (Somalia)* [2004] UKIAT 00062.

[5]   *Ahmed v Secretary of State for the Home Department* [1994] Imm AR 457, CA; *R v Immigration Appeal Tribunal, ex p Seri* (CO/2135/99) (27 June 2000, unreported); *R v Immigration Appeal Tribunal, ex p Gunn* (22 January 1998, unreported), QBD. This obligation does not extend to obvious discrepancies on matters central to the appellant's case and already drawn to the appellant's attention in the refusal letter: *R v Immigration Appeal Tribunal, ex p Williams* [1995] Imm AR 518; *Sahota v Immigration Appeal Tribunal* [1995] Imm AR 500, nor must the Tribunal foresee and put at the hearing every aspect of the evidence which goes into its findings on the facts: *R v Immigration Appeal Tribunal, ex p Hansford* [1992] Imm AR 407; *AA (Sudan)* [2004] UKIAT 00152. The Tribunal will not generally make

findings of fact based on an allegation against former representatives unless they have had an opportunity to respond to the allegation and the Tribunal is shown the response or correspondence revealing that there has been no response: BT (Nepal) [2004] UKIAT 00311.

6   *KD (Afghanistan)* [2010] UKUT 261 (IAC).

7   *R (on the application of Maheshwaran) v Secretary of State for the Home Department* [2002] EWCA Civ 173, [2004] Imm AR 176. An appellant should, for example, be told if the Tribunal does not believe his or her claim to have scars and should be given an opportunity to show them: *Sabouhi* [2002] UKIAT 06662; if the Tribunal is dissatisfied with the extent of the appellant's knowledge about the political party he or she claimed to belong to, where the inadequacy of his or her knowledge is not self-evident: *Kucher* [2002] UKIAT 07439; or if the Tribunal considers the evidence to be 'vague' *B (DR Congo)* [2003] UKIAT 00012.

8   *R (on the application of Hyseni) v Immigration Appeal Tribunal* [2002] EWHC 1239 (Admin), [2002] All ER (D) 561 (May).

9   *GY (Iran)* [2004] UKIAT 00264.

10   *Secretary of State for the Home Department v D (Iran)* [2003] UKIAT 00087.

11   *Rajah* (15159) (24 June 1997, unreported), IAT. In *Gashi v Secretary of State for the Home Department* [2002] UKIAT 03935 an appeal was allowed against an adjudicator's dismissal of a Kosovan appeal where, at the beginning of the appeal hearing, he indicated that in his view Kosovan cases lacked merit. See *Mohammed (Somalia)* [2011] UKUT 337 (IAC).

12   *Secretary of State for the Home Department v MM* (2001) (01TH00994) IAT and *MD (Pakistan)* [2009] UKAIT 00013.

13   *Muse* [2002] UKIAT 01957 where the adjudicator rejected the appellant's complaint that she was ill served by her previous solicitors because of her personal knowledge of two partners in that firm. cf *BA (Israel)* [2004] UKIAT 00118, where the adjudicator's personal knowledge of the Gaza strip had not affected the decision.

14   *R v Secretary of State for the Home Department, ex p Fortunato* [1996] Imm AR 366, QBD; *Gnanavarathan and Norbert v Special Adjudicator* [1995] Imm AR 64, CA; *R v Immigration Appeal Tribunal, ex p Kang* (CO 497/2000) (6 October 2000, unreported), QBD; *Junaid* (01TH02540), IAT. Reaching adverse conclusions on credibility on the basis of material which formed the basis of the presenting officer's cross-examination of the appellant but which was not disclosed was unfair: *Ozmico* [2002] UKIAT 00484.

15   *Laci* (2001) (01/TH/01348), IAT.

16   *Paudel* [2002] UKIAT 06868.

17   *R v Special Adjudicator, ex p Bashir* [2002] Imm AR 1, CA; *K (Rwanda)* [2003] UKIAT 00047; *SK (Sri Lanka) v Secretary of State for the Home Department* [2008] EWCA Civ 495, (2008) Times, 27 May.

18   *ML (Zambia) v Secretary of State for the Home Department* [2008] EWCA Civ 589, [2008] All ER (D) 42 (Jun).

19   *R v Immigration Appeal Tribunal, ex p Sui Rong Suen* [1997] Imm AR 355.

20   *M (Afghanistan)* [2004] UKIAT 00004.

21   *He (Bai Hai)* (00TH00744), IAT; *Mehta* (17861), IAT.

22   *Choudhury* (10646) (11 February 1994, unrerported), IAT.

23   *Ezzi* (G0003A) (29 May 1997, unreported), IAT.

24   *Kerrouche (Mohammed) v Secretary of State for the Home Department* [1997] Imm AR 610, CA; *Konan v Secretary of State for the Home Department* (IATRF 00/0020/C) (20 March 2000, unreported), CA. The majority conclusion in *R v Secretary of State for the Home Department, ex p Gawe, Abdi v Secretary of State for the Home Department* [1996] Imm AR 288, HL, of no general disclosure duty of country information, does not undermine this principle.

25   *Rahman (Shaima Osman Abdul) v Secretary of State for the Home Department* [2005] EWCA Civ 1826.

26   *R (on the application of Cindo) v Secretary of State for the Home Department* [2002] EWHC 246 (Admin), [2002] All ER (D) 181 (Feb). Failure to produce such evidence would make the Tribunal's decision, made in reliance on the 'authoritative' Tribunal decision, procedurally unfair or founded on a 'wrong factual basis'.

27   *AA (Afghanistan) v Secretary of State for the Home Department* [2007] EWCA Civ 12; *SL (Vietnam) v Secretary of State for the Home Department* [2010] EWCA Civ 225.

28   *R v Secretary of State for the Home Department, ex p Gashi* [1999] Imm AR 415, CA.

29   *G (Turkey)* [2004] UKIAT 00070.

20.101 In the context of the duty of fairness, the Tribunal has a reasonable inquisitorial function[1] to make its own inquiries in the context of full disclosure and discussion of all relevant issues at the hearing, and is entitled to control the hearing by making interventions,[2] but should exercise the power sparingly.[3] Thus, the Tribunal is entitled to put questions to a witness in order to clarify issues that it will need to deal with in the determination. The Tribunal may ask questions intended to seek an explanation for inconsistencies or to address points of concern, even if they have not been raised in the refusal letter or by the parties.[4] Whilst in general, the Tribunal's questions should be asked after the witness has been examined and cross-examined, in some cases it might be more appropriate for the questions to be asked as they arise; interruptions by the Tribunal will not necessarily cause injustice.[5] What Tribunals should not do is to develop a different case to that being pursued by the parties, ask leading questions or questions that conceal their purpose or ask questions in a hostile manner or in a way that suggests that their mind is made up.[6] Where the respondent to an appeal is unrepresented, the Tribunal should ask, either directly or through the appellant's representative, such questions as are necessary to address the issues of credibility raised in the refusal letter and those that are apparent on reading the papers; the Tribunal is not limited to issues of credibility that are raised in the reasons for refusal letter but can put questions on any issue that is not the subject of a clear and unequivocal concession.[7] The propriety of questioning by the Tribunal does not depend upon compliance or non-compliance with the *Surendran Guidelines*[8] but on whether, in all of the circumstances of the case, its questions disclose apparent bias[9] or unfairness.[10] The parties should always be permitted to put any further questions to a witness after questioning by the Tribunal.[11]

1   In *Secretary of State for the Home Department v MN and KY* [2014] UKSC 30 Lord Carnwath said 'in a specialist tribunal, particularly where parties are not represented, there is more scope, and often more need, for the judges to adopt an inquisitorial approach' (at [25]).

2   *R v Immigration Appeal Tribunal and Special Adjudicator, ex p Kumar* (CO 5073/98) (17 April 2000, unreported), QBD; *Moala* (16409) (29 June 1999, unreported), IAT; *Gimedhin* (14019) (21 October 1996, unreported), IAT.

3   There is a fine line between legitimate inquiry and stepping into the respondent's shoes; see eg *Bahar v Immigration Officer, Heathrow* [1988] Imm AR 534; *Muwyngyi* (00052) IAT; *R v Special Adjudicator, ex p Demeter* [2000] Imm AR 424, QBD. Hostile questioning led to the appearance of bias in *XS (Kosovo – adjudicator's conduct – psychiatric report) Serbia and Montenegro* [2005] UKIAT 00093.

4   *Yildizhan* [2002] UKIAT 08315; *K (Côte d'Ivoire)* [2004] UKIAT 00061; *SW (Somalia)* [2005] UKIAT 00037.

5   *Oyono* [2002] UKIAT 02034; *Ali (Shafqat)* [2002] UKIAT 05944; *SW (Somalia)* [2005] UKIAT 00037.

6   *K (Cote d'Ivoire)* [2004] UKIAT 00061; *XS (Serbia and Montenegro)* [2005] UKIAT 00093. A comment during the respondent's submissions that the appellant's account was 'like a Hollywood movie' would not lead an independent minded observer to perceive a risk of bias or unfairness: *KR (Iraq)* [2004] UKIAT 00117.

7   *Surendran* (21679); *MNM* (00/TH/02423) (1 November 2000, unreported), IAT and appended 'Surendran Guidelines'; *WN (DRC)* [2004] UKIAT 00213. In *SW (Somalia)* [2005] UKIAT 00037, the President ruled that *Surendran* and *MNM* should not be cited without *WN*, which represented an 'evolution' of the guidelines. See also *T (Algeria) v Secretary of State for the Home Department* [2003] UKIAT 00128. The Tribunal is not subject to the same obligation to ask questions about issues of credibility that do not arise from perusal of the papers but only in the course of the hearing: *R (on the application of Hyseni) v Immigration Appeal Tribunal* [2002] EWHC 1239 (Admin), [2002] All ER (D) 561 (May).

8   See fn 6 above.

9   *T (Algeria) v Secretary of State for the Home Department* [2003] UKIAT 00128 applying *Porter v Magill* [2001] UKHL 67, [2002] 2 AC 357. For examples of inappropriate questioning by the adjudicator, see *Mohammadiani-Abolvardi v Secretary of State for the Home Department* (01TH02112) (11 October 2001) and *H (Iraq)* [2003] UKIAT 00048.

¹⁰ R *(on the application of Maheshwaran) v Secretary of State for the Home Department* [2002] EWCA Civ 173, [2002] All ER (D) 184 (Feb); *SW (Somalia)* [2005] UKIAT 00037; Ahmed [2002] UKIAT 07468; and *Yildizhan* [2002] UKIAT 08315. See also *IS (Belarus)* [2004] UKIAT 00114.

¹¹ *Secretary of State for the Home Department v Yogalingam* (01TH02671) (4 January 2002), IAT.

20.102 Refusal to hear a witness, or other procedural impropriety by the Tribunal, amounts to a point of law for the purpose of an onward appeal against the decision on the appeal.¹ If on such an application an allegation is made of procedural impropriety in the conduct of a hearing before the Tribunal, it is likely to be perceived as wholly unsubstantiated if made in vague and general terms, and would only be considered arguable if it is sufficiently particularised, and is apparently made or supported by someone in a position to know what happened. Although a witness statement from a representative or a party to the proceedings would not necessarily be required at the permission stage, the application should show that such evidence would be available on the appeal.²

¹ *YB (Jamaica)* [2005] UKIAT 00029.
² *YB (Jamaica)* above; *WN (DRC)* [2004] UKIAT 00213; see also *H (Iraq)* [2003] UKIAT 00048; *Fadhul* [2002] UKIAT 06186; *Yildizhan* [2002] UKIAT 08315. Where an application for permission to appeal is based on an assertion of fact as to what happened before the Tribunal which is at odds with what is said in the determination, the allegation should be supported by evidence: *R (on the application of Bosombanguwa) v Immigration Appeal Tribunal* [2004] EWHC 1656 (Admin).

20.103 The Tribunal should not dictate to representatives which witnesses to call,¹ prevent cross-examination of a witness (although he or she may intervene to prevent unfairness).² or stop re-examination on the basis that a matter had been dealt with in chief.³ At appeal hearings it is the usual practice to exclude witnesses (other than parties) from the hearing room until they give their evidence, a practice which is now provided for in the Procedure Rules,⁴ but which is not a rule of law.⁵ In the vast majority of cases the decision whether an interpreter should be used is for the appellant and his or her advisers, and it is not the function of the Tribunal to disagree or express any view on the matter.⁶ Where an interpreter of the kind requested by an appellant is not provided, with the result that the appellant is inhibited in giving evidence, the Tribunal's adverse assessment of credibility is likely to be unsustainable.⁷ The Tribunal should immediately address any dissatisfaction about the quality of the interpretation raised by a responsible legal representative.⁸ If the Tribunal begins to hear evidence but has to adjourn the hearing owing to problems with the interpreter, it should not continue to hear the case with a new interpreter unless the parties expressly consent owing to the danger of being influenced by the tainted evidence.⁹ It would be unfair for the Tribunal to permit the respondent to call the court interpreter to give opinion evidence about the appellant's language or accent.¹⁰ The Tribunal must ensure that unrepresented appellants are aware of their entitlement to give evidence.¹¹ Women appellants alleging sexual abuse ought to be allowed an all-female Tribunal if requested.¹²

¹ Nabhani (13195) (17 April 1996, unreported), IAT; Petre (12998) (13 February 1996, unreported), IAT; Riasat (13256) (17 April 1996, unreported), IAT; Biley (11579) (22 November 1994, unreported), IAT.
² *GY (Iran)* [2004] UKIAT 00264.
³ *Kamara* (11984) (3 April 1996, unreported), IAT.

4   Tribunal Procedure (First-tier Tribunal)(Immigration and Asylum Chamber) Rules 2014 SI
    2014/2604, r 27(5); *Wadia v Secretary of State for the Home Department* [1977] Imm AR 92.
5   *Moore v Registrar of Lambeth County Court* [1969] 1 All ER 782 at 783–784, DC; *R v
    Immigration Appeal Tribunal, ex p Patel (Jebunisha)* [1996] Imm AR 161, QBD.
6   *Cavusoglu* (15357) (28 May 1997, unreported). But there is no absolute right to an interpreter
    wholly irrespective of need: *R v Special Adjudicator, ex p Naqvi* (23 February 2000,
    unreported), CA.
7   *AT* [2002] UKIAT 02883. But an allegation of incompetence or inaccurate interpretation must
    be made at the hearing: *AW (Somalia)* [2004] UKIAT 00093.
8   *Perera (Jude) v Secretary of State for the Home Department* [2004] EWCA Civ 1002; *Y
    (Afghanistan)* [2003] UKIAT 00100. It was an error of law to permit an interpreter who had
    been criticised by the appellant's interpreter to lower his voice so that he could not be heard:
    SJ (Iran) [2004] UKIAT 00131.
9   *A (Ethiopia)* [2003] UKIAT 00103. The power to transfer proceedings, contained in the 2003
    Procedure Rules, SI 2003/652, r 52, which was held to be an appropriate way of dealing with
    this situation (and others where a part-heard hearing could not be completed: see *I (Somalia)*
    [2004] UKIAT 00062), is absent from the 2005 Rules.
10 *Hydir* [2002] UKIAT 01132 See also *AA (Somalia)* [2008] UKAIT 00029.
11 *Singh (Santokh)* (13002) (22 February 1996, unreported); Tamba (13525) (12 June 1996,
    unreported).
12 *Tiganov* (11193) (29 July 1994, unreported); *Akyol* (14745) (25 March 1997, unreported),
    IAT. See Berkowitz and Jarvis, Asylum Gender Guidelines (IAA, November 2000); H Crawley,
    Refugees and gender: law and process (2001).

EVIDENCE AND FINDINGS

20.104 The Tribunal may issue a witness summons for the purposes of any appeal to require anyone in the UK to attend the hearing to answer questions or to produce relevant documents.[1] If a witness has important evidence to give but neither party wishes to call them, the Tribunal has the power to do so.[2] Where witnesses are called they may be required to give evidence on oath or affirmation,[3] and no witness can be compelled to give any evidence or produce any document which that witness could not be compelled to give or produce in a court of law.[4] The Tribunal may refuse to hear the evidence of a child,[5] vulnerable adult[6] or sensitive witness[7] where it is satisfied that the evidence is not necessary to enable the fair hearing of the case and it must refuse to allow the witness to give evidence if the witness's welfare would be prejudiced by giving evidence.[8] The Tribunal is obliged to consider how to facilitate the giving of evidence by a child, vulnerable adult or sensitive witness and it may be appropriate to direct the giving of evidence by telephone, video link or other means or to direct the appointment of a person with appropriate skills or experience in facilitating the giving of evidence.[9] Evidence obtained by means of torture, whether in the UK or abroad and by whoever obtained is inadmissible in the SIAC or in any other proceedings. In SIAC proceedings, if an appellant raises a plausible reason for believing that evidence relied on against them was obtained by torture, the Commission is bound to initiate relevant inquiries and to exclude the evidence if satisfied on a balance of probabilities that it was so obtained.[10]

1   Tribunal Procedure (First-tier Tribunal) (Immigration and Asylum Chamber) Rules 2014, SI
    2014/2604, r 15.
2   *Kesse v Secretary of State for the Home Department* [2001] EWCA Civ 177, [2001] Imm AR
    366, CA, differing from *Jamali* (TH/131186/84) (25 April 1986, unreported), in which the
    Immigration Appeal Tribunal held that the appellate authority could only call witnesses if the
    parties assented. SI 2014/2604, r 15 expressly provides for the tribunal to summons a witness
    'on its own initiative'.

3. SI 2014/2604, r 14(3).

4. SI 2014/2604, r 15(3).

5. Practice Direction: First-tier and Upper-Tribunal; Child, Vulnerable Adult and Sensitive Witnesses. Senior President of Tribunals, 30 October 2008, para 1 – a child is a person under the age of 18.

6. 'Vulnerable adult' has the same meaning as in the Safeguarding Vulnerable Groups Act 2006 – Practice Direction, para 1b.

7. 'Sensitive witness' means an adult witness where the quality of evidence given by the witness is likely to be diminished by reason of fear or distress on the part of the witness in connection with giving evidence in the case – Practice Direction, para 1c.

8. Practice Direction, para 5.

9. Practice Direction, para 6 and 7.

10. *A v Secretary of State for the Home Department (No 2)* [2005] UKHL 71, [2006] 2 AC 221, [2006] 1 All ER 575.

20.105 The 2005 Procedure Rules provided that the tribunal must not take account of any evidence that had not been made available to the parties,[1] thereby giving effect to the fundamental common law principle that 'a party has a right to know the case against him and the evidence on which it is based'.[2] In its place, the 2014 Procedure Rules[3] adopt a procedure that is inimical to that principle.[4] The rules permit the tribunal to give a direction prohibiting the disclosure of a document or information to a person, including a party to an appeal. Such a direction may be made if the tribunal is satisfied that disclosure would be likely to cause that person or some other person serious harm and that, having regard to the interests of justice, it is proportionate to give the direction.[5] A party may apply to the tribunal for a direction by providing the tribunal with a copy of the document or information and the reason why it should not be disclosed to the other party.[6] The tribunal may also direct that the document or information be disclosed to the representative of the other party if satisfied that that would be in the interests of the other party and that the representative will not make further disclosure to any person, either directly or indirectly, without the tribunal's consent.[7] Moreover, the tribunal is required to ensure that information is not disclosed contrary to the interests of national security.[8] These provisions for withholding from one party evidence that the tribunal considers is of at least doubtful legality. There would need to be express parliamentary authorisation for such a radical departure from fundamental common law principles such as that provided by NIAA 2002, ss 97–98 and the Special Immigration Appeals Commission Act 1997.[9] The enabling legislation allows the Procedure Rules to make provision for the disclosure or non-disclosure of information received during the course of proceedings[10], but does not expressly authorise, as it would have to,[11] a rule permitting non-disclosure of evidence to one of the parties to an appeal. The rules make no provision to mitigate the effects of abandoning so fundamental a principle as the right of a party to know the case against him or her, such as provision for the use of special advocates as in the Special Immigration Appeals Commission. Moreover, it is most unlikely that there will be any appellate supervision of the exercise of the power to consider evidence withheld from a party because the party with a potential interest in appealing will be kept in the dark about the fact and content of the secret evidence.

1. Asylum and Immigration Tribunal (Procedure) Rules 2005, SI 2005/230, r 51(7), subject only to NIAA 2002, s 108 which requires non-disclosure to an appellant where it is alleged that a document is a forgery and disclosure of a matter relating to the detection of forgery would be contrary to the public interest.

2. *Al Rawi v Security Service* [2011] UKSC 34, Lord Hope at [12] and generally.

3   Tribunal Procedure (First-tier Tribunal)(Immigration and Asylum Chamber) Rules 2014, SI
     2014/2604.
4   Scarman J in *Brinkley v Brinkley* [1965] P 75 at 78 said that 'for a court to take into
     consideration evidence which a party to the proceedings has had no opportunity during trial
     to see or hear, and thus to challenge, explain or comment upon, seems to us to strike at the very
     root of the judicial process', cited by Lord Kerr in *Home Office v Tariq* [2011] UKSC 35 at
     [104].
5   SI 2014/2604, r 13(2), (3).
6   SI 2014/2604, r 13(3).
7   SI 2014/2604, r 13(5) and (6).
8   SI 2014/2604, r 13(9).
9   *Al Rawi v The Security Service* [2011] UKSC 34.
10   TCEA 2007, Sch 5, para 11.
11   *R v Lord Chancellor, ex p Witham* [1998] QB 575.

20.106 In appeal hearings, the rules of evidence applicable in a court of law are relaxed. The Procedure Rules provide that the Tribunal may receive evidence that would not be admissible in a civil trial in the UK and (subject to NIAA 2002, section 85A(4)) evidence that was not available to the decision maker.[1] In general, the area of legitimate debate is about relevance and weight, not admissibility.[2] Explanatory statements[3] and refusal letters[4] have been held to be evidence. The judge's sentencing remarks in a criminal trial are admissible in a deportation appeal, along with social work, medical and probation reports prepared for the criminal courts.[5] Prosecution evidence from criminal proceedings against the appellant may be admitted where the Secretary of State relies on it to establish the same facts as had the prosecution, notwithstanding that the criminal proceedings resulted in acquittal.[6] The tribunal does not have a power to exclude relevant evidence because of how it was obtained; the safeguard in respect of prejudicial material obtained unfairly or in breach of relevant procedural protections lies with the tribunal's assessment of the weight, if any, to be given to it.[7] Where the respondent asserts a fact, little if any weight can be given to such assertion without evidence in support.[8] It is for the respondent to make good an allegation of forgery with evidence.[9] There is no overarching prohibition on advocates acting as witnesses, nor any statutory prohibition on Home Office presenting officers doing so. Where the respondent's interviewing officer appeas as advocate in an appeal, there is no procedural unfairness as such. But in the rare case where the interviewing officer is required to give evidence, it may be inappropriate for that person to present the case.[10] An entry clearance officer who is trying to establish the truth as to a claimed relationship is entitled to take into account information obtained from villagers selected at random on a visit to the sponsor's village.[11] Evidence in rebuttal may be admitted from a witness who has carried out a village visit on behalf of an appellant.[12] In cases where the Tribunal may not receive evidence of post-decision facts, as will be seen, evidence of facts not known to the decision maker is admissible.[13] The weight to be attached to such evidence is, within reasonable limits, a matter for the Tribunal.[14] But a witness's evidence supporting an appellant's case must be addressed[15] and given properly reasoned consideration.[16] In an asylum appeal the Tribunal was bound to take account of the grant of refugee status to the witness called to support the appellant's claim although the reliability and relevance of the witness' evidence was a matter for the Tribunal to determine.[17] Written evidence need not be considered unless it is either in English (or, where appropriate, Welsh) or is accompanied by a certified translation.[18]

1. Tribunal Procedure (First-tier Tribunal) (Immigration and Asylum Chamber) Rules 2014, SI 2014/2604, r 14(2). Hearsay evidence is admissible: *R v Immigration Appeal Tribunal, ex p Miah* [1987] Imm AR 143, QBD.

2. Lord Carnwath in *Secretary of State for the Home Department v MN and KY* [2014] UKSC 30 at [24].

3. *R v Immigration Appeal Tribunal, ex p Weerasuriya* [1983] 1 All ER 195, QBD.

4. *R v Secretary of State for the Home Department, ex p Gawe, Abdi v Secretary of State for the Home Department* [1996] Imm AR 288, HL, in the context of the accelerated procedure for certified appeals. These were third country appeals and it is arguable that the majority were swayed by the need for particular speed in such cases. It is unlikely that the decision would be followed today, with the far greater awareness both of the requirements of fairness and of the incidence of mistaken and misleading assertions in decision letters (as to which see **12.123** above). The respondent routinely submits evidence of country conditions in asylum appeals.

5. *Ayo v Immigration Appeal Tribunal* [1990] Imm AR 461, CA; *N (Kenya)* [2004] UKIAT 00009, upheld [2004] EWCA Civ 1094, [2004] INLR 612.

6. *R (on the application of V) v Asylum and Immigration Tribunal and Secretary of State for the Home Department (Interested Party)* [2009] EWHC 1902 (Admin); *Farquharson (Removal – proof of conduct)* [2013] UKUT 146 (IAC).

7. *R (on the application of AN (a child) and FA (a child)) v Secretary of State for the Home Department* [2012] EWCA Civ 1636 (interviews with asylum seeking children conducted in the absence of social workers and appropriate adults); *Bah (EO Turkey) – liability to deport)* [2012] UKUT 00196 (IAC) (anonymous, hearsay evidence); *MB (Admissible evidence; interview records) Iran* [2012] UKUT 19 (IAC).

8. *Gebretensae* (14794) (27 March 1997, unreported); *Lakew* (13214) (17 April 1996, unreported); *Oni* (15886) (2 December 1997, unreported), IAT.

9. *R v Immigration Appeal Tribunal, ex p Shen* [2000] INLR 389, QBD; *Chowdhury (Ahmed Hafiz)* (11721) (30 December 1994, unreported); *Findik* (17029) (12 May 1998, unreported); *Escobar* (20553) (26 March 1999, unreported); *A, B, C and D* (R17367, R21180, R16463, R21181) (3 August 1999, unreported), IAT. See, however, *Kongo-Kongo* (0064) (3 March 2000, unreported); *Waimatha* (16575) (18 August 1998, unreported), IAT; *R v Immigration Appellate Authority, ex p Mohammed (Mukhtar)* [2001] Imm AR 162, QBD, where documentary evidence was patently not genuine on its face.

10. *HK (Interviewer as advocate: unfair?) Ethiopia* [2006] UKAIT 00081.

11. *Visa Officer, Islamabad v Altaf (Mohammed)* [1979–80] Imm AR 141. A previous grant of entry clearance to a woman as wife of the sponsor, although not an estoppel, is evidence relevant to the claimed relationship when another woman later applies for admission in the same capacity: *Visa Officer, Islamabad v Bi (Channo)* [1978] Imm AR 182. Where affidavit evidence about an event is tendered by an applicant or sponsor and is disputed by the Home Office, the matter should be tested in cross-examination and evidence in rebuttal should be tendered: *Kassam v Secretary of State for the Home Department* [1976] Imm AR 20.

12. *R v Immigration Appeal Tribunal, ex p Hussain* [1982] Imm AR 74, QBD.

13. *R v Immigration Appeal Tribunal, ex p Hassanin* [1987] 1 All ER 74, [1986] 1 WLR 1448, CA.

14. *R v Immigration Appeal Tribunal, ex p Kandiya* [1989] Imm AR 491, QBD; *R v Immigration Appeal Tribunal, ex p Khan (Aurangzeb)* [1989] Imm AR 524, QBD.

15. *R (on the application of Sugur) v Secretary of State for the Home Department* (CO 279/2000) (1 November 2000, unreported), CA.

16. *R (on the application of Arzpeyma) v Secretary of State for the Home Department* [2002] EWHC 2395 (Admin), [2002] All ER (D) 21 (Nov) (dismissed on the facts, dismissal upheld at [2004] EWCA Civ 1101, [2004] All ER (D) 340 (Jul)); *AK (Turkey)* [2004] UKIAT 00230.

17. *AC (Somalia)* [2005] UKAIT 00124.

18. Asylum and Immigration Tribunal (Procedure) Rules 2005, SI 2005/230, r 52(1)(b), (2), (3), applied to fast track appeals by SI 2005/560, r 27.

Credibility of witnesses

20.107 Credibility is not in itself a valid end to the function of an immigration judge, and over-emphasis on the issue may distort his or her findings.[1] An adverse credibility finding should not be based solely on the fact that no oral evidence was called at the hearing.[2] However, credibility findings are one of the primary functions of the immigration judge, and in some cases may be the fulcrum of the decision.[3] The appellant must make a case,[4] and where credibility has been put in issue by the respondent, an appellant who does not give evidence cannot complain of an adverse credibility finding.[5] On the other hand, if there is an agreement between the parties as to the facts or a concession as to credibility it would be an error of law for the Tribunal to go behind the agreement.[6] It is an error of law to require corroboration for an appellant's evidence.[7] However, the Tribunal may take account of an unexplained failure to produce supporting evidence that should have been available to the appellant.[8] Where an allegation is made against a previous representative in order to explain a procedural failing or an earlier deficiency in the evidence, it will be difficult to establish the credibility of the allegation if evidence is not produced to show that it was put to the previous representative together with evidence of the previous representative's reply or want of reply.[9]

1   *R v Immigration Appeal Tribunal, ex p Hussain* (CO 990/1995) (25 April 1996, unreported), QBD; *Guine* (13868) (9 September 1996, unreported); *Jawaid* (17159) (20 May 1998, unreported), IAT.
2   *Ahmed (Kaleem) (12774)* (8 November 1995, unreported), IAT; *Gok (15971)* (7 January 1998, unreported); *Coskuner (16769)* (23 July 1998, unreported); *Sad-Chaouche (17423)* (19 June 1998, unreported), IAT; *Kacaj v Secretary of State for the Home Department* [2001] INLR 354 (starred), IAT. Contra when potential witness who could have given highly relevant evidence was sitting in court but was not called: *R v Secretary of State for the Home Department, ex p Kajenthra* [1998] Imm AR 158, QBD.
3   *SW (Somalia)* [2005] UKIAT 00037, where the Tribunal ruled that the extract from *Guine* (fn 1 above) that 'a decision which concentrates primarily on findings of credibility for its outcome is in general more likely to be found to be flawed' was always quoted out of context and should no longer be cited.
4   *Singh (Amrik) v Secretary of State for the Home Department* [2000] Imm AR 340, CA; *Adebola* (16731) (19 August 1998, unreported), IAT; *Nderitu* [2002] UKIAT 01058.
5   *Nassir v Secretary of State for the Home Department* (1999/5682/4) [1999] Imm AR 250, CA (permission). See also *Carcabuk and Bla (00TH0146)*, distinguishing between a concession or agreement on the facts, which the Tribunal should not disturb, and mere failure to challenge, which does not bind it.
6   *Carcabuk and Bla* above; *R (on the application of Ganidagli) v Secretary of State for the Home Department* [2001] EWHC 70 (Admin), [2001] INLR 479. So, for example, when at the end of cross-examination the Secretary of State's representative indicated that 'credibility was not an issue', it should not have been questioned: *Kabanda* (2001) (01TH01401), IAT.
7   *Saspo* (14759) (24 March 1997, unreported); *Ozer (Nazim)* (14698) (13 March 1997, unreported), IAT; *Otkay* (01TH00722) (April 2001, unreported), IAT; *Yildirim* (01TH02606) (14 November 2001, unreported), IAT; *Ates* [2002] UKIAT 06221.
8   *Jeichandrapalan* (01TH00512) (10 May 2001, unreported), IAT; *Jeyabalan* [2002] UKIAT 05992 (para 7); *Khan (Rashid)* [2002] UKIAT 06026; *C v Secretary of State for the Home Department* [2006] EWCA Civ 151, [2006] All ER (D) 122 (Feb) and *TK (Burundi) v Secretary of State for the Home Department* [2009] EWCA Civ 40, [2009] All ER (D) 29 (Feb).
9   *MM (Burundi)* [2004] UKIAT 00182*; *SV (Iran)* [2005] UKAIT 00160.

20.108 Where there is corroboration, it should be taken into account.[1] Supporting evidence should not be dismissed out of hand as 'self-serving'[2] or because of the witness' relationship with the appellant.[3] All of the evidence must be considered as part of a global assessment, and credibility should not be determined in advance of consideration of all the documentary, expert and other evidence capable of having a bearing on the issue.[4] Prejudicial evidence of little probative value should not be the basis of an adverse credibility finding.[5] Caution should be exercised in relying on past deception,[6] or on the demeanour of a witness whose language and culture is different.[7] It is perfectly possible for a witness not to be telling the truth or to be exaggerating about certain matters, but for the centre-piece of his or her story to stand[8] and the significance of lies told by an asylum seeker is pre-eminently a matter for the tribunal.[9] Late disclosure of a material fact may result from an asylum seeker's inhibition due to fear of his or her authorities[10] or cultural taboos[11] rather than indicating recent fabrication. Whether the Tribunal is entitled to make an adverse finding on the credibility of a witness whose evidence was not challenged at the hearing appears to depend on how obvious the discrepancies giving rise to the adverse finding are, or whether (in the case of an appellant) the respondent had already referred to them in the refusal letter.[12] The absence of specific challenge to a document[13] or a relationship[14] relied by an appellant might render rejection of the document or relationship unfair. In assessing credibility, the interview record should be approached with caution where there have been breaches of PACE codes[15] or defective[16] or confrontational questioning,[17] or where the record of interview was written substantially later,[18] or where the interview was a preliminary one[19] or where the applicant had felt unwell or tired,[20] or could not be represented at the interview because of the lack of LSC funding and the interview was not tape recorded.[21] Failure to give reasoned consideration to a complaint about the interpretation of the appellant's evidence at the hearing would vitiate the decision.[22]

[1]   *Immigration Officer, Heathrow v Mirani* [1990] Imm AR 132; *Atwal* (13948) (7 October 1996, unreported); *Aygun* (14091) (11 November 1996, unreported), IAT; *AK (Turkey)* [2004] UKIAT 00230.

[2]   *Quijano* (13693) (16 July 1996, unreported); *Malakar* (16540) (23 September 1998, unreported), IAT. See also the useful remarks in *Re RS* (135/92), New Zealand Refugee Status Appeals Authority (27 August 1991, unreported); *Meadows (John) v Minister for Immigration and Multicultural Affairs* [1998] 1706 FCA (23 December 1998), Canada; *R (on the application of Shire) v Secretary of State for the Home Department* [2004] EWHC 874 (Admin).

[3]   *DP (Israel) v Secretary of State for the Home Department* [2006] EWCA Civ 1375.

[4]   *MT (Credibility assessment flawed, Virjon B applied) Syria* [2004] UKIAT 00307; *Mibanga v Secretary of State for the Home Department* [2005] EWCA Civ 367; *HE (DRC – Credibility and Psychiatric Reports)* [2004] UKIAT 00321; *Malaba v Secretary of State for the Home Department* [2006] EWCA Civ 820.

[5]   *Iqbal (Pervez) v Immigration Appeal Tribunal* [1988] Imm AR 469, CA; *Ozmico* [2002] UKIAT 00484.

[6]   *R v Immigration Appeal Tribunal, ex p Miah* (12 October 1995, unreported), QBD; *Mahmood* (10629) (3 February 1994, unreported); *Majri* (12406) (9 August 1995, unreported); *Fernando* (11878) (23 February 1995, unreported); *Ibrahim* (17270) (17 June 1998, unreported); *Achiou* (2001) (01TH00159), para 10.

[7]   *Daniel* (13623) (2 July 1996, unreported); *Guarichico and Sarabia-Molina* (20230) (25 November 1999, unreported), IAT; *Luwuzi* [2002] UKIAT 07186. The Tribunal in *Khan (Rashid)* [2002] UKIAT 06026 accepted that it would be grossly unfair to judge credibility from demeanour where this might be affected by the medication taken by an appellant.

[8]   *Chiver* [1997] INLR 212, IAT; *MA (Somalia) v Secretary of State for the Home Department* [2010] UKSC 49.

[9]   *KU (Pakistan) v Secretry of State for the Home Department* [2012] EWCA Civ 107.

[10]   The Tribunal accepted this explanation in *Sharafi* [2002] UKIAT 08115.

[11]   *R (on the application of S) v Secretary of State for the Home Department* [2003] EWHC 352 (Admin), [6]; see also *R v Secretary of State for the Home Department, ex p Ejon* [1998] INLR 195.

[12]   See cases cited at **20.100** ff above; see also *Gaima v Secretary of State for the Home Department* [1989] Imm AR 65; *R v Special Adjudicator, ex p John* [1999] Imm AR 432; *R v Special Adjudicator, ex p Hassan* [2001] Imm AR 83.

13 *Secretary of State for the Home Department v Oleed* [2002] EWCA Civ 1906; [2003] INLR 179; *Luwuzi* [2002] UKIAT 07186.

14 *R (on the application of Kolcak) v Immigration Appeal Tribunal* [2001] Imm AR 666, para 25.

15 *Ziraret* (12024) (19 April 1995, unreported), IAT.

16 *R v Secretary of State for the Home Department, ex p Akdogan* [1995] Imm AR 176; *Risan* (12551) (26 September 1995, unreported), IAT.

17 *Uruthiran* (21813) (8 March 2000, unreported), IAT; see also the Tribunal's comments in *Kara* [2002] UKIAT 01083, paras 16–17.

18 *Singh (Daya Pal)* (14829) (3 April 1997, unreported), IAT. But it was wrong to disregard interview notes merely because they were not read back to the claimant or signed by him or her: *DA (Turkey)* [2004] UKIAT 00104.

19 *Salim* (13202) (17 April 1996, unreported); *Mayisokele* (13039) (23 February 1996, unreported); *Vimaleswaran* (15493) (26 August 1997, unreported); *Jeevaponkalan* (17742) (24 July 1998, unreported); *Adong* (20404) (15 November 1999, unreported), IAT. Failure to mention a matter of great importance at the initial interview may, however, be taken into account: *R v Secretary of State for the Home Department, ex p Agbonmenio* [1996] Imm AR 69, QBD (leave).

20 *Velasco* (HX00476) (11 October 1999, unreported), IAT.

21 *R (on the application of Dirshe) v Secretary of State for the Home Department* [2005] EWCA Civ 421, [2005] 1 WLR 2685. See **12.124** above.

22 *Y (Afghanistan)* [2003] UKIAT 00100.

20.109 It is inherently dangerous to place too much weight on 'plausibility' when assessing credibility because an immigration judge's judgment as to what is plausible is bound to be influenced by his or her own values and environment.[1] The Court of Appeal has warned that reliance by a decision maker on the 'inherent probability' of an account 'can be a dangerous, even a wholly inappropriate, factor to rely on in some asylum cases. Much of the evidence will be referable to societies with customs and circumstances that are very different from those of which the members of the fact-finding Tribunal have any (even second-hand) experience. Indeed, it is likely that the country that an asylum-seeker has left will be suffering from the sort of problems and dislocations with which the overwhelming majority of residents of this country will be wholly unfamiliar. The point is well made in *Hathaway on the Law of Refugee Status* (1991) at p 81: 'In assessing the general human rights information, decision makers must constantly be on guard to avoid implicitly recharacterizing the nature of the risk based on their own perceptions of reasonability'.[2] Moreover, there is a danger of judges erroneously substituting assessment of whether an occurrence is inherently likely for assessment of whether it actually took place.[3] Decisions on credibility must be reasoned, just as decisions on other aspects of the case.[4] An assessment of credibility should be made on the basis of a holistic assessment of all of the evidence in which supporting evidence (including medical and country expert reports, background evidence and and supporting witnesses) is weighed in favour of a positive finding on credibility; it is an error of approach for the Tribunal first to come to a negative assessment of credibility and then ask itself whether that assessment is displaced by any of the other material.[5] An immigration judge may rely on discrepancies in an appellant's testimony to put his or her veracity in question but they must also be evaluated in the context of the evidence as a whole; in some cases it is sufficient for the judge to identify the discrepancy and state his or her conclusion on the appellant's veracity. In other cases, the nature of the discrepancy may require further explanation of why it does or does not undermine the veracity of the testimony.[6] For credibility in the context of the burden of proof in asylum appeals, see Chapter 12.

¹ *Kasolo* (13190) (1 April 1996, unreported); *Ali (Ibrahim)* [2002] UKIAT 07001, and see the Tribunal's approach in *MM (plausibility) (DRC)* [2005] UKIAT 00019.

² *HK v Secretary of State for the Home Department* [2006] EWCA Civ 1037, [2006] All ER (D) 281 (Jul). See also *Y v Secretary of State for the Home Department* [2006] EWCA Civ 1223.

³ *A v Secretary of State for the Home Department* [2006] EWCA Civ 973 at [7].

⁴ *R v Immigration Appeal Tribunal, ex p Adin (Senol)* (CO 4533/98) (13 July 2000, unreported), QBD; *R v Secretary of State for the Home Department, ex p Chugtai* [1995] Imm AR 559; *Mecheti v Secretary of State for the Home Department* [1996] SCLR 998.

⁵ See the Court of Appeal's guidance in *Karanakaran v Secretary of State for the Home Department* [2000] Imm AR 271 and see also *R (on the application of Beqaraj) v Special Adjudicator* [2002] EWHC 1469 (Admin), [2002] All ER (D) 99 (Jun); *R (on the application of Perbalathan) v Immigration Appeal Tribunal* [2002] Imm AR 200; *R (on the application of Gautam) v Immigration Appellate Authority* [2003] EWHC 1160 (Admin); *FZ (Afghanistan)* [2004] UKIAT 00304; see also below. See also *Diaby v Secretary of State for the Home Department* [2005] EWCA Civ 651, [2005] All ER (D) 32 (Jul); *Mibanga v Secretary of State for the Home Department* [2005] EWCA Civ 367, [2005] All ER (D) 307 (Mar); *SA (Somalia) v Secretary of State for the Home Department* [2006] EWCA Civ 1302, [2006] All ER (D) 103 (Oct), confirming the principle in *Mibanga*. See also *Semu v Secretary of State for the Home Department* [2006] EWCA Civ 1153, [2006] All ER (D) 45 (Jul) and *AJ (Cameroon) v Secretary of State for the Home Department* [2007] EWCA Civ 373, [2007] All ER (D) 168 (Jun).

⁶ *HK v Secretary of State for the Home Department* [2006] EWCA Civ 1037 and see also *Y v Secretary of State for the Home Department* [2006] EWCA Civ 1223.

20.110 Section 8 of the Asylum and Immigration (Treatment of Claimants, etc) Act 2004 identifies various matters which the Tribunal is obliged to consider as damaging the credibility of an asylum seeker or human rights claimant.¹ The obligation arises even if the matter predates the coming into force of s 8.² However, the assessment of credibility remains a matter for the Tribunal considering the evidence as a whole and attaching such weight to individual features of the evidence as the Tribunal considers appropriate.³ The word 'potentially' is to be read into s 8 so that various matters are 'potentially damaging' of the appellant's credibility. Otherwise the provision would be inconsistent with the principles of legality and the separation of powers whereby the judicial decision maker is required to make his or her own decision on credibility.⁴

¹ See Chapter 12.

² *MM (Iran)* [2005] UKAIT 00115.

³ *SM (Iran)* [2005] UKAIT 00116. See also Carnwath LJ's judgment in *Y v Secretary of State for the Home Department* [2006] EWCA Civ 1223.

⁴ *JT (Cameroon) v Secretary of State for the Home Department* [2008] EWCA Civ 878, [2008] All ER (D) 348 (Jul).

Documentary evidence

20.111 All documentary evidence in support of the claim must be considered,¹ unless it is not in English or Welsh (in proceedings in Welsh or that have a connection with Wales) or accompanied by a certified translation.² The burden is on the individual relying on the document to establish that it supports his or her case and it is open to the Tribunal to find, in the context of the evidence as a whole, that the document cannot be relied on; there is no obligation on the respondent to make detailed inquiries about the document or to show that it is a forgery,³ nor is it necessary for the Tribunal to identify any evidence, either intrinsic or extrinsic to the document, showing it to be unreliable.[4] However, in exceptional circumstances, where a document is central to a protection claim and a simple process of enquiry would resolve the issue of its reliability, there may be an obligation on the Secretary of State to investigate the document. It is a matter for the tribunal to decide whether there was such an obligation and what consequences should follow from any failure to discharge the obligation.[5] Where the Secretary of State asserts that a document is a forgery, she bears the burden of proving it.[6] An allegation by an entry clearance officer that a document is forged is not entitled to evidential weight.[7] A document should not be found to be inauthentic without a challenge to its authenticity being made or without a warning to the appellant and absent a finding that a document is inauthentic, cogent reasons need to be given as to why the document does not support the appellant's case.[8] Late production of documents is not by itself a good reason for regarding them as unreliable,[9] nor by itself is the fact that what is produced is a poor photocopy.[10]

[1] Okwu (14518) (6 March 1997, unreported); *Yilmaz* (11896) (13 March 1995, unreported); *Karanakaran v Secretary of State for the Home Department* [2000] Imm AR 271.

[2] Tribunal Procedure (First-tier Tribunal) (Immigration and Asylum Chamber) Rules 2014, SI 2014/2604, r 12(5), (6).

[3] *Ahmed (Tanveer) v Secretary of State for the Home Department* [2002] UKIAT 00439; [2002] Imm AR 318; [2002] INLR 345 (starred).

[4] *R (on the application of Davila-Puga) v Immigration Appeal Tribunal* [2001] EWCA Civ 931, [2001] All ER (D) 393 (May); *Zarandy v Secretary of State for the Home Department* [2002] EWCA Civ 153, [2002] All ER (D) 355 (Jan); *Mungu v Secretary of State for the Home Department* [2003] EWCA Civ 360, [2003] All ER (D) 289 (Feb).

[5] *PJ (Sri Lanka) v Secretary of State for the Home Department* [2014] EWCA Civ 1011.

[6] *R v Immigration Appeal Tribunal, ex p Shen* [2000] INLR 389. Immigration judges are not forensic experts and should not make findings that documents have been forged on their own initiative, unless forgery is obvious: *Luwuzi* [2002] UKIAT 07186.

[7] *RP (Nigeria)* [2006] UKAIT 00086, disagreeing with *KS (Pakistan)* [2005] UKAIT 00171 which expressed the contrary conclusion.

[8] *Secretary of State for the Home Department v Oleed* [2002] EWCA Civ 1906, [2003] INLR 179, [2003] Imm AR 499; *M (Peru) v Secretary of State for the Home Department* [2003] UKIAT 00029; *HA (Iraq) v Secretary of State for the Home Department* [2006] EWCA Civ 1373.

[9] *M (Peru) v Secretary of State for the Home Department*, ibid.

[10] *O (Turkey) v Secretary of State for the Home Department* [2003] UKIAT 00006; *R (on the application of AM) v Secretary of State for the Home Department* [2011] EWCA Civ 443.

Medical and psychiatric evidence

20.112 In asylum and human rights appeals, medical and psychiatric evidence capable of supporting an appellant's claim deserves careful and specific consideration,[1] and Tribunals should not make credibility findings in isolation from it.[2] An experienced immigration judge must have regard to the possibility that the quality of a witness' evidence may be affected by his or her mental state, which might explain inconsistency and forgetfulness.[3] A lay person cannot express a view on a medical matter without the benefit of medical evidence and should not reject a doctor's prognosis, without contrary medical evidence or without giving adequate reasons for doing so.[4] Evaluation of a patient's account of his or her symptoms is a fundamental aspect of a medical practitioner's expertise and so it is not open to the Tribunal to reach a conclusion that the expert has been misled by an exaggerated or dishonest account without good and objective reason for doing so.[5] However, the tribunal is entitled to assess the weight to be given to a medical report,[6] taking into account the doctor's qualifications, specialisation and experience,[7] the quality of the doctor's reasoning[8] and the extent to which any conclusion is related to established diagnostic criteria,[9] and the material on which the opinion is based.[10] The tribunal's obligation is to consider medical evidence with appropriate care, demonstrated by giving adequate reasons; it is not bound to accept a medical expert's opinion as to causation of physical or psychiatric injury.[11] The Tribunal should not regard the account given to the doctor as being unreliable without first of all deciding whether the doctor's opinion supports a positive finding as to the credibility of the appellant,[12] but a negative inference may be drawn from inconsistencies between the history given to a doctor and the evidence given to the Secretary of State or the Tribunal.[13] An immigration judge should not reject an appellant's account of being tortured on the ground that there were no visible marks on the appellant's body unless medical evidence or the judge's own, explicitly disclosed expertise established that such marks would be present.[14] A GP's report is capable of constituting independent evidence of torture.[15] A medical report that merely documents scars or injuries without stating the doctor's opinion as to their consistency with the appellant's account will have little or no corroborative weight.[16] On the other hand, a medical practitioner's opinion as to the causation of scarring constitutes evidence of causation independent of the appellant's testimony.[17] Those preparing medical reports intended as corroborative should have regard to the Istanbul Protocol, in particular, paragraphs 186–187 on 'Examination and Evaluation following specific forms of torture'.[18] Where a doctor had given detailed evidence, corroborative of an appellant's account, about the likely causation of injuries, more was required to explain rejection of that evidence than the assertion that the injuries were equally consistent with incidents in an agrarian community not involving violence.[19] Greater weight would be given to a medical report that considered and commented on the likelihood of other possible causes for the person's injuries.[20] Where medical evidence showed that scarring could have been caused as the appellant claimed, it would be unfair to reject his or her evidence as to causation in the absence of cross-examination proposing an alternative cause.[21]

1   *Mohammed (Swaleh)* (12412) (4 August 1995, unreported); *Ibrahim v Secretary of State for the Home Department* [1998] INLR 511, IAT; *Guney* (19159) (4 August 1999, unreported); *Sivakarathas* (01056) (12 May 2000, unreported), IAT.

2   *Kitshi* (11920) (23 March 1995, unreported). It is putting the cart before the horse to make an adverse assessment of credibility, based on the appellant's oral evidence, and then reject the medical evidence he or she has produced in support: *R (on the application of Beqaraj) v Special Adjudicator* [2002] EWHC 1469 (Admin), [2002] All ER (D) 99 (Jun); *MT (Syria)* [2004] UKIAT 00307. See also *Diaby v Secretary of State for the Home Department* [2005] EWCA Civ 651, [2005] All ER (D) 32 (Jul).

3   *Mageto v Immigration Appeal Tribunal* [1996] Imm AR 56, CA; *Yahiaoui* [2002] UKIAT 03504; *Khan (Rashid)* [2002] UKIAT 06026. However, in *Singh (Amrik) v Secretary of State for the Home Department* [2000] Imm AR 340 the Court of Appeal held that psychiatric evidence of the effect of an appellant's mental state on his ability to recall reliably entitled the Tribunal to find his evidence unreliable and so reject his claim – an illustration of the double-edged nature of such evidence. The UNHCR Handbook recommends reliance on other sources of evidence in the case of mentally disturbed asylum claimants (paras 206–212). Where medical evidence shows that an appellant is suffering mental, psychological or emotional trauma or disability, it is incumbent on the judge to show that they have applied the Joint Presidential Guidance Note No 2 of 2010: 'Child, vulnerable adult and sensitive appellant guidance and, in particular, that the judge has considered whether discrepancies or

lack of clarity in the oral evidence may have been the result of the witness' age, vulnerability or sensitivity: *JL (Medical reports – credibility) China* [2013] UKUT 145 (IAC).

4   *R v Secretary of State for the Home Department, ex p Khaira* [1998] INLR 731. See also *P (Yugoslavia)* [2003] UKIAT 00017; *Secretary of State for the Home Department v S (Georgia)* [2003] UKIAT 00082; *Januzi v Secretary of State for the Home Department* [2003] EWCA Civ 1188; *R (on the application of Minani) v Immigration Appeal Tribunal* [2004] EWHC 582 (Admin), [2004] All ER (D) 410 (Feb).

5   *Y (Sri Lanka) v Secretary of State for the Home Department* [2009] EWCA Civ 362; *R (on the application of AM) v Secretary of State for the Home Department* [2012] EWCA Civ 521.

6   *SP (Yugoslavia)* [2003] UKIAT 00017; *KK v Secretary of State for the Home Department* [2005] EWCA Civ 1082, [2005] All ER (D) 214 (Jul).

7   *Demaku* [2002] UKIAT 06001; *SP (Yugoslavia)*, ibid.

8   *Jeyarajasingham* (2001) (01TH00845), IAT, para 16 (reasoning to be expected in medical reports dealing with scars). Expert psychiatrists exercise their critical faculties and experience, and should not be treated as accepting claimants' accounts uncritically: *R (on the application of Minani) v Immigration Appeal Tribunal* [2004] EWHC 582 (Admin), [2004] All ER (D) 410 (Feb); *Ademaj* [2002] UKIAT 00979.

9   *Demaku*, above; *Secretary of State for the Home Department v Lama* [2002] UKIAT 07554; *M (DRC)* [2003] UKIAT 00054.

10   *Secretary of State for the Home Department v AE and FE* [2002] UKIAT 05237 [2003] Imm AR 152. This might include consideration how many times the psychiatrist met the subject of the report and for how long, what if any medical records were seen, and the extent to which the psychiatrist relied on the subject's untested account: *Cinar* [2002] UKIAT 06624; see also *SP (Yugoslavia)* [2003] UKIAT 00017. In *HE (DRC)* [2004] UKIAT 00321 'Reported', the Tribunal urged advocates seeking to support credibility by reference to medical reports to show that the support it provides is independent of what the claimant has told the psychiatrist.

11   *SS (Sri Lanka) v Secretary of State for the Home Department* [2012] EWCA Civ 155; *IY (Turkey) v Secretary of State for the Home Department* [2012] EWCA Civ 1560 where the Court of Appeal held that the tribunal had been entitled to find that the appellant had 'hoodwinked' the psychiatrist into accepting his account.

12   *R (on the application of Gautam) v Immigration Appellate Authority* [2003] EWHC 1160 (Admin), [2003] All ER (D) 81 (May); *R (on the application of Beqaraj) v Special Adjudicator* [2002] EWHC 1469 (Admin), [2002] All ER (D) 99 (Jun); *M (DRC)* [2003] UKIAT 00054.

13   *Basak* [2002] UKIAT 03570.

14   *Reka v Secretary of State for the Home Department* [2006] EWCA Civ 552, [2006] All ER (D) 224 (May).

15   *R (on the application of D) v Secretary of State for the Home Department; R (on the application of K) v same* [2006] EWHC 980 (Admin), 150 Sol Jo LB 743, [2006] All ER (D) 300 (May).

16   *SA (Somalia) v Secretary of State for the Home Department* [2006] EWCA Civ 1302, [2006] All ER (D) 103 (Oct).

17   *R (AM) v Secretary of State for the Home Department* [2012] EWCA Civ 521.

18   *SA v Secretary of State for the Home Department*. The Istanbul Protocol is the Manual on the Effective Investigation and Documentation of Torture and Other Cruel, Inhuman or Degrading Treatment of Punishment (Submitted to the United Nations High Commissioner for Human Rights – 9 August 1999). Under the heading 'D. Examination and Evaluation following specific forms of Torture' the Istanbul Protocol says:

'186.   . . .   For each lesion and for the overall pattern of lesions, the physician should indicate the degree of consistency between it and the attribution:

(a)   Not consistent: the lesion could not have been caused by the trauma described;

(b)   Consistent with: the lesion could have been caused by the trauma described, but it is non-specific and there are many other possible causes;

(c)   Highly consistent: the lesion could have been caused by the trauma described, and there are few other possible causes;

(d)   Typical of: this is an appearance that is usually found with this type of trauma, but there are other possible causes;

(e)   Diagnostic of: this appearance could not have been caused in anyway other than that described.

187.   Ultimately, it is the overall evaluation of all lesions and not the consistency of each lesion with a particular form of torture that is important in assessing the torture story (see Chapter IV.G for a list of torture methods).'

[19] *KP (Sri Lanka) v Secretary of State for the Home Department* [2007] EWCA Civ 62, [2007] All ER (D) 91 (Jan).
[20] *RT (Sri Lanka)* [2008] UKAIT 00009.
[21] *RR (Sri Lanka)* [2010] UKUT 000274 (IAC).

Expert evidence and country background evidence

20.113 Credibility findings can only really be made on the basis of a complete understanding of the entire picture, placing a claim into the context of the background information regarding the country of origin,[1] although going into detail about the background circumstances will not always be necessary or fruitful,[2] and the Tribunal is not required to set out in detail all the background evidence it has read.[3] Instead of simply rejecting a claim to fear being persecuted because of a young appellant's inability to explain why she should be at risk, particular reliance should be placed on the background material to see whether it affords an explanation.[4] Where the background evidence is in conflict, the Tribunal and the courts have expressed a preference for independent, sourced reports,[5] but where there are divergent opinions from reputable human rights organisations about the conditions in a country, there should be an in-depth examination to see if the evidence can be reconciled,[6] and a real attempt to balance them.[7] If they cannot be reconciled, the Tribunal should give reasons for preferring one report over another.[8] The approach to the assessment of country information adopted by the European Court of Human Rights should be followed by the Tribunal in human rights and asylum cases,[9] requiring consideration of the source of the information and in particular, its independence, reliability and objectivity, the authority and reputation of its author, the method of investigation, the consistency of its conclusions with and corroboration by other sources and the presence and reporting capacity of the author of the material in the country in question.[10] Guidance about country conditions given in a UNHCR report or guidance would 'typically command very considerable respect' because of its intrinsic quality rather than the status of its author, but ultimately, its weight would be a matter for the tribunal.[11] It would be overly prescriptive to say (as the tribunal did) that advice about a country's situation from professional diplomats in a British embassy 'must be given significant weight', equivalent to that of a well-informed expert.[12] The Tribunal need not invite oral evidence from an expert witness whose report he or she is minded to reject,[13] but expert evidence[14] should not be rejected merely because it has not been tested in cross-examination,[15] or because it does not identify its sources,[16] nor should it be rejected as 'mere speculation'.[17] The Court of Appeal has been critical of the cursory and at times contemptuous way the appellate authorities have treated the evidence of reputable experts, and has pointed out that such evidence should not be lightly rejected[18] and that the Tribunal is 'bound to place heavy reliance on the views of experts and specialists'.[19] The Tribunal should not reject the opinion of an expert on grounds of the expert's 'partiality' without explaining why that label is applied to that expert.[20] In its reasoning it should clearly indicate what it has accepted from expert reports.[21] But expert witnesses' duty is to the court and it is important that they appreciate that, comply with it, believe in the truth of the facts in the report and the accuracy of the opinion given, cover all relevant matters and set out any matters affecting its validity.[22] Given the expert's obligation to provide an impartial opinion an instructing solicitor should not put leading questions to the witness.[23] In *Slimani*,[24] a starred Tribunal approved the guidance given in *The Ikarian Reefer*[25] that to be relied on, the expert needs to provide independent assistance to the Tribunal, must not assume the role of an advocate,[26] and needs to specify the facts on which his or her opinion is based. The Tribunal deprecated the practice of putting in evidence in one case expert reports prepared for a different case, unless the report is specified as a general one or the author has given his consent.[27] Foreign law is a question of fact which should be determined, in the absence of agreement between the parties, by expert evidence,[28] but in the absence of such evidence the appellate authority may review questions of foreign law for itself.[29] A tribunal should give weight to the assessment by a probation officer as to the risk of an appellant reoffending, but it would be entitled to depart from it if there were cogent, evidence-based reasons for doing so.[30] Practice directions make detailed provision about instructing experts and about how expert reports should be produced.[31]

1   UNHCR Handbook paras 42–43; *R v Immigration Appeal Tribunal, ex p Ahmed (Sardar)* [1999] INLR 473 (QBD); *Horvath v Secretary of State for the Home Department* [1999] Imm AR 121, [1999] INLR 7 (IAT); *Suleyman* (16242) (11 February 1998, unreported); *Tharunalingam* (18452) [QUERY – CITE MISSING]; *Gurung v Secretary of State for the Home Department* [2003] EWCA Civ 654, [2003] All ER (D) 14 (May). For an example of the danger of assessing credibility in isolation, see *R v Immigration Appeal Tribunal, ex p Pratheepan* (CO 1102/98) (27 April 1999, unreported), QBD (adjudicator dismissed advocate's letter on basis of ignorance of legal procedures in Sri Lanka). See also *R (on the application of Gulbudek) v Immigration Appeal Tribunal* (CO 2174/2000) (21 November 2000, unreported), where an adjudicator's conclusion that the Turkish authorities would investigate rape and torture allegations was quashed as perverse; and *R (on the application of Vuckovic) v Special Adjudicator* (CO 3021/2000) (18 December 2000, unreported) (adjudicator unfair to determine case without Home Office country assessment which lent support to appellant's case).
2   *R v Secretary of State for the Home Department, ex p Befekadu* [1999] Imm AR 467, QBD.
3   *R (on the application of Shockrollahy) v Immigration Appellate Authority* [2000] Imm AR 580, QBD.
4   *De Sousa v Secretary of State for the Home Department* [2006] EWCA Civ 183, [2006] All ER (D) 60 (Feb).
5   *Mario v Secretary of State for the Home Department* [1998] Imm AR 281, [1998] INLR 306, IAT; *Drrias v Secretary of State for the Home Department* [1997] Imm AR 346, CA (value of 'bland' FCO letter questioned); *X* (98/0474/4) 24 July 1998, CA (UNHCR report might deserve more weight than that of a national immigration authority). UNHCR reports have been seen as the most reliable: see *Ragavan* (15350) (21 August 1997, unreported); *Teshome* (15693).
6   *Hassen* (15558) (3 October 1997, unreported); see also *Lahori* (G0062) (7 October 1998, unreported), IAT.
7   *Mulumba* (14760) (24 March 1997, unreported).
8   *Thillarajah* (14606) (10 March 1997, unreported); *Vasikaran* (15241) (4 July 1997, unreported), IAT.
9   *TK (Sri Lanka) CG* [2009] UKAIT 00049.
10 *NA v United Kingdom* (Application 25904/07) (2008) 48 EHRR 337, [2008] ECHR 616.
11 *HF (Iraq) v Secretary of State for the Home Department* [2013] EWCA Civ 1276. See also *IA v Secretary of State for the Home Department* [2014] UKSC 6 as to the particular expertise and standing of UNHCR.
12 *MD (Ivory Coast) v Secretary of State for the Home Department* [2011] EWCA Civ 989.
13 *R v Secretary of State for the Home Department, ex p Khanafer* [1996] Imm AR 212.
14 On expert evidence generally, see *Secretary of State for the Home Department v MN and KY* [2014] UKSC 30.
15 *Singh (Tarlochan) v Secretary of State for the Home Department* [2000] Imm AR 36. The written evidence of an expert, even if untested in cross-examination, is entitled to the respect due to persons who possess the relevant expertise: *Kilic* [2002] UKIAT 02714. But the testimony of an expert witness who did attend court would be highly important: *Zheng* (20271) (1 April 1999, unreported).

16 It is in the nature of an expert report that the expert is the source, although reference to sources would add weight to the expert's opinion: *Secretary of State for the Home Department v Markos* [2002] UKIAT 08313. But see *Slimani* (01TH00092) (12 February 2001, unreported), (starred) IAT.

17 *Karanakaran v Secretary of State for the Home Department* [2000] Imm AR 271, CA. See also *Gomez* [2000] INLR 549; *Kapela v Secretary of State for the Home Department* [1998] Imm AR 294.

18 *Karanakaran* above; see also the Court of Appeal's observations in granting permission to appeal in *R v Immigration Appeal Tribunal, ex p Es-Eldin* (C/00/2681) (29 November 2000, unreported), subsequently allowing by consent the appeal against the QBD decision reported in [2001] Imm AR 98. See also *Singh (Tarlochan) v Secretary of State for the Home Department* [2000] Imm AR 36. For an example, see *SA (Syria) v Secretary of State for the Home Department* [2007] EWCA Civ 1390 where the court criticised the Tribunal's treatment of a letter from Amnesty International as 'unsourced', contrary to current Tribunal country guidance and therefore entitled to little weight. In the same case, the Tribunal's treatment of the reports of two experts was said to have been so cursory as not to have engaged with them at all.

19 *S v Secretary of State for the Home Department* [2002] EWCA Civ 539; [2002] INLR 416. The Tribunal has also emphasised the importance of giving proper consideration to expert reports: see eg *Misrak (Habteselassie)* (00308) (28 February 2000, unreported). More recently, in *SI (Iraq) CG* [2008] UKAIT 00094, the Tribunal said: 'In general the Tribunal takes the view that a country expert's opinion is to be given significant weight and if the Tribunal decides to come to a different view from an expert on key matters, proper reasons must be given'.

20 *Cherbal* [2002] UKIAT 02014. The Tribunal would, however, exercise particular care in assessing the weight to be attached to views expressed by an individual whose opinions were adduced on a regular basis in case his or her views were influenced, even unconsciously, by the hope of receiving further, similar instructions: *KA (Somalia) v Secretary of State for the Home Department* [2006] EWCA Civ 1324, approving *AA* [2004] UKIAT 00221.

21 *Djebari v Secretary of State for the Home Department* [2002] EWCA Civ 813, [2002] All ER (D) 184 (May). But equally, the Tribunal should not accept expert evidence uncritically, without explaining why it is preferred to a body of reputable evidence which contradicts it: *Djebbar v Secretary of State for the Home Department* [2004] EWCA Civ 804, [2004] 33 LS Gaz R 36.

22 *Thambiah* (01372) (10 May 2000, unreported), IAT. Expert reports should show the status of their author and be specifically relevant to the case: *R v Immigration Appeal Tribunal, ex p Kilinc* [1999] Imm AR 588.

23 *Y (Sri Lanka) v Secretary of State for the Home Department* [2009] EWCA Civ 362.

24 *Slimani* (01TH00092) (starred) (12 February 2001, unreported), IAT.

25 *National Justice Cia Naviera SA v Prudential Assurance Co Ltd, The Ikarian Reefer* [1993] 2 Lloyd's Rep 68 at 81–2.

26 As the expert was held to have done in *MF (Albania) v Secretary of State for the Home Department* [2014] EWCA Civ 902.

27 *Slimani* (01TH00092) (starred) (1 February 2001), IAT; *Singh (Armardeep)* (00943) (28 April 2000); *Zheng* (20271) (1 April 1999, unreported), IAT.

28 *R v Secretary of State for the Home Department, ex p Bradshaw* [1994] Imm AR 359; *Tikhonov* [1998] INLR 737, IAT.

29 *R v Special Adjudicator, ex p Turus* [1996] Imm AR 388, QBD.

30 *MA (Pakistan) vSecretary of State for the Home Department* [2011] EWCA Civ 322. In that case, the tribunal had been entitled to make a more favourable assessment of risk on the basis of the appellant's accepted evidence about his motivation to address his drug addiction; *AM v Secretary of State for the Home Department* [2012] EWCA Civ 1634: 'the OASYS assessment had been made by a trained probation officer whose job it was to assess risk and in my view was not lightly to be dismissed'.

31 Senior President of Tribunals: Immigration and Asylum Chambers of the First-tier Tribunal and the Upper Tribunal Practice Directions, 10 February 2010, Part 10.

Evidence of post-decision facts

20.114 When determining an appeal under the pre-2002 Act legislation (except one on asylum or human rights grounds), the appellate authorities were restricted to consideration of facts in existence at the date of the decision appealed against.[1] It was emphasised on a number of occasions that the appellate authorities were not some kind of super entry clearance or immigration officers, or an extension of the original decision-making function, but a process for enabling the decision to be reviewed. Evidence that was not before the original decision maker could only be considered for the purpose of determining the facts that were in existence at the time the decision was made.[2] The exception was asylum and human rights cases. In *Ravichandran*[3] the Court of Appeal held that in asylum cases, the appellate authority is an extension of the decision-making process because of the nature of the question to be asked, ie whether projected removal would bring a real risk of harm contrary to the Refugee Convention, rather than fixing on a past situation. This meant that evidence of facts which came into existence after the decision on appeal was relevant and admissible. That decision was given statutory effect in IAA 1999,[4] and was extended to cases where it was asserted that removal would breach Article 3 of the ECHR.[5] The Tribunal applied the principle to Article 8 cases in *S&K*[6] and in *Razgar*[7] the House of Lords upheld this approach to all cases in which it was asserted that human rights would be breached by removal. NIAA 2002 extended the admissibility of evidence of post-decision facts to non-asylum or human rights appeals apart from appeals against refusal of entry clearance or refusal of a certificate of entitlement,[8] in which the Tribunal is limited to consideration of the circumstances in existence at the date of the decision. In appeals concerned with refusals of leave to enter or to vary leave following an application under the Points Based Scheme, the UK Borders Act will very severely restrict the evidence that the Tribunal can consider.[9] Insofar as the appeal relies on the grounds that the decision is not in accordance with the law or Immigration Rules or a discretion should have been exercised differently, the Tribunal will only be able to consider evidence submitted with and in support of the application; evidence subsequently adduced to establish the authenticity of a document; evidence responding to the Secretary of State's reliance on rules or a discretion under the rules other than those relating to the acquisition of points (eg the general grounds for refusal under the Immigration Rules). Insofar as other grounds are relied on, eg that the decision breaches the appellant's human rights or the UK's obligations under the Refugee Convention, those restrictions will not apply. Otherwise, on an appeal under sections 82 or 83 the Tribunal may consider evidence about any matter which it thinks relevant to the substance of the decision, including evidence which concerns a matter arising after the date of the decision.[10] This means that the focus of the Tribunal's scrutiny in all immigration appeals other than those challenging refusal of entry clearance or certificate of entitlement (not just those engaging the Refugee or Human Rights Convention) has shifted from the date of decision to the date of hearing.[11] The statutory changes mean, in our view, that the appellate process really does become, in all cases, an extension of the decision-making process. Thus, evidence of facts which were unforeseeable at the date of decision can now found a successful appeal.[12] An appeal against refusal of leave to remain had to be allowed because, although at the time of the decision the appellant could not qualify under the applicable immigration rule, by the time of the hearing she had become over 65 and so satisfied the requirements of another immigration rule.[13] Where the appeal is against refusal of entry clearance or refusal of a certificate of entitlement to the right of abode, the rule remains as it was before NIAA 2002, with the Tribunal able to consider 'only the circumstances appertaining at the time of the decision'.[14] In respect of those appeals, the earlier authorities on evidence of post-decision facts remain of relevance.[15] An amended decision notice has been held to give rise to a new date of decision, thus extending the scope for factual investigation on appeal.[16] But the submission of fresh evidence to the decision maker post-decision, and the review of that evidence in a supplementary refusal letter, has been held not to give rise to a new date of decision, so that the evidence, on an entry clearance appeal, would not lose its quality of inadmissible post-decision evidence.[17] However, a number of decisions relating to entry clearance under the rules involve predictions: whether a business will succeed,[18] whether a couple will live together as man and wife,[19] whether the parties will have accommodation available,[20] whether a student will be able to pursue a course with reasonable success.[21] In these cases, evidence of post-decision facts that throw light on the decision was admissible[22] if the events were foreseeable at the time of the decision.[23] The Tribunal has held in the starred decision of *DR (Morocco)*[24] that section 85(5) now precludes the admission of evidence showing that something which was likely at the date of decision has actually happened. We believe its interpretation of the section to be unduly restrictive.[25] It did accept, however, that evidence of post-decision facts was admissible in so far as they shed light on the circumstances appertaining at the time of the decision, eg a couple's post-decision devotion being relevant to whether they had an intention to live together at the time of the decision.

[1]   *R v Immigration Appeal Tribunal, ex p Weerasuriya* [1983] 1 All ER 195, [1982] Imm AR 23, DC; *Sae-Heng v Visa Officer, Bangkok* [1979–80] Imm AR 69; *R v Secretary of State for the Home Department, ex p Miah* [1998] Imm AR 44, QBD.
[2]   *R v Immigration Appeal Tribunal, ex p Hassanin* [1987] 1 All ER 74, [1986] 1 WLR 1448, CA, per Dillon LJ.
[3]   *Ravichandran (Senathirajah) v Secretary of State for the Home Department* [1996] Imm AR 97, CA.
[4]   IAA 1999, s 77(3).
[5]   IAA 1999, s 77(4).
[6]   *Secretary of State for the Home Department v SK* [2002] UKIAT 05613 (starred).
[7]   *R (on the application of Razgar) v Secretary of State for the Home Department* [2004] UKHL 27, [2004] 3 WLR 58.
[8]   NIAA 2002, s 85(5) or, following enactment of the UK Borders Act, s 19, by a new NIAA 2002, s 85(5) and s 85A(2).
[9]   NIAA 2002, s 85A(3) and (4), to be inserted by the UK Borders Act 2007, s 19.
[10]   NIAA 2002, s 85(4).
[11]   The explanatory notes to the Act do not assist in divining the purpose of the change, which may, contrary to our argument in the text, be simply a reflection of the fact that asylum and human rights issues no longer give rise to special appeals but form grounds of appeal against in-country immigration decisions: see ss 82, 84. Read this way, in relation to non-asylum or human rights issues, s 85(4) does no more than put in statutory form the recognition in *R v Immigration Appeal Tribunal, ex p Hoque and Singh* [1988] Imm AR 216, CA that evidence of post-decision facts (such as the birth of a child in a marriage case) may cast a flood of light on the intentions of the parties at the date of decision. This remains the position for entry clearance appeals.
[12]   *CA (Nigeria)* [2004] UKIAT 00243, where evidence of acquittal of criminal charges of using a false passport was held admissible in an appeal against cancellation of leave on the ground of possession of a false passport, to show that the immigration officer's discretion should have been exercised differently. See 20.17 above.
[13]   *YZ and LX (China)* [2005] UKAIT 00157.

14 NIAA 2002, s 85(5).

15 See cases at fn 1 above, and *R v Secretary of State for the Home Department, ex p Husbadak* [1982] Imm AR 8, QBD.

16 *Rajendran (Kangeyan) v Secretary of State for the Home Department* [1989] Imm AR 512 at 519.

17 *R v Immigration Appeal Tribunal and Secretary of State for the Home Department, ex p Banu* [1999] Imm AR 161, [1999] INLR 226, QBD. Nor would the reconsideration of the original decision in the ECO's explanatory statement thereby create a new and later immigration decision: *AH (Bangladesh)* [2006] UKAIT 0028.

18 *R v Immigration Appeal Tribunal, ex p Amir Beaggi* (1982) Times, 25 May, QBD; *Secretary of State for the Home Department v Thaker* [1976] Imm AR 114.

19 *Patel (Ilyas Yakub) v Secretary of State for the Home Department* [1986] Imm AR 440, IAT.

20 *Azad (5993)*, IAT. [QUERY NO CITE]

21 *Rajendran* [1989] Imm AR 512.

22 *R v Immigration Appeal Tribunal, ex p Kwok On Tong* [1981] Imm AR 214; *R v Immigration Appeal Tribunal, ex p Amir Beaggi*, fn 16 above. The admission of post-decision evidence in these cases is, however, strictly limited to that purpose and still looks back to the date of decision.

23 *Adesegun v Entry Clearance Officer* [2002] UKIAT 02132: the sponsor becoming unable to work due to sickle cell anaemia, being unforeseeable at the time of the decision, should not have been taken into account. Post-decision evidence of existing facts is always admissible, however, to show that the situation was not what the entry clearance officer believed it to be: *Hassanin* (fn 2 above).

24 [2005] UKIAT 00038 (starred).

25 The Tribunal held that the rationale for the practise of admitting evidence of post-decision facts which were foreseeable at the date of decision has gone now that entry clearance stands as leave to enter. But with respect, that does not alter anything. The issue of entry clearance in those cases still depends on a prediction, and it is wholly unrealistic to exclude evidence that the predicted event (the sponsor obtaining a job or accommodation) took place. The restrictive interpretation amounts to a rewriting of the rules, which we do not believe was Parliament's intention.

Evidence and findings in other proceedings

20.115 There are a number of circumstances in which factual findings made by other Tribunals may be taken into account by a Tribunal including: (1) findings of fact about conditions in a particular country made in an unrelated appeal; (2) findings of fact about conditions in a particular country made by the Tribunal in a 'Country Guideline' case; (3) findings of fact made in an earlier appeal in respect of the appellant; (4) findings of fact made in the appeal of a family member or relative. Each of these will be considered below.

EVIDENCE OF LIKE FACTS IN OTHER APPEALS AND JUDGMENTS

20.116 The tribunal should not treat findings about the situation in a particular country made by the European Court of Human Rights as binding upon it. It should instead decide for itself the weight, if any, to be given to such findings by reference to the nature and quality of the country evidence that the court considered and its reasons for concluding as it did.[1] The tribunal would be entitled to have regard to an assessment of the appellant's age made by the High Court in Children Act proceedings and, whilst not bound by the court's conclusion on the issue, would be entitled to give considerable weight to it.[2] In a deportation case, the tribunal should not make findings or draw inferences about the circumstances and gravity of the appellant's offending that are inconsistent with the sentencing judgment[3] or the factual basis of a guilty plea agreed between the defendant and prosecution.[4] The family court has procedural advantages over the tribunal and particular expertise in investigating and evaluating the best interests of a child, so that a decision in family proceedings dealing with the same individuals and similar issues is likely to be of value to the tribunal.[5] Consequently, there should be co-operation and communication between the two jurisdictions with the tribunal considering adjourning an appeal to await a family court judgment.[6]

[1] *AMM and others (conflict; humanitarian crisis; returnees; FGM) Somalia CG* [2011] UKUT 0445 (IAC); *AK (Afghanistan) (Article 15(c))* [2012] UKUT 00163 (IAC).
[2] *MWA (Afghanistan) v Secretary of State for the Home Department* [2014] EWCA Civ 706.
[3] *HK (Turkey) v Secretary of State for the Home Department* [2010] EWCA Civ 583.
[4] *RK (Deportation: basis of plea) Albania* [2014] UKUT 84 (IAC).
[5] *Nimako-Boateng (Residence orders – Anton considered)* [2012] UKUT 216 (IAC).
[6] *RS (Immigration/family court liason: outcome)* [2013] UKUT 82 (IAC); *RS (Immigration and family court proceedings) India* [2012] UKUT 218 (IAC).

20.117 In asylum appeals evidence of the situation in a particular country may be common to a number of appeals and there may exist a number of determinations, for example, on whether in a particular country, members of a particular minority face persecution. The Tribunal has instituted a system of 'country guidance' cases, as to which see below, but if there is no relevant country guidance case relating to the appellant's country, is the Tribunal entitled, or obliged, to have regard to other decisions relating to that country? In *Gnanavarathan*,[1] the Court of Appeal held that adjudicators were arguably under an obligation to give full reasons, if they came to conclusions different to other adjudicators regarding country conditions. That decision is no longer apt in the light of the restrictions imposed on citation of cases before the appellate authority. In May 2003, the Tribunal stopped publishing all of its decisions and introduced a distinction between 'reported' and 'unreported' decisions. Whether a decision is to be reported or not is determined by the Tribunal and is not perceived by the Tribunal to be an issue in which the parties to the appeal have an interest.[2] The Senior President's Practice Directions provide that unreported determinations of the Tribunal may not be cited unless the appellant or a member of his or her family was a party to the proceedings in which the previous determination was issued or the Tribunal gives permission.[33] An applicant for such permission must certify that the proposition for which the determination is to be cited is not found in any reported decision of the Tribunal, the IAT or the AIT or higher authority.[4] It is no longer necessary, as it was under the AIT Practice Directions, to provide an analysis of the jurisprudence to support the certification. Permission will be given only if the Tribunal considers that it would be materially assisted by citation of the determination and the Tribunal's expectation is that such instances are likely to be rare.[5] A party citing a determination of the IAT having a neutral citation number prior to [2003] must be in a position to certify that the matter for which it is cited has not been the subject of more recent, reported determinations of the IAT or Tribunal.[6] The Tribunal would not have regard to an unreported determination cited without compliance with the Practice Direction.[7] Whether it is lawful to impose such a restraint on the citation of decisions of the Upper Tribunal is questionable given that it is a superior court of record and a characteristic of a superior court of record is that its decisions have effect as precedents for lower tribunals.[8]

[1] [1995] Imm AR 64.

2   Senior President's Practice Statements: Immigration and Asylum Chambers of the First-tier Tribunal and the Upper Tribunal, 10 February 2010, para 11.2.
3   Senior President's Practice Statements, para 11.3.
4   Senior President's Practice Statements, para 11.1 and Senior President's Practice Statement: Form of Decisions and Neutral Citation: First-tier Tribunal and Upper Tribunal on or after 3 November 2008.
5   Senior President's Practice Directions: Immigration and Asylum Chambers of the First-tier Tribunal and the Upper Tribunal, 10 February 2010, para 11.1.
6   Asylum and Immigration Tribunal Practice Direction, April 2007, para 17.7.
7   Senior President's Practice Directions, para 11.3.
8   Senior President's Practice Directions, para 11.5.

20.118 A determination is reportable if it follows a hearing or other consideration where the jurisdiction of the Tribunal was exercised by the Senior President, the Chamber President or an Upper Tribunal judge, whether or not sitting alone,[1] and a reported decision is given a neutral citation number (in the format '[year] UKUT 0000 (IAC)') and published on the Tribunal's website.[2] The Upper Tribunal (IAC) has a Reporting Committee which decides which cases should be reported. Judges and representatives may nominate decisions for consideration by the Reporting Committee. Cases in which a permanent judge of the Upper Tribunal or a visiting senior judge participated are considered suitable for reporting. The criteria for reporting decisions are that they have general significance and utility in the development of the tribunal's case law; are sufficiently well reasoned; and consistent with binding authority.[3] Surprisingly, the procedure in relation to the reporting of country guidance cases is that they are considered by the Reporting Committee before being promulgated with a view to the Reporting Committee tendering advice to the determining judges.[4] This is difficult to reconcile with the principles that appeals should be determined by the tribunal that hear them and that the parties to an appeal should be able to respond to all of the material on which the decision on the appeal will be based. However, the tribunal has endorsed the legality of the procedure.[5] The Upper Tribunal has held that tribunals must take account of its reported decisions insofar as they consider evidence that may be relevant to the case before the tribunal and that they must apply the factual findings contained in reported decisions that deal with the same factual matrix, unless there is good reason not to do so.[6] However, the Court of Appeal has held that it would be an error of law to treat a reported, but not country guidance, case as establishing a binding conclusion of fact.[7] The First-tier Tribunal is expected to follow the law as set out in reported cases unless persuaded that the decision did not take account of relevant legislative provision or a binding decision of a superior court.[8]

1   Senior President's Practice Statements, para 11.3.
2   Senior President's Practice Statements, para 11.1 and Senior President's Practice Statement: Form of Decisions and Neutral Citation: First-tier Tribunal and Upper Tribunal on or after 3 November 2008.
3   Upper Tribunal Immigration and Asylum Chamber: Guidance Note 2011, No 2: 'Reporting Decisions of the Upper Tribunal Immigration and Asylum Chamber'.
4   Upper Tribunal Immigration and Asylum Chamber: Guidance Note 2011, No 2: 'Reporting Decisions of the Upper Tribunal Immigration and Asylum Chamber', para 11.
5   *MOJ (Return to Mogadishu)* CG [2014] UKUT 442 (IAC).
6   TR (Pakistan) [2011] UKUT 33 (IAC).
7   *HK (Afghanistan) v Secretary of State for the Home Department* [2012] EWCA Civ 315.
8   Upper Tribunal Immigration and Asylum Chamber: Guidance Note 2011, No 2: 'Reporting Decisions of the Upper Tribunal Immigration and Asylum Chamber', para 10.

COUNTRY GUIDANCE DETERMINATIONS

20.119 With the increase in asylum appeals, greater emphasis has been placed upon the importance of consistency of decision making, at least as far as the impact on individual cases of general conditions in asylum seekers' countries of origin is concerned.[1] In 1997, the Court of Appeal referred to the Tribunal's expertise in the assessment of material relating to country conditions and held that careful attention had to be paid to the Tribunal's findings, although they are not findings of law to be treated as binding authority.[2] In 2002, the Court of Appeal went further, approving as 'benign and practical' the notion of a 'factual precedent' where the Tribunal decides to make an authoritative determination of some general question of fact with the intention that it should be binding as to the conditions then existing.[3] The European Court of Human Rights has acknowledged the legitimacy in principle of assessing risk to an individual returnee on the basis of a list of 'risk factors' contained in a country guidance decision so long as the decision maker properly takes account of any new country evidence.[4] Subsequently, legislative provision was made for Practice Directions by the president to require the Tribunal 'to treat a specified decision of the Tribunal as authoritative in respect of a particular matter'.[5] This has been construed as giving the 'country guidance system' a statutory basis.[6] The legislative provision has been amended so that either one or both of the FT and the UT can be required by Practice Directions of the Senior President or Chamber President to treat a determination of the FT Tribunal, the Upper Tribunal, the Asylum and Immigration Tribunal or the Immigration Appeal Tribunal as authoritative in respect of a particular matter.[7] The Senior President's Practice Direction is that reported determinations of the Tribunal, the AIT or the IAT bearing the letters 'CG' 'shall be treated as an authoritative finding on the country guidance issue identified in the determination, based upon the evidence before the [panel]' that decided it. Consequently, 'failure to follow a clear, apparently applicable country guidance case or to show why it does not apply to the case in question is likely to be regarded as ground for appeal on a point of law'.[8] Tribunals are required to treat country guidance as authoritative even if permission to appeal to the Court of Appeal against the country guidance decision has been granted.[9] The Tribunal website[10] now provides access to what the Tribunal designates as 'country guidance determinations'. The Court of Appeal has held that '[f]ailure to apply a country guidance decision unless there was good reason, explicitly stated, for not doing so would constitute an error of law in that a material consideration had been ignored or legally inadequate reasons for the decision had been given'.[11] In the House of Lords, Lord Hope endorsed the principle that country guidance decisions should be followed by immigration judges but added the qualification that 'in the end of the day each case, whether or not such guidance is available, must depend on an objective and fair assessment of its own facts'.[12] It would be an error of law for the Tribunal to determine an appeal inconsistently with relevant country guidance, even in circumstances where the country guidance was not placed before the Tribunal and even if the factual assessment made by the Tribunal was based upon a concession (inconsistent with the country guidance) made by the appellant's representative.[13] However, an error of law could not be established by reference to failure to follow a country guidance decision that post-dated the decision under challenge.[14] A country guidance decision should make clear the precise scope of the issues on which country guidance is being given, and care should be taken to ensure that the headnote (which is not part of the determination) should not conflict with the decision.[15] If an issue arises as to what is meant by something said in a country guidance determination or whether it is to be treated as part of the country guidance, the Tribunal or court is required to decide for itself the correct interpretation of the guidance; it may not hold that there is a range of legitimate interpretations that a decision maker could apply and uphold his or her decision so long as it fell within that range.[16] For the purpose of resolving such an issue, consideration may have to be given to what was and was not argued before the country guidance Tribunal and to the Tribunal's analysis and reasoning.[17] The Tribunal has refused to permit argument intended to challenge a country guidance decision relied upon in a determination unless supported by fresh evidence,[18] an approach that has received some approval from the Court of Appeal.[19] However, because the country guidance system would be productive of injustice if a legally flawed but unappealed country guidance decision was to be generally applied, a subsequent appellant may bring a challenge to the lawfulness of the country guidance.[20] On the other hand, the Court of Appeal has subjected the Tribunal's factual assessments in the making of country guidance decisions to the most detailed scrutiny.[21] Even when hearing a case where there is a relevant 'factual precedent', the Tribunal is obliged to consider and determine the facts of the individual case and to consider any evidence showing a change of circumstances since the 'factual precedent' was decided[22] or showing that a factual finding in the country guidance case was incorrect.[23]

[1] Eg *Gurung v Secretary of State for the Home Department* [2003] EWCA Civ 654, [2003] All ER (D) 14 (May); *Shirazi v Secretary of State for the Home Department* [2003] EWCA Civ 1562, [2004] 2 All ER 602, where the court held that the Tribunal should have had regard to inconsistent decisions. The court did not, however, hold that inconsistency per se is an error of law; see text and fn 8 below. See also the discussion of 'Guidance Cases' in Tribunal Justice – a New Start, Sir Robert Carnwath [2009] PL 48.

[2] *Manzeke (Bambagu) v Secretary of State for the Home Department* [1997] Imm AR 524, CA.

[3] *S v Secretary of State for the Home Department* [2002] EWCA Civ 539, [2002] INLR 416; *Krotov v Secretary of State for the Home Department* [2004] EWCA Civ 69, [2004] 1 WLR 1825. S concerned an early example of a Tribunal determination which was meant to be authoritative as regards the country situation for particular groups, such as Croatian Serbs, which it involved, or Roma in the Czech Republic: see also *Puzova (01/TH/0416)*. Buxton LJ questioned the viability of a 'Country Guideline' system where the Tribunal's jurisdiction was limited to error of law (as it was as a second-instance Tribunal under NIAA 2002 before 4 April 2005) in *Batayav v Secretary of State for the Home Department (No 2)* [2005] EWCA Civ 366 (para 23), [2005] All ER (D) 323 (Mar).

[4] *NA v United Kingdom* (Application 25904/07)(2008) 48 EHRR 337, [2008] ECHR 616, discussed in *TK (Sri Lanka) CG* [2009] UKAIT 00049.

[5] The Asylum and Immigration Act 2004, s 26(7), with effect from 4 April 2005, adding a new s 107(3) in NIAA 2002. See AIT PD (30 April 2007), para 18.

[6] *OM (Zimbabwe) CG* [2006] UKAIT 00077.

[7] By the Transfer of Functions of the Asylum and Immigration Tribunal Order 2010, SI 2010/21 amending NIAA 2002, s 107.

[8] Senior President's Practice Directions: Immigration and Asylum Chambers of the First-tier Tribunal and the Upper Tribunal, 10 February 2010, para 12.

[9] *SG (Iraq) v Secretary of State for the Home Department* [2012] EWCA Civ 940.

[10] www.tribunals.gov.uk./ImmigrationAsylum

[11] *R (Iran) v Secretary of State for the Home Department* [2005] EWCA Civ 982, (2005) Times, 19 August, [2005] All ER (D) 384 (Jul), approving Ouseley J's analysis of Tribunal country guidance in *NM (Somalia) CG* [2005] UKIAT 00076 and the AIT Practice Direction (4 April 2005). As an example, see *MT (Turkey) v Secretary of State for the Home Department* [2007] EWCA Civ 1397.

12 *Januzi v Secretary of State for the Home Department; Hamid v Same; Gaafar v Same; Mohammed v Same* [2006] UKHL 5, [2006] 3 All ER 305, [2006] 2 WLR 397 per Lord Hope at [50].

13 *Bozkurt v Secretary of State for the Home Department* [2006] EWCA Civ 289, [2006] All ER (D) 188 (Feb).

14 *AK v Secretary of State for the Home Department* [2006] EWCA Civ 1117, [2006] All ER (D) 470 (Jul); *SR (Sri Lanka) v Secretary of State for the Home Department* [2014] EWCA Civ 683.

15 *PO (Nigeria) v Secretary of State for the Home Department* [2011] EWCA Civ 132.

16 *R (on the application of Kalombo) v Secretary of State for the Home Department* [2009] EWCA Civ 302.

17 *R (Kalombo)*, ibid.

18 *MY (Eritrea)* [2005] UKAIT 00158.

19 *Ariaya v Secretary of State for the Home Department* [2006] EWCA Civ 48, (2006) Times, 20 February, [2006] All ER (D) 93 (Feb).

20 *KS (Burma) v Secretary of State for the Home Department* [2013] EWCA Civ 67.

21 Eg *S v Secretary of State for the Home Department* [2002] EWCA Civ 539, [2002] All ER (D) 212 (Apr) and *AA v Secretary of State for the Home Department* [2006] EWCA Civ 401, [2007] 2 All ER 160 and *AA (Zimbabwe) v Secretary of State for the Home Department* [2007] EWCA Civ 149.

22 *S v Secretary of State for the Home Department* [2002] EWCA Civ 539, [2002] INLR 416; *Secretary of State for the Home Department v DD (Croatia)* [2004] UKIAT 00032 (starred); *DK (Croatia)* [2003] UKIAT 00153 (starred).

23 *DSG (Afghan Sikhs: Departure from CG) Afghanistan* [2013] UKUT 148 (IAC).

Previous findings of fact in respect of the same person

20.120 Circumstances may arise, although less frequently under the one-stop system, where an individual who has had an unsuccessful appeal against an earlier decision acquires another right of appeal against a new decision. The Tribunal set out guidelines in a starred decision, *Devaseelan*, about the approach to be taken in hearing the second appeal, to the factual findings made in the first.[1] The *Devaseelan* guidelines were approved in *Djebbar*, where the Court of Appeal said that the provision of guidance on how appellate bodies should deal with the fact of an earlier unsuccessful application when deciding a later one was 'essential to ensure consistency of approach'.[2] The Court emphasised that the most important feature of the guidance is that the fundamental obligation of every immigration judge independently to decide each new application on its own individual merits was preserved; the guidelines were not written in the language of *res judicata* or estoppel.[3] The *Devaseelan* guidelines state that matters arising since the first appellate decision, and facts that were not relevant to the issues before the first immigration judge or panel can be determined by the second.[4] However the first determination is generally to be regarded by the second immigration judge or panel as an authoritative determination of the issues of fact that were before the first appellate body. Generally, the second immigration judge or panel should not revisit findings of fact made by the first on the basis of evidence that was available to the appellant at the time of the first hearing. The findings of fact made by the first appellate body may be revisited in the light of evidence that was not available to the appellant at the time of the first appeal, and they may be revisited where the circumstances of the first appeal were such that it would be right for the second appellate body to treat the first determination as if it had never been made.[5] It may also be appropriate for the second appellate body to revisit earlier credibility findings if the issue of credibility remains arguably live.[6] If the second appeal contains asylum or human rights grounds, the second appellate body in applying the *Devaseelan* guidelines would have to be mindful of the obligations to take account of all relevant material[7] and to consider the case with 'the most anxious scrutiny'.[8] A 'factual finding' announced at the conclusion of a preliminary hearing does not bind the immigration judge or panel who hears the substantive appeal.[9] It would be an error of law for an immigration judge to have regard to findings of fact made in an earlier determination if that determination was properly to be regarded as a nullity because it related to an appeal that had been abandoned.[10] However, even if all of the findings of fact in an earlier determination are vitiated owing to an error of law, the Tribunal reconsidering the appeal should receive and be entitled to consider the original determination; only in special circumstances would the interests of justice require the reconsidering Tribunal not to see the original determination.[11]

1   *Devaseelan* [2003] Imm AR 1. The guidelines apply not only to asylum and human rights appeals but also to successive appeals against entry clearance decisions: *Entry Clearance Officer, Islamabad v B (Pakistan)* [2003] UKIAT 00053. However, the *Devaseelan* guidelines apply only to successive appeals by the same individual and it would be wrong to regard them as applicable to appeals by different members of the same family: *Diyenli* [2002] UKIAT 07173. But see *TK (Georgia)* [2004] UKIAT 00149.

2   *Djebbar v Secretary of State for the Home Department* [2004] EWCA Civ 804, [2004] 33 LS Gaz R 36 at [14].

3   *Djebbar* ibid at [15].

4   The first Tribunal who heard an asylum appeal may not have made findings of fact that were relevant to the later human rights appeal: *Ayella* [2002] UKIAT 06721.

5   *Devaseelan*, fn 1 above.

6   *Ayella*, fn 2 above. Credibility findings might remain live where, for example, there was no appeal against an earlier decision dismissing an asylum appeal because of an unassailable finding that there was no Refugee Convention reason, rather than because adverse credibility findings were correct.

7   *Karanakaran v Secretary of State for the Home Department* [2000] 3 All ER 449, [2000] INLR 122, [2000] Imm AR 271, CA.

8   Dyson LJ in *R (on the application of Sivakumar) v Immigration Appeal Tribunal* [2001] EWCA Civ 1196, [2002] INLR 310 (upheld at [2003] UKHL 14, [2003] 2 All ER 1097) reminded decision makers in asylum cases that 'that is not a mantra to which only lip service should be paid. It recognises the fact that what is at stake in these cases is fundamental human rights, including the right to life itself'.

9   *L (Ethiopia)* [2003] UKIAT 00016 (adjudicator's conclusion on the 'preliminary issue' of the appellant's nationality, announced at a preliminary hearing, not binding on the adjudicator subsequently hearing the appeal).

10 *N (Cameroon)* [2005] UKAIT 00146.

11 *Swash v Secretary of State for the Home Department* [2006] EWCA Civ 1093, (2006) Times, 14 August, [2006] All ER (D) 390 (Jul).

Evidence of facts found in appeals by family members

20.121 In *Chicaiza*,[1] the Tribunal held that an adjudicator hearing the appeal of one member of a family should in certain circumstances, where their claims are closely associated with each other, take into account the determinations of appeals by other family members, although the weight to be given to the findings of fact made in the other appeals is a matter for the adjudicator. In the same case, the Tribunal pointed out that where one member of a family was granted asylum on the basis of similar considerations to those raised by the appellant, dismissal of the asylum appeal would have to be very carefully reasoned. But it is important that Tribunals do not treat earlier determinations of other family members' appeals as determinative of the particular appeal before them. In *Otshudi*,[2] Sedley LJ upheld the importance of individual justice over consistency of determinations, and mere disparity of outcomes between family members does not amount to error of law.[3] Applying the same principle, the determination of an individual's appeal was not admissible in his brother's appeal for the purpose of destroying the brother's credibility.[4] Where a family member whose evidence had been disbelieved on his own appeal gave identical evidence in his wife's appeal the immigration judge was entitled not only to have regard to the determination on his appeal but also to treat it as determinative of his credibility, although not determinative of the whole appeal.[5] The '*Devaseelan* guidelines'[6] are relevant to cases where someone who has had an appeal determined by the Tribunal gives evidence in another person's appeal. However, they need to be adapted and there may have to be more readiness to revisit factual findings made by the Tribunal that determined the witness' appeal in the light of the totality of the evidence.[7] However, the applicability of the *Devaseelan* guidelines is limited to cases that arise from the same factual matrix, eg the same relationship or the same events; an 'overlap of evidence' is not sufficient for the guidelines to apply.[8] Moreover, there should be much more scope for reopening the factual findings of the first Tribunal if the person against whom those findings are relied on was not a party to the proceedings before the first Tribunal.[9] Even in respect of whether a particular event occurred, a second Tribunal (hearing a wife's appeal) is entitled to reach a contrary conclusion to that reached by the first (which heard the husband's appeal) where such a conclusion was open to the second Tribunal on the evidence before it.[10]

[1] *Chicaiza* [2002] UKIAT 01200.
[2] *Otshudi v Secretary of State for the Home Department* [2004] EWCA Civ 893, [2004] All ER (D) 12 (Jul).
[3] *S (Sri Lanka)* [2004] UKIAT 00039.
[4] *MJ (Iran) v Secretary of State for the Home Department* [2008] EWCA Civ 564, [2008] All ER (D) 320 (Apr).
[5] *TK (Georgia)* [2004] UKIAT 00149.
[6] As to which, see the preceding paragraph.
[7] *Ocampo v Secretary of State for the Home Department* [2006] EWCA Civ 1276, [2006] 40 LS Gaz R 36.
[8] *AA (Somalia) v Secretary of State for the Home Department* [2007] EWCA Civ 1040 per Carnwath and Ward LLJ (Hooper LJ dissenting).
[9] *AA (Somalia) v Secretary of State for the Home Department* [2007] EWCA Civ 1040, [2007] All ER (D) 395 (Oct), per Carnwath and Ward LLJ (Hooper LJ dissenting).
[10] *HS (Afghanistan) v Secretary of State for the Home Department* [2009] EWCA Civ 771.

Burden and standard of proof

20.122 The rules relating to the burden of proof in appeals may be summarised as follows:

(1)   the burden of proving British citizenship or any exemption from statutory provisions is on the person who makes the assertion.[1] Usually this will be the applicant, but not always;[2]

(2)   an appellant who wishes to assert that he or she has a right of abode or is exempt and, therefore, that the decision or action should not have been taken, must prove it;[3]

(3)   most claims to enter or remain will depend on the applicant satisfying the entry clearance officer, immigration officer or Home Office of the necessary facts which will qualify them in the appropriate category, and consequently in an appeal the burden of proving such a claim is on the party making it;[4]

(4)   this applies equally to asylum and human rights or discrimination claims, where the burden of proof is on the applicant to make his or her case[5] even if the applicant is a child;[6]

(5)   the Immigration (European Economic Area) Regulations give various rights of residence to a person who is the 'spouse' of another, but define spouse so as to exclude a party to a marriage of convenience. However, there is no burden on the appellant to prove that the marriage is not one of convenience unless evidence is indicating that it may have been;[7]

(6)   where it is plain that at the date of flight or the date of the decision an asylum seeker did in fact qualify for refugee status, but the Secretary of State contends that by the date of the hearing the circumstances have changed, then by analogy with Article 1C(5) of the Refugee Convention (where proof that the circumstances of persecution have ceased to exist falls on the receiving state) there is an evidential burden on the Secretary of State to establish that the appellant can safely return home;[8]

(7)   where an internal flight option is alleged by the Secretary of State, no question of burden or standard of proof arises; the question is simply whether, the Tribunal is satisfied by the evidence that the appellant can reasonably be expected to go to and stay in the proposed place of relocation.[9] However, internal flight is not a legitimate issue unless proper notice has been given by the Secretary of State that it is to be raised;[10]

(8)   where an applicant falls into a class of persons who are acknowledged to face particular treatment, it is for the respondent to show why the applicant faces no real risk of such treatment;[11]

(9)   where the Secretary of State revokes a person's indefinite leave to enter or remain under the NIAA 2002, section 76, it is for the Secretary of State to prove the facts entitling him to make the decision,[12] ie that the person is liable to deportation but cannot be deported for legal reasons;[13] that leave was obtained by deception such that the person would have been liable to removal but cannot be removed for legal or practical reasons;[14] that the person has ceased to be a refugee, having availed him or herself of another country's protection or nationality[15]) entitling him to make the decision;

(10) where the Secretary of State seeks to deport someone under section 3(5) of the IA 1971, the Secretary of State must prove the facts necessary to establish a ground for deporting. This will also be the case where the Home Office are relying on non-disclosure of material facts to justify the refusal of entry,[16] or on any of the general grounds for refusal of entry clearance, leave to enter or remain contained in Part 9 of the Immigration Rules, such as character, conduct, associations, criminal convictions and so forth.[17] It falls on the party who asserts to prove;

(11) there will also be a heavy burden on the Secretary of State if it is sought to contradict a finding as to relationship made in a previous appeal, although the concept of *res judicata* does not apply to the determination of the immigration appellate authorities;[18]

(12)   where the respondent asserts that documents relied on by an appellant are false, it is for him or her to prove it.[19] However, possession of an apparently genuine national passport must raise an inference that the holder possesses the corresponding nationality, which it is for him or her to rebut;[20]

(13)   where an appellant establishes that an immigration decision interferes with his or her right to respect for a right protected by art 8(1) it is for the respondent to justify the decision under art 8(2).[21]

(14)   if there is an issue about whether a fee was paid in support of an application for leave to remain, the burden is on the Secretary of State to show that it was not paid.[22]

---

1   IA 1971, s 3(8).
2   An example would be where the applicant wishes to rely on a stamp on his or her passport giving indefinite leave, but the Home Office asserts that the stamp does not apply because the applicant had a diplomatic exemption at the time.
3   Asylum and Immigration Tribunal (Procedure) Rules 2005, SI 2005/230, r 53(1), applied to fast track appeals by SI 2005/560, r 27, reflecting the IA 1971, s 3(8). The rule would also include an assertion of exemption from deportation under s 7 of the IA 1971.
4   SI 2005/230, r 53(2). See *R v Secretary of State for the Home Department, ex p Mughal* [1974] QB 313, [1974] 3 All ER 796, CA. See also *Visa Officer, Islamabad v Bi (Channo)* [1978] Imm AR 182 where, although the appellant had previously been granted entry clearance as the wife of the sponsor, she still had the burden of proving she was his wife on a later occasion when she sought readmission.
5   *Adebola* (16731) (19 August 1998, unreported), IAT. So in an onward appeal, the fact that the Secretary of State, as the appellant, has to show an error of law in the decision below is quite separate from proof by an asylum seeker of the basic elements needed to satisfy the criteria of a refugee claim: *Tikhonov* [1998] INLR 737, IAT. For burden and standard of proof in asylum appeals see **12.25** ff above.
6   *HK (Afghanistan) v Secretary of State for the Home Department* [2012] EWCA Civ 315.
7   *IS (Serbia)* [2008] UKAIT 00031; *Papajorgji (EEA spouse - marriage of convenience) Greece* [2012] UKUT 00038 (IAC).
8   *Arif v Secretary of State for the Home Department* [1999] INLR 327, CA, distinguished in *Salim (Nabil) v Secretary of State for the Home Department* [2000] Imm AR 503, CA and *Dyli v Secretary of State for the Home Department* [2000] Imm AR 652 (starred). In *Sijakovic (01TH 00632)* the Tribunal said it was unhelpful to talk of a burden, whether legal or evidential, on the Secretary of State: the issue was whether there was a well-founded fear of persecution. However, in *Saad v Secretary of State for the Home Department, Diriye v Secretary of State for the Home Department, Osorio v Secretary of State for the Home Department* [2001] EWCA Civ 2008, [2002] Imm AR 471, [2002] INLR 34 the Court of Appeal referred approvingly to *Arif*. In *R (on the application of Hoxha) v Secretary of State for the Home Department* [2005] UKHL 19 the House of Lords approved *Arif* on that point. Where a person has been recognised as a refugee by another government, the burden is on the Secretary of State to show that he is no longer a refugee: *Babela* [2002] UKIAT 06124.
9   *Karanakaran v Secretary of State for the Home Department* [2000] Imm AR 271 at 305. Previously, the question had been approached on the basis that the Secretary of State must show that it would be reasonable to expect an applicant to go to another part of the country, but that the applicant had an evidential burden to put forward matters indicating that it would be unduly harsh to expect him or her to do so: *R v Immigration Appeal Tribunal, ex p Tharumakulasingham (Nadarajah)* [1997] Imm AR 550, QBD *Jowitt J* But there was some confusion about this; see *R v Secretary of State for the Home Department, ex p Salim* [1999] INLR 628, QBD, where the burden was held to be on the appellant to show that internal flight did not apply. The imposition of such a burden now would be incompatible with Article 8(1) of Council Directive 2004/83/EC ('the Qualification Directive') which requires, if asylum is to be withheld on internal flight grounds 'that the applicant can reasonably be expected to stay in that part of the country'.
10 *Daoud v Secretary of State for the Home Department* [2005] EWCA Civ 755, [2005] All ER (D) 259 (May).
11 Thus, where a Country Assessment produced by the Home Office sets out the penalties that may be imposed for draft evasion, it is for the Secretary of State to show that there was no real

risk that they would be enforced against a draft-evading asylum seeker: *Mohammed v Secretary of State for the Home Department* [2003] EWCA Civ 265, [2003] All ER (D) 18 (Mar).

[12] *RD (Algeria)* [2007] UKAIT 00066.

[13] NIAA 2002, s 76(1).

[14] NIAA 2002, s 76(2).

[15] NIAA 2002, s 76(3).

[16] Ghati (19707) (27 July 1999, unreported), IAT.

[17] *JC (China)* [2007] UKAIT 00027.

[18] *Ali (Momin) v Secretary of State for the Home Department* [1984] 1 All ER 1009, [1984] Imm AR 23, CA; *R v Immigration Appeal Tribunal, ex p Miah (Lulu)* [1987] Imm AR 143; *R v Secretary of State for the Home Department, ex p Danaie* [1998] Imm AR 84; [1998] INLE 124.

[19] *R v Immigration Appeal Tribunal, ex p Shen* [2000] INLR 389, QBD; *Makozo* (20033) (12 February 1999, unreported), IAT; *Escobar* (20553) (26 March 1999, unreported), IAT. But since the overall burden of proof is on the appellant, it is not necessary for the Secretary of State to prove forgery in order for a claim resting on documentary evidence to be dismissed: see cases cited at fn 6 above.

[20] *MW (Pakistan)* [2004] UKIAT 00136.

[21] See for example *Miao v Secretary of State for the Home Department* [2006] EWCA Civ 75, [2006] All ER (D) 215 (Feb).

[22] *Basnet (Validity of application – respondent)* [2012] UKUT 113 (IAC); *R (on the application of Zinyemba) v Secretary of State for the Home Department* [2014] EWHC 2237 (Admin).

20.123 Where the burden of proof lies on a party, he or she may adduce sufficient *prima facie* evidence to discharge that burden in the absence of reasons to the contrary or evidence in rebuttal. What is sufficient *prima facie* evidence will vary from case to case; the quality of documentation relied on as proof of events may be variable; for example later birth certificates will be less weighty than contemporaneous ones. In an asylum or Article 3 case, the Handbook indicates that evidence of past maltreatment is an excellent indicator of the fate that may await an applicant on return.[1] The Secretary of State is under no obligation to investigate unproven allegations of risk; such a duty would dilute the already lowered standard of proof.[2] Although proceedings in the tribunal are predominantly adversarial, in a human rights case, the Secretary of State has a public responsibility to assist the tribunal to decide the real issues in the case including by the production of documents in her possession that may be of assistance to an appellant; the tribunal also has an obligation to ascertain enough to make an informed decision on the critical issues.[3] Where the best interests of a child are in issue, the Secretary of State should obtain as much information as is reasonably possible to assist in determining where those best interests lie.[4] If there is a policy that may be of relevance to the issues in an appeal, the Secretary of State has a duty to place it before the Tribunal.[5]

[1] Handbook, para 45; see also *Demirkaya v Secretary of State for the Home Department* [1999] Imm AR 498, [1999] INLR 441, CA; *R v Secretary of State for the Home Department, ex p Dahmas* (17 November 1999), CA (overturning [2000] Imm AR 151). See also Council Directive 2004/83/EC on minimum standards for the qualification and status of third country nationals and stateless persons as refugees or persons who otherwise need international protection (30.9.04 OJ L304/12), the Qualification Directive, art 7(4). The court in *Demirkaya* also pointed out that the Tribunal's statement that it was 'reasonably likely that the appellant would be released after one or two days' was an incorrect application of the burden of proof. The proper question was whether there was a real risk that he would not be released.

[2] *RK (DRC)* [2004] UKIAT 00129, where the Tribunal rejected the argument that, since ECHR, art 3 contained an obligation to investigate, the appellant's return without investigating her allegation that failed asylum seekers were subjected to persecutory harm would breach art 3. In this connection, the Tribunal distinguished between the State's duty to investigate alleged

breaches by its own agents (*Aksoy v Turkey* (1996) 23 EHRR 553) and its much more limited duty to investigate conditions in the destination country, which were met by its production of CIPU and FCO reports. See also *S (Serbia and Montenegro)* [2003] UKIAT 00031; *R v Secretary of State for the Home Department, ex p Gawe, Abdi v Secretary of State for the Home Department* [1996] Imm AR 288, HL: the Secretary of State was not obliged to embark on an investigation of evidence not in his hands, to assist appellants in making their cases.

3   *Rahman (Shaima Osman Abdul) v Secretary of State for the Home Department* [2005] EWCA Civ 1826, [2005] All ER (D) 267 (Dec). See also *Mukarkar v Secretary of State for the Home Department* [2006] EWCA Civ 1045, (2006) Times, 16 August, [2006] All ER (D) 367 (Jul); and *CS (Jamaica)* [2006] UKAIT 00004.

4   *HK (Afghanistan) v Secretary of State for the Home Department* [2012] EWCA Civ 315.

5   *AA (Afghanistan) v Secretary of State for the Home Department* [2007] EWCA Civ 12, [2007] All ER (D) 250 (Jan).

Standard of proof

20.124 The standard of proof is generally that which applies in all civil proceedings – proof on balance of probabilities. This is so even when questions of citizenship and right of abode are at stake. Where the Tribunal stated that they were not 'convinced' of the appellant's means, this indicated that they were applying too high a standard of proof, more akin to that in criminal cases, and their determination was quashed.[1] There is only one civil standard of proof and that is proof that the fact in issue more probably occurred than that it did not.[2] However, the standard is flexible in its application and the more serious the allegation and the more serious the consequences if the allegation is proved, the stronger must be the evidence before the allegation will be found proved[3] and the more critically or anxiously the court will look at the facts before being satisfied as to their occurrence.[4] Thus, where fraud or corruption is alleged and the consequences for the individual may be loss of liberty correspondingly persuasive evidence is required.[5] Similarly, the facts justifying reliance on the general grounds for refusal of entry clearance and leave to enter or remain contained in Part 9 of the Immigration Rules – all of which relate to a failing or wrongdoing on the part of the appellant with serious consequences if made good (such as a re-entry ban), must be established by evidence of sufficient strength and quality and subjected to heightened examination by the Tribunal before being proved.[6] A bare assertion by an entry clearance officer that the appellant had previously been served with a decision to remove him from the UK was insufficient to prove that such a notice had been served.[7] The same applies to an allegation that documents have been forged[8] or that EURODAC fingerprint records show an that appellant had made a previous asylum claim, contrary to his or her account; a bare assertion that there was a fingerprint match would be insufficient and there would at least have to be copies of the fingerprints, details of the alleged previous asylum claim and evidence as to the general reliability of the EURODAC system.[9] Moreover, the Tribunal would also need to be satisfied as a matter of fairness that the appellant had the facility to access information that might support a meaningful rebuttal.[10] Where there has already been a binding decision of an appropriate Tribunal in favour of the applicant the standard is even higher.[11] In asylum cases where the onus is to show a well-founded fear of persecution, it is inappropriate to apply a test of balance of probabilities to what is likely to happen in the future and it will be sufficient if a reasonable likelihood of persecution is established.[12] The Court of Appeal gave guidance in *Karanakaran*[13] on how to apply this lower standard of proof, in the process illuminating the meaning of the decision in *Kaja*, in which the majority of the Tribunal had held that the lower standard applies to all aspects of proving that a person is a Convention refugee, including the assessment of accounts of past events.[14] That includes assessment of the asylum seeker's age, although when age is assessed for the purpose of determining eligibility for local authority support, the standard of proof is the balance of probabilities.[15] As far as the exclusion clauses in art 1F of the Convention are concerned, there have to be 'serious reasons for considering' that the person is guilty of one of the specified acts and that necessitates proof at least on a balance of probabilities.[16] This is dealt with in detail at **12.26** ff above. Similar considerations apply in ECHR, Article 3 cases where the onus is to show a serious risk of the relevant harm.[17] But in the absence of personal risk, it will be difficult for an appellant to show that removal would breach Article 3 unless the evidence shows a consistent pattern of gross and systematic violation of human rights in the country of return.[18] In a case concerned with Article 8 of the ECHR, the standard of proof is the balance of probabilities.[19]

1 *R v Immigration Appeal Tribunal, ex p Mehra* [1983] Imm AR 156 at 162.
2 *B (children) (sexual abuse: standard of proof)* [2008] UKHL 35.
3 *R (on the application of N) v Mental Health Review Tribunal (Northern Region)* [2005] EWCA Civ 1605, [2006] QB 468, [2006] 4 All ER 194.
4 *R (on the application of D) v Life Sentence Review Comrs (Northern Ireland)* [2008] UKHL 33, [2008] NI 292, [2008] 4 All ER 992.
5 *Khawaja v Secretary of State for the Home Department* [1984] AC 74, [1983] 1 All ER 765, HL.
6 *JC (China)* [2007] UKAIT 00027 and *NA (Pakistan)* [2009] UKAIT 00031. The mere fact that forged documents had been used by the appellant in the past was insufficient to discharge the burden of showing that false documents were relied on in the current application: *SD (India)* [2010] UKUT 276 (IAC).
7 *Singh (Paragraph 320(7A) – IS151A forms – proof)* [2014] UKUT 0162 (IAC).
8 *RP (Nigeria)* [2006] UKAIT 00086.
9 *YI (Eritrea)* [2007] UKAIT 00054.
10 *YI (Eritrea)*, ibid.
11 *Ali (Momin) v Secretary of State for the Home Department* [1984] 1 All ER 1009, [1984] Imm AR 23, CA; *R (on the application of Saribal) v Secretary of State for the Home Department* [2002] EWHC 1542 (Admin), [2002] INLR 596, [2002] All ER (D) 379 (Jul).
12 *R v Secretary of State for the Home Department, ex p Sivakumaran* [1988] AC 958. Expressions such as the 'balance of probabilities' have no place in asylum determination: *R (on the application of Xhelollari) v Immigration Appeal Tribunal* [2002] EWHC 2451 (Admin), [2002] All ER (D) 49 (Nov) (dismissed on facts).
13 *Karanakaran v Secretary of State for the Home Department* [2000] 3 All ER 449, [2000] INLR 122, [2000] Imm AR 271, CA.
14 *Kaja v Secretary of State for the Home Department* [1995] Imm AR 1, a majority decision of the Tribunal.
15 *Rawofi (Age assessment – standard of proof)* [2012] UKUT 197 (IAC).
16 *Al-Sirri v Secretary of State for the Home Department; DD (Afghanistan) v Secretary of State for the Home Department* [2012] UKSC 54 at [75].
17 *Kacaj v Secretary of State for the Home Department* (starred) (CC/23044/2000) (21 May 2001, unreported). See **12.25** above.
18 *Batayav v Secretary of State for the Home Department* [2003] EWCA Civ 1489, [2004] INLR 126, explaining *Hariri v Secretary of State for the Home Department* [2003] EWCA Civ 807, [2003] All ER (D) 340 (May); *Iqbal (Muzafar)* [2002] UKIAT 02239.
19 *Naz (subsisting marriage – standard of proof) Pakistan* [2012] UKUT 40.

Combined hearings

20.125 The Procedure Rules provide for the possibility of a combined hearing of two or more pending appeals that raise common issues.[1] In hearing a combined appeal, it is crucial that the Tribunal give separate consideration to the case for each appellant.[2] Appellants' appeals should not fail solely because they differ in their testimony at a combined hearing.[3] It is inappropriate to exclude any appellant from the hearing room from any part of the combined appeal.[4] However, where two family members had a choice between separate hearings of their appeals or a combined hearing in which one was directed to leave the hearing room whilst the other gave evidence, the direction was not unlawful.[5] If two or more appeals are heard together it is preferable to issue separate determinations, unless the appeals are interdependent.[6] Neither the Procedure Rules nor considerations of fairness require the Tribunal to adjourn the hearing of an appeal pending the determination of a family member's claim, nor is it unfair for a person whose claim has not yet been determined to give evidence in someone else's appeal.[7]

[1] Tribunal Procedures (First-tier Tribunal)(Immigration and Asylum Chamber) Rules 2014, SI 2014/2604, r 4(3)(b).
[2] *Wah (Yau Yak) v Home Office* [1982] Imm AR 16, CA; *R v Immigration Appeal Tribunal, ex p Begum (Hamida)* [1988] Imm AR 199.
[3] *Tabores and Munoz* (17819) (24 July 1998, unreported), IAT, where dismissal on the basis that they 'cannot both be telling the truth' was set aside.
[4] *Tabores and Munoz* (17819) (24 July 1998, unreported), IAT.
[5] *RS and SS (Pakistan)* [2008] UKAIT 00012.
[6] *Twum v Immigration Officer, Heathrow* [1986] Imm AR 316; *Ahmed (7903)* (unreported).
[7] *Rajan (01TH00244) (starred)*; *S (Sri Lanka)* [2004] UKIAT 00039, declining to follow *R v Secretary of State for the Home Department, ex p Kimbesa* (29 January 1997, unreported). See **20.121** above.

Hearings in public

20.126 Reflecting the principle of open justice enshrined in ECHR, art 6,[1] the general rule for immigration and asylum appeals is that hearings must take place in public.[2] However, the tribunal may give a direction that a hearing or part of a hearing is to be held in private, and in such circumstances, it may determine who is to be permitted to attend a hearing. It may also direct exclusion from a hearing or part of a hearing of any person whose conduct is disrupting or likely to disrupt a hearing; whose presence is likely to prevent another person from giving evidence or making submissions freely, or whose exclusion is necessary to give effect to a direction prohibiting disclosure of evidence.[3] The tribunal may also exclude any person where the purpose of the hearing would be defeated by the attendance of that person.[4] In addition, the tribunal may exclude a witness from a hearing until that witness gives evidence.[5] There is no power to hold a hearing in private merely because a party requests it, and it will therefore be for an appellant to justify a closed hearing by reference to one of these public interest criteria. Asylum seekers may argue that a public hearing prejudices the interests of justice in inhibiting them from giving a full account of their claim, or indeed proceeding with the hearing at all, for shame, or fear of reprisals, and those who have psychological conditions which could be exacerbated by giving evidence in open court.[6] Regrettably, many asylum seekers are not aware that the cloak of confidentiality which surrounds their claim is lifted for the appeal unless they make a case for retaining it. The Tribunal's practice of reporting asylum cases by initial only provides retrospective protection, which can be extended by direction to other witnesses, and the Tribunal may make other directions necessary for preserving confidentiality.[7]

1   'A fair and public hearing': see eg *R v Secretary of State for Health, ex p Associated Newspapers* [2001] 1 WLR 292, CA.
2   Tribunal Procedures (First-tier Tribunal) (Immigration and Asylum Chamber) Rules 2014, SI 2014/2604, r 27(1).
3   SI 2014/2604, r 27(4).
4   SI 2014/2604, r 27(4)(d).
5   SI 2014/2604, r 27(5).
6   See *R v Legal Aid Board, ex p Kaim Todner* [1999] QB 966. For general principles underlying withholding of identity, see *A-G v Leveller Magazine Ltd* [1979] AC 440; see also *R v Westminster City Council, ex p Castelli* (1995) 7 Admin LR at 845.
7   SI 2014/2604, r 4(2) which gives wide powers to regulate the conduct of hearings; see in particular r 45(4)(i).

20.127 In addition to these circumstances, there is a duty to hold a hearing in private where evidence is being given of the method of detection of a forgery of a document relied on by a party to an appeal (such as a passport, other travel document or work permit) and it is alleged that it would be contrary to the public interest to disclose the methods of detection.[1] This is a very wide power (although rarely if ever used) and it is difficult to see why it has been retained. Such evidence is given in the presence of the parties in a criminal trial, and should also be given in an immigration matter, particularly when the burden of proving such an allegation falls on the Home Office and it will be impossible to challenge it, if the appellant does not know how the Home Office are proving it.

1   Tribunal Procedures (First-tier Tribunal) (Immigration and Asylum Chamber) Rules 2014, SI 2014/2604, r 27(1), referring to NIAA 2002, s 108.

Transfer of proceedings

20.128 Under previous procedure rules, specific powers were given to a senior adjudicator to transfer an appeal which an adjudicator had started to hear, where it was not practicable for the original adjudicator to complete the hearing or give a determination justly or without undue delay.[1] This power was used where an appeal was part-heard and events conspired to prevent its return to the adjudicator who started hearing the case within a reasonable time[2] or at all. Although such specific power no longer exists, it is inherent in the general power to decide the procedure to be followed in relation to any appeal,[3] in accordance with the overriding objectives of fairness, speed and efficiency,[4] and it is dealt with in the Tribunal's Practice Direction.[5] The cases under previous rules remain relevant. Where an appeal is adjourned because of interpretation problems, the appeal should be transferred to another Tribunal unless the original Tribunal is satisfied that he or she can properly continue to hear the appeal and both of the parties expressly consent to that Tribunal continuing to hear the appeal.[6] Failure by an adjudicator to obtain a transfer order to remedy a listing error by the appellate authority which prevented the Home Office presenting officer from appearing before the adjudicator rendered the hearing that took place unfair.[7] Transfer was held not unfair and justified when there had been a delay of ten months in a part-heard appeal, although the effect was that the appellant lost the benefit of provisional positive credibility findings.[8] On transfer the new Tribunal stands in the shoes of the first Tribunal.[9]

[1] Immigration and Asylum Appeals (Procedure) Rules 2003, SI 2003/652, r 52(1).
[2] A delay of four months between hearings led to the determination being ruled unsafe in *Kissi* (11873) (27 February 1995, unreported), IAT, and five months in *Jeyanthan* (11975) (30 March 1995, unreported), IAT.
[3] Tribunal Procedures (First-tier Tribunal)(Immigration and Asylum Chamber) Rules 2014, SI 2014/2604, r 4(2).
[4] SI 2014/2604, r 2(3).
[5] ATI PD (30 April 2007), para 12.1, which enables a senior or designated immigration judge to direct transfer on the same basis as before.
[6] *A (Ethiopia)* [2003] UKIAT 00103.
[7] *Secretary of State for the Home Department v I (Somalia)* [2004] UKIAT 00062.
[8] *R v Special Adjudicator, ex p Akdogan (Hasan)* (CO 1357/99) (11 February 2000, unreported), QBD.
[9] Practice Direction 1/2005, para 12.2.

After the hearing

20.129 The Tribunal may indicate during the hearing that it is prepared to receive further evidence and/or submissions within a specified time, in order to do justice between the parties and ensure that all issues are not only ventilated but that all the requisite evidence and arguments are deployed in their support. The first guiding rule is equality of treatment; if an appellant is given extra time to submit a document which has not arrived in time for the hearing, the respondent must be afforded an opportunity to deal with it, in writing or even, if necessary, by reconvening the hearing. The course to be adopted will depend on the circumstances of the case, the approach of the parties and the Tribunal to the hearing itself.[1] The second guiding rule is that if the Tribunal has allowed time for further submissions, they must not be ignored if they are sent within the specified time.[2] If the Tribunal gives an indication at the end of the hearing that it intends to allow the appeal, it is obliged to allow further evidence or submissions if it changes its mind.[3] The Tribunal remains seised of the appeal, and so able to take account of new evidence, up until the time when its decision is formally notified to the parties.[4]

[1] *Bwamiki* (17710) (10 July 1998, unreported), IAT.
[2] *Singh (Billa)* (G0071) (21 January 1999, unreported), IAT. The admission of fresh evidence would not depend on an indication by the Tribunal at the hearing, however; if further relevant evidence becomes available between the hearing and the promulgation of the determination, it should be submitted to the Tribunal and to the other party, and if not taken into account could form the basis of an application for appeal or review (see CHAPTER 21): *E v Secretary of State for the Home Department, R v Secretary of State for the Home Department* [2004] EWCA Civ 49, [2004] INLR 268.
[3] *R v Special Adjudicator, ex p Bashir* [2002] Imm AR 1, AC; *K (Rwanda)* [2003] UKIAT 00047. The same applies where the Tribunal reconsiders a positive finding on credibility that has been communicated to the parties: *Paudel* [2002] UKIAT 06868.
[4] *E v Secretary of State for the Home Department, R v Secretary of State for the Home Department* (fn 2 above), paras 27, 92 and *SD (Russia)* [2008] UKAIT 00037.

Errors or irregularities in procedure and administrative errors

20.130 An error of procedure such as a failure to comply with a rule does not by itself invalidate any step taken in the proceedings.[1] Thus it would be an error of law for the Tribunal to treat the rule which required the Secretary of State to serve on the appellant a determination relating to an asylum claim no later than she makes an application for reconsideration[2] as being a precondition for a valid application and failure to comply as automatically invalidating the application.[3] Further, prior to determining an appeal, the Tribunal may make an order or take any other step that it considers appropriate to remedy a procedural error.[4] This would normally be done either by amendment of documents or the giving of any notice, but it is not confined to such steps.

1. Tribunal Procedures (First-tier Tribunal)(Immigration and Asylum Chamber) Rules 2014, SI 2014/2604, r 6(1).
2. SI 2005/230, r 23(5)(a)(i).
3. *NB (Guinea) v Secretary of State for the Home Department* [2008] EWCA Civ 1229, [2008] All ER (D) 121 (Nov). Thus, *HH (Iraq)* [2007] UKAIT 00036 and *RN (Zimbabwe)* [2008] UKAIT 0001 were wrongly decided. However, it would be an error of law for the Tribunal to treat an application for reconsideration where there had been non-compliance with the rule as valid without considering its discretion to make an order invalidating the application: *NB (Guinea)*.
4. SI 2005/230, r 59(1)(b).

Keeping a record of proceedings

20.131 Although the procedure rules are silent on the issue, the Senior President's Practice Statements require the Tribunal to keep a record of proceedings of any hearing and attach the record to the Tribunal's case file.[1] There is a rebuttable presumption that it is accurate.[2] A party's note of the evidence is evidence of what was said by a witness in the proceedings.[3] Where an application for permission to appeal is based on an assertion of fact as to what happened before the Tribunal which is at odds with the record, the allegation should be supported by evidence.[4]

1. Senior President of Tribunals: Practice Statements: Immigration and Asylum Chambers of the First-tier Tribunal and the Upper Tribunal, 10 February 2010, para 5.
2. *Ning* (9863), IAT.
3. *Secretary of State for the Home Department v A (Somalia)* [2003] UKIAT 143.
4. *R (on the application of Bosombanguwa) v Immigration Appeal Tribunal and Secretary of State for the Home Department* [2004] EWHC 1656 (Admin), [2004] All ER (D) 260 (Jul).

MAKING A DETERMINATION

20.132 In order to dispose of an appeal, the tribunal has to make a decision determining various matters,[1] a decision which used to be characterised in the Procedure Rules as a 'determination' ie the decision by the Tribunal in writing to allow or dismiss the appeal. It did not include a procedural, ancillary or preliminary decision.[2] The current Procedure Rules no longer refer to determinations but decisions and decisions which dispose of proceedings.[3] For present purposes, it remains apt to refer to a decision disposing of an appeal as a 'determination' because of the historical currency of the term and because the primary legislation continues to describe the tribunal's role as 'determination of appeal'.[4] If the Tribunal is not unanimous the determination is the decision of the majority and if it is equally divided, the presiding member has a casting vote.[5] The Court of Appeal has more than once deprecated the practice of only one member of a panel signing determinations as giving the impression that the Tribunal's decision making has been delegated to a single member.[6] Written notice of the determination must be provided by the tribunal to every party, together with notification of any right of appeal and how and by when such a right may be exercised.[7] The procedure under the 2005 Procedure Rules, whereby the tribunal served decisions on asylum claims on the Home Office only, leaving the Home Office to serve the determination on the appellant, has gone. Where the tribunal's decision relates to an asylum or humanitarian protection claim, the notice of decision must be accompanied by written reasons for the decision.[8] In any other matter, the tribunal 'may' provide written reasons for its decision; if it does not provide reasons, it must notify the parties of the right to apply for a written statement of reasons.[9] An application for a written statement of reasons must be received by the tribunal within 28 days of being provided with the tribunal's decision,[10] and the tribunal must then send a written statement of reasons as soon as reasonably practicable to each party.[11] If an application for permission to appeal is made to the tribunal before it has given reasons for its decision, the tribunal is to treat the application as an application for written reasons.[12] In fast track cases, the tribunal has to provide 'a notice of decision and the reasons for it'; the Fast Track Rules do not allow for written reasons to be provided after the decision.[13] The Tribunal has held that an appeal relates to an asylum claim only if the immigration decision appealed against follows an asylum claim within the meaning of section 113 of the NIAA 2002, ie a claim made to the Secretary of State at a designated place, whether or not asylum grounds are pursued before the Tribunal; conversely, even if asylum grounds are raised in the appeal, if no such claim was made to the Secretary of State, the appeal does not relate to an asylum claim. The procedure rules define asylum claim as having the same meaning as in section 113 of the NIAA 2002. Until NIAA 2002, section 86 is amended by the Immigration Act 2014, the Tribunal must allow or dismiss an appeal;[14] it cannot allow it on a conditional basis,[15] but an appeal may be allowed to the extent that the matter is remitted to the Secretary of State for consideration in accordance with the law and the correct facts as found by the Tribunal.[16] The Tribunal has indicated in a Practice Direction that where its jurisdiction is exercised by more than one member, there will be no indication whether its decision was unanimous, and dissenting views will not be included in it or otherwise communicated.[17] Although the freedom to express a dissenting view was rarely exercised in the old Immigration Appeal Tribunal, it was not banned, and this direction causes some concern in that it prevents the appellant from knowing what every defendant in a criminal case tried by a jury has the right to know, and offends the principle of open justice.

---

1   NIAA 2002, s 86(2).
2   Asylum and Immigration Tribunal (Procedure) Rules 2005, SI 2005/230, r 2, applied to fast track appeals by SI 2005/560, r 2.
3   Tribunal Procedures (First-tier Tribunal) (Immigration and Asylum Chamber) Rules 2014, SI 2014/2604, r 29.
4   NIAA 2002, s 86, heading.
5   The First-tier Tribunal and Upper Tribunal (Composition of Tribunal) Order 2008, SI 2008/2835, art 8.

6 *DM (Zambia) v Secretary of State for the Home Department* [2009] EWCA Civ 474.
7 SI 2014/2604, r 29(2).
8 SI 2014/2604, r 29(3)(a).
9 SI 2014/2604, r 29(3)(b), (4).
10 SI 2014/2604, r 29(5).
11 SI 2014/2604, r 29(6).
12 SI 2014/2604, r 33(6).
13 SI 2014/2604, Schedule, r 10(1).
14 *Hamdan* (12338) (24 July 1995, unreported), IAT: there is no power to remit to the Secretary of State as an alternative to allowing or dismissing an appeal, although the Tribunal may adjourn to enable the respondent to deal with an issue arising in the course of a hearing.
15 *Secretary of State for the Home Department v Khalil* [1993] Imm AR 481; *Aryee (8707)*, IAT.
16 *Kanahalashmi* (10007), IAT.
17 Practice Direction 1/2005, para 10.

20.133 Determinations of the Tribunal must not only get the law right and keep within the proper sphere of the appellate jurisdiction, but they must also be properly reasoned. Inadequate reasons may form the basis for a successful appeal or review under NIAA 2002. The adequacy of reasons has been dealt with in a number of decisions of the higher courts dealing with a variety of jurisdictions, including planning appeals and employment tribunals as well as immigration appellate authorities. A determination must state what the issues are, the Tribunal's decision on them, and the evidence by which it comes to that conclusion.[1] On a reasons challenge the applicant will need to show substantial prejudice, which can arise through ignorance as to the real basis of the decision.[2] In immigration appeals, as in other appeals,[3] the degree of particularity of reasoning required will vary according to the issues and it is elementary that the duty to give reasons does not require the judge to deal expressly with every point.[4] An immigration judge is not required to give reasons for findings on matters of peripheral importance and an appellate court would be anxious to avoid overturning a first instance decision for want of reasoning 'unless it really cannot understand the original judge's thought processes when he/she was making material findings'.[5] In a deportation appeal the deportee should be able to follow the basis of the conclusion, and the determination should show that the Tribunal has taken account of all the relevant factors and carried out the balancing act required by the rules and by Article 8, ECHR.[6] Among those factors is the public interest in deterring criminality, and whilst a tribunal does not have to cite any of the authorities dealing with that issue, it must show by its reasoning that it has taken that factor into account and applied the correct principles in doing so.[7] In family reunion, asylum and human rights appeals, and in other appeals where much may turn on credibility, the *locus classicus* of the Tribunal's obligation is *Mohammed Amin*:[8] 'An adjudicator should set out with some clarity what evidence was accepted, what rejected, on what evidence no conclusion could be reached and what evidence was irrelevant.' When assessing the adequacy of the Tribunal's reasons, the determination should be read as a whole and in a common-sense way,[9] but avoiding any temptation to rewrite the decision,[10] to see whether sufficient reasons, commensurate with the obligation of 'anxious scrutiny' have been given.[11] That obligation underlines the 'very special human context in which [asylum and human rights cases] are brought and the need for decisions to show by their reasoning that every factor which might tell in favour of an applicant has been properly taken into account'.[12] The reasons given should be sufficient to show why a claimant lost on a particular issue[13] and to show why evidence which might have produced a different conclusion has not done so.[14] Findings must be consistent[15] and adequate.[16] If one or some of the reasons given by the Tribunal for its decision are found to be unsustainable, the question then to be determined is whether it would nevertheless be just to let the Tribunal's decision stand; answering that question depends upon whether the Tribunal's decision would have been the same on the basis of the reasons which survived scrutiny.[17] It is not an answer to a reasons challenge that the case might have been decided in the same way but for different reasons to those given.[18]

1   *R v Immigration Appeal Tribunal, ex p Khan (Mahmud)* [1983] QB 790, [1983] 2 All ER 420, CA. But the Tribunal need not give reasons for each conclusion reached in the course of the decision: *R v Criminal Injuries Compensation Board, ex p Cook* [1996] 1 WLR 1037; *Bolton Metropolitan District Council v Secretary of State for the Environment* (1995) 71 P & CR 309; *Arulanandam (Selliah) v Secretary of State for the Home Department* [1996] Imm AR 587, CA.

2   *Save Britain's Heritage v Secretary of State for the Home Department* [1991] 1 WLR 153, HL, per Lord Bridge.

3   *Union of Construction Allied Trades and Technicians v Brain* [1981] ICR 542, CA, per Lord Denning MR.

4   *AT (Guinea) v Secretary of State for the Home Department* [2006] EWCA Civ 1889, [2007] All ER (D) 182 (Mar).

5   *R (Iran) v Secretary of State for the Home Department* [2005] EWCA Civ 982 having cited with approval *Eagil Trust Co Ltd v Pigott Brown* [1985] 3 All ER 119, CA and *English v Emery Reimbold & Strick Ltd* [2002] EWCA Civ 605, [2002] 3 All ER 385, [2002] 1 WLR 2409; *Budhathoki (Reasons for decisions)* [2014] UKUT 341 (IAC). Whilst not necessary to 'rehearse every detail or issue raised', it is necessary for judges 'to identify and resolve the key conflicts in the evidence and explain in clear and brief terms their reasons for preferring one case to the other so that the parties can understand why they have won or lost'; *Haleemudeen v Secretary of State for the Home Department* [2014] EWCA Civ 558: reasons would be adequate if they give 'sufficient detail to show the parties and the appellate tribunal or reviewing court the principles upon which the lower tribunal has acted and the reasons that led to its decision so that they are able to understand why it reached its decision'.

6   *R v Immigration Appeal Tribunal, ex p Dhaliwal* [1994] Imm AR 387, QBD.

7   *AM v Secretary of State for the Home Department* [2012] EWCA Civ 1634; *PK (Congo) v Secretary of State for the Home Department* [2013] EWCA Civ 1500.

8   *R v Immigration Appeal Tribunal, ex p Amin* [1992] Imm AR 367, QBD; see also *Singh (Jaswinder) v Secretary of State for the Home Department* 1998 SLT 1370; *Mecheti v Secretary of State for the Home Department* [1996] SCLR 998; *Senthuran v Secretary of State for the Home Department* [2004] EWCA Civ 950, [2004] 4 All ER 365; *AK (Turkey)* [2004] UKIAT 00230.

9   *R (on the application of Bouchaal) v Immigration Appeal Tribunal* [2002] EWHC 1517 (Admin), [2002] All ER (D) 264 (Jun); *R (on the application of Kolcak) v Immigration Appeal Tribunal* [2001] Imm AR 666; *R (on the application of Mohamad) v Special Adjudicator* [2002] EWHC 2496 (Admin).

10 *R (on the application of Bahrami) v Immigration Appeal Tribunal* [2003] EWHC 1453 (Admin), [2003] All ER (D) 24 (Jun); see also Davis J in *R (on the application of Tesfaye) v Immigration Appeal Tribunal* [2004] EWHC 460 (Admin), [2004] All ER (D) 377 (Feb): 'This Court is entitled to have the reasons from the adjudicator and the Tribunal and not from [counsel for the Secretary of State]'.

11 *R (on the application of Kurecaj) v Secretary of State for the Home Department* [2001] EWHC 1199 (Admin), [2001] All ER (D) 278 (Dec); *Mohammadi v Advocate-General for Scotland* 2004 SCLR 612, OH.

12 Carnwath LJ in *R (on the application of YH) v Secretary of State for the Home Department* [2010] EWCA Civ 116 at [24]. Where the decision being appealed affects the welfare of a child, the reasoning would need to demonstrate careful appraisal of the child's circumstances: *Peart v Secretary of State for the Home Department* [2012] EWCA Civ 568.

13 *Senthuran v Secretary of State for the Home Department* [2004] EWCA Civ 950; *R (on the application of Bahrami) v Immigration Appeal Tribunal* [2003] EWHC 1453 (Admin), [2003] All ER (D) 24 (Jun); *Krayem v Secretary of State for the Home Department* [2003] EWCA Civ 649, [2003] All ER (D) 80 (Apr) (reasons inadequate to show why a finding of

persecution did not follow from evidence as to general conditions for Palestinian refugees in Lebanon). See also *Tezgel v Secretary of State for the Home Department* [2004] EWCA Civ 1766.

14   *GM (Burundi) v Secretary of State for the Home Department* [2007] EWCA Civ 18. It would not be sufficient for a judge to say that he or she was attaching no weight to an important piece of evidence relied on by the appellant or to say that he or she did not believe a witness without reasons to explain those conclusions: *MK (Duty to give reasons) Pakistan* [2013] UKUT 641 (IAC). Good reasons need to be given for rejecting an expert opinion: *SS (Sri Lanka) v Secretary of State for the Home Department* [2012] EWCA Civ 155.

15   *Singh (Avtar)* (12547) (26 September 1995, unreported), IAT; *Tadesse* (15079) (19 May 1997, unreported), IAT.

16   In *R v Secretary of State for the Home Department, ex p Atputharajah* [2001] Imm AR 566, Elias J posed two tests for adequacy of reasons: (1) do the alleged defects create a genuine (as opposed to forensic) doubt whether a significant issue in dispute was properly addressed; (2) if so, is there any real doubt as to whether the decision would have been the same? See also *Januzi v Secretary of State for the Home Department* [2003] EWCA Civ 1188 (conclusion that return to Kosovo would not lead to deterioration of the claimant's mental health inadequately reasoned given that the only medical evidence showed such a deterioration would occur); *R (on the application of Kurecaj) v Secretary of State for the Home Department* [2001] EWHC 1199 (Admin), [2001] All ER (D) 278 (Dec); *R (on the application of Arzpeyma) v Secretary of State for the Home Department* [2002] EWHC 2395, [2002] All ER (D) 21 (Nov) (no finding on weight, if any, attached to the evidence of a supporting witness).

17   *HK v Secretary of State for the Home Department* [2006] EWCA Civ 1037, [2006] All ER (D) 281 (Jul).

18   *HF (Algeria) v Secretary of State for the Home Department* [2007] EWCA Civ 445, [2007] All ER (D) 302 (May).

20.134 Material facts must be the subject of clear findings.[1] A general statement that the appellant is not credible is insufficient.[2] What is sufficient reasoning will be dependant on the issues in the particular case: it may be sufficient for a Tribunal that has heard a witness to say that it accepts his or her evidence[3] or to set out the main points advanced against the witness together with the responses to them in order to show that they have been considered by the judge.[4] A positive conclusion as to the credibility of an appellant would be inadequately reasoned if reached without explaining what the judge made of significant discrepancies in the appellant's evidence.[5] However, a judge does not have to provide reasons that reconcile discrepant and evasive evidence with the core account that the judge accepts.[6] The Tribunal is not required to deal with credibility points that have not been raised in the refusal letter or in the course of cross-examination or submissions.[7] In asylum and human rights appeals it must be clear from the substance of the decision that the Tribunal applied the correct standard of proof but recitation of a particular formula is not required.[8] A mechanical recitation of a certain formula to show matters have been taken into account may be inadequate.[9] If an appellant puts forward an Article 3 case that is distinguishable from his or her Refugee Convention grounds, the Tribunal is bound to give specific reasons for rejecting the Article 3 case; it would not be sufficient to say that the Article 3 case failed for the same reasons as the refugee claim.[10] When making a decision on proportionality in an Article 8 case, it is not sufficient for the Tribunal merely to say that a decision is or is not proportionate; a properly and carefully reasoned decision is required.[11] The Court of Appeal found the Tribunal's reasoning inadequate where it failed to explain why it was 'not greatly assisted' by relevant country expert evidence;[12] failure to give adequate reasons for the conclusion that the appellant was 'living alone';[13] failure to give reasons for rejecting the evidence in the appellant's witness statement;[14] failed, in making a country guidance determination, to show that it had sufficiently addressed 'potentially important parts' of the evidence of two witnesses;[15] failure to show that a key part of a country guidance decision had been applied;[16] failure to give reasons showing what the tribunal made of a probation officer's report relevant to the risk the appellant reoffending.[17] The Court of Appeal does not have power to invite the Tribunal to supplement its reasoning as an alternative to determining whether the Tribunal had erred in law by failing to give adequate reasons.[18]

[1] Although not every single point in dispute need be the subject of a separate finding (*Rai* (00TH00048)), all material aspects of a claim should be the subject of clear findings: *Habtegiorgis* (14446) (13 January 1997, unreported); *R (on the application of Orlenko) v Immigration Appeal Tribunal* [2002] EWHC 1960 (Admin), [2002] All ER (D) 270 (Jul) (no clear finding on risk of suffering conditions shown by background evidence to be prevalent and whether conditions breached art 3); *Yelocagi v Secretary of State for the Home Department* (16 May 2000, unreported), CA; *R (on the application of Hussein) v Immigration Appeal Tribunal* [2003] EWHC 769 (Admin) (unclear whether claimant's evidence about being tortured whilst in detention was accepted or not).; *El-Rifai v Secretary of State for the Home Department* [2005] EWCA Civ 385, [2005] All ER (D) 263 (Feb).

[2] *Nicu* (11615) (7 December 1994, unreported); *Gharbi* (11791) (23 January 1995, unreported); *Ayinde* (13015) (20 February 1996, unreported); *Muthengi* (13571) (24 June 1996, unreported); *Aboud* (15127) (23 June 1997, unreported), IAT; *Kaffash* [2002] UKIAT 00549 (use of the term 'a very low credibility assessment' not sufficiently clear finding of fact). In *HJ (Iran) v Secretary of State for the Home Department* [2006] EWCA Civ 1796, [2006] All ER (D) 56 (Dec) the Court of Appeal held that the Tribunal's generic rejection of the central core of the appellant's evidence was not legally adequate; he was entitled to a specific finding in relation to the events said to have given rise to his fear of being persecuted.

[3] *RH (Ghana) v Secretary of State for the Home Department* [2007] EWCA Civ 640, [2007] All ER (D) 37 (Jun); *MS, MK and MT (Sierra Leone) v Secretary of State for the Home Department* [2010] EWCA Civ 1369.

[4] *JK (Democratic Republic of Congo) v Secretary of State for the Home Department* [2007] EWCA Civ 831.

[5] *Malaba v Secretary of State for the Home Department* [2006] EWCA Civ 820, [2006] All ER (D) 225 (Jun).

[6] *KU (Pakistan) v Secretary of State for the Home Department* [2012] EWCA Civ 107.

[7] *R (on the application of FD (Zimbabwe)) v Secretary of State for the Home Department* [2007] EWCA Civ 1220.

[8] *SR (Iran) v Secretary of State for the Home Department* [2007] EWCA Civ 460, 151 Sol Jo LB 673, [2007] All ER (D) 294 (May).

[9] *R v Immigration Appeal Tribunal, ex p Iqbal (Iram)* [1993] Imm AR 270, QBD; *Entry Clearance Officer, Islamabad v Khan* [1993] Imm AR 68; *Saini v Secretary of State for the Home Department* [1993] Imm AR 96.

[10] *RM (Somalia) v Secretary of State for the Home Department* [2007] EWCA Civ 751, [2007] All ER (D) 169 (Oct).

[11] *AG (Eritrea) v Secretary of State for the Home Department* [2007] EWCA Civ 801; *KR (Iraq) v Secretary of State for the Home Department* [2007] EWCA Civ 514, [2007] All ER (D) 426 (May); *DS (Afghanistan) v Secretary of State for the Home Department* [2007] EWCA Civ 774, [2007] All ER (D) 397 (Jul). The tribunal's reasons should show that where the appellant was long resident and came to the UK as a child, consideration had been given to the factors identified as relevant in *Uner v Netherlands* (2006) 45 EHRR 421 and *Maslov v Austria* (2007) 47 EHRR 496: see *HM (Iraq) v Secretary of State for the Home Department* [2010] EWCA Civ 1322.

[12] *DK v Secretary of State for the Home Department* [2006] EWCA Civ 682.

[13] *EK v Secretary of State for the Home Department* [2006] EWCA Civ 926, [2006] All ER (D) 31 (Jun).

[14] *Hussein v Secretary of State for the Home Department* [2006] EWCA Civ 953, [2006] All ER (D) 221 (Jun).

[15] *AA (Zimbabwe) v Secretary of State for the Home Department* [2007] EWCA Civ 149, [2007] All ER (D) 73 (Mar).

[16] *MP (Sri Lanka) v Secretary of State for the Home Department* [2011] EWCA Civ 362.

[17] *Peart v Secretary of State for the Home Department* [2012] EWCA Civ 568.

18 *Hatungimana v Secretary of State for the Home Department* [2006] EWCA Civ 231, (2006) Times, 2 March, [2006] All ER (D) 281 (Feb).

20.135 A material misdirection of fact in the determination will ground an appeal if it affects the general conclusion,[1] although a factual error on one issue does not necessarily vitiate the determination.[2] There is nothing objectionable in the Tribunal adopting the Secretary of State's decision letter, but there is a risk that any error in the letter will infect the decision,[3] and Tribunals must reach independent decisions following their own assessment of the evidence,[4] not simply ask themselves whether there was a proper basis for disagreeing with the decision maker.[5] It is incumbent on Tribunals to deal with all the issues before them.[6] In relation to appeals heard under earlier legislation, the Court of Appeal indicated that where an appeal was allowed on one ground, it was desirable that the Tribunal should decide all the other issues before it, particularly where findings of fact were involved, since they might become important on a subsequent appeal.[7] A starred Tribunal gave the opposite guidance.[8] It is clearly both wise and in accordance with the overriding objective of appeals for findings to be made on all disputed issues of fact and decisions reached on all issues raised. Moreover, there is now a statutory obligation on the Tribunal to 'determine any matter raised as a ground of appeal' so that the Tribunal may not, because it decides to allow an appeal on one ground, decline to determine the other grounds of appeal.[9] However, it is not obliged to determine grounds of appeal that have been abandoned, eg where the appellant adduces no evidence or makes no submissions in support of a particular ground.[10]

1 *Manzeke (Bambagu) v Secretary of State for the Home Department* [1997] Imm AR 524, CA; *R (on the application of Judes) v Secretary of State for the Home Department* [2001] EWCA Civ 825, [2001] All ER (D) 168 (May) (permission to appeal refused on erroneous basis that adjudicator had seen medical report); *Haile v Immigration Appeal Tribunal* [2001] EWCA Civ 663, [2002] Imm AR 170, [2002] INLR 283 (finding of credibility dependent on a mistaken view of the story told by the appellant). See also *Abdi (Dhudi Saleban) v Secretary of State for the Home Department* [1996] Imm AR 148.
2 *R v Secretary of State for the Home Department, ex p Yasun* [1998] Imm AR 215, QBD; *Wahome* (12755) (21 November 1995, unreported). Where the decision depended on the accuracy and reliability of the conclusions on credibility of the fact-finding Tribunal, and that Tribunal had made strange errors of fact such as describing a Pakistani asylum seeker as 'Egyptian' as well as giving inadequate reasons for disbelieving the appellant, the decision was unsafe: *R (on the application of Ahmed) v Secretary of State for the Home Department* [2004] EWCA Civ 552, [2004] AII ER (D) 154 (Jan).
3 *R v Immigration Appeal Tribunal, ex p Peranantham* (20 June 1996), QBD; remitted *de novo* by IAT at (13752) (29 July 1996, unreported).
4 *Xie* (14644) (14 March 1997, unreported) (adoption of Secretary of State letter rendered decision flawed); *Al-Musshadi* (11254) (15 August 1994, unreported); *Randhawa* (11514) (3 November 1994, unreported); *Atwal* (12229) (27 June 1995, unreported) (adoption of previous determination of same appeal rendered decision flawed); *Oyeleye v Entry Clearance Officer, Lagos (01TH02325)*, IAT; *Iqbal v Entry Clearance Officer, Islamabad* [2002] UKIAT 01860.
5 *A (Nigeria) v Entry Clearance Officer* [2004] UKIAT 00019.
6 *Stefanescu* (11491); *Sakota* (13576) (24 June 1996, unreported), IAT.
7 *McPherson v Secretary of State for the Home Department* [2001] EWCA Civ 1955; [2002] INLR 139. The Tribunal held in the context of 'mixed' appeals (the precursor of 'one-stop' appeals, that it was an error of law to omit consideration of one limb of the appeal: *Angus* (17706) (8 July 1998, unreported); *Dragica* (13288) (29 April 1996, unreported), IAT.
8 *Hassan (Ahmed Faraj)* [2002] UKIAT 00062.
9 NIAA 2002, s 86(2)(a); *Emunefe v Secretary of State for the Home Department* [2005] EWCA Civ 2002; *CS (Jamaica)* [2006] UKAIT 00004.

20.136 The procedure rules require the tribunal to provide notice of its decision no later than two days after concluding the hearing of an appeal in the fast track.[1] Otherwise, they do not specify a time within which the tribunal is to decide an appeal. Case law under earlier procedure rules, which similarly imposed no such time limits, held that delay in the promulgation of the determination did not by itself render a determination unsafe; it is necessary to show prejudice attributable to the delay.[2] The Tribunal has said that normally, a period of over three months between the date of hearing and promulgation is unacceptable where credibility is in issue,[3] although this is only a guide and it is not applicable where there is no prejudice, for example where the delay is administrative or where credibility findings were contemporaneously recorded, or where the decision was justified on grounds which did not depend on recollection and assessment of oral evidence[4] or where, because the nature of the evidence or other material before the Tribunal made its falsehood or absurdity plain.[5] Even a delay of nearly two and a half years would not make a determination unlawful because of the absence of any nexus between the delay and the safety of the decision.[6] Where there has been delay in promulgating a determination, the inference that something has been overlooked or forgotten by the Tribunal will be more readily drawn, particularly if there is no specific mention of it in the determination.[7]

[1] Tribunal Procedure (First-tier Tribunal)(Immigration and Asylum Chamber) Rules 2014, SI 2014/2604, Sch, r 10(2).
[2] *R (on the application of Ghorbani) v Immigration Appeal Tribunal* [2004] EWHC 510 (Admin), [2004] All ER (D) 83 (Mar); *Cobham v Frett* [2001] 1 WLR 1775 (PC).
[3] *Memorandum to Tribunal chairs*, referred to in *Waiganjo* (R15717) (17 October 1997, unreported), IAT. See *Mario v Secretary of State for the Home Department* [1998] Imm AR 281; *Omonijo* [2002] UKIAT 02643.
[4] *Sad-Chaouche (17423)* (19 June 1998, unreported), IAT; *Behre v Secretary of State for the Home Department* [2000] Imm AR 463, CA (11-month delay before promulgation did not cause prejudice as case turned on issues of law, although it brought the appellate authority into disrepute); see also *B (Albania)* [2003] UKIAT 00028.
[5] *Sambasivan v Secretary of State for the Home Department* [2000] Imm AR 85, [2000] INLR 105, CA. So a delay of nine months did not give rise to concern since it did not depend on oral evidence, there had been no material change, and nothing else had been put forward suggesting prejudice to the appellant: *R v Immigration Appeal Tribunal, ex p Shandar* [2000] Imm AR 181, QB; *Berhe* above. But in *Ehalaivan* (4275/99) 14 June 2000, CA, a delay of two months before dictating a determination should have been addressed by the Tribunal in considering leave to appeal.
[6] *RK (Algeria) v Secretary of State for the Home Department* [2007] EWCA Civ 868, [2007] All ER (D) 100 (Oct).
[7] *R (on the application of Ghorbani) v Immigration Appeal Tribunal* [2004] EWHC 510 (Admin), [2004] All ER (D) 83 (Mar).

POST-DETERMINATION POWERS OF THE TRIBUNAL

20.137 The Tribunal has a limited range of powers in respect of its decision once promulgated. Procedural irregularities (other than late service of the determination) discovered after the Tribunal's determination can normally only be dealt with by way of an appeal.[1] The power to correct slips is the only inherent power that the Tribunal has to amend, rescind or review its own decisions; any other powers must be conferred by statute.[2] The Tribunal has power to correct clerical or other accidental errors, slips and omissions by amendment of orders, notices and determinations.[3] It must serve the amended document on the parties on whom the original document was served,[4] except in fast track appeals, and if the error was contained in the determination of the appeal, time for applying for review and permission to appeal runs from the date of service of the amended determination.[5] In addition, the Tribunal has the power to set aside and re-make a decision disposing of the appeal if it considers that it is in the interests of justice to do so and there was a procedural irregularity in the proceedings, such as a document not being provided to or received by a party or the tribunal at an appropriate time, or a party or party's representative was not present at a hearing.[6] An application for a decision to be set aside has to be made within 28 days if the appellant is outside the UK or 14 days in any other case.[7] review any order, notice of decision or determination made by the Tribunal and may set it aside with a direction that the relevant proceedings be dealt with again. This power may be exercised on the ground that the order, notice of decision or determination was wrongly made as a result of an administrative error on the part of the Tribunal or its staff.

[1]   ie under Tribunals, Courts and Enforcement Act 2007, s 11 to the Upper Tribunal.
[2]   *Akewushola v Secretary of State for the Home Department* [2000] 1 WLR 2295.
[3]   Tribunals, Courts and Enforcement Act 2007, Sch 5, para 15 and SI 2014/2604, r 31. See, for example, *MF (Palestinian Territories)* [2007] UKAIT 00092.
[4]   SI 2014/2604, r 31.
[5]   SI 2014/2604, r 33(4).
[6]   SI 2014/2604, r 32(1), (2).
[7]   SI 2014/2604, r 32(3).

REVIEW

20.138 The Tribunals, Courts and Enforcement Act 2007 gives the FT a power to review a decision made by it on 'a matter in a case'.[1] The power may be exercised by the Tribunal of its own initiative or on the application of a party to the appeal[2] and if the Tribunal receives an application for permission to appeal to the UT it must consider whether to review the decision against which permission to appeal is sought before deciding the permission application.[3] The Tribunal may exercise the power only if it is satisfied that there was an error of law in the decision.[4] Having reviewed a decision, the Tribunal may correct accidental errors in the decision or record of the decision, amend reasons given for the decision or set the decision aside.[5] The Tribunal is likely to set a decision aside only if it is satisfied that the effect of the error of law was to deprive a party of a fair hearing or other opportunity to put its case or there are highly compelling reasons, which are likely to be rare, why the matter should be re-decided.[6] If the Tribunal sets the decision aside it must re-decide the matter or refer the matter to the Upper Tribunal[7] which must then re-decide the matter[8] and in doing so, may make any decision that the FT Tribunal could make if re-deciding the matter itself.[9] Findings of fact may be made for the purpose of re-deciding the matter.[10] The Act and the Procedure Rules do not define 'a matter in a case'. The Tribunal may not review 'an excluded decision'[11] other than a decision upon review to set aside a decision,[12] in which case the power of the Tribunal upon reviewing such a decision is limited to correcting accidental errors.[13] A decision may be reviewed no more than once and a decision may not be reviewed if the Tribunal had previously decided not to review it.[14] However, if a matter is re-decided following a review, the new decision may itself be reviewed.[15] The Tribunal must give written notice to the parties in writing of the outcome of any review and any right of appeal in relation to the outcome.[16] If the Tribunal had taken action following a review without first having given the parties an opportunity to make representation, the parties may apply for the action to be set aside and for the decision to be reviewed again.[17]

1   TCEA 2007, s 9(1).
2   TCEA 2007, s 9(2).
3   Tribunal Procedure (First-tier Tribunal)(Immigration and Asylum Chamber) Rules 2014, SI 2014/2604, r 34(1).
4   TCEA 2007, s 9(3)(c) and (d) and SI 2014/2604, r 35(1)(b).
5   TCEA 2007, s 9(4).
6   Senior President of Tribunals Practice Statements: Immigration and Asylum Chambers of the FT Tribunal and the Upper Tribunal, para 4.
7   TCEA 2007, s 9(5).
8   TCEA 2007, s 9(6).
9   TCEA 2007, s 9(7).
10 TCEA 2007, s 9(8).
11 Tribunals, Courts and Enforcement Act 2007, s 9(1). For the meaning of 'excluded decision' see 20.2.
12 TCEA 2007, s 9(9).
13 TCEA 2007, s 9(9).
14 TCEA 2007, s 9(1).
15 TCEA 2007, s 9(11).
16 SI 2014/2604, r 35(2).
17 SI 2014/2604, r 35(3).

PERMISSION TO APPEAL TO THE UPPER TRIBUNAL

20.139 Applications for permission to appeal to the UT must be made in the first instance to the FT Tribunal.[1] They are dealt with in CHAPTER 21 below.

1   TCEA 2007, s 11(1) and (4) and the Tribunal Procedure (Upper Tribunal) Rules 2008, SI 2008/2698, r 21(2).

Chapter 21

APPEALS TO THE UPPER TRIBUNAL, THE COURT OF APPEAL AND APPLICATIONS FOR JUDICIAL REVIEW

1895

THE UPPER TRIBUNAL

21.1 The Upper Tribunal (UT) was created by section 3(1) of the Tribunals, Courts and Enforcement Act 2007 (TCEA 2007) to exercise the functions conferred on it by the TCEA 2007 or any other Act. Its members are part of the judiciary whose continued independence is guaranteed by statute.[1] It has been given 'the same powers, rights, privileges and authority' as the High Court in England, Wales and Northern Ireland and the Court of Session in Scotland[2] and is designated a 'superior court of record'.[3] A superior court of record is one that can be presumed to act within its powers unless the contrary is shown (as opposed to one required always to demonstrate that it is acting within its jurisdiction); its decisions have effect as precedents for lower courts and tribunals and it has power to punish for contempt.[4] However, the mere fact of designation as a superior court of record does not render the UT immune from judicial review, nor does the fact that the TCEA 2007 confers on the UT standing and powers akin to those of the High Court.[5] The UT is subject to the supervisory jurisdiction of the High Court but to the limited extent appropriate to reflect the status of the new tribunal structure as 'a newly coherent and comprehensive edifice designed, among other things, to complete the long process of divorcing administrative justice from departmental policy, to ensure the application across the board of proper standards of adjudication, and to provide for the correction of legal error within rather than outside the system, with recourse on second-appeal criteria to the higher appellate courts'.[6] Thus judicial review of unappealable decisions of the UT (such as refusing to grant permission to appeal from the First-tier Tribunal) is available: see paragraph **21.67** onwards below.

[1]   Constitutional Reform Act 2005, s 3 (as amended by TCEA 2007, s 1) and Sch 14.
[2]   TCEA 2007, s 25(1).
[3]   TCEA 2007, s 3(5).
[4]   *R (Cart) v The Upper Tribunal* [2009] EWHC 3052 (Admin), para 75 and [2010] EWCA Civ 859, para 17.
[5]   *R (Cart) v The Upper Tribunal* [2010] EWCA Civ 859, para 21.
[6]   *R (Cart) v The Upper Tribunal* [2010] EWCA Civ 859, para 42.

The right of appeal and excluded decisions

21.2 There is a right of appeal to the Upper Tribunal (UT), with the permission of the First-tier Tribunal (FT) or UT, from decisions of the FT which are not 'excluded decisions'.[1] The right of appeal is given to 'any party to a case';[2] it is not restricted to the losing party.[3] Excluded decisions are decisions taken by the FT in the exercise of its power to review its own decisions[4] and decisions of the FT set aside on review by the FT.[5] In addition, the Lord Chancellor may by order specify descriptions of decisions which are excluded[6] if they are decisions which carry another right of appeal to a Court or Tribunal[7] or if they are decisions made in proceedings of a kind transferred into the FT or UT and prior to their transfer were unappealable.[8] The Lord Chancellor has made such an order in respect of decisions on bail and any procedural, ancillary or preliminary decision made in relation to an appeal under NIAA 2002, sections 82, 83 or 83A or in relation to an appeal against an EEA decision or against deprivation of British citizenship.[9] A refusal by the FT to extend time for appealing is a preliminary decision against which there is no right of appeal.[10] A decision by the FT not to make a fee award is an 'ancillary decision' and thus not appealable.[11] A decision made following a hearing, including a decision that there was no valid appeal or that for some other reason the FT did not have jurisdiction, was not a 'preliminary' and therefore 'excluded decision' but had to be made in the form of a determination and could be appealed to the UT.[12]

[1]   TCEA 2007, s 11.
[2]   TCEA 2007, s 11(2).
[3]   Reconsideration of an appeal under the now repealed section 103A of NIAA 2002 could be sought by an appellant whose appeal had been allowed but only on some of the grounds on which he or she relied. See, for example, *AS (Iran)* [2006] UKAIT 00037 where the Tribunal recognised that the appellant would be in a substantially better position if his appeal was allowed on ECHR Article 3 grounds as well as Article 8 grounds. *In EG & NG (UT rule 17: withdrawal; rule 24: scope) Ethiopia* [2013] UKUT 143 the UT held that the winning party had to make an application for permission to appeal if they considered that the appeal should have been allowed on alternative grounds and could not utilise the Reply to raise those grounds of appeal.
[4]   TCEA 2007, s 11(5)(d), discussed above at **20.138**.
[5]   TCEA 2007, s 11(5)(e).
[6]   TCEA 2007, s 11(5)(f).
[7]   TCEA 2007, s 11(6)(a).
[8]   TCEA 2007, s 11(6)(b).

9   Appeals (Excluded Decisions) Order 2009, SI 2009/275, as amended, arts 2(b) and 3(m).
10   *NA (Afghanistan)* [2010] UKUT 444 (IAC).
11   *Singh (Sandip) v Secretary of State for the Home Department* [2014] EWCA Civ 438.
12   *Abiyat (Iran)* [2011] UKUT 314 (IAC).

CONSTITUTION OF THE UPPER TRIBUNAL

21.3 The UT consists of its judges and other members[1] and, together with the FT it is presided over by the Senior President of Tribunals.[2] It is organised into Chambers, each having one or two Chambers Presidents[3] and one of which is the Immigration and Asylum Chamber.[4] Presently, the Immigration and Asylum Chamber of the UT has assigned to it all functions relating to appeals from a decision of the Immigration and Asylum Chamber of the FT and references to it by the FT in the exercise of the FT's review power.[5] The judges of the UT are the Senior President of Tribunals, the Chamber Presidents or Deputy Presidents, Social Security Commissioners, appointed judges and transferred in judges.[6] Judges may be appointed by the Queen on the recommendation of the Lord Chancellor and a person is eligible for appointment if, in England or Wales he or she is a solicitor, barrister, Fellow of the Institute of Legal Executives, a registered patent agent or registered trade mark agent and has gained legal experience as such for at least seven years;[7] in Scotland, is an advocate or solicitor of at least seven years standing; in Northern Ireland, is a barrister or solicitor of at least seven years standing[8] or is someone who has gained experience in law making that person in the opinion of the Lord Chancellor as suitable for appointment as if they had met one of the other conditions.[9] Transferred in judges are those who were members of another tribunal, the functions of which were transferred to the UT and who are made UT judges by order of the Lord Chancellor.[10] The Deputy Presidents and Senior Immigration Judges of the AIT are transferred-in judges of the UT and Designated Immigration Judges of the AIT are transferred-in deputy judges of the UT.[11] Appointed and transferred in judges and other members of the UT are assigned to at least one chamber of the UT.[12] In addition, judges of the Court of Appeal, the Court of Session and the High Court, circuit judges, county court judges, sheriffs in Scotland and district judges are ex officio judges of the UT as well as of the FT.[13] 'Other members' of the UT[14] are appointed by the Lord Chancellor, those eligible for appointment being holders of prescribed qualifications which include membership of various professions (eg medical, surveyors, accountancy) or having 'substantial experience' of various matters, one of which is 'immigration services or the law and procedure relating to immigration'.[15]

1   TCEA 2007, s 3(3).
2   TCEA 2007, s 3(4).
3   TCEA 2007, s 7.
4   First-tier Tribunal and Upper Tribunal (Chambers) Order 2008, SI 2008/2684, art 6(d).
5   SI 2008/2684, art 9A.
6   TCEA 2007, s 5(1).
7   TCEA 2007, ss 50– 52, Sch 3, para 1 and the Judicial Appointments Order 2008, SI 2008/2995.
8   TCEA 2007, Sch 3, para 1(2)(b) and (c).
9   TCEA 2007, Sch 3, para 1(2)(d).
10   TCEA 2007, ss 5(1)(c) and 31(2).
11   Transfer of Functions of the Asylum and Immigration Tribunal Order 2010, SI 2010/21, art 3.
12   TCEA 2007, Sch 4, para 12.

13 TCEA 2007, s 6.
14 TCEA 2007, ss 3(3) and 5(2).
15 TCEA 2007, Sch 3, para 2 and Qualifications for Appointment of Members to the First-tier and Upper Tribunal Order 2008, SI 2008/2692, as amended.

21.4 Any matter that has to be decided by the UT is to be decided by a single judge of the UT[1] unless the Senior President decides that the matter may be determined by one of the other members of the UT[2] or is to be determined by a panel.[3] The Senior President is to decide how many judges and how many other members are to sit on a panel.[4] A matter is to be decided by two or three UT judges if the Senior President or the Chamber President considers that the matter involves a question of law of special difficulty or an important point of principle or practice or that it is otherwise appropriate[5] and the Senior President must select one member as the 'presiding member' to chair the Tribunal.[6] In the event that the panel is equally divided, the presiding member has the casting vote.[7] Applications for permission to appeal to the UT are to be decided by one of the UT judges approved by the Senior President or the Chamber President.[8]

1 The First-tier Tribunal and Upper Tribunal (Composition of Tribunal) Order 2008, SI 2008/2835, arts 3(1) and 4(1).
2 SI 2008/2835, art 4(2).
3 SI 2008/2835, art 3(2).
4 SI 2008/2835, art 6.
5 The Senior President of Tribunals, Practice Statements: Immigration and Asylum Chambers of the First-tier Tribunal and the Upper Tribunal, 10 February 2010, para 6.2.
6 SI 2008/2385, art 7.
7 SI 2008/2385, art 8.
8 As fn 5 above, para 6.4.

POWERS OF THE UPPER TRIBUNAL

21.5 If the UT finds that the making of the decision with which the appeal is concerned involved the making of an error on a point of law it may, but need not, set aside the decision of the FT.[1] If the UT sets aside the decision of the FT then it must either remit the case to the FT to be reconsidered or it must re-make the decision itself.[2] If the UT remits the case to the FT it may also direct that the case is not to be reconsidered by the same members of the FT as made the decision to set aside and the UT may make procedural directions in connection with the reconsideration of the case by the FT.[3] If the UT decides to re-make the decision itself then it may make any decision which the FT could make if the FT was re-making the decision and may make such findings of fact as it considers appropriate.[4] The UT also has a judicial review jurisdiction.[5] See **21.5** above and **20.67** onwards below.

1 TCEA 2007, s 12(1) and (2)(a).
2 TCEA 2007, s 12 (2)(b).
3 TCEA 2007, s 12(3).
4 TCEA 2007, s 12(4).
5 See **21.79** below.

Error on a point of law

21.6 The UT has to find an error on a point of law before it can set aside the decision against which an appeal is brought. There is no additional, express requirement (as there was in order to obtain reconsideration of a decision of the Asylum and Immigration Tribunal[1]) that the error should be material although materiality is no doubt relevant to the exercise of the discretionary powers available to the UT once an error of law is established. What does an error on a point of law encompass? In *R (Iran) v Secretary of State for the Home Department*[2] the Court of Appeal gave general guidance on the most frequently encountered errors of law which it categorised as follows:

'(i)   making perverse or irrational findings on a matter or matters that were material to the outcome ("material matters");

(ii)   failing to give reasons or any adequate reasons for findings on material matters;

(iii)   failing to take into account and/or resolve conflicts of fact or opinion on material matters;

(iv)   giving weight to immaterial matters;

(v)   making a material misdirection of law on any material matter;

(vi)   committing or permitting a procedural or other irregularity capable of making a material difference to the outcome or the fairness of proceedings;

(vii) making a mistake as to a material fact which could be established by objective and uncontentious evidence, where the appellant and/or his advisers were not responsible for the mistake, and where unfairness resulted from the fact that a mistake was made'.

The references in that case to materiality reflected the statutory requirement then in existence that the error be material. The Court of Appeal had previously reviewed what might constitute an error of law in *E v Secretary of State for the Home Department*. The court held that it was generally a safe working rule that the substantive grounds for intervention were the same in the Court of Appeal on appeal and the High Court on judicial review.[3] The court accepted that an error of law could include both material breach of the rules of natural justice,[4] and error of fact based on misunderstanding or ignorance of established and relevant facts.[5] The court acknowledged that 'the time has come to accept that mistake of fact leading to unfairness is a separate head of challenge in an appeal on a point of law, at least in statutory contexts where the parties share an interest in cooperating to achieve the correct result'.[6] Asylum law, they added, was undoubtedly such an area. *E v Secretary of State for the Home Department* dealt with the situation in which the mistake arose because relevant material was not before the fact-finding Tribunal. Where the fact-finding Tribunal was in possession of all material facts, a failure to have regard to relevant evidence is an error of law,[7] and a failure to make findings on relevant facts may vitiate the decision.[8] Facts are material if in the circumstances of a particular case the decision turns on their existence.[9] Although it cannot be said to be an error of law to adopt one of a number of differing points of view of the facts, each of which may be reasonably held,[10] error may occur in the weighing of evidence, in particular, in relation to plausibility findings in asylum cases.[11] Appellate courts are not to engage 'in a microscopic search for error and should give immigration judges credit for knowing their job, even if their written determinations are imperfectly expressed'.[12] If the Tribunal finds an error of law, its decision as to whether the decision on the appeal is to be remade is likely to depend on whether the error is 'material'. An error of law is material unless the decision maker must have reached the same conclusion without the error.[13] The materiality of a procedural error or unfairness resulting in an appellant losing the opportunity to be heard would not generally depend on the underlying merits of the appeal because of the fundamental importance of the right to be heard.[14] The Upper Tribunal should follow a decision of the Administrative Court unless convinced that it is wrong.[15] Where a decision is challenged on grounds of procedural fairness, the test is not whether the impugned decision was reasonably open to its maker but whether it was fair, the requirements of procedural fairness being a question of law for the appellate court to determine.[16] However there is no absolute duty at common law to make decisions which are substantively 'fair'. The Court will only interfere with administrative decisions which are unfair in this second, ie, substantive, sense where they can be shown to be Wednesbury unreasonable, ie that no reasonable decision-maker or public body could have arrived at such a decision.

1   Asylum and Immigration Tribunal (Procedure) Rules 2005, SI 2005/230, r 31(2)(a), repealed.

2   [2005] EWCA Civ 982, (2005) Times, 19 August.

3   *E v Secretary of State for the Home Department, R v Secretary of State for the Home Department* [2004] EWCA Civ 49, [2004] INLR 264 per Carnwath LJ at [42], referring to *Railtrack plc (in Railway Administration) v Guinness Ltd* [2003] EWCA Civ 188, [2003] RVR 280; De Smith, Woolf and Jowell Judicial Review (5th edn), para 15-076). The statutory appeal with which the Court was concerned was in the Immigration and Asylum Act 1999, Sch 4, para 23 'a question of law material to the Tribunal's determination'. Note, however, Sir Robert Carnwath's observation that 'it is possible to consider how the Upper Tribunal might develop a role which goes beyond the traditional limits of judicial review, as practised by the courts. Even if the jurisdiction of the Upper Tribunal is limited to appeals on points of law, there is scope for it to develop a more extensive supervisory role, which may cross the traditional boundaries between law and fact as understood in the courts in Tribunal Justice – a New Start [2009] PL 48, 58.

4   *E v Secretary of State for the Home Department* at [38]; Council of Civil Service Unions at fn 1 above; *Gardi v Secretary of State for the Home Department* [2002] EWCA Civ 750, [2003] Imm AR 39 (annulled for want of jurisdiction at [2002] EWCA Civ 1560, [2002] INLR 557; MNM [2000] INLR 576, IAT; *R (on the application of Tataw) v Secretary of State for the Home Department* [2003] EWCA Civ 925, [2003] INLR 585.

5   *E v Secretary of State for the Home Department* at [38]; *R (on the application of Alconbury Developments Ltd) v Secretary of State for the Environment, Transport and the Regions* [2001] UKHL 23, [2003] 2 AC 295 [53] per Lord Slynn; *Secretary of State for Education and Science v Tameside Metropolitan Borough Council* [1977] AC 1014 at 1030; *Edwards (Inspector of Taxes) v Bairstow* [1956] AC 14.

6   *E v Secretary of State for the Home Department* at [66], following and explaining *R v Criminal Injuries Compensation Board, ex p A* [1999] 2 AC 330, [1999] 2 WLR 974. The UT has now expressly adopted the reasoning in *E & R: MM (Sudan) (unfairness; E & R)* [2014] UKUT 00105 (IAC).

7   *S v Secretary of State for the Home Department* [2002] EWCA Civ 539, [2002] INLR 416; *R v Secretary of State for the Home Department, ex p Parmak* (CO 702/90), (21 January 1992, unreported).

8   See eg *Minister for Immigration and Multicultural Affairs v Yusuf* [2001] HCA 30, 75 ALJR 1105; *Dhillon v Canada (Minister of Citizenship and Immigration)* [2001] FCT 1194, and cases cited at fn 7 above.

9   *R v Independent Television Commission, ex p Virgin Television Ltd* [1966] EMLR 318, cited in Demetriou and Houseman 'Review for error of fact: a brief guide' [1997] JR 27; *Minister for Immigration and Multicultural Affairs v Singh* (2000) 98 FCR 469.

10   See eg *Ndlovu v Secretary of State for the Home Department* [2004] EWCA Civ 1567, [2004] All ER (D) 395 (Jul); *CA v Secretary of State for the Home Department* [2004] EWCA Civ 1165, [2004] 34 LS Gaz R 30; *Aung (Win) v Secretary of State for the Home Department* [2004] EWCA Civ 425, [2004] All ER (D) 533 (Mar): in each case, the Court of Appeal held

that the Tribunal's disagreement with the first-instance decision of the adjudicator should not have resulted in its allowing the Secretary of State's appeal.

11 *Choudhury v Immigration Appeal Tribunal* [2001] EWHC 613 (Admin). The Canadian courts have held that plausibility findings should be made only in the clearest of cases, where the facts presented are outside the realm of what could reasonably be expected or documentary evidence demonstrates that the events could not have happened in the manner described by the claimant: *Shenoda v Canada (Minister for Citizenship and Immigration* [2003] FCT 207; *Divsalar v Canada* [2002] FCJ 875; but see *MM (plausibility) (DRC)* [2005] UKIAT 00019.

12 Sedley LJ in *NH (India) v Entry Clearance Officer* [2007] EWCA Civ 1330, (2008) INLR 154 referred to *AH (Sudan) v Secretary of State for the Home Department* [2007] UKHL 49, [2007] 3 WLR 832 where the House of Lords held that so experienced and well-qualified a tribunal could not have made the egregious and inexplicable error of law attributed to it by the Court of Appeal. Sedley LJ emphasised that in that case 'Their Lordships do not say, and cannot be taken as meaning, that the standards of decision-making or the principles of judicial scrutiny which govern immigration and asylum adjudication differ from those governing other judicial tribunal's, especially when for some asylum seekers adjudication may literally be a matter of life and death. There is no principle that the worse the apparent error is, the less ready an appellate court should be to find that it has occurred'.

13 *IA (Somalia) v Secretary of State for the Home Department* [2007] EWCA Civ 323, 151 Sol Jo LB 574. See also *MS (Iran) v Secretary of State for the Home Department* [2007] EWCA Civ 271, [2007] All ER (D) 230 (Feb). Also see *AS (India) v Secretary of State for the Home Department* [2012] EWCA Civ 229 where the Court of Appeal held that the same error of law had been made in respect of each of the two appellants, but allowed only one of the appeals, dismissing the appeal in which, on the facts, the error made no difference to the outcome.

14 *FP (Iran) and MB (Libya) v Secretary of State for the Home Department* [2007] EWCA Civ 13, (2007) Times, 26 January. See for example *MZ (Pakistan) v Secretary of State for the Home Department* [2009] EWCA Civ 919 where an appeal was allowed, notwithstanding that the case was apparently hopeless on the facts because the cumulative effect of the Tribunal's errors of law was such that the appellant had not received a judicial consideration of his case. See also *ML (Nigeria) v Secretary of State for the Home Department* [2013] EWCA Civ 844, para 10 where Moses LJ said: 'everyone, however poor their case, is entitled to a fair hearing. As part of that fair hearing, the finders of fact must listen and take into account conscientiously the arguments that are deployed in favour of a finding that the claimant is telling the truth as well as those arguments against'.

15 *R (on the application of K) v Secretary of State for the Home Department* [2010] EWHC 3102 (Admin), [2010] All ER (D) 50 (Dec) and *Bah (EO Turkey – Liability to deport)* [2012] UKUT 00196 (IAC).

16 *SH (Afghanistan) v Secretary of State for the Home Department* [2011] EWCA Civ 1284, [2011] All ER (D) 55 (Nov) and *Osborn v Parole Board* [2013] UKSC 61, para 65.

Perversity

21.7 Perversity amounting to an error of law can be established if the 'decision is one to which no reasonable decision maker, properly instructing himself on the law could have come on the evidence before him'.[1] Perversity 'is a question which has always to be scrupulously disentangled from the question whether the second decision maker simply entertains a strong disagreement with the first'.[2] It does not require 'wilful or conscious departure from the rational. A finding of fact which is wholly unsupported by the evidence is capable of amounting to an error of law by this analysis'[3] as is a finding of fact that is unfounded or erroneous.[4] Misunderstanding of evidence by an immigration judge would be an error of fact rather than an error of law. However, were the judge then to rely upon the evidence as misunderstood that would be to make a decision on the basis of no evidence which would amount to an error of law.[5] The tribunal's reliance on evidence as flimsy as an Email whose author the appellant could not cross examine in preference to the appellant's expert, who had to submit to cross examination as a condition for giving evidence, was irrational and unfair.[6]

1   Keene LJ in *Miftari v Secretary of State for the Home Department* [2005] EWCA Civ 481, [2005] All ER (D) 279 (May).
2   Sedley LJ in *RP (Zimbabwe) v Secretary of State for the Home Department* [2008] EWCA Civ 825, [2008] All ER (D) 135 (Aug). See also Sullivan LJ in *KU (Pakistan) v Secretary of State for the Home Department* [2012] EWCA Civ 107, para 17 'the fact that a contrary conclusion could properly have been reached did not mean that the Immigration Judge's conclusion in paragraph 25 was perverse'.
3   Maurice Kay LJ in *Miftari*. See for example *Adedoyun v Secretary of State for the Home Department* [2012] EWCA Civ 939.
4   *Krasniqi v Secretary of State for the Home Department* [2006] EWCA Civ 391, (2006) Times, 20 April.
5   Buxton LJ in *Miftari v Secretary of State for the Home Department*.
6   *PO (Nigeria) v Secretary of State for the Home Department* [2011] EWCA Civ 132, [2011] NLJR 327, (2011) Times, 19 April.

Failure to give adequate reasons

21.8 The previous chapter at **20.133** discusses the nature and extent of the obligation to give adequate reasons when determining an appeal.[1] When the UT considers a challenge to the FT's reasoning it is important that judicial restraint be exercised and that the UT should not too readily assume that the FT misdirected itself just because not every step in its reasoning is fully set out.[2] The nature and extent of reasons required will depend on the particular context.[3] In an asylum or human rights context, the obligation to give the most 'anxious scrutiny' to a case requires reasoning that shows 'that every factor which might tell in favour of an applicant has been properly taken into account'.[4] it may be important to distinguish between a complaint that reasons are 'inadequate' because they do not show how a decision was reached and a complaint that reasons are 'insufficient' as being indicative of a substantive, public law deficiency in the decision.[5] Failure by the FT to cite relevant authority does not establish inadequate or insufficient reasoning, provided that the FT's reasoning demonstrates that the correct principles were applied.[6]

1   See the decision by the President of the UT(IAC), McCloskey J in *MK (Duty to give reasons) Pakistan* [2013] UKUT 641 (IAC).
2   *R (on the application of JR (Jamaica)) v Secretary of State for the Home Department* [2014] EWCA Civ 477.
3   *MK (Duty to give reasons) Pakistan* [2013] UKUT 641 (IAC).
4   *ML (Nigeria) v Secretary of State for the Home Department* [2013] EWCA Civ 844, Moses LJ. Particularly careful findings are also required when considering the effect of a decision on the best interests of an affected child: *Peart v Secretary of State for the Home Department* [2012] EWCA Civ 568.
5   *Haleemudeen v Secretary of State for the Home Department* [2014] EWCA Civ 558. So for example, if that typology is used, the failure by the FT to give reasons explaining what weight, if any, it gave to the interest in maintaining effective immigration control when it decided that removal from the UK would breach article 8 was indicative of public law error in the form of failing to have regard to a relevant consideration: *JW (China) v Secretary of State for the Home Department* [2013] EWCA Civ 1526.
6   *AM v Secretary of State for the Home Department* [2012] EWCA Civ 1634; *PK (Congo) v Secretary of State for the Home Department* [2013] EWCA Civ 1500.

Proportionality

21.9 In relation to a judgment on proportionality under Article 8 of the ECHR so long as the immigration judge 'correctly directed himself as to his duty under the law', then an error of law could be found only on 'traditional public law' grounds.[1] Nevertheless, a finding as to proportionality would be 'susceptible to closer scrutiny than findings of primary fact'.[2] Whilst in some cases there may only be one permissible conclusion as to proportionality, in others a tribunal may lawfully conclude either that the decision is proportionate or disproportionate. In such cases, the European Court of Human Rights may substitute its own view of proportionality because 'it possesses the unique status of a court both of first instance and last resort'; the superior courts of the UK lack that power and are limited to determining lawfulness.[3] Whilst not being required to adopt a formulaic approach, the Tribunal must have proper and visible regard to the relevant principles and must give proper reasons for its finding on proportionality.[4] If a Tribunal allows an appeal on Article 8 grounds by taking 'what may seem an unusually generous view of the facts of a particular case' that 'does not mean that it has made an error of law'.[5]

1   R (Iran) v Secretary of State for the Home Department [2005] EWCA Civ 982, (2005) Times, 19 August, [2005] All ER (D) 384 (Jul).
2   Krasniqi v Secretary of State for the Home Department [2006] EWCA Civ 391, (2006) Times, 20 April per Sedley LJ.
3   PE (Peru) v Secretary of State for the Home Department [2011] EWCA Civ 274.
4   AG (Eritrea) v Secretary of State for the Home Department [2007] EWCA Civ 801, [2007] EWCA Civ 801.
5   Mukarkar v Secretary of State for the Home Department [2006] EWCA Civ 1045, (2006) Times, 16 August, [2006] All ER (D) 367 (Jul).

Unfairness resulting from a mistake of fact

21.10 The Court of Appeal in *E v Secretary of State for the Home Department*, having acknowledged that unfairness resulting from a mistake of fact would be an error of law held that to establish such an error would normally require the following:

'(i)   there must have been a mistake as to an existing fact, including a mistake as to the availability of evidence on a particular matter;

(ii)   it must be possible to categorise the relevant fact or evidence as "established" in the sense that it was uncontentious and objectively verifiable;

(iii)   the appellant (or his advisers) must not have been responsible for the mistake;

(iv)   the mistake must have played a material (not necessarily decisive) part in the Tribunal's reasoning'.[1]

A series of material factual errors by the tribunal as to what had been said by and on behalf of the appellant constituted an error of law.[2] An evidential dispute as to the existence of the 'existing fact' would remove the matter from the 'narrowly confined' scope of the 'mistake of fact amounting to an error of law' ground.[3] The requirement that the appellant's adviser should not have been responsible for the mistake must now apply with less, if any force in the light of the Court's subsequent decision in *FP (Iran)*.[4] New evidence to establish the existence of such a mistake could be admitted if the '*Ladd v*

Marshall principles'[5] were satisfied, although they might be departed from in exceptional circumstances where the interests of justice required.[6] Those principles are that:

(a)   the new evidence could not with reasonable diligence have been obtained for use at the trial (or hearing);

(b)   the new evidence must be such that, if given, it would probably have had an important influence on the result of the case (though it need not be decisive); and

(c)   the new evidence was apparently credible although it need not be incontrovertible.

The Court of Appeal[7] and the Tribunal[8] have held that in certain circumstances new evidence undermining the credibility of a successful appellant may be relied on to establish an error of fact amounting to an error of law. However, the Court of Appeal has subsequently indicated that the issue of whether and in what circumstances such an approach may be adopted needs to be revisited.[9] It would be an error of law for the Tribunal not to have regard to a relevant policy; if it did not consider the policy because it was not before the Tribunal it would still be an error of law owing to the Secretary of State's failure to discharge her duty to place relevant policy material before the Tribunal.[10]

1   *R (Iran) v Secretary of State for the Home Department* [2005] EWCA Civ 982, (2005) Times, 19 August, [2005] All ER (D) 384 (Jul), citing *E v Secretary of State for the Home Department* [2004] EWCA Civ 49, [2004] QB 1044, [2004] 2 WLR 1351.
2   *ML (Nigeria) v Secretary of State for the Home Department* [2013] EWCA Civ 844.
3   *R (FD (Zimbabwe)) v Secretary of State for the Home Department* [2007] EWCA Civ 1220.
4   *R (on the application of FD (Zimbabwe)) v Secretary of State for the Home Department* [2007] EWCA Civ 13. and the tribunal's decision in *MM (Unfairness; E and R) Sudan* [2014] UKUT 105 (IAC) where the mistake of fact made by the First Tier Tribunal was in finding that appellant's solicitor had not written and sent a letter to the Home Office. The mistake was made only because the appellant's solicitor had failed to put the letter in evidence.
5   A reference to *Ladd v Marshall* [1954] 3 All ER 745, [1954] 1 WLR 1489, 98 Sol Jo 870, CA.
6   *R (Iran) v Secretary of State for the Home Department* [2005] EWCA Civ 982, (2005) Times, 19 August, [2005] All ER (D) 384 (Jul).
7   *Verde v Secretary of State for the Home Department* [2004] EWCA Civ 1726, [2004] All ER (D) 75 (Dec). In *AD (Guinea) v Secretary of State for the Home Department* [2009] EWCA Civ 56 the Court of Appeal admitted new evidence about the appellant's fraudulent conduct and relied on that to dismiss the appeal it would otherwise have allowed.
8   *EA (Ghana)* [2005] UKAIT 00108.
9   *Shaheen v Secretary of State for the Home Department* [2005] EWCA Civ 1294, [2005] All ER (D) 31 (Nov); *AD (Guinea) v Secretary of State for the Home Department* [2009] EWCA Civ 56.
10   *AA (Afghanistan) v Secretary of State for the Home Department* [2007] EWCA Civ 12, (2007) Times, 2 February; *US (Nepal) v Secretary of State for the Home Department* [2009] EWCA Civ 208, [2009] All ER (D) 217 (Jan); *FH (Bangladesh) v Secretary of State for the Home Department* [2009] EWCA Civ 385 (error of law owing to Tribunal's failure to have regard to the more generous provisions of the 'long residence concession' contained in the IDIs compared with the Immigration Rules, notwithstanding that the IDIs had not been before the Tribunal).

Permission to appeal

21.11   A party to an appeal under s 82,[1] 83[2] or 83A[3] of the NIAA 2002 has to obtain permission to appeal to the UT from either the FT or the UT.[4] An application for permission has to be made to the FT first and an application may be made to the UT only if permission has been refused by the FT or the

FT has not admitted the application to it for permission to appeal.[5] An application will not be admitted to the FT if it was made out of time and the FT declines to extend time.[6] If the FT refuses to decide an application for permission to appeal for some other reason, eg because it thinks there was no appealable decision, the UT may waive the requirement[7] that the FT must first have refused permission before a permission application can be made to the UT.[8]

[1] Ie an appeal against an immigration decision as there defined.
[2] Ie an appeal against the refusal of asylum to a person who has been granted leave to enter or remain for more than one year.
[3] Ie an appeal against a decision that a person with leave to enter or remain as a refugee is not a refugee and who, following the decision, has leave but not as a refugee.
[4] TCEA 2007, s 11(2), (3) and (4).
[5] Tribunal Procedure (Upper Tribunal) Rules 2008, SI 2008/2698, r 21(2).
[6] Asylum and Immigration Tribunal (Procedure) Rules 2005, SI 2005/230, r 24(4)(b).
[7] Tribunal Procedure (Upper Tribunal) Rules 2008, r 7(2)(a).
[8] *Ved (Appealable decisions: permission applications: Basnet)* [2014] UKUT 150 (IAC).

APPLICATION TO THE FIRST-TIER TRIBUNAL FOR PERMISSION TO APPEAL

Time limits

21.12 An application for permission to appeal must be made in writing to the FT.[1] It must be received by the FT no later than 14 days after the applicant was provided with written reasons for the decision of the FT[2] unless the appellant was outside the UK, in which case the application must be received by the FT within 28 days of being provided with written reasons for the decision.[3] Where the appellant is in the detained fast track, an application for permission to appeal must be received by the FT no later than 3 days after the applicant was provided with the FT's decision.[4] If the period of 3, 14 or 28 days ends on a day other than a working day[5] then notice of appeal will have been given in time if received by the FT on the next working day.[6] If the FT has not given written reasons for its decision in a non-fast track case and the applicant has not applied for a statement of reasons, the FT must treat the application for permission to appeal as an application for a statement of reasons[7] and may either direct that the application for permission is not to be treated as an application for permission or it may determine the application.[8]

[1] Tribunal Procedure (First-tier Tribunal) (Immigration and Asylum Chamber) Rules 2014, SI 2014/2604, r 33(1).
[2] SI 2014/2604, r 33(2).
[3] SI 2014/2604, r 33(3).
[4] SI 2014/2604, Schedule, r 11.
[5] SI 2014/2604, r 1(4) defines 'working day' as any day except a Saturday or Sunday, Christmas Day, Good Friday or a bank holiday and 27th to 31st December inclusive.
[6] SI 2014/2604, r 11(2).
[7] SI 2014/2604, r 33(6)(a).
[8] SI 2014/2604, r 33(6)(b).

21.13–21.15 It is significant that time for applying for permission to appeal begins to run once the applicant has been 'provided' with written reasons for the FT's decision or notice of the decision in a fast-track case. The procedure rules specify the means by which a document is to be provided: it must be delivered or sent by post; sent via document exchange, fax, email or sent or delivered by any other method identified by the person to whom it is to be sent or by leaving it with the individual.[1] However, a document is not 'provided' until it is actually received by the person to whom it is delivered or sent; there are no presumptions of receipt or service in the current procedure rules which means that the person provided with the decision is likely to be the only person able to determine when time for applying for permission to appeal begins to run. This contrasts with appeals to the FT and applications for permission to appeal to the UT in respect of which time starts to run when the appealable decision is 'sent' to the appellant[2] or the FT's determination is 'sent' to the applicant.[3]

1   SI 2014/2604, r 12(1), (2).
2   SI 2014/2604, r 19(2).
3   SI 2014/2604, r 21(3)(aa), (ab).

Extending time for applying for permission to appeal

21.16 The previous procedure rules made express provision to deal with an application for permission to appeal made out of time; the FT could extend time if satisfied that by reason of special circumstances it would be unjust not to do so.[1] The current rules do not, but the FT's general case management powers include a power to extend the time for complying with any rule[2] and that power, exercised in accordance with the overriding objective[3] enables the FT to extend time for applying for permission to appeal. The merits of the appeal will need to be addressed on any application for permission to apply out of time.[4] An appeal remains pending under section 104 of NIAA 2002 while an application for permission to appeal to the UT could be made or is awaiting determination.[5] Section 104 does not (as it used to do) exclude the period during which an application to extend time for seeking permission to appeal or an order for reconsideration could be made as being a period during which an appeal is pending. If the FT grants permission to appeal in response to an application that is out of time but without extending time, its decision is irregular; if neither party takes a point about the irregularity then they are deemed to have waived the irregularity.[6] If the point is taken, the FT then has to decide whether to extend time; if the issue comes to light before the UT, the UT should reconstitute itself as the FT for the purpose of deciding whether to extend time.[7] When the FT decides whether to extend time it should have regard to the length of the delay;[8] the explanation for the delay in applying for permission to appeal;[9] whether the explanation is supported by sufficient evidence;[10] whether the explanation covers the whole period of delay; the strength of the grounds of appeal; the prejudice to the respondent that would be caused by extending time and the consequences of the decision.[11] The same considerations apply whichever party seeks permission to appeal.[12]

1
2   Tribunal Procedure (First-tier Tribunal) (Immigration and Asylum Chamber) Rules 2014, SI 2014/2604, r 4(3)(a).
3   SI 2014/2604, r 2.
4   *R (on the application of Makke) v Immigration Appeal Tribunal* [2005] EWCA Civ 176, (2005) Times, 5 April: a party seeking a substantial extension of time must show a real prospect of success on the appeal and it is not enough to rely on procedural points.
5   NIAA 2002, s 104(2), as substituted by SI 2010/21.

[6] *AK (Bulgaria)* [2004] UKIAT 00201 and *Boktor and Wanis* [2011] UKUT 442 (IAC).

[7] *Samir (First Tier Tribunal permission to appeal – Time)* [2013] UKUT 3 (IAC); *Mohammed (Late application – First Tier Tribunal)* [2013] UKUT 467 (IAC).

[8] The tribunal has indicated that there would need to be 'an exceptional case' to extend time where there has been 'significant delay', ie where the application is made more than 28 days out of time: *Ogundimu (Article 8 – new rules) Nigeria* [2013] UKUT 60 (IAC).

[9] The mere fact that the appellant was in detention at the time of being served with the decision is not a sufficient explanation for delay: *R (on the application of Williams) v First Tier Tribunal* [2012] EWHC 552 (Admin).

[10] An assertions in a notice of application (as opposed to a witness statement) about the date when a decision was or was not received is not evidence: *Wang and Chin (Extension of time for appealing)* [2013] UKUT 343 (IAC).

[11] *Boktor and Wanis* [2011] UKUT 442 (IAC) in which the tribunal drew upon *BO (Nigeria)* [2006] UKAIT 00035 and *TR v Asylum and Immigration Tribunal* [2010] EWHC 2055 (Admin), [2010] NLJR 1152, both of which were concerned with the principles applicable to extending time for appealing to the FT against an immigration decision.

[12] *Wang and Chin (Extension of time for appealing)* [2013] UKUT 00343 (IAC).

Form and content of the application

21.17 An application to the FT for permission to appeal to the UT must be made in writing[1] and must identify the decision of the FT to which it relates; identify the alleged error or errors of law in the decision and state the result that the party making the application is seeking and include any application for an extension of time and the reasons why an extension should be granted.[2]

[1] SI 2014/2604, r 33(1).
[2] SI 2014/2604, r 33(5).

The FT's decision on an application for permission to appeal

21.18 Upon receiving an application for permission to appeal, the FT must first consider whether to review the decision against which permission to appeal is sought.[1] If it decides not to review the decision or having reviewed the decision, to take no action, it must decide whether to give permission.[2] By contrast to the previous rules, there is no specified time within which the FT is required to make those decisions.[3] The FT may give permission to appeal on limited grounds[4] although the UT has indicated that the preferable course is to give unrestricted permission accompanied by the FT's observations as to the relative merits of the grounds.[5] The requirement to obtain permission is a 'threshold of real substance', requiring an arguable material error of law to be demonstrated.[6] However, permission should be refused on grounds of materiality only if it is plain that the error could have made no difference to the outcome, otherwise the issue of materiality should be left to be dealt with by the UT.[7] The materiality requirement need not be satisfied if there is a point of public importance that should be determined[8] or if the appellant has a sufficient interest in overturning factual findings that may bind a future decision maker, albeit ones that are not material to the outcome. The FT deciding the application for permission should consider the decision challenged with particular care when the appellant is unrepresented and in any case, should consider whether the UK's obligations under the Refugee Convention and the ECHR or the interests of justice more generally require that permission should be granted on grounds that have not been identified by the appellant.[9] Written reasons for the FT's decision must be sent to the parties (or, in the case of an appeal involving an asylum claim, the Secretary of State)[10] and if permission is given on limited grounds only, it must give reasons in relation to any grounds on which permission was refused.[11] If the FT grants permission to appeal, the application for permission stands as the notice of appeal, subject to any directions made by the FT or UT.[12] If permission is refused, the FT must notify the parties of the right to make an application for permission to the UT and the time within, and the method by which, such an application has to be made.[13]

1   SI 2014/2604, r 34(1).
2   SI 2014/2604, r 34(2).
3   SI 2005/230, r 25(3).
4   SI 2014/2604, r 34(5).
5   *Ferrer (Limited grounds of appeal; Alvi)* [2012] UKUT 304 (IAC).
6   *Nixon (Permission to appeal: grounds)* [2014] UKUT 368 (IAC).
7   'Guidance Note on Permission to appeal under paragraph 7 of Schedule 4 to the Tribunals, Courts and Enforcement Act 2007', para 16.
8   *Anoliefo (Permission to appeal)* [2013] UKUT 345 (IAC).
9   *Nixon (Permission to appeal: grounds)* [2014] UKUT 368 (IAC).
10   SI 2014/2604, r 34(3), (4).
11   SI 2014/2604, r 34(5).
12   Tribunal Procedure (Upper Tribunal) Rules 2008, SI 2008/2698, r 23(1A).
13   SI 2014/2604, r 34(4)(b).

APPLICATION TO THE UT FOR PERMISSION TO APPEAL

Time limits

21.19   An application for permission to appeal to the UT may be made to the UT only if the FT has refused permission to appeal or has refused to admit an application for permission to appeal because it was made out of time[1] or if the UT decides to waive the requirement that permission to appeal should first have been refused by the FT.[2] The time within which an application for permission has to be made to the UT begins to run on the day after the FT's decision refusing permission was sent to the appellant (ie the person applying for permission to appeal)[3] rather than from the day on which the appellant is deemed to have received the decision.[4] An appellant in the UK has seven working days after the FT's decision was sent[5] (five working days if the decision was delivered personally or sent electronically)[6] unless the appeal is in the fast track in which case the appellant has four working days[7] (or two working days if the decision was delivered personally or sent electronically).[8] Working days are any day except Saturday, Sunday, Christmas Day, Good Friday, a bank holiday,[9] the period from 27 to 31 December inclusive and, in a fast track case, 24 December, Maundy Thursday and the Tuesday after the last Monday in May.[10] If the appellant is outside the UK he or she has 56 days[11] or, if the FT's decision was sent electronically or delivered personally, 28 days.[12] The application for permission to appeal must be received by the UT by 5.00 pm on the last day of the period during which the application must be made or, if the period ends on a day which is not a working day, on the next working day.[13]

1   Tribunal Procedure (Upper Tribunal) Rules 2008, SI 2008/2698, r 21(2).

2   Under SI 2008/2698, R 7(2)(a): see *Ved (Appealable decisions: permission applications: Basnet)* [2014] UKUT 150(IAC).

3   SI 2008/2698, r 1(3).

4   SI 2008/2698, r 21(3). The rules distinguish between FT's decisions to refuse permission and decisions not to admit an application for permission. It is only the former kind of decision which commences the period within which an application to the UT must be made. Reading the rule literally, there is no time limit for making an application to the UT where the FT declined to admit the application for permission made to it.

5   SI2008/2698, r 21(3)(aa)(i).

6   SI 2008/2698, r 21(3A)(a).

7   SI 2008/2698, r 21(3)(aa)(ii).

8   SI 2008/2698, r 21(3A)(b).

9   SI 2008/2698, r 1(3).

10   SI 2008/2698, r 21(3)(ab).

11   SI 2008/2698, r 12(3A).

12   SI 2008/2698, r 21(3A)(c).

13   SI 2008/2698, r 12(1) and (2).

Out of time applications for permission to appeal

21.20 If an appellant makes an application for permission to appeal outside of the time limit specified by the Procedure Rules, the application must include a request to extend time and the reason for not having made the application in time.[1] The UT may then, in the exercise of its general case management powers, extend the time for applying for permission to appeal.[2] If it decides not to extend time, it must not admit the application for permission to appeal.[3] There are no specific provisions as to the criteria to be applied in deciding whether to extend time but the UT is required to give effect to the overriding objective of 'dealing with a case fairly and justly'[4] when it exercises any power under the Procedure Rules.[5] If the FT refused to admit an application for permission to appeal because it was out of time, the UT may admit the application if it 'considers that it is in the interests of justice for it to do so'.[6] The application to the UT must include the reason why the application to the FT was not made in time.[7] In a case where a grant of permission has to be regarded as conditional upon a decision whether time should be extended, the latter decision is part of the original decision on the application. If the application was to the FT, the decision as to time is therefore made by the FT and if the application is not admitted there is the possibility of renewal to the UT.[8] When considering an application for permission to appeal that is out of time, a judge must (i) consider all available material including the material on file and bear in mind the need for evidence to rebut the presumption of service, (ii) consider the extent of the delay and whether any explanation covers the whole of that period; (iii) give brief reasons for the discretionary decision to extend time or refuse to do so. The same principles apply whichever side is the applicant.[9] The UT should adopt a similar approach to the issue of whether time should be extended to that adopted by the FT[10] and described above.

1   Tribunal Procedure (Upper Tribunal) Rules 2008, SI 2008/2698, r 21(6)(a).

2   SI 2008/2698, r 5(3)(a).

3   SI 2008/2698, r 21(6)(b).

4   SI 2008/2698, r 2(1) and (2).

5   SI 2008/2698, r 2(3)(a).

6   SI 2008/2698, r 21(7)(a).

7   SI 2008/2698, r 21(7)(a).

8   *Samir (First Tier Tribunal permission to appeal – Time)* [2013] UKUT 3 (IAC).

9 *Wang and Chin (Extension of time for appealing)* [2013] UKUT 343 (IAC).
10 *Mohammed (Late application – First Tier Tribunal)* [2013] UKUT 467 (IAC).

Form and content of the application to the UT for permission to appeal

21.21 An application must be made in writing[1] and must state the name and address of the appellant;[2] the name and address of the appellant's representative; an address where documents for the appellant may be sent or delivered; details, including the reference number of the decision challenged; the grounds on which the appellant relies and whether the appellant wants the application to be dealt with at a hearing.[3] The appellant is required to provide with the application a copy of the decision being challenged and notice of the FT's refusal to grant permission to appeal or to admit the application for permission.[4]

1 Tribunal Procedure (Upper Tribunal) Rules 2008, SI 2008/2698, r 21(3).
2 In this context, the appellant is the person applying for permission to appeal: SI 2008/2698, r 1.
3 SI 2008/2698, r 21(4).
4 SI 2008/2698, r 21(5).

The UT's decision on an application for permission to appeal

21.22 The UT may consider an application for permission to appeal at a hearing.[1] Although the Procedure Rules give no specific indication as to the circumstances in which it will do so, it must have regard to any view expressed by a party when it decides whether to hold a hearing.[2] If the UT refuses permission to appeal it must send written notice of the refusal and the reasons for the refusal to the appellant.[3] If the UT gives permission to appeal it must send to each party written notice of the permission and of the reasons for any limitations or conditions on the permission.[4] If permission to appeal is not expressly restricted all grounds of appeal may be argued at the hearing.[5] However, some doubt has been cast on this position in *NA (UT rule 45: Singh v Belgium) Iran* [2014] UKUT 205 (IAC) when the Upper Tribunal restricted argument to the one ground in respect of which permission had been expressly granted on the basis that no notice had been given in respect of the other grounds, which would have resulted in an adjournment with costs and delay implications and two previous Judges had refused permission to appeal in respect of these grounds. Subject to any direction by the UT, the application for permission to appeal stands as the notice of appeal, copies of which must be sent to the respondent along with any document provided by the appellant. The UT may determine the appeal, if the parties consent, without obtaining any further response.[6] In UTIAC Guidance Note 2011 No 1, The President stated, at [16]:

> 'Where there is no reasonable prospect that any error of law alleged in the grounds of appeal could have made a difference to the outcome, permission to appeal should not normally be granted in the absence of some point of public importance that is otherwise in the public interest to determine'.

In *Nixon (Permission to appeal: grounds)* [2014] UKUT 368 (IAC) the current President set out some general rules of practice: every application for permission to appeal to the Upper Tribunal should identify, clearly and with all necessary particulars, the error/s of law for which the moving party contends, in recognisable and comprehensible terms which should convey at once to the Judge concerned the error/s of law said to have been committed. It should not be necessary for the permission Judge to hunt and mine in order to understand the basis and thrust of the application. Terms such as *'erred'* or *'erred in law'* or *'was wrong in law'* or *'misdirected itself in law'* are unacceptable unless accompanied by a clear specification of the error/s of law alleged and suitable brief particulars. The Judge granted permission, firstly, on the ground that the FT had arguably erred in law in its assessment of the credibility of three particular witnesses but it will very rarely be appropriate to grant permission to appeal on this kind of ground. Credibility assessments by first instance fact finding Tribunals will normally be challengeable only on the basis of irrationality (or, as it is sometimes inelegantly termed, perversity).

1 So much is evident from the requirement that an appellant must state in the application for permission to appeal whether he or she wants the application to be dealt with at a hearing. Tribunal Procedure (Upper Tribunal) Rules 2008, SI 2008/2698.
2 SI 2008/2698, r 34(2).
3 SI 2008/2698, r 22(1).
4 *Ferrer (limited appeal grounds; Alvi)* [2012] UKUT 00304 (IAC).
5 SI 2008/2698, r 22(2)(a) and (b).
6 SI 2008/2698, r 22(2)(c). *NA (UT rule 45: Singh v Belgium) Iran* [2014] UKUT 205 (IAC).

PROCEDURE ON APPEALS TO THE UPPER TRIBUNAL

Procedure Rules

21.23 The Tribunal Procedure (Upper Tribunal) Rules 2008[1] are made under section 22 and Schedule 5 to the TCEA 2007 and govern the practice and procedure to be followed by the UT.[2] They are made by the Tribunal Procedure Committee[3] which is required to exercise the power to make procedure rules with a view to securing that in proceedings before the UT and FT, justice is done; that the tribunal system is accessible and fair; that proceedings are handled quickly and efficiently; that the rules are simple and simply expressed and that they confer on members of the FT and UT responsibility for ensuring that proceedings are handled quickly and efficiently.[4] The Tribunal Procedure Committee may make rules that include provision for: functions of the UT to be exercised by its staff;[5] for time limits in respect of initiating or taking any step in proceedings;[6] for restricting the making of repeat applications in relation to the same matter;[7] for the UT to exercise its powers of its own initiative;[8] for dealing with matters without a hearing or for hearings in public or in private;[9] for conferring additional rights of audience;[10] about the production and giving of evidence;[11] for the disclosure or non-disclosure of information received during the course of proceedings and the imposition of reporting restrictions;[12] for regulating matters relating to costs;[13] for the correction of accidental errors and for the setting aside of a decision where there has been procedural irregularity;[14] for conferring on the UT such ancillary powers as are necessary for the proper discharge of its functions;[15] for the rules to make reference to practice directions;[16] and for presumptions, in particular, as to service or notification.[17]

1 SI 2008/2698.

2   TCEA 2007, s 22(1)(b).
3   TCEA 2007, s 22(2).
4   TCEA 2007, s 22(4).
5   TCEA 2007, Sch 5, para 3.
6   TCEA 2007, Sch 5, para 4.
7   TCEA 2007, Sch 5, para 5.
8   TCEA 2007, Sch 5, para 6.
9   TCEA 2007, Sch 5, para 7.
10 TCEA 2007, Sch 5, para 9.
11 TCEA 2007, Sch 5, para 10.
12 TCEA 2007, Sch 5, para 11.
13 TCEA 2007, Sch 5 para 12.
14 TCEA 2007, Sch 5, para 15.
15 TCEA 2007, Sch 5, para 16.
16 TCEA 2007, Sch 5, para 17.
17 TCEA 2007, Sch 5, para 18.

Practice Directions

21.24 The Senior President of Tribunals may give directions as to the practice and procedure of the UT and a Chamber President may give directions as to the practice and procedure of the chamber over which he or she presides. Such directions need the approval of the Lord Chancellor and also, in the case of directions by a Chamber President, of the Senior President except to the extent that they consist of guidance about the application and interpretation of the law, the making of decisions by members of the UT and the criteria for deciding which members of the UT may be chosen to decide particular categories of matter.[1]

1   TCEA 2007, s 23. The Senior President has made 'Practice Directions: Immigration and Asylum Chambers of the First-tier Tribunal and the Upper Tribunal', 10 February 2010, See also, Presidential Guidance note 2013 No 2: Video link hearings; Presidential Guidance note 2013 No 3: Guide for unrepresented claimants in Upper Tribunal Immigration and Asylum Chamber available on www.justice.gov.uk.

The overriding objective of the Procedure Rules

21.25 The overriding objective of the Procedure Rules is to enable the UT to deal with cases fairly and justly which includes: dealing with a case in ways which are proportionate to the importance of the case, the complexity of the issues, the anticipated costs and the resources of the parties; avoiding unnecessary formality and seeking flexibility in the proceedings; ensuring, so far as practicable, that the parties are able to participate fully in the proceedings; using any special expertise of the UT effectively and avoiding delay so far as compatible with proper consideration of the issues.[1] The UT must 'seek to give effect' to the overriding objective when it exercises any power under the procedure rules and when it interprets any rule or practice direction.[2] The parties to an appeal are obliged to help the UT to further the overriding objective and to co-operate with the UT generally.[3]

1   Tribunal Procedure (Upper Tribunal) Rules 2008, SI 2008/2698, r 2.
2   SI 2008/2698, r 2(3). This terminology is not consistently used throughout the rules. Rule 17A, for example, dealing with abandonment of appeals, clearly intends the references to 'appellant' to mean the person who originally appealed against an immigration decision.

³ SI 2008/2698, r 2(4).

Parties

21.26 The parties are the appellant, the respondent and any interested party in the proceedings.[1] The appellant is the person who applies for permission to appeal or makes an appeal to the UT.[2] The person who was the other party before the FT is the respondent.[3] The UT may also give a direction to add an interested party to the proceedings[4] and a person who is not a party may apply to the UT to be added as an interested party.[5] In an asylum case[6] the UK's representative of the UNHCR is entitled to participate in proceedings and to receive all documents which have to be sent to the parties if he or she gives notice to the UT that he or she wishes to participate in the proceedings.[7]

[1] Tribunal Procedure (Upper Tribunal) Rules 2008, SI 2008/2698, r 1(3).
[2] SI 2008/2698, r 1(3).
[3] SI 2008/2698, r 1(3).
[4] SI 2008/2698, r 9(1).
[5] SI 2008/2698, r 9(3).
[6] Ie proceedings before the UT arising from an appeal under NIAA 2002, ss 82, 83 or 83A in which a person claims that removing or requiring him or her to leave the UK would breach the UK's obligations under the Refugee Convention: SI 2008/2698, r 1(3).
[7] SI 2008/2698, r 9(5) and (6).

Representatives

21.27 A party may appoint a representative who is qualified to provide immigration advice or immigration services under Immigration and Asylum Act 1999, s 84.[1] In judicial review proceedings, a party may appoint as a representative only a person authorised under the Legal Services Act 2007 to undertake the conduct of litigation in the High Court.[2] The UT must be sent written notice of the representative's name and address and any such notice received by the UT must be sent to each other party.[3] Anything permitted or required to be done by a party, apart from signing a witness statement, may be done by the representative.[4] The recipient of a notice that a representative has been appointed must provide to the representative any document that he or she is required to provide to the party and need not provide them to the represented party.[5] In addition, persons notified of the appointment of a representative are entitled to assume that the appointment continues until written notice to the contrary has been received.[6] An appellant's representative before the FT will be treated as that party's representative before the UT unless the UT receives notice to the contrary.[7]

[1] Tribunal Procedure (Upper Tribunal) Rules 2008, SI 2008/2698, r 11(1). For persons qualified to provide immigration advice and immigration services see CHAPTER 1.
[2] SI 2008/2698, r 11(5A).
[3] SI 2008/2698, r 11(2) and (2A).
[4] SI 2008/2698, r 11(3).
[5] SI 2008/2698, r 11(4).
[6] SI 2008/2698, r 11(4)(b).
[7] SI 2008/2698, r 11(10).

The Upper Tribunal's case management powers

21.28 The UT may regulate its own procedure, subject to the provisions of the TCEA and any other enactment.[1] It may give a direction in relation to the conduct or disposal of proceedings at any time, including directions amending, suspending or setting aside an earlier direction.[2] Directions may in particular: extend or shorten the time for complying with any rule, practice direction or direction;[3] consolidate or hear together two or more sets of proceedings raising common issues or treat a case as a lead case;[4] permit or require a party to amend a document;[5] permit or require a party or another person to provide documents, information, evidence or submissions to the UT or a party;[6] deal with an issue as a preliminary issue;[7] hold a hearing to consider any matter including a case management issue;[8] decide the form of any hearing;[9] adjourn or postpone a hearing;[10] require a party to produce a bundle for a hearing;[11] stay proceedings;[12] transfer proceedings to another court or tribunal with jurisdiction in relation to the proceedings;[13] suspend the effect of its own decision pending an appeal or review of that decision;[14] suspend the effect of the decision of the FT pending an application for permission to appeal or an appeal against that decision;[15] require any person or body or other tribunal whose decision is the subject of proceedings before the UT to provide reasons for the decision or other information or documents in relation to the decision or any proceedings before that person, body or tribunal.[16] The UT may also direct that a fast track case is to cease being treated as a fast track case if the parties consent or the UT is satisfied that there are exceptional circumstances which suggest that the proceedings could not justly be determined if it were treated as a fast track case or the Secretary of State failed to comply with a provision of the procedure rules or a direction and the UT is satisfied that the other party would be prejudiced if the proceedings were treated as a fast track case.[17]

1 Tribunal Procedure (Upper Tribunal) Rules 2008, SI 2008/2698, r 5(1).
2 SI 2008/2698, r 5(2).
3 SI 2008/2698, r 5(3)(a).
4 SI 2008/2698, r 5(3)(b).
5 SI 2008/2698, r 5(3)(c).
6 SI 2008/2698, r 5(3)(d).
7 SI 2008/2698, r 5(3)(e).
8 SI 2008/2698, r 5(3)(f).
9 SI 2008/2698, r 5(3)(g).
10 SI 2008/2698, r 5(3)(h).
11 SI 2008/2698, r 5(3)(i).
12 SI 2008/2698, r 5(3)(j).
13 SI 2008/2698, r 5(3)(k).
14 SI 2008/2698, r 5(3)(l).
15 SI 2008/2698, r 5(3)(m).
16 SI 2008/2698, r 5(3)(n).
17 SI 2008/2698, r 5(4).

21.29 A direction may be made by the UT on its own initiative or on the application of a party. Such an application may be made by sending a written application to the UT or orally at a hearing. The application must include the reason for making the application. The UT must send written notice of any direction to the parties and to any other person affected by the direction unless it considers that there is good reason not to do so. A party or any other person sent notice of a direction may, if he or she wishes to challenge the direction, apply for another direction which amends, suspends or sets aside the direction.[1]

[1] Tribunal Procedure (Upper Tribunal) Rules, 2008/2698, r 6.

Failure to comply with procedure rules, practice directions and directions

21.30 Failure to comply with the procedure rules, a practice direction or a direction does not by itself render void the proceedings or any step taken in the proceedings.[1] However, the UT may take such action as it considers just if there has been such a failure, including: waiving the requirement or requiring the failure to be remedied.[2] Generally, the UT also has the power to strike out the whole or a part of a party's case where there has been such a failure[3] or to restrict a party's participation in the proceedings but those powers are not available in an asylum or immigration case.[4] The UT also has powers in respect of non-compliance with a requirement imposed by the FT to give evidence, produce a document or facilitate inspection of a document or thing.[5] The power is exercisable if the FT refers the non-compliance to the UT.[6] The FT's procedure rules do not presently provide for the FT to make such a referral. If they did, the current and absurd situation in which many FT judges are unwilling to make directions requiring the respondent to produce documents because they expect the directions to be disregarded with impunity might be brought to an end.

[1] Tribunal Procedure (Upper Tribunal) Rules 2008, SI 2008/2698, r 7(1).
[2] SI 2008/2698, r 7(2).
[3] SI 2008/2698, r 7(2)(c).
[4] SI 2008/2698, rr 7(2)(b) and 8(1A).
[5] SI 2008/2698, r 7(3),(4) and TCEA 2007, s 25.
[6] SI 2008/2698, r 7(3).

Calculating time

21.31 An act required to be done by the procedure rules, a practice direction or a direction on or by a particular day must be done by 5.00 pm on that day unless it is not a working day in which case the act is done in time if it is done on the next working day.[1] Working days are any day except Saturday, Sunday, Christmas Day, the period from 27 to 31 December inclusive, Good Friday and bank holidays.[2] In fast track cases, 24 December, Maundy Thursday and the Tuesday after the last Monday in May are also not counted as working days.[3]

[1] Tribunal Procedure (Upper Tribunal) Rules 2008, SI 2008/2698, r 12(1) and (2).
[2] SI 2008/2698, rr 1 and 12(3A)(a).
[3] SI 2008/2698, r 12(3A)(b).

Sending and delivery of documents

21.32 Any document to be provided to the UT must be sent by pre-paid post, document exchange or by hand to the address specified for the proceedings or to the specified fax number or by any other method the UT may permit or direct.[1] If a party provides a fax number, email address or other details for the electronic transmission of documents that party must accept delivery of documents by that method[2] unless the party informs the UT and any other party that that method is not to be used.[3] The recipient of a document sent electronically may request a hard copy of the document.[4] The UT and each party may assume, until notified to the contrary, that the address provided by a party or the party's representative is the address to which documents should be sent.[5] A document submitted to the UT that is not in English must be accompanied by a written translation[6] unless the proceedings are in Wales or have a connection with Wales in which case a document or translation may be submitted in Welsh.[7]

[1] Tribunal Procedure (Upper Tribunal) Rules 2008, SI 2008/2698, r 13(1).
[2] SI 2008/2698, r 13(2).
[3] SI 2008/2698, r 13(3).
[4] SI 2008/2698, r 13(4).
[5] SI 2008/2698, r 13(5).
[6] SI 2008/2698, r 13(6).
[7] SI 2008/2698, r 13(7).

Disclosure of documents and information

21.33 The UT may make an order prohibiting disclosure or publication of documents or information relating to the proceedings or any matter likely to lead members of the public to identify a person who the UT thinks should not be identified.[1] It may also give a direction prohibiting the disclosure of a document or information to a person if it is satisfied that such disclosure would be likely to cause that person or another person serious harm and that it is proportionate, having regard to the interests of justice, to give such a direction.[2] A party may apply for such a direction to be made and if doing so, must provide the document or information to the UT together with the reason why it should not be disclosed.[3] If the UT directs that documents or information are not to be disclosed to a party it may give a direction that it be disclosed to the party's representative if it would be in the interests of the party and the UT was satisfied that the representative would not further disclose the material without the UT's consent.[4] The UT may also give a direction, either of its own motion or on the application of a party, that certain documents or information must or may be disclosed to the UT on the basis that they will not be further disclosed to any person or specified persons.[5] In a case involving national security, the UT is required to ensure that information is not disclosed contrary to the interests of national security.[6] The UT must conduct proceedings and record its decisions and reasons so as not to undermine the effect of any order or direction given relating to disclosure or the duty not to disclose contrary to the interests of national security.[7] These rules permitting the UT to depart from the fundamental, constitutional principle that a party has the right to know the case against him or her and the evidence on which it is based are similar to the FT rules allowing the tribunal to consider secret evidence and are objectionable for the same reasons: see para **20.105**.

[1] Tribunal Procedure (Upper Tribunal) Rules 2008, SI 2008/2698, r 14(1).
[2] SI 2008/2698, r 14(2).
[3] SI 2008/2698, r 14(3).

⁴   SI 2008/2698, r 14(5) and (6).
⁵   SI 2008/2698, r 14(8).
⁶   SI 2008/2698, r 14(10).
⁷   SI 2008/2698, r 14(11).

Evidence and submissions

21.34 The UT may give directions as to the issues on which it requires evidence or submissions and the nature of the evidence or submissions it requires.[1] It may give directions requiring or permitting the parties to provide expert evidence and requiring the parties jointly to appoint a single expert.[2] It may limit the number of witnesses and give directions as to the manner in which evidence or submissions are to be provided, including orally at a hearing or in writing.[3] It may admit evidence even if it would not be admissible in a civil trial and even if it was not available to a previous decision maker.[4] It may exclude otherwise admissible evidence that was not provided within the time allowed by a direction or practice direction or that was provided in a manner that did not comply with a direction or practice direction or where it would be unfair to admit the evidence.[5] If a party wishes the UT to consider evidence that was not before the FT, the party must deliver a notice to the UT and any other party indicating the nature of the evidence and explaining why it was not submitted to the FT[6] and whether it is sought to be adduced in connection with the issue of whether the FT made an error of law or in connection with the re-making of the decision if such an error is found.[7] If a party wishes to adduce oral evidence in connection with the re-making of the decision on the appeal it must explain why in the notice and give details of the oral evidence and a time estimate.[8] When considering whether to admit such evidence, the UT must have regard to whether there has been unreasonable delay in producing the evidence.[9]

¹   Tribunal Procedure (Upper Tribunal) Rules 2008, SI 2008/2698, r 15(1)(a) and (b).
²   SI 2008/2698, r 15(1)(c).
³   SI 2008/2698, r 15(1)(d) and (e).
⁴   SI 2008/2698, r 15(2)(a).
⁵   SI 2008/2698, r 15(2)(b).
⁶   SI 2008/2698, r 15(2A)(a).
⁷   Practice Directions: Immigration and Asylum Chambers of the First-tier Tribunal and The Upper Tribunal, 10 February 2010, para 4.2.
⁸   Practice Directions: para 4.5.
⁹   SI 2008/2698, r 15(2A)(b).

Evidence that was not before the First-tier Tribunal

21.35 What considerations are relevant when the UT decides whether to admit evidence that was not before the UT? If the issue before the UT is whether to grant permission to appeal or whether the decision of the FT involved the making of an error on a point of law[1] new evidence may be relevant if it is said that the FT made a mistake of fact of a kind giving rise to unfairness.[2] New evidence to establish the existence of such a mistake should be admitted if the '*Ladd v Marshall* principles'[3] were satisfied, although they might be departed from in exceptional circumstances where the interests of justice required.[4] Those principles are that:

(a)   the new evidence could not with reasonable diligence have been obtained for use at the trial (or hearing);

(b)   the new evidence must be such that, if given, it would probably have had an important influence on the result of the case (though it need not be decisive); and

(c)   the new evidence was apparently credible although it need not be incontrovertible.

The 'reasonable diligence' requirement would have to be applied, if at all, at least in asylum and human rights cases, recognising that an appellant is not to be fixed with the errors of his or her representative.[5] The Court of Appeal[6] and the Tribunal[7] have held that in certain circumstances new evidence undermining the credibility of a successful appellant may be relied on to establish an error of fact amounting to an error of law. However, the Court of Appeal subsequently indicated that the issue of whether and in what circumstances such an approach may be adopted needs to be revisited.[8] If evidence undermining the credibility of a successful appellant is relevant and admissible to show an error of law owing to a mistake of fact, evidence establishing his or her credibility should be equally relevant and admissible. New evidence may also be relevant and indeed necessary[9] to establish procedural unfairness or some other material irregularity in the proceedings before the FT and no doubt would be admitted in the absence of some compelling reason for its exclusion. Evidence of a relevant policy that should have been produced by the Secretary of State before the FT but was not is admissible without having to satisfy *Ladd v Marshall* principles in order to show that the FT, by failing to have regard to the policy, erred in law.[10] If the UT wrongly finds that the FT erred in law and so wrongly decides to remake the decision on the appeal, the UT's decision on the appeal will not be saved by the fact that it was based upon compelling evidence that had not been seen by the FT.[11] Where there is a defect or impropriety of a procedural nature in the proceedings at first instance, this may amount to a material error of law requiring the decision of the FTT to be set aside. A successful appeal is not dependent on the demonstration of some failing on the part of the FTT. Thus an error of law may be found to have occurred in circumstances where some material evidence, through no fault of the FTT, was not considered, with resulting unfairness.[12]

[1]   TCEA 2007, s 12(1).
[2]   *E v Secretary of State for the Home Department* [2004] EWCA Civ 49, [2004] QB 1044.
[3]   A reference to *Ladd v Marshall* [1954] 3 All ER 745, [1954] 1 WLR 1489, 98 Sol Jo 870, CA.
[4]   *R (Iran) v Secretary of State for the Home Department* [2005] EWCA Civ 982, (2005) Times, 19 August.
[5]   *FP (Iran) v Secretary of State for the Home Department* [2007] EWCA Civ 13.
[6]   *Verde v Secretary of State for the Home Department* [2004] EWCA Civ 1726, [2004] All ER (D) 75 (Dec). In *AD (Guinea) v Secretary of State for the Home Department* [2009] EWCA Civ 56 the Court of Appeal admitted new evidence about the appellant's fraudulent conduct and relied on that to dismiss the appeal it would otherwise have allowed.
[7]   *EA (Ghana)* [2005] UKAIT 00108.
[8]   *Shaheen v Secretary of State for the Home Department* [2005] EWCA Civ 1294, [2005] All ER (D) 31 (Nov); *AD (Guinea) v Secretary of State for the Home Department* [2009] EWCA Civ 56.
[9]   Eg *HA (Somalia)* [2009] UKAIT 00018.
[10] *AA (Afghanistan) v Secretary of State for the Home Department* [2007] EWCA Civ 12, (2007) Times, 2 February; *US (Nepal) v Secretary of State for the Home Department* [2009] EWCA Civ 208; *FH (Bangladesh) v Secretary of State for the Home Department* [2009] EWCA Civ 385 (error of law owing to Tribunal's failure to have regard to the more generous provisions

of the 'long residence concession' contained in the IDIs compared with the Immigration Rules, notwithstanding that the IDIs had not been before the Tribunal).
11   *AM (Pakistan) v Secretary of State for the Home Department* [2011] EWCA Civ 872.
12   *MM (unfairness; E & R) Sudan* [2014] UKUT 00105 (IAC).

Summoning witnesses and orders to answer questions and produce documents

21.36 The UT may, on its own initiative or on the application of a party, issue a summons (or a citation in Scotland) requiring a party to attend as a witness or order any person to answer any questions or produce any documents in that person's possession or control which relate to any issue in the proceedings.[1] A person may not be compelled to give any evidence or produce any document that he or she could not be compelled to give or produce in a civil trial in the part of the UK where the proceedings are due to be determined.[2] The summons must give the person 14 days' notice of the hearing or such shorter period as the UT directs.[3] If the person did not have the opportunity to object to the making of the summons before it was made, he or she may apply to the UT for it to be varied or set aside.[4] Such an application must be made as soon as reasonably practicable.[5]

1   Tribunal Procedure (Upper Tribunal) Rules 2008, SI 2008/2698, r 16(1).
2   SI 2008/2698, r 16(3).
3   SI 2008/2698, r 16(2).
4   SI 2008/2698, r 16(4).
5   SI 2008/2698, r 16(5).

Notice of appeal

21.37 If the FT gives permission to appeal to the UT the application for permission to appeal that was sent to the FT stands, subject to any directions of the FT or the UT, as the notice of appeal to the UT.[1] If the UT gives permission to appeal, the application for permission to appeal that was made to the UT stands, subject to any directions of the UT, as the notice of appeal.[2] The UT may permit the appellant to amend the notice of appeal.[3] The primary legislation gives a right of appeal to the UT 'on any point of law arising from a decision'; the right of appeal is not restricted by the statute to points of law identified in the application for permission to appeal or in the notice of appeal. The Procedure Rules contain no such restriction. Nor do they provide for the scope of an appeal to be limited by the terms of or reasons for a grant of permission to appeal: they refer to limitations or conditions being attached to the grant of permission[4] but do not make express provision for their imposition and the Procedure Rules do not require reasons to be given for a grant of permission. This contrasts with the position under the procedure rules that governed reconsideration of appeals. They provided that where an immigration judge ordered reconsideration the judge's notice of decision 'must state the grounds on which the Tribunal is ordered to reconsider its decision on the appeal'[5] and the contents of that statement would then 'normally' define the scope the Tribunal's inquiry into whether there was an error of law.[6] Can it be said then[7] that the UT has jurisdiction to consider any point of law arising from a decision made by the FT whether or not identified in the notice of appeal?

1 Tribunal Procedure (Upper Tribunal) Rules 2008, SI 2008/2698, r 23(1A).
2 SI 2008/2698, r 22(2)(b).
3 SI 2008/2698, r 5(2)(c)
4 SI 2008/2698, rr 22(2)(a) and 22(4)(b). That latter provision does not apply to appeals in the Immigration and Asylum Chamber.
5 Asylum and Immigration Tribunal (Procedure) Rules 2005, SI 2005/230, r 27(2)(a), now repealed along with NIAA 2002, s 103A.
6 *DK (Serbia) v Secretary of State for the Home Department* [2006] EWCA Civ 1747.
7 As it was by the Court of Appeal in respect of the reconsideration of a decision of an appeal under section 103A of the NIAA 2002 in *Hussain v Secretary of State for the Home Department* [2006] EWCA Civ 382.

21.38 There was much litigation relating to earlier statutory provisions about whether, on an appeal from an adjudicator to the Immigration Appeal Tribunal on a point of law,[1] the Tribunal was restricted to consideration of what was contained in the grounds of appeal or whether it could consider other apparent errors of law in the adjudicator's determination. It may be that these cases will be of relevance to determining the scope of an appeal to the UT. In the context of an appeal from an adjudicator to the Immigration Appeal Tribunal on a point of law, it was clearly established that the Tribunal only had jurisdiction to consider what was legitimately to be found in the grounds of appeal as originally propounded or amended.[2] Even if it was clear that the adjudicator had made an error of law, the Tribunal did not have jurisdiction to allow an appeal if the grounds of appeal had not identified that error.[3] The Court would look at the grounds in a 'fair and reasonable fashion', not pedantically[4] or in a narrow and formalistic way[5] in order to discern whether a point of law could be found in them and an appeal would not fail simply on a point of language.[6] The Court of Appeal held that perversity had to be expressly pleaded and grounds that merely articulated a factual disagreement would not establish jurisdiction to consider perversity[7] but that strict approach was not consistently maintained.[8] An exception to the principle that inclusion of a point within the grounds of appeal was necessary to establish jurisdiction[9] was the obligation on the Tribunal to consider an obvious point of Refugee Convention law that might avail an appellant, even if not pleaded in the grounds[10]. That obligation was a 'one-way street'[11] save for the 'modest extension'[12] on behalf of the Secretary of State in relation to the possible application of the exclusion clauses in the Refugee Convention. Such an extension was said to be necessary to avoid a possible breach of the Refugee Convention that would result from recognising a person as a refugee in breach of one of the exclusion clauses.[13] The obligation to consider points not contained in the grounds extends to the UK's obligations in international law more generally, including Community law and even if the point is not 'obvious' in the sense of having a strong prospect of success.[14]

1 Under the now repealed NIAA 2002, s 101 which provided for an 'appeal to the Tribunal against the adjudicator's determination on a point of law'.
2 *Miftari v Secretary of State for the Home Department* [2005] EWCA Civ 481, [2005] All ER (D) 279 (May). See also *B v Secretary of State for the Home Department* [2005] EWCA Civ 61, [2005] All ER (D) 15 (Feb).
3 As in *Miftari* and also *H v Secretary of State for the Home Department* [2005] EWCA Civ 1603, [2005] All ER (D) 306 (Dec).
4 *Jasarevic v Secretary of State for the Home Department* [2005] EWCA Civ 1784, [2005] All ER (D) 87 (Dec) and *MA (Palestinian Territories) v Secretary of State for the Home Department* [2008] EWCA Civ 304.

5   *R (on the application of Rodriguez-Torres) v Secretary of State for the Home Department* [2005] EWCA Civ 1328, (2005) Times, 6 December.

6   *K v Secretary of State for the Home Department* [2005] EWCA Civ 1655, 149 Sol Jo LB 1455, [2005] All ER (D) 318 (Nov).

7   *Abbas v Secretary of State for the Home Department* [2005] EWCA Civ 992, [2005] All ER (D) 34 (Jul).

8   *IO (Congo) v Secretary of State for the Home Department* [2006] EWCA Civ 796.

9   *Miftari v Secretary of State for the Home Department* [2005] EWCA Civ 481, [2005] All ER (D) 279 (May).

10   *R v Secretary of State for the Home Department, ex p Robinson* [1998] QB 929, [1997] 4 All ER 210, [1997] 3 WLR 1162, CA.

11   *Miftari v Secretary of State for the Home Department* [2005] EWCA Civ 481, [2005] All ER (D) 279 (May) per Maurice Kay LJ.

12   *H v Secretary of State for the Home Department* [2005] EWCA Civ 1603, [2005] All ER (D) 306 (Dec).

13   *A (Iraq) v Secretary of State for the Home Department* [2005] EWCA Civ 1438, 149 Sol Jo LB 1492, [2005] All ER (D) 22 (Dec) – withholding from the Secretary of State the benefit of the *Robinson* principle and thereby preventing the Refugee Convention exclusion clause from being raised for the first time in the Tribunal might have led to a person being recognised as a refugee in breach of the obligation to exclude. In *GH (Afghanistan)* [2005] EWCA Civ 1603 the Court of Appeal indicated that it would be reluctant to extend the principle further to the benefit of the Secretary of State, 'not least because the inequality of resources between the government and the average asylum seeker makes it unattractive for the Secretary of State to appeal to a forensic indulgence originally formulated in favour of the asylum-seeker'.

14   *Bulale v Secretary of State for the Home Department* [2008] EWCA Civ 806.

21.39 The appeal from the adjudicator to the Immigration Appeal Tribunal given by the Nationality, Immigration and Asylum Act 2002, s 101 was replaced by section 103A which provided for the single-tier Asylum and Immigration Tribunal to reconsider its own decision if in making the original decision the Tribunal 'made an error of law'. By contrast to an appeal under s 101, the Tribunal's jurisdiction was said not to be limited by what could be found in the grounds on which reconsideration was sought or granted.[1] Although the tribunal's jurisdiction was not restricted by law to what could be found in the grounds on which reconsideration was sought or ordered, the normal rule as a matter of practice was that the reconsideration of an appeal was so limited.[2]

1   See for example *AH (Sudan)* [2006] UKAIT 00038; *DK (Serbia) v Secretary of State for the Home Department* [2006] EWCA Civ 1747; *AA v Secretary of State for the Home Department* [2006] EWCA Civ 401 and *Hussain v Secretary of State for the Home Department* [2006] EWCA Civ 382 where the Court said that 'by virtue of section 103A, the AIT has jurisdiction if there is an error of law. The section does not require the error to be pleaded in the grounds'.

2   *ZY (Turkey) v Secretary of State for the Home Department* [2011] EWCA Civ 65, [2011] All ER (D) 23 (Feb).

Response to the notice of appeal

21.40 A respondent[1] may, subject to any directions of the UT, provide a response to a notice of appeal stating whether he or she opposes the appeal[2] and the grounds on which he or she relies, including any grounds on which the respondent was unsuccessful before the FT but intends to rely on in the appeal.[3] However, the UT has held that the provision for a respondent to identify such grounds in a response does not relieve him or her of the need to obtain permission to appeal if what the respondent wants to achieve before the

UT is a materially different outcome to that obtained from the FT.[4] So, for example, a respondent may repeat grounds that were advanced unsuccessfully before the FT in support of the FT's decision to allow an appeal on a particular human rights ground; what the respondent may not do is advance a challenge to the FT's decision to dismiss the appeal on asylum grounds; to do that the respondent would need permission to appeal. Any response must be in writing and received by the UT no later than one month after the respondent was sent notice that permission to appeal had been granted[5] unless the appeal is a fast track case in which case the response must be received one day before the hearing of the appeal.[6] If the response is provided later, it must include a request for an extension of time and the reason for not having provided the response in time.[7] When the UT receives a response, it must send a copy and any accompanying documents to the appellant.[8]

[1] Ie the person who was a party before the FT other than the person appealing to the UT: Tribunal Procedure (Upper Tribunal) Rules 2008, SI 2008/2698, r 1.
[2] SI 2008/2698, r 24(3)(d).
[3] SI 2008/2698, r 24 (3)(e).
[4] *And see EG & NG (UT rule 17: withdrawal; rule 24: scope) Ethiopia* [2013] UKUT 143 at **21.2** fn 3.
[5] SI 2008/2698, r 24(2)(a).
[6] SI 2008/2698, r 24(2)(aa).
[7] SI 2008/2689, r 24(4).
[8] SI 2008/2698, r 24(5).

Appellant's reply

21.41 The appellant may reply in writing to the respondent's response to the notice of appeal.[1] The reply must be received by the UT by the earlier of one month from the date the UT sent a copy of the response to the appellant or five days before the hearing of the appeal, unless the appeal is in the fast track in which case the reply may be received on the day of the hearing.[2] The UT must send a copy of the reply and any accompanying documents to the respondent.[3] The reply does not provide the appellant with a means to open up fundamentally different grounds of appeal on which permission had not been granted; an appellant wishing to do that would need to apply to the UT for permission to amend the notice of appeal.[4]

[1] Tribunal Procedure (Upper Tribunal) Rules 2008, SI 2008/2698, r 24(1).
[2] SI 2008/2698, r 25(2A).
[3] SI 2008/2698, r 25(3).
[4] Under SI 2008/2698, r 5(2)(c); *Azimi-Moayed (Decisions affecting children; onward appeals)* [2013] UKUT 197 (IAC).

Hearing of the appeal

21.42 The UT can make any decision without a hearing but must have regard to any views expressed by the parties before deciding whether to hold a hearing and the form any such hearing is to take.[1] All hearings are to be held in public unless the UT directs that all or part of a hearing is to be in private, in which case the UT may determine who is entitled to attend the hearing.[2] Each party is entitled to attend a hearing,[3] subject to the UT's power to exclude any person from a hearing or part of a hearing.[4] It may exercise that power in respect of any person whose conduct the UT thinks is disrupting, or is likely to disrupt the hearing; whose presence the UT considers is likely to prevent another person from giving evidence or making submissions freely; who it considers should be excluded so as to prevent disclosure or publication of documents or information contrary to an order or direction prohibiting such publication or disclosure or contrary to the interests of national security;[5] whose presence would defeat the purpose of the hearing or who is under the age of 18.[6] The UT may also give a direction excluding a witness from a hearing until he or she has given evidence.[7] If a party fails to attend a hearing, the UT may proceed in the party's absence if satisfied that the party has been notified of the hearing or that reasonable steps have been taken to notify the party and it considers that it is in the interests of justice to do so.[8]

1   Tribunal Procedure (Upper Tribunal) Rules 2008, SI 2008/2698, r 34.
2   SI 2008/2698, r 37(1) and (2).
3   SI 2008/2698, r 35(1).
4   SI 2008/2698, rr 35(1) and 37(4).
5   Under SI 2008/2698, r 14.
6   The power to exclude children from hearings would have to be exercised in accordance with Article 12 of the Convention on the Rights of the Child.
7   SI 2008/2698, r 37(5).
8   SI 2008/2698, r 38.

Withdrawal of a party's case

21.43 A party may withdraw its case or any part of its case by giving written notice to the UT or orally at a hearing.[1] The UT's consent to the withdrawal of a case, other than in relation to an application for permission, is required for the withdrawal to take effect[2] and withdrawal takes effect only once the parties have received written notification of the UT's consent to the withdrawal.[3] The UT must notify each party in writing of a withdrawal.[4] A party which has withdrawn its case may apply in writing within one month of the UT receiving the notice of withdrawal or the hearing at which the case was withdrawn orally for the case to be reinstated.[5] The UT's consent is not needed for the Secretary of State to withdraw the underlying immigration decision.[6] The Secretary of State's practice of withdrawing immigration decisions just before appeals are to be heard and even after they have commenced has aggrieved the UT and appellants alike. In a careful and convincing analysis of the applicable statutory provisions the UT has held that, notwithstanding withdrawal of the immigration decision, the UT retained the powers conferred by the TCEA to hear and determine an appeal and to give directions to give effect to its decision on the appeal if it decided to withhold consent to the withdrawal of the Secretary of State's case.[7] However, the Court of Appeal has held that an appeal against an immigration decision under Nationality, Immigration and Asylum Act 2002, section 82 incorporates the further appeals brought under the TCEA[8] and if that is the case, it is difficult to contend that an appeal under the TCEA to the UT or the Court of Appeal can outlast the immigration decision.

1   Tribunal Procedure (Upper Tribunal) Rules 2008, SI 2008/2698, r 17(1).
2   SI 2008/2698, r 17(2).
3   *EG & NG (UT rule 17: withdrawal; rule 24: scope) Ethiopia* [2013] UKUT 143.
4   SI 2008/2698, r 17(5).
5   SI 2008/2698, r 17(4).

6   *SM (Withdrawal of appealed decision: effect) Pakistan* [2014] UKUT 64 (IAC). In CS (USA) [2010] UKUT 163 (IAC) the tribunal refused to consent to the Secretary of State withdrawing the immigration decision being appealed against, the Secretary of State having wrongly conceded that such consent was necessary. It did so having regard to the overriding objective: the Secretary of State's delay in seeking to withdraw the decision with the result that the appellant incurred the cost of representation at the hearing; the public interest in the UT making a reasoned decision, bringing to public attention the acknowledged error in the Secretary of State's applicable guidance that resulted in the withdrawal and the importance of identifying a possible error in a reported determination on which the FT had relied.
7   *SM (Withdrawal of appealed decision: effect) Pakistan* [2014] UKUT 64 (IAC).
8   *LB (Jamaica) v Secretary of State for the Home Department* [2011] EWCA Civ 1420.

Deemed abandonment and final determination of an appeal

21.44 An appeal against an immigration decision under NIAA 2002, s 82 is treated as abandoned if the appellant, having brought the appeal whilst in the UK leaves the country[1] or is granted leave to enter or remain (subject to provision enabling such a person to continue an appeal on asylum grounds if the leave is for more than 12 months or on race discrimination grounds and the person gives notice in accordance with tribunal procedure rules that he or she wishes to continue).[2] Similar provision is made in relation to appeals against EEA decisions brought under the EEA regulations.[3] An appeal under NIAA 2002, s 82 against certain immigration decisions is treated as 'finally determined' if a deportation order is made against the appellant.[4] Appeals to the UT are not brought under NIAA 2002, section 82 or the EEA regulations but are brought under the TCEA.[5] The Court of Appeal rejected the argument that the abandonment provisions apply only to the appeal under NIAA 2002, section 82 and have no application to further appeals to the UT and Court of Appeal under the TCEA.[6]

1   *R (on the application of MM (Ghana)) v Secretary of State for the Home Department* [2012] EWCA Civ 827.
2   NIAA 2002, s 104(4), (4A), (4B) and (4C). See Chapter 20.
3   Brought under Immigration (European Economic Area) Regulations 2006, SI 2006/1003, reg 26. See Sch 2, para 4(2).
4   NIAA 2002, s 104(5).
5   Section 11.
6   *LB (Jamaica) v Secretary of State for the Home Department* [2011] EWCA Civ 1420.

21.45 The UT procedure rules require the UT to send notice to the parties informing them 'that the appeal is being treated as abandoned or finally determined'[1] in the event of the appellant's departure from the UK, the grant of leave or a document confirming an EU law right of residence to the appellant or the making of a deportation order against the appellant. The parties are required to notify the UT if they are aware of any of those events having occurred.[2] An appellant wishing to pursue an appeal that would otherwise be treated as abandoned because of the grant of leave to enter or remain may give notice to that effect within 30 days of being sent the grant of leave or 28 days if it is given personally or electronically.[3] Those time limits may not be extended.[4] The procedure rules appear to allow any appellant wishing to pursue an appeal to which the statutory abandonment provisions apply to give notice of his or her wish to do so. They do not reflect the statutory provisions that allow for their disapplication only in respect of an appeal on race discrimination grounds or, where leave was granted for more than a year, on refugee convention grounds. The notice given by the appellant must comply with any relevant practice directions.[5]

1   Tribunal Procedure (Upper Tribunal) Rules 2008, SI 2008/2698, r 17A(2).
2   SI 2008/2698, r 17A(1).
3   SI 2008/2698, r 17A(3), (4)
4   SI 2008/2698, r 17A(5).
5   SI 2008/2698, r 17A(3). See Practice Directions: Immigration and Asylum Chambers of the First-tier Tribunal and the Upper Tribunal, para 5. The Practice Direction requires the notice to state: the appellant's full name and date of birth; the Tribunal's reference number; the Home Office reference number if applicable; the Foreign and Commonwealth Office reference number if applicable; the date on which the appellant was granted leave to enter or remain (for a period exceeding 12 months in the case of those wishing to pursue an asylum appeal) and that the appellant wishes to pursue the appeal in so far as it is brought on refugee convention or race discrimination grounds.

Notice of funding of legal services

21.46 If a party is granted funding of legal services he or she must send a copy of the funding notice[1] or legal aid certificate[2] to the UT as soon as practicable and notify every other party in writing that funding has been granted.[3]

1   If funding is granted by the Legal Services Commission or the Northern Ireland Legal Services Commission.
2   If funding is granted by the Scottish Legal Aid Board.
3   Tribunal Procedure (Upper Tribunal) Rules 2008, SI 2008/2698, r 18.

Notice of hearings

21.47 The UT must give each party entitled to attend a hearing reasonable notice of the time and place or of any change to the time and place for the hearing. The period of such notice must be at least 14 days except that in a fast-track case the minimum period of notice is one day and in other cases, shorter notice may be given if the parties agree or in urgent or exceptional cases.[1]

1   Tribunal Procedure (Upper Tribunal) Rules 2008, SI 2008/2698, r 36.

Time limits for hearing fast track cases

21.48 The UT must start the hearing of an appeal in a fast-track case no later than four days after notice of the grant of permission to appeal was sent to the appellant or two days if the notice was sent electronically or delivered personally. If the UT cannot arrange for the hearing to start within those specified times, it must set a date for the hearing as soon as is reasonably practicable.[1]

1   Tribunal Procedure (Upper Tribunal) Rules 2008, SI 2008/2698.

THE UPPER TRIBUNAL'S DECISION

21.49 The UT's powers to set aside a decision of the FT and to remake the decision or remit the case to the FT are contingent upon the UT having found that the FT's decision involved the making of an error on a point of law.[1] Therefore, as with the hearing of an application for reconsideration by the Asylum and Immigration Tribunal under the repealed NIAA 2002, s 103A, the first issue to be decided by the UT is whether there was such an error. The UT must consider all of the grounds of appeal on which permission was granted. Deciding to allow the appeal on one ground does not relieve the UT of the obligation to deal with the other grounds[2] although it need not deal with grounds that the appellant has clearly abandoned.[3] If it finds that there was not then the decision of the FT stands. If it finds that there was an error on a point of law in the making of the FT's decision the UT has a power but not an obligation to set aside the FT's decision. The legislation does not require the error of law to be material before the UT can set aside the FT's decision but in most cases, the materiality of the error is likely to be the decisive consideration for the UT in deciding whether to exercise that power[4]. It might exercise the power where the error, whilst not material, raised an issue of principle on which the UT wished to give guidance or where the making of factual findings prejudicial to the party involved an error of law albeit the finding did not affect the outcome of the appeal; if the error was material, the UT might decline to set aside the decision if it was of no practical significance to the parties but otherwise it is difficult to imagine circumstances where the UT would not set aside a decision which involved a material error of law.

[1]   TCEA 2007, s 11(1) and (2).
[2]   *JA (Afghanistan) v Secretary of State for the Home Department* [2014] EWCA Civ 450.
[3]   *Sarkar (Biplab Kumar) v Secretary of State for the Home Department* [2014] EWCA Civ 195.
[4]   *Anoliefo (Permission to appeal)* [2013] UKUT 345 (IAC).

Remitting or re-making the decision

21.50 If the UT does decide to set aside the FT's decision then it must either remit the case to the FT with directions for its reconsideration[1] or re-make the decision.[2] If the UT decides to re-make the decision it may make such findings of fact as it considers appropriate and may make any decision which the FT could make if the FT was re-making the decision.[3] When it remakes the decision, the UT is not confined to addressing the issues in respect of which the FT was found to have erred in law, nor is it confined to the issues raised in the various pleadings (reasons for refusal letter, notice of appeal, response and reply, skeleton argument) before the UT or even before the FT.[4] Thus, for example, the fact that the FT had not considered Article 8 and had made no error of law by not considering Article 8 was not an obstacle to the UT considering article 8 when it remade the decision on the appeal.[5] When remaking the decision, the UT has at its disposal the full range of powers available to the FT.[6] The UT is likely to re-make the decision rather than remit the case unless it is satisfied that the effect of the error was to deprive a party before the FT of a fair hearing[7] or other opportunity for the party's case to be put to and considered by the FT or there are highly compelling reasons why the decision should not be re-made by the UT.[8] If the case is not to be remitted to the FT, the UT will consider whether to re-make the decision by reference to the FT's findings of fact and any new documentary evidence at the same hearing as that at which it decided there was an error of law or whether further findings of fact are needed before it can do so.[9] The UT would generally expect to re-make the decision without a further hearing unless additional oral evidence is required or a party is able to satisfy the UT that there is good reason for it not being reasonably practicable to adduce the further documentary evidence in time to be considered at the hearing.[10] If the appeal has to be adjourned for a further hearing to enable the UT to remake the decision, the proceedings may be completed before the same constitution of the UT or transferred to another constitution.[11] If the appeal is transferred, the UT is required to prepare written reasons for finding an error of law which are to be sent to the parties before the next hearing and incorporated in full in the eventual determination of the UT.[12] In a fast track appeal, the parties are expected to attend with all necessary witnesses and evidence because if the UT decides to remake the decision, it would be unusual for it to adjourn for a further hearing to do so.[13]

[1]   TCEA 2007, s 12(2)(b)(i).
[2]   TCEA 2007, s 12(2)(b)(ii).
[3]   TCEA 2007, s 12(4).
[4]   *Kizhakudan (John) v Secretary of State for the Home Department* [2012] EWCA Civ 566; *NP (Sri Lanka) v Secretary of State for the Home Department* [2012] EWCA Civ 906. In both cases, the Court emphasised the importance of properly pleaded cases but that non-compliance with the procedure rules relating to pleadings was relevant in terms of procedural fairness rather than the question of whether the UT had jurisdiction to consider an issue. See also *Ferrer (Limited grounds of appeal: Alvi)* [2012] UKUT 304 (IAC).
[5]   *John Kizhakudan v Secretary of State for the Home Department* [2012] EWCA Civ 566.
[6]   *Sarkar (Biplab Kumar) v Secretary of State for the Home Department* [2014] EWCA Civ 195.
[7]   In which case there is a general rule that the appeal should be remitted to the FT because the right to a fair hearing is generally considered to rank as a right of constitutional importance and an appeal to the UT should be triggered only where that right has been fully enjoyed: *MM (Unfairness: E and R) Sudan* [2014] UKUT 105 (IAC).
[8]   Senior President's Practice Statements: Immigration and Asylum Chambers of the First-tier and the Upper Tribunal, 10 February 2010, para 7.2.
[9]   Practice Directions: Immigration and Asylum Chambers of the First-tier Tribunal and the Upper Tribunal, 10 February 2010, paras 3.1(c) and 3.4.
[10] Practice Directions: paras 3.2 and 3.3.
[11] Practice Directions: para 3.4.
[12] Practice Directions: paras 3.6 and 3.7.
[13] Practice Directions: para 3.8.

21.51 If the UT remits the case to the FT it can make three different kinds of directions. The first, which the UT must make are 'directions for [the case's] reconsideration'.[1] It is not apparent whether such directions are merely to oblige the FT to reconsider the case or whether they may also specify additional matters of substance such as what issues the FT is to consider and what facts if any are to be treated as already established. The second kind of directions relate to the composition of the FT, the UT being able to direct that the case must be reconsidered by members of the FT other than those who made the original decision.[2] The third kind are 'procedural directions in connection with the reconsideration of the case by the FT'.[3]

[1]   TCEA 2007, s 12(2)(b)(i).
[2]   TCEA 2007, s 12(3)(a).
[3]   TCEA 2007, s 12(3)(b).

Factual issues to be determined

21.52 Upon what factual basis must the UT or FT re-make or reconsider a decision whose making had been found to involve an error on a point of law? That issue, in respect of the reconsideration of decisions by the Asylum and Immigration Tribunal under provisions now repealed[1] was considered on a number of occasions by the Court of Appeal and the AIT. The starting point was that anybody asked to reconsider a decision on the grounds of an identified error of law will approach its reconsideration on the basis that any factual findings and conclusions or judgments arising from those findings which are unaffected by the error of law should not be revisited.[2] That was said to flow in part from specific features of the statutory regime, in particular, that Parliament had not provided for a rehearing of the appeal and that the same Tribunal was tasked with reconsidering its own decision.[3] However, it was also a consequence of a number of principles which are equally applicable in the statutory context in which the FT or UT has to reconsider or remake a decision. It would be wrong in principle to deprive a party of a finding in his or her favour and to dismantle an edifice of reasoning where neither was necessary in order to remedy the legal errors contained in the original decision.[4] Requiring an individual to go through the gruelling process of giving evidence again in relation to issues that had already been decided would be wasteful of the Tribunal's time and resources but also oppressive and potentially unfair to the individual.[5] However, whilst 'the normal rule' was that the reconsideration was limited to those matters which were the subject of illegality[6] it is not a bright line rule[7] and is a matter of practice, not jurisdiction, the Tribunal having a discretion as to the scope of the reconsideration once it had decided that there was an error of law.[8] With the agreement (or acquiescence[9]) of the parties the Tribunal could revisit factual findings that were otherwise outside the proper scope of the reconsideration, although the position might be different if the subject of the immigration decision was unrepresented.[10] Factual findings not affected by any error of law could be revisited on the basis of new evidence[11] or otherwise in the most exceptional circumstances.[12] Where the original Tribunal had made a positive credibility finding in respect of the appellant's account of past events, the reconsidering Tribunal's assessment, on hearing the appellant about more recent events, that he was not in fact a credible witness did not amount to new evidence entitling it to go behind the first Tribunal's conclusion as to credibility.[13]

1   NIAA 2002, s 103A and Asylum and Immigration Tribunal (Procedure) Rules 2005, SI 2005/230, rr 29–33.
2   *DK (Serbia) v Secretary of State for the Home Department* [2006] EWCA Civ 1747. See also *R (on the application of Akpinar (Irfan)) v Upper Tribunal (Immigration and Asylum Chamber); Secretary of State for the Home Department v AV (Democratic Republic of the Congo)* [2014] EWCA Civ 937 holding that the UT had not been entitled to revisit the matter of the appellant's credibility when the FT's error had no bearing on credibility at all.
3   *DK (Serbia) and AH (Sudan)* [2006] UKAIT 00038.
4   Sedley LJ, *obiter* in *Mukarkar v Secretary of State for the Home Department* [2006] EWCA Civ 1045, approved in *HF (Algeria) v Secretary of State* [2007] EWCA Civ 445.
5   Carnwath LJ in *HF (Algeria) v Secretary of State for the Home Department* [2007] EWCA Civ 445.
6   Carnwath LJ in *NJ (Iran) v Secretary of State for the Home Department* [2008] EWCA Civ 77.
7   *DM (Zambia) v Secretary of State for the Home Department* [2009] EWCA Civ 474.
8   *OB (Iraq) v Secretary of State for the Home Department* [2007] EWCA Civ 585; *LS (Uzbekistan) v Secretary of State for the Home Department* [2008] EWCA Civ 909.

9 For example, by raising no objection to cross examination which clearly put facts in issue: *Rajaratnam (Stalin) v Secretary of State for the Home Department* [2014] EWCA Civ 8.

10 *NJ (Iran) v Secretary of State for the Home Department* [2008] EWCA Civ 77.

11 As in *DM (Zambia) v Secretary of State for the Home Department* [2009] EWCA Civ 474, for example.

12 *DK (Serbia) v Secretary of State for the Home Department* [2006] EWCA Civ 17.

13 *MY (Turkey) v Secretary of State for the Home Department* [2008] EWCA Civ 477.

Consent orders

21.53 The UT may, at the request of the parties, make a consent order disposing of the proceedings and making such other provision as the parties have agreed. However, it may only do so 'if it considers it appropriate'.[1]

1 Tribunal Procedure (Upper Tribunal) Rules 2008, SI 2008/2698, r 39.

Decisions

21.54 The UT may give a decision orally at a hearing.[1] If the UT's decision finally disposes of all issues in the proceedings it must, as soon as reasonably practicable after making the decision, provide each party with a decision notice stating the decision together with written reasons for the decision (unless the decision was made by the consent of parties or they consented to the UT not giving written reasons) and notification of any rights of review or appeal against the decision.[2] In a non-fast track asylum case, instead of sending the notice of decision to the parties it has to be sent to the Secretary of State who must then send it to the other party within 30 days of being sent the notice by the UT[3] or, if the Secretary of State applies for permission to appeal, no later than the date on which that application is sent to the UT.[4] The Secretary of State is required to notify the UT when he or she has done so and if the Secretary of State fails to do that within 31 days of being sent the notice by the UT, the UT is required to send the notice of decision to the other party. The UT may provide written reasons for any decision that does not finally dispose of all the issues in the proceedings.[5]

1 Tribunal Procedure (Upper Tribunal) Rules 2008, SI 2008/2698, r 40(1).
2 SI 2008/2698, r 40(2) and (3)
3 SI 2008/2698, rr 40(2) and 40A. Rule 40A makes no reference to the UT having to provide reasons with the notice of decision or the Secretary of State having to send reasons to the other party. No doubt that is mere oversight.
4 SI 2008/2698, r 40A(5).
5 SI 2008/2698, r 40(4).

Correction, setting aside and review of decisions

21.55 The UT may at any time correct any clerical mistake or other accidental slip or omission in a decision or record of a decision by sending notification of the amended decision or a copy of the amended record to all parties and making any necessary alteration to any information published in relation to the decision.[1] In addition, the UT may set aside a decision or part of a decision which disposes of proceedings and remake the decision or the relevant part of the decision.[2] It may do so if it considers that it would be in the interests of justice and: a document relating to the proceedings was not sent to or received at an appropriate time by a party or a party's representative; a document relating to the proceedings was not sent to the UT at an appropriate time; a party or a party's representative was not present at a hearing related to the proceedings or there was some other procedural irregularity.[3] A party may apply in writing for the UT's decision to be set aside. Such an application must be received by the UT within 12 days after being sent the UT's decision if the person who brought the appeal to the FT is in the UK or 38 days if he or she is outside the UK.[4] If the notice of decision was sent electronically, the time within which the application must be made is 10 working days.[5]

[1] Tribunal Procedure (Upper Tribunal) Rules 2008, SI 2008/2698, r 42.
[2] SI 2008/2698, r 43(1).
[3] SI 2008/2698, r 43(1) and (2).
[4] SI 2008/2698, r 43(3) and (4).
[5] SI 2008/2698, r 43(5).

21.56–21.57 The TCEA gives the UT a power to review its own decisions, save 'excluded decisions', either of its own initiative or on the application of a party who has a right of appeal to the Court of Appeal.[1] It enables procedure rules to make further provision as to the kinds of decision which may be reviewed, the circumstances in and the grounds upon which a review may be carried out.[2] If the UT receives an application for permission to appeal to the Court of Appeal the UT may review the decision if, when making the decision the UT overlooked a legislative provision or binding authority that could have had a material effect on the decision or, since the UT's decision, a court made a decision binding on the UT and which could have had a material effect on the decision.[3] In the light of the review, the UT may correct accidental errors in the decision or in a record of the decision; amend reasons given for the decision or set the decision aside.[4] If it sets the decision aside then it must re-make the decision, including making such factual findings as the UT considers appropriate.[5] If the UT decides not to review the decision or reviews the decision and decides to take no action in relation to it, it must then decide the application for permission to appeal.[6] If the UT does undertake a review of its decision, it must notify the parties in writing of the outcome and of any rights of review or appeal in relation to it.[7] If the UT decides to take action in relation to a decision following a review and it does so without giving the parties an opportunity to make representations, it must give notice to the parties that they may apply for the review to be set aside and for the decision to be reviewed again.[8] The UT may treat an application for a decision to be corrected, set aside, reviewed or for permission to appeal as an application for any other one of those things.[9]

[1] TCEA 2007, s 10(1) and (2).
[2] TCEA 2007, s 10(3).
[3] Tribunal Procedure (Upper Tribunal) Rules 2008, SI 2008/2698, r 45(1).
[4] TCEA 2007, s 10(4).
[5] TCEA 2007, s 10(5) and (6).
[6] SI 2008/2698, r 45(2).
[7] SI 2008/2698, r 46(2).
[8] SI 2008/2698, r 46(3).
[9] Tribunal Procedure (Upper Tribunal) Rules 2008, SI 2008/2698, r 48 as inserted by SI 2010/2653.

Appeal to the Court of Appeal or Court of Session

21.58 Any party to an appeal to the UT has a right of appeal to the Court of Appeal or Court of Session 'on any point of law arising from a decision made by the UT' other than an excluded decision.[1] It is for the UT, before deciding an application for permission to appeal from its decision, to specify the 'relevant appellate court' for the proposed appeal, ie whichever of the Court of Appeal in England and Wales or Northern Ireland or the Court of Session appears to it to be the most appropriate.[2] Excluded decisions are decisions of the UT on applications for permission to appeal from the FT;[3] decisions of the UT to review or not to review a decision and the decisions or actions taken pursuant to a review;[4] (but the UT's new decision made after setting aside a decision on review is not an excluded decision); a decision of the UT set aside on review[5] and any procedural, ancillary or preliminary decision made in relation to an appeal against a decision to deprive the person of British citizenship,[6] an immigration decision under NIAA 2002, s 82, a refusal of asylum under NIAA 2002, s 83 or 83A or against an EEA decision.[7] The UT's decision includes its decision in respect of any directions made by the FT to give effect to the FT's decision on the appeal.[8] Permission to appeal is required[9] and permission may be given by the UT or the Court of Appeal or Court of Session.[10] An application to the Court of Appeal or Court of Session for permission to appeal may be made only if permission has been refused by the UT.[11] The Court of Appeal heard an appeal, notwithstanding that it had become academic as a result of the grant of indefinite leave to remain to the appellant because of the important public interest in the correction of errors in country guidance decisions.[12]

[1]   TCEA 2007, s 13(1).
[2]   TCEA 2007, s 13(11), (12) and (13).
[3]   TCEA 2007, s 13(8)(c).
[4]   TCEA 2007, s 13(8)(d).
[5]   TCEA 2007, s 13(8)(e).
[6]   Under the British Nationality Act 1981, s 40A.
[7]   TCEA 2007, s 13(8)(f) and Appeals (Excluded Decisions) Order 2009, SI 2009/275, art 3(m).
[8]   NIAA 2002, s 87(4).
[9]   TCEA 2007, s 13(3).
[10] TCEA 2007, s 13(4).
[11] TCEA 2007, s 13(5).
[12] *PO (Nigeria) v Secretary of State for the Home Department* [2011] EWCA Civ 132, [2011] NLJR 327, (2011) Times, 19 April.

21.59 Although the right of appeal is on any point of law arising from a decision made by the UT,[1] permission to appeal to the Court of Appeal (but not the Court of Session) is not to be granted unless the UT or the court to which the application is made considers that the proposed appeal would raise some important point of principle or practice or there is some other compelling reason for the appellate court to hear the appeal.[2] This test is substantially the same as that where an appeal was brought to the High Court or county court and permission is sought to bring a second appeal to the Court of Appeal.[3] It is applicable only where the decision of the UT was a decision on appeal from the FT[4] and so does not apply where the appeal was originally decided by the AIT.[5] The first limb of the second appeal test (important point of principle or practice) may mean that a properly arguable case or one with a real prospect of success should not be given permission even if the would-be appellant had won at first instance and even if it was clear that the decision on appeal involved the misapplication of an established legal principle.[6] In cases concerned with the UK's obligations under the Refugee Convention, the ECHR and EU law there would be a real prospect of decisions of the UT being allowed to stand which, if implemented, would put the UK in breach of its international obligations and result in persecution or violation of the appellant's human rights or community law rights.[7] In Parliament, the ministers promoting the legislation containing the second appeals test said 'there may be some cases that raise the real prospect that the decision of the Upper Tribunal will be in breach of the UK's human rights obligations. Those are precisely the sort of cases that would meet the test that is set out in section 13(6) of the Act'.[8] The Court of Appeal has given guidance as to how the second appeals test is to be applied to applications for permission to appeal from the immigration and asylum chamber of the UT.[9] A case in which there was a 'compelling reason' to hear an appeal would be one which 'cries out' for consideration by the court; normally, the prospects of success would be 'very high' or one in which the decision of the UT was 'perverse or otherwise plainly wrong' because, for example, it was 'inconsistent with authority of a higher court' or because of 'procedural failure' in the UT making it 'plainly unjust' to refuse a further appeal.[10] Whilst noting that Baroness Hale and Lord Dyson in *Cart*[11] had both acknowledged the possible relevance of the extreme consequences for the individual to a finding of a 'compelling reason', the Court held that that was not a free-standing test and that the word 'compelling' means 'legally compelling'.[12] The fact that a case involved asylum or human rights and the drastic consequences that would follow if the case was made out did not establish a 'compelling reason', notwithstanding the ministerial statements made during the passage of the 2007 Act indicating that it would.[13] That did not mean, however, that the consequences of the decision for the individual were irrelevant; the combination of 'truly drastic' or 'very adverse consequences' and a sufficiently serious legal basis for challenging the the UT's decision could establish a 'legally compelling' reason.[14] The test is stringent but flexible and capable of taking account of the particular circumstances of a case: the fact that an individual had succeeded before the FT and had an arguable case for saying the UT had erred in law would not by itself establish a 'compelling reason' but could do in combination with other circumstances.[15] Similarly, the fact that the UT set aside the FT's decision would not suffice by itself. Moreover, in such a case the reasons why the FT decision was set aside may be relevant as showing either that the UT's decision was in substance a first instance decision (because of the nature or extent of the FT's errors or because the FT had not dealt with a legal issue considered for the first time by the UT) or that the UT substantially endorsed what the FT had already decided.[16]

1   TCEA 2007, s 13(1).
2   TCEA 2007, s 13(6) and the Appeals from the Upper Tribunal to the Court of Appeal Order 2008, SI 2008/2834.
3   Access to Justice Act 1999, s 55(1) and CPR 52.13.
4   TCEA 2007, ss 13(7) and 11(1).
5   *FA (Iraq) v Secretary of State for the Home Department* [2010] EWCA Civ 827.
6   *Tanfern Ltd v Cameron-MacDonald* [2000] 2 All ER 801, [2000] 1 WLR 1311 and *Uphill v BRB (Residuary) Ltd* [2005] EWCA Civ 60, [2005] 3 All ER 264, [2005] 1 WLR 2070.
7   'It must be obvious that that cannot be right. While the United Kingdom's international obligations do not require it to provide endless opportunities for questioning the performance of those obligations in the domestic courts, good faith and practice (and, in the case of

obligations under the ECHR, Article 13 of the Convention) require that where a domestic appellate structure is provided that structure should not be deliberately withheld from cases that have a real prospect of demonstrating a breach of those obligations. And this is without reference to the position of the appellants themselves, who are faced with the prospect of being unable to challenge decisions that are arguably wrong, and which may result in their being returned to conditions of persecution, because the error has lain in applying an established principle rather than in the establishment of the principle in the first place'. 'Application of section 13(6) of the Tribunals, Courts and Enforcement Act 2007 to immigration appeals from the proposed Upper Tribunal: Opinion of Sir Richard Buxton' is accessible on the website of the Joint Council for the Welfare of Immigrants.

8   Phil Woolas, then Minister of State for Borders and Immigration in the House of Commons on 16.6.2009. See also, to similar effect, Lord West of Spithead, then Parliamentary Under-Secretary of State for the Home Office in the House of Lords, 1 April 2009.

9   *PR (Sri Lanka) v Secretary of State for the Home Department* [2011] EWCA Civ 988, [2011] All ER (D) 67 (Aug); and *JD (Congo) v Secretary of State for the Home Department* [2012] EWCA Civ 327.

10   *PR (Sri Lanka)* para 35.

11   *R (on the application of Cart) v The Upper Tribunal* [2011] UKSC 28, [2012] 1 AC 663,[2011] 4 All ER 127, [2011] STC 1659.

12   *PR (Sri Lanka)* para 36.

13   *PR (Sri Lanka)* para 41f.

14   *JD (Congo)* para 26.

15   *JD (Congo)* para 18.

16   *JD (Congo)* para 31.

Application to the Upper Tribunal for permission to appeal

21.60 An application to the UT for permission to appeal to the Court of Appeal or Court of Session must be made in writing[1] identifying the decision of the UT to which it relates, the alleged errors of law in the decision and the result sought by the party making the application[2] so as to be received by the UT within 'the appropriate period'.[3] The appropriate period begins when the person applying for permission is sent by the UT or, in an asylum case, by the Secretary of State: written notice of the decision; notification of amended reasons for or correction of the decision following a review or notification that an in-time application for the decision to be set aside has been unsuccessful.[4] The length of the appropriate period is 12 working days if the person who appealed to the FT is in the UK[5] (10 working days if the notice of the decision was sent electronically or delivered personally);[6] 7 working days if the person making the application is in detention[7] (5 working days if the decision was sent electronically or delivered personally[8]) or 38 days if the person who appealed to the FT is outside the UK at the time that the application is made[9] (or 10 working days if the notice is sent electronically or delivered personally).[10] These periods within which the application must be made contrast with the 3 months given in respect of decisions in social security and child support cases, proceedings in the War Pensions and Armed Forces Compensation Chamber, appeals against decision of the Pensions Appeal Tribunal for Scotland or Northern Ireland and proceedings under the Forfeiture Act 1982[11] and the 1 month given for applying for permission to appeal in any other kind of case.[12] If an application for permission to appeal is made out of time the application must include a request to extend time and give the reason why the application was not made in time.[13] The UT may extend time and if it does not, must refuse the application.[14]

1   Tribunal Procedure (Upper Tribunal) Rules 2008, SI 2008/2698, r 44(1).

2   SI 2008/2698, r 44(7).
3   SI 2008/2698, r 44(3A).
4   SI 2008/2698, r 44(3), (3A) and (5).
5   SI 2008/2698, r 44(3B)(a)(i).
6   SI 2008/2698, r 44(3C)(a).
7   SI 2008/2698, r 44 (3B)(a)(ii).
8   SI 2008/2698, r 44(3C)(b).
9   SI 2008/2698, r 44(3B)(b).
10 SI 2008/2698, r 44(3C)(c).
11 SI 2008/2698, r 44(3).
12 SI 2008/2698, r 44(4).
13 SI 2008/2698, r 44(6)(a).
14 SI 2008/2698, r 44(6)(b).

21.61 The UT must decide the application for permission to appeal if it does not review the decision or if it reviews the decision and decides to take no action in relation to the decision.[1] If the UT refuses permission to appeal on all or some of the grounds, it must send with the record of its decision a statement of its reasons for the refusal and notification of the right to make an application to the specified appellate court, the time within which and the method by which such an application must be made.[2] A party may apply to the Court of Appeal to vary the terms on which permission to appeal was granted by the UT as long as permission to appeal was not granted at a hearing at which the party making the application was present.[3] If permission to appeal is granted by the UT, the person who made the application must file an appellant's notice in the Court of Appeal within 14 days of being served with written notice of the grant of permission.[4] If a corrected grant of permission is subsequently served, time for filing the notice of appeal nevertheless begins to run from service of the original grant of permission.[5] The appellant's notice must be served on the respondent and the UT within seven days of filing it in the Court.[6] One reason for the requirement to serve the appellant's notice on the UT is that the UT is then required to send copies of all the documents that were before it when it considered the appeal.[7] An application to extend time for filing the appellant's notice may be made to the Court.[8]

1   Tribunal Procedure (Upper Tribunal) Rules 2008, SI 2008/2698, r 45(2).
2   SI 2008/2698, r 45(4) and (5).
3   Civil Procedure Rules, r 52.9(3) and *R (on the application of Medical Justice) v Secretary of State for the Home Department* [2011] EWCA Civ 269, [2011] 4 All ER 425, [2011] 1 WLR 2852.
4   CPR PD 52, para 21.7(3).
5   *GD (Zimbabwe) v Secretary of State for the Home Department* [2007] EWCA Civ 1565.
6   CPR 52.4(3) and PD 52, para 21.7(4).
7   PD 52, 21.7(5).
8   CPR 52.6. See *BR (Iran) v Secretary of State for the Home Department* [2007] EWCA Civ 198 for the principles that the court will apply in considering such an application by an asylum seeker and *Omar (Osman) v Secretary of State for the Home Department* [2009] EWCA Civ 383 where the delay is the Secretary of State's.

Application to the Court of Appeal for permission to appeal

21.62 If permission is refused by the UT, the applicant can apply to the Court of Appeal or Court of Session for permission.[1] In England and Wales the procedure is governed by Civil Procedure Rules, Part 52 and the accompanying Practice Direction. The appellant's notice which will include the application for permission must be lodged with the Court of Appeal within 14 days of the appellant being served with the Tribunal's refusal of permission.[2] The grounds of appeal should be a concise identification of the respects in which the UT is said to have erred rather than a skeleton argument.[3] The court may extend time for the application.[4] The appellant's notice must be served on the respondent and the Tribunal within seven days of being filed with the Court.[5] The application is dealt with by a single judge on the papers in the first instance, renewable to the full court[6] upon a request being filed within seven days of service of the refusal of permission[7] unless the Court considers the application 'totally without merit' and orders that the application may not be renewed orally.[8] The single judge might issue a preliminary 'minded to refuse' decision and list the matter for hearing before him or herself. If so, the applicant should address the reasons for the judge being 'minded to refuse'.[9] If permission is refused on consideration of the papers and the application is to be reconsidered at a hearing, the appellant's advocate must, at least four days before the hearing, file a statement of the points he or she proposes to raise at the hearing and the reasons why permission should be granted notwithstanding the reasons for refusal on the papers.[10] The court may not grant permission to appeal unless it considers that the proposed appeal would raise some important point of principle or practice or there is some other compelling reason for the court to hear the appeal.[11] However, if the decision of the Upper Tribunal was made on appeal from a decision of the Asylum and Immigration Tribunal this second appeals test does not apply[12] and permission may be given where the Court considers that the appeal would have a real prospect of success or there is some other compelling reason why the appeal should be heard.[13] It may limit the issues to be argued and impose conditions on the grant of permission.[14] An appeal under NIAA 2002, s 82 is not finally determined during the period in which an application for permission to appeal to the Court of Appeal may be made or is awaiting determination or permission to appeal has been granted and determination of the appeal is awaited[15] and whilst the section 82 appeal is pending there is a statutory bar on removal.[16] An application for permission lodged out of time would not prevent removal until permission was granted, so in such circumstances a stay should be sought from the court.[17] An appeal to the Court of Appeal is not deemed abandoned if the appellant leaves the UK.[18]

[1] TCEA 2007, s 13(4) and (5).
[2] CPR PD 52, para 21.7(3).
[3] *Wanjiku v Secretary of State for the Home Department* [2011] EWCA Civ 264, [2011] All ER (D) 153 (Mar).
[4] CPR 3.1(2)(a) and CPR 52.6; *A v Secretary of State for the Home Department* [2003] EWCA Civ 175, [2003] INLR 249. For an example of refusal to extend, where no good reason was proffered and no extension of time sought before the time limit, see *R (on the applilcaiton of Harris (Darrel)) v Secretary of State for the Home Department* [2002] EWCA Civ 100 (appeal in judicial review). As to the approach the court will take to applications to extend time for applying for permission to appeal, see *YD (Turkey) v Secretary of State for the Home Department* [2006] EWCA Civ 52, [2006] 1 WLR 1646, (2006) Times, 28 February and the observations on the decision in *BR (Iran) v Secretary of State for the Home Department* [2007] EWCA Civ 198.
[5] CPR 52.4(3) and CPR PD 52, para 21.7(4).
[6] CPR 52.3(4).
[7] CPR 52.3(5).
[8] CPR 52.3(4A).
[9] *Sad-Chaouche v Secretary of State for the Home Department* ((29 March 2000, unreported), CA).

10 PD 52, para 4.14A.
11 TCEA 2007, s 13(6) and Appeals from the Upper Tribunal to the Court of Appeal Order 2008, SI 2008/2834. See **21.58** above for second appeals.
12 *FA (Iraq) v Secretary of State for the Home Department* [2010] EWCA Civ 827.
13 CPR 52.3(6).
14 CPR 52.3(7).
15 NIAA 2002, s 104(2).
16 NIAA 2002, s 78.
17 CPR 52.7(b), indicates that an appeal to the Court of Appeal, other than from the Immigration and Asylum Chamber of the UT does not operate as a stay of the order or decision under appeal, but this wording does not necessarily mean that an out of time appeal from the Tribunal automatically stays the decision.
18 *Shirazi v Secretary of State for the Home Department* [2003] EWCA Civ 1562, [2004] INLR 92. Although the case was decided under the IAA 1999 appeals regime, the appeals provisions under the NIAA 2002 and the TCEA are not materially different for these purposes.

Abandonment of an appeal to the Court of Appeal

21.63 Appeals to the Court of Appeal, even though brought under TCEA 2007, section 13 and not NIAA 2002, section 82 are treated as abandoned if the person who brought the original appeal under NIAA 2002, section 82 leaves the UK or is granted leave to enter or remain (unless the person gives notice of his or her wish to continue the appeal on race discrimination or asylum grounds).[1] The Court of Appeal rejected the argument that the statutory abandonment provisions were inapplicable because they applied only to appeals under NIAA 2002, section 82 and not to an appeal brought under TCEA 2007, section 13, not NIAA 2002, section 82 and it is only the latter to which the abandonment provisions in NIAA 2002, section 104 apply.[2]

1 Under NIAA 2002, s 104(4) or (4A).
2 *LB (Jamaica) v Secretary of State for the Home Department* [2011] EWCA Civ 1420 and *R R (on the application of MM (Ghana)) v Secretary of State for the Home Department* [2012] EWCA Civ 827.

Scope of the court's jurisdiction

21.64 The scope of the court's jurisdiction was said in *E v Secretary of State for the Home Department*[1] to be the same as that of the Administrative Court in judicial review, and was considered at **21.6** above. The principles governing the admission of fresh evidence on appeal have been considered at **21.35** above. The court may, on agreed facts, decide that an asylum claimant fulfils the criteria for refugee status, as an alternative to remitting a successful appeal to the Tribunal.[2] The court will not hear academic appeals (ie where a respondent has abandoned a claim, as happened in *Dahir*,[3] or an appellant cannot be found, having been unlawfully removed from the country, as happened in *Re M*),[4] unless there is a good reason in the public interest for doing so, for example, the case raises questions of general importance which can be decided irrespective of the facts of individual appeals and would affect a large number of similar cases.[5] Nor will it hear an appeal on a point not argued before the Tribunal by agreement but raised before it in order to obtain a remittal to the Tribunal.[6] The doctrine of binding precedent applies to the Court of Appeal.[7] Generally, the point of law on which there is a right to appeal to the Court of Appeal must arise from the tribunal's determination rather than being one that was not raised before the tribunal.[8] However, the issue of whether there had been jurisdiction to hear the appeal could be raised in the Court of Appeal whether or not the point had been raised below.[9] The 'Robinson doctrine' obliges the Court to exercise its powers to ensure the UK's compliance not only with the Refugee Convention but with its international obligations more generally, including those under Community law. Thus it may be required to consider a point that was not raised before the Tribunal once the point has occurred to the Court even if the point is not 'obvious' in the sense of having a strong prospect of success.[10] The Court's power to consider grounds that were not raised in the UT is not restricted to issues concerning international law.[11]

1 *E v Secretary of State for the Home Department, R v Secretary of State for the Home Department* [2004] EWCA Civ 49, [2004] INLR 264. The distinction formerly drawn in cases such as *Macharia v Immigration Appeal Tribunal* [2000] Imm AR 190, between administrative law grounds, including procedural impropriety, and questions of law, which were believed to be narrower, has become obsolete, as procedural and evidential matters are seen as errors of law potentially vitiating decisions.

2 As the House of Lords did in *Islam v Secretary of State for the Home Department (United Nations High Comr for Refugees intervening)* [1999] 2 AC 629.

3 *Secretary of State for the Home Department v Abdi and Dahir* [1995] Imm AR 570, CA. But an appeal to the Court of Appeal is not deemed abandoned if the appellant leaves the UK: *Shirazi v Secretary of State for the Home Department* [2003] EWCA Civ 1562, [2004] INLR 92, 21.63 above.

4 *Re M* [1994] 1 AC 377, where the issue was whether the Secretary of State was in contempt of court for removing and failing to return to the jurisdiction an asylum seeker in respect of whom an undertaking had been given not to remove him.

5 *R v Secretary of State for the Home Department, ex p Salem* [1999] 1 AC 450, HL.

6 *Srimanoharan v Secretary of State for the Home Department* (13 June 2000, unreported); *Zaitz v Secretary of State for the Home Department* [2000] INLR 346.

7 See *HM v Secretary of State for the Home Department* [2003] EWCA Civ 583, [2003] Imm AR 470.

8 *SA (Pakistan) v Secretary of State for the Home Department* [2010] EWCA Civ 1269; *Sapkota (Ramesh) v Secretary of State for the Home Department* [2011] EWCA Civ 1320, [2011] All ER (D) 141 (Nov) .and *Secretary of State for the Home Department v FV (Italy)* [2012] EWCA Civ 1155

9 *Virk (Pavandeep) v Secretary of State for the Home Department* [2013] EWCA Civ 652.

10 *Bulale v Secretary of State for the Home Department* [2008] EWCA Civ 806, [2008] 3 CMLR 738, applying *Robinson (Anthonypillai Francis) v Secretary of State for the Home Department and Immigration Appeal Tribunal* [1997] Imm AR 568

11 See for example *MB (Bangladesh) (by her mother and litigation friend JB) v Secretary of State for the Home Department* [2013] EWCA Civ 220 where the Court allowed an appeal owing to the UT's failure to consider a statutory provision (Legitimacy Act 1976, s 1) which was identified by the Court, not the parties.

21.65 In *AH (Sudan) v Secretary of State for the Home Department* Baroness Hale of Richmond said of the Asylum and Immigration Tribunal:[1]

'This is an expert tribunal charged with administering a complex area of law in challenging circumstances. To paraphrase a view I have expressed about such expert tribunals in another context, the ordinary courts should approach appeals from them with an appropriate degree of caution; it is probable that in understanding and applying the law in their specialised field the tribunal will have got it right: see *Cooke v Secretary of State for Social Security* [2001] EWCA Civ 734, [2002] 3 All ER 279, para 16. They and they alone are the judges of the facts. It is not enough that their decision on those facts may seem harsh to people who have not heard and read the evidence and arguments which they have heard and read. Their decisions should be respected unless it is quite clear that they have misdirected themselves in law. Appellate courts should not rush to find such misdirections simply because they might have reached a different conclusion on the facts or expressed themselves differently. I cannot believe that this eminent Tribunal had indeed confused the three tests or neglected to apply the correct relocation test.'

These remarks concern the interface between a non-specialist court and a specialist tribunal and so they had no application where one constitution of the Asylum and Immigration Tribunal was reconsidering a decision made by another[2] and should have no application where the UT is considering an appeal from the FT. They have been cited and followed repeatedly in the context of appeals from the Tribunal to the Court of Appeal[3] dismissed as inappropriate attempts to complain about factual determinations. However, they do not alter the principles governing appeals from the Tribunal on points of law that were comprehensively and authoritatively stated in *R (Iran) v Secretary of State for the Home Department*.[4] Whilst Baroness Hale says that decisions of the Tribunal should be respected unless 'it is quite clear that they have misdirected themselves in law'[5] Carnwath LJ has questioned whether she thereby intended to modify the approach of the Court of Appeal: 'If it is "unclear" from a decision whether an error has been made, that is normally taken as an indication of materially defective reasoning which in itself may be a ground for intervention'.[6] In *NH (India)* Lord Justice Sedley said[7] that Baroness Hale:

'intended to lay down no new principle of law . . . but to ensure that appellate practice is realistic and not zealous to find fault. Their Lordships do not say, and cannot be taken as meaning, that the standards of decision making or the principles of judicial scrutiny which govern immigration and asylum adjudication differ from those governing other judicial tribunals, especially where for some asylum-seekers adjudication may literally be a matter of life and death. There is no principle that the worse the apparent error is, the less ready an appellate court should be to find that it has occurred.'

Lord Neuberger, whilst recognising the need to be wary of interfering with the conclusions of the fact finding Tribunal nevertheless highlighted the particular difficulties of the fact finding exercise in the asylum context and the 'potentially severe, even catastrophic consequences of a mistaken rejection of an appeal where fear of ill-treatment or worse is alleged' as justifying 'a particularly thorough reading of any decision of the Asylum and Immigration Tribunal'.[8] In the light of the guidance given in *AH (Sudan)* the Court of Appeal has continued to find material errors of law by the Tribunal in making factual conclusions and judgments. For example, given the objective evidence about the suppression of dissent by the Eritrean authorities, the Tribunal's refusal to accept that they had the means and inclination to monitor opposition activities in the UK without affirmative evidence to that effect risked losing contact with reality;[9] it was perverse to find that a church would adequately support a returnee to Uganda without evidence about that church and to find that being driven into prostitution did not make internal relocation unduly harsh and to give no weight to a psychiatric report.[10]

1   *AH (Sudan) v Secretary of State for the Home Department* [2007] UKHL 49, [2008] 1 AC 678, para 30.
2   *OH (Serbia) v Secretary of State for the Home Department* [2008] EWCA Civ 694, [2008] All ER (D) 435 (Apr).
3   Eg *OD (Ivory Coast) v Secretary of State for the Home Department* [2008] EWCA Civ 1299, [2008] All ER (D) 08 (Dec and *BK (Democratic of Congo) v Secretary of State for the Home Department* [2008] EWCA Civ 1322, [2008] All ER (D) 43 (Dec).

4   [2005] EWCA Civ 982, (2005) Times, 19 August. See *SK (Sierra Leone) v Secretary of State for the Home Department* [2008] EWCA Civ 853 and *AA (Uganda) v Secretary of State for the Home Department* [2008] EWCA Civ 579, [2008] All ER (D) 300 (May) (per Carnwath LJ).

5   And this was said to be the test in *AS and DD (Libya) v Secretary of State for the Home Department* [2008] EWCA Civ 289, (2008) Times, 16 April, [2009] 1 LRC 704, albeit without dissent from either party.

6   *AA (Uganda) v Secretary of State for the Home Department* 2008] EWCA Civ 579, [2008] All ER (D) 300 (May).

7   *NH (India) v Entry Clearance Officer* [2007] EWCA Civ 1330, [2007] All ER (D) 199 (Dec), approved in *SK (Sierra Leone)*.

8   *SS (Iran) v Secretary of State for the Home Department* [2008] EWCA Civ 310, [2008] All ER (D) 140 (Apr).

9   *YB (Eritrea) v Secretary of State for the Home Department* [2008] EWCA Civ 360, [2008] All ER (D) 195 (Apr).

10   *AA (Uganda) v Secretary of State for the Home Department* [2008] EWCA Cvi 579.

The court's decision on the appeal

21.66 If the court finds that the decision of the UT involved the making of an error on a point of law it has similar powers to those of the UT deciding an appeal from the FT.[1] It may set aside the decision of the UT and if it does must either remit the case to the UT or the FT or re-make the decision itself.[2] If it remits the case to the UT or FT it may make directions about who is to hear the appeal and give procedural directions.[3] If the case is remitted to the UT the UT may further remit the case to the FT.[4] If the court decides to remake the decision it may make any decision that the UT or FT could make if remaking the decision and may make such findings of fact as it considers appropriate.[5] Whilst the Court of Appeal has power to substitute its own decision on the appeal for that of the tribunal, as a general rule it will do so only when there are clear findings of fact by the tribunal which are undisputed and as a matter of law admit of only one answer to the appeal.[6] As far as costs are concerned, the starting point is that the successful party is entitled to be paid his or her costs by the losing party, including where an appeal is allowed by consent[7] and even where the losing party was clearly not responsible for the legal error in the UT's decision that necessitated the appeal being brought.[8]

1   TCEA 2007, s 14.

2   TCEA 2007, s 14(2). For the court's powers to limit the ambit of what is remitted to the UT see *ND (Guinea) v Secretary of State for the Home Department* [2008] EWCA Civ 458 and *VH (Malawi) v Secretary of State for the Home Department* [2009] EWCA Civ 645.

3   TCEA 2007, s 14(3).

4   TCEA 2007, s 14(5).

5   TCEA 2007, s 14(4).

6   *KR (Nepal) v Secretary of State for the Home Department* [2010] EWCA Civ 1619, [2010] All ER (D) 180 (Nov).

7   *AL (Albania) v Secretary of State for the Home Department* [2012] EWCA Civ 710.

8   *AN (Afghanistan) v Secretary of State for the Home Department* [2012] EWCA Civ 1333.

Judicial review

21.67 A claim for judicial review is a claim to review the lawfulness of an enactment or a decision, action or failure to act in relation to the exercise of a public function.[1] Claims for judicial review used to be heard (at least in the first instance) by the High Court in the branch known since November 2000 as the Administrative Court. The UT, rather than the Administrative Court, is now the primary forum for immigration judicial reviews following the Direction of the Lord Chief Justice on 21 August 2013 under section 19 of the TCEA 2007 which provides that any judicial review applications in respect of decisions made under the Immigration Acts or otherwise relating to leave to enter or remain in the United Kingdom outside the Rules be heard in the Upper Tribunal from 1 November 2013. The only judicial review applications which should continue to be lodged and heard in the Administrative Court are those which comprise or include:

(i) a challenge to the validity of primary or subordinate legislation or of Immigration Rules;

(ii) a challenge to the lawfulness of detention[2] (but an application does not do so by reason only of the fact that it challenges a decision in relation to bail);

(iii) a challenge to a decision concerning inclusion on the register of licensed Sponsors maintained by the United Kingdom Border Agency, or any authorisation of such Sponsors;

(iv) a challenge to a decision as to citizenship under the British Nationality Act 1981 or any other provision of the law for the time being in force which determines British citizenship, the status of a British national (Overseas), British Overseas citizenship or the status of a British subject;

(v) a challenge to a decision made under or by virtue of section 4 (accommodation centres) or Part VI (support for asylum seekers) of the Immigration and Asylum Act 1999;

(vi) a challenge to a decision made under or by virtue of Part II (accommodation centres) or Part III (other support and assistance) of the Nationality, Immigration and Asylum Act 2002;

(vii) a challenge to a decision of the Upper Tribunal;

(viii) a challenge to a decision of the Special Immigration Appeals Commission;

(ix) an application for a declaration of incompatibility under section 4 of the Human Rights Act 1998.

The Tribunal Procedure (Amendment No 4) Rules 2013, SI 2013/2067came into force simultaneously, amending the Tribunal Procedure (Upper Tribunal) Rules 2008, SI 2008/2698 so as to reflect the changes made by the transfer of judicial review to the Upper Tribunal. A further Practice Direction of 24 October 2013 made provision for the changes to be applied retrospectively to any outstanding fresh claim judicial review applications lodged prior to 1 November 2013 to be transferred to the Upper Tribunal (IAC).

---

[1] Civil Procedure Rules, 54.1(2)

[2] Mr Justice Cranston has sounded a word of warning against lodging a JR application in the Administrative Court rather than the UT by virtue of adding on an unlawful detention challenge, which could constitute an abuse of process in the absence of obvious distinct merit in that aspect.

21.68 Most decisions in the context of immigration are potentially subject to judicial review, whether those of an entry clearance officer, an immigration officer, the Secretary of State or a criminal court dealing with immigration offences.[1] In *Javed* the Court of Appeal confirmed that a statutory instrument which had been approved by both Houses of Parliament was vulnerable to judicial review.[2] Decisions of the Secretary of State are reviewable, including prerogative acts such as the grant or refusal of a passport,[3] and even where statute makes express provision to the contrary.[4] Equally, failures and delays by administrative bodies are challengeable by judicial review.[5] In recent years, judicial review has increasingly been used to challenge policies and procedures, such as service of adverse decisions on appellants via the Secretary of State,[6] the removal of benefits from categories of asylum claimants,[7] the system in place to penalise unwitting carriers of clandestine entrants,[8] the failure of the Secretary of State to publicise a policy providing support to rejected asylum claimants,[9] detention of asylum claimants to process their claims,[10] the use of fast track procedures at Oakington and Harmondsworth removal centres,[11] racially discriminatory procedures,[12] the giving of reduced or no notice of removal directions to certain categories of individual,[13] a change in the Immigration Rules to the detriment of post-graduate doctors,[14] the failure to make tape recordings of asylum interviews,[15] the raising of the level of competence in English language required of those seeking entry as students,[16] the withholding of permission to work from failed asylum seekers pursuing fresh claims.[17] Judicial review has become an important tool for seeking to ensure minimum standards of fairness and consistency in decision-making.[18] The rules of standing in judicial review are much more generous than those in (for example) the European Court of Human Rights,[19] enabling organisations with a legitimate interest in the subject matter, such as the Joint Council for the Welfare of Immigrants, the Immigration Law Practitioners' Association, the Refugee Legal Centre and Amnesty International among others to bring actions.

1   *R v Uxbridge Magistrates' Court, ex p Adimi* [1999] 4 All ER 520 challenge to the conviction of asylum claimants as contrary to the Refugee Convention.
2   *R (on the application of Javed) v Secretary of State for the Home Department* [2001] EWCA Civ 789, [2002] QB 129, [2001] 3 WLR 323, followed in *R (on the application of Husan) v Secretary of State for the Home Department* [2005] EWHC 189 (Admin), (2005) Times, 1 March in respect of the designation of Bangladesh as a safe country for the purpose of NIAA 2002, s 94 by statutory instrument.
3   *R v Secretary of State for Foreign and Commonwealth Affairs, ex p Everett* [1989] QB 811, [1989] 1 All ER 655, CA. In *R (on the application of Abbasi) v Secretary of State for Foreign and Commonwealth Affairs* [2002] EWCA Civ 1598, (2002) Times, 8 November, the Court of Appeal re-emphasised that 'it is no answer to a judicial review claim to say that the source of power . . . is the prerogative. It is the subject matter that is determinative.' However, the court will not rule on questions of international law which affect foreign sovereign states, or questions of foreign policy: *R (on the application of Campaign for Nuclear Disarmament) v Prime Minister* [2002] EWHC 2712.
4   *R v Secretary of State for the Home Department, ex p Ejaz* [1994] QB 496; *R v Secretary of State for the Home Department, ex p Fayed* [1997] 1 All ER 228, [1997] INLR 138, CA (statutory exclusion of judicial review of decisions on grant or withholding of nationality under former legislation did not oust court's jurisdiction where decision was unlawful on administrative law grounds).
5   See eg *R v Secretary of State for the Home Department, ex p Phansopkar* [1976] QB 606; *Teh Cheng Poh (alias Char Meh) v Public Prosecutor, Malaysia* [1980] AC 458, PC; *Engineers' and Managers' Association v Advisory, Conciliation and Arbitration Service* [1980] 1 WLR 302; *R v Secretary of State for the Home Department, ex p Mersin (Deniz)* [2000] INLR 511; *R (on the application of Anufrijeva) v Secretary of State for the Home Department* [2003] UKHL 36, [2003] Imm AR 570, [2003] INLR 521; *R (on the application of FH) v Secretary of State for the Home Department* [2007] EWHC 1571 (Admin). *R (on the application of MK) v Secretary of State for the Home Department* [2010] EWCA Civ 115 (damages claim in respect of delay in deciding an asylum claim).

6   *R (on the application of Bubaker) v Lord Chancellor* [2002] EWCA Civ 1107, [2002] Imm AR 552 (permission).
7   *R v Secretary of State for Social Security, ex p Joint Council for the Welfare of Immigrants* [1996] 4 All ER 385, [1997] 1 WLR 275.
8   *International Transport Roth GmbH v Secretary of State for the Home Department* [2002] EWCA Civ 158, [2002] 3 WLR 344.
9   *R (on the application of Salih) v Secretary of State for the Home Department* [2003] EWHC 2273 (Admin).
10 *R (on the application of Saadi) v Secretary of State for the Home Department* [2002] UKHL 41, [2002] 1 WLR 3131, [2002] INLR 523.
11 *R (on the application of the Refugee Legal Centre) v Secretary of State for the Home Department* [2004] EWCA Civ 1481, [2004] All ER (D) 580 (Mar).
12 *R (on the application of the Tamil Information Centre) v Secretary of State for the Home Department* [2002] EWHC 2155 (Admin); *European Roma Rights Centre v Immigration Officer at Prague Airport* [2003] EWCA Civ 666, [2003] INLR 374, rvsd [2004] UKHL 55, [2005] 2 WLR 1.
13 *R (on the application of Medical Justice) v Secretary of State for the Home Department* [2010] EWHC 1925 (Admin).
14 *R (on the application of BAPIO Action Ltd) v Secretary of State for the Home Department* [2008] UKHL 27.
15 *R (on the application of Dirshe) v Secretary of State for the Home Department* [2005] EWCA Civ 421.
16 *R (on the application of English UK Ltd) v Secretary of State for the Home Department* [2010] EWHC 1726 (Admin).
17 *R (on the application of ZO (Somalia)) v Secretary of State for the Home Department* [2010] UKSC 36.
18 See *R (on the application of the Refugee Legal Centre) v Secretary of State for the Home Department* [2004] EWCA Civ 1481, [2004] All ER (D) 580 (Mar) (fn 11 above); *Mapah v Secretary of State for the Home Department* [2003] EWHC 306 (Admin), [2003] Imm AR 395.
19 The restrictive rules on standing in claims under the Human Rights Act 1998 have not proved an obstacle to bringing public interest claims, as had been feared; see **7.26** above.

21.69 An important and developing area of judicial review relates to the present relevance of past wrongs by the Secretary of State for the purpose of establishing entitlement to relief in respect of a current decision. The principles of fairness and consistency are said to underlie the statutory scheme by which immigration control operates and therefore it is open to the Court to conclude that a legally relevant factor in the exercise of a statutory discretion is the correction of injustice.[1] The leading case is *Rashid*[2] in which the claimant, having lost his appeal against refusal of asylum, discovered that the Secretary of State had a policy which should have been applied to his claim and would have resulted in his being recognised as a refugee had it been applied. He made an application to the Secretary of State to reconsider the refusal of asylum in the light of the policy. The application was refused and the refusal defended in the subsequent judicial review on the grounds that by the time that renewed application was made, the policy had been withdrawn; that circumstances in Iraq had so changed that the claimant no longer had a fear of being persecuted; that he had had sanctuary from persecution in the UK, albeit his refugee status was unrecognised and that it was an important and well established[3] that claims for refugee status were to be determined according to circumstances in existence at the date of the determination of rather than the claim for asylum. The Court held that there had been 'conspicuous unfairness' amounting to 'abuse of power' due to the 'flagrant and prolonged incompetence' of the Secretary of State whereby he had failed to apply his policy when deciding the claimant's asylum claim; he had presented his case to the adjudicator and Tribunal not only without reference to his policy but inconsistently with his policy; he offered no explanation for his conduct and he decided to grant asylum to procedurally linked and materially indistinguishable claimants. The Court decided that the appropriate remedy was a grant of indefinite leave to remain. The absence of a history of cumulative errors such as there had been in *Rashid* led the Court to reject the allegation that there had been an 'abuse of power' made by an Afghan whose asylum claim had been refused without regard to the then applicable policy of granting exceptional leave to remain to failed Afghan asylum seekers.[4] However, in its earlier decision, *Secretary of State for the Home Department v R (S)*[5] the Court held that such a history of flagrant incompetence was unnecessary to establish an abuse of power and that unlawfulness within the meaning of well-established public law principles[6] was sufficient to require the Secretary of State to consider whether the historical injustice should be remedied by a grant of leave to remain and in the absence of countervailing factors, such a grant might be the only legitimate outcome of such consideration. Where the decision that led to the claimant losing the benefit of that same policy was wrong but not unlawful, the claimant was not entitled to be put into the position he would have been in had the correct decision been made.[7]

[1] *R (on the application of S) v Secretary of State for the Home Department* [2007] EWCA Civ 546.

[2] *R (on the application of Rashid) v Secretary of State for the Home Department* [2005] EWCA Civ 744, (2005) Times, 12 July, [2005] All ER (D) 152 (Jun).

[3] By *Ravichandran (Senathirajah) v Secretary of State for the Home Department* [1996] Imm AR 97.

[4] *R (on the application of ZK (Afghanistan)) v Secretary of State for the Home Department* [2007] EWCA Civ 615, [2007] All ER (D) 342 (Jun).

[5] [2007] EWCA Civ 546, decided just over a week before *R (ZK Afghanistan)* and not considered in that case.

[6] In this case, deciding not to determine the claimant's asylum claim pursuant to a Public Service Agreement with the Treasury and without scope for consideration of individual circumstances, was arbitrary, unfair and a fettering of the Secretary of State's discretion.

[7] *DS (Afghanistan) v Secretary of State for the Home Department* [2007] EWCA Civ 774, [2007] All ER (D) 397 (Jul). In that case, the Secretary of State did not believe the claimant was Afghan and therefore did not give him exceptional leave to remain as he would have done, had he accepted his nationality. The decision that the claimant was not Afghan was held to be rational and legally permissible. By the time the Secretary of State accepted that the claimant was Afghan, the policy had been withdrawn. See also *R (on the application of MM) v Secretary of State for the Home Department; R (on the application of SS) v Secretary of State for the Home Department* [2009] EWCA Civ 833; *SL (Vietnam) v Secretary of State for the Home Department* [2010] EWCA Civ 225 and *R (on the application of Teluwo) v Secretary of State for the Home Department* [2009] EWHC 2762 (Admin); *R (on the application of AA (Afghanistan) v Secretary of State for the Home Department* [2012] EWCA Civ 1643; *R (on the application of Gurung) v Secretary of State for the Home Department* [2013] EWCA Civ 8; *R (on the application of Jabarkhail) v Secretary of State for the Home Department* [2014] EWHC 1821 (Admin).

Statutory appeals and judicial review

21.70 As we have indicated above, the scope of the appellate courts' review of Tribunal decisions has been held to be co-extensive with that of the Administrative Court on judicial review.[1] The issue of whether a challenge may be pursued by way of appeal or judicial review now depends entirely on the availability of a statutory remedy. If such a remedy exists, it must be used. If not, the remedy, if any, lies in judicial review. Where a statutory right of appeal exists against an immigration decision, judicial review cannot be used instead merely because the right can only be exercised out-of-country or is otherwise less convenient.[2] Whether an application for judicial review will be entertained, notwithstanding the existence of a statutory right of appeal, is a matter of judicial discretion. The discretion should be exercised in favour of the claimant if an immigration decision is challenged on the basis that the power to make the decision was not exercisable because of issues of precedent fact relating to the claimant's identity or nationality. Otherwise, save in special or exceptional circumstances, the court would refuse to exercise discretion in the claimant's favour in deference to the Parliamentary intention that the appellant's remedy should generally be exercised out of country.[3] Where the appeal right is defective, eg a decision that a human rights or asylum claim is clearly unfounded, so that an appeal does not suspend removal to a country alleged by the claimant to be unsafe), judicial review is available.[4] A similar principle applies in relation to interim decisions made by the tribunal. So for example, a Tribunal's refusal to transfer a fast track appeal to the normal appeal track may ground a statutory appeal against eventual dismissal of the appeal if the appellant can show that the refusal prejudiced his or her substantive appeal under the fast track. In such a case judicial review of the decision of the Tribunal would not lie.[5] But the Secretary of State's refusal to transfer the person out of the fast track at the refugee determination stage could ground judicial review proceedings, since no statutory remedy exists except an appeal on asylum grounds, which, as the Court of Appeal recognised in *Refugee Legal Centre*, could be irrevocably flawed from the outset by the unfairness of the circumstances of the initial interview.[6] Interim decisions of the FT may also be challenged by judicial review if the statutory appeal would not be capable of remedying the consequences of the procedural failings before the FT.[7]

1 See 21.6 above.
2 *R v Secretary of State for the Home Department, ex p Swati* [1986] 1 All ER 717, [1986] Imm AR 88, *Rehman v Secretary of State for the Home Department* [1987] Imm AR 602, CA; *R v Secretary of State for the Home Department, ex p Ozkurtulus* [1986] Imm AR 80, QBD; *R v Secretary of State for the Home Department, ex p Fernando (Nirupa Kaushal)* [1987] Imm AR 377, QBD; *R (on the application of Sivasubramaniam) v Wandworth County Court* [2002] EWCA Civ 1738, [2003] 2 All ER 160 (perm). But the court held judicial review appropriate to quash a decision to deport a claimant, despite the availability of a statutory appeal, where the decision was reached improperly, without regard to the determination by the Tribunal that the claimant was a refugee, the high threshold required to establish fraud and the absence of cogent evidence of fraud in *R (on the application of Saribal) v Secretary of State for the Home Department* [2002] EWHC 1542 (Admin), [2002] INLR 596.
3 *R (on the application of Lim) v Secretary of State for the Home Department* [2007] EWCA Civ 773, [2007] All ER (D) 402 (Jul). However, in *R (on the application of Yu) v Secretary of State for the Home Department* [2008] EWHC 3072 (Admin) the Court applied *Lim* but held that the subject of the decision under Immigration and Asylum Act 1999, s 10 could judicially review the exercise of the power to make the decision as opposed to the decision itself. Subsequent cases have rejected the distinction between the decision and the decision to make the decision and have taken the hard line insisted on by *Lim*. See *R (on the application of Bilal Jan) v Secretary of State for the Home Department* [2014] UKUT 265 (IAC) and *R (on the application of Khan (Azmat Rauf)) v Secretary of State for the Home Department* [2014] EWHC 2494 (Admin), both disapproving *R (on the application of Thapa) v Secretary of State for the Home Department* [2014] EWHC 659 (Admin) which had held that the decision to make a removal decision as opposed to a decision appealable in country could be challenged by judicial review, particularly having regard to the unfairness and harsh consequences of making a decision that could only be appealed out of country.
4 *IR v Secretary of State for the Home Department, ex p Canbolat* [1997] Imm AR 442, CA; *R (on the application of L) v Secretary of State for the Home Department* [2003] EWCA Civ 25, [2003] Imm AR 330, [2003] INLR 224.

5   R (on the application of Wani) v Secretary of State for the Home Department [2005] EWHC
    2815 (Admin) and R (on the application of AM (Cameroon)) v Asylum and Immigration
    Tribunal [2008] EWCA Civ 100.
6   R (on the application of the Refugee Legal Centre) v Secretary of State for the Home
    Department [2004] EWCA Civ 1481, [2004] All ER (D) 580 (Mar).
7   R (AM Cameroon) v Secretary of State for the Home Department [2008] EWCA Civ 100.

Judicial review of refusal of permission to appeal by the Upper Tribunal

21.71 A decision by the UT refusing to grant permission to appeal to itself is in principle susceptible to judicial review.[1] However, a heightened threshold for obtaining permission to apply for judicial review has been imposed,[2] justified by the enhanced expertise and status accorded to the UT within the integrated tribunal structure created by the TCEA; the new relationship between the tribunal and court systems expressed in the 'second appeals test' for appeals from the UT to the court of appeal; the provision for judicial scrutiny of FTT decisions first by an FT judge and then by a UT judge in the context of applications for permission to appeal and in the interests of reducing demands on the time and resources of the High Court.[3] Notwithstanding such considerations, continued High Court supervision of the UT has been retained because of the risk that otherwise the UT would develop 'local law' and that bad law would fossilise and bearing in mind the potential gravity of the consequences of erroneous decisions.[4] The threshold adopted is the same as the 'second appeals test' for appeals from the UT to the Court of Appeal. Permission to apply for judicial review of a refusal of permission to appeal by the UT will be granted only if there is an arguable case that the refusal of permission by the UT and the decision of the FT from which permission to appeal was sought were wrong in law and either the claim raises an important point of principle or practice or there is some other compelling reason to hear the claim.[5] Once permission to apply for judicial review has been granted, the 'second appeals' test no longer applies and the court makes the substantive decision on the claim by applying ordinary judicial review principles.[6] Applications for permission to apply for judicial review of UT decisions refusing permission to appeal are decided on the papers only; there is no right to an oral hearing where permission is refused and whilst permission to appeal to the Court of Appeal from a refusal of permission on the papers may be sought, that application will also be considered on the papers only.[7]

1   R (on the application of Cart) v Upper Tribunal [2011] UKSC 28.
2   R (Cart) v The Upper Tribunal [2011] UKSC 28 and CPR 54.7A.
3   R (Cart) v The Upper Tribunal [2011] UKSC 28.
4   R (Cart) v The Upper Tribunal [2011] UKSC 28.
5   CPR 54.7A(7).
6   R (on the application of HS) v Upper Tribunal (Immigration and Asylum Chamber) (IAC)
    [2012] EWHC 3126 (Admin); R (on the application of AA (Iran)) v Upper Tribunal
    (Immigration and Asylum Chamber) (IAC) [2013] EWCA Civ 1523; Khatoon v Entry
    Clearance Officer, Islamabad and Upper Tribunal (Immigration and Asylum Chamber)
    [2013] EWHC 972 (Admin).
7   R (on the application of Parekh) v Upper Tribunal (Immigration Asylum Chamber) [2013]
    EWCA Civ 679.

Procedure in the Administrative Court

21.72 An application for judicial review must be made promptly[1] and in any event within three months of the decision complained of.[2] However, if the application is for judicial review of a decision of the UT refusing permission to appeal, the application must be filed no later than 16 days after the date on which the UT's decision was sent to the applicant.[3] A pre-action protocol should normally be complied with, involving a letter of claim to a proposed defendant, and reasons must be given for failure to comply.[4] The three months' time limit cannot be artificially extended by making further representations which contain no new material in order to generate a fresh formal decision; time starts to run at the date of the operative decision.[5] On the other hand, Lord Woolf said in *Ahmad and Simba*[6] that in the case of asylum claimants the court would normally be circumspect about being too rigorous in relation to delay, appreciating that to refuse an application solely on the ground of delay may have very grave consequences. This would apply equally to human rights claims. A late applicant for judicial review cannot rely on matters that have occurred during the period of delay, however.[7] The Civil Procedure Rules now require all applications for permission to be considered on the papers initially.[8] An application for permission may be renewed at a hearing[9] unless the decision challenged is a refusal of the UT to grant permission to appeal[10] or as well as refusing permission, the court states that 'the application is totally without merit'.[11] A copy of the claim form and supporting documents must be served on the defendant,[12] who must be given an opportunity to respond, by filing an acknowledgement of service, before permission is granted.[13] In urgent cases, time limits may be abridged and in cases of exceptional urgency, interim relief may be granted, on telephone application if necessary, pending lodging of the acknowledgment and sometimes on an undertaking to lodge the application.[14] However, if urgent consideration is sought, the court will insist upon completion in full of the relevant application form including justification of the need for urgent or immediate consideration; an explanation of when the need for making the application became apparent and of any delay in bringing the application and details of steps taken to communicate with the defendant, failing which the application may be refused or not considered and the legal representative may be ordered to attend before the court to explain any non-compliance.[11] The defendant may not apply to be set aside permission once granted.[12] Permission may be limited to one or more of the grounds, and if it is so limited, the claimant should not seek to re-open the refusal of permission on those grounds at the substantive hearing.[13] Refusal of permission may be appealed to the Court of Appeal, and if that court gives permission for the application but dismisses the appeal, to the House of Lords.[14]

1   Civil Procedure Rules (CPR) r 54.5, a requirement which was held proportionate and lawful, and not restrictive of rights of access to a court in *Lam v United Kingdom* (Application 41671/98) (5 July 2001, unreported), ECtHR. See also *R (on the application of Burkett) v Hammersmith London Borough Council* [2002] 1 WLR 1593. In *R (on the application of Agnello) v Hounslow London Borough Council* [2003] EWHC 3112 (Admin) the court held that a claim brought within the three month time limit benefitted from a rebuttable presumption that it was brought promptly, in the absence of evidence of prejudice to the defendant or a third party. However in *R v Secretary of State for the Home Department, ex p Ondiek* (CO 4/2000) (25 February 2000, unreported), QBD, Owen J discharged an injunction preventing the applicant's removal when he failed to seek judicial review promptly of the Tribunal's decision that his appeal was out of time but had let a month go by, despite

previous proceedings being compromised on the basis that he would not be removed while the appeal was pending. The applicant had a history of delays in making applications.

2   CPR r 54.5. A five-year delay in challenging a decision to treat the claimant as an illegal entrant was held fatal to the application in *R v Secretary of State for the Home Department, ex p Ullah* [2002] Imm AR 62 (perm). Once permission has been granted without any objection based on delay, it is too late for the respondent to seek to argue on the substantive hearing that the application should not be allowed to proceed, although delay may be relevant to the issue of relief: *R v Criminal Injuries Compensation Board, ex p A* [1999] 2 AC 330; [1999] 2 WLR 974, HL.

3   CPR 54.7A(3).

4   The protocol is inappropriate where the defendant does not have the legal power to change the decision being challenged, eg decisions issued by a court or Tribunal, nor is it appropriate in urgent cases, eg where directions have been set, or are in force, for the claimant's removal from the UK, or where there is an urgent need for an interim order to compel a public body to act where it has unlawfully refused to do so (eg the refusal of NASS to provide support or accommodation to an asylum claimant): see 'Pre-Action Protocol for Judicial Review', on DCA website.

5   *R v Secretary of State for the Home Department, ex p Foster* (13 October 1998, unreported), QBD.

6   *Ahmad and Simba v Secretary of State for the Home Department* [1999] Imm AR 356, CA.

7   *Almad* and *Simba* above.

8   CPR r 54.12. If permission is refused, or limited to certain grounds only, the application may be renewed orally, or the judge may adjourn the permission hearing to an oral hearing: r 54.12(3). Neither the defendant nor any interested party need attend a permission hearing unless directed to by the judge and the court will not generally make a costs order against the claimant where the defendant does attend a hearing: Practice Direction 54, 8.5–8.6.

9   CPR 54.12(3).

10 CPR 54.7A(8).

11 CPR 54.12(7).

12 CPR r 54.7–9. Any interested party should also be served; if the defendant is the Tribunal, the Secretary of State should always be served as an interested party.

13 CPR 54.8; *R (on the application of Webb) v Bristol City Council* [2001] EWHC 696 (Admin). Where a claimant was on his fourth application seeking to judicially review his proposed removal, it was appropriate to direct an urgent oral hearing of the permission application rather than adopting the usual, longer procedure: *Dahmani v Secretary of State for the Home Department* [2003] EWHC 882 (QB), [2003] Imm AR 479.

14 *R (on the application of Webb) v Bristol City Council* above. The claim form now includes a section to be completed if urgent consideration of the application is required.

11 *R (on the application of Hamid) v Secretary of State for the Home Department* [2012] EWHC 3070 (Admin); *R (on the application of Butt) v Secretary of State for the Home Department* [2014] EWHC 264 (Admin); *R (on the application of Kharug) v Upper Tribunal (Immigration Asylum Chamber)* [2014] EWHC 2037 (Admin). The UT has indicated that its expectations are the same and it will operate a similar procedure: *R (on the application of Okondu) v Secretary of State for the Home Department* [2014] UKUT 377 (IAC).

12 CPR r 54.13.

13 The right course is to appeal to the Court of Appeal against refusal of permission on the rejected grounds: *R (on the application of Opoku) v Principal of Southwark College* [2002] EWHC 2092 (Admin), [2003] 1 WLR 234.

14 R (on the application of Burkett) v Hammersmith and Fulham LBC [2002] UKHL 23, [2002] 1 WLR 1593.

Challenging removal directions, third country and non-suspensive appeal cases

21.73 The Home Office has a policy contained in the Enforcement Instructions and Guidance about how it will respond to actual or possible applications for judicial review in cases where removal directions have been or are to be given[1] and there is specific provision in the Civil Procedure Rules about judicial review challenges to removal directions.[2] There is no requirement to comply with the pre-action protocol in these circumstances. The Home Office accepts that there should be sufficient time between notification and enforcement of removal directions so as to enable the person to seek legal advice and apply for judicial review. The Home Office will give, a minimum period of 72 hours' notice of removal directions, including at least two working days and of which the last 24 hours must be a working day should be allowed between notification and enforcement of removal directions.[3] In third-country and non-suspensive appeals cases a minimum of five working days should be allowed between setting of removal directions and removal.[4] A minimum of five working days' notice will be given where the removal is by charter flight.[5] In port cases, 72 hours' notice need only be given if removal has not taken place within seven days of refusal of leave to enter.[6] Similarly in cases of 'failed removal' where further removal directions are set within ten days.[7] Removal will not normally be deferred in response to a threat of judicial review.[8] Removal will be deferred if a claim for judicial review is issued and a copy of the claim as issued by the court and the detailed statement of grounds are received by the Home Office[9] unless within the previous three months there was a judicial review or statutory appeal relating to the same grounds and issues or a judicial review or appeal in which those issues could have been raised; or a stay on removal relating to the current JR has already been refused, and no subsequent application for a stay has been granted; or the individual is being removed by special arrangements (including by charter flight).[10] An injunction may be necessary to stop removal in those cases and where permission to apply for judicial review has been refused by the High Court and permission to appeal is sought from the Court of Appeal.[11] The 2010 version of the EIG made no exceptions to the rule that notice of removal directions be given, following the Medical Justice case[12] contrary to previous versions which did provide for reduced or no notice of removal directions in 'exceptional' cases which included unaccompanied children. However, the current version provides that in cases where there is a risk to safety or a significant risk of disruption, the exact details of the flight and time of departure may be withheld and limited notice given using form IS151G.[13] No definition of a 'risk to safety' or 'a significant risk of disruption' are provided. If removal takes place despite an injunction or the grant of permission to appeal, the Secretary of State 's policy is to make every effort to return the person to the UK.[14] The court will not necessarily order the Secretary of State to bring a person granted permission to apply for judicial review back to the UK; whether it will do so will be a matter for the court's discretion.[15] Even if an injunction or permission to appeal is refused and removal takes place, the judicial review can (and should) be continued if there is substantive merit to the application.[16]

---

1   Enforcement Instructions and Guidance (EIG), Chapter 60: 'Judicial Review and Injunctions: 10 December 2013, last amended 14.7.14.
2   Civil Procedure Rules, Practice Direction 54A, Section II (PD 54A).
3   EIG, 60.2.1.
4   EIG 60.2.3.
5   EIG 60.2.5.
6   EIG 60.3.1.6.
7   EIG 60.3.2.
8   EIG 60.4 and 60.5.
9   EIG 60.4.1.
10 EIG 60.6.
11 R (on the application of Pharis (Ben)) v Secretary of State for the Home Department [2004] EWCA Civ 654, [2004] 3 All ER 310.

12 *R (on the application of Medical Justice) v Secretary of State for the Home Department* [2010] EWHC 1925 (Admin).

13 EIG 60 2.

14 EIG 60 14.3 and 14.4.

15 For example, *R (on the application of YZ (China)) v Secretary of State for the Home Department* [2012] EWCA Civ 1022; *R (on the application of F) v Upper Tribunal (Immigration and Asylum Chamber)* [2014] EWHC 676 (Admin).

16 See eg *R (on the application of Tawakoli) v Secretary of State for the Home Department* IJR [2014] UKUT 00235 (IAC).

21.74 When, following the issue of proceedings, the Secretary of State withdraws the decision under review, or other events supervene, should the court continue to hear the application? In *Canbolat*[1] and in *Abdi and Dahir*[2] the Court of Appeal heard the applications although in the former case there was no longer any question of the applicant's removal and in the latter, one of the persons who was the object of the application had disappeared, because of the general importance of the issues and the number of other cases affected by the legal point at issue. The principles are set out in *Salem*,[3] apply equally to appeals to the Court of Appeal and to judicial review applications. Whether judicial review of a refusal of leave to enter as a visitor should be pursued after the applicant has returned home and the Home Office has undertaken to decide any further application on its merits has been the subject of conflicting decisions,[4] but in *Zhou* the Court of Appeal allowed an application by a student to proceed although it had become academic in that he had been able through issue of the proceedings to remain beyond the period for which he had been granted leave to enter, on the basis that success would strengthen his position in applying for further leave to remain to complete the studies.[5] In *Alabi* the Court of Appeal dealt with an agreement to reconsider the decision under review. Simon Brown LJ held that it would be inappropriate in all but the rarest of cases involving a point of general importance and wide application to proceed to a substantive hearing while the decision-maker is undertaking to consider a decision afresh. Generally, such an agreement would exhaust whatever rights an applicant had in the challenge and bring an end to proceedings. But, he continued, where a *Wednesbury* irrationality challenge may lie against any future adverse decision however it comes to be reasoned, the right course is to put the judicial review on hold, with no further evidence and no steps to bring to substantive hearing, and a fresh decision should be reached as soon as possible, so that the future course of proceedings can be reviewed.[6] In *Turgut* the court gave further guidance as to the approach to be followed where the Secretary of State makes a new decision in response to the claim for judicial review. Further litigation in respect of the original decision would be fruitless: 'in general it will be convenient to substitute the second decision for the first decision as being the decision challenged in the proceedings', allowing the claimant to amend his or her grounds accordingly.[7] In judicial review claims in respect of immigration matters, the Court is frequently faced with a moving target. If the respondent makes a new decision prior to a decision on the application for permission, the Court will normally consider the lawfulness of the new decision rather than dismissing the claim in respect of the superseded decision as having become academic.[8] If the parties cannot agree that the applicant may use the leave already obtained to advance a challenge the respondent thinks impossible, the respondent should apply to set aside the leave and strike out the proceedings.[9]

1 *R v Secretary of State for the Home Department, ex p Canbolat* [1997] Imm AR 442, CA.
2 *Secretary of State for the Home Department v Abdi and Dahir* [1995] Imm AR 570, CA.
3 *R v Secretary of State for the Home Department, ex p Salem* [1999] 1 AC 450, HL. In *R (on the application of Yaseetharan (Selluthurai)) v Secretary of State for the Home Department and CIO Stansted* [2002] EWHC 1467 (QB), [2003] Imm AR 62, a change of policy midway through the proceedings to allow legal representatives to be present for screening interviews at Stansted meant that pursuit of a challenge to the previous policy, which was now academic, was not justified.
4 In *R v Secretary of State for the Home Department, ex p Kekana* [1998] Imm AR 136, the judge refused to hear the application. In the earlier case of *R v Immigration Officer, ex p Honegan* (13 March 1995), QBD, the application was heard, the refusal of leave to enter quashed and subsequently, damages of £17,000 awarded for the detention arising from the unlawful refusal. We suggest that wherever a decision has potentially prejudicial implications for future applications, a challenge cannot reasonably be pre-emptively rejected as academic.
5 *R (on the application of Zhou) v Secretary of State for the Home Department* [2003] EWCA Civ 51, [2003] INLR 211, para 3.
6 *R v Secretary of State for the Home Department, ex p Alabi* [1997] INLR 124, CA.
7 *R v Secretary of State for the Home Department, ex p Turgut* [2000] EWCA Civ 22.
8 *R (on the application for CA) v Secretary of State for the Home Department* [2011] EWCA Civ 1144.
9 *Turgut*, above.

Evidence

21.75 In removal cases the High Court can investigate the truth of an allegation that entry was obtained by deception or was otherwise illegal, because illegal entry is a precedent fact to the exercise of the power to remove[1] (although no longer to the exercise of the power to detain).[2] This has already been dealt with in CHAPTER 17. Where the claimant seeks a declaration that he or she is a British citizen, the court will investigate that issue in its precedent fact jurisdiction.[3] In other cases the court's role is not a fact-finding one, although evidence will be carefully scrutinised in asylum and human rights cases.[4] Where the Secretary of State must establish the existence of precedent facts, the court will hear oral evidence and cross-examination if necessary,[5] but hearsay evidence is admissible.[6] So interviews in relation to variation of leave, for entry clearance and at the port may be admitted, as may confidential medical records which resolve the issue of whether someone is an impostor.[7] Discovery should be unnecessary in an application for judicial review, since it is the obligation of the respondent public body in its evidence to make frank disclosure to the court of the decision-making process. The absence of a requirement to give reasons cannot be prayed in aid to avoid discovery or the usual 'cards on the table' approach.[8]

1 *Khawaja v Secretary of State for the Home Department* [1984] AC 74, [1983] 1 All ER 765, HL.
2 IA 1971, Sch 2, para 16(2), as amended by IAA 1999, s 140.
3 *R (on the application of Harrison) v Secretary of State for the Home Department* [2003] EWCA Civ 432, [2003] INLR 284.
4 *Bugdaycay v Secretary of State for the Home Department* [1987] AC 514; *R v Secretary of State for the Home Department, ex p Turgut* [2000] EWCA Civ 22, [2001] 1 All ER 719, [2000] Imm AR 306, [2000] INLR 292, CA.
5 *Khawaja v Secretary of State for the Home Department* [1984] AC 74; *R v Secretary of State for the Home Department, ex p Yasmeen* (CO 2930/99) (29 September 1999, unreported), QBD. The reviewing court has the power to direct cross-examination where it is necessary to do justice, although the CPR gives no express power: *R (on the application of G) v Ealing*

London Borough Council [2002] EWHC 250 (Admin), (2002) Times, 18 March, [2002] ACD 48; *R (on the application of Wilkinson) v Responsible Medical Officer Broadmoor Hospital* [2001] EWCA Civ 1545, [2002] 1 WLR 419, 65 BMLR 15. But the case of *Wilkinson* is not a charter for routine applications for oral evidence in human rights cases: *R (on the application of N) v M* [2002] EWCA Civ 1789, [2003] 1 WLR 562.

6 *R v Secretary of State for the Home Department, ex p Yilmaz* [1993] Imm AR 359; *R v Secretary of State for the Home Department, ex p Rahman* [1997] Imm AR 197, CA.

7 *R v Secretary of State for the Home Department, ex p Taj* (CO 1084/99) (20 October 1999, unreported), QBD. This clearly engages ECHR, art 8 privacy issues, see *Z v Finland* (1997) 25 EHRR 371, and there would have to be a balancing exercise to see whether the interference was necessary in the circumstances.

8 *R v Secretary of State for the Home Department, ex p Fayed* [1997] INLR 138, CA. But see *R v Secretary of State for the Home Department, ex p BH* [1990] COD 445, where Roch J ordered discovery of documents relevant to an operation at Istanbul airport in which the claimant was prevented from boarding a flight to London, where the judge was satisfied that the defendant's affidavits did not disclose the whole story.

21.76 In *R v Secretary of State for the Home Department, ex p Turgut*,[1] a case decided before the coming into force of the Human Rights Act 1998, the Court of Appeal examined the standard of review and the correct approach to the evidence required in a human rights case. It held that on an ECHR, art 3 challenge the court had an obligation to subject the Secretary of State's decision to rigorous examination by reference to the underlying factual material on which the decision was based. Although the court's role was still supervisory, it would pay no special deference to the Secretary of State's conclusions on the facts, since the right involved is absolute and fundamental. The court was hardly less well placed than the decision-maker to evaluate the risk once the relevant material was before it, and the discretionary area of judgment of the Secretary of State was decidedly narrow. Since the material date for the assessment of risk is the time of the court's consideration of the case (following *Chahal*),[2] the Secretary of State had to reconsider the decision repeatedly, and the High Court would not shut out evidence, might order disclosure of evidence, and was not limited to the evidence before the Secretary of State at the time of the decision.[3] And in *Daly*[4] the House of Lords affirmed that the *Wednesbury* test of irrationality has no place in cases engaging fundamental human rights, a view reaffirmed in the Court of Appeal in *Huang*.[5]

1 [2000] Imm AR 306, CA.

2 *Chahal v United Kingdom* (1996) 23 EHRR 413, para 97: 'the notion of an effective remedy under Article 13 requires independent scrutiny of the claim that there exist substantial grounds for fearing a real risk of treatment contrary to Article 3.'

3 In *E v Secretary of State for the Home Department, R v Secretary of State for the Home Department* [2004] EWCA Civ 49, [2004] 2 WLR 1351 the Court of Appeal contrasted the Secretary of State's position, as someone with a continuing responsibility up to the point of removal, with that of the Tribunal, whose task was to make one discrete decision on the evidence before it at the time, in order to explain why on an application for judicial review of a decision to remove, post-decision material could continue to be submitted to the Secretary of State and considered by the Court.

4 *R (on the application of Daly) v Secretary of State for the Home Department* [2001] UKHL 26, [2001] 2 WLR 1622.

5 *Huang v Secretary of State for the Home Department* [2005] EWCA Civ 105, (2005) 149 Sol Jo LB 297.

Relief

21.77 The most common order sought in the immigration context in judicial review is a quashing order to quash a decision or removal directions, but orders may be sought requiring the performance of a duty (such as an order to provide NASS support to a claimant), or restraining the defendant from doing something (such as an injunction preventing the defendant from removing the claimant).[1] Interim relief may be sought in urgent cases, including an order to return someone to the jurisdiction who has been wrongfully removed from it.[2] A declaration may be sought (for example, that the claimant is a British citizen[3] or even a refugee.[4] But it is not the function of the court to make orders as to how the Secretary of State should run his department, and the court refused to make a declaration about the general position regarding delays in granting asylum in *Arbab*.[5] The court has jurisdiction to grant relief in the form of an advisory declaration, but will not do so save for demonstrably good reasons.[6] Damages are also available in judicial review proceedings, if they have been specifically sought on the claim form.[7]

[1] See CPR r 54.2.
[2] The order is expressed in terms such as 'the Secretary of State to take all reasonable steps' or 'to use his best endeavours' to secure the return of the claimant to the UK. In *R (on the application of Changuizi) v Secretary of State for the Home Department* [2002] EWHC 2569 (Admin), [2003] Imm AR 355, an undertaking not to remove the claimant from the jurisdiction was breached, and the judge concluded that the claimant should be returned. An application by the Secretary of State to be relieved of the undertaking to return the claimant pending an appeal to the Court of Appeal was rejected at [2003] EWCA Civ 165. See also *R v Secretary of State for the Home Department, ex p Shanmuganathan* (11 March 1999, unreported), CA; *R (on the application of Ahmed (Goran Kadr)) v Secretary of State for the Home Department* [2009] EWHC 2676 (Admin) where return was ordered on the basis of an Article 8 breach.
[3] CPR r 54.2; *R (on the application of Harrison) v Secretary of State for the Home Department* [2003] EWCA Civ 432, [2003] INLR 284.
[4] *R (on the application of Rashid) v Secretary of State for the Home Department* [2004] EWHC 2465 (Admin), (2004) Times, 17 November.
[5] *R v Secretary of State for the Home Department, ex p Arbab* [2002] EWHC 1249 (Admin), [2002] Imm AR 536, following *R v Secretary of State for the Home Department, ex p Fire Brigades Union* [1995] 2 WLR 464; see also *R v Secretary of State for the Home Department and Secretary of State for Social Security, ex p Paulo* [2001] Imm AR 645, to similar effect.
[6] *R (on the application of Campaign for Nuclear Disarmament) v Prime Minister* [2002] EWHC 2712 (Admin), para 47.
[7] CPR r 54.3. In cases involving judicial review of detention, a prayer for damages in the claim form will prevent the application from being dismissed as academic if the claimant is released: see eg *AFP Nadarajah* [2002] EWHC 748 (Admin). But the Court of Appeal held in *Anufrijeva v Southwark London Borough Council* [2003] EWCA Civ 1406, [2004] 1 All ER 833 that permission to apply for judicial review would be granted in respect of damages for maladministration affecting human rights only if persuaded that a complaint procedure, eg through the Ombudsman, was not more appropriate.

21.78 Costs normally follow the event on a judicial review which goes to full hearing. In cases where a non-governmental organisation brings a claim in the public interest, pre-emptive or protective costs orders may be sought, limiting or even preventing a costs order against the claimant in the event of dismissal of the claim.[1] Save in exceptional circumstances, the costs of the defendant or interested party's attendance at an oral permission hearing should not be awarded against an unsuccessful claimant.[2]. The defendant may be liable for the claimant's costs if the claim is withdrawn because the defendant concedes the relief sought before the claim is decided and even before the question of permission is decided. The starting point is that a successful claimant who followed the Pre Action Protocol by issuing an adequately formulated letter of claim is entitled to his or her costs. The defendant would have to persuade the court to depart from that rule and will find it hard to do so if the claimant, but not the defendant, complied with the Pre Action Protocol. The principle that costs orders should not discourage parties from settling claims has effect at the Pre Action Protocol stage and is not a principle that a defendant can subsequently rely on to avoid costs liability when making a concession that should have been made earlier.[3] Even if the claimant has not complied with the pre-action protocol but it is evident that he or she would not have secured relief from the defendant without issuing proceedings, the claimant should still be entitled to costs from the defendant who concedes the relief sought.[4]

[1] In *R (on the application of Campaign for Nuclear Disarmament) v Prime Minister* [2002] EWHC 2712 (Admin), (2002) Times, 27 December, the court made a pre-emptive costs order capping the claimant's liability; in the light of the genuine public importance of the issues, it was right to give CND the certainty required to pursue them. In *R (on the application of the Refugee Legal Centre) v Secretary of State for the Home Department* [2004] EWCA Civ 1481, the Court of Appeal made a protective costs order protecting the claimant from paying the defendant's costs on appeal from dismissal of its judicial review claim.

[2] CPR PD 54 (JR) 8.6; *R (on the application of Mount Cook Land Ltd) v Westminster City Council* [2003] EWCA Civ 1346, (2003) 43 EGCS 137, where the court held there was no good reason not to follow the guidance in the Practice Direction in the absence of exceptional circumstances, such as a hopeless case or abuse of judicial review for collateral ends, although a successful defendant at the permission stage who has complied with the pre-action protocol and has filed an acknowledgement of service should generally recover the costs of doing so from the claimant, approving *R (on the application of Leach) v Local Administration Comr* [2001] EWHC 455 (Admin), [2001] 4 PRL 28.

[3] *R (on the application of Bahta) v Secretary of State for the Home Department* [2011] EWCA Civ 895, [2011] All ER (D) 244 (Jul).

[4] *R (on the application of KR) v Secretary of State for the Home Department* [2012] EWCA Civ 1555.

JUDICIAL REVIEW IN THE UPPER TRIBUNAL

21.79 The TCEA 2007 confers on the UT a judicial review jurisdiction whereby it can give the public law remedies (mandatory orders, prohibiting orders, quashing orders, declarations and injunctions) available from the High Court upon an application for judicial review.[1] The UT may also award damages if the application for judicial review includes such a claim and damages would have been awarded had the claim been brought in the High Court[2] and it may award costs.[3] The remedies have the same effect and are enforceable as if made by the High Court[4] and are to be granted in accordance with the same principles as would govern an application in the High Court.[5] The Lord Chief Justice has made two directions specifying classes of applications for judicial review that are to be heard by the UT rather than the Administrative Court with the consequence that most judicial reviews relating to immigration decisions are to be heard by the UT.

[1] TCEA 2007, s 15(1).

[2] TCEA 2007, s 15(6).

[3] TCEA 2007, s 29, including making orders for 'wasted costs' in accordance with the principles in *Ridehalgh v Horsefield* [1994] EWCA Civ 40 if it considers that costs were incurred as a result of an 'improper, unreasonable or negligent act or omission on the part of any legal or other representative'. In *R (on the application of Okondu) v Secretary of State for the Home Department* [2014] UKUT 377 (IAC) wasted costs were ordered against the solicitor with

conduct of a claim for judicial review which relied on assertions shown to be misleading by the evidence adduced in support of the claim. The tribunal observed that 'Applicants with weak cases are entitled to seek to advance their case and have it adjudicated upon; that is a fundamental aspect of having a right of access to a court. But there is a wealth of difference between the advancing of a case that is held to be unarguable in a fair, professional and proper manner and . . . . the advancing of unarguable cases in a professionally improper manner'.

4   TCEA 2007, s 15(3).
5   TCEA 2007, s 16(4) and (5).

21.80 As in the High Court, permission to make the application is required[1] and 'undue delay' in bringing the application may result in refusal of permission or relief.[2] Similar provision is made in the UT's procedure rules to that in the Civil Procedure Rules in respect of applications for judicial review including: as to the form and content of the written application;[3] a three-month time limit for making the application[4] which the UT may extend on application;[5] for acknowledgment of service by the respondent;[6] for the refusal or partial refusal of permission on the papers to be reconsidered at a hearing;[7] for the respondent and any other person who provided an acknowledgment of service to respond to the application after a grant of permission;[8] for the applicant to apply for permission to amend his or her grounds;[9] and for the parties and any other person to whom the UT gives permission to submit evidence and make oral and written representations.[10] The UT's general case management powers and the provisions about hearings described above also apply. As a consequence of undue delays by the Secretary of State for the Home Department in responding by way of an Acknowledgment of Service, the UT has decided that this need not be done for 6 weeks (rather than 3) unless an application is made for urgent consideration or expedition but if no AOS is received the application will then be decided on the papers without it and if permission is refused but renewed at an oral hearing, the SSHD will be vulnerable to a costs order.[11]

1   TCEA 2007, s 16(2).
2   TCEA 2007, s 16(4) and (5).
3   Tribunal Procedure (Upper Tribunal) Rules 2008, SI 2008/2698, r 28.
4   SI 2008/2698, r 28(2).
5   SI 2008/2698, rr 5(3)(a) and 28(7).
6   SI 2008/2698, r 29.
7   SI 2008/2698, r 30(4).
8   SI 2008/2698, r 31.
9   SI 2008/2698, r 32.
10   SI 2008/2698, r 33.
11   *R (on the application of Kumar) v Secretary of State for the Home Department (acknowledgement of service; Tribunal arrangements)* [2014] UKUT 104 (IAC).

21.81 The Senior President of Tribunals has made Practice Directions, concerned with applications for judicial review in the Upper Tribunal.[1] The most recent are dated 1 November 2013[2] which provide that applications are to be made on the form on the UT's website[3]. The application to be accompanied by any written evidence relied on, copies of relevant statutory material and a list of essential reading;[4] the applicant has to file two copies of a paginated and indexed bundle of the documents required by the PD and the Procedure Rules[5] and the UT to decide the question of permission without a hearing, in the first instance.[6] The fee is currently £140 to lodge the application; £350 to renew at an oral hearing and £700 for a substantive hearing; for making another application on notice (£80) or by consent (£45) and for photocopying of documents.[7] A fee remission may be applied for on form EX160 if the applicant is in receipt of benefits[8] and has a low gross monthly income[9] and part remission is also possible. Reduced fees may be payable depending on the party's disposable income.[10] The party's partner's income is treated as being the party's income for the purpose of determining liability for fees.[11] Fees may also be reduced or remitted if the Lord Chancellor is satisfied that owing to exceptional circumstances, payment would involve 'undue financial hardship'.[12] The UT may not accept an application for permission to bring proceedings unless it is accompanied by the fee or the UT accepts an undertaking that the fee will be paid.[13] The application must be lodged with the Upper Tribunal in London or at one of the regional centres.[14]

[1] Practice Directions: Fresh claim judicial review in the Immigration and Asylum Chamber of the Upper Tribunal, 17 October 2011 ('PD') supplemented in a further Practice Statement dated 26 April 2013.
[2] Immigration Judicial Review in the Immigration & Asylum Chamber of the Upper Tribunal 1 November 2013 www.judiciary.gov.uk/wp-content/uploads/2013/11/utiac-immigration-claim-01112013.pdf.
[3] PD 3.1. Currently, form T480. Guidance notes are available [T481].
[4] PD 4.
[5] PD 5.
[6] PD 6.
[7] The Upper Tribunal (Immigration and Asylum Chamber) (Judicial Review) (England and Wales) Fees (Amendment) Order 2011, SI 2011/2344, Sch 2, as amended by SI 2014/878 in force from 22.4.14.
[8] JSA, ESA, IS, Universal Credit, State Pension or Scottish Legal Aid.
[9] £1085 for a single person without children.
[10] SI 2011/2344 Sch 2, para 5.
[11] SI 2011/2344, Sch 2, para 6.
[12] SI 2011/2344, Sch 2, para 8.
[13] Tribunal Procedure (Upper Tribunal) Rules 2008, SI 2008/2698, r 28A(1), as inserted by SI 2011/2343.
[14] Upper Tribunal Immigration and Asylum Chamber Field House 15-25 Breams Buildings London EC4A 1DZ or Birmingham Civil Justice Centre, Priory Courts, 5th Floor, 33 Bull Street, Birmingham, B4 6DS; Cardiff Civil Justice Centre, 2 Park Street, Cardiff, CF10 1ET; Leeds Combined Court, 1 Oxford Row, Leeds, LS1 3BG or Manchester Civil Justice Centre, 1 Bridge Street West, Manchester, M60 9DJ.

21.82 There is provision for the applicant to request that the tribunal deal urgently with an application for permission and to seek an interim injunction.[1] If the UT refuses permission or grants permission on limited grounds without a hearing, it will reconsider its decision at a hearing if it receives an application to do so within 9 days of sending written notice of the decision to the applicant.[2] The applicant is required to serve any respondent and interested party with copies of the application and accompanying documents within 9 days of making the application and must serve the UT with a written statement of when and how they were served.[3] An applicant may amend an application for judicial review, including by advancing additional grounds, but if the result of the amendment is that the application would have to be transferred to the High Court, the UT's permission is required.[4] The PD requires the filing and service of skeleton arguments before the substantive hearing of an application.[5] A party may be represented only by a person authorized to conduct litigation in the High Court and, at a hearing, by a person with rights of audience in the

High Court.[6]

1   Practice Direction 11 of the Immigration Judicial Review in the IAC of the UT PD and see PD 12. There is currently no clear procedure for the oral renewal of an application for urgent consideration and it would clearly be of assistance to practitioners if the UT were to make provision for this in the PD eg 'In urgent consideration cases the UT will endeavour to list an application the same day it is made and in any event before the time removal is due to take place.'

2   Tribunal Procedure (Upper Tribunal) Rules 2008, r 30, as amended by SI 2011/2343, giving the 9 day time limit, rather than the usual 14 days, for fresh claim proceedings.

3   Tribunal Procedure (Upper Tribunal) Rules 2008, r 28A(2), as inserted by SI 2011/2343.

4   Tribunal Procedure (Upper Tribunal) Rules 2008, r 33A, as inserted by SI 2011/2343.

5   PD 8.

6   Tribunal Procedure (Upper Tribunal) Rules 2008, r 11 (5A) and (5B) as amended by SI 2011/2343.

Chapter 22

SPECIAL IMMIGRATION APPEALS COMMISSION

BACKGROUND AND STRUCTURE OF THE SPECIAL IMMIGRATION APPEALS COMMISSION

22.1 The Special Immigration Appeals Commission (SIAC) was created by the Special Immigration Appeals Commission Act 1997 and established on 3 August 1998. Before this, immigration decisions made on the basis of national security or political grounds were subject to the rather mysterious and extra-statutory advisory procedure known as the 'three wise men', whose outstanding feature was its failure to meet elementary rules of natural justice. No particulars about the case to be met were given to the appellant, not even the names of witnesses, there was no right to representation, its rulings were not binding and the advice tendered to the Secretary of State at the end of the procedure was not disclosed.[1] In *Chahal v United Kingdom*[2] the European Court of Human Rights concluded that the procedural shortcomings of the advisory panel meant that it could not be considered to be a 'court' for the purposes of Article 5(4)) (which guarantees the right to have the lawfulness of detention decided speedily by a court) and even together with Habeaus Corpus, judicial review and bail, it did not collectively provide the substantial measure of procedural protection required by Article 5(4). The Court also held that the panel and judicial review were not an effective remedy for the purposes of Article 3 and 13 of the ECHR because of their inability independently to review the justifications for the decision. The Court, whilst recognising constraints that national security could legitimately place on legal proceedings, could not permit the executive to attempt to free itself from effective control by the domestic courts. The Court also pointed to the possibility of alternative arrangements originating in Canada which 'both accommodate legitimate security concerns . . . and yet accord the individual a substantial measure of procedural justice'.[3] The Court referred to a number of features of the Canadian system, notably the holding of hearings *in camera*, the disclosure of as much of the case against the applicant as possible, and the use of security cleared counsel instructed by the Court to test the strength of the State's case.[4] The Special Immigration Appeals Commission was the UK government's response. It now appears that there was a misunderstanding of the nature of procedures operated in Canada which has since adopted the special advocate process developed in the 1997 Act.[5] The Strasbourg court moreover has since found the Commission's processes to be incompatible with the procedural requirements of Articles 5(4) and 6(1) of the ECHR.[6]

[1]   The procedure is set out in detail in the fourth edition of this book, at 15.55–15.56.
[2]   *Chahal v United Kingdom* (1996) 23 EHRR 413.
[3]   (1996) 23 EHRR 413, para 131. For a description of the previous Canadian SIRC system, see *Charkaoui v Minister of Citizenship and Immigration* 2007 SCC 9, paras 71–79), 24 BHRC 489; see also Professor Murray Rankin, 'The Security Intelligence Review Committee: Reconciling National Security with Procedural Fairness' (1990), 3 CJALP 173, at p 179. In 1988, Parliament added section 40(1) to the Immigration Act 1971 to empower the Minister and the Solicitor General to issue security certificates in respect of foreign nationals. Section 40(1) effectively bypassed the SIRC investigation process where foreign nationals were concerned, instead referring the certificate to a designated judge of the Federal Court for subsequent review. The Canadian Supreme Court referred to the *Chahal* decision, stating at paragraph 75 that: 'The court in *Chahal* commented favourably on the idea of security-cleared counsel instructed by the court, identifying it as being Canadian in origin (perhaps referring to the procedure developed by SIRC).'
[4]   (1996) 23 EHRR 413, para 144.
[5]   See *There and back again: the strange journey of special advocates and the comparative law methodology* Jenkins, D *Columbia Human Rights Law Review*, v 42, 2011.
[6]   *A v United Kingdom* (2009) 49 EHRR 625, Grand Chamber.

22.2 The Lord Chancellor (who is also the Secretary of State for Justice) appoints members of the Special Immigration Appeals Commission.[1] It is 'duly constituted' by three members, of whom one holds or has held high judicial office,[2] and one is or has been a judge of the immigration and asylum chamber of either the First-tier Tribunal or the Upper Tribunal.[3] The third member of the Commission needs no particular qualification by statute, but during the passage of the Bill the minister indicated that the third member would 'have some experience of national security matters and will be familiar with the evidence that is likely to be presented to the commission'.[4] In recent experience, particular familiarity on the part of the 'Security member' with the national security matter in issue has resulted in recusal.

[1]   Special Immigration Appeals Commission Act 1997, Sch 1, para 1.
[2]   SIACA 1997, Sch 1, para 5(a). This means a High Court or Court of Appeal judge. The current Chairman of the Commission is Mr Justice Irwin. A number of other High Court Judges have been appointed to sit in the Commission having regard to the need to accommodate *de novo* remittals and the number of hearings generated by the Commission's recently expanded

jurisdiction to review decisions to refuse to naturalise or to exclude a person under ss 2C and 2D of the Special Immigration Appeals Commission Act (SIACA 1997) (amended by s 15 of the Justice and Security Act 2013).

3 SIACA 1997, Sch 1, para 5(b) as amended by Asylum and Immigration (Treatment of Claimants, etc) Act 2004, Sch 2, para 12(1) and by Transfer of Functions of the Asylum and Immigration Tribunal Order 2010, SI 2010/21, Art 5(1), Sch 1, paras 14 and 16.

4 301 HC Official Report (6th series) col 1033, 26 November 1997.

JURISDICTION

22.3 The SIAC hears appeals against immigration decisions where appellants are excluded from the normal system of appeals to the First-tier Tribunal owing to the political or national security issues raised by the decision. The right of appeal to the First-tier Tribunal may be excluded as a result of certification by the Secretary of State and any appeal must instead be brought to SIAC.[1] Since the changes introduced by s 15 of the Justice and Security Act 2013, the Commission also has a review jurisdiction in respects of certain decisions by the Secretary of State to direct that a person be excluded or that an application for naturalisation as a British citizen be refused.

1 Nationality, Immigration and Asylum Act 2002, ss 97, 97A, 98.

APPEALS

22.4 The recent changes to appeal rights provided by the Immigration Act 2014, addressed in detail in Chapters 19 and 20, by which:

(a)   the rights of appeal to the FTT (IAC) and the grounds on which they may be brought are limited to 'protection', human rights or revocation of protection decisions, EEA decisions or deprivations of citizenship; and

(b)   appeals can be certified as 'out of country' appeals on the grounds that removal pending the appeal will not cause 'serious irreversible harm' are reflected in parallel provisions for SIAC appeals. The circumstances in which an appeal is directed to SIAC rather than the FTT are set out in NIAA 2002, s 97. They are decisions in respect of which the Secretary of State certifies that a decision was made on the grounds that the person's exclusion or removal from the United Kingdom is:

    (i)   in the interests of national security; or

    (ii)   in the interests of the relationship between the United Kingdom and another country

or, or in addition, the Secretary of State certifies that the decision was taken wholly or partly in reliance on information which in her opinion should not be made public:

    (i)   in the interests of national security;

    (ii)   in the interests of the relationship between the United Kingdom and another country; or

    (iii) otherwise in the public interest.

The decisions that must be appealed to the SIAC rather than to the First-tier Tribunal are:

(1)   a personal decision of the Secretary of State taken wholly or partly on the ground that the person's removal or exclusion from the United Kingdom is in the interests of national security or in the interests of the relationship between the United Kingdom and another country;[1]

(2)   a decision taken in accordance with a personal direction of the Secretary of State, identifying the person to whom the decision relates and wholly or partly in the interests of national security or in the interests of the relationship between the United Kingdom and another country;[2]

(3)   a decision taken wholly or partly in reliance on information which the Secretary of State personally certifies should not be made public for national security, diplomatic or other public interest reasons;[3]

(4)   a decision to deprive a person of his or her citizenship taken wholly or partly in reliance on information which the Secretary of State certifies should not be made public for national security, diplomatic or other public interest reasons.[4]

[1]   NIAA 2002, s 97(1)(a), (2) and (4) in the case of immigration decisions, refusals of asylum and curtailment of, or refusal to, extend leave as a refugee; in the case of EEA decisions, the Immigration (European Economic Area) Regulations 2006, SI 2006/1003, reg 28(1), (2)(a), (3) and (5).

[2]   NIAA 2002, s 97(1)(b), (2) and (4) in the case of immigration decisions, refusals of asylum and curtailment of or refusal to extend leave as a refugee; in the case of EEA decisions, the Immigration (European Economic Area) Regulations 2006, SI 2006/1003, reg 28(1), (2)(b), (3) and (5).

[3]   NIAA 2002, s 97(3) and (4) in the case of immigration decisions, refusals of asylum and curtailment of, or refusal to, extend leave as a refugee; in the case of EEA decisions, the Immigration (European Economic Area) Regulations 2006, SI 2006/1003, reg 28(1), (4) and (5).

[4]   British Nationality Act 1981, s 40A(2), as inserted by NIAA 2002, s 4.

22.5 Many of the statutory provisions which apply in respect of appeals before the First-tier Tribunal also apply in respect of appeals to the SIAC, including the statutory extension of leave pending a variation decision, an appeal or an application for administrative review,[1] the prohibition of removal while an appeal is pending,[2] the prohibition on giving effect to a variation or revocation of leave, while an appeal against the decision to make the order, variation or revocation could be brought or is pending,[3] the statutory grounds on which an appeal may be brought[4] and on which the appeal must be allowed,[5] the matters and evidence to be considered on the appeal,[6] the power to give directions to give effect to the decision,[7] exclusion of a second appeal in respect of matters which should have been raised in an earlier appeal or one-stop notice,[8] the definition of a 'pending appeal',[9] and the obligation to give notice of the decision.[10] An appeal against the rejection of an asylum claim will be treated as abandoned if the appellant leaves the United Kingdom.[11] The circumstances in which there is a right to an in-country appeal before SIAC mirror those which give rise to a similar right before the First-tier Tribunal.[12] Appellants to the SIAC are now entitled to a grant of controlled legal representation. Since 25 June 2013, the amended s 97A of NIAA 2002 (introduced by the Crime and Courts Act 2013) has provided for a process of certification giving a further power to the Secretary of State to curtail in-country appeal rights. This power is now effectively being rolled out to all deportation appeals by s 15 et seq of the Immigration Act 2014 and the Immigration (European Economic Area) (Amendment) (No 2) Regulations

2014, SI 2014/1976 (in force 28 July 2014).

1   Under ss 3C and 3D of the Immigration Act 1971; Special Immigration Appeals Commission Act 1997, s 2(2)(a).
2   Under the Nationality, Immigration and Asylum Act 2002, s 78; Special Immigration Appeals Commission Act 1997, s 2(2)(b).
3   Special Immigration Appeals Commission Act 1997, s 2(2)(c), (d). NIAA 2002, s 82(3) was repealed on 31 August 2006 by the Immigration, Asylum and Nationality Act 2006, s 11(6) except in relation to a decision made before that date: SI 2006/2226, arts 3, 4(5), Schs 1 and 2.
4   Under NIAA 2002, s 84: Special Immigration Appeals Commission Act 1997, s 2(2)(e).
5   Under NIAA 2002, s 86: Special Immigration Appeals Commission Act 1997, s 2(2)(g).
6   Under NIAA 2002, s 85: Special Immigration Appeals Commission Act 1997, s 2(2)(f).
7   Under NIAA 2002, s 87: Special Immigration Appeals Commission Act 1997, s 2(2)(h).
8   Under NIAA 2002, s 96, see CHAPTER 12 above: Special Immigration Appeals Commission Act 1997, s 2(2)(i).
9   Under NIAA 2002, s 104: Special Immigration Appeals Commission Act 1997, s 2(2)(j).
10   Under NIAA 2002, s 105: Special Immigration Appeals Commission Act 1997, s 2(2)(k).
11   Special Immigration Appeals Commission Act 1997, s 2(4).
12   Special Immigration Appeals Commission Act 1997, s 2(5).

REVIEW

22.6 Section 15 of the Justice and Security Act 2013 introduced ss 2C and 2D of the Special Immigration Appeals Commission Act 1997 which provide for a new jurisdiction in SIAC to review and set aside:

(1)   a direction by the Secretary of State, acting in person, about the exclusion[1] from the UK of a non-EEA national made wholly or partly on the ground that the exclusion is conducive to the public good which does not attract a right of appeal and which has been certified by the Secretary of State (acting in person) as having been made wholly or partly in reliance on information which, in the opinion of the Secretary of State, should not be made public:

(i)   in the interests of national security;
(ii)   in the interests of the relationship between the UK and another country;
(iii)   otherwise in the public interest.

(2)   a decision to refuse to issue a certificate of naturalisation as a British citizen under s 6 of the British Nationality Act 1981 (BNA 1981) or to refuse to register as a British citizen under BNA 1981, s 41A, which is similarly certified by the Secretary of State.[2]

The Commission must, in determining whether the direction should be set aside, apply the principles which apply in judicial review proceedings.[3] If the Commission decides that a direction to exclude or decision to refuse naturalisation should be set aside, it may make any order or relief that may be given in judicial review proceedings.[4] That leaves the obvious lacuna of no jurisdiction to grant interim relief. This was raised before the Divisional Court in *Ignaoua*[5] but the court contemplated that in cases where interim relief or other unavailable remedy was sought, the parallel judicial review jurisdiction could be invoked. This jurisdiction remains because the Court of Appeal struck down the part of the Commencement Order[6] to the Justice and Security Act 2013 which purported to terminate Mr Ignaoua's judicial review claim against exclusion which had been issued in 2010.[7] However, in subsequent rulings the Court of Appeal[8] and Divisional Court have held that the statutory steer is plainly that extant claims for judicial review in affected exclusion or citizenship cases are to be heard in SIAC where the availability of a closed material procedure will avoid the problem of untriability that arises when the Secretary of State successfully seeks to withhold evidence from a party in judicial review. This flows from judgments in the Supreme Court[9] and Administrative Court[10] that the court has no inherent power, even by consent of the parties, to devise a closed material procedure which must be done by Parliament. The Justice and Security Act 2013 now also provides a statutory basis for a closed material procedure in judicial review.[11]

As the effect of the new review jurisdiction in SIAC is said to be to provide an alternative remedy to judicial review,[12] extant challenges in the Administrative Court by way of judicial review to decisions to exclude or refuse to register or naturalise will normally be stayed where the Secretary of State issues a certified direction or decision under ss 2C or 2D of the Special Immigration Appeals Commission Act 1997. However, extant claims for judicial review which had been stayed may be unstayed for the purpose of granting relief unavailable in SIAC's review jurisdiction and the Administrative Court may entertain cases where the relief sought cannot be obtained in SIAC's review jurisdiction.

1. Special Immigration Appeals Commission Act 1997, s 2C.
2. Special Immigration Appeals Commission Act 1997, s 2D.
3. Special Immigration Appeals Commission Act 1997, ss 2C(3) and 2D(3).
4. Special Immigration Appeals Commission Act 1997, ss 2C(4) and 2D(4).
5. *R (on the application of Ignaoua) v Secretary of State for the Home Department* [2014] EWHC 1382 (Admin), para 37.
6. Justice and Security Act 2013 (Commencement, Transitional and Saving Provisions) Order 2013, SI 2013/1482.
7. *R (on the application of Ignaoua) v The Secretary of State for the Home Department* [2013] EWCA Civ 1498.
8. *AHK v The Secretary of State for the Home Department* [2014] EWCA Civ 151.
9. *Al Rawi v The Security Service* [2011] UKSC 34, [2012] 1 AC 531.
10. *AHK v Secretary of State for the Home Department* [2013] EWHC 1426 (Admin).
11. Justice and Security Act 2013, s 6.
12. [2014] EWHC 1382 (Admin).

Procedure on SIAC review

22.7 The Commission has sought to lay down the procedural and substantive ground rules for the exercise of its new review jurisdiction. The scope and intensity of review in the light of the impact on the effectiveness of any review of the closed material procedure was considered in the first tranche of review cases in 2014.[1] The Secretary of State urged in argument that the Commission limit its consideration to the rationality of a decision based on a memorandum in summary form before a Home Office decision-maker. The Commission decided that in both s 2C and s 2D reviews it will adopt the following approach in reliance, in particular on the principles of common law fairness and its duty under rule 4(3) of its Procedure Rules to satisfy itself that the material available to it enables it properly to determine proceedings:

(a)   The factual basis for the judgment exercised by the Secretary of State must be 'scrutinised very carefully or "anxiously" by the Commission' (§30). Justification for this heightened scrutiny does not derive from any engagement of human rights, but the common law duty of fairness to compensate for the fact that the determinative material is likely to be withheld from the appellant.

(b)   'It is still a review, not an appeal on the facts. If a close and anxious review of the evidence produces the outcome that the facts or factual inferences reached by the Secretary of State were reasonable, then there should be no interference on that ground, even if the Commission would reach different conclusions' (§31).

(c)   'Once the facts and inferences of fact have been reviewed, and if the factual or evidential conclusions drawn by the Secretary of State are found to be reasonable, the Commission should proceed to review the judgments made by the Secretary of State based on that factual picture. In the review of fact there is no place for "deference" to the Secretary of State. In the consideration of a judgement based on the reviewed fact, public law principles do support a degree of deference to the decision of the Secretary of State, for well established reasons. The Minister has democratic responsibility and answers to Parliament; the Minister is entitled to formulate and implement policy; the Minister has expert advice to assist her conclusions. Here, the task of the Commission is to interfere when and if the Secretary of State has been unreasonable, allowing for due deference paid' (§32).

(d)   'If and when a proper basis is laid demonstrating that the decision engages Convention rights, the Commission will go on to consider whether an otherwise reasonable decision represents a disproportionate interference with the relevant Convention rights' (§33).

(e)   'It will not be sufficient for the Commission and Special Advocates to be shown only a summary prepared for the Home Office official, plus any other documents not before the summary writer but taken into account by the Home Office official taking the decision in the name of the Minister' (§36).

(f)   'In the absence of further obligations arising from properly admitted discrimination claims under domestic or EU law, neither domestic law nor Strasbourg authority requires a minimum level of disclosure to the Appellant, where the case does not involve personal liberty' (§48).

This last finding relates not to disclosure to the Commission – in order to carry out its function of 'anxious scrutiny' of the factual basis of a decision under review – but onward disclosure to the appellant by operation of the 'rule 38' process. See **22.14** et seq below which deals in more detail with the principles applicable to disclosure and in special cases (where the right to liberty is engaged or Community law principles are in play). Applicants for review are known as 'appellants' as set out in the Procedure Rules. The Commission has adopted the prefix SN/followed by either anonymised initials or numbers, the name if not anonymised and the year of issue as the form in which review cases will be identified. See below the Commission's approach to anonymisation in the section on Practice and Procedure at **22.16**.

[1] See *AHK v Secretary of State for the Home Department* (SN/2/2014, SN/3/2014, SN/4/2014 and SN/5/2014) (judgment 18 July 2014 unreported) and *Ignaoua v Secretary of State for the Home Department* (SIAC, judgment 31 July 2014).

Review of certain deportation decisions

22.8 Section 18 of the Immigration Act 2014 provides for a further s 2E to be inserted into the Special Immigration Appeals Commission Act 1997. At the time of writing, no date had been appointed for commencement. The new s 2E will provide for a SIAC review of deportation decisions which have been certified under ss 97 or 97A(1) of NIAA 2002 and where there is no right of appeal or where owing to the limited appeal rights, a decision 'gives rise to issues which may not be raised on such an appeal'. That is because, under the Immigration Act 2014, appeal rights are limited to protection and human rights decisions and grounds. There is thus no scope to challenge by way of appeal the justification for deportation including any assertion that a person's removal or exclusion is conducive to the public good by reason of national security. As noted above, SIAC has since June 2013 been seized of a review jurisdiction where the Secretary of State has certified under the amended s 97A of NIAA 2002[1] that a person liable to deportation may be deported pending his appeal as he would not 'face a real risk of serious irreversible harm if removed to the country or territory to which (he) is proposed to be removed'.

[1] In force from 25 June 2013, inserted by the Crime and Courts Act 2013.

PRESENCE OF APPELLANTS IN THE UK

22.9 Section 79 of NIAA 2002, which prevents the making of a deportation order while an appeal against the decision to make the order could be brought or is pending, is disapplied where the Secretary of State certifies that the decision to make the deportation order in respect of a person was taken on the grounds that his removal from the United Kingdom is in the interests of national security.[1] An appeal to SIAC may only be brought from within the United Kingdom if the equivalent right applied had the appeal been to the First-tier Tribunal.[2] The person may, however, appeal against the decision to make a deportation order from within the UK if he or she makes a human rights claim unless the Secretary of State has certified that removal pending the appeal would not be unlawful under s 6 of the Human Rights Act[3] on the grounds that removal would not cause a real risk of serious irreversible harm to the appellant or that all or part of the human rights claim was clearly unfounded.[4]

[1] NIAA 2002, s 97A(1), (1A), (2)(a), (b).
[2] NIAA 2002, s 97A(2)(c)(i), (ii); Special Immigration Appeals Commission Act 1997, s 2(5).
[3] NIAA 2002, s 97A(2B).
[4] Under NIAA 2002, s 97A(2C).

22.10 The SIAC had been the designated court to hear appeals[1] and reviews[2] under the Anti-Terrorism, Crime and Security Act 2001 against the certification of a foreign national as a suspected international terrorist,[3] and against indefinite detention of such persons by derogation from Article 5 of ECHR.[4] In *A* the House of Lords held that the provisions of the 2001 Act which allowed the indefinite detention of foreign nationals were disproportionate, discriminatory and unlawful and made a declaration of incompatibility with Article 5 of ECHR.[5] The provisions in ss 21 and 23 of the 2001 Act expired in March 2005. The procedure for certification of a claim for asylum provided for in s 33 of the 2001 Act remained until it was repealed and replaced with s 55 of the Immigration, Asylum and Nationality Act 2006.

[1] Section 25 of the Anti-terrorism, Crime and Security Act 2001 (ACSA 2001).

[2] ACSA 2001, s 26.

[3] Ie under s 21 of that Act. The Commission was required to cancel the certificate if it believes that the Secretary of State did not have reasonable grounds for the belief or suspicion relied on in issuing the certificate, or for some other reason the certificate should not have been issued.

[4] ACSA 2001, s 30. A derogation order was made in the exercise of the Secretary of State's power under s 14 of the Human Rights Act 1998 on 11 November 2001. The order was rejected by the House of Lords in *A v Secretary of State for the Home Department* [2004] UKHL 56, [2005] 2 AC 68 as incompatible with Article 15 of ECHR because although it was accepted that there was a public emergency, the measures adopted in ss 21 and 23 of the 2001 Act, which were confined to foreign nationals, did not meet the requirements of necessity and proportionality. In *A v United Kingdom* (Application No 3455/05) (2009) 49 EHRR 625, (2009) Times, 20 February, Strasbourg itself held that the 2001 Act had breached Article 5(1) but also concluded that SIAC had failed to provide sufficient procedural protection for the purposes of Article 5(4) in so far as the essence of the case against the detainees had not been disclosed and he had not been able to give effective instructions to the special advocate.

[5] *A v Secretary of State for the Home Department* [2004] UKHL 56, [2005] 2 AC 68.

PROCEDURE AND EVIDENCE BEFORE THE SPECIAL IMMIGRATION APPEALS COMMISSION

Procedure on appeals

22.11 As noted above, the Commission's jurisdiction on an appeal against an appealable decision or a decision to refuse asylum is the same as that of the First-tier Tribunal, in that it must allow the appeal if the decision was not in accordance with the law, including the immigration rules, or a discretion conferred by the rules should have been exercised differently, but otherwise it must dismiss the appeal.[1] The Court of Appeal in *Rehman*[2] agreed with the Commission that its role was a full merits review including reviewing both the facts and the exercise of discretion,[3] but disagreed with them over their definition of the national interest and the deference which should be shown to the decision of the Secretary of State on these matters (see **22.12**, below). It is to be noted that the House of Lords in *A* whilst upholding SIAC's conclusions that the provisions in the 2001 Act were unlawful because they were discriminatory, went further and held that SIAC had afforded too great a degree of deference to the Secretary of State in judging the proportionality of the measures and in particular to the choice by the government of an immigration measure to control a national security threat.[4]

The Lord Chancellor is empowered to make rules for the regulation of the exercise of appeal rights and for prescribing the practice and procedure to be followed in appeals, including rules making provision for the withholding of evidence from the appellant, the exclusion of appellants and their representatives from hearings and the appointment of special advocates.[5] The balancing exercise which has to be performed, and to which the Lord Chancellor is obliged to have regard in making procedural rules, is between the need for a proper review of an executive decision and the need to secure that information is not disclosed contrary to the public interest.[6] The Statute gives no precedence to the public interest. However, the Special Immigration Appeals Commission (Procedure) Rules 2003, require the Commission, as its general duty, to secure that information is not disclosed contrary to the interests of national security, the international relations of the United Kingdom, the detection and prevention of crime, or in any other circumstances where disclosure is likely to harm the public interest.[7] Subject to that clear proviso, the Commission must satisfy itself that the material available to it enables it to properly determine proceedings.[8] In *R (on the application of Cart) v The Upper Tribunal; U v Special Immigration Appeals Commission; XC v Special Immigration Appeals Commission,*[9] the Divisional Court ruled that on an application for bail SIAC was required to read this provision compatibly with Article 5(4) and to ensure that there was a core irreducible minimum of disclosure necessary for the appellant to effectively rebut the allegations against him applying the reasoning of the House of Lords in *AF (No 3)*[10] and Strasbourg in *A v United Kingdom.*[11] However, in *W (Algeria) v Secretary of State for the Home Department,*[12] the Court of Appeal rejected arguments that rule 4(3) could and should be read subject to the similar common law right to a fair trial which requires sufficient disclosure of the case against the appellant. The Court accepted that the common law did require such disclosure to be made but concluded that the rule was clear and unambiguous and intra vires of the statute. Parliament had deliberately legislated to exclude this fundamental aspect of the right to a fair hearing. Similarly, where an appeal or review engages EU law (eg the deportation of an EU national) then the same procedural protections as provided by Article 6 apply and the essence of the case against the appellant must be disclosed to him if the Secretary of State wishes to defend the appeal.[13]

When an appealable decision is made and certified, notice of appeal must be given by filing it simultaneously with the Commission and the Secretary of State.[14] Where an appellant is in detention, the notice must be filed either in the same way, or with the custodian who must then forward it to the Commission and the Secretary of State.[15] The time limit for appealing for those in detention is five days after service of the decision, otherwise if in-country, ten days, and out of country, 28 days.[16] For non-suspensive appeals, the time limit for appealing is 28 days after the appellant's departure from the United Kingdom.[17] The Commission has a discretion to extend time for the filing of a notice of appeal by operation of rule 8(5) 'if satisfied that by reason of special circumstances it would be unjust not to do so'. In *L1 v Secretary of State for the Home Department* [2013] EWCA Civ 906 the Court of Appeal held that a deliberate plan by the Secretary of State to delay service of a decision already taken in principle to coincide with L1's temporary absence from his home in the UK was in itself a 'special circumstance' such that time for the filing of a notice of appeal should be extended. Where an appeal to the First-tier Tribunal lapses due to the issue of a certificate under NIAA 2002, s 97, a new notice of appeal must be given to the Commission with the same time limits for 'original' appeals before the Commission.[18] The notice of appeal must state the grounds of appeal with reasons in support.[19] An appellant may vary the grounds of appeal with the leave of the Commission and must serve a copy of the varied grounds on the Secretary of State.[20] An appeal may be withdrawn by the appellant orally at a hearing or by written notice to the Commission.[21] If the Secretary of State withdraws the decision under appeal, then the appeal will be treated as withdrawn.[22] Every appeal must be determined at a hearing, except where the appeal is abandoned, treated as finally determined, withdrawn by the appellant, where the Secretary of State consents to the appeal being allowed, or where the appellant is outside the United Kingdom or it is impracticable to give him notice of appeal and in either case he is unrepresented.[23] On an asylum appeal UNHCR is entitled to be treated as a party, but on the same terms as the appellant as regards access to closed material.[24] The Procedure Rules also contain provision for representation, the giving of directions, the filing and service of documents, notification of hearings, adjournments, summoning of witnesses and combined hearings, in similar terms to those rules governing appeals to the Asylum and Immigration Tribunal.[25]

Following the expansion of the Commission's role to include a review jurisdiction, the Procedure Rules also make provision for applications for review.

Service of deprivation decisions is governed by reg 10 of the British Nationality (General) Regulations 2003, SI 2003/548. Service may be to the 'last known address' where the deprivee's whereabouts are not known the Secretary of State. Service of immigration decisions is governed by the Immigration (Notices) Regulations 2003, SI 2003/658. The notice must give accurate information regarding appeal rights: *E1/(OS Russia) v Secretary of State for the Home Department* [2012] EWCA Civ 357.

1   Nationality, Immigration and Asylum Act 2002, s 86(3), Special Immigration Appeals Commission Act 1997, s 2(2)(g).

2   *Secretary of State for the Home Department v Rehman (Shafiq Ur)* [2000] INLR 531, CA, upheld by the House of Lords at [2001] UKHL 47, [2003] 1 AC 153. For the Commission decision, see [1999] INLR 517.

3   This was also the approach applied by SIAC under the 2001 Act appeals and approved by the House of Lords in *A v Secretary of State for the Home Department* [2004] UKHL 56, [2005] 2 AC 68, [2005] 3 All ER 169 (see **22.10**, fn 4).

4   A, fn 3 above.

5   Special Immigration Appeals Commission Act 1997, s 5(1) and (3). Practice and procedure is governed by the Special Immigration Commission Appeals (Procedure) Rules 2003, SI 2003/1034, as amended by the Special Immigration Appeals Commission (Procedure) (Amendment) Rules 2007, SI 2007/1285 and the Special Immigration Appeals Commission (Procedure) (Amendment No 2) Rules 2007, SI 2007/3370.

6   Special Immigration Appeals Commission Act 1997, s 5(6).

7   Special Immigration Commission Appeals (Procedure) Rules 2003, SI 2003/1034, r 4(1). In *Y and Othman v Secretary of State for the Home Department* (SC/36, 15/2002), Judgment on disclosure following interlocutory application for directions, 12 July 2006, the Commission held that 'public interest' did not include a public interest that someone should not be returned to face torture, and further, that rule 4 did not embody a balancing exercise between the risk to the protected interest and the need of an appellant to know some aspect of the case relied on against him, or indeed which might be helpful to him.

8   SI 2003/1034, r 4(3).

9   [2009] EWHC 3052 (Admin), [2010] 1 All ER 908, [2010] 2 FCR 309.

10   *Secretary of State for the Home Department v AF* [2009] UKHL 28, [2009] 3 All ER 643 [2009] 3 WLR 74. The House of Lords ruled that in control order proceedings under the Prevention of Terrorism Act 2005 following the reasons of the EctHR in *A and Ors v UK* (challenge in Strasbourg to the detention under the 2001 Act) in respect of minimum standards

of procedural fairness for the purpose of Article 5(4) and Article 6, that national security could not justify denial of the essence of a fair hearing and core irreducible minimum of the case against the appellant was necessary in order to provide the special advocate with effective instructions to rebut the case. In the absence of this minimum degree of disclosure the special advocate could not provide the substantial measure of procedural protection required.

11 *(Application No 3455/05)*, (2009) 49 EHRR 625, (2009) Times, 20 February.

12 [2010] EWCA Civ 898.

13 *ZZ (France) v Secretary of State for the Home Department (No 2)* [2014] EWCA Civ 7.

14 SI 2003/1034, r 7(2) and (4).

15 SI 2003/1034, r 7(3) and (5).

16 SI 2003/1034, r 8(1).

17 SI 2003/1034, r 8(2).

18 SI 2003/1034, r 8(3) and (4).

19 SI 2003/1034, r 9. The notice of appeal is not in a prescribed form but must contain the appellant's name, address, representative and grounds, and must be signed by the appellant or representative, and dated: rr 9(2), (3), 14(6), (7). If signed by the representative, the representative must certify that the notice has been completed in accordance with the appellant's instructions, and must attach a copy of the decision appealed: r 9(4).

20 SI 2003/1034, r 11.

21 SI 2003/1034, r 11A(1).

22 SI 2003/1034, r 11A(2).

23 SI 2003/1034, r 12.

24 SI 2003/1034 r 32(2), (3).

25 See SI 2003/1034, rr 32–33 (parties and representation), 39–40 (directions; the power is always subject to the obligation that information is not disclosed contrary to the public interest as per rule 4; on non-compliance the Commission may issue an 'unless' order requiring compliance with a stated period, in default of which the appeal proceeds without the relevant evidence, or will result in a strike out of the notice of appeal or Secretary of State's reply as the case may be), 41 (notification of hearing), 42 (adjournments), 44–5 (evidence and summoning of witnesses), 46 (combined hearings), 49–50 (filing and service of documents), 51 (calculation of time), 52 (signature of documents), 53 (procedural errors), 54 (correction of slips).

22.12 In the light of the general duty on the Commission not to disclose information contrary to the interests of national security, diplomatic relations, the detection and prevention of crime, or the public interest, the special advocate system has been devised. When the Secretary of State is served with a notice of appeal or application under the 1997 Act, then, unless it is intended to concede the appeal or not to object to the disclosure of any material on which the decision is based, the relevant law officer[1] must be notified of the proceedings,[2] with a view to appointing a special advocate. This is a security-vetted lawyer who represents the appellant's interests on the appeal but is not instructed by or responsible to the appellant.[3] The special advocate is entitled to see the 'closed material' made available to SIAC, to make private submissions and discuss with the Home Office's legal team items in the closed material which should be disclosed, to argue the issue of disclosure before SIAC where no agreement on disclosure has been reached in prior discussions with the Crown lawyers, to make any other submissions at any hearing from which appellants and their representatives are excluded,[4] to adduce evidence from and cross-examine witnesses at such hearings and make written submissions.[5] The special advocate may communicate with the appellant or his representatives at any time before the Secretary of State serves 'closed material'.[6] After this time, such communication is prohibited unless the Commission otherwise directs.[7] The special advocate can request such a direction, but must notify the Secretary of State of the request, in response to which the Secretary of State must, within a period specified by the Commission, file with the Commission and serve on the special advocate notice of any objection to the proposed communication.[8] The appellant can communicate with the special advocate after the service of closed material but only in writing through a legal representative, and the special advocate may not reply, apart from sending a written acknowledgement, without a direction from the Commission which will normally be consequent upon security clearance by the Secretary of State's representatives who will necessarily become aware of its contents.[9] The House of Lords in *RB (Algeria) v Secretary of State for the Home Department*[10] upheld this process as lawful and compatible with Convention rights. It rejected arguments that Article 6 applied to deportation appeals and concluded that there was no breach of procedural fairness in cases where reliance was placed on Article 3 ECHR and closed material was utilised. The Court did, however, hold that where diplomatic assurances where relied upon to obviate otherwise existing Article 3 risks, the assurances themselves and the key conversations or documents relating to assurances had to be in the open. Despite this ruling the Secretary of State has since attempted to rely upon wholly secret diplomatic assurances not disclosed in the open material in national security deportations to Pakistan.[11]

1   The Attorney-General in England and Wales, the Lord Advocate in Scotland and the Attorney General for Northern Ireland in Northern Ireland: Special Immigration Appeals Commission Act 1997, s 6(2).
2   Special Immigration Commission Appeals (Procedure) Rules 2003, SI 2003/1034, r 34.
3   Special Immigration Appeals Commission Act 1997, s 6(1) and (4). The Courts have commented on the nebulous nature of their position and special advocates have explained to the courts the fundamental limitations of their role in *RB (Algeria) v Secretary of State for the Home Department* [2009] UKHL 10, [2009] 4 All ER 1045, [2009] 2 WLR 512 and given evidence to like effect to Parliament.
4   In *N v Secretary of State for the Home Department* [2006] EWCA Civ 299 (28 March 2006), the Court of Appeal gave permission to appeal against the findings of SIAC on legal submissions made by the special advocates in closed session and shortly thereafter the Home Office conceded the case and revoked a deportation order made against the appellant.
5   SI 2003/1034, r 35.
6   SI 2003/1034, r 36(1).
7   SI 2003/1034, r 36(2).
8   SI 2003/1034, r 36(4) and (5).
9   SI 2003/1034, r 36(6). The Secretary of State is not to make forensic use of such communications: *BG v Secretary of State for the Home Department* [2011] EWHC 1478 (Admin).
10 [2009] UKHL 10, [2009] 4 All ER 1045 [2009] 2 WLR 512, fn 3 above.
11 *Abid Nasser (XC) v Secretary of State for the Home Department* (SC/77/2005), 18 May 2010, unreported).

22.13 After the filing of the notice of appeal, the Commission will fix a directions hearing as soon as reasonably practicable, at which parties and their representatives and special advocates may attend.[1] At this hearing, the Commission may give directions as to the order in which, and the time within which various documents are to be filed and served.[2] Where the Secretary of State intends to oppose an appeal, she must file with the Commission a statement of the evidence on which she relies in opposition to the appeal, and any exculpatory material of which she is aware.[3] The statement must be disclosed to the appellant or his representative unless the Secretary of State objects.[4] The statement must always be served on the special advocate.[5] Uniquely, the Commission may 'strike out' a notice of appeal or the Secretary of State's reply if they disclose no reasonable grounds for bringing or defending the appeal respectively, or may strike out a notice of appeal if it appears to be an abuse of the Commission's process.[6] Where the appellant wishes to rely on evidence in support of his appeal, he must file with the Commission, and serve on the Secretary of State and special advocate a statement of that evidence.[7] Such a statement triggers a duty upon the Secretary of State to make a reasonable search for exculpatory material.[8] The appellant or the special advocate may apply to the Commission for a direction requiring the Secretary of State to file further information about his or her case, or other information.[9] Such an application must indicate why the information is necessary for the determination of the appeal, and the Commission may make the direction where it considers that the information sought is necessary and can be provided without disproportionate cost, time or effort.[10] Any statement, material or information arising from a search or in response to a direction must be served on the special advocate and the appellant unless the Secretary of State objects to such disclosure to the appellant or his representative.[11] The duty to file material or statements of evidence is a continuing one until the appeal has been determined.[12]

1   Special Immigration Commission Appeals (Procedure) Rules 2003, SI 2003/1034, r 9A(1).
2   SI 2003/1034, r 9A(2) and (3), namely documents under rr 10–10A and rr 37–38 (see below). At this hearing, the Commission may also give directions in relation to bail applications and objections by the Secretary of State in relation to requests by the special advocate for communication post service of 'closed material', and in relation to disclosure.
3   SI 2003/1034, r 10(1). The procedure rules call these documents the 'Secretary of State's reply'.
4   SI 2003/1034, r 10(2). Where the Secretary of State objects to such disclosure, rules 37 and 38 apply: r 10(3).
5   SI 2003/1034, r 10(4).
6   SI 2003/1034, r 11B.
7   SI 2003/1034, r 10A(1).
8   SI 2003/1034, r 10A(2). Any such exculpatory material should be filed with the Commission: r 10(2)(c). The Secretary of State must notify the appellant of the extent of the search, however, where the Secretary of State considers that the disclosure of particular information in such notification would be contrary to the public interest he or she must omit that information from the notification and serve the notification including that information on the special advocate: r 10A(4). Relevant factors in deciding the reasonableness of the search include the number of documents involved, the nature and complexity of the proceedings, whether the Secretary of State controls the documents, the ease and expense of retrieval and the significance of any document: r 10A(3). In the context of national security deportations, the Secretary of State has accepted that this is material which advanced an Appellant's case or undermined her own, in relation to safety on return as well as in relation to national security: *Y and Othman v Secretary of State for the Home Department* (SC/36, 15/2002), Judgment on disclosure following interlocutory application for directions, 12 July 2006.
9   SI 2003/1034, r 10A(6).
10 SI 2003/1034, r 10A(6) and (7).
11 SI 2003/1034, r 10A(8). Where the Secretary of State objects to such disclosure, rules 37 and 38 apply: r 10A(9).
12 SI 2003/1034, r 10A(10), subject to the any disclosure objection by the Secretary of State: r 10A(11).

Closed material and disclosure

22.14 'Closed material' is defined as material upon which the Secretary of State wishes to rely; material which adversely affects his or her case or supports the appellant's case, or material which she must file pursuant to a direction, but which she objects to being disclosed to the appellant or his representative.[1] The Secretary of State must file with the Commission and serve on the special advocate the closed material and a statement of his or her reasons for objecting to its disclosure.[2] The Secretary of State is also required to serve, if and to the extent that it is possible to do so without disclosing information contrary to the public interest, a statement of the closed material in a form which can be served on the appellant.[3] In practice the Secretary of State almost always takes the position that this cannot be done. In the light of the trenchant observations of the Supreme Court in *Bank Mellat*[4] regarding over-reliance by the Secretary of State on closed material, the practice of the Secretary of State may be under greater scrutiny. The Commission's procedures have sufficient flexibility to ensure that appellants can test at every stage whether the public interest in non-disclosure has become replaced with a practice which has hardened into a rule. Where closed material which has been redacted on grounds other than legal professional privilege is served on the special advocate, the unredacted material must be filed with the Commission together with an explanation for the redactions.[5] The Commission will then give a direction as to what the Secretary of State may redact.[6] Where the Secretary of State objects to the disclosure of any material to the appellant or his representatives or objects to a special advocate's request for post 'closed material' communication with the appellant or his representative, the Commission must fix a hearing for the Secretary of State and the special advocate to make oral representations.[7] This is referred to as a 'rule 38' hearing which neither the appellant nor his representative may attend.[8] In non-EU appeals, the following procedure applies. The Commission should test the Secretary of State's assertion that material should not be disclosed. It may uphold or overrule the Secretary of State's objection, but must always uphold the Secretary of State's objection on closed material where it considers that disclosure would be contrary to the public interest.[9] If the Secretary of State's objection is upheld, the Commission must consider whether to direct the Secretary of State to serve a summary of the closed material on the appellant, and must approve such summary to ensure that disclosure of its contents is not contrary to the public interest.[10] If the Secretary of State's objection is overruled or service on the appellant of a summary of the closed material is directed, the Secretary of State will not be required to serve the summary or that material.[11] If she chooses not to do so the Commission may, after hearing representations from the Secretary of State and the special advocate, direct that the Secretary of State shall not rely on such points in his or her case or shall make concessions or take such other steps, as the Commission may specify.[12] The Commission has a general power to exclude an appellant and his representative from a hearing or part of the hearing in order to secure that information is not disclosed contrary to the public interest (namely when closed evidence is being heard) or 'for any other good reason'.[13] In *BB v Secretary of State for the Home Department*,[14] the Commission held that in theory, as a court of superior record it could regulate its own procedure, and hence it had the general powers of direction which were broad enough to direct that certain hearings be held 'in private', ie including the appellant and his representatives, but excluding the public and press, or that certain material be 'restricted open material', ie disclosed to an appellant's representative with the consent of the appellant not to seek sight of documents or to be present at parts of a hearing when particular matters were discussed. The Commission held however, that the clear terms of Rule 4 of the Procedure Rules and the 'bright line' which existed within the entire structure of the Commission, the special advocate system and the Procedure Rules, between 'open' and 'closed' material meant, that this sharp division had to be observed in practice, that in reality 'restricted open material' and 'in private' hearings were tantamount to making 'closed' material 'open', and hence that there were no circumstances in which these powers could ever be deployed.[15] Since then, however, such restricted disclosure and private hearings have occurred in SIAC[16] and in Control Order proceedings. In *RB (Algeria) v Secretary of State for the Home Department; OO (Jordan) v Secretary of State*, the House of Lords rejected the proposition that closed material could only be relied upon where the interests of national security required non-disclosure; it was clear that the Procedure Rules permitted other public interest considerations (eg the interests of relations with another state) to justify non-disclosure of evidence both in relation to any national security case but also in relation to the issue of risk on return.[17] Ironically, given that one of the principal issues before the House of Lords was the reliability of government assurances, the Secretary of State's case that use of closed material need not be limited to situations where it was necessary in the interests of national security breached the assurance to the contrary that she had given to Parliament.[18] It is to be noted that in *Chahal* the ECtHR clearly did not contemplate the use of secret evidence in respect of Article 3 issues.

[1] Special Immigration Commission Appeals (Procedure) Rules 2003, SI 2003/1034, r 37(1).
[2] SI 2003/1034, r 37(3)(a) and (b).
[3] SI 2003/1034, r 37(3)(c).
[4] [2013] UKSC 38 at §§70-74
[5] SI 2003/1034, r 37(4A)(a).
[6] SI 2003/1034, r 37(4A)(b).
[7] SI 2003/1034, r 38(2). The Commission need not hold a hearing if (a) the special advocate does not challenge the objection, (b) the Commission has previously upheld an objection relating to the same or substantially the same material or communication, and is satisfied that it would be just to uphold the objection without a hearing, or (c) the Secretary of State and special advocate consent to the Commission deciding the issue without a hearing. If the special advocate does not challenge the objection, he or she must give notice of that fact to the Commission and the Secretary of State within 14 days after receipt of notice of a post closed material communication objection or receipt of closed material
[8] SI 2003/1034, r 38(5).
[9] SI 2003/1034, r 38(6) and (7).
[10] SI 2003/1034, r 38(8).
[11] SI 2003/1034, r 38(9)(a).
[12] SI 2003/1034, r 38(9)(b)(i). Where the Secretary of State defies a Commission ruling on disclosure, the Commission appears to have very broad powers to compel the Secretary of State to act in a certain manner. This provision came into force on 7 May 2007. Its predecessor simply allowed the Secretary of State not to rely on the material in the face of an overruled objection therefore not to serve on the appellant notwithstanding a direction to do so. The amendment may have been as a result of the Commission's ruling in *Y and Othman v Secretary of State for the Home Department* (SC/36, 15/2002), Judgment on disclosure following interlocutory application for directions, 12 July 2006: Whilst the Commission was not required to resolve the issue of whether the Secretary of State was permitted to withdraw material in respect of which his objection to open disclosure had been overruled by the Commission, where that material was helpful to the appellant, it stated that there would be strong concerns by the Commission and that adverse inferences could be drawn. It further stated that 'the Commission would be surprised to see its judgment as to what did not constitute a risk to a protected interest overridden, where there is no balance to be struck, particularly over material helpful to an Appellant'.
[13] SI 2003/1034, r 43(1) and (2).
[14] *BB v Secretary of State for the Home Department* (SC/36, 15/2002), Judgment on closed material following interlocutory application, 14 November 2006.
[15] Similar proposals put forward by Liberty intervening in *RB (Algeria) v Secretary of State for the Home Department; Othman (Jordan) v Secretary of State* [2009] UKHL 10, [2009] 4 All ER 1045, [2009] 2 WLR 512 were rejected in the House of Lords.

¹⁶ In two deportation appeals the Secretary of State inadvertently disclosed closed material to the appellant's representatives and SIAC decided in both cases that this material could be utilised on their behalf but in private hearings with confidentiality undertakings.

¹⁷ [2009] UKHL 10, [2009] 2 WLR 512 applying r 4 of the Special Immigration Appeals Commission (Procedure) Rules 2003, SI 2003/1034 and rejecting the argument that the rule was ultra vires the rule making power under Special Immigration Appeals Commission Act 1997, s 5.

¹⁸ *RB* para 80 for the assurance given by the Minister to Parliament.

The approach in cases engaging EU law and article 6

22.15 In *ZZ (France) v Secretary of State for the Home Department (No 2)*,[1] the Court of Appeal confirmed following the judgment of the Court of Justice of the European Union (CJEU) in the same case[2] that where the state authority refused to permit a citizen of the European Union admission to the United Kingdom on grounds of public security, the national court had to ensure, as a minimum requirement, that he was informed of the essence of the grounds for the decision. While the manner in which that was done had to take due account of the necessary confidentiality of the related evidence against him, the need to protect such confidentiality was not capable of justifying non-disclosure of the essence of the grounds. The Court of Appeal considered the meaning and effect of the CJEU's judgment. ZZ submitted that in an EU case the national court was required to balance the interests of the state against the interests of the individual in determining whether and to what extent there should be anything less than precise and full disclosure of grounds and evidence where national security was invoked, but that there was in any event a core minimum level of disclosure which could not be less than the essence of the grounds on which the decision was based. The Secretary of State's position was that a national court which had proper oversight of the decision to exclude on grounds of national security and, in particular, whose procedure ensures that the person was provided with as much information as possible as to the reasons for his exclusion was enough – disclosure of the essence of the grounds always had to take account of the confidentiality of the evidence, so that if such disclosure would undermine the confidentiality of the evidence, it was not, as a matter of EU law, necessary to make the disclosure. The court held that the CJEU's judgment laid down with reasonable clarity that the essence of the grounds on which the decision was based had *always* to be disclosed to the person concerned. That was a minimum requirement which could not yield to the demands of national security having regard to Article 47 of the Charter of Fundamental Rights of the European Union which conferred a fundamental right to an effective remedy. The requirements of national security might impose some limitations but there was no suggestion that a person's procedural rights in an EU case might have to give way altogether to national security considerations. The court drew a distinction between the CJEU's approach to 'the grounds' and 'the related evidence' which formed the basis for a decision. In the light of the need to comply with Article 47 of the Charter, the procedure had to ensure to the greatest possible extent that the adversarial principle was complied with so as to enable the person to put forward an effective defence. In a judgment handed down by the Commission on 8 August 2014,[3] SIAC held that it would apply the 'plain English' meaning to the phrase 'the essence of the grounds' and acknowledged that in future cases the CJEU judgment means that SIAC must determine in an EU case whether there is justification within EU legal principles to withhold full and detailed reasons in any event. This will entail ensuring that in an EU case the Secretary of State makes clear which of the bases for certification under s 97 of the Special Immigration Appeals Act is in play. Lastly, the Commission made clear that the impact of the judgment on Procedure Rule 4(1) (the Commission's duty to ensure no disclosure where it is likely to harm the public interest) was not that rule 4(1) did not apply in EU cases, but that it would have to be 'read down' and is only qualified so far as is necessary to comply with EU law.

1   [2014] EWCA Civ 7.
2   [2013] QB 1136.
3   ZZ v Secretary of State for the Home Department SC/63/2007.

Protection for witnesses in cases of sensitive evidence

22.16 In *W (Algeria) v Secretary of State for the Home Department*,[1] the Supreme Court considered whether the appellants, in a deportation with assurances case, should be granted an absolute and irrevocable order that protected the identity of witnesses who were able to give evidence directly relevant to the issue of risk on return to Algeria. The appellants sought an order which would have prevented disclosure of those witnesses' identities to the Secretary of State. The witnesses would not give their evidence unless it could be guaranteed that their identity and what they had to say – since it would identify them – would be withheld from the authorities. The Secretary of State refused to be bound not to disclose this information in the interests of foreign relations. The Procedure Rules did not make provision for such a 'reverse closed' situation. The Supreme Court considered that the Secretary of State's fundamental objection to the proposed order, based on her concerns about being obliged to withhold vital information relating to national security from a foreign state, thereby imperilling future diplomatic relations, was unpersuasive as it was a substantial defence to any diplomatic complaint by a foreign state that the Secretary of State is subject to a final and absolute court order prohibiting her from acting differently. There were also a number of recent international instruments urging states to ensure that witnesses are protected against ill-treatment or intimidation, particularly in a human rights context. The Supreme Court held that the imperative need was to maximise SIAC's chances of arriving at the correct decision on the issue before them concerning the safety of the appellants on return to Algeria and, therefore, for SIAC to obtain all such evidence as may contribute to this task. Accordingly, it was open to SIAC to make absolute and irreversible ex parte orders of the kind sought in this case and in future cases where it may be appropriate to do so. The power to make such orders should however be used most sparingly. Before making one of the proposed ex parte orders, SIAC should require the very fullest disclosure from the applicant for such an order of:

(a)   the proposed evidence from A's proposed witness;
(b)   the particular circumstances in which the witness claims to fear reprisals; and

(c)   how the applicant and his legal advisers came to hear about the proposed evidence and what if any steps they have taken to encourage the witness to give that evidence in the usual way subject to the usual steps generally taken to safeguard witnesses in such circumstances (eg anonymity orders and hearings in private).

SIAC should only then, in the interests of justice, grant such an order if it:

(i)   is satisfied that a witness can give evidence which appears to be capable of belief and which could be decisive or at least highly material on the issue of safety of return; and

(ii)   has no reason to doubt that the witness genuinely and reasonably fears that he and/or others close to him would face reprisals if his identity and the evidence that he is willing to give were disclosed to the relevant foreign state.

The Court, in permitting the making of such *without notice* orders in the circumstances of this case noted that the scope of the orders sought here should not be regarded as 'levelling the playing field' between the parties because the Secretary of State in cases before SIAC acts in the wider public interest and not as an interested party. The same considerations and the same result would follow if the case – engaging as it does here the rights of the appellants under Article 3 of the ECHR – raised a question under Article 2 of the same. However, if the ground on which an appellant is resisting deportation is an alleged risk of breach of some other article of the ECHR (eg Article 8), the balance will almost certainly be struck the other way. In those circumstances it would be inappropriate to make an ex parte order to protect the confidentiality of a witness. As a consequence it is possible that a single case may have several categories of evidence: open, closed, anonymised and protected or confidential. In practice thus far, 'W' orders are rarely made and must be carefully and thoroughly supported by evidence. It remains to be seen what impact the UK government's recent disclosure[2] of policies regarding the use by the Security Services of material protected by Legal Professional Privilege will have on SIAC practice. In a recent decision[3] the Commission has held that complaints about the policies and practices involved in the obtaining and use of such information are for the Investigatory Powers Tribunal, not SIAC. The Commission continued:

> 'However, that does not preclude an application in SIAC for an abuse of process, where such application is founded in the specific facts revealed to SIAC. SIAC must have the power to protect itself from abuse. If, on the facts, it could be shown in a given case that information was obtained in breach of the safeguards, obtained deliberately in an unlawful manner, then that might well be a relevant matter for SIAC in an abuse of process application.'

[1]   [2012] UKSC 8, [2012] 2 AC 115.
[2]   *Belhadj v Security Service* (IPT/13/132-9/H) (6 November 2014, unreported).
[3]   See the Commission's ruling in *ZZ v Secretary of State for the Home Department* [2014] UKSIAC B1 (14 November 2014).

'National security' deportations

22.17 Following the expiry of the provisions of the Anti-Terrorism, Crime and Security Act 2001 which allowed for the indefinite detention of foreign nationals, the vast majority of cases before the Commission are national security deportation cases. They begin with the Secretary of State decision to deport the appellant on the grounds that deportation is deemed to be 'conducive to the public good',[1] and then certifying under the NIAA 2002, s 97, that the decision was taken in the interests of national security. Such appeals generally fall into two halves, first, the 'national security case', and second, issues relating to safety on return. In *Rehman*[2] the House of Lords agreed with the Court of Appeal that the Commission had taken too narrow a view of what could constitute a threat to national security. It was held that a global approach had to be taken to the question of what the interests of national security were, that the action did not have to be either directly or immediately against the UK, that action against a foreign state may be capable of indirectly affecting the security of the UK, and that there would be significant deference given to the Secretary of State's view on this.[3] Their Lordships further agreed with the Court of Appeal that the concept of a 'standard of proof' was not particularly helpful in the national security deportation concept. Where the focus of the enquiry was the assessment of future risk, proof of past facts to the civil standard was not necessary to reach the conclusion that a person poses a danger to national security, and that the question was to be answered by a cumulative evaluation of all the evidence in relation to the actual and potential activities and connections of the person concerned and the importance of the security interest at stake. The Commission has held that Sedley LJ's approach to evidence in *Karanakaran v Secretary of State for the Home Department*[4] was of equal force in the assessment of danger to national security as it was to risk under the Refugee Convention.[5] However, SIAC has held that where specific acts which have already occurred are relied upon, they should be proved to the civil standard of proof.[6] Few appellants have succeeded in the national security case.[7]

---

[1] Immigration Act 1971, s 3(5).

[2] *Secretary of State for the Home Department v Rehman (Shafiq Ur)* [2000] INLR 531, CA, upheld by the House of Lords at [2001] UKHL 47, [2003] 1 AC 153. For the Commission decision, see [1999] INLR 517.

[3] Lord Hoffman at paragraph 62: '*Postscript.* I wrote this speech some three months before the recent events in New York and Washington. They are a reminder that in matters of national security, the cost of failure can be high. This seems to me to underline the need for the judicial arm of government to respect the decisions of ministers of the Crown on the question of whether support for terrorist activities in a foreign country constitutes a threat to national security. It is not only that the executive has access to special information and expertise in these matters. It is also that such decisions, with serious potential results for the community, require a legitimacy which can be conferred only by entrusting them to persons responsible to the community through the democratic process. If the people are to accept the consequences of such decisions, they must be made by persons whom the people have elected and whom they can remove'.

[4] *Karanakaran v Secretary of State for the Home Department* [2000] Imm AR 271.

[5] *Y v Secretary of State for the Home Department* (SC/36/2005), 24 August 2006.

[6] *ZZ v Secretary of State for the Home Department* (SC/63/2007) 30 July 2008, *EV v Secretary of State for the Home Department* (SC/67/2008), 7 April 2009 and *OL v Secretary of State for the Home Department* (SC/86/2009), 27 May 2010.

[7] *Moloud Sihali v Secretary of State for the Home Department* (SC/38/2007), 14 May 2007. *T v Secretary of State for the Home Department* (SC/31/2005), 22 March 2010.

22.18 In appeals where the national security case has been made out appellants will invariably be denied the protection, to which they otherwise would have been entitled, under the Refugee Convention.[1] Such appellants therefore only have the safety net of the ECHR. It is often the case that those being deported are at risk of torture and ill-treatment in their home country. However this has not deterred the Secretary of State from seeking to deport such persons. The Secretary of State has attempted to achieve this by seeking assurances, in the form of Memoranda of Understanding (MOUs) with countries such as Algeria,[2] Jordan[3] Libya[4] and Ethiopia.[5] These are assurances from the governments of the receiving state that they will respect the human rights of deportees. The very fact that diplomatic assurances are required amounts to a recognition by the Secretary of State that but for such assurances, the profile of the appellants taken in conjunction with the poor human rights situation in those countries would lead to them being at risk of having their human rights breached, by being seriously ill-treated or tortured. The consensus amongst the leading NGOs, and shared by the UN Special Rapporteur on Torture and the UN High Commissioner for Human Rights,[6] is that diplomatic assurances cannot be relied on to prevent torture or ill treatment. However, other than in the case of Libya, the Commission has accepted that diplomatic assurances from the Algerian and Jordanian governments mean that there are no substantial grounds for believing that there is a real risk that deportees from those countries will be subjected to treatment contrary to Article 3 ECHR. In *MT (Algeria) and Ors*[7] the Court of Appeal held that the legitimacy of diplomatic assurances depended on the facts of each case, rather than upon any legal principle which outlawed reliance on them *per se*. In doing so, the Court relied on the European Court of Human Rights decision in *Chahal v United Kingdom*,[8] stating that the conclusion on Article 3 of the ECHR in that case was reached after an analysis of the facts of the case and of the particular vulnerability of Mr Chahal, rather than by the application of any rule of law or thumb. Seen within the wider context of the substantial evidence which now exists in relation to the use of 'extraordinary rendition'[9] the effectiveness of MUMs must be in some doubt and their use by the Secretary of State and their ratification by the Commission in the case of countries with a proven track record of torture continues to be a matter of considerable concern. The approach to be taken by SIAC to the issue of assurances was considered by the House of Lords in *RB (Algeria) v Secretary of State for the Home Department; OO (Jordan) v Secretary of State*.[10] Their Lordships endorsed the approach of the Court of Appeal in *MT (Algeria)*, holding that whilst assurances from countries which have a track record of endemic torture should be treated with scepticism, the question of whether assurances could be relied upon was a matter of fact for determination by SIAC and that SIAC had lawfully concluded that the particular assurances from Algeria and Jordan, although not guarantees that no harm would occur, could be relied upon to obviate the real risk[11] of an Article 3 breach that otherwise existed. Assurances were utilised for the first time in a non-national security removal before SIAC in the case of *Sihali*[12] despite the clear terms of the negotiations between the UK and Algeria and statements to Parliament, and other international bodies including the UN that the use of diplomatic assurances was to be confined to an exceptional category of national security cases.[13] SIAC ruled that there was no policy covering the situation where a person like Mr Sihali had succeeded in overturning the national security case on an appeal but an assurance had in the past been negotiated in respect of his return, albeit on the erroneous premise that he was a national security risk.

¹ See CHAPTER 12 in relation to exclusion and expulsion of refugees.

² *Y v Secretary of State for the Home Department* (SC/36/2005), 24 August 2006, where the Commission accepted that diplomatic assurances offered by the Algerian government were satisfactory such that the appellant was not at risk. This decision was subject to an appeal to the Court of Appeal: *MT (Algeria) v Secretary of State for the Home Department; RB (Algeria) v Secretary of State for the Home Department; U (Algeria) v Secretary of State for the Home Department* [2007] EWCA Civ 808, [2008] QB 533, and was allowed and was remitted back to the Commission. The appeal was again dismissed by the Commission in the conjoined appeals of *Y, BB & U v Secretary of State for the Home Department* (SC/21/36/39/2005), 2 November 2007. Since the initial decision in *Y*, a number of Algerians have had appeals dismissed on the basis of the diplomatic assurances from the Algerian government.

³ *Omar Othman v Secretary of State for the Home Department* (SC/15/2005), 26 February 2007, where the Commission accepted that diplomatic assurances offered by the Jordanian government were satisfactory such that the appellant was not at risk. This decision was followed in the appeal of another Jordanian national: *VV v Secretary of State for the Home Department* (SC/59/2006), 2 November 2007.

⁴ *DD and AS v Secretary of State for the Home Department* (SC/42, 50/2005), 27 April 2007. In these appeals, the Commission rejected the assurances given by the Libyan government as to the safety of the appellants, and therefore found that the deportations would breach Article 3. The Secretary of State unsuccessfully appealed to the Court of Appeal, who held that SIAC's conclusion was open to it: *AS & DD (Libya) v Secretary of State for the Home Department* [2008] EWCA Civ 289.

⁵ *XX v Secretary of State for the Home Department* [2012] EWCA Civ 742, [2013] QB 656, [2012] 4 All ER 692.

⁶ See paras 292–303 of *Omar Othman*, fn 3 above.

⁷ *MT (Algeria) v Secretary of State for the Home Department* [2007] EWCA Civ 808, (2007) Times, 3 August.

⁸ *Chahal v United Kingdom* (1996) 23 EHRR 413. The ECtHR has, in a number of cases, considered the weight to be attached to diplomatic assurances in the assessment of whether expulsion would result in a breach of Article 3 ECHR. In *Saadi v Italy* [2008] INLR 621, in a case concerning expulsion to Tunisia, the Grand Chamber of the Court stated that 'The weight to be given to assurances from the receiving State depends, in each case, on the circumstances obtaining at the material time' (para 148). With regard to expulsion to Uzbekistan, see: *Mamatkulov and Askarov v Turkey* (2005) 41 EHRR 25, *Ismoilov v Russia Application 2947/06)* [2008] 49 EHRR 1128, ECtHR and *Muminov v Russia* [2008] ECHR 1683; expulsion to Turkmenistan: *Soldatenko v Ukraine* [2008] ECHR 1142 and *Ryabikin v Russia* (2008) 48 EHRR 1322, ECtHR; expulsion to Kazakhstan: *Kaboulov v Ukraine* [2009] ECHR 1903 and *Baysakov v Ukraine* [2010] ECHR 221, In *Ben Khem v Italy* *(February 2009)* and *Abdelahi v Italy and Ors (March 2009)* which were decided after *RB*, the ECtHR has rejected assurances from Tunisia which are in very similar terms to the Algerian assurances negotiated with the UK placing significant weight on the lack of any independent means of verifying the conditions of the returnee. See also *Al-Sadoon and Mufdhi v United Kingdom* [2010] ECHR 285 relating to assurances within the context of transfer of detainees from British custody in Iraq to the custody of Iraqi forces.

⁹ See paras 320–333 of *Omar Othman*, fn 3 above.

¹⁰ *RB (Algeria) v Secretary of State for the Home Department; Othman (Jordan) v Secretary of State for the Home Department* [2009] UKHL 10, [2009] 2 WLR 512.

¹¹ *Sihali v Secretary of State for the Home Department* (SC38/2005), 27 March 2010.

¹² Response by the United Kingdom to Recommendations by the United Nations Committee against Torture following its Examination of the United Kingdom's 4th Periodic Report on 17 and 18 November 2004: '50. In certain circumstances, the Government will seek to remove a foreign national from the UK following receipt of assurances from the government of the country to which the person is to be removed regarding the future treatment of that person. Although the Government would only seek to do this in exceptional circumstances, it believes that seeking such assurances is a sensible measure in some cases where the presence of the person in the UK is not conducive to the public good, or where it considers that the person represents a security risk.'

13 The House of Lords also held that there was no principle that such assurances must eliminate
all risk of inhuman treatment before they could be relied upon; what mattered was whether on
an analysis of all the relevant circumstances, including the assurances, there were no
substantial grounds for believing that a deportee will be at real risk (paras 114). This may not
be consistent with the approach of the ECtHR in *Khemais* and *Abdelahi* which required that
the assurances 'eliminate' the risk – see fn 8 above.

Evidence obtained by torture

22.19 The Commission may receive evidence which is not admissible in a
court of law,[1] and the Commission and the Court of Appeal unpardonably
held that in an appeal under the Anti-Terrorism, Crime and Security Act 2001,
this may include evidence obtained through torture.[2] These decisions were
however emphatically overruled by the House of Lords in *A and Ors v
Secretary of State for the Home Department*.[3] The House held that the Commission could not receive evidence that had or might have been procured by
torture inflicted by officials of a foreign state without the complicity of the
British authorities.[4] The more difficult point arose in relation to the burden and
standard of proving that the evidence had been obtained by torture. The
majority, guided by the wording of Article 15 of the 1984 Convention against
Torture requiring the exclusion of statements 'established' to have been
obtained by torture, held that the Commission should refuse to admit evidence
relied on by the Secretary of State if it concluded on a balance of probabilities
that the evidence had been obtained by torture, but that if the Commission was
left in doubt as to whether the evidence had been obtained by torture, then it
should admit it, but it had to bear its doubt in mind when evaluating the
evidence. The majority did not suggest that the appellant is expected to
shoulder the entire burden of demonstrating that a particular piece of evidence
was obtained by torture. Such a burden would, the majority accepted, be
unrealistic in the particular context of the Commission where the appellant
may not even know what material has been adduced. Lord Hope[5] suggested
that an appellant should be required only to raise the issue by pointing to the
fact that the information which is to be used against him may have come from
a country known or suspected to practice torture. Lord Rodger[6] suggested that
the investigation into the sources of the evidence would then be shared by the
Secretary of State and the Commission. Whilst the outright condemnation of
the reliance on evidence obtained by torture is welcomed, the decision of the
majority as to the standard of proof may well have the effect of undermining
the real effectiveness of the condemnation. The minority (Lords Bingham,
Nicholls and Hoffmann) felt that the Commission should refuse to admit
evidence if it was unable to conclude that there was not a real risk that the
evidence had been obtained by torture.[7] Since the ruling, the Secretary of State
has adopted a 'pragmatic approach', whereby reliance on material which the
Special Advocates argue, or may argue, may have been obtained by torture is
withdrawn.[8]

1   SI 2003/1034, r 44(3). Section 5(7) of the Special Immigration Appeals Commission Act 1997
provided that the exclusionary rule of evidence in the Interception of Communications Act
1985, s 9 did not apply in proceedings before the Commission, but this section was repealed
by the Regulation of Investigatory Powers Act 2000, s 82.
2   *A, B, C and D v Secretary of State for the Home Department* (SC/1, 6, 7, 9, 10/2002)
(2 October 2003, unreported) upheld in CA as *A v Secretary of State for the Home
Department* [2004] EWCA Civ 1123. The majority (Neuberger LJ dissenting) of the Court of

Appeal held that evidence obtained by torture was admissible before the Special Immigration Appeals Commission, provided the torture was not that of the Secretary of State or his officers.

3   *A v Secretary of State for the Home Department* [2005] UKHL 71, [2006] 2 AC 221.

4   The thrust of the ruling is encapsulated by Lord Hoffmann at paragraph 82: 'The use of torture is dishonourable. It corrupts and degrades the state which uses it and the legal system which accepts it'.

5   At para 116.

6   Per Lord Rodger at paragraph 143: 'On behalf of the Home Secretary, Mr Burnett QC explained how those in the relevant departments who were preparing a case for a SIAC hearing would sift through the material, on the lookout for anything that might suggest that torture had been used. The Home Secretary accepted that he was under a duty to put any such material before the Commission. With the aid of the relevant intelligence services, doubtless as much as possible will be done. And SIAC itself will wish to take an active role in suggesting possible lines of investigation'.

7   In a powerful dissent on this issue, Lord Bingham stated at para 59: 'This is a test which, in the real world, can never be satisfied. The foreign torturer does not boast of his trade. The security services, as the Secretary of State has made clear, do not wish to imperil their relations with regimes where torture is practised. The special advocates have no means or resources to investigate. The detainee is in the dark. It is inconsistent with the most rudimentary notions of fairness to blindfold a man and then impose a standard which only the sighted could hope to meet. The result will be that, despite the universal abhorrence expressed for torture and its fruits, evidence procured by torture will be laid before SIAC because its source will not have been 'established'. For an interesting discussion of the circumstances of that judgment, see Lord Bingham, *The Rule of Law*.

8   *Omar Othman v Secretary of State for the Home Department* (SC/15/2005), 26 February 2007 at para 73.

Fairness of proceedings before the Special Immigration Appeals Commission

22.20 Since its inception, the Commission has been plagued by accusations that its procedures are inherently unfair to appellants who often cannot see the vast bulk of the evidence against them, and that the unfairness is not remedied by the appointment of special advocates who cannot cross-examine or make submissions on instructions, since as soon as the special advocate receives the 'closed material' his or her contact with the appellant is at an end. This is a submission which has been roundly rejected by the Commission itself, the Court of Appeal and the House of Lords.[1] The argument that Article 6 of the ECHR applies to proceedings before the Commission[2] has been rejected on the basis that deportation proceedings and decisions regarding the entry, stay and deportation of aliens do not concern the determination of an applicant's civil rights or obligations, even though profoundly and directly impacting on other Convention rights.[3] In maintaining this position in relation to proceedings before SIAC, the House of Lords distinguished them from control order proceedings which, so a majority of the House of Lords held,[4] were subject to Article 6. More recently, their Lordships have held that in order to satisfy the requirements of Article 6 in control order proceedings in the High Court, the controlee must be given sufficient information about the allegations against him to enable him to give effective instructions in relation to those allegations, notwithstanding that the detail or the sources of the evidence forming the basis of the allegations is not disclosed. Where, however, the open material consists purely of general assertions and the case against the controlee is based solely or to a decisive degree on closed materials the requirements of a fair trial will not be satisfied, however cogent the case based on the closed materials may be.[5] Further attempts to transpose such minimum standards of fairness to SIAC proceedings have been repeatedly rebuffed by the Commission[6] within the context of deportation appeals, save in respect of EU cases. An argument that no lesser procedural obligations arise in Article 8 cases as in Article 6 was rejected by the Strasbourg Court at the admissibility stage.[7] The Court of Appeal in *W (Algeria) v Secretary of State for the Home Department*[8] whilst recognising that the proceedings in SIAC may breach the equivalent fundamental right at common law to a fair hearing, this was mandated by Parliament through s 5 of the 1997 Act and procedural rule 4. However, when it comes to SIAC bail hearings where deprivation of liberty is in issue, the minimum standard of fairness applicable in control order cases applies.[9]

[1]   *RB (Algeria) v Secretary of State for the Home Department; Othman (Jordan) v Secretary of State for the Home Department* [2009] UKHL 10, [2009] 2 WLR 512.

[2]   *PP v Secretary of State for the Home Department* (SC/54/2006), 23 November 2007 at para 4.

[3]   *Maaouia v France* (2000) 33 EHRR 1037, para 40, 9 BHRC 205, ECtHR and *RB (Algeria) v Secretary of State for the Home Department; Othman (Jordan) v Secretary of State for the Home Department* [2009] UKHL 10, [2009] 2 WLR 512.

[4]   *Secretary of State for the Home Department v MB; Secretary of State for the Home Department v AF* [2007] UKHL 46, [2008] 1 AC 440.

[5]   *Secretary of State for the Home Department v AF* [2009] UKHL 28, [2009] 3 All ER 643, [2009] 3 WLR 74 following the decision of the Grand Chamber of the ECtHR in *A v United Kingdom* (2009) 49 EHRR 29.

[6]   See *OO v Secretary of State for the Home Department* (SC/51/2006), 27 June 2008; *ZZ v Secretary of State for the Home Department* (SC/63/2007), 30 July 2008; *IR v Secretary of State for the Home Department* (SC/70/2008), 30 October 2009; and *GT v Secretary of State for the Home Department* (SC/68/2008), 21 December 2009. The Court of Appeal has, however, granted permission to appeal, albeit reluctantly, on the question of whether domestic law may yet impose an obligation of disclosure as a matter of procedural fairness on the issue of whether the appellant is a risk to national security in this country (but not on the issue of risk on return), within the context of SIAC proceedings: *Z v Secretary of State for the Home Department* [2009] EWCA Civ 1287.

[7]   *IR & GT v United Kingdom* (2014) 58 EHRR SE14.

[8]   [2010] EWCA Civ 898, [2010] All ER (D) 321 (Jul).

[9]   *R (on the application of Cart) v Upper Tribunal; U v Special Immigration Appeals Commission; XC v Special Immigration Appeals Commission* [2009] EWHC 3052 (Admin), [2010] 1 All ER 908, [2010] 2 WLR 1012 followed by the bail determination in *U, XC and UF v Secretary of State for the Home Department* (SC/77/2009; SC/80/2009; SC/32/2005), 21 December 2009.

Determinations

22.21 The Commission must record its decision and the reasons for it.[1] It must serve its written determination on the parties within a reasonable time but its duty to give reasons is circumscribed once more by public interest considerations. The determination must contain reasons 'to the extent that it is possible to do so without disclosing information contrary to the public interest',[2] and where the determination does not include the full reasons for the decision, the Commission must serve a separate determination, including those full reasons, on the Secretary of State and the special advocate.[3] The rules provide that the special advocate may apply to the Commission to amend both determinations on the ground that the separate determination contains material the disclosure of which would not be contrary to the public interest.[4] Such an application must be served on the Secretary of State[5] and the Commission must give the special advocate and the Secretary of State an opportunity to make representations and may determine the application with or without a hearing.[6] Where the Commission proposes to serve on the appellant its determination, it must first serve notice on the Secretary of State of its intention to do so.[7] The Secretary of State may, within five days of being served with such notice apply to the Commission to amend the determination if it is considered that notification to the appellant of any matter contained in the determination would cause information to be disclosed contrary to the public interest.[8] The Commission if forbidden from serving the determination on the appellant before the time for the Secretary of State to make the application has expired, or where such application is made, before it has been determined.[9]

1   Special Immigration Appeals Commission (Procedure) Rules 2003, SI 2003/1034, r 47(2).
2   SI 2003/1034, r 47(3).
3   SI 2003/1034, r 47(4). This raises questions as to the duty of a special advocate to put forward grounds of appeal based on closed material.
4   SI 2003/1034, r 47(5).
5   SI 2003/1034, r 47(6).
6   SI 2003/1034, r 47(7).
7   SI 2003/1034, r 48(1) and (2).
8   SI 2003/1034, r 48(3). Such application must be served simultaneously on the special advocate: r 48(4). The Commission must give the special advocate and Secretary of State an opportunity to make representations and may determine the application with or without a hearing: r 48(5).
9   SI 2003/1034, r 48(6).

Onward appeals

22.22 Any party to an appeal before the Commission may bring a further appeal to the appropriate appeal court on any question of law material to the final determination of an appeal.[1] In relation to a determination made by the Commission in England and Wales, the appropriate court is the Court of Appeal, in Scotland the Court of Session and in Northern Ireland to the Court of Appeal in Northern Ireland.[2] Such an appeal can only be brought with the leave of the Commission or if such leave is refused, with the leave of the appropriate appeal court.[3] An application for leave to appeal must be filed with the Commission in writing.[4] The appellant must file the application, if in detention, within five days of service of the Commission's determination or otherwise within 10 days.[5] Where the Secretary of State makes an application to amend the determination under r 48 of the Procedure Rules, he must file any application for permission to appeal with the Commission no later than 10 days after the hearing of the amendment application, or where there is no hearing the day on which he received notification of the decision on the application.[6] Where the Secretary of State does not make such an application, any application for permission to appeal must be filed no later than 15 days after receiving the determination.[7] The Commission may accept a late application if it is satisfied that by reason of special circumstances, it would be unjust to do so.[8] The Commission may decide an application for leave without a hearing unless it considers there are special circumstances which make a hearing necessary or desirable.[9] The House of Lords has rejected the notion that compatibility with the Convention is itself a question of law.[10] The Court of Appeal does not have an unrestricted jurisdiction to review the facts that underpin SIAC's conclusions, as a specialist tribunal, on whether deportation will result in a violation of the Convention, and its role on appeals under

SIACA 1997, s 7(1) is a secondary, reviewing function limited to traditional questions of law.

Whilst SIAC is a court of superior record[11] the Divisional Court[12] has held that its decisions are still amenable to judicial review for excess of jurisdiction in both the *pre* and *post-Anisminic sense*, and that section 1(4) of the Special Immigration Appeals Commission Act 1997 fell foul of the *Anisminic* principle and could not oust judicial review of SIAC's decisions in respect of bail.[13] However, a final determination of an appeal by SIAC is appealable to the Court of Appeal and the decision in *U* does not open the way for SIAC's appealable determinations to be judicially reviewed, nor can it be used to challenge interlocutory decisions on the way to making such a determination in the absence of gross error by SIAC. In *U*, the decision amenable to challenge was SIAC's revocation and refusal of bail, although the court stated that judicial review, in the absence of a clear sharp-edged error of law, could not be used as a surrogate means of appeal against bail decisions.[14]

1   Special Immigration Appeals Commission Act 1997, s 7(1).
2   SIACA 1997, s 7(3).
3   SIACA 1997, s 7(2).
4   Special Immigration Appeals Commission (Procedure) Rules 2003, SI 2003/1034, r 27(1). The application must state the grounds of appeal and be signed by the applicant or his representative and dated: r 27(3). The applicant must serve a copy of the application notice on every other party: r 27(4).
5   SI 2003/1034, r 27(2).
6   SI 2003/1034, r 27(2A)(a).
7   SI 2003/1034, r 27(2A)(b).
8   SI 2003/1034, r 27(2B).
9   SI 2003/1034, r 27(5).
10   *RB (Algeria) v Secretary of State for the Home Department; Othman (Jordan) v Secretary of State for the Home Department* [2009] UKHL 10, [2009] 2 WLR 512.
11   Special Immigration Appeals Commission Act 1997, s 1(3).
12   *R (on the application of Cart) v Upper Tribunal; U v Special Immigration Appeals Commission; XC v Special Immigration Appeals Commission* [2009] EWHC 3052 (Admin), [2010] 1 All ER 908, [2010] 2 WLR 1012.
13   *U*, paras 82–83, per Laws LJ.
14   *U*, para 85, per Laws LJ. On a further application for revocation in *U* and the remitted hearing in *XC*, SIAC reviewed its approach in principle to the issue of bail reaffirming its long established practice of itself reviewing whether the national security and abscond risk could be met by strict conditions of bail but concluded that the inability to take account of certain forms of closed material meant that in future it would adopt a more 'precautionary approach' to the grant of bail: *R (on the application of Cart; U and; XC v Special Immigration Appeals Commission; Upper Tribunal* (21 December 2009). SIAC maintained both the decision to revoke U's bail and to refuse bail to XC. U again judicially reviewed this decision and whilst the Divisional Court upheld SIAC's ruling it raised serious questions about the legality of the 'precautionary approach' but found that it had not in fact been determinative of the revocation in U's case: *R (on the application of U) v Special Immigration Appeals Commission* [2010] EWHC 813 (Admin), [2010] All ER (D) 178 (Apr).

Bail

22.23 Bail before SIAC is governed by the bail provisions contained in Sch 2 to the Immigration Act 1971 (see CHAPTER 18, above), as applied[1] and modified[2] by the Special Immigration Appeals Commission Act 1997. The application by someone held under the Immigration Acts must be made in writing to SIAC and in addition to the usual particulars (name, date of birth, etc) it should also state the amount of any recognisance the applicant will agree to be bound by and the names and details of any sureties.[3] On receipt of an application SIAC must 'as soon as reasonably practicable' serve the Secretary of State with a copy and fix a date for a hearing.[4] If the application is contested it is then the duty of the Secretary of State to file a written statement of his or her reasons for contesting the application.[5] If the Secretary of State objects to the statement being disclosed to the applicant or his representative, then the rules relating to closed material apply,[6] namely that the closed material can only be relied on if a special advocate has been appointed to represent the interests of the bail applicant and he or she has been served with the closed material and a statement by the Secretary of State of her reasons for objecting to its disclosure.[7] Once this has happened the special advocate is no longer able to communicate or take instructions from the applicant or the applicant's legal advisers without the leave of the Commission,[8] but must nevertheless decide whether to object to the non-disclosure. If he or she does so there may have to be a secret 'rule 38' hearing on this issue, and SIAC must then make a finding.[9] After any disclosure procedure is concluded the bail application may be heard. Again, there may have to be open and closed sessions before the Commission makes its decision on the bail application. The decision must be in writing and SIAC must give its reasons 'if and to the extent that it is possible to do so without disclosing information contrary to the public interest'.[10] The minimum standards of procedural fairness which pertain to control order proceedings also apply to bail hearings before SIAC, namely that the applicant must be given sufficient information about the grounds upon which the grant of bail is opposed and/or its revocation sought.[11] This has become known shortly as 'AF No 3' disclosure. This additional fairness requirement arises because the Article 5 right to liberty and Article 6 of the ECHR procedural obligations are in play in a bail hearing. On a hearing to consider variation of bail conditions where deprivation of liberty and thus Article 5 safeguards are not in issue, there is no entitlement to a 'gist' or 'AF No 3' disclosure, and neither Article 6 nor 8 of the ECHR provide a route to enhanced procedural safeguards over and above that afforded by way of the normal SIAC Procedure.[12] This approach has subsequently been approved by the Strasbourg court in *IR & GT v United Kingdom*,[13] an admissibility decision. Whilst there is no statutory test for granting or withholding bail, SIAC has consistently held that the risk of absconding and the risk to national security, including that posed were the appellant to abscond, are factors of great importance.[14] When bail is granted in an alleged terrorist case it is usually only granted subject to the most stringent of conditions. A person on bail may be arrested by an immigration officer or police officer if he (a) anticipates that the person will break a condition of bail, (b) suspects that a condition is being or has been broken, or (c) is notified in writing by a surety that the person is likely to break a condition.[15] Such a person must be brought before SIAC within 24 hours.[16] SIAC then has to form a view as to whether the person has broken or is likely to break any condition on which he was released in order then to decide whether or not bail is to be revoked.[17] The likelihood of a prospective breach of condition is established if there are 'substantial grounds for believing' that the person will breach a condition of their bail.[18] In *R (on the application of Othman) v Special Immigration Appeals Commission*[19] the Divisional Court held that SIAC had jurisdiction and was well-placed to determine the lawfulness of detention on a bail application; the existence of SIAC's bail jurisdiction did not oust the supervisory jurisdiction of the High court, which retained jurisdiction to hear applications for judicial review of bail decisions (as with all unappealable decisions including decisions on an interlocutory matter)[20] but it did mean that the court would not normally substitute its own view unless some 'hard-edged or florid' error of law or approach was demonstrated.

1   SIACA 1997, s 3.
2   SIACA 1997, Sch 3.
3   SI 2003/1034, r 29, as modified by r 31 in its application to Scotland.
4   SI 2003/1034, r 30(1).
5   SI 2003/1034, r 30(2).
6   SI 2003/1034, r 30(3).
7   SI 2003/1034, r 37(2) and (3).
8   SI 2003/1034, r 36.
9   SI 2003/1034, r 38.
10   SI 2003/1034, r 30(4).
11   *R (on the application of Cart) v Upper Tribunal; U v Special Immigration Appeals Commission; XC v Special Immigration Appeals Commission* [2009] EWHC 3052 (Admin), [2010] 1 All ER 908, [2010] 2 WLR 1012 followed by the bail decision in *U, XC and UF v Secretary of State for the Home Department* (SC/77/2009; SC/80/2009; SC/32/2005), 21 December 2009. See also *Secretary of State for the Home Department v AF* [2010] 2 AC 269.
12   *R (on the application of BB) v Special Immigration Appeals Commission* [2012] EWCA Civ 1499. The point at which conditions amounting to a deprivation of liberty become a restriction which does not trigger Article 5 protections has been put by the court at circa 16 hrs (although the impact of restrictions should be viewed cumulatively: see *Secretary of State for the Home Department v JJ* [2007] UKHL 45, [2008] 1 AC 385.
13   (2014) 58 EHRR SE14.
14   See, for example, *Othman v Secretary of State for the Home Department* (SC/15/2005), 2 December 2008 (SIAC).
15   Immigration Act 1971, Sch 2, para 24(1)(a), (b) as applied and modified by the Special Immigration Appeals Act 1997, s 3(1), Sch 3.
16   Immigration Act 1971, Sch 2, para 24(2) as applied and modified by the Special Immigration Appeals Act 1997, s 3(1), Sch 3.
17   Immigration Act 1971, Sch 2, para 24(3)(a) as applied.
18   *Othman v Secretary of State for the Home Department* (SC/15/2005), 2 December 2008 (SIAC). The legality of the Secretary of State's decision to detain a number of appellants immediately after a hearing by SIAC to refuse to revoke bail following the judgment of the House of Lords in *RB* is soon to be determined by the High Court.
19   [2012] EWHC 2349 (Admin)
20   See *Cart* [2009] EWHC 3052 (Admin), fn 11 above.

Index

[all references are to paragraph number]

a

Index

Index